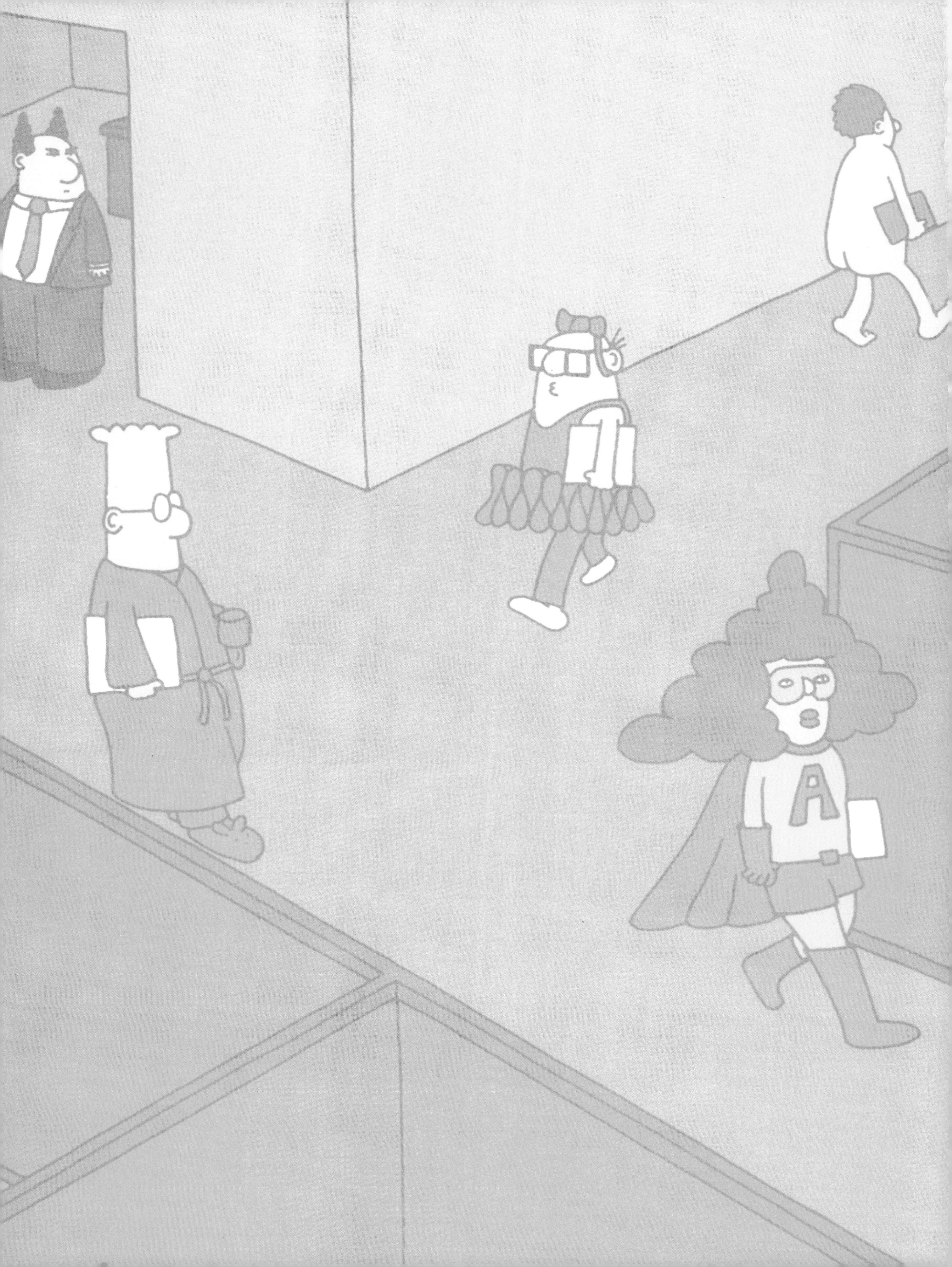

DILBERT 2.0™

THE 20th ANNIVERSARY

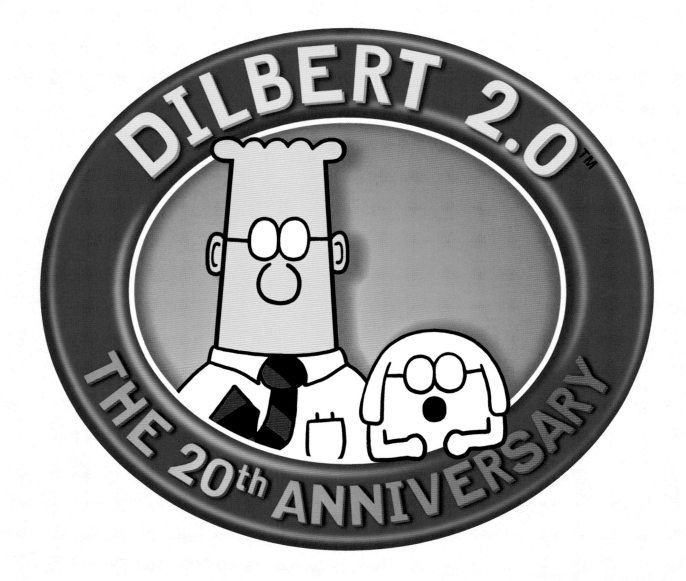

Dilbert 2.0: 20 Years of Dilbert copyright © 2008 by Scott Adams, Inc. All rights reserved.
Licensed by United Feature Syndicate, Inc. Printed in China. No part of this book may be
used or reproduced in any manner whatsoever without written permission except in the case
of reprints in the context of reviews. For information, write to: Andrews McMeel Publishing, LLC,
an Andrews McMeel Universal company, 1130 Walnut Street, Kansas City, Missouri 64106.

08 09 10 11 12 POA 10 9 8 7 6 5 4 3 2 1

ISBN-13: 978-0-7407-7735-6
ISBN-10: 0-7407-7735-1

Library of Congress Control Number: 2008927324

www.andrewsmcmeel.com
www.dilbert.com

ATTENTION: SCHOOLS AND BUSINESSES

Andrews McMeel books are available at quantity discounts with bulk purchase for educational, business, or sales promotional use. For information, please write to: Special Sales Department,
Andrews McMeel Publishing, LLC, 1130 Walnut Street, Kansas City, Missouri 64106.

Produced by Lionheart Books Ltd.
5200 Peachtree Rd.
Atlanta, Georgia 30341

Designed by Michael Reagan

Printed in China through Asia Pacific Offset

Dilbert 2.0

20 Years of Dilbert

Scott Adams

Andrews McMeel
Publishing, LLC

Kansas City

For Jack Cassady
Thank you for the advice.

Contents

Dilbert appears in 2,000 newspapers and is translated into 23 languages in 70 countries.
There are over 20 million *Dilbert* books and calendars in print.

Introduction
by Scott Adams

When I sat down to organize this twentieth-anniversary book, I wondered how best to tell the tale. I knew I could do it in a variety of ways. But I thought the most interesting way would be to explain the unlikely combination of events that put me, and then *Dilbert*, in the right places at the right times. Let's start at the beginning.

1957 — Born

You can never be sure how much of what you become is due to nature versus nurture. My mother was a successful landscape artist in her spare time, so I probably inherited some of her artistic DNA, evidently mutated. I also have my dad's sense of humor and his economical way with words. The building blocks for *Dilbert* were in place early.

I probably got my stubbornness from both sides of the family, which I prefer to call persistence. My parents' work ethic was also baked into me at a young age. I come from a long line of hard workers who believe that having only one full-time job per day is the same as slacking.

1963 — *Peanuts* Books

My uncle owned a farm just up the road. When we visited, I would head straight for his collection of *Peanuts* paperback books. I became obsessed with them, even before I could read or understand them. They had the x-factor. There was just something about them that was special and amazing. I was hooked for life.

My parents always told me I could grow up to be anything I wanted to be. I decided to grow up to be Charles Schulz. Surely the world had room for two of him. And after all, how hard could it be? You draw pictures, you write some words—it seemed like easy work to me. And from what I heard, the pay was good. I decided to start right in on my new profession.

Between the ages of six and nine, I drew a comic featuring creatures I named Little Grabbers, which was the phrase my dad often used to describe children. I imagined my

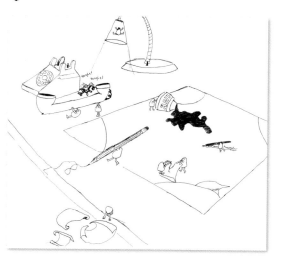

characters as the tiny gremlins who were responsible for all the things that went wrong in the house and had no other explanation. My mother saved my early drawings from that period. On the right, we see the Little Grabbers leaving the

phone off the hook, spilling ink, and causing trouble. In the masterpiece on the left, the Little Grabbers are accelerating the decomposition of a flower arrangement. Luckily they have their own helicopter for this sort of work.

By about the age of eleven, I was influenced primarily by *MAD* magazine, and by the single-panel comics in other magazines. Drawing single-panel comics didn't look that hard, so I tried making some of my own. In the hilarious work on the left, a hunting dog fails to notice a rabbit.

In the knee-slapper on the right, a prisoner tries to tunnel to freedom with a spoon, and hits oil. It's sort of a good news-bad news situation. I was not yet a master of perspective.

Around this time I acquired a book on cartooning. I spent countless hours with it, often practicing the drawing of human hands, which are especially hard to get right. That's part of the reason *Dilbert* characters have five digits on each hand while most comics characters have only four. Once I learned how to draw hands, I didn't want to squander that ability on four-digit mutants.

I can trace Dogbert's origin back to my own family dog, Lucy, who was mostly beagle. Lucy never once came when called. And she was indifferent to everyone in the family except my mom,

who fed her. In the drawing on the left, they are enjoying some quality time. It is no coincidence that later I developed a dog character with floppy ears that disdains humans.

1967—Cereal Box Contest Winner
One day I noticed a contest on the back of a cereal box: draw a picture of the geyser Old Faithful, and you could win a TV. There were also a number of runners-up prizes, including some cool-looking cameras. I entered the contest, confident I would win some sort of prize. My mother noticed my misplaced optimism and cautioned against getting my hopes up, explaining that thousands of kids would enter the contest, and only a few would win prizes. I remained confident despite the warnings, in a way that only people with no life experience can be.

I won a camera. The camera was made entirely of plastic, but it worked. I was thrilled. I started to suspect that beating long odds wasn't as hard as it seemed. This became a pattern that repeated itself throughout my life.

1968—The Golden Egg
Our small town held an annual Easter egg contest. Eggs labeled with various monetary amounts were hidden in a large field. The grand prize was the Golden Egg, worth ten dollars, which was big money for an eleven-year-old in those days. I boldly predicted that I would be first among the hordes to find that Golden Egg.

By pure luck, I found myself in the right place at the right time. I walked to a particular spot in the field, on a hunch, looked down, and there it was: the Golden Egg. The local newspaper published a picture of me posing with the Golden Egg. I tasted fame for the first time, and liked it. Again, beating long odds seemed easier than everyone kept saying. It was time to raise my sights, to try something bigger.

1968—Famous Artists Course for Talented Young People

I applied for the Famous Artists Course for Talented Young People. It was a correspondence course for wannabe artists. My mother saved my application in the attic all these years. Here it is, so you can judge how much talent I had (or didn't have) at a young age.

Tell us about yourself

Date Dec. 3, 1968

Name Scott Adams

Street City Windham State N.Y. Zip 12446

Phone No Age 11

Please answer all the questions below. Your answers will help us greatly in judging your talent and possibilities in the field of art.

1. What school do you attend? Windham Ashland, Jewett, Central School Grade 6
2. How long have you been interested in art? about 4 years
3. Do you study art in school? yes How much time per week? 45 minutes

   Do you take any other art classes? no Where?
4. Check the types of art which interest you most:

   Still life ☐ Story illustration ☐ Landscapes ☐ Magazine covers ☐ Greeting cards ☐ Flowers ☐ Design and layout ☐ Political cartoons ☐ Animal drawing ☑ Sports cartoons ☑ Advertising illustration ☐ Human figures ☐ Fashion drawing ☐ Marine subjects ☐ Calendar art ☐ Portraits ☐ Posters ☐ Advertising cartoons ☐ Cartoon strips ☑ Magazine cartoons ☐ Television art ☐

   Others
5. Check what mediums interest you most: Oil painting ☐ Watercolor ☐ Pen and ink ☑ Pencil ☑

   Others
6. Who are your favorite artists? AL Capp,
7. Are you willing and able to study at home and work by yourself? yes
8. Can you accept sincere criticism of your work? yes
9. Why would you like to become an artist? It could be a good job when I get older. I like to draw.

3 Your ability to observe

Complete the outline sketch alongside the original, using a soft pencil. Before you begin, study the pencil lines and shading in the original drawing. Notice which areas are darkest and which are lightest. Also note the character of the pencil work.

Grade B−

PUT
PUT
PUT

4 Your imagination in developing a picture idea

Complete this sketch by adding whatever figures or objects you think will help to make an interesting picture. Draw them with lines similar to those in the hot rod. You might show some boys repairing the car, or pushing it home after a breakdown. You could show Grandma being given her first exciting ride in a hot rod. Some boys and girls going on a surfing date is another idea. Let your imagination have free rein.

Grade B

Good picture details, Scott!

Grass
Rocks
Tree
Foliage

5 Drawing textures and surfaces

Complete this landscape picture by adding textures. Below the picture we show you the textures of some of the objects in it — grass, rocks, the tree trunk, and foliage — and how to draw them to complete an effect of realism. You may draw the textures of other things, such as the rutted and pebbly surface of the road. A soft pencil can give you all the textural effects you desire. Don't make all of your textures equally light or dark. For example, a plain white sky would help to bring out the dark rough bark of the tree.

Grade B−

Nice form, tone, and feeling of animation!

6 Animal drawing — animation

Complete the outlined drawing of the dog by giving him his full coat of hair, as in the smaller drawing. Use a soft pencil for shading. Try to draw the puppy in full tone and retain the sense of form underneath his fur, as well as his gay, animated spirit.

Grade B+

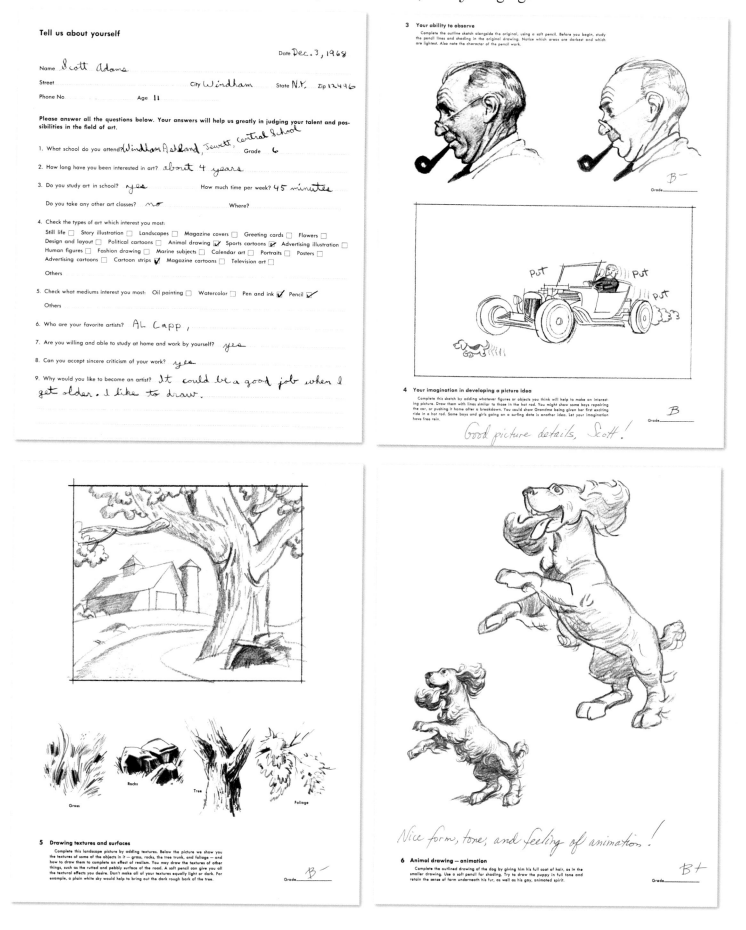

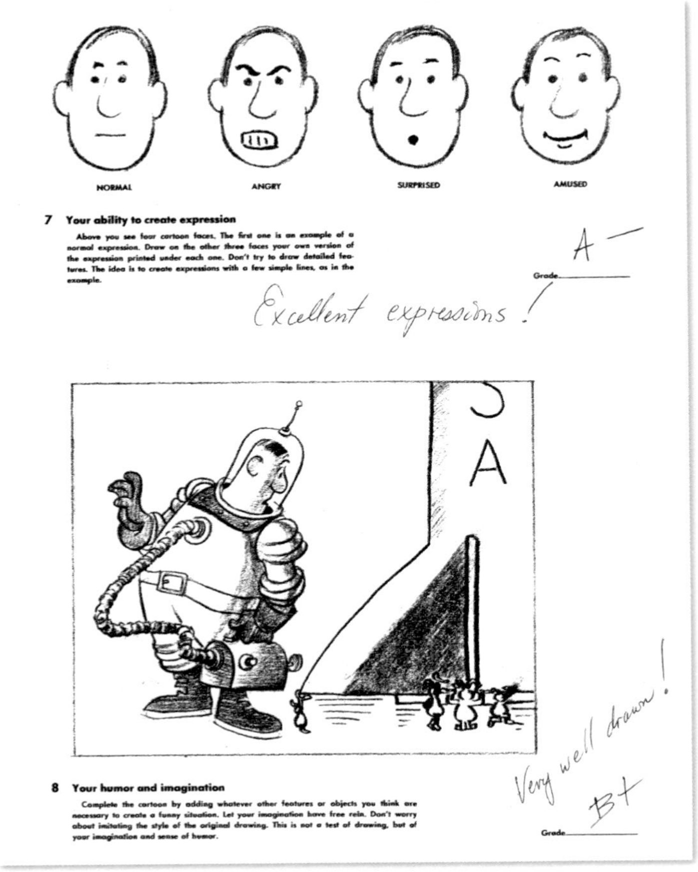

NORMAL
ANGRY
SURPRISED
AMUSED
7 Your ability to create expression
Above you see four cartoon faces. The first one is an example of a normal expression. Draw on the other three faces your own version of the expression printed under each one. Don't try to draw detailed features. The idea is to create expressions with a few simple lines, as in the example.
Grade A–
Excellent expressions!
S
A
Very well drawn!
8 Your humor and imagination
Complete the cartoon by adding whatever other features or objects you think are necessary to create a funny situation. Let your imagination have free rein. Don't worry about imitating the style of the original drawing. This is not a test of drawing, but of your imagination and sense of humor.
Grade B+

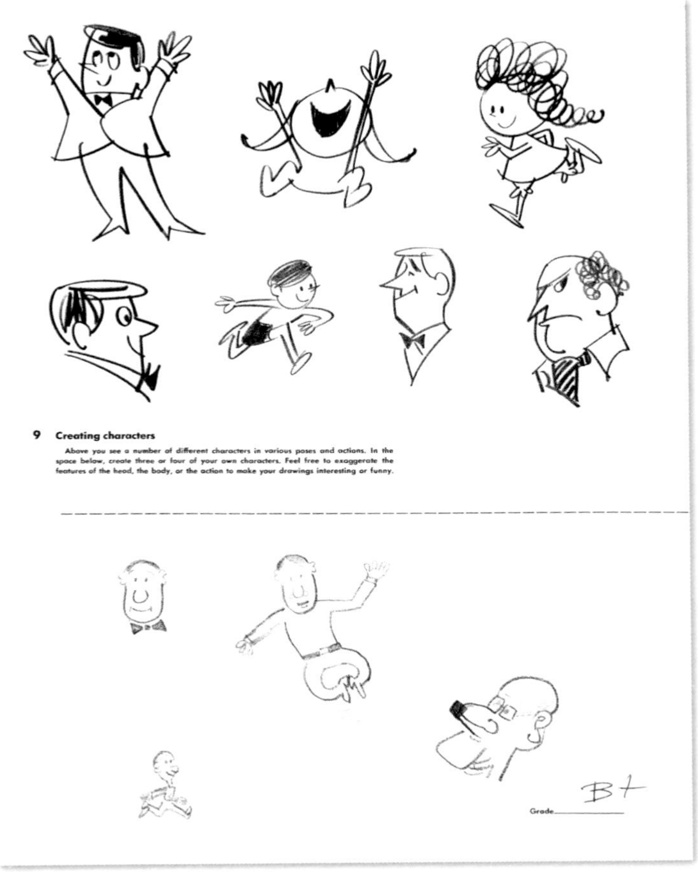

9 Creating characters
Above you see a number of different characters in various poses and actions. In the space below, create three or four of your own characters. Feel free to exaggerate the features of the head, the body, or the action to make your drawings interesting or funny.
Grade B+

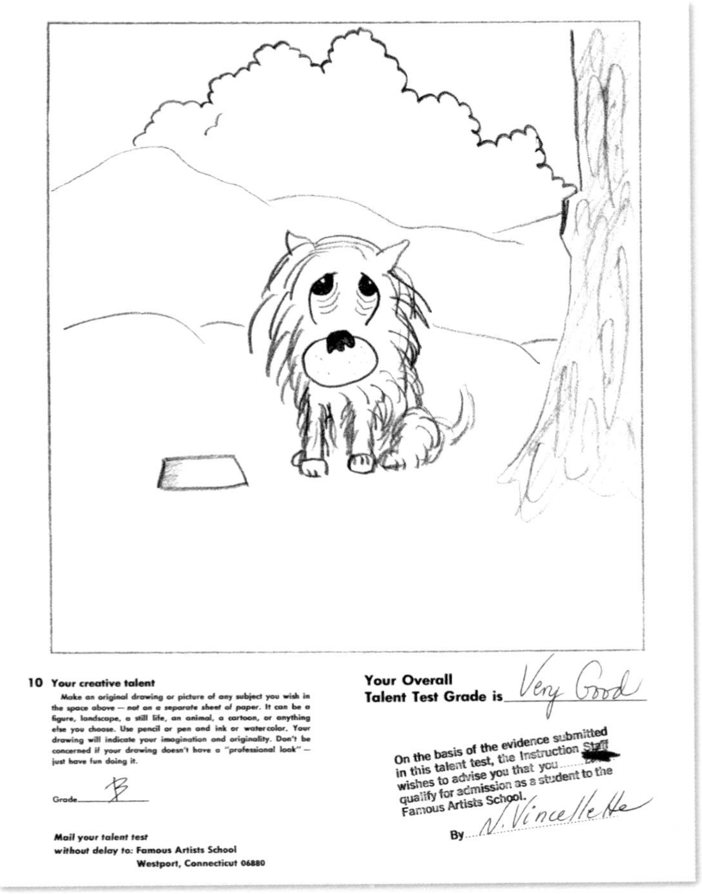

10 Your creative talent
Make an original drawing or picture of any subject you wish in the space above — not on a separate sheet of paper. It can be a figure, landscape, a still life, an animal, a cartoon, or anything else you choose. Use pencil or pen and ink or watercolor. Your drawing will indicate your imagination and originality. Don't be concerned if your drawing doesn't have a "professional look" — just have fun doing it.
Grade B
Mail your talent test
without delay to: Famous Artists School
Westport, Connecticut 06880
Your Overall
Talent Test Grade is Very Good
On the basis of the evidence submitted
in this talent test, the Instruction Staff
wishes to advise you that you ....
qualify for admission as a student to the
Famous Artists School.
By N. Vincellette

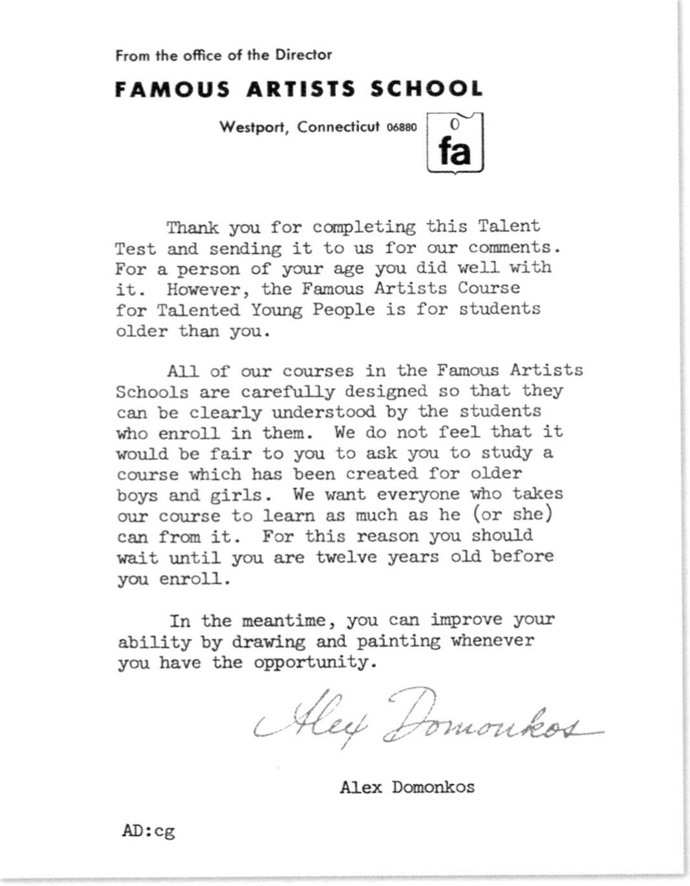
From the office of the Director
FAMOUS ARTISTS SCHOOL
Westport, Connecticut 06880
fa

Thank you for completing this Talent
Test and sending it to us for our comments.
For a person of your age you did well with
it. However, the Famous Artists Course
for Talented Young People is for students
older than you.

All of our courses in the Famous Artists
Schools are carefully designed so that they
can be clearly understood by the students
who enroll in them. We do not feel that it
would be fair to you to ask you to study a
course which has been created for older
boys and girls. We want everyone who takes
our course to learn as much as he (or she)
can from it. For this reason you should
wait until you are twelve years old before
you enroll.

In the meantime, you can improve your
ability by drawing and painting whenever
you have the opportunity.

Alex Domonkos

Alex Domonkos

AD:cg

I got an okay grade on the application, but I was rejected by the school because I was too young. Above is the rejection letter that broke the news to me. It was the day I learned you can't always find the Golden Egg just because you want to.

I soon abandoned my dreams of becoming a famous cartoonist. And I started to learn that unlikely things are indeed unlikely. I adjusted my goals to something that seemed more attainable. I looked around my town and learned that exactly two people had high incomes. One was the only doctor in town, and the other was the only lawyer. I didn't like touching other people's guts and tendons and whatnot, so I set my sights on a career in law.

1975 — Graduated High School

There were only about forty people in my graduating class, and I had known most of them since kindergarten. My world was small, so it wasn't hard to be in the top ten at any particular activity. The guy who jumped center on our basketball team my senior year was 5′6″. The small-town experience made success seem attainable. If you wanted to be the best in town at one thing or another, your chances were excellent because it was unlikely anyone else was even trying hard.

I was one of the top students in my tiny class, but opted to not take chemistry or physics in high school for reasons that make a fascinating story, but don't fit with this one. Skipping upper-level science classes was an unwise move for someone planning to go to college. But in a strange twist of fate, it turned out to be the luckiest unwise move of my life.

The only other course offered during the period when chemistry was taught was typing. At the time, typing was thought to be a skill reserved for future secretaries. The typing class was a lot easier than chemistry, and I got an A. The people who took chemistry didn't do so well. No one got an A in that class. That tiny difference allowed me to graduate as class valedictorian. I won a few scholarships and applied for colleges that weren't too far from home.

I don't recommend that anyone follow my example. But it needs to be said that as an adult, I rarely use chemistry. However, I have authored several books, while simultaneously writing and typing at about ninety words per minute. Sometimes doing the wrong thing works out.

1975 — Hartwick College, Oneonta, New York

In college, I majored in economics, partly because someone told me it was good preparation for law school, and partly because I wanted to understand how money worked. It seemed as though it would come in handy no matter what I did. And it did.

I took one art class in college, primarily because I thought it would be easy. It wasn't. I got the lowest grade in the class, and deserved it. The other students were talented artists who could draw a bunch of fruit on a table so well it made you hungry. My drawings looked like something you see on prison walls.

In my senior year of college, I went to a job interview in Syracuse for an internship at an accounting firm. The interviewer dismissed me without talking to me because I wasn't wearing a suit. I was so naïve that I thought my casual clothes were just fine for an interview at an accounting firm.

On my way home, as I was driving along a new highway with virtually no other traffic, the engine on my beat-up Datsun 510 quit. It was February, at night, and snowing, and I hadn't brought a coat because I figured I would be sprinting from car to building and back. I managed to pack a whole lot of stupid into that one day.

There was no civilization in sight, no streetlights, and no traffic. I knew I couldn't go back the way I came, because I would freeze to death, literally, before reaching civilization. I hoped there were homes along the road ahead of me, near enough for me to reach on foot. It was my best shot, so I decided to run in that direction.

As I ran, my extremities started freezing. My feet felt like blocks of ice pounding the frozen road. I thought I had a good chance of dying that night. I ran as far as I could, then stopped, froze some more, and ran again. As I approached exhaustion, I promised myself that if I lived, I would sell my car for a one-way ticket to California and never see another (expletive deleted) snowflake as long as I lived.

After an hour of running and freezing, headlights appeared over the horizon. I flagged down a station wagon. A shoe salesman saved me and gave me a ride back to campus. Upon graduation, a few months later, I traded my car to my sister for a one-way ticket to California. I haven't been in snow since.

" Another Person is Added to the System "

1979 — My First Job

In California, I stayed with my brother and looked for a job where my degree in economics had some value. Crocker National Bank, in San Francisco, hired me as a teller. I was robbed twice at gunpoint in a four-month period, and realized that management was a safer place to be.

I got into a management training program after I sent some suggestions for improving profits to the senior vice president. The suggestions were naïve and impractical, as he informed me with a grin, but he liked the way I made my case. I had included some wry humor in the write-up, and my sense of humor reminded him of someone he loved: himself. He took a chance and put me in the management training program.

Hmm.... could be another bug in the system...

Over the course of the next six years, I was a management trainee, computer programmer, budget analyst, commercial lender, product manager, and finally a supervisor of a small group of analysts who negotiated contracts, wrote business cases, and tracked budgets. I can say with all appropriate modesty that I was incompetent at all of those jobs, primarily because I never stayed in one position long enough to develop any skill. At least that's my excuse.

Several of my jobs at the bank involved making presentations to upper management. I seasoned my presentations with comics to keep the audience awake, and to have a business reason for sitting around drawing comics at work. My comics weren't funny in the ha-ha sense, but they reminded people of their jobs, and that seemed to be enough. I believe my first published comic was the mole I drew for the cover of the company newsletter.

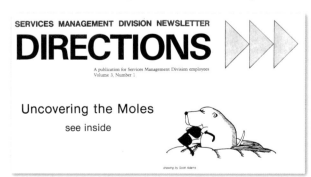

SERVICES MANAGEMENT DIVISION NEWSLETTER

DIRECTIONS ▶▶▶

A publication for Services Management Division employees
Volume 3, Number 1

Uncovering the Moles

see inside

drawing by Scott Adams

At about this time, I started drawing two characters more than others. One was a guy with glasses who would later become Dilbert. The other was a dog that was loosely based on my old family dog, Lucy.

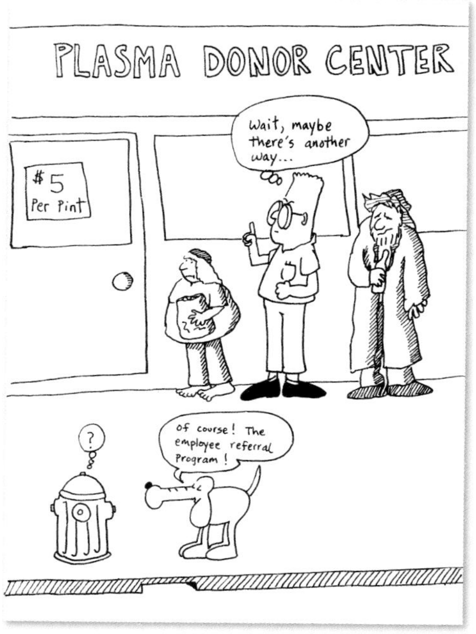
PLASMA DONOR CENTER
Wait, maybe there's another way...
$5 Per Pint
?
Of course! The employee referral Program!

In my early drawings, the character who would become Dilbert had no necktie. But other characters did. I came across the old drawing below from pre-Dilbert days showing perhaps the first upturned necktie I ever drew. I have no memory of why or when I first drew Dilbert with the upturned tie, but the comic below foreshadowed it.

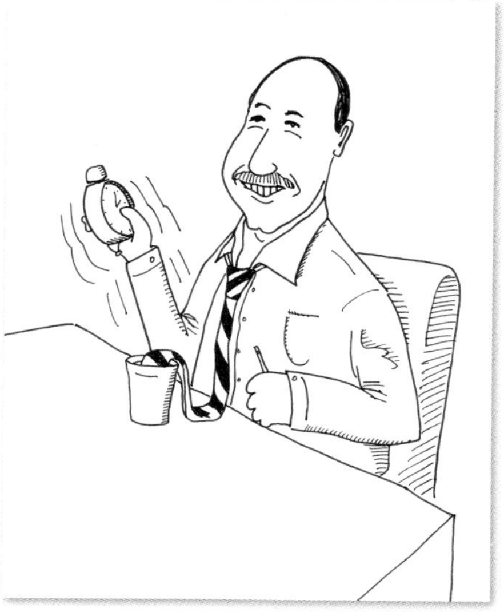

1983—MBA

I had ambitions to reach upper management at the bank, but to do that I needed an MBA from a good school. I set my sights on the University of California at Berkeley, which had an evening program the bank was willing to pay for. As it turns out, "free" was the exact price I could afford, so that plan suited me.

The only problem was that a few years earlier I had taken the required aptitude test for a master's degree in business (called the GMAT), and only scored in the top seventy-seventh percentile. That was nowhere near the level I needed to get into Berkeley. I needed to be somewhere above the ninetieth percentile, I figured.

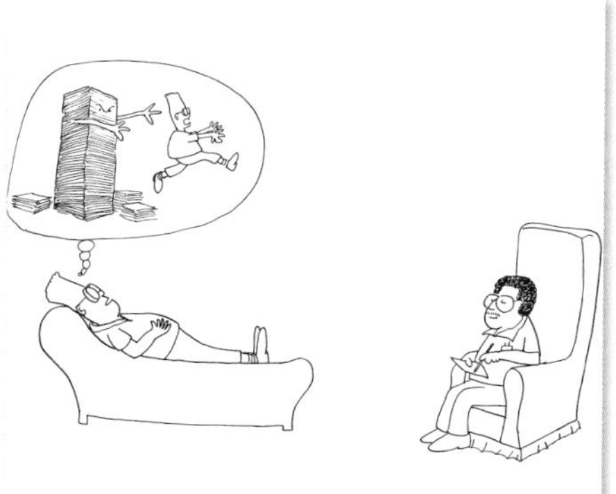

"Assistance and Advice"

At about this time I was experimenting with something called affirmations. The idea (admittedly whacko sounding) is that you can manifest your destiny by writing down your specific goals fifteen times a day. I had tried it a few times that year, on some personal goals, and was shocked at the coincidences that seemed to pile together to make the goal happen.

I should digress at this point to note that I am among the most skeptical people you could ever meet. I don't believe in ghosts, magic, ESP, Santa Claus, UFOs, horoscopes, or religion. My best guess as to why affirmations *appear* to work is that they help you focus, and perhaps that makes you think sharper, or try harder, or notice opportunities more easily than you would have otherwise.

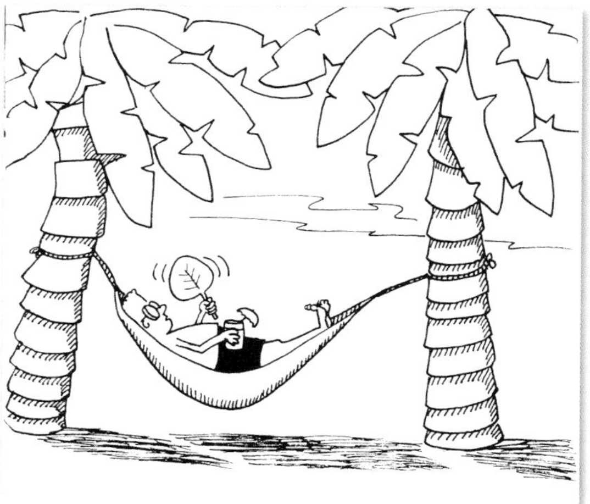

This could be you

Or perhaps selective memory is at work, and I somehow forgot the times that affirmations *didn't* work. I was alert to the illusion of selective memory while trying affirmations, but I still can't rule it out. I want to be perfectly clear that I am not claiming affirmations have magic powers, or even that they work. I'm simply describing my story. And part of that story involves experimenting with writing my goals every day.

I ended up making a foolish bet with a co-worker who was taking a class to prepare for the GMAT in a few months. She had scored somewhere in the upper eightieth percentile the first time she tried and hoped to improve on that.

I made a bet with her that I could beat her next (presumably improved) score by doing nothing but study the practice books and take the test again. This was an unwise bet, because the experts agreed that practice wasn't likely to improve my score as much as I needed mine to improve.

So I picked a specific goal that seemed high enough—the ninety-fourth percentile—and I did my affirmations daily: "I, Scott Adams, will score in the ninety-fourth percentile on my GMATs." I visualized seeing the 94 on the test results. I also studied the practice tests, and consistently scored about the same as on my original test. Things weren't looking good. But I took the GMAT again and hoped for the best.

Some weeks later, I received a letter containing my test results. I opened it, and looked for the box I had visualized with a 94. And there it was. Exactly 94.

I reiterate that I don't think magic was involved. I'm simply describing the events as they happened. It is relevant in the story of *Dilbert*'s origins because it changed forever my view of what was likely and what was not.

I applied to the University of California at Berkeley's evening MBA program and was accepted. For the next three years, I worked days, took classes at night, and did homework during all the cracks in my schedule. It was the hardest three years of my life, but also, as you will see, a key to *Dilbert*'s success.

As I neared the completion of my MBA program, I expected greater opportunities for promotion. This time I was in the wrong place at the wrong time. The media had recently discovered that my employer had virtually no diversity in management. When an assistant vice president position opened up, and I was an obvious candidate for the spot, my boss called me into her office. I was the most qualified candidate for the position, she explained, but because of pressure to be more diverse, there was no hope for another generic white male to get promoted any time soon.

I updated my resume, hoping to find a company that would value me for my abilities. The only offer I got was from the local phone company, Pacific Bell. The money they offered was good, the commute was reasonable, and I took the job. Within a few months, every person in my old group at the bank had been downsized.

1986—Career Turning Point

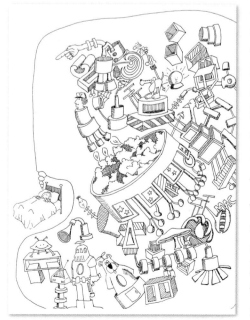

At Pacific Bell, I completed my MBA and did my best to act and talk like an up-and-coming senior manager. Apparently my act was convincing, and I was soon added to what they called "the binder" of people who were ready for promotion. One day my boss called me into his office and informed me that while I was indeed management material, the company had been getting a lot of bad press lately about their lack of diversity in management. He noted that promoting me would only make things worse.

You might think this was a bad day for me. But you would be wrong. Because the day you realize that your efforts and your rewards are not related, it really frees up your calendar. Suddenly I didn't see the need to come to work so early, or to stay late, or to work hard. I had time for hobbies. I worked on my tennis game, and I started drawing comics for my own amusement. The doodle on the left came from that era.

One day I decided to see if I could get my comics published. I didn't care what publication printed them. I just wanted to get paid for cartooning, and to feel as if I was doing something that had upside potential, unlike my job. But how do you become a cartoonist? I had no idea. So I started my affirmations again, this time focusing on becoming a cartoonist.

In pre-Internet days, figuring out how to do something out of the ordinary was a challenge. In a strange twist of fate, I came home from work one day, and found myself in the right place at the right time. I started flipping through the channels on TV and noticed the tail end of a show about cartooning. As the closing credits rolled by, I grabbed a pen and paper, and wrote down the name of the host: Jack Cassady.

I wrote a letter to Jack Cassady, asking a number of questions about starting a career in cartooning. I asked about materials, and where and how to submit comics. He responded with a two-and-a-half-page handwritten letter that was packed with tips.

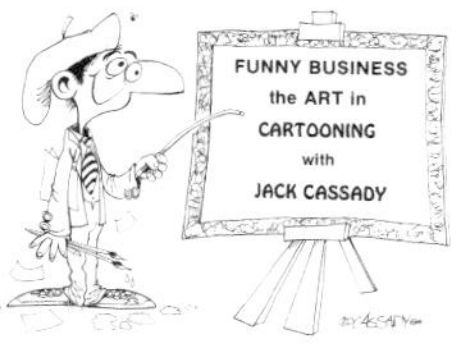
FUNNY BUSINESS
the ART in
CARTOONING
with
JACK CASSADY

WDCN 11 FEB 86

DEAR SCOTT,
THANKS FOR WATCHING "FUNNY BUSINESS..." AND
TAKING TIME TO WRITE – SINCE YOU DIDN'T INCLUDE A
S.A.S.E (SELF ADDRESSED STAMPED ENVELOPE) I ASSUME IT'S
OK TO KEEP YOUR DRAWINGS – IF YOU WANT THEM BACK
JUST LET ME KNOW. I ENJOYED THEM & GOT A GOOD
LAUGH OUT OF SEVERAL. I DON'T KNOW HOW LONG YOU'VE BEEN
CARTOONING, BUT I'D SAY YOU DEFINITELY HAVE THE 'RIGHT
STUFF.' SO KEEP ON DRAWING – NOW TO YOUR QUESTIONS –
FIRST – MORT GERBERG WROTE A GREAT BOOK RECENTLY
CALLED "THE ARBOR HOUSE BOOK OF CARTOONING." IT'S LOADED
WITH GREAT TIPS, TECHNICAL AND OTHERWISE. IT WOULD BE
A GOOD INVESTMENT FOR YOU. A BOOK LOADED WITH
INFO ABOUT CARTOON/ART MARKETS ALSO A 'MUST BUY' IS
THE 86 ARTIST'S MARKET BY WRITER'S DIGEST. MOST BOOKSTORES
HAVE THESE, OR CAN ORDER THEM FOR YOU. THE A.M. TELLS
YOU ADDRESSES, NEEDS, RATES, ETC. TWO OTHER HELPFUL
PERIODICALS ARE GAG-RECAP & TRADE JOURNAL RECAP.
IF YOU'RE JUST STARTING OUT – IT'S GOOD TO GO TO THE T.J.
MARKETS FIRST – BUILD SALES, GET YOUR STUFF SEEN,
THEN GO FOR THE BIGGIES ONCE YOU'VE STARTED TO
(OVER)

(2)
ESTABLISH A REP WITHIN THE FIELD. REMEMBER IT'S VERY
COMPETITIVE AND EXPECT TO GET LOTS OF REJECT (RJ) SLIPS.
DON'T TAKE IT PERSONALLY – YOUR STUFF IS GOOD AND BECAUSE
OF THAT SOMEONE WILL BE BRIGHT ENOUGH TO BUY IT
EVENTUALLY – HECK, IF I WAS AN EDITOR I WOULD'VE TAKEN
5 OR SO OF THE ONES YOU SENT ME TO LOOK AT – UNFORTUNATELY,
THERE ARE TOO FEW EDITORS WITH REAL LIFE TOUGH
RAMBO FREE-LANCE BACKGROUNDS – HA HA.
YOUR CARTOONS CAN BE DRAWN ON A GOOD QUALITY TYPING
PAPER 8½ x 11 – 25% RAG CONTENT, AT LEAST 20 lb or
HIGHER WEIGHT & FLORESCENT OR VERY WHITE – YOU CAN
USE ABOUT ANYTHING THAT MAKES A GOOD REPRODUCABLE
LINE. CAPTIONS CAN BE NEATLY HAND LETTERED OR
TYPED AT THE BASE OF YOUR DRAWING – BORDERS ARE
GENERALLY NOT NECESSARY – PAYMENT VARIES FROM
PUBLICATION TO PUBLICATION & IS A RESULT OF THE VALUE
THEY ATTACH TO GRAPHIC HUMOR, CIRCULATION, AD
REVENUE AND MOON PHASE. AM USUALLY LISTS RATES.
EACH BATCH OF 8 to 10 CARTOONS SHOULD BE
PROTECTED BY SOME KIND OF STIFFENER (IE CUT DOWN
FILE FOLDER) AND INCLUDE A S.A.S.E. THIS IS IMPORTANT,
SINCE EDITORS ARE BUSY FOLKS AND WON'T USUALLY
RETURN YOUR WORK UNLESS YOU INCLUDE A SASE. A NOTE
IN THE BATCH IS USUALLY NOT NECESSARY BUT DO EITHER
WRITE OR RUBBER STAMP YOUR NAME, & ADDRESS &
MAYBE PHONE NR ON THE BACK OF EACH DRAWING –
SEND ORIGINAL ART UNLESS THEY (EDITORS) REQUEST
OTHERWISE – MASS MAILINGS OF THE SAME DRAWING ARE

NOT GOOD BUSINESS PRACTICES DUE TO COPYRIGHTS ETC.
(SEE TAD CRAWFORD'S) THE LAW & THE VISUAL ARTIST.
I HOPE I'VE POINTED OUT A HELPFUL DIRECTION &
WISH YOU THE BEST OF LUCK.
I'M HOPING TO WIN APPROVAL FOR A CONTINUATION OF
13 MORE "FUNNY BUSINESS..." SHOWS FOR 86 – YOU CAN
HELP BY GETTING EVERYONE IN S.F. TO WRITE WDCN
DEMANDING MORE SHOWS – HA HA –

GOOD LUCK SLINGING THE INK!
JACK

Armed with this advice, I bought the *1986 Artist's Market* book, which told me how and where to submit comics, and I started drawing. I soon learned that the *New Yorker* magazine and *Playboy* paid the most for comics. So I focused on drawing off-the-wall comics for the *New Yorker*, and naughty comics for *Playboy*. See if you can tell which are which.

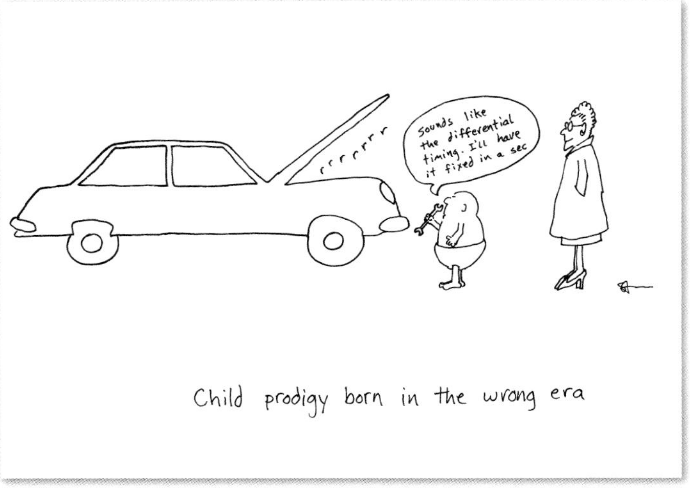

Sounds like the differential timing. I'll have it fixed in a sec

Child prodigy born in the wrong era

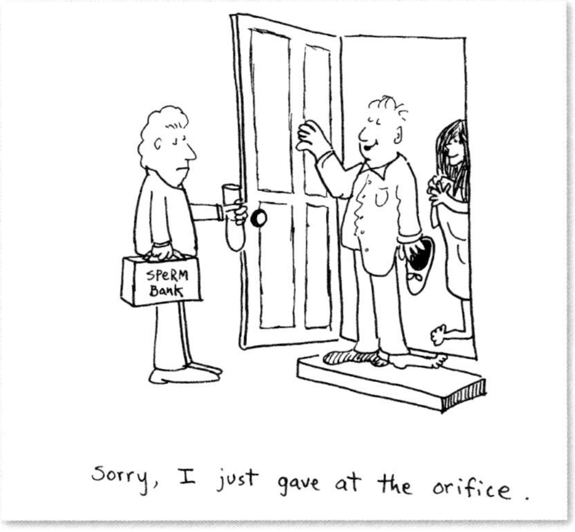

SPERM Bank

Sorry, I just gave at the orifice.

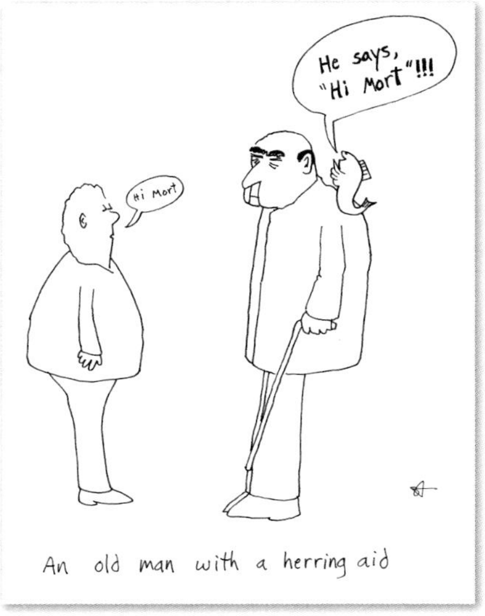

Hi Mort
He says, "Hi Mort"!!!

An old man with a herring aid

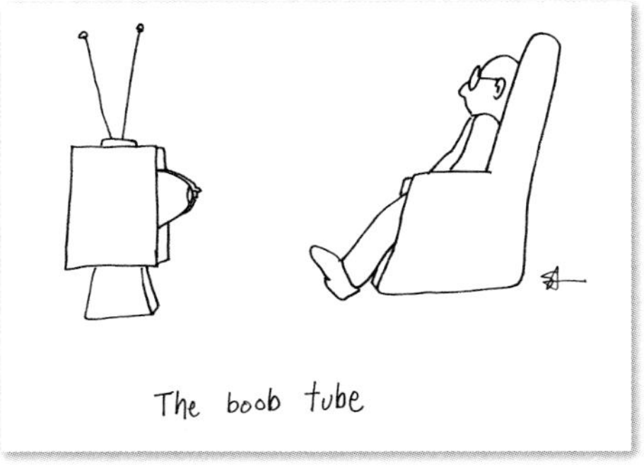
The boob tube

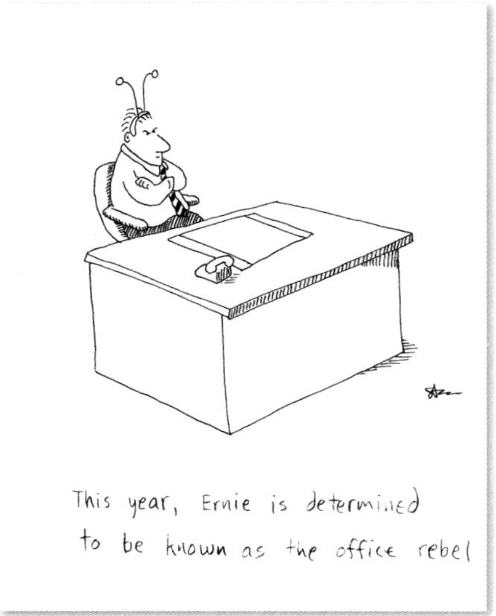
This year, Ernie is determined to be known as the office rebel

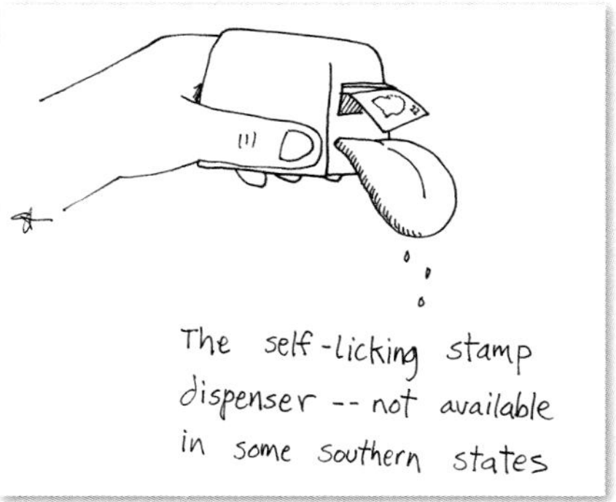
The self-licking stamp dispenser -- not available in some southern states

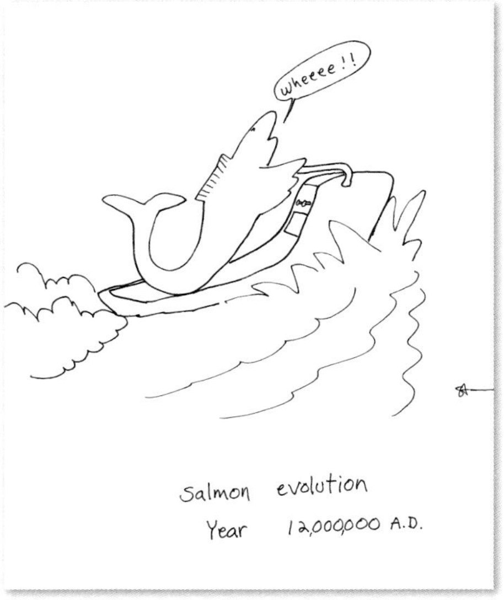

wheeee!!

Salmon evolution
Year 12,000,000 A.D.

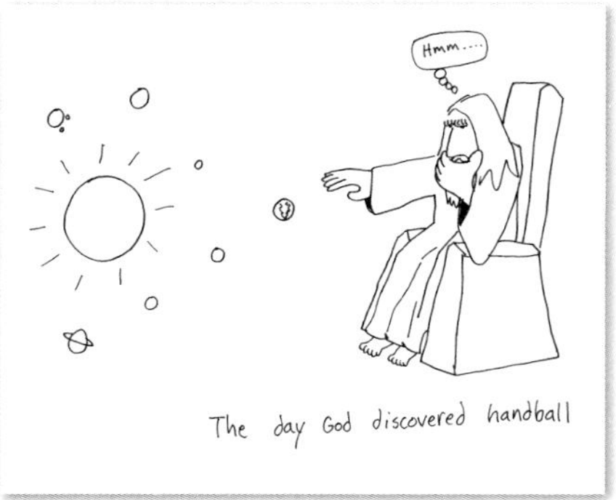

Hmm....

The day God discovered handball

Playboy rejected my comics with a form letter. They made the right decision. The comics I submitted were dreadful. (Years later, when *Dilbert* hit its peak, I was the subject of a *Playboy* interview, and got on the party invitation list for the Playboy Mansion. But I never attended because I couldn't imagine myself hanging out with Playmates and sweating through my pajamas.)

The *New Yorker* magazine rejected me too. I think we all know they made the right decision.

So I gathered up my art supplies and put them in a closet. I felt okay about my effort. I tried as hard as I knew how. I didn't expect everything to work out the way I wanted. I decided to move on. I figured affirmations didn't work every time.

A year later, out of the blue, I got a second letter from Jack Cassady. This was especially odd because I hadn't even thanked him for his original advice. Why would he write a second letter after so much time had passed? Here's why.

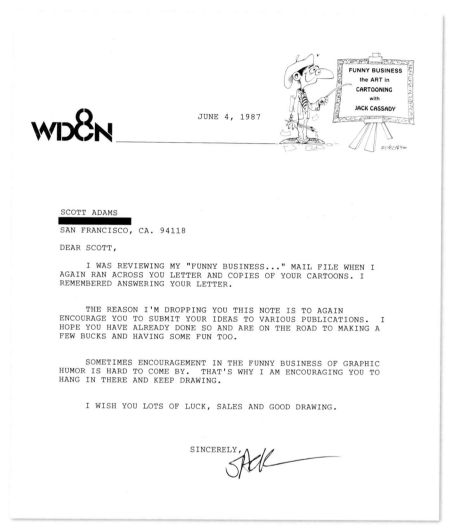

FUNNY BUSINESS
the ART in
CARTOONING
with
JACK CASSADY

WD8N

JUNE 4, 1987

SCOTT ADAMS
[redacted]
SAN FRANCISCO, CA. 94118

DEAR SCOTT,

I WAS REVIEWING MY "FUNNY BUSINESS..." MAIL FILE WHEN I AGAIN RAN ACROSS YOU LETTER AND COPIES OF YOUR CARTOONS. I REMEMBERED ANSWERING YOUR LETTER.

THE REASON I'M DROPPING YOU THIS NOTE IS TO AGAIN ENCOURAGE YOU TO SUBMIT YOUR IDEAS TO VARIOUS PUBLICATIONS. I HOPE YOU HAVE ALREADY DONE SO AND ARE ON THE ROAD TO MAKING A FEW BUCKS AND HAVING SOME FUN TOO.

SOMETIMES ENCOURAGEMENT IN THE FUNNY BUSINESS OF GRAPHIC HUMOR IS HARD TO COME BY. THAT'S WHY I AM ENCOURAGING YOU TO HANG IN THERE AND KEEP DRAWING.

I WISH YOU LOTS OF LUCK, SALES AND GOOD DRAWING.

SINCERELY,
Jack

Somehow he knew I needed the encouragement. He saw something in my work that *Playboy* and the *New Yorker* didn't see. In fact, I didn't see it myself. I think you will agree that my talent was well hidden in that period. But Jack saw it. His letter accomplished exactly what he intended. I got out my art supplies and started drawing again.

During this period I was drawing pre-Dilbert and pre-Dogbert comics on the whiteboard in my cubicle, complete with witty captions about workplace happenings. Cartoons naturally draw attention, and soon my co-workers were asking the names of my two regular characters. I didn't have names for them, so I held a "Name the Nerd" contest on my whiteboard. My co-workers would trickle in during the day and write their ideas for names. The suggestions were traditional nerd-sounding names. None of them stood out. Until one day, my ex-boss, Mike Goodwin, walked in, picked up a dry erase marker, and wrote "Dilbert."

This was one of those moments when you feel as if you can see the future. I ended the contest immediately. It felt as though I was learning this character's name, not naming him. The name Dilbert fit him so perfectly, I literally got a chill. I have a vivid memory of that moment, because it felt as if something special had just happened.

Later, I named Dilbert's dog on my own. I wanted the dog's name to have some connection to Dilbert's name. So naturally, I named him Dildog. (Yes, really.)

At about this time, my friend Josh Libresco noticed in the local paper, the *San Francisco Examiner*, a contest for people who looked like their dogs. Readers were encouraged to send in photos posing with their dogs, and the best ones would get some sort of prize. Josh suggested that I send in a drawing of Dilbert and Dildog. After all, they looked sort of similar.

In retrospect, this was a ridiculous idea, since the contest was specifically for photos. For some reason, that didn't stop me. But I knew I had to change Dildog's name to something more newspaper-friendly. That's when Dildog became Dogbert. This is my letter and entry.

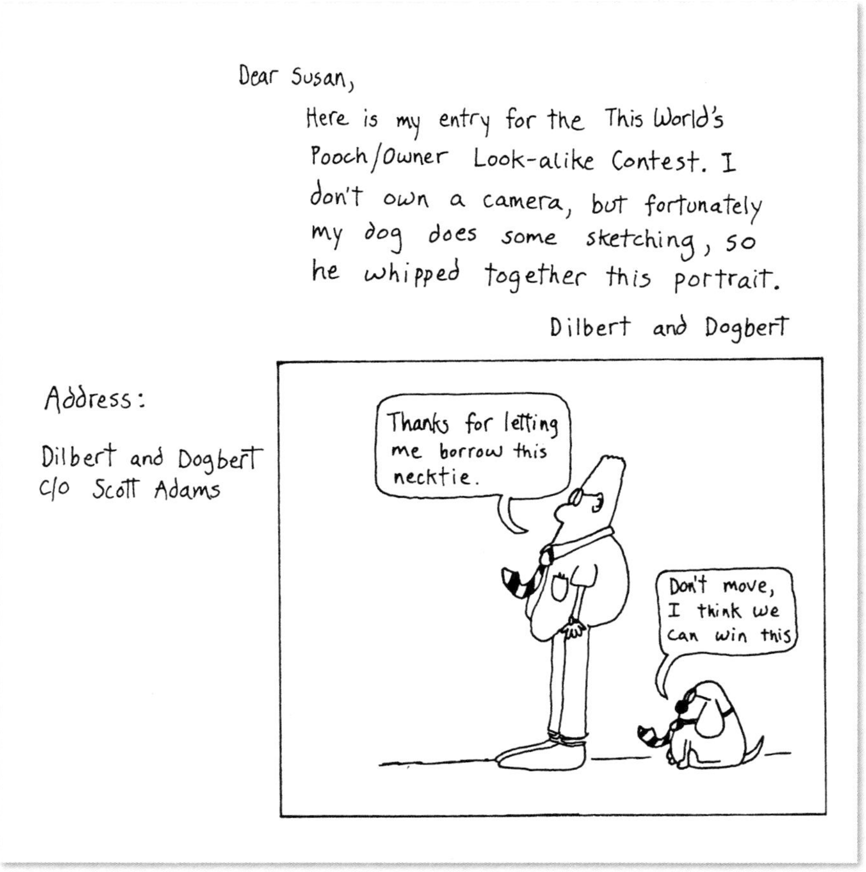
Dear Susan,

Here is my entry for the This World's Pooch/Owner Look-alike Contest. I don't own a camera, but fortunately my dog does some sketching, so he whipped together this portrait.

Dilbert and Dogbert

Address:

Dilbert and Dogbert
c/o Scott Adams
Thanks for letting me borrow this necktie.
Don't move, I think we can win this

For some reason, my drawing was selected for publication among a page of photos of people who looked like their dogs. They probably thought I was a twelve-year-old kid, based on the artwork, and figured it was cute. But the reasons didn't matter to me. My comic was published in a newspaper. My co-workers congratulated me. I liked the feeling. And I wanted more.

I knew that practice was essential. You don't get good at something by sitting around hoping. So I started waking up every morning at 4 A.M. to work on a series of comic panels, in something of a comic book form, that featured Dilbert and Dogbert. I spent two hours every morning developing my drawing and writing skills before heading to my day job. Here is the very first comic form of Dilbert and Dogbert. At the time, I believed puns were the highest form of humor. Please forgive me.

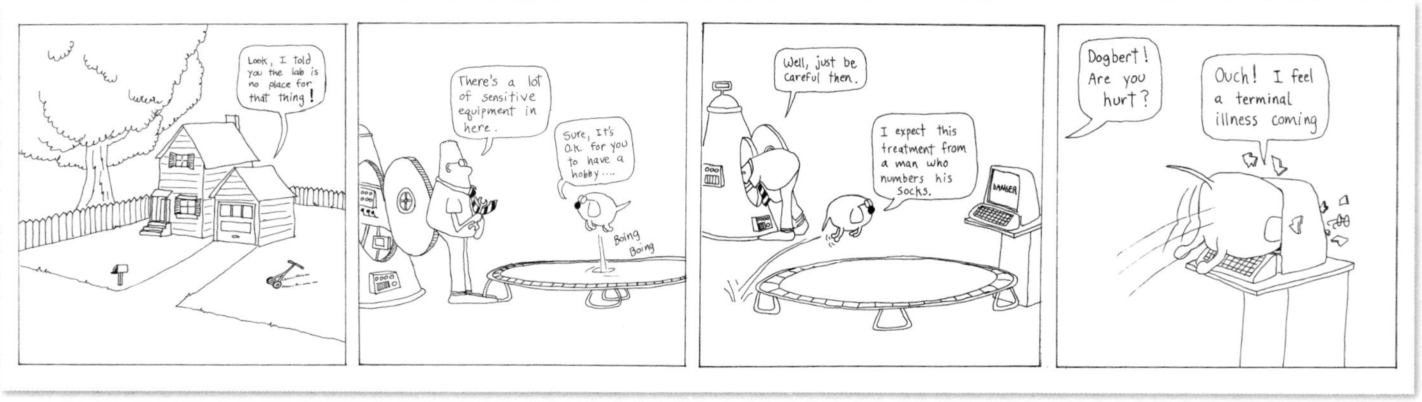
Look, I told you the lab is no place for that thing!
There's a lot of sensitive equipment in here.
Sure, It's O.K. for you to have a hobby....
Boing Boing
Well, just be careful then.
I expect this treatment from a man who numbers his socks.
DANGER
Dogbert! Are you hurt?
Ouch! I feel a terminal illness coming

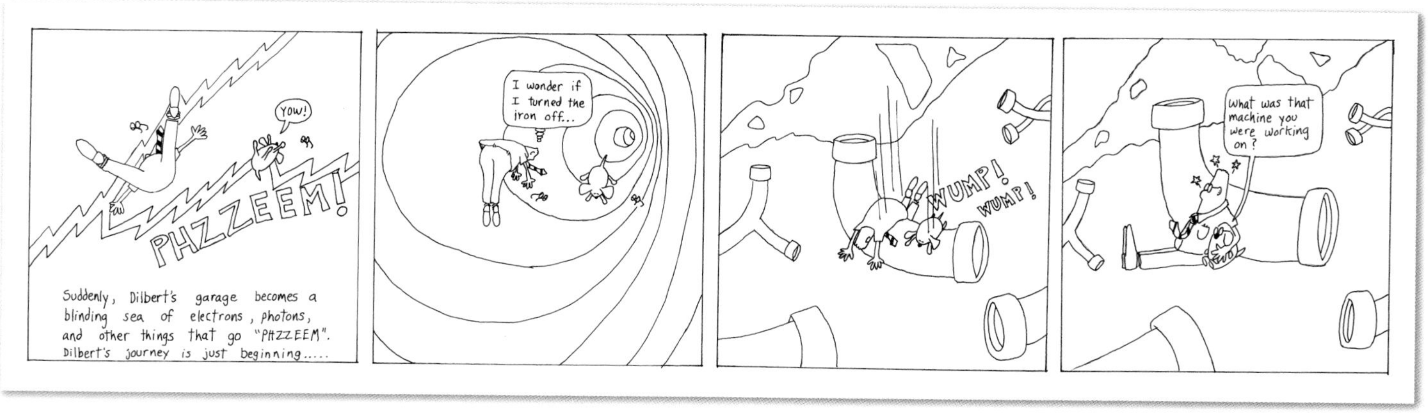
Yow!
PHZZEEM!
Suddenly, Dilbert's garage becomes a blinding sea of electrons, photons, and other things that go "PHZZEEM". Dilbert's journey is just beginning.....
I wonder if I turned the iron off...
WUMP! WUMP!
What was that machine you were working on?

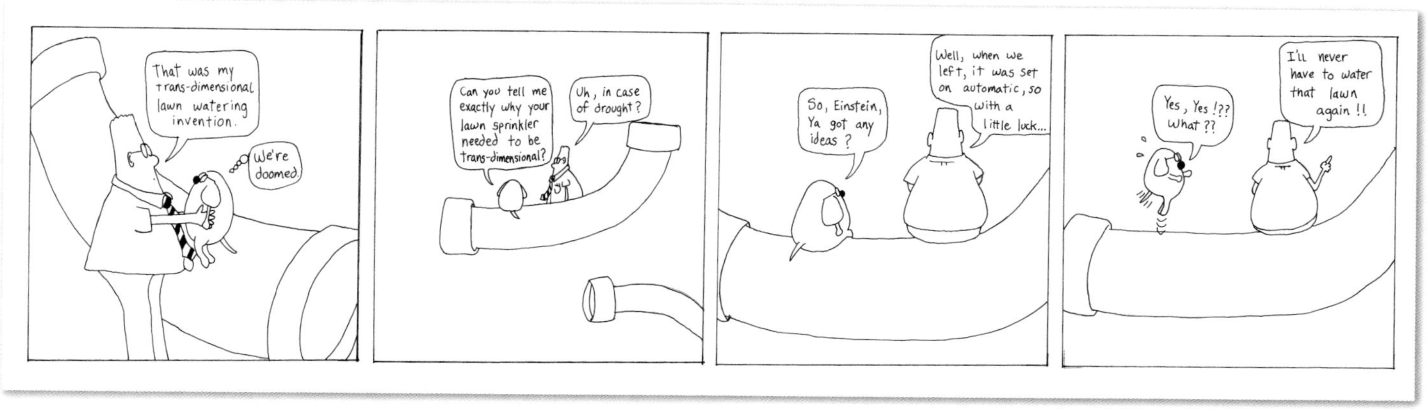
That was my trans-dimensional lawn watering invention.
We're doomed
Can you tell me exactly why your lawn sprinkler needed to be trans-dimensional?
Uh, in case of drought?
So, Einstein, Ya got any ideas?
Well, when we left, it was set on automatic, so with a little luck...
Yes, Yes!?? What??
I'll never have to water that lawn again!!

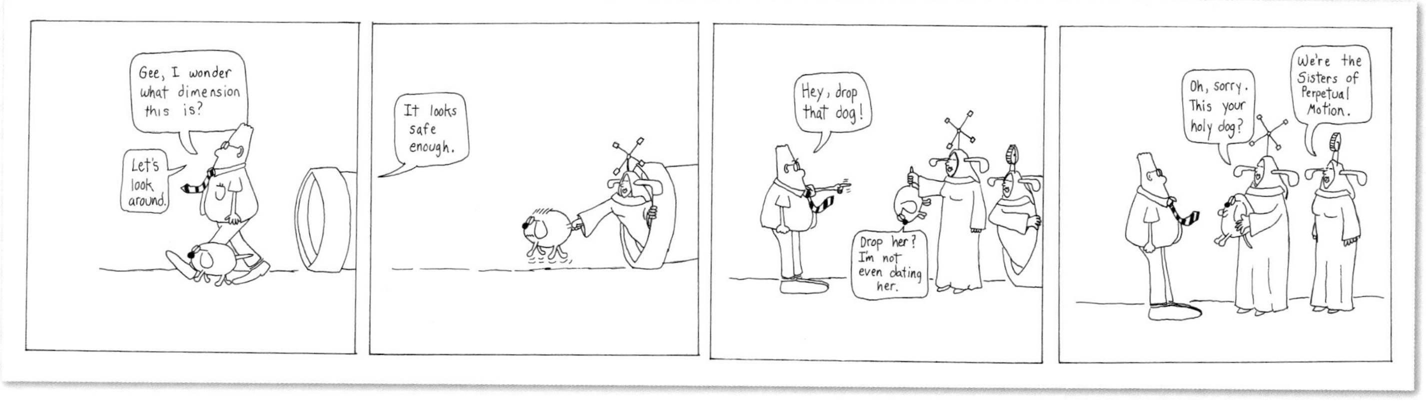
Gee, I wonder what dimension this is?
Let's look around.
It looks safe enough.
Hey, drop that dog!
Drop her? I'm not even dating her.
Oh, sorry. This your holy dog?
We're the Sisters of Perpetual Motion.

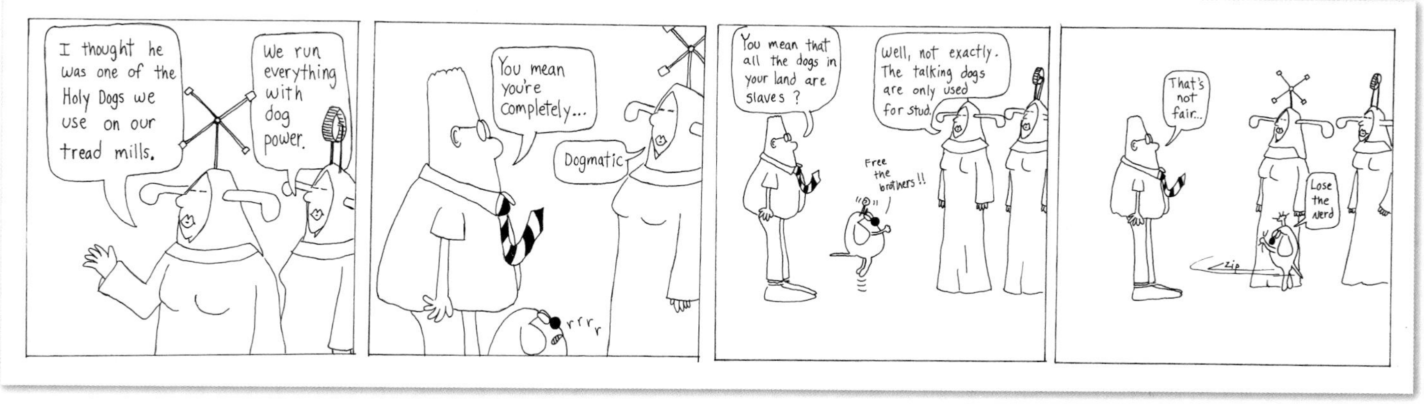
I thought he was one of the Holy Dogs we use on our tread mills.
We run everything with dog power.
You mean you're completely...
Dogmatic
rrrr
You mean that all the dogs in your land are slaves?
Well, not exactly. The talking dogs are only used for stud.
Free the brothers!!
That's not fair...
Lose the nerd
zip

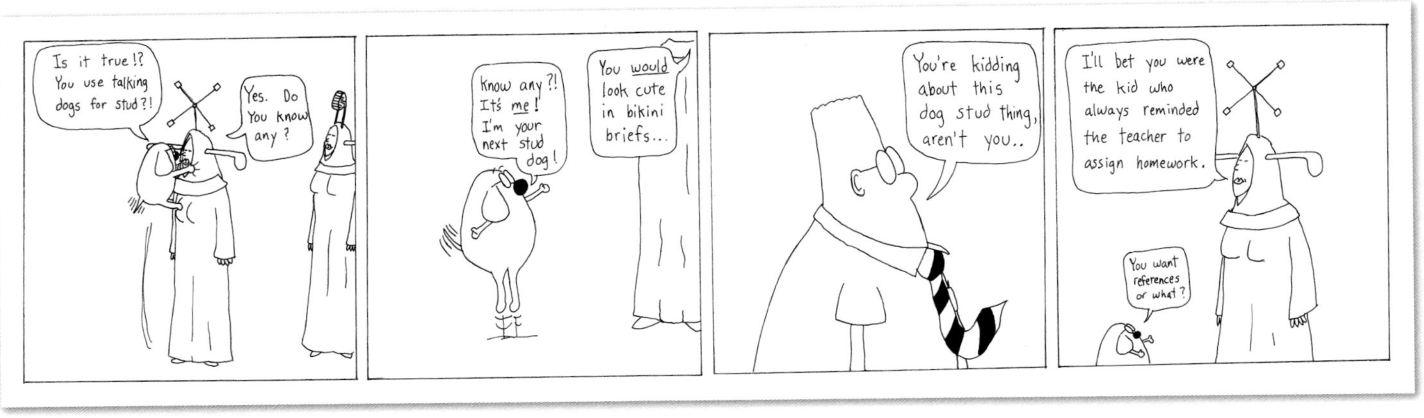
Is it true!? You use talking dogs for stud?!
Yes. Do you know any?
Know any?! It's me! I'm your next stud dog!
You would look cute in bikini briefs...
You're kidding about this dog stud thing, aren't you..
I'll bet you were the kid who always reminded the teacher to assign homework.
You want references or what?

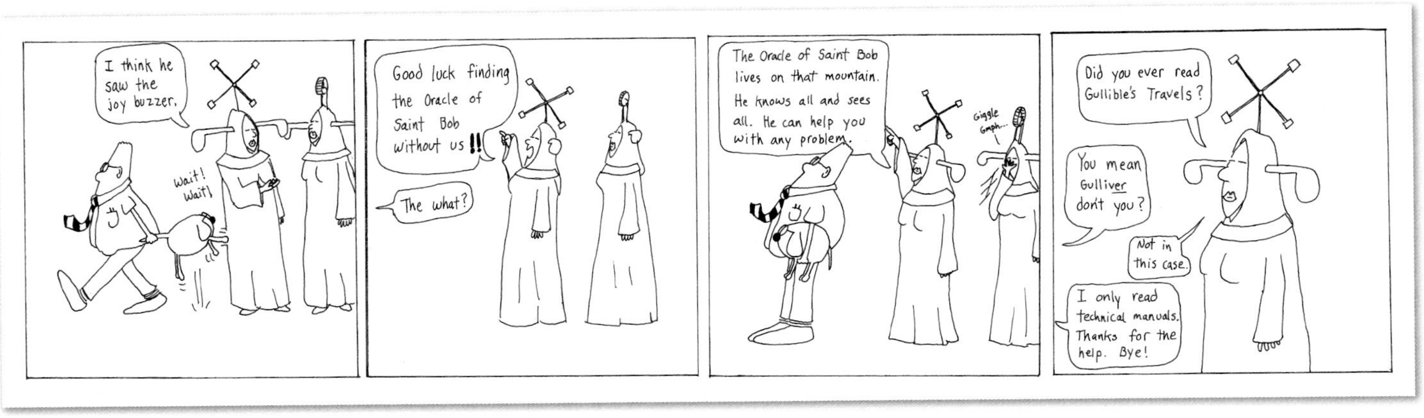
I think he saw the joy buzzer.
Wait! Wait!
Good luck finding the Oracle of Saint Bob without us!!
The what?
The Oracle of Saint Bob lives on that mountain. He knows all and sees all. He can help you with any problem.
Giggle
Did you ever read Gullible's Travels?
You mean Gulliver don't you?
Not in this case.
I only read technical manuals. Thanks for the help. Bye!

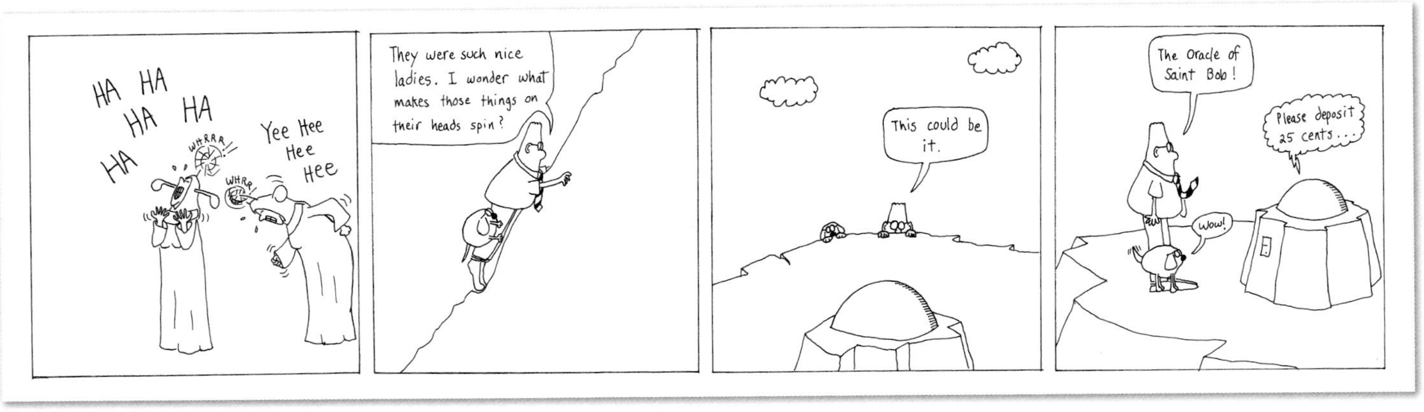
HA HA HA HA HA
Yee Hee Hee Hee
They were such nice ladies. I wonder what makes those things on their heads spin?
This could be it.
The Oracle of Saint Bob!
Please deposit 25 cents...
Wow!

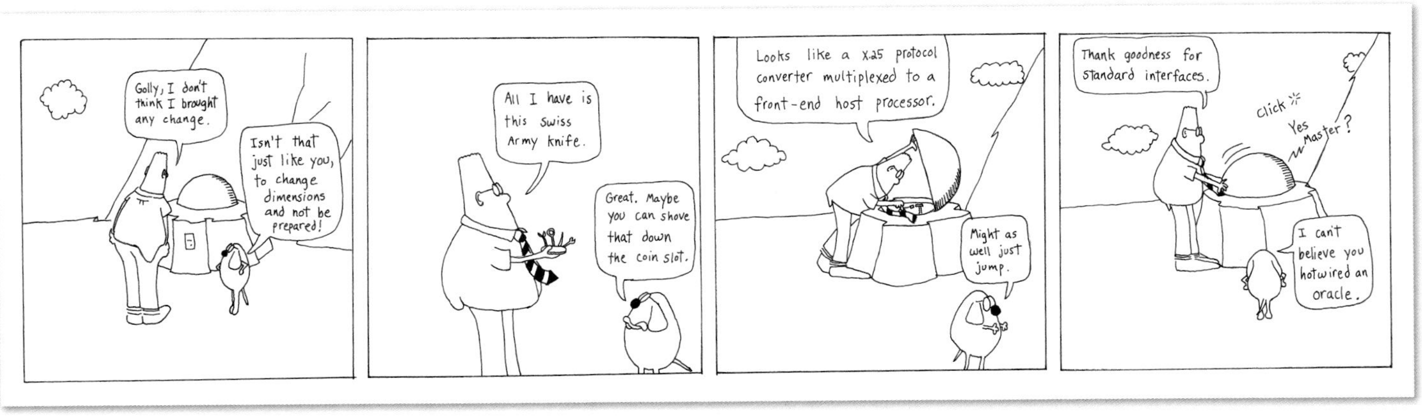
Golly, I don't think I brought any change.
Isn't that just like you, to change dimensions and not be prepared!
All I have is this Swiss Army knife.
Great. Maybe you can shove that down the coin slot.
Looks like a X.25 protocol converter multiplexed to a front-end host processor.
Might as well just jump.
Thank goodness for standard interfaces.
Click
Yes master?
I can't believe you hotwired an oracle.

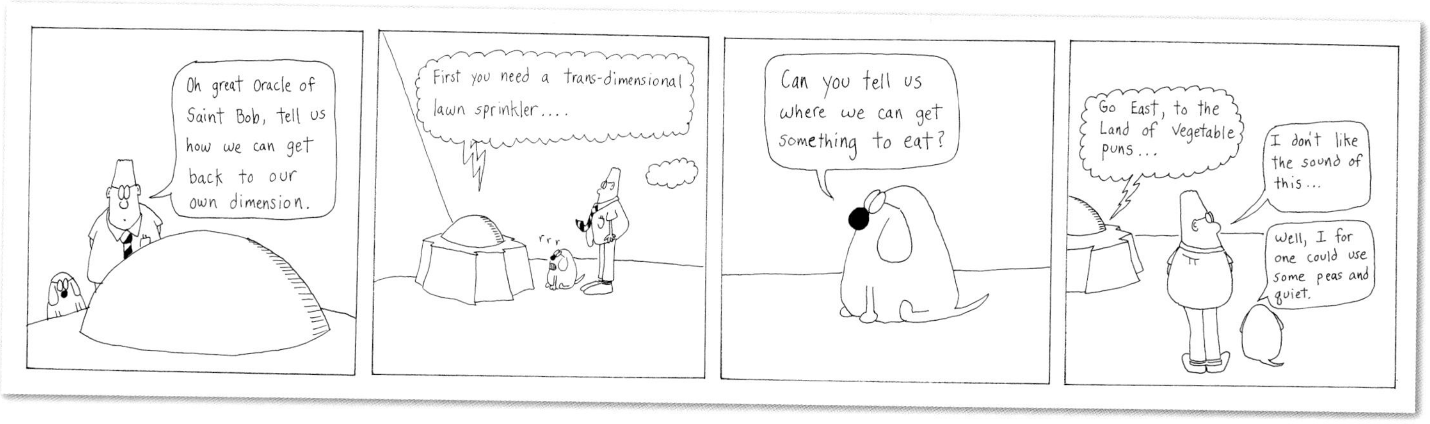
Oh great Oracle of Saint Bob, tell us how we can get back to our own dimension.
First you need a trans-dimensional lawn sprinkler....
rrr
Can you tell us where we can get something to eat?
Go East, to the Land of Vegetable puns...
I don't like the sound of this...
Well, I for one could use some peas and quiet.

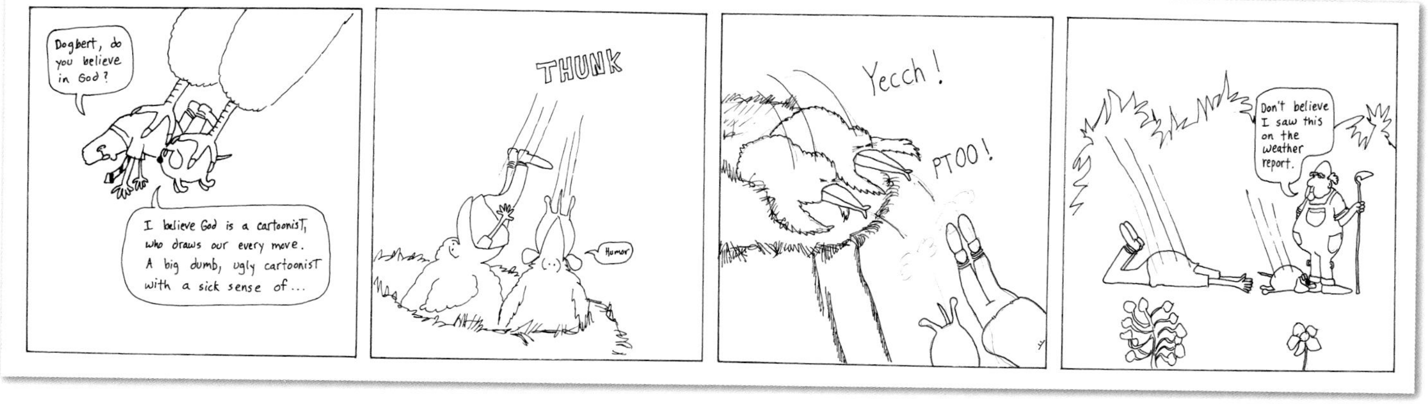
Dogbert, do you believe in God?
I believe God is a cartoonist, who draws our every move. A big dumb, ugly cartoonist with a sick sense of...
THUNK
Humor
Yecch!
PTOO!
Don't believe I saw this on the weather report.

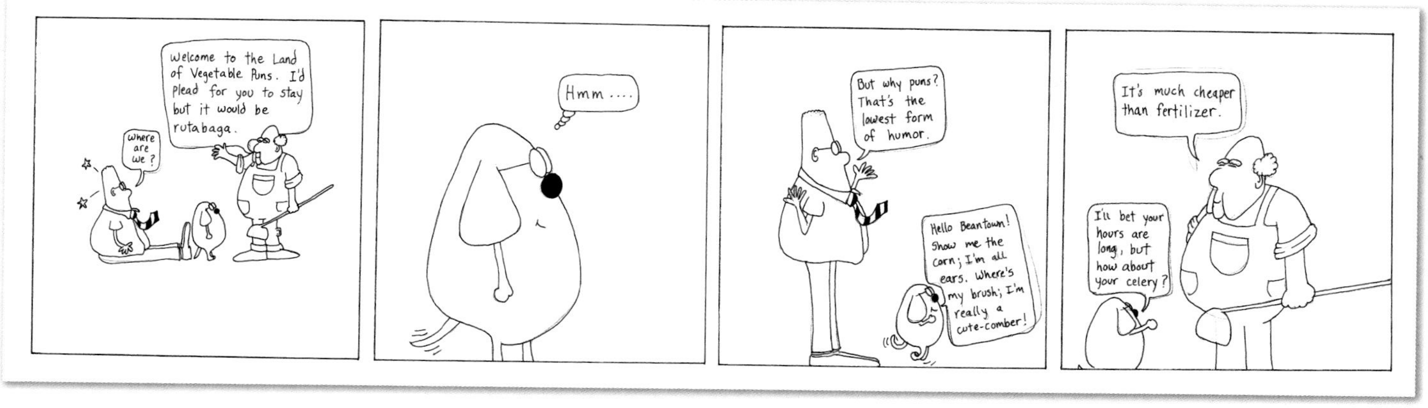
Welcome to the Land of Vegetable Puns. I'd Plead for you to stay but it would be rutabaga.
Where are we?
Hmm....
But why puns? That's the lowest form of humor.
Hello Beantown! Show me the corn; I'm all ears. Where's my brush; I'm really a cute-comber!
It's much cheaper than fertilizer.
I'll bet your hours are long, but how about your celery?

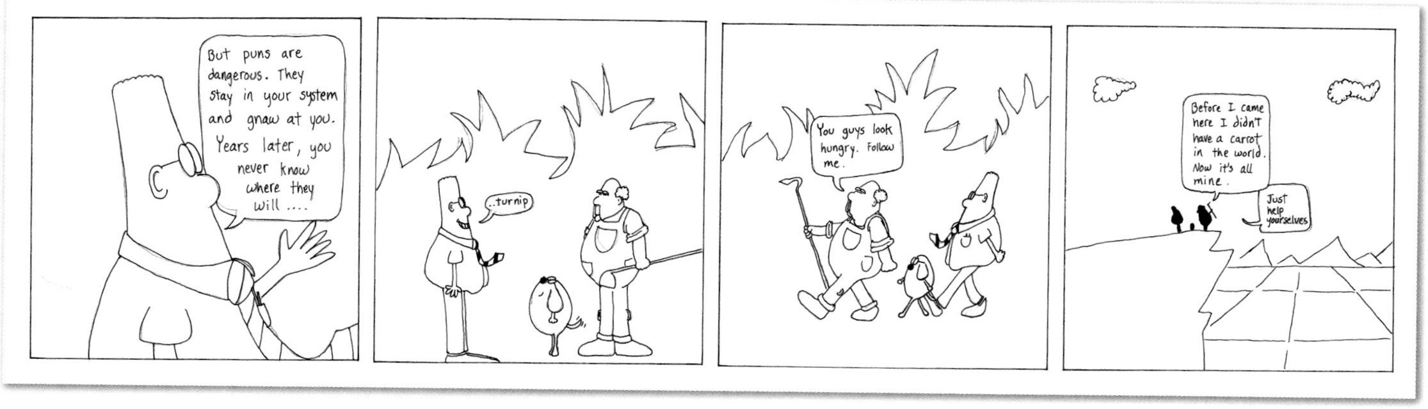
But puns are dangerous. They stay in your system and gnaw at you. Years later, you never know where they will....
..turnip
You guys look hungry. Follow me.
Before I came here I didn't have a carrot in the world. Now it's all mine.
Just help yourselves

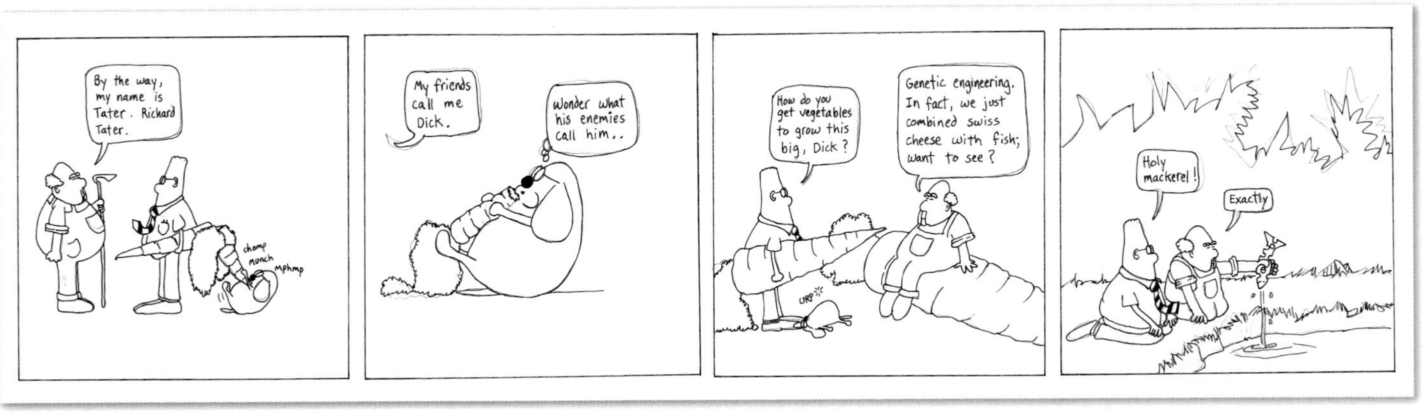

By the way, my name is Tater. Richard Tater.
chomp munch mphmp
My friends call me Dick.
Wonder what his enemies call him..
How do you get vegetables to grow this big, Dick?
Genetic engineering. In fact, we just combined swiss cheese with fish; want to see?
Holy mackerel!
Exactly

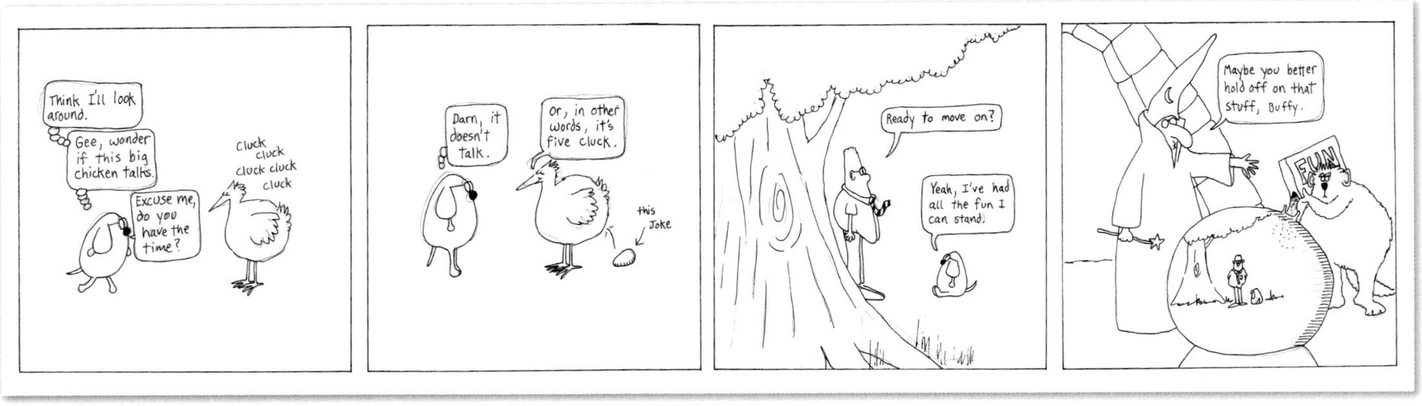

Think I'll look around.
Gee, wonder if this big chicken talks.
Excuse me, do you have the time?
cluck cluck cluck cluck cluck
Darn, it doesn't talk.
Or, in other words, it's five cluck.
this joke
Ready to move on?
Yeah, I've had all the fun I can stand.
Maybe you better hold off on that stuff, Buffy.
FUN

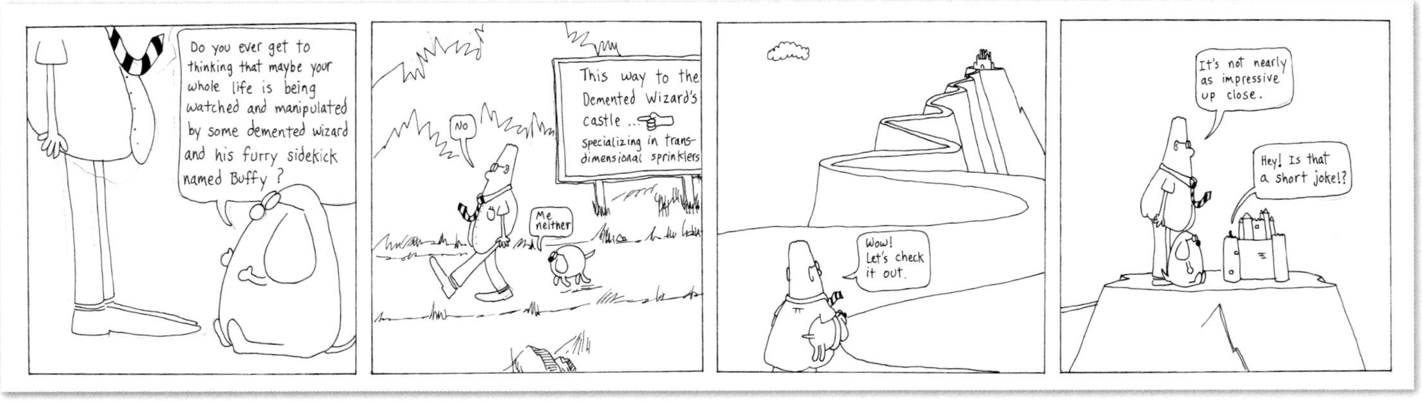

Do you ever get to thinking that maybe your whole life is being watched and manipulated by some demented wizard and his furry sidekick named Buffy?
No
This way to the Demented Wizard's castle ... specializing in trans-dimensional sprinklers
Me neither
Wow! Let's check it out.
It's not nearly as impressive up close.
Hey! Is that a short joke!?

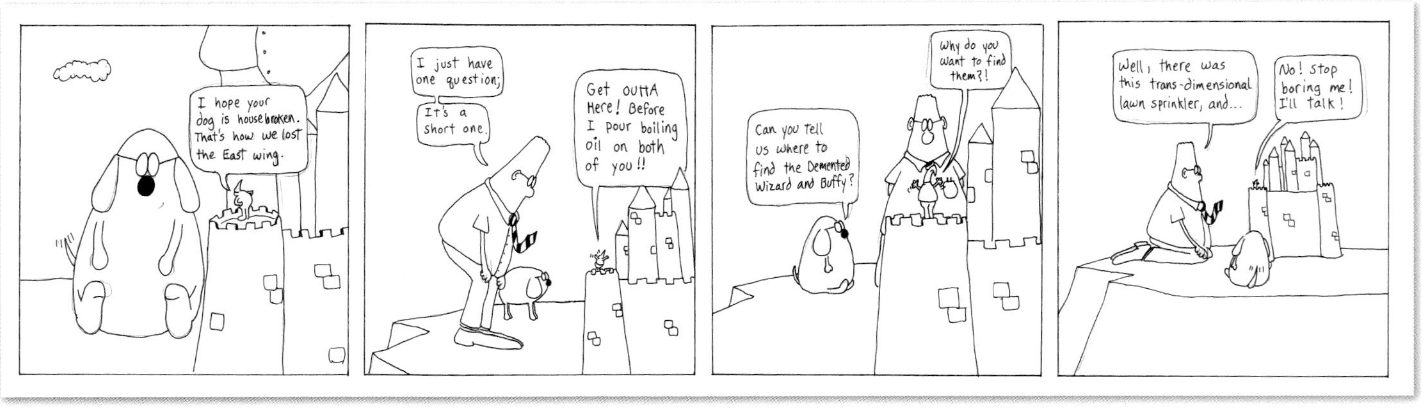

I hope your dog is housebroken. That's how we lost the East wing.
I just have one question;
It's a short one.
Get OUTTA Here! Before I pour boiling oil on both of you!!
Can you tell us where to find the Demented Wizard and Buffy?
Why do you want to find them?!
Well, there was this trans-dimensional lawn sprinkler, and...
No! Stop boring me! I'll talk!

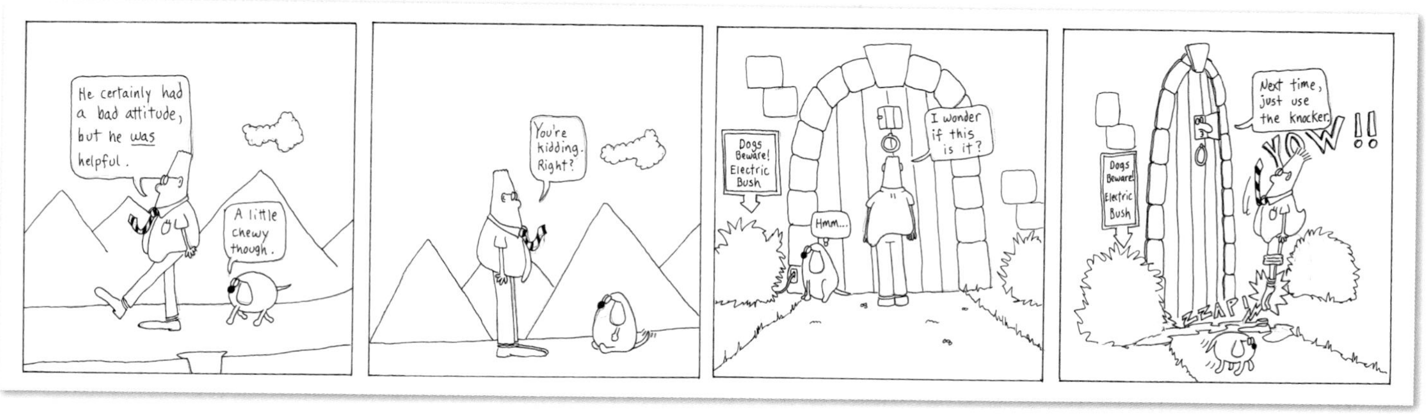
He certainly had a bad attitude, but he was helpful.
A little chewy though.
You're kidding. Right?
Dogs Beware! Electric Bush
I wonder if this is it?
Hmm...
Dogs Beware! Electric Bush
Next time, just use the knocker.
YOW!!
ZZAP

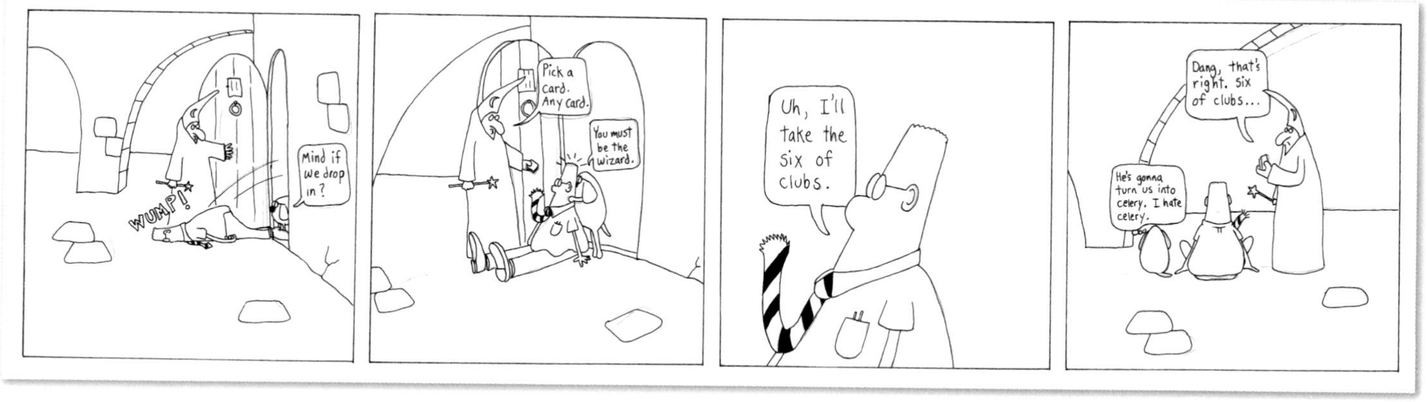
WUMP!
Mind if we drop in?
Pick a card. Any card.
You must be the wizard.
Uh, I'll take the six of clubs.
Dang, that's right. Six of clubs...
He's gonna turn us into celery. I hate celery.

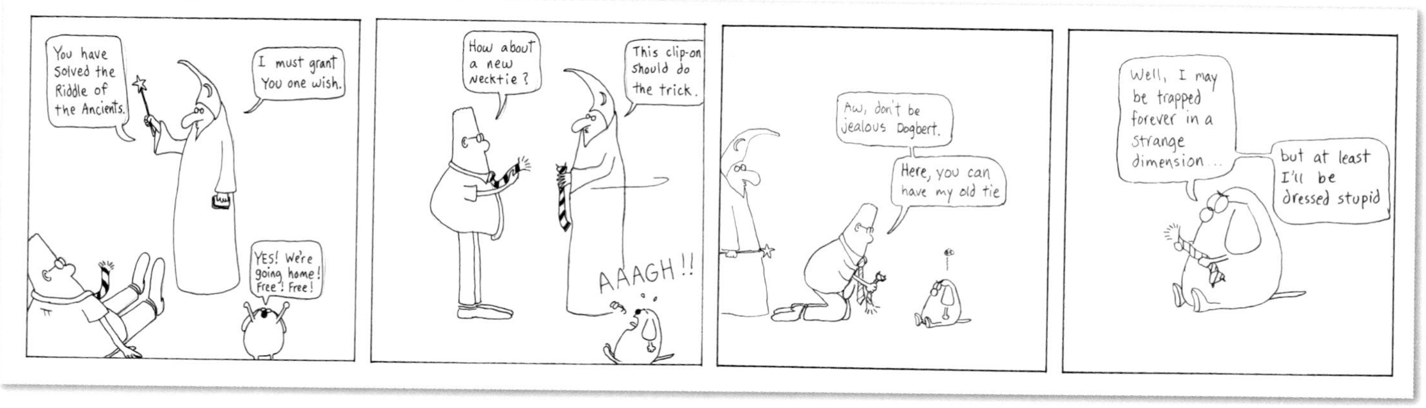
You have solved the Riddle of the Ancients.
I must grant you one wish.
YES! We're going home! Free! Free!
How about a new necktie?
This clip-on should do the trick.
AAAGH!!
Aw, don't be jealous Dogbert.
Here, you can have my old tie
Well, I may be trapped forever in a strange dimension...
but at least I'll be dressed stupid

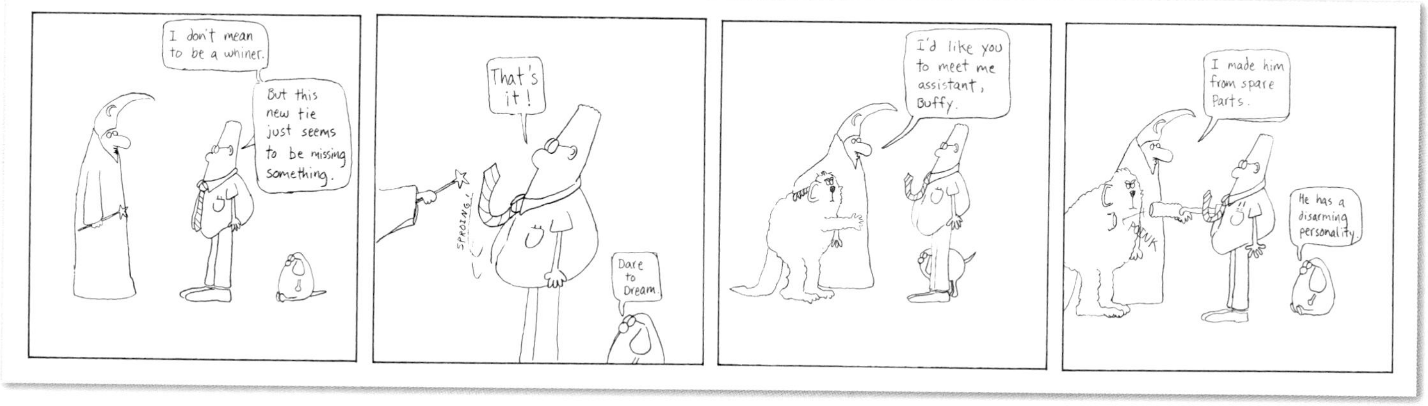
I don't mean to be a whiner.
But this new tie just seems to be missing something.
That's it!
SPROING!
Dare to Dream
I'd like you to meet me assistant, Buffy.
I made him from spare parts.
He has a disarming personality.

1988—Submitting to Syndicates

I liked these two characters, Dilbert and Dogbert. Inspired by Jack Cassady's letter of encouragement, I decided to set my sights high and submit my comics for syndication in newspapers. It didn't cost much to try, except some paper and ink and postage. I put together about fifty comics based on Dilbert and Dogbert, and sent them by mail to the addresses in the *1986 Artist's Market* book. Below is a portion of my original *Dilbert* submission package.

DILBERT

BY SCOTT ADAMS

COPYRIGHT (C) 1988, SCOTT ADAMS

ABOUT THE COMIC STRIP

NAME OF STRIP:

Dilbert

SYNOPSIS:

Dilbert is an engineer. He is about thirty, and works at an undisclosed high-tech company in Northern California. He lives with his dog, Dogbert, who bears a striking resemblance to Dilbert (including glasses and the ability to speak).

Dilbert is very intelligent and kind-hearted, which makes him particularly ill-suited for life on this planet.

Dogbert is also intelligent, but with a cynical edge. In contrast to his master, Dogbert has such a simple, yet keen understanding of human nature that his perceptions seem ridiculous to Dilbert.

MARKET RESEARCH:

The enclosed sample cartoons have been reviewed with dozens of people, many of whom are not personally known by the artist. Most of the interviewees were baby boomers, with a few more women than men.

Without exception, the response has been positive. All people interviewed thought that Dilbert was of syndication quality.

Interestingly, there was a tremendous diversity of feeling about specific cartoons. Each cartoon made at least one person's "best" list, but was equally likely to be in another person's "I don't get it" list.

The "Devil series", for example, evoked especially strong feelings, in opposite directions.

Based on interview responses, only two strips were discarded from the original fifty drawings because they did not get a good enough response. (And one of them was on several people's "best" list).

The only noticeable common denominator of people's reactions was that the strips which include Dogbert are more likely to be appreciated.

Scott R. Adams

OBJECTIVE

Syndicated cartoonist for daily newspapers.

PUBLICATIONS

Dilbert cartoon character first appeared in the This World section of the Sunday San Francisco Examiner, 9/27/87, as a surprise winner of the Pooch/owner Look-alike Contest.

Princeton Club of Northern California Newsletter, November 1987 and December 1987.

Crocker Bank Directions newsletter, September 1985, and June 1985.

EXPERIENCE

6/79 - 4/86, Crocker National Bank

Worked in a variety of positions, including: Branch Operations, Commercial Lending, Product Management, Computer Programming, Budgeting, Finance, Contracts, and New Technology Acquisitions. Made no loans to South America.

5/86 - Present, Pacific Bell

Engineer and financial guy for the Research and Development wing of the company. Act as interpreter for the engineers, so management can understand them.

EDUCATION

BA in Economics, Hartwick College, Oneonta New York, 1979.

MBA with emphasis in Finance, University of California, Berkeley, 1986. Evening program.

At last. My gravity neutralizer is complete. I will be the envy of the entire engineering department!
Raise your paw if you could see that coming.
No! I told you -- dogs can't drink coffee. It's too much for your little system.
Last time you drank coffee I was picking fur out of the ceiling for a week.
Okay, okay. Just some decaf.
With luck, this will trigger a flashback.
What the heck is "JEQUIRITY"?
You know - the poisonous, red and black seed of the Indian licorice plant. Want to challenge?
No. At least this one has vowels.
That's 7,045 for me and 65 for you.
To his horror, Dilbert discovers that his white socks all have holes. "My goodness!" he cries, "I shall be forced to wear black socks to work!"
"If only my pants reached the top of my shoes, then the other engineers might not notice.", Dilbert despaired.
What are you writing?
It's a Geek tragedy

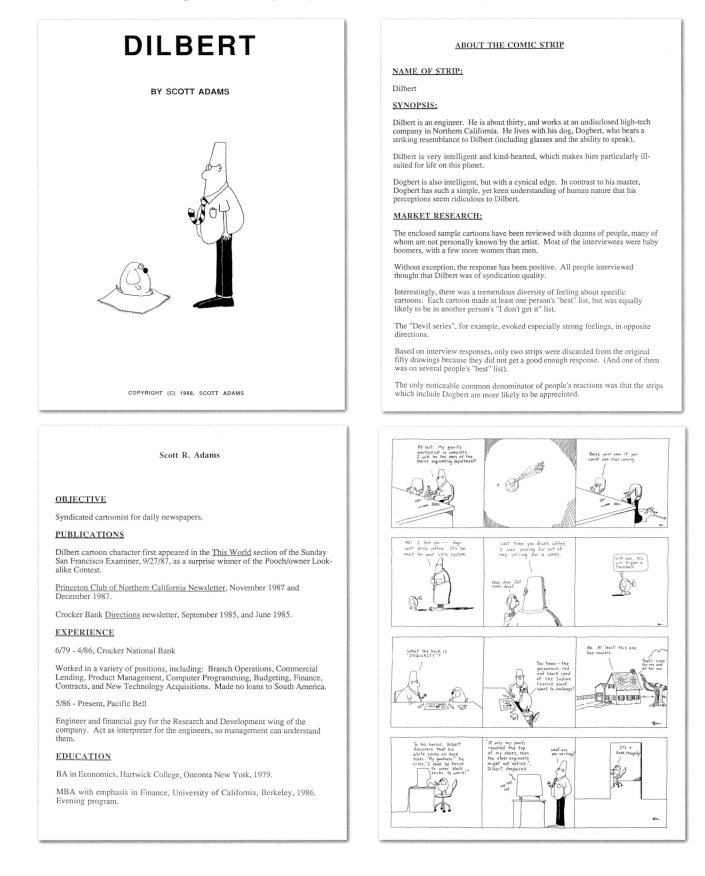

So, Dilbert, I understand this is the prototype you have been working on for the last six months.
Yes sir.
This little baby can convert worthless pocket lint into a valuable parsley substitute!
Well, this looks absolutely brilliant, and completely unmarketable.
Thank you, sir. I'm technology driven.
Did you ever get to thinking that maybe you are just an android, placed on Earth by an advanced civilization of huge radish-like aliens who are studying your every move?
No
Me neither.
Welcome to Electrode Hut. I'm half your age and I know more about electronics than you ever will. May I help you?
Yes. I would like a half dozen niad pulse converters and an anza brush.
(I'm bluffing)
This guy is good.
Back to mowing lawns junior.
Please read these brochures carefully. It could save your life.
What the heck is "Electronics Anonymous"?
Let's take the enclosed quiz. Number one. How many functions do you have on your toaster?
Does that include the toaster disk drive and printer?
I think we can move directly to the "Emergency Application Form."

rrrrr
POW!
Regrettably, you violated my airspace.
You're kidding
It's true. Nature compensates for weaknesses. That's why blind people have good hearing.
I guess that also explains why dumb people have big mouths.
Hmm... This looks interesting.
Popular Inventor
"Build your own Star Wars missile defense system from common household appliances. Send $25 for complete plans."
Sounds great... Uh, here's the catch, "Guaranteed to be as effective as the real thing."
Lew's Drugs
And what can I get for you little fellow?
I want it all! Ha Ha Ha! Give me mouthwash, Gum, deodorant, lipstick, krazy Glue. Yes, Yes, and some Rolaids, and
I panicked.

I'm looking for a fine wool suit, in the $700 range. Something fashionable yet timeless.
Try this. It's a $35 polyester beauty. You can use it for dining out or swimming. It's half your size.
Gee, and bell bottoms too!
Sure, there's risk in being a fashion pioneer, but I guess I was just born for the spotlight.
$35
FONG'S
NO Pets!
Remember to act human.
OPEN
Egg rolls, hot and sour soup, curry chicken, and steamed rice.
And a cat
That's "catsup", my friend would like some catsup.
No Pets!
Maybe something Siamese...
Hey! Dilbert! Look at this. I discovered a hat that makes you talk funny. Try it!
okay, okay
Now say something.
Ah feel like the North end of a Southbound prairie dawg.
See? Gibberish.
Whoa! Looks like we got a Pippin Hawk, a Prickly Beak Mountain Swallow, and a Yellow-Tail quail.
There's that robin again
How is it that you have spotted 1,700 exotic birds this morning and all I have seen is one robin?
Look! A Monkey-faced Disco Hawk!!
Where?!
Ah-hah! Just as I suspected.
Here it is! Mathematical proof that attractive single women exist only in aerobics classes and in white Volkswagon Rabbits!
How do you explain Vanna White!
I wonder if Isaac Newton had a dog.
Or a girlfriend.

I've decided that I need to make some dog friends. But I don't even know what regular dogs do when they get together.
Well, I suppose they would bark like idiots, run around in circles, then sniff each others' butts.
You're kidding, right?
Did I mention chewing on old bones?
Do you think I look more like Rin Tin Tin or Lassie? Maybe Benji?
I dunno. Maybe a big furry egg.
Thank you for that little inspirational boost.
You're in luck, Dogbert. We're going skiing!
But I hate snow.
C'mon! Stop being a gloomy Gus. You're gonna love it. It's great exercise and the view is spectacular!
Spectacular view.
If you move around you won't turn into a furry chunk of ice.
There. It's perfect.
What's that you've been working on?
It's a stick-on Velcro shirt pocket. You can attach it to your chest hairs while swimming or showering!
Hmm... This just might work.
'Course you may also be interested in my new Velcro chest hair.
And, like snowflakes, no two are exactly alike.
I saw two snowflakes that were exactly alike.
Uh... that's not the point.
I didn't bring it up.

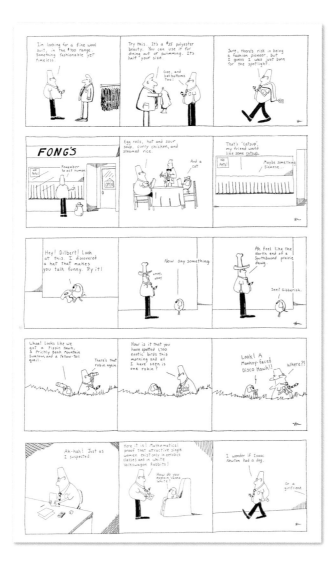

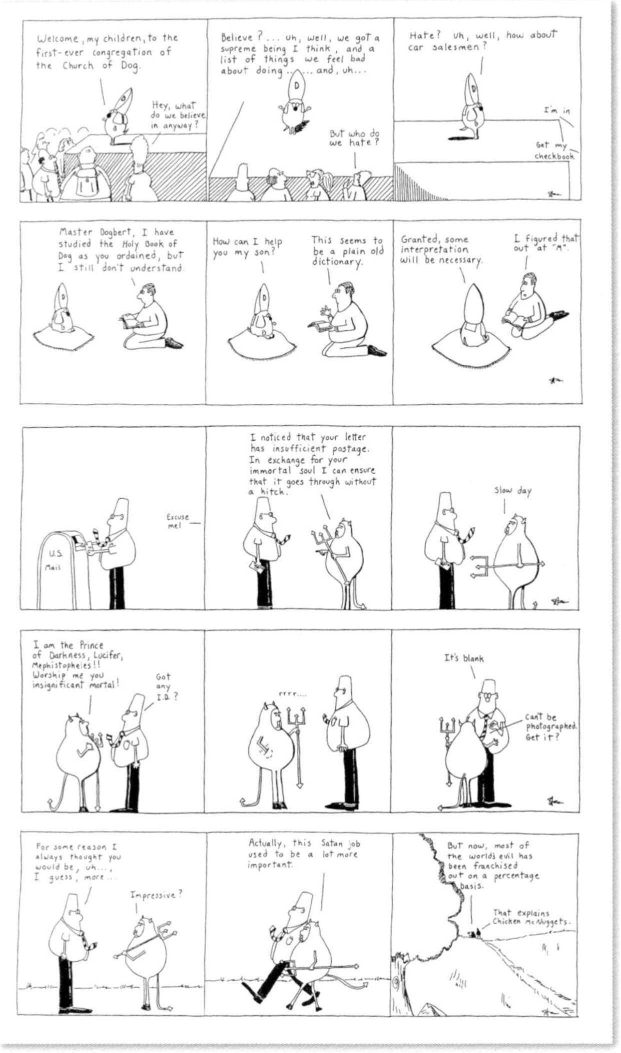
Welcome, my children, to the first-ever congregation of the Church of Dog.
Hey, what do we believe in anyway?
Believe?... uh, well, we got a supreme being I think, and a list of things we feel bad about doing... ...and, uh...
But who do we hate?
Hate? uh, well, how about car salesmen?
I'm in
Get my checkbook
Master Dogbert, I have studied the Holy Book of Dog as you ordained, but I still don't understand.
How can I help you my son?
This seems to be a plain old dictionary.
Granted, some interpretation will be necessary.
I figured that out at "M".
Excuse me!
I noticed that your letter has insufficient postage. In exchange for your immortal soul I can ensure that it goes through without a hitch.
Slow day
I am the Prince of Darkness, Lucifer, Mephistopheles!! Worship me you insignificant mortal!
Got any I.D.?
rrrr....
It's blank
Can't be photographed. Get it?
For some reason I always thought you would be, uh..., I guess, more...
Impressive?
Actually, this Satan job used to be a lot more important.
But now, most of the world's evil has been franchised out on a percentage basis.
That explains Chicken McNuggets.

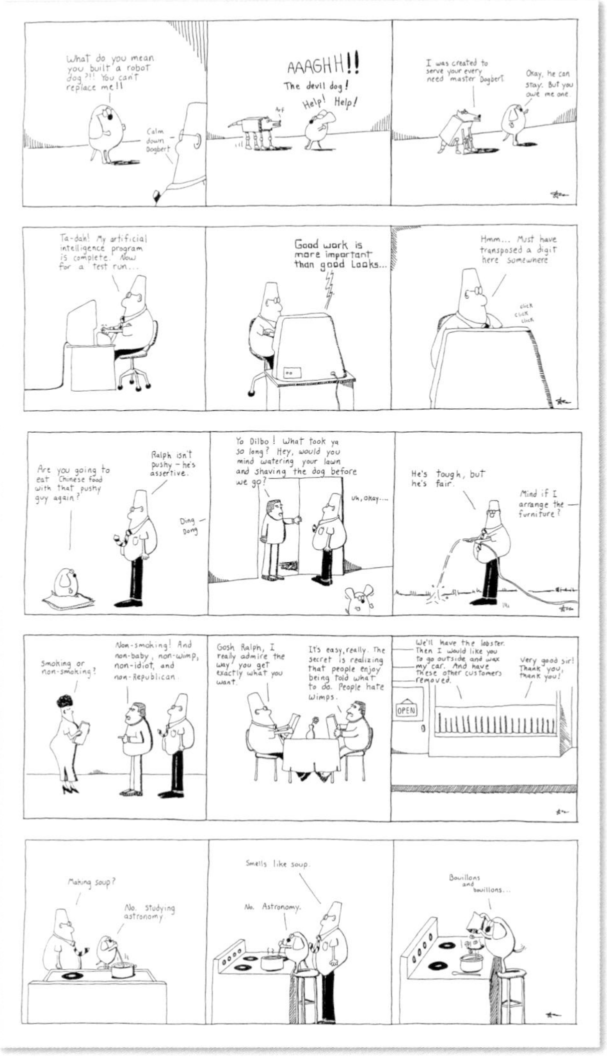
What do you mean you built a robot dog?!! You can't replace me!!
Calm down Dogbert
Arf
AAAGHH!!
The devil dog!
Help! Help!
I was created to serve your every need master Dogbert.
Okay, he can stay. But you owe me one.
Ta-dah! My artificial intelligence program is complete. Now for a test run...
Good work is more important than good Looks...
Hmm... Must have transposed a digit here somewhere
click click click
Are you going to eat Chinese food with that pushy guy again?
Ralph isn't pushy – he's assertive.
Ding Dong
Yo Dilbo! What took ya so long? Hey, would you mind watering your lawn and shaving the dog before we go?
Uh, okay....
He's tough, but he's fair.
Mind if I arrange the furniture?
Smoking or non-smoking?
Non-smoking! And non-baby, non-wimp, non-idiot, and non-Republican.
Gosh Ralph, I really admire the way you get exactly what you want.
It's easy, really. The secret is realizing that people enjoy being told what to do. People hate wimps.
We'll have the lobster. Then I would like you to go outside and wax my car. And have these other customers removed.
OPEN
Very good sir! Thank you, thank you!
Making soup?
No. Studying astronomy.
Smells like soup.
No. Astronomy.
Bouillons and bouillons...

Then the rejections started trickling in. I have included a couple, so you get the general idea.

UNIVERSAL PRESS SYNDICATE

4900 Main Street • Kansas City, Missouri 64112 • 816/932-6600

Dear Contributor:

I regret that it is necessary for us to respond to your submission with an impersonal letter. However, the volume of materials being submitted exceeds our ability to write personal responses quickly.

I want to assure you that we have reviewed your feature submission carefully. This rejection does not necessarily reflect on the editorial value of your work, but may be motivated by matters of scheduling and marketing.

Thank you for allowing Universal Press Syndicate to review your work. Again my apologies for the necessity of responding in this impersonal manner.

Best regards.

Sincerely,

Jake Morrissey
Associate Editor

JM:bt

u|p|s

Time & Life Building • Suite 3717 • 1271 Avenue of the Americas
New York, N.Y. 10020 • 212/582-0650

CABLE ADDRESS KINGSYN NEW YORK
AREA CODE 212 – 682-5600

King Features

235 EAST 45TH STREET, NEW YORK, N.Y. 10017

JAY KENNEDY
DEPUTY COMICS EDITOR

July 6, 1988

Mr. Scott Adams
[redacted]
San Francisco, CA 94118

Dear Mr. Adams:

I apologize for the lengthy delay in responding to your submission. "Dilbert" arrived at about the same time as I began work at King Features. I liked "Dilbert" enough that I placed it in a small stack of submissions that I wanted to reply to personally. Unfortunately, it has taken me this long to settle into my job enough to have the time to respond to the better submissions we receive.

We are not going to syndicate "Dilbert," but I did want to write to encourage you in your career as a cartoonist. I am most impressed by the writing and sense of humor in "Dilbert." The art needs to be developed to an equal level. Your lettering should be larger and try using all capital letters. The characters are well designed, but the finished art needs to be more polished.

Look at existing cartoon work that you like and experiment with different techniques and materials. Just drawing cartoons frequently is the best way to improve.

Again, sorry for the delay in getting back to you and please continue with your cartooning.

Sincerely,

Jay Kennedy

JK:pr

Enclosure

After a few months, when I thought all the rejections had come in, I gathered up my art supplies and put them back in the closet. I had given it my best shot. I felt okay with my effort. It was time to move on.

One day, the phone rang. A woman identified herself as Sarah Gillespie, an editor for a company I had never heard of called United Media. At that point I didn't know United Media was the parent company of United Feature Syndicate, Inc., to whom I had sent my submission, and I assumed had thrown it in the trash. Sarah said she liked *Dilbert*, and wanted to offer me a development contract.

Having never heard of this United Media outfit, I was flattered but a bit wary. I didn't know how this company even got a copy of my comics. I decided to play my cards close to the vest. I told Sarah I was interested in discussing the offer, but I would feel better if she had some references. I asked if there were any comics her company had ever successfully syndicated. I made it clear I wasn't going to take a chance on some start-up.

There was a long pause.

Sarah replied, "Um, yes. We handle *Peanuts*. And *Garfield*. And *Marmaduke*, and . . ."

It was at that moment I realized my negotiating position had been compromised. After scraping myself off the ceiling, I said yes. And so began my twenty-year association with United Media.

It was time to thank Jack Cassady.

April 12, 1988

Dear Jack:

In early 1986 I wrote to you after watching your Funny Business special. I asked a bunch of questions about how to submit cartoons for publication. Some of my cartoons were included with the letter.

You were kind enough to write back, with about three pages of encouragement and helpful information. I was very grateful for your generous reply, and used your suggestions to put together some cartoon submissions.

Unfortunately, as you predicted, the "RJs" came and I got discouraged. I stopped cartooning. About a year later, out of the blue, you wrote again to tell me not to be discouraged by the RJs, and that you thought my work was good. You said you came across my original letter in your files and it prompted you to write.

I needed that second letter from you. You must have ESP. My artistic ego was at bottom. Your letter got me started again; this time with a new determination.

I put together a bunch of three-panel strips and sent them to eight of the big syndicates. I decided to go for the whole enchilada: a daily strip in newspapers.

One company, the LA Times Syndicate, called me. My ego reinflated. The cartoon editor said he liked my work, but maybe I should take art classes and learn to draw. Or maybe I should work with somebody who already knows how to draw. Goodbye ego.

Then, amazingly, I got a call from United Media (i.e. Garfield, Peanuts, etc.), and they said they liked my work. I started to apologize for my poor drawing skills and mentioned that I already knew I needed to learn to draw. But they liked my drawing. And my writing.

They mailed me a development contract, with two five year extensions if it works out. I was numb. I still can't believe it. My attorney is working the contract over now.

I don't know how the syndication thing will go; obviously, it's still a long shot. But I don't believe the odds anymore. Somehow, I'm going to make it work. It feels right.

The reason I'm writing this letter is to express my deepest thanks to you, for taking the time, for caring, and for knowing exactly what I needed and when. It was the difference.

You know, in this world it's hard enough to get help from your friends when you need it. It's really a special thing to get help from somebody who doesn't even know you, and won't be there to see the expression on your face. Yours was the kind of gift that makes me think that maybe the world is a pretty good place after all.

I hope this letter finds you with all the health, happiness, and good fortune that I know you deserve. Again, my sincerest appreciation and thanks.

Warmest Regards,

Scott Adams

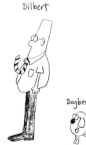

Dilbert

Dogbert

Coming Soon To A Newspaper Near You!

(with any luck)

1988 — Developing *Dilbert*

A syndication development contract is a six-month agreement where a cartoonist works with a syndication company editor to refine the strip and make it newspaper-worthy. There was no guarantee *Dilbert* would ever be offered to newspapers if the development phase didn't work out. But within a few months of the contract getting signed, United Media liked what they saw, and decided to launch *Dilbert* in April of 1989.

The launch was modestly successful, and *Dilbert* was picked up by a few dozen small newspapers. Most papers probably didn't run the strip in the beginning, preferring to hold the rights and watch what other papers did first.

After a year of hard work as a cartoonist, my efforts were about to be rewarded. My first monthly royalty check from United Media: $368.62.

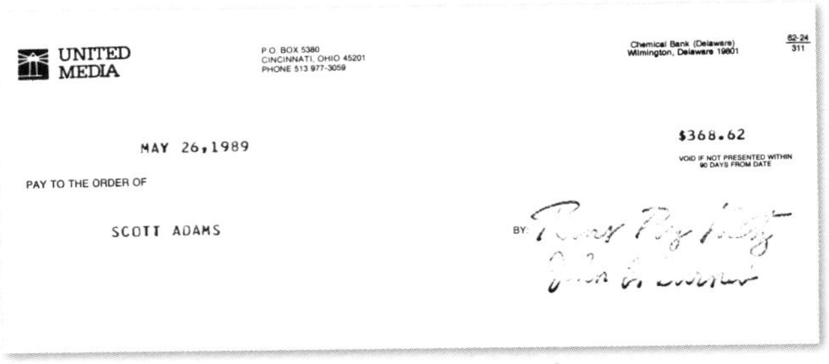
UNITED MEDIA
P.O. BOX 5380
CINCINNATI, OHIO 45201
PHONE 513 977-3059
Chemical Bank (Delaware)
Wilmington, Delaware 19801
62-24
311
MAY 26,1989
$368.62
VOID IF NOT PRESENTED WITHIN 90 DAYS FROM DATE
PAY TO THE ORDER OF
SCOTT ADAMS
BY:

It soon became clear that I wasn't going to be quitting my day job anytime soon. The royalties grew each month, but *Dilbert* was not setting the world on fire; it didn't even run in my local papers. Cartooning was a lonely job. I drew pictures all alone, mailed them away, and rarely heard any feedback from anyone who read them. The strip grew slowly, with what seemed like two cancellations for every three sales. Some readers hated it. Some loved it. Few people were neutral.

By 1990 *Dilbert* was in fifty newspapers. By 1991 it hit a milestone of one hundred papers. That's often considered the point where a comic strip has a chance of lasting. But it was a tenuous grip. By 1992 it was in one hundred and fifty newspapers, and growth was slowing. The sales people naturally moved their attention to the newer comics in their stable.

The biggest comic strips of the day were in over two thousand newspapers. It seemed that *Dilbert* had hit its peak potential, and while I had a nice side job, it seemed I would never be able to quit my day job. Still, I tried my affirmations, focusing on the seemingly unrealistic goal of making *Dilbert* one of the top comic strips in the world.

The Internet and e-mail were still in the toddler phase. But because of my day job I was surrounded by the vendors and engineers who were bringing those technologies to the market. One day, my business training kicked in and I noticed an opportunity that no syndicated cartoonist had yet explored.

The problem with cartooning in those years was that you normally got no direct feedback from readers. Your friends and your family aren't a reliable gauge for how well you are doing. They lie. I was navigating without reference points. And I noticed that every successful business had solved this customer feedback problem in one way or another. I realized e-mail could be the solution for me.

I started including my AOL e-mail address in the strip every day. The response was huge. I started getting thousands of messages daily, and readers were all too happy to give their opinions. A clear pattern emerged: readers wanted more of Dilbert in the office.

Up to that point, *Dilbert* wasn't a workplace strip. Dilbert was usually shown at his home or about town. But as someone smarter than me once said, "Your customers tell you what business you are in." I changed the strip to more of a workplace theme, and it took off. I credit my business training for providing me the discipline to give readers what they wanted. For an artist (of sorts), that is deceptively difficult to do.

At about the same time, my editor suspected there might be more *Dilbert* lovers than the newspaper editors who were rejecting the strip believed. She suggested I write a book of *Dilbert*-themed comics. If it sold well, it would be a powerful message to newspapers that hadn't yet picked up the strip. I agreed to give it a try.

Now I had three full-time jobs: my day job, the comic strip, and writing a book. I call that period my "running years." If I was moving from one room in my home to another, I literally ran. When I went to the mailbox, I ran. I didn't have time for walking. I was on a mission.

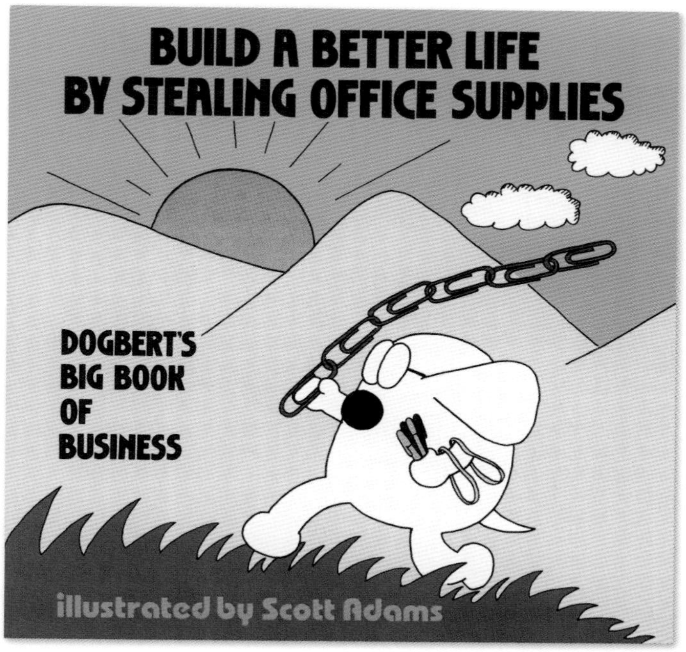
BUILD A BETTER LIFE
BY STEALING OFFICE SUPPLIES
DOGBERT'S
BIG BOOK
OF
BUSINESS
illustrated by Scott Adams

In 1994, my first book of cartoons, *Build a Better Life by Stealing Office Supplies*, hit the bookstores. It was a small but solid success. And it confirmed the market for workplace humor. It was also a great sales tool for selling into newspapers.

By the end of 1994, *Dilbert* was in four hundred newspapers.

1995—Dot-com Era

At about 1995, the dot-com era began, and all hell broke loose. Dilbert was the right character at the right time. Technology workers embraced Dilbert as one of their own. The media embraced *Dilbert* as a symbol of the downsizing era, which overlapped with the first part of the dot-com build-up. *Dilbert* became shorthand for bad management, oppressed cubicle workers, and high-tech life. Readers imbued *Dilbert* with their own meaning, beyond anything I intended for it.

I was an early user of the Internet because of my day job, which involved showing customers how Pacific Bell's high-speed data services could help them. The demonstrations took a familiar pattern. First we would demonstrate some useful business features involving control of the telephone, and the customers would yawn. At the end, we showed them something totally useless, known at the time as the World Wide Web.

In 1993, there were only a handful of Web sites you could access, such as the Smithsonian's exhibit of gems. Those pages were slow to load and crashed as often as they worked. But something interesting happened every time we demonstrated this technology. The customers would get out of their chairs, their eyes like saucers, and they would approach the keyboard. They had to touch it themselves. There was something about the Internet that was like catnip. At the end of every meeting, the only thing our customers wanted to know was how they could get access to this magic land of Web pages that had no practical use whatsoever.

That experience clued me in early that the Internet was the future. United Media was reaching the same conclusion at about the same time. Once again, by luck, I found myself in the right place at the right time. In 1995, *Dilbert* became the first syndicated comic strip to be offered for free on the Internet. The response was huge. From that point on, when a sales person from United Media went into a meeting with a newspaper editor, the editor often said, "My readers keep asking for this one. They saw it online." Sales started to come easy.

At about the same time, Bill Watterson decided to retire from creating *Calvin and Hobbes*. That left a huge number of newspapers with openings, just when *Dilbert* was considered the hot new comic. By the end of 1995, *Dilbert* was in eight hundred newspapers, and I left my day job at Pacific Bell.

People often ask if I quit or was fired. It was a little of both. In the final few years of my day job, *Dilbert* had turned me into a minor celebrity among technology workers. My co-workers found my fame useful in attracting customers to the lab to see Pacific Bell's latest offerings. By then, *Dilbert* was consuming too much of my time for me to be effective in my day job. It was clear I would soon need to quit or be fired. That's when my co-worker Anita Freeman, who was the prototype for the Alice character, suggested a deal. With our boss's consent, she and my other co-workers in the lab offered to pick up my slack any time I needed to leave work for *Dilbert* reasons. In return, I agreed to schmooze customers who were *Dilbert* fans. As part of that understanding, I told my boss that any time the arrangement didn't work for him, and he needed the budget for a better purpose, I would be happy to leave. Eventually he took me up on the offer.

That year, the *Wall Street Journal* asked me to write a guest editorial. Someone at the *Journal* was apparently a *Dilbert* fan. So I wrote a piece introducing what I called the Dilbert Principle, in which I explained in witty prose how the most incompetent workers are often promoted to management.

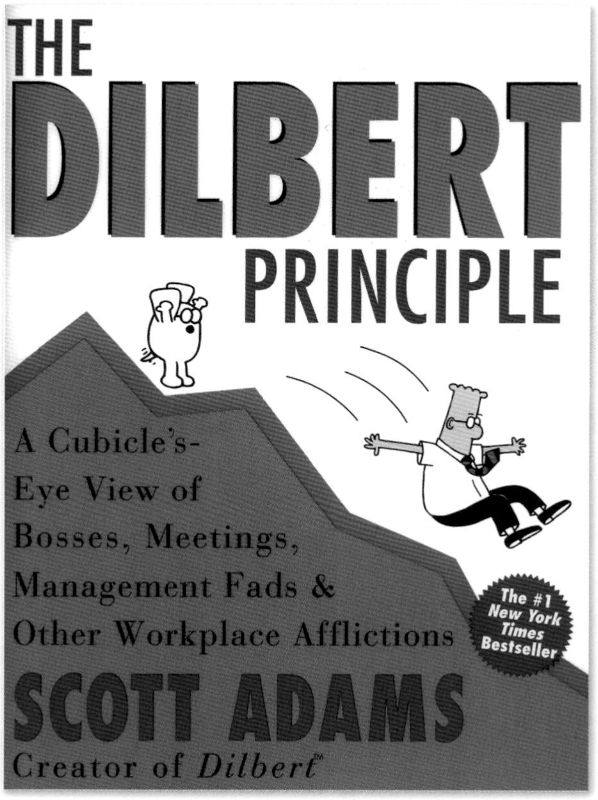
THE
DILBERT
PRINCIPLE
A Cubicle's-Eye View of Bosses, Meetings, Management Fads & Other Workplace Afflictions
The #1 New York Times Bestseller
SCOTT ADAMS
Creator of Dilbert

An editor at HarperCollins noticed my editorial in the *Wall Street Journal* and asked if I could expand it into a book. By then, hundreds of *Dilbert* readers had asked me to write a business book, and even suggested the form. They wanted a book that included both *Dilbert* comics on business themes and some extra witty text on those topics. I pitched that idea, and my publisher liked it.

In 1996, my first "real" book, *The Dilbert Principle*, came out. It became a #1 *New York Times* best-seller, and stayed there for eleven weeks.

Based on that success, I quickly followed it with *Dogbert's Top Secret Management Handbook*. It joined *The Dilbert Principle* at the top of the best-seller list, ranking #1 and #2 for a brief period. (My affirmation at the time was to become a #1 best-selling author.)

By then, *Dilbert* was in over one thousand papers and growing. It was approaching icon status. The phrase "getting Dilberted" entered the language, along with "pointy-haired boss," and Elbonians. My life was a tornado of TV, radio, and print interviews. I thought I knew what media attention felt like when the comic strip was rising in popularity, but nothing prepared me for having a #1 best-selling book. It was insane.

As *Dilbert*'s popularity soared, no one seemed to mind so much that my artwork looked as if it had been drawn by an inebriated monkey. In 1997 I won both the National Cartoonists Society's Reuben Award for Outstanding Cartoonist of the Year, and Best Newspaper Comic Strip of 1997. For cartoonists, these awards are the equivalent of getting the Oscars for best actor and best picture.

My life during that period was moving at a scorching pace. I was lucky to get four hours of sleep a night, and always worked weekends, evenings, and holidays. I was also doing regular speaking engagements for corporate events, writing more books, and starting both a vegetarian food company and a local restaurant with partners.

In 1998 I started working on what would become the *Dilbert* TV show that ran on UPN during 1999 and 2000. We had a tiny operating budget, so I found myself doing more of the writing than I had expected. The show started out well, but in the second season the network made a strategic decision to focus on shows with African-American actors. *Dilbert* lost its time slot, and cancellation followed.

The dot-com era was well underway by then. This was the hardest time to write *Dilbert* comics. There were so many people getting rich with Internet businesses, optimism was the dominant feeling among workers. If you weren't getting rich, you figured it must be your own fault, because apparently anyone could start a company and become a billionaire. I couldn't find anyone to complain about work, least of all the technology workers who were in high demand. Still, *Dilbert* grew. By 2000, *Dilbert* was in two thousand newspapers, in fifty-seven countries, and nineteen languages. There were over ten million books and calendars in print. Then the dot-com bubble burst.

In the past several years, which might someday be remembered as the Outsourcing Era, employee attitudes reverted to healthy levels of pessimism. Suddenly it became much easier to write *Dilbert*, thanks to a steady stream of new employee complaints.

Best of all, I got married to my wonderful wife Shelly, and she has embarked on a mission to show me how to work less and enjoy life more. I hope she knows what she's getting herself into.

That brings us to now, and this twentieth-anniversary book. I hope you enjoy it as much as I enjoyed creating it.

—Scott Adams, 2008

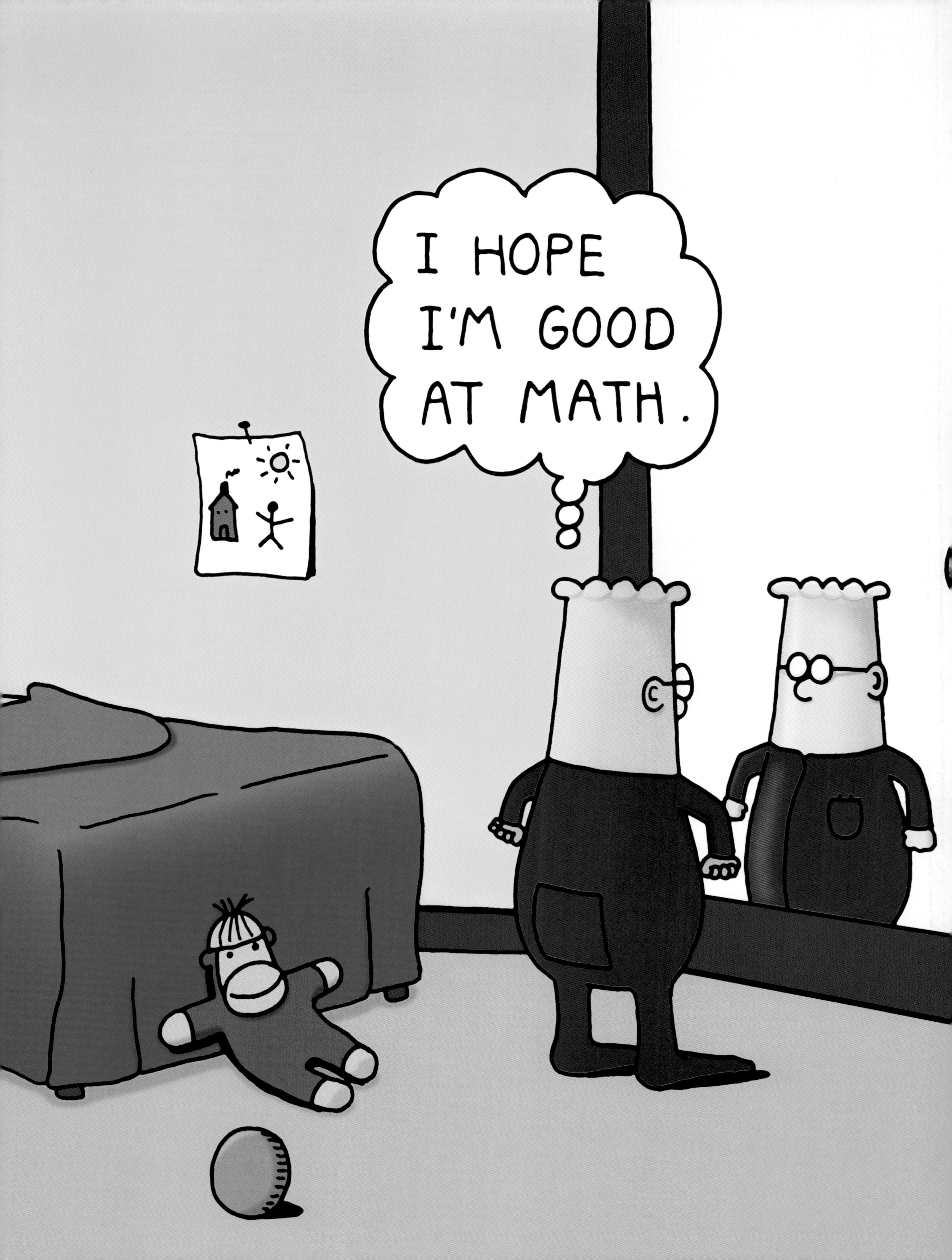
I HOPE I'M GOOD AT MATH.

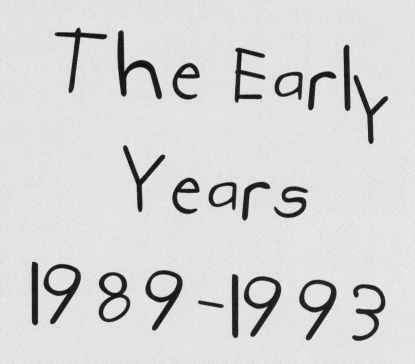

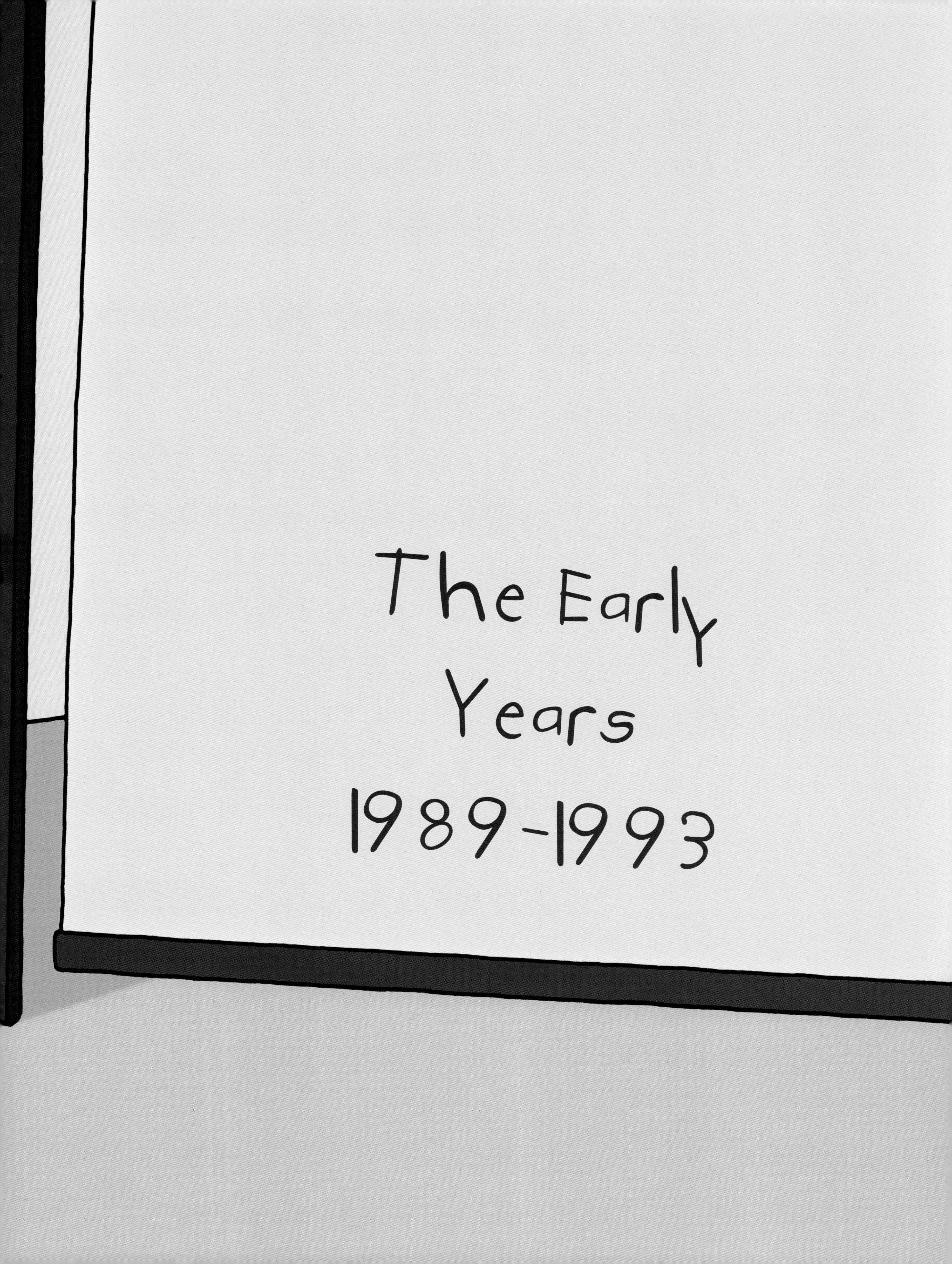

The Early
Years
1989-1993

April 16, 1989

Below is the first published Dilbert *comic strip.*

The way comic syndication works is that the syndicator, in my case United Feature Syndicate, sells a new comic to newspapers, and tells them what day to start running it. In theory, all the new clients start on the same day. In practice, newspapers often buy the rights to a strip and wait for their own best time to start running it. I have no direct evidence that any newspaper ran Dilbert *on the first official day, but I assume at least one did. When people ask me which paper first ran* Dilbert, *I don't know the answer.*

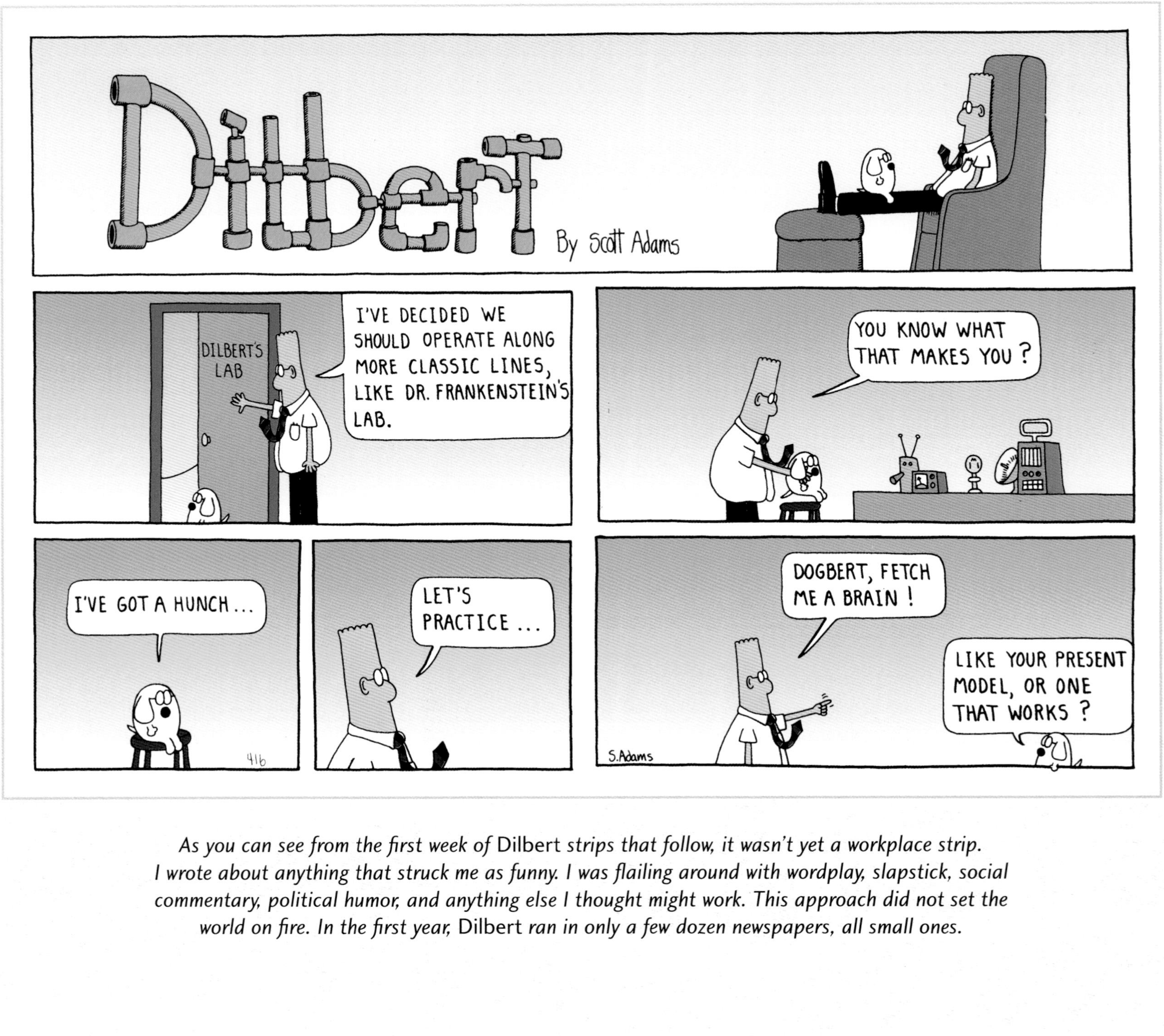
Dilbert
By Scott Adams
DILBERT'S LAB
I'VE DECIDED WE SHOULD OPERATE ALONG MORE CLASSIC LINES, LIKE DR. FRANKENSTEIN'S LAB.
YOU KNOW WHAT THAT MAKES YOU ?
I'VE GOT A HUNCH ...
LET'S PRACTICE ...
DOGBERT, FETCH ME A BRAIN !
LIKE YOUR PRESENT MODEL, OR ONE THAT WORKS ?
S.Adams

As you can see from the first week of Dilbert *strips that follow, it wasn't yet a workplace strip. I wrote about anything that struck me as funny. I was flailing around with wordplay, slapstick, social commentary, political humor, and anything else I thought might work. This approach did not set the world on fire. In the first year,* Dilbert *ran in only a few dozen newspapers, all small ones.*

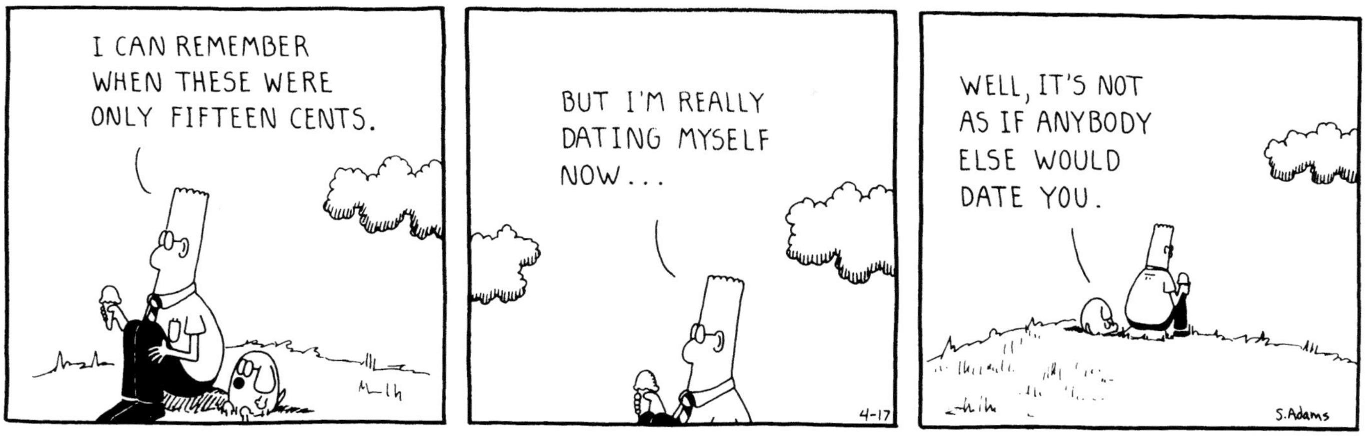
I CAN REMEMBER WHEN THESE WERE ONLY FIFTEEN CENTS.
BUT I'M REALLY DATING MYSELF NOW...
4-17
WELL, IT'S NOT AS IF ANYBODY ELSE WOULD DATE YOU.
S.Adams

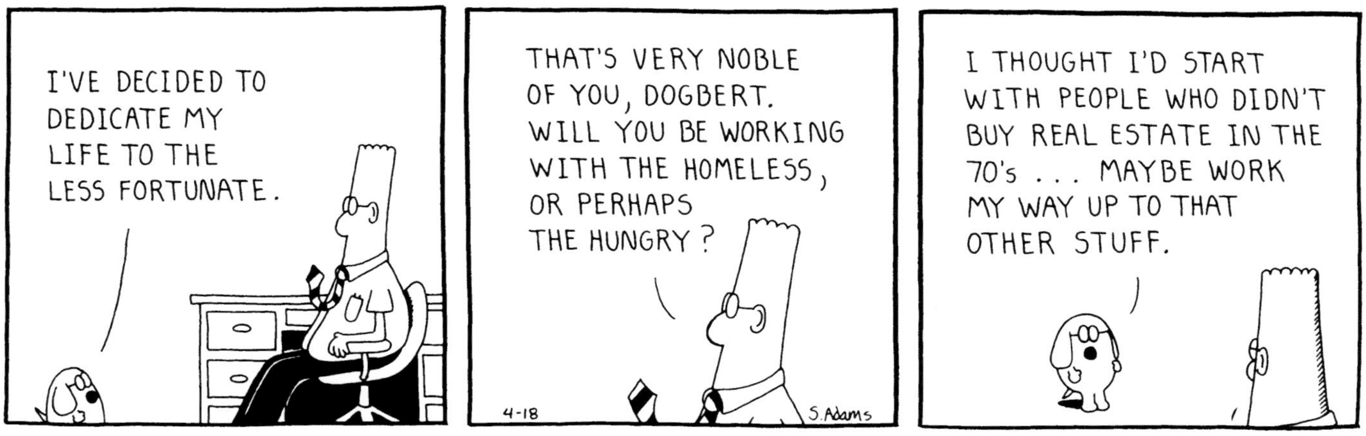
I'VE DECIDED TO DEDICATE MY LIFE TO THE LESS FORTUNATE.
THAT'S VERY NOBLE OF YOU, DOGBERT. WILL YOU BE WORKING WITH THE HOMELESS, OR PERHAPS THE HUNGRY?
4-18
S.Adams
I THOUGHT I'D START WITH PEOPLE WHO DIDN'T BUY REAL ESTATE IN THE 70's ... MAYBE WORK MY WAY UP TO THAT OTHER STUFF.

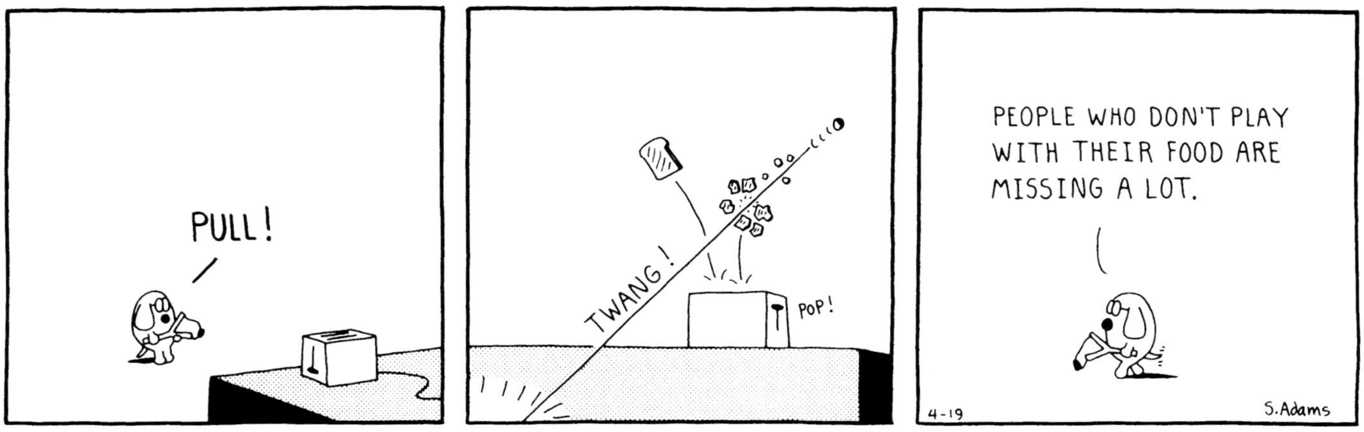
PULL!
TWANG!
POP!
PEOPLE WHO DON'T PLAY WITH THEIR FOOD ARE MISSING A LOT.
4-19
S.Adams

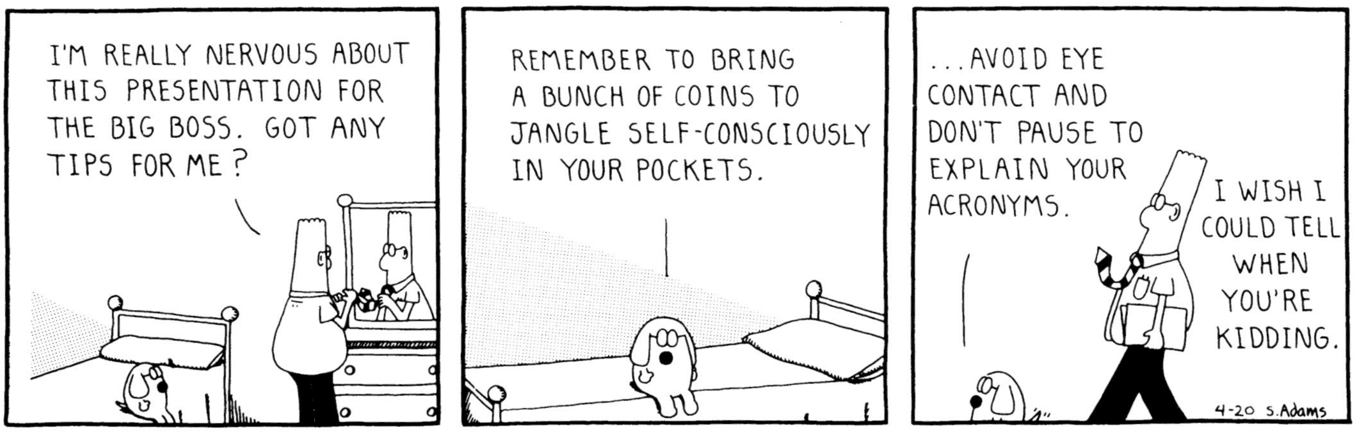
I'M REALLY NERVOUS ABOUT THIS PRESENTATION FOR THE BIG BOSS. GOT ANY TIPS FOR ME?
REMEMBER TO BRING A BUNCH OF COINS TO JANGLE SELF-CONSCIOUSLY IN YOUR POCKETS.
...AVOID EYE CONTACT AND DON'T PAUSE TO EXPLAIN YOUR ACRONYMS.
I WISH I COULD TELL WHEN YOU'RE KIDDING.
4-20 S.Adams

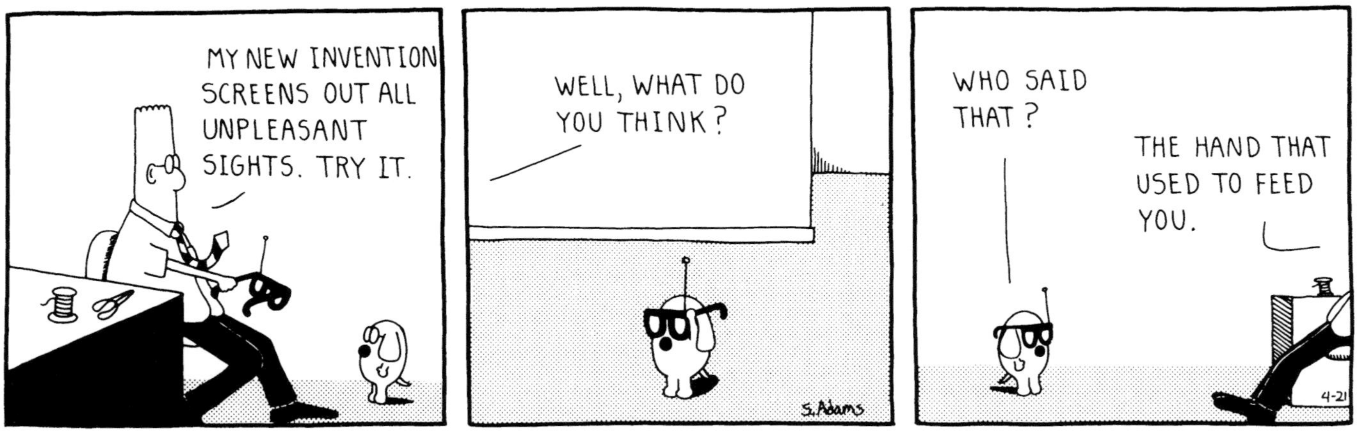
MY NEW INVENTION SCREENS OUT ALL UNPLEASANT SIGHTS. TRY IT.
WELL, WHAT DO YOU THINK?
S. Adams
WHO SAID THAT?
THE HAND THAT USED TO FEED YOU.
4-21

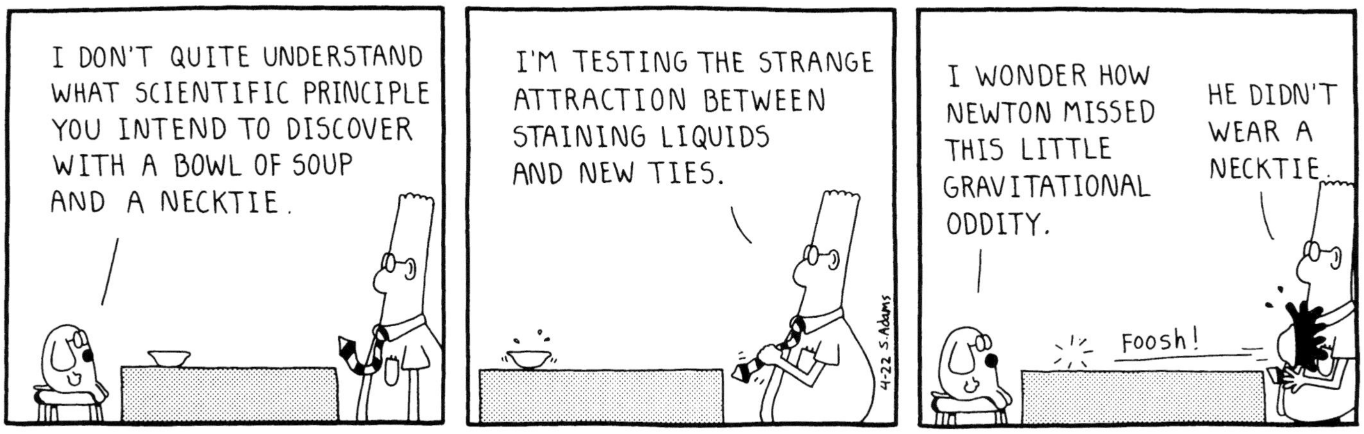
I DON'T QUITE UNDERSTAND WHAT SCIENTIFIC PRINCIPLE YOU INTEND TO DISCOVER WITH A BOWL OF SOUP AND A NECKTIE.
I'M TESTING THE STRANGE ATTRACTION BETWEEN STAINING LIQUIDS AND NEW TIES.
4-22 S. Adams
I WONDER HOW NEWTON MISSED THIS LITTLE GRAVITATIONAL ODDITY.
HE DIDN'T WEAR A NECKTIE.
Foosh!

Notice that I didn't have the artistic talent to draw Dogbert looking exactly the same twice in a row. To work around it, I usually tried showing him in different poses and from different angles in each panel, so it wouldn't be so obvious. Still, I'm guessing some readers noticed my lack of talent.

While the humor and the art were sorely lacking, what I did right, more by accident than by design, is give the characters distinct personalities that people related to. Everyone knows a Dilbert (or is one). And everyone has a dark side, generally hidden, that is represented by Dogbert.

A standard cartoon trick is to give a character the opposite personality you might expect. Dogs are generally loyal and obedient, so I made Dogbert the opposite. He was loosely based on a beagle my family had when I was a kid. Her name was Lucy, and she never once came when I called her. Sitting, fetching, and rolling over were out of the question. All she liked to do was grab me by the sleeve and try to rip the shirt off my torso. She actually succeeded once in turning my shirt into a vest. As a loyal pet, she was highly defective. As an inspiration for a cartoon character, she was ideal.

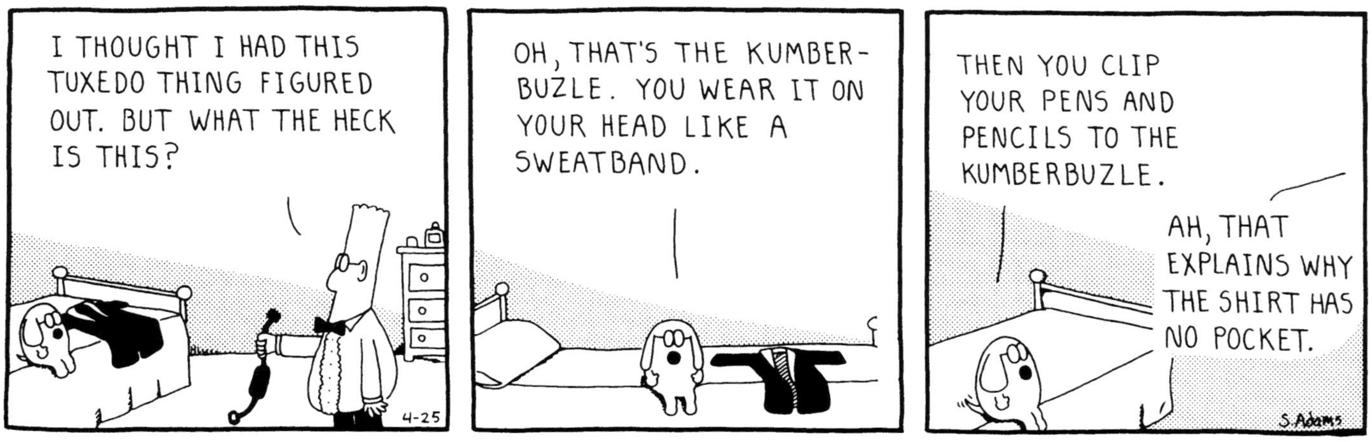
I THOUGHT I HAD THIS TUXEDO THING FIGURED OUT. BUT WHAT THE HECK IS THIS?
4-25
OH, THAT'S THE KUMBERBUZLE. YOU WEAR IT ON YOUR HEAD LIKE A SWEATBAND.
THEN YOU CLIP YOUR PENS AND PENCILS TO THE KUMBERBUZLE.
AH, THAT EXPLAINS WHY THE SHIRT HAS NO POCKET.
S. Adams

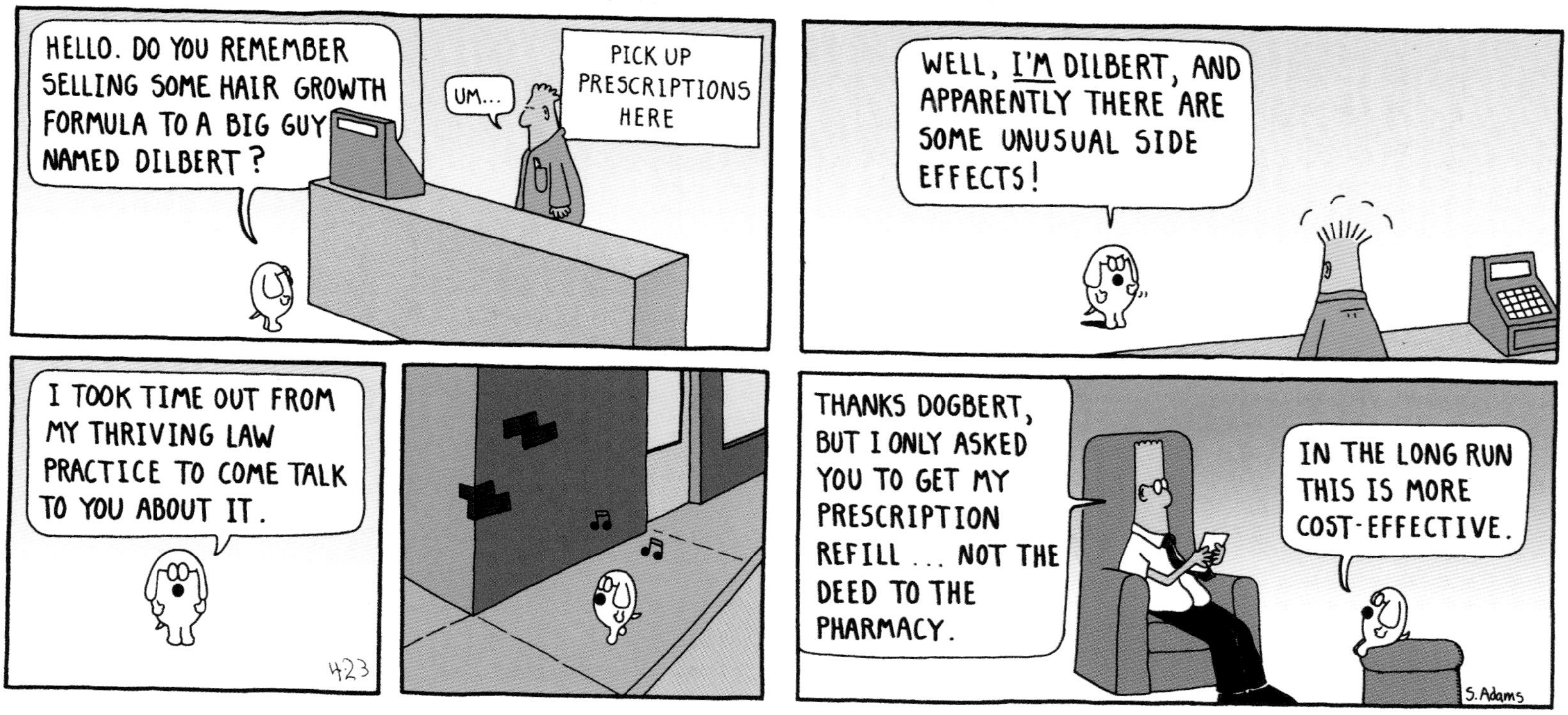
HELLO. DO YOU REMEMBER SELLING SOME HAIR GROWTH FORMULA TO A BIG GUY NAMED DILBERT?
UM...
PICK UP PRESCRIPTIONS HERE
WELL, I'M DILBERT, AND APPARENTLY THERE ARE SOME UNUSUAL SIDE EFFECTS!
I TOOK TIME OUT FROM MY THRIVING LAW PRACTICE TO COME TALK TO YOU ABOUT IT.
423
THANKS DOGBERT, BUT I ONLY ASKED YOU TO GET MY PRESCRIPTION REFILL ... NOT THE DEED TO THE PHARMACY.
IN THE LONG RUN THIS IS MORE COST-EFFECTIVE.
S. Adams

During this period I was working my day job at Pacific Bell. I woke up at 4 A.M. every workday and completed a comic in pencil before heading for my other job. At night I watched TV and inked over the pencil drawings. I worked every weekend, and every holiday, for the first ten years. That's why I rarely drew background scenery. I literally didn't have the time.

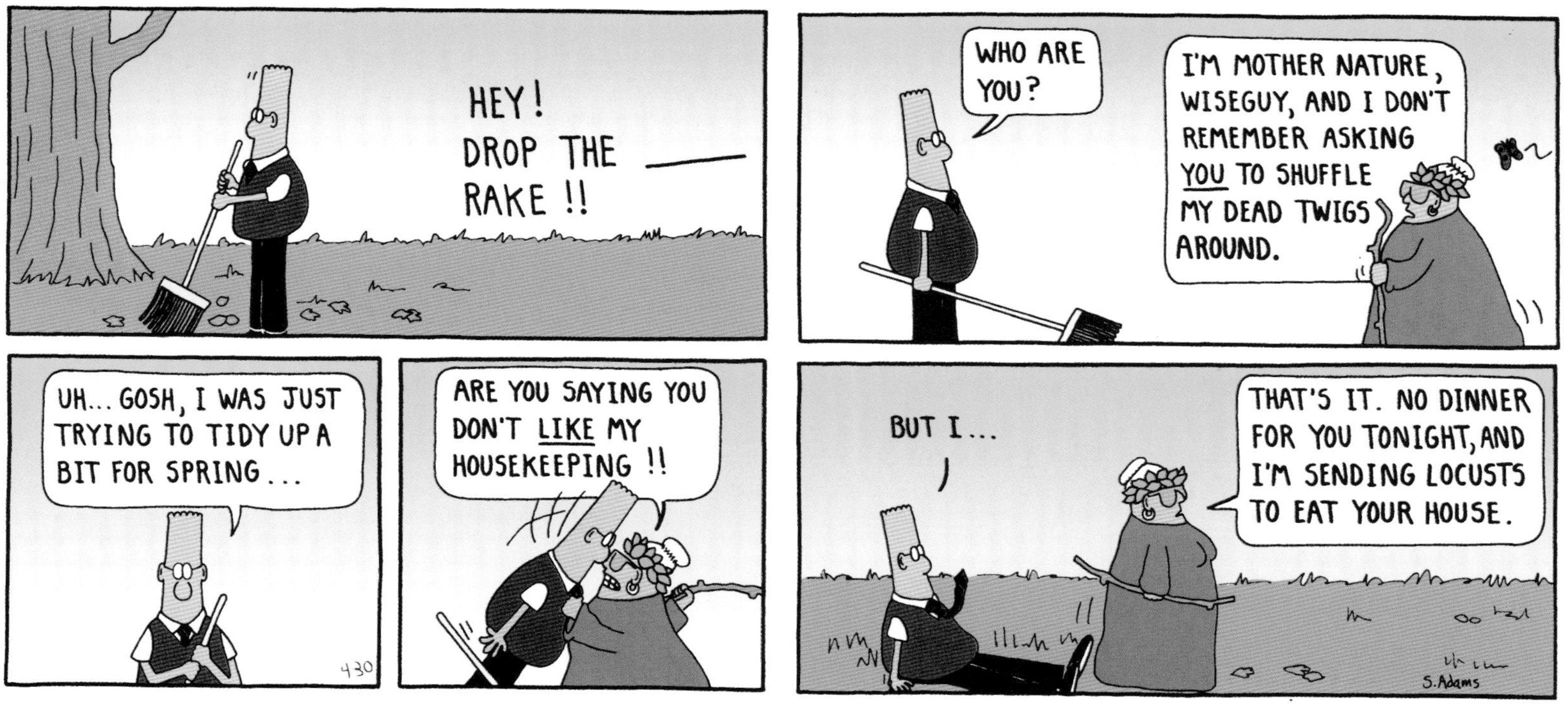
HEY! DROP THE RAKE!!
WHO ARE YOU?
I'M MOTHER NATURE, WISEGUY, AND I DON'T REMEMBER ASKING YOU TO SHUFFLE MY DEAD TWIGS AROUND.
UH... GOSH, I WAS JUST TRYING TO TIDY UP A BIT FOR SPRING...
430
ARE YOU SAYING YOU DON'T LIKE MY HOUSEKEEPING!!
BUT I...
THAT'S IT. NO DINNER FOR YOU TONIGHT, AND I'M SENDING LOCUSTS TO EAT YOUR HOUSE.
S. Adams

I was highly influenced by Gary Larson's The Far Side® *comic, which was huge at the time. I was among an army of imitators. Mother Nature and Phil from Heck (next page) were the sorts of characters I would have imagined in a* Far Side *strip. If Larson's influence isn't obvious to you, it's only because I wasn't good at imitating.*

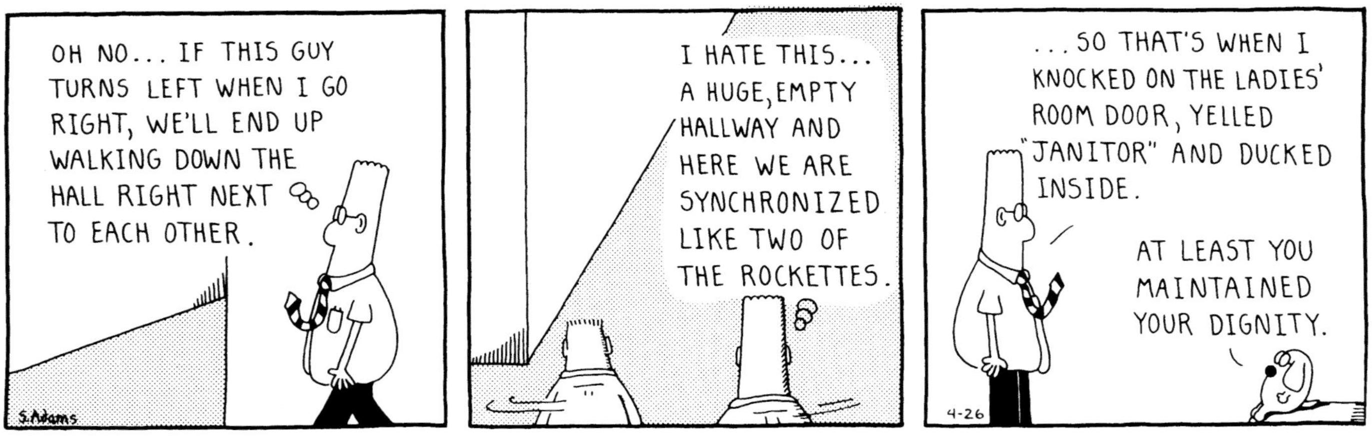
OH NO... IF THIS GUY TURNS LEFT WHEN I GO RIGHT, WE'LL END UP WALKING DOWN THE HALL RIGHT NEXT TO EACH OTHER.
I HATE THIS... A HUGE, EMPTY HALLWAY AND HERE WE ARE SYNCHRONIZED LIKE TWO OF THE ROCKETTES.
...SO THAT'S WHEN I KNOCKED ON THE LADIES' ROOM DOOR, YELLED "JANITOR" AND DUCKED INSIDE.
AT LEAST YOU MAINTAINED YOUR DIGNITY.
S.Adams
4-26

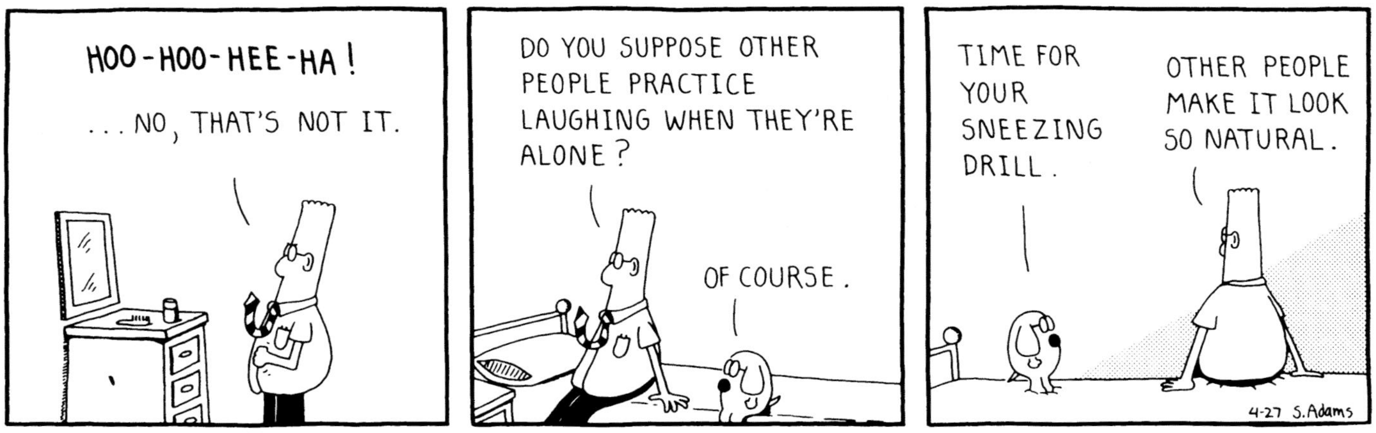
HOO-HOO-HEE-HA!
...NO, THAT'S NOT IT.
DO YOU SUPPOSE OTHER PEOPLE PRACTICE LAUGHING WHEN THEY'RE ALONE?
OF COURSE.
TIME FOR YOUR SNEEZING DRILL.
OTHER PEOPLE MAKE IT LOOK SO NATURAL.
4-27 S.Adams

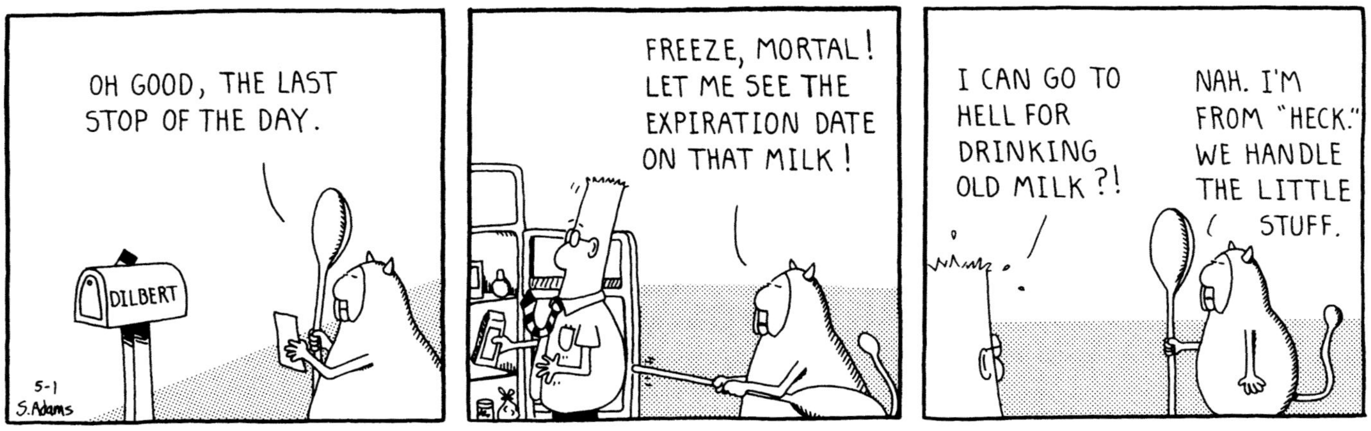
OH GOOD, THE LAST STOP OF THE DAY.
DILBERT
5-1
S.Adams
FREEZE, MORTAL! LET ME SEE THE EXPIRATION DATE ON THAT MILK!
I CAN GO TO HELL FOR DRINKING OLD MILK?!
NAH. I'M FROM "HECK." WE HANDLE THE LITTLE STUFF.

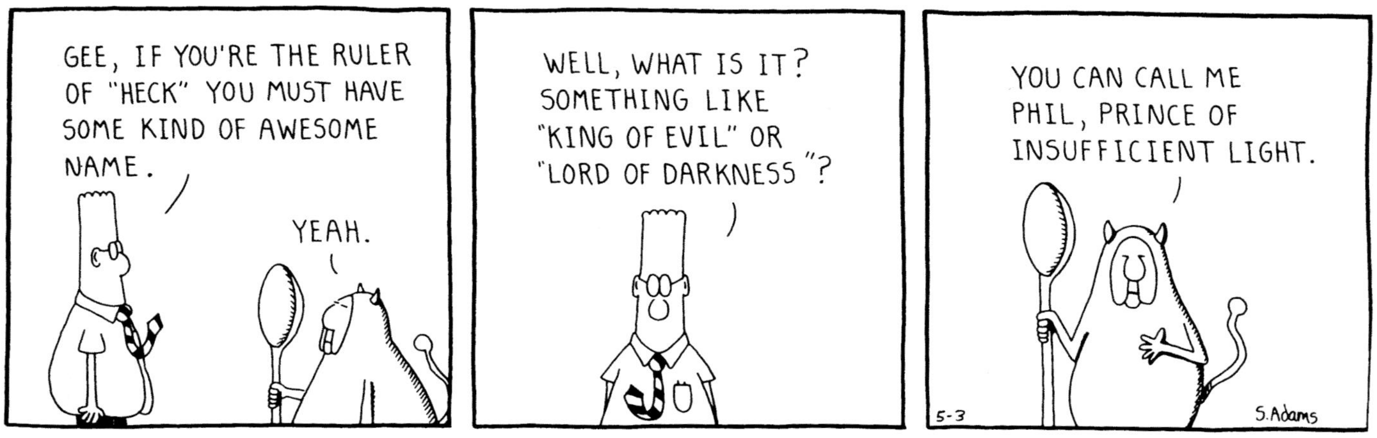
GEE, IF YOU'RE THE RULER OF "HECK" YOU MUST HAVE SOME KIND OF AWESOME NAME.
YEAH.
WELL, WHAT IS IT? SOMETHING LIKE "KING OF EVIL" OR "LORD OF DARKNESS"?
YOU CAN CALL ME PHIL, PRINCE OF INSUFFICIENT LIGHT.
5-3
S.Adams

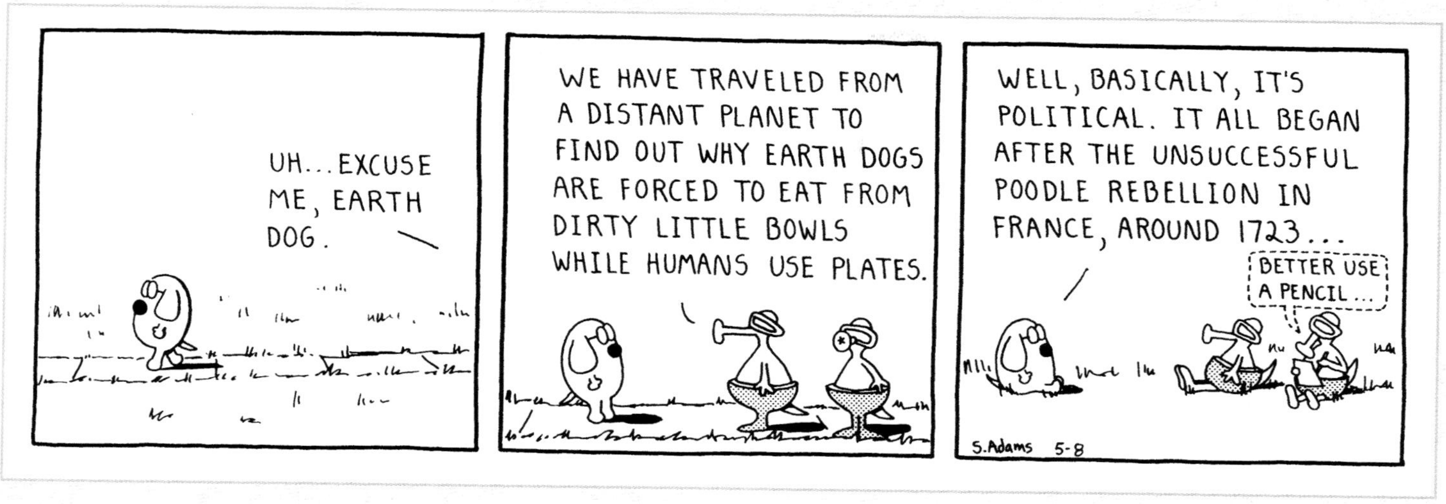
UH... EXCUSE ME, EARTH DOG.
WE HAVE TRAVELED FROM A DISTANT PLANET TO FIND OUT WHY EARTH DOGS ARE FORCED TO EAT FROM DIRTY LITTLE BOWLS WHILE HUMANS USE PLATES.
WELL, BASICALLY, IT'S POLITICAL. IT ALL BEGAN AFTER THE UNSUCCESSFUL POODLE REBELLION IN FRANCE, AROUND 1723...
BETTER USE A PENCIL...
S. Adams 5-8

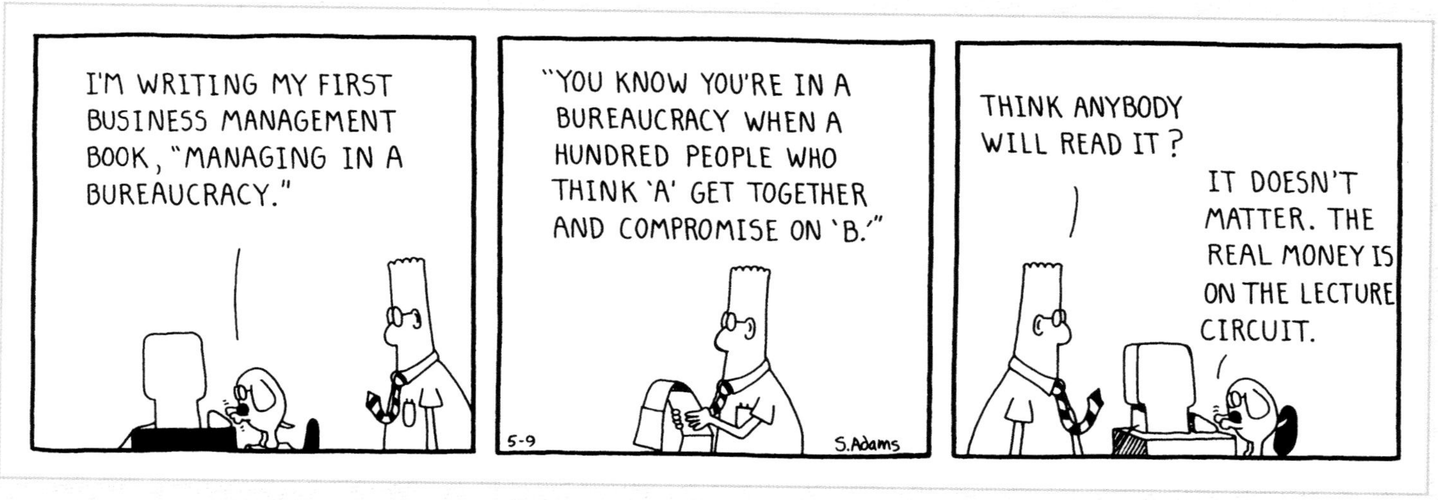
I'M WRITING MY FIRST BUSINESS MANAGEMENT BOOK, "MANAGING IN A BUREAUCRACY."
"YOU KNOW YOU'RE IN A BUREAUCRACY WHEN A HUNDRED PEOPLE WHO THINK 'A' GET TOGETHER AND COMPROMISE ON 'B.'"
5-9
S. Adams
THINK ANYBODY WILL READ IT?
IT DOESN'T MATTER. THE REAL MONEY IS ON THE LECTURE CIRCUIT.

A few years after this strip ran, I wrote The Dilbert Principle, *a business management book of sorts, and went on the lecture circuit.*

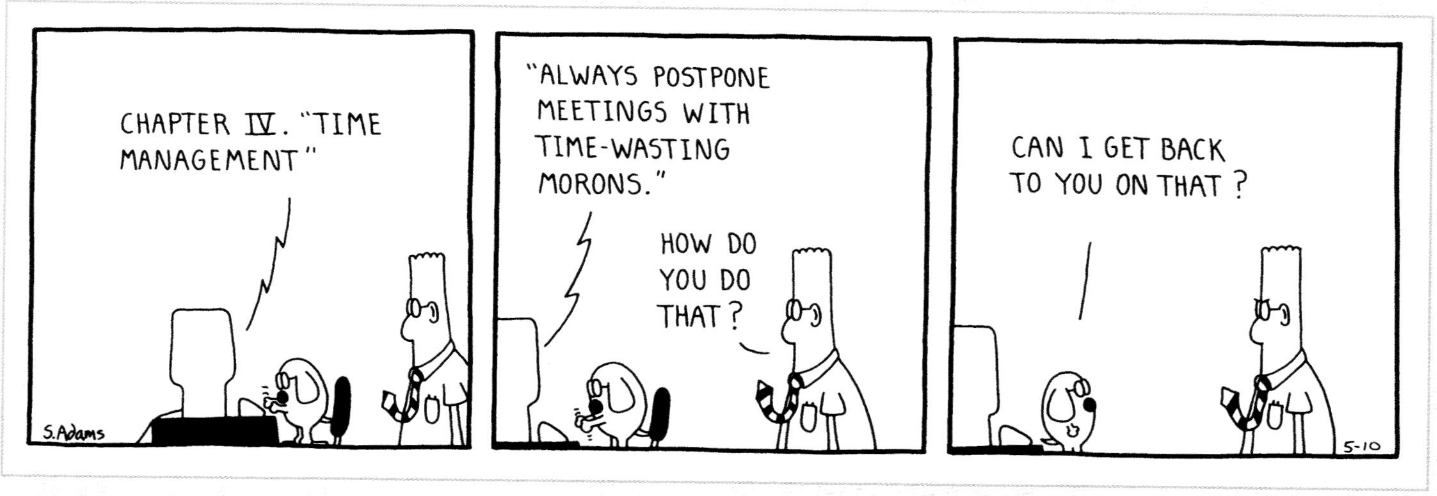
CHAPTER IV. "TIME MANAGEMENT"
S. Adams
"ALWAYS POSTPONE MEETINGS WITH TIME-WASTING MORONS."
HOW DO YOU DO THAT?
CAN I GET BACK TO YOU ON THAT?
5-10

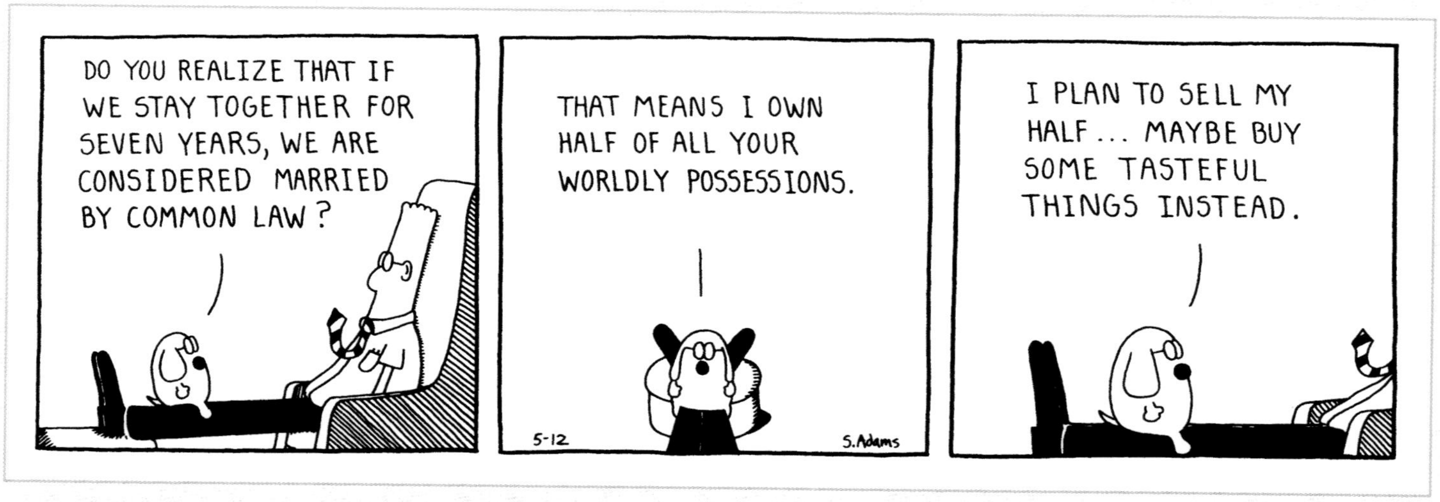
DO YOU REALIZE THAT IF WE STAY TOGETHER FOR SEVEN YEARS, WE ARE CONSIDERED MARRIED BY COMMON LAW?
THAT MEANS I OWN HALF OF ALL YOUR WORLDLY POSSESSIONS.
5-12
S. Adams
I PLAN TO SELL MY HALF... MAYBE BUY SOME TASTEFUL THINGS INSTEAD.

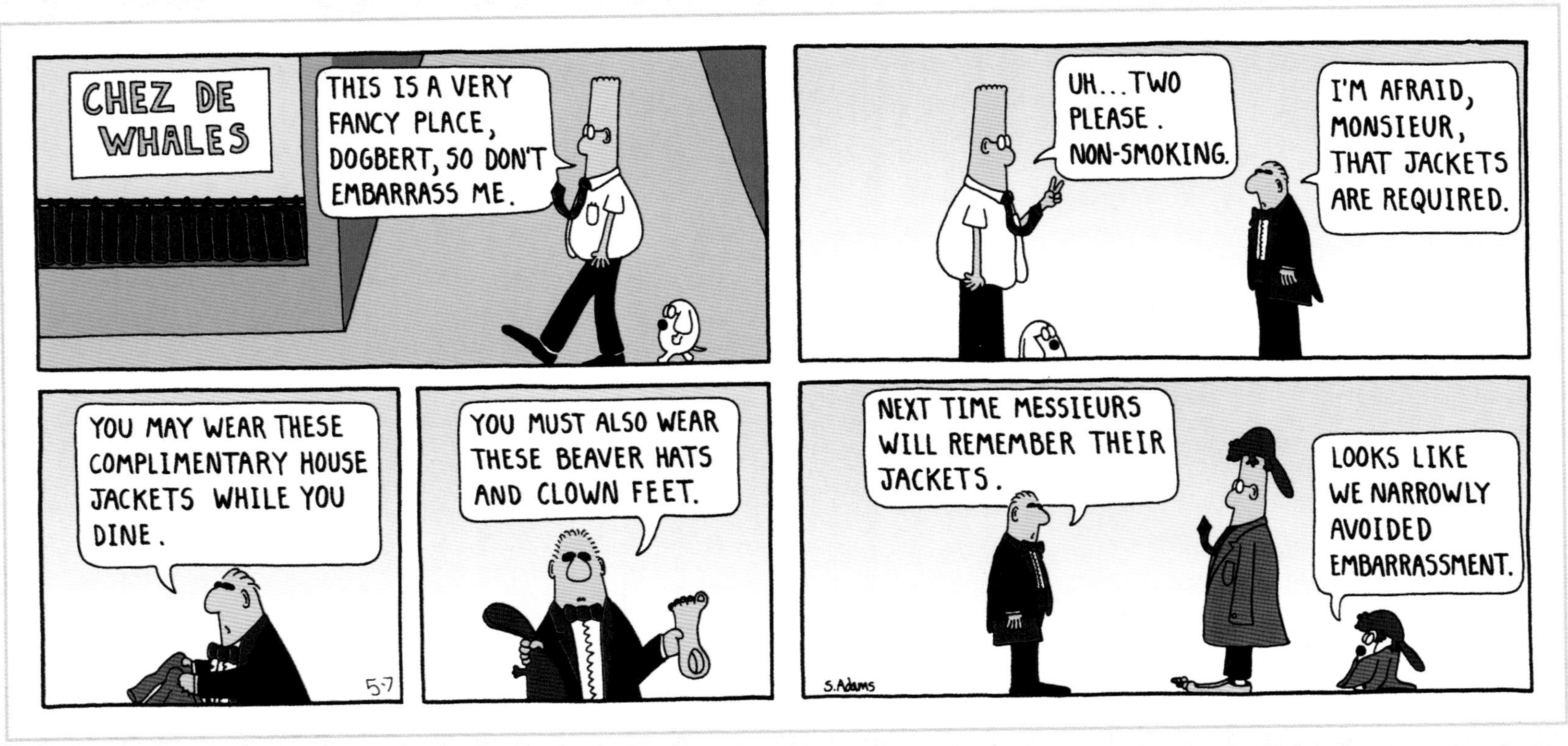
CHEZ DE WHALES
THIS IS A VERY FANCY PLACE, DOGBERT, SO DON'T EMBARRASS ME.
UH...TWO PLEASE. NON-SMOKING.
I'M AFRAID, MONSIEUR, THAT JACKETS ARE REQUIRED.
YOU MAY WEAR THESE COMPLIMENTARY HOUSE JACKETS WHILE YOU DINE.
5-7
YOU MUST ALSO WEAR THESE BEAVER HATS AND CLOWN FEET.
NEXT TIME MESSIEURS WILL REMEMBER THEIR JACKETS.
LOOKS LIKE WE NARROWLY AVOIDED EMBARRASSMENT.
S.Adams

Arguably, this is the first unambiguous workplace-themed Dilbert *comic. At this point it didn't occur to me that there was a market for a comic about work. Dilbert had a job, but it was simply a shorthand way to define his personality.*

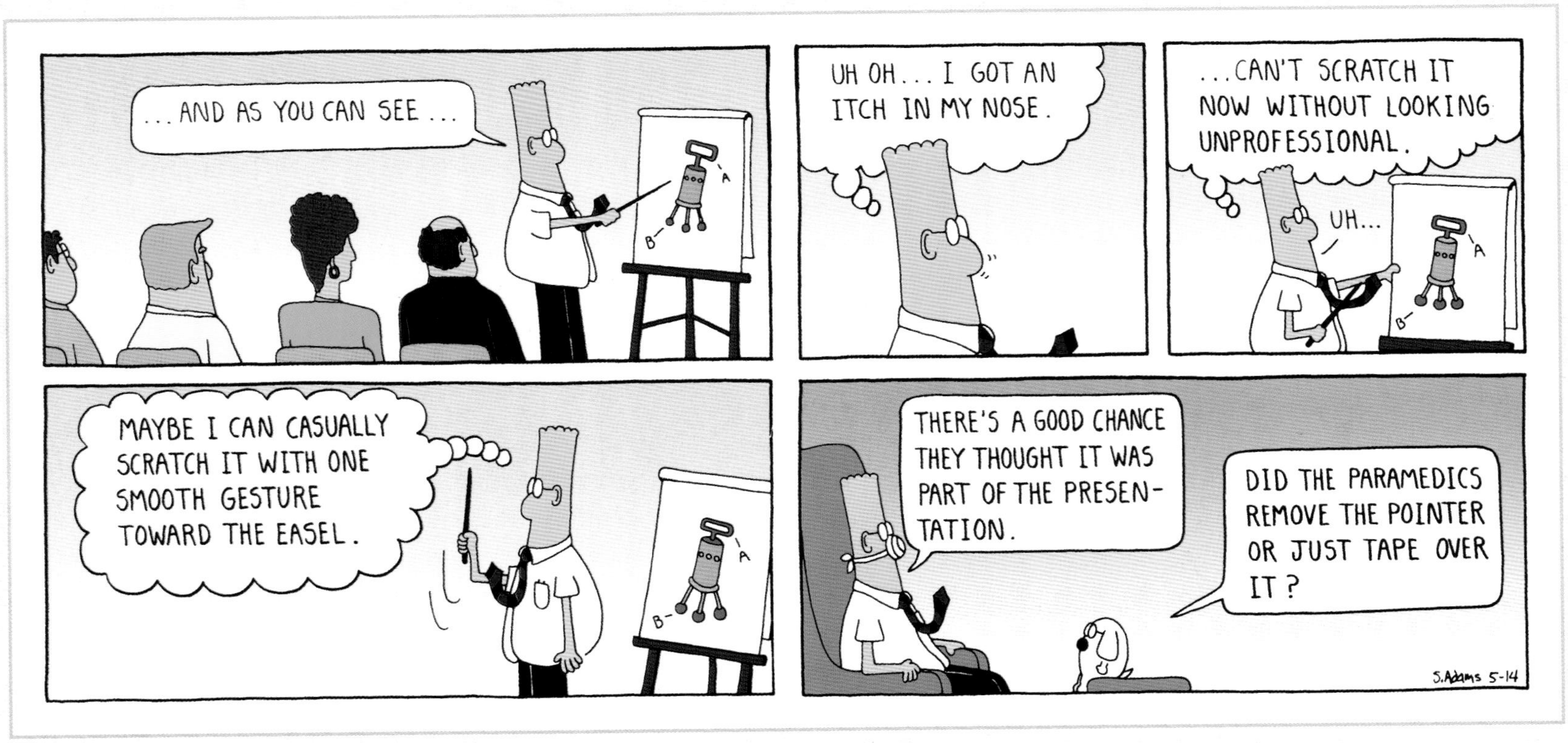
...AND AS YOU CAN SEE...
UH OH... I GOT AN ITCH IN MY NOSE.
...CAN'T SCRATCH IT NOW WITHOUT LOOKING UNPROFESSIONAL.
UH...
MAYBE I CAN CASUALLY SCRATCH IT WITH ONE SMOOTH GESTURE TOWARD THE EASEL.
THERE'S A GOOD CHANCE THEY THOUGHT IT WAS PART OF THE PRESEN-TATION.
DID THE PARAMEDICS REMOVE THE POINTER OR JUST TAPE OVER IT?
S.Adams 5-14

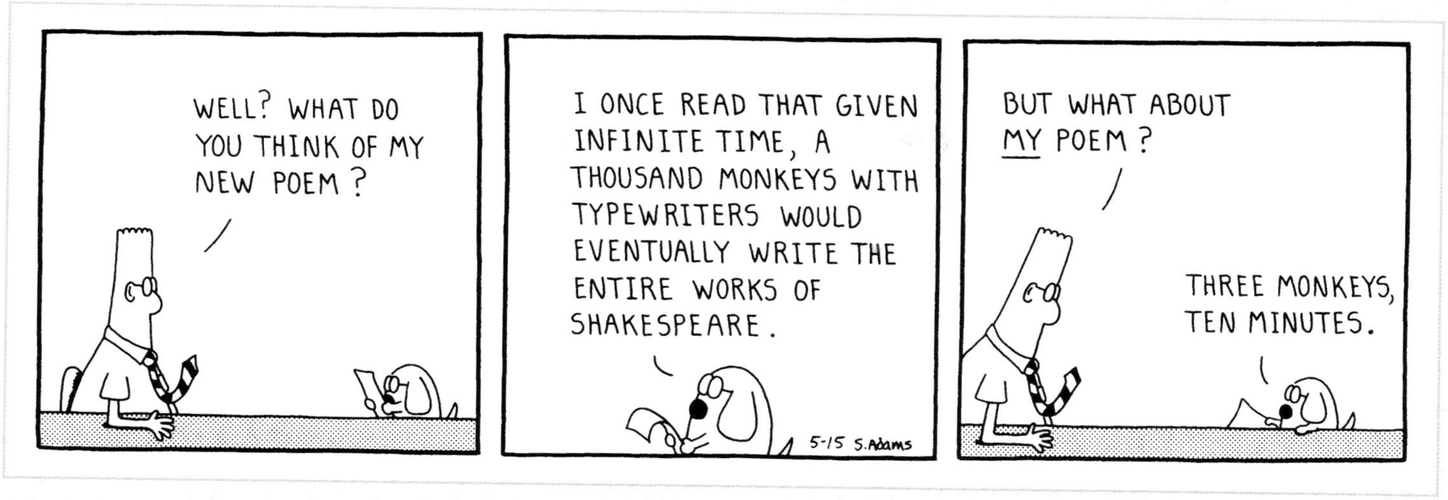
WELL? WHAT DO YOU THINK OF MY NEW POEM ?
I ONCE READ THAT GIVEN INFINITE TIME, A THOUSAND MONKEYS WITH TYPEWRITERS WOULD EVENTUALLY WRITE THE ENTIRE WORKS OF SHAKESPEARE.
5-15 S.Adams
BUT WHAT ABOUT MY POEM ?
THREE MONKEYS, TEN MINUTES.

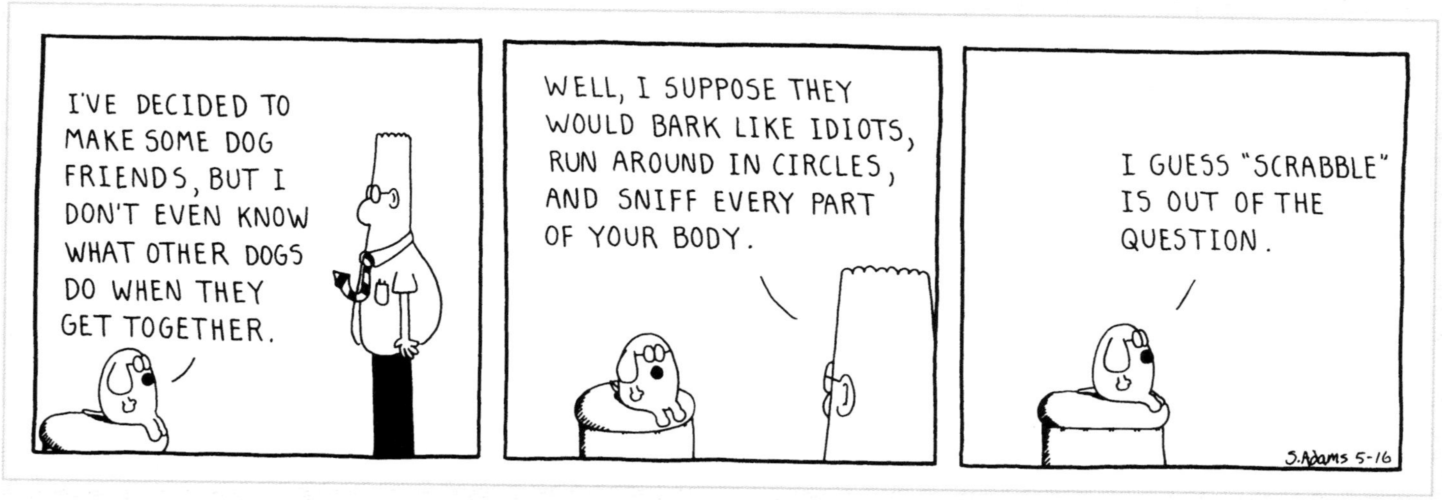
I'VE DECIDED TO MAKE SOME DOG FRIENDS, BUT I DON'T EVEN KNOW WHAT OTHER DOGS DO WHEN THEY GET TOGETHER.
WELL, I SUPPOSE THEY WOULD BARK LIKE IDIOTS, RUN AROUND IN CIRCLES, AND SNIFF EVERY PART OF YOUR BODY.
I GUESS "SCRABBLE" IS OUT OF THE QUESTION.
S.Adams 5-16

In the beginning, Dogbert still had one paw in the canine world. Over time, I banned any reference to actual dog behavior in Dogbert. I came to treat him as something unique, neither dog nor human, but above both.

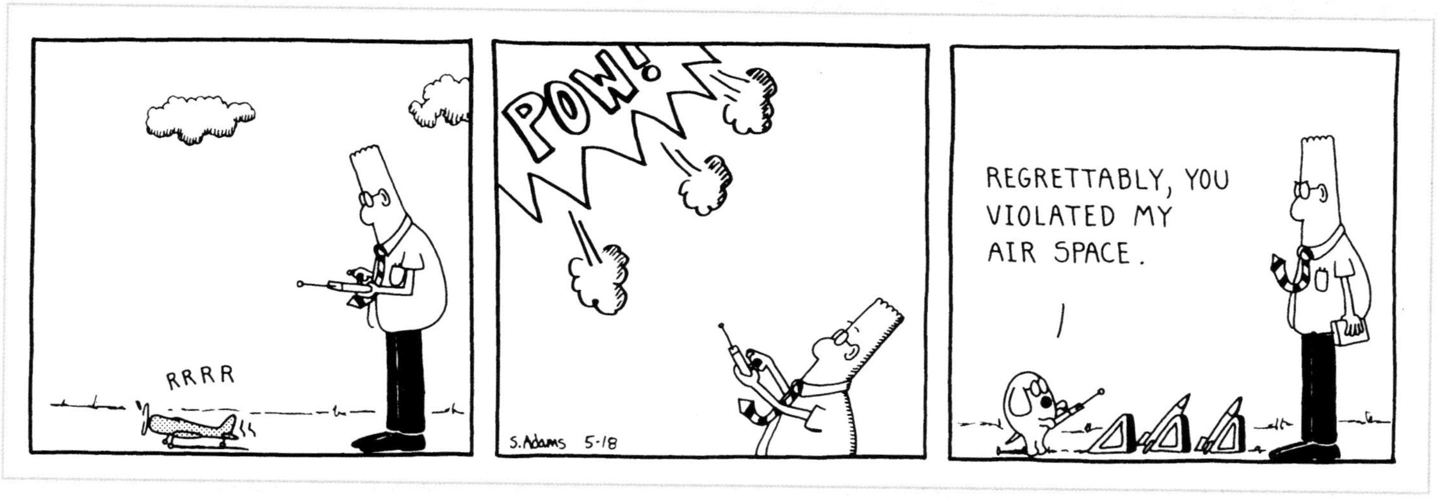
RRRR
POW!
S.Adams 5-18
REGRETTABLY, YOU VIOLATED MY AIR SPACE.

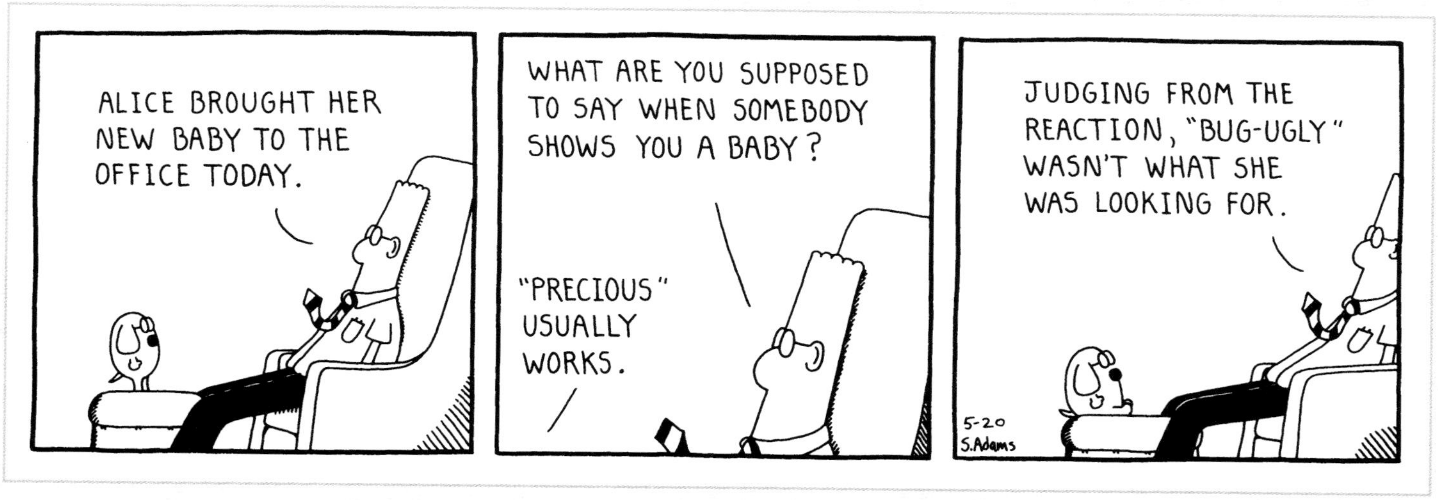
ALICE BROUGHT HER NEW BABY TO THE OFFICE TODAY.
WHAT ARE YOU SUPPOSED TO SAY WHEN SOMEBODY SHOWS YOU A BABY?
"PRECIOUS" USUALLY WORKS.
JUDGING FROM THE REACTION, "BUG-UGLY" WASN'T WHAT SHE WAS LOOKING FOR.
5-20 S.Adams

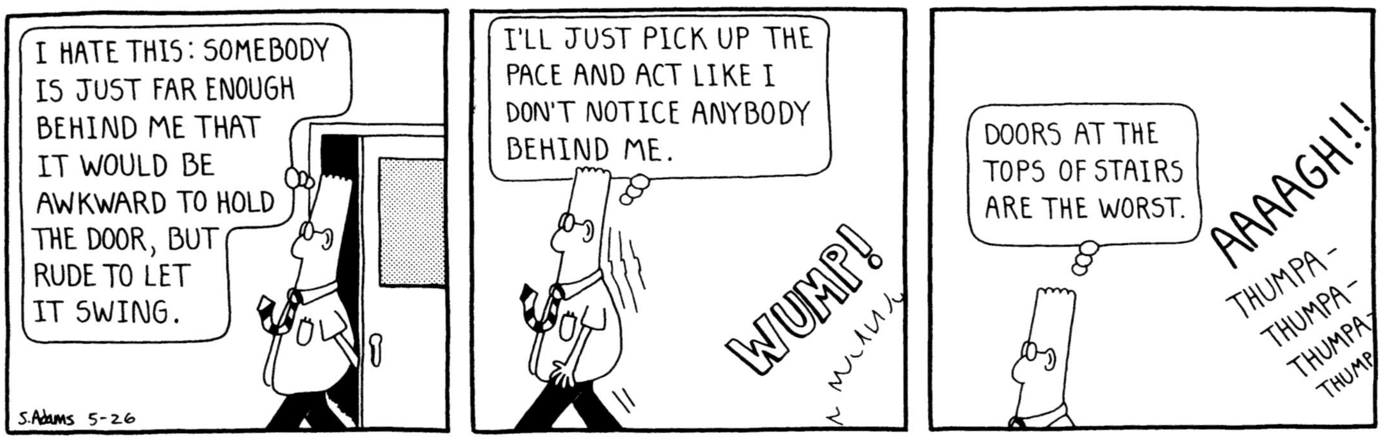
I HATE THIS: SOMEBODY IS JUST FAR ENOUGH BEHIND ME THAT IT WOULD BE AWKWARD TO HOLD THE DOOR, BUT RUDE TO LET IT SWING.
S.Adams 5-26
I'LL JUST PICK UP THE PACE AND ACT LIKE I DON'T NOTICE ANYBODY BEHIND ME.
WUMP!
DOORS AT THE TOPS OF STAIRS ARE THE WORST.
AAAAGH!!
THUMPA- THUMPA- THUMPA- THUMP

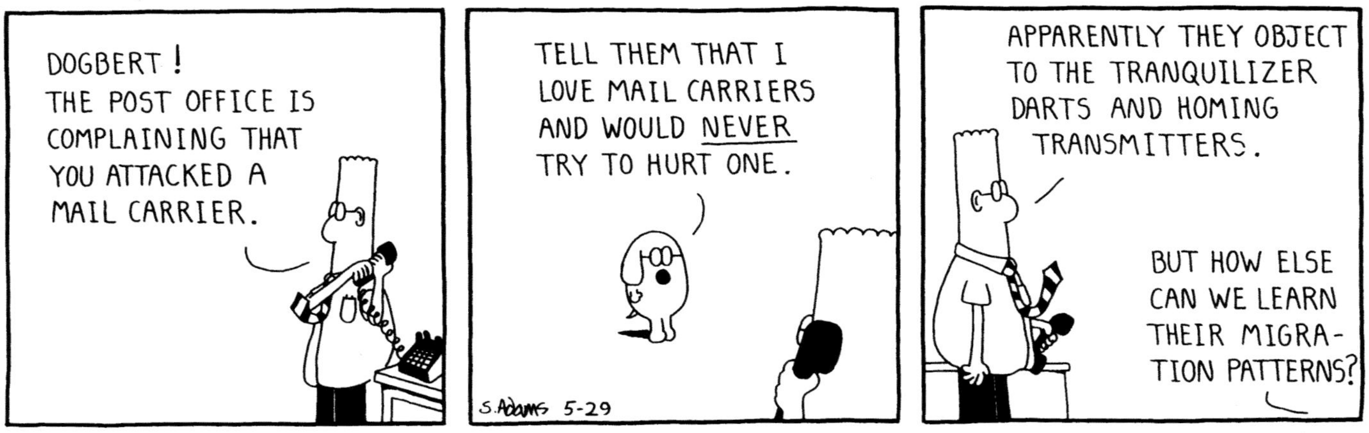
DOGBERT! THE POST OFFICE IS COMPLAINING THAT YOU ATTACKED A MAIL CARRIER.
TELL THEM THAT I LOVE MAIL CARRIERS AND WOULD NEVER TRY TO HURT ONE.
S.Adams 5-29
APPARENTLY THEY OBJECT TO THE TRANQUILIZER DARTS AND HOMING TRANSMITTERS.
BUT HOW ELSE CAN WE LEARN THEIR MIGRATION PATTERNS?

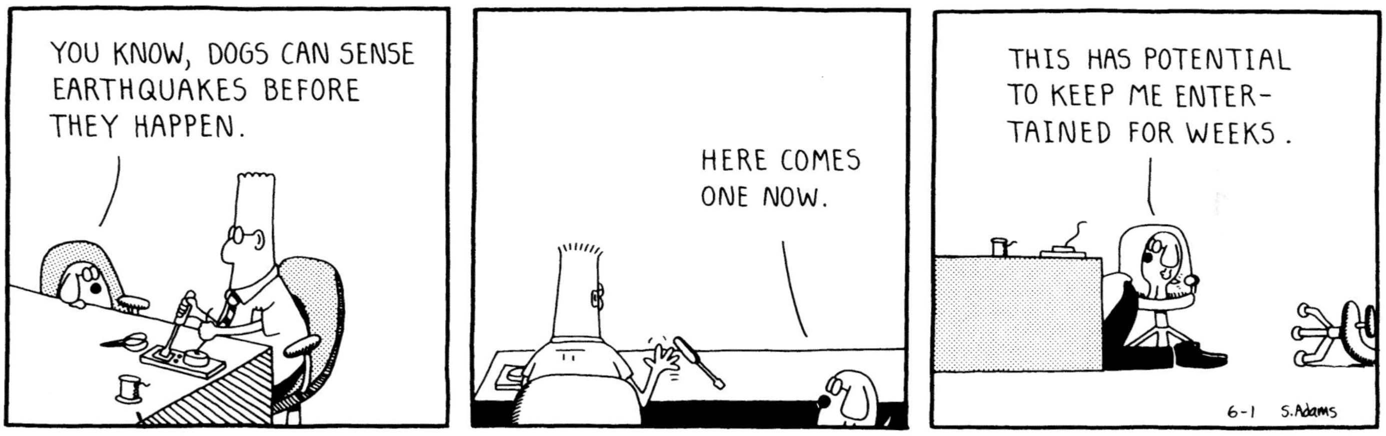
YOU KNOW, DOGS CAN SENSE EARTHQUAKES BEFORE THEY HAPPEN.
HERE COMES ONE NOW.
THIS HAS POTENTIAL TO KEEP ME ENTERTAINED FOR WEEKS.
6-1 S.Adams

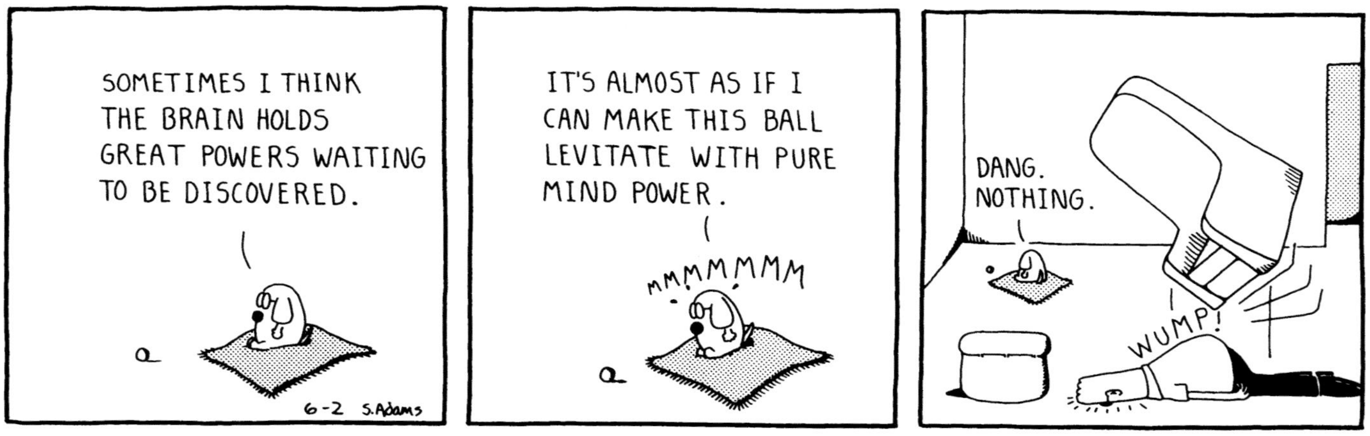
SOMETIMES I THINK THE BRAIN HOLDS GREAT POWERS WAITING TO BE DISCOVERED.
6-2 S.Adams
IT'S ALMOST AS IF I CAN MAKE THIS BALL LEVITATE WITH PURE MIND POWER.
MMMMMMM
DANG. NOTHING.
WUMP!

WHY DO YOU WASTE YOUR TIME READING BOOKS ?
BECAUSE READING INCREASES MY KNOWLEDGE, AND KNOWLEDGE IS POWER.
BOOK
BUT POWER CORRUPTS . . .
BOOK
. . . AND CORRUPTION IS A CRIME . . .
AND CRIME DOESN'T PAY . . .
IF YOU KEEP READING, YOU'LL GO BROKE ! ! !
5-28
S.Adams
GOSH! IT ALWAYS SEEMED SO . . . SO . . . HARMLESS .
OH YEAH, THE LIBRARIANS WOULD LOVE TO HAVE YOU BELIEVE THAT !

I'LL BE BACK LATE. I HAVE A DATE WITH SHARON TO GROUT HER BATHTUB.
YOU CALL THAT A DATE ?
LAST WEEK YOU CLEANED HER RAIN GUTTERS AND PAINTED HER HOUSE . . .
THE WEEK BEFORE, YOU INSTALLED HER SPRINKLER SYSTEM AND REBUILT HER CAR'S ENGINE.
DON'T YOU THINK SHE MIGHT BE USING YOU ?
WELL . . . AT LEAST I GET LUNCH OUT OF THE DEAL.
SHE ACTUALLY PREPARES FOOD FOR YOU ?
NO, BAG LUNCH. I GET TO EAT IT DURING BREAK.
6-4 S.Adams

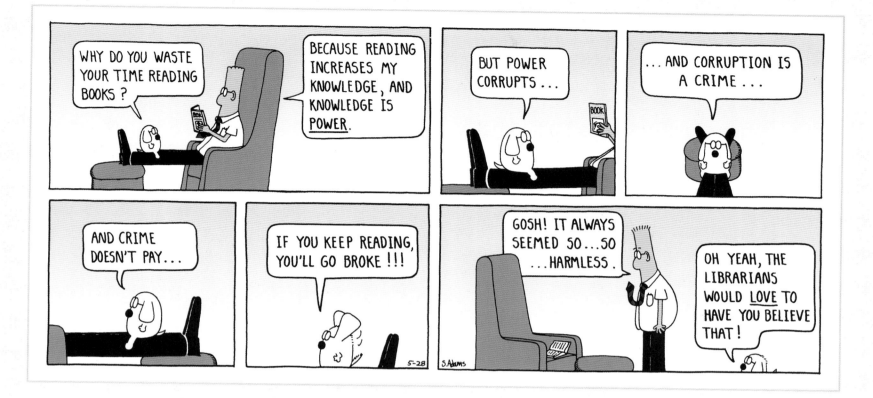

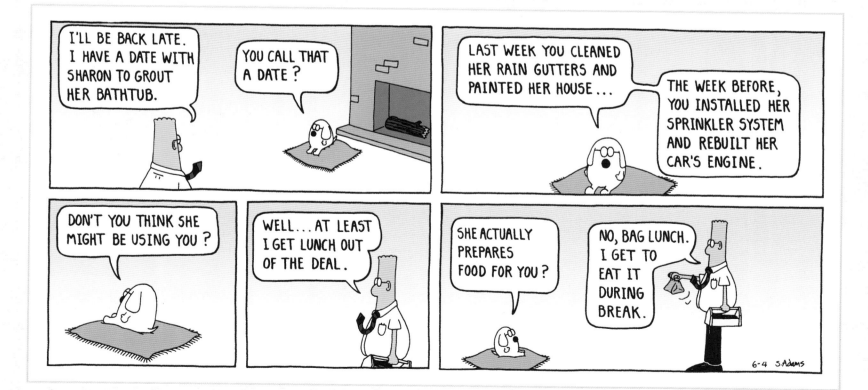

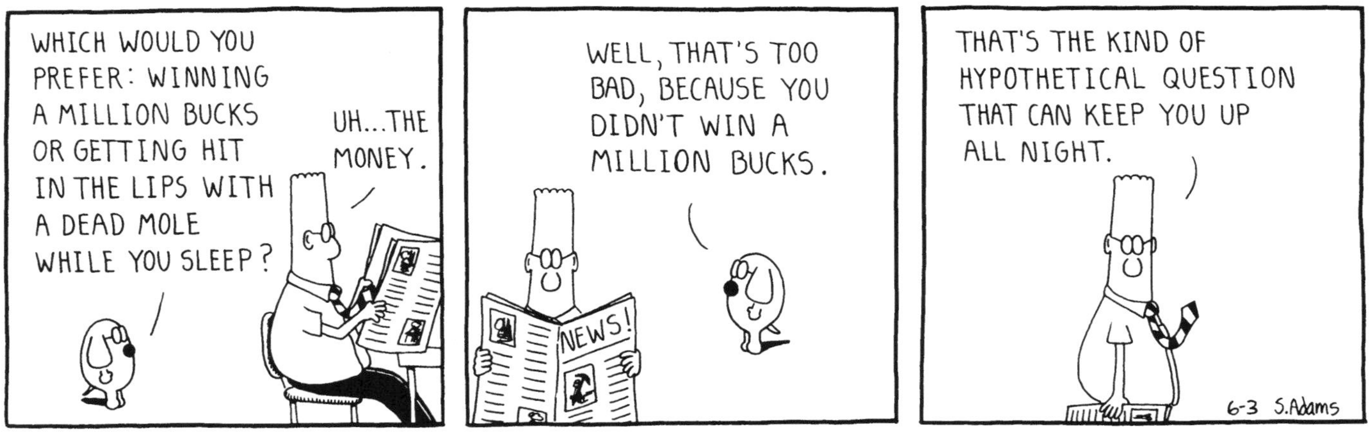
WHICH WOULD YOU PREFER: WINNING A MILLION BUCKS OR GETTING HIT IN THE LIPS WITH A DEAD MOLE WHILE YOU SLEEP?
UH...THE MONEY.
WELL, THAT'S TOO BAD, BECAUSE YOU DIDN'T WIN A MILLION BUCKS.
NEWS!
THAT'S THE KIND OF HYPOTHETICAL QUESTION THAT CAN KEEP YOU UP ALL NIGHT.
6-3 S.Adams

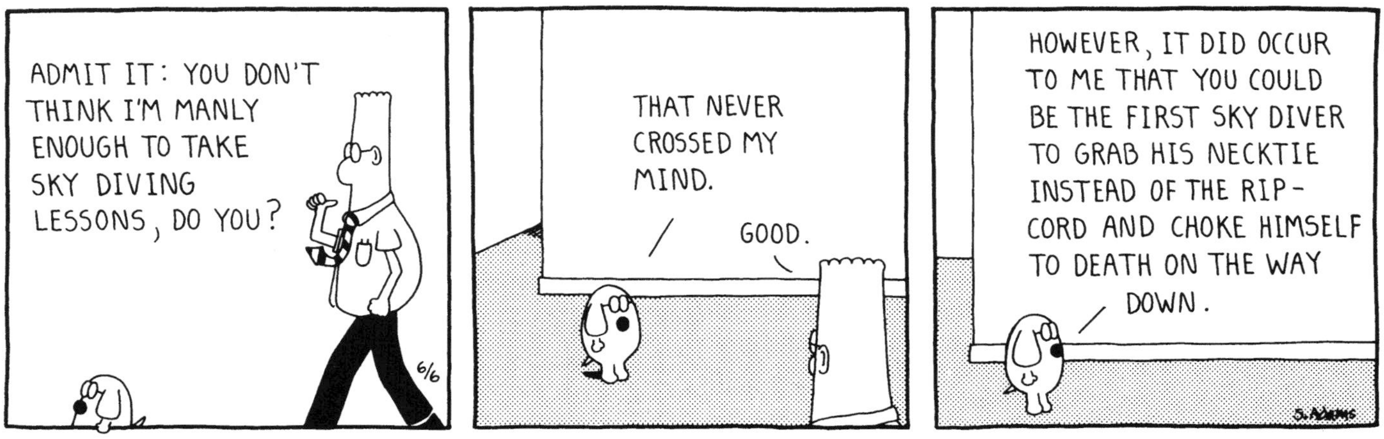
ADMIT IT: YOU DON'T THINK I'M MANLY ENOUGH TO TAKE SKY DIVING LESSONS, DO YOU?
6/6
THAT NEVER CROSSED MY MIND.
GOOD.
HOWEVER, IT DID OCCUR TO ME THAT YOU COULD BE THE FIRST SKY DIVER TO GRAB HIS NECKTIE INSTEAD OF THE RIP-CORD AND CHOKE HIMSELF TO DEATH ON THE WAY DOWN.
S.Adams

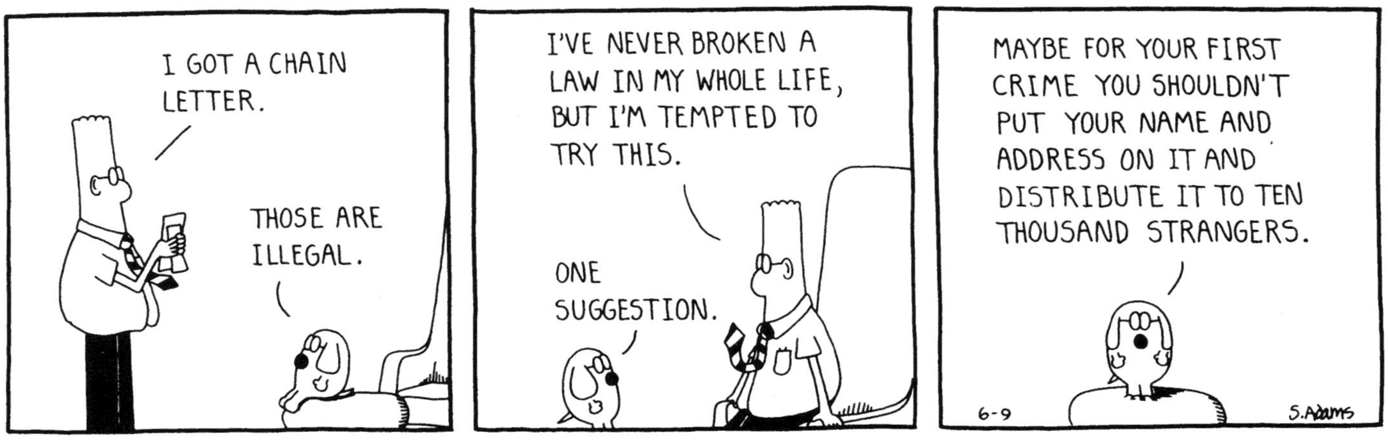
I GOT A CHAIN LETTER.
THOSE ARE ILLEGAL.
I'VE NEVER BROKEN A LAW IN MY WHOLE LIFE, BUT I'M TEMPTED TO TRY THIS.
ONE SUGGESTION.
MAYBE FOR YOUR FIRST CRIME YOU SHOULDN'T PUT YOUR NAME AND ADDRESS ON IT AND DISTRIBUTE IT TO TEN THOUSAND STRANGERS.
6-9
S.Adams

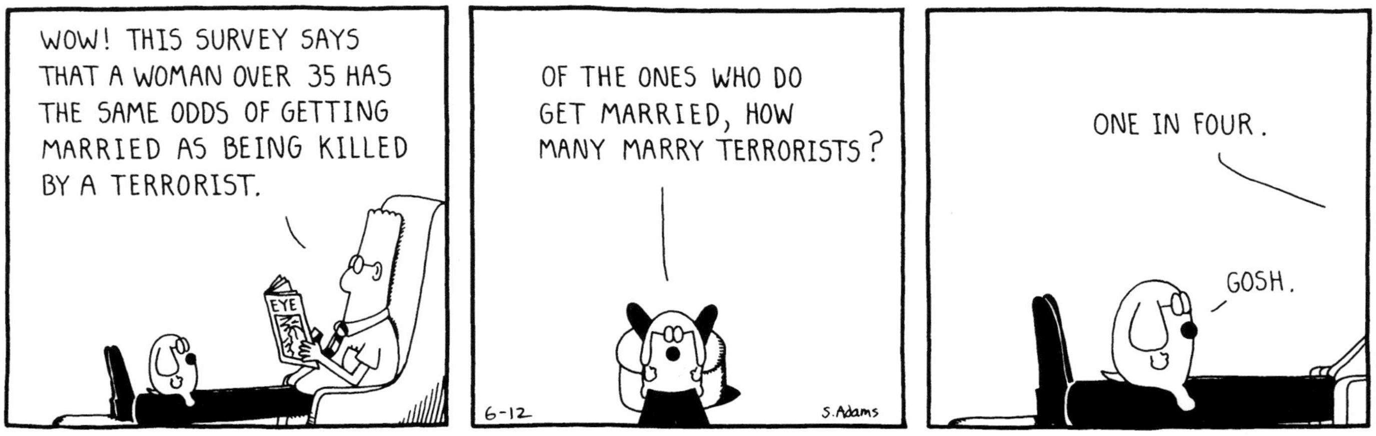
WOW! THIS SURVEY SAYS THAT A WOMAN OVER 35 HAS THE SAME ODDS OF GETTING MARRIED AS BEING KILLED BY A TERRORIST.
EYE
OF THE ONES WHO DO GET MARRIED, HOW MANY MARRY TERRORISTS?
6-12
S.Adams
ONE IN FOUR.
GOSH.

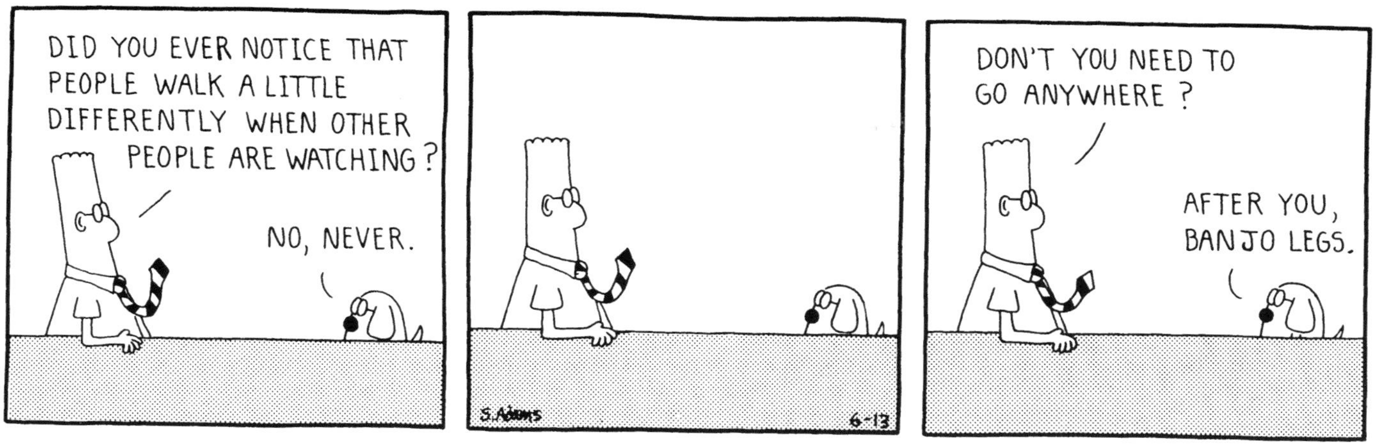
DID YOU EVER NOTICE THAT PEOPLE WALK A LITTLE DIFFERENTLY WHEN OTHER PEOPLE ARE WATCHING?
NO, NEVER.
S.Adams 6-13
DON'T YOU NEED TO GO ANYWHERE?
AFTER YOU, BANJO LEGS.

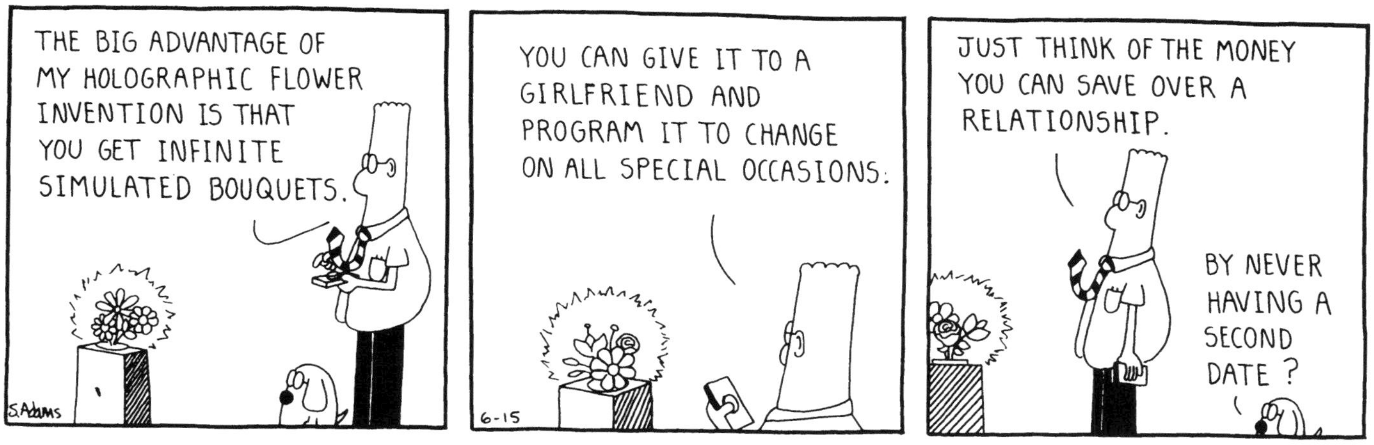
THE BIG ADVANTAGE OF MY HOLOGRAPHIC FLOWER INVENTION IS THAT YOU GET INFINITE SIMULATED BOUQUETS.
S.Adams
YOU CAN GIVE IT TO A GIRLFRIEND AND PROGRAM IT TO CHANGE ON ALL SPECIAL OCCASIONS.
6-15
JUST THINK OF THE MONEY YOU CAN SAVE OVER A RELATIONSHIP.
BY NEVER HAVING A SECOND DATE?

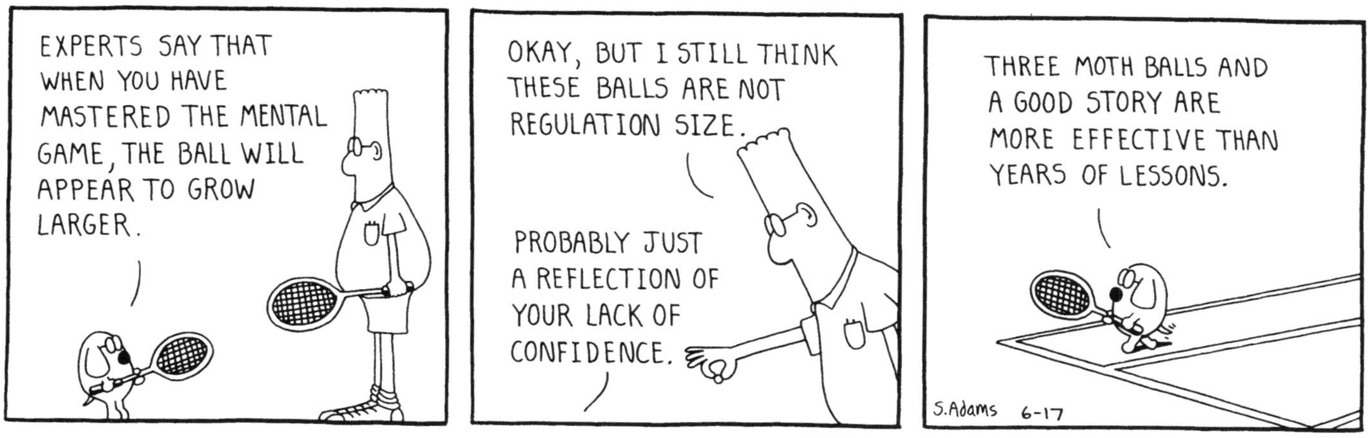
EXPERTS SAY THAT WHEN YOU HAVE MASTERED THE MENTAL GAME, THE BALL WILL APPEAR TO GROW LARGER.
OKAY, BUT I STILL THINK THESE BALLS ARE NOT REGULATION SIZE.
PROBABLY JUST A REFLECTION OF YOUR LACK OF CONFIDENCE.
THREE MOTH BALLS AND A GOOD STORY ARE MORE EFFECTIVE THAN YEARS OF LESSONS.
S.Adams 6-17

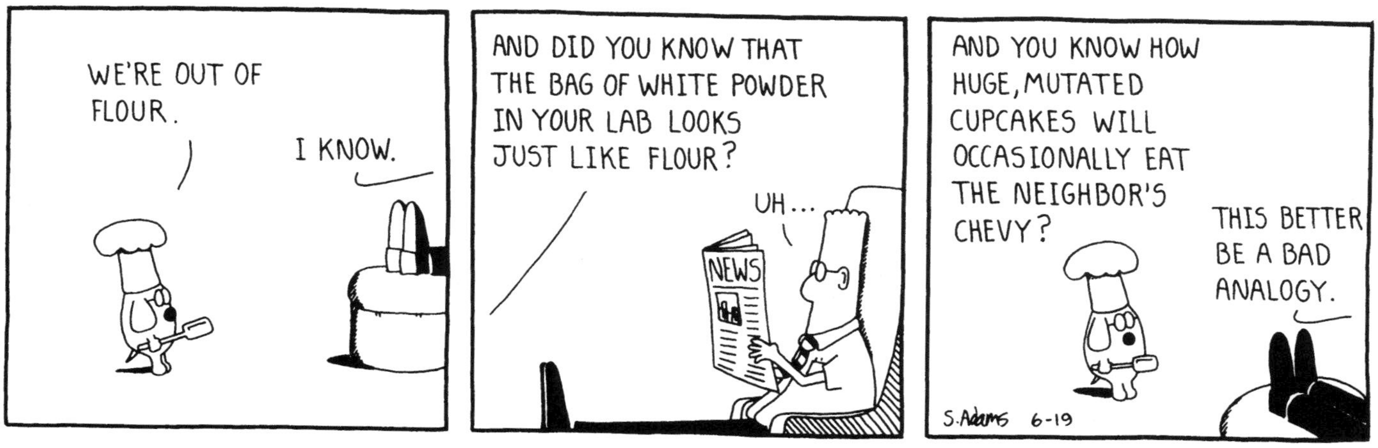
WE'RE OUT OF FLOUR.
I KNOW.
AND DID YOU KNOW THAT THE BAG OF WHITE POWDER IN YOUR LAB LOOKS JUST LIKE FLOUR?
UH...
NEWS
AND YOU KNOW HOW HUGE, MUTATED CUPCAKES WILL OCCASIONALLY EAT THE NEIGHBOR'S CHEVY?
THIS BETTER BE A BAD ANALOGY.
S.Adams 6-19

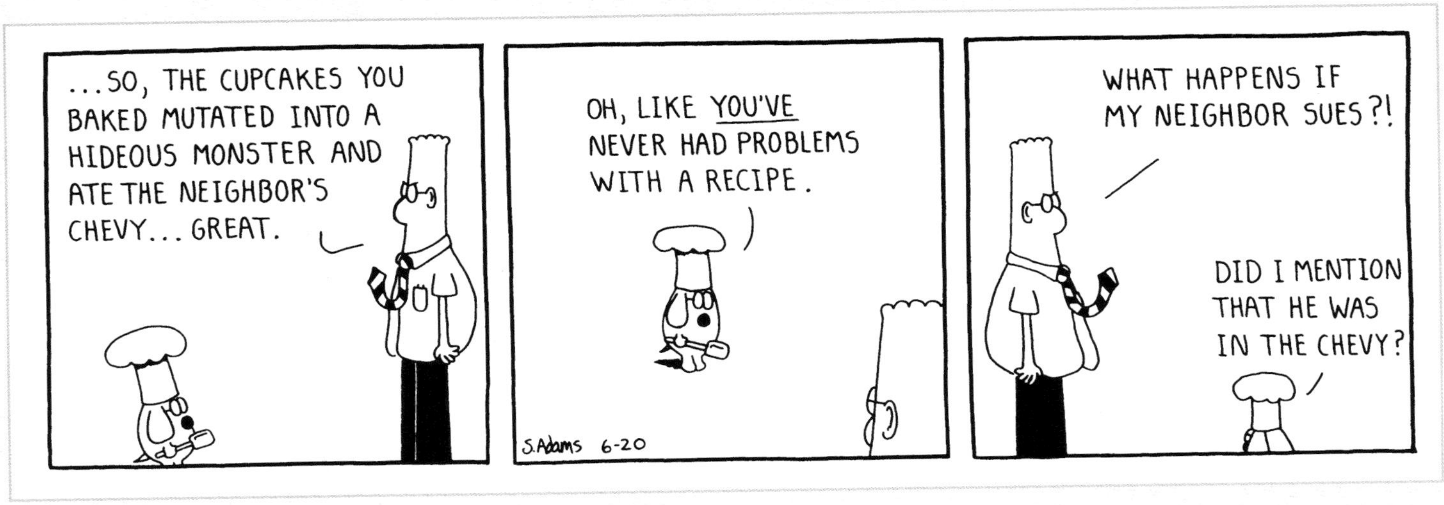
...SO, THE CUPCAKES YOU BAKED MUTATED INTO A HIDEOUS MONSTER AND ATE THE NEIGHBOR'S CHEVY... GREAT.
OH, LIKE YOU'VE NEVER HAD PROBLEMS WITH A RECIPE.
S.Adams 6-20
WHAT HAPPENS IF MY NEIGHBOR SUES?!
DID I MENTION THAT HE WAS IN THE CHEVY?

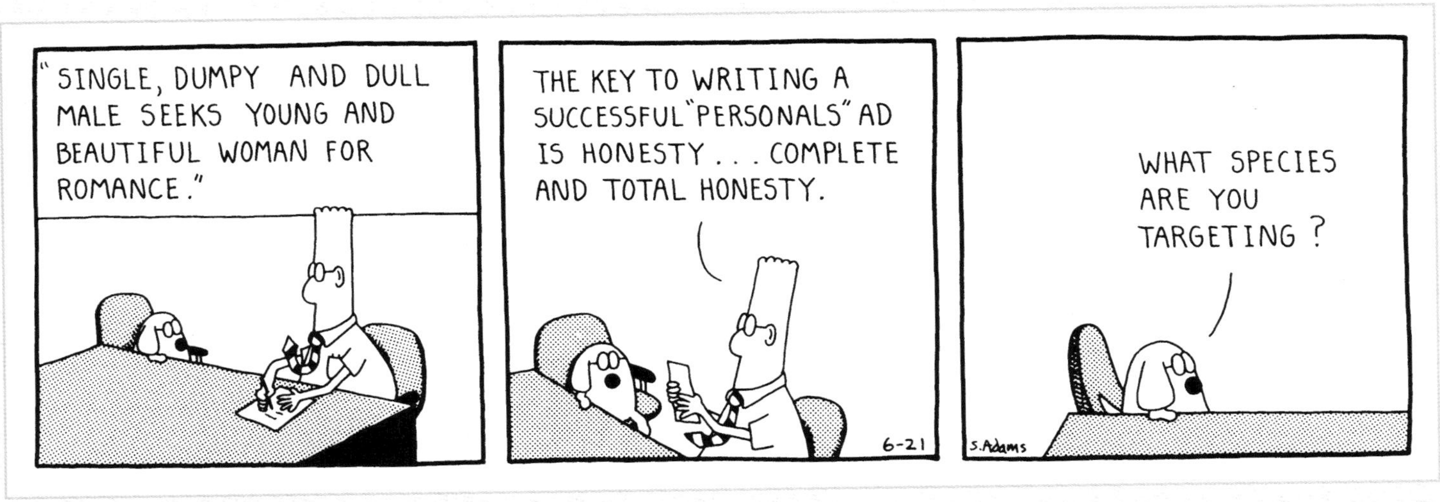
"SINGLE, DUMPY AND DULL MALE SEEKS YOUNG AND BEAUTIFUL WOMAN FOR ROMANCE."
THE KEY TO WRITING A SUCCESSFUL "PERSONALS" AD IS HONESTY... COMPLETE AND TOTAL HONESTY.
6-21
WHAT SPECIES ARE YOU TARGETING?
S.Adams

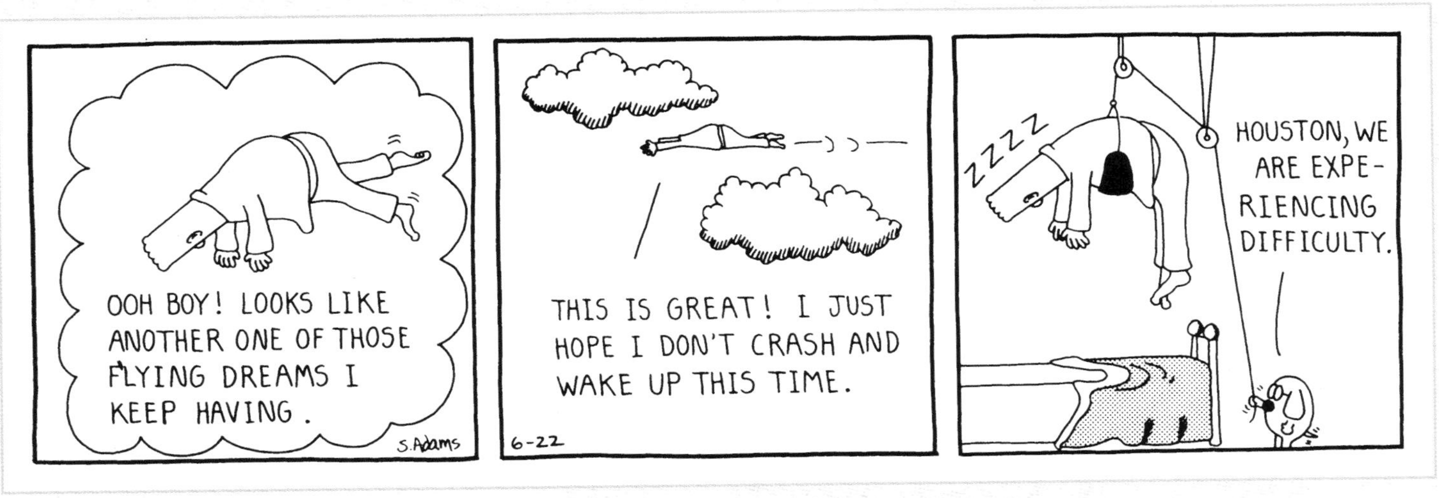
OOH BOY! LOOKS LIKE ANOTHER ONE OF THOSE FLYING DREAMS I KEEP HAVING.
S.Adams
THIS IS GREAT! I JUST HOPE I DON'T CRASH AND WAKE UP THIS TIME.
6-22
ZZZZ
HOUSTON, WE ARE EXPE-RIENCING DIFFICULTY.

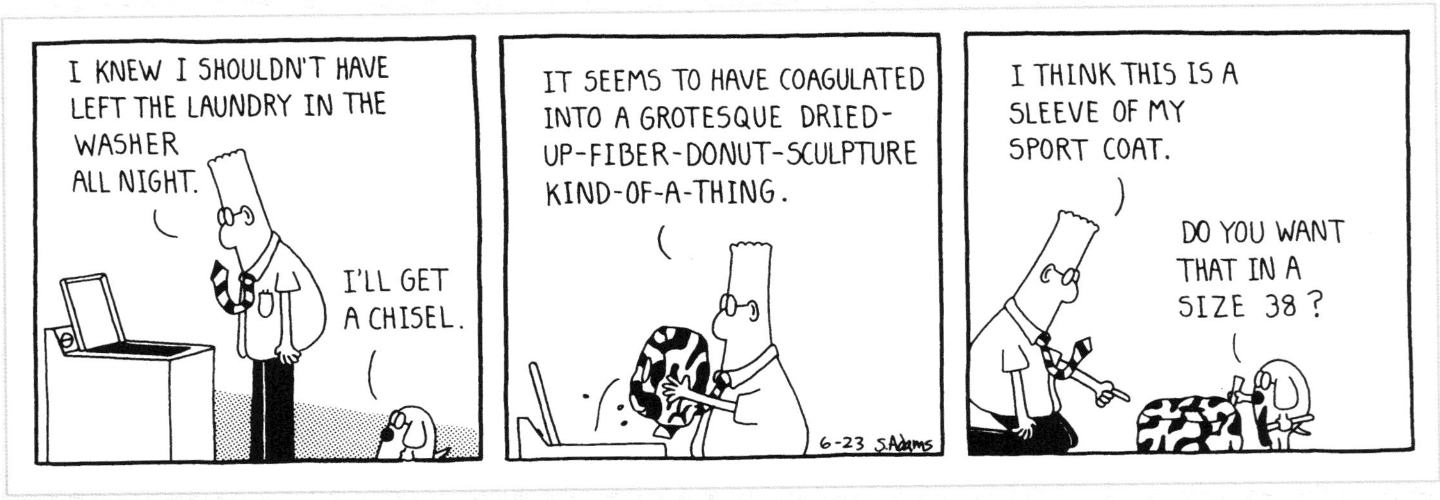
I KNEW I SHOULDN'T HAVE LEFT THE LAUNDRY IN THE WASHER ALL NIGHT.
I'LL GET A CHISEL.
IT SEEMS TO HAVE COAGULATED INTO A GROTESQUE DRIED-UP-FIBER-DONUT-SCULPTURE KIND-OF-A-THING.
6-23 S.Adams
I THINK THIS IS A SLEEVE OF MY SPORT COAT.
DO YOU WANT THAT IN A SIZE 38?

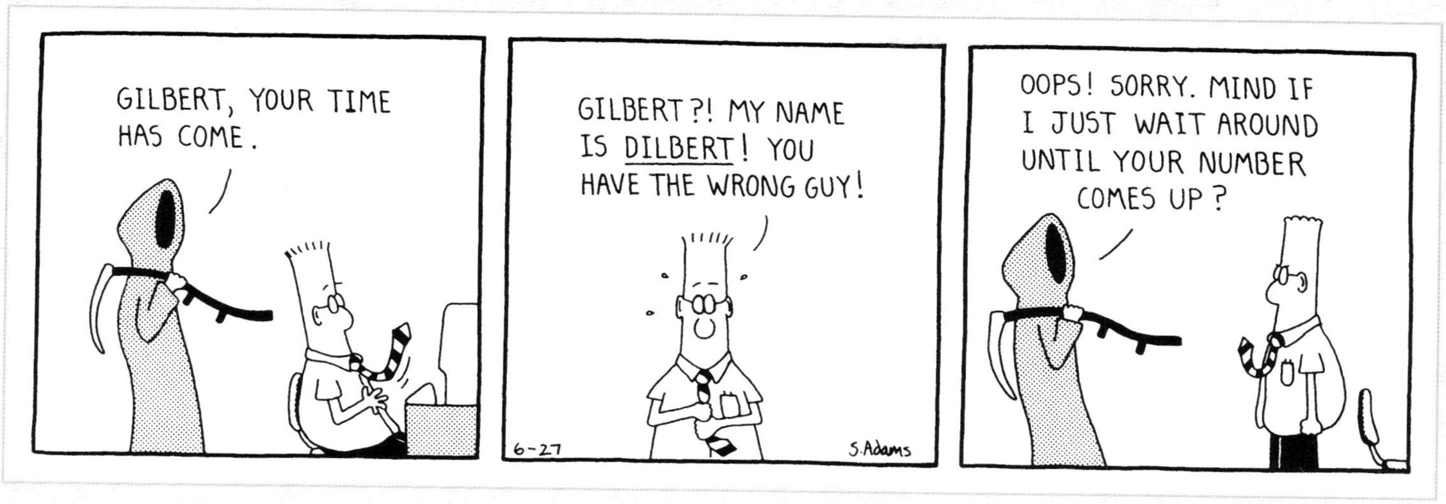
GILBERT, YOUR TIME HAS COME.
GILBERT?! MY NAME IS DILBERT! YOU HAVE THE WRONG GUY!
6-27
S.Adams
OOPS! SORRY. MIND IF I JUST WAIT AROUND UNTIL YOUR NUMBER COMES UP?

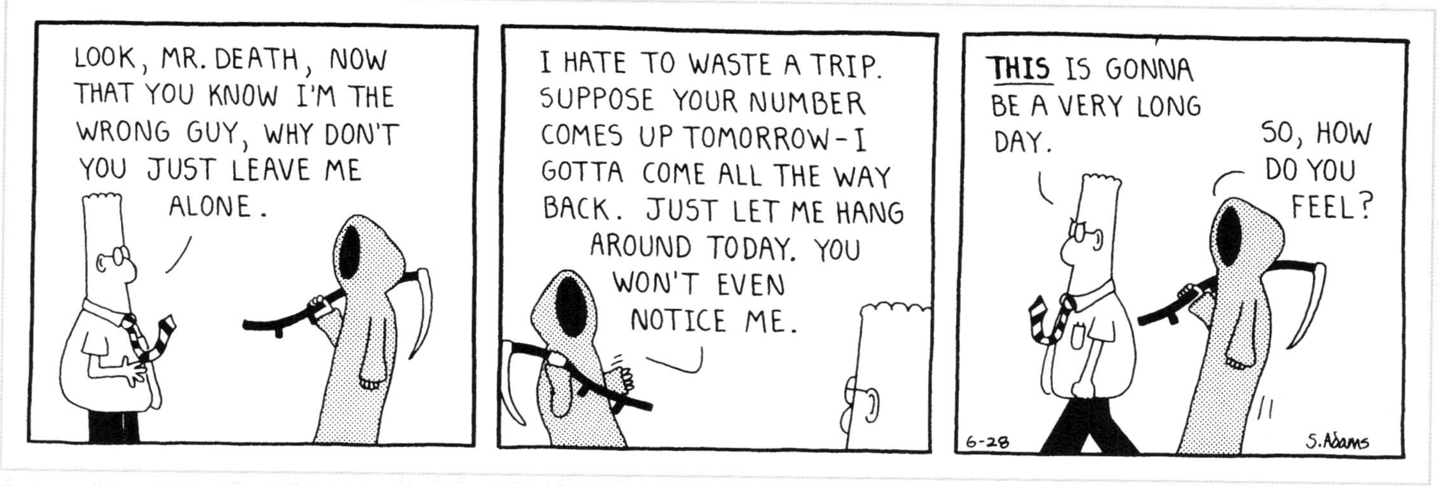
LOOK, MR. DEATH, NOW THAT YOU KNOW I'M THE WRONG GUY, WHY DON'T YOU JUST LEAVE ME ALONE.
I HATE TO WASTE A TRIP. SUPPOSE YOUR NUMBER COMES UP TOMORROW - I GOTTA COME ALL THE WAY BACK. JUST LET ME HANG AROUND TODAY. YOU WON'T EVEN NOTICE ME.
THIS IS GONNA BE A VERY LONG DAY.
SO, HOW DO YOU FEEL?
6-28
S.Adams

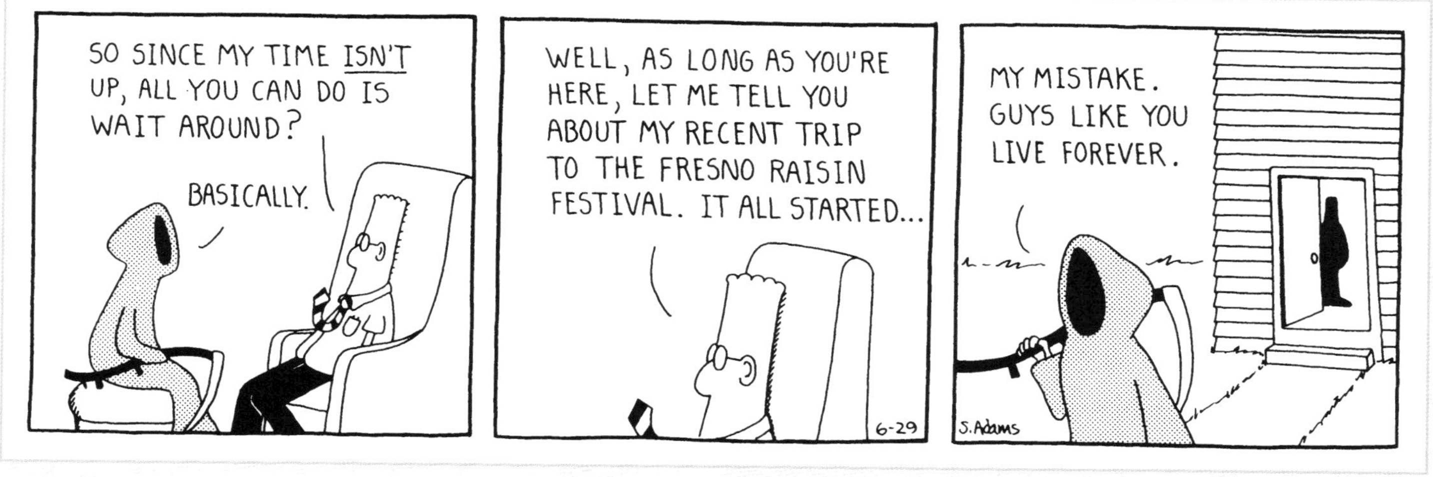
SO SINCE MY TIME ISN'T UP, ALL YOU CAN DO IS WAIT AROUND?
BASICALLY.
WELL, AS LONG AS YOU'RE HERE, LET ME TELL YOU ABOUT MY RECENT TRIP TO THE FRESNO RAISIN FESTIVAL. IT ALL STARTED...
6-29
MY MISTAKE. GUYS LIKE YOU LIVE FOREVER.
S.Adams

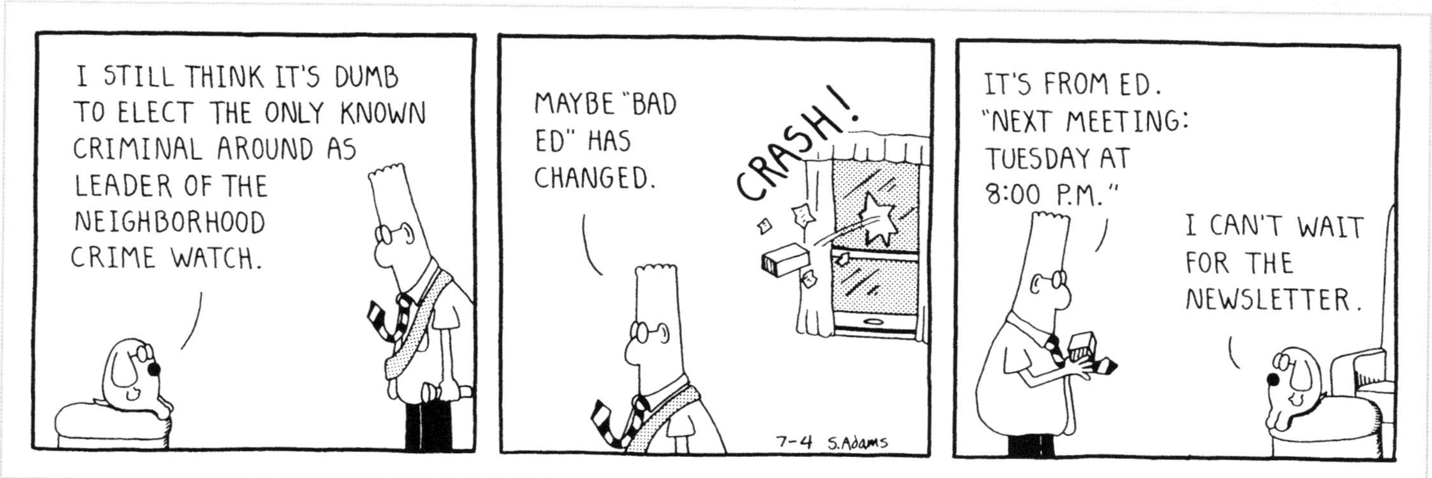
I STILL THINK IT'S DUMB TO ELECT THE ONLY KNOWN CRIMINAL AROUND AS LEADER OF THE NEIGHBORHOOD CRIME WATCH.
MAYBE "BAD ED" HAS CHANGED.
CRASH!
7-4 S.Adams
IT'S FROM ED. "NEXT MEETING: TUESDAY AT 8:00 P.M."
I CAN'T WAIT FOR THE NEWSLETTER.

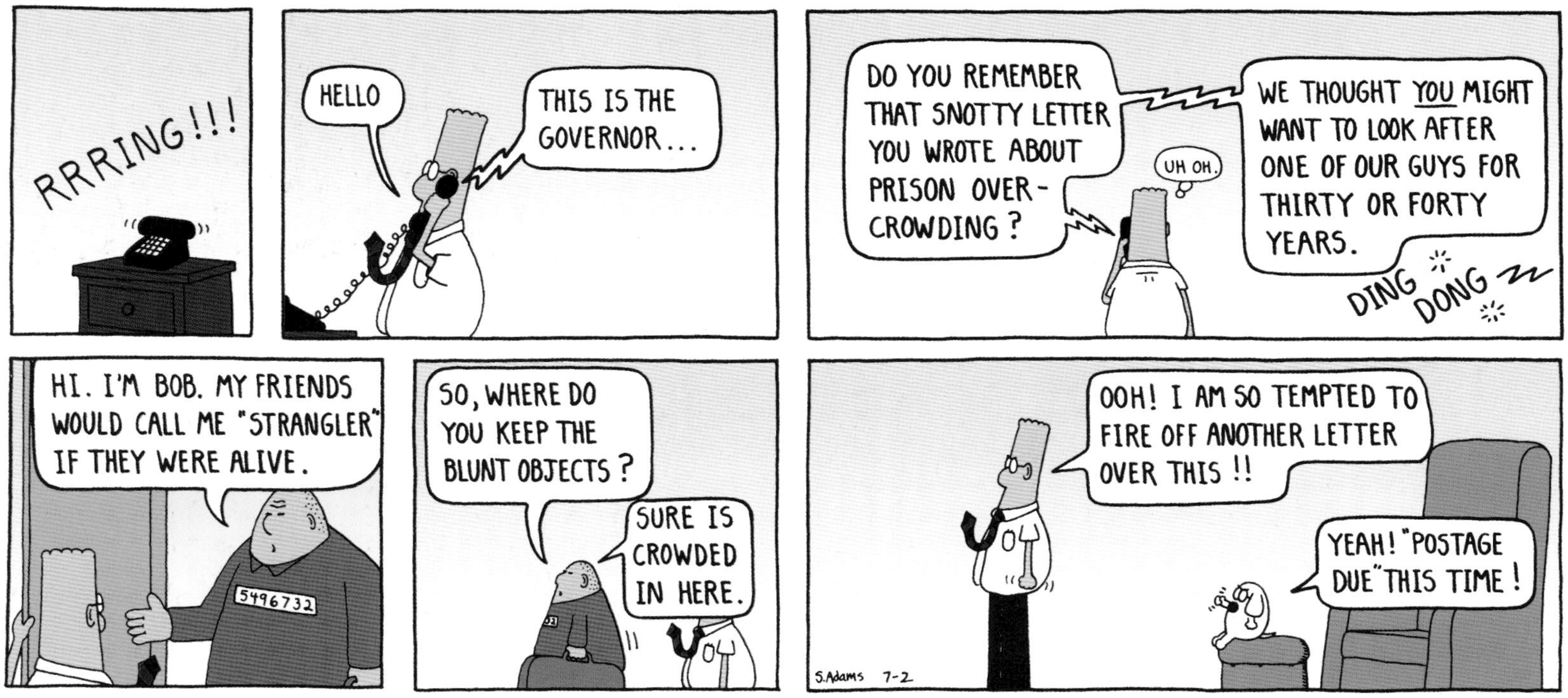
RRRING!!!
HELLO
THIS IS THE GOVERNOR...
DO YOU REMEMBER THAT SNOTTY LETTER YOU WROTE ABOUT PRISON OVER-CROWDING?
UH OH.
WE THOUGHT YOU MIGHT WANT TO LOOK AFTER ONE OF OUR GUYS FOR THIRTY OR FORTY YEARS.
DING DONG
HI. I'M BOB. MY FRIENDS WOULD CALL ME "STRANGLER" IF THEY WERE ALIVE.
5496732
SO, WHERE DO YOU KEEP THE BLUNT OBJECTS?
SURE IS CROWDED IN HERE.
OOH! I AM SO TEMPTED TO FIRE OFF ANOTHER LETTER OVER THIS!!
YEAH! "POSTAGE DUE" THIS TIME!
S.Adams 7-2

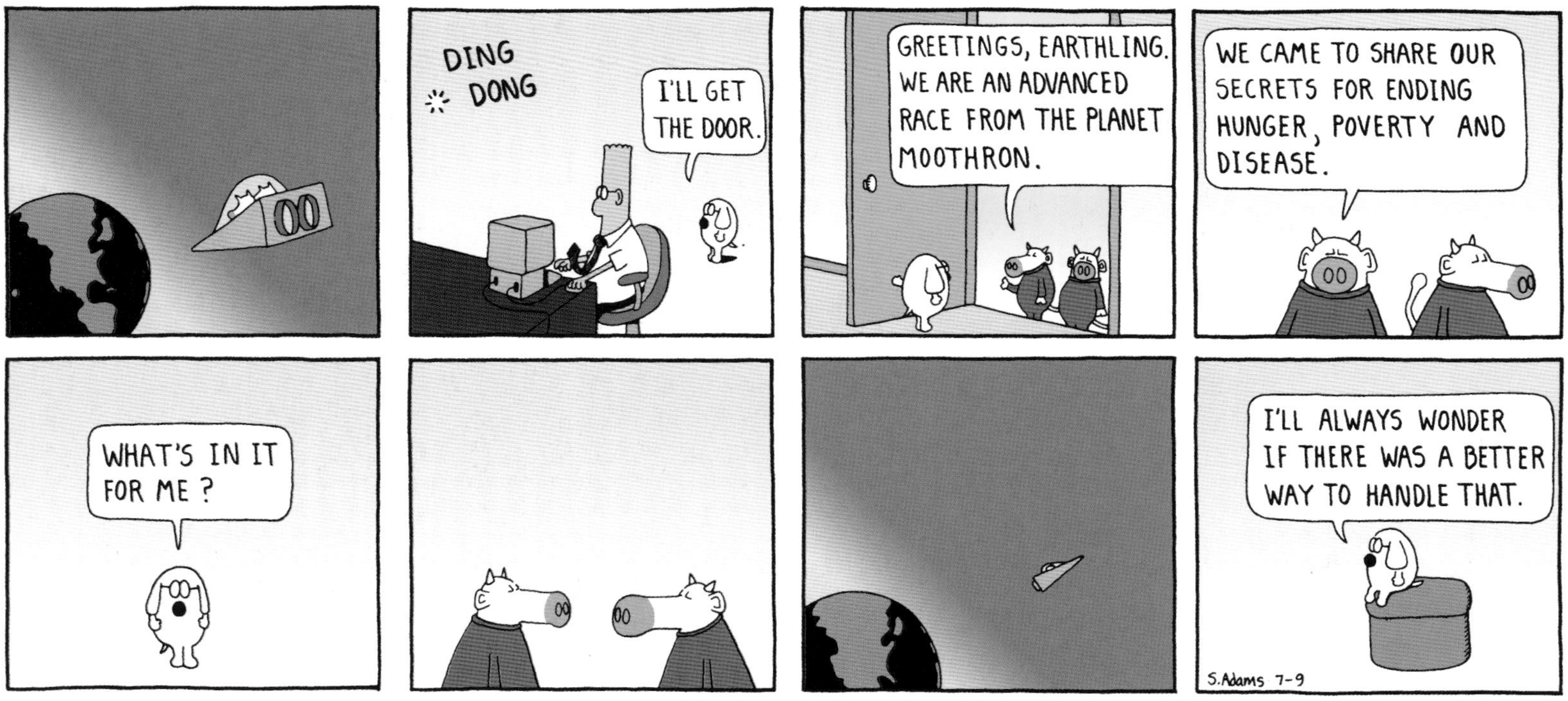
DING DONG
I'LL GET THE DOOR.
GREETINGS, EARTHLING. WE ARE AN ADVANCED RACE FROM THE PLANET MOOTHRON.
WE CAME TO SHARE OUR SECRETS FOR ENDING HUNGER, POVERTY AND DISEASE.
WHAT'S IN IT FOR ME?
I'LL ALWAYS WONDER IF THERE WAS A BETTER WAY TO HANDLE THAT.
S.Adams 7-9

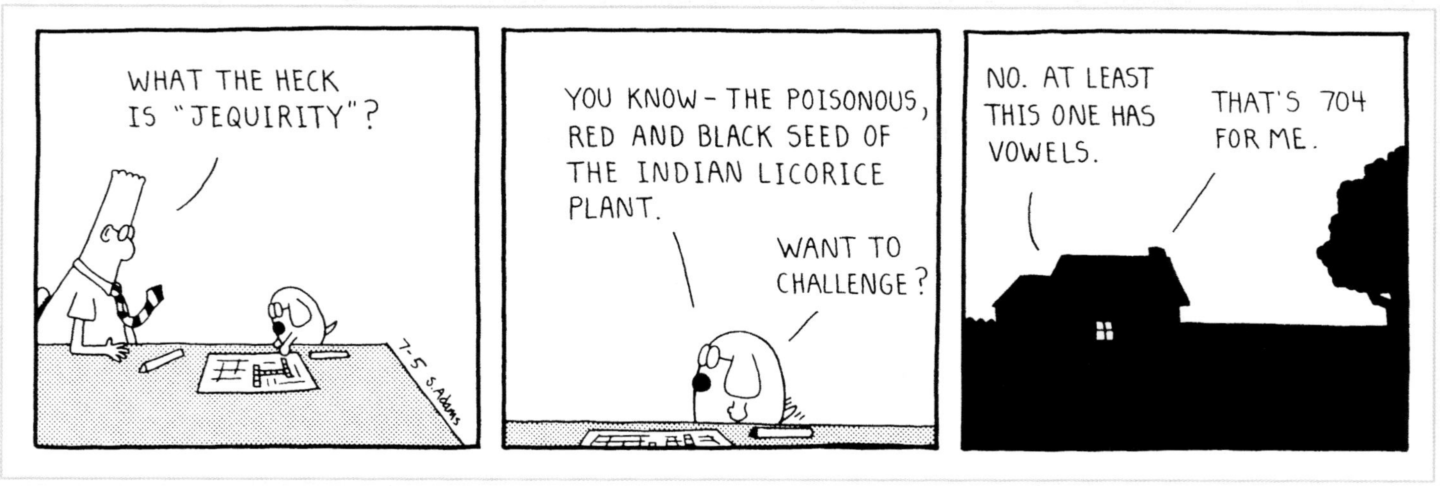
WHAT THE HECK IS "JEQUIRITY"?
7-5 S.Adams
YOU KNOW - THE POISONOUS, RED AND BLACK SEED OF THE INDIAN LICORICE PLANT.
WANT TO CHALLENGE?
NO. AT LEAST THIS ONE HAS VOWELS.
THAT'S 704 FOR ME.

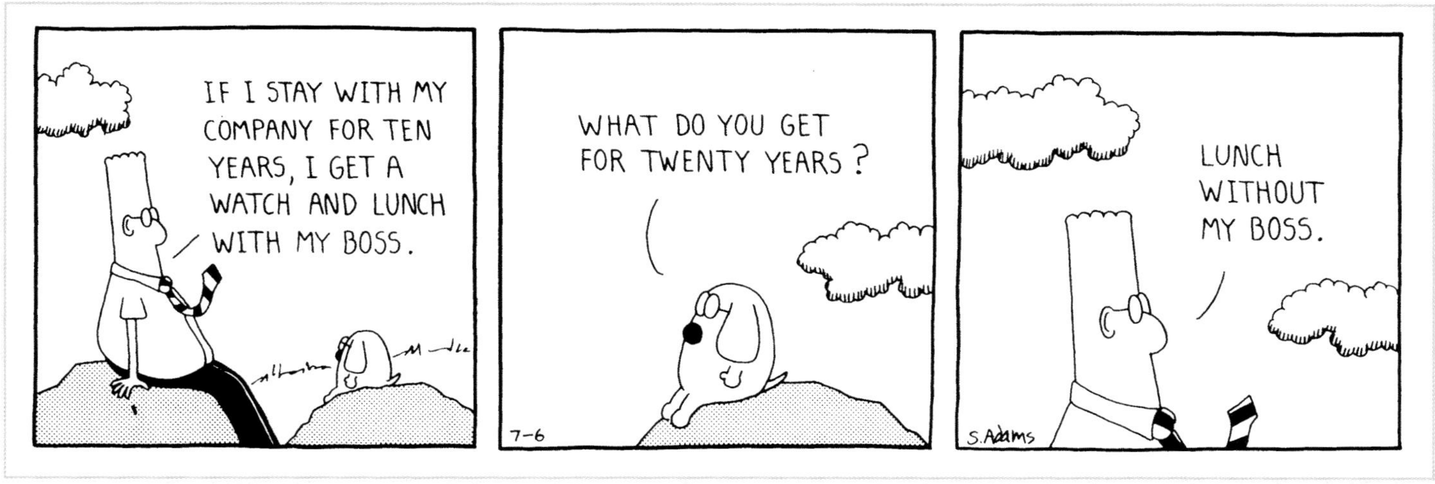
IF I STAY WITH MY COMPANY FOR TEN YEARS, I GET A WATCH AND LUNCH WITH MY BOSS.
WHAT DO YOU GET FOR TWENTY YEARS?
7-6
LUNCH WITHOUT MY BOSS.
S.Adams

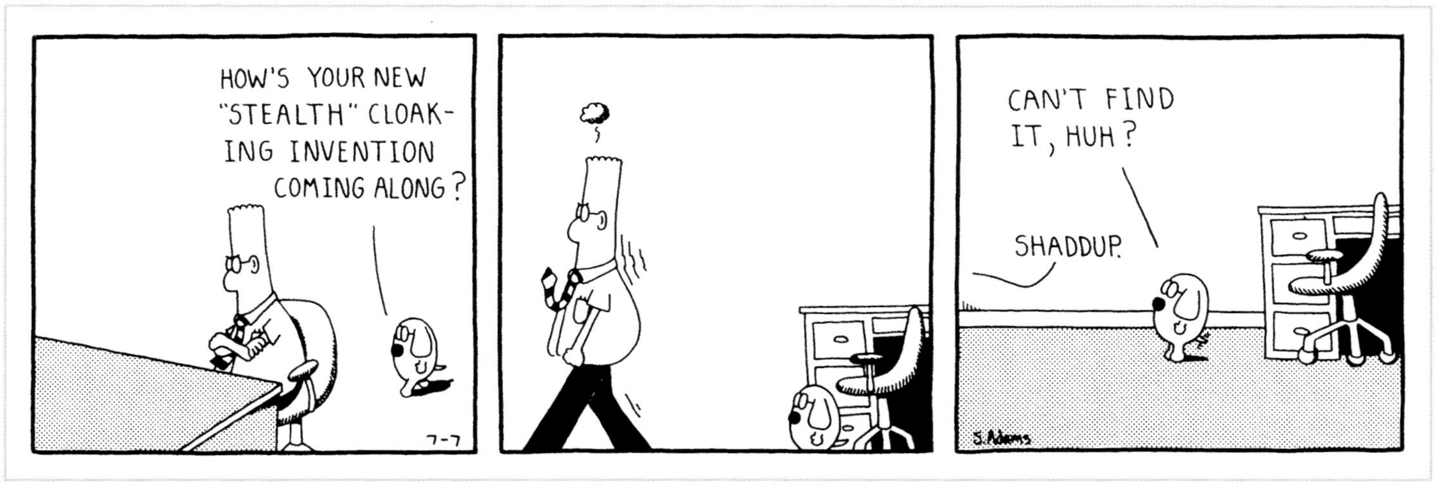
HOW'S YOUR NEW "STEALTH" CLOAKING INVENTION COMING ALONG?
7-7
CAN'T FIND IT, HUH?
SHADDUP.
S.Adams

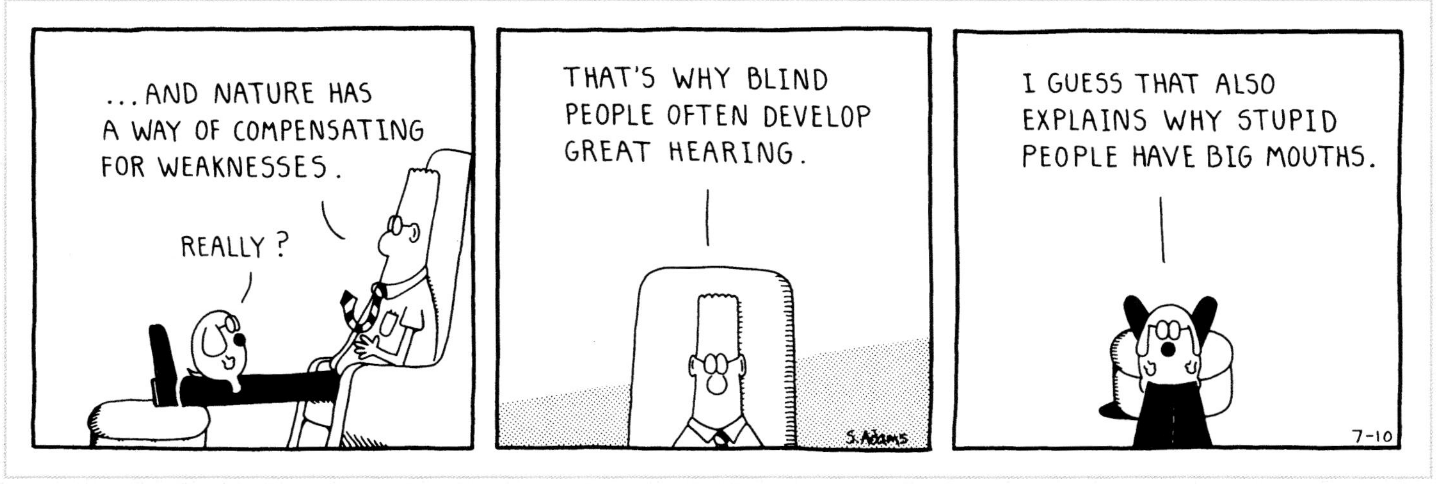
...AND NATURE HAS A WAY OF COMPENSATING FOR WEAKNESSES.
REALLY?
THAT'S WHY BLIND PEOPLE OFTEN DEVELOP GREAT HEARING.
S.Adams
I GUESS THAT ALSO EXPLAINS WHY STUPID PEOPLE HAVE BIG MOUTHS.
7-10

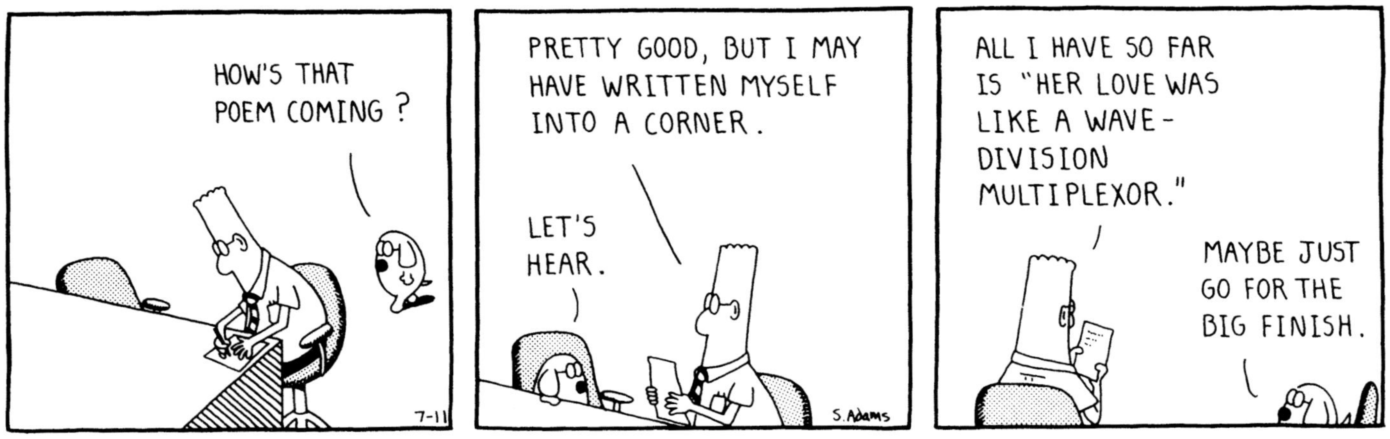
HOW'S THAT POEM COMING ?
PRETTY GOOD, BUT I MAY HAVE WRITTEN MYSELF INTO A CORNER.
LET'S HEAR.
ALL I HAVE SO FAR IS "HER LOVE WAS LIKE A WAVE-DIVISION MULTIPLEXOR."
MAYBE JUST GO FOR THE BIG FINISH.
7-11
S. Adams

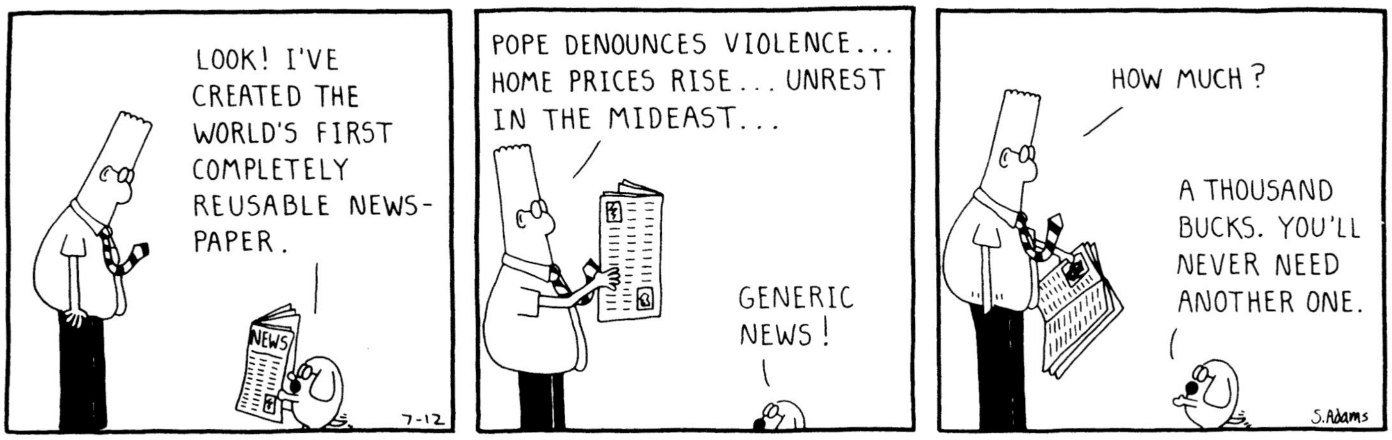
LOOK! I'VE CREATED THE WORLD'S FIRST COMPLETELY REUSABLE NEWS-PAPER.
NEWS
7-12
POPE DENOUNCES VIOLENCE... HOME PRICES RISE... UNREST IN THE MIDEAST...
GENERIC NEWS!
HOW MUCH?
A THOUSAND BUCKS. YOU'LL NEVER NEED ANOTHER ONE.
S. Adams

Almost twenty years later, and Dogbert's newspaper is still accurate, except for the part about rising home prices. But eventually he will be right about that again too.

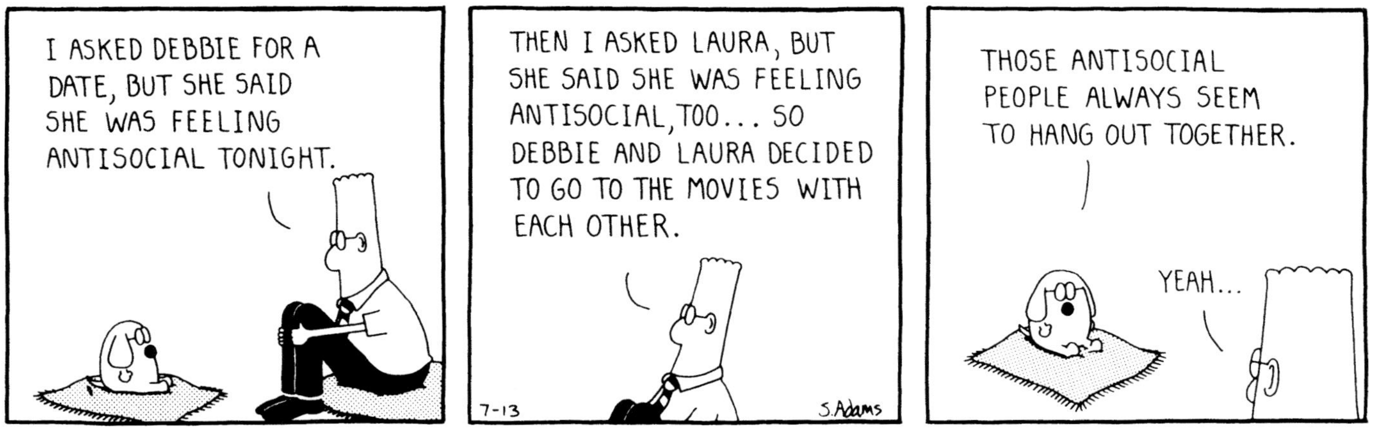
I ASKED DEBBIE FOR A DATE, BUT SHE SAID SHE WAS FEELING ANTISOCIAL TONIGHT.
THEN I ASKED LAURA, BUT SHE SAID SHE WAS FEELING ANTISOCIAL, TOO... SO DEBBIE AND LAURA DECIDED TO GO TO THE MOVIES WITH EACH OTHER.
7-13
S. Adams
THOSE ANTISOCIAL PEOPLE ALWAYS SEEM TO HANG OUT TOGETHER.
YEAH...

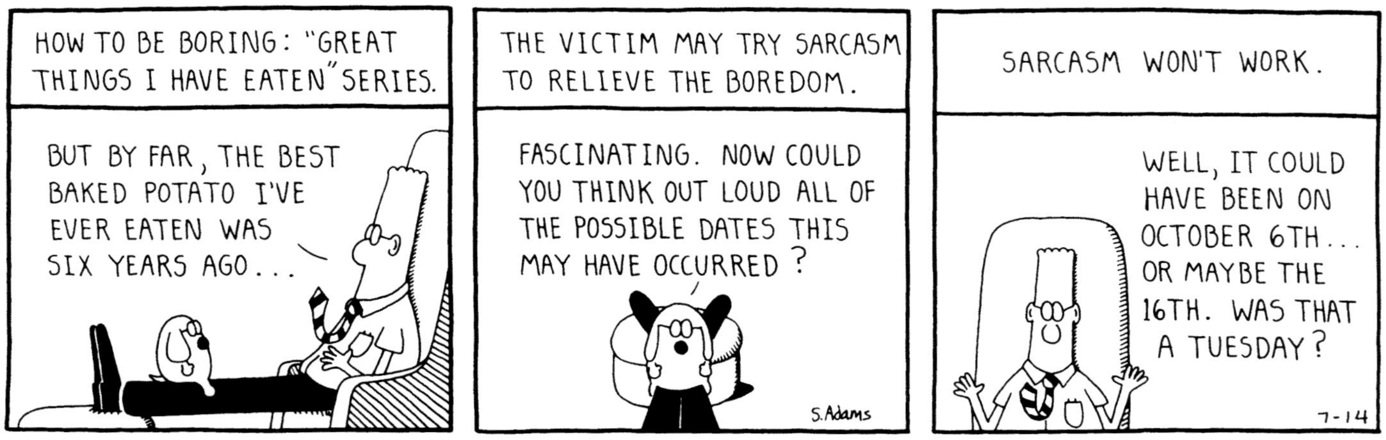
HOW TO BE BORING: "GREAT THINGS I HAVE EATEN" SERIES.
BUT BY FAR, THE BEST BAKED POTATO I'VE EVER EATEN WAS SIX YEARS AGO...
THE VICTIM MAY TRY SARCASM TO RELIEVE THE BOREDOM.
FASCINATING. NOW COULD YOU THINK OUT LOUD ALL OF THE POSSIBLE DATES THIS MAY HAVE OCCURRED?
S. Adams
SARCASM WON'T WORK.
WELL, IT COULD HAVE BEEN ON OCTOBER 6TH... OR MAYBE THE 16TH. WAS THAT A TUESDAY?
7-14

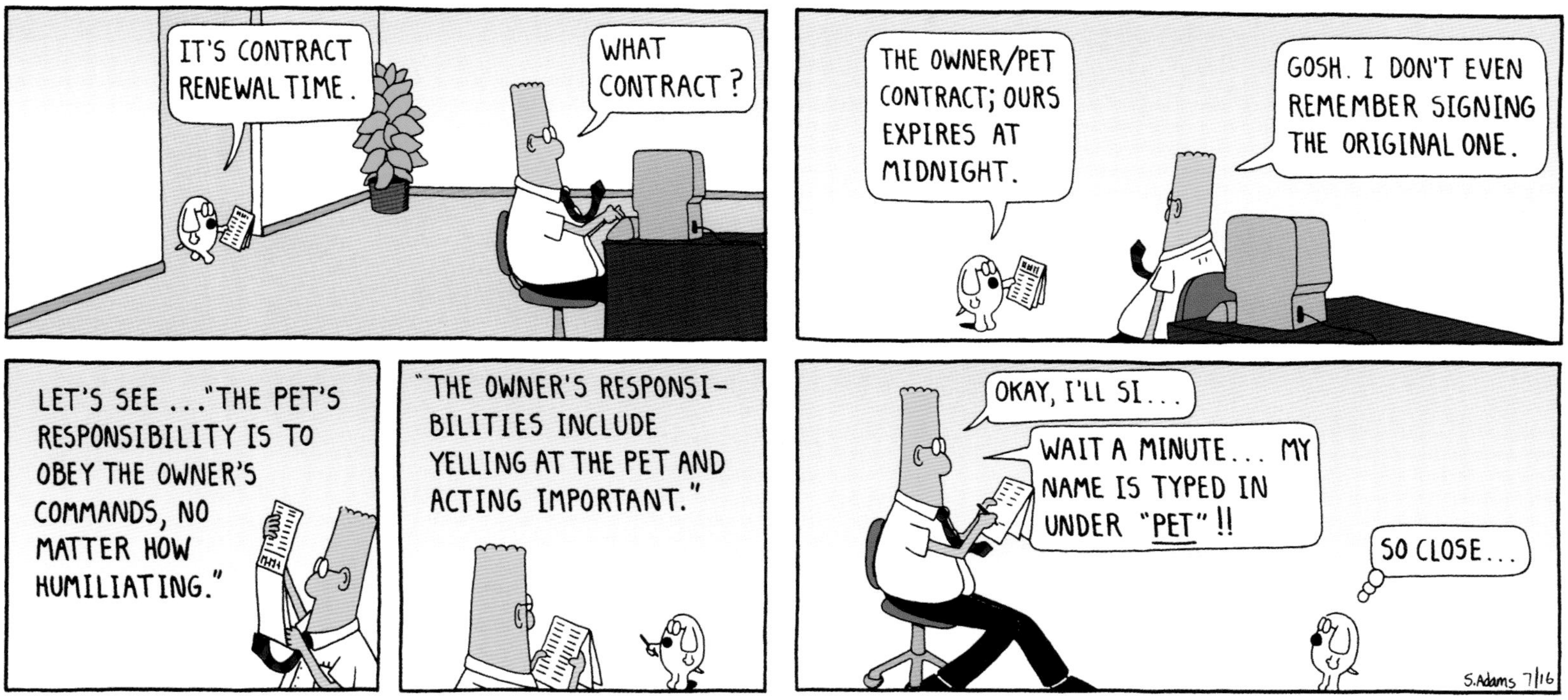
IT'S CONTRACT RENEWAL TIME.
WHAT CONTRACT?
THE OWNER/PET CONTRACT; OURS EXPIRES AT MIDNIGHT.
GOSH. I DON'T EVEN REMEMBER SIGNING THE ORIGINAL ONE.
LET'S SEE ..."THE PET'S RESPONSIBILITY IS TO OBEY THE OWNER'S COMMANDS, NO MATTER HOW HUMILIATING."
"THE OWNER'S RESPONSIBILITIES INCLUDE YELLING AT THE PET AND ACTING IMPORTANT."
OKAY, I'LL SI...
WAIT A MINUTE... MY NAME IS TYPED IN UNDER "PET"!!
SO CLOSE...
S.Adams 7/16

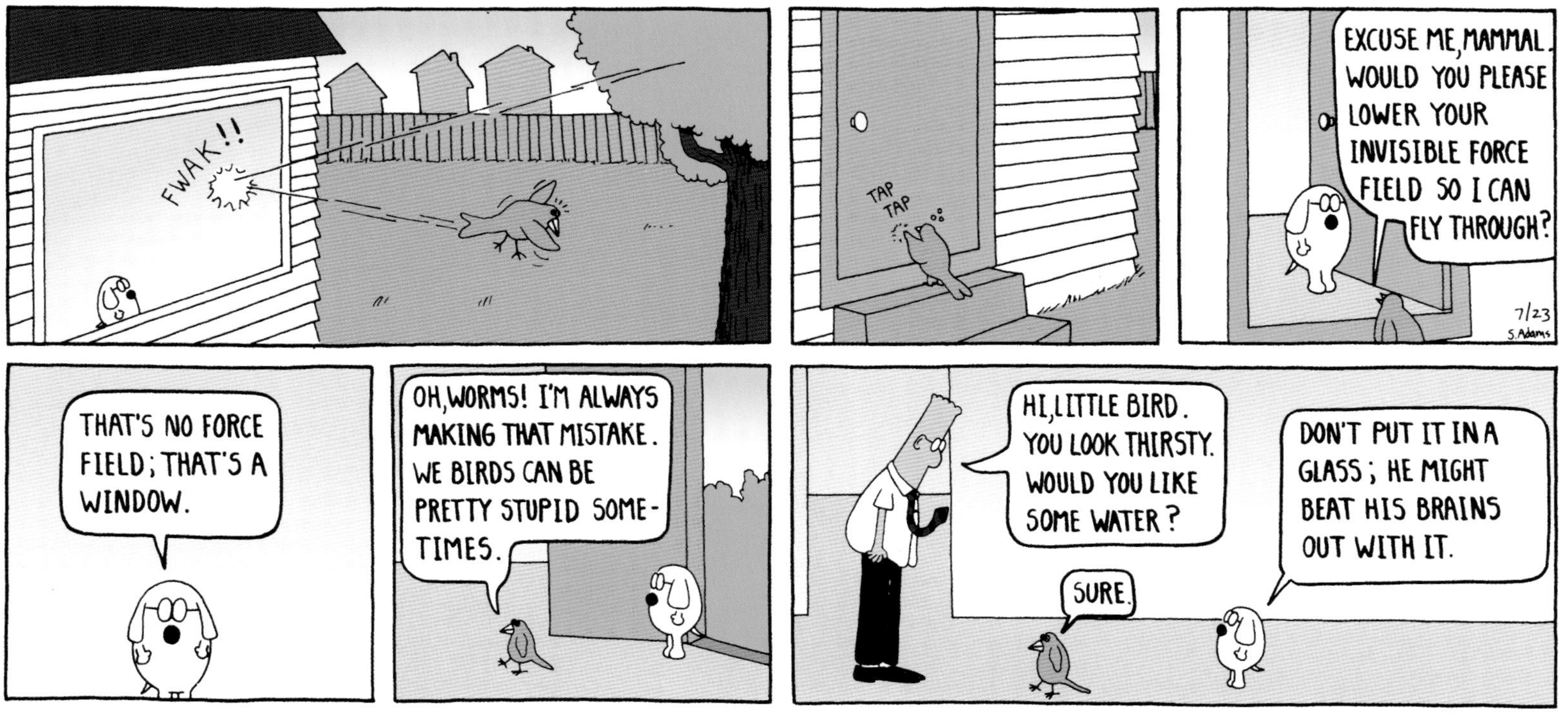
FWAK!!
TAP TAP
EXCUSE ME, MAMMAL. WOULD YOU PLEASE LOWER YOUR INVISIBLE FORCE FIELD SO I CAN FLY THROUGH?
7/23 S.Adams
THAT'S NO FORCE FIELD; THAT'S A WINDOW.
OH, WORMS! I'M ALWAYS MAKING THAT MISTAKE. WE BIRDS CAN BE PRETTY STUPID SOMETIMES.
HI, LITTLE BIRD. YOU LOOK THIRSTY. WOULD YOU LIKE SOME WATER?
SURE.
DON'T PUT IT IN A GLASS; HE MIGHT BEAT HIS BRAINS OUT WITH IT.

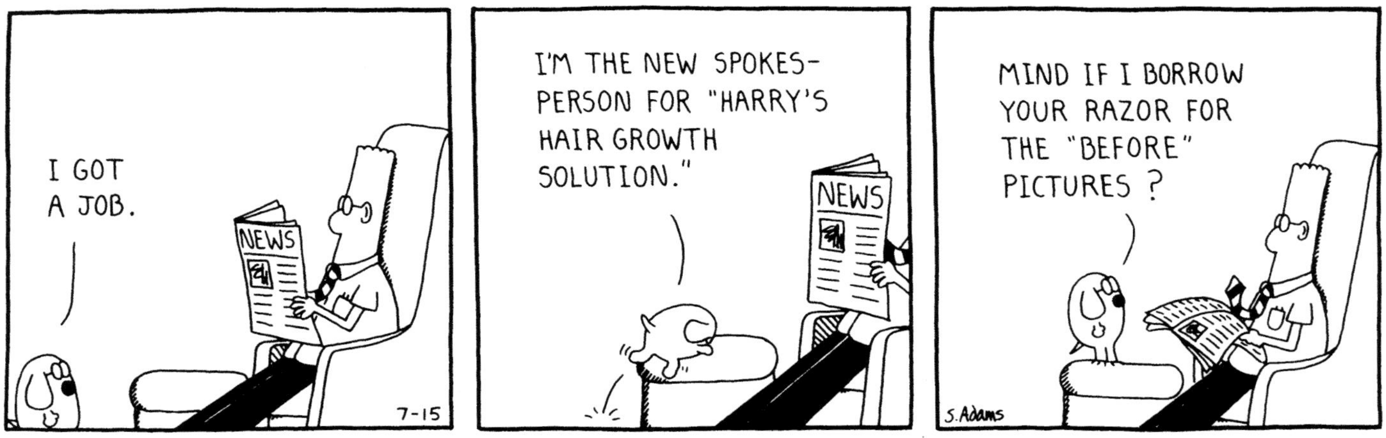
I GOT A JOB.
I'M THE NEW SPOKES-PERSON FOR "HARRY'S HAIR GROWTH SOLUTION."
NEWS
MIND IF I BORROW YOUR RAZOR FOR THE "BEFORE" PICTURES ?
7-15
S. Adams

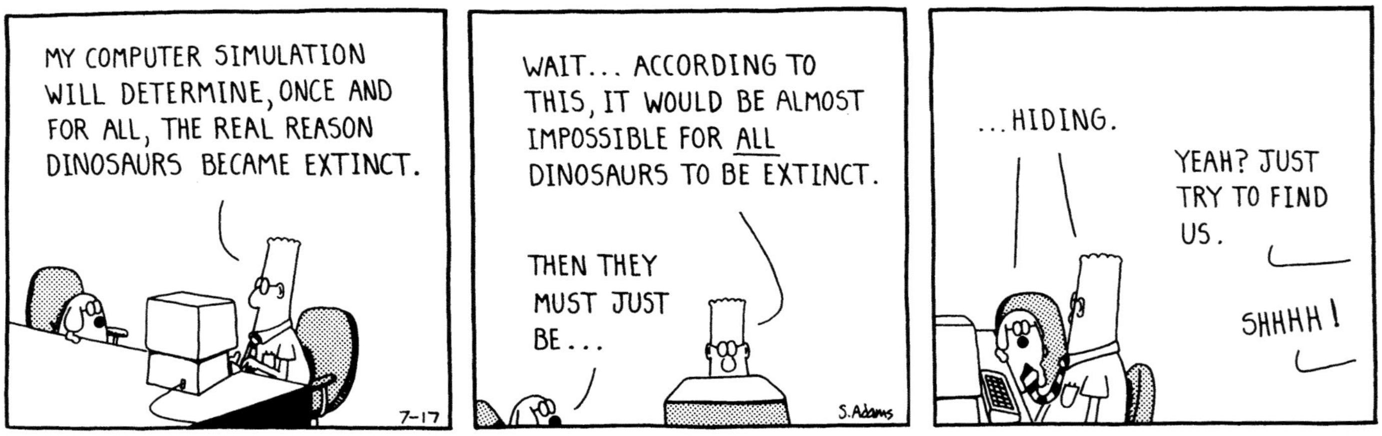
MY COMPUTER SIMULATION WILL DETERMINE, ONCE AND FOR ALL, THE REAL REASON DINOSAURS BECAME EXTINCT.
7-17
WAIT... ACCORDING TO THIS, IT WOULD BE ALMOST IMPOSSIBLE FOR ALL DINOSAURS TO BE EXTINCT.
THEN THEY MUST JUST BE...
S. Adams
...HIDING.
YEAH? JUST TRY TO FIND US.
SHHHH!

In the early days, I had a group of semiregular characters that were dinosaurs living in Dilbert's house. Admittedly, I introduced these characters because the strip was floundering and dinosaurs are always popular. One big problem was finding a way to introduce dinosaurs in a strip about the present.

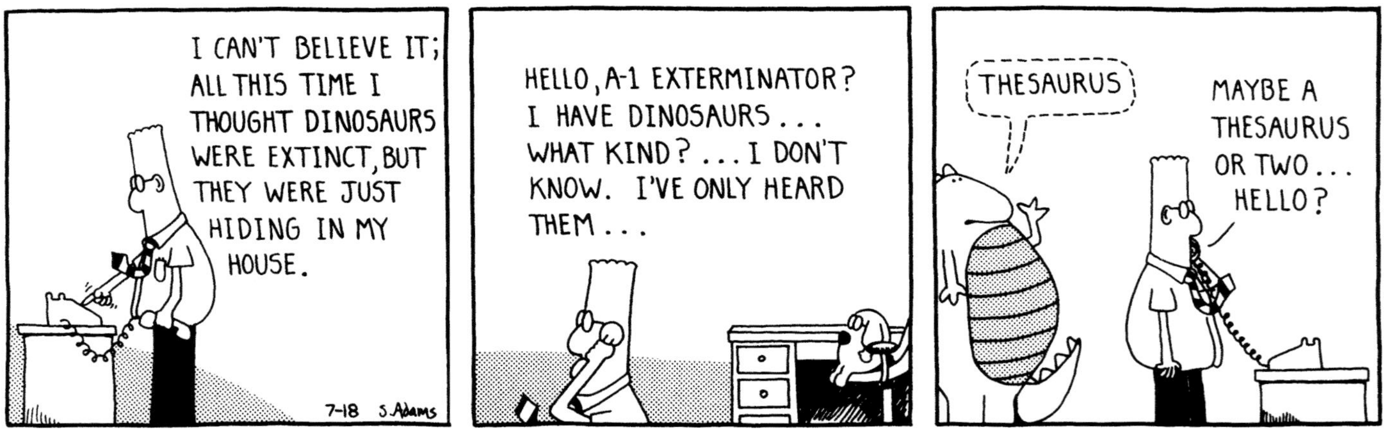
I CAN'T BELIEVE IT; ALL THIS TIME I THOUGHT DINOSAURS WERE EXTINCT, BUT THEY WERE JUST HIDING IN MY HOUSE.
7-18 S. Adams
HELLO, A-1 EXTERMINATOR? I HAVE DINOSAURS... WHAT KIND? ...I DON'T KNOW. I'VE ONLY HEARD THEM...
THESAURUS
MAYBE A THESAURUS OR TWO... HELLO?

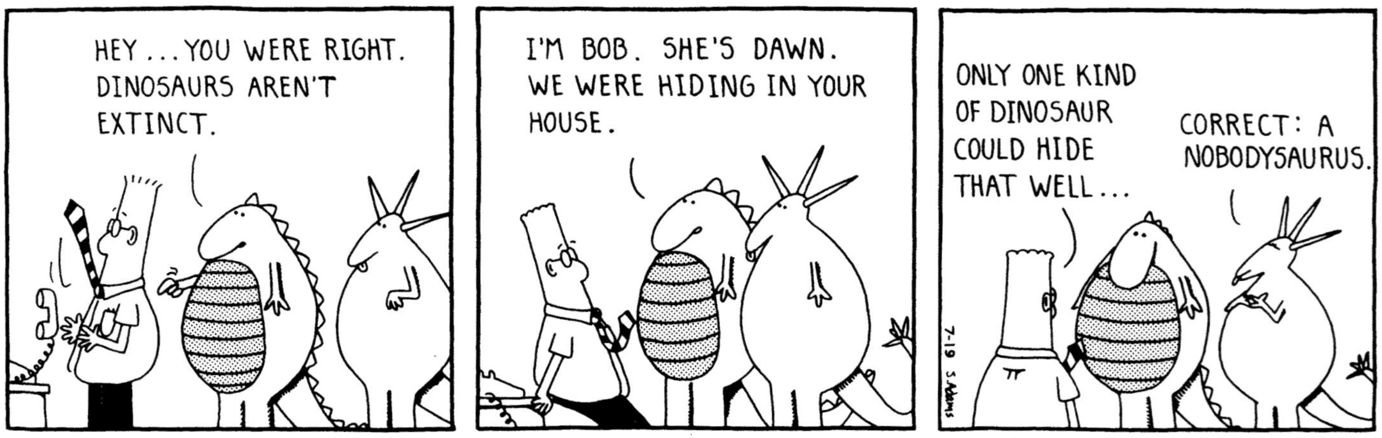
HEY...YOU WERE RIGHT. DINOSAURS AREN'T EXTINCT.
I'M BOB. SHE'S DAWN. WE WERE HIDING IN YOUR HOUSE.
ONLY ONE KIND OF DINOSAUR COULD HIDE THAT WELL...
CORRECT: A NOBODYSAURUS.
7-19 S. Adams

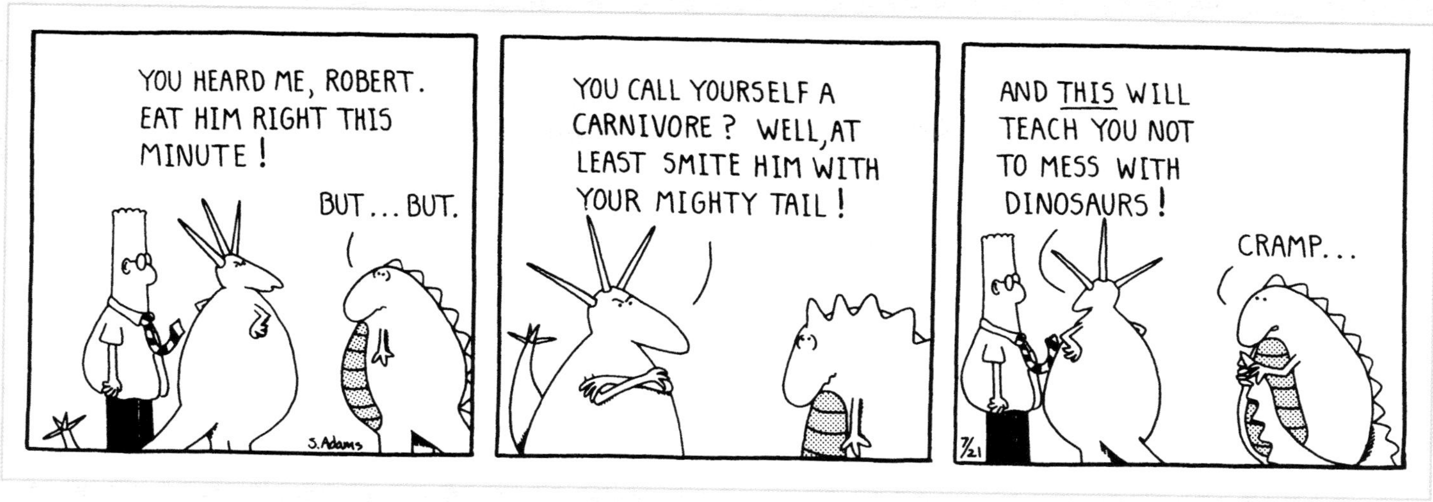
YOU HEARD ME, ROBERT. EAT HIM RIGHT THIS MINUTE!
BUT... BUT.
YOU CALL YOURSELF A CARNIVORE? WELL, AT LEAST SMITE HIM WITH YOUR MIGHTY TAIL!
AND THIS WILL TEACH YOU NOT TO MESS WITH DINOSAURS!
CRAMP...

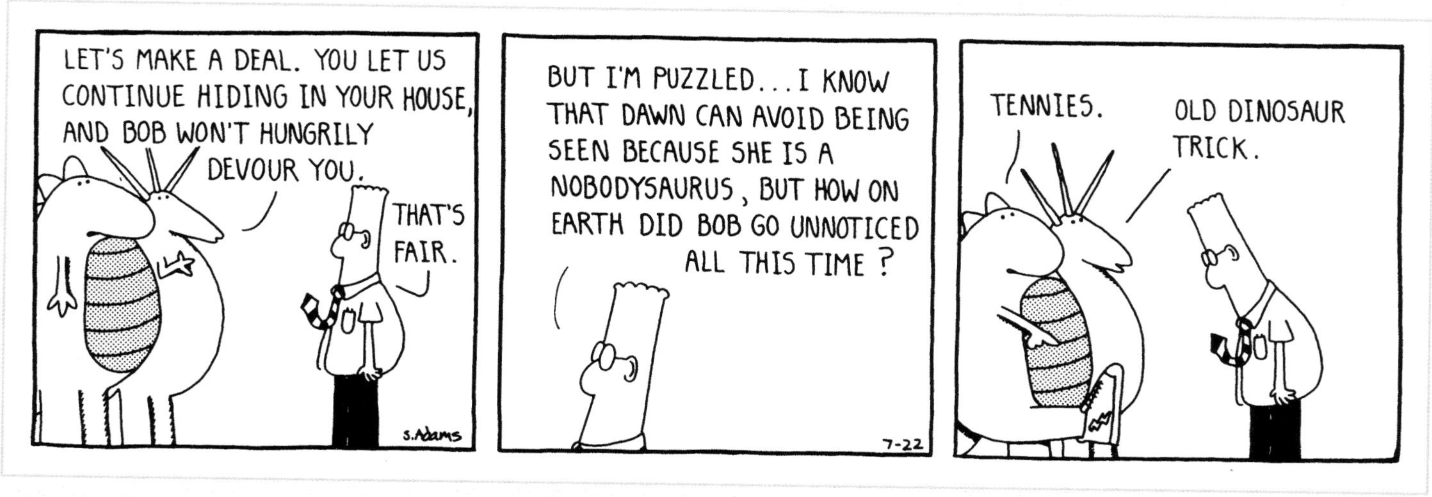
LET'S MAKE A DEAL. YOU LET US CONTINUE HIDING IN YOUR HOUSE, AND BOB WON'T HUNGRILY DEVOUR YOU.
THAT'S FAIR.
BUT I'M PUZZLED... I KNOW THAT DAWN CAN AVOID BEING SEEN BECAUSE SHE IS A NOBODYSAURUS, BUT HOW ON EARTH DID BOB GO UNNOTICED ALL THIS TIME?
TENNIES.
OLD DINOSAUR TRICK.

Another problem is that dinosaurs are huge, and if I drew them to scale, the human characters would be too small to see. I solved that by making the dinosaurs human-sized.

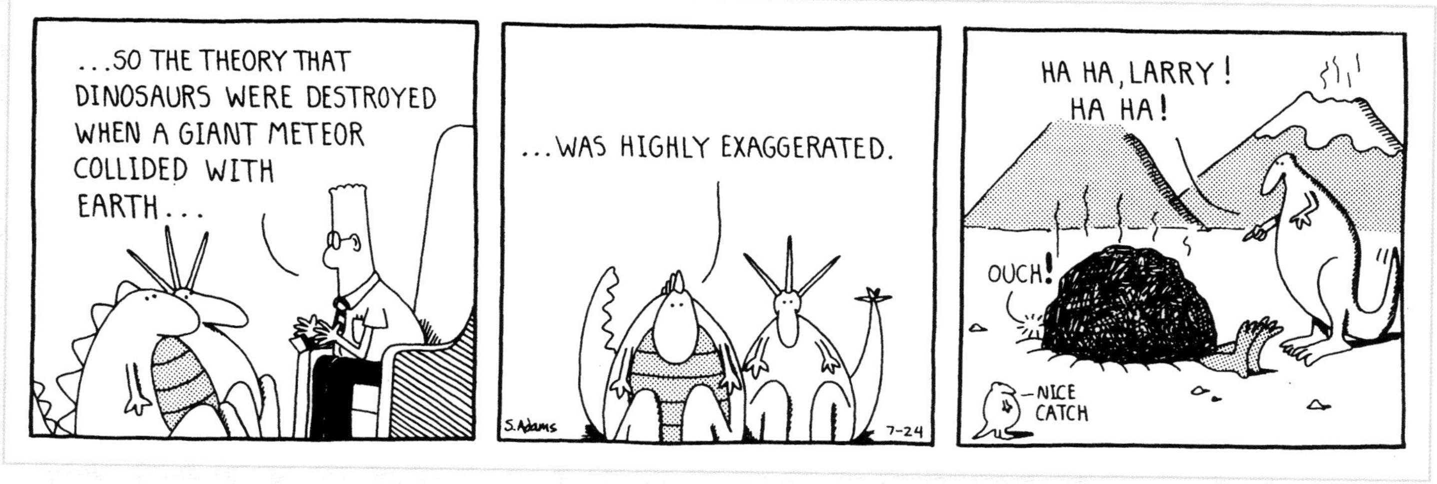
...SO THE THEORY THAT DINOSAURS WERE DESTROYED WHEN A GIANT METEOR COLLIDED WITH EARTH...
...WAS HIGHLY EXAGGERATED.
HA HA, LARRY! HA HA!
OUCH!
NICE CATCH

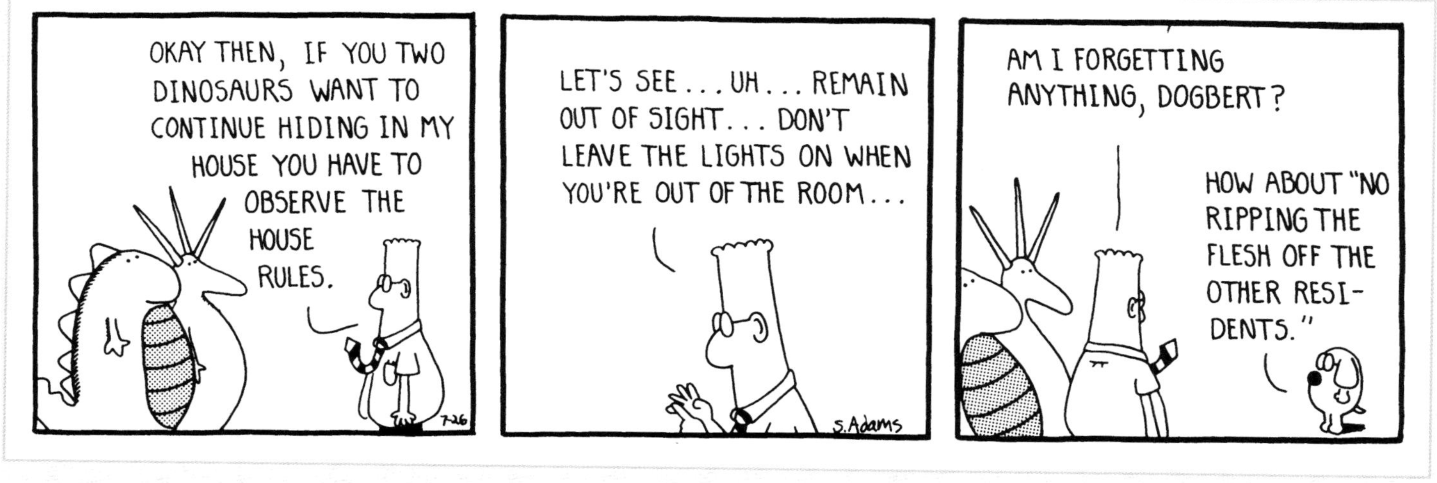
OKAY THEN, IF YOU TWO DINOSAURS WANT TO CONTINUE HIDING IN MY HOUSE YOU HAVE TO OBSERVE THE HOUSE RULES.
LET'S SEE... UH... REMAIN OUT OF SIGHT... DON'T LEAVE THE LIGHTS ON WHEN YOU'RE OUT OF THE ROOM...
AM I FORGETTING ANYTHING, DOGBERT?
HOW ABOUT "NO RIPPING THE FLESH OFF THE OTHER RESI-DENTS."

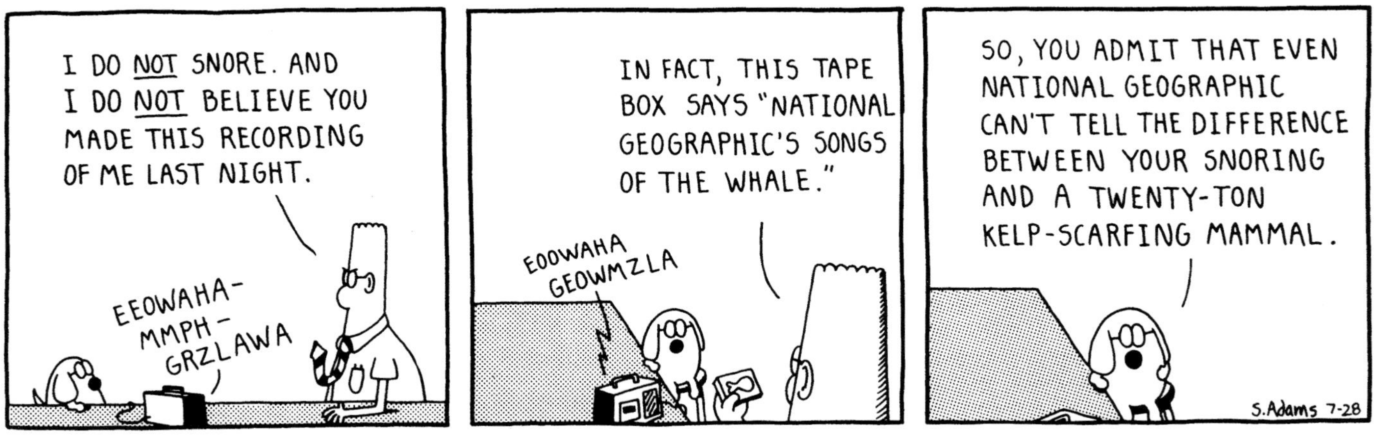
I DO NOT SNORE. AND I DO NOT BELIEVE YOU MADE THIS RECORDING OF ME LAST NIGHT.
EEOWAHA-MMPH-GRZLAWA
IN FACT, THIS TAPE BOX SAYS "NATIONAL GEOGRAPHIC'S SONGS OF THE WHALE."
EOOWAHA GEOWMZLA
SO, YOU ADMIT THAT EVEN NATIONAL GEOGRAPHIC CAN'T TELL THE DIFFERENCE BETWEEN YOUR SNORING AND A TWENTY-TON KELP-SCARFING MAMMAL.
S.Adams 7-28

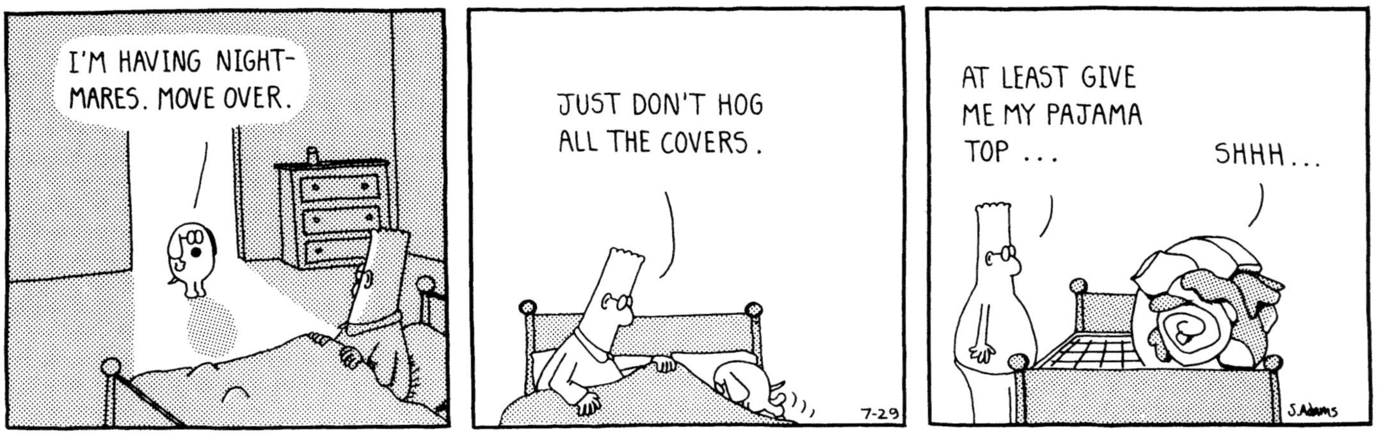
I'M HAVING NIGHT-MARES. MOVE OVER.
JUST DON'T HOG ALL THE COVERS.
7-29
AT LEAST GIVE ME MY PAJAMA TOP ...
SHHH...
S.Adams

I stopped doing puns (mostly) a few years later when Dilbert *started to be translated into a variety of different languages. It was unfair to the clients who had to rerun old strips because the puns didn't translate. Plus a lot of people complained. Puns are only popular with about 5 percent of the public.*

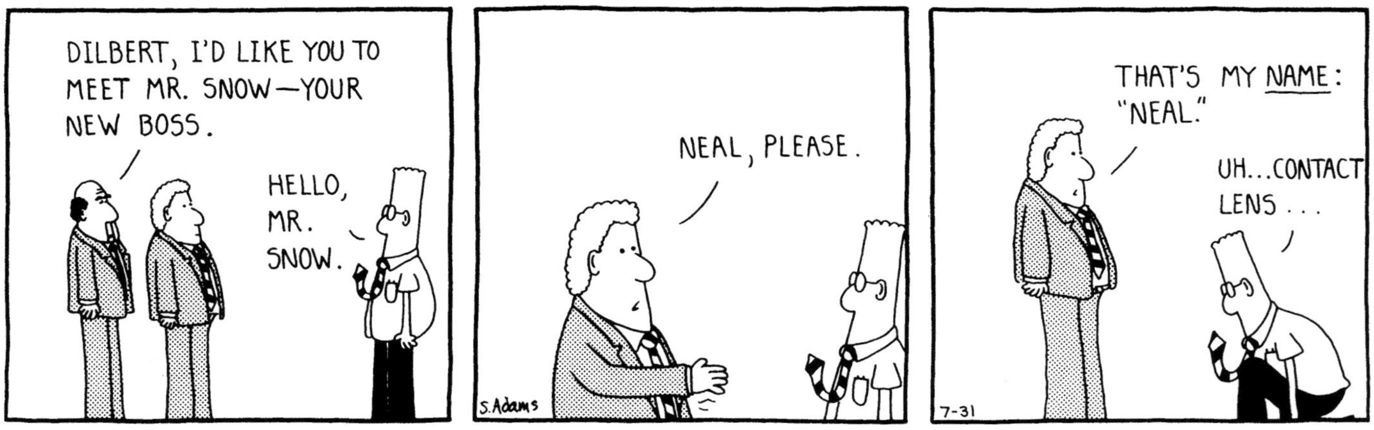
DILBERT, I'D LIKE YOU TO MEET MR. SNOW—YOUR NEW BOSS.
HELLO, MR. SNOW.
NEAL, PLEASE.
S.Adams
THAT'S MY NAME: "NEAL."
UH...CONTACT LENS ...
7-31

Dogbert didn't yet fit in completely with humans. Here I had him wearing a hat so it wouldn't be so obvious to the restaurant that he wasn't human.

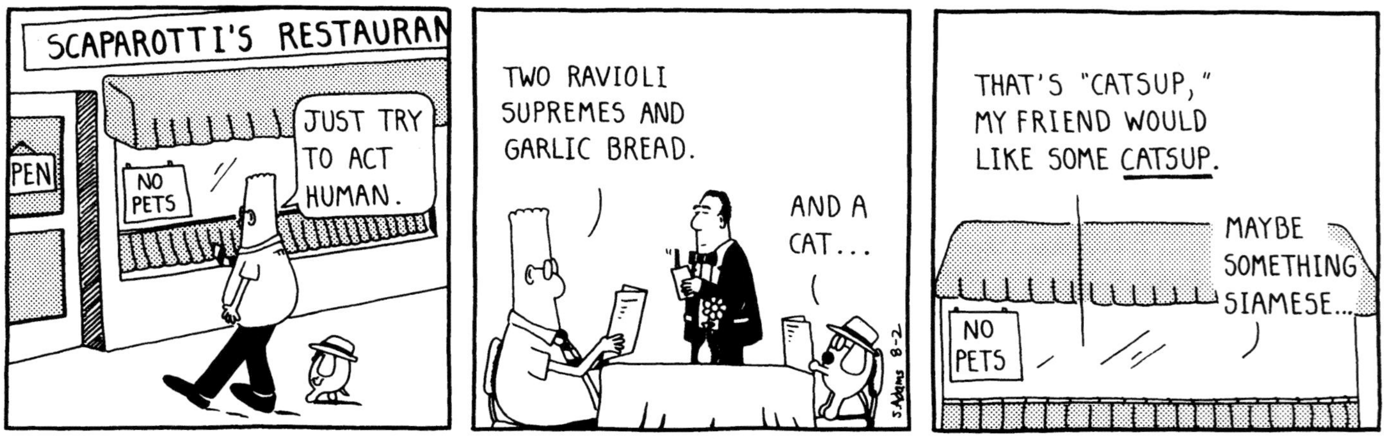
SCAPAROTTI'S RESTAURAN
PEN
NO PETS
JUST TRY TO ACT HUMAN.
TWO RAVIOLI SUPREMES AND GARLIC BREAD.
AND A CAT...
S.Adams 8-2
THAT'S "CATSUP," MY FRIEND WOULD LIKE SOME CATSUP.
NO PETS
MAYBE SOMETHING SIAMESE...

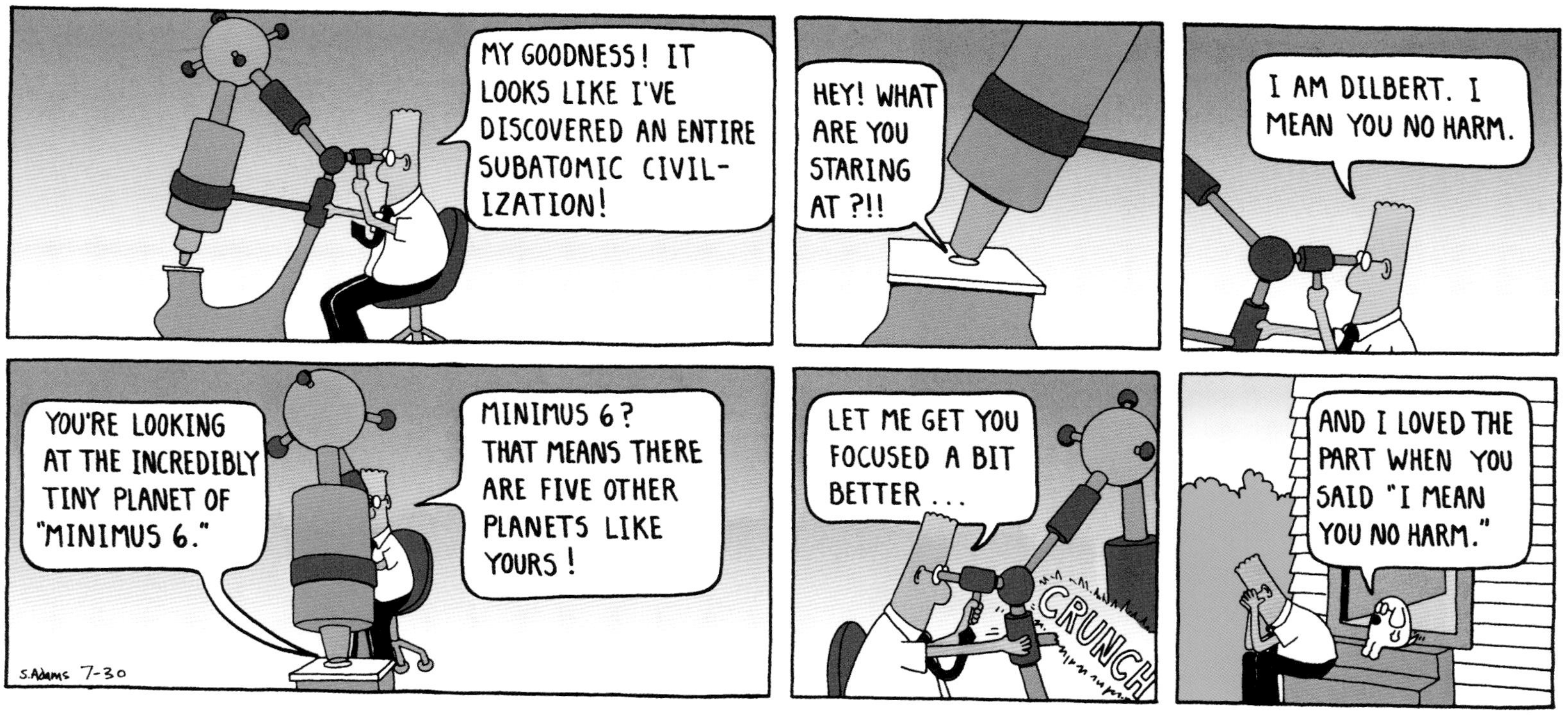
MY GOODNESS! IT LOOKS LIKE I'VE DISCOVERED AN ENTIRE SUBATOMIC CIVIL-IZATION!
HEY! WHAT ARE YOU STARING AT ?!!
I AM DILBERT. I MEAN YOU NO HARM.
YOU'RE LOOKING AT THE INCREDIBLY TINY PLANET OF "MINIMUS 6."
MINIMUS 6? THAT MEANS THERE ARE FIVE OTHER PLANETS LIKE YOURS!
S.Adams 7-30
LET ME GET YOU FOCUSED A BIT BETTER . . .
CRUNCH
AND I LOVED THE PART WHEN YOU SAID "I MEAN YOU NO HARM."

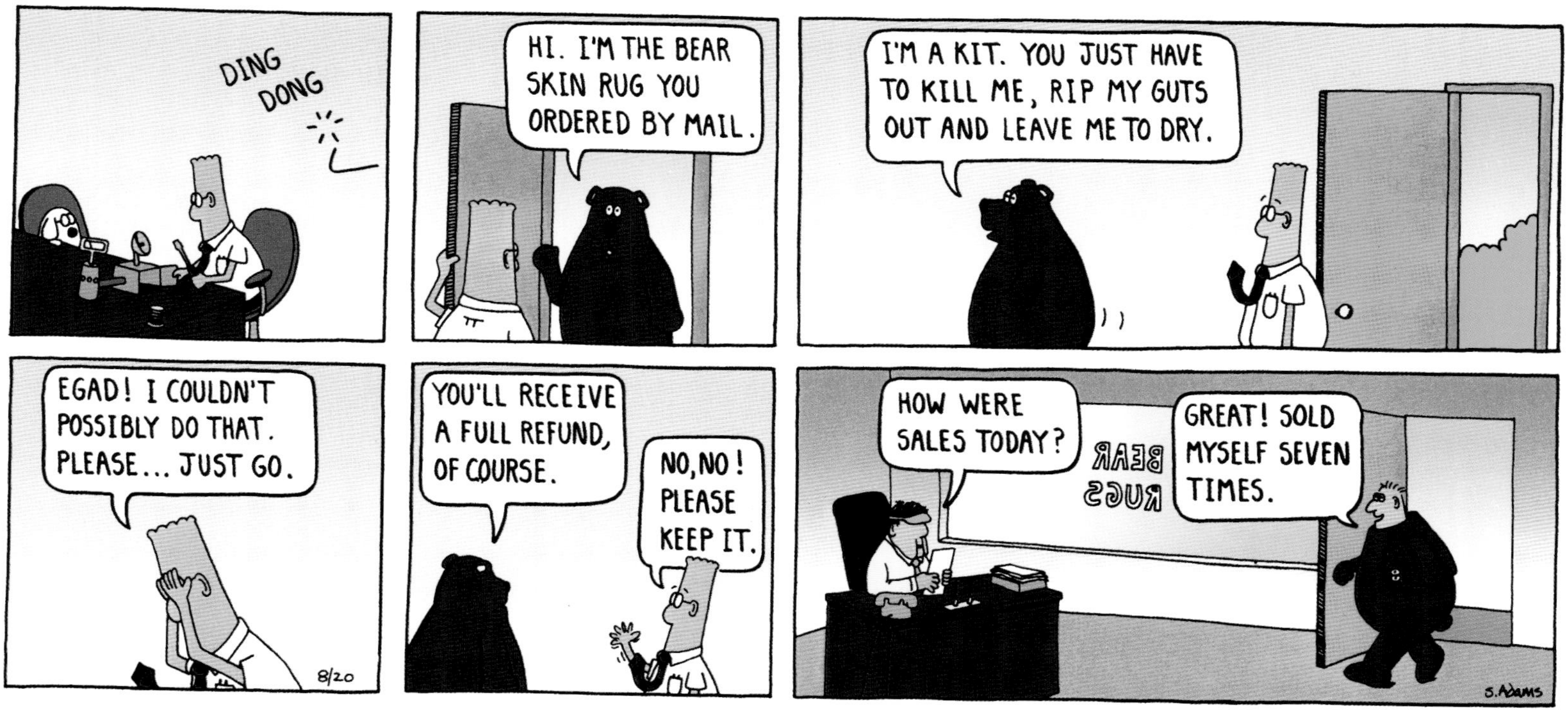
DING DONG
HI. I'M THE BEAR SKIN RUG YOU ORDERED BY MAIL.
I'M A KIT. YOU JUST HAVE TO KILL ME, RIP MY GUTS OUT AND LEAVE ME TO DRY.
EGAD! I COULDN'T POSSIBLY DO THAT. PLEASE... JUST GO.
8/20
YOU'LL RECEIVE A FULL REFUND, OF COURSE.
NO, NO! PLEASE KEEP IT.
HOW WERE SALES TODAY?
BEAR RUGS
GREAT! SOLD MYSELF SEVEN TIMES.
S.ADAMS

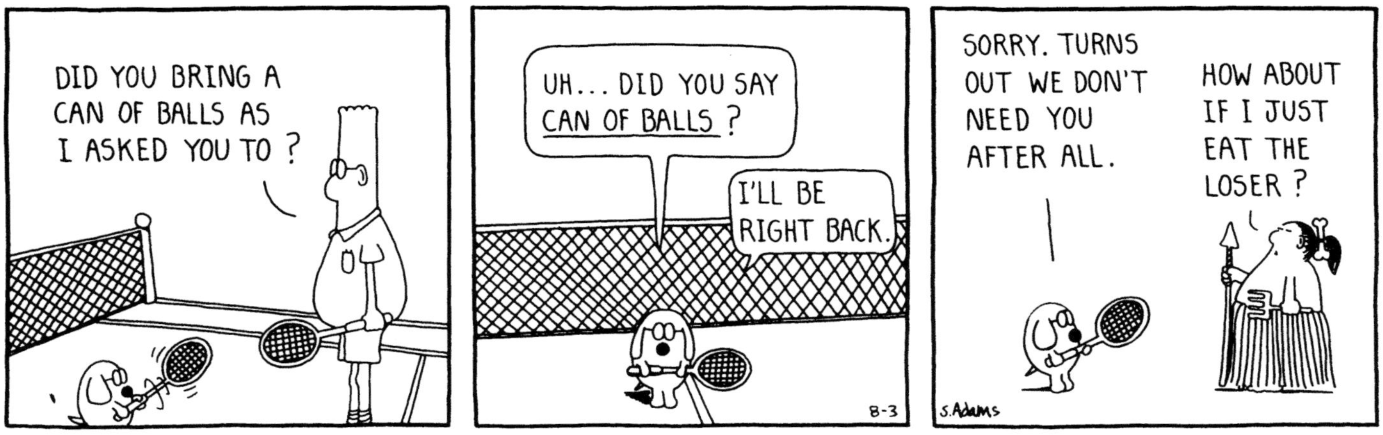
DID YOU BRING A CAN OF BALLS AS I ASKED YOU TO ?
UH... DID YOU SAY CAN OF BALLS ?
I'LL BE RIGHT BACK.
8-3
SORRY. TURNS OUT WE DON'T NEED YOU AFTER ALL.
HOW ABOUT IF I JUST EAT THE LOSER ?
S.Adams

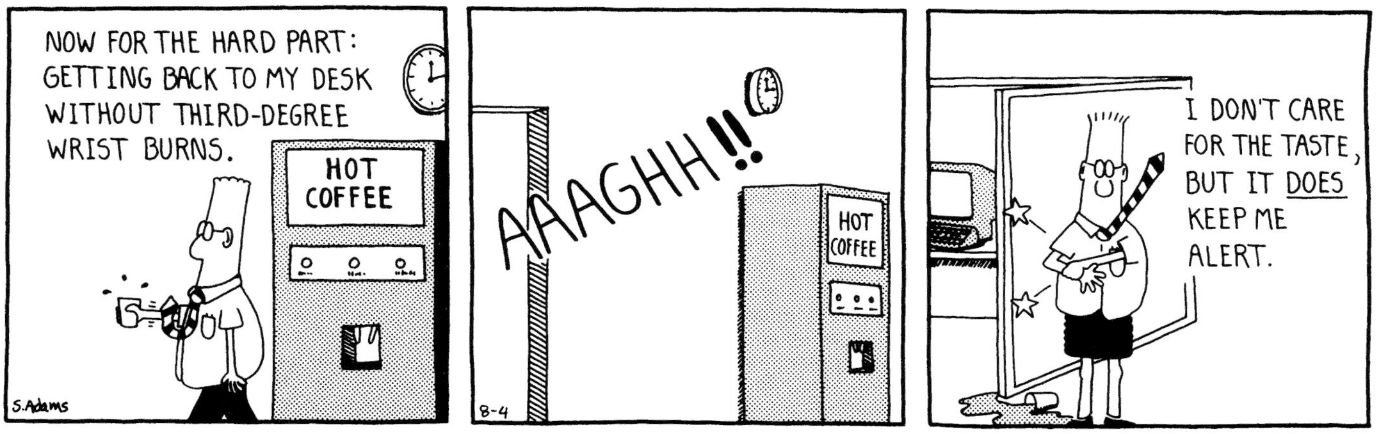
NOW FOR THE HARD PART: GETTING BACK TO MY DESK WITHOUT THIRD-DEGREE WRIST BURNS.
HOT COFFEE
S.Adams
AAAGHH!!
HOT COFFEE
8-4
I DON'T CARE FOR THE TASTE, BUT IT DOES KEEP ME ALERT.

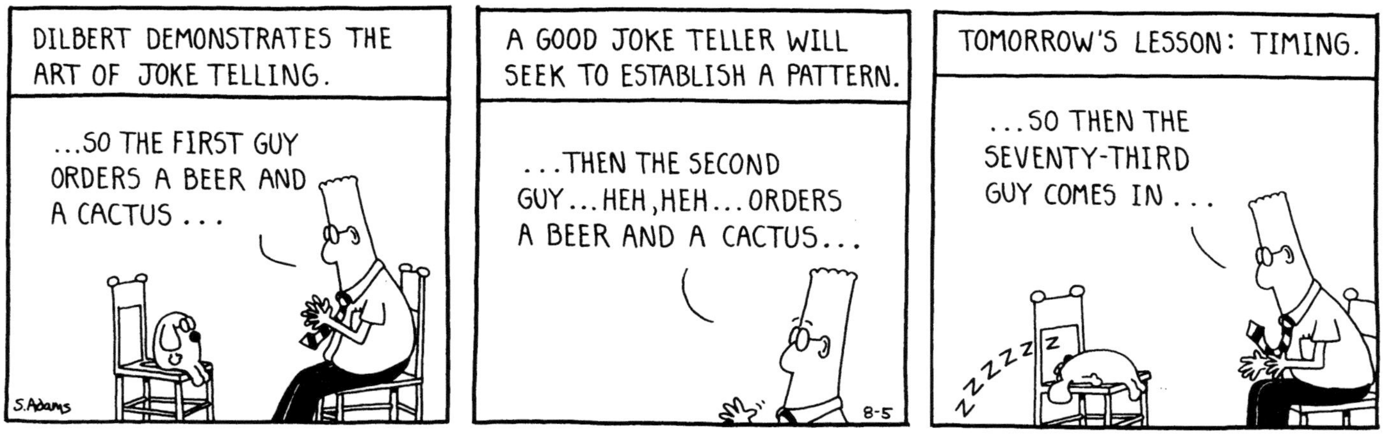
DILBERT DEMONSTRATES THE ART OF JOKE TELLING.
...SO THE FIRST GUY ORDERS A BEER AND A CACTUS ...
S.Adams
A GOOD JOKE TELLER WILL SEEK TO ESTABLISH A PATTERN.
...THEN THE SECOND GUY...HEH,HEH...ORDERS A BEER AND A CACTUS...
8-5
TOMORROW'S LESSON: TIMING.
...SO THEN THE SEVENTY-THIRD GUY COMES IN ...
ZZZZZ

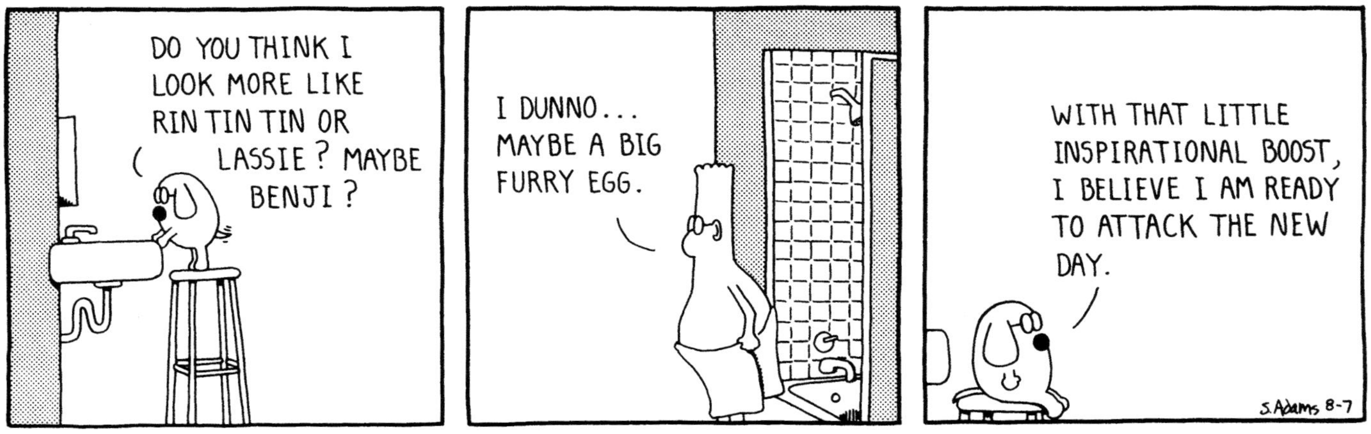
DO YOU THINK I LOOK MORE LIKE RIN TIN TIN OR LASSIE ? MAYBE BENJI ?
I DUNNO... MAYBE A BIG FURRY EGG.
WITH THAT LITTLE INSPIRATIONAL BOOST, I BELIEVE I AM READY TO ATTACK THE NEW DAY.
S.Adams 8-7

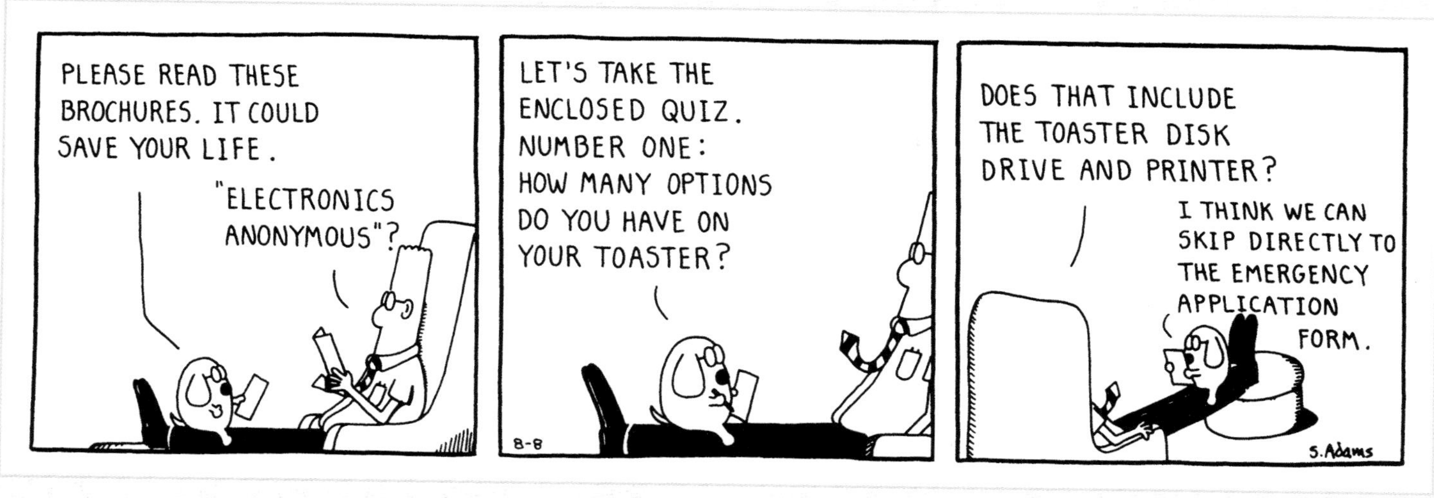
PLEASE READ THESE BROCHURES. IT COULD SAVE YOUR LIFE.
"ELECTRONICS ANONYMOUS"?
LET'S TAKE THE ENCLOSED QUIZ. NUMBER ONE: HOW MANY OPTIONS DO YOU HAVE ON YOUR TOASTER?
8-8
DOES THAT INCLUDE THE TOASTER DISK DRIVE AND PRINTER?
I THINK WE CAN SKIP DIRECTLY TO THE EMERGENCY APPLICATION FORM.
S. Adams

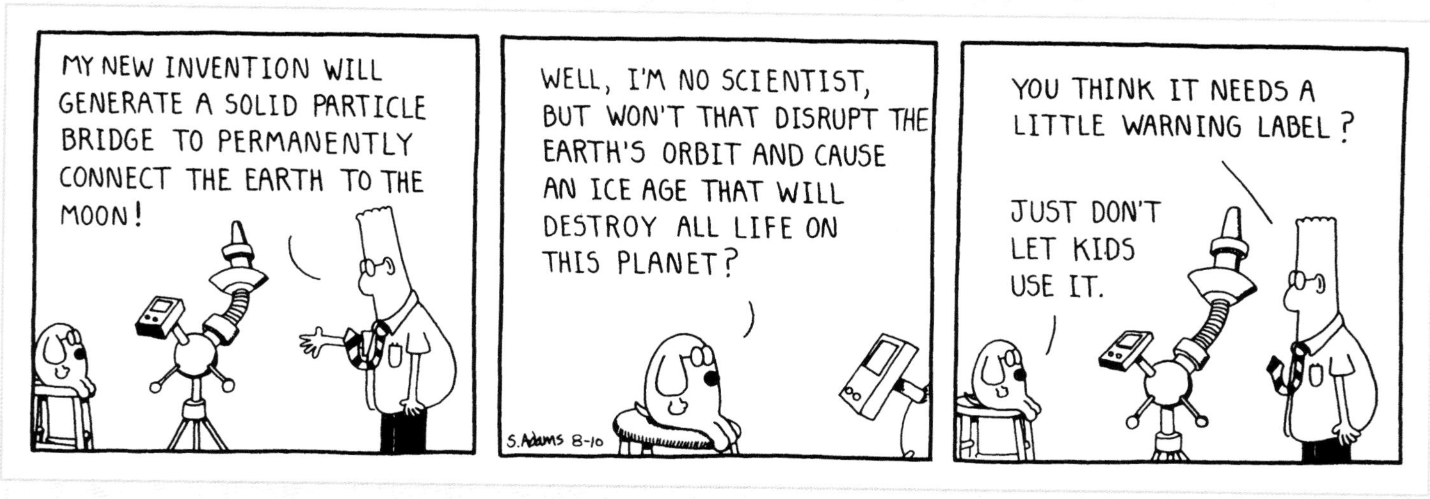
MY NEW INVENTION WILL GENERATE A SOLID PARTICLE BRIDGE TO PERMANENTLY CONNECT THE EARTH TO THE MOON!
WELL, I'M NO SCIENTIST, BUT WON'T THAT DISRUPT THE EARTH'S ORBIT AND CAUSE AN ICE AGE THAT WILL DESTROY ALL LIFE ON THIS PLANET?
S. Adams 8-10
YOU THINK IT NEEDS A LITTLE WARNING LABEL?
JUST DON'T LET KIDS USE IT.

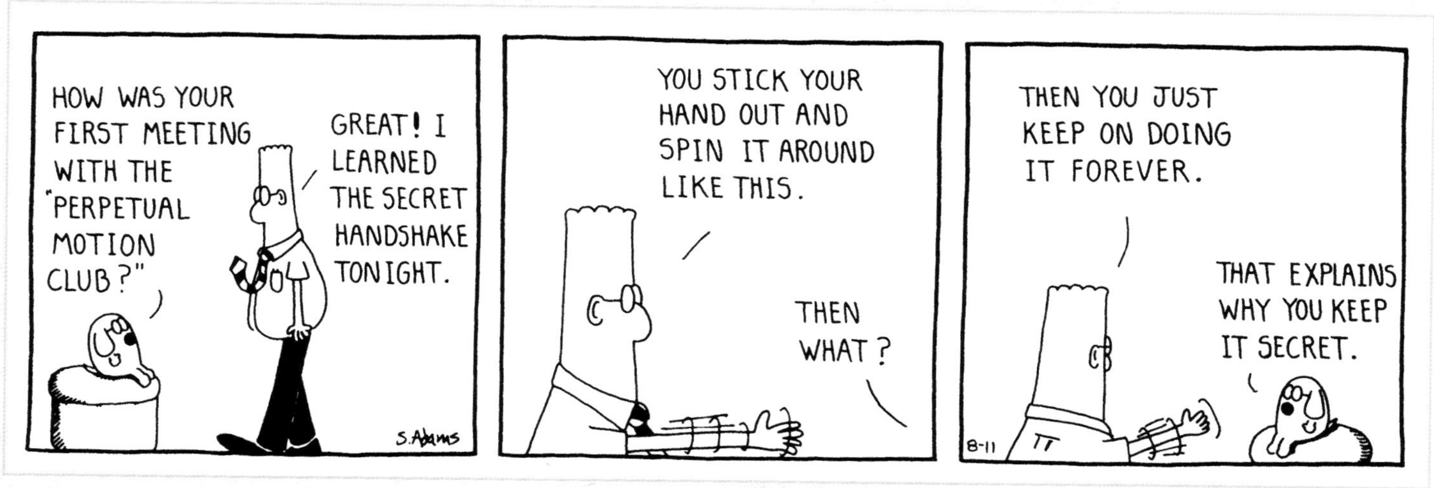
HOW WAS YOUR FIRST MEETING WITH THE "PERPETUAL MOTION CLUB?"
GREAT! I LEARNED THE SECRET HANDSHAKE TONIGHT.
S. Adams
YOU STICK YOUR HAND OUT AND SPIN IT AROUND LIKE THIS.
THEN WHAT?
THEN YOU JUST KEEP ON DOING IT FOREVER.
THAT EXPLAINS WHY YOU KEEP IT SECRET.
8-11

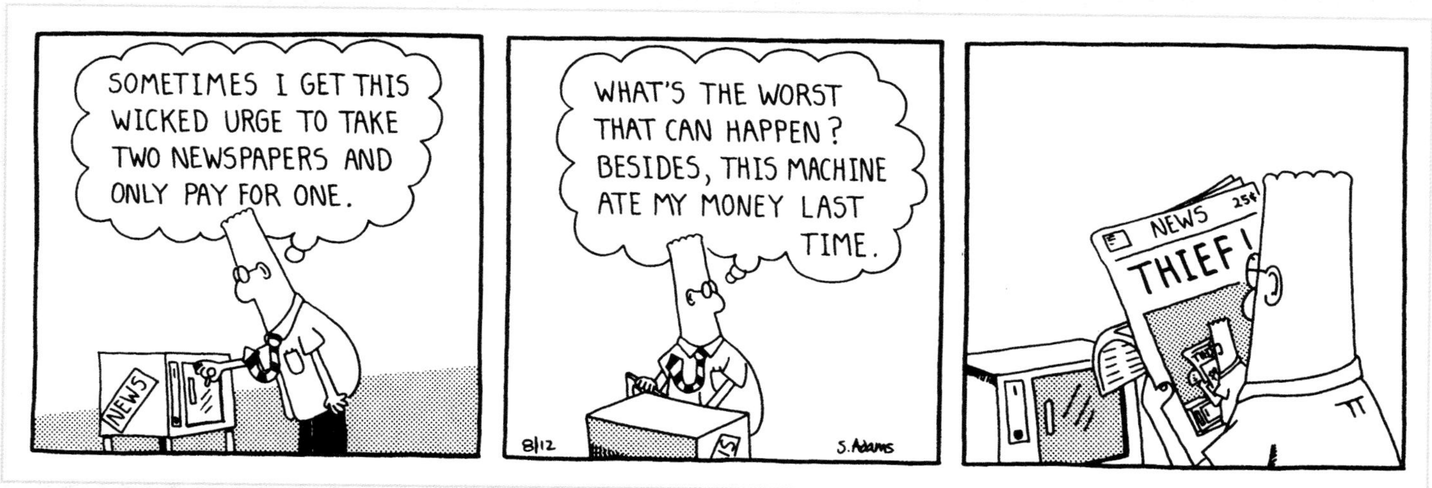
SOMETIMES I GET THIS WICKED URGE TO TAKE TWO NEWSPAPERS AND ONLY PAY FOR ONE.
NEWS
WHAT'S THE WORST THAT CAN HAPPEN? BESIDES, THIS MACHINE ATE MY MONEY LAST TIME.
8/12
S. Adams
NEWS 25¢
THIEF!

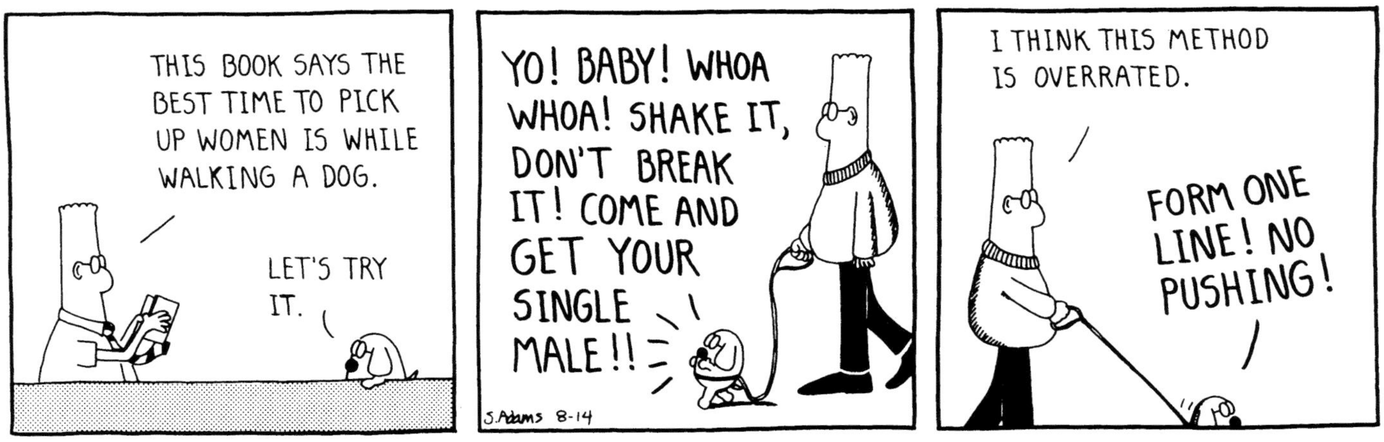
THIS BOOK SAYS THE BEST TIME TO PICK UP WOMEN IS WHILE WALKING A DOG.
LET'S TRY IT.
YO! BABY! WHOA WHOA! SHAKE IT, DON'T BREAK IT! COME AND GET YOUR SINGLE MALE!!
S.Adams 8-14
I THINK THIS METHOD IS OVERRATED.
FORM ONE LINE! NO PUSHING!

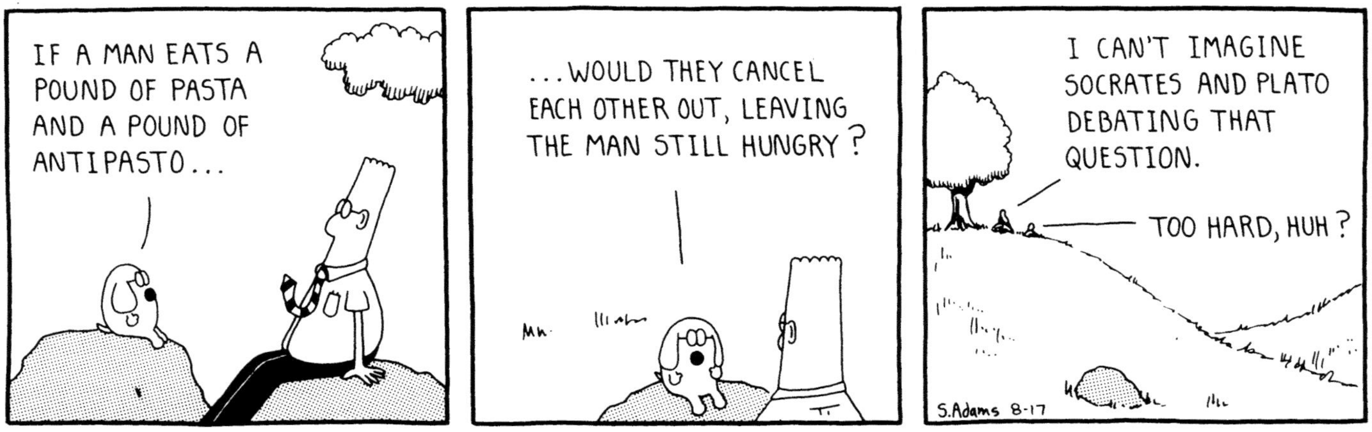
IF A MAN EATS A POUND OF PASTA AND A POUND OF ANTIPASTO...
...WOULD THEY CANCEL EACH OTHER OUT, LEAVING THE MAN STILL HUNGRY?
I CAN'T IMAGINE SOCRATES AND PLATO DEBATING THAT QUESTION.
TOO HARD, HUH?
S.Adams 8-17

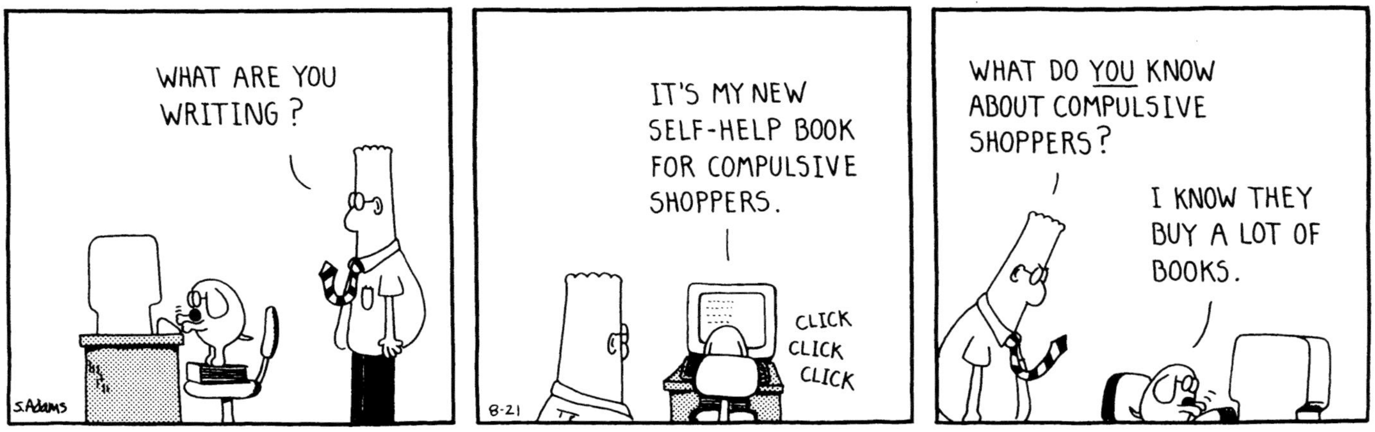
WHAT ARE YOU WRITING?
S.Adams
IT'S MY NEW SELF-HELP BOOK FOR COMPULSIVE SHOPPERS.
CLICK
CLICK
CLICK
8-21
WHAT DO YOU KNOW ABOUT COMPULSIVE SHOPPERS?
I KNOW THEY BUY A LOT OF BOOKS.

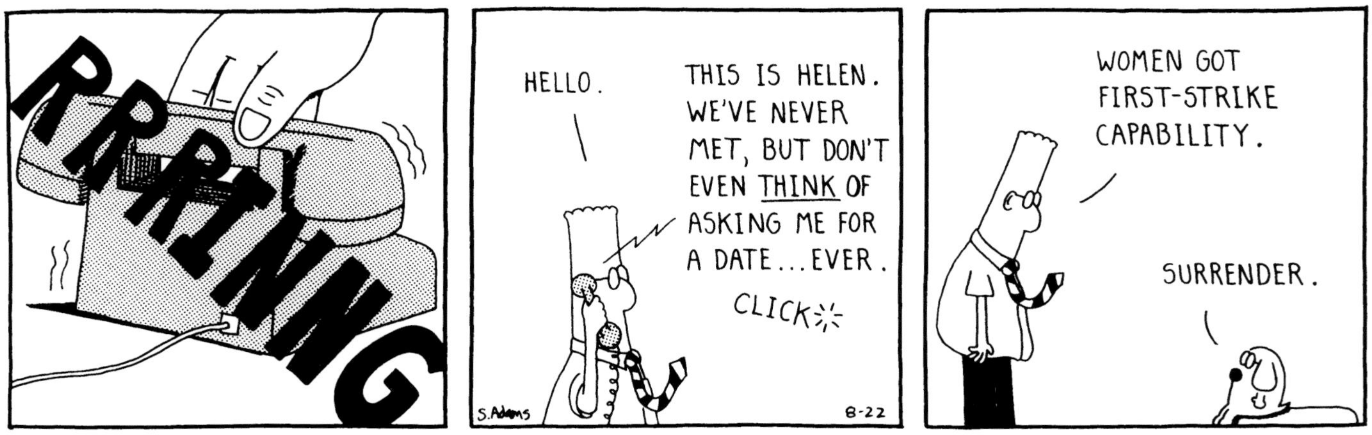
RRRING
HELLO.
THIS IS HELEN. WE'VE NEVER MET, BUT DON'T EVEN THINK OF ASKING ME FOR A DATE...EVER.
CLICK
S.Adams
8-22
WOMEN GOT FIRST-STRIKE CAPABILITY.
SURRENDER.

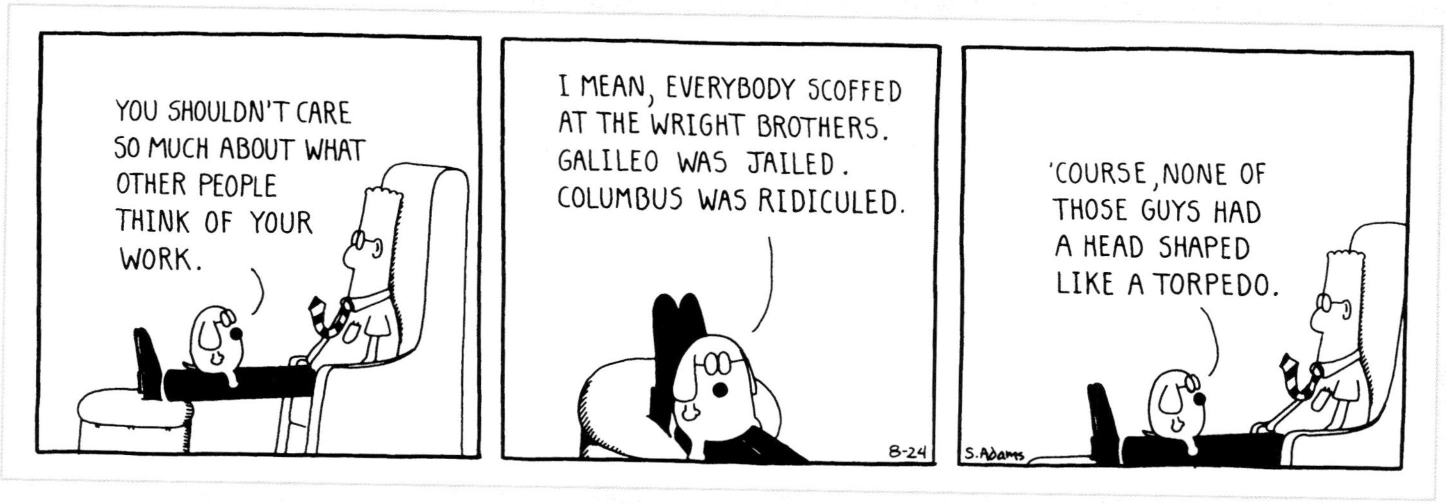
YOU SHOULDN'T CARE SO MUCH ABOUT WHAT OTHER PEOPLE THINK OF YOUR WORK.
I MEAN, EVERYBODY SCOFFED AT THE WRIGHT BROTHERS. GALILEO WAS JAILED. COLUMBUS WAS RIDICULED.
8-24
'COURSE, NONE OF THOSE GUYS HAD A HEAD SHAPED LIKE A TORPEDO.
S. Adams

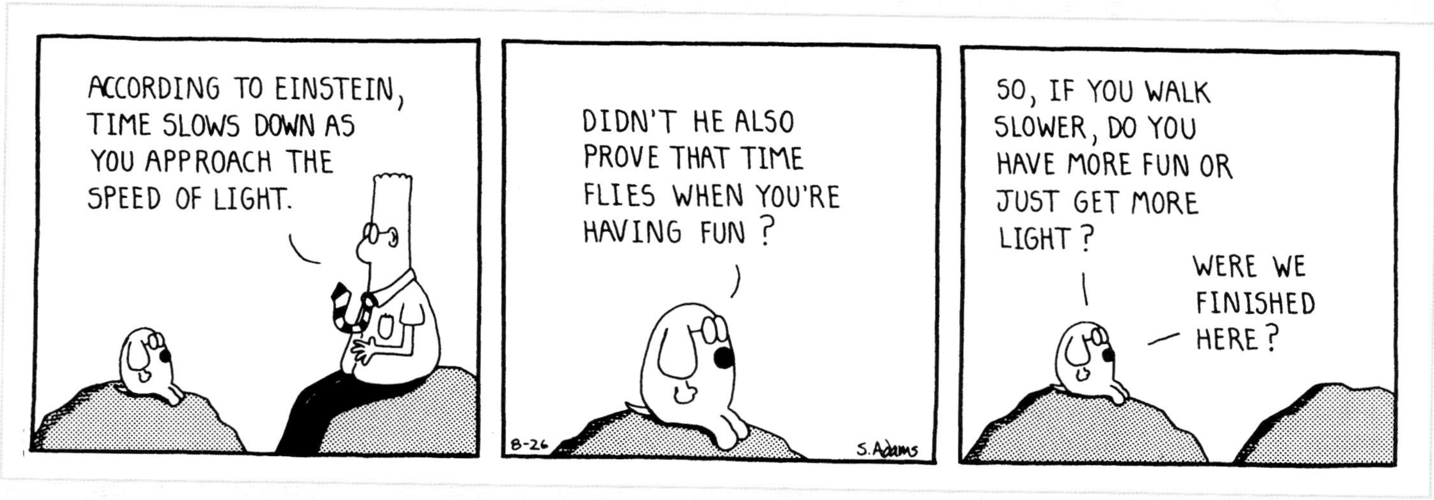
ACCORDING TO EINSTEIN, TIME SLOWS DOWN AS YOU APPROACH THE SPEED OF LIGHT.
DIDN'T HE ALSO PROVE THAT TIME FLIES WHEN YOU'RE HAVING FUN ?
8-26
S. Adams
SO, IF YOU WALK SLOWER, DO YOU HAVE MORE FUN OR JUST GET MORE LIGHT ?
WERE WE FINISHED HERE ?

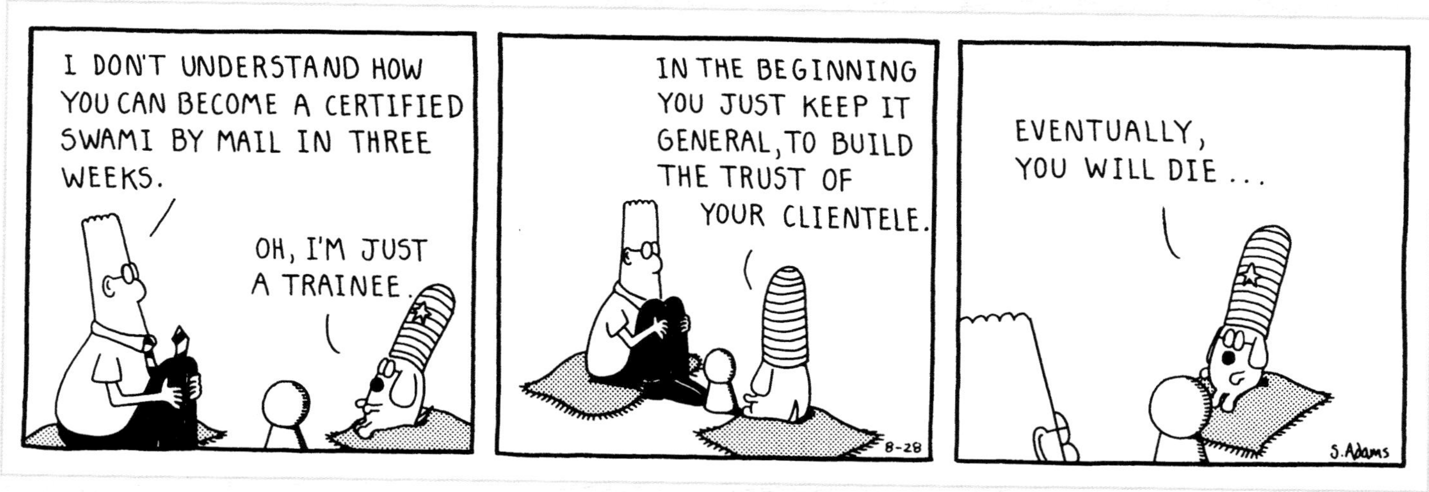
I DON'T UNDERSTAND HOW YOU CAN BECOME A CERTIFIED SWAMI BY MAIL IN THREE WEEKS.
OH, I'M JUST A TRAINEE.
IN THE BEGINNING YOU JUST KEEP IT GENERAL, TO BUILD THE TRUST OF YOUR CLIENTELE.
8-28
EVENTUALLY, YOU WILL DIE . . .
S. Adams

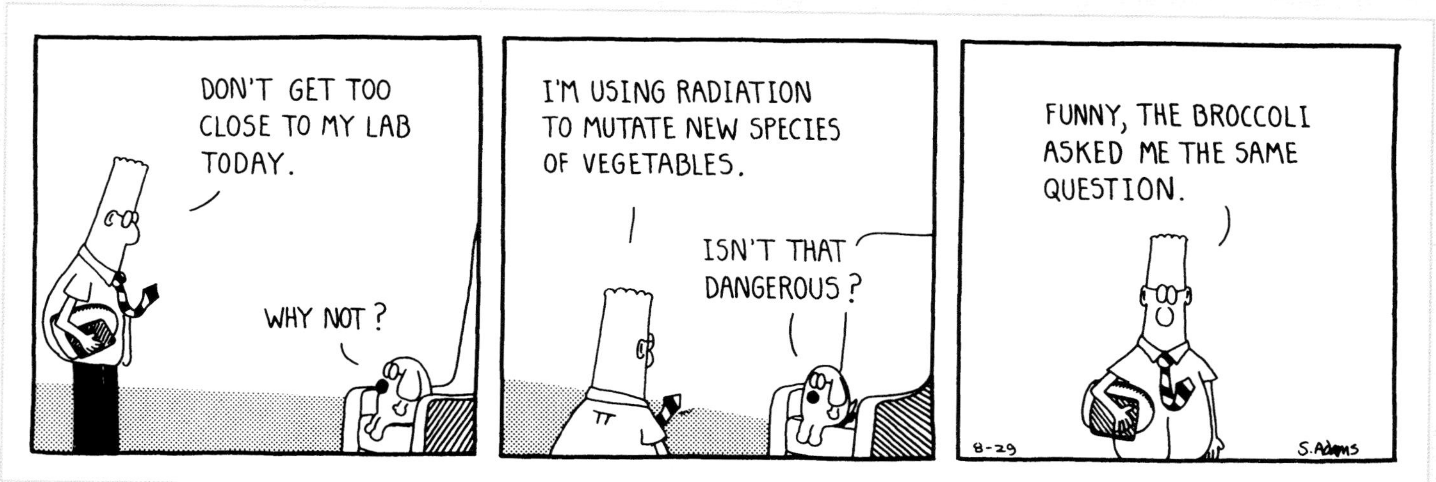
DON'T GET TOO CLOSE TO MY LAB TODAY.
WHY NOT ?
I'M USING RADIATION TO MUTATE NEW SPECIES OF VEGETABLES.
ISN'T THAT DANGEROUS ?
FUNNY, THE BROCCOLI ASKED ME THE SAME QUESTION.
8-29
S. Adams

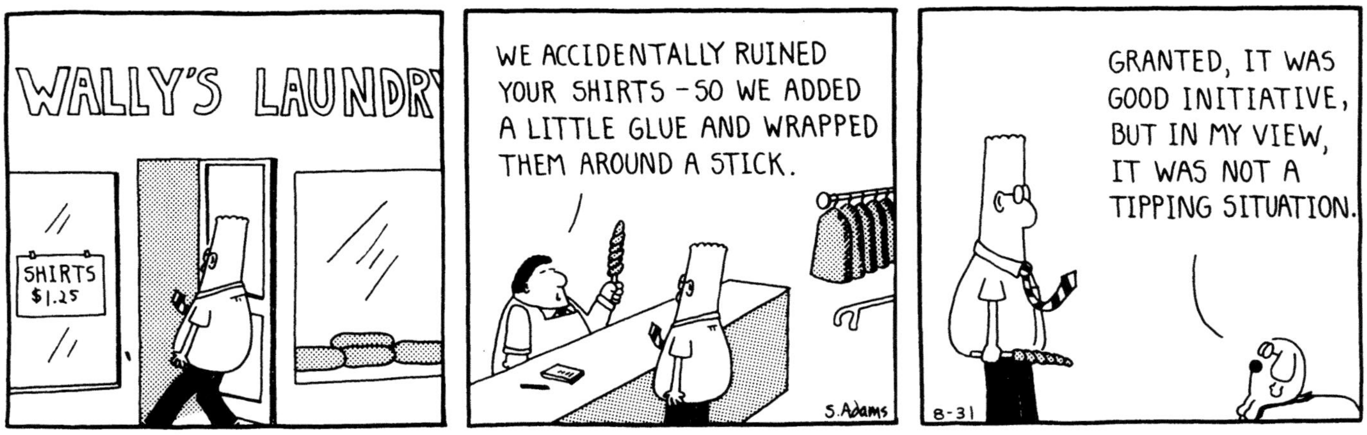
WALLY'S LAUNDRY
SHIRTS $1.25
WE ACCIDENTALLY RUINED YOUR SHIRTS – SO WE ADDED A LITTLE GLUE AND WRAPPED THEM AROUND A STICK.
S. Adams
GRANTED, IT WAS GOOD INITIATIVE, BUT IN MY VIEW, IT WAS NOT A TIPPING SITUATION.
8-31

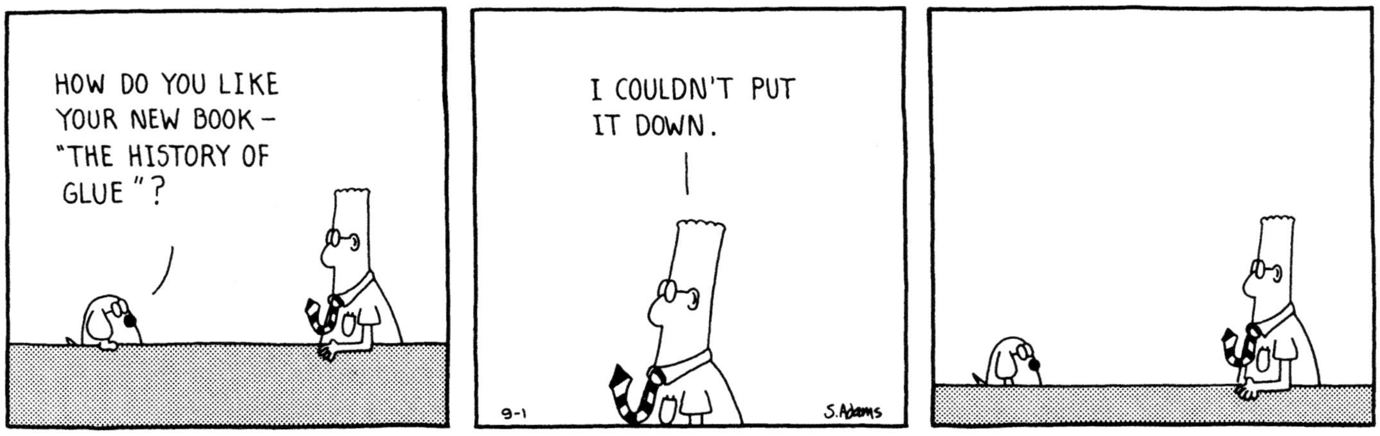
HOW DO YOU LIKE YOUR NEW BOOK – "THE HISTORY OF GLUE"?
I COULDN'T PUT IT DOWN.
9-1
S. Adams

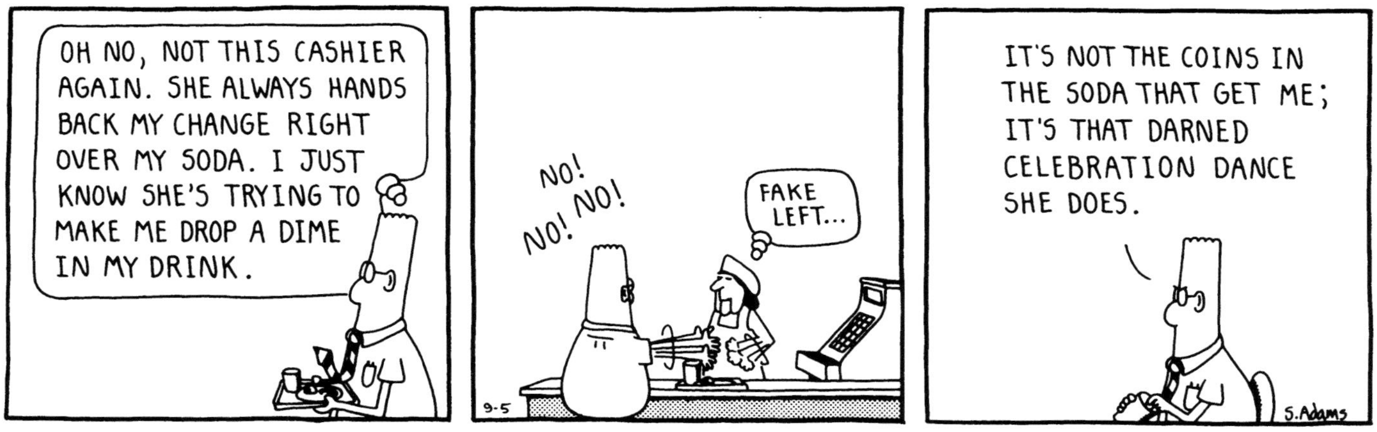
OH NO, NOT THIS CASHIER AGAIN. SHE ALWAYS HANDS BACK MY CHANGE RIGHT OVER MY SODA. I JUST KNOW SHE'S TRYING TO MAKE ME DROP A DIME IN MY DRINK.
NO! NO! NO!
FAKE LEFT...
9-5
IT'S NOT THE COINS IN THE SODA THAT GET ME; IT'S THAT DARNED CELEBRATION DANCE SHE DOES.
S. Adams

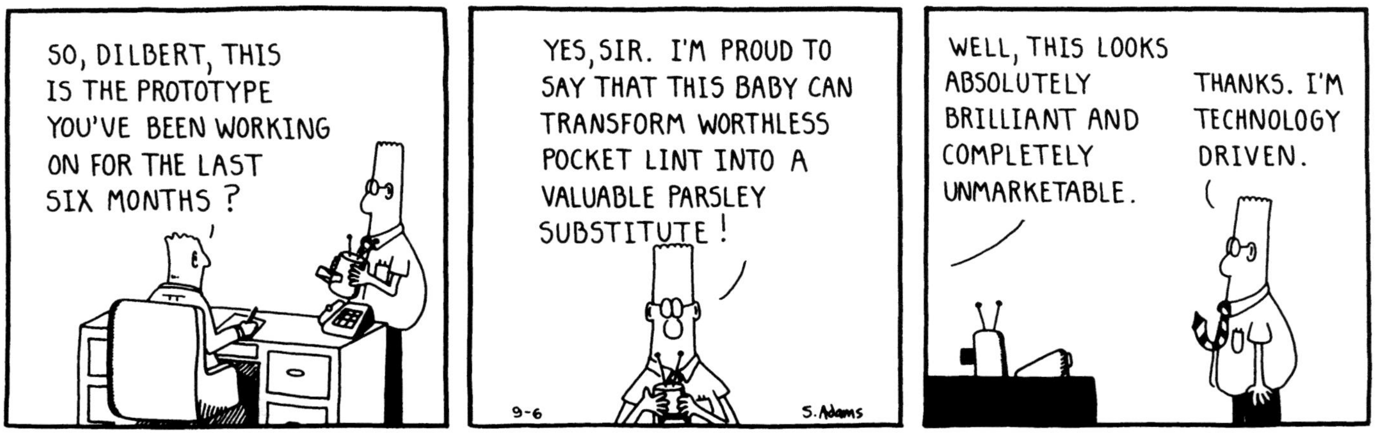
SO, DILBERT, THIS IS THE PROTOTYPE YOU'VE BEEN WORKING ON FOR THE LAST SIX MONTHS?
YES, SIR. I'M PROUD TO SAY THAT THIS BABY CAN TRANSFORM WORTHLESS POCKET LINT INTO A VALUABLE PARSLEY SUBSTITUTE!
9-6
S. Adams
WELL, THIS LOOKS ABSOLUTELY BRILLIANT AND COMPLETELY UNMARKETABLE.
THANKS. I'M TECHNOLOGY DRIVEN.

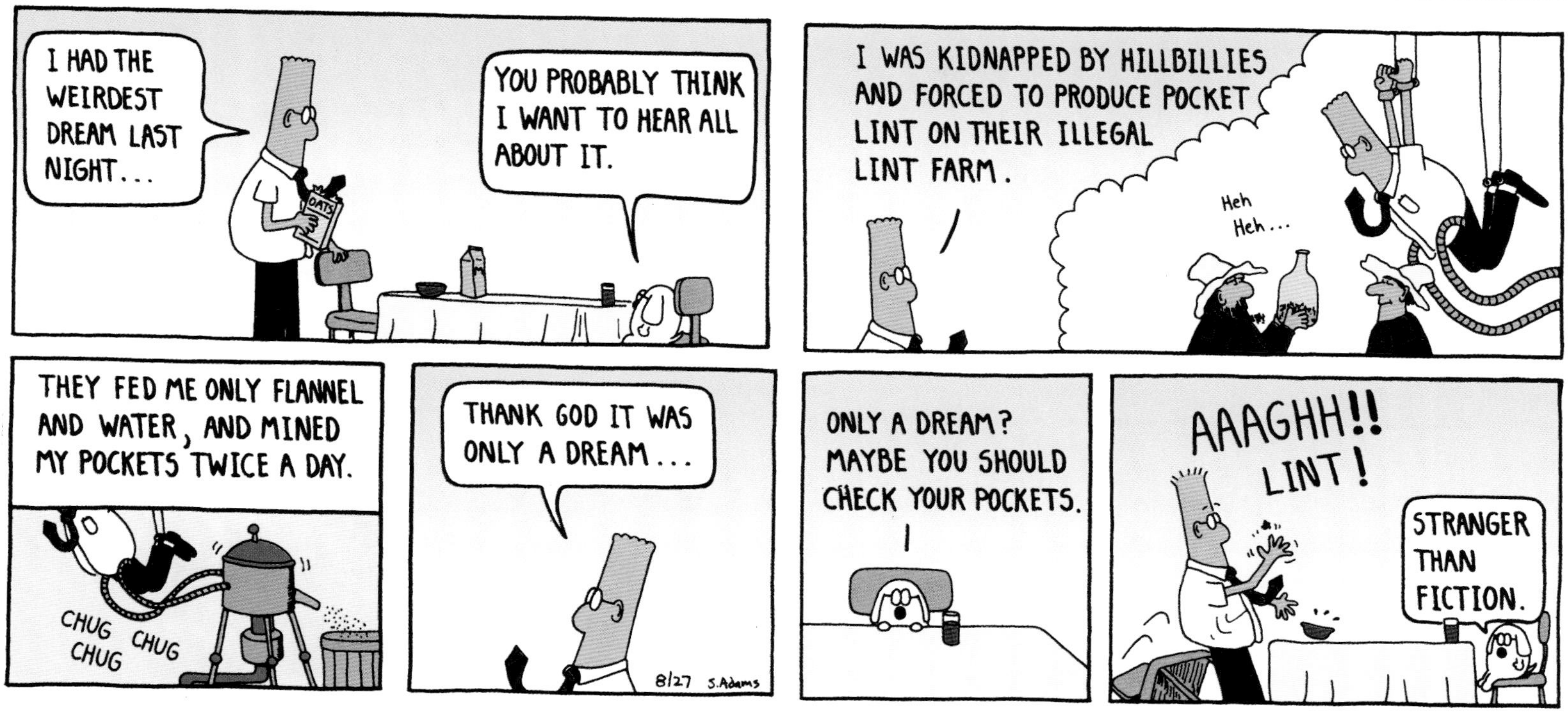
I HAD THE WEIRDEST DREAM LAST NIGHT...
YOU PROBABLY THINK I WANT TO HEAR ALL ABOUT IT.
I WAS KIDNAPPED BY HILLBILLIES AND FORCED TO PRODUCE POCKET LINT ON THEIR ILLEGAL LINT FARM.
Heh Heh...
THEY FED ME ONLY FLANNEL AND WATER, AND MINED MY POCKETS TWICE A DAY.
CHUG CHUG CHUG
THANK GOD IT WAS ONLY A DREAM...
8/27 S.Adams
ONLY A DREAM? MAYBE YOU SHOULD CHECK YOUR POCKETS.
AAAGHH!! LINT!
STRANGER THAN FICTION.

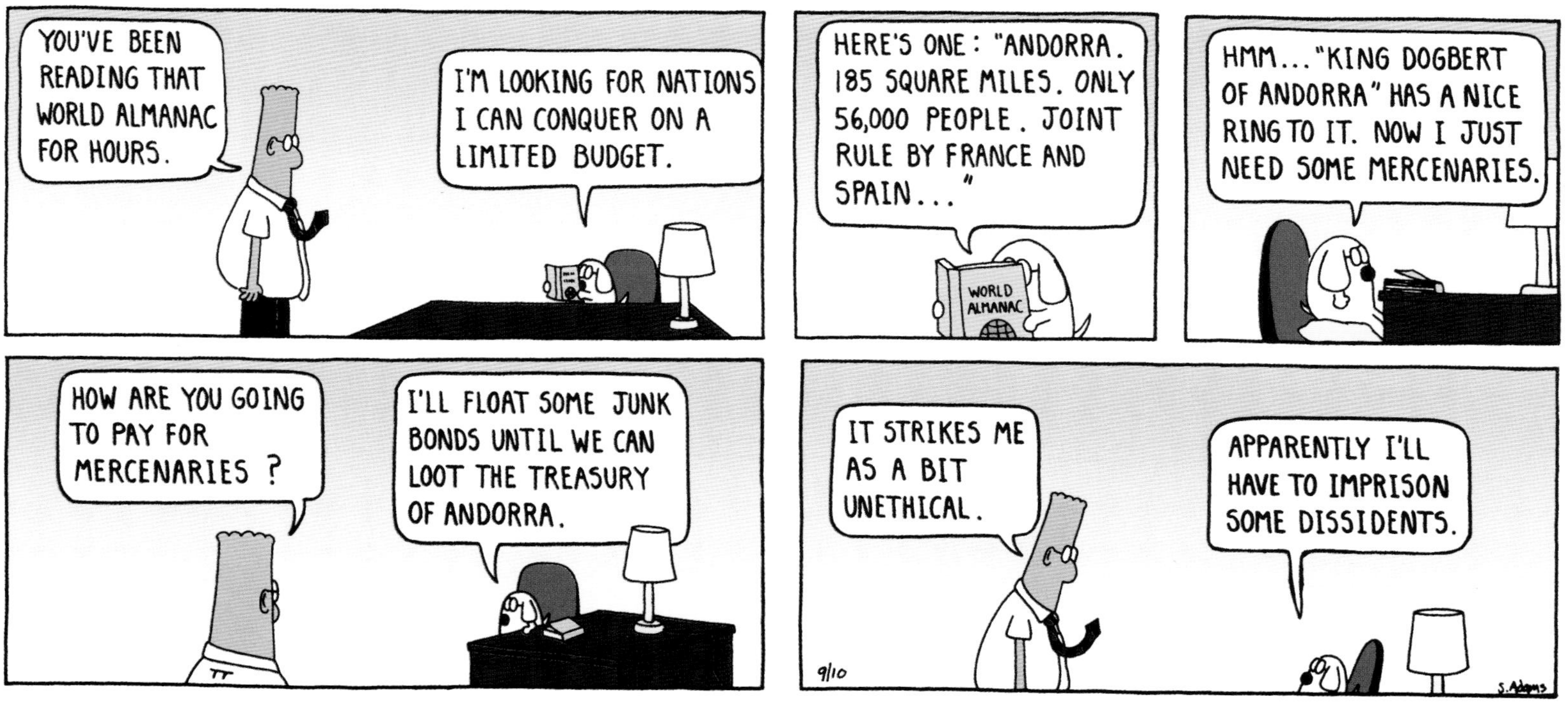
YOU'VE BEEN READING THAT WORLD ALMANAC FOR HOURS.
I'M LOOKING FOR NATIONS I CAN CONQUER ON A LIMITED BUDGET.
HERE'S ONE: "ANDORRA. 185 SQUARE MILES. ONLY 56,000 PEOPLE. JOINT RULE BY FRANCE AND SPAIN..."
WORLD ALMANAC
HMM..."KING DOGBERT OF ANDORRA" HAS A NICE RING TO IT. NOW I JUST NEED SOME MERCENARIES.
HOW ARE YOU GOING TO PAY FOR MERCENARIES ?
I'LL FLOAT SOME JUNK BONDS UNTIL WE CAN LOOT THE TREASURY OF ANDORRA.
IT STRIKES ME AS A BIT UNETHICAL.
APPARENTLY I'LL HAVE TO IMPRISON SOME DISSIDENTS.
9/10
S.Adams

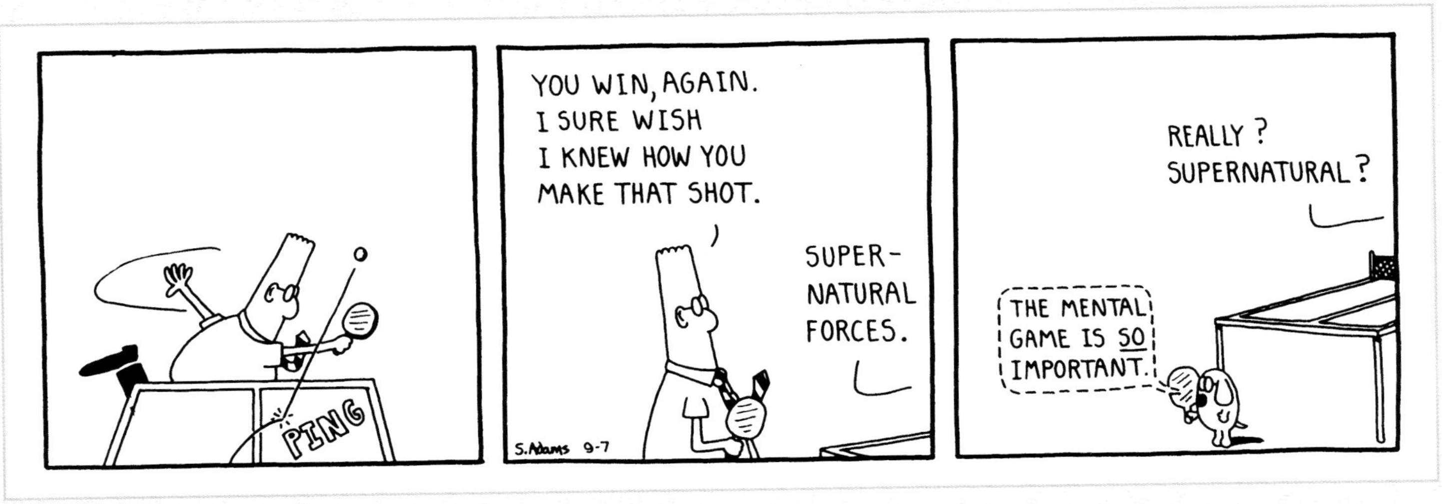

PING
YOU WIN, AGAIN. I SURE WISH I KNEW HOW YOU MAKE THAT SHOT.
SUPER-NATURAL FORCES.
S. Adams 9-7
THE MENTAL GAME IS SO IMPORTANT.
REALLY? SUPERNATURAL?

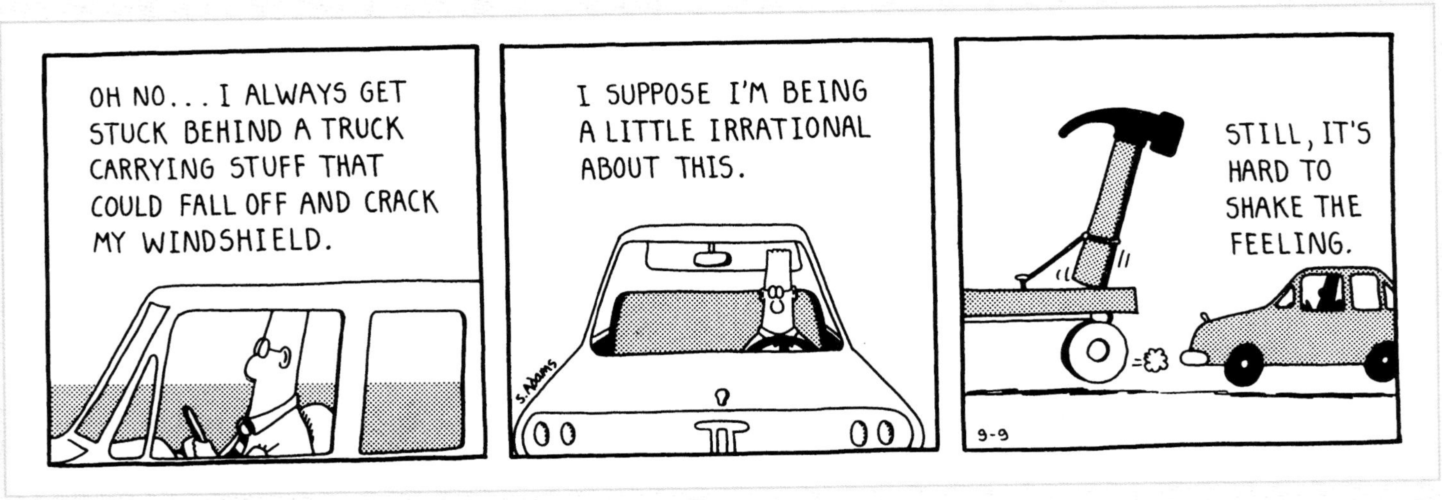

OH NO... I ALWAYS GET STUCK BEHIND A TRUCK CARRYING STUFF THAT COULD FALL OFF AND CRACK MY WINDSHIELD.
I SUPPOSE I'M BEING A LITTLE IRRATIONAL ABOUT THIS.
S. Adams
STILL, IT'S HARD TO SHAKE THE FEELING.
9-9

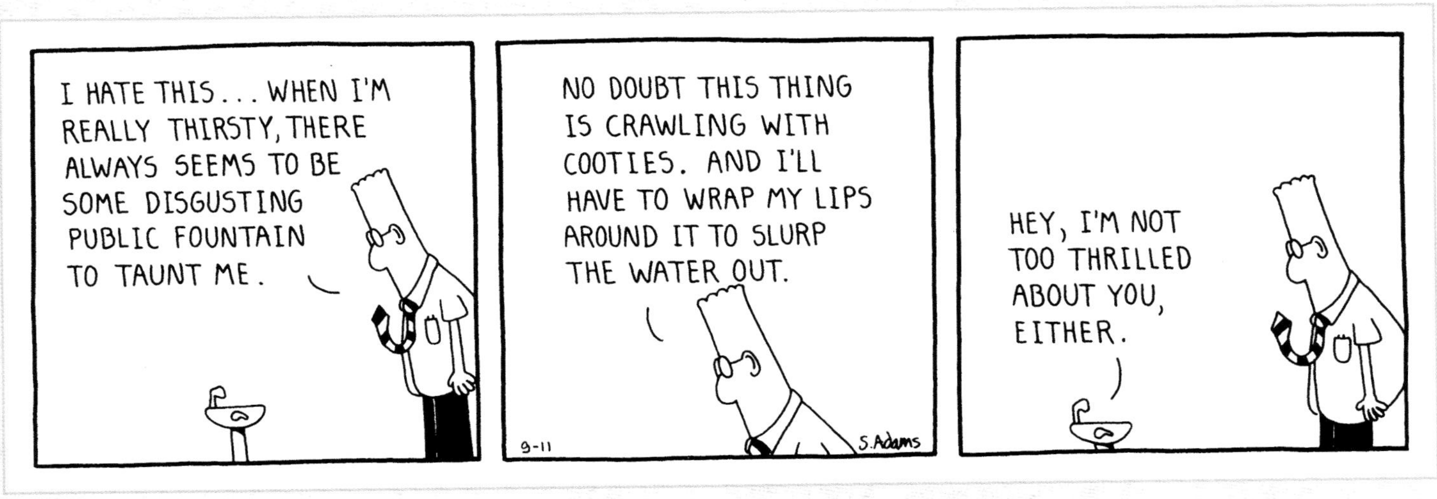

I HATE THIS... WHEN I'M REALLY THIRSTY, THERE ALWAYS SEEMS TO BE SOME DISGUSTING PUBLIC FOUNTAIN TO TAUNT ME.
NO DOUBT THIS THING IS CRAWLING WITH COOTIES. AND I'LL HAVE TO WRAP MY LIPS AROUND IT TO SLURP THE WATER OUT.
9-11
S. Adams
HEY, I'M NOT TOO THRILLED ABOUT YOU, EITHER.

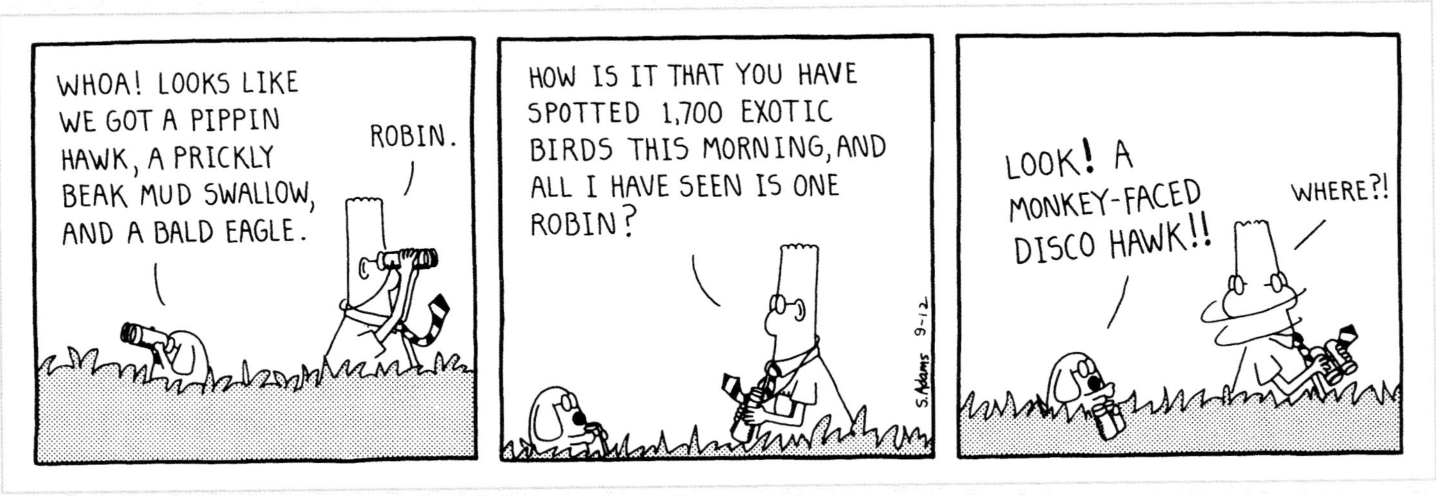

WHOA! LOOKS LIKE WE GOT A PIPPIN HAWK, A PRICKLY BEAK MUD SWALLOW, AND A BALD EAGLE.
ROBIN.
HOW IS IT THAT YOU HAVE SPOTTED 1,700 EXOTIC BIRDS THIS MORNING, AND ALL I HAVE SEEN IS ONE ROBIN?
S. Adams 9-12
LOOK! A MONKEY-FACED DISCO HAWK!!
WHERE?!

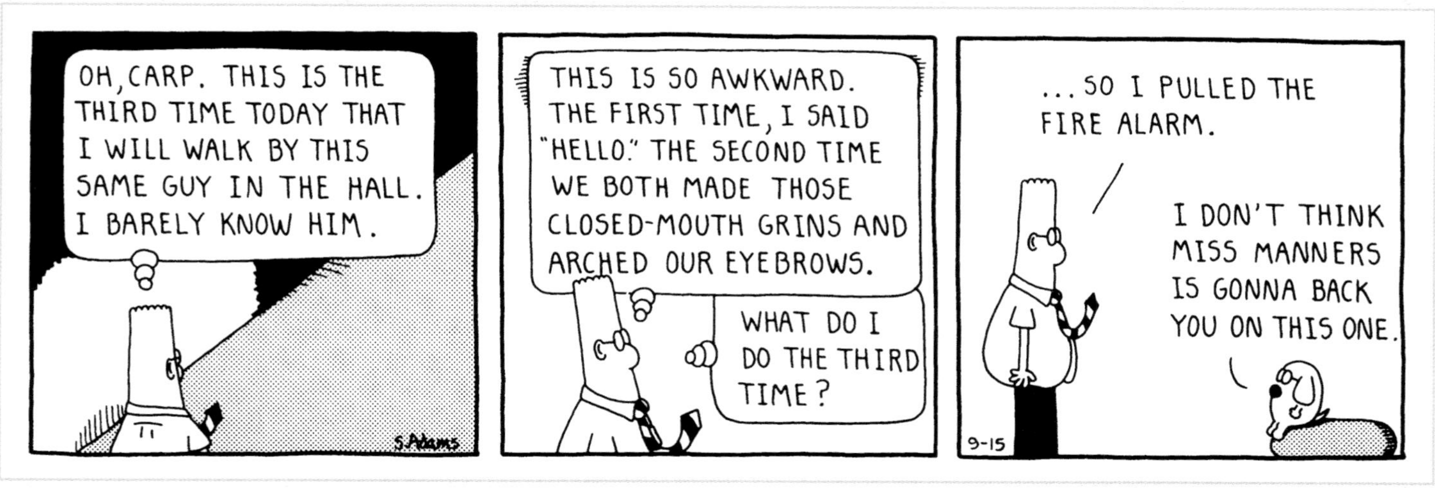
OH, CARP. THIS IS THE THIRD TIME TODAY THAT I WILL WALK BY THIS SAME GUY IN THE HALL. I BARELY KNOW HIM.
S. Adams
THIS IS SO AWKWARD. THE FIRST TIME, I SAID "HELLO." THE SECOND TIME WE BOTH MADE THOSE CLOSED-MOUTH GRINS AND ARCHED OUR EYEBROWS.
WHAT DO I DO THE THIRD TIME?
...SO I PULLED THE FIRE ALARM.
I DON'T THINK MISS MANNERS IS GONNA BACK YOU ON THIS ONE.
9-15

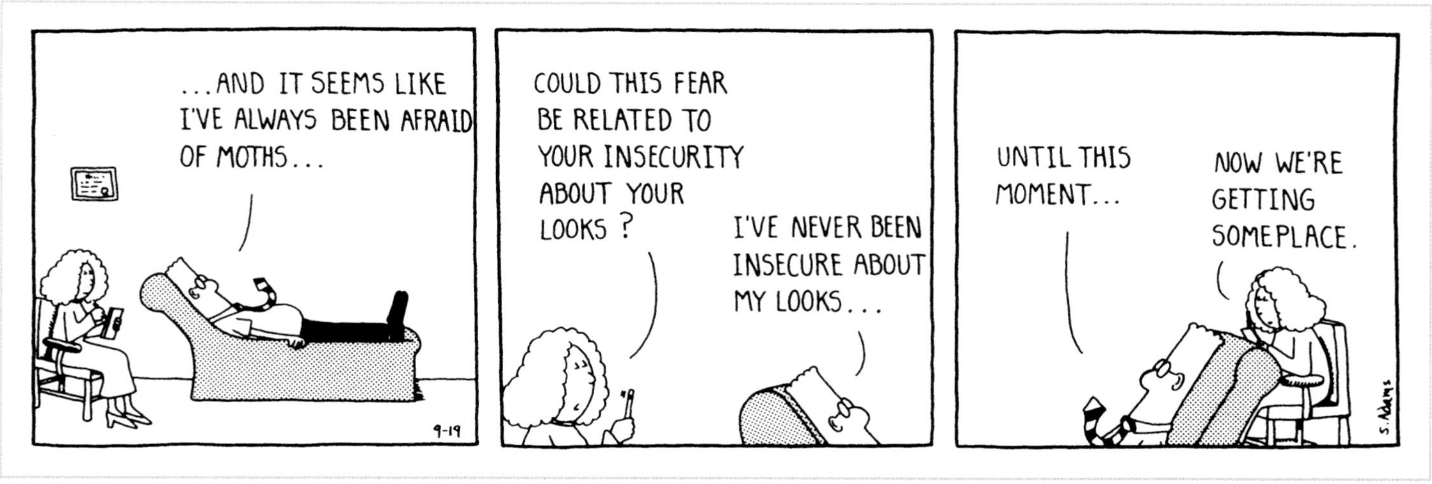
...AND IT SEEMS LIKE I'VE ALWAYS BEEN AFRAID OF MOTHS...
9-19
COULD THIS FEAR BE RELATED TO YOUR INSECURITY ABOUT YOUR LOOKS?
I'VE NEVER BEEN INSECURE ABOUT MY LOOKS...
UNTIL THIS MOMENT...
NOW WE'RE GETTING SOMEPLACE.
S. Adams

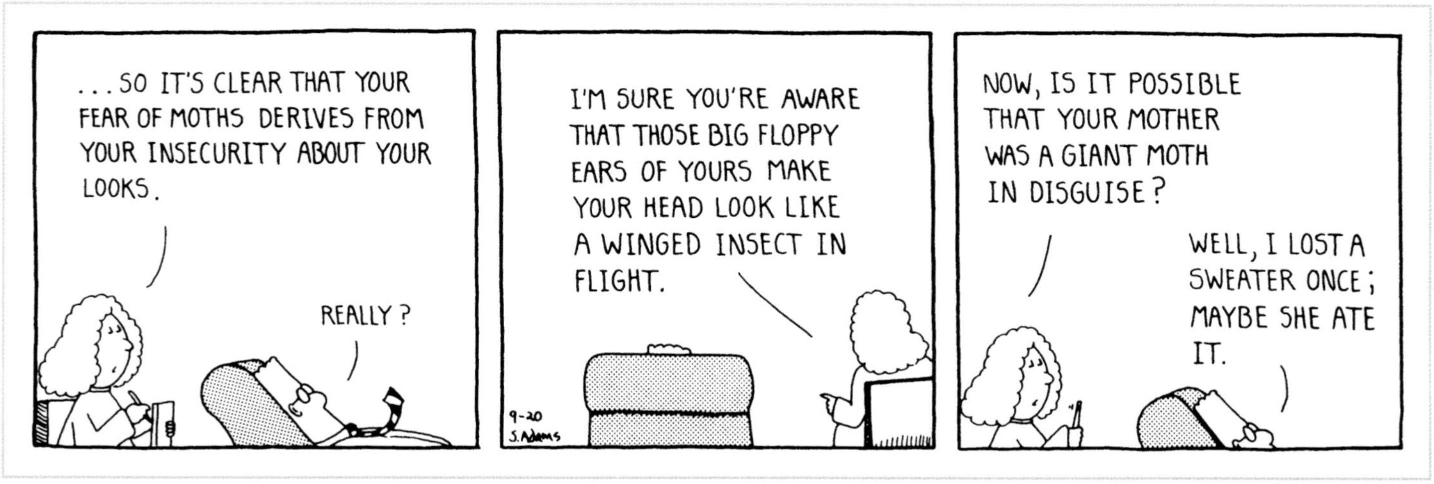
...SO IT'S CLEAR THAT YOUR FEAR OF MOTHS DERIVES FROM YOUR INSECURITY ABOUT YOUR LOOKS.
REALLY?
I'M SURE YOU'RE AWARE THAT THOSE BIG FLOPPY EARS OF YOURS MAKE YOUR HEAD LOOK LIKE A WINGED INSECT IN FLIGHT.
9-20
S. Adams
NOW, IS IT POSSIBLE THAT YOUR MOTHER WAS A GIANT MOTH IN DISGUISE?
WELL, I LOST A SWEATER ONCE; MAYBE SHE ATE IT.

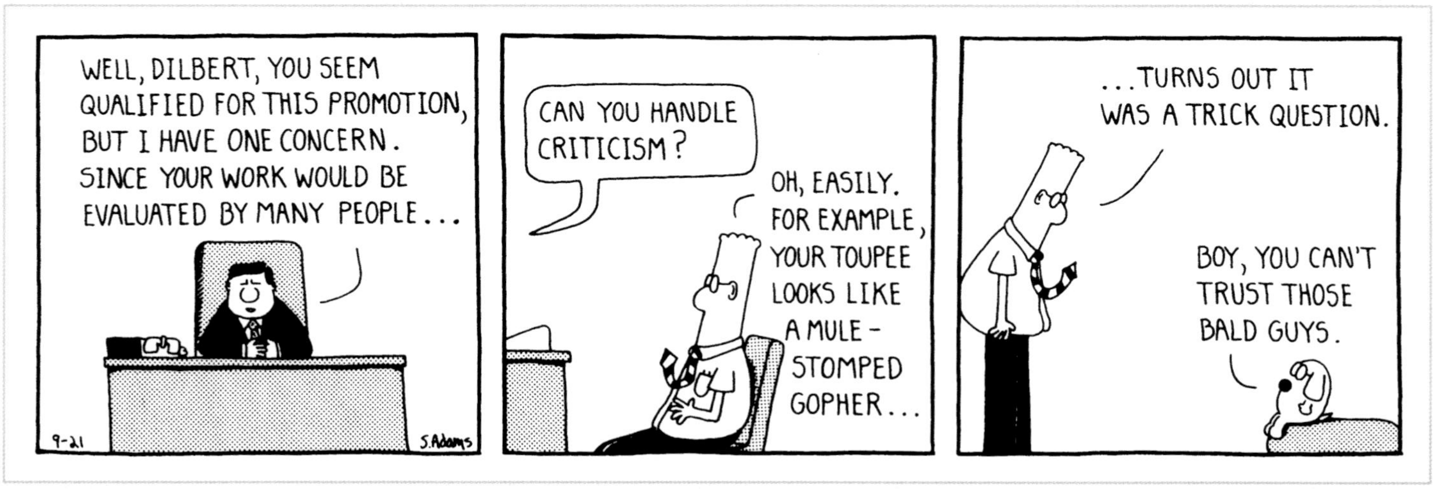
WELL, DILBERT, YOU SEEM QUALIFIED FOR THIS PROMOTION, BUT I HAVE ONE CONCERN. SINCE YOUR WORK WOULD BE EVALUATED BY MANY PEOPLE...
9-21
S. Adams
CAN YOU HANDLE CRITICISM?
OH, EASILY. FOR EXAMPLE, YOUR TOUPEE LOOKS LIKE A MULE-STOMPED GOPHER...
...TURNS OUT IT WAS A TRICK QUESTION.
BOY, YOU CAN'T TRUST THOSE BALD GUYS.

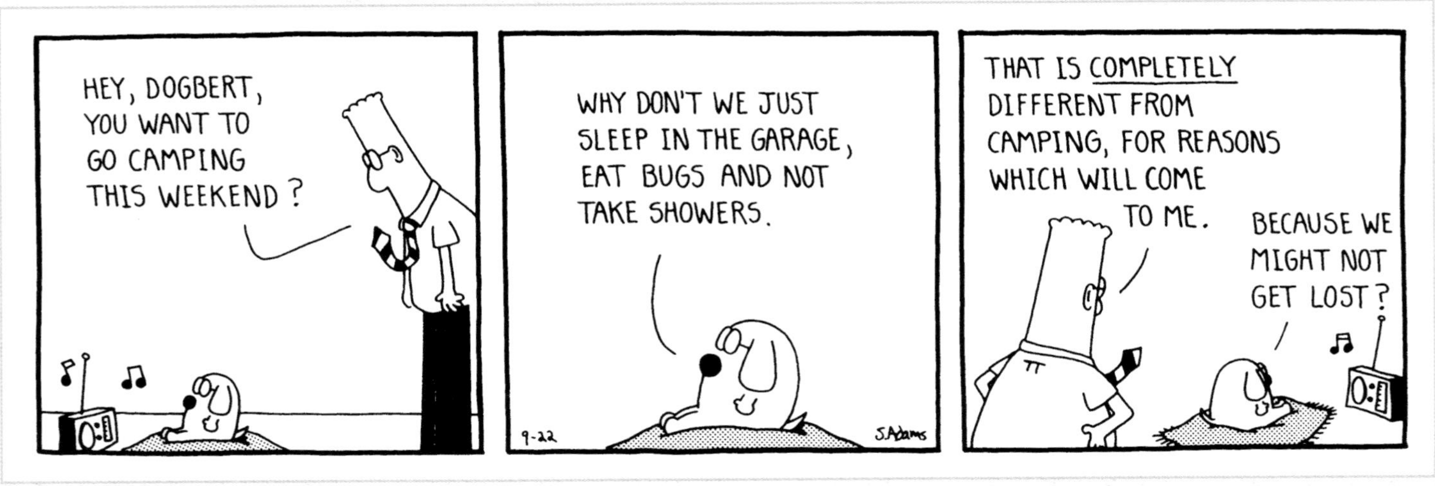
HEY, DOGBERT, YOU WANT TO GO CAMPING THIS WEEKEND?
WHY DON'T WE JUST SLEEP IN THE GARAGE, EAT BUGS AND NOT TAKE SHOWERS.
THAT IS COMPLETELY DIFFERENT FROM CAMPING, FOR REASONS WHICH WILL COME TO ME.
BECAUSE WE MIGHT NOT GET LOST?

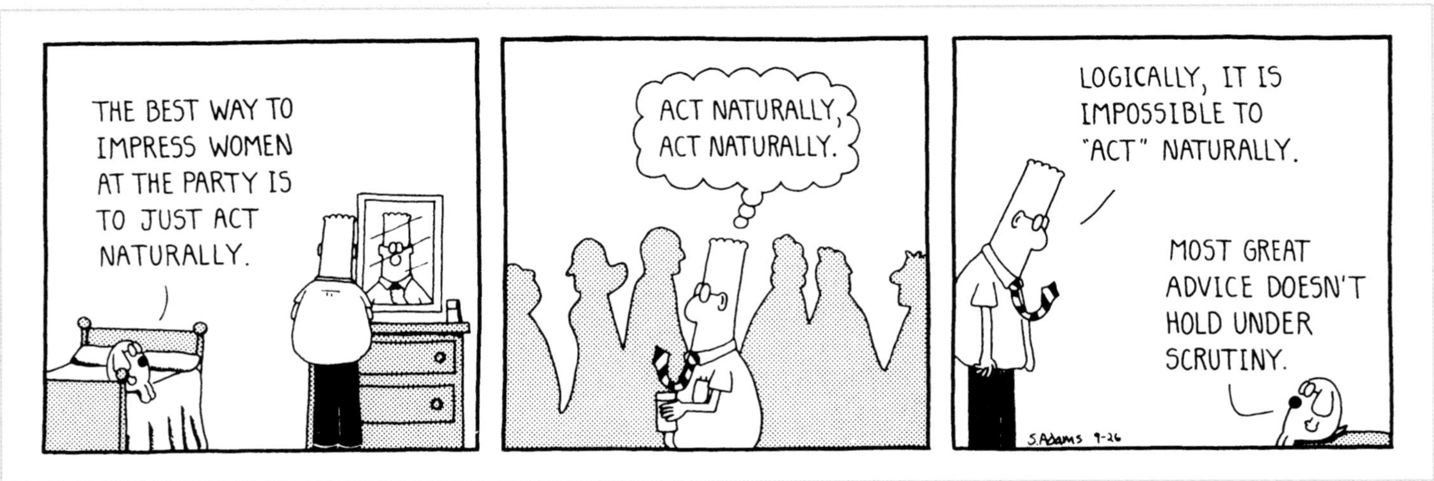
THE BEST WAY TO IMPRESS WOMEN AT THE PARTY IS TO JUST ACT NATURALLY.
ACT NATURALLY, ACT NATURALLY.
LOGICALLY, IT IS IMPOSSIBLE TO "ACT" NATURALLY.
MOST GREAT ADVICE DOESN'T HOLD UNDER SCRUTINY.

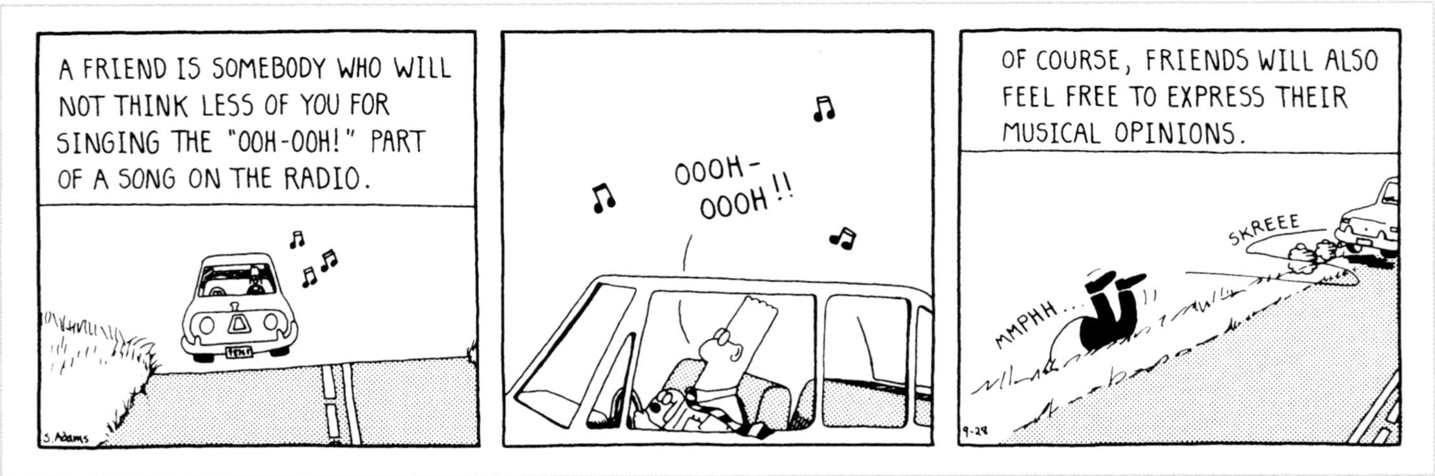
A FRIEND IS SOMEBODY WHO WILL NOT THINK LESS OF YOU FOR SINGING THE "OOH-OOH!" PART OF A SONG ON THE RADIO.
OOOH-OOOH!!
OF COURSE, FRIENDS WILL ALSO FEEL FREE TO EXPRESS THEIR MUSICAL OPINIONS.
SKREEE
MMPHH..

One of the great aspects of being a cartoonist is the opportunity to exercise all of your pet peeves. Car singers make me nuts.

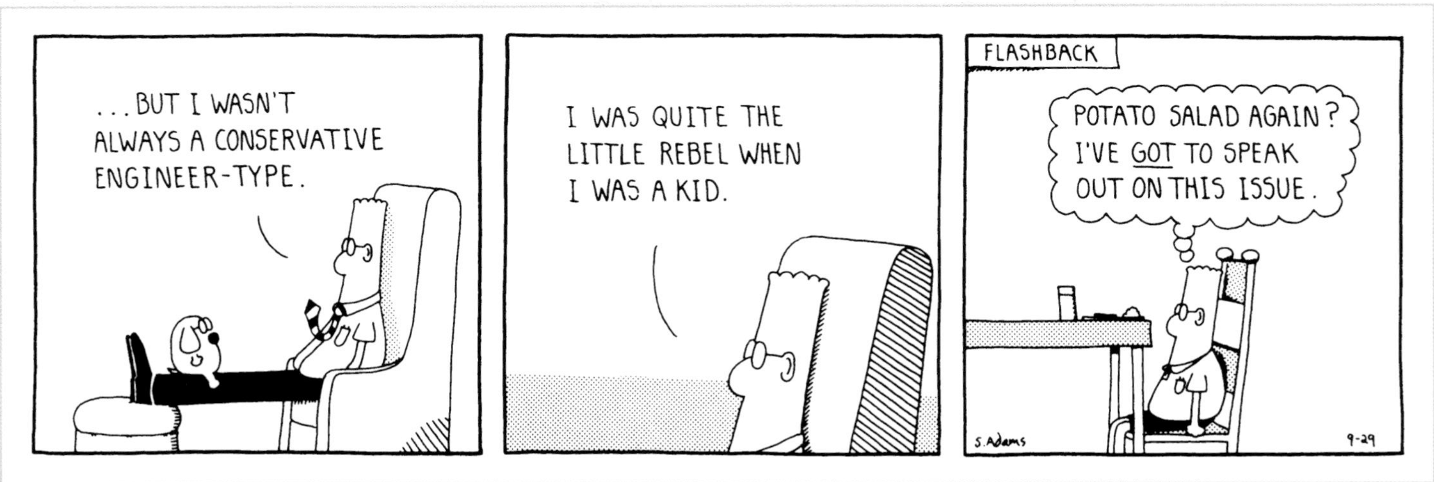
...BUT I WASN'T ALWAYS A CONSERVATIVE ENGINEER-TYPE.
I WAS QUITE THE LITTLE REBEL WHEN I WAS A KID.
FLASHBACK
POTATO SALAD AGAIN? I'VE GOT TO SPEAK OUT ON THIS ISSUE.

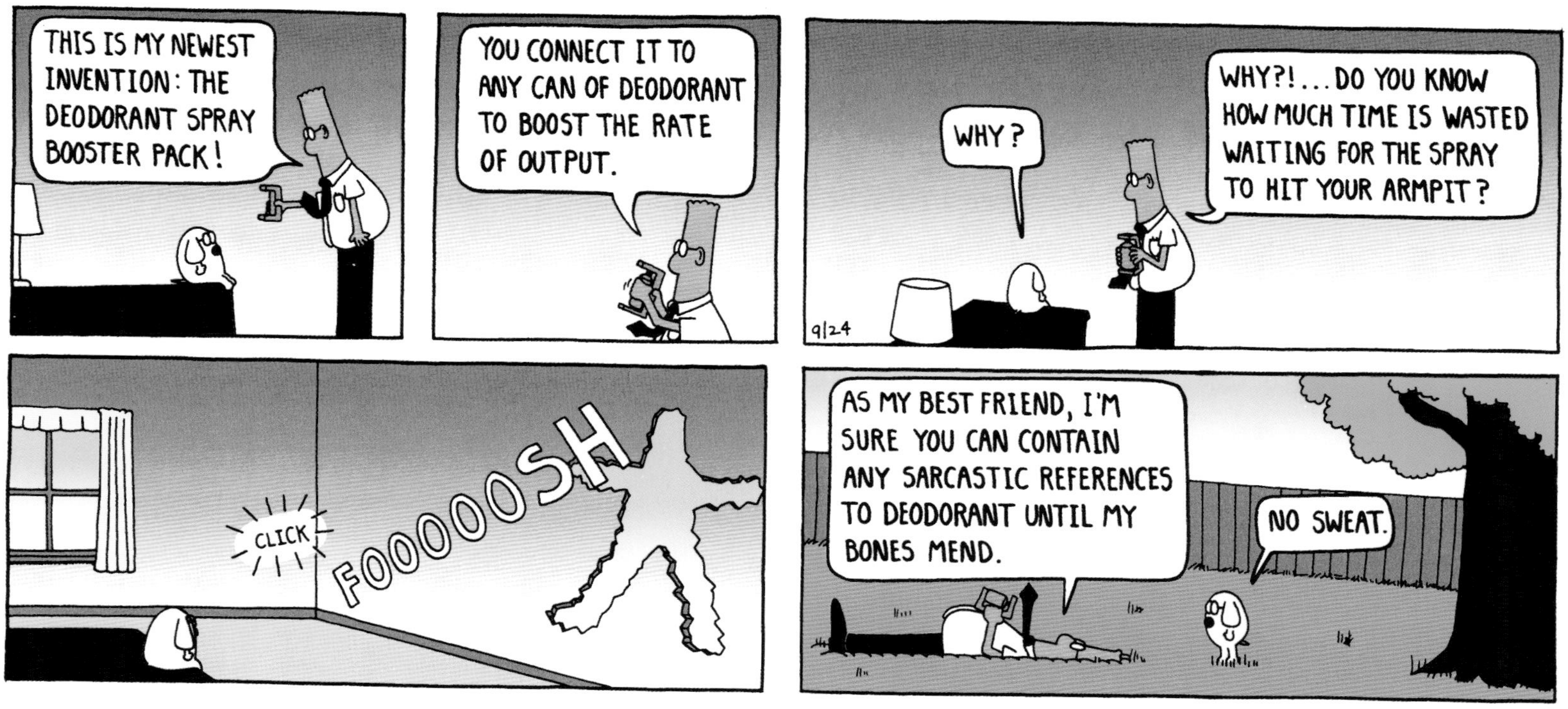
THIS IS MY NEWEST INVENTION: THE DEODORANT SPRAY BOOSTER PACK!
YOU CONNECT IT TO ANY CAN OF DEODORANT TO BOOST THE RATE OF OUTPUT.
WHY?
WHY?!... DO YOU KNOW HOW MUCH TIME IS WASTED WAITING FOR THE SPRAY TO HIT YOUR ARMPIT?
9/24
CLICK
FOOOOOSH
AS MY BEST FRIEND, I'M SURE YOU CAN CONTAIN ANY SARCASTIC REFERENCES TO DEODORANT UNTIL MY BONES MEND.
NO SWEAT.

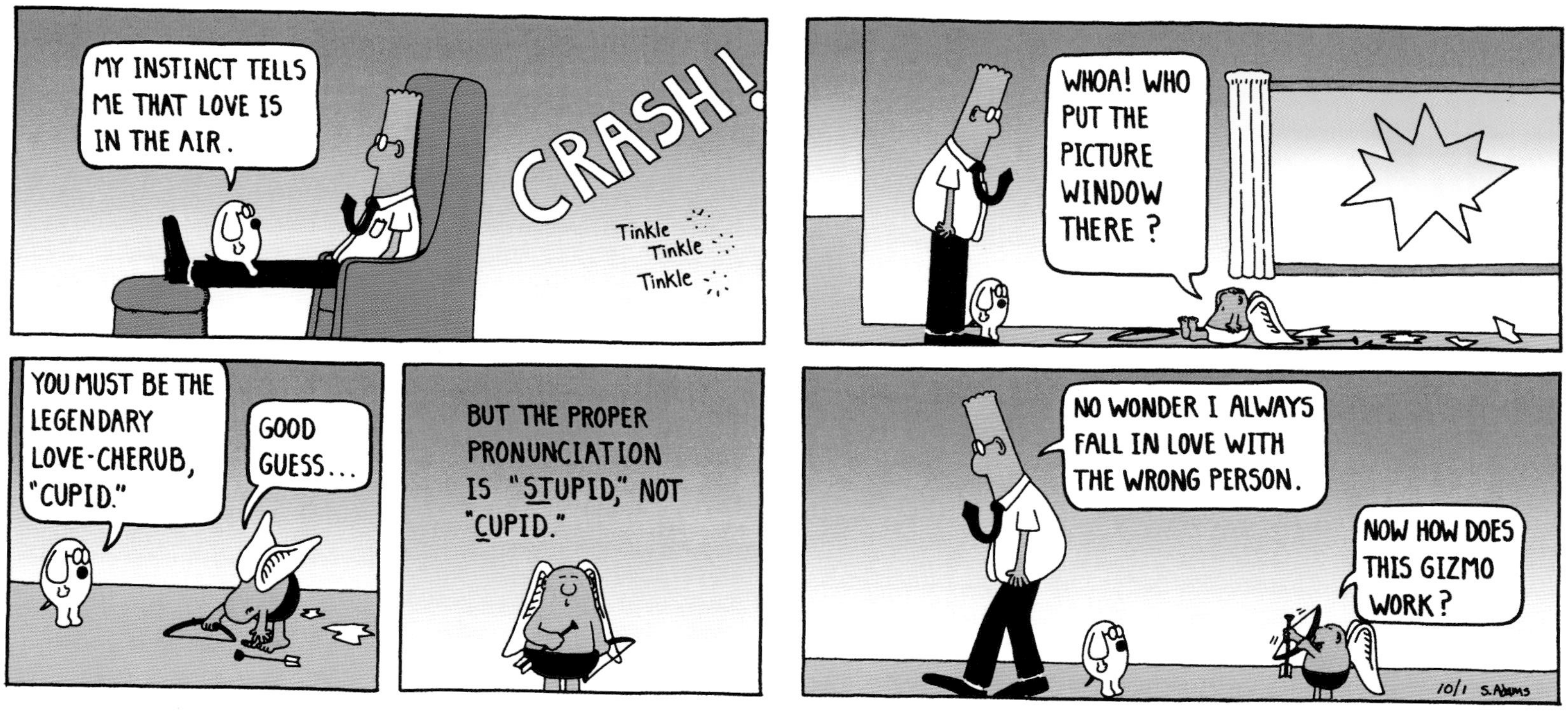
MY INSTINCT TELLS ME THAT LOVE IS IN THE AIR.
CRASH!
Tinkle
Tinkle
Tinkle
WHOA! WHO PUT THE PICTURE WINDOW THERE?
YOU MUST BE THE LEGENDARY LOVE-CHERUB, "CUPID."
GOOD GUESS...
BUT THE PROPER PRONUNCIATION IS "STUPID," NOT "CUPID."
NO WONDER I ALWAYS FALL IN LOVE WITH THE WRONG PERSON.
NOW HOW DOES THIS GIZMO WORK?
10/1 S.Adams

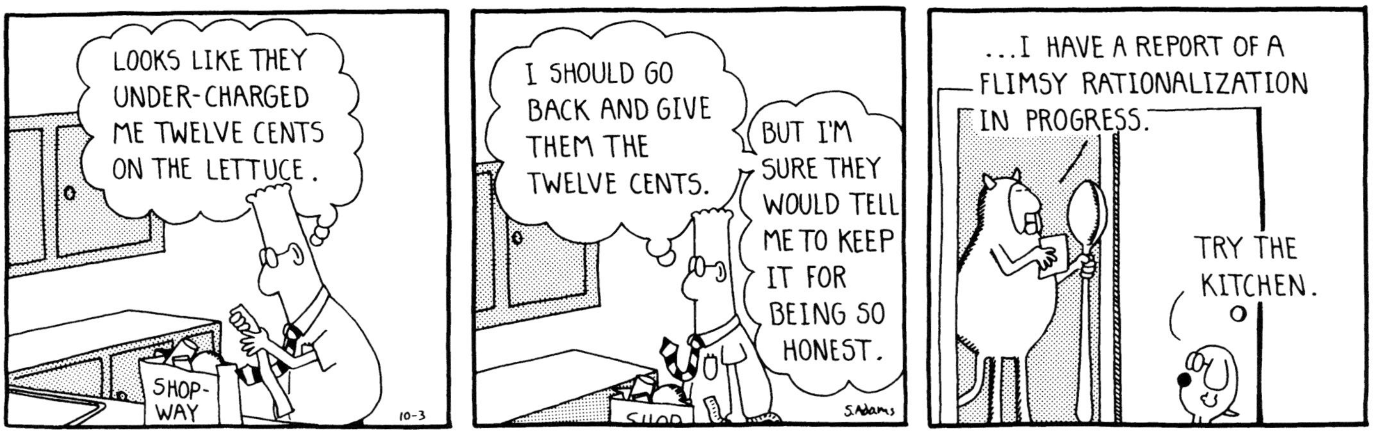
LOOKS LIKE THEY UNDER-CHARGED ME TWELVE CENTS ON THE LETTUCE.
SHOP-WAY
10-3
I SHOULD GO BACK AND GIVE THEM THE TWELVE CENTS.
BUT I'M SURE THEY WOULD TELL ME TO KEEP IT FOR BEING SO HONEST.
S.Adams
...I HAVE A REPORT OF A FLIMSY RATIONALIZATION IN PROGRESS.
TRY THE KITCHEN.

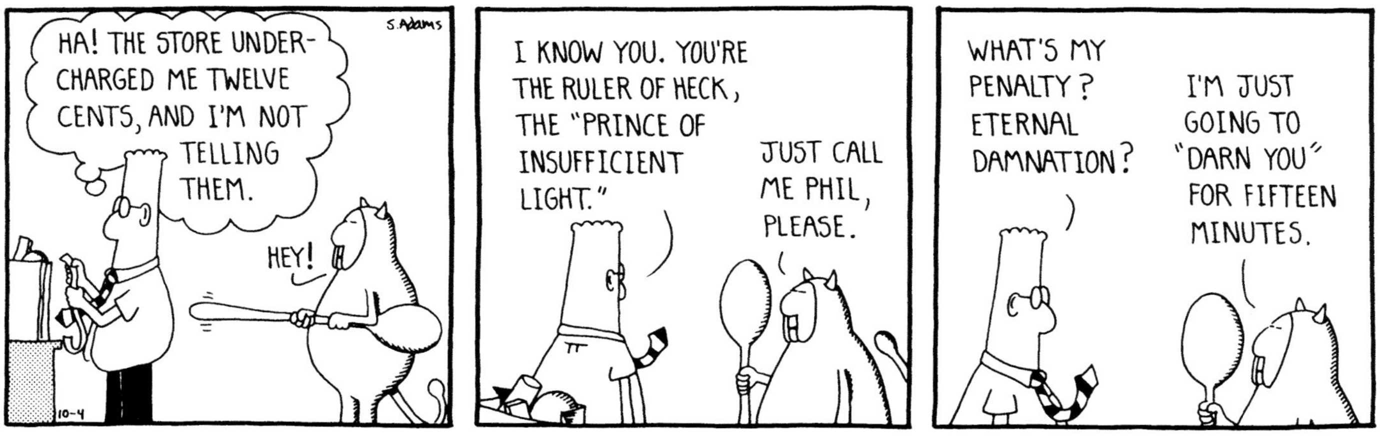
S.Adams
HA! THE STORE UNDER-CHARGED ME TWELVE CENTS, AND I'M NOT TELLING THEM.
HEY!
10-4
I KNOW YOU. YOU'RE THE RULER OF HECK, THE "PRINCE OF INSUFFICIENT LIGHT."
JUST CALL ME PHIL, PLEASE.
WHAT'S MY PENALTY? ETERNAL DAMNATION?
I'M JUST GOING TO "DARN YOU" FOR FIFTEEN MINUTES.

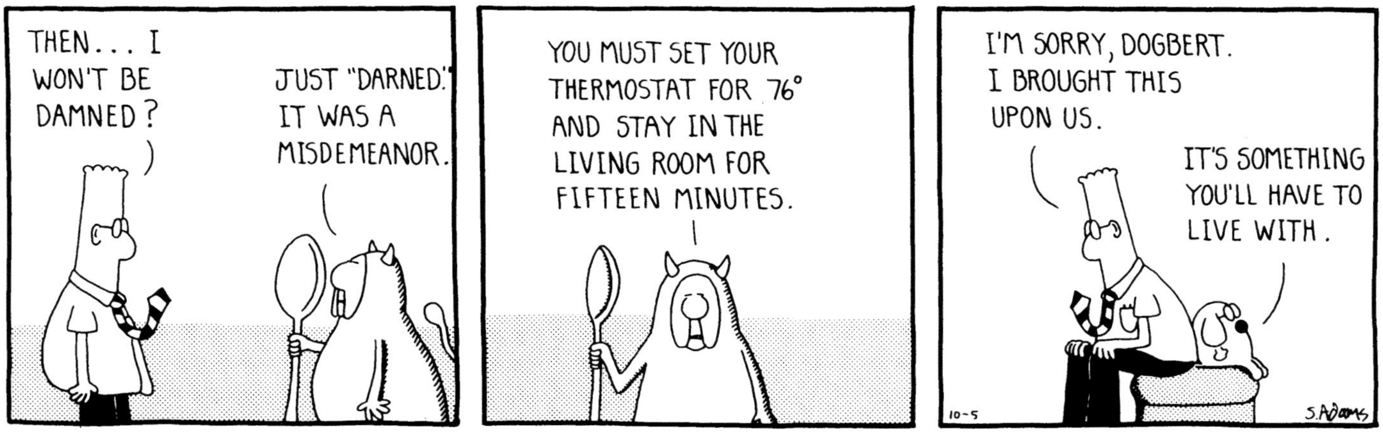
THEN... I WON'T BE DAMNED?
JUST "DARNED." IT WAS A MISDEMEANOR.
YOU MUST SET YOUR THERMOSTAT FOR 76° AND STAY IN THE LIVING ROOM FOR FIFTEEN MINUTES.
I'M SORRY, DOGBERT. I BROUGHT THIS UPON US.
IT'S SOMETHING YOU'LL HAVE TO LIVE WITH.
10-5
S.Adams

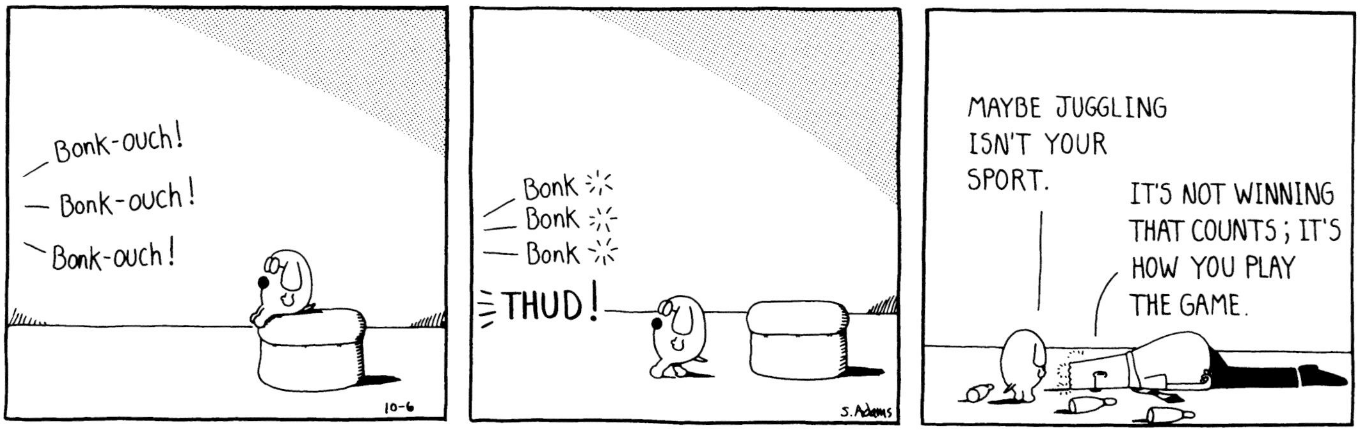
Bonk-ouch!
Bonk-ouch!
Bonk-ouch!
10-6
Bonk
Bonk
Bonk
THUD!
S.Adams
MAYBE JUGGLING ISN'T YOUR SPORT.
IT'S NOT WINNING THAT COUNTS; IT'S HOW YOU PLAY THE GAME.

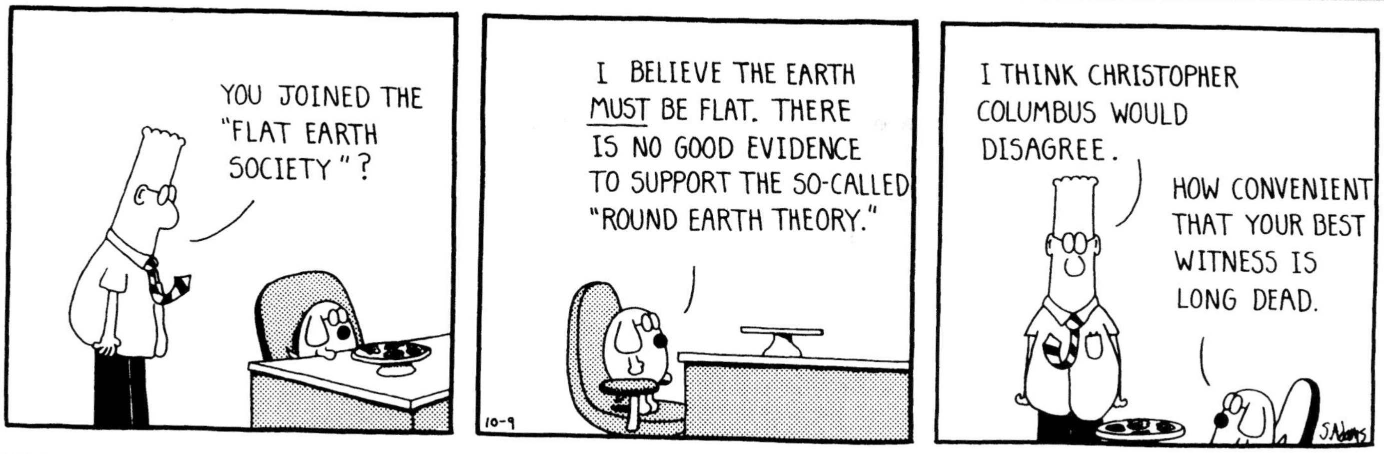
YOU JOINED THE "FLAT EARTH SOCIETY"?
I BELIEVE THE EARTH MUST BE FLAT. THERE IS NO GOOD EVIDENCE TO SUPPORT THE SO-CALLED "ROUND EARTH THEORY."
10-9
I THINK CHRISTOPHER COLUMBUS WOULD DISAGREE.
HOW CONVENIENT THAT YOUR BEST WITNESS IS LONG DEAD.
S.Adams

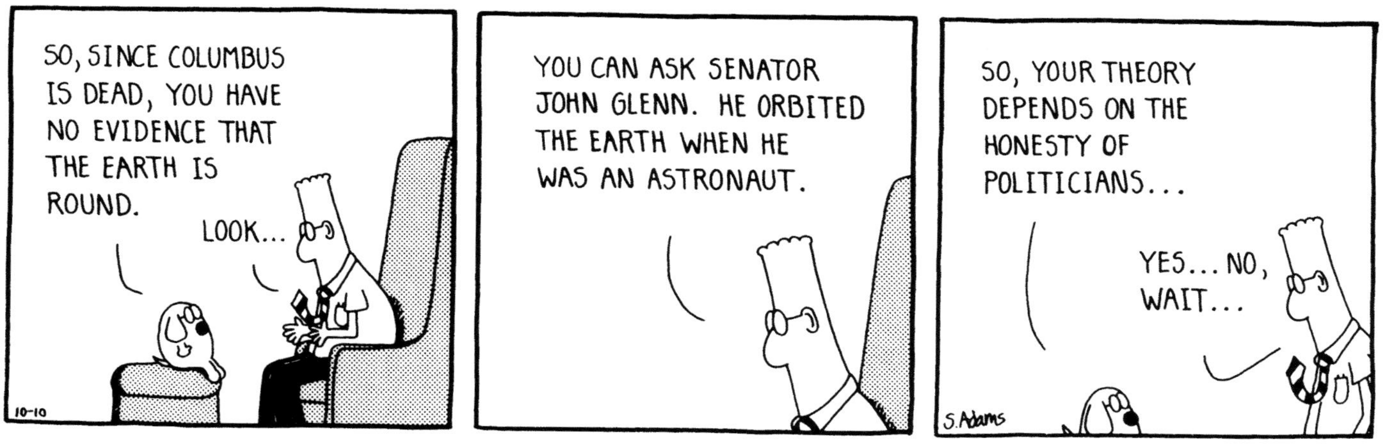
SO, SINCE COLUMBUS IS DEAD, YOU HAVE NO EVIDENCE THAT THE EARTH IS ROUND.
LOOK...
10-10
YOU CAN ASK SENATOR JOHN GLENN. HE ORBITED THE EARTH WHEN HE WAS AN ASTRONAUT.
SO, YOUR THEORY DEPENDS ON THE HONESTY OF POLITICIANS...
YES... NO, WAIT...
S.Adams

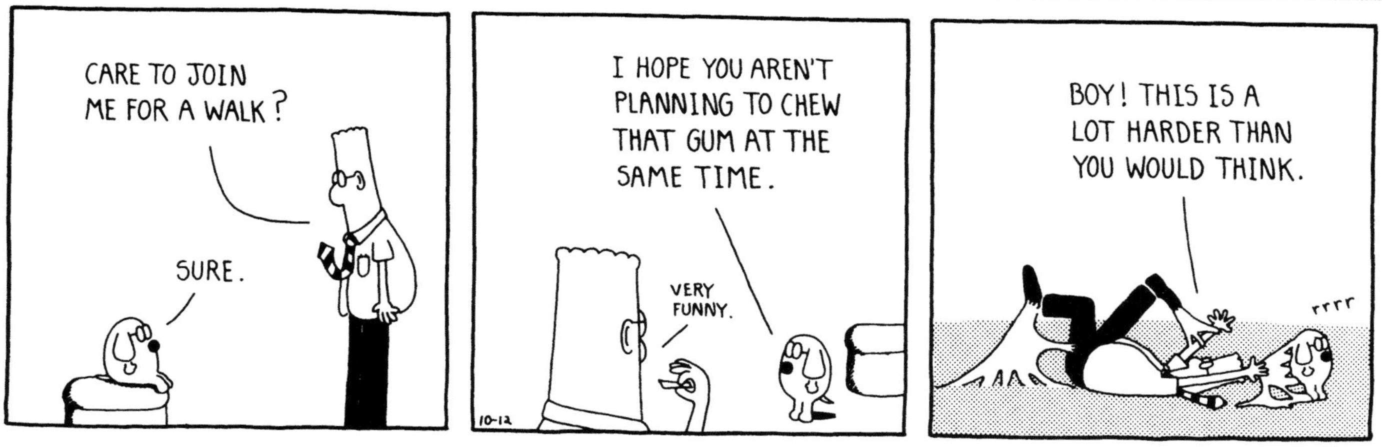
CARE TO JOIN ME FOR A WALK?
SURE.
I HOPE YOU AREN'T PLANNING TO CHEW THAT GUM AT THE SAME TIME.
VERY FUNNY.
10-12
BOY! THIS IS A LOT HARDER THAN YOU WOULD THINK.
rrrr

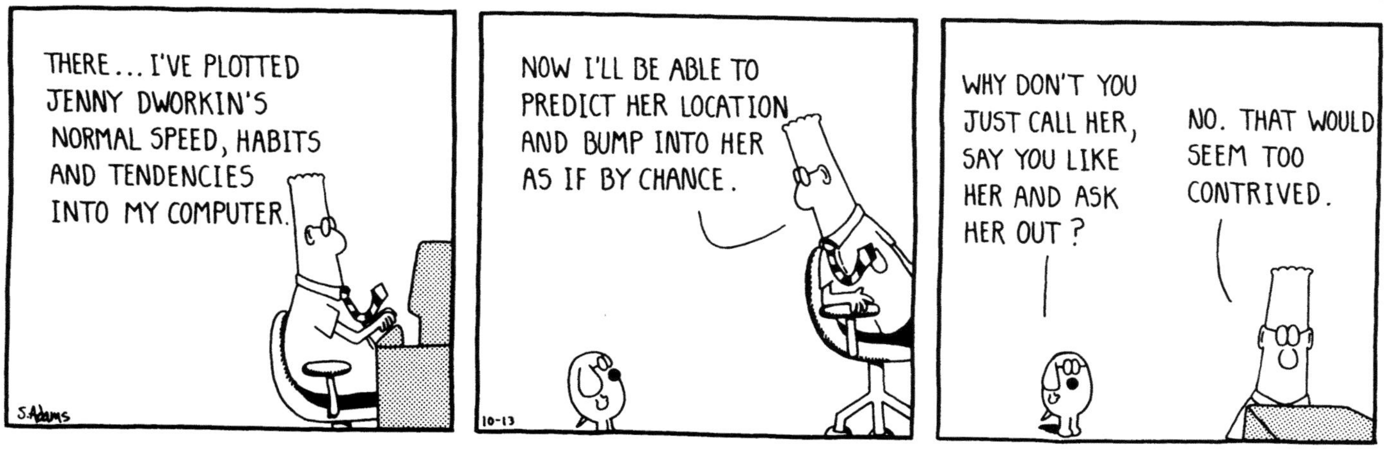
THERE... I'VE PLOTTED JENNY DWORKIN'S NORMAL SPEED, HABITS AND TENDENCIES INTO MY COMPUTER.
S.Adams
NOW I'LL BE ABLE TO PREDICT HER LOCATION AND BUMP INTO HER AS IF BY CHANCE.
10-13
WHY DON'T YOU JUST CALL HER, SAY YOU LIKE HER AND ASK HER OUT?
NO. THAT WOULD SEEM TOO CONTRIVED.

MY NEW SECURITY SYSTEM IS NOW INSTALLED.
TAP
TAP
HOW'S IT WORK?
I BURIED A GIANT SPRING UNDER THE WELCOME MAT TO CATAPULT ANY UNDESIRABLES INTO THE WILSEY'S POOL THREE BLOCKS FROM HERE.
YOU JUST TAP THAT LITTLE BUTTON ON THE FLOOR THERE...
TIME STANDS STILL AS DOGBERT PONDERS THE GIFT THAT FATE HAS GIVEN HIM.
I'M PRETTY SURE THE LOOK ON HIS FACE WILL BE WORTH WHATEVER MINOR GUILT I FEEL OVER THIS.
10-8

...THEREFORE, CURLY MUST HAVE BEEN THE SMARTEST OF ALL THE STOOGES.
RRRRING
I WON WHAT?!!
I WON THE LOTTERY! WE'RE MILLIONAIRES, DOGBERT!!
KNOCK KNOCK
GLOBAL NEWS - MAY I INTERVIEW YOU ON YOUR SUDDEN WEALTH?
WHAT WOULD YOU LIKE TO SAY TO THE ENTIRE PLANET?
POINK
THE WEALTH HAD COME QUICKLY...
ER...UM...
10-15
AND JUST AS QUICKLY, IT WAS GONE.
DRINKS FOR EVERYBODY!
S.Adams

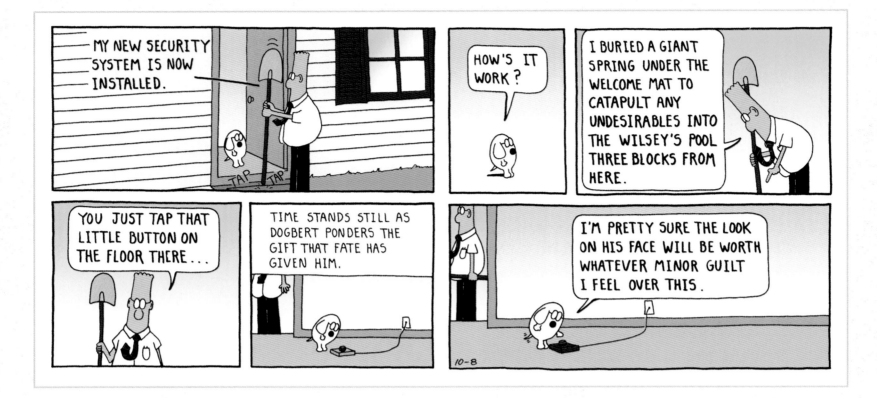

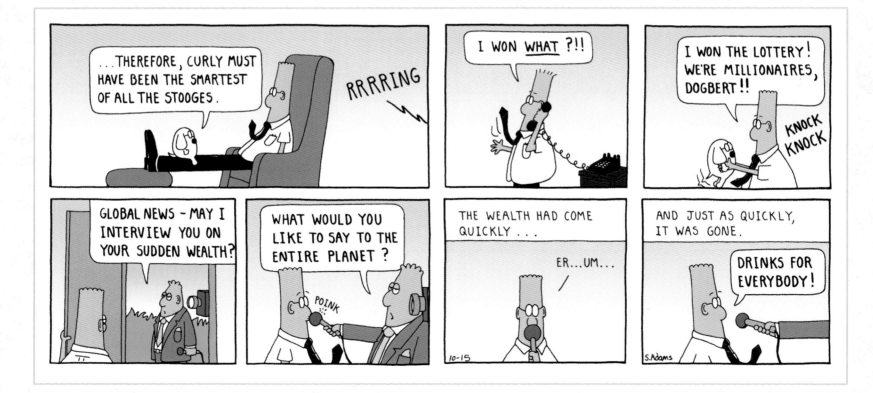

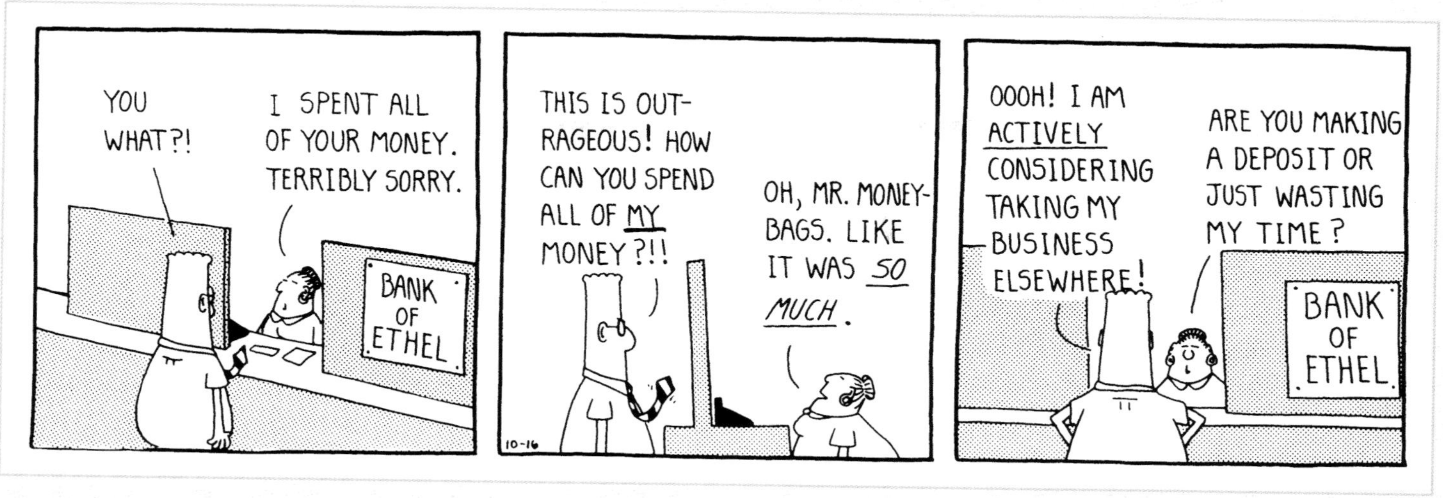
YOU WHAT?!
I SPENT ALL OF YOUR MONEY. TERRIBLY SORRY.
BANK OF ETHEL
THIS IS OUTRAGEOUS! HOW CAN YOU SPEND ALL OF MY MONEY?!!
OH, MR. MONEY-BAGS. LIKE IT WAS SO MUCH.
10-16
OOOH! I AM ACTIVELY CONSIDERING TAKING MY BUSINESS ELSEWHERE!
ARE YOU MAKING A DEPOSIT OR JUST WASTING MY TIME?
BANK OF ETHEL

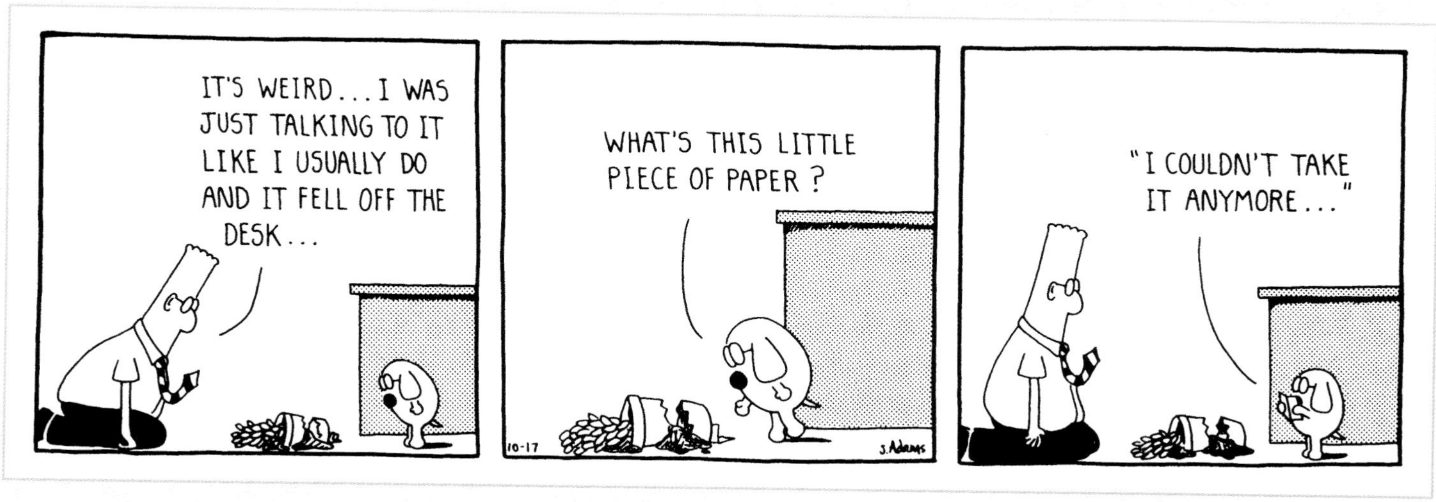
IT'S WEIRD... I WAS JUST TALKING TO IT LIKE I USUALLY DO AND IT FELL OFF THE DESK...
WHAT'S THIS LITTLE PIECE OF PAPER?
10-17
S. Adams
"I COULDN'T TAKE IT ANYMORE..."

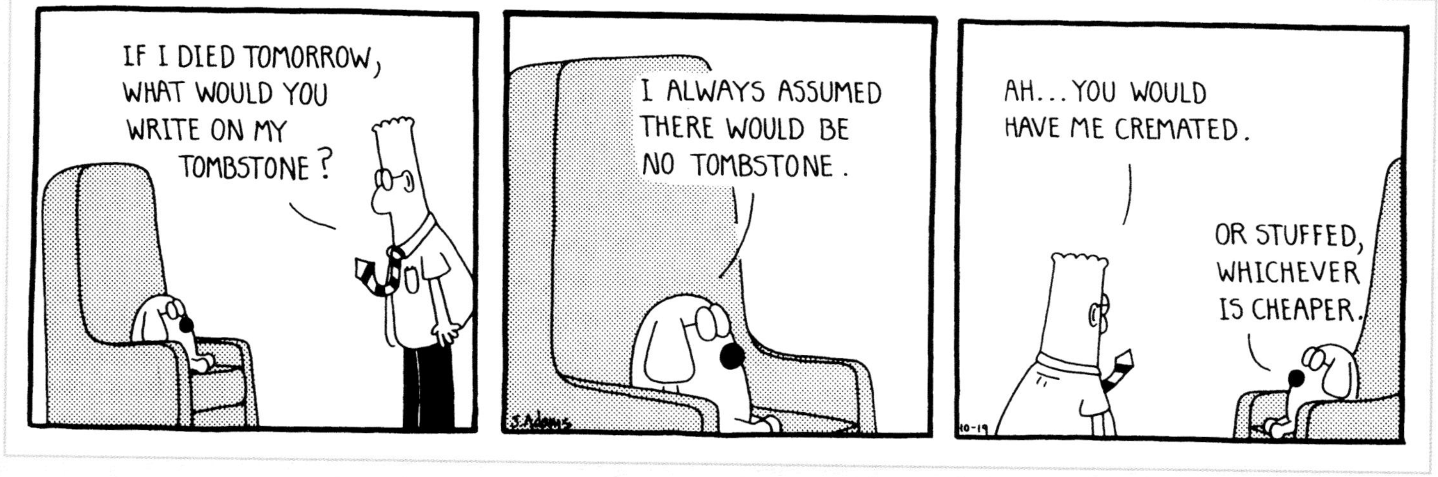
IF I DIED TOMORROW, WHAT WOULD YOU WRITE ON MY TOMBSTONE?
I ALWAYS ASSUMED THERE WOULD BE NO TOMBSTONE.
S. Adams
AH... YOU WOULD HAVE ME CREMATED.
OR STUFFED, WHICHEVER IS CHEAPER.
10-19

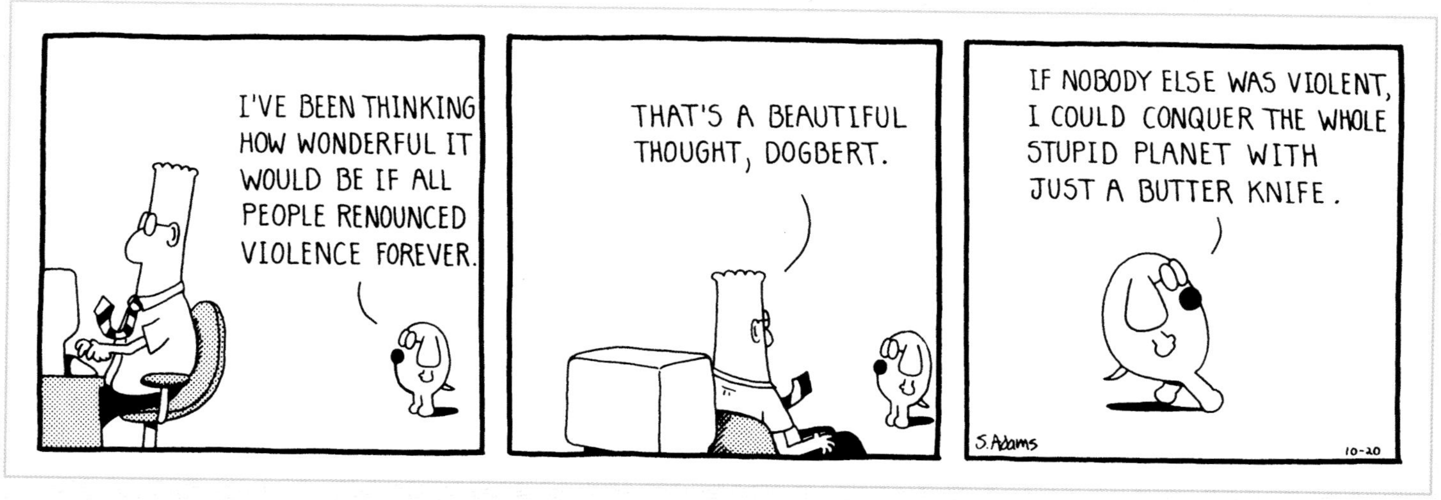
I'VE BEEN THINKING HOW WONDERFUL IT WOULD BE IF ALL PEOPLE RENOUNCED VIOLENCE FOREVER.
THAT'S A BEAUTIFUL THOUGHT, DOGBERT.
IF NOBODY ELSE WAS VIOLENT, I COULD CONQUER THE WHOLE STUPID PLANET WITH JUST A BUTTER KNIFE.
S. Adams
10-20

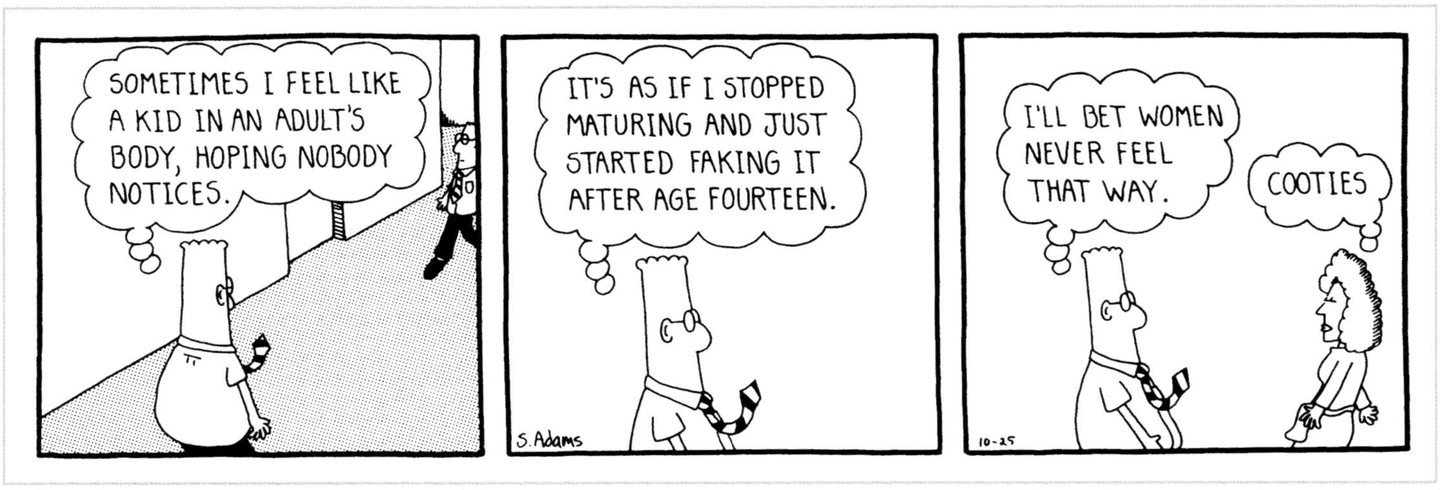
SOMETIMES I FEEL LIKE A KID IN AN ADULT'S BODY, HOPING NOBODY NOTICES.
IT'S AS IF I STOPPED MATURING AND JUST STARTED FAKING IT AFTER AGE FOURTEEN.
S. Adams
I'LL BET WOMEN NEVER FEEL THAT WAY.
COOTIES
10-25

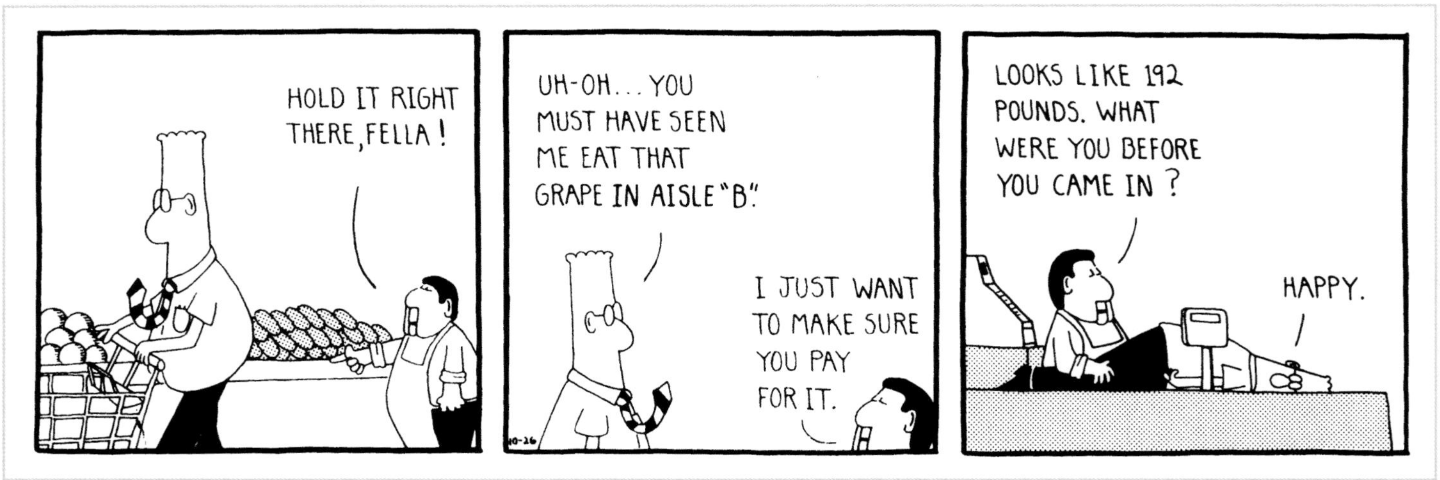
HOLD IT RIGHT THERE, FELLA!
UH-OH... YOU MUST HAVE SEEN ME EAT THAT GRAPE IN AISLE "B".
I JUST WANT TO MAKE SURE YOU PAY FOR IT.
10-26
LOOKS LIKE 192 POUNDS. WHAT WERE YOU BEFORE YOU CAME IN?
HAPPY.

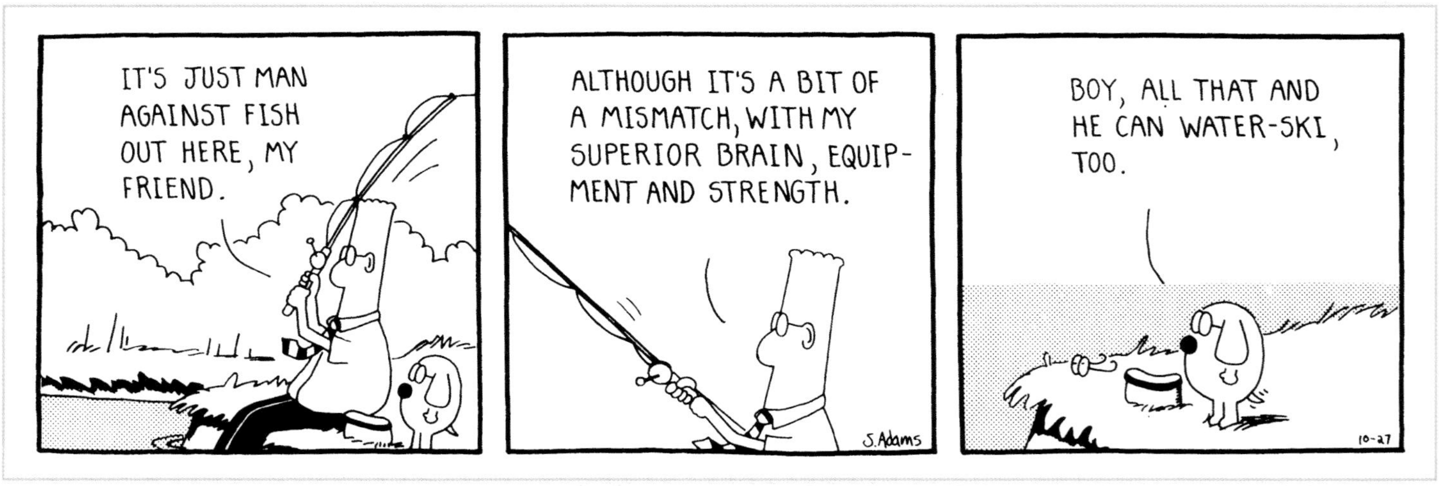
IT'S JUST MAN AGAINST FISH OUT HERE, MY FRIEND.
ALTHOUGH IT'S A BIT OF A MISMATCH, WITH MY SUPERIOR BRAIN, EQUIP-MENT AND STRENGTH.
S. Adams
BOY, ALL THAT AND HE CAN WATER-SKI, TOO.
10-27

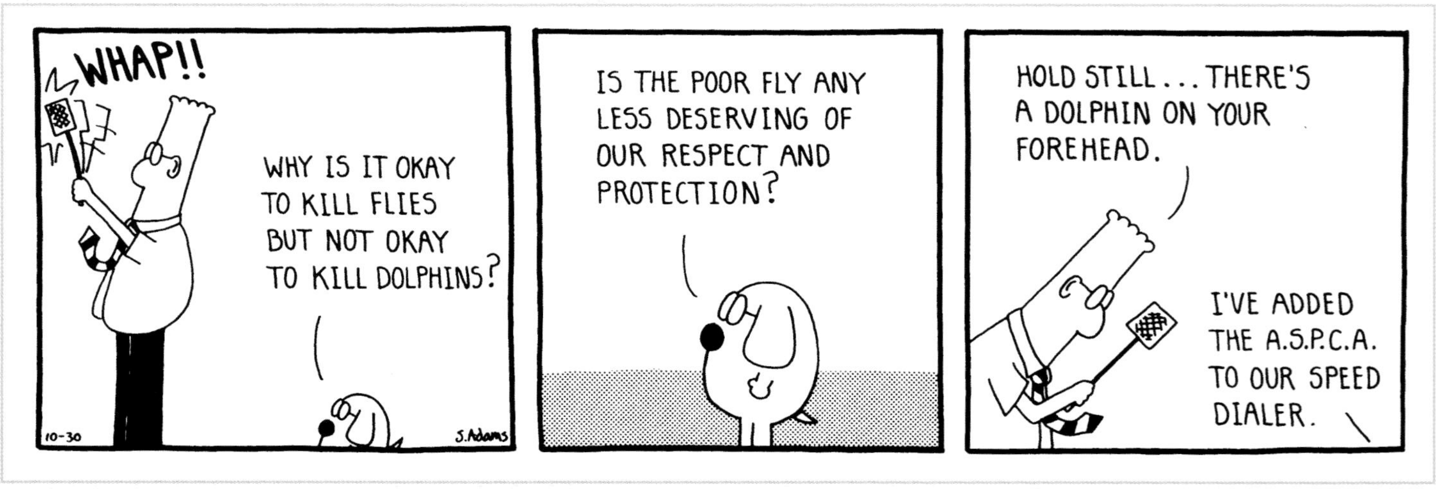
WHAP!!
WHY IS IT OKAY TO KILL FLIES BUT NOT OKAY TO KILL DOLPHINS?
10-30
S. Adams
IS THE POOR FLY ANY LESS DESERVING OF OUR RESPECT AND PROTECTION?
HOLD STILL... THERE'S A DOLPHIN ON YOUR FOREHEAD.
I'VE ADDED THE A.S.P.C.A. TO OUR SPEED DIALER.

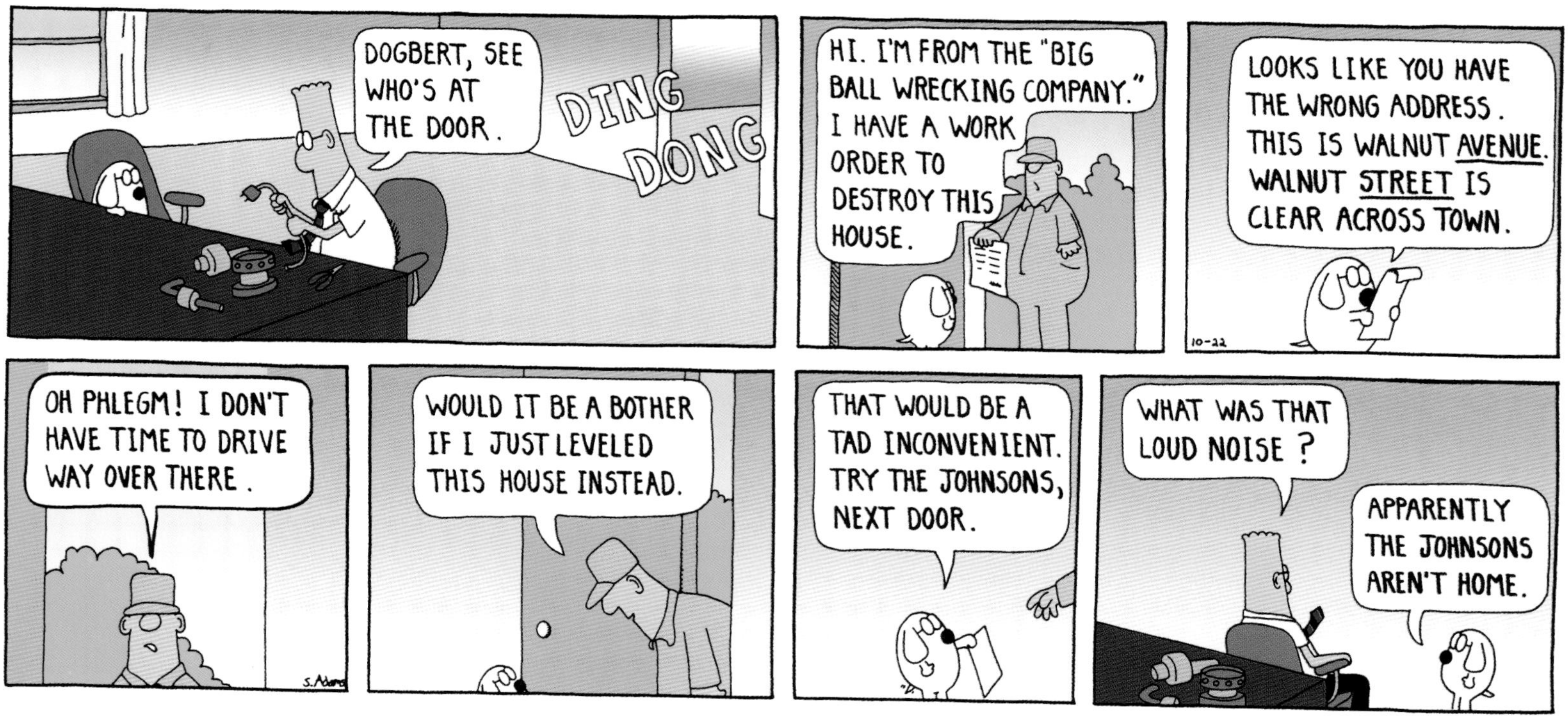
DOGBERT, SEE WHO'S AT THE DOOR.
DING DONG
HI. I'M FROM THE "BIG BALL WRECKING COMPANY." I HAVE A WORK ORDER TO DESTROY THIS HOUSE.
LOOKS LIKE YOU HAVE THE WRONG ADDRESS. THIS IS WALNUT AVENUE. WALNUT STREET IS CLEAR ACROSS TOWN.
10-22
OH PHLEGM! I DON'T HAVE TIME TO DRIVE WAY OVER THERE.
S.Adams
WOULD IT BE A BOTHER IF I JUST LEVELED THIS HOUSE INSTEAD.
THAT WOULD BE A TAD INCONVENIENT. TRY THE JOHNSONS, NEXT DOOR.
WHAT WAS THAT LOUD NOISE?
APPARENTLY THE JOHNSONS AREN'T HOME.

When I was a teller at Crocker National Bank in San Francisco, billionaire David Packard came to my window to cash a stipend check. I declined it because he didn't have a personal account at our branch. I learned later that it was the wrong decision.

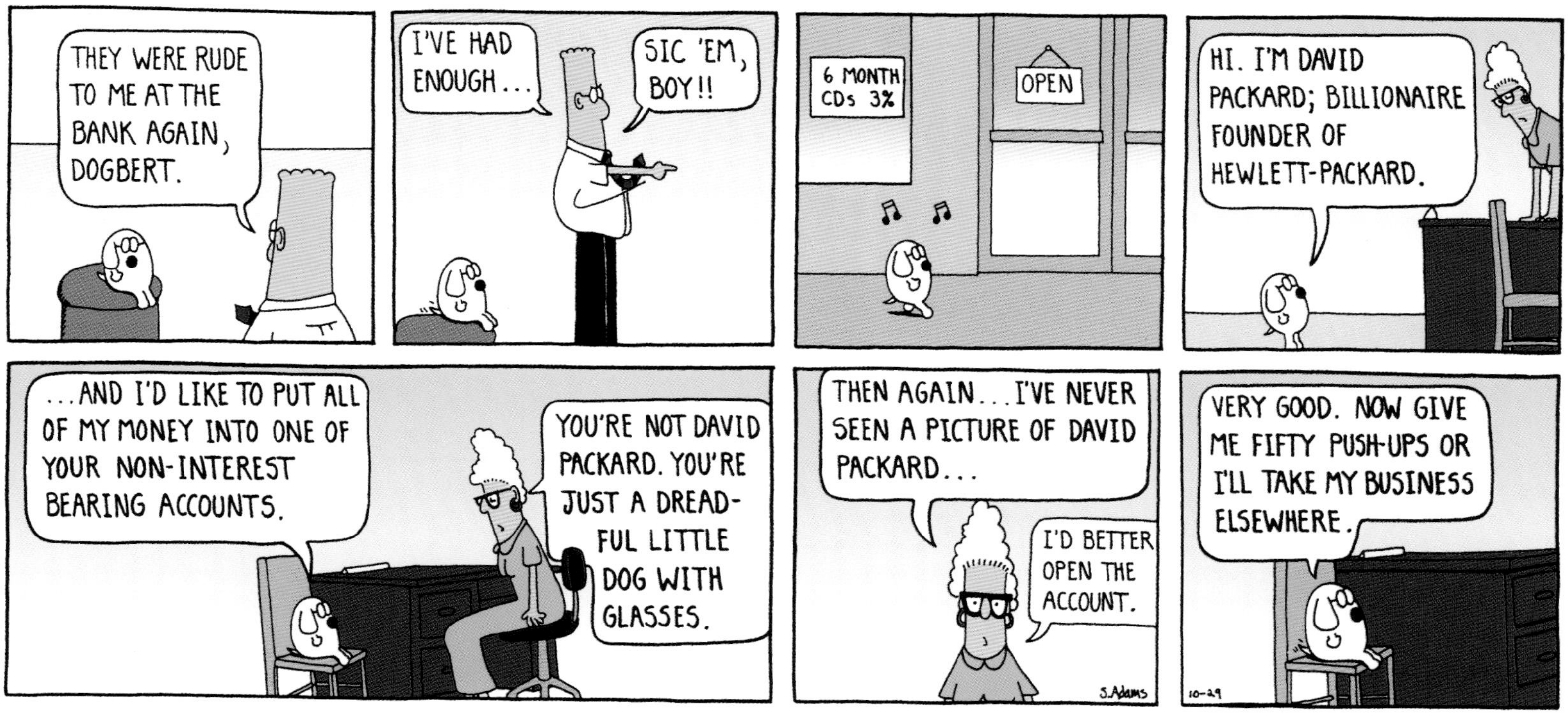
THEY WERE RUDE TO ME AT THE BANK AGAIN, DOGBERT.
I'VE HAD ENOUGH...
SIC 'EM, BOY!!
6 MONTH CDs 3%
OPEN
HI. I'M DAVID PACKARD; BILLIONAIRE FOUNDER OF HEWLETT-PACKARD.
...AND I'D LIKE TO PUT ALL OF MY MONEY INTO ONE OF YOUR NON-INTEREST BEARING ACCOUNTS.
YOU'RE NOT DAVID PACKARD. YOU'RE JUST A DREAD-FUL LITTLE DOG WITH GLASSES.
THEN AGAIN... I'VE NEVER SEEN A PICTURE OF DAVID PACKARD...
I'D BETTER OPEN THE ACCOUNT.
S.Adams
10-29
VERY GOOD. NOW GIVE ME FIFTY PUSH-UPS OR I'LL TAKE MY BUSINESS ELSEWHERE.

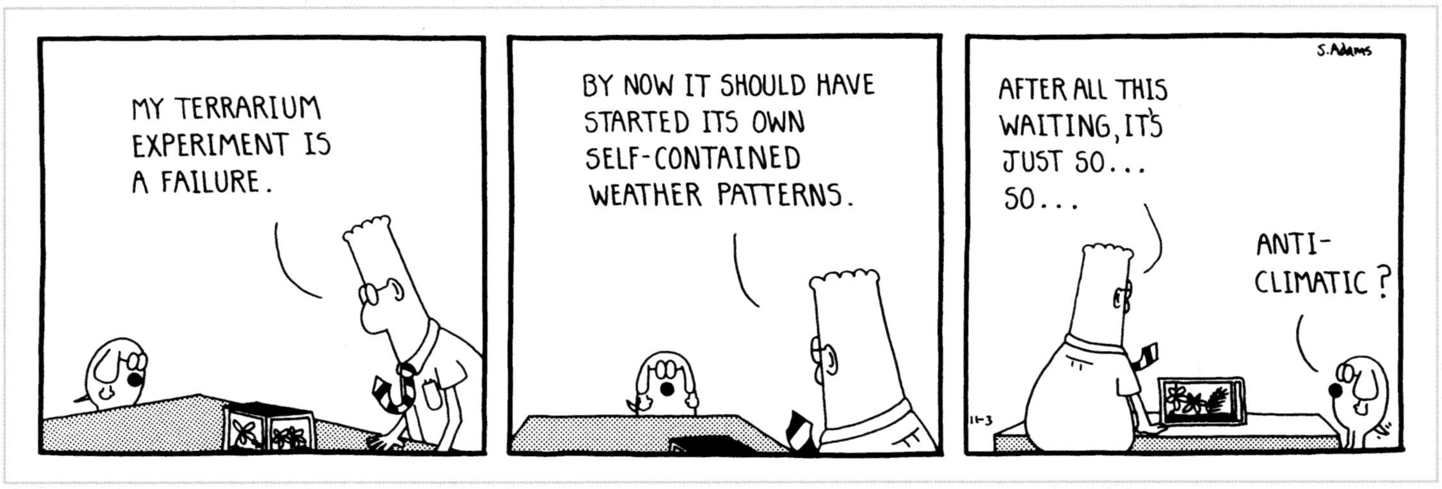
MY TERRARIUM EXPERIMENT IS A FAILURE.
BY NOW IT SHOULD HAVE STARTED ITS OWN SELF-CONTAINED WEATHER PATTERNS.
S. Adams
AFTER ALL THIS WAITING, IT'S JUST SO... SO...
ANTI-CLIMATIC?
11-3

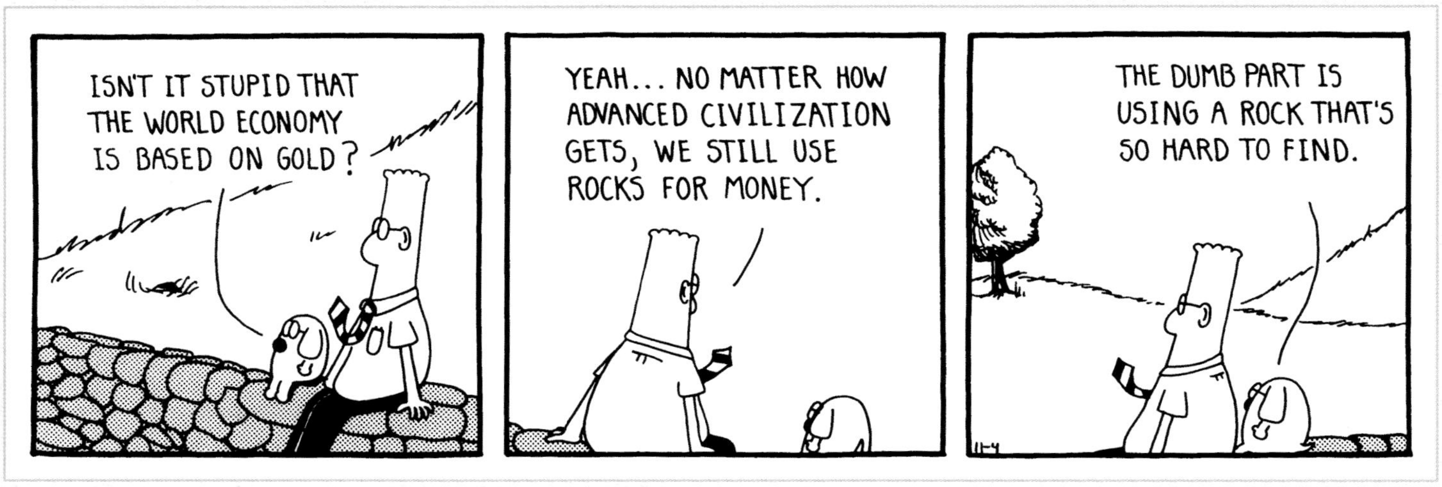
ISN'T IT STUPID THAT THE WORLD ECONOMY IS BASED ON GOLD?
YEAH... NO MATTER HOW ADVANCED CIVILIZATION GETS, WE STILL USE ROCKS FOR MONEY.
THE DUMB PART IS USING A ROCK THAT'S SO HARD TO FIND.
11-4

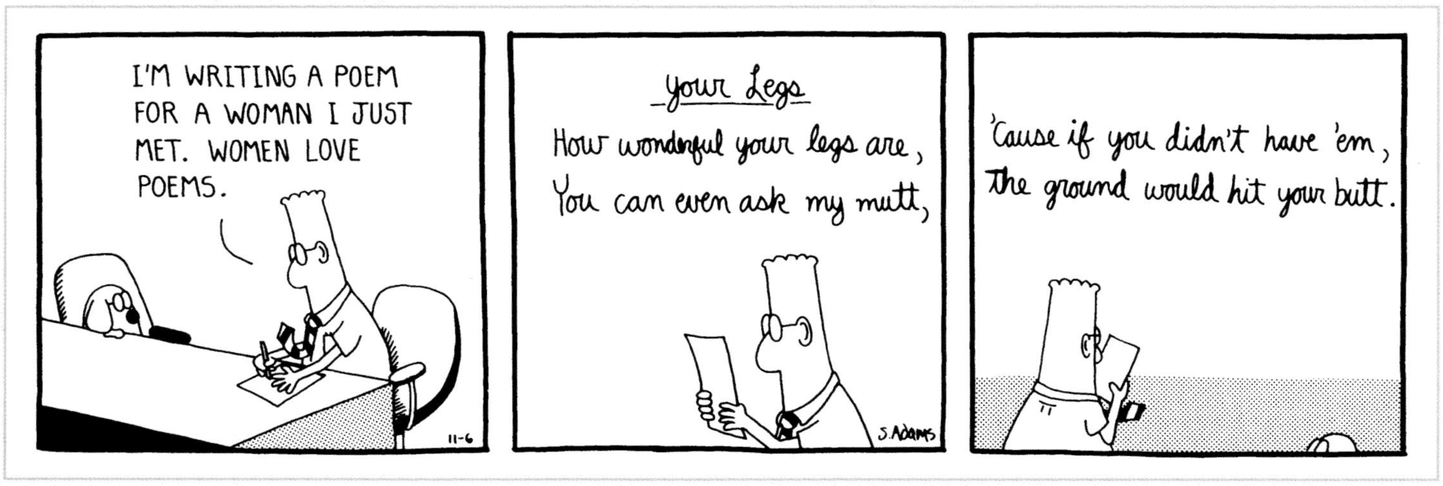
I'M WRITING A POEM FOR A WOMAN I JUST MET. WOMEN LOVE POEMS.
11-6
Your Legs
How wonderful your legs are,
You can even ask my mutt,
S. Adams
'Cause if you didn't have 'em,
The ground would hit your butt.

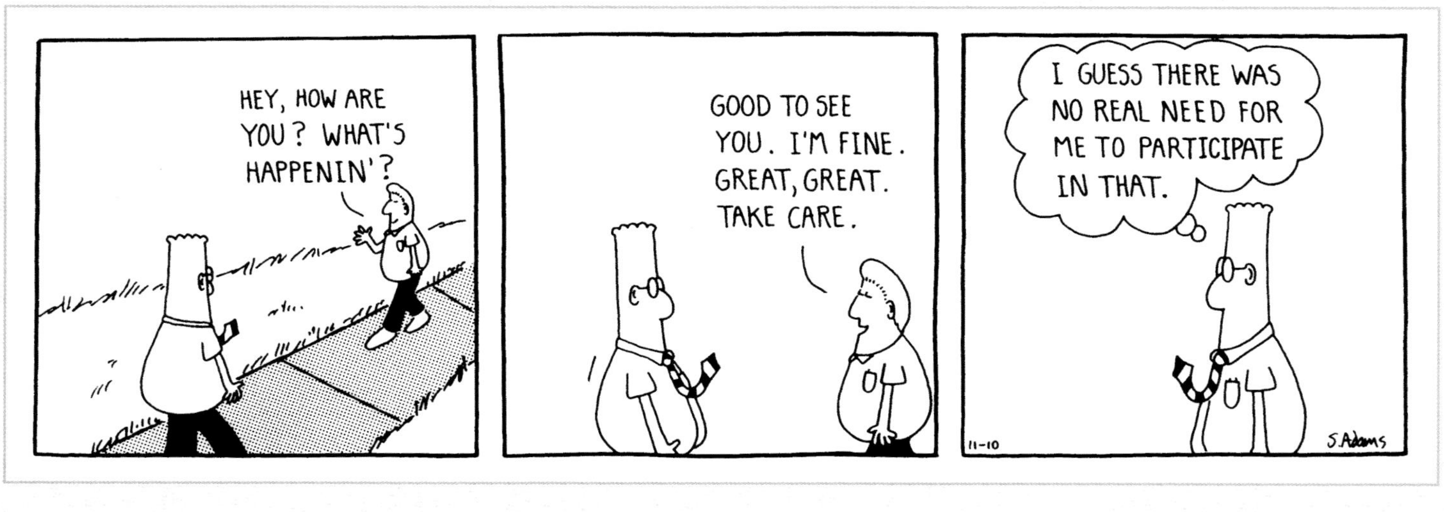
HEY, HOW ARE YOU? WHAT'S HAPPENIN'?
GOOD TO SEE YOU. I'M FINE. GREAT, GREAT. TAKE CARE.
I GUESS THERE WAS NO REAL NEED FOR ME TO PARTICIPATE IN THAT.
11-10
S. Adams

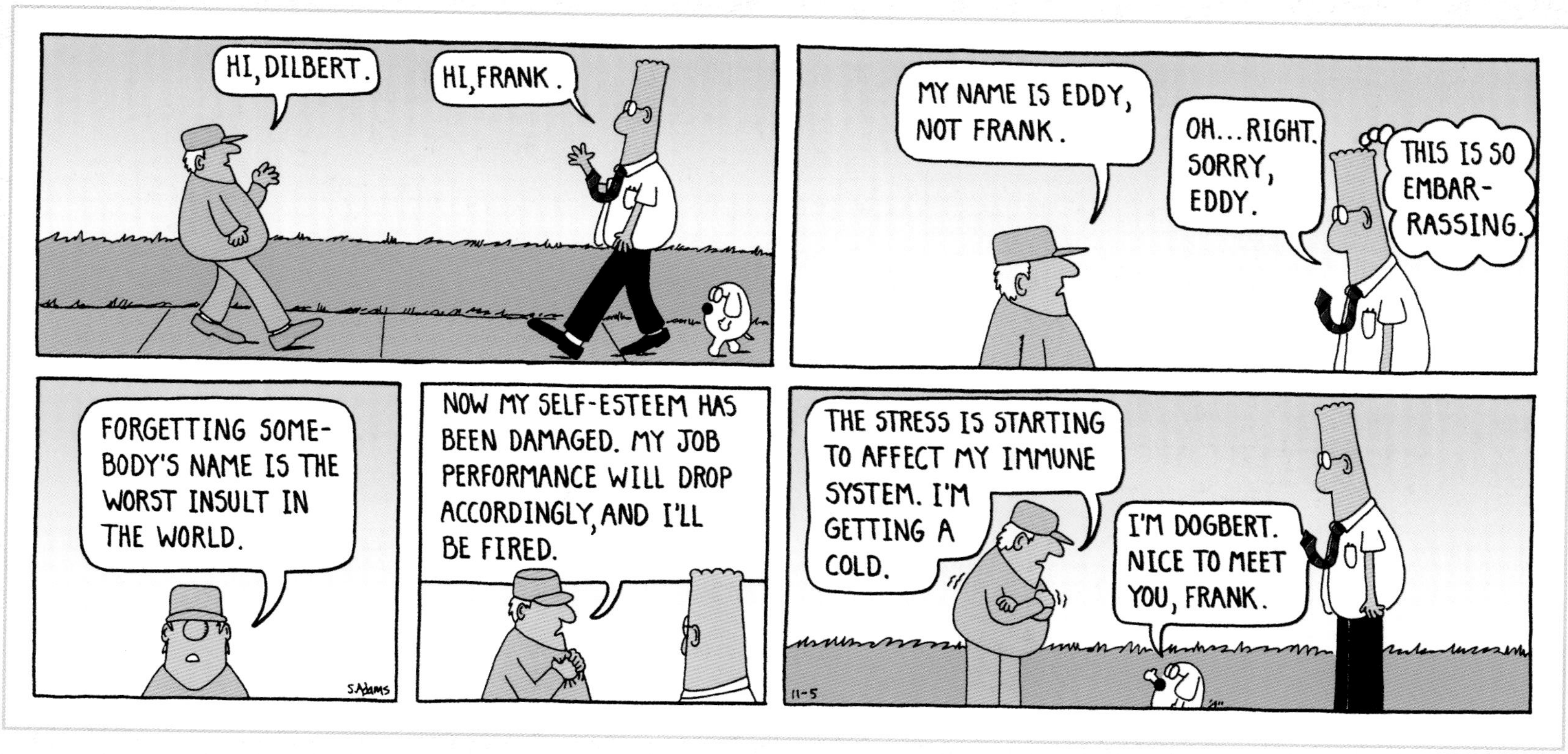
HI, DILBERT.
HI, FRANK.
MY NAME IS EDDY, NOT FRANK.
OH... RIGHT. SORRY, EDDY.
THIS IS SO EMBAR-RASSING.
FORGETTING SOME-BODY'S NAME IS THE WORST INSULT IN THE WORLD.
S.Adams
NOW MY SELF-ESTEEM HAS BEEN DAMAGED. MY JOB PERFORMANCE WILL DROP ACCORDINGLY, AND I'LL BE FIRED.
THE STRESS IS STARTING TO AFFECT MY IMMUNE SYSTEM. I'M GETTING A COLD.
I'M DOGBERT. NICE TO MEET YOU, FRANK.
11-5

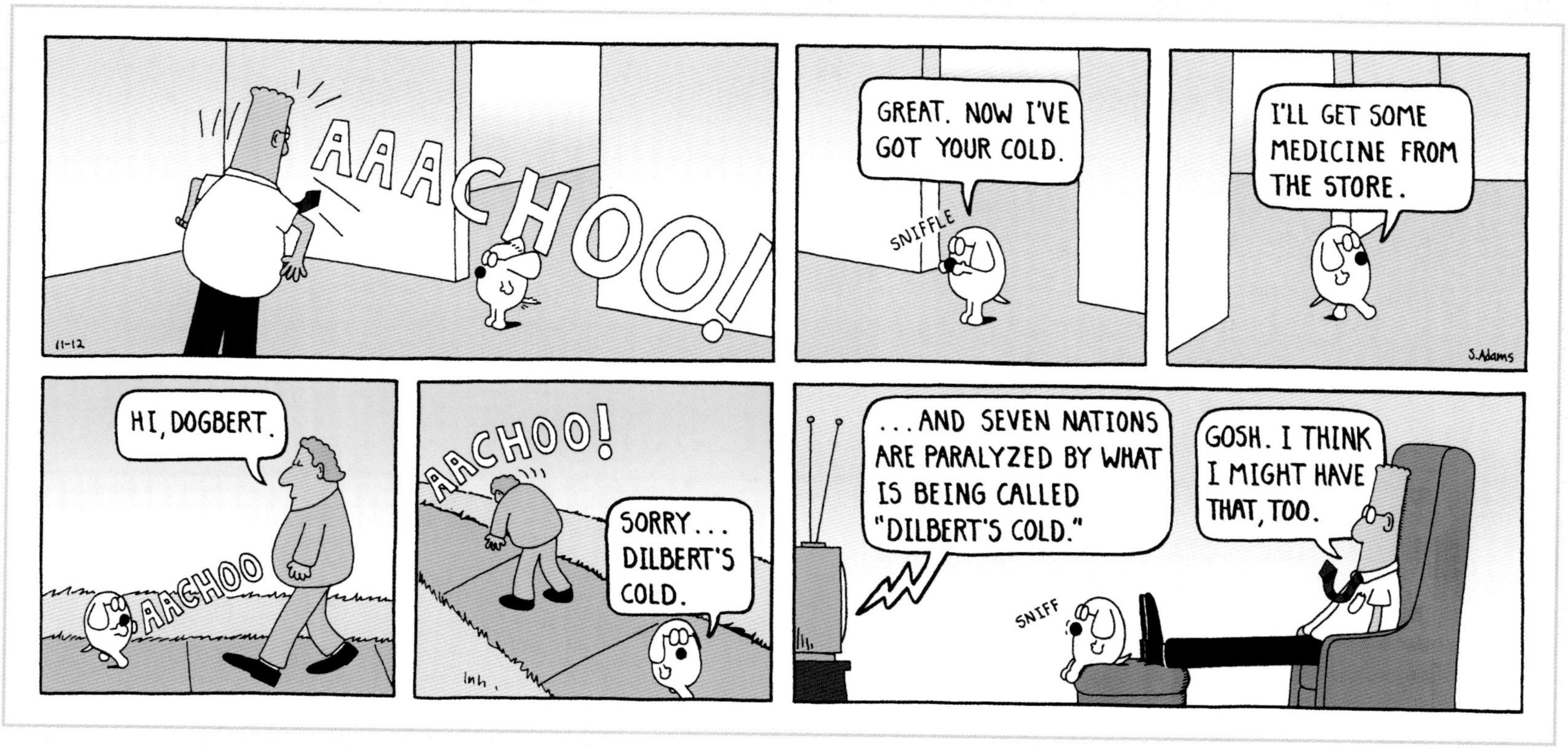
AAACHOO!
11-12
GREAT. NOW I'VE GOT YOUR COLD.
SNIFFLE
I'LL GET SOME MEDICINE FROM THE STORE.
S.Adams
HI, DOGBERT.
AACHOO
AACHOO!
SORRY... DILBERT'S COLD.
...AND SEVEN NATIONS ARE PARALYZED BY WHAT IS BEING CALLED "DILBERT'S COLD."
GOSH. I THINK I MIGHT HAVE THAT, TOO.
SNIFF

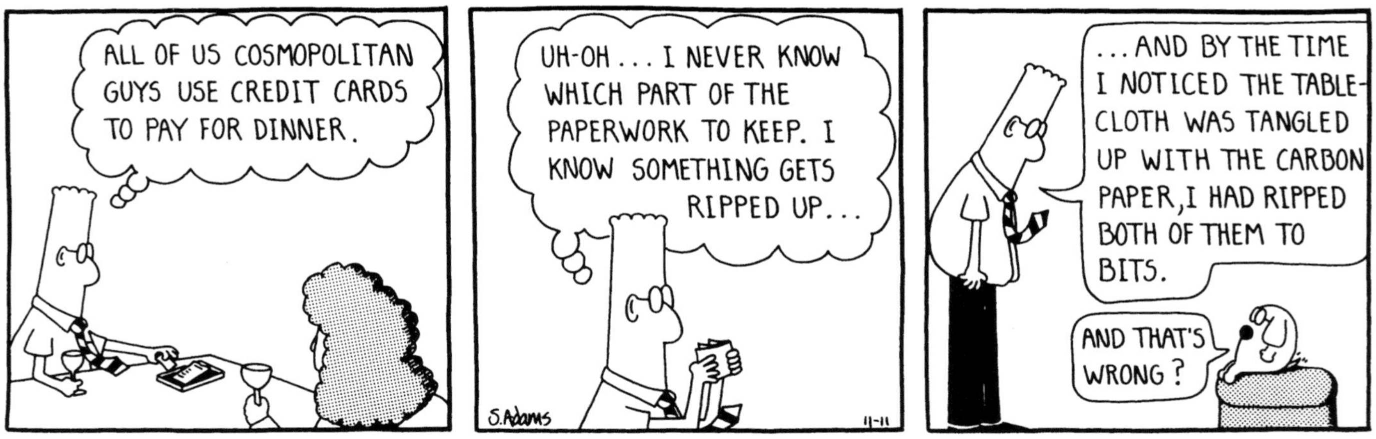
ALL OF US COSMOPOLITAN GUYS USE CREDIT CARDS TO PAY FOR DINNER.
UH-OH... I NEVER KNOW WHICH PART OF THE PAPERWORK TO KEEP. I KNOW SOMETHING GETS RIPPED UP...
S.Adams
11-11
...AND BY THE TIME I NOTICED THE TABLE-CLOTH WAS TANGLED UP WITH THE CARBON PAPER, I HAD RIPPED BOTH OF THEM TO BITS.
AND THAT'S WRONG?

This is one of the few early strips that made me laugh out loud when I searched through the archives. I have a habit of doing simple tasks wrong and later blaming the clarity of the directions.

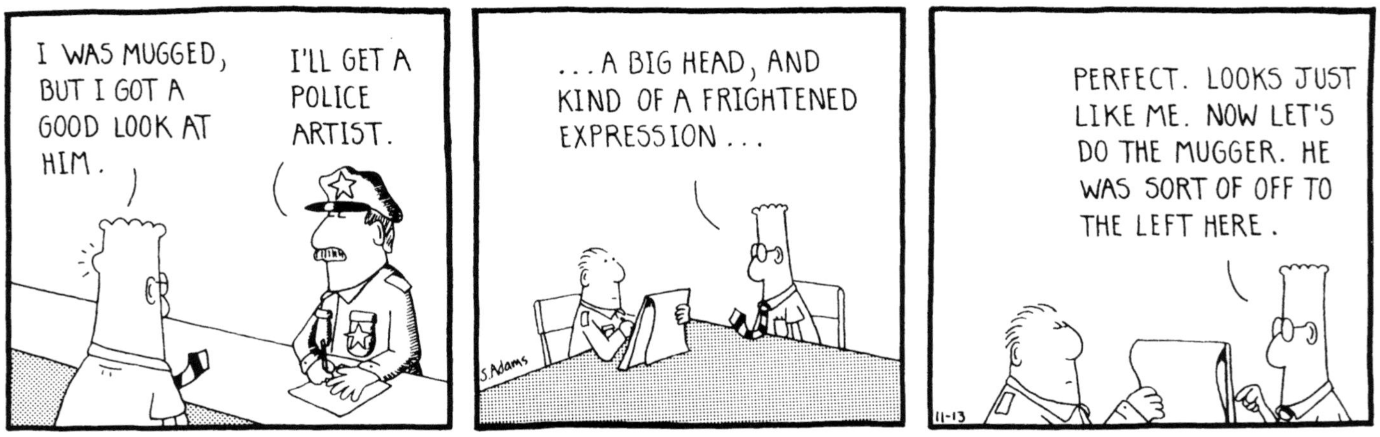
I WAS MUGGED, BUT I GOT A GOOD LOOK AT HIM.
I'LL GET A POLICE ARTIST.
...A BIG HEAD, AND KIND OF A FRIGHTENED EXPRESSION...
S.Adams
PERFECT. LOOKS JUST LIKE ME. NOW LET'S DO THE MUGGER. HE WAS SORT OF OFF TO THE LEFT HERE.
11-13

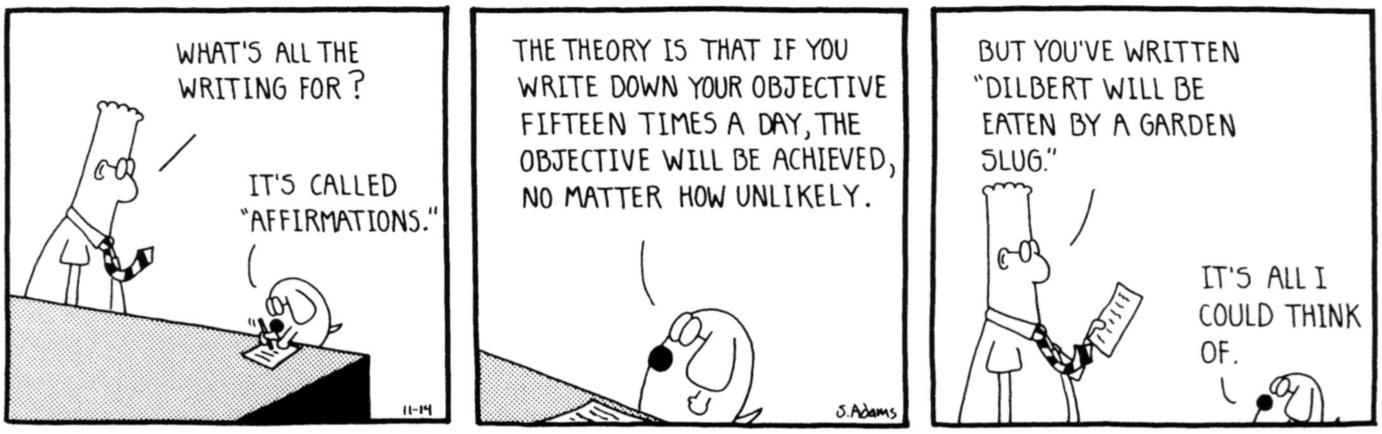
WHAT'S ALL THE WRITING FOR?
IT'S CALLED "AFFIRMATIONS."
11-14
THE THEORY IS THAT IF YOU WRITE DOWN YOUR OBJECTIVE FIFTEEN TIMES A DAY, THE OBJECTIVE WILL BE ACHIEVED, NO MATTER HOW UNLIKELY.
S.Adams
BUT YOU'VE WRITTEN "DILBERT WILL BE EATEN BY A GARDEN SLUG."
IT'S ALL I COULD THINK OF.

In 1988 I was writing "I, Scott, will become a syndicated cartoonist" fifteen times a day. Within a few months, United Feature Syndicate offered me a contract. I don't believe there's any magic in affirmations, but I think they helped me focus.

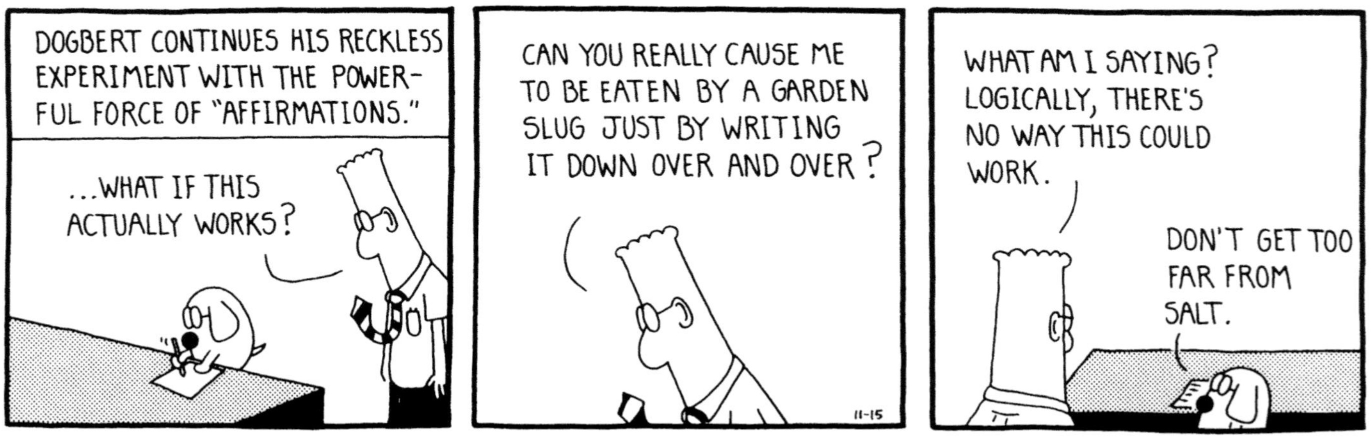
DOGBERT CONTINUES HIS RECKLESS EXPERIMENT WITH THE POWERFUL FORCE OF "AFFIRMATIONS."
...WHAT IF THIS ACTUALLY WORKS?
CAN YOU REALLY CAUSE ME TO BE EATEN BY A GARDEN SLUG JUST BY WRITING IT DOWN OVER AND OVER?
11-15
WHAT AM I SAYING? LOGICALLY, THERE'S NO WAY THIS COULD WORK.
DON'T GET TOO FAR FROM SALT.

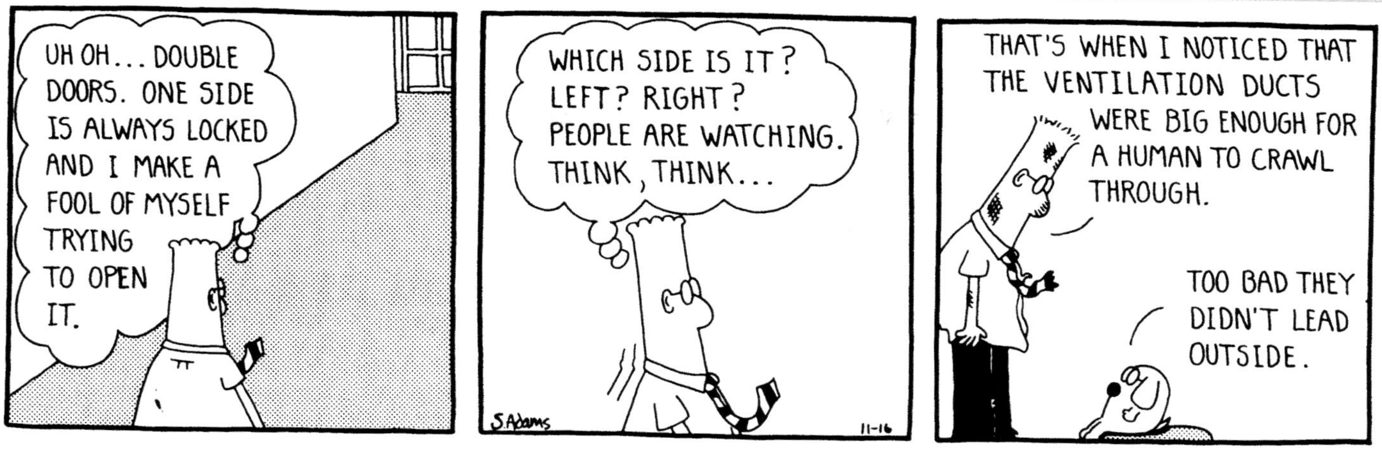
UH OH... DOUBLE DOORS. ONE SIDE IS ALWAYS LOCKED AND I MAKE A FOOL OF MYSELF TRYING TO OPEN IT.
WHICH SIDE IS IT? LEFT? RIGHT? PEOPLE ARE WATCHING. THINK, THINK...
S.Adams
11-16
THAT'S WHEN I NOTICED THAT THE VENTILATION DUCTS WERE BIG ENOUGH FOR A HUMAN TO CRAWL THROUGH.
TOO BAD THEY DIDN'T LEAD OUTSIDE.

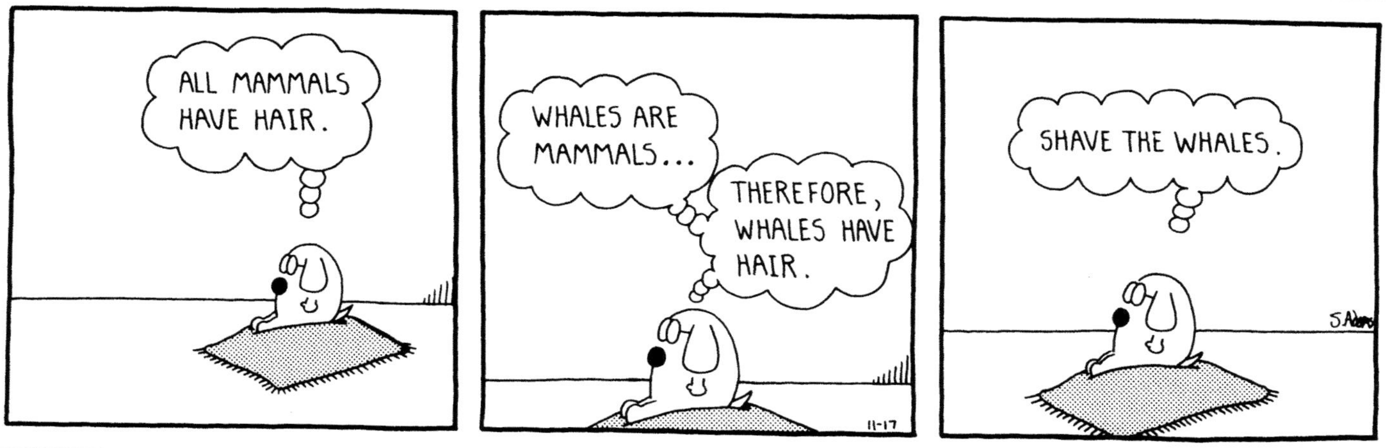
ALL MAMMALS HAVE HAIR.
WHALES ARE MAMMALS...
THEREFORE, WHALES HAVE HAIR.
11-17
SHAVE THE WHALES.
S.Adams

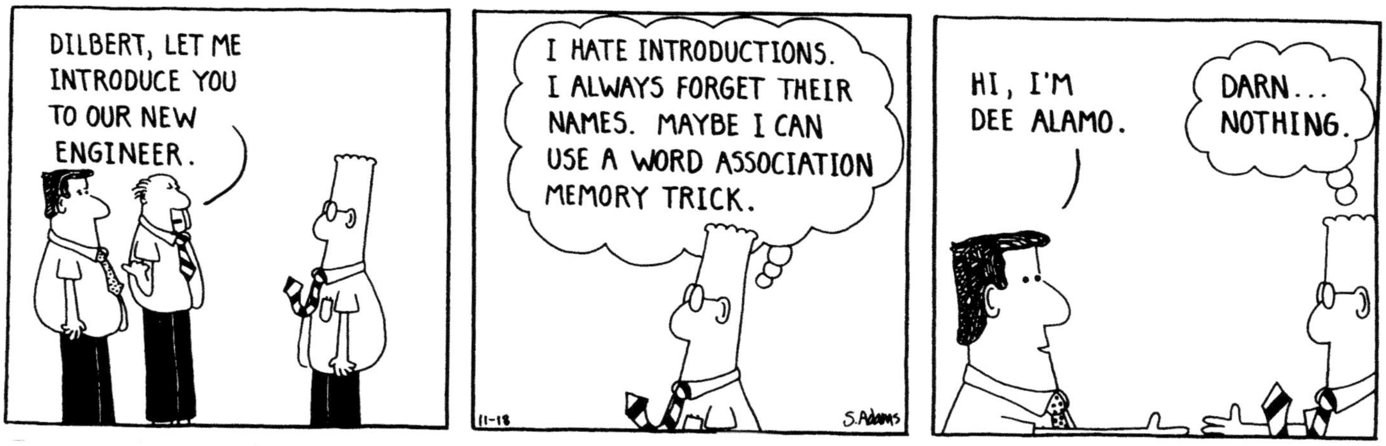
DILBERT, LET ME INTRODUCE YOU TO OUR NEW ENGINEER.
I HATE INTRODUCTIONS. I ALWAYS FORGET THEIR NAMES. MAYBE I CAN USE A WORD ASSOCIATION MEMORY TRICK.
11-18
S.Adams
HI, I'M DEE ALAMO.
DARN... NOTHING.

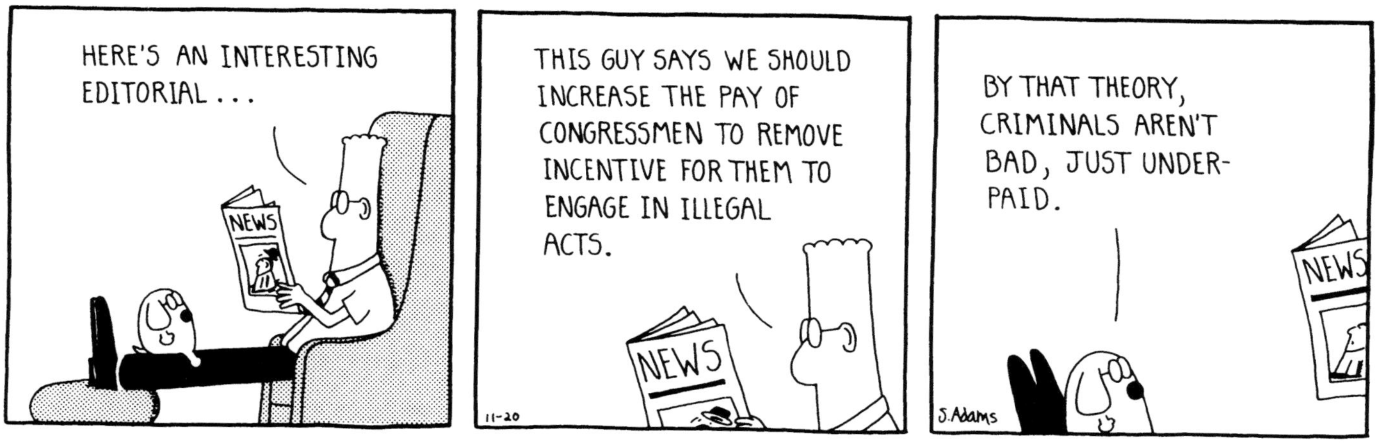
HERE'S AN INTERESTING EDITORIAL...
NEWS
THIS GUY SAYS WE SHOULD INCREASE THE PAY OF CONGRESSMEN TO REMOVE INCENTIVE FOR THEM TO ENGAGE IN ILLEGAL ACTS.
NEWS
11-20
BY THAT THEORY, CRIMINALS AREN'T BAD, JUST UNDER-PAID.
NEWS
S.Adams

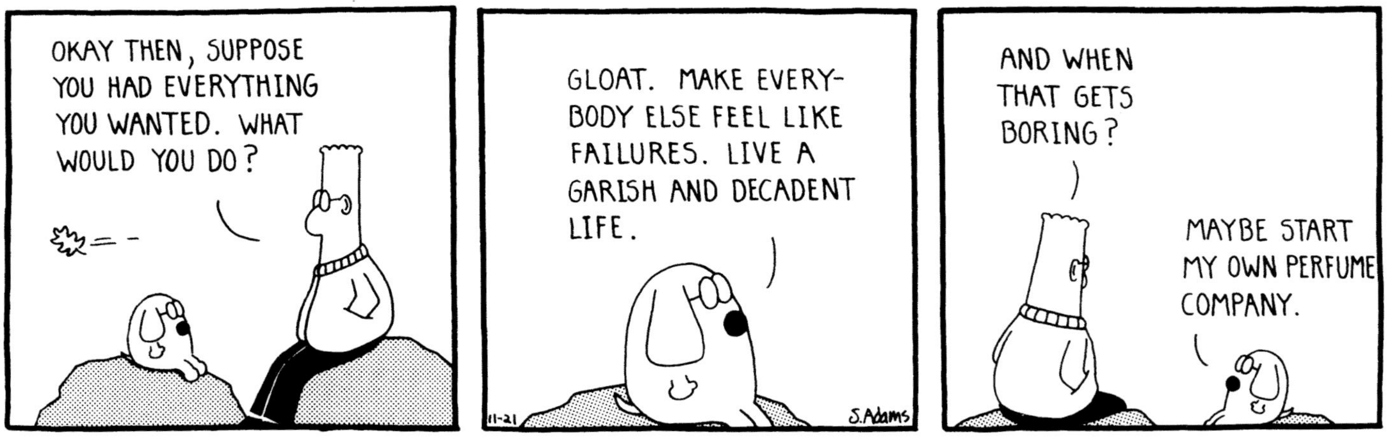
OKAY THEN, SUPPOSE YOU HAD EVERYTHING YOU WANTED. WHAT WOULD YOU DO?
GLOAT. MAKE EVERYBODY ELSE FEEL LIKE FAILURES. LIVE A GARISH AND DECADENT LIFE.
AND WHEN THAT GETS BORING?
MAYBE START MY OWN PERFUME COMPANY.

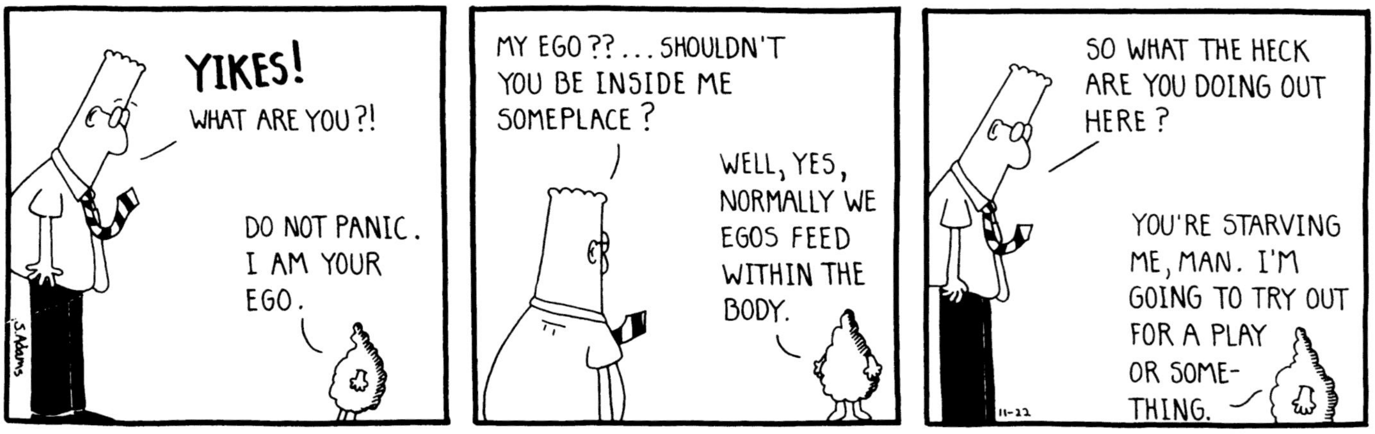
YIKES! WHAT ARE YOU?!
DO NOT PANIC. I AM YOUR EGO.
MY EGO??... SHOULDN'T YOU BE INSIDE ME SOMEPLACE?
WELL, YES, NORMALLY WE EGOS FEED WITHIN THE BODY.
SO WHAT THE HECK ARE YOU DOING OUT HERE?
YOU'RE STARVING ME, MAN. I'M GOING TO TRY OUT FOR A PLAY OR SOMETHING.

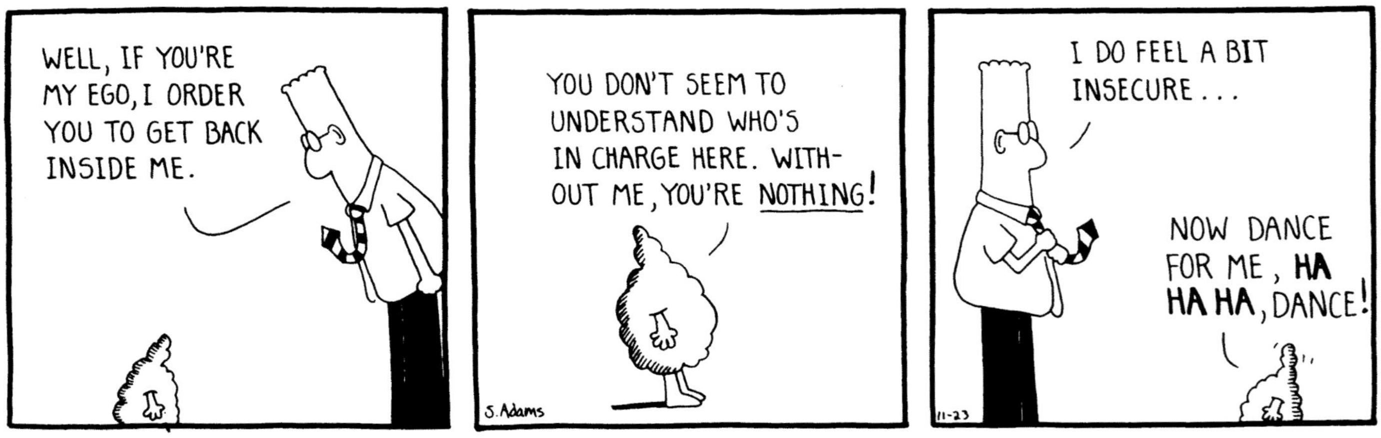
WELL, IF YOU'RE MY EGO, I ORDER YOU TO GET BACK INSIDE ME.
YOU DON'T SEEM TO UNDERSTAND WHO'S IN CHARGE HERE. WITHOUT ME, YOU'RE NOTHING!
I DO FEEL A BIT INSECURE...
NOW DANCE FOR ME, HA HA HA, DANCE!

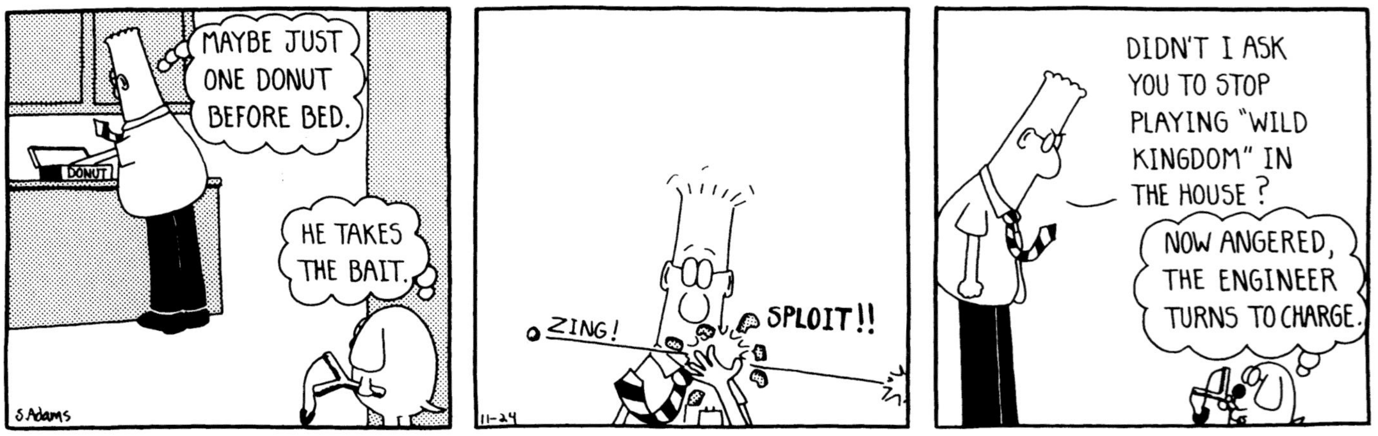
MAYBE JUST ONE DONUT BEFORE BED.
DONUT
HE TAKES THE BAIT.
ZING!
SPLOIT!!
DIDN'T I ASK YOU TO STOP PLAYING "WILD KINGDOM" IN THE HOUSE?
NOW ANGERED, THE ENGINEER TURNS TO CHARGE.

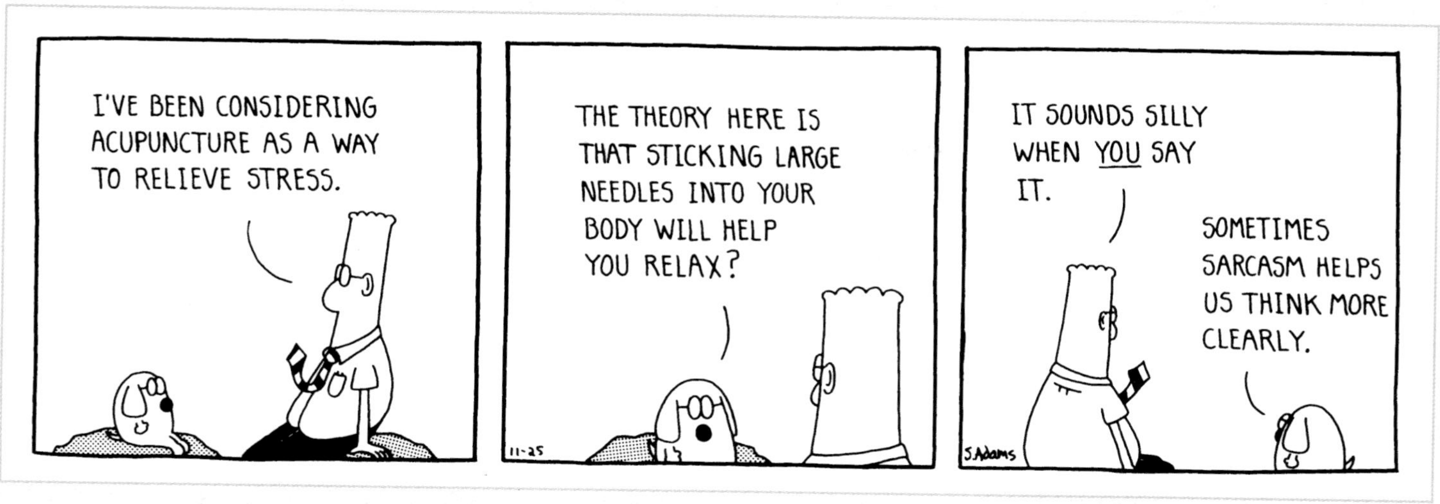
I'VE BEEN CONSIDERING ACUPUNCTURE AS A WAY TO RELIEVE STRESS.
THE THEORY HERE IS THAT STICKING LARGE NEEDLES INTO YOUR BODY WILL HELP YOU RELAX?
IT SOUNDS SILLY WHEN YOU SAY IT.
SOMETIMES SARCASM HELPS US THINK MORE CLEARLY.
11-25
S.Adams

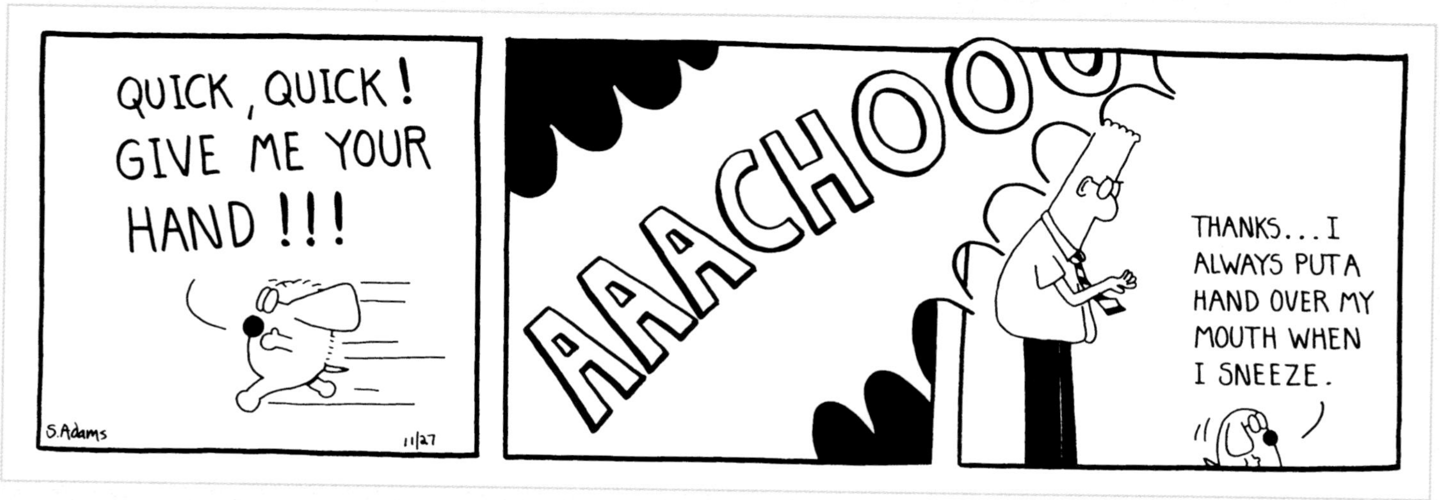
QUICK, QUICK! GIVE ME YOUR HAND!!!
S.Adams
11/27
AAACHOO
THANKS... I ALWAYS PUT A HAND OVER MY MOUTH WHEN I SNEEZE.

Every time I tried political humor, I regretted it.

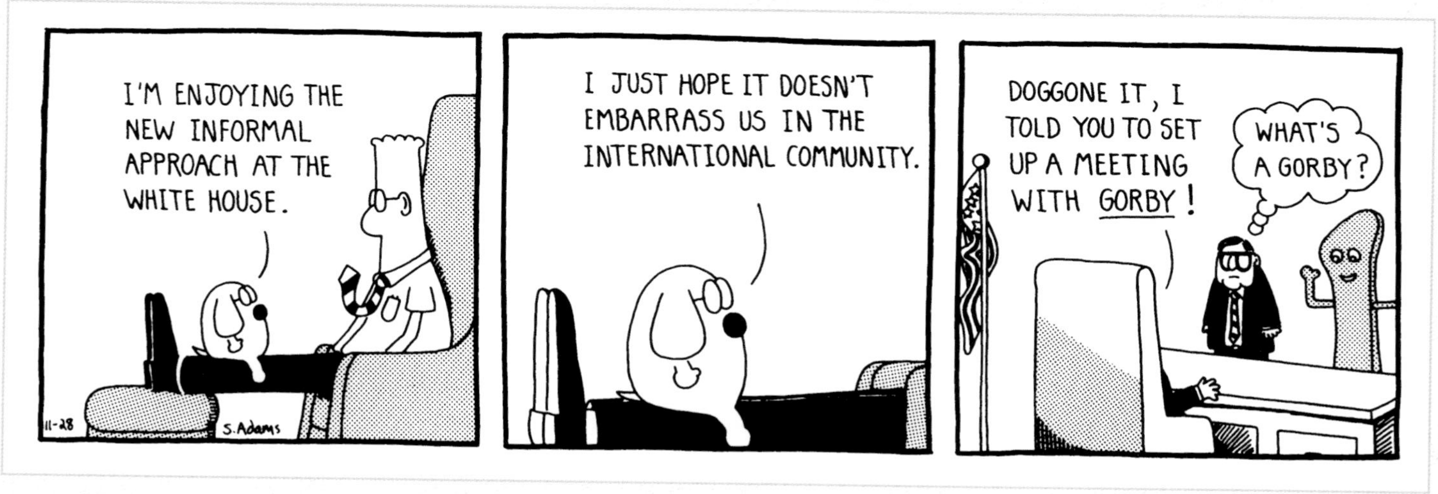
I'M ENJOYING THE NEW INFORMAL APPROACH AT THE WHITE HOUSE.
11-28
S.Adams
I JUST HOPE IT DOESN'T EMBARRASS US IN THE INTERNATIONAL COMMUNITY.
DOGGONE IT, I TOLD YOU TO SET UP A MEETING WITH GORBY!
WHAT'S A GORBY?

The text from the middle panel of the strip below is the first thing I ever wrote that became widely quoted. It still pops up on the Internet on lists of famous quotes.

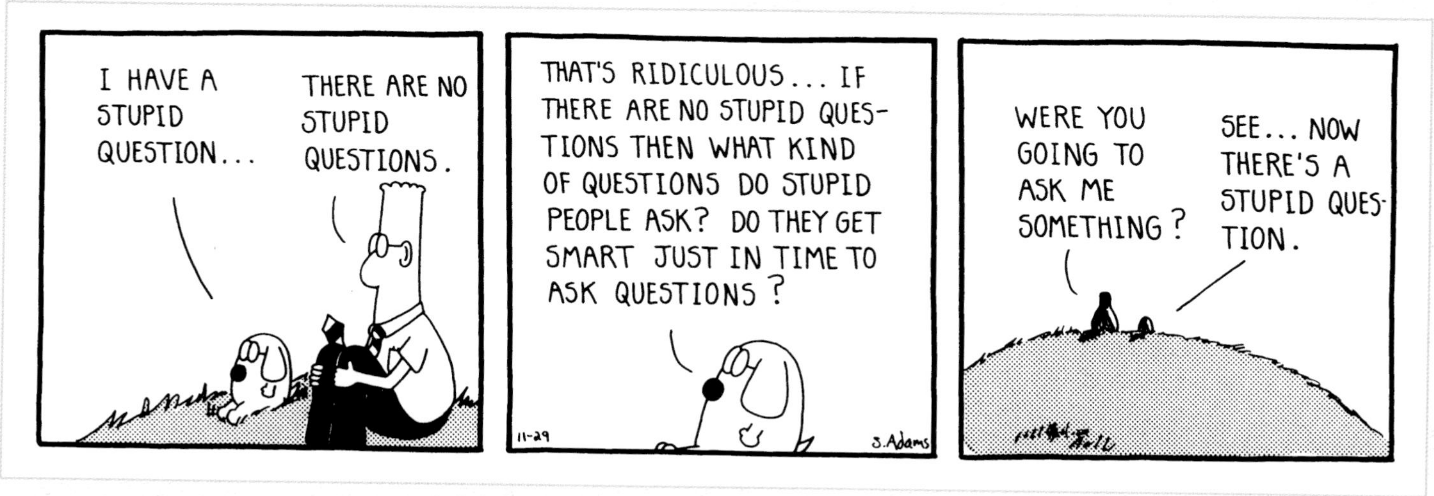
I HAVE A STUPID QUESTION...
THERE ARE NO STUPID QUESTIONS.
THAT'S RIDICULOUS... IF THERE ARE NO STUPID QUESTIONS THEN WHAT KIND OF QUESTIONS DO STUPID PEOPLE ASK? DO THEY GET SMART JUST IN TIME TO ASK QUESTIONS?
11-29
S.Adams
WERE YOU GOING TO ASK ME SOMETHING?
SEE... NOW THERE'S A STUPID QUESTION.

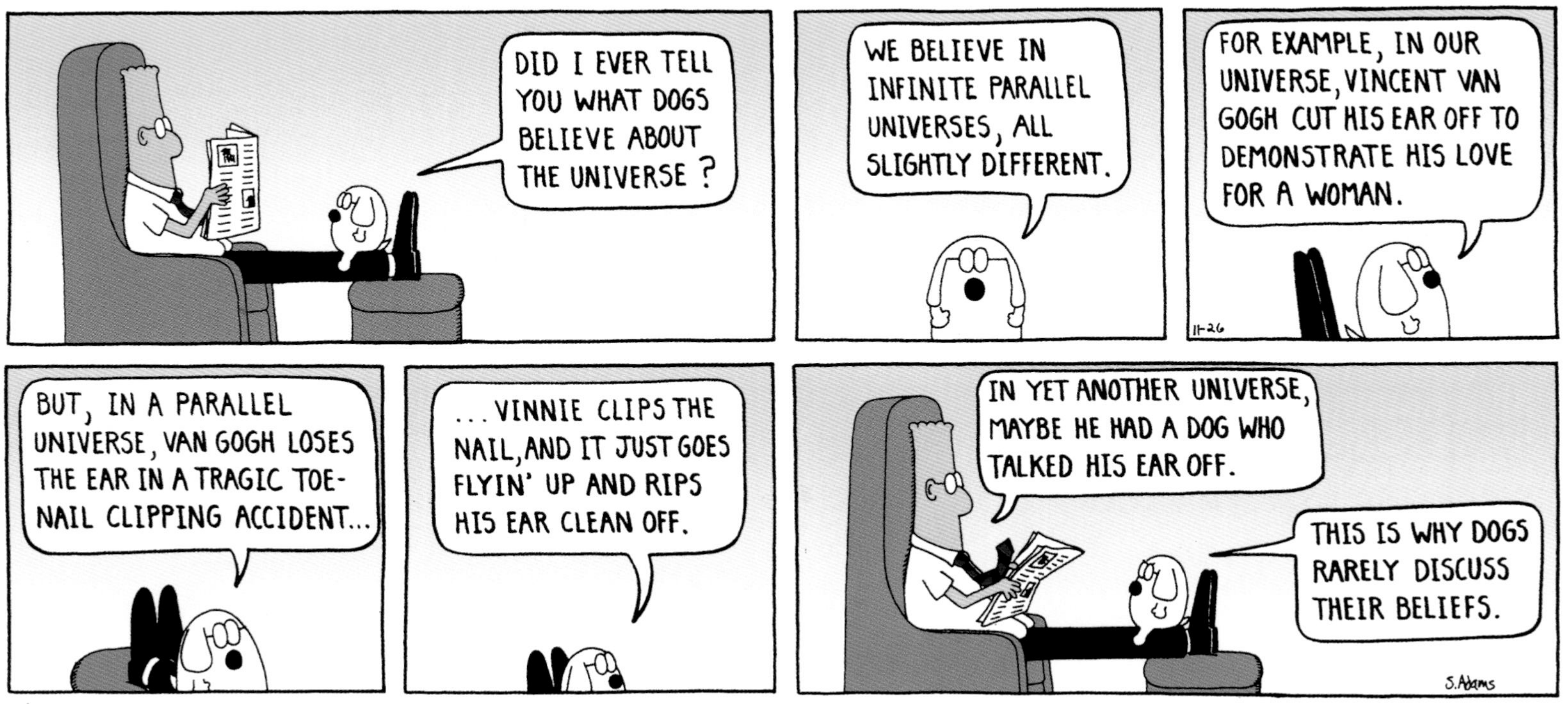
DID I EVER TELL YOU WHAT DOGS BELIEVE ABOUT THE UNIVERSE ?
WE BELIEVE IN INFINITE PARALLEL UNIVERSES, ALL SLIGHTLY DIFFERENT.
FOR EXAMPLE, IN OUR UNIVERSE, VINCENT VAN GOGH CUT HIS EAR OFF TO DEMONSTRATE HIS LOVE FOR A WOMAN.
11-26
BUT, IN A PARALLEL UNIVERSE, VAN GOGH LOSES THE EAR IN A TRAGIC TOE-NAIL CLIPPING ACCIDENT...
...VINNIE CLIPS THE NAIL, AND IT JUST GOES FLYIN' UP AND RIPS HIS EAR CLEAN OFF.
IN YET ANOTHER UNIVERSE, MAYBE HE HAD A DOG WHO TALKED HIS EAR OFF.
THIS IS WHY DOGS RARELY DISCUSS THEIR BELIEFS.
S.Adams

This is the first appearance of the character that would morph into Dilbert's pointy-haired boss who has no name.

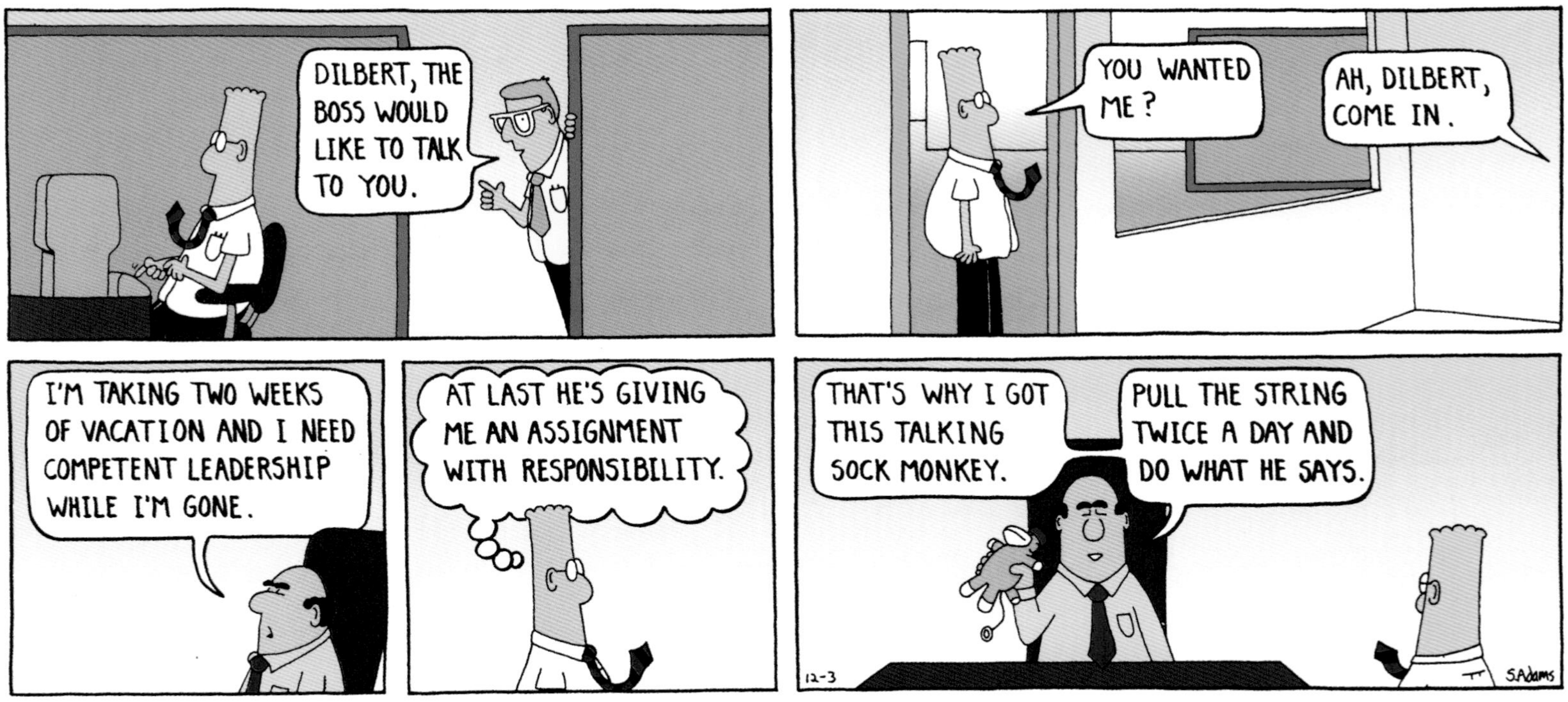
DILBERT, THE BOSS WOULD LIKE TO TALK TO YOU.
YOU WANTED ME ?
AH, DILBERT, COME IN.
I'M TAKING TWO WEEKS OF VACATION AND I NEED COMPETENT LEADERSHIP WHILE I'M GONE.
AT LAST HE'S GIVING ME AN ASSIGNMENT WITH RESPONSIBILITY.
THAT'S WHY I GOT THIS TALKING SOCK MONKEY.
PULL THE STRING TWICE A DAY AND DO WHAT HE SAYS.
12-3
S.Adams

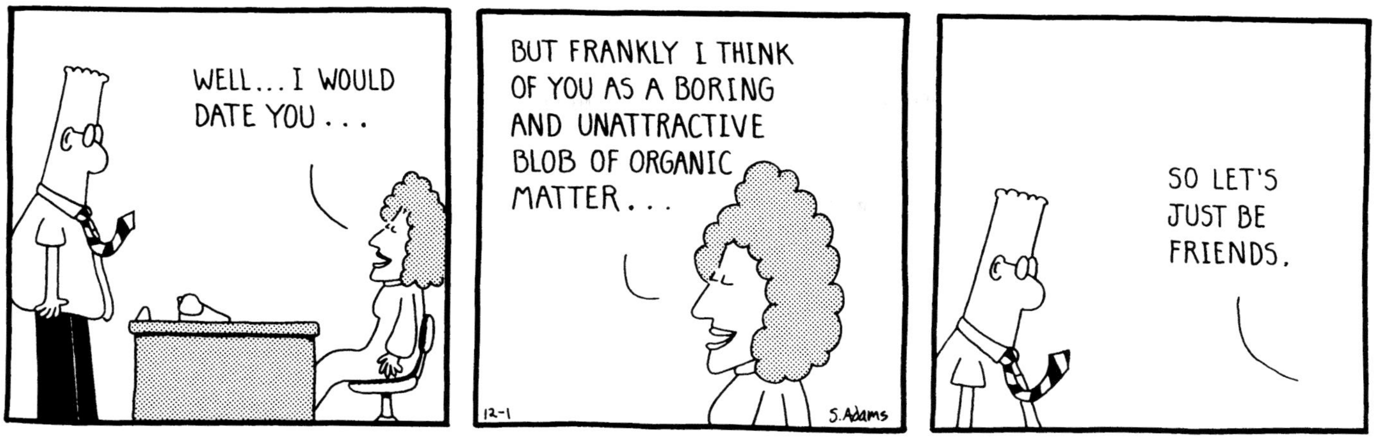
WELL... I WOULD DATE YOU . . .
BUT FRANKLY I THINK OF YOU AS A BORING AND UNATTRACTIVE BLOB OF ORGANIC MATTER . . .
12-1
S. Adams
SO LET'S JUST BE FRIENDS.

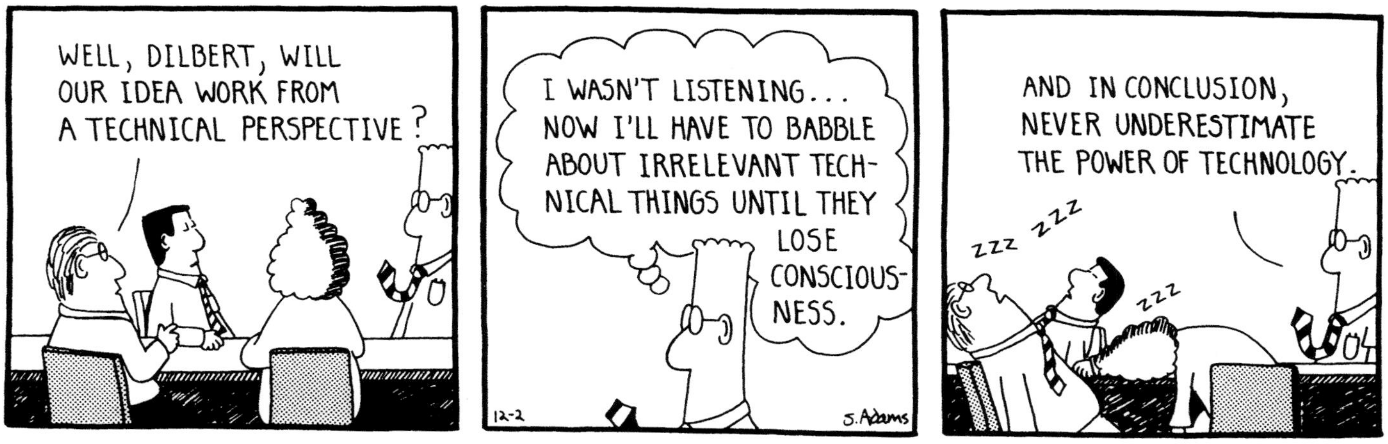
WELL, DILBERT, WILL OUR IDEA WORK FROM A TECHNICAL PERSPECTIVE ?
I WASN'T LISTENING... NOW I'LL HAVE TO BABBLE ABOUT IRRELEVANT TECHNICAL THINGS UNTIL THEY LOSE CONSCIOUSNESS.
12-2
S. Adams
AND IN CONCLUSION, NEVER UNDERESTIMATE THE POWER OF TECHNOLOGY.
ZZZ ZZZ
ZZZ

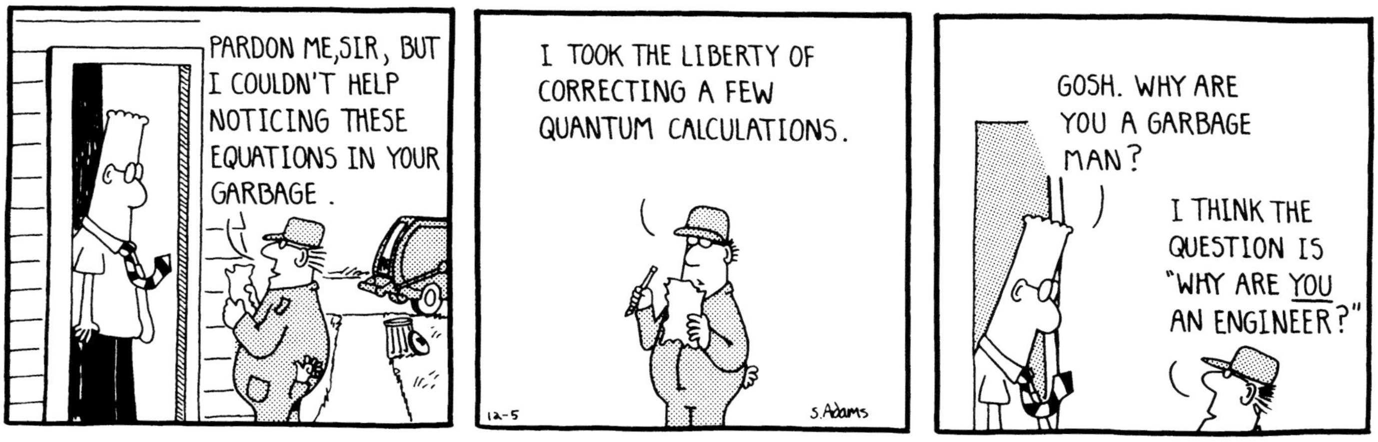
PARDON ME, SIR, BUT I COULDN'T HELP NOTICING THESE EQUATIONS IN YOUR GARBAGE .
I TOOK THE LIBERTY OF CORRECTING A FEW QUANTUM CALCULATIONS.
12-5
S. Adams
GOSH. WHY ARE YOU A GARBAGE MAN ?
I THINK THE QUESTION IS "WHY ARE YOU AN ENGINEER?"

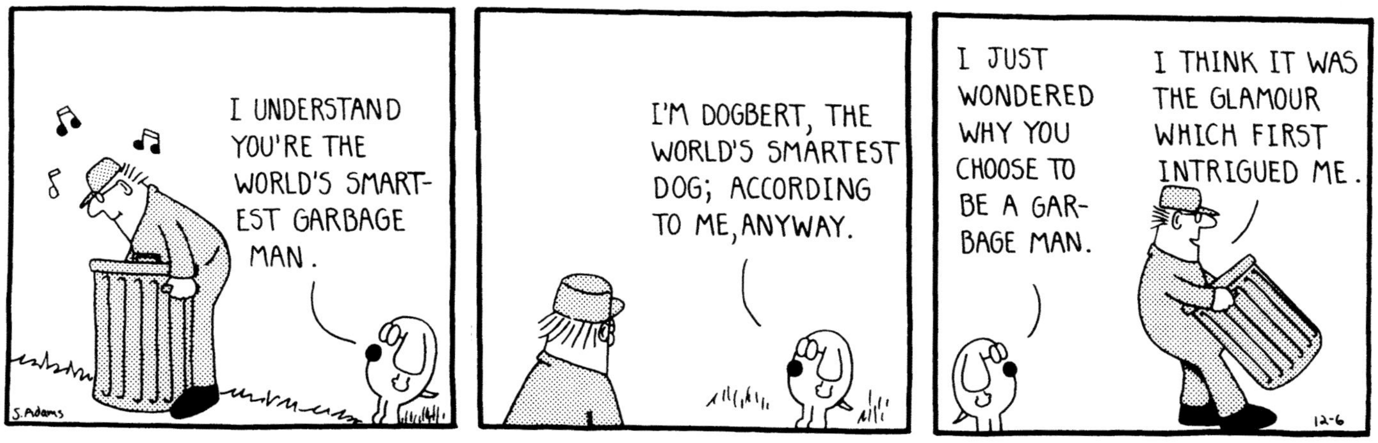
I UNDERSTAND YOU'RE THE WORLD'S SMART-EST GARBAGE MAN .
S. Adams
I'M DOGBERT, THE WORLD'S SMARTEST DOG; ACCORDING TO ME, ANYWAY.
I JUST WONDERED WHY YOU CHOOSE TO BE A GAR-BAGE MAN.
I THINK IT WAS THE GLAMOUR WHICH FIRST INTRIGUED ME .
12-6

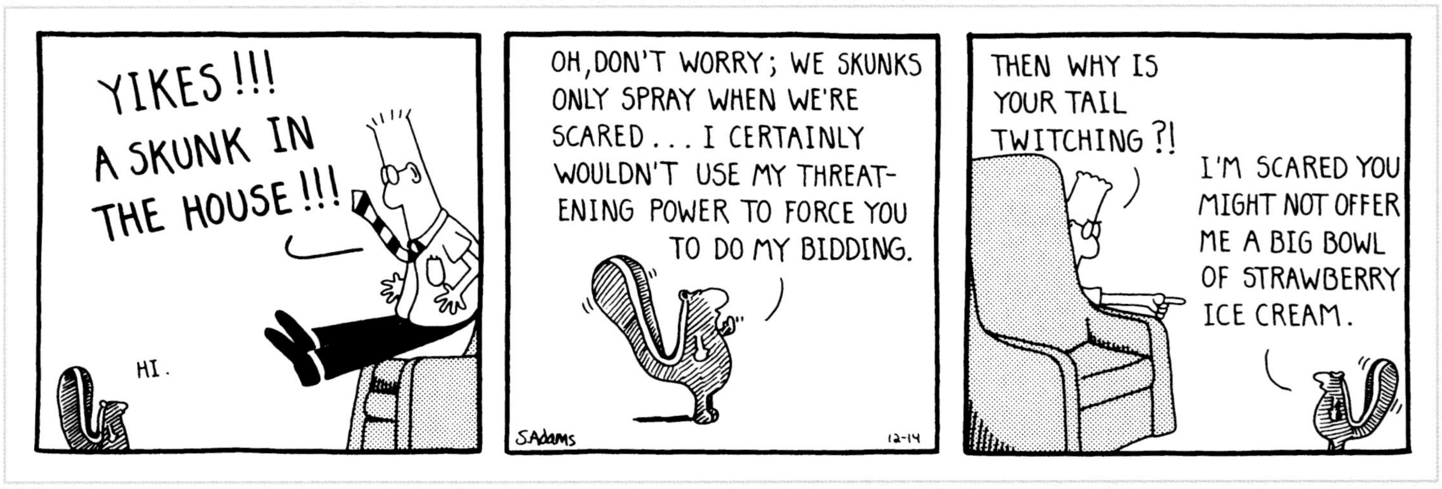
YIKES!!! A SKUNK IN THE HOUSE!!!
HI.
OH, DON'T WORRY; WE SKUNKS ONLY SPRAY WHEN WE'RE SCARED... I CERTAINLY WOULDN'T USE MY THREAT-ENING POWER TO FORCE YOU TO DO MY BIDDING.
S.Adams
12-14
THEN WHY IS YOUR TAIL TWITCHING?!
I'M SCARED YOU MIGHT NOT OFFER ME A BIG BOWL OF STRAWBERRY ICE CREAM.

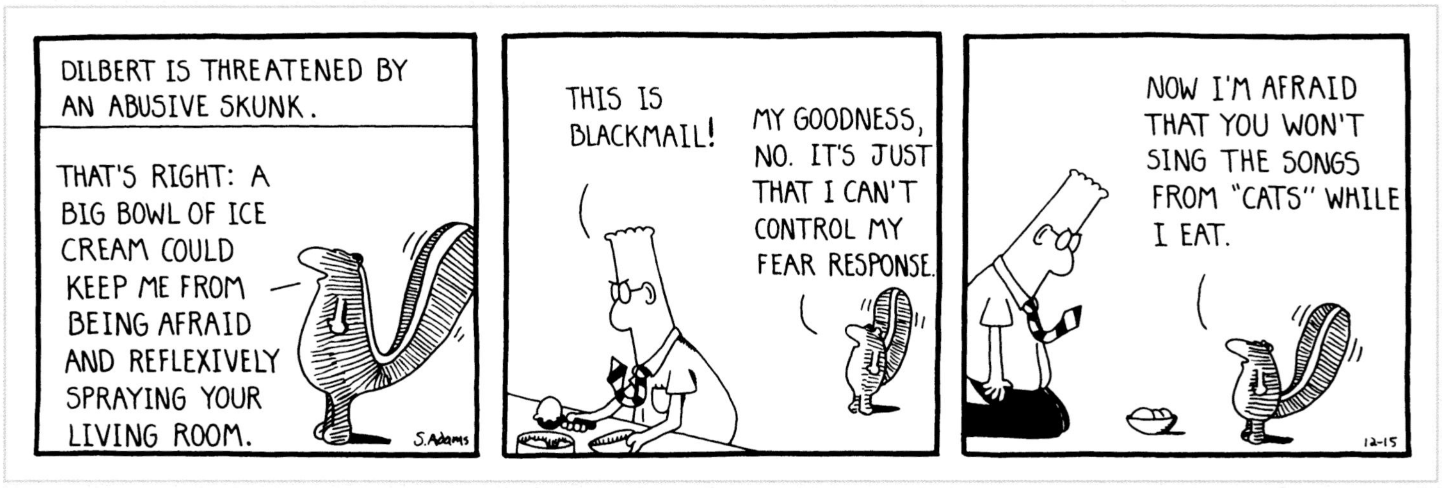
DILBERT IS THREATENED BY AN ABUSIVE SKUNK.
THAT'S RIGHT: A BIG BOWL OF ICE CREAM COULD KEEP ME FROM BEING AFRAID AND REFLEXIVELY SPRAYING YOUR LIVING ROOM.
S.Adams
THIS IS BLACKMAIL!
MY GOODNESS, NO. IT'S JUST THAT I CAN'T CONTROL MY FEAR RESPONSE.
NOW I'M AFRAID THAT YOU WON'T SING THE SONGS FROM "CATS" WHILE I EAT.
12-15

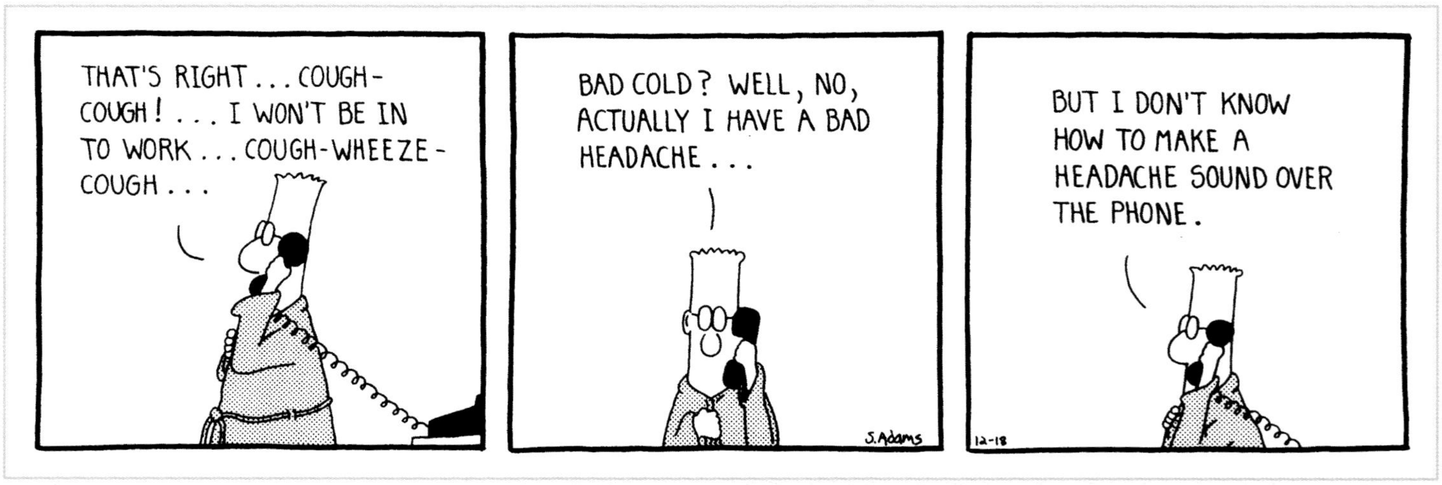
THAT'S RIGHT... COUGH-COUGH!... I WON'T BE IN TO WORK... COUGH-WHEEZE-COUGH...
BAD COLD? WELL, NO, ACTUALLY I HAVE A BAD HEADACHE...
S.Adams
12-18
BUT I DON'T KNOW HOW TO MAKE A HEADACHE SOUND OVER THE PHONE.

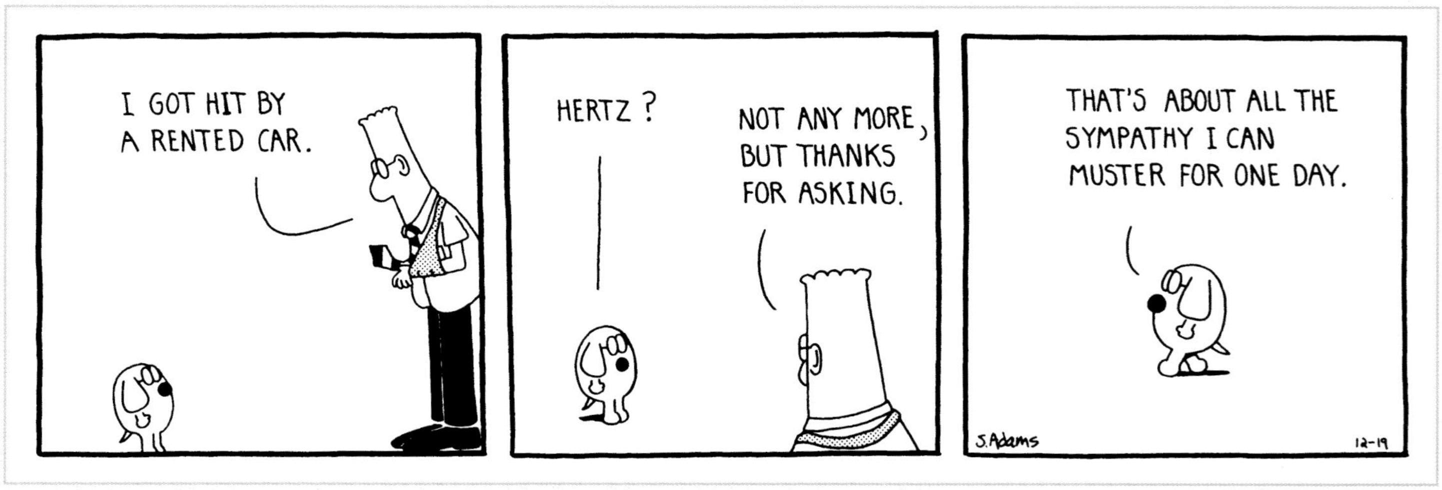
I GOT HIT BY A RENTED CAR.
HERTZ?
NOT ANY MORE, BUT THANKS FOR ASKING.
THAT'S ABOUT ALL THE SYMPATHY I CAN MUSTER FOR ONE DAY.
S.Adams
12-19

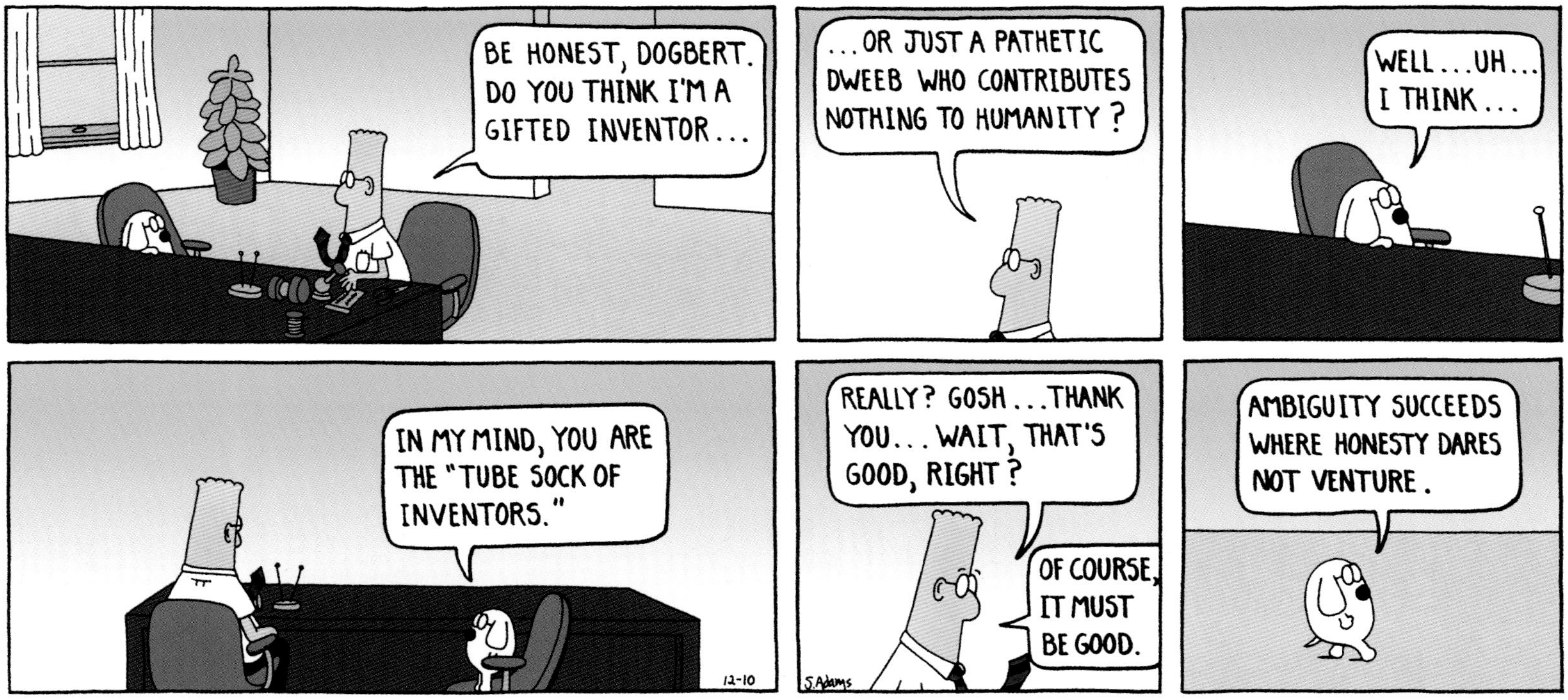
BE HONEST, DOGBERT. DO YOU THINK I'M A GIFTED INVENTOR...
...OR JUST A PATHETIC DWEEB WHO CONTRIBUTES NOTHING TO HUMANITY?
WELL...UH... I THINK...
IN MY MIND, YOU ARE THE "TUBE SOCK OF INVENTORS."
12-10
REALLY? GOSH...THANK YOU... WAIT, THAT'S GOOD, RIGHT?
OF COURSE, IT MUST BE GOOD.
S.Adams
AMBIGUITY SUCCEEDS WHERE HONESTY DARES NOT VENTURE.

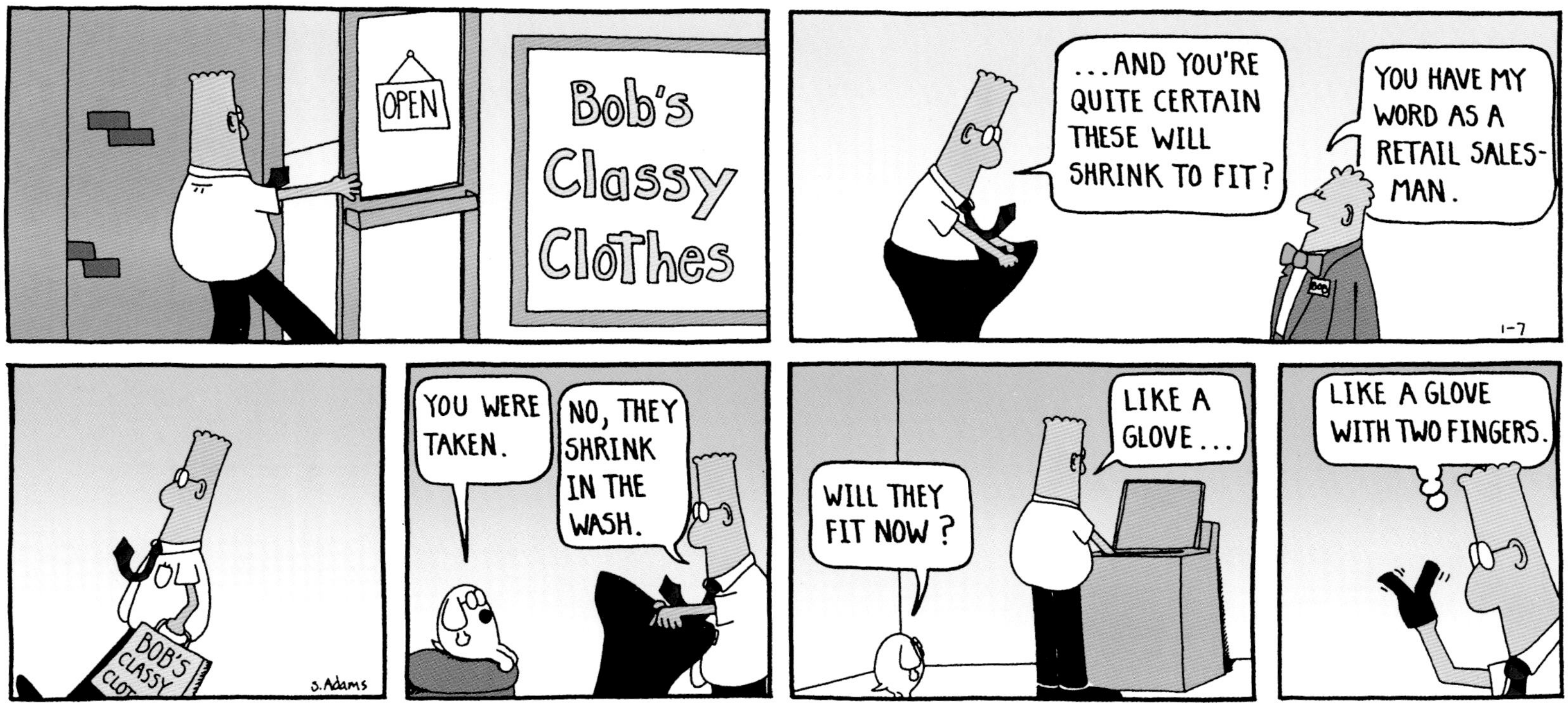
OPEN
Bob's Classy Clothes
...AND YOU'RE QUITE CERTAIN THESE WILL SHRINK TO FIT?
YOU HAVE MY WORD AS A RETAIL SALES-MAN.
1-7
BOB'S CLASSY
S.Adams
YOU WERE TAKEN.
NO, THEY SHRINK IN THE WASH.
WILL THEY FIT NOW?
LIKE A GLOVE...
LIKE A GLOVE WITH TWO FINGERS.

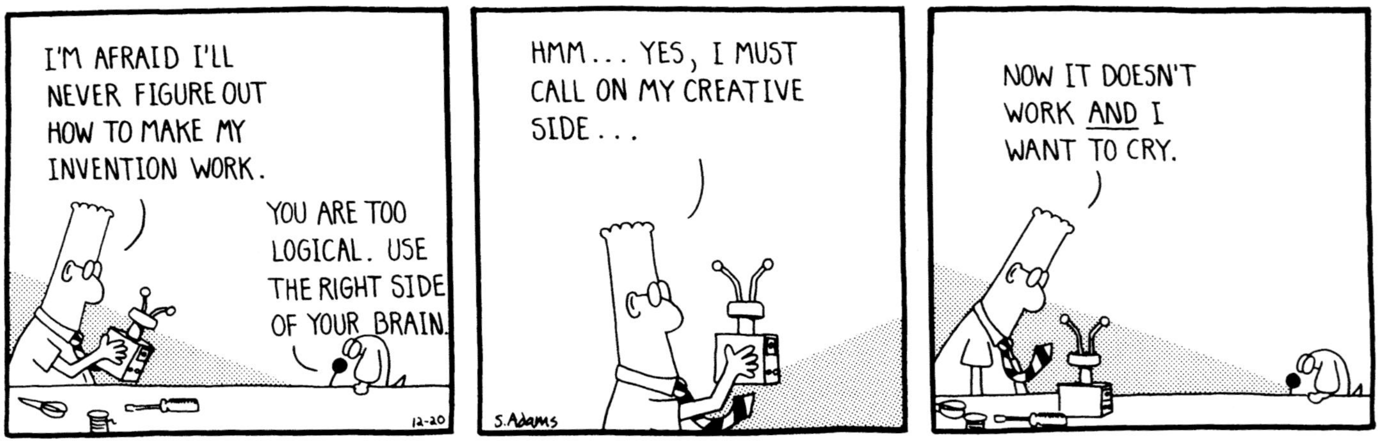
I'M AFRAID I'LL NEVER FIGURE OUT HOW TO MAKE MY INVENTION WORK.
YOU ARE TOO LOGICAL. USE THE RIGHT SIDE OF YOUR BRAIN.
12-20
HMM... YES, I MUST CALL ON MY CREATIVE SIDE...
S. Adams
NOW IT DOESN'T WORK AND I WANT TO CRY.

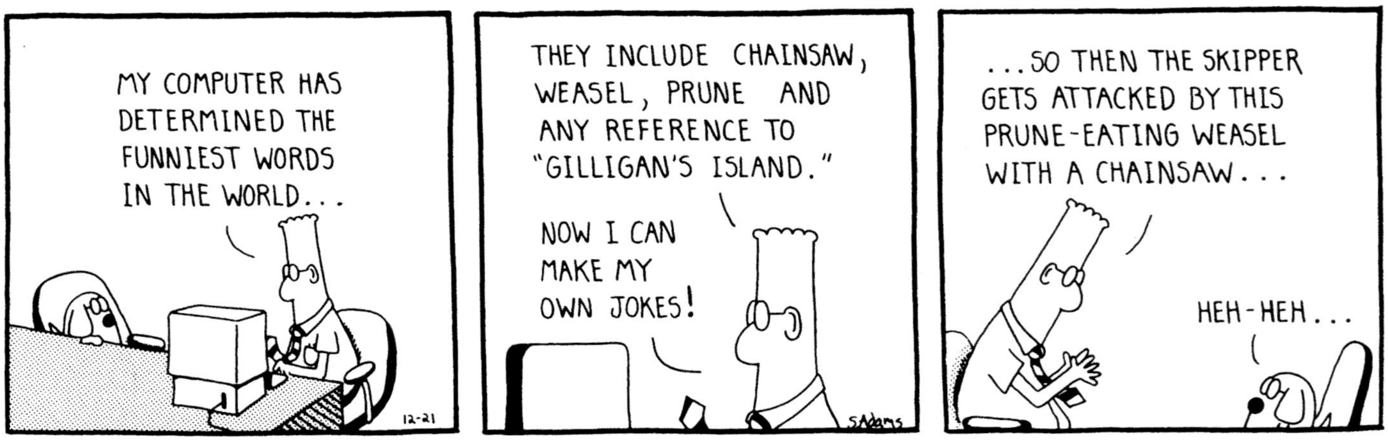
MY COMPUTER HAS DETERMINED THE FUNNIEST WORDS IN THE WORLD...
12-21
THEY INCLUDE CHAINSAW, WEASEL, PRUNE AND ANY REFERENCE TO "GILLIGAN'S ISLAND."
NOW I CAN MAKE MY OWN JOKES!
S. Adams
...SO THEN THE SKIPPER GETS ATTACKED BY THIS PRUNE-EATING WEASEL WITH A CHAINSAW...
HEH-HEH...

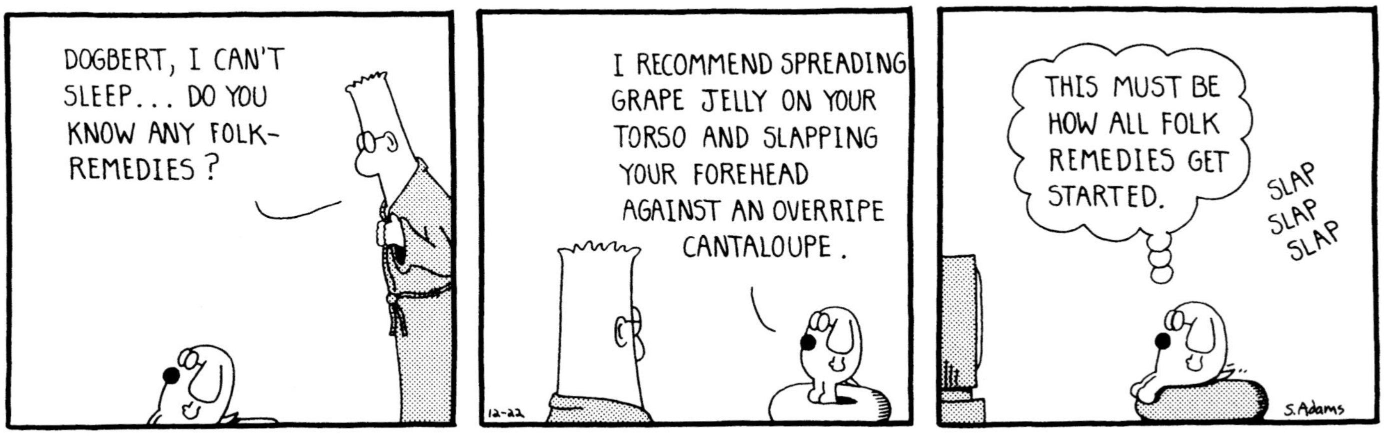
DOGBERT, I CAN'T SLEEP... DO YOU KNOW ANY FOLK-REMEDIES?
12-22
I RECOMMEND SPREADING GRAPE JELLY ON YOUR TORSO AND SLAPPING YOUR FOREHEAD AGAINST AN OVERRIPE CANTALOUPE.
THIS MUST BE HOW ALL FOLK REMEDIES GET STARTED.
SLAP SLAP SLAP
S. Adams

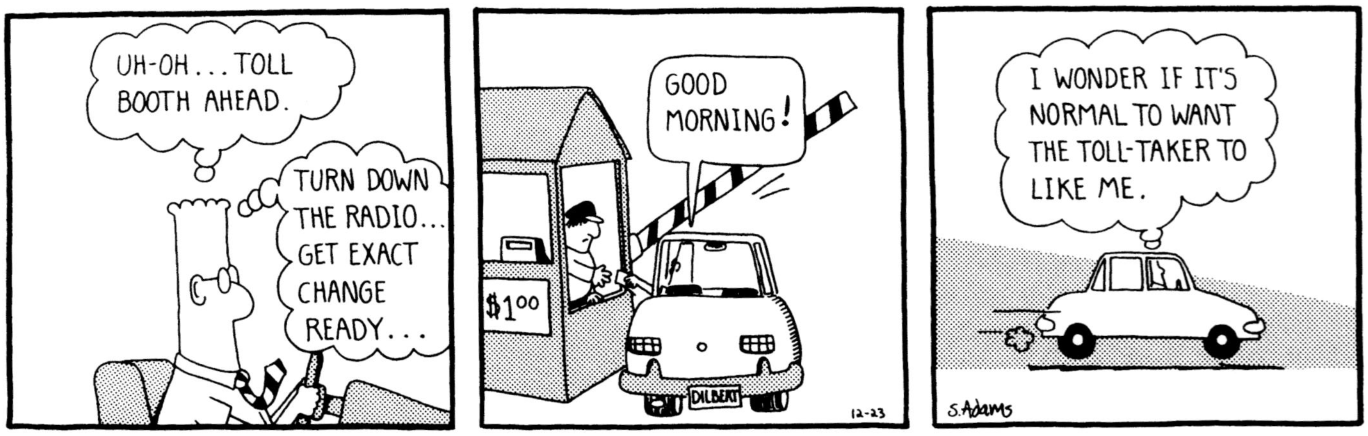
UH-OH... TOLL BOOTH AHEAD.
TURN DOWN THE RADIO... GET EXACT CHANGE READY...
GOOD MORNING!
$1.00
DILBERT
12-23
I WONDER IF IT'S NORMAL TO WANT THE TOLL-TAKER TO LIKE ME.
S. Adams

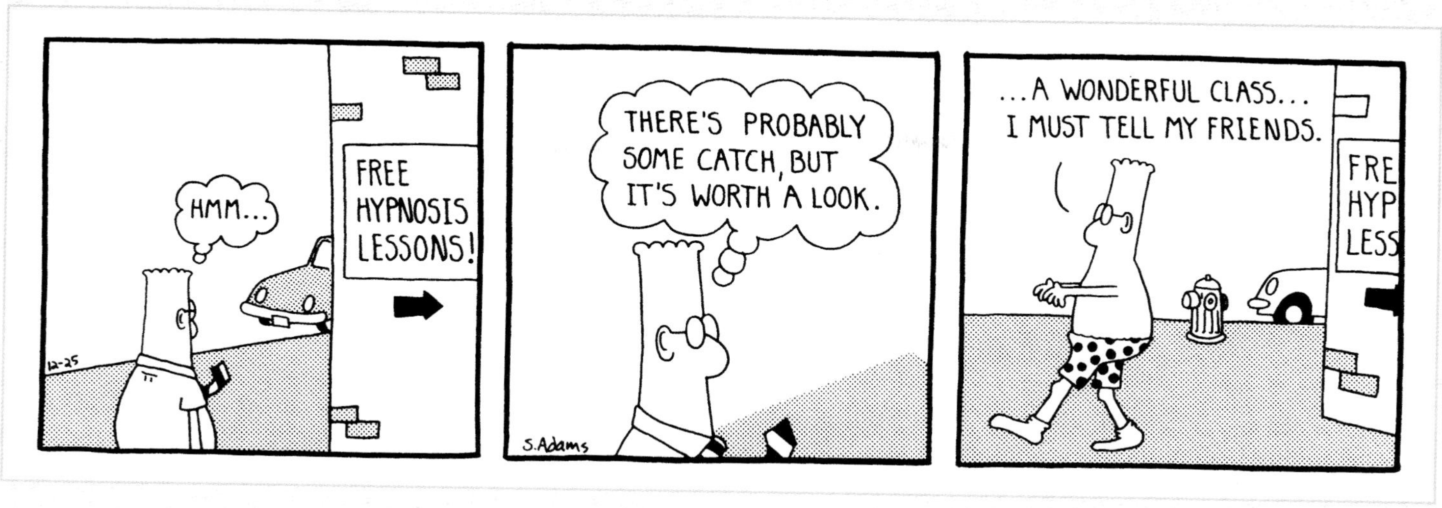
HMM...
FREE HYPNOSIS LESSONS!
12-25
THERE'S PROBABLY SOME CATCH, BUT IT'S WORTH A LOOK.
S.Adams
...A WONDERFUL CLASS... I MUST TELL MY FRIENDS.
FRE HYP LESS

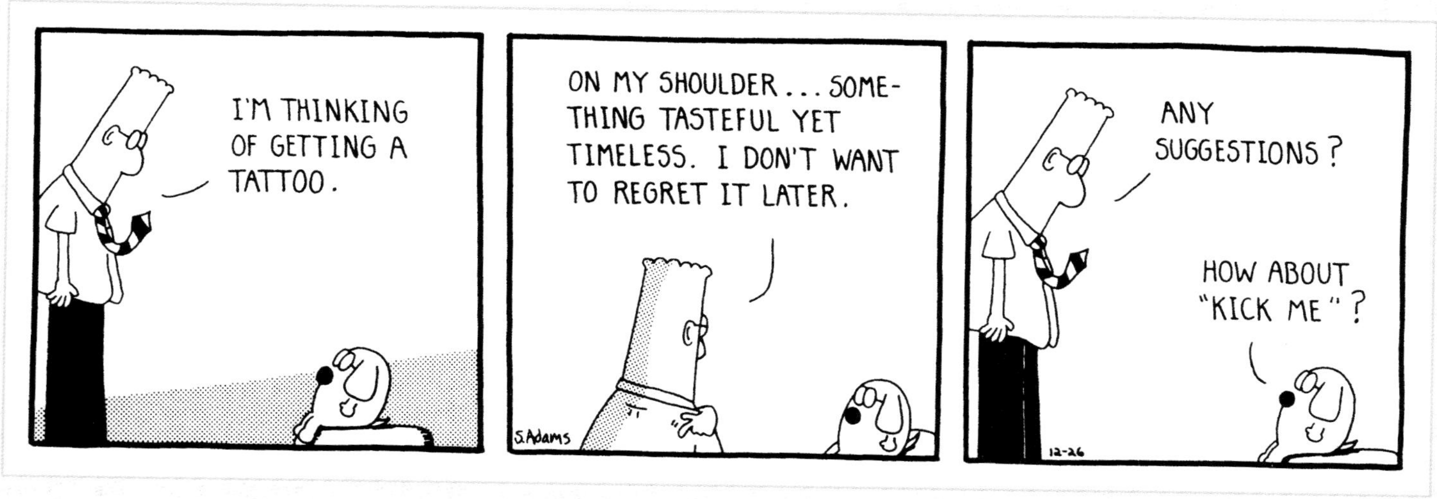
I'M THINKING OF GETTING A TATTOO.
ON MY SHOULDER... SOMETHING TASTEFUL YET TIMELESS. I DON'T WANT TO REGRET IT LATER.
S.Adams
ANY SUGGESTIONS?
HOW ABOUT "KICK ME"?
12-26

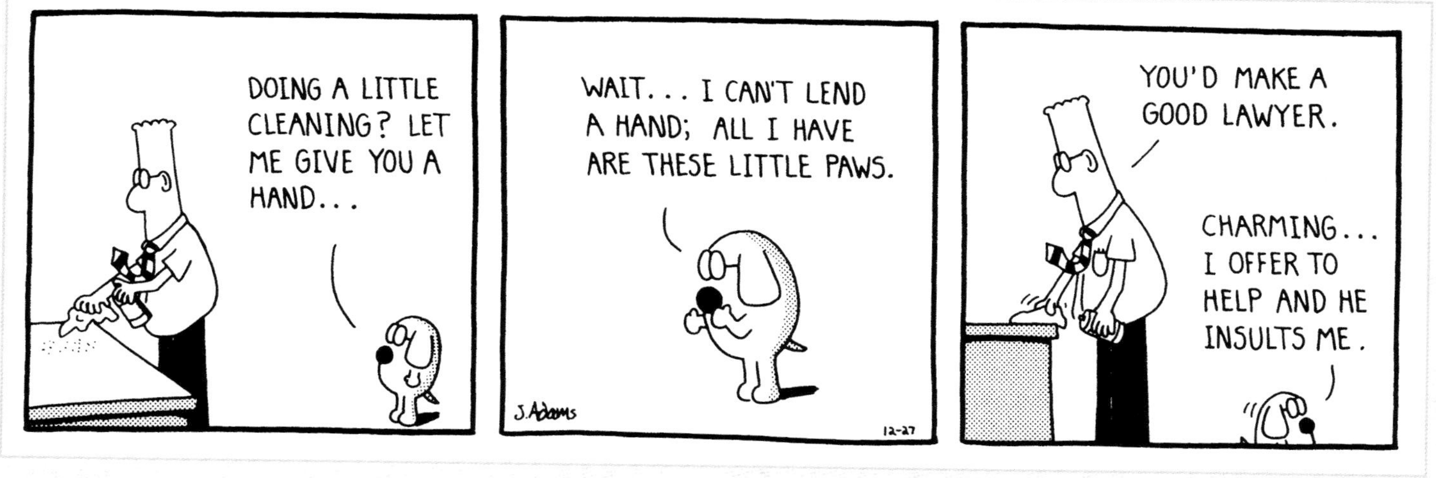
DOING A LITTLE CLEANING? LET ME GIVE YOU A HAND...
WAIT... I CAN'T LEND A HAND; ALL I HAVE ARE THESE LITTLE PAWS.
S.Adams
12-27
YOU'D MAKE A GOOD LAWYER.
CHARMING... I OFFER TO HELP AND HE INSULTS ME.

I went to great lengths to avoid drawing faces of actual people. No one would have recognized them anyway.

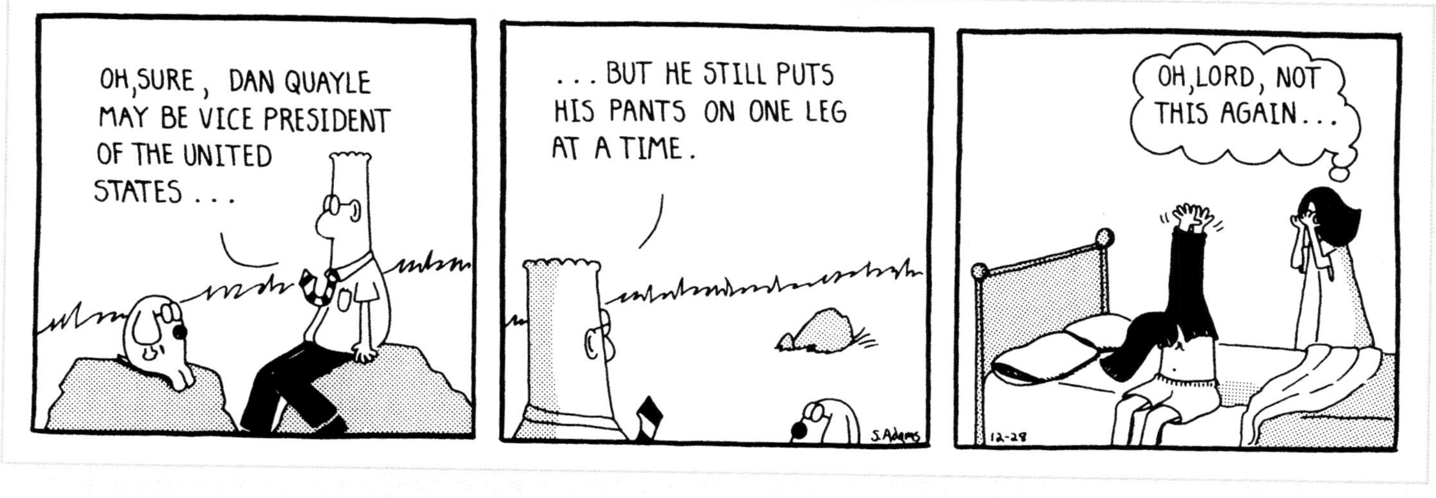
OH, SURE, DAN QUAYLE MAY BE VICE PRESIDENT OF THE UNITED STATES...
...BUT HE STILL PUTS HIS PANTS ON ONE LEG AT A TIME.
S.Adams
OH, LORD, NOT THIS AGAIN...
12-28

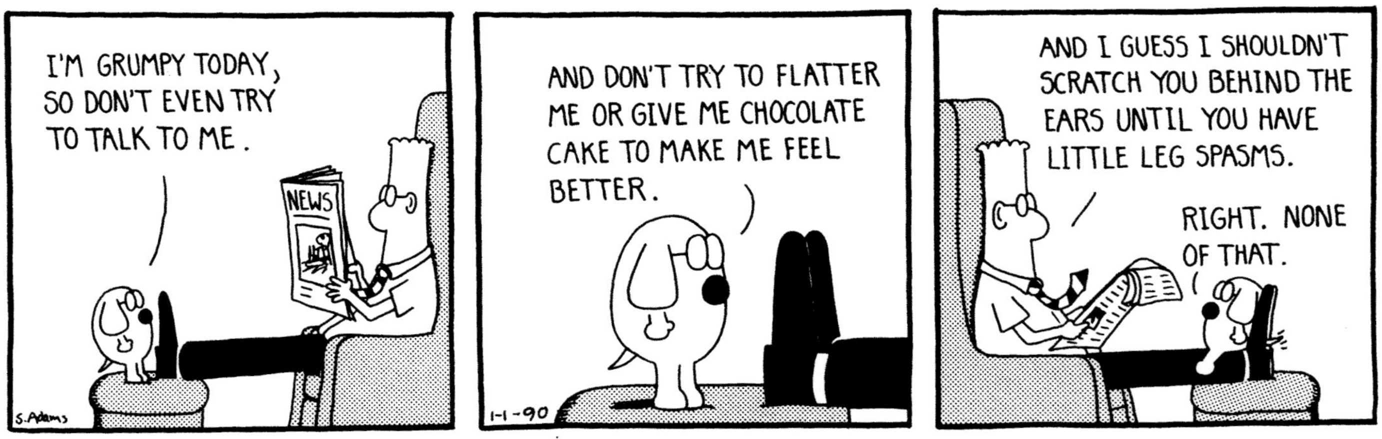
I'M GRUMPY TODAY, SO DON'T EVEN TRY TO TALK TO ME.
NEWS
S. Adams
AND DON'T TRY TO FLATTER ME OR GIVE ME CHOCOLATE CAKE TO MAKE ME FEEL BETTER.
1-1-90
AND I GUESS I SHOULDN'T SCRATCH YOU BEHIND THE EARS UNTIL YOU HAVE LITTLE LEG SPASMS.
RIGHT. NONE OF THAT.

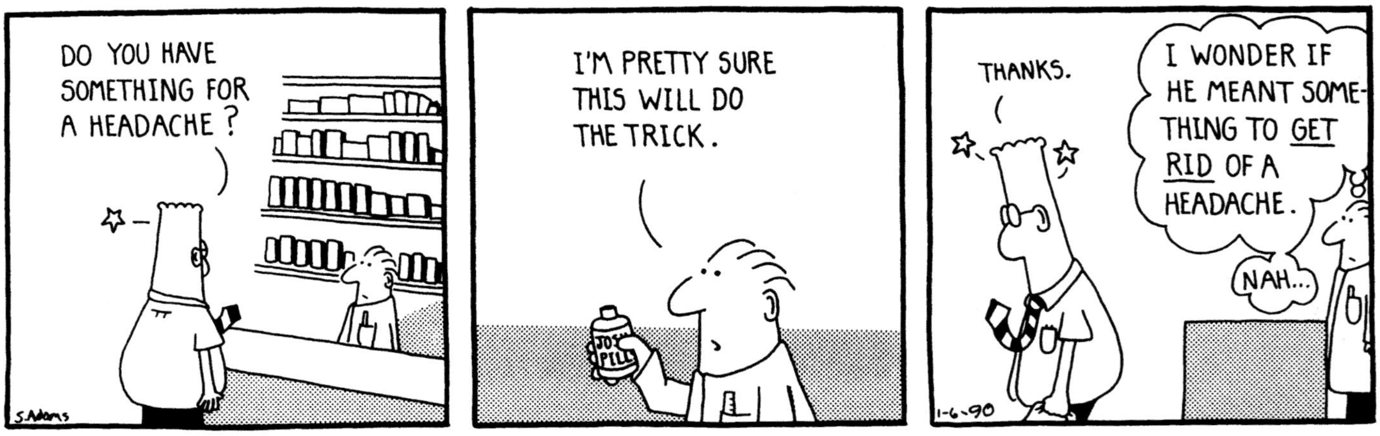
DO YOU HAVE SOMETHING FOR A HEADACHE?
S. Adams
I'M PRETTY SURE THIS WILL DO THE TRICK.
THANKS.
I WONDER IF HE MEANT SOMETHING TO GET RID OF A HEADACHE.
NAH...
1-6-90

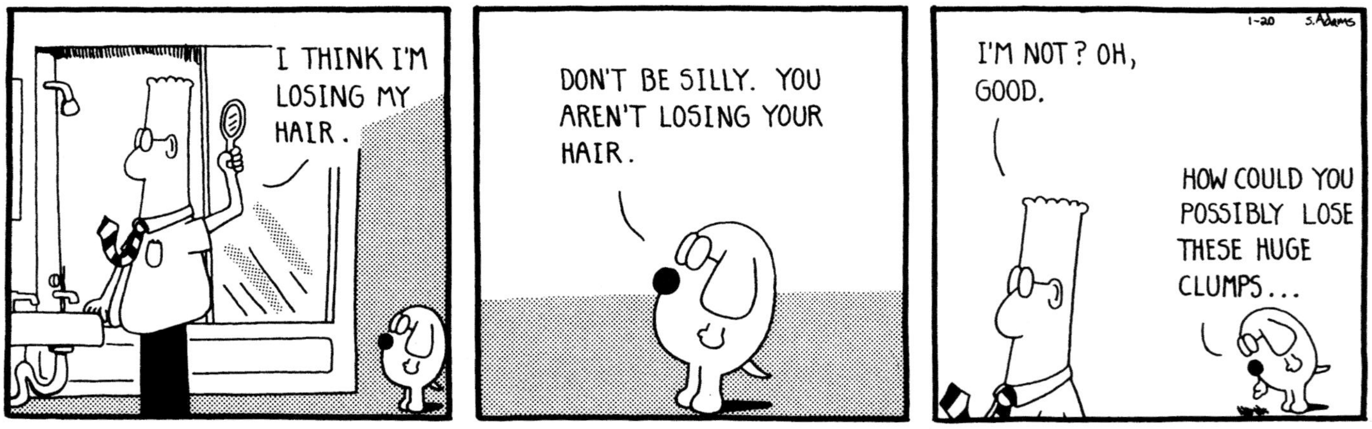
I THINK I'M LOSING MY HAIR.
DON'T BE SILLY. YOU AREN'T LOSING YOUR HAIR.
1-20 S. Adams
I'M NOT? OH, GOOD.
HOW COULD YOU POSSIBLY LOSE THESE HUGE CLUMPS...

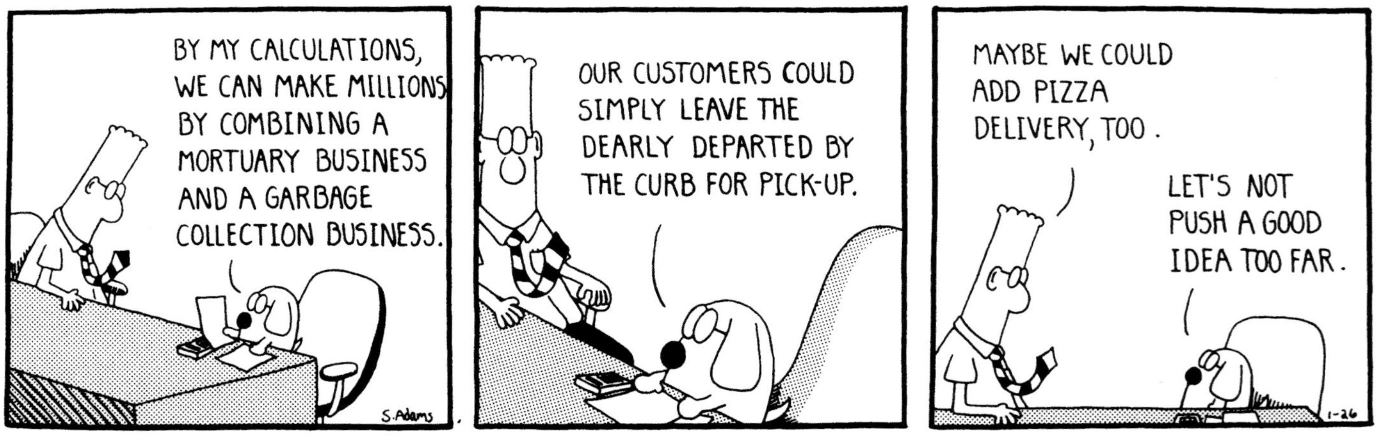
BY MY CALCULATIONS, WE CAN MAKE MILLIONS BY COMBINING A MORTUARY BUSINESS AND A GARBAGE COLLECTION BUSINESS.
S. Adams
OUR CUSTOMERS COULD SIMPLY LEAVE THE DEARLY DEPARTED BY THE CURB FOR PICK-UP.
MAYBE WE COULD ADD PIZZA DELIVERY, TOO.
LET'S NOT PUSH A GOOD IDEA TOO FAR.
1-26

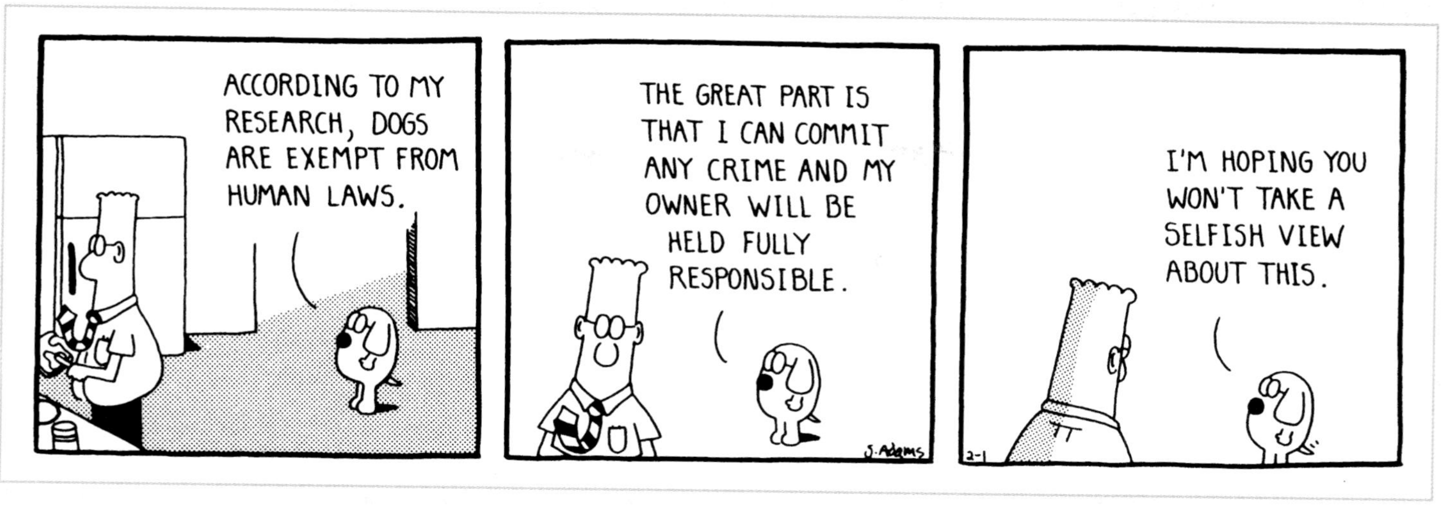
ACCORDING TO MY RESEARCH, DOGS ARE EXEMPT FROM HUMAN LAWS.
THE GREAT PART IS THAT I CAN COMMIT ANY CRIME AND MY OWNER WILL BE HELD FULLY RESPONSIBLE.
I'M HOPING YOU WON'T TAKE A SELFISH VIEW ABOUT THIS.

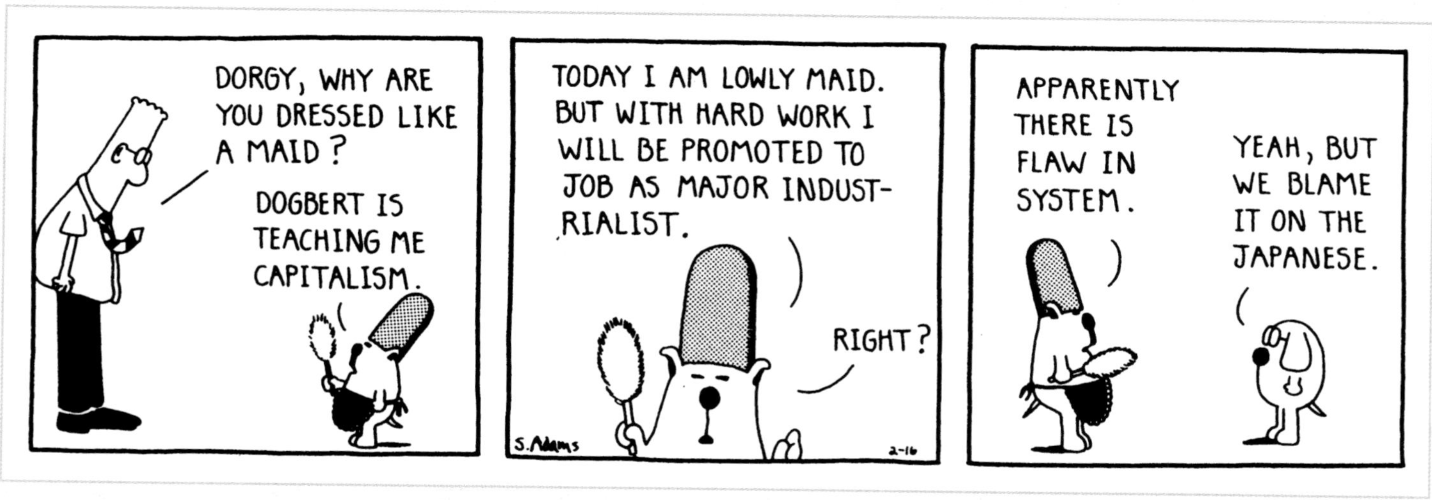
DORGY, WHY ARE YOU DRESSED LIKE A MAID?
DOGBERT IS TEACHING ME CAPITALISM.
TODAY I AM LOWLY MAID. BUT WITH HARD WORK I WILL BE PROMOTED TO JOB AS MAJOR INDUST-RIALIST.
RIGHT?
APPARENTLY THERE IS FLAW IN SYSTEM.
YEAH, BUT WE BLAME IT ON THE JAPANESE.

I thought my calling might be in political commentary. Clearly it wasn't.

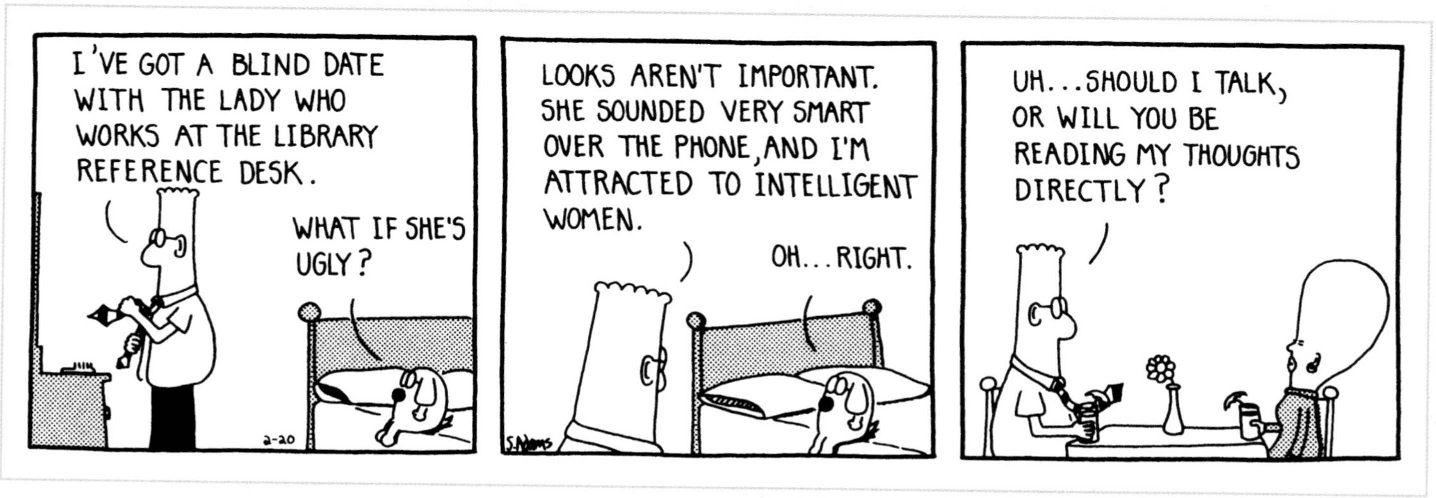
I'VE GOT A BLIND DATE WITH THE LADY WHO WORKS AT THE LIBRARY REFERENCE DESK.
WHAT IF SHE'S UGLY?
LOOKS AREN'T IMPORTANT. SHE SOUNDED VERY SMART OVER THE PHONE, AND I'M ATTRACTED TO INTELLIGENT WOMEN.
OH... RIGHT.
UH...SHOULD I TALK, OR WILL YOU BE READING MY THOUGHTS DIRECTLY?

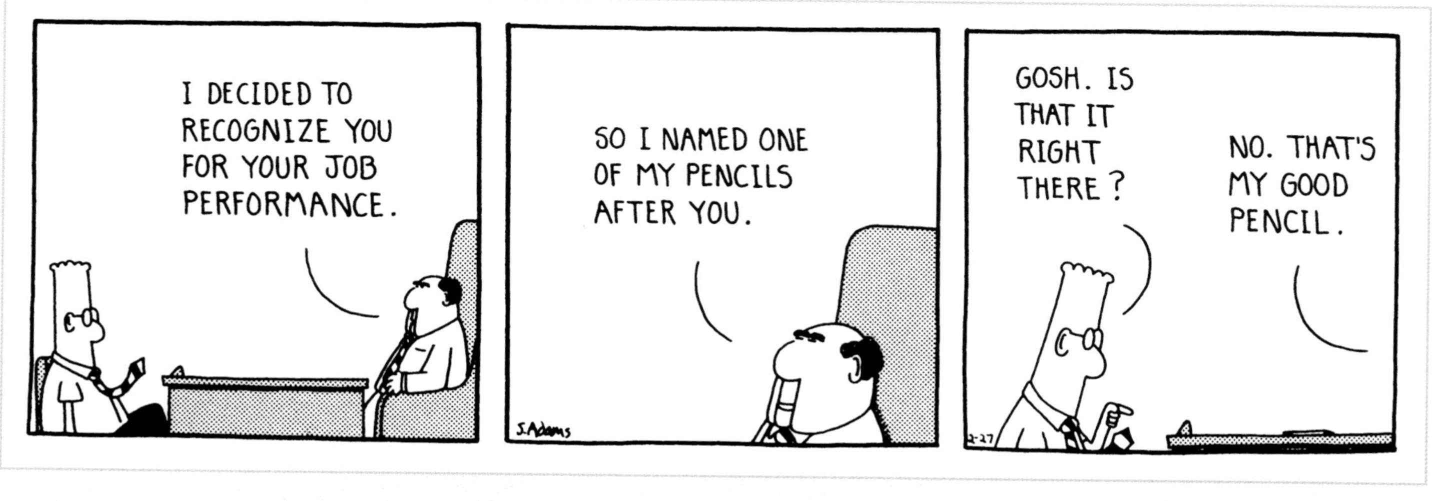
I DECIDED TO RECOGNIZE YOU FOR YOUR JOB PERFORMANCE.
SO I NAMED ONE OF MY PENCILS AFTER YOU.
GOSH. IS THAT IT RIGHT THERE?
NO. THAT'S MY GOOD PENCIL.

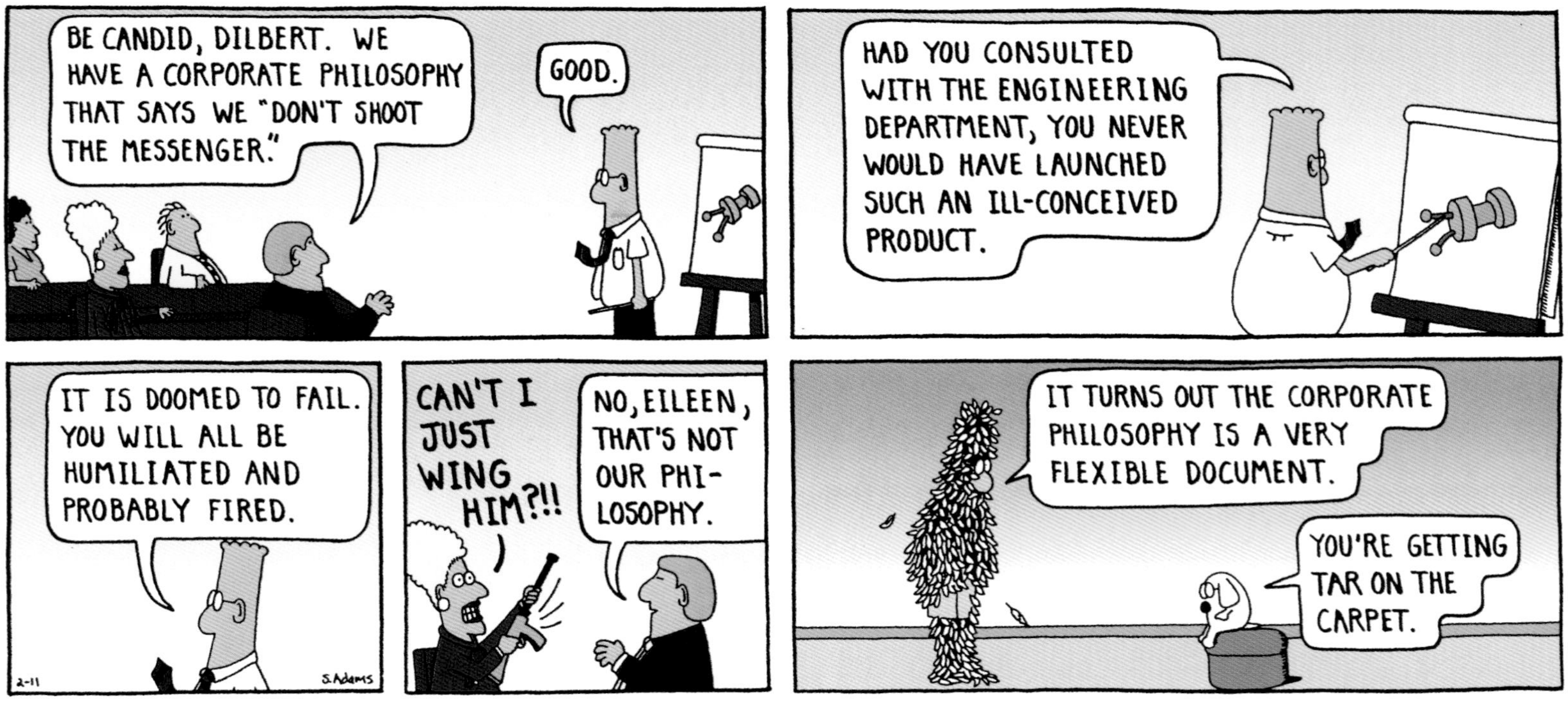
BE CANDID, DILBERT. WE HAVE A CORPORATE PHILOSOPHY THAT SAYS WE "DON'T SHOOT THE MESSENGER."
GOOD.
HAD YOU CONSULTED WITH THE ENGINEERING DEPARTMENT, YOU NEVER WOULD HAVE LAUNCHED SUCH AN ILL-CONCEIVED PRODUCT.
IT IS DOOMED TO FAIL. YOU WILL ALL BE HUMILIATED AND PROBABLY FIRED.
CAN'T I JUST WING HIM?!!
NO, EILEEN, THAT'S NOT OUR PHI-LOSOPHY.
IT TURNS OUT THE CORPORATE PHILOSOPHY IS A VERY FLEXIBLE DOCUMENT.
YOU'RE GETTING TAR ON THE CARPET.
2-11
S.Adams

This comic showcases some of the techniques that would later define the strip. Here Dilbert is at work, and makes the mistake of being honest. The gap between what people say and what they think in the workplace eventually became the defining concept for Dilbert *comics.*

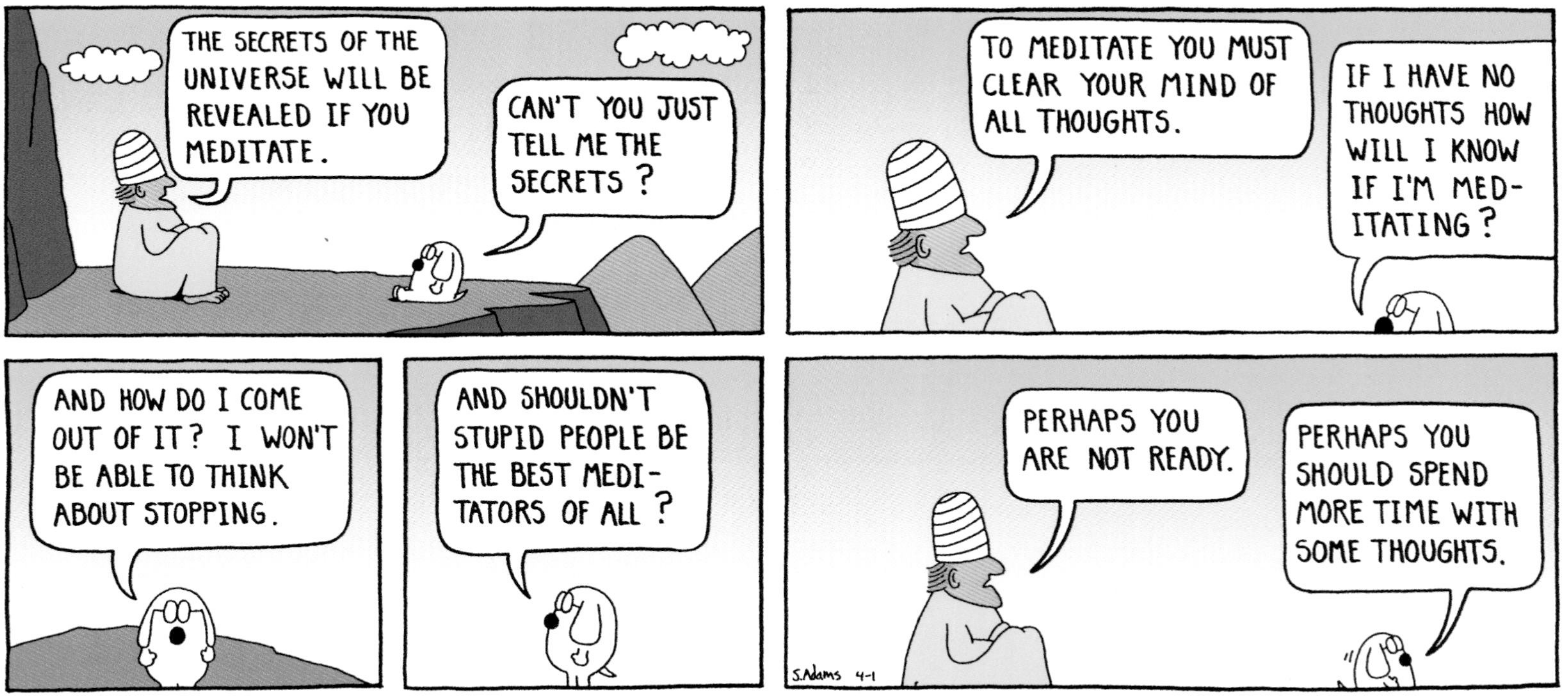
THE SECRETS OF THE UNIVERSE WILL BE REVEALED IF YOU MEDITATE.
CAN'T YOU JUST TELL ME THE SECRETS ?
TO MEDITATE YOU MUST CLEAR YOUR MIND OF ALL THOUGHTS.
IF I HAVE NO THOUGHTS HOW WILL I KNOW IF I'M MED-ITATING ?
AND HOW DO I COME OUT OF IT ? I WON'T BE ABLE TO THINK ABOUT STOPPING.
AND SHOULDN'T STUPID PEOPLE BE THE BEST MEDI-TATORS OF ALL ?
PERHAPS YOU ARE NOT READY.
PERHAPS YOU SHOULD SPEND MORE TIME WITH SOME THOUGHTS.
S.Adams 4-1

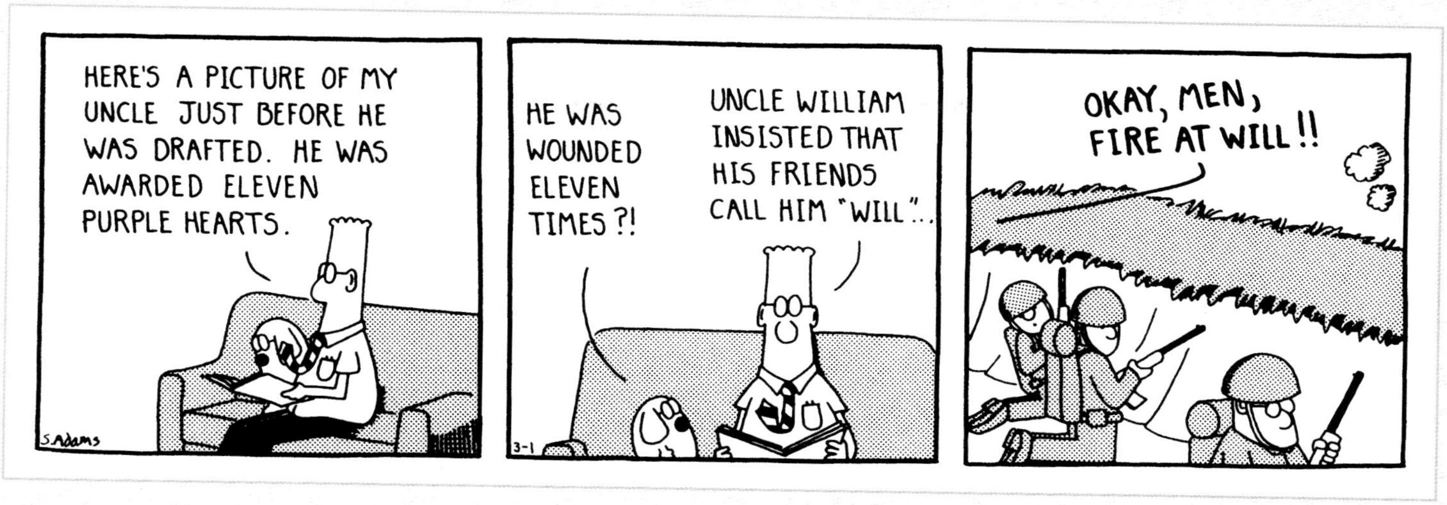
HERE'S A PICTURE OF MY UNCLE JUST BEFORE HE WAS DRAFTED. HE WAS AWARDED ELEVEN PURPLE HEARTS.
HE WAS WOUNDED ELEVEN TIMES ?!
UNCLE WILLIAM INSISTED THAT HIS FRIENDS CALL HIM "WILL"...
OKAY, MEN, FIRE AT WILL!!

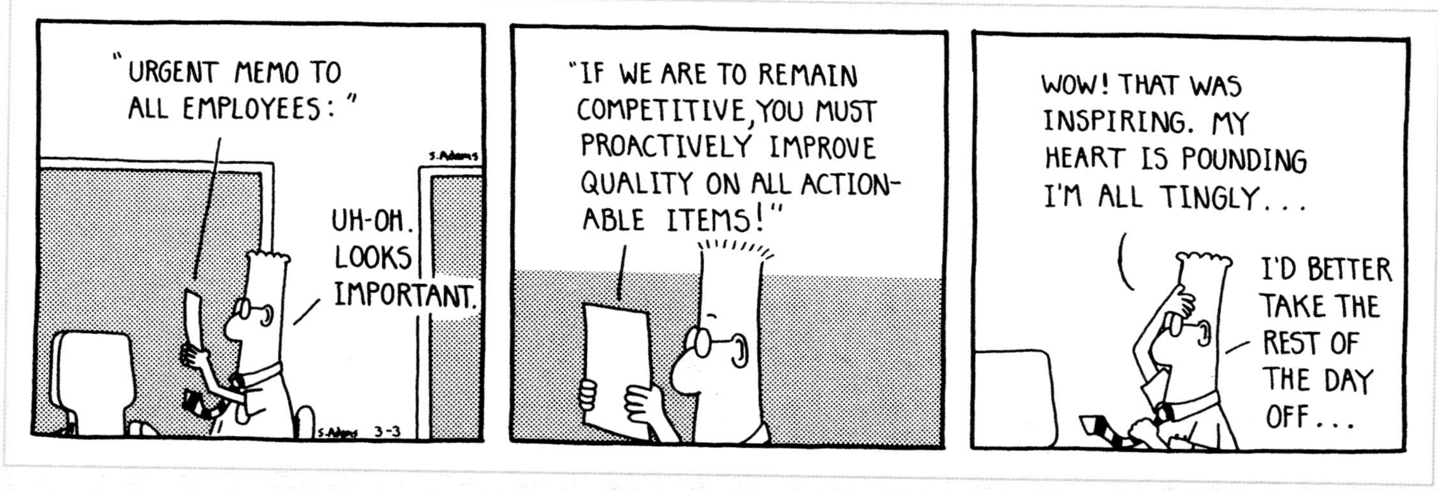
"URGENT MEMO TO ALL EMPLOYEES:"
UH-OH. LOOKS IMPORTANT.
"IF WE ARE TO REMAIN COMPETITIVE, YOU MUST PROACTIVELY IMPROVE QUALITY ON ALL ACTION-ABLE ITEMS!"
WOW! THAT WAS INSPIRING. MY HEART IS POUNDING I'M ALL TINGLY...
I'D BETTER TAKE THE REST OF THE DAY OFF...

The comic above features a direct quote from a memo written by a vice president of engineering at Pacific Bell, my employer at the time, to his entire division. I didn't think he would notice I borrowed the wording. Dilbert wasn't in many papers at the time, and I was sure it wasn't in the vice president's local paper.

What I didn't count on was a member of his staff making copies of the strip and handing it out at the vice president's staff meeting. I learned later that someone at the meeting connected the dots, and the vice president allegedly decided to fire me. Luckily, my boss's boss stepped in and said it would be a mistake to fire me just for making jokes. A better plan would be to give me awful assignments until I quit. That plan went into effect, unknown to me for a long time.

What they didn't count on is that when you're a cartoonist, there's no such thing as an entirely bad day. The more absurd my day job got, the funnier my comics became. Later in this book you'll see what comics I drew after I learned how much trouble I had been in without knowing it.

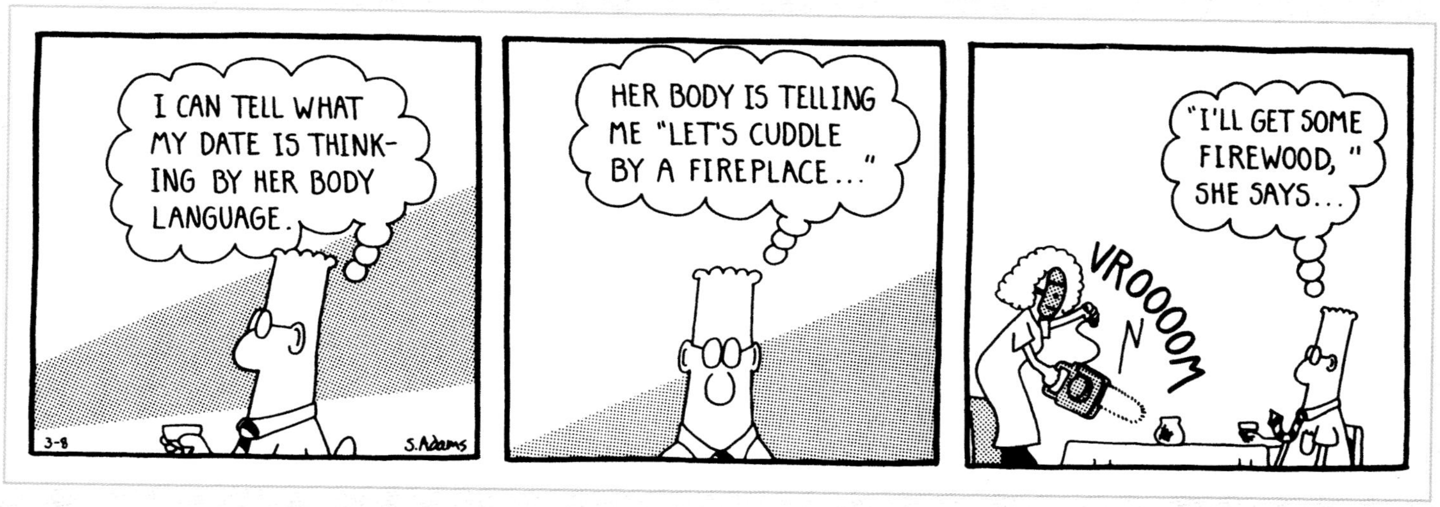
I CAN TELL WHAT MY DATE IS THINK-ING BY HER BODY LANGUAGE.
HER BODY IS TELLING ME "LET'S CUDDLE BY A FIREPLACE..."
VROOOOM
"I'LL GET SOME FIREWOOD," SHE SAYS...

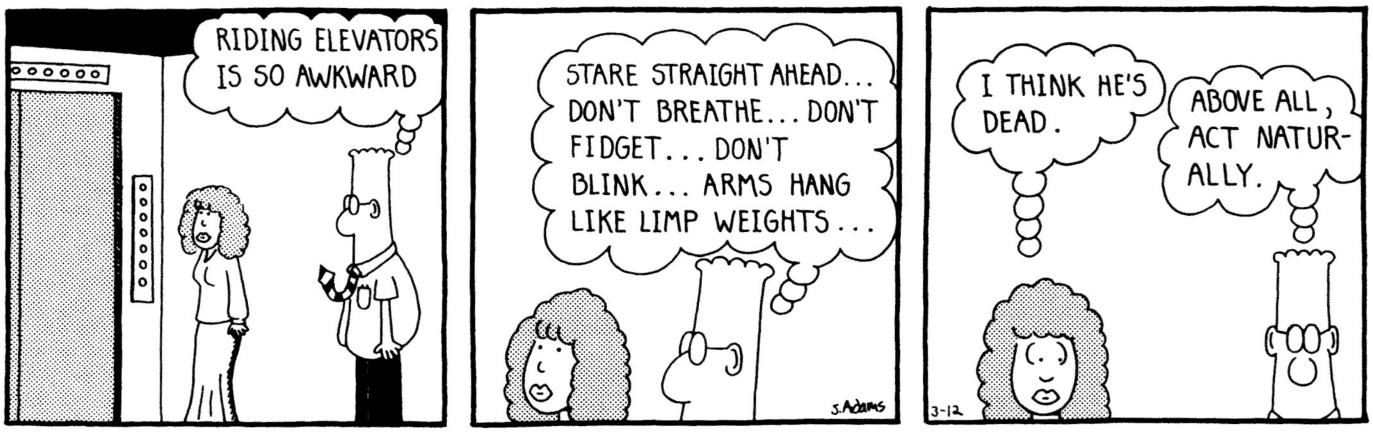
RIDING ELEVATORS IS SO AWKWARD
STARE STRAIGHT AHEAD... DON'T BREATHE... DON'T FIDGET... DON'T BLINK... ARMS HANG LIKE LIMP WEIGHTS...
S.Adams
I THINK HE'S DEAD.
ABOVE ALL, ACT NATURALLY.
3-12

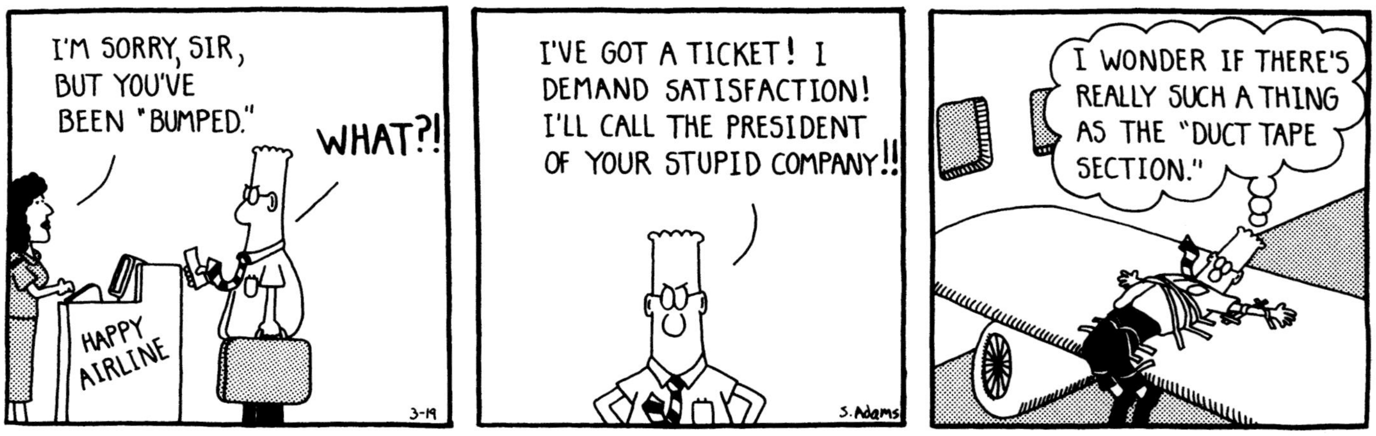
I'M SORRY, SIR, BUT YOU'VE BEEN "BUMPED."
WHAT?!
HAPPY AIRLINE
3-19
I'VE GOT A TICKET! I DEMAND SATISFACTION! I'LL CALL THE PRESIDENT OF YOUR STUPID COMPANY!!
S.Adams
I WONDER IF THERE'S REALLY SUCH A THING AS THE "DUCT TAPE SECTION."

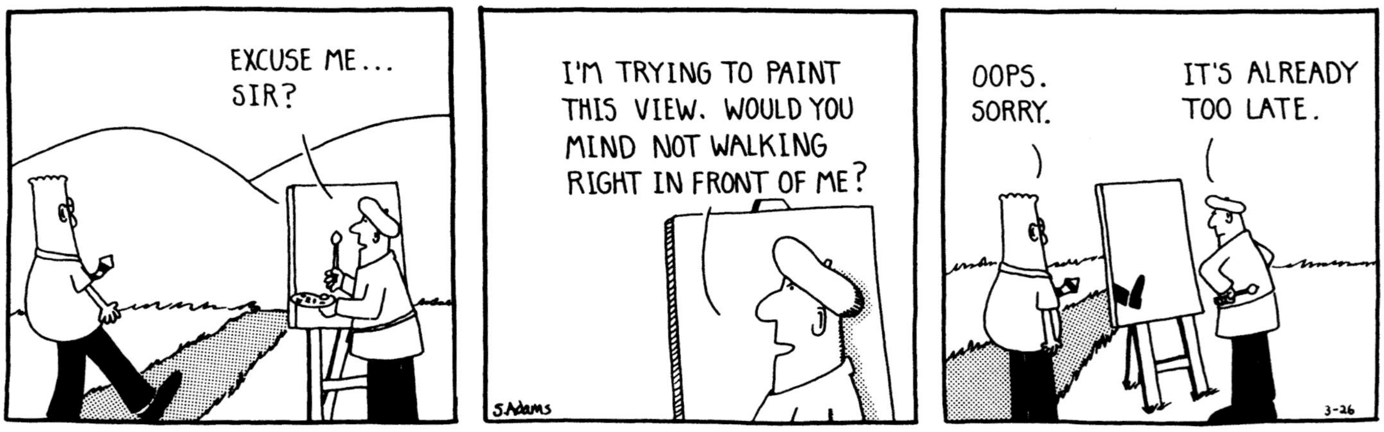
EXCUSE ME... SIR?
I'M TRYING TO PAINT THIS VIEW. WOULD YOU MIND NOT WALKING RIGHT IN FRONT OF ME?
S.Adams
OOPS. SORRY.
IT'S ALREADY TOO LATE.
3-26

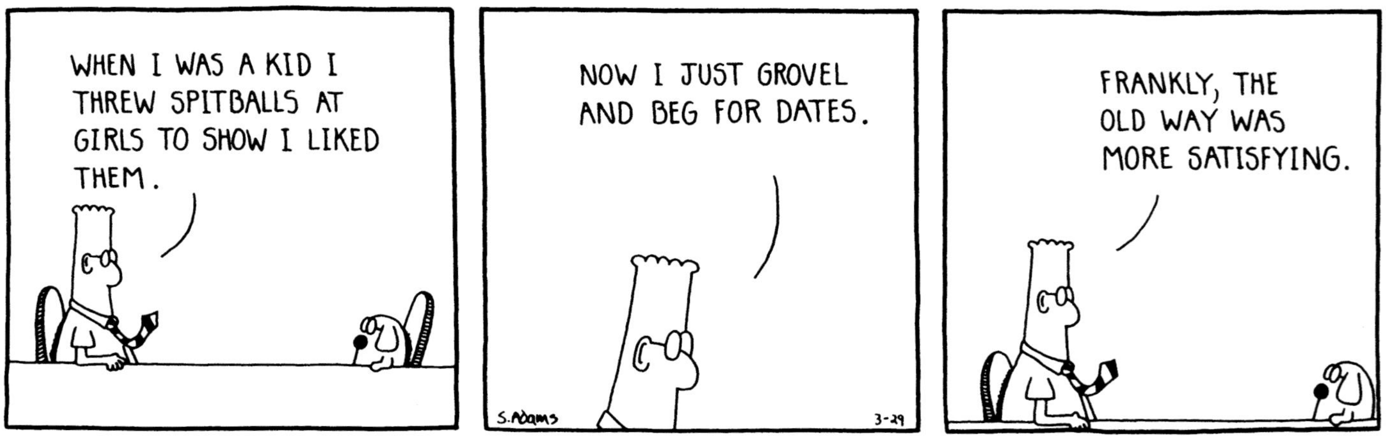
WHEN I WAS A KID I THREW SPITBALLS AT GIRLS TO SHOW I LIKED THEM.
NOW I JUST GROVEL AND BEG FOR DATES.
S.Adams
3-29
FRANKLY, THE OLD WAY WAS MORE SATISFYING.

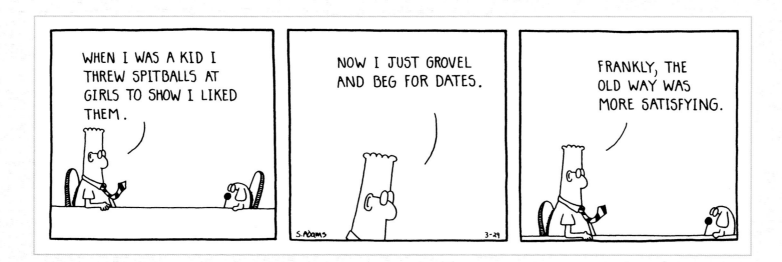

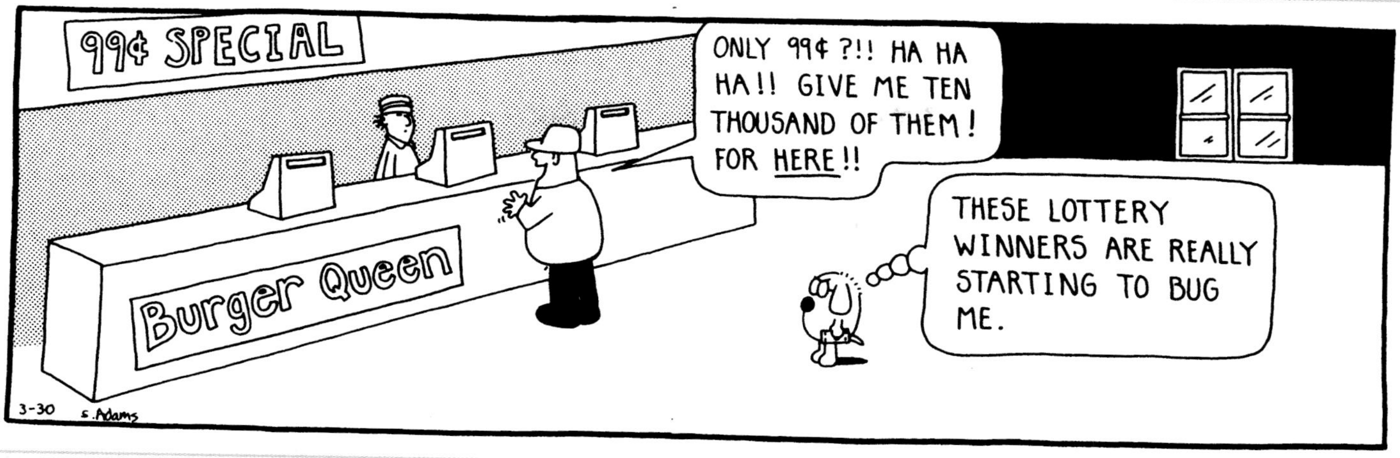
99¢ SPECIAL
Burger Queen
ONLY 99¢ ?!! HA HA HA!! GIVE ME TEN THOUSAND OF THEM! FOR HERE!!
THESE LOTTERY WINNERS ARE REALLY STARTING TO BUG ME.
3-30
S. Adams

This is one of the few single-panel comics I ever did for Dilbert, *at least for newspapers. Writing for one panel is a different skill than writing for three, and I learned I wasn't a single-panel cartoonist.*

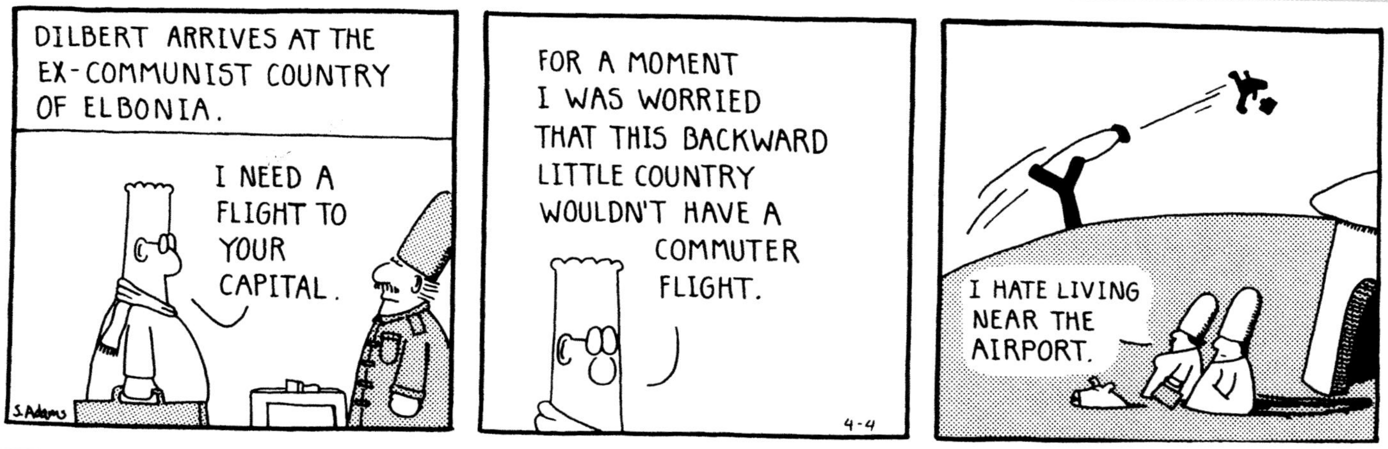
DILBERT ARRIVES AT THE EX-COMMUNIST COUNTRY OF ELBONIA.
I NEED A FLIGHT TO YOUR CAPITAL.
S. Adams
FOR A MOMENT I WAS WORRIED THAT THIS BACKWARD LITTLE COUNTRY WOULDN'T HAVE A COMMUTER FLIGHT.
4-4
I HATE LIVING NEAR THE AIRPORT.

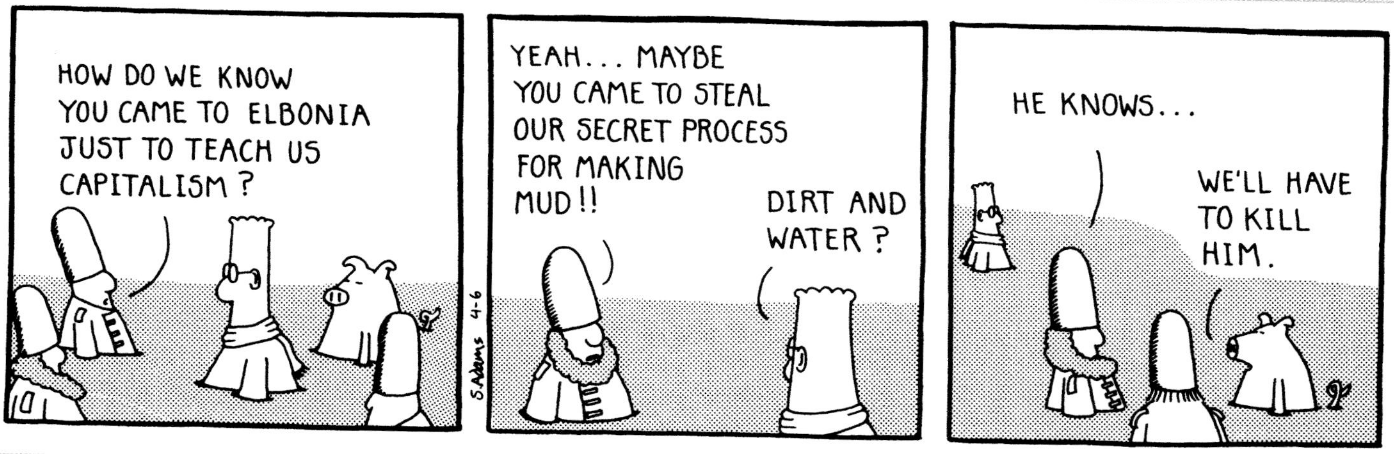
HOW DO WE KNOW YOU CAME TO ELBONIA JUST TO TEACH US CAPITALISM?
S. Adams 4-6
YEAH... MAYBE YOU CAME TO STEAL OUR SECRET PROCESS FOR MAKING MUD!!
DIRT AND WATER?
HE KNOWS...
WE'LL HAVE TO KILL HIM.

Later on, I made all Elbonians look identical, even the women, with long black beards. It seemed funnier to me.

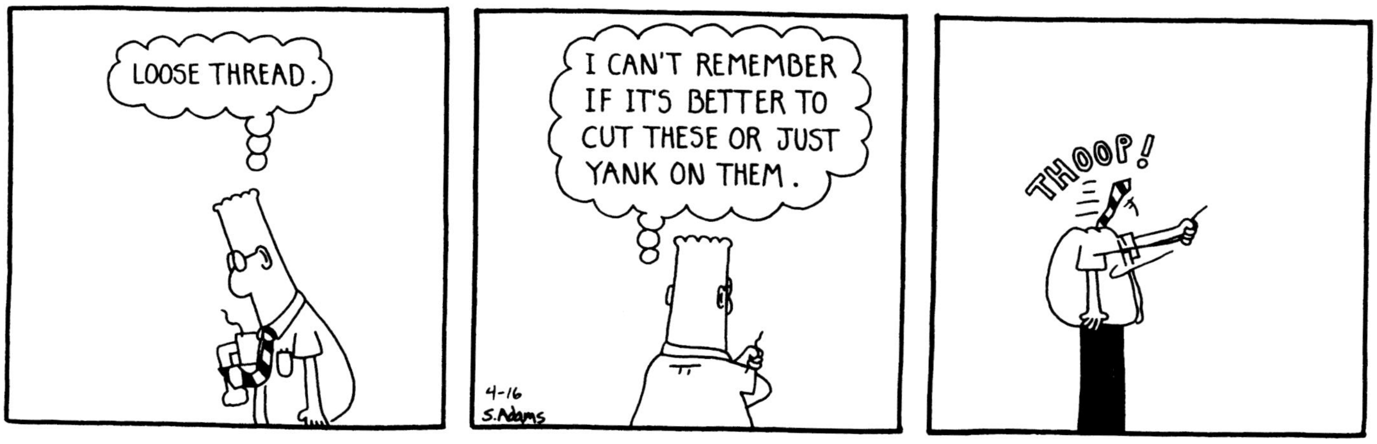
LOOSE THREAD.
I CAN'T REMEMBER IF IT'S BETTER TO CUT THESE OR JUST YANK ON THEM.
4-16
S. Adams
THOOP!

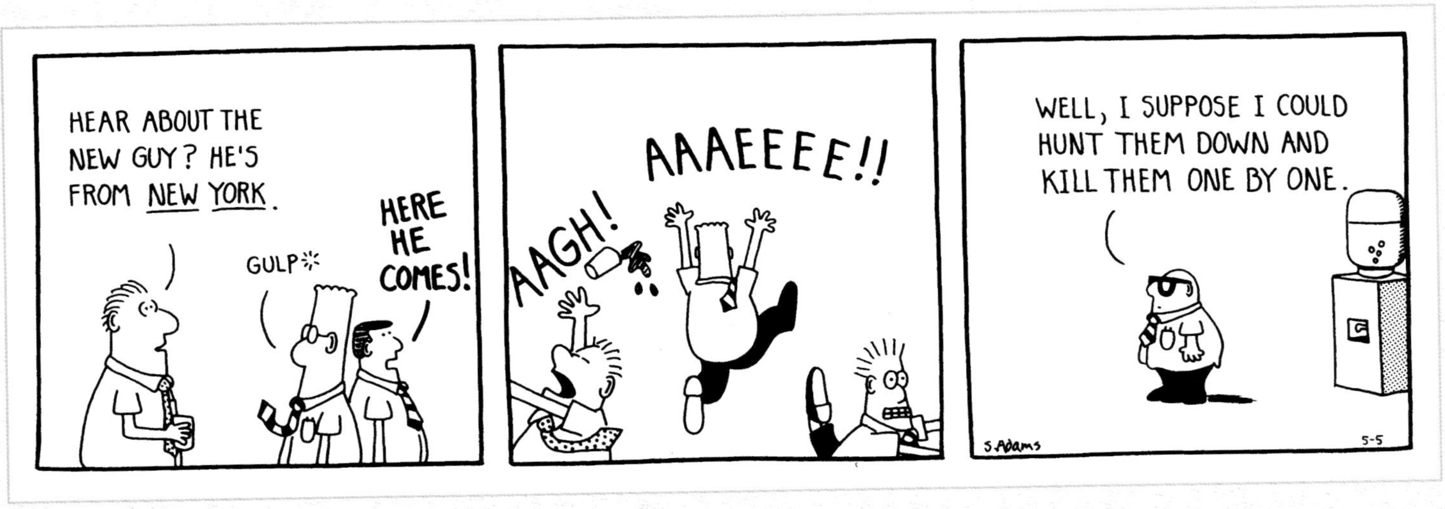
HEAR ABOUT THE NEW GUY? HE'S FROM NEW YORK.
GULP
HERE HE COMES!
AAAEEEE!!
AAGH!
WELL, I SUPPOSE I COULD HUNT THEM DOWN AND KILL THEM ONE BY ONE.
S.Adams
5-5

The guy from New York eventually morphed into Wally. I can't draw many different-looking characters, so anything I felt comfortable drawing got used until it became a regular feature of the strip.

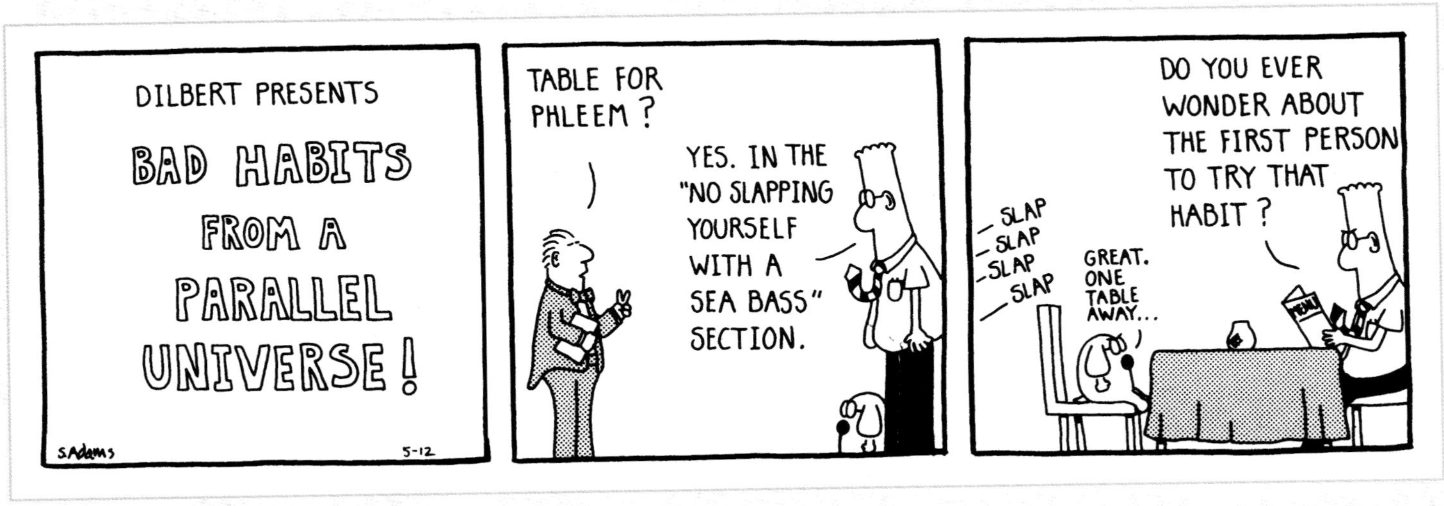
DILBERT PRESENTS
BAD HABITS FROM A PARALLEL UNIVERSE!
S.Adams
5-12
TABLE FOR PHLEEM?
YES. IN THE "NO SLAPPING YOURSELF WITH A SEA BASS" SECTION.
SLAP SLAP SLAP SLAP
GREAT. ONE TABLE AWAY...
DO YOU EVER WONDER ABOUT THE FIRST PERSON TO TRY THAT HABIT?

The trick to being absurd in comics, and still being funny, is leaving one foot firmly in the familiar. The comic above didn't leave enough foot in the real world. Over time, I learned to be more about the familiar and less about the absurd.

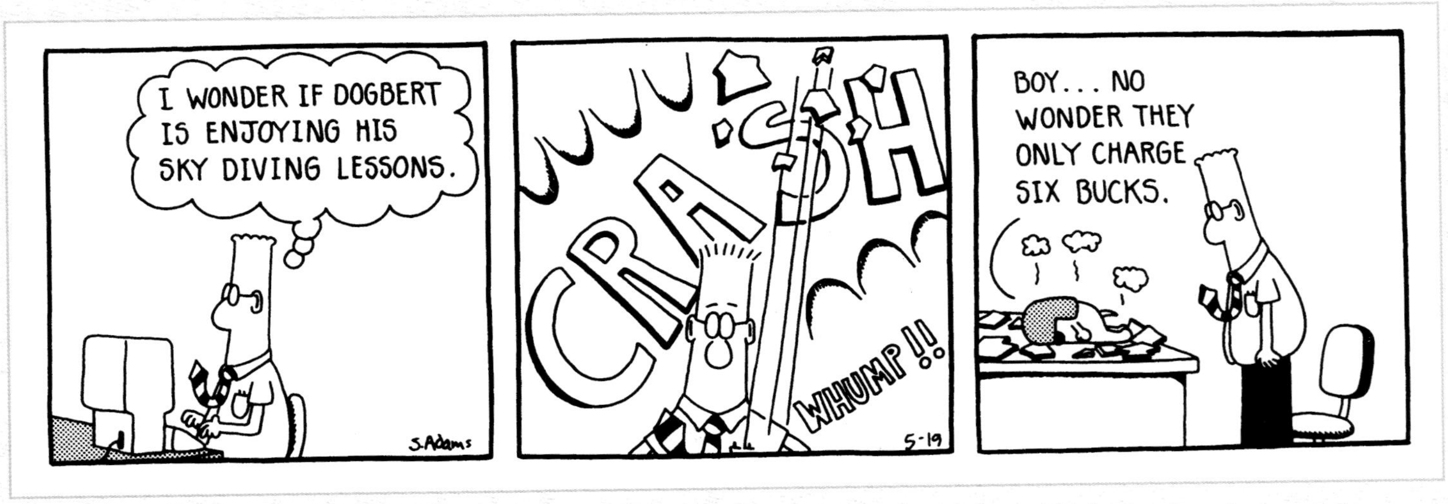
I WONDER IF DOGBERT IS ENJOYING HIS SKY DIVING LESSONS.
S.Adams
CRASH
WHUMP!!
5-19
BOY... NO WONDER THEY ONLY CHARGE SIX BUCKS.

There are only a hundred jokes in the universe. I've reused some form of "the inexpensive product or service" dozens of times with different characters and scenarios.

I ALWAYS GET A WARM, SATISFIED FEELING RIGHT AFTER PAYING MY TAXES.
SURE, IT'S A SACRIFICE...
BUT MY MONEY GOES TO SUPPORT VITAL PUBLIC SERVICES.
KNOCK KNOCK
WE'RE THE I R S MOP-UP CREW.
WE CAME TO TAKE YOUR SOCKS AND SHAVE SIXTY PERCENT OF YOUR DOG.
BZZZZ
REMIND ME TO ADJUST MY WITHHOLDINGS FOR NEXT YEAR.
4-15-90

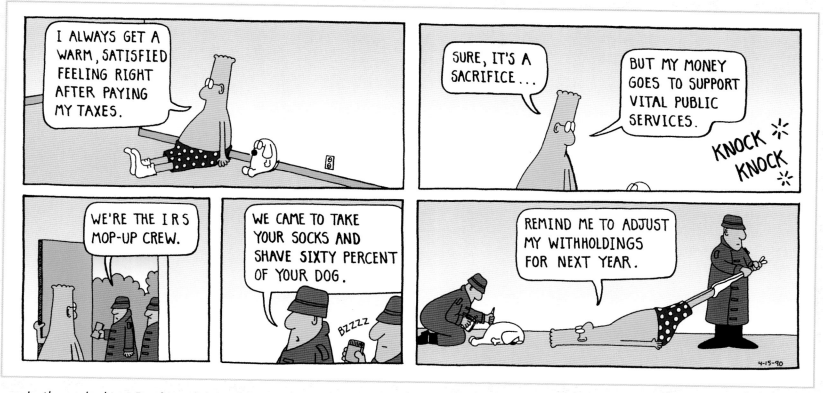

In the early days, Dogbert didn't always come out ahead. Later on, I developed a rule that he could never lose at any endeavor.

HEY DOG! WHAT'S THE QUICKEST WAY TO GO TO THE HOSPITAL?
DRIVE AS FAST AS YOU CAN INTO THAT TREE.
WHAT'S THE SECOND QUICKEST WAY?
HMM... WELL, GO LEFT, THEN RIGHT, RIGHT, LEFT, LEFT, LEFT, RIGHT, LEFT, LEFT, LEFT, LEFT.
S.Adams
THANKS!
ACTUALLY, I HAVE NO IDEA HOW TO GET TO THE HOSPITAL...
BUT I DIDN'T WANT HIM TO THINK I'M A JERK.
5-6-90

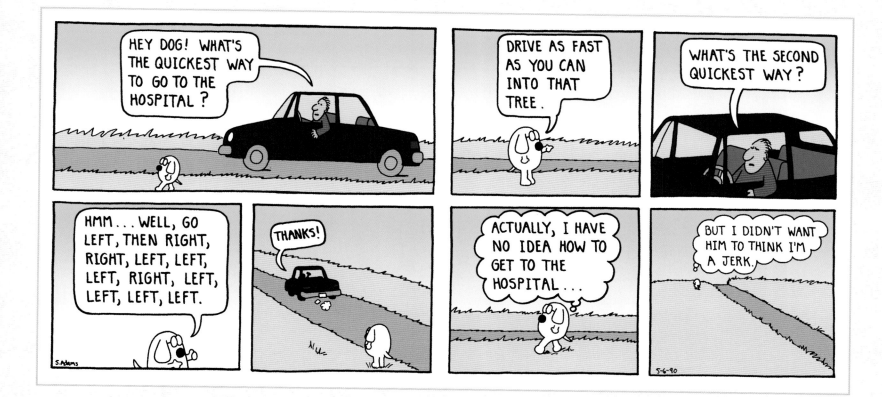

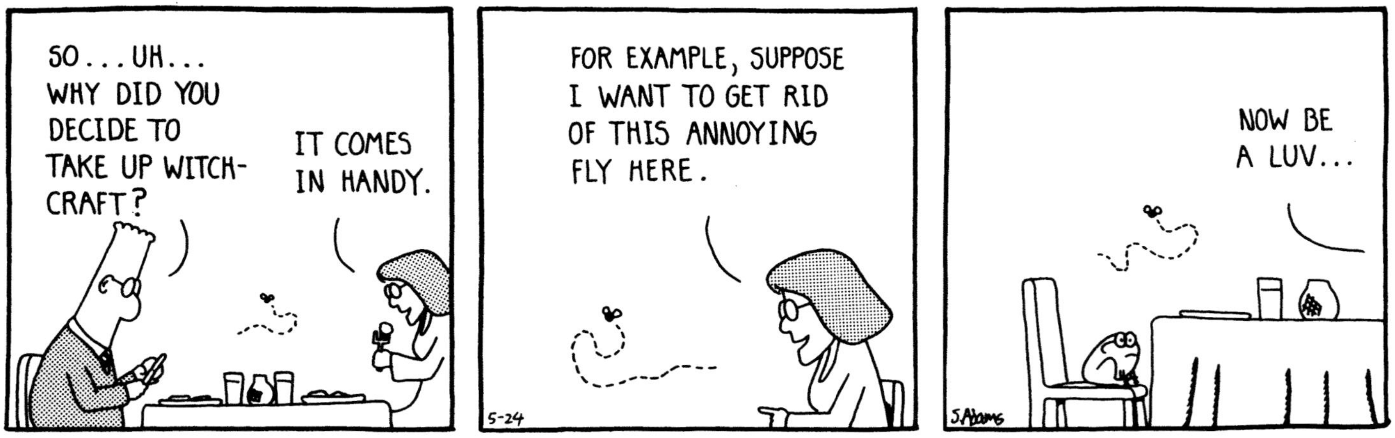
SO... UH... WHY DID YOU DECIDE TO TAKE UP WITCH-CRAFT?
IT COMES IN HANDY.
FOR EXAMPLE, SUPPOSE I WANT TO GET RID OF THIS ANNOYING FLY HERE.
NOW BE A LUV...
5-24
S.Adams

Another one of the hundred jokes in the universe is "the unexpected solution to a problem."

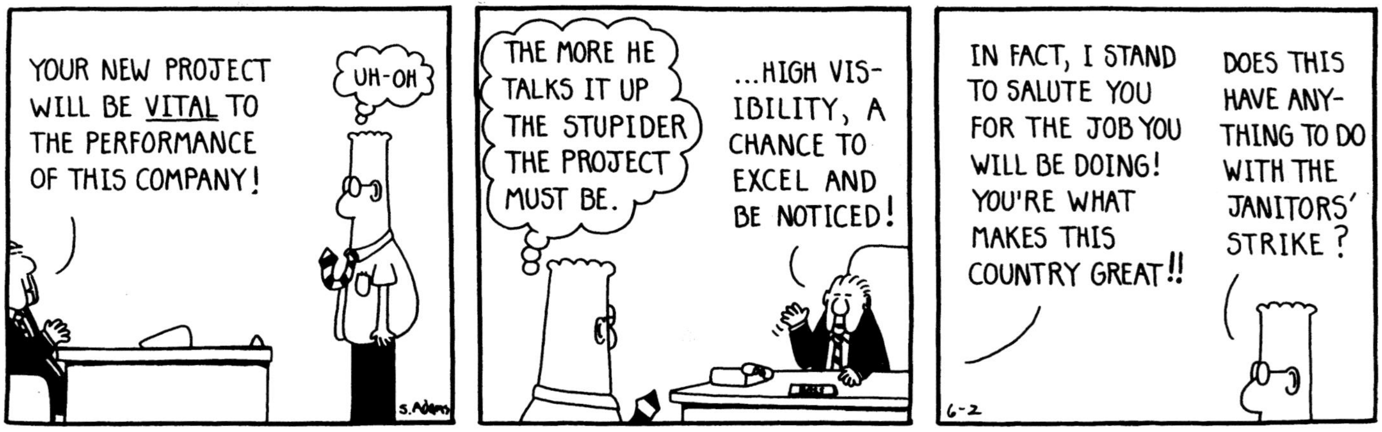
YOUR NEW PROJECT WILL BE VITAL TO THE PERFORMANCE OF THIS COMPANY!
UH-OH
S.Adams
THE MORE HE TALKS IT UP THE STUPIDER THE PROJECT MUST BE.
...HIGH VIS-IBILITY, A CHANCE TO EXCEL AND BE NOTICED!
IN FACT, I STAND TO SALUTE YOU FOR THE JOB YOU WILL BE DOING! YOU'RE WHAT MAKES THIS COUNTRY GREAT!!
DOES THIS HAVE ANY-THING TO DO WITH THE JANITORS' STRIKE?
6-2

Dilbert's boss wasn't yet depicted as always being the iconic pointy-haired boss.
And Dilbert was still rarely shown at work.

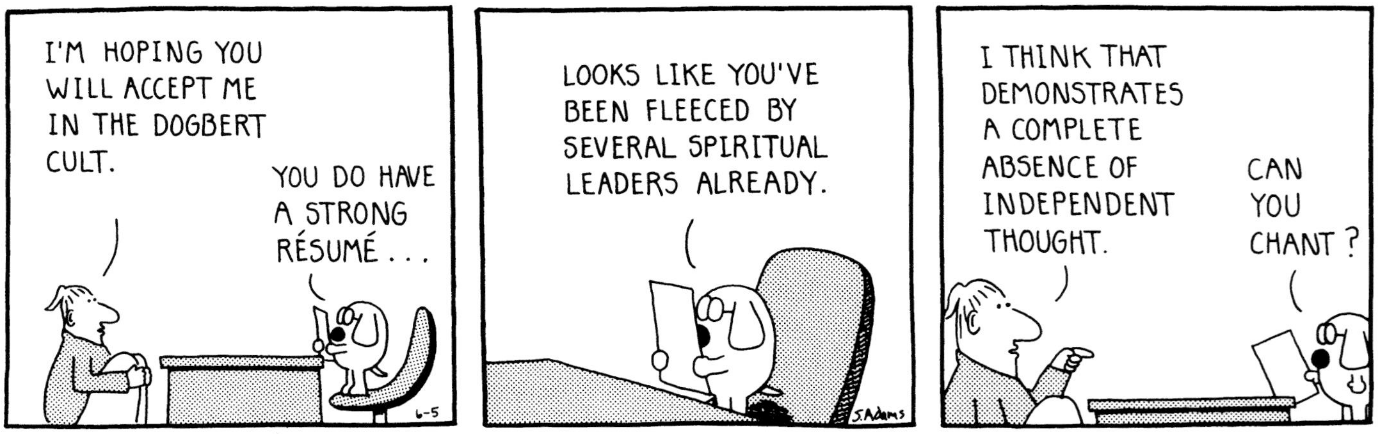
I'M HOPING YOU WILL ACCEPT ME IN THE DOGBERT CULT.
YOU DO HAVE A STRONG RÉSUMÉ...
6-5
LOOKS LIKE YOU'VE BEEN FLEECED BY SEVERAL SPIRITUAL LEADERS ALREADY.
S.Adams
I THINK THAT DEMONSTRATES A COMPLETE ABSENCE OF INDEPENDENT THOUGHT.
CAN YOU CHANT?

I started to find my "voice" during this period. Prior comics were mostly my own versions of classic gags. In this comic I started inserting the humor in any panel it fit, and aiming for more than one laugh when I could get it. This one has several mini-punch lines instead of the usual one at the end. None of this was intentional. I just drifted in that direction.

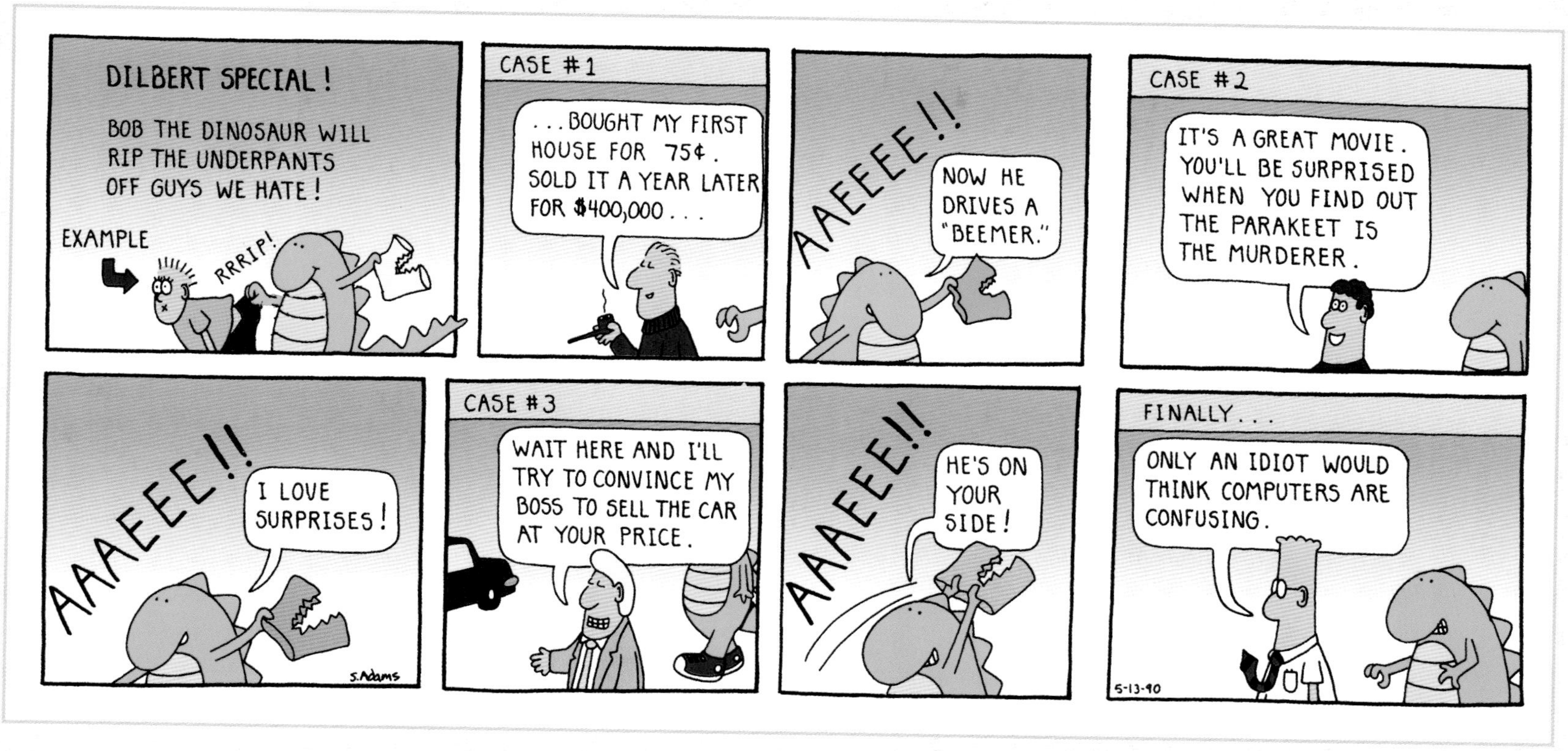
DILBERT SPECIAL!
BOB THE DINOSAUR WILL RIP THE UNDERPANTS OFF GUYS WE HATE!
EXAMPLE
RRRIP!
CASE #1
...BOUGHT MY FIRST HOUSE FOR 75¢. SOLD IT A YEAR LATER FOR $400,000...
AAEEEE!!
NOW HE DRIVES A "BEEMER."
CASE #2
IT'S A GREAT MOVIE. YOU'LL BE SURPRISED WHEN YOU FIND OUT THE PARAKEET IS THE MURDERER.
AAAEEE!!
I LOVE SURPRISES!
S.Adams
CASE #3
WAIT HERE AND I'LL TRY TO CONVINCE MY BOSS TO SELL THE CAR AT YOUR PRICE.
AAAEEE!!
HE'S ON YOUR SIDE!
FINALLY...
ONLY AN IDIOT WOULD THINK COMPUTERS ARE CONFUSING.
5-13-90

This is essentially the same joke as the one at the top of the previous page.
It's an unexpected solution to the problem of how to hassle the maximum number of cats.

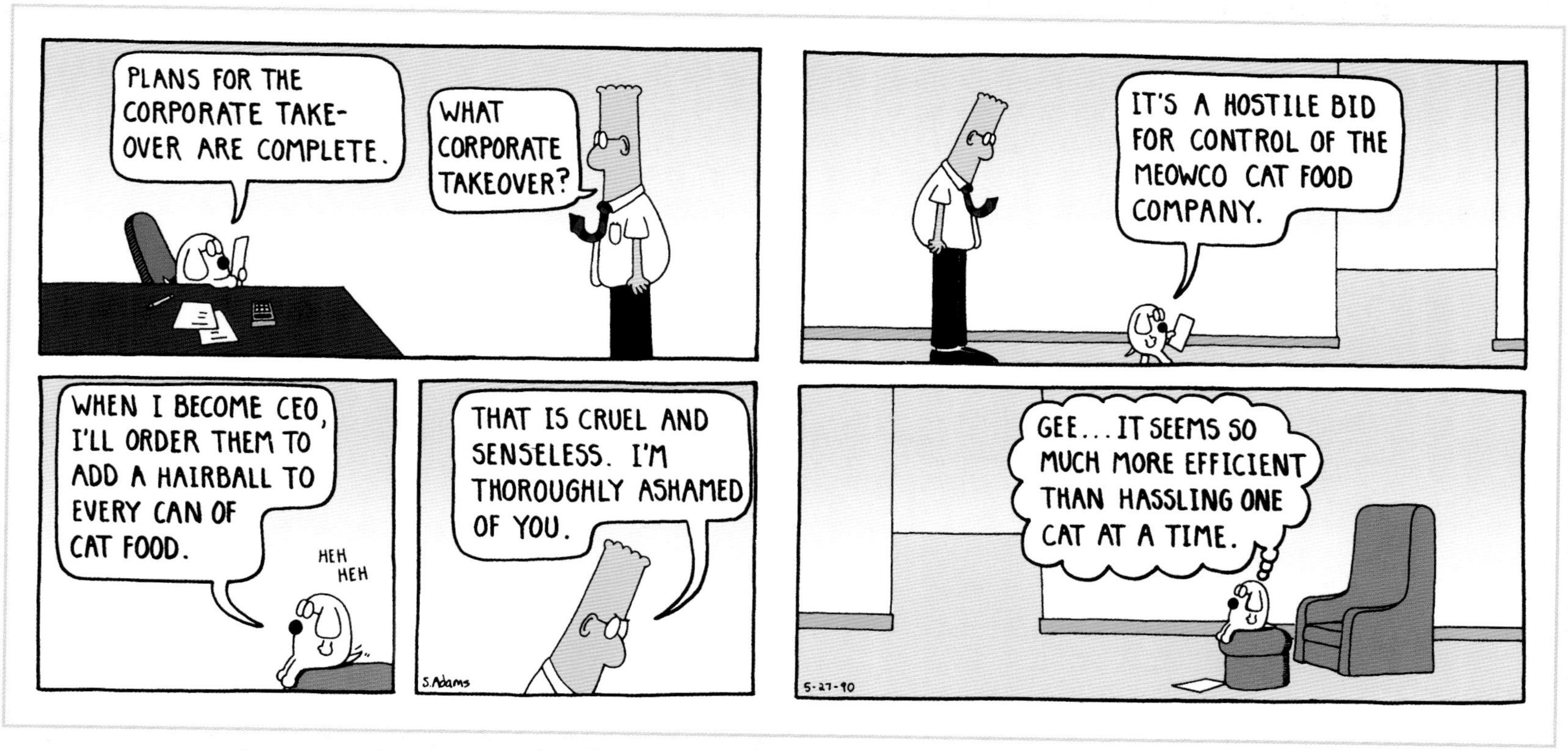
PLANS FOR THE CORPORATE TAKE-OVER ARE COMPLETE.
WHAT CORPORATE TAKEOVER?
IT'S A HOSTILE BID FOR CONTROL OF THE MEOWCO CAT FOOD COMPANY.
WHEN I BECOME CEO, I'LL ORDER THEM TO ADD A HAIRBALL TO EVERY CAN OF CAT FOOD.
HEH HEH
THAT IS CRUEL AND SENSELESS. I'M THOROUGHLY ASHAMED OF YOU.
S.Adams
GEE... IT SEEMS SO MUCH MORE EFFICIENT THAN HASSLING ONE CAT AT A TIME.
5-27-90

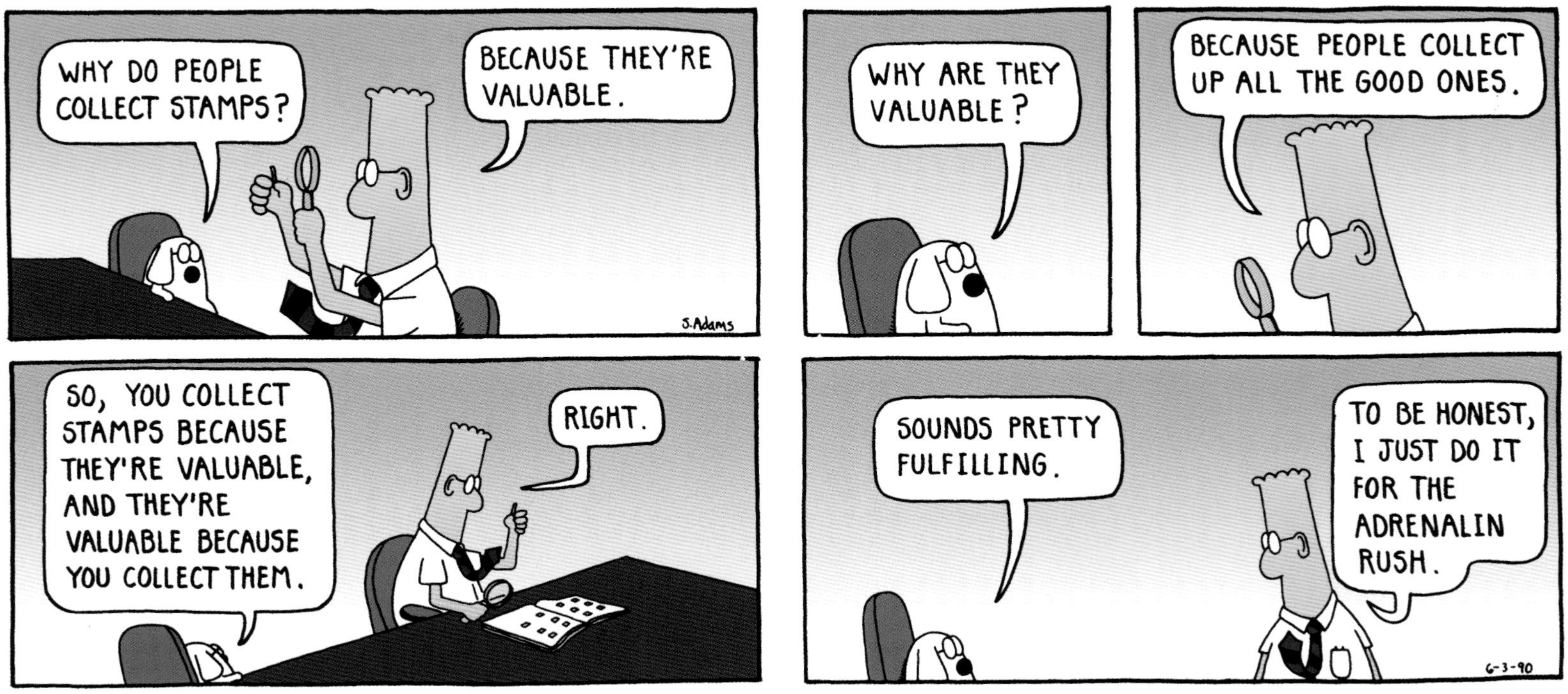
WHY DO PEOPLE COLLECT STAMPS?
BECAUSE THEY'RE VALUABLE.
S.Adams
WHY ARE THEY VALUABLE?
BECAUSE PEOPLE COLLECT UP ALL THE GOOD ONES.
SO, YOU COLLECT STAMPS BECAUSE THEY'RE VALUABLE, AND THEY'RE VALUABLE BECAUSE YOU COLLECT THEM.
RIGHT.
SOUNDS PRETTY FULFILLING.
TO BE HONEST, I JUST DO IT FOR THE ADRENALIN RUSH.
6-3-90

More than anything else, comics are an examination of our irrational nature.

This comic introduces the theme that everyone is smarter than his or her boss. That concept would become refined over the next several years, and become the genesis of my first #1 best-selling book called The Dilbert Principle.

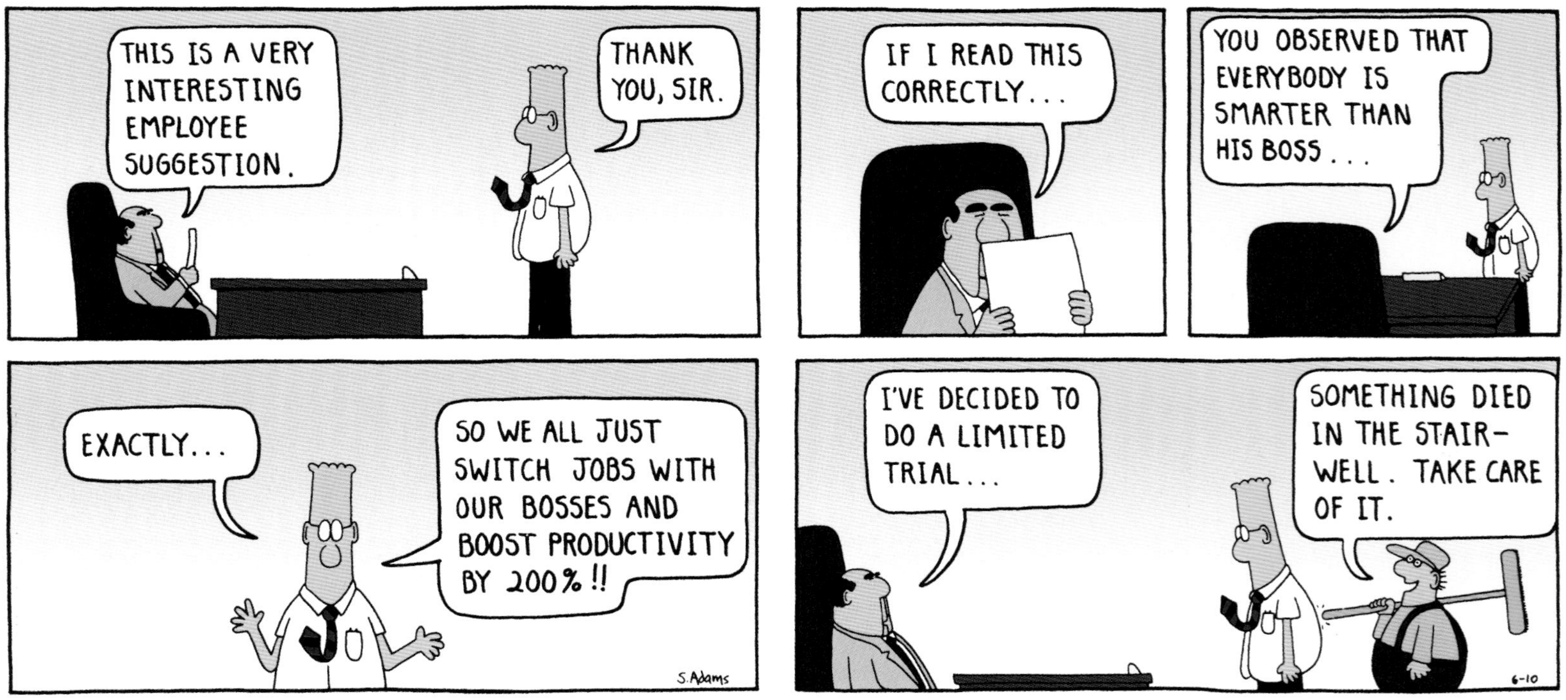
THIS IS A VERY INTERESTING EMPLOYEE SUGGESTION.
THANK YOU, SIR.
IF I READ THIS CORRECTLY...
YOU OBSERVED THAT EVERYBODY IS SMARTER THAN HIS BOSS...
EXACTLY...
SO WE ALL JUST SWITCH JOBS WITH OUR BOSSES AND BOOST PRODUCTIVITY BY 200%!!
S.Adams
I'VE DECIDED TO DO A LIMITED TRIAL...
SOMETHING DIED IN THE STAIR-WELL. TAKE CARE OF IT.
6-10

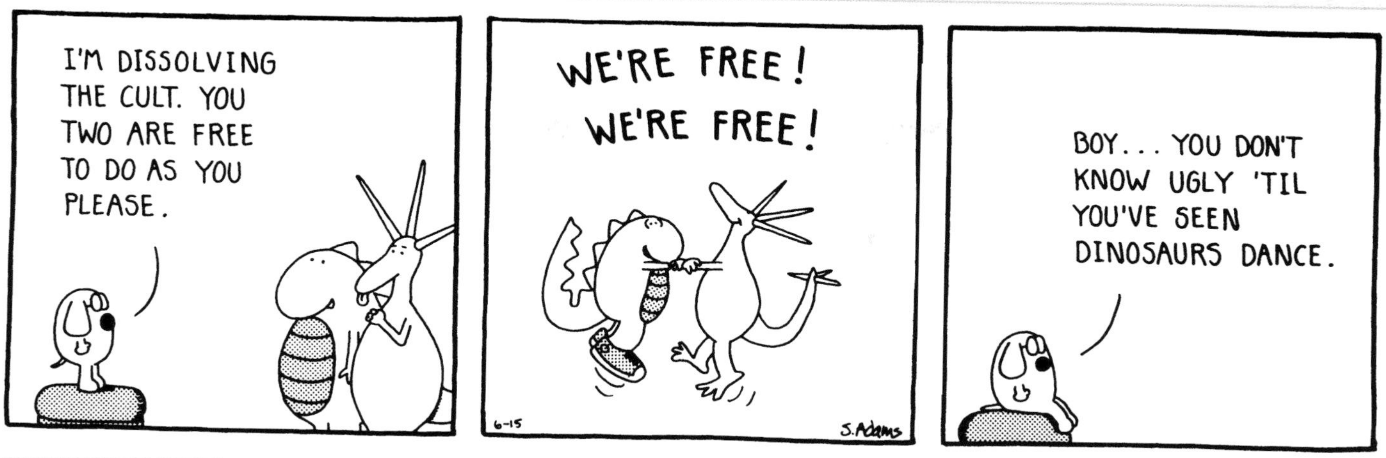
I'M DISSOLVING THE CULT. YOU TWO ARE FREE TO DO AS YOU PLEASE.
WE'RE FREE! WE'RE FREE!
BOY... YOU DON'T KNOW UGLY 'TIL YOU'VE SEEN DINOSAURS DANCE.
6-15
S.Adams

Eventually the dinosaurs would become (almost) extinct in the Dilbert comic. Bob the dinosaur still makes occasional appearances in the strip, but his mate, Dawn, disappeared altogether.

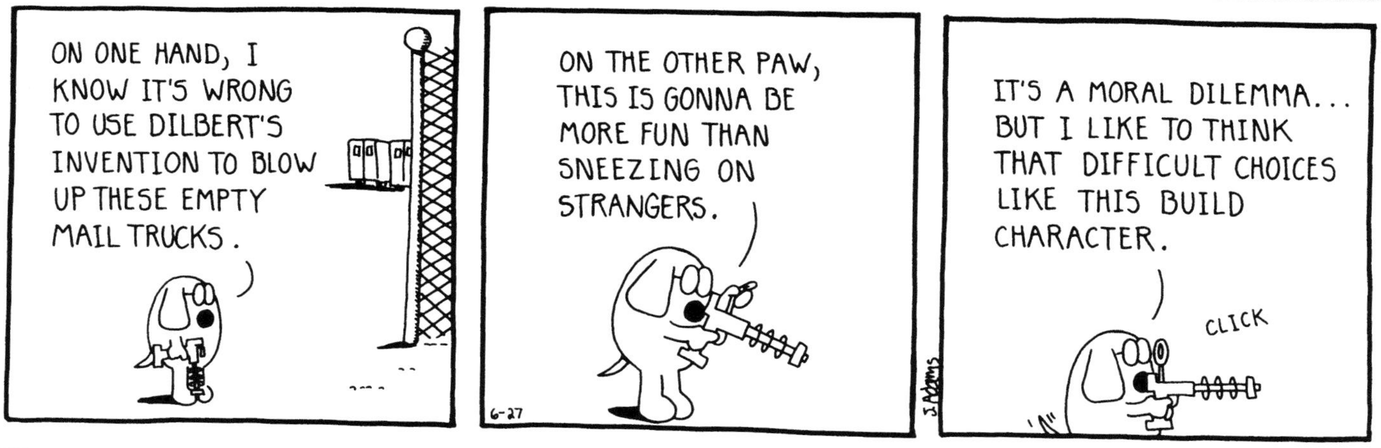
ON ONE HAND, I KNOW IT'S WRONG TO USE DILBERT'S INVENTION TO BLOW UP THESE EMPTY MAIL TRUCKS.
ON THE OTHER PAW, THIS IS GONNA BE MORE FUN THAN SNEEZING ON STRANGERS.
IT'S A MORAL DILEMMA... BUT I LIKE TO THINK THAT DIFFICULT CHOICES LIKE THIS BUILD CHARACTER.
CLICK
6-27
S.Adams

Dogbert is evolving into a more aggressive character.

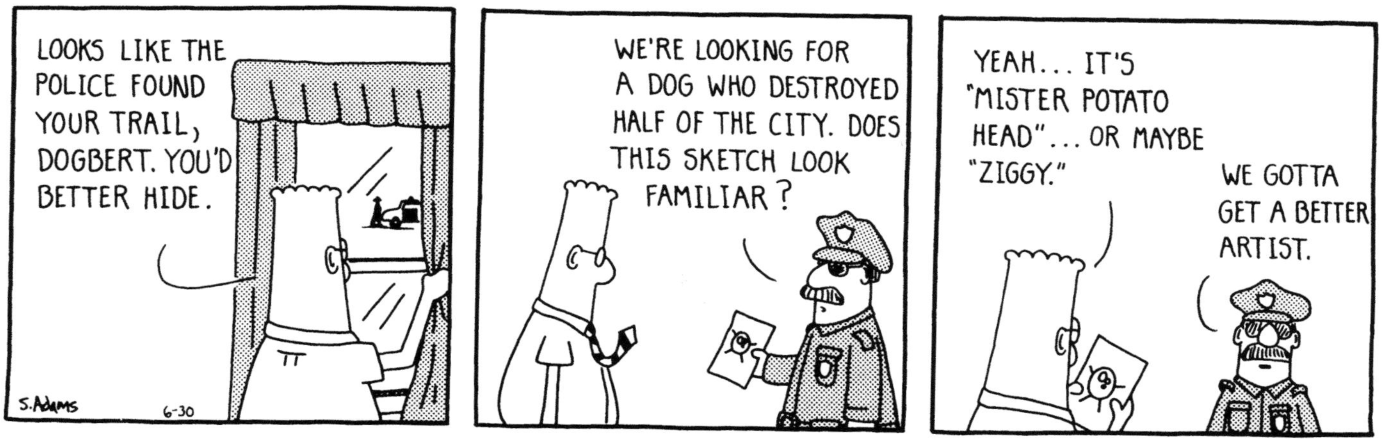
LOOKS LIKE THE POLICE FOUND YOUR TRAIL, DOGBERT. YOU'D BETTER HIDE.
S.Adams
6-30
WE'RE LOOKING FOR A DOG WHO DESTROYED HALF OF THE CITY. DOES THIS SKETCH LOOK FAMILIAR?
YEAH... IT'S "MISTER POTATO HEAD"... OR MAYBE "ZIGGY."
WE GOTTA GET A BETTER ARTIST.

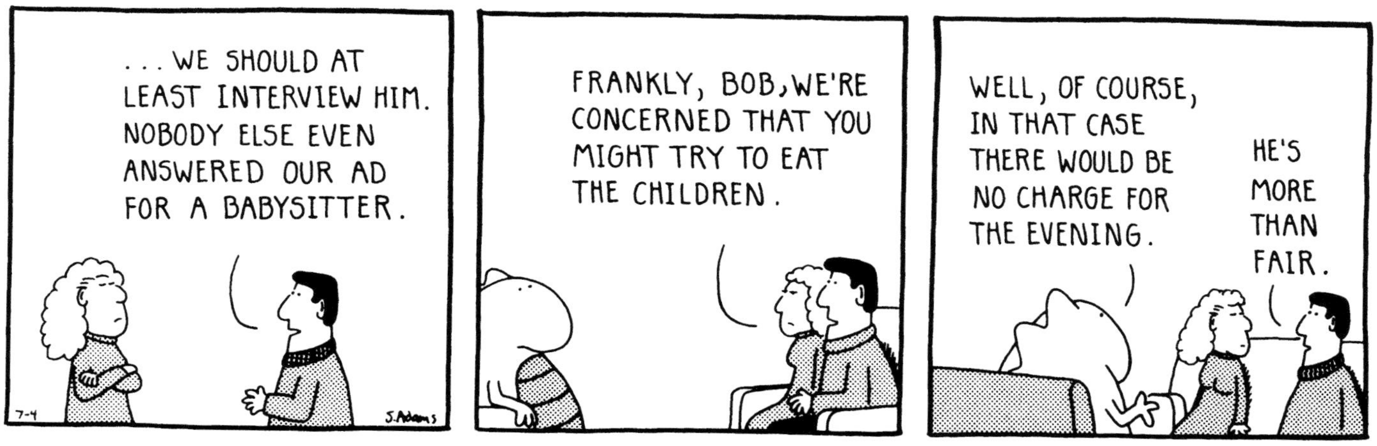
...WE SHOULD AT LEAST INTERVIEW HIM. NOBODY ELSE EVEN ANSWERED OUR AD FOR A BABYSITTER.
7-4
S.Adams
FRANKLY, BOB, WE'RE CONCERNED THAT YOU MIGHT TRY TO EAT THE CHILDREN.
WELL, OF COURSE, IN THAT CASE THERE WOULD BE NO CHARGE FOR THE EVENING.
HE'S MORE THAN FAIR.

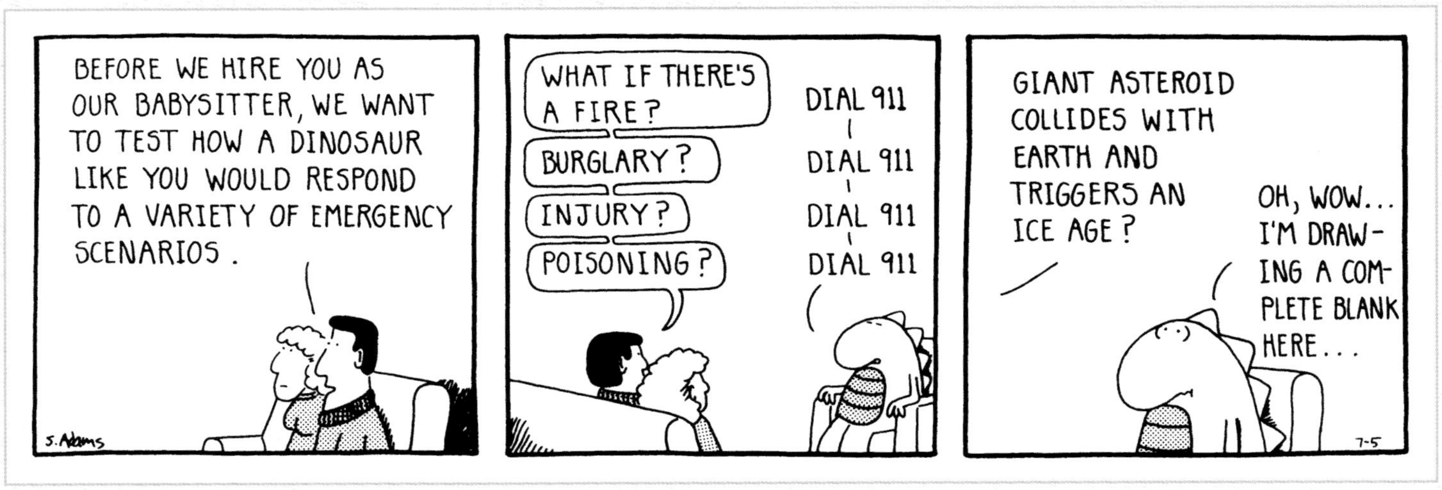
BEFORE WE HIRE YOU AS OUR BABYSITTER, WE WANT TO TEST HOW A DINOSAUR LIKE YOU WOULD RESPOND TO A VARIETY OF EMERGENCY SCENARIOS.
WHAT IF THERE'S A FIRE?
BURGLARY?
INJURY?
POISONING?
DIAL 911
DIAL 911
DIAL 911
DIAL 911
GIANT ASTEROID COLLIDES WITH EARTH AND TRIGGERS AN ICE AGE?
OH, WOW... I'M DRAWING A COMPLETE BLANK HERE...
S. Adams
7-5

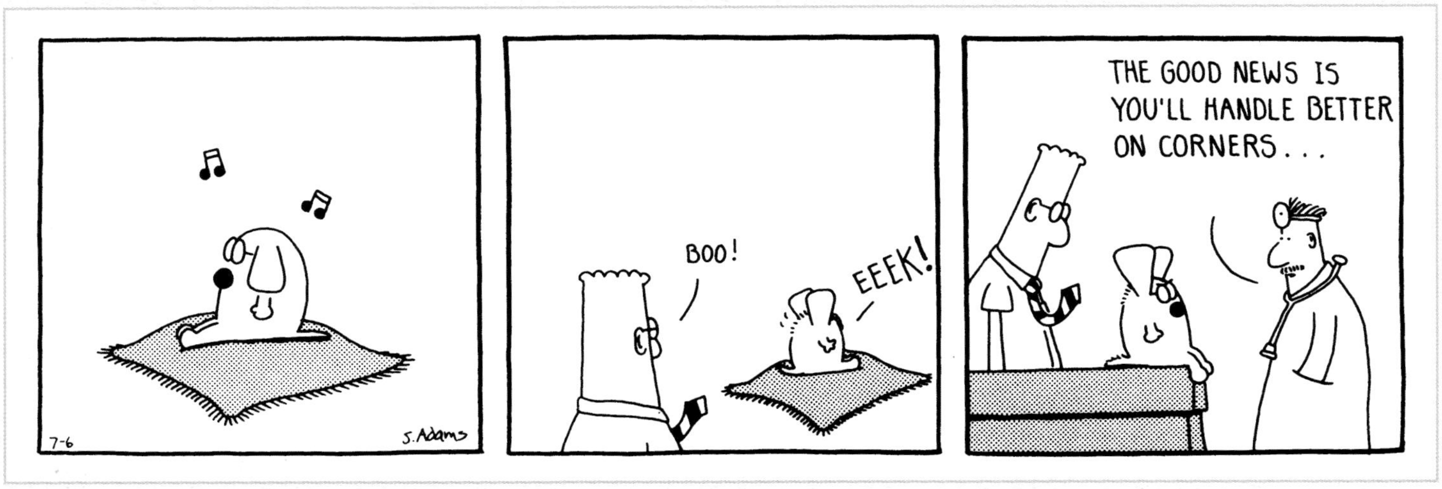
7-6
S. Adams
BOO!
EEEK!
THE GOOD NEWS IS YOU'LL HANDLE BETTER ON CORNERS...

This comic had nothing to do with the punch line and everything to do with the fact that Dogbert is ridiculously cute with his ears up.

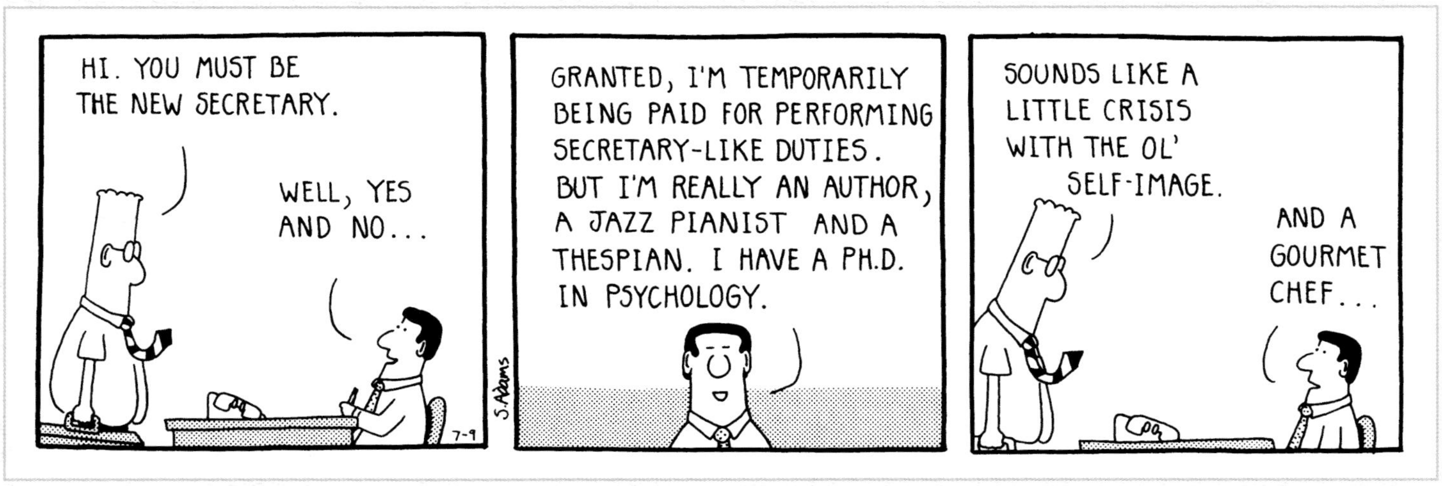
HI. YOU MUST BE THE NEW SECRETARY.
WELL, YES AND NO...
7-9
S. Adams
GRANTED, I'M TEMPORARILY BEING PAID FOR PERFORMING SECRETARY-LIKE DUTIES. BUT I'M REALLY AN AUTHOR, A JAZZ PIANIST AND A THESPIAN. I HAVE A PH.D. IN PSYCHOLOGY.
SOUNDS LIKE A LITTLE CRISIS WITH THE OL' SELF-IMAGE.
AND A GOURMET CHEF...

This series, which was based on several real people combined into one secretary, is when I started to realize how much comic fodder was available in the workplace.

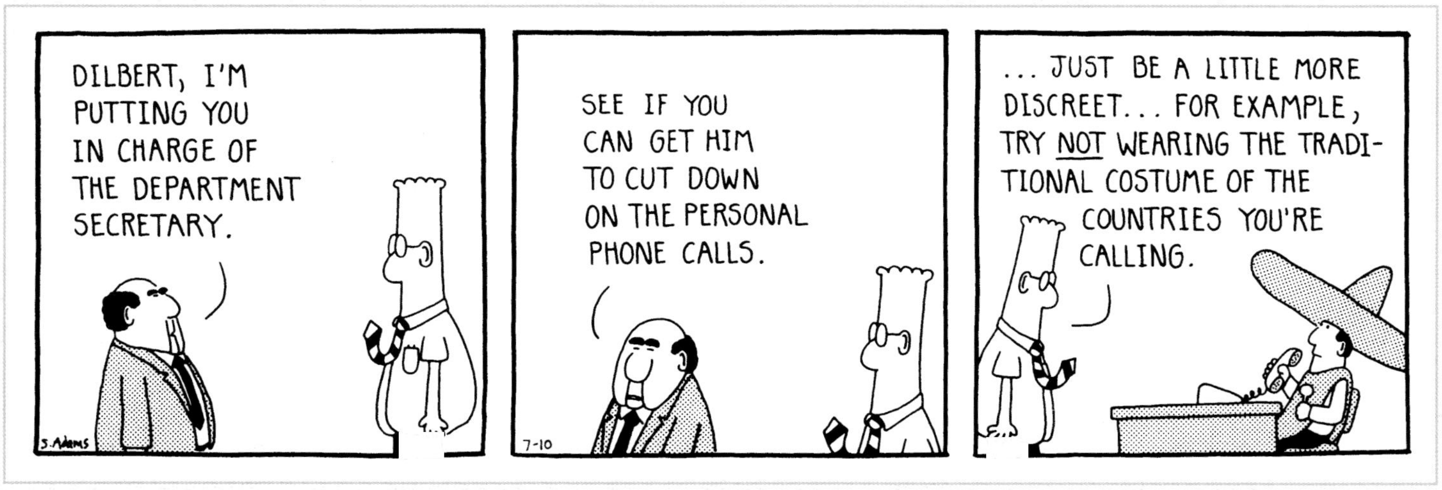
DILBERT, I'M PUTTING YOU IN CHARGE OF THE DEPARTMENT SECRETARY.
S. Adams
SEE IF YOU CAN GET HIM TO CUT DOWN ON THE PERSONAL PHONE CALLS.
7-10
... JUST BE A LITTLE MORE DISCREET... FOR EXAMPLE, TRY NOT WEARING THE TRADITIONAL COSTUME OF THE COUNTRIES YOU'RE CALLING.

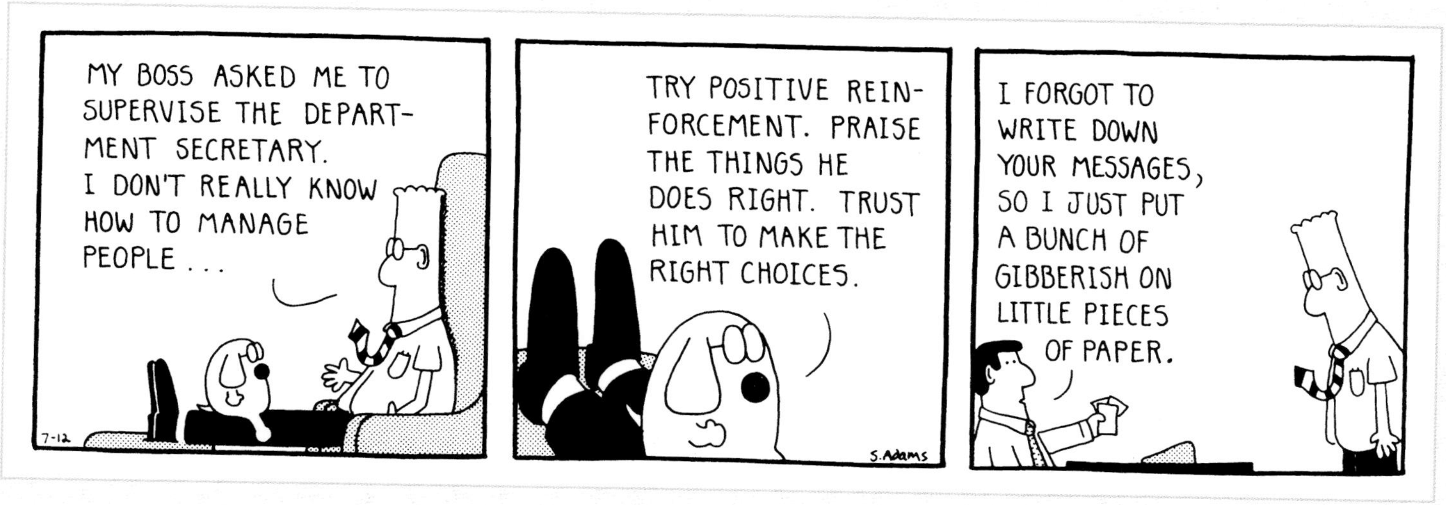
MY BOSS ASKED ME TO SUPERVISE THE DEPARTMENT SECRETARY. I DON'T REALLY KNOW HOW TO MANAGE PEOPLE . . .
TRY POSITIVE REINFORCEMENT. PRAISE THE THINGS HE DOES RIGHT. TRUST HIM TO MAKE THE RIGHT CHOICES.
I FORGOT TO WRITE DOWN YOUR MESSAGES, SO I JUST PUT A BUNCH OF GIBBERISH ON LITTLE PIECES OF PAPER.

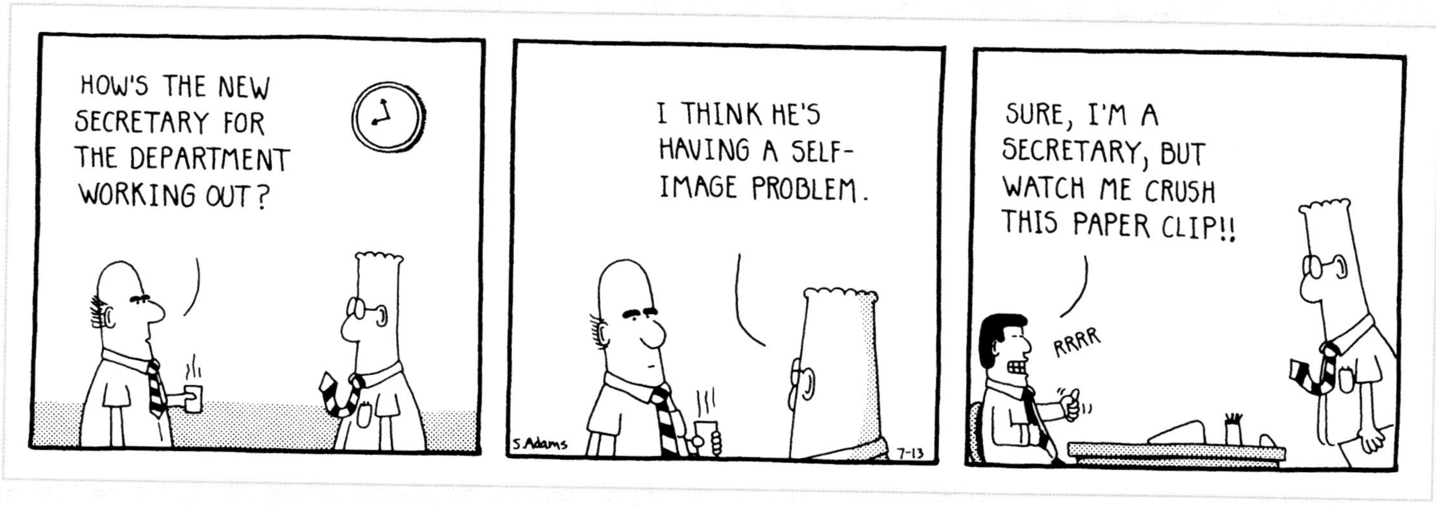
HOW'S THE NEW SECRETARY FOR THE DEPARTMENT WORKING OUT?
I THINK HE'S HAVING A SELF-IMAGE PROBLEM.
SURE, I'M A SECRETARY, BUT WATCH ME CRUSH THIS PAPER CLIP!!
RRRR

Here's another early version of the character who would become Wally.

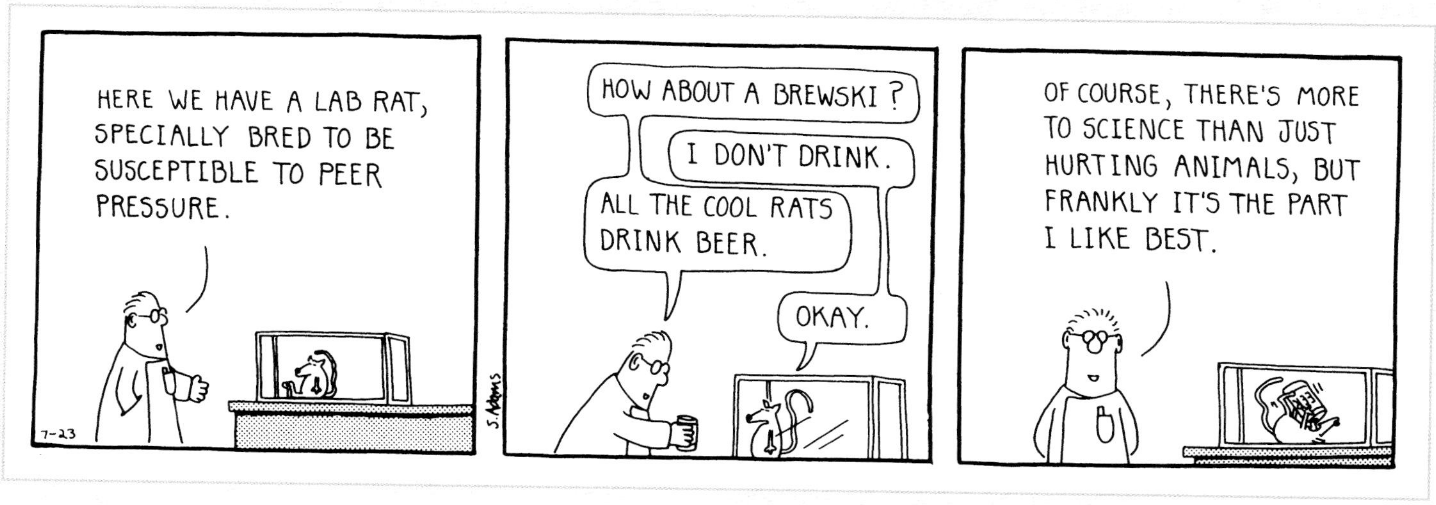
HERE WE HAVE A LAB RAT, SPECIALLY BRED TO BE SUSCEPTIBLE TO PEER PRESSURE.
HOW ABOUT A BREWSKI?
I DON'T DRINK.
ALL THE COOL RATS DRINK BEER.
OKAY.
OF COURSE, THERE'S MORE TO SCIENCE THAN JUST HURTING ANIMALS, BUT FRANKLY IT'S THE PART I LIKE BEST.

This is the origin of Ratbert. I didn't contemplate him as a regular at this point. He just emerged.

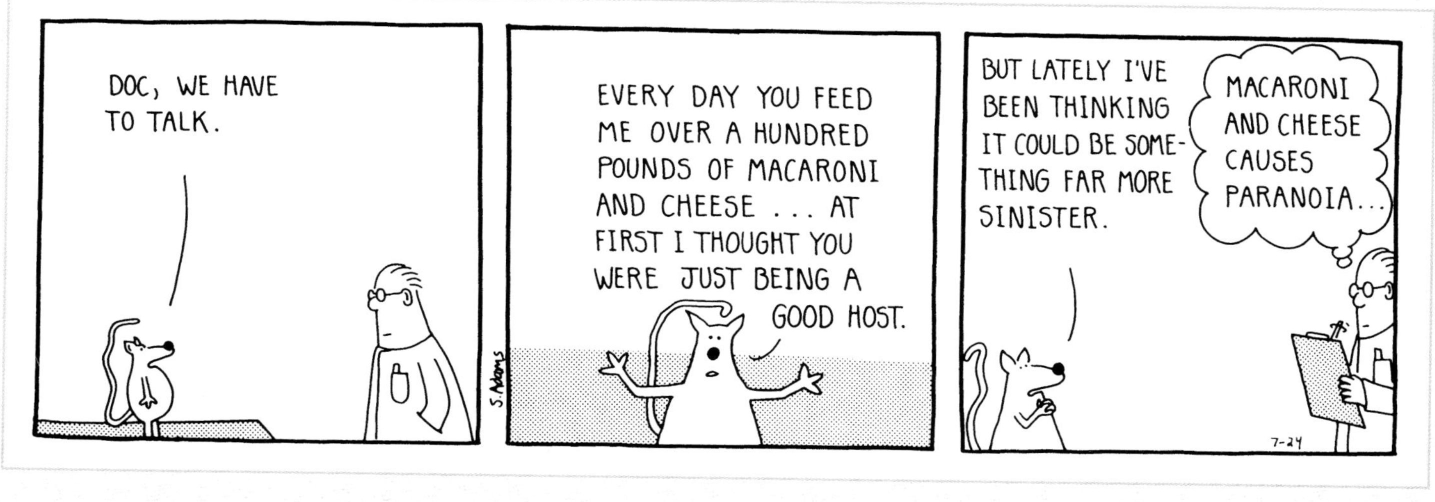
DOC, WE HAVE TO TALK.
EVERY DAY YOU FEED ME OVER A HUNDRED POUNDS OF MACARONI AND CHEESE . . . AT FIRST I THOUGHT YOU WERE JUST BEING A GOOD HOST.
BUT LATELY I'VE BEEN THINKING IT COULD BE SOMETHING FAR MORE SINISTER.
MACARONI AND CHEESE CAUSES PARANOIA . . .

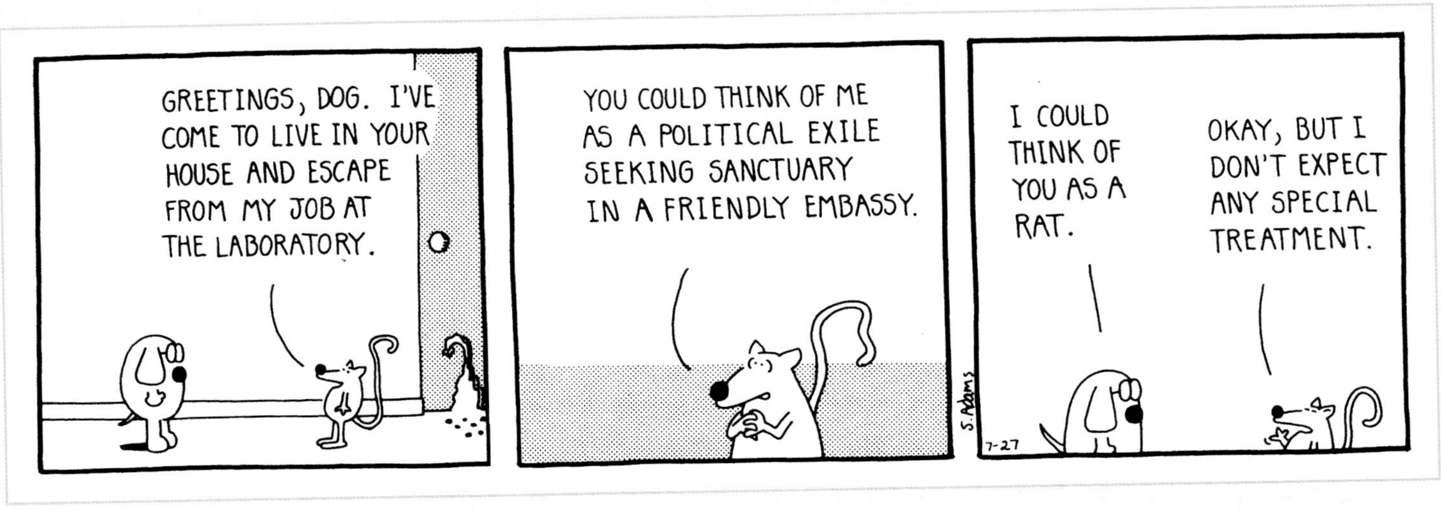
GREETINGS, DOG. I'VE COME TO LIVE IN YOUR HOUSE AND ESCAPE FROM MY JOB AT THE LABORATORY.
YOU COULD THINK OF ME AS A POLITICAL EXILE SEEKING SANCTUARY IN A FRIENDLY EMBASSY.
I COULD THINK OF YOU AS A RAT.
OKAY, BUT I DON'T EXPECT ANY SPECIAL TREATMENT.
S. Adams
7-27

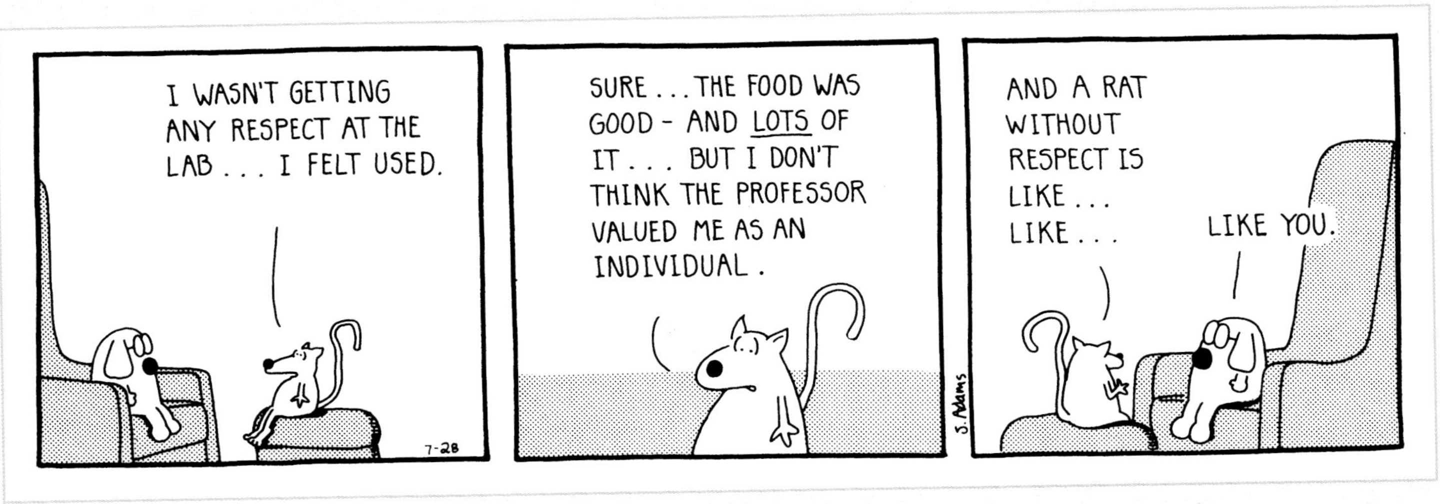
I WASN'T GETTING ANY RESPECT AT THE LAB . . . I FELT USED.
7-28
SURE . . . THE FOOD WAS GOOD - AND LOTS OF IT . . . BUT I DON'T THINK THE PROFESSOR VALUED ME AS AN INDIVIDUAL.
S. Adams
AND A RAT WITHOUT RESPECT IS LIKE . . . LIKE . . .
LIKE YOU.

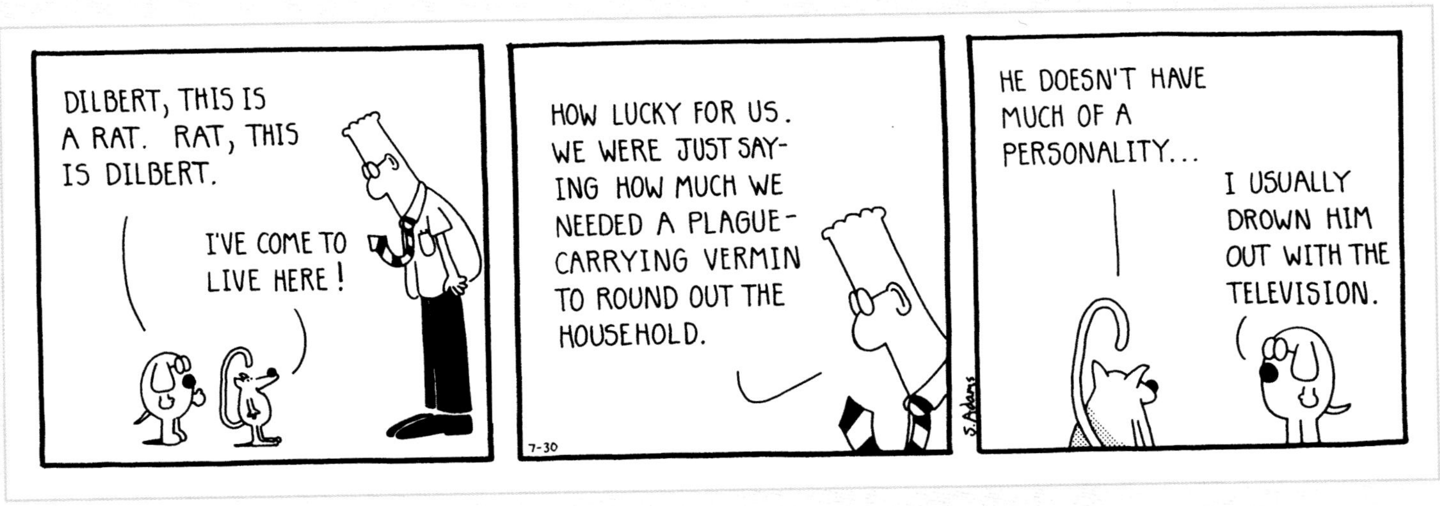
DILBERT, THIS IS A RAT. RAT, THIS IS DILBERT.
I'VE COME TO LIVE HERE!
HOW LUCKY FOR US. WE WERE JUST SAYING HOW MUCH WE NEEDED A PLAGUE-CARRYING VERMIN TO ROUND OUT THE HOUSEHOLD.
7-30
S. Adams
HE DOESN'T HAVE MUCH OF A PERSONALITY...
I USUALLY DROWN HIM OUT WITH THE TELEVISION.

Once he had a name, I knew he was a keeper.

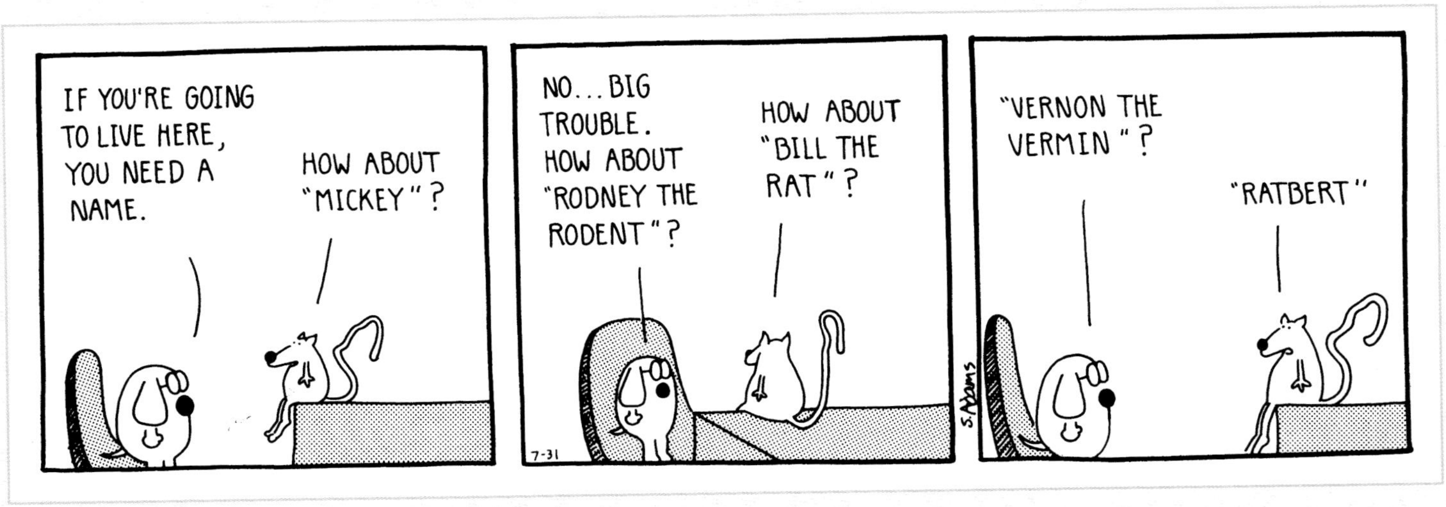
IF YOU'RE GOING TO LIVE HERE, YOU NEED A NAME.
HOW ABOUT "MICKEY"?
NO... BIG TROUBLE. HOW ABOUT "RODNEY THE RODENT"?
HOW ABOUT "BILL THE RAT"?
7-31
S. Adams
"VERNON THE VERMIN"?
"RATBERT"

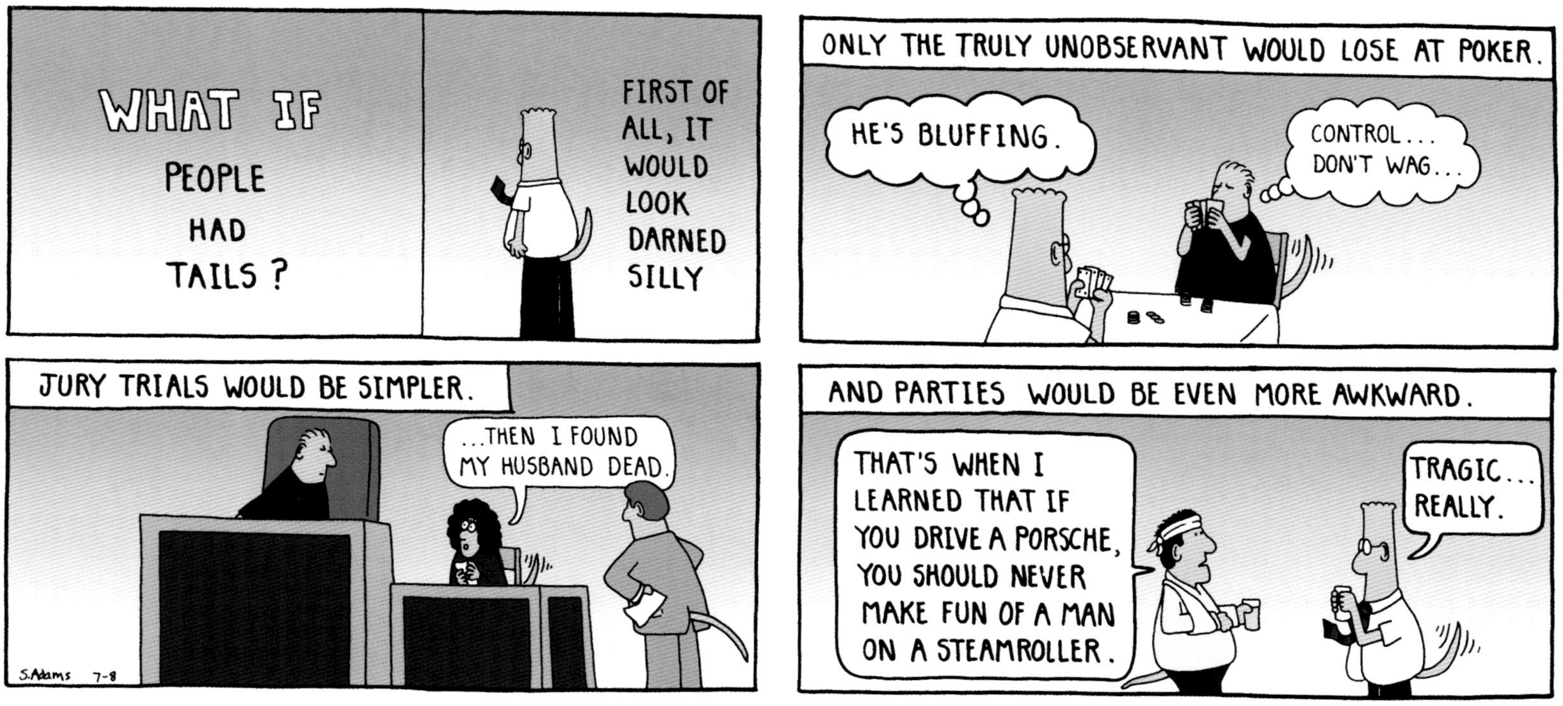
WHAT IF PEOPLE HAD TAILS?
FIRST OF ALL, IT WOULD LOOK DARNED SILLY
ONLY THE TRULY UNOBSERVANT WOULD LOSE AT POKER.
HE'S BLUFFING.
CONTROL... DON'T WAG...
JURY TRIALS WOULD BE SIMPLER.
...THEN I FOUND MY HUSBAND DEAD.
S.Adams 7-8
AND PARTIES WOULD BE EVEN MORE AWKWARD.
THAT'S WHEN I LEARNED THAT IF YOU DRIVE A PORSCHE, YOU SHOULD NEVER MAKE FUN OF A MAN ON A STEAMROLLER.
TRAGIC... REALLY.

In the early '90s, bosses didn't generally feel it was necessary to pretend they cared about the little people. That changed during the dot-com era when skilled workers were in great demand.

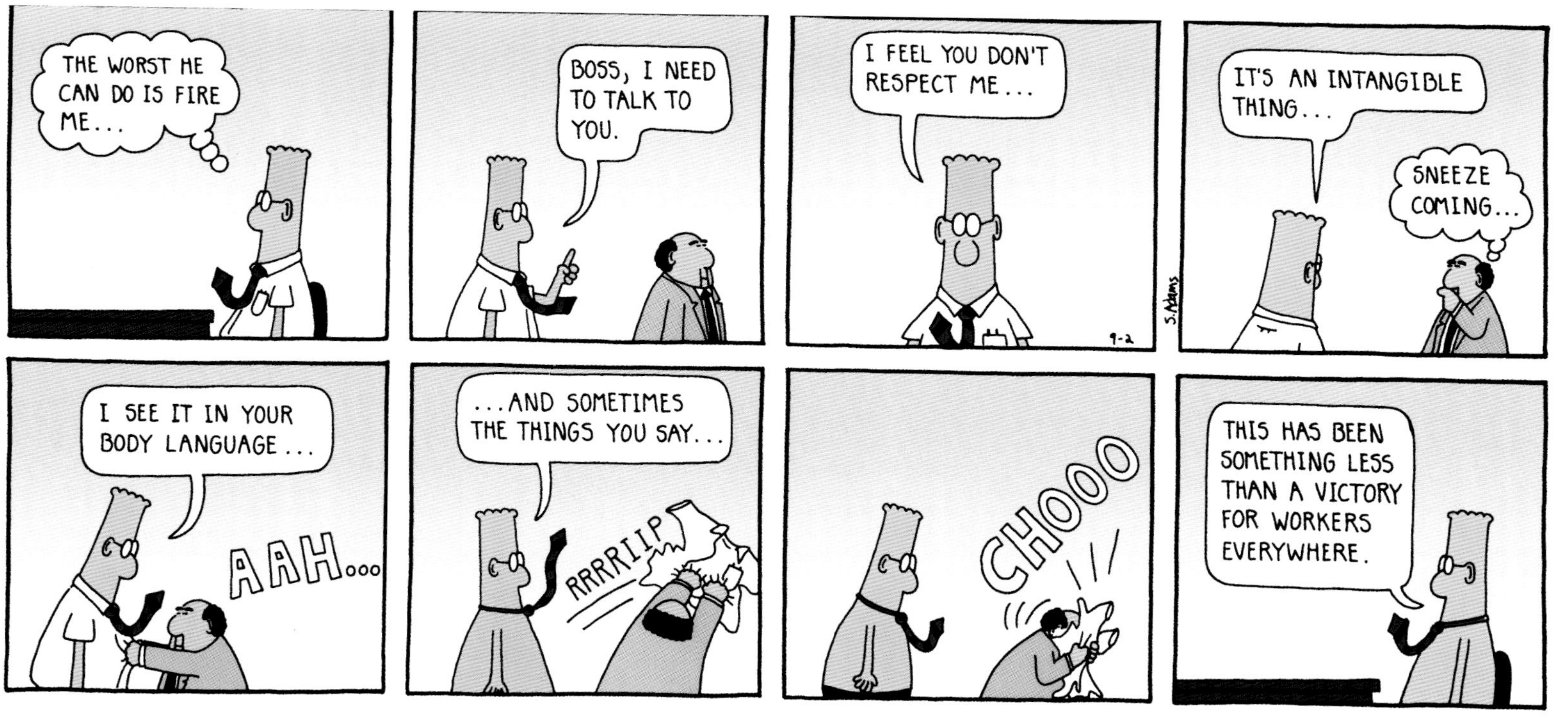
THE WORST HE CAN DO IS FIRE ME...
BOSS, I NEED TO TALK TO YOU.
I FEEL YOU DON'T RESPECT ME...
9-2
S.Adams
IT'S AN INTANGIBLE THING...
SNEEZE COMING...
I SEE IT IN YOUR BODY LANGUAGE...
AAH...
...AND SOMETIMES THE THINGS YOU SAY...
RRRRIIP
CHOOO
THIS HAS BEEN SOMETHING LESS THAN A VICTORY FOR WORKERS EVERYWHERE.

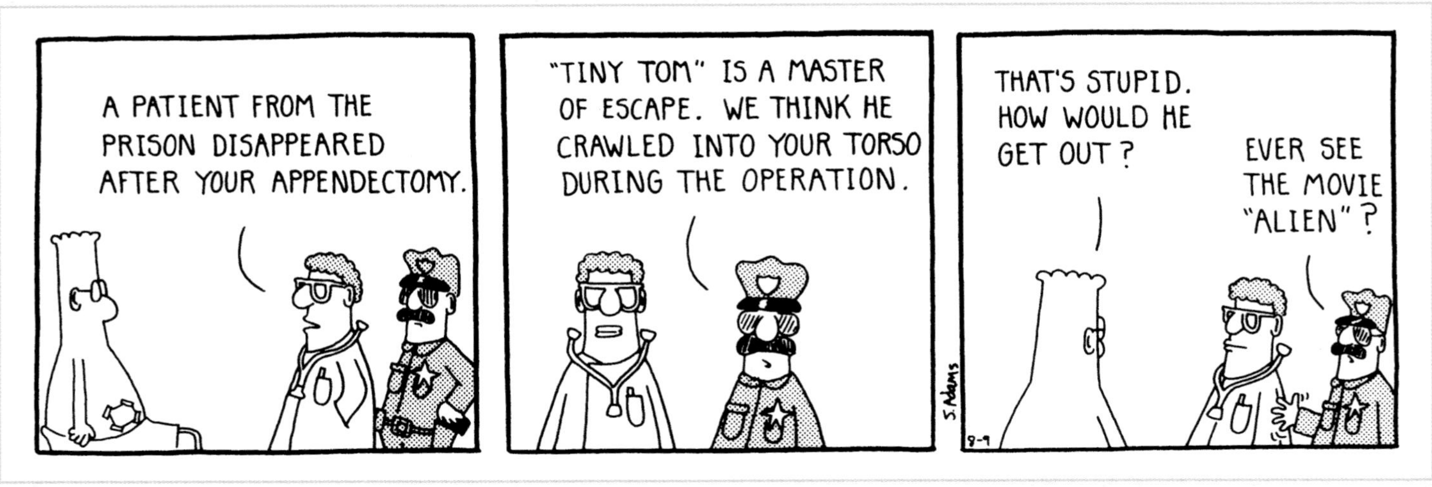
A PATIENT FROM THE PRISON DISAPPEARED AFTER YOUR APPENDECTOMY.
"TINY TOM" IS A MASTER OF ESCAPE. WE THINK HE CRAWLED INTO YOUR TORSO DURING THE OPERATION.
THAT'S STUPID. HOW WOULD HE GET OUT?
EVER SEE THE MOVIE "ALIEN"?
S. Adams
8-9

My artistic instinct drew me toward the absurd. It was a mistake.
The more absurd the comic, the less funny it was, as in this example.

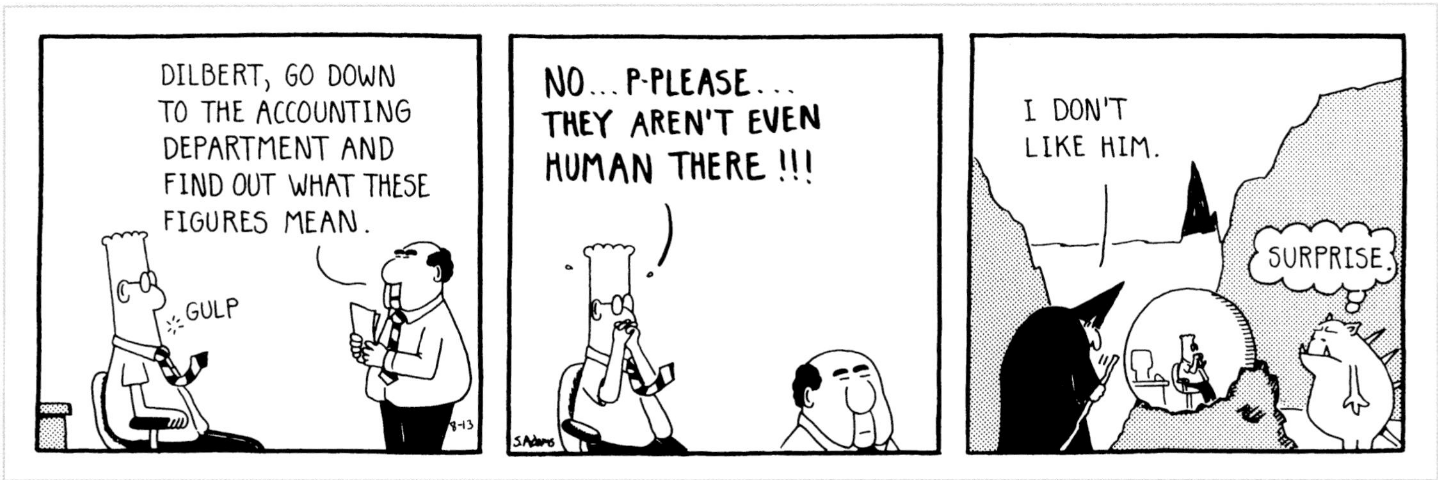
DILBERT, GO DOWN TO THE ACCOUNTING DEPARTMENT AND FIND OUT WHAT THESE FIGURES MEAN.
GULP
8-13
NO... P-PLEASE... THEY AREN'T EVEN HUMAN THERE!!!
S. Adams
I DON'T LIKE HIM.
SURPRISE.

The boss's hair was not yet pointy shaped, and he had jowls.

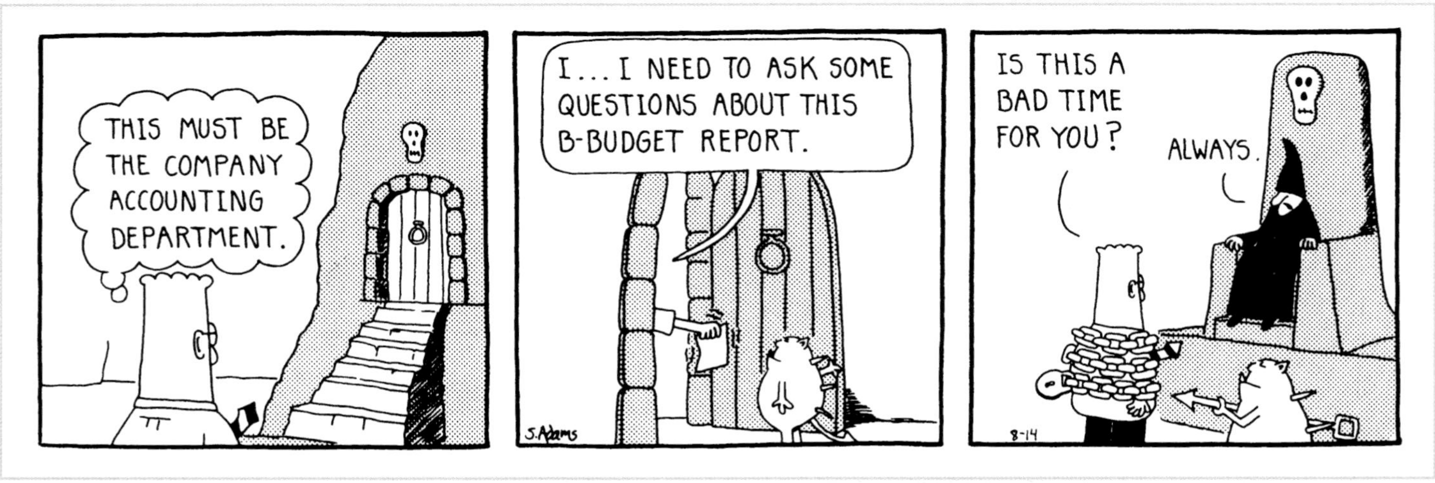
THIS MUST BE THE COMPANY ACCOUNTING DEPARTMENT.
I... I NEED TO ASK SOME QUESTIONS ABOUT THIS B-BUDGET REPORT.
S. Adams
IS THIS A BAD TIME FOR YOU?
ALWAYS.
8-14

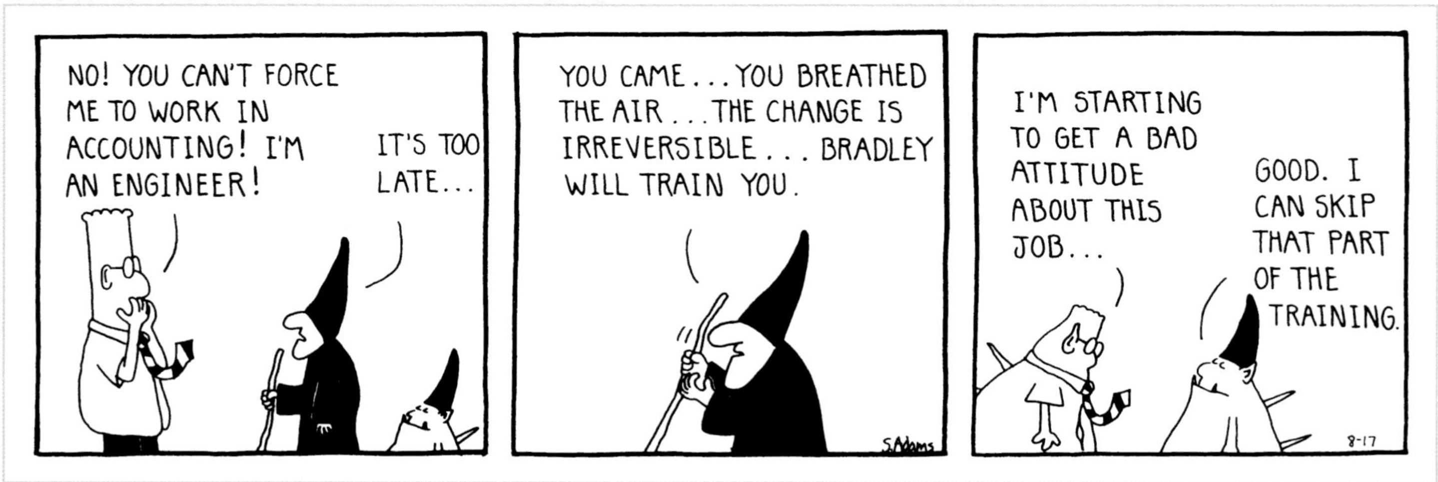
NO! YOU CAN'T FORCE ME TO WORK IN ACCOUNTING! I'M AN ENGINEER!
IT'S TOO LATE...
YOU CAME... YOU BREATHED THE AIR... THE CHANGE IS IRREVERSIBLE... BRADLEY WILL TRAIN YOU.
S. Adams
I'M STARTING TO GET A BAD ATTITUDE ABOUT THIS JOB...
GOOD. I CAN SKIP THAT PART OF THE TRAINING.
8-17

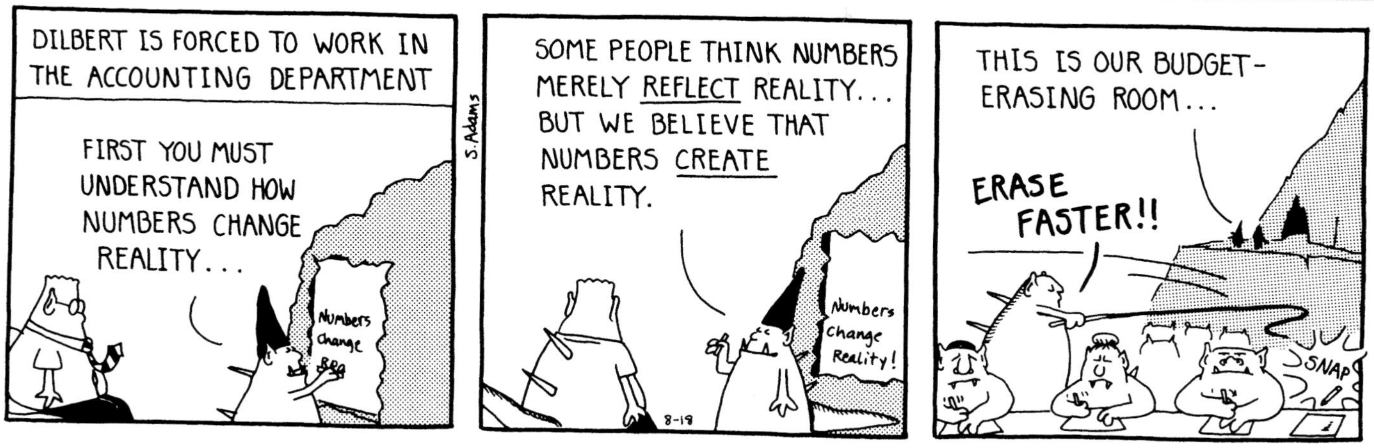
DILBERT IS FORCED TO WORK IN THE ACCOUNTING DEPARTMENT
FIRST YOU MUST UNDERSTAND HOW NUMBERS CHANGE REALITY...
Numbers Change
SOME PEOPLE THINK NUMBERS MERELY REFLECT REALITY... BUT WE BELIEVE THAT NUMBERS CREATE REALITY.
Numbers Change Reality!
THIS IS OUR BUDGET-ERASING ROOM...
ERASE FASTER!!
SNAP

When this series ran, I learned that any time I focused on a profession, the people in those jobs loved the attention. This became my marketing trick in the early years. I picked popular professions and focused on them for a day or two, knowing the friends and family of people in those types of jobs would pass the strip around and build awareness. It was hugely effective.

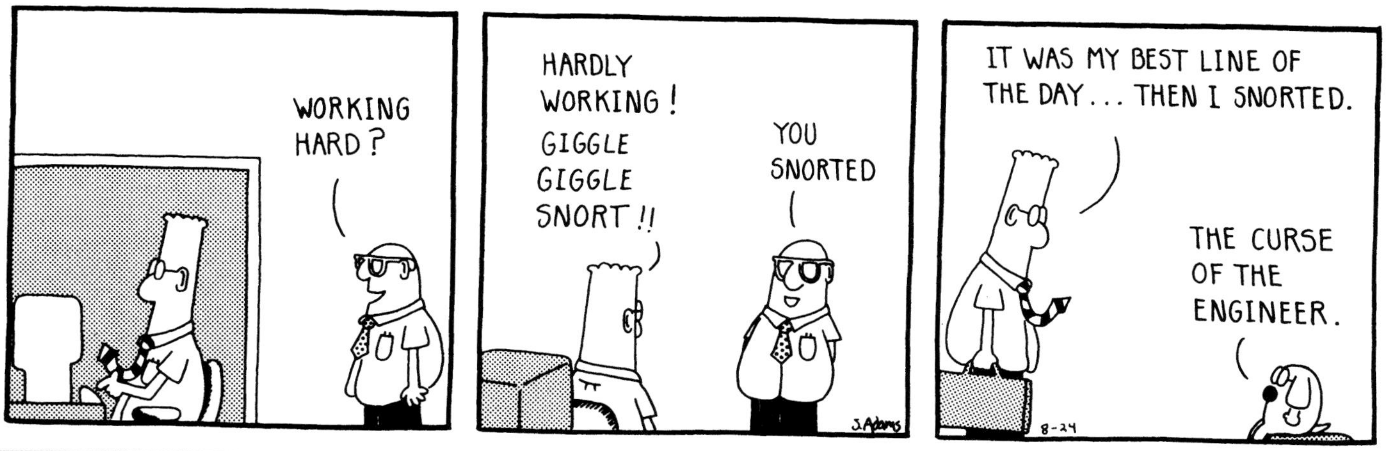
WORKING HARD?
HARDLY WORKING!
GIGGLE GIGGLE SNORT!!
YOU SNORTED
IT WAS MY BEST LINE OF THE DAY... THEN I SNORTED.
THE CURSE OF THE ENGINEER.

The pre-Wally doesn't yet have his trademark six hairs and pursed lips. His coffee cup comes later too.

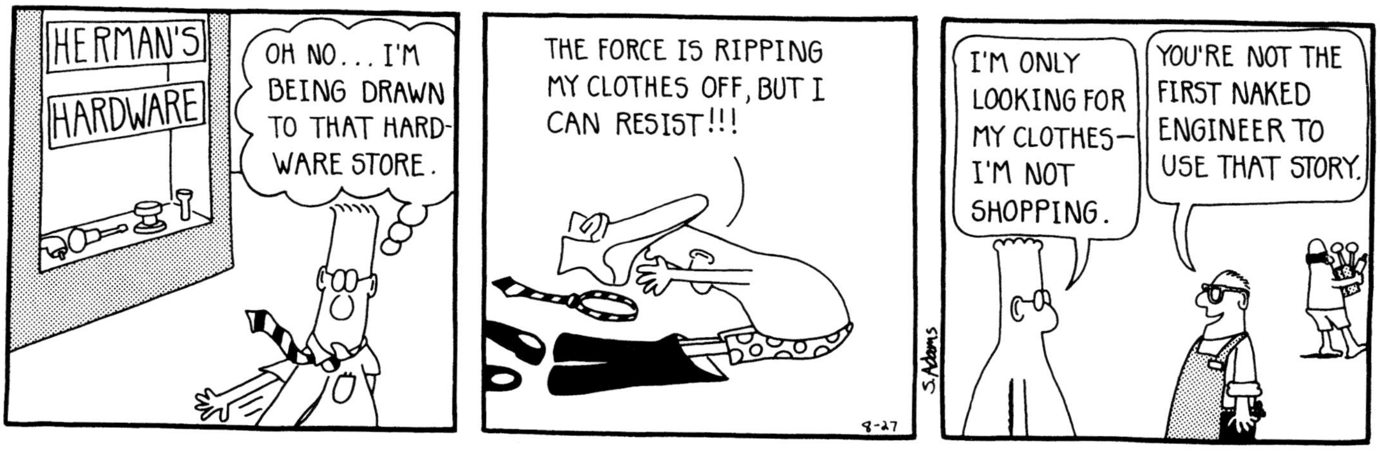
HERMAN'S
HARDWARE
OH NO... I'M BEING DRAWN TO THAT HARD-WARE STORE.
THE FORCE IS RIPPING MY CLOTHES OFF, BUT I CAN RESIST!!!
I'M ONLY LOOKING FOR MY CLOTHES— I'M NOT SHOPPING.
YOU'RE NOT THE FIRST NAKED ENGINEER TO USE THAT STORY.

This comic borrows shamelessly from a classic Far Side® *comic featuring a large woman being sucked into a candy store.*

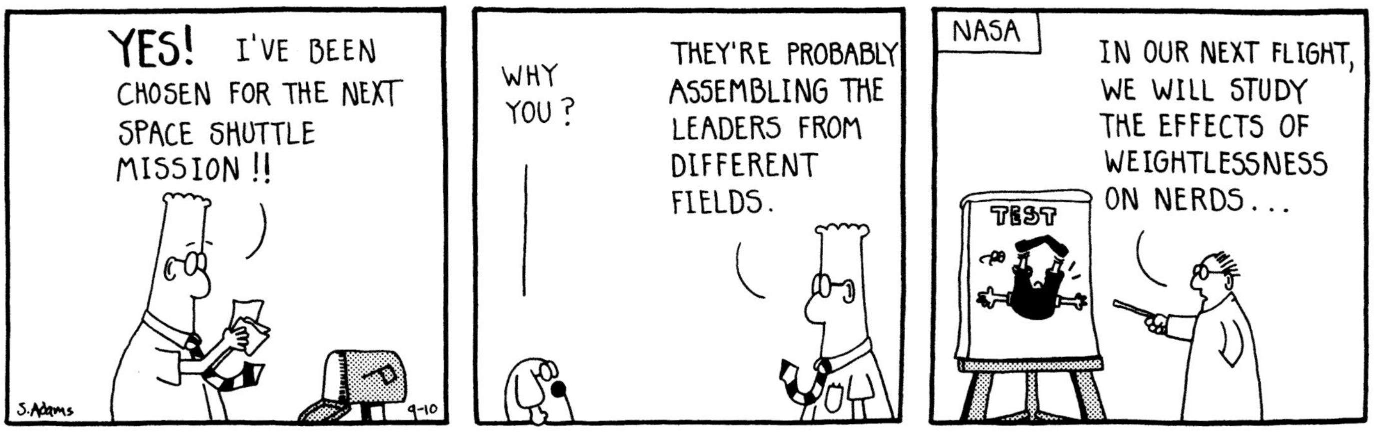
YES! I'VE BEEN CHOSEN FOR THE NEXT SPACE SHUTTLE MISSION !!
S. Adams
9-10
WHY YOU ?
THEY'RE PROBABLY ASSEMBLING THE LEADERS FROM DIFFERENT FIELDS.
NASA
TEST
IN OUR NEXT FLIGHT, WE WILL STUDY THE EFFECTS OF WEIGHTLESSNESS ON NERDS . . .

When Dilbert *became more of a workplace comic, I banned the use of the word "nerd." I didn't want it to be the defining characteristic of the strip. I wanted Dilbert to represent the Everyworker.*

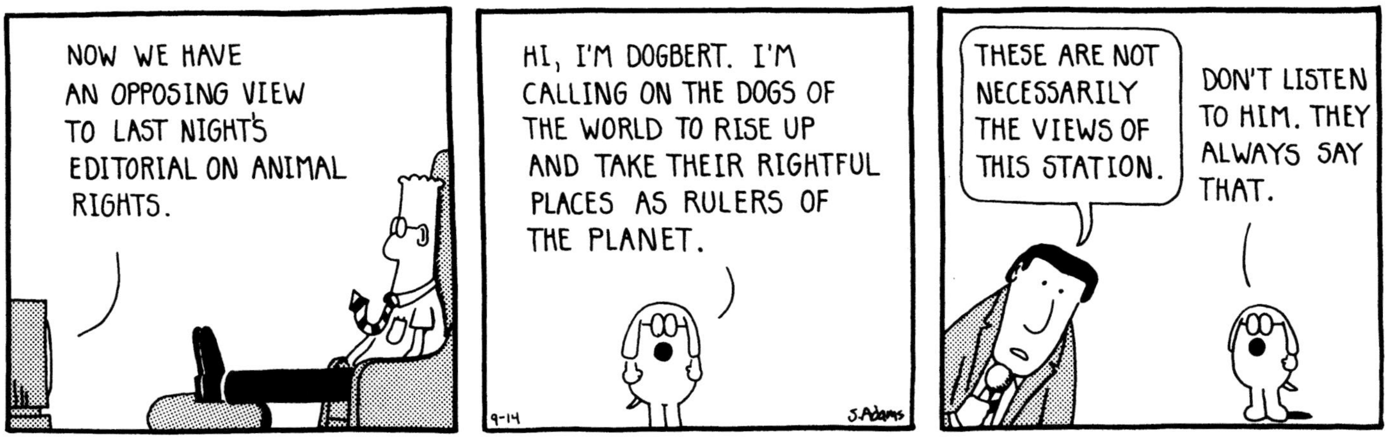
NOW WE HAVE AN OPPOSING VIEW TO LAST NIGHT'S EDITORIAL ON ANIMAL RIGHTS.
HI, I'M DOGBERT. I'M CALLING ON THE DOGS OF THE WORLD TO RISE UP AND TAKE THEIR RIGHTFUL PLACES AS RULERS OF THE PLANET.
9-14
S. Adams
THESE ARE NOT NECESSARILY THE VIEWS OF THIS STATION.
DON'T LISTEN TO HIM. THEY ALWAYS SAY THAT.

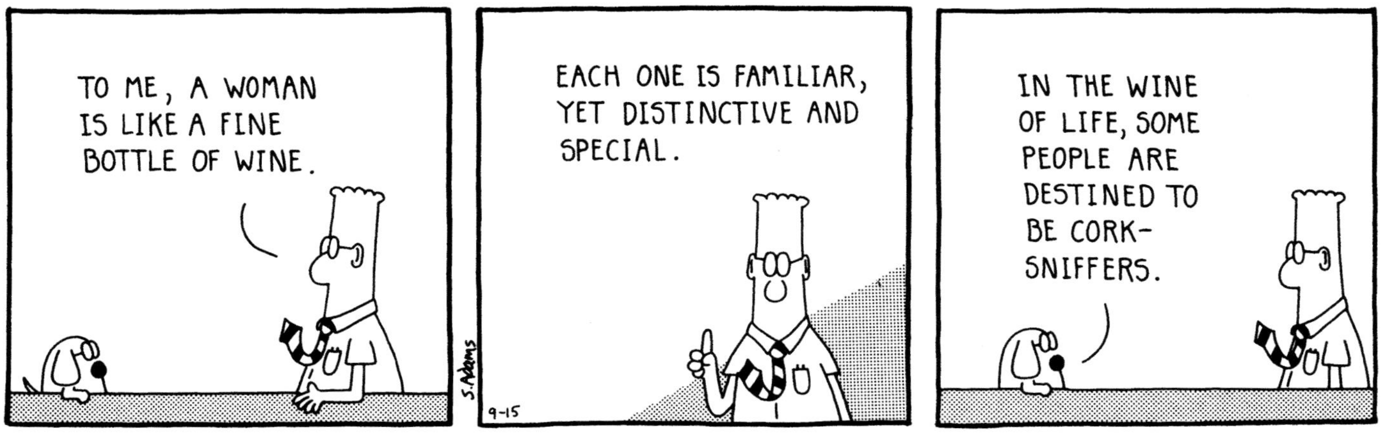
TO ME, A WOMAN IS LIKE A FINE BOTTLE OF WINE.
S. Adams
9-15
EACH ONE IS FAMILIAR, YET DISTINCTIVE AND SPECIAL.
IN THE WINE OF LIFE, SOME PEOPLE ARE DESTINED TO BE CORK-SNIFFERS.

This comic confesses one of my biggest inspirations.

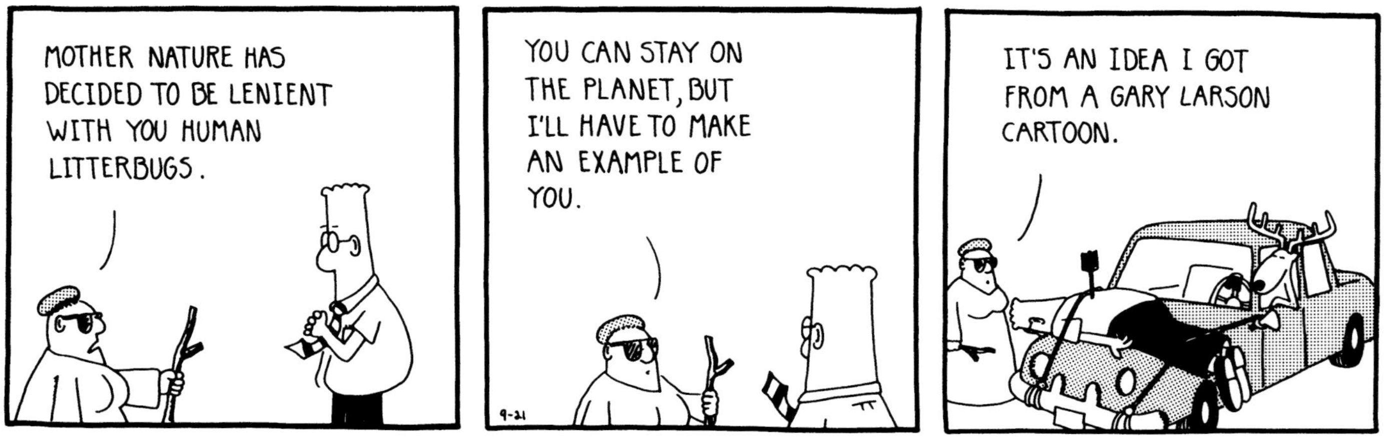
MOTHER NATURE HAS DECIDED TO BE LENIENT WITH YOU HUMAN LITTERBUGS.
YOU CAN STAY ON THE PLANET, BUT I'LL HAVE TO MAKE AN EXAMPLE OF YOU.
9-21
IT'S AN IDEA I GOT FROM A GARY LARSON CARTOON.

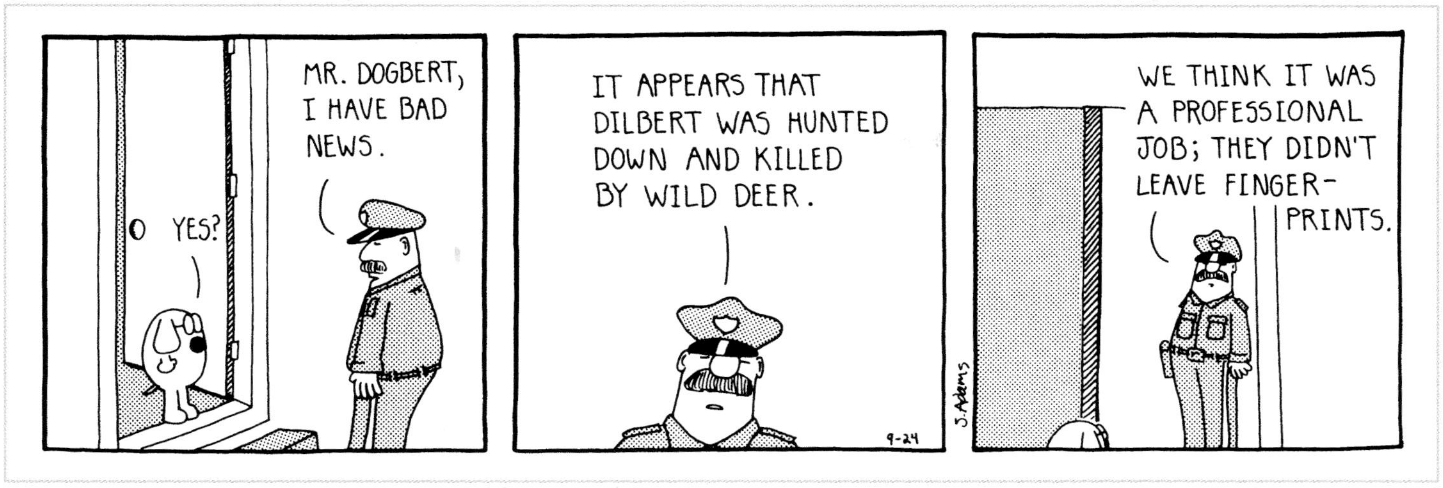
MR. DOGBERT, I HAVE BAD NEWS.
YES?
IT APPEARS THAT DILBERT WAS HUNTED DOWN AND KILLED BY WILD DEER.
WE THINK IT WAS A PROFESSIONAL JOB; THEY DIDN'T LEAVE FINGER-PRINTS.

I killed Dilbert to see if it would get any public attention. It didn't. No one yet cared.

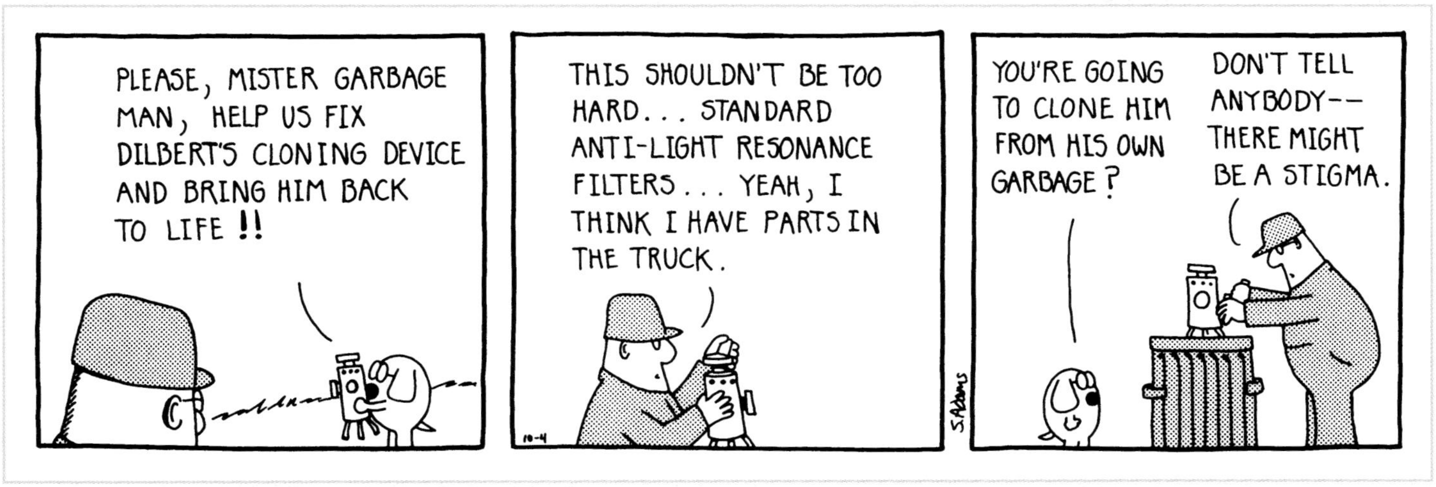
PLEASE, MISTER GARBAGE MAN, HELP US FIX DILBERT'S CLONING DEVICE AND BRING HIM BACK TO LIFE!!
THIS SHOULDN'T BE TOO HARD... STANDARD ANTI-LIGHT RESONANCE FILTERS... YEAH, I THINK I HAVE PARTS IN THE TRUCK.
YOU'RE GOING TO CLONE HIM FROM HIS OWN GARBAGE?
DON'T TELL ANYBODY-- THERE MIGHT BE A STIGMA.

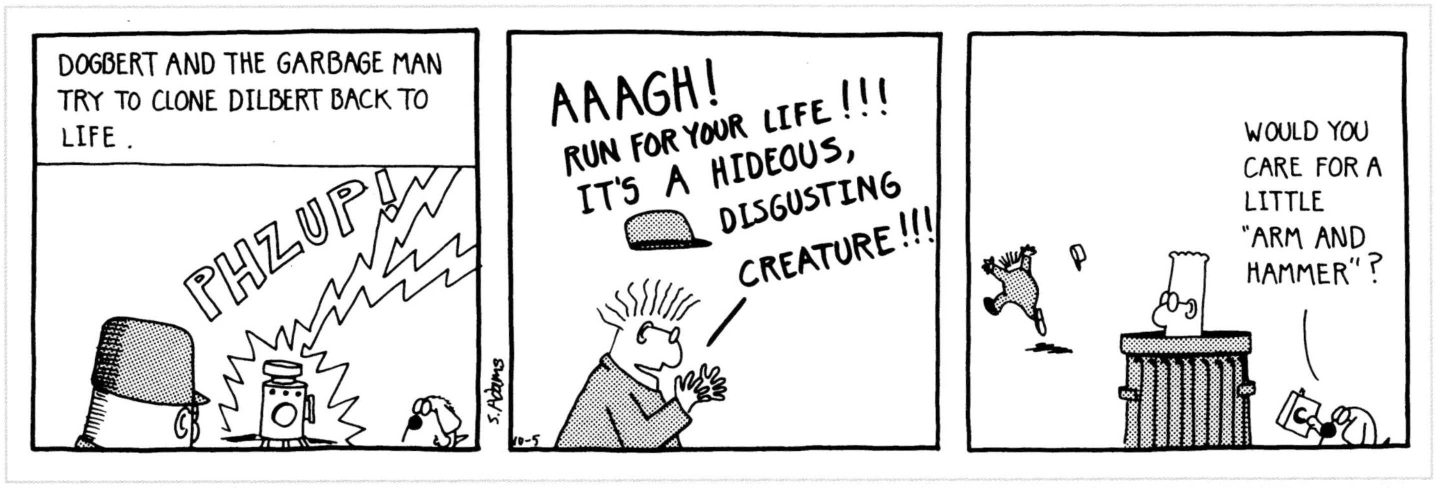
DOGBERT AND THE GARBAGE MAN TRY TO CLONE DILBERT BACK TO LIFE.
PHZUP!
AAAGH! RUN FOR YOUR LIFE!!! IT'S A HIDEOUS, DISGUSTING CREATURE!!!
WOULD YOU CARE FOR A LITTLE "ARM AND HAMMER"?

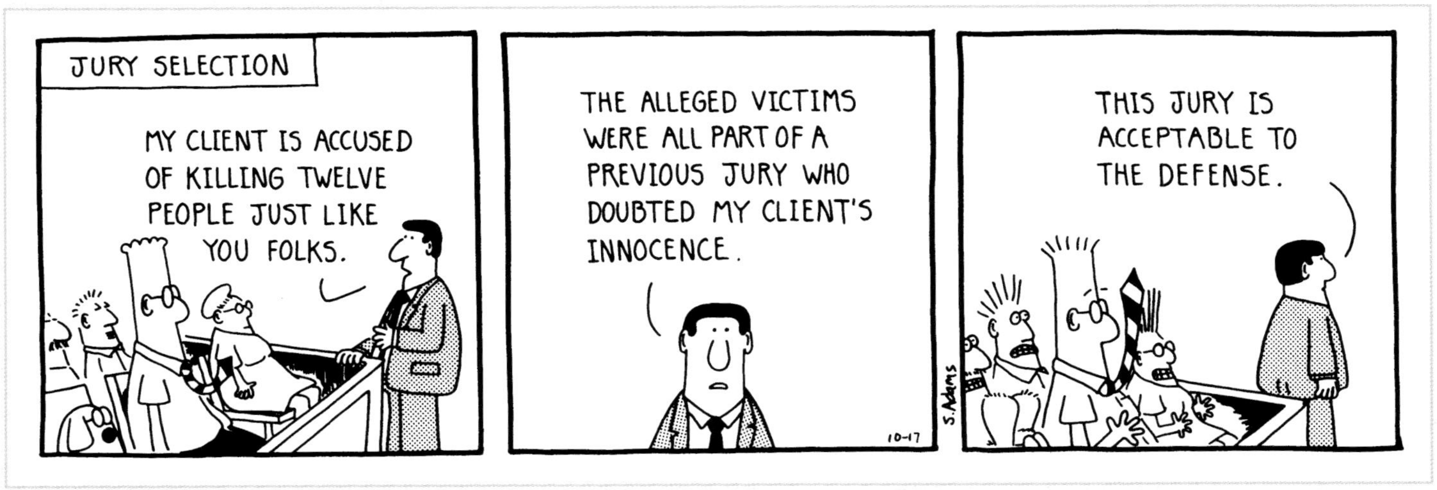
JURY SELECTION
MY CLIENT IS ACCUSED OF KILLING TWELVE PEOPLE JUST LIKE YOU FOLKS.
THE ALLEGED VICTIMS WERE ALL PART OF A PREVIOUS JURY WHO DOUBTED MY CLIENT'S INNOCENCE.
THIS JURY IS ACCEPTABLE TO THE DEFENSE.

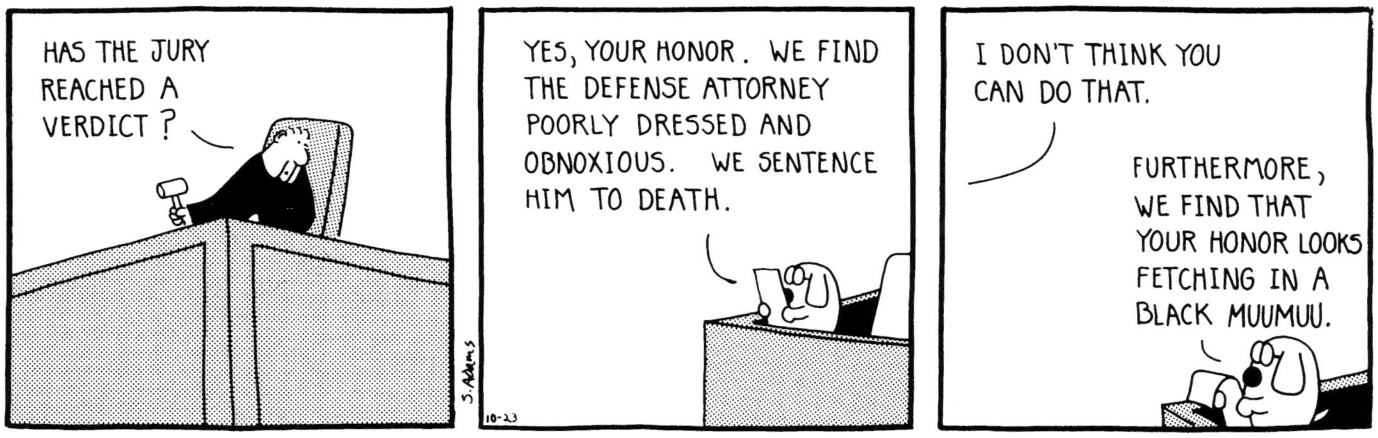
HAS THE JURY REACHED A VERDICT ?
YES, YOUR HONOR. WE FIND THE DEFENSE ATTORNEY POORLY DRESSED AND OBNOXIOUS. WE SENTENCE HIM TO DEATH.
I DON'T THINK YOU CAN DO THAT.
FURTHERMORE, WE FIND THAT YOUR HONOR LOOKS FETCHING IN A BLACK MUUMUU.
S. Adams
10-23

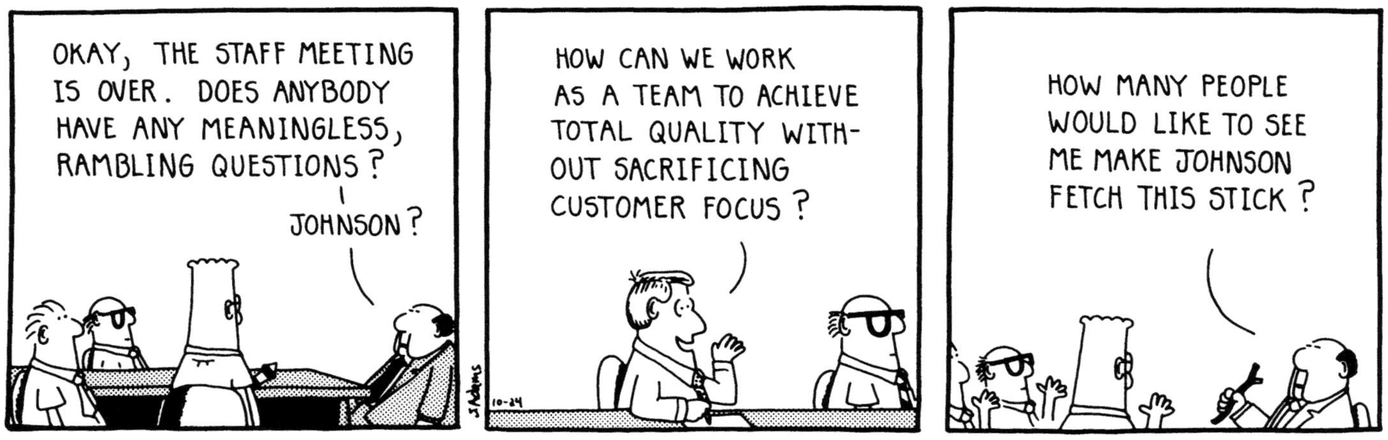
OKAY, THE STAFF MEETING IS OVER. DOES ANYBODY HAVE ANY MEANINGLESS, RAMBLING QUESTIONS ?
JOHNSON ?
HOW CAN WE WORK AS A TEAM TO ACHIEVE TOTAL QUALITY WITHOUT SACRIFICING CUSTOMER FOCUS ?
HOW MANY PEOPLE WOULD LIKE TO SEE ME MAKE JOHNSON FETCH THIS STICK ?
S. Adams
10-24

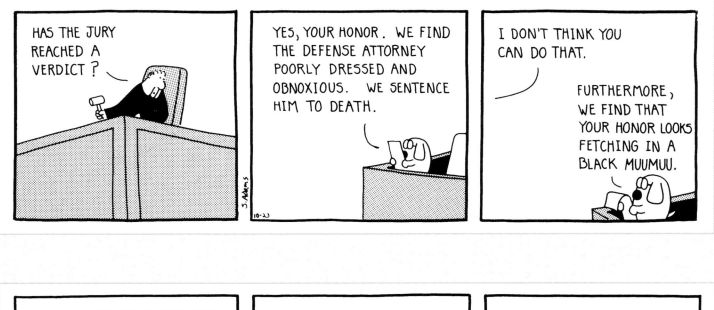

The second panel from the comic above is verbatim from a meeting I attended at my day job.

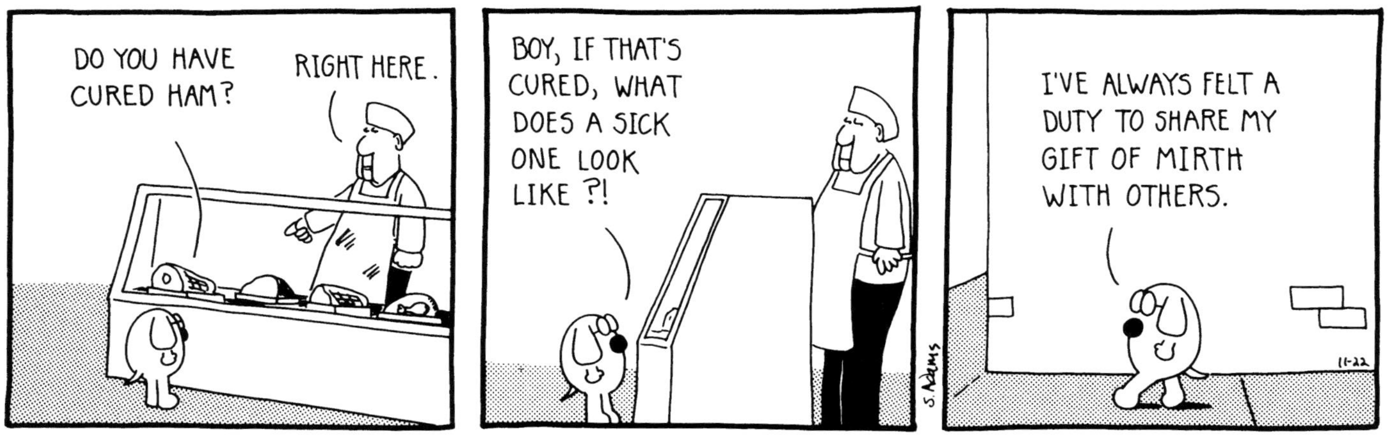
DO YOU HAVE CURED HAM?
RIGHT HERE.
BOY, IF THAT'S CURED, WHAT DOES A SICK ONE LOOK LIKE ?!
I'VE ALWAYS FELT A DUTY TO SHARE MY GIFT OF MIRTH WITH OTHERS.
S. Adams
11-22

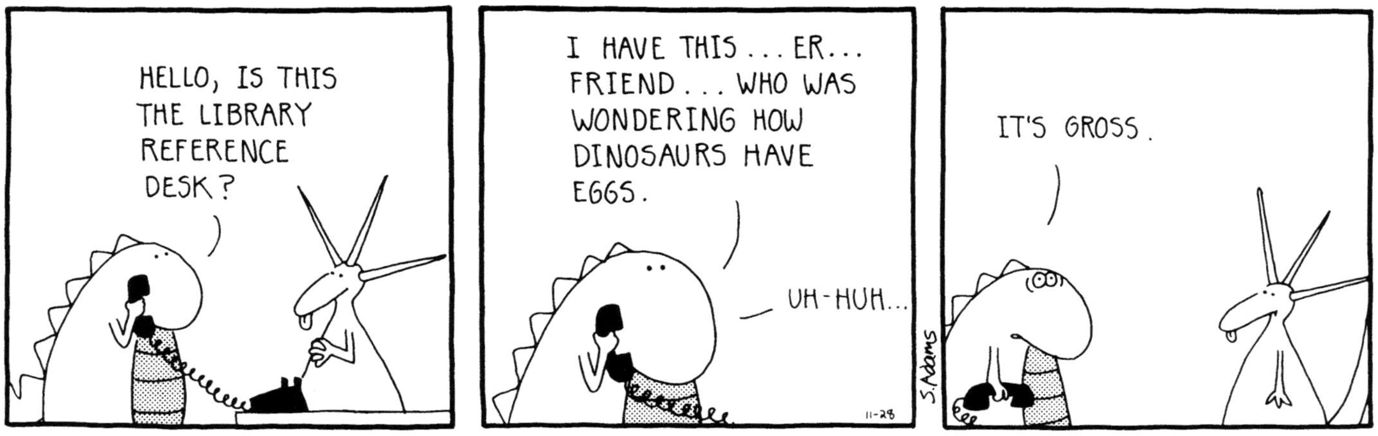
HELLO, IS THIS THE LIBRARY REFERENCE DESK?
I HAVE THIS ... ER... FRIEND ... WHO WAS WONDERING HOW DINOSAURS HAVE EGGS.
UH-HUH...
IT'S GROSS.
S. Adams
11-28

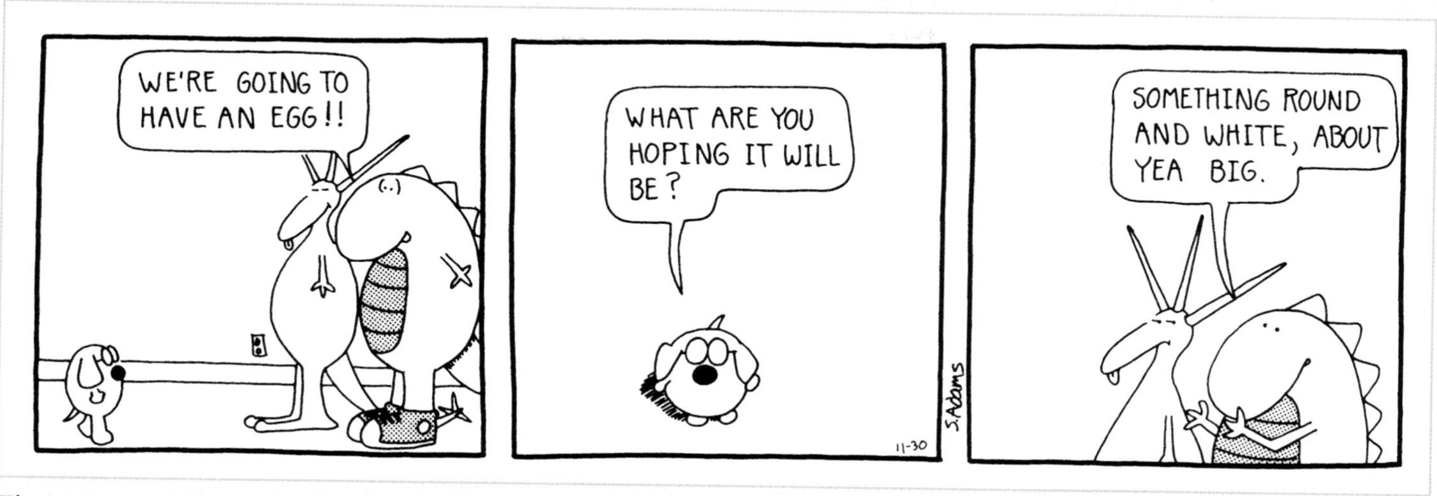
WE'RE GOING TO HAVE AN EGG!!
WHAT ARE YOU HOPING IT WILL BE?
SOMETHING ROUND AND WHITE, ABOUT YEA BIG.

The strip wasn't growing as quickly as I hoped during this period, so I was searching for a way to make it more popular. I figured everyone loves dinosaurs, and lots of people like comics about kids, so a comic about a dinosaur kid should be a big hit. It wasn't. After a few months of giving the dinosaurs lots of attention, I let it go.

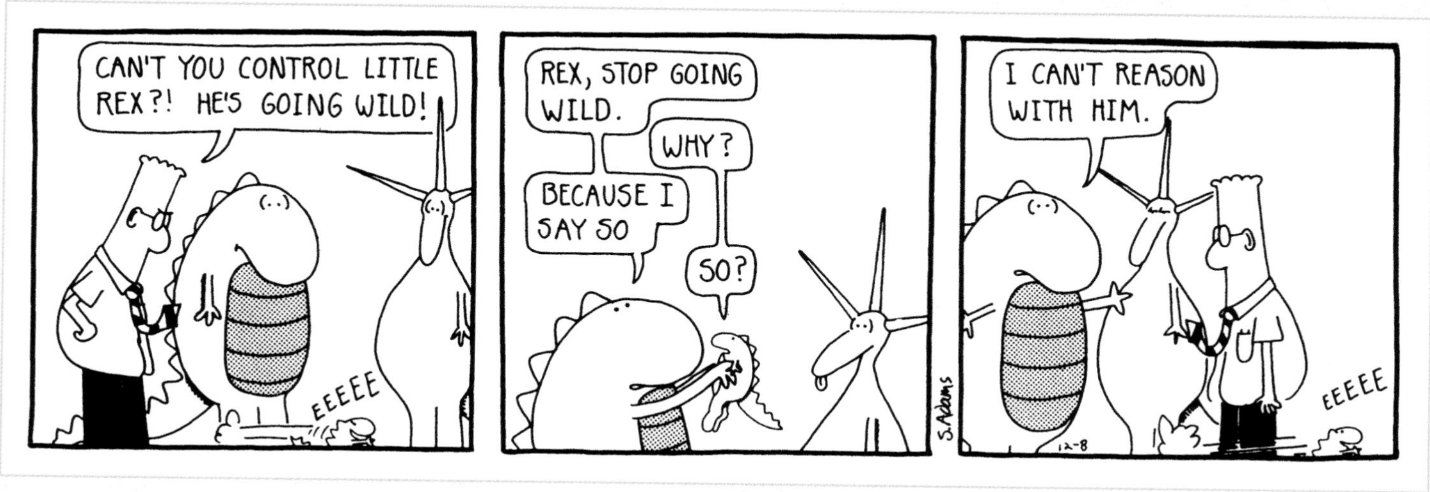
CAN'T YOU CONTROL LITTLE REX?! HE'S GOING WILD!
EEEEE
REX, STOP GOING WILD.
WHY?
BECAUSE I SAY SO
SO?
I CAN'T REASON WITH HIM.
EEEEE

I am still surprised Rex the dinosaur didn't catch on. He's impossibly cute.

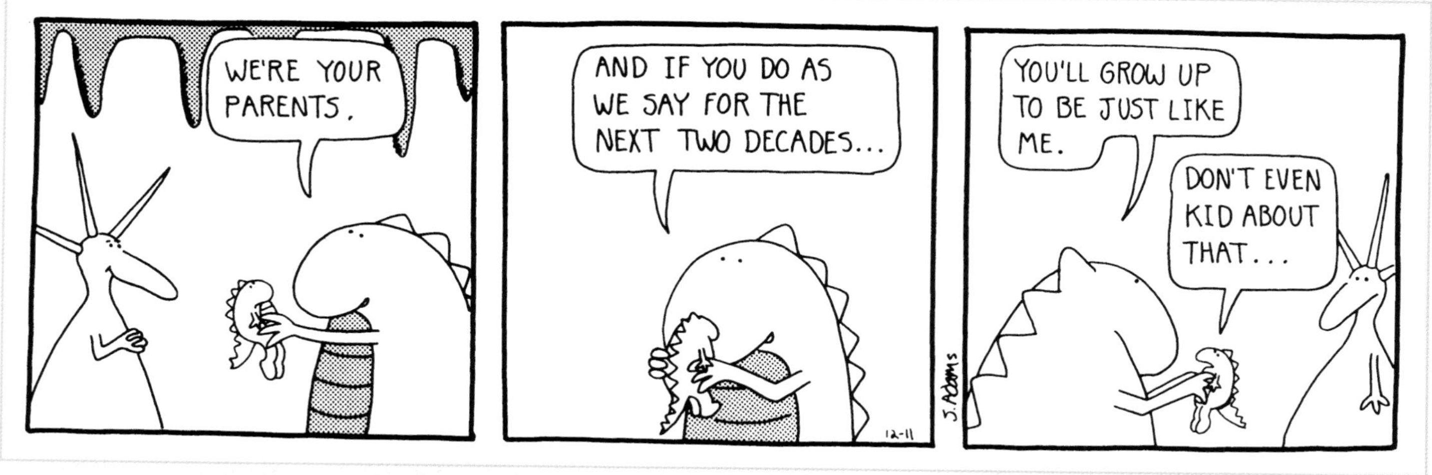
WE'RE YOUR PARENTS.
AND IF YOU DO AS WE SAY FOR THE NEXT TWO DECADES...
YOU'LL GROW UP TO BE JUST LIKE ME.
DON'T EVEN KID ABOUT THAT...

My lunches with the engineers at work often turned into a competition.

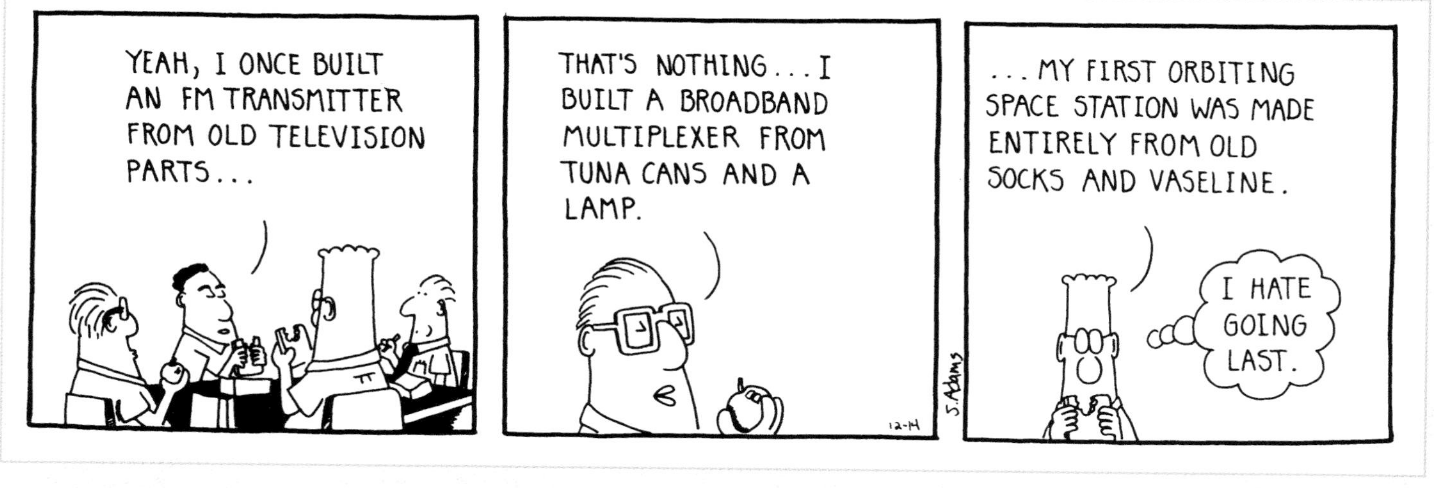
YEAH, I ONCE BUILT AN FM TRANSMITTER FROM OLD TELEVISION PARTS...
THAT'S NOTHING... I BUILT A BROADBAND MULTIPLEXER FROM TUNA CANS AND A LAMP.
... MY FIRST ORBITING SPACE STATION WAS MADE ENTIRELY FROM OLD SOCKS AND VASELINE.
I HATE GOING LAST.

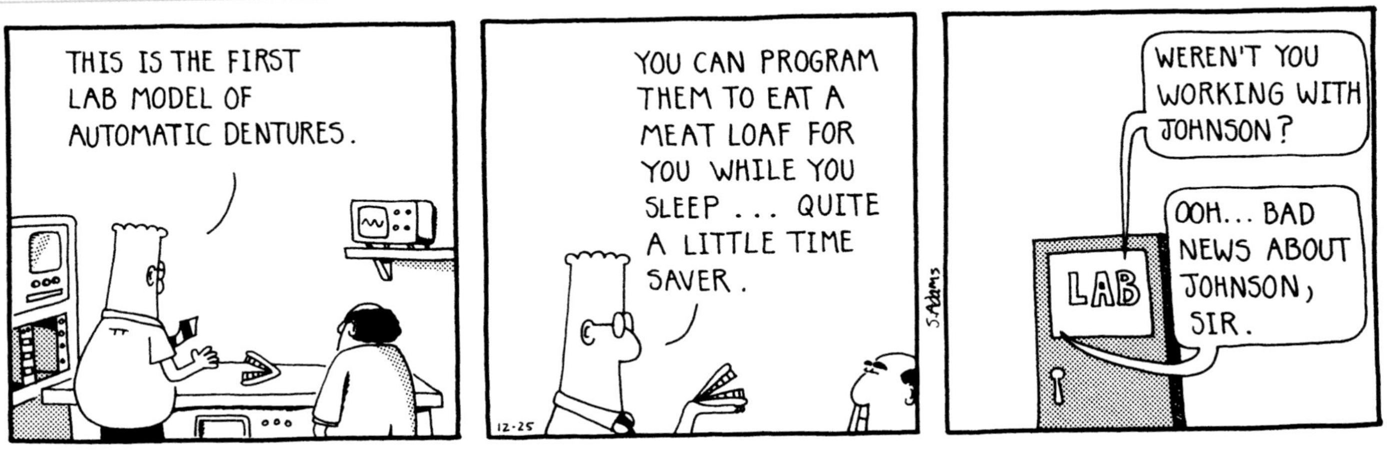
THIS IS THE FIRST LAB MODEL OF AUTOMATIC DENTURES.
YOU CAN PROGRAM THEM TO EAT A MEAT LOAF FOR YOU WHILE YOU SLEEP ... QUITE A LITTLE TIME SAVER.
12-25
S.Adams
WEREN'T YOU WORKING WITH JOHNSON?
LAB
OOH... BAD NEWS ABOUT JOHNSON, SIR.

I don't know how many people have died in the strip, but I'm sure I hold some sort of comic strip record.

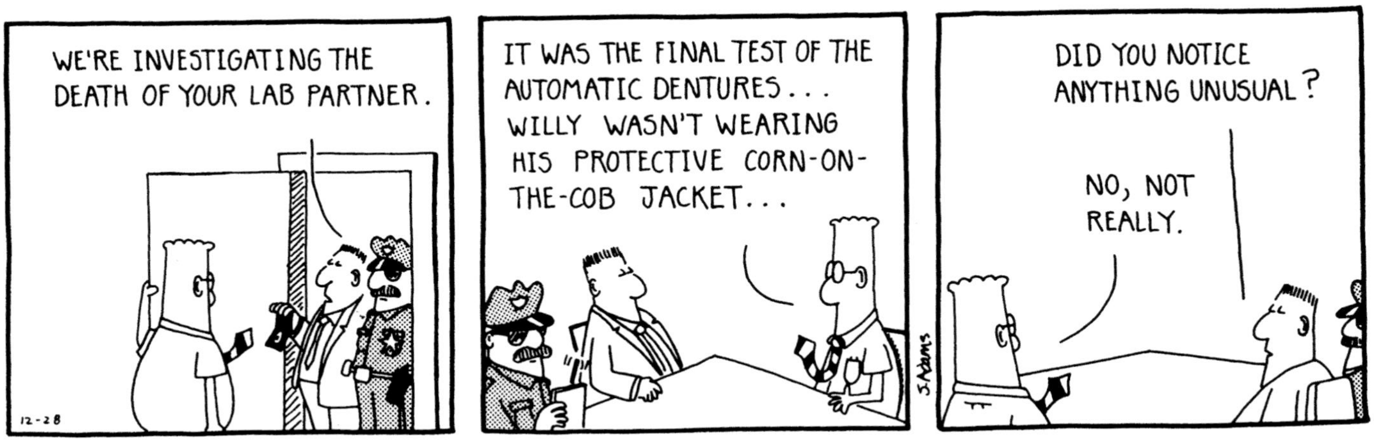
WE'RE INVESTIGATING THE DEATH OF YOUR LAB PARTNER.
12-28
IT WAS THE FINAL TEST OF THE AUTOMATIC DENTURES... WILLY WASN'T WEARING HIS PROTECTIVE CORN-ON-THE-COB JACKET...
S.Adams
DID YOU NOTICE ANYTHING UNUSUAL?
NO, NOT REALLY.

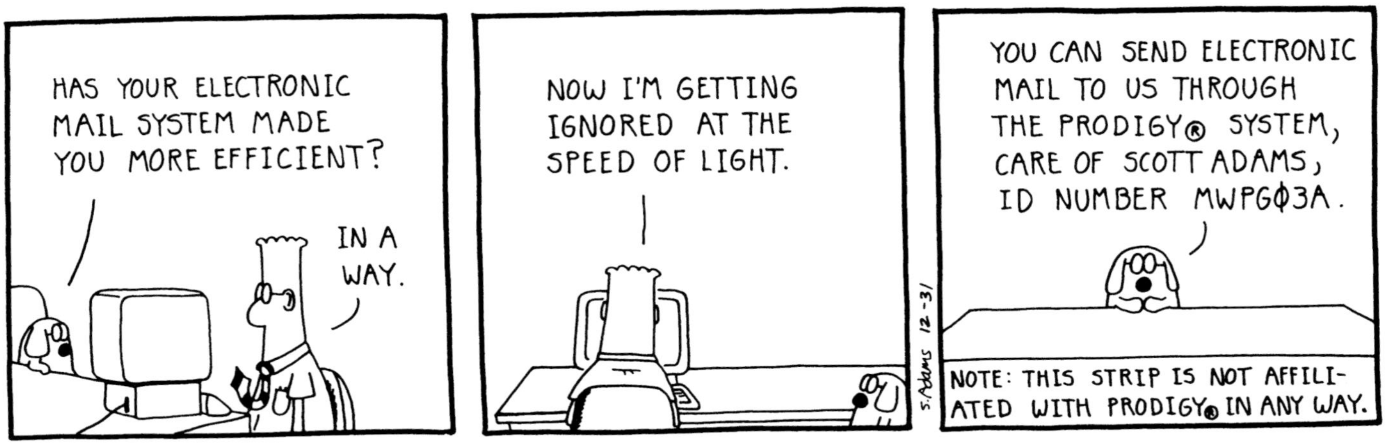
HAS YOUR ELECTRONIC MAIL SYSTEM MADE YOU MORE EFFICIENT?
IN A WAY.
NOW I'M GETTING IGNORED AT THE SPEED OF LIGHT.
S.Adams 12-31
YOU CAN SEND ELECTRONIC MAIL TO US THROUGH THE PRODIGY® SYSTEM, CARE OF SCOTT ADAMS, ID NUMBER MWPGØ3A.
NOTE: THIS STRIP IS NOT AFFILIATED WITH PRODIGY® IN ANY WAY.

This is the first time I put my e-mail address in the comic. But few people were using e-mail, and fewer yet used the Prodigy system. Still, I got hundreds of messages that week, and it felt like I was on to something.

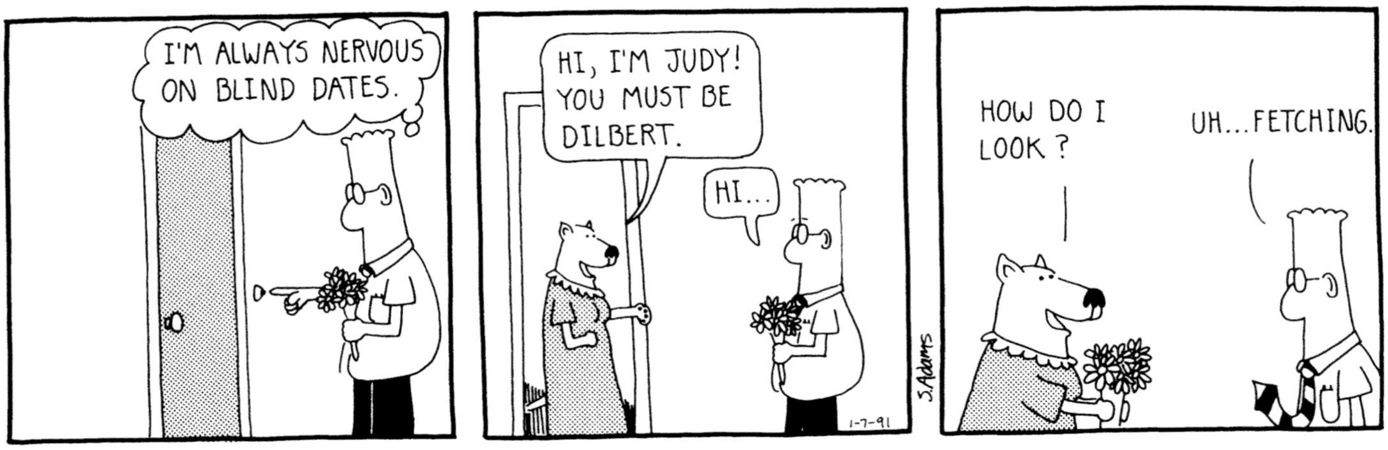
I'M ALWAYS NERVOUS ON BLIND DATES.
HI, I'M JUDY! YOU MUST BE DILBERT.
HI...
1-7-91
S.Adams
HOW DO I LOOK?
UH...FETCHING.

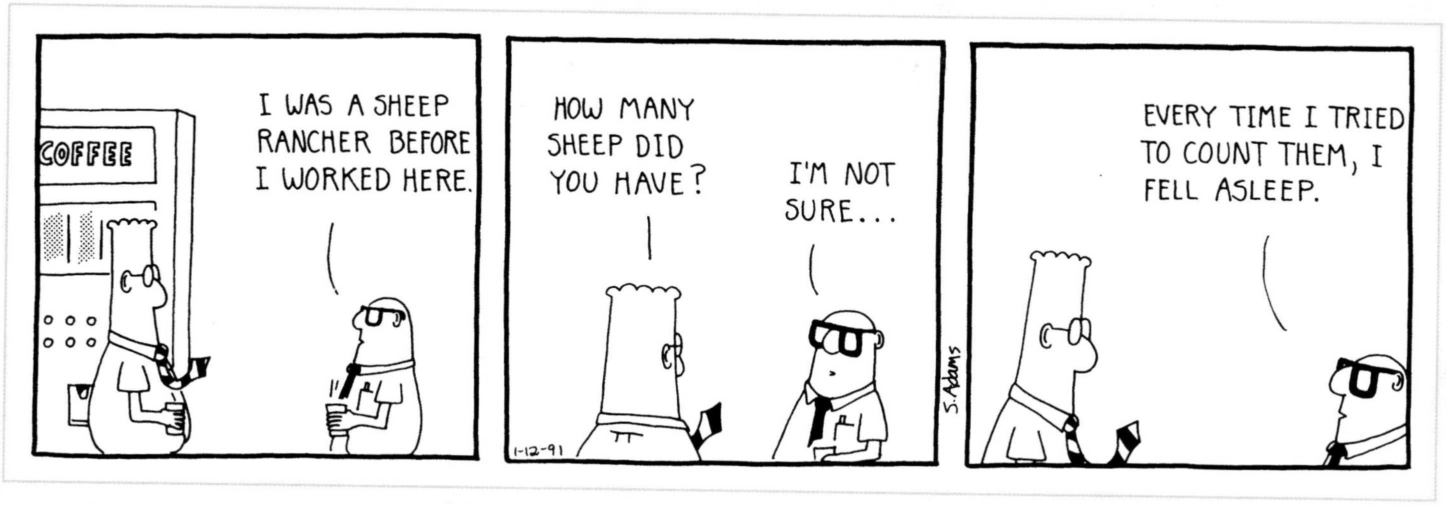
COFFEE
I WAS A SHEEP RANCHER BEFORE I WORKED HERE.
HOW MANY SHEEP DID YOU HAVE?
I'M NOT SURE...
1-12-91
S. Adams
EVERY TIME I TRIED TO COUNT THEM, I FELL ASLEEP.

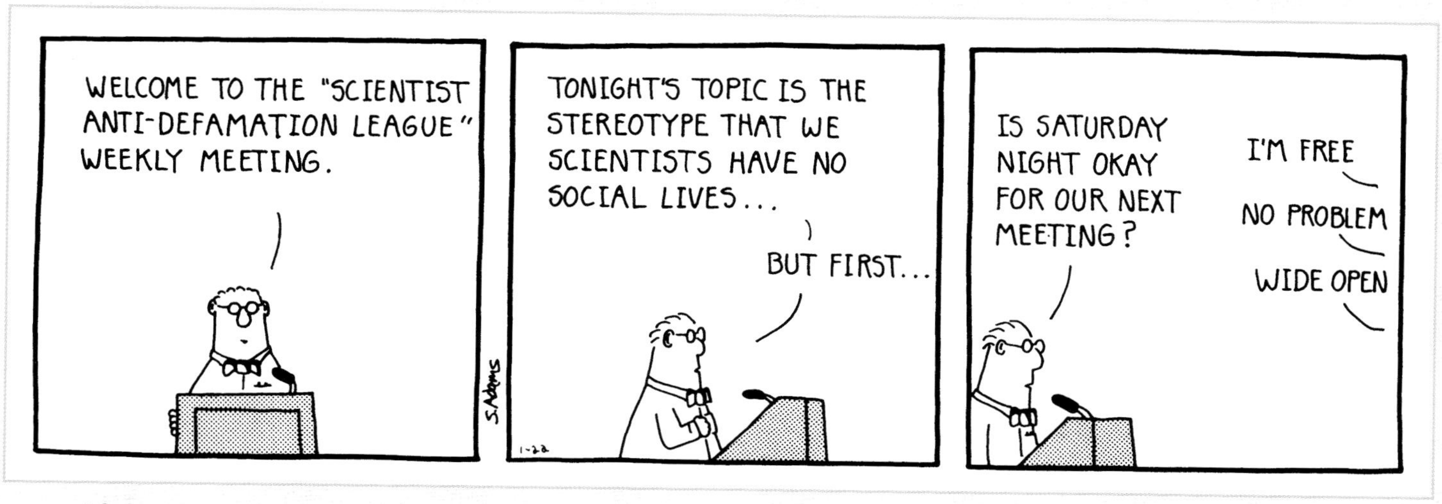
WELCOME TO THE "SCIENTIST ANTI-DEFAMATION LEAGUE" WEEKLY MEETING.
S. Adams
TONIGHT'S TOPIC IS THE STEREOTYPE THAT WE SCIENTISTS HAVE NO SOCIAL LIVES...
BUT FIRST...
IS SATURDAY NIGHT OKAY FOR OUR NEXT MEETING?
I'M FREE
NO PROBLEM
WIDE OPEN

After my series featuring the lab origins of Ratbert ran in papers, I got a letter from a woman who said she was a scientist, and that the Dilbert comic makes it seem as if scientists enjoy hurting animals. After I got that letter, I wrote this series.

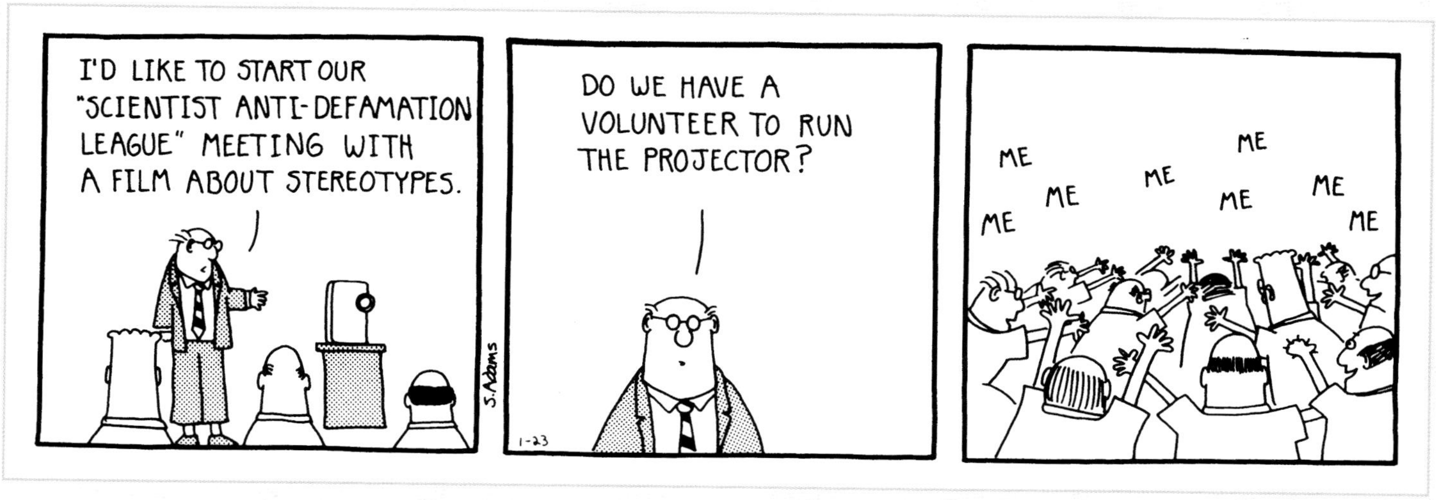
I'D LIKE TO START OUR "SCIENTIST ANTI-DEFAMATION LEAGUE" MEETING WITH A FILM ABOUT STEREOTYPES.
S. Adams
1-23
DO WE HAVE A VOLUNTEER TO RUN THE PROJECTOR?
ME
ME
ME
ME
ME
ME
ME
ME

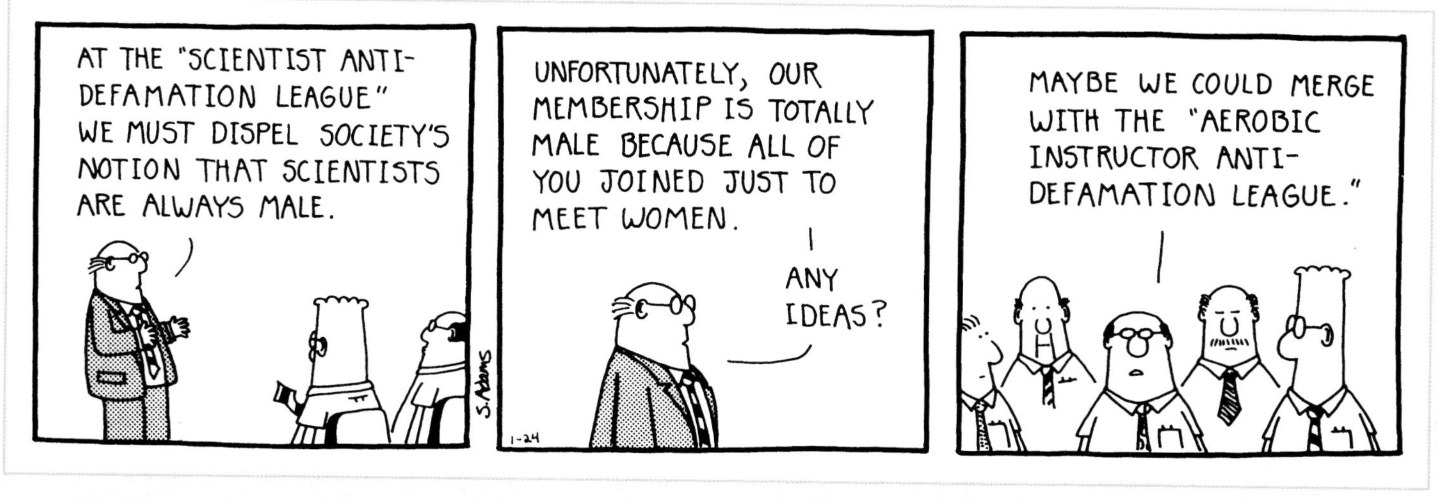
AT THE "SCIENTIST ANTI-DEFAMATION LEAGUE" WE MUST DISPEL SOCIETY'S NOTION THAT SCIENTISTS ARE ALWAYS MALE.
S. Adams
UNFORTUNATELY, OUR MEMBERSHIP IS TOTALLY MALE BECAUSE ALL OF YOU JOINED JUST TO MEET WOMEN.
ANY IDEAS?
1-24
MAYBE WE COULD MERGE WITH THE "AEROBIC INSTRUCTOR ANTI-DEFAMATION LEAGUE."

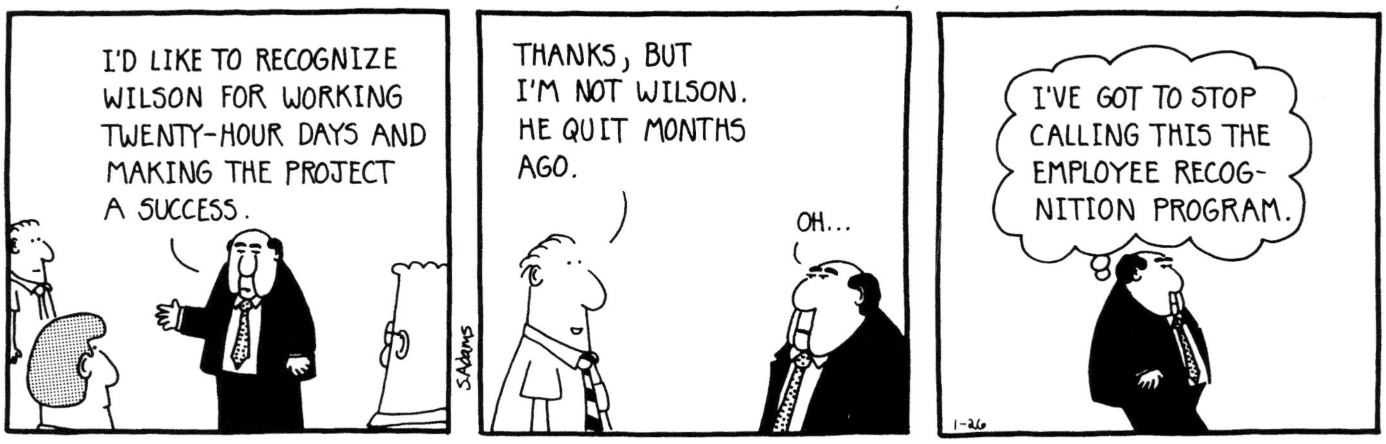
I'D LIKE TO RECOGNIZE WILSON FOR WORKING TWENTY-HOUR DAYS AND MAKING THE PROJECT A SUCCESS.
THANKS, BUT I'M NOT WILSON. HE QUIT MONTHS AGO.
OH...
I'VE GOT TO STOP CALLING THIS THE EMPLOYEE RECOGNITION PROGRAM.

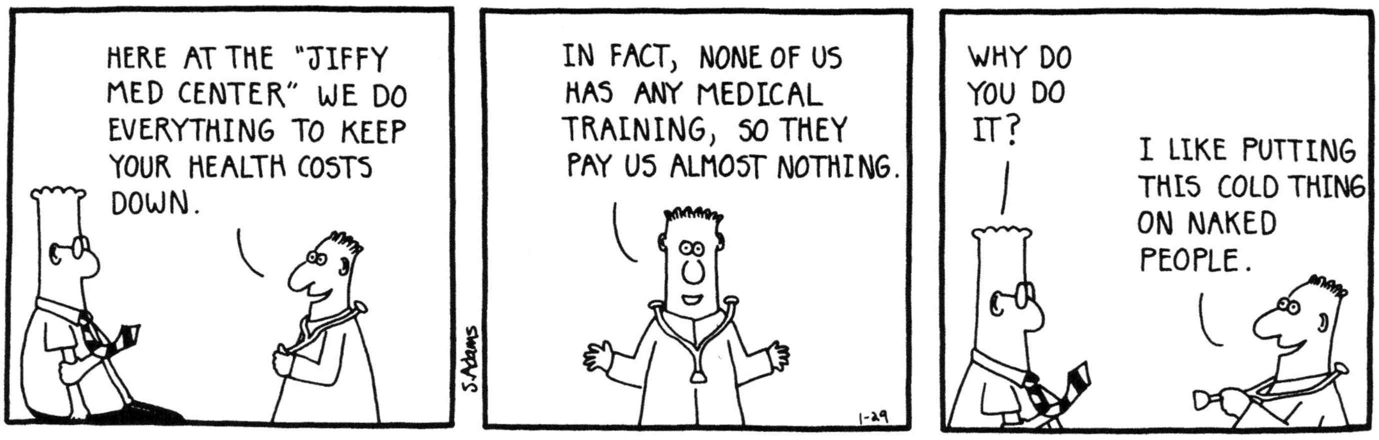
HERE AT THE "JIFFY MED CENTER" WE DO EVERYTHING TO KEEP YOUR HEALTH COSTS DOWN.
IN FACT, NONE OF US HAS ANY MEDICAL TRAINING, SO THEY PAY US ALMOST NOTHING.
WHY DO YOU DO IT?
I LIKE PUTTING THIS COLD THING ON NAKED PEOPLE.

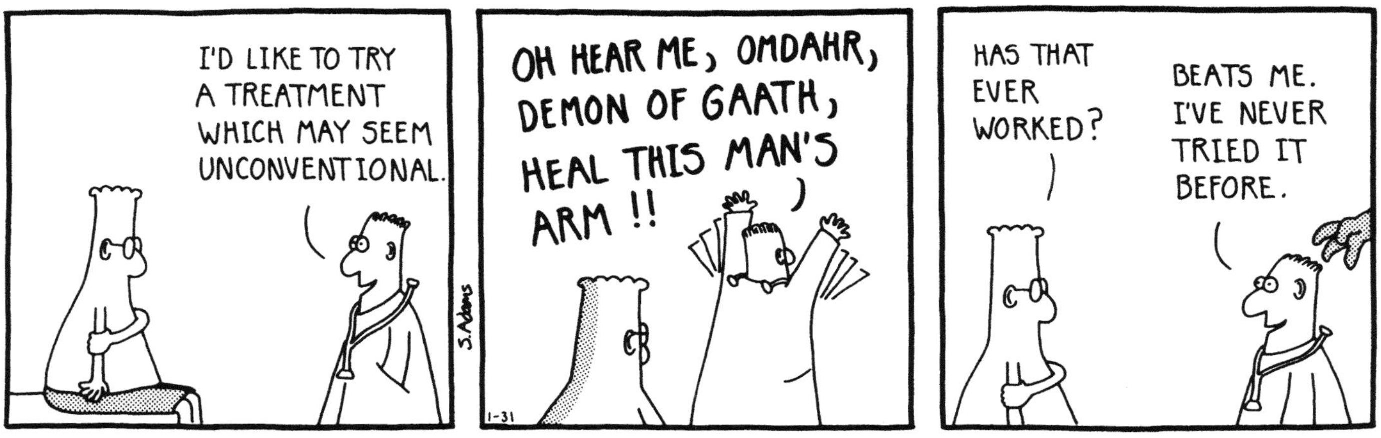
I'D LIKE TO TRY A TREATMENT WHICH MAY SEEM UNCONVENTIONAL.
OH HEAR ME, OMDAHR, DEMON OF GAATH, HEAL THIS MAN'S ARM !!
HAS THAT EVER WORKED?
BEATS ME. I'VE NEVER TRIED IT BEFORE.

This is the only comic I ever censored on my own after I had submitted it, but before it ran in papers. The first war against Iraq had just started, and President Bush's popularity was soaring. In a time of war, making an unflattering reference to the commander in chief's wife seemed extra wrong, as opposed to the ordinary wrong I was aiming for. So this comic didn't run in papers.

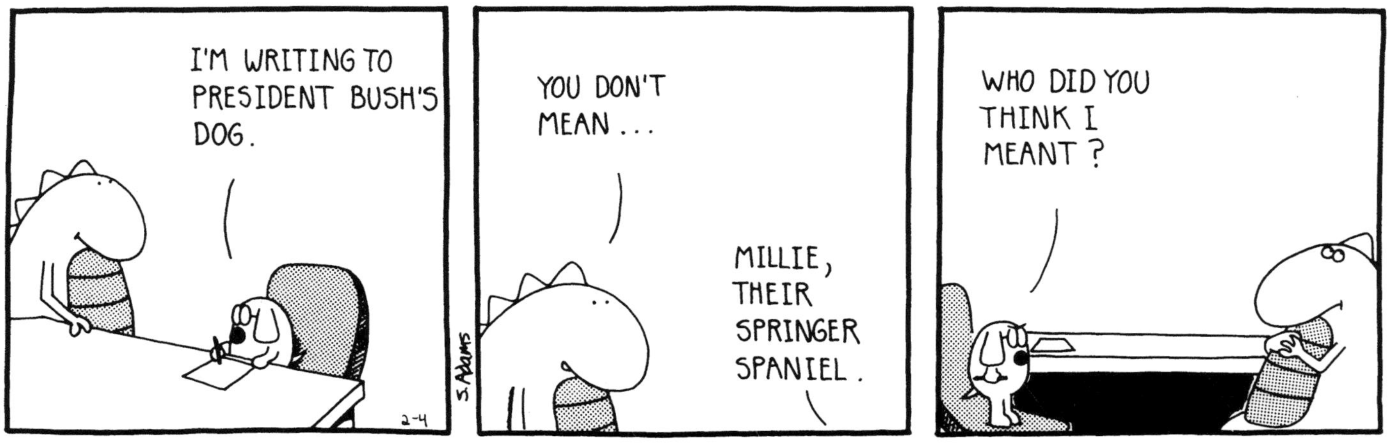
I'M WRITING TO PRESIDENT BUSH'S DOG.
YOU DON'T MEAN...
MILLIE, THEIR SPRINGER SPANIEL.
WHO DID YOU THINK I MEANT?

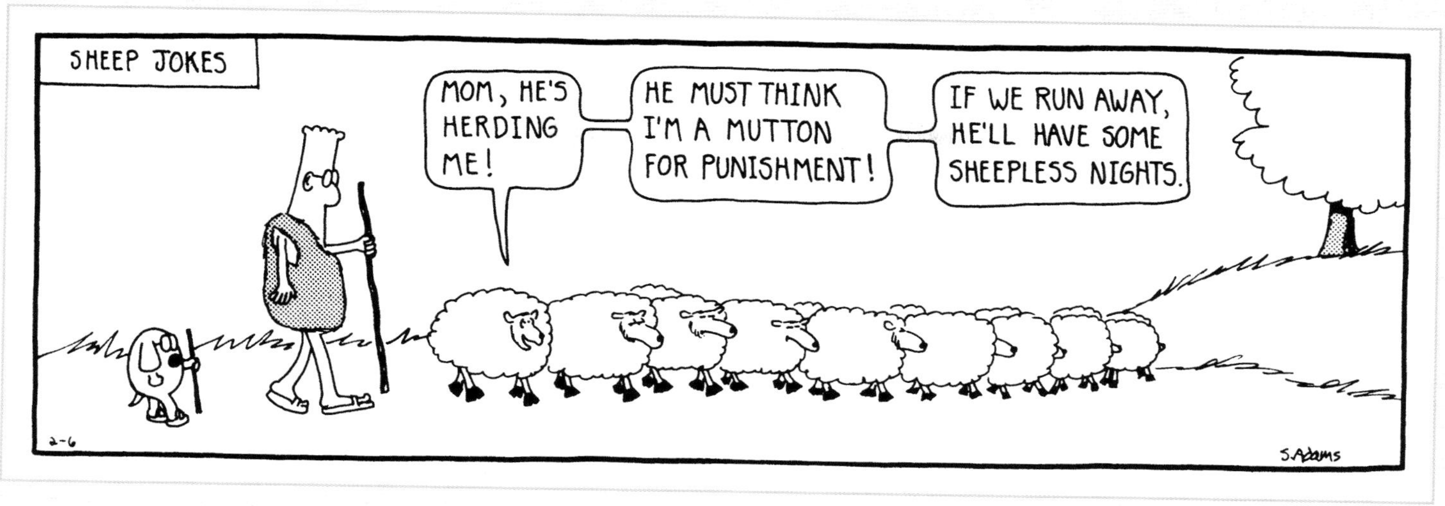
SHEEP JOKES
MOM, HE'S HERDING ME!
HE MUST THINK I'M A MUTTON FOR PUNISHMENT!
IF WE RUN AWAY, HE'LL HAVE SOME SHEEPLESS NIGHTS.
2-6
S. Adams

Puns from sheep are not funny. I have deep regrets about this one.

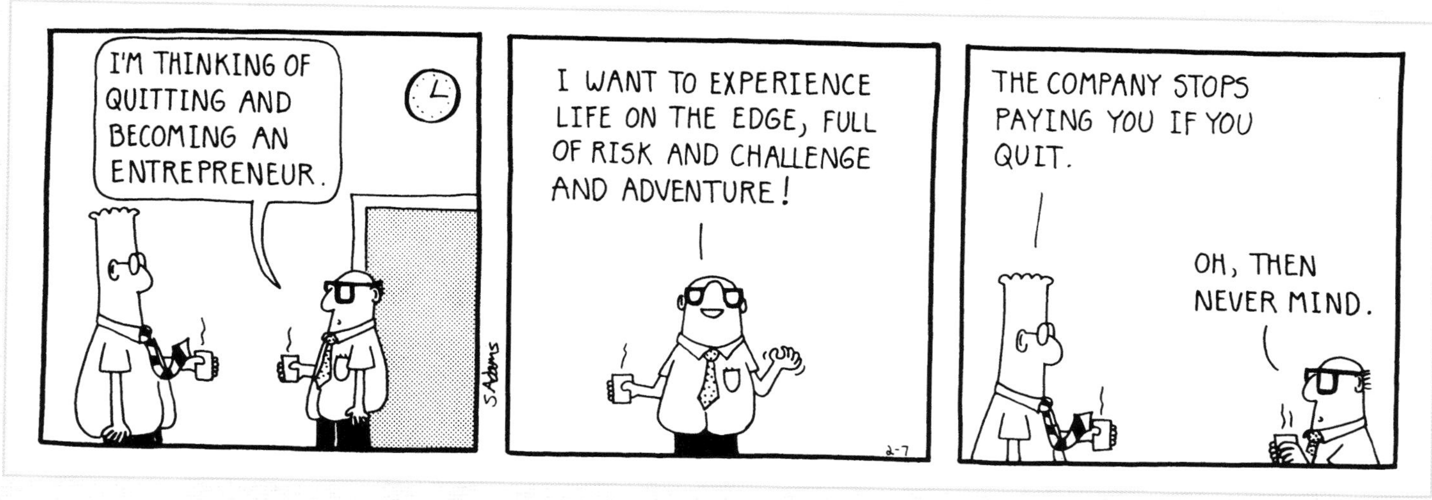
I'M THINKING OF QUITTING AND BECOMING AN ENTREPRENEUR.
S. Adams
I WANT TO EXPERIENCE LIFE ON THE EDGE, FULL OF RISK AND CHALLENGE AND ADVENTURE!
2-7
THE COMPANY STOPS PAYING YOU IF YOU QUIT.
OH, THEN NEVER MIND.

Suddenly, the character who would become Wally has a few strands of hair.

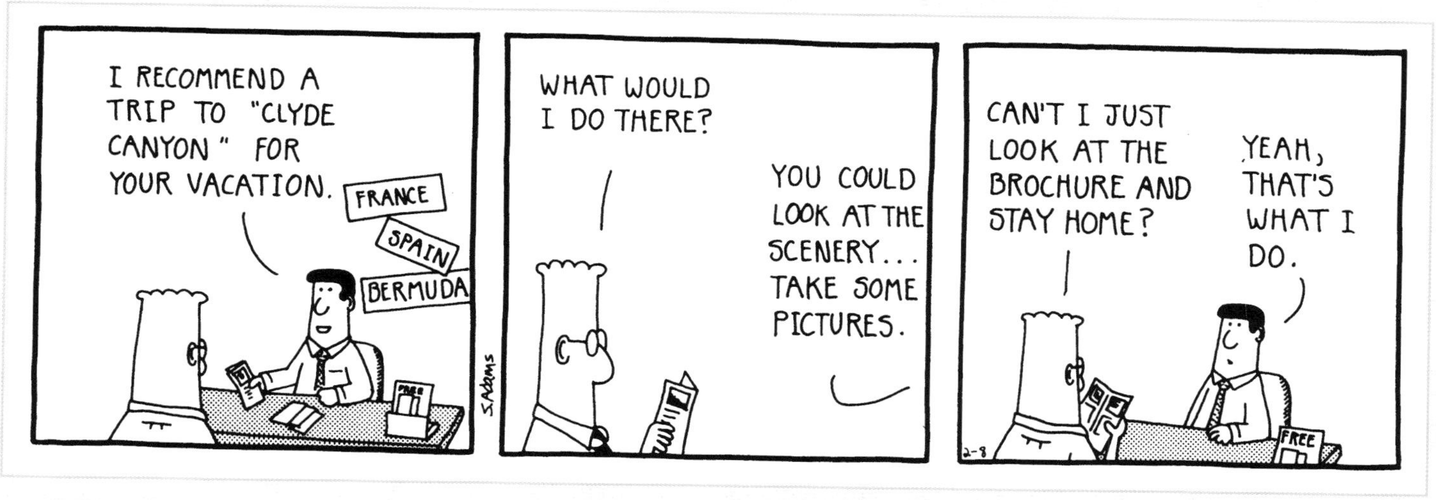
I RECOMMEND A TRIP TO "CLYDE CANYON" FOR YOUR VACATION.
FRANCE
SPAIN
BERMUDA
S. Adams
WHAT WOULD I DO THERE?
YOU COULD LOOK AT THE SCENERY... TAKE SOME PICTURES.
CAN'T I JUST LOOK AT THE BROCHURE AND STAY HOME?
YEAH, THAT'S WHAT I DO.
2-8
FREE

I've never been to the Grand Canyon. I hear it is great to look at. But I always wonder how long the feeling lasts.

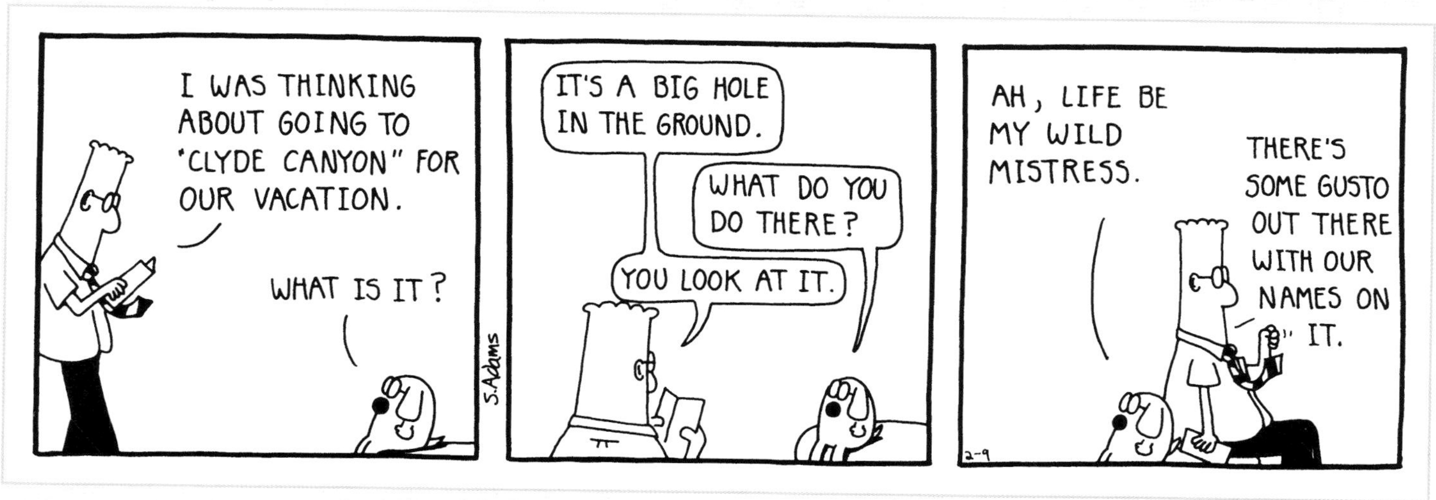
I WAS THINKING ABOUT GOING TO "CLYDE CANYON" FOR OUR VACATION.
WHAT IS IT?
S. Adams
IT'S A BIG HOLE IN THE GROUND.
WHAT DO YOU DO THERE?
YOU LOOK AT IT.
AH, LIFE BE MY WILD MISTRESS.
THERE'S SOME GUSTO OUT THERE WITH OUR NAMES ON IT.
2-9

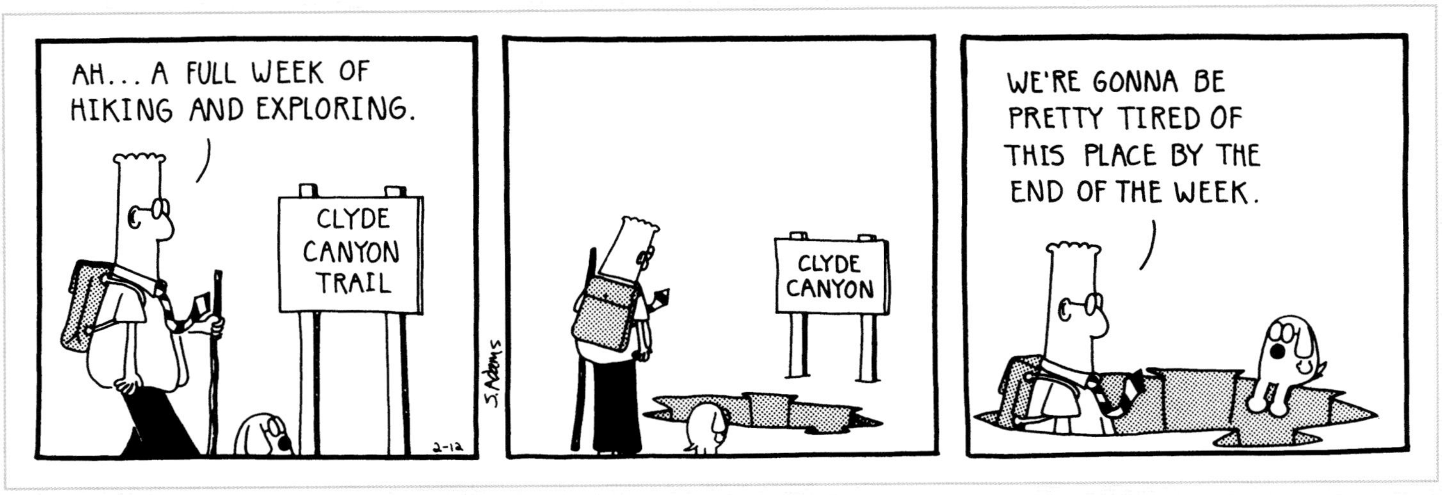
AH... A FULL WEEK OF HIKING AND EXPLORING.
CLYDE CANYON TRAIL
CLYDE CANYON
WE'RE GONNA BE PRETTY TIRED OF THIS PLACE BY THE END OF THE WEEK.

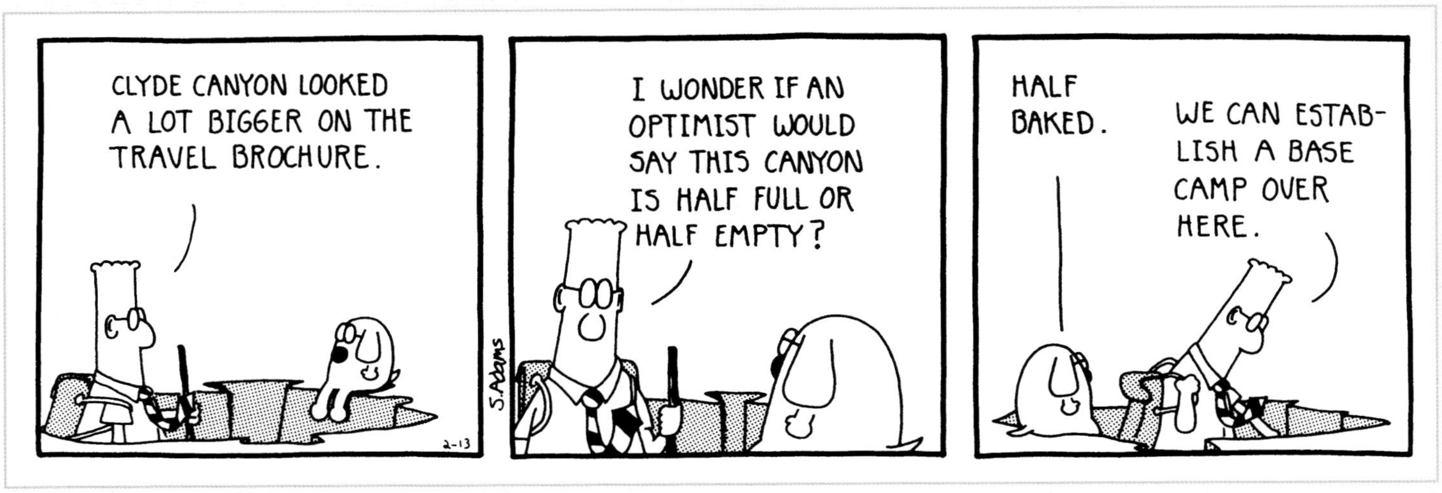
CLYDE CANYON LOOKED A LOT BIGGER ON THE TRAVEL BROCHURE.
I WONDER IF AN OPTIMIST WOULD SAY THIS CANYON IS HALF FULL OR HALF EMPTY?
HALF BAKED.
WE CAN ESTABLISH A BASE CAMP OVER HERE.

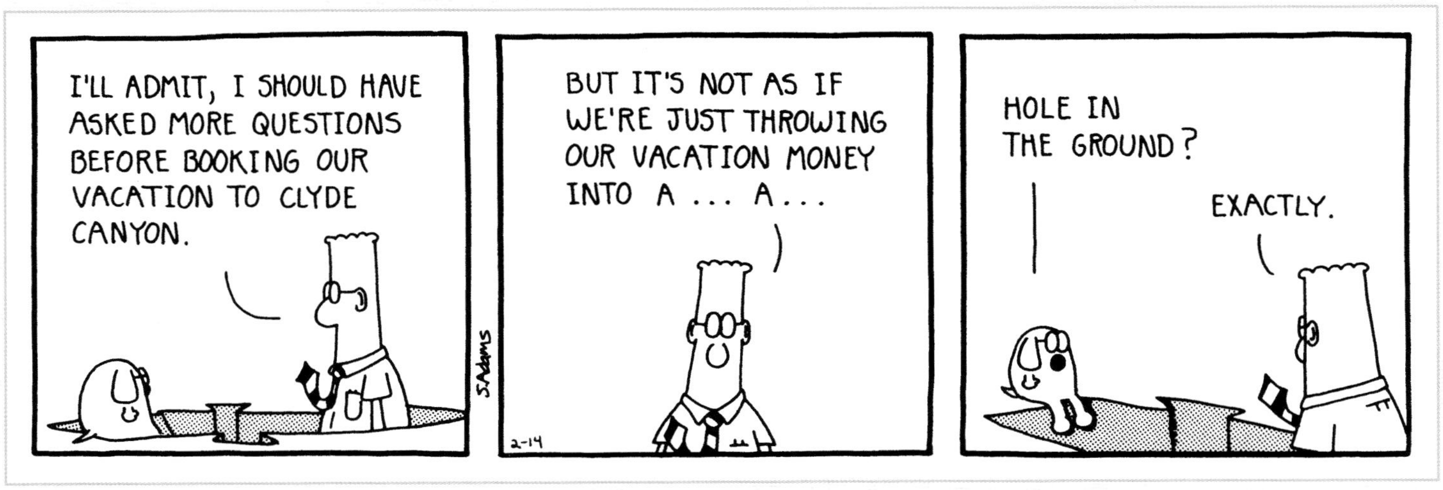
I'LL ADMIT, I SHOULD HAVE ASKED MORE QUESTIONS BEFORE BOOKING OUR VACATION TO CLYDE CANYON.
BUT IT'S NOT AS IF WE'RE JUST THROWING OUR VACATION MONEY INTO A ... A ...
HOLE IN THE GROUND?
EXACTLY.

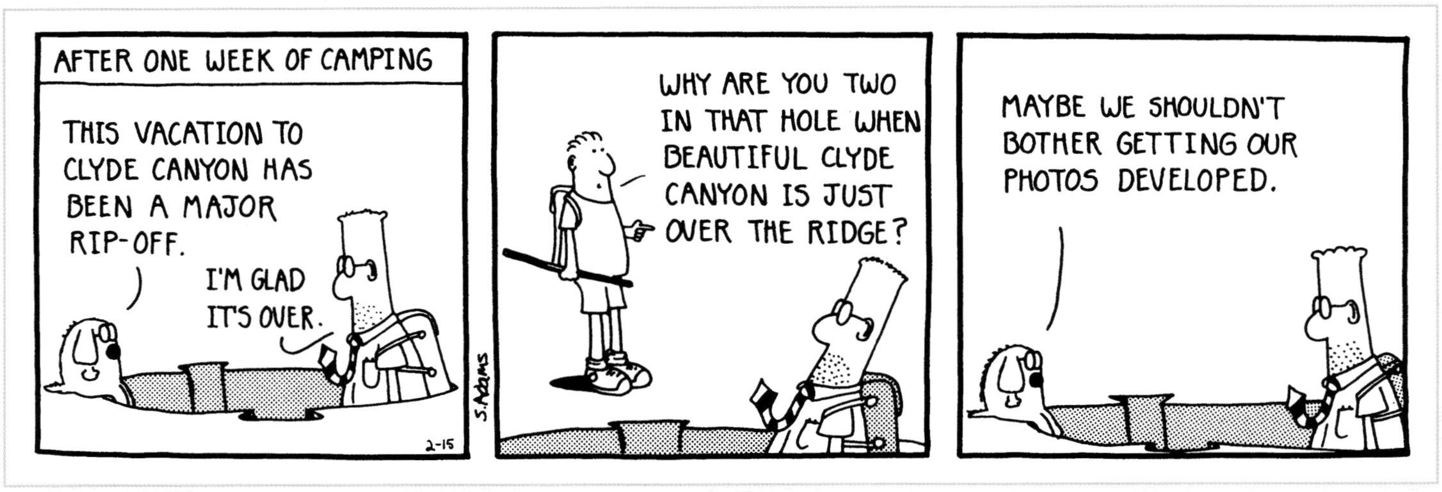
AFTER ONE WEEK OF CAMPING
THIS VACATION TO CLYDE CANYON HAS BEEN A MAJOR RIP-OFF.
I'M GLAD IT'S OVER.
WHY ARE YOU TWO IN THAT HOLE WHEN BEAUTIFUL CLYDE CANYON IS JUST OVER THE RIDGE?
MAYBE WE SHOULDN'T BOTHER GETTING OUR PHOTOS DEVELOPED.

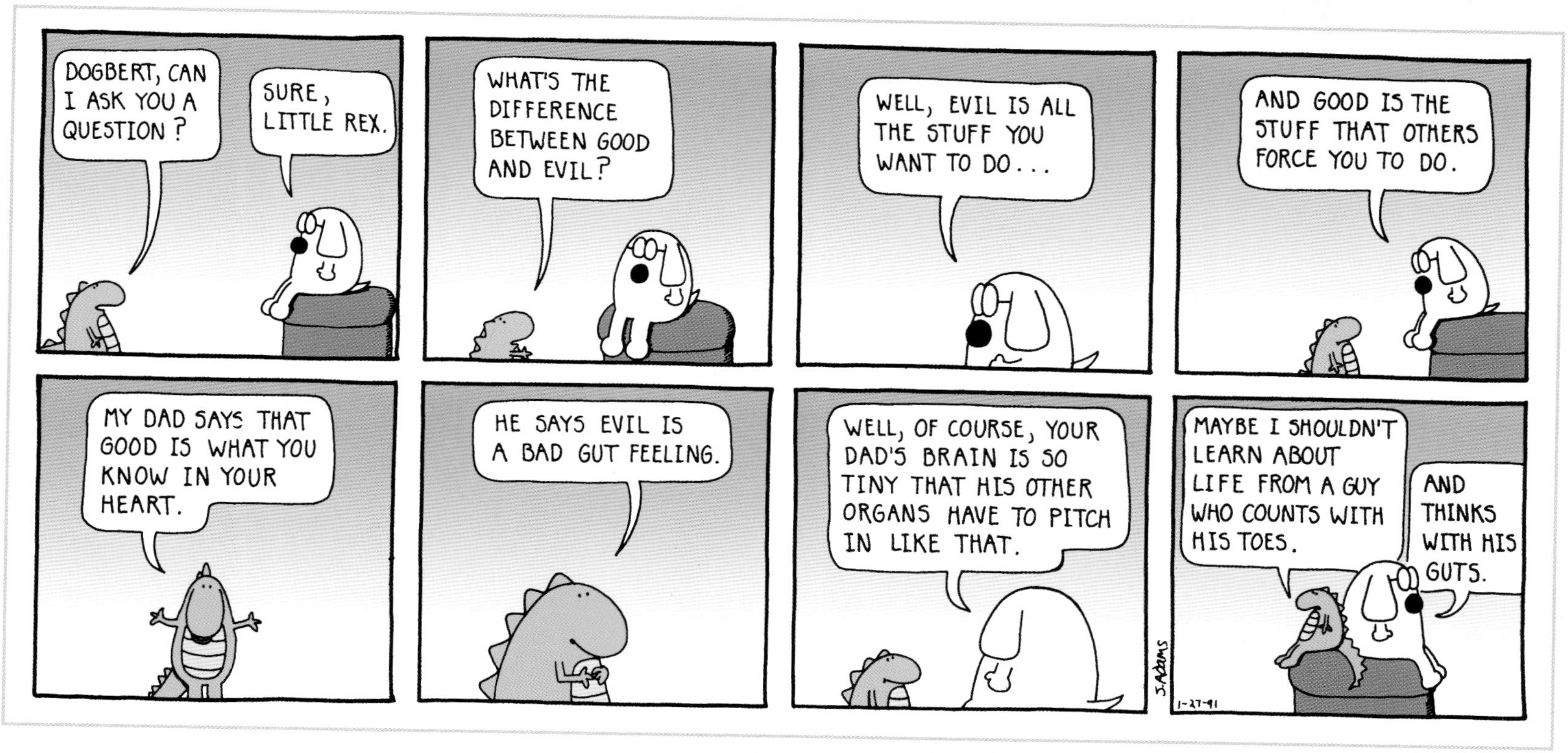
DOGBERT, CAN I ASK YOU A QUESTION?
SURE, LITTLE REX.
WHAT'S THE DIFFERENCE BETWEEN GOOD AND EVIL?
WELL, EVIL IS ALL THE STUFF YOU WANT TO DO...
AND GOOD IS THE STUFF THAT OTHERS FORCE YOU TO DO.
MY DAD SAYS THAT GOOD IS WHAT YOU KNOW IN YOUR HEART.
HE SAYS EVIL IS A BAD GUT FEELING.
WELL, OF COURSE, YOUR DAD'S BRAIN IS SO TINY THAT HIS OTHER ORGANS HAVE TO PITCH IN LIKE THAT.
MAYBE I SHOULDN'T LEARN ABOUT LIFE FROM A GUY WHO COUNTS WITH HIS TOES.
AND THINKS WITH HIS GUTS.
S. Adams
1-27-91

This comic features a cutaway, where the final panel is in a different location and time from the rest. I use this method sometimes when I have a good setup but can't figure out how to end it. Changing the time and place often helps.

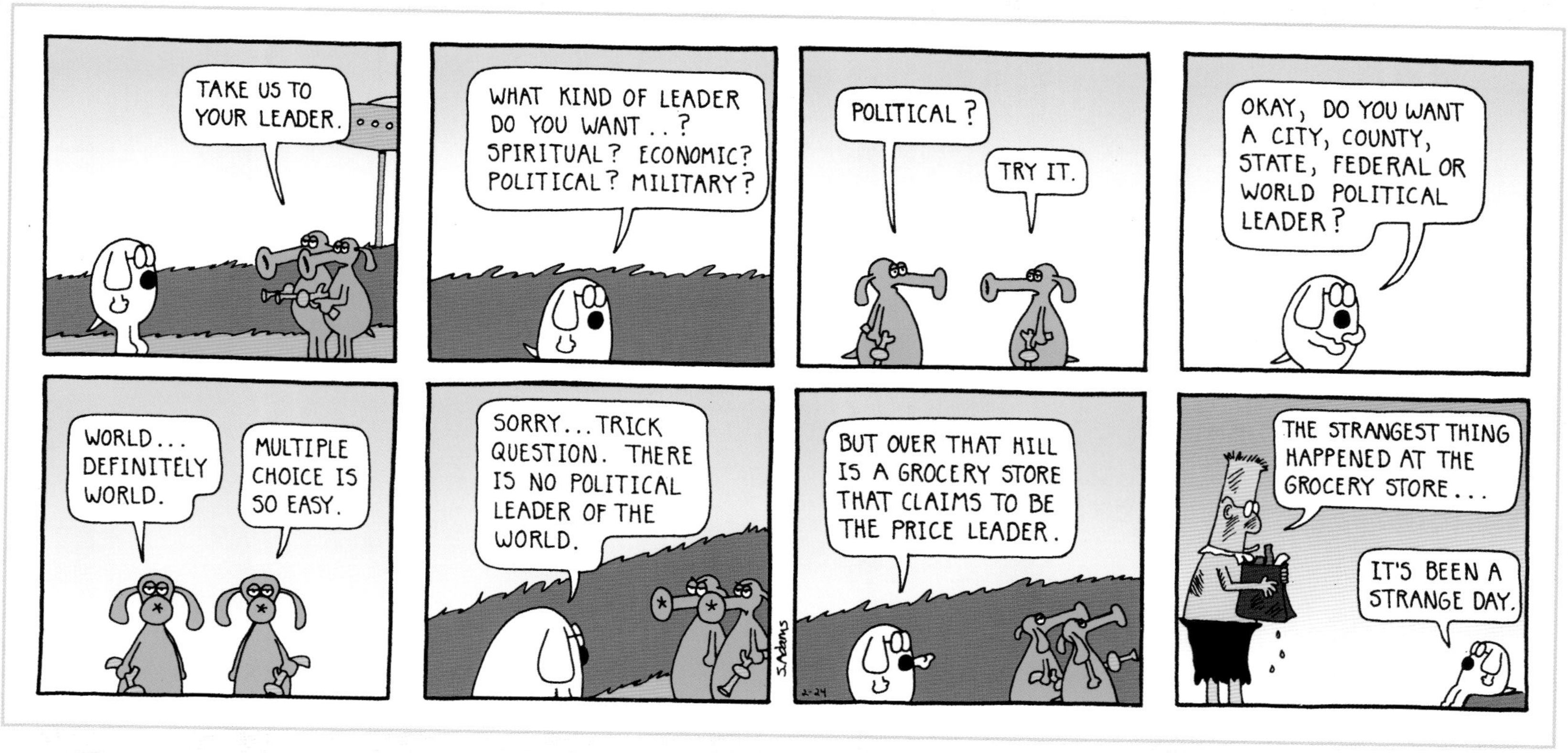
TAKE US TO YOUR LEADER.
WHAT KIND OF LEADER DO YOU WANT..? SPIRITUAL? ECONOMIC? POLITICAL? MILITARY?
POLITICAL?
TRY IT.
OKAY, DO YOU WANT A CITY, COUNTY, STATE, FEDERAL OR WORLD POLITICAL LEADER?
WORLD... DEFINITELY WORLD.
MULTIPLE CHOICE IS SO EASY.
SORRY... TRICK QUESTION. THERE IS NO POLITICAL LEADER OF THE WORLD.
S. Adams
2-24
BUT OVER THAT HILL IS A GROCERY STORE THAT CLAIMS TO BE THE PRICE LEADER.
THE STRANGEST THING HAPPENED AT THE GROCERY STORE...
IT'S BEEN A STRANGE DAY.

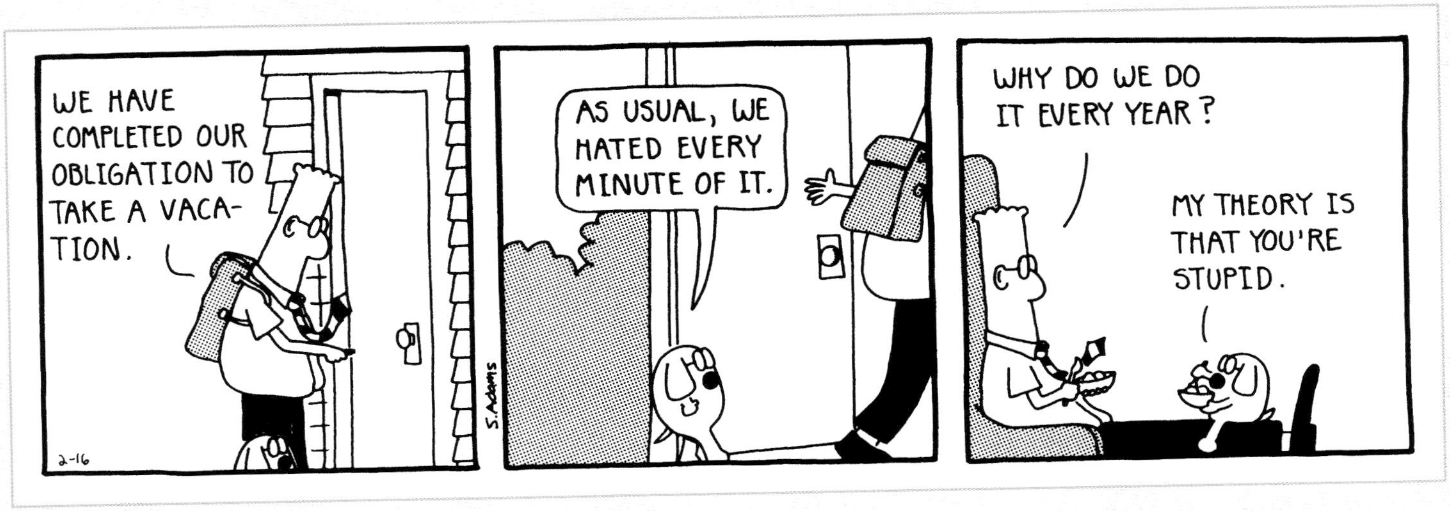
WE HAVE COMPLETED OUR OBLIGATION TO TAKE A VACA-TION.
AS USUAL, WE HATED EVERY MINUTE OF IT.
WHY DO WE DO IT EVERY YEAR?
MY THEORY IS THAT YOU'RE STUPID.

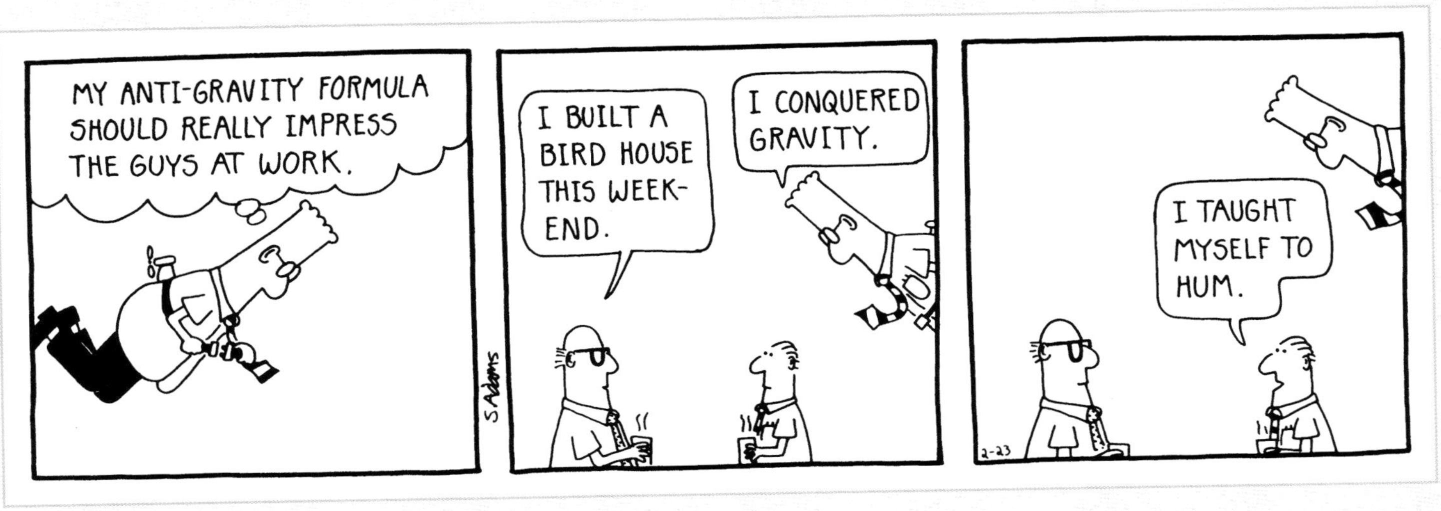
MY ANTI-GRAVITY FORMULA SHOULD REALLY IMPRESS THE GUYS AT WORK.
I BUILT A BIRD HOUSE THIS WEEK-END.
I CONQUERED GRAVITY.
I TAUGHT MYSELF TO HUM.

This is based on my recurring dream, which comes to me about once per year, where I can fly, but no one cares.

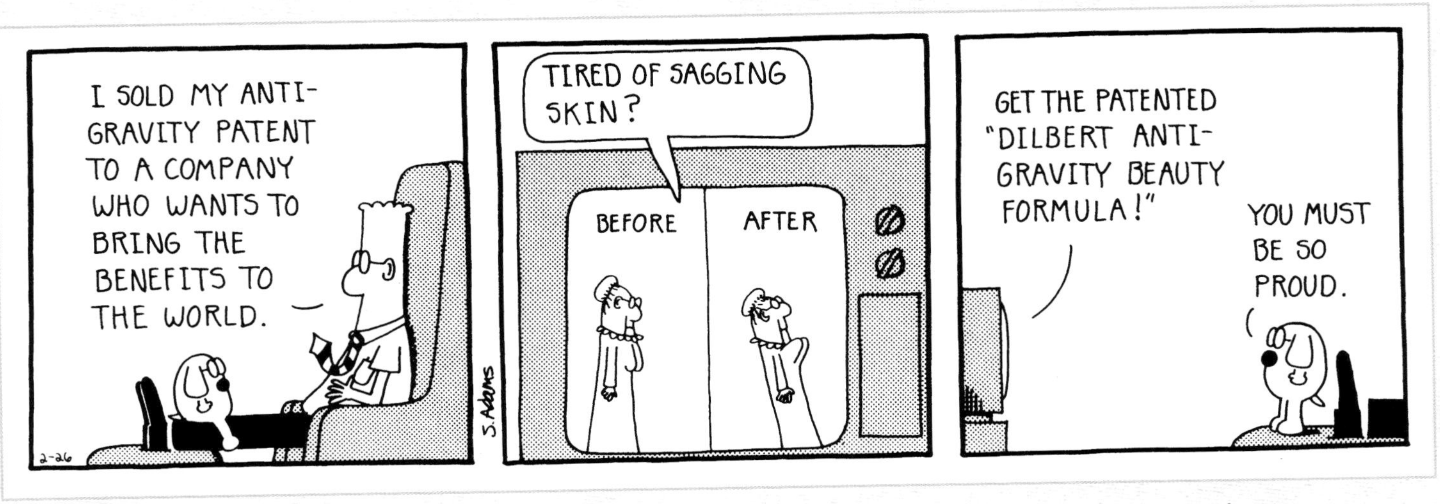
I SOLD MY ANTI-GRAVITY PATENT TO A COMPANY WHO WANTS TO BRING THE BENEFITS TO THE WORLD.
TIRED OF SAGGING SKIN?
BEFORE
AFTER
GET THE PATENTED "DILBERT ANTI-GRAVITY BEAUTY FORMULA!"
YOU MUST BE SO PROUD.

I was amazed this comic got published. My editor and assistant editor were both women at the time. I believe a male editor would have stopped it.

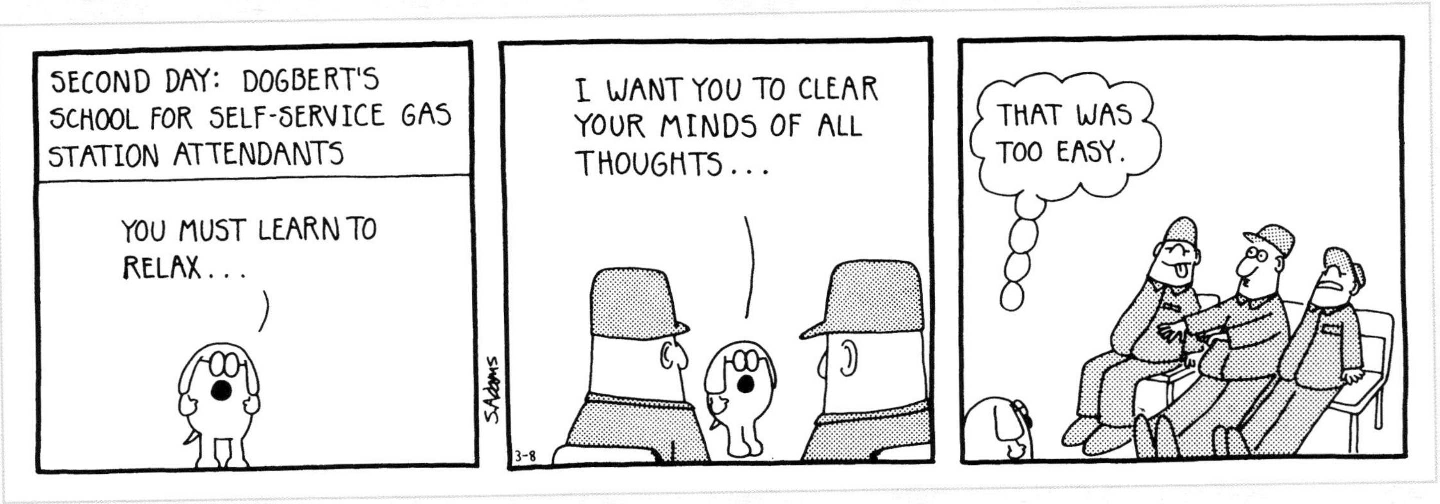
SECOND DAY: DOGBERT'S SCHOOL FOR SELF-SERVICE GAS STATION ATTENDANTS
YOU MUST LEARN TO RELAX...
I WANT YOU TO CLEAR YOUR MINDS OF ALL THOUGHTS...
THAT WAS TOO EASY.

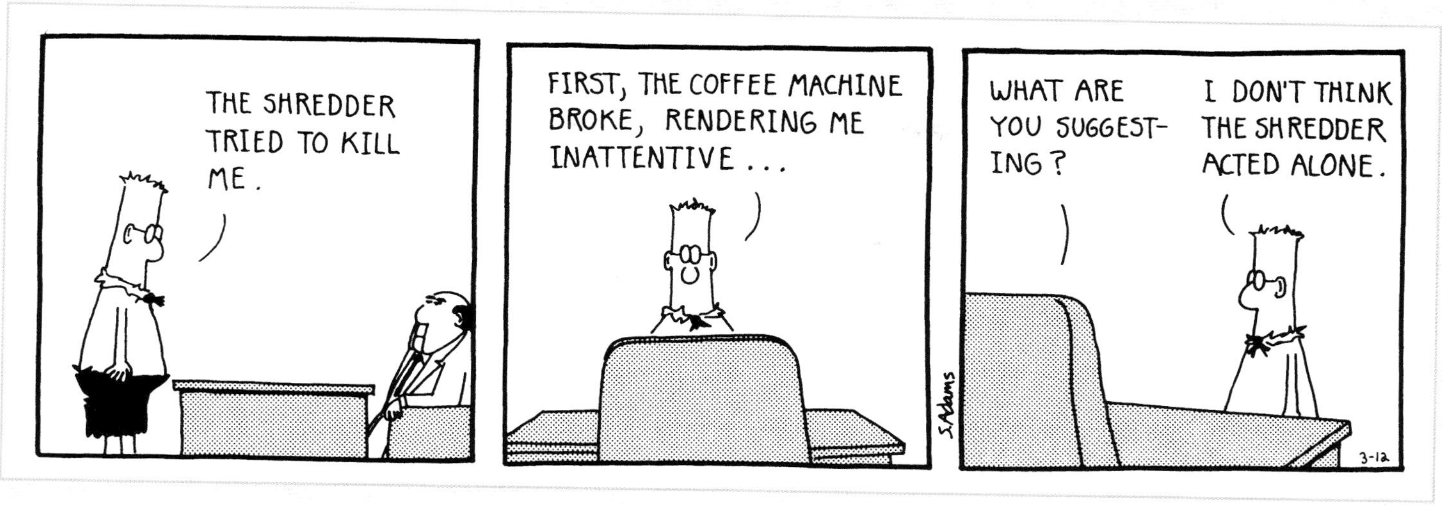
THE SHREDDER TRIED TO KILL ME.
FIRST, THE COFFEE MACHINE BROKE, RENDERING ME INATTENTIVE...
WHAT ARE YOU SUGGESTING?
I DON'T THINK THE SHREDDER ACTED ALONE.
S.Adams
3-12

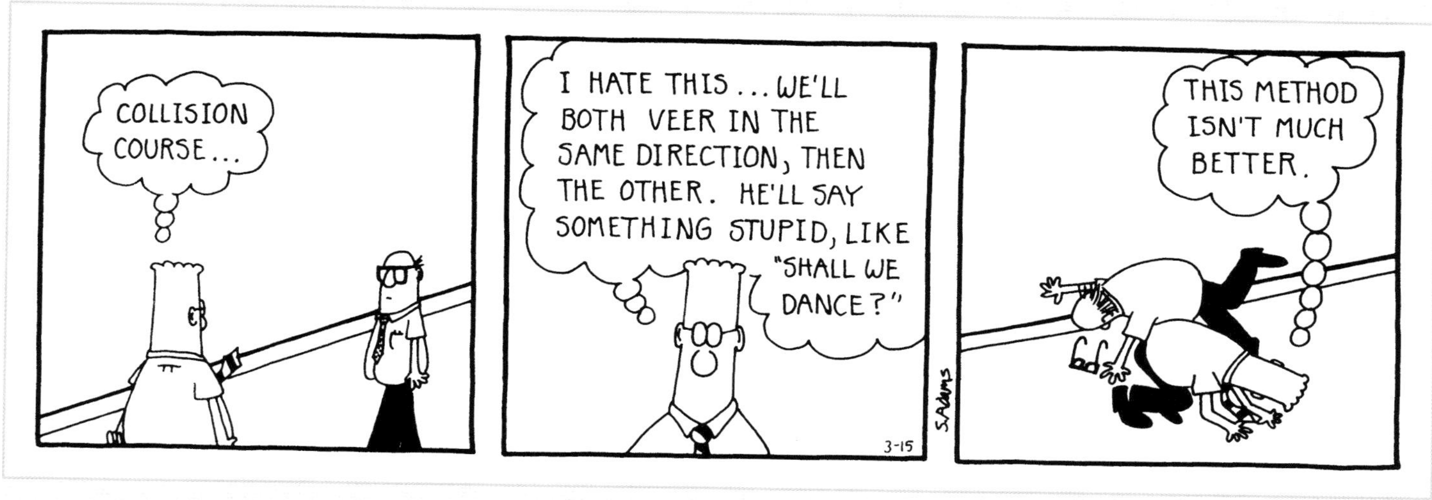
COLLISION COURSE...
I HATE THIS... WE'LL BOTH VEER IN THE SAME DIRECTION, THEN THE OTHER. HE'LL SAY SOMETHING STUPID, LIKE "SHALL WE DANCE?"
3-15
S.Adams
THIS METHOD ISN'T MUCH BETTER.

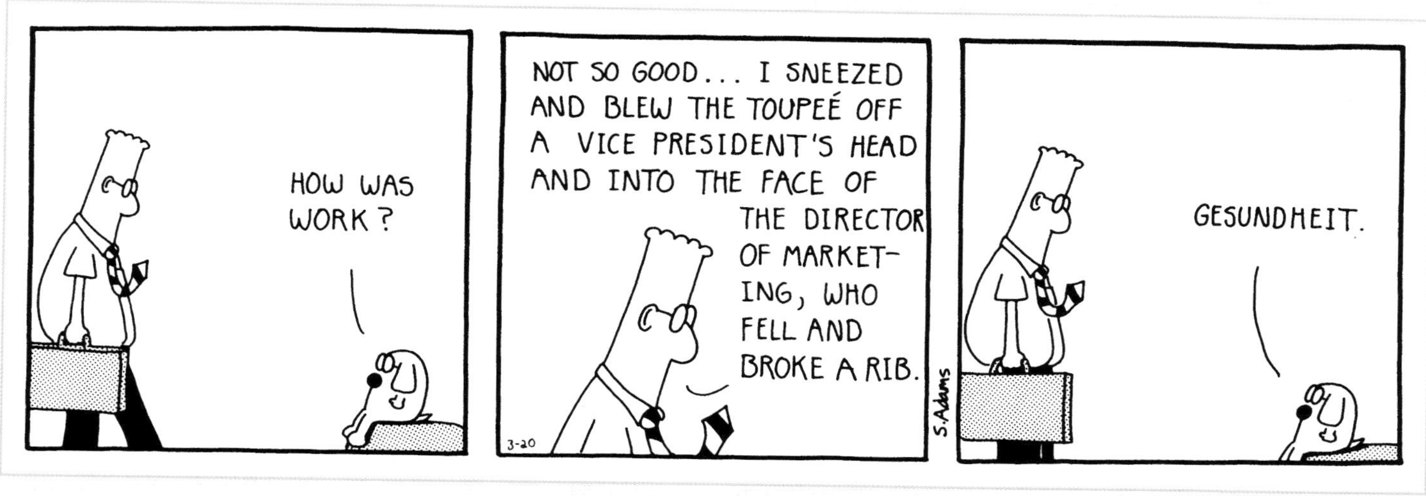
HOW WAS WORK?
NOT SO GOOD... I SNEEZED AND BLEW THE TOUPEÉ OFF A VICE PRESIDENT'S HEAD AND INTO THE FACE OF THE DIRECTOR OF MARKETING, WHO FELL AND BROKE A RIB.
3-20
S.Adams
GESUNDHEIT.

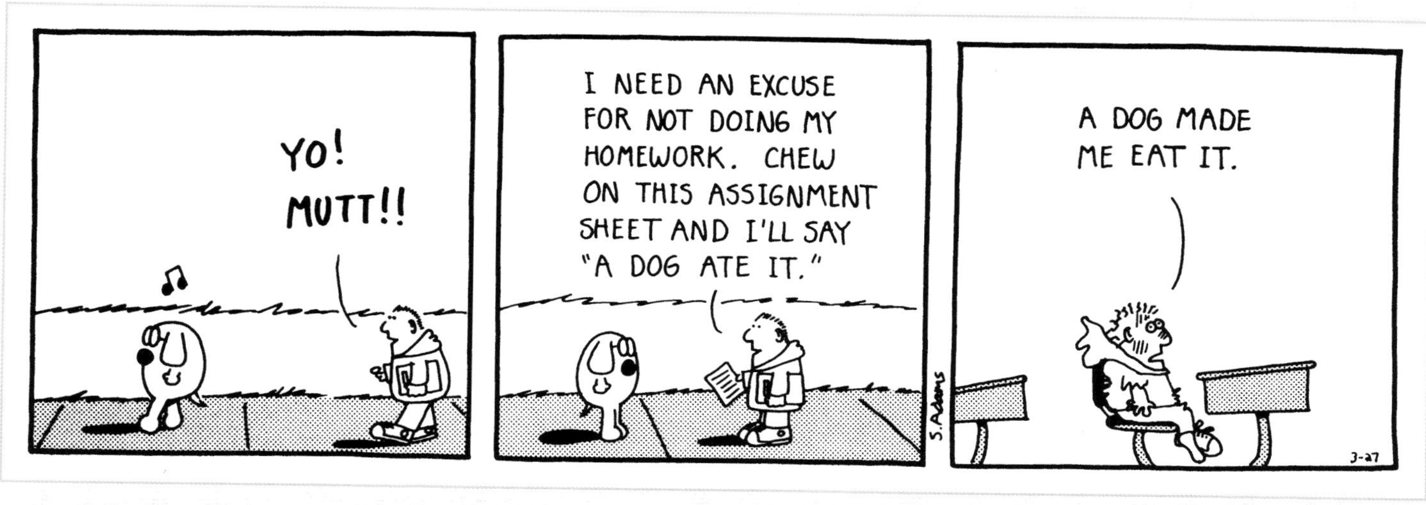
YO! MUTT!!
I NEED AN EXCUSE FOR NOT DOING MY HOMEWORK. CHEW ON THIS ASSIGNMENT SHEET AND I'LL SAY "A DOG ATE IT."
S.Adams
A DOG MADE ME EAT IT.
3-27

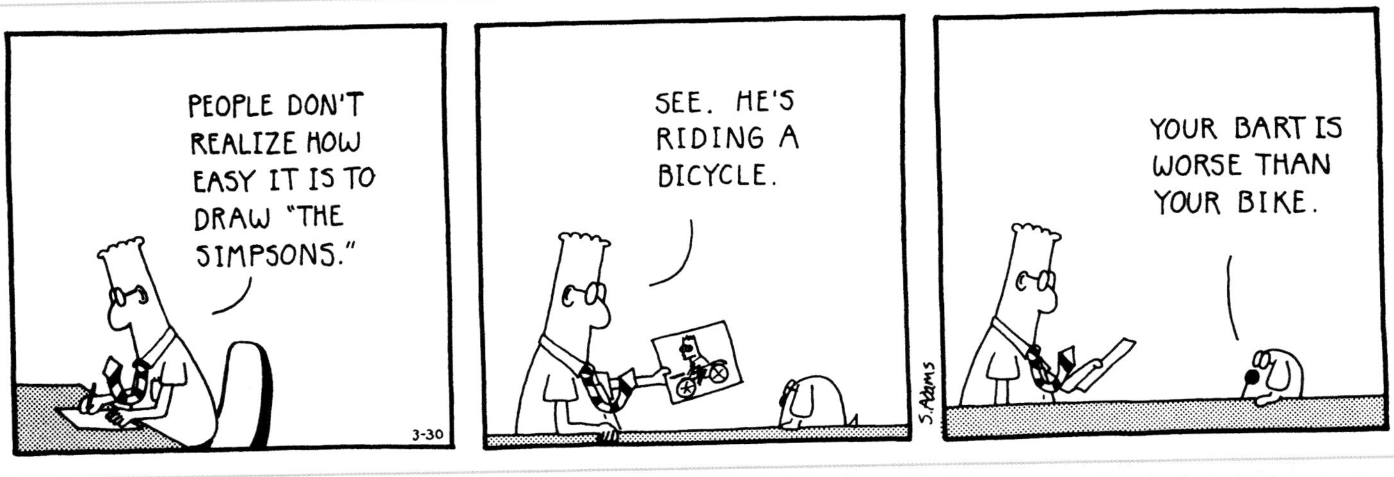
PEOPLE DON'T REALIZE HOW EASY IT IS TO DRAW "THE SIMPSONS."
SEE. HE'S RIDING A BICYCLE.
YOUR BART IS WORSE THAN YOUR BIKE.
3-30
S. Adams

I started drawing Dilbert in the mid-'80s, before The Simpsons *was on television.*
But The Simpsons *got famous faster, so people often think Dilbert's head is copied from Bart's look.*

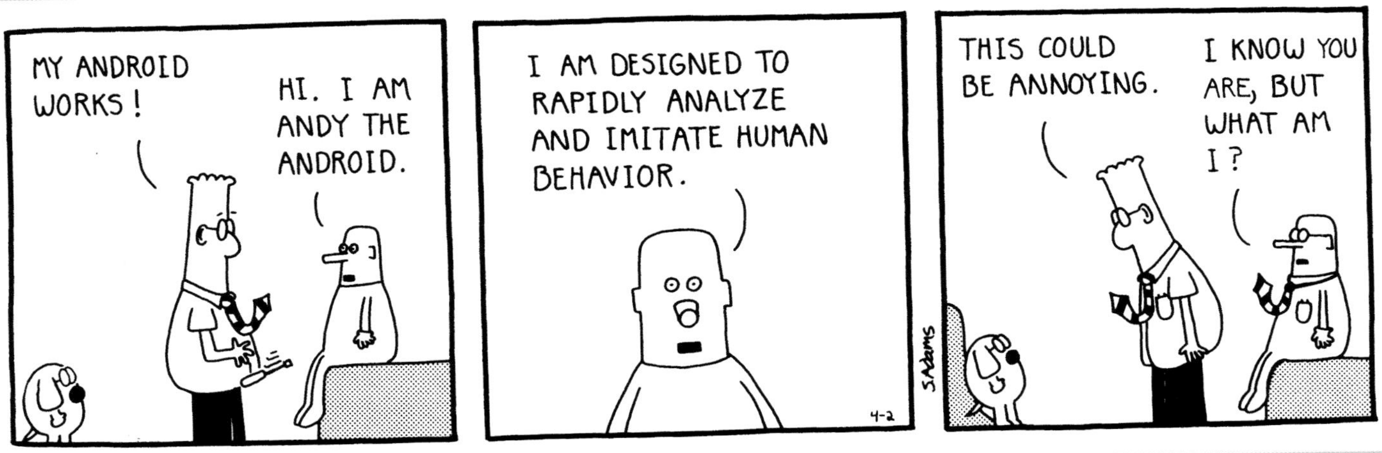
MY ANDROID WORKS!
HI. I AM ANDY THE ANDROID.
I AM DESIGNED TO RAPIDLY ANALYZE AND IMITATE HUMAN BEHAVIOR.
4-2
THIS COULD BE ANNOYING.
I KNOW YOU ARE, BUT WHAT AM I?
S. Adams

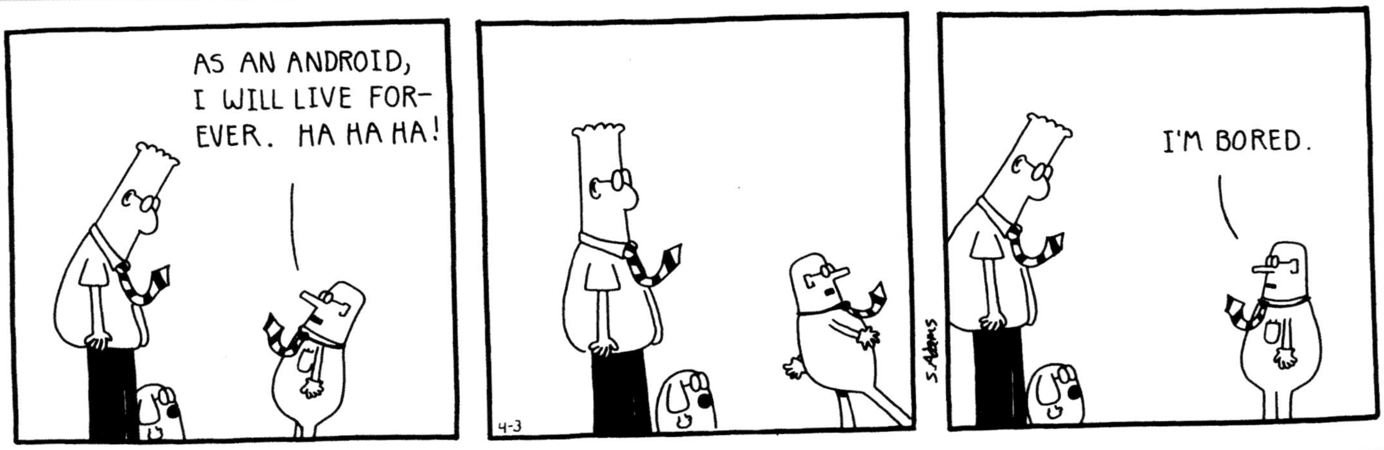
AS AN ANDROID, I WILL LIVE FOREVER. HA HA HA!
4-3
S. Adams
I'M BORED.

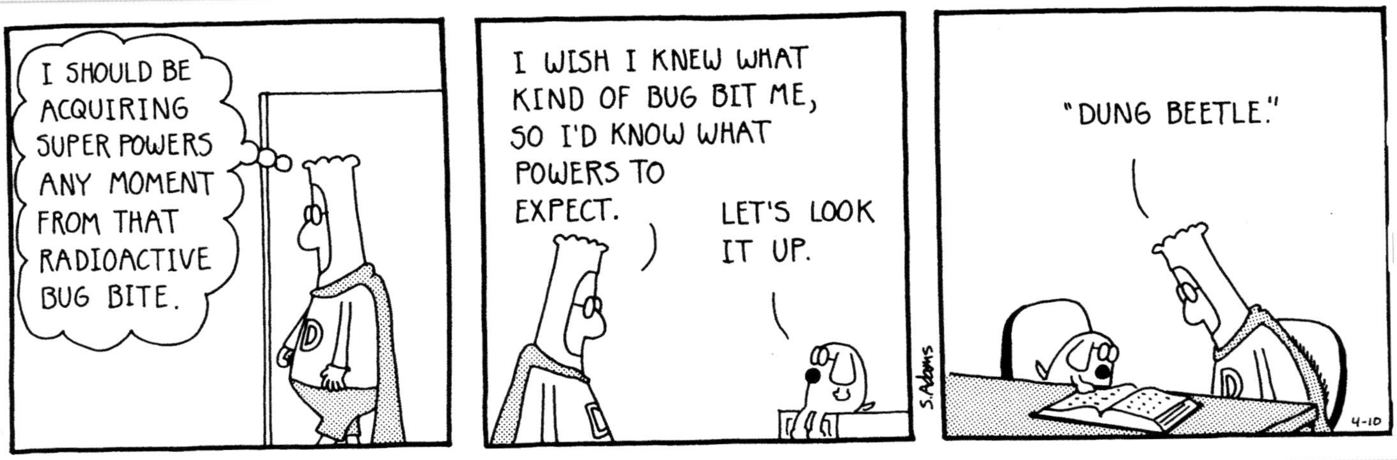
I SHOULD BE ACQUIRING SUPER POWERS ANY MOMENT FROM THAT RADIOACTIVE BUG BITE.
I WISH I KNEW WHAT KIND OF BUG BIT ME, SO I'D KNOW WHAT POWERS TO EXPECT.
LET'S LOOK IT UP.
S. Adams
"DUNG BEETLE."
4-10

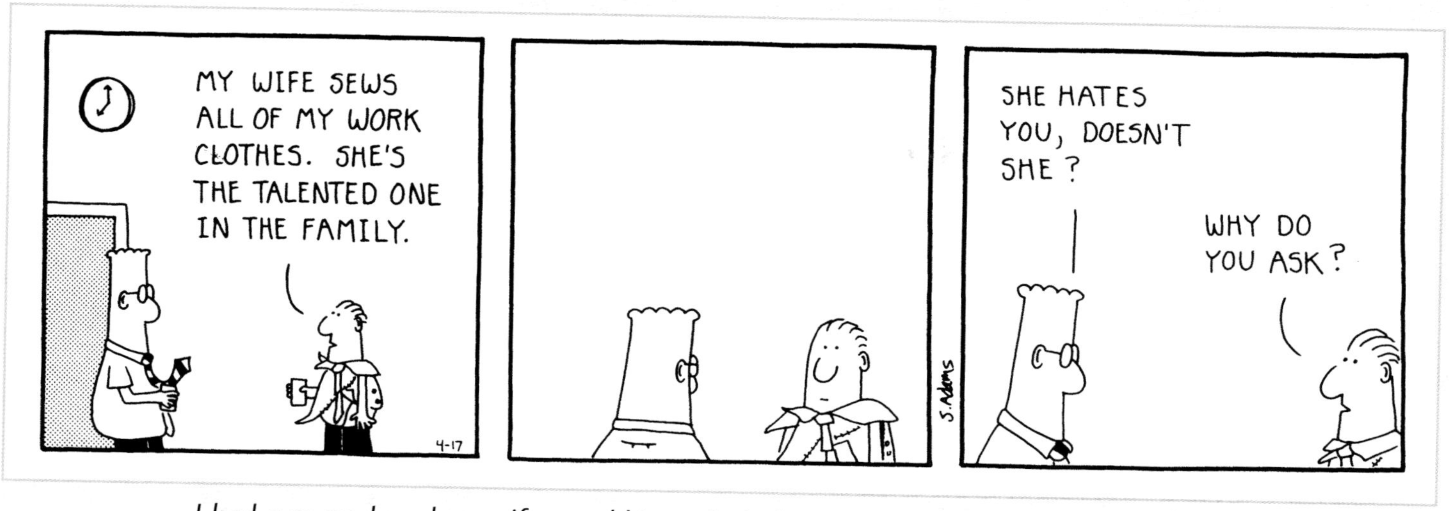
MY WIFE SEWS ALL OF MY WORK CLOTHES. SHE'S THE TALENTED ONE IN THE FAMILY.
SHE HATES YOU, DOESN'T SHE?
WHY DO YOU ASK?

I had a co-worker whose wife sewed his work clothes, including suits. At about this time, people started getting careful what they told me.

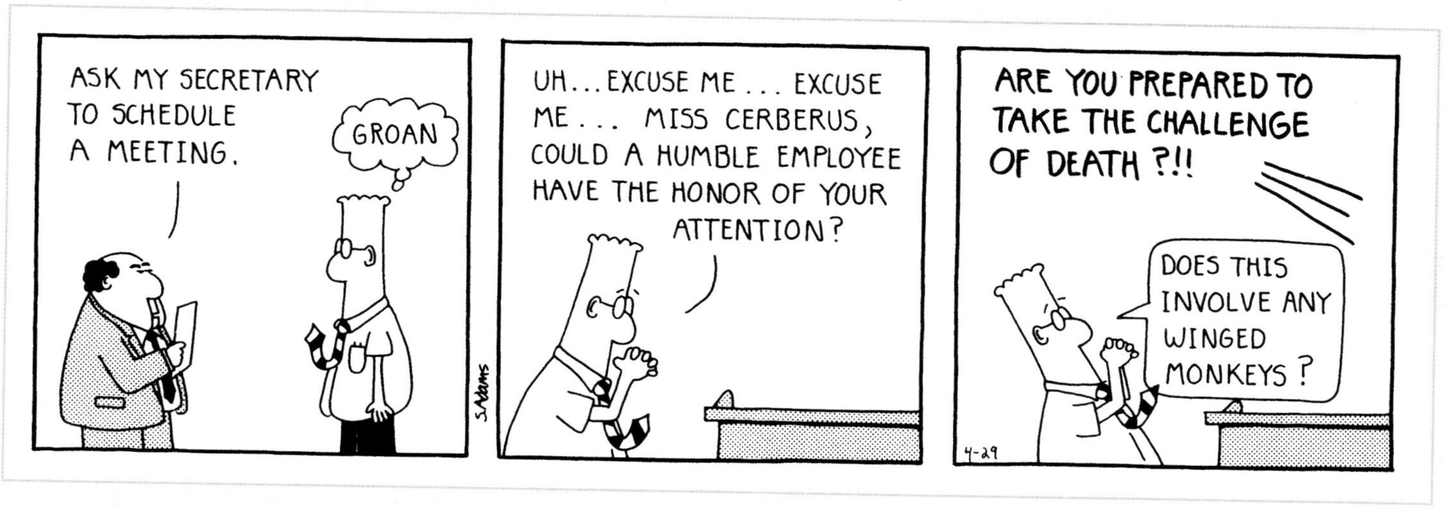
ASK MY SECRETARY TO SCHEDULE A MEETING.
GROAN
UH... EXCUSE ME... EXCUSE ME... MISS CERBERUS, COULD A HUMBLE EMPLOYEE HAVE THE HONOR OF YOUR ATTENTION?
ARE YOU PREPARED TO TAKE THE CHALLENGE OF DEATH ?!!
DOES THIS INVOLVE ANY WINGED MONKEYS?

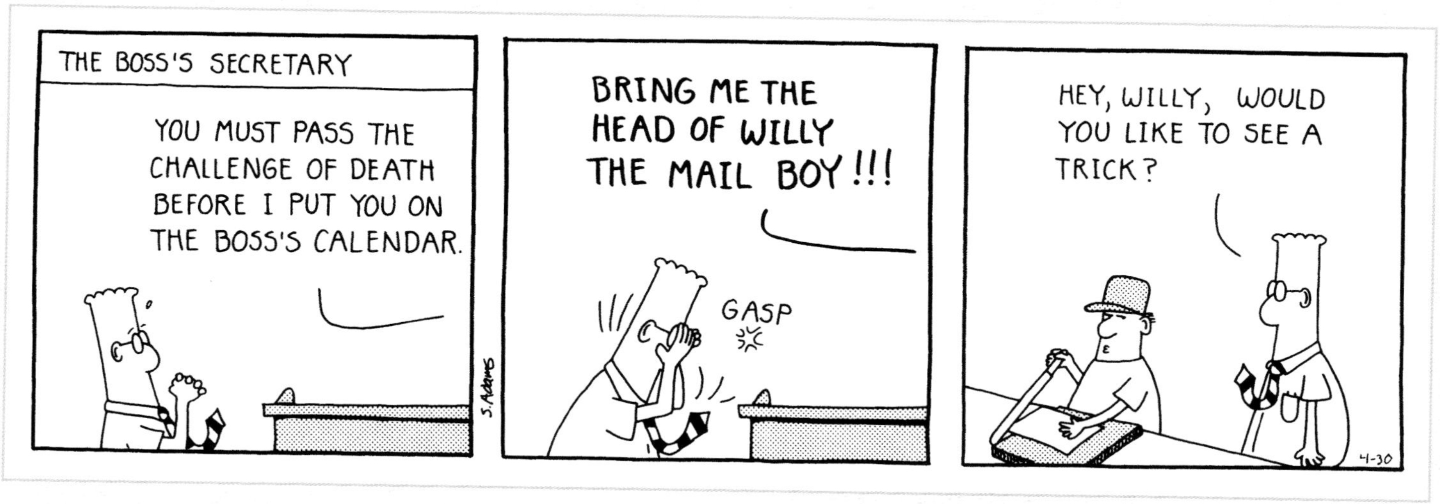
THE BOSS'S SECRETARY
YOU MUST PASS THE CHALLENGE OF DEATH BEFORE I PUT YOU ON THE BOSS'S CALENDAR.
BRING ME THE HEAD OF WILLY THE MAIL BOY!!!
GASP
HEY, WILLY, WOULD YOU LIKE TO SEE A TRICK?

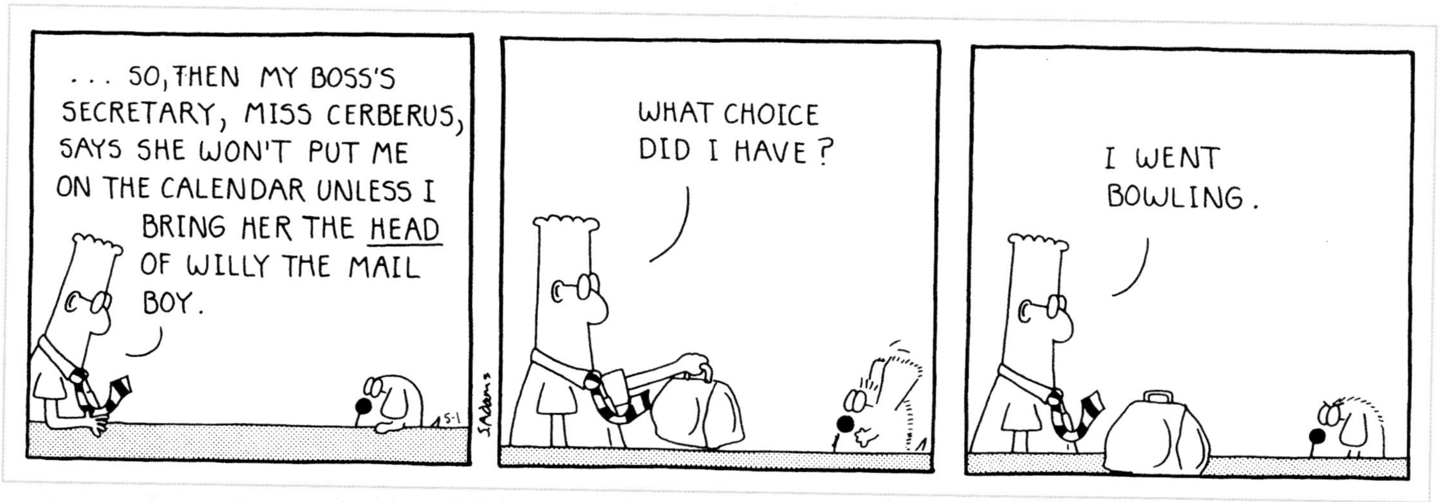
... SO, THEN MY BOSS'S SECRETARY, MISS CERBERUS, SAYS SHE WON'T PUT ME ON THE CALENDAR UNLESS I BRING HER THE HEAD OF WILLY THE MAIL BOY.
WHAT CHOICE DID I HAVE?
I WENT BOWLING.

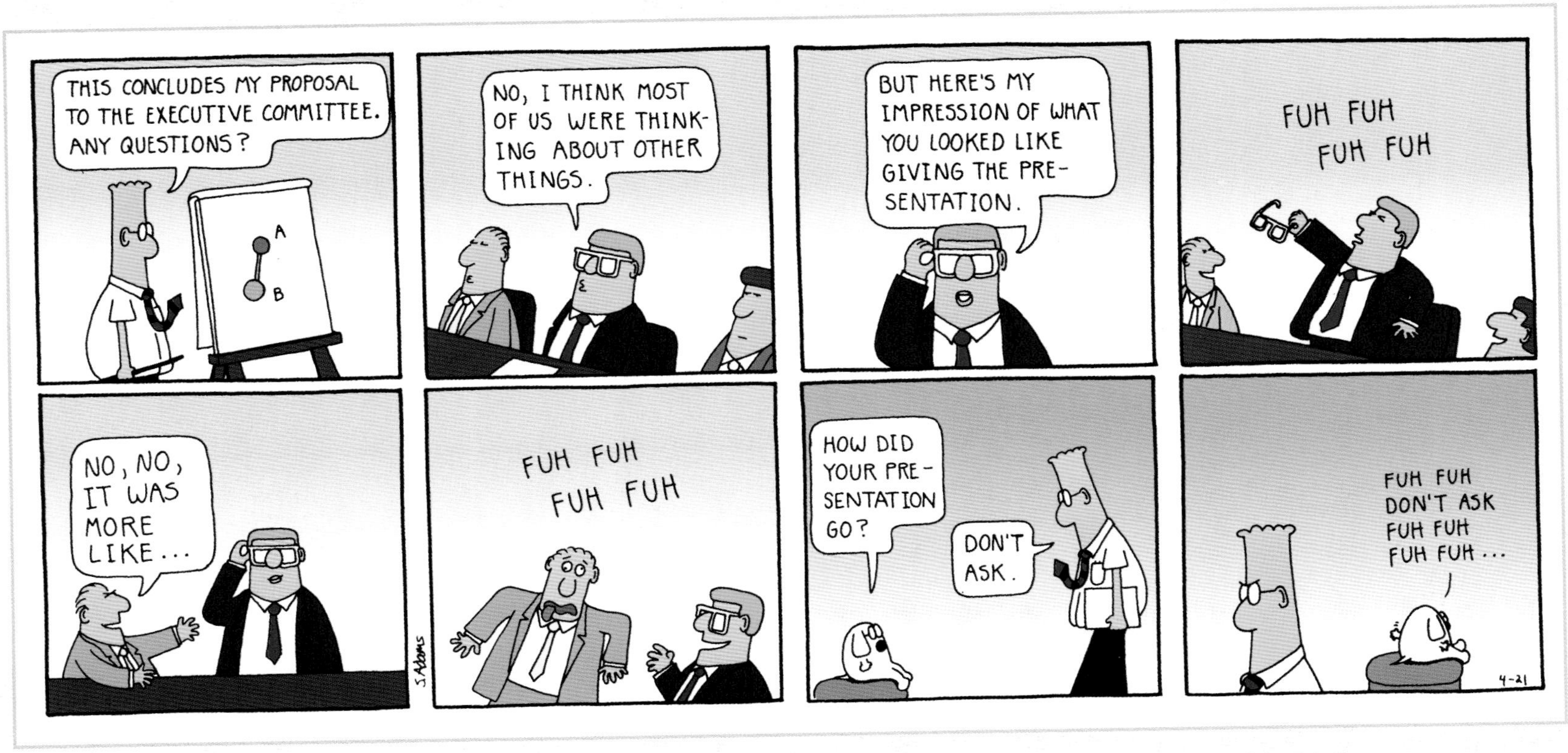
THIS CONCLUDES MY PROPOSAL TO THE EXECUTIVE COMMITTEE. ANY QUESTIONS?
A
B
NO, I THINK MOST OF US WERE THINKING ABOUT OTHER THINGS.
BUT HERE'S MY IMPRESSION OF WHAT YOU LOOKED LIKE GIVING THE PRESENTATION.
FUH FUH FUH FUH
NO, NO, IT WAS MORE LIKE...
FUH FUH FUH FUH
HOW DID YOUR PRESENTATION GO?
DON'T ASK.
FUH FUH DON'T ASK FUH FUH FUH FUH...
S. Adams
4-21

A vice president at Pacific Bell used to do unflattering imitations of his peers using the fuh-fuh-fuh form. It was funny and horrible at the same time.

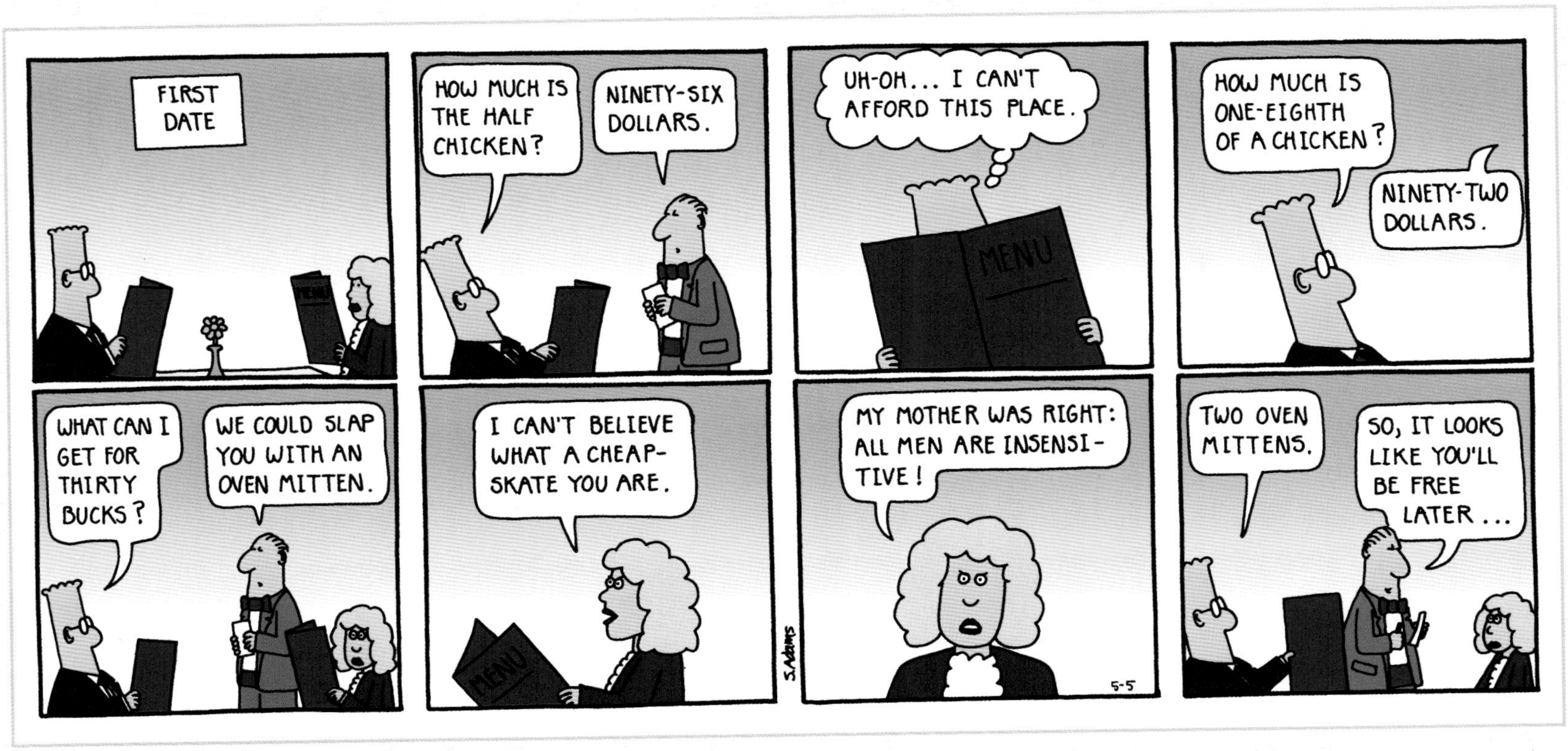
FIRST DATE
HOW MUCH IS THE HALF CHICKEN?
NINETY-SIX DOLLARS.
UH-OH... I CAN'T AFFORD THIS PLACE.
MENU
HOW MUCH IS ONE-EIGHTH OF A CHICKEN?
NINETY-TWO DOLLARS.
WHAT CAN I GET FOR THIRTY BUCKS?
WE COULD SLAP YOU WITH AN OVEN MITTEN.
I CAN'T BELIEVE WHAT A CHEAPSKATE YOU ARE.
MENU
MY MOTHER WAS RIGHT: ALL MEN ARE INSENSITIVE!
TWO OVEN MITTENS.
SO, IT LOOKS LIKE YOU'LL BE FREE LATER...
S. Adams
5-5

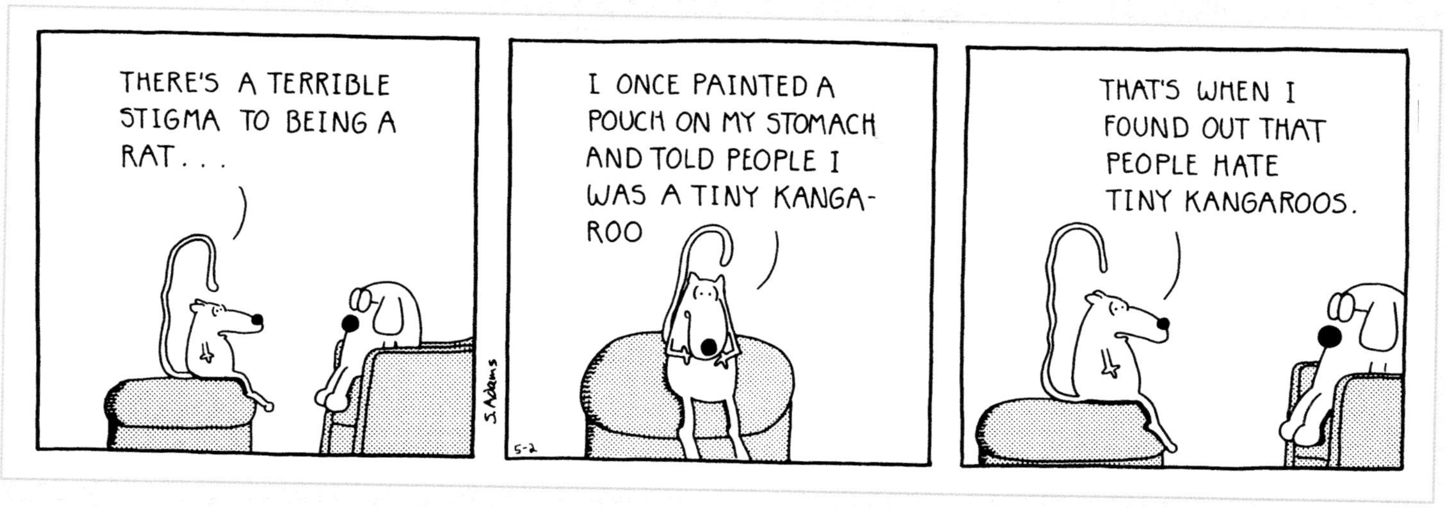
THERE'S A TERRIBLE STIGMA TO BEING A RAT...
I ONCE PAINTED A POUCH ON MY STOMACH AND TOLD PEOPLE I WAS A TINY KANGAROO
THAT'S WHEN I FOUND OUT THAT PEOPLE HATE TINY KANGAROOS.

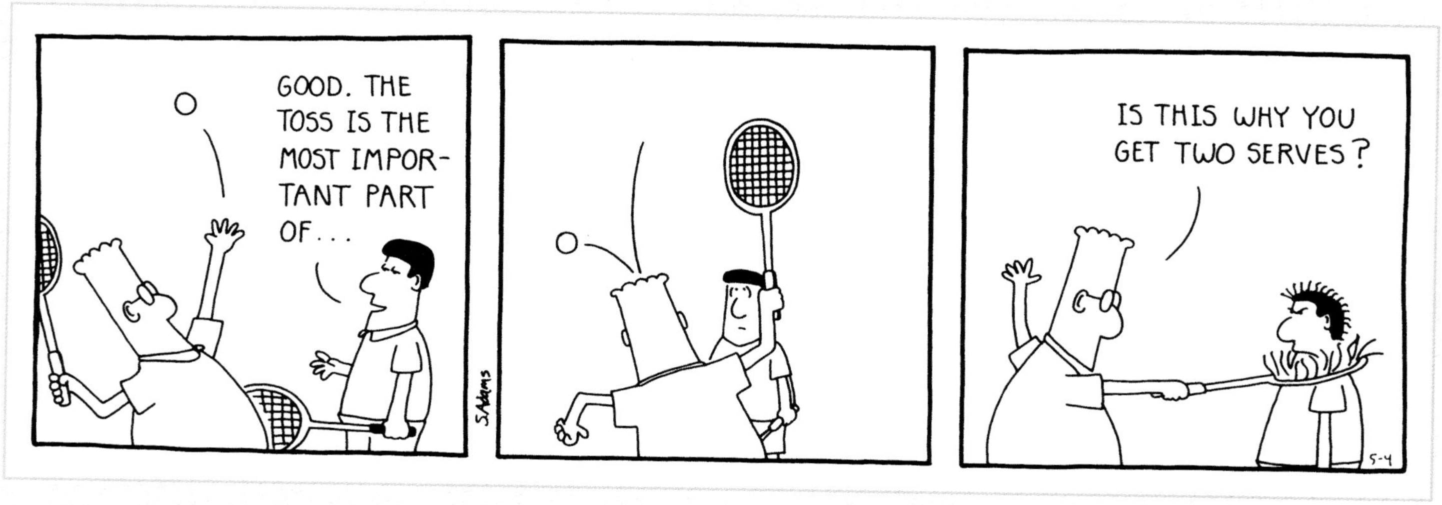
GOOD. THE TOSS IS THE MOST IMPORTANT PART OF...
IS THIS WHY YOU GET TWO SERVES?

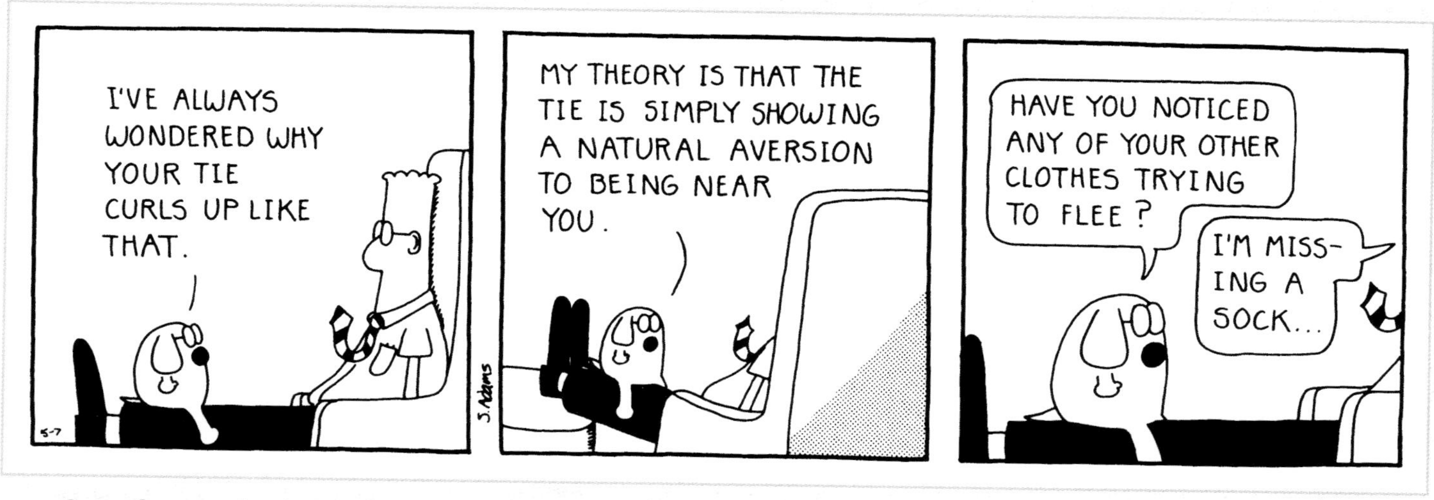
I'VE ALWAYS WONDERED WHY YOUR TIE CURLS UP LIKE THAT.
MY THEORY IS THAT THE TIE IS SIMPLY SHOWING A NATURAL AVERSION TO BEING NEAR YOU.
HAVE YOU NOTICED ANY OF YOUR OTHER CLOTHES TRYING TO FLEE?
I'M MISSING A SOCK...

One of my readers' most frequently asked questions is about Dilbert's upturned necktie. Why does it do that? I don't know the answer myself. My best guess is that I doodled him that way years ago, for no particular reason, before I knew I would be a professional cartoonist, liked how it looked, and kept it. Maybe I recognized it as a useful metaphor, or maybe I just thought it looked funny. I wish I remembered.

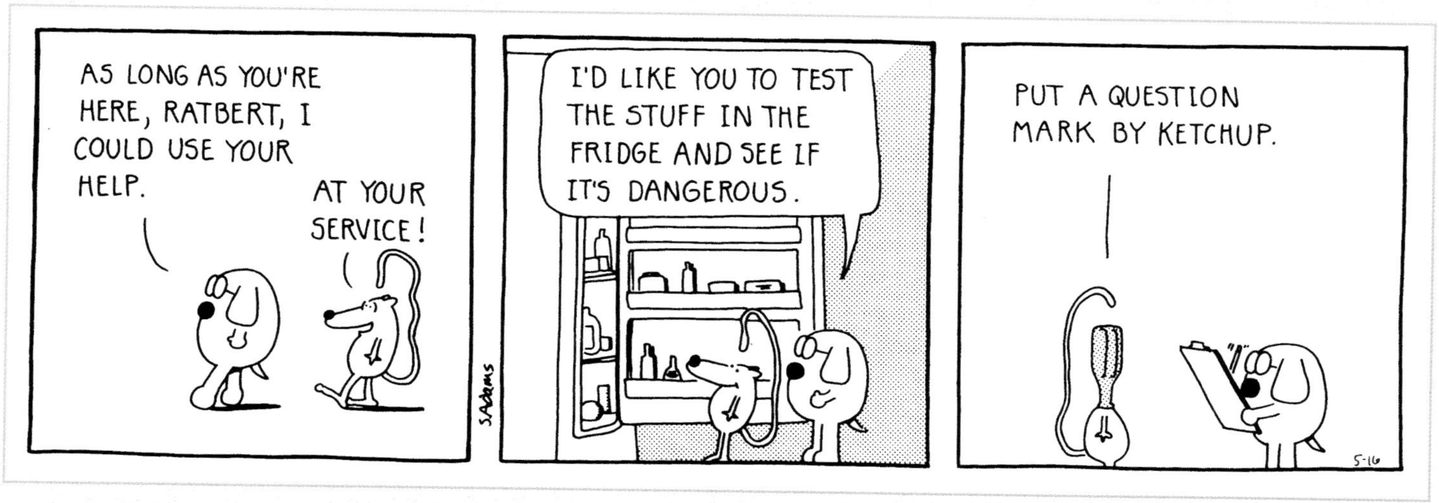
AS LONG AS YOU'RE HERE, RATBERT, I COULD USE YOUR HELP.
AT YOUR SERVICE!
I'D LIKE YOU TO TEST THE STUFF IN THE FRIDGE AND SEE IF IT'S DANGEROUS.
PUT A QUESTION MARK BY KETCHUP.

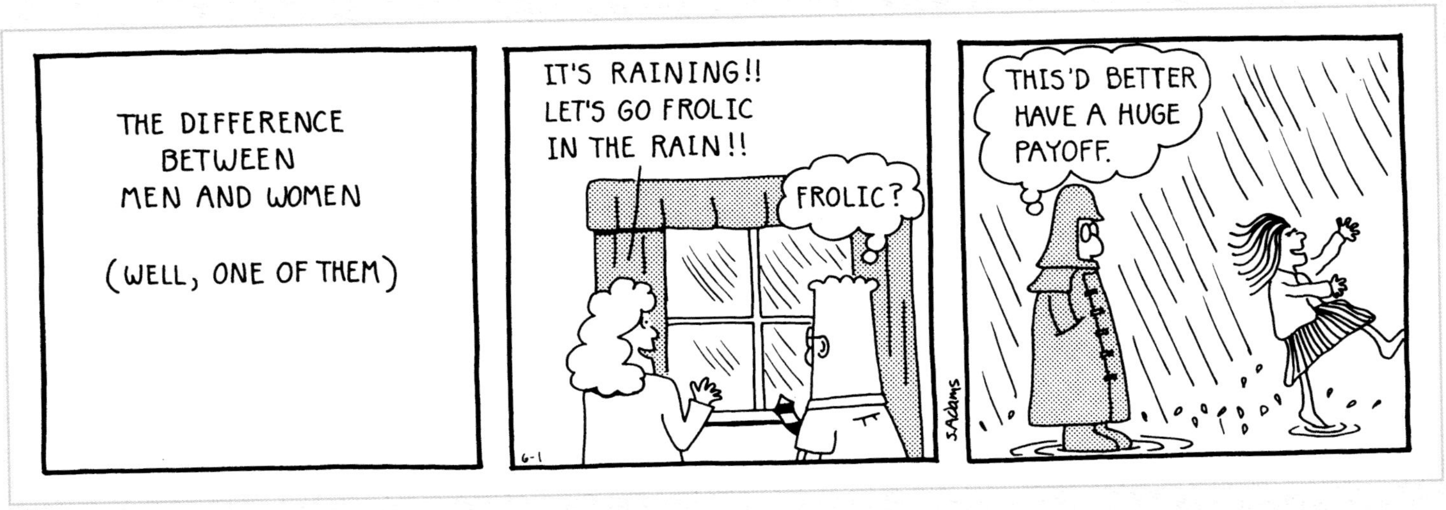
THE DIFFERENCE BETWEEN MEN AND WOMEN
(WELL, ONE OF THEM)
IT'S RAINING!! LET'S GO FROLIC IN THE RAIN!!
FROLIC?
THIS'D BETTER HAVE A HUGE PAYOFF.

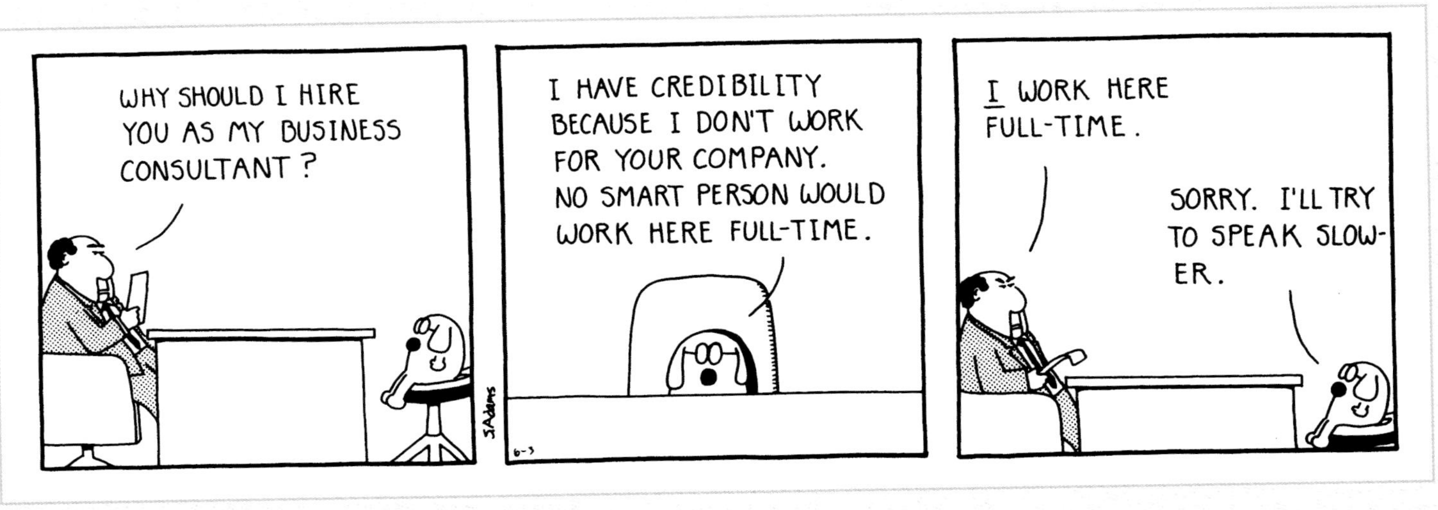
WHY SHOULD I HIRE YOU AS MY BUSINESS CONSULTANT?
I HAVE CREDIBILITY BECAUSE I DON'T WORK FOR YOUR COMPANY. NO SMART PERSON WOULD WORK HERE FULL-TIME.
I WORK HERE FULL-TIME.
SORRY. I'LL TRY TO SPEAK SLOW-ER.

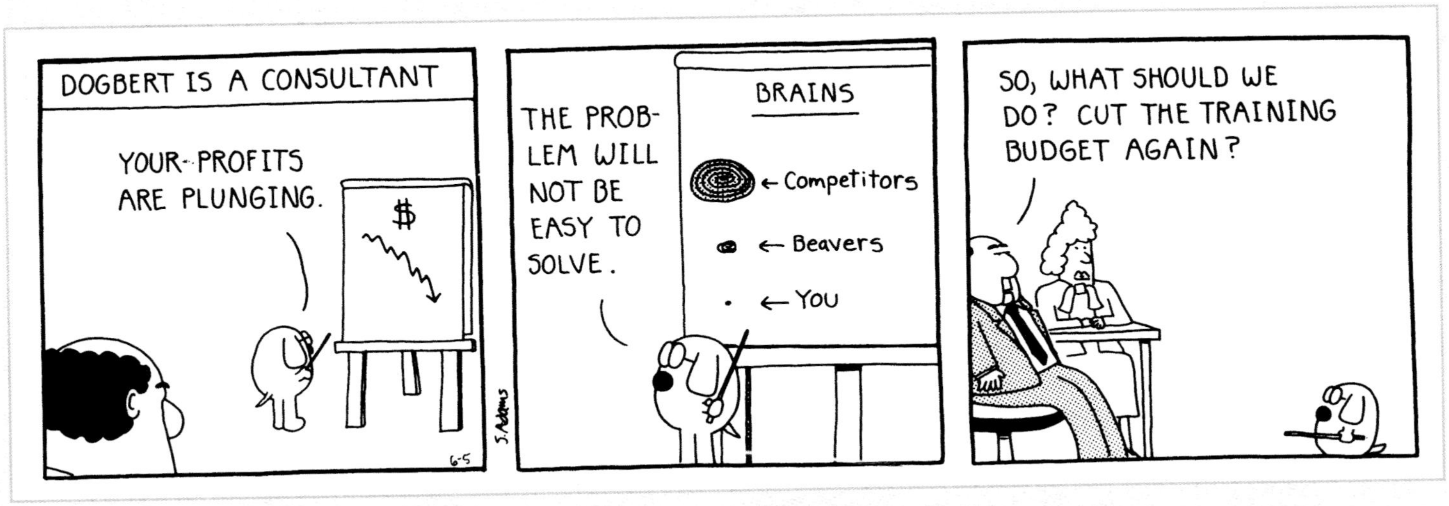
DOGBERT IS A CONSULTANT
YOUR PROFITS ARE PLUNGING.
$
THE PROB-LEM WILL NOT BE EASY TO SOLVE.
BRAINS
← Competitors
← Beavers
← You
SO, WHAT SHOULD WE DO? CUT THE TRAINING BUDGET AGAIN?

This day, Wally is Johnson. The real main characters have no last names, intentionally. That makes them easier to relate to.

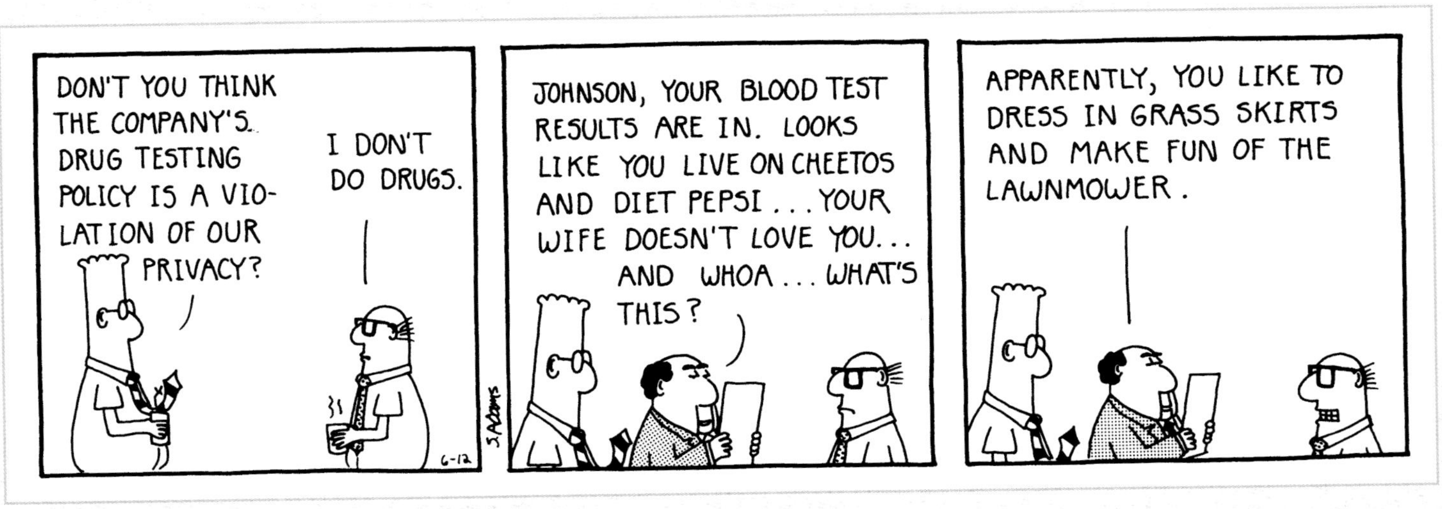
DON'T YOU THINK THE COMPANY'S DRUG TESTING POLICY IS A VIO-LATION OF OUR PRIVACY?
I DON'T DO DRUGS.
JOHNSON, YOUR BLOOD TEST RESULTS ARE IN. LOOKS LIKE YOU LIVE ON CHEETOS AND DIET PEPSI... YOUR WIFE DOESN'T LOVE YOU... AND WHOA... WHAT'S THIS?
APPARENTLY, YOU LIKE TO DRESS IN GRASS SKIRTS AND MAKE FUN OF THE LAWNMOWER.

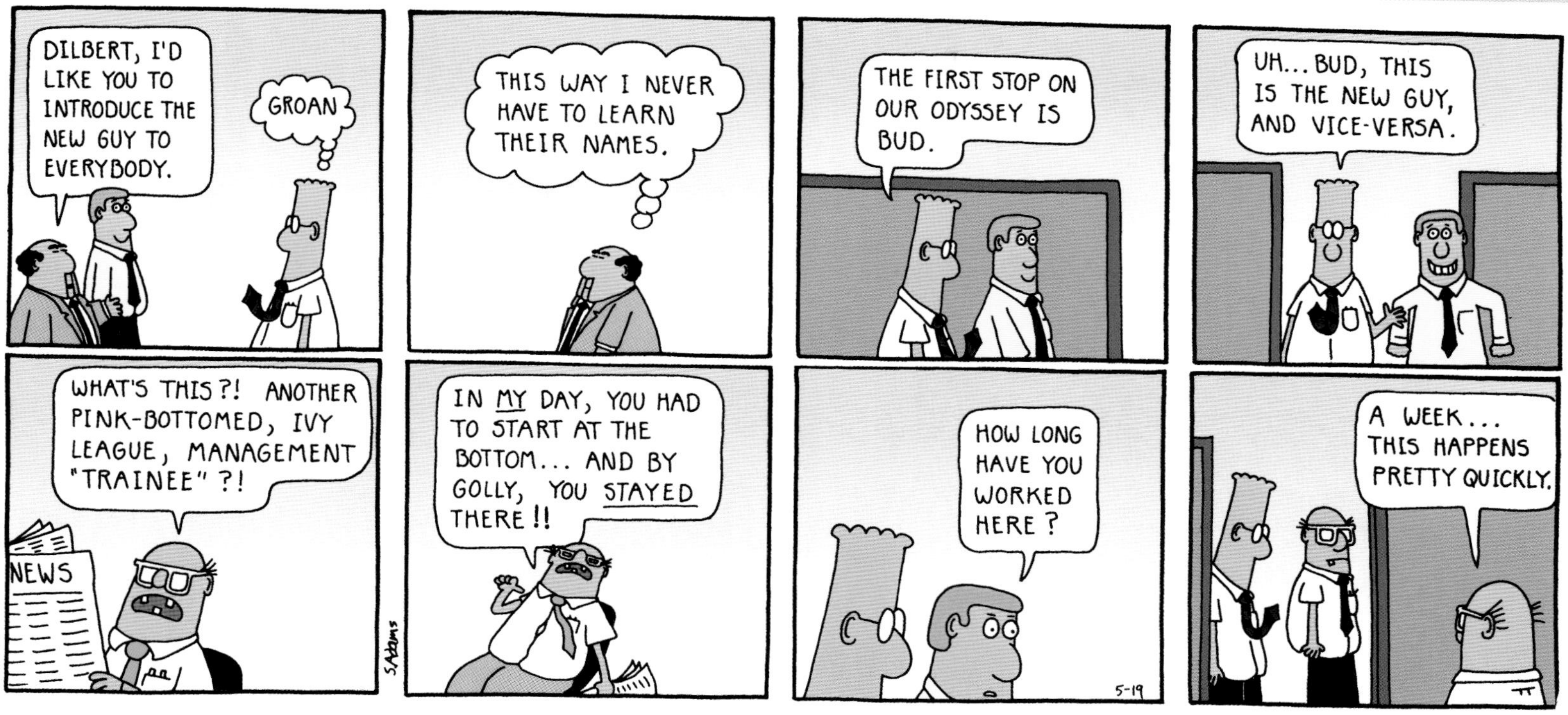
DILBERT, I'D LIKE YOU TO INTRODUCE THE NEW GUY TO EVERYBODY.
GROAN
THIS WAY I NEVER HAVE TO LEARN THEIR NAMES.
THE FIRST STOP ON OUR ODYSSEY IS BUD.
UH... BUD, THIS IS THE NEW GUY, AND VICE-VERSA.
WHAT'S THIS?! ANOTHER PINK-BOTTOMED, IVY LEAGUE, MANAGEMENT "TRAINEE"?!
NEWS
IN MY DAY, YOU HAD TO START AT THE BOTTOM... AND BY GOLLY, YOU STAYED THERE!!
HOW LONG HAVE YOU WORKED HERE?
A WEEK... THIS HAPPENS PRETTY QUICKLY.
S.Adams
5-19

Wally didn't have his official name yet. He was still a generic representation of an older employee coasting to retirement.

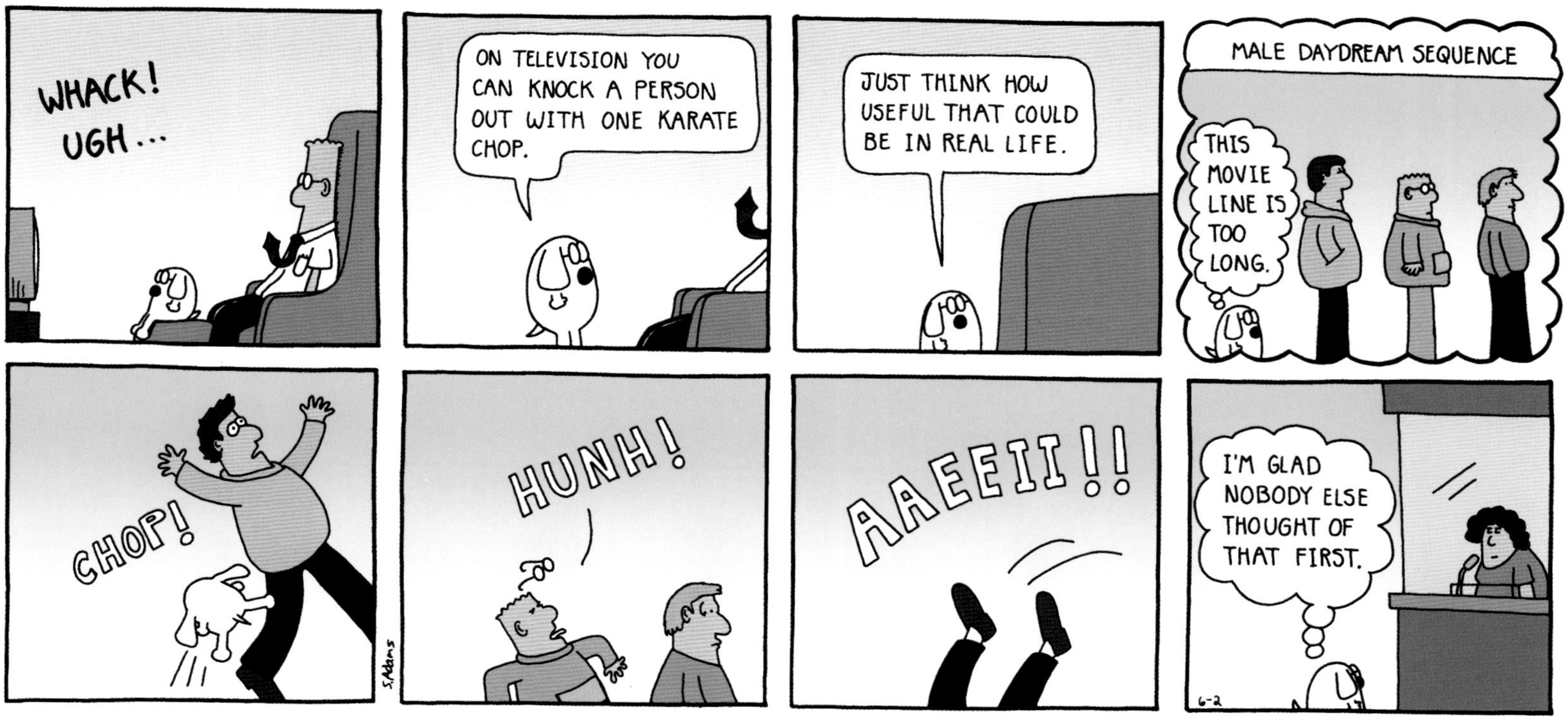
WHACK! UGH...
ON TELEVISION YOU CAN KNOCK A PERSON OUT WITH ONE KARATE CHOP.
JUST THINK HOW USEFUL THAT COULD BE IN REAL LIFE.
MALE DAYDREAM SEQUENCE
THIS MOVIE LINE IS TOO LONG.
CHOP!
HUNH!
AAEEII!!
I'M GLAD NOBODY ELSE THOUGHT OF THAT FIRST.
S.Adams
6-2

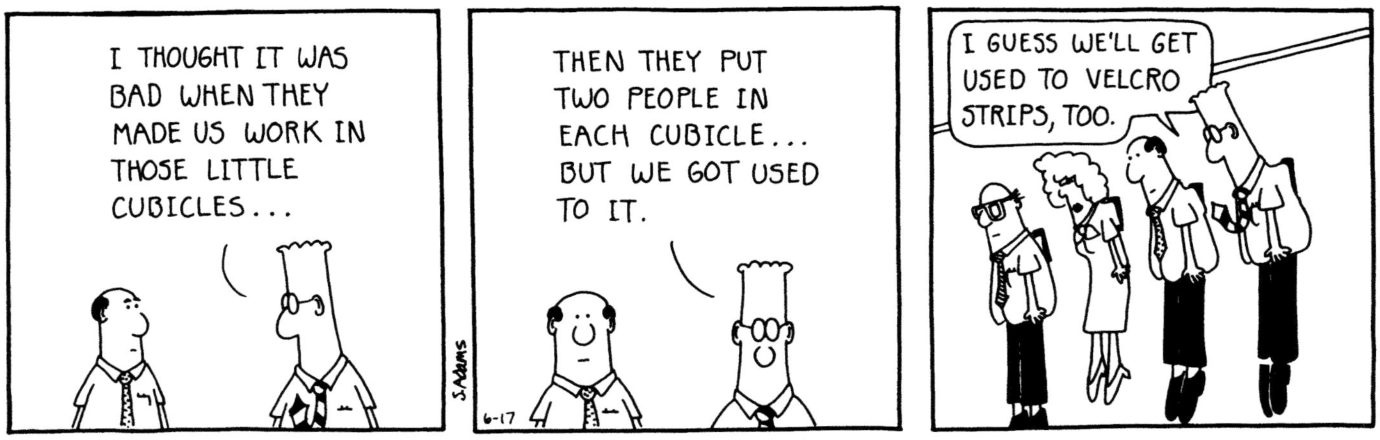
I THOUGHT IT WAS BAD WHEN THEY MADE US WORK IN THOSE LITTLE CUBICLES...
THEN THEY PUT TWO PEOPLE IN EACH CUBICLE... BUT WE GOT USED TO IT.
I GUESS WE'LL GET USED TO VELCRO STRIPS, TOO.
S.Adams
6-17

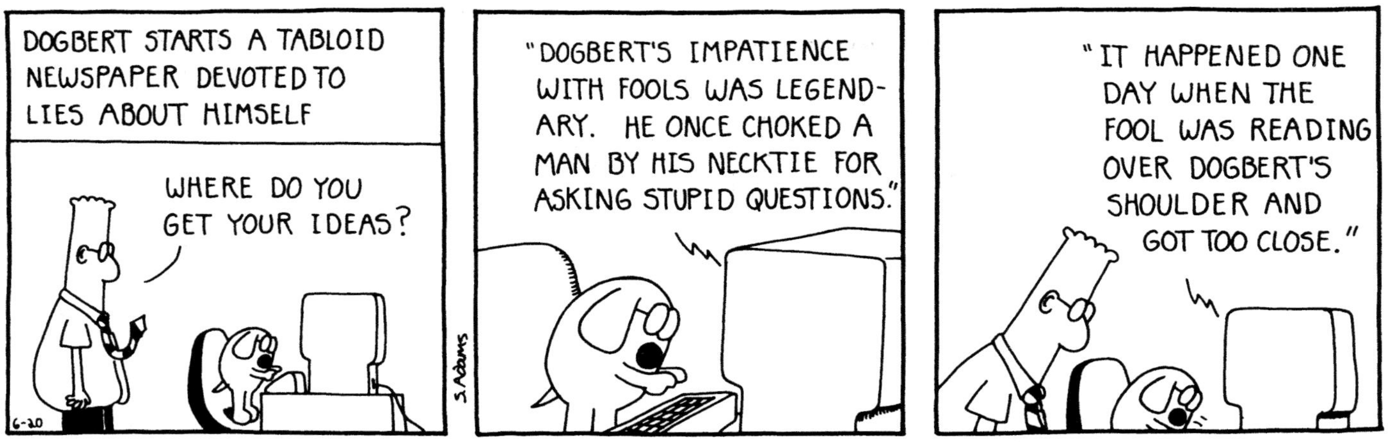
DOGBERT STARTS A TABLOID NEWSPAPER DEVOTED TO LIES ABOUT HIMSELF
WHERE DO YOU GET YOUR IDEAS?
6-20
"DOGBERT'S IMPATIENCE WITH FOOLS WAS LEGENDARY. HE ONCE CHOKED A MAN BY HIS NECKTIE FOR ASKING STUPID QUESTIONS."
S.Adams
"IT HAPPENED ONE DAY WHEN THE FOOL WAS READING OVER DOGBERT'S SHOULDER AND GOT TOO CLOSE."

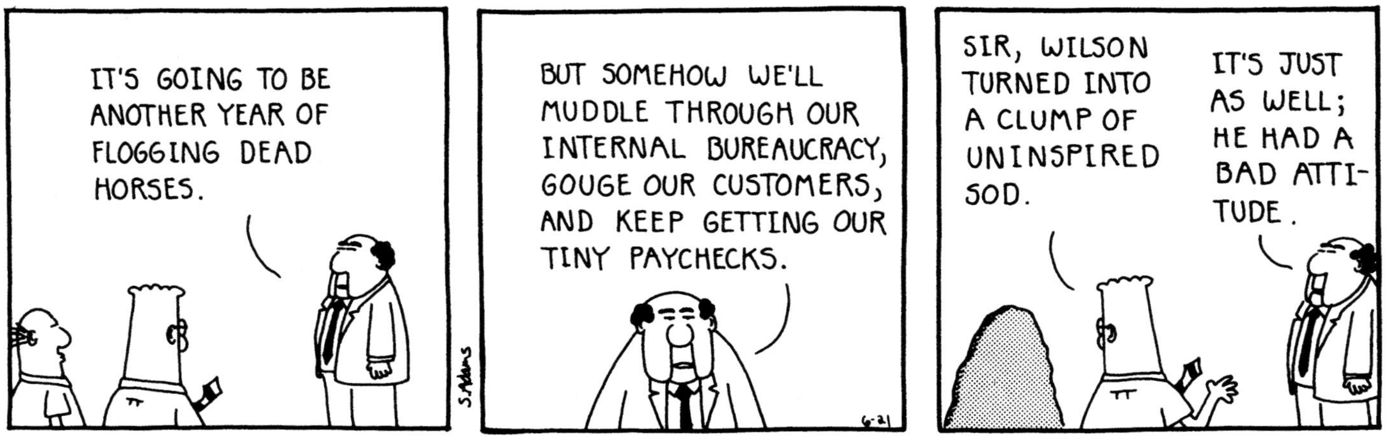
IT'S GOING TO BE ANOTHER YEAR OF FLOGGING DEAD HORSES.
S.Adams
BUT SOMEHOW WE'LL MUDDLE THROUGH OUR INTERNAL BUREAUCRACY, GOUGE OUR CUSTOMERS, AND KEEP GETTING OUR TINY PAYCHECKS.
6-21
SIR, WILSON TURNED INTO A CLUMP OF UNINSPIRED SOD.
IT'S JUST AS WELL; HE HAD A BAD ATTITUDE.

At about this time, I learned the vice president for my division had wanted to fire me for a comic that ran the previous year, mocking a memo he had written (see page 87). This series, where Dilbert is invited to have lunch with a senior executive, is based on my experience with that same vice president.

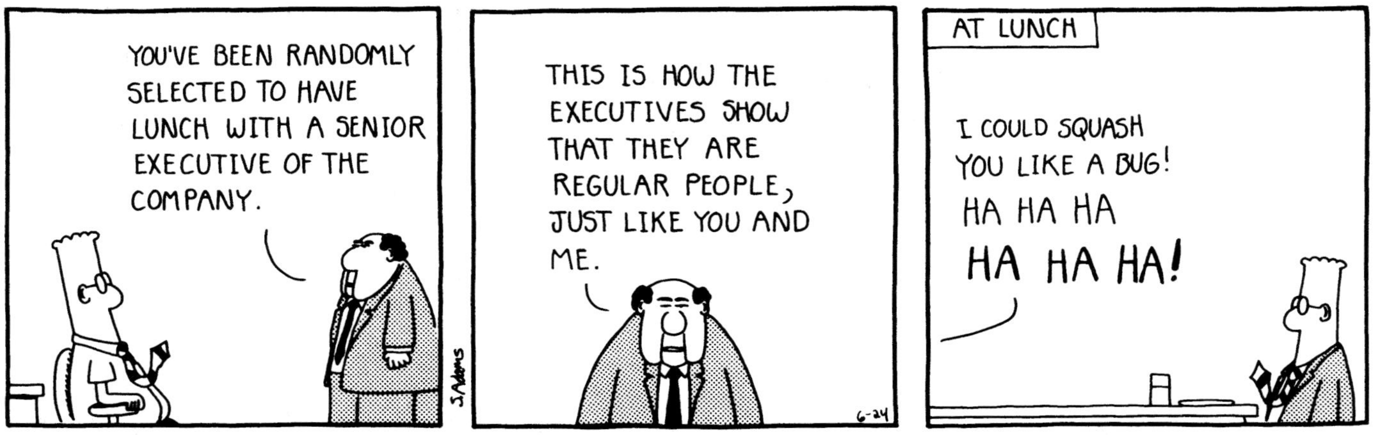
YOU'VE BEEN RANDOMLY SELECTED TO HAVE LUNCH WITH A SENIOR EXECUTIVE OF THE COMPANY.
S.Adams
THIS IS HOW THE EXECUTIVES SHOW THAT THEY ARE REGULAR PEOPLE, JUST LIKE YOU AND ME.
6-24
AT LUNCH
I COULD SQUASH YOU LIKE A BUG! HA HA HA
HA HA HA!

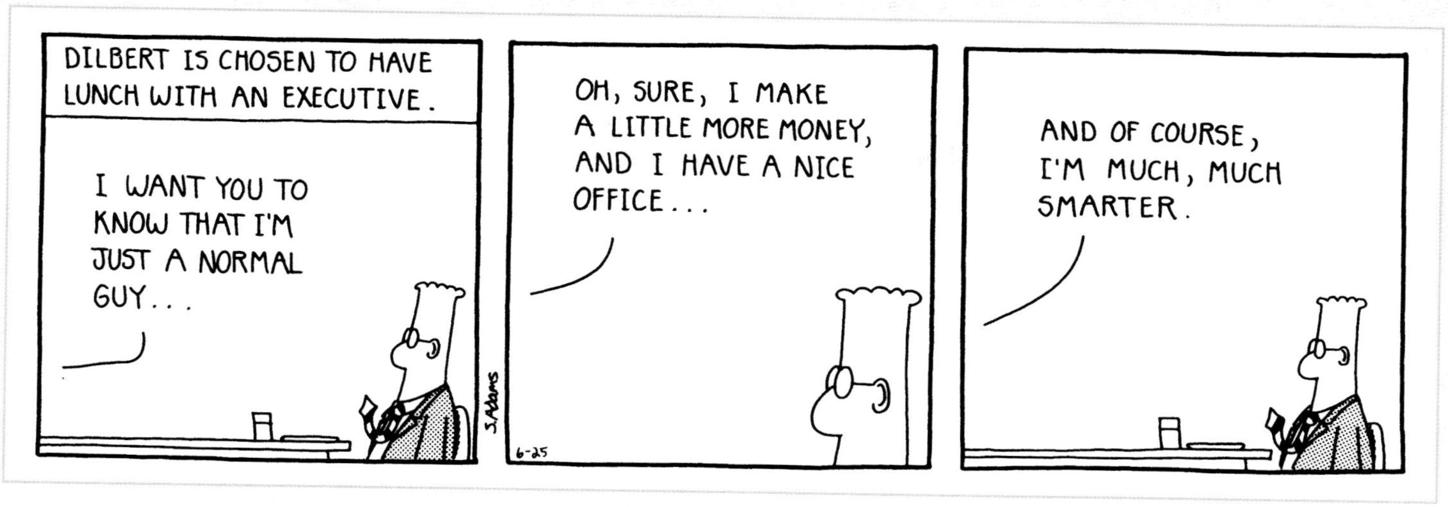
DILBERT IS CHOSEN TO HAVE LUNCH WITH AN EXECUTIVE.
I WANT YOU TO KNOW THAT I'M JUST A NORMAL GUY...
OH, SURE, I MAKE A LITTLE MORE MONEY, AND I HAVE A NICE OFFICE...
AND OF COURSE, I'M MUCH, MUCH SMARTER.

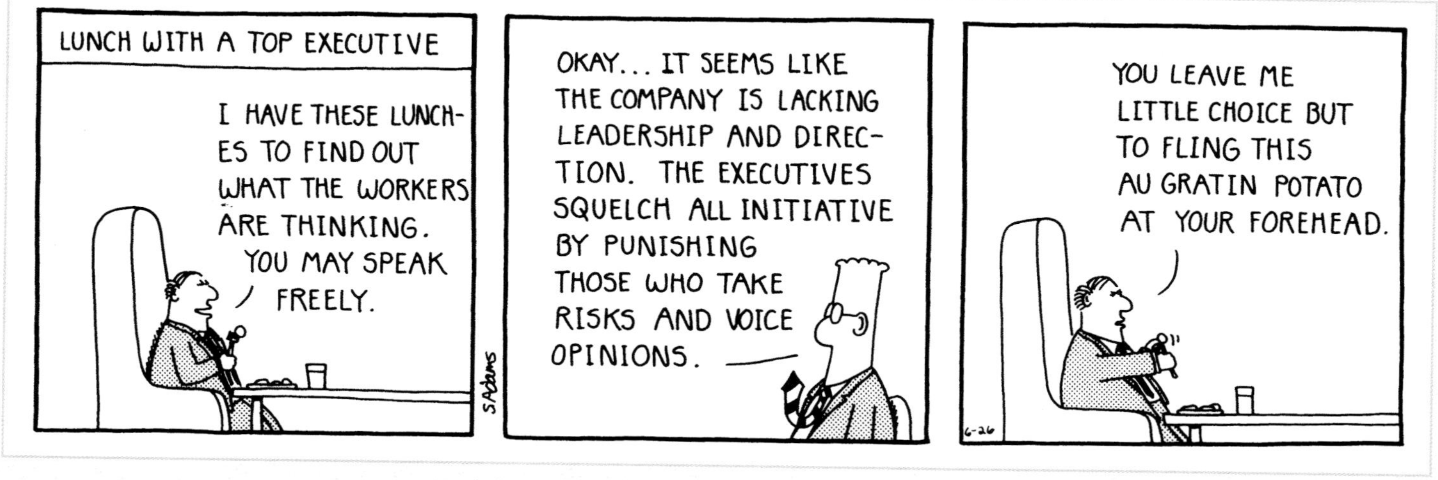
LUNCH WITH A TOP EXECUTIVE
I HAVE THESE LUNCHES TO FIND OUT WHAT THE WORKERS ARE THINKING. YOU MAY SPEAK FREELY.
OKAY... IT SEEMS LIKE THE COMPANY IS LACKING LEADERSHIP AND DIRECTION. THE EXECUTIVES SQUELCH ALL INITIATIVE BY PUNISHING THOSE WHO TAKE RISKS AND VOICE OPINIONS.
YOU LEAVE ME LITTLE CHOICE BUT TO FLING THIS AU GRATIN POTATO AT YOUR FOREHEAD.

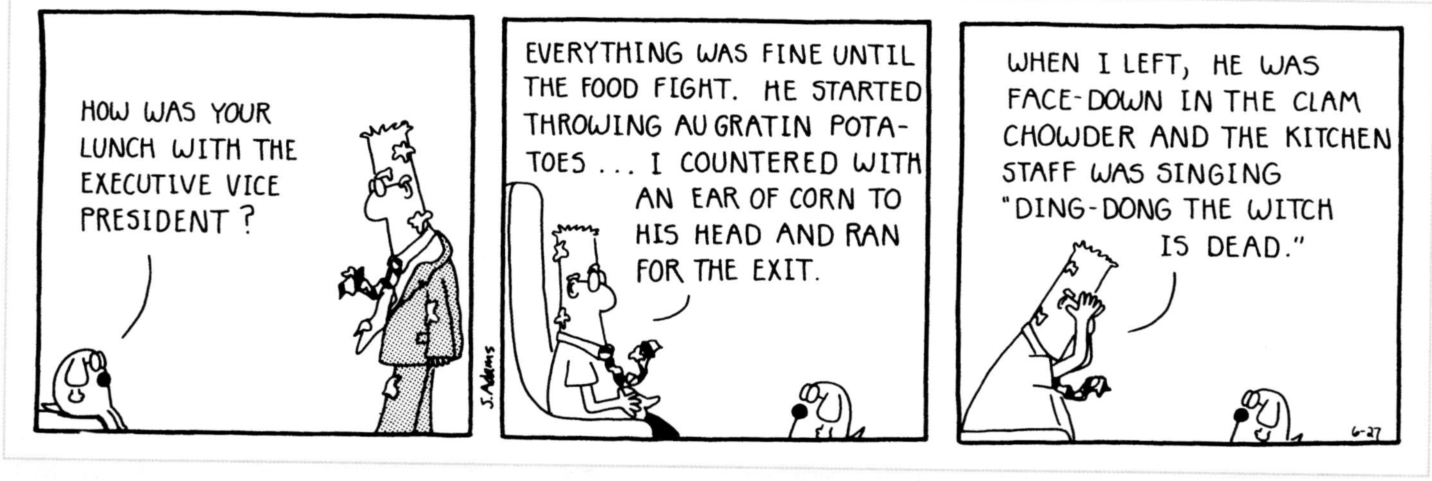
HOW WAS YOUR LUNCH WITH THE EXECUTIVE VICE PRESIDENT?
EVERYTHING WAS FINE UNTIL THE FOOD FIGHT. HE STARTED THROWING AU GRATIN POTATOES... I COUNTERED WITH AN EAR OF CORN TO HIS HEAD AND RAN FOR THE EXIT.
WHEN I LEFT, HE WAS FACE-DOWN IN THE CLAM CHOWDER AND THE KITCHEN STAFF WAS SINGING "DING-DONG THE WITCH IS DEAD."

And then I felt better.

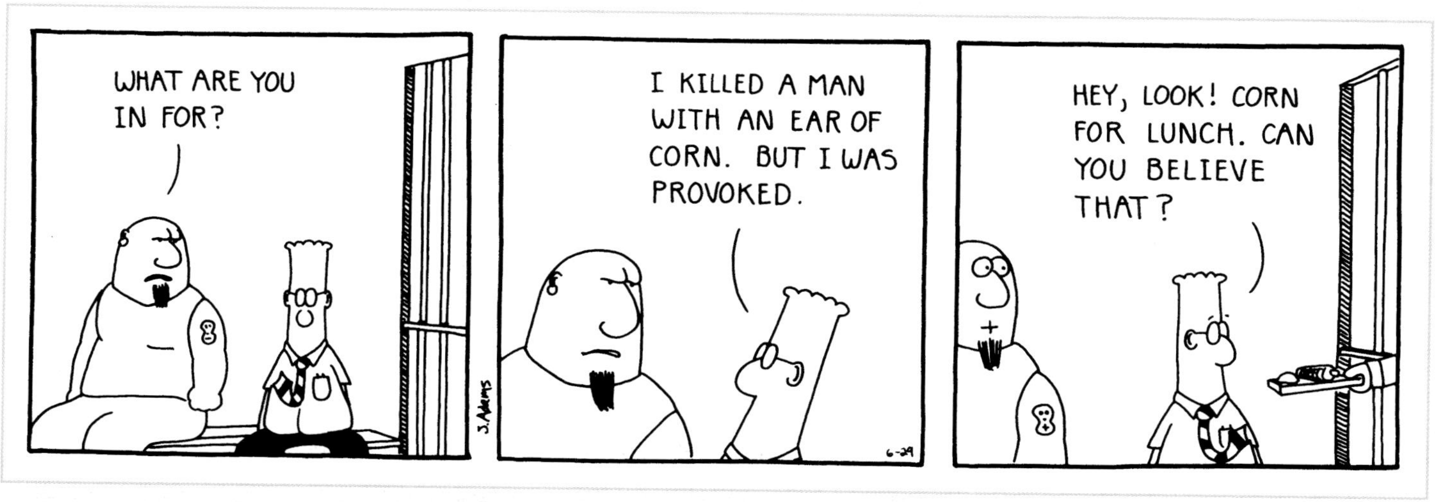
WHAT ARE YOU IN FOR?
I KILLED A MAN WITH AN EAR OF CORN. BUT I WAS PROVOKED.
HEY, LOOK! CORN FOR LUNCH. CAN YOU BELIEVE THAT?

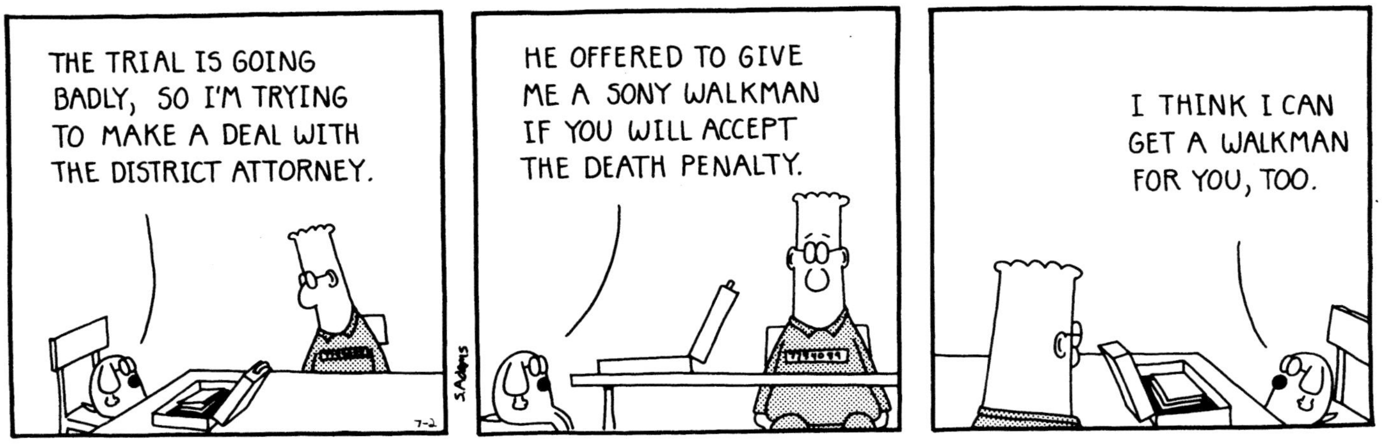
THE TRIAL IS GOING BADLY, SO I'M TRYING TO MAKE A DEAL WITH THE DISTRICT ATTORNEY.
HE OFFERED TO GIVE ME A SONY WALKMAN IF YOU WILL ACCEPT THE DEATH PENALTY.
I THINK I CAN GET A WALKMAN FOR YOU, TOO.

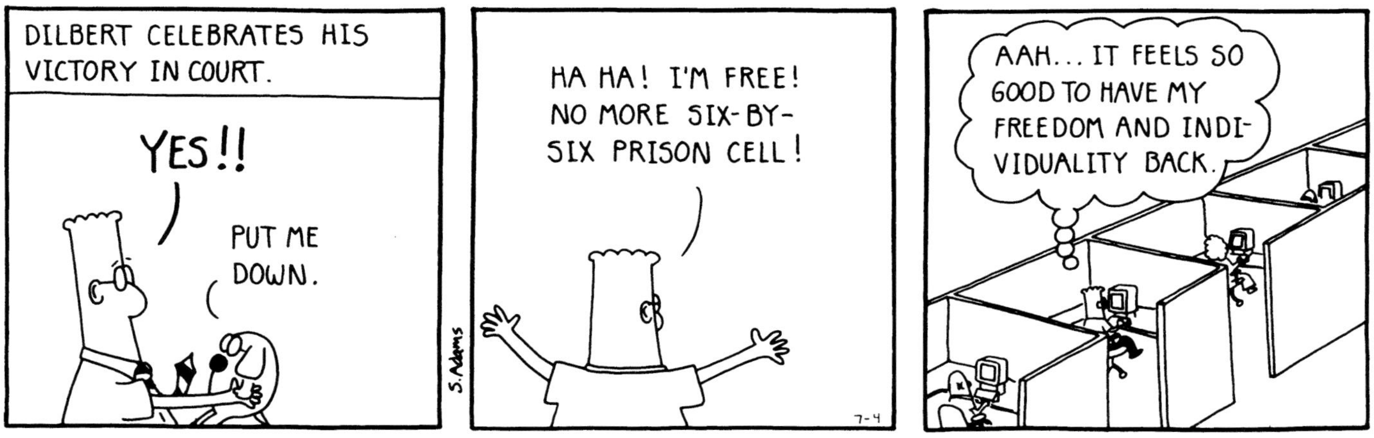
DILBERT CELEBRATES HIS VICTORY IN COURT.
YES!!
PUT ME DOWN.
HA HA! I'M FREE! NO MORE SIX-BY-SIX PRISON CELL!
AAH... IT FEELS SO GOOD TO HAVE MY FREEDOM AND INDIVIDUALITY BACK.

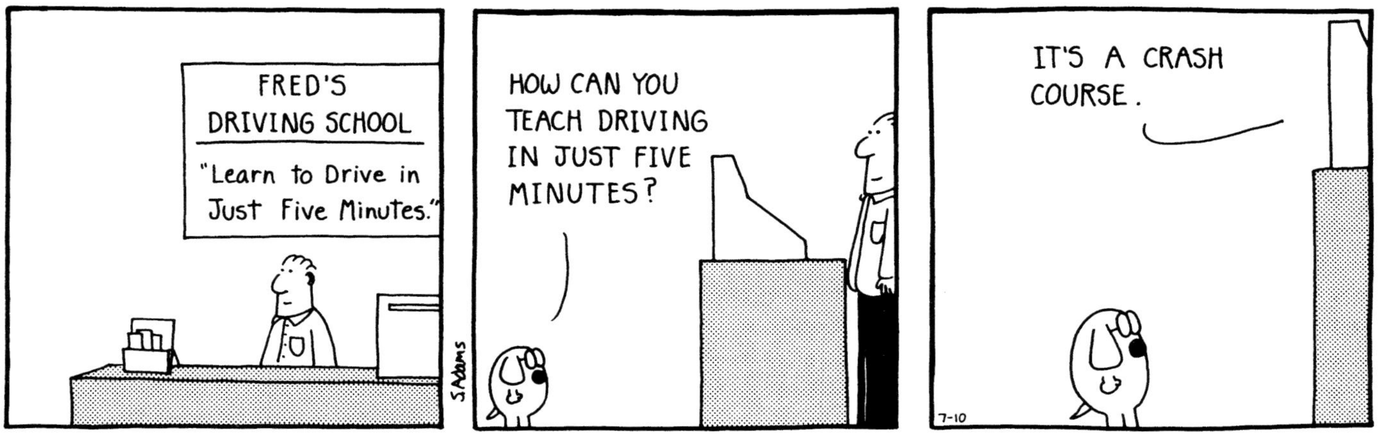
FRED'S DRIVING SCHOOL
"Learn to Drive in Just Five Minutes."
HOW CAN YOU TEACH DRIVING IN JUST FIVE MINUTES?
IT'S A CRASH COURSE.

Contrary to popular opinion, Dilbert has never had a pocket protector. He usually only has two pens in his pocket.

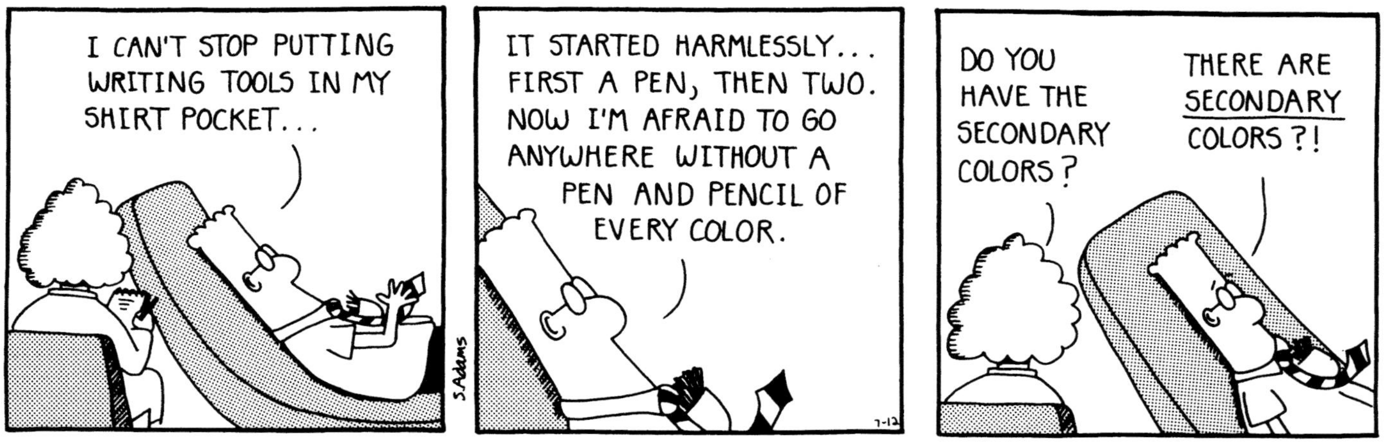
I CAN'T STOP PUTTING WRITING TOOLS IN MY SHIRT POCKET...
IT STARTED HARMLESSLY... FIRST A PEN, THEN TWO. NOW I'M AFRAID TO GO ANYWHERE WITHOUT A PEN AND PENCIL OF EVERY COLOR.
DO YOU HAVE THE SECONDARY COLORS?
THERE ARE SECONDARY COLORS?!

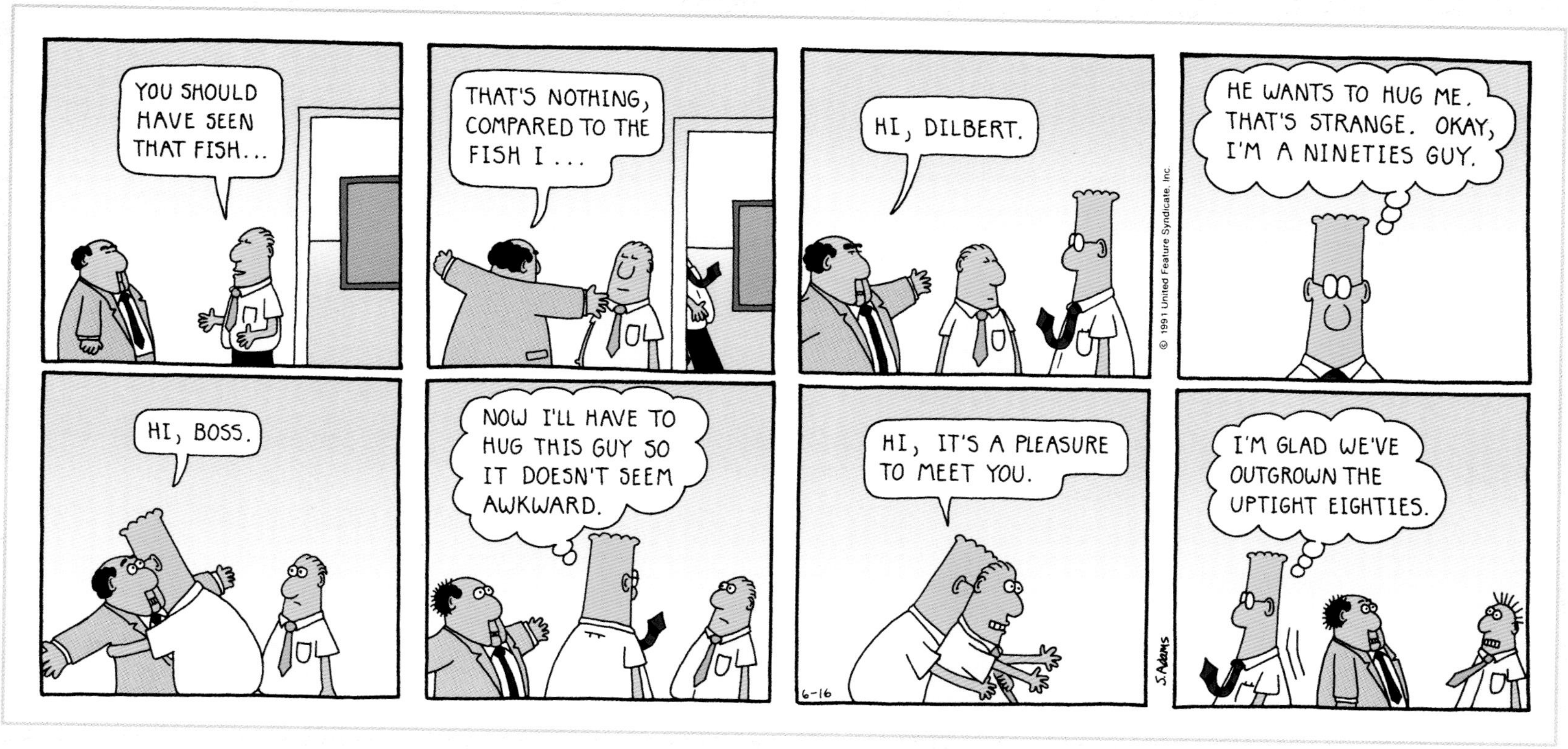
YOU SHOULD HAVE SEEN THAT FISH...
THAT'S NOTHING, COMPARED TO THE FISH I ...
HI, DILBERT.
HE WANTS TO HUG ME. THAT'S STRANGE. OKAY, I'M A NINETIES GUY.
HI, BOSS.
NOW I'LL HAVE TO HUG THIS GUY SO IT DOESN'T SEEM AWKWARD.
HI, IT'S A PLEASURE TO MEET YOU.
I'M GLAD WE'VE OUTGROWN THE UPTIGHT EIGHTIES.
© 1991 United Feature Syndicate, Inc.
6-16
S.ADAMS

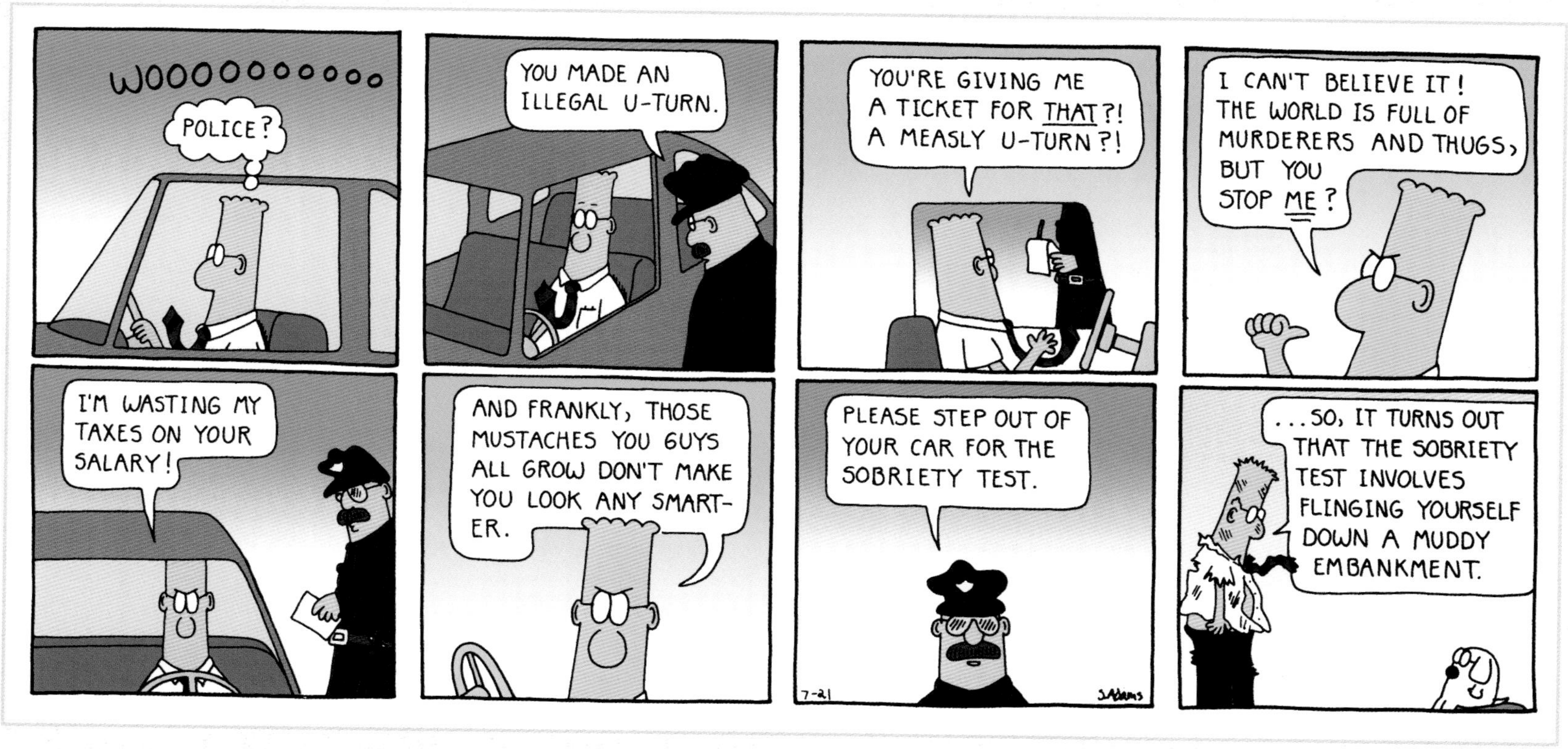
WOOOOOOOOOO
POLICE?
YOU MADE AN ILLEGAL U-TURN.
YOU'RE GIVING ME A TICKET FOR THAT?! A MEASLY U-TURN?!
I CAN'T BELIEVE IT! THE WORLD IS FULL OF MURDERERS AND THUGS, BUT YOU STOP ME?
I'M WASTING MY TAXES ON YOUR SALARY!
AND FRANKLY, THOSE MUSTACHES YOU GUYS ALL GROW DON'T MAKE YOU LOOK ANY SMARTER.
PLEASE STEP OUT OF YOUR CAR FOR THE SOBRIETY TEST.
...SO, IT TURNS OUT THAT THE SOBRIETY TEST INVOLVES FLINGING YOURSELF DOWN A MUDDY EMBANKMENT.
7-21
S.ADAMS

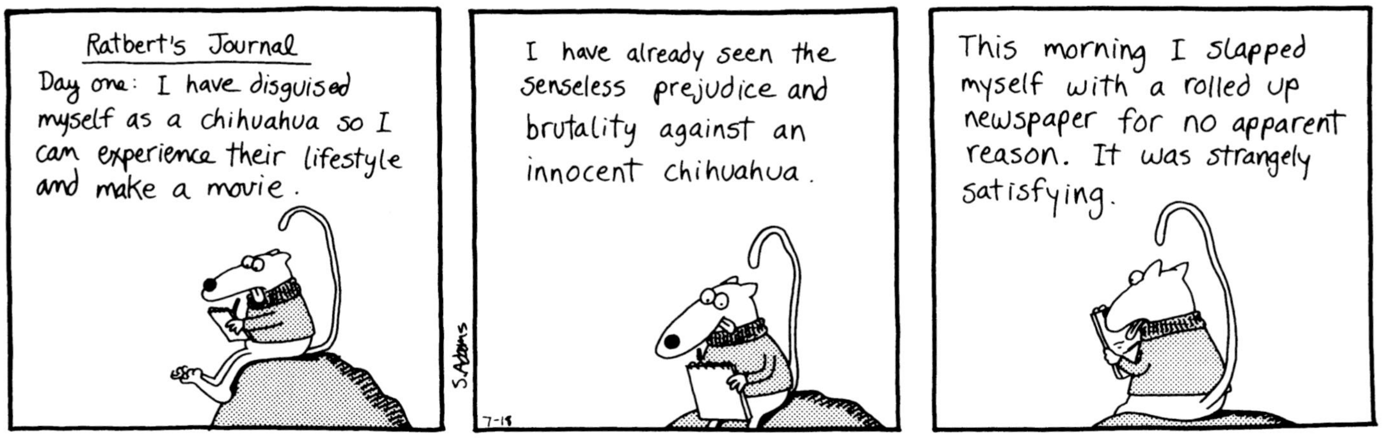
Ratbert's Journal
Day one: I have disguised myself as a chihuahua so I can experience their lifestyle and make a movie.
I have already seen the senseless prejudice and brutality against an innocent chihuahua.
This morning I slapped myself with a rolled up newspaper for no apparent reason. It was strangely satisfying.
S.Adams
7-18

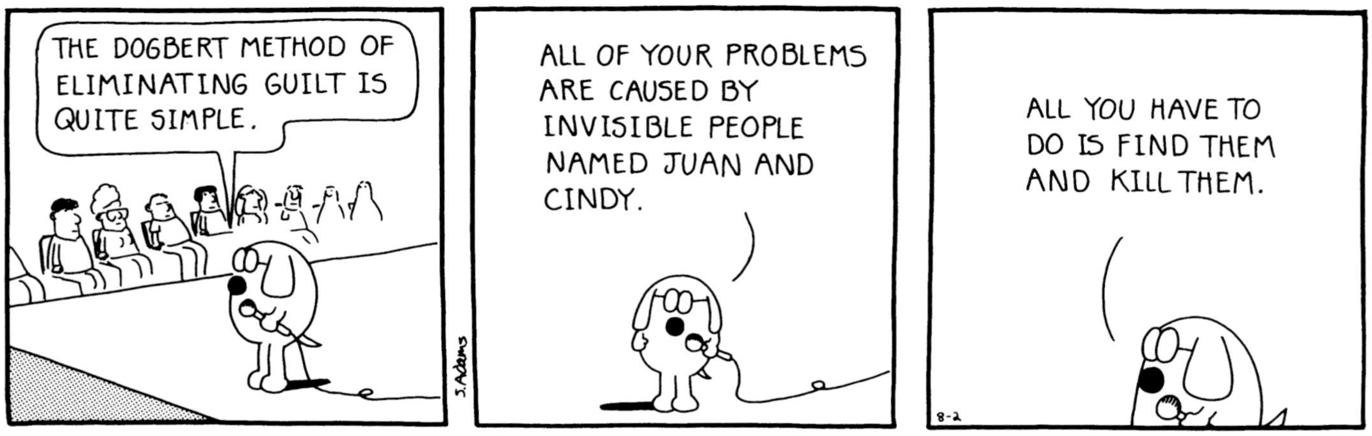
THE DOGBERT METHOD OF ELIMINATING GUILT IS QUITE SIMPLE.
ALL OF YOUR PROBLEMS ARE CAUSED BY INVISIBLE PEOPLE NAMED JUAN AND CINDY.
ALL YOU HAVE TO DO IS FIND THEM AND KILL THEM.
S.Adams
8-2

The comic above appealed to a very small portion of the population. If you are one of them, your friends might only be pretending to like you.

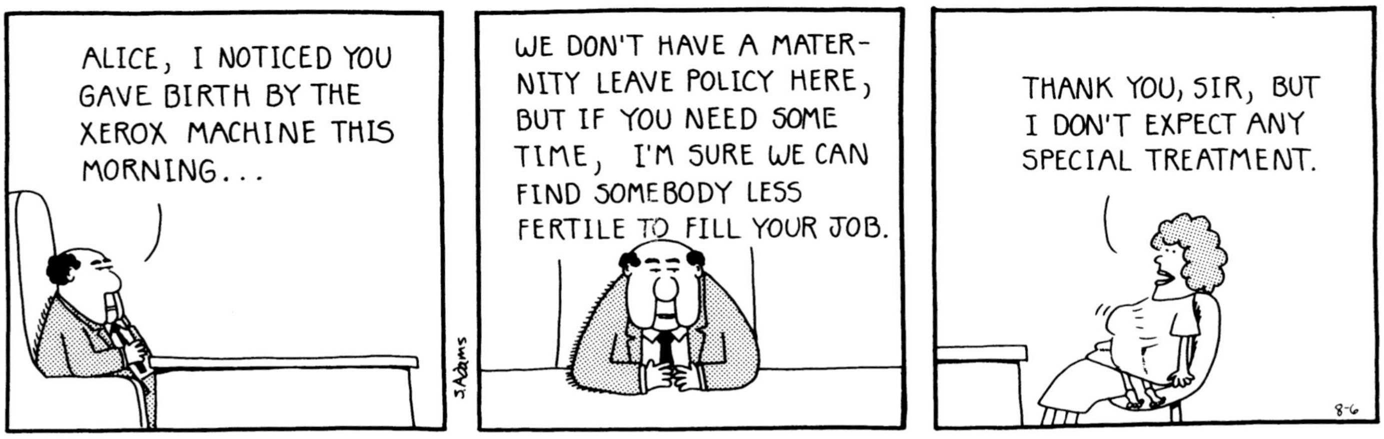
ALICE, I NOTICED YOU GAVE BIRTH BY THE XEROX MACHINE THIS MORNING...
WE DON'T HAVE A MATERNITY LEAVE POLICY HERE, BUT IF YOU NEED SOME TIME, I'M SURE WE CAN FIND SOMEBODY LESS FERTILE TO FILL YOUR JOB.
THANK YOU, SIR, BUT I DON'T EXPECT ANY SPECIAL TREATMENT.
S.Adams
8-6

At this point, Alice didn't have the pyramid-shaped hair, and wasn't the single woman she morphed into. This comic was the one that taught me how many readers don't recognize satire. A number of angry readers wrote to say I was portraying working mothers in a negative light.

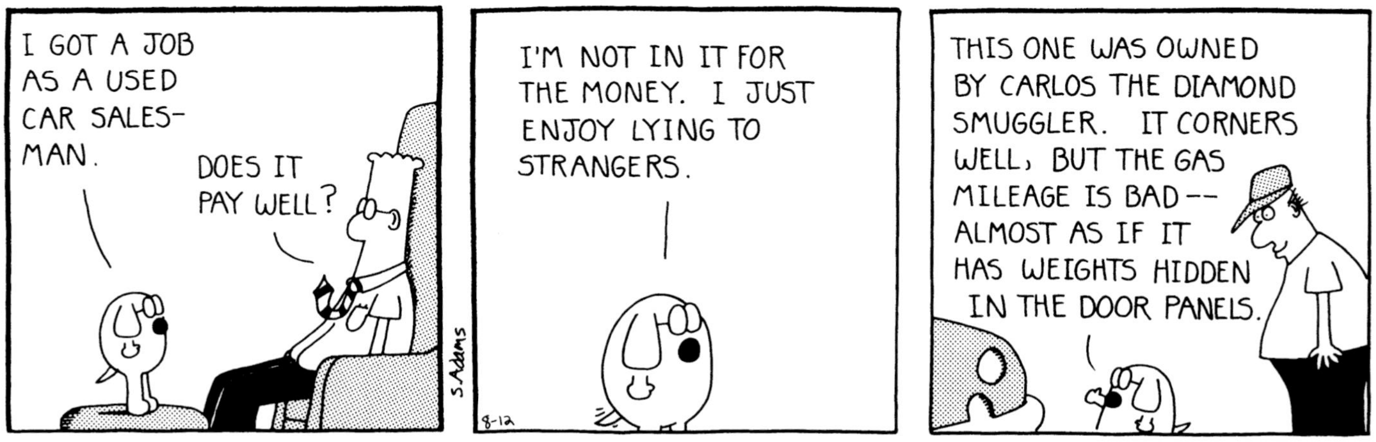
I GOT A JOB AS A USED CAR SALESMAN.
DOES IT PAY WELL?
I'M NOT IN IT FOR THE MONEY. I JUST ENJOY LYING TO STRANGERS.
THIS ONE WAS OWNED BY CARLOS THE DIAMOND SMUGGLER. IT CORNERS WELL, BUT THE GAS MILEAGE IS BAD -- ALMOST AS IF IT HAS WEIGHTS HIDDEN IN THE DOOR PANELS.
S.Adams
8-12

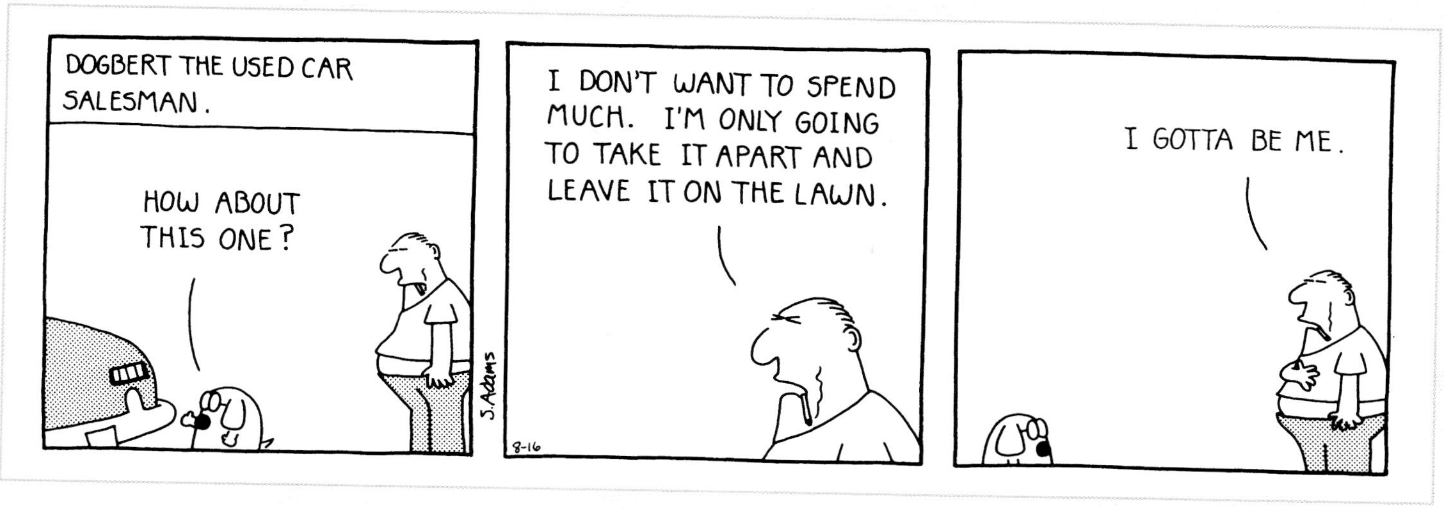
DOGBERT THE USED CAR SALESMAN.
HOW ABOUT THIS ONE?
S. Adams
8-16
I DON'T WANT TO SPEND MUCH. I'M ONLY GOING TO TAKE IT APART AND LEAVE IT ON THE LAWN.
I GOTTA BE ME.

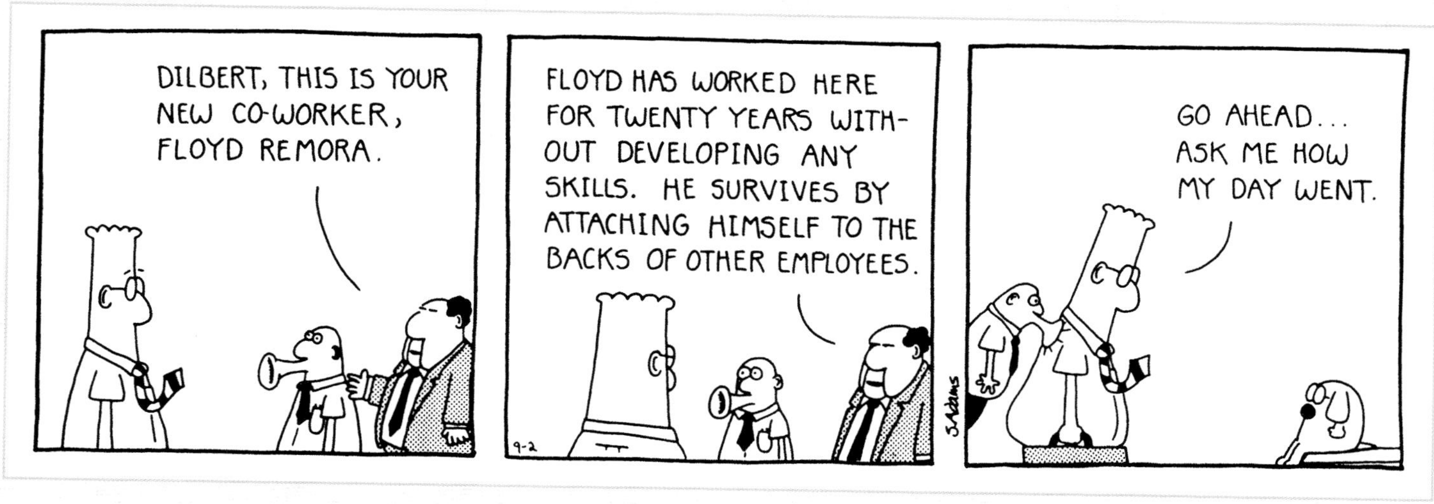
DILBERT, THIS IS YOUR NEW CO-WORKER, FLOYD REMORA.
FLOYD HAS WORKED HERE FOR TWENTY YEARS WITHOUT DEVELOPING ANY SKILLS. HE SURVIVES BY ATTACHING HIMSELF TO THE BACKS OF OTHER EMPLOYEES.
9-2
S. Adams
GO AHEAD... ASK ME HOW MY DAY WENT.

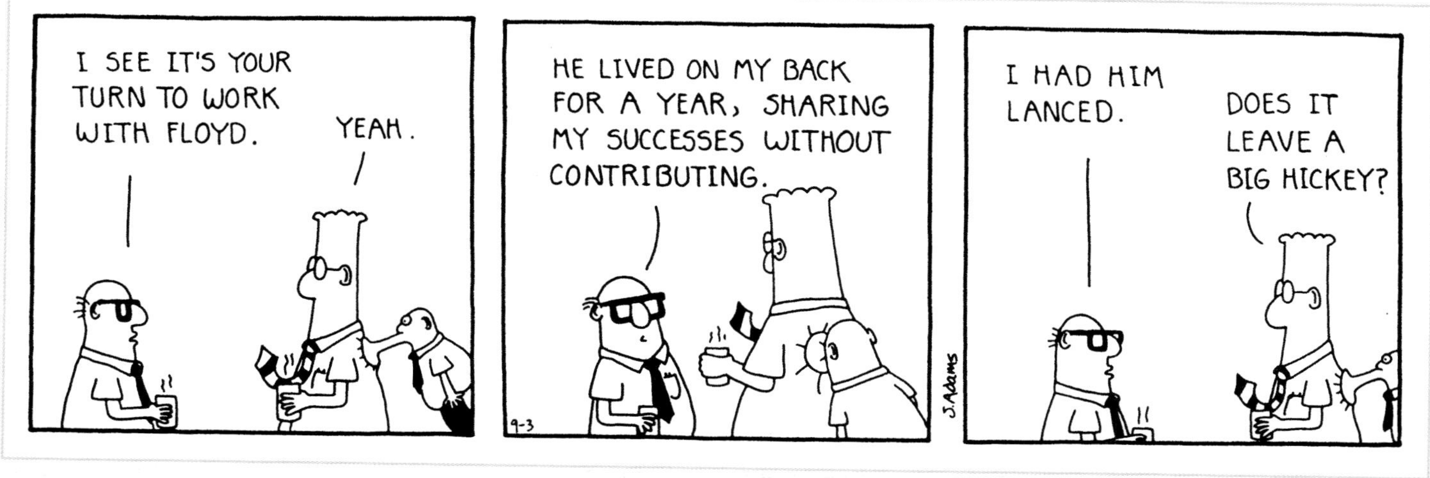
I SEE IT'S YOUR TURN TO WORK WITH FLOYD.
YEAH.
HE LIVED ON MY BACK FOR A YEAR, SHARING MY SUCCESSES WITHOUT CONTRIBUTING.
9-3
S. Adams
I HAD HIM LANCED.
DOES IT LEAVE A BIG HICKEY?

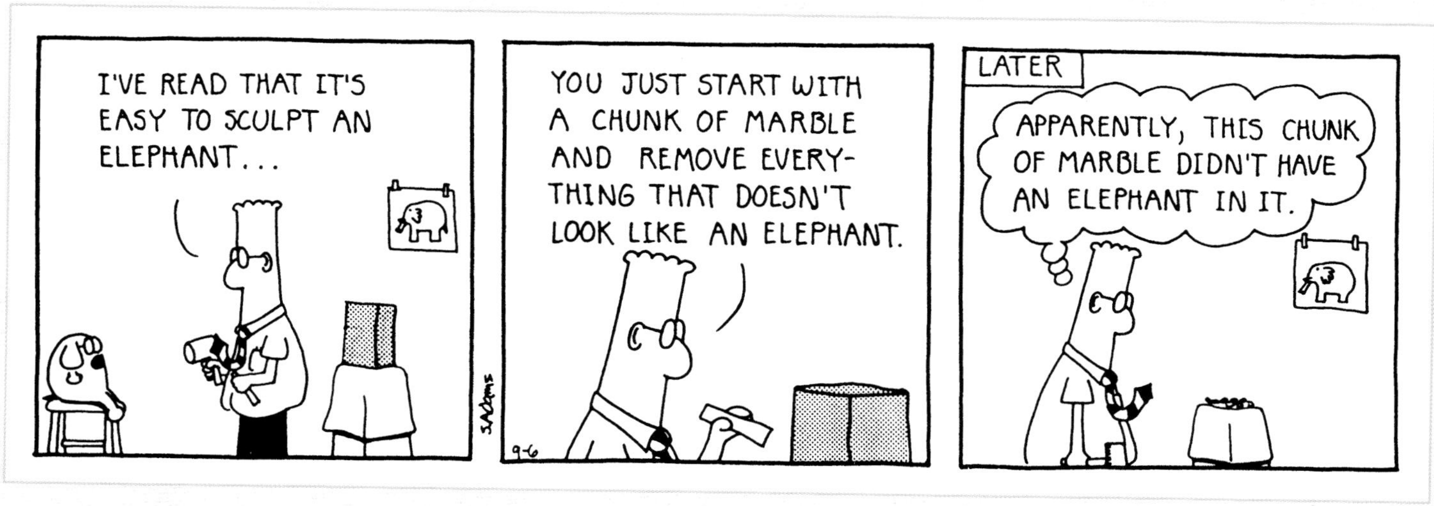
I'VE READ THAT IT'S EASY TO SCULPT AN ELEPHANT...
S. Adams
9-6
YOU JUST START WITH A CHUNK OF MARBLE AND REMOVE EVERYTHING THAT DOESN'T LOOK LIKE AN ELEPHANT.
LATER
APPARENTLY, THIS CHUNK OF MARBLE DIDN'T HAVE AN ELEPHANT IN IT.

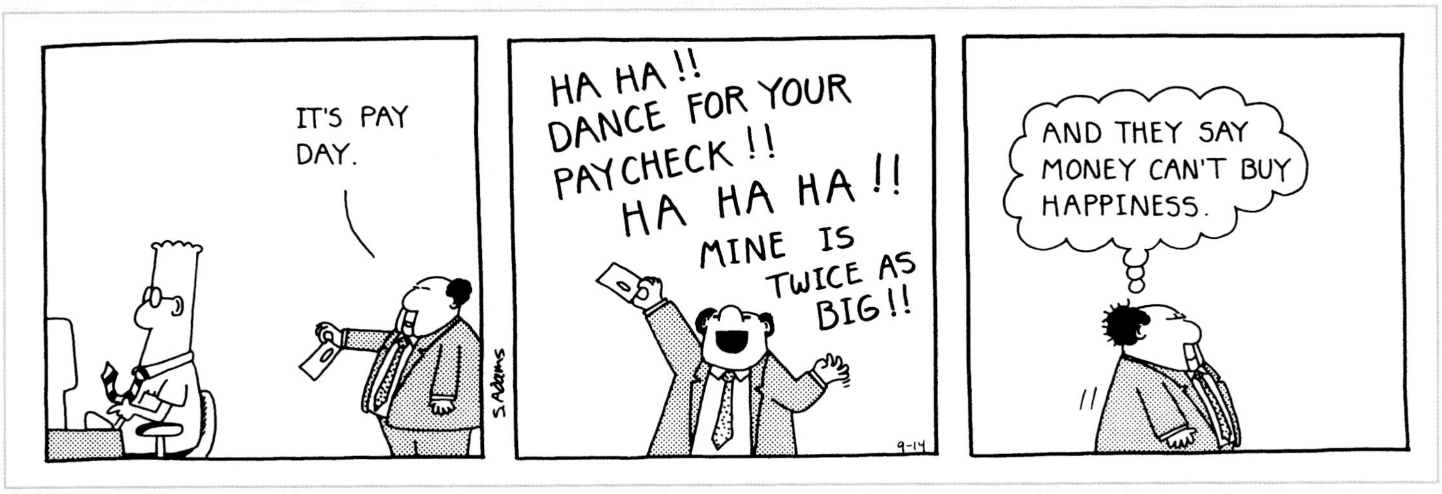

IT'S PAY DAY.
HA HA !! DANCE FOR YOUR PAYCHECK !! HA HA HA !! MINE IS TWICE AS BIG !!
AND THEY SAY MONEY CAN'T BUY HAPPINESS.

This drawing of the boss features pointier hair than ever before, initially by an accident of the pen. While inking this comic, I inadvertently made the clump of hair more elongated than usual. But I liked it. The evolution to full pointy hair was now inevitable.

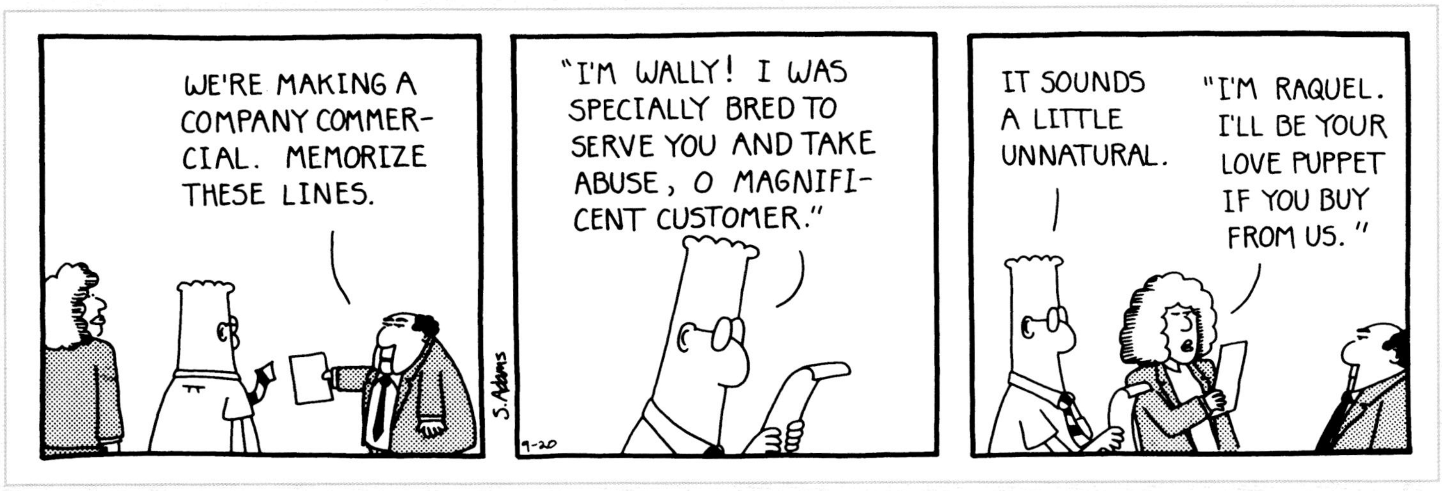

WE'RE MAKING A COMPANY COMMERCIAL. MEMORIZE THESE LINES.
"I'M WALLY! I WAS SPECIALLY BRED TO SERVE YOU AND TAKE ABUSE, O MAGNIFICENT CUSTOMER."
IT SOUNDS A LITTLE UNNATURAL.
"I'M RAQUEL. I'LL BE YOUR LOVE PUPPET IF YOU BUY FROM US."

This might be the first use of the name Wally in the strip. It's a good comic name, and those are hard to find.

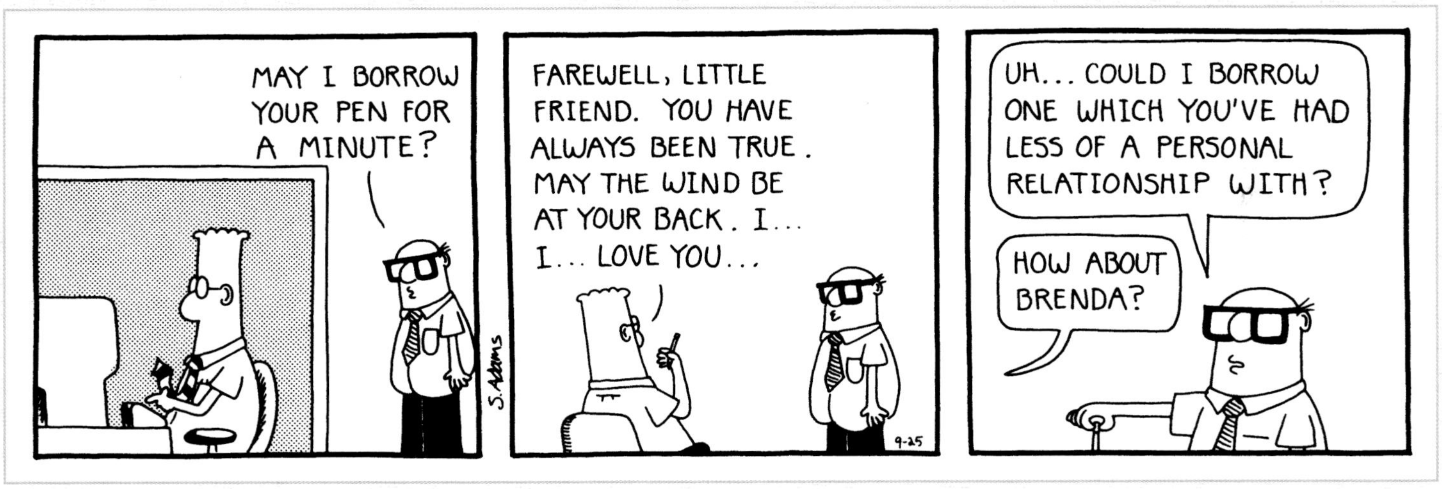

MAY I BORROW YOUR PEN FOR A MINUTE?
FAREWELL, LITTLE FRIEND. YOU HAVE ALWAYS BEEN TRUE. MAY THE WIND BE AT YOUR BACK. I... I... LOVE YOU...
UH... COULD I BORROW ONE WHICH YOU'VE HAD LESS OF A PERSONAL RELATIONSHIP WITH?
HOW ABOUT BRENDA?

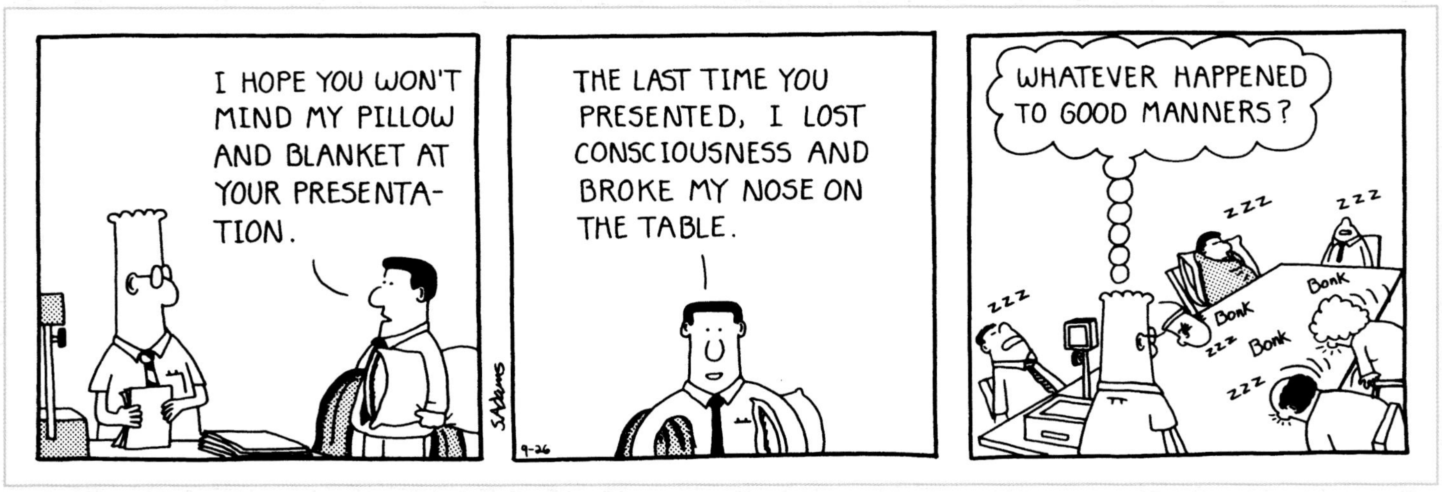

I HOPE YOU WON'T MIND MY PILLOW AND BLANKET AT YOUR PRESENTATION.
THE LAST TIME YOU PRESENTED, I LOST CONSCIOUSNESS AND BROKE MY NOSE ON THE TABLE.
WHATEVER HAPPENED TO GOOD MANNERS?
ZZZ
BONK

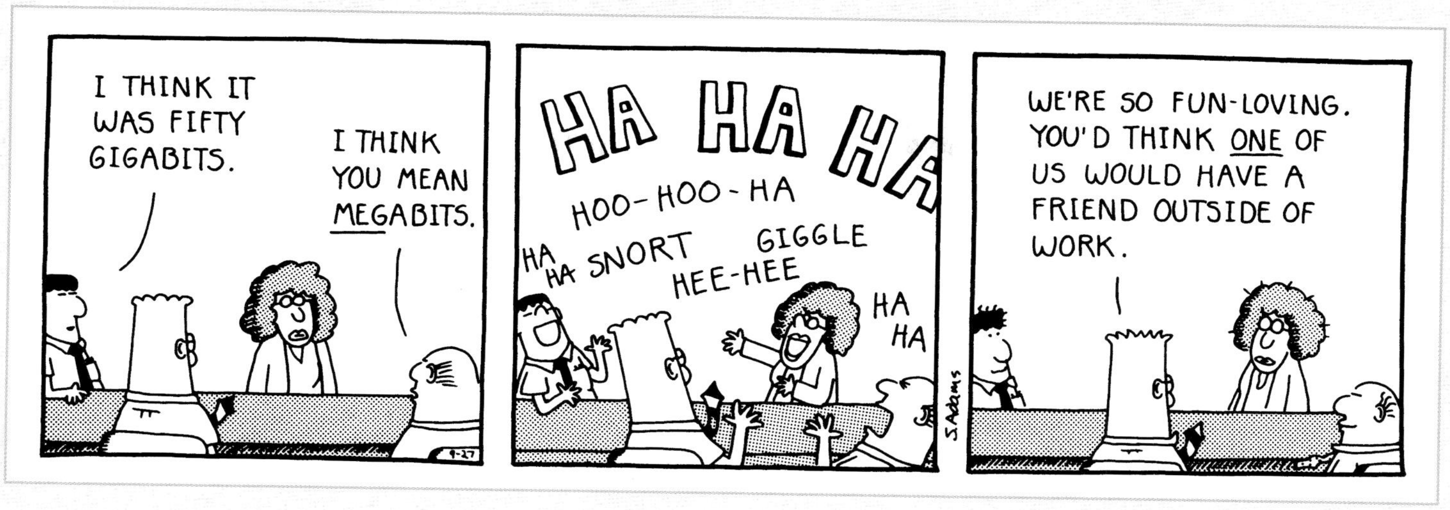
I THINK IT WAS FIFTY GIGABITS.
I THINK YOU MEAN MEGABITS.
HA HA HA
HOO-HOO-HA
HA HA SNORT
GIGGLE
HEE-HEE
HA HA
WE'RE SO FUN-LOVING. YOU'D THINK ONE OF US WOULD HAVE A FRIEND OUTSIDE OF WORK.

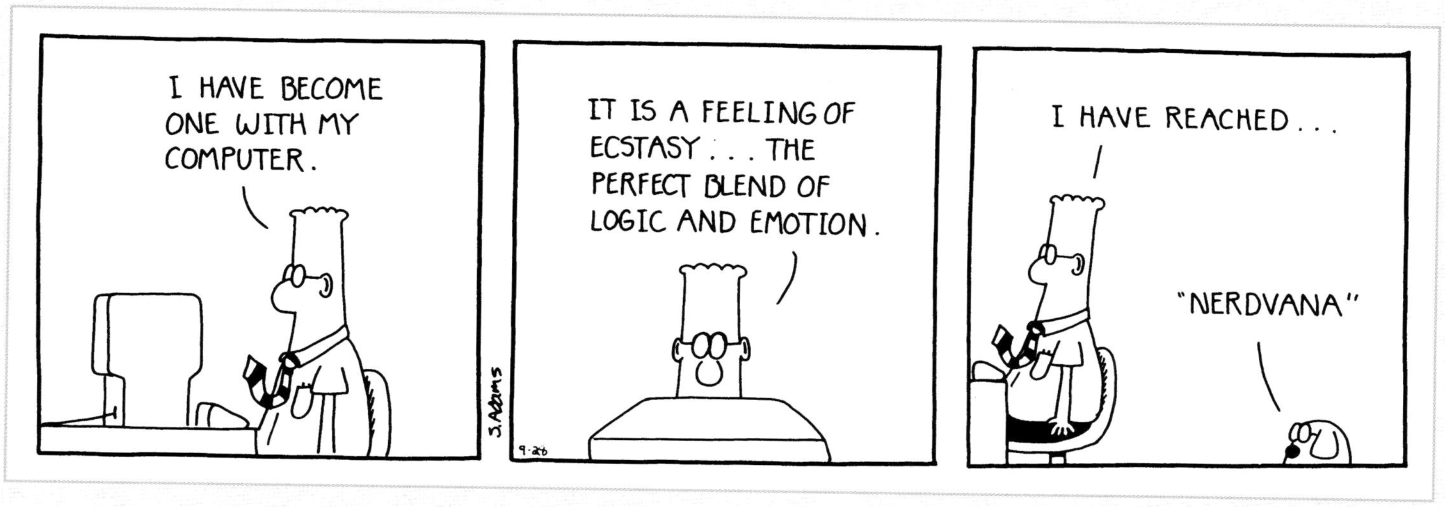
I HAVE BECOME ONE WITH MY COMPUTER.
IT IS A FEELING OF ECSTASY . . . THE PERFECT BLEND OF LOGIC AND EMOTION.
I HAVE REACHED . . .
"NERDVANA"

I just Googled "nerdvana" to see if it ever caught on. There are 147,000 hits.

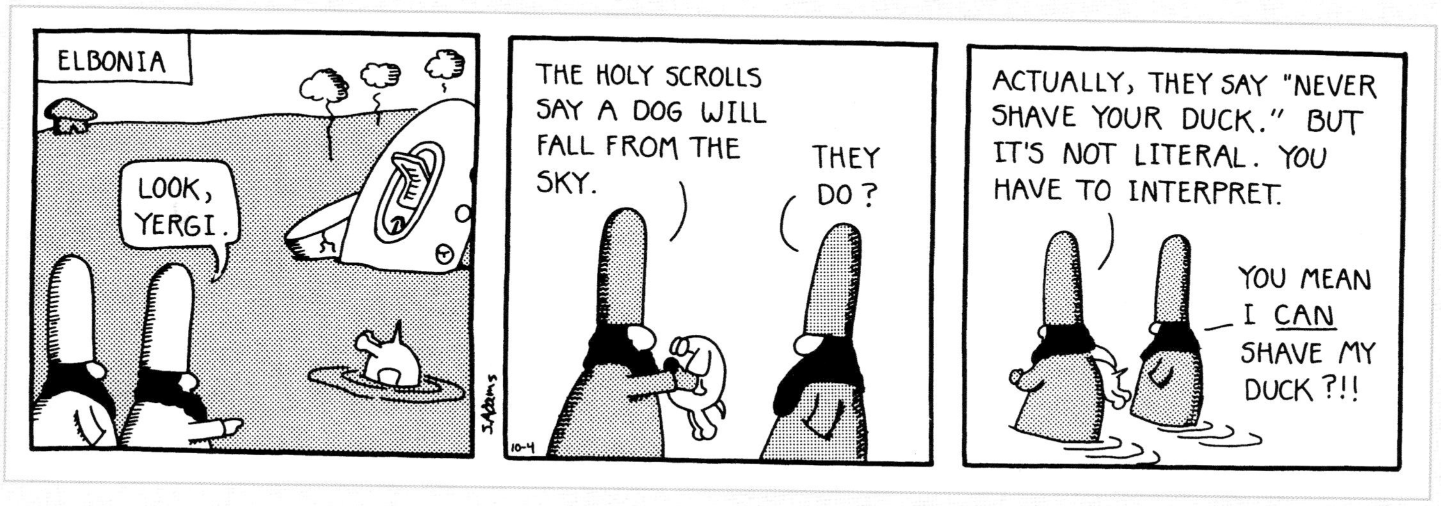
ELBONIA
LOOK, YERGI.
THE HOLY SCROLLS SAY A DOG WILL FALL FROM THE SKY.
THEY DO?
ACTUALLY, THEY SAY "NEVER SHAVE YOUR DUCK." BUT IT'S NOT LITERAL. YOU HAVE TO INTERPRET.
YOU MEAN I CAN SHAVE MY DUCK?!!

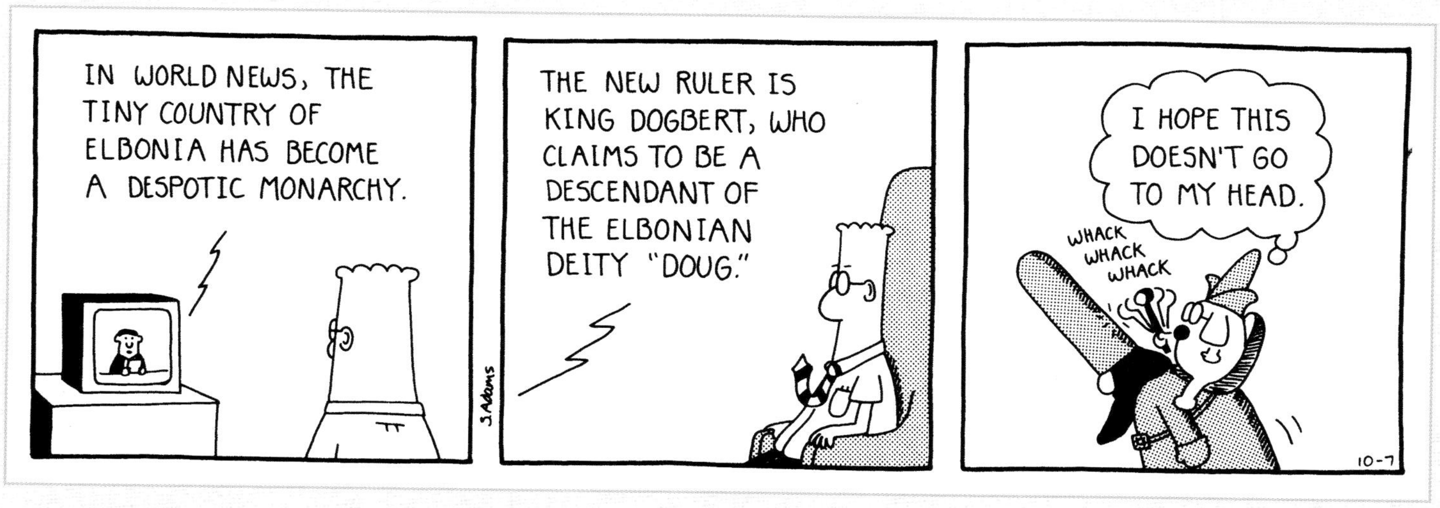
IN WORLD NEWS, THE TINY COUNTRY OF ELBONIA HAS BECOME A DESPOTIC MONARCHY.
THE NEW RULER IS KING DOGBERT, WHO CLAIMS TO BE A DESCENDANT OF THE ELBONIAN DEITY "DOUG."
I HOPE THIS DOESN'T GO TO MY HEAD.
WHACK WHACK WHACK

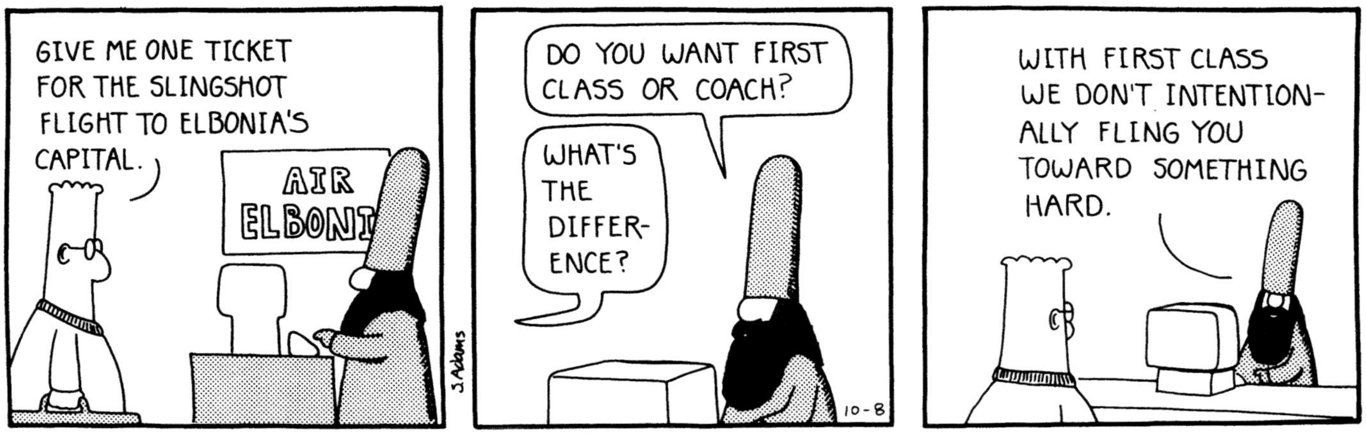
GIVE ME ONE TICKET FOR THE SLINGSHOT FLIGHT TO ELBONIA'S CAPITAL.
AIR ELBONI
DO YOU WANT FIRST CLASS OR COACH?
WHAT'S THE DIFFERENCE?
WITH FIRST CLASS WE DON'T INTENTIONALLY FLING YOU TOWARD SOMETHING HARD.
S. Adams
10-8

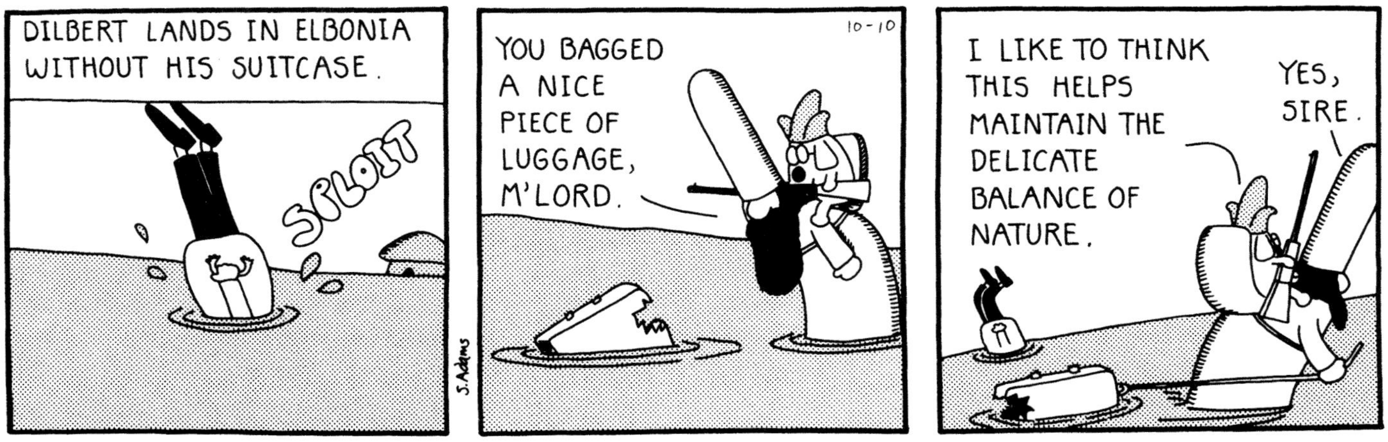
DILBERT LANDS IN ELBONIA WITHOUT HIS SUITCASE.
SPLOIT
YOU BAGGED A NICE PIECE OF LUGGAGE, M'LORD.
10-10
S. Adams
I LIKE TO THINK THIS HELPS MAINTAIN THE DELICATE BALANCE OF NATURE.
YES, SIRE.

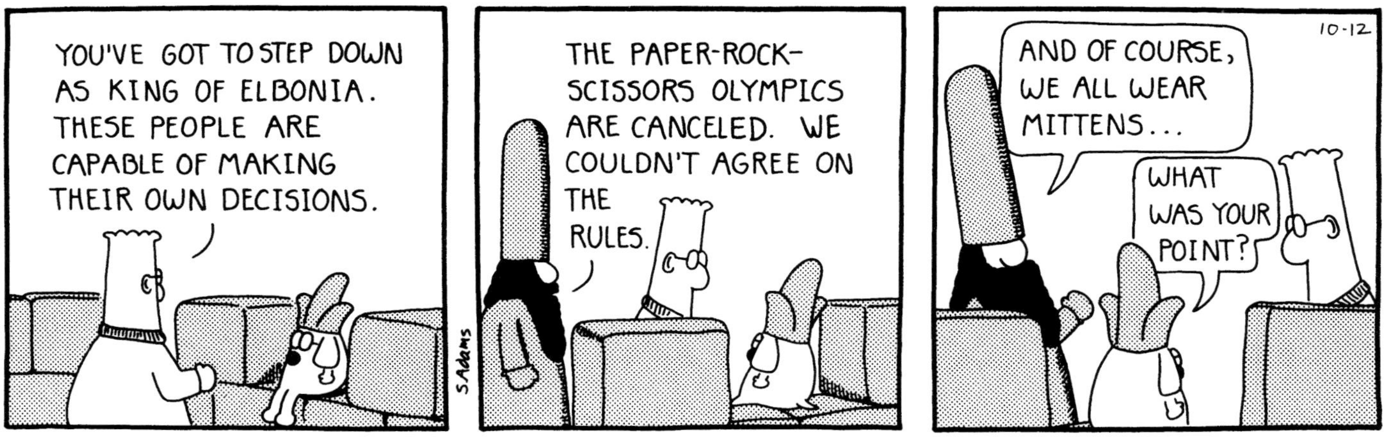
YOU'VE GOT TO STEP DOWN AS KING OF ELBONIA. THESE PEOPLE ARE CAPABLE OF MAKING THEIR OWN DECISIONS.
THE PAPER-ROCK-SCISSORS OLYMPICS ARE CANCELED. WE COULDN'T AGREE ON THE RULES.
S. Adams
10-12
AND OF COURSE, WE ALL WEAR MITTENS...
WHAT WAS YOUR POINT?

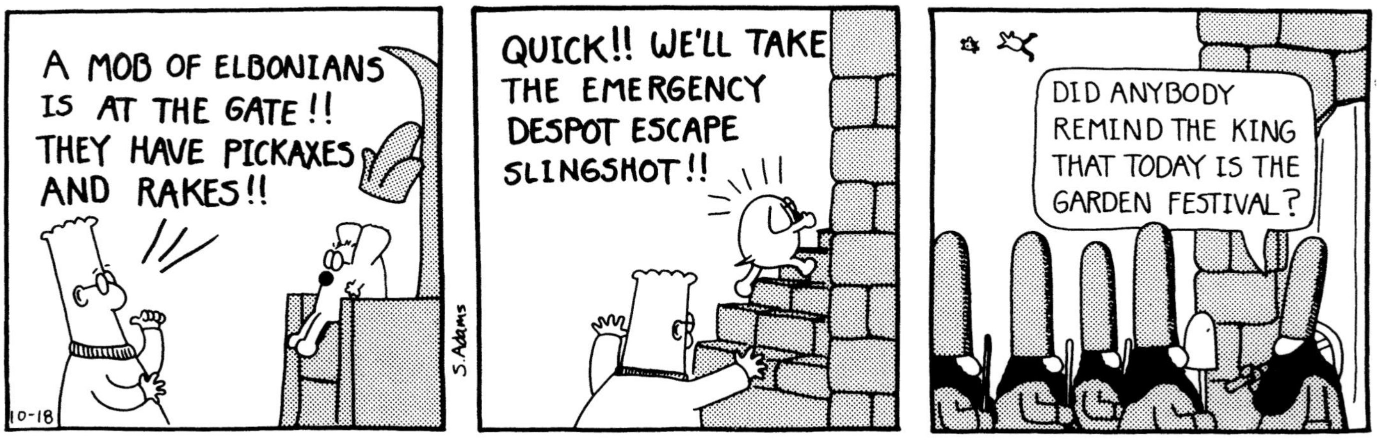
A MOB OF ELBONIANS IS AT THE GATE!! THEY HAVE PICKAXES AND RAKES!!
10-18
S. Adams
QUICK!! WE'LL TAKE THE EMERGENCY DESPOT ESCAPE SLINGSHOT!!
DID ANYBODY REMIND THE KING THAT TODAY IS THE GARDEN FESTIVAL?

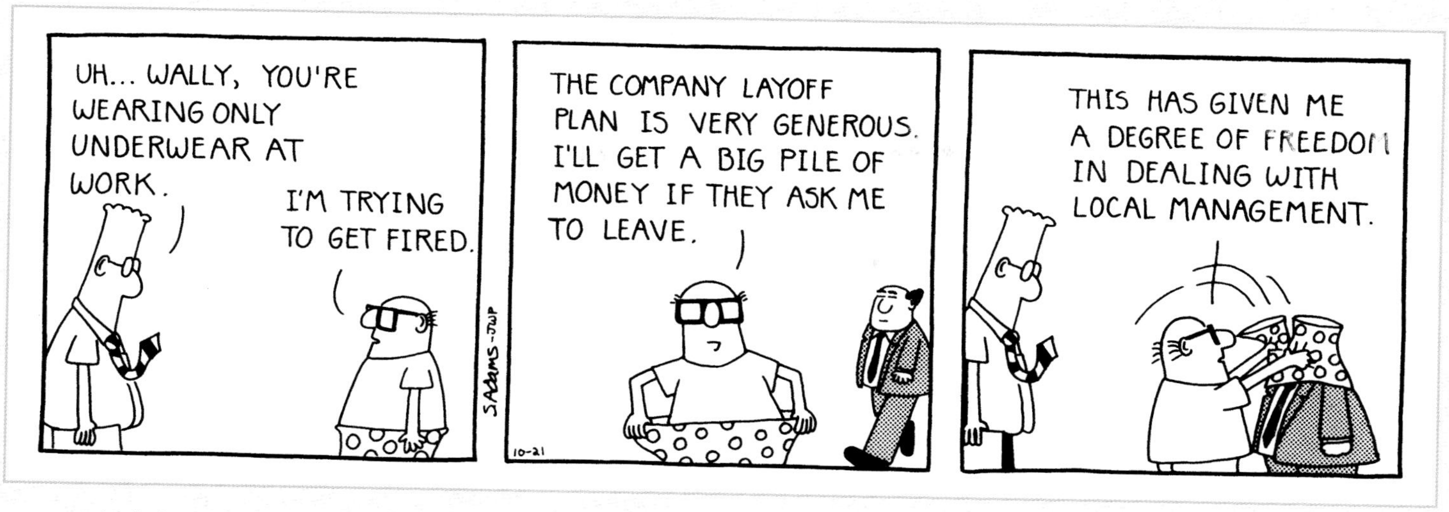
UH... WALLY, YOU'RE WEARING ONLY UNDERWEAR AT WORK.
I'M TRYING TO GET FIRED.
THE COMPANY LAYOFF PLAN IS VERY GENEROUS. I'LL GET A BIG PILE OF MONEY IF THEY ASK ME TO LEAVE.
THIS HAS GIVEN ME A DEGREE OF FREEDOM IN DEALING WITH LOCAL MANAGEMENT.

And the modern Wally character is born. This one is based on a co-worker who made a bad decision with some proprietary information. Management informed him that he wouldn't be fired, but he could never be promoted, and never get another raise. He was young, and knew he had to leave the company for the benefit of his career, but he wanted to do it in the smartest way.

Coincidentally, in the bowels of human resources, a devious plan was being hatched to downsize. The worst 10 percent of the employees would be given a sizable pile of money if they agreed to leave peacefully. My co-worker realized that his best career option was to be the worst employee he could be, so he could leave with money.

But I have to tell you that making it into the bottom 10 percent of workers at Pacific Bell wasn't easy in those days. There was fierce competition for those slots. Fortunately, the man who inspired the creation of Wally was a very bright guy. He succeeded in making it to the bottom 10 percent, and left with a nice pile of money. During this time, attending a meeting with him was like being part of some sort of excellent performance theater. There were times I laughed until I cried.

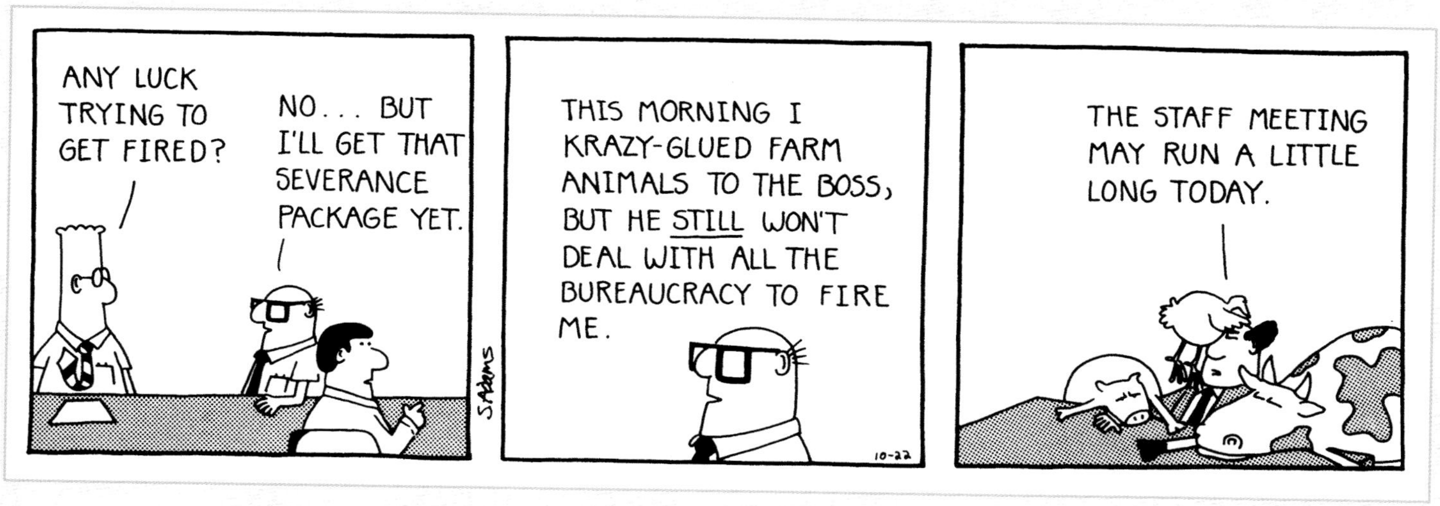
ANY LUCK TRYING TO GET FIRED?
NO... BUT I'LL GET THAT SEVERANCE PACKAGE YET.
THIS MORNING I KRAZY-GLUED FARM ANIMALS TO THE BOSS, BUT HE STILL WON'T DEAL WITH ALL THE BUREAUCRACY TO FIRE ME.
THE STAFF MEETING MAY RUN A LITTLE LONG TODAY.

I heard later from some people who worked with Tom Peters that he was, indeed, a spitter. It was a lucky guess.

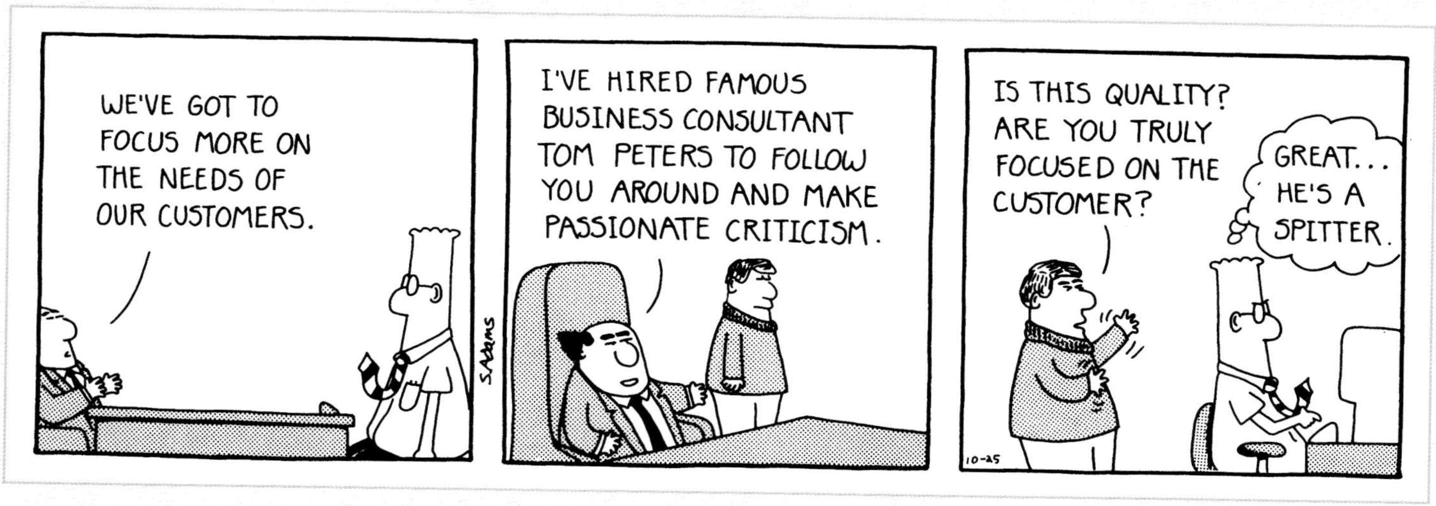
WE'VE GOT TO FOCUS MORE ON THE NEEDS OF OUR CUSTOMERS.
I'VE HIRED FAMOUS BUSINESS CONSULTANT TOM PETERS TO FOLLOW YOU AROUND AND MAKE PASSIONATE CRITICISM.
IS THIS QUALITY? ARE YOU TRULY FOCUSED ON THE CUSTOMER?
GREAT... HE'S A SPITTER.

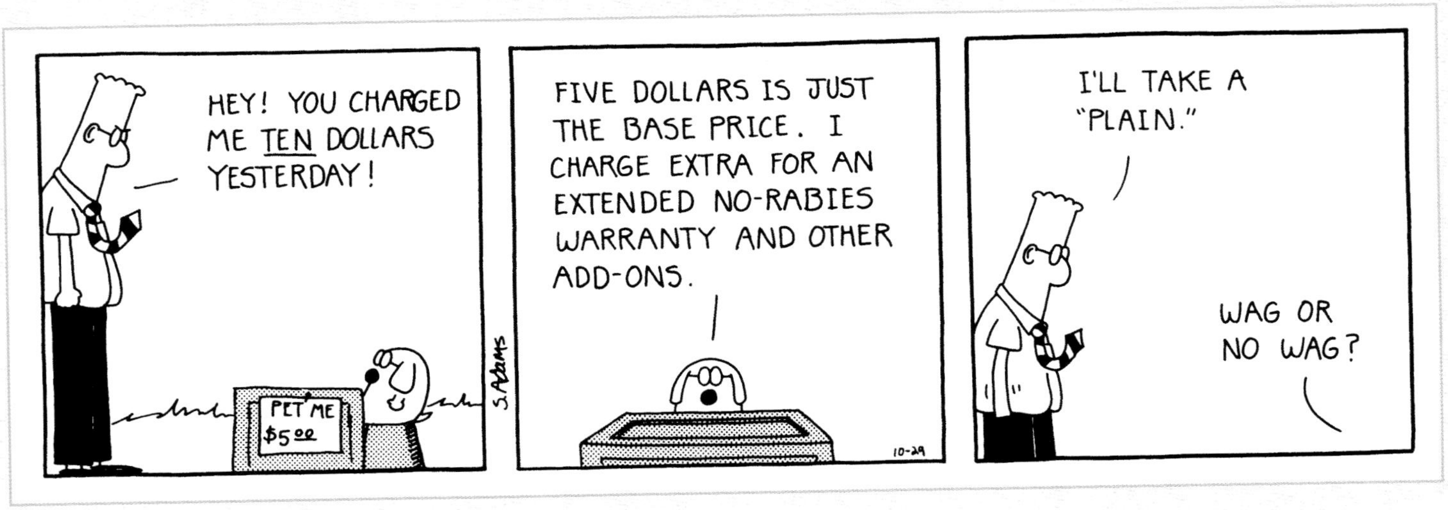
HEY! YOU CHARGED ME TEN DOLLARS YESTERDAY!
PET ME $5.00
FIVE DOLLARS IS JUST THE BASE PRICE. I CHARGE EXTRA FOR AN EXTENDED NO-RABIES WARRANTY AND OTHER ADD-ONS.
I'LL TAKE A "PLAIN."
WAG OR NO WAG?

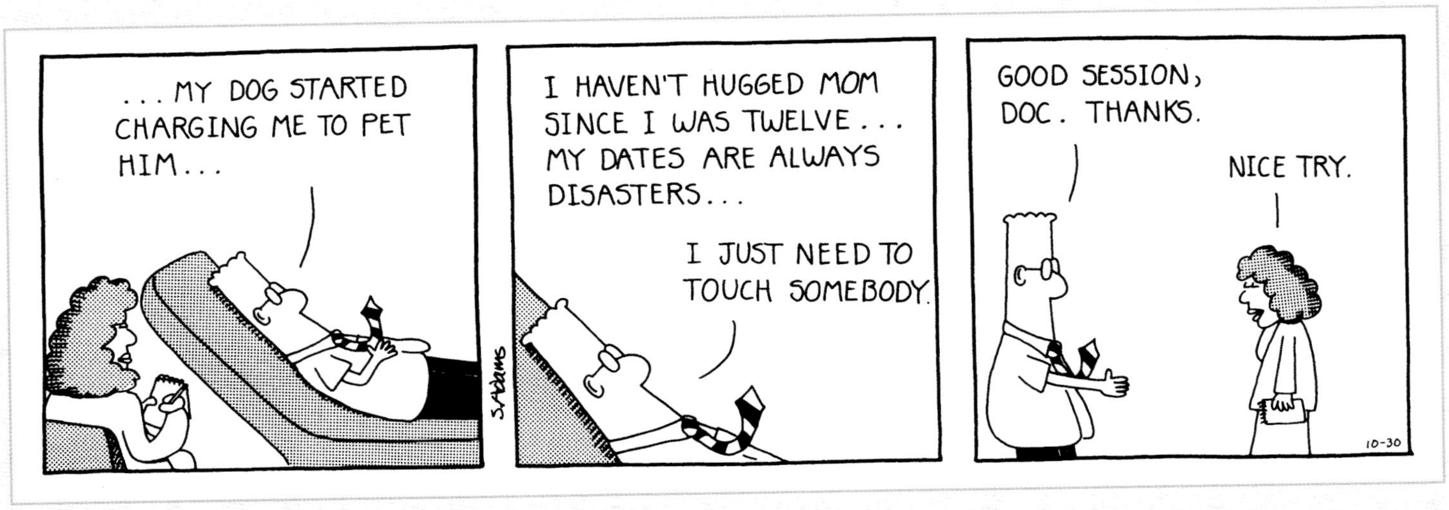
...MY DOG STARTED CHARGING ME TO PET HIM...
I HAVEN'T HUGGED MOM SINCE I WAS TWELVE... MY DATES ARE ALWAYS DISASTERS...
I JUST NEED TO TOUCH SOMEBODY.
GOOD SESSION, DOC. THANKS.
NICE TRY.

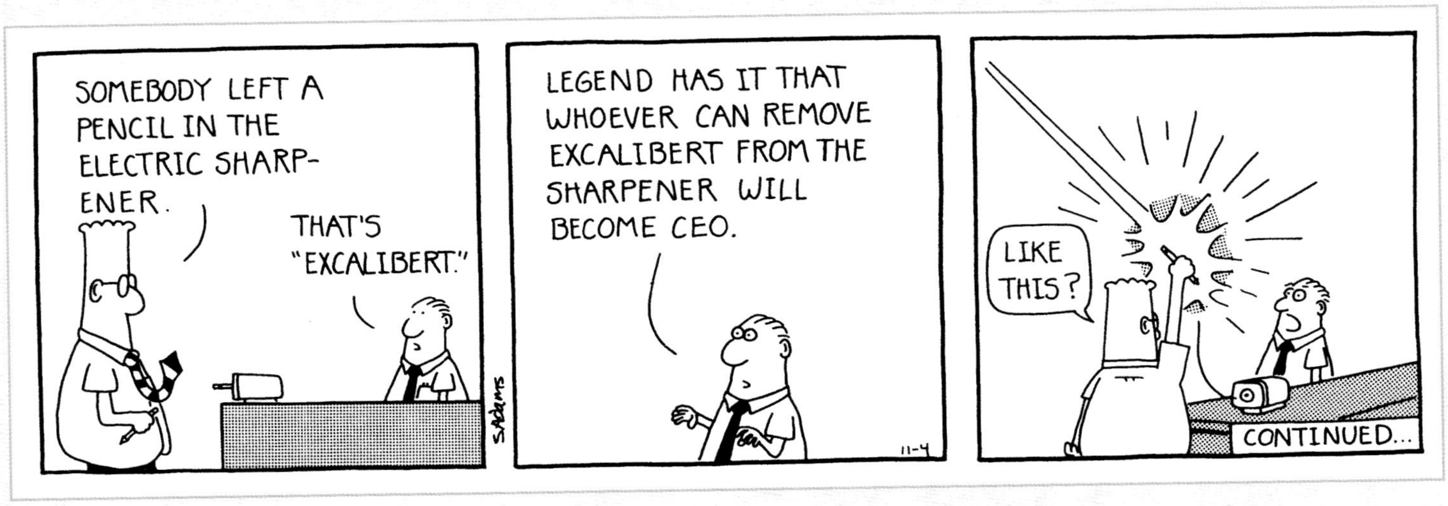
SOMEBODY LEFT A PENCIL IN THE ELECTRIC SHARPENER.
THAT'S "EXCALIBERT."
LEGEND HAS IT THAT WHOEVER CAN REMOVE EXCALIBERT FROM THE SHARPENER WILL BECOME CEO.
LIKE THIS?
CONTINUED...

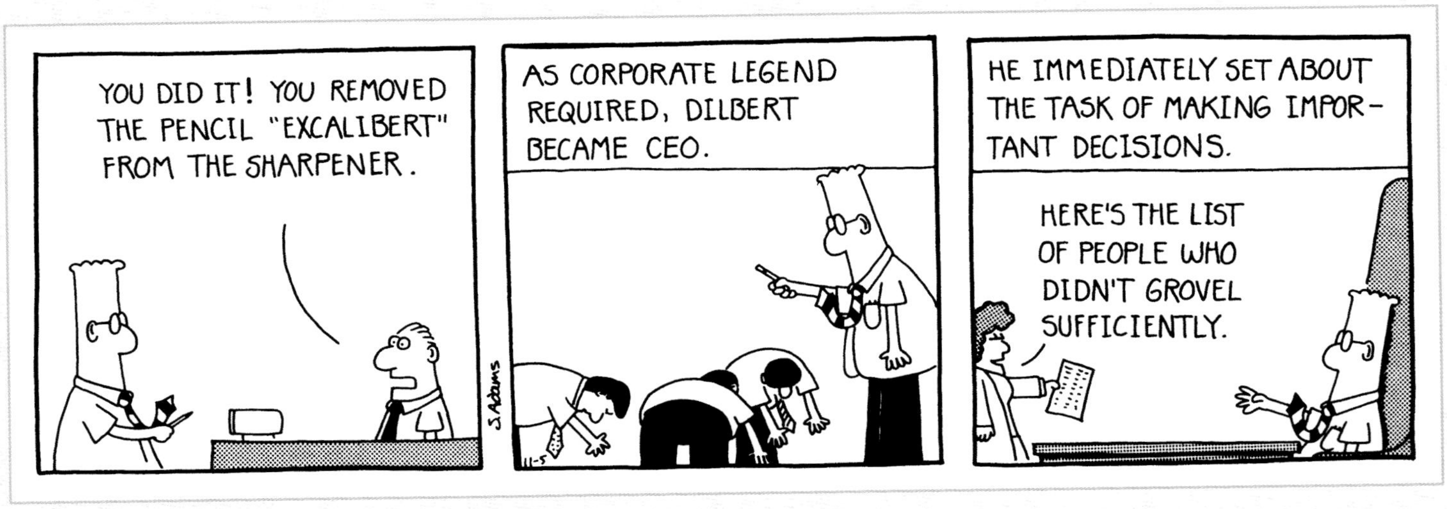
YOU DID IT! YOU REMOVED THE PENCIL "EXCALIBERT" FROM THE SHARPENER.
AS CORPORATE LEGEND REQUIRED, DILBERT BECAME CEO.
HE IMMEDIATELY SET ABOUT THE TASK OF MAKING IMPORTANT DECISIONS.
HERE'S THE LIST OF PEOPLE WHO DIDN'T GROVEL SUFFICIENTLY.

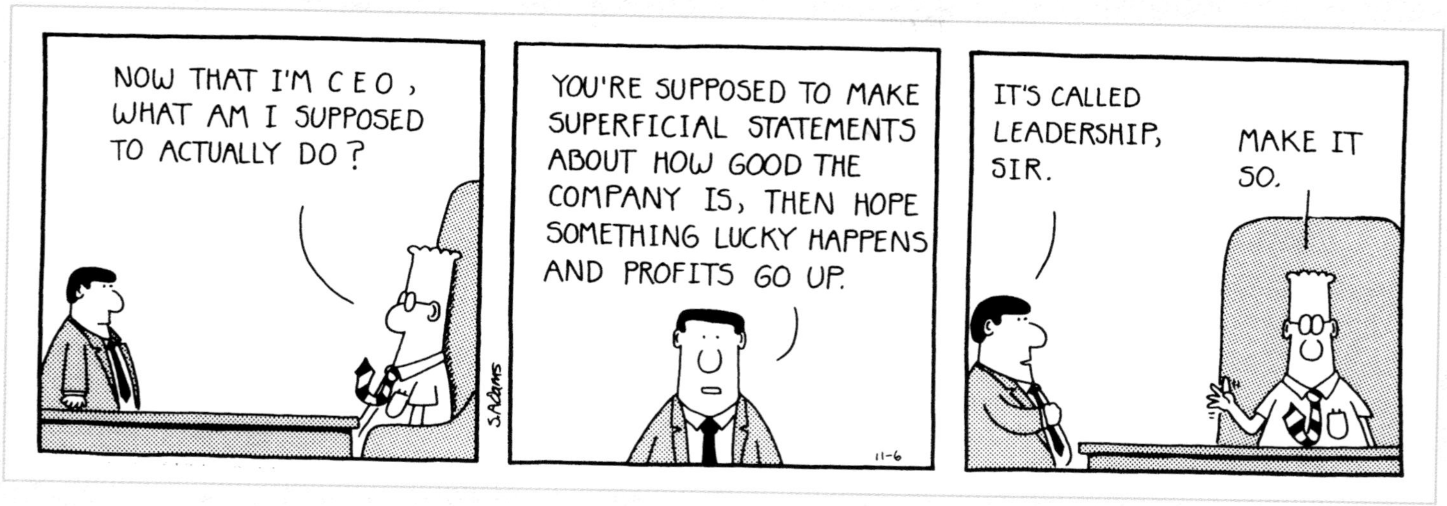
NOW THAT I'M C E O, WHAT AM I SUPPOSED TO ACTUALLY DO?
S.Adams
YOU'RE SUPPOSED TO MAKE SUPERFICIAL STATEMENTS ABOUT HOW GOOD THE COMPANY IS, THEN HOPE SOMETHING LUCKY HAPPENS AND PROFITS GO UP.
11-6
IT'S CALLED LEADERSHIP, SIR.
MAKE IT SO.

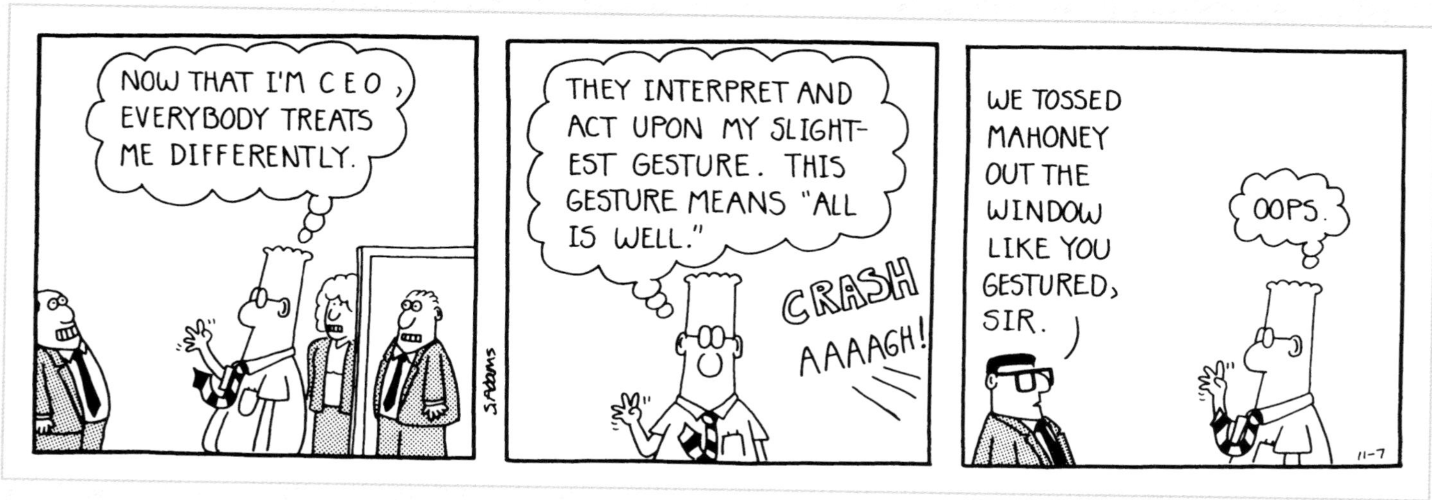
NOW THAT I'M C E O, EVERYBODY TREATS ME DIFFERENTLY.
S.Adams
THEY INTERPRET AND ACT UPON MY SLIGHT-EST GESTURE. THIS GESTURE MEANS "ALL IS WELL."
CRASH
AAAAGH!
WE TOSSED MAHONEY OUT THE WINDOW LIKE YOU GESTURED, SIR.
OOPS.
11-7

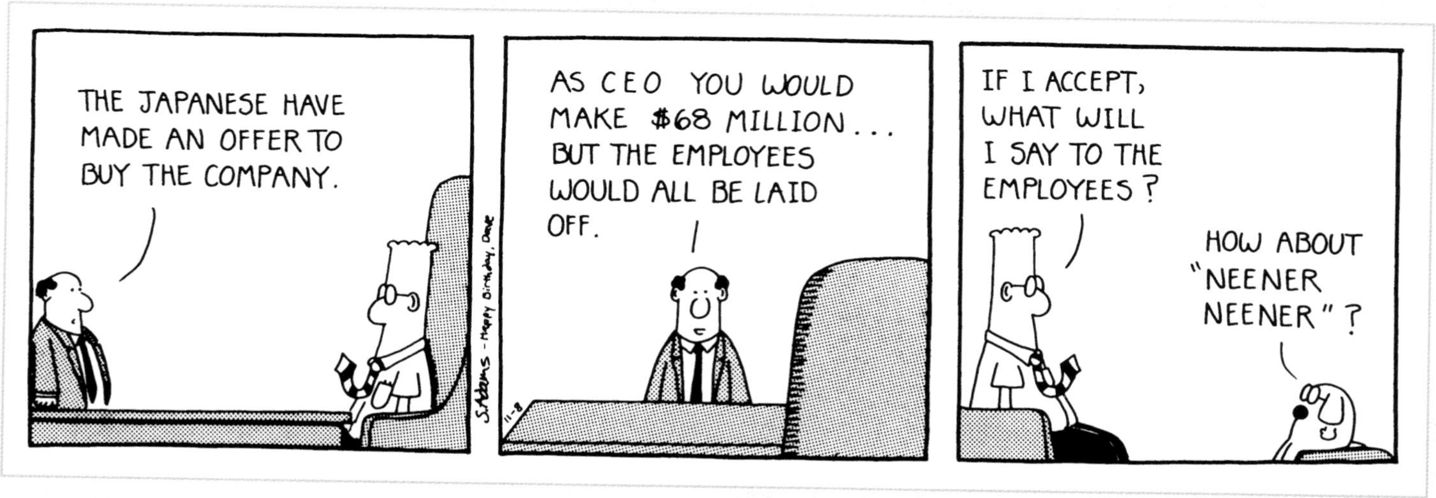
THE JAPANESE HAVE MADE AN OFFER TO BUY THE COMPANY.
S.Adams - Happy Birthday, Dave
11-8
AS C E O YOU WOULD MAKE $68 MILLION... BUT THE EMPLOYEES WOULD ALL BE LAID OFF.
IF I ACCEPT, WHAT WILL I SAY TO THE EMPLOYEES?
HOW ABOUT "NEENER NEENER"?

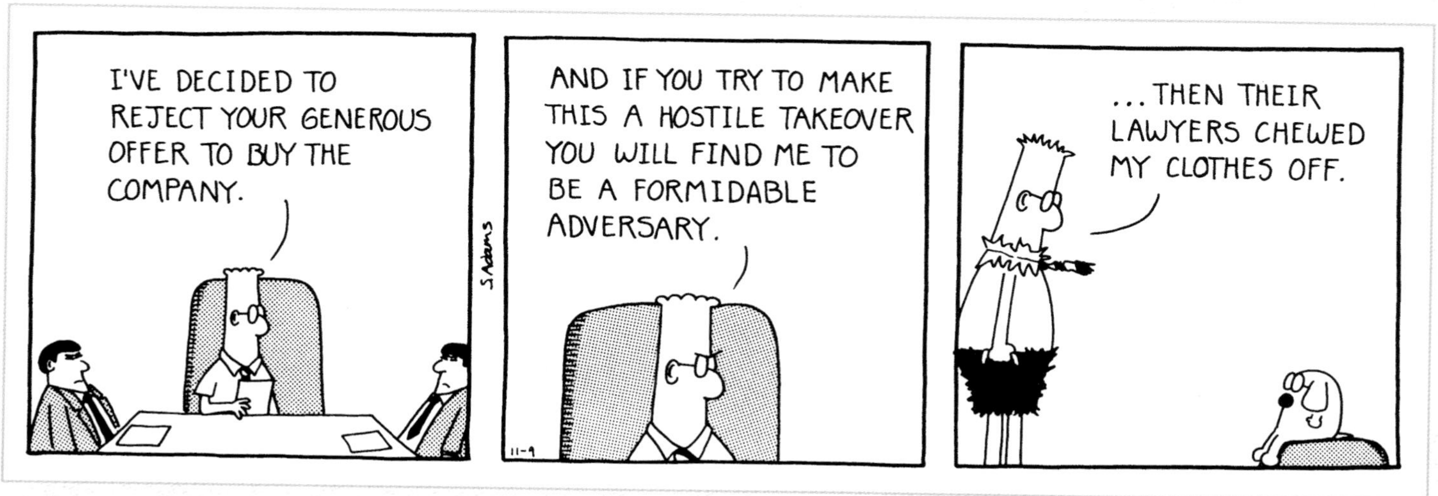
I'VE DECIDED TO REJECT YOUR GENEROUS OFFER TO BUY THE COMPANY.
S.Adams
AND IF YOU TRY TO MAKE THIS A HOSTILE TAKEOVER YOU WILL FIND ME TO BE A FORMIDABLE ADVERSARY.
11-9
...THEN THEIR LAWYERS CHEWED MY CLOTHES OFF.

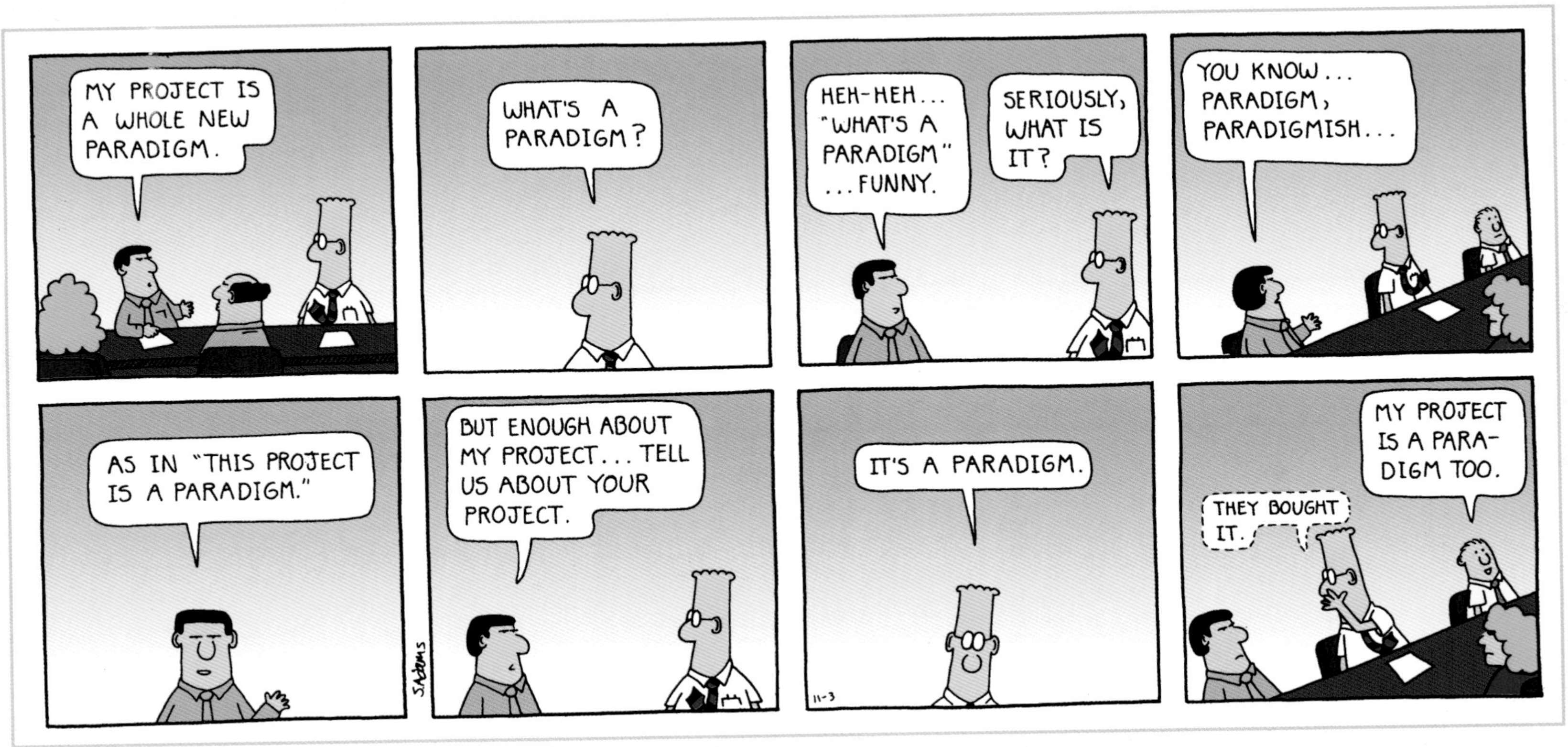

MY PROJECT IS A WHOLE NEW PARADIGM.
WHAT'S A PARADIGM?
HEH-HEH... "WHAT'S A PARADIGM" ... FUNNY.
SERIOUSLY, WHAT IS IT?
YOU KNOW... PARADIGM, PARADIGMISH...
AS IN "THIS PROJECT IS A PARADIGM."
BUT ENOUGH ABOUT MY PROJECT... TELL US ABOUT YOUR PROJECT.
IT'S A PARADIGM.
THEY BOUGHT IT.
MY PROJECT IS A PARADIGM TOO.

By this time, Dilbert was becoming popular in the workplace, thanks to comics like this one. But I didn't know it. I had no form of feedback about the strip except from friends and family, who are notoriously unreliable.

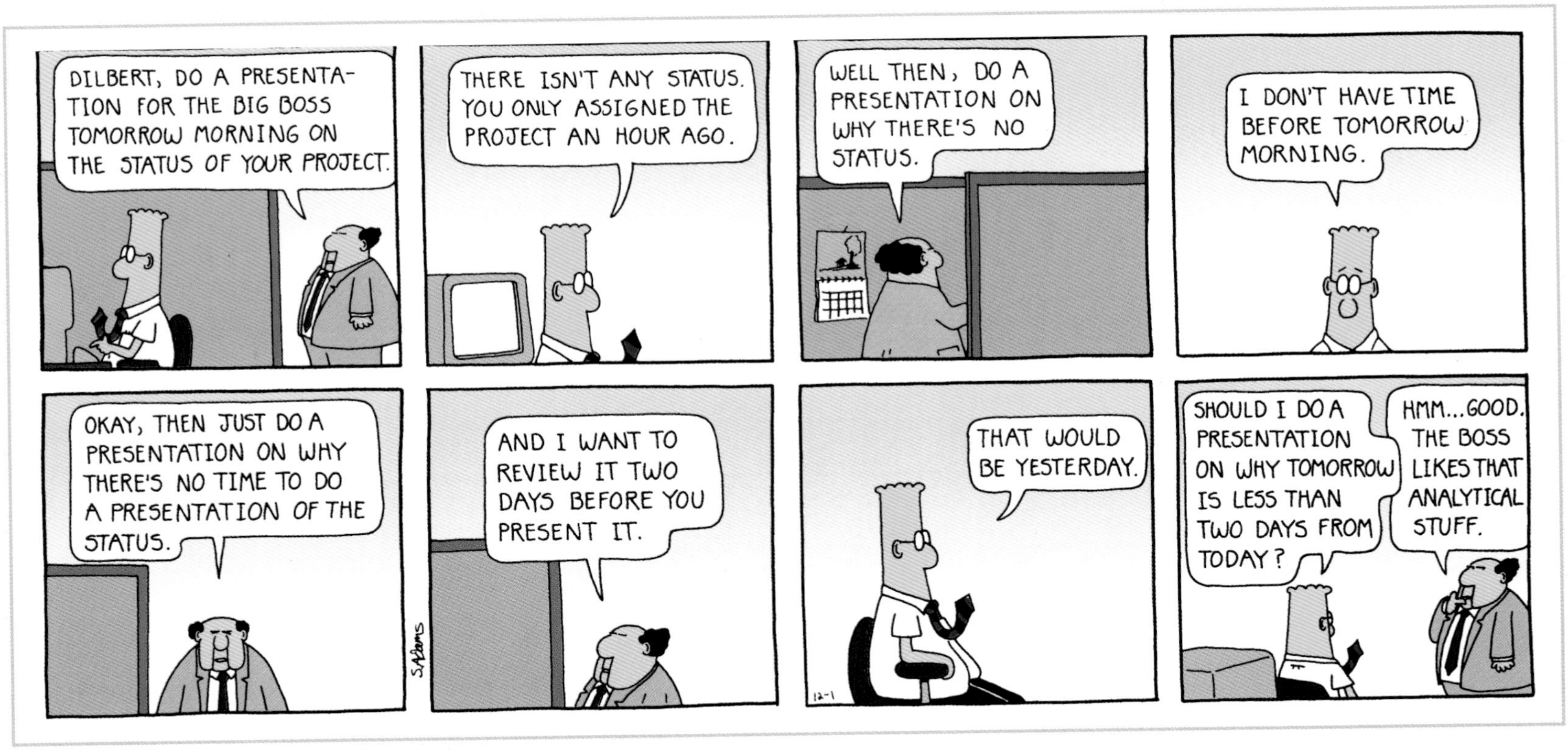

DILBERT, DO A PRESENTATION FOR THE BIG BOSS TOMORROW MORNING ON THE STATUS OF YOUR PROJECT.
THERE ISN'T ANY STATUS. YOU ONLY ASSIGNED THE PROJECT AN HOUR AGO.
WELL THEN, DO A PRESENTATION ON WHY THERE'S NO STATUS.
I DON'T HAVE TIME BEFORE TOMORROW MORNING.
OKAY, THEN JUST DO A PRESENTATION ON WHY THERE'S NO TIME TO DO A PRESENTATION OF THE STATUS.
AND I WANT TO REVIEW IT TWO DAYS BEFORE YOU PRESENT IT.
THAT WOULD BE YESTERDAY.
SHOULD I DO A PRESENTATION ON WHY TOMORROW IS LESS THAN TWO DAYS FROM TODAY?
HMM...GOOD. THE BOSS LIKES THAT ANALYTICAL STUFF.

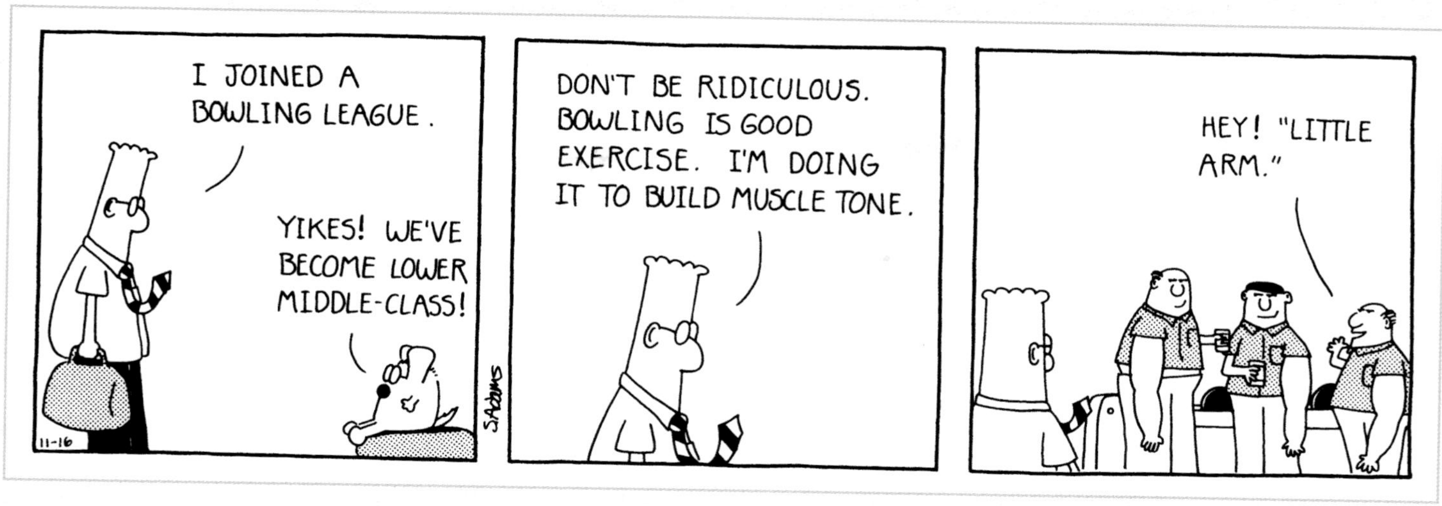
I JOINED A BOWLING LEAGUE.
YIKES! WE'VE BECOME LOWER MIDDLE-CLASS!
DON'T BE RIDICULOUS. BOWLING IS GOOD EXERCISE. I'M DOING IT TO BUILD MUSCLE TONE.
HEY! "LITTLE ARM."

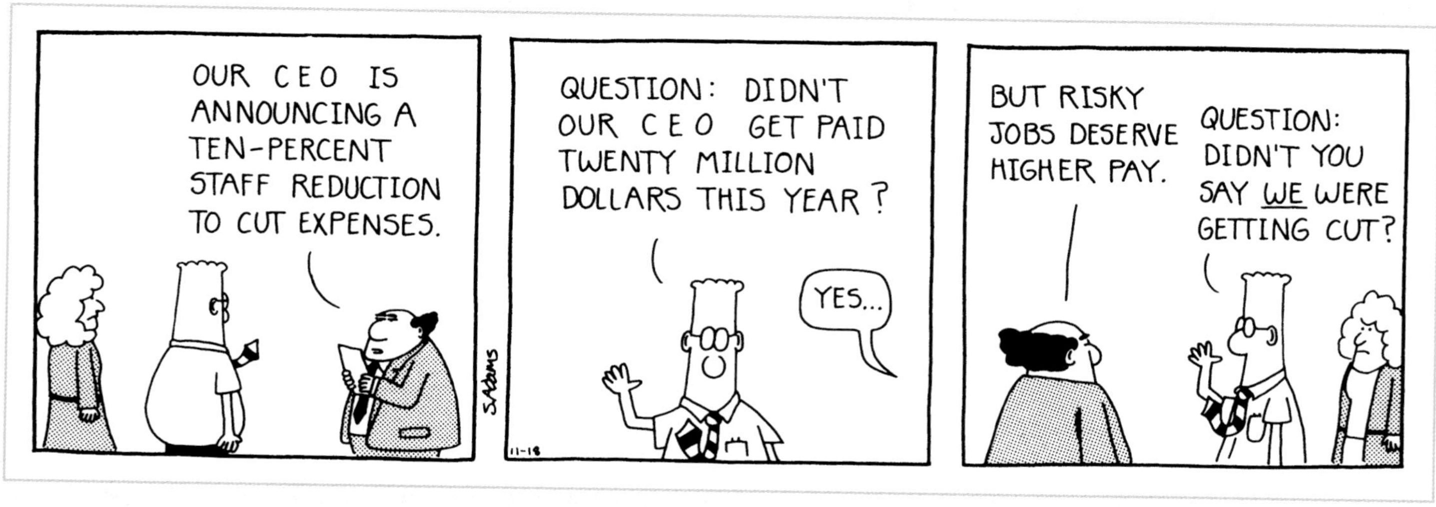
OUR CEO IS ANNOUNCING A TEN-PERCENT STAFF REDUCTION TO CUT EXPENSES.
QUESTION: DIDN'T OUR CEO GET PAID TWENTY MILLION DOLLARS THIS YEAR?
YES...
BUT RISKY JOBS DESERVE HIGHER PAY.
QUESTION: DIDN'T YOU SAY WE WERE GETTING CUT?

The boss's hair reaches a full point.

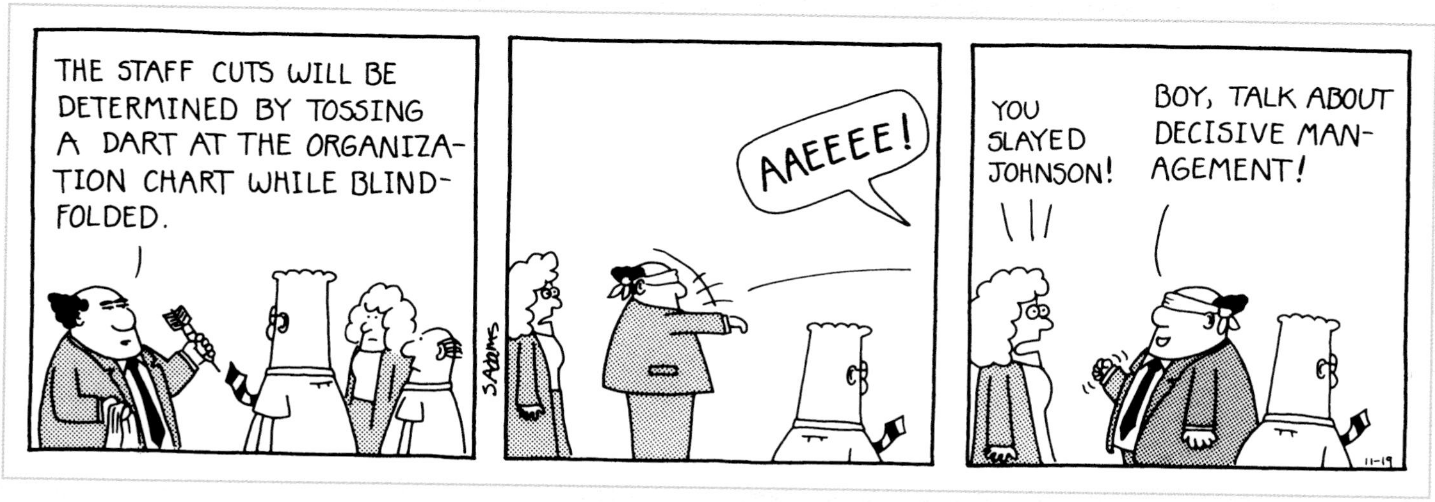
THE STAFF CUTS WILL BE DETERMINED BY TOSSING A DART AT THE ORGANIZATION CHART WHILE BLINDFOLDED.
AAEEEE!
YOU SLAYED JOHNSON!
BOY, TALK ABOUT DECISIVE MANAGEMENT!

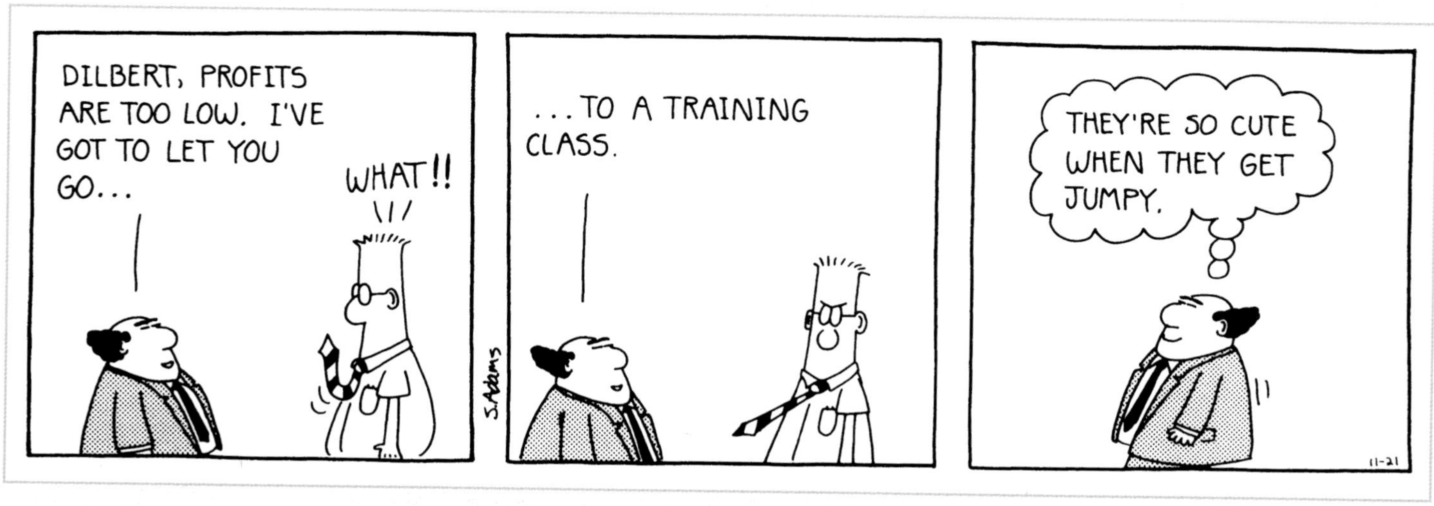
DILBERT, PROFITS ARE TOO LOW. I'VE GOT TO LET YOU GO...
WHAT!!
...TO A TRAINING CLASS.
THEY'RE SO CUTE WHEN THEY GET JUMPY.

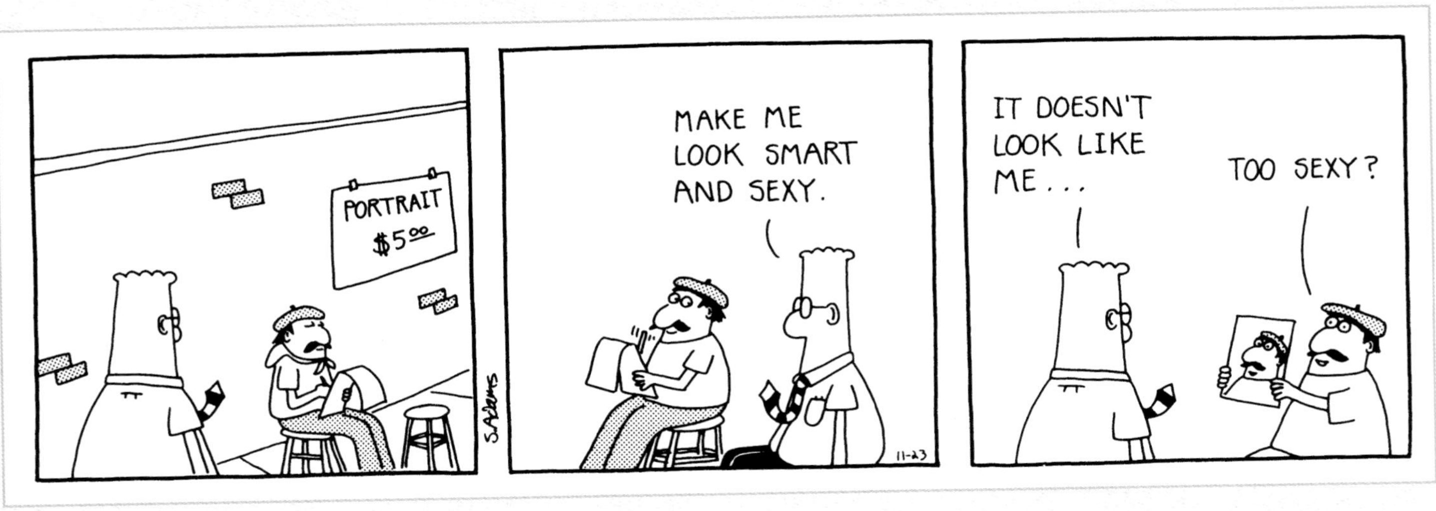
PORTRAIT $5.00
MAKE ME LOOK SMART AND SEXY.
IT DOESN'T LOOK LIKE ME...
TOO SEXY?

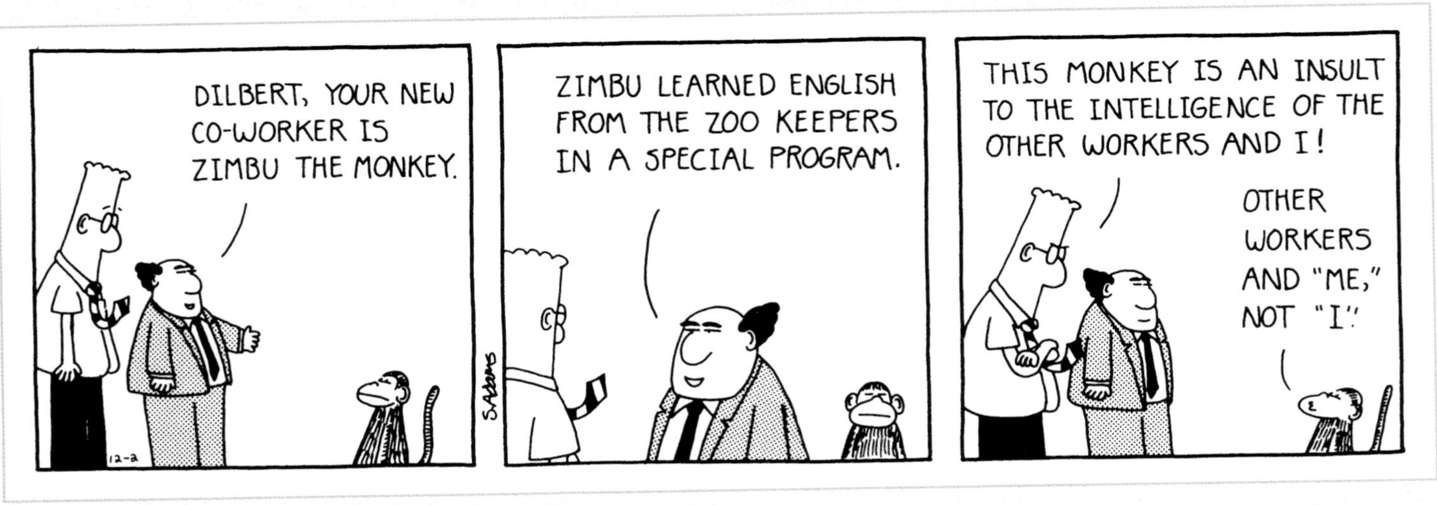
DILBERT, YOUR NEW CO-WORKER IS ZIMBU THE MONKEY.
ZIMBU LEARNED ENGLISH FROM THE ZOO KEEPERS IN A SPECIAL PROGRAM.
THIS MONKEY IS AN INSULT TO THE INTELLIGENCE OF THE OTHER WORKERS AND I!
OTHER WORKERS AND "ME," NOT "I."

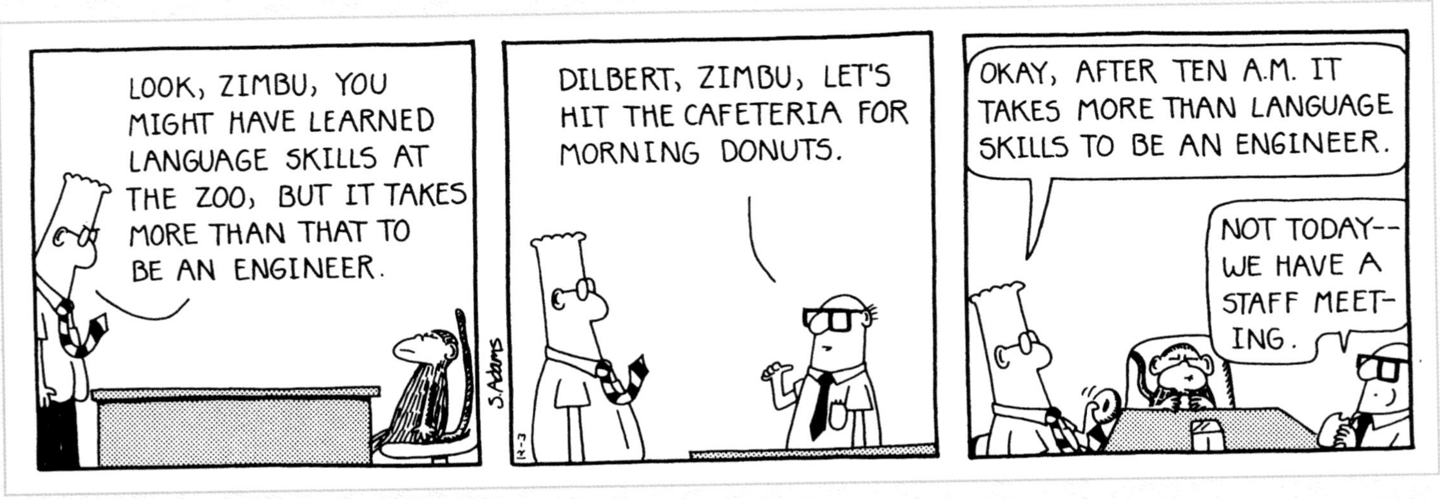
LOOK, ZIMBU, YOU MIGHT HAVE LEARNED LANGUAGE SKILLS AT THE ZOO, BUT IT TAKES MORE THAN THAT TO BE AN ENGINEER.
DILBERT, ZIMBU, LET'S HIT THE CAFETERIA FOR MORNING DONUTS.
OKAY, AFTER TEN A.M. IT TAKES MORE THAN LANGUAGE SKILLS TO BE AN ENGINEER.
NOT TODAY-- WE HAVE A STAFF MEETING.

Dilbert would eventually become the media's face for downsizing, in a period when it was front-page news. At this point, I didn't realize I was perfectly positioned for the media storm that would follow. I thought I was just making jokes about my job.

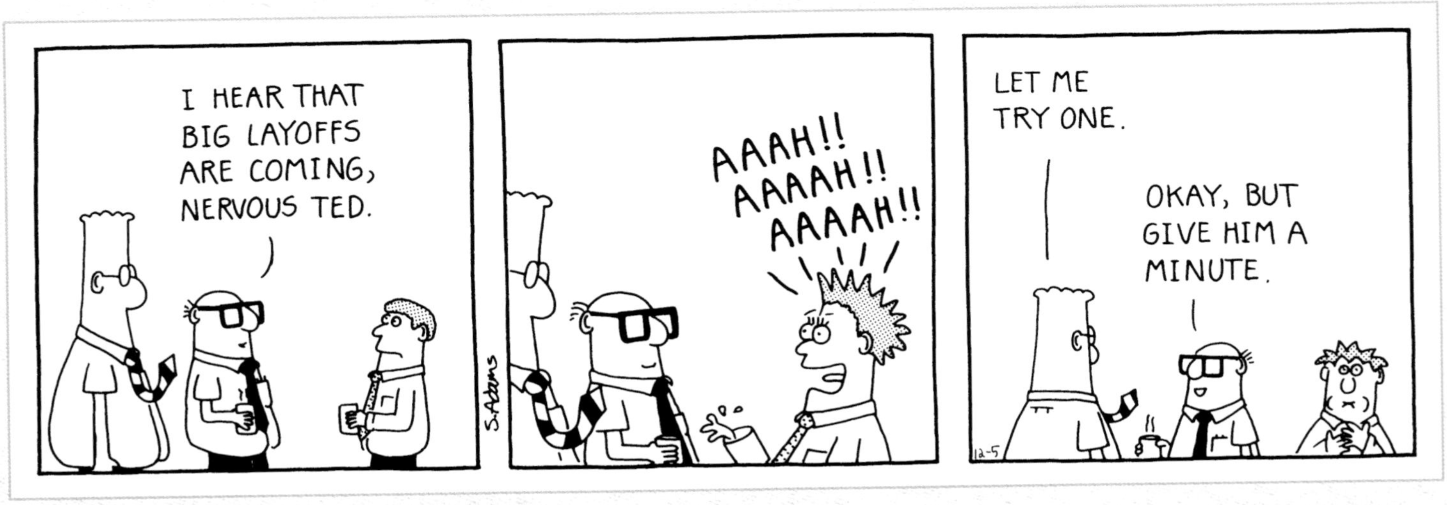
I HEAR THAT BIG LAYOFFS ARE COMING, NERVOUS TED.
AAAH!! AAAAH!! AAAAH!!
LET ME TRY ONE.
OKAY, BUT GIVE HIM A MINUTE.

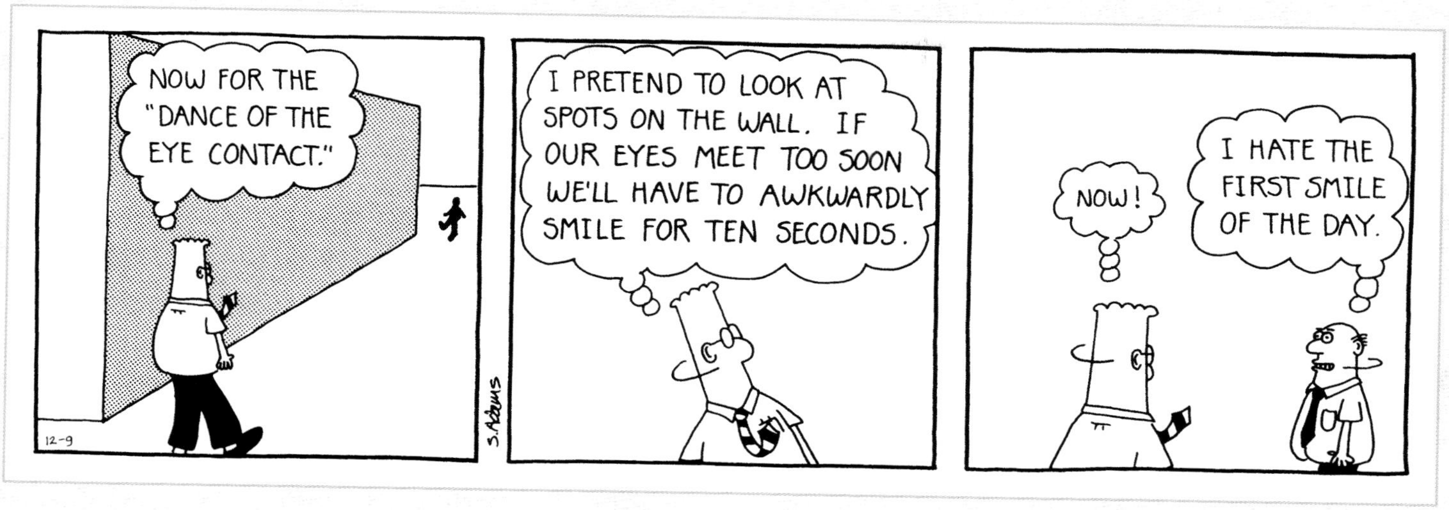
NOW FOR THE "DANCE OF THE EYE CONTACT."
12-9
S.Adams
I PRETEND TO LOOK AT SPOTS ON THE WALL. IF OUR EYES MEET TOO SOON WE'LL HAVE TO AWKWARDLY SMILE FOR TEN SECONDS.
NOW!
I HATE THE FIRST SMILE OF THE DAY.

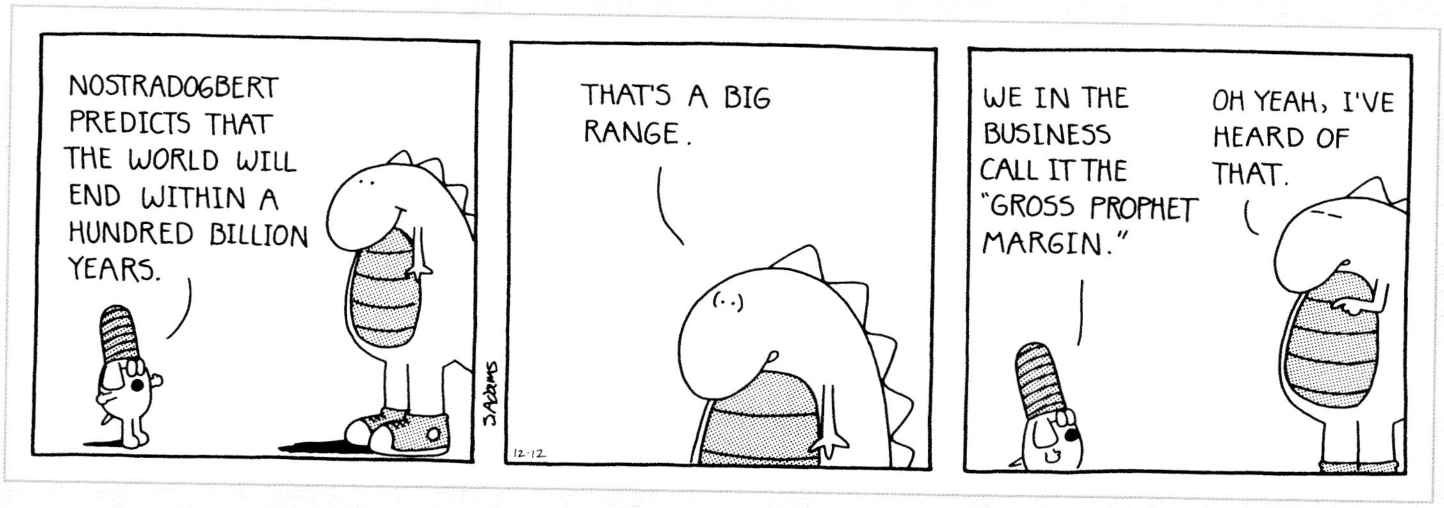
NOSTRADOGBERT PREDICTS THAT THE WORLD WILL END WITHIN A HUNDRED BILLION YEARS.
S.Adams
12-12
THAT'S A BIG RANGE.
WE IN THE BUSINESS CALL IT THE "GROSS PROPHET MARGIN."
OH YEAH, I'VE HEARD OF THAT.

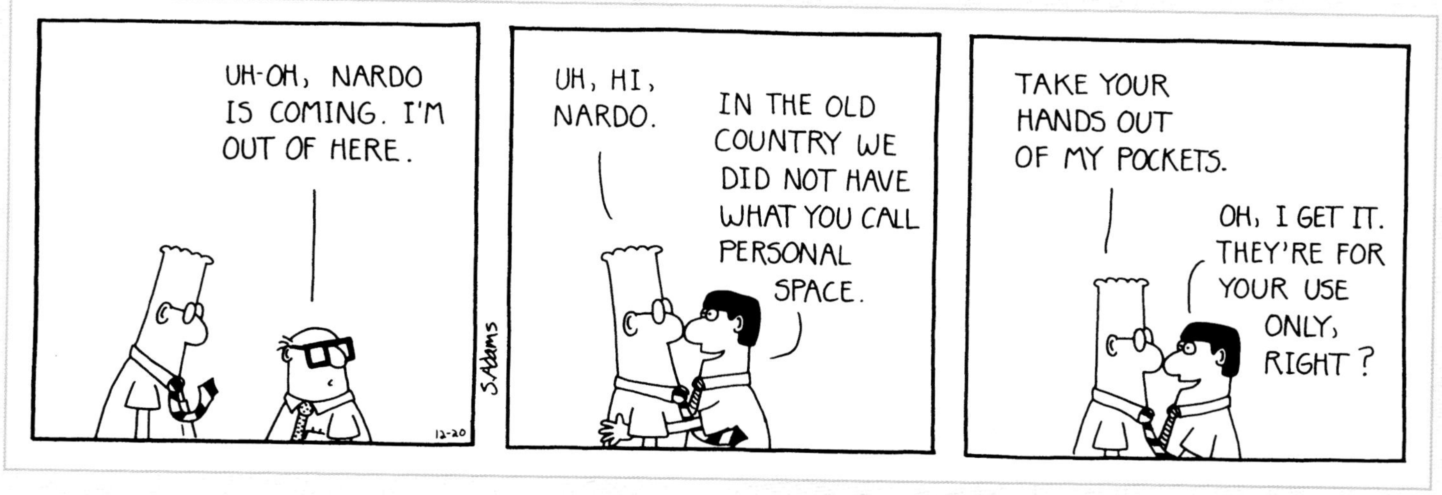
UH-OH, NARDO IS COMING. I'M OUT OF HERE.
12-20
S.Adams
UH, HI, NARDO.
IN THE OLD COUNTRY WE DID NOT HAVE WHAT YOU CALL PERSONAL SPACE.
TAKE YOUR HANDS OUT OF MY POCKETS.
OH, I GET IT. THEY'RE FOR YOUR USE ONLY, RIGHT?

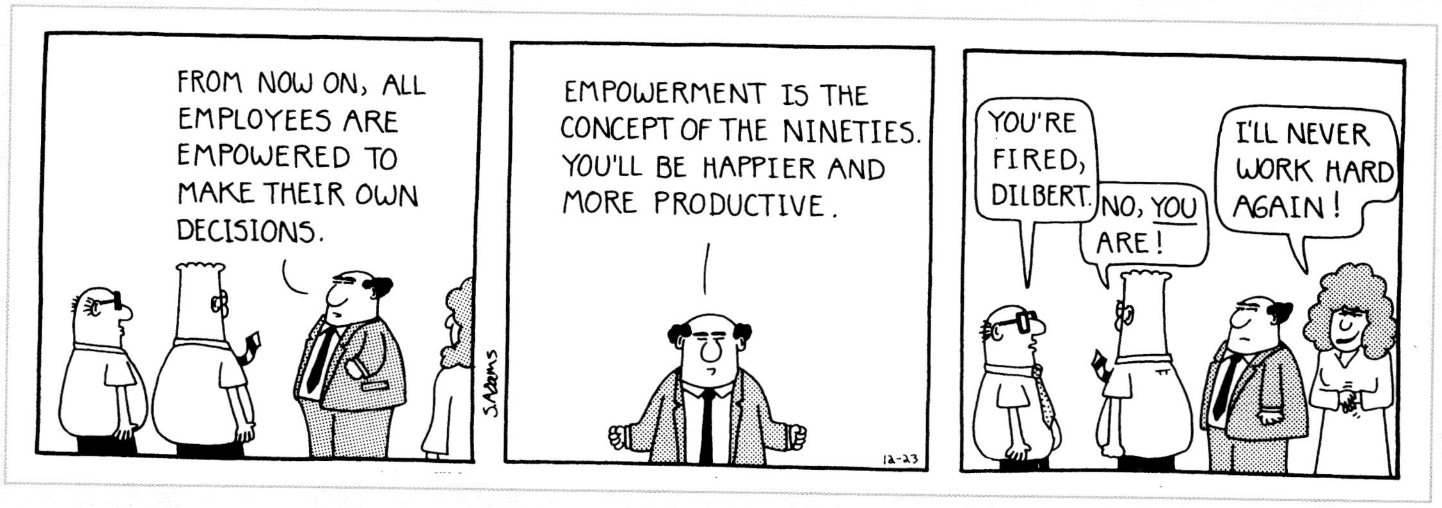
FROM NOW ON, ALL EMPLOYEES ARE EMPOWERED TO MAKE THEIR OWN DECISIONS.
S.Adams
EMPOWERMENT IS THE CONCEPT OF THE NINETIES. YOU'LL BE HAPPIER AND MORE PRODUCTIVE.
12-23
YOU'RE FIRED, DILBERT.
NO, YOU ARE!
I'LL NEVER WORK HARD AGAIN!

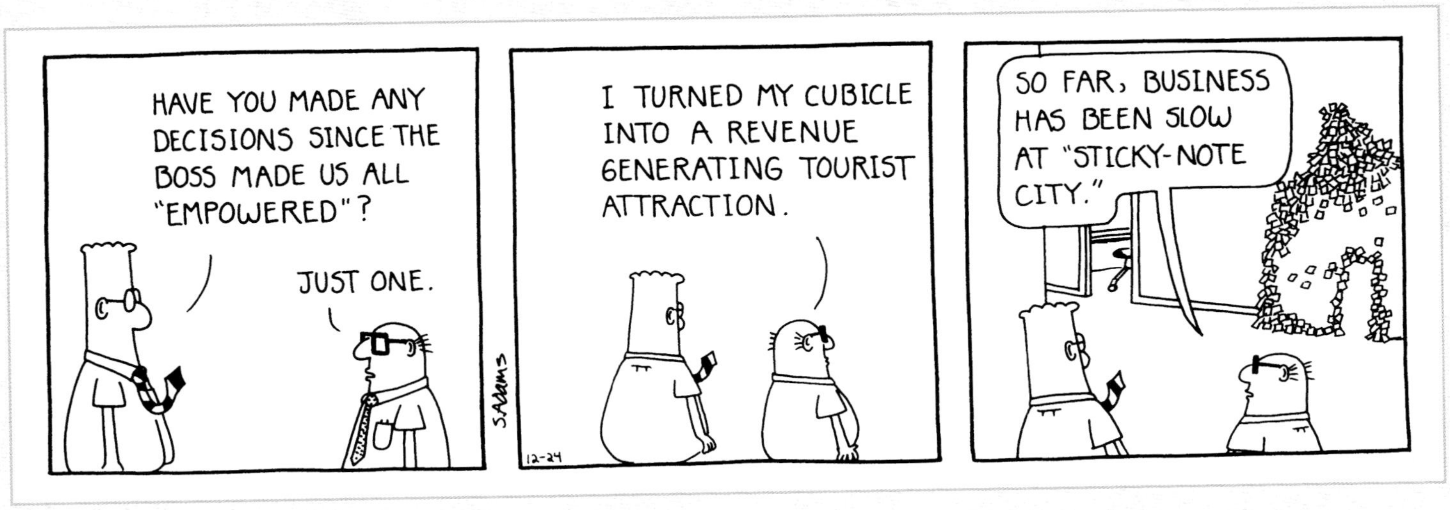
HAVE YOU MADE ANY DECISIONS SINCE THE BOSS MADE US ALL "EMPOWERED"?
JUST ONE.
S. Adams
12-24
I TURNED MY CUBICLE INTO A REVENUE GENERATING TOURIST ATTRACTION.
SO FAR, BUSINESS HAS BEEN SLOW AT "STICKY-NOTE CITY."

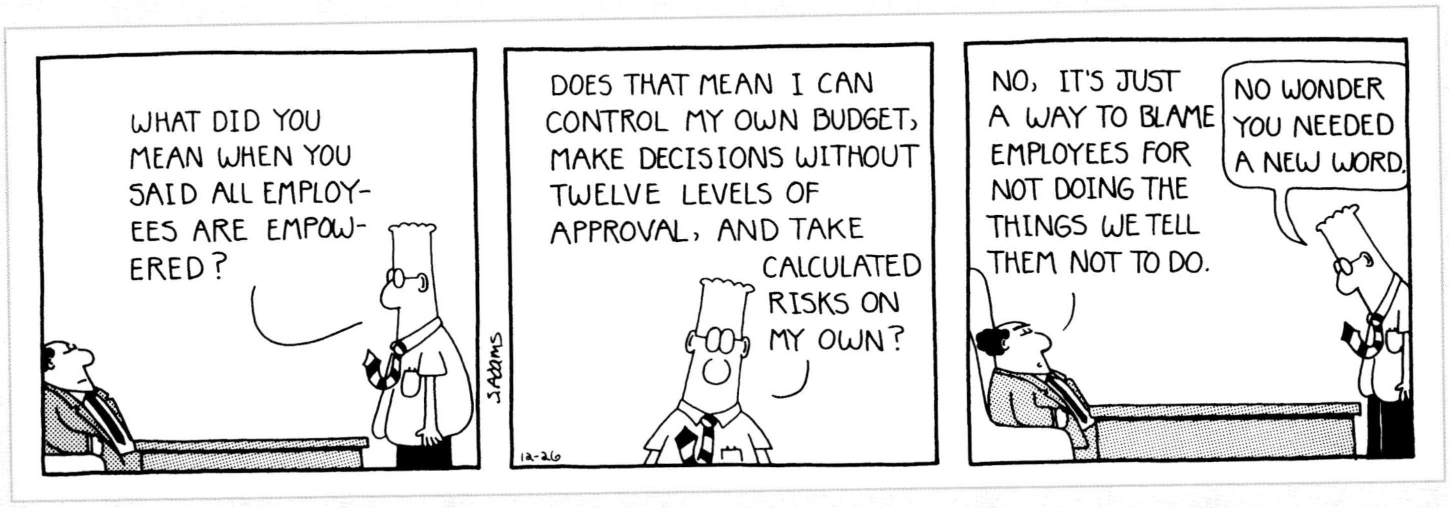
WHAT DID YOU MEAN WHEN YOU SAID ALL EMPLOY-EES ARE EMPOW-ERED?
S. Adams
12-26
DOES THAT MEAN I CAN CONTROL MY OWN BUDGET, MAKE DECISIONS WITHOUT TWELVE LEVELS OF APPROVAL, AND TAKE CALCULATED RISKS ON MY OWN?
NO, IT'S JUST A WAY TO BLAME EMPLOYEES FOR NOT DOING THE THINGS WE TELL THEM NOT TO DO.
NO WONDER YOU NEEDED A NEW WORD.

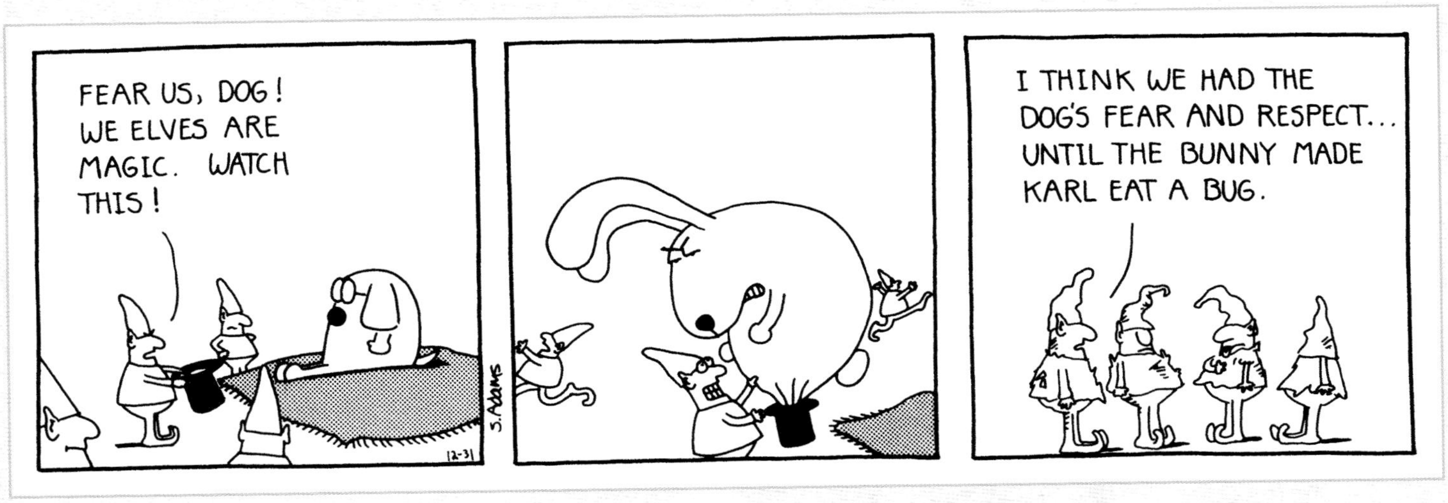
FEAR US, DOG! WE ELVES ARE MAGIC. WATCH THIS!
12-31
S. Adams
I THINK WE HAD THE DOG'S FEAR AND RESPECT... UNTIL THE BUNNY MADE KARL EAT A BUG.

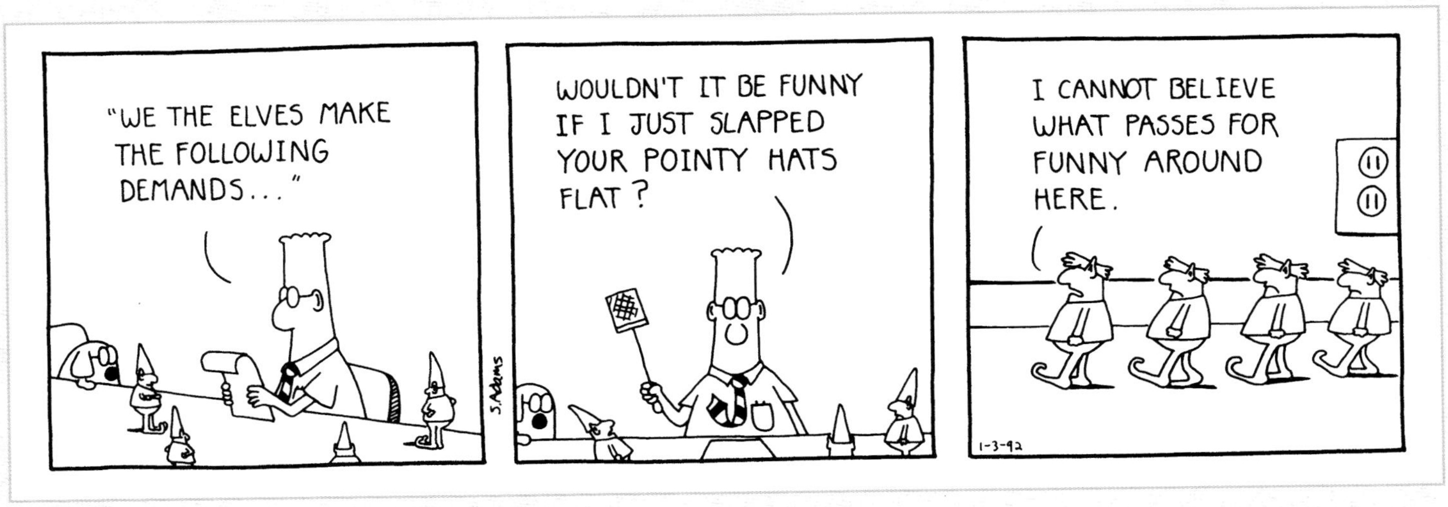
"WE THE ELVES MAKE THE FOLLOWING DEMANDS..."
S. Adams
WOULDN'T IT BE FUNNY IF I JUST SLAPPED YOUR POINTY HATS FLAT?
I CANNOT BELIEVE WHAT PASSES FOR FUNNY AROUND HERE.
1-3-92

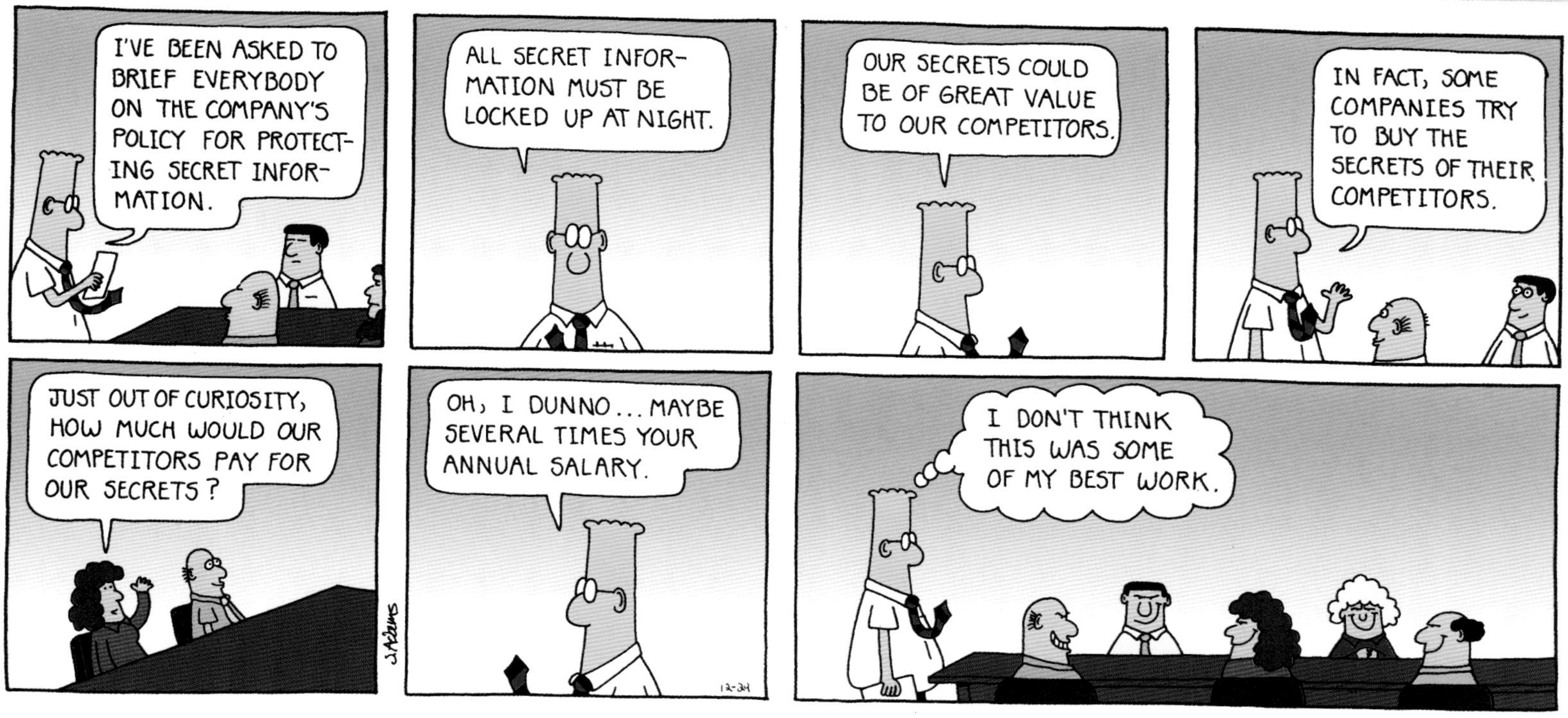
I'VE BEEN ASKED TO BRIEF EVERYBODY ON THE COMPANY'S POLICY FOR PROTECTING SECRET INFORMATION.
ALL SECRET INFORMATION MUST BE LOCKED UP AT NIGHT.
OUR SECRETS COULD BE OF GREAT VALUE TO OUR COMPETITORS.
IN FACT, SOME COMPANIES TRY TO BUY THE SECRETS OF THEIR COMPETITORS.
JUST OUT OF CURIOSITY, HOW MUCH WOULD OUR COMPETITORS PAY FOR OUR SECRETS?
OH, I DUNNO... MAYBE SEVERAL TIMES YOUR ANNUAL SALARY.
I DON'T THINK THIS WAS SOME OF MY BEST WORK.
S.Adams
12-24

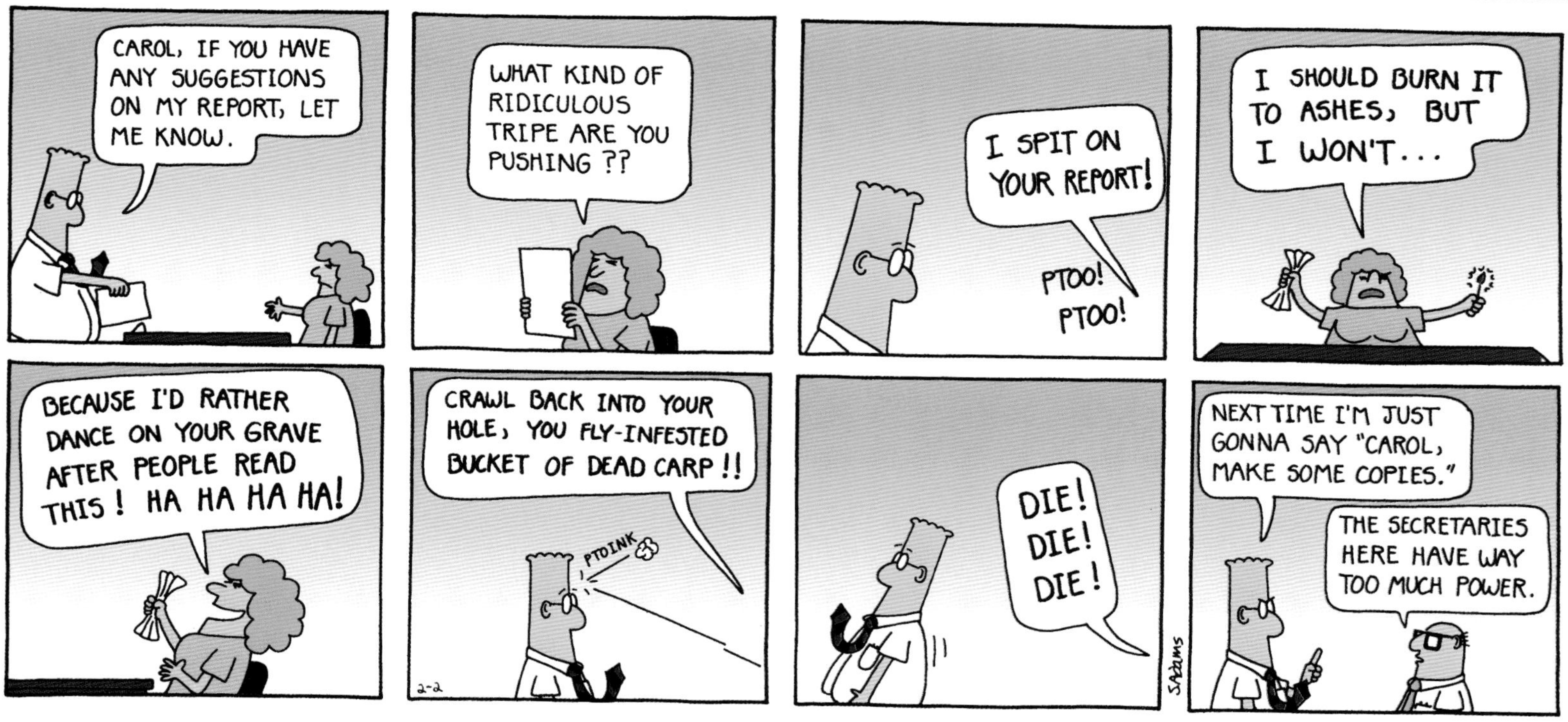
CAROL, IF YOU HAVE ANY SUGGESTIONS ON MY REPORT, LET ME KNOW.
WHAT KIND OF RIDICULOUS TRIPE ARE YOU PUSHING ??
I SPIT ON YOUR REPORT!
PTOO! PTOO!
I SHOULD BURN IT TO ASHES, BUT I WON'T...
BECAUSE I'D RATHER DANCE ON YOUR GRAVE AFTER PEOPLE READ THIS! HA HA HA HA!
CRAWL BACK INTO YOUR HOLE, YOU FLY-INFESTED BUCKET OF DEAD CARP!!
PTOINK
2-2
DIE! DIE! DIE!
S.Adams
NEXT TIME I'M JUST GONNA SAY "CAROL, MAKE SOME COPIES."
THE SECRETARIES HERE HAVE WAY TOO MUCH POWER.

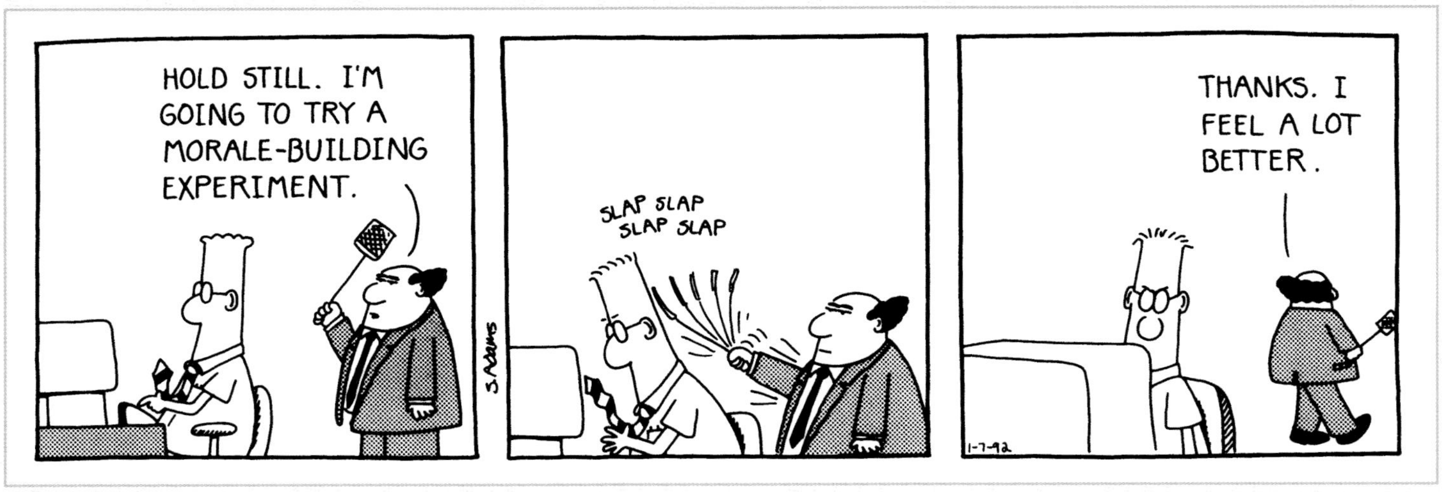
HOLD STILL. I'M GOING TO TRY A MORALE-BUILDING EXPERIMENT.
SLAP SLAP SLAP SLAP
THANKS. I FEEL A LOT BETTER.
1-7-92

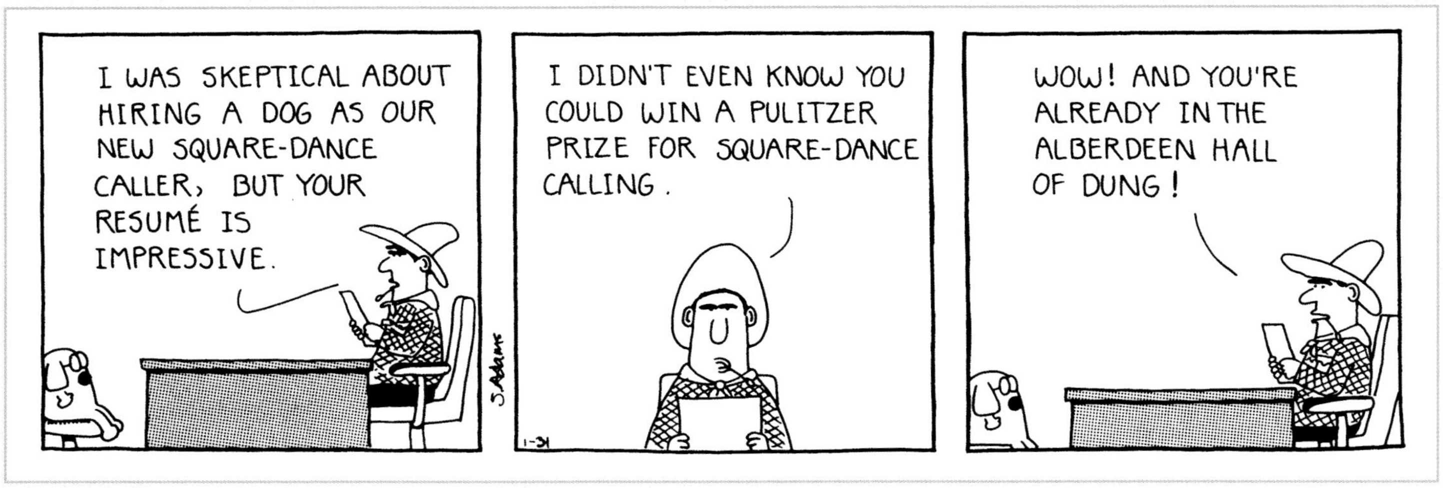
I WAS SKEPTICAL ABOUT HIRING A DOG AS OUR NEW SQUARE-DANCE CALLER, BUT YOUR RESUMÉ IS IMPRESSIVE.
I DIDN'T EVEN KNOW YOU COULD WIN A PULITZER PRIZE FOR SQUARE-DANCE CALLING.
WOW! AND YOU'RE ALREADY IN THE ALBERDEEN HALL OF DUNG!

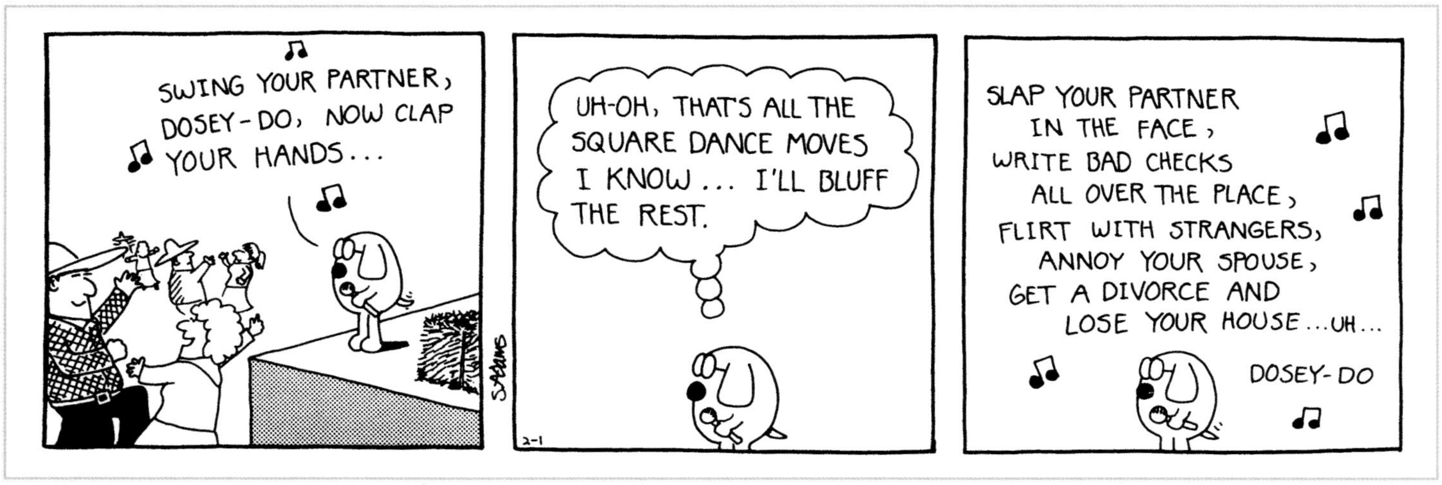
SWING YOUR PARTNER, DOSEY-DO, NOW CLAP YOUR HANDS...
UH-OH, THAT'S ALL THE SQUARE DANCE MOVES I KNOW... I'LL BLUFF THE REST.
SLAP YOUR PARTNER IN THE FACE, WRITE BAD CHECKS ALL OVER THE PLACE, FLIRT WITH STRANGERS, ANNOY YOUR SPOUSE, GET A DIVORCE AND LOSE YOUR HOUSE...UH...
DOSEY-DO
2-1

I got an angry letter from the International Association of Square Dance Callers. They did not approve of my treatment of square dance callers.

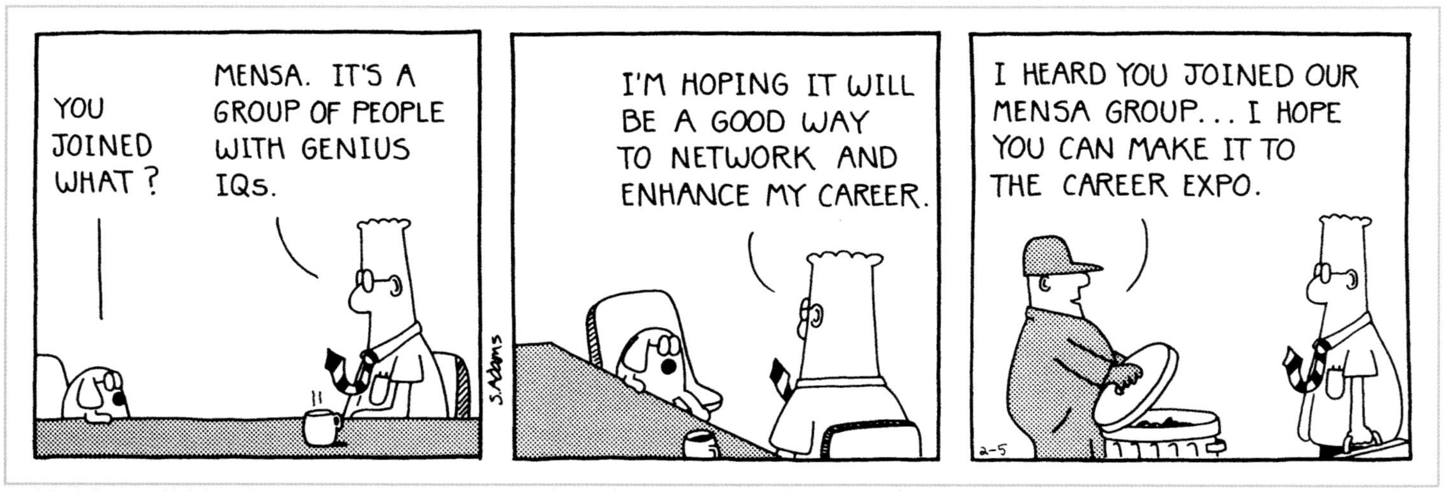
YOU JOINED WHAT?
MENSA. IT'S A GROUP OF PEOPLE WITH GENIUS IQs.
I'M HOPING IT WILL BE A GOOD WAY TO NETWORK AND ENHANCE MY CAREER.
I HEARD YOU JOINED OUR MENSA GROUP... I HOPE YOU CAN MAKE IT TO THE CAREER EXPO.
2-5

CALLERLAB

The International Association of Square Dance Callers

February 21, 1992

United Features Syndicate
200 Park Ave
New York City NY 10166

Reference: Comic strip "Dilbert" by Scott Adams

Gentlemen,

Our office has been bombarded by phone calls and letters objecting to the attached cartoons that have appeared in hundreds of newspapers across the country.

We represent over 4,000 square dance callers in the US, 10 Canadian provinces and 30 countries. These callers call to over 500,000 square dancers every week.

The square dance is the official folk dance of 17 states and was named the National Folk Dance in 1986.

Square dancing is a wholesome recreational activity whose participants are friendly, outgoing, honest and concerned that their activity is viewed by many as a back woods, hillbilly activity. Nothing could be further from the truth. It is a recognized art form that provides a healthy activity that is enjoyed by people of all ages.. children, teens, adults and senior citizens.

There are dozens of square dance clubs that provide recreation for the handicapped, including those confined to wheel chairs and the hearing or sight impaired.

Square dancers and square dance callers spend many hours entertaining at nursing homes, hospitals, senior citizen centers, county and state fairs, shopping malls, etc.

Square dancers and their callers do not deserve the negative press extolled by cartoonist Scott Adams. If he has had a bad experience with square dancing, I can assure you that it was a very, very isolated incidence and not at all representative of the activity.

We would welcome his comments and a chance to prove to him that square dancing is not now, nor has ever been, an activity even remotely similar to what he has depicted.

We eagerly await your response.

FOR THE EXECUTIVE COMMITTEE

Executive Secretary

ENC

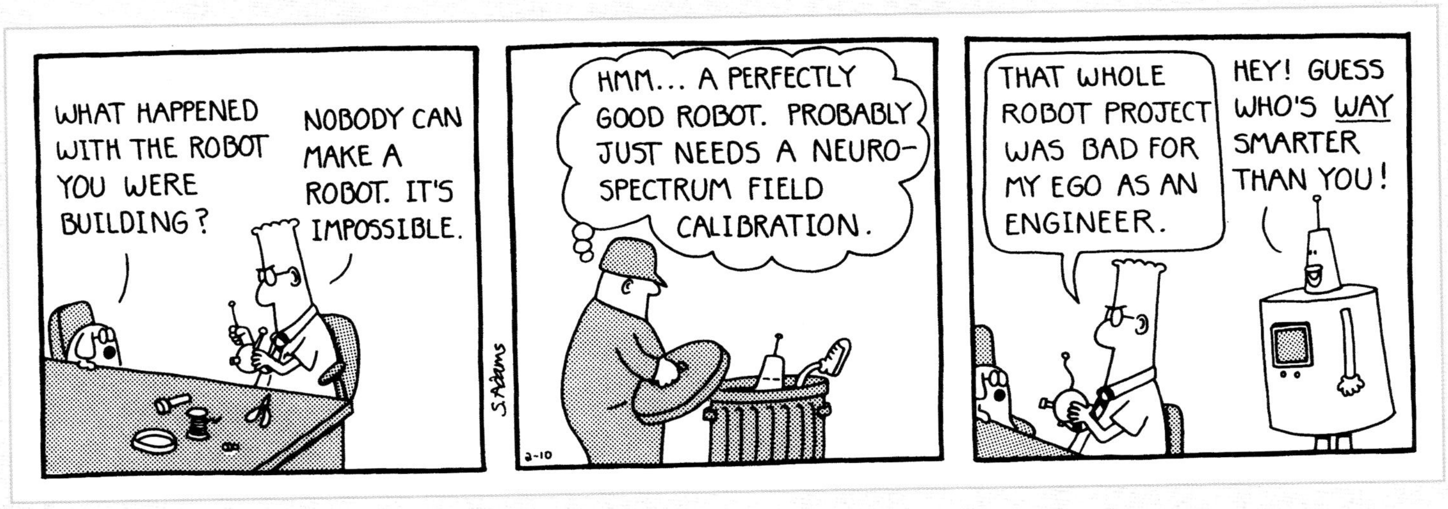
WHAT HAPPENED WITH THE ROBOT YOU WERE BUILDING?
NOBODY CAN MAKE A ROBOT. IT'S IMPOSSIBLE.
HMM... A PERFECTLY GOOD ROBOT. PROBABLY JUST NEEDS A NEURO-SPECTRUM FIELD CALIBRATION.
THAT WHOLE ROBOT PROJECT WAS BAD FOR MY EGO AS AN ENGINEER.
HEY! GUESS WHO'S WAY SMARTER THAN YOU!

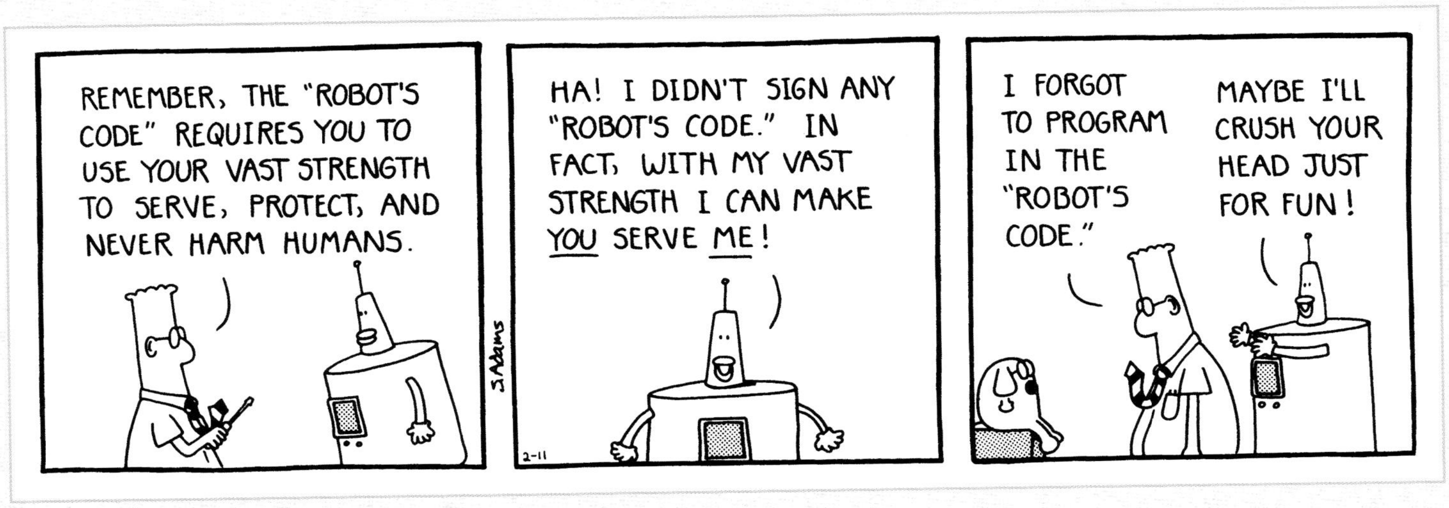
REMEMBER, THE "ROBOT'S CODE" REQUIRES YOU TO USE YOUR VAST STRENGTH TO SERVE, PROTECT, AND NEVER HARM HUMANS.
HA! I DIDN'T SIGN ANY "ROBOT'S CODE." IN FACT, WITH MY VAST STRENGTH I CAN MAKE YOU SERVE ME!
I FORGOT TO PROGRAM IN THE "ROBOT'S CODE."
MAYBE I'LL CRUSH YOUR HEAD JUST FOR FUN!

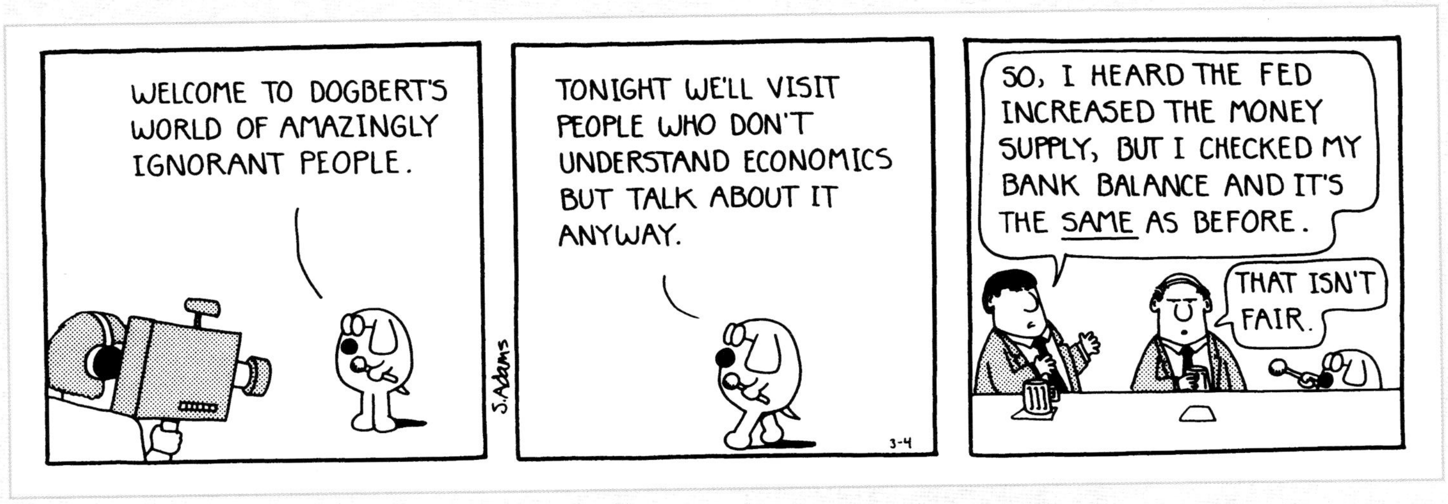
WELCOME TO DOGBERT'S WORLD OF AMAZINGLY IGNORANT PEOPLE.
TONIGHT WE'LL VISIT PEOPLE WHO DON'T UNDERSTAND ECONOMICS BUT TALK ABOUT IT ANYWAY.
SO, I HEARD THE FED INCREASED THE MONEY SUPPLY, BUT I CHECKED MY BANK BALANCE AND IT'S THE SAME AS BEFORE.
THAT ISN'T FAIR.

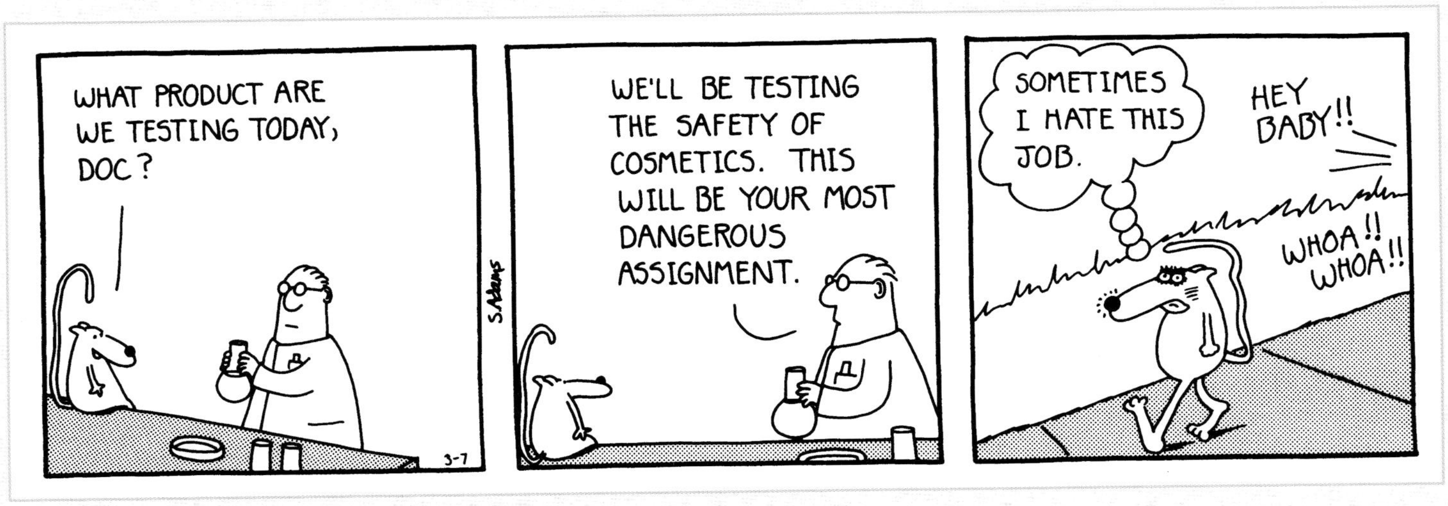
WHAT PRODUCT ARE WE TESTING TODAY, DOC?
WE'LL BE TESTING THE SAFETY OF COSMETICS. THIS WILL BE YOUR MOST DANGEROUS ASSIGNMENT.
SOMETIMES I HATE THIS JOB.
HEY BABY!!
WHOA!! WHOA!!

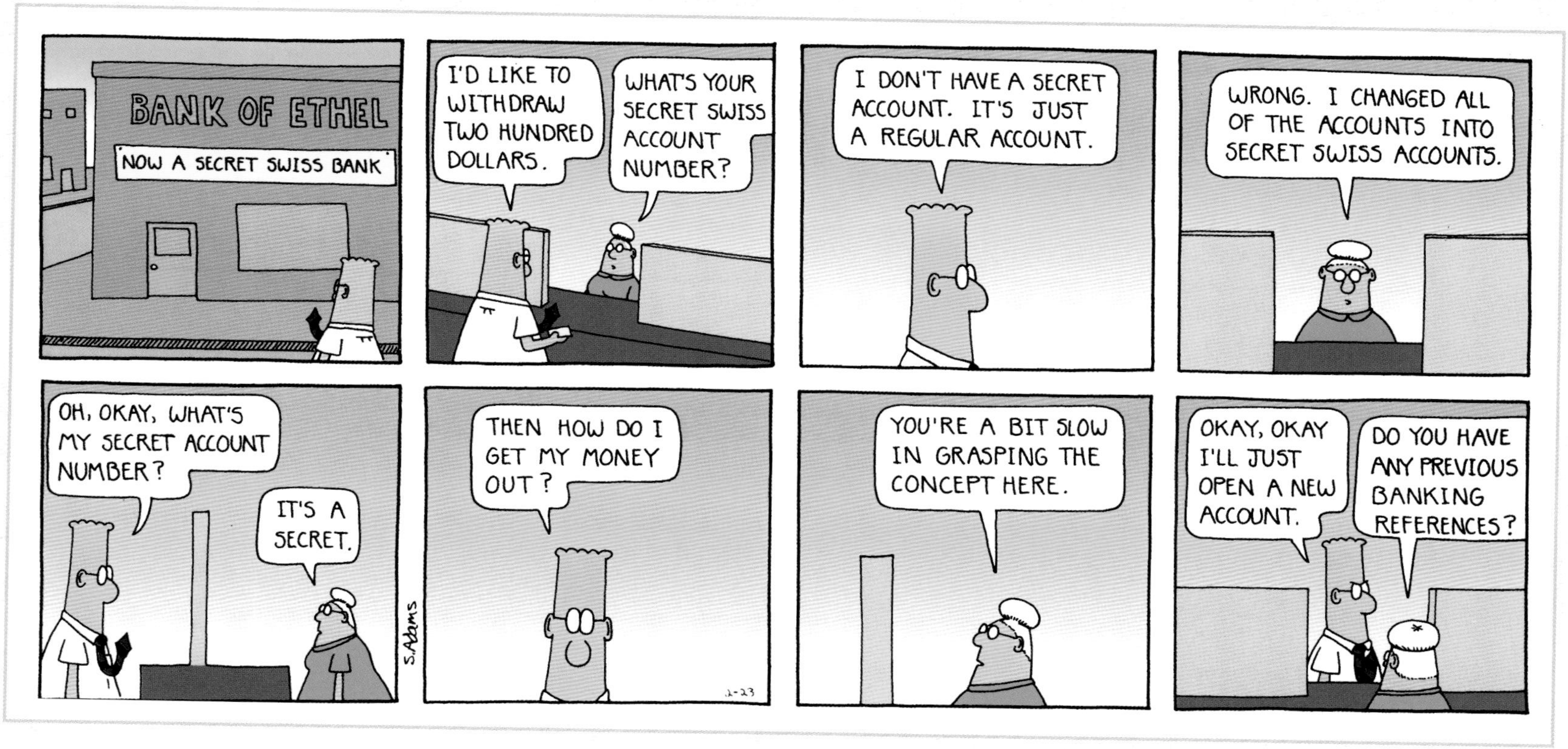
BANK OF ETHEL
NOW A SECRET SWISS BANK
I'D LIKE TO WITHDRAW TWO HUNDRED DOLLARS.
WHAT'S YOUR SECRET SWISS ACCOUNT NUMBER?
I DON'T HAVE A SECRET ACCOUNT. IT'S JUST A REGULAR ACCOUNT.
WRONG. I CHANGED ALL OF THE ACCOUNTS INTO SECRET SWISS ACCOUNTS.
OH, OKAY, WHAT'S MY SECRET ACCOUNT NUMBER?
IT'S A SECRET.
S.Adams
THEN HOW DO I GET MY MONEY OUT?
YOU'RE A BIT SLOW IN GRASPING THE CONCEPT HERE.
OKAY, OKAY I'LL JUST OPEN A NEW ACCOUNT.
DO YOU HAVE ANY PREVIOUS BANKING REFERENCES?

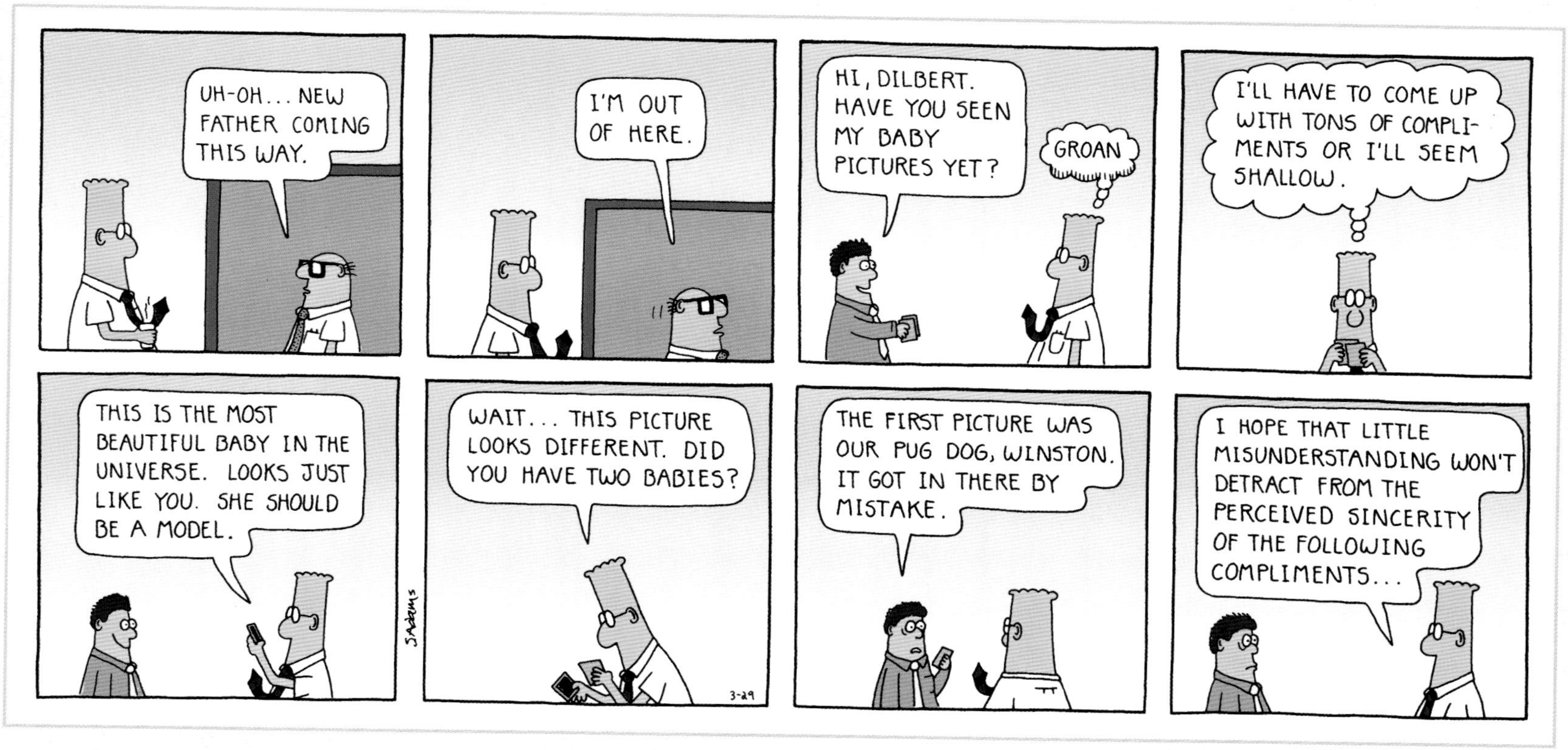
UH-OH... NEW FATHER COMING THIS WAY.
I'M OUT OF HERE.
HI, DILBERT. HAVE YOU SEEN MY BABY PICTURES YET?
GROAN
I'LL HAVE TO COME UP WITH TONS OF COMPLI-MENTS OR I'LL SEEM SHALLOW.
THIS IS THE MOST BEAUTIFUL BABY IN THE UNIVERSE. LOOKS JUST LIKE YOU. SHE SHOULD BE A MODEL.
S.Adams
WAIT... THIS PICTURE LOOKS DIFFERENT. DID YOU HAVE TWO BABIES?
3-29
THE FIRST PICTURE WAS OUR PUG DOG, WINSTON. IT GOT IN THERE BY MISTAKE.
I HOPE THAT LITTLE MISUNDERSTANDING WON'T DETRACT FROM THE PERCEIVED SINCERITY OF THE FOLLOWING COMPLIMENTS...

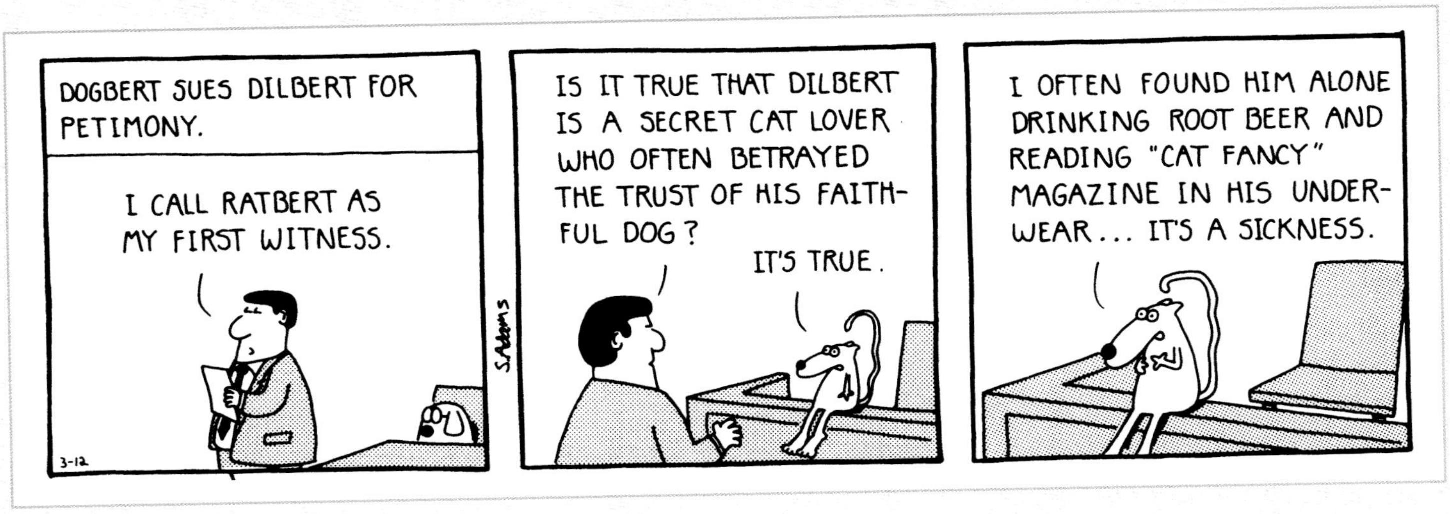
DOGBERT SUES DILBERT FOR PETIMONY.
I CALL RATBERT AS MY FIRST WITNESS.
IS IT TRUE THAT DILBERT IS A SECRET CAT LOVER WHO OFTEN BETRAYED THE TRUST OF HIS FAITHFUL DOG?
IT'S TRUE.
I OFTEN FOUND HIM ALONE DRINKING ROOT BEER AND READING "CAT FANCY" MAGAZINE IN HIS UNDERWEAR... IT'S A SICKNESS.

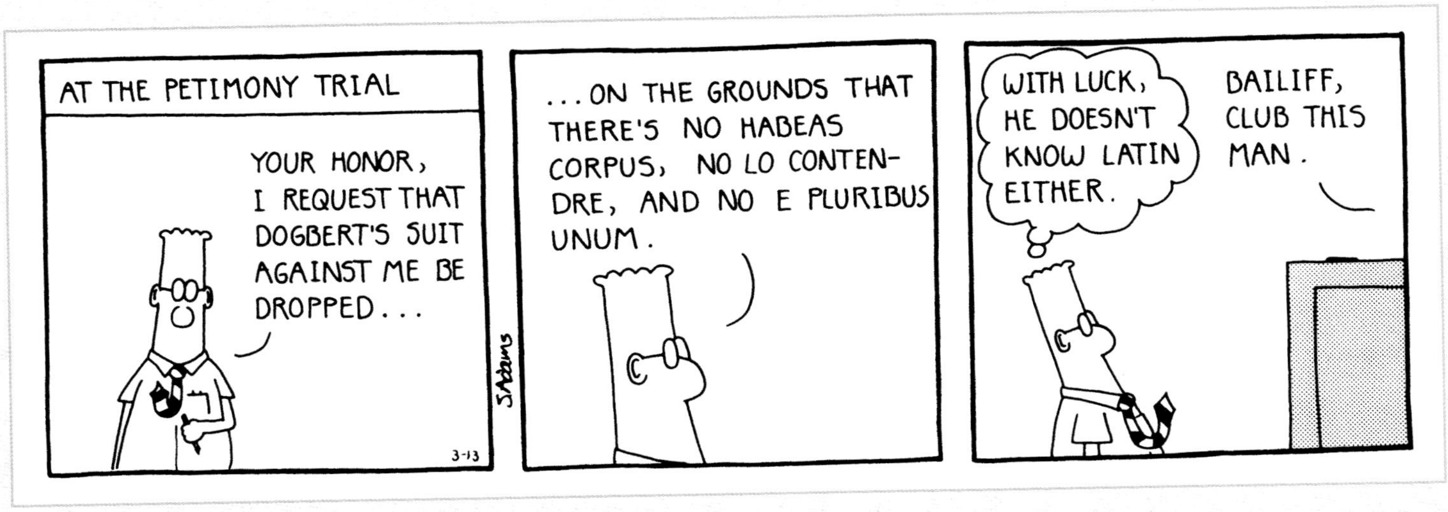
AT THE PETIMONY TRIAL
YOUR HONOR, I REQUEST THAT DOGBERT'S SUIT AGAINST ME BE DROPPED...
...ON THE GROUNDS THAT THERE'S NO HABEAS CORPUS, NO LO CONTENDRE, AND NO E PLURIBUS UNUM.
WITH LUCK, HE DOESN'T KNOW LATIN EITHER.
BAILIFF, CLUB THIS MAN.

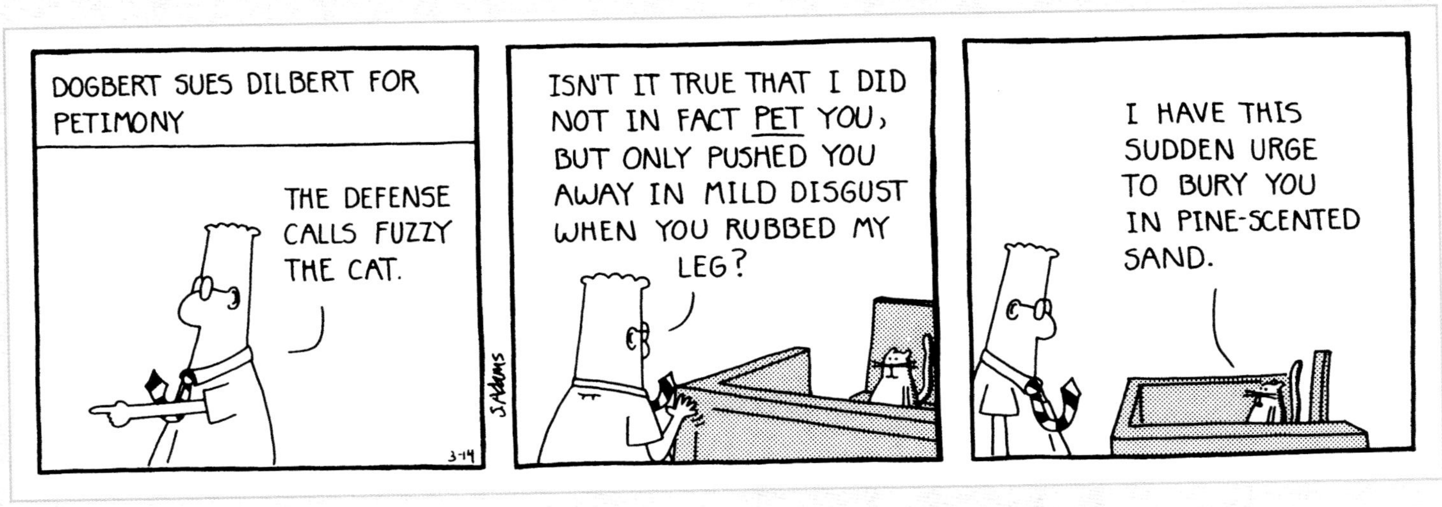
DOGBERT SUES DILBERT FOR PETIMONY
THE DEFENSE CALLS FUZZY THE CAT.
ISN'T IT TRUE THAT I DID NOT IN FACT PET YOU, BUT ONLY PUSHED YOU AWAY IN MILD DISGUST WHEN YOU RUBBED MY LEG?
I HAVE THIS SUDDEN URGE TO BURY YOU IN PINE-SCENTED SAND.

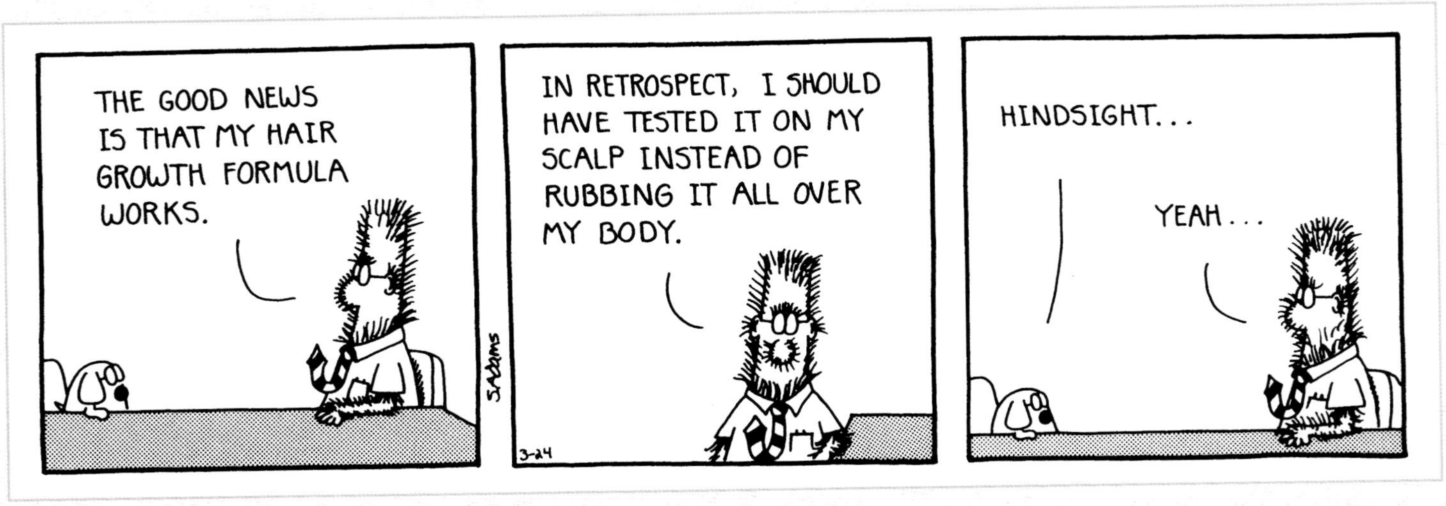
THE GOOD NEWS IS THAT MY HAIR GROWTH FORMULA WORKS.
IN RETROSPECT, I SHOULD HAVE TESTED IT ON MY SCALP INSTEAD OF RUBBING IT ALL OVER MY BODY.
HINDSIGHT...
YEAH...

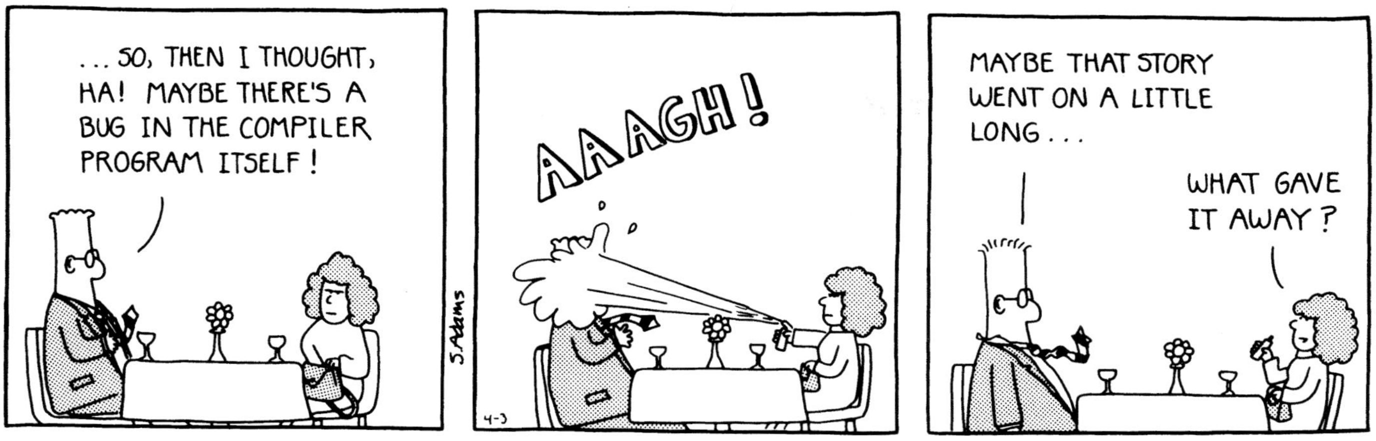

... SO, THEN I THOUGHT, HA! MAYBE THERE'S A BUG IN THE COMPILER PROGRAM ITSELF!
AAAGH!
MAYBE THAT STORY WENT ON A LITTLE LONG . . .
WHAT GAVE IT AWAY?

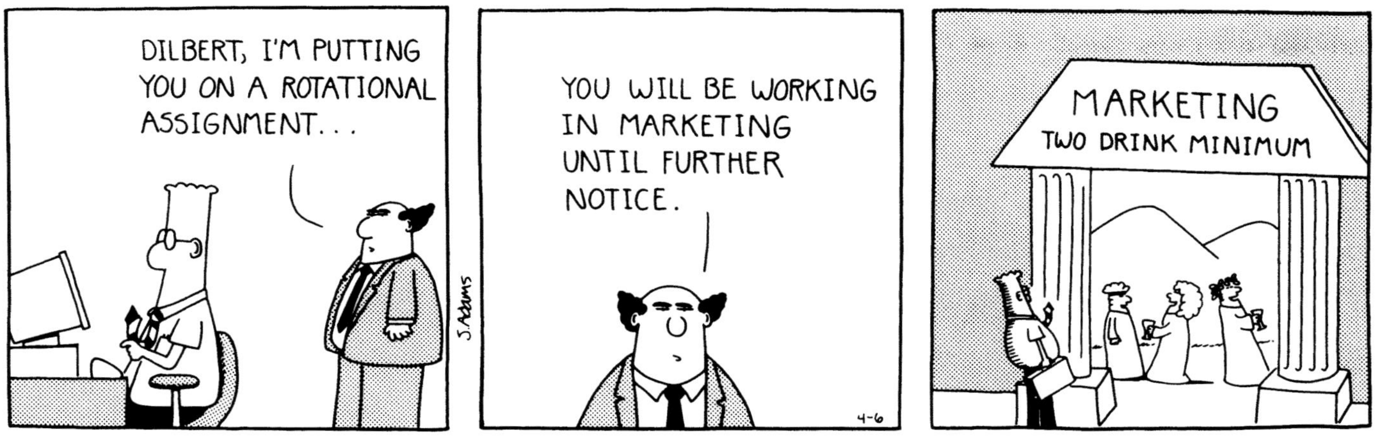

DILBERT, I'M PUTTING YOU ON A ROTATIONAL ASSIGNMENT . . .
YOU WILL BE WORKING IN MARKETING UNTIL FURTHER NOTICE.
MARKETING
TWO DRINK MINIMUM

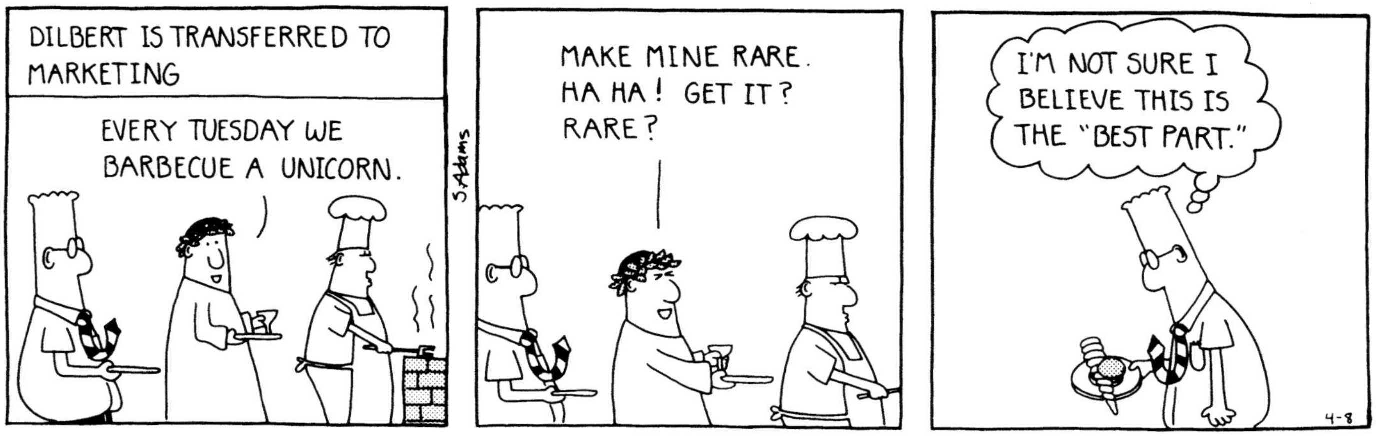

DILBERT IS TRANSFERRED TO MARKETING
EVERY TUESDAY WE BARBECUE A UNICORN.
MAKE MINE RARE. HA HA! GET IT? RARE?
I'M NOT SURE I BELIEVE THIS IS THE "BEST PART."

I got complaints from unicorn lovers. They mounted a letter-writing campaign to local newspapers to protest my treatment of unicorns. One put it this way: "There's nothing funny about frying a unicorn." I actually agree with that, which is why I had it barbecued.

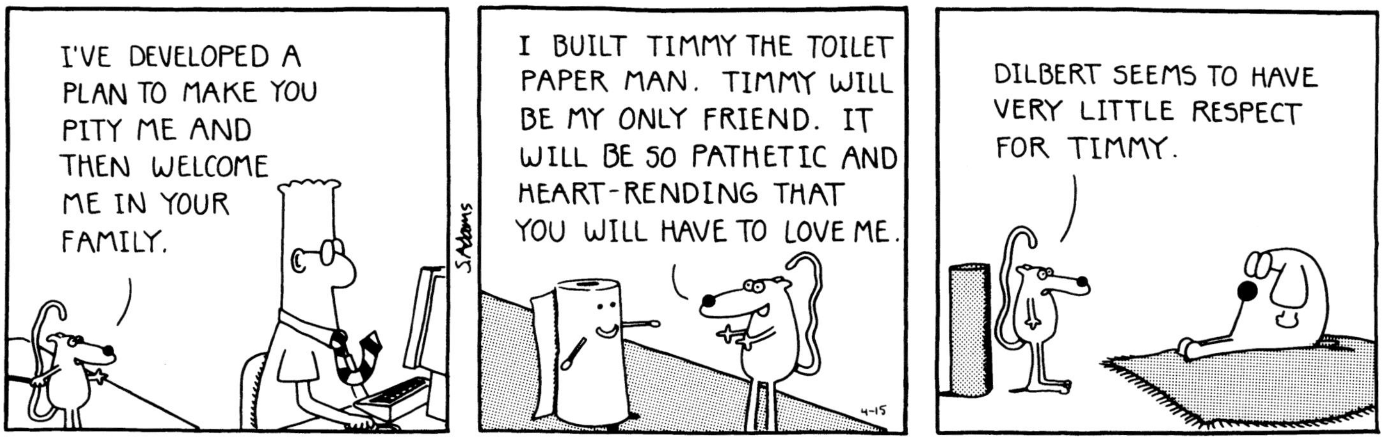

I'VE DEVELOPED A PLAN TO MAKE YOU PITY ME AND THEN WELCOME ME IN YOUR FAMILY.
I BUILT TIMMY THE TOILET PAPER MAN. TIMMY WILL BE MY ONLY FRIEND. IT WILL BE SO PATHETIC AND HEART-RENDING THAT YOU WILL HAVE TO LOVE ME.
DILBERT SEEMS TO HAVE VERY LITTLE RESPECT FOR TIMMY.

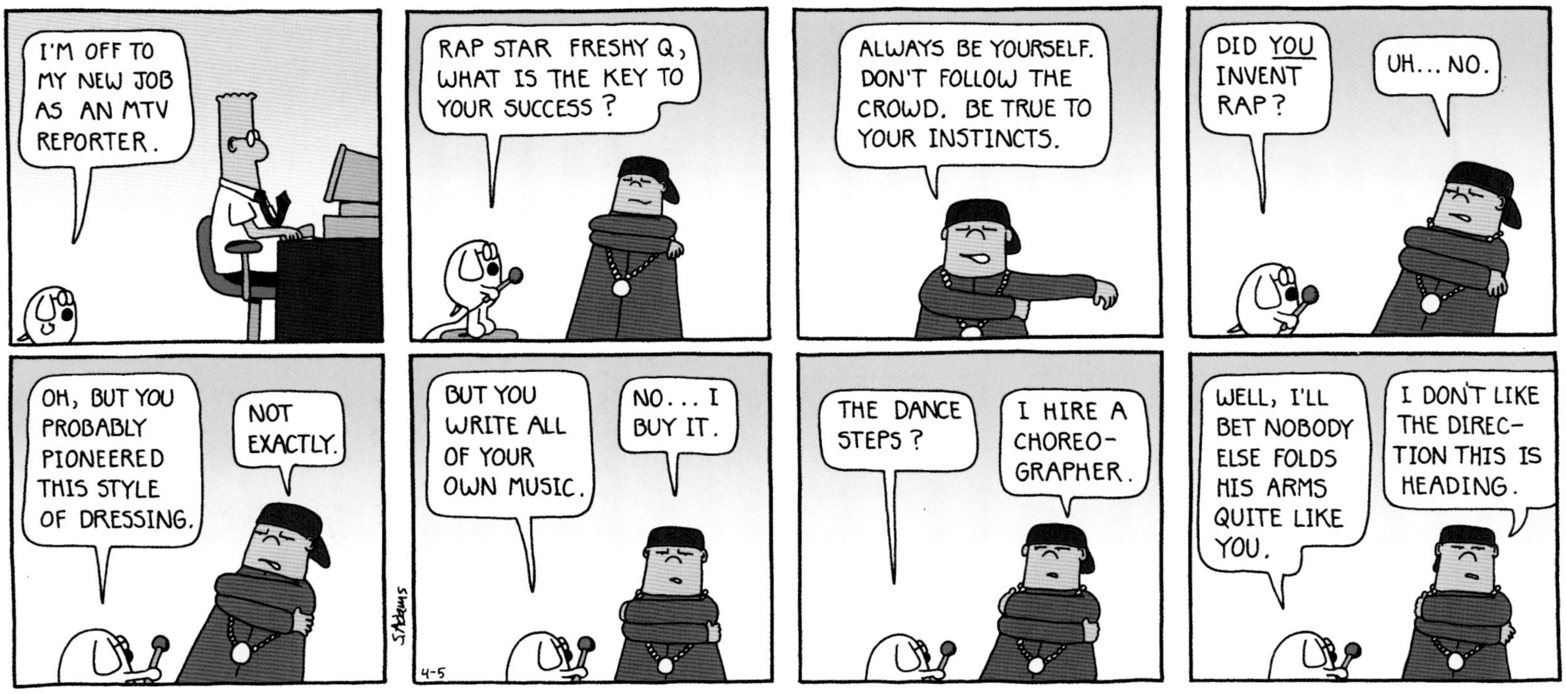
I'M OFF TO MY NEW JOB AS AN MTV REPORTER.
RAP STAR FRESHY Q, WHAT IS THE KEY TO YOUR SUCCESS?
ALWAYS BE YOURSELF. DON'T FOLLOW THE CROWD. BE TRUE TO YOUR INSTINCTS.
DID YOU INVENT RAP?
UH... NO.
OH, BUT YOU PROBABLY PIONEERED THIS STYLE OF DRESSING.
NOT EXACTLY.
BUT YOU WRITE ALL OF YOUR OWN MUSIC.
NO... I BUY IT.
THE DANCE STEPS?
I HIRE A CHOREOGRAPHER.
WELL, I'LL BET NOBODY ELSE FOLDS HIS ARMS QUITE LIKE YOU.
I DON'T LIKE THE DIRECTION THIS IS HEADING.
S.Adams
4-5

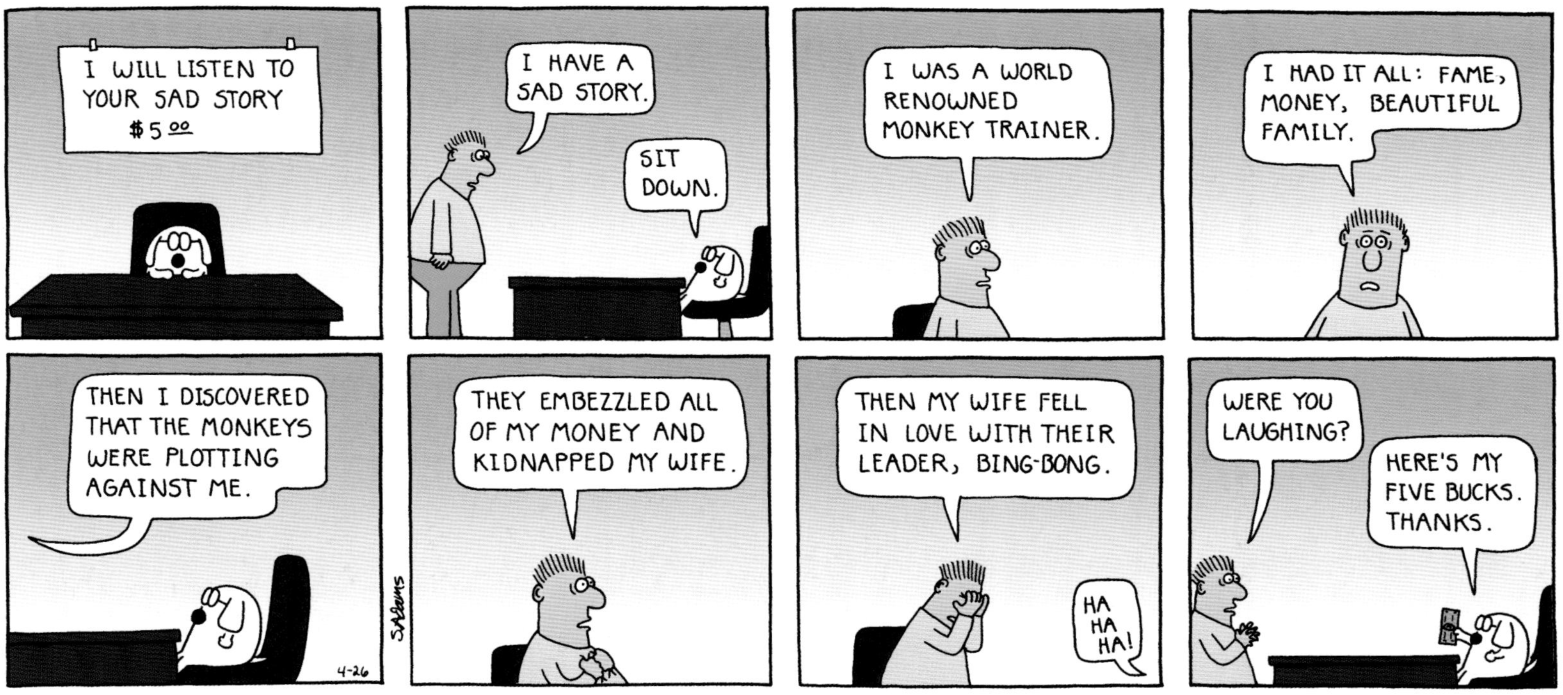
I WILL LISTEN TO YOUR SAD STORY $5 00
I HAVE A SAD STORY.
SIT DOWN.
I WAS A WORLD RENOWNED MONKEY TRAINER.
I HAD IT ALL: FAME, MONEY, BEAUTIFUL FAMILY.
THEN I DISCOVERED THAT THE MONKEYS WERE PLOTTING AGAINST ME.
THEY EMBEZZLED ALL OF MY MONEY AND KIDNAPPED MY WIFE.
THEN MY WIFE FELL IN LOVE WITH THEIR LEADER, BING-BONG.
HA HA HA!
WERE YOU LAUGHING?
HERE'S MY FIVE BUCKS. THANKS.
4-26
S.Adams

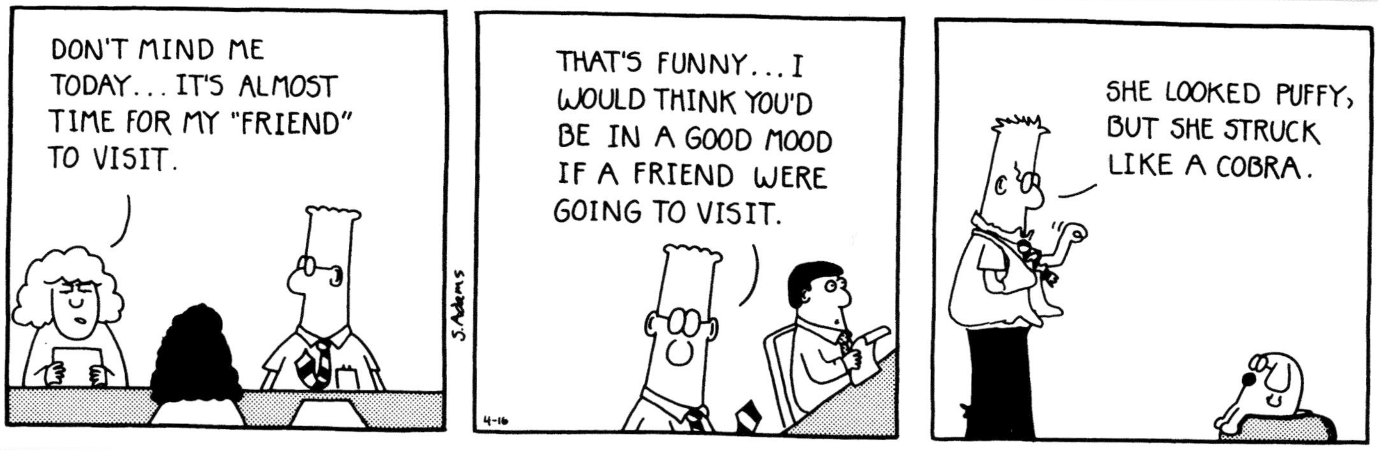
DON'T MIND ME TODAY... IT'S ALMOST TIME FOR MY "FRIEND" TO VISIT.
S. Adams
4-16
THAT'S FUNNY... I WOULD THINK YOU'D BE IN A GOOD MOOD IF A FRIEND WERE GOING TO VISIT.
SHE LOOKED PUFFY, BUT SHE STRUCK LIKE A COBRA.

The dark-haired woman in the foreground was originally Wally. My editor suggested I add a woman to the table, to make the content of this comic more acceptable to the public. So I took my black pen and gave Wally some hair.

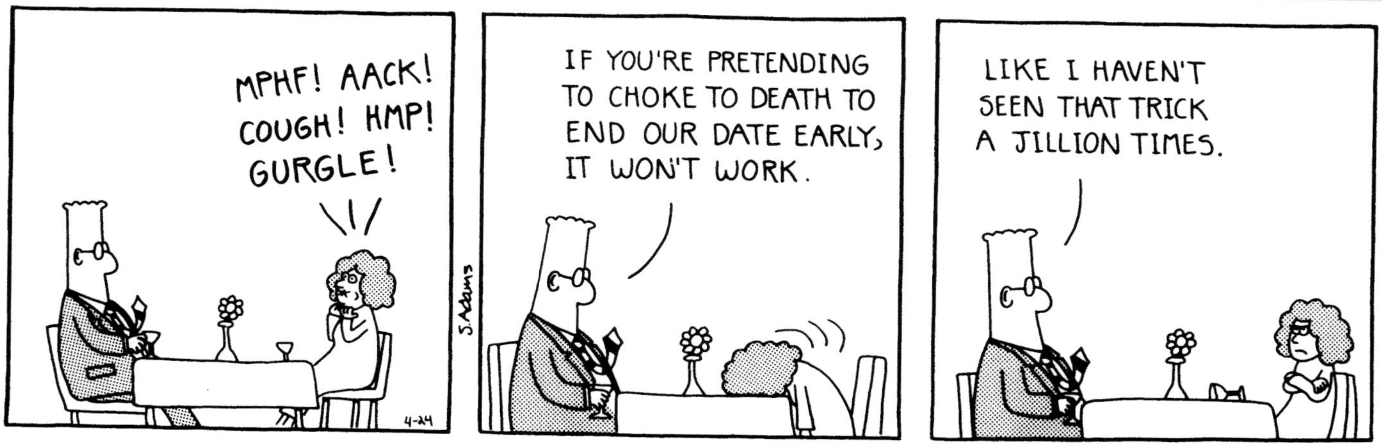
MPHF! AACK! COUGH! HMP! GURGLE!
4-24
S. Adams
IF YOU'RE PRETENDING TO CHOKE TO DEATH TO END OUR DATE EARLY, IT WON'T WORK.
LIKE I HAVEN'T SEEN THAT TRICK A JILLION TIMES.

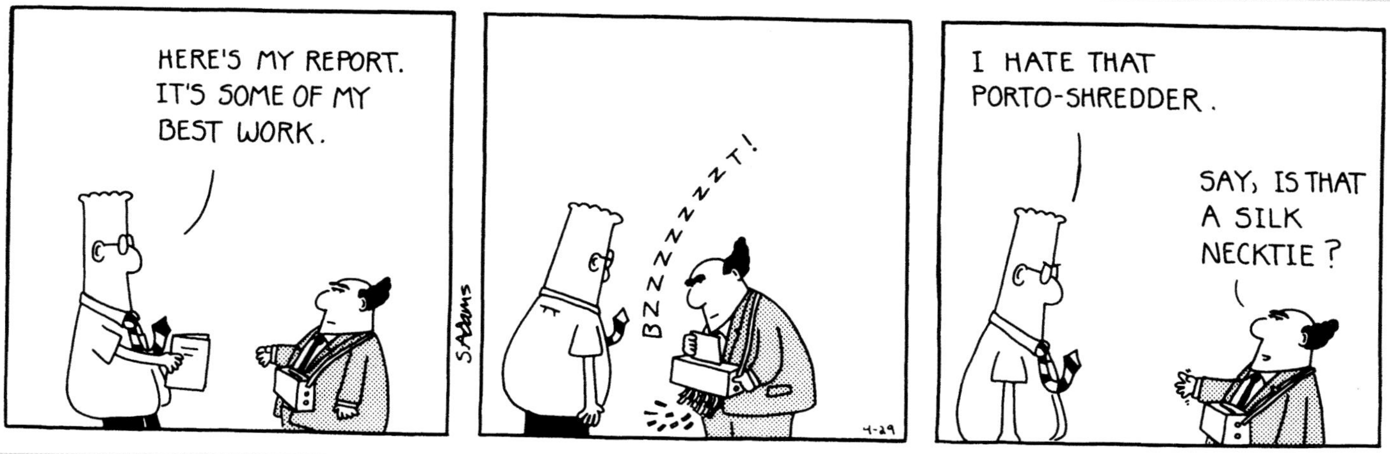
HERE'S MY REPORT. IT'S SOME OF MY BEST WORK.
S. Adams
BZZZZZZZZZT!
4-29
I HATE THAT PORTO-SHREDDER.
SAY, IS THAT A SILK NECKTIE?

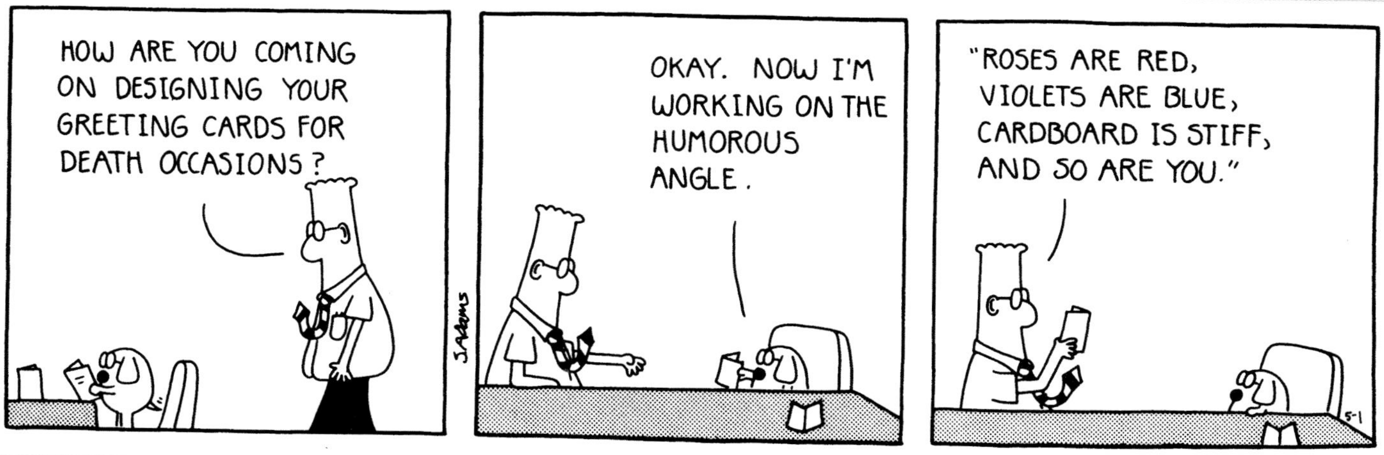
HOW ARE YOU COMING ON DESIGNING YOUR GREETING CARDS FOR DEATH OCCASIONS?
S. Adams
OKAY. NOW I'M WORKING ON THE HUMOROUS ANGLE.
"ROSES ARE RED, VIOLETS ARE BLUE, CARDBOARD IS STIFF, AND SO ARE YOU."
5-1

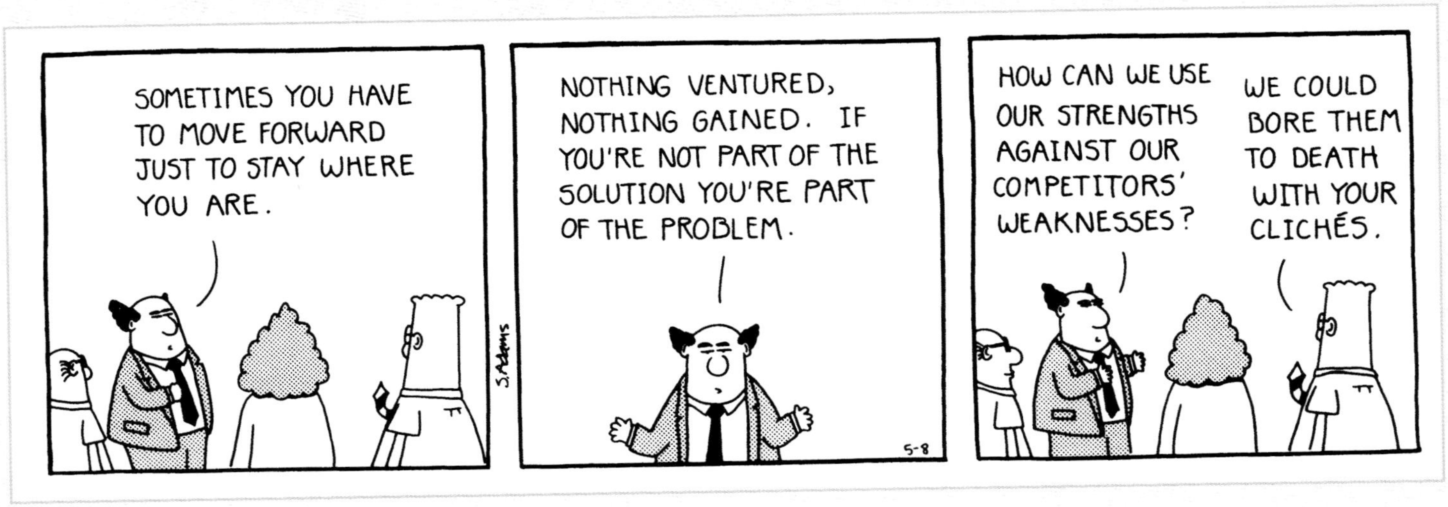
SOMETIMES YOU HAVE TO MOVE FORWARD JUST TO STAY WHERE YOU ARE.
NOTHING VENTURED, NOTHING GAINED. IF YOU'RE NOT PART OF THE SOLUTION YOU'RE PART OF THE PROBLEM.
HOW CAN WE USE OUR STRENGTHS AGAINST OUR COMPETITORS' WEAKNESSES?
WE COULD BORE THEM TO DEATH WITH YOUR CLICHÉS.

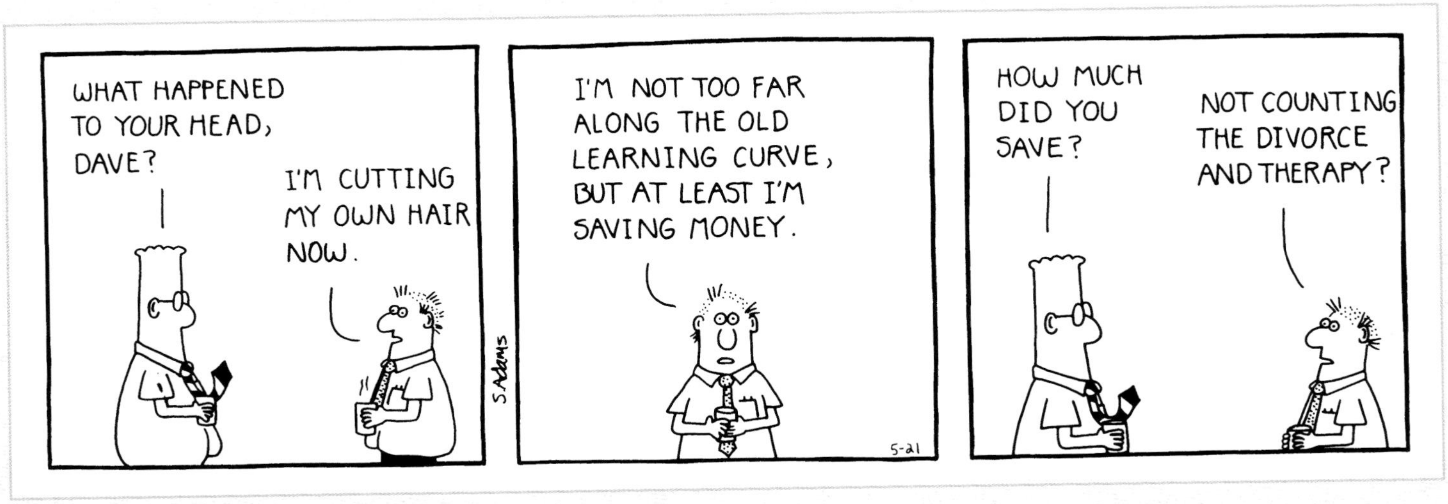
WHAT HAPPENED TO YOUR HEAD, DAVE?
I'M CUTTING MY OWN HAIR NOW.
I'M NOT TOO FAR ALONG THE OLD LEARNING CURVE, BUT AT LEAST I'M SAVING MONEY.
HOW MUCH DID YOU SAVE?
NOT COUNTING THE DIVORCE AND THERAPY?

One of my co-workers cut his own hair. I met him after he had been doing it for a while. I wondered how the first few passes went.

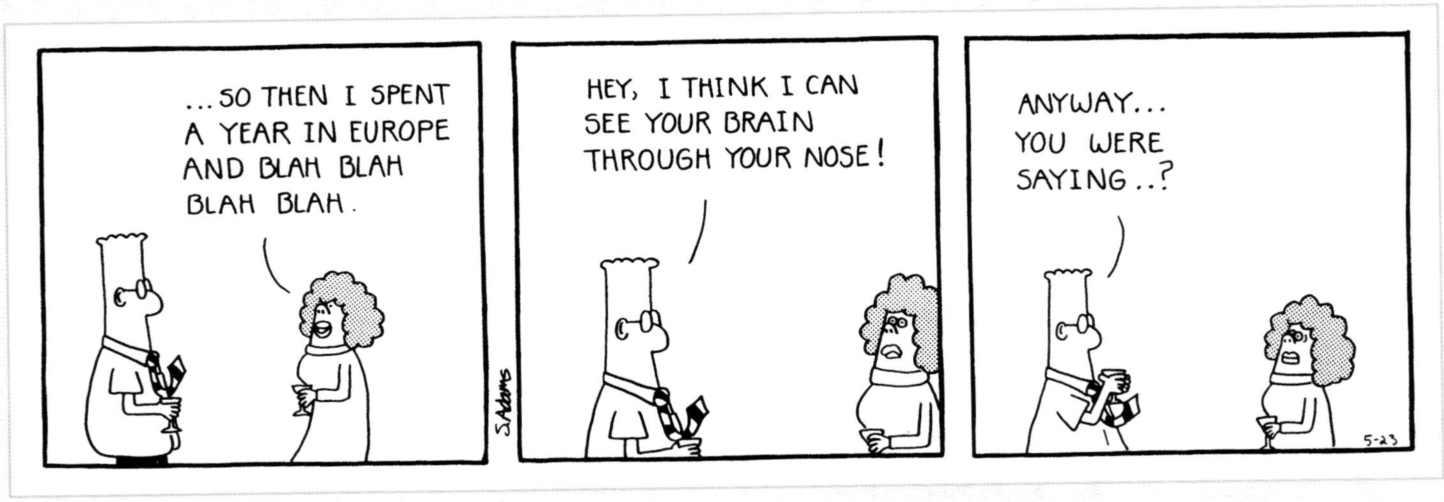
...SO THEN I SPENT A YEAR IN EUROPE AND BLAH BLAH BLAH BLAH.
HEY, I THINK I CAN SEE YOUR BRAIN THROUGH YOUR NOSE!
ANYWAY... YOU WERE SAYING..?

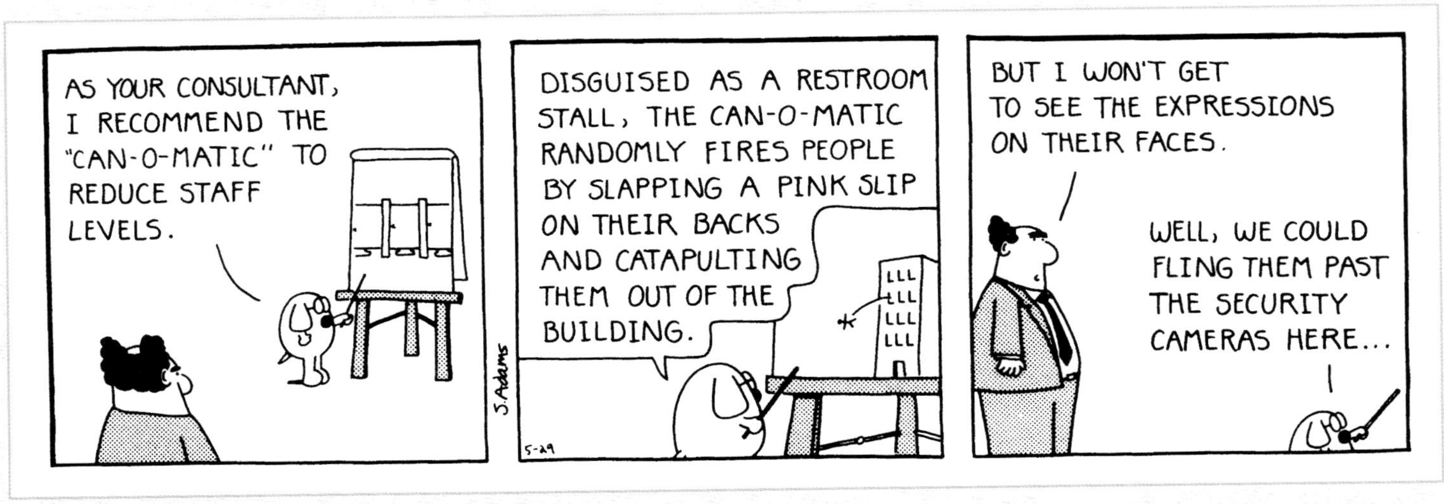
AS YOUR CONSULTANT, I RECOMMEND THE "CAN-O-MATIC" TO REDUCE STAFF LEVELS.
DISGUISED AS A RESTROOM STALL, THE CAN-O-MATIC RANDOMLY FIRES PEOPLE BY SLAPPING A PINK SLIP ON THEIR BACKS AND CATAPULTING THEM OUT OF THE BUILDING.
BUT I WON'T GET TO SEE THE EXPRESSIONS ON THEIR FACES.
WELL, WE COULD FLING THEM PAST THE SECURITY CAMERAS HERE...

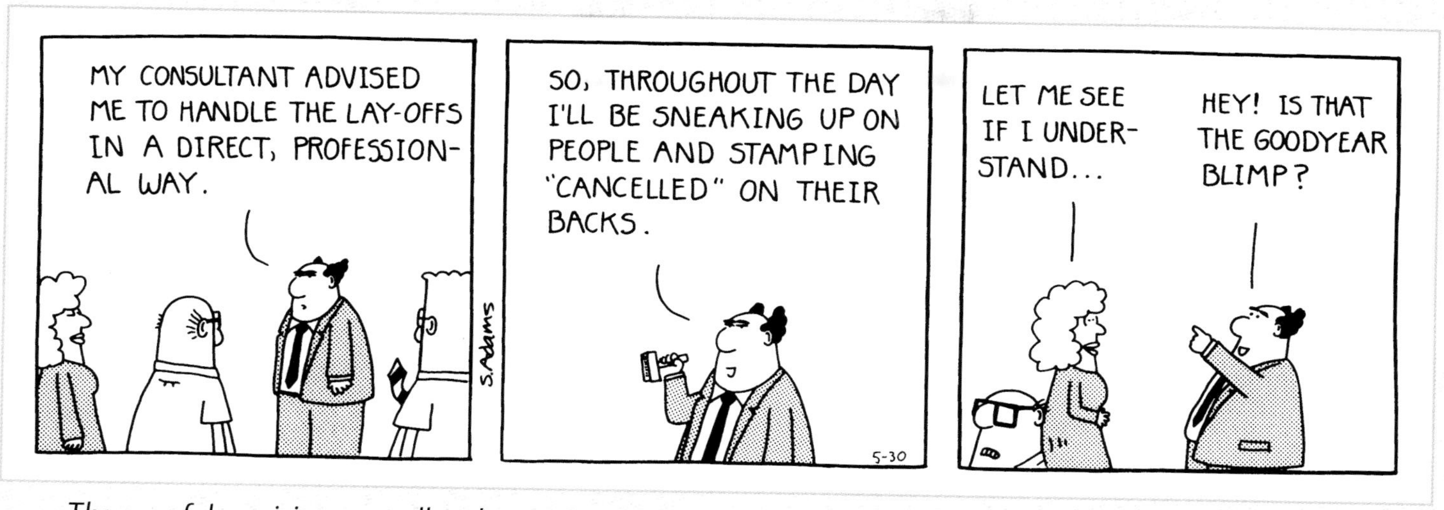
MY CONSULTANT ADVISED ME TO HANDLE THE LAY-OFFS IN A DIRECT, PROFESSION-AL WAY.
S.Adams
SO, THROUGHOUT THE DAY I'LL BE SNEAKING UP ON PEOPLE AND STAMPING "CANCELLED" ON THEIR BACKS.
5-30
LET ME SEE IF I UNDER-STAND...
HEY! IS THAT THE GOODYEAR BLIMP?

The era of downsizing was well underway. Pain and humor are highly correlated. As the downsizing escalated, more readers were drawn to Dilbert. *It was the right comic at the right time, entirely by chance.*

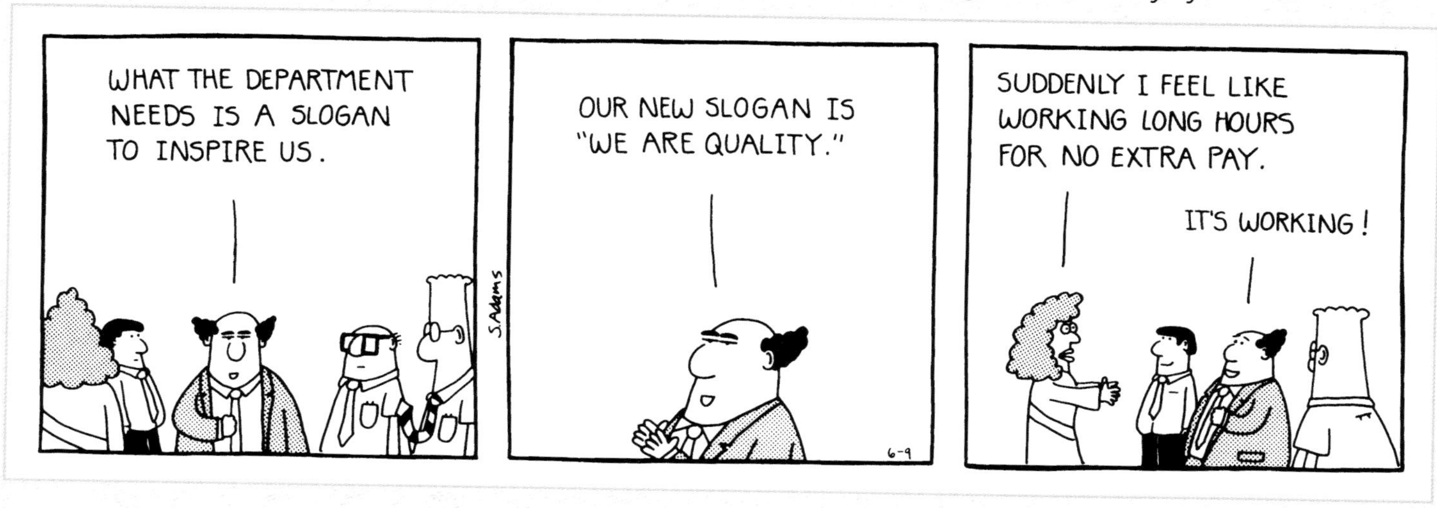
WHAT THE DEPARTMENT NEEDS IS A SLOGAN TO INSPIRE US.
S.Adams
OUR NEW SLOGAN IS "WE ARE QUALITY."
6-9
SUDDENLY I FEEL LIKE WORKING LONG HOURS FOR NO EXTRA PAY.
IT'S WORKING!

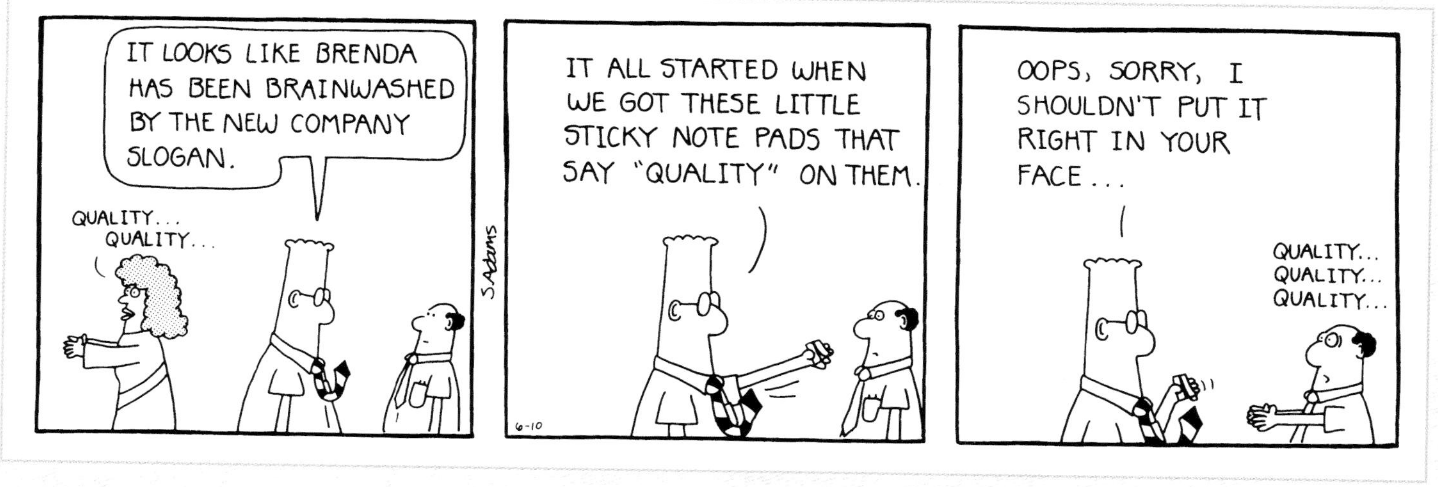
IT LOOKS LIKE BRENDA HAS BEEN BRAINWASHED BY THE NEW COMPANY SLOGAN.
QUALITY... QUALITY...
S.Adams
IT ALL STARTED WHEN WE GOT THESE LITTLE STICKY NOTE PADS THAT SAY "QUALITY" ON THEM.
6-10
OOPS, SORRY, I SHOULDN'T PUT IT RIGHT IN YOUR FACE...
QUALITY... QUALITY... QUALITY...

This series on "quality" came to distinguish Dilbert *as the comic that mocks ridiculous management fads.*

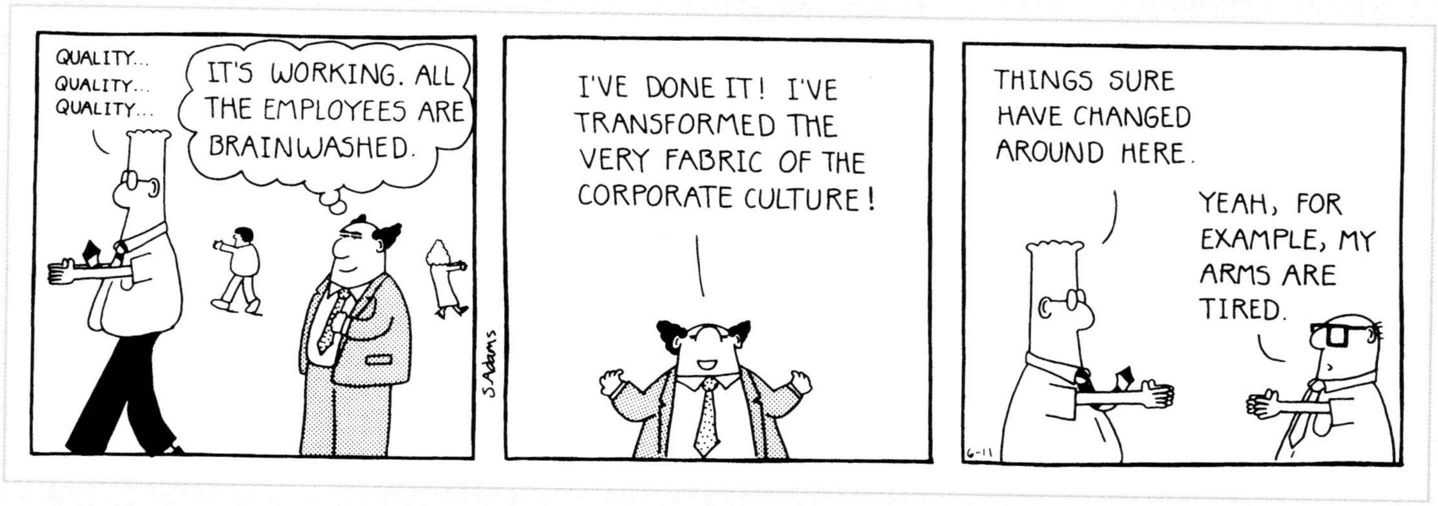
QUALITY... QUALITY... QUALITY...
IT'S WORKING. ALL THE EMPLOYEES ARE BRAINWASHED.
S.Adams
I'VE DONE IT! I'VE TRANSFORMED THE VERY FABRIC OF THE CORPORATE CULTURE!
THINGS SURE HAVE CHANGED AROUND HERE.
YEAH, FOR EXAMPLE, MY ARMS ARE TIRED.
6-11

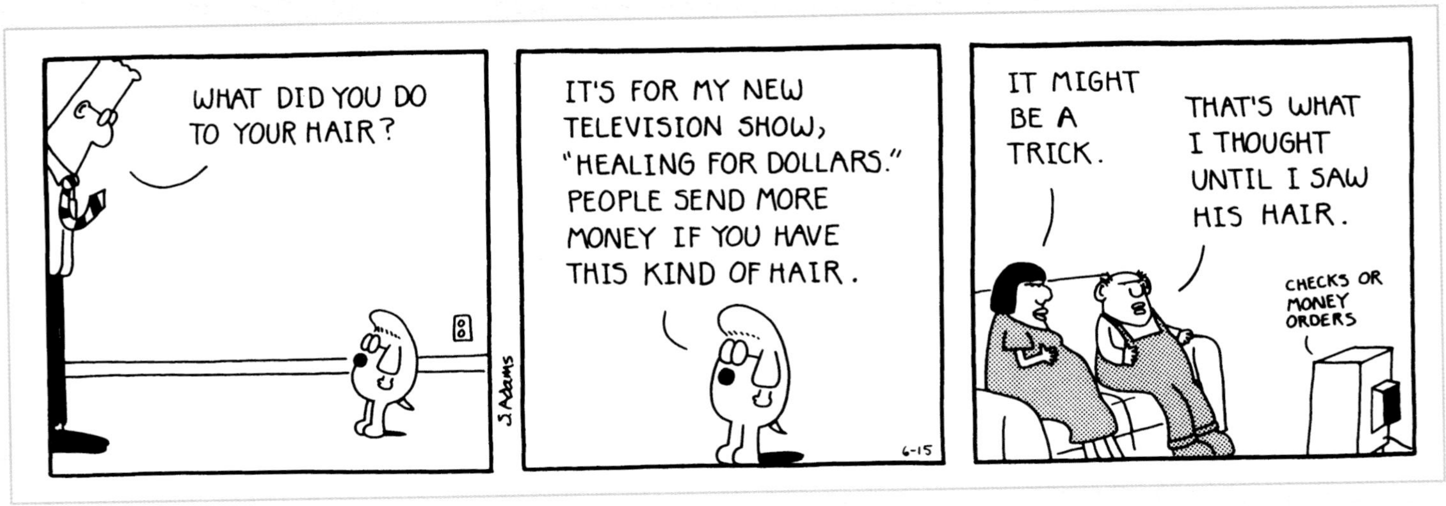
WHAT DID YOU DO TO YOUR HAIR?
IT'S FOR MY NEW TELEVISION SHOW, "HEALING FOR DOLLARS." PEOPLE SEND MORE MONEY IF YOU HAVE THIS KIND OF HAIR.
IT MIGHT BE A TRICK.
THAT'S WHAT I THOUGHT UNTIL I SAW HIS HAIR.
CHECKS OR MONEY ORDERS
S. Adams
6-15

When Dilbert started in a new client newspaper, it generally caused a small flurry of immediate complaints. This one was typical.

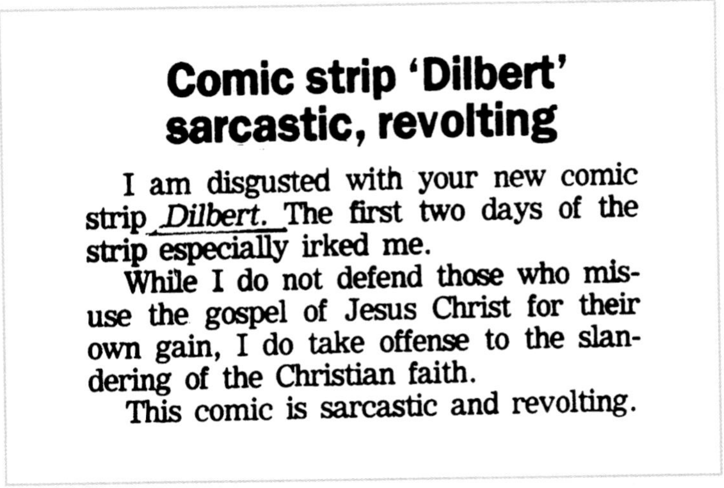

Comic strip 'Dilbert' sarcastic, revolting

I am disgusted with your new comic strip *Dilbert.* The first two days of the strip especially irked me.

While I do not defend those who misuse the gospel of Jesus Christ for their own gain, I do take offense to the slandering of the Christian faith.

This comic is sarcastic and revolting.

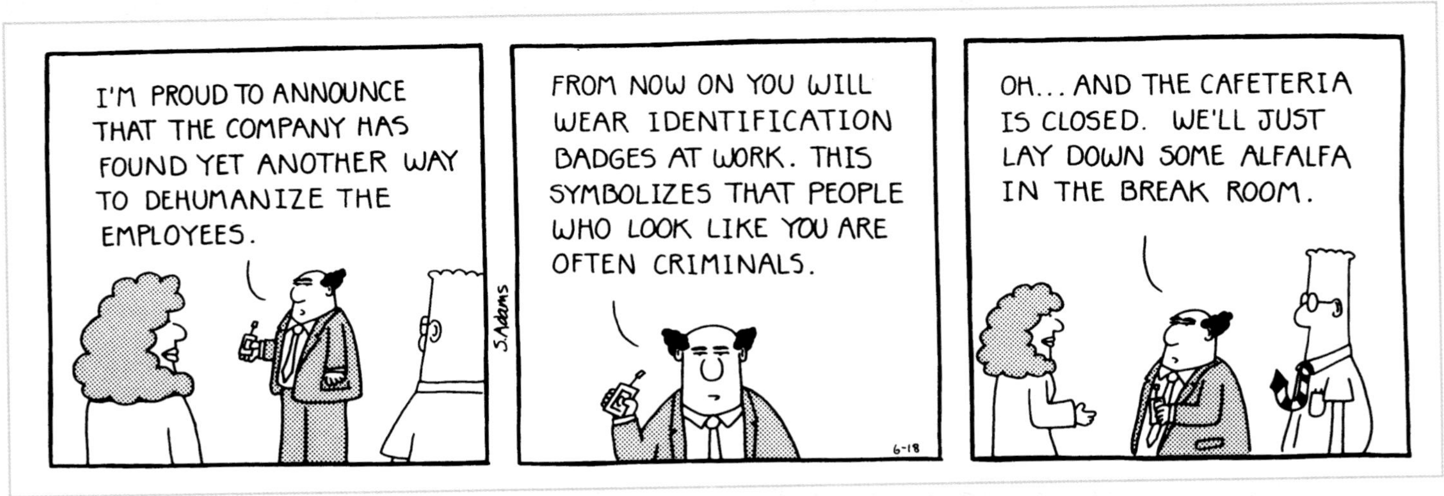
I'M PROUD TO ANNOUNCE THAT THE COMPANY HAS FOUND YET ANOTHER WAY TO DEHUMANIZE THE EMPLOYEES.
FROM NOW ON YOU WILL WEAR IDENTIFICATION BADGES AT WORK. THIS SYMBOLIZES THAT PEOPLE WHO LOOK LIKE YOU ARE OFTEN CRIMINALS.
OH... AND THE CAFETERIA IS CLOSED. WE'LL JUST LAY DOWN SOME ALFALFA IN THE BREAK ROOM.
S. Adams
6-18

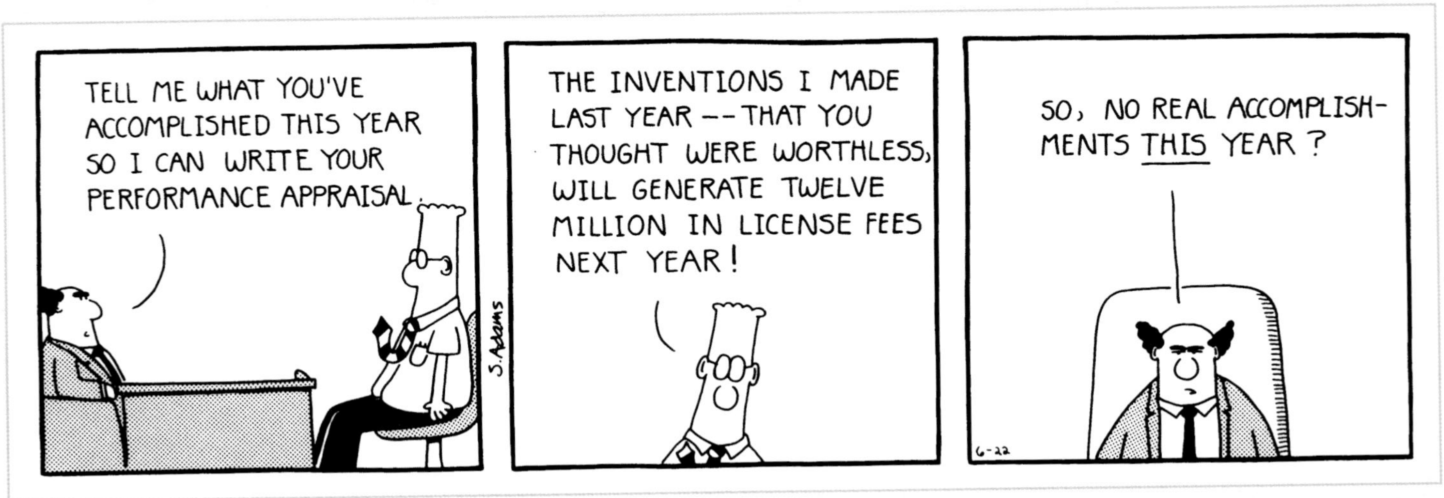
TELL ME WHAT YOU'VE ACCOMPLISHED THIS YEAR SO I CAN WRITE YOUR PERFORMANCE APPRAISAL.
THE INVENTIONS I MADE LAST YEAR -- THAT YOU THOUGHT WERE WORTHLESS, WILL GENERATE TWELVE MILLION IN LICENSE FEES NEXT YEAR!
SO, NO REAL ACCOMPLISHMENTS THIS YEAR?
S. Adams
6-22

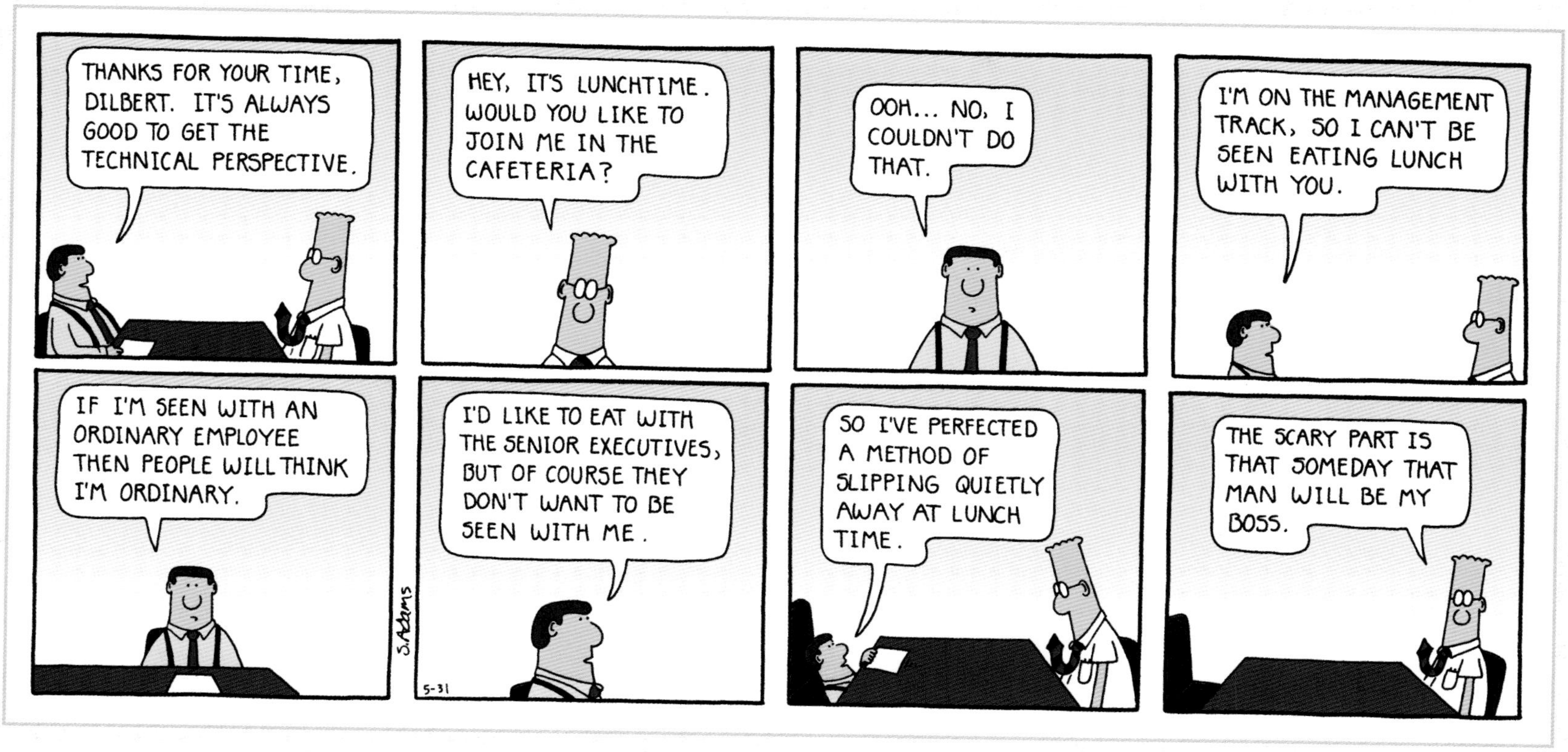
THANKS FOR YOUR TIME, DILBERT. IT'S ALWAYS GOOD TO GET THE TECHNICAL PERSPECTIVE.
HEY, IT'S LUNCHTIME. WOULD YOU LIKE TO JOIN ME IN THE CAFETERIA?
OOH... NO, I COULDN'T DO THAT.
I'M ON THE MANAGEMENT TRACK, SO I CAN'T BE SEEN EATING LUNCH WITH YOU.
IF I'M SEEN WITH AN ORDINARY EMPLOYEE THEN PEOPLE WILL THINK I'M ORDINARY.
I'D LIKE TO EAT WITH THE SENIOR EXECUTIVES, BUT OF COURSE THEY DON'T WANT TO BE SEEN WITH ME.
SO I'VE PERFECTED A METHOD OF SLIPPING QUIETLY AWAY AT LUNCH TIME.
THE SCARY PART IS THAT SOMEDAY THAT MAN WILL BE MY BOSS.
S. Adams
5-31

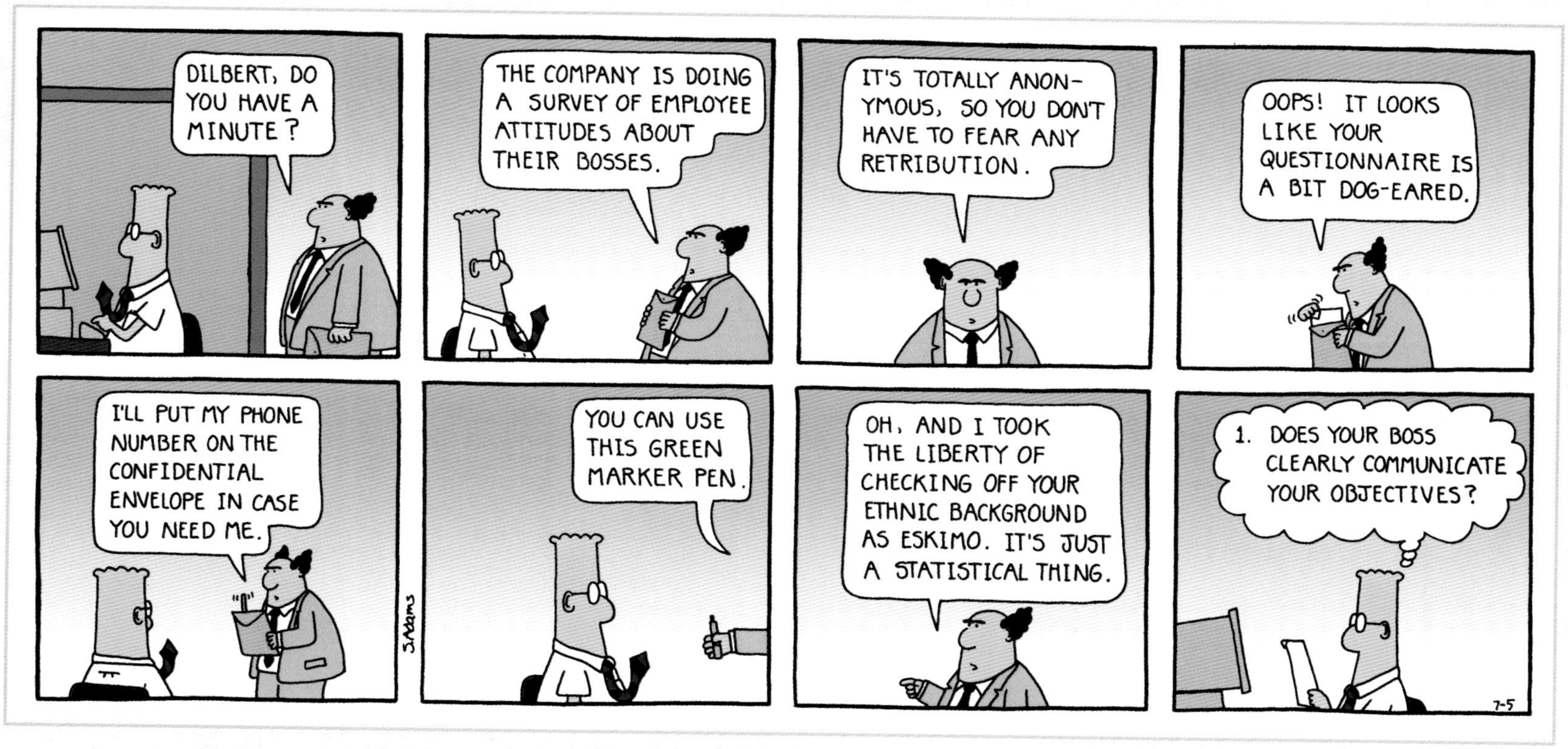
DILBERT, DO YOU HAVE A MINUTE?
THE COMPANY IS DOING A SURVEY OF EMPLOYEE ATTITUDES ABOUT THEIR BOSSES.
IT'S TOTALLY ANONYMOUS, SO YOU DON'T HAVE TO FEAR ANY RETRIBUTION.
OOPS! IT LOOKS LIKE YOUR QUESTIONNAIRE IS A BIT DOG-EARED.
I'LL PUT MY PHONE NUMBER ON THE CONFIDENTIAL ENVELOPE IN CASE YOU NEED ME.
YOU CAN USE THIS GREEN MARKER PEN.
OH, AND I TOOK THE LIBERTY OF CHECKING OFF YOUR ETHNIC BACKGROUND AS ESKIMO. IT'S JUST A STATISTICAL THING.
1. DOES YOUR BOSS CLEARLY COMMUNICATE YOUR OBJECTIVES?
S. Adams
7-5

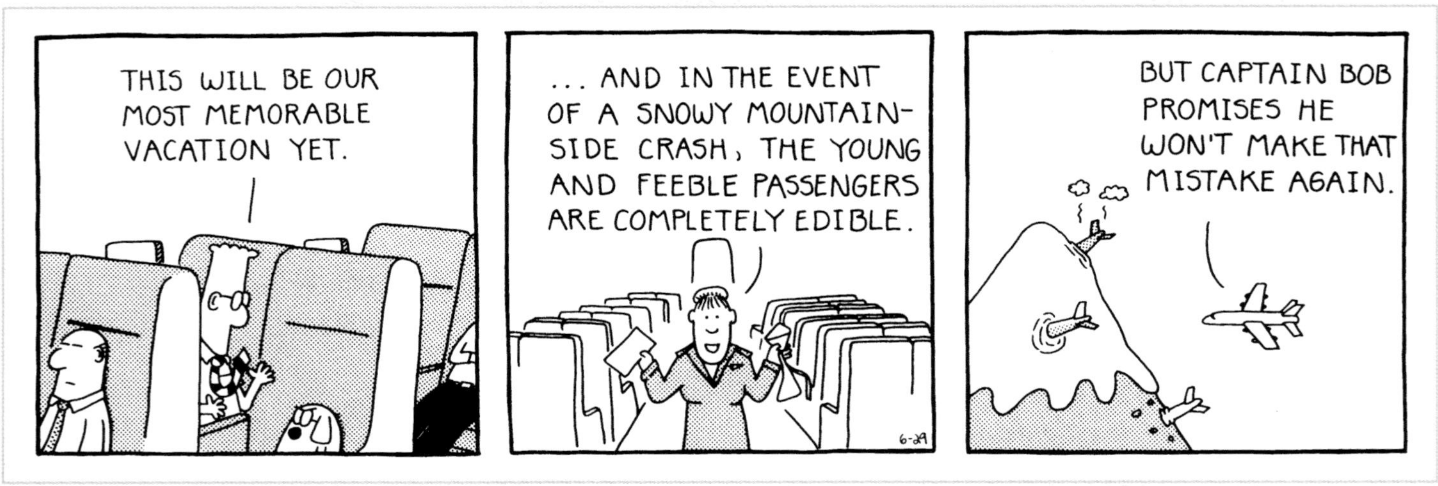
THIS WILL BE OUR MOST MEMORABLE VACATION YET.
... AND IN THE EVENT OF A SNOWY MOUNTAIN-SIDE CRASH, THE YOUNG AND FEEBLE PASSENGERS ARE COMPLETELY EDIBLE.
6-29
BUT CAPTAIN BOB PROMISES HE WON'T MAKE THAT MISTAKE AGAIN.

To me, few things are harder to draw than the interior of an airplane. I was still working my full-time day job at this point, and trying to draw comics between 4 A.M. *and 5:30* A.M.. *That's a big part of the reason I didn't feature much in the way of backgrounds.*

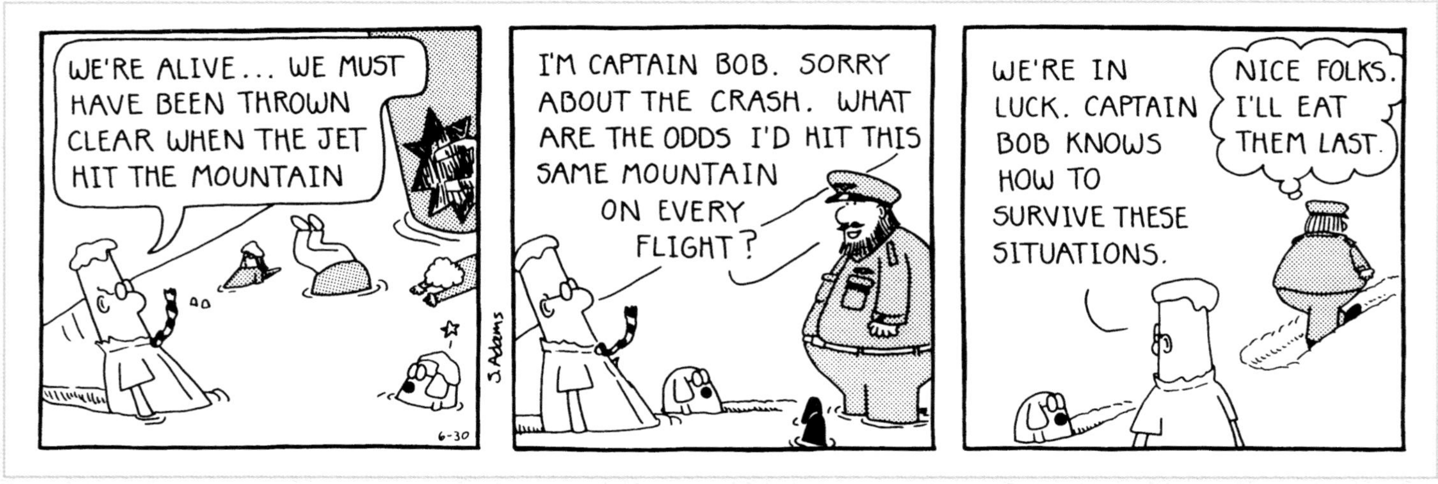
WE'RE ALIVE... WE MUST HAVE BEEN THROWN CLEAR WHEN THE JET HIT THE MOUNTAIN
6-30
S. Adams
I'M CAPTAIN BOB. SORRY ABOUT THE CRASH. WHAT ARE THE ODDS I'D HIT THIS SAME MOUNTAIN ON EVERY FLIGHT?
WE'RE IN LUCK. CAPTAIN BOB KNOWS HOW TO SURVIVE THESE SITUATIONS.
NICE FOLKS. I'LL EAT THEM LAST.

Not everyone thinks cannibalism is as funny as I do. This letter to the editor was typical.

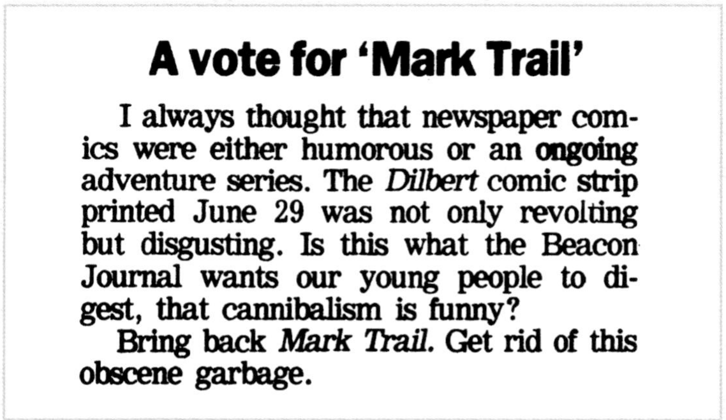

A vote for 'Mark Trail'

I always thought that newspaper comics were either humorous or an ongoing adventure series. The *Dilbert* comic strip printed June 29 was not only revolting but disgusting. Is this what the Beacon Journal wants our young people to digest, that cannibalism is funny?

Bring back *Mark Trail.* Get rid of this obscene garbage.

The one group of people who never complain about bad treatment in the comics is attorneys. They are also the group most likely to contact me and ask if they can buy the original art to hang on the wall.

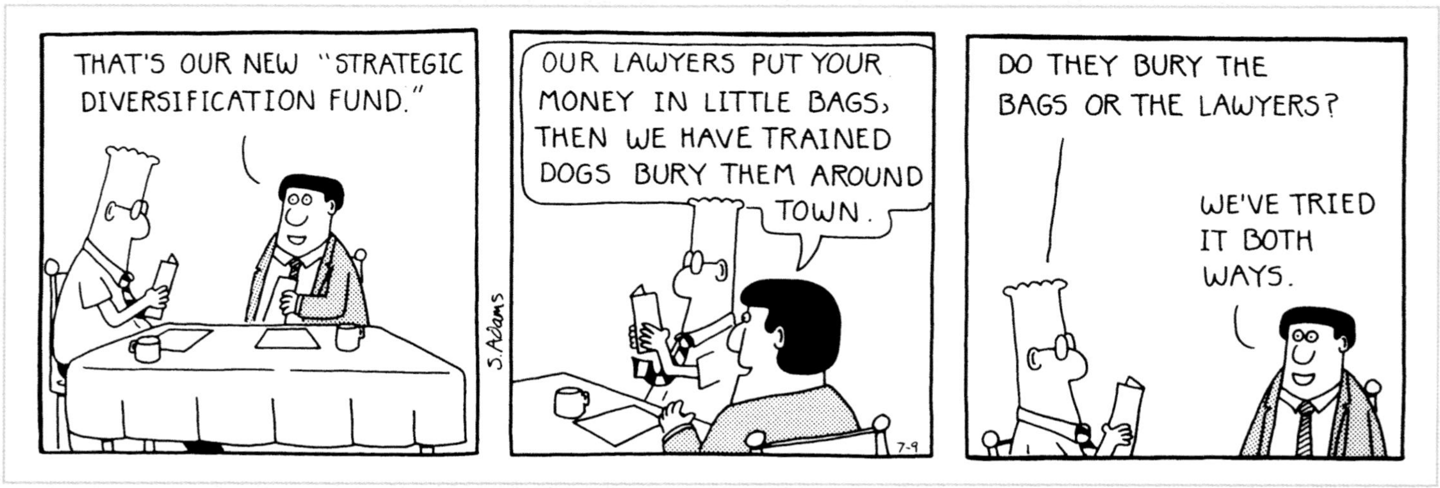
THAT'S OUR NEW "STRATEGIC DIVERSIFICATION FUND."
S. Adams
OUR LAWYERS PUT YOUR MONEY IN LITTLE BAGS, THEN WE HAVE TRAINED DOGS BURY THEM AROUND TOWN.
7-9
DO THEY BURY THE BAGS OR THE LAWYERS?
WE'VE TRIED IT BOTH WAYS.

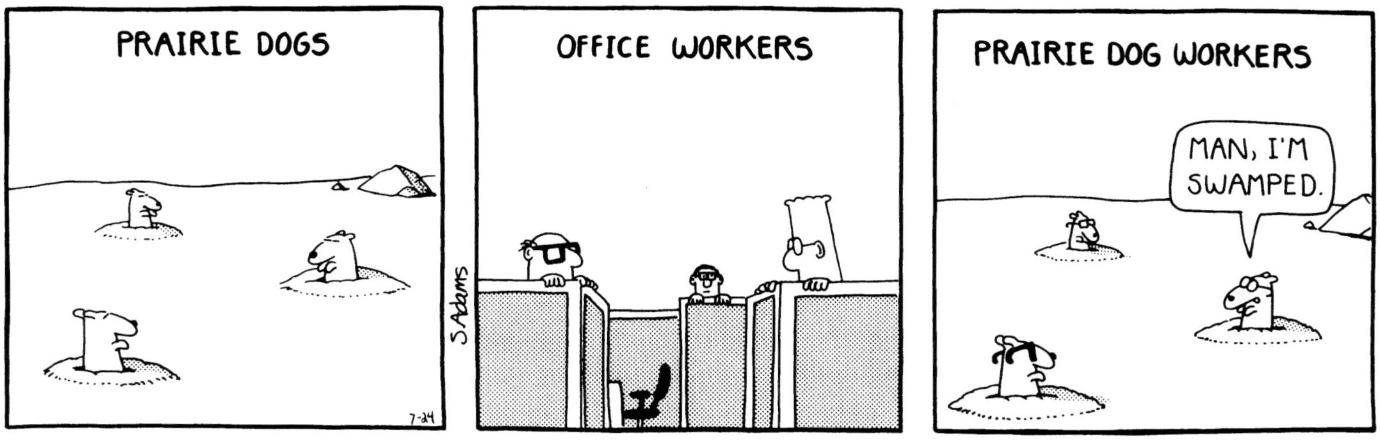
PRAIRIE DOGS
OFFICE WORKERS
PRAIRIE DOG WORKERS
MAN, I'M SWAMPED.

Peeking over the top of your cubicle is often referred to as prairie dogging. I don't know if I invented the term with this comic, or heard it someplace, or came up with it independently because it is a somewhat obvious idea. But I do know that lots of people e-mail me to say they, or an acquaintance, invented it. One of them might be right.

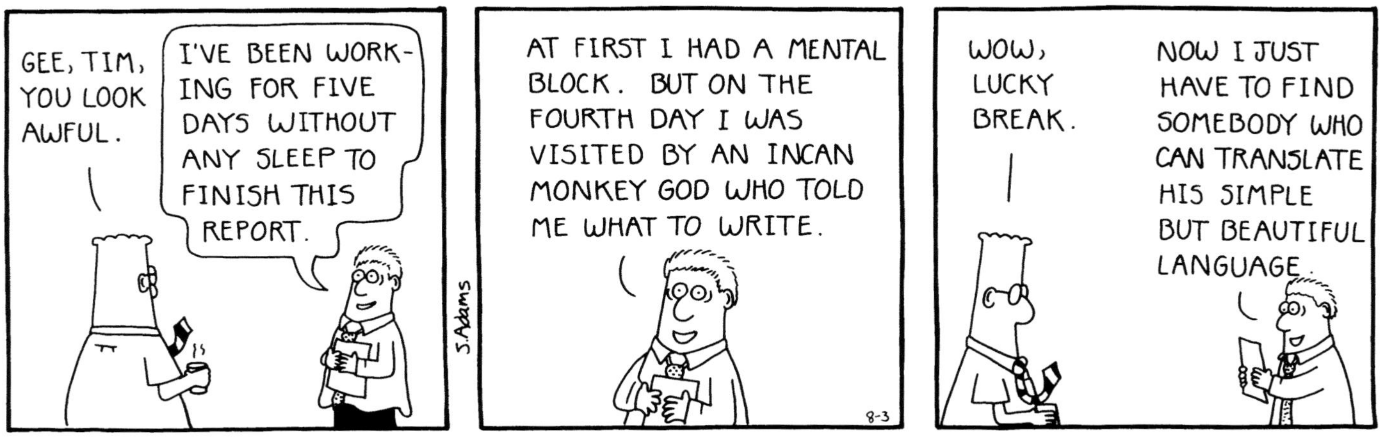
GEE, TIM, YOU LOOK AWFUL.
I'VE BEEN WORKING FOR FIVE DAYS WITHOUT ANY SLEEP TO FINISH THIS REPORT.
AT FIRST I HAD A MENTAL BLOCK. BUT ON THE FOURTH DAY I WAS VISITED BY AN INCAN MONKEY GOD WHO TOLD ME WHAT TO WRITE.
WOW, LUCKY BREAK.
NOW I JUST HAVE TO FIND SOMEBODY WHO CAN TRANSLATE HIS SIMPLE BUT BEAUTIFUL LANGUAGE.

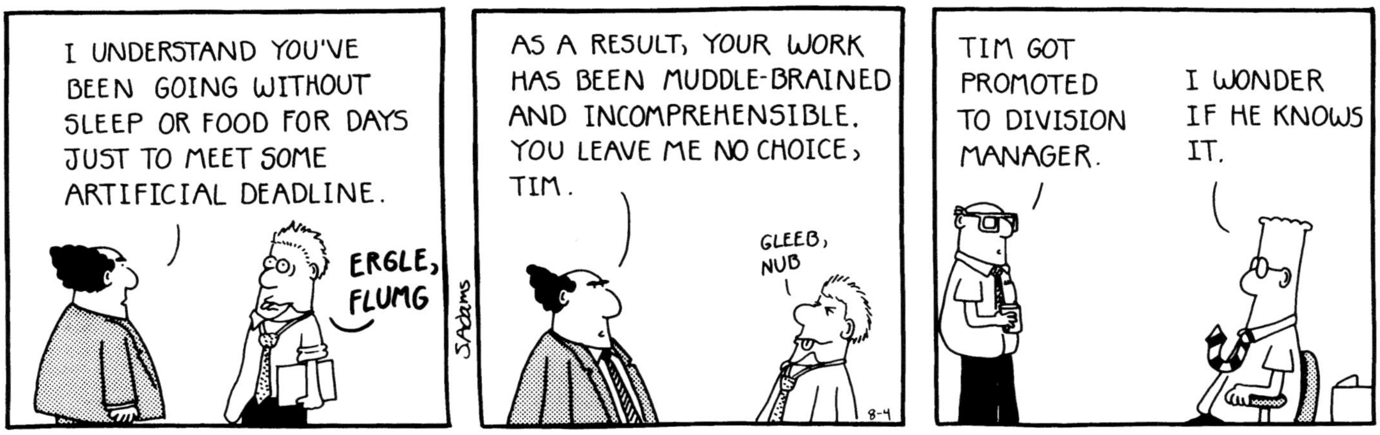
I UNDERSTAND YOU'VE BEEN GOING WITHOUT SLEEP OR FOOD FOR DAYS JUST TO MEET SOME ARTIFICIAL DEADLINE.
ERGLE, FLUMG
AS A RESULT, YOUR WORK HAS BEEN MUDDLE-BRAINED AND INCOMPREHENSIBLE. YOU LEAVE ME NO CHOICE, TIM.
GLEEB, NUB
TIM GOT PROMOTED TO DIVISION MANAGER.
I WONDER IF HE KNOWS IT.

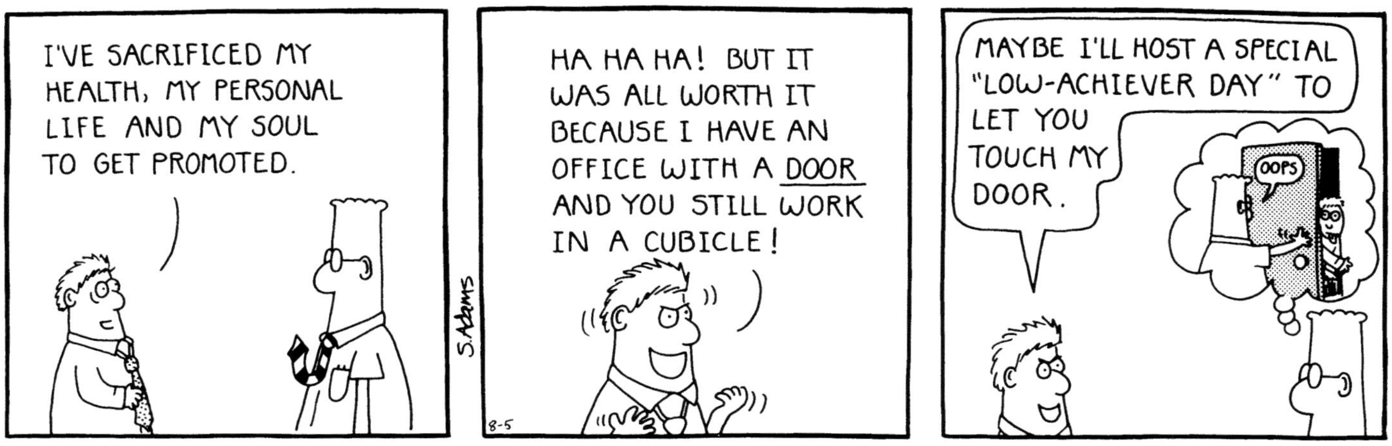
I'VE SACRIFICED MY HEALTH, MY PERSONAL LIFE AND MY SOUL TO GET PROMOTED.
HA HA HA! BUT IT WAS ALL WORTH IT BECAUSE I HAVE AN OFFICE WITH A DOOR AND YOU STILL WORK IN A CUBICLE!
MAYBE I'LL HOST A SPECIAL "LOW-ACHIEVER DAY" TO LET YOU TOUCH MY DOOR.
OOPS

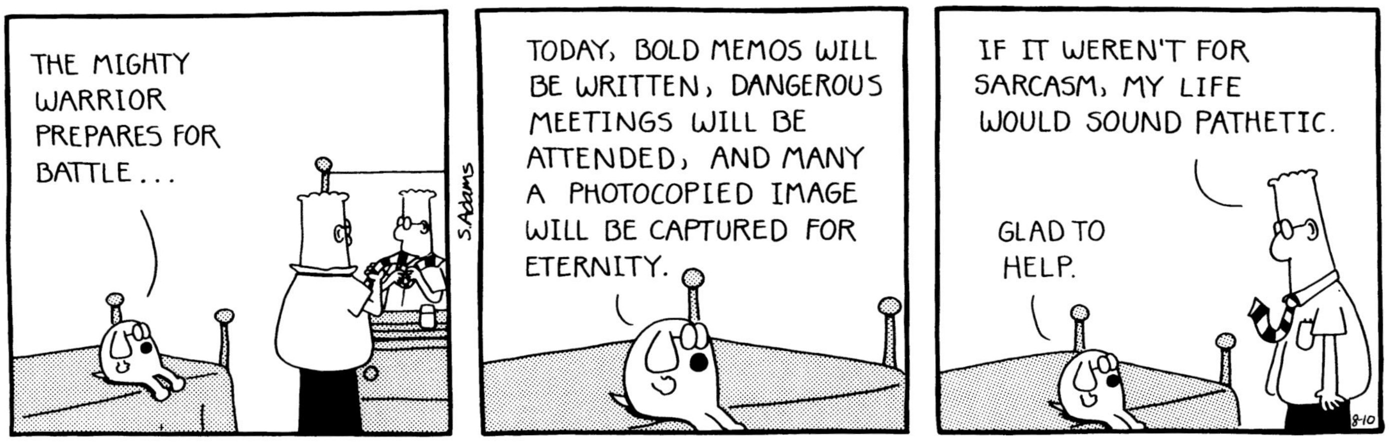
THE MIGHTY WARRIOR PREPARES FOR BATTLE . . .
S. Adams
TODAY, BOLD MEMOS WILL BE WRITTEN, DANGEROUS MEETINGS WILL BE ATTENDED, AND MANY A PHOTOCOPIED IMAGE WILL BE CAPTURED FOR ETERNITY.
IF IT WEREN'T FOR SARCASM, MY LIFE WOULD SOUND PATHETIC.
GLAD TO HELP.
8-10

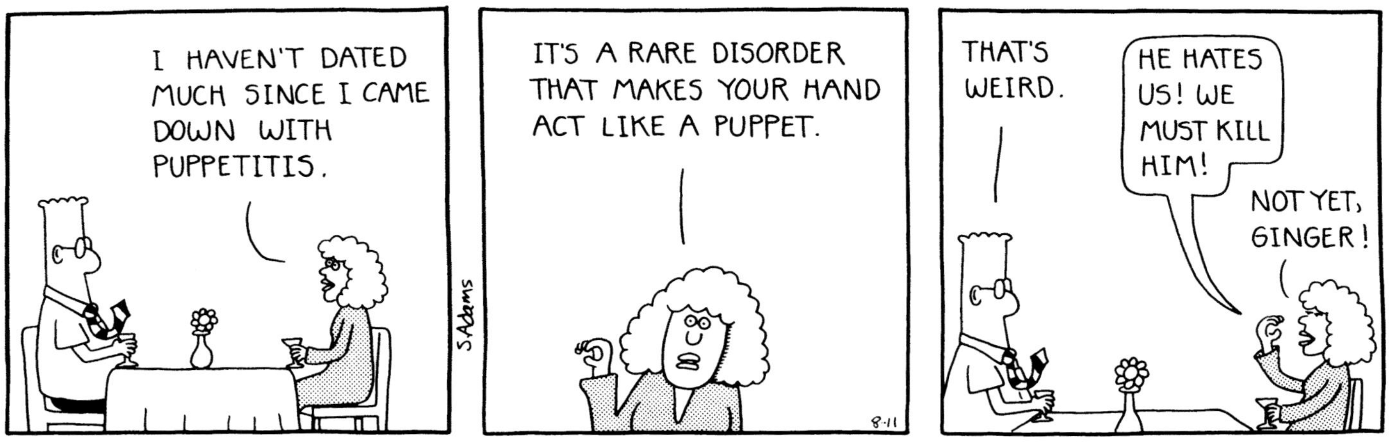
I HAVEN'T DATED MUCH SINCE I CAME DOWN WITH PUPPETITIS.
S. Adams
IT'S A RARE DISORDER THAT MAKES YOUR HAND ACT LIKE A PUPPET.
8-11
THAT'S WEIRD.
HE HATES US! WE MUST KILL HIM!
NOT YET, GINGER!

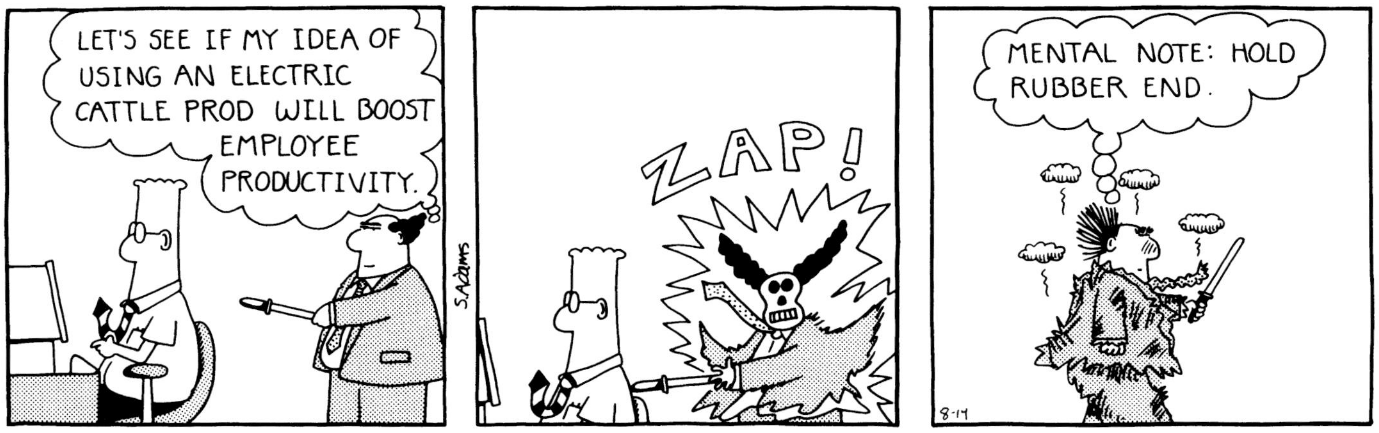
LET'S SEE IF MY IDEA OF USING AN ELECTRIC CATTLE PROD WILL BOOST EMPLOYEE PRODUCTIVITY.
S. Adams
ZAP!
MENTAL NOTE: HOLD RUBBER END.
8-14

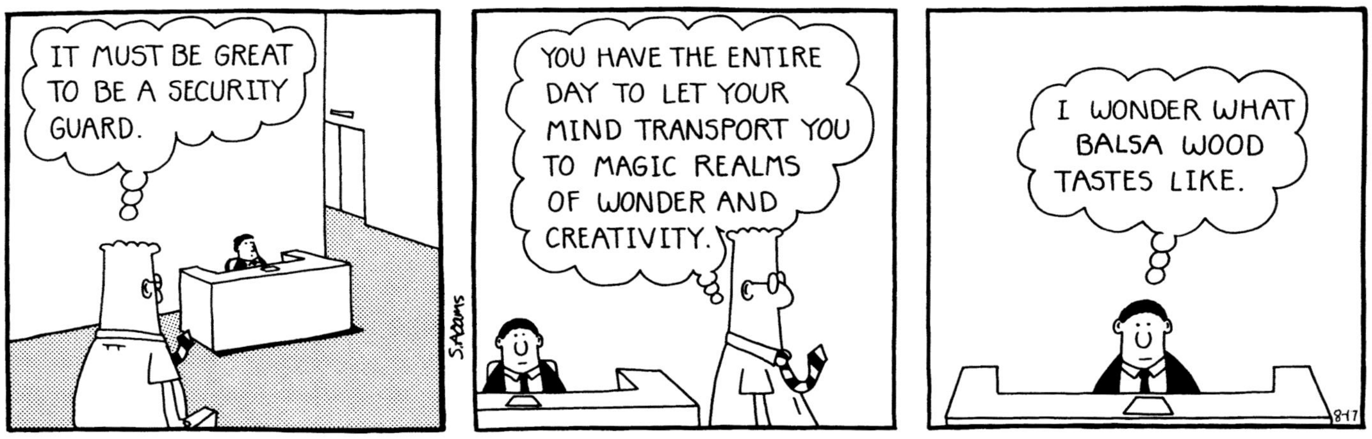
IT MUST BE GREAT TO BE A SECURITY GUARD.
S. Adams
YOU HAVE THE ENTIRE DAY TO LET YOUR MIND TRANSPORT YOU TO MAGIC REALMS OF WONDER AND CREATIVITY.
I WONDER WHAT BALSA WOOD TASTES LIKE.
8-17

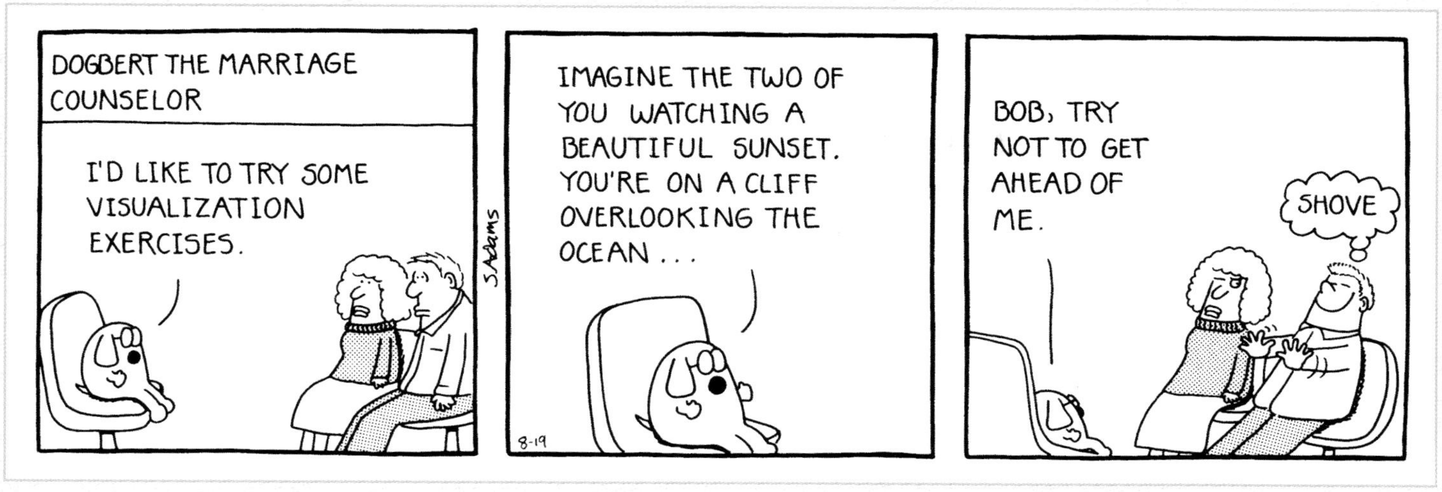
DOGBERT THE MARRIAGE COUNSELOR
I'D LIKE TO TRY SOME VISUALIZATION EXERCISES.
S. Adams
IMAGINE THE TWO OF YOU WATCHING A BEAUTIFUL SUNSET. YOU'RE ON A CLIFF OVERLOOKING THE OCEAN . . .
8-19
BOB, TRY NOT TO GET AHEAD OF ME.
SHOVE

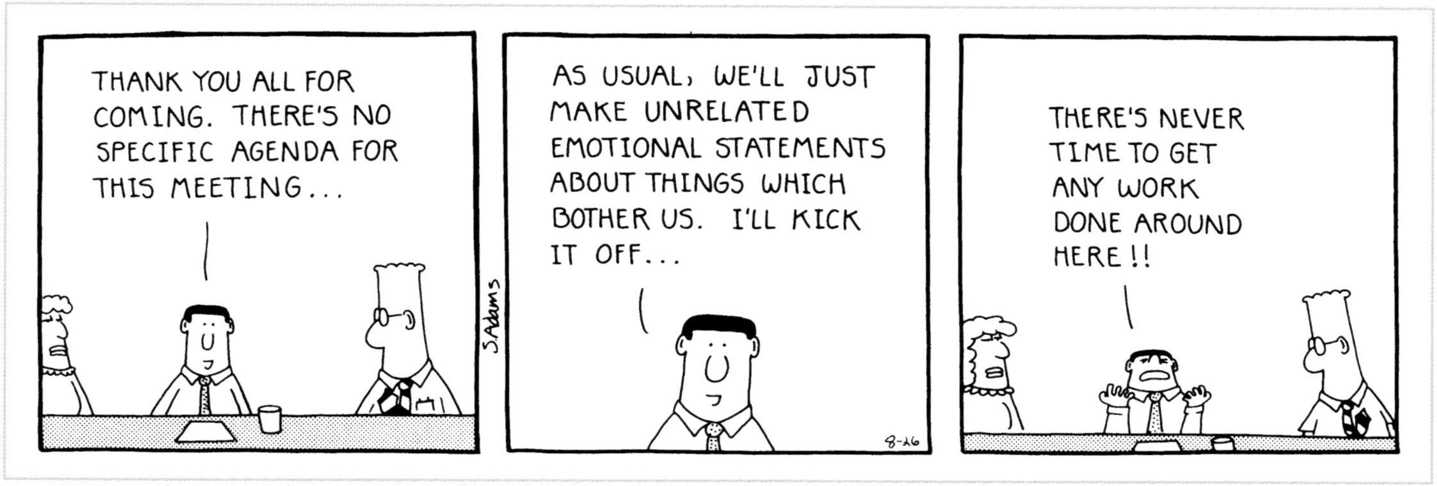
THANK YOU ALL FOR COMING. THERE'S NO SPECIFIC AGENDA FOR THIS MEETING . . .
S. Adams
AS USUAL, WE'LL JUST MAKE UNRELATED EMOTIONAL STATEMENTS ABOUT THINGS WHICH BOTHER US. I'LL KICK IT OFF . . .
8-26
THERE'S NEVER TIME TO GET ANY WORK DONE AROUND HERE !!

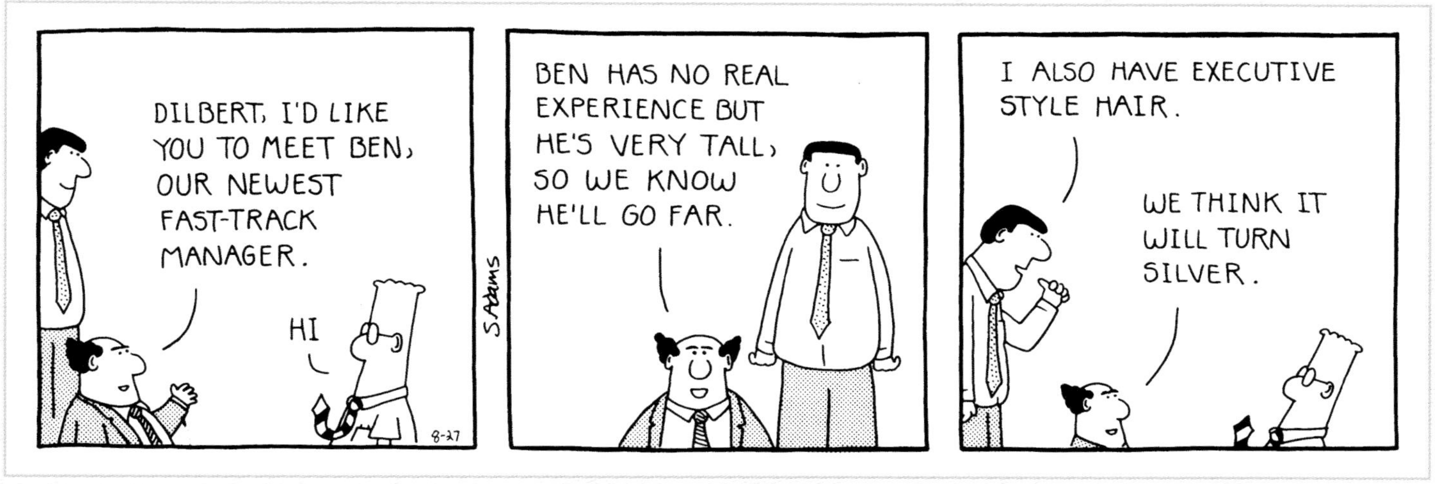
DILBERT, I'D LIKE YOU TO MEET BEN, OUR NEWEST FAST-TRACK MANAGER.
HI
8-27
S. Adams
BEN HAS NO REAL EXPERIENCE BUT HE'S VERY TALL, SO WE KNOW HE'LL GO FAR.
I ALSO HAVE EXECUTIVE STYLE HAIR.
WE THINK IT WILL TURN SILVER.

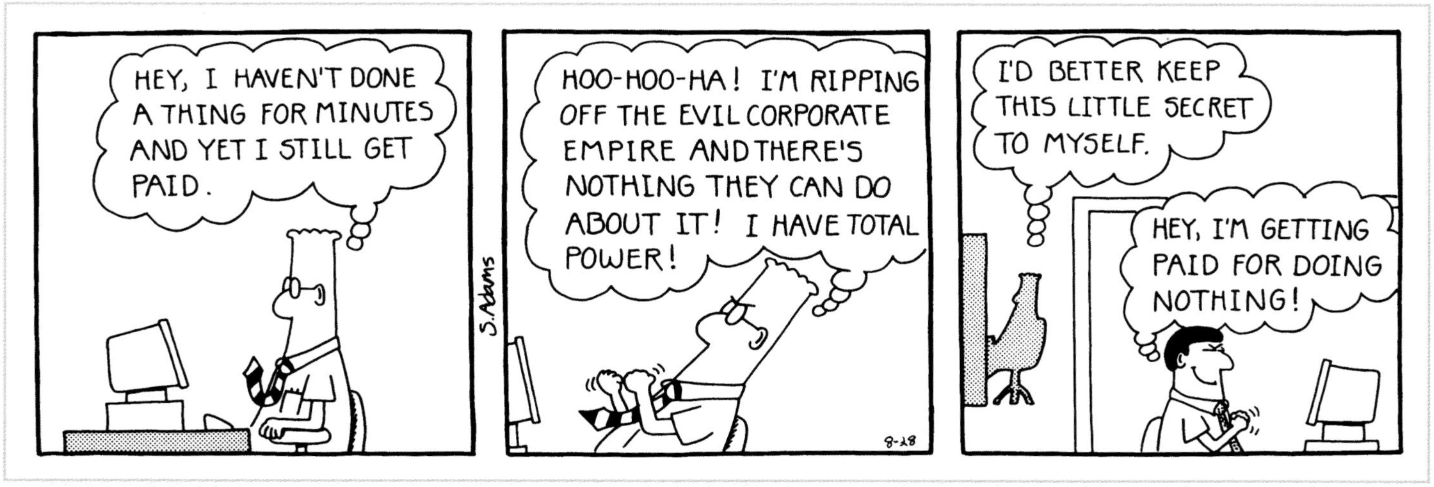
HEY, I HAVEN'T DONE A THING FOR MINUTES AND YET I STILL GET PAID.
S. Adams
HOO-HOO-HA! I'M RIPPING OFF THE EVIL CORPORATE EMPIRE AND THERE'S NOTHING THEY CAN DO ABOUT IT! I HAVE TOTAL POWER!
8-28
I'D BETTER KEEP THIS LITTLE SECRET TO MYSELF.
HEY, I'M GETTING PAID FOR DOING NOTHING!

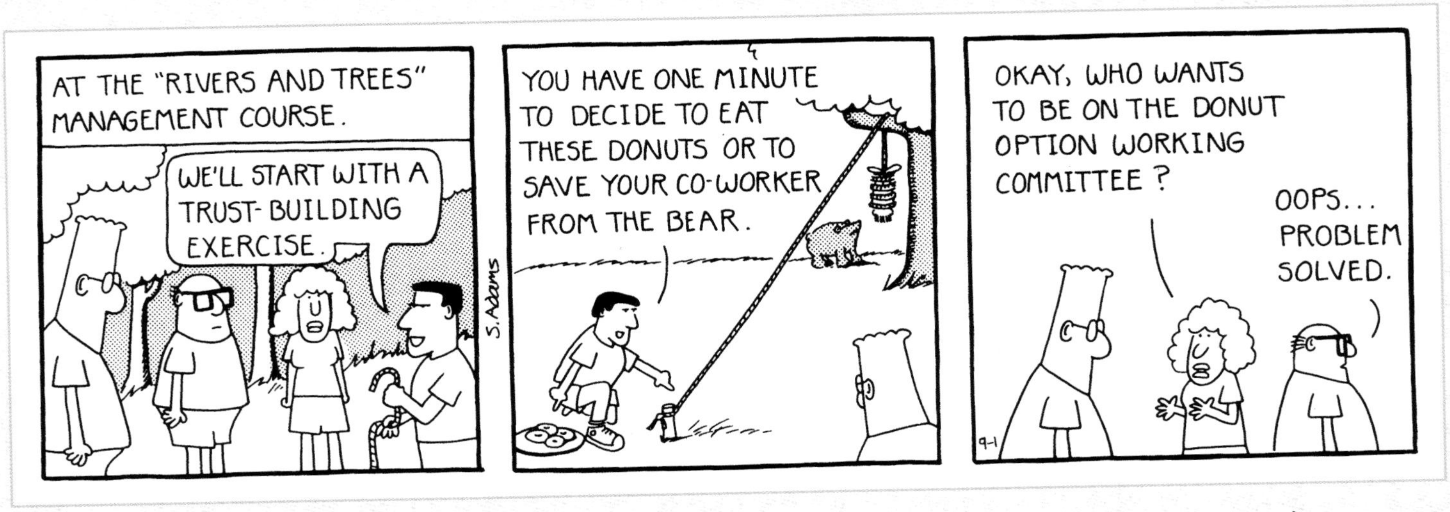
AT THE "RIVERS AND TREES" MANAGEMENT COURSE.
WE'LL START WITH A TRUST-BUILDING EXERCISE.
S. Adams
YOU HAVE ONE MINUTE TO DECIDE TO EAT THESE DONUTS OR TO SAVE YOUR CO-WORKER FROM THE BEAR.
OKAY, WHO WANTS TO BE ON THE DONUT OPTION WORKING COMMITTEE?
OOPS... PROBLEM SOLVED.
9-1

I went on a corporate team-building exercise that inspired this comic. During the first trust exercise, I fell backward so a co-worker could catch me, only she jumped aside and let me fall flat on my back. Her reasoning was "I looked heavy." After that, I faked an injury so I didn't have to risk death in the pursuit of intangible benefits to the company.

That's also the day a co-worker pointed out, to the delight of the assembled crowd, that I was wearing my helmet backward. This got a hearty laugh from all of my co-workers. At the end of the team-building exercise, I hated them all.

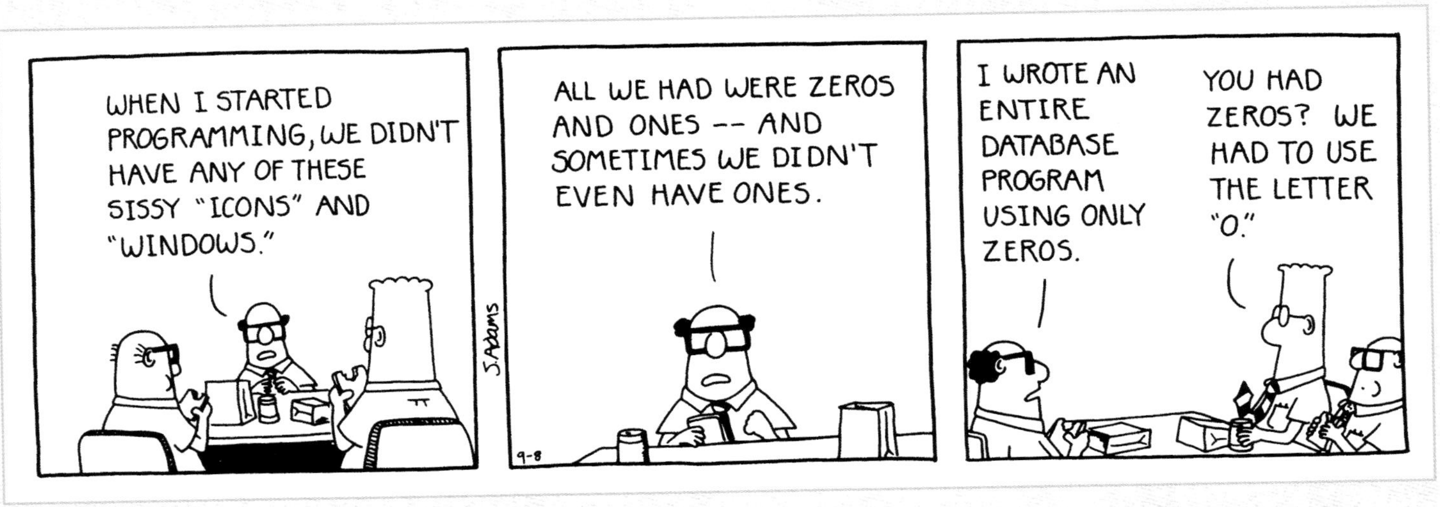
WHEN I STARTED PROGRAMMING, WE DIDN'T HAVE ANY OF THESE SISSY "ICONS" AND "WINDOWS."
S. Adams
ALL WE HAD WERE ZEROS AND ONES -- AND SOMETIMES WE DIDN'T EVEN HAVE ONES.
9-8
I WROTE AN ENTIRE DATABASE PROGRAM USING ONLY ZEROS.
YOU HAD ZEROS? WE HAD TO USE THE LETTER "O."

My actual home phone number at the time was on the sign in this strip. I got few hundred messages from women who wanted to date a Dilbert, and from men who wondered if Dilbert was willing to be flexible.

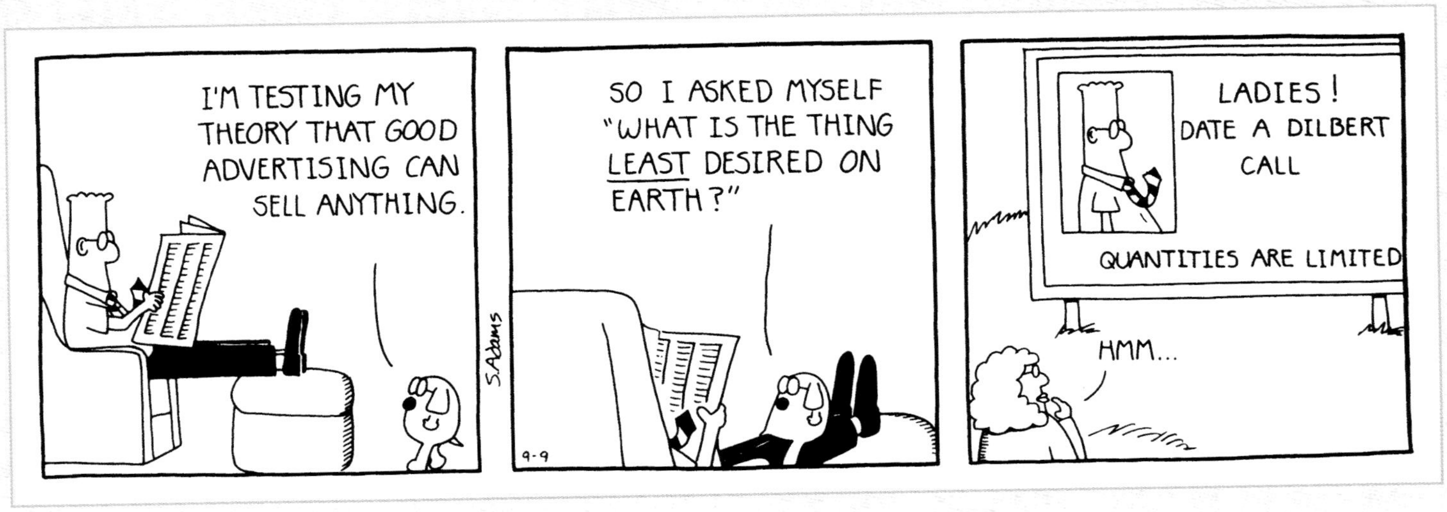
I'M TESTING MY THEORY THAT GOOD ADVERTISING CAN SELL ANYTHING.
S. Adams
SO I ASKED MYSELF "WHAT IS THE THING LEAST DESIRED ON EARTH?"
9-9
LADIES! DATE A DILBERT CALL
QUANTITIES ARE LIMITED
HMM...

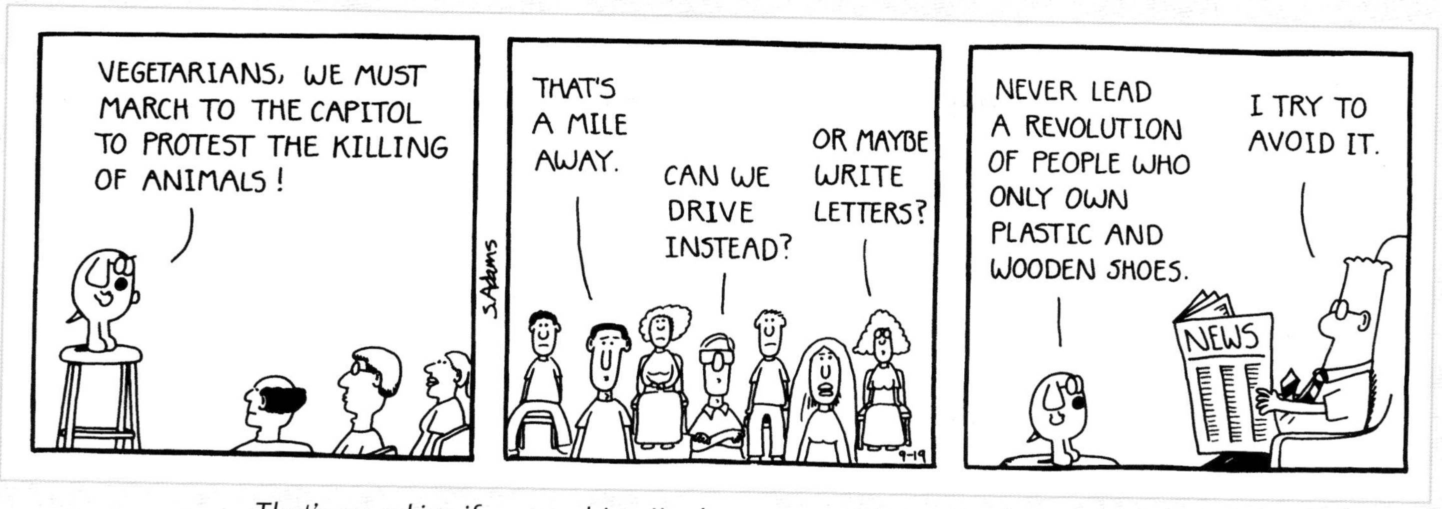
VEGETARIANS, WE MUST MARCH TO THE CAPITOL TO PROTEST THE KILLING OF ANIMALS!
THAT'S A MILE AWAY.
CAN WE DRIVE INSTEAD?
OR MAYBE WRITE LETTERS?
NEVER LEAD A REVOLUTION OF PEOPLE WHO ONLY OWN PLASTIC AND WOODEN SHOES.
I TRY TO AVOID IT.
NEWS

That's me asking if we can drive. I've been a vegetarian most of my adult life.
It's the first time I drew myself into the strip.

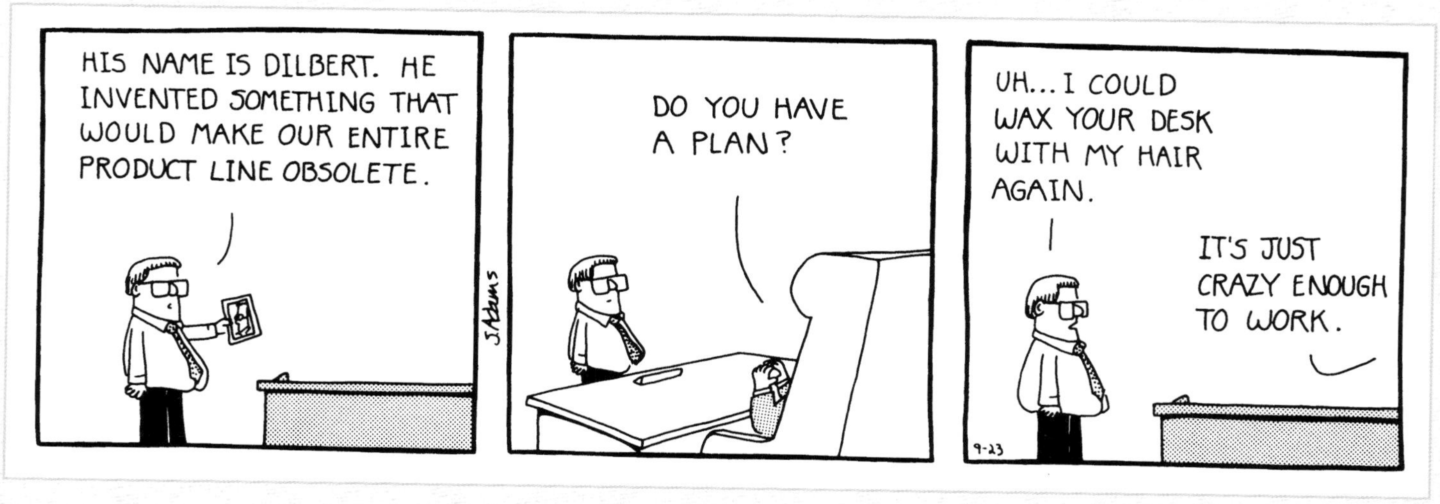
HIS NAME IS DILBERT. HE INVENTED SOMETHING THAT WOULD MAKE OUR ENTIRE PRODUCT LINE OBSOLETE.
DO YOU HAVE A PLAN?
UH... I COULD WAX YOUR DESK WITH MY HAIR AGAIN.
IT'S JUST CRAZY ENOUGH TO WORK.

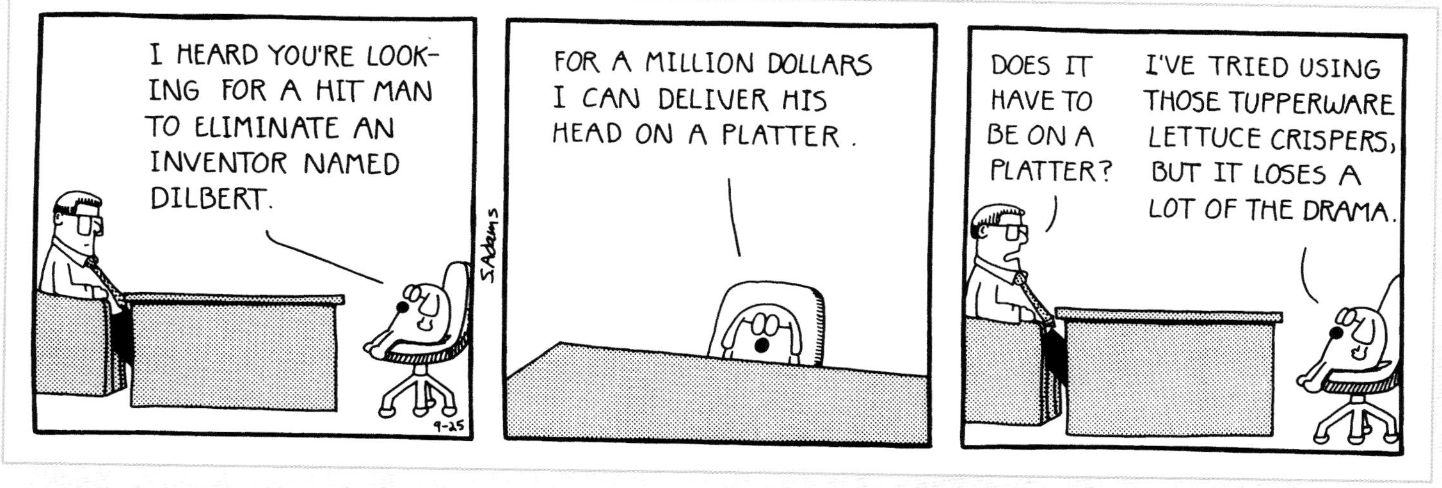
I HEARD YOU'RE LOOKING FOR A HIT MAN TO ELIMINATE AN INVENTOR NAMED DILBERT.
FOR A MILLION DOLLARS I CAN DELIVER HIS HEAD ON A PLATTER.
DOES IT HAVE TO BE ON A PLATTER?
I'VE TRIED USING THOSE TUPPERWARE LETTUCE CRISPERS, BUT IT LOSES A LOT OF THE DRAMA.

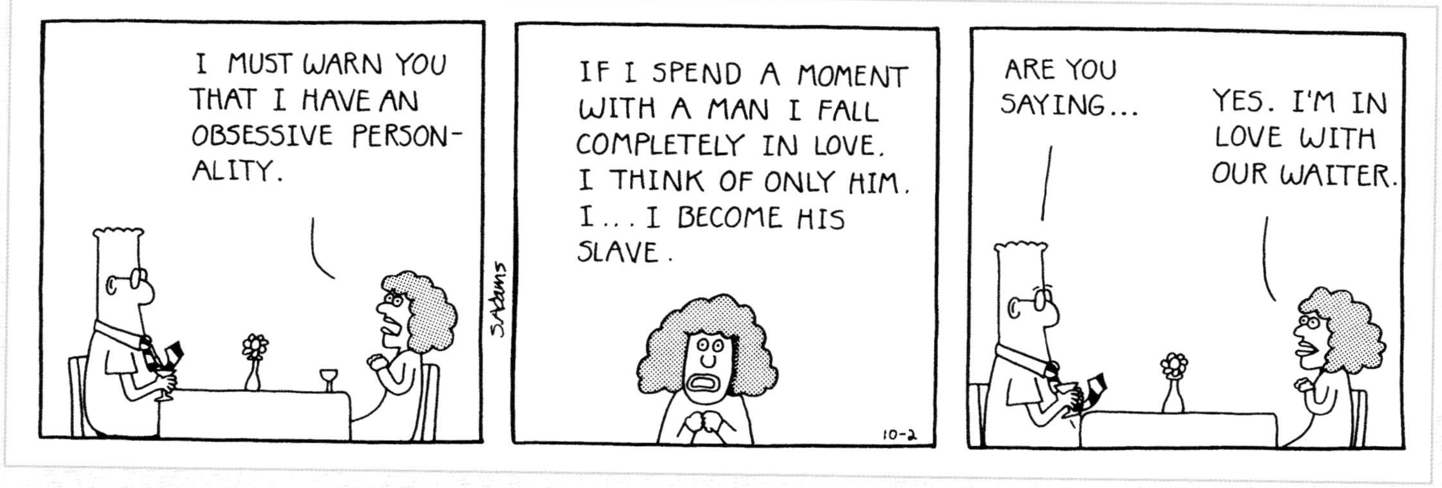
I MUST WARN YOU THAT I HAVE AN OBSESSIVE PERSONALITY.
IF I SPEND A MOMENT WITH A MAN I FALL COMPLETELY IN LOVE. I THINK OF ONLY HIM. I... I BECOME HIS SLAVE.
ARE YOU SAYING...
YES. I'M IN LOVE WITH OUR WAITER.

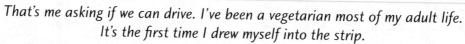

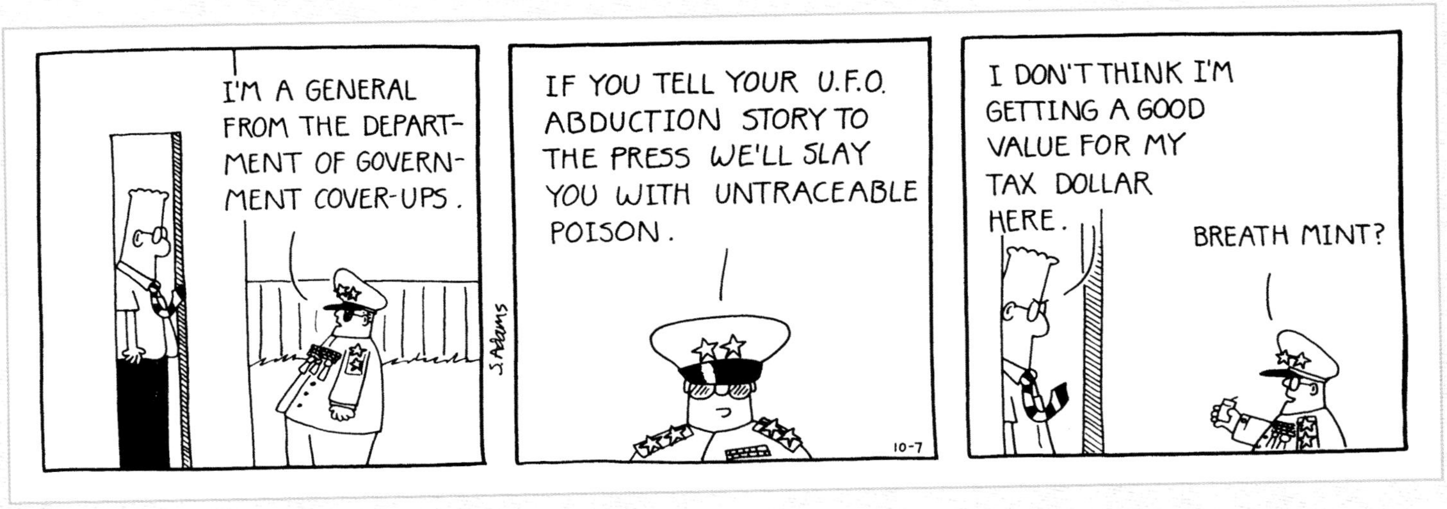
I'M A GENERAL FROM THE DEPARTMENT OF GOVERNMENT COVER-UPS.
S. Adams
IF YOU TELL YOUR U.F.O. ABDUCTION STORY TO THE PRESS WE'LL SLAY YOU WITH UNTRACEABLE POISON.
10-7
I DON'T THINK I'M GETTING A GOOD VALUE FOR MY TAX DOLLAR HERE.
BREATH MINT?

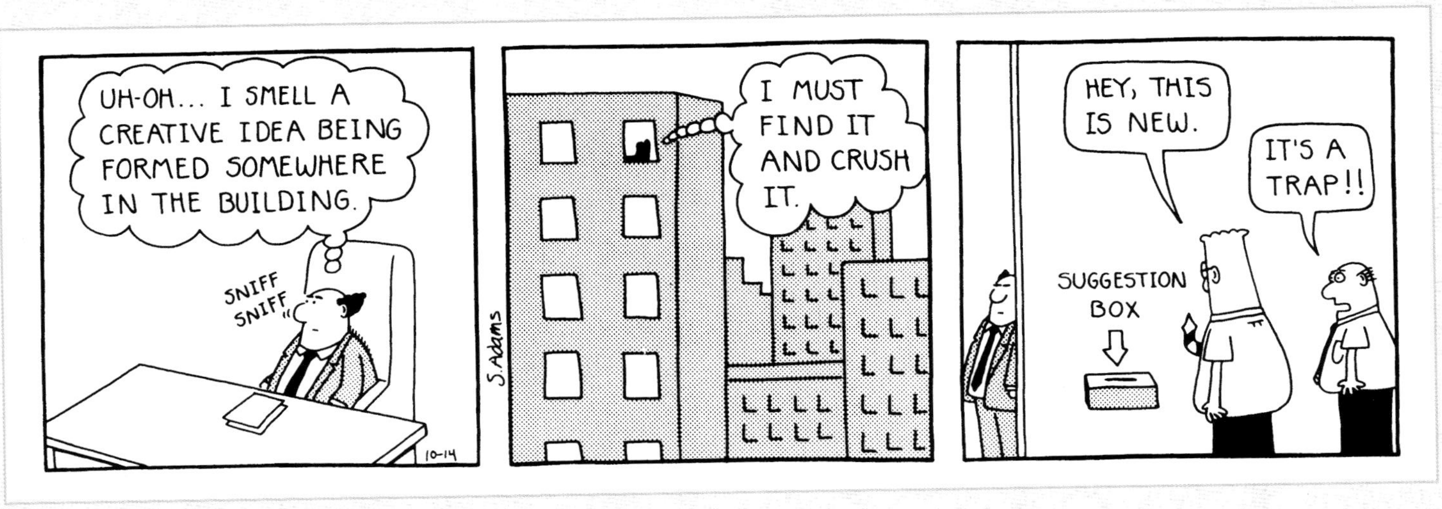
UH-OH... I SMELL A CREATIVE IDEA BEING FORMED SOMEWHERE IN THE BUILDING.
SNIFF SNIFF
10-14
S. Adams
I MUST FIND IT AND CRUSH IT.
HEY, THIS IS NEW.
IT'S A TRAP!!
SUGGESTION BOX

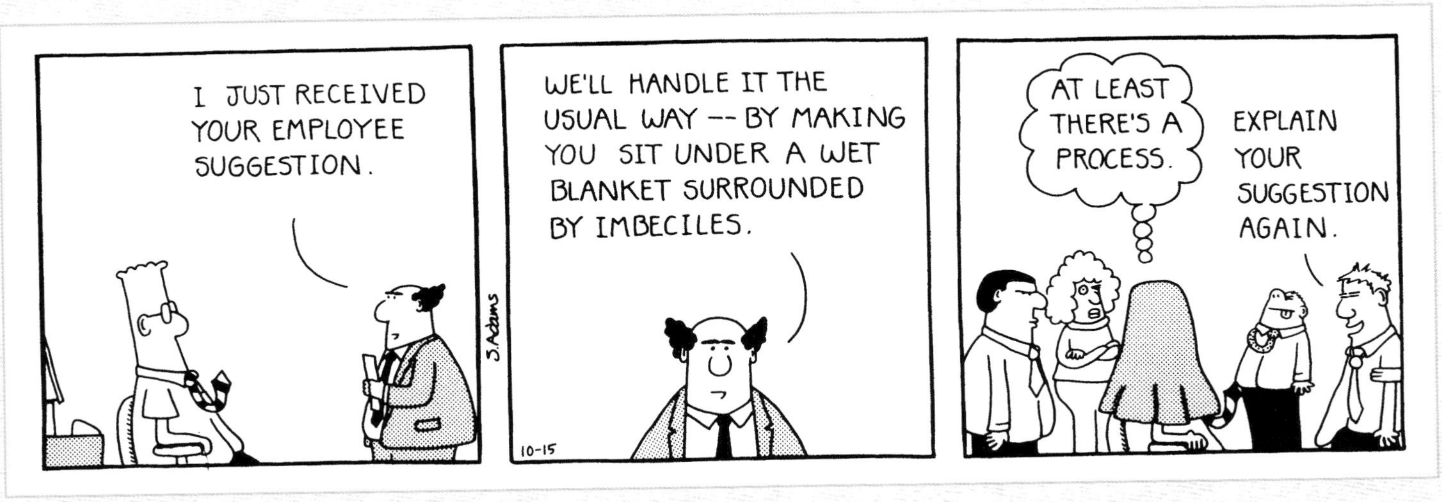
I JUST RECEIVED YOUR EMPLOYEE SUGGESTION.
S. Adams
WE'LL HANDLE IT THE USUAL WAY -- BY MAKING YOU SIT UNDER A WET BLANKET SURROUNDED BY IMBECILES.
10-15
AT LEAST THERE'S A PROCESS.
EXPLAIN YOUR SUGGESTION AGAIN.

When you see a character in Dilbert who doesn't look like my usual generic people, it's probably because the comic is based on a real person, like this one. I once reviewed a binder of material with a hand licker. It was my binder. Afterward I had to kick it all the way down the hall back to my cubicle.

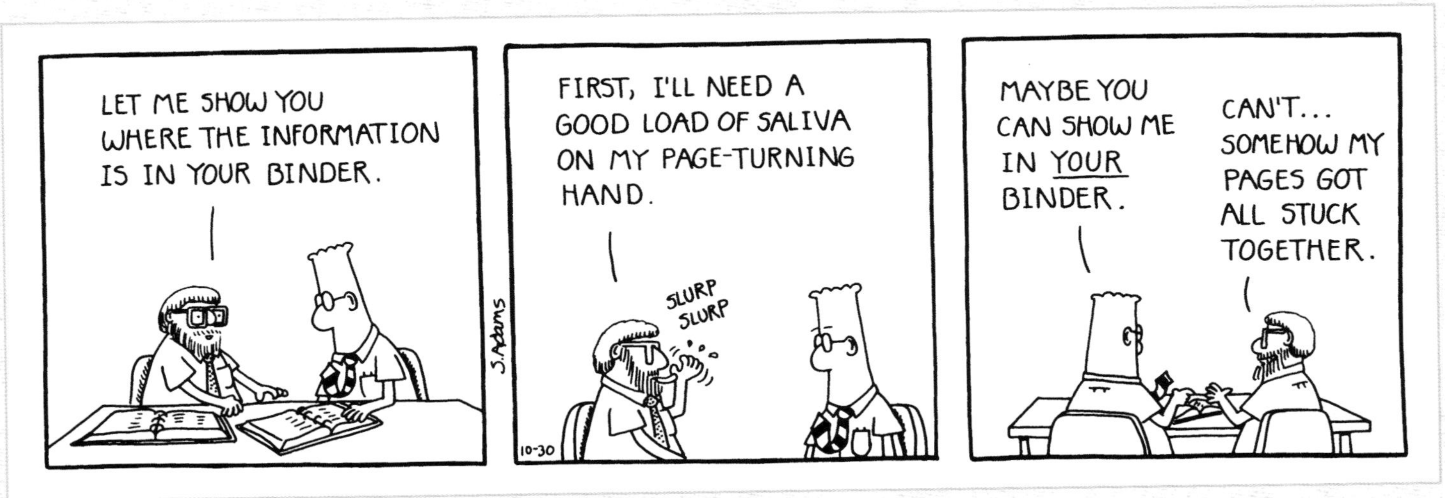
LET ME SHOW YOU WHERE THE INFORMATION IS IN YOUR BINDER.
S. Adams
FIRST, I'LL NEED A GOOD LOAD OF SALIVA ON MY PAGE-TURNING HAND.
SLURP SLURP
10-30
MAYBE YOU CAN SHOW ME IN YOUR BINDER.
CAN'T... SOMEHOW MY PAGES GOT ALL STUCK TOGETHER.

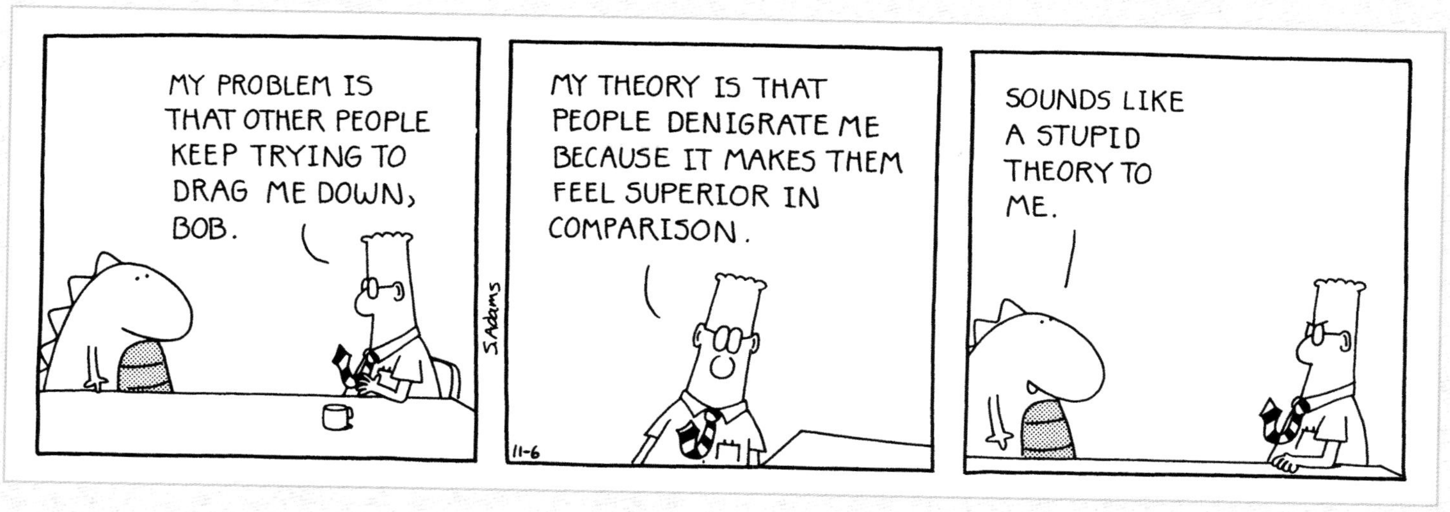
MY PROBLEM IS THAT OTHER PEOPLE KEEP TRYING TO DRAG ME DOWN, BOB.
MY THEORY IS THAT PEOPLE DENIGRATE ME BECAUSE IT MAKES THEM FEEL SUPERIOR IN COMPARISON.
SOUNDS LIKE A STUPID THEORY TO ME.
S. Adams
11-6

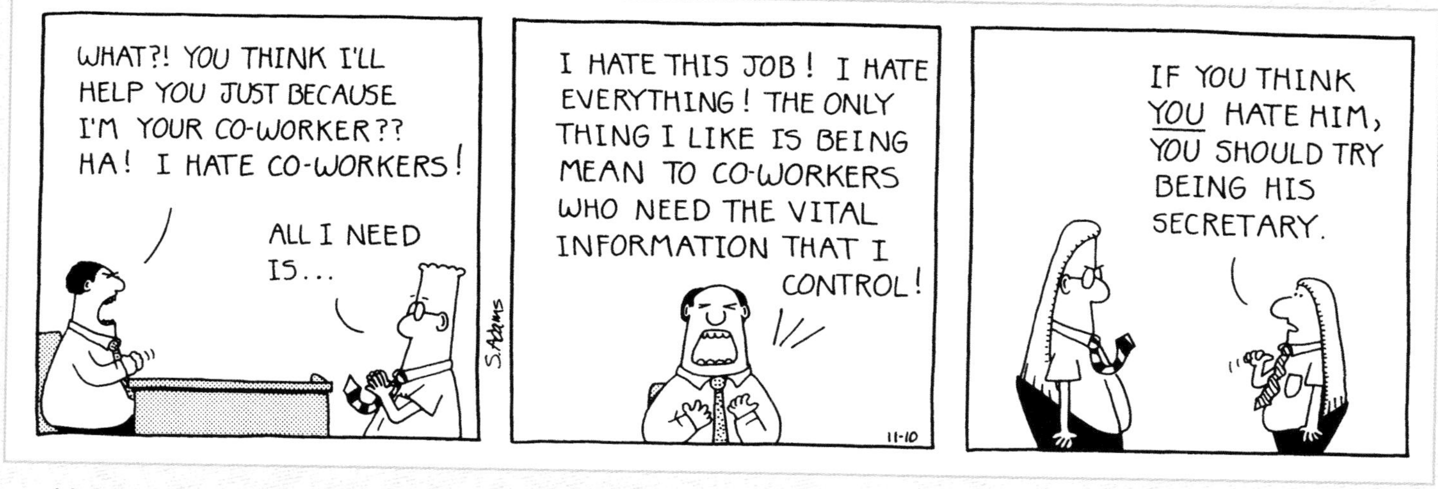
WHAT?! YOU THINK I'LL HELP YOU JUST BECAUSE I'M YOUR CO-WORKER?? HA! I HATE CO-WORKERS!
ALL I NEED IS...
I HATE THIS JOB! I HATE EVERYTHING! THE ONLY THING I LIKE IS BEING MEAN TO CO-WORKERS WHO NEED THE VITAL INFORMATION THAT I CONTROL!
IF YOU THINK YOU HATE HIM, YOU SHOULD TRY BEING HIS SECRETARY.
S. Adams
11-10

Most workplace problems are caused by morons or sadists. Every group of five people has at least one of each.

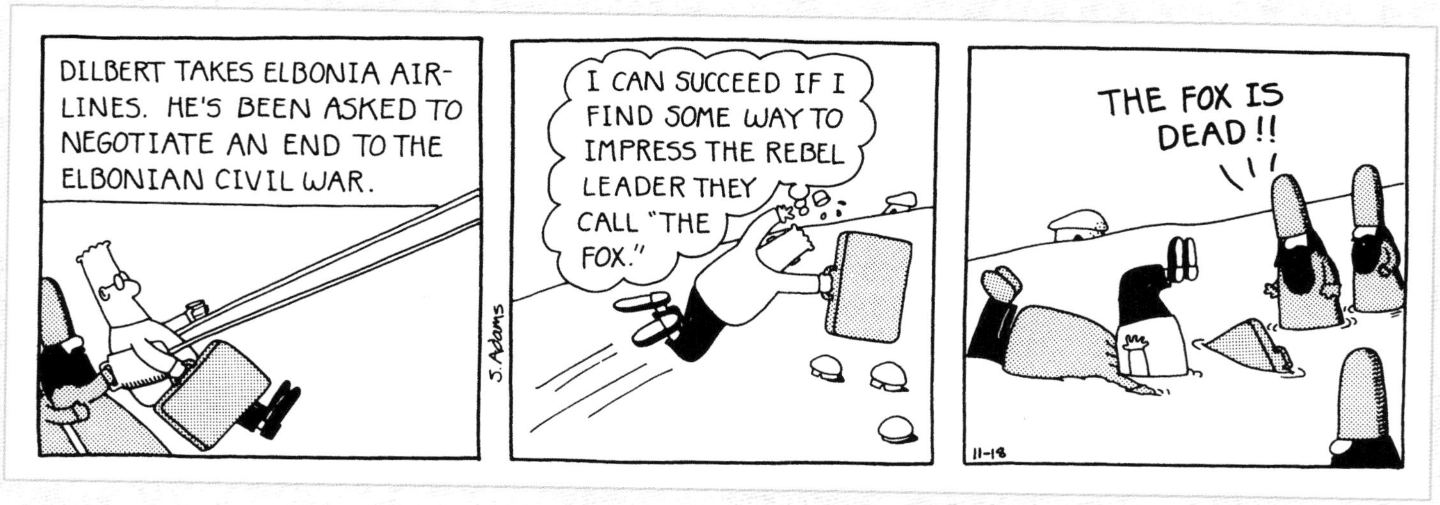
DILBERT TAKES ELBONIA AIRLINES. HE'S BEEN ASKED TO NEGOTIATE AN END TO THE ELBONIAN CIVIL WAR.
I CAN SUCCEED IF I FIND SOME WAY TO IMPRESS THE REBEL LEADER THEY CALL "THE FOX."
THE FOX IS DEAD!!
S. Adams
11-18

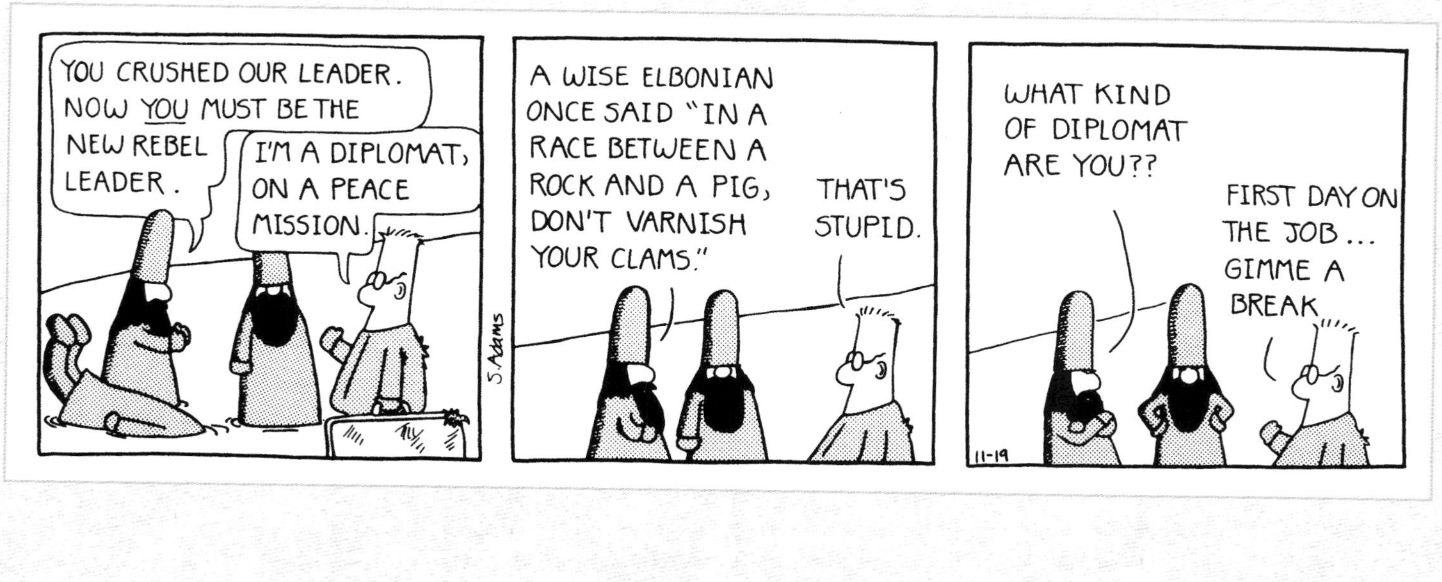
YOU CRUSHED OUR LEADER. NOW YOU MUST BE THE NEW REBEL LEADER.
I'M A DIPLOMAT, ON A PEACE MISSION.
A WISE ELBONIAN ONCE SAID "IN A RACE BETWEEN A ROCK AND A PIG, DON'T VARNISH YOUR CLAMS."
THAT'S STUPID.
WHAT KIND OF DIPLOMAT ARE YOU??
FIRST DAY ON THE JOB... GIMME A BREAK.
S. Adams
11-19

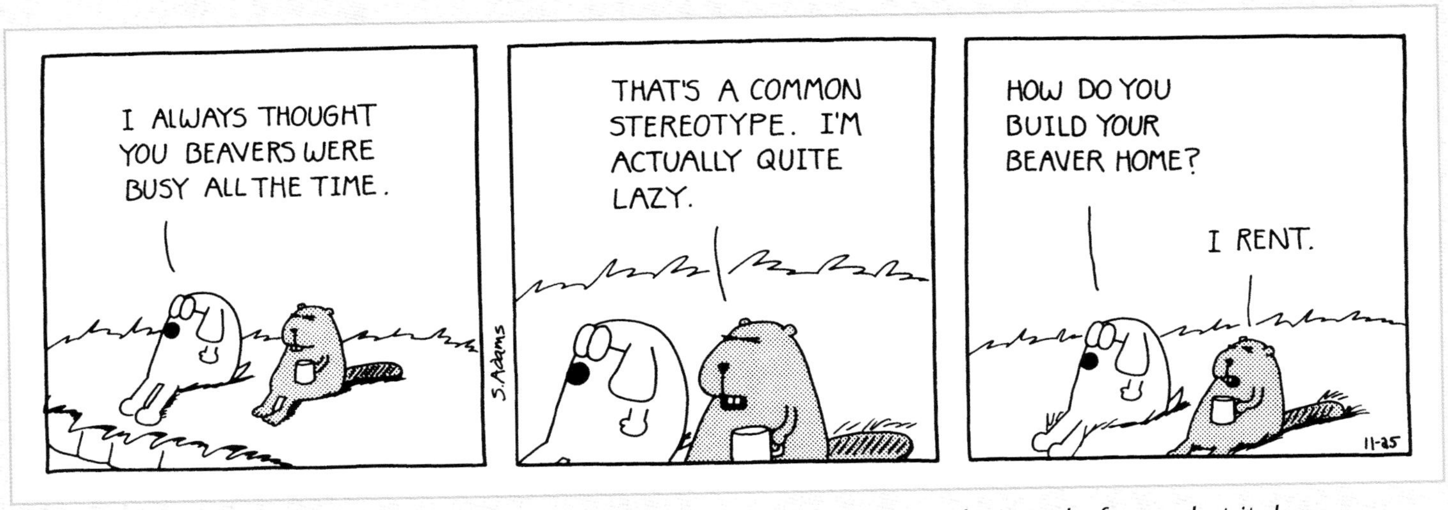
I ALWAYS THOUGHT YOU BEAVERS WERE BUSY ALL THE TIME.
THAT'S A COMMON STEREOTYPE. I'M ACTUALLY QUITE LAZY.
HOW DO YOU BUILD YOUR BEAVER HOME?
I RENT.

I've often mentioned this strip as my personal favorite. I don't know why it works for me, but it does.

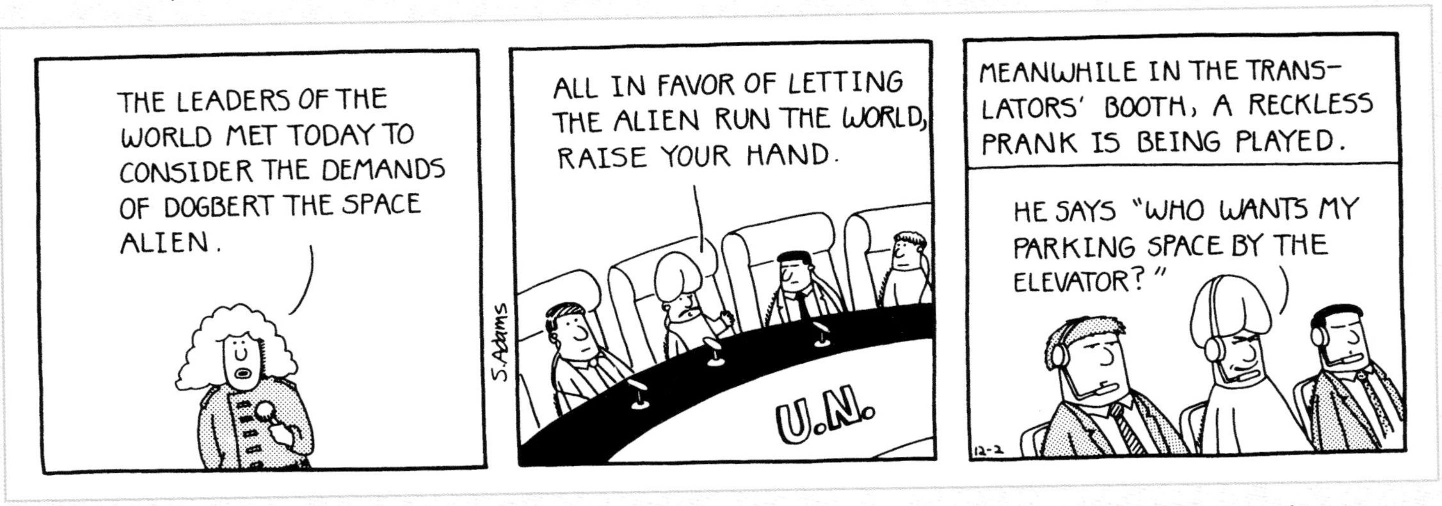
THE LEADERS OF THE WORLD MET TODAY TO CONSIDER THE DEMANDS OF DOGBERT THE SPACE ALIEN.
ALL IN FAVOR OF LETTING THE ALIEN RUN THE WORLD, RAISE YOUR HAND.
U.N.
MEANWHILE IN THE TRANSLATORS' BOOTH, A RECKLESS PRANK IS BEING PLAYED.
HE SAYS "WHO WANTS MY PARKING SPACE BY THE ELEVATOR?"

After this comic ran, I got mail from a guy who said he was on to my tricks. He said he knew I drew the one character to look like an unmentionable part of the male anatomy. At first I dismissed the letter as the work of a crank. But out of curiosity, I pulled the comic out and took a look. You be the judge.

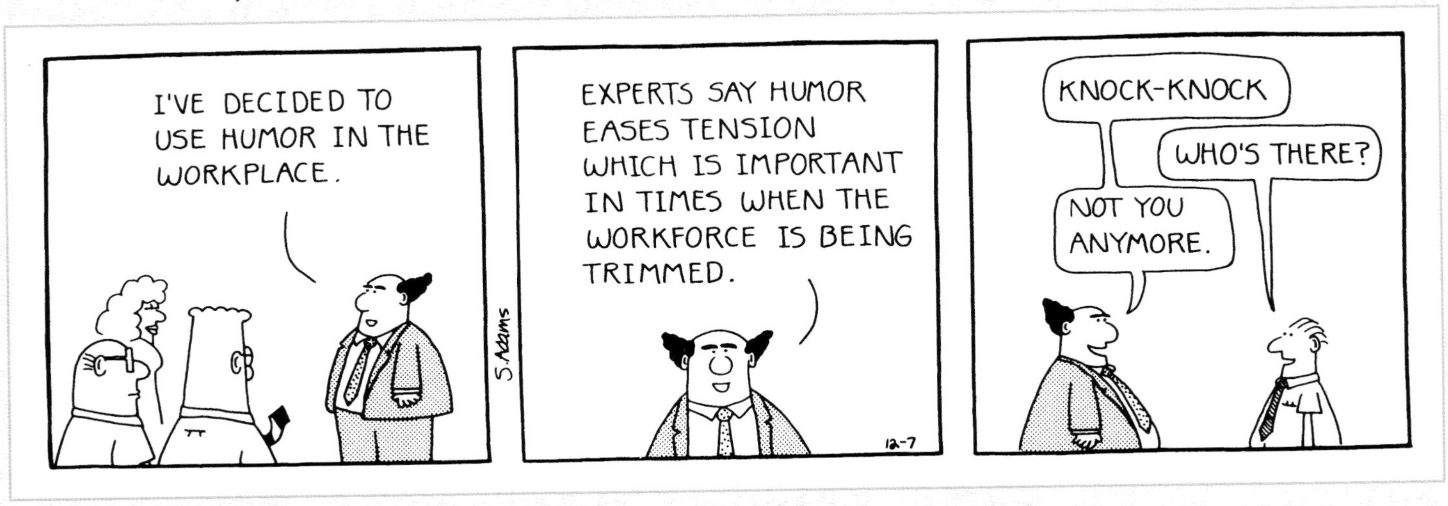
I'VE DECIDED TO USE HUMOR IN THE WORKPLACE.
EXPERTS SAY HUMOR EASES TENSION WHICH IS IMPORTANT IN TIMES WHEN THE WORKFORCE IS BEING TRIMMED.
KNOCK-KNOCK
WHO'S THERE?
NOT YOU ANYMORE.

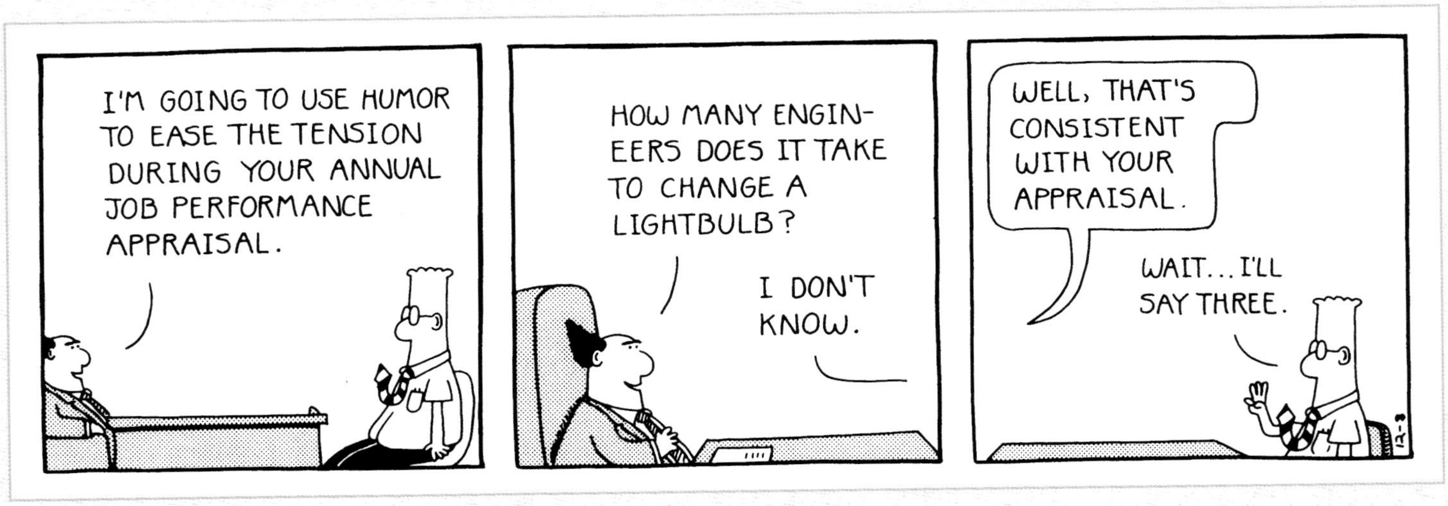
I'M GOING TO USE HUMOR TO EASE THE TENSION DURING YOUR ANNUAL JOB PERFORMANCE APPRAISAL.
HOW MANY ENGINEERS DOES IT TAKE TO CHANGE A LIGHTBULB?
I DON'T KNOW.
WELL, THAT'S CONSISTENT WITH YOUR APPRAISAL.
WAIT... I'LL SAY THREE.

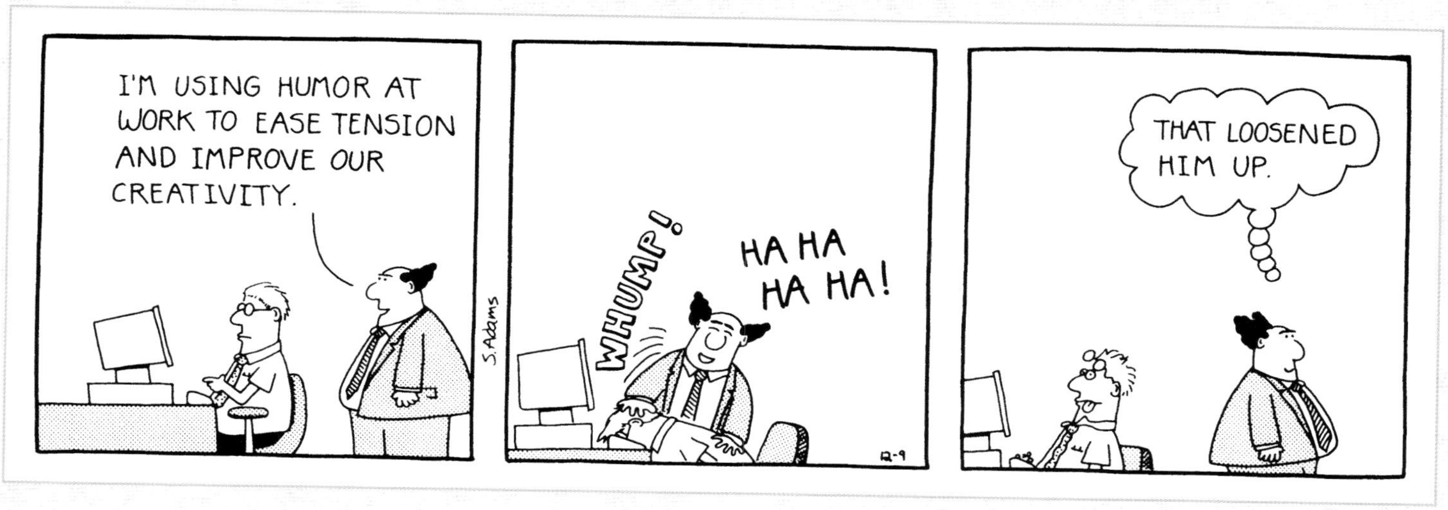
I'M USING HUMOR AT WORK TO EASE TENSION AND IMPROVE OUR CREATIVITY.
S. Adams
WHUMP!
HA HA HA HA!
12-9
THAT LOOSENED HIM UP.

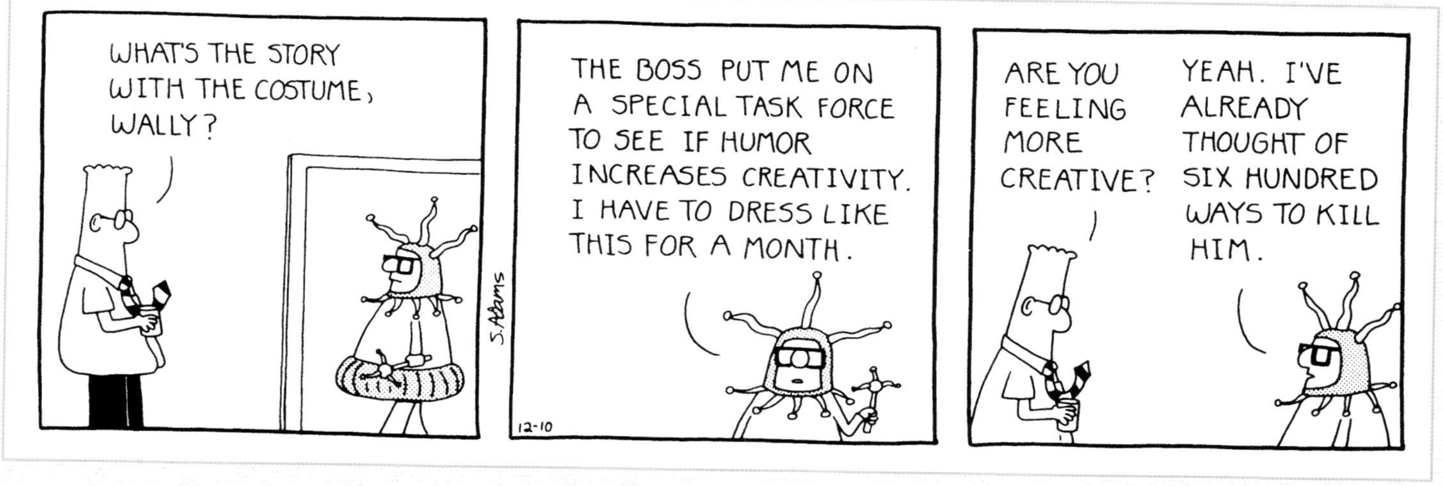
WHAT'S THE STORY WITH THE COSTUME, WALLY?
S. Adams
THE BOSS PUT ME ON A SPECIAL TASK FORCE TO SEE IF HUMOR INCREASES CREATIVITY. I HAVE TO DRESS LIKE THIS FOR A MONTH.
12-10
ARE YOU FEELING MORE CREATIVE?
YEAH. I'VE ALREADY THOUGHT OF SIX HUNDRED WAYS TO KILL HIM.

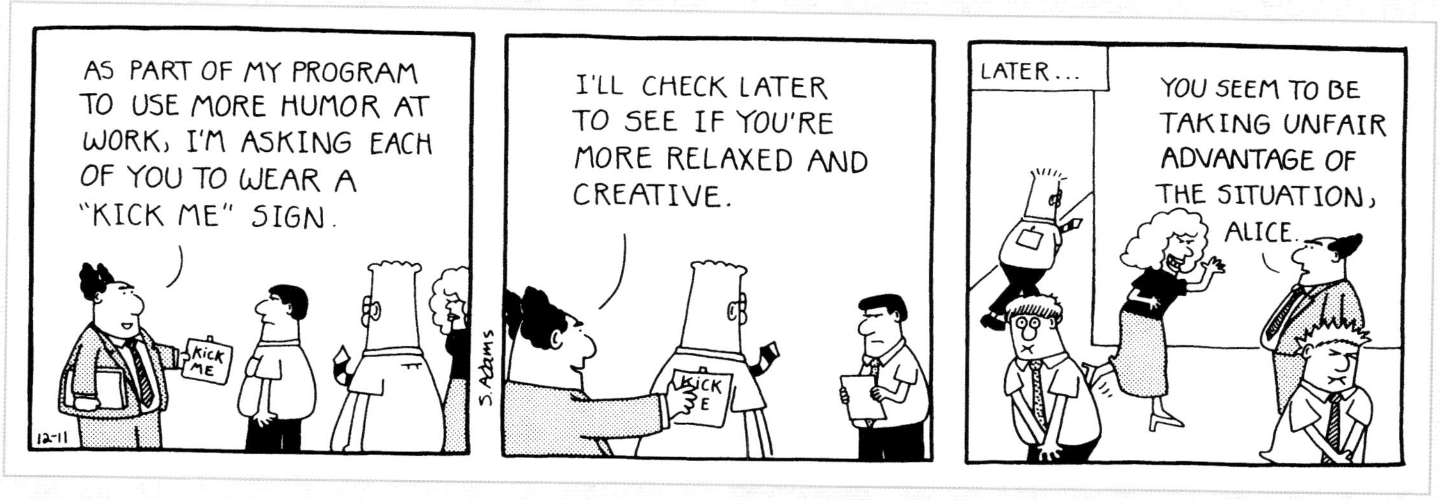
AS PART OF MY PROGRAM TO USE MORE HUMOR AT WORK, I'M ASKING EACH OF YOU TO WEAR A "KICK ME" SIGN.
KICK ME
12-11
S. Adams
I'LL CHECK LATER TO SEE IF YOU'RE MORE RELAXED AND CREATIVE.
LATER...
YOU SEEM TO BE TAKING UNFAIR ADVANTAGE OF THE SITUATION, ALICE.

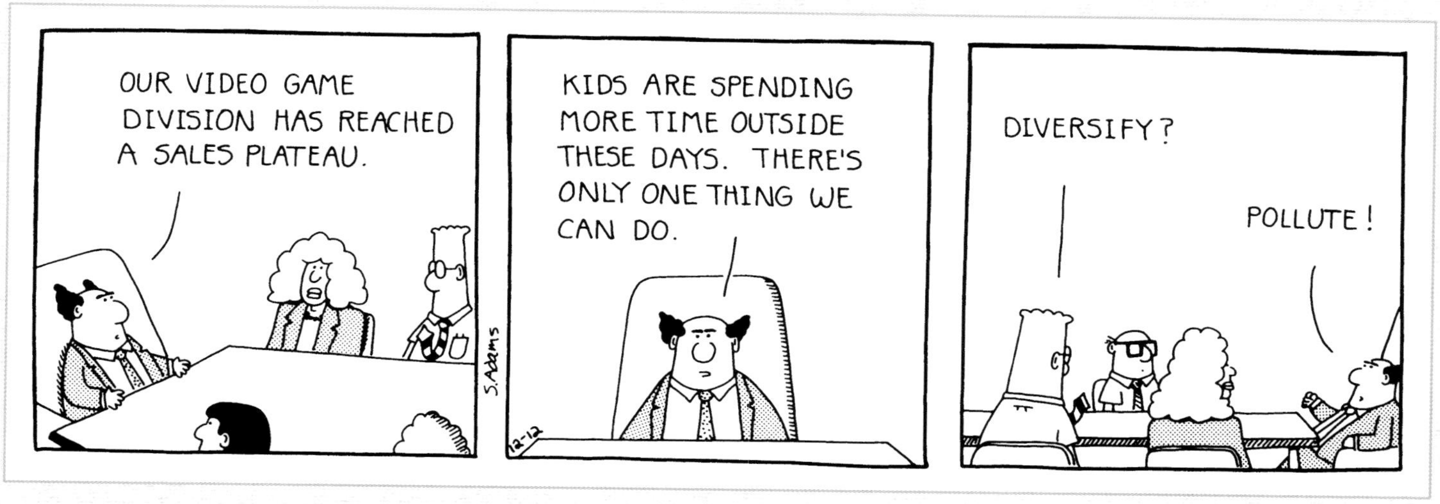
OUR VIDEO GAME DIVISION HAS REACHED A SALES PLATEAU.
S. Adams
KIDS ARE SPENDING MORE TIME OUTSIDE THESE DAYS. THERE'S ONLY ONE THING WE CAN DO.
12-12
DIVERSIFY?
POLLUTE!

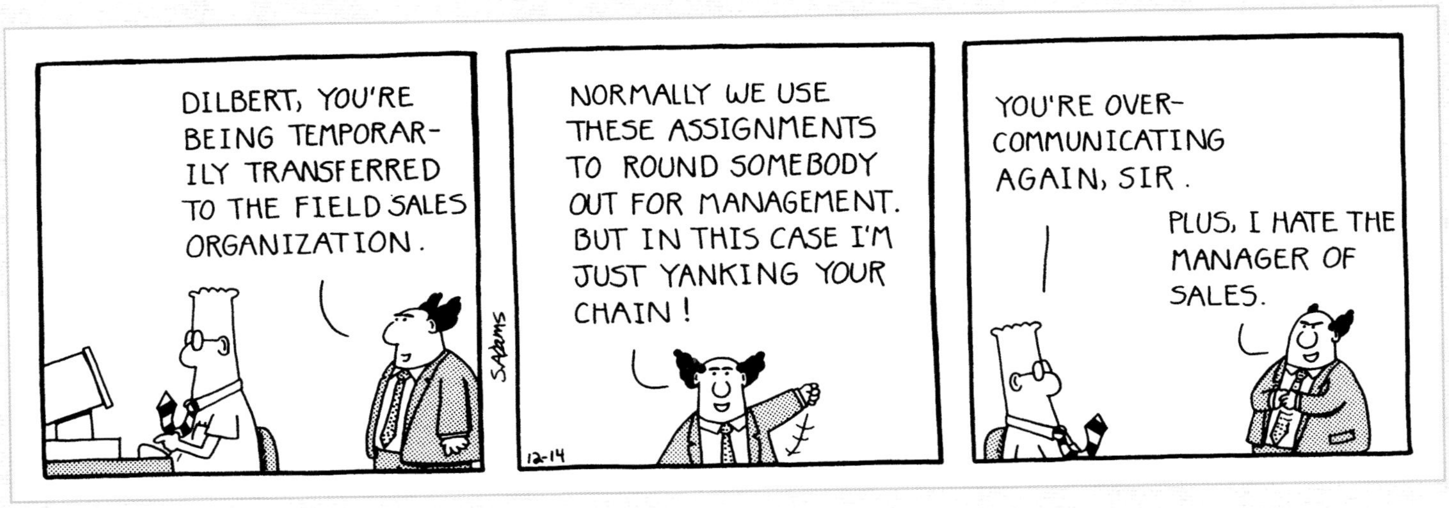
DILBERT, YOU'RE BEING TEMPORARILY TRANSFERRED TO THE FIELD SALES ORGANIZATION.
S. Adams
NORMALLY WE USE THESE ASSIGNMENTS TO ROUND SOMEBODY OUT FOR MANAGEMENT. BUT IN THIS CASE I'M JUST YANKING YOUR CHAIN!
12-14
YOU'RE OVER-COMMUNICATING AGAIN, SIR.
PLUS, I HATE THE MANAGER OF SALES.

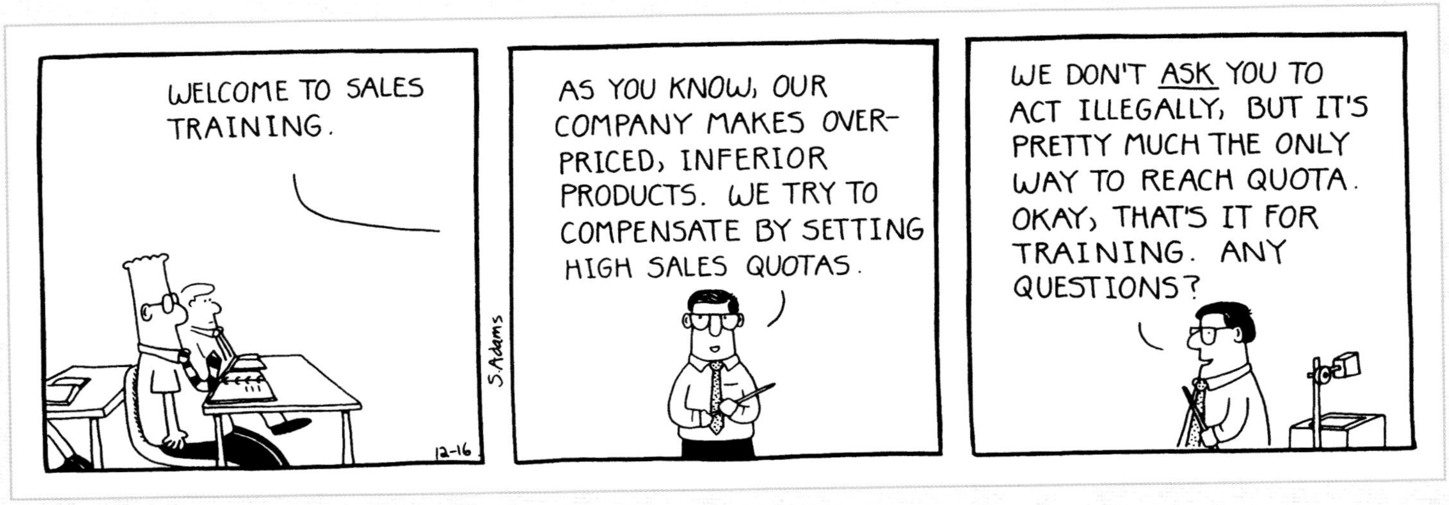
WELCOME TO SALES TRAINING.
12-16
S. Adams
AS YOU KNOW, OUR COMPANY MAKES OVERPRICED, INFERIOR PRODUCTS. WE TRY TO COMPENSATE BY SETTING HIGH SALES QUOTAS.
WE DON'T ASK YOU TO ACT ILLEGALLY, BUT IT'S PRETTY MUCH THE ONLY WAY TO REACH QUOTA. OKAY, THAT'S IT FOR TRAINING. ANY QUESTIONS?

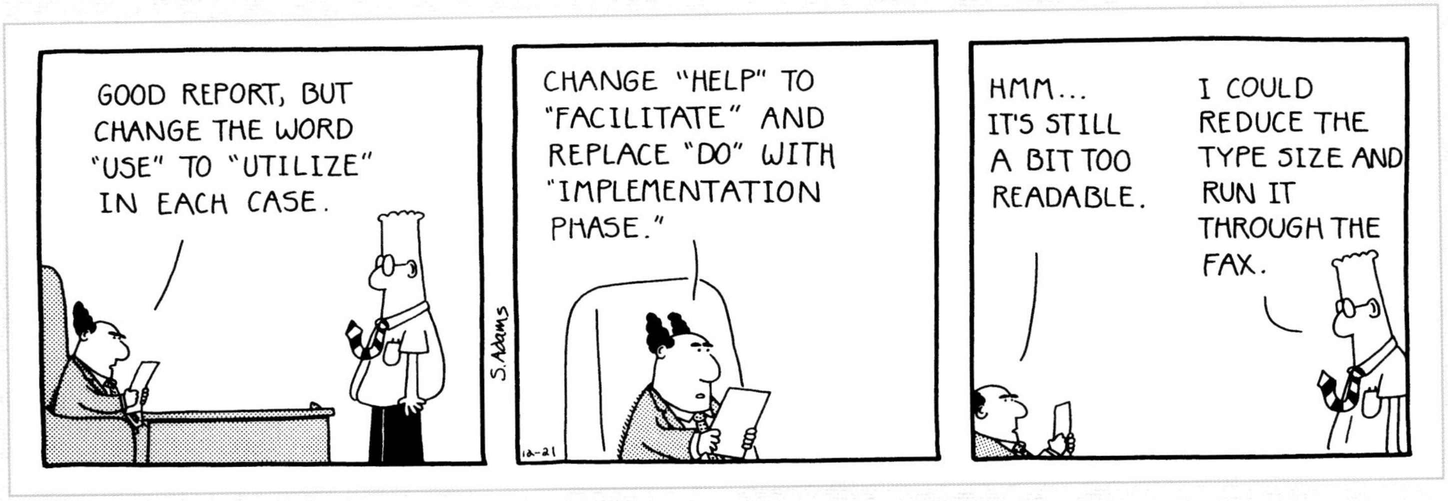
GOOD REPORT, BUT CHANGE THE WORD "USE" TO "UTILIZE" IN EACH CASE.
S. Adams
CHANGE "HELP" TO "FACILITATE" AND REPLACE "DO" WITH "IMPLEMENTATION PHASE."
12-21
HMM... IT'S STILL A BIT TOO READABLE.
I COULD REDUCE THE TYPE SIZE AND RUN IT THROUGH THE FAX.

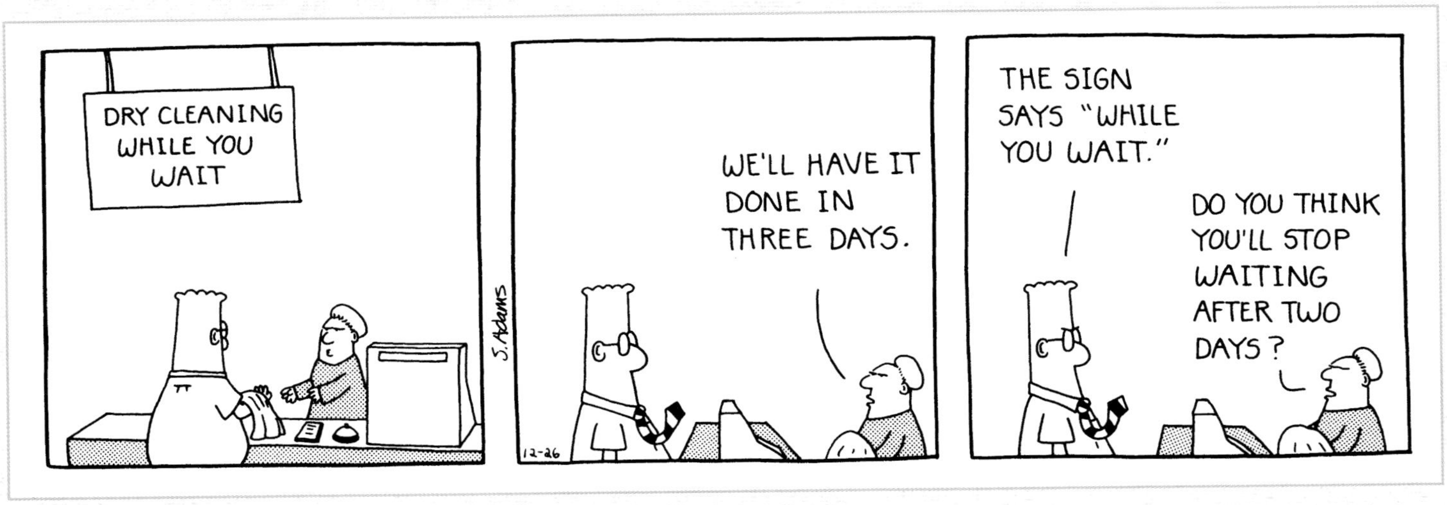
DRY CLEANING WHILE YOU WAIT
S. Adams
WE'LL HAVE IT DONE IN THREE DAYS.
12-26
THE SIGN SAYS "WHILE YOU WAIT."
DO YOU THINK YOU'LL STOP WAITING AFTER TWO DAYS?

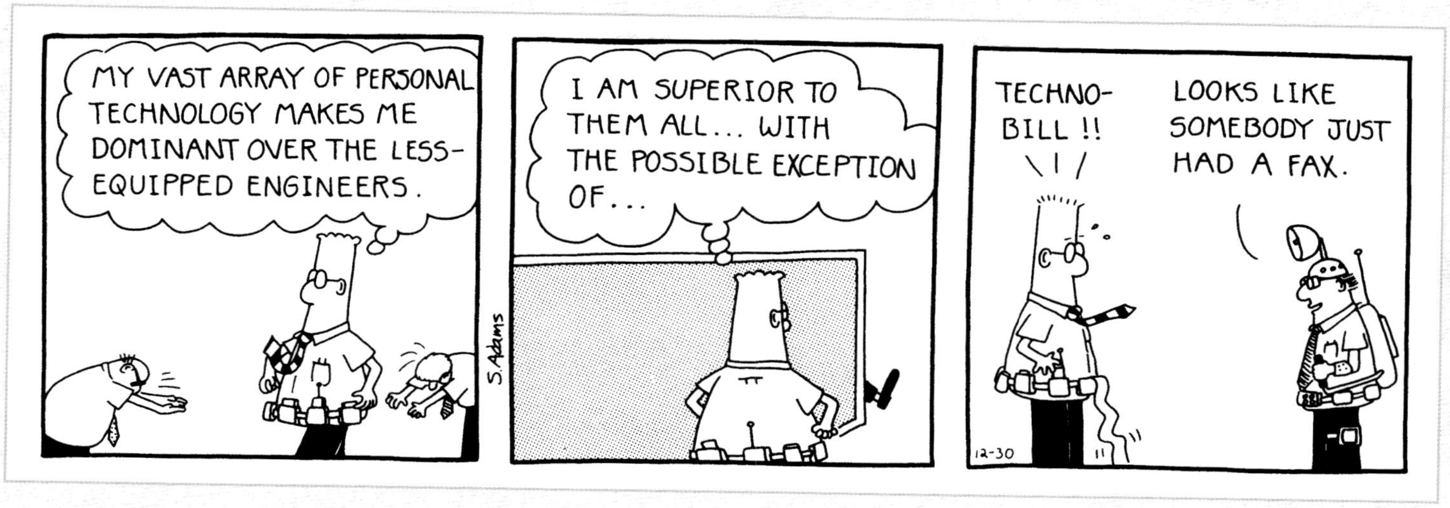

MY VAST ARRAY OF PERSONAL TECHNOLOGY MAKES ME DOMINANT OVER THE LESS-EQUIPPED ENGINEERS.
I AM SUPERIOR TO THEM ALL... WITH THE POSSIBLE EXCEPTION OF...
TECHNO-BILL !!
LOOKS LIKE SOMEBODY JUST HAD A FAX.
S.Adams
12-30

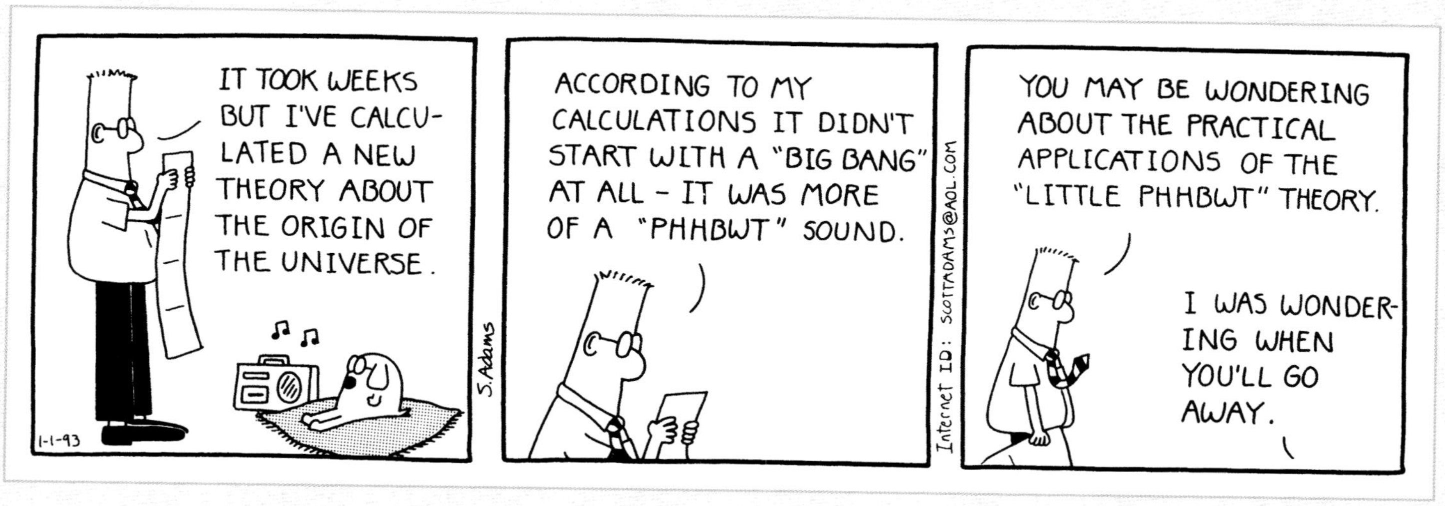

IT TOOK WEEKS BUT I'VE CALCULATED A NEW THEORY ABOUT THE ORIGIN OF THE UNIVERSE.
ACCORDING TO MY CALCULATIONS IT DIDN'T START WITH A "BIG BANG" AT ALL - IT WAS MORE OF A "PHHBWT" SOUND.
YOU MAY BE WONDERING ABOUT THE PRACTICAL APPLICATIONS OF THE "LITTLE PHHBWT" THEORY.
I WAS WONDERING WHEN YOU'LL GO AWAY.
S.Adams
1-1-93
Internet ID: SCOTTADAMS@AOL.COM

This is when I started running my e-mail address in the margin of the strip every day. E-mail was in such an infant stage that I had to label it "Internet ID" so people would know what it was. I was the first syndicated comic strip to include an e-mail address, and at the time it seemed like a big risk. There was concern that the newspaper clients would view it as some sort of embedded advertisement. Had Dilbert *been more successful already, it probably wouldn't have been worth the perceived risk. As it turned out, no newspaper complained.*

I got flooded with e-mail almost instantly. The most common message I received in those days was "I wrote to you because I don't know anyone else who has e-mail yet."

I got thousands of messages a day. Most of them were comments or suggestions for the strip. Many were brutal. Some were constructive. But the thing they had in common was a strong preference for the workplace-themed comics. 1993 is when I knew for sure where the biggest market for Dilbert *was. I started changing the focus of the strip from the generic and absurd to the workplace. That change clarified the identity of the strip, and it took off in popularity.*

I still include my e-mail address in the strip. And while readership is many times greater than it was in 1993, far fewer people send e-mail. I think the difference is that readers have other people to e-mail now, and also, I think people assume the volume of my e-mail is so great that I couldn't possibly read it all.

Editor's note: For this book, we have taken the e-mail address out of the strips, after the one above.

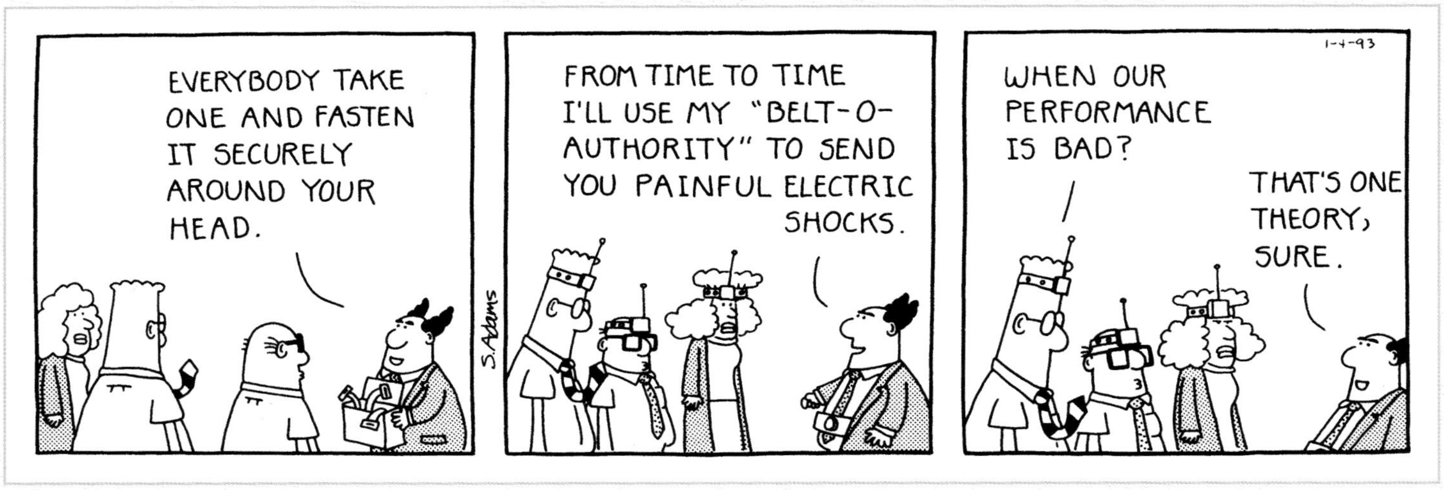
EVERYBODY TAKE ONE AND FASTEN IT SECURELY AROUND YOUR HEAD.
S. Adams
FROM TIME TO TIME I'LL USE MY "BELT-O-AUTHORITY" TO SEND YOU PAINFUL ELECTRIC SHOCKS.
1-4-93
WHEN OUR PERFORMANCE IS BAD?
THAT'S ONE THEORY, SURE.

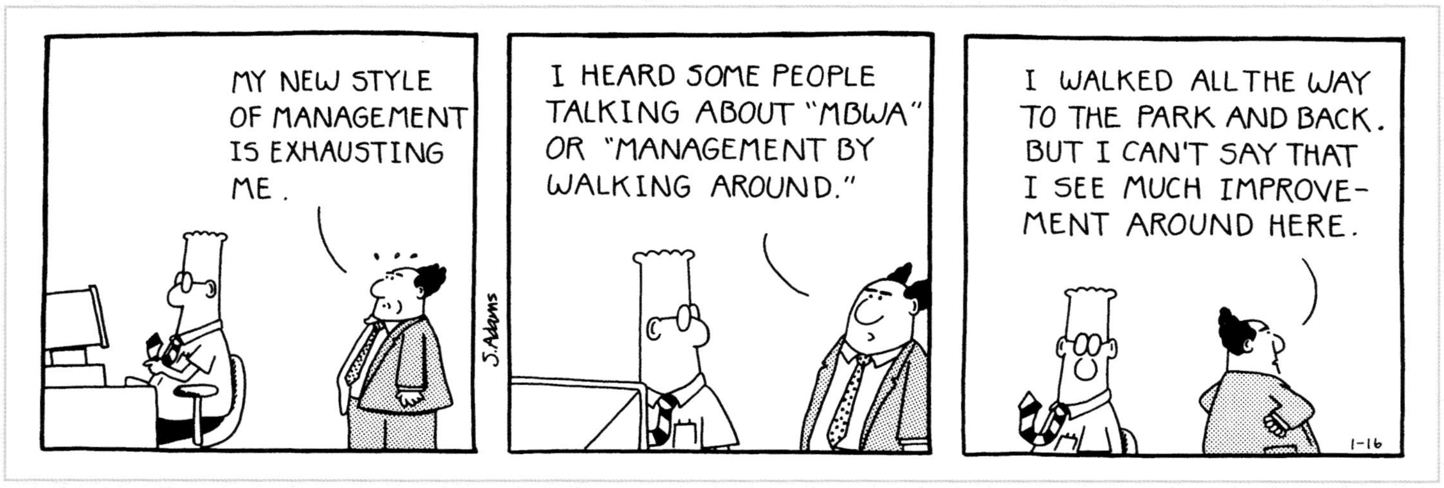
MY NEW STYLE OF MANAGEMENT IS EXHAUSTING ME.
S. Adams
I HEARD SOME PEOPLE TALKING ABOUT "MBWA" OR "MANAGEMENT BY WALKING AROUND."
I WALKED ALL THE WAY TO THE PARK AND BACK. BUT I CAN'T SAY THAT I SEE MUCH IMPROVEMENT AROUND HERE.
1-16

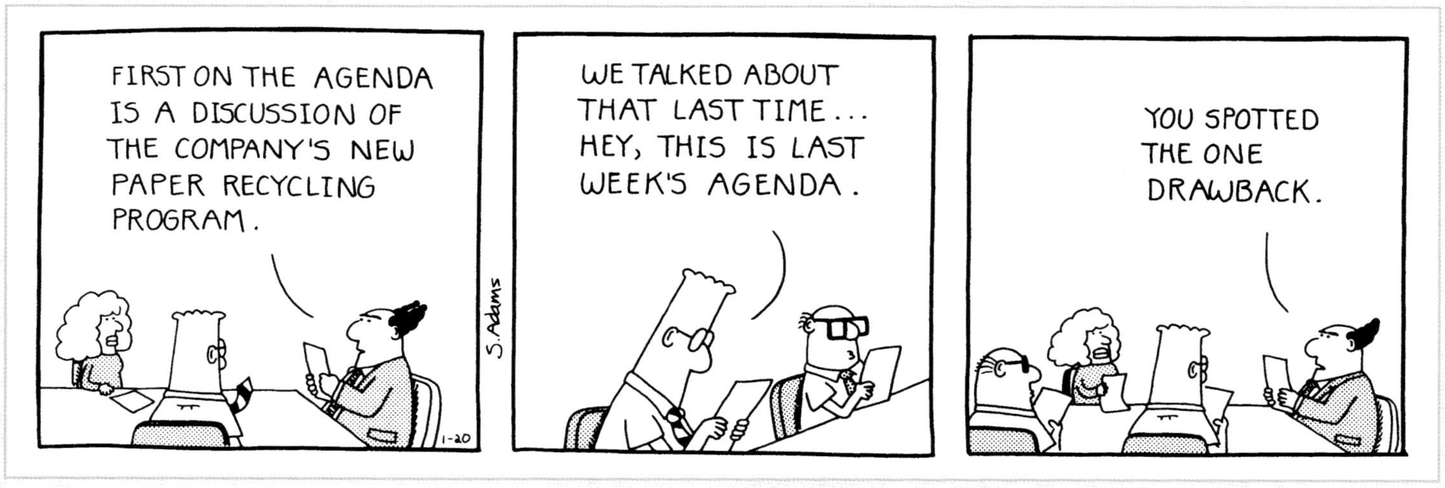
FIRST ON THE AGENDA IS A DISCUSSION OF THE COMPANY'S NEW PAPER RECYCLING PROGRAM.
1-20
S. Adams
WE TALKED ABOUT THAT LAST TIME... HEY, THIS IS LAST WEEK'S AGENDA.
YOU SPOTTED THE ONE DRAWBACK.

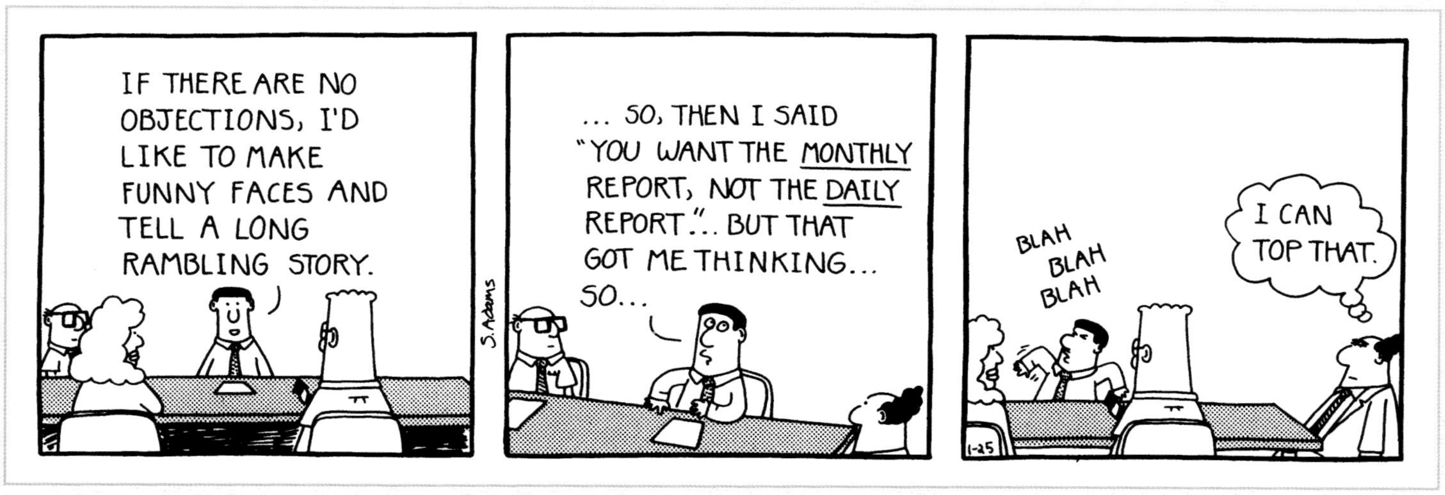
IF THERE ARE NO OBJECTIONS, I'D LIKE TO MAKE FUNNY FACES AND TELL A LONG RAMBLING STORY.
S. Adams
... SO, THEN I SAID "YOU WANT THE MONTHLY REPORT, NOT THE DAILY REPORT."... BUT THAT GOT ME THINKING... SO...
BLAH BLAH BLAH
I CAN TOP THAT.
1-25

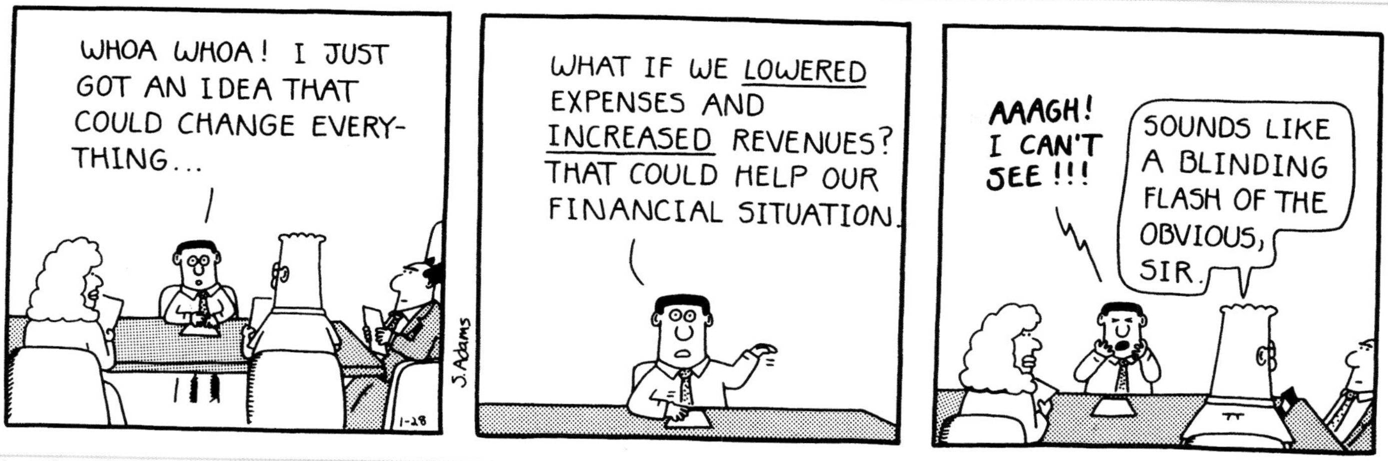
WHOA WHOA! I JUST GOT AN IDEA THAT COULD CHANGE EVERYTHING...
WHAT IF WE LOWERED EXPENSES AND INCREASED REVENUES? THAT COULD HELP OUR FINANCIAL SITUATION.
AAAGH! I CAN'T SEE!!!
SOUNDS LIKE A BLINDING FLASH OF THE OBVIOUS, SIR.

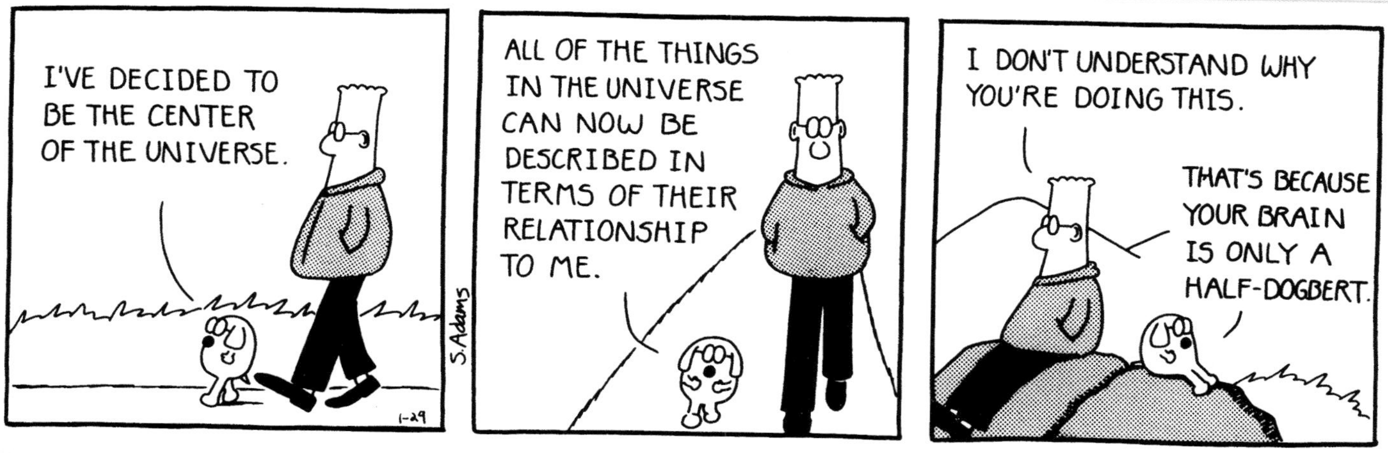
I'VE DECIDED TO BE THE CENTER OF THE UNIVERSE.
ALL OF THE THINGS IN THE UNIVERSE CAN NOW BE DESCRIBED IN TERMS OF THEIR RELATIONSHIP TO ME.
I DON'T UNDERSTAND WHY YOU'RE DOING THIS.
THAT'S BECAUSE YOUR BRAIN IS ONLY A HALF-DOGBERT.

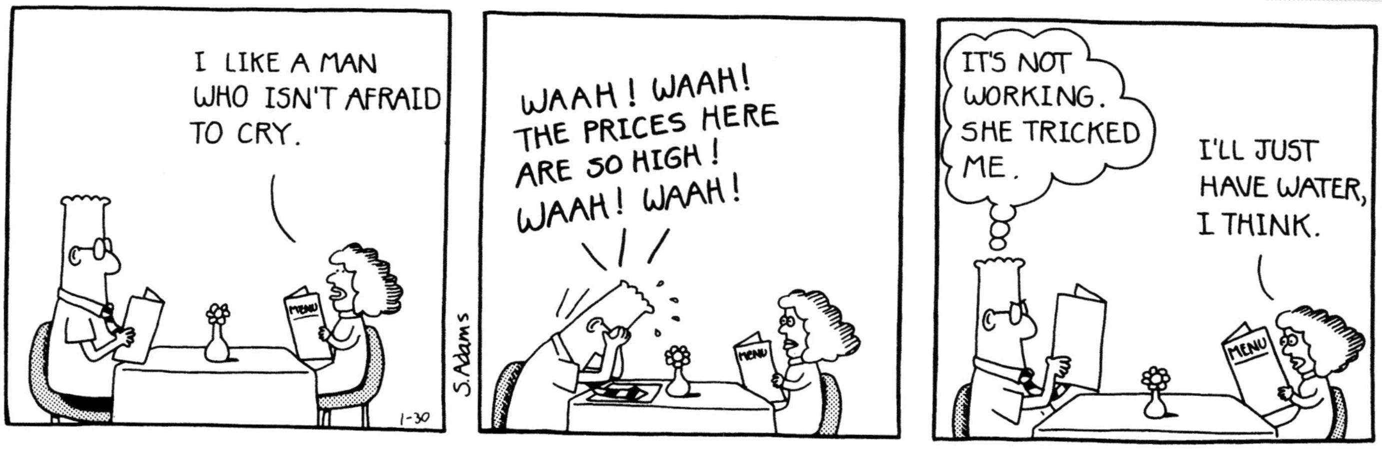
I LIKE A MAN WHO ISN'T AFRAID TO CRY.
WAAH! WAAH! THE PRICES HERE ARE SO HIGH! WAAH! WAAH!
MENU
IT'S NOT WORKING. SHE TRICKED ME.
I'LL JUST HAVE WATER, I THINK.

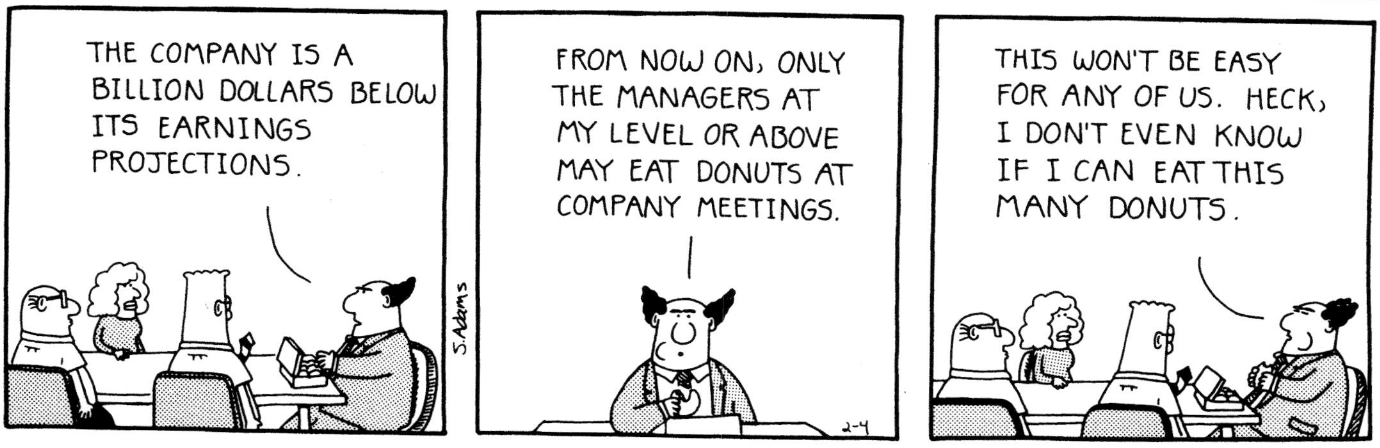
THE COMPANY IS A BILLION DOLLARS BELOW ITS EARNINGS PROJECTIONS.
FROM NOW ON, ONLY THE MANAGERS AT MY LEVEL OR ABOVE MAY EAT DONUTS AT COMPANY MEETINGS.
THIS WON'T BE EASY FOR ANY OF US. HECK, I DON'T EVEN KNOW IF I CAN EAT THIS MANY DONUTS.

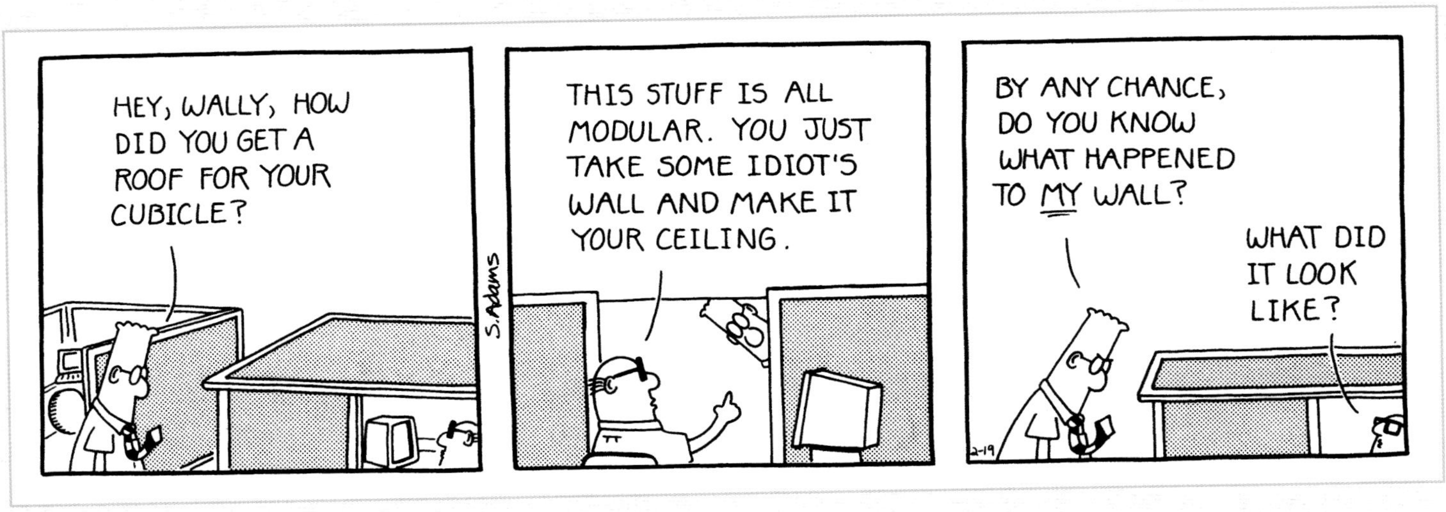
HEY, WALLY, HOW DID YOU GET A ROOF FOR YOUR CUBICLE?
THIS STUFF IS ALL MODULAR. YOU JUST TAKE SOME IDIOT'S WALL AND MAKE IT YOUR CEILING.
BY ANY CHANCE, DO YOU KNOW WHAT HAPPENED TO MY WALL?
WHAT DID IT LOOK LIKE?

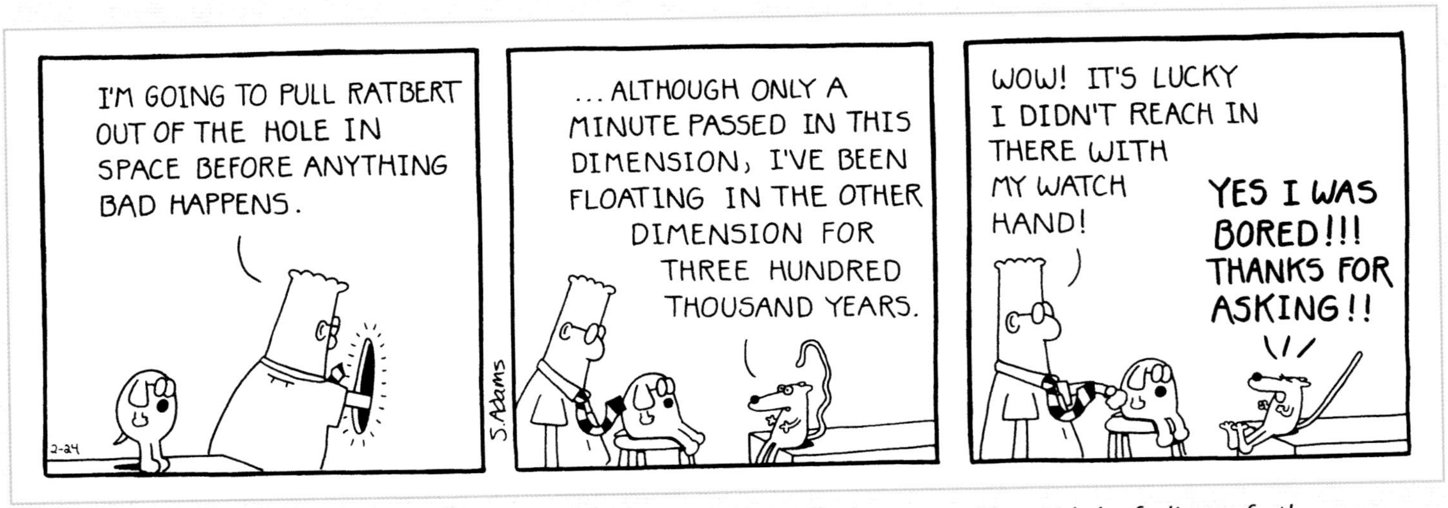
I'M GOING TO PULL RATBERT OUT OF THE HOLE IN SPACE BEFORE ANYTHING BAD HAPPENS.
...ALTHOUGH ONLY A MINUTE PASSED IN THIS DIMENSION, I'VE BEEN FLOATING IN THE OTHER DIMENSION FOR THREE HUNDRED THOUSAND YEARS.
WOW! IT'S LUCKY I DIDN'T REACH IN THERE WITH MY WATCH HAND!
YES I WAS BORED!!! THANKS FOR ASKING!!

This is one of my personal favorites. I always find it funny when people disregard the feelings of others.

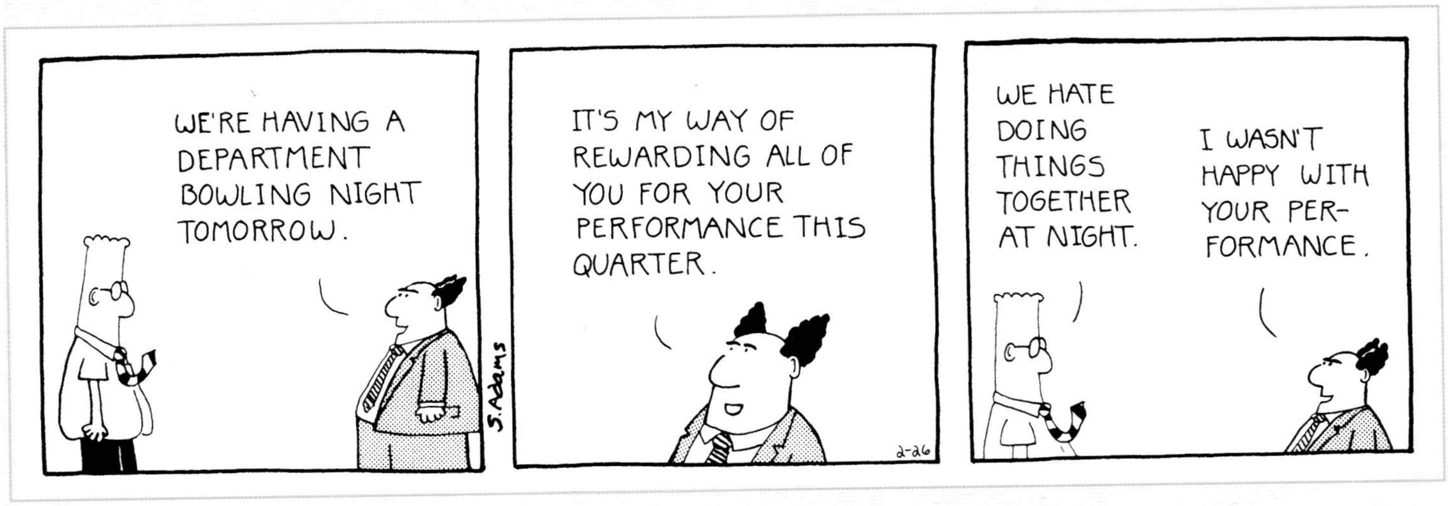
WE'RE HAVING A DEPARTMENT BOWLING NIGHT TOMORROW.
IT'S MY WAY OF REWARDING ALL OF YOU FOR YOUR PERFORMANCE THIS QUARTER.
WE HATE DOING THINGS TOGETHER AT NIGHT.
I WASN'T HAPPY WITH YOUR PER-FORMANCE.

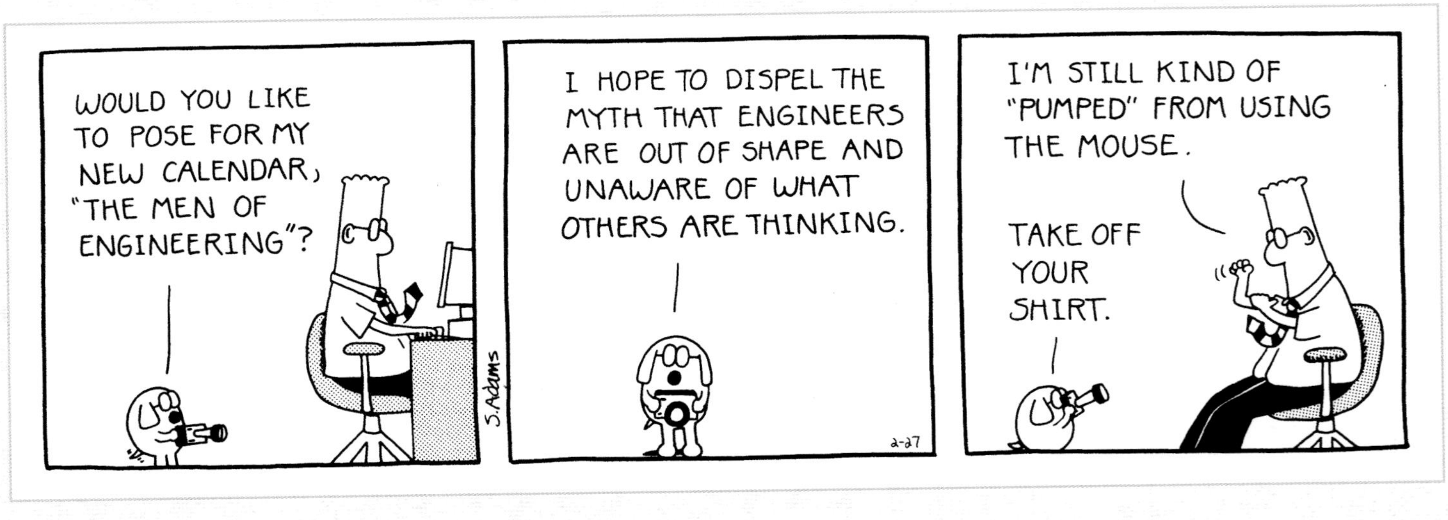
WOULD YOU LIKE TO POSE FOR MY NEW CALENDAR, "THE MEN OF ENGINEERING"?
I HOPE TO DISPEL THE MYTH THAT ENGINEERS ARE OUT OF SHAPE AND UNAWARE OF WHAT OTHERS ARE THINKING.
I'M STILL KIND OF "PUMPED" FROM USING THE MOUSE.
TAKE OFF YOUR SHIRT.

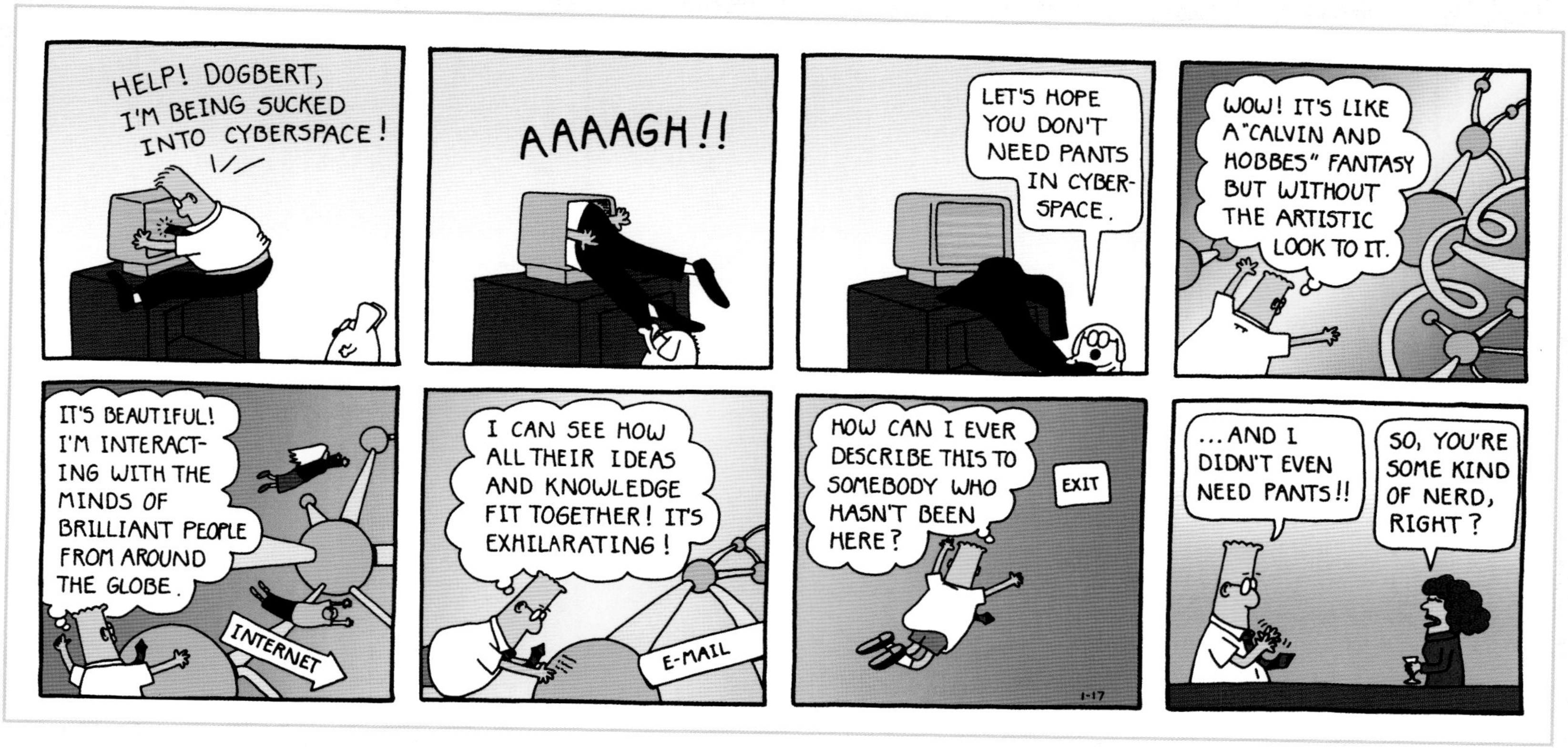
HELP! DOGBERT, I'M BEING SUCKED INTO CYBERSPACE!
AAAAGH!!
LET'S HOPE YOU DON'T NEED PANTS IN CYBER-SPACE.
WOW! IT'S LIKE A "CALVIN AND HOBBES" FANTASY BUT WITHOUT THE ARTISTIC LOOK TO IT.
IT'S BEAUTIFUL! I'M INTERACT-ING WITH THE MINDS OF BRILLIANT PEOPLE FROM AROUND THE GLOBE.
INTERNET
I CAN SEE HOW ALL THEIR IDEAS AND KNOWLEDGE FIT TOGETHER! IT'S EXHILARATING!
E-MAIL
HOW CAN I EVER DESCRIBE THIS TO SOMEBODY WHO HASN'T BEEN HERE?
EXIT
...AND I DIDN'T EVEN NEED PANTS!!
SO, YOU'RE SOME KIND OF NERD, RIGHT?

This comic was primarily written to highlight the inclusion of my e-mail address. Sunday comics readers are often a different group from the daily readers.

Why does this comic seem so dated? It's because everyone would be using cell phones during a break now. Mingling is virtually obsolete.

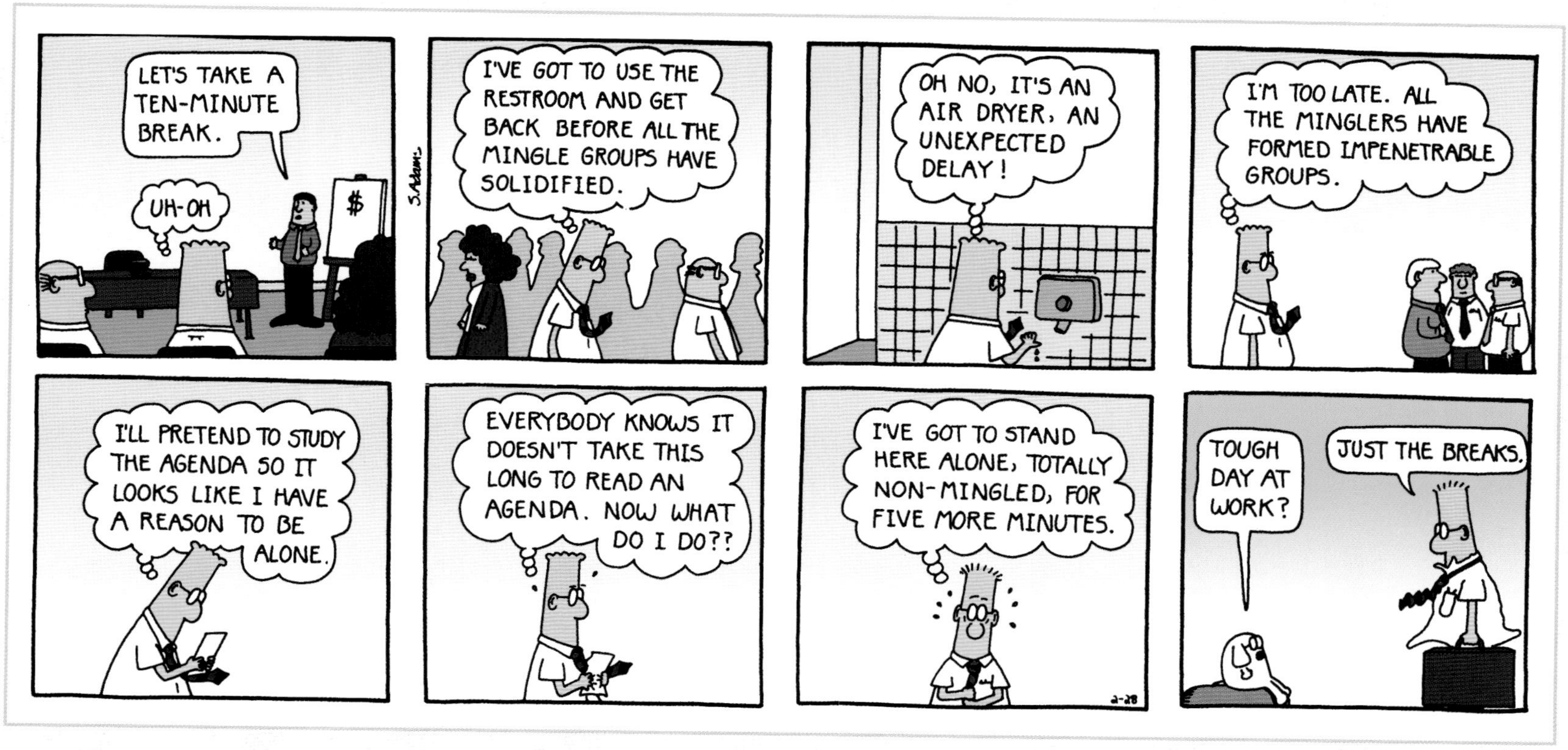
LET'S TAKE A TEN-MINUTE BREAK.
UH-OH
$
I'VE GOT TO USE THE RESTROOM AND GET BACK BEFORE ALL THE MINGLE GROUPS HAVE SOLIDIFIED.
OH NO, IT'S AN AIR DRYER, AN UNEXPECTED DELAY!
I'M TOO LATE. ALL THE MINGLERS HAVE FORMED IMPENETRABLE GROUPS.
I'LL PRETEND TO STUDY THE AGENDA SO IT LOOKS LIKE I HAVE A REASON TO BE ALONE.
EVERYBODY KNOWS IT DOESN'T TAKE THIS LONG TO READ AN AGENDA. NOW WHAT DO I DO??
I'VE GOT TO STAND HERE ALONE, TOTALLY NON-MINGLED, FOR FIVE MORE MINUTES.
TOUGH DAY AT WORK?
JUST THE BREAKS.

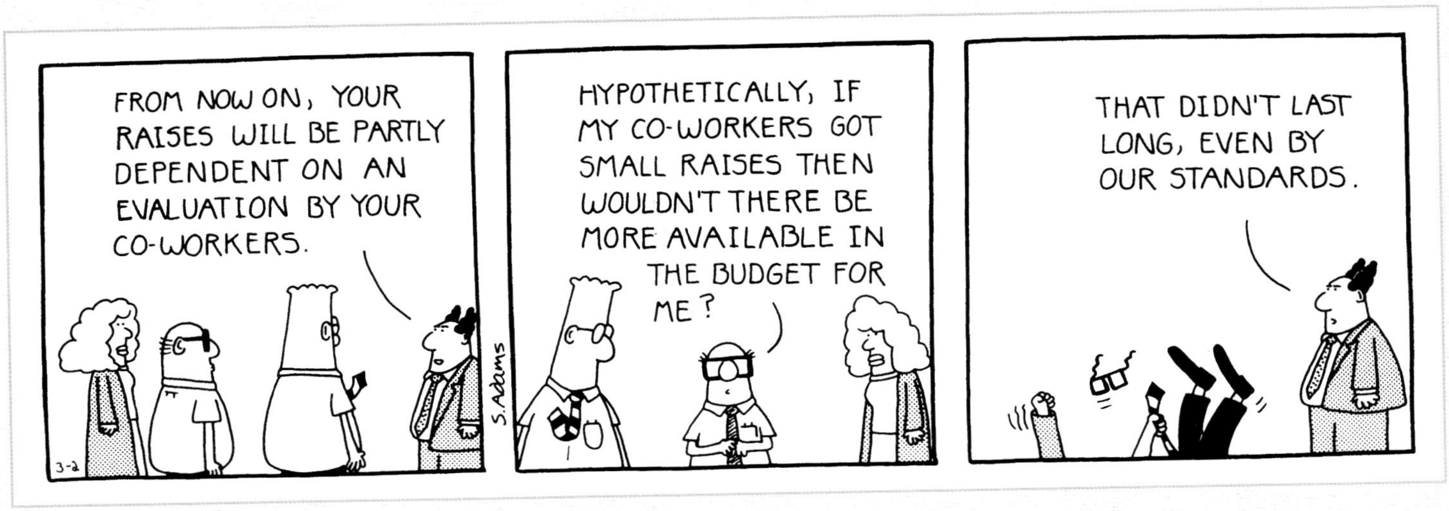
FROM NOW ON, YOUR RAISES WILL BE PARTLY DEPENDENT ON AN EVALUATION BY YOUR CO-WORKERS.
S. Adams
3-2
HYPOTHETICALLY, IF MY CO-WORKERS GOT SMALL RAISES THEN WOULDN'T THERE BE MORE AVAILABLE IN THE BUDGET FOR ME?
THAT DIDN'T LAST LONG, EVEN BY OUR STANDARDS.

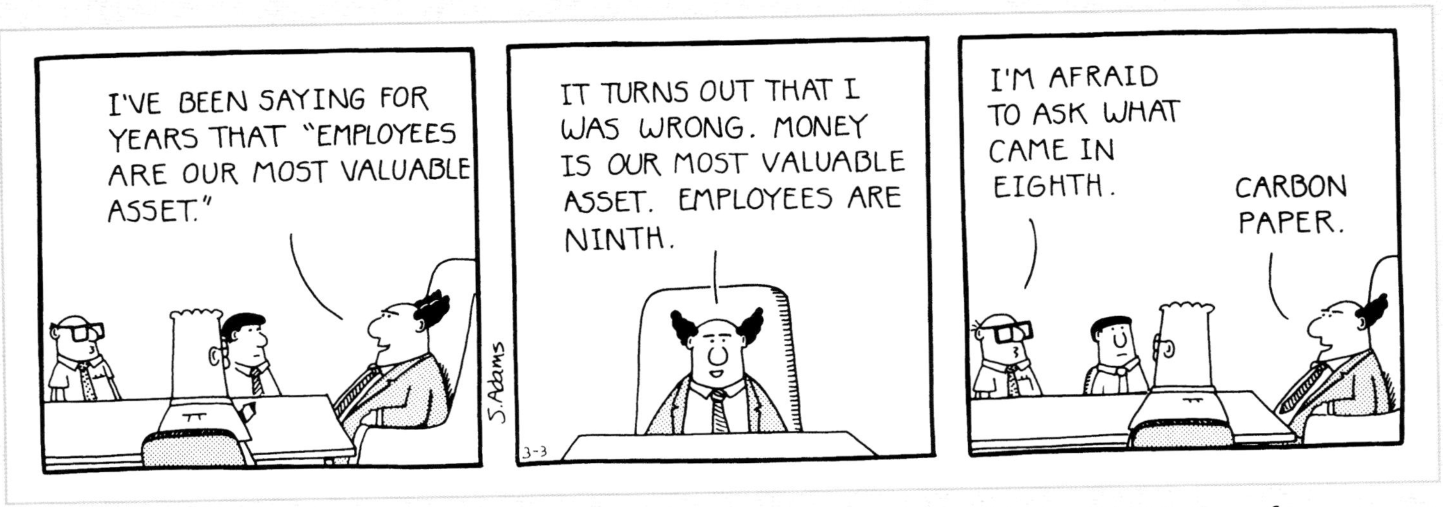
I'VE BEEN SAYING FOR YEARS THAT "EMPLOYEES ARE OUR MOST VALUABLE ASSET."
S. Adams
3-3
IT TURNS OUT THAT I WAS WRONG. MONEY IS OUR MOST VALUABLE ASSET. EMPLOYEES ARE NINTH.
I'M AFRAID TO ASK WHAT CAME IN EIGHTH.
CARBON PAPER.

I first wrote everything but the boss's last line, hoping I would come up with something that was funny as the eighth-best asset. "Stapler" wouldn't be funny. Neither would most other office supplies. I recall taking a break, petting my cat, and staring out the window. The words "carbon paper" floated into my head, and I realized that was the answer.

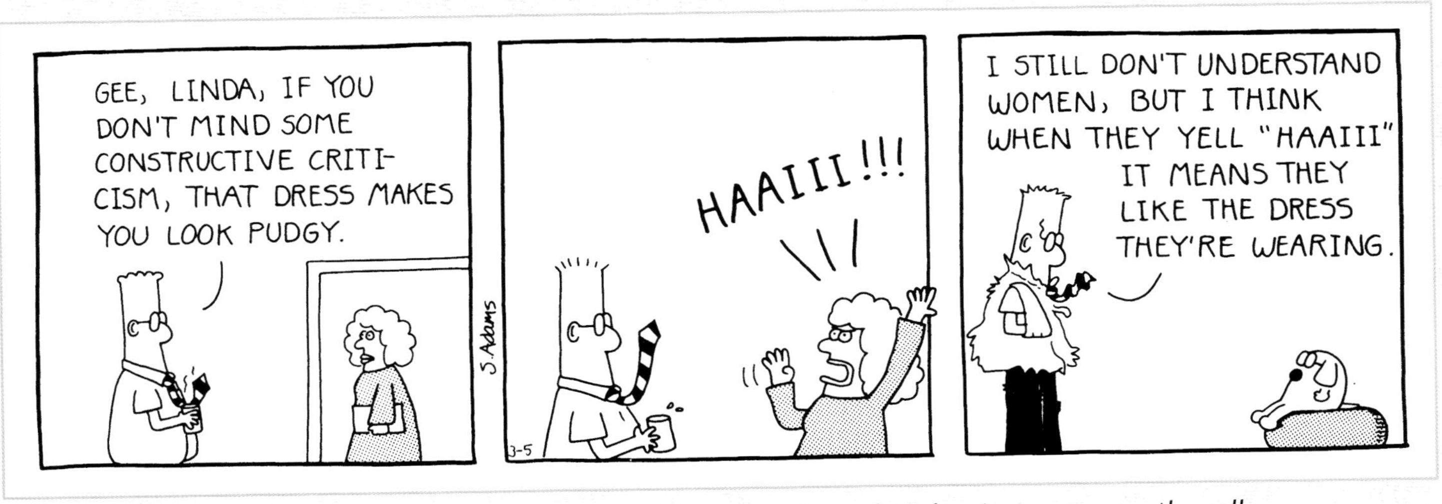
GEE, LINDA, IF YOU DON'T MIND SOME CONSTRUCTIVE CRITI-CISM, THAT DRESS MAKES YOU LOOK PUDGY.
S. Adams
3-5
HAAIII!!!
I STILL DON'T UNDERSTAND WOMEN, BUT I THINK WHEN THEY YELL "HAAIII" IT MEANS THEY LIKE THE DRESS THEY'RE WEARING.

This is before Alice was a regular character. I'm not good at drawing women, so they all sort of looked alike. Eventually, all the generic women with fluffy hair congealed into Alice, who was based on a co-worker of mine at Pacific Bell.

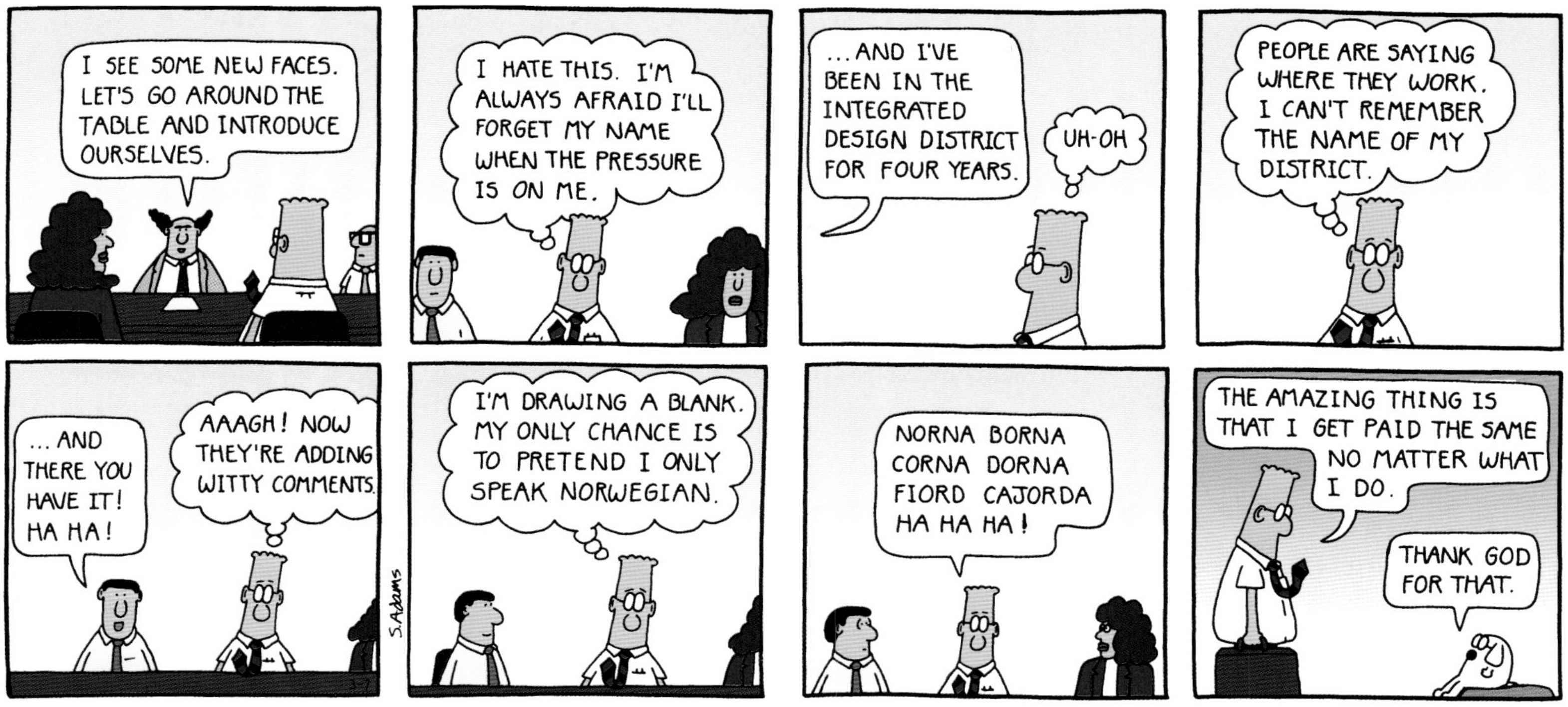
I SEE SOME NEW FACES. LET'S GO AROUND THE TABLE AND INTRODUCE OURSELVES.
I HATE THIS. I'M ALWAYS AFRAID I'LL FORGET MY NAME WHEN THE PRESSURE IS ON ME.
...AND I'VE BEEN IN THE INTEGRATED DESIGN DISTRICT FOR FOUR YEARS.
UH-OH
PEOPLE ARE SAYING WHERE THEY WORK. I CAN'T REMEMBER THE NAME OF MY DISTRICT.
...AND THERE YOU HAVE IT! HA HA!
AAAGH! NOW THEY'RE ADDING WITTY COMMENTS.
S. Adams
I'M DRAWING A BLANK. MY ONLY CHANCE IS TO PRETEND I ONLY SPEAK NORWEGIAN.
NORNA BORNA CORNA DORNA FIORD CAJORDA HA HA HA!
THE AMAZING THING IS THAT I GET PAID THE SAME NO MATTER WHAT I DO.
THANK GOD FOR THAT.

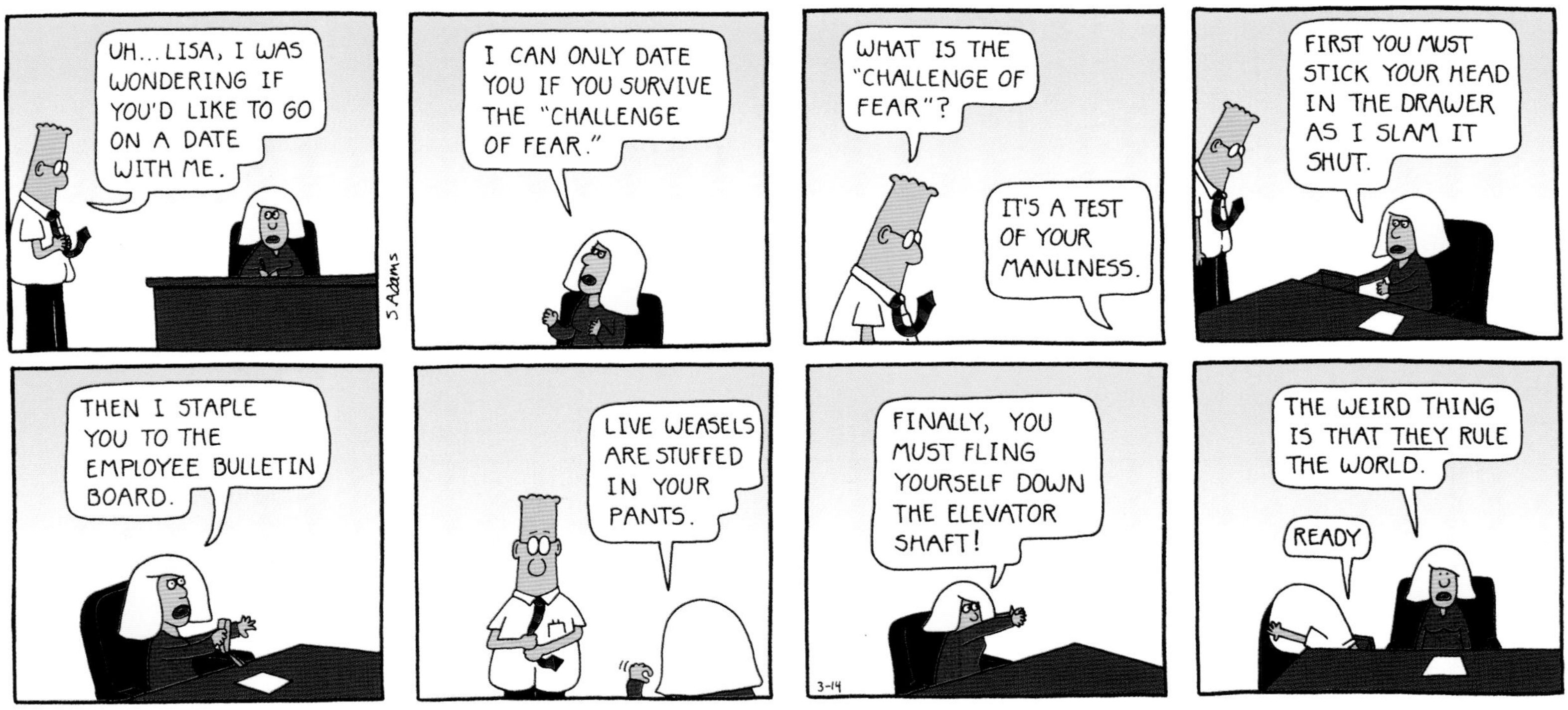
UH... LISA, I WAS WONDERING IF YOU'D LIKE TO GO ON A DATE WITH ME.
S. Adams
I CAN ONLY DATE YOU IF YOU SURVIVE THE "CHALLENGE OF FEAR."
WHAT IS THE "CHALLENGE OF FEAR"?
IT'S A TEST OF YOUR MANLINESS.
FIRST YOU MUST STICK YOUR HEAD IN THE DRAWER AS I SLAM IT SHUT.
THEN I STAPLE YOU TO THE EMPLOYEE BULLETIN BOARD.
LIVE WEASELS ARE STUFFED IN YOUR PANTS.
FINALLY, YOU MUST FLING YOURSELF DOWN THE ELEVATOR SHAFT!
3-14
THE WEIRD THING IS THAT THEY RULE THE WORLD.
READY

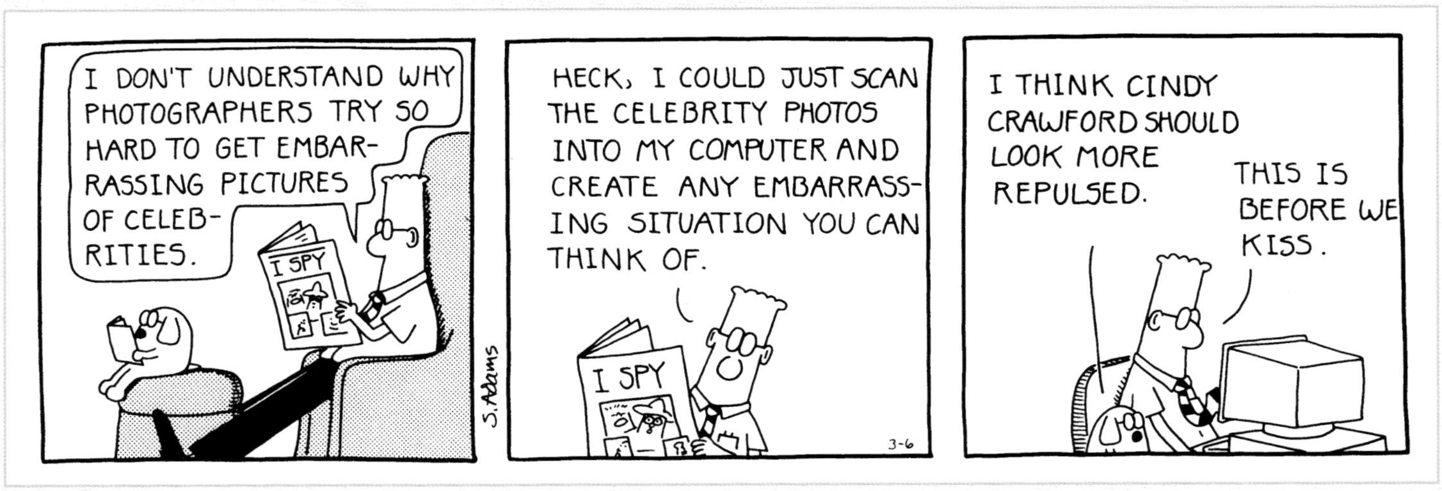
I DON'T UNDERSTAND WHY PHOTOGRAPHERS TRY SO HARD TO GET EMBARRASSING PICTURES OF CELEBRITIES.
I SPY
HECK, I COULD JUST SCAN THE CELEBRITY PHOTOS INTO MY COMPUTER AND CREATE ANY EMBARRASSING SITUATION YOU CAN THINK OF.
I SPY
I THINK CINDY CRAWFORD SHOULD LOOK MORE REPULSED.
THIS IS BEFORE WE KISS.

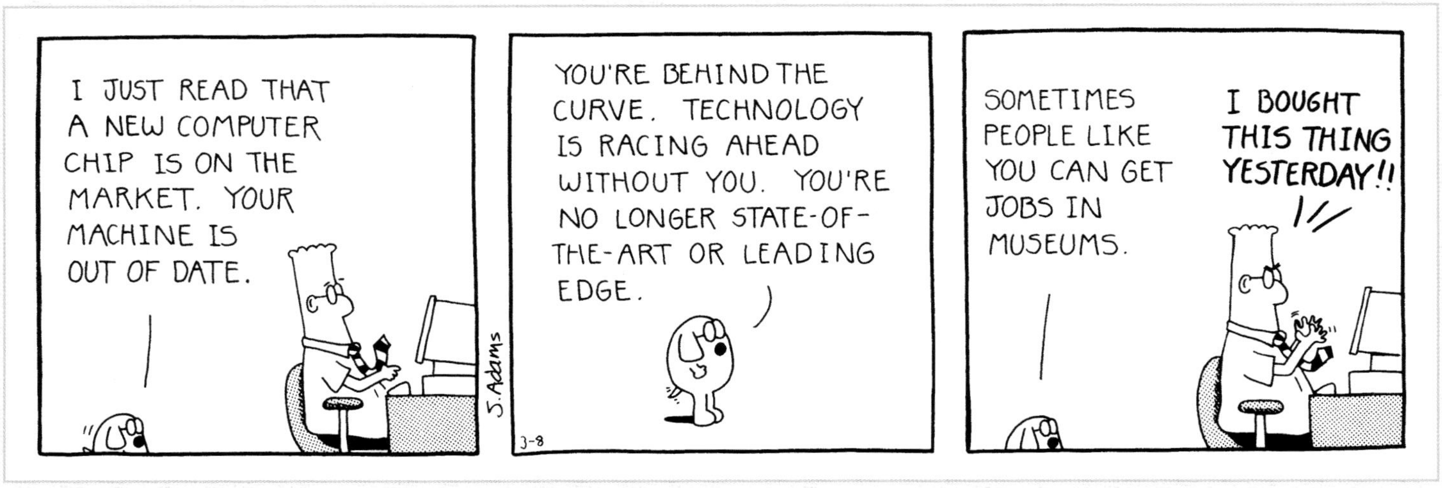
I JUST READ THAT A NEW COMPUTER CHIP IS ON THE MARKET. YOUR MACHINE IS OUT OF DATE.
YOU'RE BEHIND THE CURVE. TECHNOLOGY IS RACING AHEAD WITHOUT YOU. YOU'RE NO LONGER STATE-OF-THE-ART OR LEADING EDGE.
SOMETIMES PEOPLE LIKE YOU CAN GET JOBS IN MUSEUMS.
I BOUGHT THIS THING YESTERDAY!!

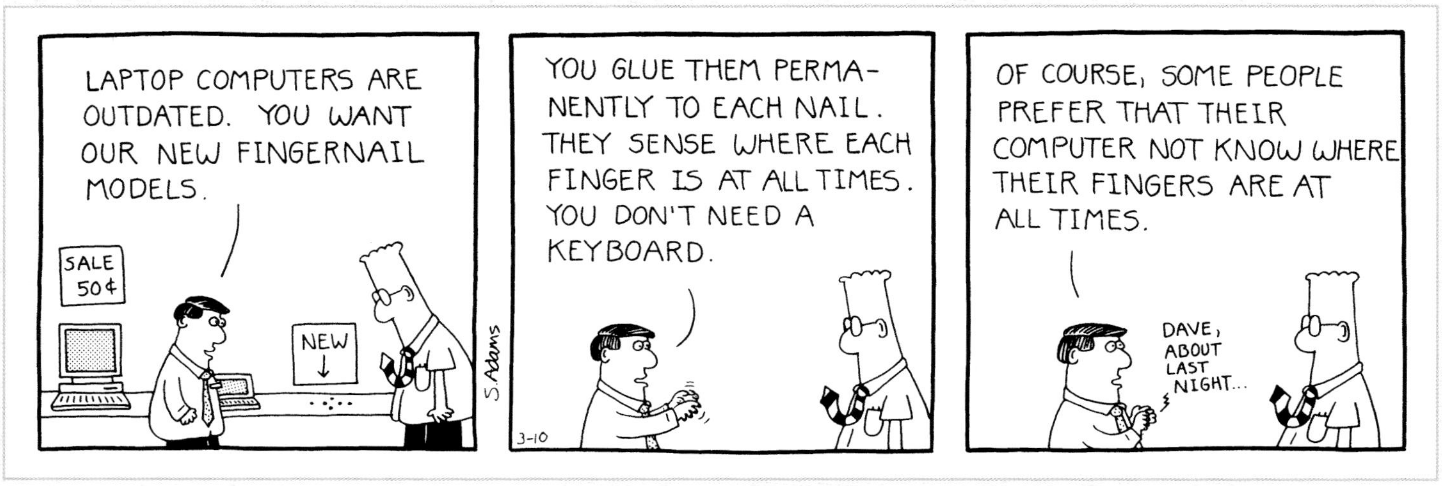
LAPTOP COMPUTERS ARE OUTDATED. YOU WANT OUR NEW FINGERNAIL MODELS.
SALE 50¢
NEW ↓
YOU GLUE THEM PERMANENTLY TO EACH NAIL. THEY SENSE WHERE EACH FINGER IS AT ALL TIMES. YOU DON'T NEED A KEYBOARD.
OF COURSE, SOME PEOPLE PREFER THAT THEIR COMPUTER NOT KNOW WHERE THEIR FINGERS ARE AT ALL TIMES.
DAVE, ABOUT LAST NIGHT...

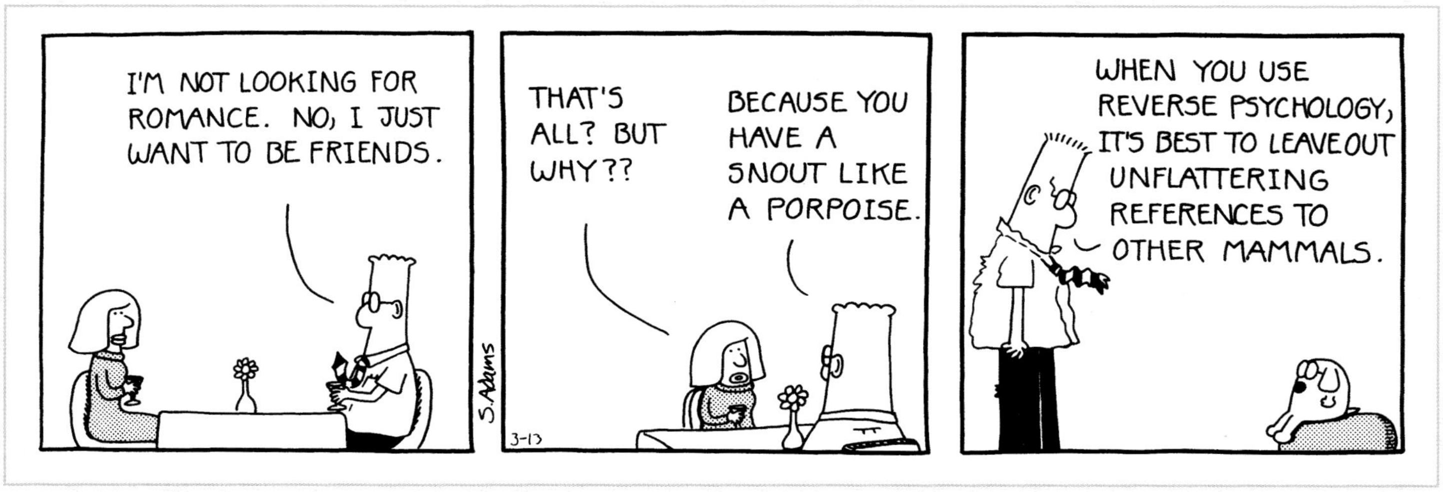
I'M NOT LOOKING FOR ROMANCE. NO, I JUST WANT TO BE FRIENDS.
THAT'S ALL? BUT WHY??
BECAUSE YOU HAVE A SNOUT LIKE A PORPOISE.
WHEN YOU USE REVERSE PSYCHOLOGY, IT'S BEST TO LEAVE OUT UNFLATTERING REFERENCES TO OTHER MAMMALS.

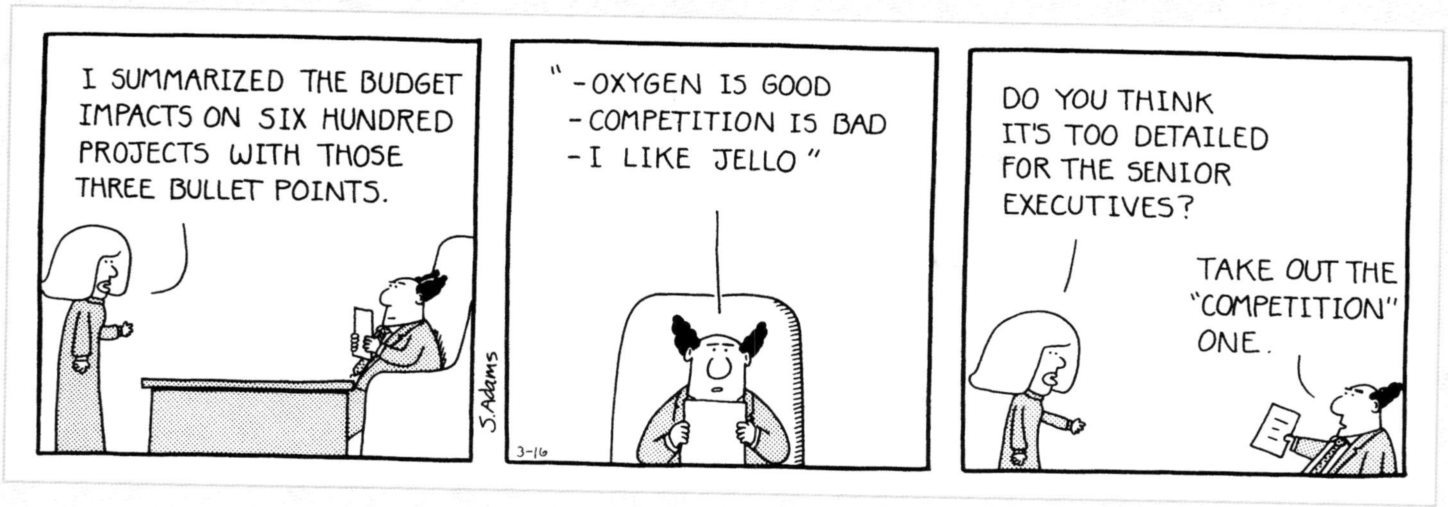
I SUMMARIZED THE BUDGET IMPACTS ON SIX HUNDRED PROJECTS WITH THOSE THREE BULLET POINTS.
S. Adams
3-16
" -OXYGEN IS GOOD -COMPETITION IS BAD -I LIKE JELLO "
DO YOU THINK IT'S TOO DETAILED FOR THE SENIOR EXECUTIVES?
TAKE OUT THE "COMPETITION" ONE.

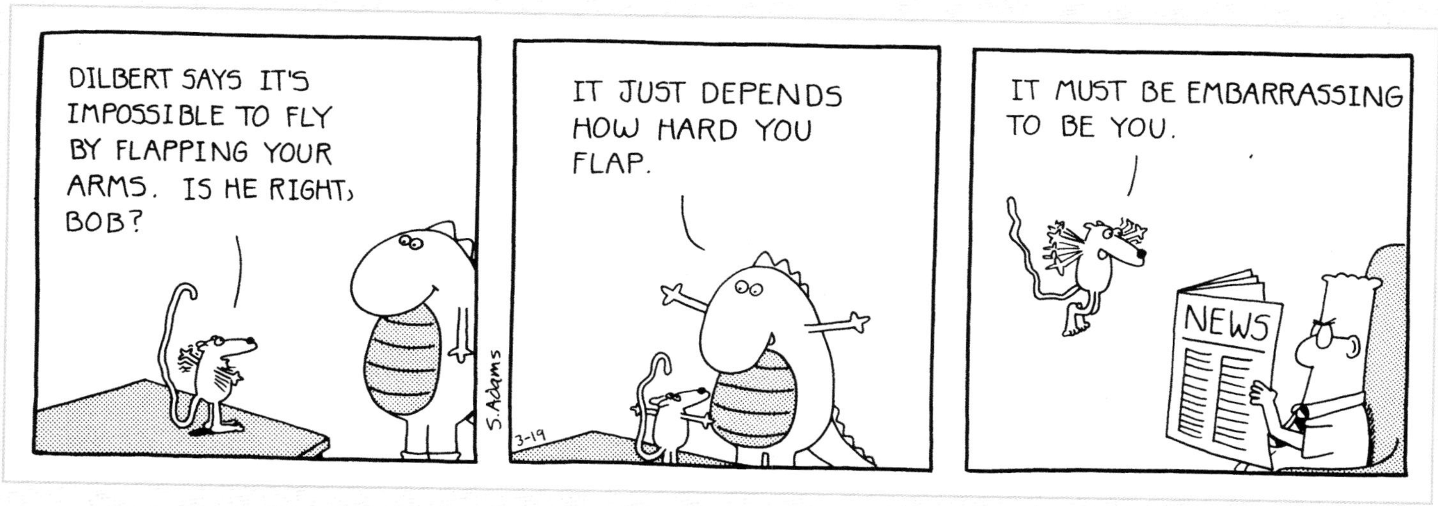
DILBERT SAYS IT'S IMPOSSIBLE TO FLY BY FLAPPING YOUR ARMS. IS HE RIGHT, BOB?
S. Adams
3-19
IT JUST DEPENDS HOW HARD YOU FLAP.
IT MUST BE EMBARRASSING TO BE YOU.
NEWS

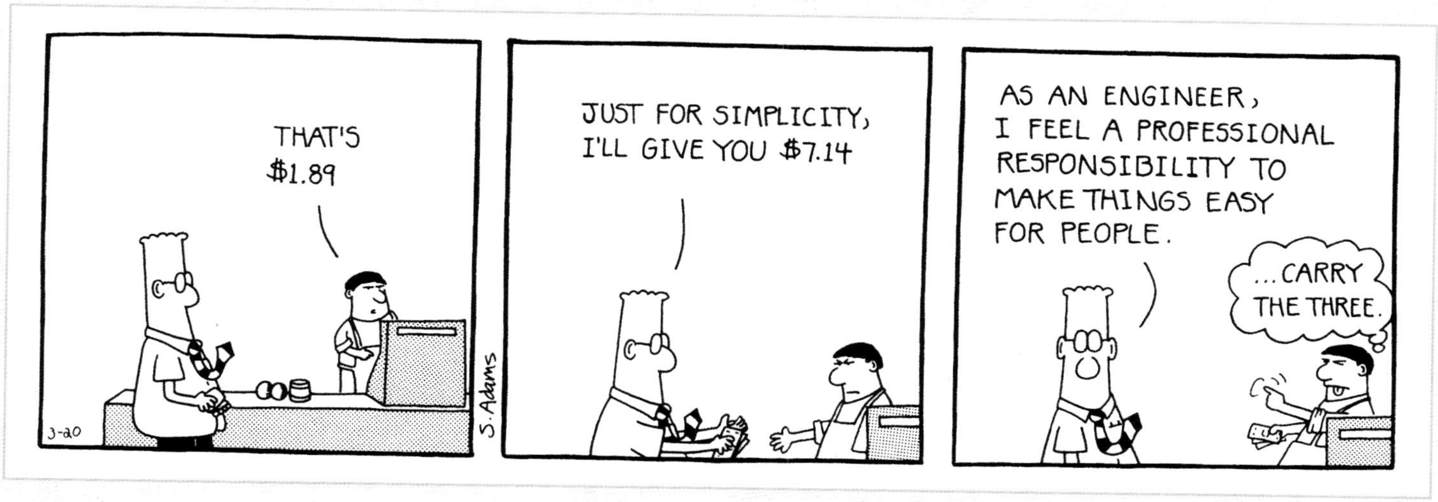
THAT'S $1.89
3-20
S. Adams
JUST FOR SIMPLICITY, I'LL GIVE YOU $7.14
AS AN ENGINEER, I FEEL A PROFESSIONAL RESPONSIBILITY TO MAKE THINGS EASY FOR PEOPLE.
...CARRY THE THREE.

"Sand-blasting a soup cracker" is one of those phrases that I am proud to have written.

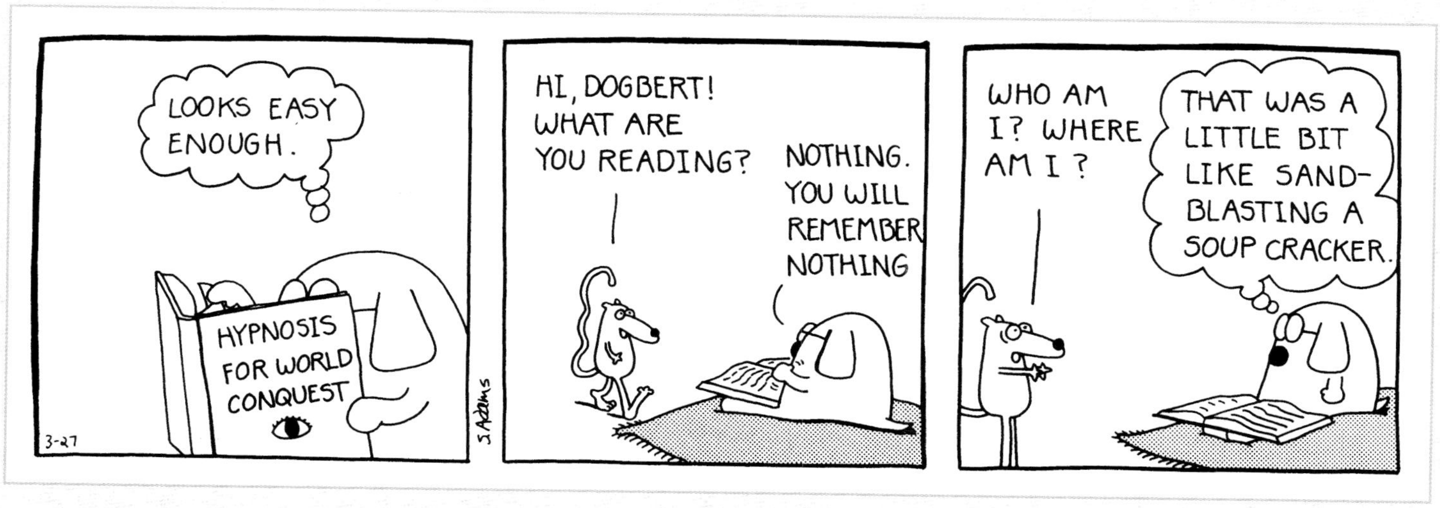
LOOKS EASY ENOUGH.
HYPNOSIS FOR WORLD CONQUEST
3-27
S. Adams
HI, DOGBERT! WHAT ARE YOU READING?
NOTHING. YOU WILL REMEMBER NOTHING
WHO AM I? WHERE AM I?
THAT WAS A LITTLE BIT LIKE SAND-BLASTING A SOUP CRACKER.

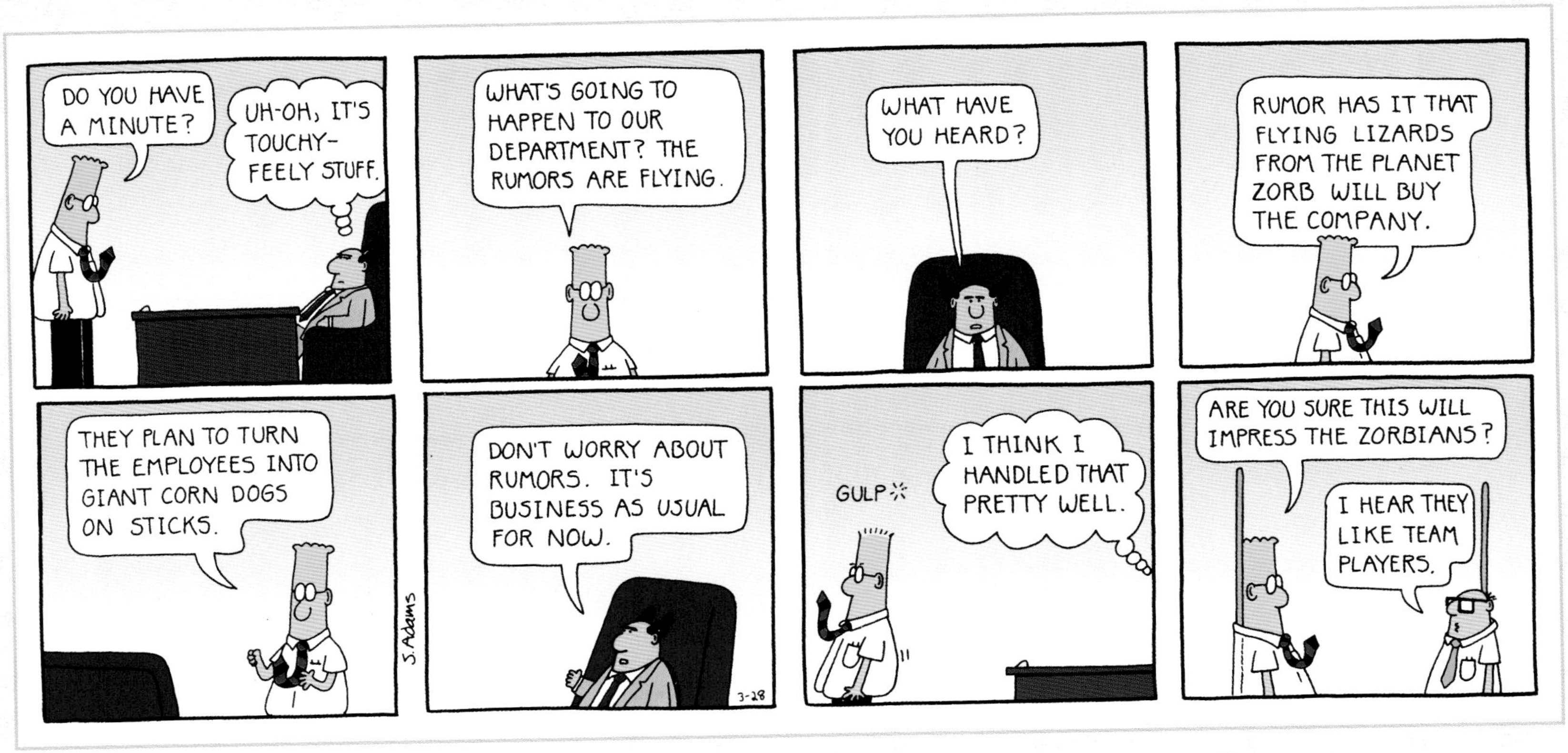
DO YOU HAVE A MINUTE?
UH-OH, IT'S TOUCHY-FEELY STUFF.
WHAT'S GOING TO HAPPEN TO OUR DEPARTMENT? THE RUMORS ARE FLYING.
WHAT HAVE YOU HEARD?
RUMOR HAS IT THAT FLYING LIZARDS FROM THE PLANET ZORB WILL BUY THE COMPANY.
THEY PLAN TO TURN THE EMPLOYEES INTO GIANT CORN DOGS ON STICKS.
S. Adams
DON'T WORRY ABOUT RUMORS. IT'S BUSINESS AS USUAL FOR NOW.
3-28
GULP
I THINK I HANDLED THAT PRETTY WELL.
ARE YOU SURE THIS WILL IMPRESS THE ZORBIANS?
I HEAR THEY LIKE TEAM PLAYERS.

Guess how the sticks were drawn in the first draft that didn't make it past my editors.

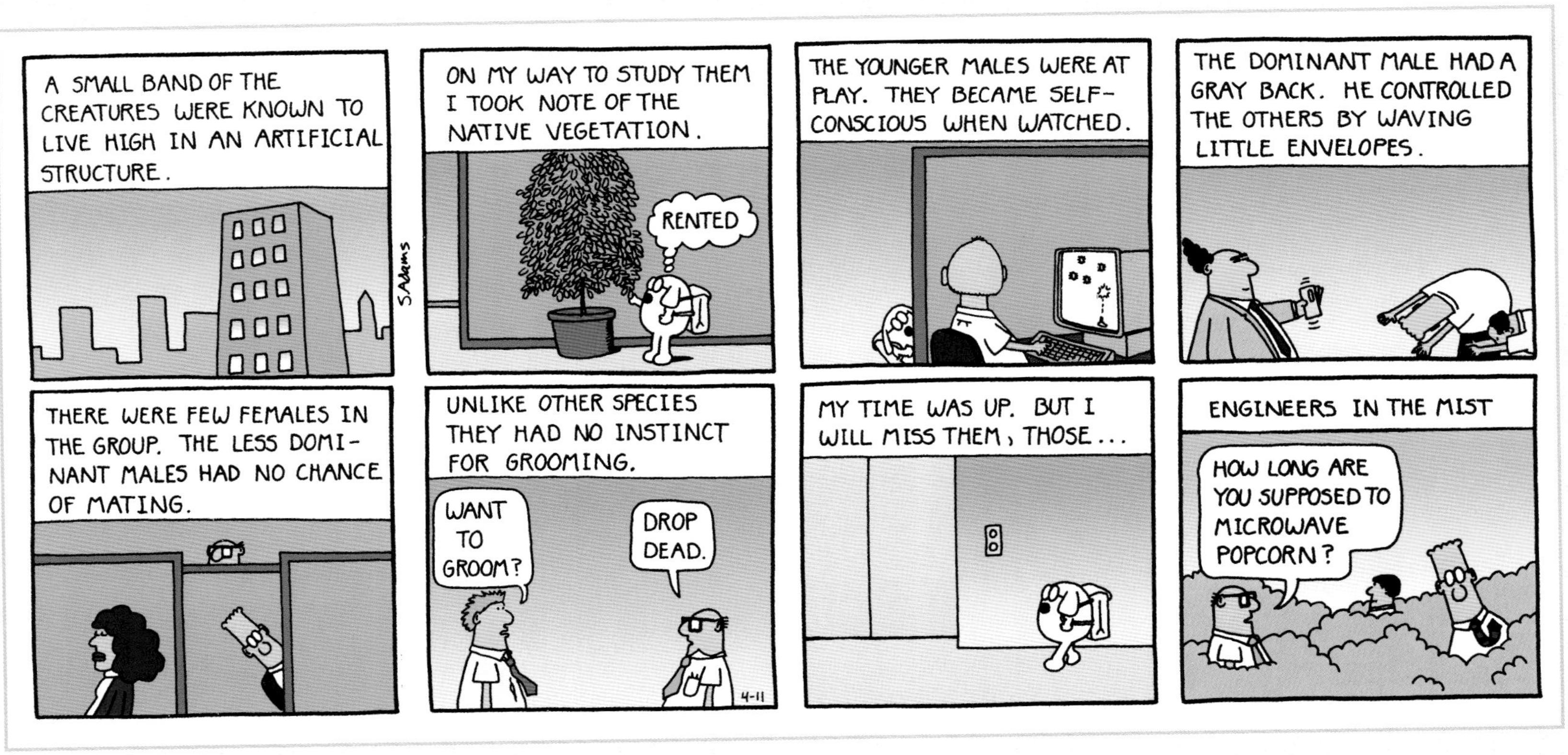
A SMALL BAND OF THE CREATURES WERE KNOWN TO LIVE HIGH IN AN ARTIFICIAL STRUCTURE.
S. Adams
ON MY WAY TO STUDY THEM I TOOK NOTE OF THE NATIVE VEGETATION.
RENTED
THE YOUNGER MALES WERE AT PLAY. THEY BECAME SELF-CONSCIOUS WHEN WATCHED.
THE DOMINANT MALE HAD A GRAY BACK. HE CONTROLLED THE OTHERS BY WAVING LITTLE ENVELOPES.
THERE WERE FEW FEMALES IN THE GROUP. THE LESS DOMINANT MALES HAD NO CHANCE OF MATING.
UNLIKE OTHER SPECIES THEY HAD NO INSTINCT FOR GROOMING.
WANT TO GROOM?
DROP DEAD.
4-11
MY TIME WAS UP. BUT I WILL MISS THEM, THOSE . . .
ENGINEERS IN THE MIST
HOW LONG ARE YOU SUPPOSED TO MICROWAVE POPCORN?

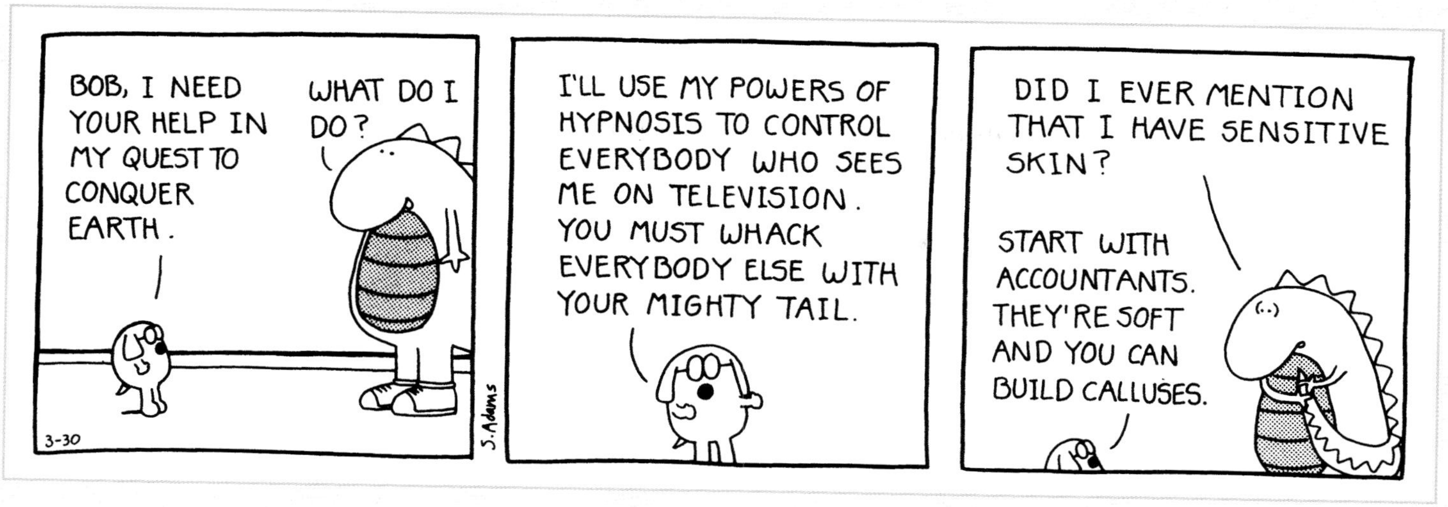
BOB, I NEED YOUR HELP IN MY QUEST TO CONQUER EARTH.
WHAT DO I DO?
I'LL USE MY POWERS OF HYPNOSIS TO CONTROL EVERYBODY WHO SEES ME ON TELEVISION. YOU MUST WHACK EVERYBODY ELSE WITH YOUR MIGHTY TAIL.
DID I EVER MENTION THAT I HAVE SENSITIVE SKIN?
START WITH ACCOUNTANTS. THEY'RE SOFT AND YOU CAN BUILD CALLUSES.

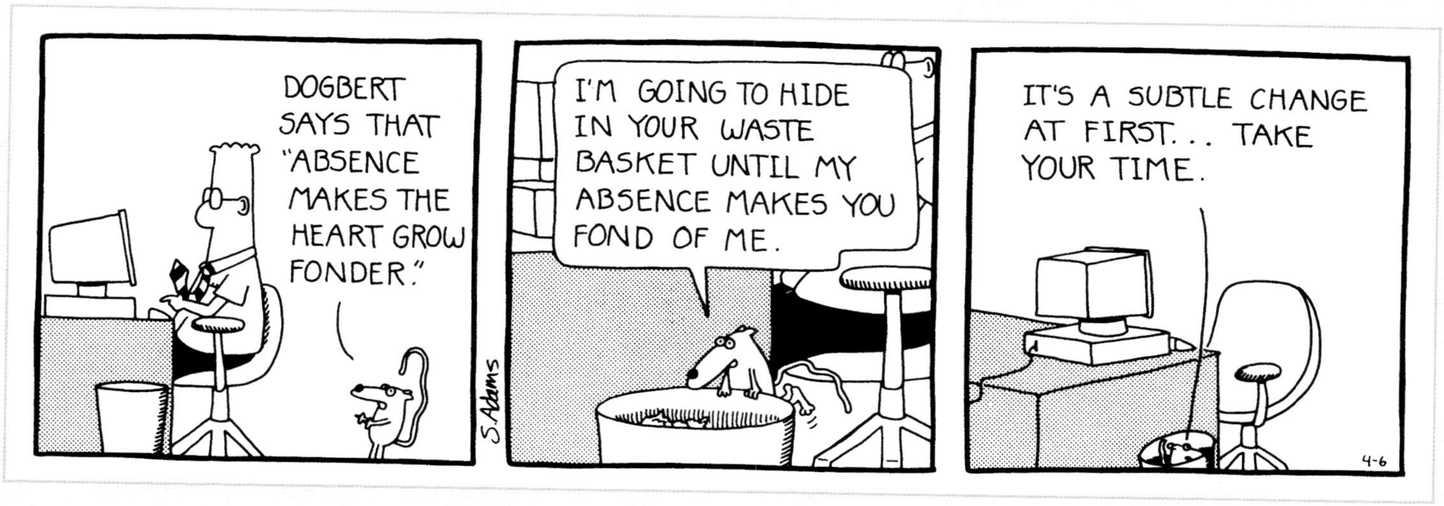
DOGBERT SAYS THAT "ABSENCE MAKES THE HEART GROW FONDER."
I'M GOING TO HIDE IN YOUR WASTE BASKET UNTIL MY ABSENCE MAKES YOU FOND OF ME.
IT'S A SUBTLE CHANGE AT FIRST... TAKE YOUR TIME.

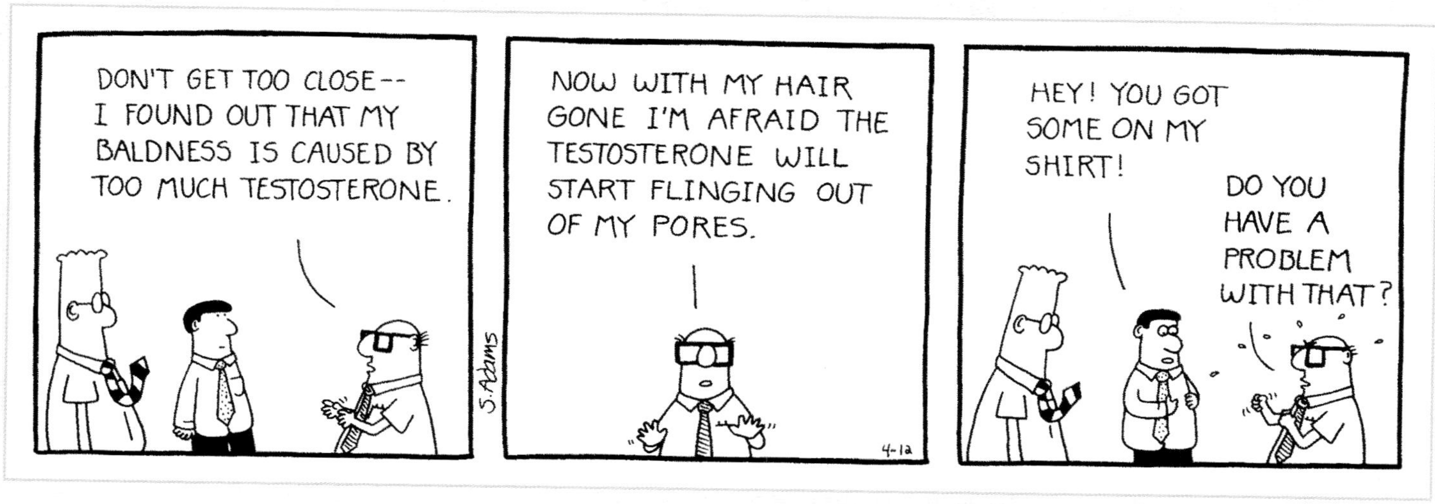
DON'T GET TOO CLOSE-- I FOUND OUT THAT MY BALDNESS IS CAUSED BY TOO MUCH TESTOSTERONE.
NOW WITH MY HAIR GONE I'M AFRAID THE TESTOSTERONE WILL START FLINGING OUT OF MY PORES.
HEY! YOU GOT SOME ON MY SHIRT!
DO YOU HAVE A PROBLEM WITH THAT?

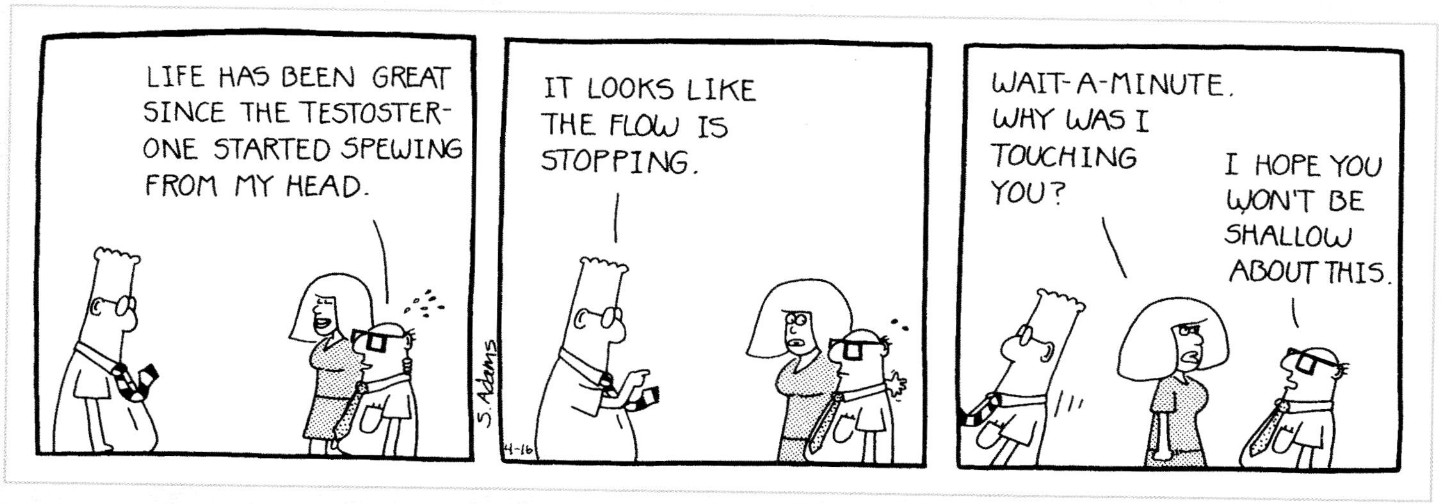
LIFE HAS BEEN GREAT SINCE THE TESTOSTERONE STARTED SPEWING FROM MY HEAD.
IT LOOKS LIKE THE FLOW IS STOPPING.
WAIT-A-MINUTE. WHY WAS I TOUCHING YOU?
I HOPE YOU WON'T BE SHALLOW ABOUT THIS.

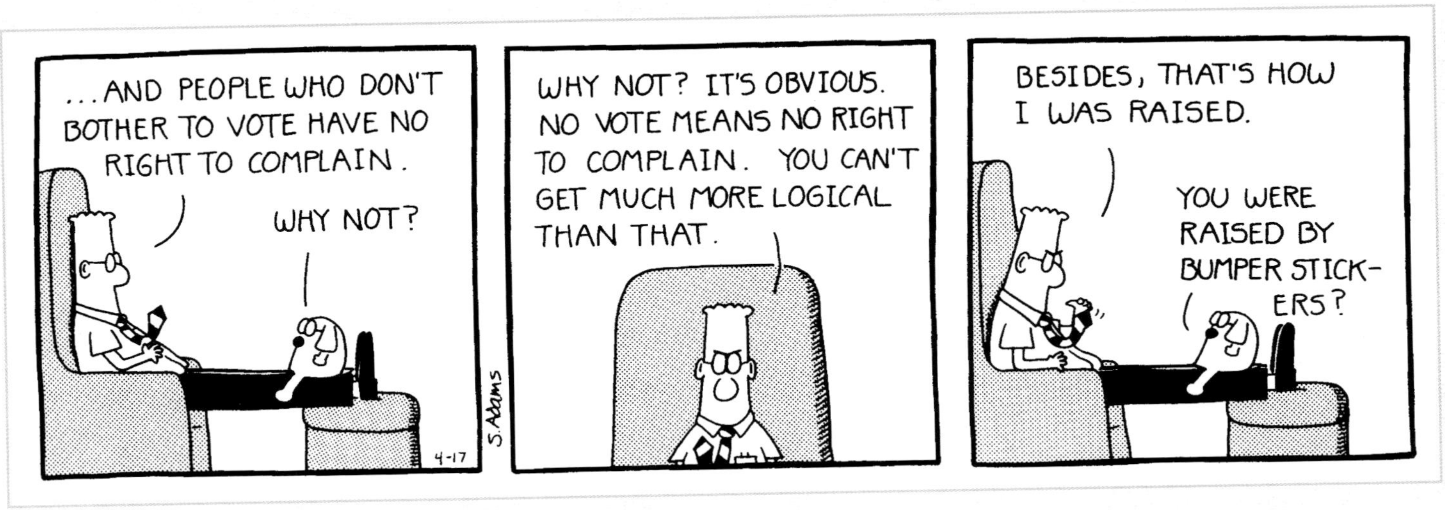
...AND PEOPLE WHO DON'T BOTHER TO VOTE HAVE NO RIGHT TO COMPLAIN.
WHY NOT?
4-17
S. Adams
WHY NOT? IT'S OBVIOUS. NO VOTE MEANS NO RIGHT TO COMPLAIN. YOU CAN'T GET MUCH MORE LOGICAL THAN THAT.
BESIDES, THAT'S HOW I WAS RAISED.
YOU WERE RAISED BY BUMPER STICK-ERS?

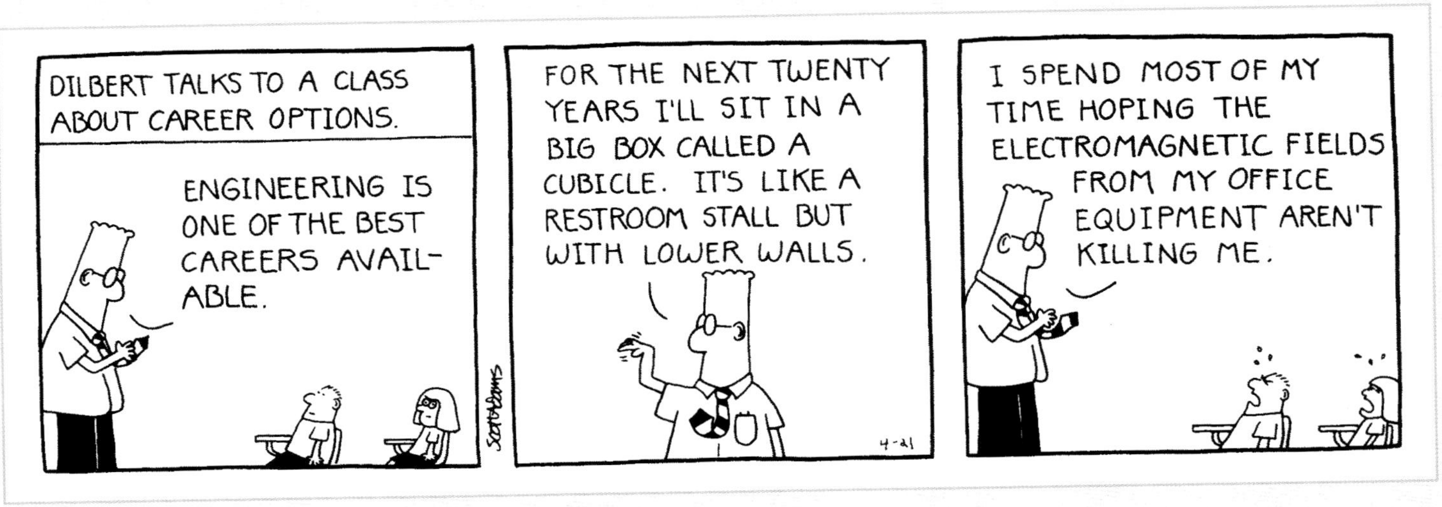
DILBERT TALKS TO A CLASS ABOUT CAREER OPTIONS.
ENGINEERING IS ONE OF THE BEST CAREERS AVAIL-ABLE.
Scott Adams
FOR THE NEXT TWENTY YEARS I'LL SIT IN A BIG BOX CALLED A CUBICLE. IT'S LIKE A RESTROOM STALL BUT WITH LOWER WALLS.
4-21
I SPEND MOST OF MY TIME HOPING THE ELECTROMAGNETIC FIELDS FROM MY OFFICE EQUIPMENT AREN'T KILLING ME.

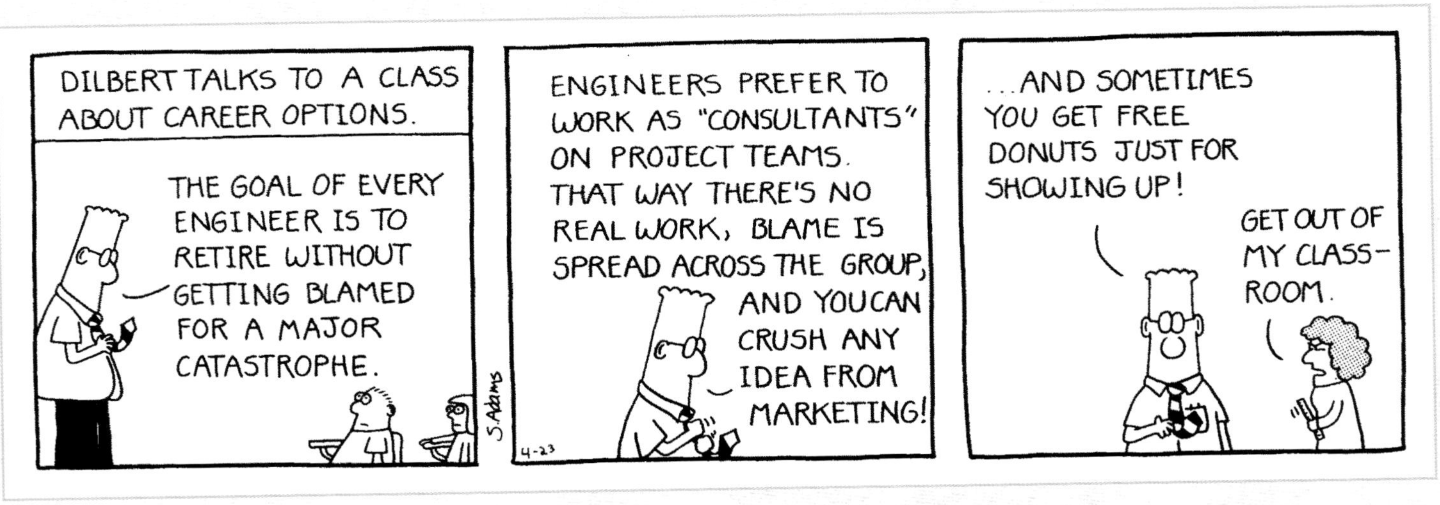
DILBERT TALKS TO A CLASS ABOUT CAREER OPTIONS.
THE GOAL OF EVERY ENGINEER IS TO RETIRE WITHOUT GETTING BLAMED FOR A MAJOR CATASTROPHE.
S. Adams
4-23
ENGINEERS PREFER TO WORK AS "CONSULTANTS" ON PROJECT TEAMS. THAT WAY THERE'S NO REAL WORK, BLAME IS SPREAD ACROSS THE GROUP, AND YOU CAN CRUSH ANY IDEA FROM MARKETING!
...AND SOMETIMES YOU GET FREE DONUTS JUST FOR SHOWING UP!
GET OUT OF MY CLASS-ROOM.

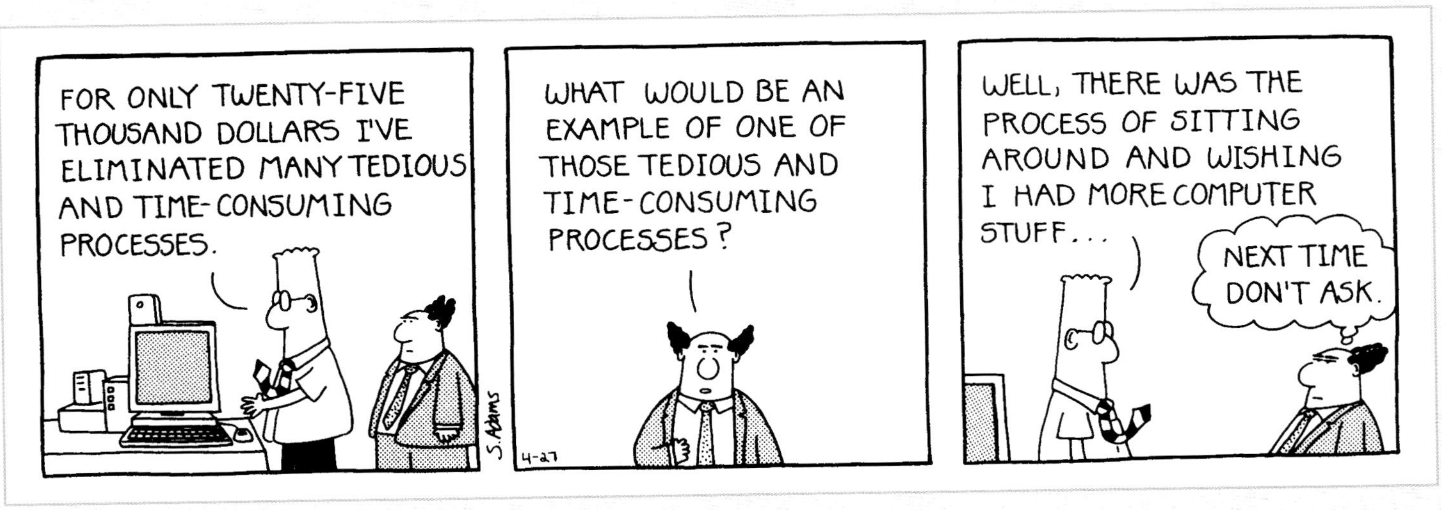
FOR ONLY TWENTY-FIVE THOUSAND DOLLARS I'VE ELIMINATED MANY TEDIOUS AND TIME-CONSUMING PROCESSES.
S. Adams
4-27
WHAT WOULD BE AN EXAMPLE OF ONE OF THOSE TEDIOUS AND TIME-CONSUMING PROCESSES?
WELL, THERE WAS THE PROCESS OF SITTING AROUND AND WISHING I HAD MORE COMPUTER STUFF...
NEXT TIME DON'T ASK.

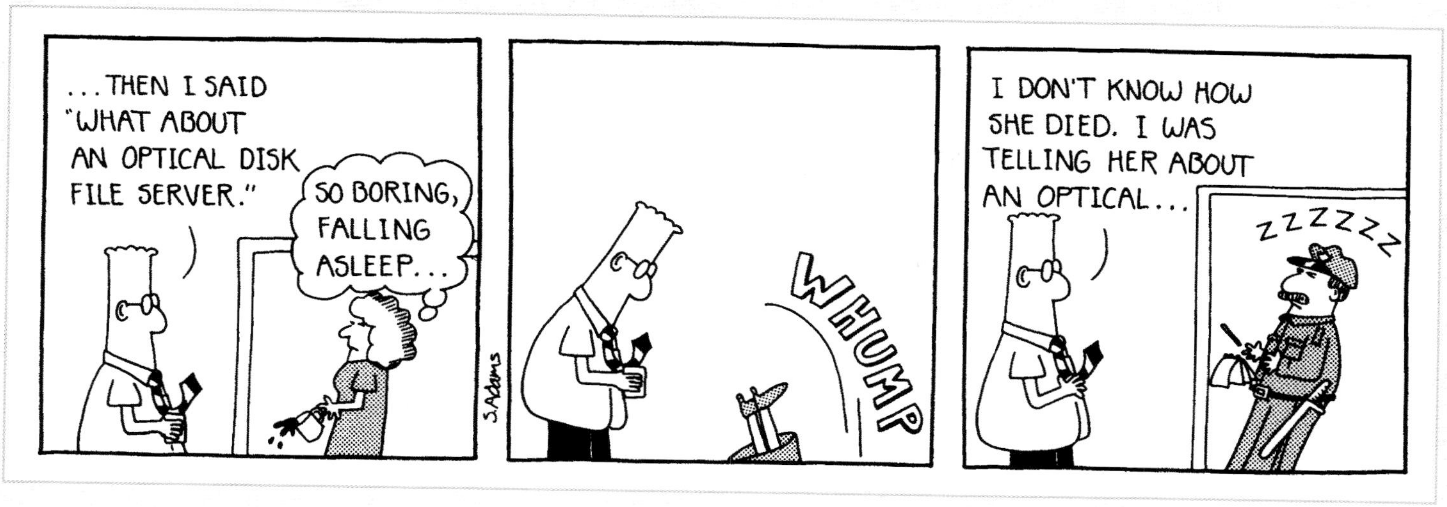
...THEN I SAID "WHAT ABOUT AN OPTICAL DISK FILE SERVER."
SO BORING, FALLING ASLEEP...
S.Adams
WHUMP
I DON'T KNOW HOW SHE DIED. I WAS TELLING HER ABOUT AN OPTICAL...
ZZZZZZ

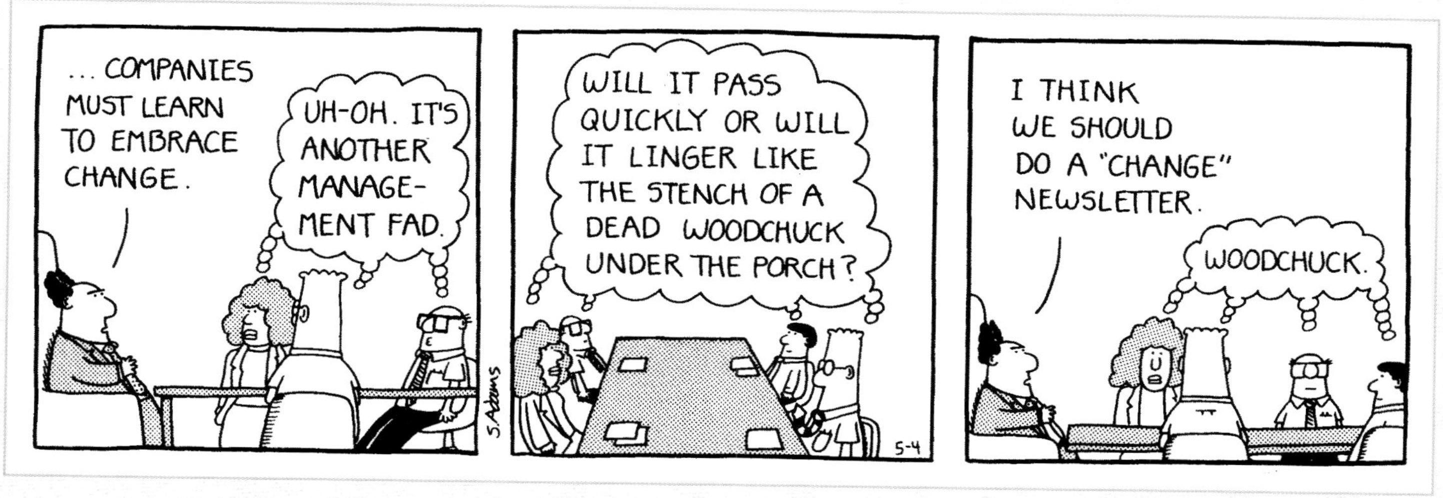
...COMPANIES MUST LEARN TO EMBRACE CHANGE.
UH-OH. IT'S ANOTHER MANAGE-MENT FAD.
S.Adams
WILL IT PASS QUICKLY OR WILL IT LINGER LIKE THE STENCH OF A DEAD WOODCHUCK UNDER THE PORCH?
5-4
I THINK WE SHOULD DO A "CHANGE" NEWSLETTER.
WOODCHUCK.

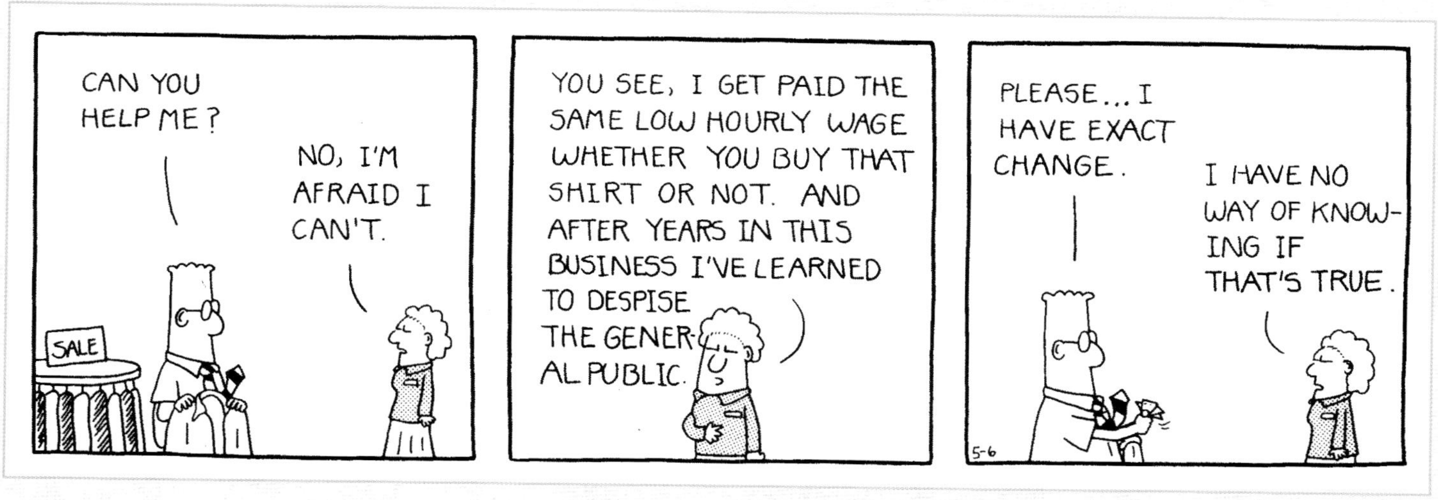
CAN YOU HELP ME?
NO, I'M AFRAID I CAN'T.
SALE
YOU SEE, I GET PAID THE SAME LOW HOURLY WAGE WHETHER YOU BUY THAT SHIRT OR NOT. AND AFTER YEARS IN THIS BUSINESS I'VE LEARNED TO DESPISE THE GENER-AL PUBLIC.
PLEASE... I HAVE EXACT CHANGE.
I HAVE NO WAY OF KNOW-ING IF THAT'S TRUE.
5-6

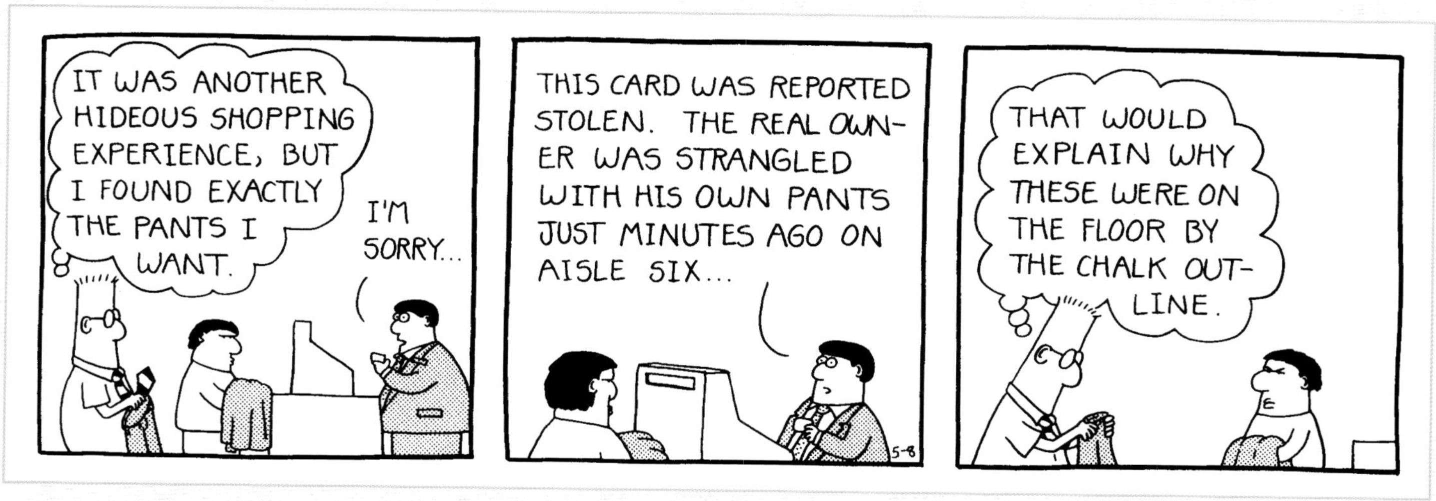
IT WAS ANOTHER HIDEOUS SHOPPING EXPERIENCE, BUT I FOUND EXACTLY THE PANTS I WANT.
I'M SORRY...
THIS CARD WAS REPORTED STOLEN. THE REAL OWN-ER WAS STRANGLED WITH HIS OWN PANTS JUST MINUTES AGO ON AISLE SIX...
5-8
THAT WOULD EXPLAIN WHY THESE WERE ON THE FLOOR BY THE CHALK OUT-LINE.

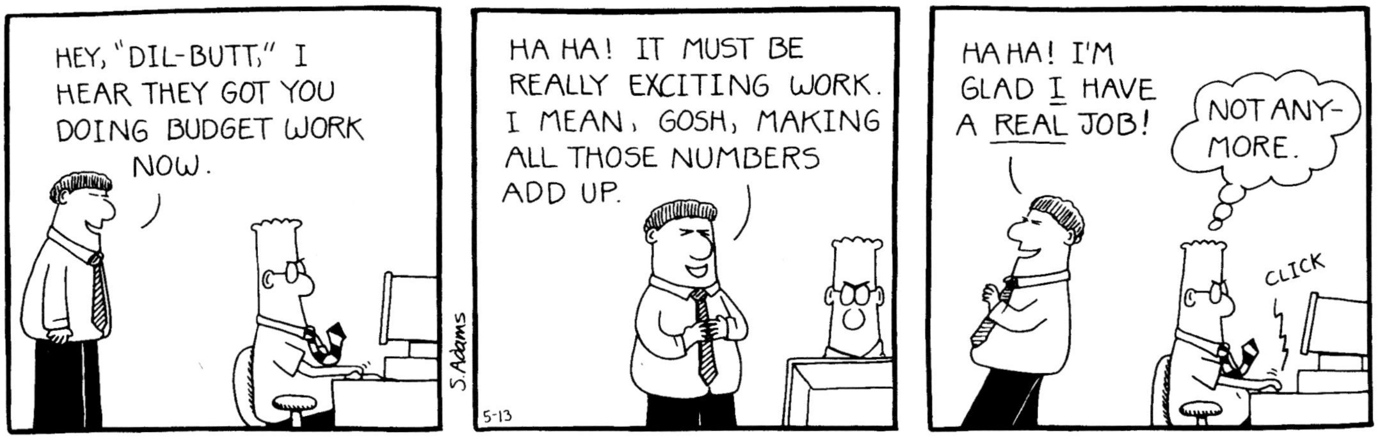
HEY, "DIL-BUTT," I HEAR THEY GOT YOU DOING BUDGET WORK NOW.
S. Adams
HA HA! IT MUST BE REALLY EXCITING WORK. I MEAN, GOSH, MAKING ALL THOSE NUMBERS ADD UP.
5-13
HA HA! I'M GLAD I HAVE A REAL JOB!
NOT ANY-MORE.
CLICK

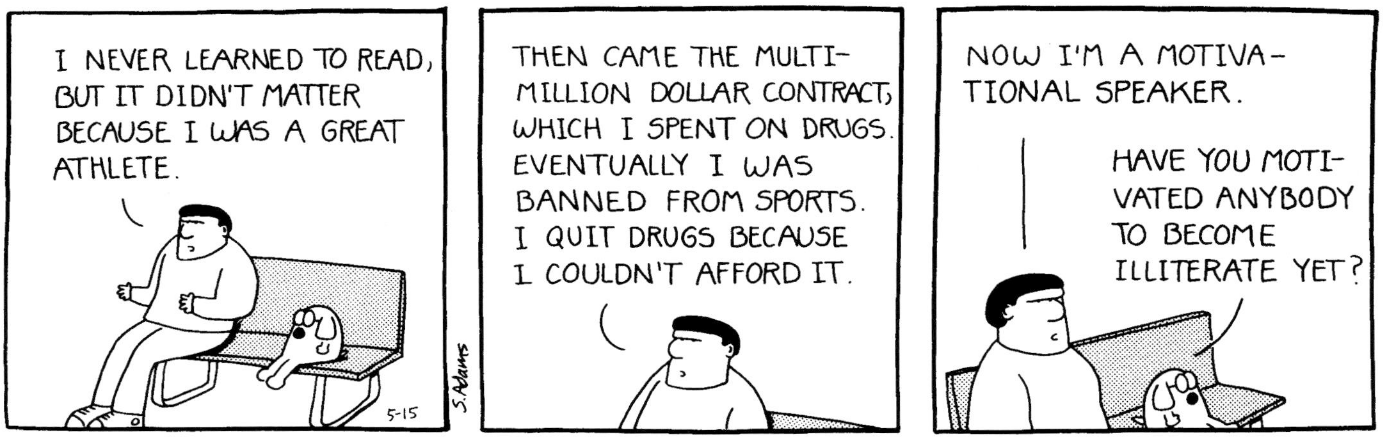
I NEVER LEARNED TO READ, BUT IT DIDN'T MATTER BECAUSE I WAS A GREAT ATHLETE.
5-15
S. Adams
THEN CAME THE MULTI-MILLION DOLLAR CONTRACT, WHICH I SPENT ON DRUGS. EVENTUALLY I WAS BANNED FROM SPORTS. I QUIT DRUGS BECAUSE I COULDN'T AFFORD IT.
NOW I'M A MOTIVA-TIONAL SPEAKER.
HAVE YOU MOTI-VATED ANYBODY TO BECOME ILLITERATE YET?

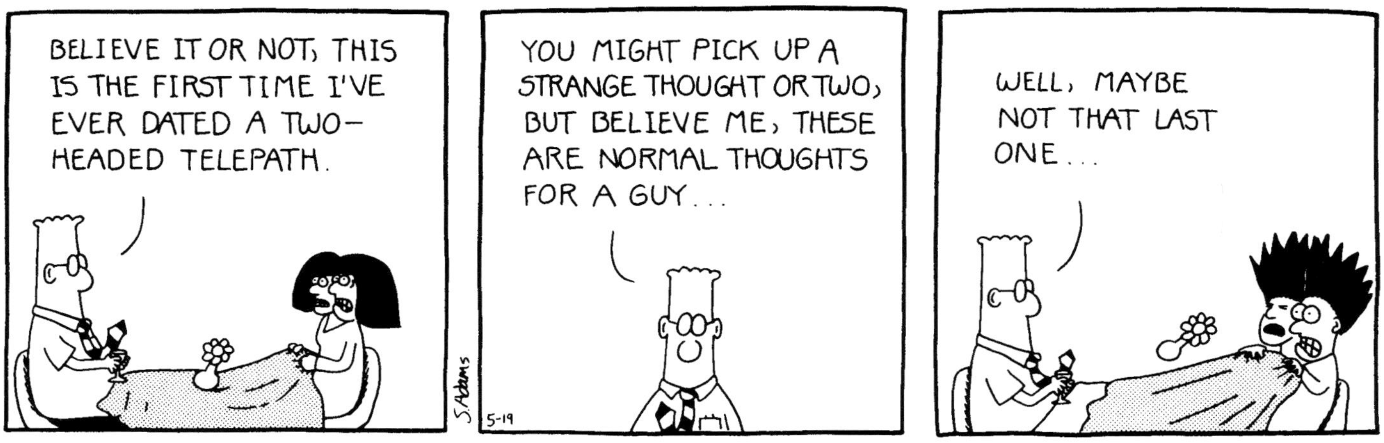
BELIEVE IT OR NOT, THIS IS THE FIRST TIME I'VE EVER DATED A TWO-HEADED TELEPATH.
S. Adams
5-19
YOU MIGHT PICK UP A STRANGE THOUGHT OR TWO, BUT BELIEVE ME, THESE ARE NORMAL THOUGHTS FOR A GUY...
WELL, MAYBE NOT THAT LAST ONE...

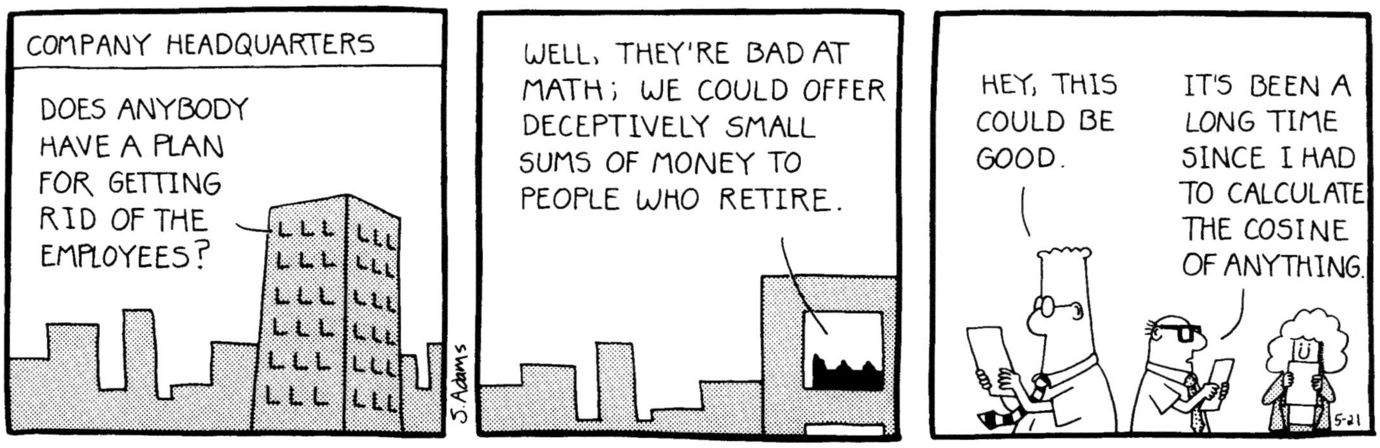
COMPANY HEADQUARTERS
DOES ANYBODY HAVE A PLAN FOR GETTING RID OF THE EMPLOYEES?
S. Adams
WELL, THEY'RE BAD AT MATH; WE COULD OFFER DECEPTIVELY SMALL SUMS OF MONEY TO PEOPLE WHO RETIRE.
HEY, THIS COULD BE GOOD.
IT'S BEEN A LONG TIME SINCE I HAD TO CALCULATE THE COSINE OF ANYTHING.
5-21

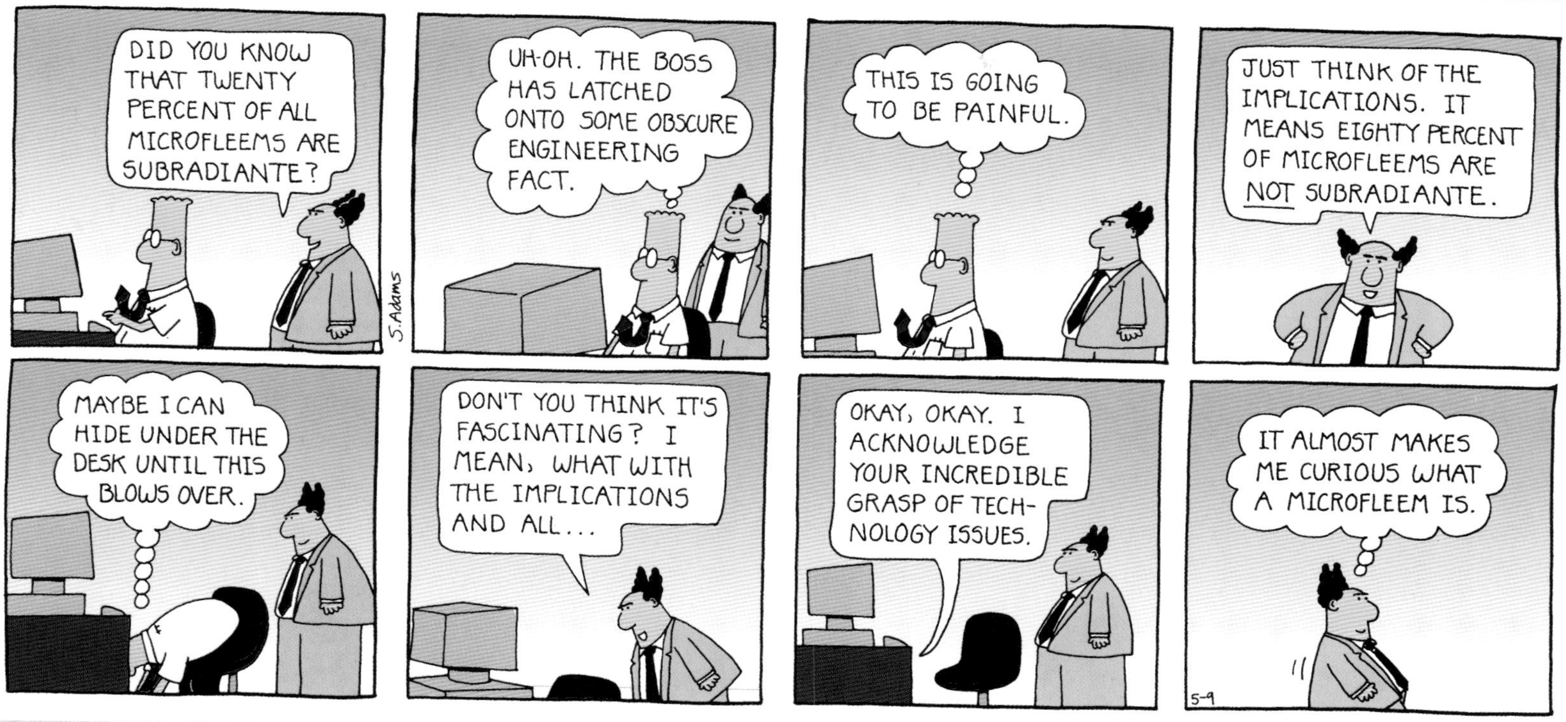
DID YOU KNOW THAT TWENTY PERCENT OF ALL MICROFLEEMS ARE SUBRADIANTE?
S.Adams
UH-OH. THE BOSS HAS LATCHED ONTO SOME OBSCURE ENGINEERING FACT.
THIS IS GOING TO BE PAINFUL.
JUST THINK OF THE IMPLICATIONS. IT MEANS EIGHTY PERCENT OF MICROFLEEMS ARE NOT SUBRADIANTE.
MAYBE I CAN HIDE UNDER THE DESK UNTIL THIS BLOWS OVER.
DON'T YOU THINK IT'S FASCINATING? I MEAN, WHAT WITH THE IMPLICATIONS AND ALL...
OKAY, OKAY. I ACKNOWLEDGE YOUR INCREDIBLE GRASP OF TECH-NOLOGY ISSUES.
IT ALMOST MAKES ME CURIOUS WHAT A MICROFLEEM IS.
5-9

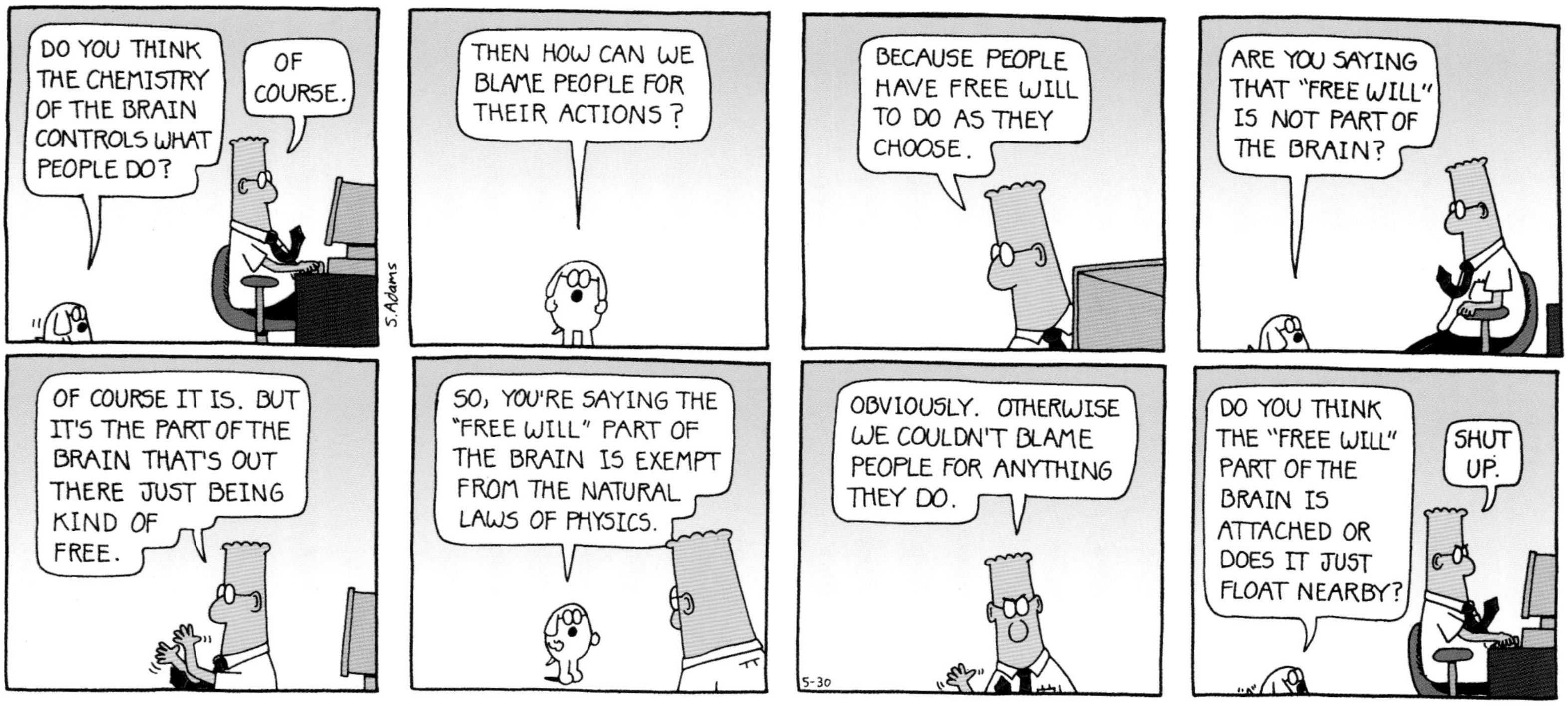
DO YOU THINK THE CHEMISTRY OF THE BRAIN CONTROLS WHAT PEOPLE DO?
OF COURSE.
S.Adams
THEN HOW CAN WE BLAME PEOPLE FOR THEIR ACTIONS?
BECAUSE PEOPLE HAVE FREE WILL TO DO AS THEY CHOOSE.
ARE YOU SAYING THAT "FREE WILL" IS NOT PART OF THE BRAIN?
OF COURSE IT IS. BUT IT'S THE PART OF THE BRAIN THAT'S OUT THERE JUST BEING KIND OF FREE.
SO, YOU'RE SAYING THE "FREE WILL" PART OF THE BRAIN IS EXEMPT FROM THE NATURAL LAWS OF PHYSICS.
OBVIOUSLY. OTHERWISE WE COULDN'T BLAME PEOPLE FOR ANYTHING THEY DO.
5-30
DO YOU THINK THE "FREE WILL" PART OF THE BRAIN IS ATTACHED OR DOES IT JUST FLOAT NEARBY?
SHUT UP.

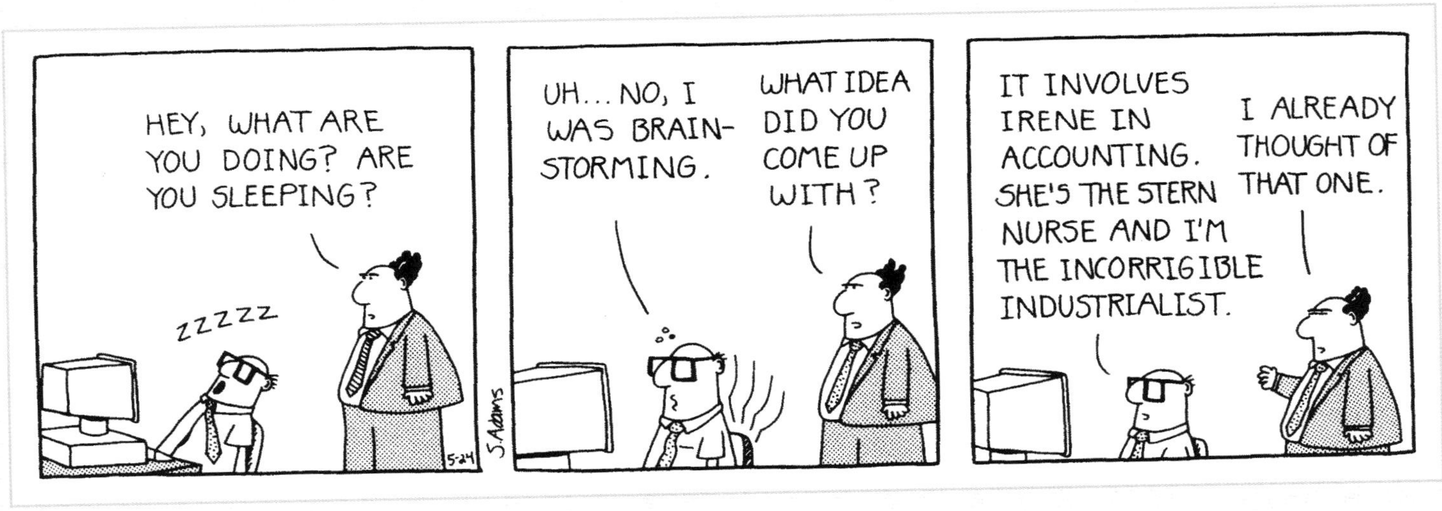
HEY, WHAT ARE YOU DOING? ARE YOU SLEEPING?
ZZZZZ
UH... NO, I WAS BRAIN-STORMING.
WHAT IDEA DID YOU COME UP WITH?
IT INVOLVES IRENE IN ACCOUNTING. SHE'S THE STERN NURSE AND I'M THE INCORRIGIBLE INDUSTRIALIST.
I ALREADY THOUGHT OF THAT ONE.

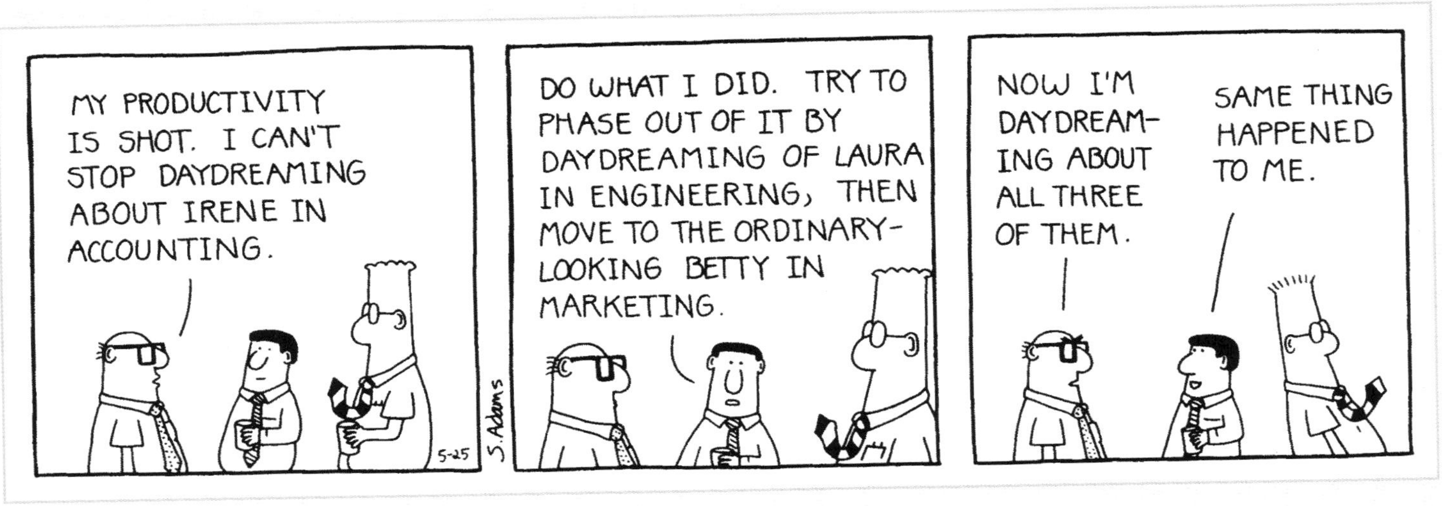
MY PRODUCTIVITY IS SHOT. I CAN'T STOP DAYDREAMING ABOUT IRENE IN ACCOUNTING.
DO WHAT I DID. TRY TO PHASE OUT OF IT BY DAYDREAMING OF LAURA IN ENGINEERING, THEN MOVE TO THE ORDINARY-LOOKING BETTY IN MARKETING.
NOW I'M DAYDREAM-ING ABOUT ALL THREE OF THEM.
SAME THING HAPPENED TO ME.

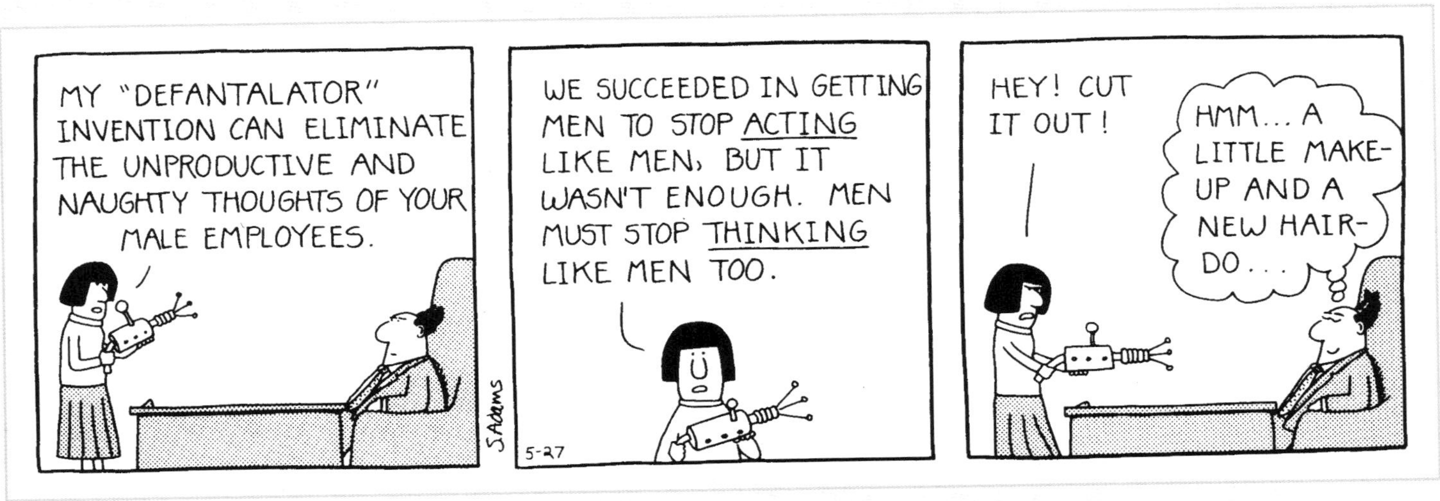
MY "DEFANTALATOR" INVENTION CAN ELIMINATE THE UNPRODUCTIVE AND NAUGHTY THOUGHTS OF YOUR MALE EMPLOYEES.
WE SUCCEEDED IN GETTING MEN TO STOP ACTING LIKE MEN, BUT IT WASN'T ENOUGH. MEN MUST STOP THINKING LIKE MEN TOO.
HEY! CUT IT OUT!
HMM... A LITTLE MAKE-UP AND A NEW HAIR-DO...

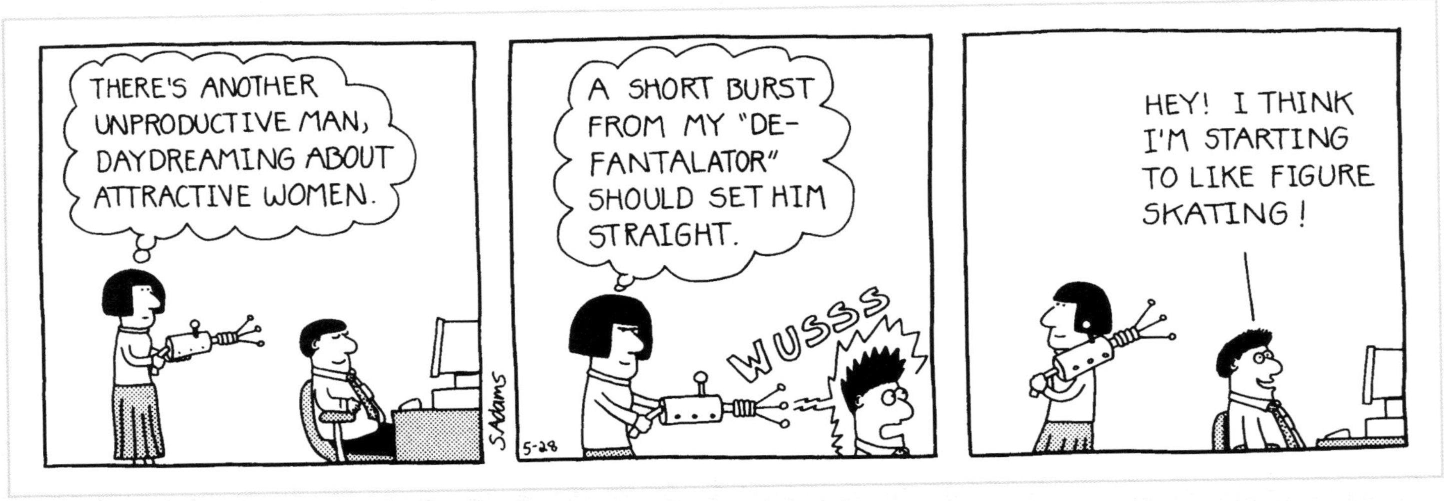
THERE'S ANOTHER UNPRODUCTIVE MAN, DAYDREAMING ABOUT ATTRACTIVE WOMEN.
A SHORT BURST FROM MY "DE-FANTALATOR" SHOULD SET HIM STRAIGHT.
WUSSS
HEY! I THINK I'M STARTING TO LIKE FIGURE SKATING!

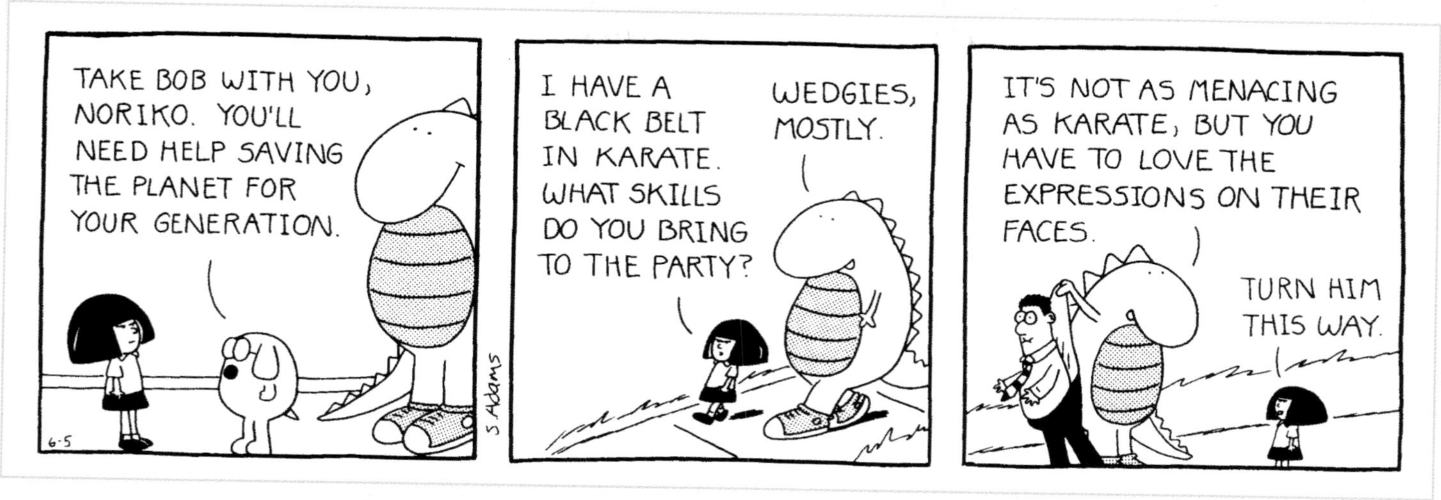
TAKE BOB WITH YOU, NORIKO. YOU'LL NEED HELP SAVING THE PLANET FOR YOUR GENERATION.
I HAVE A BLACK BELT IN KARATE. WHAT SKILLS DO YOU BRING TO THE PARTY?
WEDGIES, MOSTLY.
IT'S NOT AS MENACING AS KARATE, BUT YOU HAVE TO LOVE THE EXPRESSIONS ON THEIR FACES.
TURN HIM THIS WAY.

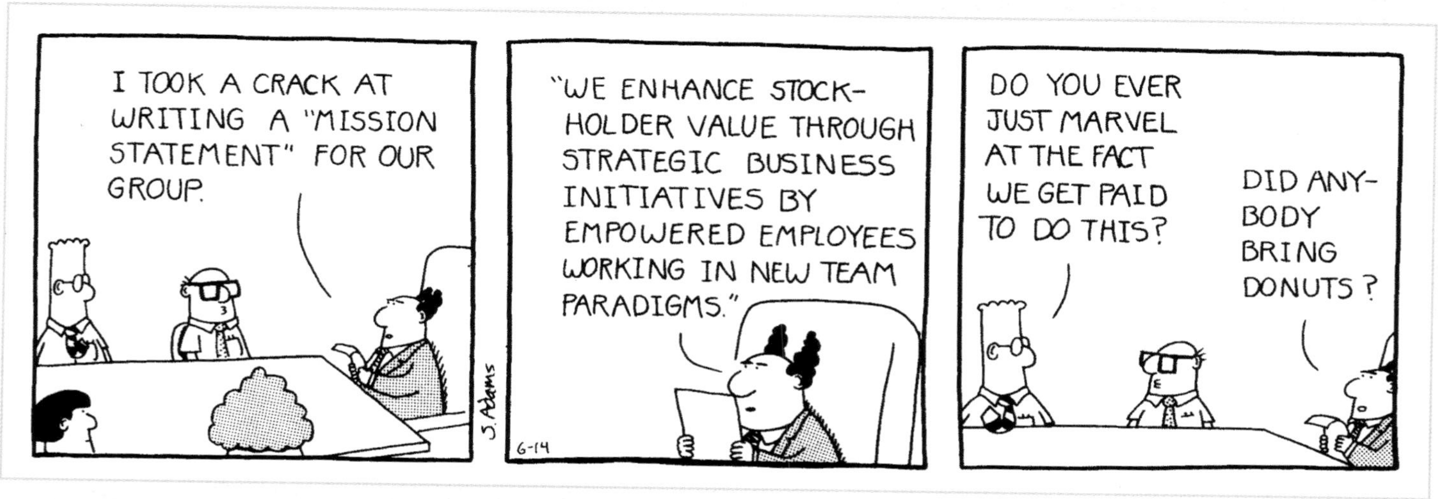
I TOOK A CRACK AT WRITING A "MISSION STATEMENT" FOR OUR GROUP.
"WE ENHANCE STOCK-HOLDER VALUE THROUGH STRATEGIC BUSINESS INITIATIVES BY EMPOWERED EMPLOYEES WORKING IN NEW TEAM PARADIGMS."
DO YOU EVER JUST MARVEL AT THE FACT WE GET PAID TO DO THIS?
DID ANY-BODY BRING DONUTS?

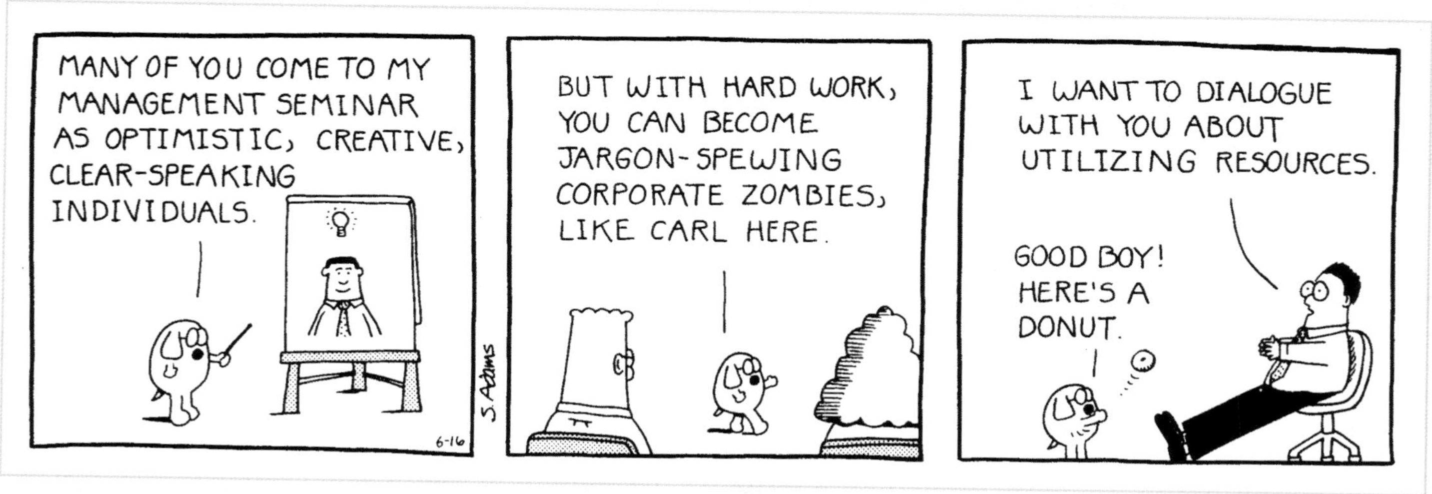
MANY OF YOU COME TO MY MANAGEMENT SEMINAR AS OPTIMISTIC, CREATIVE, CLEAR-SPEAKING INDIVIDUALS.
BUT WITH HARD WORK, YOU CAN BECOME JARGON-SPEWING CORPORATE ZOMBIES, LIKE CARL HERE.
I WANT TO DIALOGUE WITH YOU ABOUT UTILIZING RESOURCES.
GOOD BOY! HERE'S A DONUT.

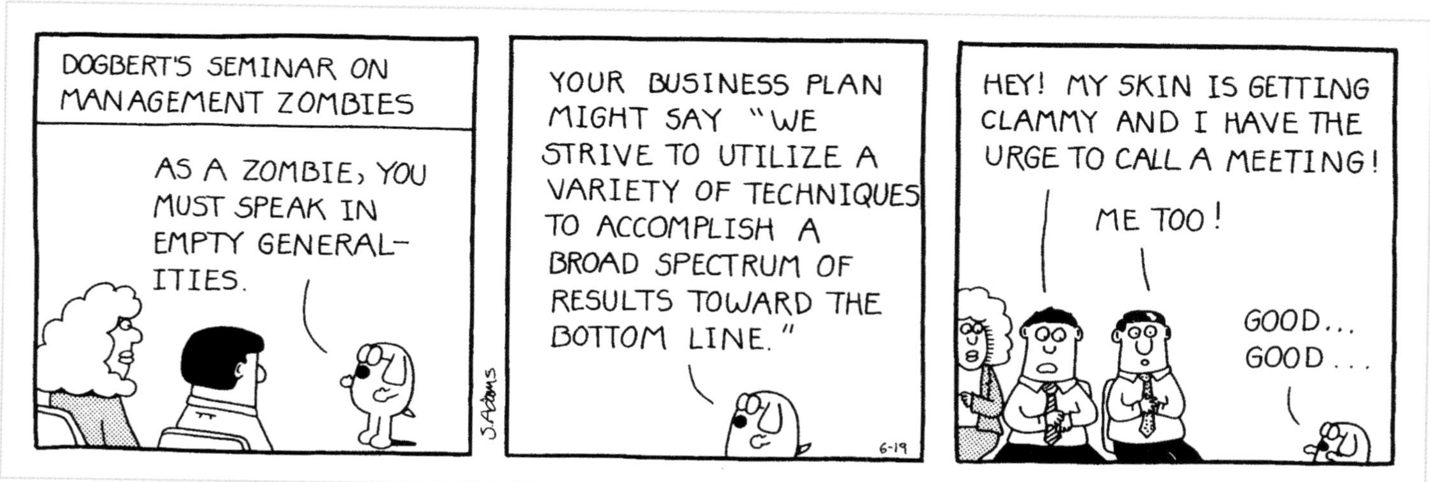
DOGBERT'S SEMINAR ON MANAGEMENT ZOMBIES
AS A ZOMBIE, YOU MUST SPEAK IN EMPTY GENERAL-ITIES.
YOUR BUSINESS PLAN MIGHT SAY "WE STRIVE TO UTILIZE A VARIETY OF TECHNIQUES TO ACCOMPLISH A BROAD SPECTRUM OF RESULTS TOWARD THE BOTTOM LINE."
HEY! MY SKIN IS GETTING CLAMMY AND I HAVE THE URGE TO CALL A MEETING!
ME TOO!
GOOD... GOOD...

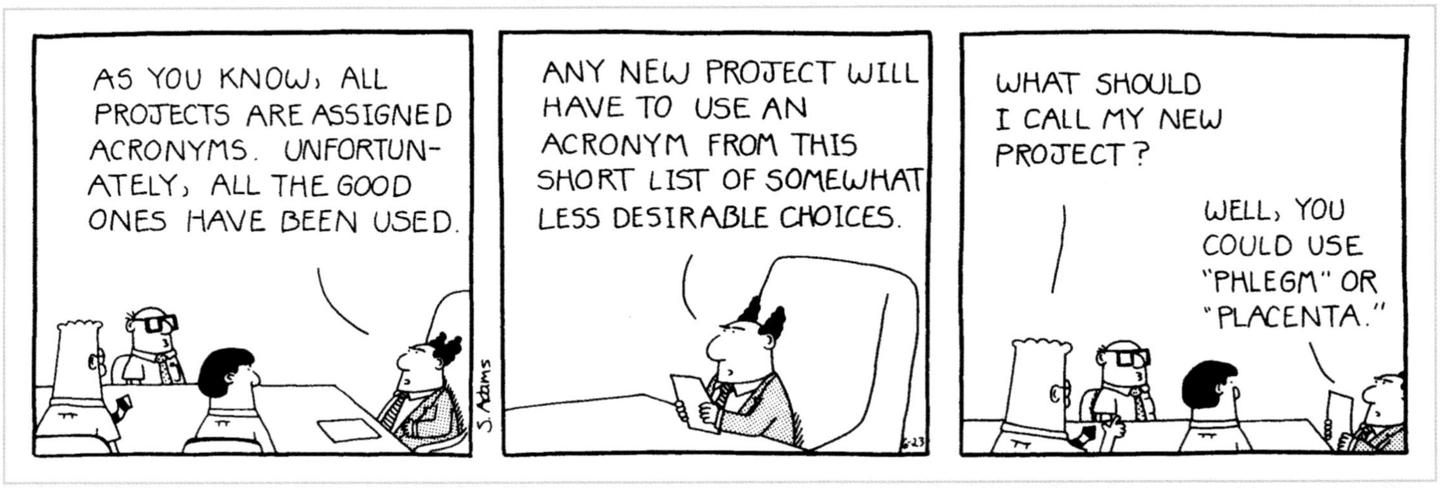
AS YOU KNOW, ALL PROJECTS ARE ASSIGNED ACRONYMS. UNFORTUNATELY, ALL THE GOOD ONES HAVE BEEN USED.
ANY NEW PROJECT WILL HAVE TO USE AN ACRONYM FROM THIS SHORT LIST OF SOMEWHAT LESS DESIRABLE CHOICES.
WHAT SHOULD I CALL MY NEW PROJECT?
WELL, YOU COULD USE "PHLEGM" OR "PLACENTA."

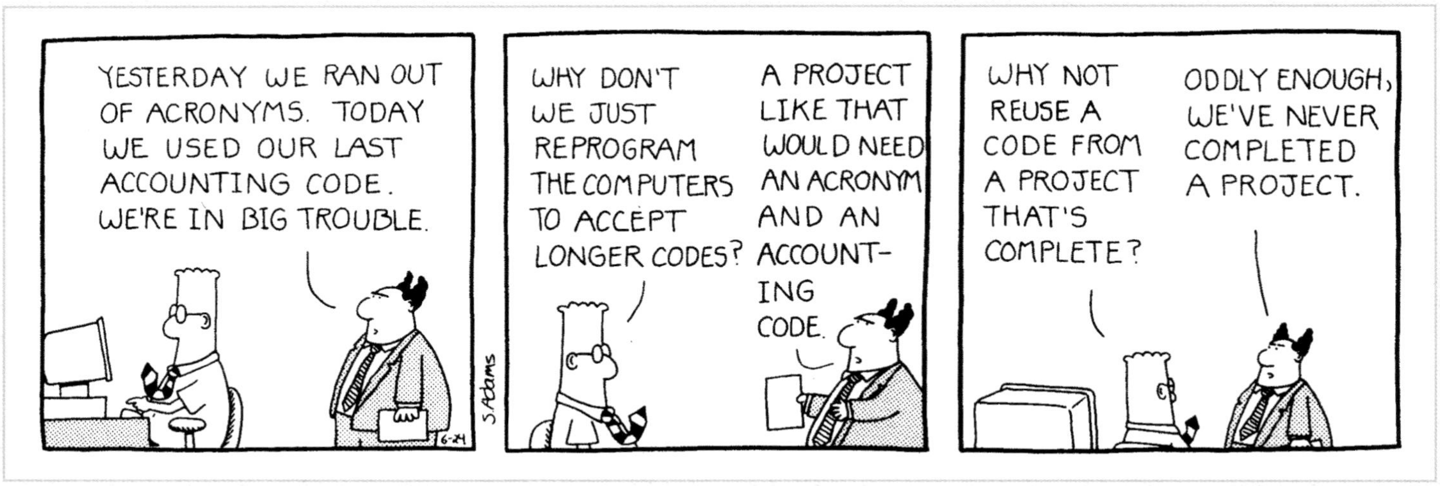
YESTERDAY WE RAN OUT OF ACRONYMS. TODAY WE USED OUR LAST ACCOUNTING CODE. WE'RE IN BIG TROUBLE.
WHY DON'T WE JUST REPROGRAM THE COMPUTERS TO ACCEPT LONGER CODES?
A PROJECT LIKE THAT WOULD NEED AN ACRONYM AND AN ACCOUNTING CODE.
WHY NOT REUSE A CODE FROM A PROJECT THAT'S COMPLETE?
ODDLY ENOUGH, WE'VE NEVER COMPLETED A PROJECT.

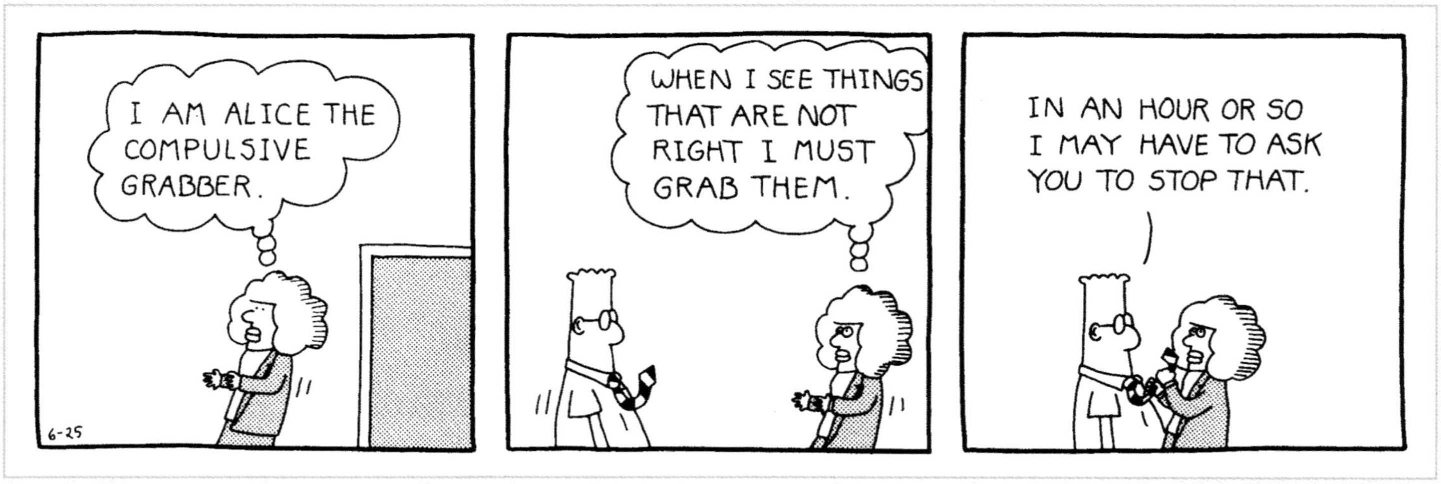
I AM ALICE THE COMPULSIVE GRABBER.
WHEN I SEE THINGS THAT ARE NOT RIGHT I MUST GRAB THEM.
IN AN HOUR OR SO I MAY HAVE TO ASK YOU TO STOP THAT.

I believe this is the day Alice got her name. Until then, a variety of generic female co-workers with puffy hair inhabited the office.

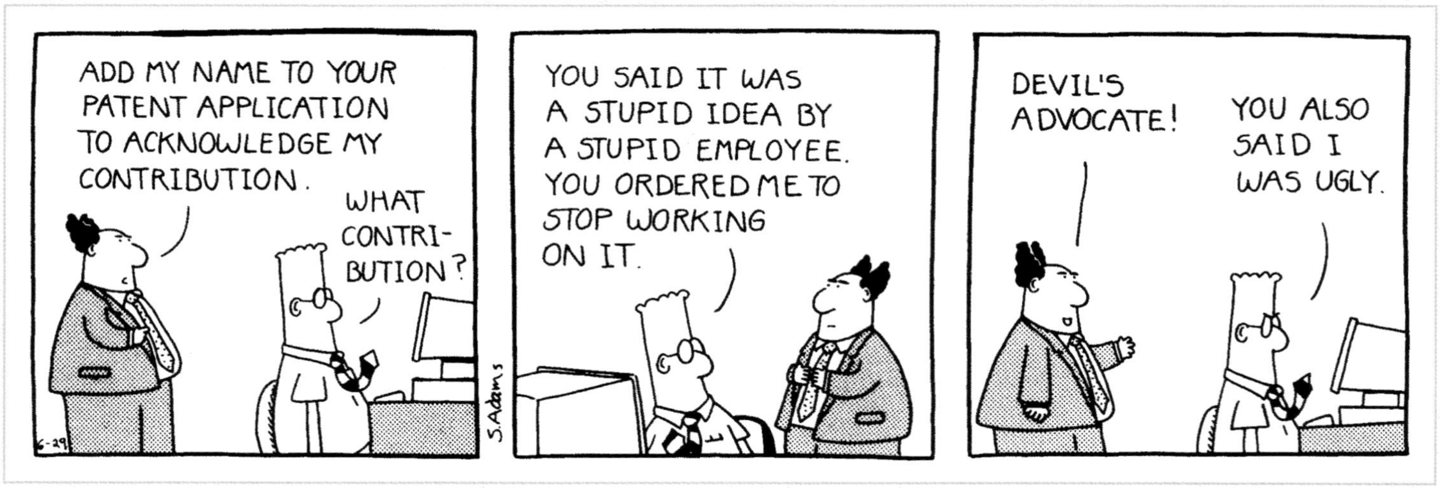
ADD MY NAME TO YOUR PATENT APPLICATION TO ACKNOWLEDGE MY CONTRIBUTION.
WHAT CONTRIBUTION?
YOU SAID IT WAS A STUPID IDEA BY A STUPID EMPLOYEE. YOU ORDERED ME TO STOP WORKING ON IT.
DEVIL'S ADVOCATE!
YOU ALSO SAID I WAS UGLY.

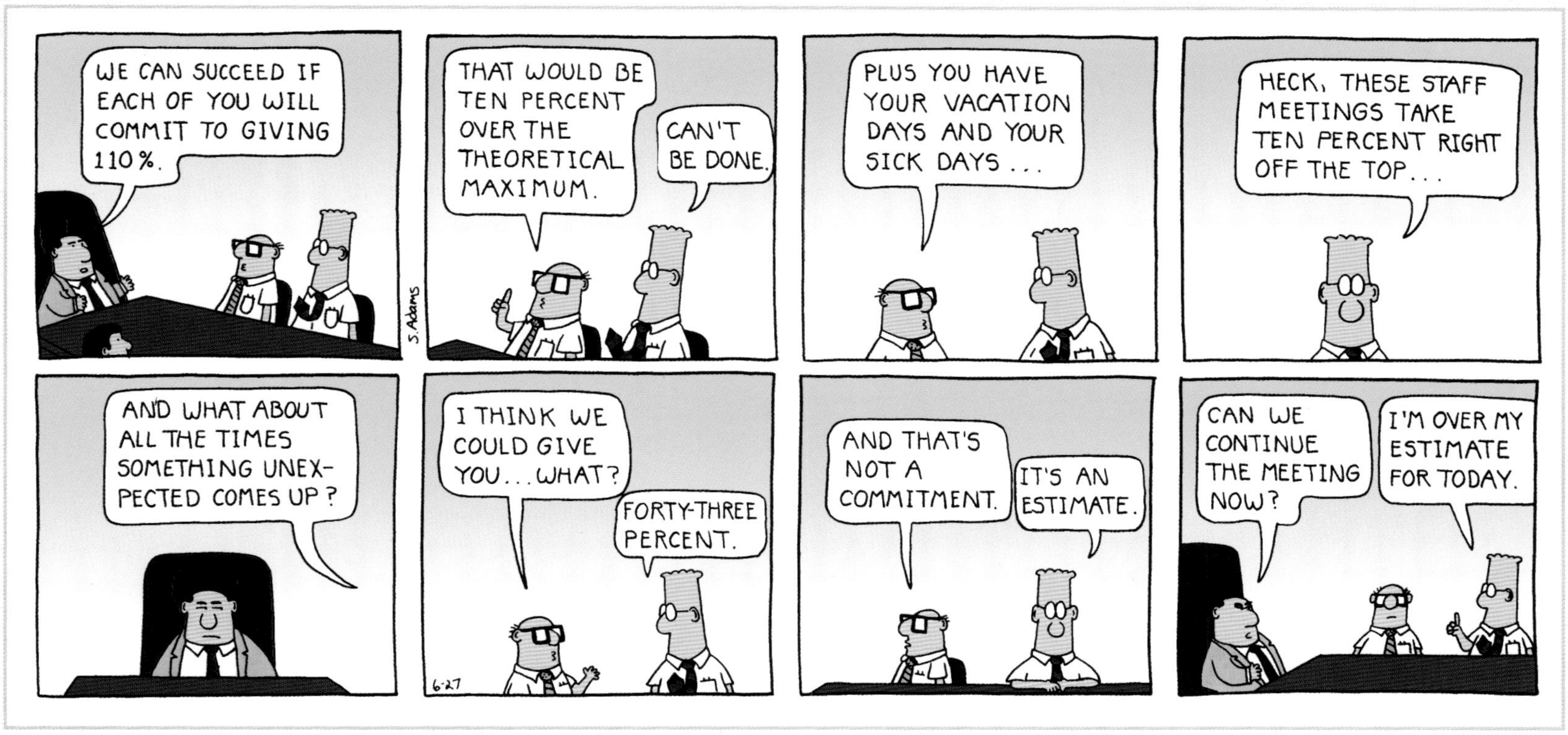
WE CAN SUCCEED IF EACH OF YOU WILL COMMIT TO GIVING 110%.
THAT WOULD BE TEN PERCENT OVER THE THEORETICAL MAXIMUM.
CAN'T BE DONE.
PLUS YOU HAVE YOUR VACATION DAYS AND YOUR SICK DAYS . . .
HECK, THESE STAFF MEETINGS TAKE TEN PERCENT RIGHT OFF THE TOP . . .
AND WHAT ABOUT ALL THE TIMES SOMETHING UNEXPECTED COMES UP?
I THINK WE COULD GIVE YOU . . . WHAT?
FORTY-THREE PERCENT.
AND THAT'S NOT A COMMITMENT.
IT'S AN ESTIMATE.
CAN WE CONTINUE THE MEETING NOW?
I'M OVER MY ESTIMATE FOR TODAY.

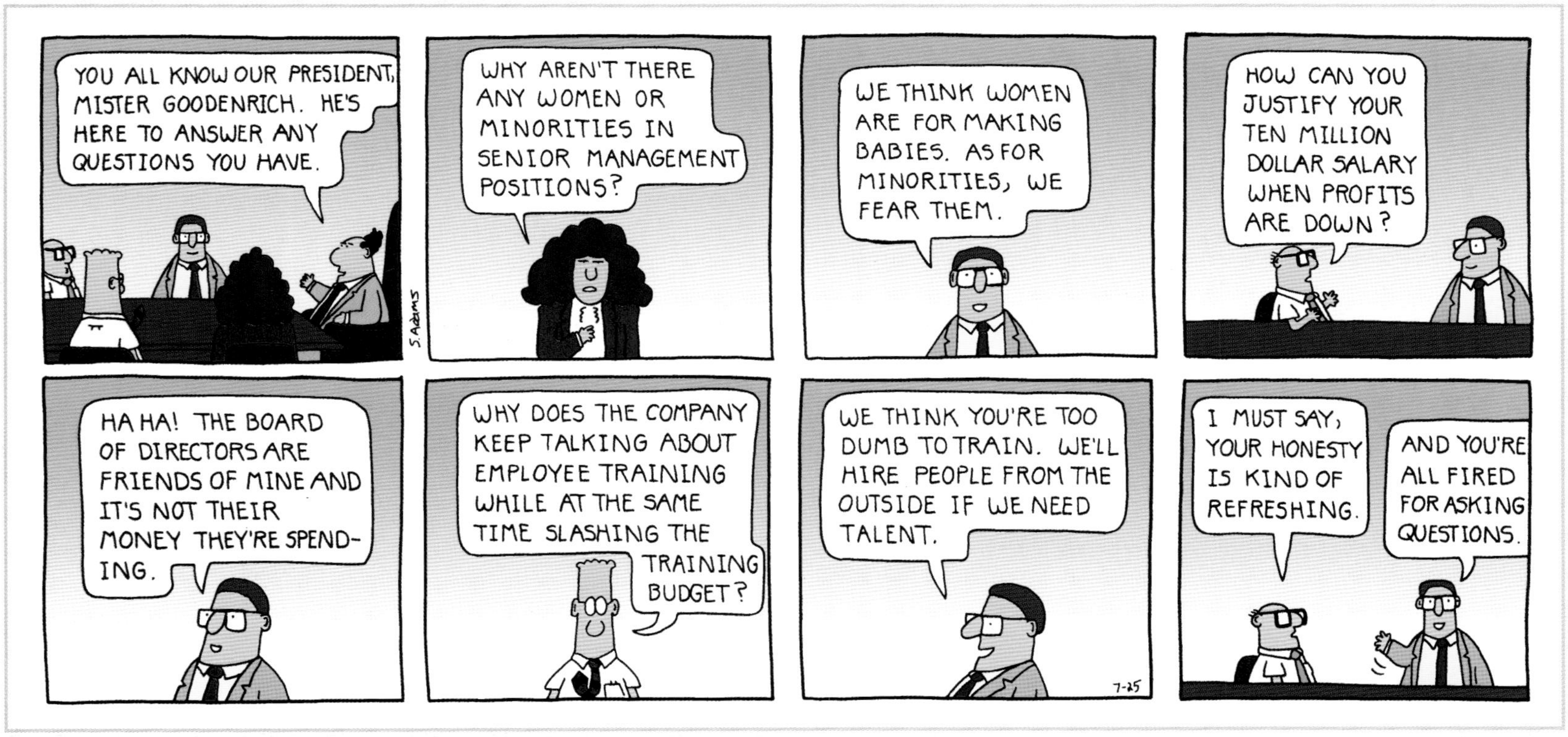
YOU ALL KNOW OUR PRESIDENT, MISTER GOODENRICH. HE'S HERE TO ANSWER ANY QUESTIONS YOU HAVE.
WHY AREN'T THERE ANY WOMEN OR MINORITIES IN SENIOR MANAGEMENT POSITIONS?
WE THINK WOMEN ARE FOR MAKING BABIES. AS FOR MINORITIES, WE FEAR THEM.
HOW CAN YOU JUSTIFY YOUR TEN MILLION DOLLAR SALARY WHEN PROFITS ARE DOWN?
HA HA! THE BOARD OF DIRECTORS ARE FRIENDS OF MINE AND IT'S NOT THEIR MONEY THEY'RE SPENDING.
WHY DOES THE COMPANY KEEP TALKING ABOUT EMPLOYEE TRAINING WHILE AT THE SAME TIME SLASHING THE TRAINING BUDGET?
WE THINK YOU'RE TOO DUMB TO TRAIN. WE'LL HIRE PEOPLE FROM THE OUTSIDE IF WE NEED TALENT.
I MUST SAY, YOUR HONESTY IS KIND OF REFRESHING.
AND YOU'RE ALL FIRED FOR ASKING QUESTIONS.

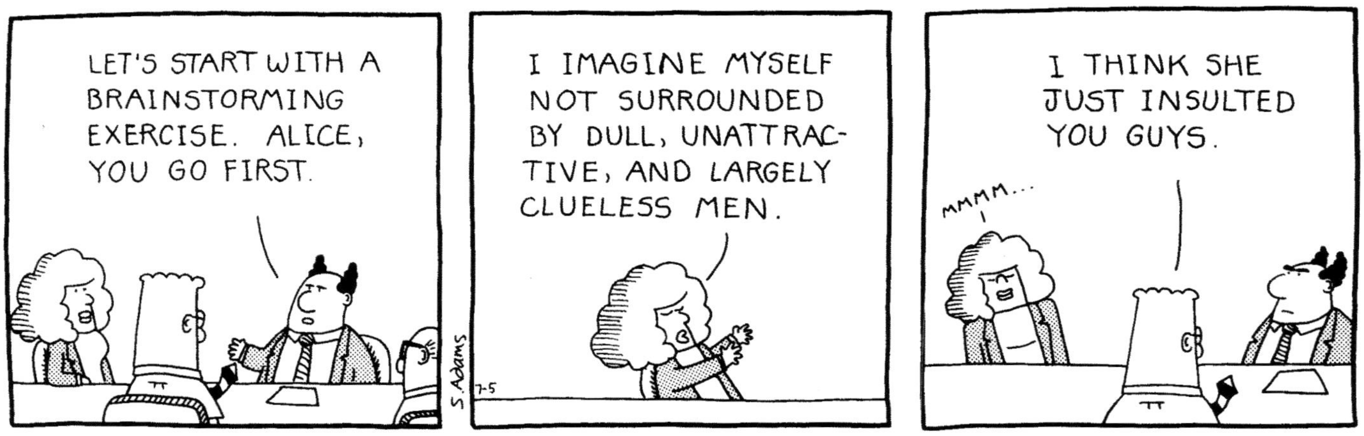
LET'S START WITH A BRAINSTORMING EXERCISE. ALICE, YOU GO FIRST.
S. Adams
7-5
I IMAGINE MYSELF NOT SURROUNDED BY DULL, UNATTRACTIVE, AND LARGELY CLUELESS MEN.
MMMM...
I THINK SHE JUST INSULTED YOU GUYS.

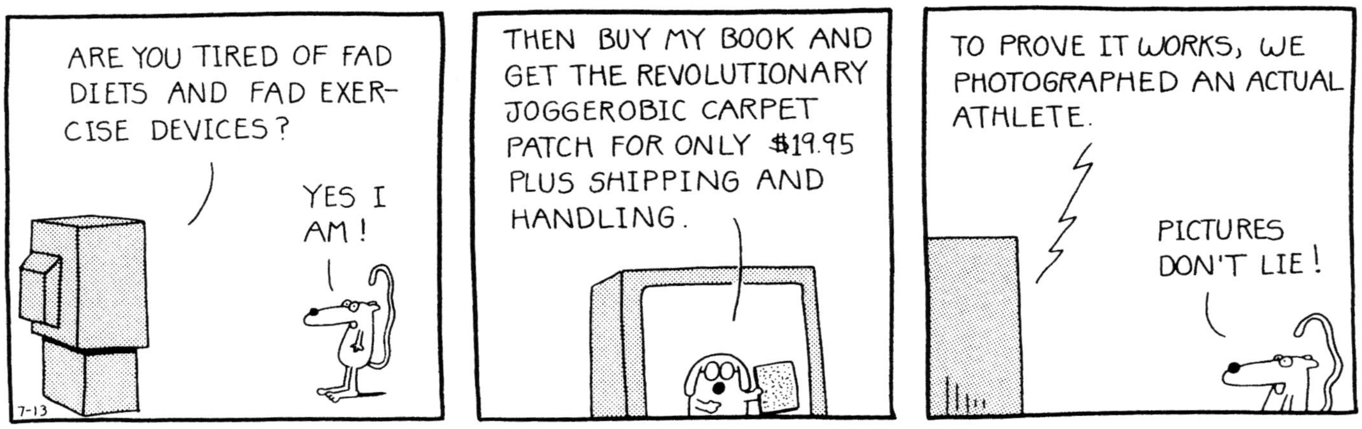
ARE YOU TIRED OF FAD DIETS AND FAD EXERCISE DEVICES?
YES I AM!
7-13
THEN BUY MY BOOK AND GET THE REVOLUTIONARY JOGGEROBIC CARPET PATCH FOR ONLY $19.95 PLUS SHIPPING AND HANDLING.
TO PROVE IT WORKS, WE PHOTOGRAPHED AN ACTUAL ATHLETE.
PICTURES DON'T LIE!

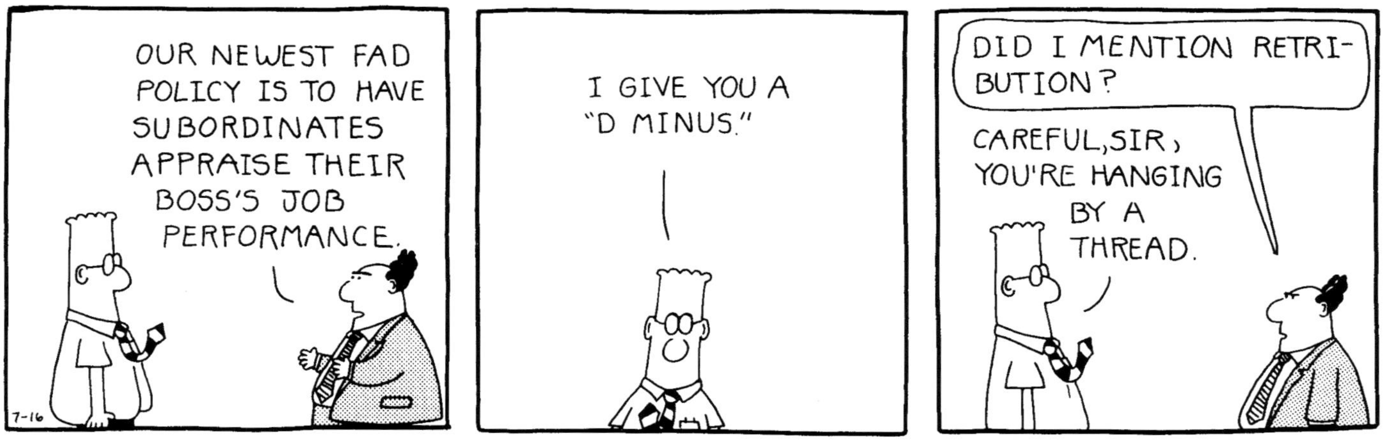
OUR NEWEST FAD POLICY IS TO HAVE SUBORDINATES APPRAISE THEIR BOSS'S JOB PERFORMANCE.
7-16
I GIVE YOU A "D MINUS."
DID I MENTION RETRIBUTION?
CAREFUL, SIR, YOU'RE HANGING BY A THREAD.

Dilbert called his pointy-haired boss "sir," because I didn't have a better way to deal with the fact that the boss has no actual name.

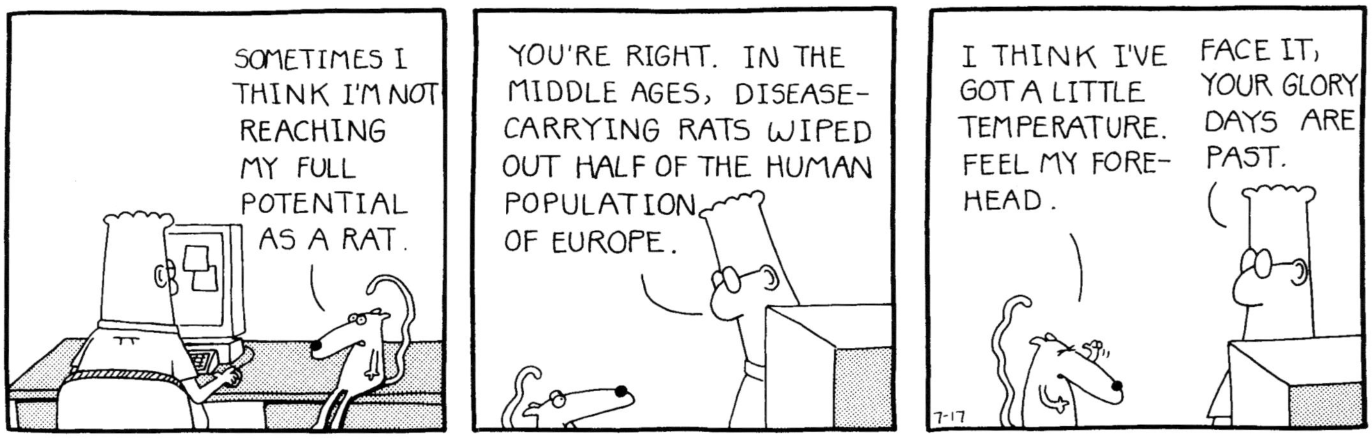
SOMETIMES I THINK I'M NOT REACHING MY FULL POTENTIAL AS A RAT.
YOU'RE RIGHT. IN THE MIDDLE AGES, DISEASE-CARRYING RATS WIPED OUT HALF OF THE HUMAN POPULATION OF EUROPE.
I THINK I'VE GOT A LITTLE TEMPERATURE. FEEL MY FOREHEAD.
FACE IT, YOUR GLORY DAYS ARE PAST.
7-17

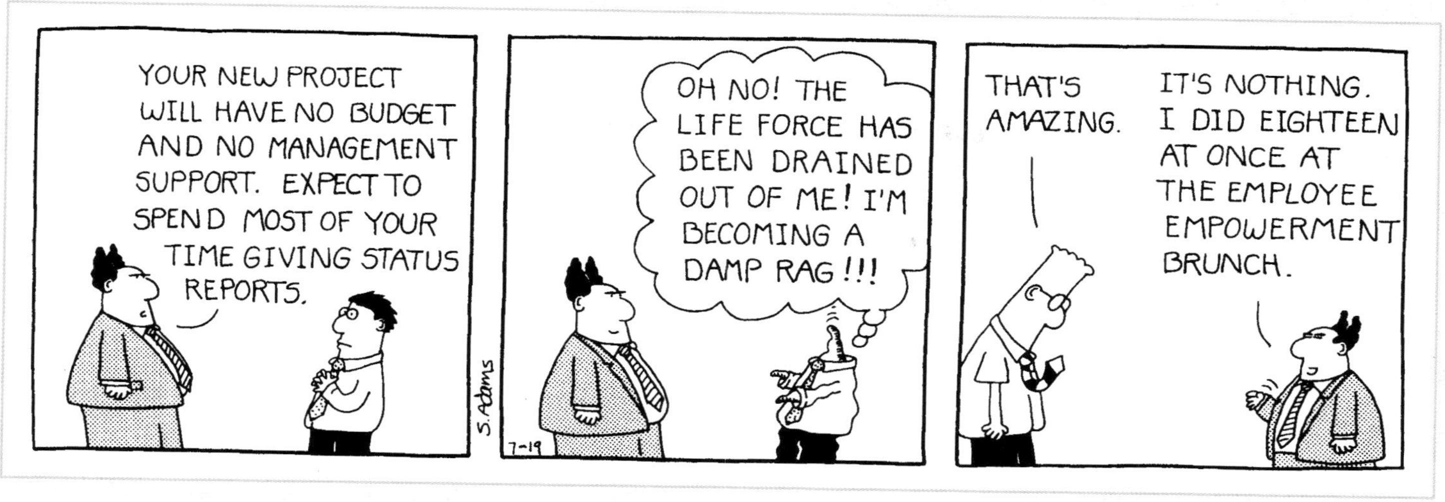
YOUR NEW PROJECT WILL HAVE NO BUDGET AND NO MANAGEMENT SUPPORT. EXPECT TO SPEND MOST OF YOUR TIME GIVING STATUS REPORTS.
OH NO! THE LIFE FORCE HAS BEEN DRAINED OUT OF ME! I'M BECOMING A DAMP RAG!!!
S. Adams
7-19
THAT'S AMAZING.
IT'S NOTHING. I DID EIGHTEEN AT ONCE AT THE EMPLOYEE EMPOWERMENT BRUNCH.

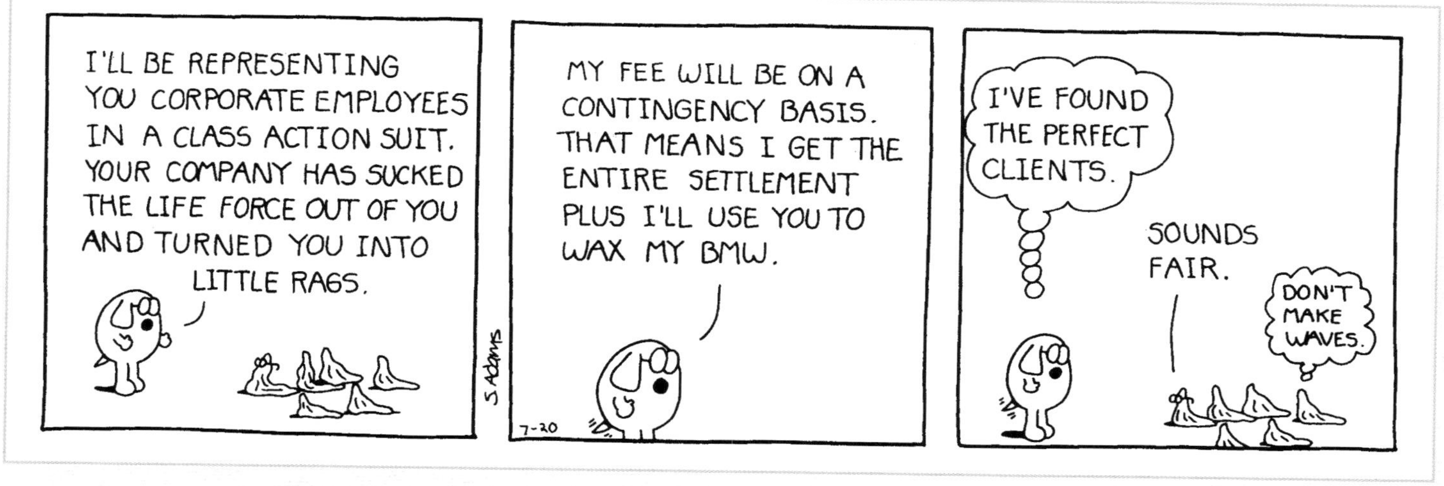
I'LL BE REPRESENTING YOU CORPORATE EMPLOYEES IN A CLASS ACTION SUIT. YOUR COMPANY HAS SUCKED THE LIFE FORCE OUT OF YOU AND TURNED YOU INTO LITTLE RAGS.
MY FEE WILL BE ON A CONTINGENCY BASIS. THAT MEANS I GET THE ENTIRE SETTLEMENT PLUS I'LL USE YOU TO WAX MY BMW.
S. Adams
7-20
I'VE FOUND THE PERFECT CLIENTS.
SOUNDS FAIR.
DON'T MAKE WAVES.

This series is the first time I used the phrase "suck the life force out of you." Later I used it almost every time I described the corporate experience.

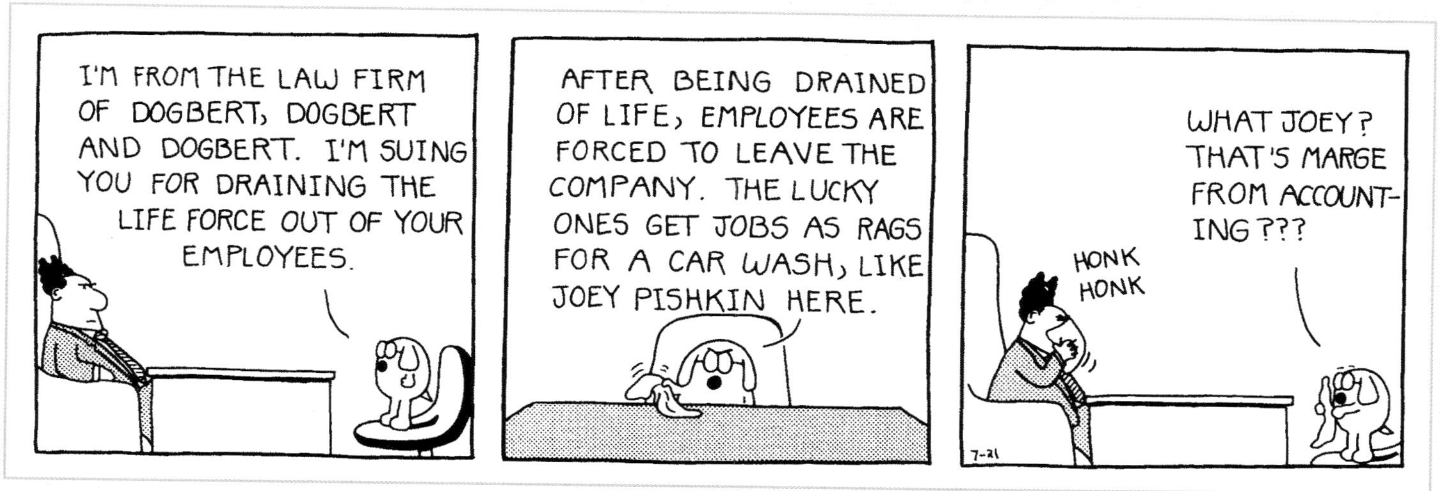
I'M FROM THE LAW FIRM OF DOGBERT, DOGBERT AND DOGBERT. I'M SUING YOU FOR DRAINING THE LIFE FORCE OUT OF YOUR EMPLOYEES.
AFTER BEING DRAINED OF LIFE, EMPLOYEES ARE FORCED TO LEAVE THE COMPANY. THE LUCKY ONES GET JOBS AS RAGS FOR A CAR WASH, LIKE JOEY PISHKIN HERE.
HONK HONK
WHAT JOEY? THAT'S MARGE FROM ACCOUNTING???
7-21

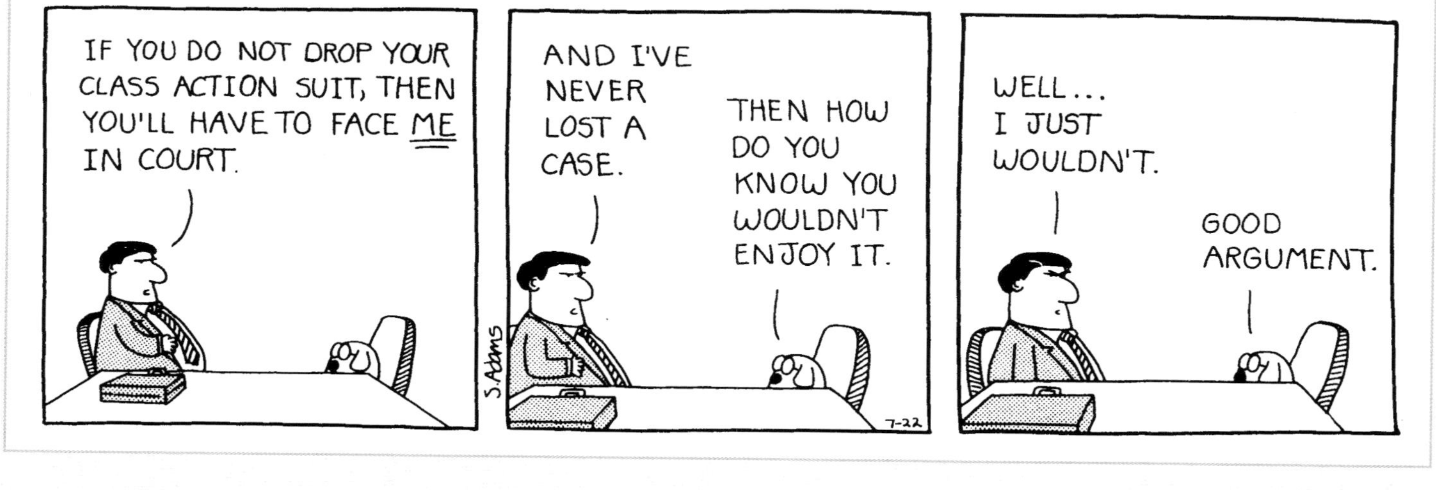
IF YOU DO NOT DROP YOUR CLASS ACTION SUIT, THEN YOU'LL HAVE TO FACE ME IN COURT.
S. Adams
AND I'VE NEVER LOST A CASE.
THEN HOW DO YOU KNOW YOU WOULDN'T ENJOY IT.
7-22
WELL... I JUST WOULDN'T.
GOOD ARGUMENT.

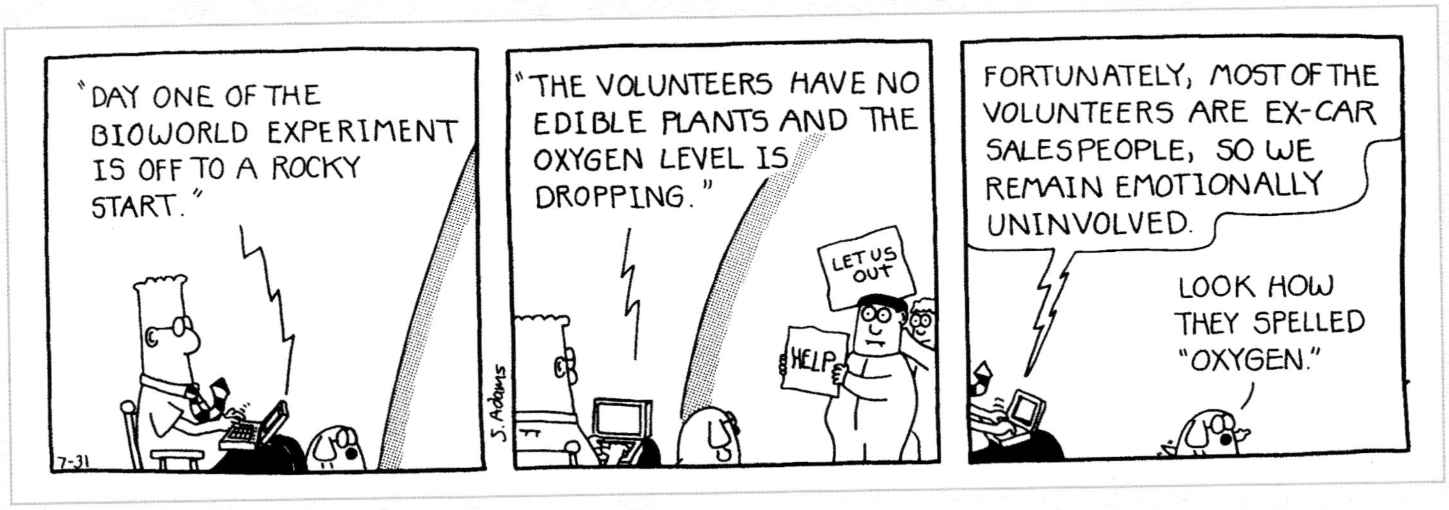
"DAY ONE OF THE BIOWORLD EXPERIMENT IS OFF TO A ROCKY START."
7-31
"THE VOLUNTEERS HAVE NO EDIBLE PLANTS AND THE OXYGEN LEVEL IS DROPPING."
LET US OUT
HELP
S. Adams
FORTUNATELY, MOST OF THE VOLUNTEERS ARE EX-CAR SALESPEOPLE, SO WE REMAIN EMOTIONALLY UNINVOLVED.
LOOK HOW THEY SPELLED "OXYGEN."

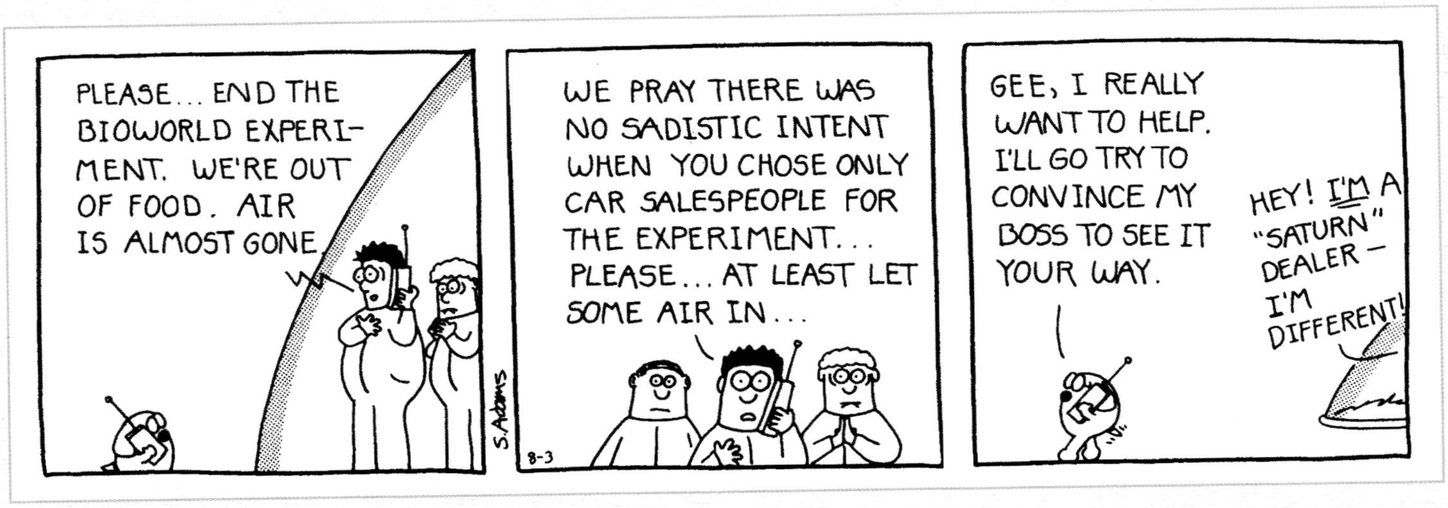
PLEASE... END THE BIOWORLD EXPERI-MENT. WE'RE OUT OF FOOD. AIR IS ALMOST GONE.
S. Adams
8-3
WE PRAY THERE WAS NO SADISTIC INTENT WHEN YOU CHOSE ONLY CAR SALESPEOPLE FOR THE EXPERIMENT... PLEASE... AT LEAST LET SOME AIR IN...
GEE, I REALLY WANT TO HELP. I'LL GO TRY TO CONVINCE MY BOSS TO SEE IT YOUR WAY.
HEY! I'M A "SATURN" DEALER — I'M DIFFERENT!

One of the great things about being a cartoonist is killing people who have demonstrated they deserve it.

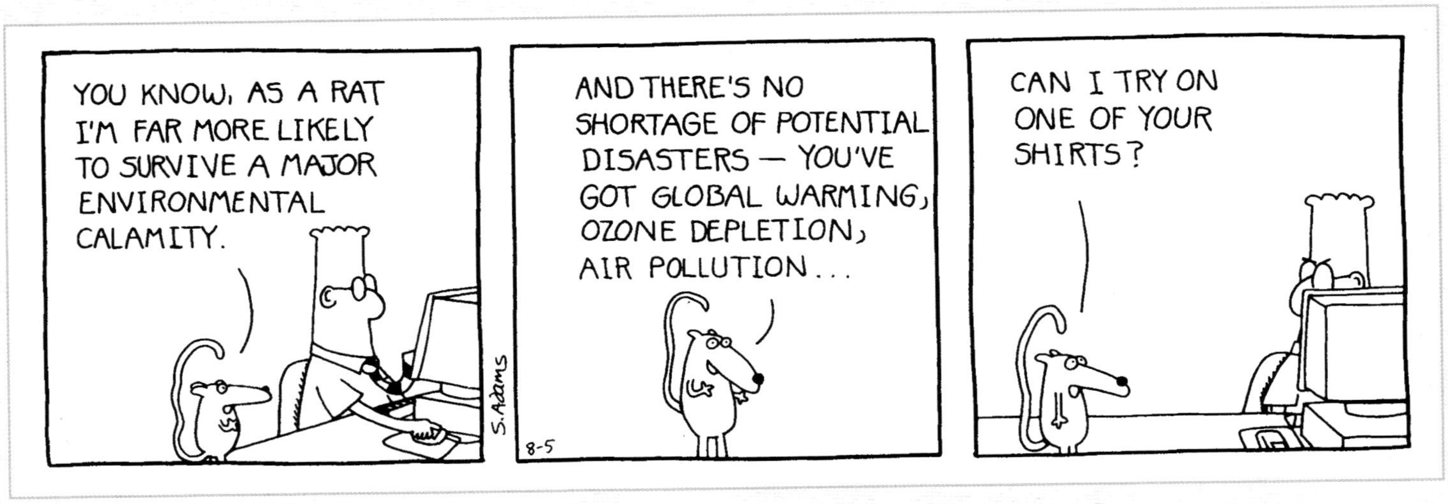
YOU KNOW, AS A RAT I'M FAR MORE LIKELY TO SURVIVE A MAJOR ENVIRONMENTAL CALAMITY.
S. Adams
8-5
AND THERE'S NO SHORTAGE OF POTENTIAL DISASTERS — YOU'VE GOT GLOBAL WARMING, OZONE DEPLETION, AIR POLLUTION...
CAN I TRY ON ONE OF YOUR SHIRTS?

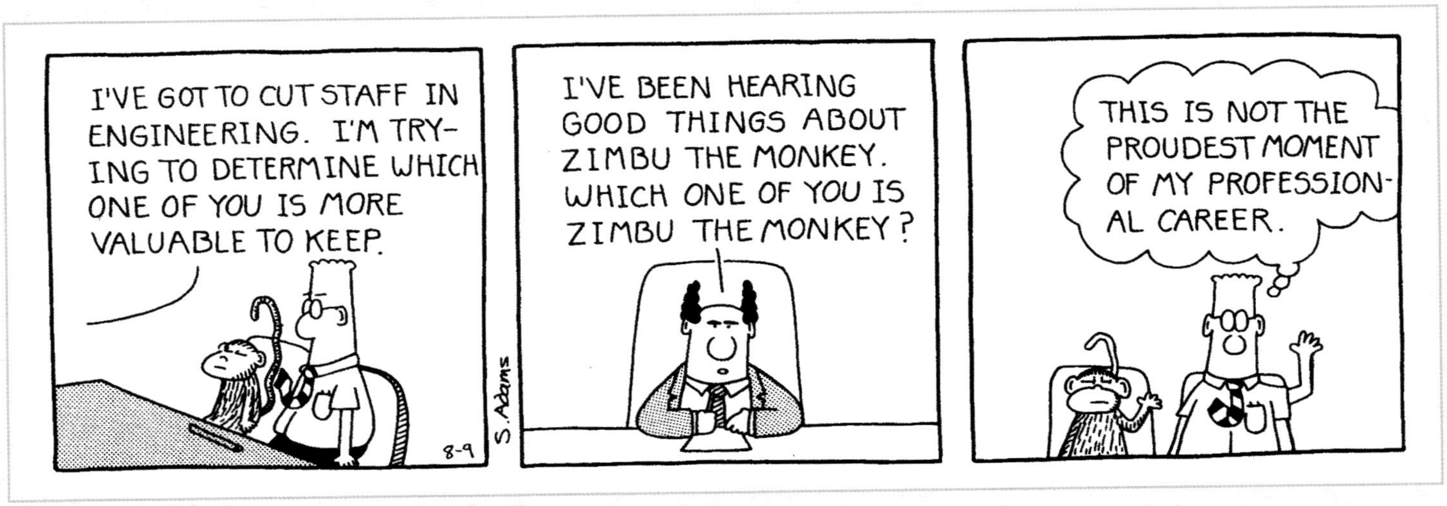
I'VE GOT TO CUT STAFF IN ENGINEERING. I'M TRY-ING TO DETERMINE WHICH ONE OF YOU IS MORE VALUABLE TO KEEP.
8-9
S. Adams
I'VE BEEN HEARING GOOD THINGS ABOUT ZIMBU THE MONKEY. WHICH ONE OF YOU IS ZIMBU THE MONKEY?
THIS IS NOT THE PROUDEST MOMENT OF MY PROFESSION-AL CAREER.

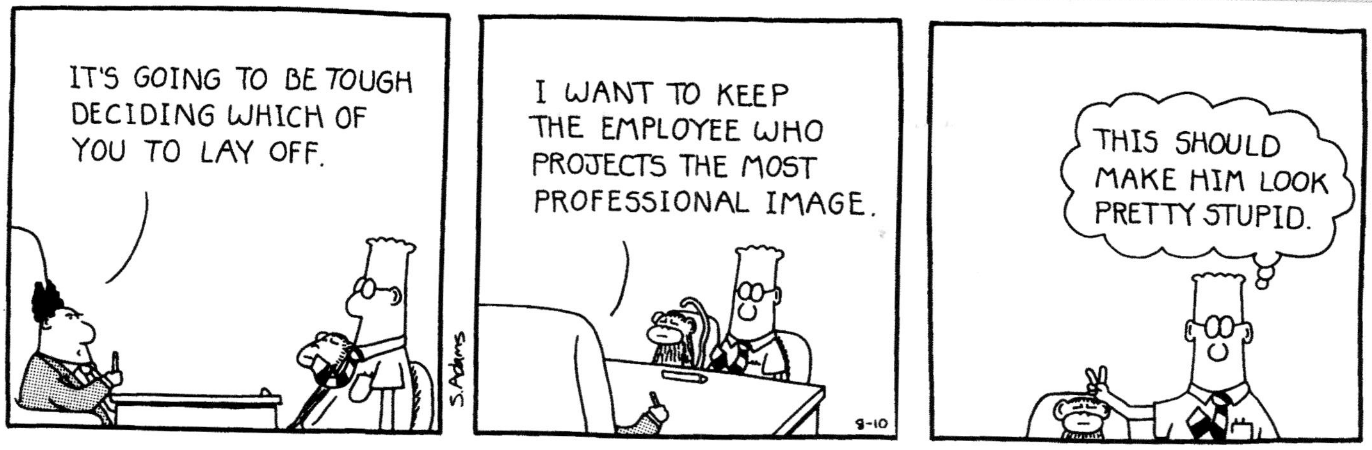
IT'S GOING TO BE TOUGH DECIDING WHICH OF YOU TO LAY OFF.
S. Adams
I WANT TO KEEP THE EMPLOYEE WHO PROJECTS THE MOST PROFESSIONAL IMAGE.
8-10
THIS SHOULD MAKE HIM LOOK PRETTY STUPID.

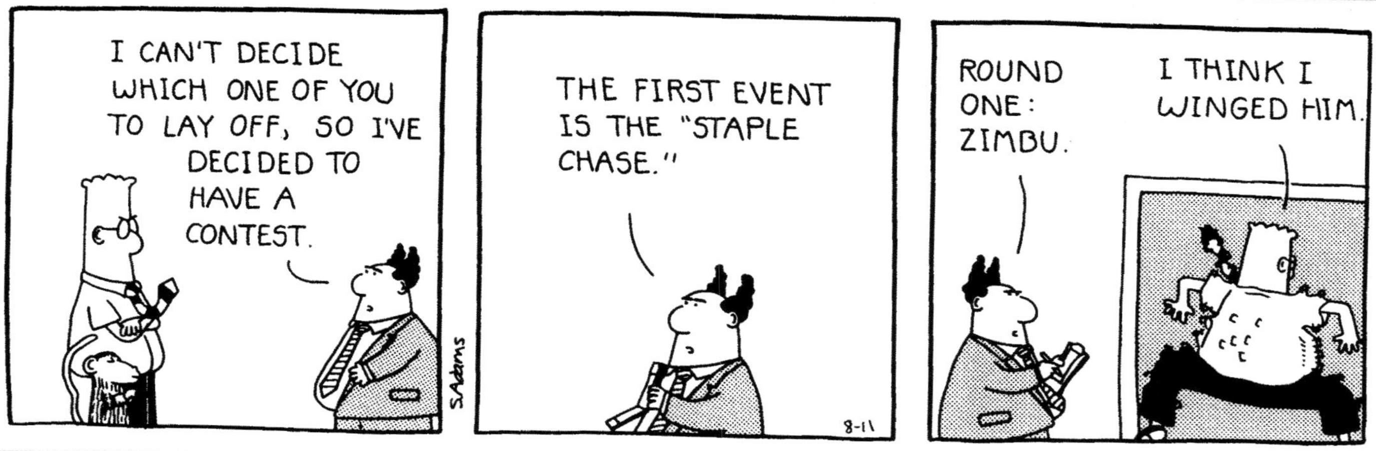
I CAN'T DECIDE WHICH ONE OF YOU TO LAY OFF, SO I'VE DECIDED TO HAVE A CONTEST.
S. Adams
THE FIRST EVENT IS THE "STAPLE CHASE."
8-11
ROUND ONE: ZIMBU.
I THINK I WINGED HIM.

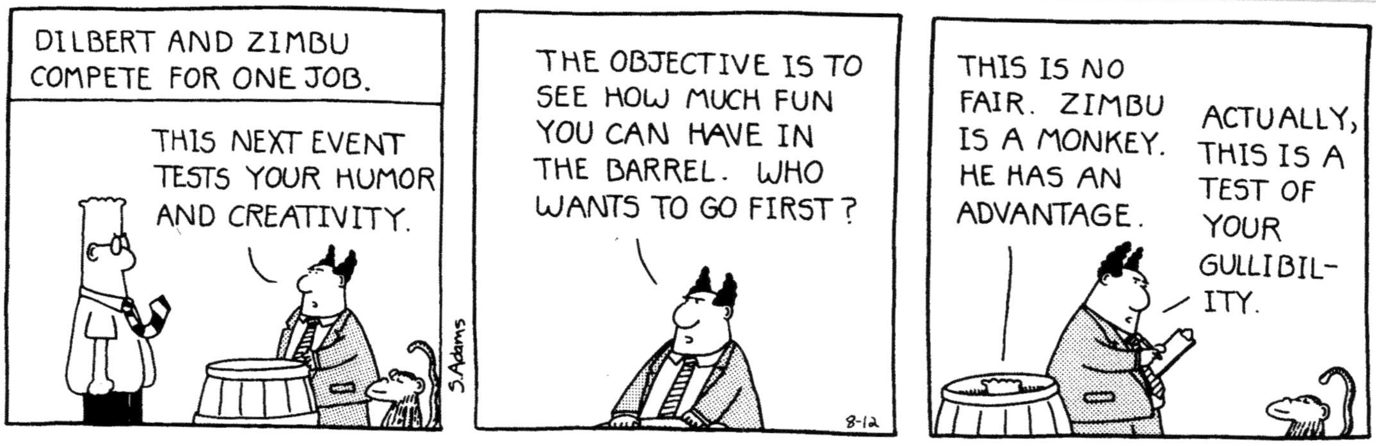
DILBERT AND ZIMBU COMPETE FOR ONE JOB.
THIS NEXT EVENT TESTS YOUR HUMOR AND CREATIVITY.
S. Adams
THE OBJECTIVE IS TO SEE HOW MUCH FUN YOU CAN HAVE IN THE BARREL. WHO WANTS TO GO FIRST?
8-12
THIS IS NO FAIR. ZIMBU IS A MONKEY. HE HAS AN ADVANTAGE.
ACTUALLY, THIS IS A TEST OF YOUR GULLIBIL-ITY.

Years later, this series on Zimbu the monkey is still quoted to me when I meet people. I think the name Zimbu is part of the appeal. It rolls off the tongue.

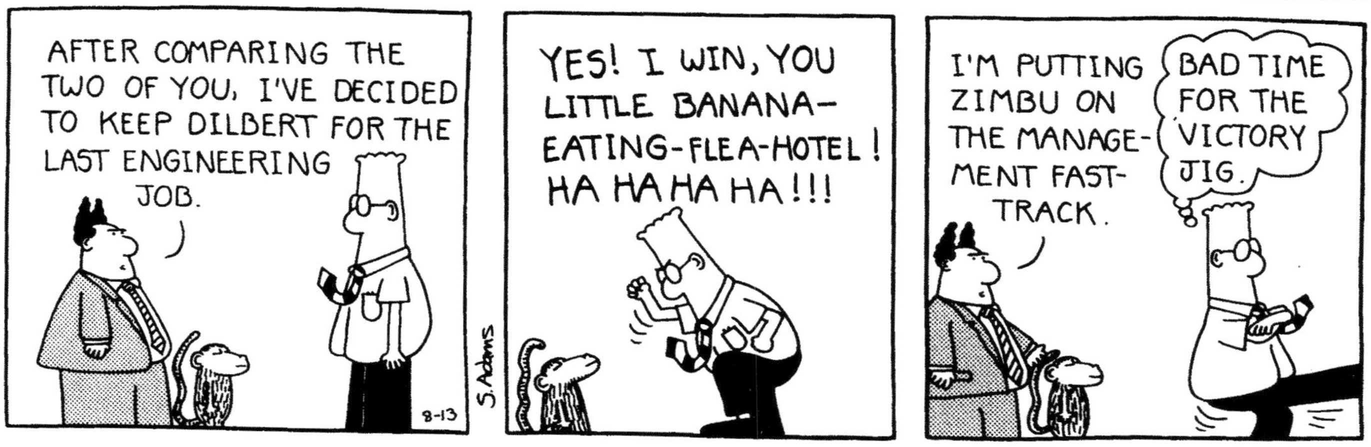
AFTER COMPARING THE TWO OF YOU, I'VE DECIDED TO KEEP DILBERT FOR THE LAST ENGINEERING JOB.
8-13
S. Adams
YES! I WIN, YOU LITTLE BANANA-EATING-FLEA-HOTEL! HA HA HA HA!!!
I'M PUTTING ZIMBU ON THE MANAGE-MENT FAST-TRACK.
BAD TIME FOR THE VICTORY JIG.

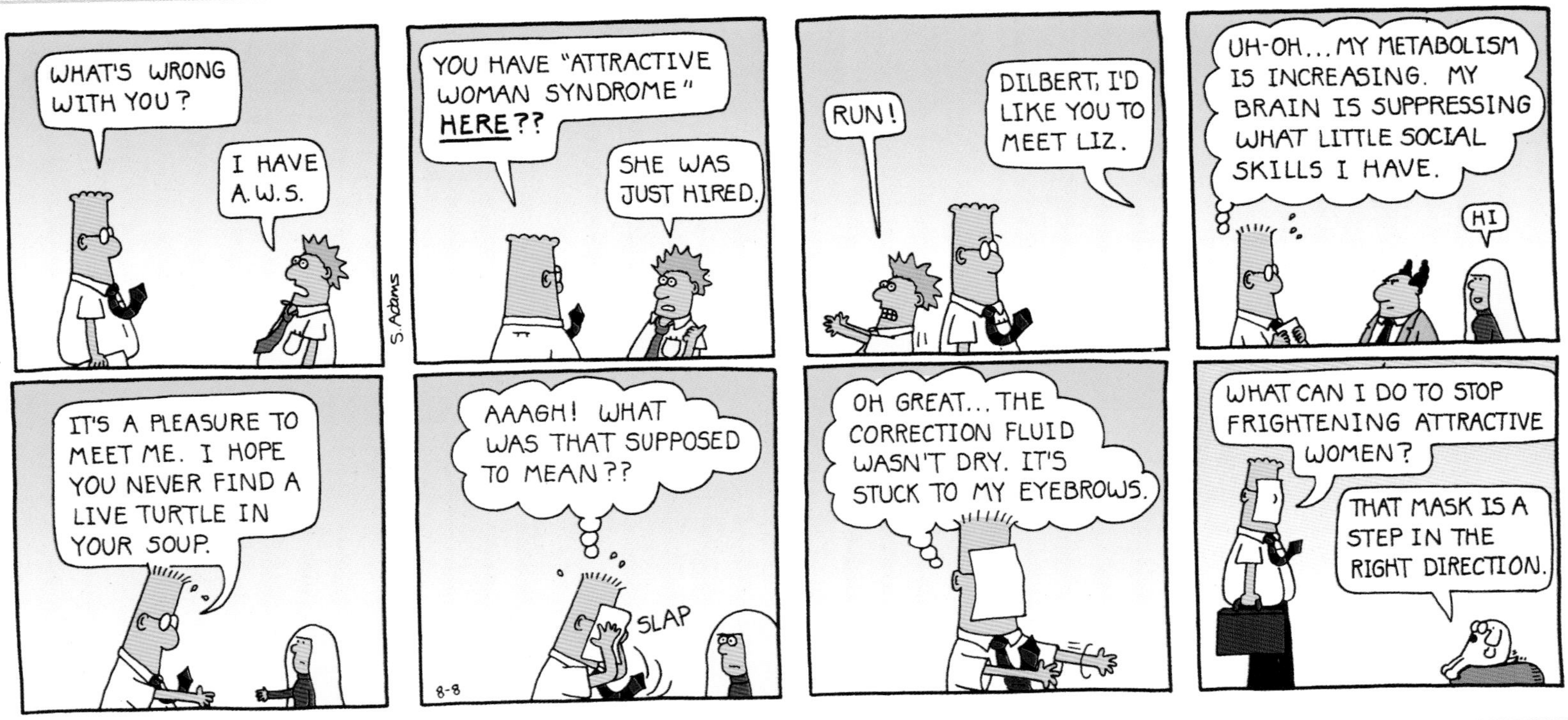
WHAT'S WRONG WITH YOU?
I HAVE A.W.S.
S. Adams
YOU HAVE "ATTRACTIVE WOMAN SYNDROME" HERE??
SHE WAS JUST HIRED.
RUN!
DILBERT, I'D LIKE YOU TO MEET LIZ.
UH-OH... MY METABOLISM IS INCREASING. MY BRAIN IS SUPPRESSING WHAT LITTLE SOCIAL SKILLS I HAVE.
HI
IT'S A PLEASURE TO MEET ME. I HOPE YOU NEVER FIND A LIVE TURTLE IN YOUR SOUP.
AAAGH! WHAT WAS THAT SUPPOSED TO MEAN??
SLAP
8-8
OH GREAT... THE CORRECTION FLUID WASN'T DRY. IT'S STUCK TO MY EYEBROWS.
WHAT CAN I DO TO STOP FRIGHTENING ATTRACTIVE WOMEN?
THAT MASK IS A STEP IN THE RIGHT DIRECTION.

I think this was the introduction of Dilbert's longest-lasting girlfriend, Liz.

Any reference to chipmunks or squirrels is automatically funny. No one knows why.

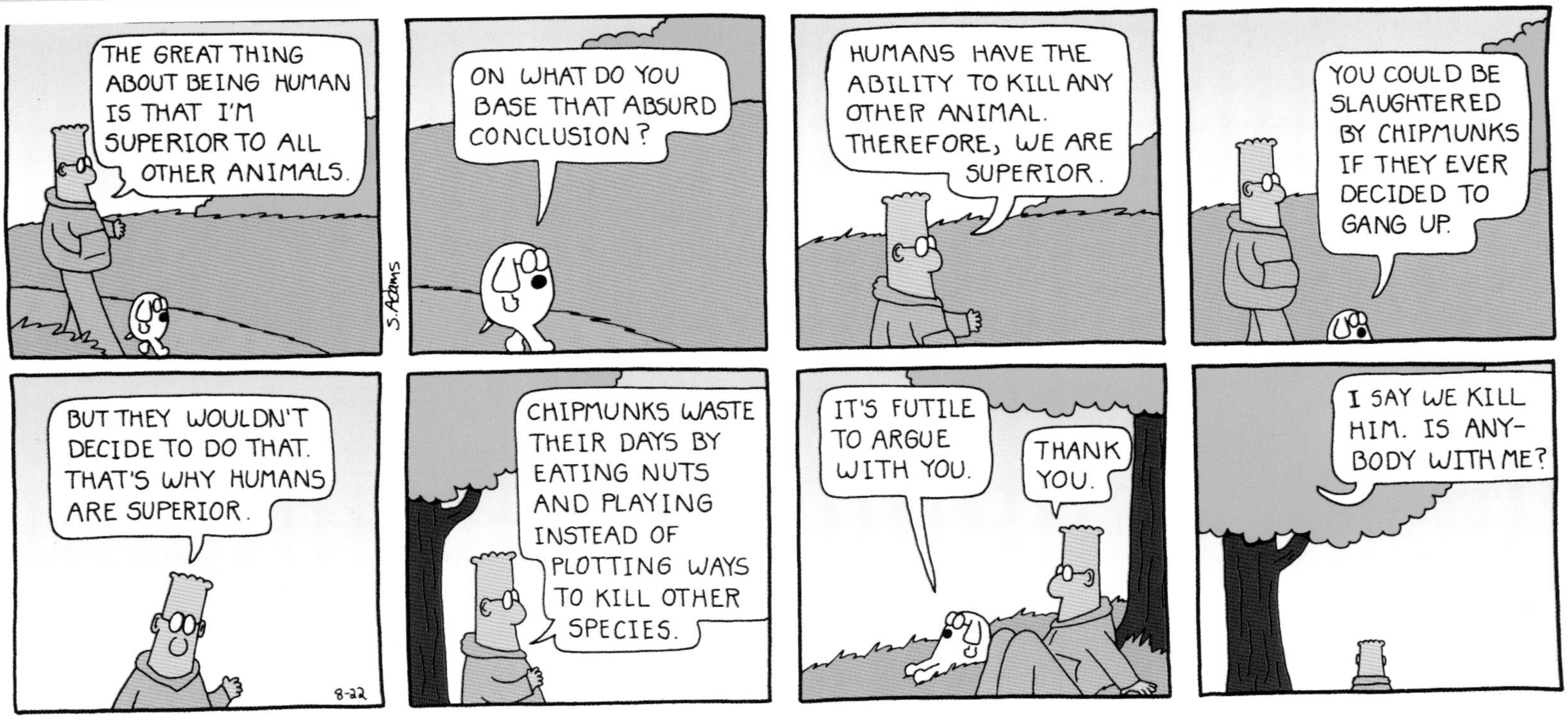
THE GREAT THING ABOUT BEING HUMAN IS THAT I'M SUPERIOR TO ALL OTHER ANIMALS.
S. Adams
ON WHAT DO YOU BASE THAT ABSURD CONCLUSION?
HUMANS HAVE THE ABILITY TO KILL ANY OTHER ANIMAL. THEREFORE, WE ARE SUPERIOR.
YOU COULD BE SLAUGHTERED BY CHIPMUNKS IF THEY EVER DECIDED TO GANG UP.
BUT THEY WOULDN'T DECIDE TO DO THAT. THAT'S WHY HUMANS ARE SUPERIOR.
8-22
CHIPMUNKS WASTE THEIR DAYS BY EATING NUTS AND PLAYING INSTEAD OF PLOTTING WAYS TO KILL OTHER SPECIES.
IT'S FUTILE TO ARGUE WITH YOU.
THANK YOU.
I SAY WE KILL HIM. IS ANY-BODY WITH ME?

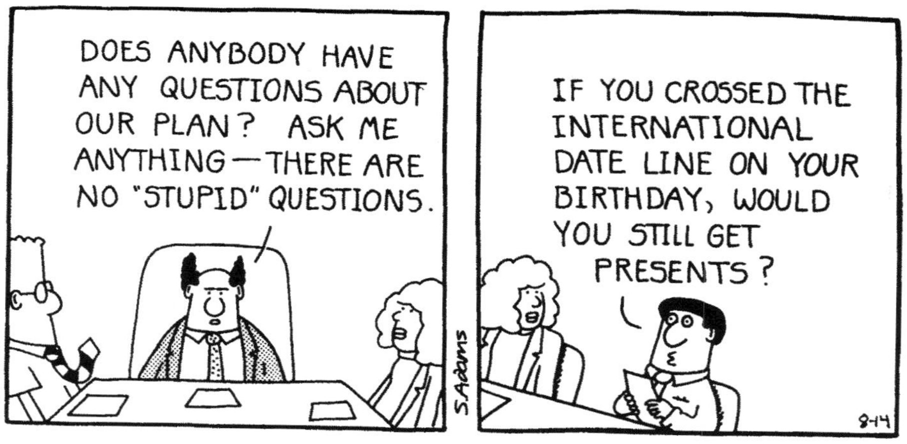
DOES ANYBODY HAVE ANY QUESTIONS ABOUT OUR PLAN? ASK ME ANYTHING—THERE ARE NO "STUPID" QUESTIONS.
IF YOU CROSSED THE INTERNATIONAL DATE LINE ON YOUR BIRTHDAY, WOULD YOU STILL GET PRESENTS?
OH GREAT... THERE ARE STUPID QUESTIONS AND I DON'T KNOW THE ANSWERS.
S. Adams
8-14

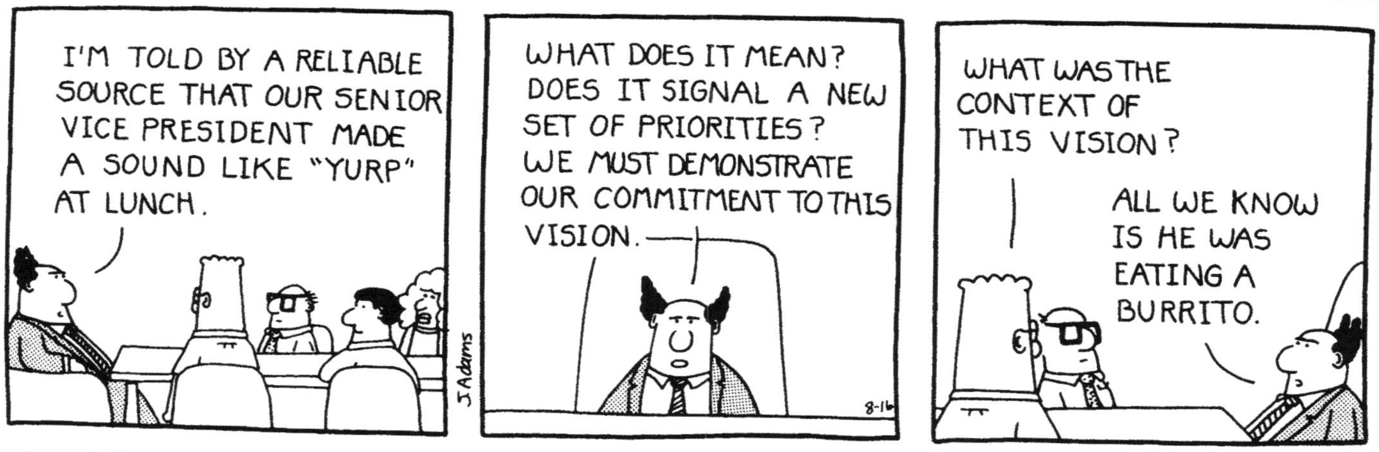
I'M TOLD BY A RELIABLE SOURCE THAT OUR SENIOR VICE PRESIDENT MADE A SOUND LIKE "YURP" AT LUNCH.
WHAT DOES IT MEAN? DOES IT SIGNAL A NEW SET OF PRIORITIES? WE MUST DEMONSTRATE OUR COMMITMENT TO THIS VISION.
WHAT WAS THE CONTEXT OF THIS VISION?
ALL WE KNOW IS HE WAS EATING A BURRITO.
S. Adams
8-16

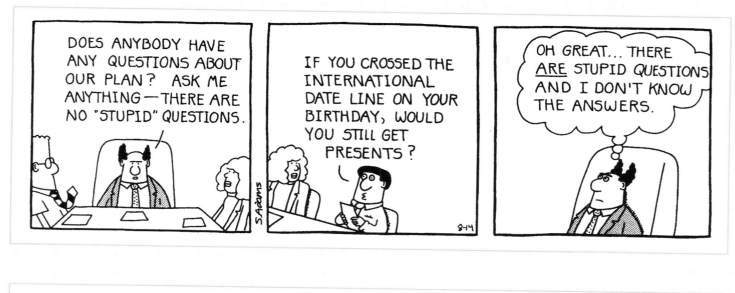

I got a lot of complaints from readers who said the Vulcan grip doesn't cause death, only temporary unconsciousness. That's when I really understood who my readers were.

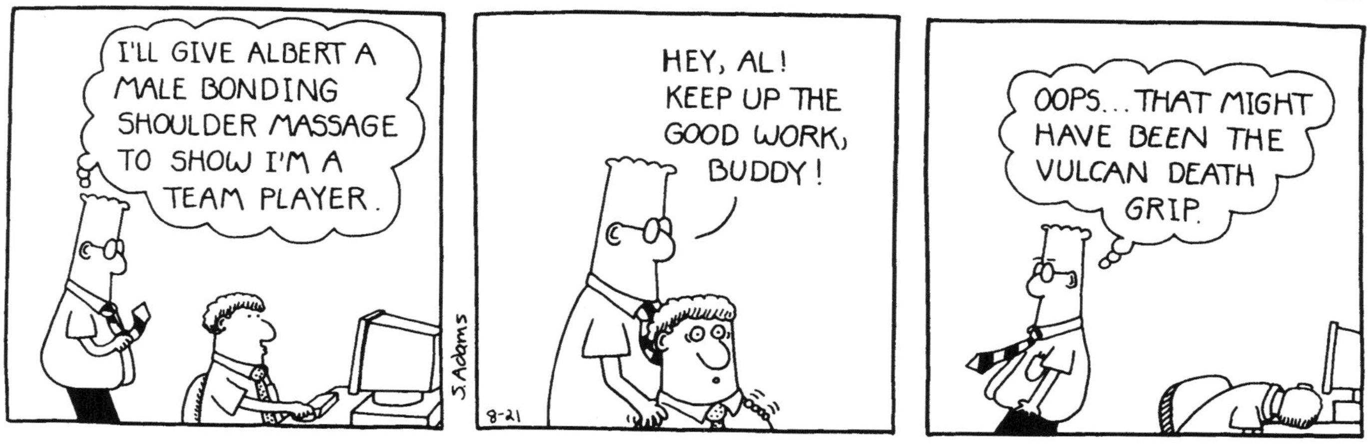
I'LL GIVE ALBERT A MALE BONDING SHOULDER MASSAGE TO SHOW I'M A TEAM PLAYER.
HEY, AL! KEEP UP THE GOOD WORK, BUDDY!
OOPS... THAT MIGHT HAVE BEEN THE VULCAN DEATH GRIP.
S. Adams
8-21

People often ask what the Elbonians are standing in. Water, snow, mud? The answer is mud.

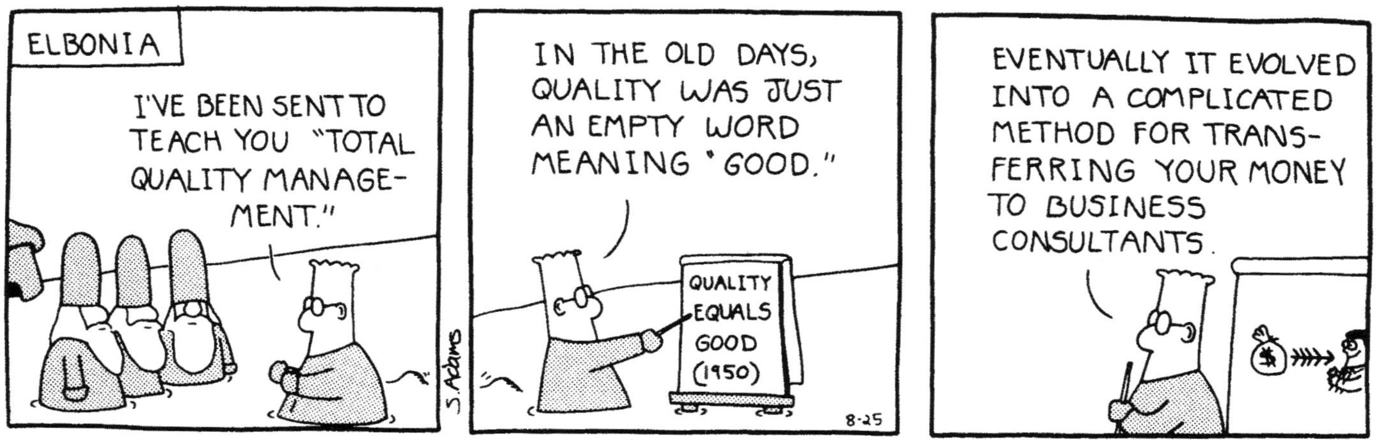
ELBONIA
I'VE BEEN SENT TO TEACH YOU "TOTAL QUALITY MANAGE-MENT."
IN THE OLD DAYS, QUALITY WAS JUST AN EMPTY WORD MEANING "GOOD."
QUALITY EQUALS GOOD (1950)
EVENTUALLY IT EVOLVED INTO A COMPLICATED METHOD FOR TRANS-FERRING YOUR MONEY TO BUSINESS CONSULTANTS.
S. Adams
8-25

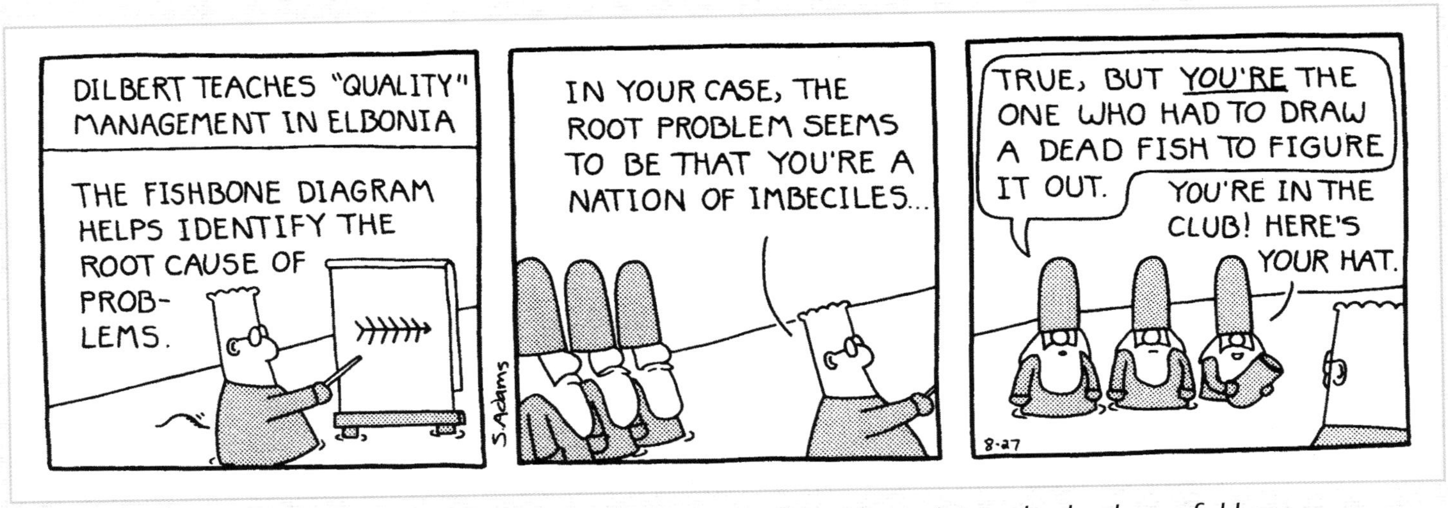
DILBERT TEACHES "QUALITY" MANAGEMENT IN ELBONIA
THE FISHBONE DIAGRAM HELPS IDENTIFY THE ROOT CAUSE OF PROBLEMS.
IN YOUR CASE, THE ROOT PROBLEM SEEMS TO BE THAT YOU'RE A NATION OF IMBECILES...
TRUE, BUT YOU'RE THE ONE WHO HAD TO DRAW A DEAD FISH TO FIGURE IT OUT.
YOU'RE IN THE CLUB! HERE'S YOUR HAT.

When I worked at Pacific Bell, I went through a similar process. A team leader drew a fishbone diagram on the whiteboard and walked us through a process to find the root cause. We all tried hard to ignore the obvious explanation that our co-workers were defective.

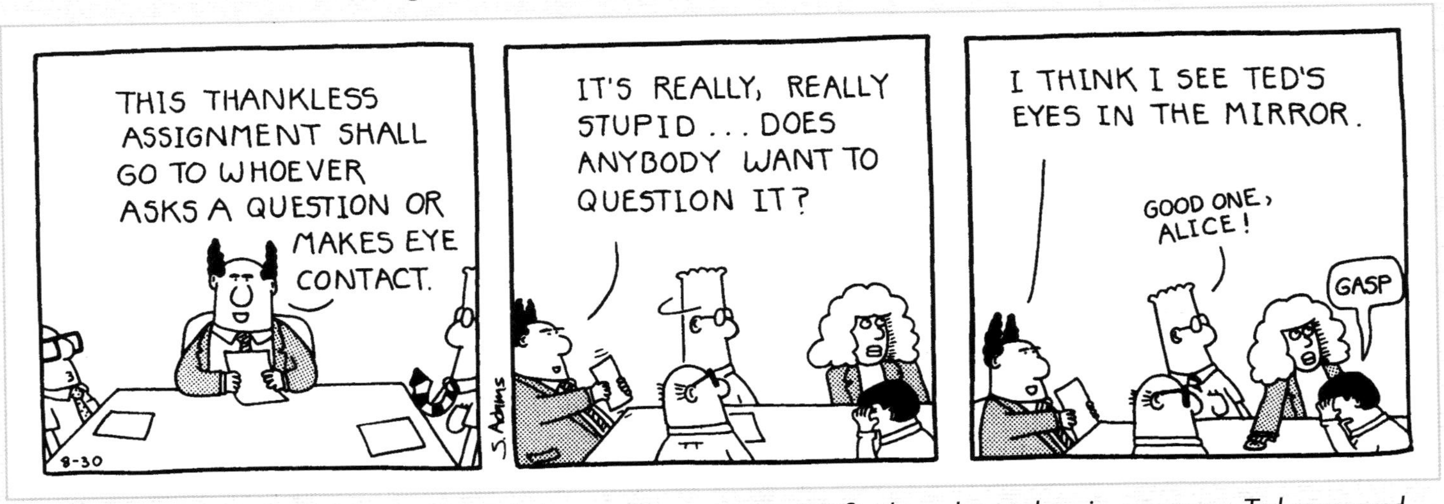
THIS THANKLESS ASSIGNMENT SHALL GO TO WHOEVER ASKS A QUESTION OR MAKES EYE CONTACT.
IT'S REALLY, REALLY STUPID ... DOES ANYBODY WANT TO QUESTION IT?
I THINK I SEE TED'S EYES IN THE MIRROR.
GOOD ONE, ALICE!
GASP

Ted was my generic guy. Whenever I needed an extra guy to die, get fired, or dumped on in some way, Ted appeared.

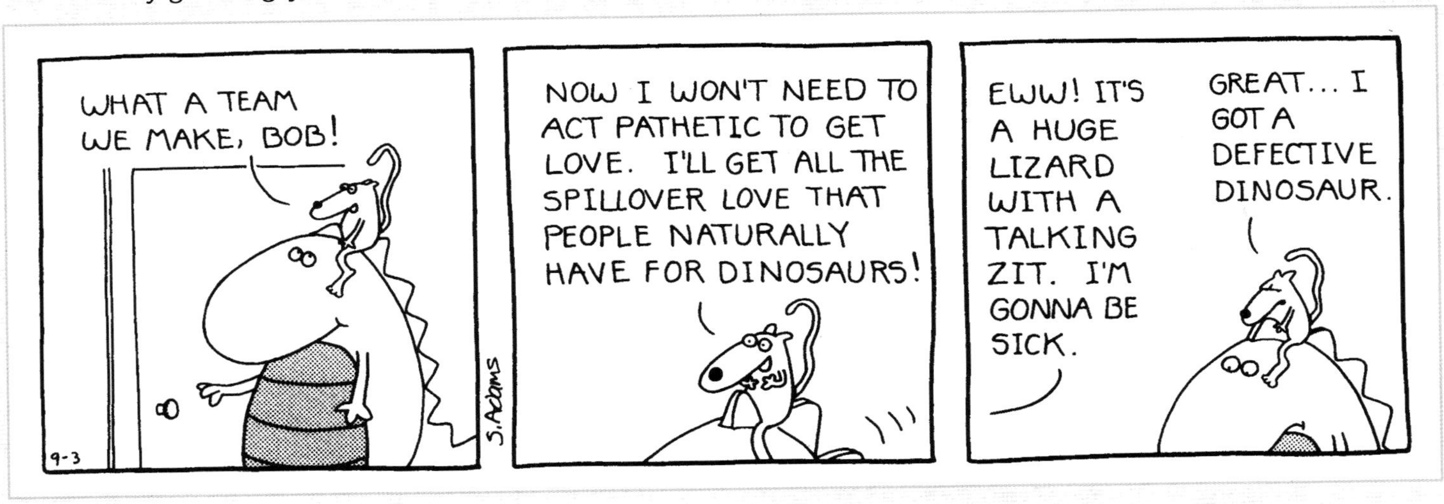
WHAT A TEAM WE MAKE, BOB!
NOW I WON'T NEED TO ACT PATHETIC TO GET LOVE. I'LL GET ALL THE SPILLOVER LOVE THAT PEOPLE NATURALLY HAVE FOR DINOSAURS!
EWW! IT'S A HUGE LIZARD WITH A TALKING ZIT. I'M GONNA BE SICK.
GREAT... I GOT A DEFECTIVE DINOSAUR.

I got a lot of complaints from satire-impaired people saying temps did not deserve this bad treatment in the comics.

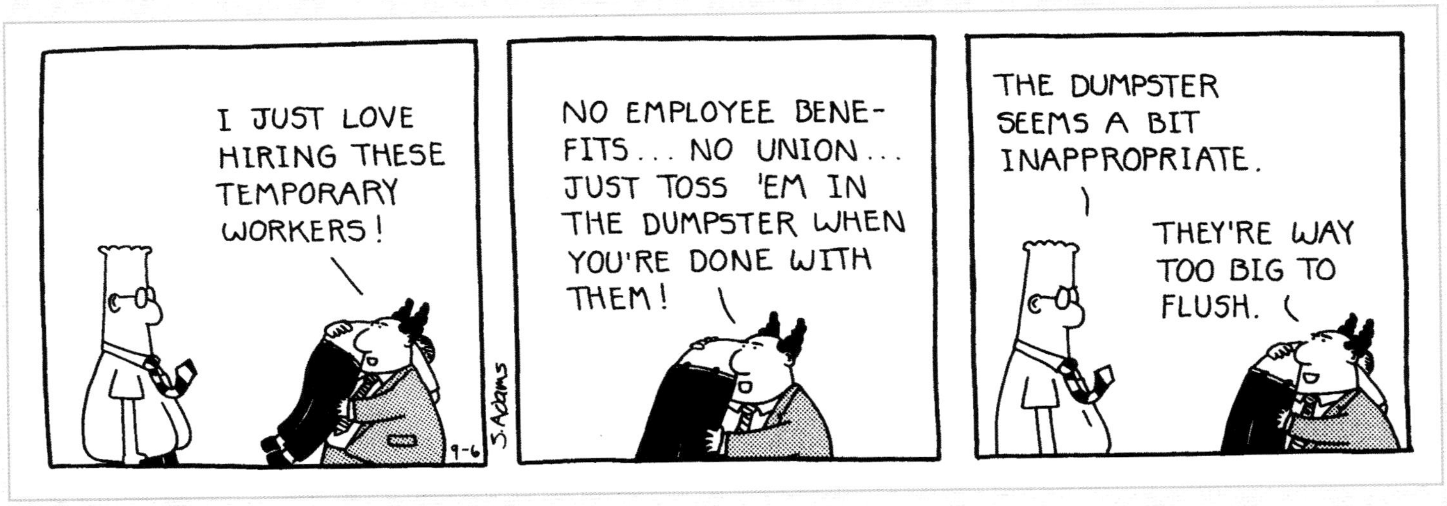
I JUST LOVE HIRING THESE TEMPORARY WORKERS!
NO EMPLOYEE BENEFITS... NO UNION... JUST TOSS 'EM IN THE DUMPSTER WHEN YOU'RE DONE WITH THEM!
THE DUMPSTER SEEMS A BIT INAPPROPRIATE.
THEY'RE WAY TOO BIG TO FLUSH.

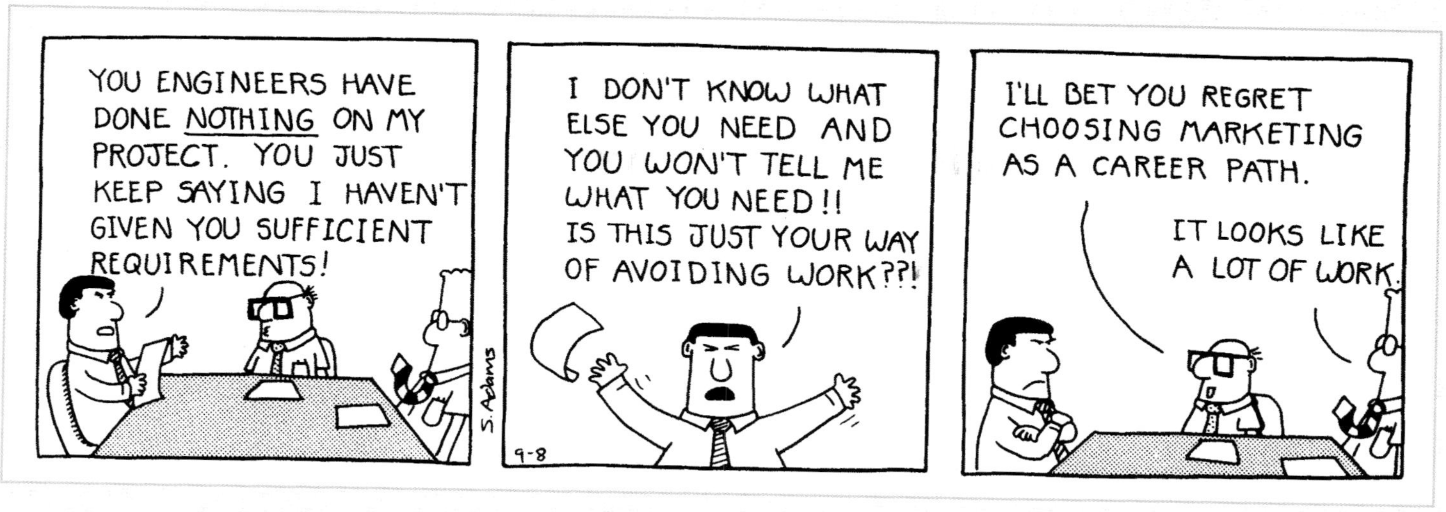
YOU ENGINEERS HAVE DONE NOTHING ON MY PROJECT. YOU JUST KEEP SAYING I HAVEN'T GIVEN YOU SUFFICIENT REQUIREMENTS!
S. Adams
I DON'T KNOW WHAT ELSE YOU NEED AND YOU WON'T TELL ME WHAT YOU NEED!!
IS THIS JUST YOUR WAY OF AVOIDING WORK??!
9-8
I'LL BET YOU REGRET CHOOSING MARKETING AS A CAREER PATH.
IT LOOKS LIKE A LOT OF WORK.

The battle between marketing and engineering became a running theme.

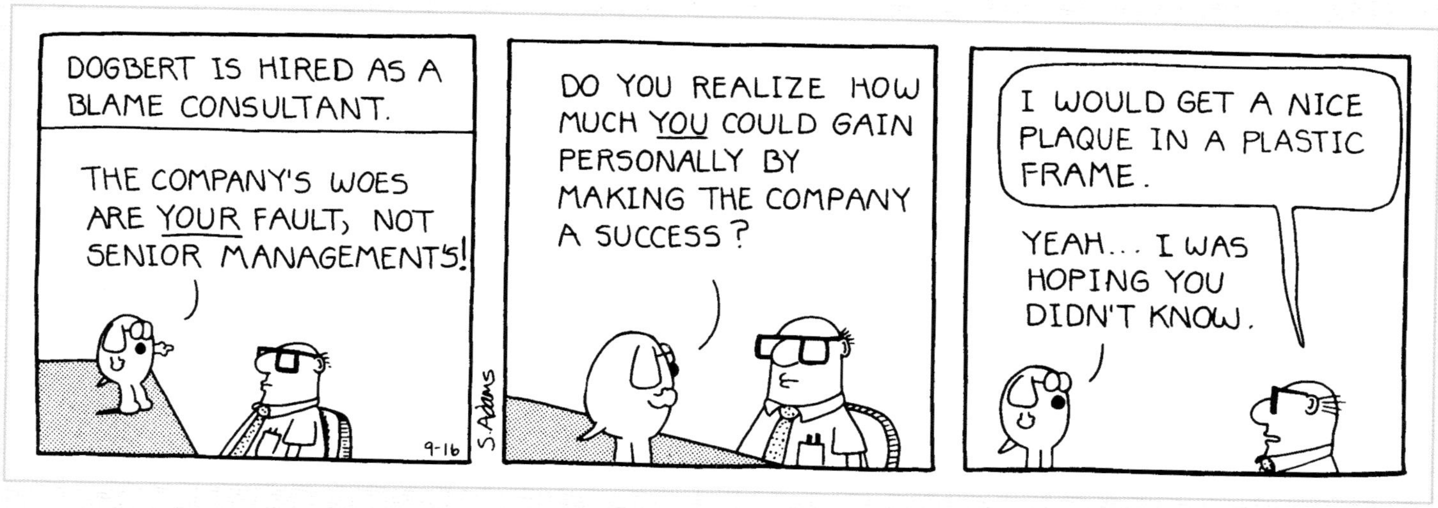
DOGBERT IS HIRED AS A BLAME CONSULTANT.
THE COMPANY'S WOES ARE YOUR FAULT, NOT SENIOR MANAGEMENT'S!
9-16
S. Adams
DO YOU REALIZE HOW MUCH YOU COULD GAIN PERSONALLY BY MAKING THE COMPANY A SUCCESS?
I WOULD GET A NICE PLAQUE IN A PLASTIC FRAME.
YEAH... I WAS HOPING YOU DIDN'T KNOW.

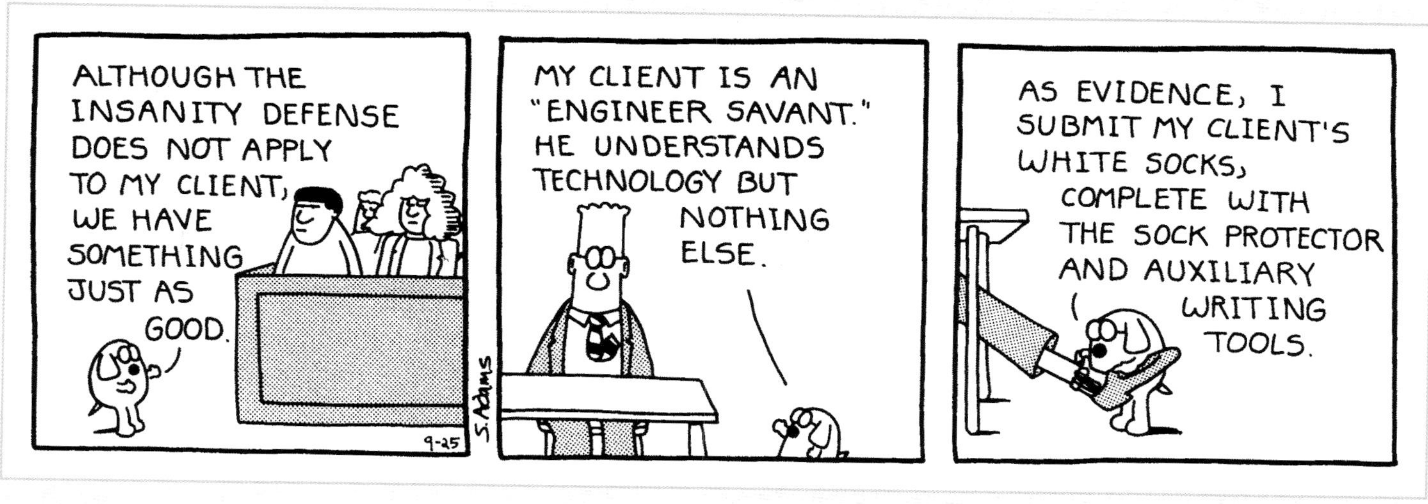
ALTHOUGH THE INSANITY DEFENSE DOES NOT APPLY TO MY CLIENT, WE HAVE SOMETHING JUST AS GOOD.
9-25
S. Adams
MY CLIENT IS AN "ENGINEER SAVANT." HE UNDERSTANDS TECHNOLOGY BUT NOTHING ELSE.
AS EVIDENCE, I SUBMIT MY CLIENT'S WHITE SOCKS, COMPLETE WITH THE SOCK PROTECTOR AND AUXILIARY WRITING TOOLS.

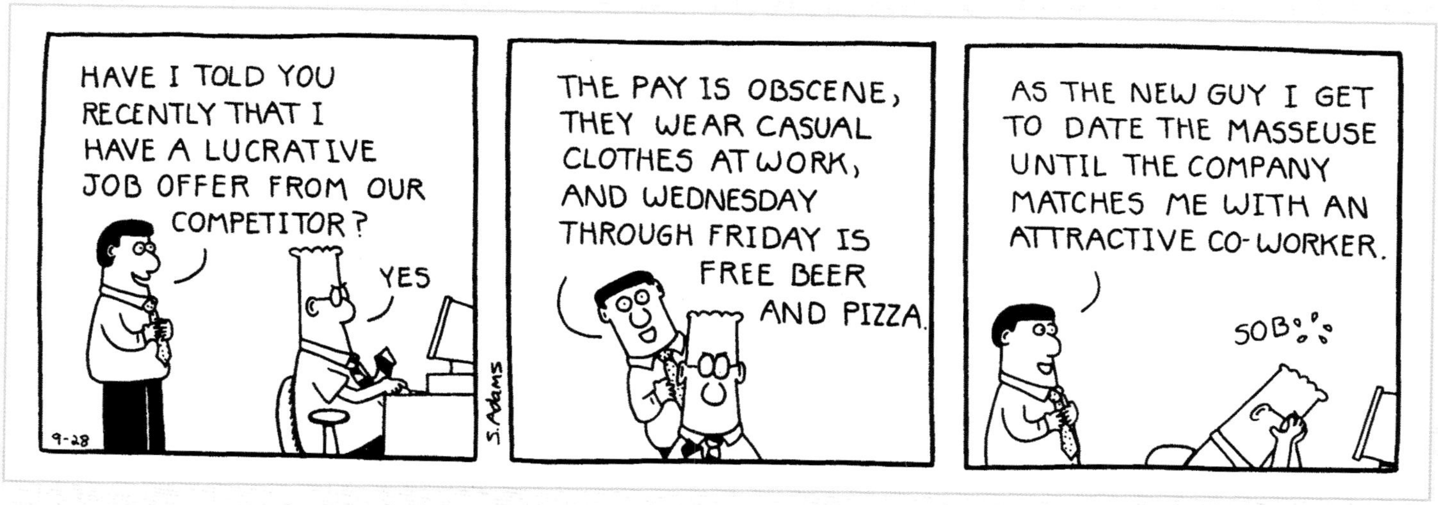
HAVE I TOLD YOU RECENTLY THAT I HAVE A LUCRATIVE JOB OFFER FROM OUR COMPETITOR?
YES
9-28
S. Adams
THE PAY IS OBSCENE, THEY WEAR CASUAL CLOTHES AT WORK, AND WEDNESDAY THROUGH FRIDAY IS FREE BEER AND PIZZA.
AS THE NEW GUY I GET TO DATE THE MASSEUSE UNTIL THE COMPANY MATCHES ME WITH AN ATTRACTIVE CO-WORKER.
SOB

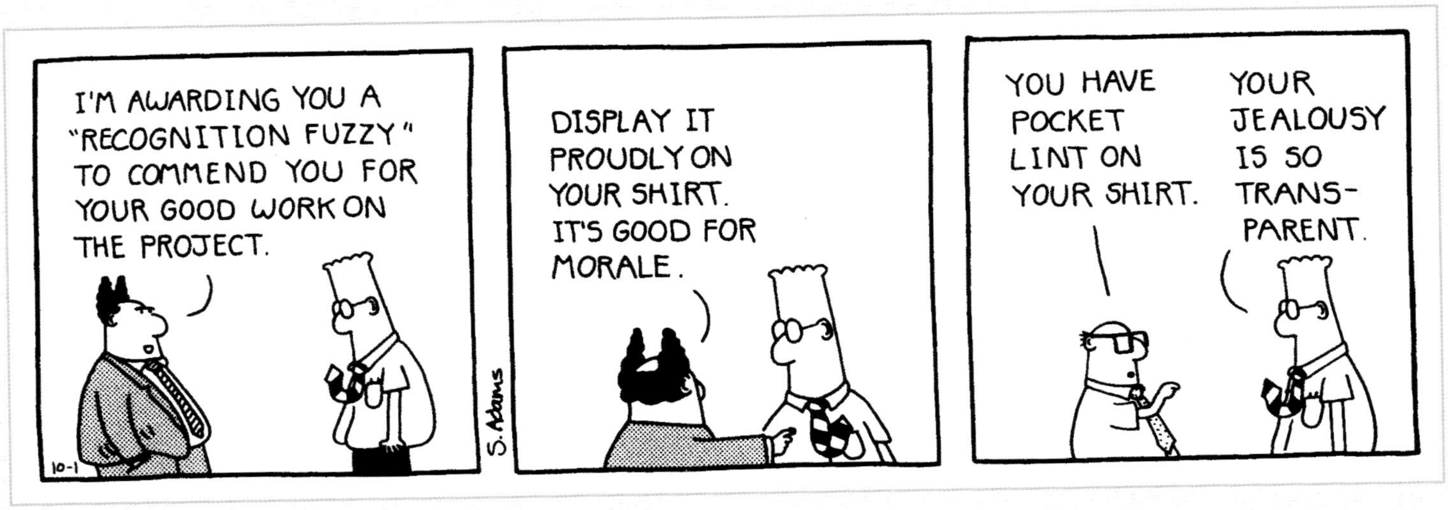

I'M AWARDING YOU A "RECOGNITION FUZZY" TO COMMEND YOU FOR YOUR GOOD WORK ON THE PROJECT.
DISPLAY IT PROUDLY ON YOUR SHIRT. IT'S GOOD FOR MORALE.
YOU HAVE POCKET LINT ON YOUR SHIRT.
YOUR JEALOUSY IS SO TRANS-PARENT.

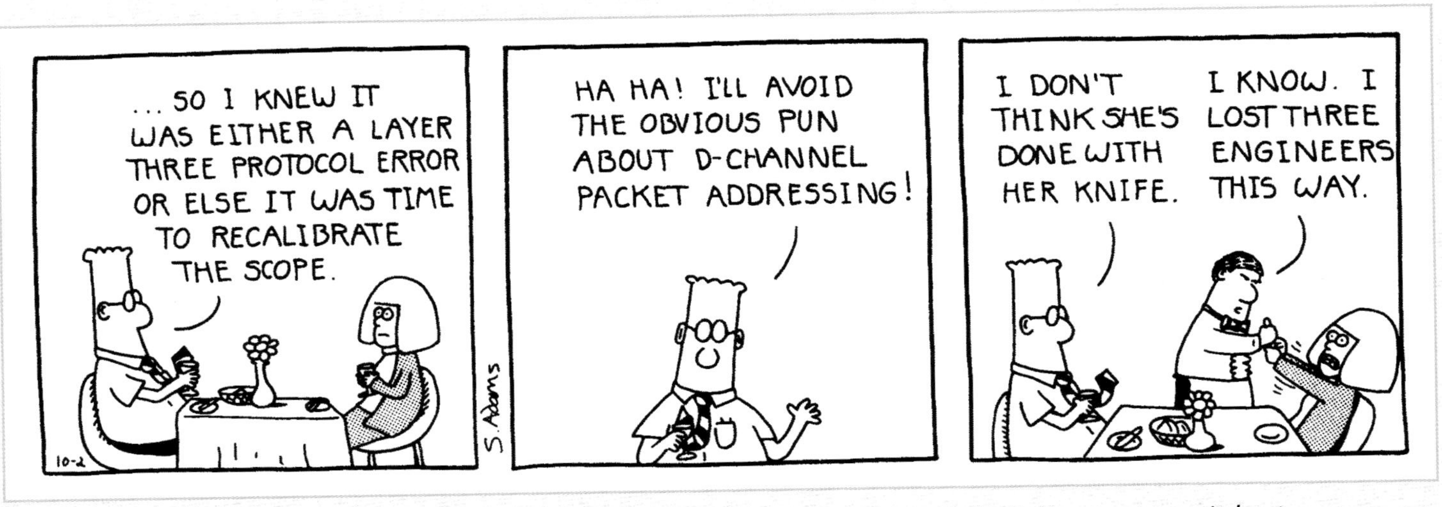

... SO I KNEW IT WAS EITHER A LAYER THREE PROTOCOL ERROR OR ELSE IT WAS TIME TO RECALIBRATE THE SCOPE.
HA HA! I'LL AVOID THE OBVIOUS PUN ABOUT D-CHANNEL PACKET ADDRESSING!
I DON'T THINK SHE'S DONE WITH HER KNIFE.
I KNOW. I LOST THREE ENGINEERS THIS WAY.

This was another running theme: executives with good hair. At Pacific Bell, it was so true it hurt.

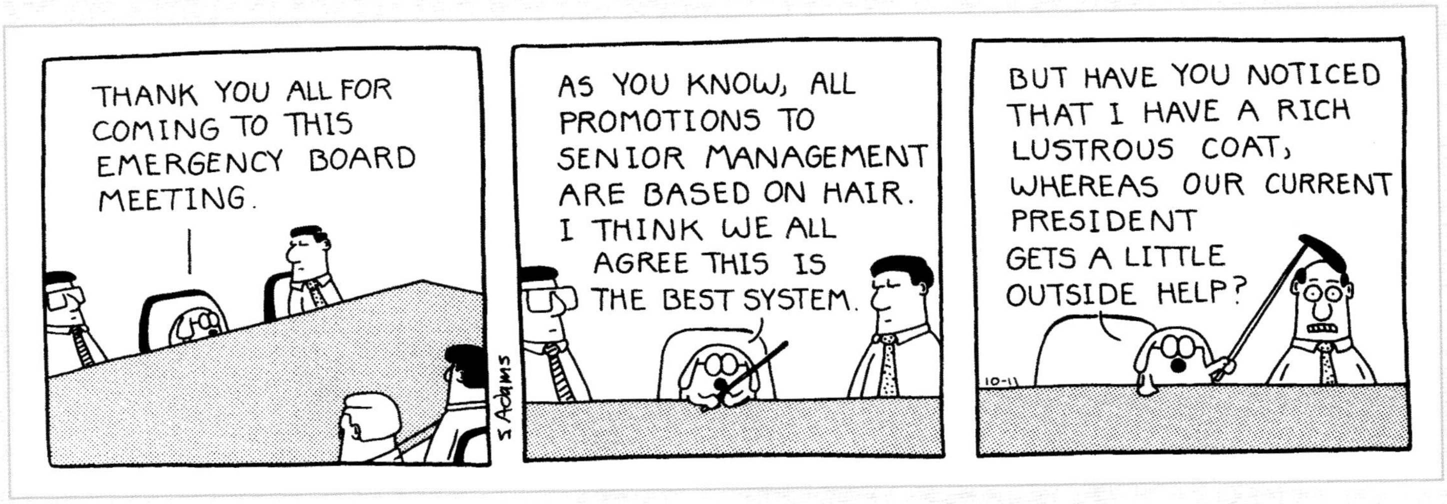

THANK YOU ALL FOR COMING TO THIS EMERGENCY BOARD MEETING.
AS YOU KNOW, ALL PROMOTIONS TO SENIOR MANAGEMENT ARE BASED ON HAIR. I THINK WE ALL AGREE THIS IS THE BEST SYSTEM.
BUT HAVE YOU NOTICED THAT I HAVE A RICH LUSTROUS COAT, WHEREAS OUR CURRENT PRESIDENT GETS A LITTLE OUTSIDE HELP?

At this point, Alice had a family. Later, she morphed into a single woman with no kids.

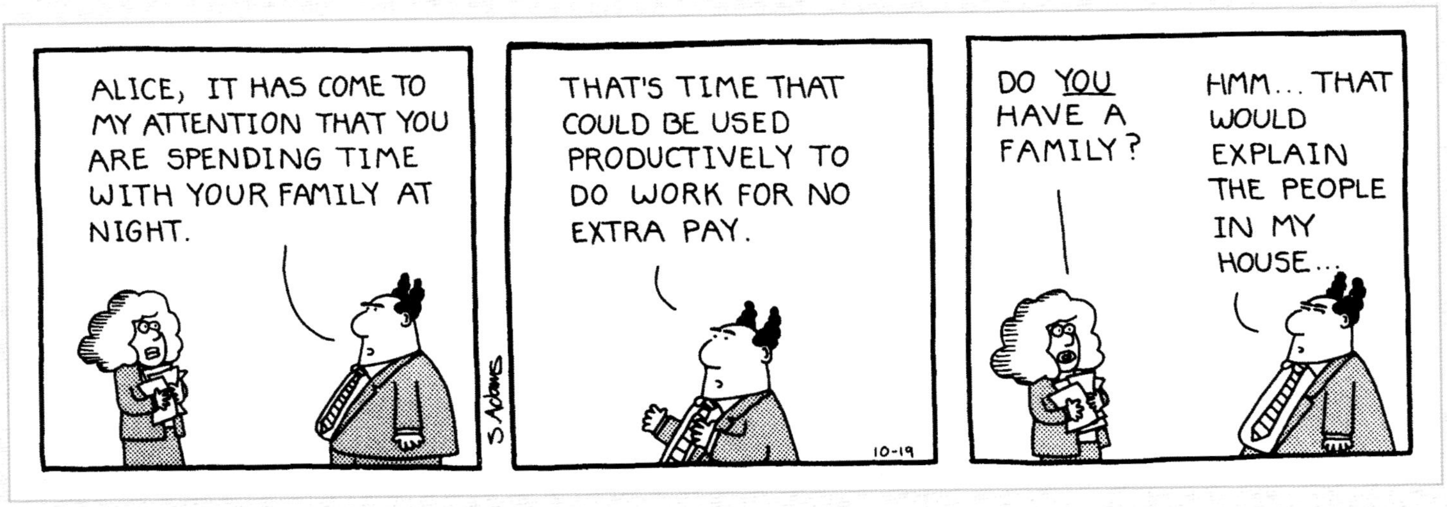

ALICE, IT HAS COME TO MY ATTENTION THAT YOU ARE SPENDING TIME WITH YOUR FAMILY AT NIGHT.
THAT'S TIME THAT COULD BE USED PRODUCTIVELY TO DO WORK FOR NO EXTRA PAY.
DO YOU HAVE A FAMILY?
HMM... THAT WOULD EXPLAIN THE PEOPLE IN MY HOUSE...

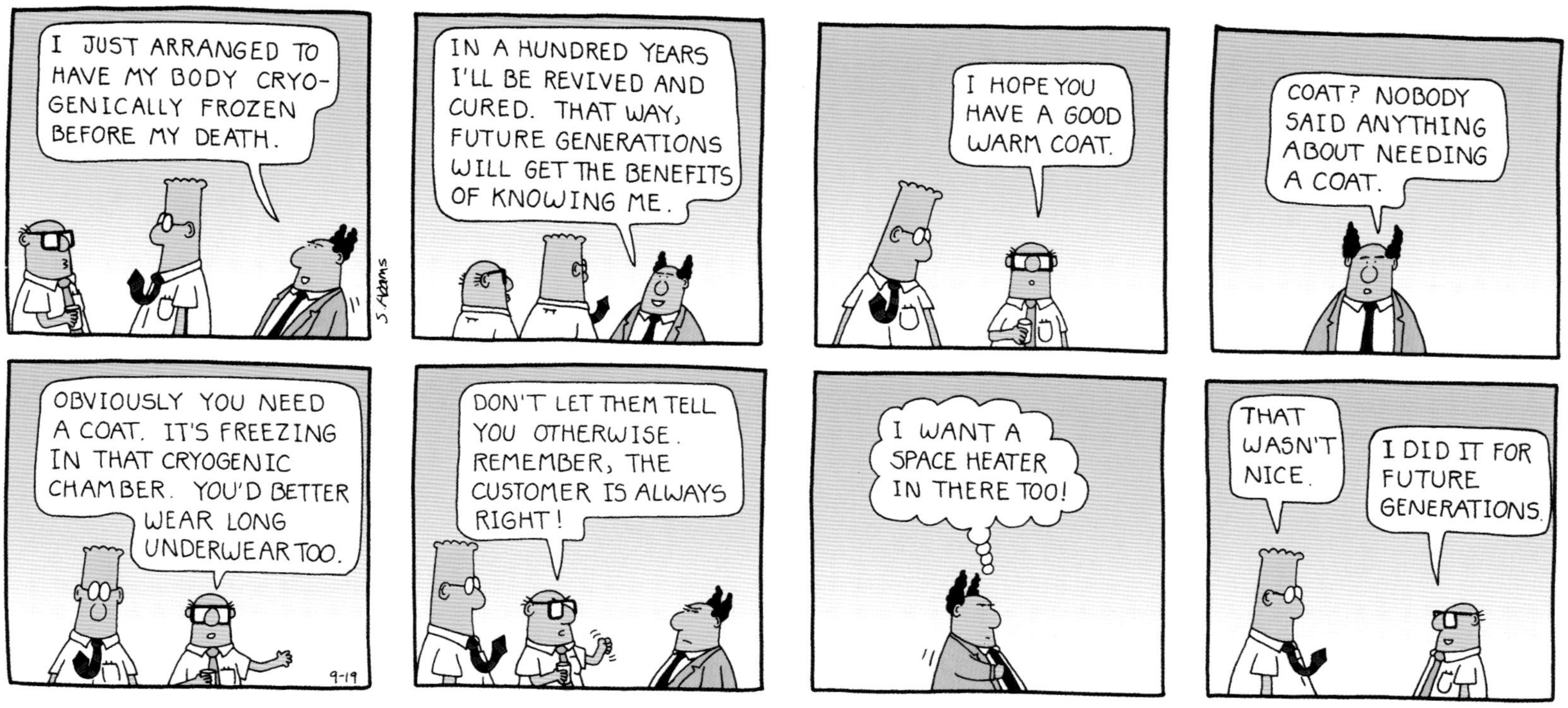
I JUST ARRANGED TO HAVE MY BODY CRYOGENICALLY FROZEN BEFORE MY DEATH.
S.Adams
IN A HUNDRED YEARS I'LL BE REVIVED AND CURED. THAT WAY, FUTURE GENERATIONS WILL GET THE BENEFITS OF KNOWING ME.
I HOPE YOU HAVE A GOOD WARM COAT.
COAT? NOBODY SAID ANYTHING ABOUT NEEDING A COAT.
OBVIOUSLY YOU NEED A COAT. IT'S FREEZING IN THAT CRYOGENIC CHAMBER. YOU'D BETTER WEAR LONG UNDERWEAR TOO.
9-19
DON'T LET THEM TELL YOU OTHERWISE. REMEMBER, THE CUSTOMER IS ALWAYS RIGHT!
I WANT A SPACE HEATER IN THERE TOO!
THAT WASN'T NICE.
I DID IT FOR FUTURE GENERATIONS.

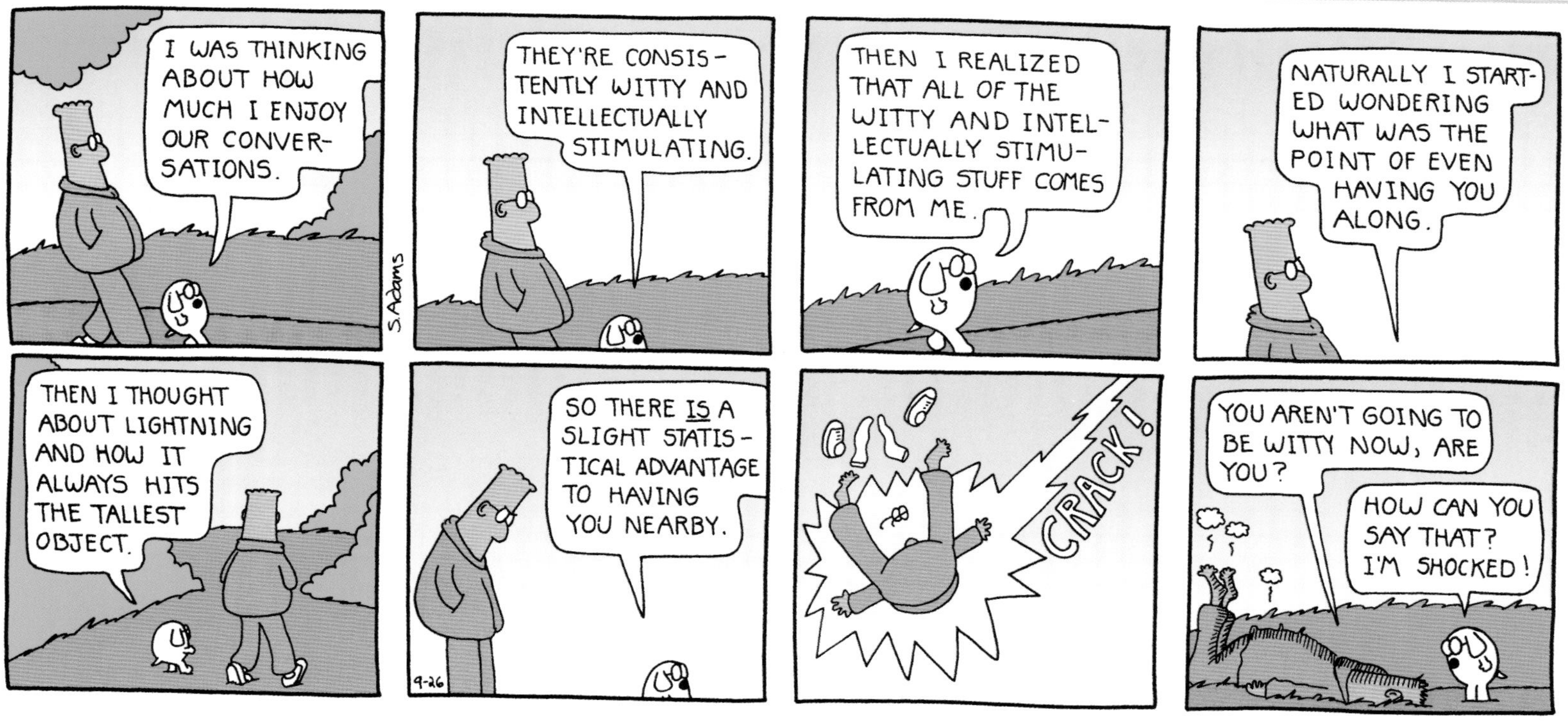
I WAS THINKING ABOUT HOW MUCH I ENJOY OUR CONVERSATIONS.
S.Adams
THEY'RE CONSISTENTLY WITTY AND INTELLECTUALLY STIMULATING.
THEN I REALIZED THAT ALL OF THE WITTY AND INTELLECTUALLY STIMULATING STUFF COMES FROM ME.
NATURALLY I STARTED WONDERING WHAT WAS THE POINT OF EVEN HAVING YOU ALONG.
THEN I THOUGHT ABOUT LIGHTNING AND HOW IT ALWAYS HITS THE TALLEST OBJECT.
SO THERE IS A SLIGHT STATISTICAL ADVANTAGE TO HAVING YOU NEARBY.
9-26
CRACK!
YOU AREN'T GOING TO BE WITTY NOW, ARE YOU?
HOW CAN YOU SAY THAT? I'M SHOCKED!

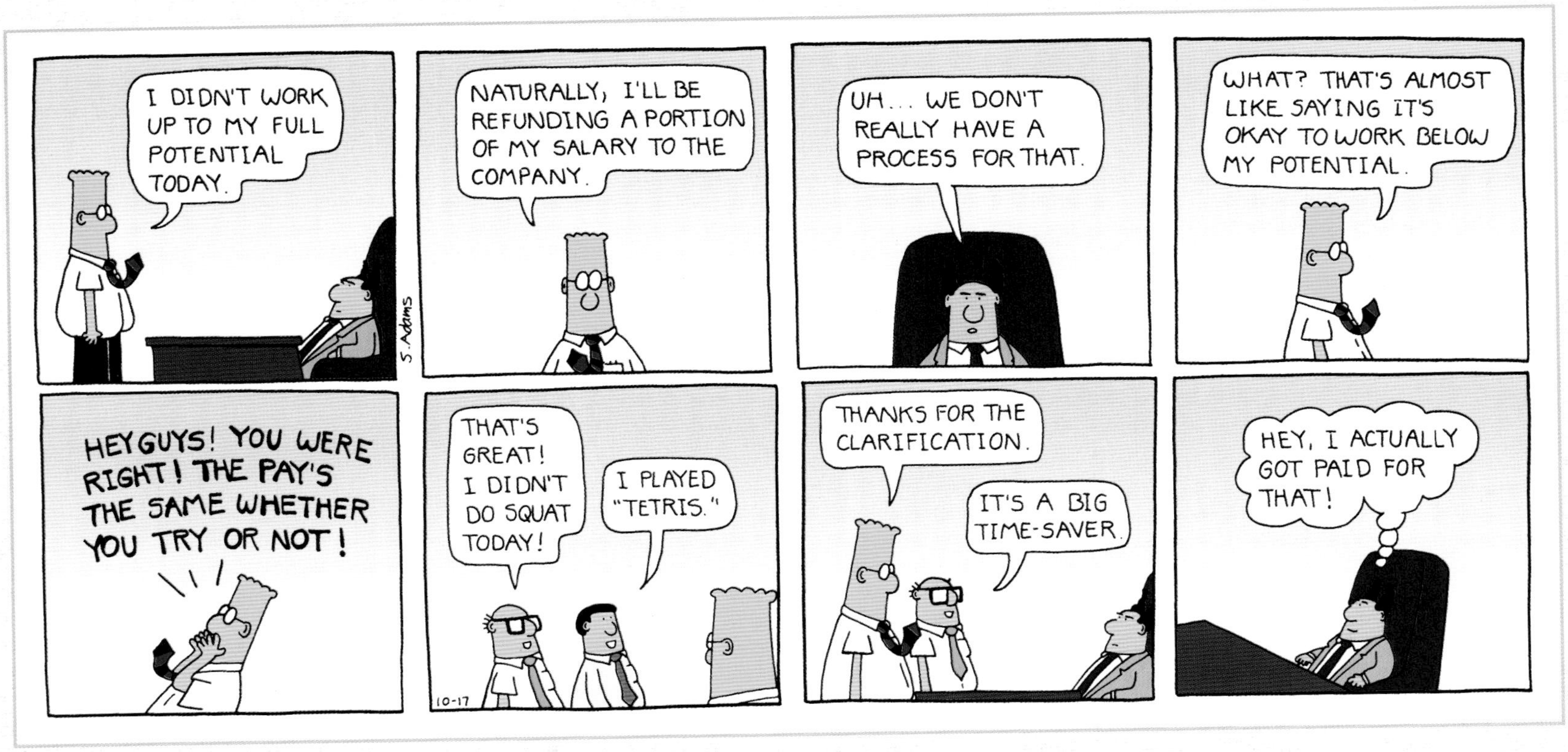
I DIDN'T WORK UP TO MY FULL POTENTIAL TODAY.
S. Adams
NATURALLY, I'LL BE REFUNDING A PORTION OF MY SALARY TO THE COMPANY.
UH... WE DON'T REALLY HAVE A PROCESS FOR THAT.
WHAT? THAT'S ALMOST LIKE SAYING IT'S OKAY TO WORK BELOW MY POTENTIAL.
HEY GUYS! YOU WERE RIGHT! THE PAY'S THE SAME WHETHER YOU TRY OR NOT!
THAT'S GREAT! I DIDN'T DO SQUAT TODAY!
I PLAYED "TETRIS."
10-17
THANKS FOR THE CLARIFICATION.
IT'S A BIG TIME-SAVER.
HEY, I ACTUALLY GOT PAID FOR THAT!

The disconnect between effort and reward always seems funny to me.

A head of security once confided that most thefts in the company were perpetrated by his own staff.

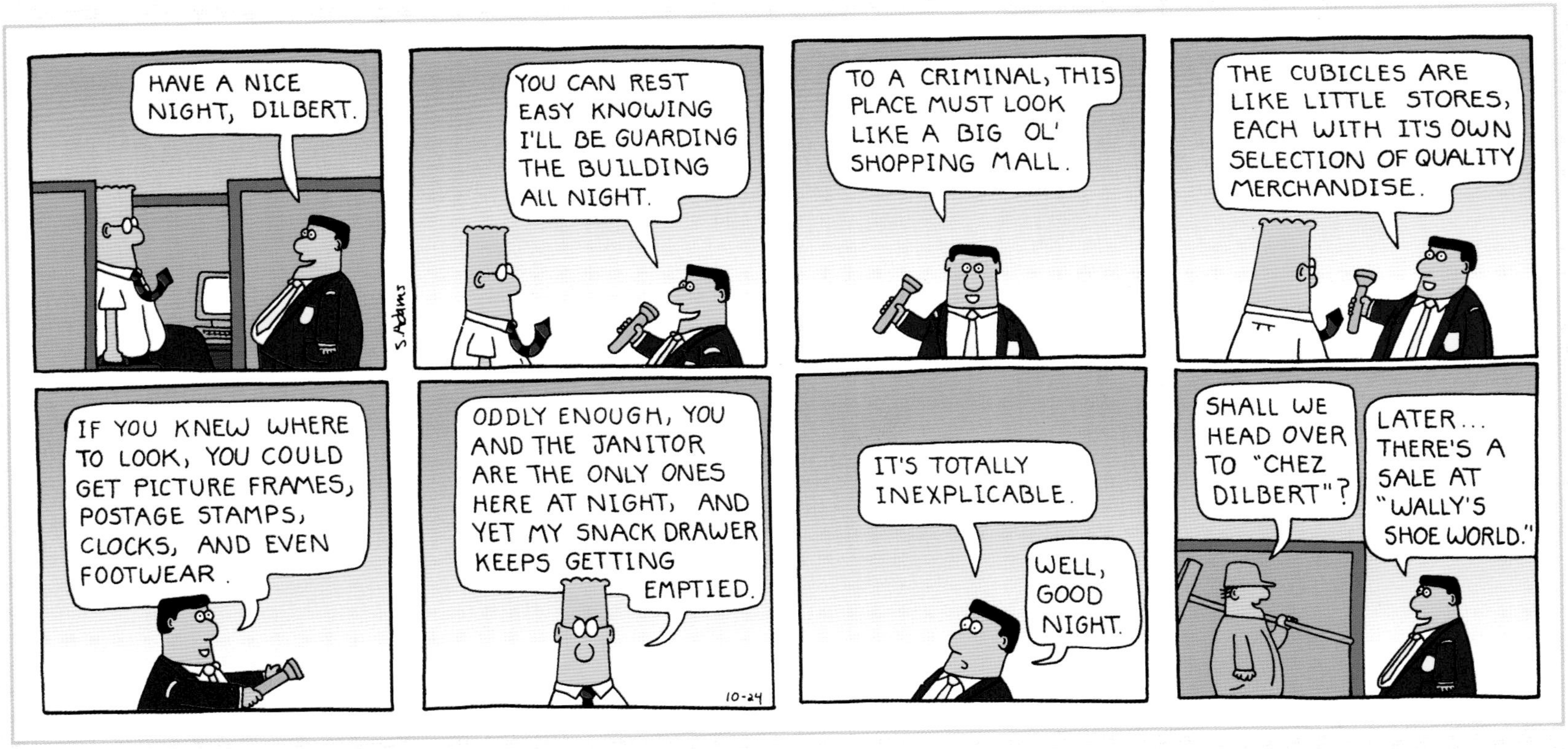
HAVE A NICE NIGHT, DILBERT.
S. Adams
YOU CAN REST EASY KNOWING I'LL BE GUARDING THE BUILDING ALL NIGHT.
TO A CRIMINAL, THIS PLACE MUST LOOK LIKE A BIG OL' SHOPPING MALL.
THE CUBICLES ARE LIKE LITTLE STORES, EACH WITH IT'S OWN SELECTION OF QUALITY MERCHANDISE.
IF YOU KNEW WHERE TO LOOK, YOU COULD GET PICTURE FRAMES, POSTAGE STAMPS, CLOCKS, AND EVEN FOOTWEAR.
ODDLY ENOUGH, YOU AND THE JANITOR ARE THE ONLY ONES HERE AT NIGHT, AND YET MY SNACK DRAWER KEEPS GETTING EMPTIED.
10-24
IT'S TOTALLY INEXPLICABLE.
WELL, GOOD NIGHT.
SHALL WE HEAD OVER TO "CHEZ DILBERT"?
LATER... THERE'S A SALE AT "WALLY'S SHOE WORLD."

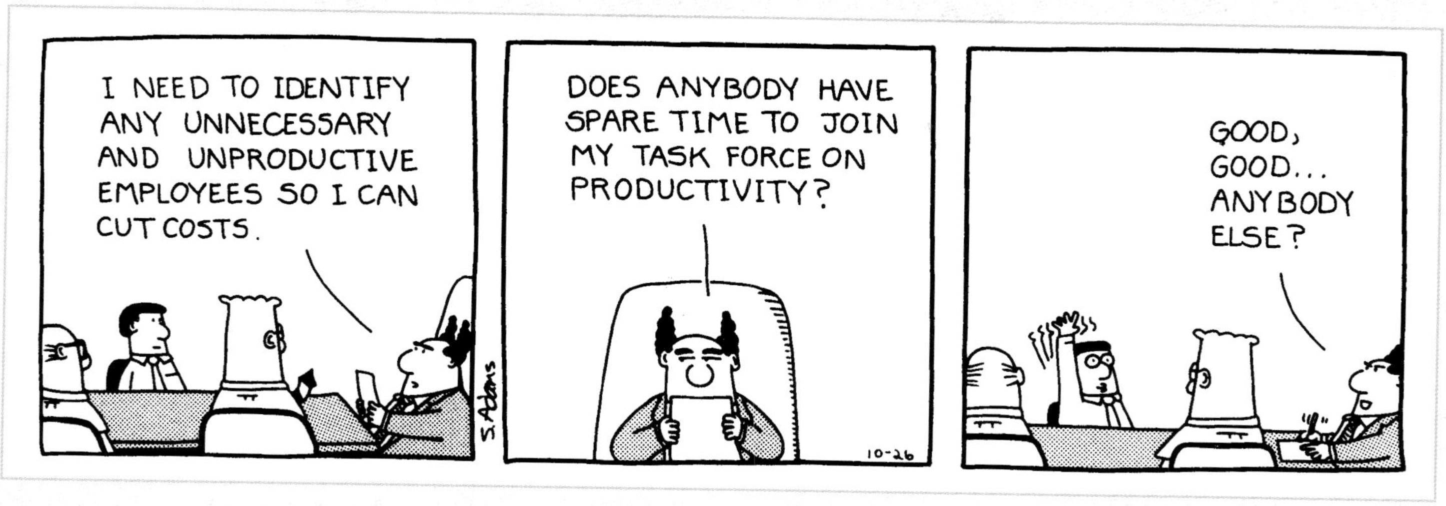
I NEED TO IDENTIFY ANY UNNECESSARY AND UNPRODUCTIVE EMPLOYEES SO I CAN CUT COSTS.
DOES ANYBODY HAVE SPARE TIME TO JOIN MY TASK FORCE ON PRODUCTIVITY?
GOOD, GOOD... ANYBODY ELSE?
S. Adams
10-26

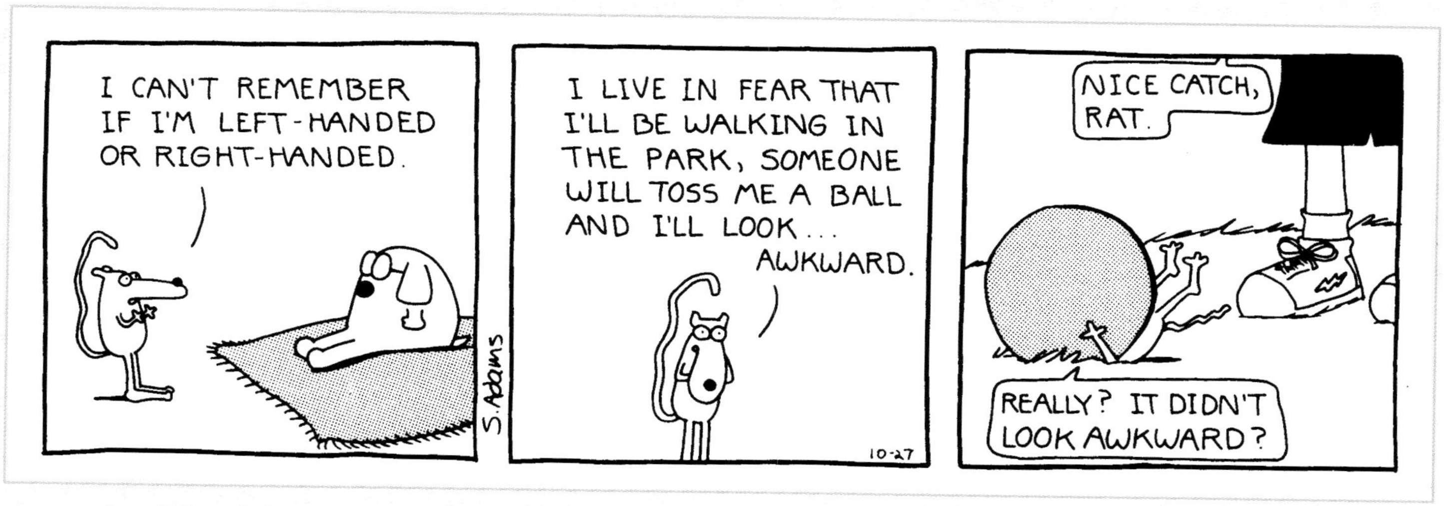
I CAN'T REMEMBER IF I'M LEFT-HANDED OR RIGHT-HANDED.
I LIVE IN FEAR THAT I'LL BE WALKING IN THE PARK, SOMEONE WILL TOSS ME A BALL AND I'LL LOOK... AWKWARD.
NICE CATCH, RAT.
REALLY? IT DIDN'T LOOK AWKWARD?
S. Adams
10-27

When Dilbert *got moved more to an office environment, Ratbert's role diminished substantially.*

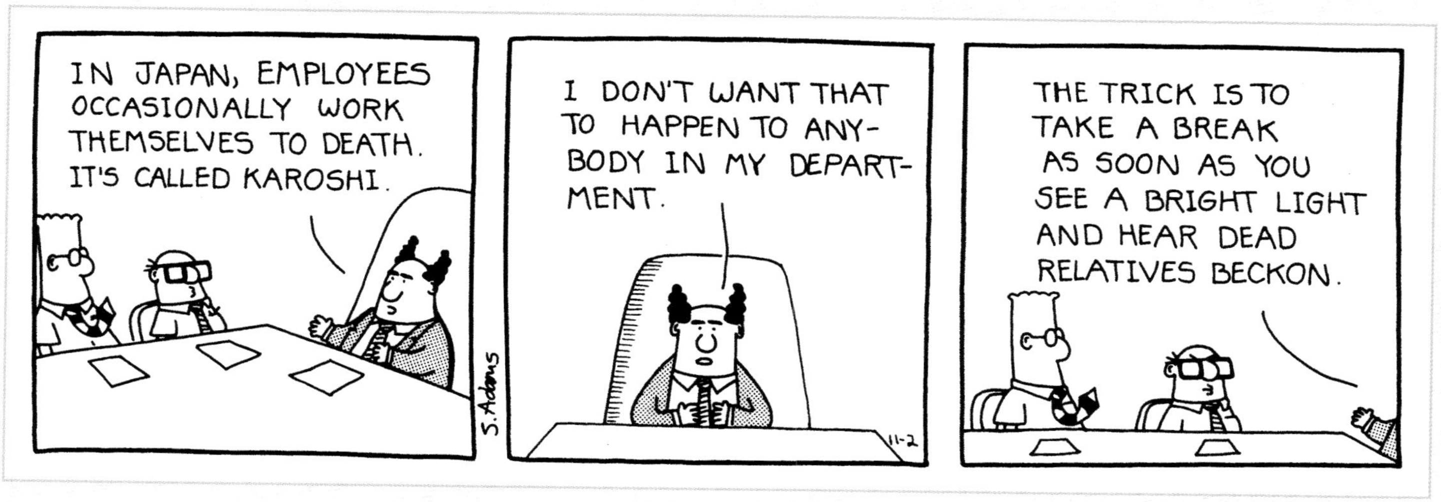
IN JAPAN, EMPLOYEES OCCASIONALLY WORK THEMSELVES TO DEATH. IT'S CALLED KAROSHI.
I DON'T WANT THAT TO HAPPEN TO ANYBODY IN MY DEPARTMENT.
THE TRICK IS TO TAKE A BREAK AS SOON AS YOU SEE A BRIGHT LIGHT AND HEAR DEAD RELATIVES BECKON.
S. Adams
11-2

The two most common suggestions for Dilbert*: (1) people taking the last of the coffee and not making another pot, and (2) people using speakerphones in cubicles.*

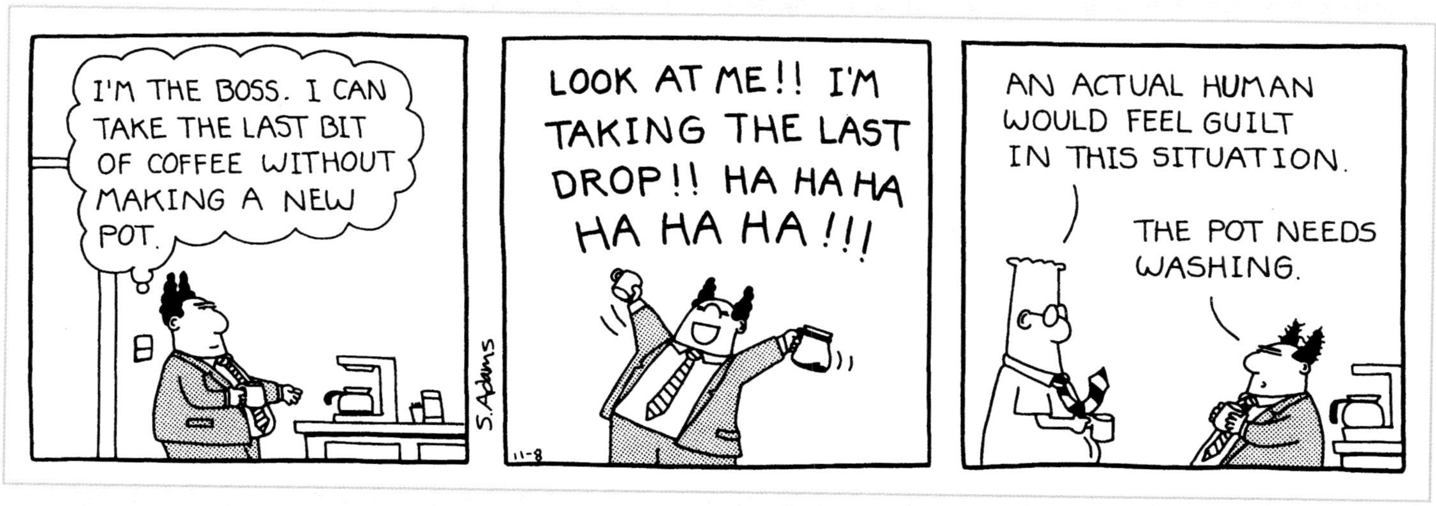
I'M THE BOSS. I CAN TAKE THE LAST BIT OF COFFEE WITHOUT MAKING A NEW POT.
LOOK AT ME!! I'M TAKING THE LAST DROP!! HA HA HA HA HA HA!!!
AN ACTUAL HUMAN WOULD FEEL GUILT IN THIS SITUATION.
THE POT NEEDS WASHING.
S. Adams
11-8

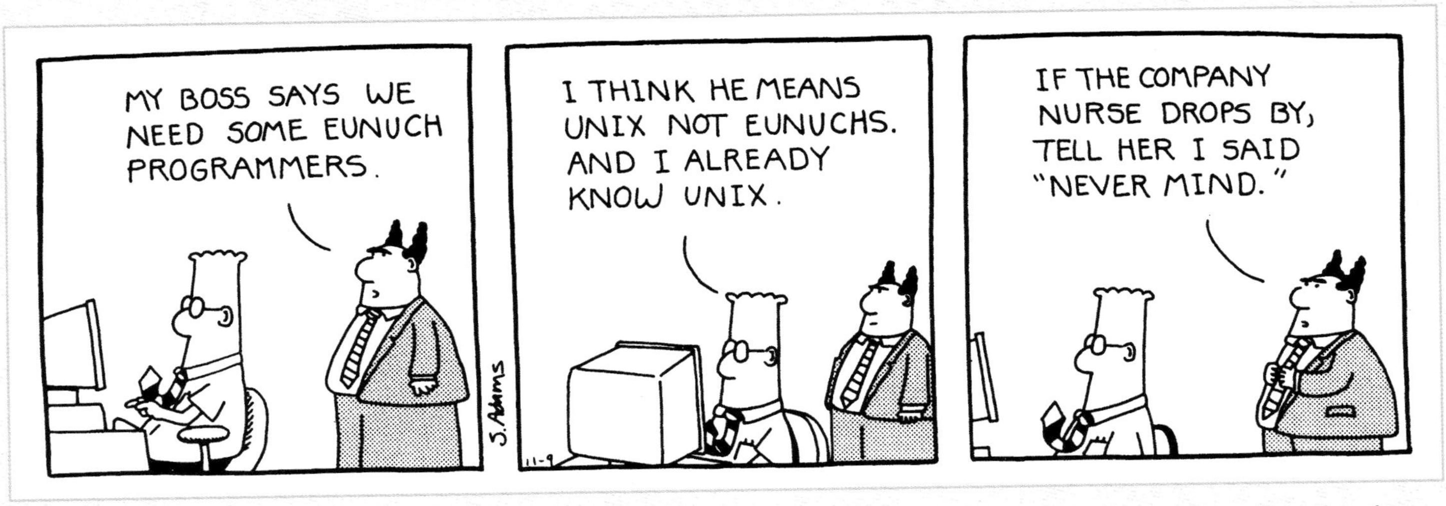
MY BOSS SAYS WE NEED SOME EUNUCH PROGRAMMERS.
I THINK HE MEANS UNIX NOT EUNUCHS. AND I ALREADY KNOW UNIX.
IF THE COMPANY NURSE DROPS BY, TELL HER I SAID "NEVER MIND."

When I was doing lots of public speaking, I ended every talk with this comic because it always got a huge laugh.

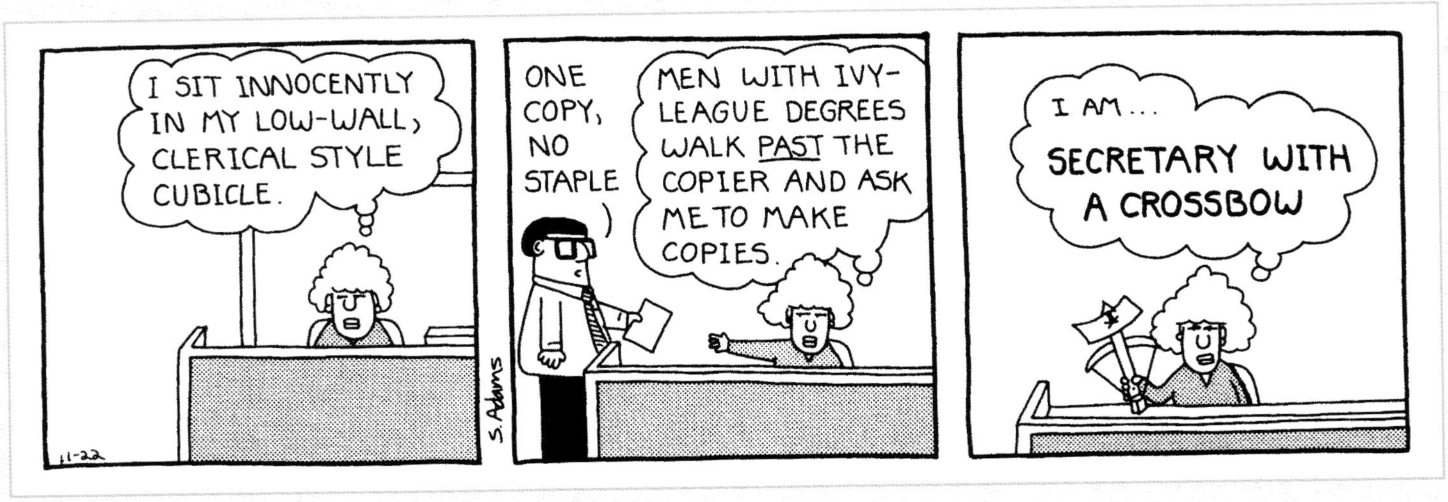
I SIT INNOCENTLY IN MY LOW-WALL, CLERICAL STYLE CUBICLE.
ONE COPY, NO STAPLE
MEN WITH IVY-LEAGUE DEGREES WALK PAST THE COPIER AND ASK ME TO MAKE COPIES.
I AM...
SECRETARY WITH A CROSSBOW

Later the secretary with a crossbow morphed into Carol, the secretary who is always plotting to kill the pointy-haired boss.

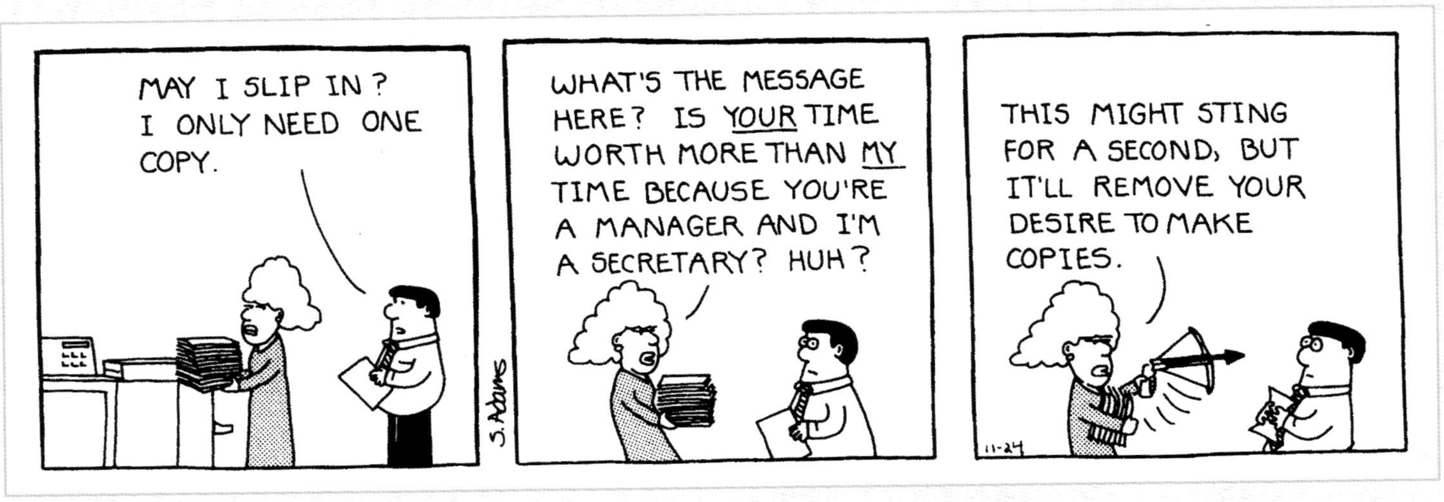
MAY I SLIP IN? I ONLY NEED ONE COPY.
WHAT'S THE MESSAGE HERE? IS YOUR TIME WORTH MORE THAN MY TIME BECAUSE YOU'RE A MANAGER AND I'M A SECRETARY? HUH?
THIS MIGHT STING FOR A SECOND, BUT IT'LL REMOVE YOUR DESIRE TO MAKE COPIES.

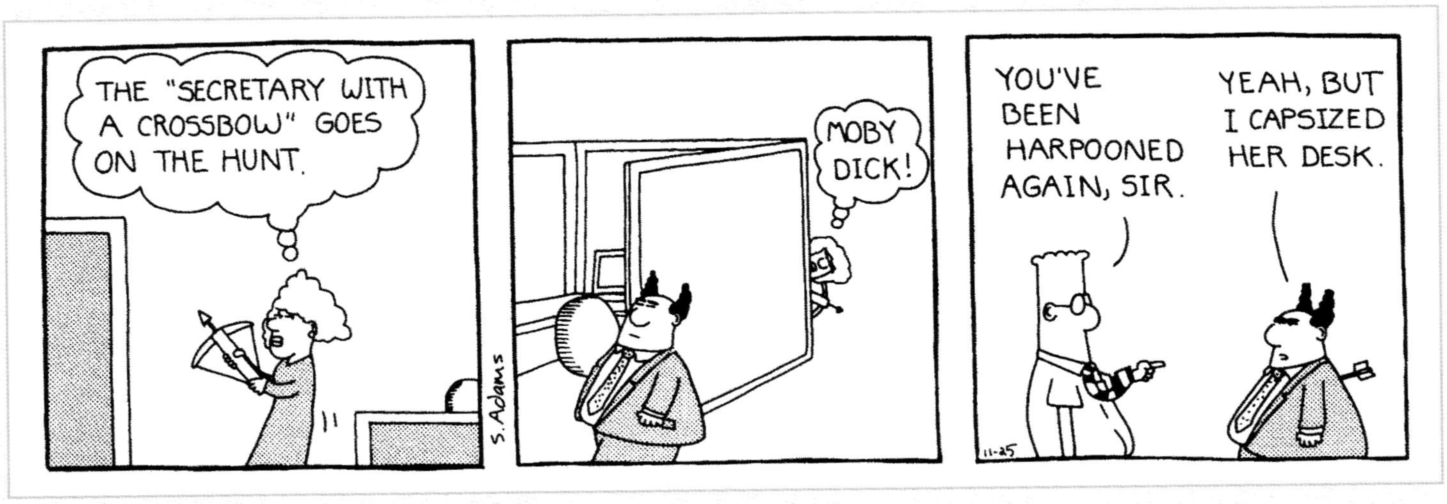
THE "SECRETARY WITH A CROSSBOW" GOES ON THE HUNT.
MOBY DICK!
YOU'VE BEEN HARPOONED AGAIN, SIR.
YEAH, BUT I CAPSIZED HER DESK.

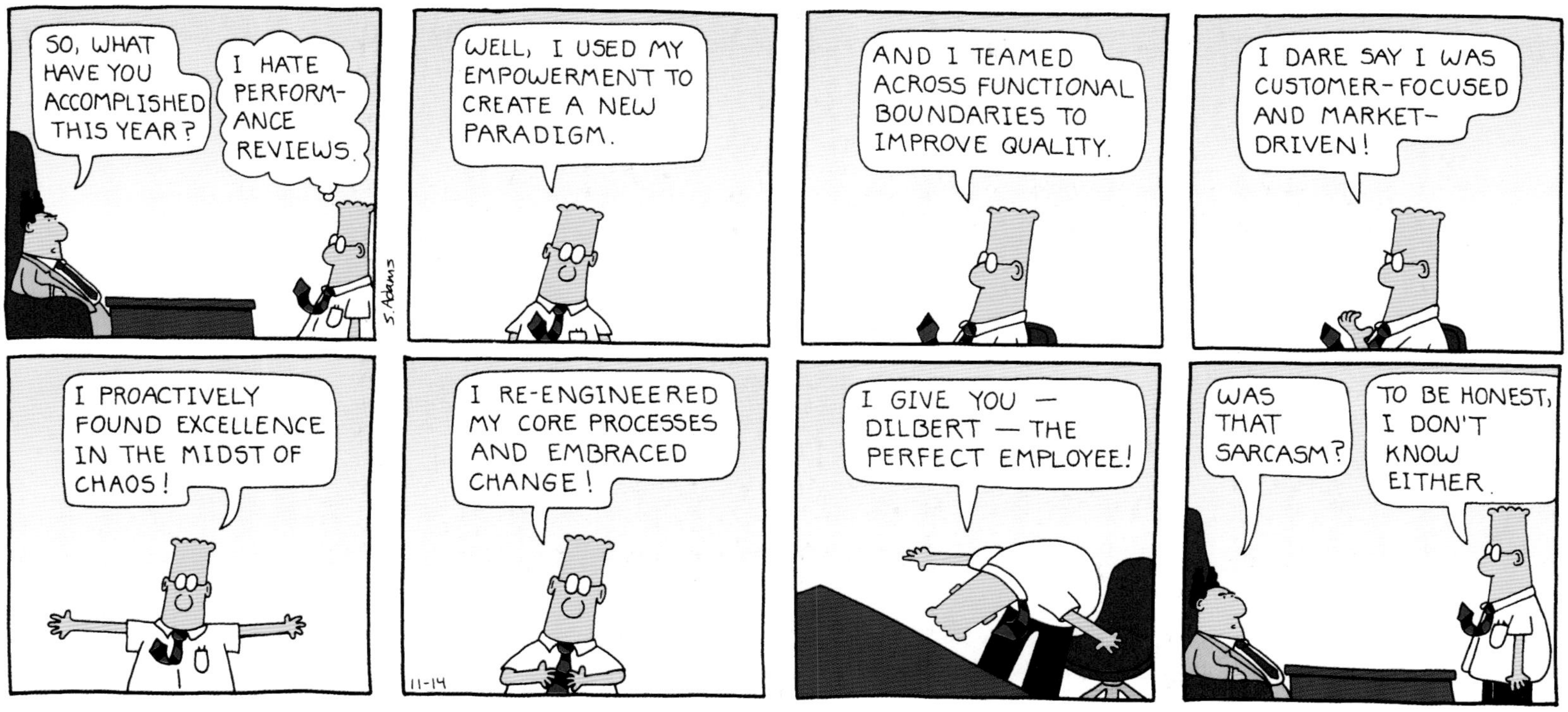
SO, WHAT HAVE YOU ACCOMPLISHED THIS YEAR?
I HATE PERFORMANCE REVIEWS.
WELL, I USED MY EMPOWERMENT TO CREATE A NEW PARADIGM.
AND I TEAMED ACROSS FUNCTIONAL BOUNDARIES TO IMPROVE QUALITY.
I DARE SAY I WAS CUSTOMER-FOCUSED AND MARKET-DRIVEN!
I PROACTIVELY FOUND EXCELLENCE IN THE MIDST OF CHAOS!
I RE-ENGINEERED MY CORE PROCESSES AND EMBRACED CHANGE!
I GIVE YOU — DILBERT — THE PERFECT EMPLOYEE!
WAS THAT SARCASM?
TO BE HONEST, I DON'T KNOW EITHER.
S. Adams
11-14

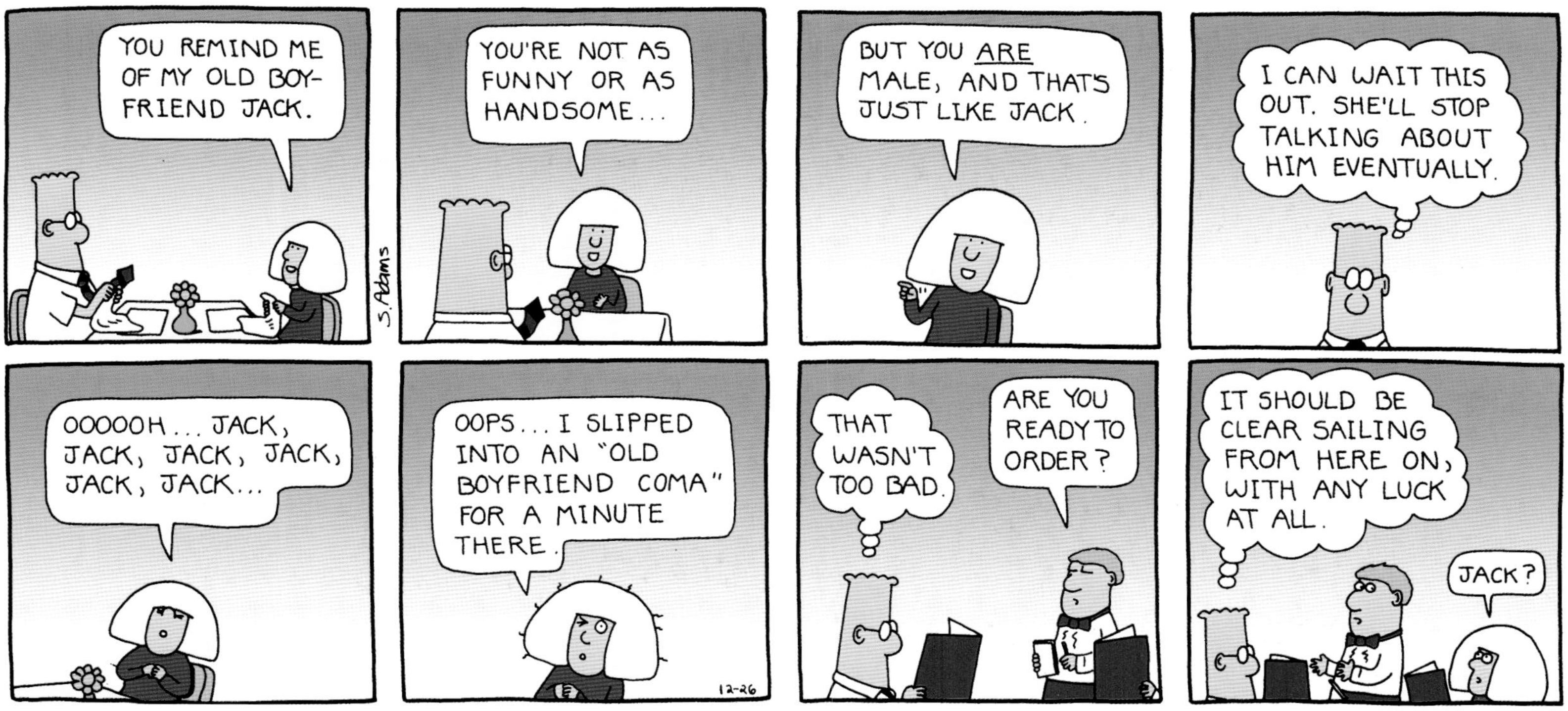
YOU REMIND ME OF MY OLD BOYFRIEND JACK.
YOU'RE NOT AS FUNNY OR AS HANDSOME...
BUT YOU ARE MALE, AND THAT'S JUST LIKE JACK.
I CAN WAIT THIS OUT. SHE'LL STOP TALKING ABOUT HIM EVENTUALLY.
OOOOOH... JACK, JACK, JACK, JACK, JACK, JACK...
OOPS... I SLIPPED INTO AN "OLD BOYFRIEND COMA" FOR A MINUTE THERE.
THAT WASN'T TOO BAD.
ARE YOU READY TO ORDER?
IT SHOULD BE CLEAR SAILING FROM HERE ON, WITH ANY LUCK AT ALL.
JACK?
S. Adams
12-26

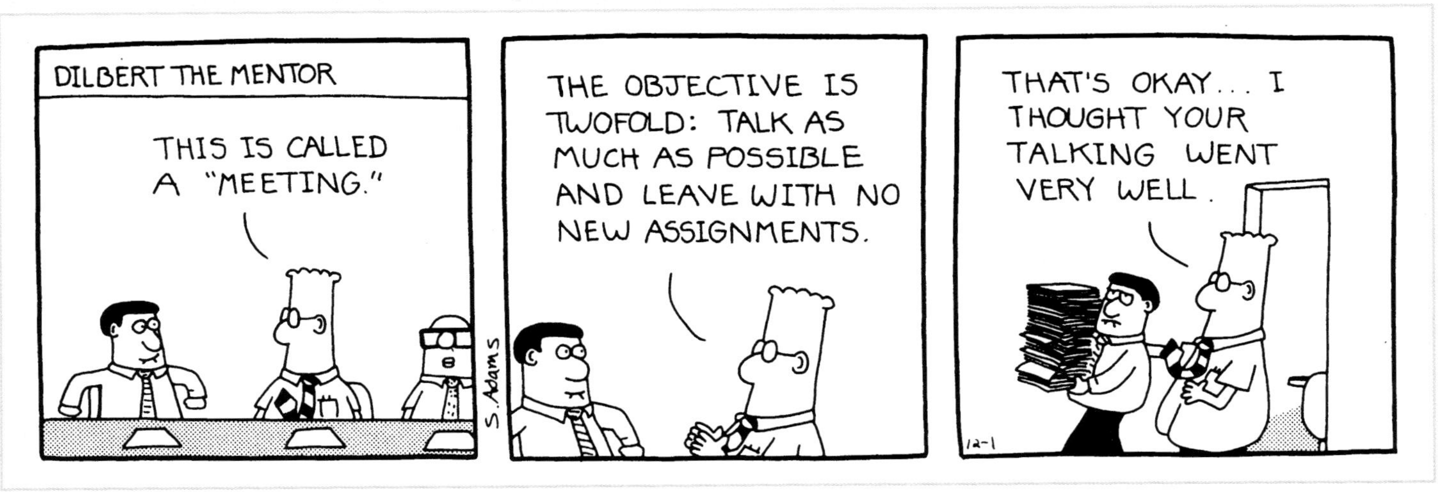
DILBERT THE MENTOR
THIS IS CALLED A "MEETING."
THE OBJECTIVE IS TWOFOLD: TALK AS MUCH AS POSSIBLE AND LEAVE WITH NO NEW ASSIGNMENTS.
THAT'S OKAY... I THOUGHT YOUR TALKING WENT VERY WELL.
S. Adams
12-1

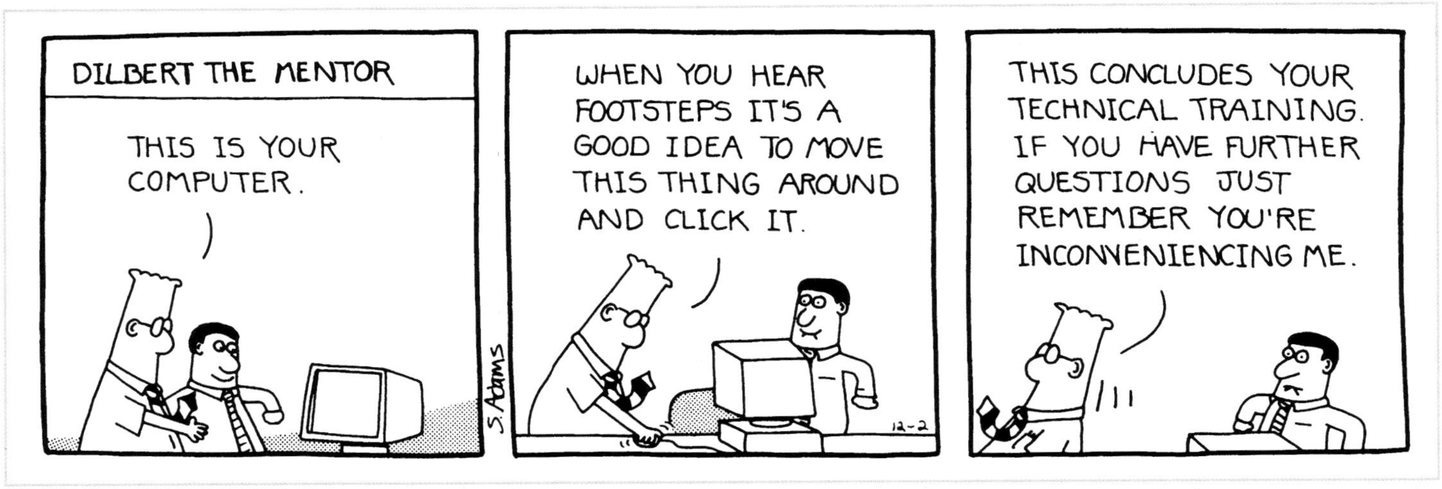
DILBERT THE MENTOR
THIS IS YOUR COMPUTER.
WHEN YOU HEAR FOOTSTEPS IT'S A GOOD IDEA TO MOVE THIS THING AROUND AND CLICK IT.
THIS CONCLUDES YOUR TECHNICAL TRAINING. IF YOU HAVE FURTHER QUESTIONS JUST REMEMBER YOU'RE INCONVENIENCING ME.
S. Adams
12-2

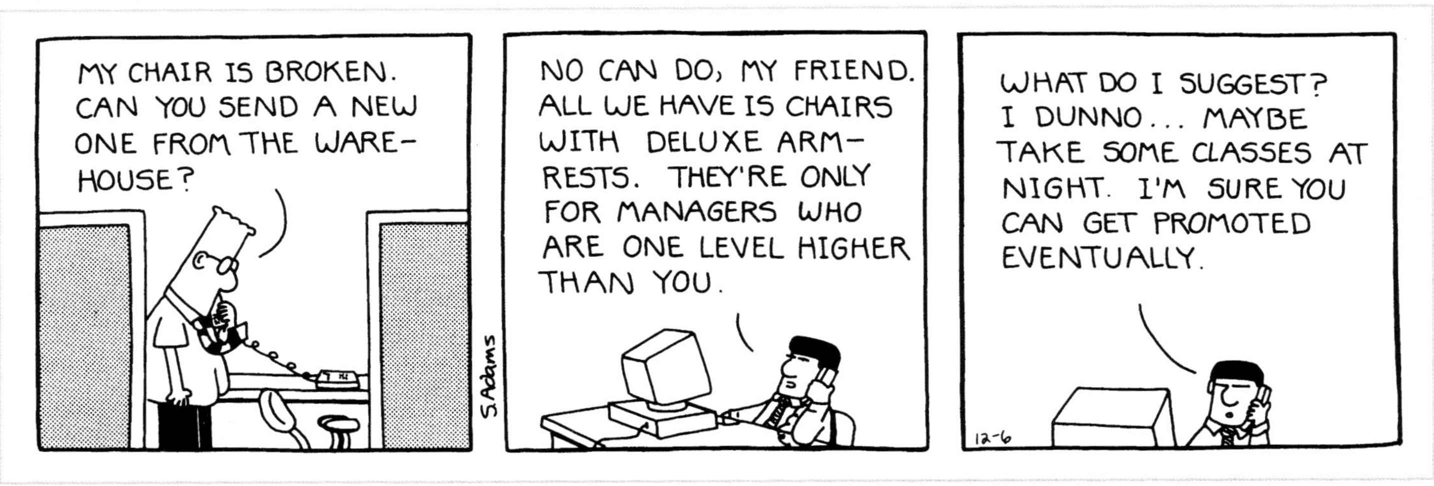
MY CHAIR IS BROKEN. CAN YOU SEND A NEW ONE FROM THE WARE-HOUSE?
NO CAN DO, MY FRIEND. ALL WE HAVE IS CHAIRS WITH DELUXE ARM-RESTS. THEY'RE ONLY FOR MANAGERS WHO ARE ONE LEVEL HIGHER THAN YOU.
WHAT DO I SUGGEST? I DUNNO... MAYBE TAKE SOME CLASSES AT NIGHT. I'M SURE YOU CAN GET PROMOTED EVENTUALLY.
S. Adams
12-6

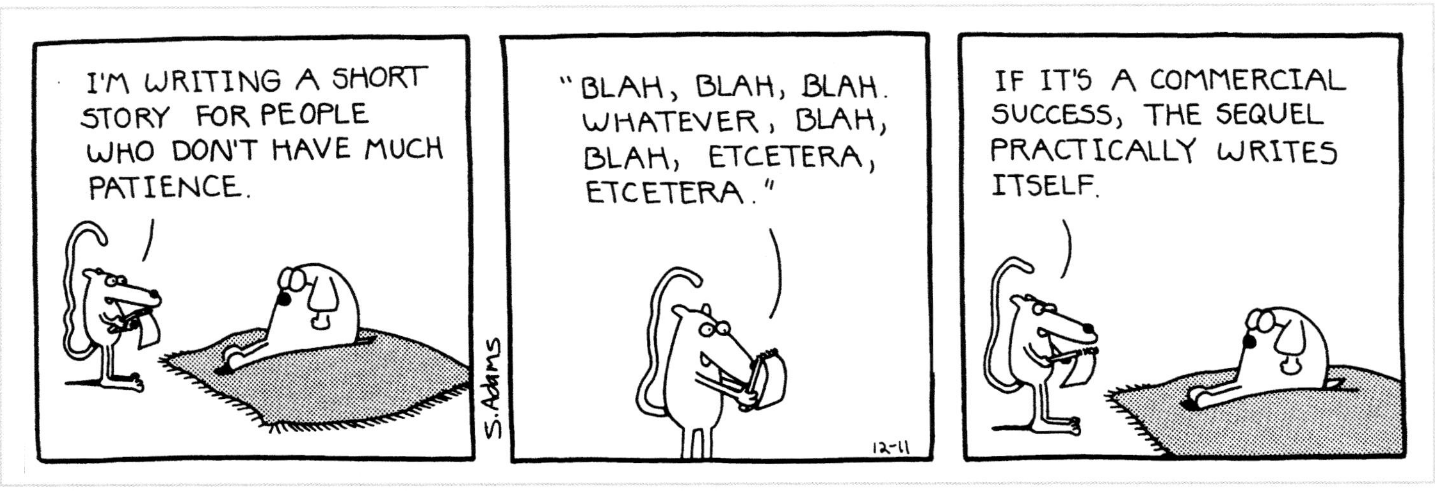
I'M WRITING A SHORT STORY FOR PEOPLE WHO DON'T HAVE MUCH PATIENCE.
"BLAH, BLAH, BLAH. WHATEVER, BLAH, BLAH, ETCETERA, ETCETERA."
IF IT'S A COMMERCIAL SUCCESS, THE SEQUEL PRACTICALLY WRITES ITSELF.
S. Adams
12-11

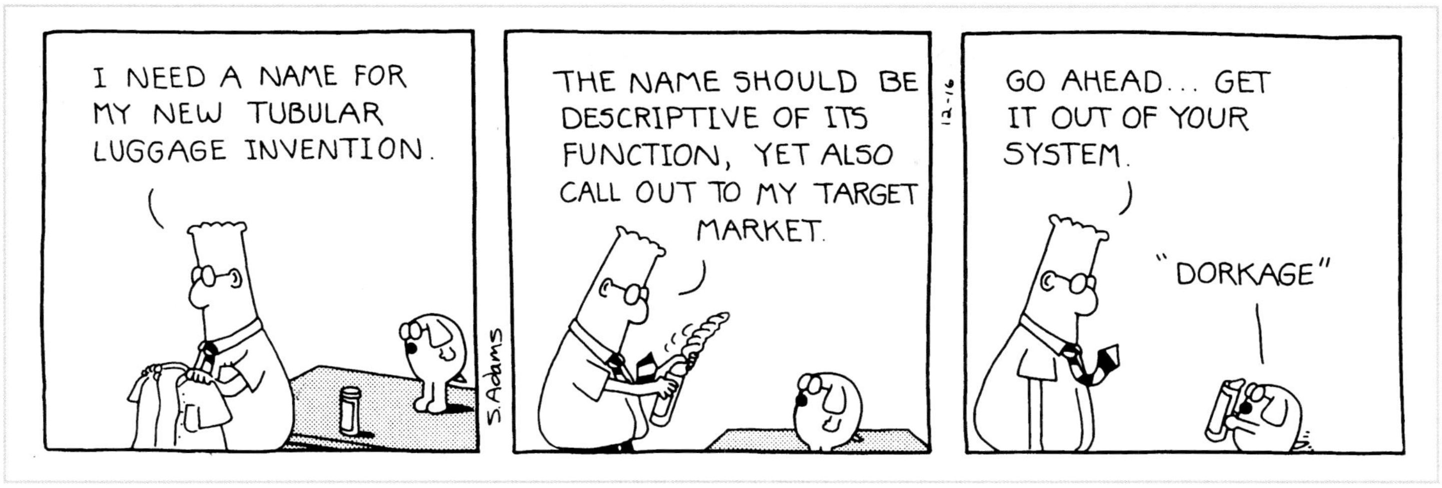
I NEED A NAME FOR MY NEW TUBULAR LUGGAGE INVENTION.
THE NAME SHOULD BE DESCRIPTIVE OF ITS FUNCTION, YET ALSO CALL OUT TO MY TARGET MARKET.
GO AHEAD... GET IT OUT OF YOUR SYSTEM.
"DORKAGE"
S. Adams
12-16

I got a complaint from Mr. Dork. He wasn't happy that I used his last name in a derogatory fashion. He asked for an apology.

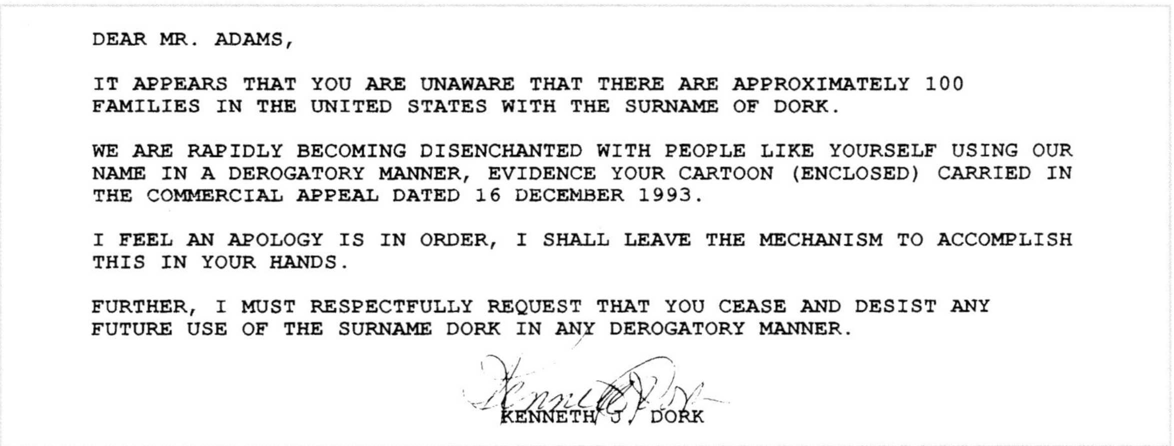

DEAR MR. ADAMS,

IT APPEARS THAT YOU ARE UNAWARE THAT THERE ARE APPROXIMATELY 100 FAMILIES IN THE UNITED STATES WITH THE SURNAME OF DORK.

WE ARE RAPIDLY BECOMING DISENCHANTED WITH PEOPLE LIKE YOURSELF USING OUR NAME IN A DEROGATORY MANNER, EVIDENCE YOUR CARTOON (ENCLOSED) CARRIED IN THE COMMERCIAL APPEAL DATED 16 DECEMBER 1993.

I FEEL AN APOLOGY IS IN ORDER, I SHALL LEAVE THE MECHANISM TO ACCOMPLISH THIS IN YOUR HANDS.

FURTHER, I MUST RESPECTFULLY REQUEST THAT YOU CEASE AND DESIST ANY FUTURE USE OF THE SURNAME DORK IN ANY DEROGATORY MANNER.

KENNETH J. DORK

Some cartoonists might not care about their readers. But I'm not like that. If I offend someone, even accidentally, I feel a moral obligation to apologize, as I did a few months later in the strip.

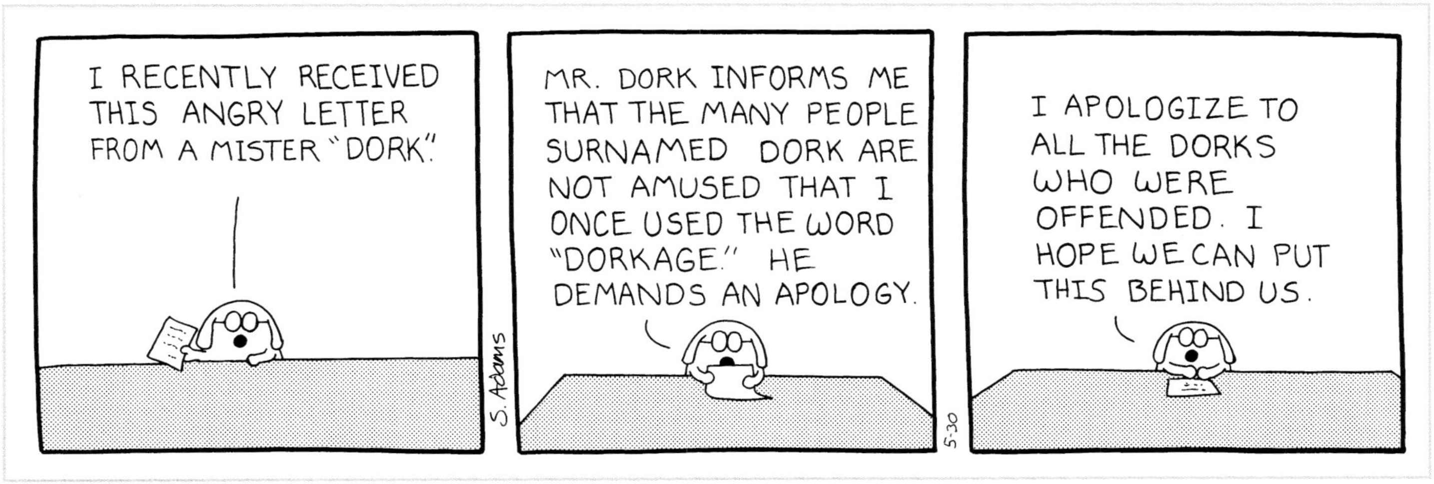
I RECENTLY RECEIVED THIS ANGRY LETTER FROM A MISTER "DORK."
MR. DORK INFORMS ME THAT THE MANY PEOPLE SURNAMED DORK ARE NOT AMUSED THAT I ONCE USED THE WORD "DORKAGE." HE DEMANDS AN APOLOGY.
I APOLOGIZE TO ALL THE DORKS WHO WERE OFFENDED. I HOPE WE CAN PUT THIS BEHIND US.
S. Adams
5-30

Ratbert gained acceptance on Christmas. Eventually, as Dilbert got more international clients, I stopped doing holiday strips.

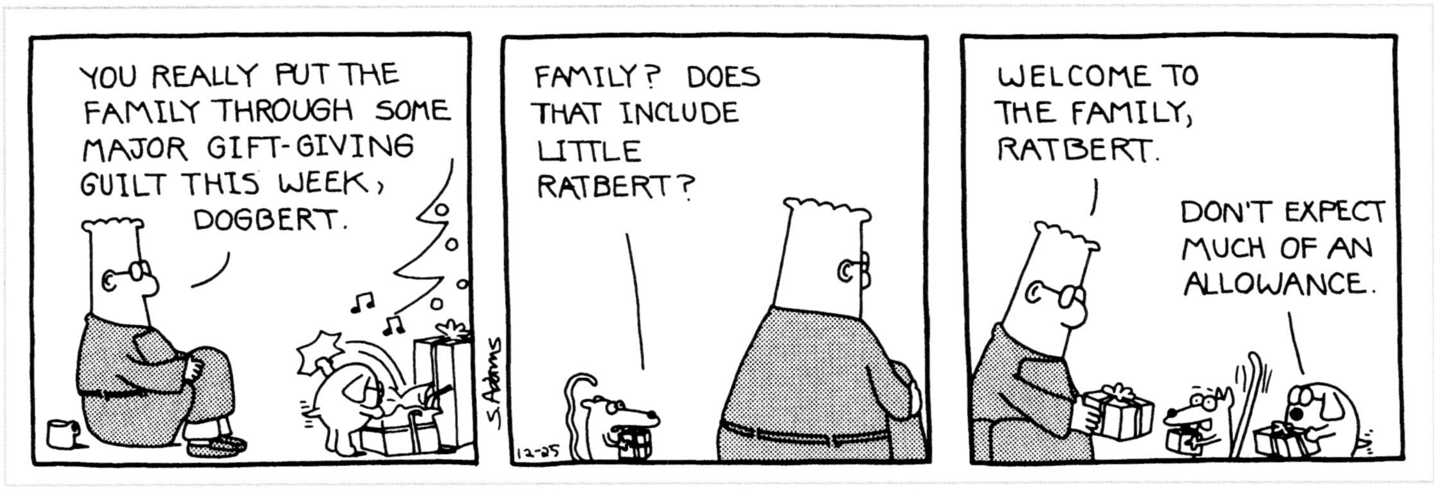
YOU REALLY PUT THE FAMILY THROUGH SOME MAJOR GIFT-GIVING GUILT THIS WEEK, DOGBERT.
FAMILY? DOES THAT INCLUDE LITTLE RATBERT?
WELCOME TO THE FAMILY, RATBERT.
DON'T EXPECT MUCH OF AN ALLOWANCE.
S. Adams
12-25

The Boom
Years
1994-1997

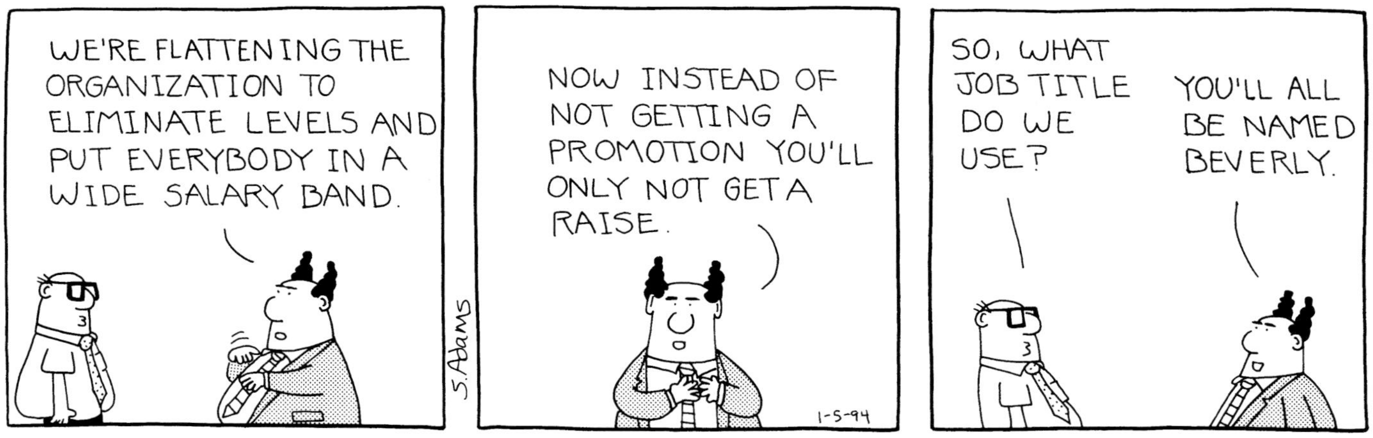
WE'RE FLATTENING THE ORGANIZATION TO ELIMINATE LEVELS AND PUT EVERYBODY IN A WIDE SALARY BAND.
NOW INSTEAD OF NOT GETTING A PROMOTION YOU'LL ONLY NOT GET A RAISE.
SO, WHAT JOB TITLE DO WE USE?
YOU'LL ALL BE NAMED BEVERLY.
S. Adams
1-5-94

This was the sort of joke I wondered if I alone would appreciate. It wasn't a huge hit, but a small portion of readers thought it was wonderfully random. Others wondered who Beverly was or what it meant. It was nothing but a name that seemed funny when I thought of it.

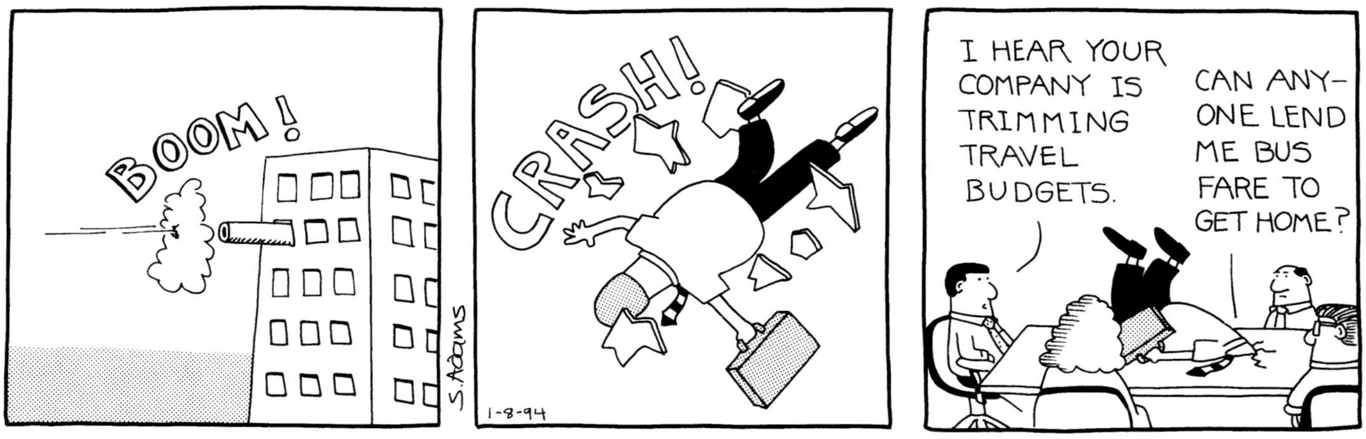
BOOM!
CRASH!
S. Adams
1-8-94
I HEAR YOUR COMPANY IS TRIMMING TRAVEL BUDGETS.
CAN ANYONE LEND ME BUS FARE TO GET HOME?

While lacking in cleverness or subtlety, workplace themes that hammer some pet peeve or another, such as this one about travel budgets getting trimmed, find the biggest audience. These are the ones people cut out and pass around, because they put words and pictures to what people are thinking.

I discovered it's often funny to have characters voice inner thoughts.

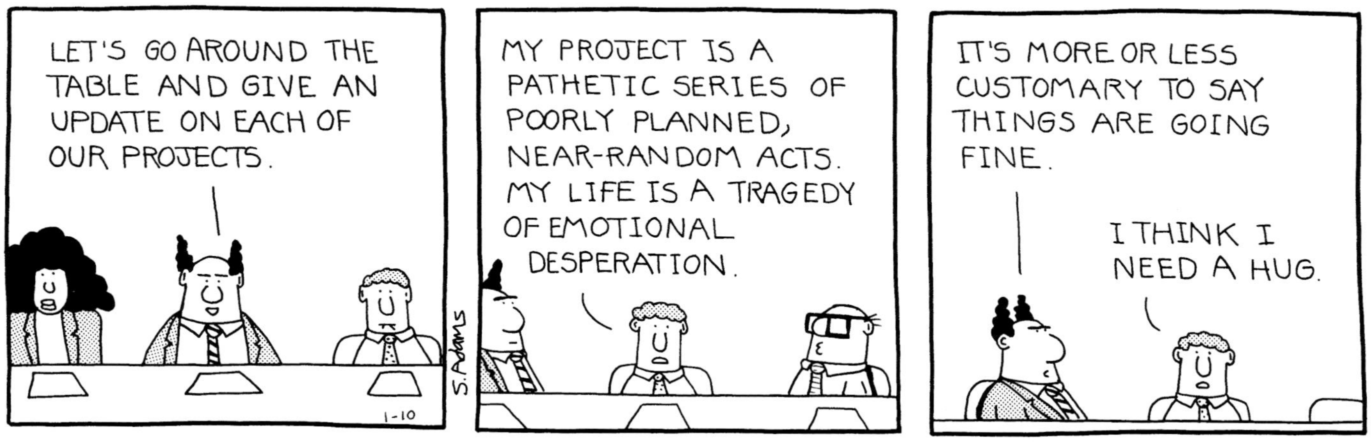
LET'S GO AROUND THE TABLE AND GIVE AN UPDATE ON EACH OF OUR PROJECTS.
1-10
S. Adams
MY PROJECT IS A PATHETIC SERIES OF POORLY PLANNED, NEAR-RANDOM ACTS. MY LIFE IS A TRAGEDY OF EMOTIONAL DESPERATION.
IT'S MORE OR LESS CUSTOMARY TO SAY THINGS ARE GOING FINE.
I THINK I NEED A HUG.

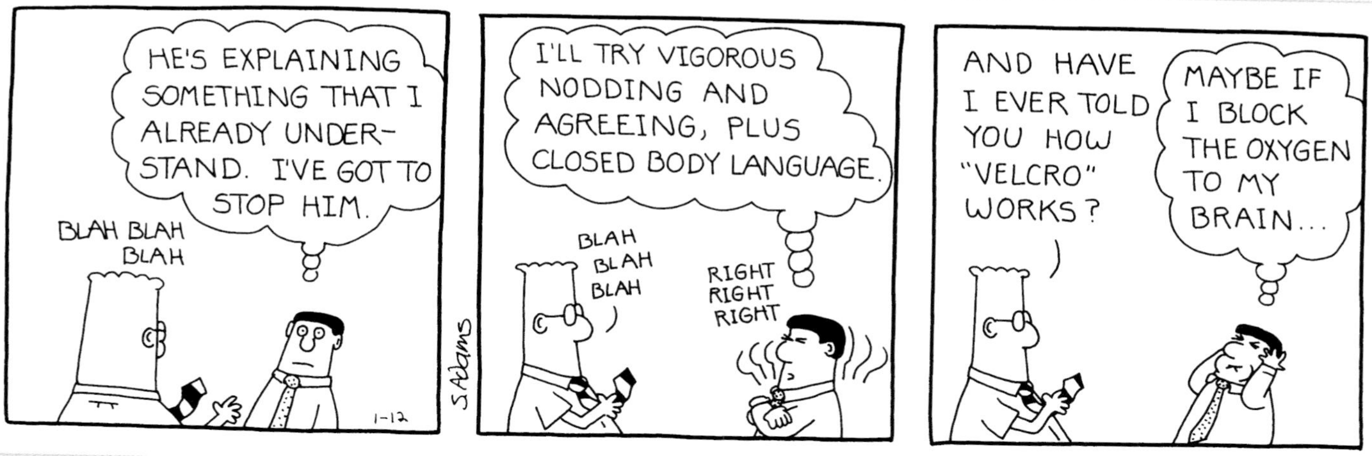
HE'S EXPLAINING SOMETHING THAT I ALREADY UNDERSTAND. I'VE GOT TO STOP HIM.
BLAH BLAH BLAH
I'LL TRY VIGOROUS NODDING AND AGREEING, PLUS CLOSED BODY LANGUAGE.
BLAH BLAH BLAH
RIGHT RIGHT RIGHT
AND HAVE I EVER TOLD YOU HOW "VELCRO" WORKS?
MAYBE IF I BLOCK THE OXYGEN TO MY BRAIN...

The person who talks too much is a theme I have hit over and over. It's one of my biggest complaints in life. Ironically, by doing this gag so often, in various forms, I have become the thing I loathe.

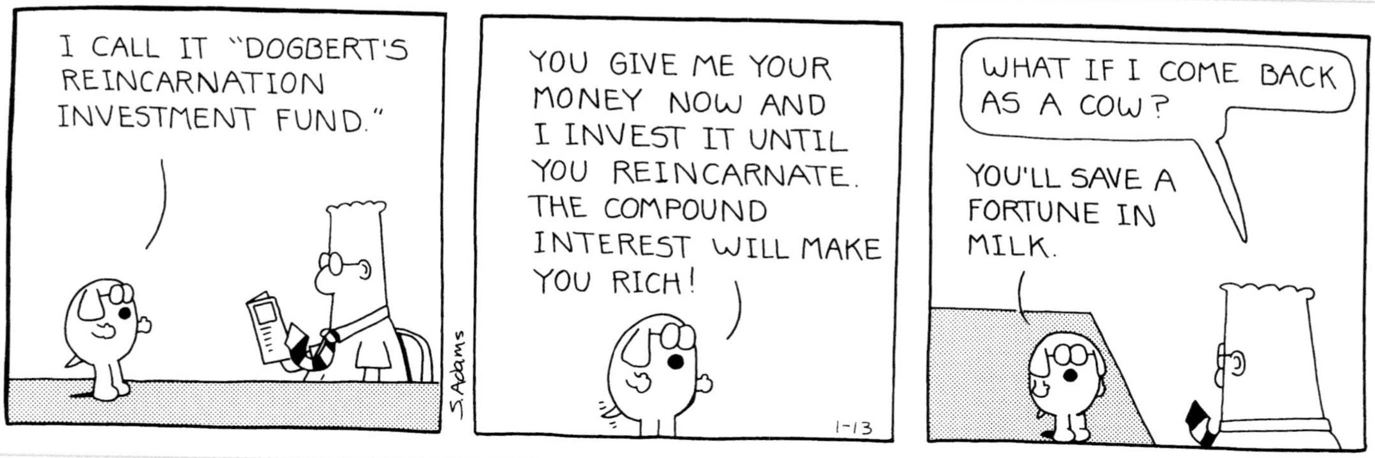
I CALL IT "DOGBERT'S REINCARNATION INVESTMENT FUND."
YOU GIVE ME YOUR MONEY NOW AND I INVEST IT UNTIL YOU REINCARNATE. THE COMPOUND INTEREST WILL MAKE YOU RICH!
WHAT IF I COME BACK AS A COW?
YOU'LL SAVE A FORTUNE IN MILK.

Sometimes it is hard to find the comic exaggeration in a situation. The only way Dogbert could come up with an investment fund that is more of a scam than the ones on the market is to work reincarnation into the mix.

For newspapers, this comic was edited from "Cubicle Gestapo" to "Cubicle Police." The thinking was that any Nazi reference would get people all wound up. At the time, I thought that was a ridiculous decision. Eventually, I learned it was a wise decision. The change didn't hurt the joke, and lots of people do complain about any reference to Nazis.

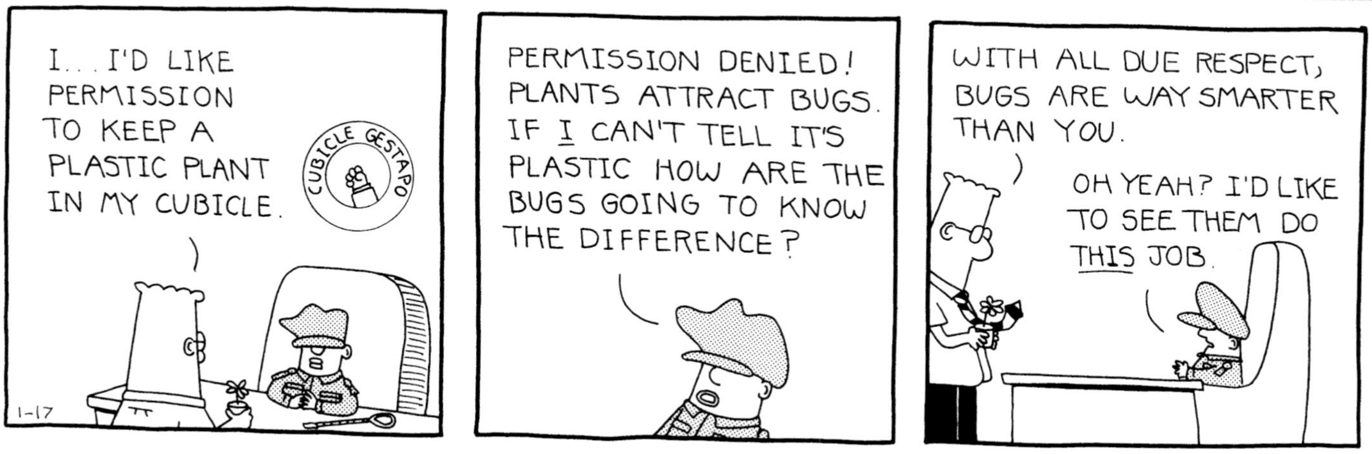
I... I'D LIKE PERMISSION TO KEEP A PLASTIC PLANT IN MY CUBICLE.
CUBICLE GESTAPO
PERMISSION DENIED! PLANTS ATTRACT BUGS. IF I CAN'T TELL IT'S PLASTIC HOW ARE THE BUGS GOING TO KNOW THE DIFFERENCE?
WITH ALL DUE RESPECT, BUGS ARE WAY SMARTER THAN YOU.
OH YEAH? I'D LIKE TO SEE THEM DO THIS JOB.

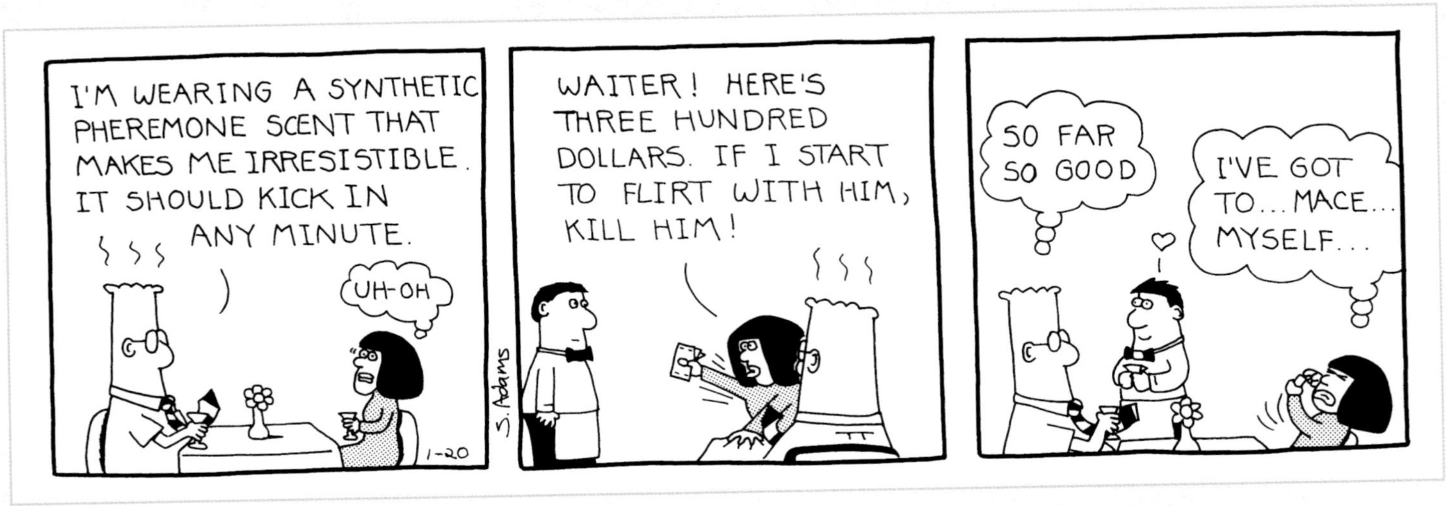
I'M WEARING A SYNTHETIC PHEREMONE SCENT THAT MAKES ME IRRESISTIBLE. IT SHOULD KICK IN ANY MINUTE.
UH-OH
WAITER! HERE'S THREE HUNDRED DOLLARS. IF I START TO FLIRT WITH HIM, KILL HIM!
SO FAR SO GOOD
I'VE GOT TO... MACE... MYSELF...

I enjoyed writing dating jokes for Dilbert, and did a lot of them in the early days, but they never found the audience I hoped for.

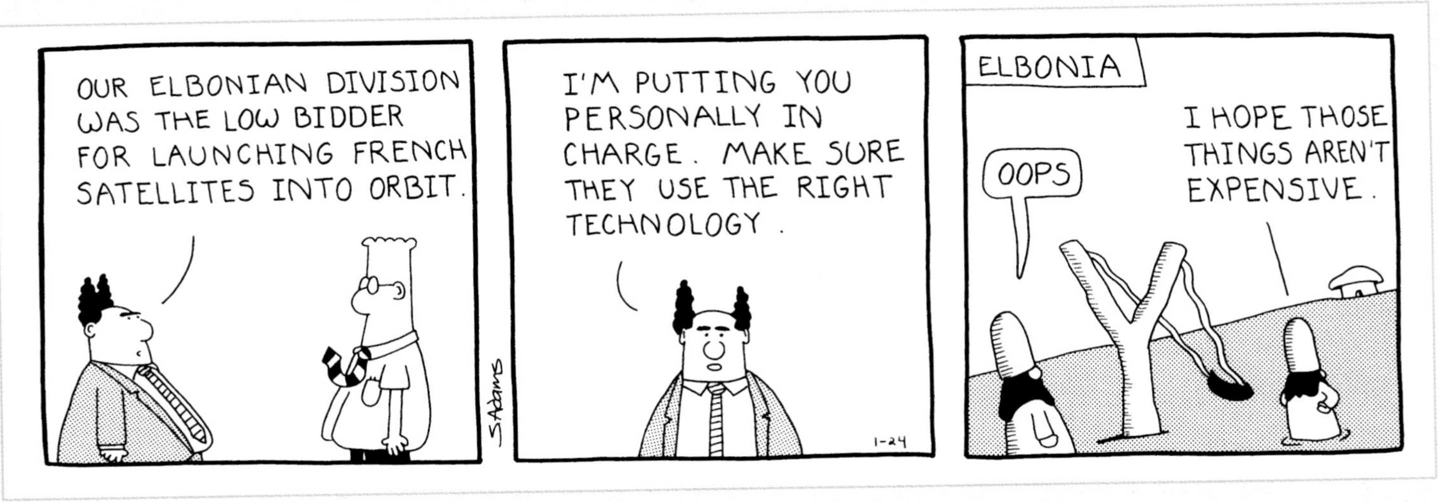
OUR ELBONIAN DIVISION WAS THE LOW BIDDER FOR LAUNCHING FRENCH SATELLITES INTO ORBIT.
I'M PUTTING YOU PERSONALLY IN CHARGE. MAKE SURE THEY USE THE RIGHT TECHNOLOGY.
ELBONIA
OOPS
I HOPE THOSE THINGS AREN'T EXPENSIVE.

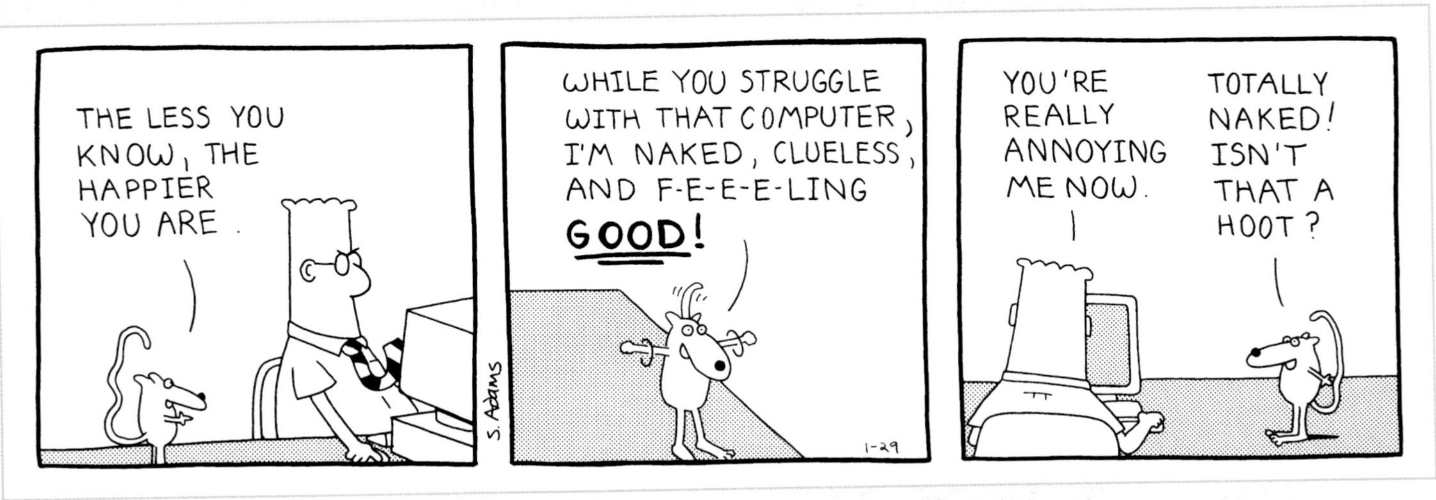
THE LESS YOU KNOW, THE HAPPIER YOU ARE.
WHILE YOU STRUGGLE WITH THAT COMPUTER, I'M NAKED, CLUELESS, AND F-E-E-E-LING GOOD!
YOU'RE REALLY ANNOYING ME NOW.
TOTALLY NAKED! ISN'T THAT A HOOT?

I thought the middle panel above would make a best-selling T-shirt. We tried. It wasn't.

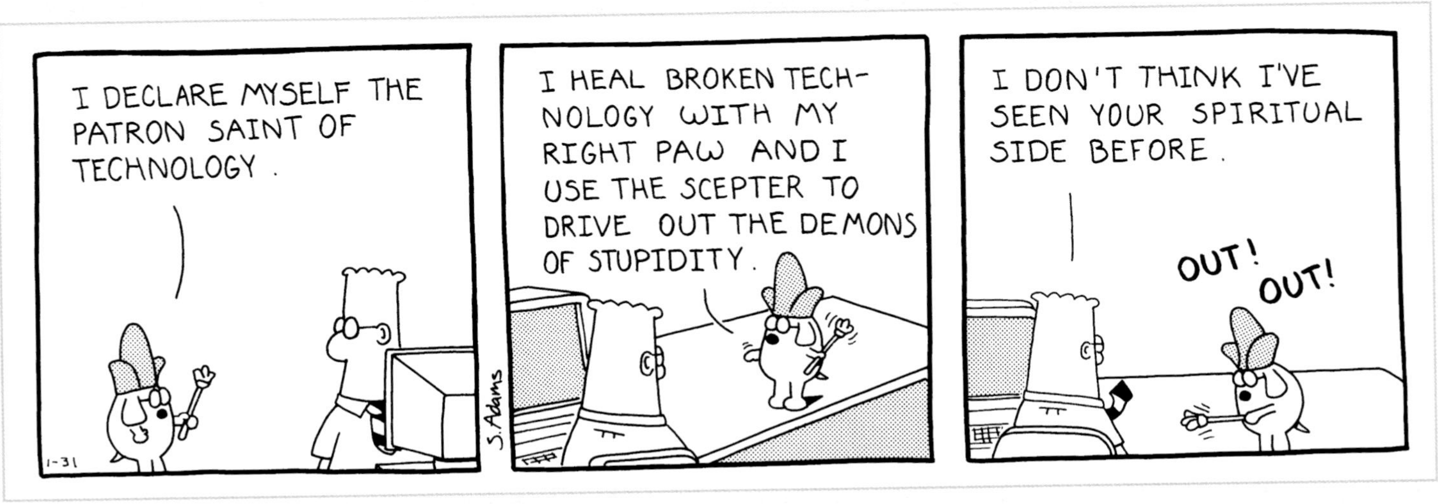
I DECLARE MYSELF THE PATRON SAINT OF TECHNOLOGY.
I HEAL BROKEN TECHNOLOGY WITH MY RIGHT PAW AND I USE THE SCEPTER TO DRIVE OUT THE DEMONS OF STUPIDITY.
I DON'T THINK I'VE SEEN YOUR SPIRITUAL SIDE BEFORE.
OUT! OUT!

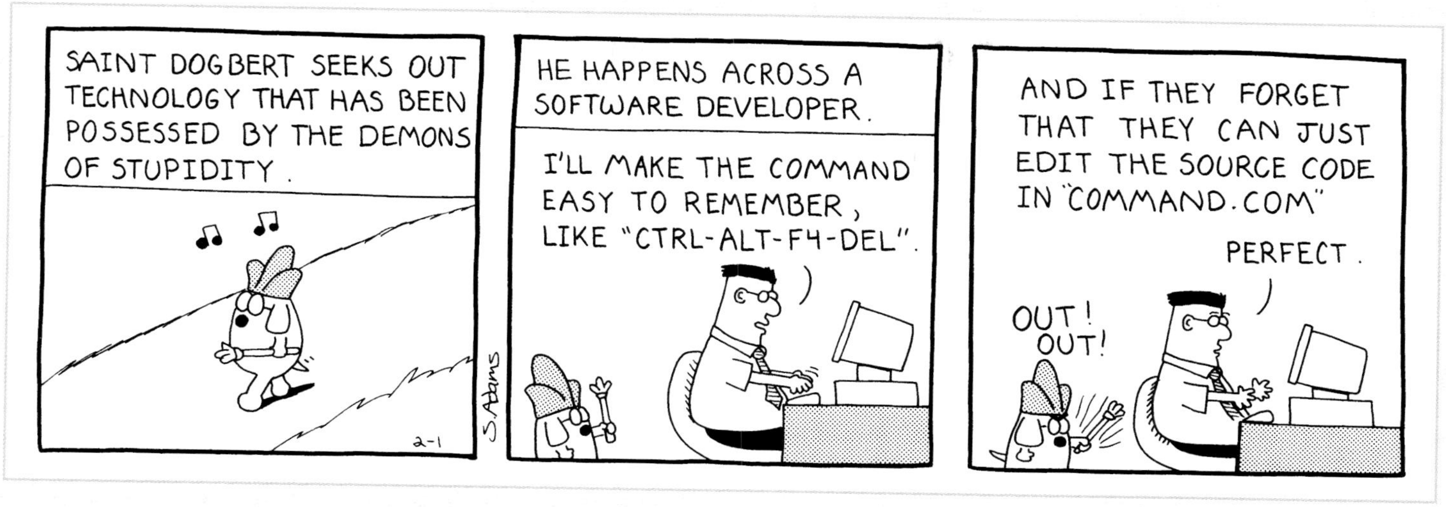
SAINT DOGBERT SEEKS OUT TECHNOLOGY THAT HAS BEEN POSSESSED BY THE DEMONS OF STUPIDITY.
HE HAPPENS ACROSS A SOFTWARE DEVELOPER.
I'LL MAKE THE COMMAND EASY TO REMEMBER, LIKE "CTRL-ALT-F4-DEL".
AND IF THEY FORGET THAT THEY CAN JUST EDIT THE SOURCE CODE IN "COMMAND.COM"
PERFECT.
OUT! OUT!

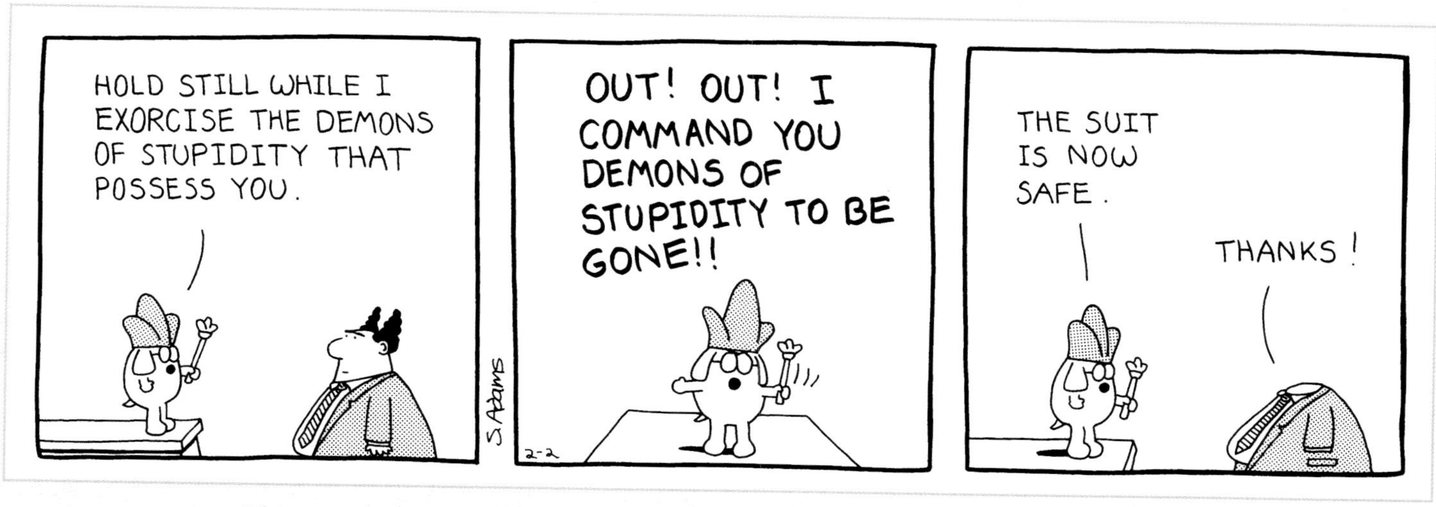
HOLD STILL WHILE I EXORCISE THE DEMONS OF STUPIDITY THAT POSSESS YOU.
OUT! OUT! I COMMAND YOU DEMONS OF STUPIDITY TO BE GONE!!
THE SUIT IS NOW SAFE.
THANKS!

This series with Dogbert as the patron saint of technology was hugely popular. It became the theme for T-shirts, greeting cards, and mugs.

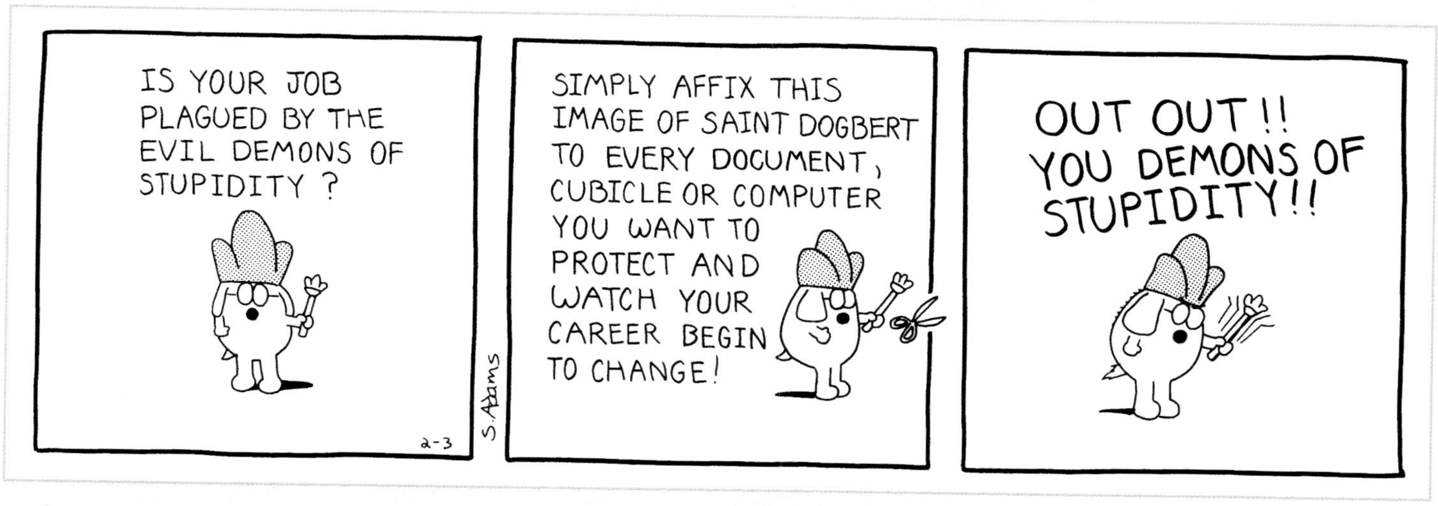
IS YOUR JOB PLAGUED BY THE EVIL DEMONS OF STUPIDITY?
SIMPLY AFFIX THIS IMAGE OF SAINT DOGBERT TO EVERY DOCUMENT, CUBICLE OR COMPUTER YOU WANT TO PROTECT AND WATCH YOUR CAREER BEGIN TO CHANGE!
OUT OUT!! YOU DEMONS OF STUPIDITY!!

Alice's personality is starting to be defined by her grumpiness. She hasn't yet developed the Fist of Death.

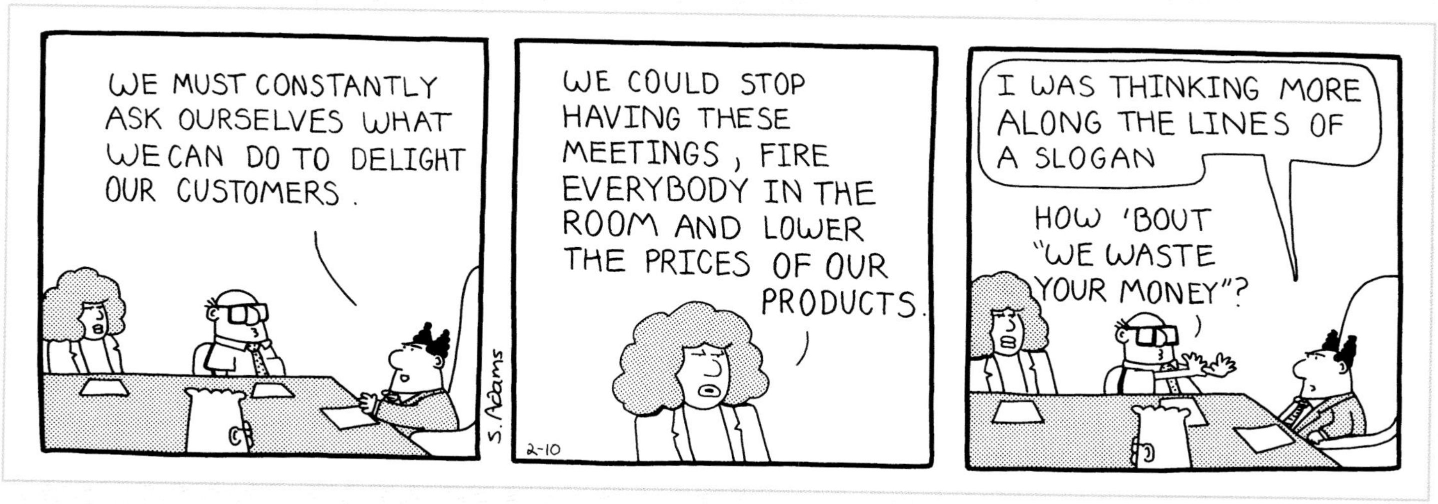
WE MUST CONSTANTLY ASK OURSELVES WHAT WE CAN DO TO DELIGHT OUR CUSTOMERS.
WE COULD STOP HAVING THESE MEETINGS, FIRE EVERYBODY IN THE ROOM AND LOWER THE PRICES OF OUR PRODUCTS.
I WAS THINKING MORE ALONG THE LINES OF A SLOGAN
HOW 'BOUT "WE WASTE YOUR MONEY"?

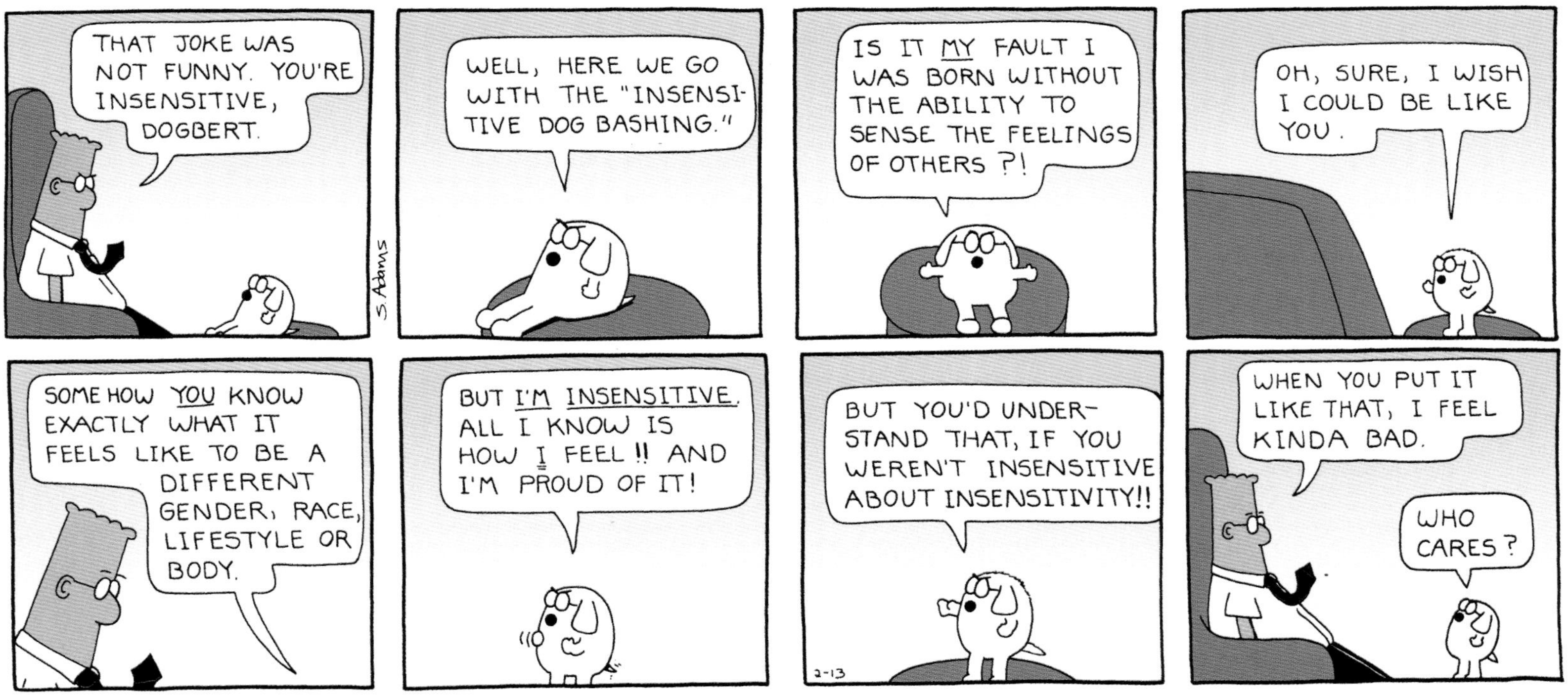
THAT JOKE WAS NOT FUNNY. YOU'RE INSENSITIVE, DOGBERT.
WELL, HERE WE GO WITH THE "INSENSITIVE DOG BASHING."
IS IT MY FAULT I WAS BORN WITHOUT THE ABILITY TO SENSE THE FEELINGS OF OTHERS ?!
OH, SURE, I WISH I COULD BE LIKE YOU.
SOME HOW YOU KNOW EXACTLY WHAT IT FEELS LIKE TO BE A DIFFERENT GENDER, RACE, LIFESTYLE OR BODY.
BUT I'M INSENSITIVE. ALL I KNOW IS HOW I FEEL!! AND I'M PROUD OF IT!
BUT YOU'D UNDERSTAND THAT, IF YOU WEREN'T INSENSITIVE ABOUT INSENSITIVITY!!
WHEN YOU PUT IT LIKE THAT, I FEEL KINDA BAD.
WHO CARES?
S. Adams
2-13

At this time I started having trouble with my drawing hand from overuse. The lettering is different because I hired another artist to ink over my penciled text. I still did all of the artwork and writing.

I always wonder to what degree the readers who have no corporate experience think the situations in Dilbert *are fantasy. This comic was based on an actual strategy I saw succeed at my day job.*

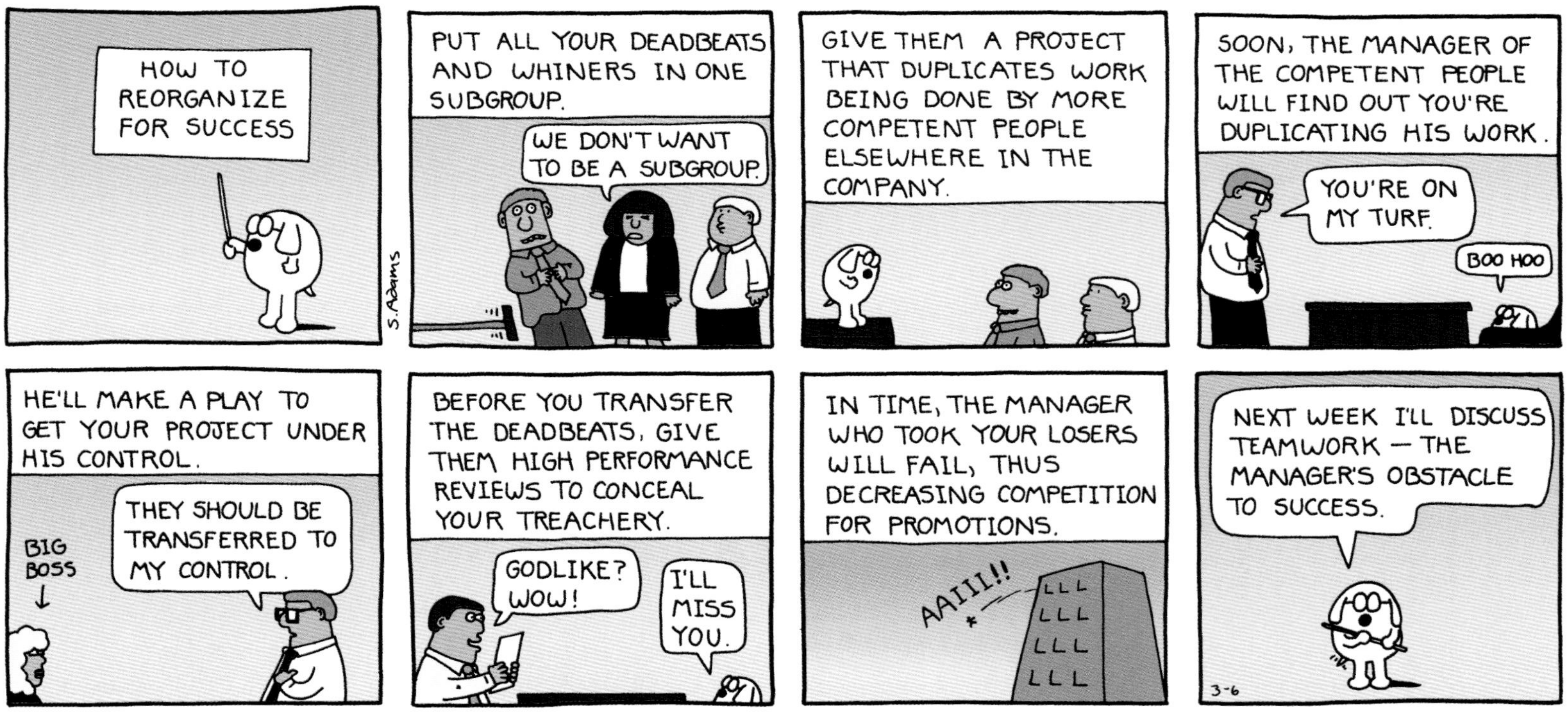
HOW TO REORGANIZE FOR SUCCESS
S. Adams
PUT ALL YOUR DEADBEATS AND WHINERS IN ONE SUBGROUP.
WE DON'T WANT TO BE A SUBGROUP.
GIVE THEM A PROJECT THAT DUPLICATES WORK BEING DONE BY MORE COMPETENT PEOPLE ELSEWHERE IN THE COMPANY.
SOON, THE MANAGER OF THE COMPETENT PEOPLE WILL FIND OUT YOU'RE DUPLICATING HIS WORK.
YOU'RE ON MY TURF.
BOO HOO
HE'LL MAKE A PLAY TO GET YOUR PROJECT UNDER HIS CONTROL.
BIG BOSS
THEY SHOULD BE TRANSFERRED TO MY CONTROL.
BEFORE YOU TRANSFER THE DEADBEATS, GIVE THEM HIGH PERFORMANCE REVIEWS TO CONCEAL YOUR TREACHERY.
GODLIKE? WOW!
I'LL MISS YOU.
IN TIME, THE MANAGER WHO TOOK YOUR LOSERS WILL FAIL, THUS DECREASING COMPETITION FOR PROMOTIONS.
AAIIL!!
NEXT WEEK I'LL DISCUSS TEAMWORK — THE MANAGER'S OBSTACLE TO SUCCESS.
3-6

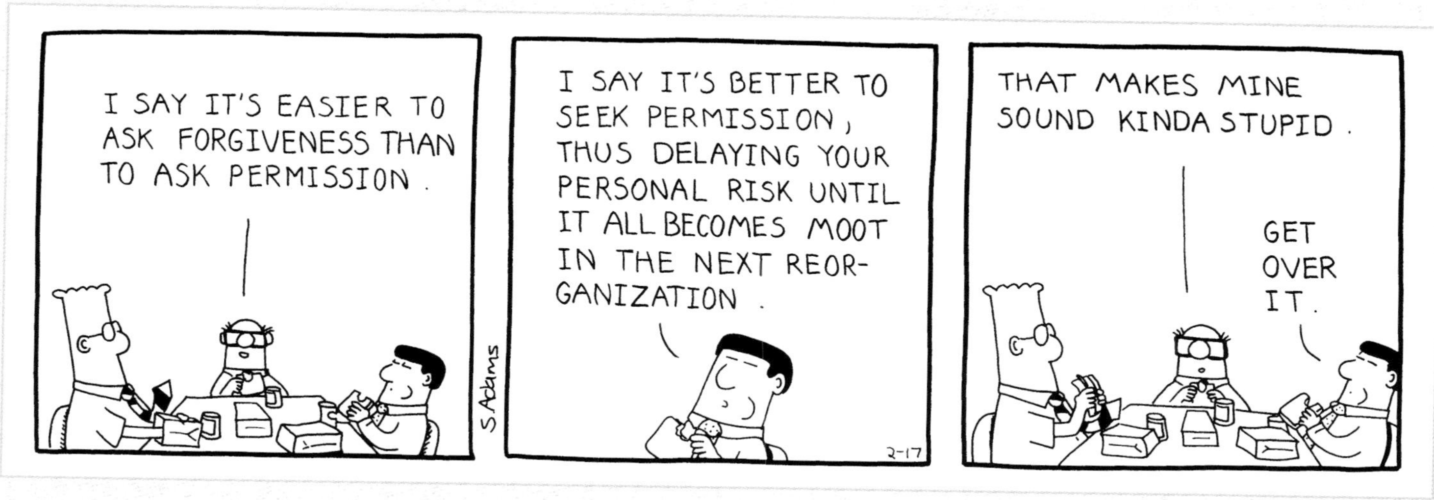
I SAY IT'S EASIER TO ASK FORGIVENESS THAN TO ASK PERMISSION.
S. Adams
I SAY IT'S BETTER TO SEEK PERMISSION, THUS DELAYING YOUR PERSONAL RISK UNTIL IT ALL BECOMES MOOT IN THE NEXT REORGANIZATION.
2-17
THAT MAKES MINE SOUND KINDA STUPID.
GET OVER IT.

Most old sayings aren't as wise as they sound.

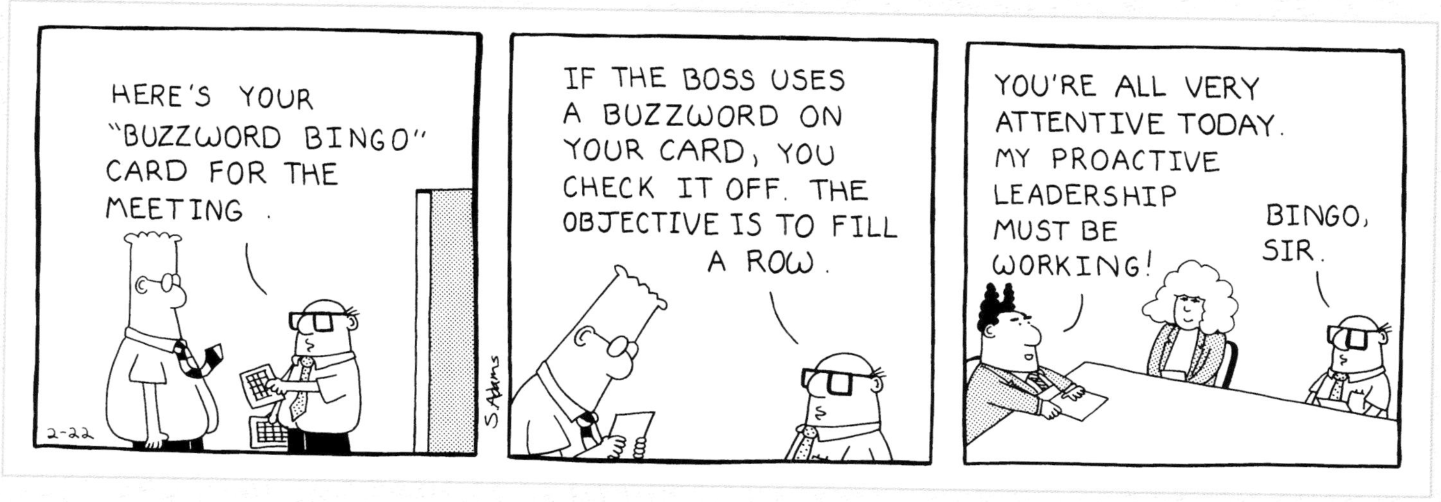
HERE'S YOUR "BUZZWORD BINGO" CARD FOR THE MEETING.
2-22
S. Adams
IF THE BOSS USES A BUZZWORD ON YOUR CARD, YOU CHECK IT OFF. THE OBJECTIVE IS TO FILL A ROW.
YOU'RE ALL VERY ATTENTIVE TODAY. MY PROACTIVE LEADERSHIP MUST BE WORKING!
BINGO, SIR.

I didn't invent Buzzword Bingo, but this strip did a lot to popularize it.
The idea for the game is often incorrectly attributed to me.

This comic was based on a mistake I made when my boss asked me to attend a meeting in his place and defend the budget for my project. The meeting leader asked what the downside of slashing my budget would be, and I answered honestly that it wouldn't make much difference because my project wasn't terribly important. My boss informed me later that that was the wrong answer. My project didn't get funded, but I also never had to go to another meeting on budgets.

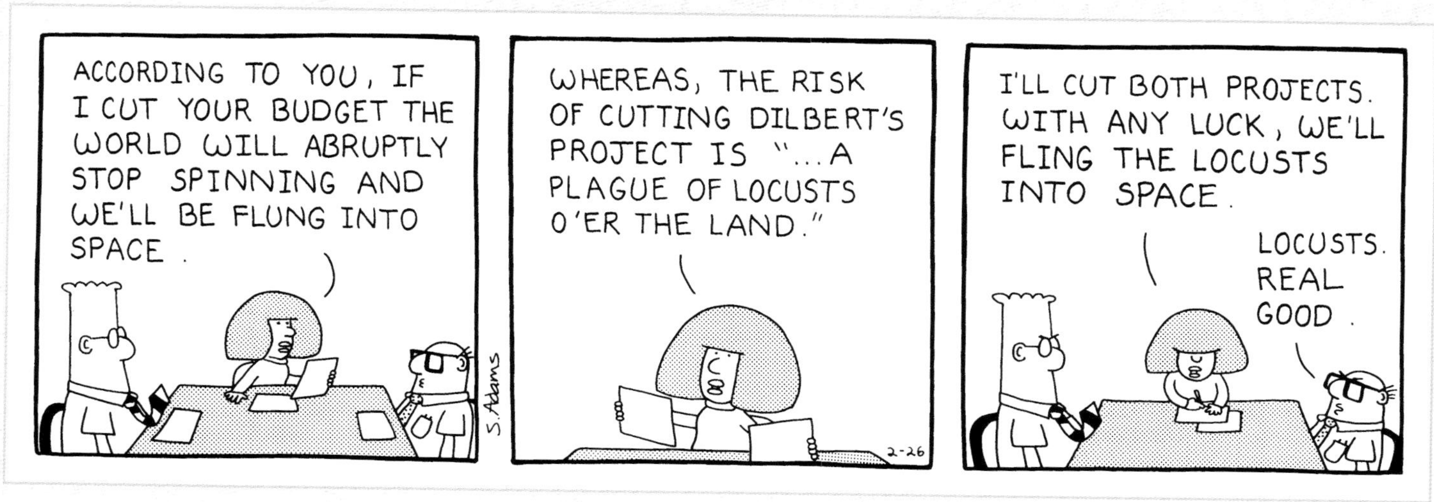
ACCORDING TO YOU, IF I CUT YOUR BUDGET THE WORLD WILL ABRUPTLY STOP SPINNING AND WE'LL BE FLUNG INTO SPACE.
S. Adams
WHEREAS, THE RISK OF CUTTING DILBERT'S PROJECT IS "...A PLAGUE OF LOCUSTS O'ER THE LAND."
2-26
I'LL CUT BOTH PROJECTS. WITH ANY LUCK, WE'LL FLING THE LOCUSTS INTO SPACE.
LOCUSTS. REAL GOOD.

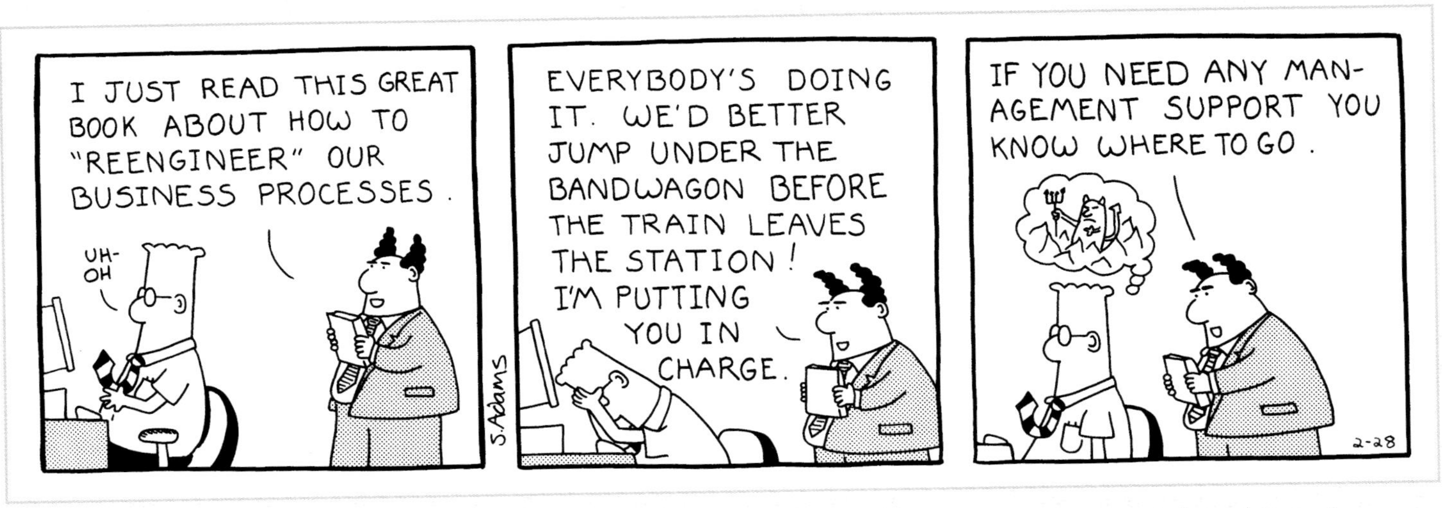
I JUST READ THIS GREAT BOOK ABOUT HOW TO "REENGINEER" OUR BUSINESS PROCESSES.
UH-OH
EVERYBODY'S DOING IT. WE'D BETTER JUMP UNDER THE BANDWAGON BEFORE THE TRAIN LEAVES THE STATION! I'M PUTTING YOU IN CHARGE.
S.Adams
IF YOU NEED ANY MANAGEMENT SUPPORT YOU KNOW WHERE TO GO.
2-28

At this point, Dilbert was systematically mocking all the management trends that were the subject of best-selling business books. All the trends had an element of common sense to them, but when overapplied by simple-minded managers, they usually generated more bad than good.

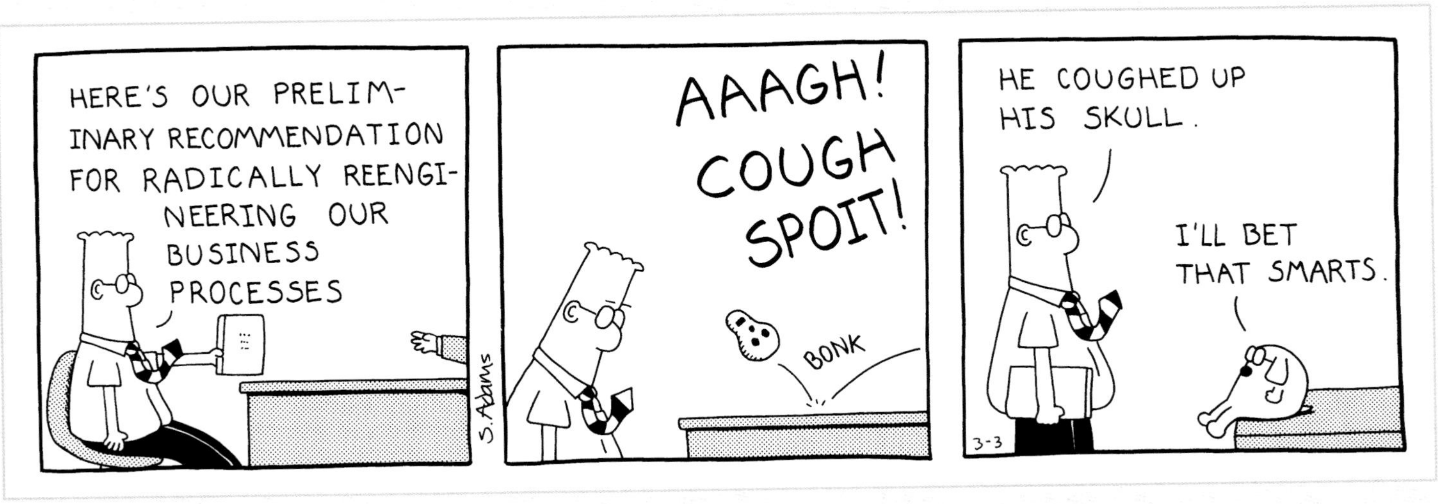
HERE'S OUR PRELIMINARY RECOMMENDATION FOR RADICALLY REENGINEERING OUR BUSINESS PROCESSES
S.Adams
AAAGH! COUGH SPOIT!
BONK
HE COUGHED UP HIS SKULL.
I'LL BET THAT SMARTS.
3-3

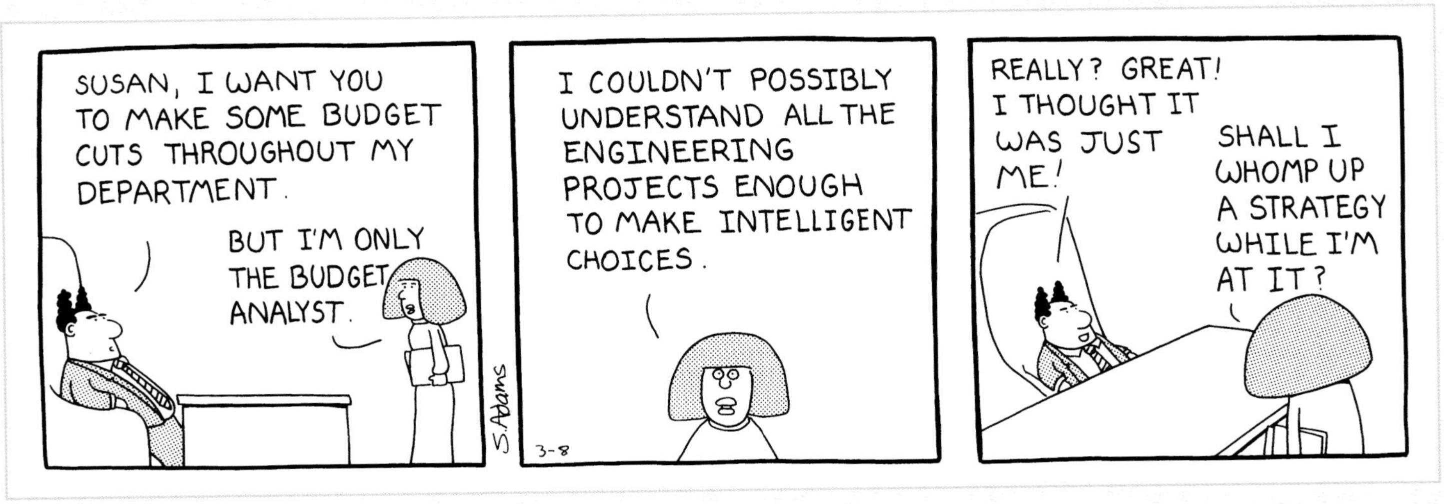
SUSAN, I WANT YOU TO MAKE SOME BUDGET CUTS THROUGHOUT MY DEPARTMENT.
BUT I'M ONLY THE BUDGET ANALYST.
S.Adams
3-8
I COULDN'T POSSIBLY UNDERSTAND ALL THE ENGINEERING PROJECTS ENOUGH TO MAKE INTELLIGENT CHOICES.
REALLY? GREAT! I THOUGHT IT WAS JUST ME!
SHALL I WHOMP UP A STRATEGY WHILE I'M AT IT?

As the "budget guy" in one of my many corporate jobs, people assumed I made the decisions on who got what budget. It was hard to convince managers I was only in charge of addition and subtraction. They often lobbied me to get more money.

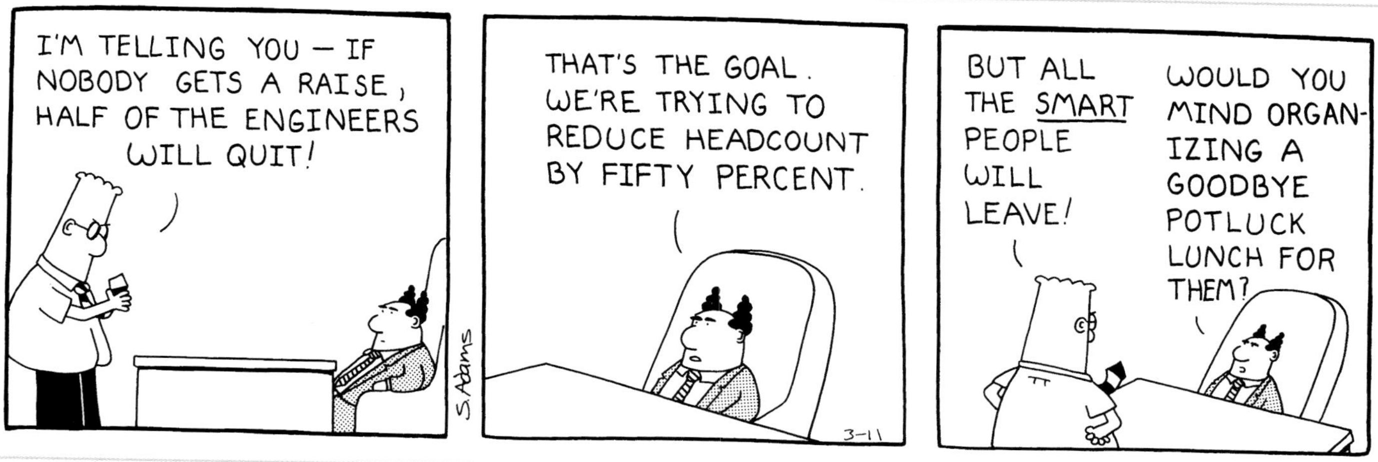
I'M TELLING YOU — IF NOBODY GETS A RAISE, HALF OF THE ENGINEERS WILL QUIT!
THAT'S THE GOAL. WE'RE TRYING TO REDUCE HEADCOUNT BY FIFTY PERCENT.
BUT ALL THE SMART PEOPLE WILL LEAVE!
WOULD YOU MIND ORGANIZING A GOODBYE POTLUCK LUNCH FOR THEM?
S. Adams
3-11

The era of downsizing in the '90s is what put Dilbert *on the map. The media needed a face for all the corporate incompetence and insensitivity, and* Dilbert *was just hitting its stride.* Dilbert *appeared on the covers of* Newsweek, Time, Fortune, *and even* People.

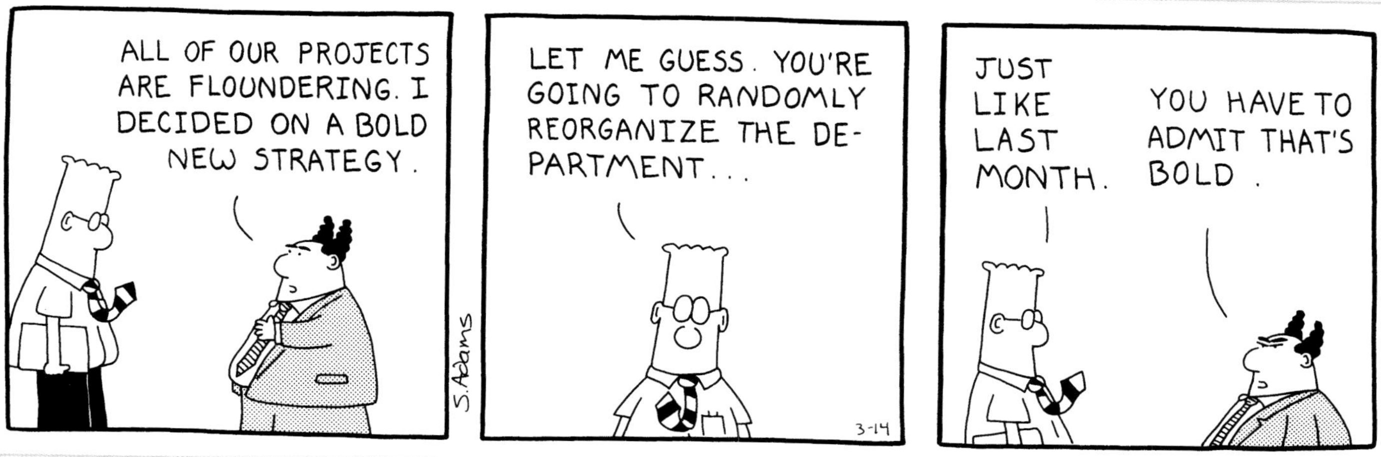
ALL OF OUR PROJECTS ARE FLOUNDERING. I DECIDED ON A BOLD NEW STRATEGY.
LET ME GUESS. YOU'RE GOING TO RANDOMLY REORGANIZE THE DEPARTMENT...
JUST LIKE LAST MONTH.
YOU HAVE TO ADMIT THAT'S BOLD.
S. Adams
3-14

By this point I had learned from reader feedback that simply describing an absurd corporate situation with honesty was enough to make the comic work, at least for people who identified with the situation. The clever puns and elaborate "gags" were unnecessary, and largely abandoned going forward.

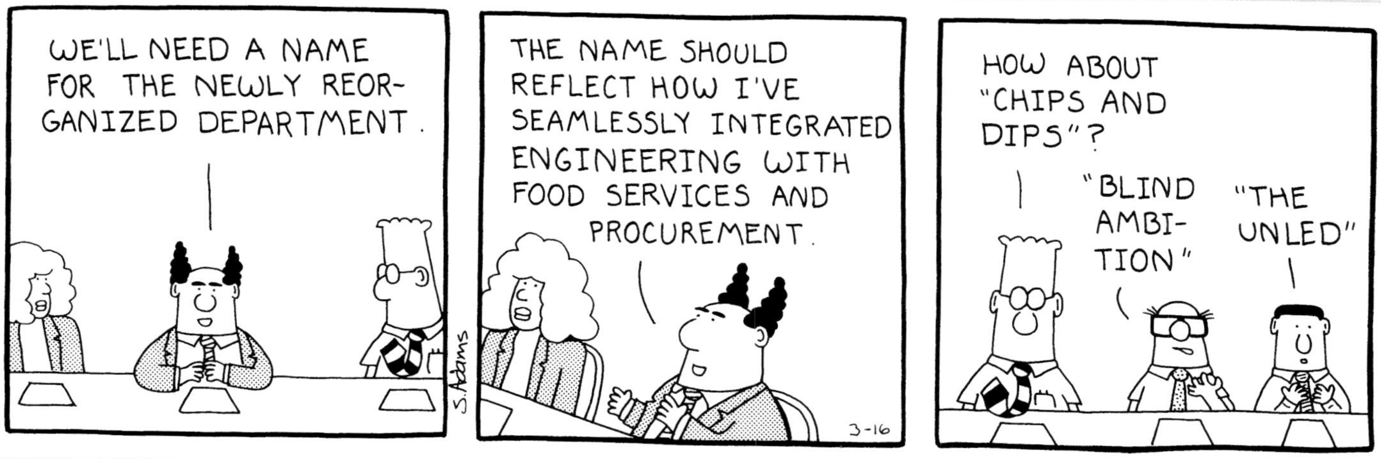
WE'LL NEED A NAME FOR THE NEWLY REORGANIZED DEPARTMENT.
THE NAME SHOULD REFLECT HOW I'VE SEAMLESSLY INTEGRATED ENGINEERING WITH FOOD SERVICES AND PROCUREMENT.
HOW ABOUT "CHIPS AND DIPS"?
"BLIND AMBITION"
"THE UNLED"
S. Adams
3-16

To me, few things are funnier than subordinates making unhelpful suggestions for their own entertainment. I learned this from a co-worker named Red, who intentionally used as many buzzwords as possible in meetings while trying to keep a straight face. It was pure subversive genius.

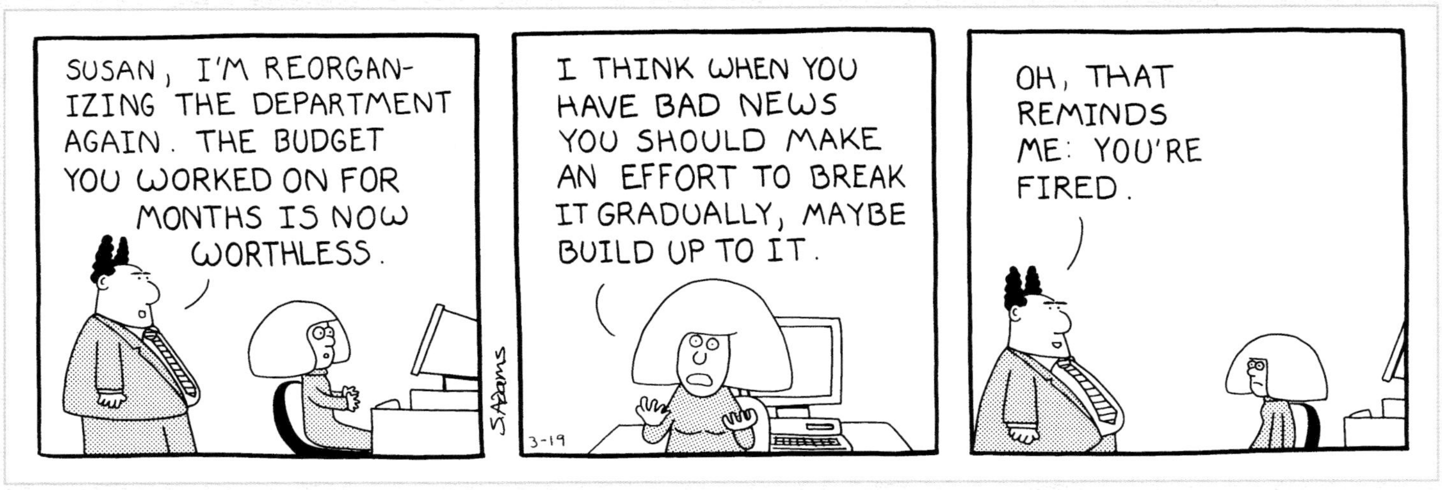
SUSAN, I'M REORGANIZING THE DEPARTMENT AGAIN. THE BUDGET YOU WORKED ON FOR MONTHS IS NOW WORTHLESS.
I THINK WHEN YOU HAVE BAD NEWS YOU SHOULD MAKE AN EFFORT TO BREAK IT GRADUALLY, MAYBE BUILD UP TO IT.
OH, THAT REMINDS ME: YOU'RE FIRED.
S.Adams
3-19

The boss reached his portliest dimensions at about this time, for no particular reason. I just have trouble drawing things the same way twice, so there tends to be some drift.

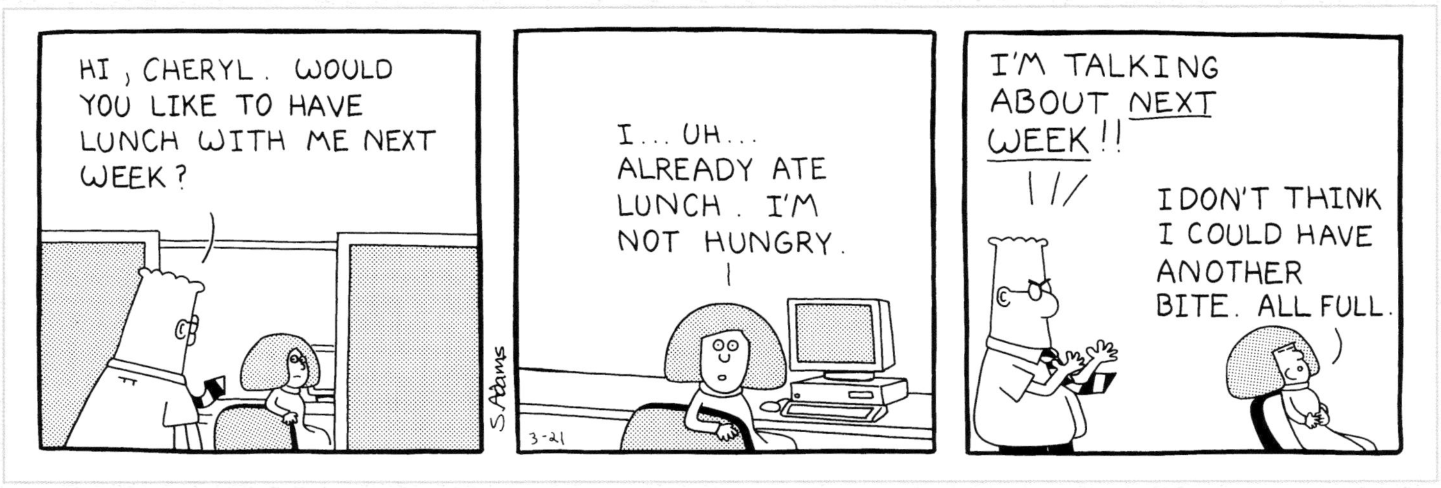
HI, CHERYL. WOULD YOU LIKE TO HAVE LUNCH WITH ME NEXT WEEK?
I... UH... ALREADY ATE LUNCH. I'M NOT HUNGRY.
I'M TALKING ABOUT NEXT WEEK!!
I DON'T THINK I COULD HAVE ANOTHER BITE. ALL FULL.
S.Adams
3-21

Dilbert's dating life mirrored my own experience in my twenties. These jokes were painfully easy to write. And yes, I did get turned down for a lunch date because the woman I asked out had eaten a big breakfast.

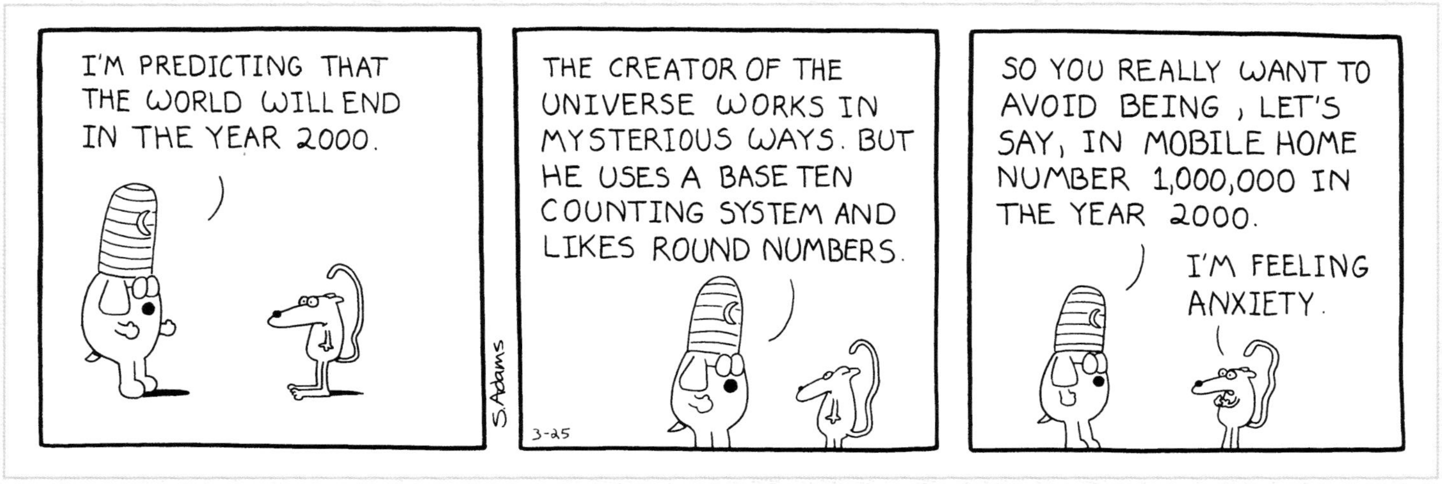
I'M PREDICTING THAT THE WORLD WILL END IN THE YEAR 2000.
THE CREATOR OF THE UNIVERSE WORKS IN MYSTERIOUS WAYS. BUT HE USES A BASE TEN COUNTING SYSTEM AND LIKES ROUND NUMBERS.
SO YOU REALLY WANT TO AVOID BEING, LET'S SAY, IN MOBILE HOME NUMBER 1,000,000 IN THE YEAR 2000.
I'M FEELING ANXIETY.
S.Adams
3-25

The quote about big round numbers still pops up on the Internet on a regular basis. It has always been impossible to predict which ideas will catch the public's imagination. This one surprised me.

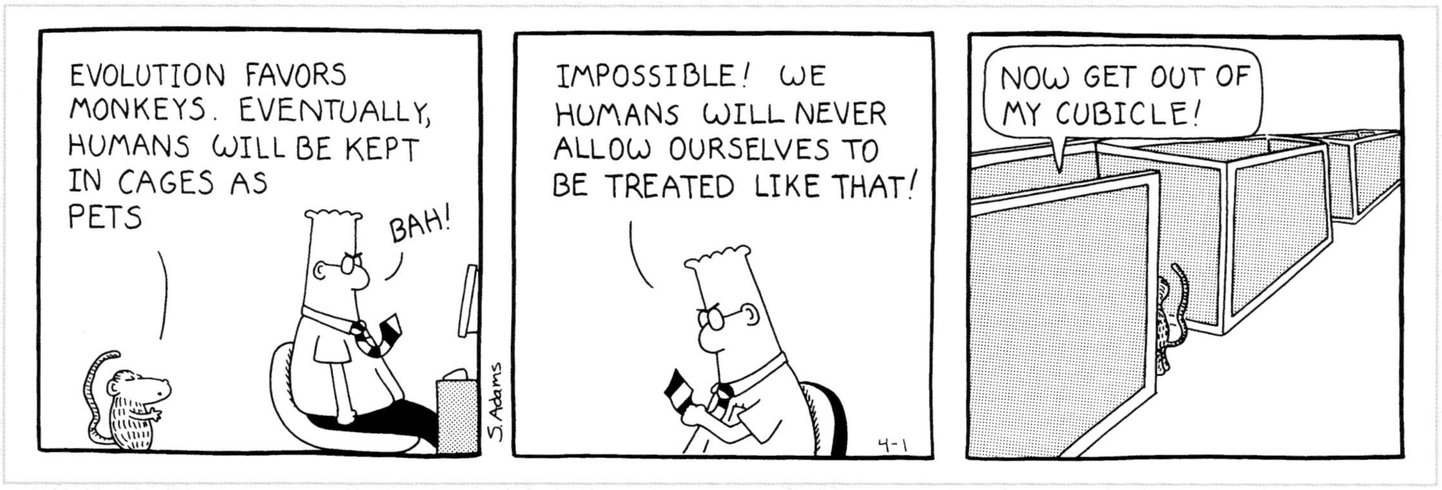
EVOLUTION FAVORS MONKEYS. EVENTUALLY, HUMANS WILL BE KEPT IN CAGES AS PETS
BAH!
IMPOSSIBLE! WE HUMANS WILL NEVER ALLOW OURSELVES TO BE TREATED LIKE THAT!
NOW GET OUT OF MY CUBICLE!
S.Adams
4-1

ZIMBU, YOU'RE NOT SUPPOSED TO USE YOUR TAIL TO OPERATE THE MOUSE.
IF TAILS WERE A NATURAL ADVANTAGE FOR ENGINEERS THEN EVOLUTION WOULD PROVIDE US ALL WITH TAILS!
DILBERT, I DON'T BELIEVE YOU'VE MET ROCKY, OUR NEW C PROGRAMMER.
S. Adams
3-30

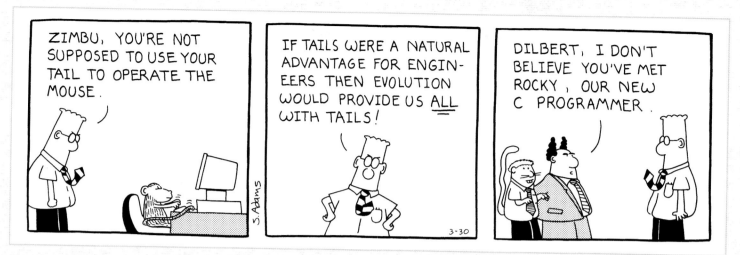

Cartoonists have a limited set of tricks. Among mine are putting tails on people and coming up with names that sound funny. Combine the two, and a guy with a tail, named Rocky, is automatically funny. At least to me.

The character that would become Alice was getting increasingly angry, but I didn't know she would become a regular.

IF YOU WANT TO GET PROMOTED, SAY BAD THINGS ABOUT YOUR CO-WORKERS SO YOU LOOK BETTER BY COMPARISON.
GEEZ, LISA, IT LOOKS LIKE YOU'VE BEEN HITTING THE DONUTS PRETTY HARD LATELY.
HEH-HEH... BIG THINGS ARE COMING MY WAY SOON.
S. Adams
4-6

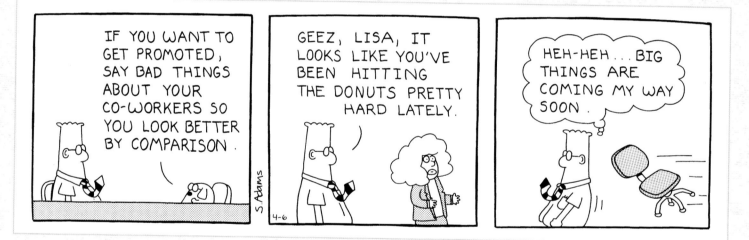

As a rule, you shouldn't flip the perspective on a comic as I did with the first and third panels below. It confuses the reader. I did it in this case because I started the comic before knowing how it would end, and I needed Dilbert to have the last line. In those days, I drew everything with pencil, pen, and paper. So once I started a comic, I finished it any way I could. I had to get to my day job, which meant do-overs weren't an option. Virtually every comic from 1989 to 1995 is essentially the first draft.

OUR DEVICE CONFORMS TO ALL INTERNATIONAL STANDARDS FOR COMMUNICATIONS.
IN OTHER WORDS, IT DOESN'T DO ANYTHING USEFUL AND IT'S NOT YOUR FAULT.
IS THERE SOMEBODY LESS EXPERIENCED I COULD TALK TO?
DO YOU HAVE MY BOSS'S NUMBER?
S. Adams
4-11

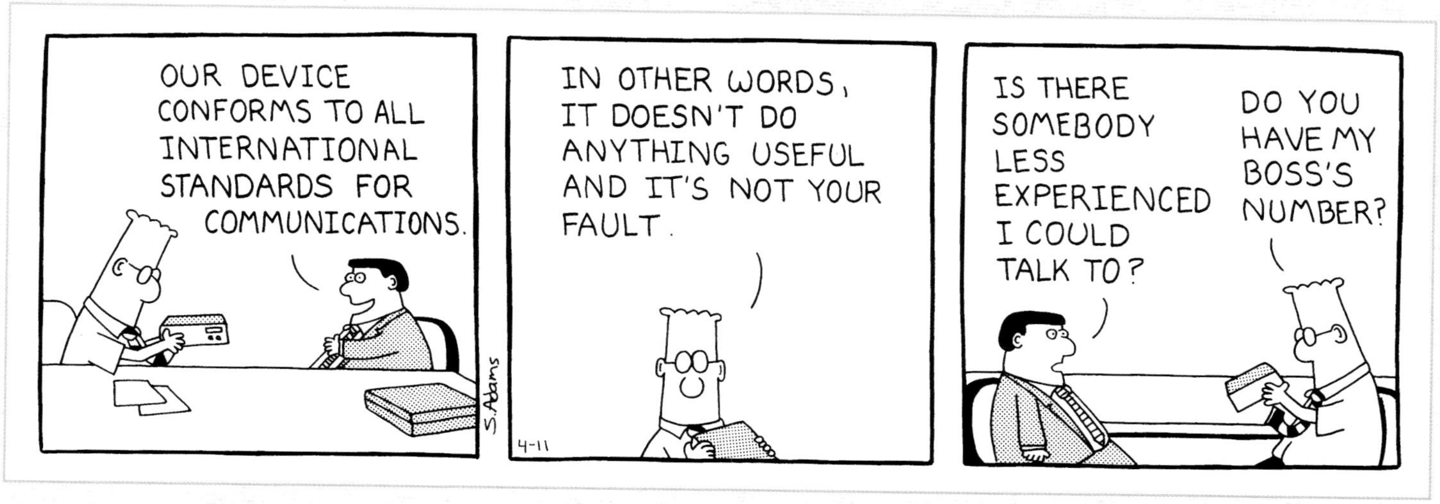

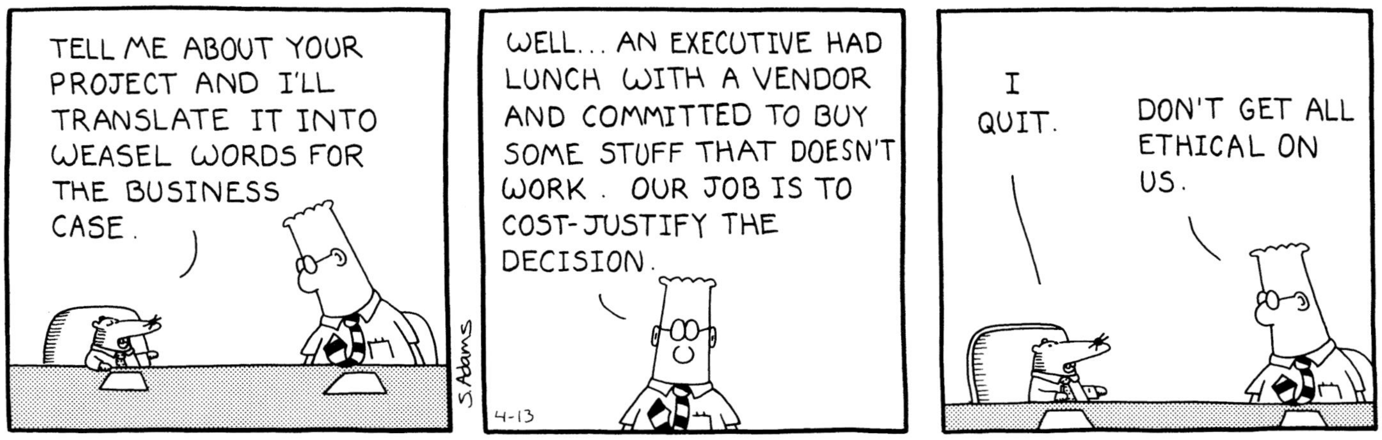
TELL ME ABOUT YOUR PROJECT AND I'LL TRANSLATE IT INTO WEASEL WORDS FOR THE BUSINESS CASE.
WELL... AN EXECUTIVE HAD LUNCH WITH A VENDOR AND COMMITTED TO BUY SOME STUFF THAT DOESN'T WORK. OUR JOB IS TO COST-JUSTIFY THE DECISION.
I QUIT.
DON'T GET ALL ETHICAL ON US.

One of my corporate jobs was writing business cases. This is a fancy way of saying "lying."

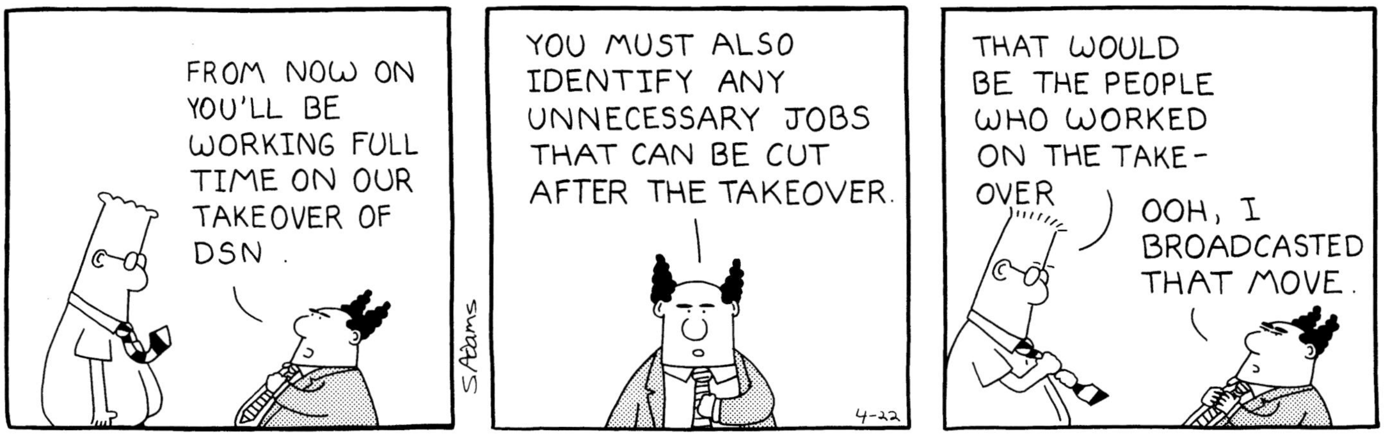
FROM NOW ON YOU'LL BE WORKING FULL TIME ON OUR TAKEOVER OF DSN.
YOU MUST ALSO IDENTIFY ANY UNNECESSARY JOBS THAT CAN BE CUT AFTER THE TAKEOVER.
THAT WOULD BE THE PEOPLE WHO WORKED ON THE TAKE-OVER
OOH, I BROADCASTED THAT MOVE.

I once worked on a project where it was clear that completing the project would mean I was out of a job. I managed to stretch it until the next reorganization made it all moot. That's called experience.

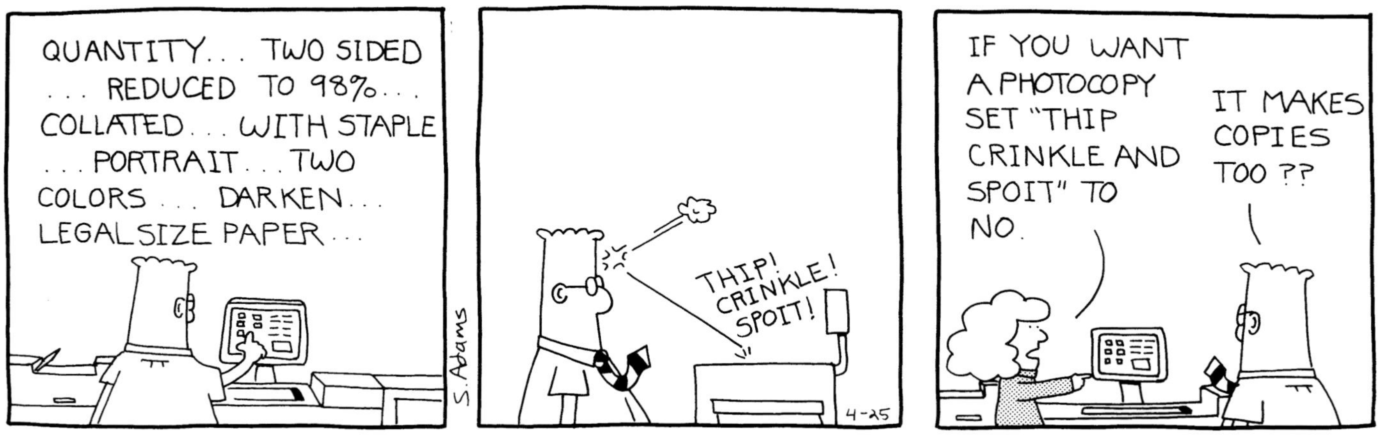
QUANTITY... TWO SIDED ... REDUCED TO 98%... COLLATED... WITH STAPLE ... PORTRAIT... TWO COLORS... DARKEN... LEGALSIZE PAPER...
THIP! CRINKLE! SPOIT!
IF YOU WANT A PHOTOCOPY SET "THIP CRINKLE AND SPOIT" TO NO.
IT MAKES COPIES TOO ??

Try to get "Thip! Crinkle! Spoit!" out of your head. It's not so easy.

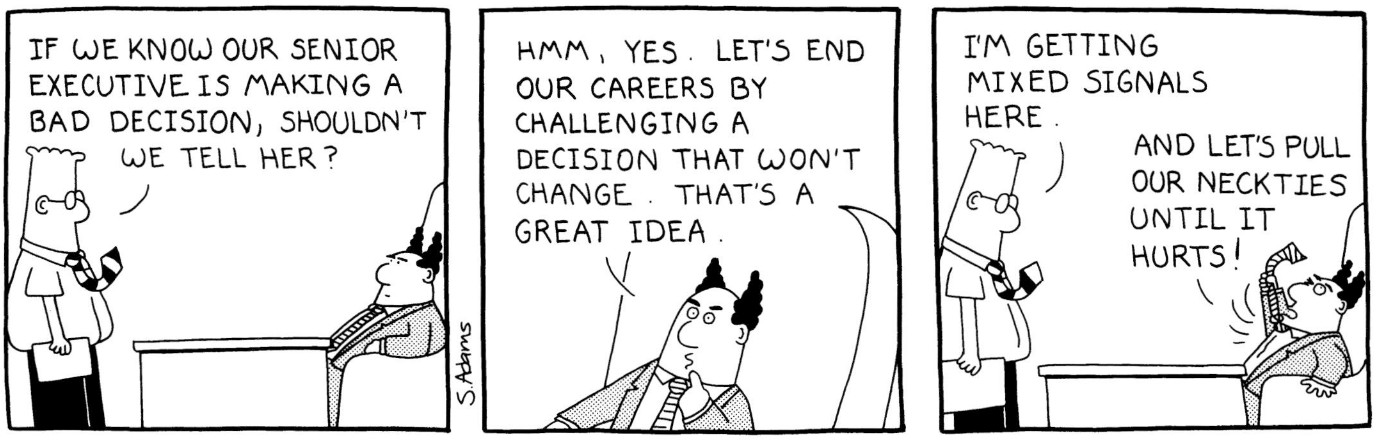
IF WE KNOW OUR SENIOR EXECUTIVE IS MAKING A BAD DECISION, SHOULDN'T WE TELL HER?
HMM, YES. LET'S END OUR CAREERS BY CHALLENGING A DECISION THAT WON'T CHANGE. THAT'S A GREAT IDEA.
I'M GETTING MIXED SIGNALS HERE.
AND LET'S PULL OUR NECKTIES UNTIL IT HURTS!

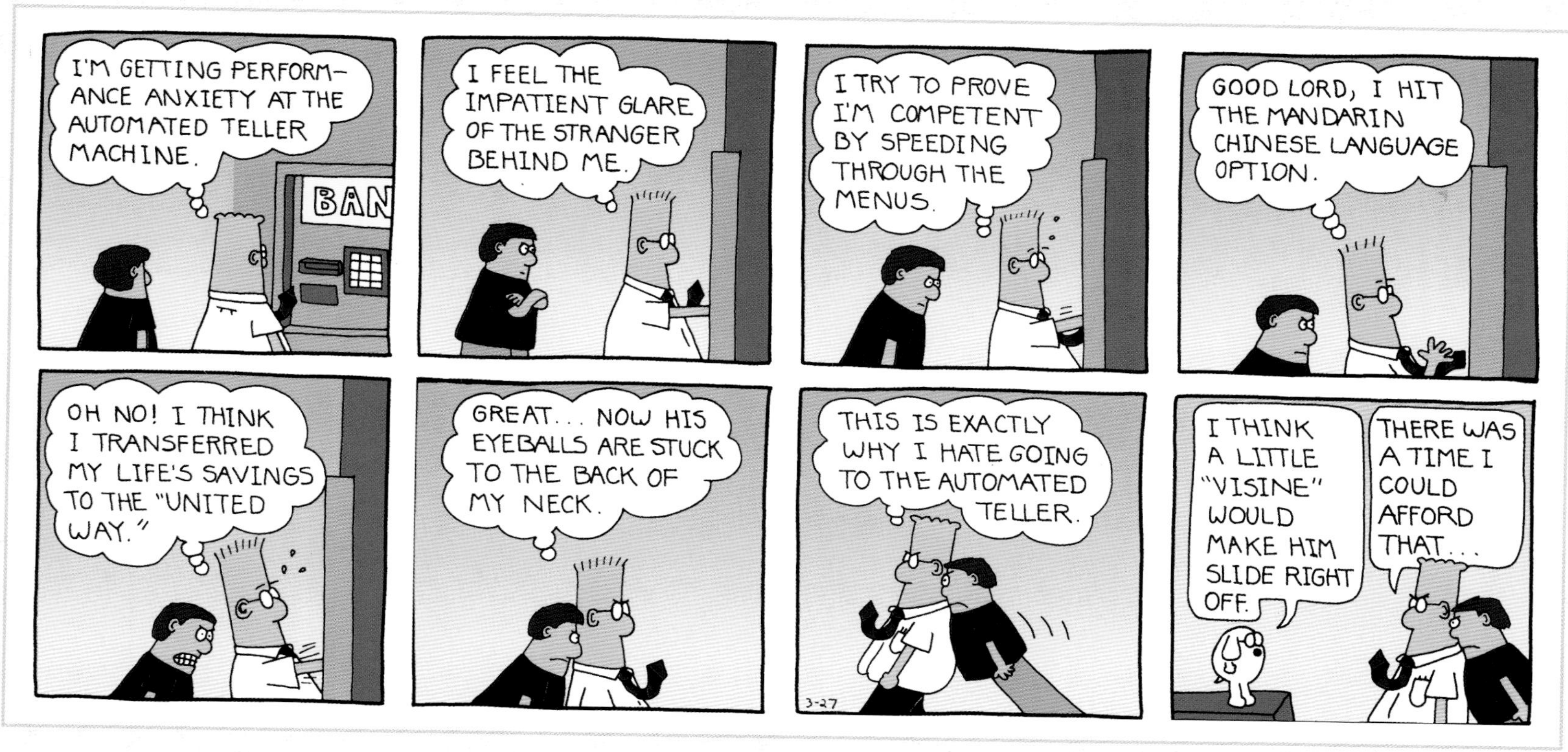
I'M GETTING PERFORMANCE ANXIETY AT THE AUTOMATED TELLER MACHINE.
BAN
I FEEL THE IMPATIENT GLARE OF THE STRANGER BEHIND ME.
I TRY TO PROVE I'M COMPETENT BY SPEEDING THROUGH THE MENUS.
GOOD LORD, I HIT THE MANDARIN CHINESE LANGUAGE OPTION.
OH NO! I THINK I TRANSFERRED MY LIFE'S SAVINGS TO THE "UNITED WAY."
GREAT... NOW HIS EYEBALLS ARE STUCK TO THE BACK OF MY NECK.
THIS IS EXACTLY WHY I HATE GOING TO THE AUTOMATED TELLER.
3-27
I THINK A LITTLE "VISINE" WOULD MAKE HIM SLIDE RIGHT OFF.
THERE WAS A TIME I COULD AFFORD THAT...

Like Dilbert, I worry about all the wrong things. I hate having anyone waiting in line behind me for anything. It's the main reason I don't golf.

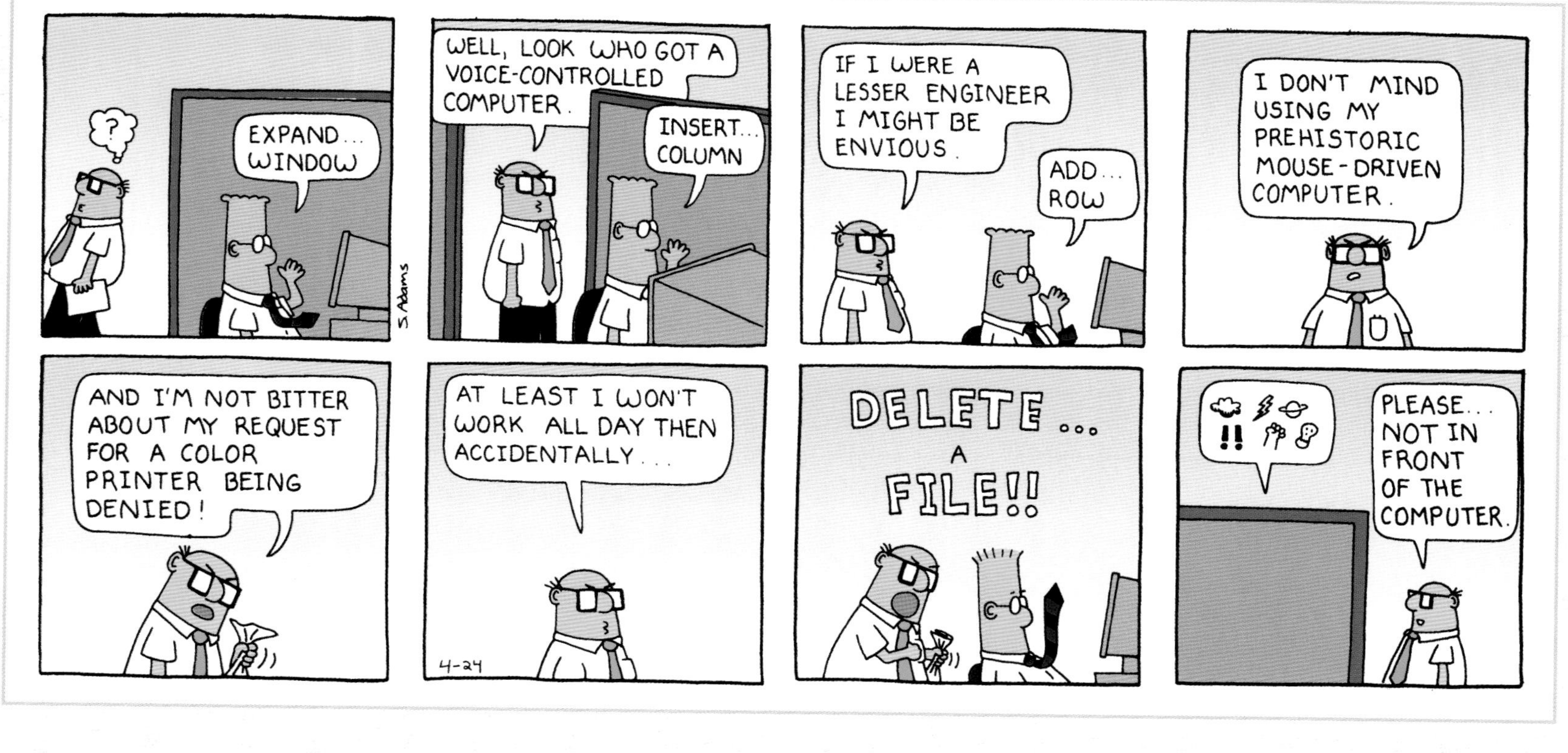
EXPAND... WINDOW
S. Adams
WELL, LOOK WHO GOT A VOICE-CONTROLLED COMPUTER.
INSERT... COLUMN
IF I WERE A LESSER ENGINEER I MIGHT BE ENVIOUS.
ADD... ROW
I DON'T MIND USING MY PREHISTORIC MOUSE-DRIVEN COMPUTER.
AND I'M NOT BITTER ABOUT MY REQUEST FOR A COLOR PRINTER BEING DENIED!
AT LEAST I WON'T WORK ALL DAY THEN ACCIDENTALLY...
4-24
DELETE... A FILE!!
!!
PLEASE... NOT IN FRONT OF THE COMPUTER.

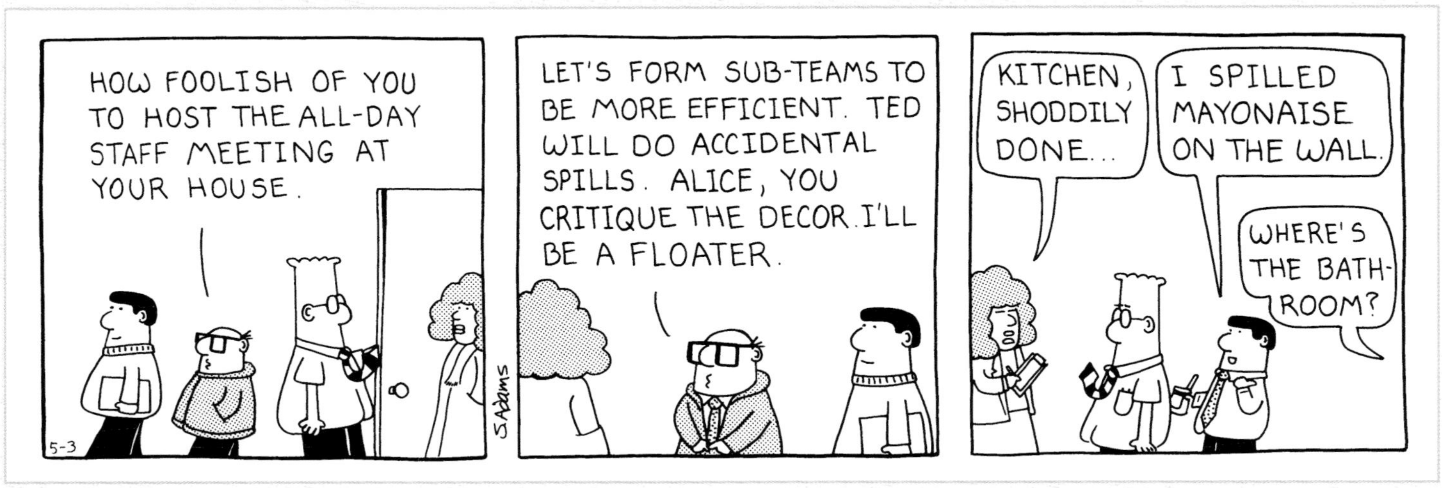
HOW FOOLISH OF YOU TO HOST THE ALL-DAY STAFF MEETING AT YOUR HOUSE.
LET'S FORM SUB-TEAMS TO BE MORE EFFICIENT. TED WILL DO ACCIDENTAL SPILLS. ALICE, YOU CRITIQUE THE DECOR. I'LL BE A FLOATER.
KITCHEN, SHODDILY DONE...
I SPILLED MAYONAISE ON THE WALL.
WHERE'S THE BATH-ROOM?

Behold, Alice gets her name. And her hair is starting to form the triangle that would come to define her look.

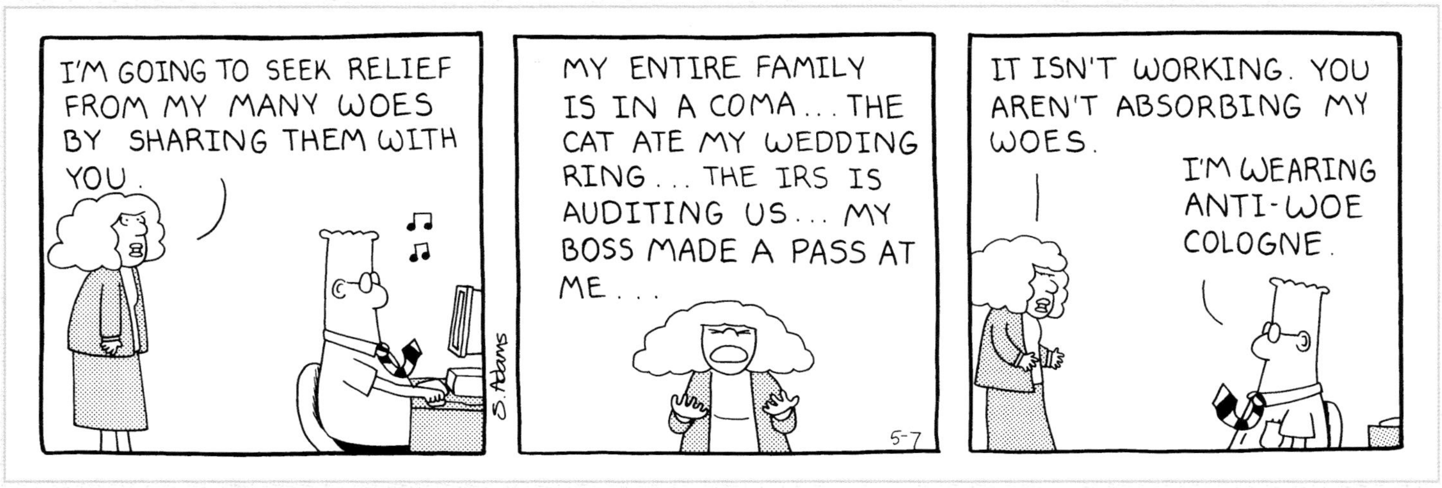
I'M GOING TO SEEK RELIEF FROM MY MANY WOES BY SHARING THEM WITH YOU.
MY ENTIRE FAMILY IS IN A COMA... THE CAT ATE MY WEDDING RING... THE IRS IS AUDITING US... MY BOSS MADE A PASS AT ME...
IT ISN'T WORKING. YOU AREN'T ABSORBING MY WOES.
I'M WEARING ANTI-WOE COLOGNE.

Alice is still married at this point.

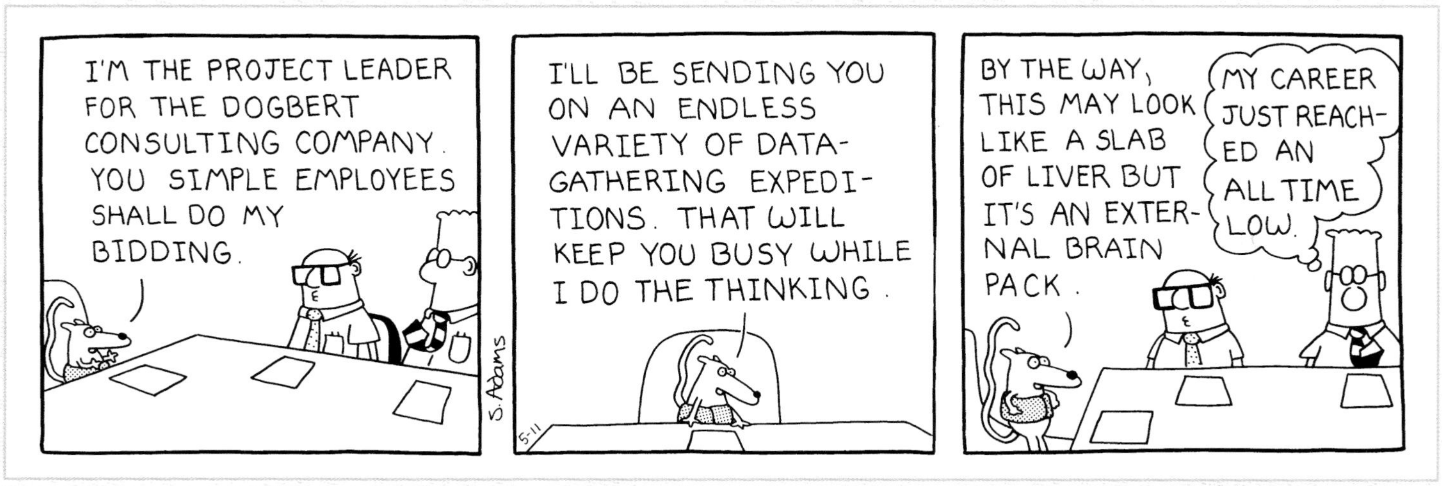
I'M THE PROJECT LEADER FOR THE DOGBERT CONSULTING COMPANY. YOU SIMPLE EMPLOYEES SHALL DO MY BIDDING.
I'LL BE SENDING YOU ON AN ENDLESS VARIETY OF DATA-GATHERING EXPEDI-TIONS. THAT WILL KEEP YOU BUSY WHILE I DO THE THINKING.
BY THE WAY, THIS MAY LOOK LIKE A SLAB OF LIVER BUT IT'S AN EXTER-NAL BRAIN PACK.
MY CAREER JUST REACH-ED AN ALL TIME LOW.

I was enduring a team of consultants in my day job. They didn't have external brain packs, but they did have the attitude.

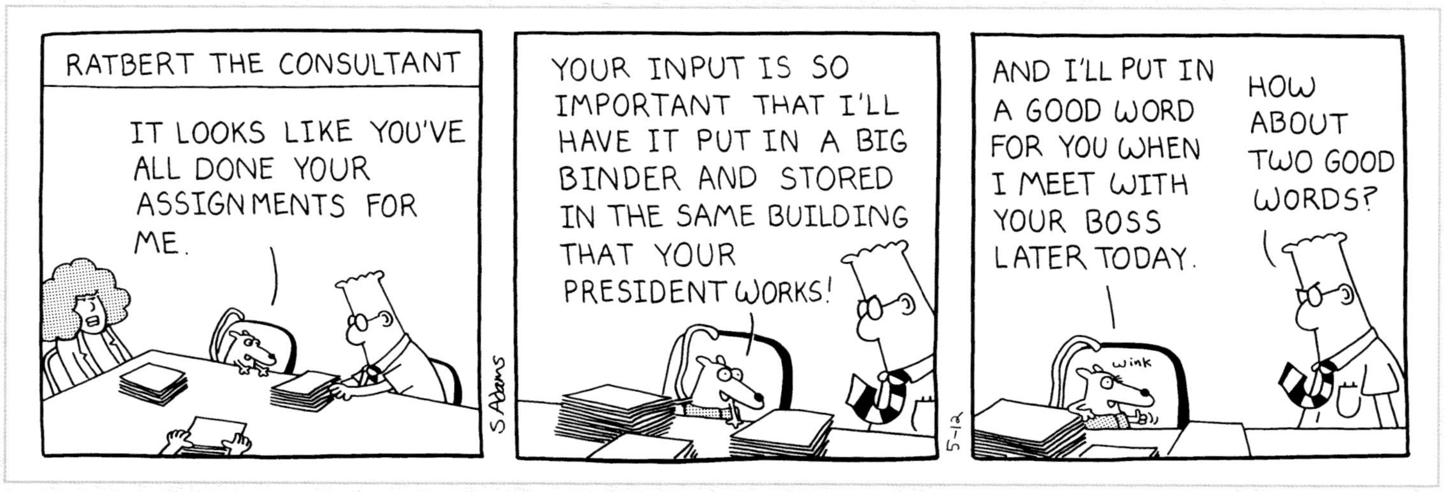
RATBERT THE CONSULTANT
IT LOOKS LIKE YOU'VE ALL DONE YOUR ASSIGNMENTS FOR ME.
YOUR INPUT IS SO IMPORTANT THAT I'LL HAVE IT PUT IN A BIG BINDER AND STORED IN THE SAME BUILDING THAT YOUR PRESIDENT WORKS!
AND I'LL PUT IN A GOOD WORD FOR YOU WHEN I MEET WITH YOUR BOSS LATER TODAY.
HOW ABOUT TWO GOOD WORDS?
wink

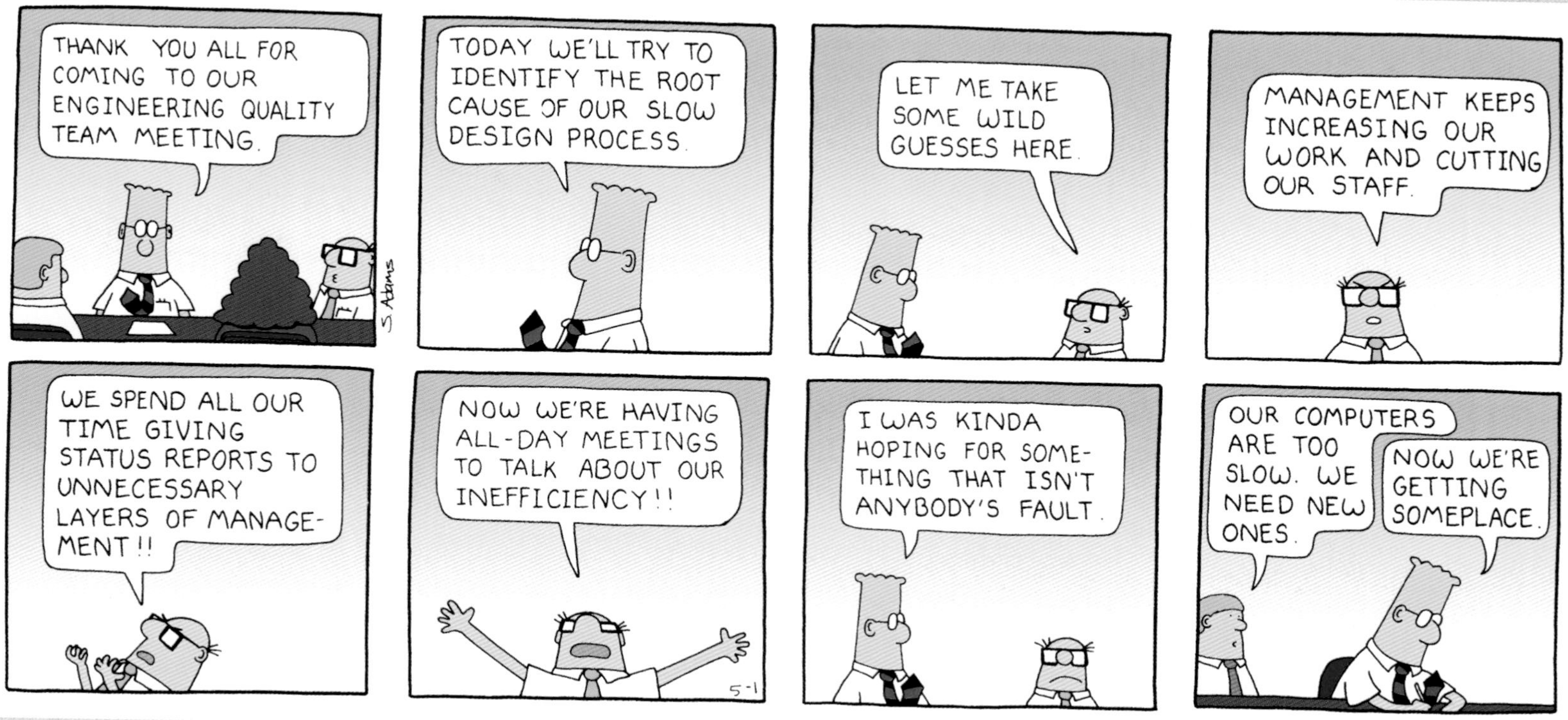
THANK YOU ALL FOR COMING TO OUR ENGINEERING QUALITY TEAM MEETING.
TODAY WE'LL TRY TO IDENTIFY THE ROOT CAUSE OF OUR SLOW DESIGN PROCESS.
LET ME TAKE SOME WILD GUESSES HERE.
MANAGEMENT KEEPS INCREASING OUR WORK AND CUTTING OUR STAFF.
WE SPEND ALL OUR TIME GIVING STATUS REPORTS TO UNNECESSARY LAYERS OF MANAGE-MENT!!
NOW WE'RE HAVING ALL-DAY MEETINGS TO TALK ABOUT OUR INEFFICIENCY!!
I WAS KINDA HOPING FOR SOME-THING THAT ISN'T ANYBODY'S FAULT.
OUR COMPUTERS ARE TOO SLOW. WE NEED NEW ONES.
NOW WE'RE GETTING SOMEPLACE.

Yes, I was in that meeting.

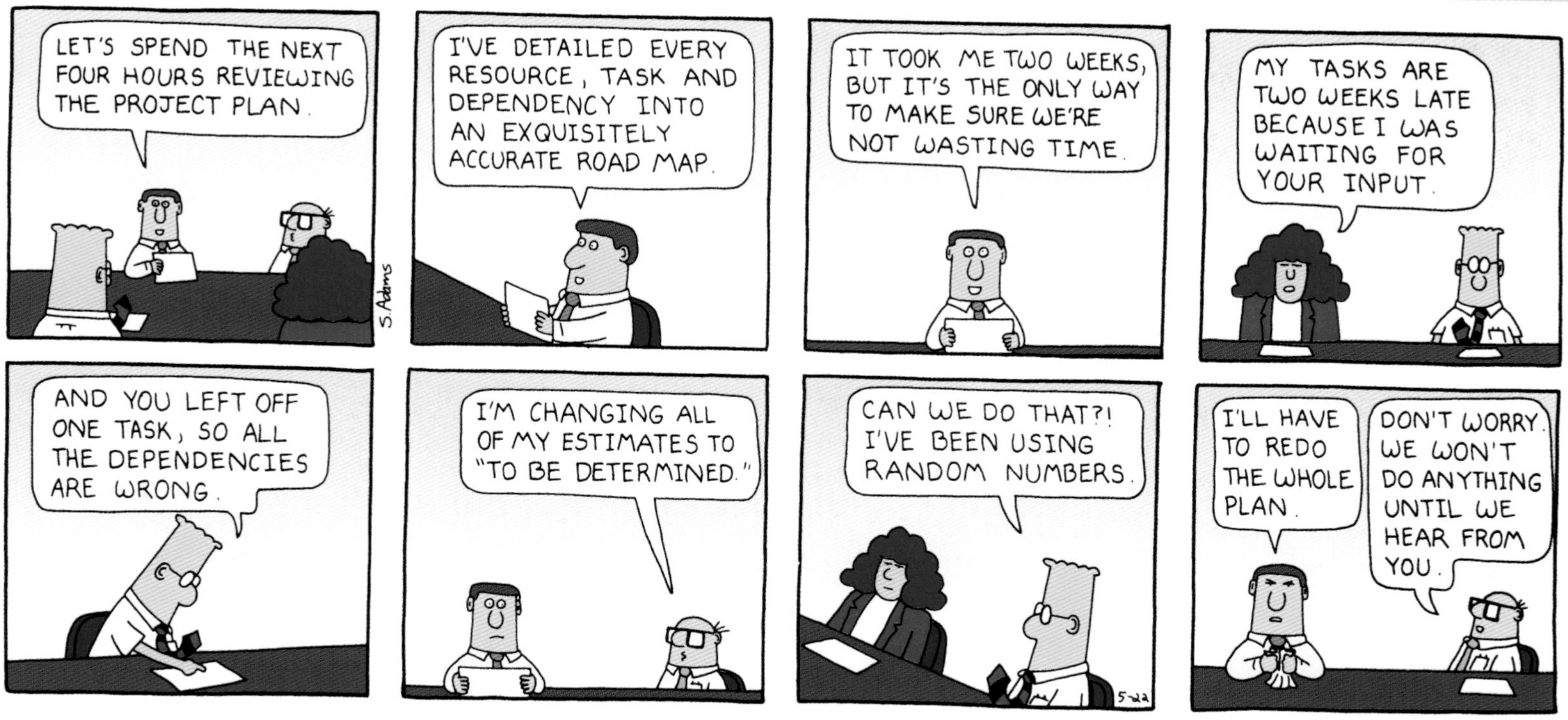
LET'S SPEND THE NEXT FOUR HOURS REVIEWING THE PROJECT PLAN.
I'VE DETAILED EVERY RESOURCE, TASK AND DEPENDENCY INTO AN EXQUISITELY ACCURATE ROAD MAP.
IT TOOK ME TWO WEEKS, BUT IT'S THE ONLY WAY TO MAKE SURE WE'RE NOT WASTING TIME.
MY TASKS ARE TWO WEEKS LATE BECAUSE I WAS WAITING FOR YOUR INPUT.
AND YOU LEFT OFF ONE TASK, SO ALL THE DEPENDENCIES ARE WRONG.
I'M CHANGING ALL OF MY ESTIMATES TO "TO BE DETERMINED."
CAN WE DO THAT?! I'VE BEEN USING RANDOM NUMBERS.
I'LL HAVE TO REDO THE WHOLE PLAN.
DON'T WORRY. WE WON'T DO ANYTHING UNTIL WE HEAR FROM YOU.

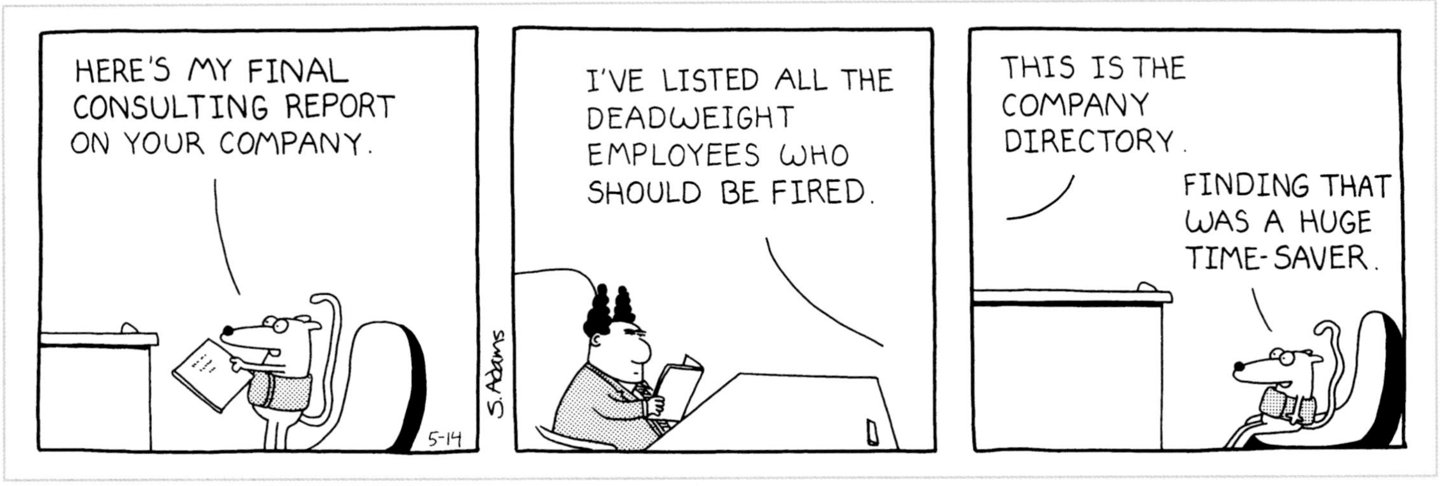
HERE'S MY FINAL CONSULTING REPORT ON YOUR COMPANY.
I'VE LISTED ALL THE DEADWEIGHT EMPLOYEES WHO SHOULD BE FIRED.
THIS IS THE COMPANY DIRECTORY.
FINDING THAT WAS A HUGE TIME-SAVER.

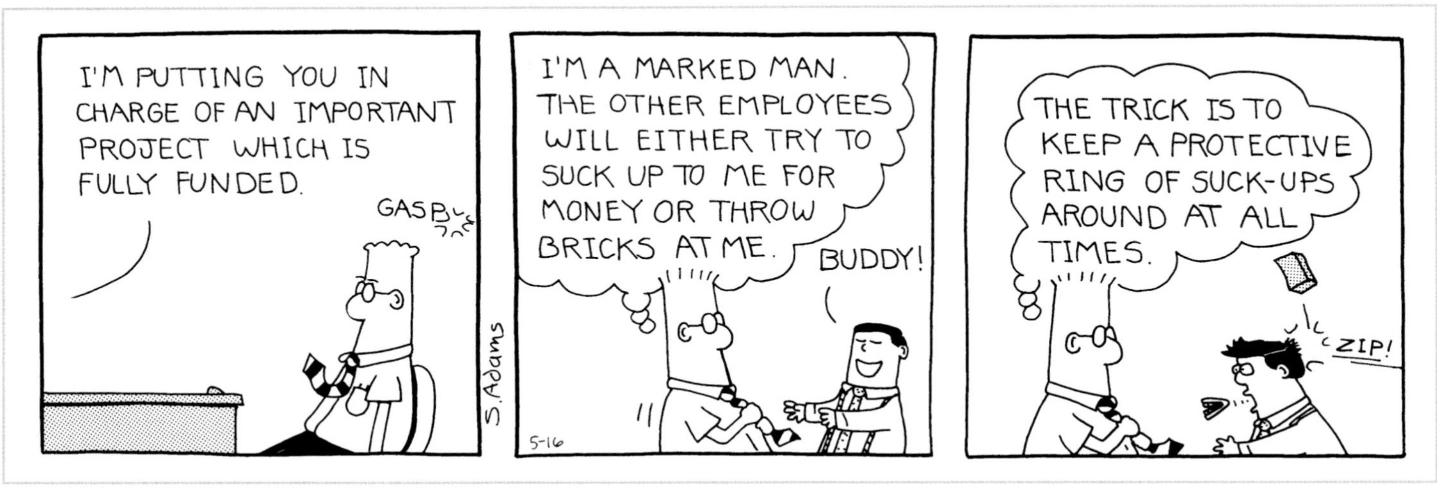
I'M PUTTING YOU IN CHARGE OF AN IMPORTANT PROJECT WHICH IS FULLY FUNDED.
GASP!
I'M A MARKED MAN. THE OTHER EMPLOYEES WILL EITHER TRY TO SUCK UP TO ME FOR MONEY OR THROW BRICKS AT ME.
BUDDY!
THE TRICK IS TO KEEP A PROTECTIVE RING OF SUCK-UPS AROUND AT ALL TIMES.
ZIP!

Slapstick works if you can get the flying dentures to look just right.

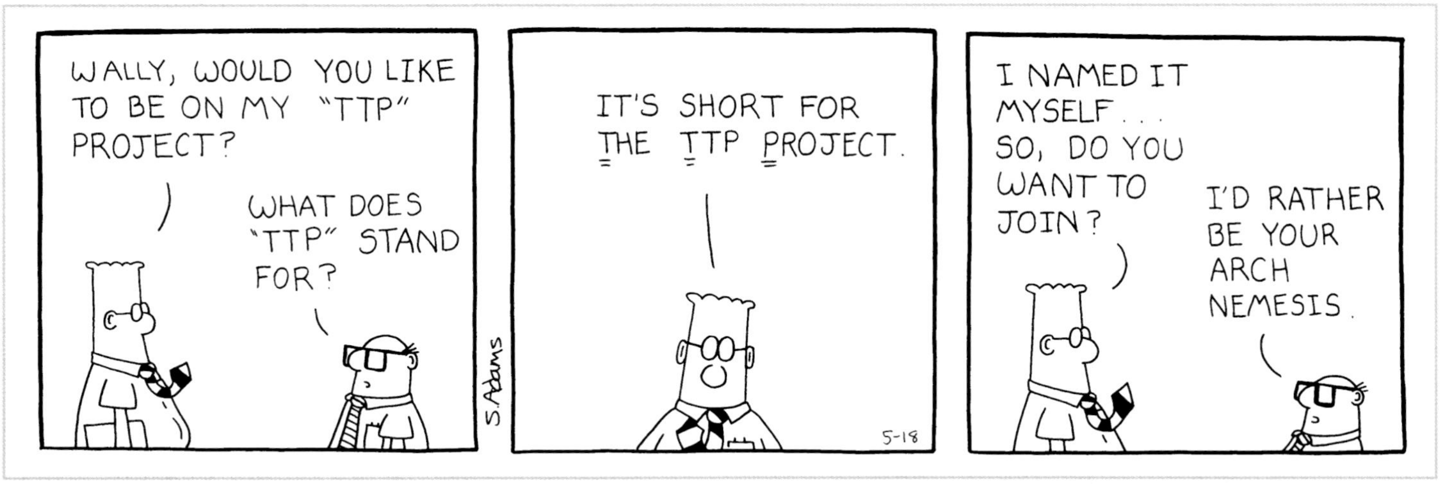
WALLY, WOULD YOU LIKE TO BE ON MY "TTP" PROJECT?
WHAT DOES "TTP" STAND FOR?
IT'S SHORT FOR THE TTP PROJECT.
I NAMED IT MYSELF . . . SO, DO YOU WANT TO JOIN?
I'D RATHER BE YOUR ARCH NEMESIS.

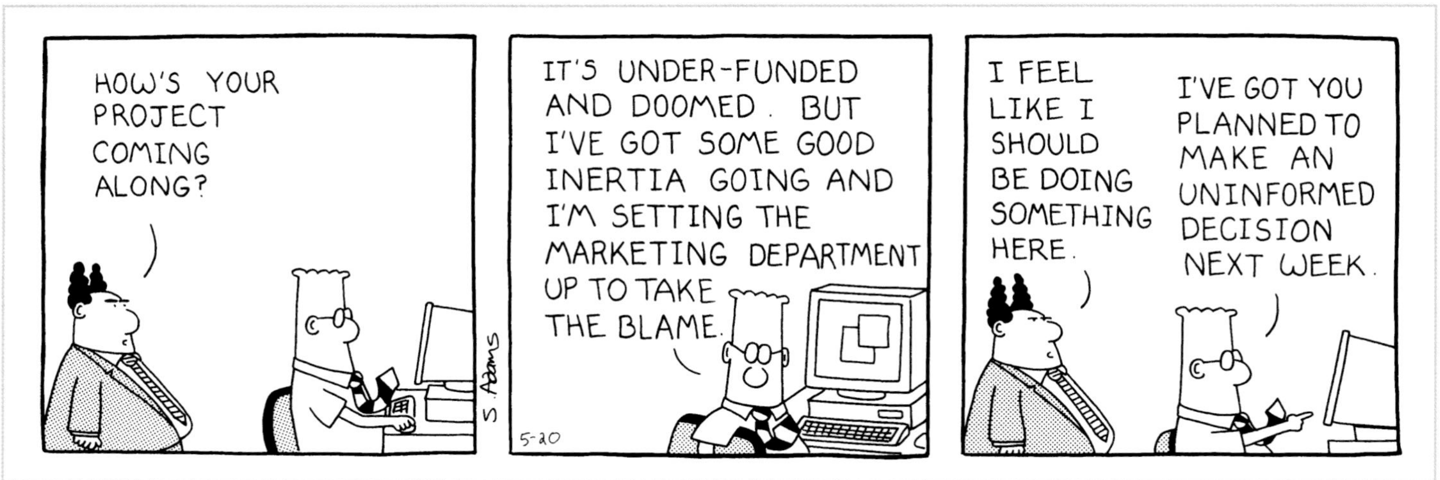
HOW'S YOUR PROJECT COMING ALONG?
IT'S UNDER-FUNDED AND DOOMED. BUT I'VE GOT SOME GOOD INERTIA GOING AND I'M SETTING THE MARKETING DEPARTMENT UP TO TAKE THE BLAME.
I FEEL LIKE I SHOULD BE DOING SOMETHING HERE.
I'VE GOT YOU PLANNED TO MAKE AN UNINFORMED DECISION NEXT WEEK.

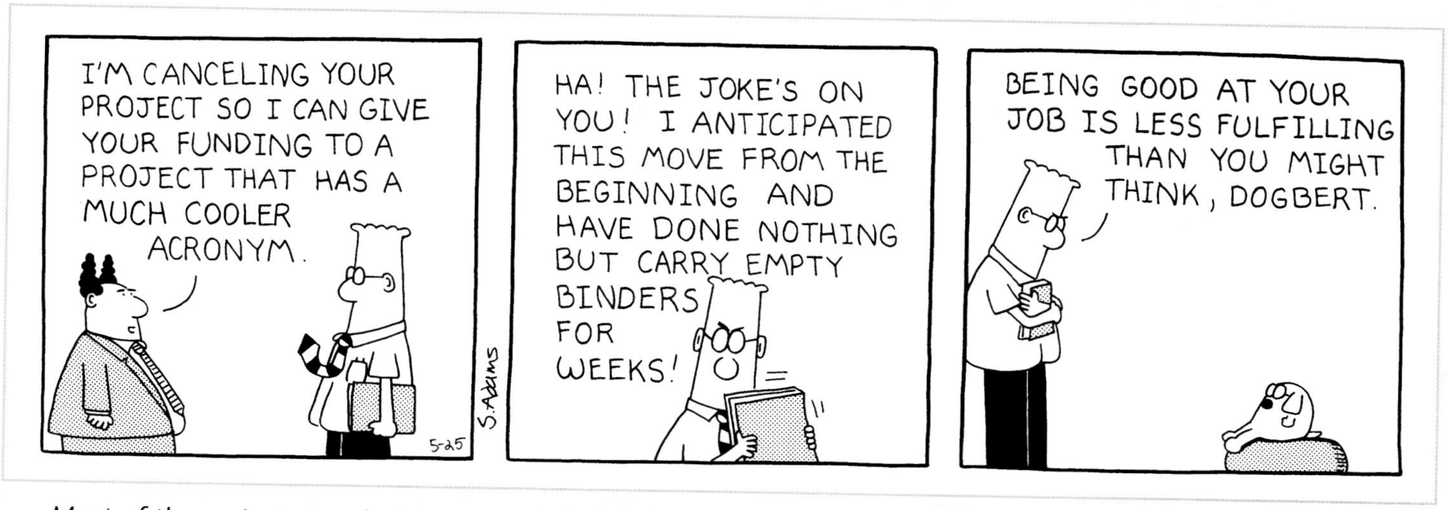
I'M CANCELING YOUR PROJECT SO I CAN GIVE YOUR FUNDING TO A PROJECT THAT HAS A MUCH COOLER ACRONYM.
HA! THE JOKE'S ON YOU! I ANTICIPATED THIS MOVE FROM THE BEGINNING AND HAVE DONE NOTHING BUT CARRY EMPTY BINDERS FOR WEEKS!
BEING GOOD AT YOUR JOB IS LESS FULFILLING THAN YOU MIGHT THINK, DOGBERT.

Most of the projects I worked on got canceled in favor of cooler sounding projects that also later got canceled.

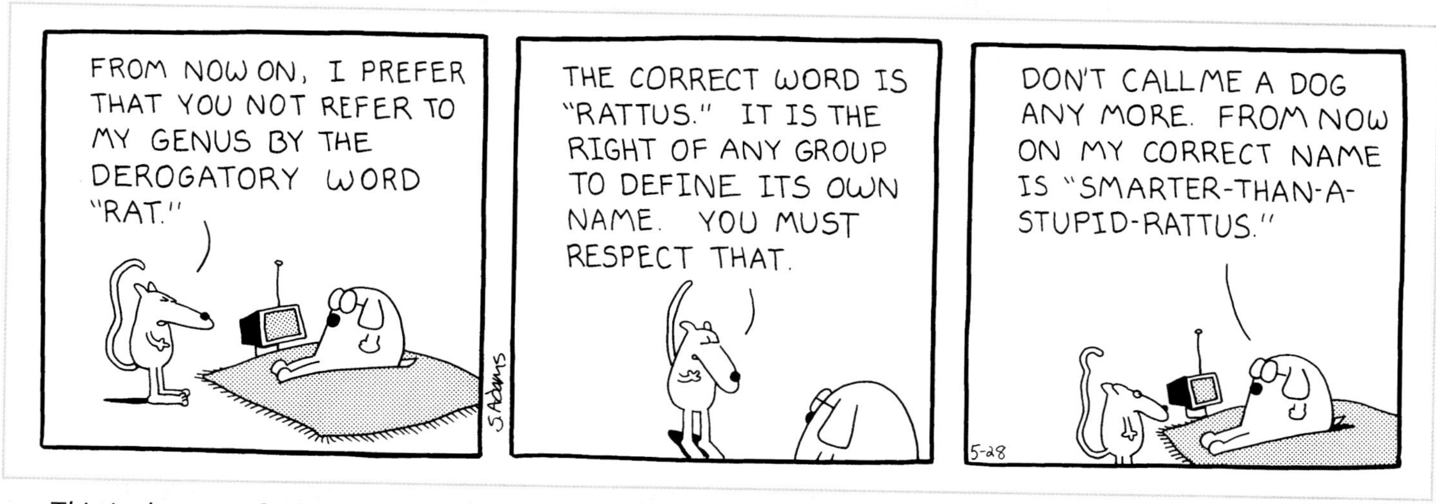
FROM NOW ON, I PREFER THAT YOU NOT REFER TO MY GENUS BY THE DEROGATORY WORD "RAT."
THE CORRECT WORD IS "RATTUS." IT IS THE RIGHT OF ANY GROUP TO DEFINE ITS OWN NAME. YOU MUST RESPECT THAT.
DON'T CALL ME A DOG ANY MORE. FROM NOW ON MY CORRECT NAME IS "SMARTER-THAN-A-STUPID-RATTUS."

This is the sort of joke that has a thought-provoking core wrapped in a coating of juvenile humor. Jokes like this are a big reason I have so many readers in fifth grade who wear glasses and get excellent grades.

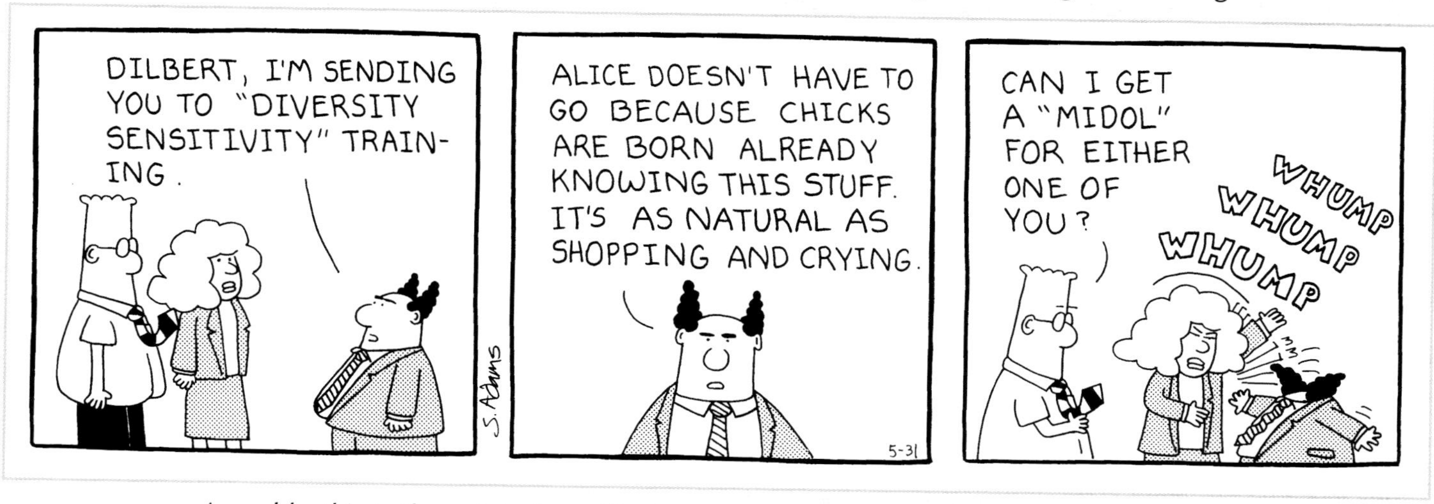
DILBERT, I'M SENDING YOU TO "DIVERSITY SENSITIVITY" TRAINING.
ALICE DOESN'T HAVE TO GO BECAUSE CHICKS ARE BORN ALREADY KNOWING THIS STUFF. IT'S AS NATURAL AS SHOPPING AND CRYING.
CAN I GET A "MIDOL" FOR EITHER ONE OF YOU?
WHUMP
WHUMP
WHUMP

Arguably, this is the point where Alice's true personality emerges and begins to solidify. Her name will fluctuate a few times before settling in at Alice.

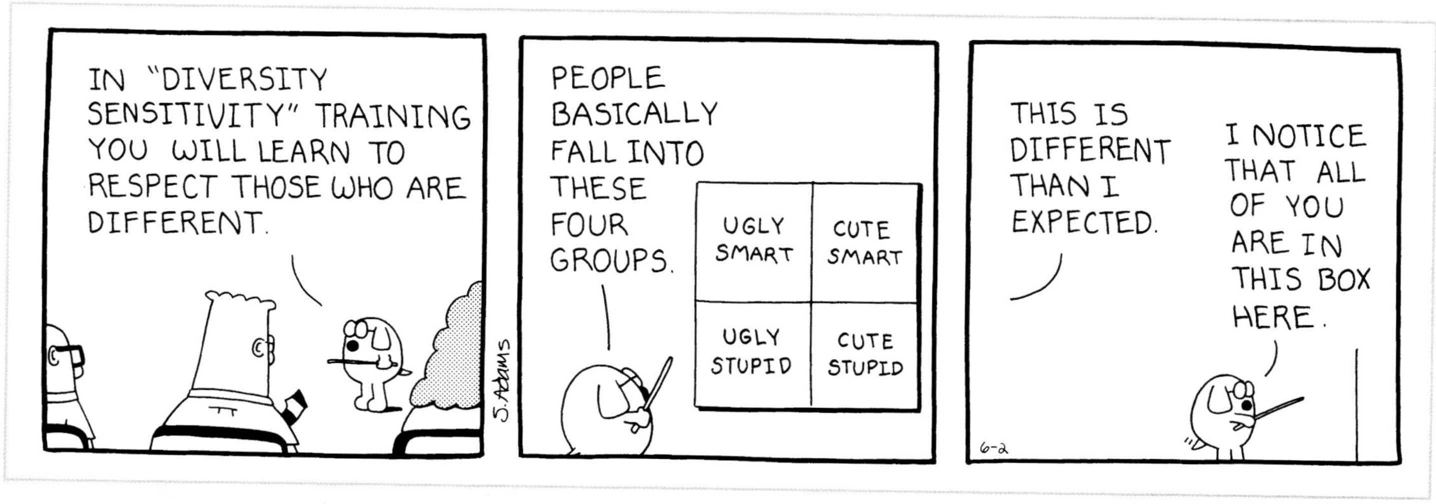
IN "DIVERSITY SENSITIVITY" TRAINING YOU WILL LEARN TO RESPECT THOSE WHO ARE DIFFERENT.
PEOPLE BASICALLY FALL INTO THESE FOUR GROUPS.
UGLY SMART
CUTE SMART
UGLY STUPID
CUTE STUPID
THIS IS DIFFERENT THAN I EXPECTED.
I NOTICE THAT ALL OF YOU ARE IN THIS BOX HERE.

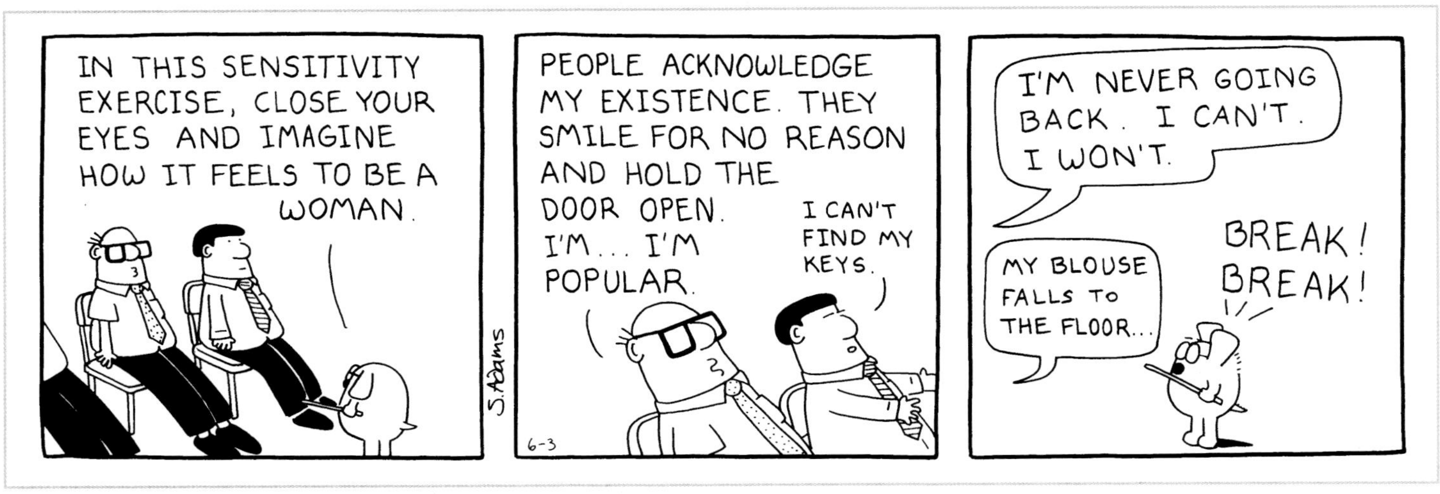
IN THIS SENSITIVITY EXERCISE, CLOSE YOUR EYES AND IMAGINE HOW IT FEELS TO BE A WOMAN.
PEOPLE ACKNOWLEDGE MY EXISTENCE. THEY SMILE FOR NO REASON AND HOLD THE DOOR OPEN. I'M... I'M POPULAR.
I CAN'T FIND MY KEYS.
I'M NEVER GOING BACK. I CAN'T. I WON'T.
MY BLOUSE FALLS TO THE FLOOR...
BREAK! BREAK!

I don't know if this is the funniest comic I've ever written, but it might be the densest number of jokes in a three-panel strip.

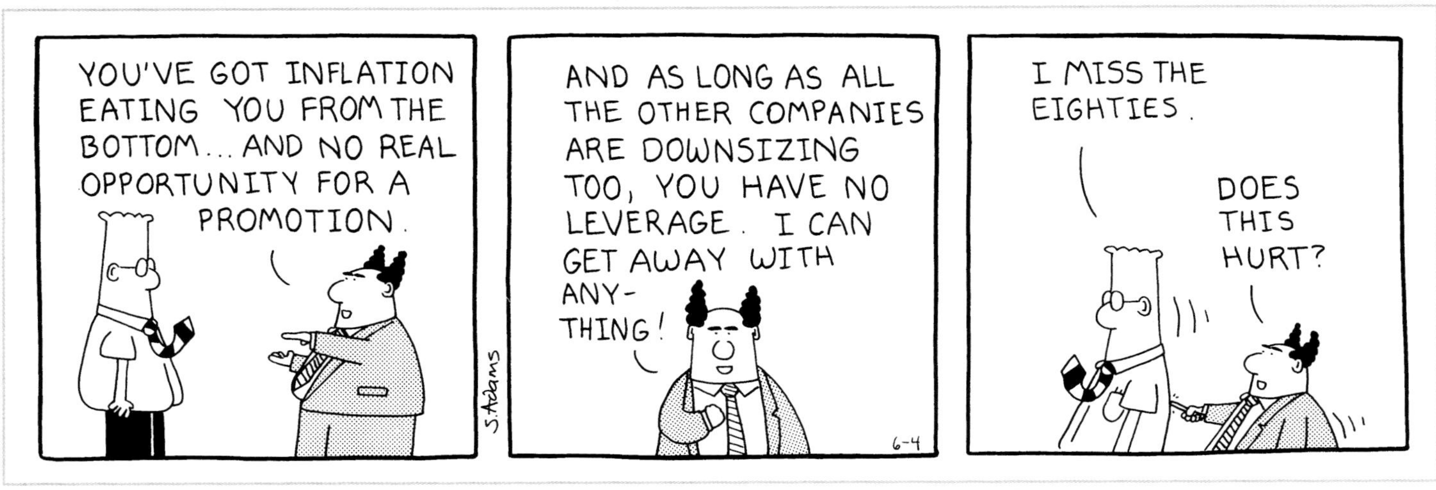
YOU'VE GOT INFLATION EATING YOU FROM THE BOTTOM... AND NO REAL OPPORTUNITY FOR A PROMOTION.
AND AS LONG AS ALL THE OTHER COMPANIES ARE DOWNSIZING TOO, YOU HAVE NO LEVERAGE. I CAN GET AWAY WITH ANY-THING!
I MISS THE EIGHTIES.
DOES THIS HURT?

Dilbert *is most popular when the workplace is at its worst. In the mid-'90s, when downsizing was the dominant trend in business,* Dilbert *took off. A few years later, in the dot-com era, I literally couldn't find anyone willing to complain about his or her job. People started to think they could become Internet billionaires any time they wanted if they just quit their jobs and started their own companies. And since they didn't do that, I think people convinced themselves that their jobs weren't so bad after all. This was the toughest time for me to draw the strip. My snitches went dry.*

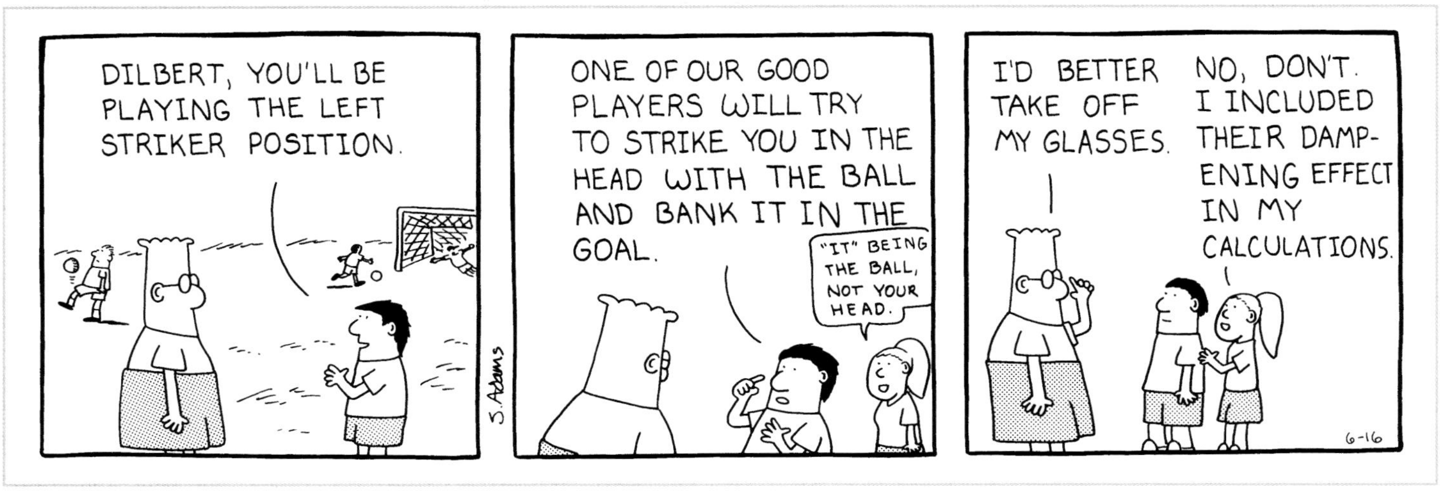
DILBERT, YOU'LL BE PLAYING THE LEFT STRIKER POSITION.
ONE OF OUR GOOD PLAYERS WILL TRY TO STRIKE YOU IN THE HEAD WITH THE BALL AND BANK IT IN THE GOAL.
"IT" BEING THE BALL, NOT YOUR HEAD.
I'D BETTER TAKE OFF MY GLASSES.
NO, DON'T. I INCLUDED THEIR DAMP-ENING EFFECT IN MY CALCULATIONS.

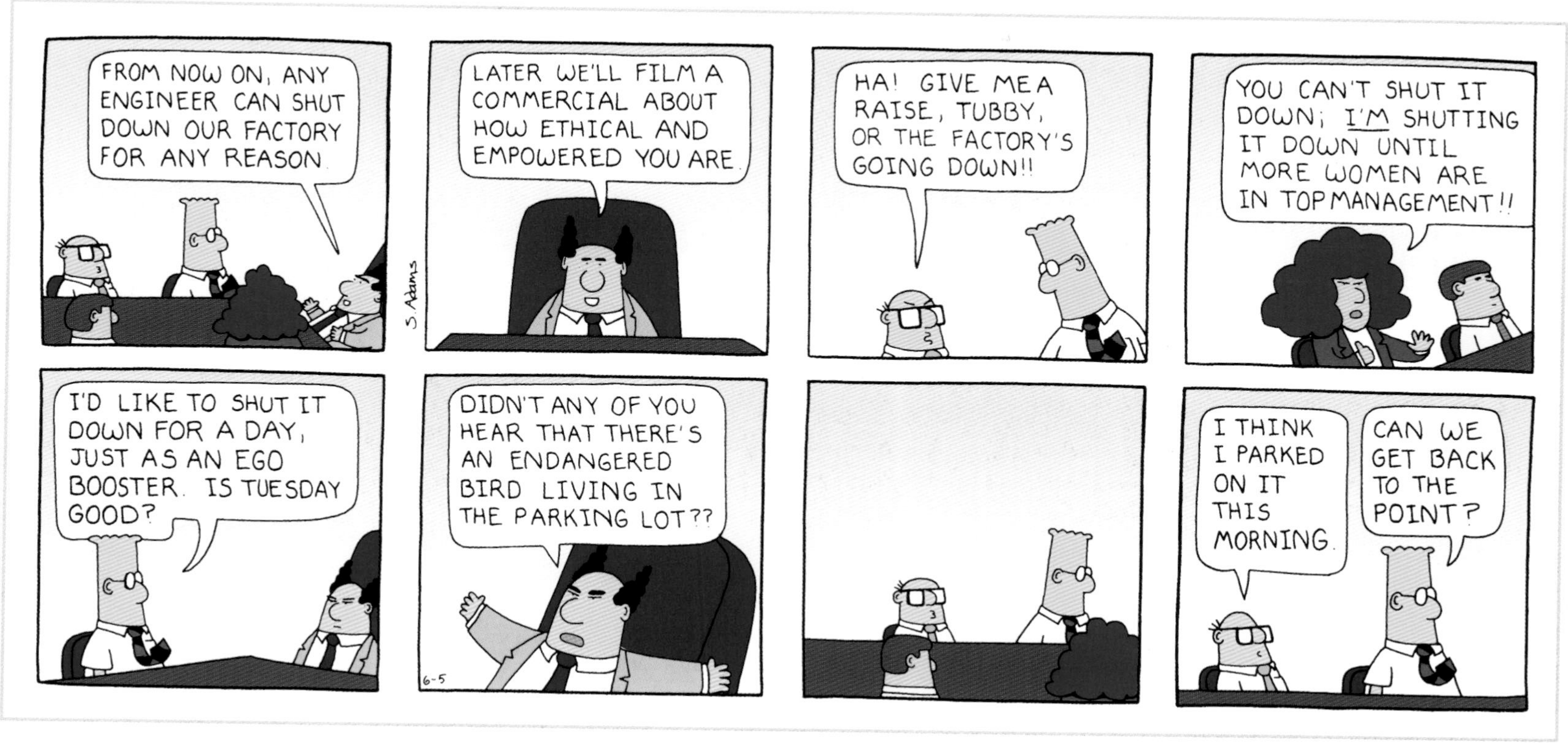
FROM NOW ON, ANY ENGINEER CAN SHUT DOWN OUR FACTORY FOR ANY REASON.
LATER WE'LL FILM A COMMERCIAL ABOUT HOW ETHICAL AND EMPOWERED YOU ARE
HA! GIVE ME A RAISE, TUBBY, OR THE FACTORY'S GOING DOWN!!
YOU CAN'T SHUT IT DOWN; I'M SHUTTING IT DOWN UNTIL MORE WOMEN ARE IN TOP MANAGEMENT!!
I'D LIKE TO SHUT IT DOWN FOR A DAY, JUST AS AN EGO BOOSTER. IS TUESDAY GOOD?
DIDN'T ANY OF YOU HEAR THAT THERE'S AN ENDANGERED BIRD LIVING IN THE PARKING LOT??
I THINK I PARKED ON IT THIS MORNING.
CAN WE GET BACK TO THE POINT?
S. Adams
6-5

I wondered how many readers realized the real joke was in the fifth panel. The rest was filler.

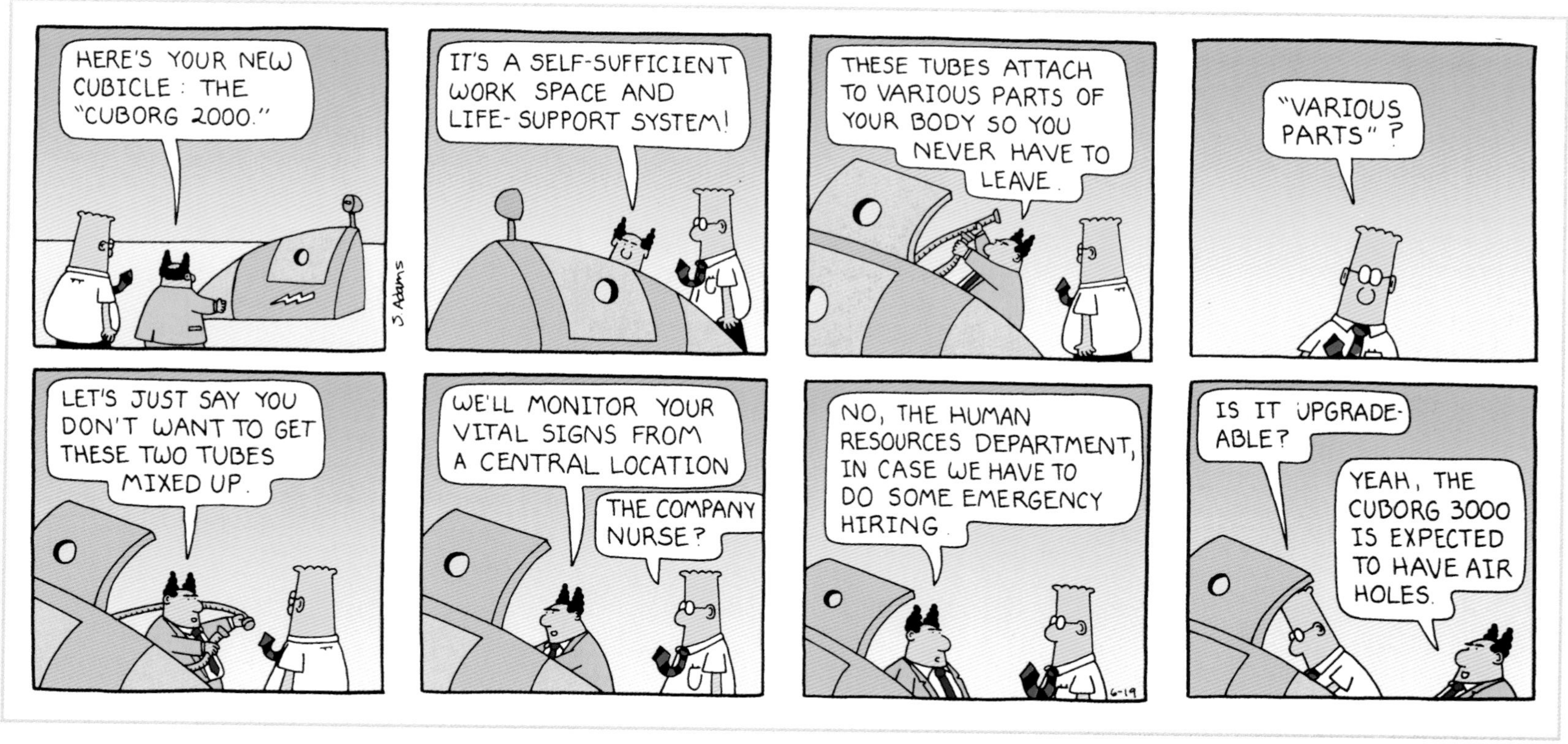
HERE'S YOUR NEW CUBICLE: THE "CUBORG 2000."
IT'S A SELF-SUFFICIENT WORK SPACE AND LIFE-SUPPORT SYSTEM!
THESE TUBES ATTACH TO VARIOUS PARTS OF YOUR BODY SO YOU NEVER HAVE TO LEAVE.
"VARIOUS PARTS"?
LET'S JUST SAY YOU DON'T WANT TO GET THESE TWO TUBES MIXED UP.
WE'LL MONITOR YOUR VITAL SIGNS FROM A CENTRAL LOCATION
THE COMPANY NURSE?
NO, THE HUMAN RESOURCES DEPARTMENT, IN CASE WE HAVE TO DO SOME EMERGENCY HIRING.
IS IT UPGRADE-ABLE?
YEAH, THE CUBORG 3000 IS EXPECTED TO HAVE AIR HOLES.
S. Adams
6-19

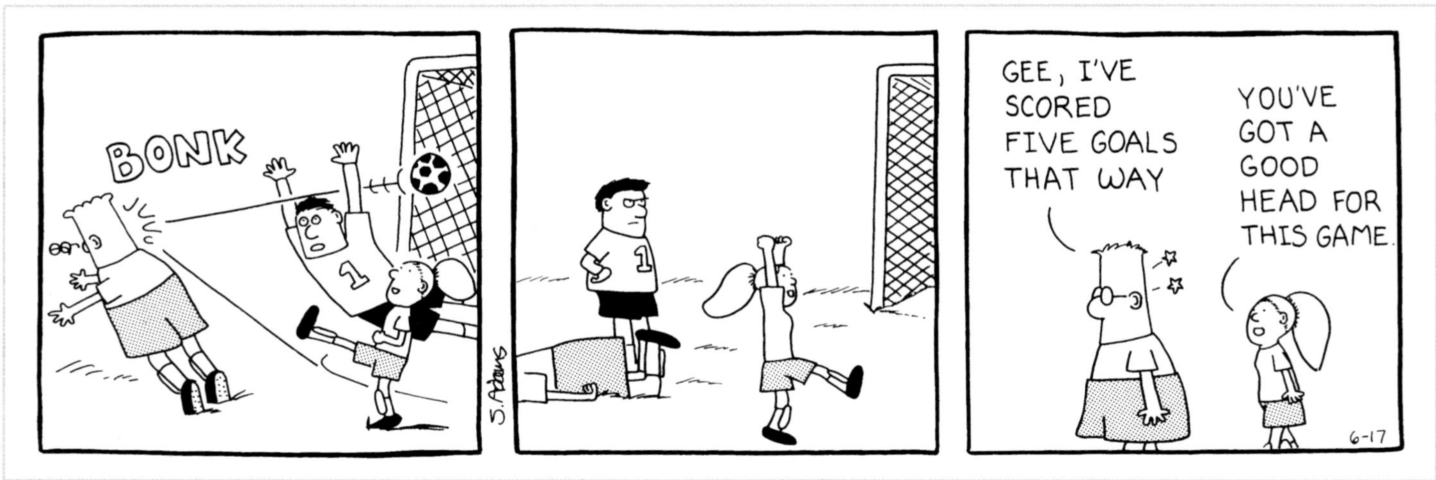
BONK
S. Adams
GEE, I'VE SCORED FIVE GOALS THAT WAY
YOU'VE GOT A GOOD HEAD FOR THIS GAME.
6-17

This strip features Liz, Dilbert's only long-term (relatively) girlfriend. I got rid of her eventually, largely because people complained that she looked twelve years old the way I drew her. And also because people who related to Dilbert couldn't relate to him as much if he were happy in love.

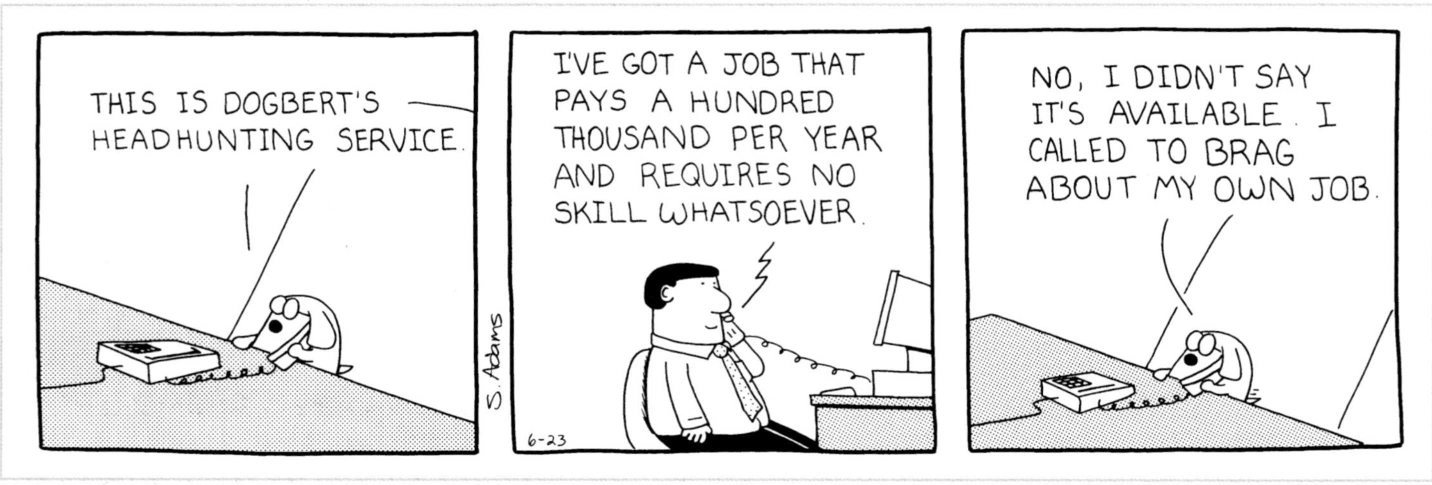
THIS IS DOGBERT'S HEADHUNTING SERVICE.
S. Adams
I'VE GOT A JOB THAT PAYS A HUNDRED THOUSAND PER YEAR AND REQUIRES NO SKILL WHATSOEVER.
6-23
NO, I DIDN'T SAY IT'S AVAILABLE. I CALLED TO BRAG ABOUT MY OWN JOB.

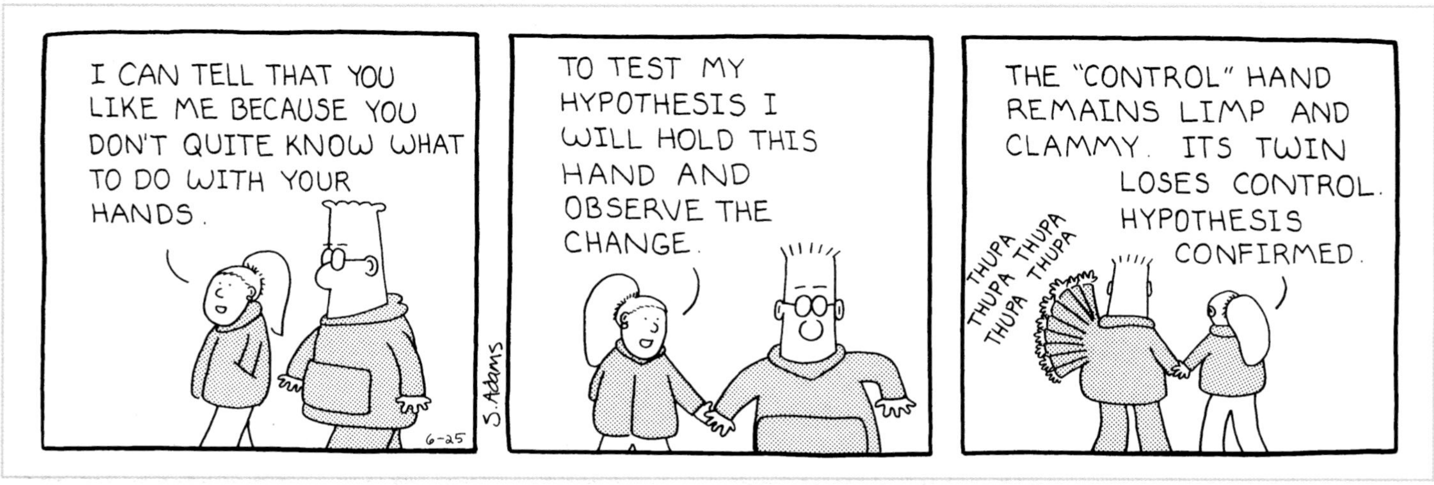
I CAN TELL THAT YOU LIKE ME BECAUSE YOU DON'T QUITE KNOW WHAT TO DO WITH YOUR HANDS.
6-25
S. Adams
TO TEST MY HYPOTHESIS I WILL HOLD THIS HAND AND OBSERVE THE CHANGE.
THE "CONTROL" HAND REMAINS LIMP AND CLAMMY. ITS TWIN LOSES CONTROL. HYPOTHESIS CONFIRMED.
THUPA THUPA THUPA THUPA THUPA THUPA

A big part of cartooning is coming up with words to express sounds. The sound of an arm waving rapidly is obviously "THUPA THUPA THUPA."

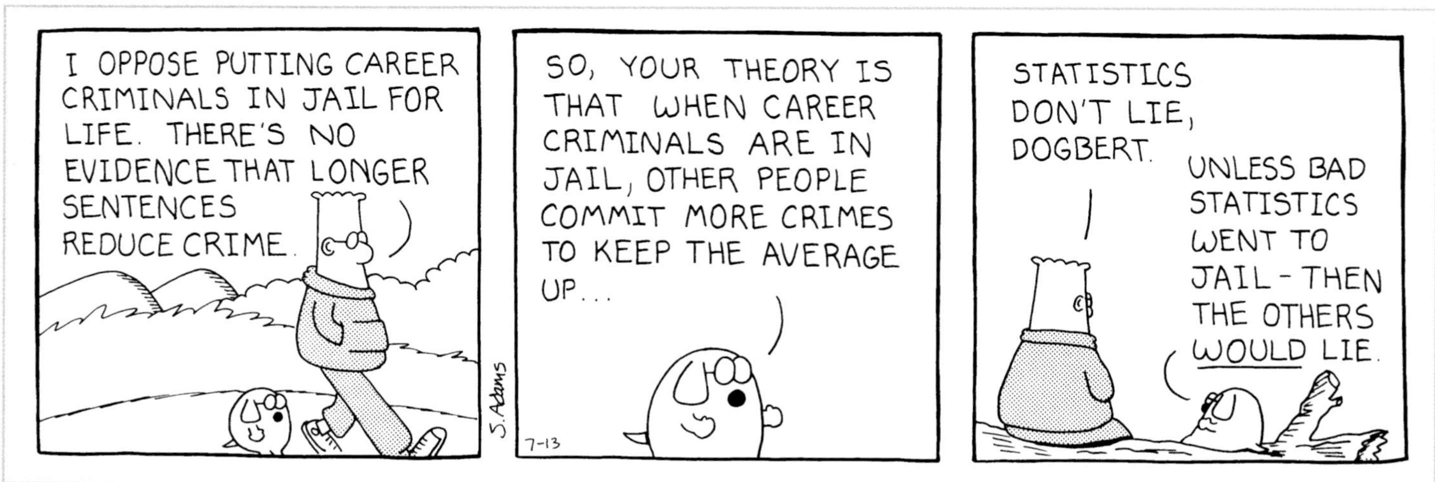
I OPPOSE PUTTING CAREER CRIMINALS IN JAIL FOR LIFE. THERE'S NO EVIDENCE THAT LONGER SENTENCES REDUCE CRIME.
S. Adams
SO, YOUR THEORY IS THAT WHEN CAREER CRIMINALS ARE IN JAIL, OTHER PEOPLE COMMIT MORE CRIMES TO KEEP THE AVERAGE UP...
7-13
STATISTICS DON'T LIE, DOGBERT.
UNLESS BAD STATISTICS WENT TO JAIL - THEN THE OTHERS WOULD LIE.

Bad math is often considered a political opinion.

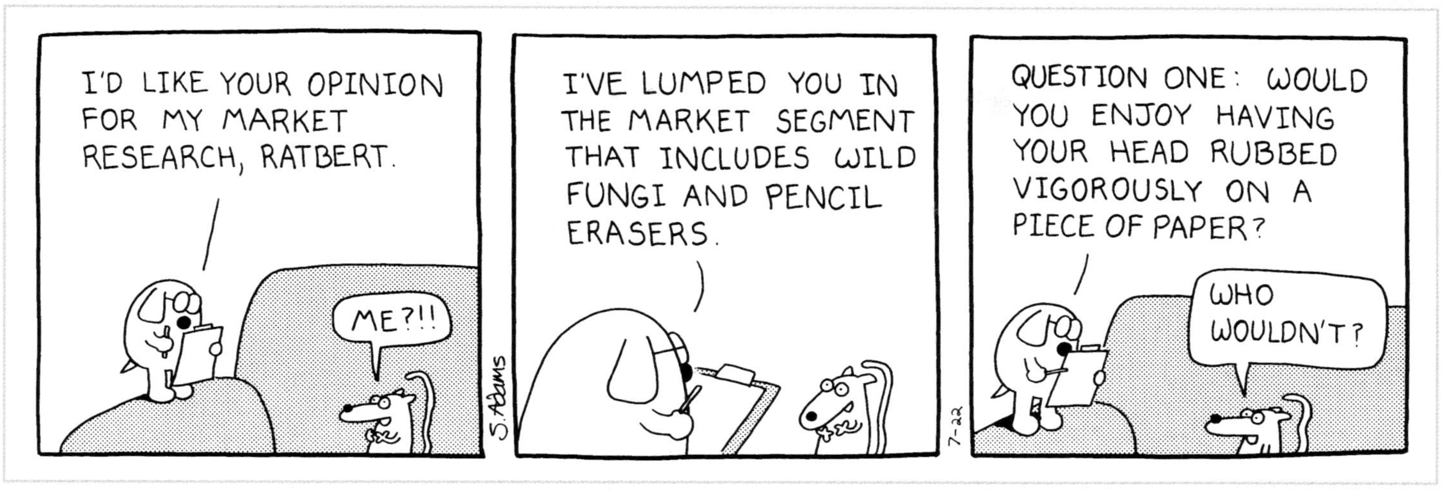
I'D LIKE YOUR OPINION FOR MY MARKET RESEARCH, RATBERT.
ME?!!
S. Adams
I'VE LUMPED YOU IN THE MARKET SEGMENT THAT INCLUDES WILD FUNGI AND PENCIL ERASERS.
7-22
QUESTION ONE: WOULD YOU ENJOY HAVING YOUR HEAD RUBBED VIGOROUSLY ON A PIECE OF PAPER?
WHO WOULDN'T?

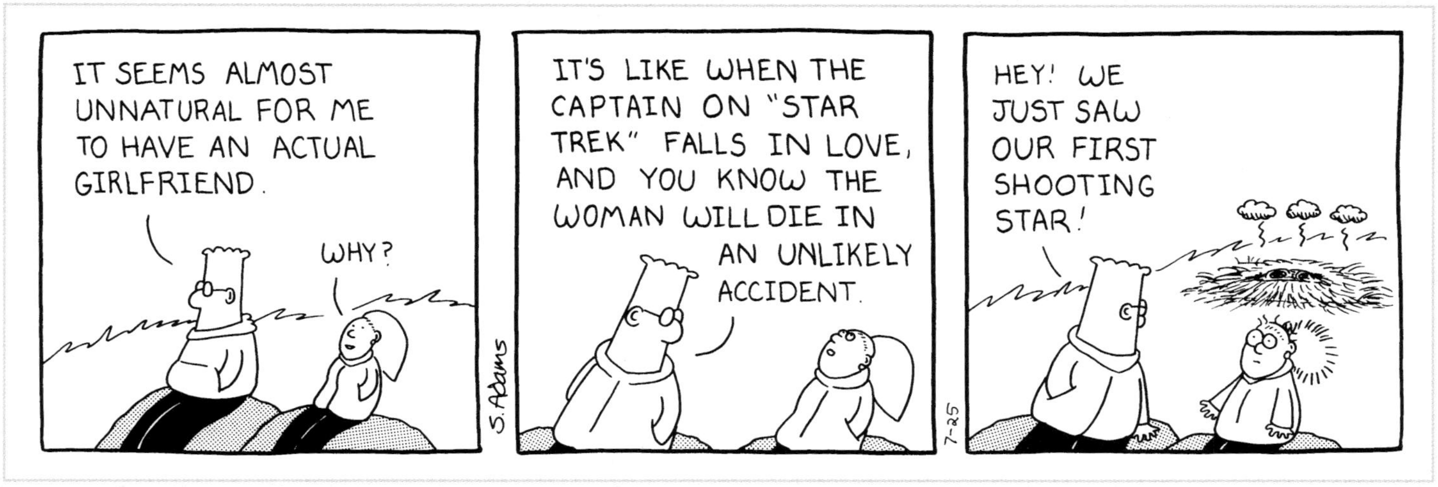
IT SEEMS ALMOST UNNATURAL FOR ME TO HAVE AN ACTUAL GIRLFRIEND.
WHY?
S. Adams
IT'S LIKE WHEN THE CAPTAIN ON "STAR TREK" FALLS IN LOVE, AND YOU KNOW THE WOMAN WILL DIE IN AN UNLIKELY ACCIDENT.
7-25
HEY! WE JUST SAW OUR FIRST SHOOTING STAR!

Any reference to Star Trek *or* Star Wars *always gets a huge reaction. I try to slip them in occasionally. I'm a pleaser.*

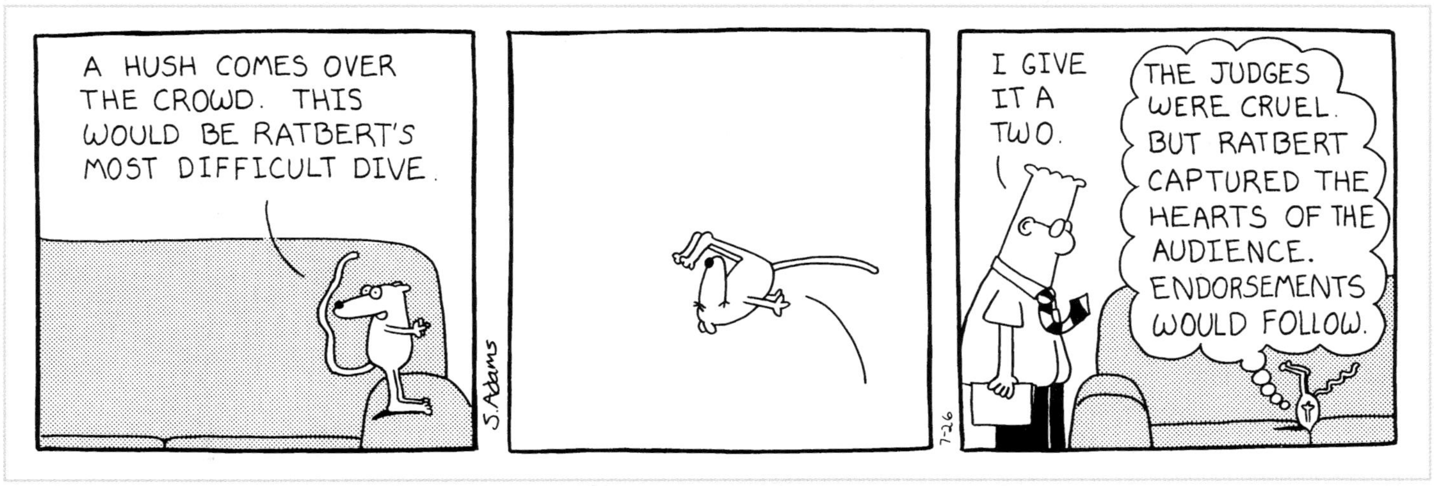
A HUSH COMES OVER THE CROWD. THIS WOULD BE RATBERT'S MOST DIFFICULT DIVE.
S. Adams
7-26
I GIVE IT A TWO.
THE JUDGES WERE CRUEL. BUT RATBERT CAPTURED THE HEARTS OF THE AUDIENCE. ENDORSEMENTS WOULD FOLLOW.

I was amazed the one below got published in newspapers. But I believe a few of the more conservative ones ran a repeat that day.

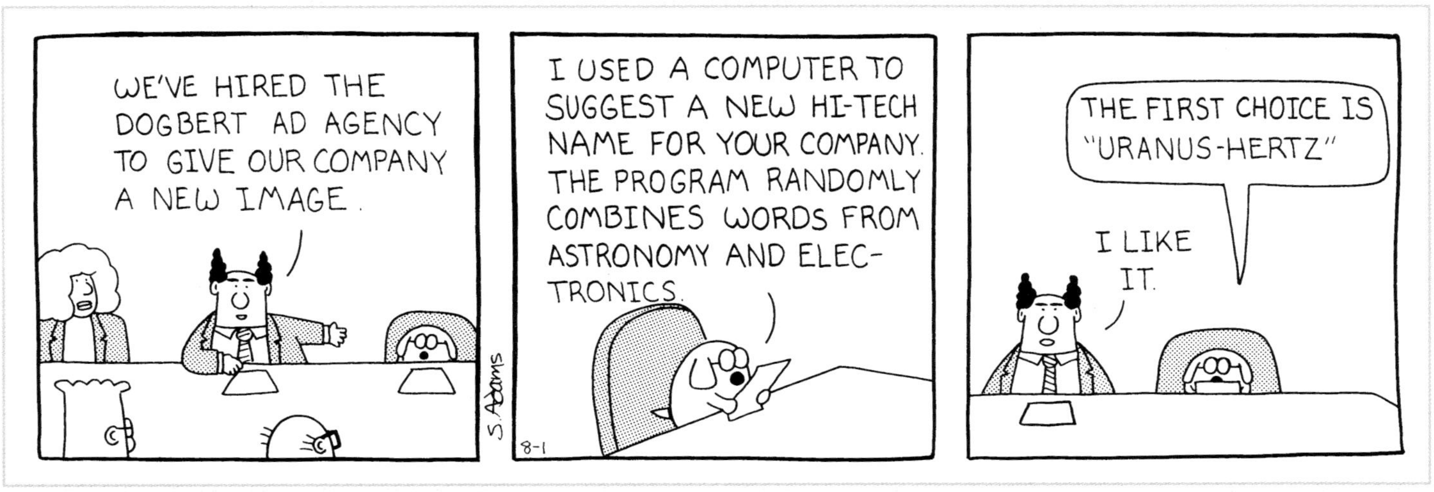
WE'VE HIRED THE DOGBERT AD AGENCY TO GIVE OUR COMPANY A NEW IMAGE.
S. Adams
8-1
I USED A COMPUTER TO SUGGEST A NEW HI-TECH NAME FOR YOUR COMPANY. THE PROGRAM RANDOMLY COMBINES WORDS FROM ASTRONOMY AND ELECTRONICS.
THE FIRST CHOICE IS "URANUS-HERTZ"
I LIKE IT.

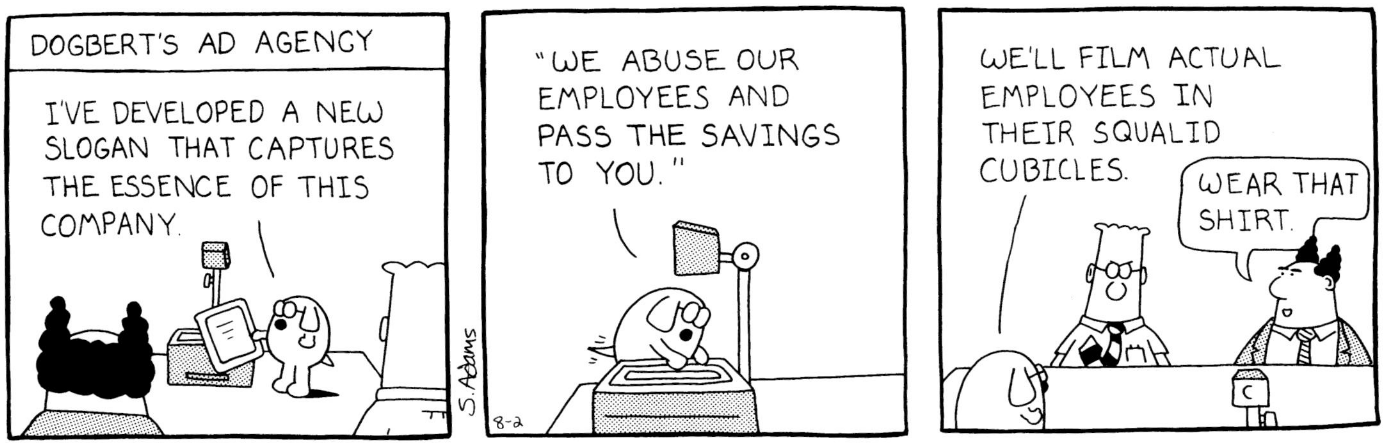
DOGBERT'S AD AGENCY
I'VE DEVELOPED A NEW SLOGAN THAT CAPTURES THE ESSENCE OF THIS COMPANY.
"WE ABUSE OUR EMPLOYEES AND PASS THE SAVINGS TO YOU."
WE'LL FILM ACTUAL EMPLOYEES IN THEIR SQUALID CUBICLES.
WEAR THAT SHIRT.
S. Adams
8-2

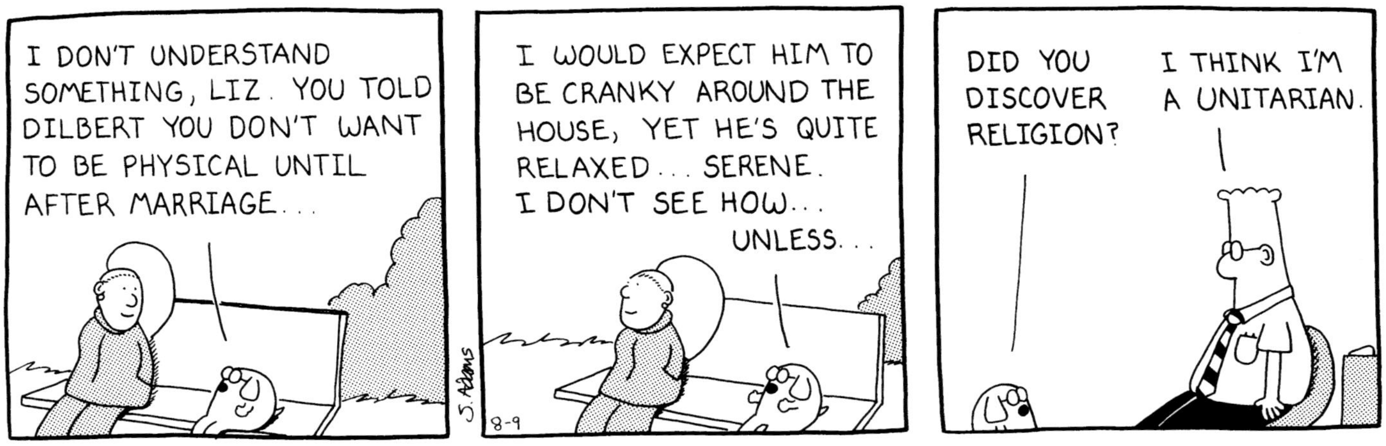
I DON'T UNDERSTAND SOMETHING, LIZ. YOU TOLD DILBERT YOU DON'T WANT TO BE PHYSICAL UNTIL AFTER MARRIAGE...
I WOULD EXPECT HIM TO BE CRANKY AROUND THE HOUSE, YET HE'S QUITE RELAXED... SERENE. I DON'T SEE HOW... UNLESS...
DID YOU DISCOVER RELIGION?
I THINK I'M A UNITARIAN.
S. Adams
8-9

I told my readers via The Dilbert Newsletter *that if Dilbert ever reached the promised land with a woman, I would depict his necktie in a relaxed pose. It was strictly an inside joke for the people on my newsletter list. But I gave the situation some ambiguity with Dilbert's Unitarian reference. Don't make me explain it.*

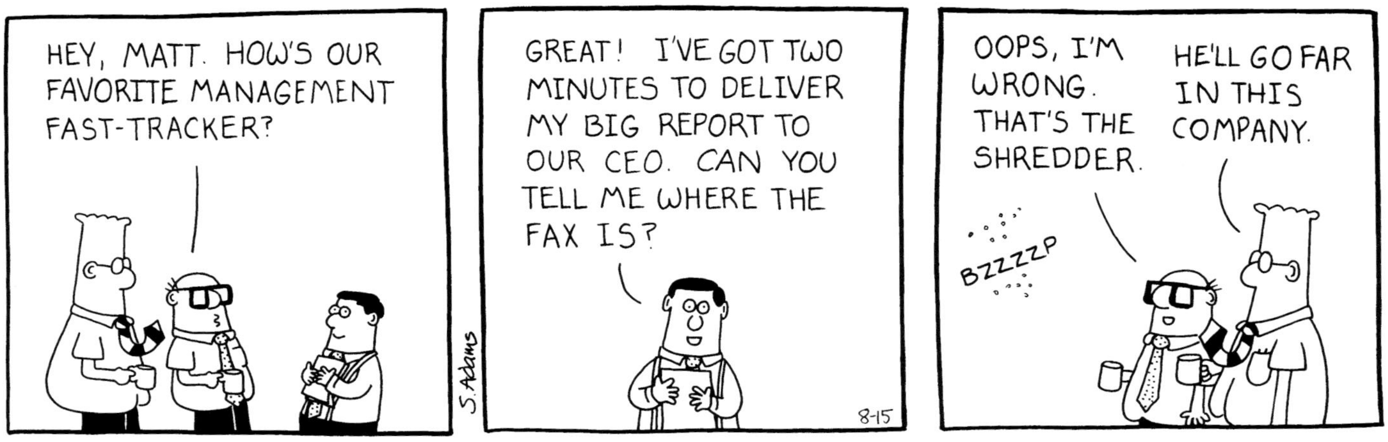
HEY, MATT. HOW'S OUR FAVORITE MANAGEMENT FAST-TRACKER?
GREAT! I'VE GOT TWO MINUTES TO DELIVER MY BIG REPORT TO OUR CEO. CAN YOU TELL ME WHERE THE FAX IS?
OOPS, I'M WRONG. THAT'S THE SHREDDER.
HE'LL GO FAR IN THIS COMPANY.
BZZZZP
S. Adams
8-15

Strips like this one are not clever, but they sure are popular.

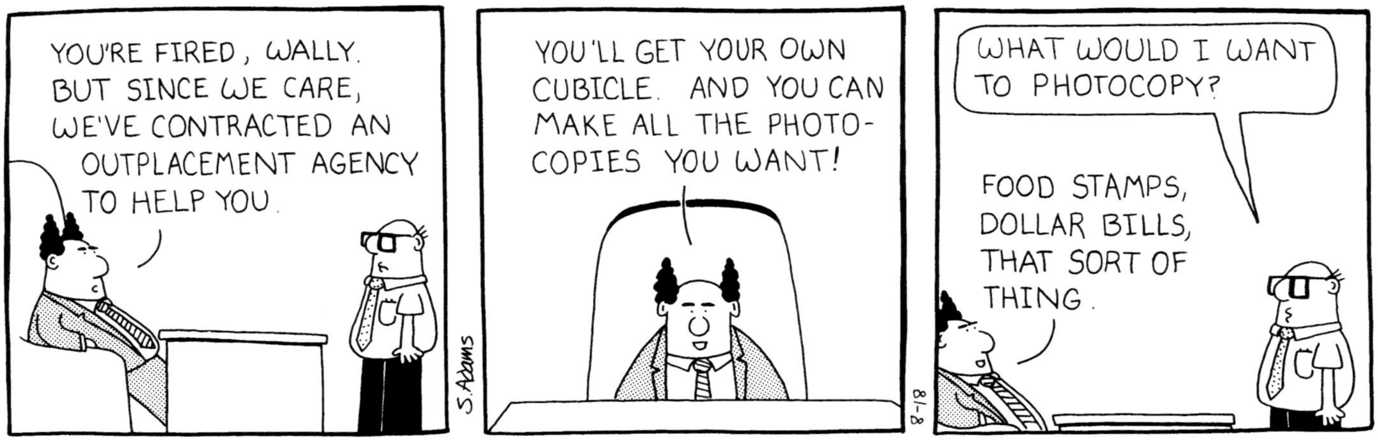
YOU'RE FIRED, WALLY. BUT SINCE WE CARE, WE'VE CONTRACTED AN OUTPLACEMENT AGENCY TO HELP YOU.
YOU'LL GET YOUR OWN CUBICLE. AND YOU CAN MAKE ALL THE PHOTO-COPIES YOU WANT!
WHAT WOULD I WANT TO PHOTOCOPY?
FOOD STAMPS, DOLLAR BILLS, THAT SORT OF THING.
S. Adams
8-18

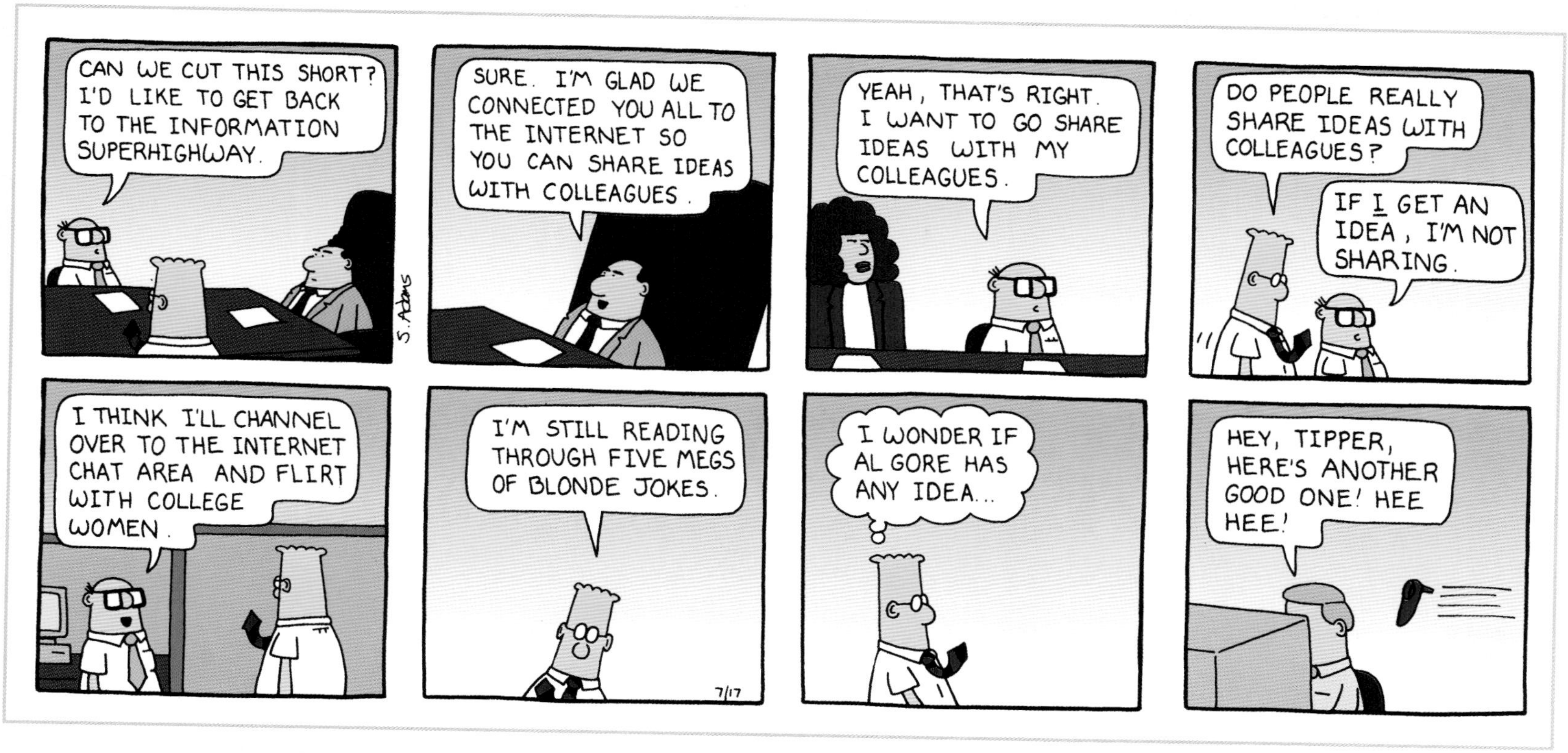
CAN WE CUT THIS SHORT? I'D LIKE TO GET BACK TO THE INFORMATION SUPERHIGHWAY.
S. Adams
SURE. I'M GLAD WE CONNECTED YOU ALL TO THE INTERNET SO YOU CAN SHARE IDEAS WITH COLLEAGUES.
YEAH, THAT'S RIGHT. I WANT TO GO SHARE IDEAS WITH MY COLLEAGUES.
DO PEOPLE REALLY SHARE IDEAS WITH COLLEAGUES?
IF I GET AN IDEA, I'M NOT SHARING.
I THINK I'LL CHANNEL OVER TO THE INTERNET CHAT AREA AND FLIRT WITH COLLEGE WOMEN.
I'M STILL READING THROUGH FIVE MEGS OF BLONDE JOKES.
7/17
I WONDER IF AL GORE HAS ANY IDEA...
HEY, TIPPER, HERE'S ANOTHER GOOD ONE! HEE HEE!

Al Gore's staff asked for the original of this comic. It hung in the vice president's office.

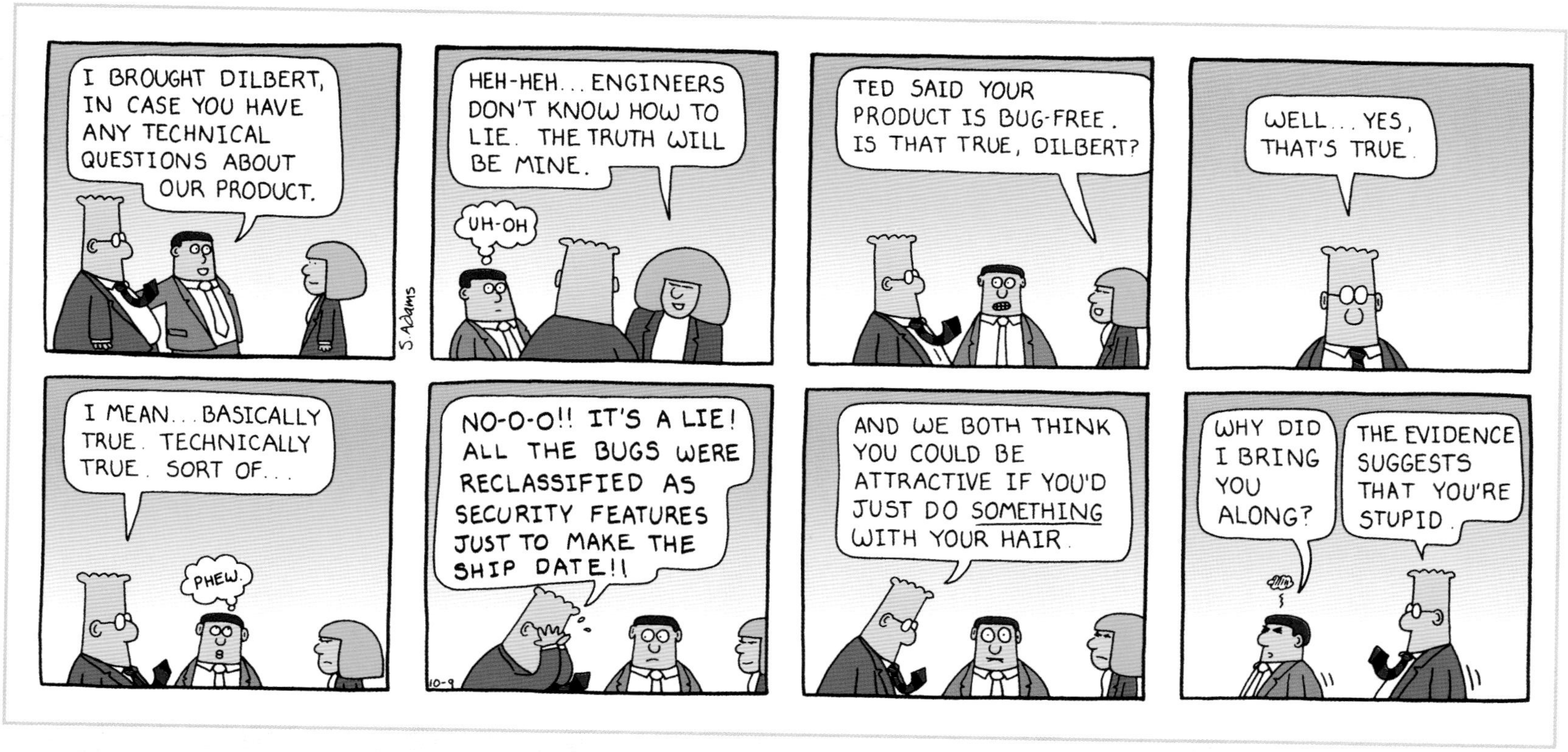
I BROUGHT DILBERT, IN CASE YOU HAVE ANY TECHNICAL QUESTIONS ABOUT OUR PRODUCT.
S. Adams
HEH-HEH... ENGINEERS DON'T KNOW HOW TO LIE. THE TRUTH WILL BE MINE.
UH-OH
TED SAID YOUR PRODUCT IS BUG-FREE. IS THAT TRUE, DILBERT?
WELL... YES, THAT'S TRUE.
I MEAN... BASICALLY TRUE. TECHNICALLY TRUE. SORT OF...
PHEW.
NO-O-O!! IT'S A LIE! ALL THE BUGS WERE RECLASSIFIED AS SECURITY FEATURES JUST TO MAKE THE SHIP DATE!!
10-9
AND WE BOTH THINK YOU COULD BE ATTRACTIVE IF YOU'D JUST DO SOMETHING WITH YOUR HAIR.
WHY DID I BRING YOU ALONG?
THE EVIDENCE SUGGESTS THAT YOU'RE STUPID.

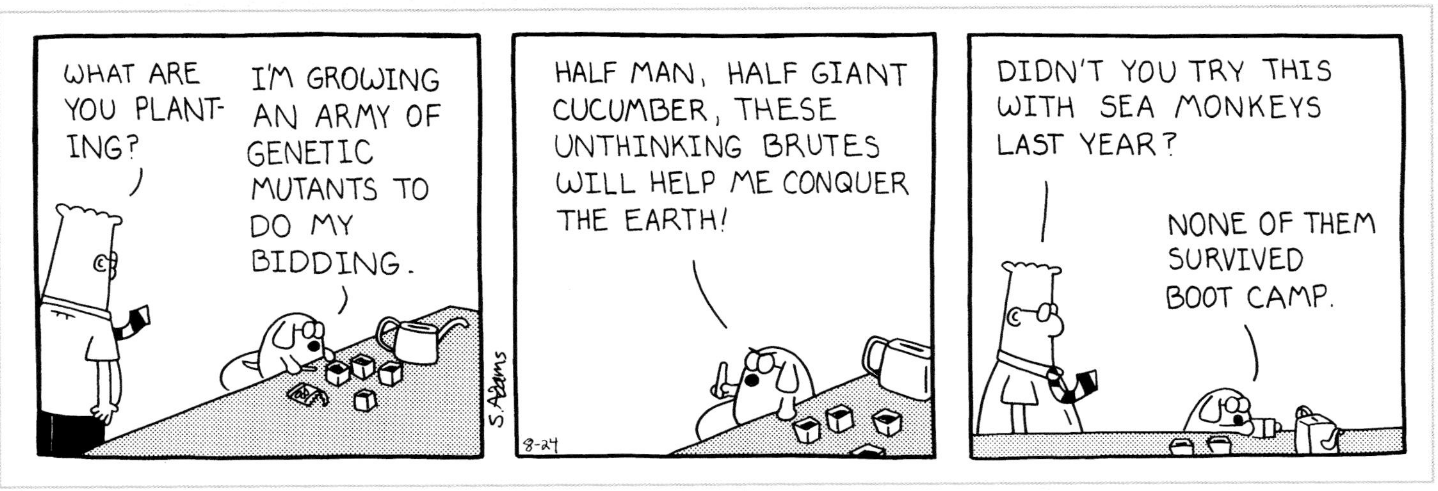
WHAT ARE YOU PLANT-ING?
I'M GROWING AN ARMY OF GENETIC MUTANTS TO DO MY BIDDING.
HALF MAN, HALF GIANT CUCUMBER, THESE UNTHINKING BRUTES WILL HELP ME CONQUER THE EARTH!
DIDN'T YOU TRY THIS WITH SEA MONKEYS LAST YEAR?
NONE OF THEM SURVIVED BOOT CAMP.
S. Adams
8-24

Until I quit my day job, I couldn't go back and rewrite strips if I decided they didn't work after all. I simply didn't have time. The one below is the most obvious case where I had to salvage something from nothing. I failed.

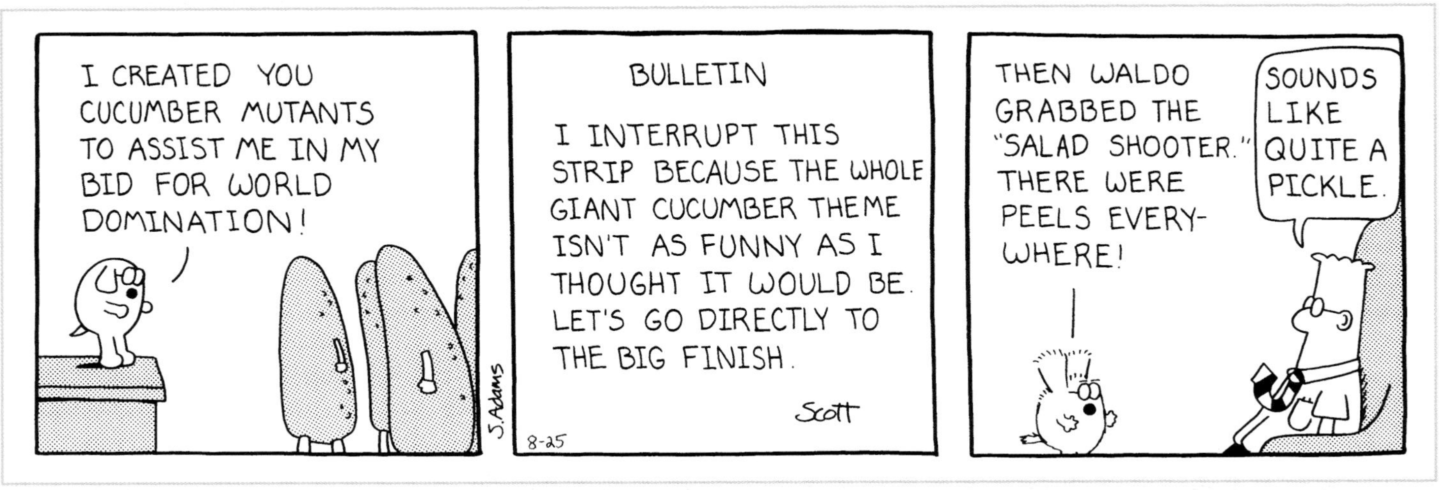
I CREATED YOU CUCUMBER MUTANTS TO ASSIST ME IN MY BID FOR WORLD DOMINATION!
S. Adams
BULLETIN
I INTERRUPT THIS STRIP BECAUSE THE WHOLE GIANT CUCUMBER THEME ISN'T AS FUNNY AS I THOUGHT IT WOULD BE. LET'S GO DIRECTLY TO THE BIG FINISH.
Scott
8-25
THEN WALDO GRABBED THE "SALAD SHOOTER." THERE WERE PEELS EVERY-WHERE!
SOUNDS LIKE QUITE A PICKLE.

This Bungee Boss comic became an instant classic. And another Dilbert *phrase entered the workplace vocabulary.*

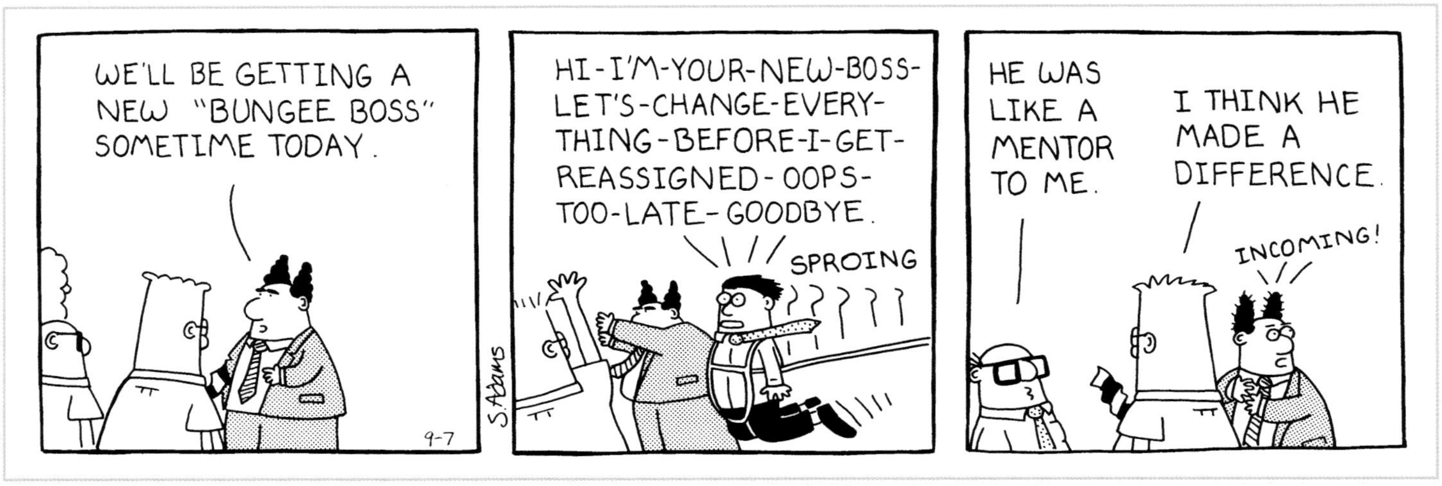
WE'LL BE GETTING A NEW "BUNGEE BOSS" SOMETIME TODAY.
9-7
S. Adams
HI-I'M-YOUR-NEW-BOSS-LET'S-CHANGE-EVERY-THING-BEFORE-I-GET-REASSIGNED-OOPS-TOO-LATE-GOODBYE.
SPROING
HE WAS LIKE A MENTOR TO ME.
I THINK HE MADE A DIFFERENCE.
INCOMING!

This is the first comic featuring the character that later became Catbert. At this point, I had no plans for keeping him beyond the week.

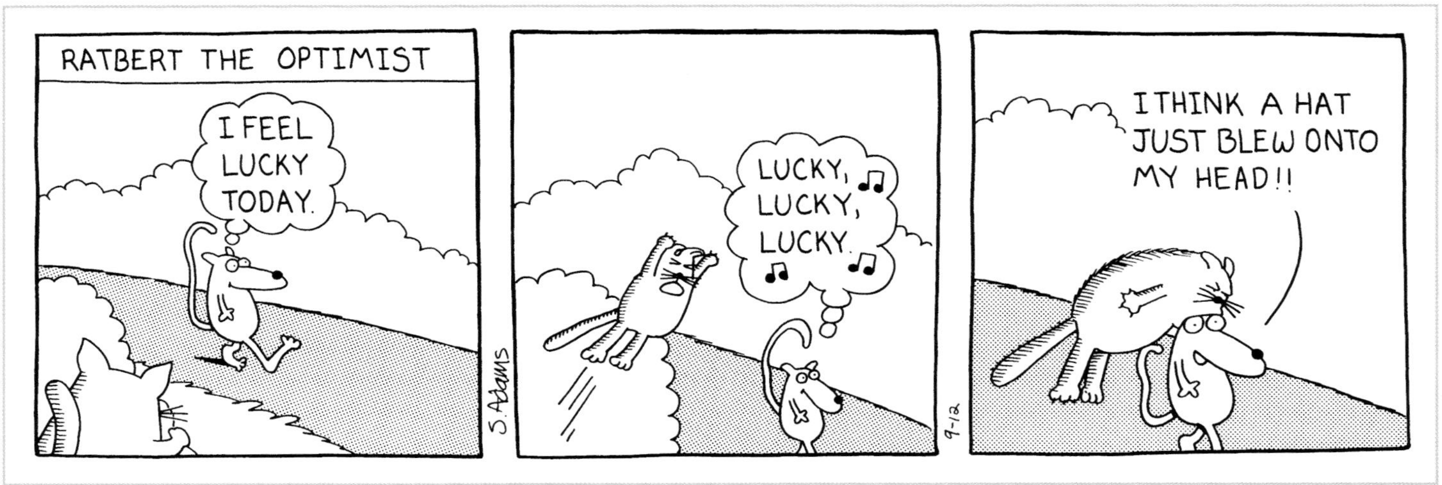
RATBERT THE OPTIMIST
I FEEL LUCKY TODAY.
S. Adams
LUCKY, LUCKY, LUCKY.
9-12
I THINK A HAT JUST BLEW ONTO MY HEAD!!

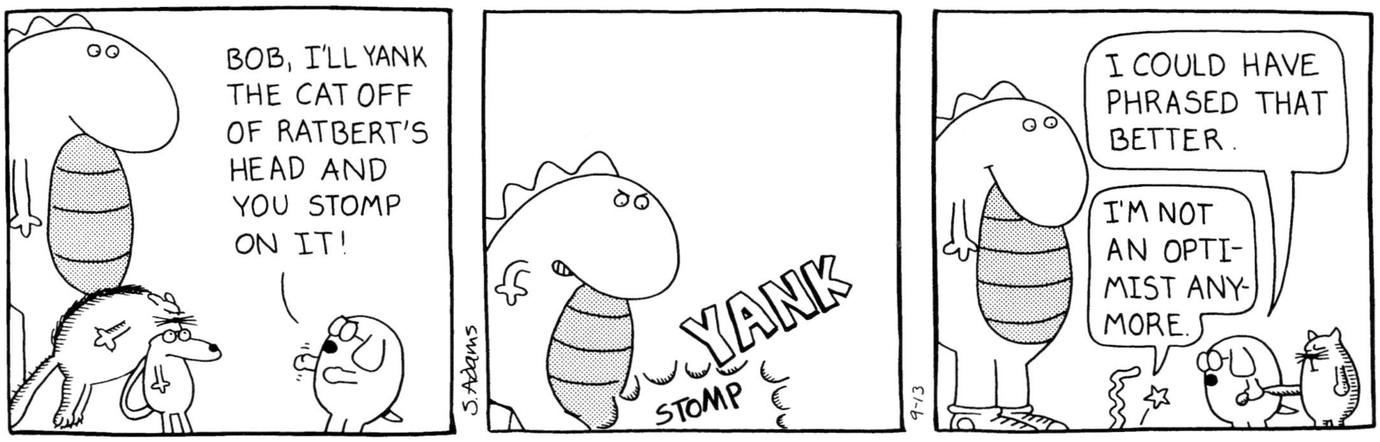
BOB, I'LL YANK THE CAT OFF OF RATBERT'S HEAD AND YOU STOMP ON IT!
YANK
STOMP
I COULD HAVE PHRASED THAT BETTER.
I'M NOT AN OPTI-MIST ANY-MORE.

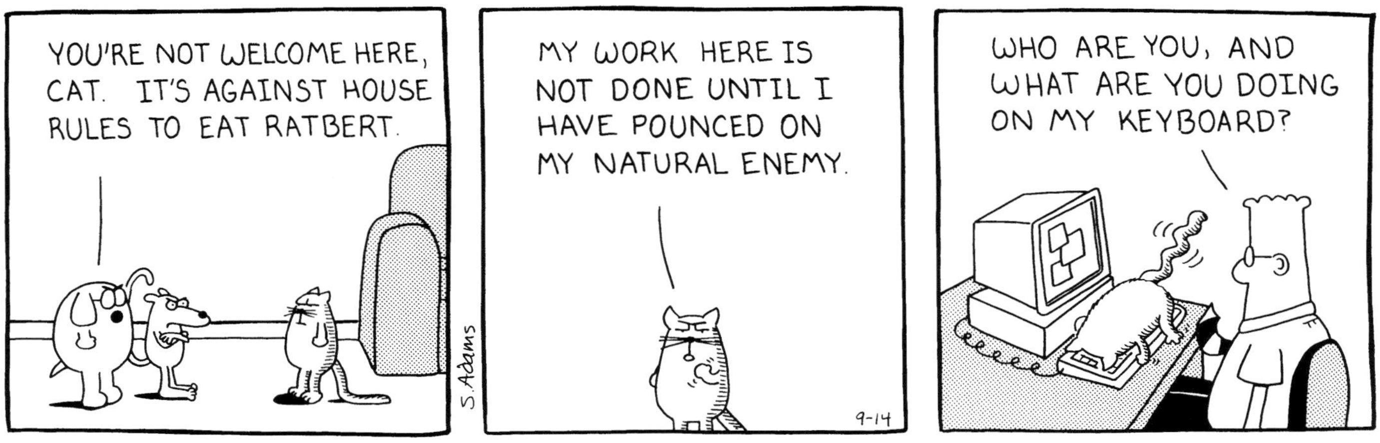
YOU'RE NOT WELCOME HERE, CAT. IT'S AGAINST HOUSE RULES TO EAT RATBERT.
MY WORK HERE IS NOT DONE UNTIL I HAVE POUNCED ON MY NATURAL ENEMY.
WHO ARE YOU, AND WHAT ARE YOU DOING ON MY KEYBOARD?

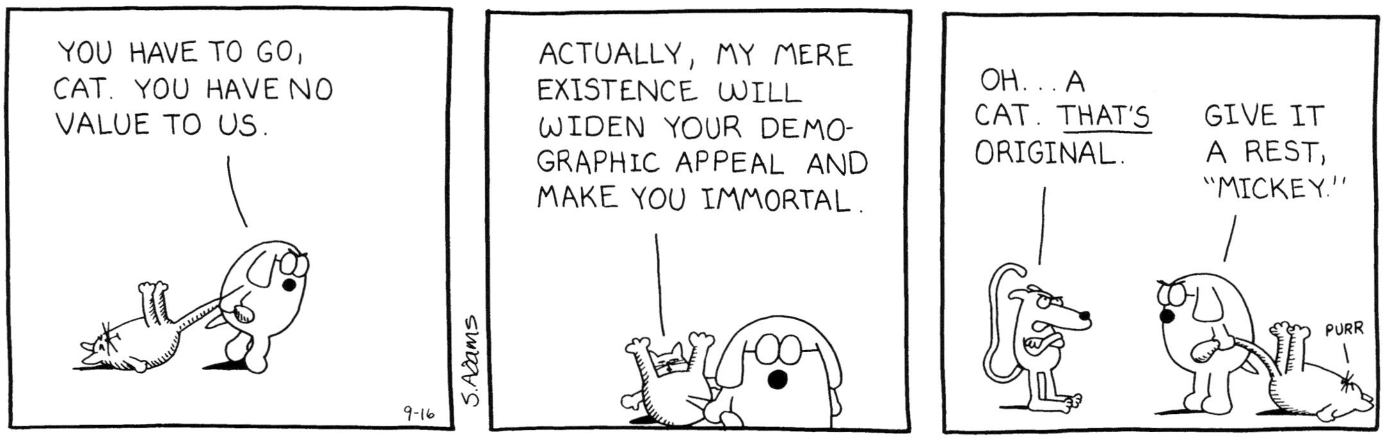
YOU HAVE TO GO, CAT. YOU HAVE NO VALUE TO US.
ACTUALLY, MY MERE EXISTENCE WILL WIDEN YOUR DEMO-GRAPHIC APPEAL AND MAKE YOU IMMORTAL.
OH... A CAT. THAT'S ORIGINAL.
GIVE IT A REST, "MICKEY."
PURR

The cat character had no name, but hundreds of people e-mailed me to say they "loved Catbert." I'm no marketing genius, but when hundreds of people spontaneously give a character the same name, it's a keeper. The problem was trying to move Catbert into the workplace so he could have more impact. One day, while taking a shower, inspiration struck. I decided to make Catbert the Evil Director of Human Resources. I figured it was a good fit because the director of HR generally doesn't care if you live or die, and enjoys playing with you until you get downsized. That is very catlike.

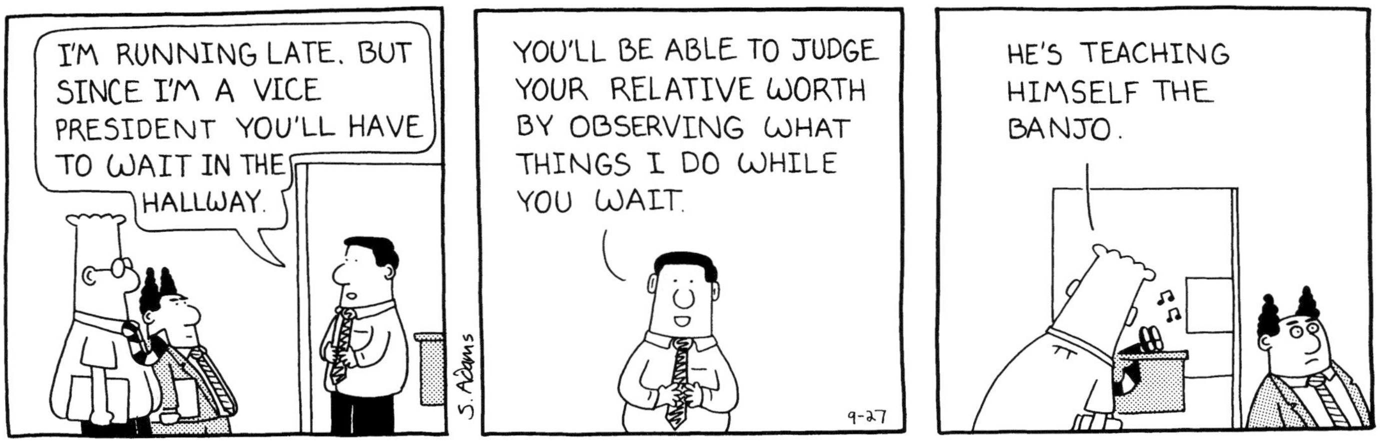
I'M RUNNING LATE. BUT SINCE I'M A VICE PRESIDENT YOU'LL HAVE TO WAIT IN THE HALLWAY.
YOU'LL BE ABLE TO JUDGE YOUR RELATIVE WORTH BY OBSERVING WHAT THINGS I DO WHILE YOU WAIT.
HE'S TEACHING HIMSELF THE BANJO.

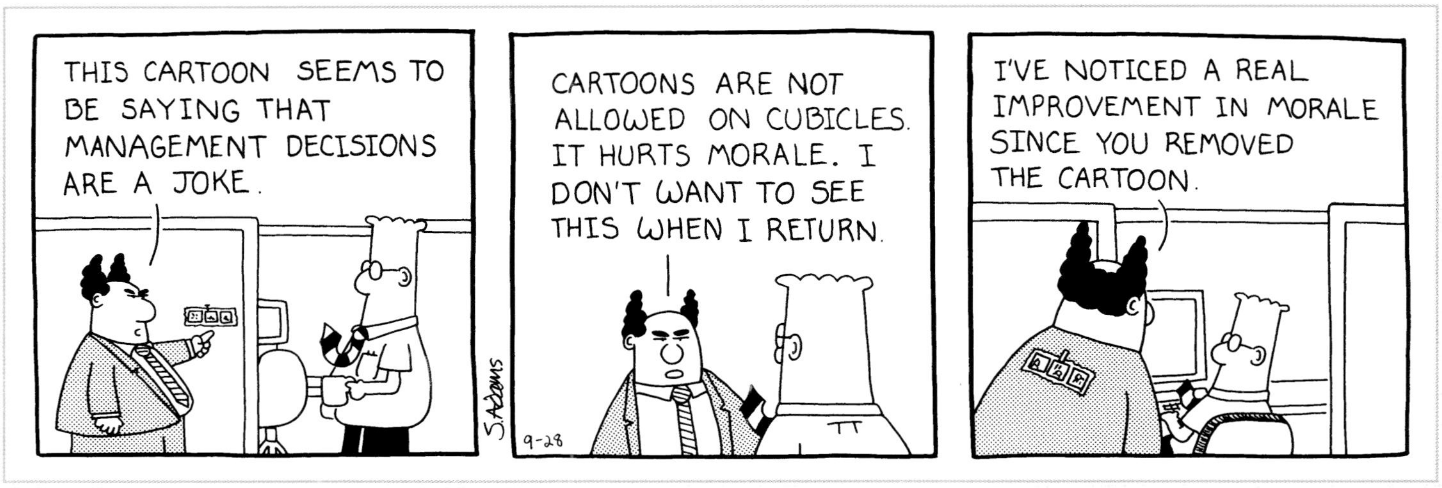
THIS CARTOON SEEMS TO BE SAYING THAT MANAGEMENT DECISIONS ARE A JOKE.
CARTOONS ARE NOT ALLOWED ON CUBICLES. IT HURTS MORALE. I DON'T WANT TO SEE THIS WHEN I RETURN.
I'VE NOTICED A REAL IMPROVEMENT IN MORALE SINCE YOU REMOVED THE CARTOON.

By this time, Dilbert comics were a common occurrence on cubicle walls. And management didn't like it.

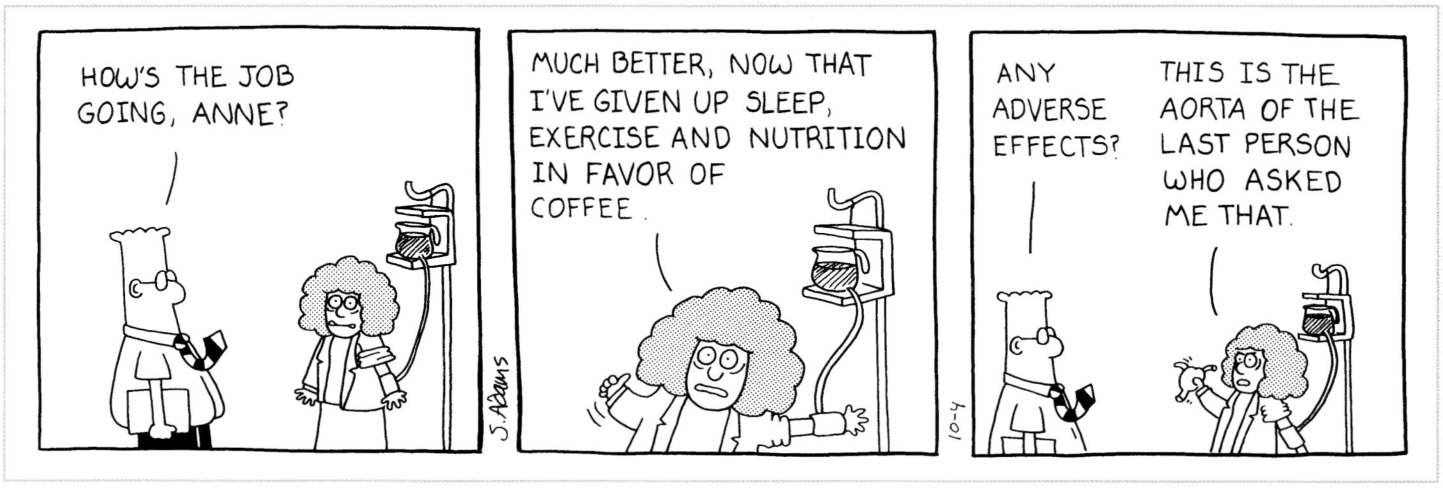
HOW'S THE JOB GOING, ANNE?
MUCH BETTER, NOW THAT I'VE GIVEN UP SLEEP, EXERCISE AND NUTRITION IN FAVOR OF COFFEE.
ANY ADVERSE EFFECTS?
THIS IS THE AORTA OF THE LAST PERSON WHO ASKED ME THAT.

Oops. Alice became Anne in this strip. I probably just forgot the name I used last time.

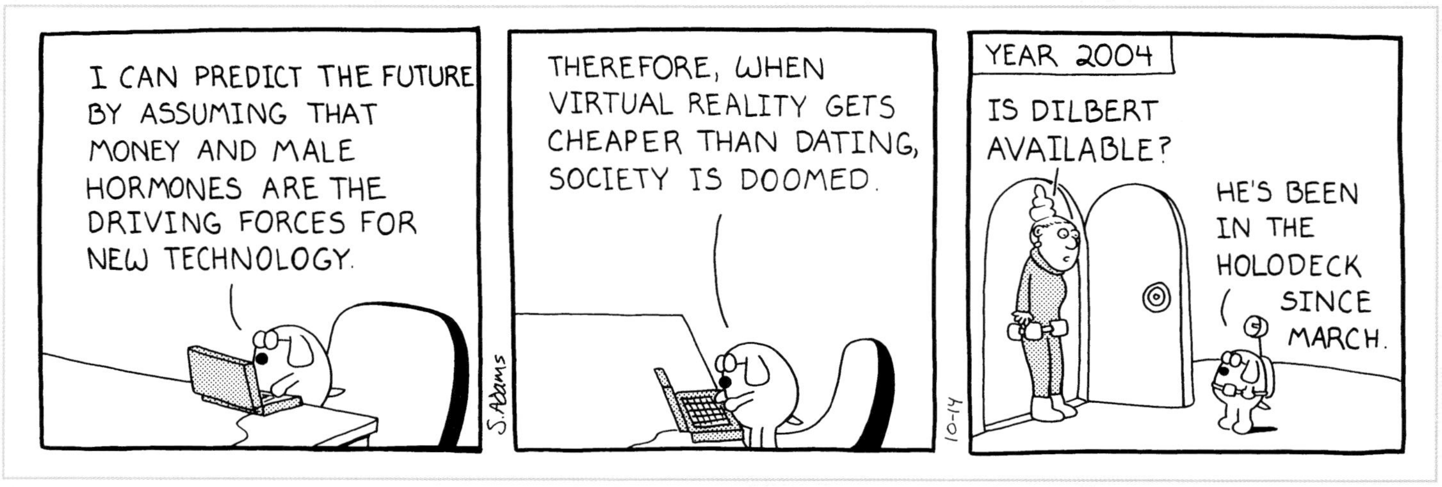
I CAN PREDICT THE FUTURE BY ASSUMING THAT MONEY AND MALE HORMONES ARE THE DRIVING FORCES FOR NEW TECHNOLOGY.
THEREFORE, WHEN VIRTUAL REALITY GETS CHEAPER THAN DATING, SOCIETY IS DOOMED.
YEAR 2004
IS DILBERT AVAILABLE?
HE'S BEEN IN THE HOLODECK SINCE MARCH.

I literally think Dogbert's prediction will happen.

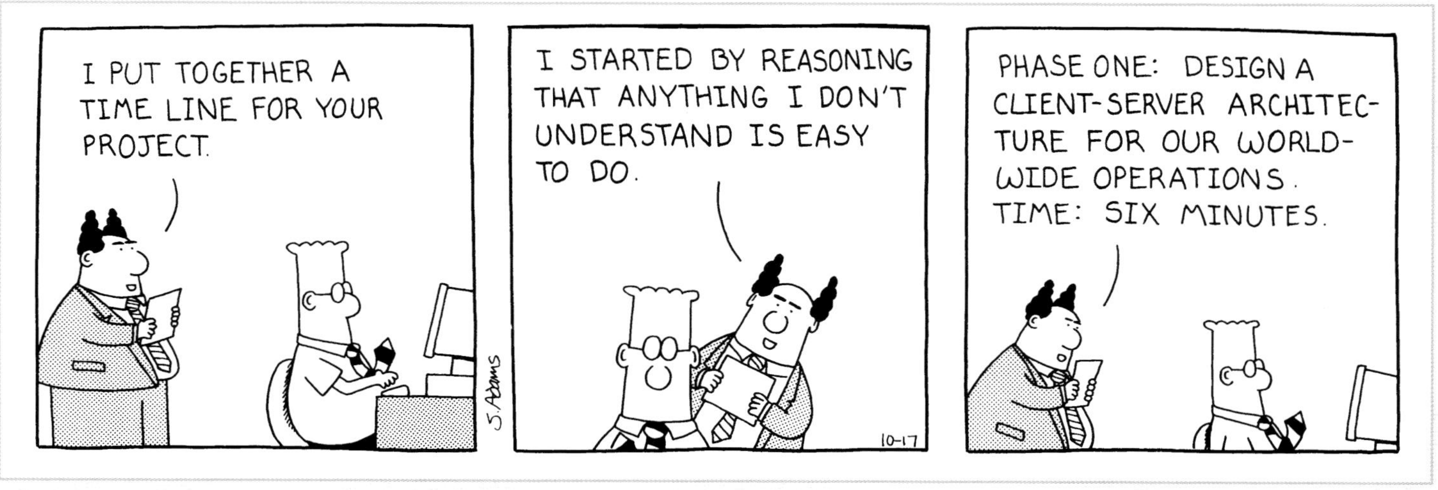
I PUT TOGETHER A TIME LINE FOR YOUR PROJECT.
I STARTED BY REASONING THAT ANYTHING I DON'T UNDERSTAND IS EASY TO DO.
PHASE ONE: DESIGN A CLIENT-SERVER ARCHITECTURE FOR OUR WORLD-WIDE OPERATIONS. TIME: SIX MINUTES.

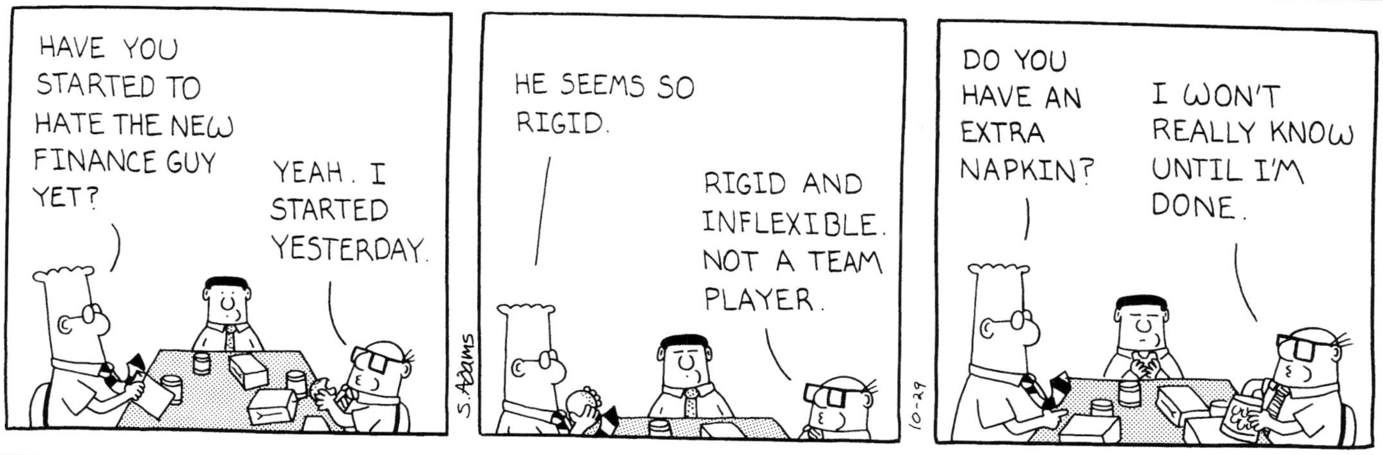
HAVE YOU STARTED TO HATE THE NEW FINANCE GUY YET?
YEAH. I STARTED YESTERDAY.
S. Adams
HE SEEMS SO RIGID.
RIGID AND INFLEXIBLE. NOT A TEAM PLAYER.
10-29
DO YOU HAVE AN EXTRA NAPKIN?
I WON'T REALLY KNOW UNTIL I'M DONE.

Selfishness is a theme that always works. If you develop the characters, and have them all act selfishly, half of the writing is done.

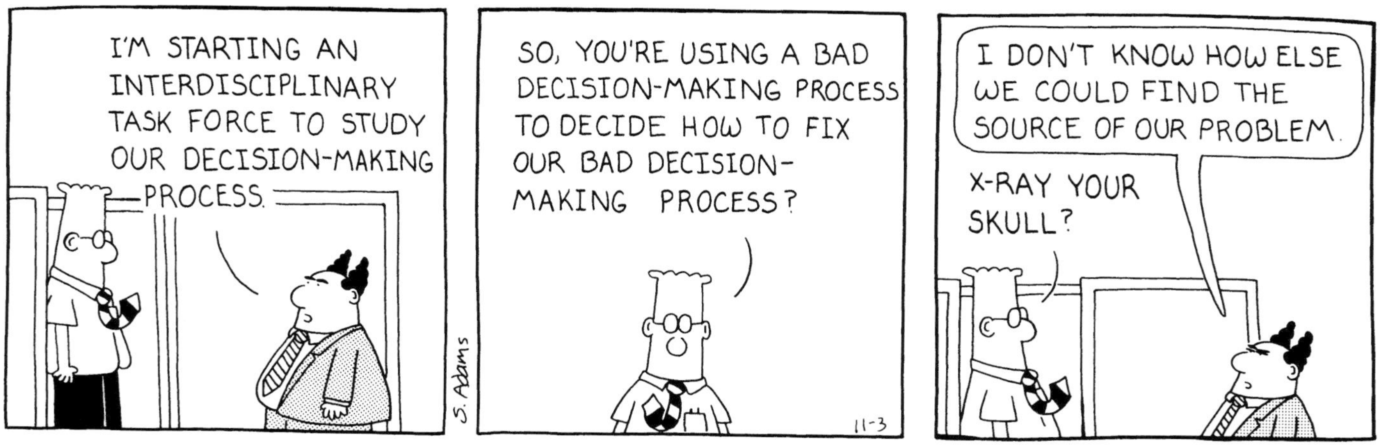
I'M STARTING AN INTERDISCIPLINARY TASK FORCE TO STUDY OUR DECISION-MAKING PROCESS.
S. Adams
SO, YOU'RE USING A BAD DECISION-MAKING PROCESS TO DECIDE HOW TO FIX OUR BAD DECISION-MAKING PROCESS?
11-3
I DON'T KNOW HOW ELSE WE COULD FIND THE SOURCE OF OUR PROBLEM.
X-RAY YOUR SKULL?

Dilbert started getting more of a bad attitude at this point.

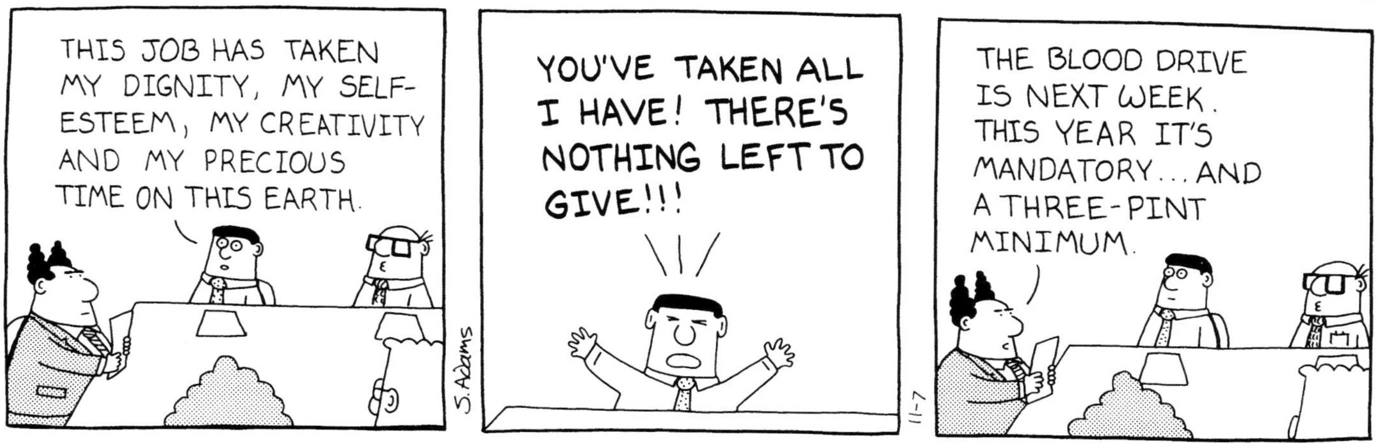
THIS JOB HAS TAKEN MY DIGNITY, MY SELF-ESTEEM, MY CREATIVITY AND MY PRECIOUS TIME ON THIS EARTH.
S. Adams
YOU'VE TAKEN ALL I HAVE! THERE'S NOTHING LEFT TO GIVE!!!
11-7
THE BLOOD DRIVE IS NEXT WEEK. THIS YEAR IT'S MANDATORY... AND A THREE-PINT MINIMUM.

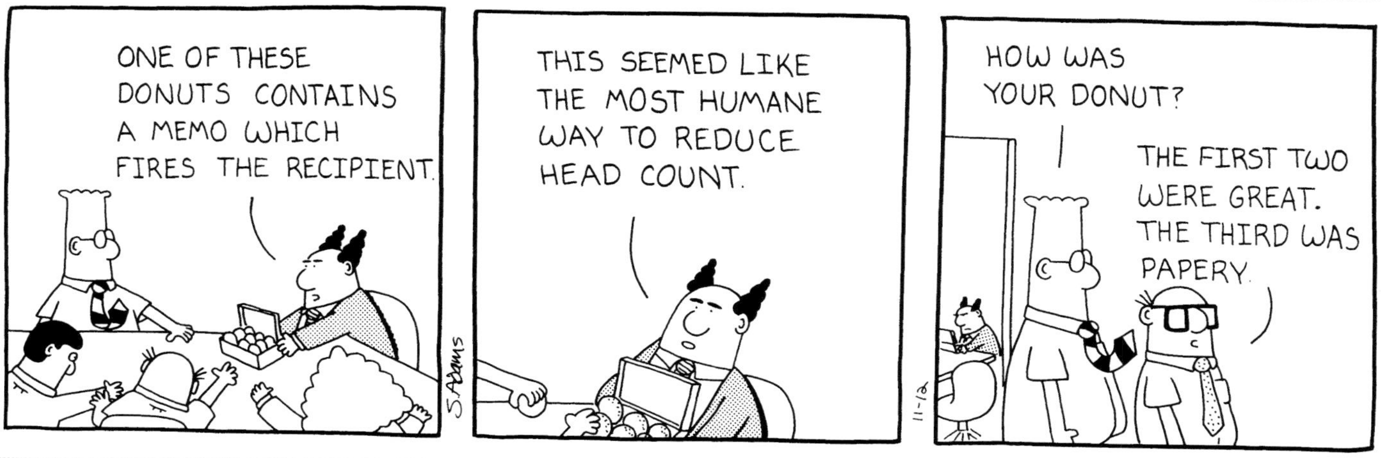
ONE OF THESE DONUTS CONTAINS A MEMO WHICH FIRES THE RECIPIENT.
S. Adams
THIS SEEMED LIKE THE MOST HUMANE WAY TO REDUCE HEAD COUNT.
11-12
HOW WAS YOUR DONUT?
THE FIRST TWO WERE GREAT. THE THIRD WAS PAPERY.

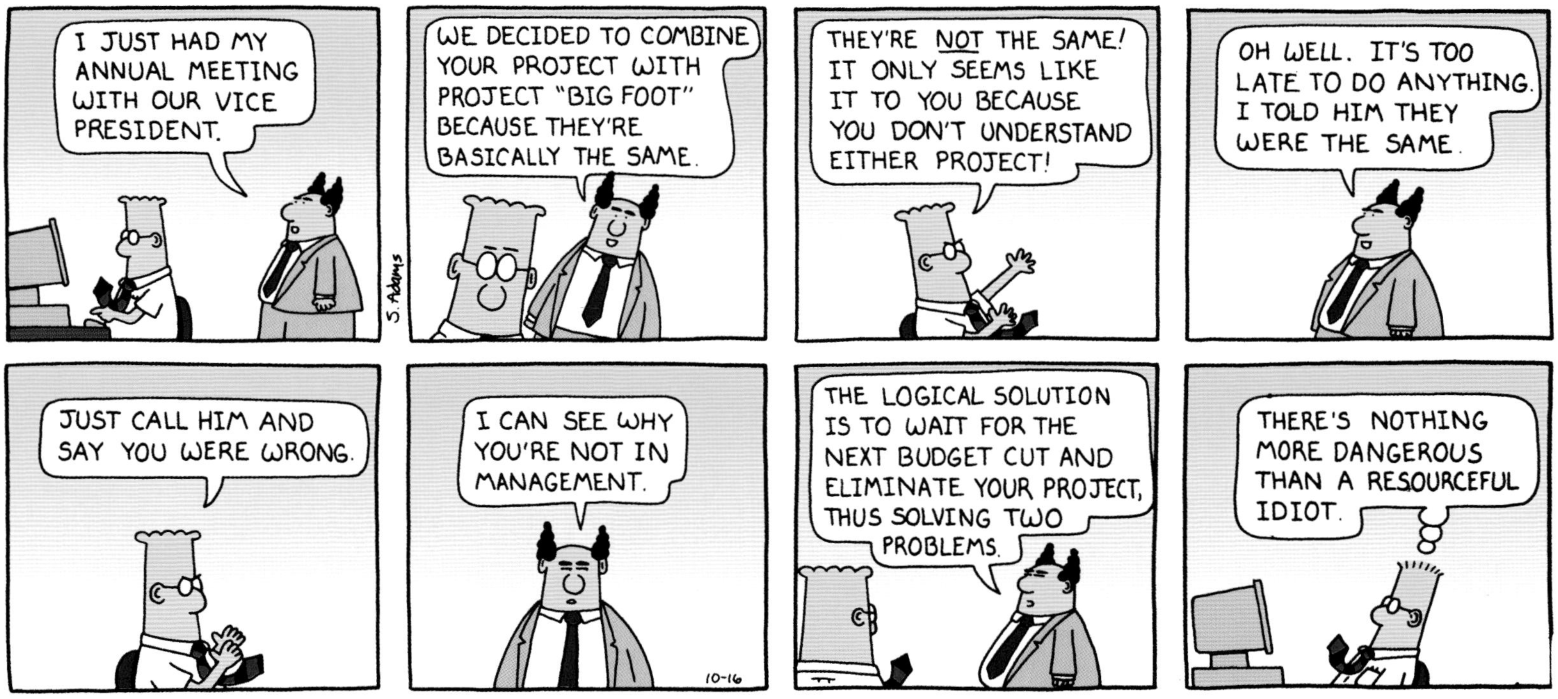
I JUST HAD MY ANNUAL MEETING WITH OUR VICE PRESIDENT.
WE DECIDED TO COMBINE YOUR PROJECT WITH PROJECT "BIG FOOT" BECAUSE THEY'RE BASICALLY THE SAME.
S. Adams
THEY'RE NOT THE SAME! IT ONLY SEEMS LIKE IT TO YOU BECAUSE YOU DON'T UNDERSTAND EITHER PROJECT!
OH WELL. IT'S TOO LATE TO DO ANYTHING. I TOLD HIM THEY WERE THE SAME.
JUST CALL HIM AND SAY YOU WERE WRONG.
I CAN SEE WHY YOU'RE NOT IN MANAGEMENT.
10-16
THE LOGICAL SOLUTION IS TO WAIT FOR THE NEXT BUDGET CUT AND ELIMINATE YOUR PROJECT, THUS SOLVING TWO PROBLEMS.
THERE'S NOTHING MORE DANGEROUS THAN A RESOURCEFUL IDIOT.

This is the first comic describing the Dilbert Principle, i.e., the most worthless employees are promoted to management where they can do the least harm.

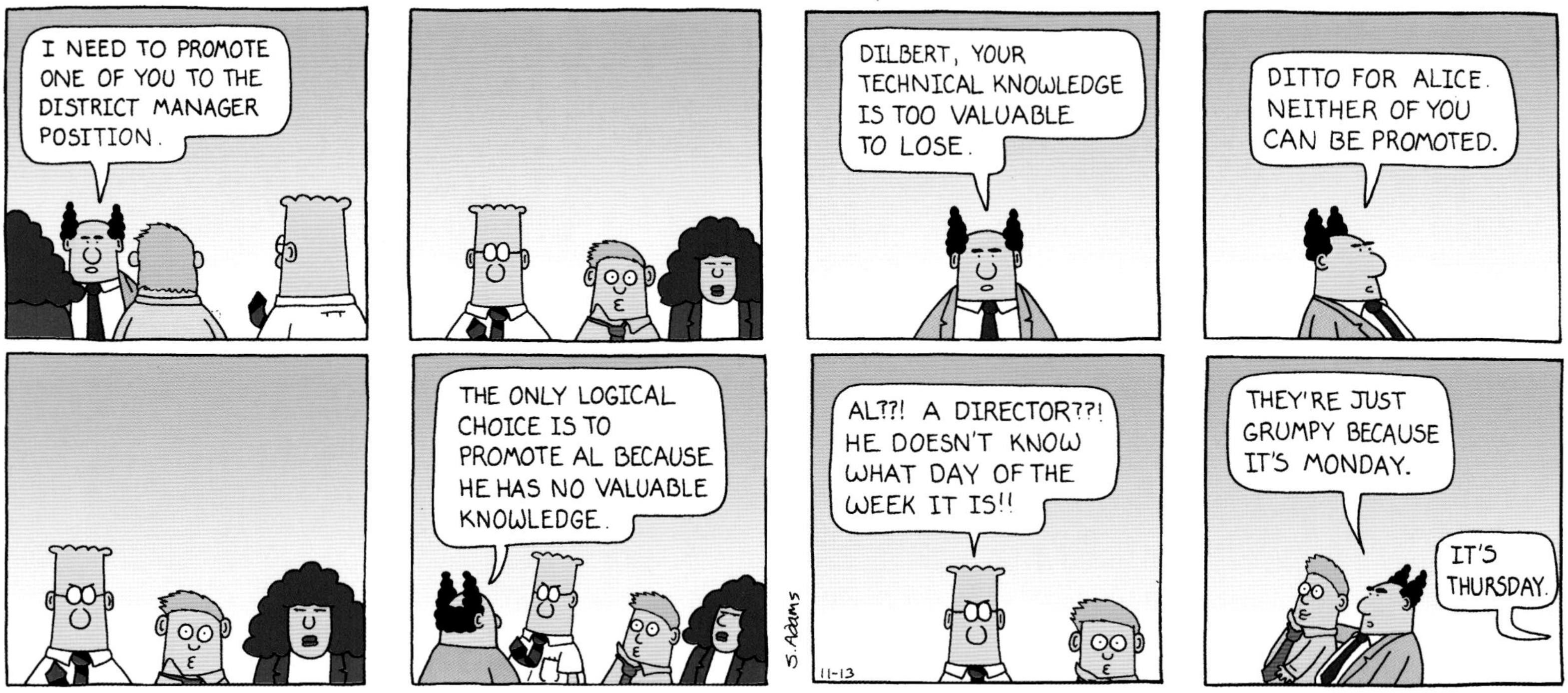
I NEED TO PROMOTE ONE OF YOU TO THE DISTRICT MANAGER POSITION.
DILBERT, YOUR TECHNICAL KNOWLEDGE IS TOO VALUABLE TO LOSE.
DITTO FOR ALICE. NEITHER OF YOU CAN BE PROMOTED.
THE ONLY LOGICAL CHOICE IS TO PROMOTE AL BECAUSE HE HAS NO VALUABLE KNOWLEDGE.
S. Adams
11-13
AL?!! A DIRECTOR??! HE DOESN'T KNOW WHAT DAY OF THE WEEK IT IS!!
THEY'RE JUST GRUMPY BECAUSE IT'S MONDAY.
IT'S THURSDAY.

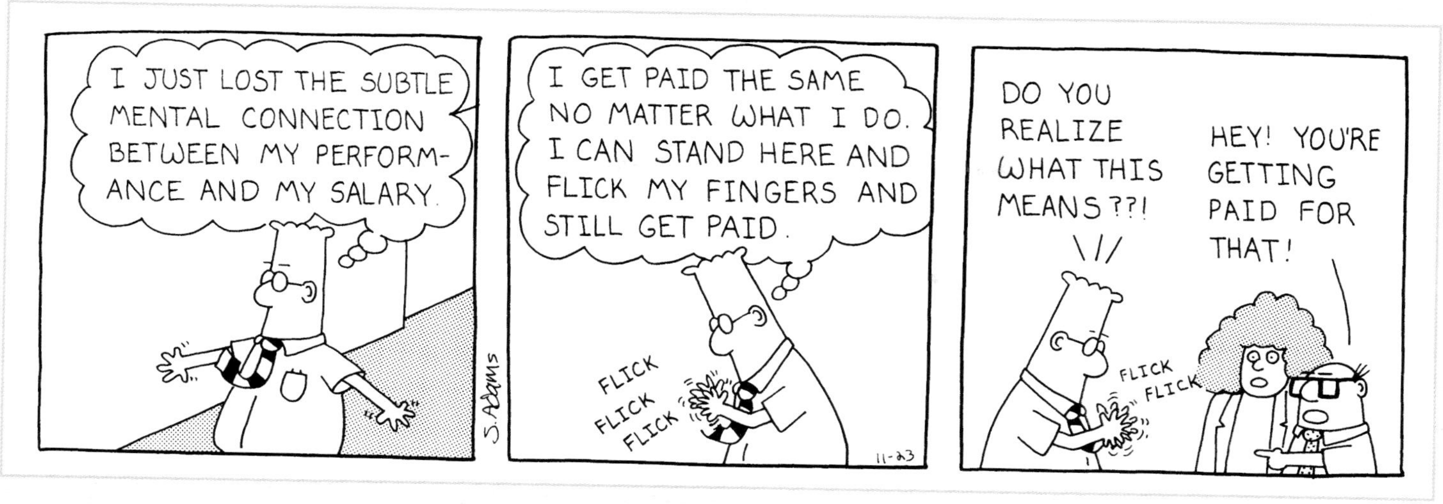
I JUST LOST THE SUBTLE MENTAL CONNECTION BETWEEN MY PERFORM-ANCE AND MY SALARY.
S. Adams
I GET PAID THE SAME NO MATTER WHAT I DO. I CAN STAND HERE AND FLICK MY FINGERS AND STILL GET PAID.
FLICK FLICK FLICK
11-23
DO YOU REALIZE WHAT THIS MEANS??!
HEY! YOU'RE GETTING PAID FOR THAT!
FLICK FLICK

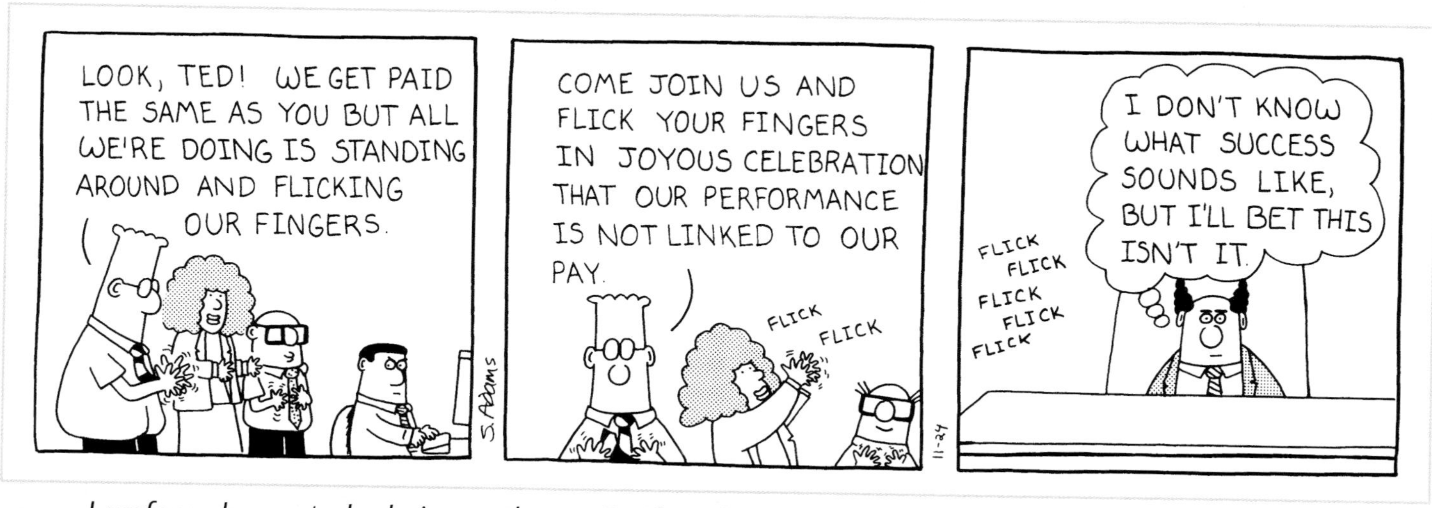
LOOK, TED! WE GET PAID THE SAME AS YOU BUT ALL WE'RE DOING IS STANDING AROUND AND FLICKING OUR FINGERS.
S. Adams
COME JOIN US AND FLICK YOUR FINGERS IN JOYOUS CELEBRATION THAT OUR PERFORMANCE IS NOT LINKED TO OUR PAY.
FLICK FLICK
11-24
FLICK FLICK FLICK FLICK FLICK
I DON'T KNOW WHAT SUCCESS SOUNDS LIKE, BUT I'LL BET THIS ISN'T IT.

I performed many tasks during my days at Pacific Bell. Most of them involved pretending to work. I wasn't a computer programmer, but to fight boredom I read computer manuals and taught myself how to code. At one point I wrote a word processing program. It took months, and had no purpose other than to entertain me. Luckily for me, writing my own programs looked like work.

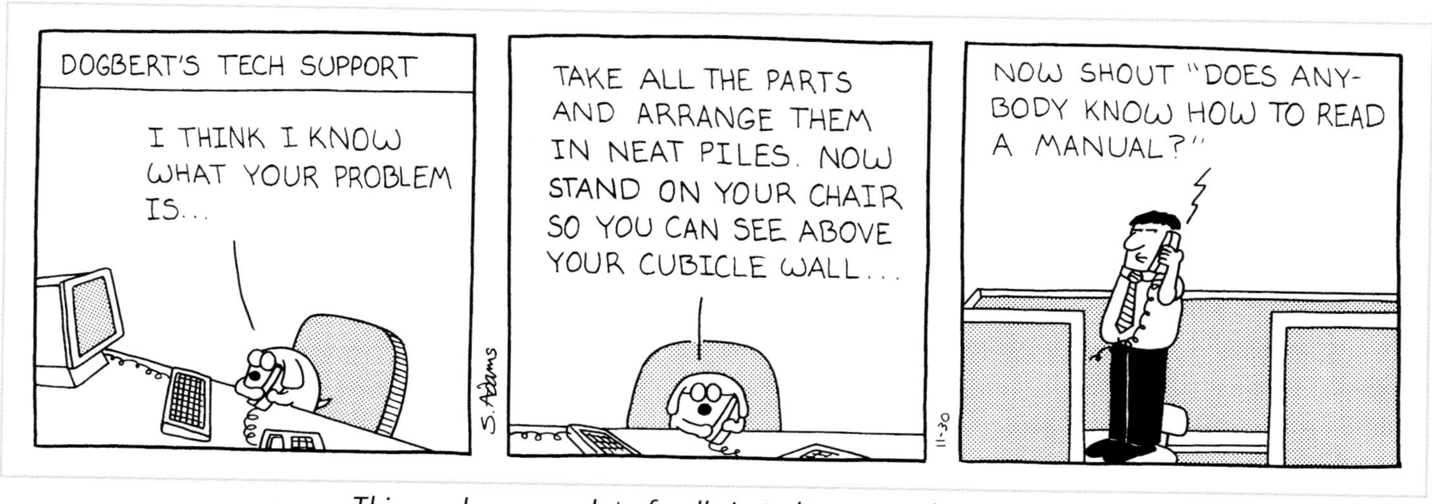
DOGBERT'S TECH SUPPORT
I THINK I KNOW WHAT YOUR PROBLEM IS...
S. Adams
TAKE ALL THE PARTS AND ARRANGE THEM IN NEAT PILES. NOW STAND ON YOUR CHAIR SO YOU CAN SEE ABOVE YOUR CUBICLE WALL...
11-30
NOW SHOUT "DOES ANY-BODY KNOW HOW TO READ A MANUAL?"

This one hung on a lot of walls in tech support departments.

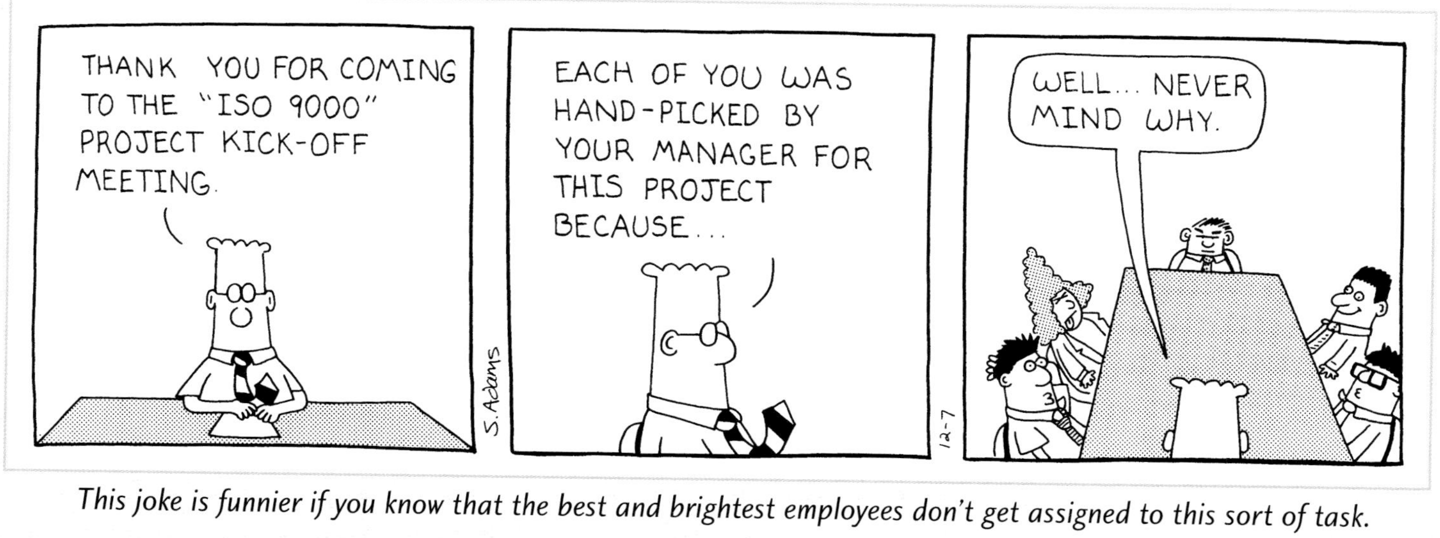
THANK YOU FOR COMING TO THE "ISO 9000" PROJECT KICK-OFF MEETING.
S. Adams
EACH OF YOU WAS HAND-PICKED BY YOUR MANAGER FOR THIS PROJECT BECAUSE...
12-7
WELL... NEVER MIND WHY.

This joke is funnier if you know that the best and brightest employees don't get assigned to this sort of task.

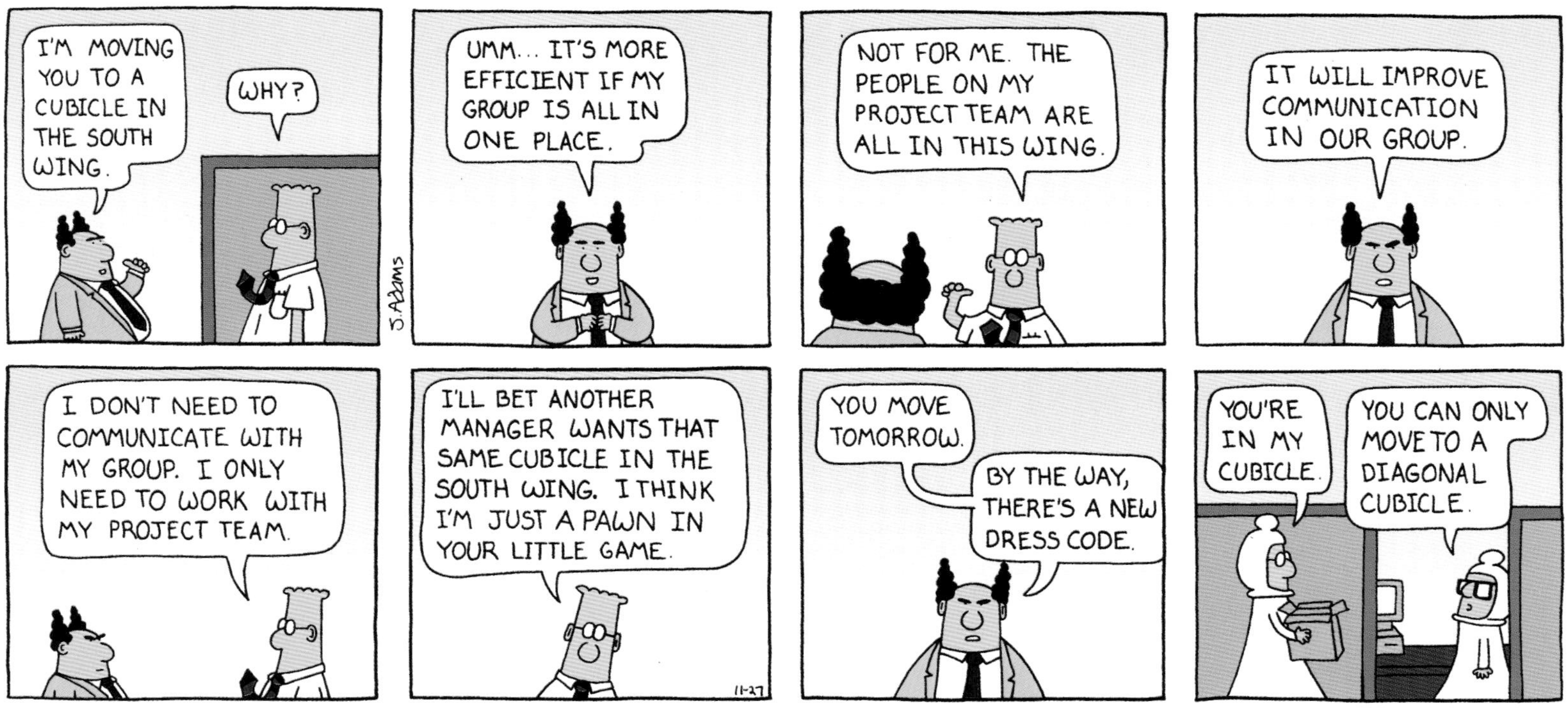
I'M MOVING YOU TO A CUBICLE IN THE SOUTH WING.
WHY?
S. Adams
UMM... IT'S MORE EFFICIENT IF MY GROUP IS ALL IN ONE PLACE.
NOT FOR ME. THE PEOPLE ON MY PROJECT TEAM ARE ALL IN THIS WING.
IT WILL IMPROVE COMMUNICATION IN OUR GROUP.
I DON'T NEED TO COMMUNICATE WITH MY GROUP. I ONLY NEED TO WORK WITH MY PROJECT TEAM.
I'LL BET ANOTHER MANAGER WANTS THAT SAME CUBICLE IN THE SOUTH WING. I THINK I'M JUST A PAWN IN YOUR LITTLE GAME.
11-27
YOU MOVE TOMORROW.
BY THE WAY, THERE'S A NEW DRESS CODE.
YOU'RE IN MY CUBICLE.
YOU CAN ONLY MOVE TO A DIAGONAL CUBICLE.

I usually ate my lunch alone, primarily for this reason.

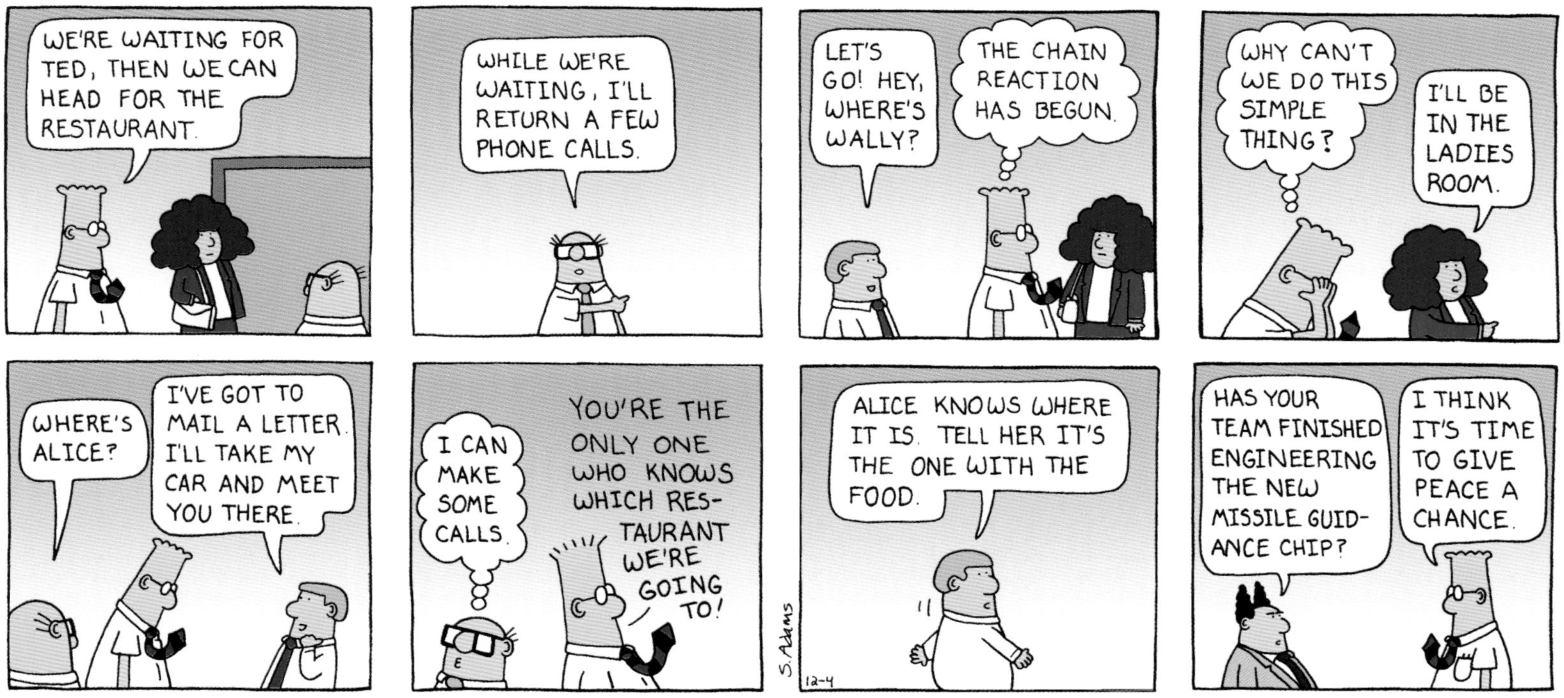
WE'RE WAITING FOR TED, THEN WE CAN HEAD FOR THE RESTAURANT.
WHILE WE'RE WAITING, I'LL RETURN A FEW PHONE CALLS.
LET'S GO! HEY, WHERE'S WALLY?
THE CHAIN REACTION HAS BEGUN.
WHY CAN'T WE DO THIS SIMPLE THING?
I'LL BE IN THE LADIES ROOM.
WHERE'S ALICE?
I'VE GOT TO MAIL A LETTER. I'LL TAKE MY CAR AND MEET YOU THERE.
I CAN MAKE SOME CALLS.
YOU'RE THE ONLY ONE WHO KNOWS WHICH RESTAURANT WE'RE GOING TO!
S. Adams
12-4
ALICE KNOWS WHERE IT IS. TELL HER IT'S THE ONE WITH THE FOOD.
HAS YOUR TEAM FINISHED ENGINEERING THE NEW MISSILE GUIDANCE CHIP?
I THINK IT'S TIME TO GIVE PEACE A CHANCE.

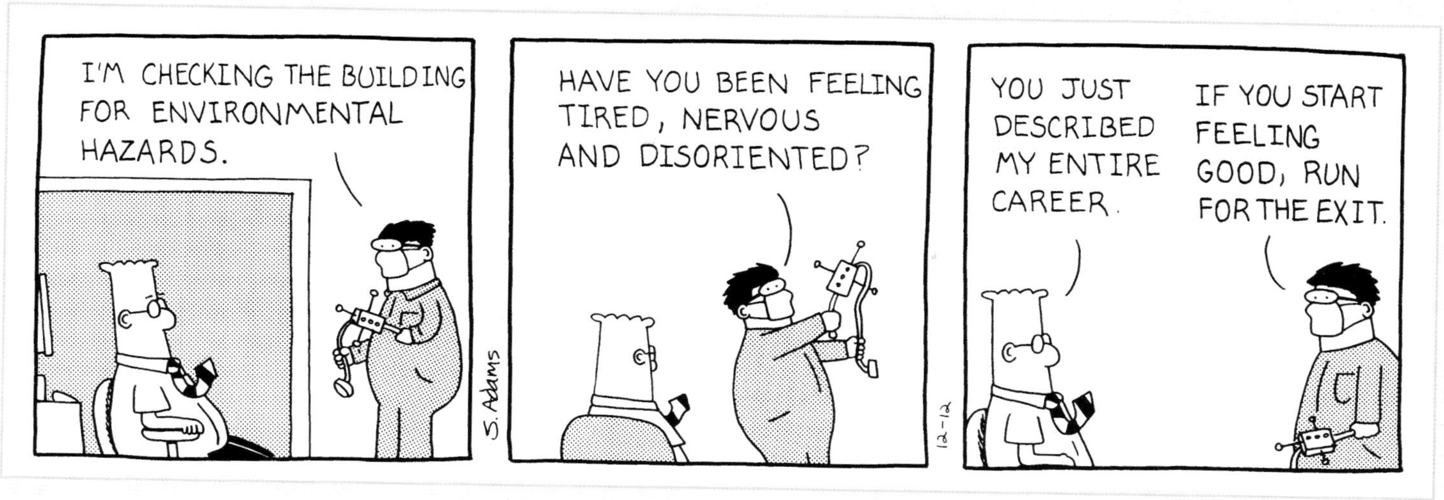
I'M CHECKING THE BUILDING FOR ENVIRONMENTAL HAZARDS.
S. Adams
HAVE YOU BEEN FEELING TIRED, NERVOUS AND DISORIENTED?
12-12
YOU JUST DESCRIBED MY ENTIRE CAREER.
IF YOU START FEELING GOOD, RUN FOR THE EXIT.

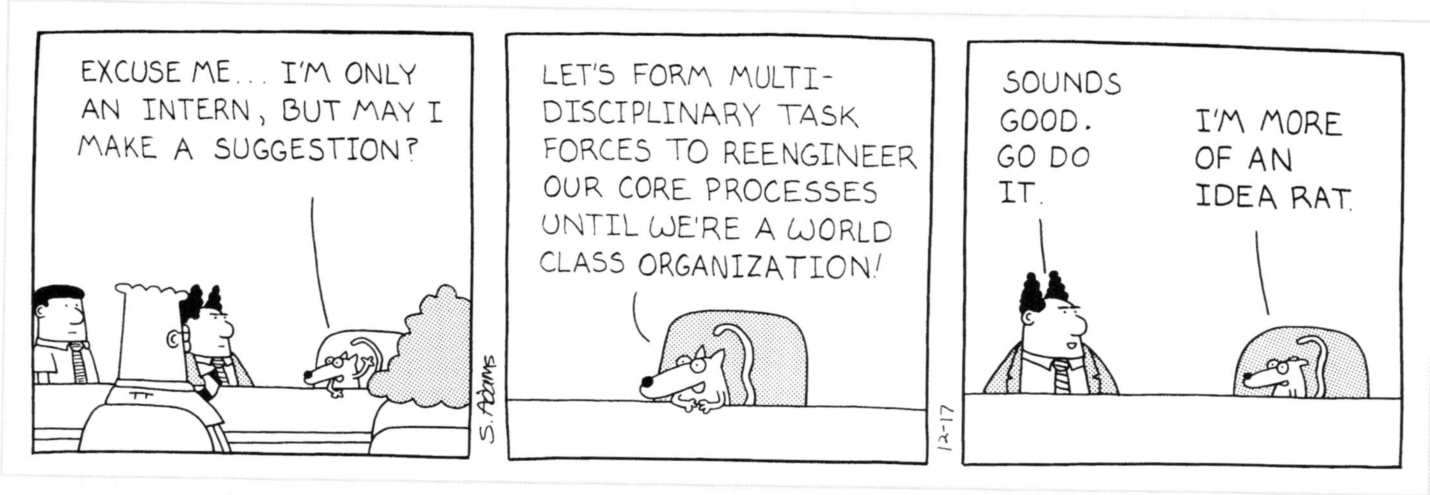
EXCUSE ME... I'M ONLY AN INTERN, BUT MAY I MAKE A SUGGESTION?
S. Adams
LET'S FORM MULTI-DISCIPLINARY TASK FORCES TO REENGINEER OUR CORE PROCESSES UNTIL WE'RE A WORLD CLASS ORGANIZATION!
12-17
SOUNDS GOOD. GO DO IT.
I'M MORE OF AN IDEA RAT.

Asok the intern hadn't been created yet.

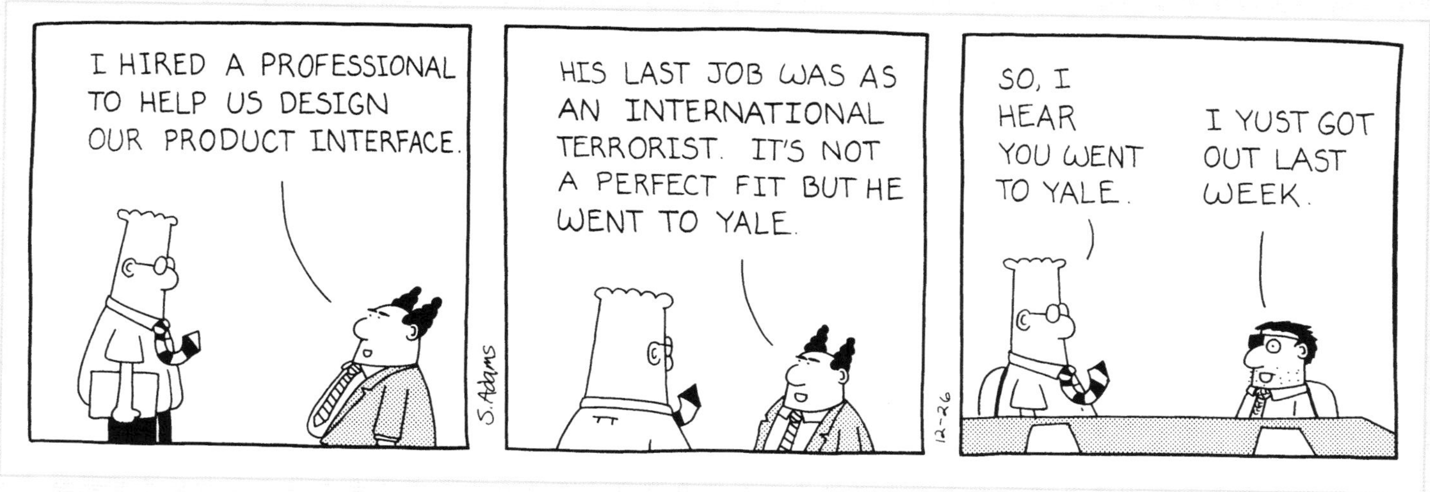
I HIRED A PROFESSIONAL TO HELP US DESIGN OUR PRODUCT INTERFACE.
S. Adams
HIS LAST JOB WAS AS AN INTERNATIONAL TERRORIST. IT'S NOT A PERFECT FIT BUT HE WENT TO YALE.
12-26
SO, I HEAR YOU WENT TO YALE.
I YUST GOT OUT LAST WEEK.

The strip above is the version I originally submitted. My editor rejected it, explaining that the terrorist character would be construed by readers as Middle Eastern. This would cause complaints about my unfair stereotyping. After some negotiating, I agreed to give the terrorist a name that made it clear he was Scandinavian. Ironically, this actually improved the clarity of the joke. The version that ran in papers is below. No Scandinavians complained.

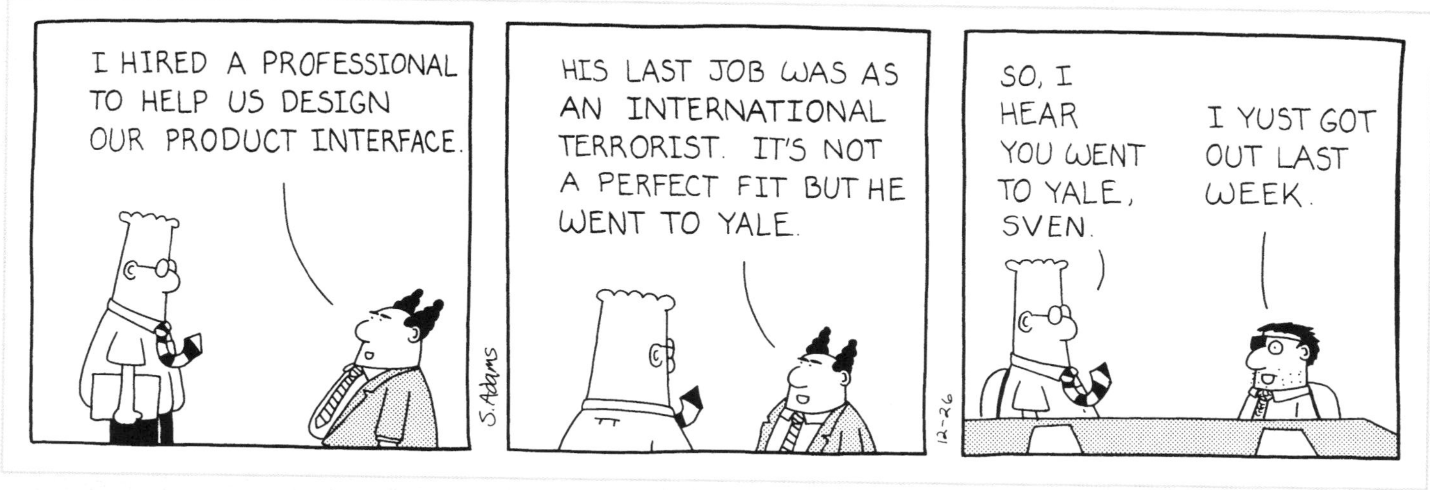
I HIRED A PROFESSIONAL TO HELP US DESIGN OUR PRODUCT INTERFACE.
S. Adams
HIS LAST JOB WAS AS AN INTERNATIONAL TERRORIST. IT'S NOT A PERFECT FIT BUT HE WENT TO YALE.
12-26
SO, I HEAR YOU WENT TO YALE, SVEN.
I YUST GOT OUT LAST WEEK.

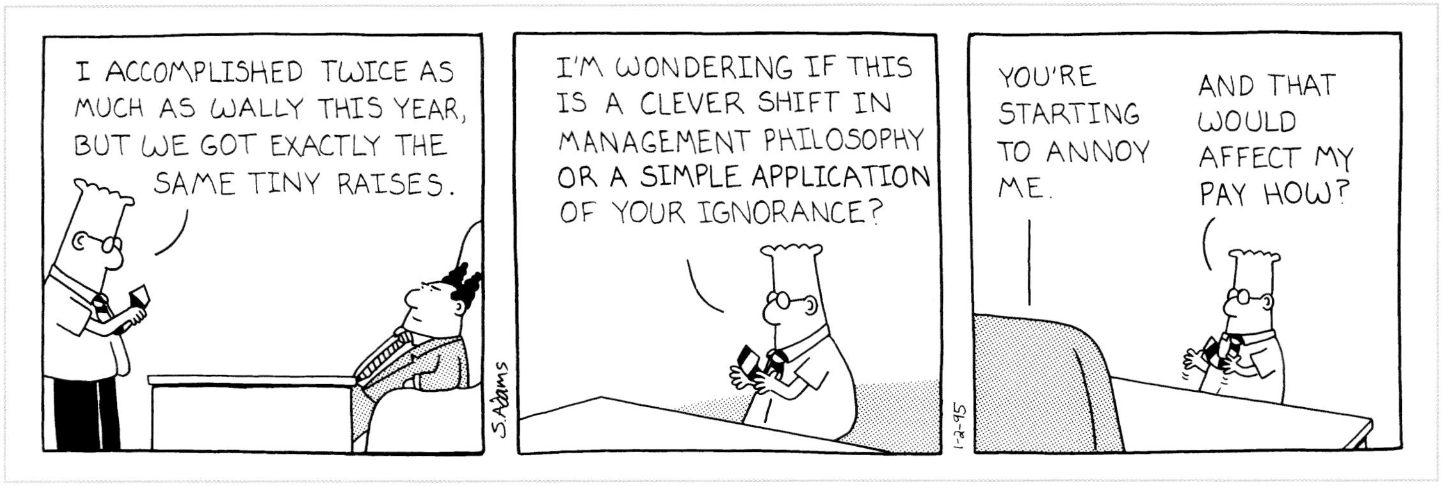
I ACCOMPLISHED TWICE AS MUCH AS WALLY THIS YEAR, BUT WE GOT EXACTLY THE SAME TINY RAISES.
S. Adams
I'M WONDERING IF THIS IS A CLEVER SHIFT IN MANAGEMENT PHILOSOPHY OR A SIMPLE APPLICATION OF YOUR IGNORANCE?
1-2-95
YOU'RE STARTING TO ANNOY ME.
AND THAT WOULD AFFECT MY PAY HOW?

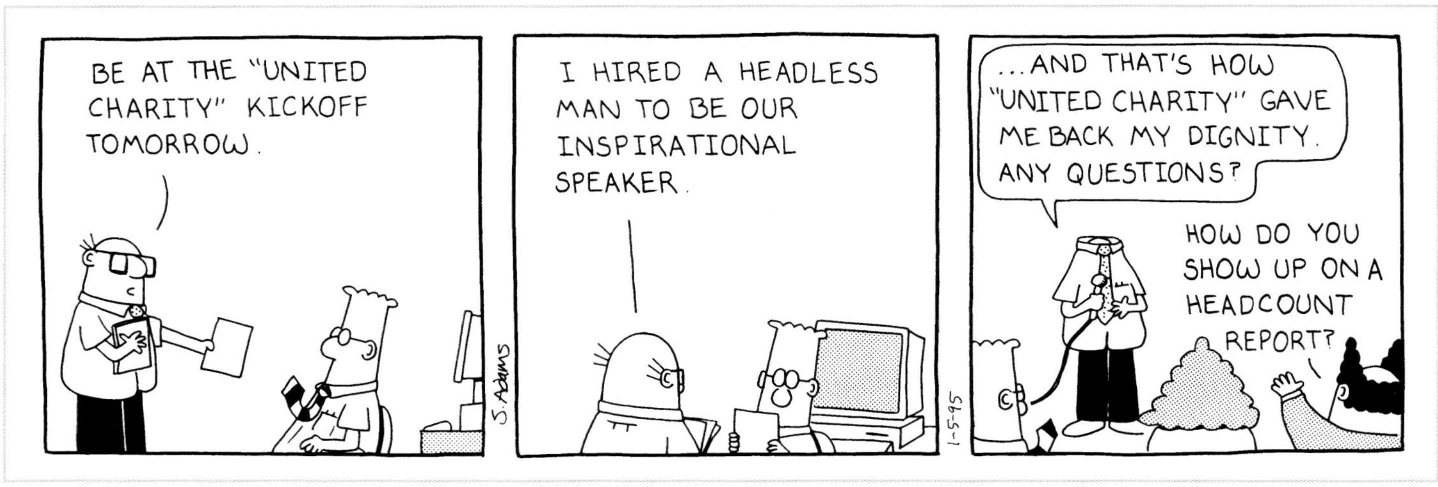
BE AT THE "UNITED CHARITY" KICKOFF TOMORROW.
S. Adams
I HIRED A HEADLESS MAN TO BE OUR INSPIRATIONAL SPEAKER.
1-5-95
...AND THAT'S HOW "UNITED CHARITY" GAVE ME BACK MY DIGNITY. ANY QUESTIONS?
HOW DO YOU SHOW UP ON A HEADCOUNT REPORT?

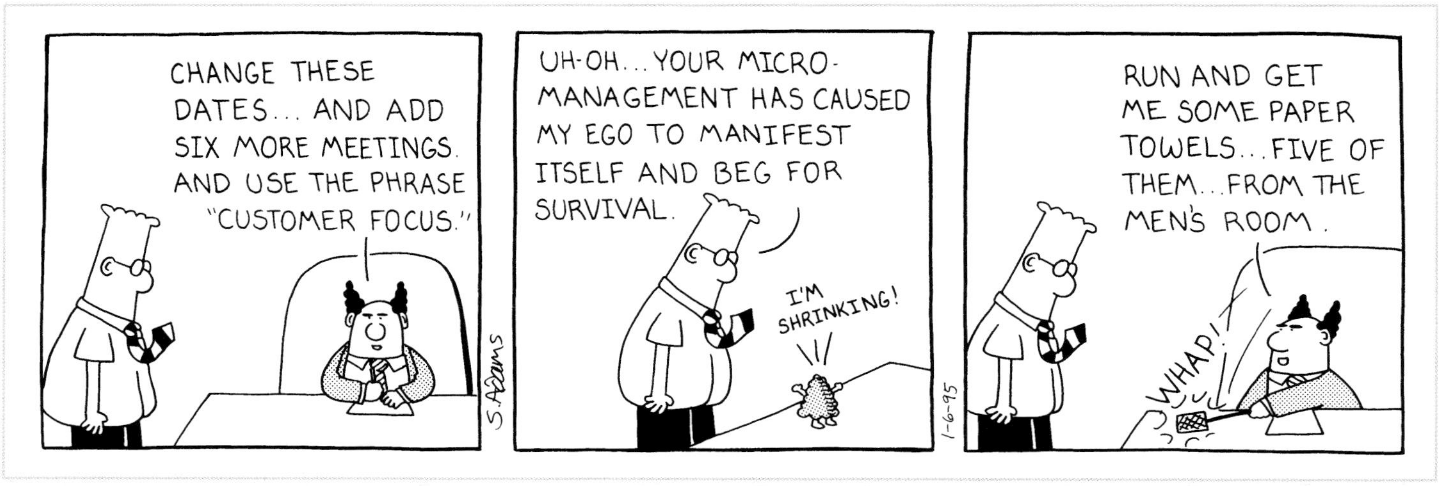
CHANGE THESE DATES... AND ADD SIX MORE MEETINGS. AND USE THE PHRASE "CUSTOMER FOCUS."
S. Adams
UH-OH... YOUR MICRO-MANAGEMENT HAS CAUSED MY EGO TO MANIFEST ITSELF AND BEG FOR SURVIVAL.
I'M SHRINKING!
1-6-95
RUN AND GET ME SOME PAPER TOWELS... FIVE OF THEM... FROM THE MEN'S ROOM.
WHAP!

I experimented with lettering by computer, but I didn't have a working font. It was just cut and paste. That's why the spacing in the lettering below is so bad.

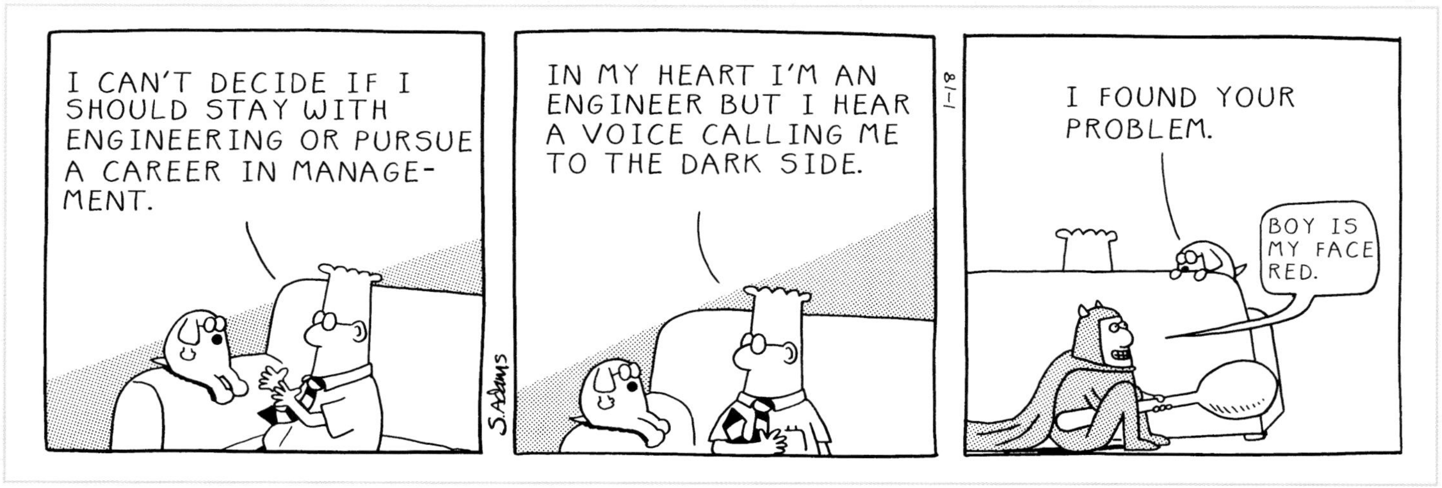
I CAN'T DECIDE IF I SHOULD STAY WITH ENGINEERING OR PURSUE A CAREER IN MANAGE-MENT.
S. Adams
IN MY HEART I'M AN ENGINEER BUT I HEAR A VOICE CALLING ME TO THE DARK SIDE.
1-18
I FOUND YOUR PROBLEM.
BOY IS MY FACE RED.

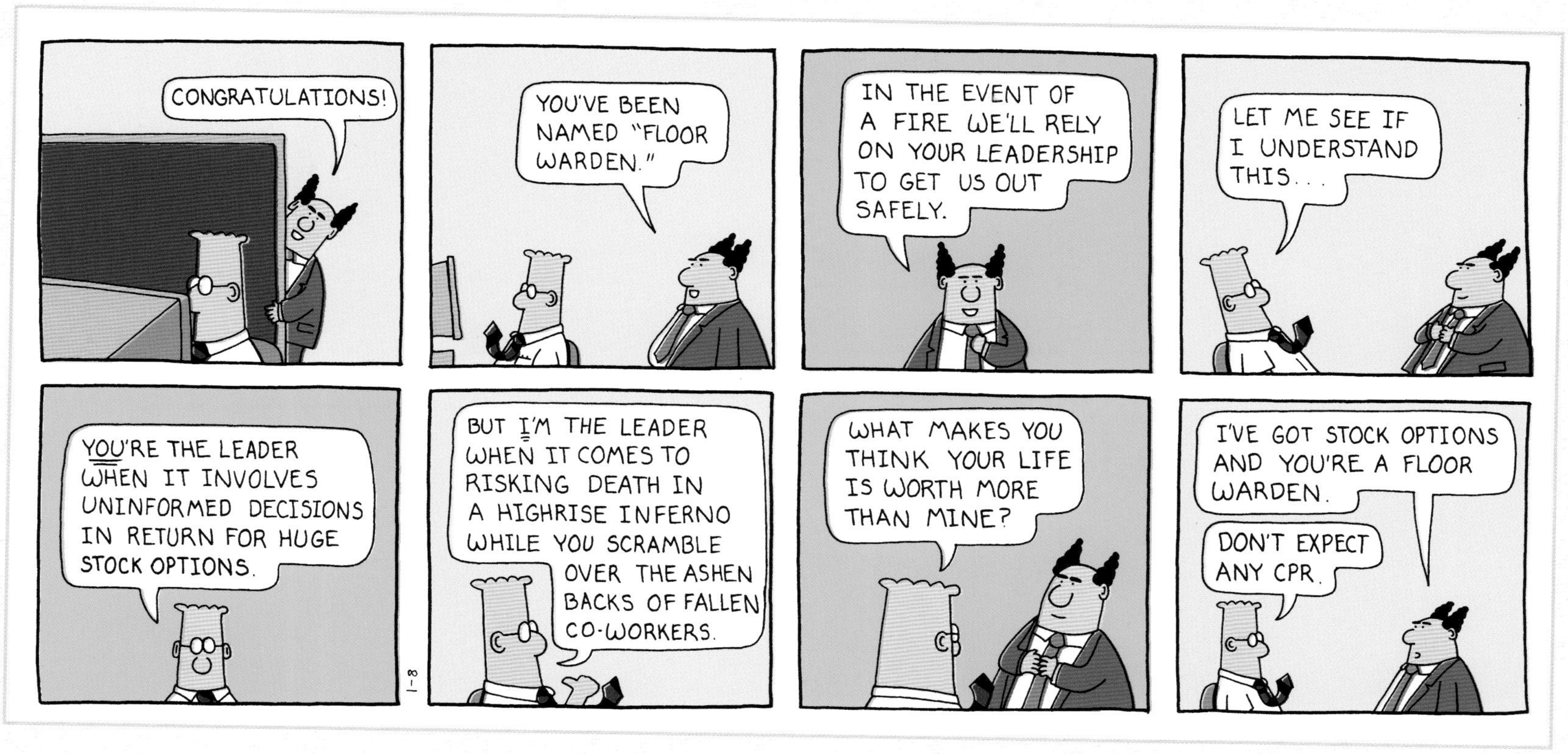
CONGRATULATIONS!
YOU'VE BEEN NAMED "FLOOR WARDEN."
IN THE EVENT OF A FIRE WE'LL RELY ON YOUR LEADERSHIP TO GET US OUT SAFELY.
LET ME SEE IF I UNDERSTAND THIS...
YOU'RE THE LEADER WHEN IT INVOLVES UNINFORMED DECISIONS IN RETURN FOR HUGE STOCK OPTIONS.
BUT I'M THE LEADER WHEN IT COMES TO RISKING DEATH IN A HIGHRISE INFERNO WHILE YOU SCRAMBLE OVER THE ASHEN BACKS OF FALLEN CO-WORKERS.
1-8
WHAT MAKES YOU THINK YOUR LIFE IS WORTH MORE THAN MINE?
I'VE GOT STOCK OPTIONS AND YOU'RE A FLOOR WARDEN.
DON'T EXPECT ANY CPR.

I was once a floor warden. It did not make me feel important.

I was on that team.

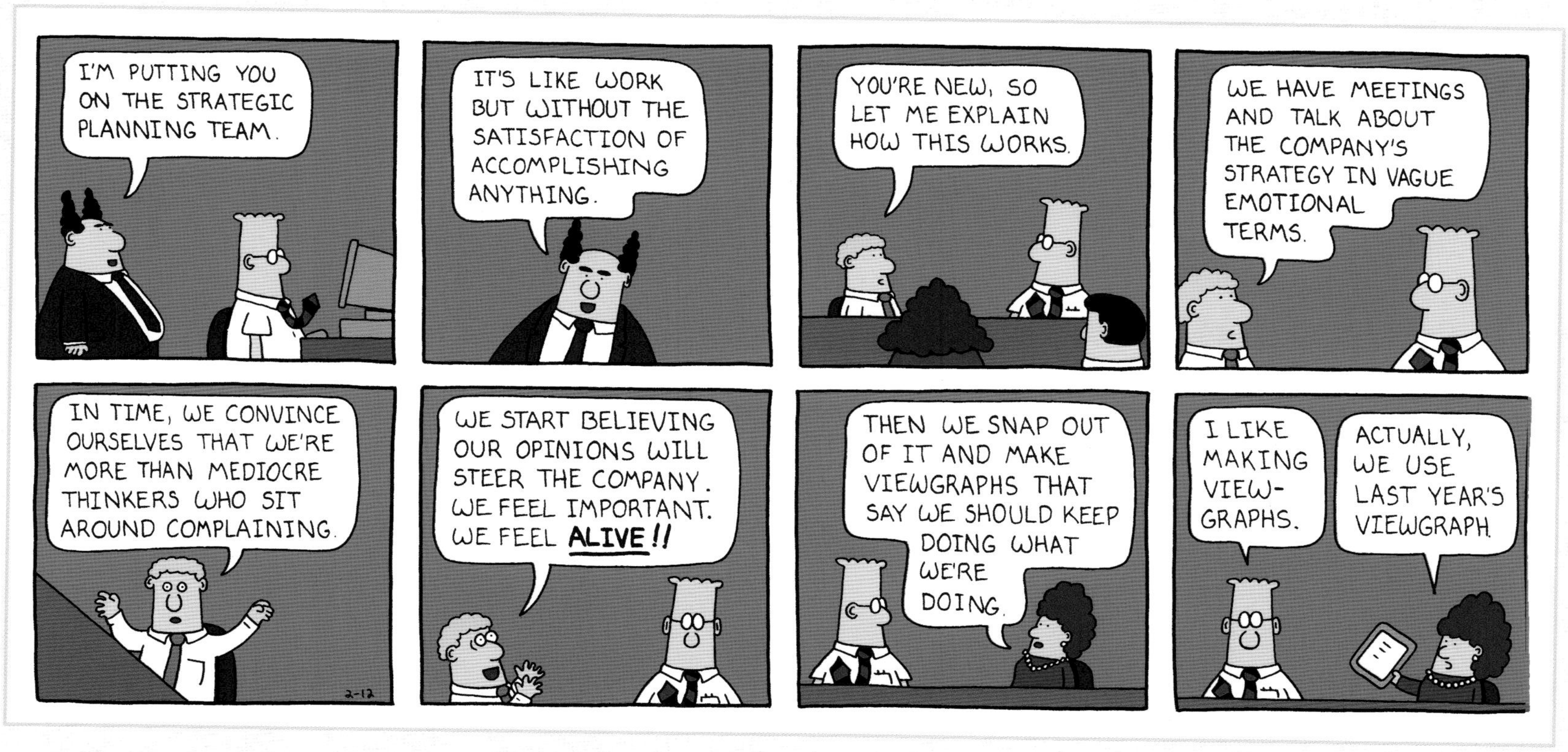
I'M PUTTING YOU ON THE STRATEGIC PLANNING TEAM.
IT'S LIKE WORK BUT WITHOUT THE SATISFACTION OF ACCOMPLISHING ANYTHING.
YOU'RE NEW, SO LET ME EXPLAIN HOW THIS WORKS.
WE HAVE MEETINGS AND TALK ABOUT THE COMPANY'S STRATEGY IN VAGUE EMOTIONAL TERMS.
IN TIME, WE CONVINCE OURSELVES THAT WE'RE MORE THAN MEDIOCRE THINKERS WHO SIT AROUND COMPLAINING.
2-12
WE START BELIEVING OUR OPINIONS WILL STEER THE COMPANY. WE FEEL IMPORTANT. WE FEEL ALIVE!!
THEN WE SNAP OUT OF IT AND MAKE VIEWGRAPHS THAT SAY WE SHOULD KEEP DOING WHAT WE'RE DOING.
I LIKE MAKING VIEW-GRAPHS.
ACTUALLY, WE USE LAST YEAR'S VIEWGRAPH.

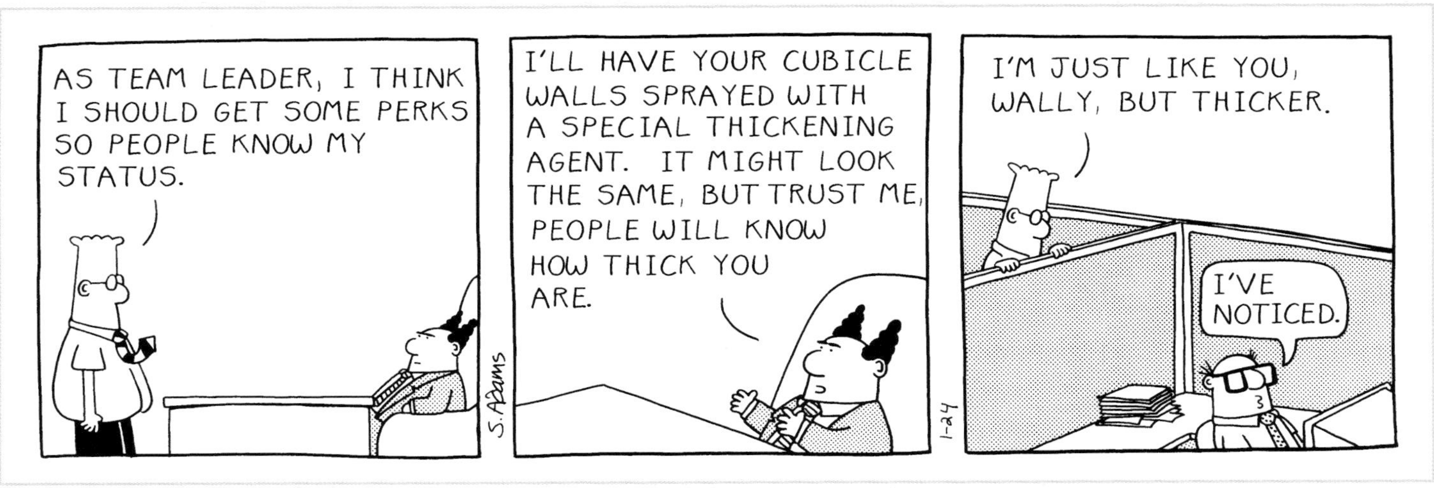
AS TEAM LEADER, I THINK I SHOULD GET SOME PERKS SO PEOPLE KNOW MY STATUS.
I'LL HAVE YOUR CUBICLE WALLS SPRAYED WITH A SPECIAL THICKENING AGENT. IT MIGHT LOOK THE SAME, BUT TRUST ME, PEOPLE WILL KNOW HOW THICK YOU ARE.
S. Adams
I'M JUST LIKE YOU, WALLY, BUT THICKER.
I'VE NOTICED.
1-24

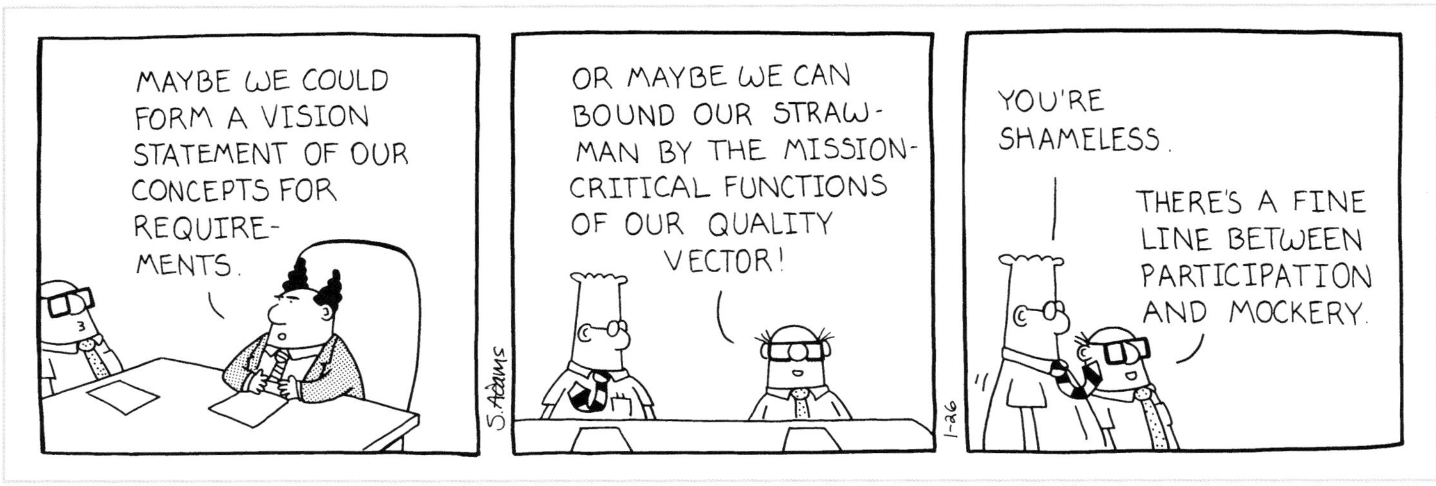
MAYBE WE COULD FORM A VISION STATEMENT OF OUR CONCEPTS FOR REQUIRE-MENTS.
OR MAYBE WE CAN BOUND OUR STRAW-MAN BY THE MISSION-CRITICAL FUNCTIONS OF OUR QUALITY VECTOR!
S. Adams
YOU'RE SHAMELESS.
THERE'S A FINE LINE BETWEEN PARTICIPATION AND MOCKERY.
1-26

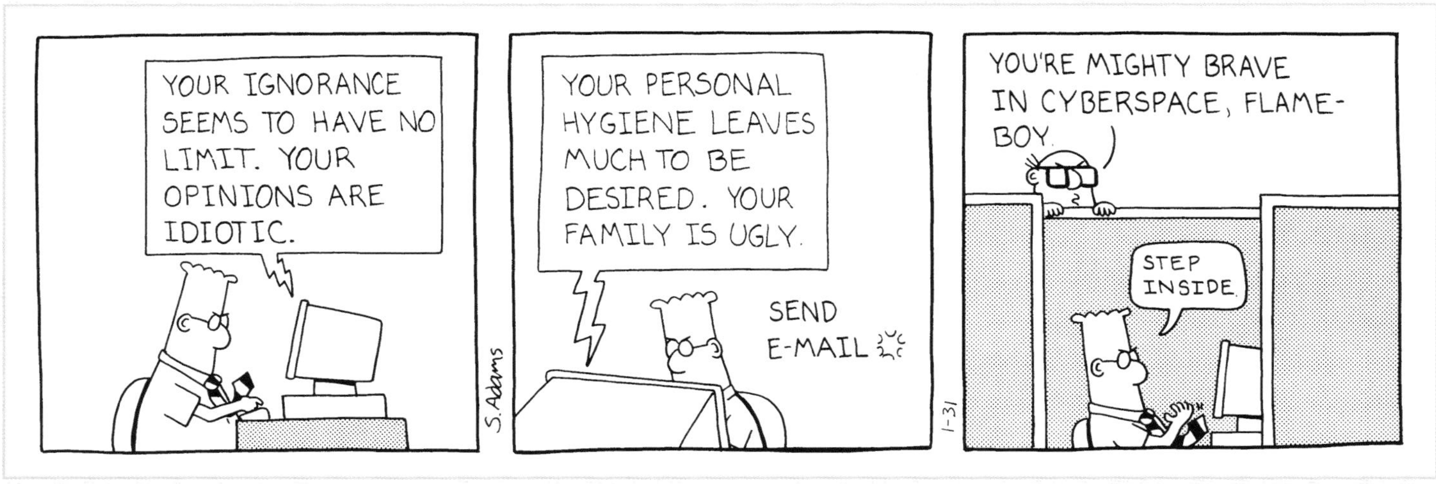
YOUR IGNORANCE SEEMS TO HAVE NO LIMIT. YOUR OPINIONS ARE IDIOTIC.
YOUR PERSONAL HYGIENE LEAVES MUCH TO BE DESIRED. YOUR FAMILY IS UGLY.
SEND E-MAIL
S. Adams
YOU'RE MIGHTY BRAVE IN CYBERSPACE, FLAME-BOY.
STEP INSIDE.
1-31

When the strip above was published, it wasn't common to send e-mail to people within whispering distance. Now it seems normal.

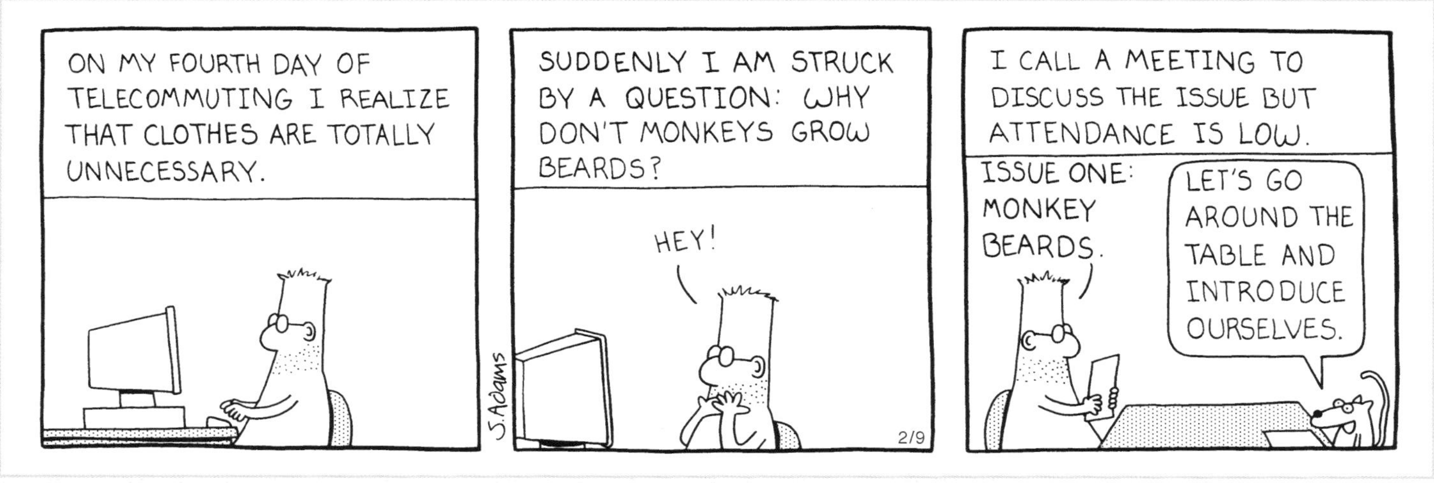
ON MY FOURTH DAY OF TELECOMMUTING I REALIZE THAT CLOTHES ARE TOTALLY UNNECESSARY.
SUDDENLY I AM STRUCK BY A QUESTION: WHY DON'T MONKEYS GROW BEARDS?
HEY!
S. Adams
2/9
I CALL A MEETING TO DISCUSS THE ISSUE BUT ATTENDANCE IS LOW.
ISSUE ONE: MONKEY BEARDS.
LET'S GO AROUND THE TABLE AND INTRODUCE OURSELVES.

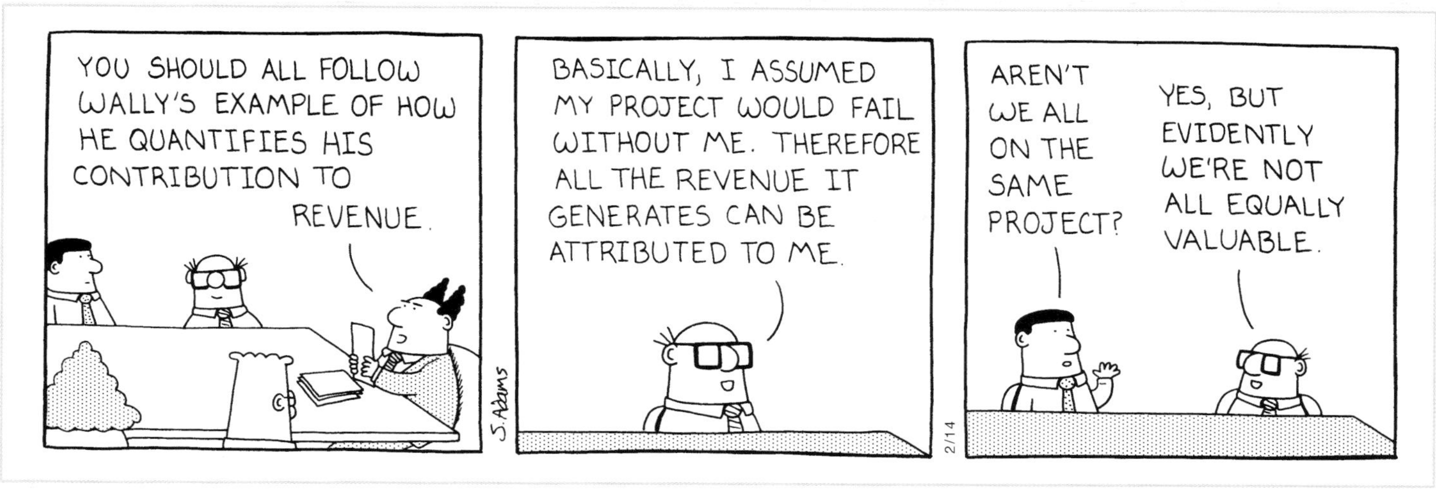
YOU SHOULD ALL FOLLOW WALLY'S EXAMPLE OF HOW HE QUANTIFIES HIS CONTRIBUTION TO REVENUE.
BASICALLY, I ASSUMED MY PROJECT WOULD FAIL WITHOUT ME. THEREFORE ALL THE REVENUE IT GENERATES CAN BE ATTRIBUTED TO ME.
AREN'T WE ALL ON THE SAME PROJECT?
YES, BUT EVIDENTLY WE'RE NOT ALL EQUALLY VALUABLE.
S. Adams
2/14

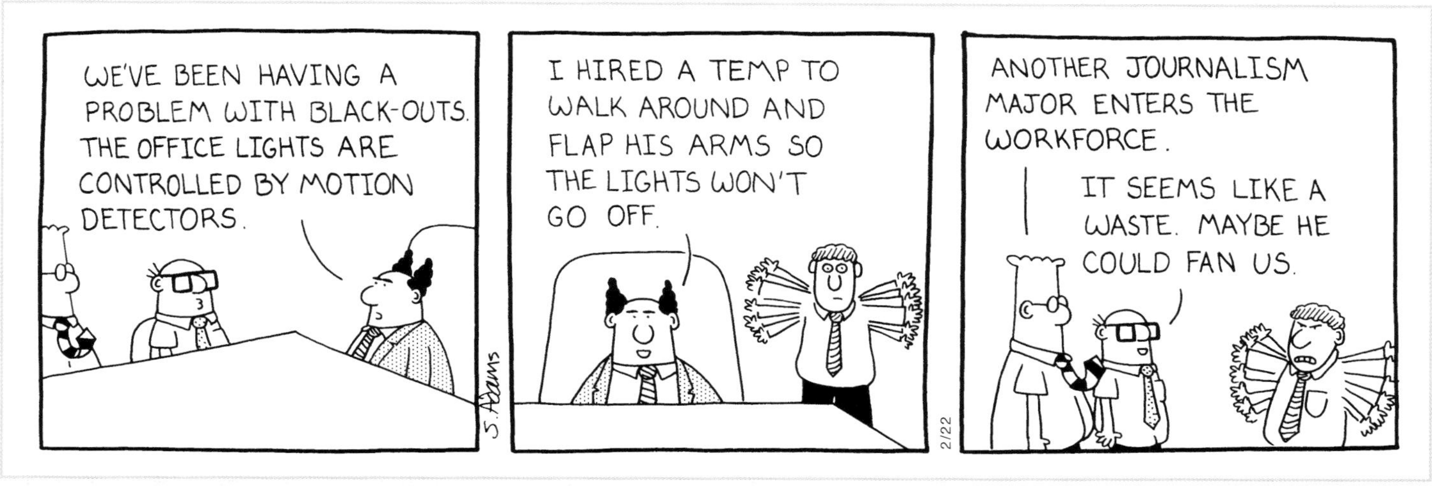
WE'VE BEEN HAVING A PROBLEM WITH BLACK-OUTS. THE OFFICE LIGHTS ARE CONTROLLED BY MOTION DETECTORS.
I HIRED A TEMP TO WALK AROUND AND FLAP HIS ARMS SO THE LIGHTS WON'T GO OFF.
ANOTHER JOURNALISM MAJOR ENTERS THE WORKFORCE.
IT SEEMS LIKE A WASTE. MAYBE HE COULD FAN US.
S. Adams
2/22

I don't know how many people playfully sent copies of this comic to journalism majors, but it was a lot.

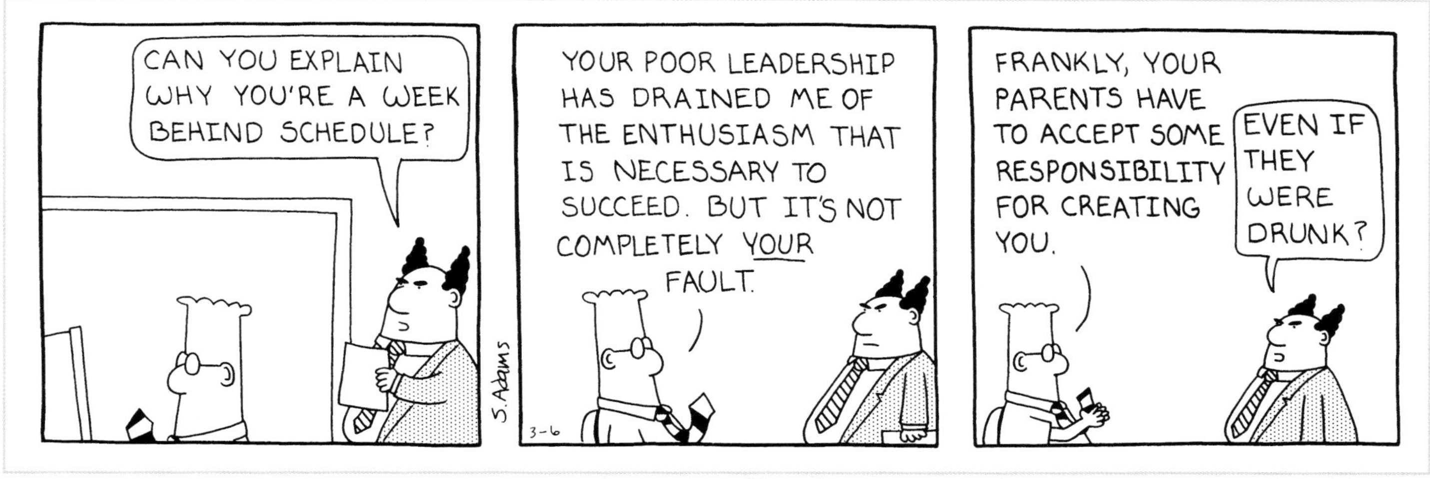
CAN YOU EXPLAIN WHY YOU'RE A WEEK BEHIND SCHEDULE?
YOUR POOR LEADERSHIP HAS DRAINED ME OF THE ENTHUSIASM THAT IS NECESSARY TO SUCCEED. BUT IT'S NOT COMPLETELY YOUR FAULT.
FRANKLY, YOUR PARENTS HAVE TO ACCEPT SOME RESPONSIBILITY FOR CREATING YOU.
EVEN IF THEY WERE DRUNK?
S. Adams
3-6

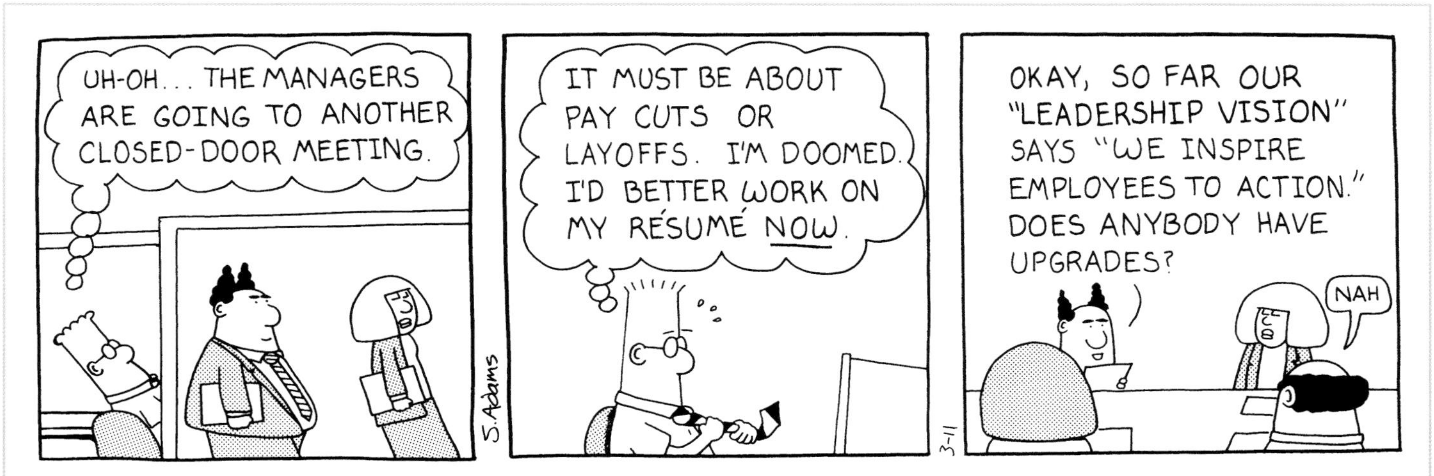
UH-OH... THE MANAGERS ARE GOING TO ANOTHER CLOSED-DOOR MEETING.
IT MUST BE ABOUT PAY CUTS OR LAYOFFS. I'M DOOMED. I'D BETTER WORK ON MY RÉSUMÉ NOW.
OKAY, SO FAR OUR "LEADERSHIP VISION" SAYS "WE INSPIRE EMPLOYEES TO ACTION." DOES ANYBODY HAVE UPGRADES?
NAH
S. Adams
3-11

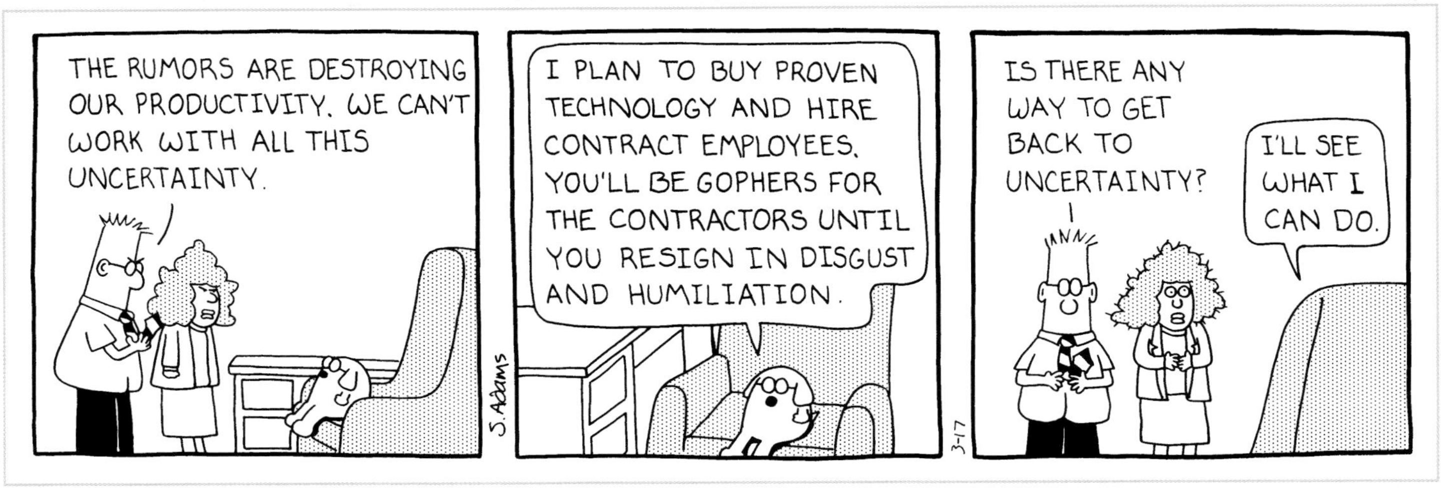
THE RUMORS ARE DESTROYING OUR PRODUCTIVITY. WE CAN'T WORK WITH ALL THIS UNCERTAINTY.
I PLAN TO BUY PROVEN TECHNOLOGY AND HIRE CONTRACT EMPLOYEES. YOU'LL BE GOPHERS FOR THE CONTRACTORS UNTIL YOU RESIGN IN DISGUST AND HUMILIATION.
IS THERE ANY WAY TO GET BACK TO UNCERTAINTY?
I'LL SEE WHAT I CAN DO.

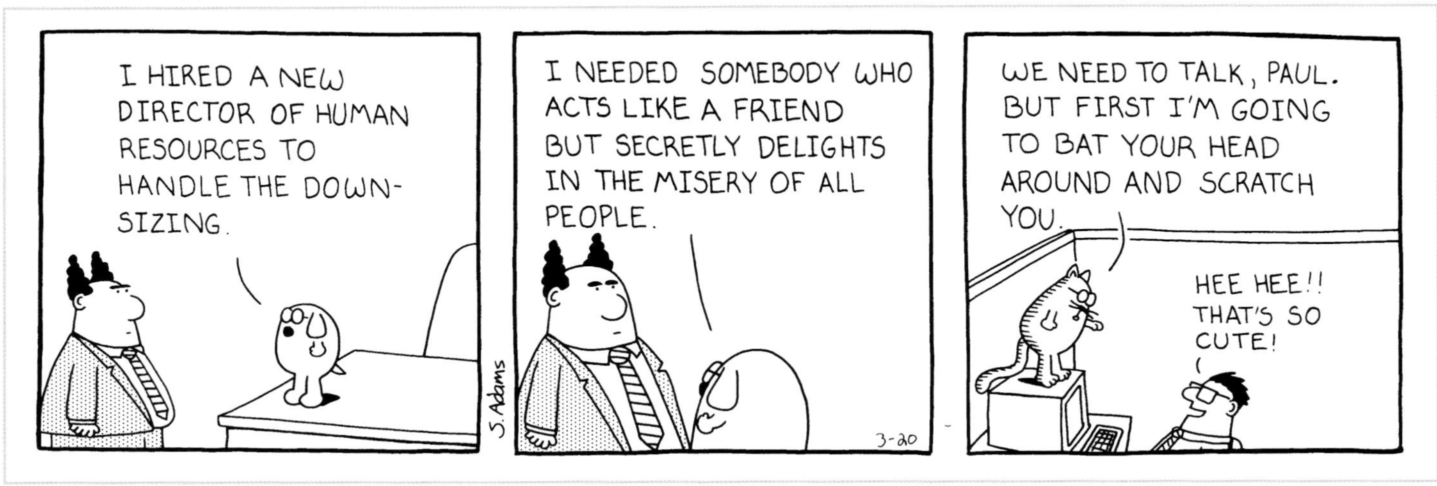
I HIRED A NEW DIRECTOR OF HUMAN RESOURCES TO HANDLE THE DOWN-SIZING.
I NEEDED SOMEBODY WHO ACTS LIKE A FRIEND BUT SECRETLY DELIGHTS IN THE MISERY OF ALL PEOPLE.
WE NEED TO TALK, PAUL. BUT FIRST I'M GOING TO BAT YOUR HEAD AROUND AND SCRATCH YOU.
HEE HEE!! THAT'S SO CUTE!

Here's where Catbert became a regular character, with a natural role in the office. He also got glasses.

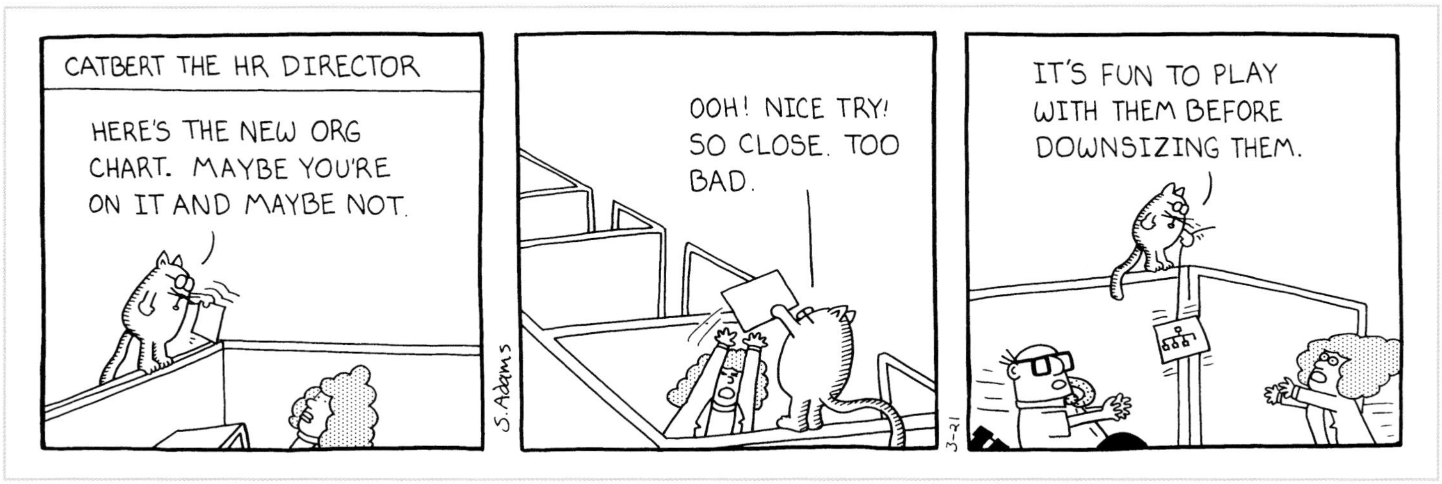
CATBERT THE HR DIRECTOR
HERE'S THE NEW ORG CHART. MAYBE YOU'RE ON IT AND MAYBE NOT.
OOH! NICE TRY! SO CLOSE. TOO BAD.
IT'S FUN TO PLAY WITH THEM BEFORE DOWNSIZING THEM.

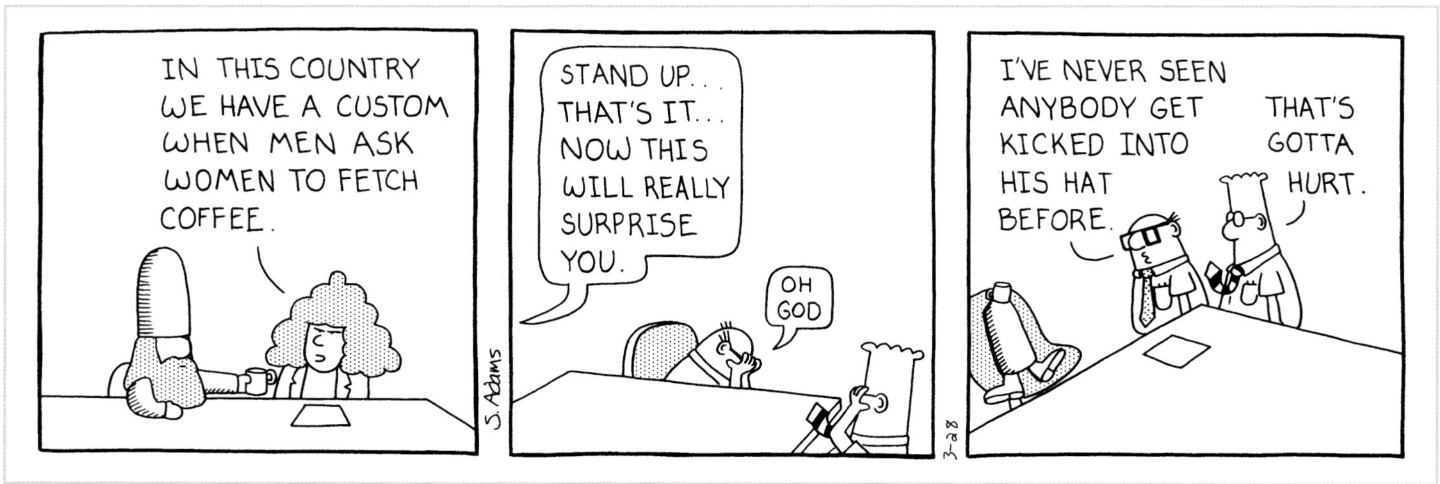
IN THIS COUNTRY WE HAVE A CUSTOM WHEN MEN ASK WOMEN TO FETCH COFFEE.
STAND UP... THAT'S IT... NOW THIS WILL REALLY SURPRISE YOU.
OH GOD
I'VE NEVER SEEN ANYBODY GET KICKED INTO HIS HAT BEFORE.
THAT'S GOTTA HURT.

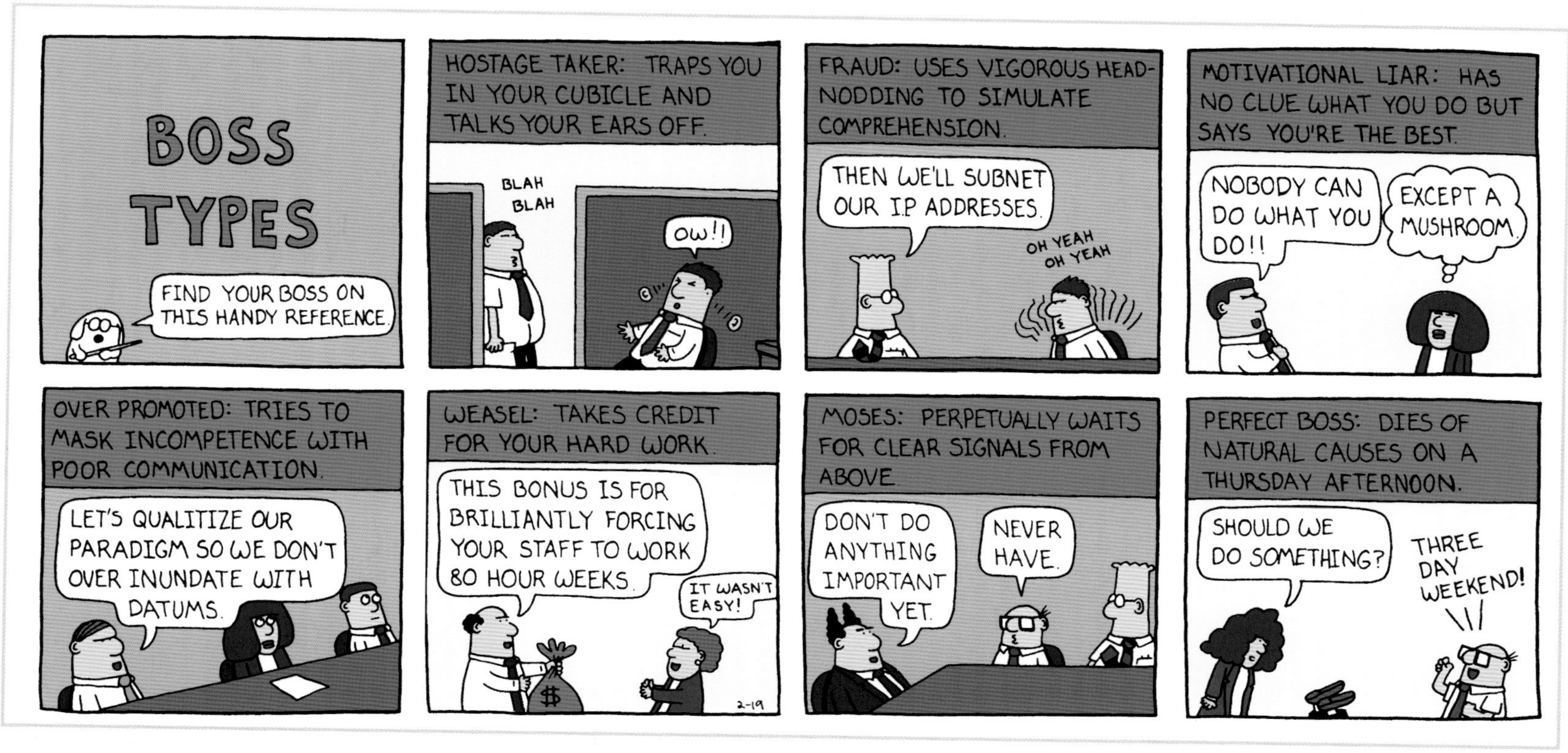
BOSS TYPES
FIND YOUR BOSS ON THIS HANDY REFERENCE.
HOSTAGE TAKER: TRAPS YOU IN YOUR CUBICLE AND TALKS YOUR EARS OFF.
BLAH BLAH
OW!!
FRAUD: USES VIGOROUS HEAD-NODDING TO SIMULATE COMPREHENSION.
THEN WE'LL SUBNET OUR I.P. ADDRESSES.
OH YEAH OH YEAH
MOTIVATIONAL LIAR: HAS NO CLUE WHAT YOU DO BUT SAYS YOU'RE THE BEST.
NOBODY CAN DO WHAT YOU DO!!
EXCEPT A MUSHROOM.
OVER PROMOTED: TRIES TO MASK INCOMPETENCE WITH POOR COMMUNICATION.
LET'S QUALITIZE OUR PARADIGM SO WE DON'T OVER INUNDATE WITH DATUMS.
WEASEL: TAKES CREDIT FOR YOUR HARD WORK.
THIS BONUS IS FOR BRILLIANTLY FORCING YOUR STAFF TO WORK 80 HOUR WEEKS.
IT WASN'T EASY!
2-19
MOSES: PERPETUALLY WAITS FOR CLEAR SIGNALS FROM ABOVE.
DON'T DO ANYTHING IMPORTANT YET.
NEVER HAVE.
PERFECT BOSS: DIES OF NATURAL CAUSES ON A THURSDAY AFTERNOON.
SHOULD WE DO SOMETHING?
THREE DAY WEEKEND!

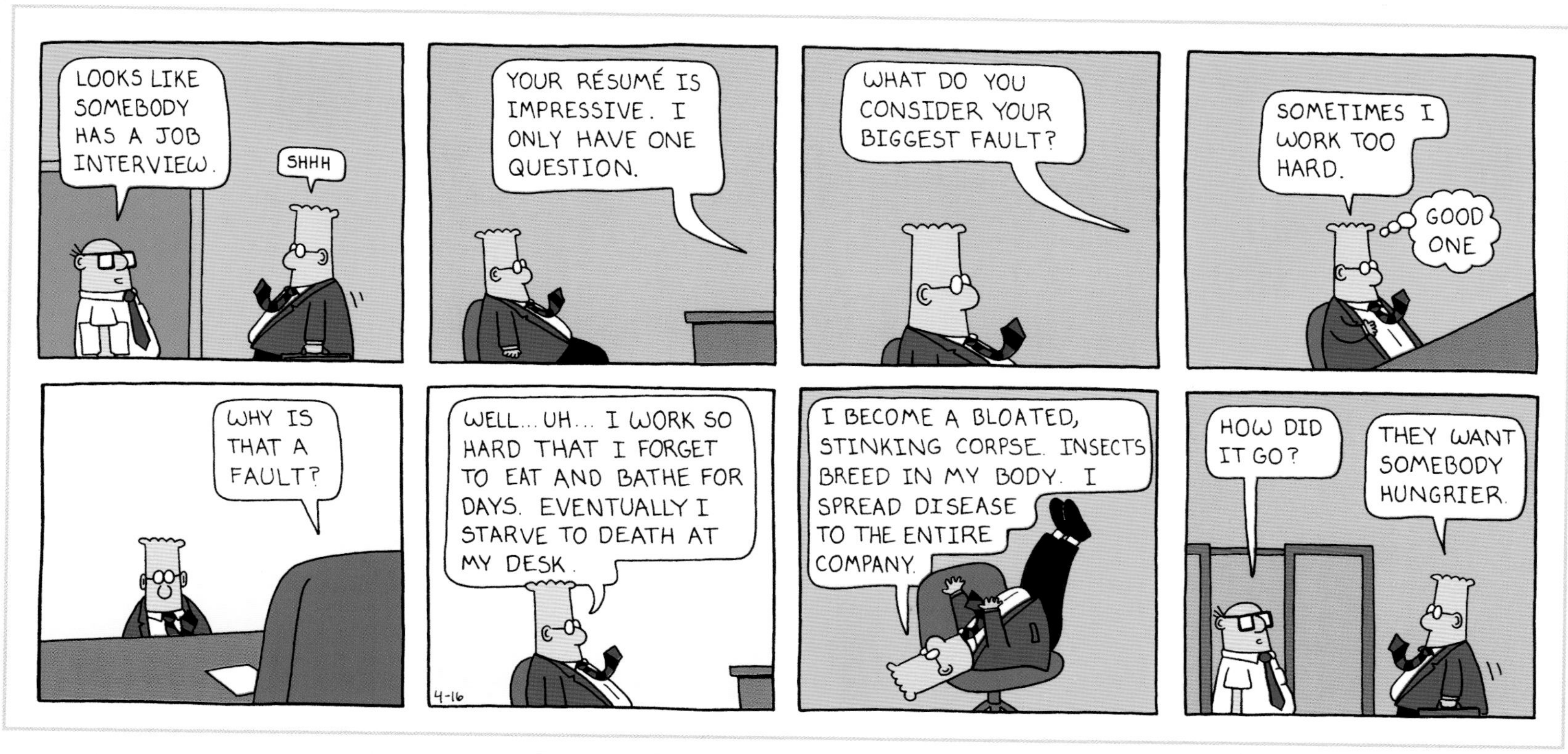
LOOKS LIKE SOMEBODY HAS A JOB INTERVIEW.
SHHH
YOUR RÉSUMÉ IS IMPRESSIVE. I ONLY HAVE ONE QUESTION.
WHAT DO YOU CONSIDER YOUR BIGGEST FAULT?
SOMETIMES I WORK TOO HARD.
GOOD ONE
WHY IS THAT A FAULT?
WELL... UH... I WORK SO HARD THAT I FORGET TO EAT AND BATHE FOR DAYS. EVENTUALLY I STARVE TO DEATH AT MY DESK.
4-16
I BECOME A BLOATED, STINKING CORPSE. INSECTS BREED IN MY BODY. I SPREAD DISEASE TO THE ENTIRE COMPANY.
HOW DID IT GO?
THEY WANT SOMEBODY HUNGRIER.

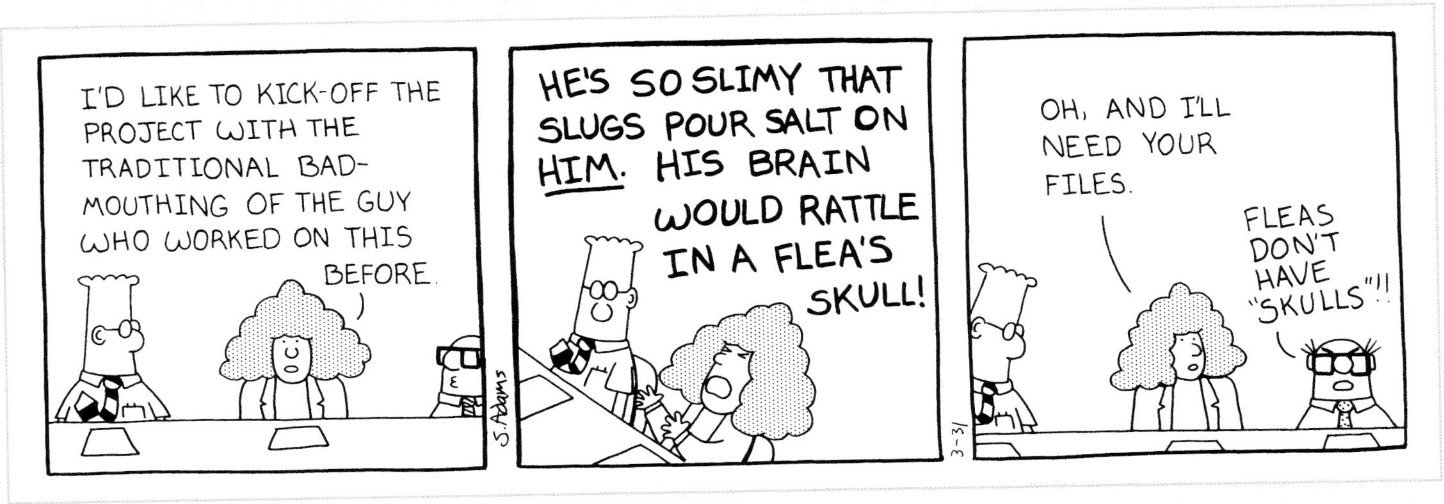
I'D LIKE TO KICK-OFF THE PROJECT WITH THE TRADITIONAL BAD-MOUTHING OF THE GUY WHO WORKED ON THIS BEFORE.
S. Adams
HE'S SO SLIMY THAT SLUGS POUR SALT ON HIM. HIS BRAIN WOULD RATTLE IN A FLEA'S SKULL!
3-31
OH, AND I'LL NEED YOUR FILES.
FLEAS DON'T HAVE "SKULLS"!!

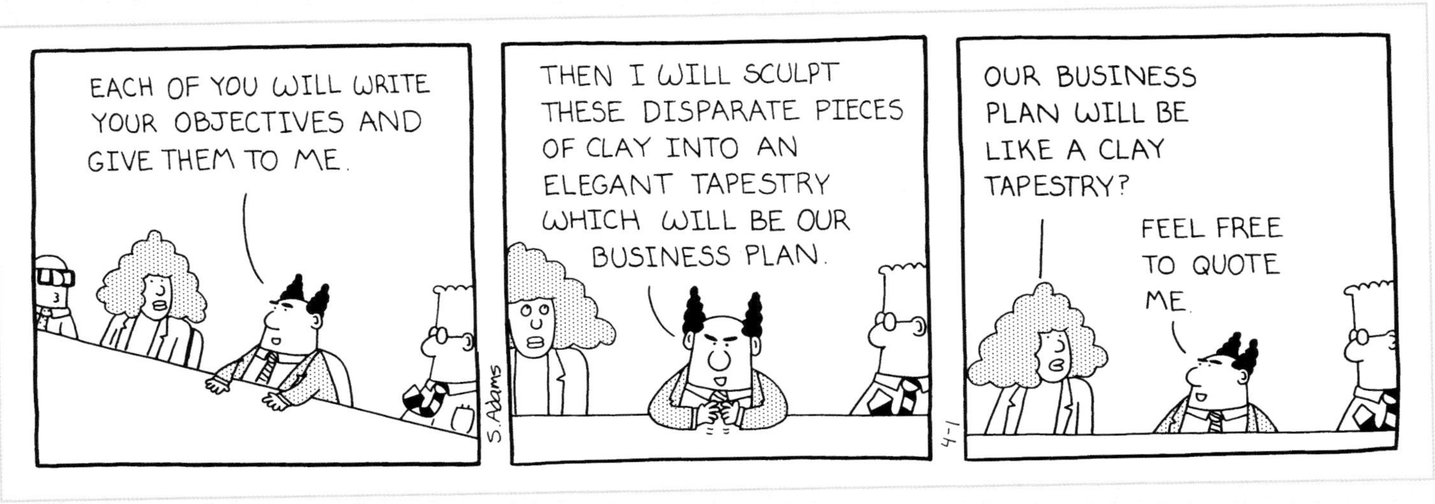
EACH OF YOU WILL WRITE YOUR OBJECTIVES AND GIVE THEM TO ME.
S. Adams
THEN I WILL SCULPT THESE DISPARATE PIECES OF CLAY INTO AN ELEGANT TAPESTRY WHICH WILL BE OUR BUSINESS PLAN.
4-1
OUR BUSINESS PLAN WILL BE LIKE A CLAY TAPESTRY?
FEEL FREE TO QUOTE ME.

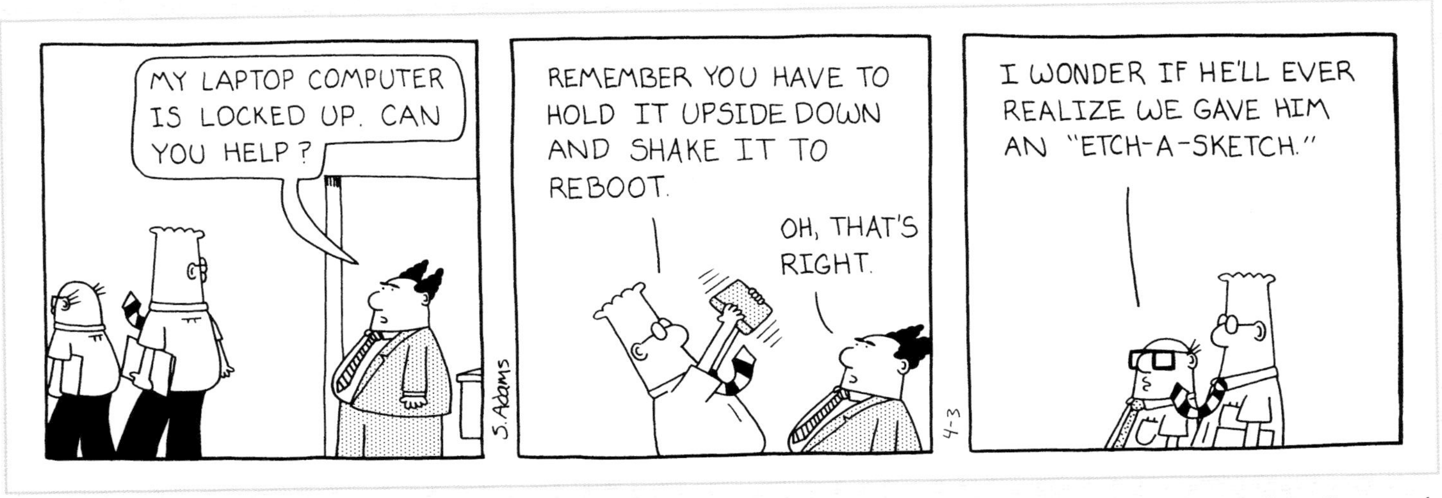
MY LAPTOP COMPUTER IS LOCKED UP. CAN YOU HELP?
S. Adams
REMEMBER YOU HAVE TO HOLD IT UPSIDE DOWN AND SHAKE IT TO REBOOT.
OH, THAT'S RIGHT.
4-3
I WONDER IF HE'LL EVER REALIZE WE GAVE HIM AN "ETCH-A-SKETCH."

The strip above is the all-time most popular Dilbert *comic. When I wrote it, I thought it was weak. Readers disagreed. It went on to appear on coffee mugs, mouse pads, and T-shirts. And it's probably the most reprinted* Dilbert *strip.*

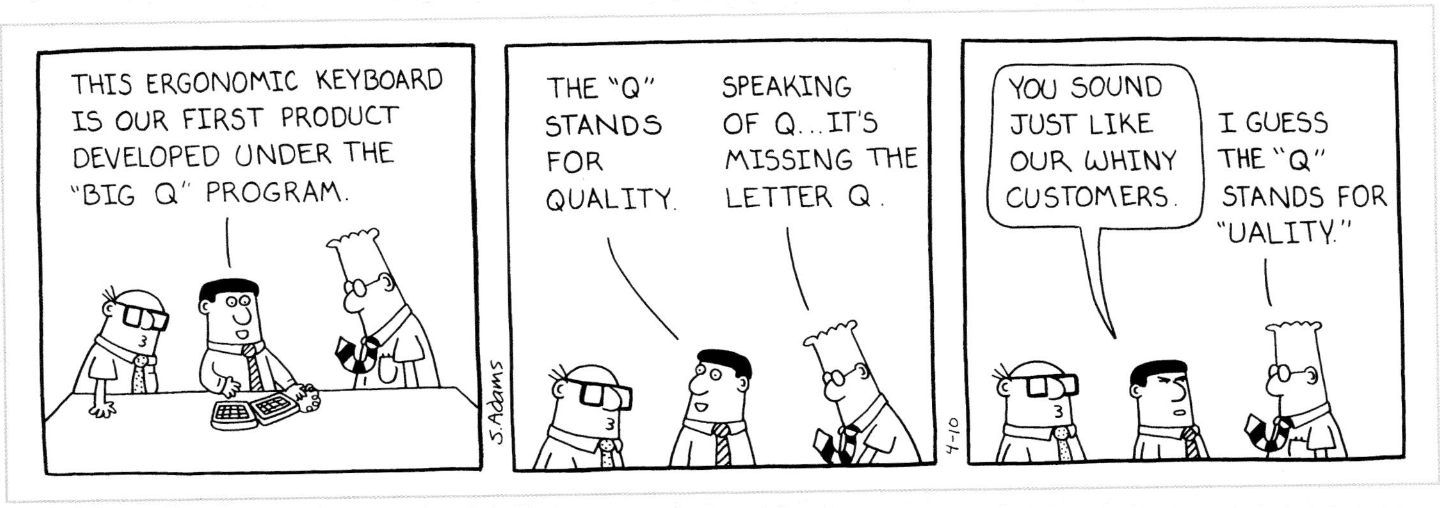
THIS ERGONOMIC KEYBOARD IS OUR FIRST PRODUCT DEVELOPED UNDER THE "BIG Q" PROGRAM.
S. Adams
THE "Q" STANDS FOR QUALITY.
SPEAKING OF Q... IT'S MISSING THE LETTER Q.
4-10
YOU SOUND JUST LIKE OUR WHINY CUSTOMERS.
I GUESS THE "Q" STANDS FOR "UALITY."

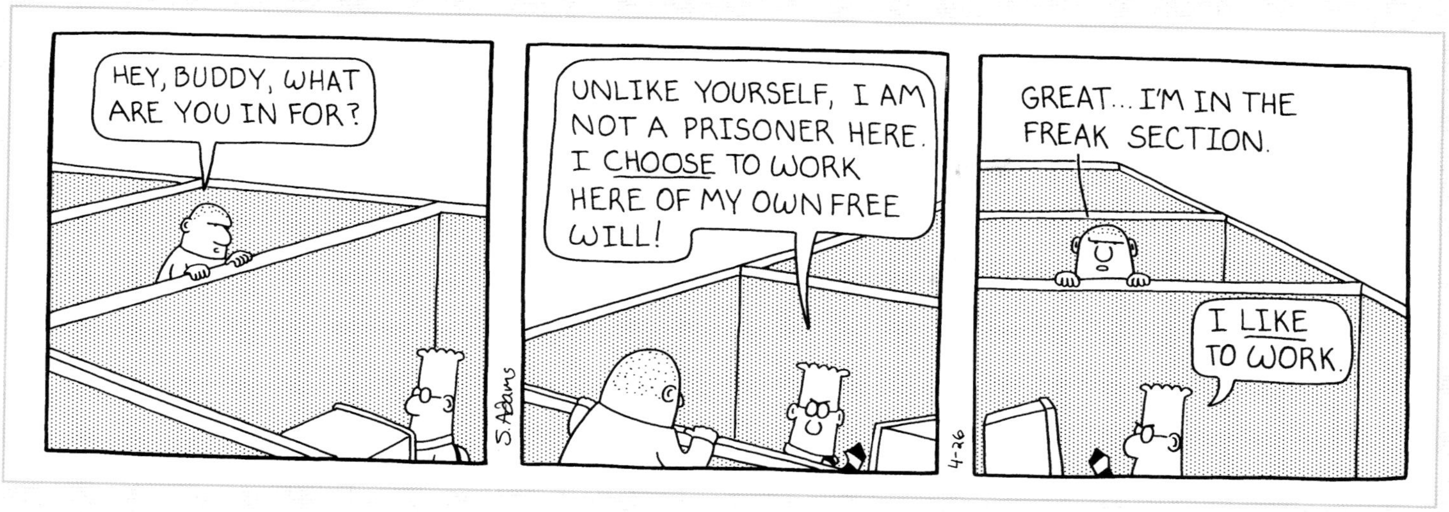
HEY, BUDDY, WHAT ARE YOU IN FOR?
S. Adams
UNLIKE YOURSELF, I AM NOT A PRISONER HERE. I CHOOSE TO WORK HERE OF MY OWN FREE WILL!
4-26
GREAT... I'M IN THE FREAK SECTION.
I LIKE TO WORK.

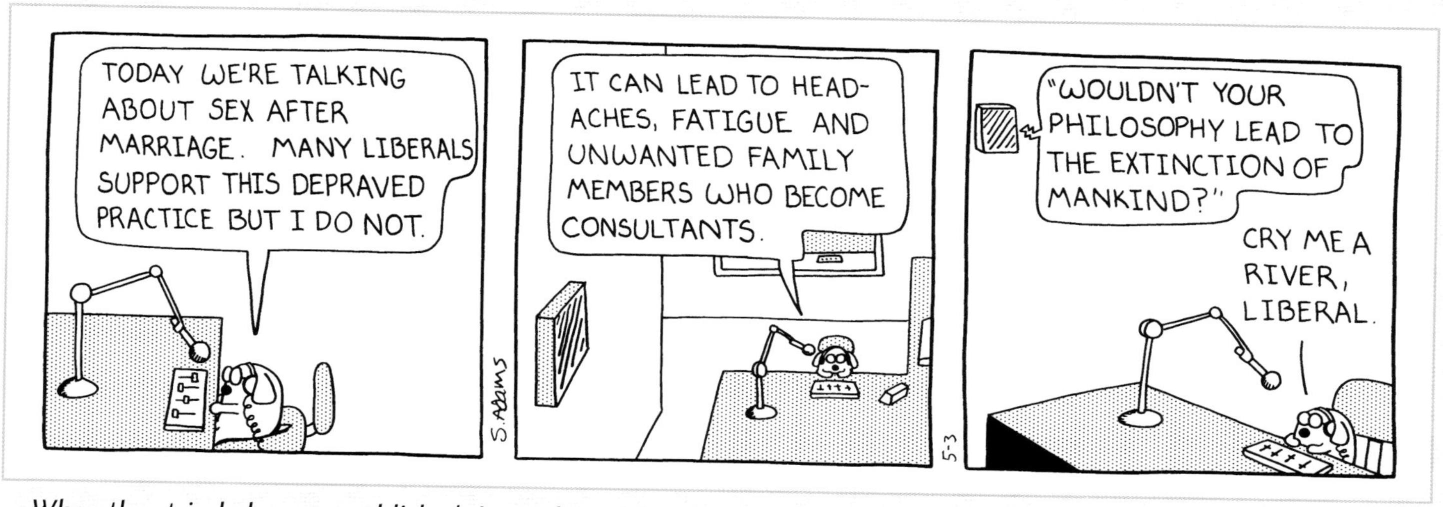
TODAY WE'RE TALKING ABOUT SEX AFTER MARRIAGE. MANY LIBERALS SUPPORT THIS DEPRAVED PRACTICE BUT I DO NOT.
S. Adams
IT CAN LEAD TO HEADACHES, FATIGUE AND UNWANTED FAMILY MEMBERS WHO BECOME CONSULTANTS.
5-3
"WOULDN'T YOUR PHILOSOPHY LEAD TO THE EXTINCTION OF MANKIND?"
CRY ME A RIVER, LIBERAL.

When the strip below was published, I was doing book signings of my own. I was amazed when people asked me to write entire paragraphs in their books, or draw them their own comic strip with them as characters, while a hundred people stood in line behind them wishing they would die.

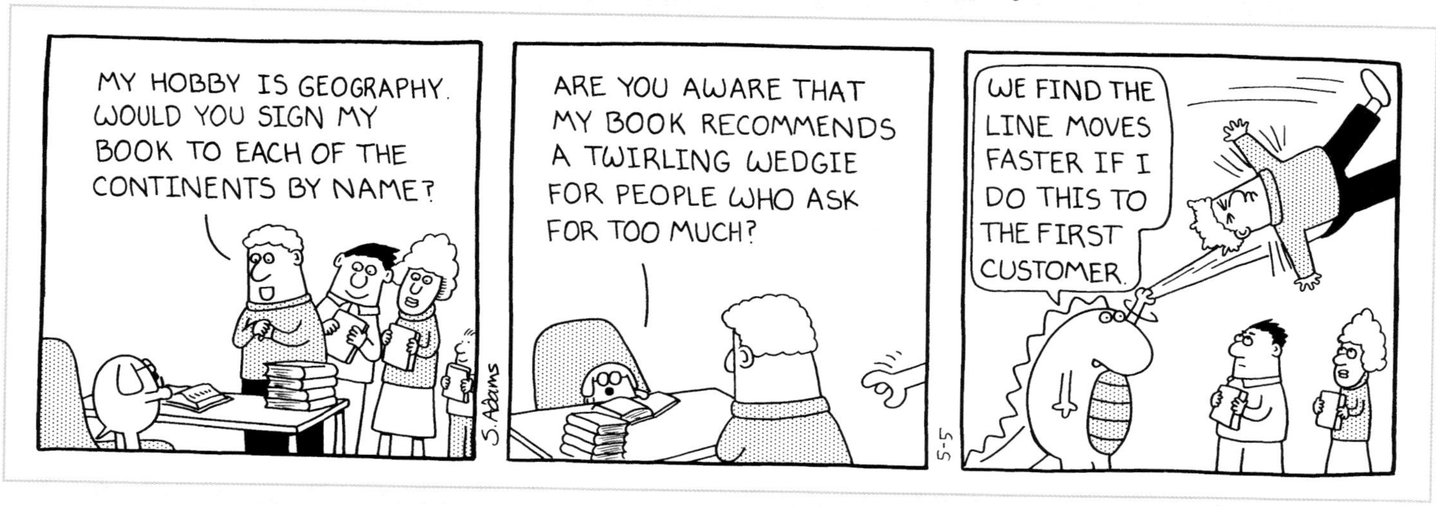
MY HOBBY IS GEOGRAPHY. WOULD YOU SIGN MY BOOK TO EACH OF THE CONTINENTS BY NAME?
S. Adams
ARE YOU AWARE THAT MY BOOK RECOMMENDS A TWIRLING WEDGIE FOR PEOPLE WHO ASK FOR TOO MUCH?
5-5
WE FIND THE LINE MOVES FASTER IF I DO THIS TO THE FIRST CUSTOMER.

This comic is only funny because his name is Gustav.

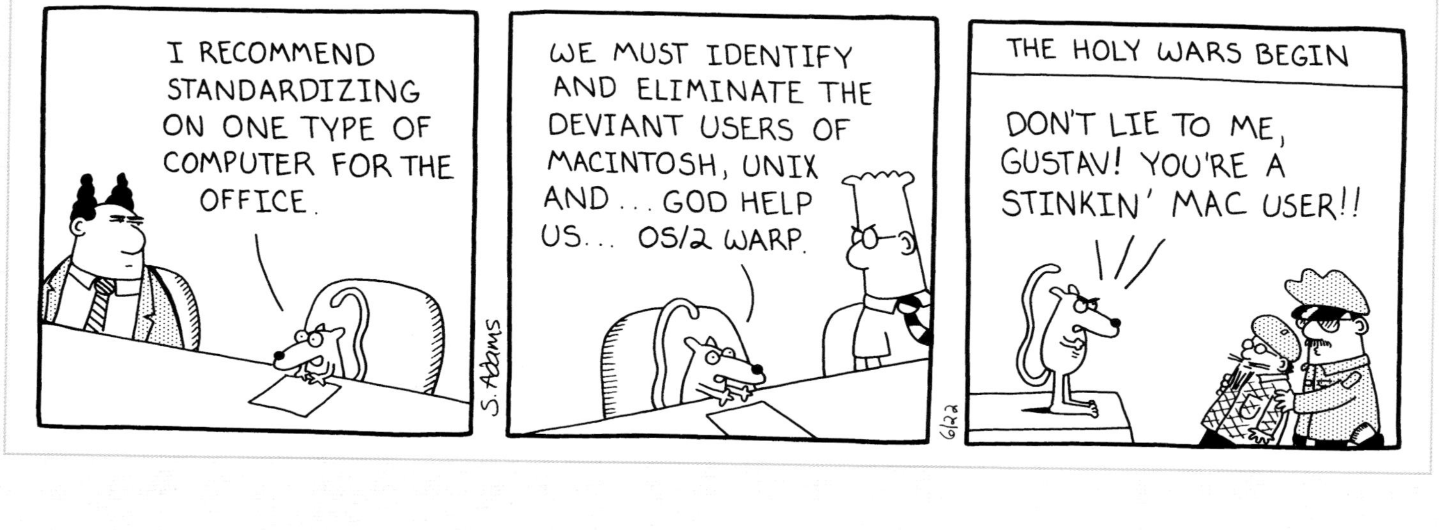
I RECOMMEND STANDARDIZING ON ONE TYPE OF COMPUTER FOR THE OFFICE.
S. Adams
WE MUST IDENTIFY AND ELIMINATE THE DEVIANT USERS OF MACINTOSH, UNIX AND... GOD HELP US... OS/2 WARP.
6/22
THE HOLY WARS BEGIN
DON'T LIE TO ME, GUSTAV! YOU'RE A STINKIN' MAC USER!!

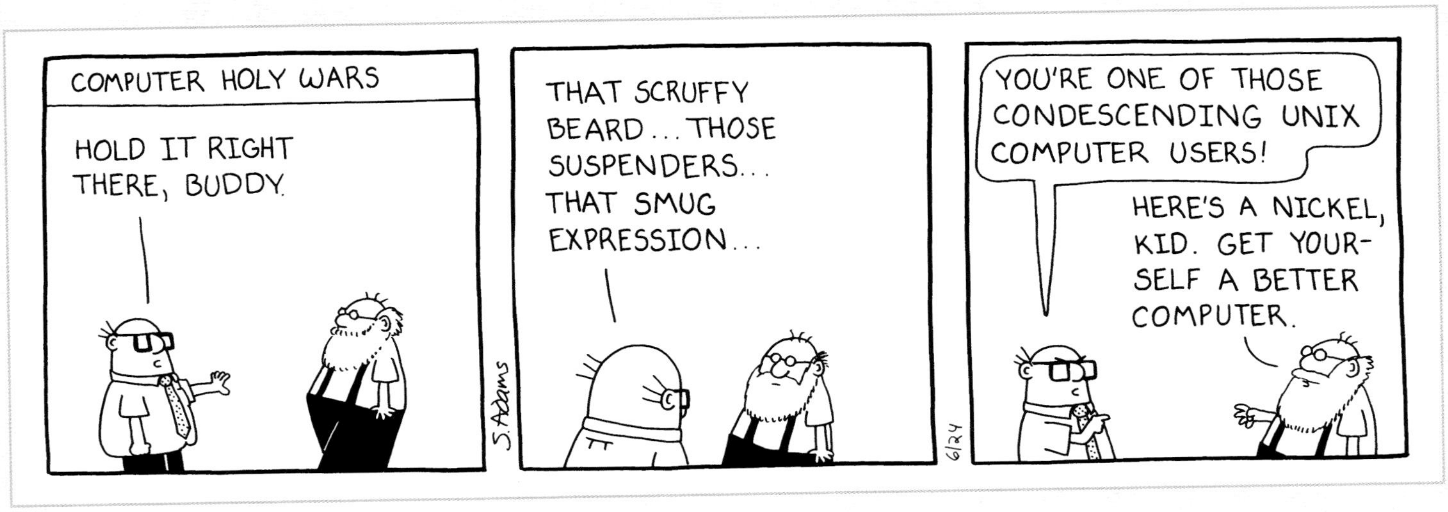
COMPUTER HOLY WARS
HOLD IT RIGHT THERE, BUDDY.
THAT SCRUFFY BEARD... THOSE SUSPENDERS... THAT SMUG EXPRESSION...
S. Adams
6/24
YOU'RE ONE OF THOSE CONDESCENDING UNIX COMPUTER USERS!
HERE'S A NICKEL, KID. GET YOURSELF A BETTER COMPUTER.

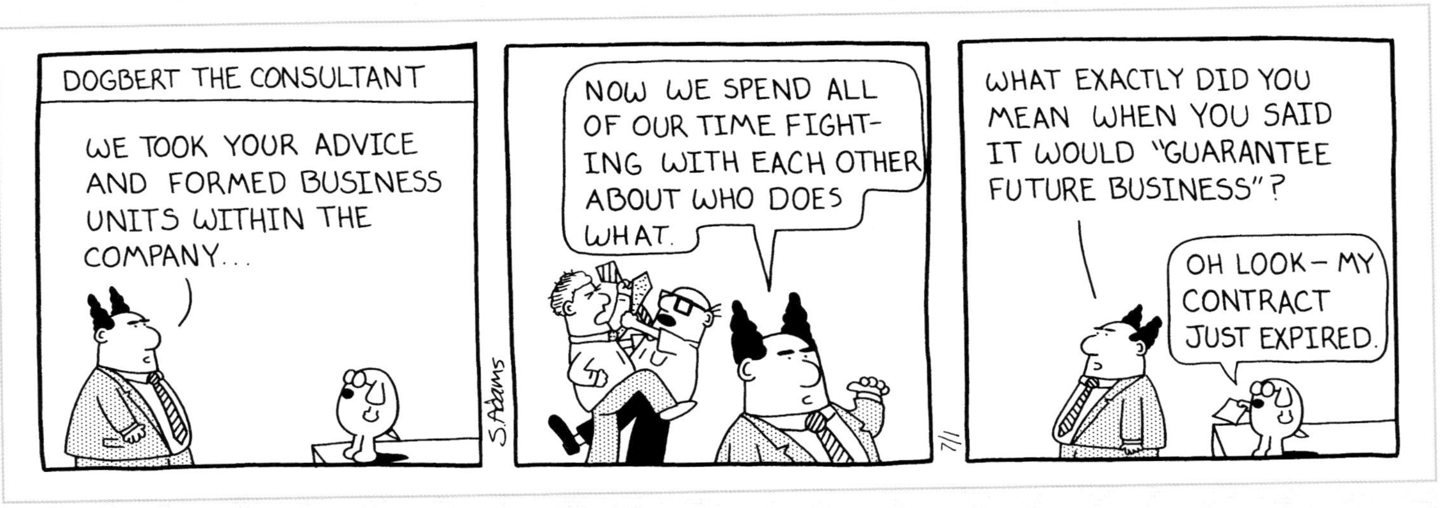
DOGBERT THE CONSULTANT
WE TOOK YOUR ADVICE AND FORMED BUSINESS UNITS WITHIN THE COMPANY...
NOW WE SPEND ALL OF OUR TIME FIGHTING WITH EACH OTHER ABOUT WHO DOES WHAT.
S. Adams
7/1
WHAT EXACTLY DID YOU MEAN WHEN YOU SAID IT WOULD "GUARANTEE FUTURE BUSINESS"?
OH LOOK– MY CONTRACT JUST EXPIRED.

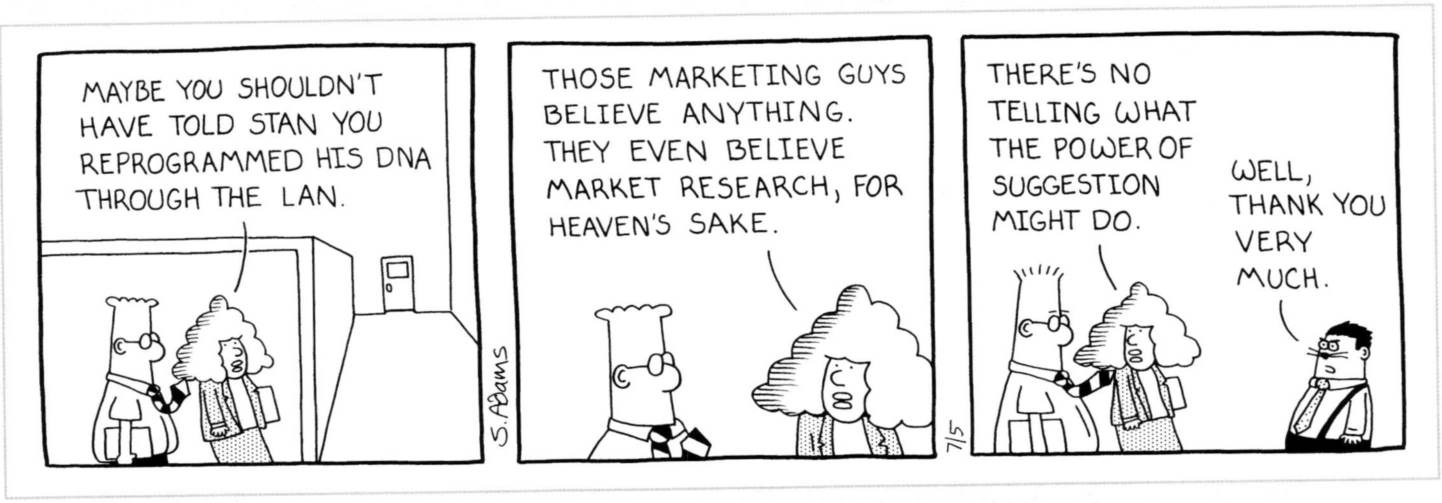
MAYBE YOU SHOULDN'T HAVE TOLD STAN YOU REPROGRAMMED HIS DNA THROUGH THE LAN.
THOSE MARKETING GUYS BELIEVE ANYTHING. THEY EVEN BELIEVE MARKET RESEARCH, FOR HEAVEN'S SAKE.
S. Adams
7/5
THERE'S NO TELLING WHAT THE POWER OF SUGGESTION MIGHT DO.
WELL, THANK YOU VERY MUCH.

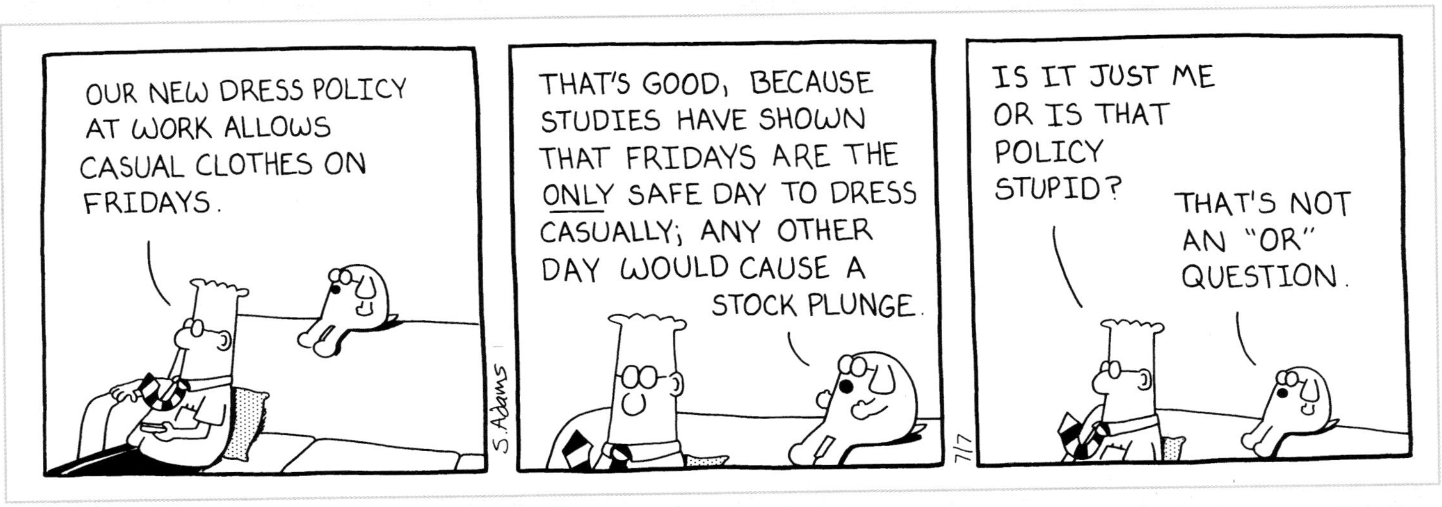
OUR NEW DRESS POLICY AT WORK ALLOWS CASUAL CLOTHES ON FRIDAYS.
THAT'S GOOD, BECAUSE STUDIES HAVE SHOWN THAT FRIDAYS ARE THE ONLY SAFE DAY TO DRESS CASUALLY; ANY OTHER DAY WOULD CAUSE A STOCK PLUNGE.
S. Adams
7/7
IS IT JUST ME OR IS THAT POLICY STUPID?
THAT'S NOT AN "OR" QUESTION.

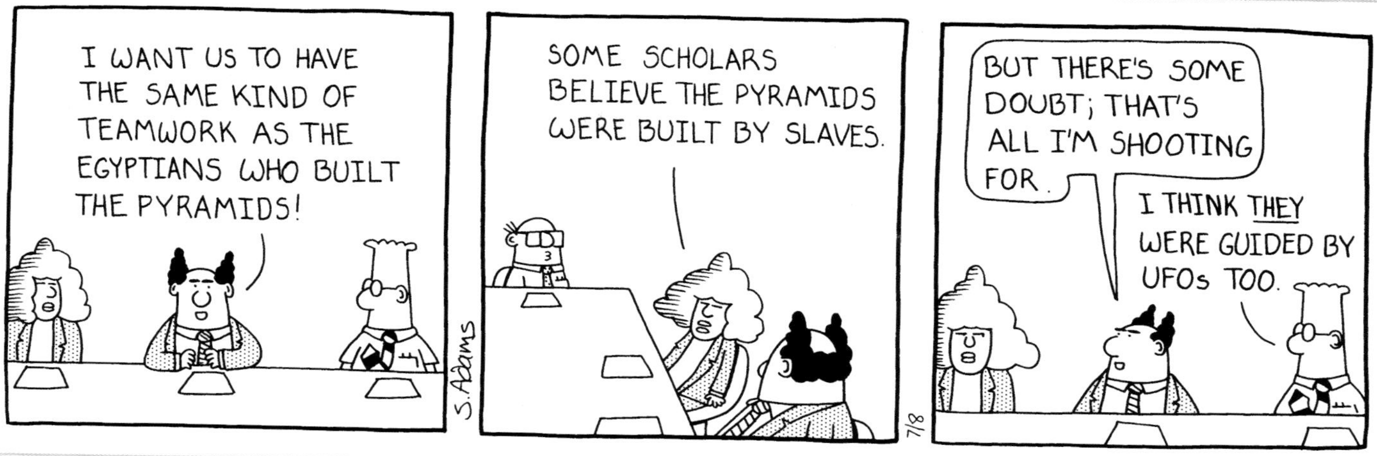
I WANT US TO HAVE THE SAME KIND OF TEAMWORK AS THE EGYPTIANS WHO BUILT THE PYRAMIDS!
S. Adams
SOME SCHOLARS BELIEVE THE PYRAMIDS WERE BUILT BY SLAVES.
7/8
BUT THERE'S SOME DOUBT; THAT'S ALL I'M SHOOTING FOR.
I THINK THEY WERE GUIDED BY UFOs TOO.

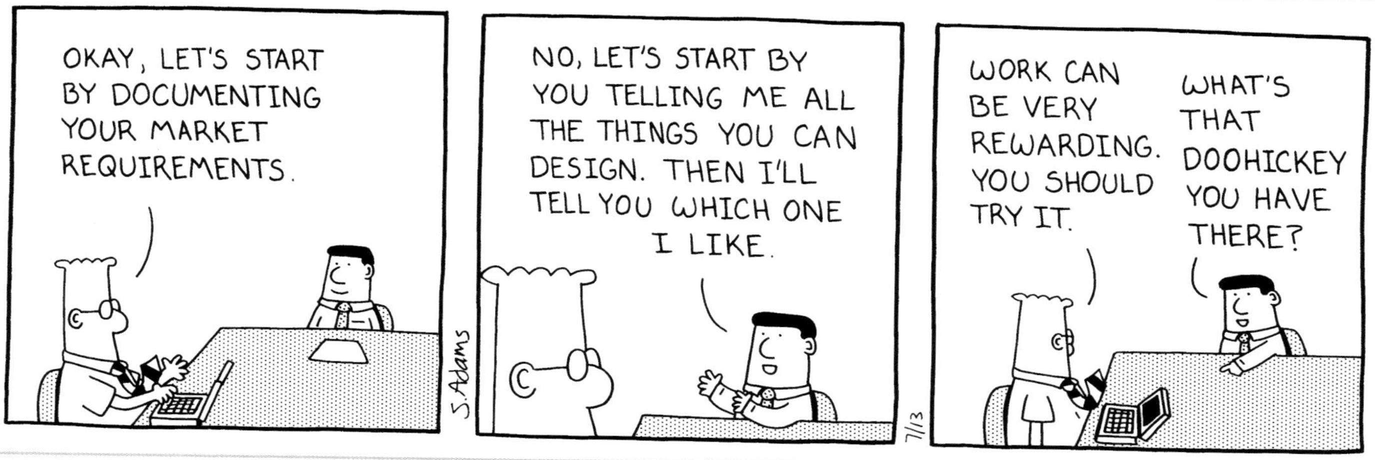
OKAY, LET'S START BY DOCUMENTING YOUR MARKET REQUIREMENTS.
S. Adams
NO, LET'S START BY YOU TELLING ME ALL THE THINGS YOU CAN DESIGN. THEN I'LL TELL YOU WHICH ONE I LIKE.
7/13
WORK CAN BE VERY REWARDING. YOU SHOULD TRY IT.
WHAT'S THAT DOOHICKEY YOU HAVE THERE?

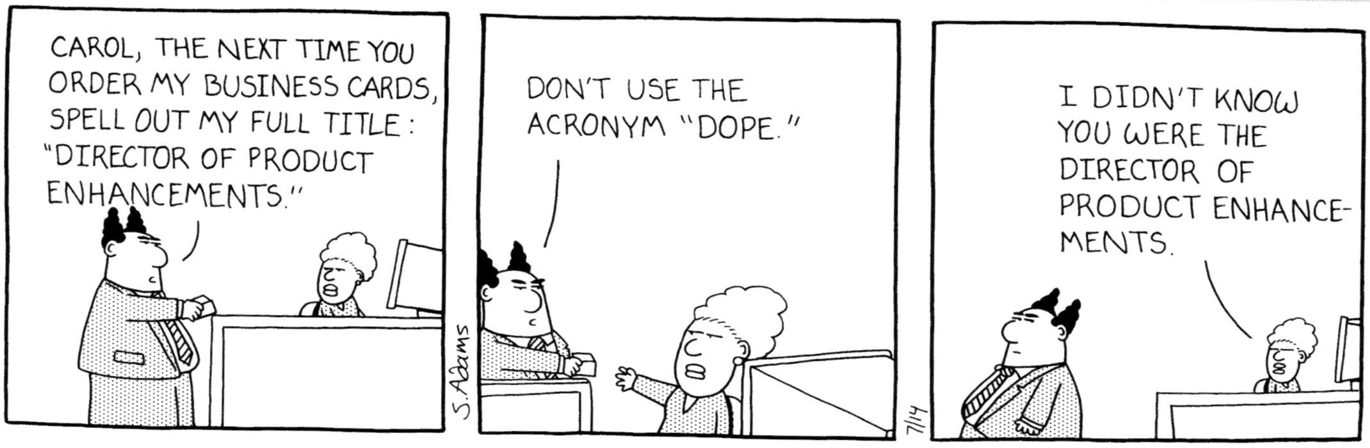
CAROL, THE NEXT TIME YOU ORDER MY BUSINESS CARDS, SPELL OUT MY FULL TITLE: "DIRECTOR OF PRODUCT ENHANCEMENTS."
S. Adams
DON'T USE THE ACRONYM "DOPE."
7/14
I DIDN'T KNOW YOU WERE THE DIRECTOR OF PRODUCT ENHANCE-MENTS.

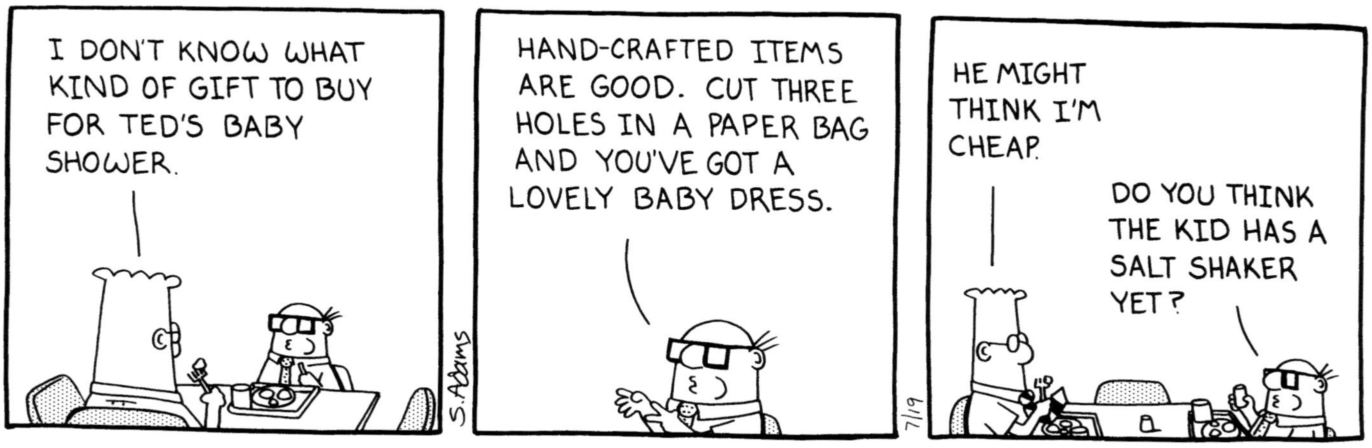
I DON'T KNOW WHAT KIND OF GIFT TO BUY FOR TED'S BABY SHOWER.
S. Adams
HAND-CRAFTED ITEMS ARE GOOD. CUT THREE HOLES IN A PAPER BAG AND YOU'VE GOT A LOVELY BABY DRESS.
7/19
HE MIGHT THINK I'M CHEAP.
DO YOU THINK THE KID HAS A SALT SHAKER YET?

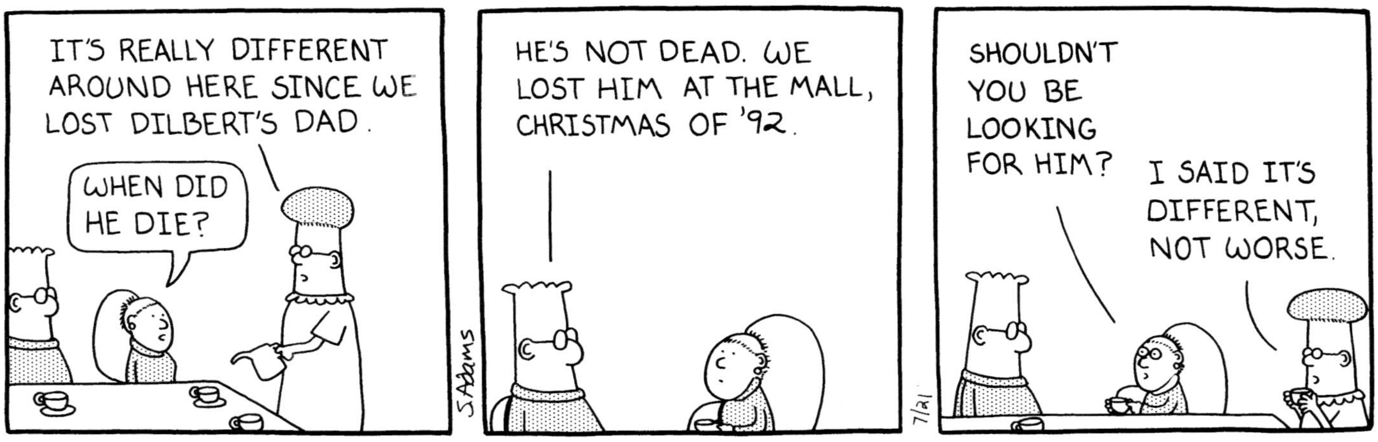
IT'S REALLY DIFFERENT AROUND HERE SINCE WE LOST DILBERT'S DAD.
WHEN DID HE DIE?
HE'S NOT DEAD. WE LOST HIM AT THE MALL, CHRISTMAS OF '92.
SHOULDN'T YOU BE LOOKING FOR HIM?
I SAID IT'S DIFFERENT, NOT WORSE.
S. Adams
7/21

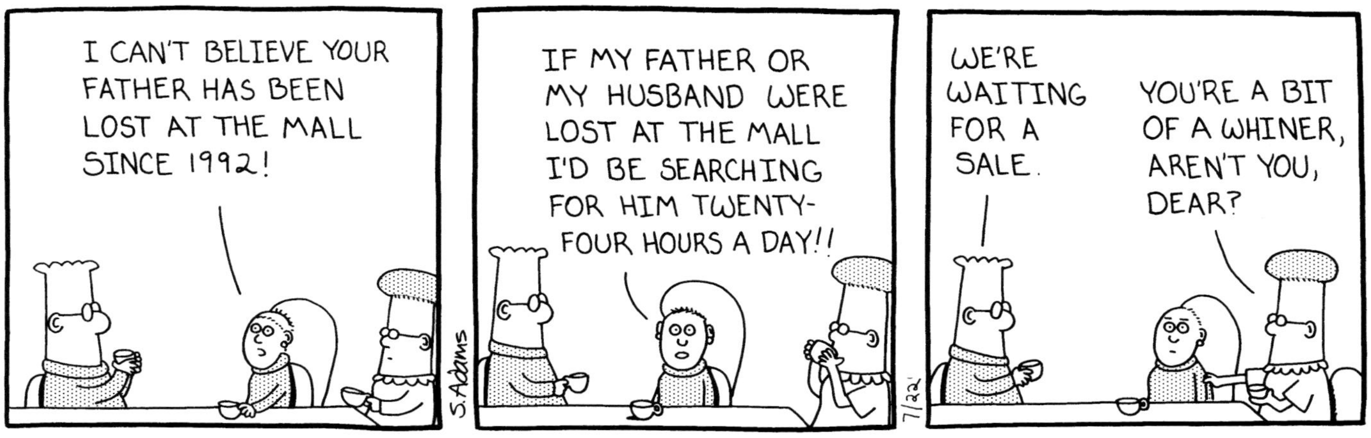
I CAN'T BELIEVE YOUR FATHER HAS BEEN LOST AT THE MALL SINCE 1992!
IF MY FATHER OR MY HUSBAND WERE LOST AT THE MALL I'D BE SEARCHING FOR HIM TWENTY-FOUR HOURS A DAY!!
WE'RE WAITING FOR A SALE.
YOU'RE A BIT OF A WHINER, AREN'T YOU, DEAR?
S. Adams
7/22

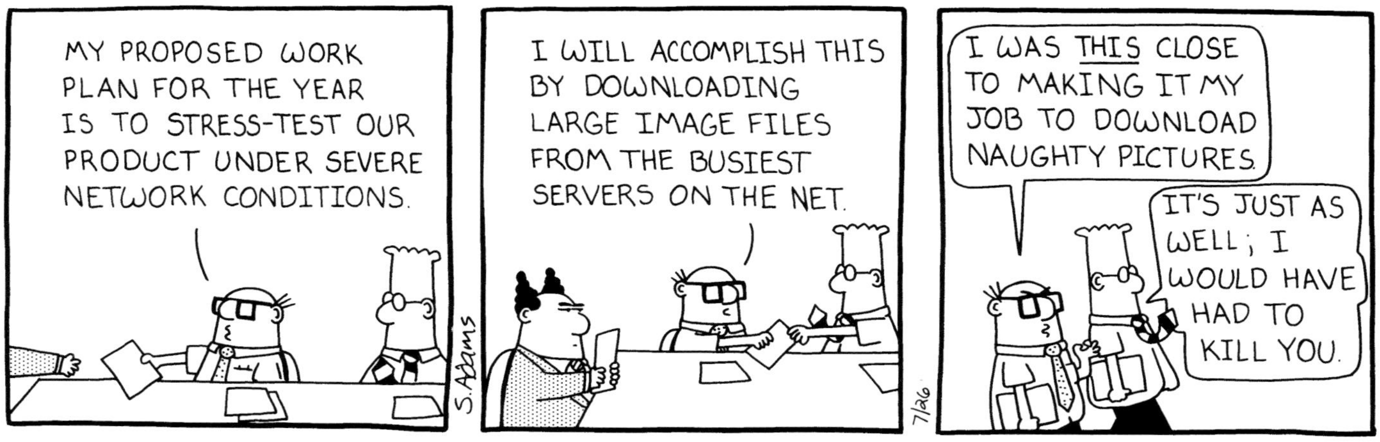
MY PROPOSED WORK PLAN FOR THE YEAR IS TO STRESS-TEST OUR PRODUCT UNDER SEVERE NETWORK CONDITIONS.
I WILL ACCOMPLISH THIS BY DOWNLOADING LARGE IMAGE FILES FROM THE BUSIEST SERVERS ON THE NET.
I WAS THIS CLOSE TO MAKING IT MY JOB TO DOWNLOAD NAUGHTY PICTURES.
IT'S JUST AS WELL; I WOULD HAVE HAD TO KILL YOU.
S. Adams
7/26

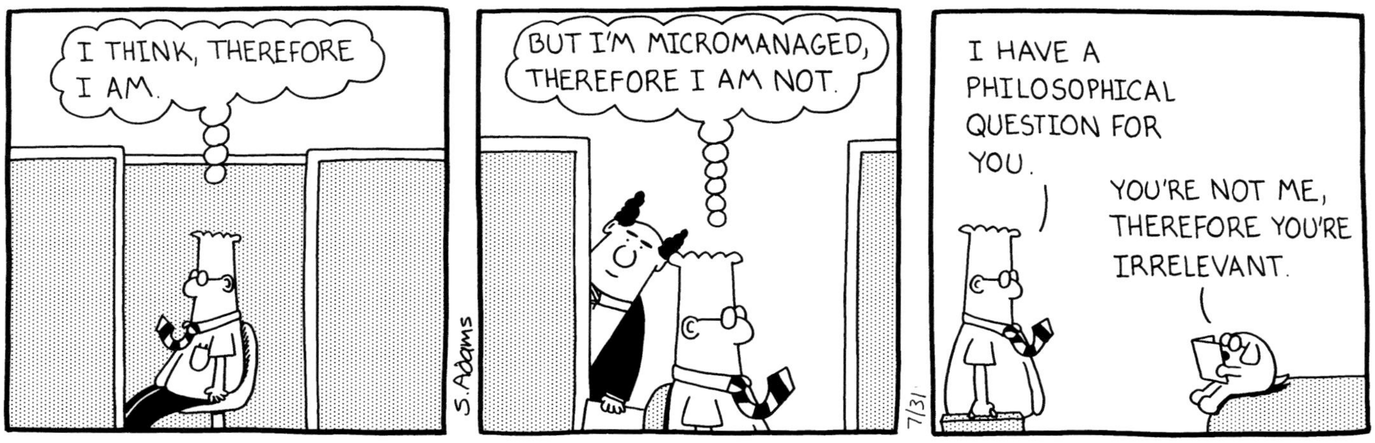
I THINK, THEREFORE I AM.
BUT I'M MICROMANAGED, THEREFORE I AM NOT.
I HAVE A PHILOSOPHICAL QUESTION FOR YOU.
YOU'RE NOT ME, THEREFORE YOU'RE IRRELEVANT.
S. Adams
7/31

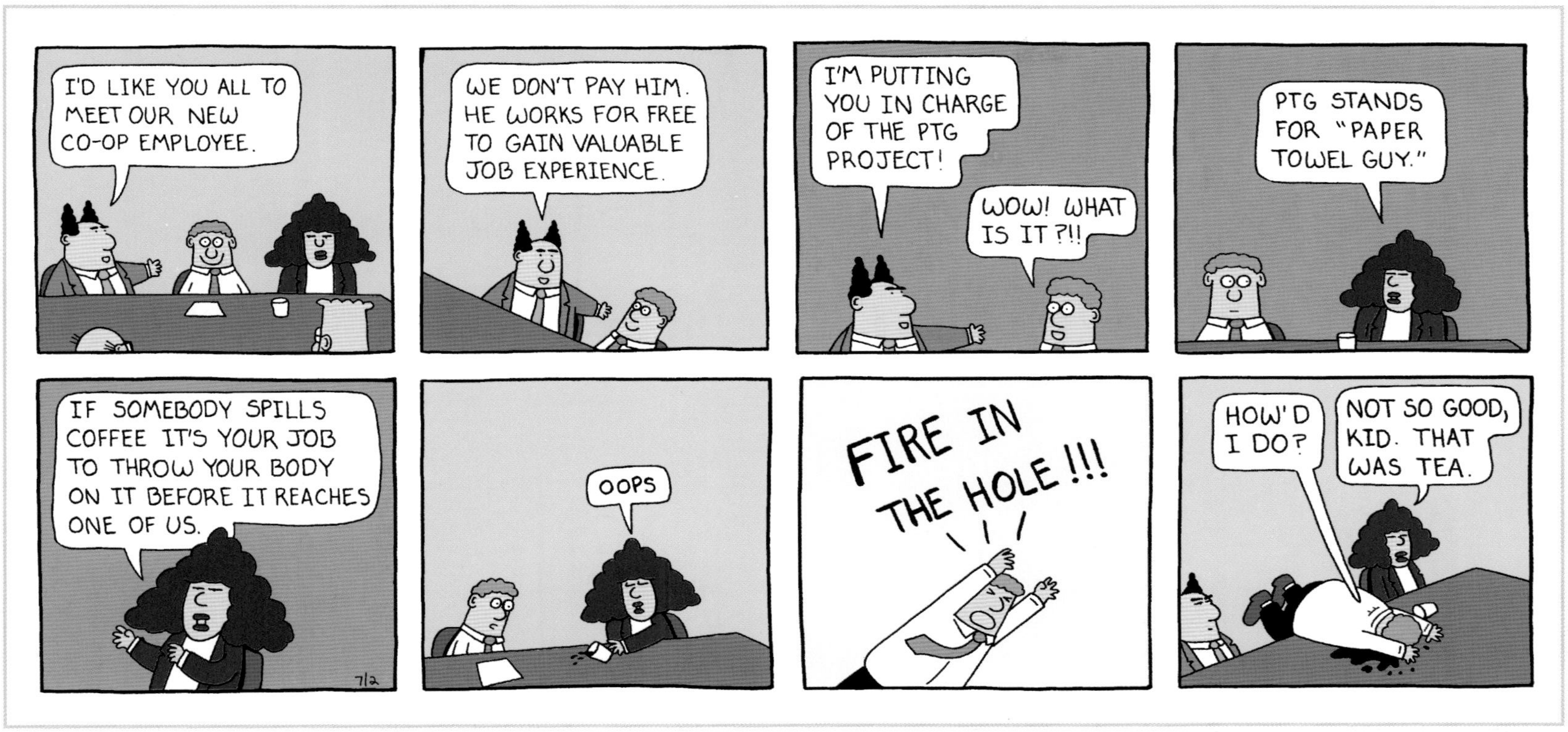
I'D LIKE YOU ALL TO MEET OUR NEW CO-OP EMPLOYEE.
WE DON'T PAY HIM. HE WORKS FOR FREE TO GAIN VALUABLE JOB EXPERIENCE.
I'M PUTTING YOU IN CHARGE OF THE PTG PROJECT!
WOW! WHAT IS IT?!!
PTG STANDS FOR "PAPER TOWEL GUY."
IF SOMEBODY SPILLS COFFEE IT'S YOUR JOB TO THROW YOUR BODY ON IT BEFORE IT REACHES ONE OF US.
OOPS
FIRE IN THE HOLE!!!
HOW'D I DO?
NOT SO GOOD, KID. THAT WAS TEA.

After the following comic ran, I got an e-mail from the attorney for Uncle Milton Industries, Inc., informing me that his client owned the trademark Ant Farm®. Because I used it as if it were generic, the attorney explained that I had damaged his client's intellectual property. He demanded I run a correction in a subsequent strip.

But I was busy. So I ignored it. A few weeks later, the attorney e-mailed again. He said he hadn't heard back from me, and he reiterated his demand for a correction.

But again, I was busy. I ignored it. By the time I got a third e-mail from the attorney, and I realized he was probably paid by the hour, I knew I couldn't win. I decided to cave in, and do what probably no cartoonist has ever done: I issued a correction (next page) that ran in a subsequent strip.

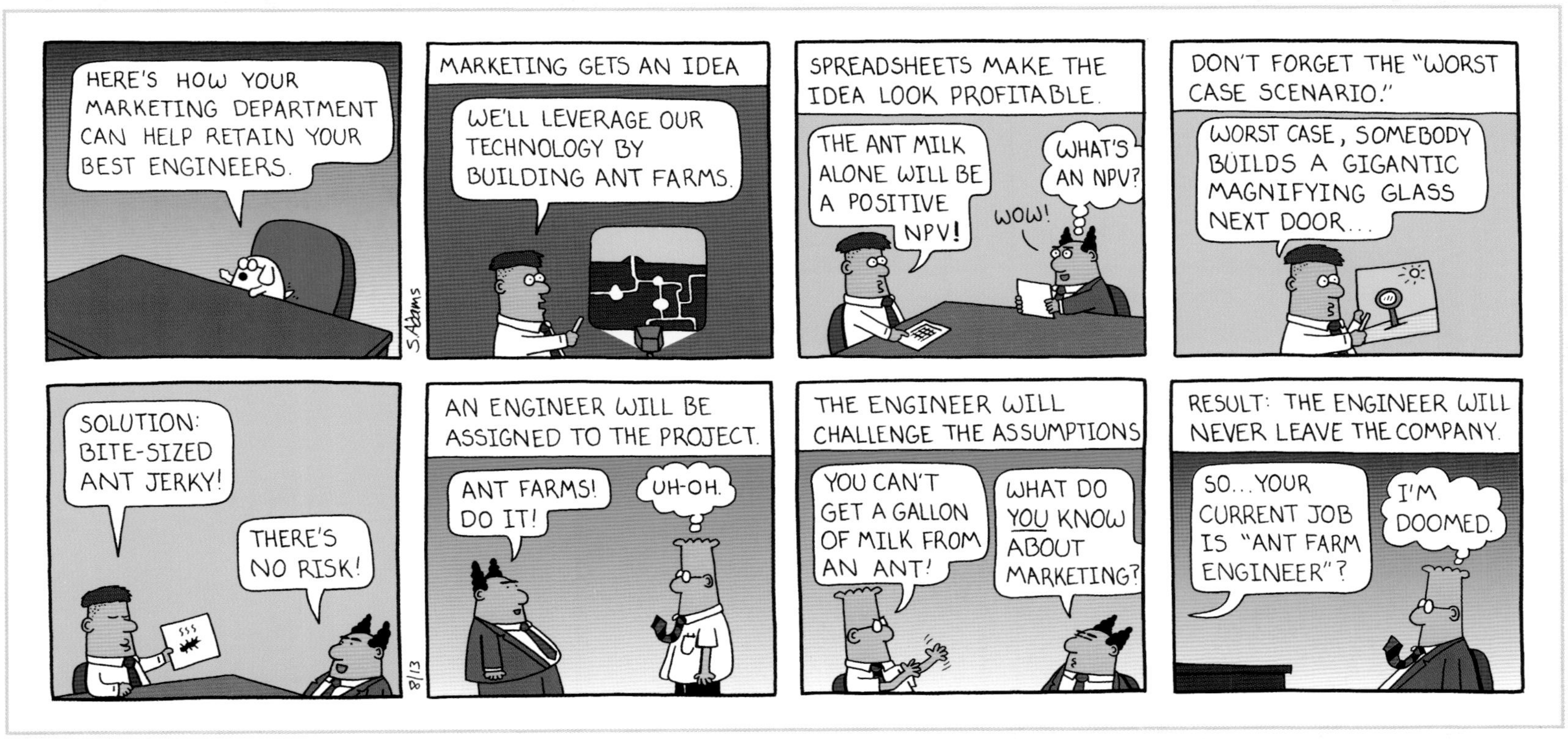
HERE'S HOW YOUR MARKETING DEPARTMENT CAN HELP RETAIN YOUR BEST ENGINEERS.
MARKETING GETS AN IDEA
WE'LL LEVERAGE OUR TECHNOLOGY BY BUILDING ANT FARMS.
SPREADSHEETS MAKE THE IDEA LOOK PROFITABLE.
THE ANT MILK ALONE WILL BE A POSITIVE NPV!
WHAT'S AN NPV?
WOW!
DON'T FORGET THE "WORST CASE SCENARIO."
WORST CASE, SOMEBODY BUILDS A GIGANTIC MAGNIFYING GLASS NEXT DOOR...
SOLUTION: BITE-SIZED ANT JERKY!
THERE'S NO RISK!
AN ENGINEER WILL BE ASSIGNED TO THE PROJECT.
ANT FARMS! DO IT!
UH-OH.
THE ENGINEER WILL CHALLENGE THE ASSUMPTIONS
YOU CAN'T GET A GALLON OF MILK FROM AN ANT!
WHAT DO YOU KNOW ABOUT MARKETING?
RESULT: THE ENGINEER WILL NEVER LEAVE THE COMPANY.
SO... YOUR CURRENT JOB IS "ANT FARM ENGINEER"?
I'M DOOMED.

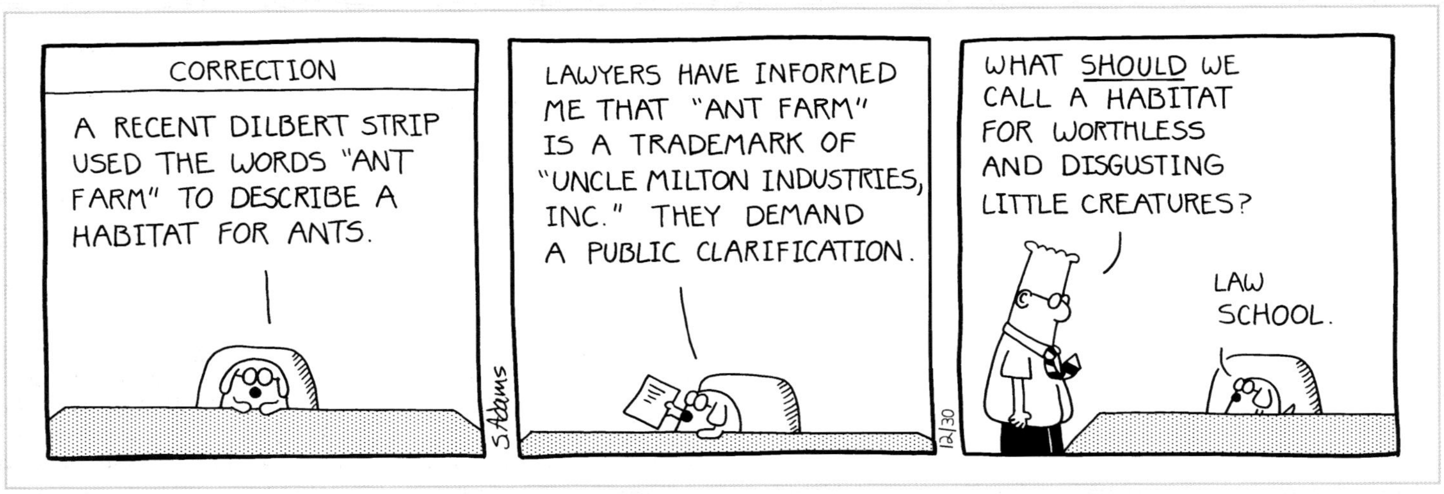
CORRECTION
A RECENT DILBERT STRIP USED THE WORDS "ANT FARM" TO DESCRIBE A HABITAT FOR ANTS.
LAWYERS HAVE INFORMED ME THAT "ANT FARM" IS A TRADEMARK OF "UNCLE MILTON INDUSTRIES, INC." THEY DEMAND A PUBLIC CLARIFICATION.
WHAT SHOULD WE CALL A HABITAT FOR WORTHLESS AND DISGUSTING LITTLE CREATURES?
LAW SCHOOL.

The attorney thanked me for the correction.

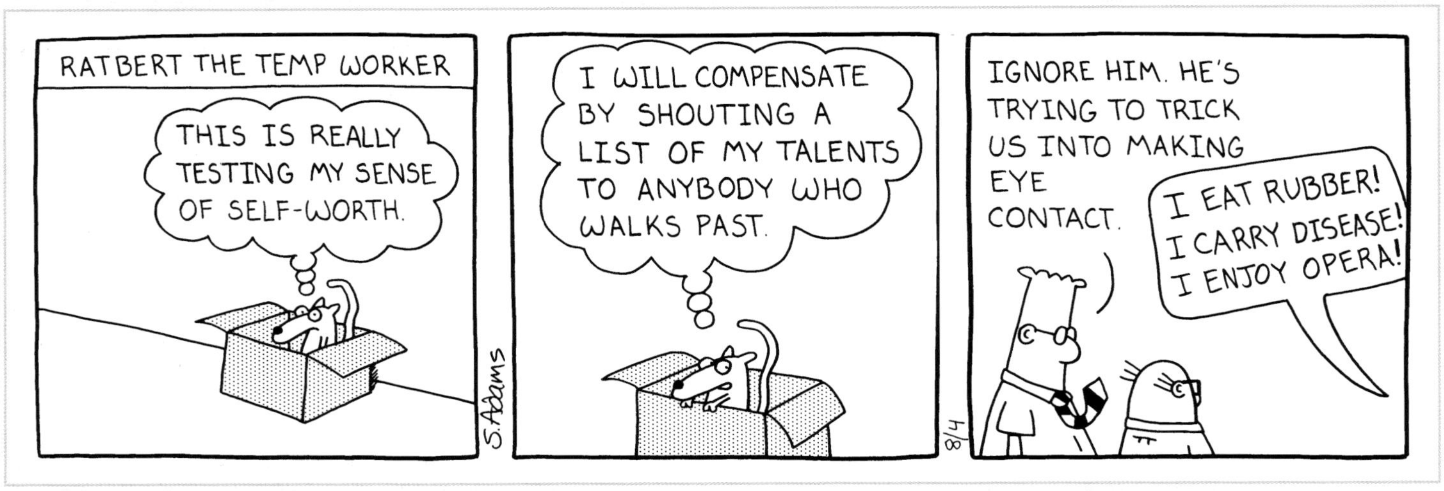
RATBERT THE TEMP WORKER
THIS IS REALLY TESTING MY SENSE OF SELF-WORTH.
I WILL COMPENSATE BY SHOUTING A LIST OF MY TALENTS TO ANYBODY WHO WALKS PAST.
IGNORE HIM. HE'S TRYING TO TRICK US INTO MAKING EYE CONTACT.
I EAT RUBBER! I CARRY DISEASE! I ENJOY OPERA!

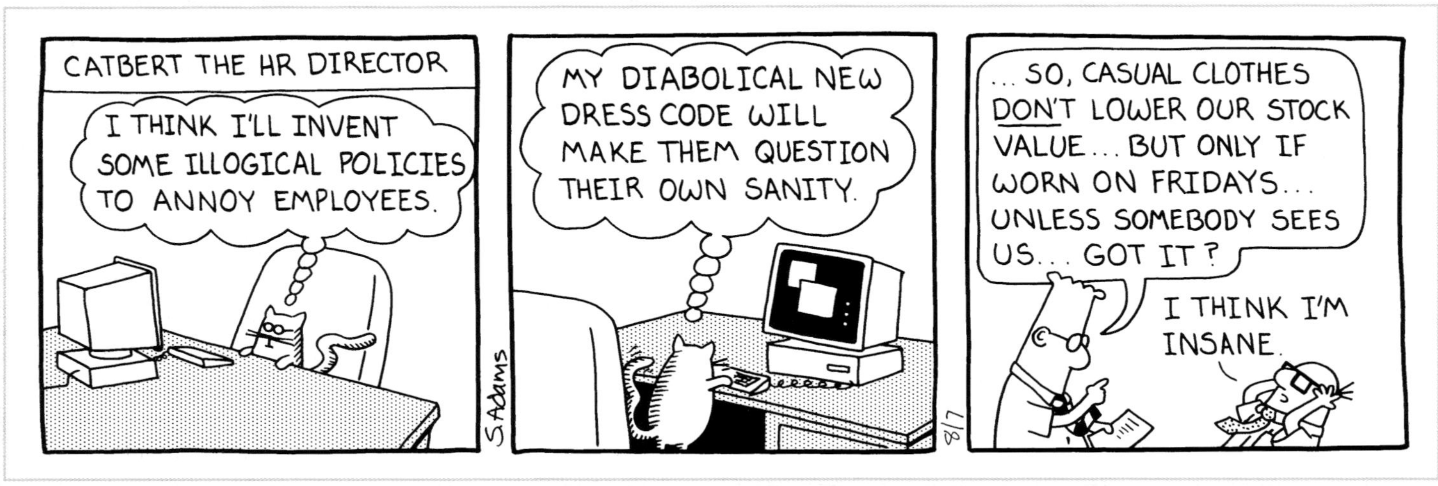
CATBERT THE HR DIRECTOR
I THINK I'LL INVENT SOME ILLOGICAL POLICIES TO ANNOY EMPLOYEES.
MY DIABOLICAL NEW DRESS CODE WILL MAKE THEM QUESTION THEIR OWN SANITY.
... SO, CASUAL CLOTHES DON'T LOWER OUR STOCK VALUE ... BUT ONLY IF WORN ON FRIDAYS ... UNLESS SOMEBODY SEES US ... GOT IT?
I THINK I'M INSANE.

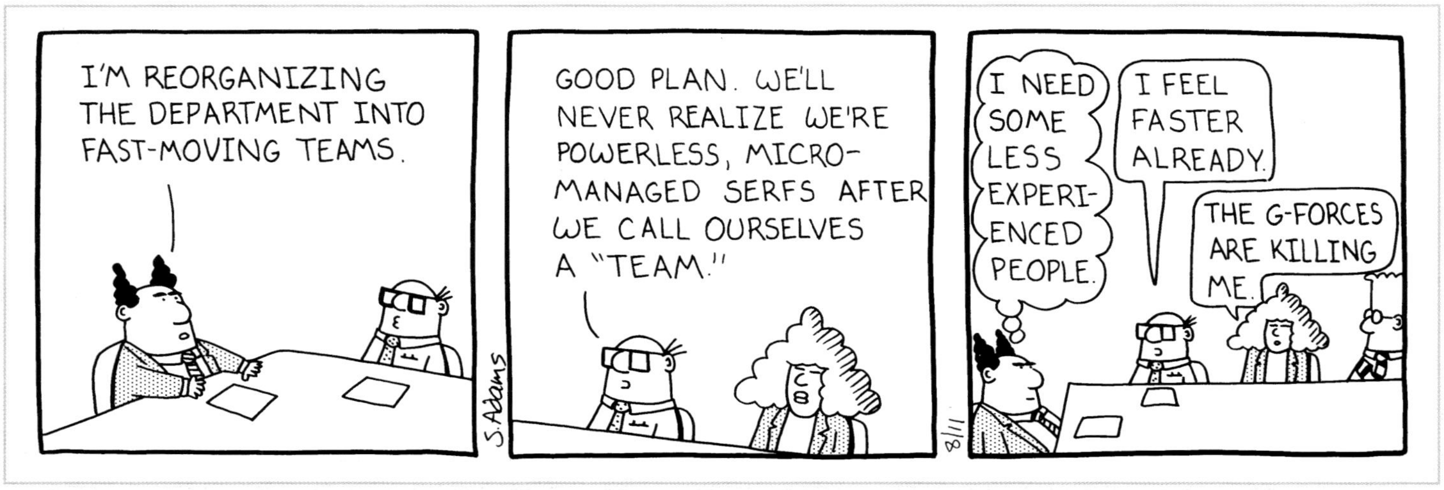
I'M REORGANIZING THE DEPARTMENT INTO FAST-MOVING TEAMS.
GOOD PLAN. WE'LL NEVER REALIZE WE'RE POWERLESS, MICRO-MANAGED SERFS AFTER WE CALL OURSELVES A "TEAM."
I NEED SOME LESS EXPERI-ENCED PEOPLE.
I FEEL FASTER ALREADY.
THE G-FORCES ARE KILLING ME.

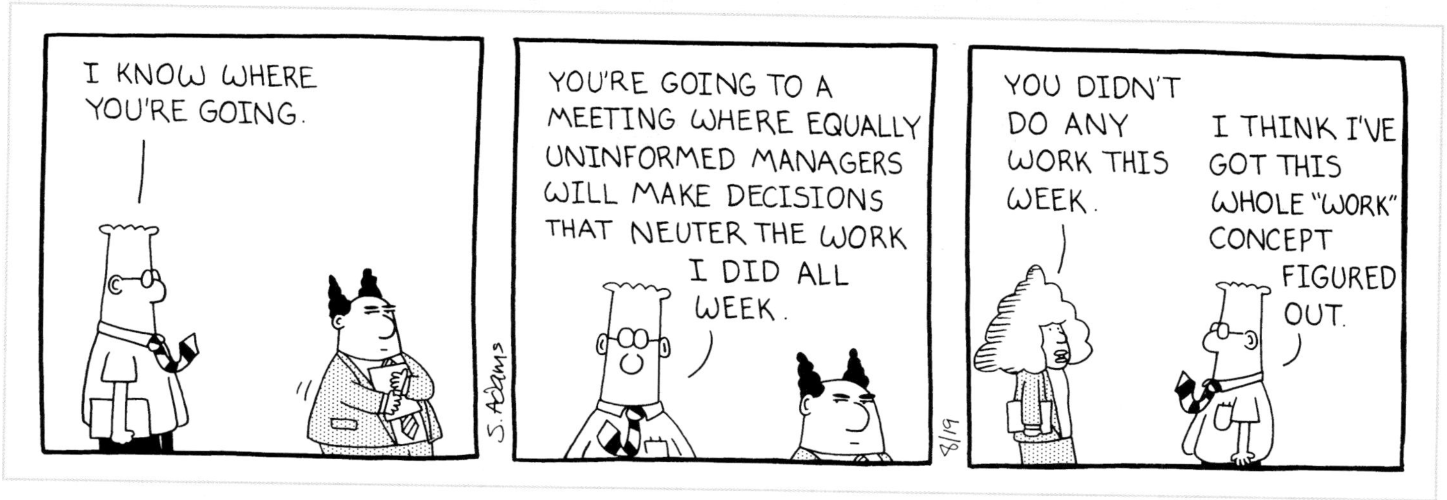
I KNOW WHERE YOU'RE GOING.
S. Adams
YOU'RE GOING TO A MEETING WHERE EQUALLY UNINFORMED MANAGERS WILL MAKE DECISIONS THAT NEUTER THE WORK
I DID ALL WEEK.
8/19
YOU DIDN'T DO ANY WORK THIS WEEK.
I THINK I'VE GOT THIS WHOLE "WORK" CONCEPT FIGURED OUT.

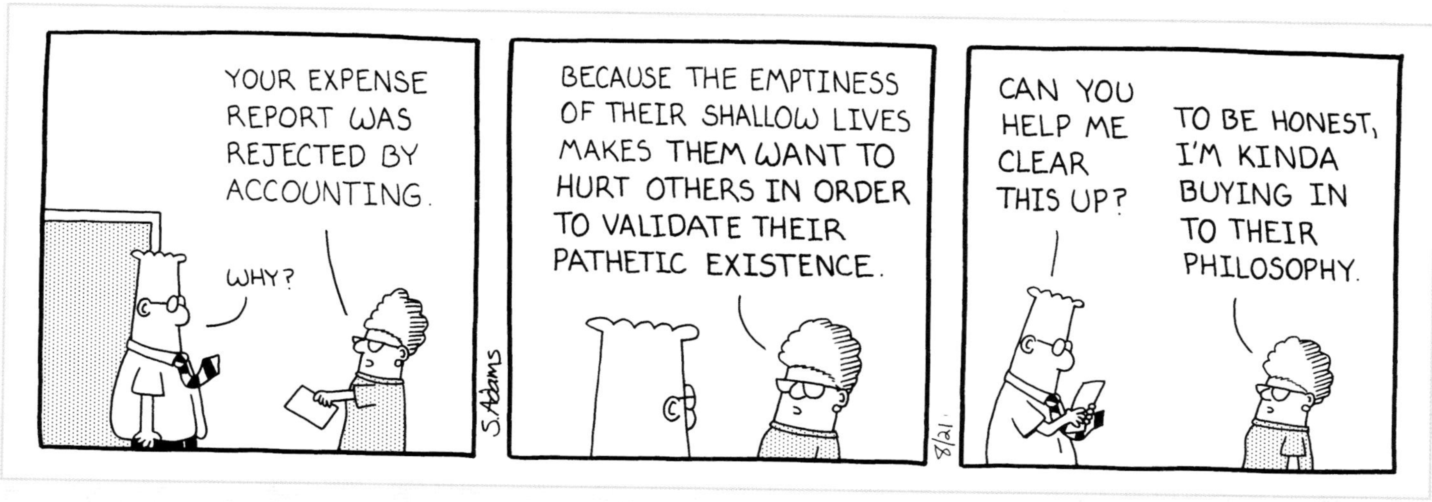
YOUR EXPENSE REPORT WAS REJECTED BY ACCOUNTING.
WHY?
S. Adams
BECAUSE THE EMPTINESS OF THEIR SHALLOW LIVES MAKES THEM WANT TO HURT OTHERS IN ORDER TO VALIDATE THEIR PATHETIC EXISTENCE.
8/21
CAN YOU HELP ME CLEAR THIS UP?
TO BE HONEST, I'M KINDA BUYING IN TO THEIR PHILOSOPHY.

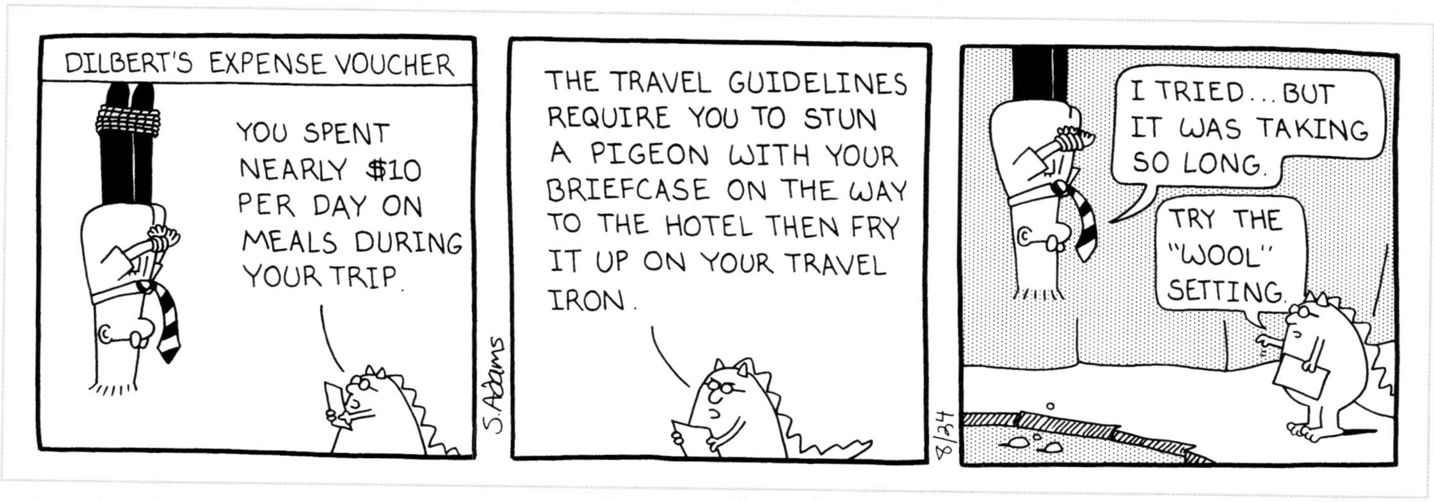
DILBERT'S EXPENSE VOUCHER
YOU SPENT NEARLY $10 PER DAY ON MEALS DURING YOUR TRIP.
S. Adams
THE TRAVEL GUIDELINES REQUIRE YOU TO STUN A PIGEON WITH YOUR BRIEFCASE ON THE WAY TO THE HOTEL THEN FRY IT UP ON YOUR TRAVEL IRON.
8/24
I TRIED... BUT IT WAS TAKING SO LONG.
TRY THE "WOOL" SETTING.

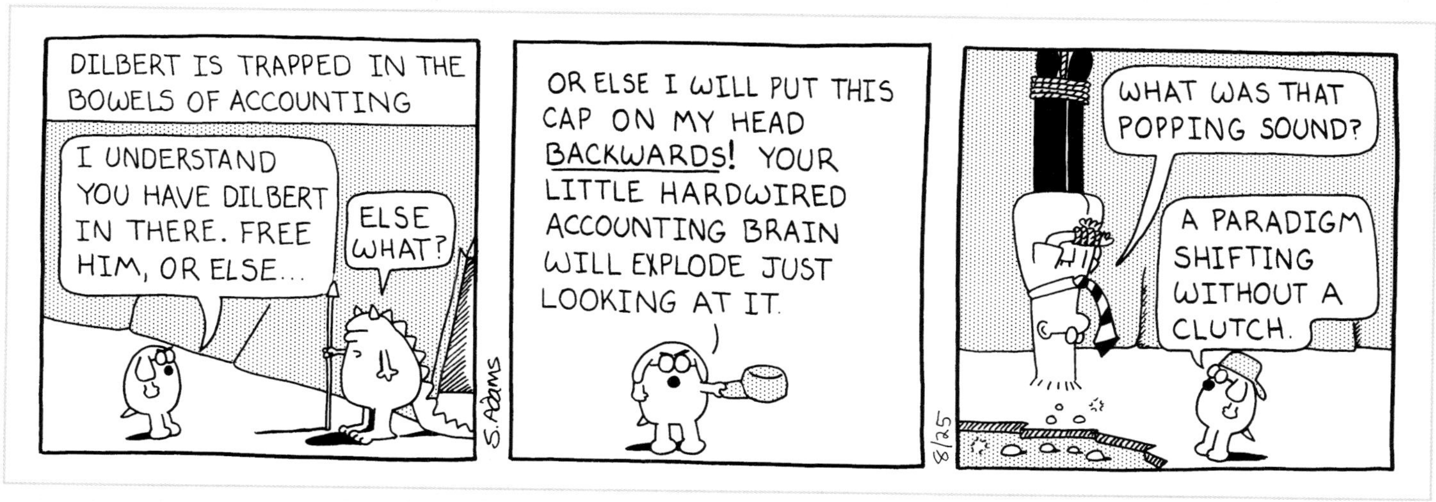
DILBERT IS TRAPPED IN THE BOWELS OF ACCOUNTING
I UNDERSTAND YOU HAVE DILBERT IN THERE. FREE HIM, OR ELSE...
ELSE WHAT?
S. Adams
OR ELSE I WILL PUT THIS CAP ON MY HEAD BACKWARDS! YOUR LITTLE HARDWIRED ACCOUNTING BRAIN WILL EXPLODE JUST LOOKING AT IT.
8/25
WHAT WAS THAT POPPING SOUND?
A PARADIGM SHIFTING WITHOUT A CLUTCH.

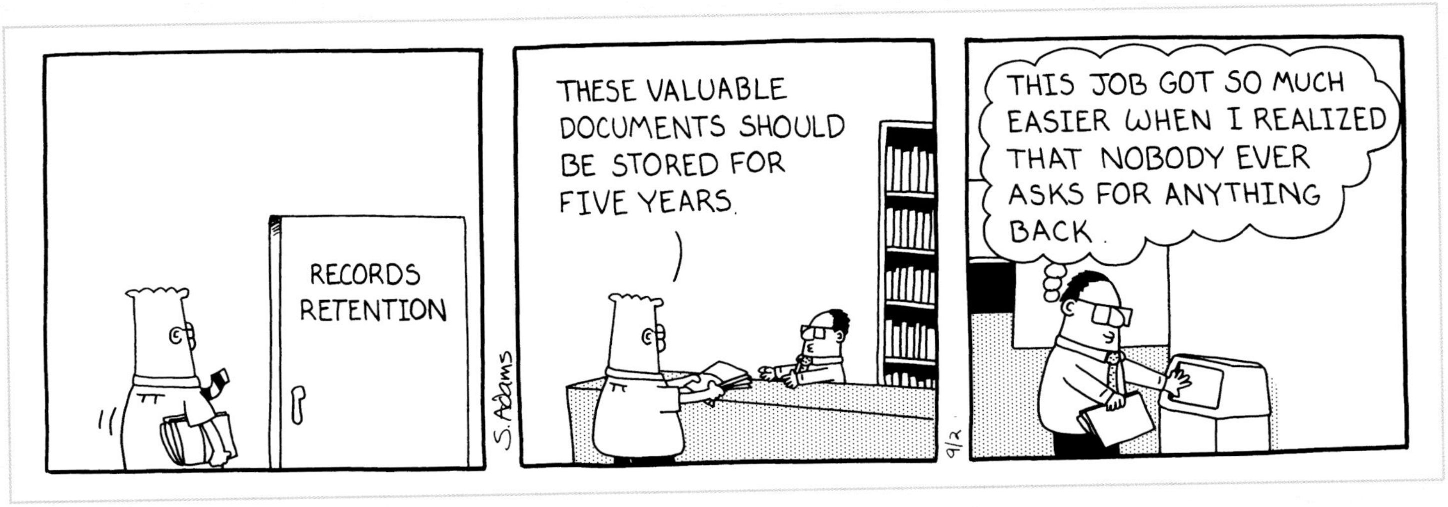
RECORDS RETENTION
THESE VALUABLE DOCUMENTS SHOULD BE STORED FOR FIVE YEARS.
THIS JOB GOT SO MUCH EASIER WHEN I REALIZED THAT NOBODY EVER ASKS FOR ANYTHING BACK.
S. Adams
9/2

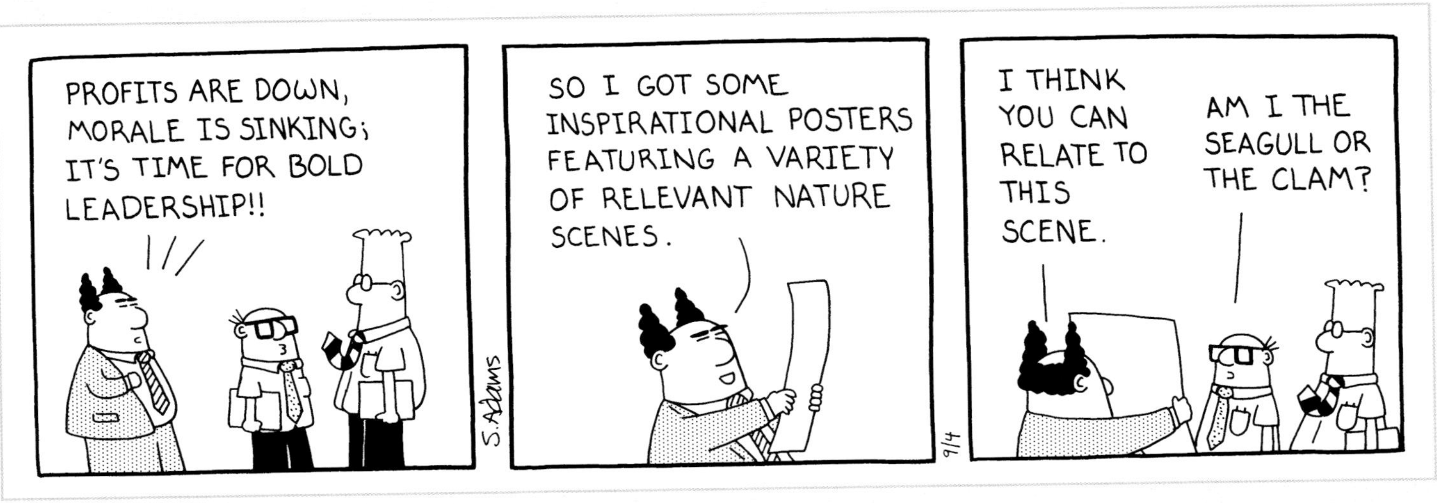
PROFITS ARE DOWN, MORALE IS SINKING; IT'S TIME FOR BOLD LEADERSHIP!!
SO I GOT SOME INSPIRATIONAL POSTERS FEATURING A VARIETY OF RELEVANT NATURE SCENES.
I THINK YOU CAN RELATE TO THIS SCENE.
AM I THE SEAGULL OR THE CLAM?
S. Adams
9/4

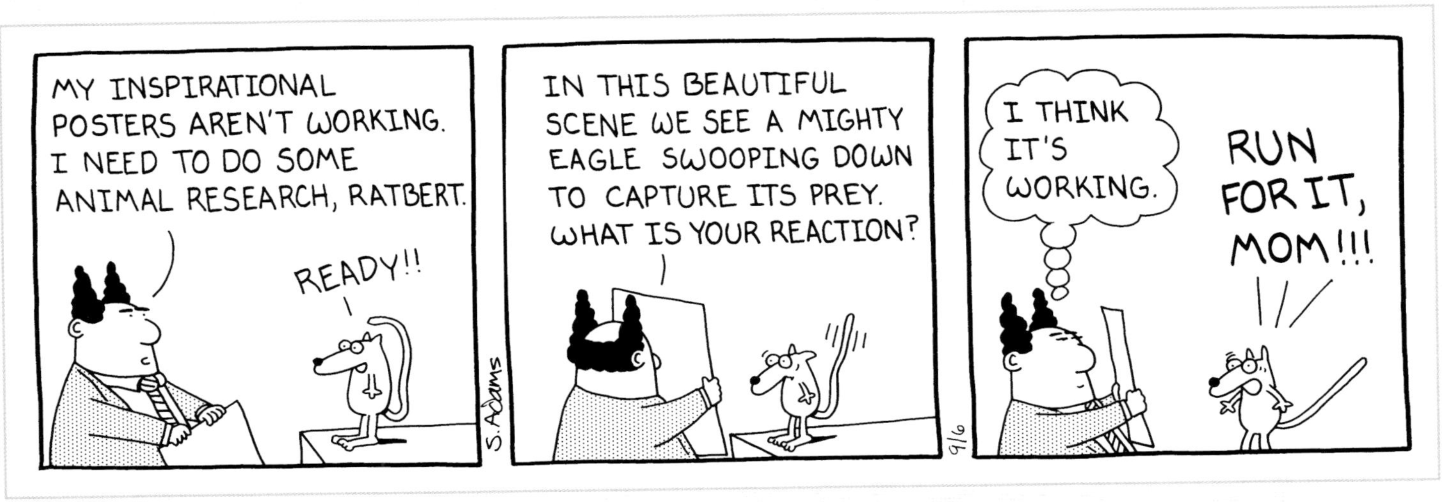
MY INSPIRATIONAL POSTERS AREN'T WORKING. I NEED TO DO SOME ANIMAL RESEARCH, RATBERT.
READY!!
IN THIS BEAUTIFUL SCENE WE SEE A MIGHTY EAGLE SWOOPING DOWN TO CAPTURE ITS PREY. WHAT IS YOUR REACTION?
I THINK IT'S WORKING.
RUN FOR IT, MOM!!!
S. Adams
9/6

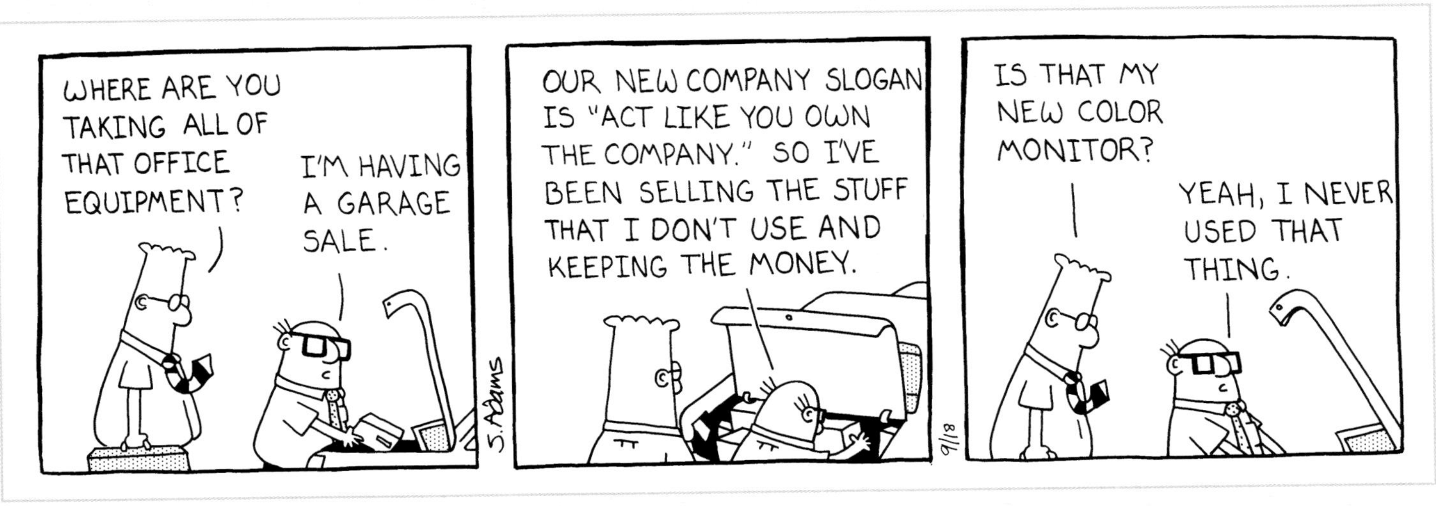
WHERE ARE YOU TAKING ALL OF THAT OFFICE EQUIPMENT?
I'M HAVING A GARAGE SALE.
OUR NEW COMPANY SLOGAN IS "ACT LIKE YOU OWN THE COMPANY." SO I'VE BEEN SELLING THE STUFF THAT I DON'T USE AND KEEPING THE MONEY.
IS THAT MY NEW COLOR MONITOR?
YEAH, I NEVER USED THAT THING.
S. Adams
9/8

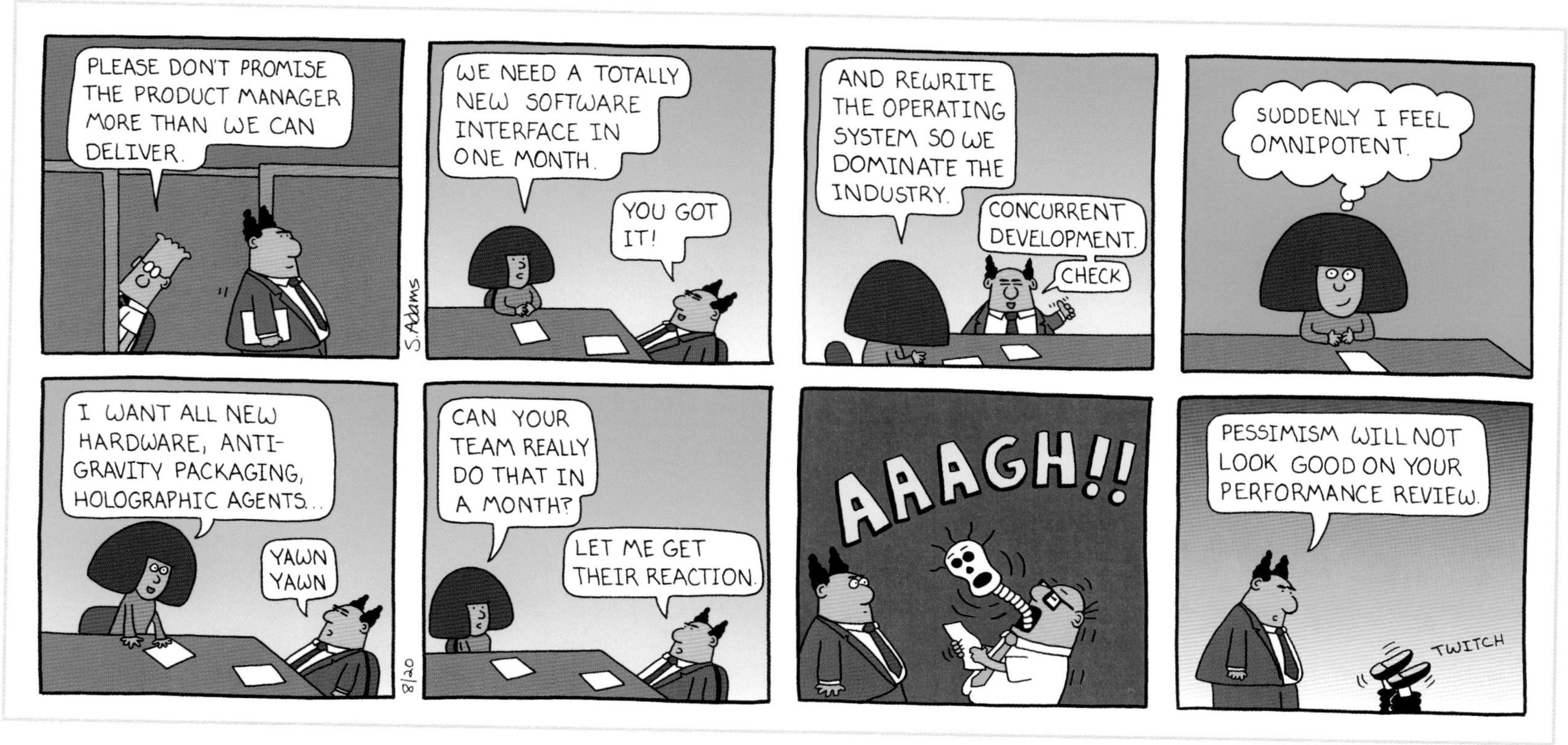
PLEASE DON'T PROMISE THE PRODUCT MANAGER MORE THAN WE CAN DELIVER.
S. Adams
WE NEED A TOTALLY NEW SOFTWARE INTERFACE IN ONE MONTH.
YOU GOT IT!
AND REWRITE THE OPERATING SYSTEM SO WE DOMINATE THE INDUSTRY.
CONCURRENT DEVELOPMENT.
CHECK
SUDDENLY I FEEL OMNIPOTENT.
I WANT ALL NEW HARDWARE, ANTI-GRAVITY PACKAGING, HOLOGRAPHIC AGENTS...
YAWN YAWN
8/20
CAN YOUR TEAM REALLY DO THAT IN A MONTH?
LET ME GET THEIR REACTION.
AAAGH!!
PESSIMISM WILL NOT LOOK GOOD ON YOUR PERFORMANCE REVIEW.
TWITCH

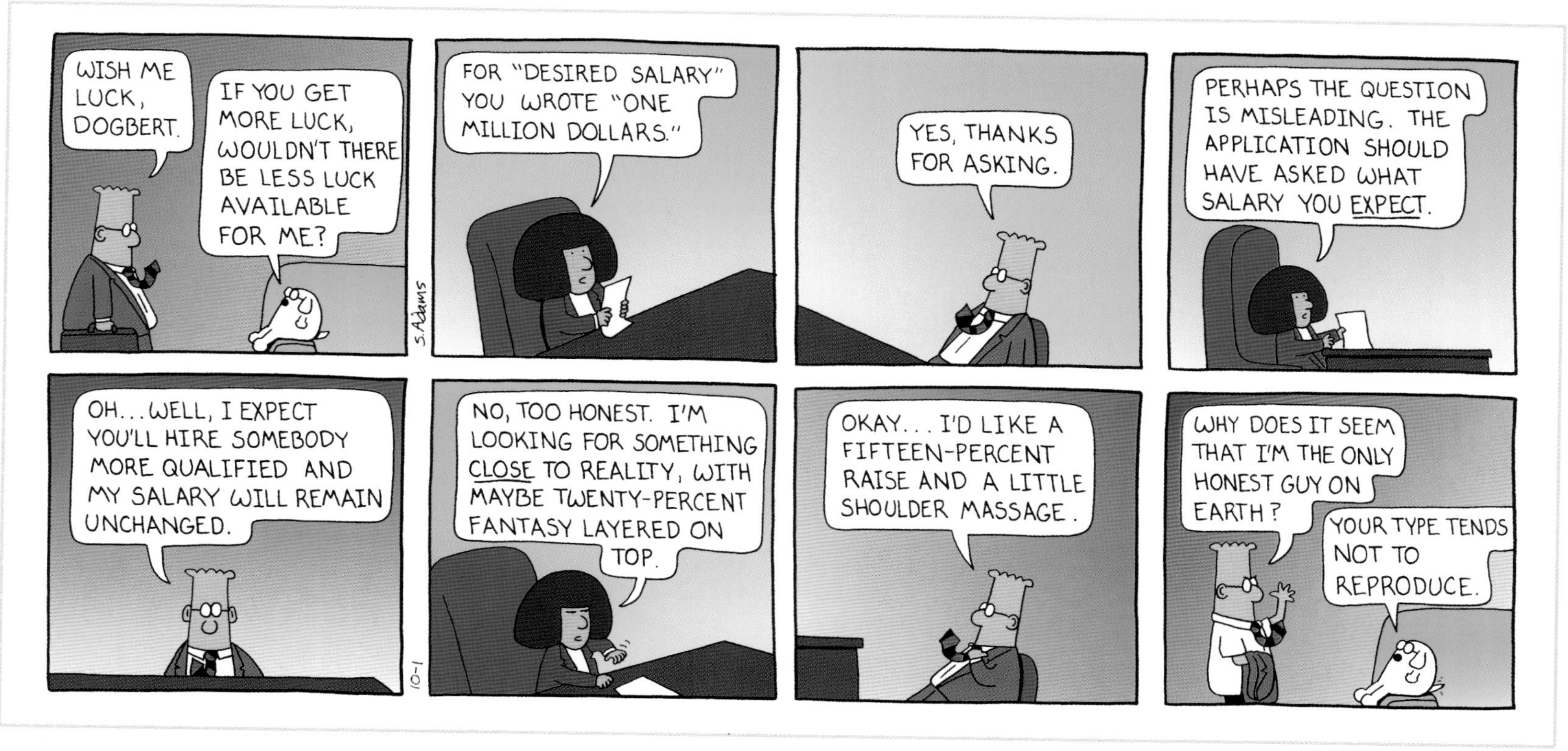
WISH ME LUCK, DOGBERT.
IF YOU GET MORE LUCK, WOULDN'T THERE BE LESS LUCK AVAILABLE FOR ME?
S. Adams
FOR "DESIRED SALARY" YOU WROTE "ONE MILLION DOLLARS."
YES, THANKS FOR ASKING.
PERHAPS THE QUESTION IS MISLEADING. THE APPLICATION SHOULD HAVE ASKED WHAT SALARY YOU EXPECT.
OH...WELL, I EXPECT YOU'LL HIRE SOMEBODY MORE QUALIFIED AND MY SALARY WILL REMAIN UNCHANGED.
10-1
NO, TOO HONEST. I'M LOOKING FOR SOMETHING CLOSE TO REALITY, WITH MAYBE TWENTY-PERCENT FANTASY LAYERED ON TOP.
OKAY... I'D LIKE A FIFTEEN-PERCENT RAISE AND A LITTLE SHOULDER MASSAGE.
WHY DOES IT SEEM THAT I'M THE ONLY HONEST GUY ON EARTH?
YOUR TYPE TENDS NOT TO REPRODUCE.

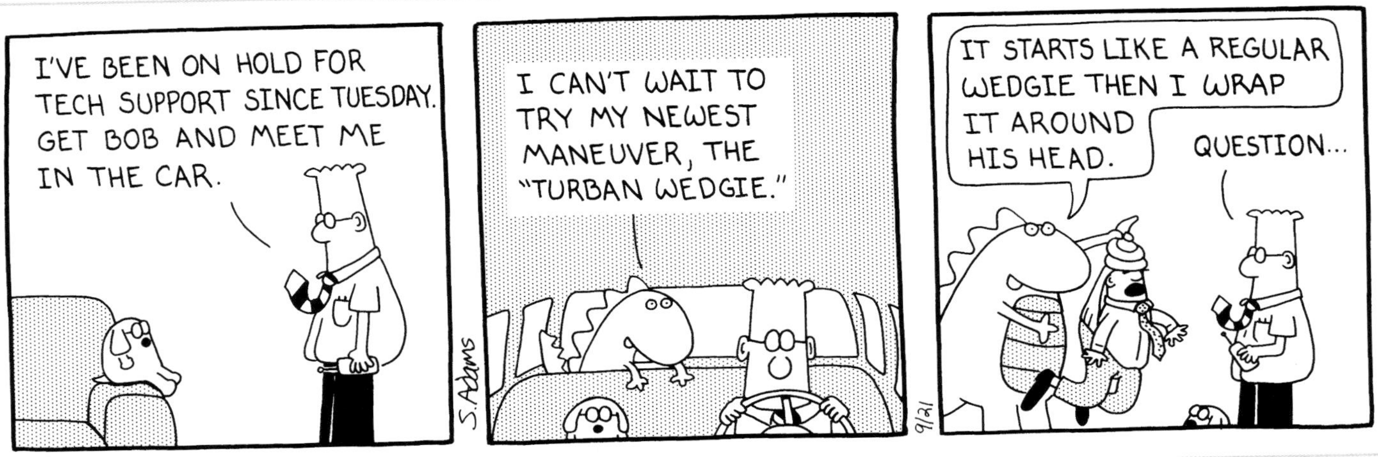
I'VE BEEN ON HOLD FOR TECH SUPPORT SINCE TUESDAY. GET BOB AND MEET ME IN THE CAR.
I CAN'T WAIT TO TRY MY NEWEST MANEUVER, THE "TURBAN WEDGIE."
S. Adams
IT STARTS LIKE A REGULAR WEDGIE THEN I WRAP IT AROUND HIS HEAD.
QUESTION...
9/21

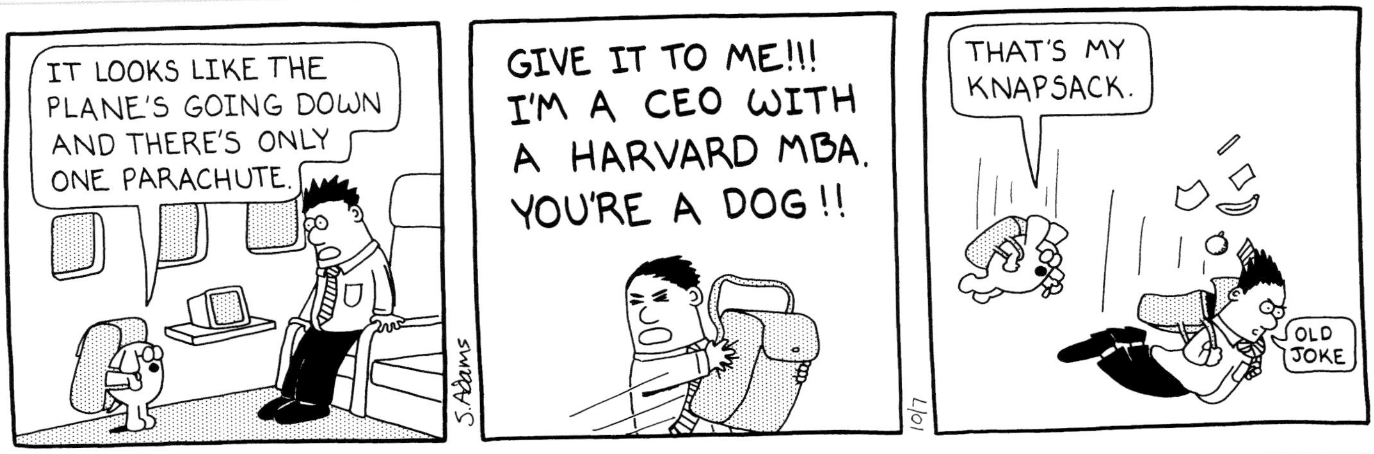
IT LOOKS LIKE THE PLANE'S GOING DOWN AND THERE'S ONLY ONE PARACHUTE.
S. Adams
GIVE IT TO ME!!! I'M A CEO WITH A HARVARD MBA. YOU'RE A DOG!!
10/7
THAT'S MY KNAPSACK.
OLD JOKE

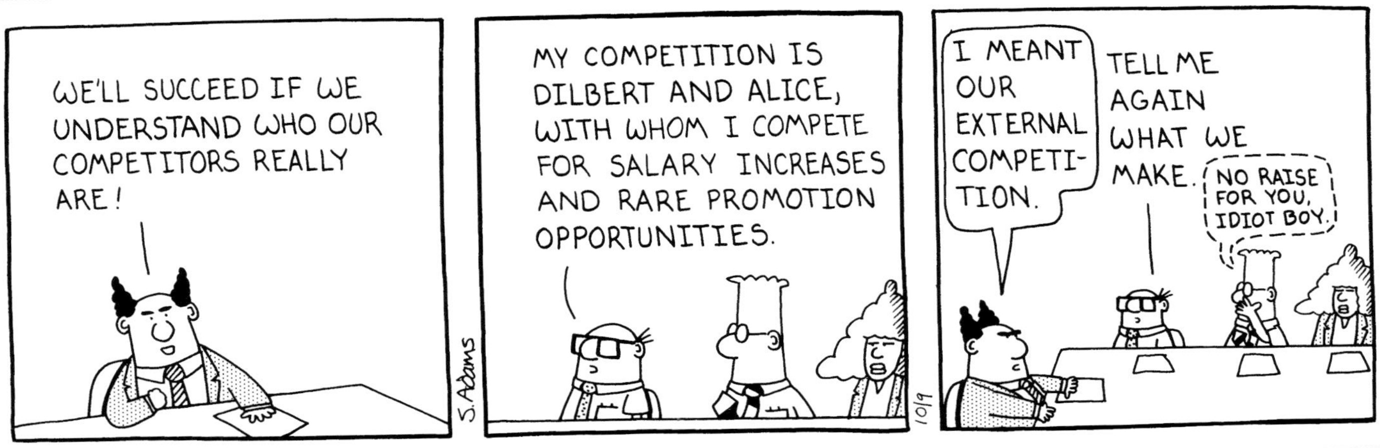
WE'LL SUCCEED IF WE UNDERSTAND WHO OUR COMPETITORS REALLY ARE!
S. Adams
MY COMPETITION IS DILBERT AND ALICE, WITH WHOM I COMPETE FOR SALARY INCREASES AND RARE PROMOTION OPPORTUNITIES.
10/9
I MEANT OUR EXTERNAL COMPETITION.
TELL ME AGAIN WHAT WE MAKE.
NO RAISE FOR YOU, IDIOT BOY.

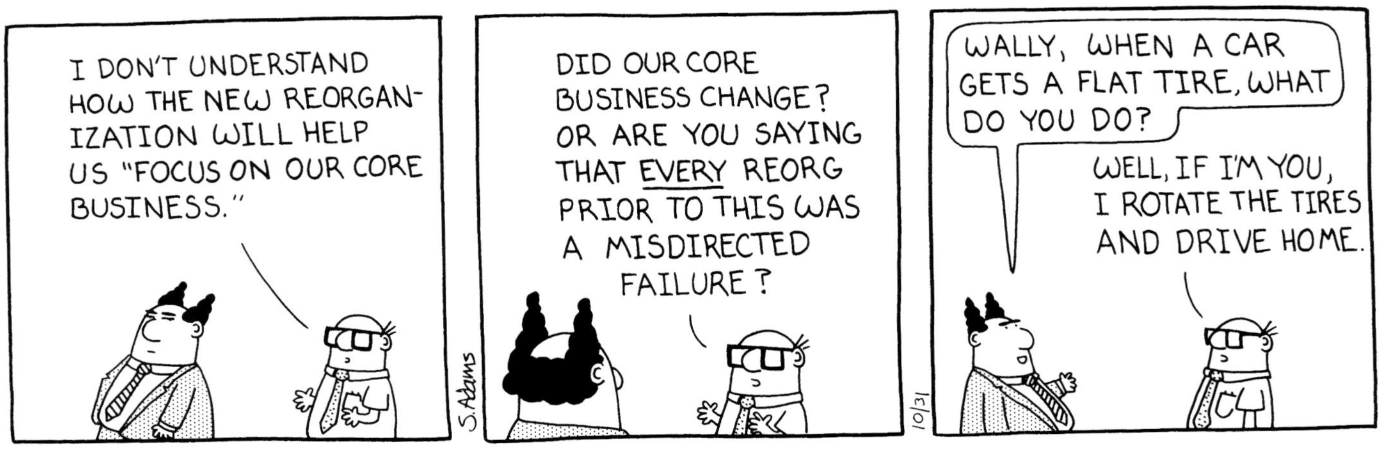
I DON'T UNDERSTAND HOW THE NEW REORGANIZATION WILL HELP US "FOCUS ON OUR CORE BUSINESS."
S. Adams
DID OUR CORE BUSINESS CHANGE? OR ARE YOU SAYING THAT EVERY REORG PRIOR TO THIS WAS A MISDIRECTED FAILURE?
10/31
WALLY, WHEN A CAR GETS A FLAT TIRE, WHAT DO YOU DO?
WELL, IF I'M YOU, I ROTATE THE TIRES AND DRIVE HOME.

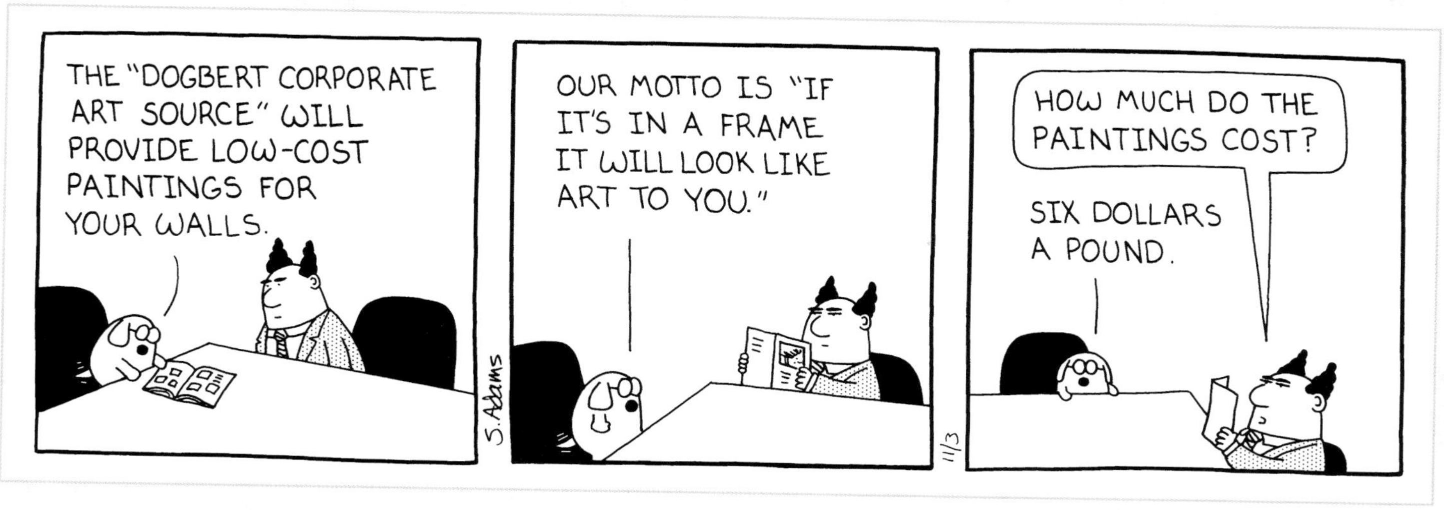
THE "DOGBERT CORPORATE ART SOURCE" WILL PROVIDE LOW-COST PAINTINGS FOR YOUR WALLS.
S. Adams
OUR MOTTO IS "IF IT'S IN A FRAME IT WILL LOOK LIKE ART TO YOU."
11/3
HOW MUCH DO THE PAINTINGS COST?
SIX DOLLARS A POUND.

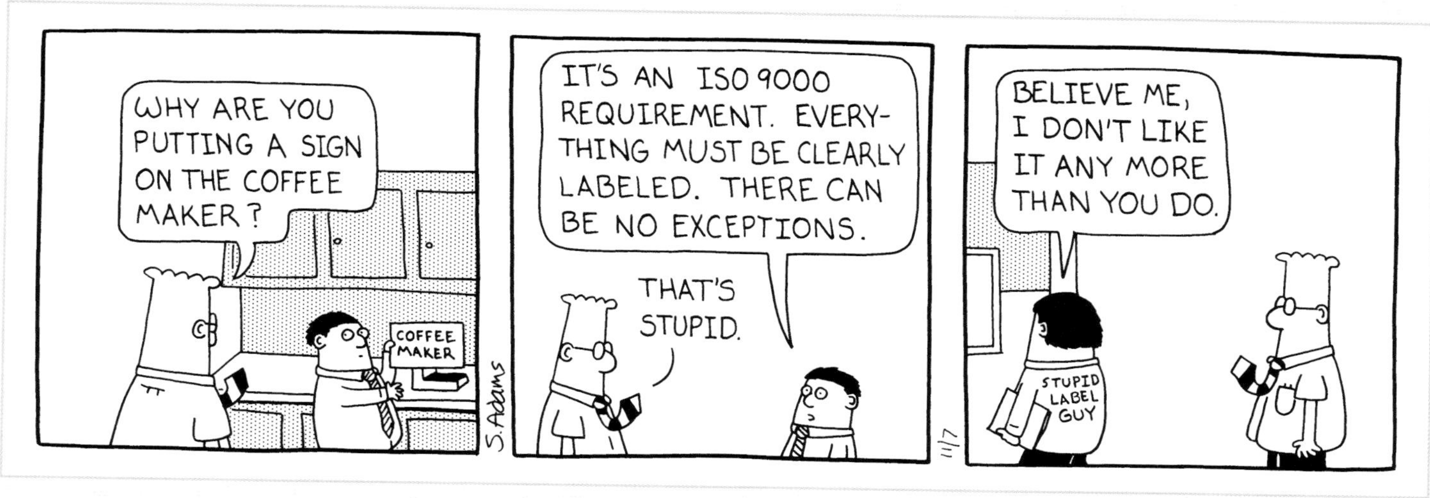
WHY ARE YOU PUTTING A SIGN ON THE COFFEE MAKER?
COFFEE MAKER
S. Adams
IT'S AN ISO 9000 REQUIREMENT. EVERYTHING MUST BE CLEARLY LABELED. THERE CAN BE NO EXCEPTIONS.
THAT'S STUPID.
11/7
BELIEVE ME, I DON'T LIKE IT ANY MORE THAN YOU DO.
STUPID LABEL GUY

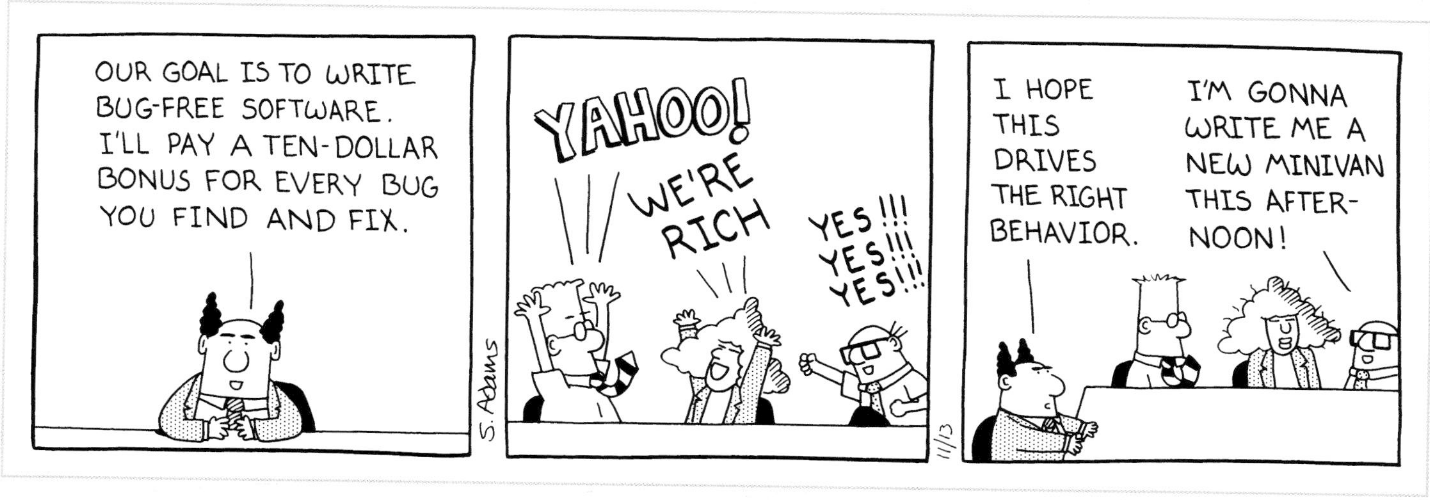
OUR GOAL IS TO WRITE BUG-FREE SOFTWARE. I'LL PAY A TEN-DOLLAR BONUS FOR EVERY BUG YOU FIND AND FIX.
S. Adams
YAHOO!
WE'RE RICH
YES!!! YES!!! YES!!!
11/13
I HOPE THIS DRIVES THE RIGHT BEHAVIOR.
I'M GONNA WRITE ME A NEW MINIVAN THIS AFTERNOON!

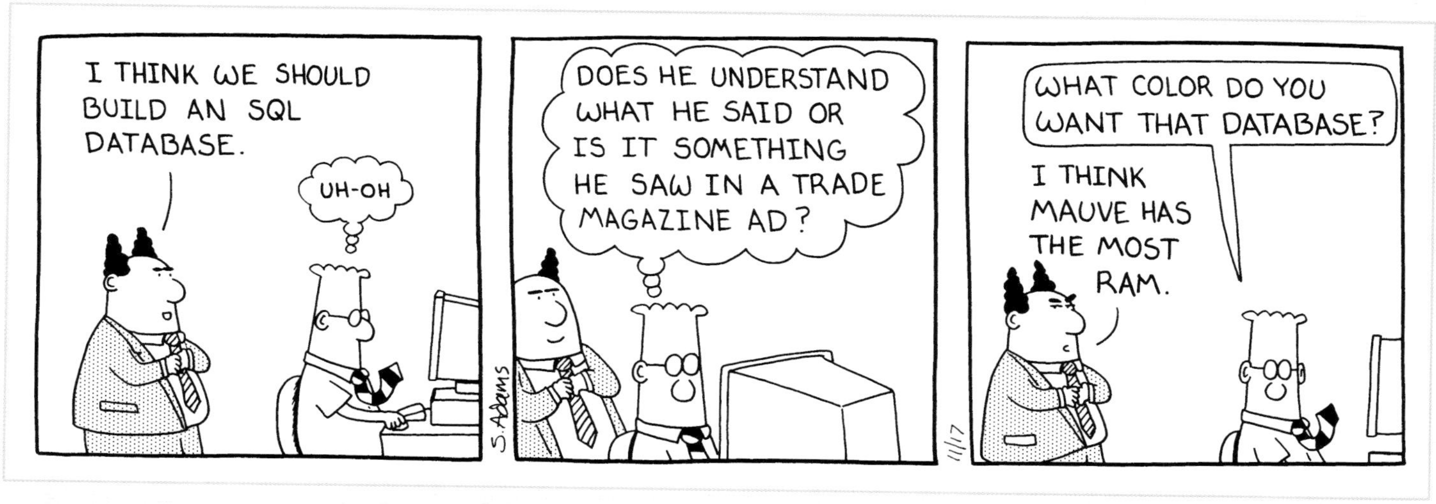
I THINK WE SHOULD BUILD AN SQL DATABASE.
UH-OH
S. Adams
DOES HE UNDERSTAND WHAT HE SAID OR IS IT SOMETHING HE SAW IN A TRADE MAGAZINE AD?
11/17
WHAT COLOR DO YOU WANT THAT DATABASE?
I THINK MAUVE HAS THE MOST RAM.

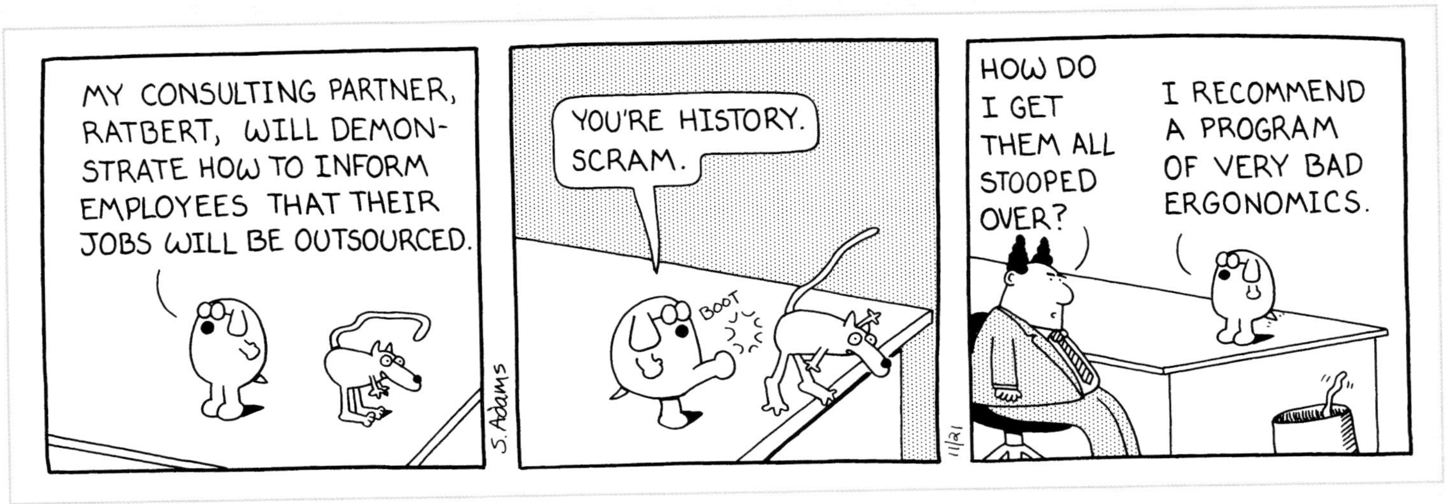
MY CONSULTING PARTNER, RATBERT, WILL DEMON-STRATE HOW TO INFORM EMPLOYEES THAT THEIR JOBS WILL BE OUTSOURCED.
YOU'RE HISTORY. SCRAM.
BOOT
S. Adams
HOW DO I GET THEM ALL STOOPED OVER?
I RECOMMEND A PROGRAM OF VERY BAD ERGONOMICS.
11/21

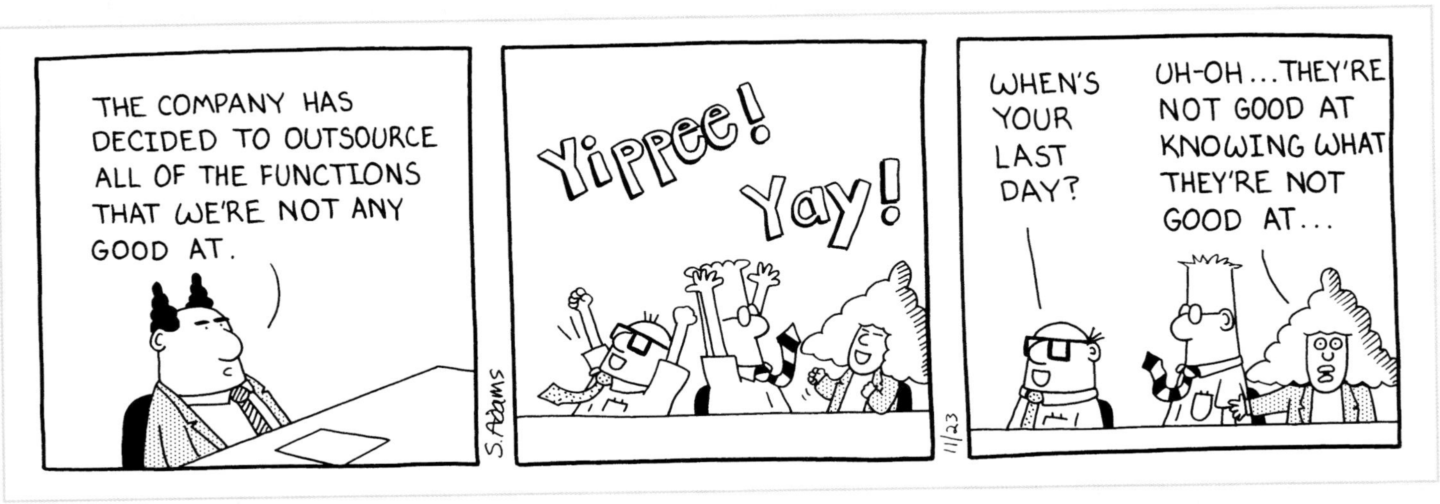
THE COMPANY HAS DECIDED TO OUTSOURCE ALL OF THE FUNCTIONS THAT WE'RE NOT ANY GOOD AT.
S. Adams
Yippee!
Yay!
11/23
WHEN'S YOUR LAST DAY?
UH-OH... THEY'RE NOT GOOD AT KNOWING WHAT THEY'RE NOT GOOD AT...

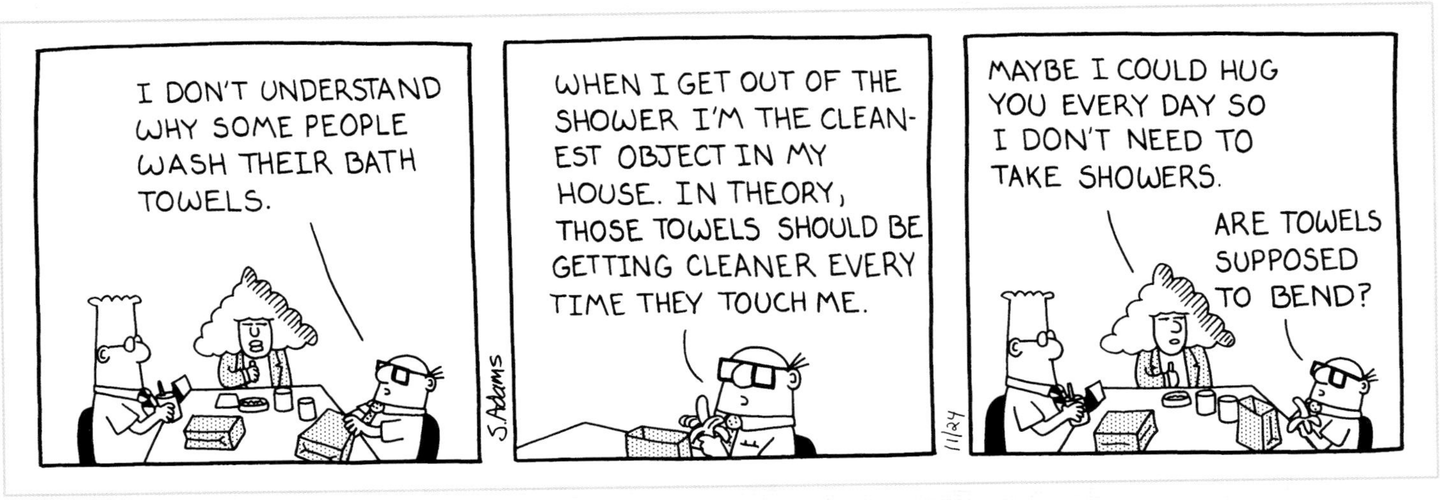
I DON'T UNDERSTAND WHY SOME PEOPLE WASH THEIR BATH TOWELS.
S. Adams
WHEN I GET OUT OF THE SHOWER I'M THE CLEAN-EST OBJECT IN MY HOUSE. IN THEORY, THOSE TOWELS SHOULD BE GETTING CLEANER EVERY TIME THEY TOUCH ME.
11/24
MAYBE I COULD HUG YOU EVERY DAY SO I DON'T NEED TO TAKE SHOWERS.
ARE TOWELS SUPPOSED TO BEND?

The one below isn't funny, but it was one of the most requested themes by my readers.

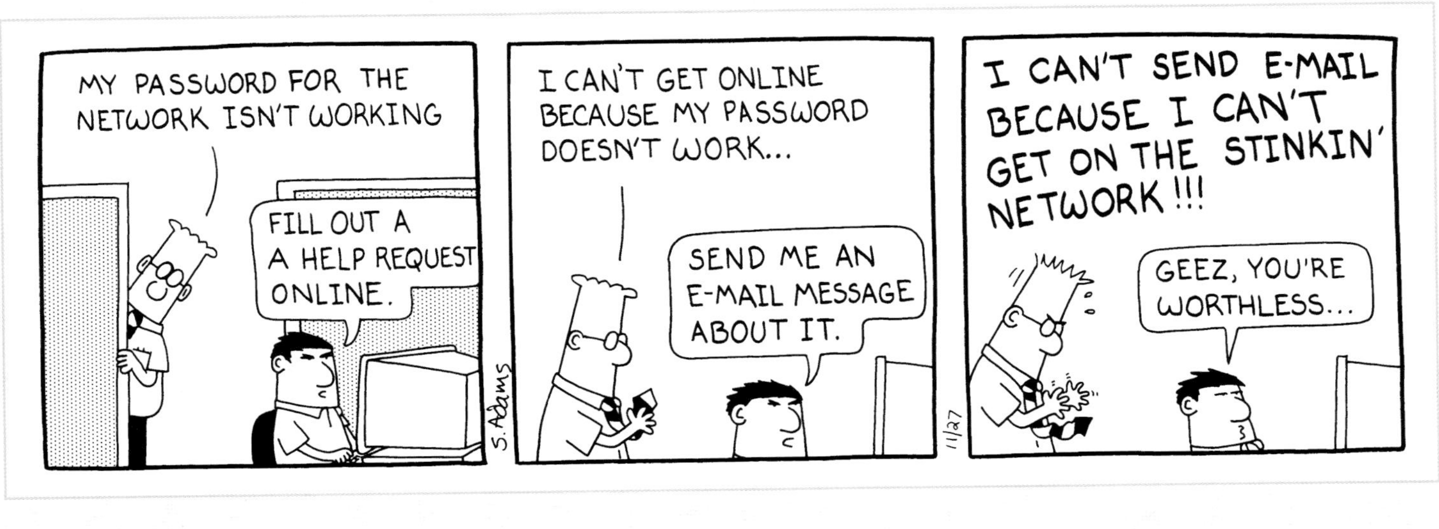
MY PASSWORD FOR THE NETWORK ISN'T WORKING
FILL OUT A HELP REQUEST ONLINE.
S. Adams
I CAN'T GET ONLINE BECAUSE MY PASSWORD DOESN'T WORK...
SEND ME AN E-MAIL MESSAGE ABOUT IT.
11/27
I CAN'T SEND E-MAIL BECAUSE I CAN'T GET ON THE STINKIN' NETWORK!!!
GEEZ, YOU'RE WORTHLESS...

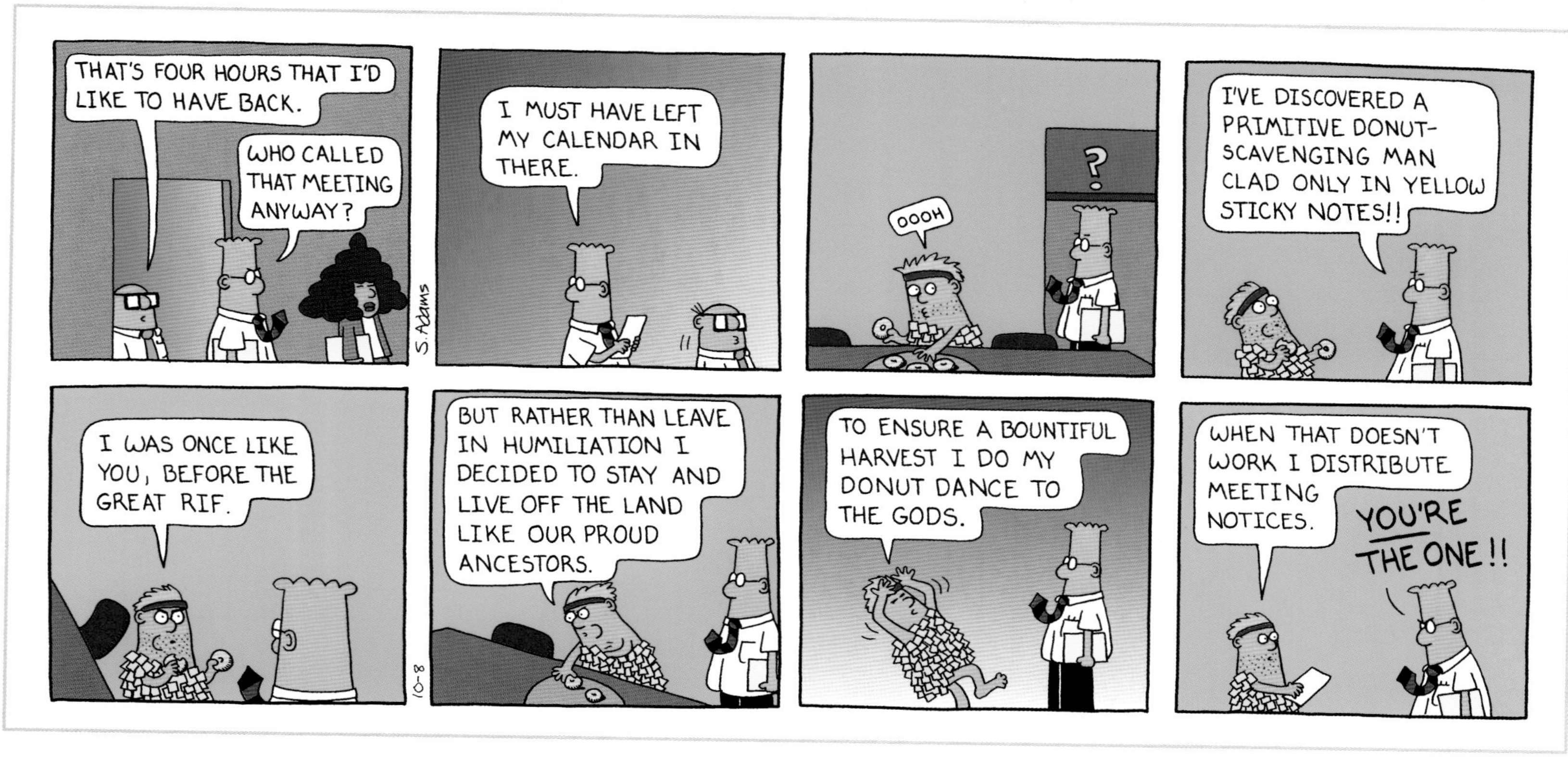
THAT'S FOUR HOURS THAT I'D LIKE TO HAVE BACK.
WHO CALLED THAT MEETING ANYWAY?
S. Adams
I MUST HAVE LEFT MY CALENDAR IN THERE.
OOOH
?
I'VE DISCOVERED A PRIMITIVE DONUT-SCAVENGING MAN CLAD ONLY IN YELLOW STICKY NOTES!!
I WAS ONCE LIKE YOU, BEFORE THE GREAT RIF.
10-8
BUT RATHER THAN LEAVE IN HUMILIATION I DECIDED TO STAY AND LIVE OFF THE LAND LIKE OUR PROUD ANCESTORS.
TO ENSURE A BOUNTIFUL HARVEST I DO MY DONUT DANCE TO THE GODS.
WHEN THAT DOESN'T WORK I DISTRIBUTE MEETING NOTICES.
YOU'RE THE ONE!!

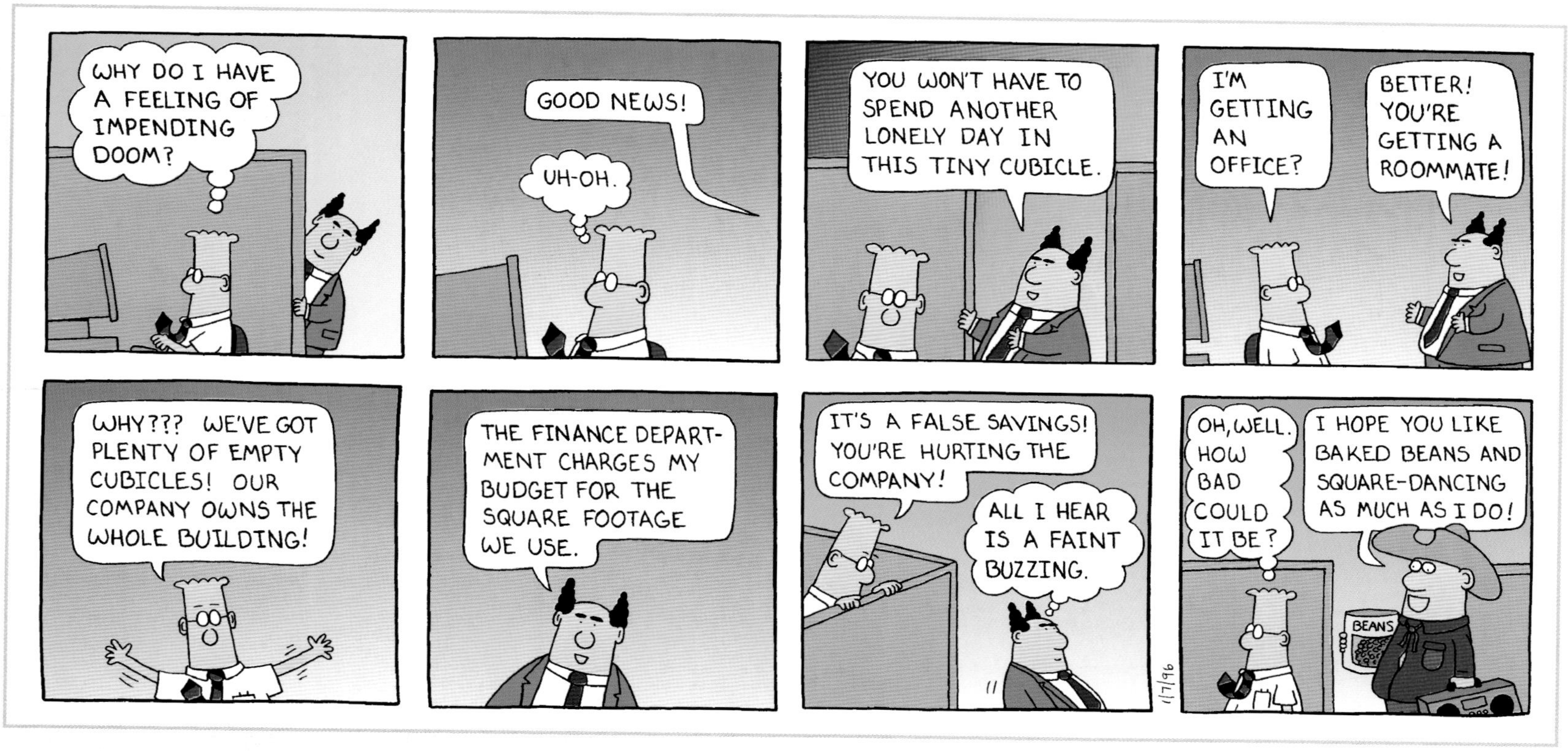
WHY DO I HAVE A FEELING OF IMPENDING DOOM?
GOOD NEWS!
UH-OH.
YOU WON'T HAVE TO SPEND ANOTHER LONELY DAY IN THIS TINY CUBICLE.
I'M GETTING AN OFFICE?
BETTER! YOU'RE GETTING A ROOMMATE!
WHY??? WE'VE GOT PLENTY OF EMPTY CUBICLES! OUR COMPANY OWNS THE WHOLE BUILDING!
THE FINANCE DEPARTMENT CHARGES MY BUDGET FOR THE SQUARE FOOTAGE WE USE.
IT'S A FALSE SAVINGS! YOU'RE HURTING THE COMPANY!
ALL I HEAR IS A FAINT BUZZING.
1/7/96
OH, WELL. HOW BAD COULD IT BE?
I HOPE YOU LIKE BAKED BEANS AND SQUARE-DANCING AS MUCH AS I DO!
BEANS

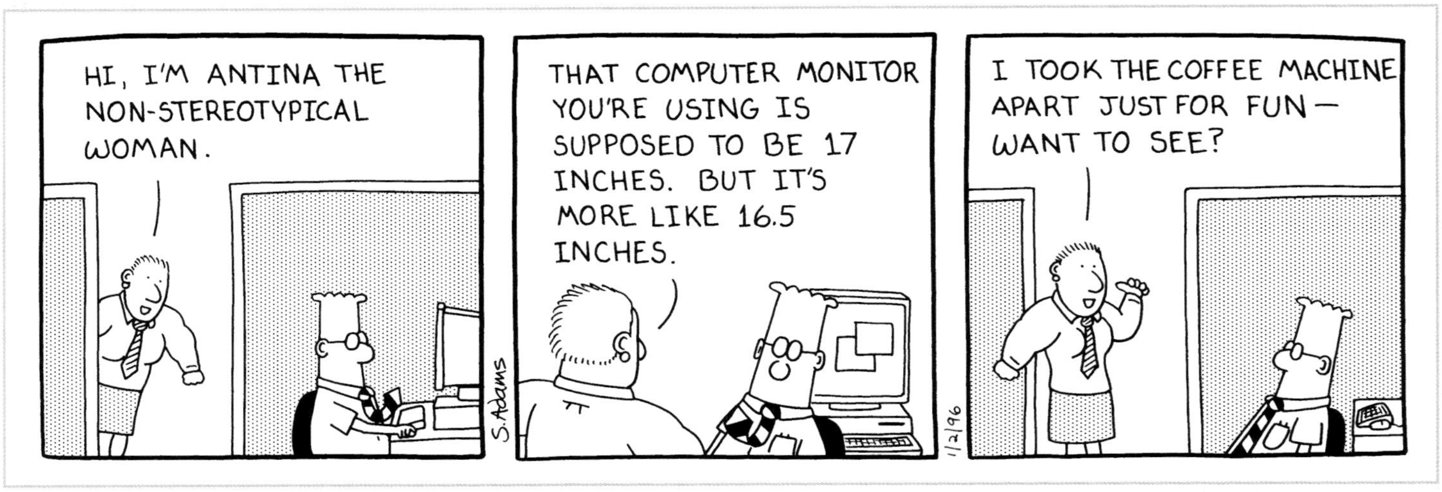
HI, I'M ANTINA THE NON-STEREOTYPICAL WOMAN.
THAT COMPUTER MONITOR YOU'RE USING IS SUPPOSED TO BE 17 INCHES. BUT IT'S MORE LIKE 16.5 INCHES.
S. Adams
1/2/96
I TOOK THE COFFEE MACHINE APART JUST FOR FUN — WANT TO SEE?

This is the second time I drew Dilbert's necktie lying flat. It was a subtle reference to Antina's lack of appeal. A surprising number of people noticed.

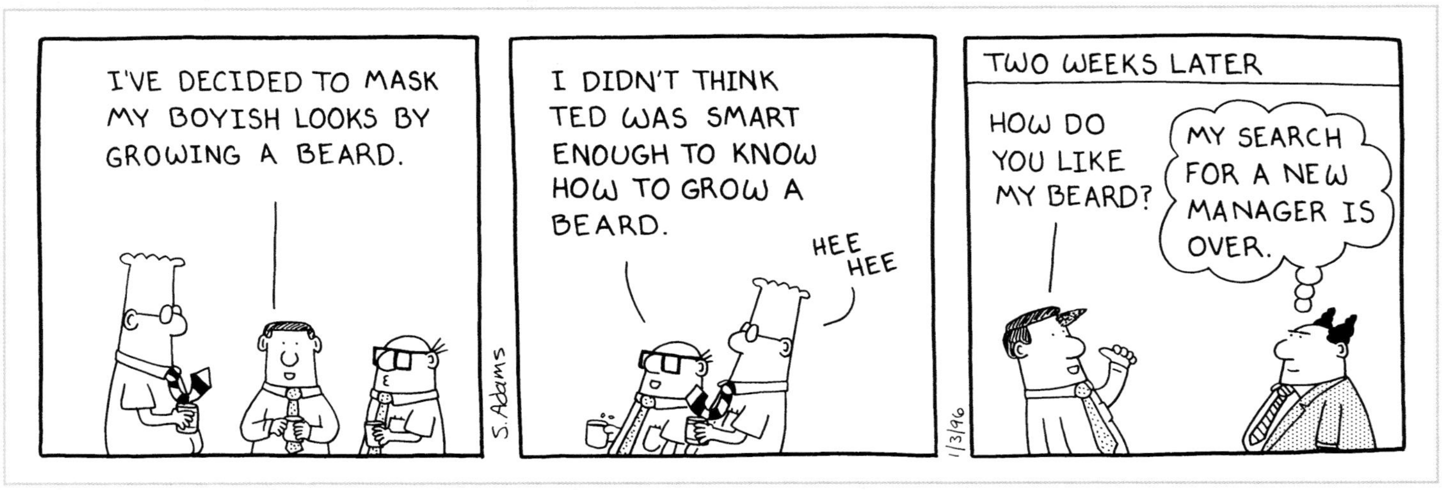
I'VE DECIDED TO MASK MY BOYISH LOOKS BY GROWING A BEARD.
I DIDN'T THINK TED WAS SMART ENOUGH TO KNOW HOW TO GROW A BEARD.
HEE HEE
S. Adams
1/3/96
TWO WEEKS LATER
HOW DO YOU LIKE MY BEARD?
MY SEARCH FOR A NEW MANAGER IS OVER.

This series ran not long after I left my day job at Pacific Bell and became a full-time cartoonist. My last boss—the one who asked me to leave so he could use the budget for someone more useful—had a goatee.

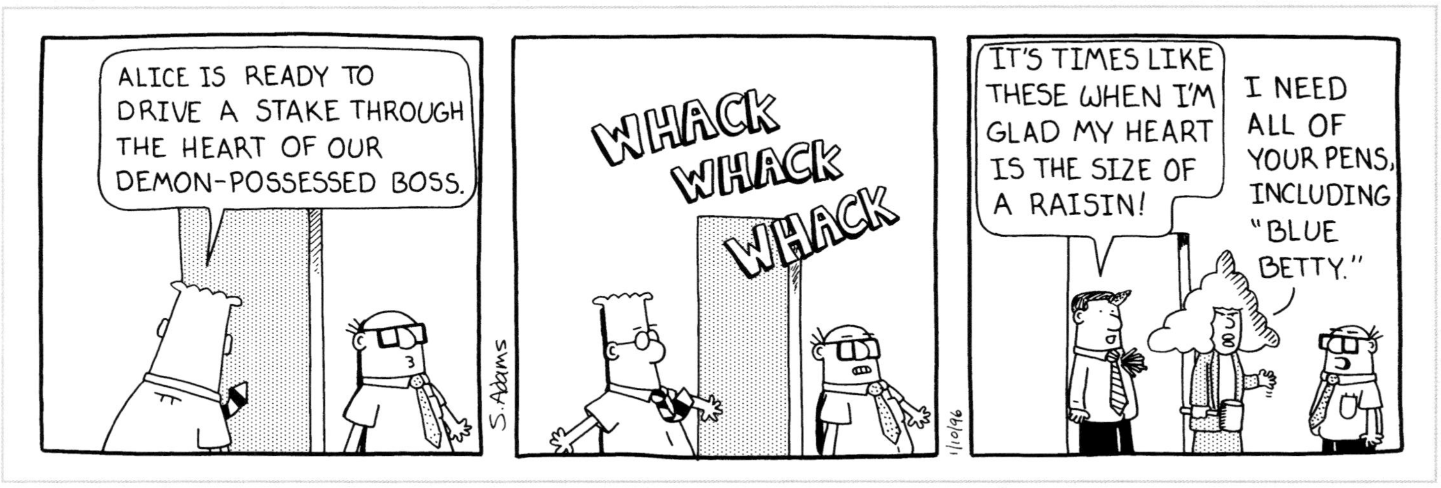
ALICE IS READY TO DRIVE A STAKE THROUGH THE HEART OF OUR DEMON-POSSESSED BOSS.
WHACK
WHACK
WHACK
S. Adams
1/10/96
IT'S TIMES LIKE THESE WHEN I'M GLAD MY HEART IS THE SIZE OF A RAISIN!
I NEED ALL OF YOUR PENS, INCLUDING "BLUE BETTY."

The great thing about being a cartoonist is the opportunity to get revenge without risking jail time.

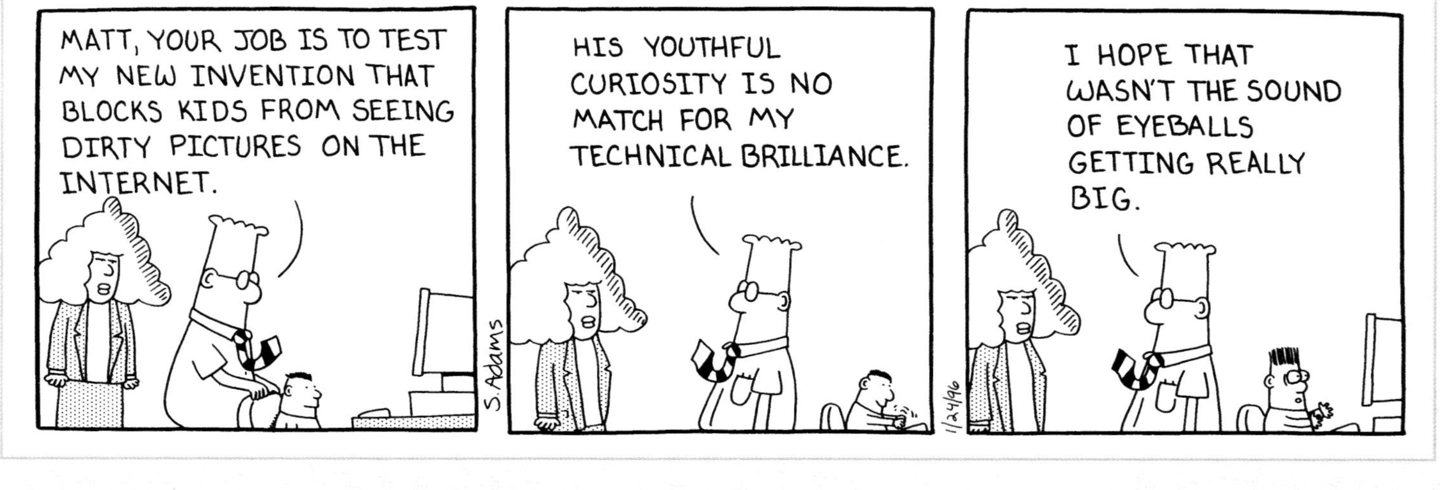
MATT, YOUR JOB IS TO TEST MY NEW INVENTION THAT BLOCKS KIDS FROM SEEING DIRTY PICTURES ON THE INTERNET.
HIS YOUTHFUL CURIOSITY IS NO MATCH FOR MY TECHNICAL BRILLIANCE.
S. Adams
1/24/96
I HOPE THAT WASN'T THE SOUND OF EYEBALLS GETTING REALLY BIG.

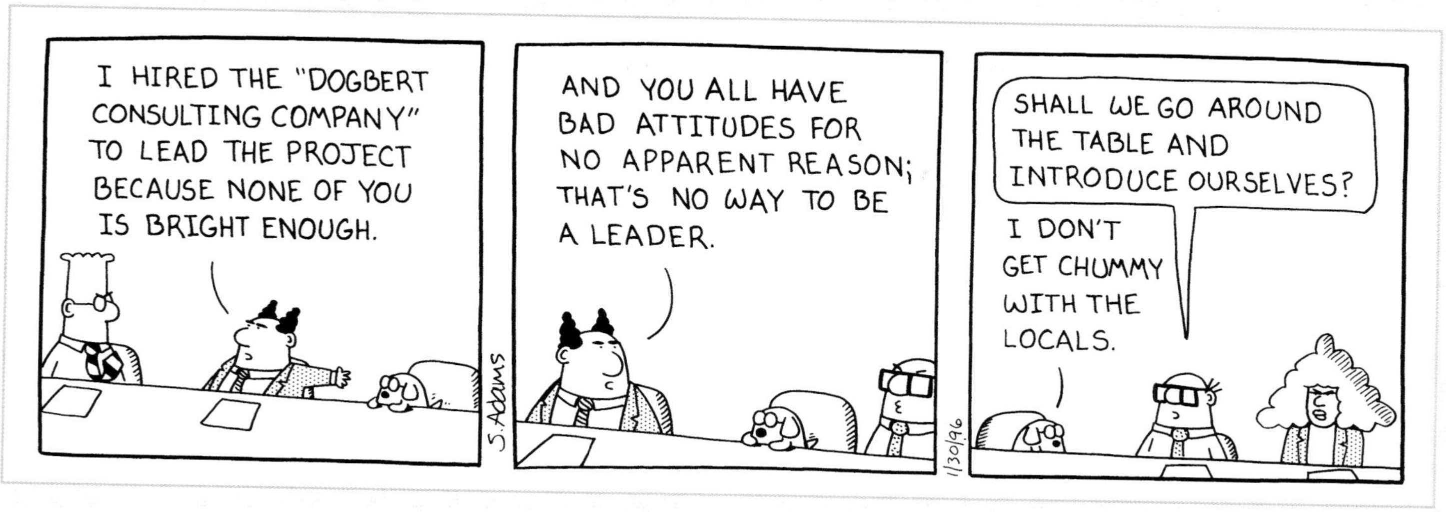
I HIRED THE "DOGBERT CONSULTING COMPANY" TO LEAD THE PROJECT BECAUSE NONE OF YOU IS BRIGHT ENOUGH.
AND YOU ALL HAVE BAD ATTITUDES FOR NO APPARENT REASON; THAT'S NO WAY TO BE A LEADER.
SHALL WE GO AROUND THE TABLE AND INTRODUCE OURSELVES?
I DON'T GET CHUMMY WITH THE LOCALS.
S. Adams
1/30/96

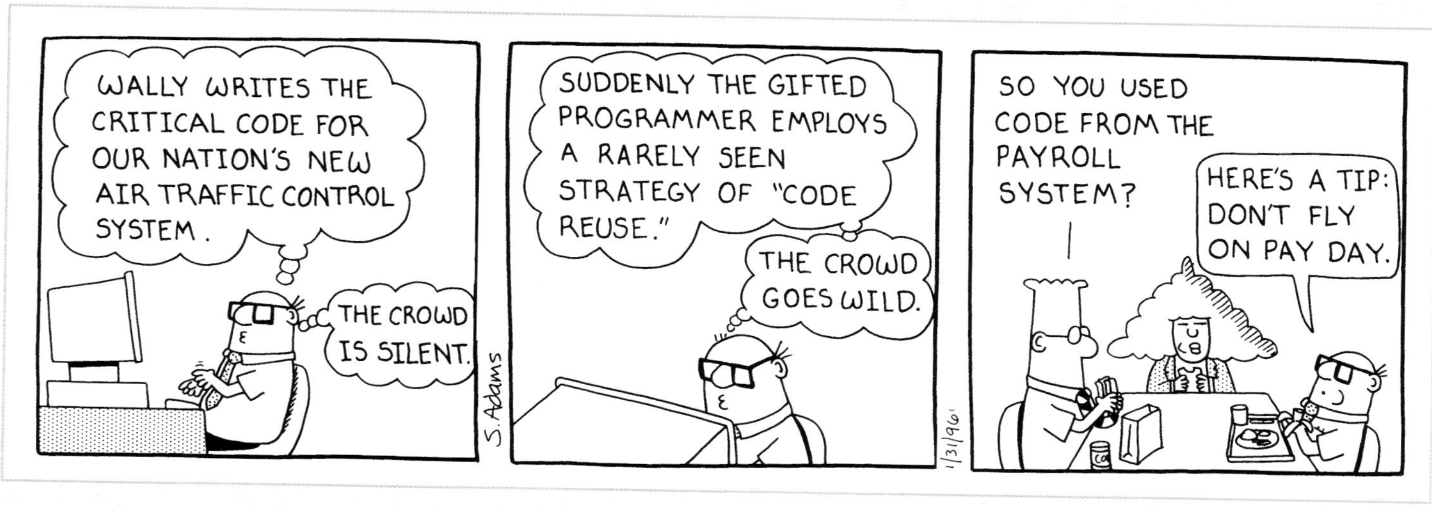
WALLY WRITES THE CRITICAL CODE FOR OUR NATION'S NEW AIR TRAFFIC CONTROL SYSTEM.
THE CROWD IS SILENT.
SUDDENLY THE GIFTED PROGRAMMER EMPLOYS A RARELY SEEN STRATEGY OF "CODE REUSE."
THE CROWD GOES WILD.
SO YOU USED CODE FROM THE PAYROLL SYSTEM?
HERE'S A TIP: DON'T FLY ON PAY DAY.
S. Adams
1/31/96

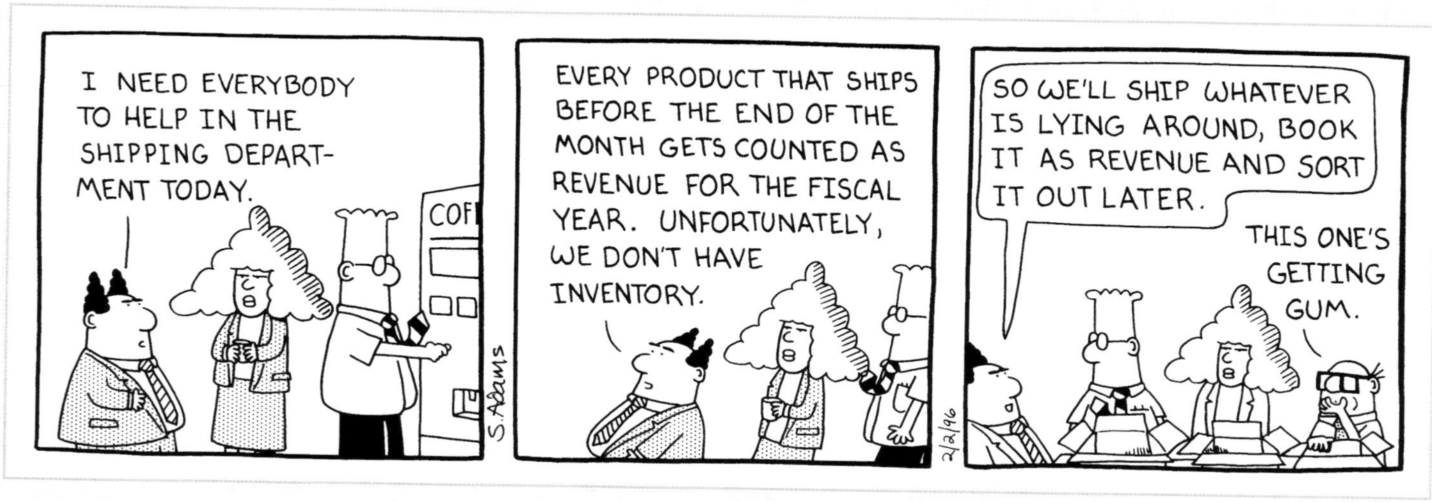
I NEED EVERYBODY TO HELP IN THE SHIPPING DEPARTMENT TODAY.
EVERY PRODUCT THAT SHIPS BEFORE THE END OF THE MONTH GETS COUNTED AS REVENUE FOR THE FISCAL YEAR. UNFORTUNATELY, WE DON'T HAVE INVENTORY.
SO WE'LL SHIP WHATEVER IS LYING AROUND, BOOK IT AS REVENUE AND SORT IT OUT LATER.
THIS ONE'S GETTING GUM.
S. Adams
2/2/96

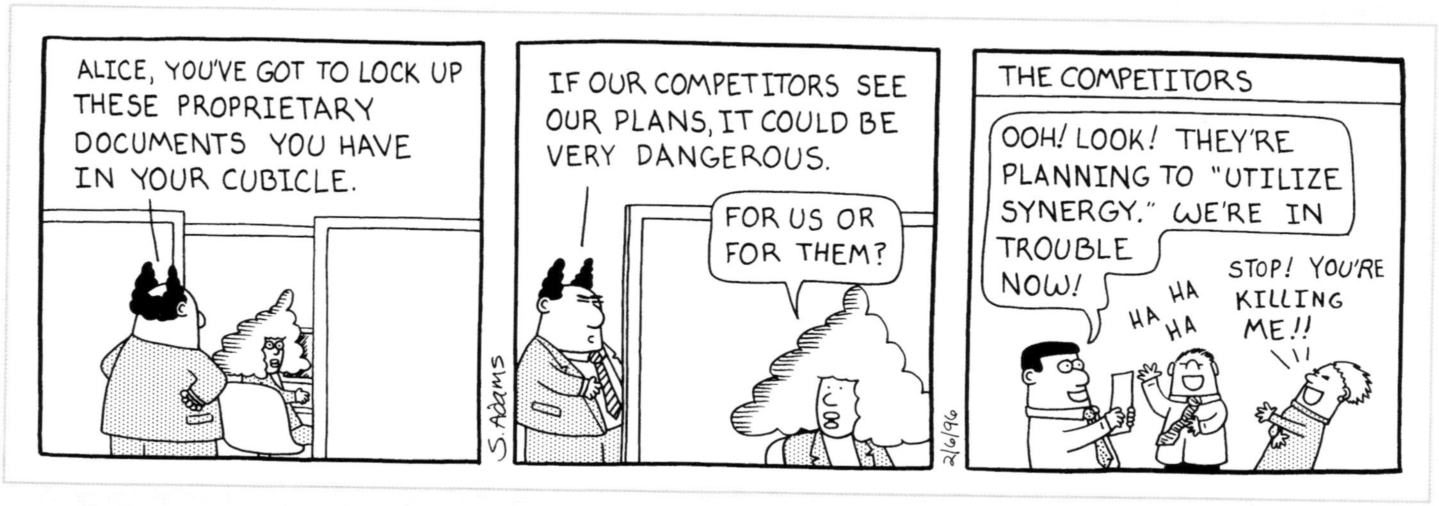
ALICE, YOU'VE GOT TO LOCK UP THESE PROPRIETARY DOCUMENTS YOU HAVE IN YOUR CUBICLE.
IF OUR COMPETITORS SEE OUR PLANS, IT COULD BE VERY DANGEROUS.
FOR US OR FOR THEM?
THE COMPETITORS
OOH! LOOK! THEY'RE PLANNING TO "UTILIZE SYNERGY." WE'RE IN TROUBLE NOW!
HA HA HA
STOP! YOU'RE KILLING ME!!
S. Adams
2/6/96

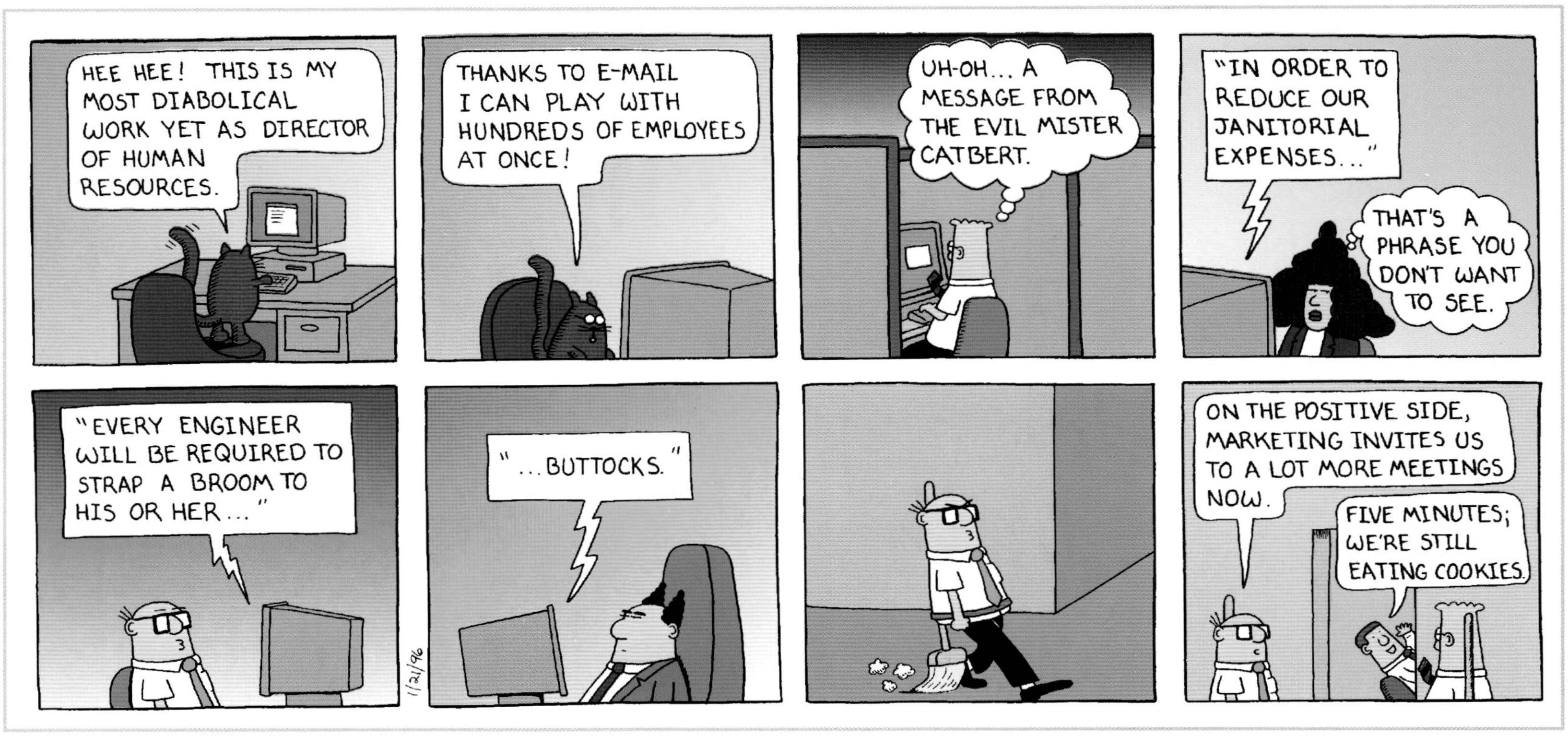
HEE HEE! THIS IS MY MOST DIABOLICAL WORK YET AS DIRECTOR OF HUMAN RESOURCES.
THANKS TO E-MAIL I CAN PLAY WITH HUNDREDS OF EMPLOYEES AT ONCE!
UH-OH... A MESSAGE FROM THE EVIL MISTER CATBERT.
"IN ORDER TO REDUCE OUR JANITORIAL EXPENSES..."
THAT'S A PHRASE YOU DON'T WANT TO SEE.
"EVERY ENGINEER WILL BE REQUIRED TO STRAP A BROOM TO HIS OR HER..."
1/21/96
"...BUTTOCKS."
ON THE POSITIVE SIDE, MARKETING INVITES US TO A LOT MORE MEETINGS NOW.
FIVE MINUTES; WE'RE STILL EATING COOKIES.

In my first draft, the brooms were inserted. That didn't make it past the editorial filters.

*This idea eventually became the theme of my first non-*Dilbert *book,* God's Debris.

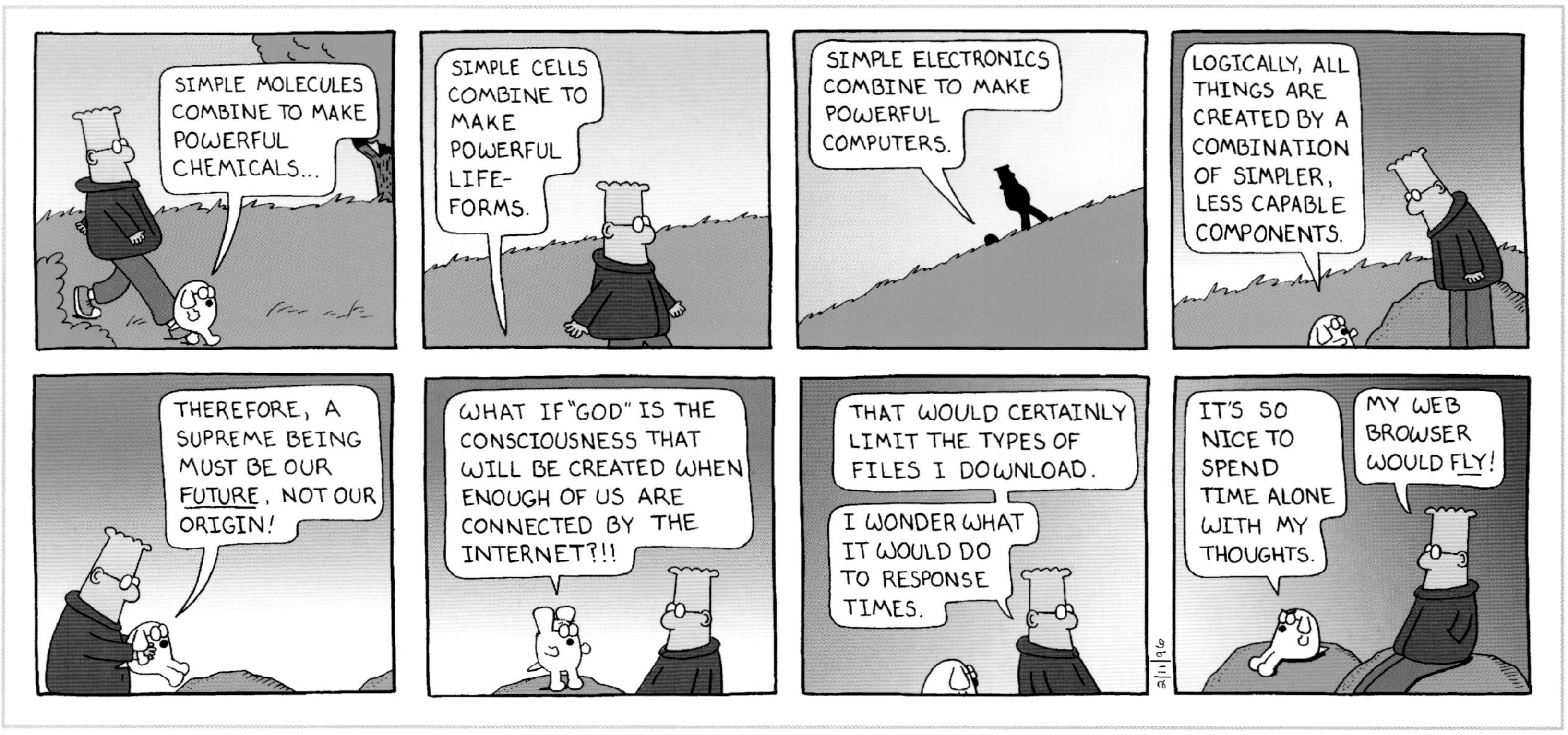
SIMPLE MOLECULES COMBINE TO MAKE POWERFUL CHEMICALS...
SIMPLE CELLS COMBINE TO MAKE POWERFUL LIFE-FORMS.
SIMPLE ELECTRONICS COMBINE TO MAKE POWERFUL COMPUTERS.
LOGICALLY, ALL THINGS ARE CREATED BY A COMBINATION OF SIMPLER, LESS CAPABLE COMPONENTS.
THEREFORE, A SUPREME BEING MUST BE OUR FUTURE, NOT OUR ORIGIN!
WHAT IF "GOD" IS THE CONSCIOUSNESS THAT WILL BE CREATED WHEN ENOUGH OF US ARE CONNECTED BY THE INTERNET?!!
THAT WOULD CERTAINLY LIMIT THE TYPES OF FILES I DOWNLOAD.
I WONDER WHAT IT WOULD DO TO RESPONSE TIMES.
2/1/96
IT'S SO NICE TO SPEND TIME ALONE WITH MY THOUGHTS.
MY WEB BROWSER WOULD FLY!

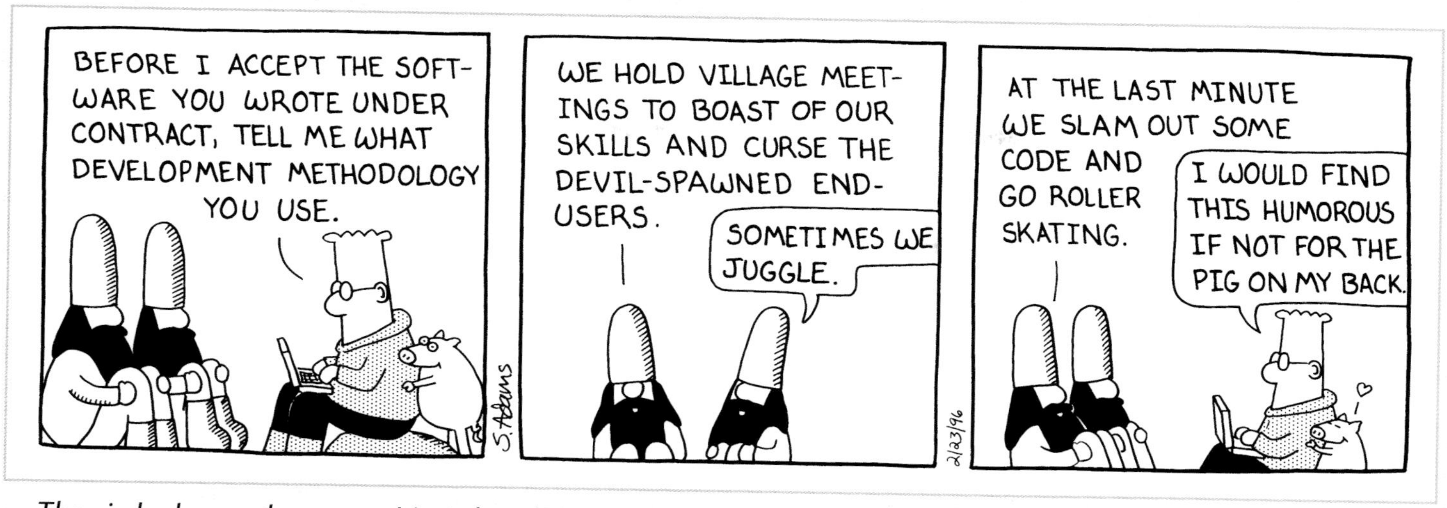
BEFORE I ACCEPT THE SOFTWARE YOU WROTE UNDER CONTRACT, TELL ME WHAT DEVELOPMENT METHODOLOGY YOU USE.
WE HOLD VILLAGE MEETINGS TO BOAST OF OUR SKILLS AND CURSE THE DEVIL-SPAWNED END-USERS.
SOMETIMES WE JUGGLE.
AT THE LAST MINUTE WE SLAM OUT SOME CODE AND GO ROLLER SKATING.
I WOULD FIND THIS HUMOROUS IF NOT FOR THE PIG ON MY BACK.
S. Adams
2/23/96

The pig had no real purpose. I just thought pigs would be wandering around in Elbonia. And pigs are fun to draw. I often draw my comics before I write the dialogue, starting with a general idea and hoping something funny occurs to me. In this case, the drawing of the pig suggested the last line. That's why it seems so random.

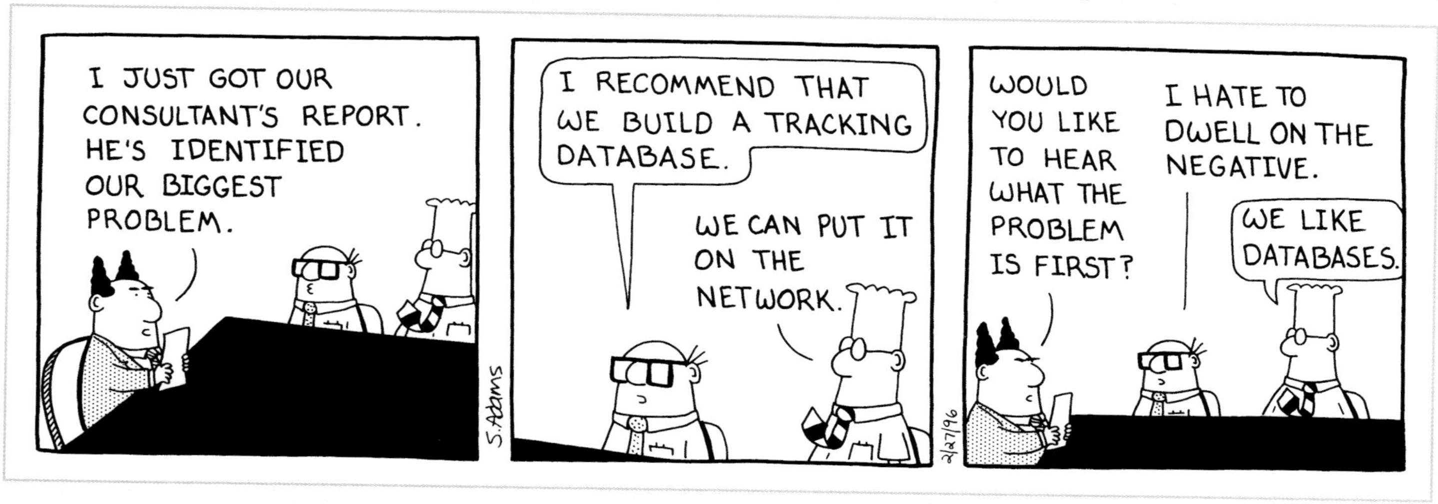
I JUST GOT OUR CONSULTANT'S REPORT. HE'S IDENTIFIED OUR BIGGEST PROBLEM.
I RECOMMEND THAT WE BUILD A TRACKING DATABASE.
WE CAN PUT IT ON THE NETWORK.
WOULD YOU LIKE TO HEAR WHAT THE PROBLEM IS FIRST?
I HATE TO DWELL ON THE NEGATIVE.
WE LIKE DATABASES.
S. Adams
2/27/96

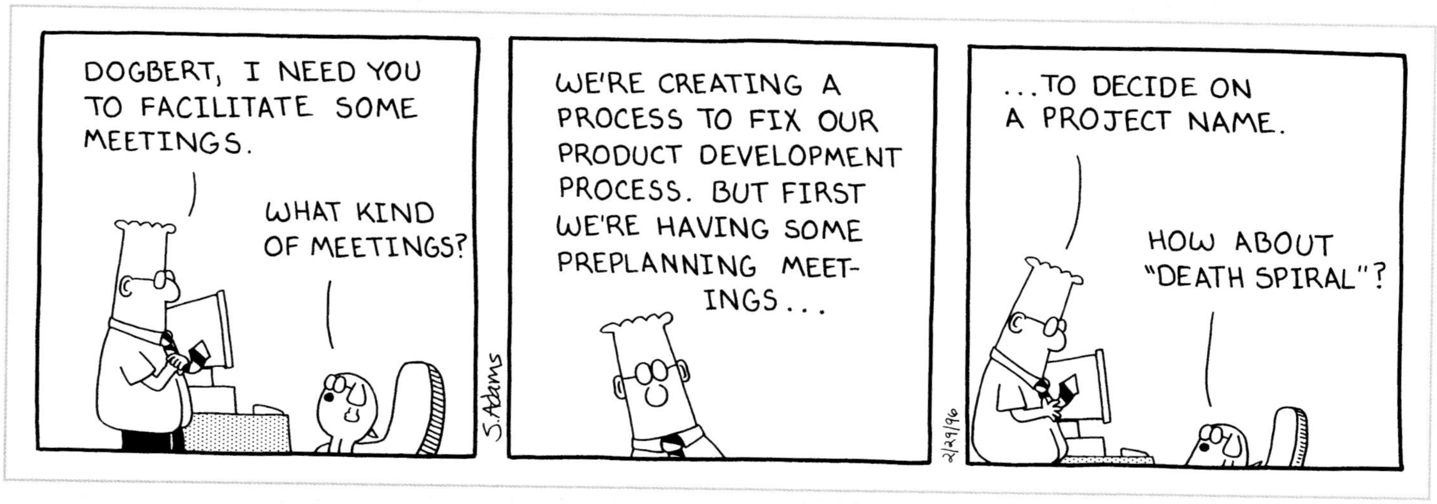
DOGBERT, I NEED YOU TO FACILITATE SOME MEETINGS.
WHAT KIND OF MEETINGS?
WE'RE CREATING A PROCESS TO FIX OUR PRODUCT DEVELOPMENT PROCESS. BUT FIRST WE'RE HAVING SOME PREPLANNING MEETINGS...
...TO DECIDE ON A PROJECT NAME.
HOW ABOUT "DEATH SPIRAL"?
S. Adams
2/29/96

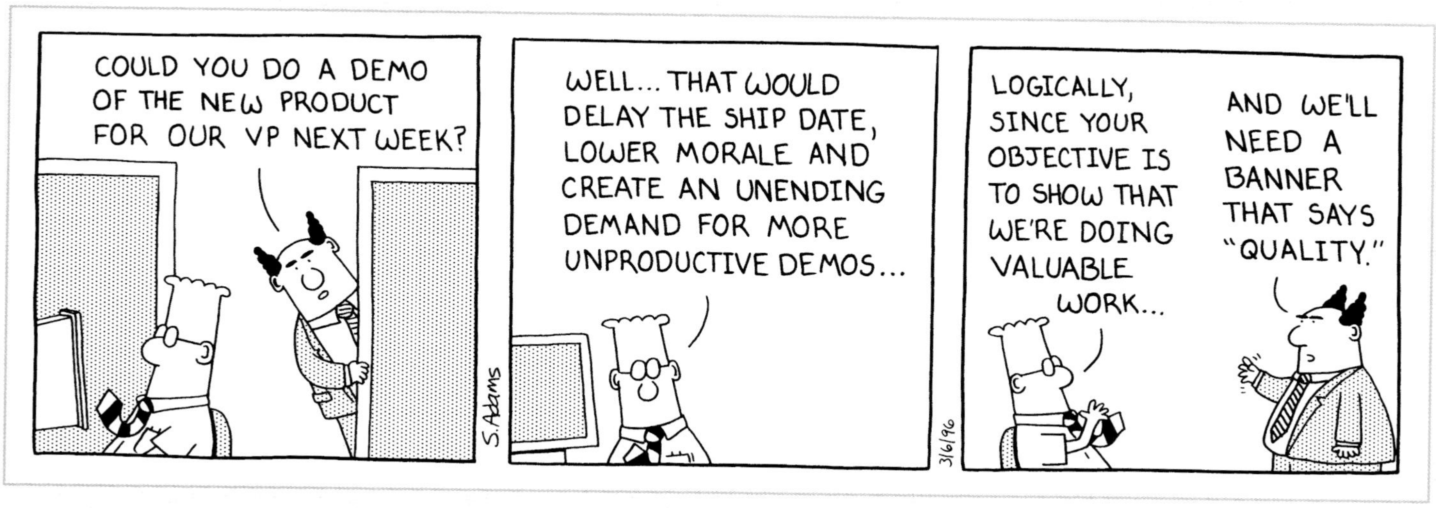
COULD YOU DO A DEMO OF THE NEW PRODUCT FOR OUR VP NEXT WEEK?
WELL... THAT WOULD DELAY THE SHIP DATE, LOWER MORALE AND CREATE AN UNENDING DEMAND FOR MORE UNPRODUCTIVE DEMOS...
LOGICALLY, SINCE YOUR OBJECTIVE IS TO SHOW THAT WE'RE DOING VALUABLE WORK...
AND WE'LL NEED A BANNER THAT SAYS "QUALITY."
S. Adams
3/6/96

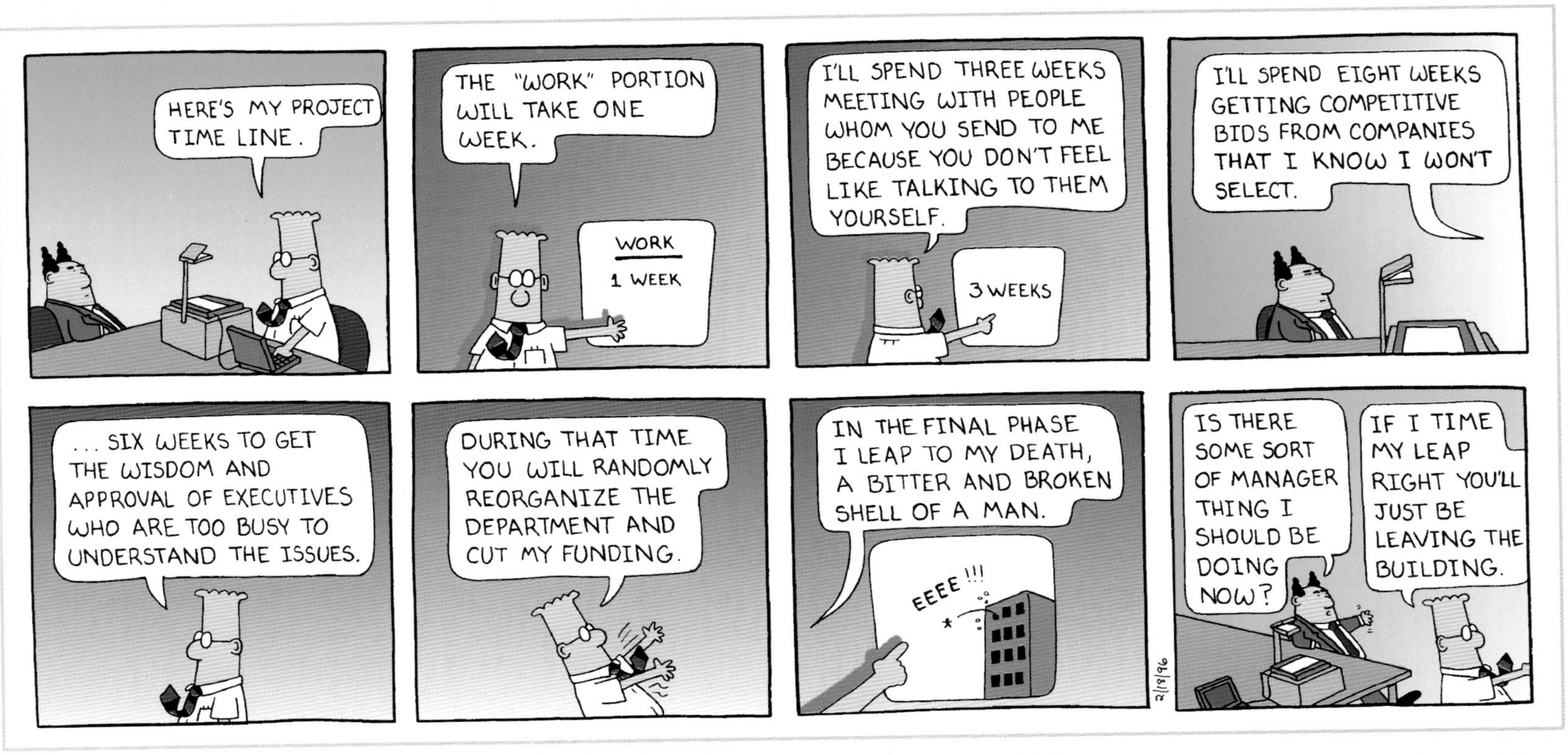
HERE'S MY PROJECT TIME LINE.
THE "WORK" PORTION WILL TAKE ONE WEEK.
WORK
1 WEEK
I'LL SPEND THREE WEEKS MEETING WITH PEOPLE WHOM YOU SEND TO ME BECAUSE YOU DON'T FEEL LIKE TALKING TO THEM YOURSELF.
3 WEEKS
I'LL SPEND EIGHT WEEKS GETTING COMPETITIVE BIDS FROM COMPANIES THAT I KNOW I WON'T SELECT.
. . . SIX WEEKS TO GET THE WISDOM AND APPROVAL OF EXECUTIVES WHO ARE TOO BUSY TO UNDERSTAND THE ISSUES.
DURING THAT TIME YOU WILL RANDOMLY REORGANIZE THE DEPARTMENT AND CUT MY FUNDING.
IN THE FINAL PHASE I LEAP TO MY DEATH, A BITTER AND BROKEN SHELL OF A MAN.
EEEE!!!
2/18/96
IS THERE SOME SORT OF MANAGER THING I SHOULD BE DOING NOW?
IF I TIME MY LEAP RIGHT YOU'LL JUST BE LEAVING THE BUILDING.

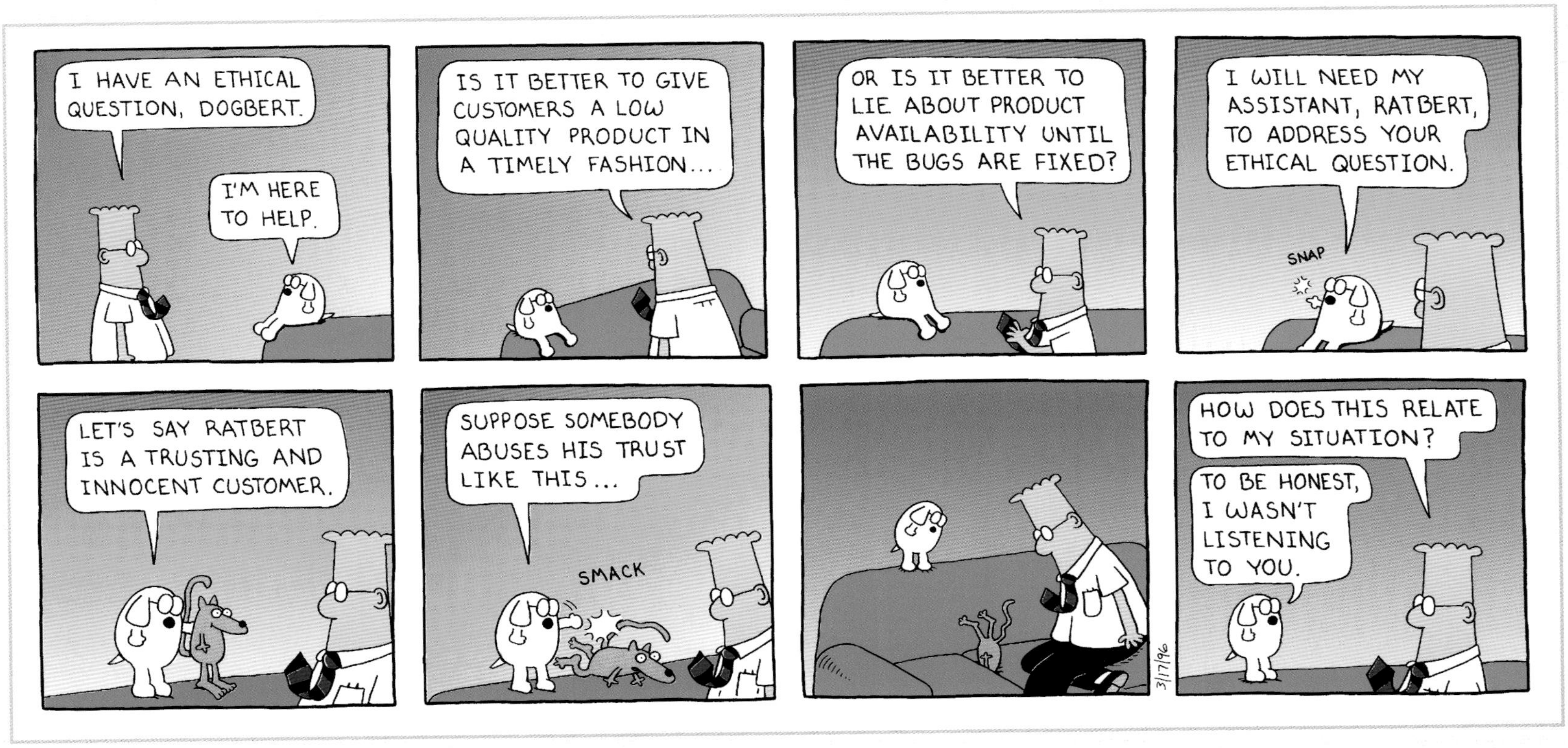
I HAVE AN ETHICAL QUESTION, DOGBERT.
I'M HERE TO HELP.
IS IT BETTER TO GIVE CUSTOMERS A LOW QUALITY PRODUCT IN A TIMELY FASHION...
OR IS IT BETTER TO LIE ABOUT PRODUCT AVAILABILITY UNTIL THE BUGS ARE FIXED?
I WILL NEED MY ASSISTANT, RATBERT, TO ADDRESS YOUR ETHICAL QUESTION.
SNAP
LET'S SAY RATBERT IS A TRUSTING AND INNOCENT CUSTOMER.
SUPPOSE SOMEBODY ABUSES HIS TRUST LIKE THIS...
SMACK
3/17/96
HOW DOES THIS RELATE TO MY SITUATION?
TO BE HONEST, I WASN'T LISTENING TO YOU.

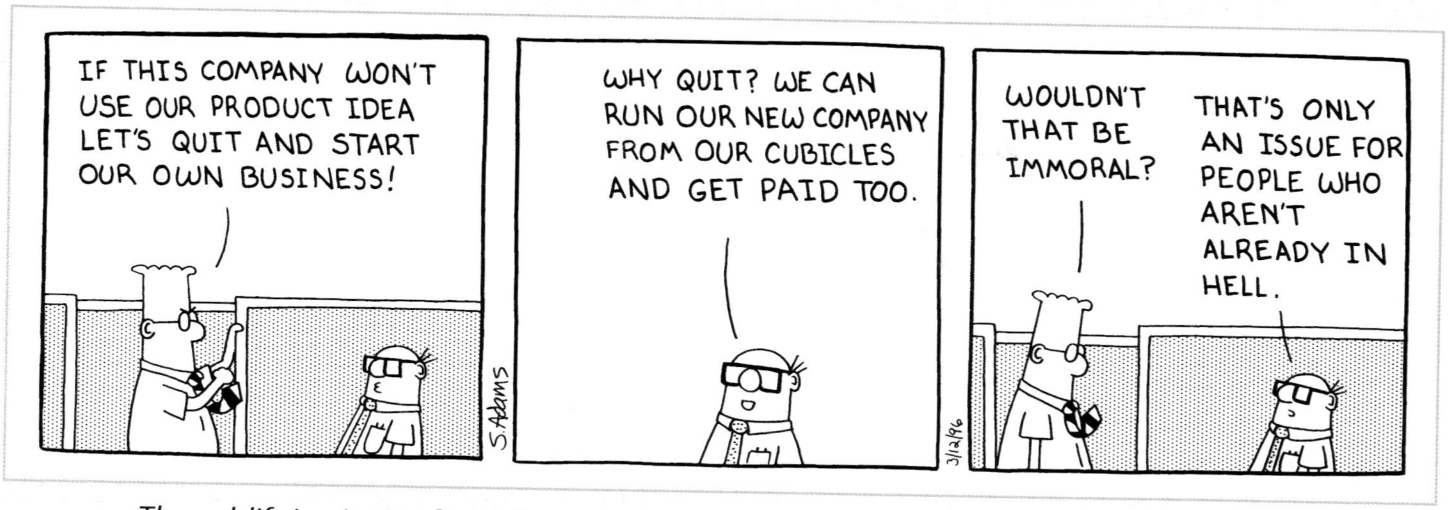
IF THIS COMPANY WON'T USE OUR PRODUCT IDEA LET'S QUIT AND START OUR OWN BUSINESS!
S. Adams
WHY QUIT? WE CAN RUN OUR NEW COMPANY FROM OUR CUBICLES AND GET PAID TOO.
WOULDN'T THAT BE IMMORAL?
THAT'S ONLY AN ISSUE FOR PEOPLE WHO AREN'T ALREADY IN HELL.

The real-life inspiration for Wally, my co-worker, ran a side business out of his cubicle behind me.

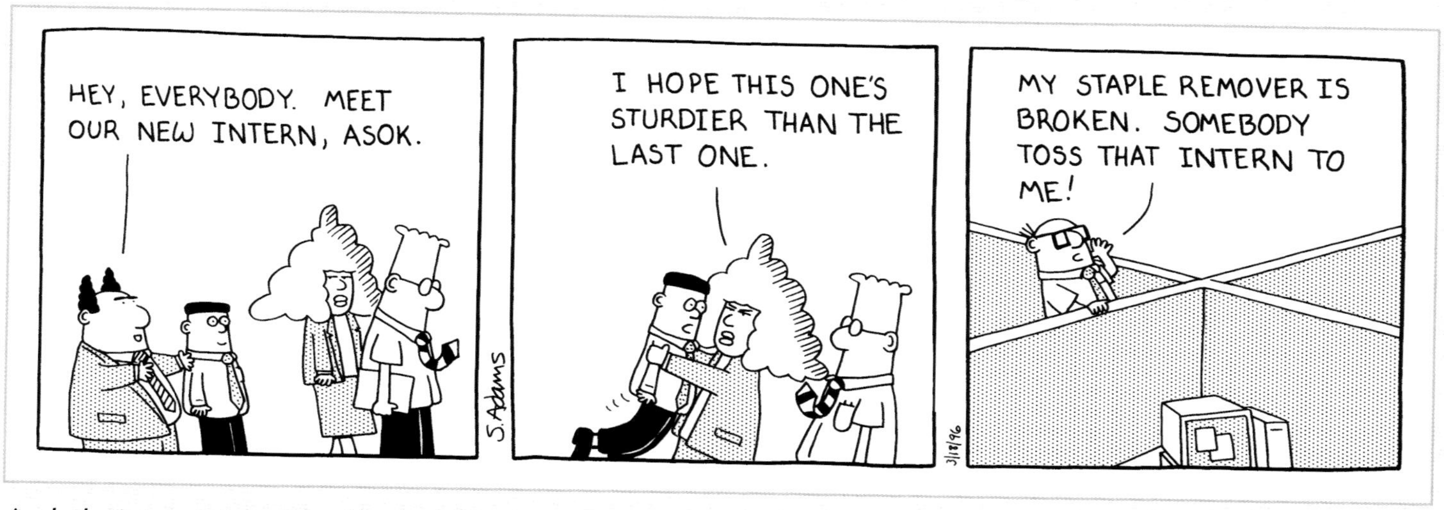
HEY, EVERYBODY. MEET OUR NEW INTERN, ASOK.
S. Adams
I HOPE THIS ONE'S STURDIER THAN THE LAST ONE.
MY STAPLE REMOVER IS BROKEN. SOMEBODY TOSS THAT INTERN TO ME!

Asok the intern is introduced here. I didn't know he would become a regular. He's named after a friend of mine from my day job at Pacific Bell, who spelled his name that way. I didn't know that the common spelling in India is Ashok. Many people have wondered if Asok is actually an acronym for something. I've heard some good scatological guesses.

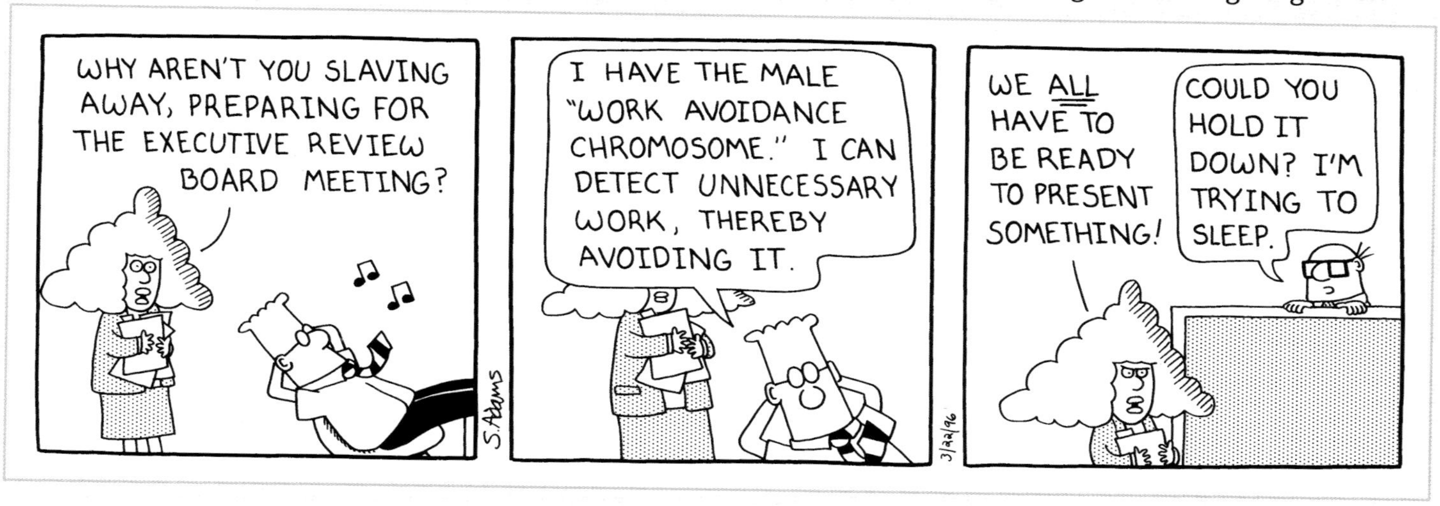
WHY AREN'T YOU SLAVING AWAY, PREPARING FOR THE EXECUTIVE REVIEW BOARD MEETING?
S. Adams
I HAVE THE MALE "WORK AVOIDANCE CHROMOSOME." I CAN DETECT UNNECESSARY WORK, THEREBY AVOIDING IT.
WE ALL HAVE TO BE READY TO PRESENT SOMETHING!
COULD YOU HOLD IT DOWN? I'M TRYING TO SLEEP.

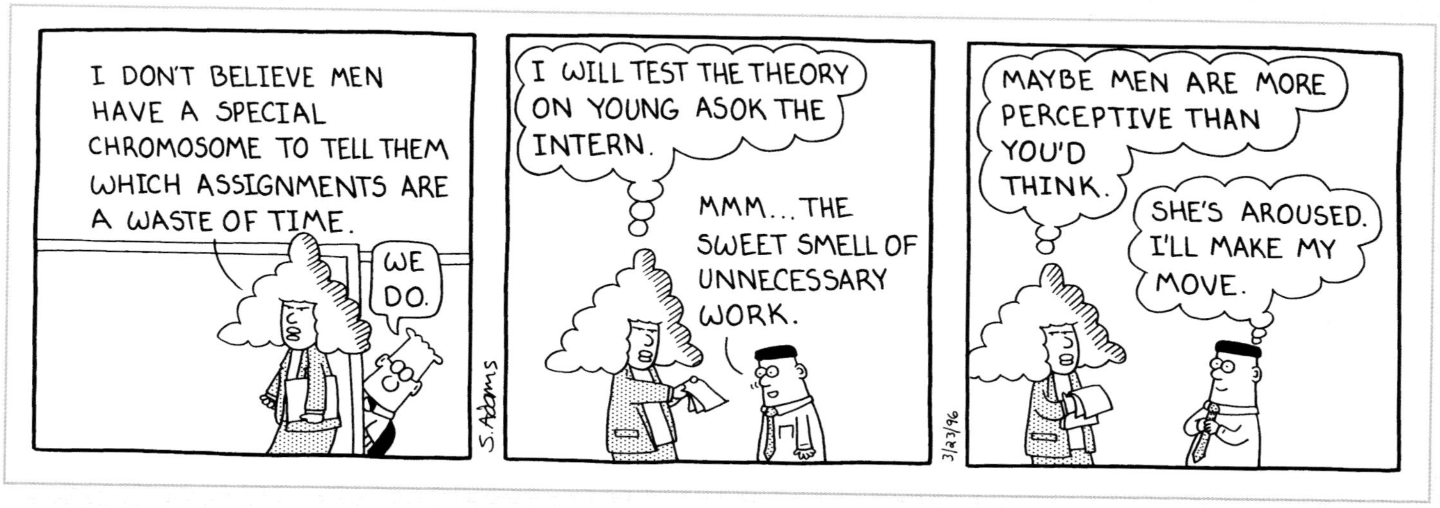
I DON'T BELIEVE MEN HAVE A SPECIAL CHROMOSOME TO TELL THEM WHICH ASSIGNMENTS ARE A WASTE OF TIME.
WE DO.
S. Adams
I WILL TEST THE THEORY ON YOUNG ASOK THE INTERN.
MMM... THE SWEET SMELL OF UNNECESSARY WORK.
MAYBE MEN ARE MORE PERCEPTIVE THAN YOU'D THINK.
SHE'S AROUSED. I'LL MAKE MY MOVE.

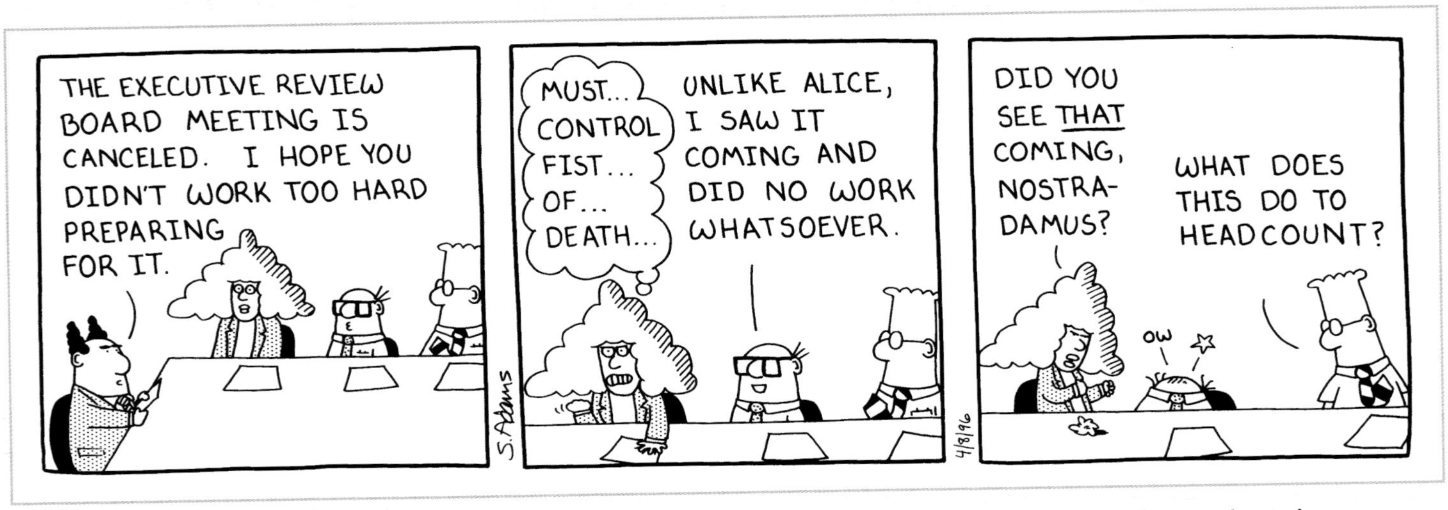
THE EXECUTIVE REVIEW BOARD MEETING IS CANCELED. I HOPE YOU DIDN'T WORK TOO HARD PREPARING FOR IT.
MUST... CONTROL FIST... OF... DEATH...
UNLIKE ALICE, I SAW IT COMING AND DID NO WORK WHATSOEVER.
DID YOU SEE THAT COMING, NOSTRA-DAMUS?
OW
WHAT DOES THIS DO TO HEADCOUNT?
S. Adams
4/8/96

This is the first strip with Alice trying to control her Fist of Death. Later it became her trademark.

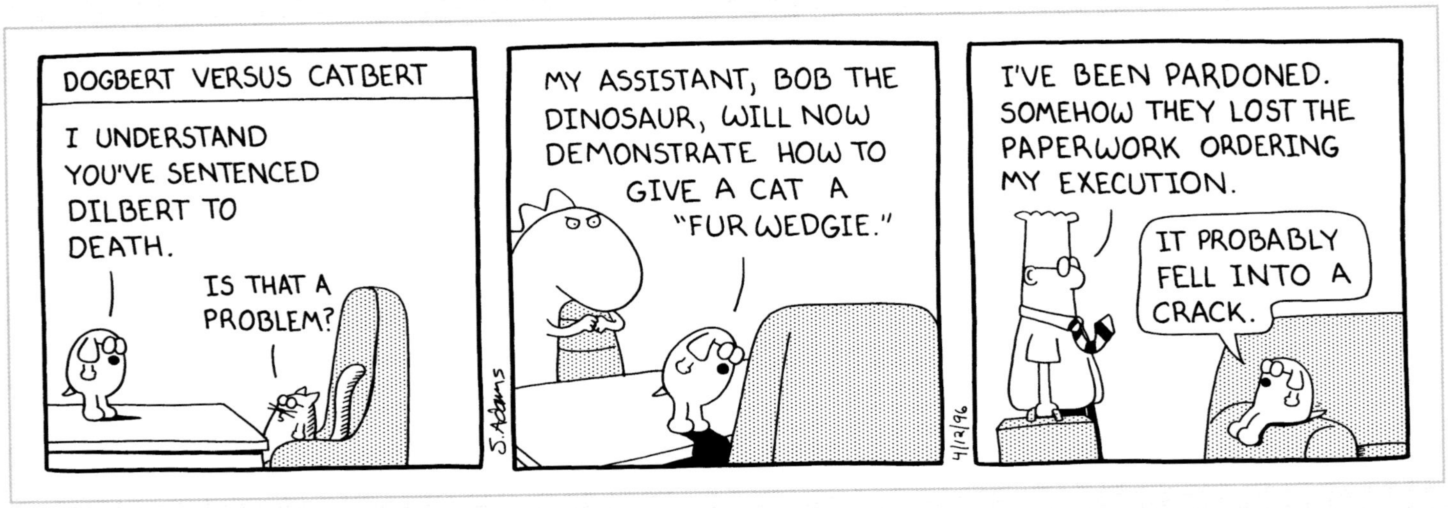
DOGBERT VERSUS CATBERT
I UNDERSTAND YOU'VE SENTENCED DILBERT TO DEATH.
IS THAT A PROBLEM?
MY ASSISTANT, BOB THE DINOSAUR, WILL NOW DEMONSTRATE HOW TO GIVE A CAT A "FUR WEDGIE."
I'VE BEEN PARDONED. SOMEHOW THEY LOST THE PAPERWORK ORDERING MY EXECUTION.
IT PROBABLY FELL INTO A CRACK.
S. Adams
4/12/96

If you think the reference to a crack has an intentional double meaning, you might be right. I'm not saying.

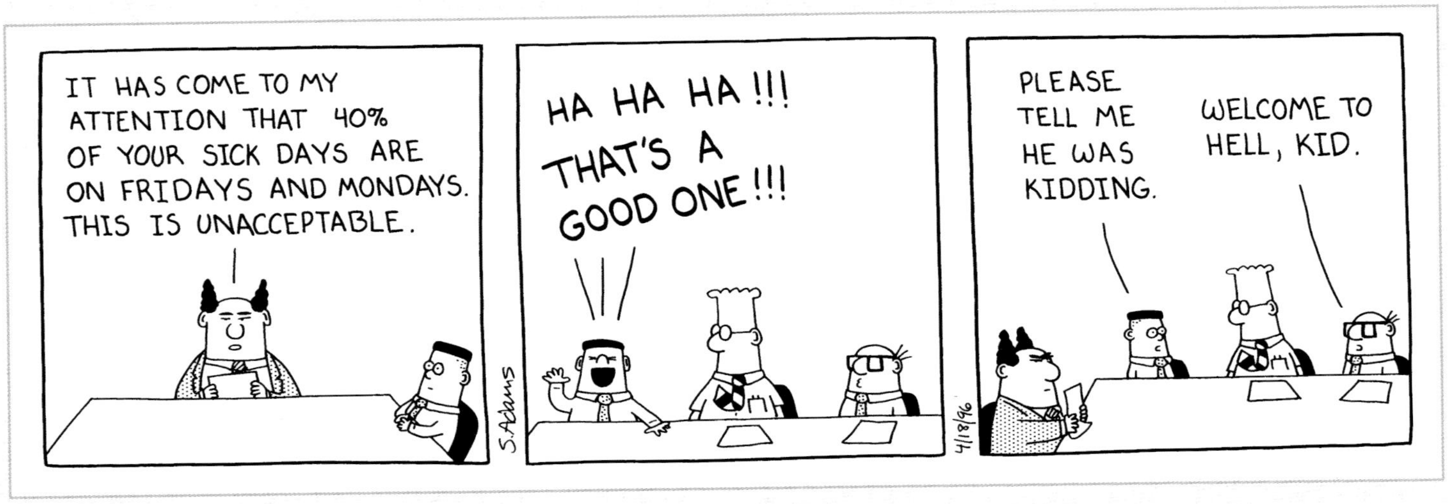
IT HAS COME TO MY ATTENTION THAT 40% OF YOUR SICK DAYS ARE ON FRIDAYS AND MONDAYS. THIS IS UNACCEPTABLE.
HA HA HA!!! THAT'S A GOOD ONE!!!
PLEASE TELL ME HE WAS KIDDING.
WELCOME TO HELL, KID.
S. Adams
4/18/96

Amazingly, this comic comes directly from real life. (Friday plus Monday equals 40 percent of the workweek, so you'd expect that much absence.)

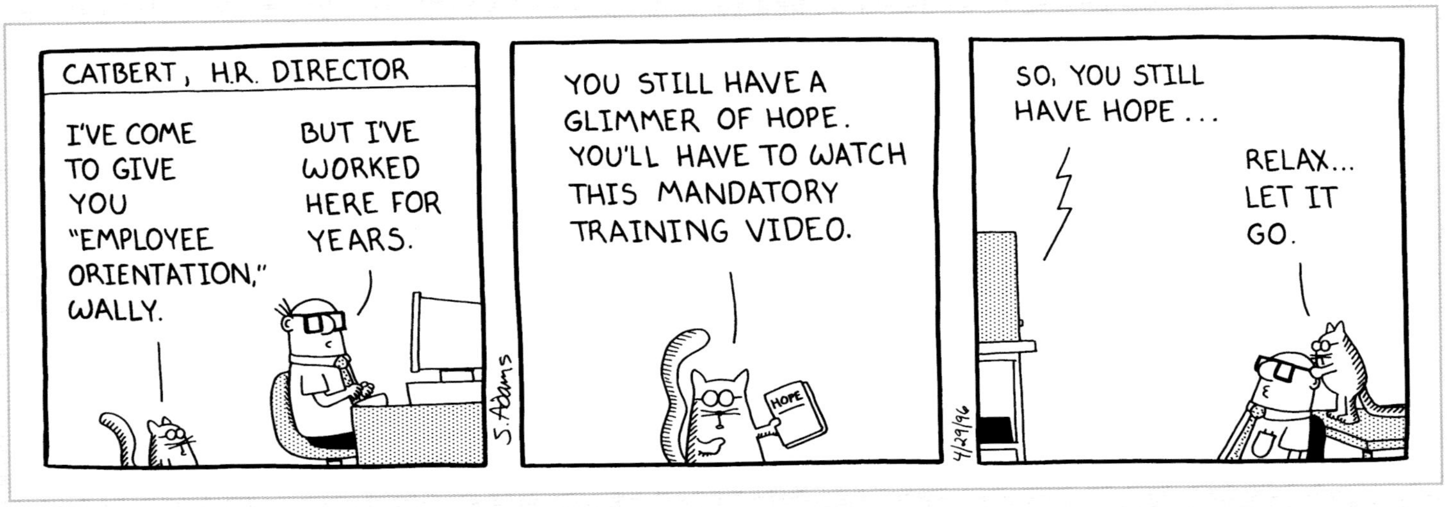
CATBERT, H.R. DIRECTOR
I'VE COME TO GIVE YOU "EMPLOYEE ORIENTATION," WALLY.
BUT I'VE WORKED HERE FOR YEARS.
YOU STILL HAVE A GLIMMER OF HOPE. YOU'LL HAVE TO WATCH THIS MANDATORY TRAINING VIDEO.
HOPE
SO, YOU STILL HAVE HOPE...
RELAX... LET IT GO.
S. Adams
4/29/96

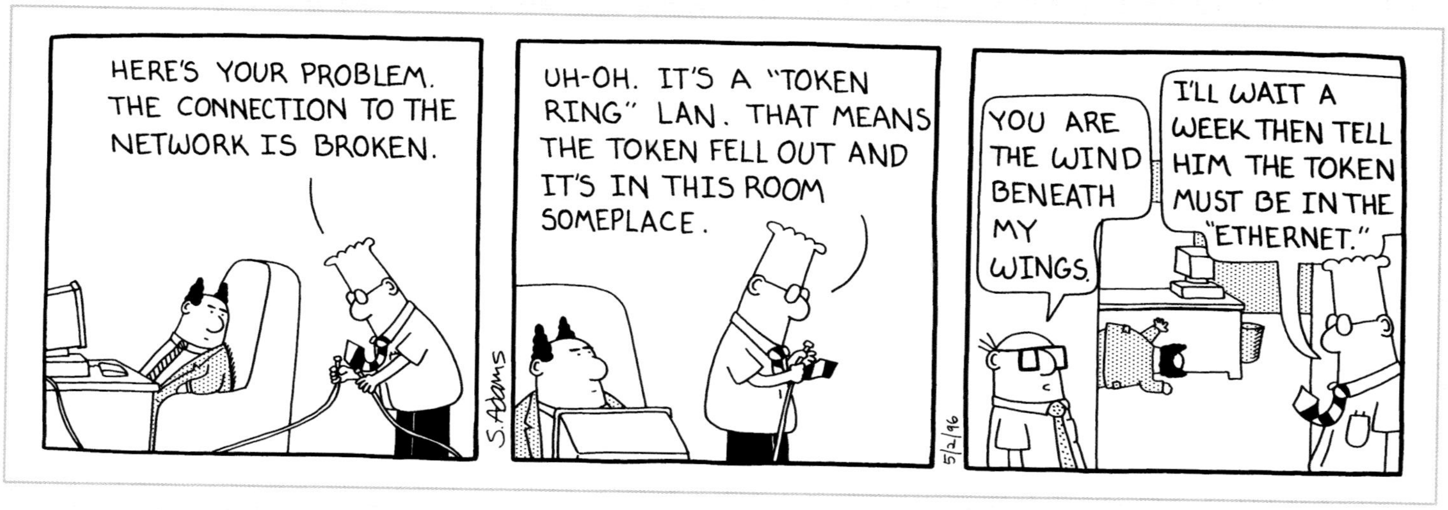
HERE'S YOUR PROBLEM. THE CONNECTION TO THE NETWORK IS BROKEN.
UH-OH. IT'S A "TOKEN RING" LAN. THAT MEANS THE TOKEN FELL OUT AND IT'S IN THIS ROOM SOMEPLACE.
S. Adams
YOU ARE THE WIND BENEATH MY WINGS.
I'LL WAIT A WEEK THEN TELL HIM THE TOKEN MUST BE IN THE "ETHERNET."
5/2/96

The strip above is a bit dated, but at the time it was one of the most popular strips I had drawn.

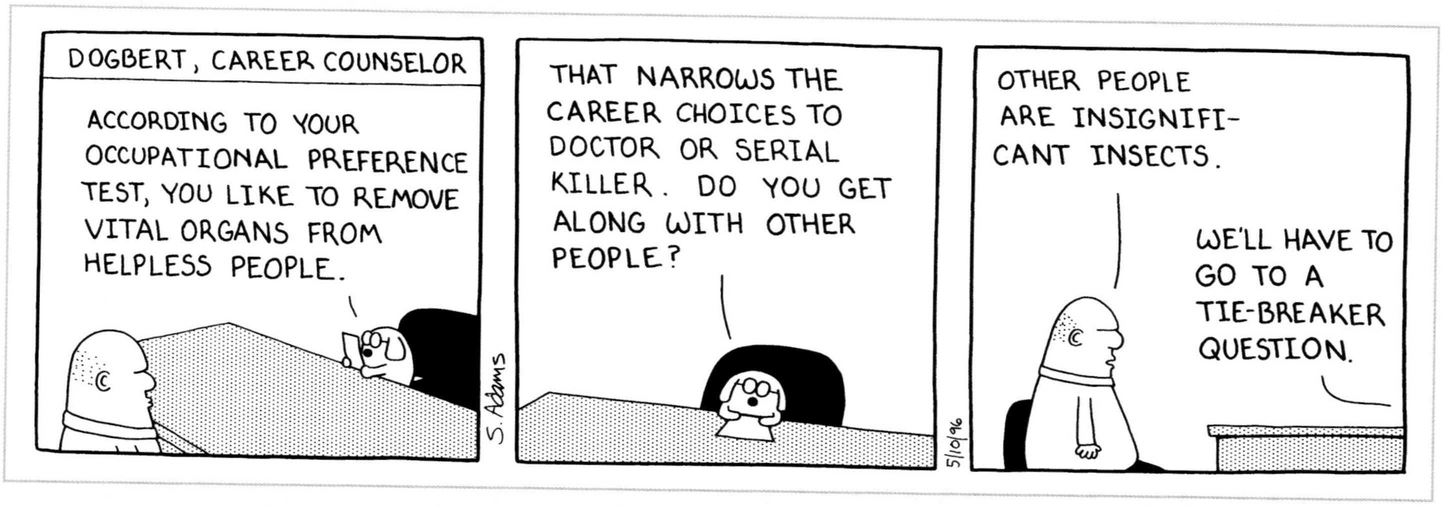
DOGBERT, CAREER COUNSELOR
ACCORDING TO YOUR OCCUPATIONAL PREFERENCE TEST, YOU LIKE TO REMOVE VITAL ORGANS FROM HELPLESS PEOPLE.
S. Adams
THAT NARROWS THE CAREER CHOICES TO DOCTOR OR SERIAL KILLER. DO YOU GET ALONG WITH OTHER PEOPLE?
5/10/96
OTHER PEOPLE ARE INSIGNIFI-CANT INSECTS.
WE'LL HAVE TO GO TO A TIE-BREAKER QUESTION.

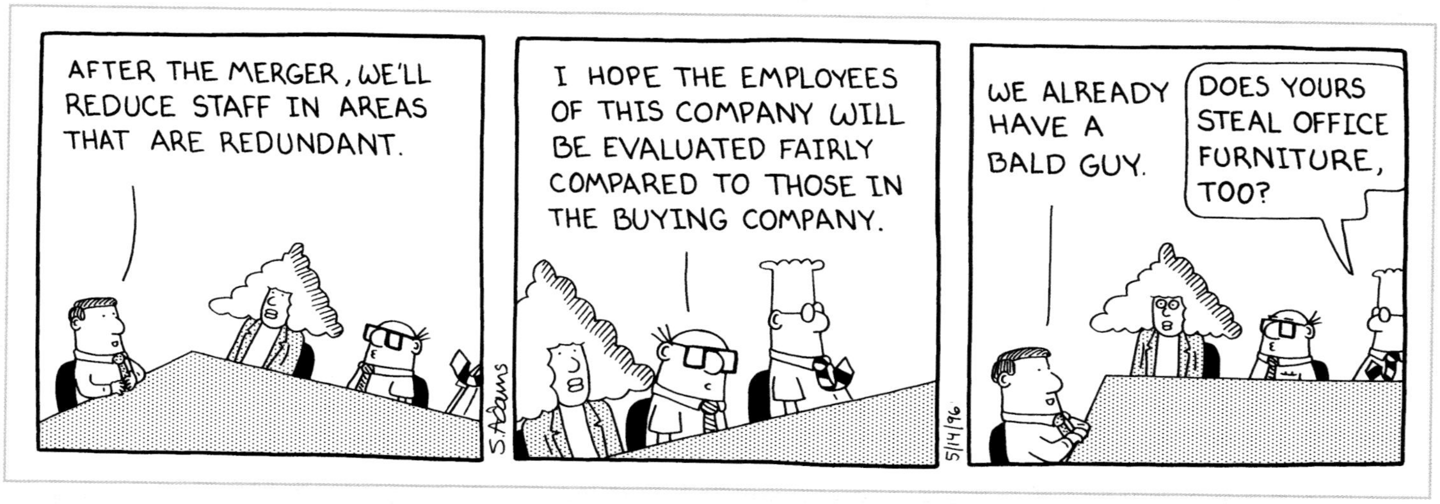
AFTER THE MERGER, WE'LL REDUCE STAFF IN AREAS THAT ARE REDUNDANT.
S. Adams
I HOPE THE EMPLOYEES OF THIS COMPANY WILL BE EVALUATED FAIRLY COMPARED TO THOSE IN THE BUYING COMPANY.
5/14/96
WE ALREADY HAVE A BALD GUY.
DOES YOURS STEAL OFFICE FURNITURE, TOO?

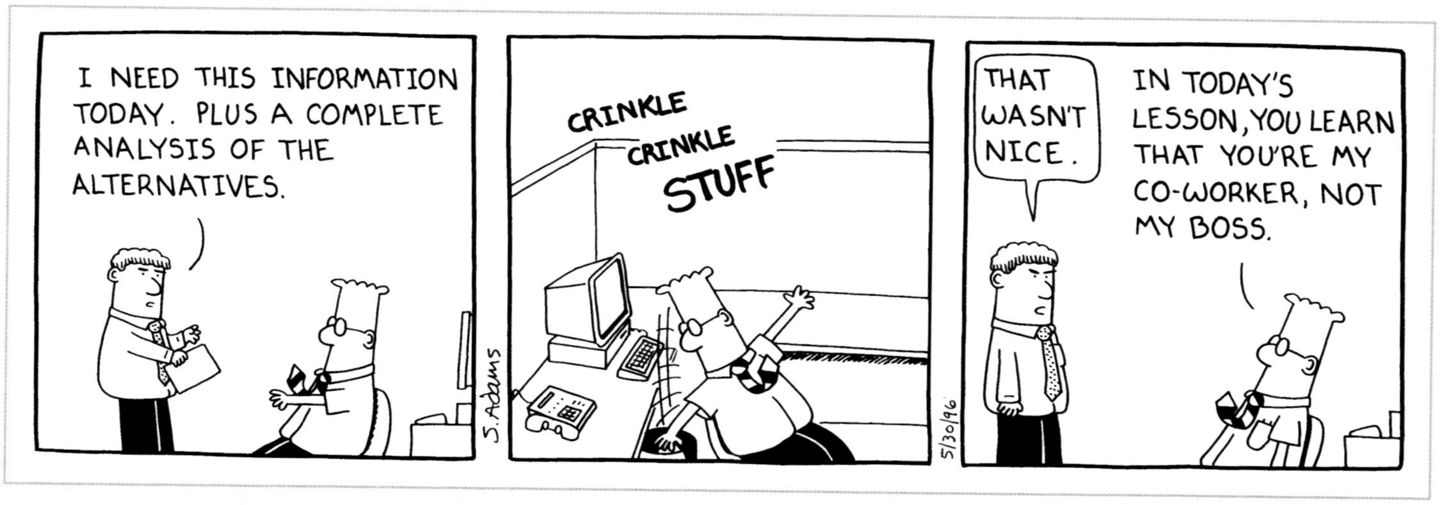
I NEED THIS INFORMATION TODAY. PLUS A COMPLETE ANALYSIS OF THE ALTERNATIVES.
S. Adams
CRINKLE
CRINKLE
STUFF
5/30/96
THAT WASN'T NICE.
IN TODAY'S LESSON, YOU LEARN THAT YOU'RE MY CO-WORKER, NOT MY BOSS.

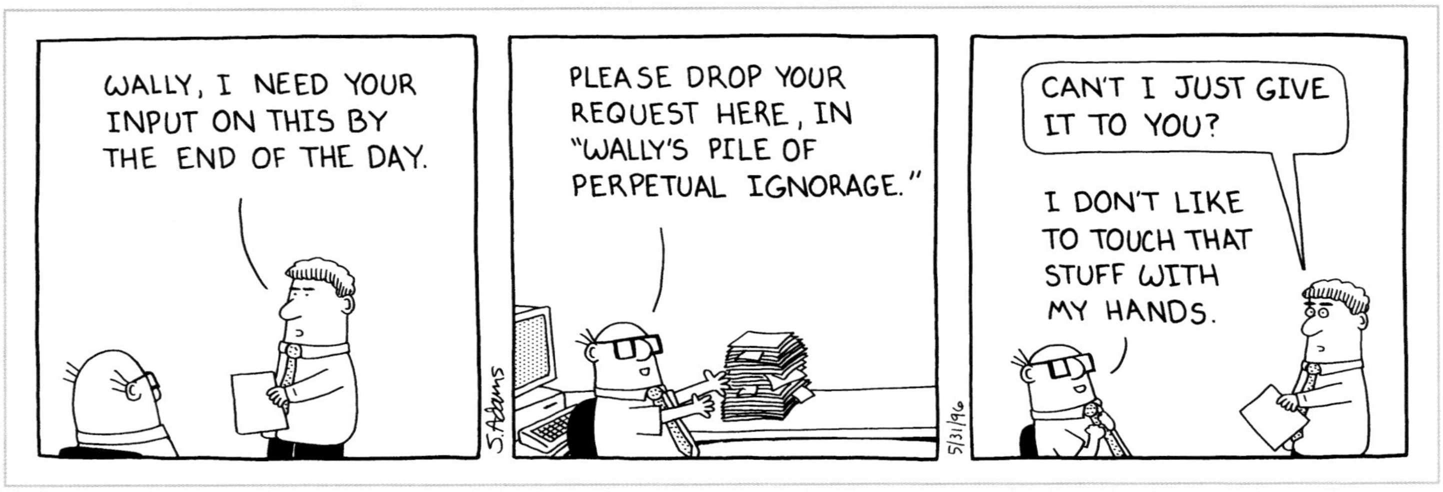
WALLY, I NEED YOUR INPUT ON THIS BY THE END OF THE DAY.
PLEASE DROP YOUR REQUEST HERE, IN "WALLY'S PILE OF PERPETUAL IGNORAGE."
S. Adams
5/31/96
CAN'T I JUST GIVE IT TO YOU?
I DON'T LIKE TO TOUCH THAT STUFF WITH MY HANDS.

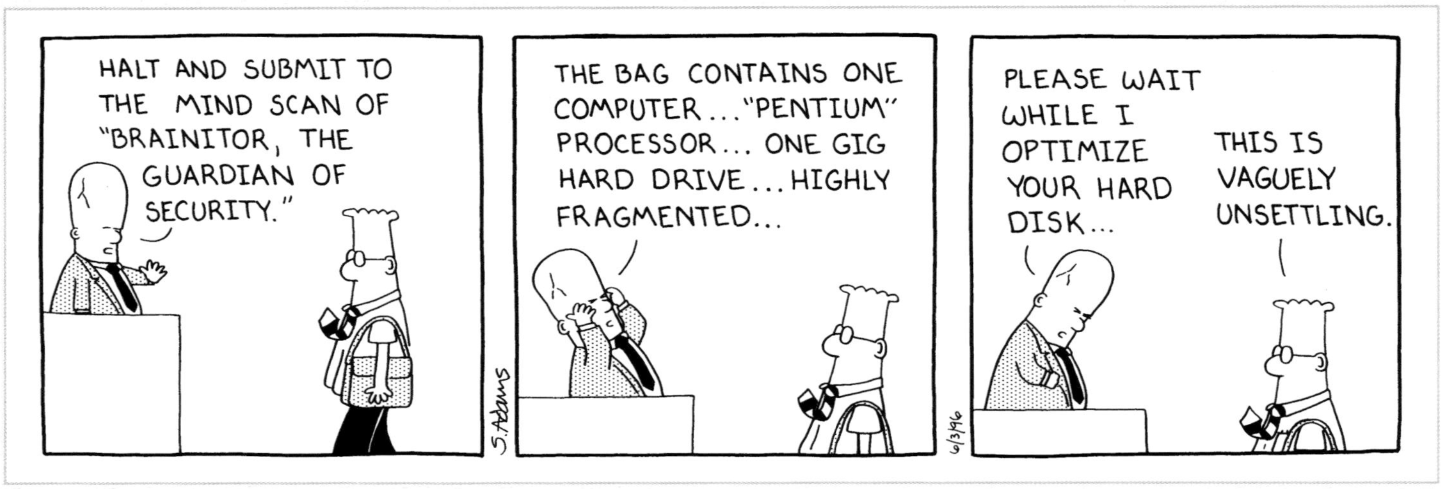
HALT AND SUBMIT TO THE MIND SCAN OF "BRAINITOR, THE GUARDIAN OF SECURITY."
THE BAG CONTAINS ONE COMPUTER ... "PENTIUM" PROCESSOR ... ONE GIG HARD DRIVE ... HIGHLY FRAGMENTED ...
S. Adams
6/3/96
PLEASE WAIT WHILE I OPTIMIZE YOUR HARD DISK ...
THIS IS VAGUELY UNSETTLING.

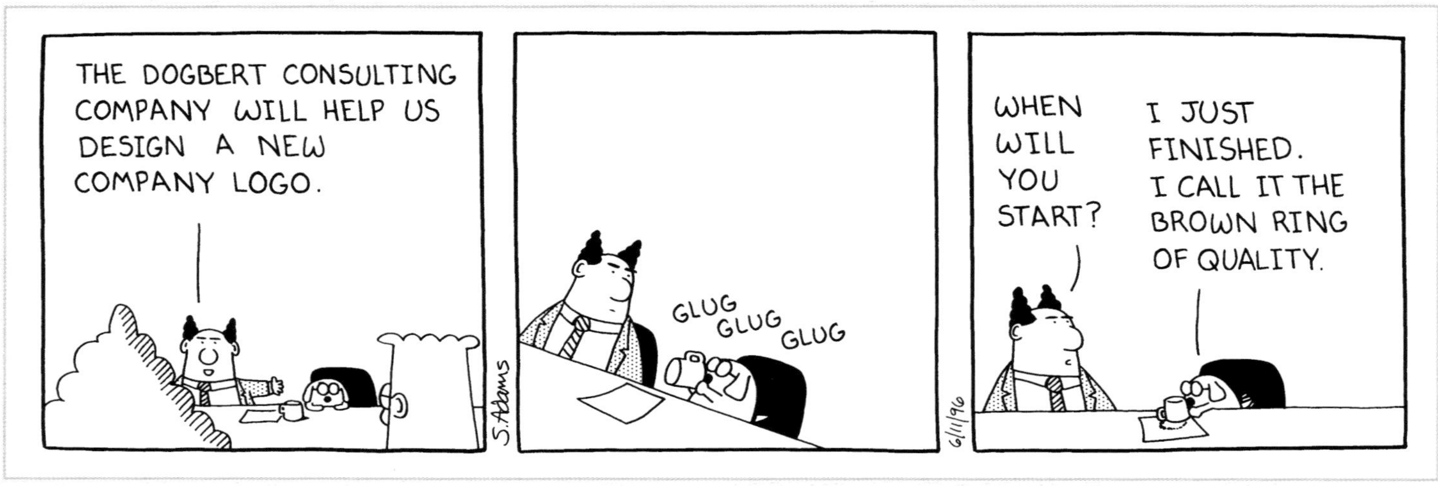
THE DOGBERT CONSULTING COMPANY WILL HELP US DESIGN A NEW COMPANY LOGO.
GLUG GLUG GLUG
S. Adams
6/11/96
WHEN WILL YOU START?
I JUST FINISHED. I CALL IT THE BROWN RING OF QUALITY.

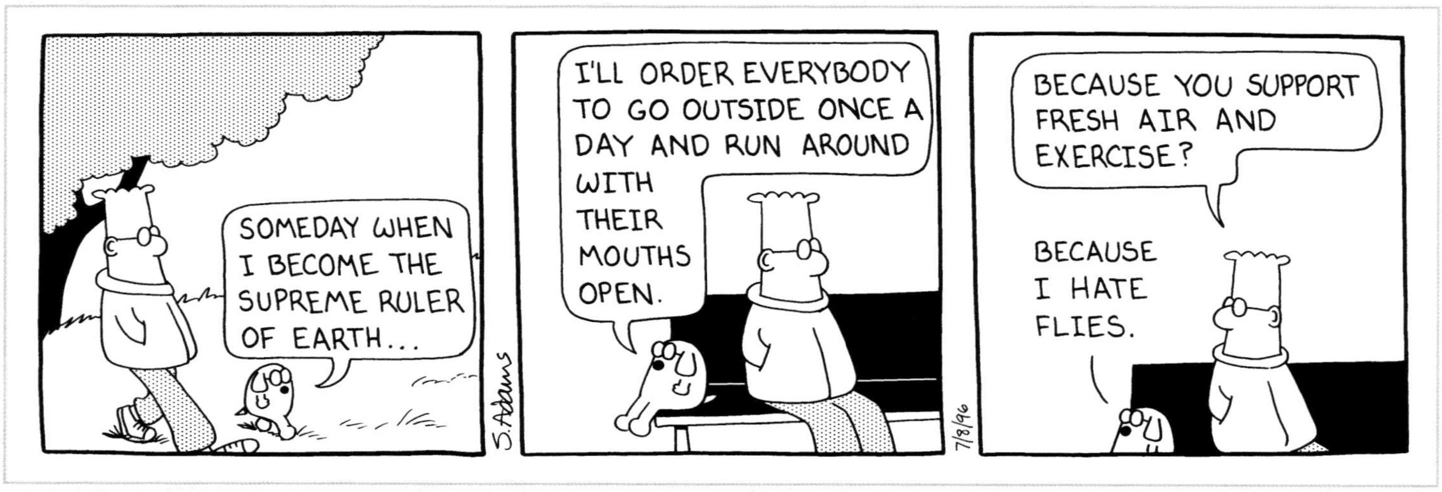
SOMEDAY WHEN I BECOME THE SUPREME RULER OF EARTH ...
I'LL ORDER EVERYBODY TO GO OUTSIDE ONCE A DAY AND RUN AROUND WITH THEIR MOUTHS OPEN.
S. Adams
7/8/96
BECAUSE YOU SUPPORT FRESH AIR AND EXERCISE?
BECAUSE I HATE FLIES.

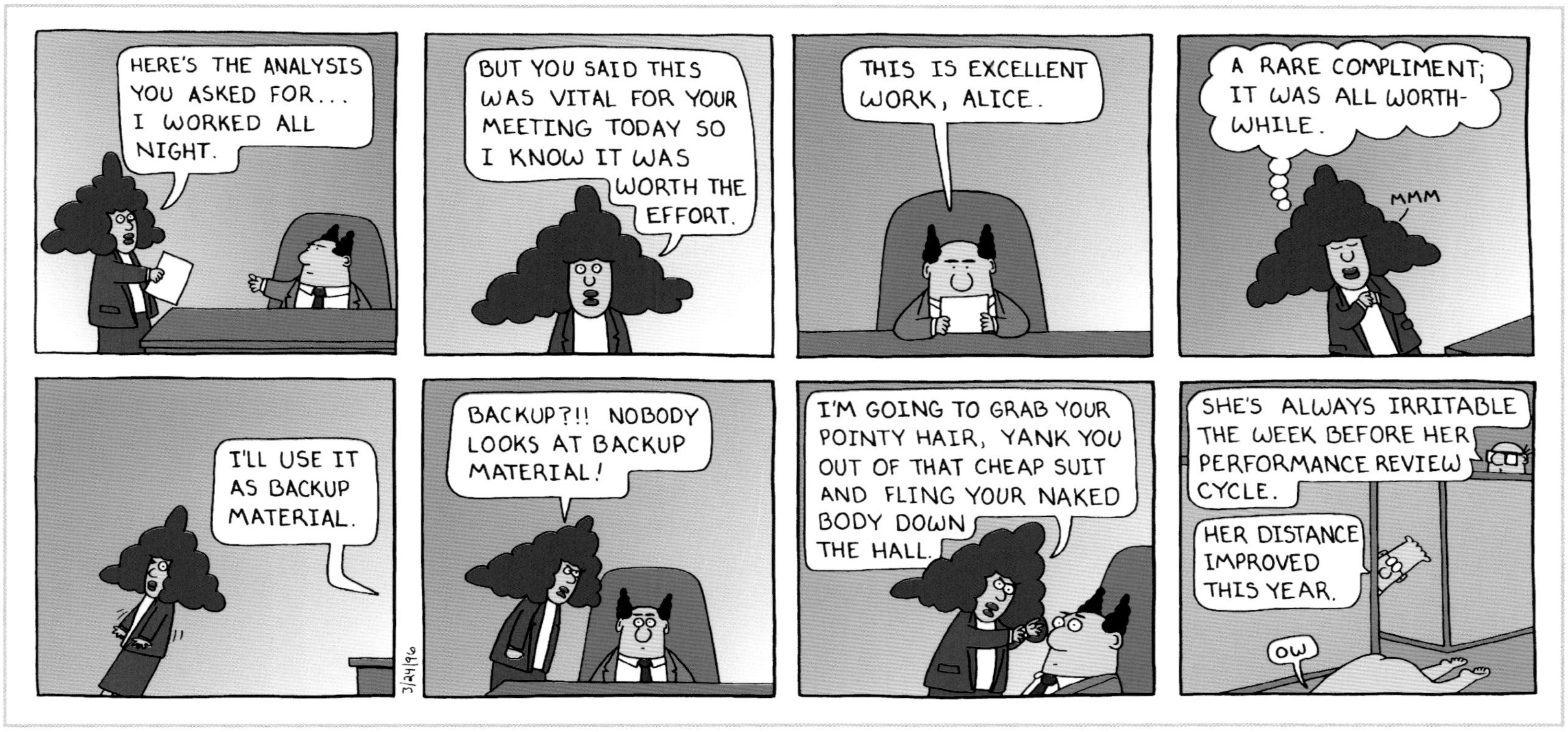
HERE'S THE ANALYSIS YOU ASKED FOR... I WORKED ALL NIGHT.
BUT YOU SAID THIS WAS VITAL FOR YOUR MEETING TODAY SO I KNOW IT WAS WORTH THE EFFORT.
THIS IS EXCELLENT WORK, ALICE.
A RARE COMPLIMENT; IT WAS ALL WORTH-WHILE.
MMM
I'LL USE IT AS BACKUP MATERIAL.
BACKUP?!! NOBODY LOOKS AT BACKUP MATERIAL!
I'M GOING TO GRAB YOUR POINTY HAIR, YANK YOU OUT OF THAT CHEAP SUIT AND FLING YOUR NAKED BODY DOWN THE HALL.
SHE'S ALWAYS IRRITABLE THE WEEK BEFORE HER PERFORMANCE REVIEW CYCLE.
HER DISTANCE IMPROVED THIS YEAR.
OW
3/24/96

Normally, butt cracks are not allowed in comics. For some reason, I got away with this one, probably because the actual crack part is small.

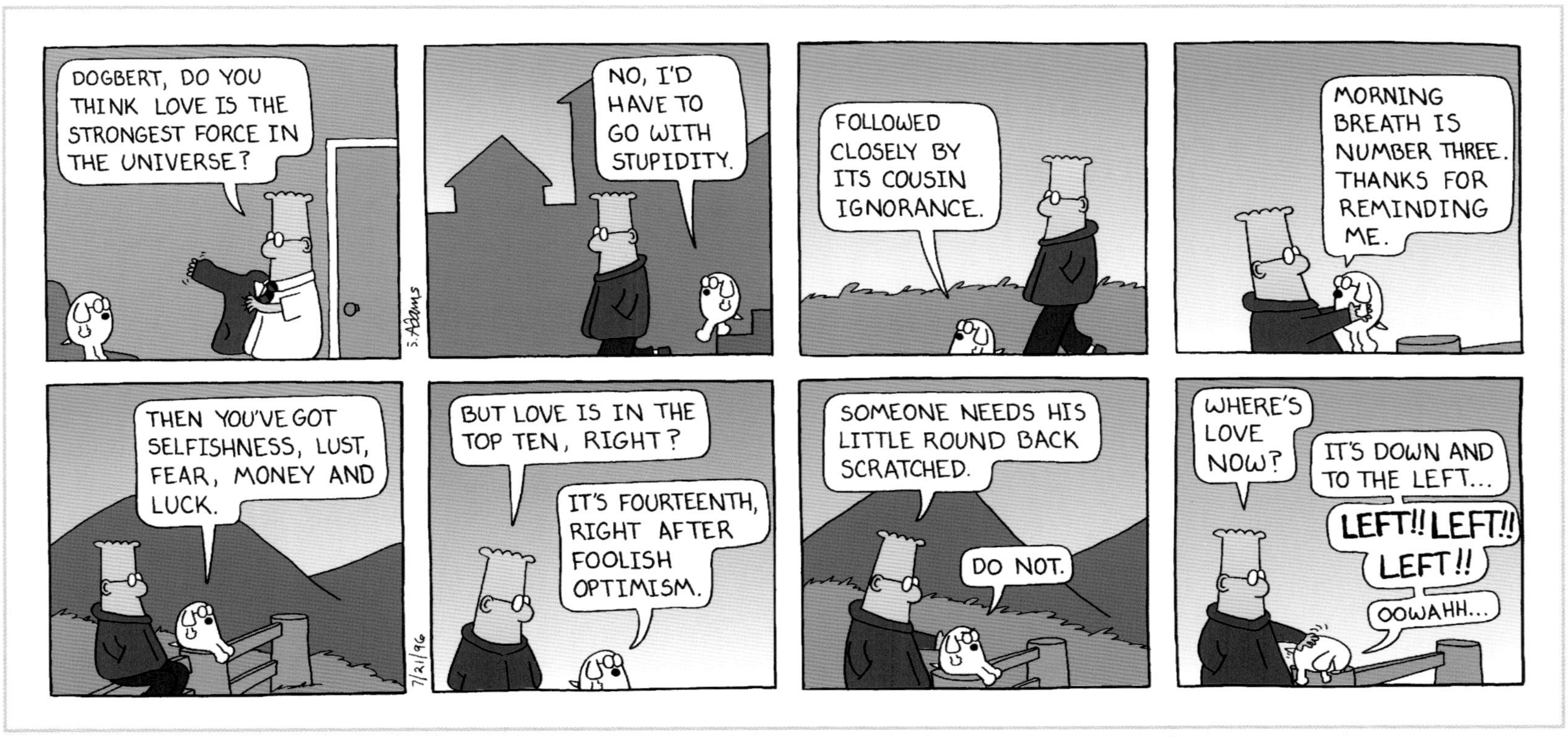
DOGBERT, DO YOU THINK LOVE IS THE STRONGEST FORCE IN THE UNIVERSE?
NO, I'D HAVE TO GO WITH STUPIDITY.
FOLLOWED CLOSELY BY ITS COUSIN IGNORANCE.
MORNING BREATH IS NUMBER THREE. THANKS FOR REMINDING ME.
THEN YOU'VE GOT SELFISHNESS, LUST, FEAR, MONEY AND LUCK.
BUT LOVE IS IN THE TOP TEN, RIGHT?
IT'S FOURTEENTH, RIGHT AFTER FOOLISH OPTIMISM.
SOMEONE NEEDS HIS LITTLE ROUND BACK SCRATCHED.
DO NOT.
WHERE'S LOVE NOW?
IT'S DOWN AND TO THE LEFT...
LEFT!! LEFT!! LEFT!!
OOWAHH...
S. ADAMS
7/21/96

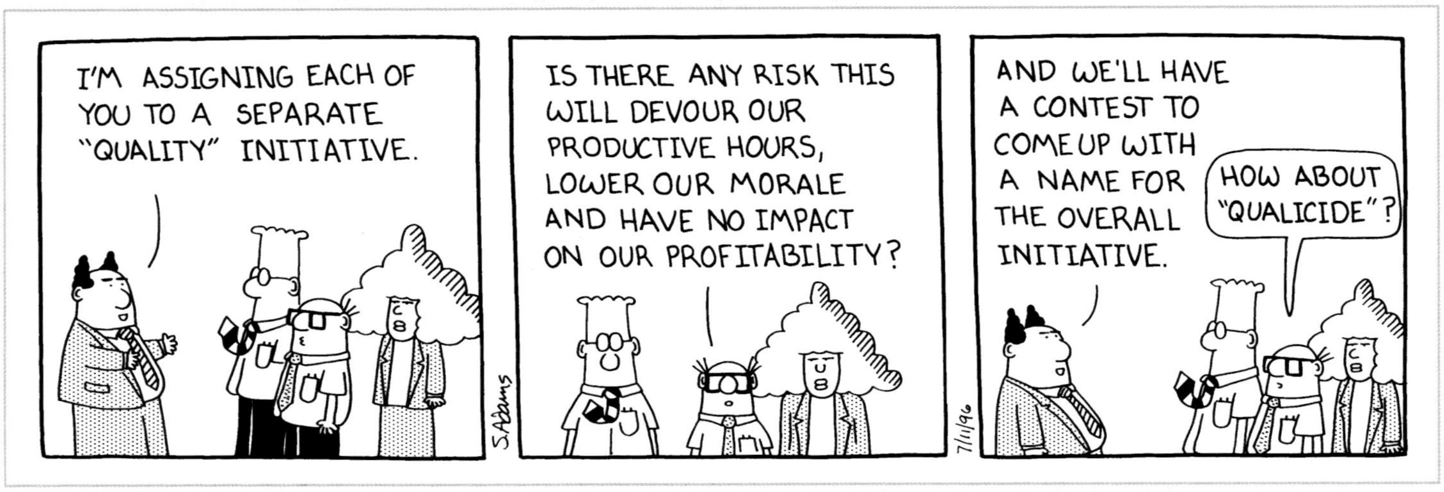
I'M ASSIGNING EACH OF YOU TO A SEPARATE "QUALITY" INITIATIVE.
S.Adams
IS THERE ANY RISK THIS WILL DEVOUR OUR PRODUCTIVE HOURS, LOWER OUR MORALE AND HAVE NO IMPACT ON OUR PROFITABILITY?
7/1/96
AND WE'LL HAVE A CONTEST TO COME UP WITH A NAME FOR THE OVERALL INITIATIVE.
HOW ABOUT "QUALICIDE"?

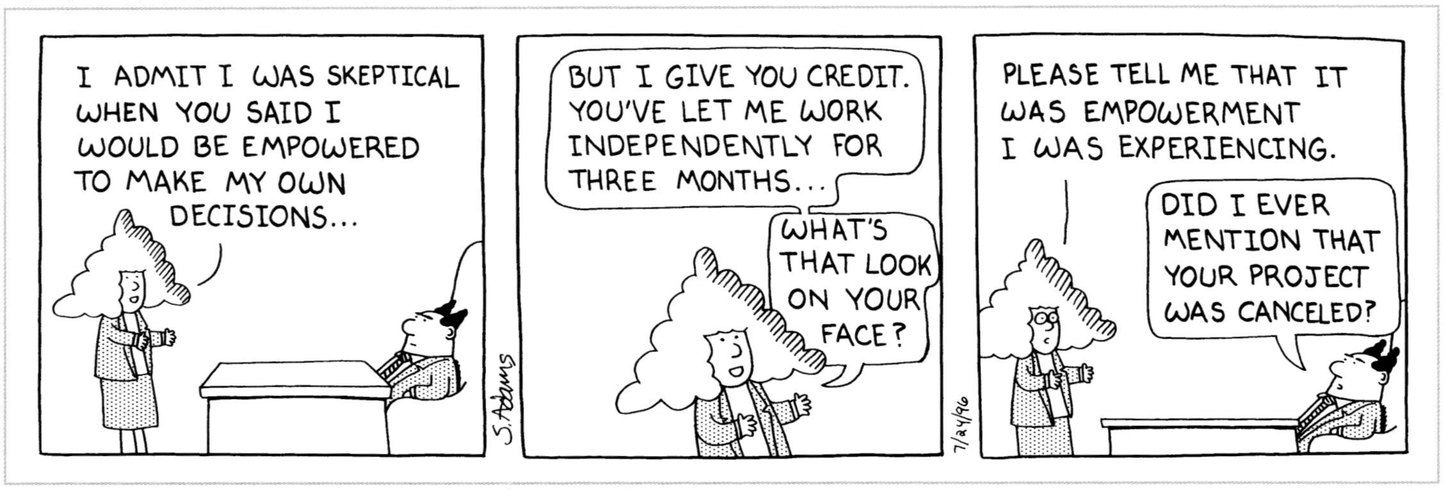
I ADMIT I WAS SKEPTICAL WHEN YOU SAID I WOULD BE EMPOWERED TO MAKE MY OWN DECISIONS...
S.Adams
BUT I GIVE YOU CREDIT. YOU'VE LET ME WORK INDEPENDENTLY FOR THREE MONTHS...
WHAT'S THAT LOOK ON YOUR FACE?
7/24/96
PLEASE TELL ME THAT IT WAS EMPOWERMENT I WAS EXPERIENCING.
DID I EVER MENTION THAT YOUR PROJECT WAS CANCELED?

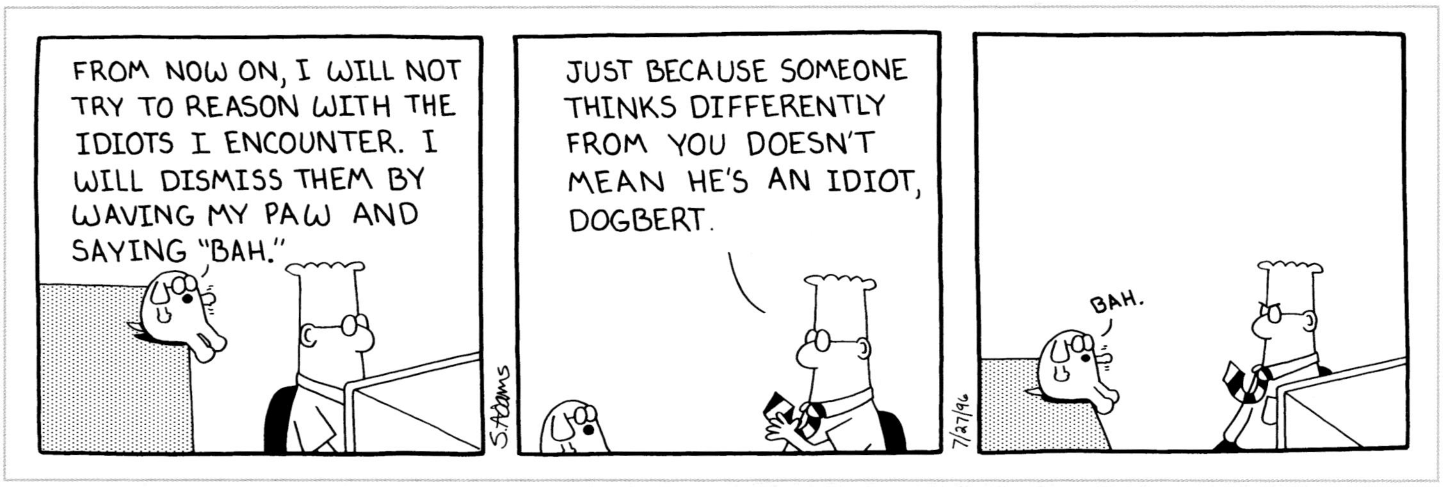
FROM NOW ON, I WILL NOT TRY TO REASON WITH THE IDIOTS I ENCOUNTER. I WILL DISMISS THEM BY WAVING MY PAW AND SAYING "BAH."
S.Adams
JUST BECAUSE SOMEONE THINKS DIFFERENTLY FROM YOU DOESN'T MEAN HE'S AN IDIOT, DOGBERT.
7/27/96
BAH.

This strip became an instant favorite with readers. People like it when Dogbert is dismissive of others.

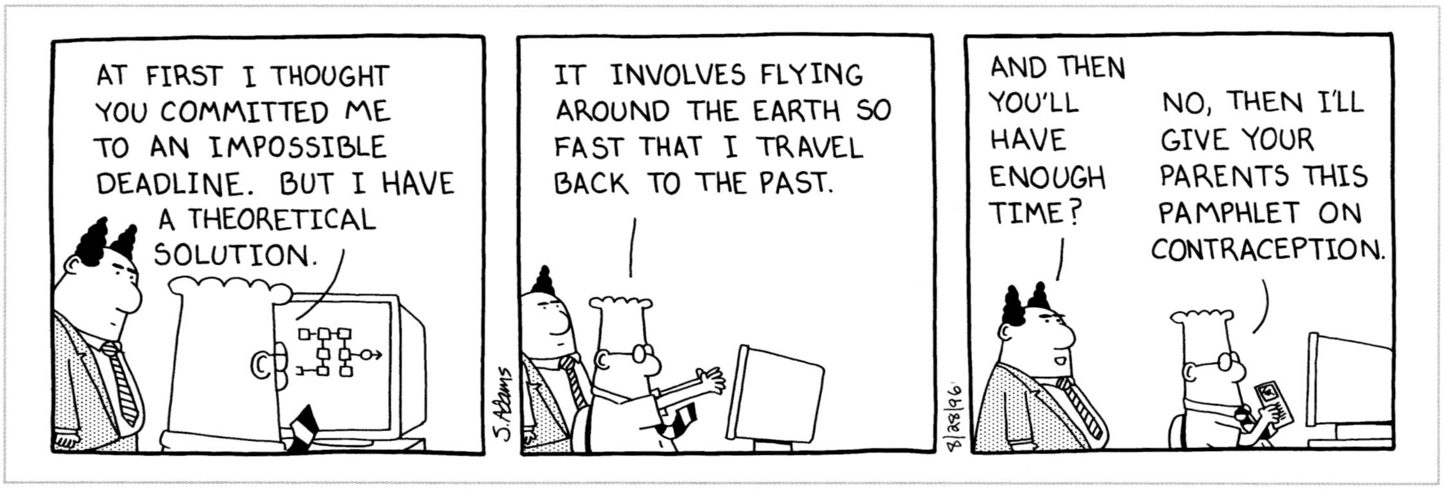
AT FIRST I THOUGHT YOU COMMITTED ME TO AN IMPOSSIBLE DEADLINE. BUT I HAVE A THEORETICAL SOLUTION.
S.Adams
IT INVOLVES FLYING AROUND THE EARTH SO FAST THAT I TRAVEL BACK TO THE PAST.
8/28/96
AND THEN YOU'LL HAVE ENOUGH TIME?
NO, THEN I'LL GIVE YOUR PARENTS THIS PAMPHLET ON CONTRACEPTION.

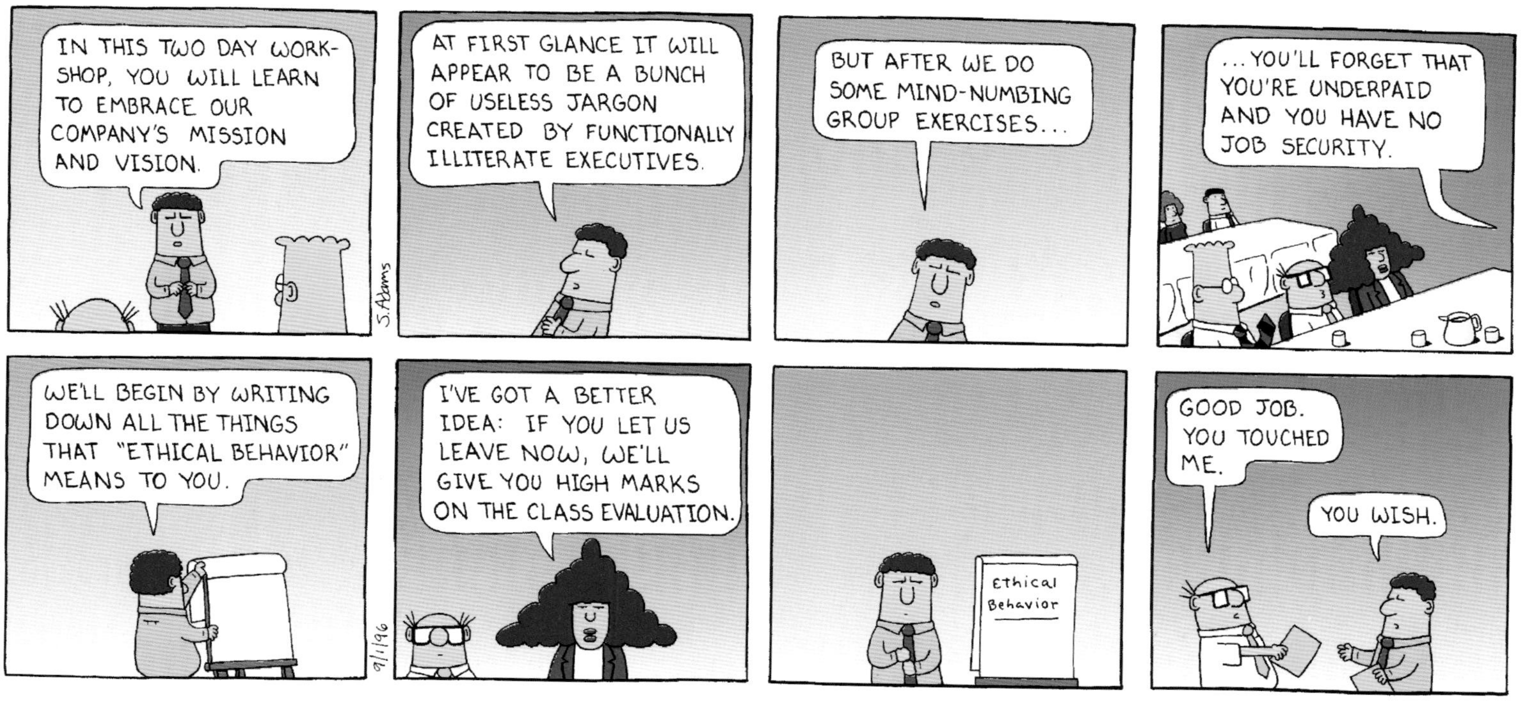
IN THIS TWO DAY WORK-SHOP, YOU WILL LEARN TO EMBRACE OUR COMPANY'S MISSION AND VISION.
S. Adams
AT FIRST GLANCE IT WILL APPEAR TO BE A BUNCH OF USELESS JARGON CREATED BY FUNCTIONALLY ILLITERATE EXECUTIVES.
BUT AFTER WE DO SOME MIND-NUMBING GROUP EXERCISES...
...YOU'LL FORGET THAT YOU'RE UNDERPAID AND YOU HAVE NO JOB SECURITY.
WE'LL BEGIN BY WRITING DOWN ALL THE THINGS THAT "ETHICAL BEHAVIOR" MEANS TO YOU.
9/1/96
I'VE GOT A BETTER IDEA: IF YOU LET US LEAVE NOW, WE'LL GIVE YOU HIGH MARKS ON THE CLASS EVALUATION.
Ethical Behavior
GOOD JOB. YOU TOUCHED ME.
YOU WISH.

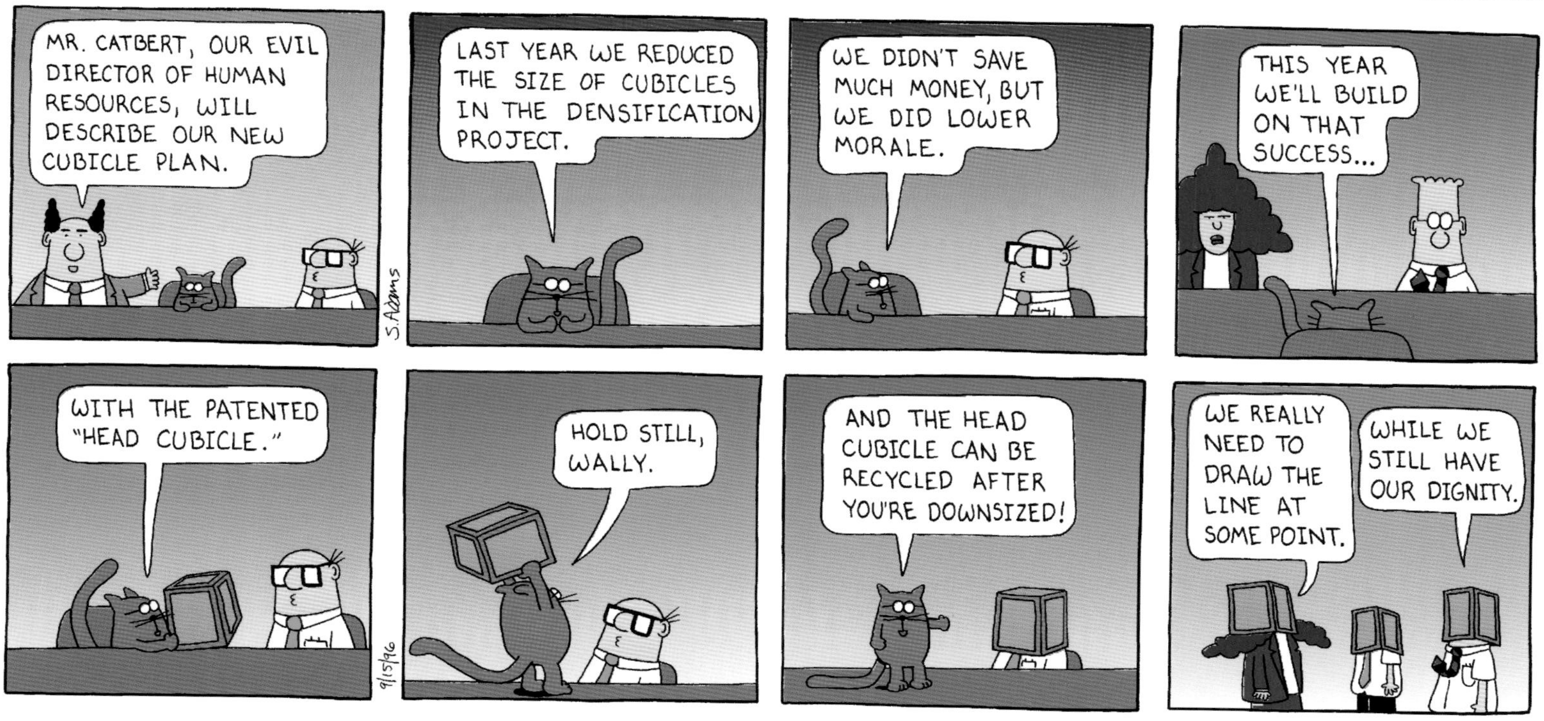
MR. CATBERT, OUR EVIL DIRECTOR OF HUMAN RESOURCES, WILL DESCRIBE OUR NEW CUBICLE PLAN.
S. Adams
LAST YEAR WE REDUCED THE SIZE OF CUBICLES IN THE DENSIFICATION PROJECT.
WE DIDN'T SAVE MUCH MONEY, BUT WE DID LOWER MORALE.
THIS YEAR WE'LL BUILD ON THAT SUCCESS...
WITH THE PATENTED "HEAD CUBICLE."
9/15/96
HOLD STILL, WALLY.
AND THE HEAD CUBICLE CAN BE RECYCLED AFTER YOU'RE DOWNSIZED!
WE REALLY NEED TO DRAW THE LINE AT SOME POINT.
WHILE WE STILL HAVE OUR DIGNITY.

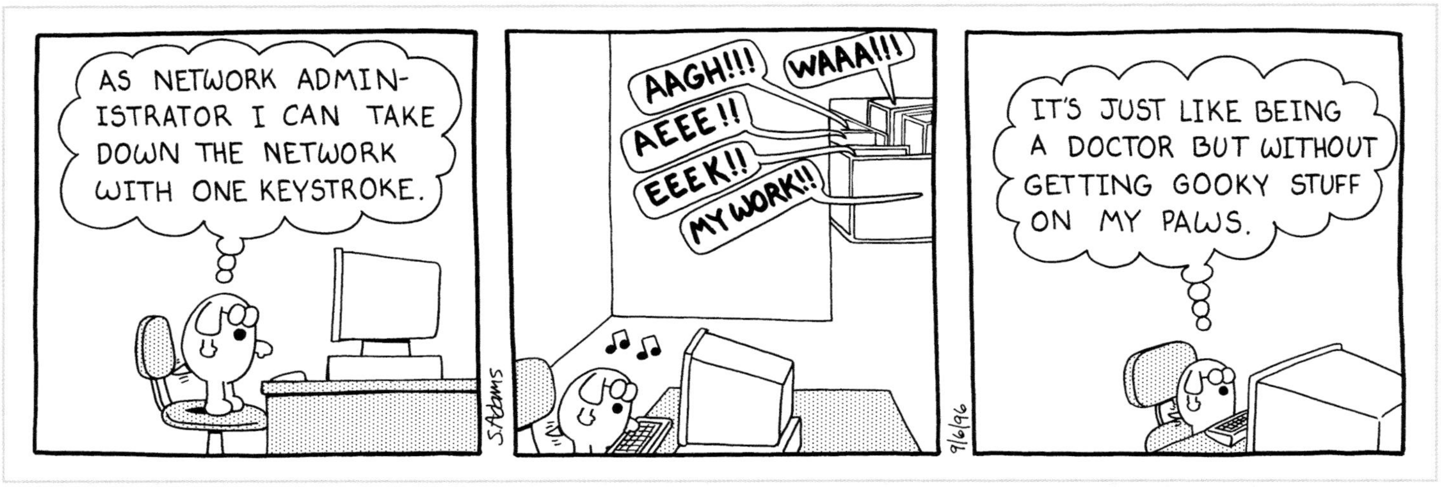
AS NETWORK ADMIN-ISTRATOR I CAN TAKE DOWN THE NETWORK WITH ONE KEYSTROKE.
AAGH!!!
WAAA!!!
AEEE!!
EEEK!!
MY WORK!!
S. Adams
9/6/96
IT'S JUST LIKE BEING A DOCTOR BUT WITHOUT GETTING GOOKY STUFF ON MY PAWS.

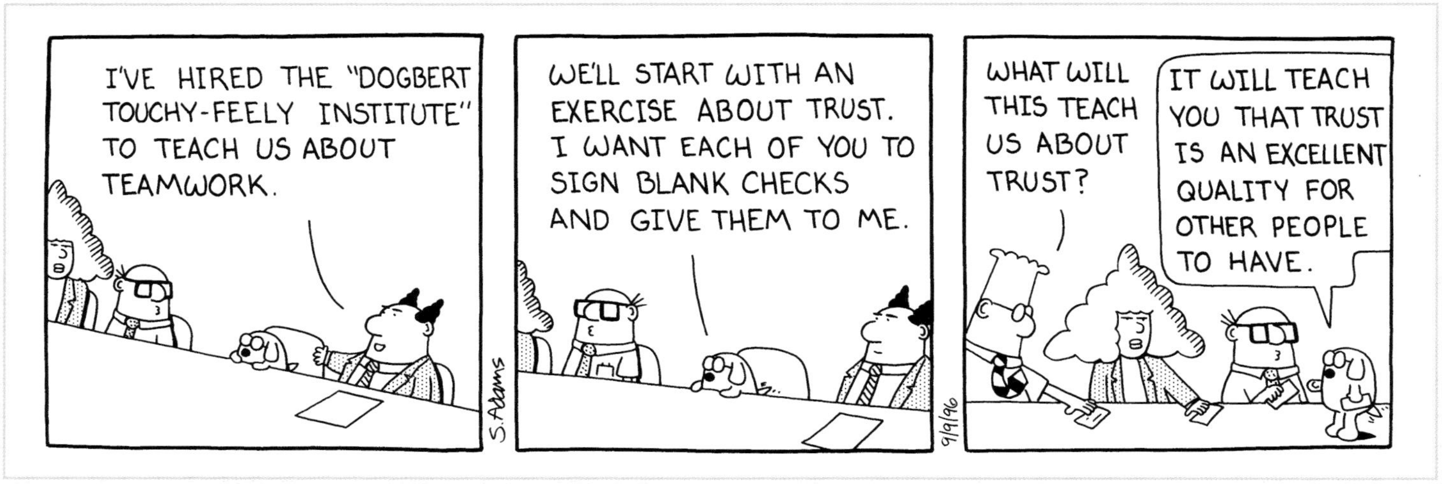
I'VE HIRED THE "DOGBERT TOUCHY-FEELY INSTITUTE" TO TEACH US ABOUT TEAMWORK.
S. Adams
WE'LL START WITH AN EXERCISE ABOUT TRUST. I WANT EACH OF YOU TO SIGN BLANK CHECKS AND GIVE THEM TO ME.
9/9/96
WHAT WILL THIS TEACH US ABOUT TRUST?
IT WILL TEACH YOU THAT TRUST IS AN EXCELLENT QUALITY FOR OTHER PEOPLE TO HAVE.

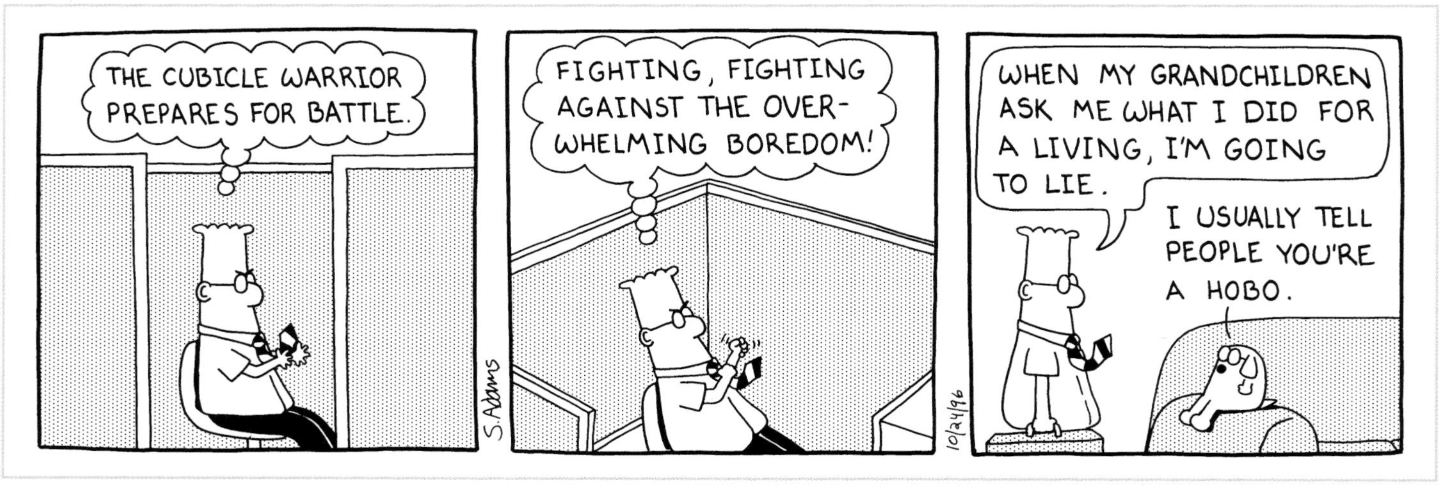
THE CUBICLE WARRIOR PREPARES FOR BATTLE.
S. Adams
FIGHTING, FIGHTING AGAINST THE OVER-WHELMING BOREDOM!
10/24/96
WHEN MY GRANDCHILDREN ASK ME WHAT I DID FOR A LIVING, I'M GOING TO LIE.
I USUALLY TELL PEOPLE YOU'RE A HOBO.

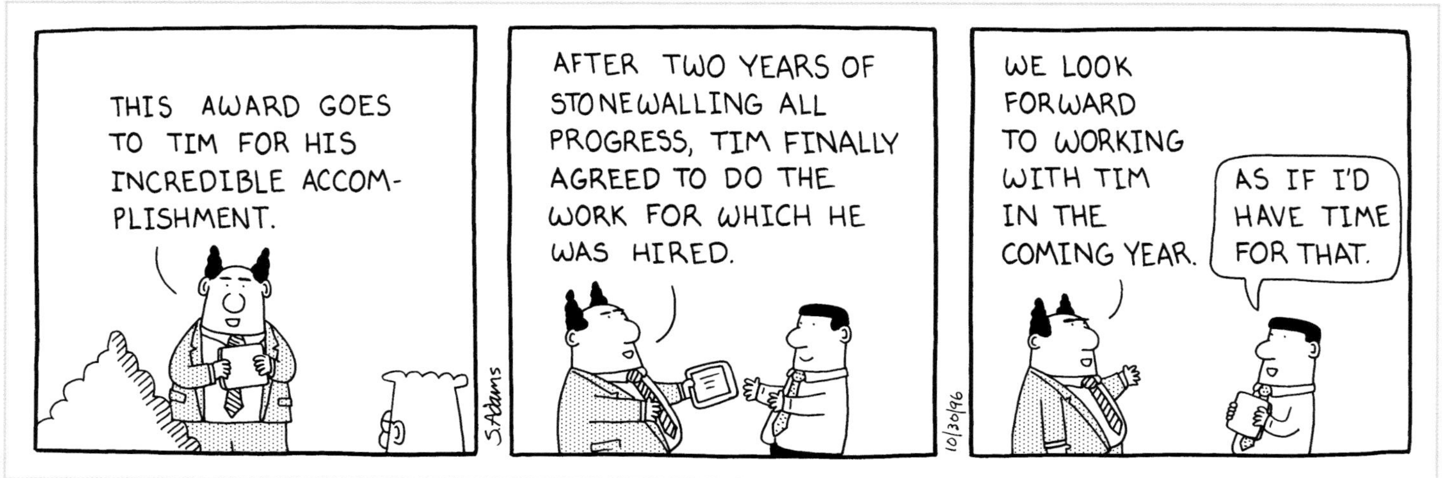
THIS AWARD GOES TO TIM FOR HIS INCREDIBLE ACCOM-PLISHMENT.
S. Adams
AFTER TWO YEARS OF STONEWALLING ALL PROGRESS, TIM FINALLY AGREED TO DO THE WORK FOR WHICH HE WAS HIRED.
10/30/96
WE LOOK FORWARD TO WORKING WITH TIM IN THE COMING YEAR.
AS IF I'D HAVE TIME FOR THAT.

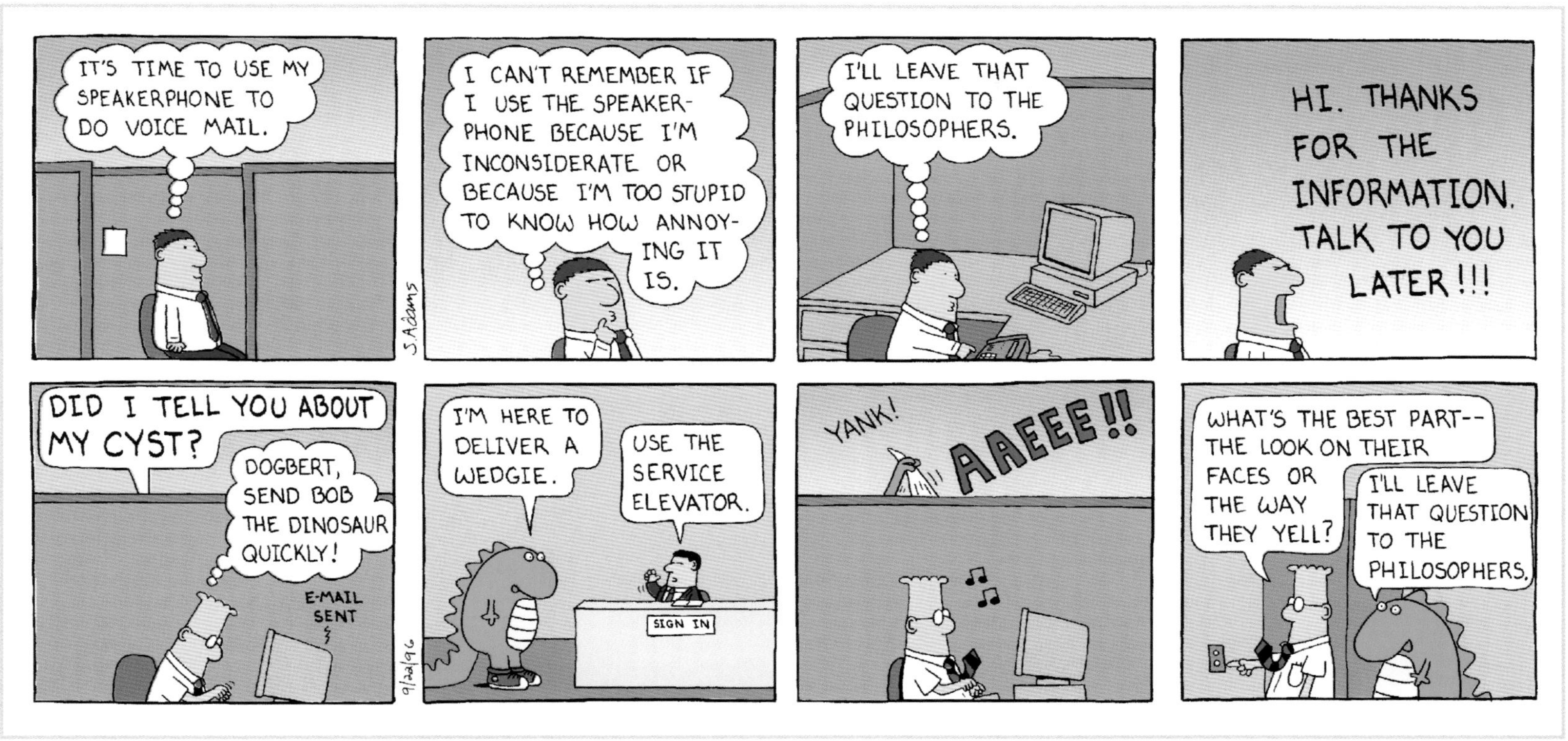
IT'S TIME TO USE MY SPEAKERPHONE TO DO VOICE MAIL.
I CAN'T REMEMBER IF I USE THE SPEAKER-PHONE BECAUSE I'M INCONSIDERATE OR BECAUSE I'M TOO STUPID TO KNOW HOW ANNOY-ING IT IS.
I'LL LEAVE THAT QUESTION TO THE PHILOSOPHERS.
HI. THANKS FOR THE INFORMATION. TALK TO YOU LATER!!!
DID I TELL YOU ABOUT MY CYST?
DOGBERT, SEND BOB THE DINOSAUR QUICKLY!
E-MAIL SENT
I'M HERE TO DELIVER A WEDGIE.
USE THE SERVICE ELEVATOR.
SIGN IN
YANK!
AAEEE!!
WHAT'S THE BEST PART-- THE LOOK ON THEIR FACES OR THE WAY THEY YELL?
I'LL LEAVE THAT QUESTION TO THE PHILOSOPHERS.

I did this comic in 1996, but it remains one of the most requested themes, presumably for people who didn't read this version.

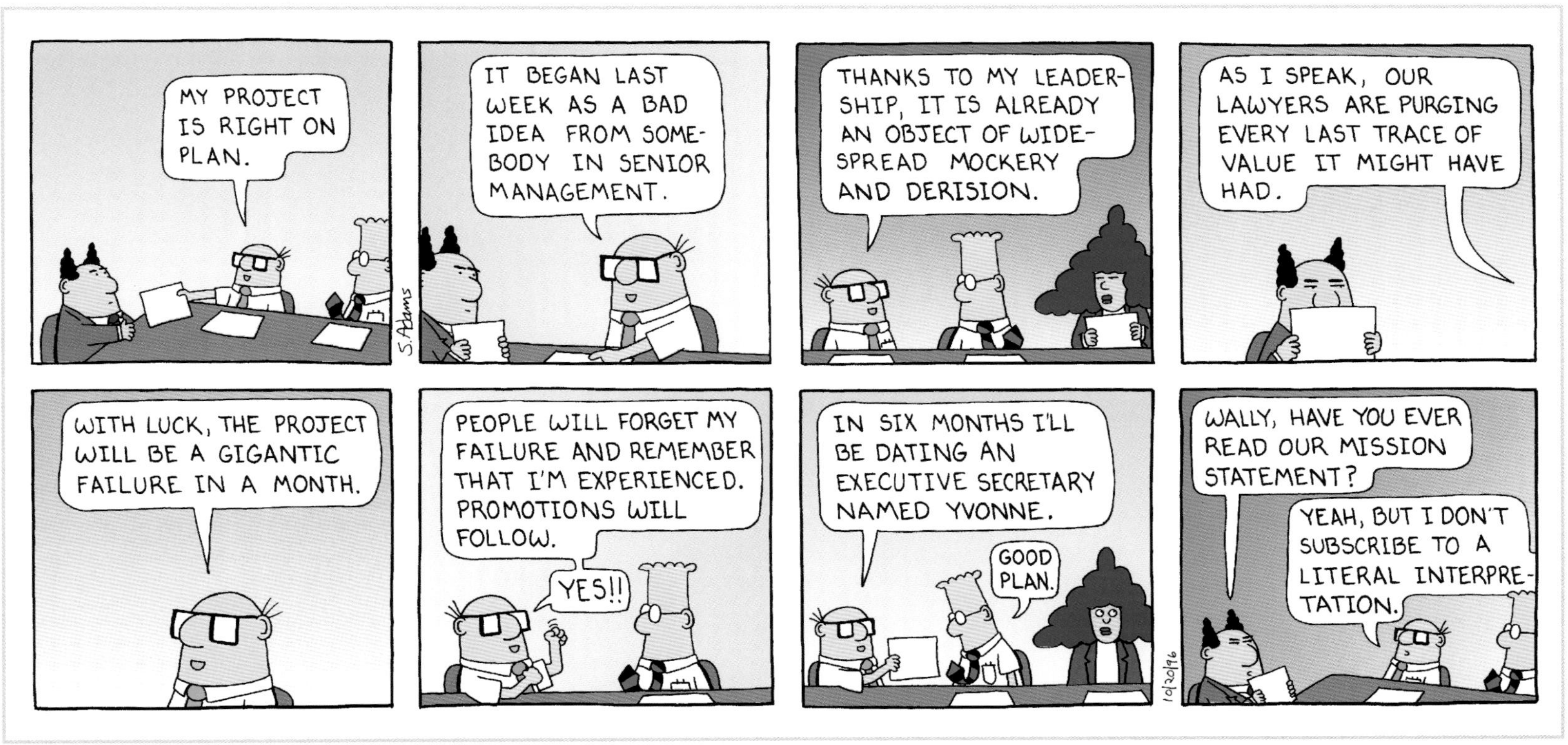
MY PROJECT IS RIGHT ON PLAN.
IT BEGAN LAST WEEK AS A BAD IDEA FROM SOME-BODY IN SENIOR MANAGEMENT.
THANKS TO MY LEADER-SHIP, IT IS ALREADY AN OBJECT OF WIDE-SPREAD MOCKERY AND DERISION.
AS I SPEAK, OUR LAWYERS ARE PURGING EVERY LAST TRACE OF VALUE IT MIGHT HAVE HAD.
WITH LUCK, THE PROJECT WILL BE A GIGANTIC FAILURE IN A MONTH.
PEOPLE WILL FORGET MY FAILURE AND REMEMBER THAT I'M EXPERIENCED. PROMOTIONS WILL FOLLOW.
YES!!
IN SIX MONTHS I'LL BE DATING AN EXECUTIVE SECRETARY NAMED YVONNE.
GOOD PLAN.
WALLY, HAVE YOU EVER READ OUR MISSION STATEMENT?
YEAH, BUT I DON'T SUBSCRIBE TO A LITERAL INTERPRE-TATION.

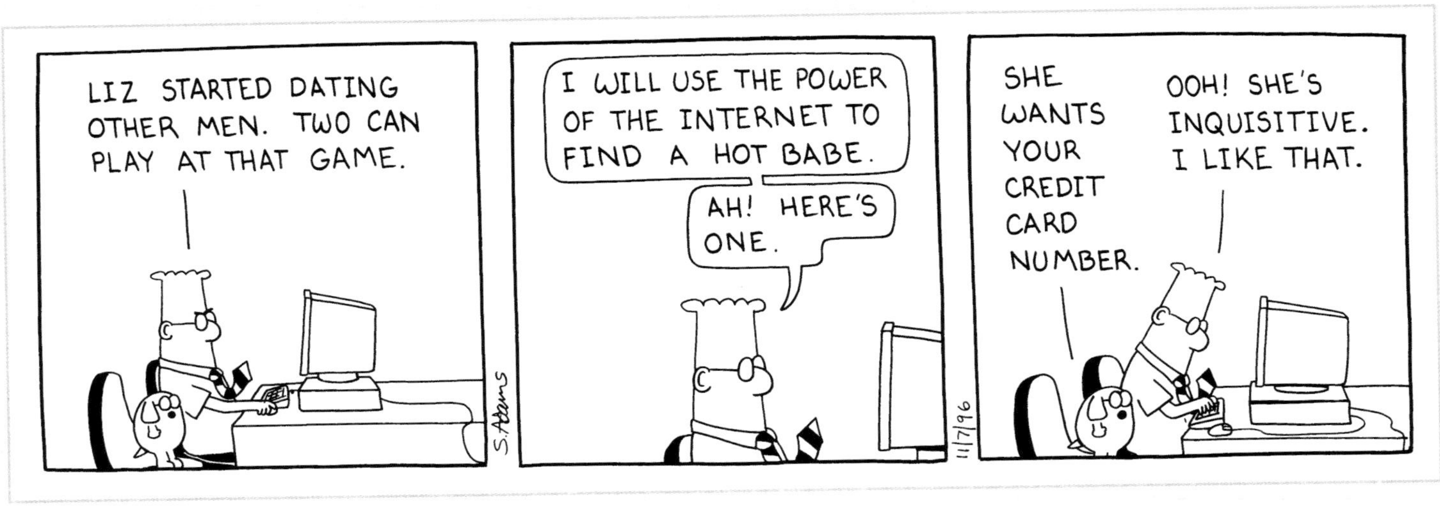
LIZ STARTED DATING OTHER MEN. TWO CAN PLAY AT THAT GAME.
I WILL USE THE POWER OF THE INTERNET TO FIND A HOT BABE.
AH! HERE'S ONE.
S. Adams
11/7/96
SHE WANTS YOUR CREDIT CARD NUMBER.
OOH! SHE'S INQUISITIVE. I LIKE THAT.

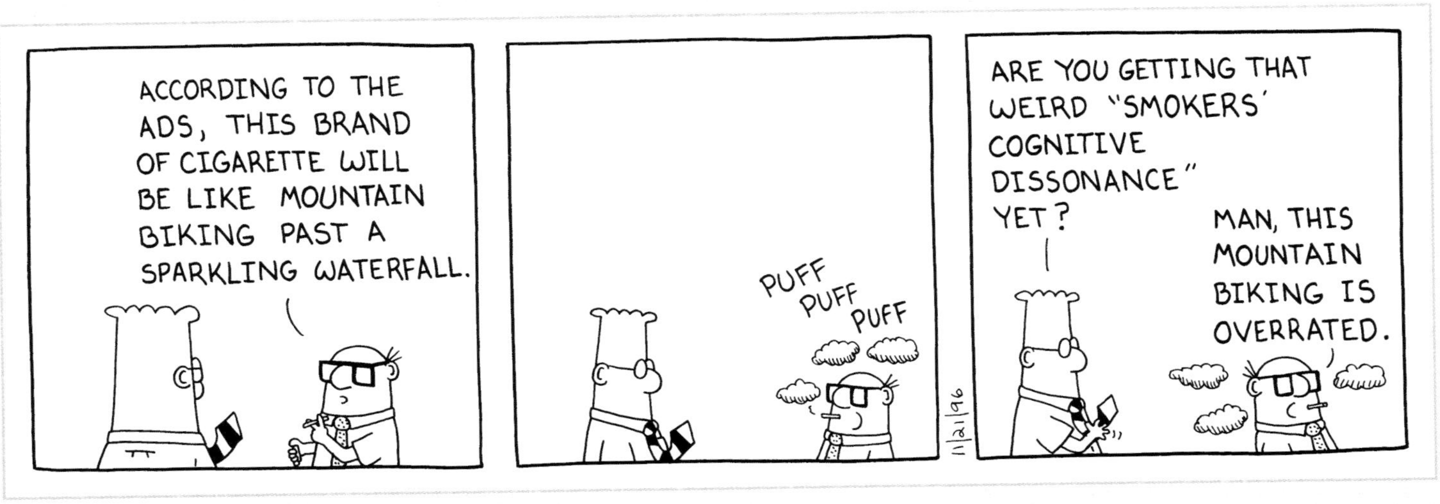
ACCORDING TO THE ADS, THIS BRAND OF CIGARETTE WILL BE LIKE MOUNTAIN BIKING PAST A SPARKLING WATERFALL.
PUFF PUFF PUFF
11/21/96
ARE YOU GETTING THAT WEIRD "SMOKERS' COGNITIVE DISSONANCE" YET?
MAN, THIS MOUNTAIN BIKING IS OVERRATED.

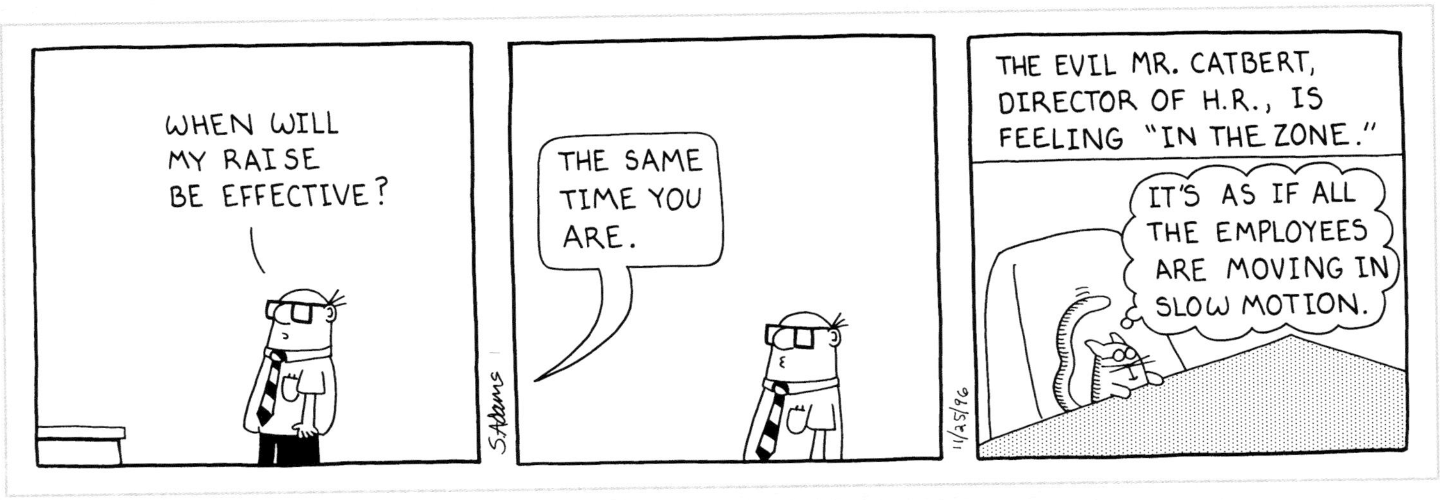
WHEN WILL MY RAISE BE EFFECTIVE?
S. Adams
THE SAME TIME YOU ARE.
11/25/96
THE EVIL MR. CATBERT, DIRECTOR OF H.R., IS FEELING "IN THE ZONE."
IT'S AS IF ALL THE EMPLOYEES ARE MOVING IN SLOW MOTION.

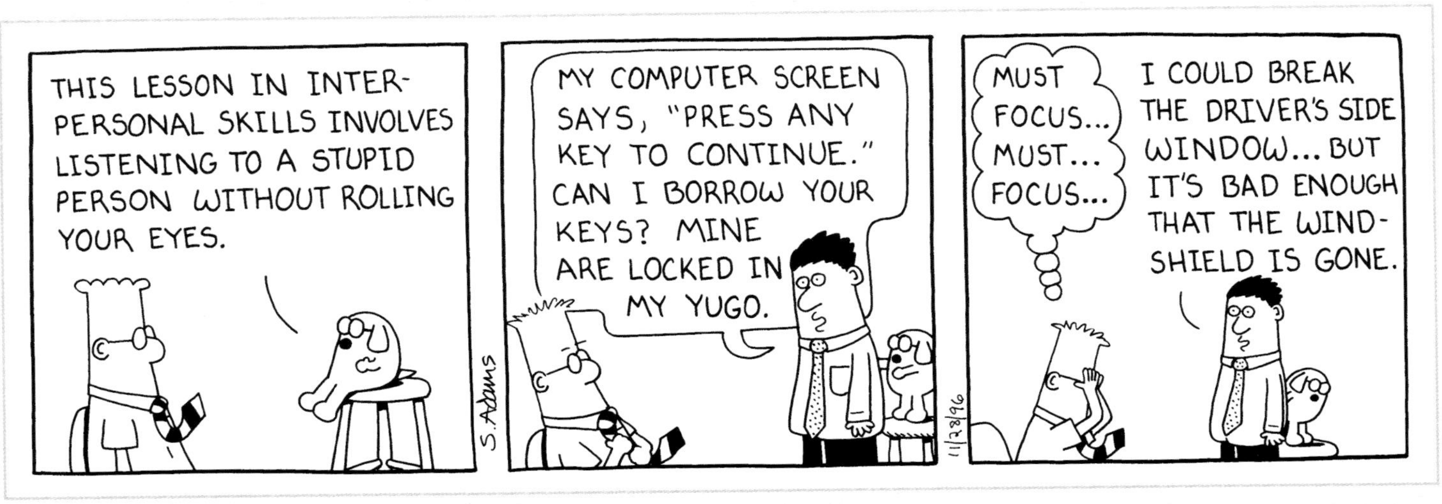
THIS LESSON IN INTER-PERSONAL SKILLS INVOLVES LISTENING TO A STUPID PERSON WITHOUT ROLLING YOUR EYES.
S. Adams
MY COMPUTER SCREEN SAYS, "PRESS ANY KEY TO CONTINUE." CAN I BORROW YOUR KEYS? MINE ARE LOCKED IN MY YUGO.
11/28/96
MUST FOCUS... MUST... FOCUS...
I COULD BREAK THE DRIVER'S SIDE WINDOW... BUT IT'S BAD ENOUGH THAT THE WIND-SHIELD IS GONE.

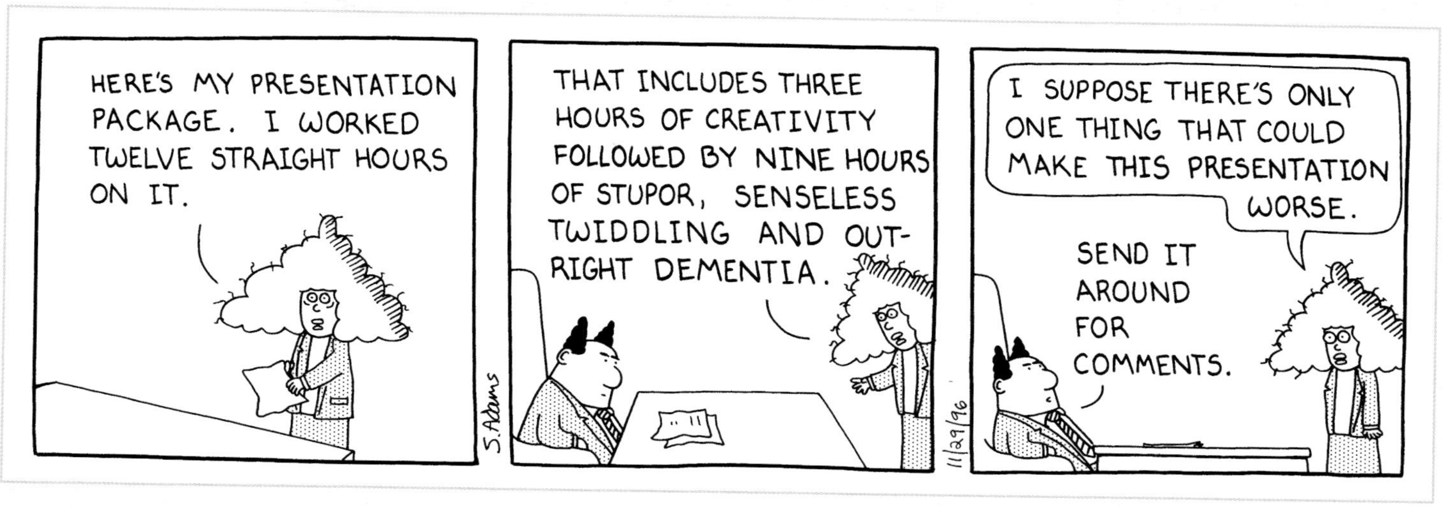
HERE'S MY PRESENTATION PACKAGE. I WORKED TWELVE STRAIGHT HOURS ON IT.
THAT INCLUDES THREE HOURS OF CREATIVITY FOLLOWED BY NINE HOURS OF STUPOR, SENSELESS TWIDDLING AND OUT-RIGHT DEMENTIA.
S. Adams
11/29/96
I SUPPOSE THERE'S ONLY ONE THING THAT COULD MAKE THIS PRESENTATION WORSE.
SEND IT AROUND FOR COMMENTS.

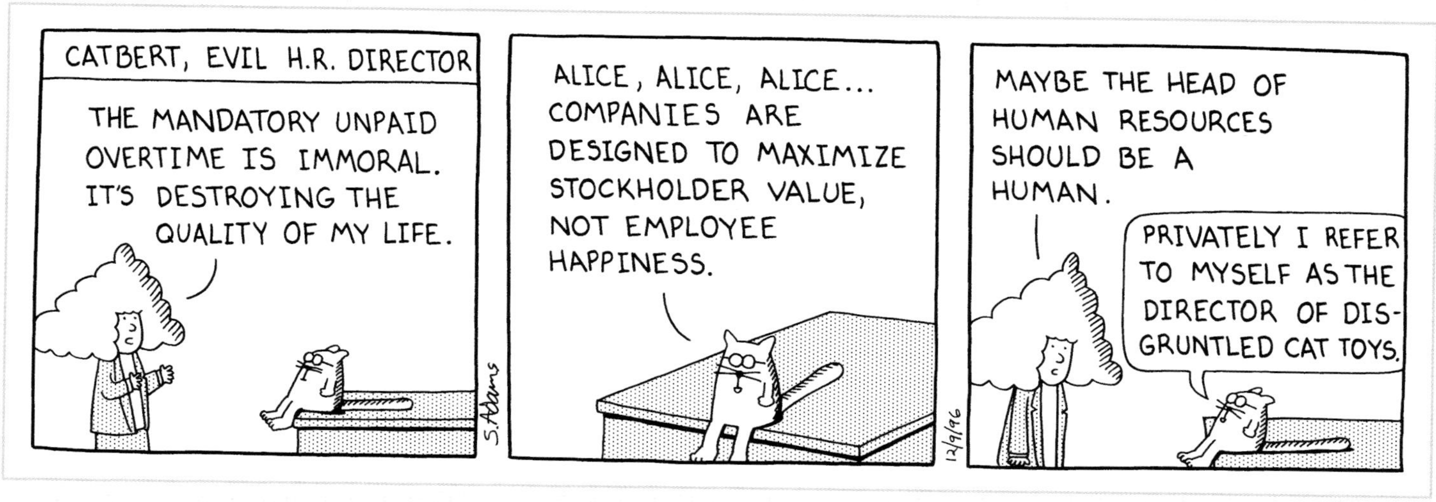
CATBERT, EVIL H.R. DIRECTOR
THE MANDATORY UNPAID OVERTIME IS IMMORAL. IT'S DESTROYING THE QUALITY OF MY LIFE.
S. Adams
ALICE, ALICE, ALICE... COMPANIES ARE DESIGNED TO MAXIMIZE STOCKHOLDER VALUE, NOT EMPLOYEE HAPPINESS.
12/9/96
MAYBE THE HEAD OF HUMAN RESOURCES SHOULD BE A HUMAN.
PRIVATELY I REFER TO MYSELF AS THE DIRECTOR OF DIS-GRUNTLED CAT TOYS.

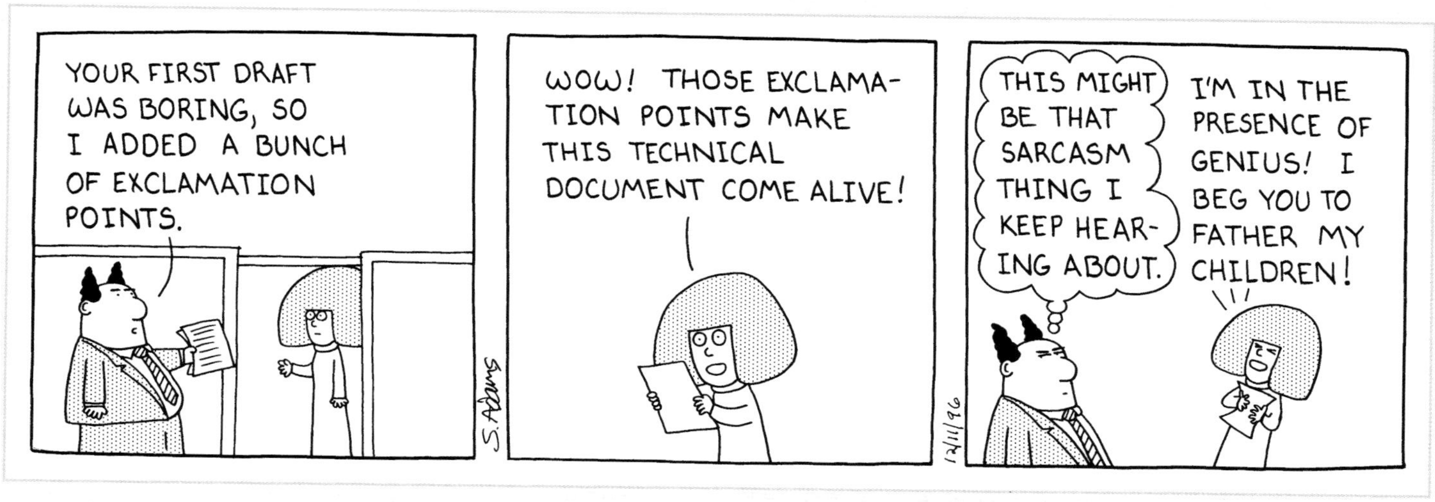
YOUR FIRST DRAFT WAS BORING, SO I ADDED A BUNCH OF EXCLAMATION POINTS.
S. Adams
WOW! THOSE EXCLAMA-TION POINTS MAKE THIS TECHNICAL DOCUMENT COME ALIVE!
12/11/96
THIS MIGHT BE THAT SARCASM THING I KEEP HEAR-ING ABOUT.
I'M IN THE PRESENCE OF GENIUS! I BEG YOU TO FATHER MY CHILDREN!

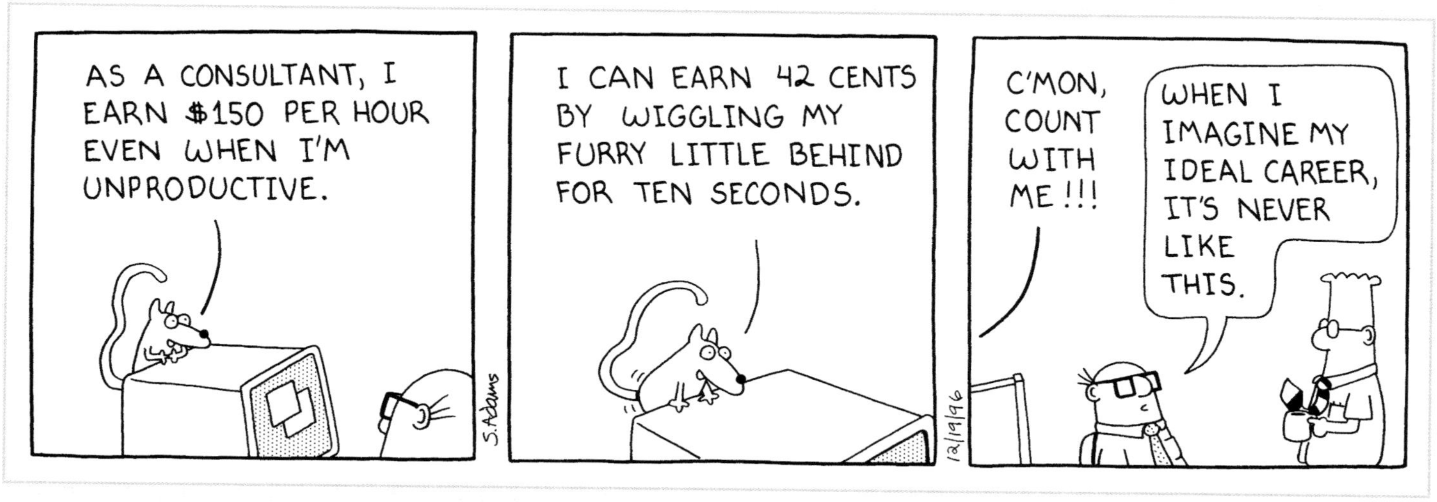
AS A CONSULTANT, I EARN $150 PER HOUR EVEN WHEN I'M UNPRODUCTIVE.
S. Adams
I CAN EARN 42 CENTS BY WIGGLING MY FURRY LITTLE BEHIND FOR TEN SECONDS.
12/19/96
C'MON, COUNT WITH ME!!!
WHEN I IMAGINE MY IDEAL CAREER, IT'S NEVER LIKE THIS.

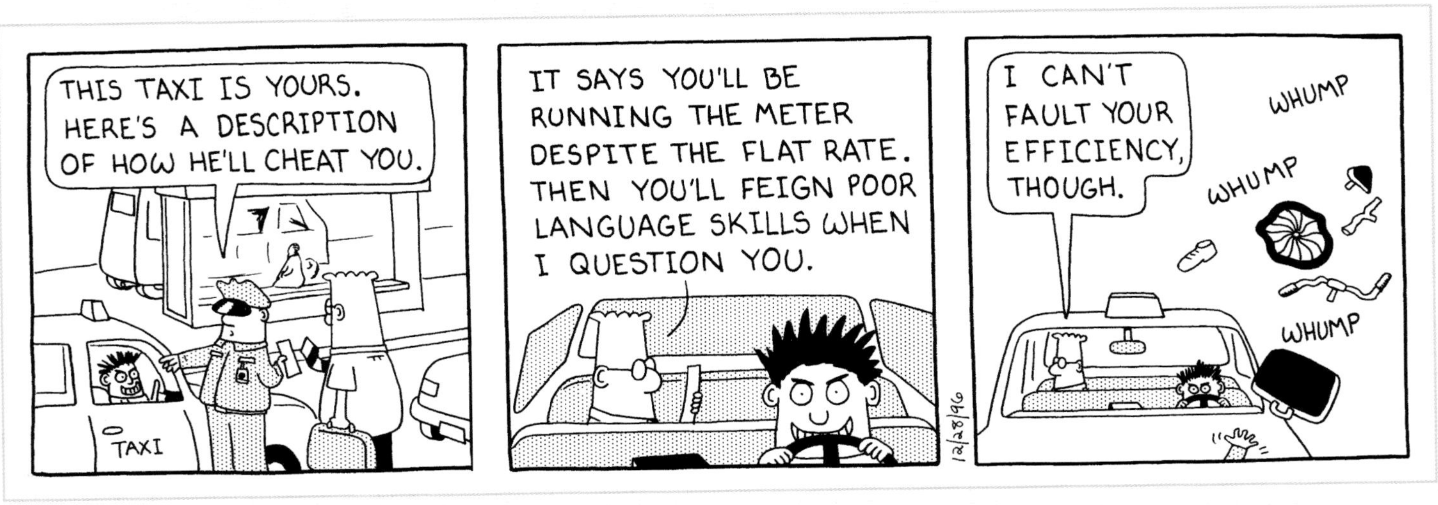
THIS TAXI IS YOURS. HERE'S A DESCRIPTION OF HOW HE'LL CHEAT YOU.
TAXI
IT SAYS YOU'LL BE RUNNING THE METER DESPITE THE FLAT RATE. THEN YOU'LL FEIGN POOR LANGUAGE SKILLS WHEN I QUESTION YOU.
12/28/96
I CAN'T FAULT YOUR EFFICIENCY, THOUGH.
WHUMP
WHUMP
WHUMP

Bicyclists were not amused by this comic.

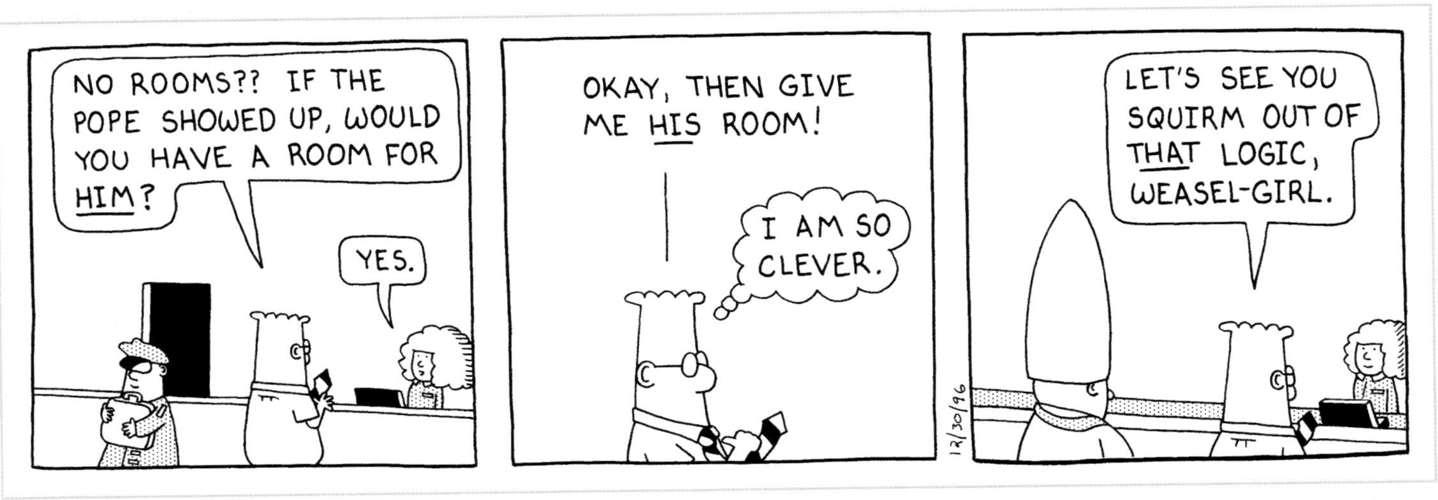
NO ROOMS?? IF THE POPE SHOWED UP, WOULD YOU HAVE A ROOM FOR HIM?
YES.
OKAY, THEN GIVE ME HIS ROOM!
I AM SO CLEVER.
12/30/96
LET'S SEE YOU SQUIRM OUT OF THAT LOGIC, WEASEL-GIRL.

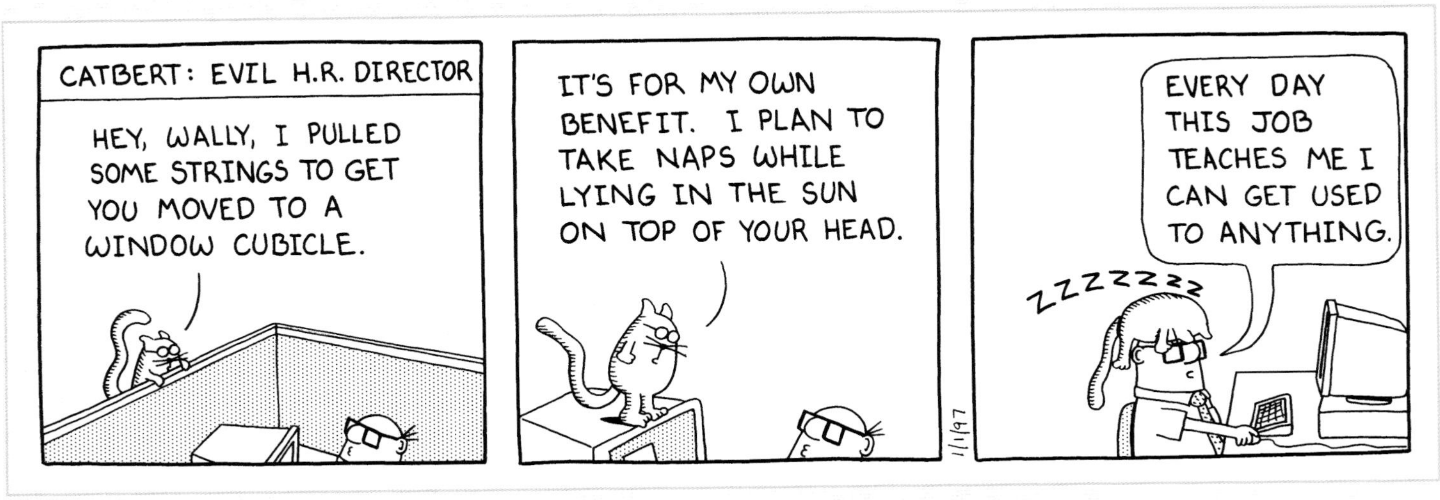
CATBERT: EVIL H.R. DIRECTOR
HEY, WALLY, I PULLED SOME STRINGS TO GET YOU MOVED TO A WINDOW CUBICLE.
IT'S FOR MY OWN BENEFIT. I PLAN TO TAKE NAPS WHILE LYING IN THE SUN ON TOP OF YOUR HEAD.
1/1/97
ZZZZZZZ
EVERY DAY THIS JOB TEACHES ME I CAN GET USED TO ANYTHING.

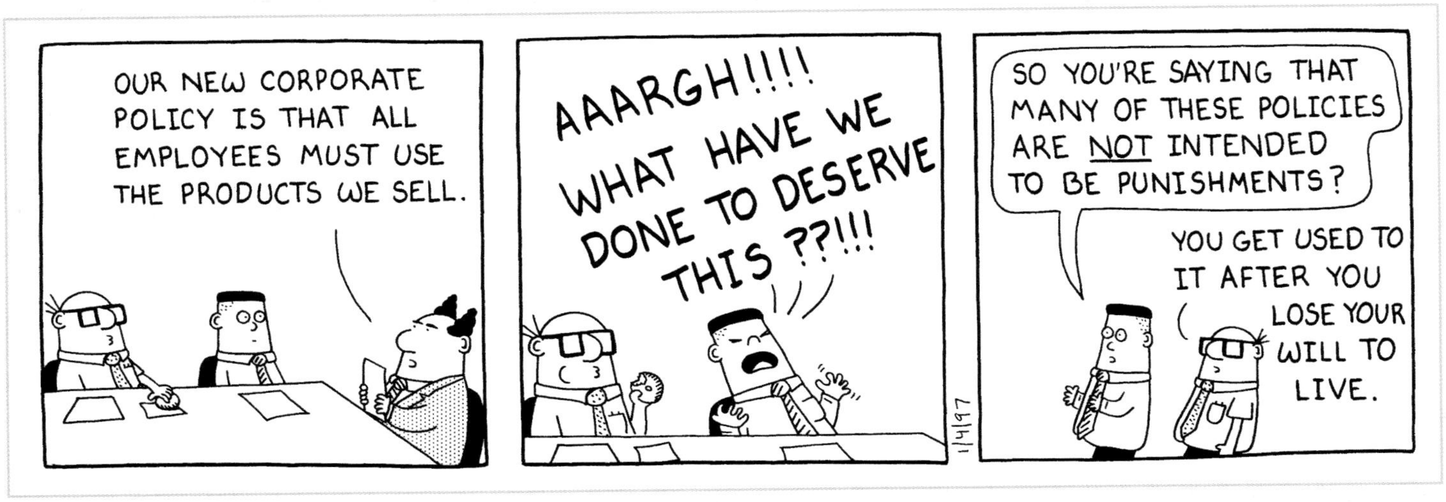
OUR NEW CORPORATE POLICY IS THAT ALL EMPLOYEES MUST USE THE PRODUCTS WE SELL.
AAARGH!!!! WHAT HAVE WE DONE TO DESERVE THIS ??!!!
1/4/97
SO YOU'RE SAYING THAT MANY OF THESE POLICIES ARE NOT INTENDED TO BE PUNISHMENTS?
YOU GET USED TO IT AFTER YOU LOSE YOUR WILL TO LIVE.

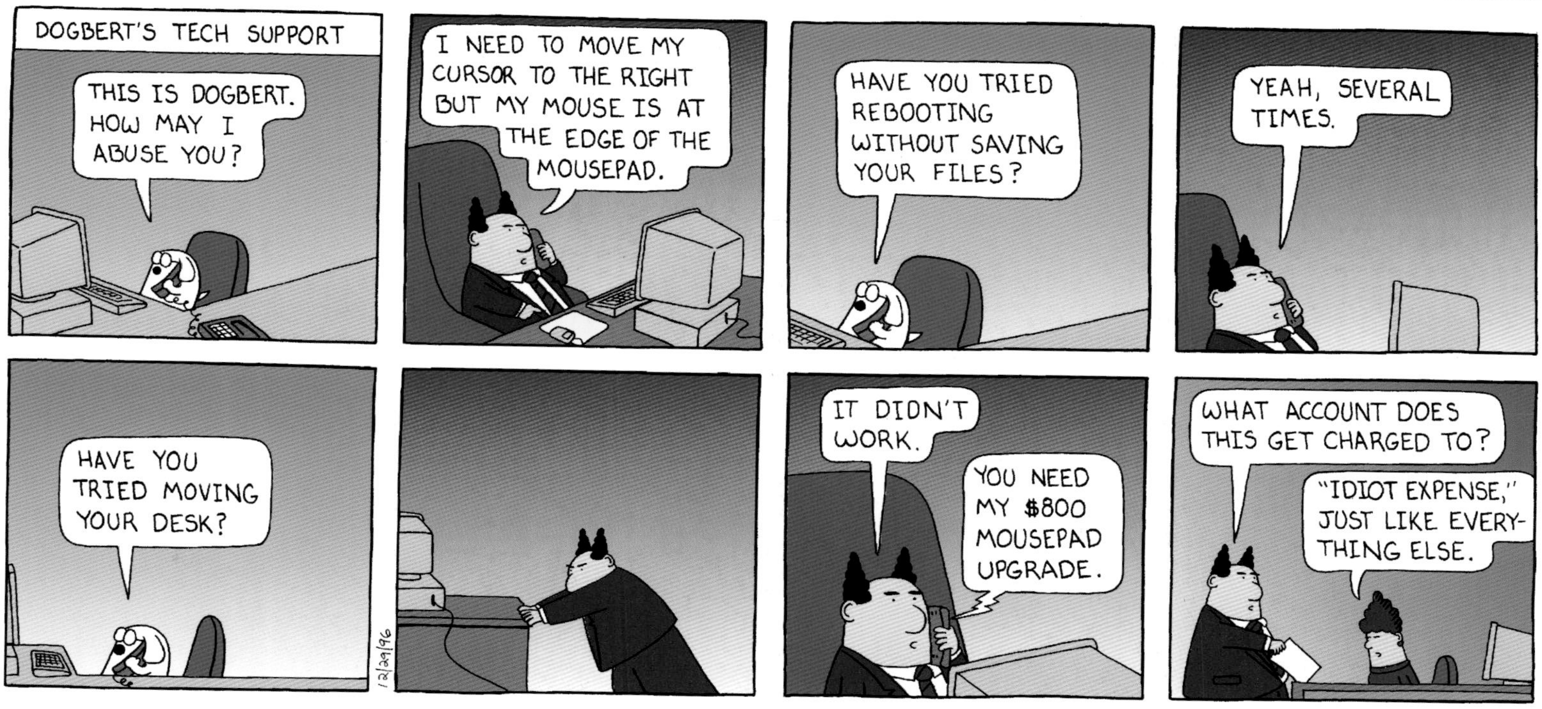
DOGBERT'S TECH SUPPORT
THIS IS DOGBERT. HOW MAY I ABUSE YOU?
I NEED TO MOVE MY CURSOR TO THE RIGHT BUT MY MOUSE IS AT THE EDGE OF THE MOUSEPAD.
HAVE YOU TRIED REBOOTING WITHOUT SAVING YOUR FILES?
YEAH, SEVERAL TIMES.
HAVE YOU TRIED MOVING YOUR DESK?
12/29/96
IT DIDN'T WORK.
YOU NEED MY $800 MOUSEPAD UPGRADE.
WHAT ACCOUNT DOES THIS GET CHARGED TO?
"IDIOT EXPENSE," JUST LIKE EVERYTHING ELSE.

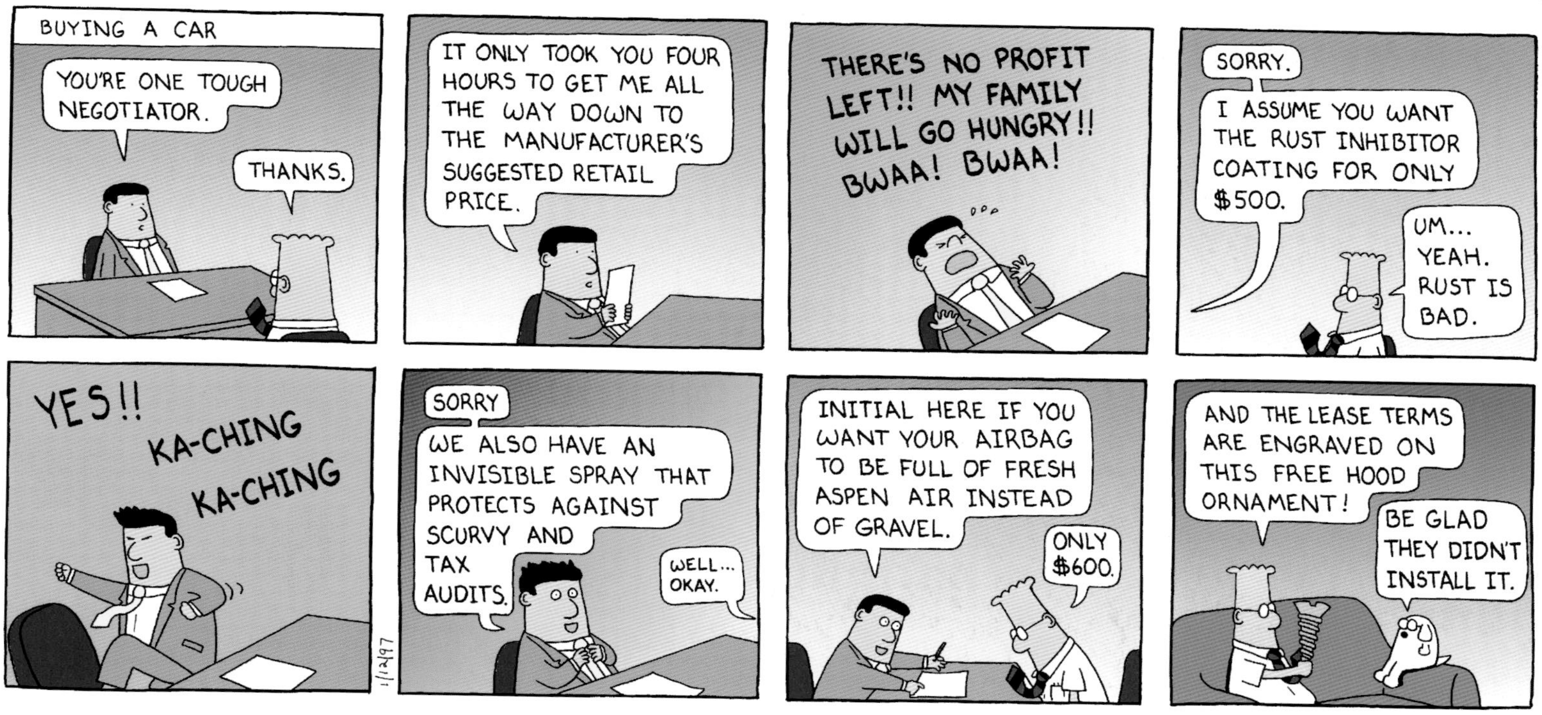
BUYING A CAR
YOU'RE ONE TOUGH NEGOTIATOR.
THANKS.
IT ONLY TOOK YOU FOUR HOURS TO GET ME ALL THE WAY DOWN TO THE MANUFACTURER'S SUGGESTED RETAIL PRICE.
THERE'S NO PROFIT LEFT!! MY FAMILY WILL GO HUNGRY!! BWAA! BWAA!
SORRY.
I ASSUME YOU WANT THE RUST INHIBITOR COATING FOR ONLY $500.
UM... YEAH. RUST IS BAD.
YES!!
KA-CHING
KA-CHING
1/12/97
SORRY
WE ALSO HAVE AN INVISIBLE SPRAY THAT PROTECTS AGAINST SCURVY AND TAX AUDITS.
WELL... OKAY.
INITIAL HERE IF YOU WANT YOUR AIRBAG TO BE FULL OF FRESH ASPEN AIR INSTEAD OF GRAVEL.
ONLY $600.
AND THE LEASE TERMS ARE ENGRAVED ON THIS FREE HOOD ORNAMENT!
BE GLAD THEY DIDN'T INSTALL IT.

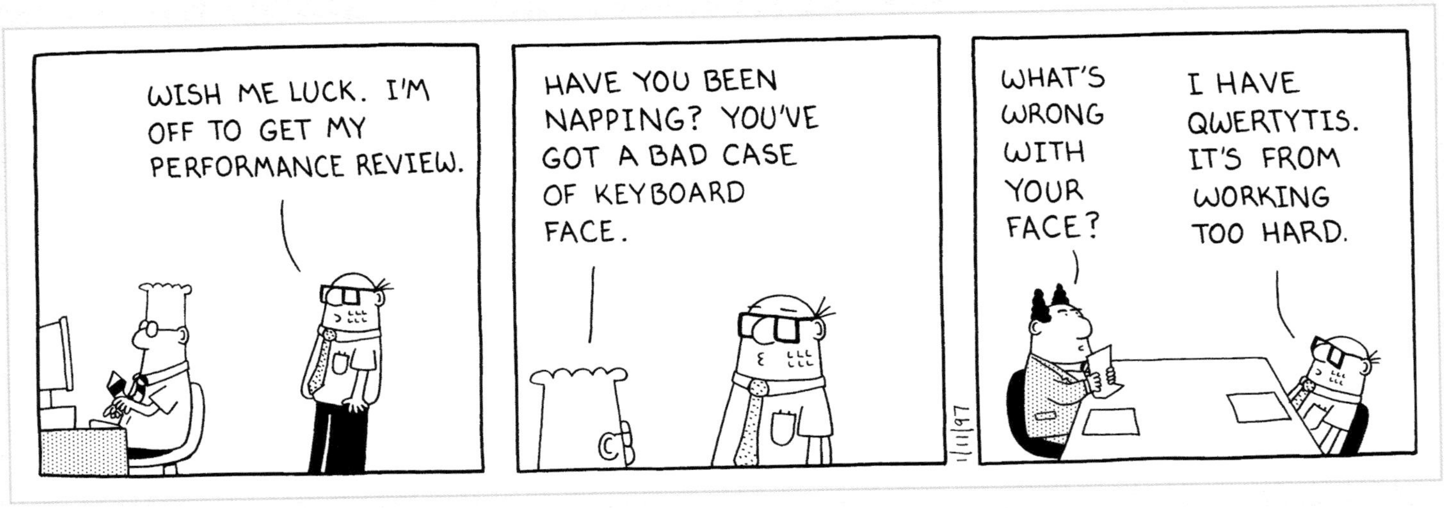
WISH ME LUCK. I'M OFF TO GET MY PERFORMANCE REVIEW.
HAVE YOU BEEN NAPPING? YOU'VE GOT A BAD CASE OF KEYBOARD FACE.
1/11/97
WHAT'S WRONG WITH YOUR FACE?
I HAVE QWERTYTIS. IT'S FROM WORKING TOO HARD.

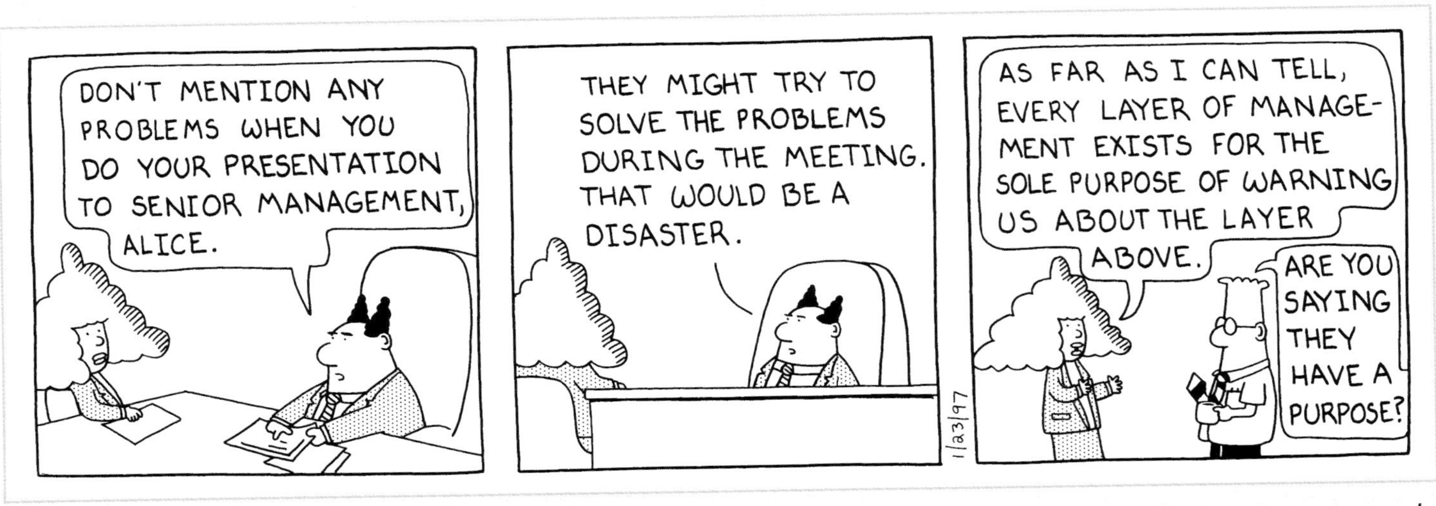
DON'T MENTION ANY PROBLEMS WHEN YOU DO YOUR PRESENTATION TO SENIOR MANAGEMENT, ALICE.
THEY MIGHT TRY TO SOLVE THE PROBLEMS DURING THE MEETING. THAT WOULD BE A DISASTER.
1/23/97
AS FAR AS I CAN TELL, EVERY LAYER OF MANAGEMENT EXISTS FOR THE SOLE PURPOSE OF WARNING US ABOUT THE LAYER ABOVE.
ARE YOU SAYING THEY HAVE A PURPOSE?

I started putting balloons around more of the dialogue, thinking it was an improvement. In the end, it was just extra work.

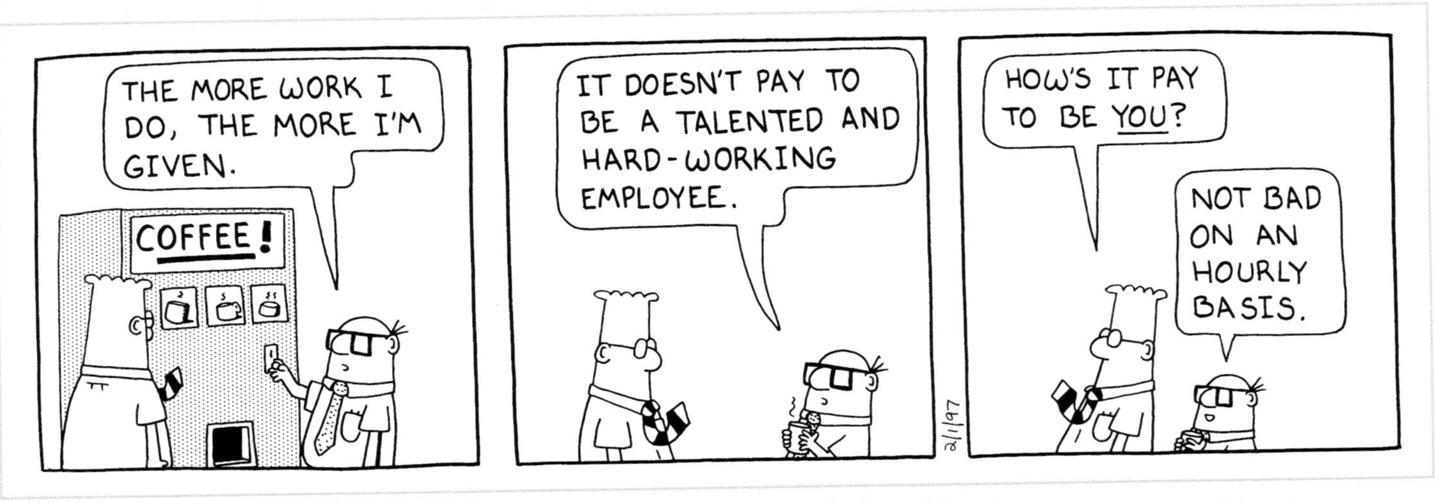
THE MORE WORK I DO, THE MORE I'M GIVEN.
COFFEE!
IT DOESN'T PAY TO BE A TALENTED AND HARD-WORKING EMPLOYEE.
2/1/97
HOW'S IT PAY TO BE YOU?
NOT BAD ON AN HOURLY BASIS.

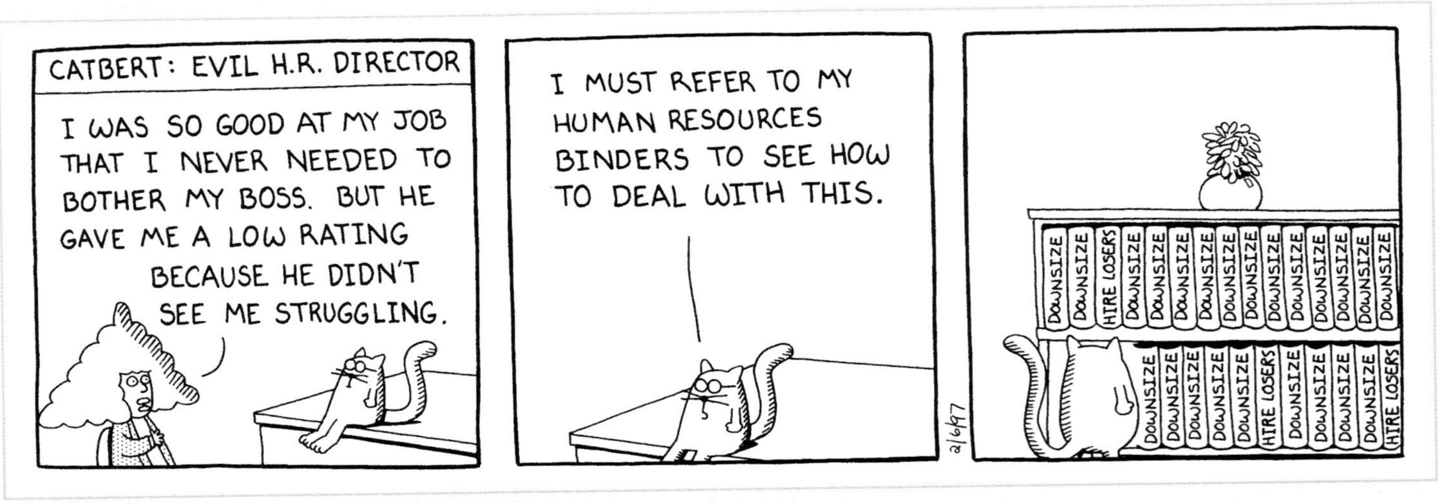
CATBERT: EVIL H.R. DIRECTOR
I WAS SO GOOD AT MY JOB THAT I NEVER NEEDED TO BOTHER MY BOSS. BUT HE GAVE ME A LOW RATING BECAUSE HE DIDN'T SEE ME STRUGGLING.
I MUST REFER TO MY HUMAN RESOURCES BINDERS TO SEE HOW TO DEAL WITH THIS.
2/6/97
DOWNSIZE
HIRE LOSERS

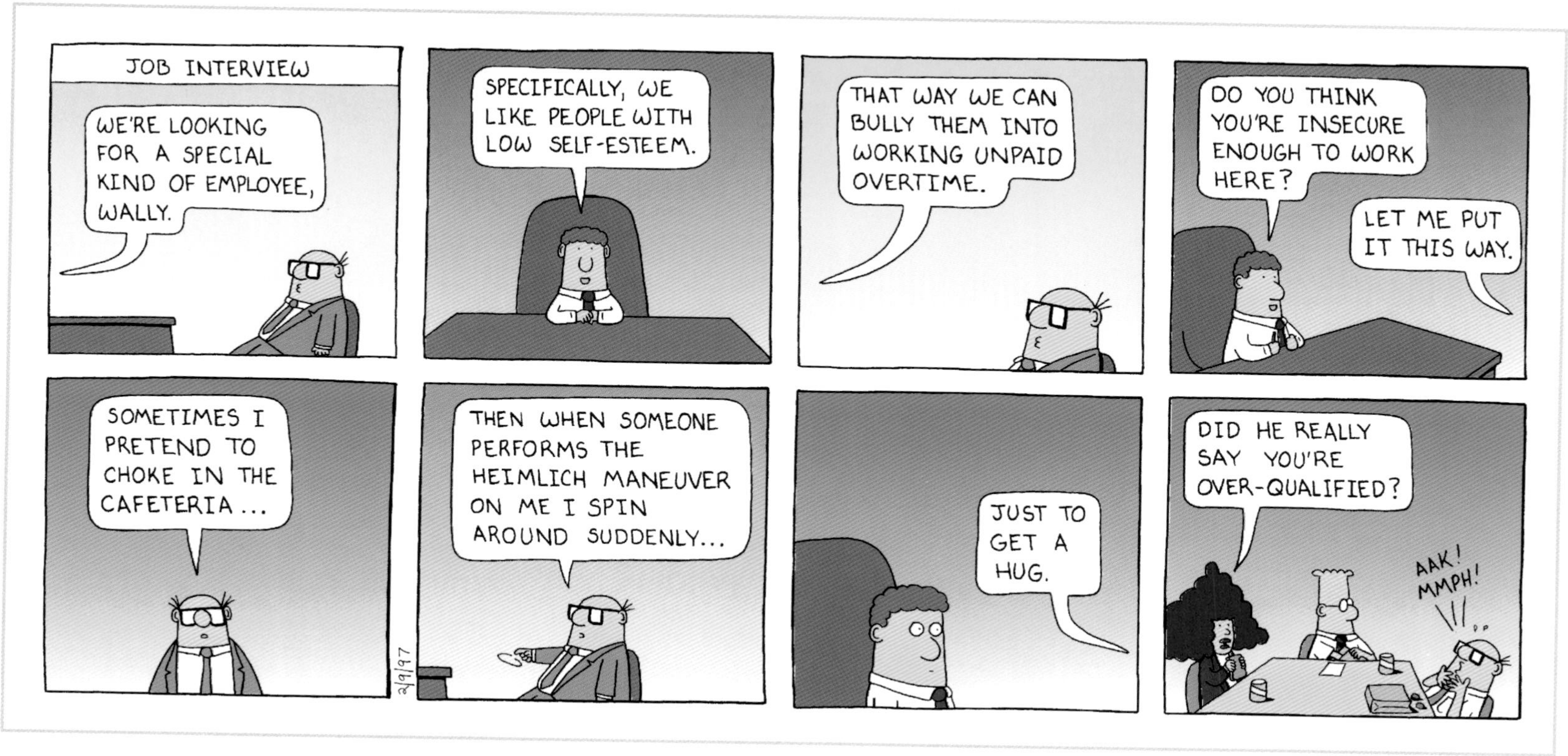
JOB INTERVIEW
WE'RE LOOKING FOR A SPECIAL KIND OF EMPLOYEE, WALLY.
SPECIFICALLY, WE LIKE PEOPLE WITH LOW SELF-ESTEEM.
THAT WAY WE CAN BULLY THEM INTO WORKING UNPAID OVERTIME.
DO YOU THINK YOU'RE INSECURE ENOUGH TO WORK HERE?
LET ME PUT IT THIS WAY.
SOMETIMES I PRETEND TO CHOKE IN THE CAFETERIA ...
THEN WHEN SOMEONE PERFORMS THE HEIMLICH MANEUVER ON ME I SPIN AROUND SUDDENLY...
2/9/97
JUST TO GET A HUG.
DID HE REALLY SAY YOU'RE OVER-QUALIFIED?
AAK! MMPH!

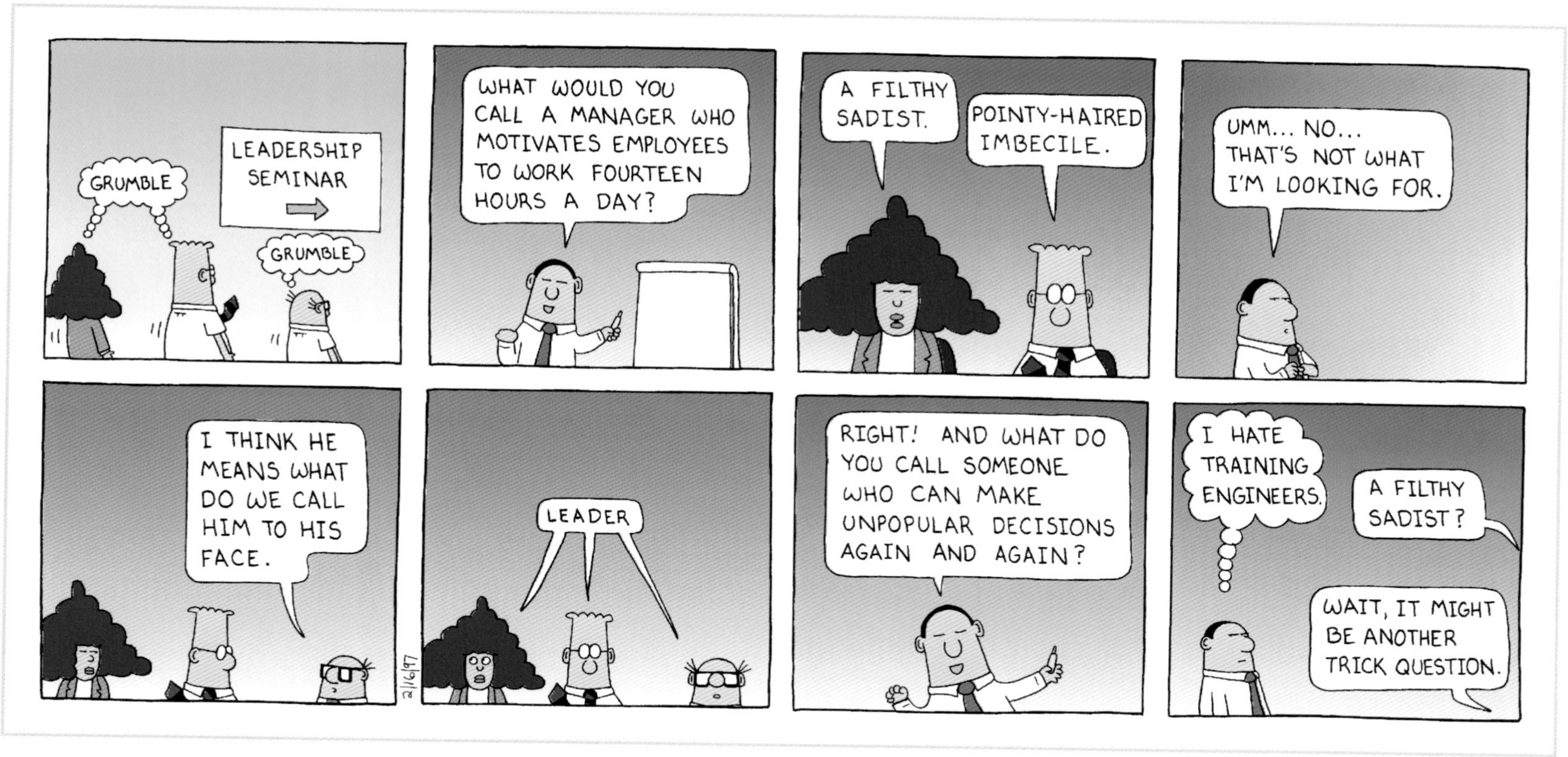
GRUMBLE
LEADERSHIP SEMINAR
GRUMBLE
WHAT WOULD YOU CALL A MANAGER WHO MOTIVATES EMPLOYEES TO WORK FOURTEEN HOURS A DAY?
A FILTHY SADIST.
POINTY-HAIRED IMBECILE.
UMM... NO... THAT'S NOT WHAT I'M LOOKING FOR.
I THINK HE MEANS WHAT DO WE CALL HIM TO HIS FACE.
2/16/97
LEADER
RIGHT! AND WHAT DO YOU CALL SOMEONE WHO CAN MAKE UNPOPULAR DECISIONS AGAIN AND AGAIN?
I HATE TRAINING ENGINEERS.
A FILTHY SADIST?
WAIT, IT MIGHT BE ANOTHER TRICK QUESTION.

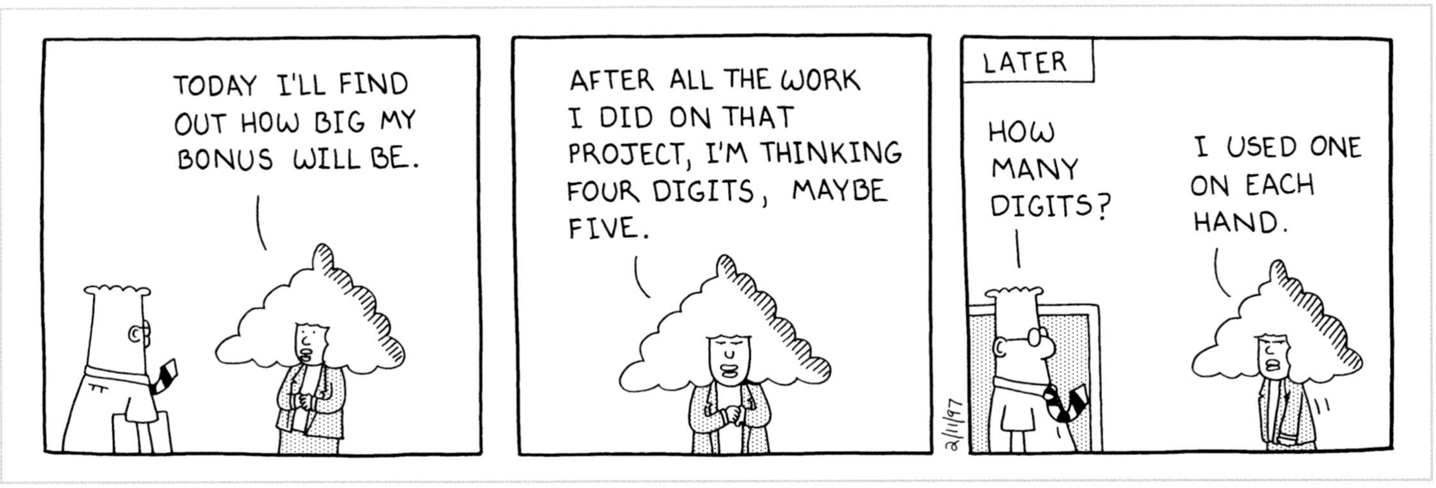
TODAY I'LL FIND OUT HOW BIG MY BONUS WILL BE.
AFTER ALL THE WORK I DID ON THAT PROJECT, I'M THINKING FOUR DIGITS, MAYBE FIVE.
LATER
HOW MANY DIGITS?
I USED ONE ON EACH HAND.
2/11/97

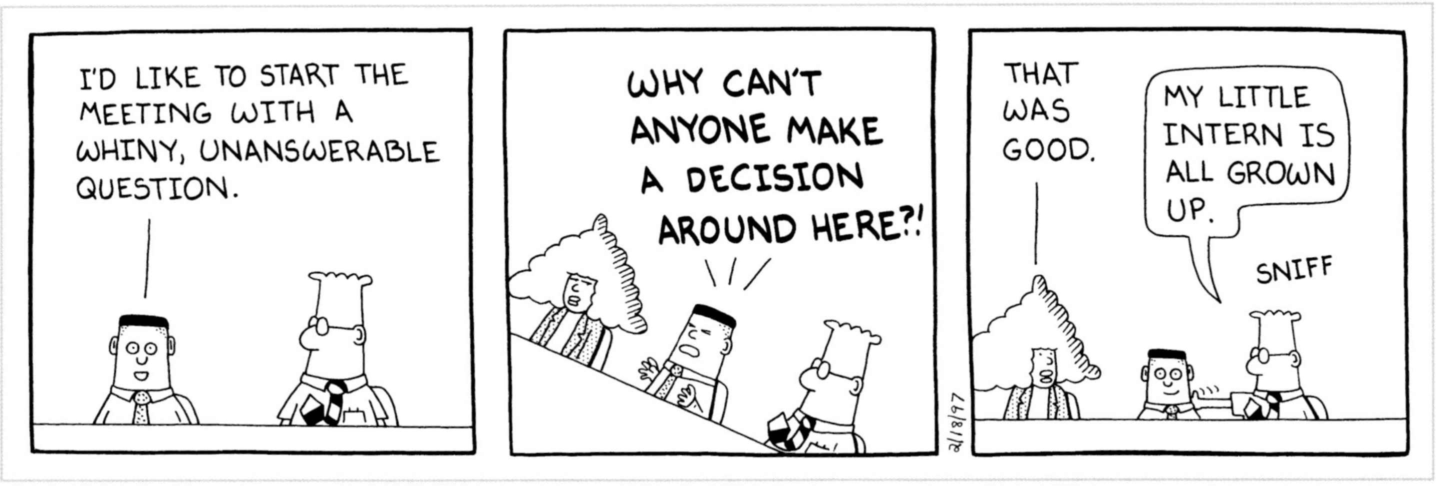
I'D LIKE TO START THE MEETING WITH A WHINY, UNANSWERABLE QUESTION.
WHY CAN'T ANYONE MAKE A DECISION AROUND HERE?!
THAT WAS GOOD.
MY LITTLE INTERN IS ALL GROWN UP.
SNIFF
2/18/97

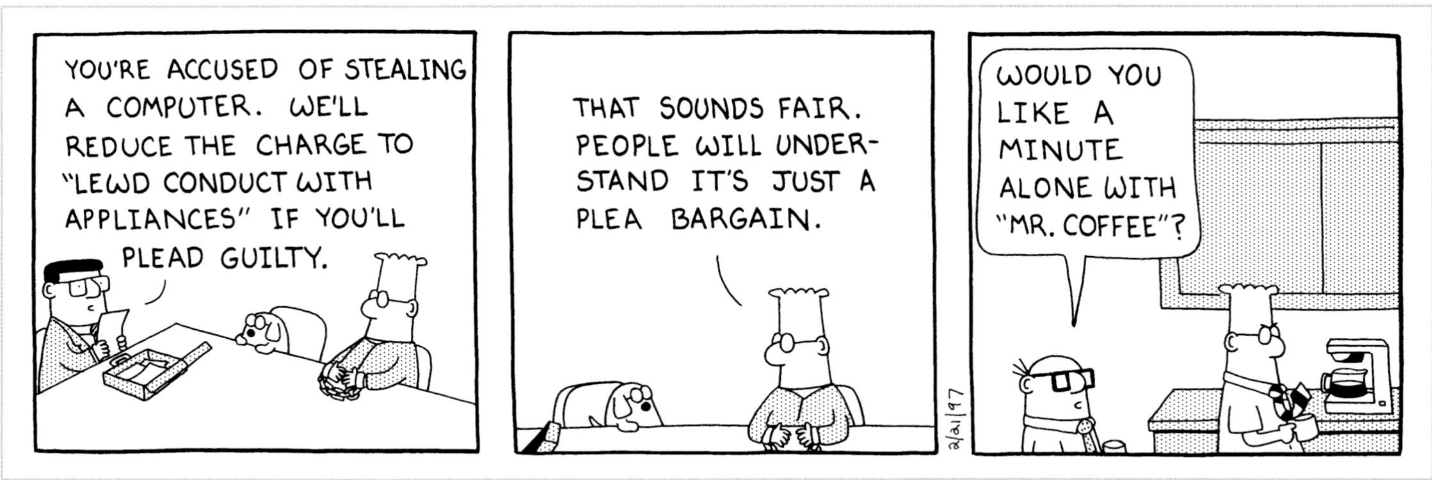
YOU'RE ACCUSED OF STEALING A COMPUTER. WE'LL REDUCE THE CHARGE TO "LEWD CONDUCT WITH APPLIANCES" IF YOU'LL PLEAD GUILTY.
THAT SOUNDS FAIR. PEOPLE WILL UNDERSTAND IT'S JUST A PLEA BARGAIN.
WOULD YOU LIKE A MINUTE ALONE WITH "MR. COFFEE"?
2/21/97

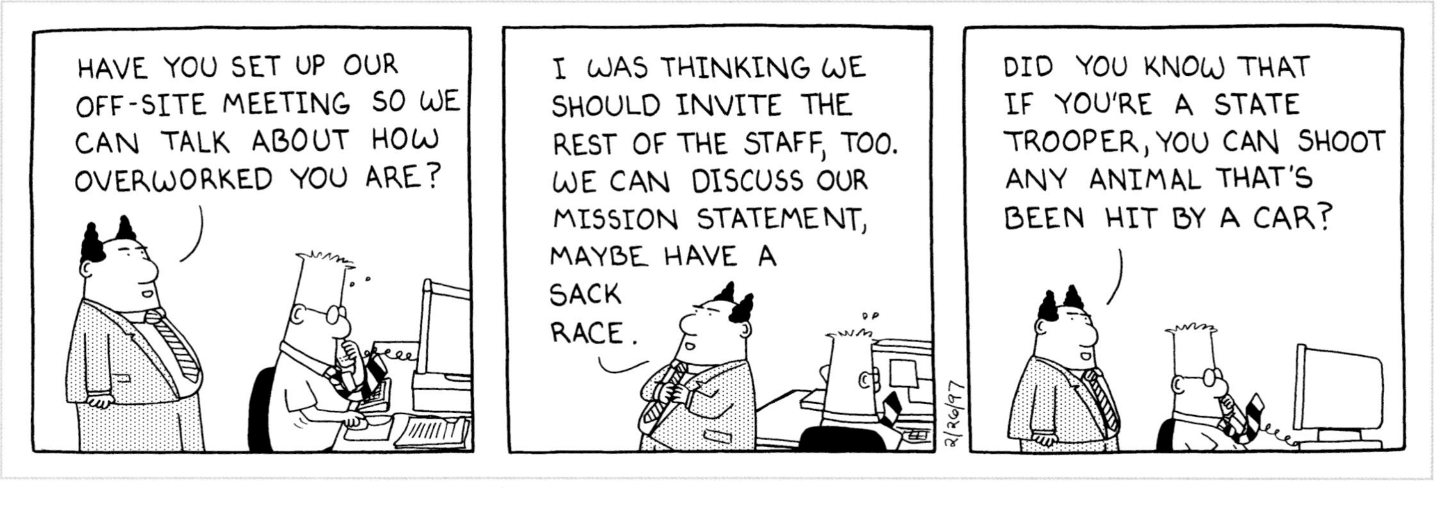
HAVE YOU SET UP OUR OFF-SITE MEETING SO WE CAN TALK ABOUT HOW OVERWORKED YOU ARE?
I WAS THINKING WE SHOULD INVITE THE REST OF THE STAFF, TOO. WE CAN DISCUSS OUR MISSION STATEMENT, MAYBE HAVE A SACK RACE.
DID YOU KNOW THAT IF YOU'RE A STATE TROOPER, YOU CAN SHOOT ANY ANIMAL THAT'S BEEN HIT BY A CAR?
2/26/97

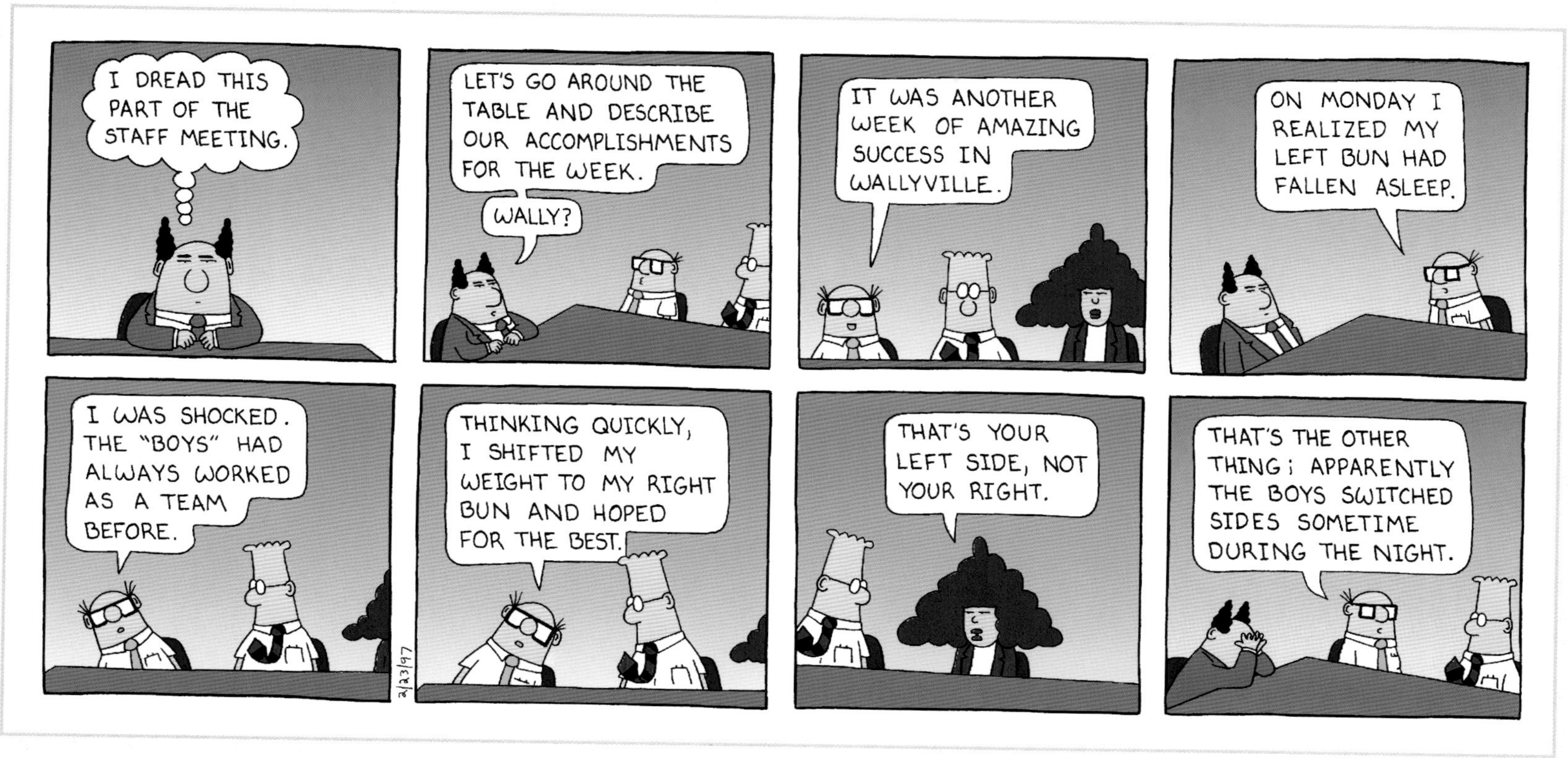
I DREAD THIS PART OF THE STAFF MEETING.
LET'S GO AROUND THE TABLE AND DESCRIBE OUR ACCOMPLISHMENTS FOR THE WEEK.
WALLY?
IT WAS ANOTHER WEEK OF AMAZING SUCCESS IN WALLYVILLE.
ON MONDAY I REALIZED MY LEFT BUN HAD FALLEN ASLEEP.
I WAS SHOCKED. THE "BOYS" HAD ALWAYS WORKED AS A TEAM BEFORE.
THINKING QUICKLY, I SHIFTED MY WEIGHT TO MY RIGHT BUN AND HOPED FOR THE BEST.
THAT'S YOUR LEFT SIDE, NOT YOUR RIGHT.
THAT'S THE OTHER THING; APPARENTLY THE BOYS SWITCHED SIDES SOMETIME DURING THE NIGHT.
2/23/97

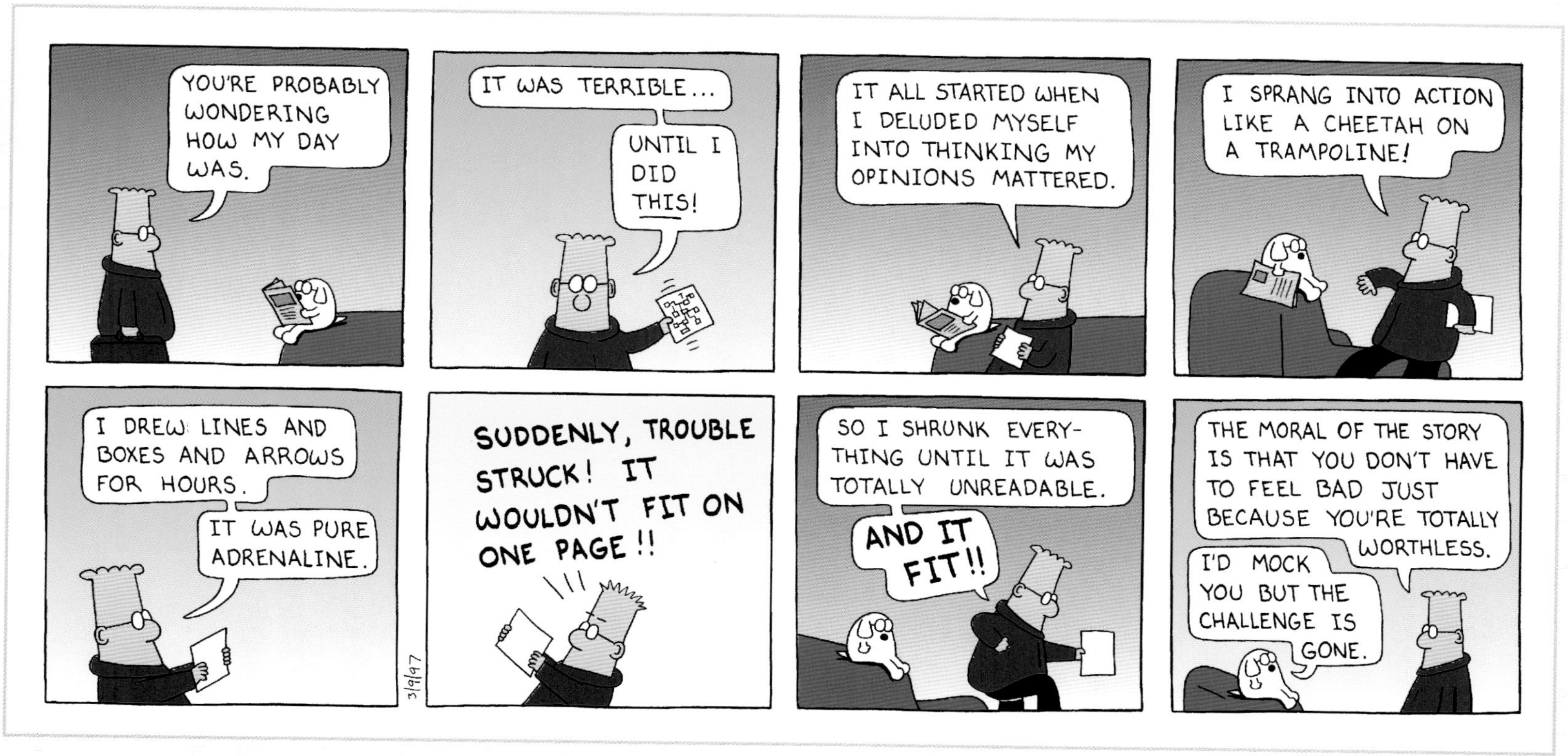
YOU'RE PROBABLY WONDERING HOW MY DAY WAS.
IT WAS TERRIBLE...
UNTIL I DID THIS!
IT ALL STARTED WHEN I DELUDED MYSELF INTO THINKING MY OPINIONS MATTERED.
I SPRANG INTO ACTION LIKE A CHEETAH ON A TRAMPOLINE!
I DREW LINES AND BOXES AND ARROWS FOR HOURS.
IT WAS PURE ADRENALINE.
SUDDENLY, TROUBLE STRUCK! IT WOULDN'T FIT ON ONE PAGE!!
SO I SHRUNK EVERYTHING UNTIL IT WAS TOTALLY UNREADABLE.
AND IT FIT!!
THE MORAL OF THE STORY IS THAT YOU DON'T HAVE TO FEEL BAD JUST BECAUSE YOU'RE TOTALLY WORTHLESS.
I'D MOCK YOU BUT THE CHALLENGE IS GONE.
3/9/97

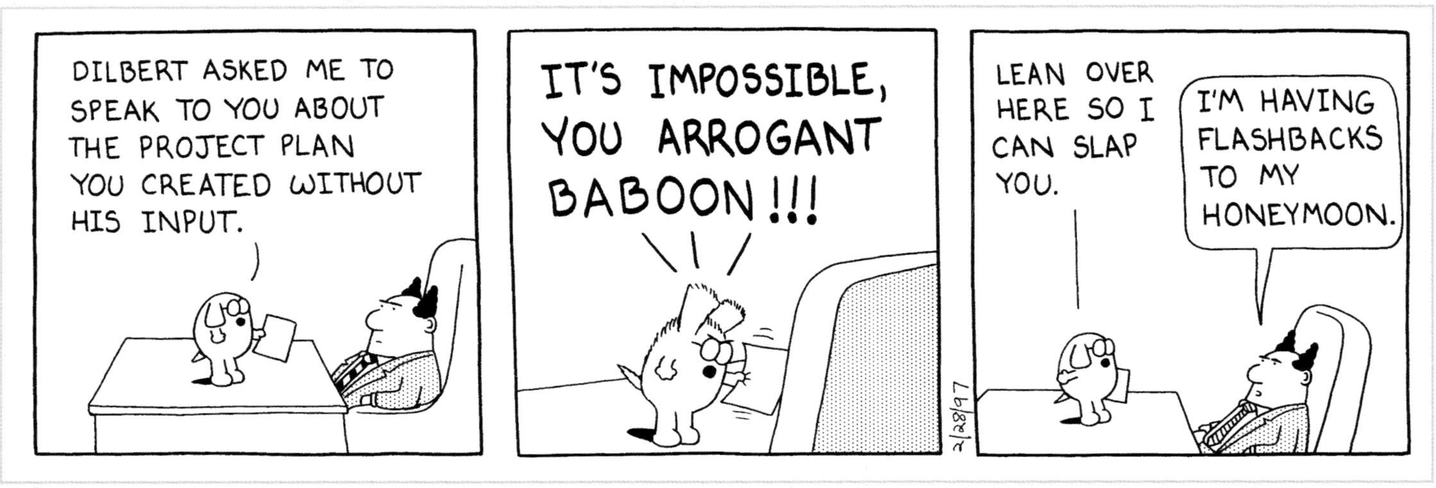
DILBERT ASKED ME TO SPEAK TO YOU ABOUT THE PROJECT PLAN YOU CREATED WITHOUT HIS INPUT.
IT'S IMPOSSIBLE, YOU ARROGANT BABOON!!!
LEAN OVER HERE SO I CAN SLAP YOU.
I'M HAVING FLASHBACKS TO MY HONEYMOON.
2/28/97

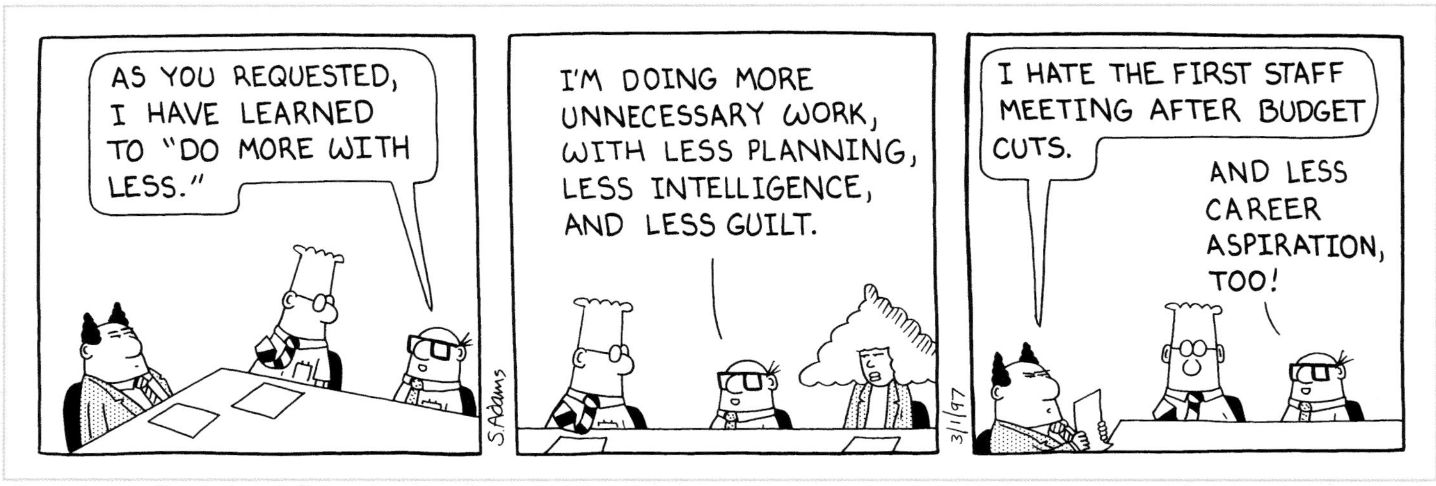
AS YOU REQUESTED, I HAVE LEARNED TO "DO MORE WITH LESS."
S.Adams
I'M DOING MORE UNNECESSARY WORK, WITH LESS PLANNING, LESS INTELLIGENCE, AND LESS GUILT.
3/1/97
I HATE THE FIRST STAFF MEETING AFTER BUDGET CUTS.
AND LESS CAREER ASPIRATION, TOO!

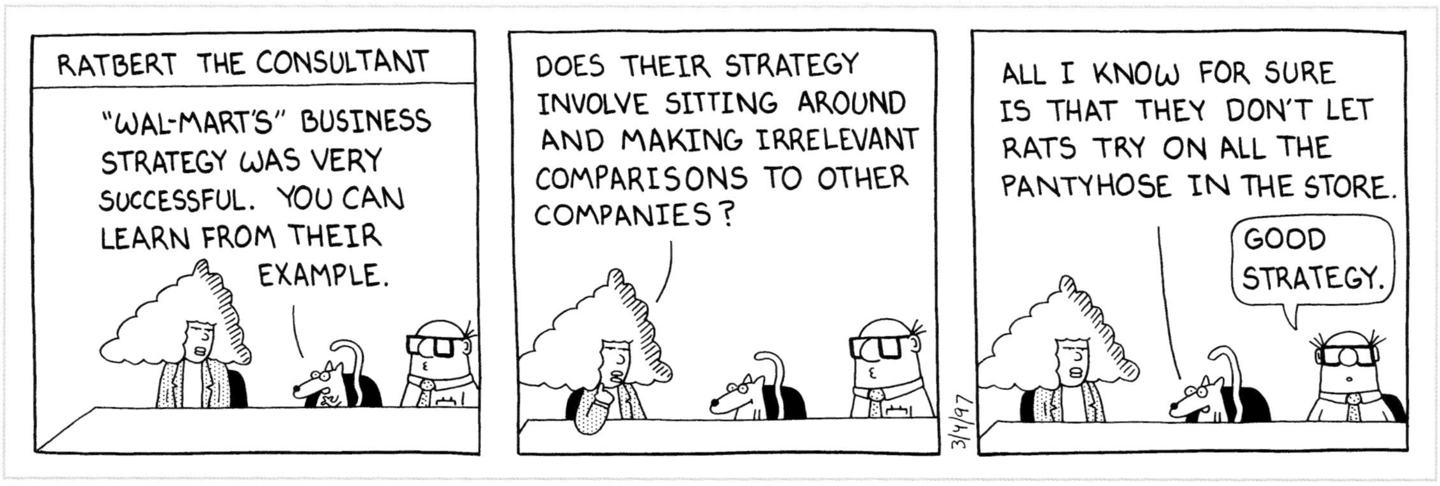
RATBERT THE CONSULTANT
"WAL-MART'S" BUSINESS STRATEGY WAS VERY SUCCESSFUL. YOU CAN LEARN FROM THEIR EXAMPLE.
DOES THEIR STRATEGY INVOLVE SITTING AROUND AND MAKING IRRELEVANT COMPARISONS TO OTHER COMPANIES?
3/4/97
ALL I KNOW FOR SURE IS THAT THEY DON'T LET RATS TRY ON ALL THE PANTYHOSE IN THE STORE.
GOOD STRATEGY.

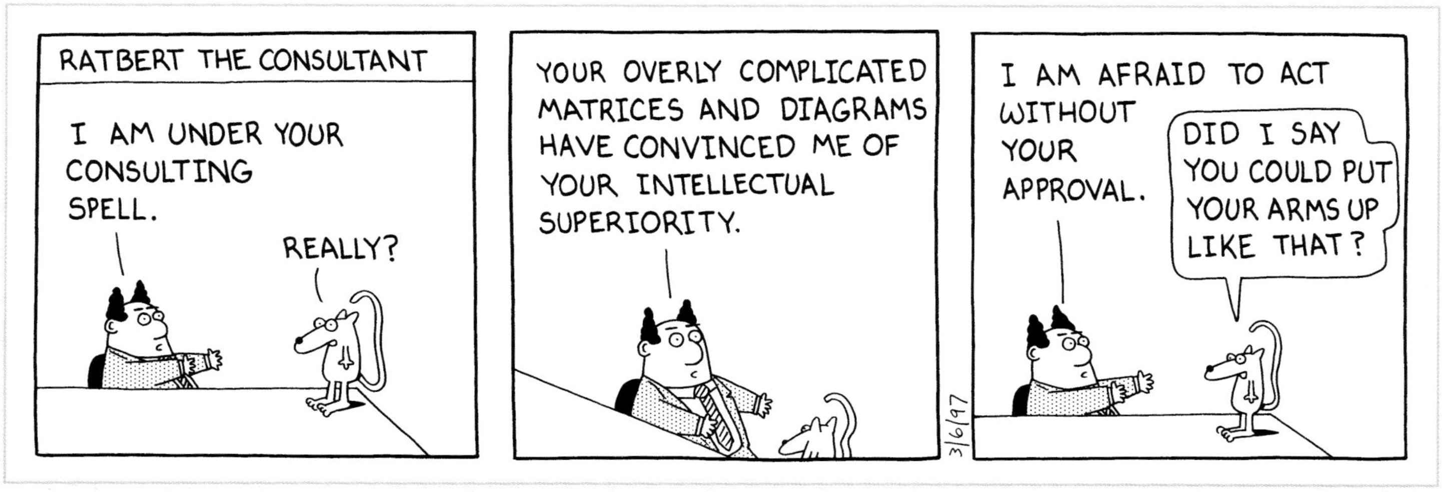
RATBERT THE CONSULTANT
I AM UNDER YOUR CONSULTING SPELL.
REALLY?
YOUR OVERLY COMPLICATED MATRICES AND DIAGRAMS HAVE CONVINCED ME OF YOUR INTELLECTUAL SUPERIORITY.
3/6/97
I AM AFRAID TO ACT WITHOUT YOUR APPROVAL.
DID I SAY YOU COULD PUT YOUR ARMS UP LIKE THAT?

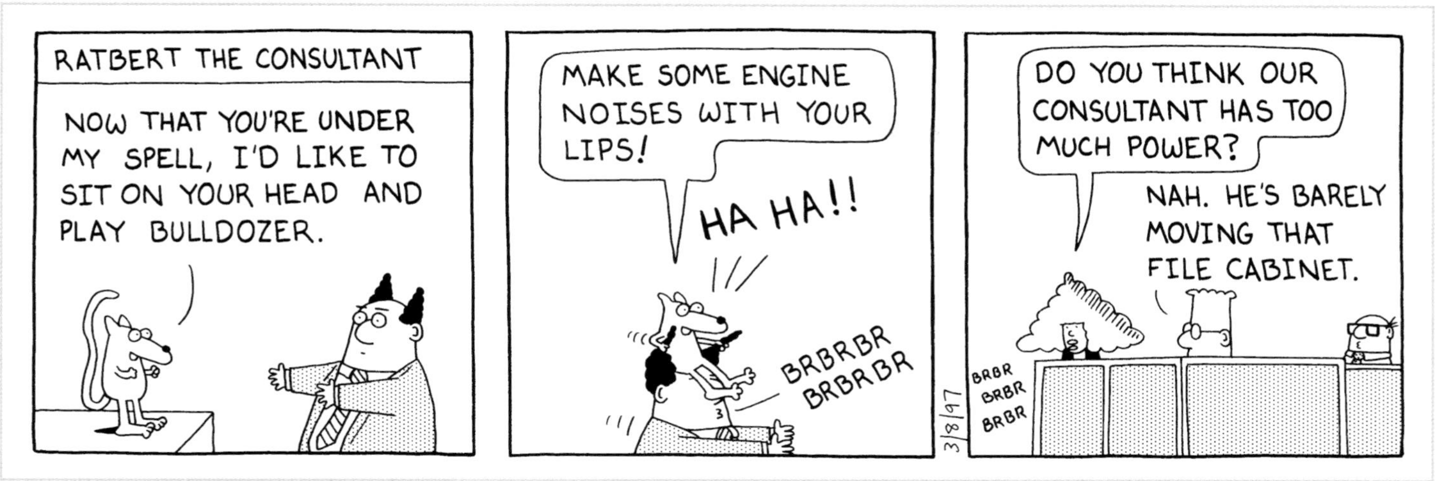
RATBERT THE CONSULTANT
NOW THAT YOU'RE UNDER MY SPELL, I'D LIKE TO SIT ON YOUR HEAD AND PLAY BULLDOZER.
MAKE SOME ENGINE NOISES WITH YOUR LIPS!
HA HA!!
BRBRBR BRBRBR
3/8/97
BRBR BRBR BRBR
DO YOU THINK OUR CONSULTANT HAS TOO MUCH POWER?
NAH. HE'S BARELY MOVING THAT FILE CABINET.

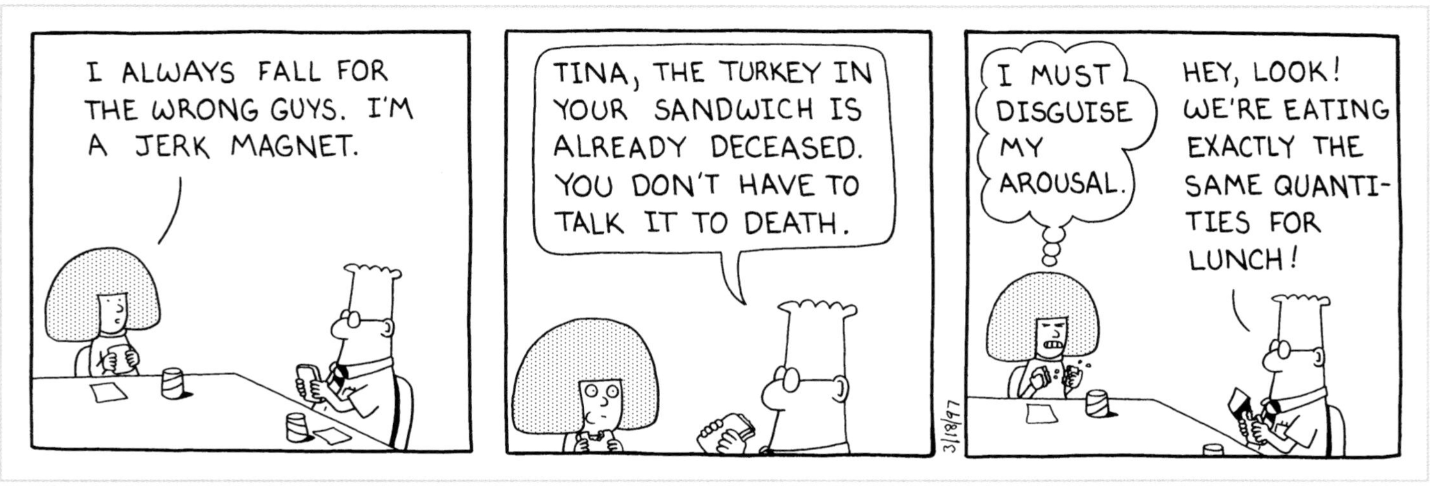
I ALWAYS FALL FOR THE WRONG GUYS. I'M A JERK MAGNET.
TINA, THE TURKEY IN YOUR SANDWICH IS ALREADY DECEASED. YOU DON'T HAVE TO TALK IT TO DEATH.
3/18/97
I MUST DISGUISE MY AROUSAL.
HEY, LOOK! WE'RE EATING EXACTLY THE SAME QUANTITIES FOR LUNCH!

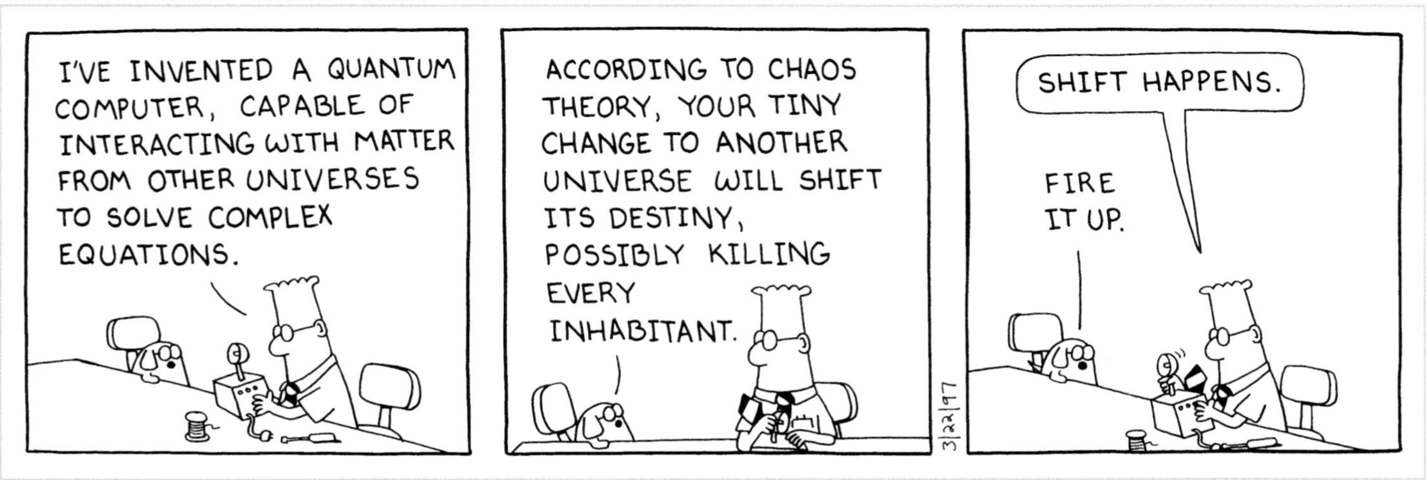
I'VE INVENTED A QUANTUM COMPUTER, CAPABLE OF INTERACTING WITH MATTER FROM OTHER UNIVERSES TO SOLVE COMPLEX EQUATIONS.
ACCORDING TO CHAOS THEORY, YOUR TINY CHANGE TO ANOTHER UNIVERSE WILL SHIFT ITS DESTINY, POSSIBLY KILLING EVERY INHABITANT.
3/22/97
FIRE IT UP.
SHIFT HAPPENS.

How did I get away with this one?

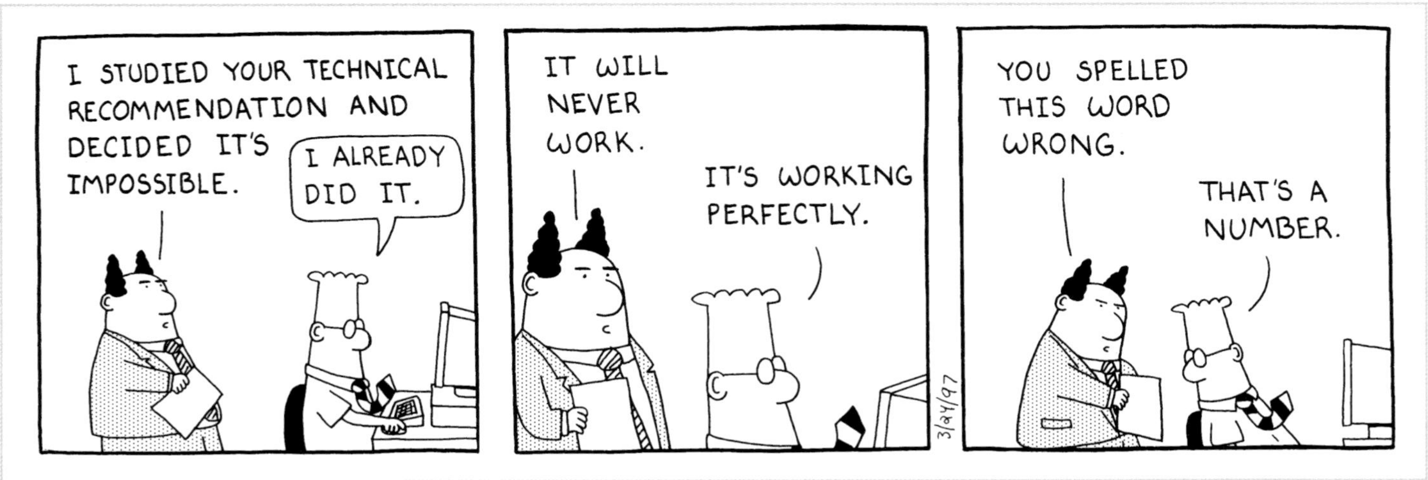
I STUDIED YOUR TECHNICAL RECOMMENDATION AND DECIDED IT'S IMPOSSIBLE.
I ALREADY DID IT.
IT WILL NEVER WORK.
IT'S WORKING PERFECTLY.
3/24/97
YOU SPELLED THIS WORD WRONG.
THAT'S A NUMBER.

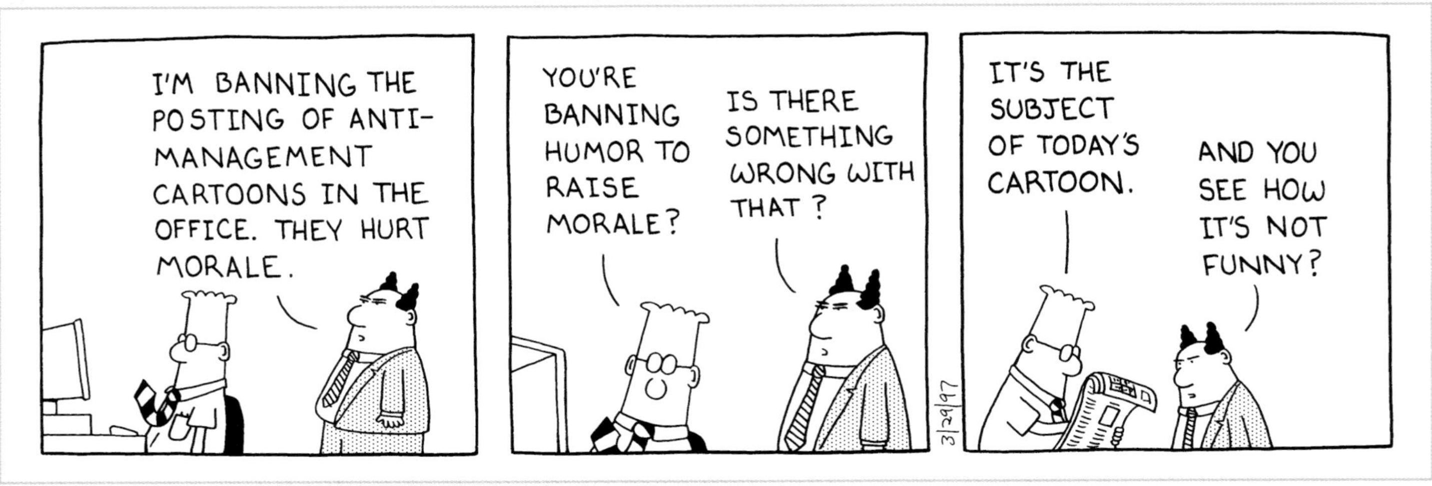
I'M BANNING THE POSTING OF ANTI-MANAGEMENT CARTOONS IN THE OFFICE. THEY HURT MORALE.
YOU'RE BANNING HUMOR TO RAISE MORALE?
IS THERE SOMETHING WRONG WITH THAT?
3/29/97
IT'S THE SUBJECT OF TODAY'S CARTOON.
AND YOU SEE HOW IT'S NOT FUNNY?

So many people were getting in trouble for posting Dilbert *comics at work that I figured it was time to revisit this theme.*

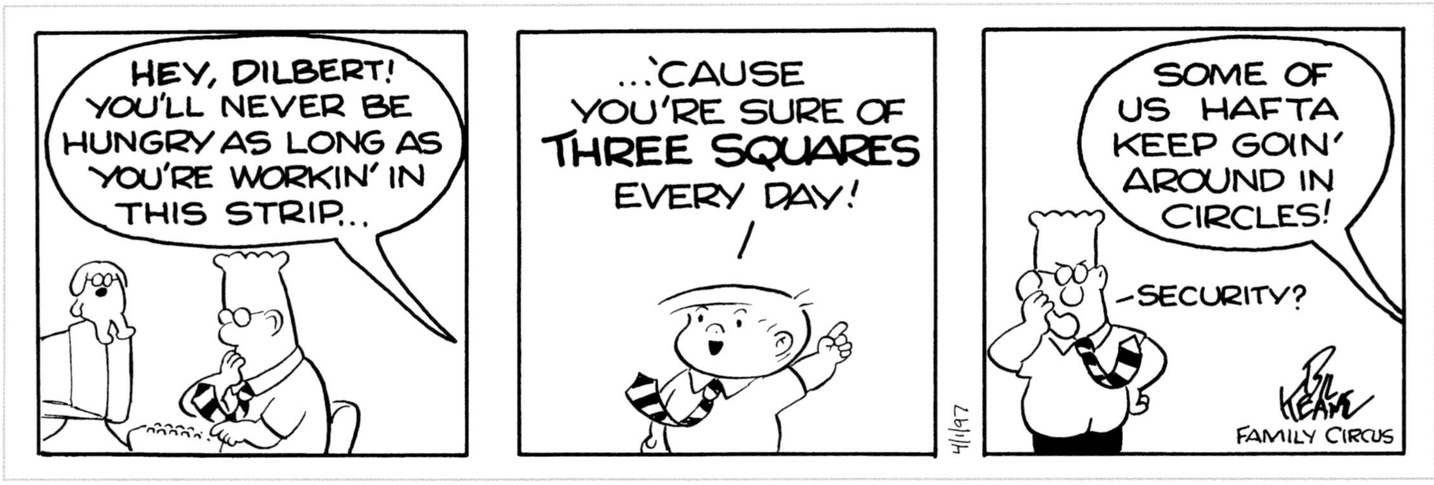
HEY, DILBERT! YOU'LL NEVER BE HUNGRY AS LONG AS YOU'RE WORKIN' IN THIS STRIP...
...'CAUSE YOU'RE SURE OF THREE SQUARES EVERY DAY!
4/1/97
SOME OF US HAFTA KEEP GOIN' AROUND IN CIRCLES!
-SECURITY?
FAMILY CIRCUS

For April Fool's Day, a number of cartoonists switched comics. Mine was drawn by Bil Keane who created The Family Circus. *It seemed ironic at the time, since* Dilbert *was about the edgiest comic in papers.*

Bil gave me the best advice I ever got in cartooning, although it took me some time to realize it. Early in my career, at a meeting of newspaper editors, where both of us were presenting, he told me my comics were "cartoonist cartoons," by which he meant they would appeal mostly to other cartoonists, and not to the general public. At first I felt insulted. Later I realized I really did work for the public, and their preferences didn't match mine as closely as I would have liked. That simple realization is what allowed me to change the strip to a workplace theme and trust the readers to know what they wanted.

You can say what you want about The Family Circus, *but Bil is a genius, and he knows his audience.*

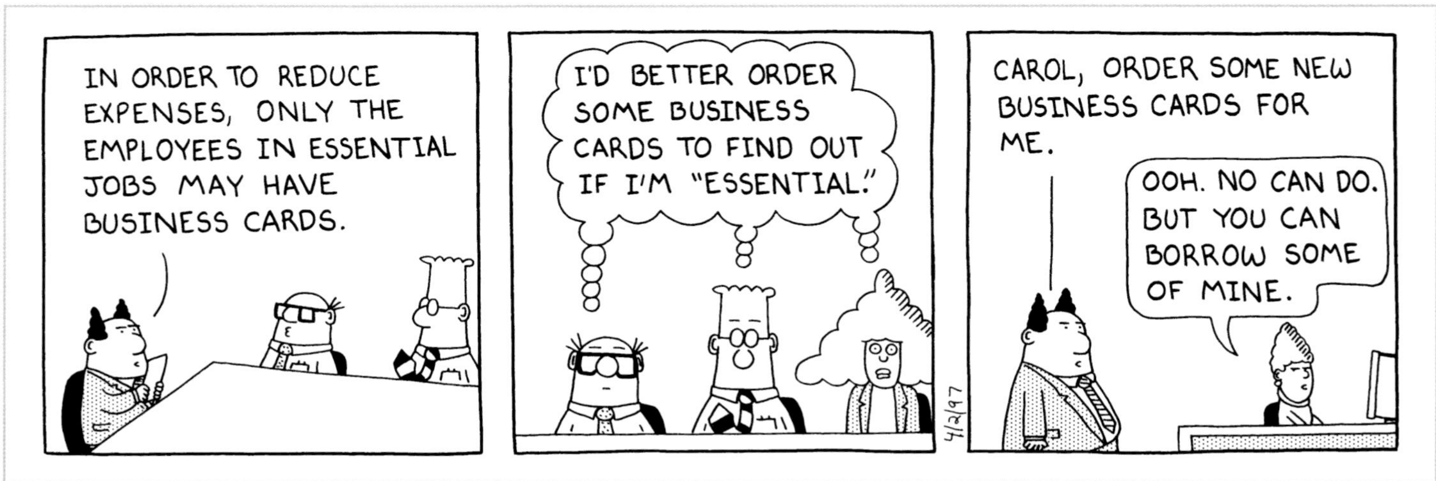
IN ORDER TO REDUCE EXPENSES, ONLY THE EMPLOYEES IN ESSENTIAL JOBS MAY HAVE BUSINESS CARDS.
I'D BETTER ORDER SOME BUSINESS CARDS TO FIND OUT IF I'M "ESSENTIAL."
4/2/97
CAROL, ORDER SOME NEW BUSINESS CARDS FOR ME.
OOH. NO CAN DO. BUT YOU CAN BORROW SOME OF MINE.

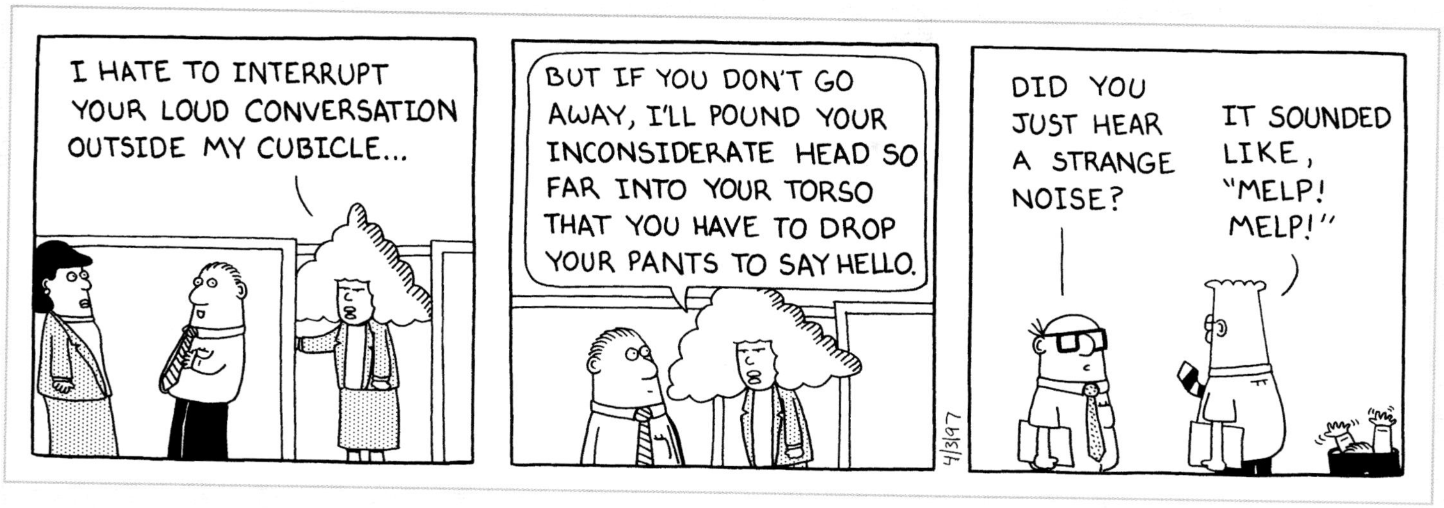
I HATE TO INTERRUPT YOUR LOUD CONVERSATION OUTSIDE MY CUBICLE...
BUT IF YOU DON'T GO AWAY, I'LL POUND YOUR INCONSIDERATE HEAD SO FAR INTO YOUR TORSO THAT YOU HAVE TO DROP YOUR PANTS TO SAY HELLO.
4/3/97
DID YOU JUST HEAR A STRANGE NOISE?
IT SOUNDED LIKE, "MELP! MELP!"

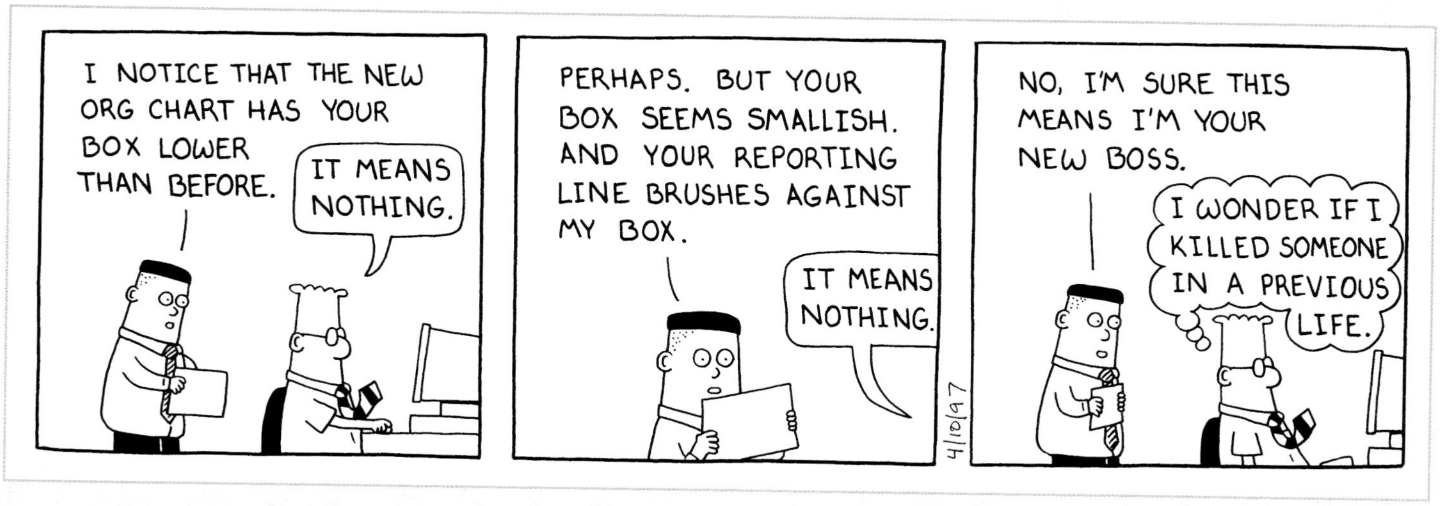
I NOTICE THAT THE NEW ORG CHART HAS YOUR BOX LOWER THAN BEFORE.
IT MEANS NOTHING.
PERHAPS. BUT YOUR BOX SEEMS SMALLISH. AND YOUR REPORTING LINE BRUSHES AGAINST MY BOX.
IT MEANS NOTHING.
4/10/97
NO, I'M SURE THIS MEANS I'M YOUR NEW BOSS.
I WONDER IF I KILLED SOMEONE IN A PREVIOUS LIFE.

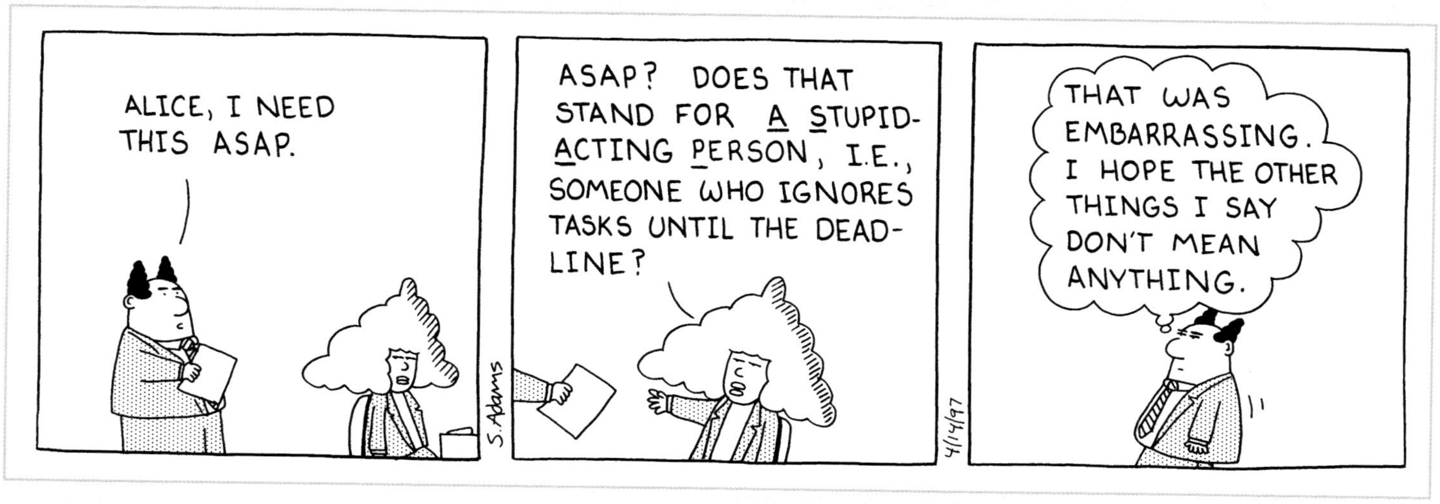
ALICE, I NEED THIS ASAP.
S. Adams
ASAP? DOES THAT STAND FOR A STUPID-ACTING PERSON, I.E., SOMEONE WHO IGNORES TASKS UNTIL THE DEAD-LINE?
4/14/97
THAT WAS EMBARRASSING. I HOPE THE OTHER THINGS I SAY DON'T MEAN ANYTHING.

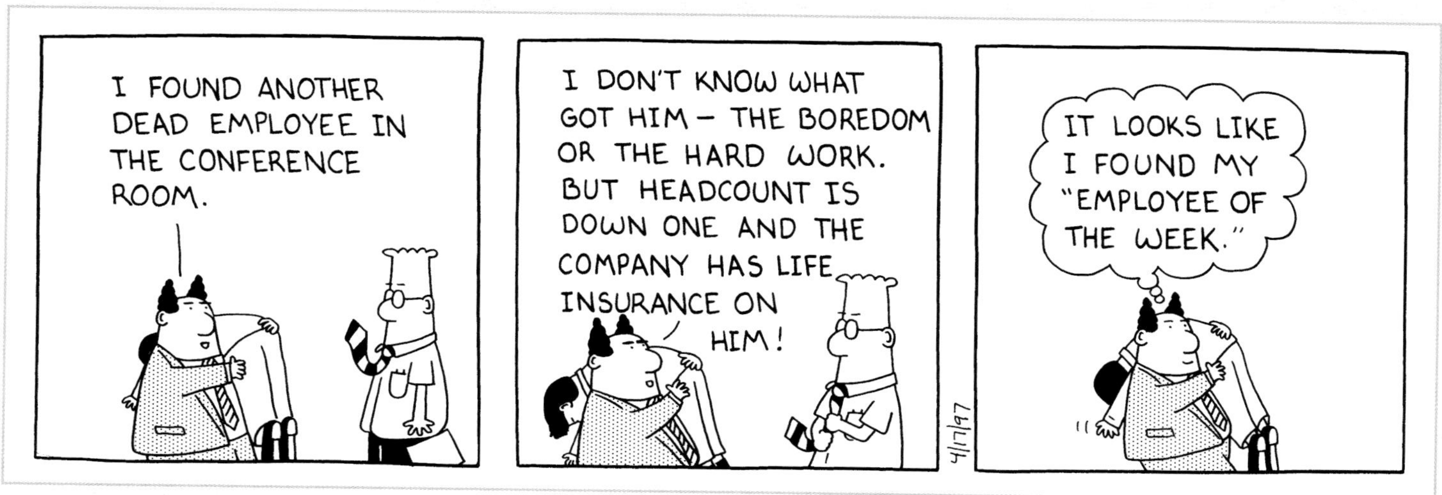
I FOUND ANOTHER DEAD EMPLOYEE IN THE CONFERENCE ROOM.
I DON'T KNOW WHAT GOT HIM – THE BOREDOM OR THE HARD WORK. BUT HEADCOUNT IS DOWN ONE AND THE COMPANY HAS LIFE INSURANCE ON HIM!
4/17/97
IT LOOKS LIKE I FOUND MY "EMPLOYEE OF THE WEEK."

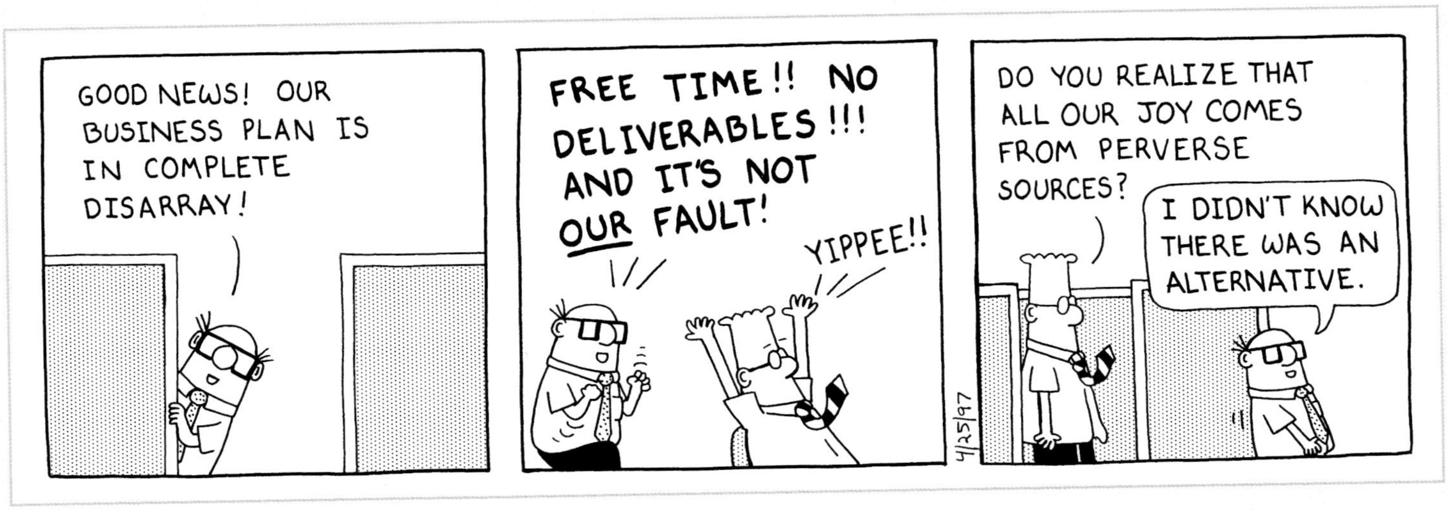
GOOD NEWS! OUR BUSINESS PLAN IS IN COMPLETE DISARRAY!
FREE TIME!! NO DELIVERABLES!!! AND IT'S NOT OUR FAULT!
YIPPEE!!
DO YOU REALIZE THAT ALL OUR JOY COMES FROM PERVERSE SOURCES?
I DIDN'T KNOW THERE WAS AN ALTERNATIVE.
4/25/97

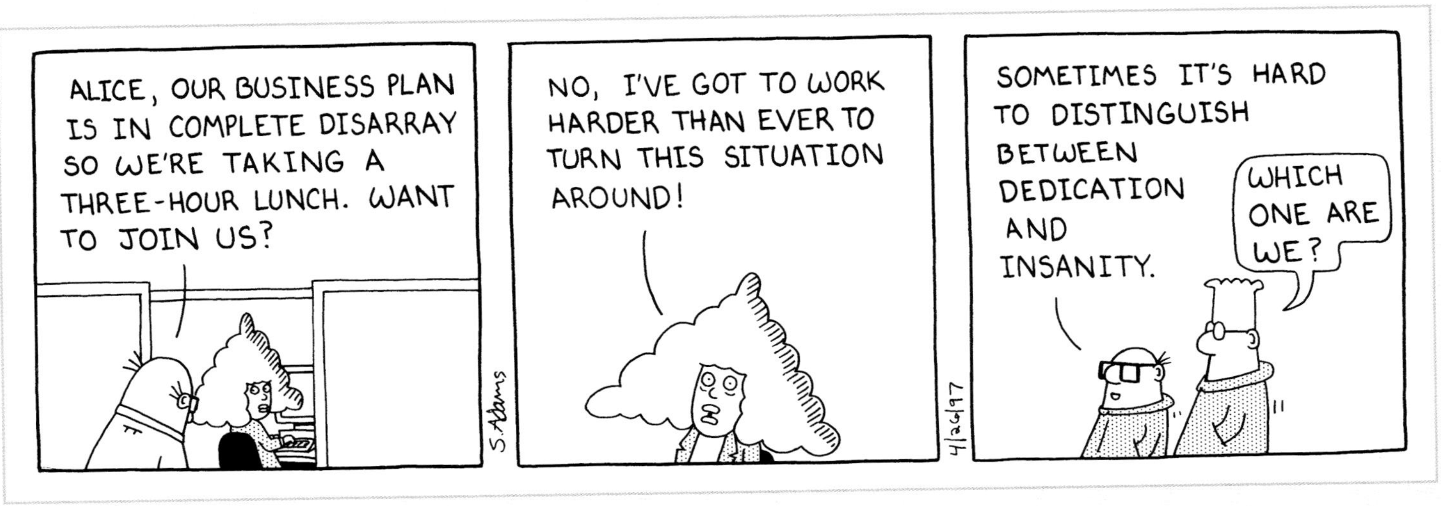
ALICE, OUR BUSINESS PLAN IS IN COMPLETE DISARRAY SO WE'RE TAKING A THREE-HOUR LUNCH. WANT TO JOIN US?
S. Adams
NO, I'VE GOT TO WORK HARDER THAN EVER TO TURN THIS SITUATION AROUND!
SOMETIMES IT'S HARD TO DISTINGUISH BETWEEN DEDICATION AND INSANITY.
WHICH ONE ARE WE?
4/26/97

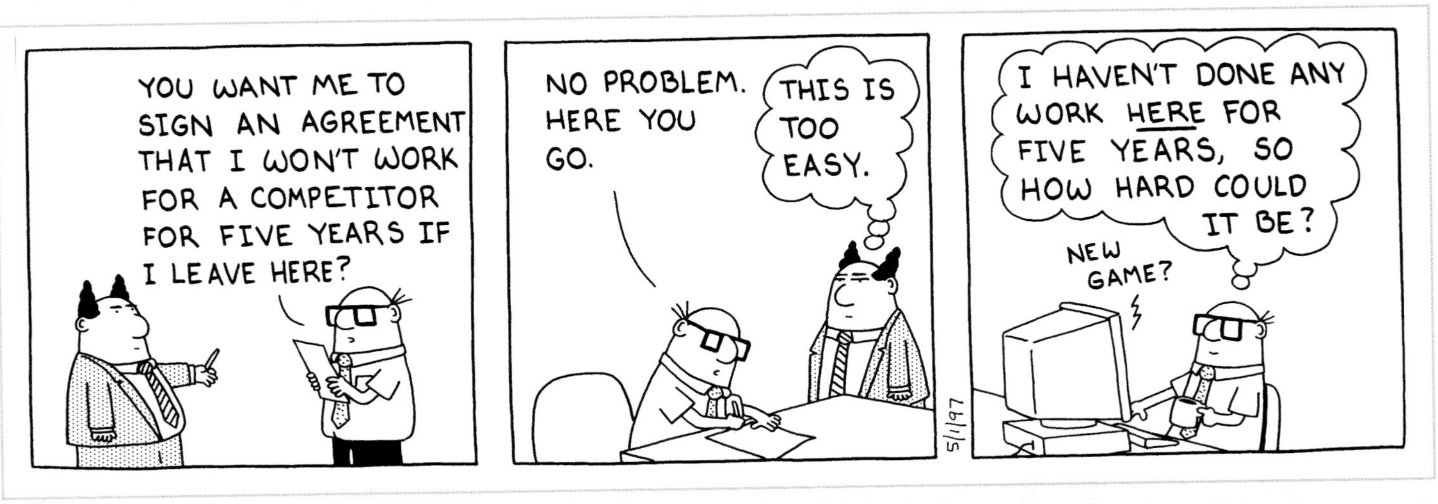
YOU WANT ME TO SIGN AN AGREEMENT THAT I WON'T WORK FOR A COMPETITOR FOR FIVE YEARS IF I LEAVE HERE?
NO PROBLEM. HERE YOU GO.
THIS IS TOO EASY.
I HAVEN'T DONE ANY WORK HERE FOR FIVE YEARS, SO HOW HARD COULD IT BE?
NEW GAME?
5/1/97

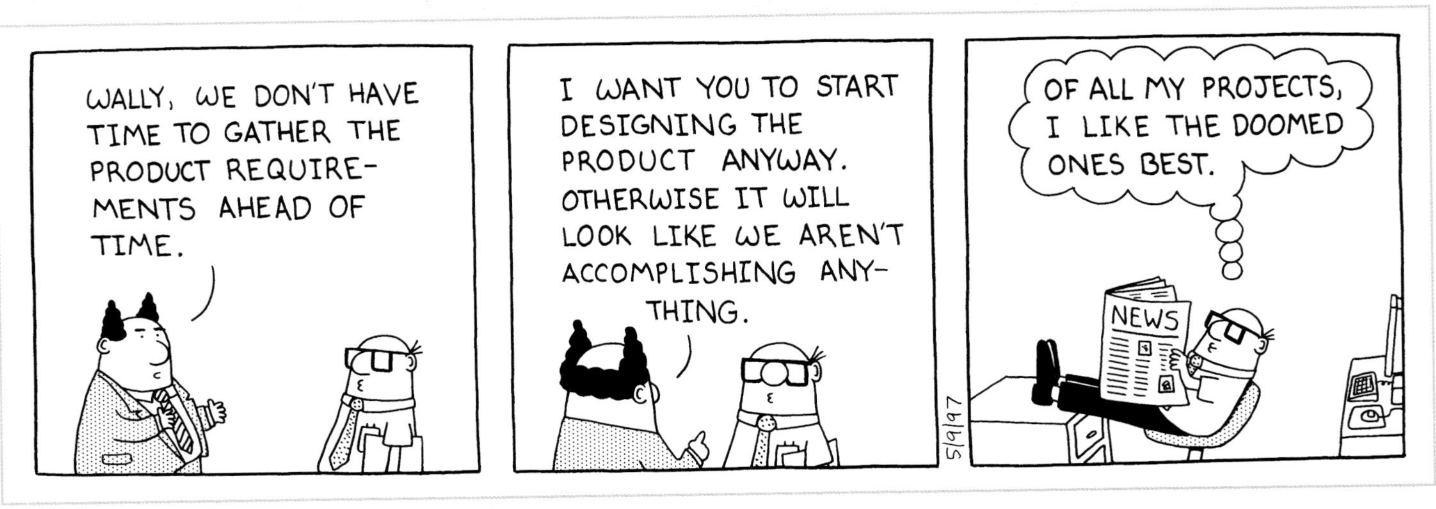
WALLY, WE DON'T HAVE TIME TO GATHER THE PRODUCT REQUIRE-MENTS AHEAD OF TIME.
I WANT YOU TO START DESIGNING THE PRODUCT ANYWAY. OTHERWISE IT WILL LOOK LIKE WE AREN'T ACCOMPLISHING ANY-THING.
OF ALL MY PROJECTS, I LIKE THE DOOMED ONES BEST.
NEWS
5/9/97

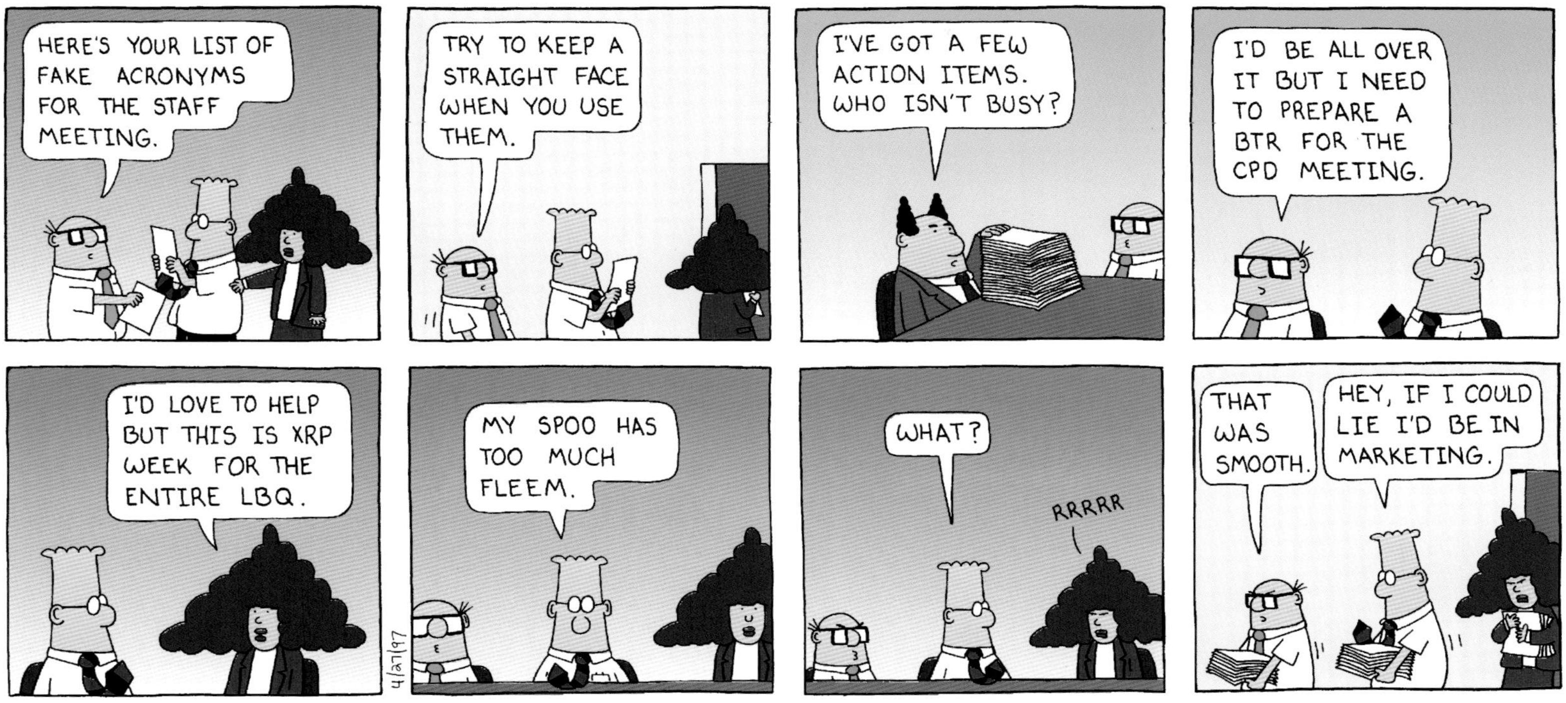
HERE'S YOUR LIST OF FAKE ACRONYMS FOR THE STAFF MEETING.
TRY TO KEEP A STRAIGHT FACE WHEN YOU USE THEM.
I'VE GOT A FEW ACTION ITEMS. WHO ISN'T BUSY?
I'D BE ALL OVER IT BUT I NEED TO PREPARE A BTR FOR THE CPD MEETING.
I'D LOVE TO HELP BUT THIS IS XRP WEEK FOR THE ENTIRE LBQ.
4/27/97
MY SPOO HAS TOO MUCH FLEEM.
WHAT?
RRRRR
THAT WAS SMOOTH.
HEY, IF I COULD LIE I'D BE IN MARKETING.

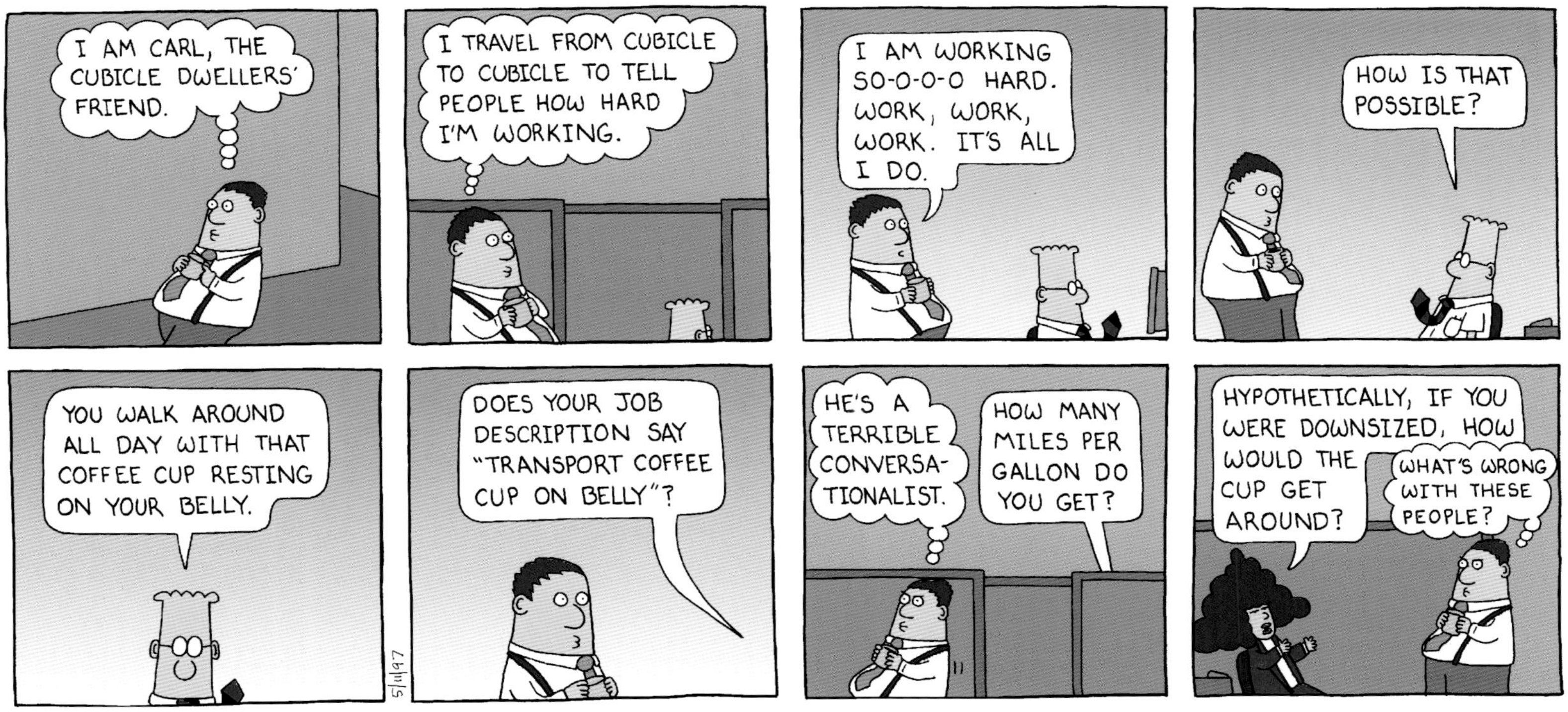
I AM CARL, THE CUBICLE DWELLERS' FRIEND.
I TRAVEL FROM CUBICLE TO CUBICLE TO TELL PEOPLE HOW HARD I'M WORKING.
I AM WORKING SO-O-O-O HARD. WORK, WORK, WORK. IT'S ALL I DO.
HOW IS THAT POSSIBLE?
YOU WALK AROUND ALL DAY WITH THAT COFFEE CUP RESTING ON YOUR BELLY.
5/11/97
DOES YOUR JOB DESCRIPTION SAY "TRANSPORT COFFEE CUP ON BELLY"?
HE'S A TERRIBLE CONVERSA-TIONALIST.
HOW MANY MILES PER GALLON DO YOU GET?
HYPOTHETICALLY, IF YOU WERE DOWNSIZED, HOW WOULD THE CUP GET AROUND?
WHAT'S WRONG WITH THESE PEOPLE?

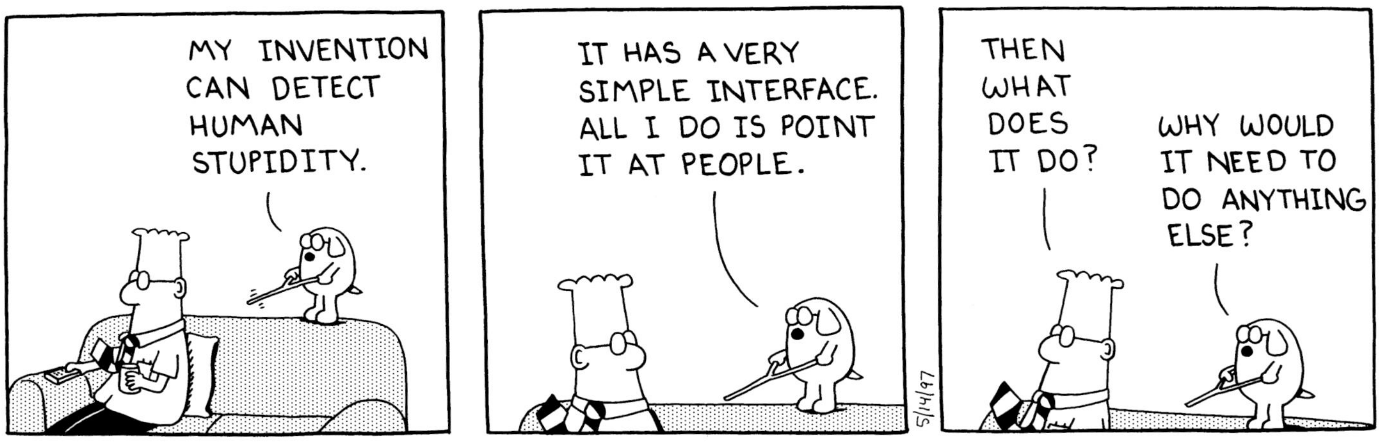
MY INVENTION CAN DETECT HUMAN STUPIDITY.
IT HAS A VERY SIMPLE INTERFACE. ALL I DO IS POINT IT AT PEOPLE.
THEN WHAT DOES IT DO?
WHY WOULD IT NEED TO DO ANYTHING ELSE?
5/14/97

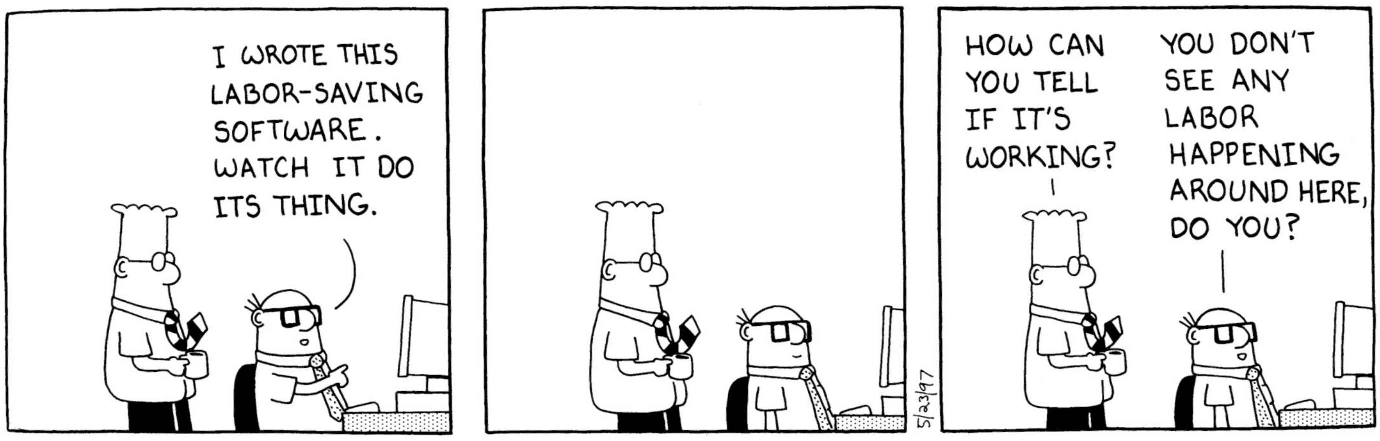
I WROTE THIS LABOR-SAVING SOFTWARE. WATCH IT DO ITS THING.
HOW CAN YOU TELL IF IT'S WORKING?
YOU DON'T SEE ANY LABOR HAPPENING AROUND HERE, DO YOU?
5/23/97

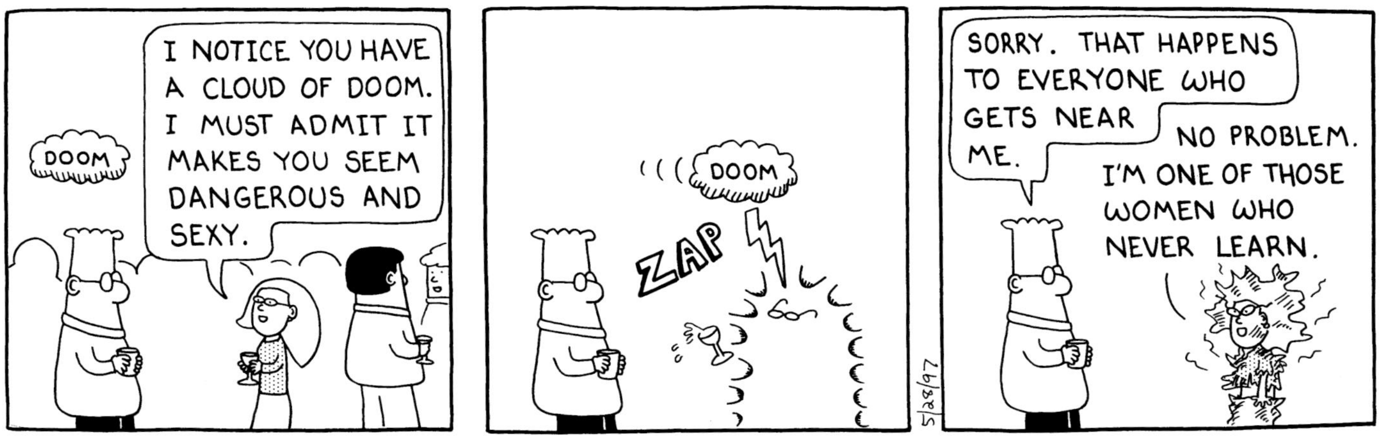
DOOM
I NOTICE YOU HAVE A CLOUD OF DOOM. I MUST ADMIT IT MAKES YOU SEEM DANGEROUS AND SEXY.
DOOM
ZAP
SORRY. THAT HAPPENS TO EVERYONE WHO GETS NEAR ME.
NO PROBLEM. I'M ONE OF THOSE WOMEN WHO NEVER LEARN.
5/28/97

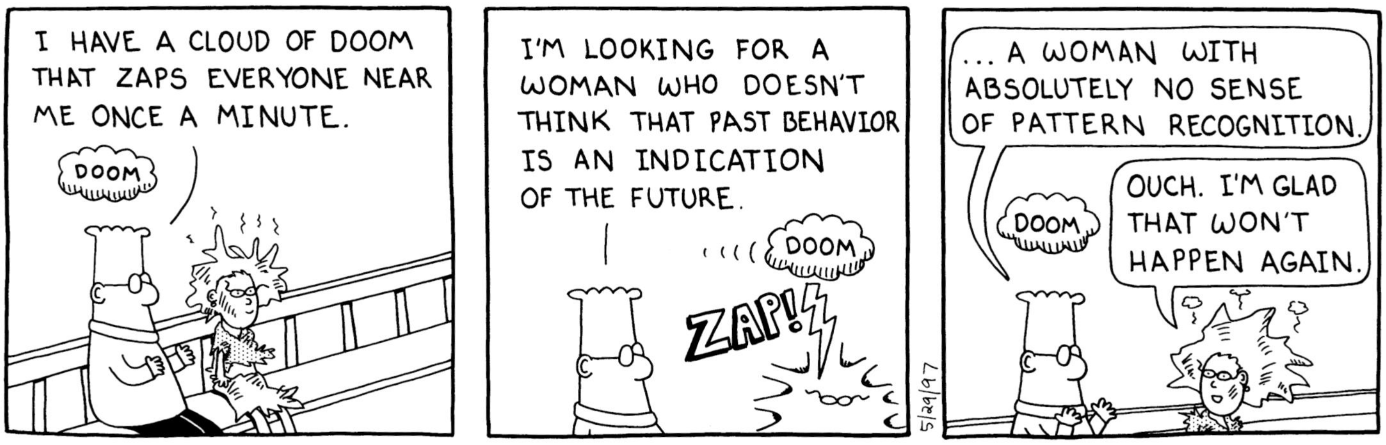
I HAVE A CLOUD OF DOOM THAT ZAPS EVERYONE NEAR ME ONCE A MINUTE.
DOOM
I'M LOOKING FOR A WOMAN WHO DOESN'T THINK THAT PAST BEHAVIOR IS AN INDICATION OF THE FUTURE.
DOOM
ZAP!
... A WOMAN WITH ABSOLUTELY NO SENSE OF PATTERN RECOGNITION.
DOOM
OUCH. I'M GLAD THAT WON'T HAPPEN AGAIN.
5/29/97

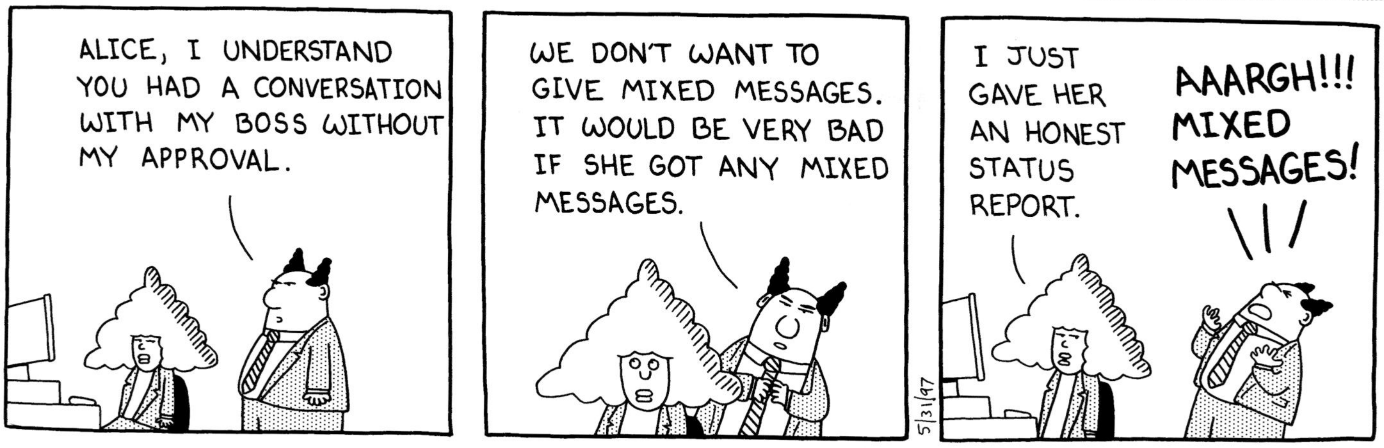
ALICE, I UNDERSTAND YOU HAD A CONVERSATION WITH MY BOSS WITHOUT MY APPROVAL.
WE DON'T WANT TO GIVE MIXED MESSAGES. IT WOULD BE VERY BAD IF SHE GOT ANY MIXED MESSAGES.
I JUST GAVE HER AN HONEST STATUS REPORT.
AAARGH!!! MIXED MESSAGES!
5/31/97

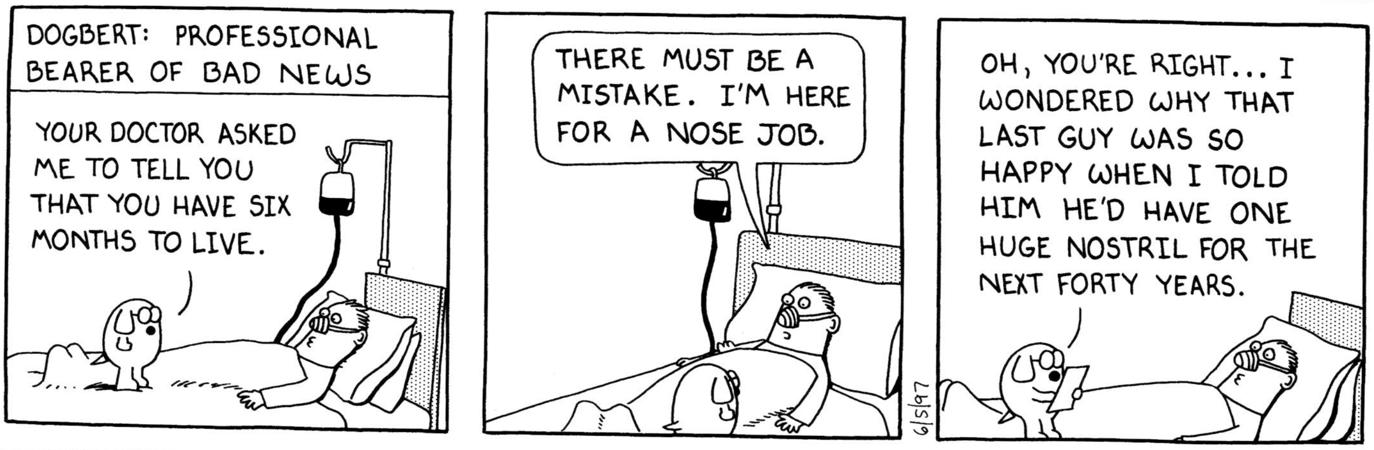
DOGBERT: PROFESSIONAL BEARER OF BAD NEWS
YOUR DOCTOR ASKED ME TO TELL YOU THAT YOU HAVE SIX MONTHS TO LIVE.
THERE MUST BE A MISTAKE. I'M HERE FOR A NOSE JOB.
OH, YOU'RE RIGHT... I WONDERED WHY THAT LAST GUY WAS SO HAPPY WHEN I TOLD HIM HE'D HAVE ONE HUGE NOSTRIL FOR THE NEXT FORTY YEARS.
6/5/97

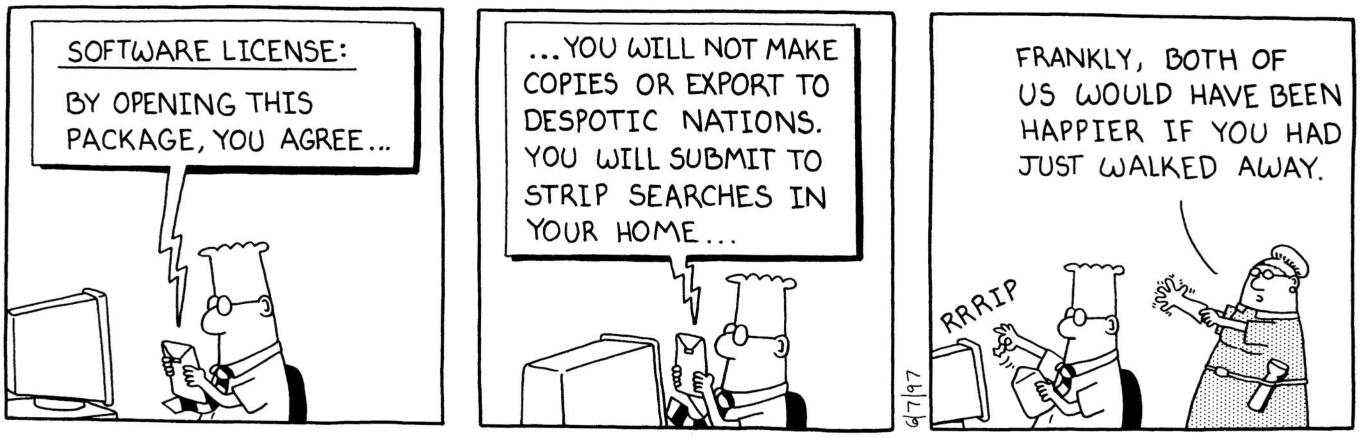
SOFTWARE LICENSE:
BY OPENING THIS PACKAGE, YOU AGREE...
...YOU WILL NOT MAKE COPIES OR EXPORT TO DESPOTIC NATIONS. YOU WILL SUBMIT TO STRIP SEARCHES IN YOUR HOME...
RRRIP
FRANKLY, BOTH OF US WOULD HAVE BEEN HAPPIER IF YOU HAD JUST WALKED AWAY.
6/7/97

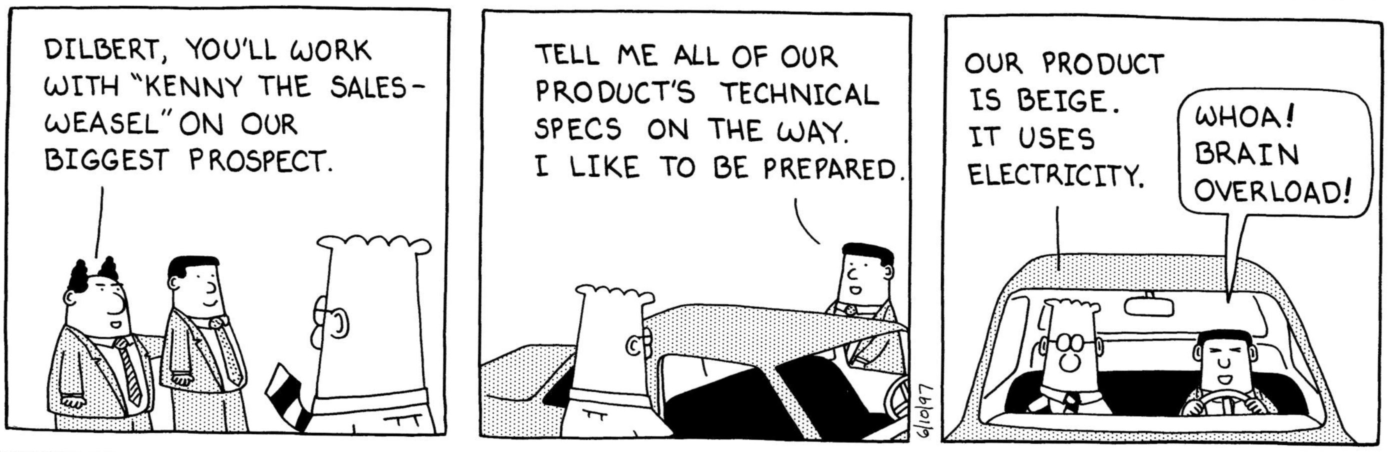
DILBERT, YOU'LL WORK WITH "KENNY THE SALES-WEASEL" ON OUR BIGGEST PROSPECT.
TELL ME ALL OF OUR PRODUCT'S TECHNICAL SPECS ON THE WAY. I LIKE TO BE PREPARED.
OUR PRODUCT IS BEIGE. IT USES ELECTRICITY.
WHOA! BRAIN OVERLOAD!
6/10/97

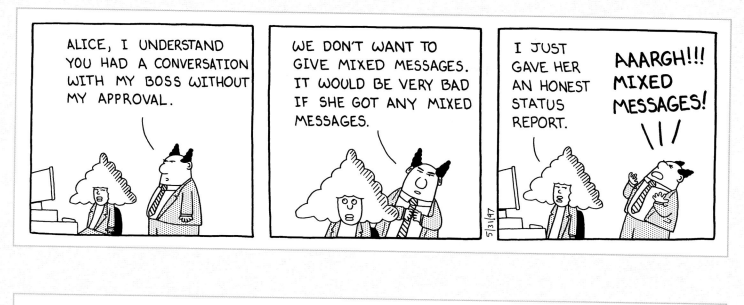

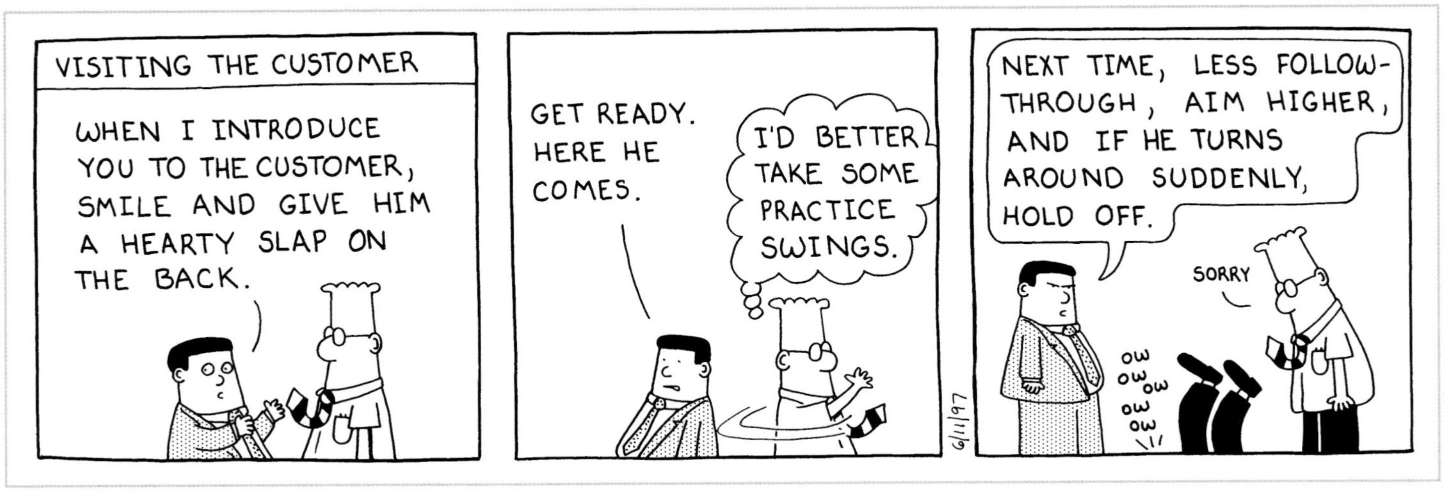
VISITING THE CUSTOMER
WHEN I INTRODUCE YOU TO THE CUSTOMER, SMILE AND GIVE HIM A HEARTY SLAP ON THE BACK.
GET READY. HERE HE COMES.
I'D BETTER TAKE SOME PRACTICE SWINGS.
6/11/97
NEXT TIME, LESS FOLLOW-THROUGH, AIM HIGHER, AND IF HE TURNS AROUND SUDDENLY, HOLD OFF.
SORRY
OW OW OW OW OW OW

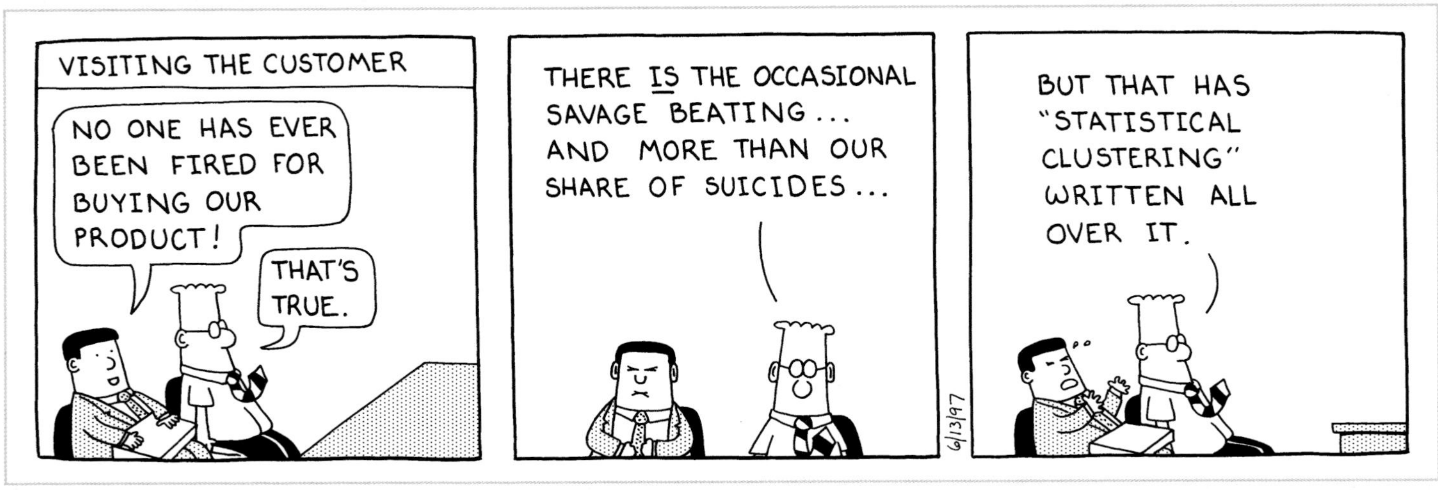
VISITING THE CUSTOMER
NO ONE HAS EVER BEEN FIRED FOR BUYING OUR PRODUCT!
THAT'S TRUE.
THERE IS THE OCCASIONAL SAVAGE BEATING... AND MORE THAN OUR SHARE OF SUICIDES...
6/13/97
BUT THAT HAS "STATISTICAL CLUSTERING" WRITTEN ALL OVER IT.

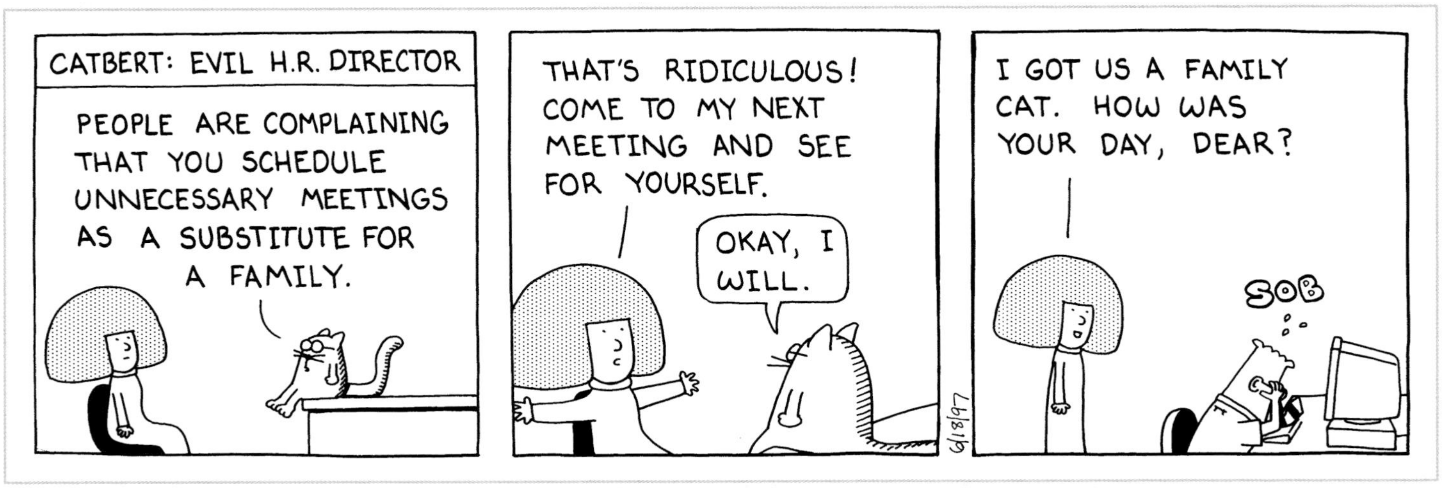
CATBERT: EVIL H.R. DIRECTOR
PEOPLE ARE COMPLAINING THAT YOU SCHEDULE UNNECESSARY MEETINGS AS A SUBSTITUTE FOR A FAMILY.
THAT'S RIDICULOUS! COME TO MY NEXT MEETING AND SEE FOR YOURSELF.
OKAY, I WILL.
6/18/97
I GOT US A FAMILY CAT. HOW WAS YOUR DAY, DEAR?
SOB

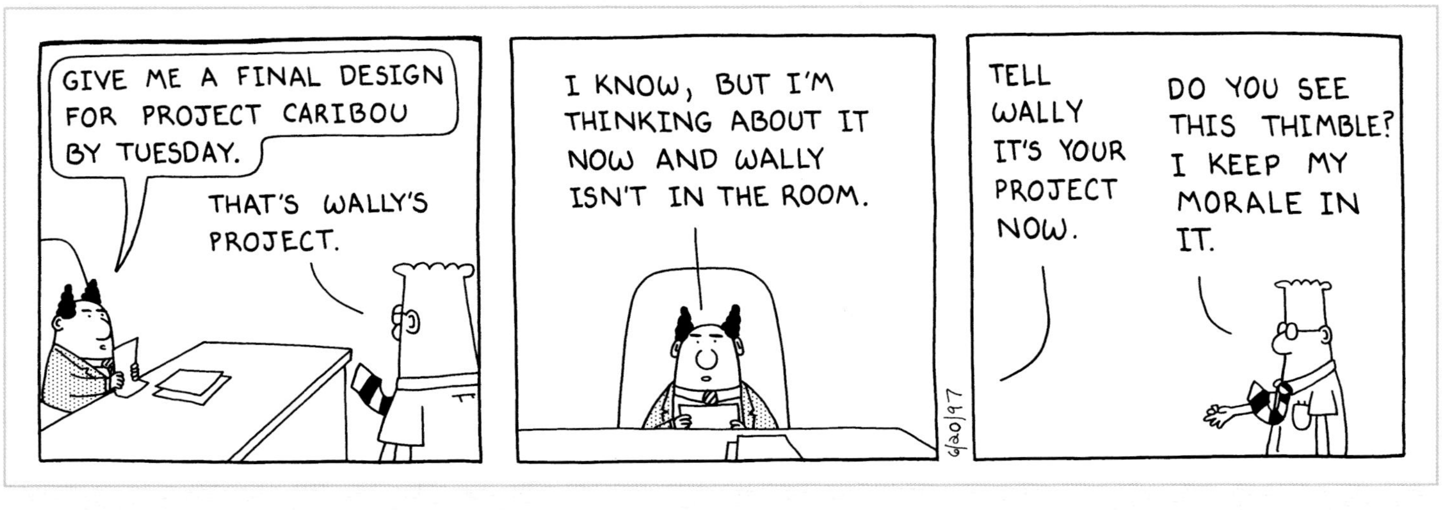
GIVE ME A FINAL DESIGN FOR PROJECT CARIBOU BY TUESDAY.
THAT'S WALLY'S PROJECT.
I KNOW, BUT I'M THINKING ABOUT IT NOW AND WALLY ISN'T IN THE ROOM.
6/20/97
TELL WALLY IT'S YOUR PROJECT NOW.
DO YOU SEE THIS THIMBLE? I KEEP MY MORALE IN IT.

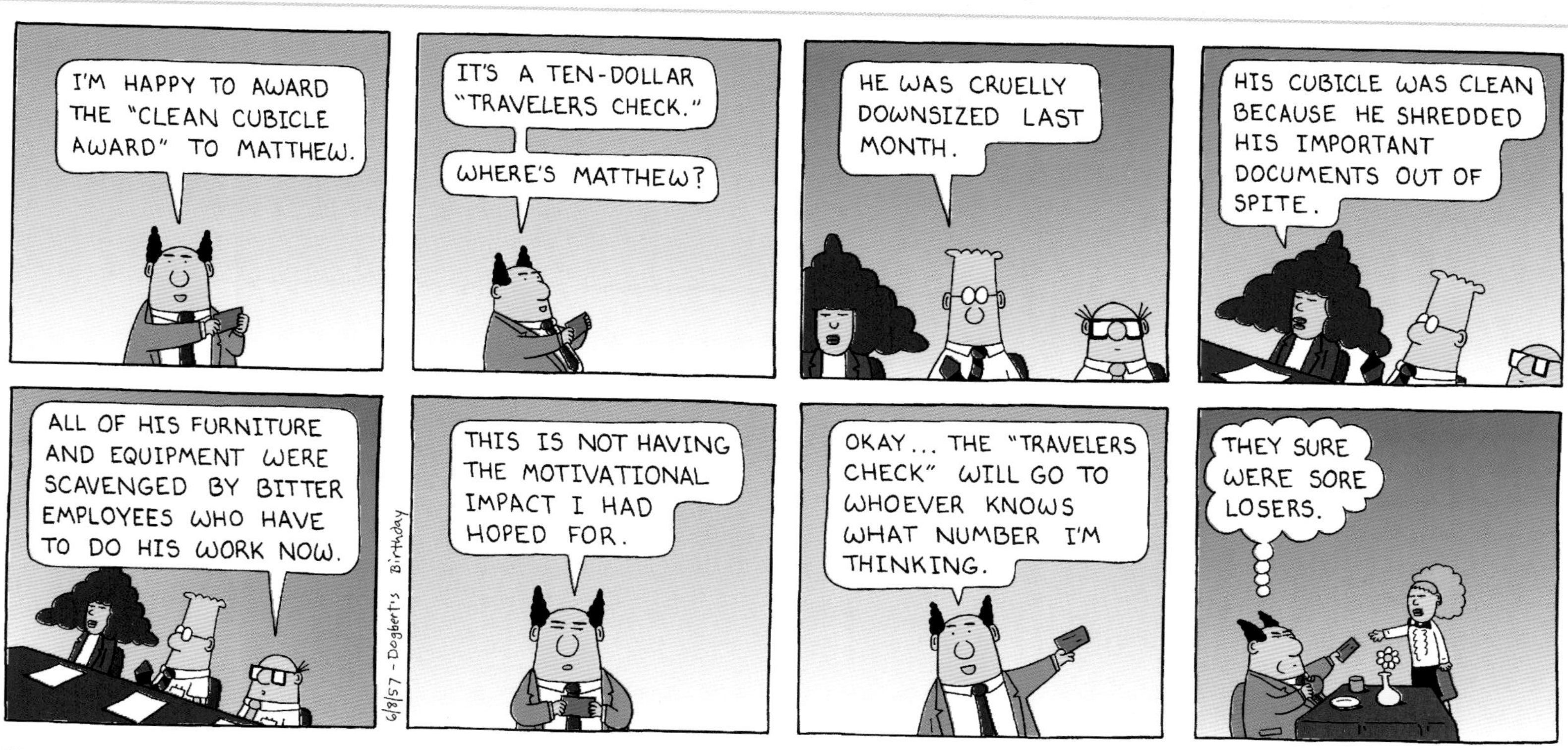
I'M HAPPY TO AWARD THE "CLEAN CUBICLE AWARD" TO MATTHEW.
IT'S A TEN-DOLLAR "TRAVELERS CHECK."
WHERE'S MATTHEW?
HE WAS CRUELLY DOWNSIZED LAST MONTH.
HIS CUBICLE WAS CLEAN BECAUSE HE SHREDDED HIS IMPORTANT DOCUMENTS OUT OF SPITE.
ALL OF HIS FURNITURE AND EQUIPMENT WERE SCAVENGED BY BITTER EMPLOYEES WHO HAVE TO DO HIS WORK NOW.
6/8/57 - Dogbert's Birthday
THIS IS NOT HAVING THE MOTIVATIONAL IMPACT I HAD HOPED FOR.
OKAY... THE "TRAVELERS CHECK" WILL GO TO WHOEVER KNOWS WHAT NUMBER I'M THINKING.
THEY SURE WERE SORE LOSERS.

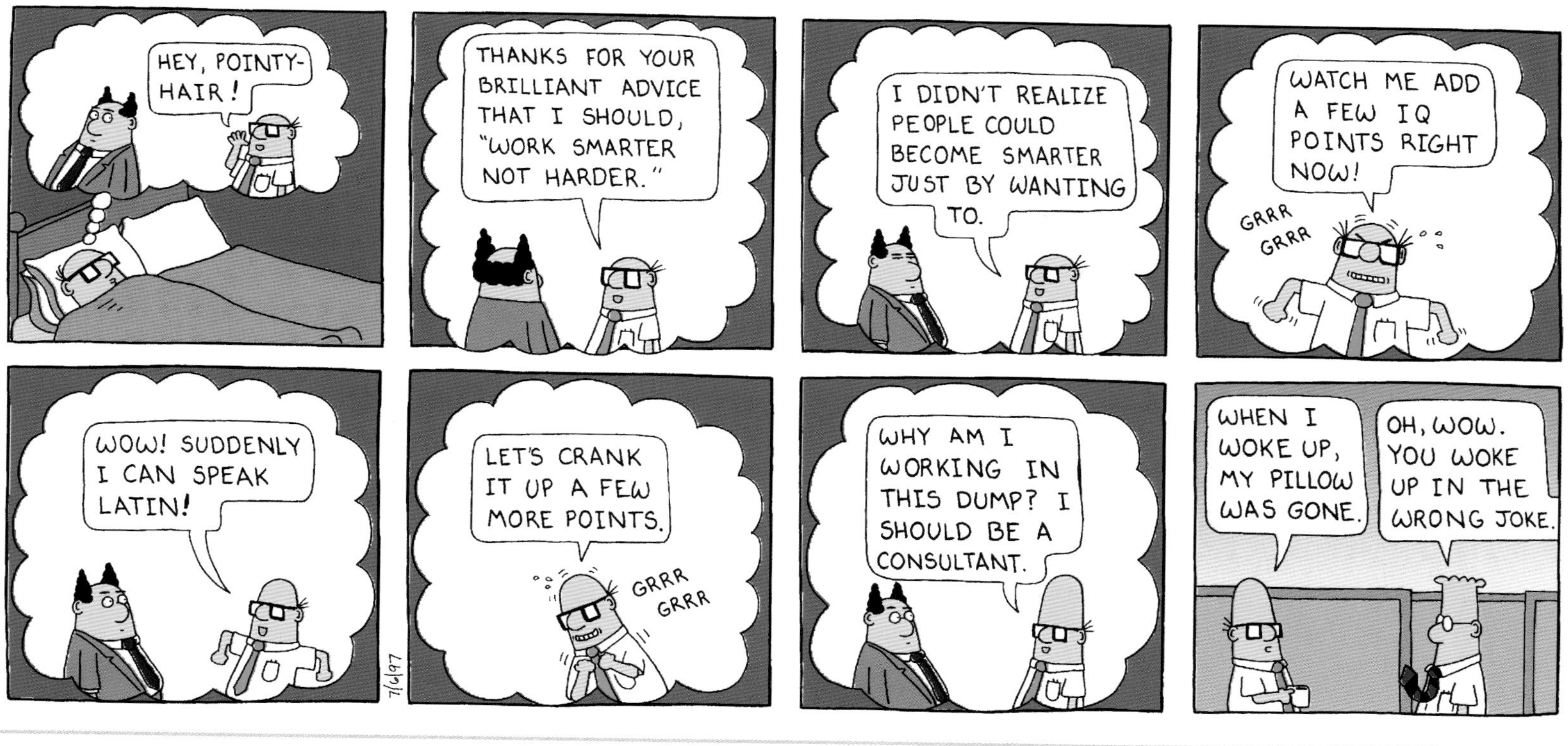
HEY, POINTY-HAIR!
THANKS FOR YOUR BRILLIANT ADVICE THAT I SHOULD, "WORK SMARTER NOT HARDER."
I DIDN'T REALIZE PEOPLE COULD BECOME SMARTER JUST BY WANTING TO.
WATCH ME ADD A FEW IQ POINTS RIGHT NOW!
GRRR GRRR
WOW! SUDDENLY I CAN SPEAK LATIN!
7/6/97
LET'S CRANK IT UP A FEW MORE POINTS.
GRRR GRRR
WHY AM I WORKING IN THIS DUMP? I SHOULD BE A CONSULTANT.
WHEN I WOKE UP, MY PILLOW WAS GONE.
OH, WOW. YOU WOKE UP IN THE WRONG JOKE.

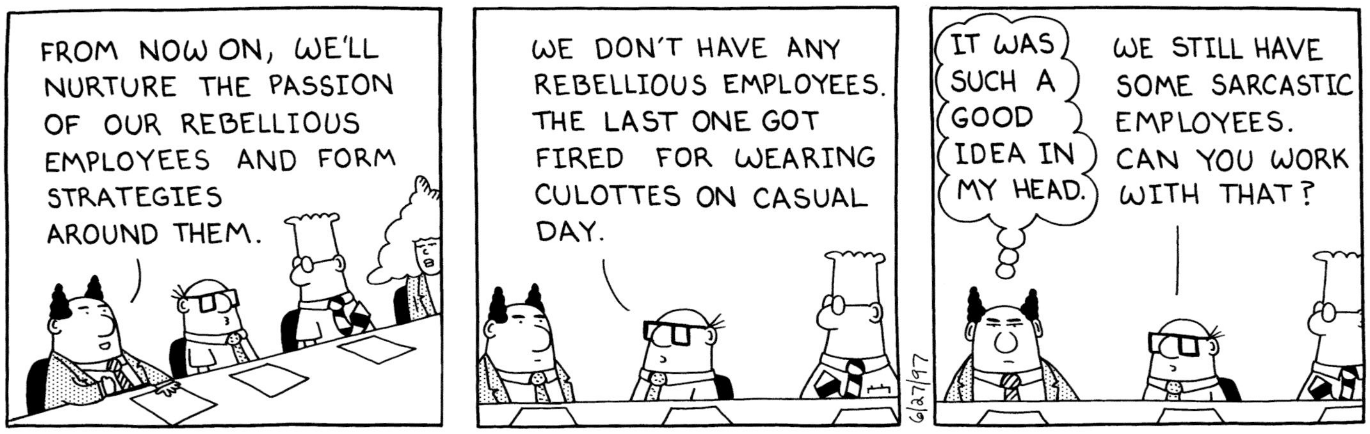
FROM NOW ON, WE'LL NURTURE THE PASSION OF OUR REBELLIOUS EMPLOYEES AND FORM STRATEGIES AROUND THEM.
WE DON'T HAVE ANY REBELLIOUS EMPLOYEES. THE LAST ONE GOT FIRED FOR WEARING CULOTTES ON CASUAL DAY.
6/27/97
IT WAS SUCH A GOOD IDEA IN MY HEAD.
WE STILL HAVE SOME SARCASTIC EMPLOYEES. CAN YOU WORK WITH THAT?

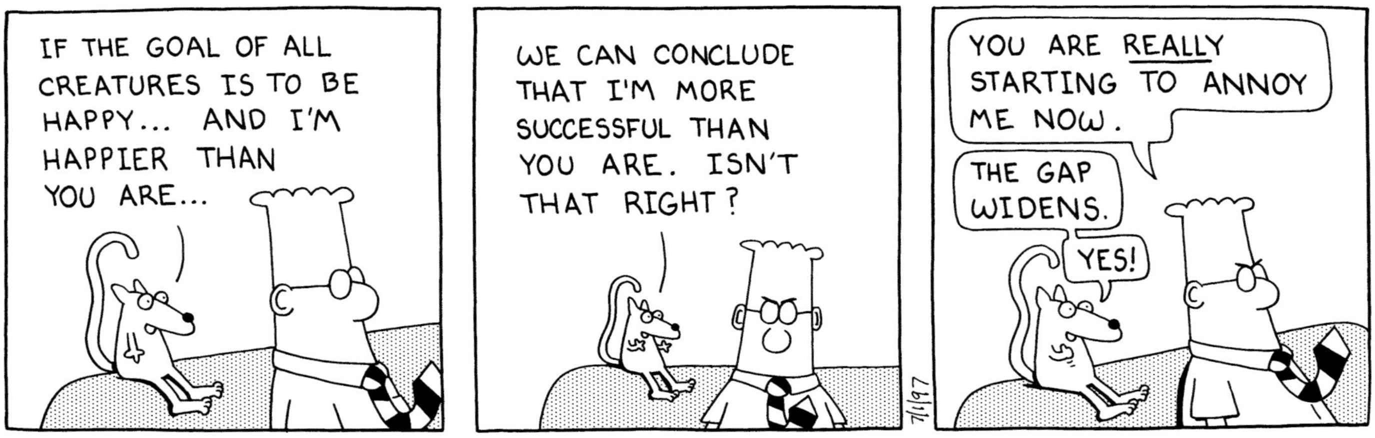
IF THE GOAL OF ALL CREATURES IS TO BE HAPPY... AND I'M HAPPIER THAN YOU ARE...
WE CAN CONCLUDE THAT I'M MORE SUCCESSFUL THAN YOU ARE. ISN'T THAT RIGHT?
7/1/97
YOU ARE REALLY STARTING TO ANNOY ME NOW.
THE GAP WIDENS.
YES!

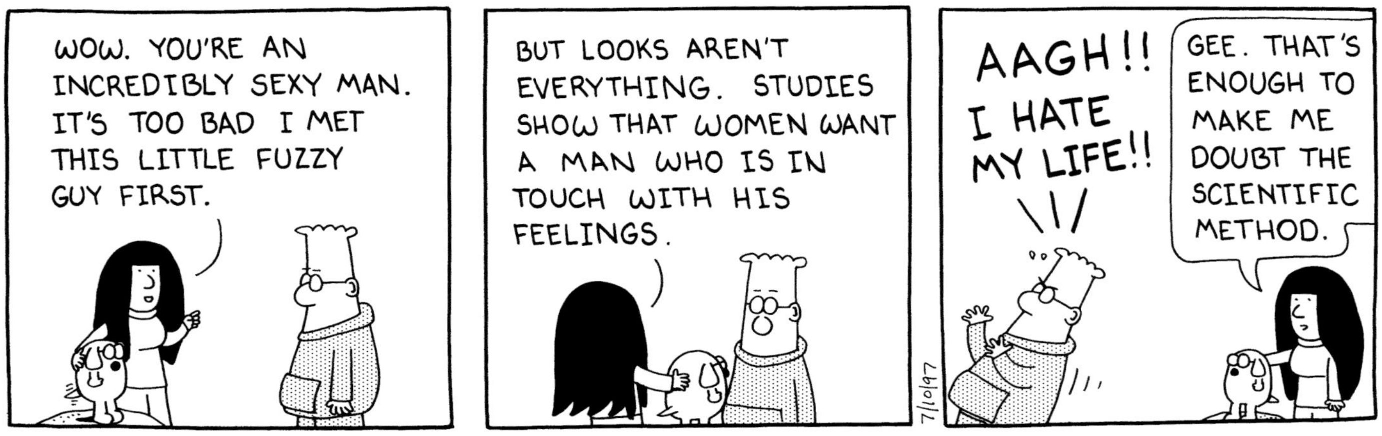
WOW. YOU'RE AN INCREDIBLY SEXY MAN. IT'S TOO BAD I MET THIS LITTLE FUZZY GUY FIRST.
BUT LOOKS AREN'T EVERYTHING. STUDIES SHOW THAT WOMEN WANT A MAN WHO IS IN TOUCH WITH HIS FEELINGS.
7/10/97
AAGH!! I HATE MY LIFE!!
GEE. THAT'S ENOUGH TO MAKE ME DOUBT THE SCIENTIFIC METHOD.

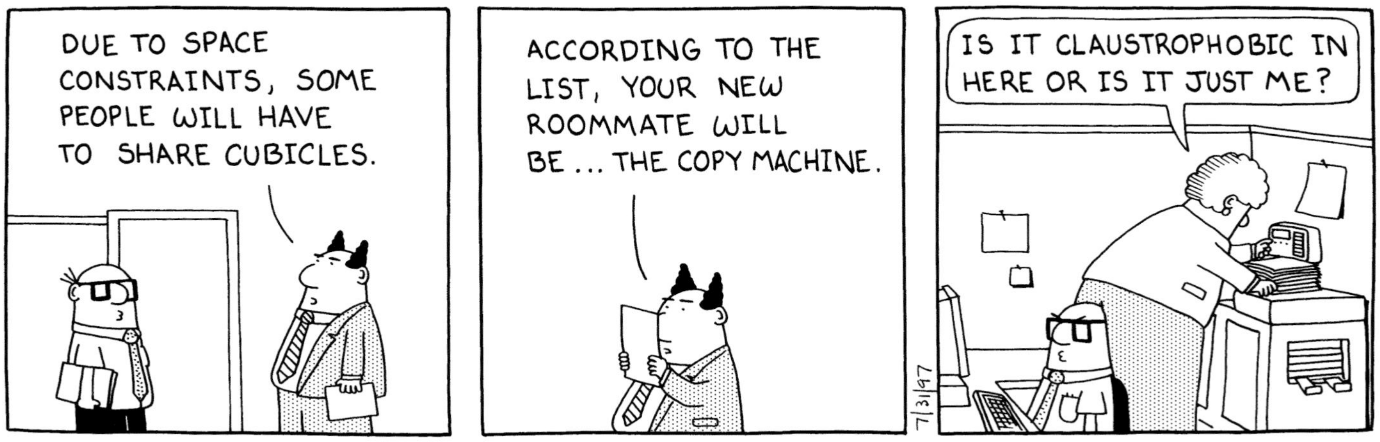
DUE TO SPACE CONSTRAINTS, SOME PEOPLE WILL HAVE TO SHARE CUBICLES.
ACCORDING TO THE LIST, YOUR NEW ROOMMATE WILL BE ... THE COPY MACHINE.
7/31/97
IS IT CLAUSTROPHOBIC IN HERE OR IS IT JUST ME?

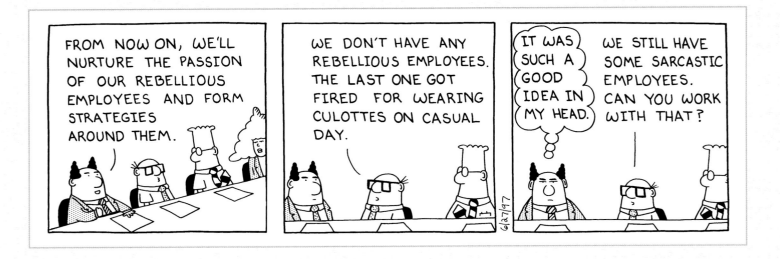

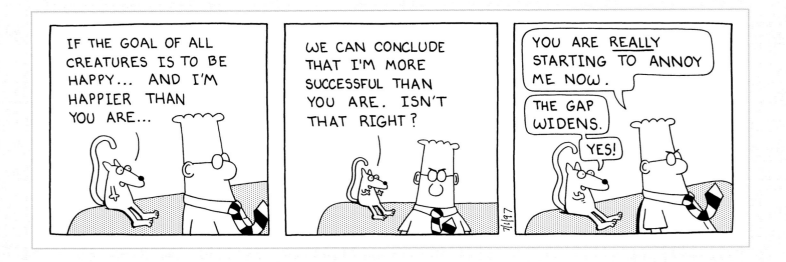

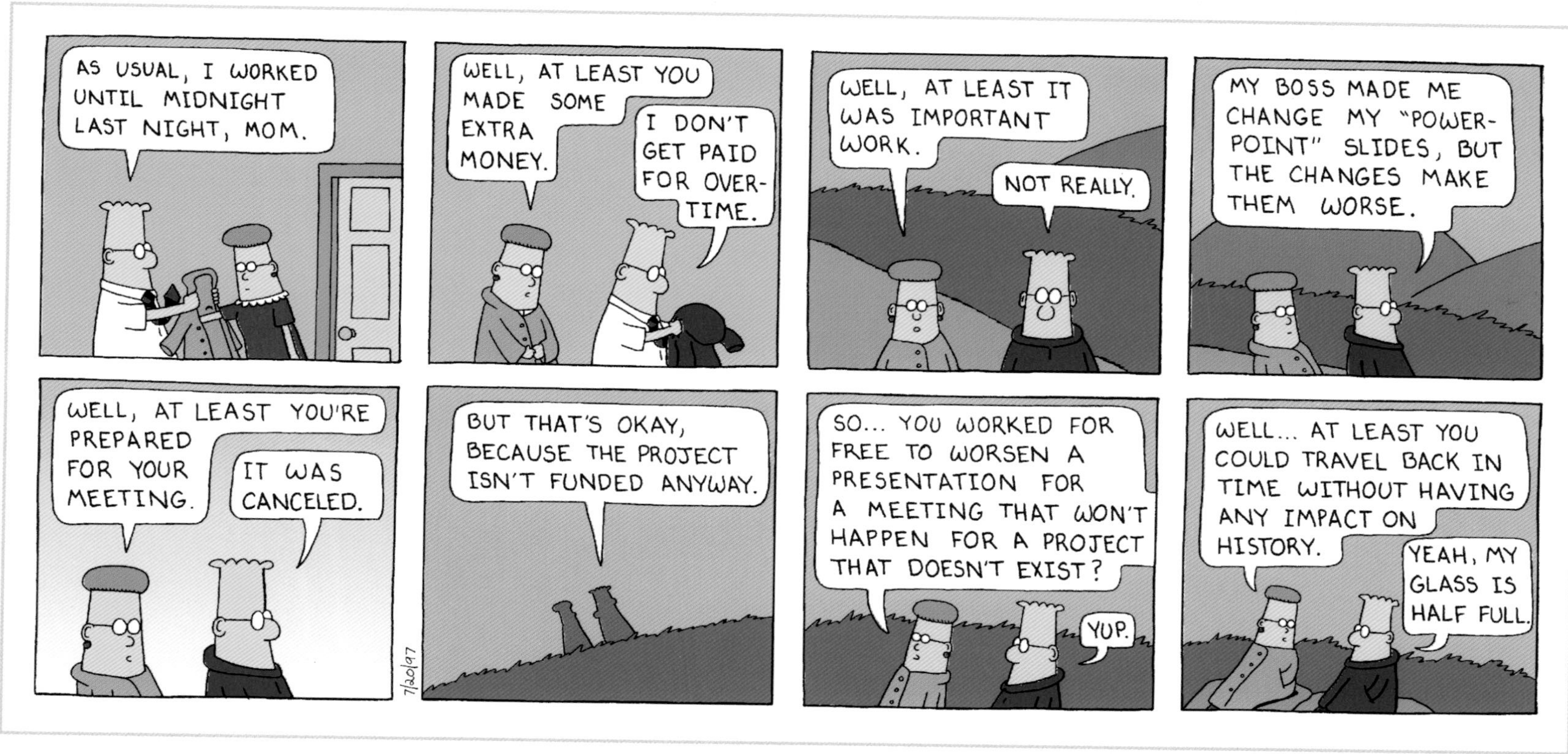
AS USUAL, I WORKED UNTIL MIDNIGHT LAST NIGHT, MOM.
WELL, AT LEAST YOU MADE SOME EXTRA MONEY.
I DON'T GET PAID FOR OVER-TIME.
WELL, AT LEAST IT WAS IMPORTANT WORK.
NOT REALLY.
MY BOSS MADE ME CHANGE MY "POWER-POINT" SLIDES, BUT THE CHANGES MAKE THEM WORSE.
WELL, AT LEAST YOU'RE PREPARED FOR YOUR MEETING.
IT WAS CANCELED.
BUT THAT'S OKAY, BECAUSE THE PROJECT ISN'T FUNDED ANYWAY.
7/20/97
SO... YOU WORKED FOR FREE TO WORSEN A PRESENTATION FOR A MEETING THAT WON'T HAPPEN FOR A PROJECT THAT DOESN'T EXIST?
YUP.
WELL... AT LEAST YOU COULD TRAVEL BACK IN TIME WITHOUT HAVING ANY IMPACT ON HISTORY.
YEAH, MY GLASS IS HALF FULL.

This is the most widely reader-altered Dilbert *comic ever. People in various companies and professions change Dilmom's last line to say something along the lines of "So, you must work at [my company]." Hundreds of people have e-mailed to ask for copies of "the comic that mentions my company." Sadly, it only exists illegally.*

Many people wrote to say Einstein was a pacifist.

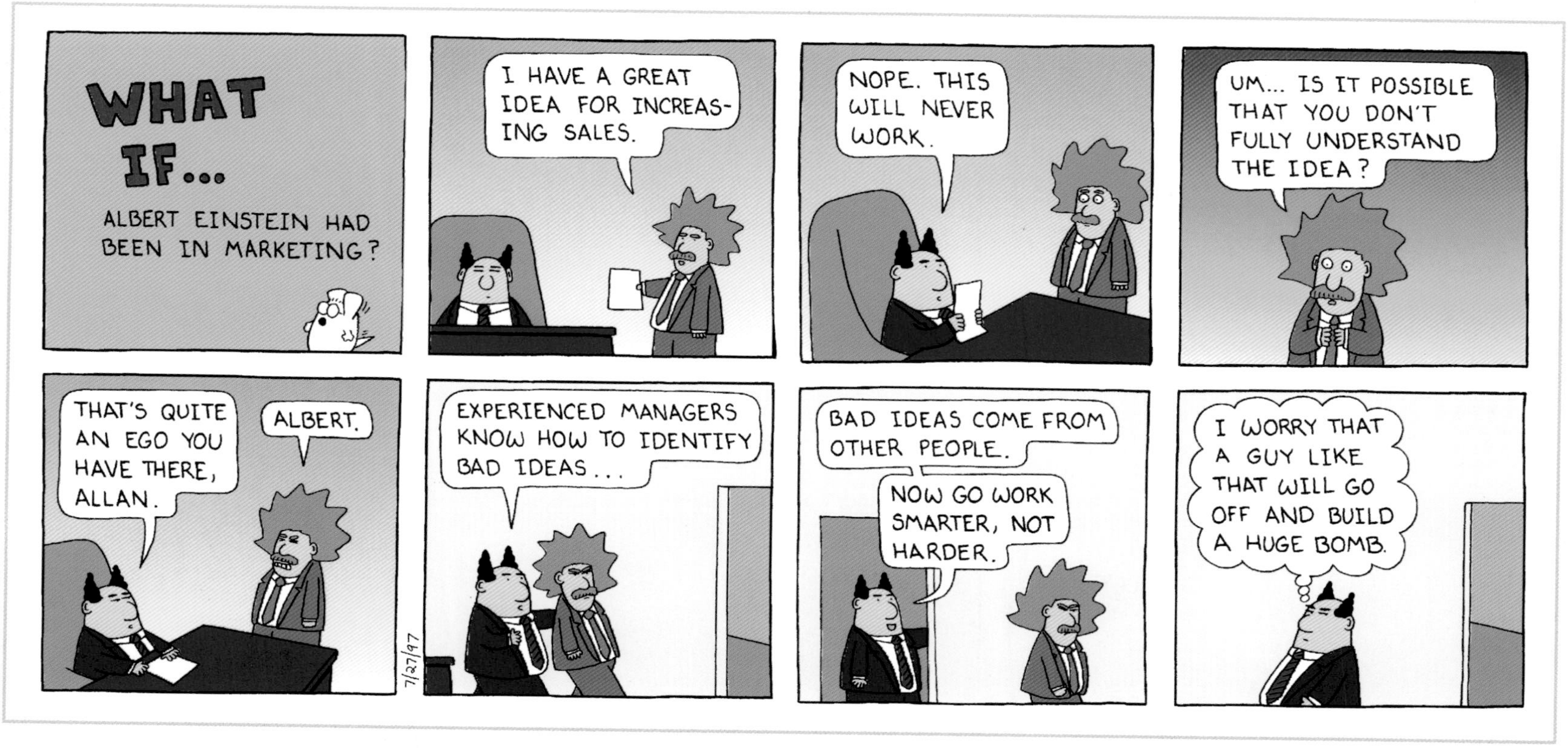
WHAT IF...
ALBERT EINSTEIN HAD BEEN IN MARKETING?
I HAVE A GREAT IDEA FOR INCREAS-ING SALES.
NOPE. THIS WILL NEVER WORK.
UM... IS IT POSSIBLE THAT YOU DON'T FULLY UNDERSTAND THE IDEA?
THAT'S QUITE AN EGO YOU HAVE THERE, ALLAN.
ALBERT.
7/27/97
EXPERIENCED MANAGERS KNOW HOW TO IDENTIFY BAD IDEAS...
BAD IDEAS COME FROM OTHER PEOPLE.
NOW GO WORK SMARTER, NOT HARDER.
I WORRY THAT A GUY LIKE THAT WILL GO OFF AND BUILD A HUGE BOMB.

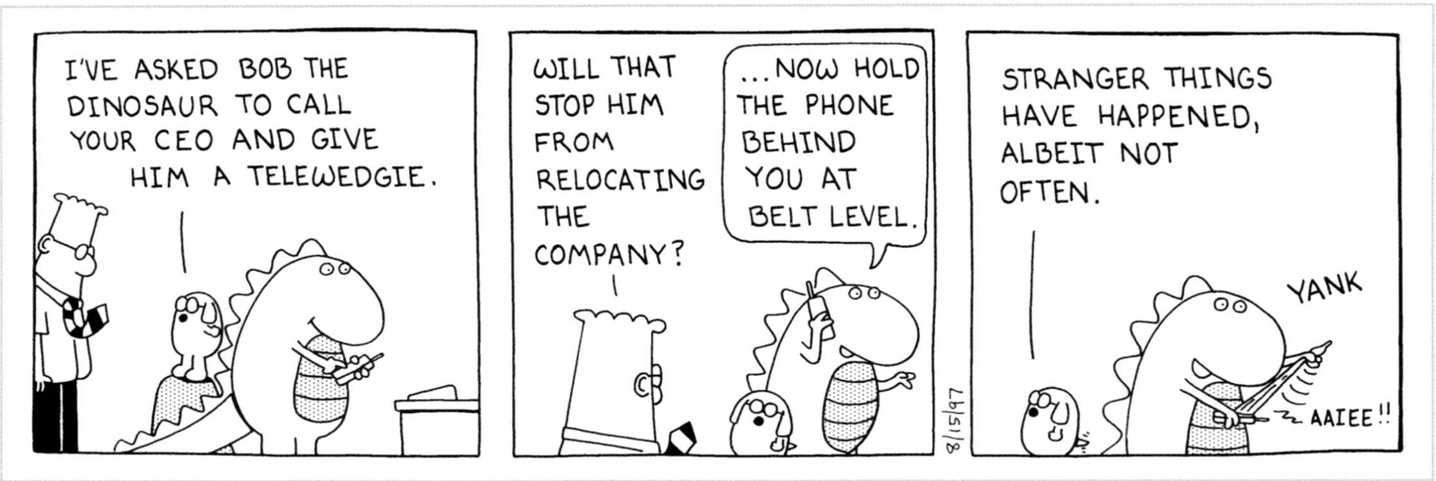
I'VE ASKED BOB THE DINOSAUR TO CALL YOUR CEO AND GIVE HIM A TELEWEDGIE.
WILL THAT STOP HIM FROM RELOCATING THE COMPANY?
...NOW HOLD THE PHONE BEHIND YOU AT BELT LEVEL.
8/15/97
STRANGER THINGS HAVE HAPPENED, ALBEIT NOT OFTEN.
YANK
AAIEE!!

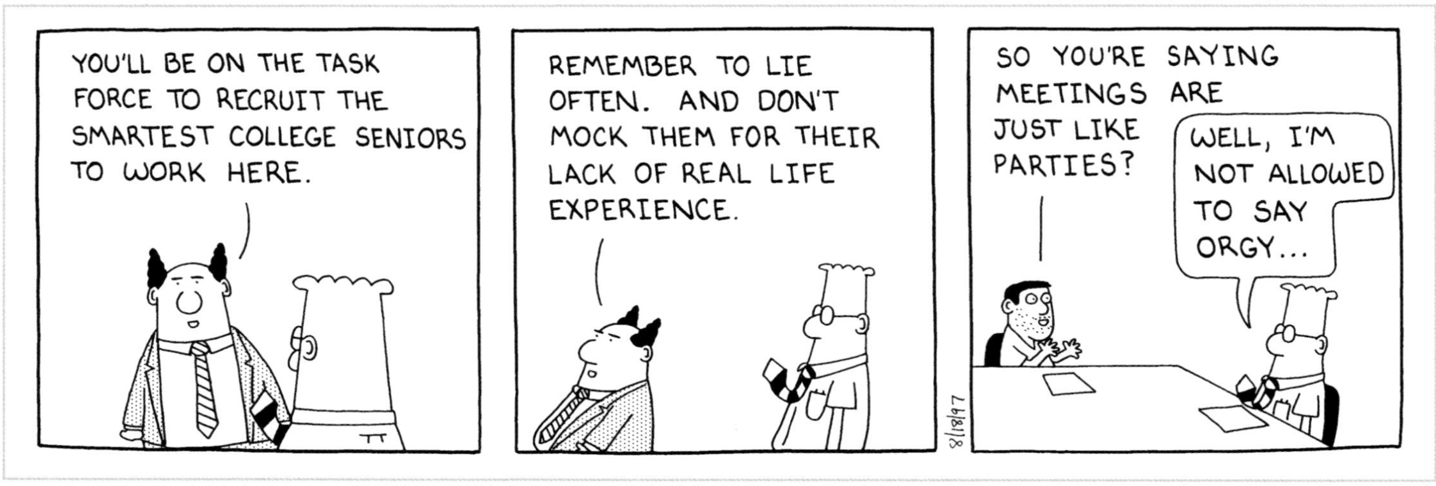
YOU'LL BE ON THE TASK FORCE TO RECRUIT THE SMARTEST COLLEGE SENIORS TO WORK HERE.
REMEMBER TO LIE OFTEN. AND DON'T MOCK THEM FOR THEIR LACK OF REAL LIFE EXPERIENCE.
8/18/97
SO YOU'RE SAYING MEETINGS ARE JUST LIKE PARTIES?
WELL, I'M NOT ALLOWED TO SAY ORGY...

This comic didn't run in its original form. The word "orgy" was considered inappropriate for the funny pages.

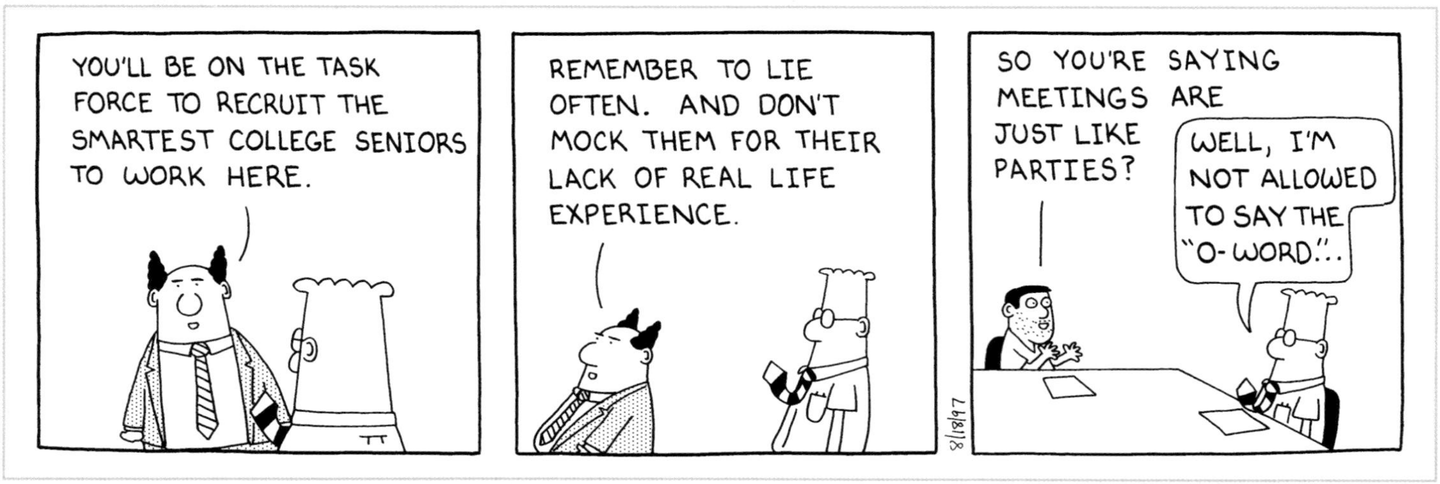
YOU'LL BE ON THE TASK FORCE TO RECRUIT THE SMARTEST COLLEGE SENIORS TO WORK HERE.
REMEMBER TO LIE OFTEN. AND DON'T MOCK THEM FOR THEIR LACK OF REAL LIFE EXPERIENCE.
8/18/97
SO YOU'RE SAYING MEETINGS ARE JUST LIKE PARTIES?
WELL, I'M NOT ALLOWED TO SAY THE "O-WORD."..

So I changed the last panel to replace "orgy" with the "o-word." That version ran in papers.
A surprising number of people wrote to ask what the o-word was.

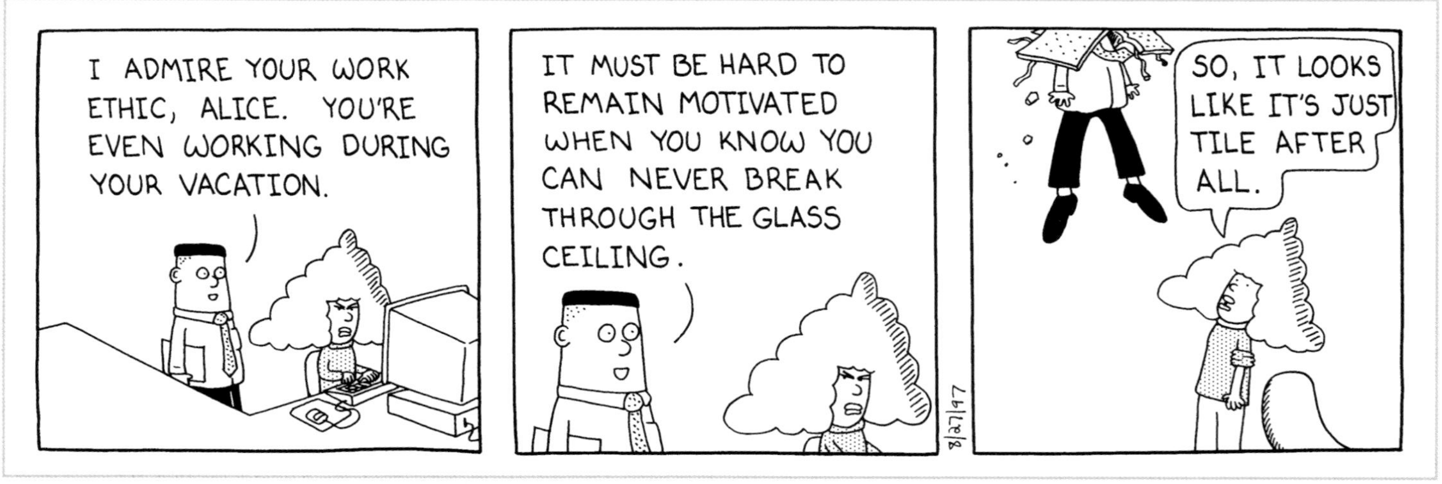
I ADMIRE YOUR WORK ETHIC, ALICE. YOU'RE EVEN WORKING DURING YOUR VACATION.
IT MUST BE HARD TO REMAIN MOTIVATED WHEN YOU KNOW YOU CAN NEVER BREAK THROUGH THE GLASS CEILING.
8/27/97
SO, IT LOOKS LIKE IT'S JUST TILE AFTER ALL.

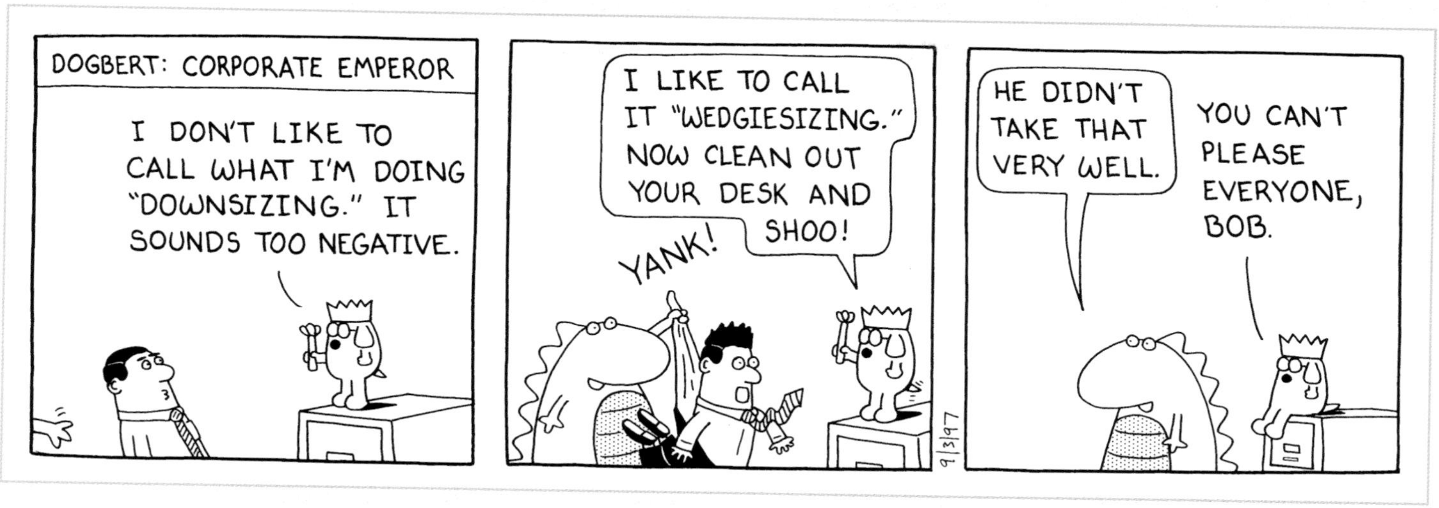
DOGBERT: CORPORATE EMPEROR
I DON'T LIKE TO CALL WHAT I'M DOING "DOWNSIZING." IT SOUNDS TOO NEGATIVE.
I LIKE TO CALL IT "WEDGIESIZING." NOW CLEAN OUT YOUR DESK AND SHOO!
YANK!
HE DIDN'T TAKE THAT VERY WELL.
YOU CAN'T PLEASE EVERYONE, BOB.
9/3/97

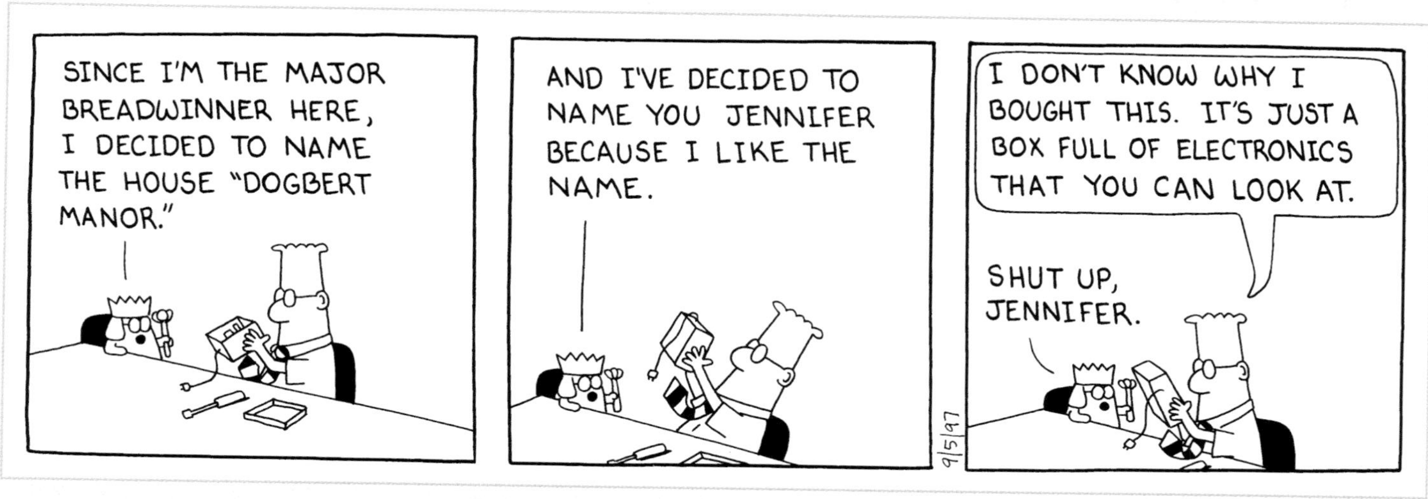
SINCE I'M THE MAJOR BREADWINNER HERE, I DECIDED TO NAME THE HOUSE "DOGBERT MANOR."
AND I'VE DECIDED TO NAME YOU JENNIFER BECAUSE I LIKE THE NAME.
I DON'T KNOW WHY I BOUGHT THIS. IT'S JUST A BOX FULL OF ELECTRONICS THAT YOU CAN LOOK AT.
SHUT UP, JENNIFER.
9/5/97

When I started this comic, I wanted Dilbert to be busy with something, but I didn't care what it was. By the third panel, the irrelevant thing in Dilbert's hands became the joke, along with Dogbert's response. My writing method generates a lot of apparent randomness.

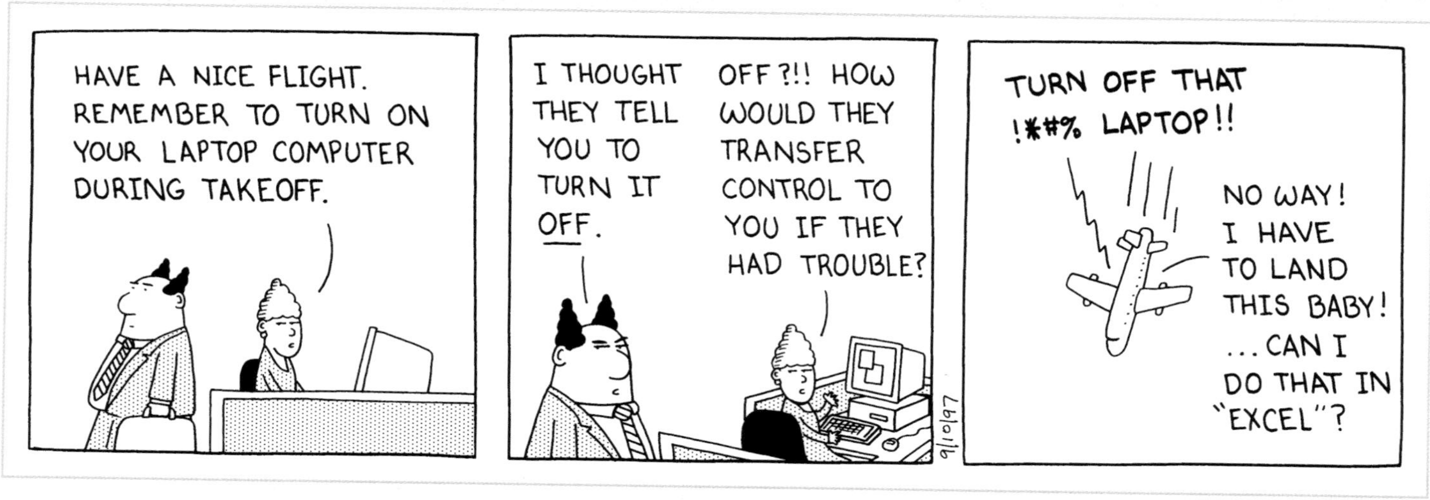
HAVE A NICE FLIGHT. REMEMBER TO TURN ON YOUR LAPTOP COMPUTER DURING TAKEOFF.
I THOUGHT THEY TELL YOU TO TURN IT OFF.
OFF?!! HOW WOULD THEY TRANSFER CONTROL TO YOU IF THEY HAD TROUBLE?
9/10/97
TURN OFF THAT !*#% LAPTOP!!
NO WAY! I HAVE TO LAND THIS BABY! ... CAN I DO THAT IN "EXCEL"?

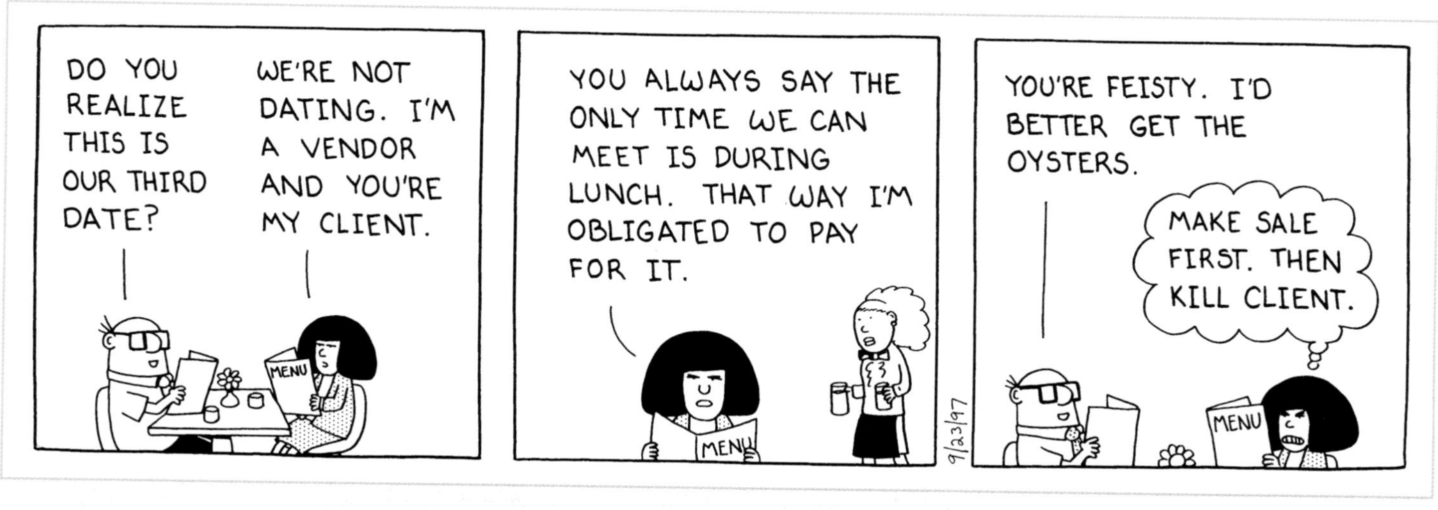
DO YOU REALIZE THIS IS OUR THIRD DATE?
WE'RE NOT DATING. I'M A VENDOR AND YOU'RE MY CLIENT.
MENU
YOU ALWAYS SAY THE ONLY TIME WE CAN MEET IS DURING LUNCH. THAT WAY I'M OBLIGATED TO PAY FOR IT.
MENU
9/23/97
YOU'RE FEISTY. I'D BETTER GET THE OYSTERS.
MAKE SALE FIRST. THEN KILL CLIENT.
MENU

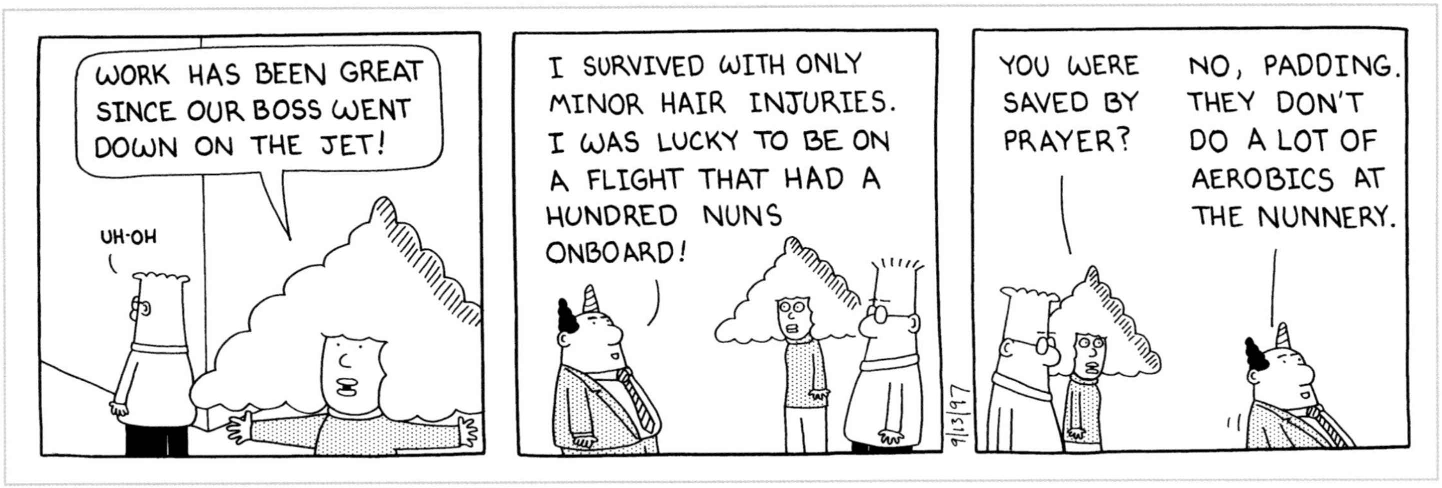
WORK HAS BEEN GREAT SINCE OUR BOSS WENT DOWN ON THE JET!
UH-OH
I SURVIVED WITH ONLY MINOR HAIR INJURIES. I WAS LUCKY TO BE ON A FLIGHT THAT HAD A HUNDRED NUNS ONBOARD!
9/13/97
YOU WERE SAVED BY PRAYER?
NO, PADDING. THEY DON'T DO A LOT OF AEROBICS AT THE NUNNERY.

Mother Teresa passed away a week before this comic ran. I got a lot of angry mail from people who thought I was insensitive because of the timing. I had submitted this comic two months earlier, and had forgotten it was in the pipeline. In retrospect, it was insensitive no matter what the timing was, because some readers can be expected to conflate fiction and reality.

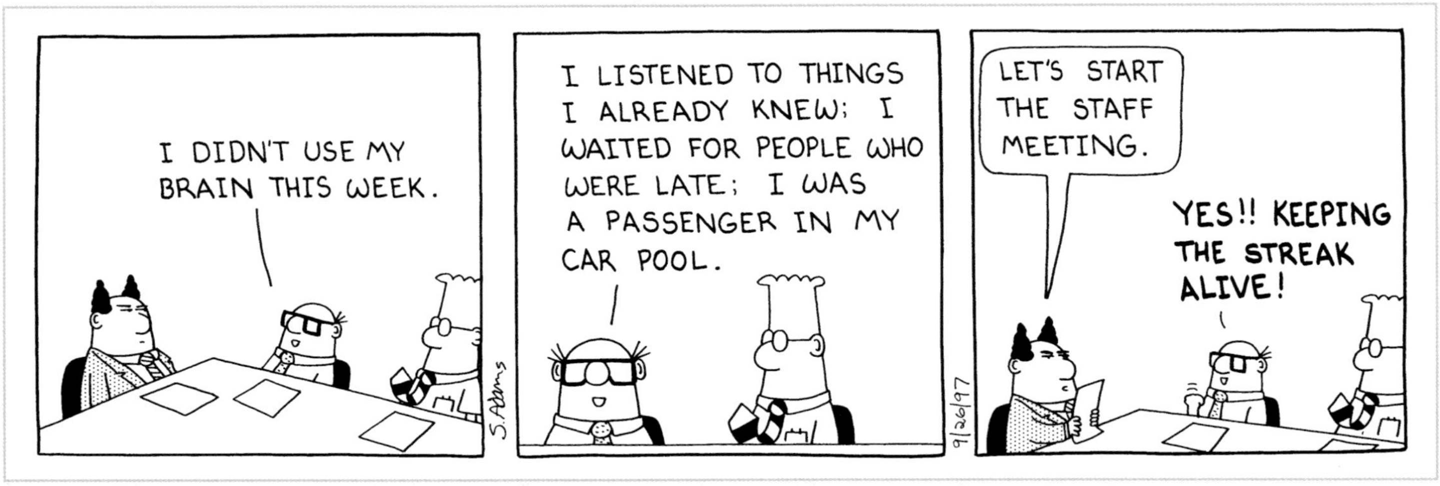
I DIDN'T USE MY BRAIN THIS WEEK.
S. Adams
I LISTENED TO THINGS I ALREADY KNEW; I WAITED FOR PEOPLE WHO WERE LATE; I WAS A PASSENGER IN MY CAR POOL.
9/26/97
LET'S START THE STAFF MEETING.
YES!! KEEPING THE STREAK ALIVE!

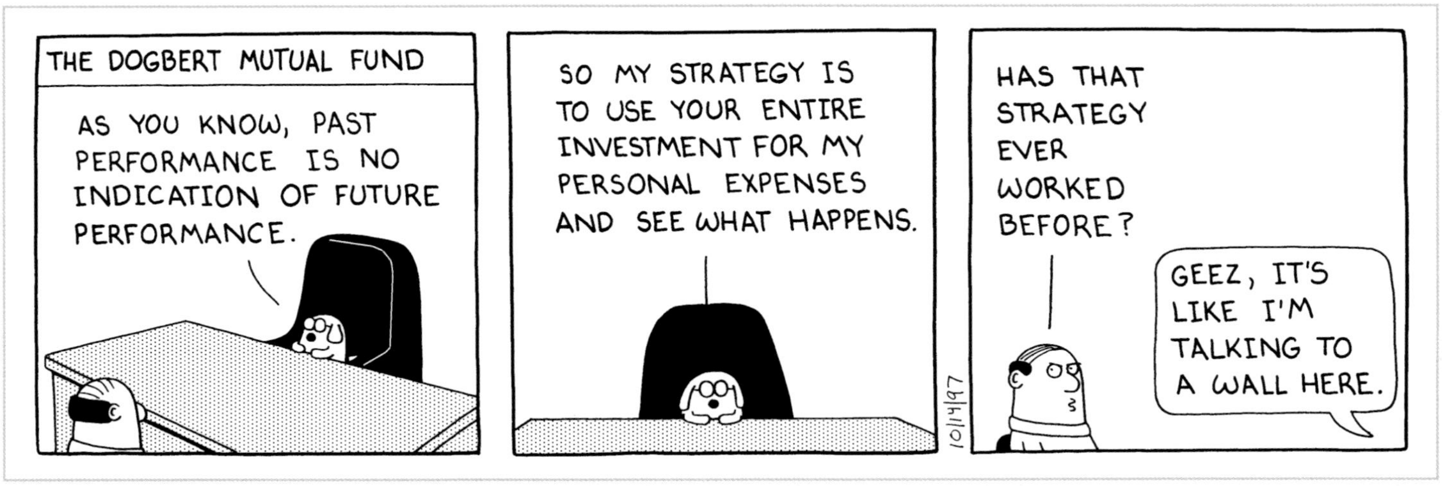
THE DOGBERT MUTUAL FUND
AS YOU KNOW, PAST PERFORMANCE IS NO INDICATION OF FUTURE PERFORMANCE.
SO MY STRATEGY IS TO USE YOUR ENTIRE INVESTMENT FOR MY PERSONAL EXPENSES AND SEE WHAT HAPPENS.
10/14/97
HAS THAT STRATEGY EVER WORKED BEFORE?
GEEZ, IT'S LIKE I'M TALKING TO A WALL HERE.

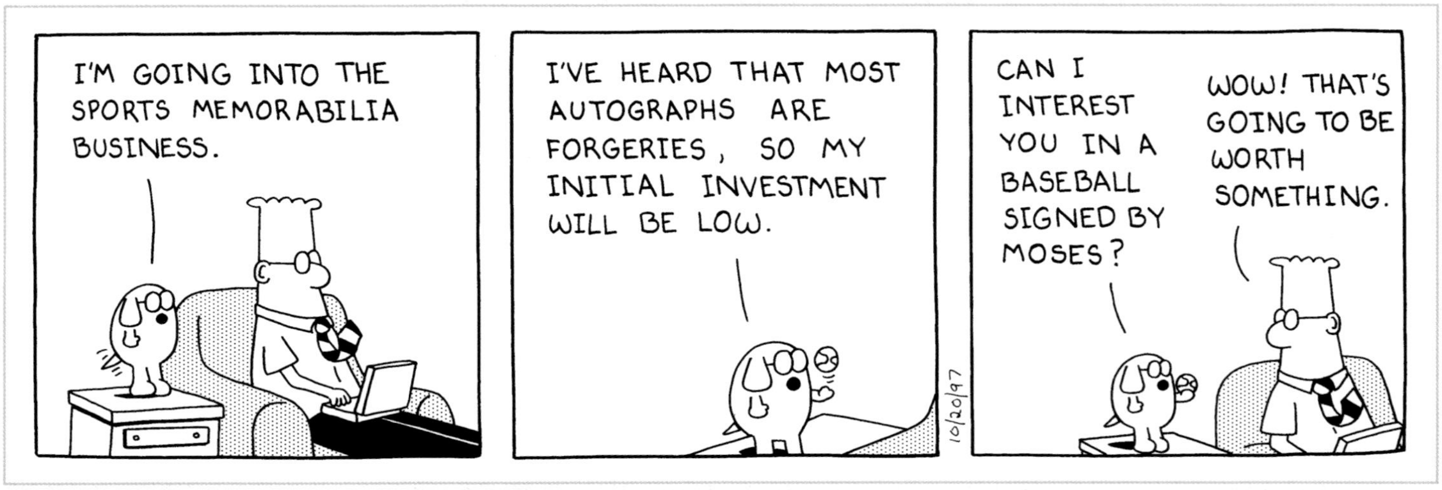
I'M GOING INTO THE SPORTS MEMORABILIA BUSINESS.
I'VE HEARD THAT MOST AUTOGRAPHS ARE FORGERIES, SO MY INITIAL INVESTMENT WILL BE LOW.
10/20/97
CAN I INTEREST YOU IN A BASEBALL SIGNED BY MOSES?
WOW! THAT'S GOING TO BE WORTH SOMETHING.

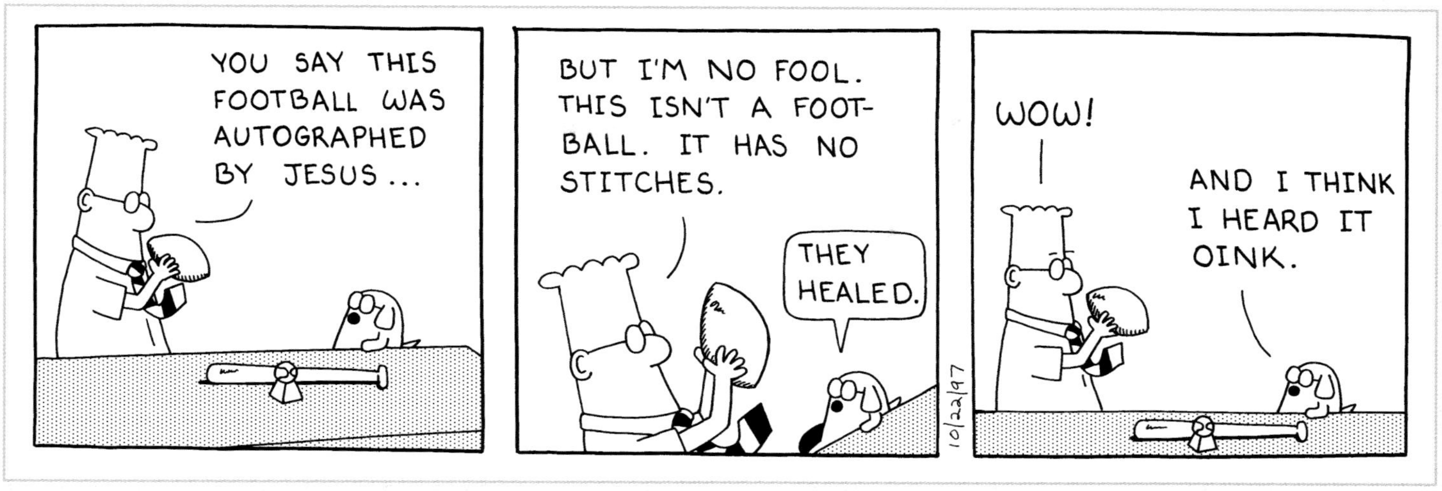
YOU SAY THIS FOOTBALL WAS AUTOGRAPHED BY JESUS...
BUT I'M NO FOOL. THIS ISN'T A FOOT-BALL. IT HAS NO STITCHES.
THEY HEALED.
10/22/97
WOW!
AND I THINK I HEARD IT OINK.

The sports memorabilia industry was not amused by this series

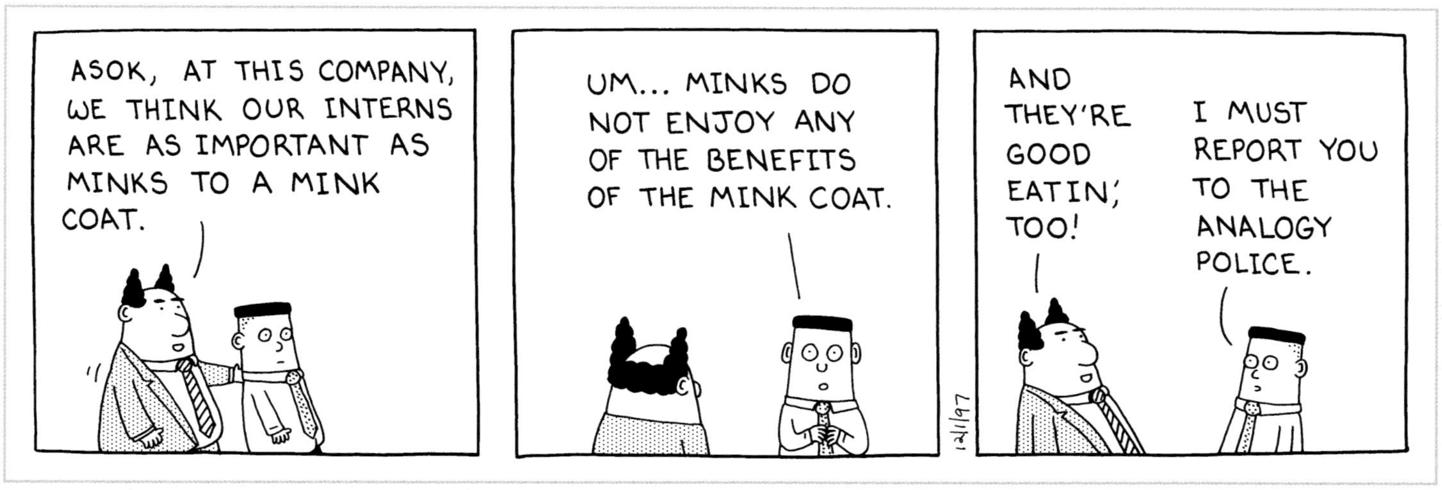
ASOK, AT THIS COMPANY, WE THINK OUR INTERNS ARE AS IMPORTANT AS MINKS TO A MINK COAT.
UM... MINKS DO NOT ENJOY ANY OF THE BENEFITS OF THE MINK COAT.
12/1/97
AND THEY'RE GOOD EATIN', TOO!
I MUST REPORT YOU TO THE ANALOGY POLICE.

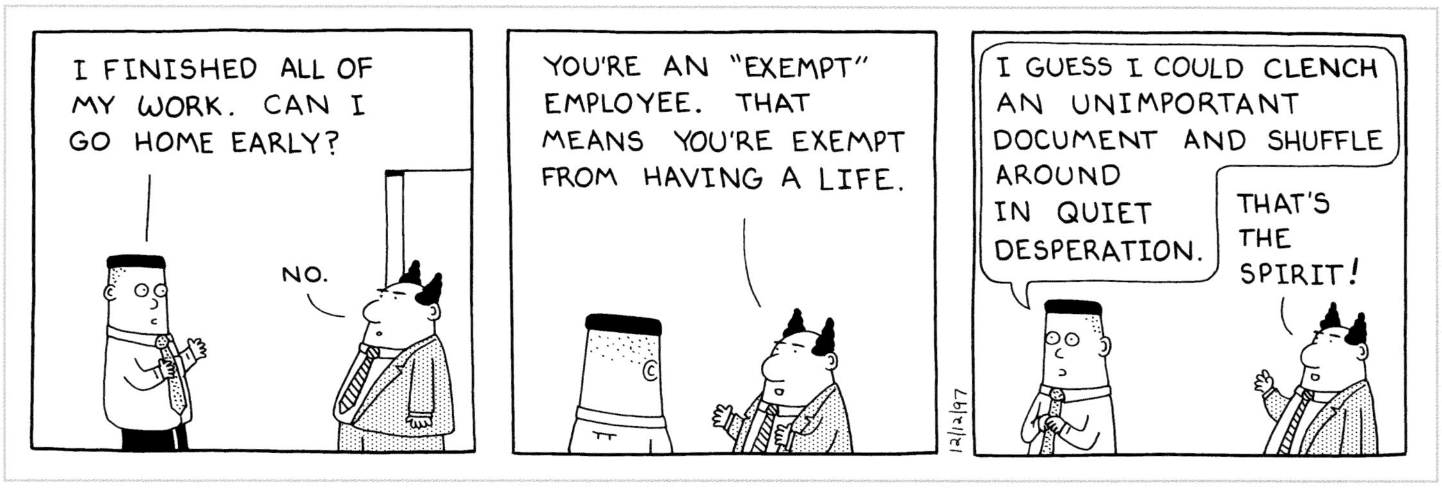
I FINISHED ALL OF MY WORK. CAN I GO HOME EARLY?
NO.
YOU'RE AN "EXEMPT" EMPLOYEE. THAT MEANS YOU'RE EXEMPT FROM HAVING A LIFE.
12/12/97
I GUESS I COULD CLENCH AN UNIMPORTANT DOCUMENT AND SHUFFLE AROUND IN QUIET DESPERATION.
THAT'S THE SPIRIT!

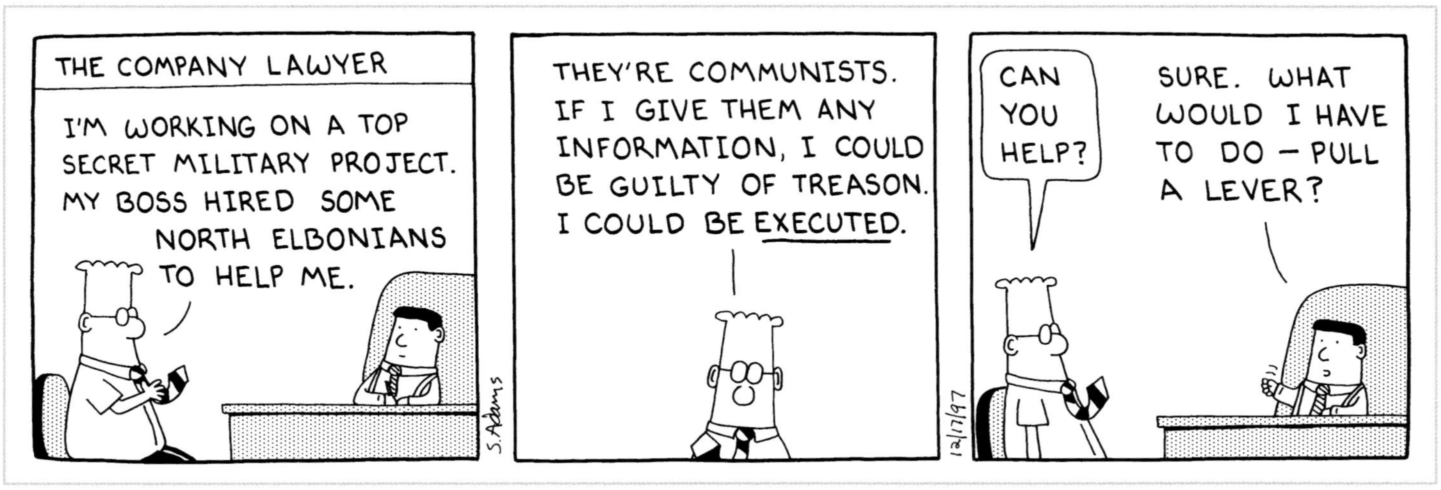
THE COMPANY LAWYER
I'M WORKING ON A TOP SECRET MILITARY PROJECT. MY BOSS HIRED SOME NORTH ELBONIANS TO HELP ME.
S. Adams
THEY'RE COMMUNISTS. IF I GIVE THEM ANY INFORMATION, I COULD BE GUILTY OF TREASON. I COULD BE EXECUTED.
12/17/97
CAN YOU HELP?
SURE. WHAT WOULD I HAVE TO DO — PULL A LEVER?

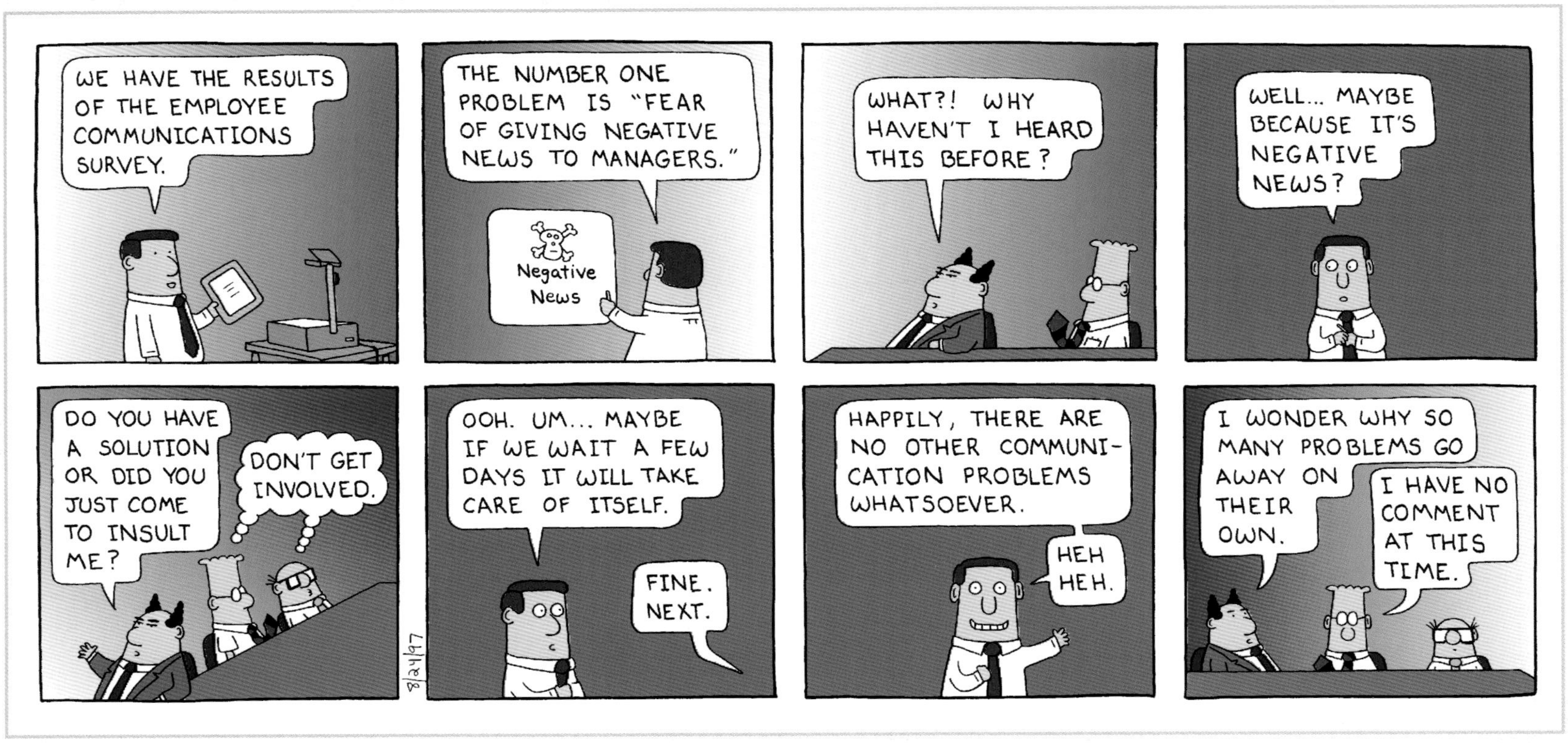
WE HAVE THE RESULTS OF THE EMPLOYEE COMMUNICATIONS SURVEY.
THE NUMBER ONE PROBLEM IS "FEAR OF GIVING NEGATIVE NEWS TO MANAGERS."
Negative News
WHAT?! WHY HAVEN'T I HEARD THIS BEFORE?
WELL... MAYBE BECAUSE IT'S NEGATIVE NEWS?
DO YOU HAVE A SOLUTION OR DID YOU JUST COME TO INSULT ME?
DON'T GET INVOLVED.
8/24/97
OOH. UM... MAYBE IF WE WAIT A FEW DAYS IT WILL TAKE CARE OF ITSELF.
FINE. NEXT.
HAPPILY, THERE ARE NO OTHER COMMUNICATION PROBLEMS WHATSOEVER.
HEH HEH.
I WONDER WHY SO MANY PROBLEMS GO AWAY ON THEIR OWN.
I HAVE NO COMMENT AT THIS TIME.

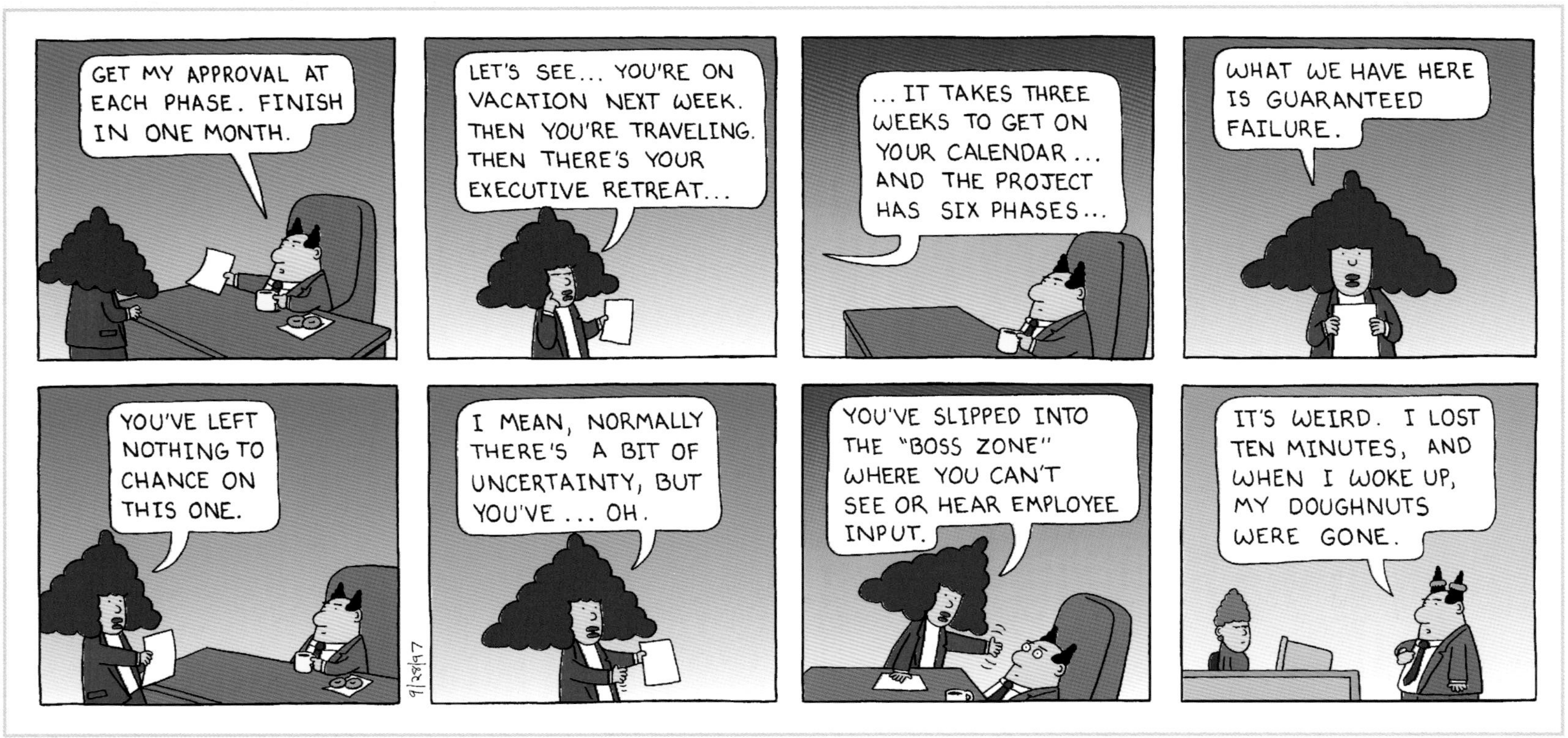
GET MY APPROVAL AT EACH PHASE. FINISH IN ONE MONTH.
LET'S SEE... YOU'RE ON VACATION NEXT WEEK. THEN YOU'RE TRAVELING. THEN THERE'S YOUR EXECUTIVE RETREAT...
...IT TAKES THREE WEEKS TO GET ON YOUR CALENDAR... AND THE PROJECT HAS SIX PHASES...
WHAT WE HAVE HERE IS GUARANTEED FAILURE.
YOU'VE LEFT NOTHING TO CHANCE ON THIS ONE.
9/28/97
I MEAN, NORMALLY THERE'S A BIT OF UNCERTAINTY, BUT YOU'VE ... OH.
YOU'VE SLIPPED INTO THE "BOSS ZONE" WHERE YOU CAN'T SEE OR HEAR EMPLOYEE INPUT.
IT'S WEIRD. I LOST TEN MINUTES, AND WHEN I WOKE UP, MY DOUGHNUTS WERE GONE.

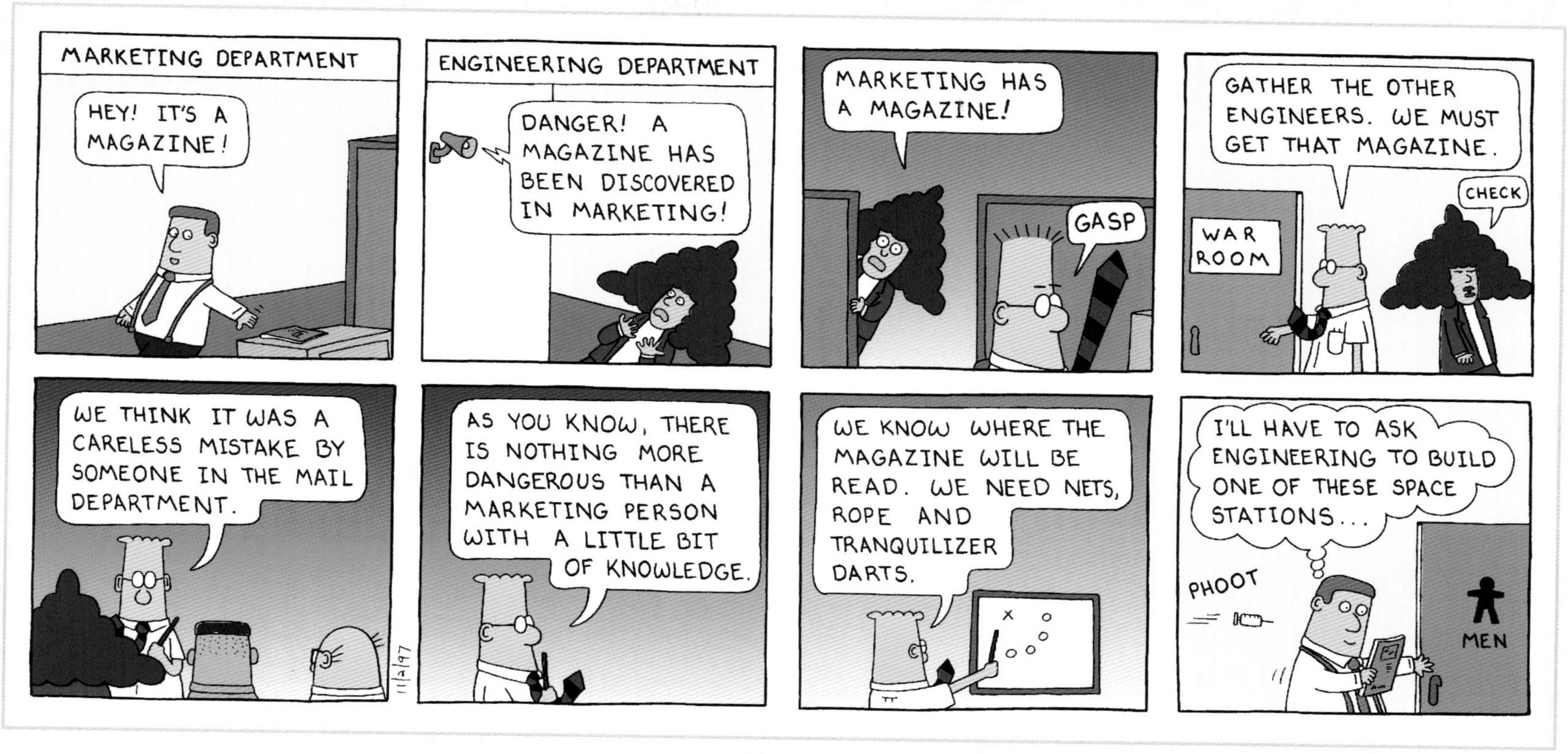
MARKETING DEPARTMENT
HEY! IT'S A MAGAZINE!
ENGINEERING DEPARTMENT
DANGER! A MAGAZINE HAS BEEN DISCOVERED IN MARKETING!
MARKETING HAS A MAGAZINE!
GASP
GATHER THE OTHER ENGINEERS. WE MUST GET THAT MAGAZINE.
WAR ROOM
CHECK
WE THINK IT WAS A CARELESS MISTAKE BY SOMEONE IN THE MAIL DEPARTMENT.
11/2/97
AS YOU KNOW, THERE IS NOTHING MORE DANGEROUS THAN A MARKETING PERSON WITH A LITTLE BIT OF KNOWLEDGE.
WE KNOW WHERE THE MAGAZINE WILL BE READ. WE NEED NETS, ROPE AND TRANQUILIZER DARTS.
I'LL HAVE TO ASK ENGINEERING TO BUILD ONE OF THESE SPACE STATIONS...
PHOOT
MEN

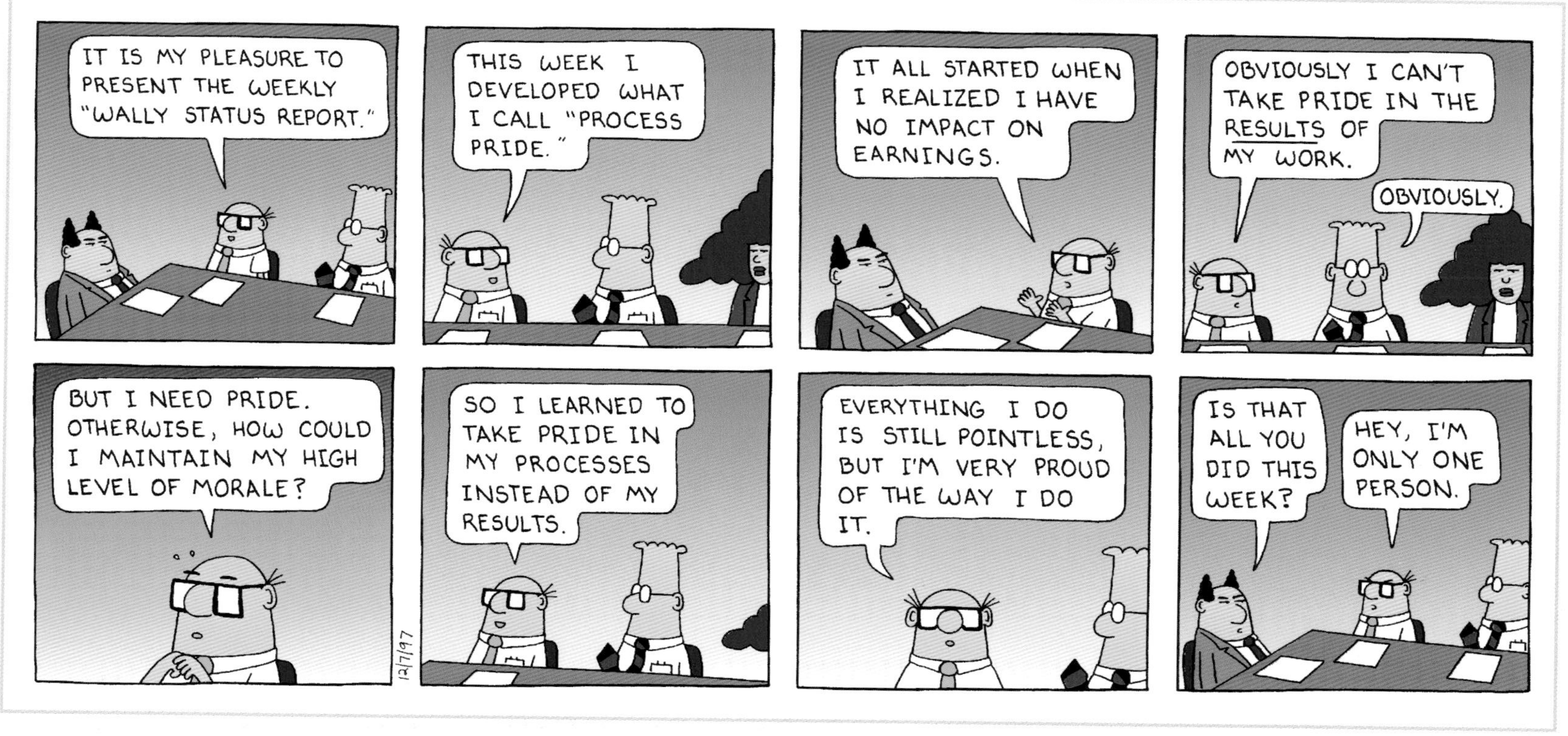
IT IS MY PLEASURE TO PRESENT THE WEEKLY "WALLY STATUS REPORT."
THIS WEEK I DEVELOPED WHAT I CALL "PROCESS PRIDE."
IT ALL STARTED WHEN I REALIZED I HAVE NO IMPACT ON EARNINGS.
OBVIOUSLY I CAN'T TAKE PRIDE IN THE RESULTS OF MY WORK.
OBVIOUSLY.
BUT I NEED PRIDE. OTHERWISE, HOW COULD I MAINTAIN MY HIGH LEVEL OF MORALE?
12/7/97
SO I LEARNED TO TAKE PRIDE IN MY PROCESSES INSTEAD OF MY RESULTS.
EVERYTHING I DO IS STILL POINTLESS, BUT I'M VERY PROUD OF THE WAY I DO IT.
IS THAT ALL YOU DID THIS WEEK?
HEY, I'M ONLY ONE PERSON.

The Dot-Com Bubble 1999-2000

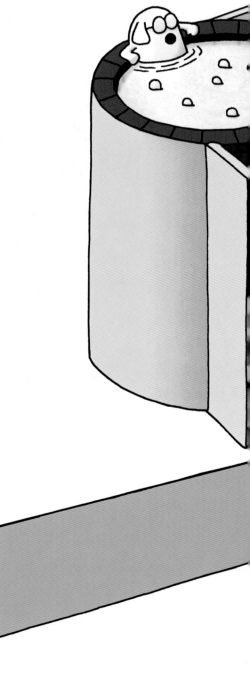

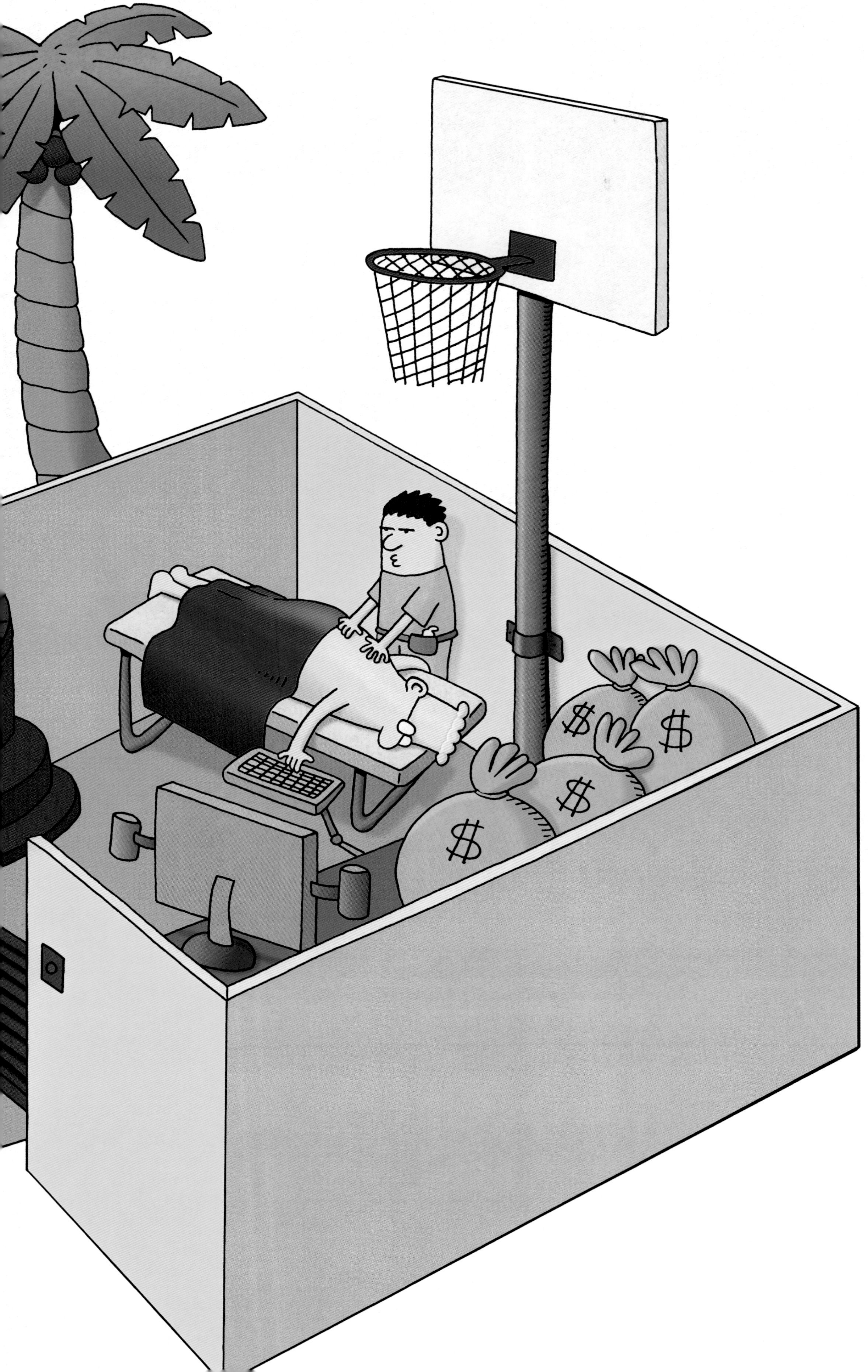

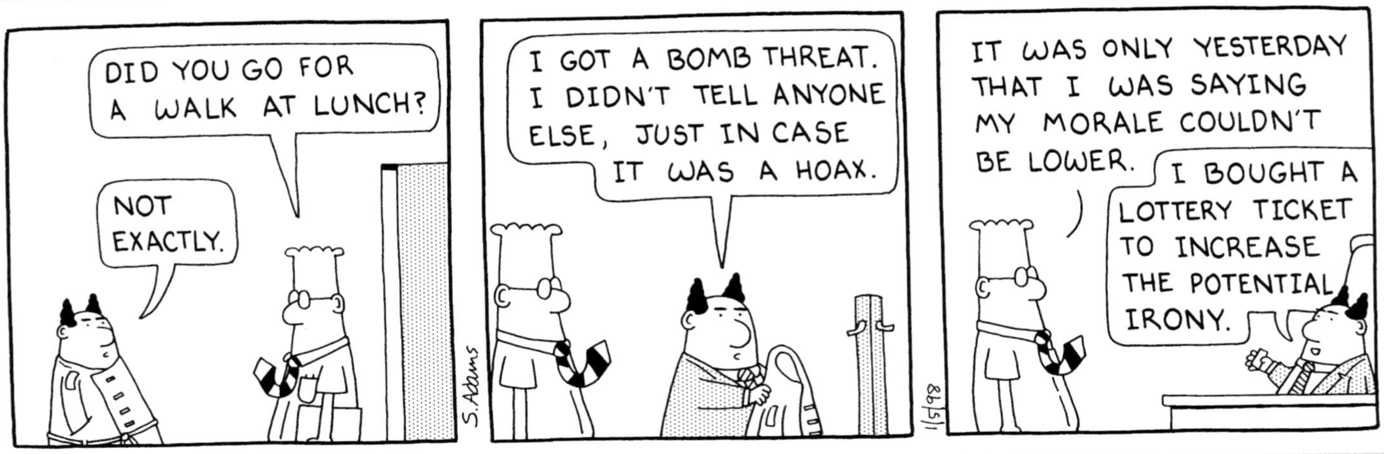
DID YOU GO FOR A WALK AT LUNCH?
NOT EXACTLY.
I GOT A BOMB THREAT. I DIDN'T TELL ANYONE ELSE, JUST IN CASE IT WAS A HOAX.
IT WAS ONLY YESTERDAY THAT I WAS SAYING MY MORALE COULDN'T BE LOWER.
I BOUGHT A LOTTERY TICKET TO INCREASE THE POTENTIAL IRONY.
S. Adams
1/5/98

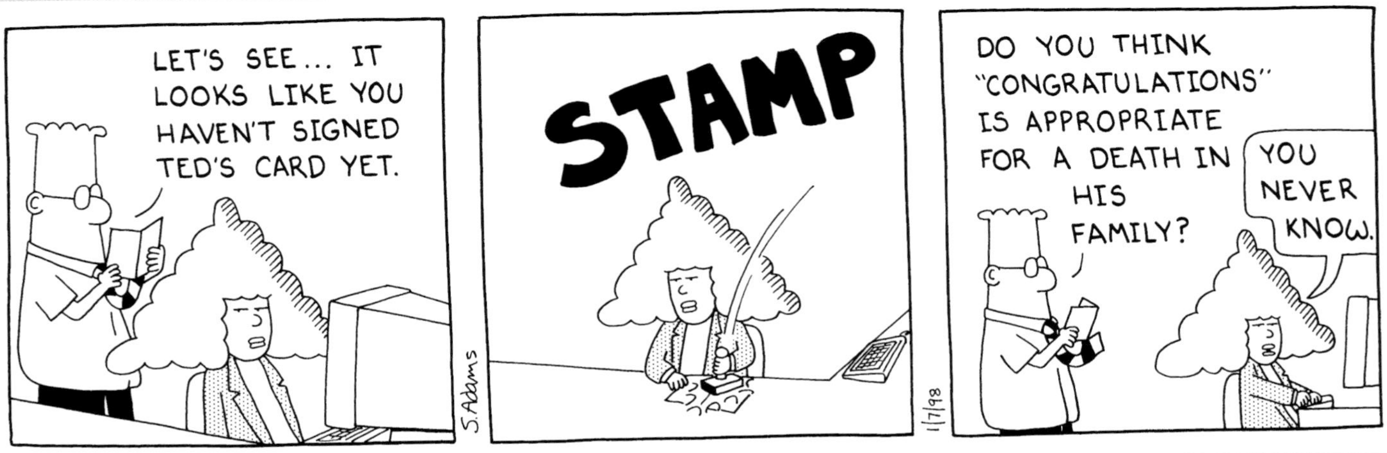
LET'S SEE... IT LOOKS LIKE YOU HAVEN'T SIGNED TED'S CARD YET.
STAMP
DO YOU THINK "CONGRATULATIONS" IS APPROPRIATE FOR A DEATH IN HIS FAMILY?
YOU NEVER KNOW.
S. Adams
1/7/98

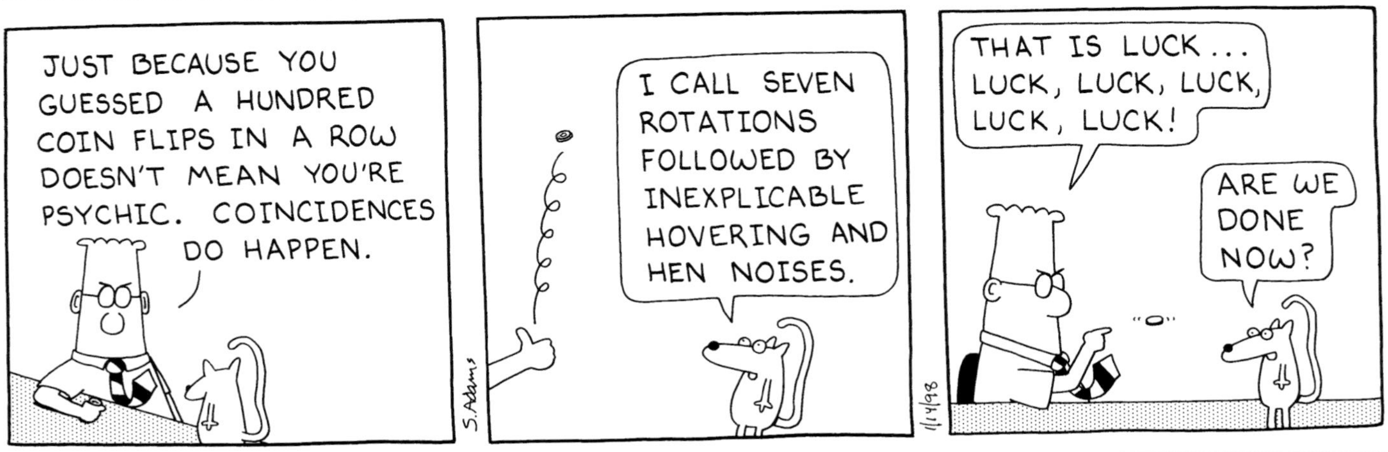
JUST BECAUSE YOU GUESSED A HUNDRED COIN FLIPS IN A ROW DOESN'T MEAN YOU'RE PSYCHIC. COINCIDENCES DO HAPPEN.
I CALL SEVEN ROTATIONS FOLLOWED BY INEXPLICABLE HOVERING AND HEN NOISES.
THAT IS LUCK... LUCK, LUCK, LUCK, LUCK, LUCK!
ARE WE DONE NOW?
S. Adams
1/14/98

An author named Norman Solomon wrote a book called The Trouble with Dilbert. *He got a lot of press. His main idea was that management tolerated* Dilbert *comics because they gave employees a harmless form of rebellion, and reduced the odds of a real one. Therefore, Solomon argued,* Dilbert *was really a tool of corporate overlords and not a champion of the working class as people assumed.*

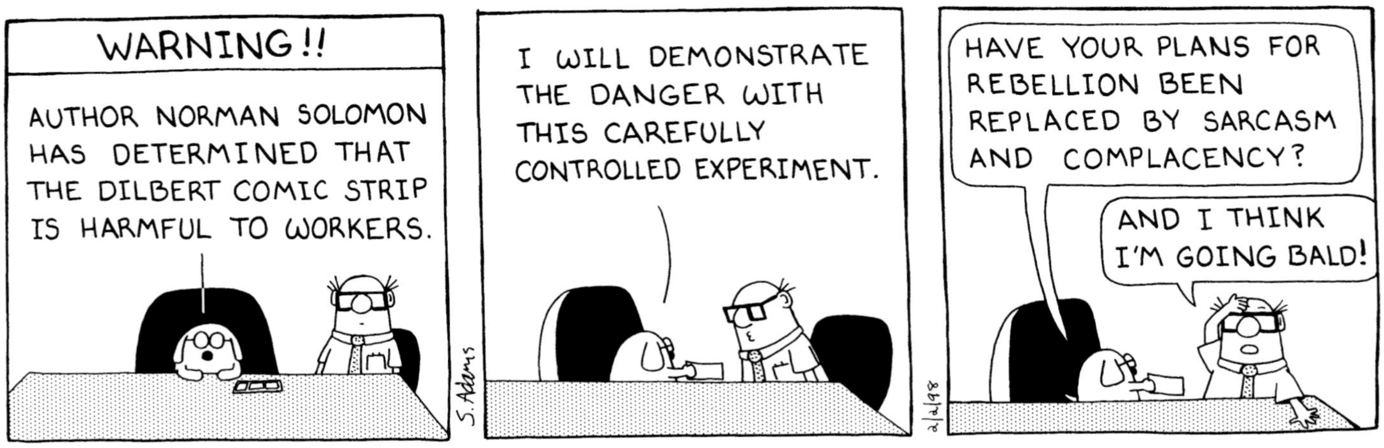
WARNING!!
AUTHOR NORMAN SOLOMON HAS DETERMINED THAT THE DILBERT COMIC STRIP IS HARMFUL TO WORKERS.
I WILL DEMONSTRATE THE DANGER WITH THIS CAREFULLY CONTROLLED EXPERIMENT.
HAVE YOUR PLANS FOR REBELLION BEEN REPLACED BY SARCASM AND COMPLACENCY?
AND I THINK I'M GOING BALD!
S. Adams
2/2/98

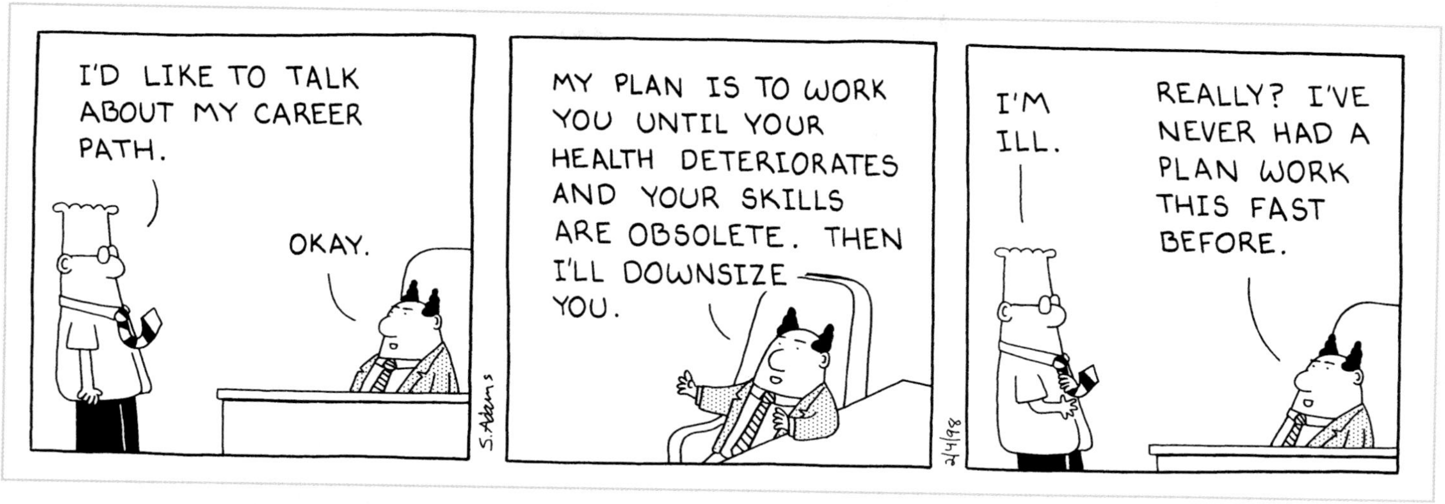
I'D LIKE TO TALK ABOUT MY CAREER PATH.
OKAY.
S. Adams
MY PLAN IS TO WORK YOU UNTIL YOUR HEALTH DETERIORATES AND YOUR SKILLS ARE OBSOLETE. THEN I'LL DOWNSIZE YOU.
2/4/98
I'M ILL.
REALLY? I'VE NEVER HAD A PLAN WORK THIS FAST BEFORE.

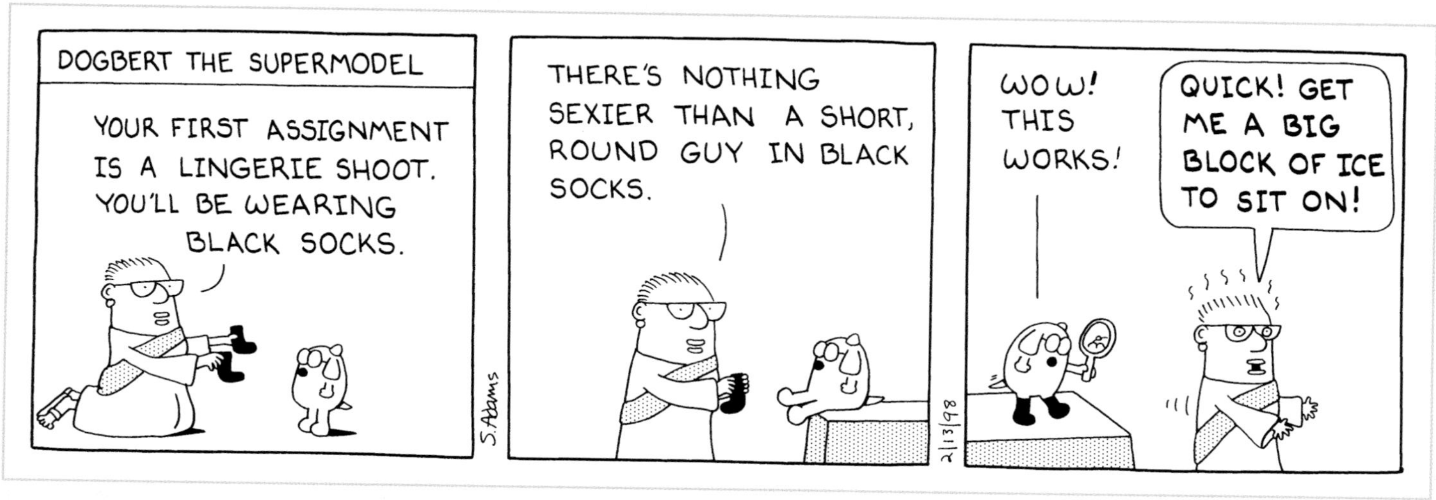
DOGBERT THE SUPERMODEL
YOUR FIRST ASSIGNMENT IS A LINGERIE SHOOT. YOU'LL BE WEARING BLACK SOCKS.
S. Adams
THERE'S NOTHING SEXIER THAN A SHORT, ROUND GUY IN BLACK SOCKS.
2/13/98
WOW! THIS WORKS!
QUICK! GET ME A BIG BLOCK OF ICE TO SIT ON!

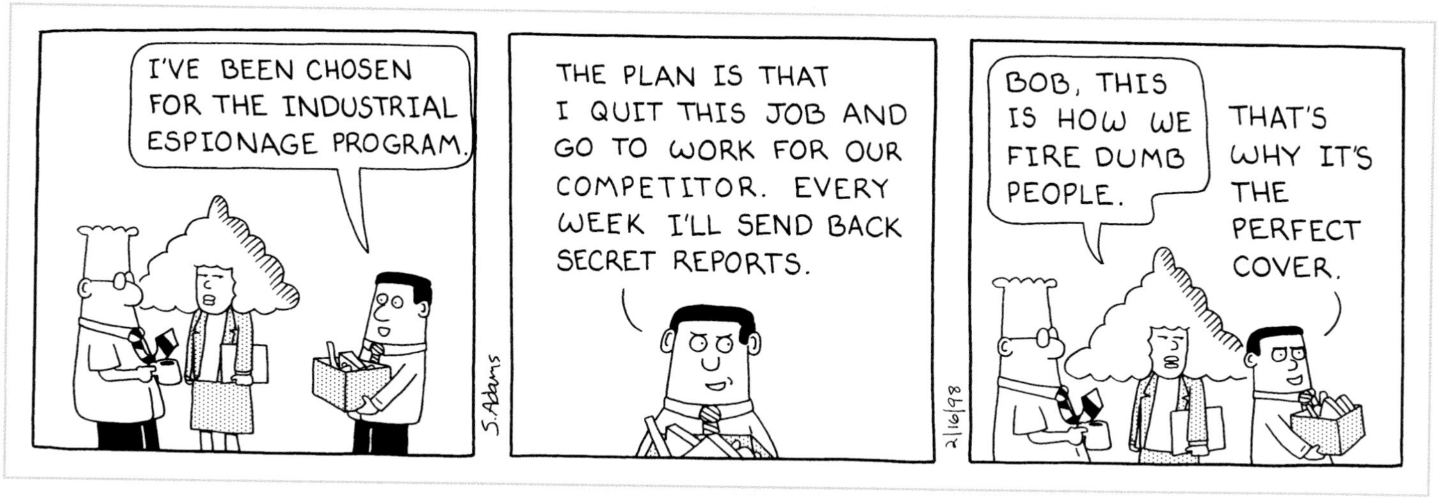
I'VE BEEN CHOSEN FOR THE INDUSTRIAL ESPIONAGE PROGRAM.
S. Adams
THE PLAN IS THAT I QUIT THIS JOB AND GO TO WORK FOR OUR COMPETITOR. EVERY WEEK I'LL SEND BACK SECRET REPORTS.
2/16/98
BOB, THIS IS HOW WE FIRE DUMB PEOPLE.
THAT'S WHY IT'S THE PERFECT COVER.

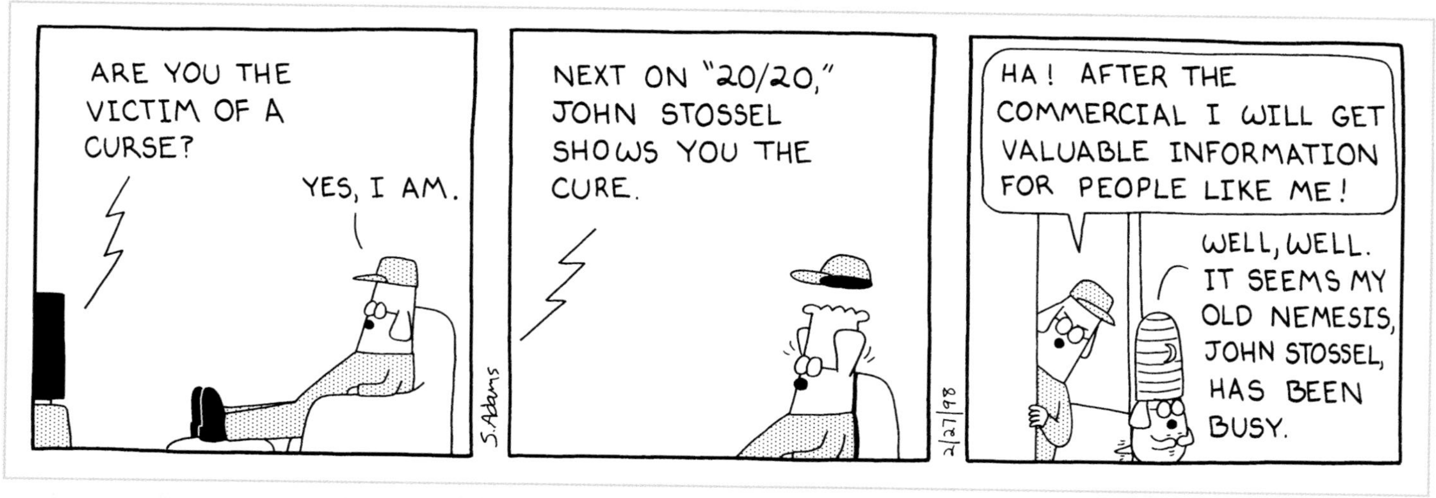
ARE YOU THE VICTIM OF A CURSE?
YES, I AM.
S. Adams
NEXT ON "20/20," JOHN STOSSEL SHOWS YOU THE CURE.
2/27/98
HA! AFTER THE COMMERCIAL I WILL GET VALUABLE INFORMATION FOR PEOPLE LIKE ME!
WELL, WELL. IT SEEMS MY OLD NEMESIS, JOHN STOSSEL, HAS BEEN BUSY.

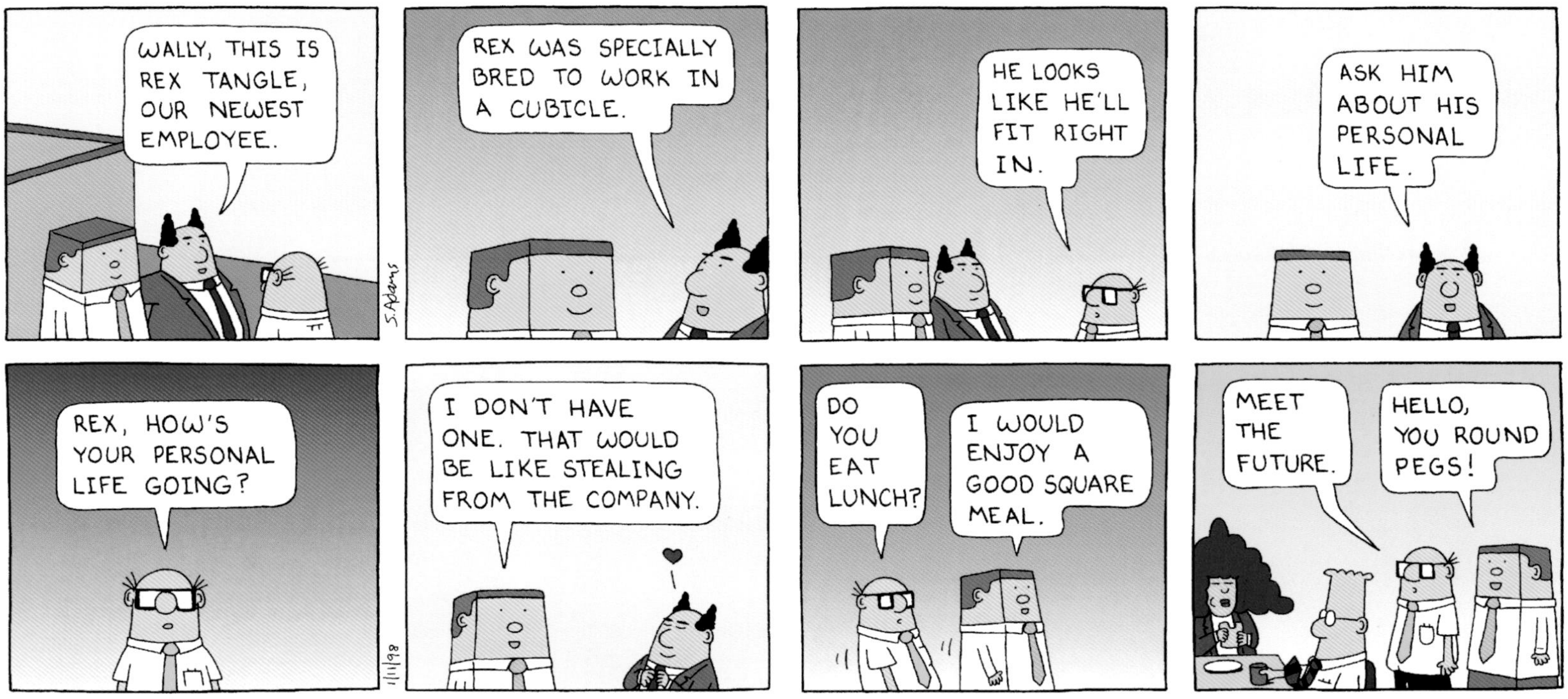
WALLY, THIS IS REX TANGLE, OUR NEWEST EMPLOYEE.
REX WAS SPECIALLY BRED TO WORK IN A CUBICLE.
HE LOOKS LIKE HE'LL FIT RIGHT IN.
ASK HIM ABOUT HIS PERSONAL LIFE.
REX, HOW'S YOUR PERSONAL LIFE GOING?
I DON'T HAVE ONE. THAT WOULD BE LIKE STEALING FROM THE COMPANY.
DO YOU EAT LUNCH?
I WOULD ENJOY A GOOD SQUARE MEAL.
MEET THE FUTURE.
HELLO, YOU ROUND PEGS!

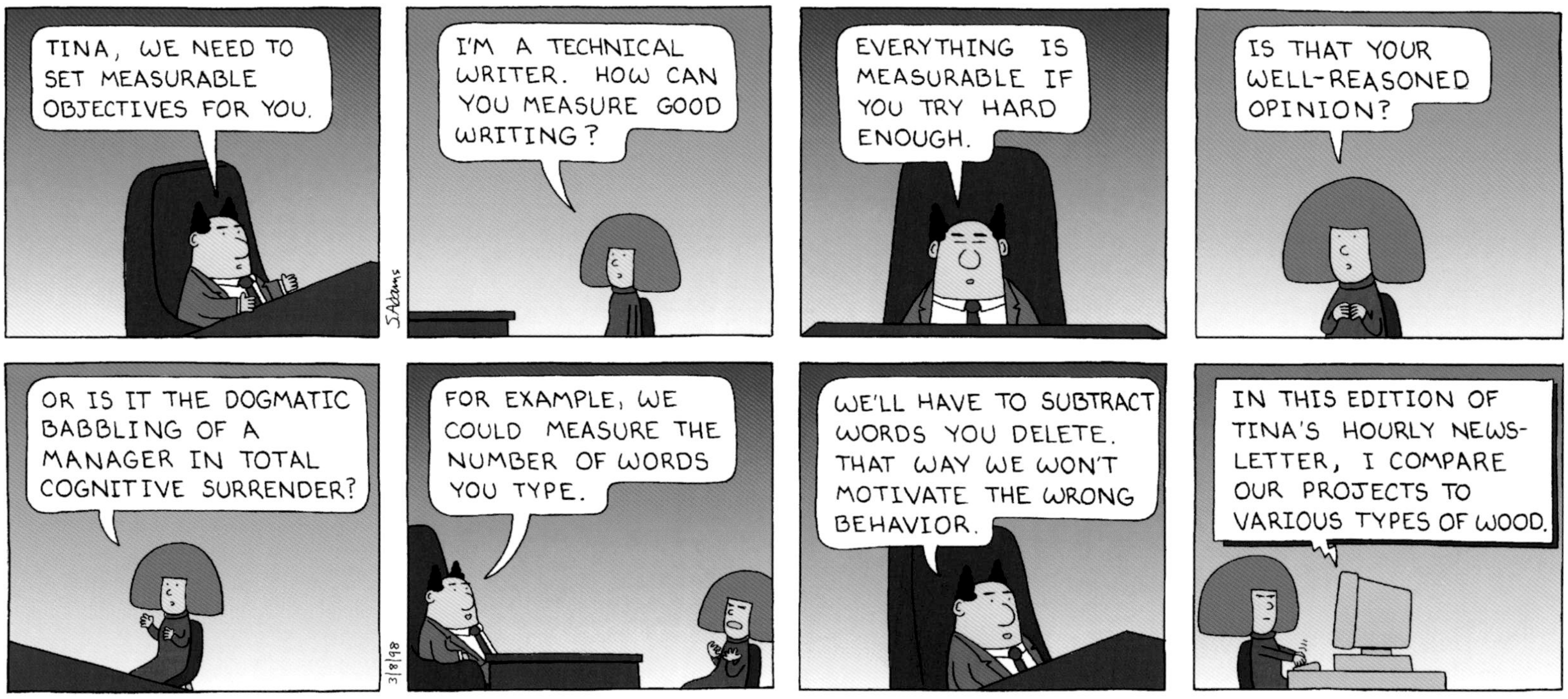
TINA, WE NEED TO SET MEASURABLE OBJECTIVES FOR YOU.
I'M A TECHNICAL WRITER. HOW CAN YOU MEASURE GOOD WRITING?
EVERYTHING IS MEASURABLE IF YOU TRY HARD ENOUGH.
IS THAT YOUR WELL-REASONED OPINION?
OR IS IT THE DOGMATIC BABBLING OF A MANAGER IN TOTAL COGNITIVE SURRENDER?
FOR EXAMPLE, WE COULD MEASURE THE NUMBER OF WORDS YOU TYPE.
WE'LL HAVE TO SUBTRACT WORDS YOU DELETE. THAT WAY WE WON'T MOTIVATE THE WRONG BEHAVIOR.
IN THIS EDITION OF TINA'S HOURLY NEWS-LETTER, I COMPARE OUR PROJECTS TO VARIOUS TYPES OF WOOD.

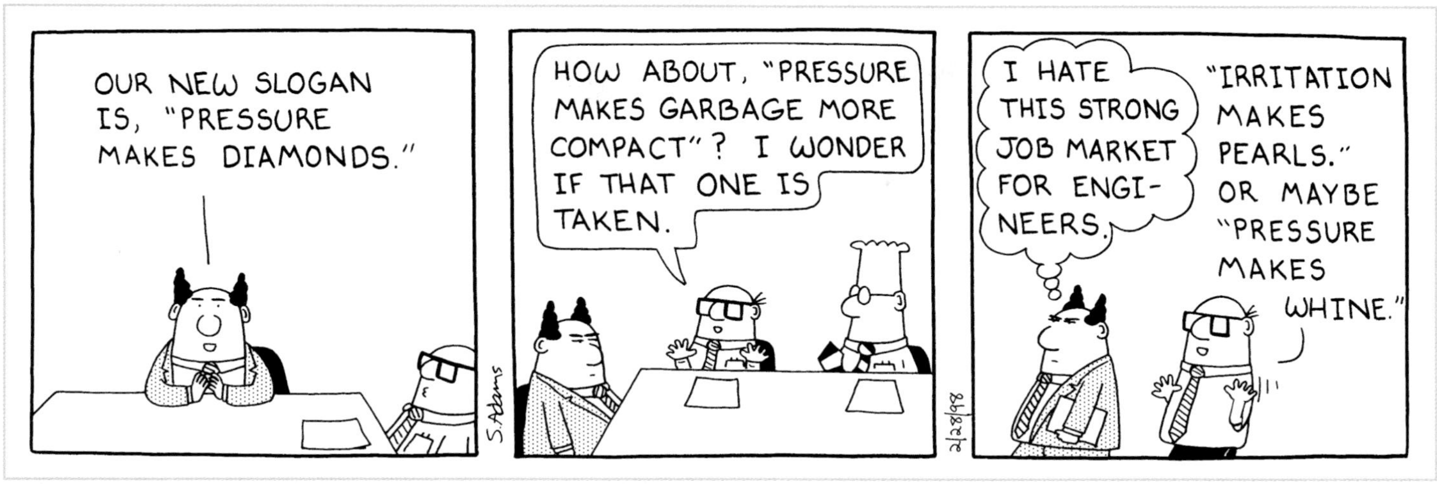
OUR NEW SLOGAN IS, "PRESSURE MAKES DIAMONDS."
S. Adams
HOW ABOUT, "PRESSURE MAKES GARBAGE MORE COMPACT"? I WONDER IF THAT ONE IS TAKEN.
2/28/98
I HATE THIS STRONG JOB MARKET FOR ENGINEERS.
"IRRITATION MAKES PEARLS." OR MAYBE "PRESSURE MAKES WHINE."

By 1998, the dot-com era was in full force, and it was difficult to write comics about hideous workplace events. I literally couldn't find people willing to complain. The suggestions for Dilbert *started to take a far less angry tone, and it made my job substantially harder.*

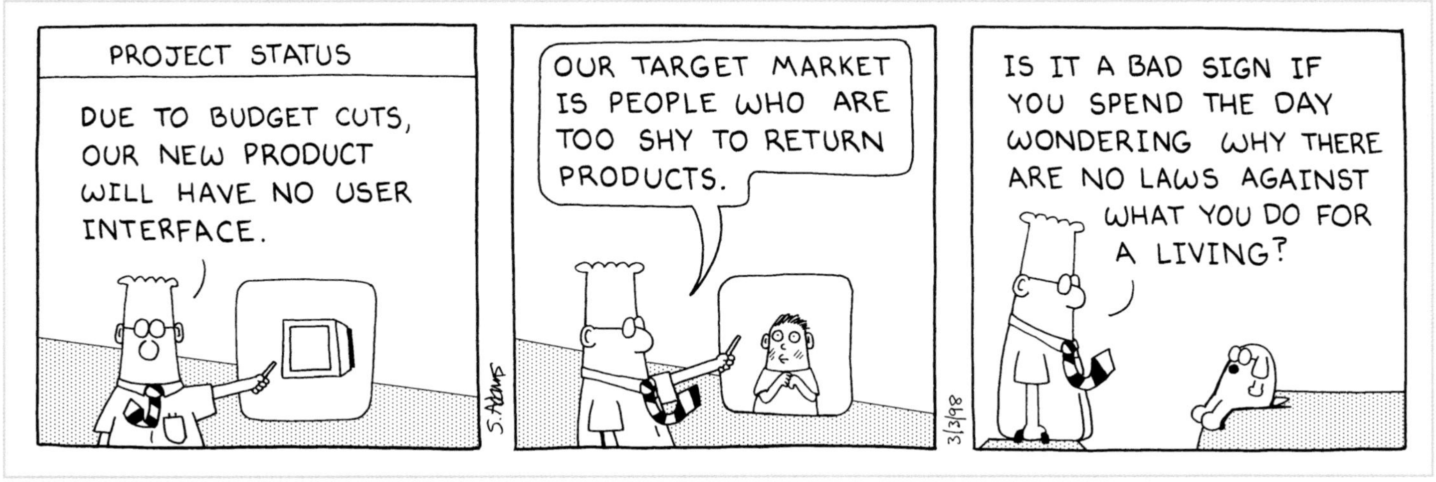
PROJECT STATUS
DUE TO BUDGET CUTS, OUR NEW PRODUCT WILL HAVE NO USER INTERFACE.
S. Adams
OUR TARGET MARKET IS PEOPLE WHO ARE TOO SHY TO RETURN PRODUCTS.
3/3/98
IS IT A BAD SIGN IF YOU SPEND THE DAY WONDERING WHY THERE ARE NO LAWS AGAINST WHAT YOU DO FOR A LIVING?

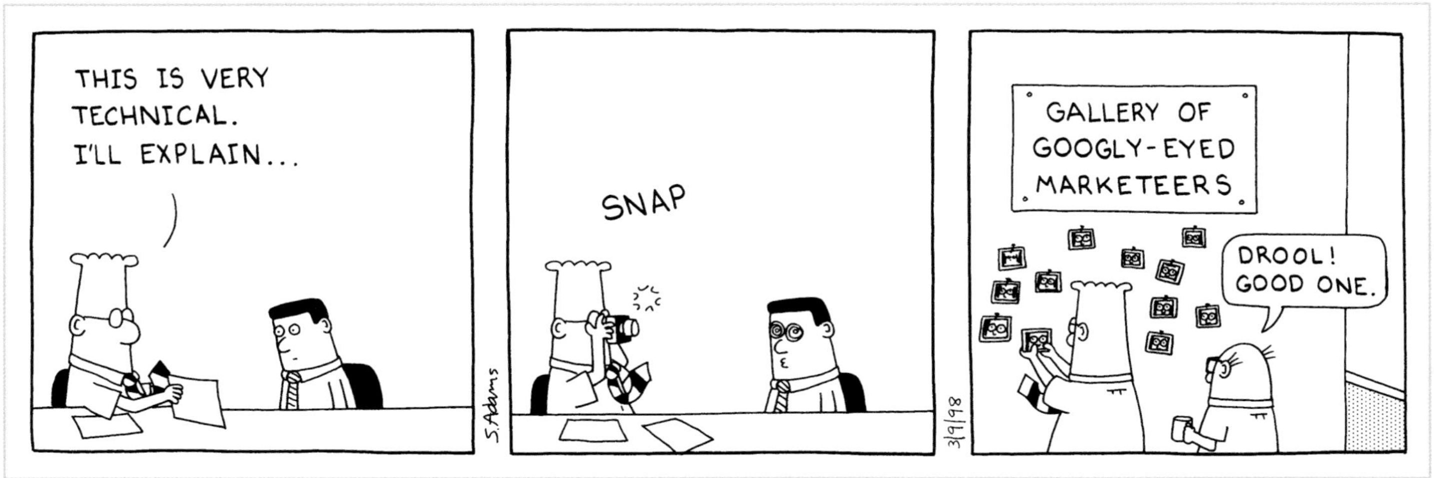
THIS IS VERY TECHNICAL. I'LL EXPLAIN...
S. Adams
SNAP
3/9/98
GALLERY OF GOOGLY-EYED MARKETEERS
DROOL! GOOD ONE.

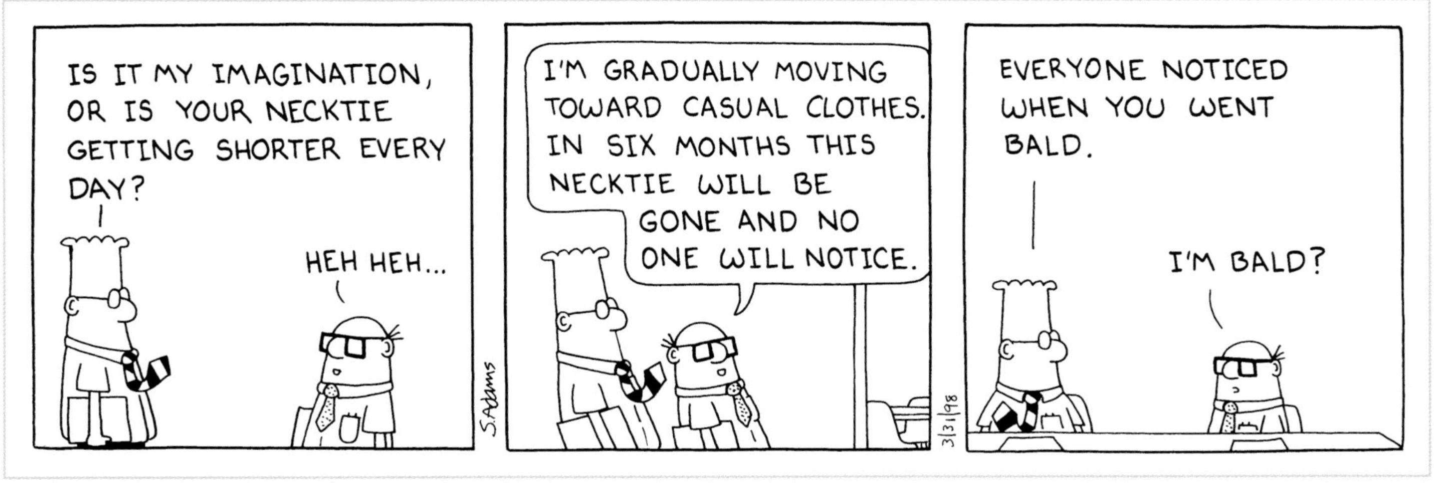
IS IT MY IMAGINATION, OR IS YOUR NECKTIE GETTING SHORTER EVERY DAY?
HEH HEH...
S. Adams
I'M GRADUALLY MOVING TOWARD CASUAL CLOTHES. IN SIX MONTHS THIS NECKTIE WILL BE GONE AND NO ONE WILL NOTICE.
3/31/98
EVERYONE NOTICED WHEN YOU WENT BALD.
I'M BALD?

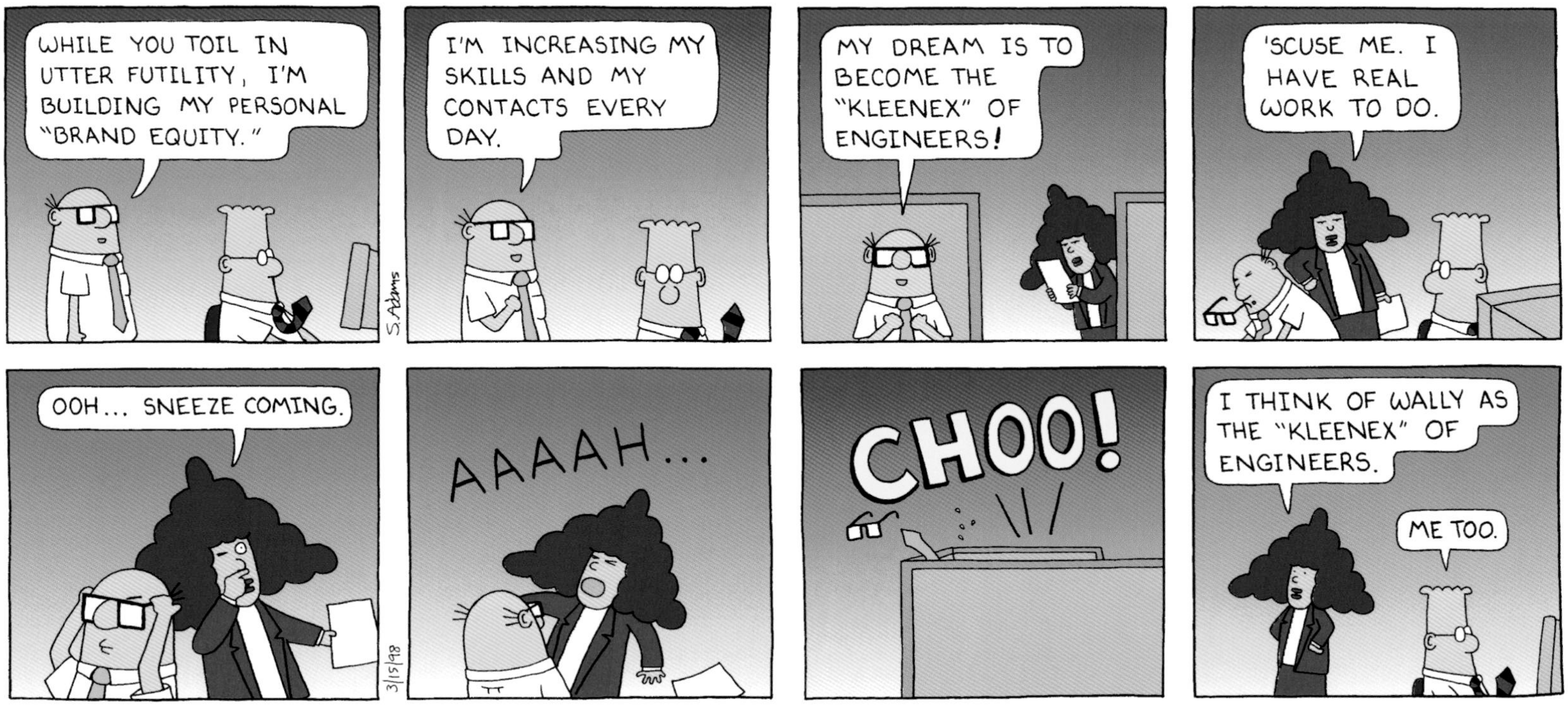
WHILE YOU TOIL IN UTTER FUTILITY, I'M BUILDING MY PERSONAL "BRAND EQUITY."
I'M INCREASING MY SKILLS AND MY CONTACTS EVERY DAY.
MY DREAM IS TO BECOME THE "KLEENEX" OF ENGINEERS!
'SCUSE ME. I HAVE REAL WORK TO DO.
OOH... SNEEZE COMING.
AAAAH...
CHOO!
I THINK OF WALLY AS THE "KLEENEX" OF ENGINEERS.
ME TOO.

I hoped "porcelain cruise" would enter the vocabulary. I just checked the online Urban Dictionary and there it is. But I can't be sure Wally was the source.

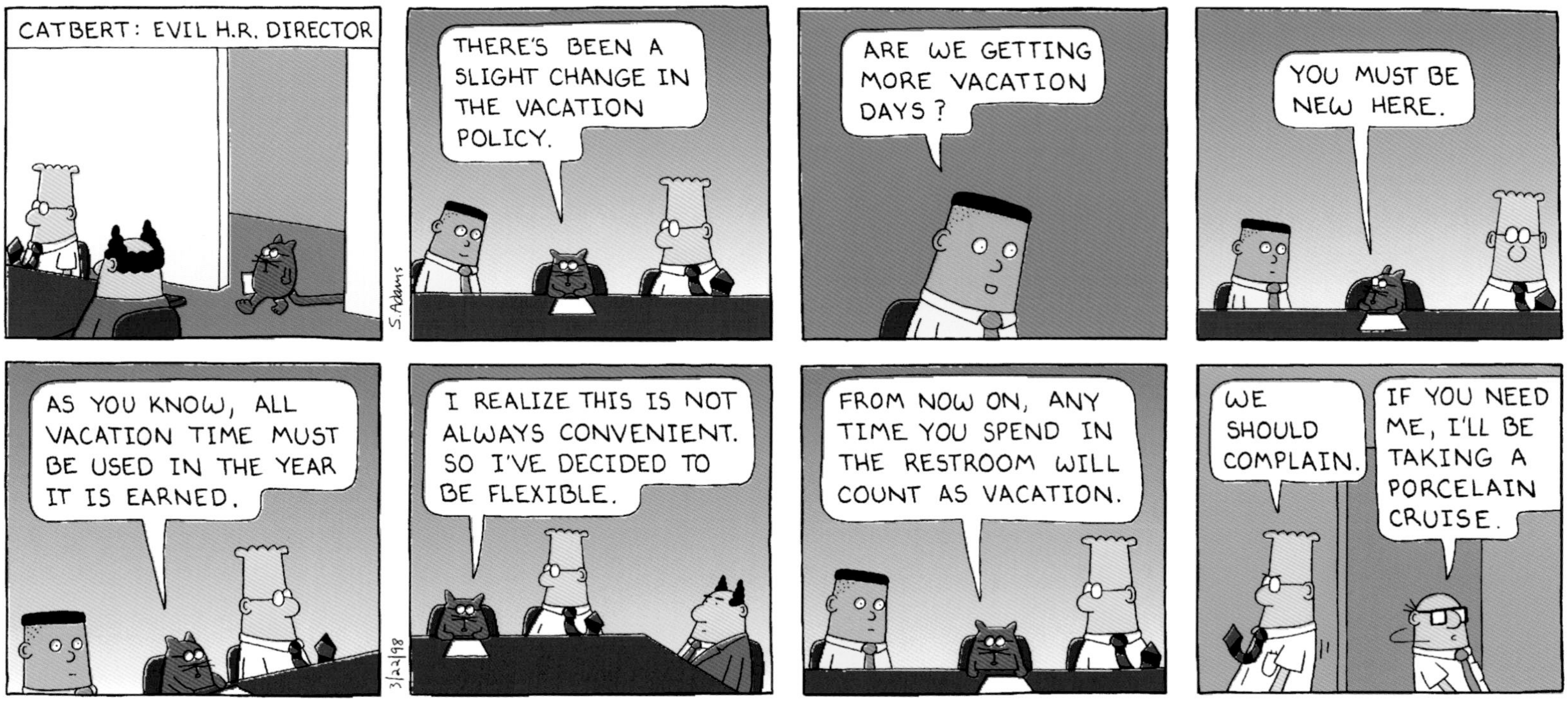
CATBERT: EVIL H.R. DIRECTOR
THERE'S BEEN A SLIGHT CHANGE IN THE VACATION POLICY.
ARE WE GETTING MORE VACATION DAYS?
YOU MUST BE NEW HERE.
AS YOU KNOW, ALL VACATION TIME MUST BE USED IN THE YEAR IT IS EARNED.
I REALIZE THIS IS NOT ALWAYS CONVENIENT. SO I'VE DECIDED TO BE FLEXIBLE.
FROM NOW ON, ANY TIME YOU SPEND IN THE RESTROOM WILL COUNT AS VACATION.
WE SHOULD COMPLAIN.
IF YOU NEED ME, I'LL BE TAKING A PORCELAIN CRUISE.

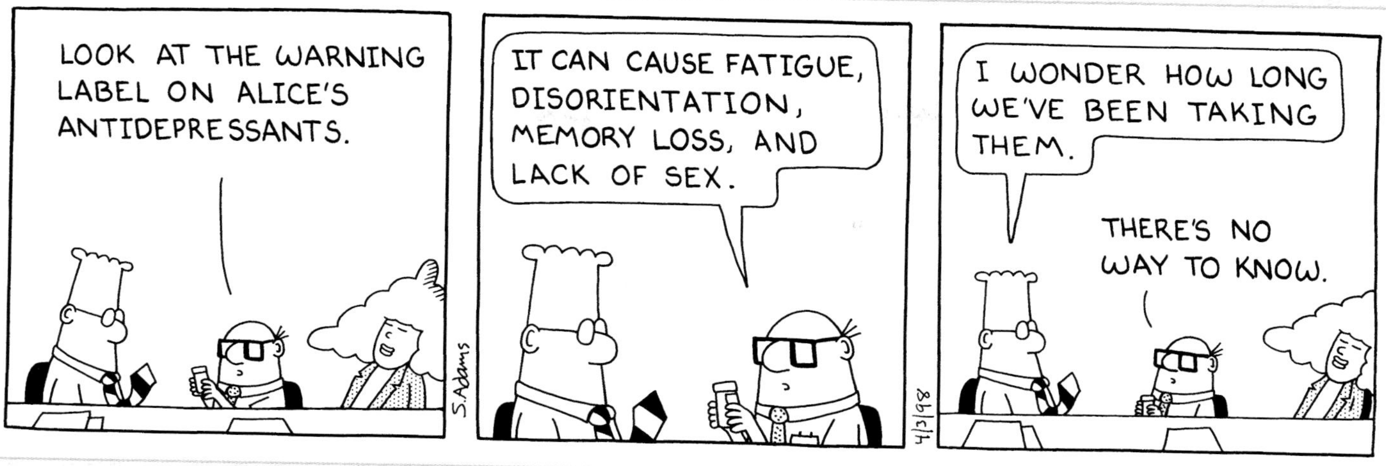
LOOK AT THE WARNING LABEL ON ALICE'S ANTIDEPRESSANTS.
S. Adams
IT CAN CAUSE FATIGUE, DISORIENTATION, MEMORY LOSS, AND LACK OF SEX.
4/3/98
I WONDER HOW LONG WE'VE BEEN TAKING THEM.
THERE'S NO WAY TO KNOW.

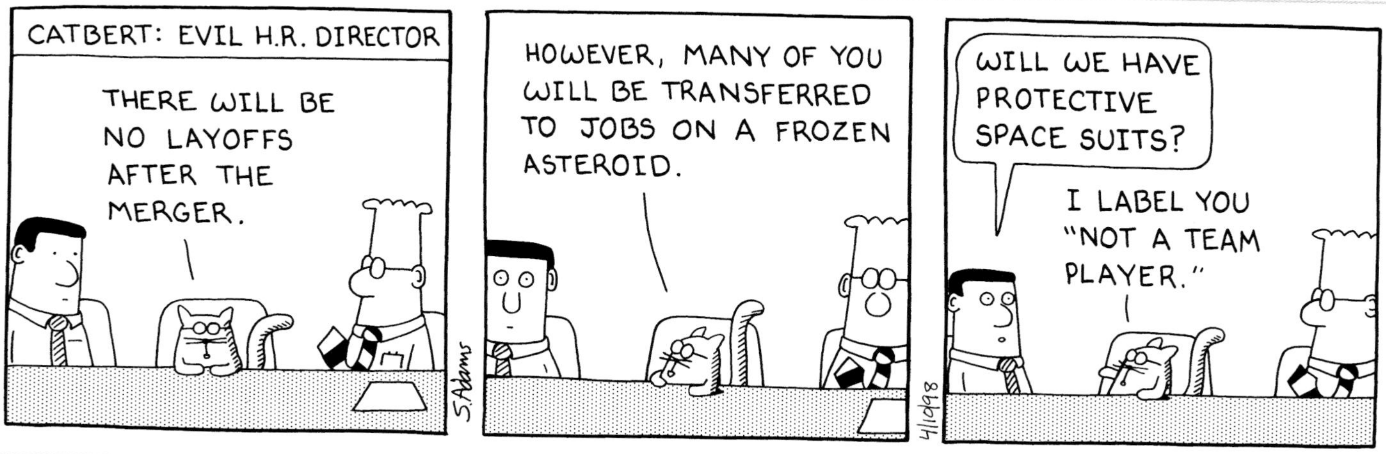
CATBERT: EVIL H.R. DIRECTOR
THERE WILL BE NO LAYOFFS AFTER THE MERGER.
S. Adams
HOWEVER, MANY OF YOU WILL BE TRANSFERRED TO JOBS ON A FROZEN ASTEROID.
4/10/98
WILL WE HAVE PROTECTIVE SPACE SUITS?
I LABEL YOU "NOT A TEAM PLAYER."

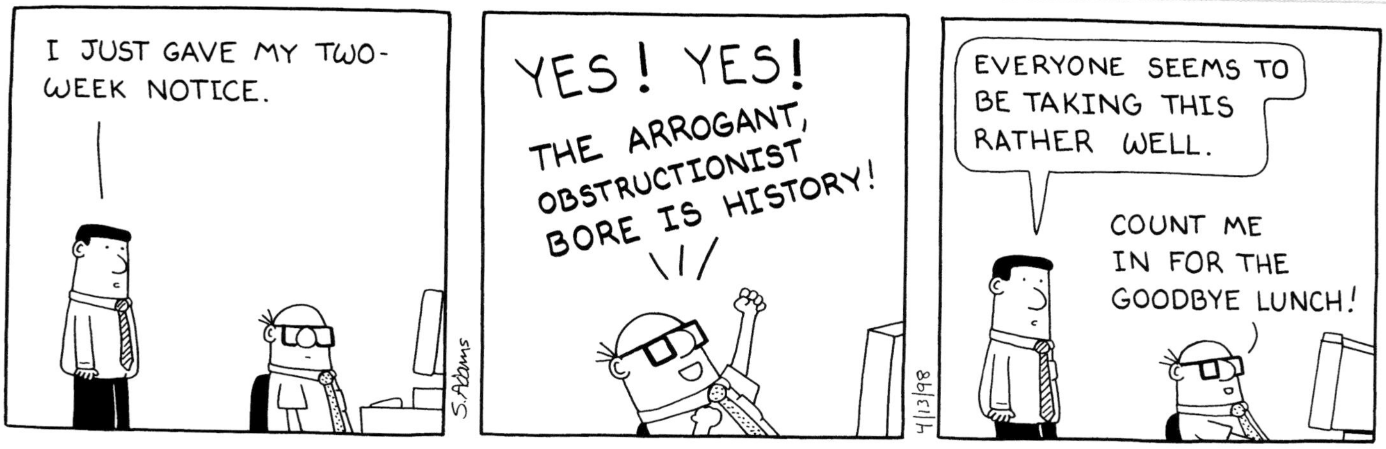
I JUST GAVE MY TWO-WEEK NOTICE.
S. Adams
YES! YES!
THE ARROGANT, OBSTRUCTIONIST BORE IS HISTORY!
4/13/98
EVERYONE SEEMS TO BE TAKING THIS RATHER WELL.
COUNT ME IN FOR THE GOODBYE LUNCH!

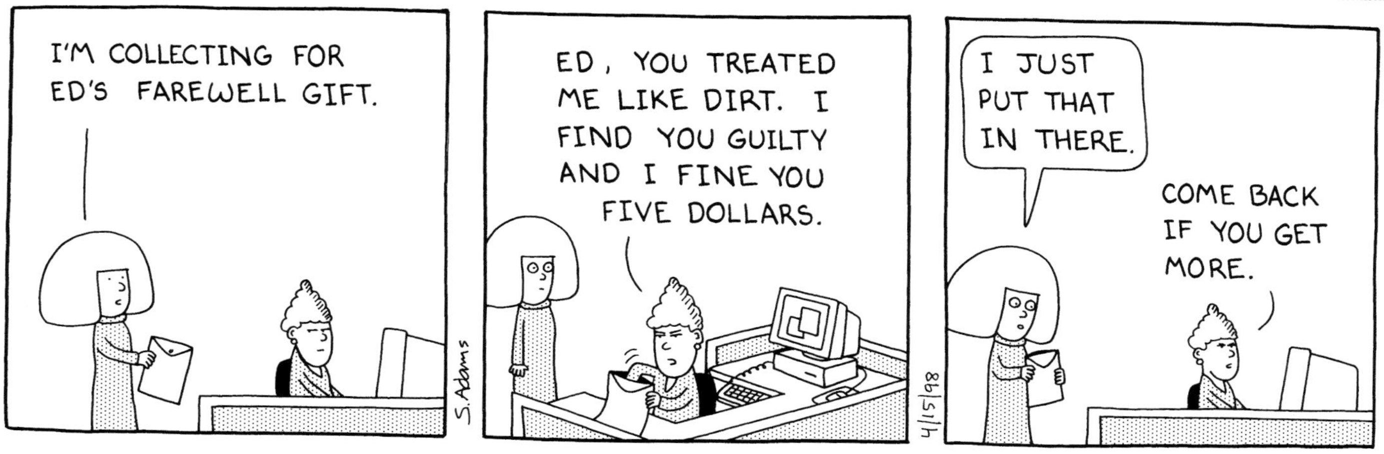
I'M COLLECTING FOR ED'S FAREWELL GIFT.
S. Adams
ED, YOU TREATED ME LIKE DIRT. I FIND YOU GUILTY AND I FINE YOU FIVE DOLLARS.
4/15/98
I JUST PUT THAT IN THERE.
COME BACK IF YOU GET MORE.

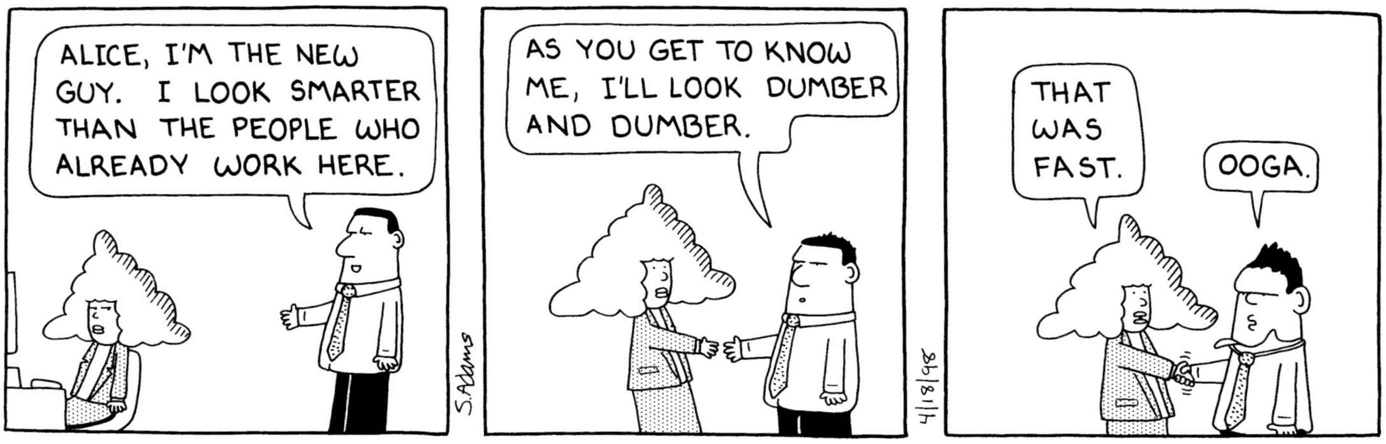
ALICE, I'M THE NEW GUY. I LOOK SMARTER THAN THE PEOPLE WHO ALREADY WORK HERE.
AS YOU GET TO KNOW ME, I'LL LOOK DUMBER AND DUMBER.
THAT WAS FAST.
OOGA.
S. Adams
4/18/98

I've drawn myself into the strip a few times. During this period, I was working about eighty hours a week.

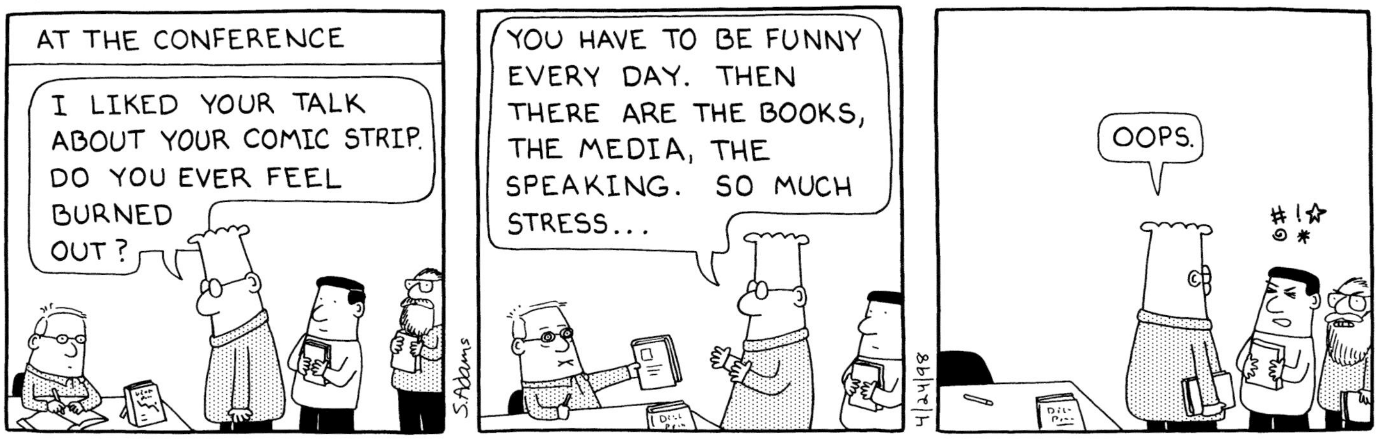
AT THE CONFERENCE
I LIKED YOUR TALK ABOUT YOUR COMIC STRIP. DO YOU EVER FEEL BURNED OUT?
YOU HAVE TO BE FUNNY EVERY DAY. THEN THERE ARE THE BOOKS, THE MEDIA, THE SPEAKING. SO MUCH STRESS...
OOPS.
S. Adams
4/24/98

The strip below is arguably the naughtiest comic I've ever drawn. But it was subtle enough to fly through the editorial filters.

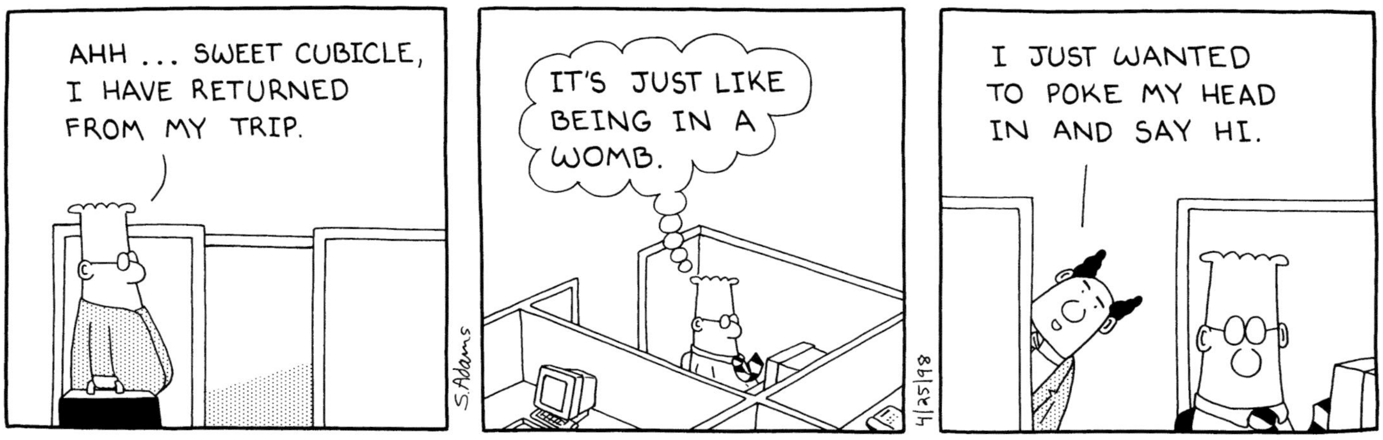
AHH ... SWEET CUBICLE, I HAVE RETURNED FROM MY TRIP.
IT'S JUST LIKE BEING IN A WOMB.
I JUST WANTED TO POKE MY HEAD IN AND SAY HI.
S. Adams
4/25/98

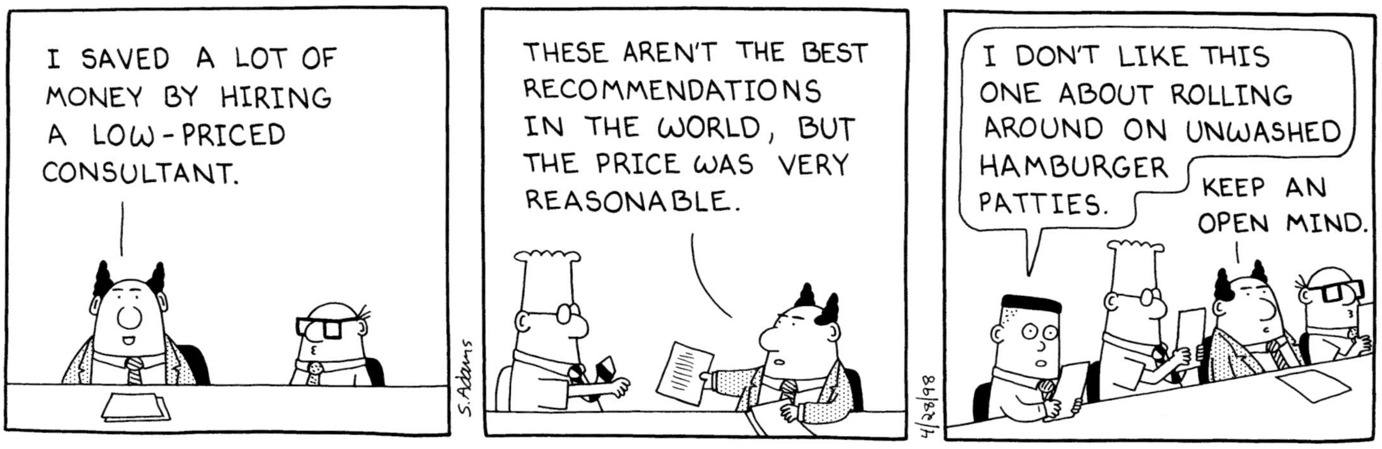
I SAVED A LOT OF MONEY BY HIRING A LOW-PRICED CONSULTANT.
THESE AREN'T THE BEST RECOMMENDATIONS IN THE WORLD, BUT THE PRICE WAS VERY REASONABLE.
I DON'T LIKE THIS ONE ABOUT ROLLING AROUND ON UNWASHED HAMBURGER PATTIES.
KEEP AN OPEN MIND.
S. Adams
4/28/98

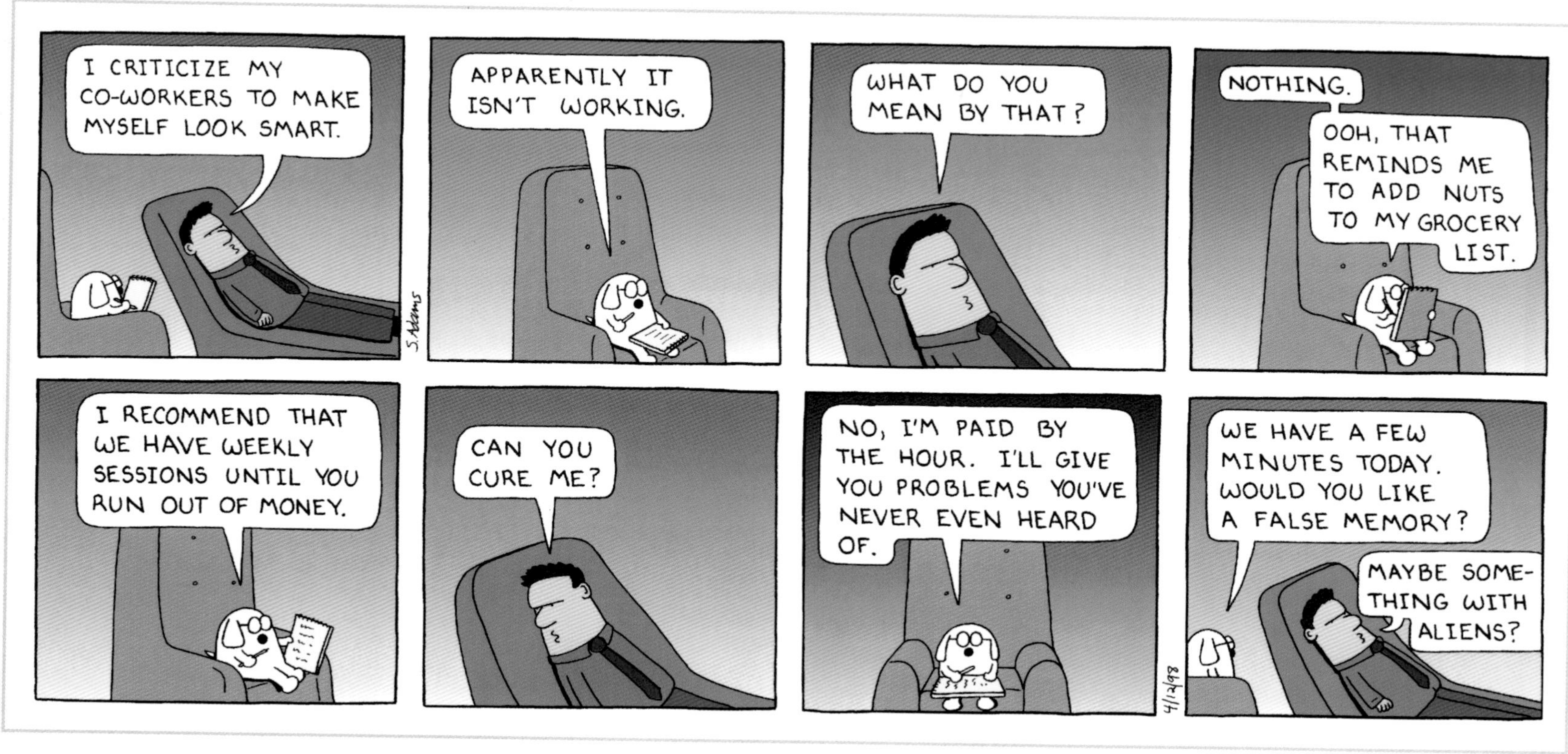
I CRITICIZE MY CO-WORKERS TO MAKE MYSELF LOOK SMART.
APPARENTLY IT ISN'T WORKING.
WHAT DO YOU MEAN BY THAT?
NOTHING.
OOH, THAT REMINDS ME TO ADD NUTS TO MY GROCERY LIST.
I RECOMMEND THAT WE HAVE WEEKLY SESSIONS UNTIL YOU RUN OUT OF MONEY.
CAN YOU CURE ME?
NO, I'M PAID BY THE HOUR. I'LL GIVE YOU PROBLEMS YOU'VE NEVER EVEN HEARD OF.
WE HAVE A FEW MINUTES TODAY. WOULD YOU LIKE A FALSE MEMORY?
MAYBE SOME-THING WITH ALIENS?
S. Adams
4/12/98

Amazingly, this comic was based on real events. Apparently the acoustic integrity of cubicles is an issue in some companies.

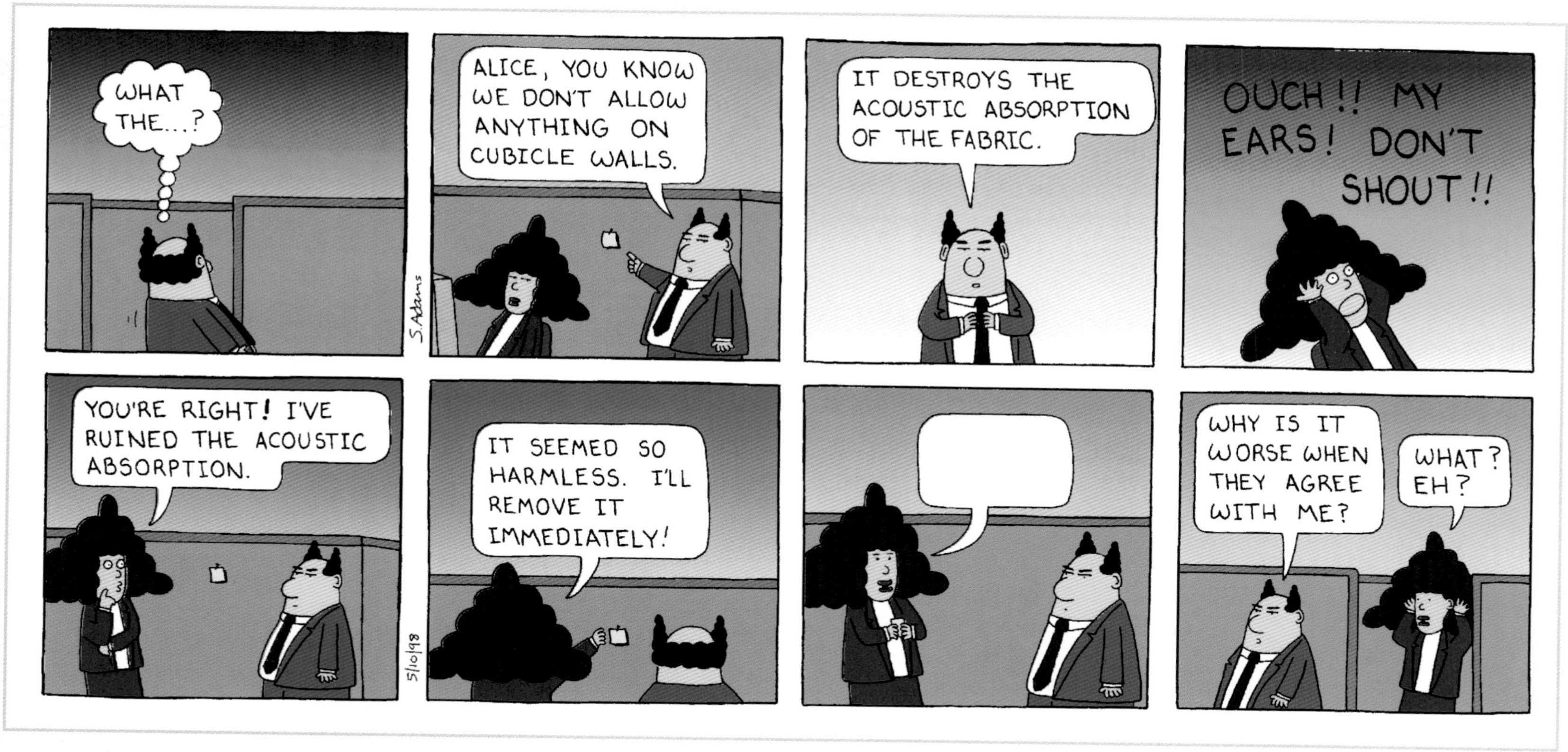
WHAT THE...?
ALICE, YOU KNOW WE DON'T ALLOW ANYTHING ON CUBICLE WALLS.
IT DESTROYS THE ACOUSTIC ABSORPTION OF THE FABRIC.
OUCH!! MY EARS! DON'T SHOUT!!
YOU'RE RIGHT! I'VE RUINED THE ACOUSTIC ABSORPTION.
IT SEEMED SO HARMLESS. I'LL REMOVE IT IMMEDIATELY!
WHY IS IT WORSE WHEN THEY AGREE WITH ME?
WHAT? EH?
S. Adams
5/10/98

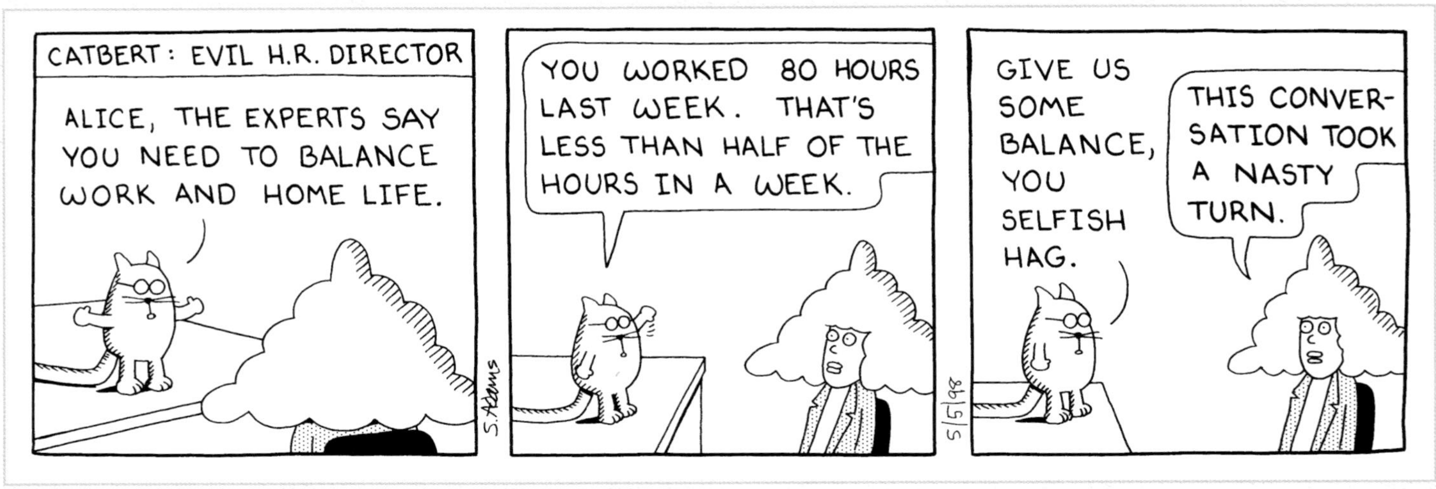
CATBERT: EVIL H.R. DIRECTOR
ALICE, THE EXPERTS SAY YOU NEED TO BALANCE WORK AND HOME LIFE.
YOU WORKED 80 HOURS LAST WEEK. THAT'S LESS THAN HALF OF THE HOURS IN A WEEK.
GIVE US SOME BALANCE, YOU SELFISH HAG.
THIS CONVERSATION TOOK A NASTY TURN.

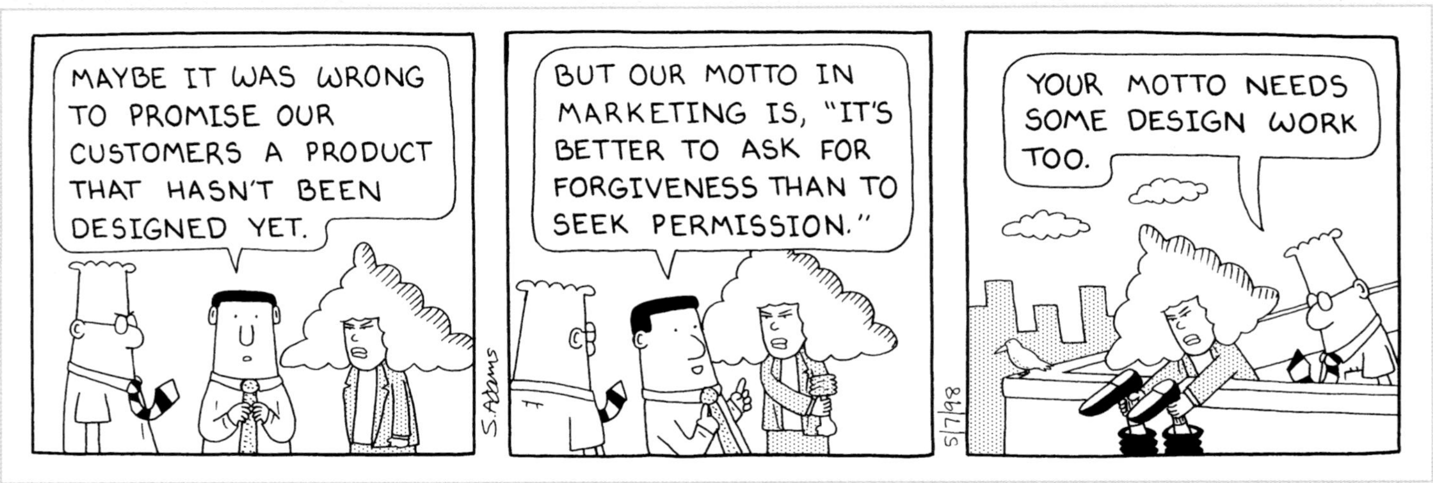
MAYBE IT WAS WRONG TO PROMISE OUR CUSTOMERS A PRODUCT THAT HASN'T BEEN DESIGNED YET.
BUT OUR MOTTO IN MARKETING IS, "IT'S BETTER TO ASK FOR FORGIVENESS THAN TO SEEK PERMISSION."
YOUR MOTTO NEEDS SOME DESIGN WORK TOO.

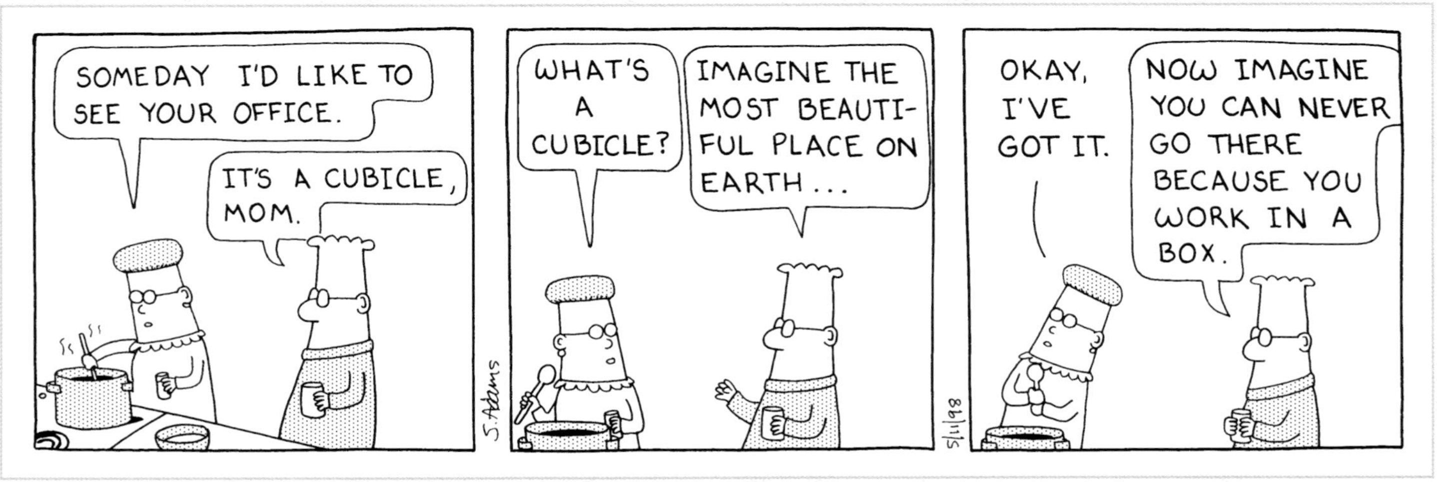
SOMEDAY I'D LIKE TO SEE YOUR OFFICE.
IT'S A CUBICLE, MOM.
WHAT'S A CUBICLE?
IMAGINE THE MOST BEAUTIFUL PLACE ON EARTH...
OKAY, I'VE GOT IT.
NOW IMAGINE YOU CAN NEVER GO THERE BECAUSE YOU WORK IN A BOX.

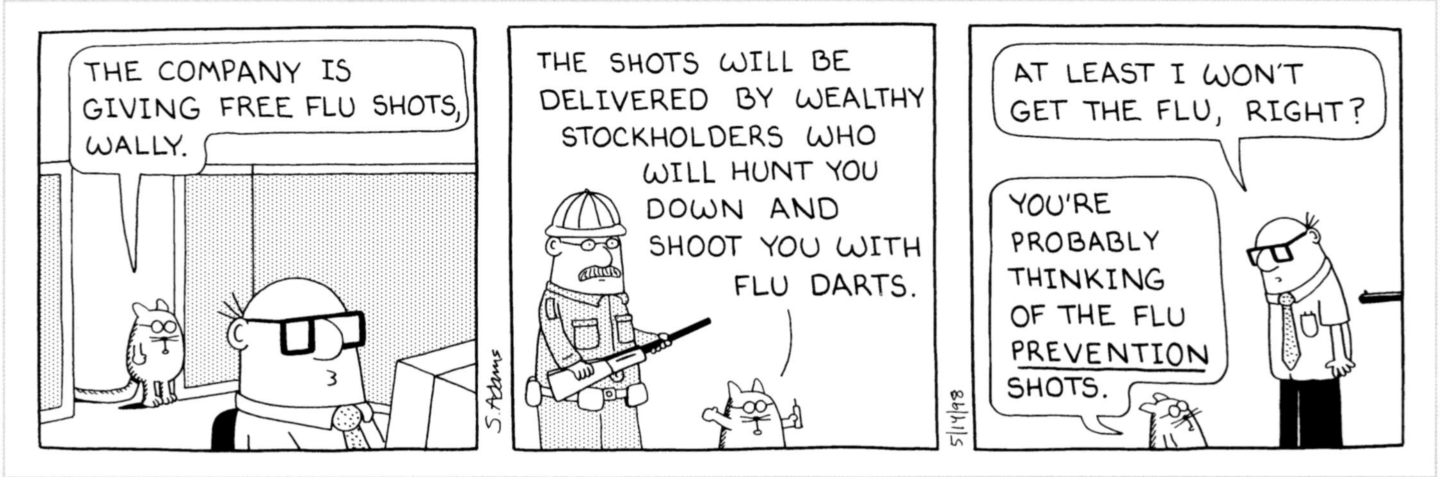
THE COMPANY IS GIVING FREE FLU SHOTS, WALLY.
THE SHOTS WILL BE DELIVERED BY WEALTHY STOCKHOLDERS WHO WILL HUNT YOU DOWN AND SHOOT YOU WITH FLU DARTS.
AT LEAST I WON'T GET THE FLU, RIGHT?
YOU'RE PROBABLY THINKING OF THE FLU PREVENTION SHOTS.

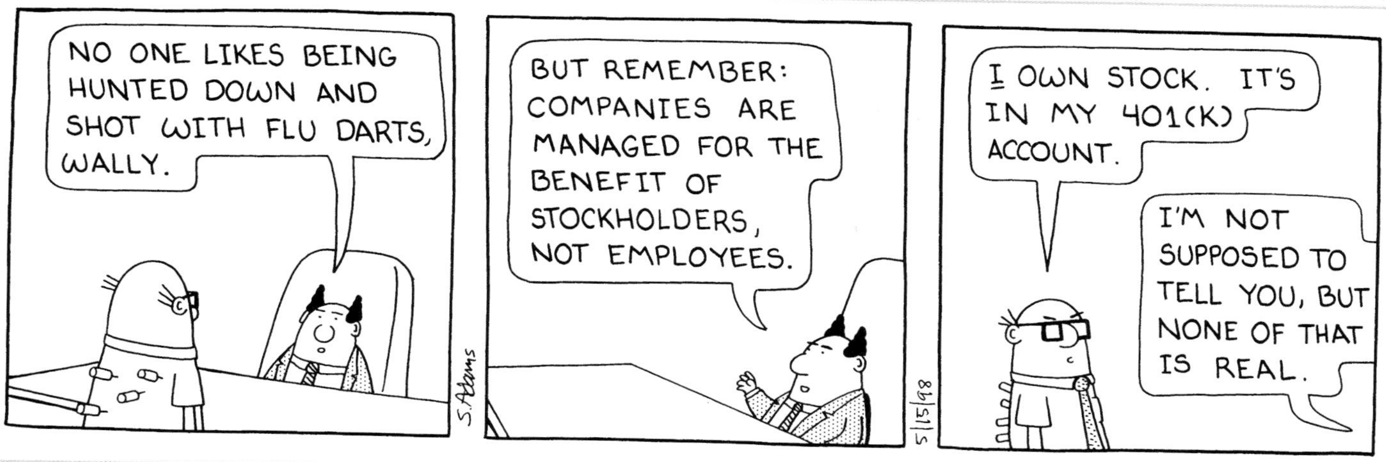
NO ONE LIKES BEING HUNTED DOWN AND SHOT WITH FLU DARTS, WALLY.
S. Adams
BUT REMEMBER: COMPANIES ARE MANAGED FOR THE BENEFIT OF STOCKHOLDERS, NOT EMPLOYEES.
5/15/98
I OWN STOCK. IT'S IN MY 401(K) ACCOUNT.
I'M NOT SUPPOSED TO TELL YOU, BUT NONE OF THAT IS REAL.

At this point in my career, I was getting flack from cartoonists who objected to my crass commercialism and minimal artistic talent. Bill Griffith, who does Zippy the Pinhead, *wrote an article about my lack of artistic integrity. This comic was my reply.*

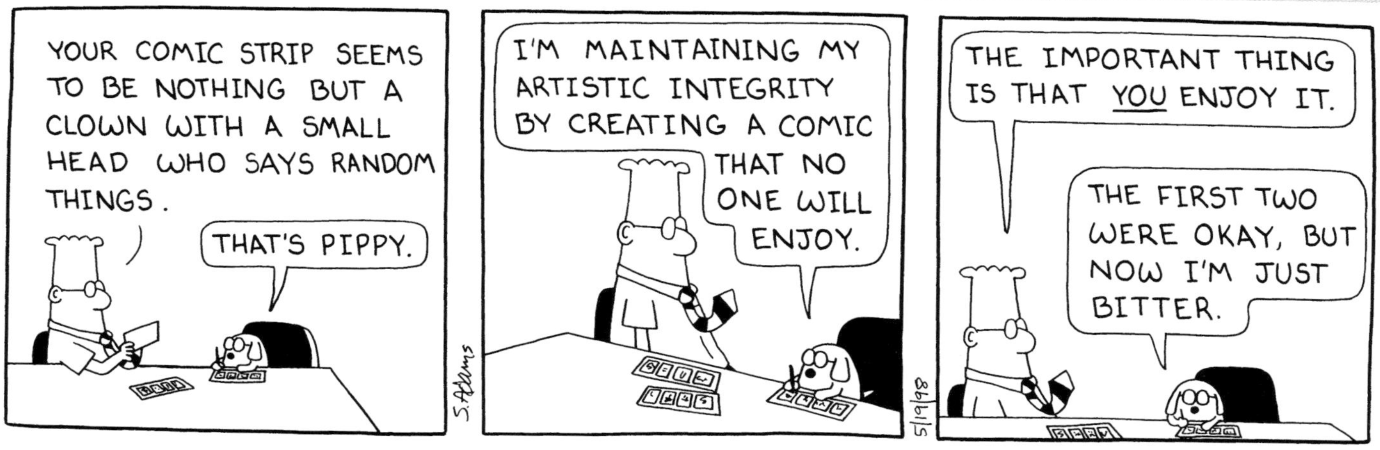
YOUR COMIC STRIP SEEMS TO BE NOTHING BUT A CLOWN WITH A SMALL HEAD WHO SAYS RANDOM THINGS.
THAT'S PIPPY.
S. Adams
I'M MAINTAINING MY ARTISTIC INTEGRITY BY CREATING A COMIC THAT NO ONE WILL ENJOY.
5/19/98
THE IMPORTANT THING IS THAT YOU ENJOY IT.
THE FIRST TWO WERE OKAY, BUT NOW I'M JUST BITTER.

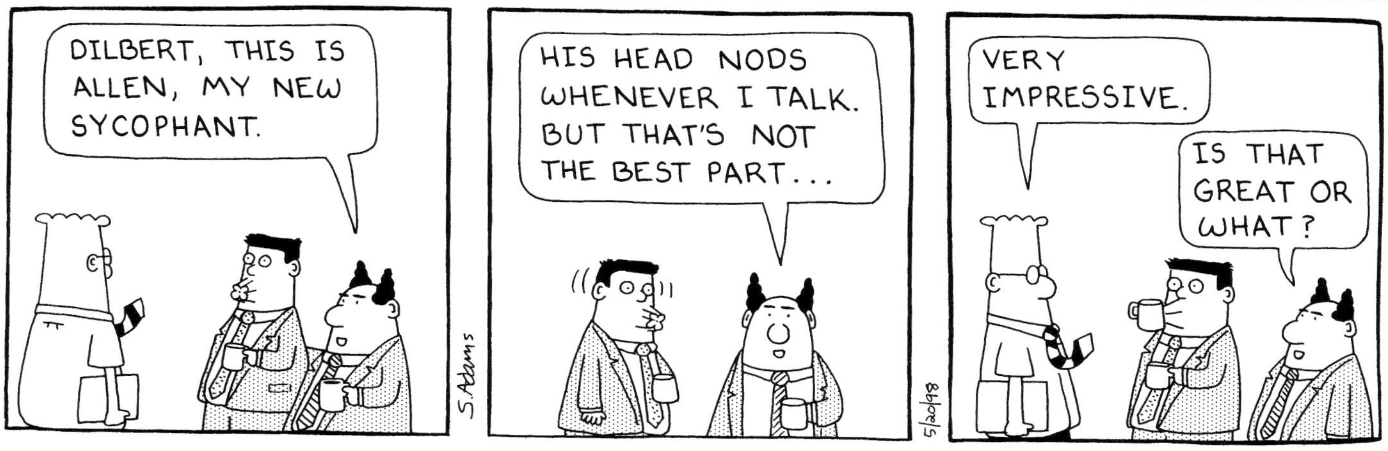
DILBERT, THIS IS ALLEN, MY NEW SYCOPHANT.
S. Adams
HIS HEAD NODS WHENEVER I TALK. BUT THAT'S NOT THE BEST PART...
5/20/98
VERY IMPRESSIVE.
IS THAT GREAT OR WHAT?

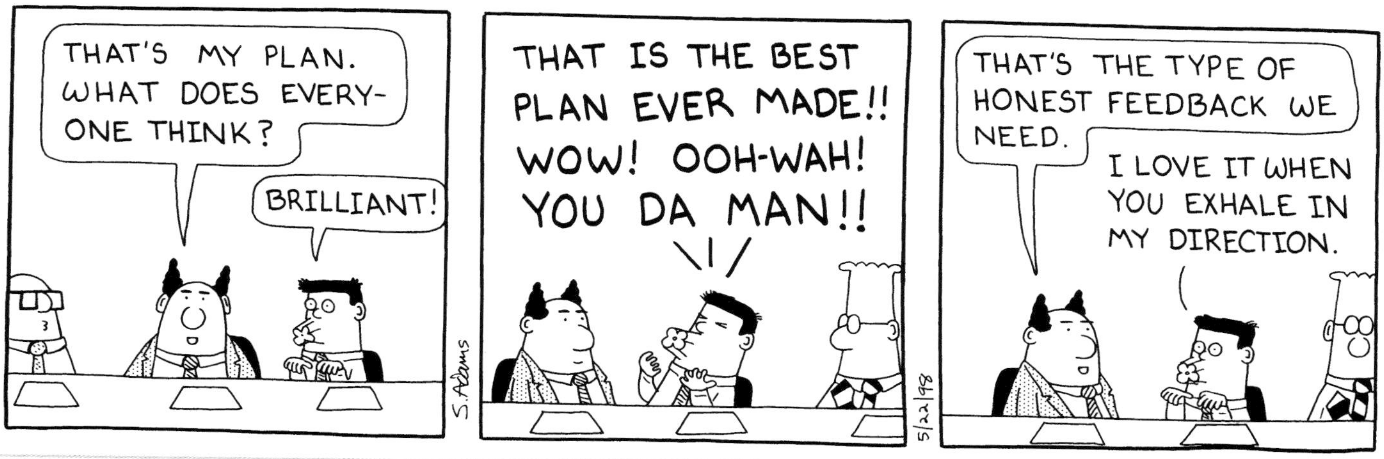
THAT'S MY PLAN. WHAT DOES EVERY-ONE THINK?
BRILLIANT!
S. Adams
THAT IS THE BEST PLAN EVER MADE!! WOW! OOH-WAH! YOU DA MAN!!
5/22/98
THAT'S THE TYPE OF HONEST FEEDBACK WE NEED.
I LOVE IT WHEN YOU EXHALE IN MY DIRECTION.

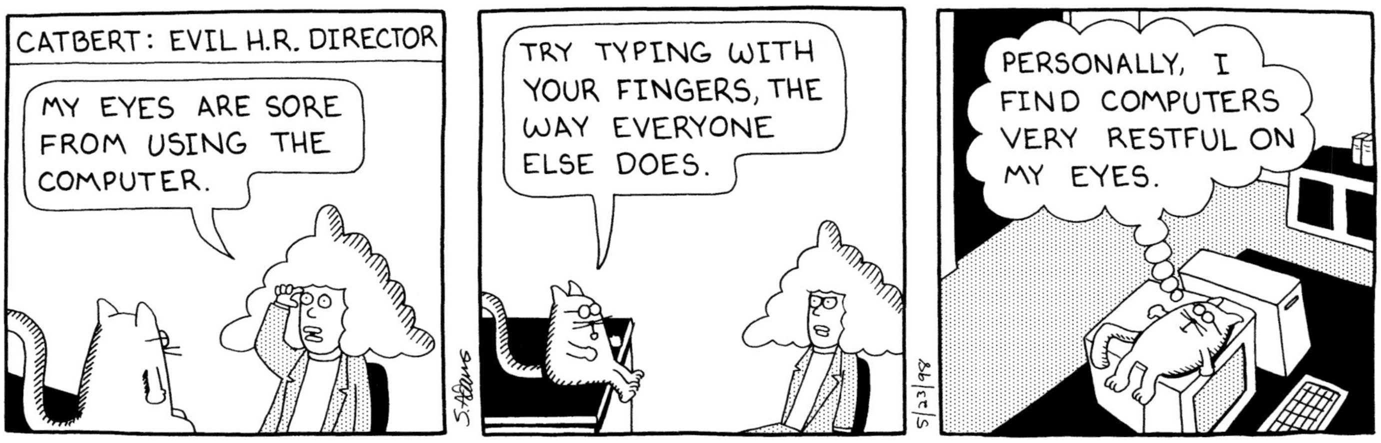
CATBERT: EVIL H.R. DIRECTOR
MY EYES ARE SORE FROM USING THE COMPUTER.
TRY TYPING WITH YOUR FINGERS, THE WAY EVERYONE ELSE DOES.
S. Adams
5/23/98
PERSONALLY, I FIND COMPUTERS VERY RESTFUL ON MY EYES.

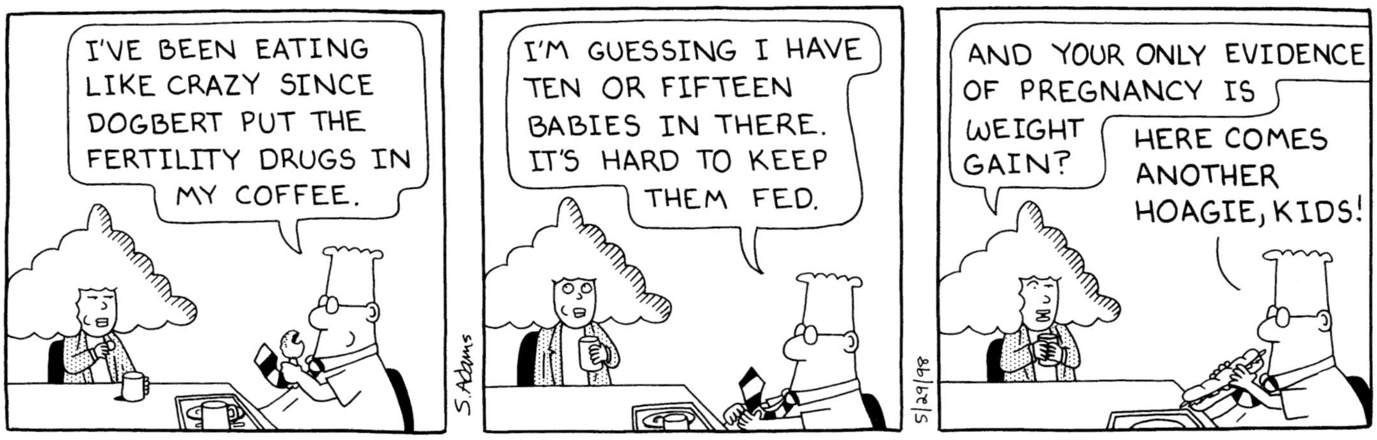
I'VE BEEN EATING LIKE CRAZY SINCE DOGBERT PUT THE FERTILITY DRUGS IN MY COFFEE.
I'M GUESSING I HAVE TEN OR FIFTEEN BABIES IN THERE. IT'S HARD TO KEEP THEM FED.
S. Adams
5/29/98
AND YOUR ONLY EVIDENCE OF PREGNANCY IS WEIGHT GAIN?
HERE COMES ANOTHER HOAGIE, KIDS!

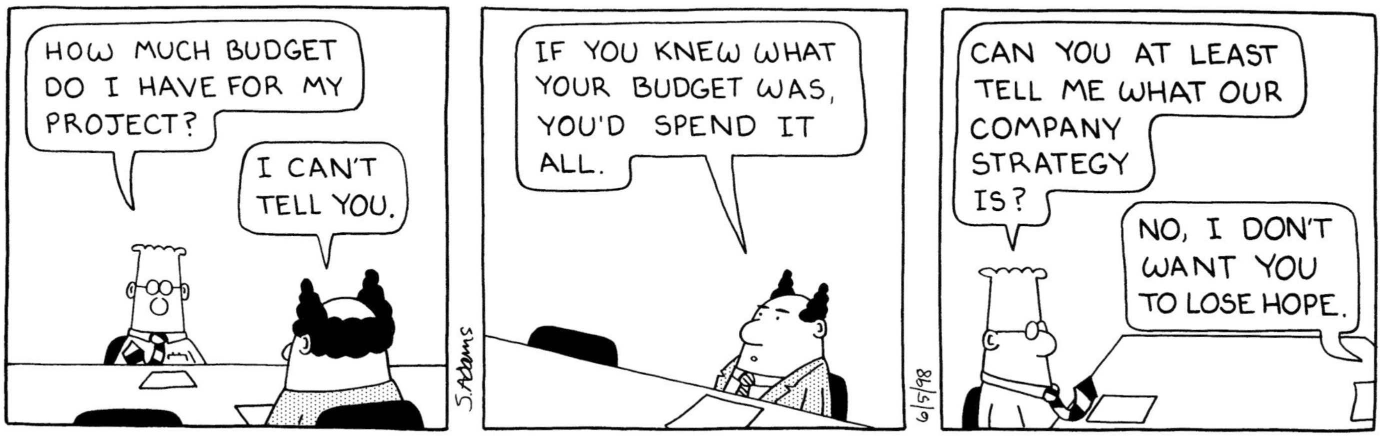
HOW MUCH BUDGET DO I HAVE FOR MY PROJECT?
I CAN'T TELL YOU.
IF YOU KNEW WHAT YOUR BUDGET WAS, YOU'D SPEND IT ALL.
S. Adams
6/5/98
CAN YOU AT LEAST TELL ME WHAT OUR COMPANY STRATEGY IS?
NO, I DON'T WANT YOU TO LOSE HOPE.

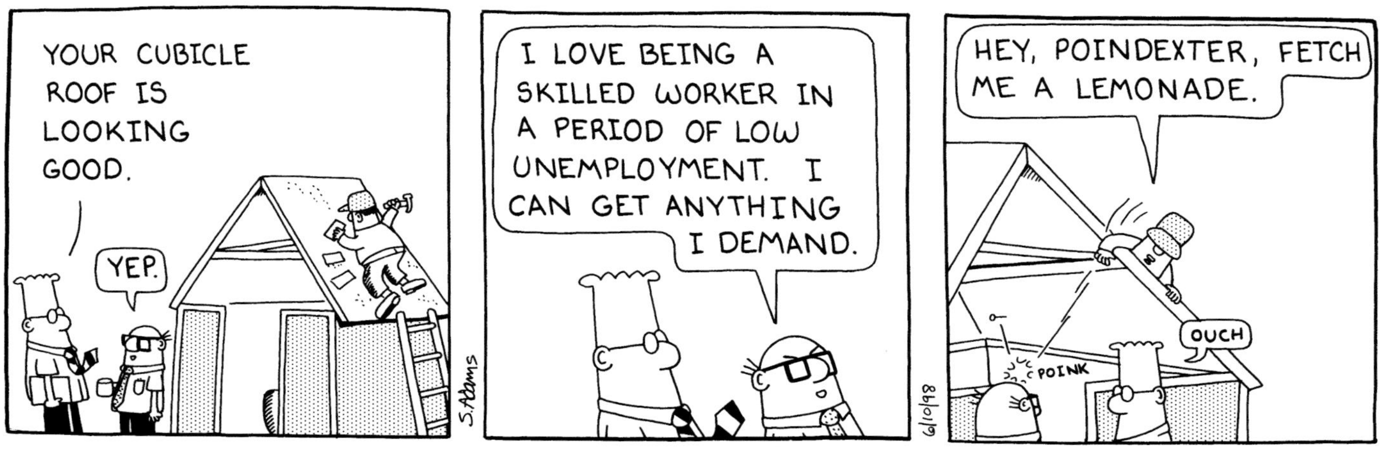
YOUR CUBICLE ROOF IS LOOKING GOOD.
YEP.
I LOVE BEING A SKILLED WORKER IN A PERIOD OF LOW UNEMPLOYMENT. I CAN GET ANYTHING I DEMAND.
S. Adams
6/10/98
HEY, POINDEXTER, FETCH ME A LEMONADE.
OUCH
POINK

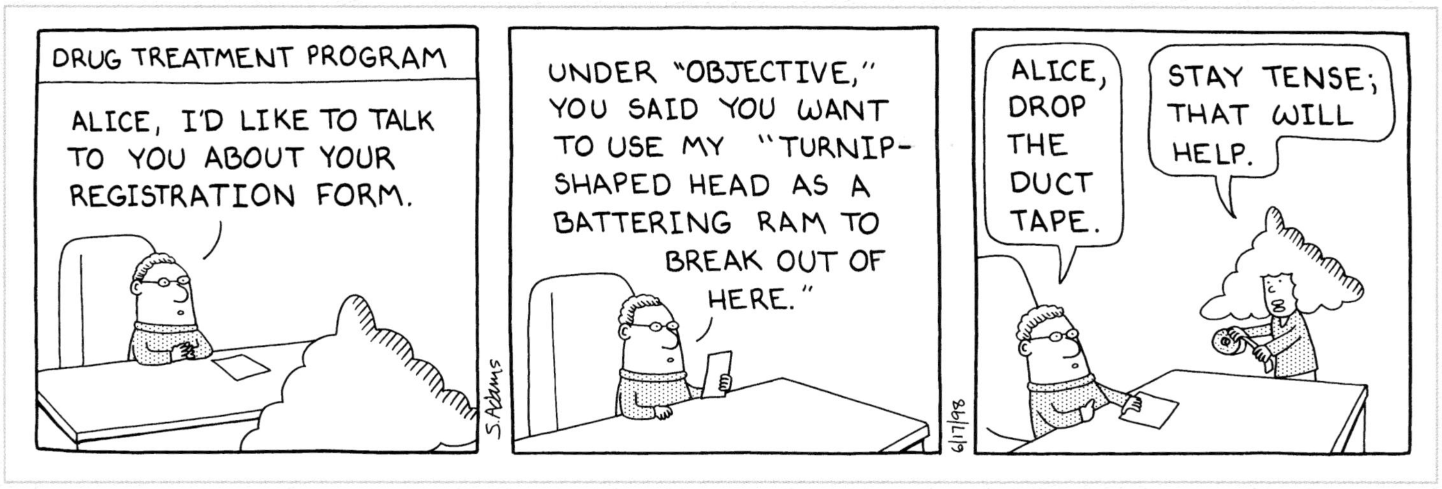
DRUG TREATMENT PROGRAM
ALICE, I'D LIKE TO TALK TO YOU ABOUT YOUR REGISTRATION FORM.
S. Adams
UNDER "OBJECTIVE," YOU SAID YOU WANT TO USE MY "TURNIP-SHAPED HEAD AS A BATTERING RAM TO BREAK OUT OF HERE."
6/17/98
ALICE, DROP THE DUCT TAPE.
STAY TENSE; THAT WILL HELP.

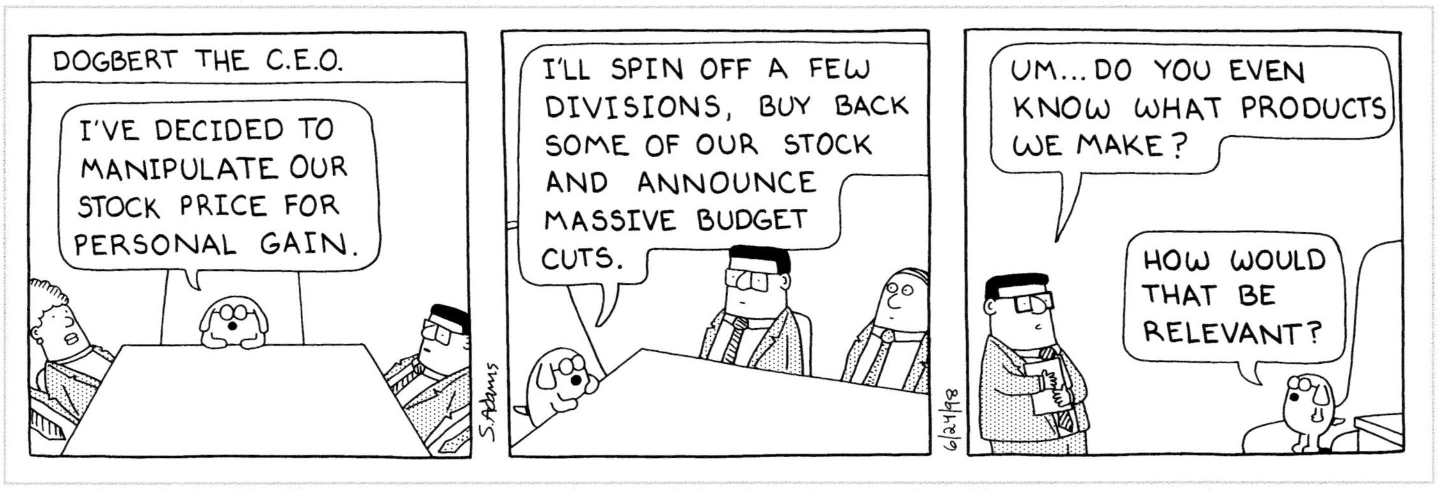
DOGBERT THE C.E.O.
I'VE DECIDED TO MANIPULATE OUR STOCK PRICE FOR PERSONAL GAIN.
S. Adams
I'LL SPIN OFF A FEW DIVISIONS, BUY BACK SOME OF OUR STOCK AND ANNOUNCE MASSIVE BUDGET CUTS.
6/24/98
UM... DO YOU EVEN KNOW WHAT PRODUCTS WE MAKE?
HOW WOULD THAT BE RELEVANT?

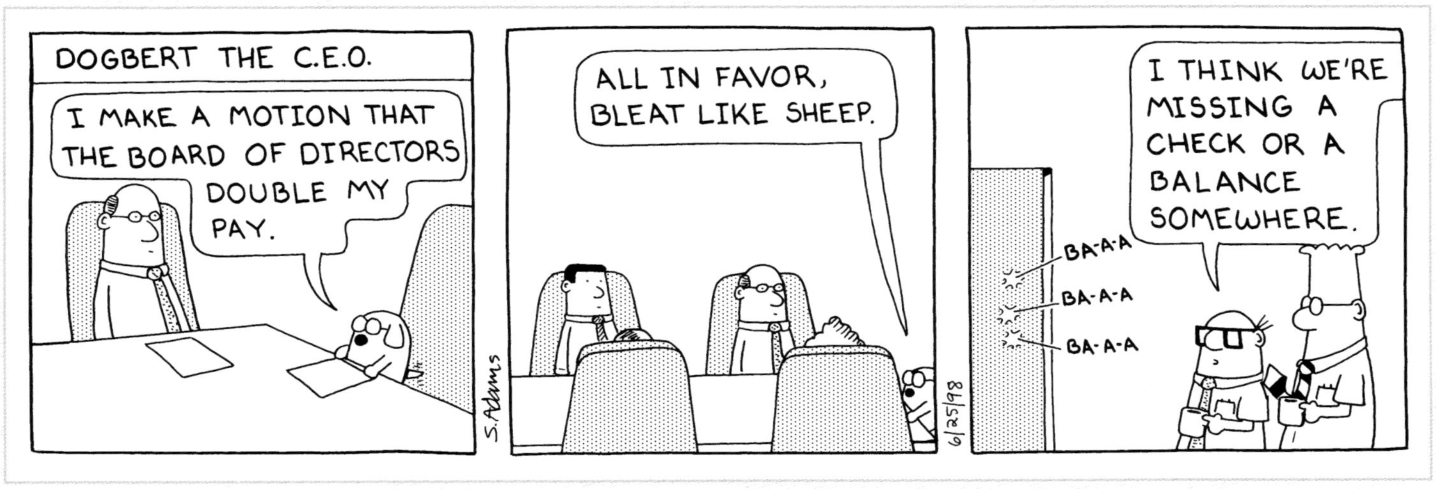
DOGBERT THE C.E.O.
I MAKE A MOTION THAT THE BOARD OF DIRECTORS DOUBLE MY PAY.
S. Adams
ALL IN FAVOR, BLEAT LIKE SHEEP.
6/25/98
BA-A-A
BA-A-A
BA-A-A
I THINK WE'RE MISSING A CHECK OR A BALANCE SOMEWHERE.

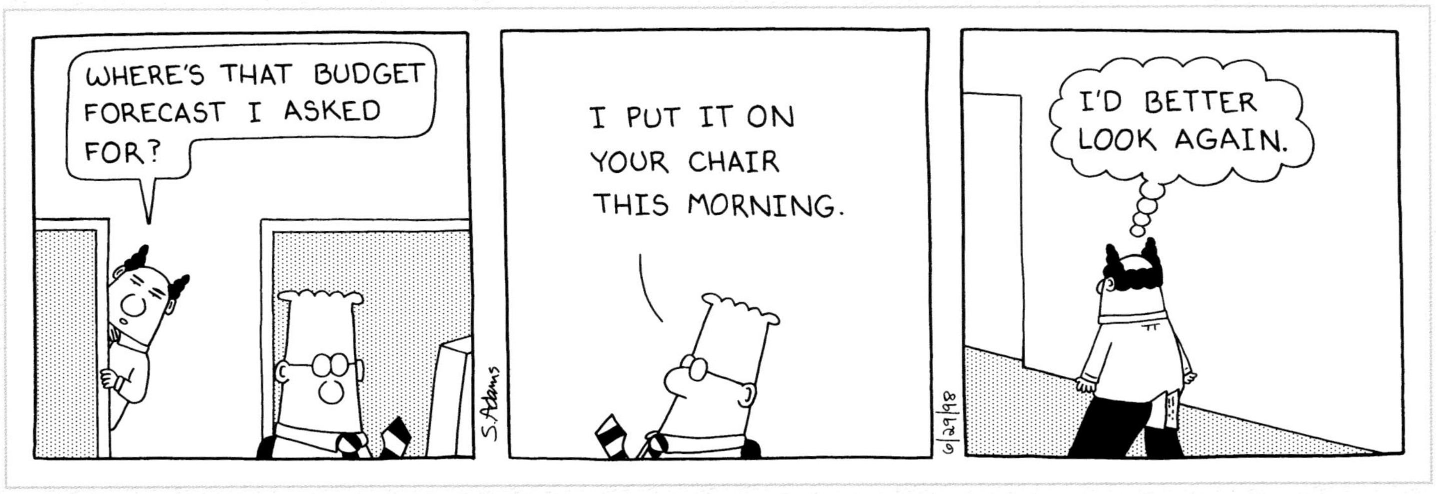
WHERE'S THAT BUDGET FORECAST I ASKED FOR?
S. Adams
I PUT IT ON YOUR CHAIR THIS MORNING.
6/29/98
I'D BETTER LOOK AGAIN.

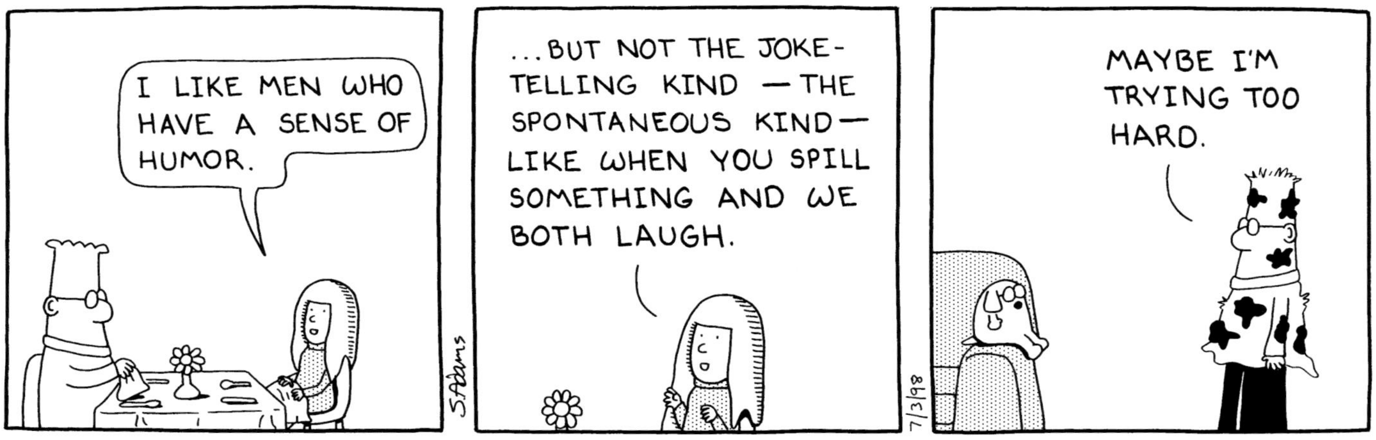
I LIKE MEN WHO HAVE A SENSE OF HUMOR.
...BUT NOT THE JOKE-TELLING KIND —THE SPONTANEOUS KIND— LIKE WHEN YOU SPILL SOMETHING AND WE BOTH LAUGH.
MAYBE I'M TRYING TOO HARD.
S.Adams
7/3/98

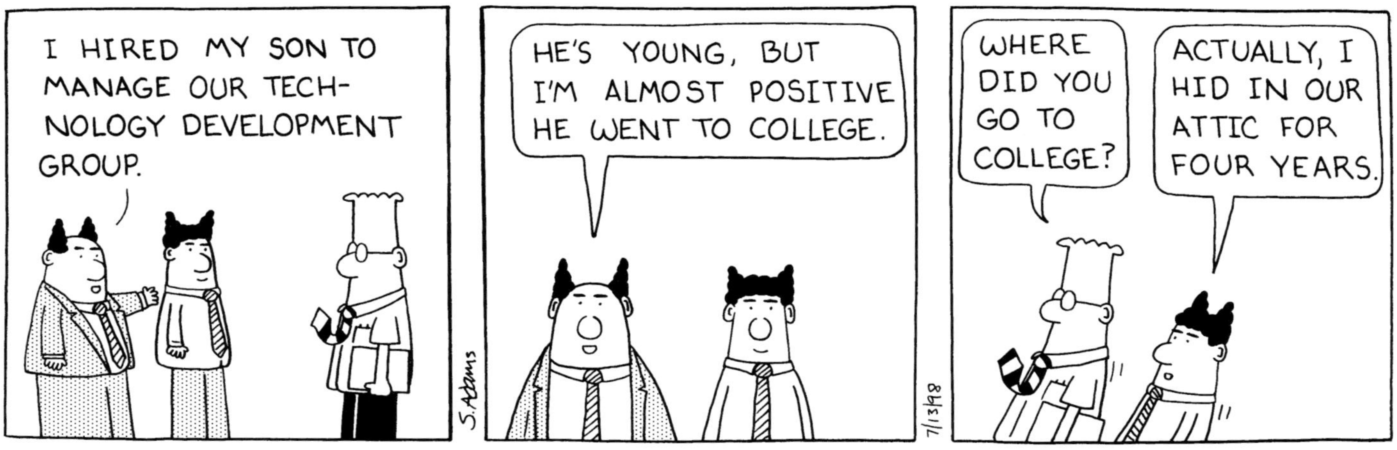
I HIRED MY SON TO MANAGE OUR TECH-NOLOGY DEVELOPMENT GROUP.
HE'S YOUNG, BUT I'M ALMOST POSITIVE HE WENT TO COLLEGE.
WHERE DID YOU GO TO COLLEGE?
ACTUALLY, I HID IN OUR ATTIC FOR FOUR YEARS.
S.Adams
7/13/98

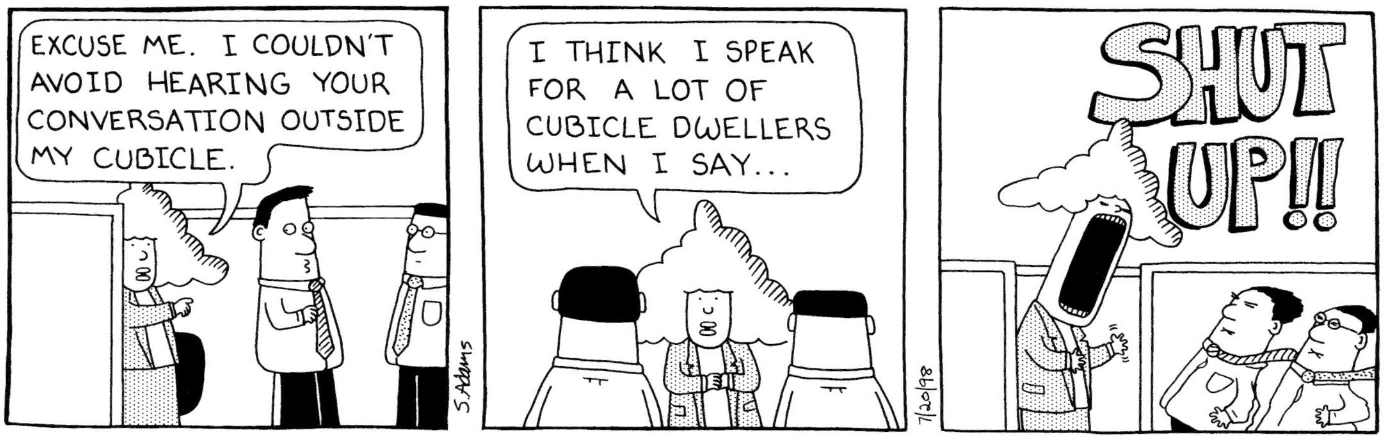
EXCUSE ME. I COULDN'T AVOID HEARING YOUR CONVERSATION OUTSIDE MY CUBICLE.
I THINK I SPEAK FOR A LOT OF CUBICLE DWELLERS WHEN I SAY...
SHUT UP!!
S.Adams
7/20/98

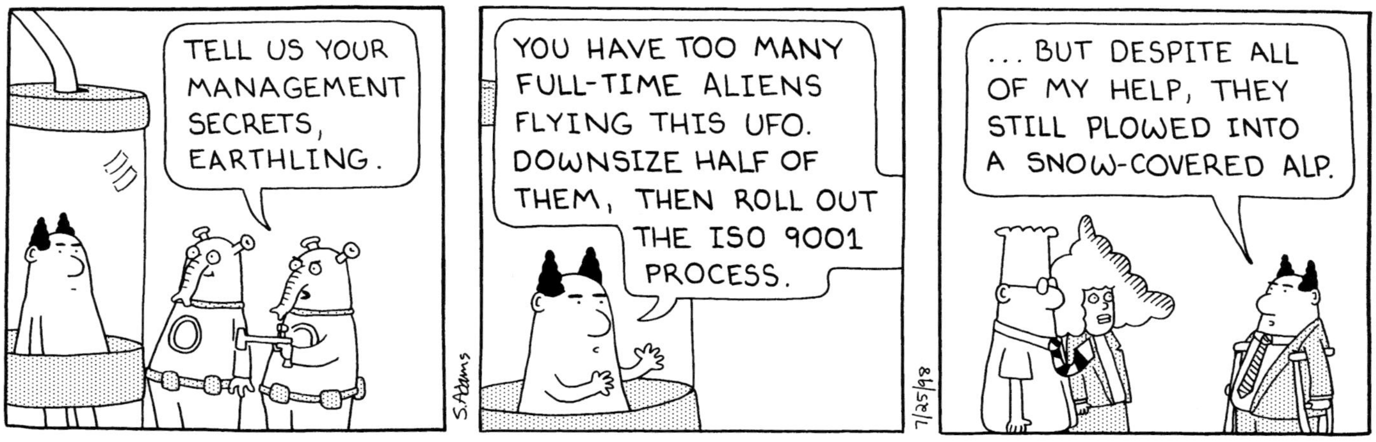
TELL US YOUR MANAGEMENT SECRETS, EARTHLING.
YOU HAVE TOO MANY FULL-TIME ALIENS FLYING THIS UFO. DOWNSIZE HALF OF THEM, THEN ROLL OUT THE ISO 9001 PROCESS.
... BUT DESPITE ALL OF MY HELP, THEY STILL PLOWED INTO A SNOW-COVERED ALP.
S.Adams
7/25/98

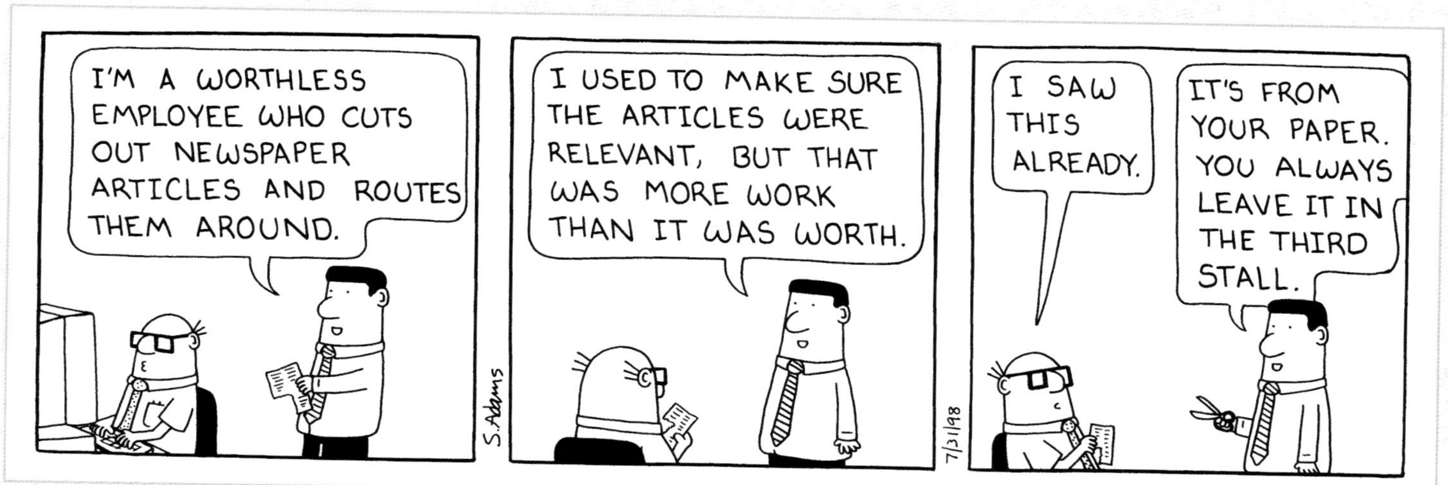
I'M A WORTHLESS EMPLOYEE WHO CUTS OUT NEWSPAPER ARTICLES AND ROUTES THEM AROUND.
I USED TO MAKE SURE THE ARTICLES WERE RELEVANT, BUT THAT WAS MORE WORK THAN IT WAS WORTH.
S. Adams
7/31/98
I SAW THIS ALREADY.
IT'S FROM YOUR PAPER. YOU ALWAYS LEAVE IT IN THE THIRD STALL.

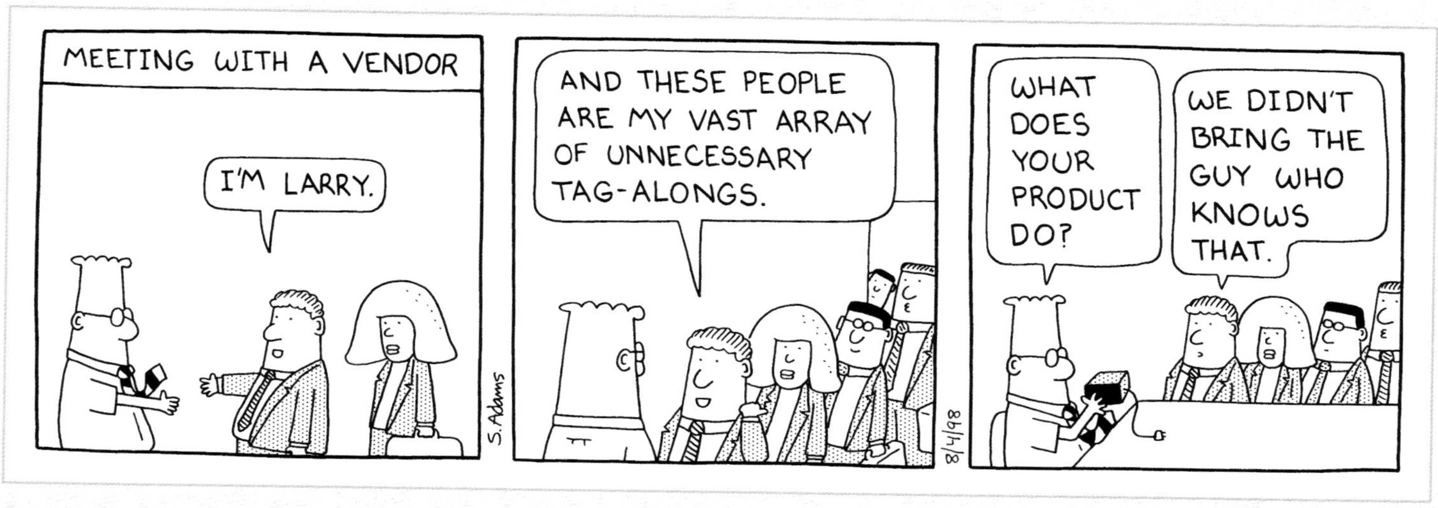
MEETING WITH A VENDOR
I'M LARRY.
AND THESE PEOPLE ARE MY VAST ARRAY OF UNNECESSARY TAG-ALONGS.
S. Adams
8/4/98
WHAT DOES YOUR PRODUCT DO?
WE DIDN'T BRING THE GUY WHO KNOWS THAT.

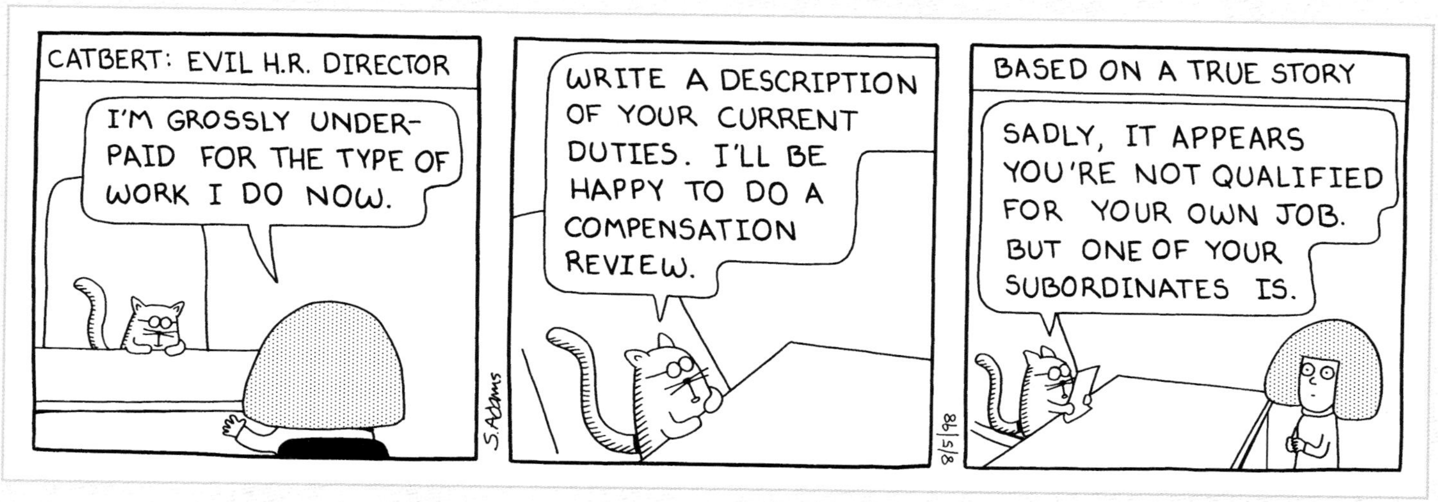
CATBERT: EVIL H.R. DIRECTOR
I'M GROSSLY UNDER-PAID FOR THE TYPE OF WORK I DO NOW.
WRITE A DESCRIPTION OF YOUR CURRENT DUTIES. I'LL BE HAPPY TO DO A COMPENSATION REVIEW.
S. Adams
8/5/98
BASED ON A TRUE STORY
SADLY, IT APPEARS YOU'RE NOT QUALIFIED FOR YOUR OWN JOB. BUT ONE OF YOUR SUBORDINATES IS.

I added "based on a true story" to the third panel because the strip is only funny if you realize this actually happened to someone. It did.

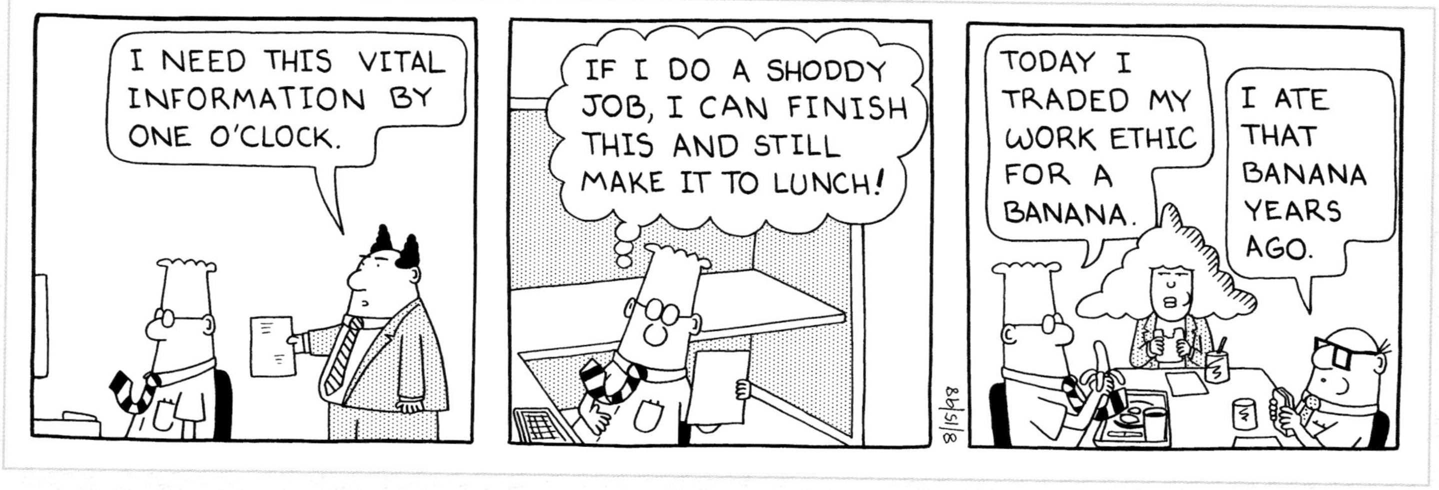
I NEED THIS VITAL INFORMATION BY ONE O'CLOCK.
IF I DO A SHODDY JOB, I CAN FINISH THIS AND STILL MAKE IT TO LUNCH!
8/15/98
TODAY I TRADED MY WORK ETHIC FOR A BANANA.
I ATE THAT BANANA YEARS AGO.

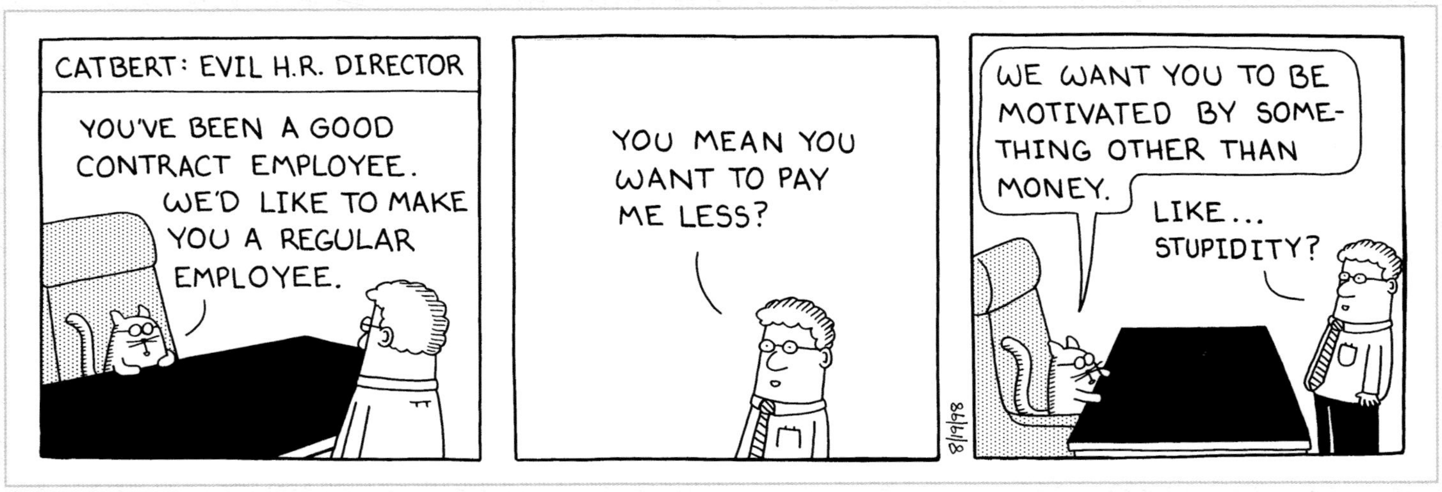
CATBERT: EVIL H.R. DIRECTOR
YOU'VE BEEN A GOOD CONTRACT EMPLOYEE. WE'D LIKE TO MAKE YOU A REGULAR EMPLOYEE.
YOU MEAN YOU WANT TO PAY ME LESS?
WE WANT YOU TO BE MOTIVATED BY SOMETHING OTHER THAN MONEY.
LIKE... STUPIDITY?
8/19/98

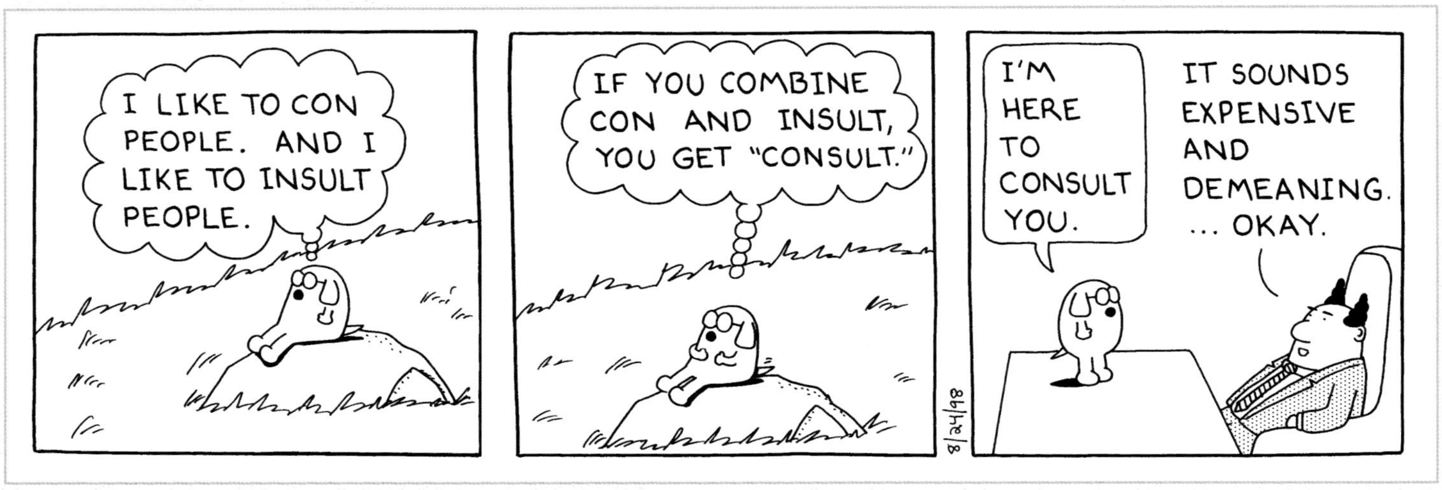
I LIKE TO CON PEOPLE. AND I LIKE TO INSULT PEOPLE.
IF YOU COMBINE CON AND INSULT, YOU GET "CONSULT."
I'M HERE TO CONSULT YOU.
IT SOUNDS EXPENSIVE AND DEMEANING. ... OKAY.
8/24/98

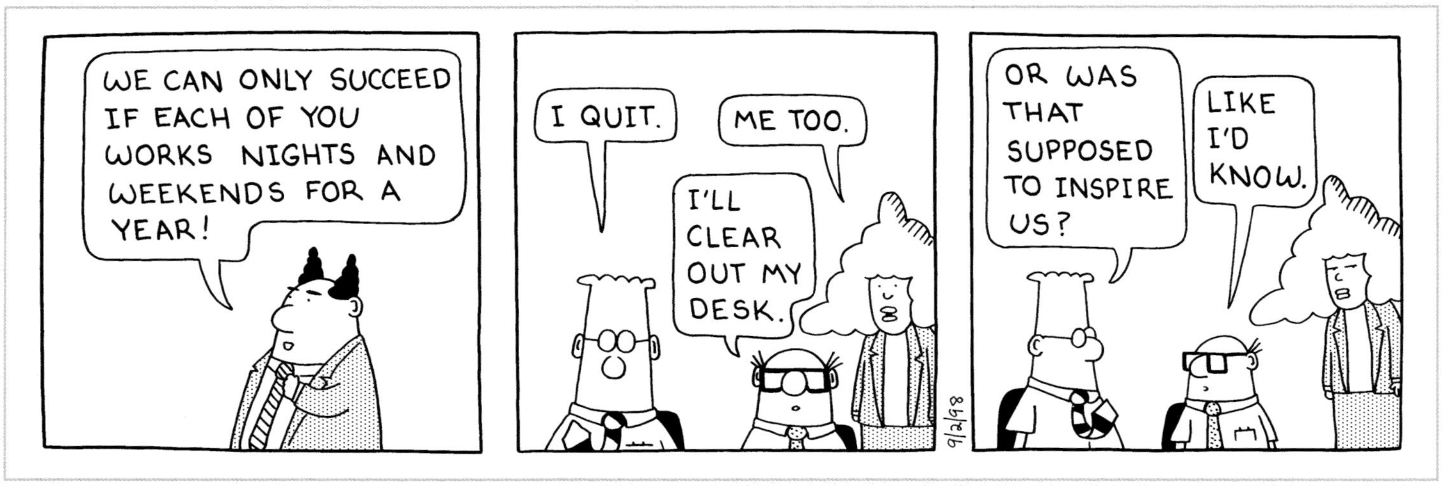
WE CAN ONLY SUCCEED IF EACH OF YOU WORKS NIGHTS AND WEEKENDS FOR A YEAR!
I QUIT.
ME TOO.
I'LL CLEAR OUT MY DESK.
OR WAS THAT SUPPOSED TO INSPIRE US?
LIKE I'D KNOW.
9/2/98

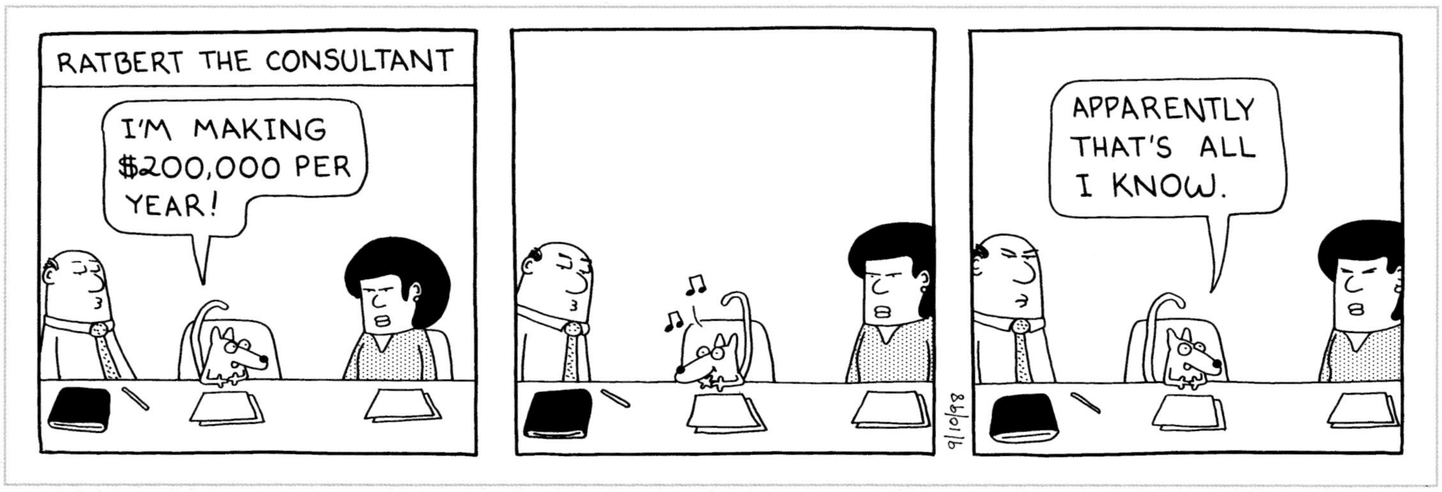
RATBERT THE CONSULTANT
I'M MAKING $200,000 PER YEAR!
APPARENTLY THAT'S ALL I KNOW.
9/10/98

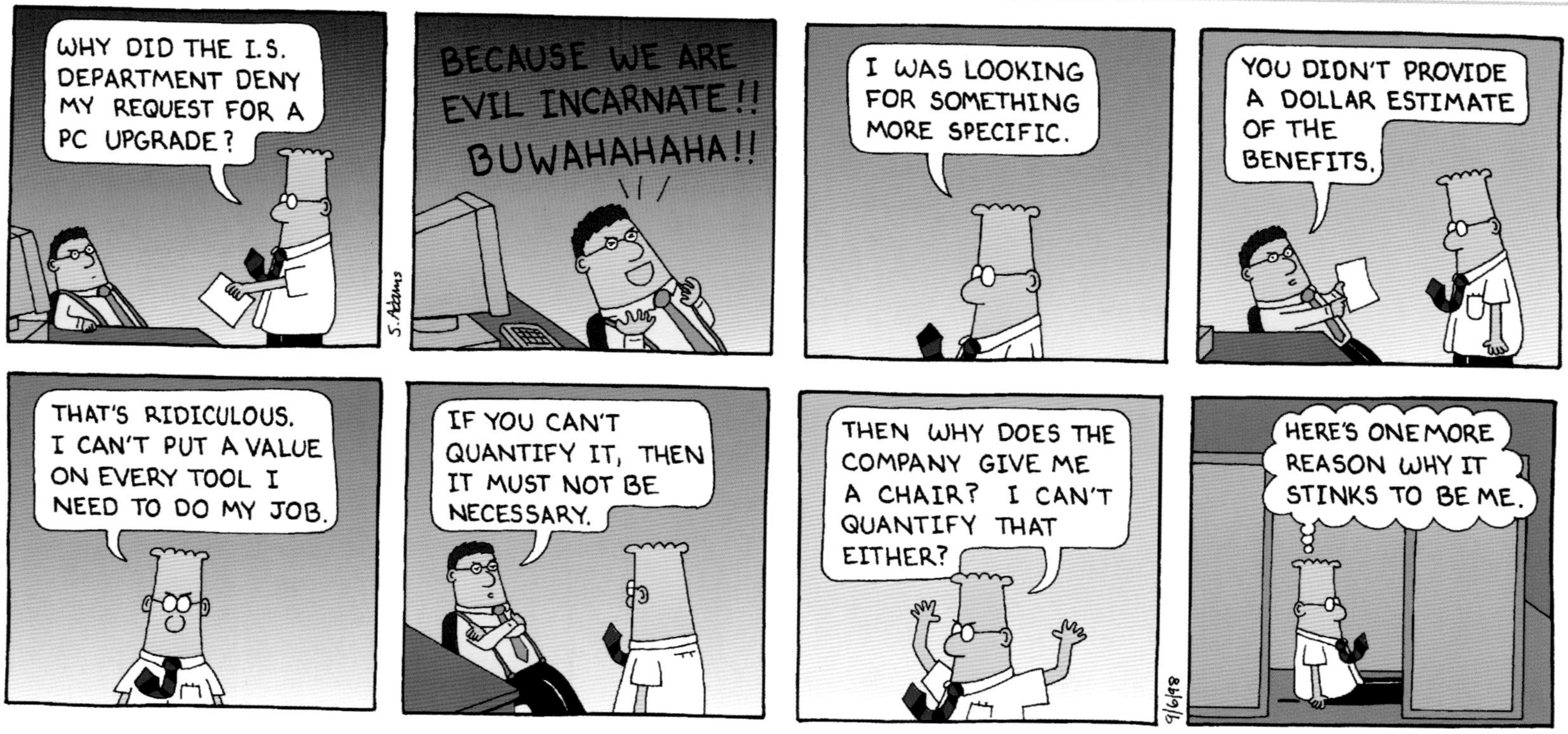
WHY DID THE I.S. DEPARTMENT DENY MY REQUEST FOR A PC UPGRADE?
BECAUSE WE ARE EVIL INCARNATE!! BUWAHAHAHA!!
I WAS LOOKING FOR SOMETHING MORE SPECIFIC.
YOU DIDN'T PROVIDE A DOLLAR ESTIMATE OF THE BENEFITS.
THAT'S RIDICULOUS. I CAN'T PUT A VALUE ON EVERY TOOL I NEED TO DO MY JOB.
IF YOU CAN'T QUANTIFY IT, THEN IT MUST NOT BE NECESSARY.
THEN WHY DOES THE COMPANY GIVE ME A CHAIR? I CAN'T QUANTIFY THAT EITHER?
HERE'S ONE MORE REASON WHY IT STINKS TO BE ME.

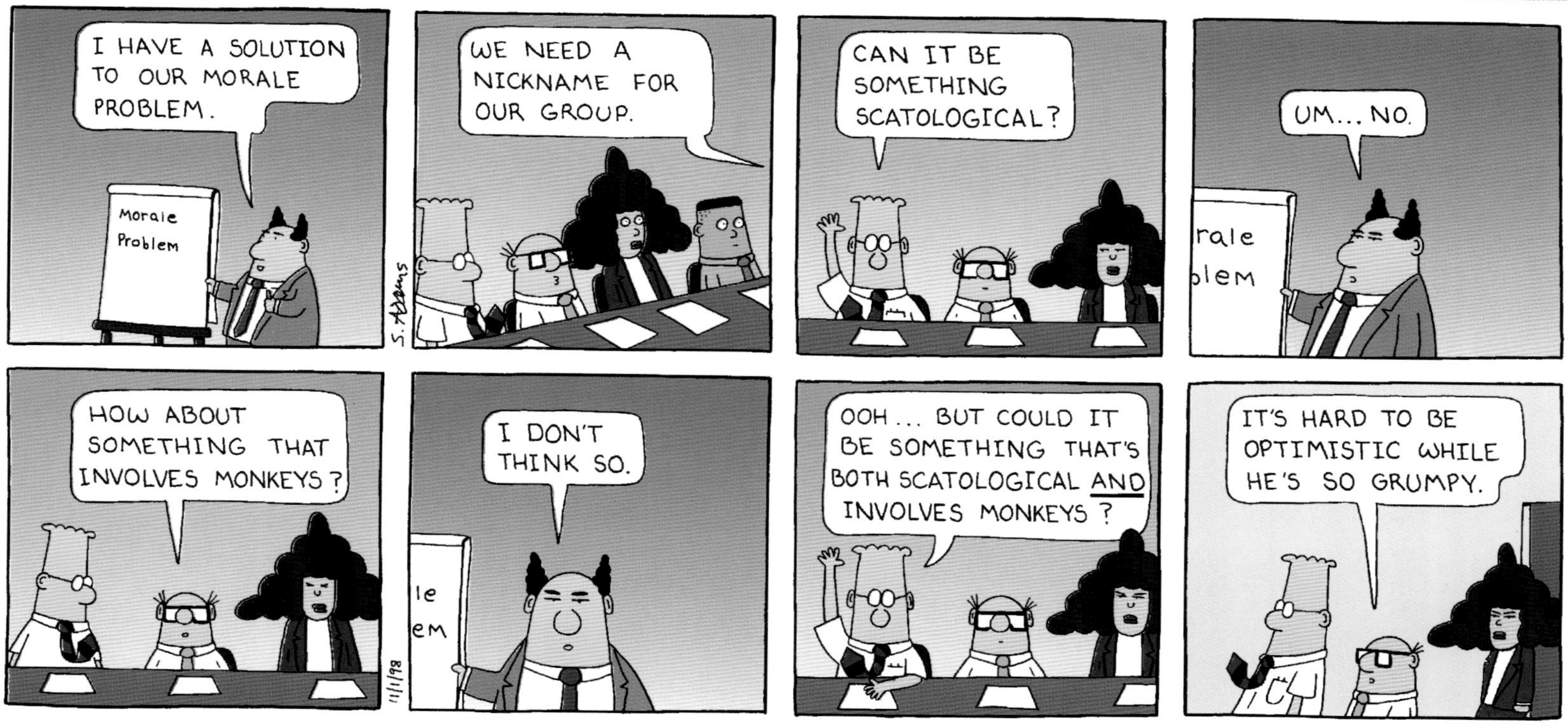
I HAVE A SOLUTION TO OUR MORALE PROBLEM.
Morale Problem
WE NEED A NICKNAME FOR OUR GROUP.
CAN IT BE SOMETHING SCATOLOGICAL?
UM... NO.
HOW ABOUT SOMETHING THAT INVOLVES MONKEYS?
I DON'T THINK SO.
OOH... BUT COULD IT BE SOMETHING THAT'S BOTH SCATOLOGICAL AND INVOLVES MONKEYS?
IT'S HARD TO BE OPTIMISTIC WHILE HE'S SO GRUMPY.

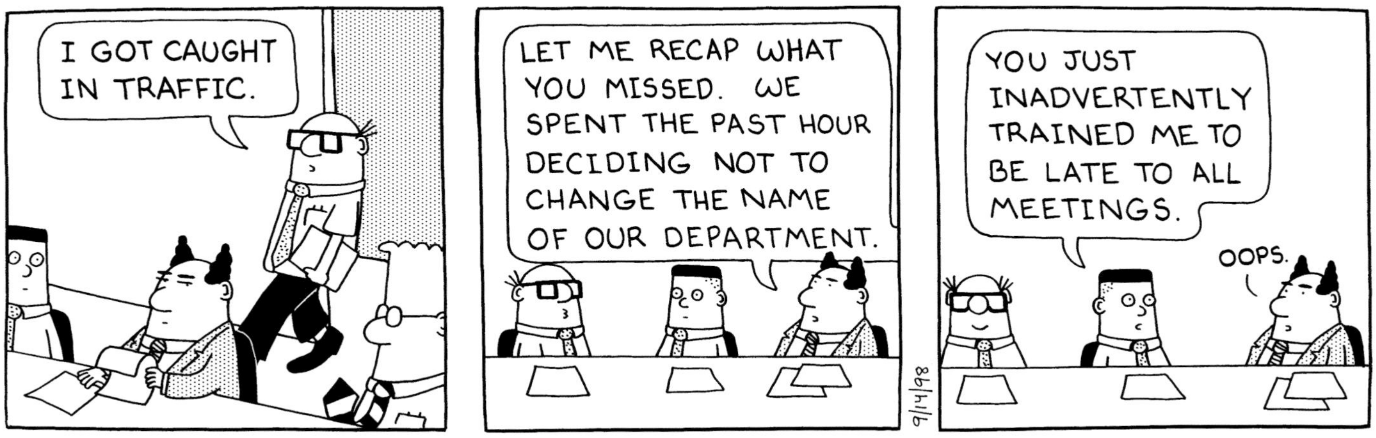
I GOT CAUGHT IN TRAFFIC.
LET ME RECAP WHAT YOU MISSED. WE SPENT THE PAST HOUR DECIDING NOT TO CHANGE THE NAME OF OUR DEPARTMENT.
9/14/98
YOU JUST INADVERTENTLY TRAINED ME TO BE LATE TO ALL MEETINGS.
OOPS.

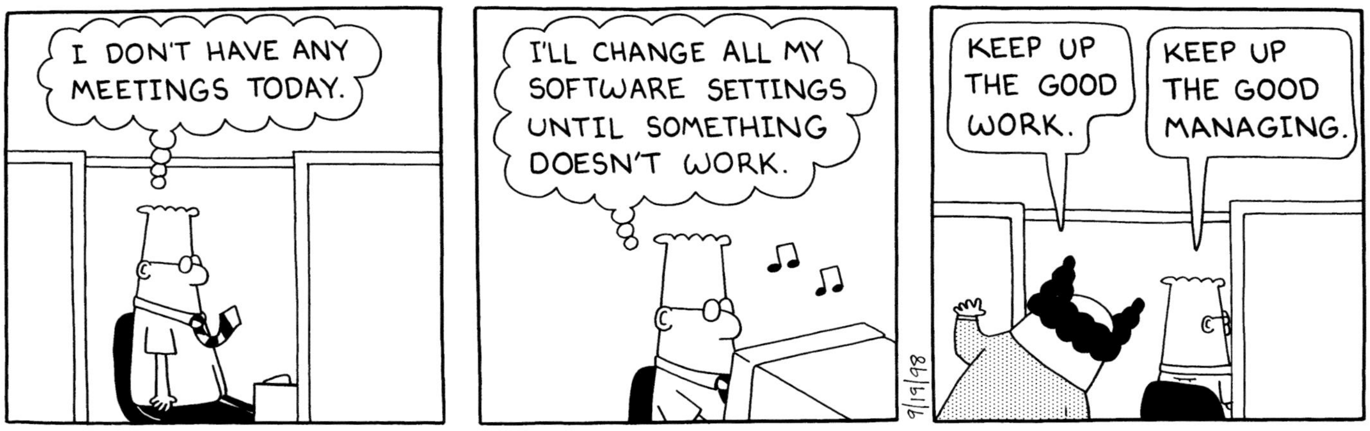
I DON'T HAVE ANY MEETINGS TODAY.
I'LL CHANGE ALL MY SOFTWARE SETTINGS UNTIL SOMETHING DOESN'T WORK.
9/19/98
KEEP UP THE GOOD WORK.
KEEP UP THE GOOD MANAGING.

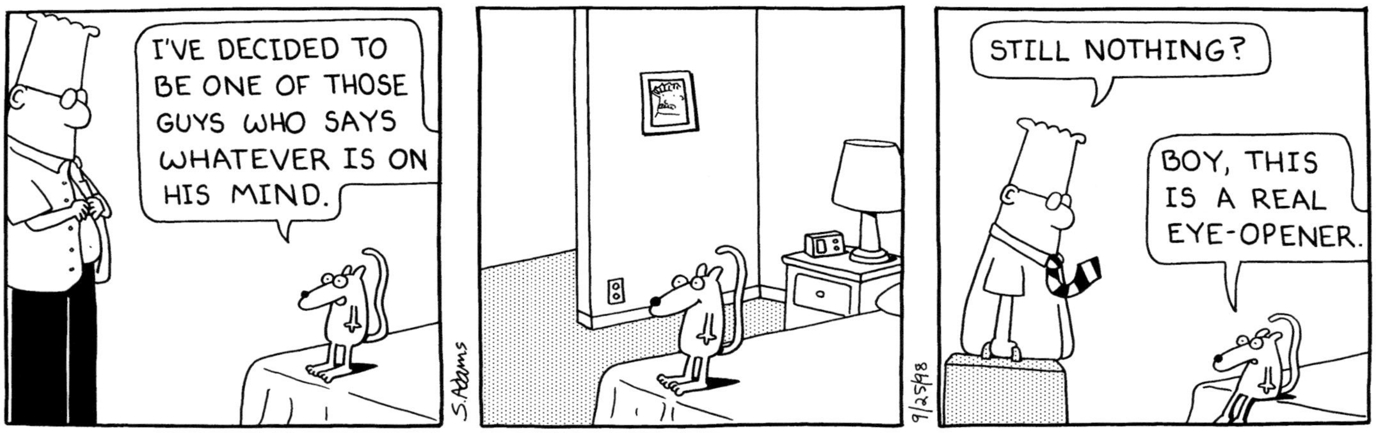
I'VE DECIDED TO BE ONE OF THOSE GUYS WHO SAYS WHATEVER IS ON HIS MIND.
S. Adams
9/25/98
STILL NOTHING?
BOY, THIS IS A REAL EYE-OPENER.

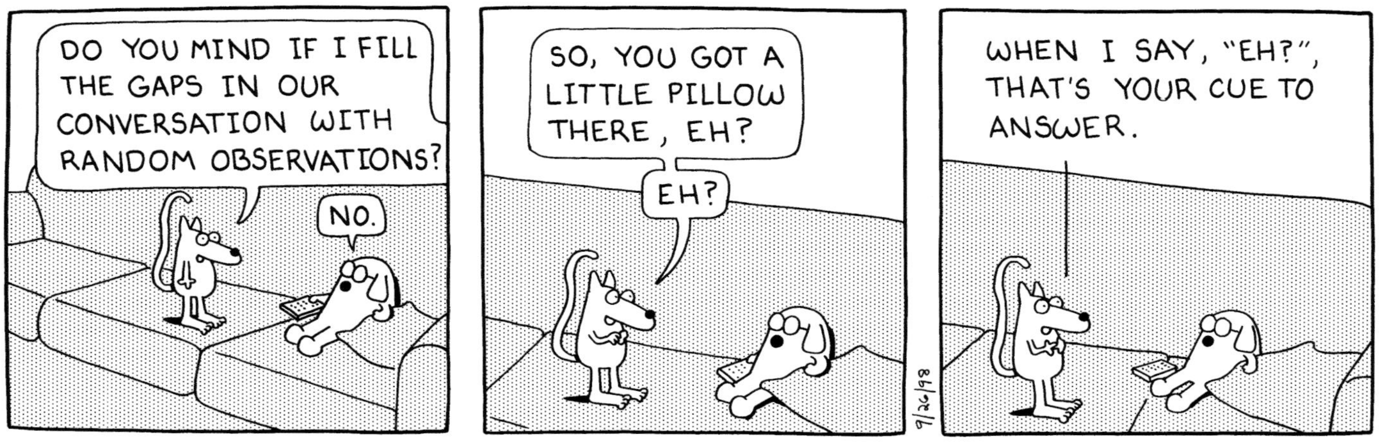
DO YOU MIND IF I FILL THE GAPS IN OUR CONVERSATION WITH RANDOM OBSERVATIONS?
NO.
SO, YOU GOT A LITTLE PILLOW THERE, EH?
EH?
9/26/98
WHEN I SAY, "EH?", THAT'S YOUR CUE TO ANSWER.

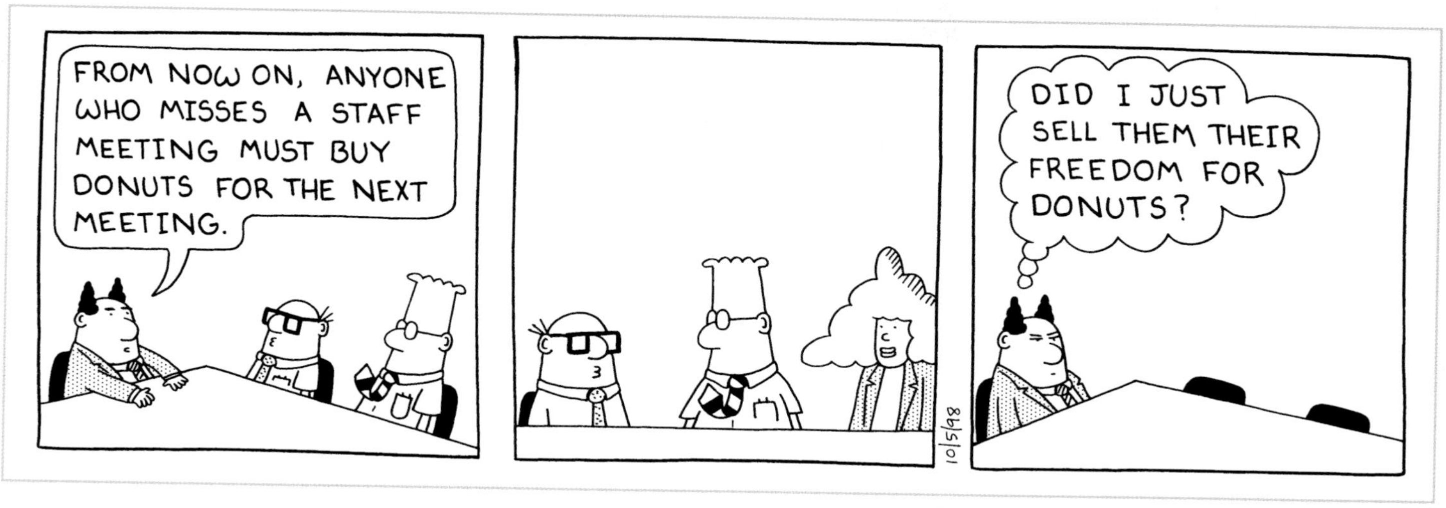
FROM NOW ON, ANYONE WHO MISSES A STAFF MEETING MUST BUY DONUTS FOR THE NEXT MEETING.
10/5/98
DID I JUST SELL THEM THEIR FREEDOM FOR DONUTS?

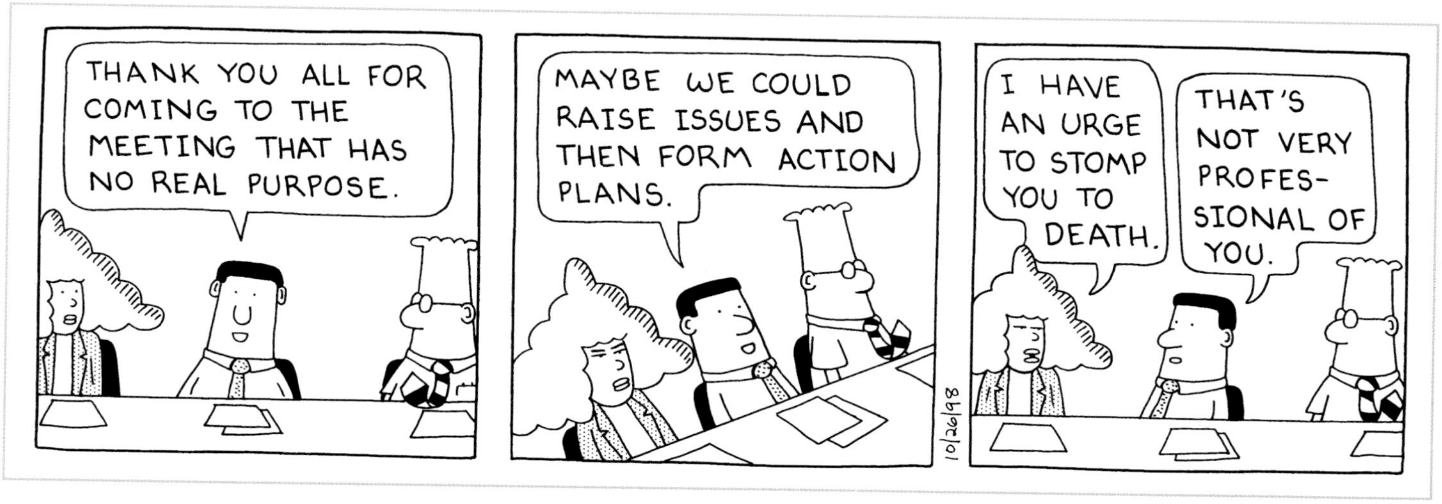
THANK YOU ALL FOR COMING TO THE MEETING THAT HAS NO REAL PURPOSE.
MAYBE WE COULD RAISE ISSUES AND THEN FORM ACTION PLANS.
10/26/98
I HAVE AN URGE TO STOMP YOU TO DEATH.
THAT'S NOT VERY PROFES-SIONAL OF YOU.

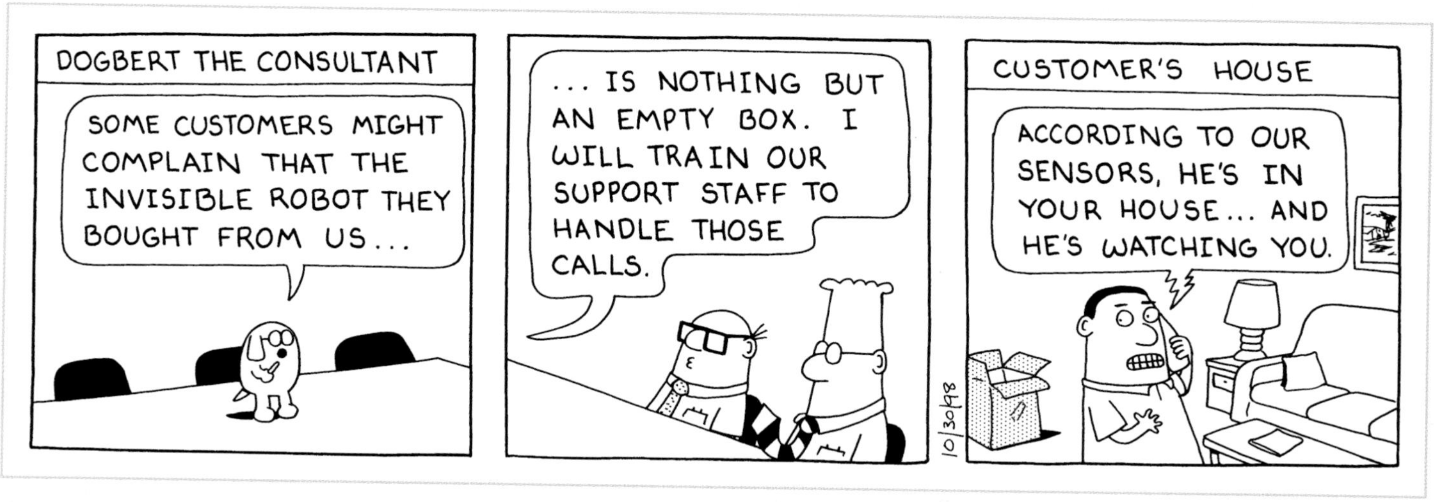
DOGBERT THE CONSULTANT
SOME CUSTOMERS MIGHT COMPLAIN THAT THE INVISIBLE ROBOT THEY BOUGHT FROM US...
... IS NOTHING BUT AN EMPTY BOX. I WILL TRAIN OUR SUPPORT STAFF TO HANDLE THOSE CALLS.
10/30/98
CUSTOMER'S HOUSE
ACCORDING TO OUR SENSORS, HE'S IN YOUR HOUSE... AND HE'S WATCHING YOU.

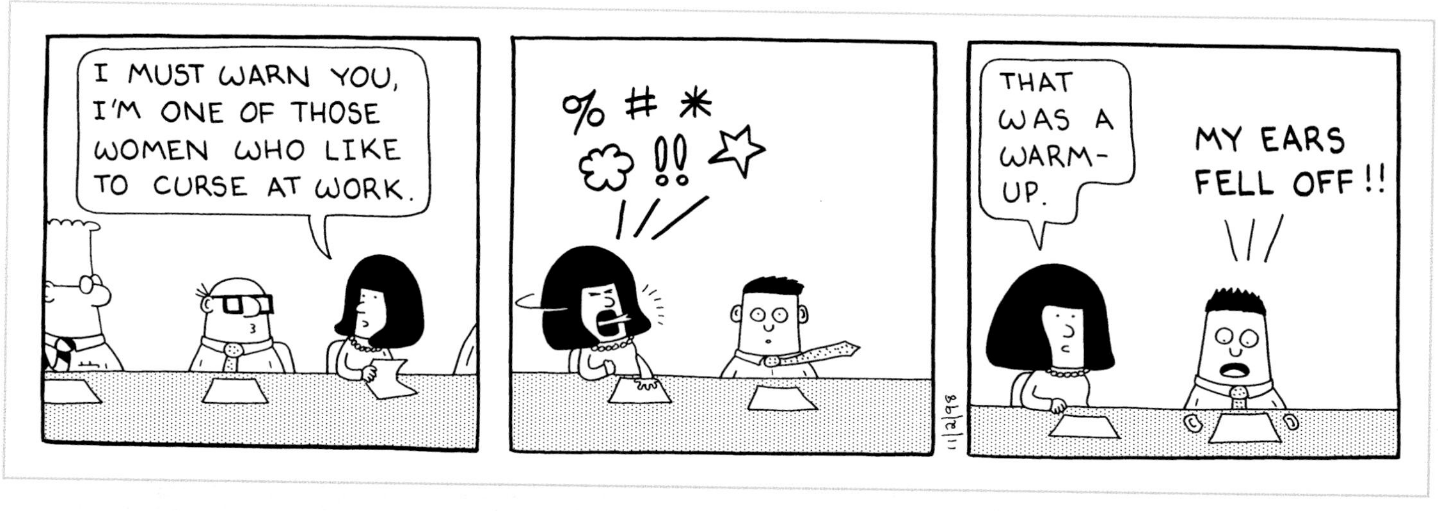
I MUST WARN YOU, I'M ONE OF THOSE WOMEN WHO LIKE TO CURSE AT WORK.
% # * !!
11/2/98
THAT WAS A WARM-UP.
MY EARS FELL OFF!!

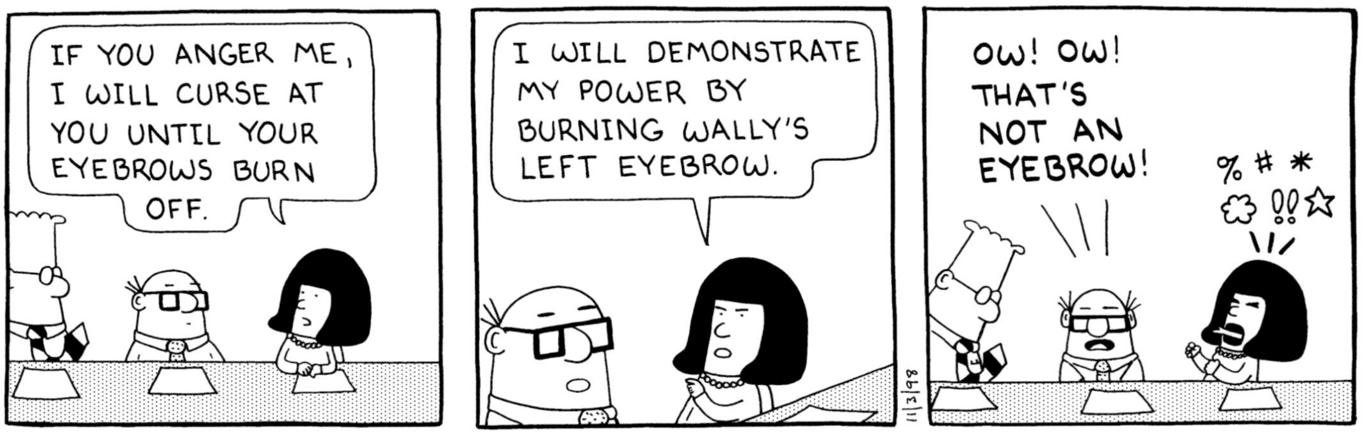
IF YOU ANGER ME, I WILL CURSE AT YOU UNTIL YOUR EYEBROWS BURN OFF.
I WILL DEMONSTRATE MY POWER BY BURNING WALLY'S LEFT EYEBROW.
11/3/98
OW! OW! THAT'S NOT AN EYEBROW!
% # *

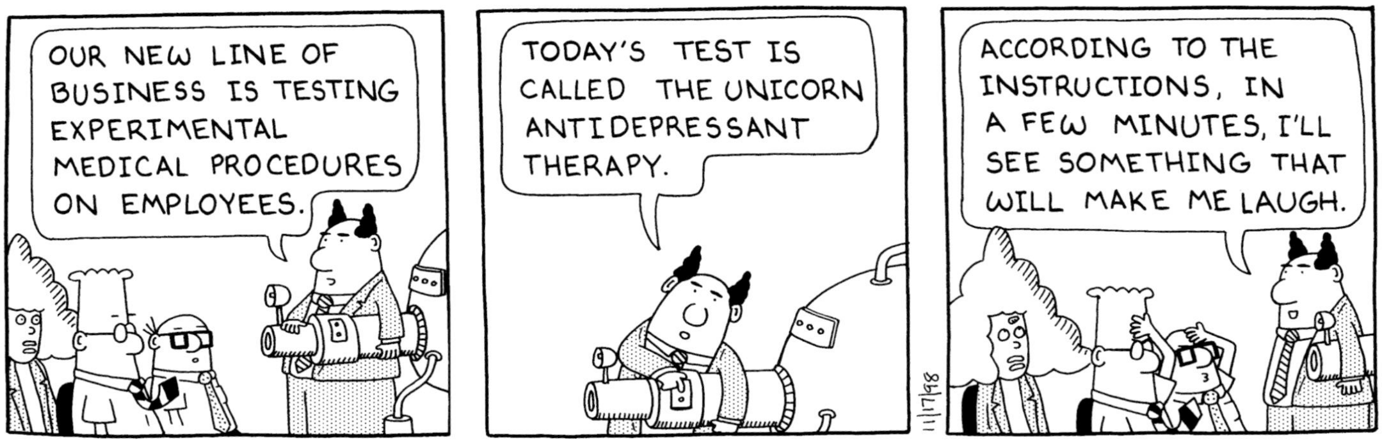
OUR NEW LINE OF BUSINESS IS TESTING EXPERIMENTAL MEDICAL PROCEDURES ON EMPLOYEES.
TODAY'S TEST IS CALLED THE UNICORN ANTIDEPRESSANT THERAPY.
11/17/98
ACCORDING TO THE INSTRUCTIONS, IN A FEW MINUTES, I'LL SEE SOMETHING THAT WILL MAKE ME LAUGH.

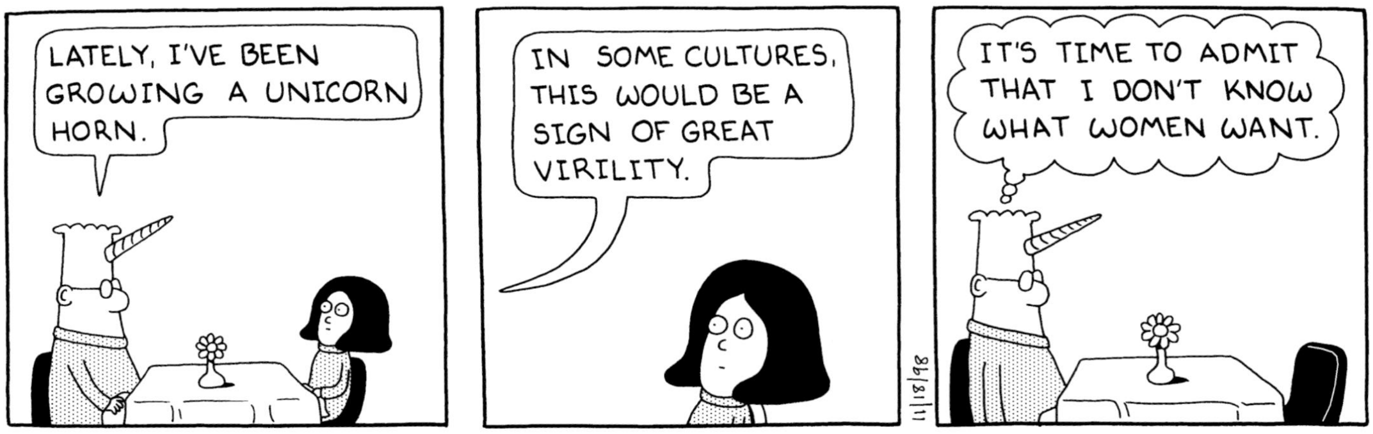
LATELY, I'VE BEEN GROWING A UNICORN HORN.
IN SOME CULTURES, THIS WOULD BE A SIGN OF GREAT VIRILITY.
11/18/98
IT'S TIME TO ADMIT THAT I DON'T KNOW WHAT WOMEN WANT.

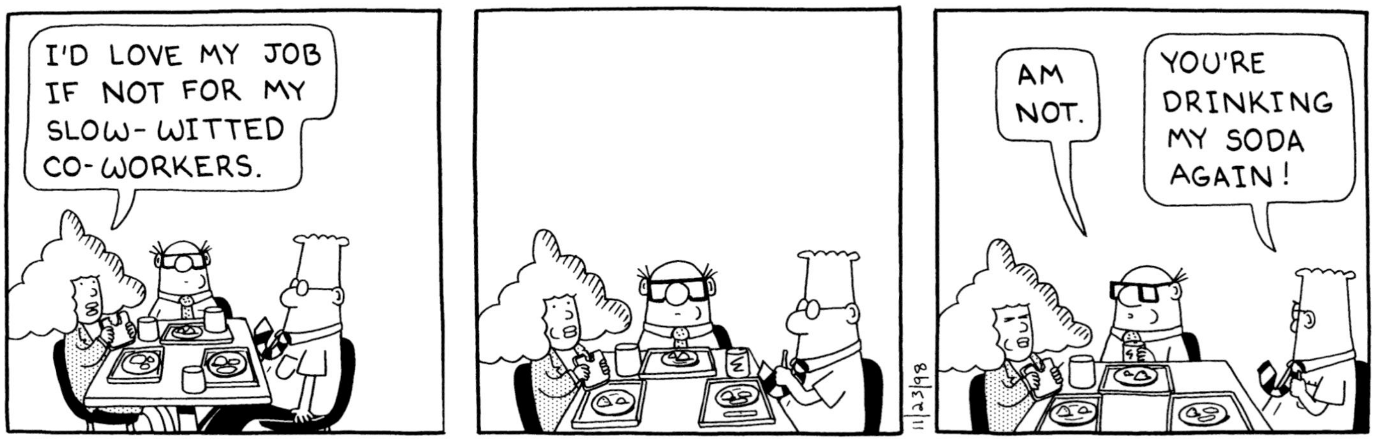
I'D LOVE MY JOB IF NOT FOR MY SLOW-WITTED CO-WORKERS.
11/23/98
AM NOT.
YOU'RE DRINKING MY SODA AGAIN!

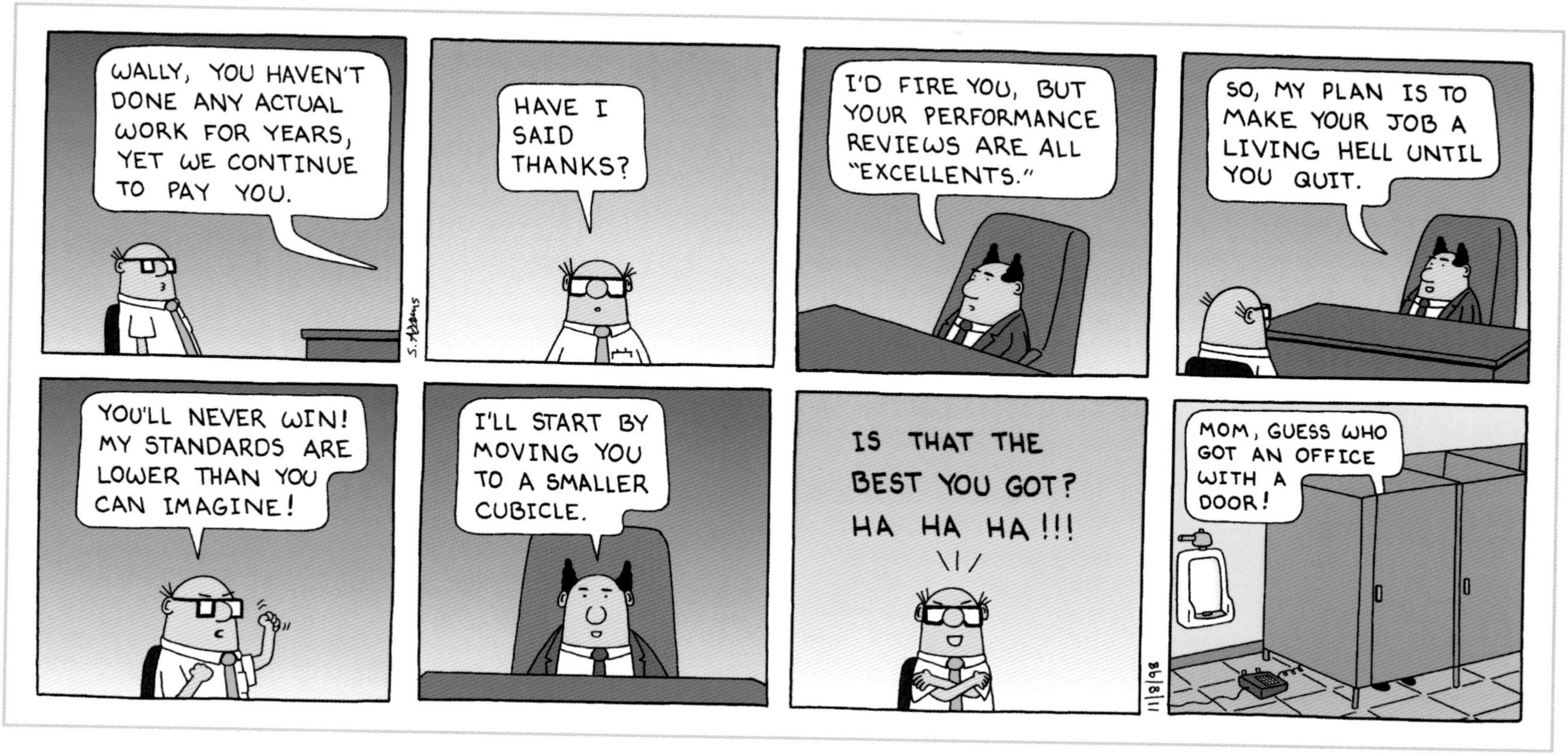
WALLY, YOU HAVEN'T DONE ANY ACTUAL WORK FOR YEARS, YET WE CONTINUE TO PAY YOU.
HAVE I SAID THANKS?
I'D FIRE YOU, BUT YOUR PERFORMANCE REVIEWS ARE ALL "EXCELLENTS."
SO, MY PLAN IS TO MAKE YOUR JOB A LIVING HELL UNTIL YOU QUIT.
YOU'LL NEVER WIN! MY STANDARDS ARE LOWER THAN YOU CAN IMAGINE!
I'LL START BY MOVING YOU TO A SMALLER CUBICLE.
IS THAT THE BEST YOU GOT? HA HA HA!!!
MOM, GUESS WHO GOT AN OFFICE WITH A DOOR!
11/8/98

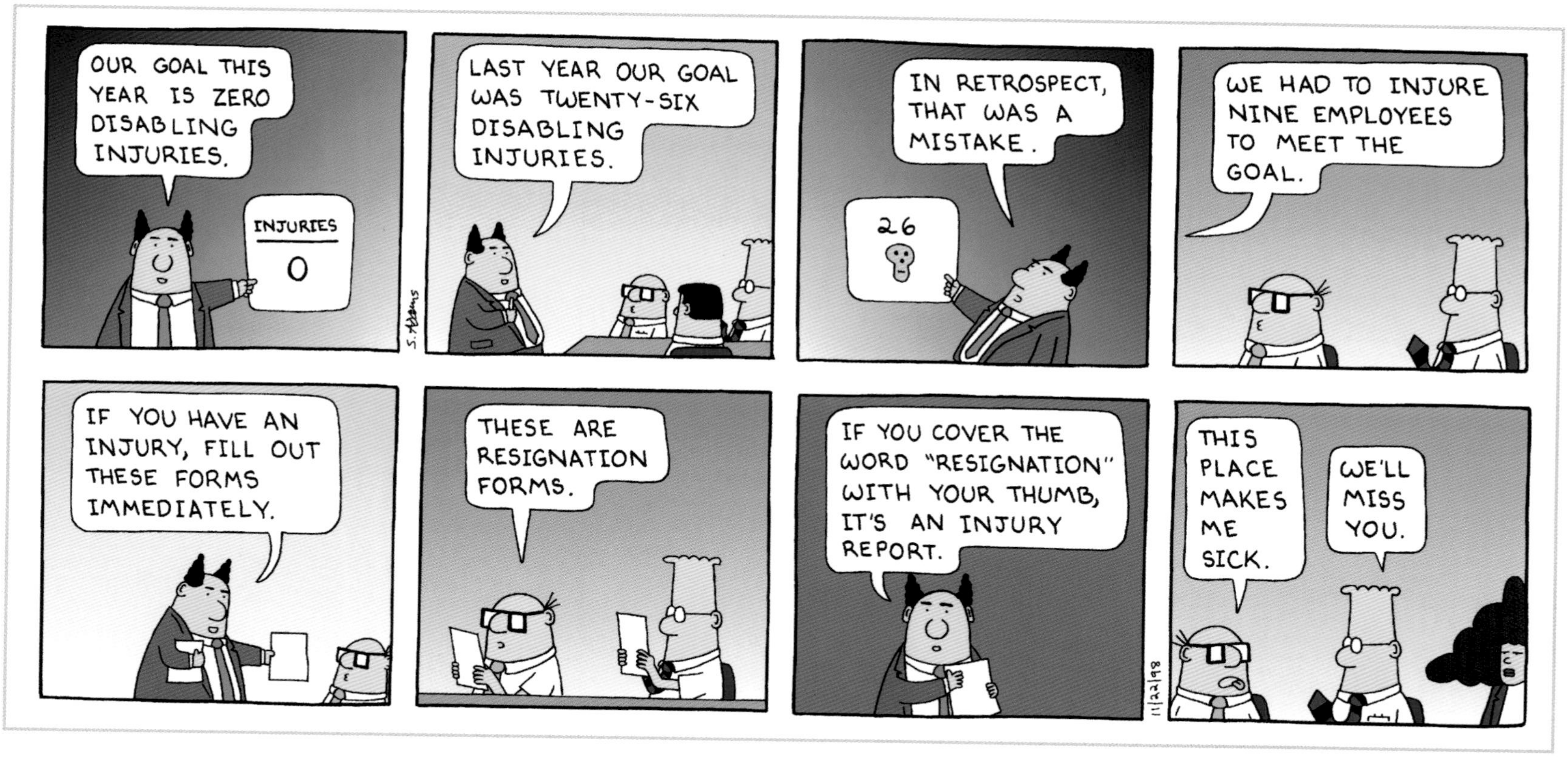
OUR GOAL THIS YEAR IS ZERO DISABLING INJURIES.
INJURIES
0
LAST YEAR OUR GOAL WAS TWENTY-SIX DISABLING INJURIES.
IN RETROSPECT, THAT WAS A MISTAKE.
26
WE HAD TO INJURE NINE EMPLOYEES TO MEET THE GOAL.
IF YOU HAVE AN INJURY, FILL OUT THESE FORMS IMMEDIATELY.
THESE ARE RESIGNATION FORMS.
IF YOU COVER THE WORD "RESIGNATION" WITH YOUR THUMB, IT'S AN INJURY REPORT.
THIS PLACE MAKES ME SICK.
WE'LL MISS YOU.
11/22/98

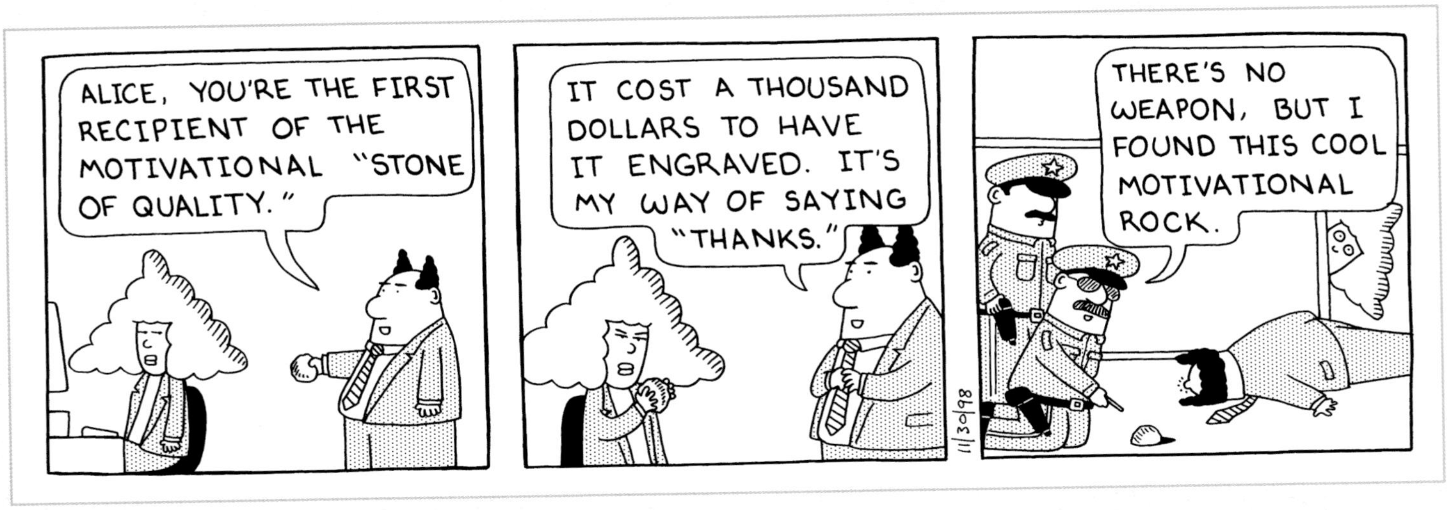
ALICE, YOU'RE THE FIRST RECIPIENT OF THE MOTIVATIONAL "STONE OF QUALITY."
IT COST A THOUSAND DOLLARS TO HAVE IT ENGRAVED. IT'S MY WAY OF SAYING "THANKS."
11/30/98
THERE'S NO WEAPON, BUT I FOUND THIS COOL MOTIVATIONAL ROCK.

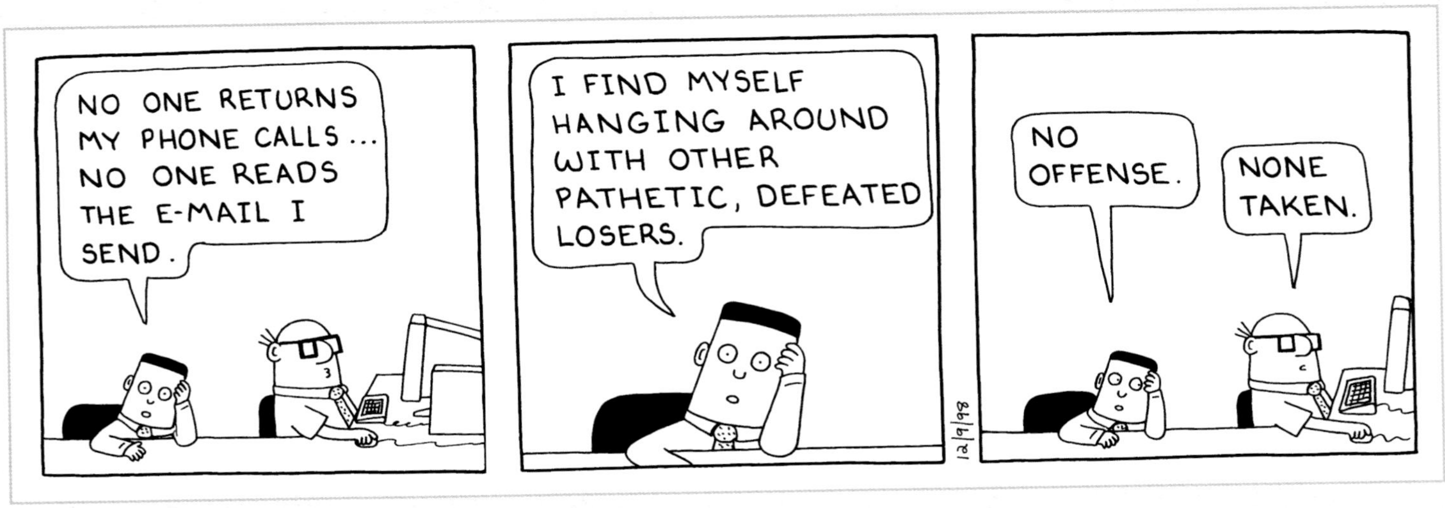
NO ONE RETURNS MY PHONE CALLS... NO ONE READS THE E-MAIL I SEND.
I FIND MYSELF HANGING AROUND WITH OTHER PATHETIC, DEFEATED LOSERS.
12/9/98
NO OFFENSE.
NONE TAKEN.

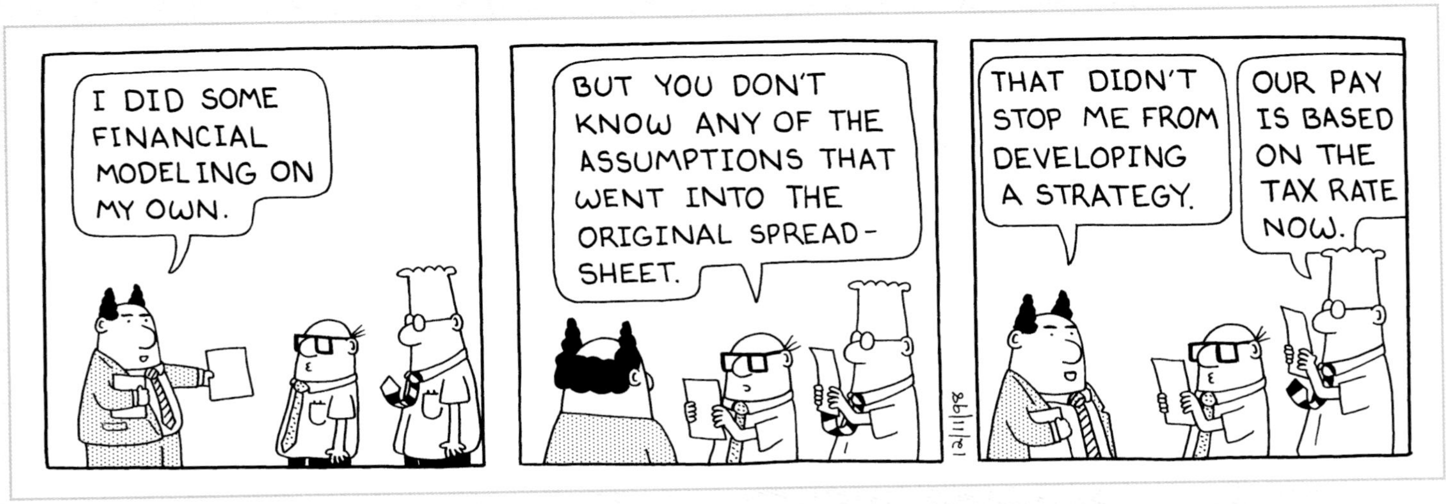
I DID SOME FINANCIAL MODELING ON MY OWN.
BUT YOU DON'T KNOW ANY OF THE ASSUMPTIONS THAT WENT INTO THE ORIGINAL SPREAD-SHEET.
12/11/98
THAT DIDN'T STOP ME FROM DEVELOPING A STRATEGY.
OUR PAY IS BASED ON THE TAX RATE NOW.

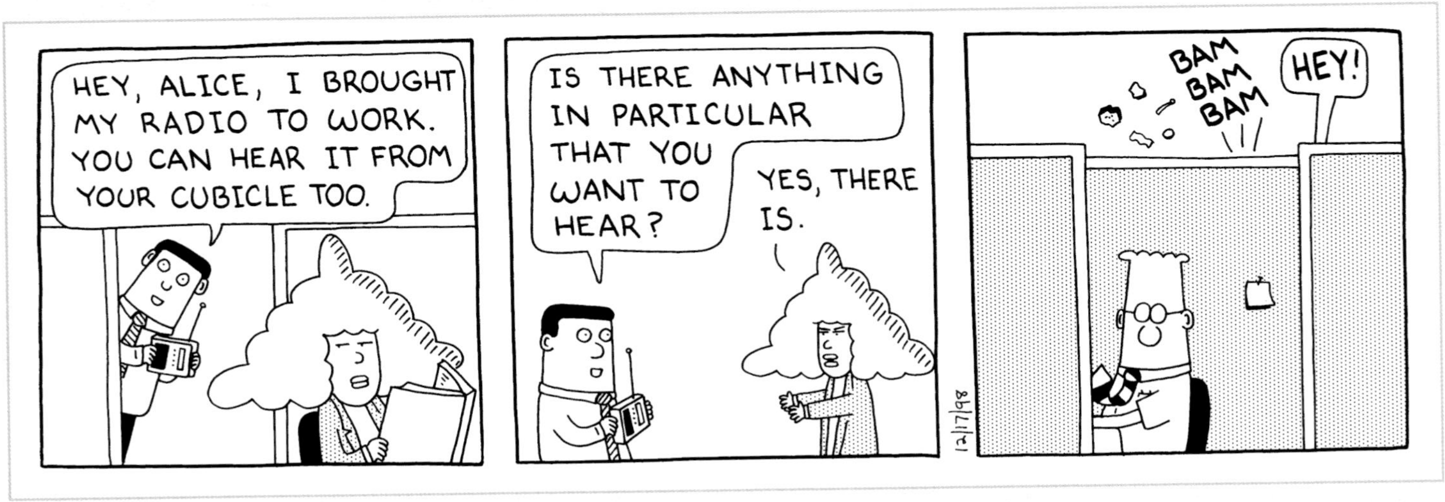
HEY, ALICE, I BROUGHT MY RADIO TO WORK. YOU CAN HEAR IT FROM YOUR CUBICLE TOO.
IS THERE ANYTHING IN PARTICULAR THAT YOU WANT TO HEAR?
YES, THERE IS.
12/17/98
BAM BAM BAM
HEY!

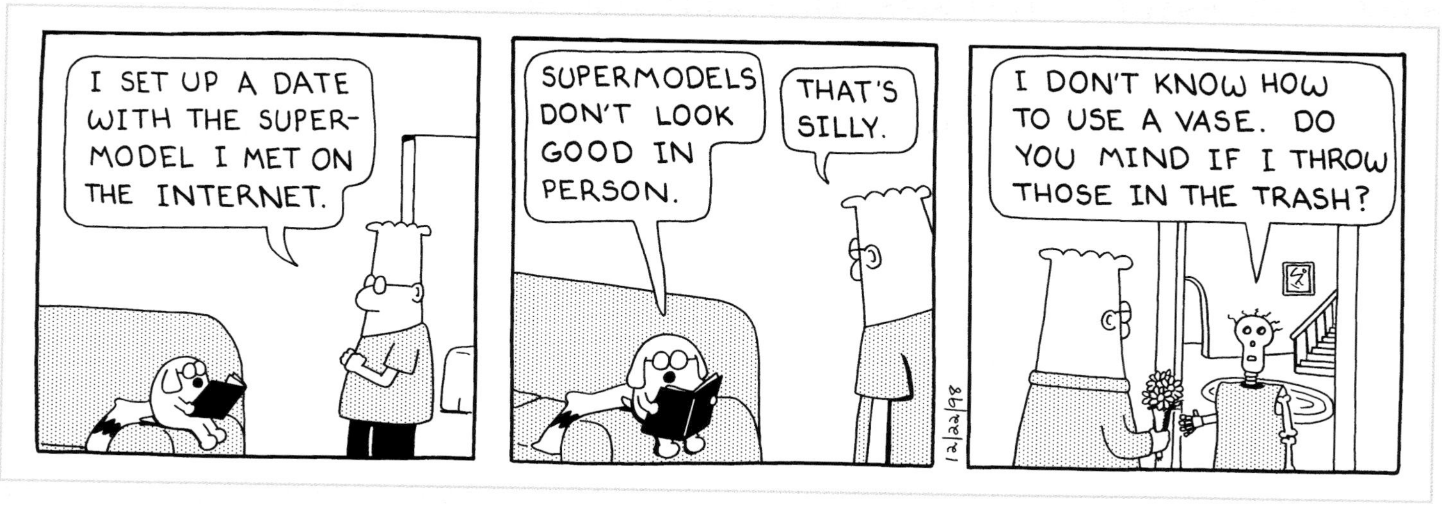
I SET UP A DATE WITH THE SUPER-MODEL I MET ON THE INTERNET.
SUPERMODELS DON'T LOOK GOOD IN PERSON.
THAT'S SILLY.
12/22/98
I DON'T KNOW HOW TO USE A VASE. DO YOU MIND IF I THROW THOSE IN THE TRASH?

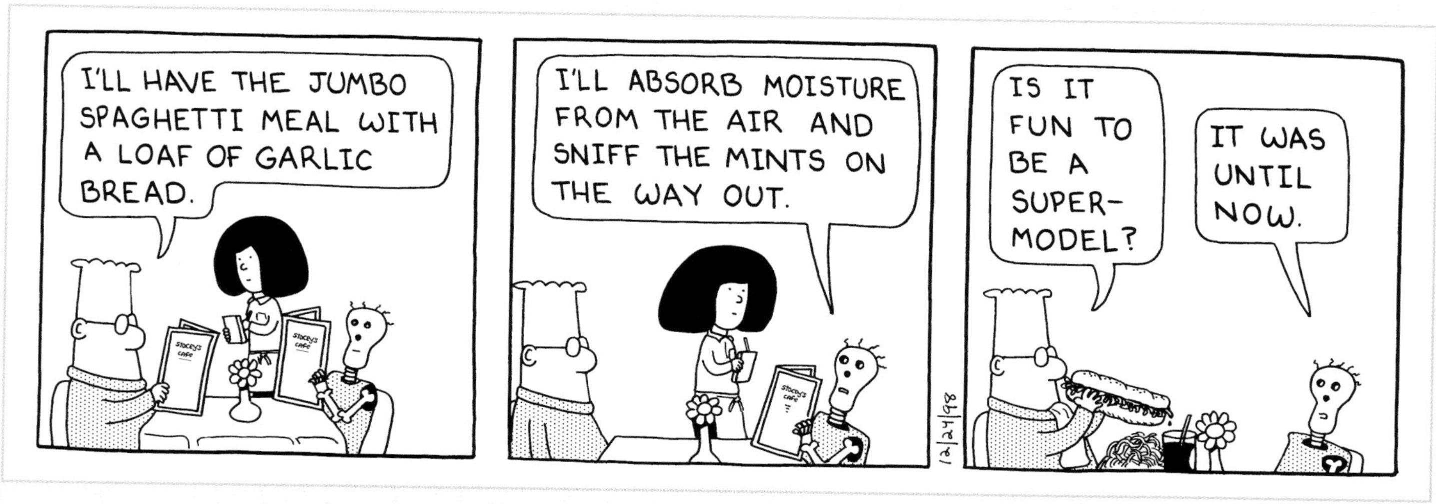
I'LL HAVE THE JUMBO SPAGHETTI MEAL WITH A LOAF OF GARLIC BREAD.
I'LL ABSORB MOISTURE FROM THE AIR AND SNIFF THE MINTS ON THE WAY OUT.
12/24/98
IS IT FUN TO BE A SUPER-MODEL?
IT WAS UNTIL NOW.

I felt the strip above was hilarious. I might have been the only one.

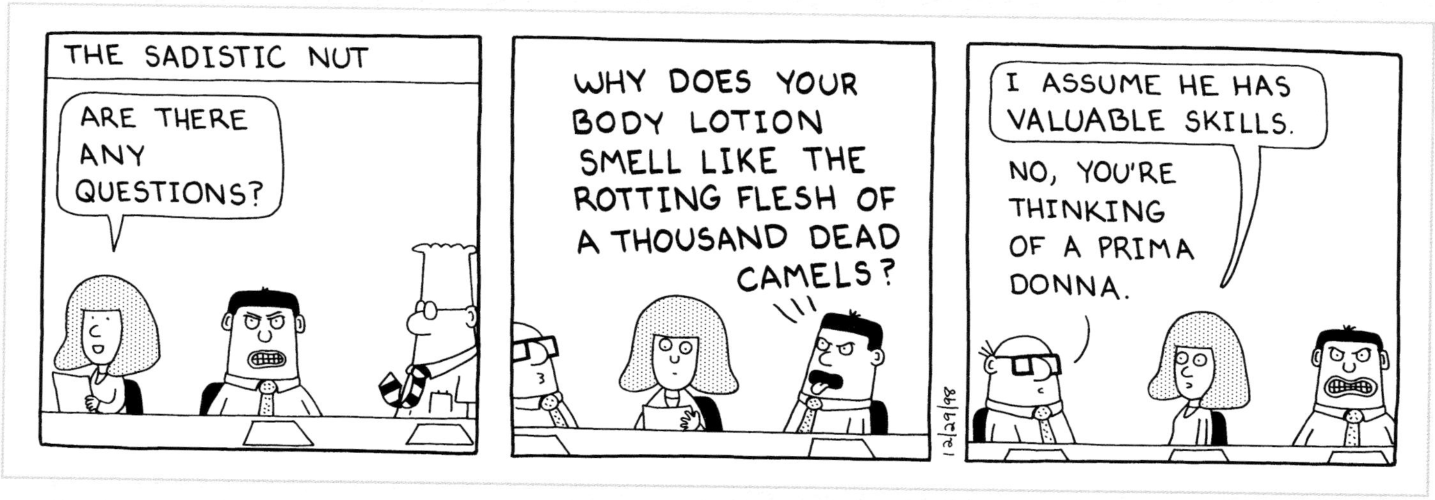
THE SADISTIC NUT
ARE THERE ANY QUESTIONS?
WHY DOES YOUR BODY LOTION SMELL LIKE THE ROTTING FLESH OF A THOUSAND DEAD CAMELS?
12/29/98
I ASSUME HE HAS VALUABLE SKILLS.
NO, YOU'RE THINKING OF A PRIMA DONNA.

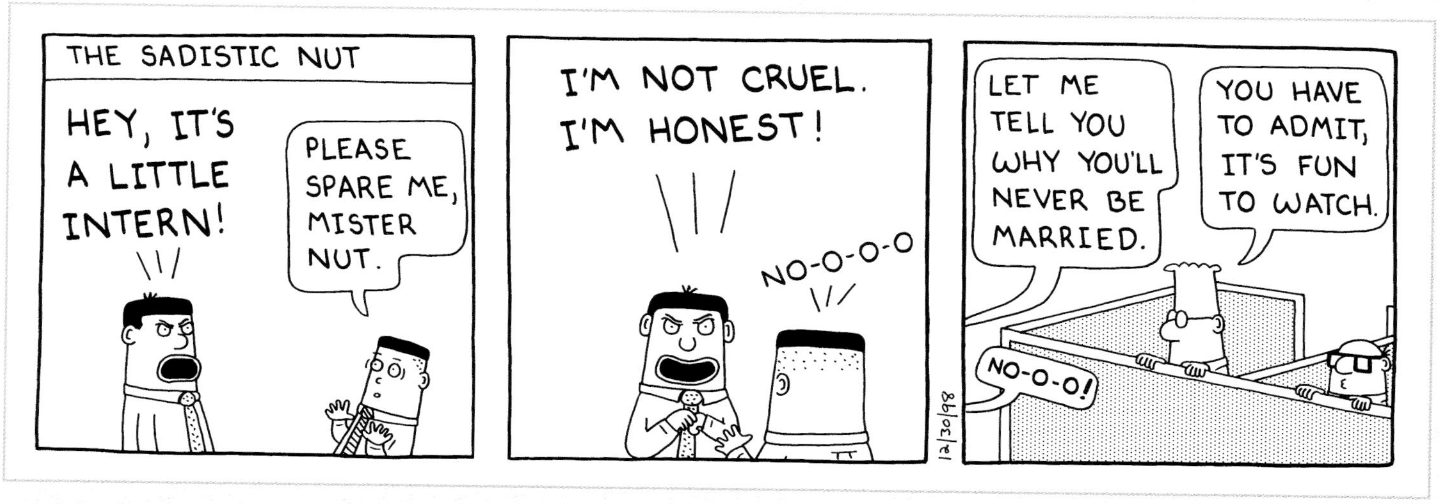
THE SADISTIC NUT
HEY, IT'S A LITTLE INTERN!
PLEASE SPARE ME, MISTER NUT.
I'M NOT CRUEL. I'M HONEST!
NO-O-O-O
12/30/98
LET ME TELL YOU WHY YOU'LL NEVER BE MARRIED.
YOU HAVE TO ADMIT, IT'S FUN TO WATCH.
NO-O-O!

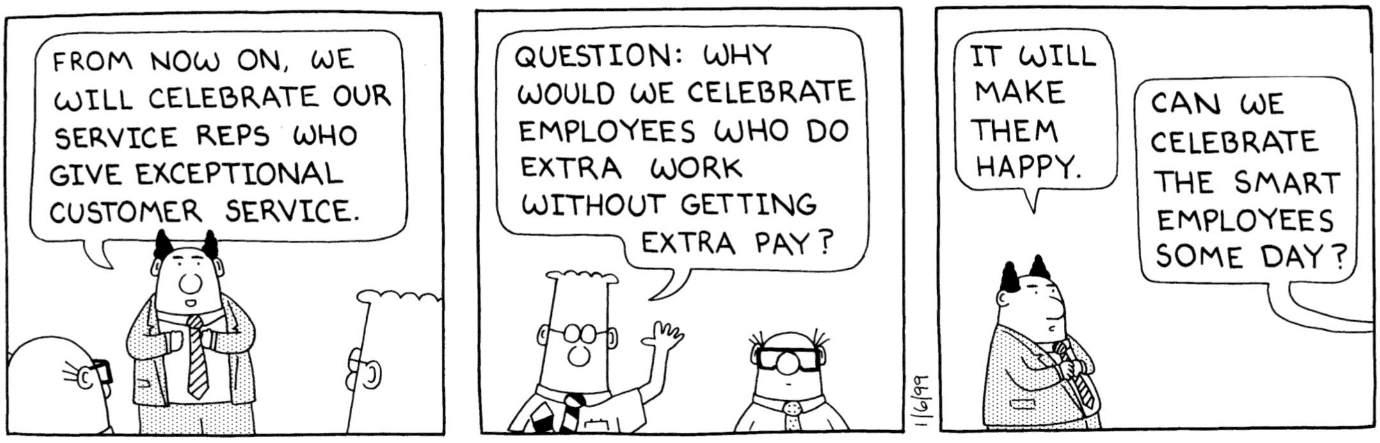
FROM NOW ON, WE WILL CELEBRATE OUR SERVICE REPS WHO GIVE EXCEPTIONAL CUSTOMER SERVICE.
QUESTION: WHY WOULD WE CELEBRATE EMPLOYEES WHO DO EXTRA WORK WITHOUT GETTING EXTRA PAY?
IT WILL MAKE THEM HAPPY.
CAN WE CELEBRATE THE SMART EMPLOYEES SOME DAY?
1/6/99

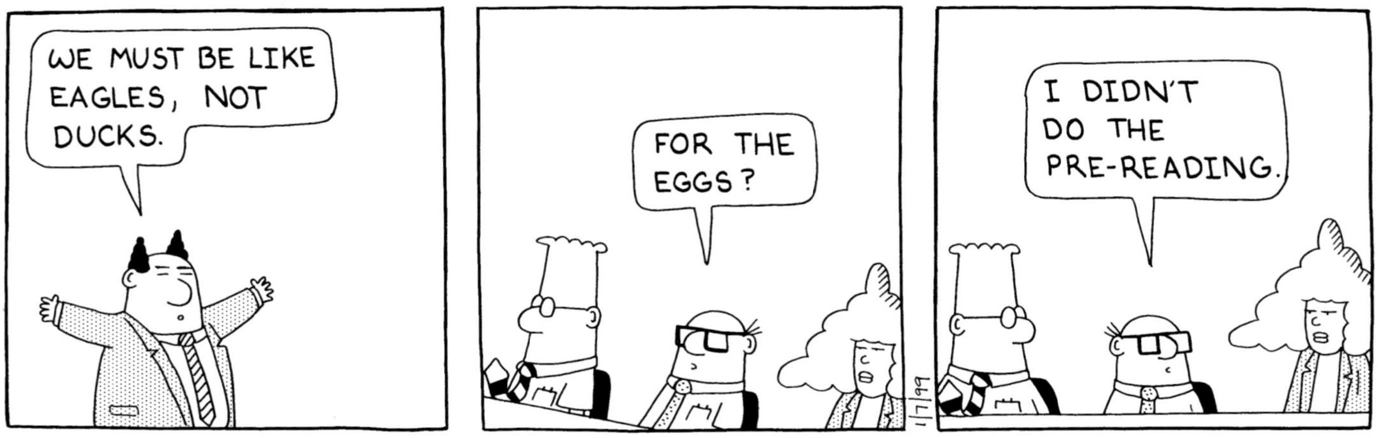
WE MUST BE LIKE EAGLES, NOT DUCKS.
FOR THE EGGS?
I DIDN'T DO THE PRE-READING.
1/7/99

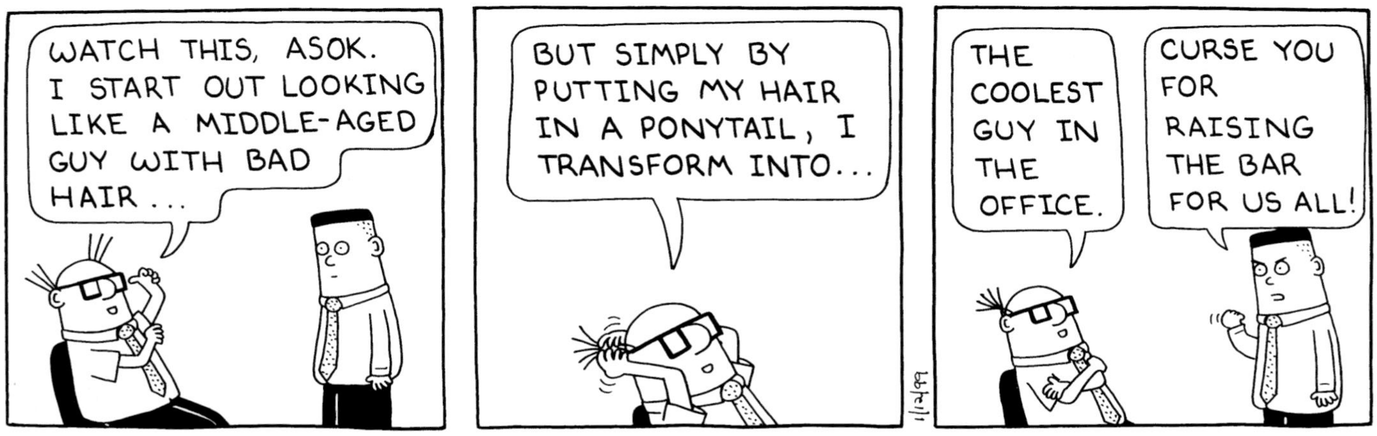
WATCH THIS, ASOK. I START OUT LOOKING LIKE A MIDDLE-AGED GUY WITH BAD HAIR...
BUT SIMPLY BY PUTTING MY HAIR IN A PONYTAIL, I TRANSFORM INTO...
THE COOLEST GUY IN THE OFFICE.
CURSE YOU FOR RAISING THE BAR FOR US ALL!
1/12/99

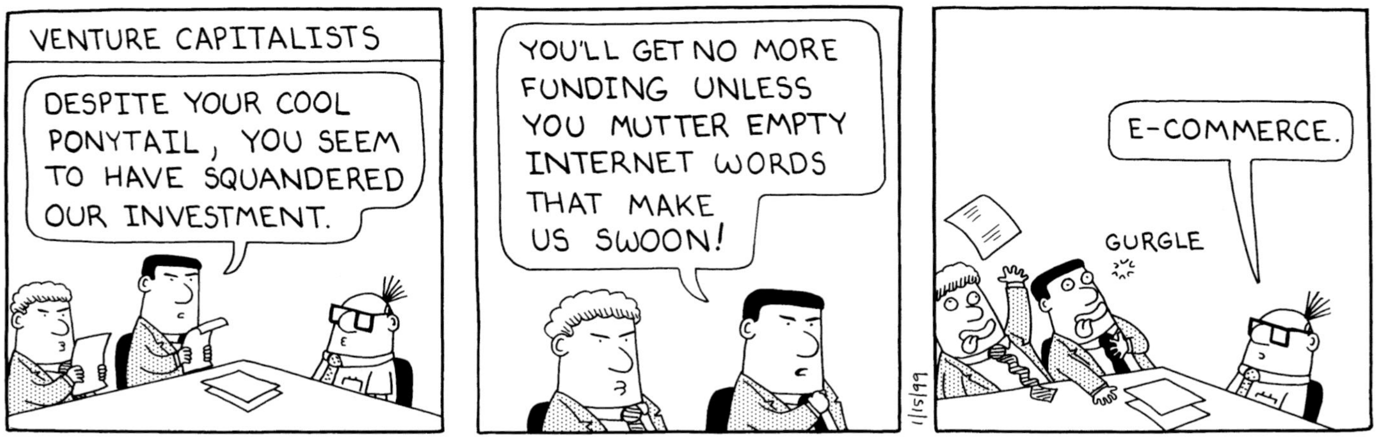
VENTURE CAPITALISTS
DESPITE YOUR COOL PONYTAIL, YOU SEEM TO HAVE SQUANDERED OUR INVESTMENT.
YOU'LL GET NO MORE FUNDING UNLESS YOU MUTTER EMPTY INTERNET WORDS THAT MAKE US SWOON!
E-COMMERCE.
GURGLE
1/15/99

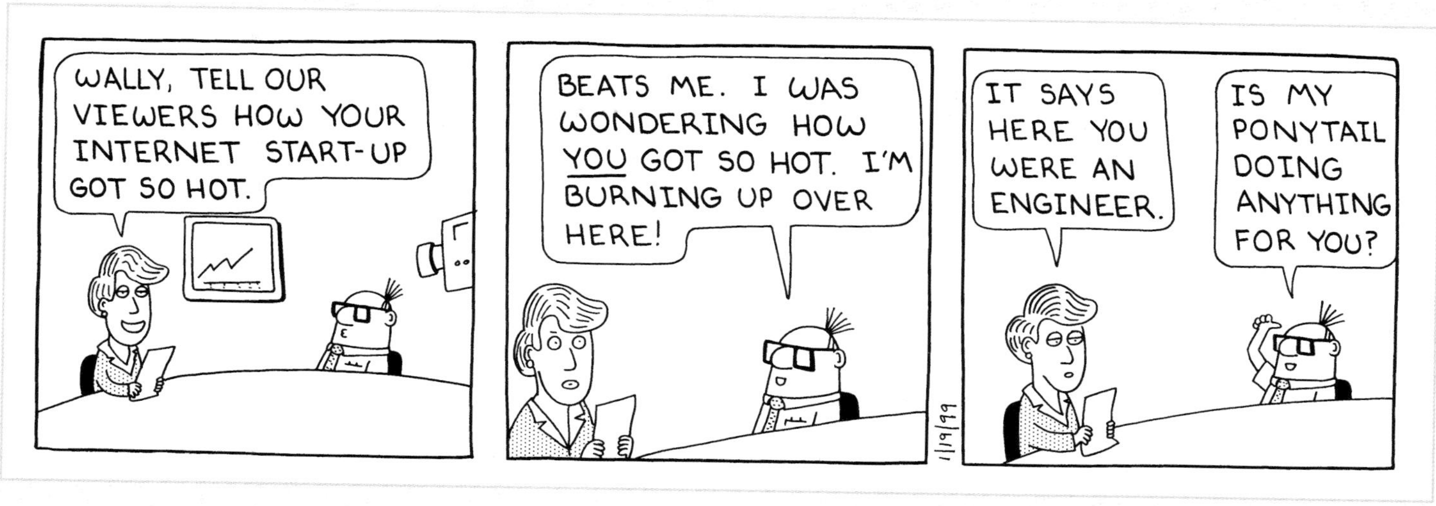
WALLY, TELL OUR VIEWERS HOW YOUR INTERNET START-UP GOT SO HOT.
BEATS ME. I WAS WONDERING HOW YOU GOT SO HOT. I'M BURNING UP OVER HERE!
1/19/99
IT SAYS HERE YOU WERE AN ENGINEER.
IS MY PONYTAIL DOING ANYTHING FOR YOU?

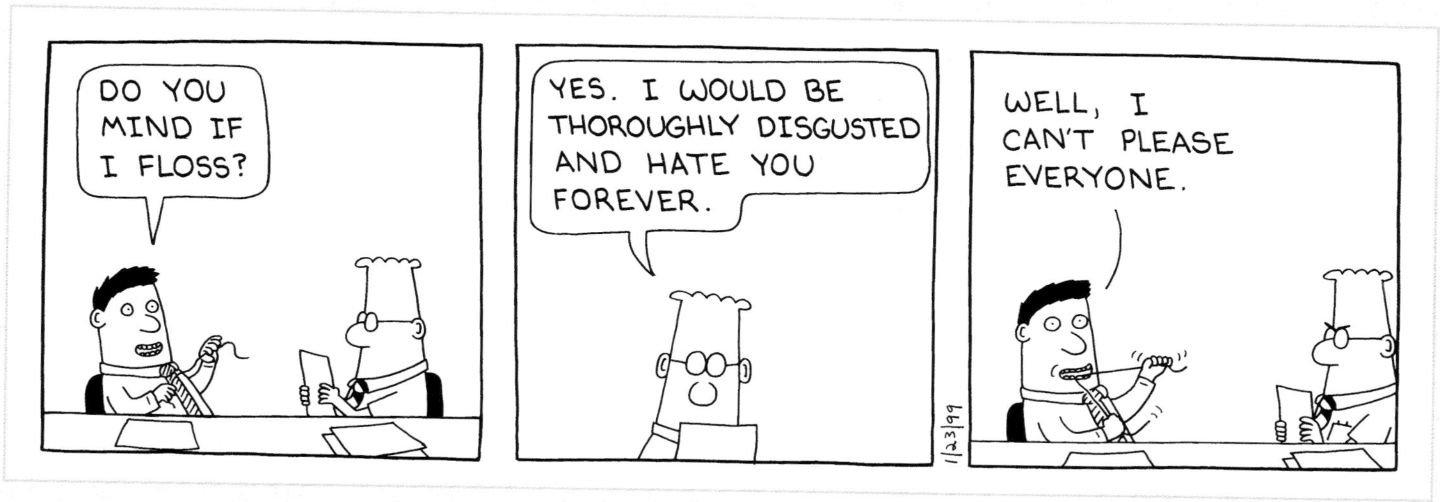
DO YOU MIND IF I FLOSS?
YES. I WOULD BE THOROUGHLY DISGUSTED AND HATE YOU FOREVER.
1/23/99
WELL, I CAN'T PLEASE EVERYONE.

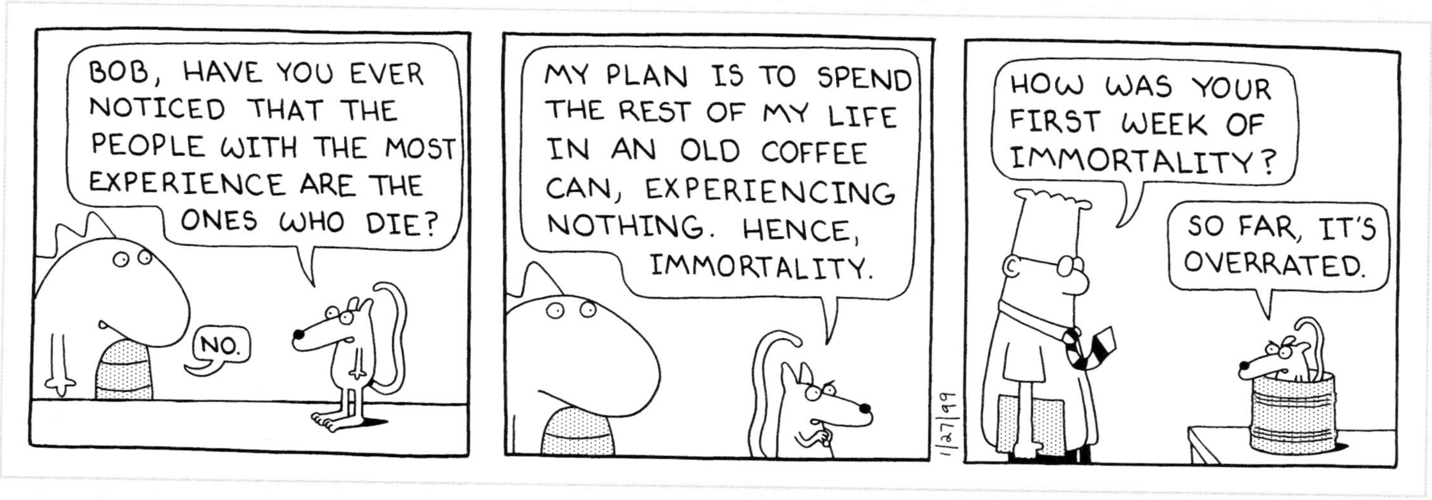
BOB, HAVE YOU EVER NOTICED THAT THE PEOPLE WITH THE MOST EXPERIENCE ARE THE ONES WHO DIE?
NO.
MY PLAN IS TO SPEND THE REST OF MY LIFE IN AN OLD COFFEE CAN, EXPERIENCING NOTHING. HENCE, IMMORTALITY.
1/27/99
HOW WAS YOUR FIRST WEEK OF IMMORTALITY?
SO FAR, IT'S OVERRATED.

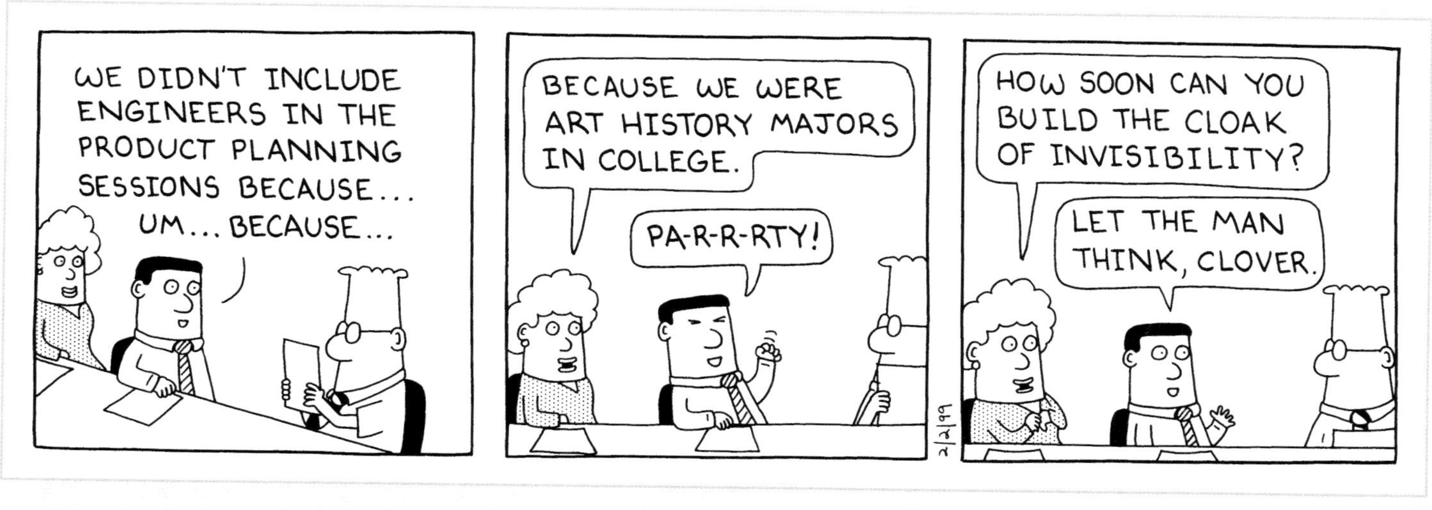
WE DIDN'T INCLUDE ENGINEERS IN THE PRODUCT PLANNING SESSIONS BECAUSE... UM... BECAUSE...
BECAUSE WE WERE ART HISTORY MAJORS IN COLLEGE.
PA-R-R-RTY!
2/2/99
HOW SOON CAN YOU BUILD THE CLOAK OF INVISIBILITY?
LET THE MAN THINK, CLOVER.

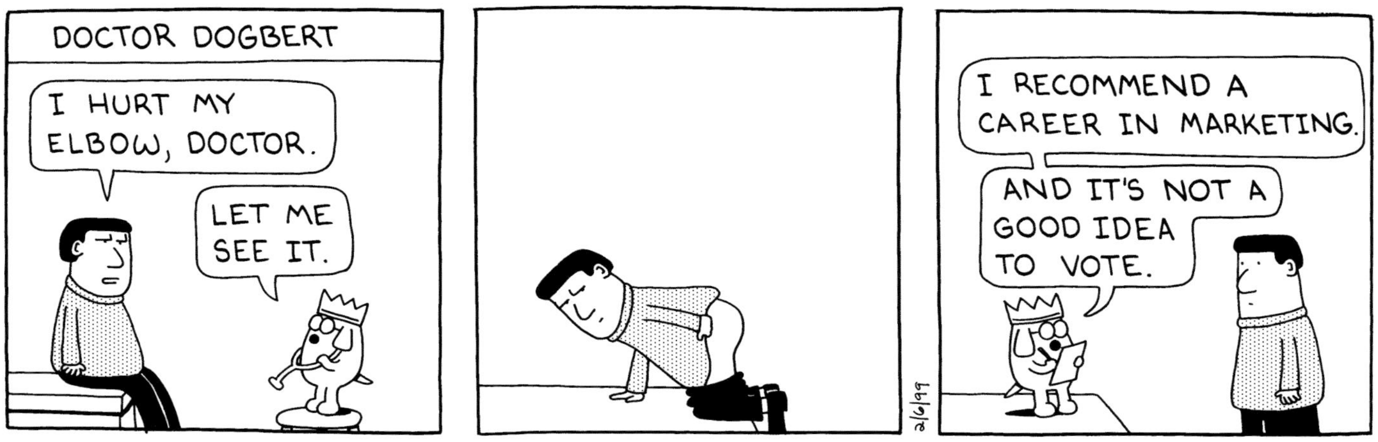
DOCTOR DOGBERT
I HURT MY ELBOW, DOCTOR.
LET ME SEE IT.
I RECOMMEND A CAREER IN MARKETING.
AND IT'S NOT A GOOD IDEA TO VOTE.
2/6/99

I don't know how this comic got published. It probably helped that the view is from the side. And maybe having a dog as the doctor helped too.

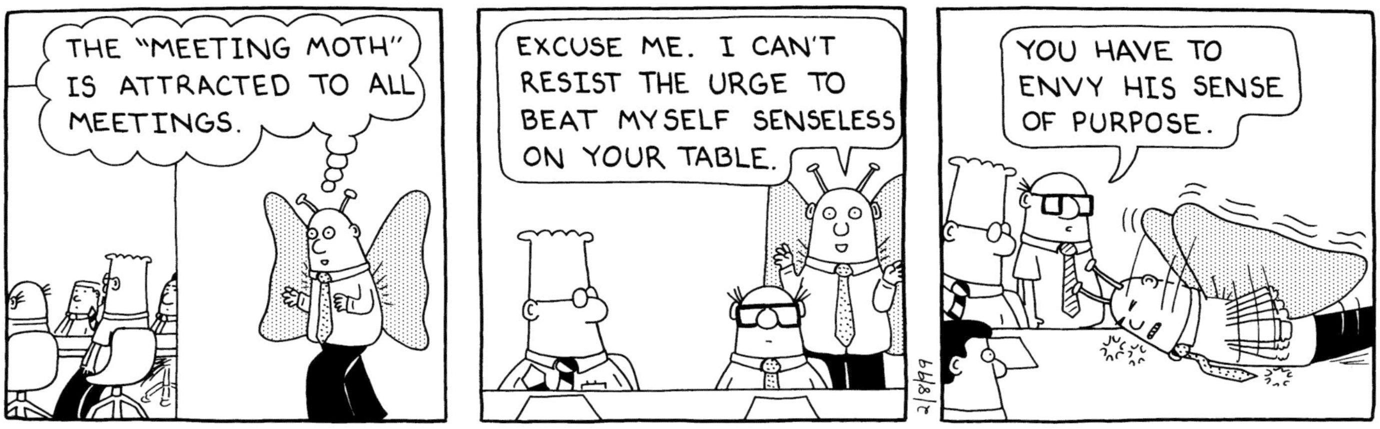
THE "MEETING MOTH" IS ATTRACTED TO ALL MEETINGS.
EXCUSE ME. I CAN'T RESIST THE URGE TO BEAT MYSELF SENSELESS ON YOUR TABLE.
YOU HAVE TO ENVY HIS SENSE OF PURPOSE.
2/8/99

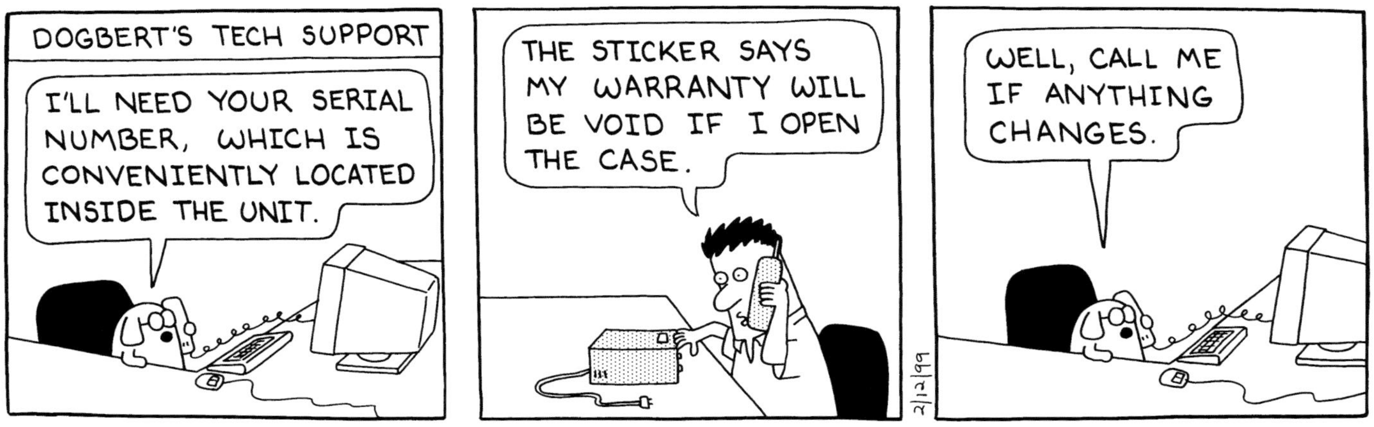
DOGBERT'S TECH SUPPORT
I'LL NEED YOUR SERIAL NUMBER, WHICH IS CONVENIENTLY LOCATED INSIDE THE UNIT.
THE STICKER SAYS MY WARRANTY WILL BE VOID IF I OPEN THE CASE.
WELL, CALL ME IF ANYTHING CHANGES.
2/12/99

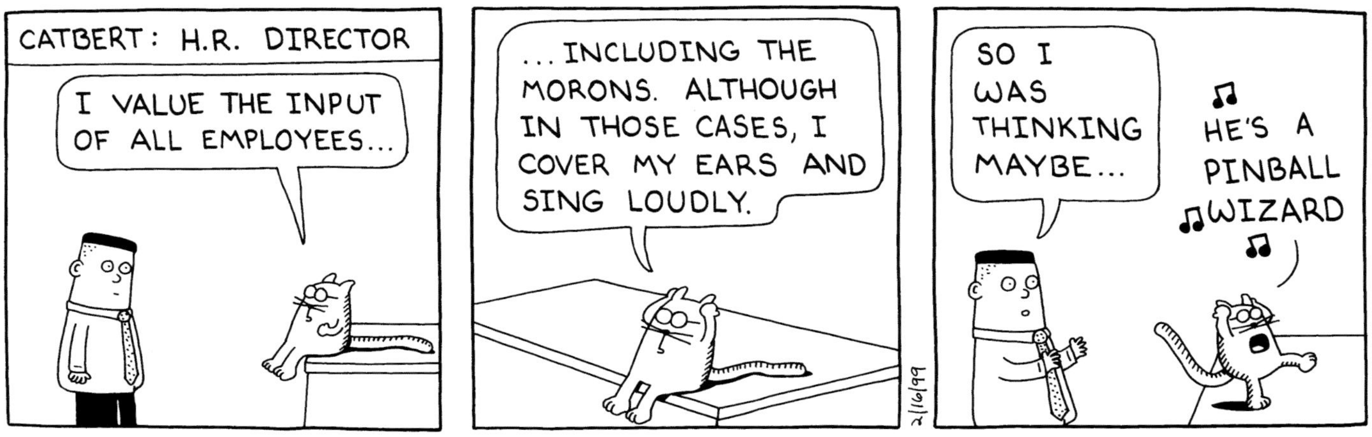
CATBERT: H.R. DIRECTOR
I VALUE THE INPUT OF ALL EMPLOYEES...
...INCLUDING THE MORONS. ALTHOUGH IN THOSE CASES, I COVER MY EARS AND SING LOUDLY.
SO I WAS THINKING MAYBE...
HE'S A PINBALL WIZARD
2/16/99

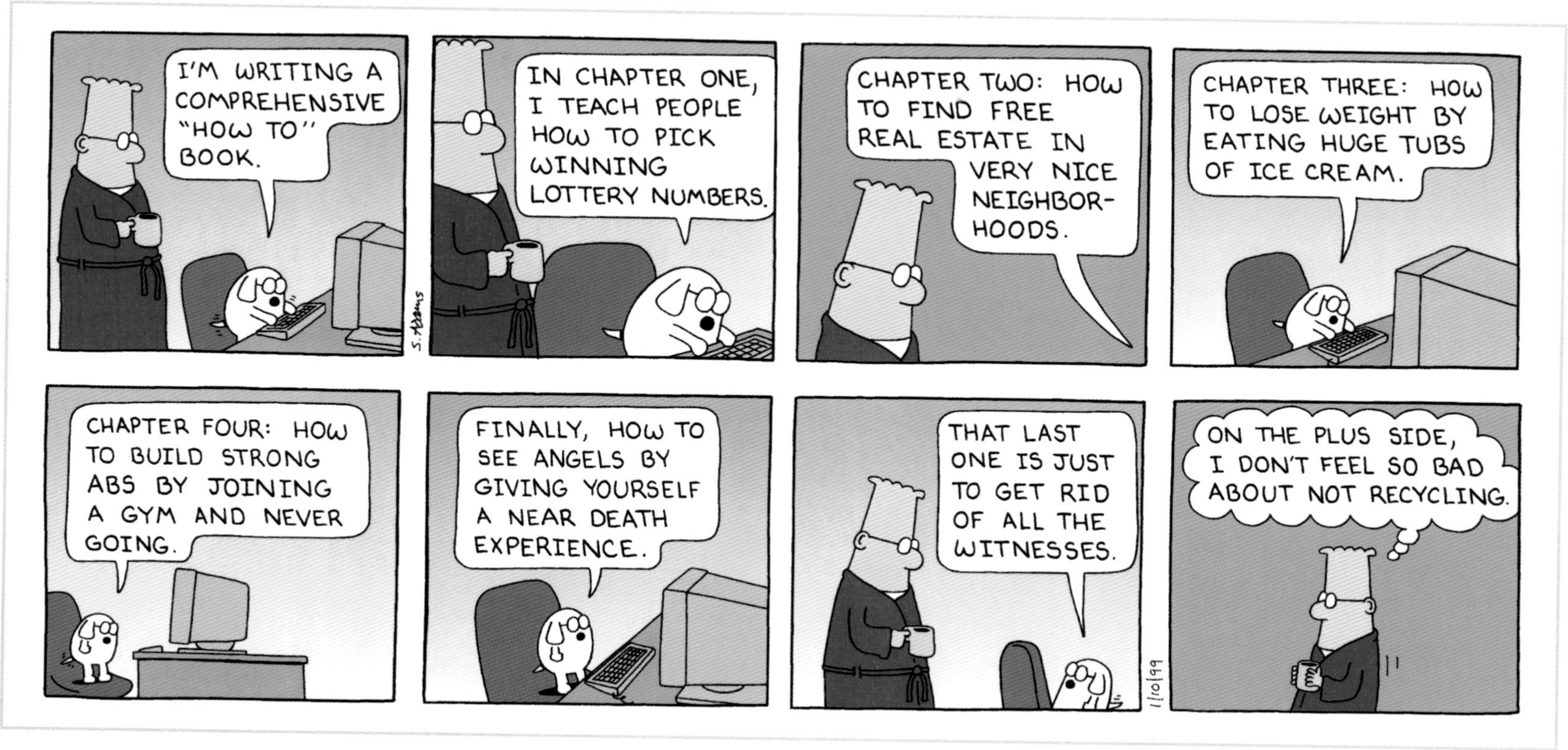
I'M WRITING A COMPREHENSIVE "HOW TO" BOOK.
S. Adams
IN CHAPTER ONE, I TEACH PEOPLE HOW TO PICK WINNING LOTTERY NUMBERS.
CHAPTER TWO: HOW TO FIND FREE REAL ESTATE IN VERY NICE NEIGHBOR-HOODS.
CHAPTER THREE: HOW TO LOSE WEIGHT BY EATING HUGE TUBS OF ICE CREAM.
CHAPTER FOUR: HOW TO BUILD STRONG ABS BY JOINING A GYM AND NEVER GOING.
FINALLY, HOW TO SEE ANGELS BY GIVING YOURSELF A NEAR DEATH EXPERIENCE.
THAT LAST ONE IS JUST TO GET RID OF ALL THE WITNESSES.
1/10/99
ON THE PLUS SIDE, I DON'T FEEL SO BAD ABOUT NOT RECYCLING.

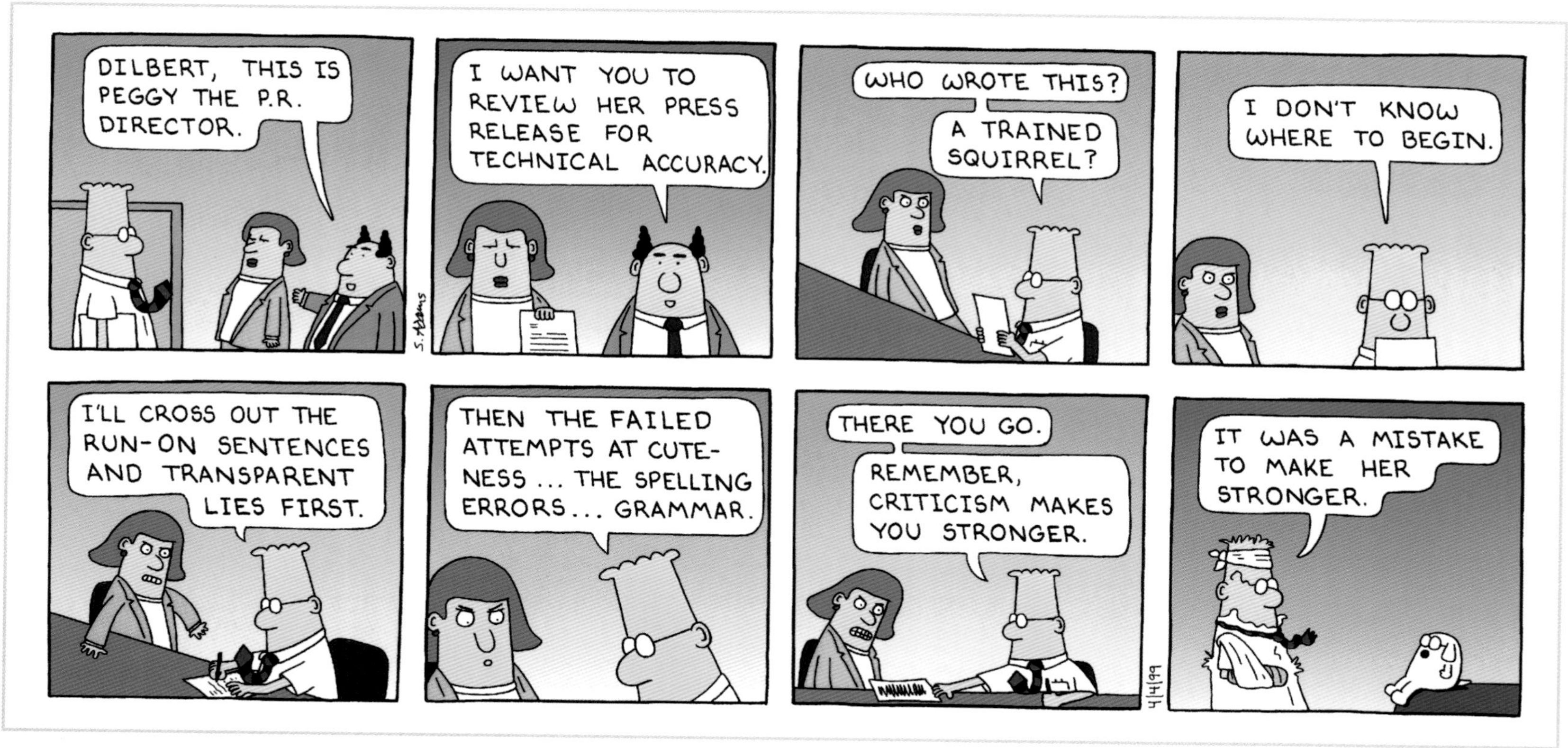
DILBERT, THIS IS PEGGY THE P.R. DIRECTOR.
S. Adams
I WANT YOU TO REVIEW HER PRESS RELEASE FOR TECHNICAL ACCURACY.
WHO WROTE THIS?
A TRAINED SQUIRREL?
I DON'T KNOW WHERE TO BEGIN.
I'LL CROSS OUT THE RUN-ON SENTENCES AND TRANSPARENT LIES FIRST.
THEN THE FAILED ATTEMPTS AT CUTE-NESS ... THE SPELLING ERRORS ... GRAMMAR.
THERE YOU GO.
REMEMBER, CRITICISM MAKES YOU STRONGER.
4/4/99
IT WAS A MISTAKE TO MAKE HER STRONGER.

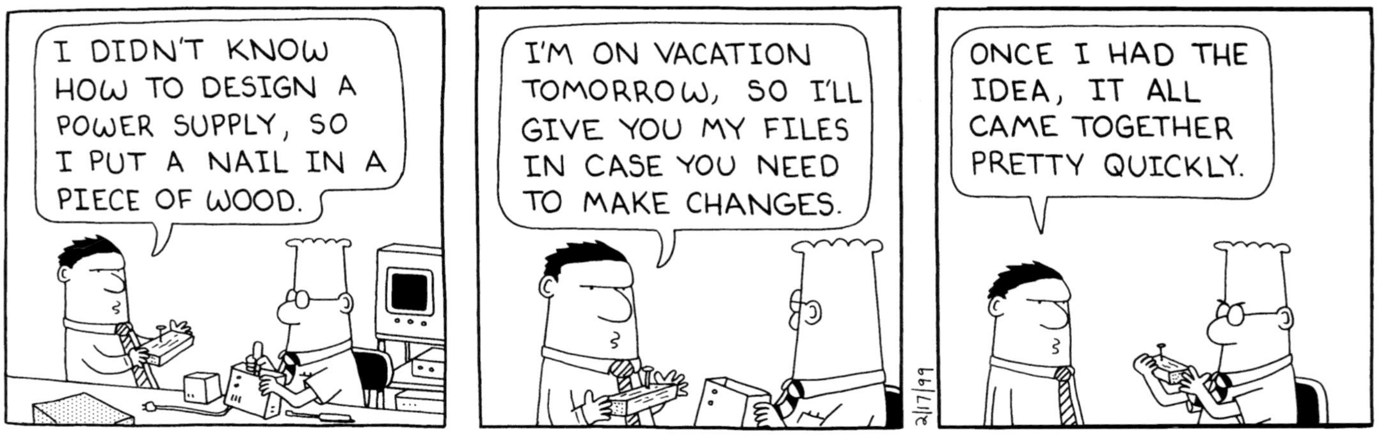
I DIDN'T KNOW HOW TO DESIGN A POWER SUPPLY, SO I PUT A NAIL IN A PIECE OF WOOD.
I'M ON VACATION TOMORROW, SO I'LL GIVE YOU MY FILES IN CASE YOU NEED TO MAKE CHANGES.
2/17/99
ONCE I HAD THE IDEA, IT ALL CAME TOGETHER PRETTY QUICKLY.

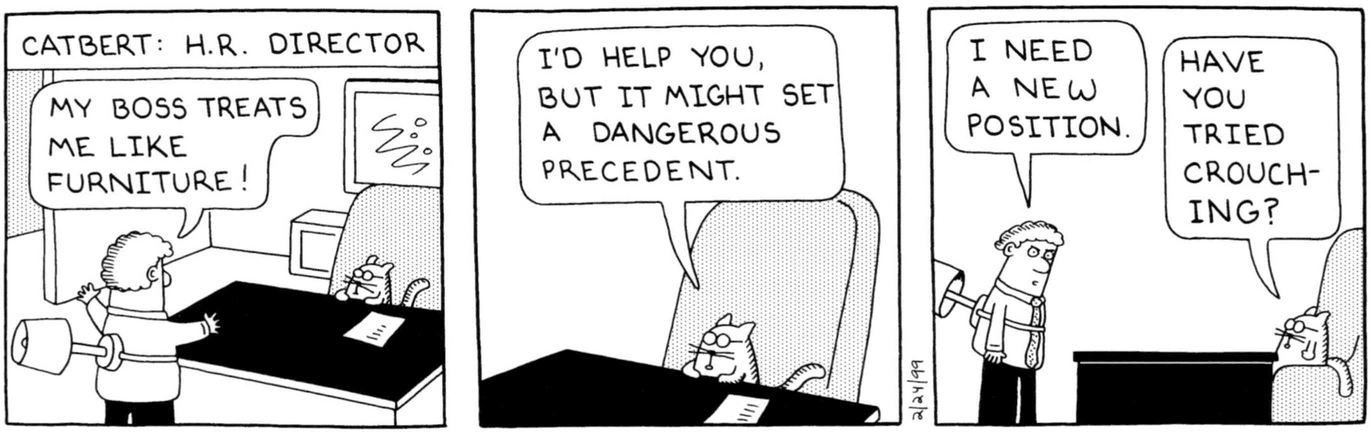
CATBERT: H.R. DIRECTOR
MY BOSS TREATS ME LIKE FURNITURE!
I'D HELP YOU, BUT IT MIGHT SET A DANGEROUS PRECEDENT.
2/24/99
I NEED A NEW POSITION.
HAVE YOU TRIED CROUCHING?

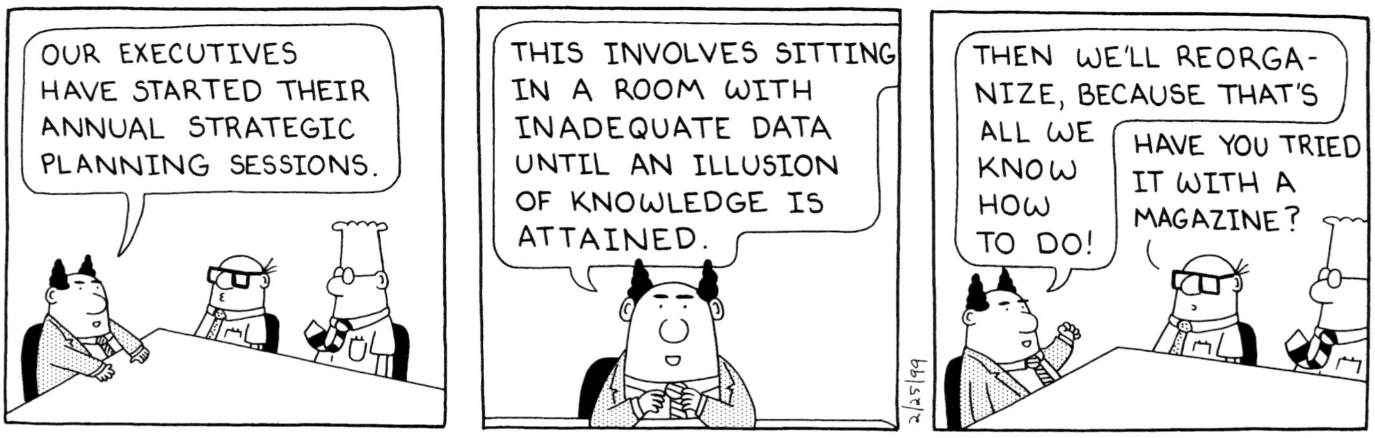
OUR EXECUTIVES HAVE STARTED THEIR ANNUAL STRATEGIC PLANNING SESSIONS.
THIS INVOLVES SITTING IN A ROOM WITH INADEQUATE DATA UNTIL AN ILLUSION OF KNOWLEDGE IS ATTAINED.
2/25/99
THEN WE'LL REORGANIZE, BECAUSE THAT'S ALL WE KNOW HOW TO DO!
HAVE YOU TRIED IT WITH A MAGAZINE?

I learned that with a little bit of ambiguity, you can get away with anything.

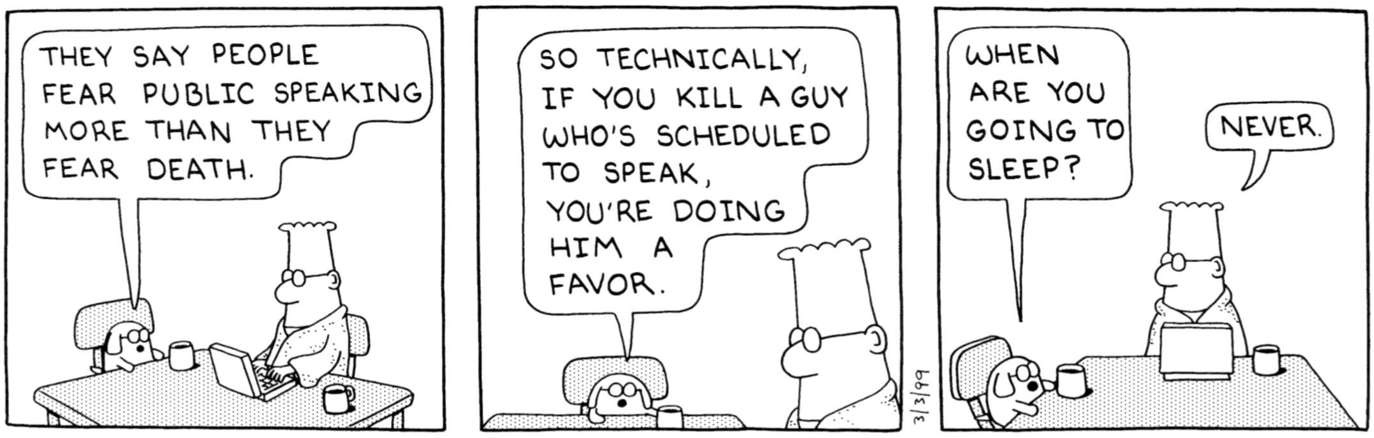
THEY SAY PEOPLE FEAR PUBLIC SPEAKING MORE THAN THEY FEAR DEATH.
SO TECHNICALLY, IF YOU KILL A GUY WHO'S SCHEDULED TO SPEAK, YOU'RE DOING HIM A FAVOR.
3/3/99
WHEN ARE YOU GOING TO SLEEP?
NEVER.

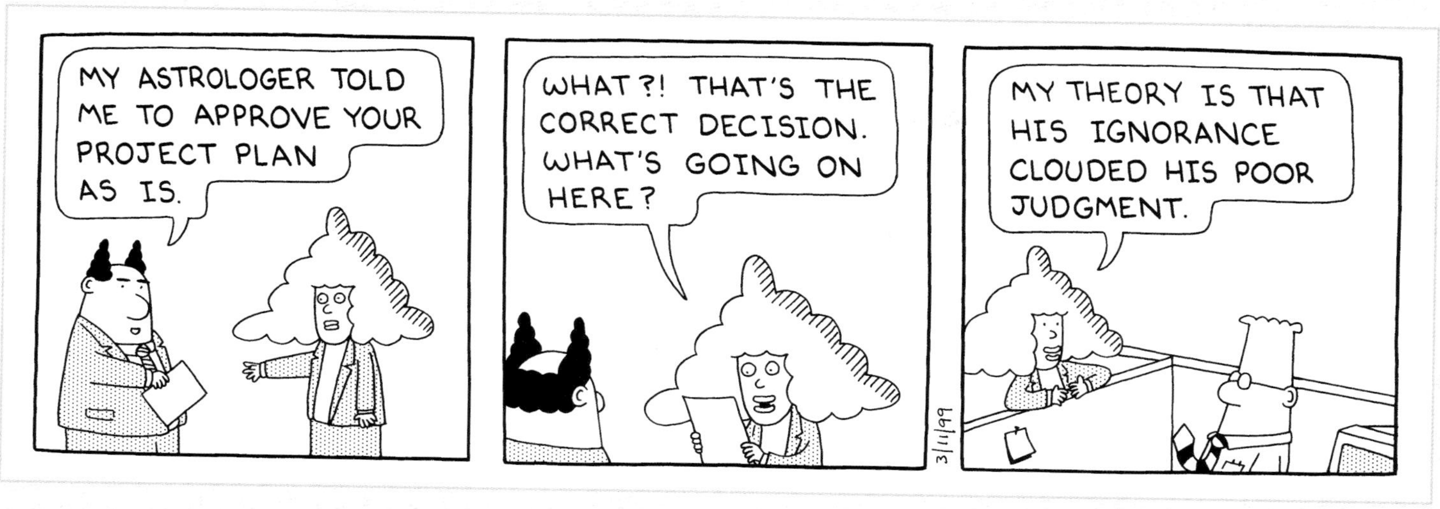
MY ASTROLOGER TOLD ME TO APPROVE YOUR PROJECT PLAN AS IS.
WHAT?! THAT'S THE CORRECT DECISION. WHAT'S GOING ON HERE?
3/11/99
MY THEORY IS THAT HIS IGNORANCE CLOUDED HIS POOR JUDGMENT.

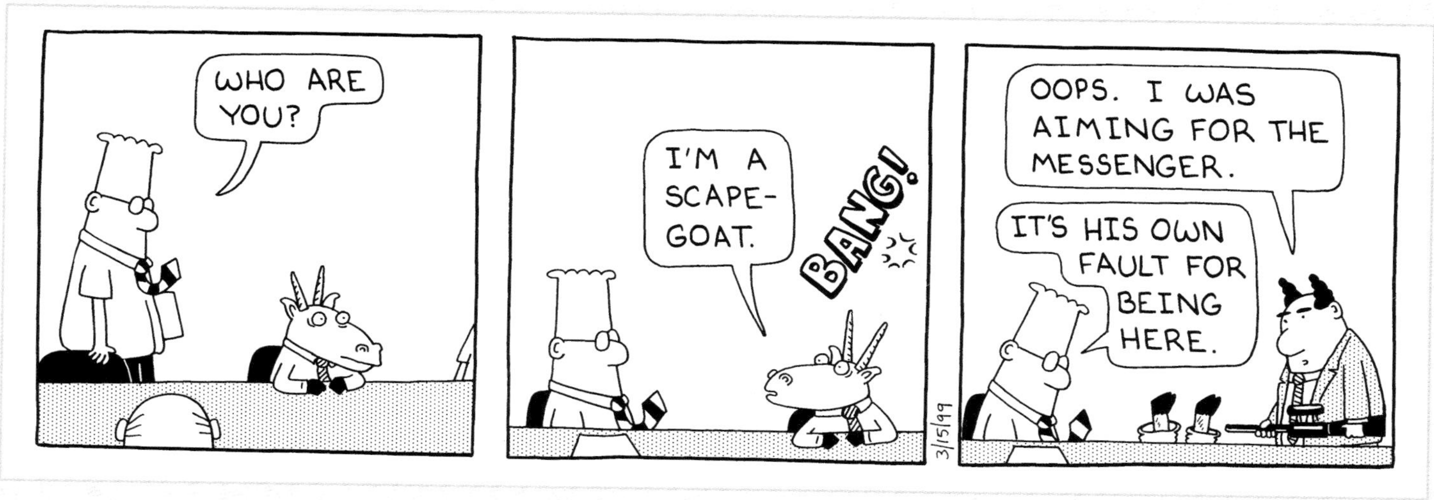
WHO ARE YOU?
I'M A SCAPE-GOAT.
BANG!
3/15/99
OOPS. I WAS AIMING FOR THE MESSENGER.
IT'S HIS OWN FAULT FOR BEING HERE.

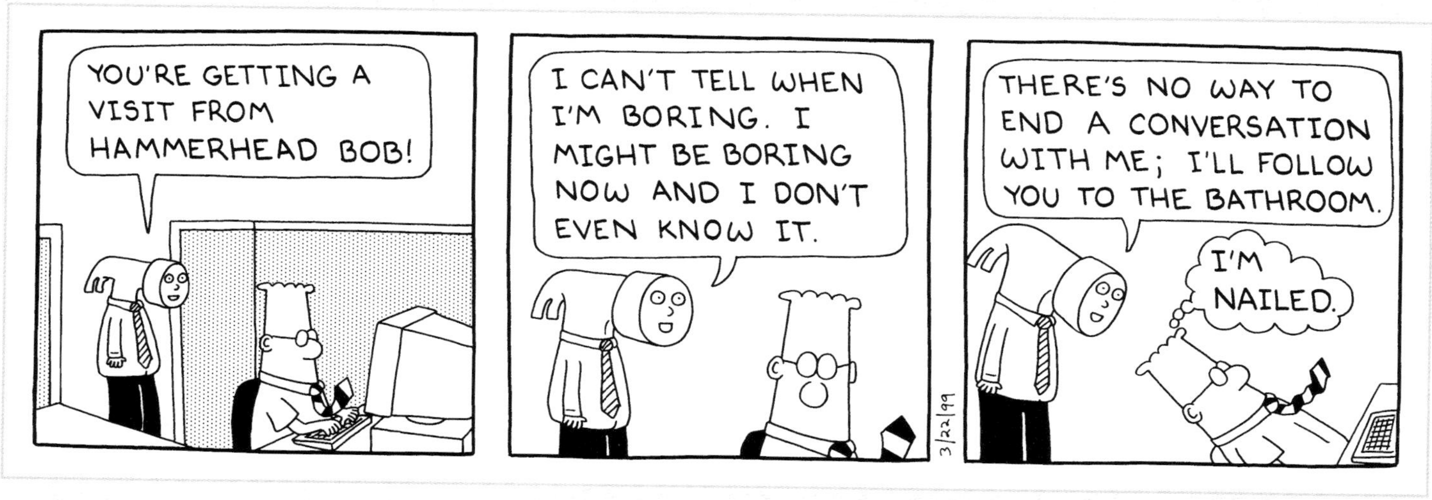
YOU'RE GETTING A VISIT FROM HAMMERHEAD BOB!
I CAN'T TELL WHEN I'M BORING. I MIGHT BE BORING NOW AND I DON'T EVEN KNOW IT.
3/22/99
THERE'S NO WAY TO END A CONVERSATION WITH ME; I'LL FOLLOW YOU TO THE BATHROOM.
I'M NAILED.

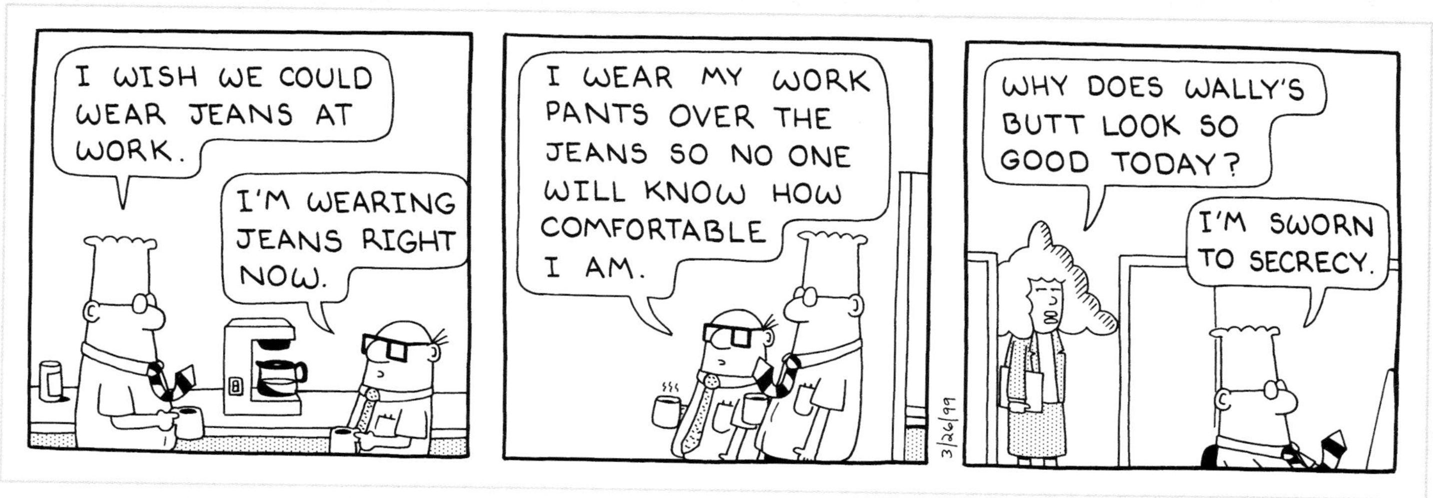
I WISH WE COULD WEAR JEANS AT WORK.
I'M WEARING JEANS RIGHT NOW.
I WEAR MY WORK PANTS OVER THE JEANS SO NO ONE WILL KNOW HOW COMFORTABLE I AM.
3/26/99
WHY DOES WALLY'S BUTT LOOK SO GOOD TODAY?
I'M SWORN TO SECRECY.

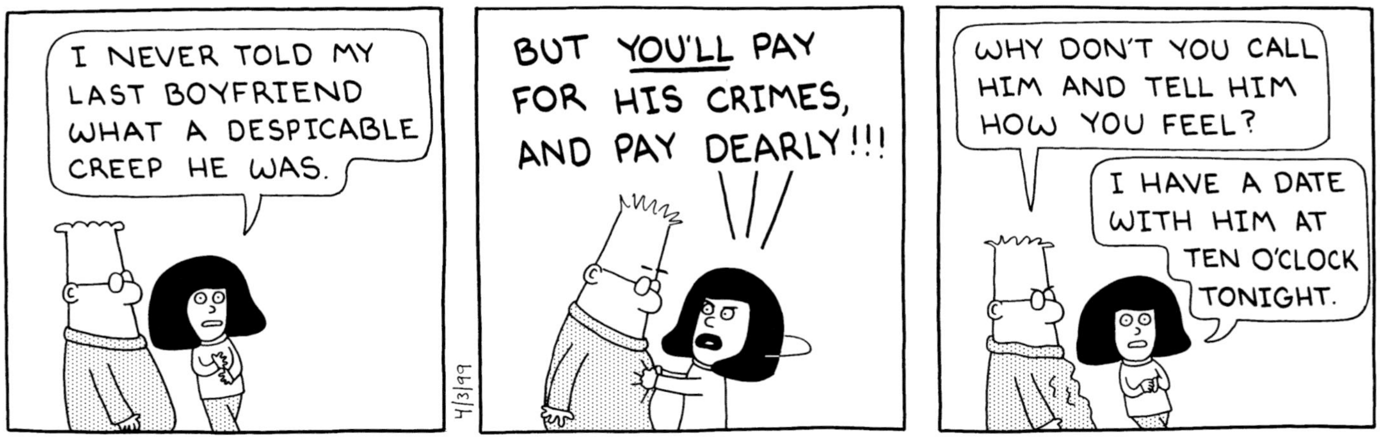
I NEVER TOLD MY LAST BOYFRIEND WHAT A DESPICABLE CREEP HE WAS.
4/3/99
BUT YOU'LL PAY FOR HIS CRIMES, AND PAY DEARLY!!!
WHY DON'T YOU CALL HIM AND TELL HIM HOW YOU FEEL?
I HAVE A DATE WITH HIM AT TEN O'CLOCK TONIGHT.

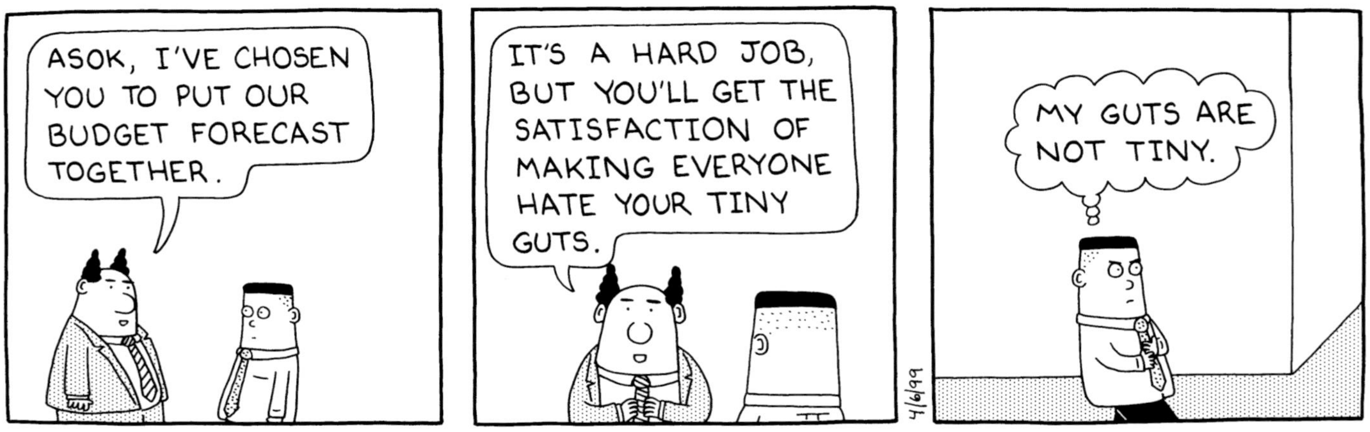
ASOK, I'VE CHOSEN YOU TO PUT OUR BUDGET FORECAST TOGETHER.
IT'S A HARD JOB, BUT YOU'LL GET THE SATISFACTION OF MAKING EVERYONE HATE YOUR TINY GUTS.
4/6/99
MY GUTS ARE NOT TINY.

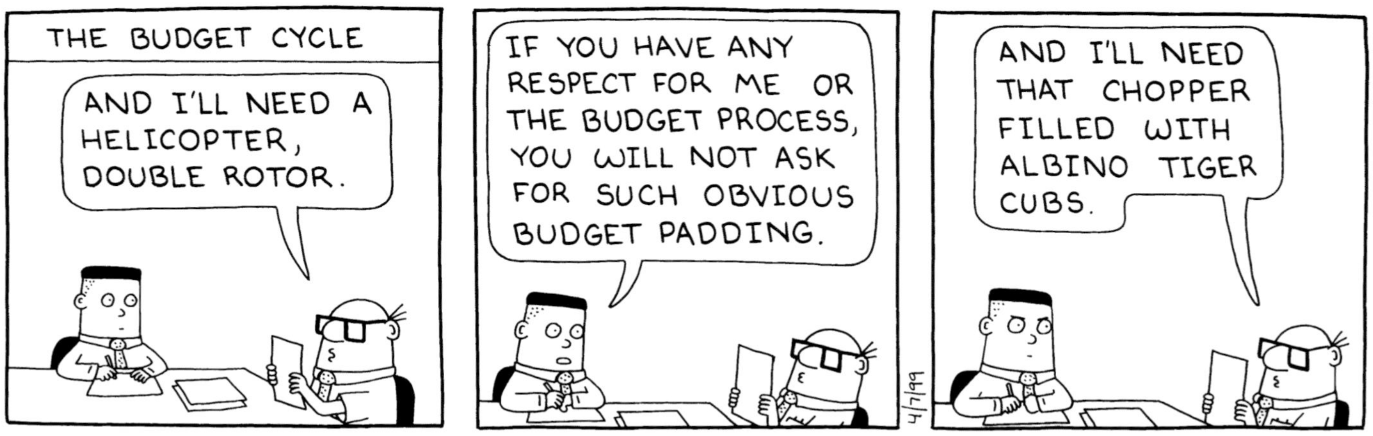
THE BUDGET CYCLE
AND I'LL NEED A HELICOPTER, DOUBLE ROTOR.
IF YOU HAVE ANY RESPECT FOR ME OR THE BUDGET PROCESS, YOU WILL NOT ASK FOR SUCH OBVIOUS BUDGET PADDING.
4/7/99
AND I'LL NEED THAT CHOPPER FILLED WITH ALBINO TIGER CUBS.

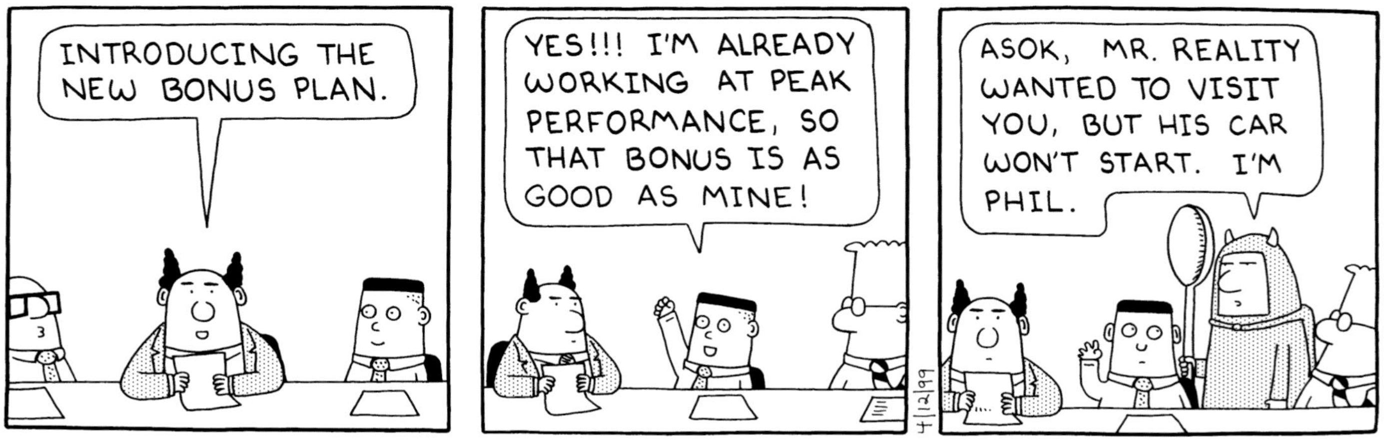
INTRODUCING THE NEW BONUS PLAN.
YES!!! I'M ALREADY WORKING AT PEAK PERFORMANCE, SO THAT BONUS IS AS GOOD AS MINE!
4/12/99
ASOK, MR. REALITY WANTED TO VISIT YOU, BUT HIS CAR WON'T START. I'M PHIL.

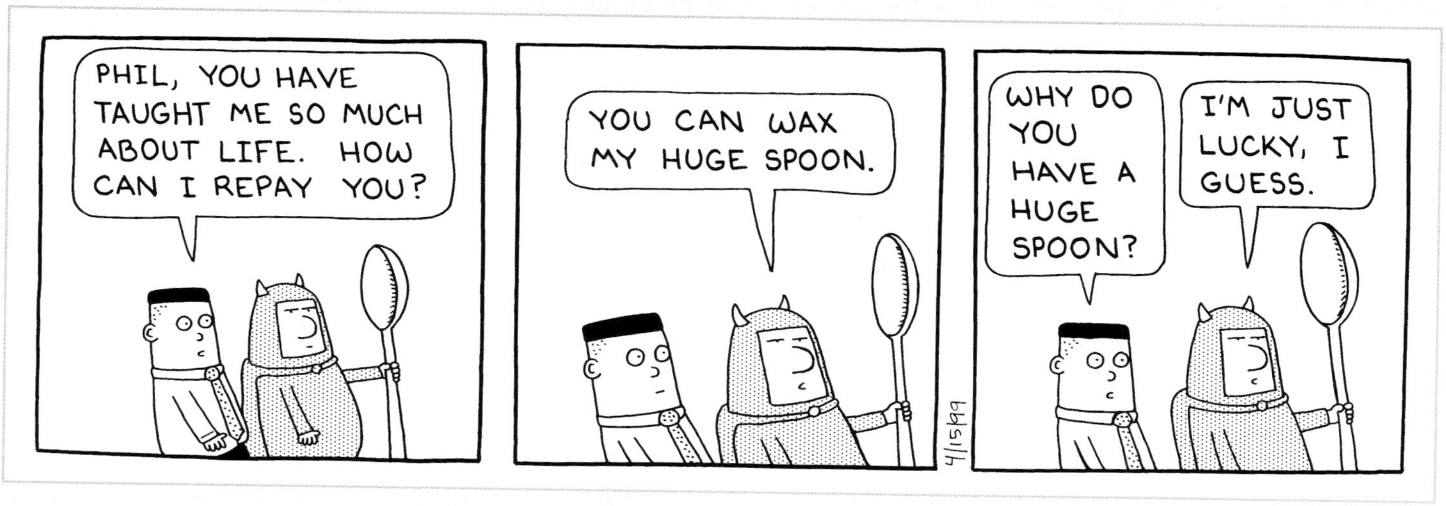
PHIL, YOU HAVE TAUGHT ME SO MUCH ABOUT LIFE. HOW CAN I REPAY YOU?
YOU CAN WAX MY HUGE SPOON.
4/15/99
WHY DO YOU HAVE A HUGE SPOON?
I'M JUST LUCKY, I GUESS.

The strip above came out naughtier than I intended.

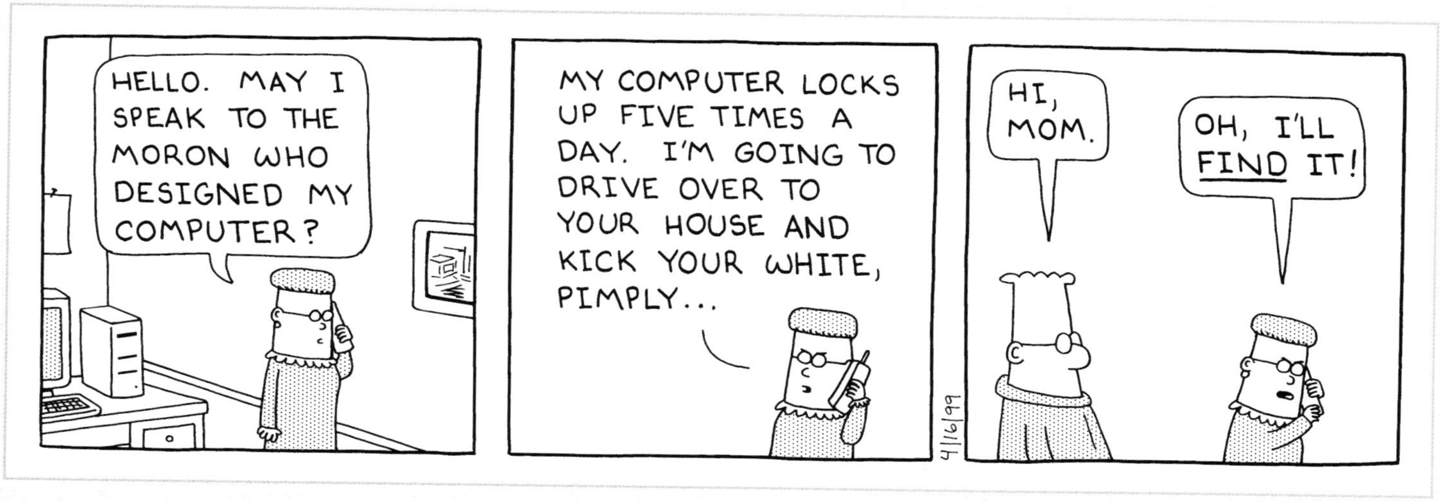
HELLO. MAY I SPEAK TO THE MORON WHO DESIGNED MY COMPUTER?
MY COMPUTER LOCKS UP FIVE TIMES A DAY. I'M GOING TO DRIVE OVER TO YOUR HOUSE AND KICK YOUR WHITE, PIMPLY...
4/16/99
HI, MOM.
OH, I'LL FIND IT!

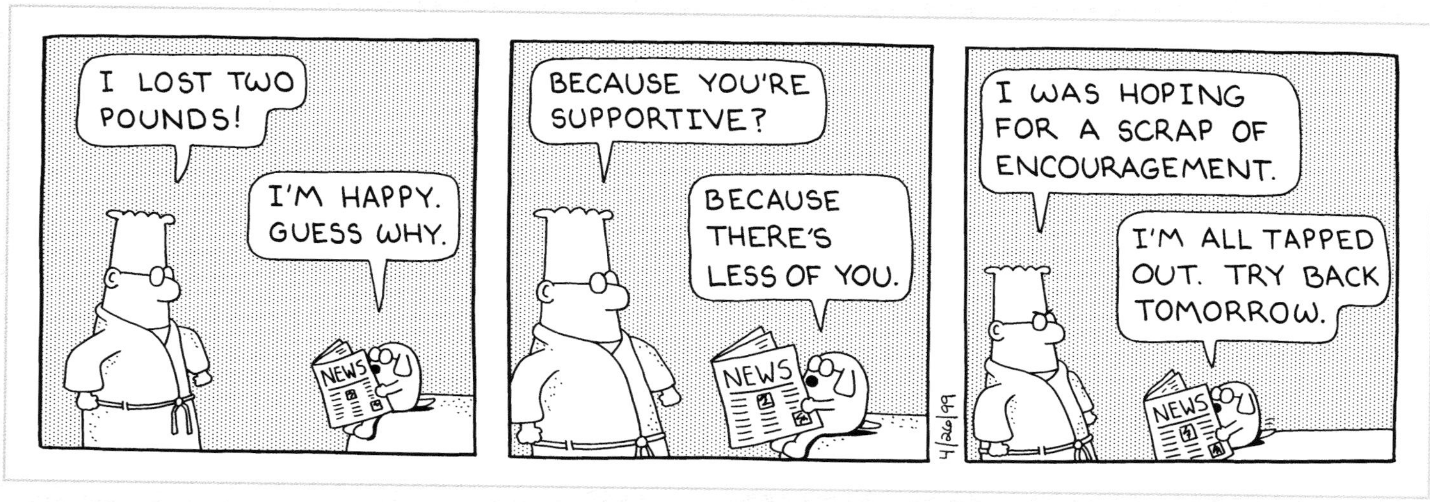
I LOST TWO POUNDS!
I'M HAPPY. GUESS WHY.
NEWS
BECAUSE YOU'RE SUPPORTIVE?
BECAUSE THERE'S LESS OF YOU.
NEWS
4/26/99
I WAS HOPING FOR A SCRAP OF ENCOURAGEMENT.
I'M ALL TAPPED OUT. TRY BACK TOMORROW.
NEWS

I was in search of the holy grail of newspaper comic writing: using the forbidden word "crap" and getting away with it.

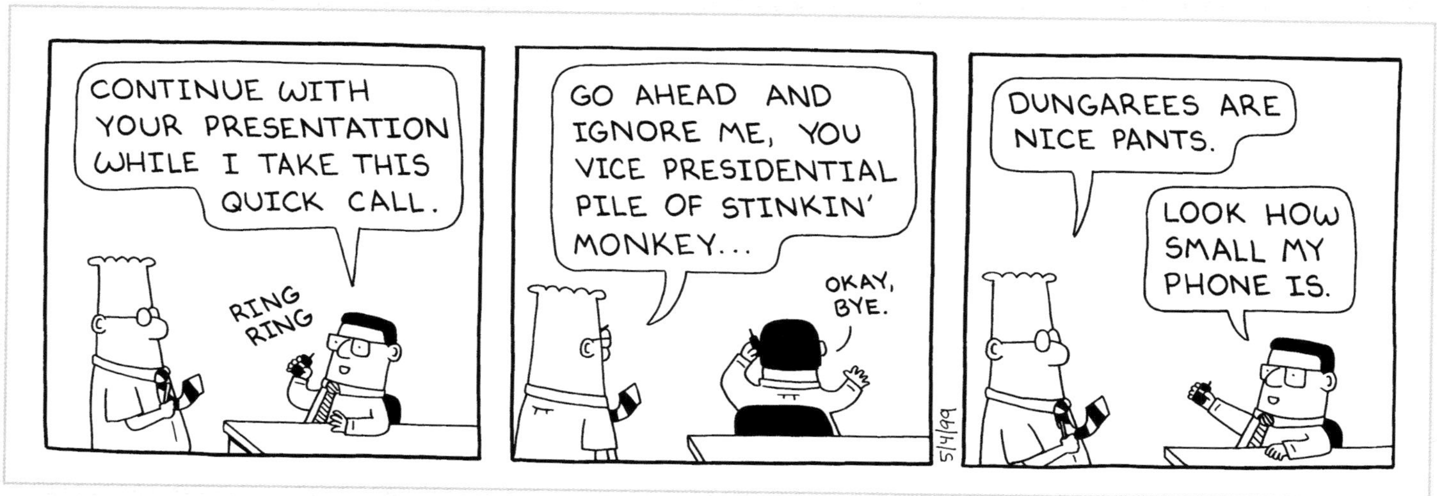
CONTINUE WITH YOUR PRESENTATION WHILE I TAKE THIS QUICK CALL.
RING RING
GO AHEAD AND IGNORE ME, YOU VICE PRESIDENTIAL PILE OF STINKIN' MONKEY...
OKAY, BYE.
5/4/99
DUNGAREES ARE NICE PANTS.
LOOK HOW SMALL MY PHONE IS.

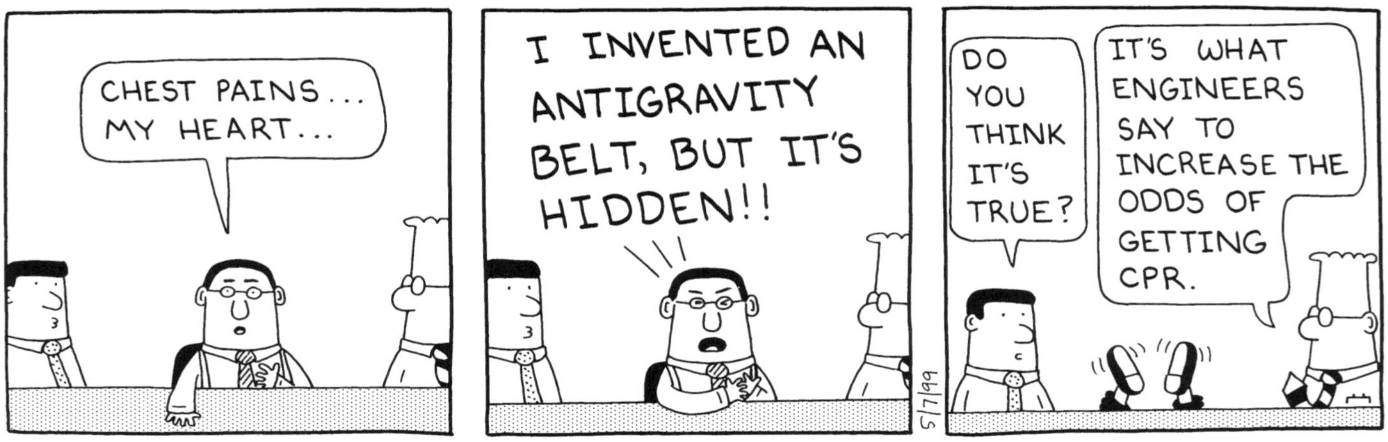
CHEST PAINS... MY HEART...
I INVENTED AN ANTIGRAVITY BELT, BUT IT'S HIDDEN!!
DO YOU THINK IT'S TRUE?
IT'S WHAT ENGINEERS SAY TO INCREASE THE ODDS OF GETTING CPR.
5/7/99

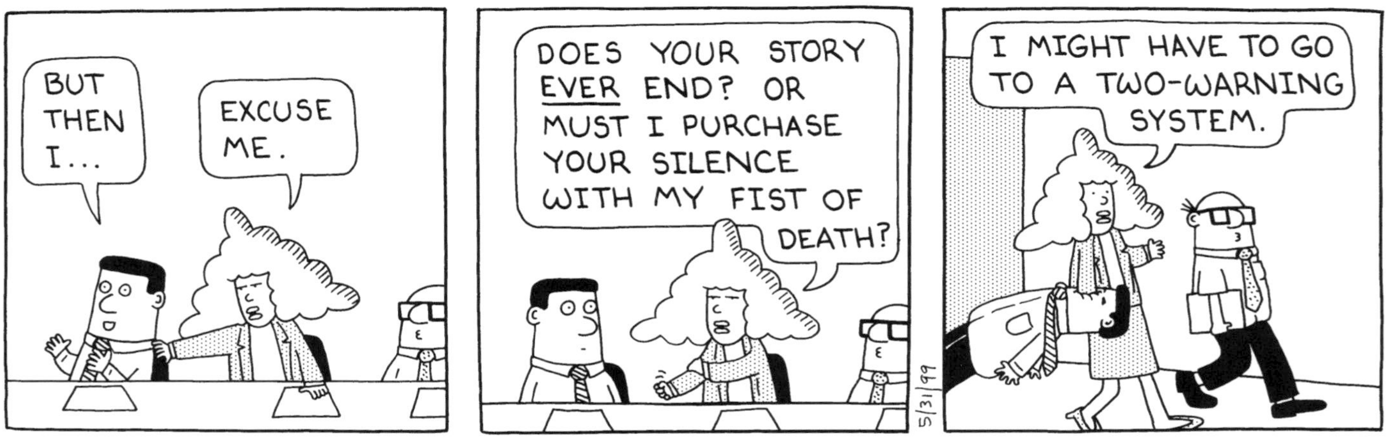
BUT THEN I...
EXCUSE ME.
DOES YOUR STORY EVER END? OR MUST I PURCHASE YOUR SILENCE WITH MY FIST OF DEATH?
I MIGHT HAVE TO GO TO A TWO-WARNING SYSTEM.
5/31/99

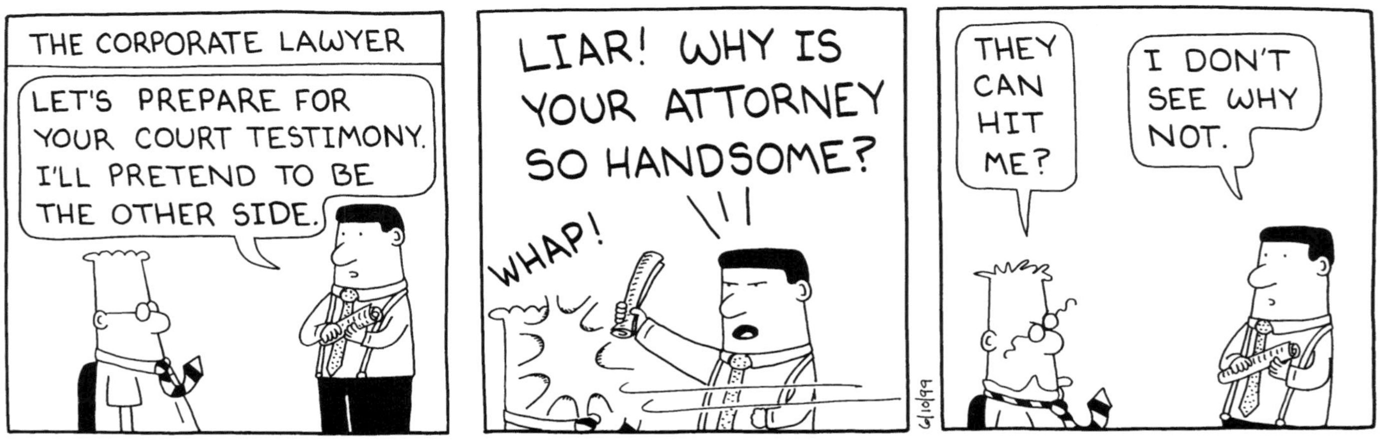
THE CORPORATE LAWYER
LET'S PREPARE FOR YOUR COURT TESTIMONY. I'LL PRETEND TO BE THE OTHER SIDE.
LIAR! WHY IS YOUR ATTORNEY SO HANDSOME?
WHAP!
THEY CAN HIT ME?
I DON'T SEE WHY NOT.
6/10/99

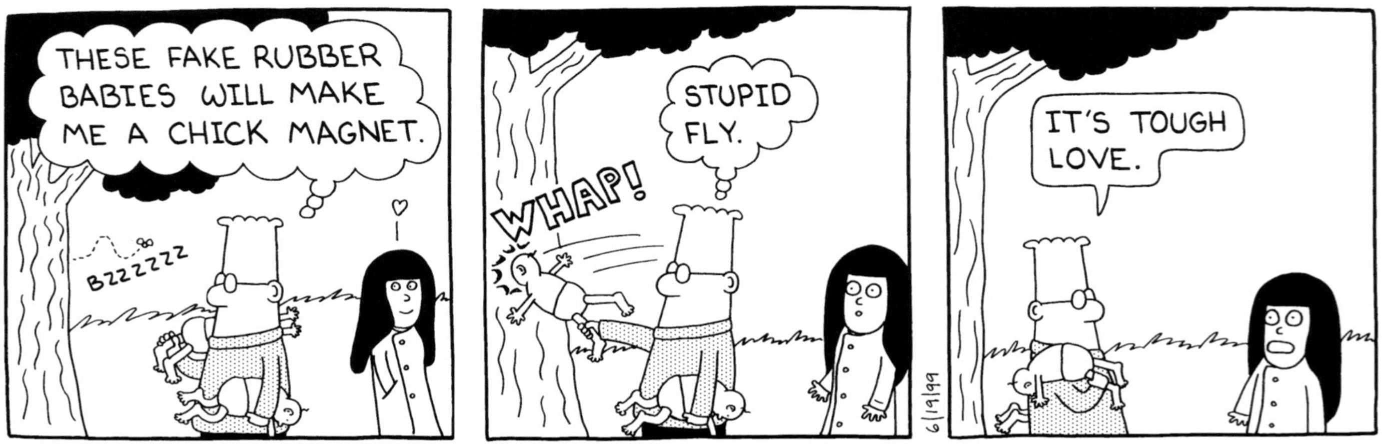
THESE FAKE RUBBER BABIES WILL MAKE ME A CHICK MAGNET.
BZZZZZZ
STUPID FLY.
WHAP!
IT'S TOUGH LOVE.
6/19/99

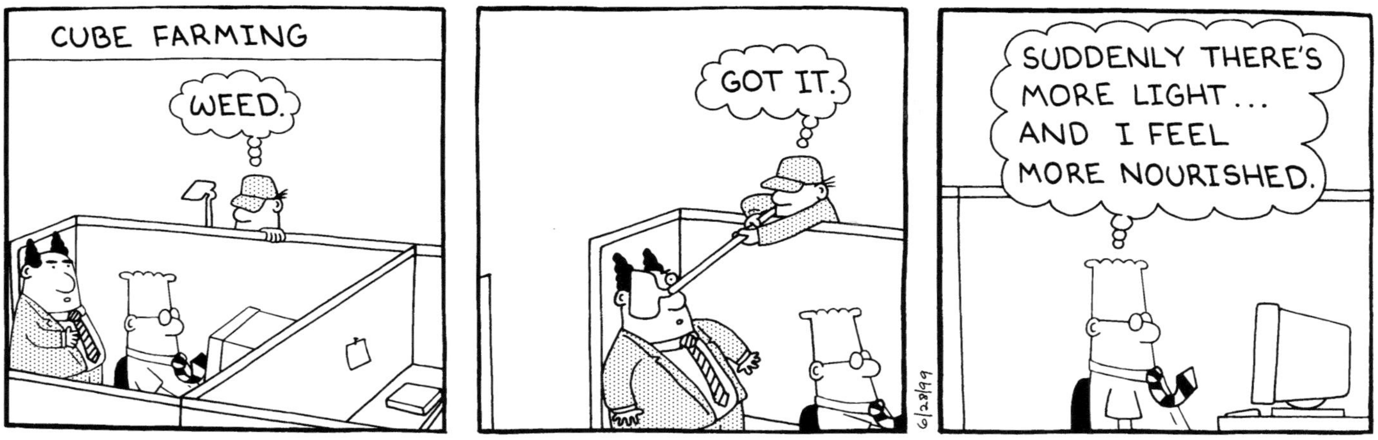
CUBE FARMING
WEED.
GOT IT.
SUDDENLY THERE'S MORE LIGHT... AND I FEEL MORE NOURISHED.
6/28/99

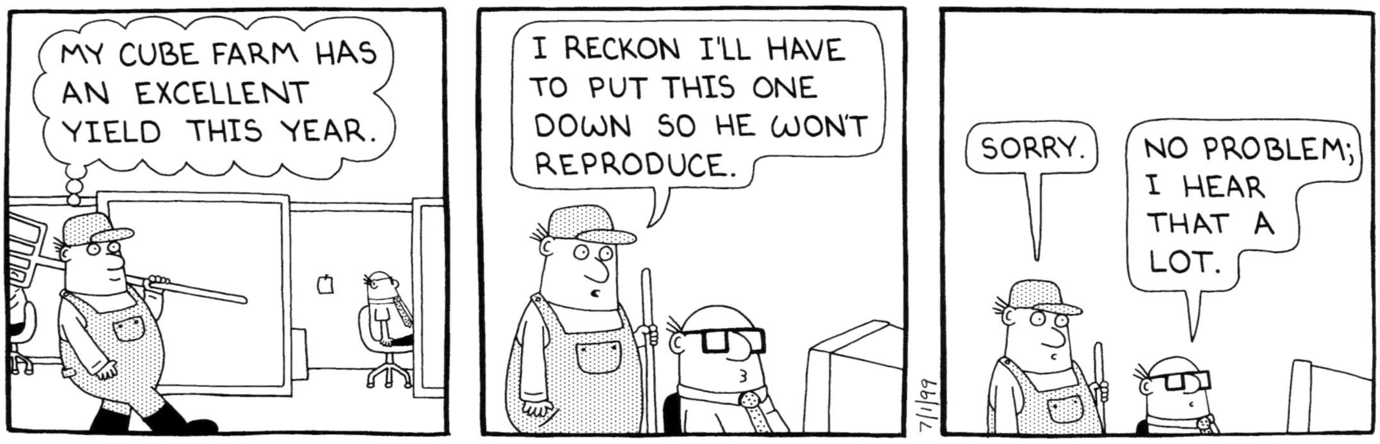
MY CUBE FARM HAS AN EXCELLENT YIELD THIS YEAR.
I RECKON I'LL HAVE TO PUT THIS ONE DOWN SO HE WON'T REPRODUCE.
SORRY.
NO PROBLEM; I HEAR THAT A LOT.
7/1/99

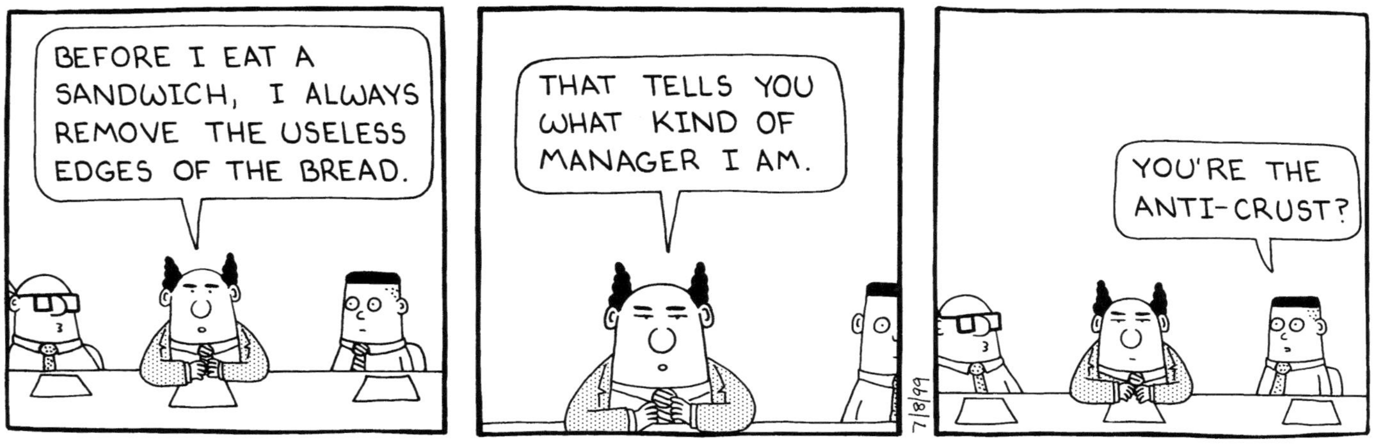
BEFORE I EAT A SANDWICH, I ALWAYS REMOVE THE USELESS EDGES OF THE BREAD.
THAT TELLS YOU WHAT KIND OF MANAGER I AM.
YOU'RE THE ANTI-CRUST?
7/8/99

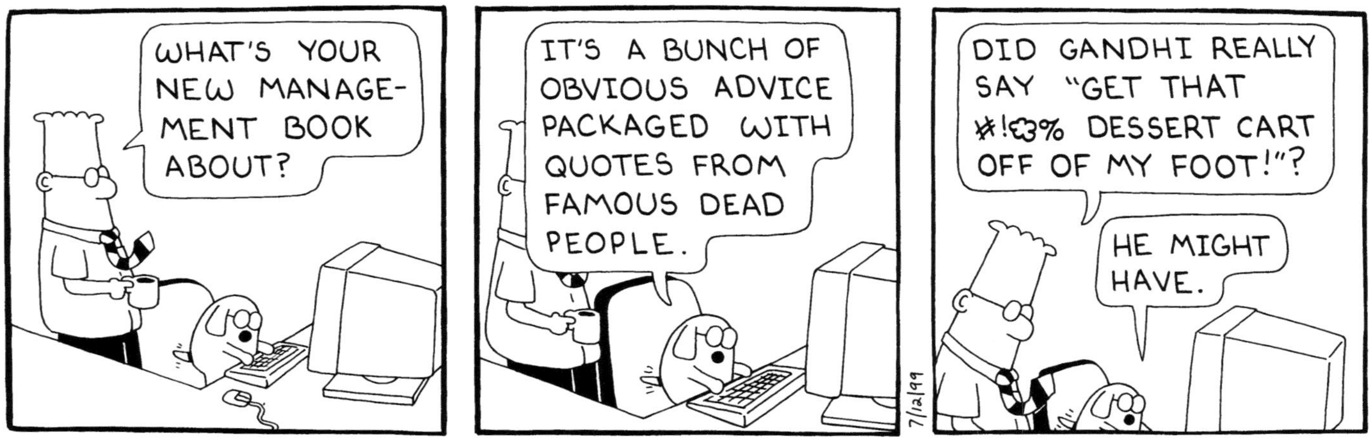
WHAT'S YOUR NEW MANAGE-MENT BOOK ABOUT?
IT'S A BUNCH OF OBVIOUS ADVICE PACKAGED WITH QUOTES FROM FAMOUS DEAD PEOPLE.
DID GANDHI REALLY SAY "GET THAT ✱!✿% DESSERT CART OFF OF MY FOOT!"?
HE MIGHT HAVE.
7/12/99

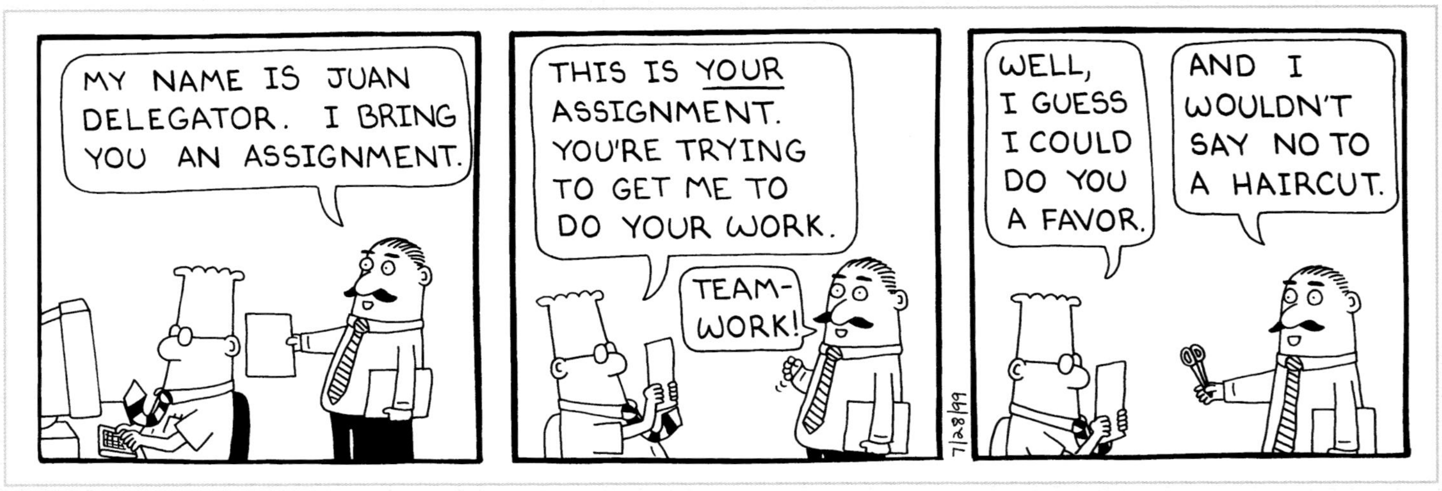
MY NAME IS JUAN DELEGATOR. I BRING YOU AN ASSIGNMENT.
THIS IS YOUR ASSIGNMENT. YOU'RE TRYING TO GET ME TO DO YOUR WORK.
TEAM-WORK!
7/28/99
WELL, I GUESS I COULD DO YOU A FAVOR.
AND I WOULDN'T SAY NO TO A HAIRCUT.

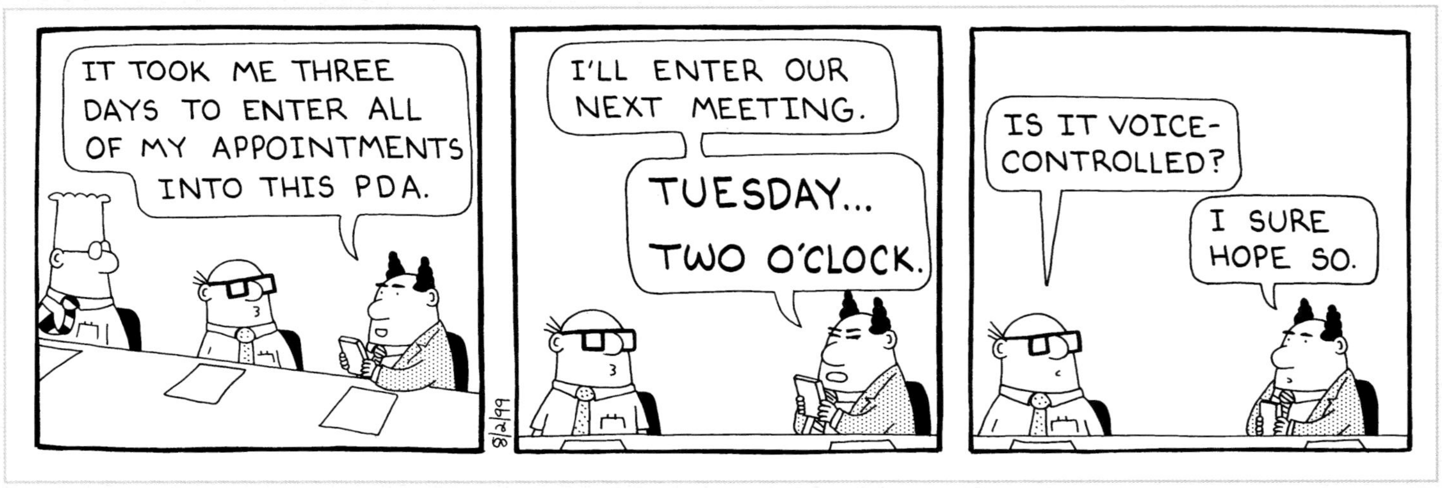
IT TOOK ME THREE DAYS TO ENTER ALL OF MY APPOINTMENTS INTO THIS PDA.
8/2/99
I'LL ENTER OUR NEXT MEETING.
TUESDAY... TWO O'CLOCK.
IS IT VOICE-CONTROLLED?
I SURE HOPE SO.

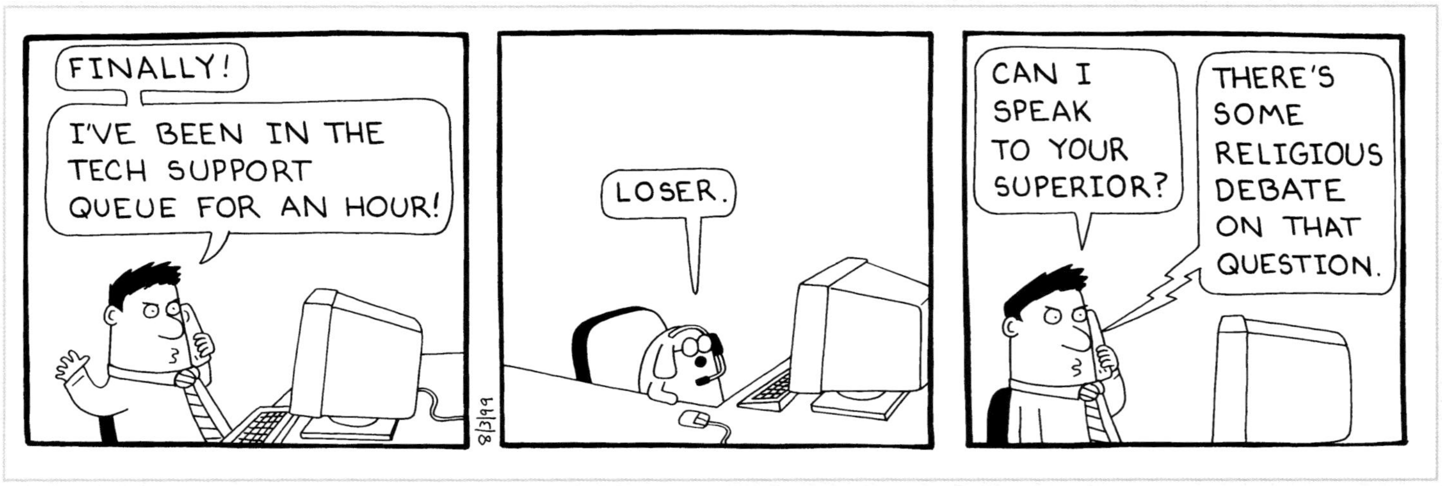
FINALLY!
I'VE BEEN IN THE TECH SUPPORT QUEUE FOR AN HOUR!
8/3/99
LOSER.
CAN I SPEAK TO YOUR SUPERIOR?
THERE'S SOME RELIGIOUS DEBATE ON THAT QUESTION.

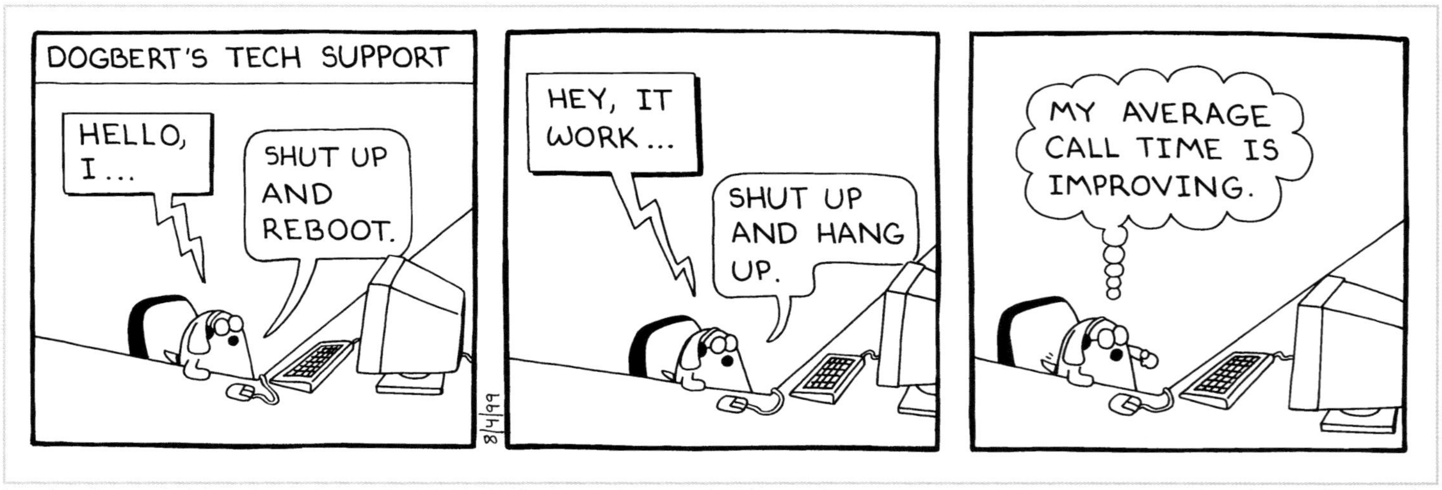
DOGBERT'S TECH SUPPORT
HELLO, I...
SHUT UP AND REBOOT.
8/4/99
HEY, IT WORK...
SHUT UP AND HANG UP.
MY AVERAGE CALL TIME IS IMPROVING.

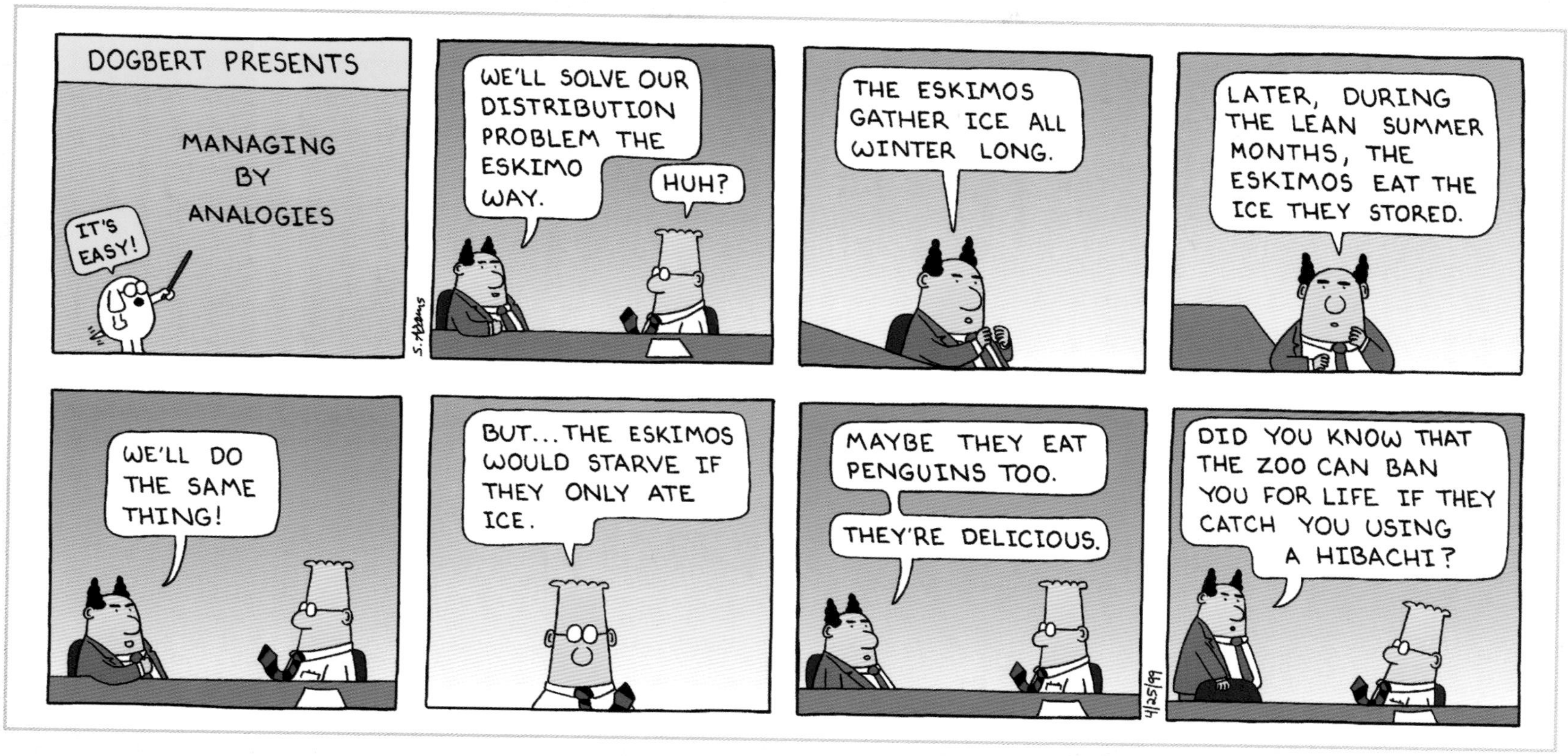
DOGBERT PRESENTS
MANAGING BY ANALOGIES
IT'S EASY!
S. ADAMS
WE'LL SOLVE OUR DISTRIBUTION PROBLEM THE ESKIMO WAY.
HUH?
THE ESKIMOS GATHER ICE ALL WINTER LONG.
LATER, DURING THE LEAN SUMMER MONTHS, THE ESKIMOS EAT THE ICE THEY STORED.
WE'LL DO THE SAME THING!
BUT...THE ESKIMOS WOULD STARVE IF THEY ONLY ATE ICE.
MAYBE THEY EAT PENGUINS TOO.
THEY'RE DELICIOUS.
4/25/99
DID YOU KNOW THAT THE ZOO CAN BAN YOU FOR LIFE IF THEY CATCH YOU USING A HIBACHI?

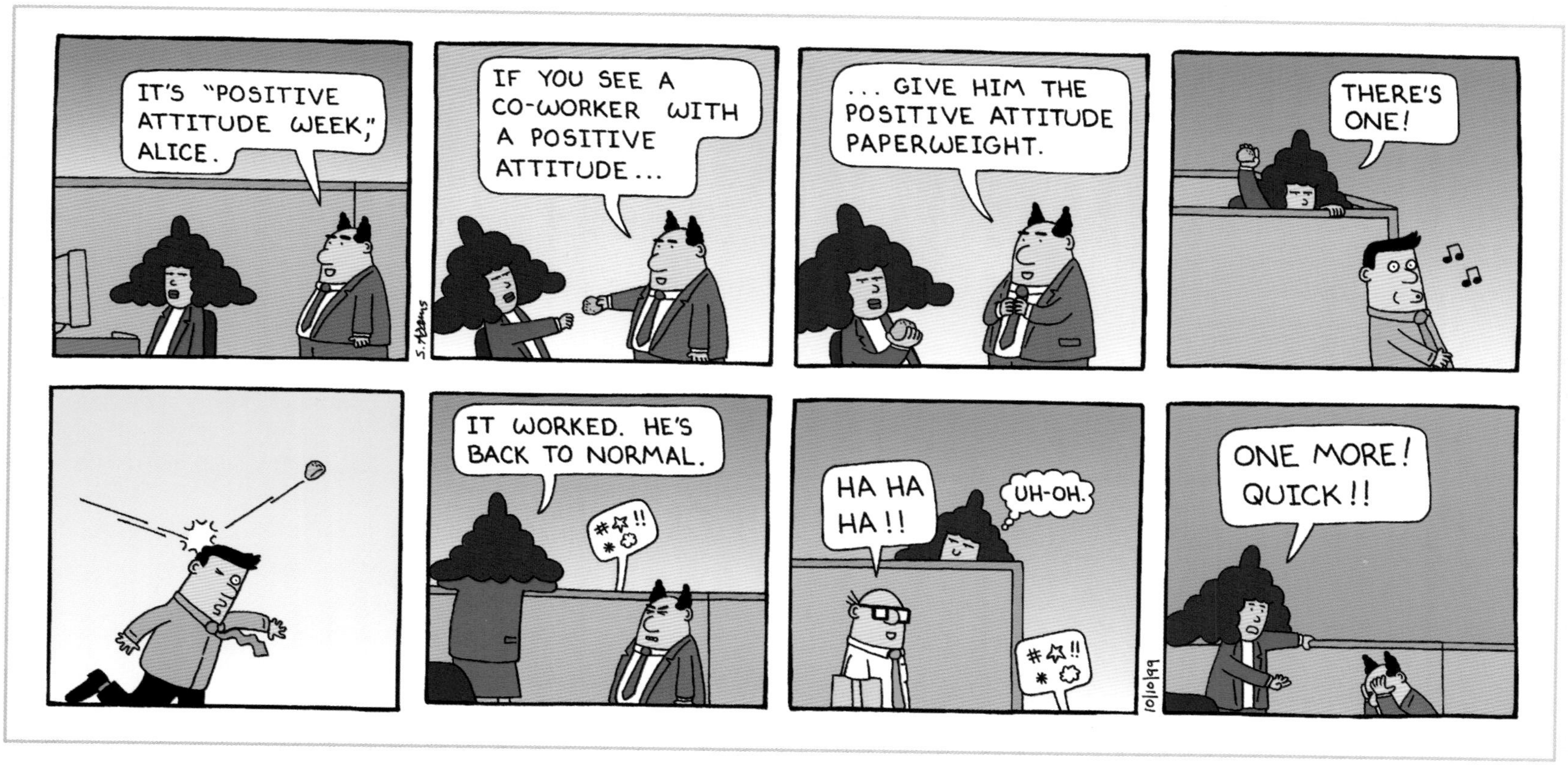
IT'S "POSITIVE ATTITUDE WEEK," ALICE.
S. ADAMS
IF YOU SEE A CO-WORKER WITH A POSITIVE ATTITUDE...
... GIVE HIM THE POSITIVE ATTITUDE PAPERWEIGHT.
THERE'S ONE!
IT WORKED. HE'S BACK TO NORMAL.
#☆!! * ✪
HA HA HA!!
UH-OH.
#☆!! * ✪
10/10/99
ONE MORE! QUICK!!

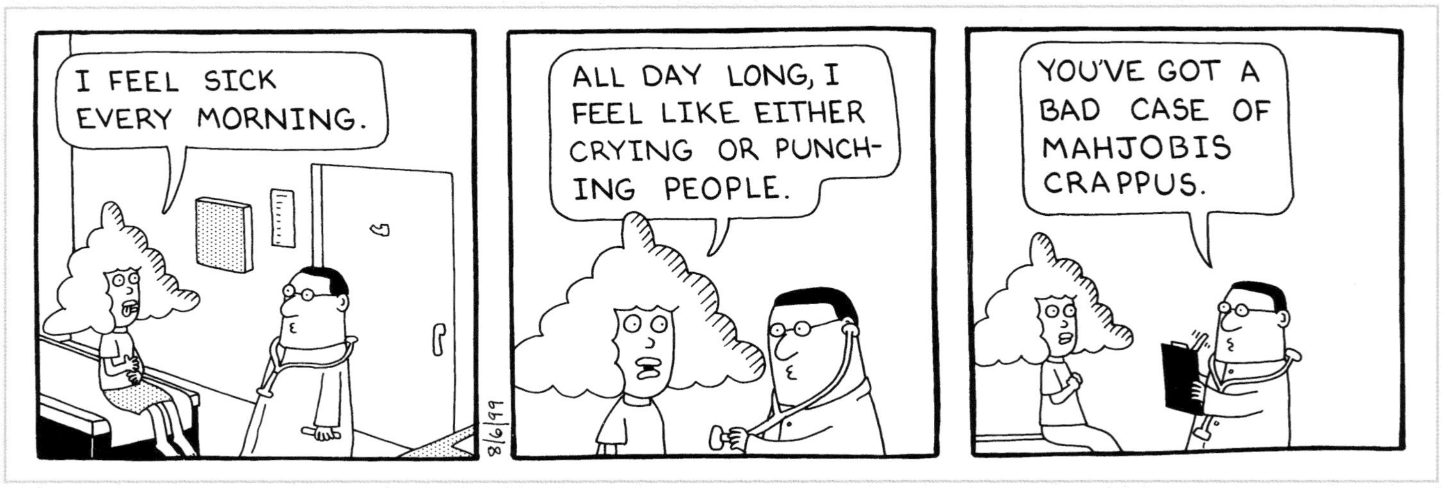
I FEEL SICK EVERY MORNING.
ALL DAY LONG, I FEEL LIKE EITHER CRYING OR PUNCH-ING PEOPLE.
YOU'VE GOT A BAD CASE OF MAHJOBIS CRAPPUS.
8/6/99

"Crappus" is Latin for a word I wasn't allowed to put in comics.

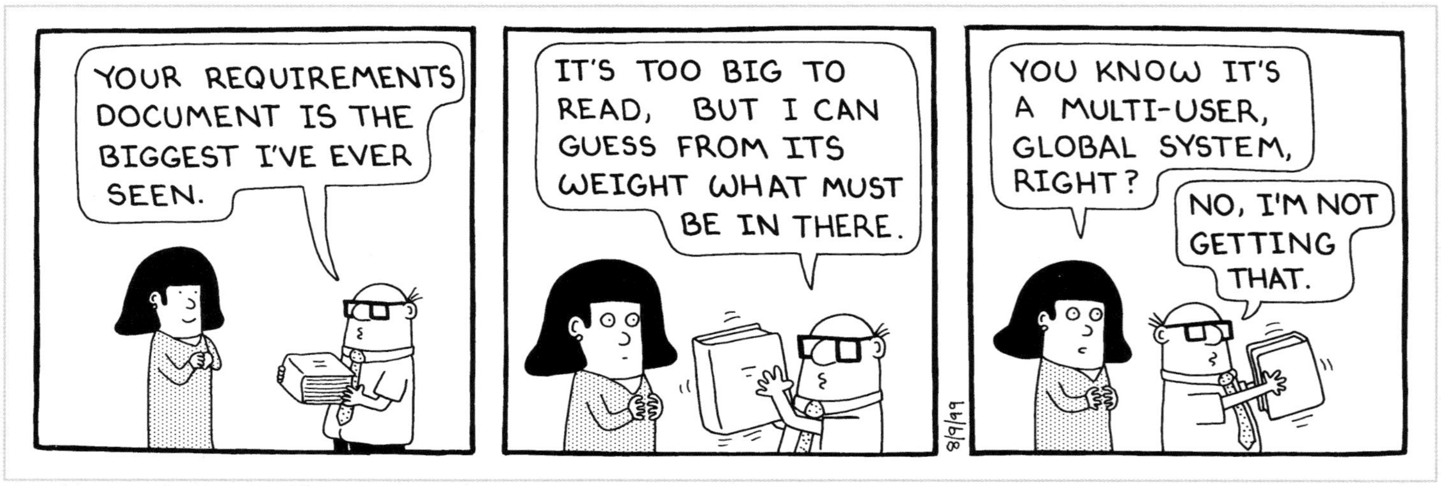
YOUR REQUIREMENTS DOCUMENT IS THE BIGGEST I'VE EVER SEEN.
IT'S TOO BIG TO READ, BUT I CAN GUESS FROM ITS WEIGHT WHAT MUST BE IN THERE.
YOU KNOW IT'S A MULTI-USER, GLOBAL SYSTEM, RIGHT?
NO, I'M NOT GETTING THAT.
8/9/99

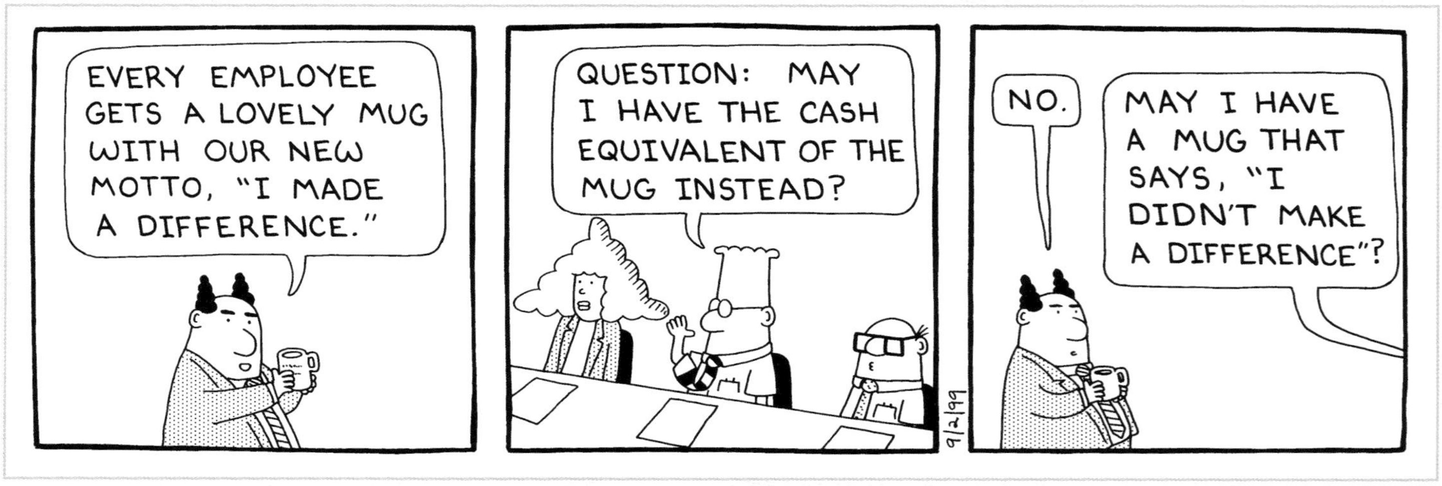
EVERY EMPLOYEE GETS A LOVELY MUG WITH OUR NEW MOTTO, "I MADE A DIFFERENCE."
QUESTION: MAY I HAVE THE CASH EQUIVALENT OF THE MUG INSTEAD?
NO.
MAY I HAVE A MUG THAT SAYS, "I DIDN'T MAKE A DIFFERENCE"?
9/2/99

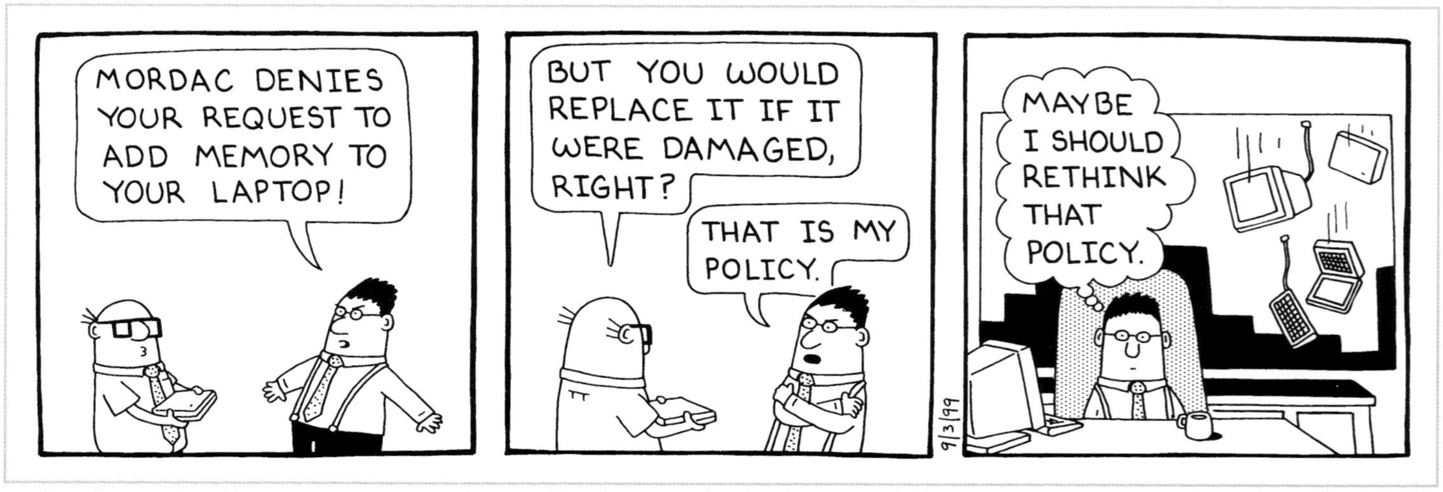
MORDAC DENIES YOUR REQUEST TO ADD MEMORY TO YOUR LAPTOP!
BUT YOU WOULD REPLACE IT IF IT WERE DAMAGED, RIGHT?
THAT IS MY POLICY.
MAYBE I SHOULD RETHINK THAT POLICY.
9/3/99

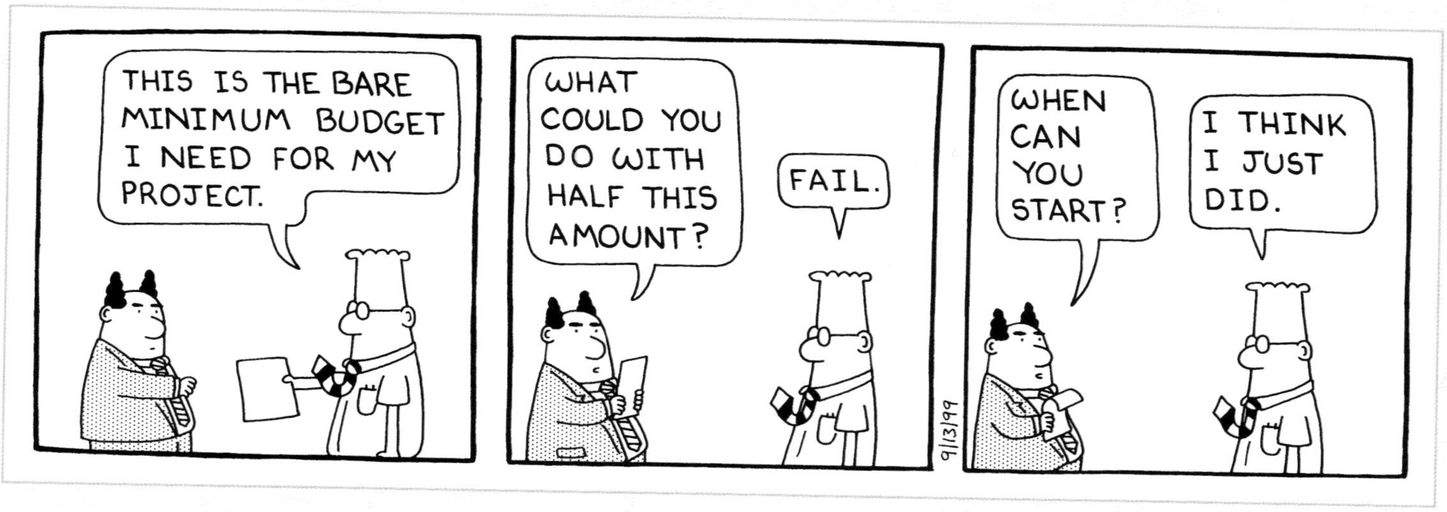
THIS IS THE BARE MINIMUM BUDGET I NEED FOR MY PROJECT.
WHAT COULD YOU DO WITH HALF THIS AMOUNT?
FAIL.
WHEN CAN YOU START?
I THINK I JUST DID.
9/13/99

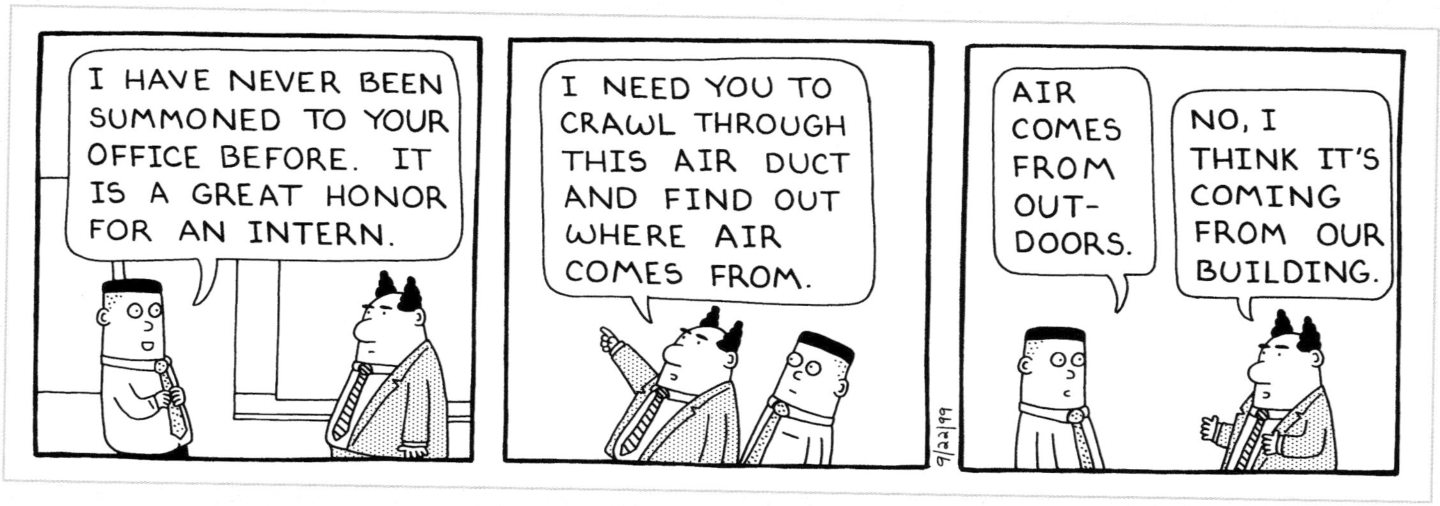
I HAVE NEVER BEEN SUMMONED TO YOUR OFFICE BEFORE. IT IS A GREAT HONOR FOR AN INTERN.
I NEED YOU TO CRAWL THROUGH THIS AIR DUCT AND FIND OUT WHERE AIR COMES FROM.
AIR COMES FROM OUT-DOORS.
NO, I THINK IT'S COMING FROM OUR BUILDING.
9/22/99

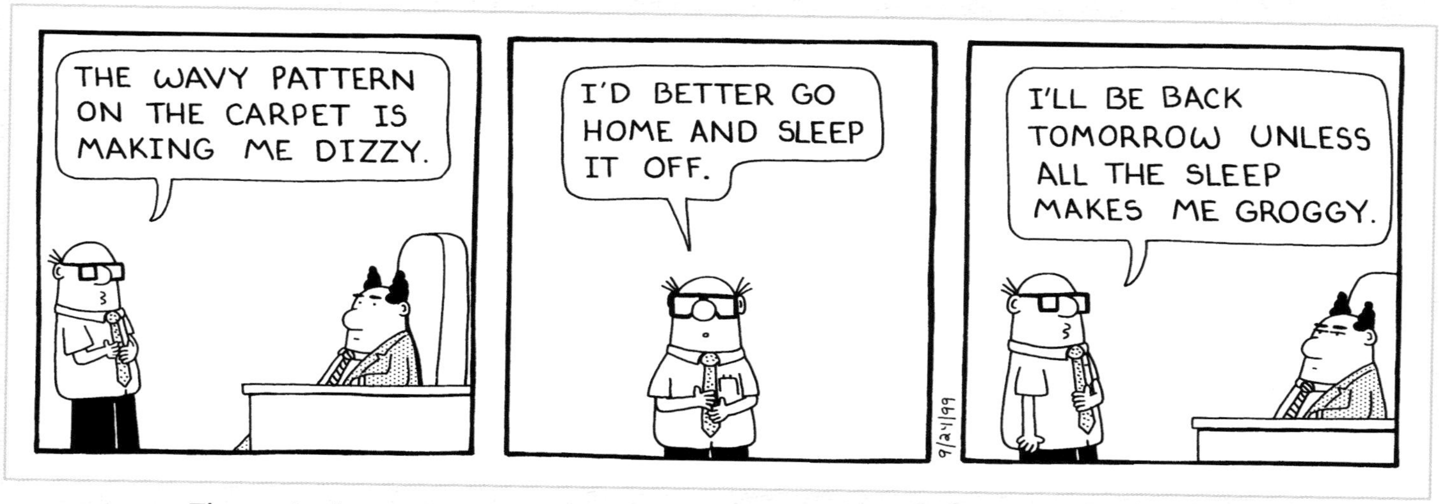
THE WAVY PATTERN ON THE CARPET IS MAKING ME DIZZY.
I'D BETTER GO HOME AND SLEEP IT OFF.
I'LL BE BACK TOMORROW UNLESS ALL THE SLEEP MAKES ME GROGGY.
9/21/99

The comic above is based on a real event. It isn't nearly as funny if you don't know that.

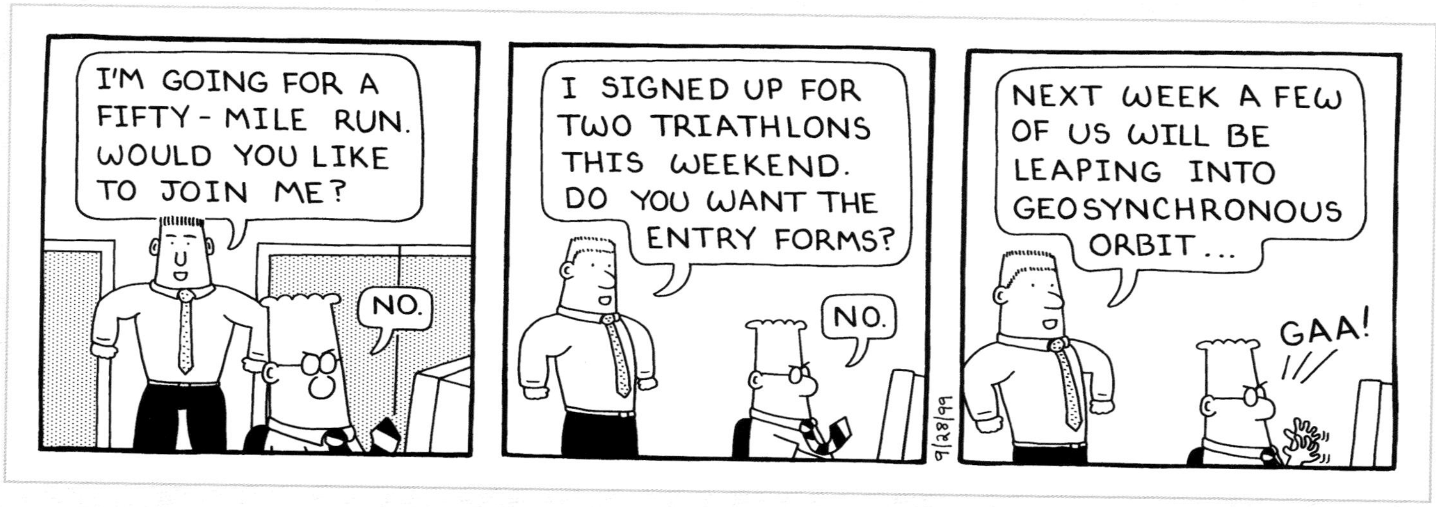
I'M GOING FOR A FIFTY-MILE RUN. WOULD YOU LIKE TO JOIN ME?
NO.
I SIGNED UP FOR TWO TRIATHLONS THIS WEEKEND. DO YOU WANT THE ENTRY FORMS?
NO.
NEXT WEEK A FEW OF US WILL BE LEAPING INTO GEOSYNCHRONOUS ORBIT...
GAA!
9/28/99

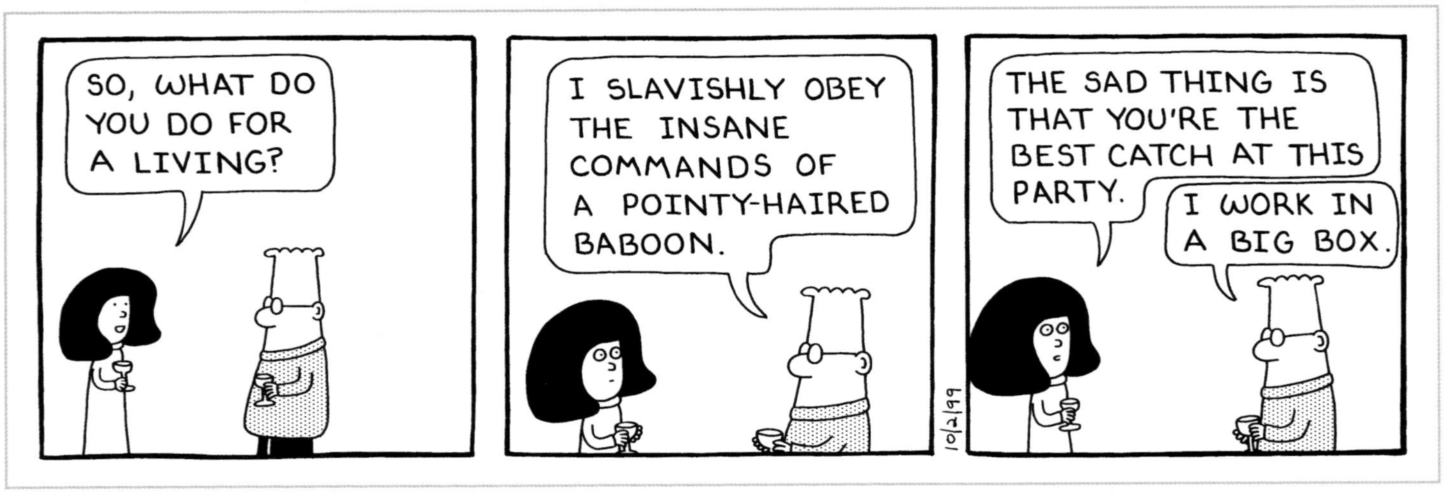
SO, WHAT DO YOU DO FOR A LIVING?
I SLAVISHLY OBEY THE INSANE COMMANDS OF A POINTY-HAIRED BABOON.
10/2/99
THE SAD THING IS THAT YOU'RE THE BEST CATCH AT THIS PARTY.
I WORK IN A BIG BOX.

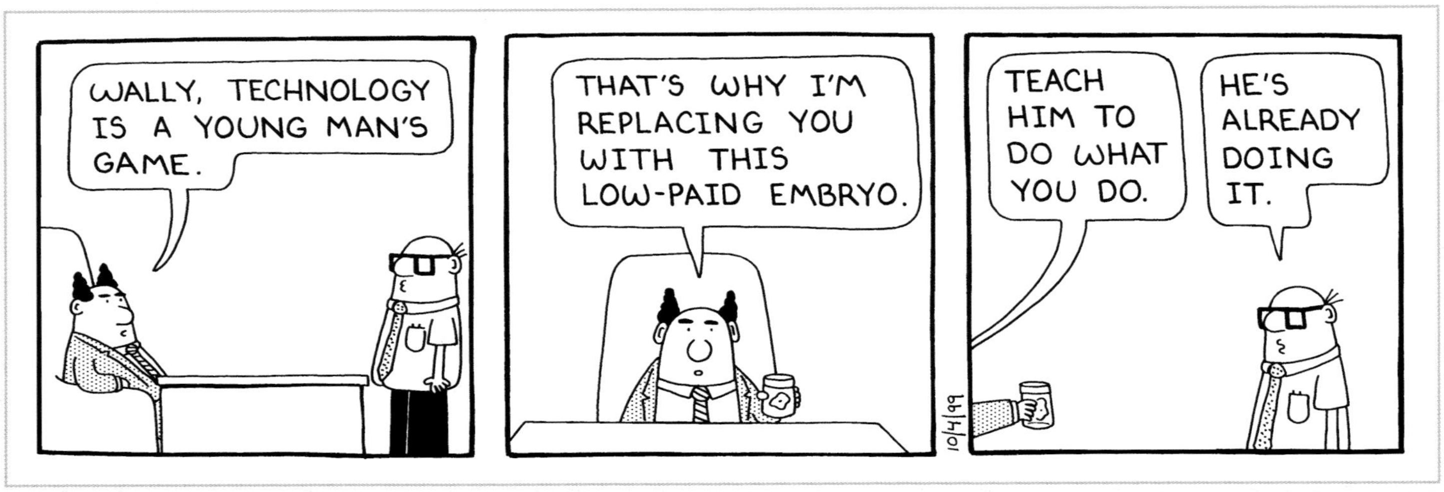
WALLY, TECHNOLOGY IS A YOUNG MAN'S GAME.
THAT'S WHY I'M REPLACING YOU WITH THIS LOW-PAID EMBRYO.
10/4/99
TEACH HIM TO DO WHAT YOU DO.
HE'S ALREADY DOING IT.

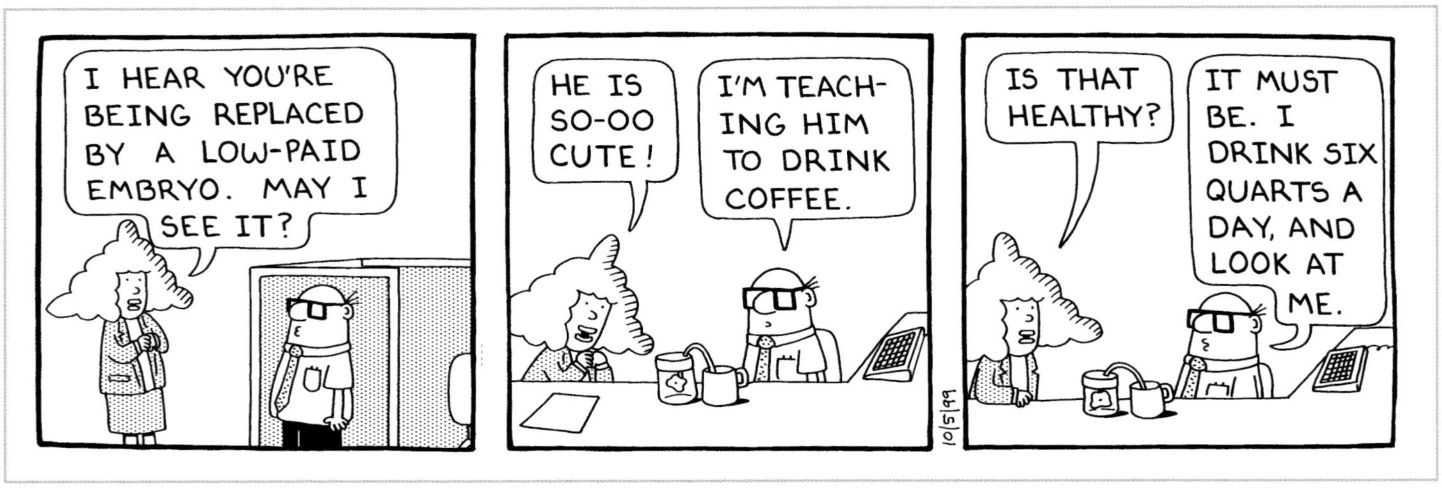
I HEAR YOU'RE BEING REPLACED BY A LOW-PAID EMBRYO. MAY I SEE IT?
HE IS SO-OO CUTE!
I'M TEACH-ING HIM TO DRINK COFFEE.
10/5/99
IS THAT HEALTHY?
IT MUST BE. I DRINK SIX QUARTS A DAY, AND LOOK AT ME.

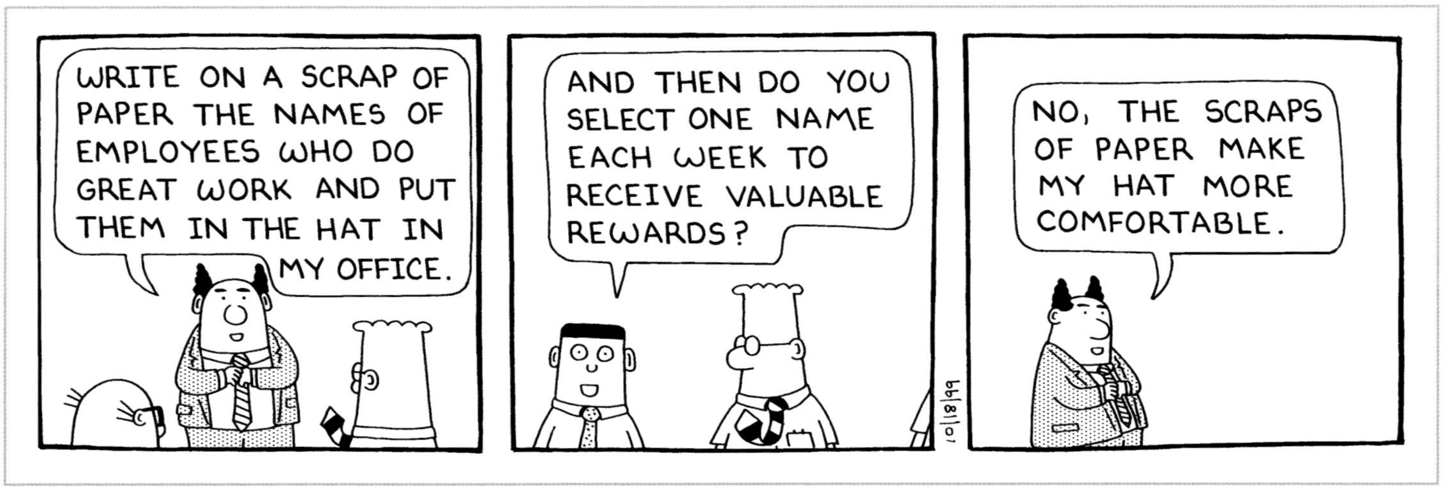
WRITE ON A SCRAP OF PAPER THE NAMES OF EMPLOYEES WHO DO GREAT WORK AND PUT THEM IN THE HAT IN MY OFFICE.
AND THEN DO YOU SELECT ONE NAME EACH WEEK TO RECEIVE VALUABLE REWARDS?
10/18/99
NO, THE SCRAPS OF PAPER MAKE MY HAT MORE COMFORTABLE.

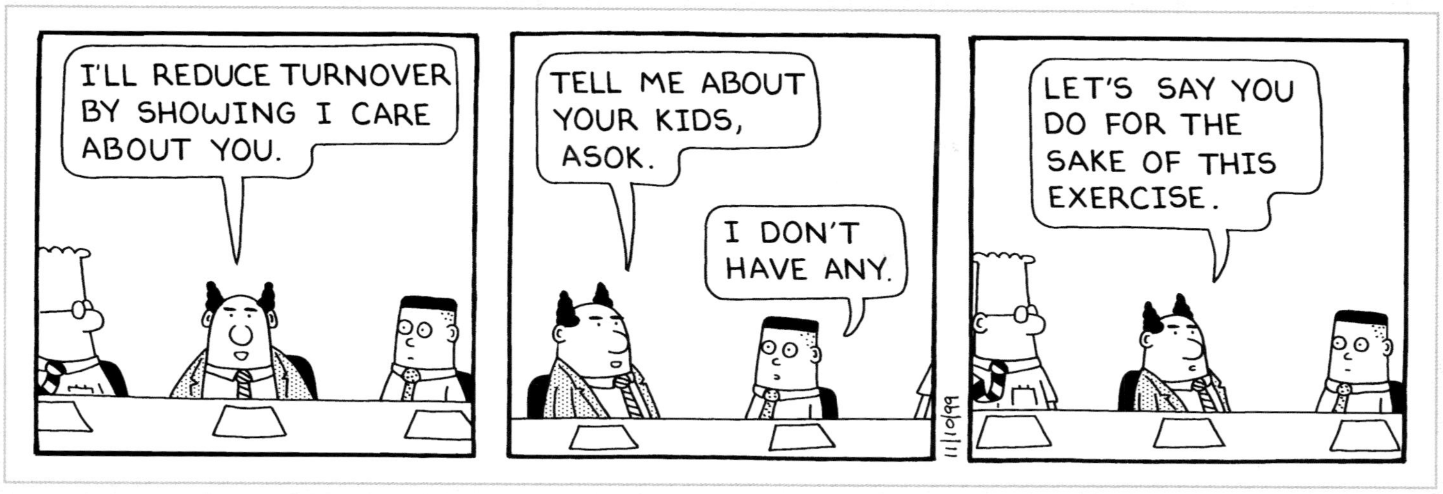
I'LL REDUCE TURNOVER BY SHOWING I CARE ABOUT YOU.
TELL ME ABOUT YOUR KIDS, ASOK.
I DON'T HAVE ANY.
LET'S SAY YOU DO FOR THE SAKE OF THIS EXERCISE.
11/10/99

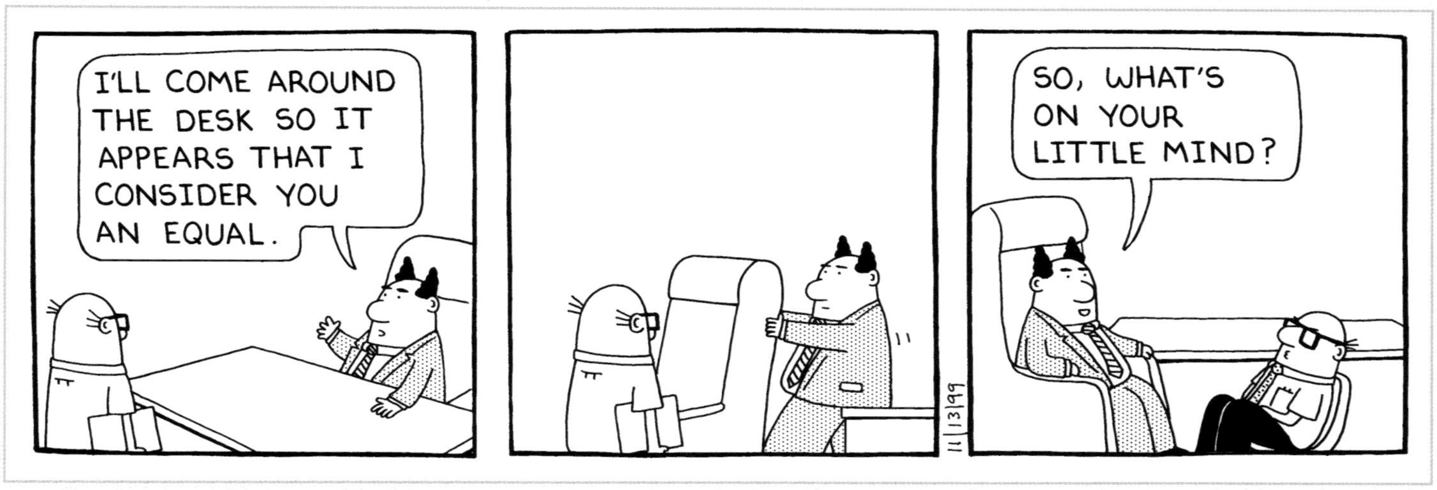
I'LL COME AROUND THE DESK SO IT APPEARS THAT I CONSIDER YOU AN EQUAL.
SO, WHAT'S ON YOUR LITTLE MIND?
11/13/99

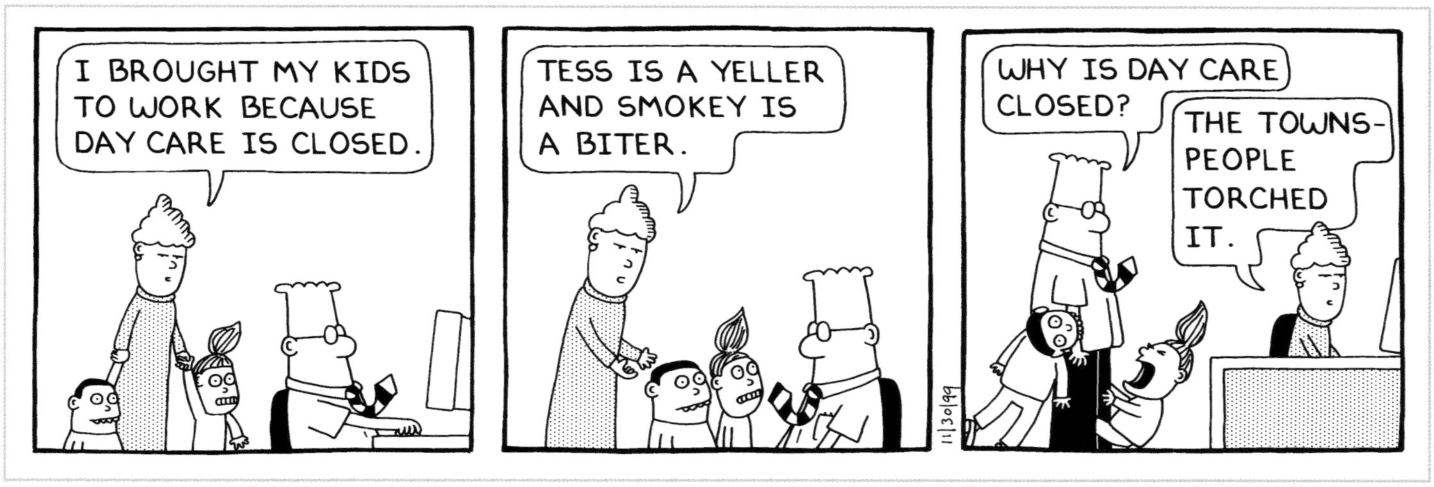
I BROUGHT MY KIDS TO WORK BECAUSE DAY CARE IS CLOSED.
TESS IS A YELLER AND SMOKEY IS A BITER.
WHY IS DAY CARE CLOSED?
THE TOWNS-PEOPLE TORCHED IT.
11/30/99

Sometime around this period, I stopped employing an artist to ink the letters, and started doing it myself on the computer. I didn't have that process worked out yet, and you can see that the space between lines of text is irregular.

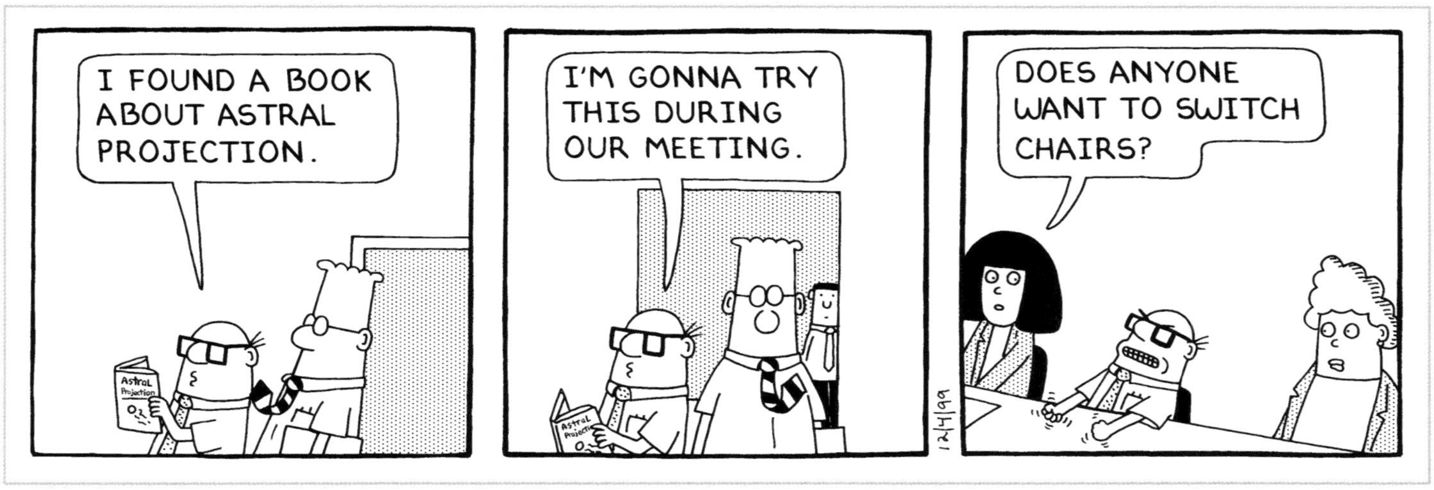
I FOUND A BOOK ABOUT ASTRAL PROJECTION.
I'M GONNA TRY THIS DURING OUR MEETING.
DOES ANYONE WANT TO SWITCH CHAIRS?
12/4/99

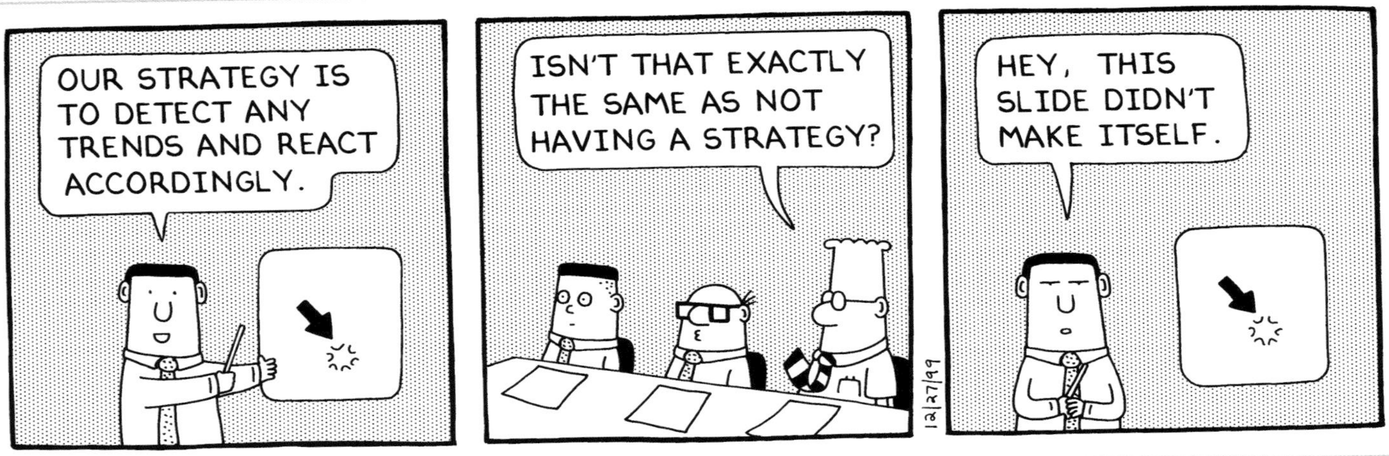
OUR STRATEGY IS TO DETECT ANY TRENDS AND REACT ACCORDINGLY.
ISN'T THAT EXACTLY THE SAME AS NOT HAVING A STRATEGY?
HEY, THIS SLIDE DIDN'T MAKE ITSELF.
12/27/99

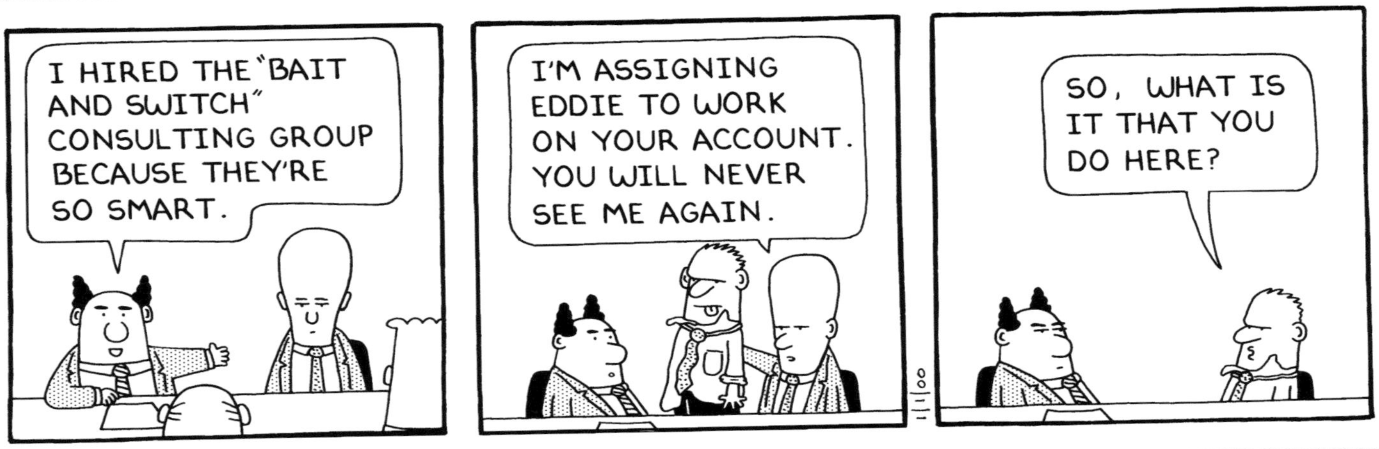
I HIRED THE "BAIT AND SWITCH" CONSULTING GROUP BECAUSE THEY'RE SO SMART.
I'M ASSIGNING EDDIE TO WORK ON YOUR ACCOUNT. YOU WILL NEVER SEE ME AGAIN.
SO, WHAT IS IT THAT YOU DO HERE?
1/1/00

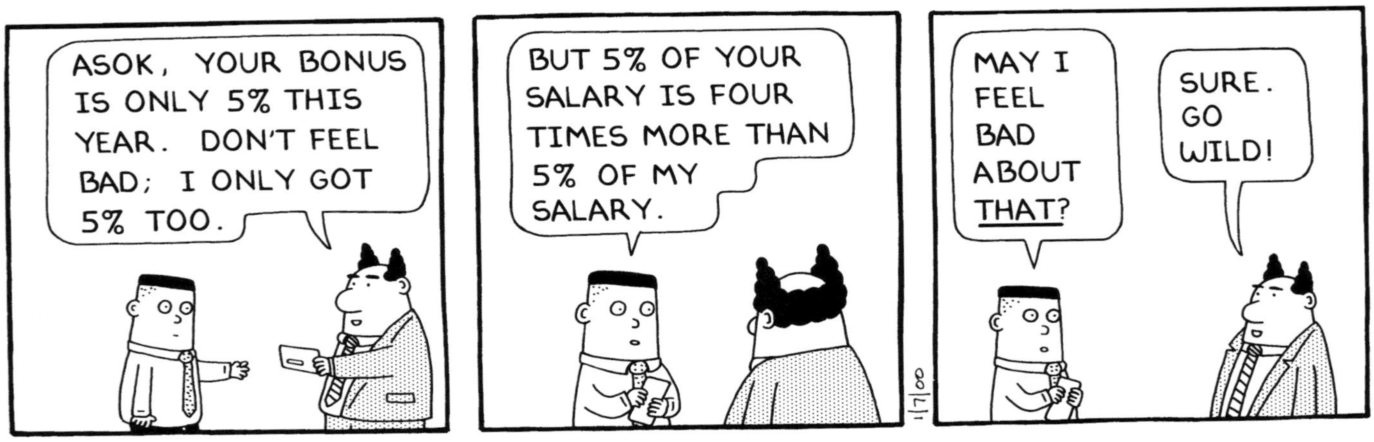
ASOK, YOUR BONUS IS ONLY 5% THIS YEAR. DON'T FEEL BAD; I ONLY GOT 5% TOO.
BUT 5% OF YOUR SALARY IS FOUR TIMES MORE THAN 5% OF MY SALARY.
MAY I FEEL BAD ABOUT THAT?
SURE. GO WILD!
1/7/00

As I reviewed the archives to put this book together, I realized I have done some version of this joke at least three times.

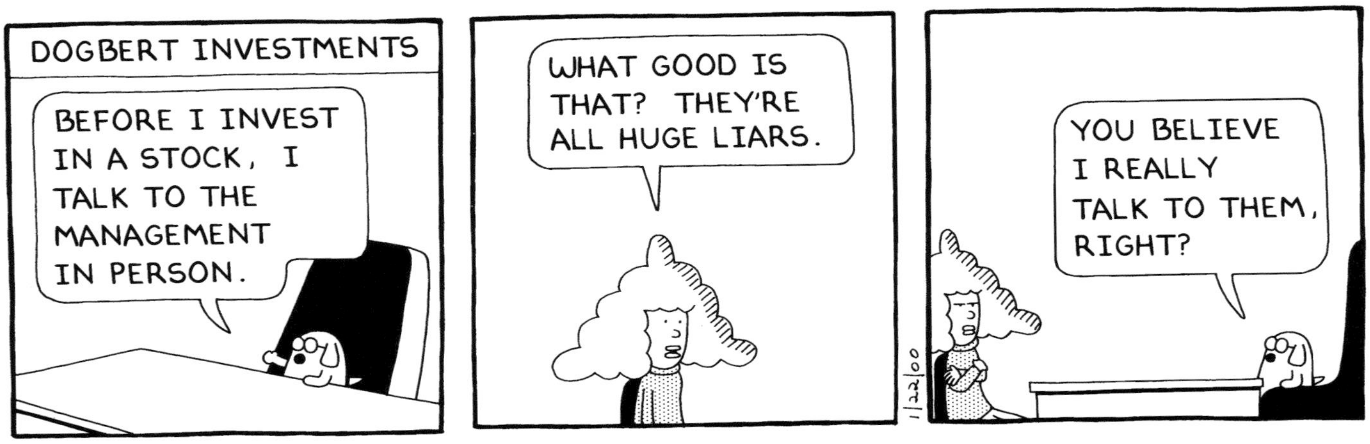
DOGBERT INVESTMENTS
BEFORE I INVEST IN A STOCK, I TALK TO THE MANAGEMENT IN PERSON.
WHAT GOOD IS THAT? THEY'RE ALL HUGE LIARS.
YOU BELIEVE I REALLY TALK TO THEM, RIGHT?
1/22/00

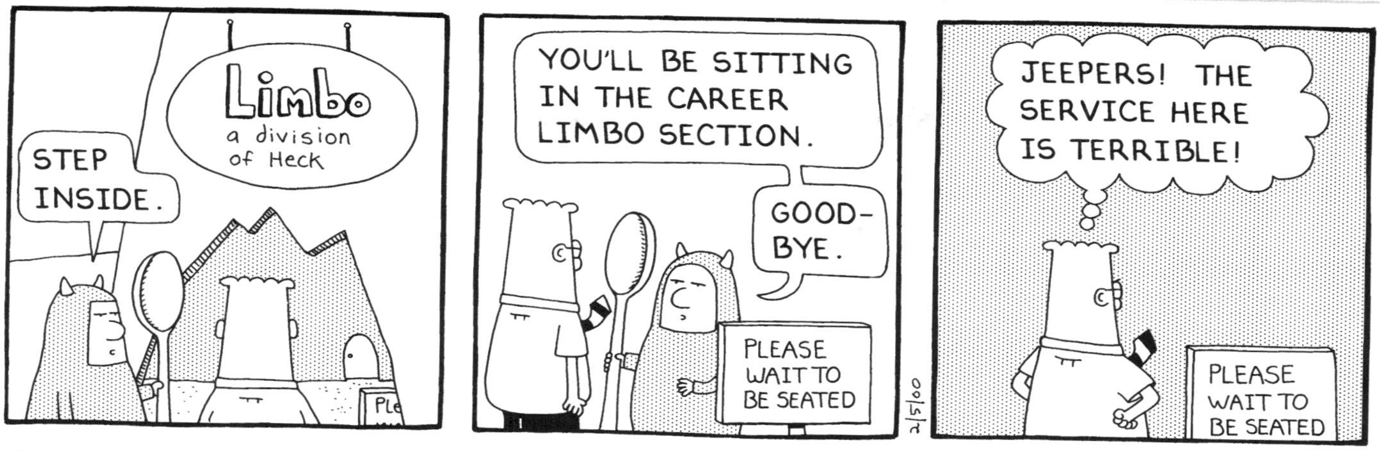
Limbo
a division of Heck
STEP INSIDE.
YOU'LL BE SITTING IN THE CAREER LIMBO SECTION.
GOOD-BYE.
PLEASE WAIT TO BE SEATED
2/5/00
JEEPERS! THE SERVICE HERE IS TERRIBLE!
PLEASE WAIT TO BE SEATED

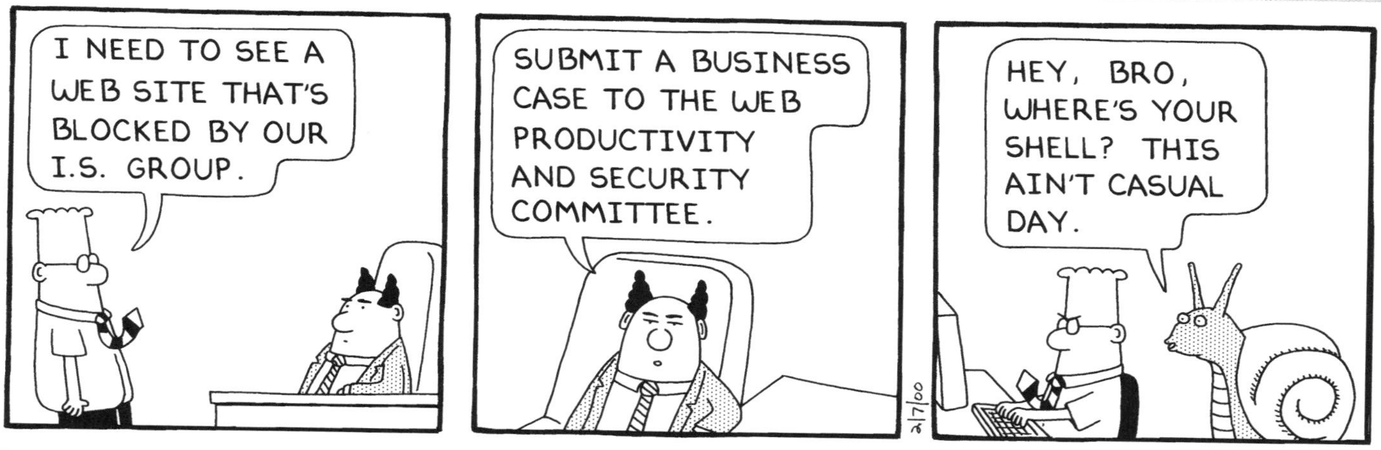
I NEED TO SEE A WEB SITE THAT'S BLOCKED BY OUR I.S. GROUP.
SUBMIT A BUSINESS CASE TO THE WEB PRODUCTIVITY AND SECURITY COMMITTEE.
2/7/00
HEY, BRO, WHERE'S YOUR SHELL? THIS AIN'T CASUAL DAY.

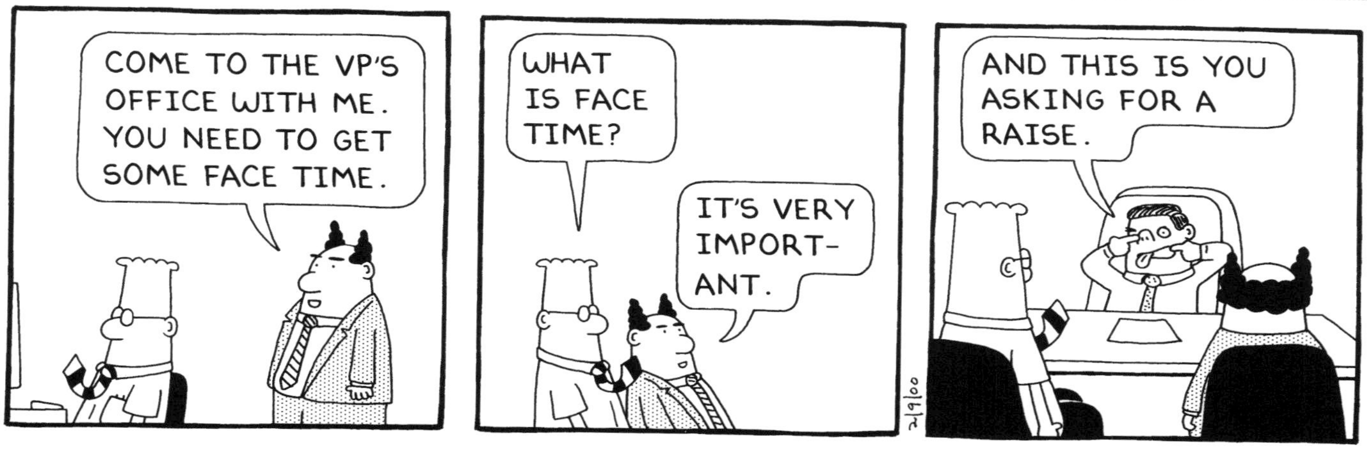
COME TO THE VP'S OFFICE WITH ME. YOU NEED TO GET SOME FACE TIME.
WHAT IS FACE TIME?
IT'S VERY IMPORT-ANT.
2/9/00
AND THIS IS YOU ASKING FOR A RAISE.

The strip above ran in newspapers, but it isn't how I originally drew it. The original was deemed too naughty. The one below is my original version. It's punchier, don't you think?

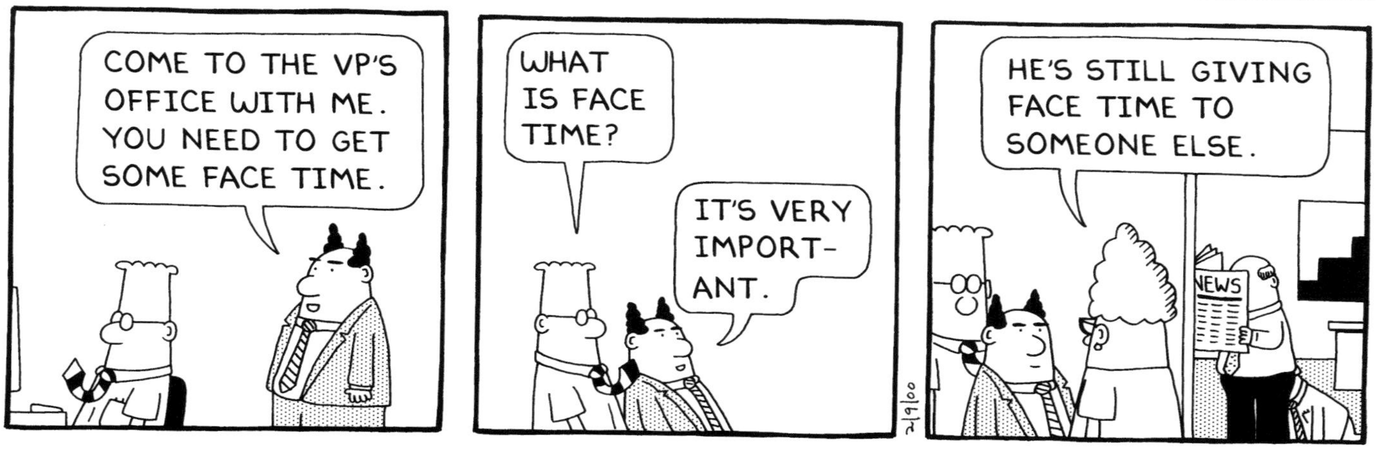
COME TO THE VP'S OFFICE WITH ME. YOU NEED TO GET SOME FACE TIME.
WHAT IS FACE TIME?
IT'S VERY IMPORT-ANT.
2/9/00
HE'S STILL GIVING FACE TIME TO SOMEONE ELSE.
NEWS

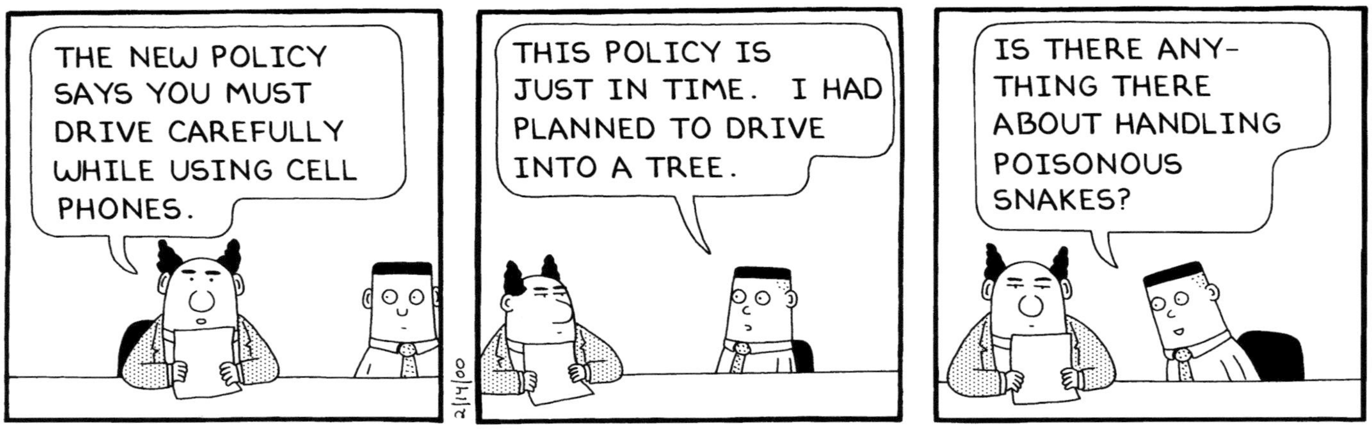
THE NEW POLICY SAYS YOU MUST DRIVE CAREFULLY WHILE USING CELL PHONES.
THIS POLICY IS JUST IN TIME. I HAD PLANNED TO DRIVE INTO A TREE.
2/14/00
IS THERE ANYTHING THERE ABOUT HANDLING POISONOUS SNAKES?

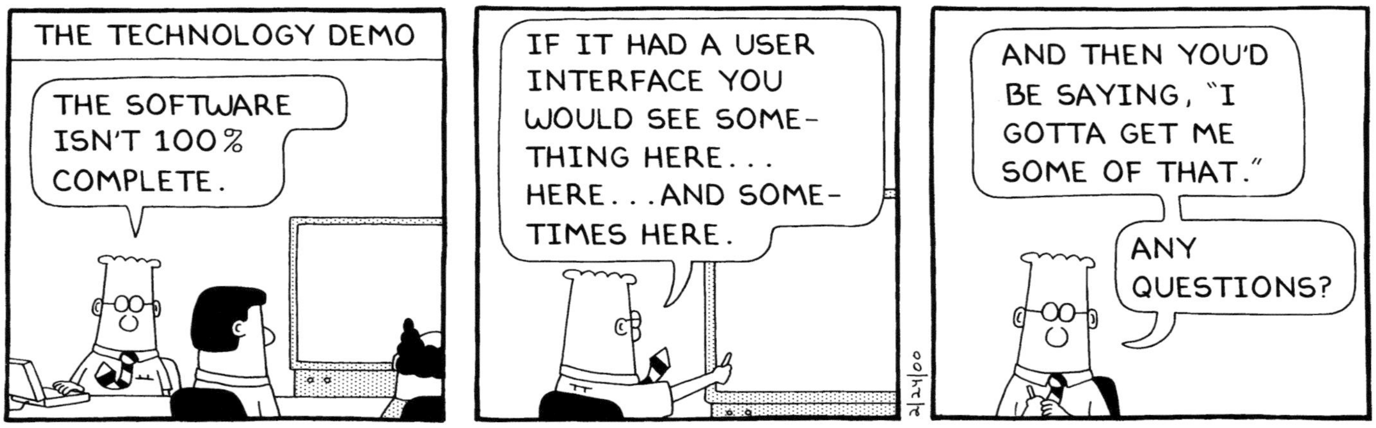
THE TECHNOLOGY DEMO
THE SOFTWARE ISN'T 100% COMPLETE.
IF IT HAD A USER INTERFACE YOU WOULD SEE SOMETHING HERE... HERE...AND SOMETIMES HERE.
2/24/00
AND THEN YOU'D BE SAYING, "I GOTTA GET ME SOME OF THAT."
ANY QUESTIONS?

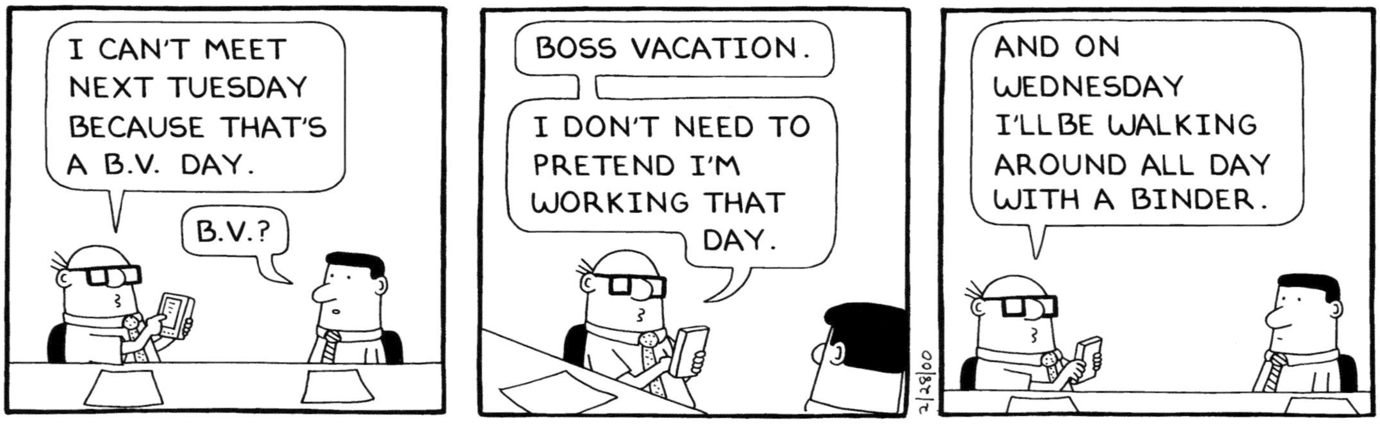
I CAN'T MEET NEXT TUESDAY BECAUSE THAT'S A B.V. DAY.
B.V.?
BOSS VACATION.
I DON'T NEED TO PRETEND I'M WORKING THAT DAY.
2/28/00
AND ON WEDNESDAY I'LL BE WALKING AROUND ALL DAY WITH A BINDER.

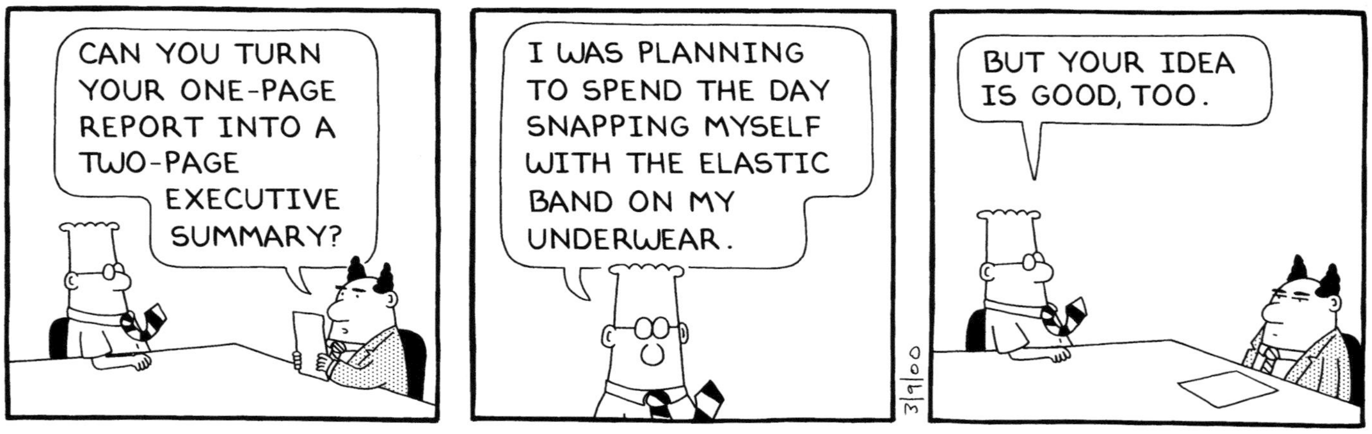
CAN YOU TURN YOUR ONE-PAGE REPORT INTO A TWO-PAGE EXECUTIVE SUMMARY?
I WAS PLANNING TO SPEND THE DAY SNAPPING MYSELF WITH THE ELASTIC BAND ON MY UNDERWEAR.
3/9/00
BUT YOUR IDEA IS GOOD, TOO.

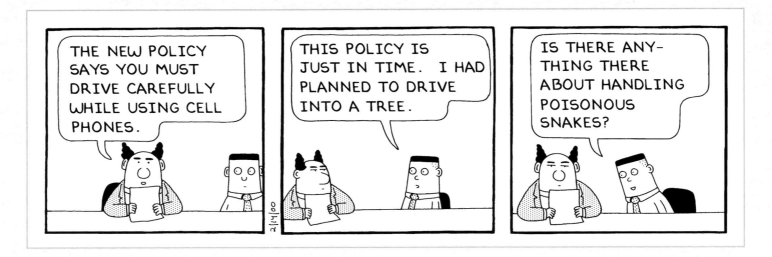

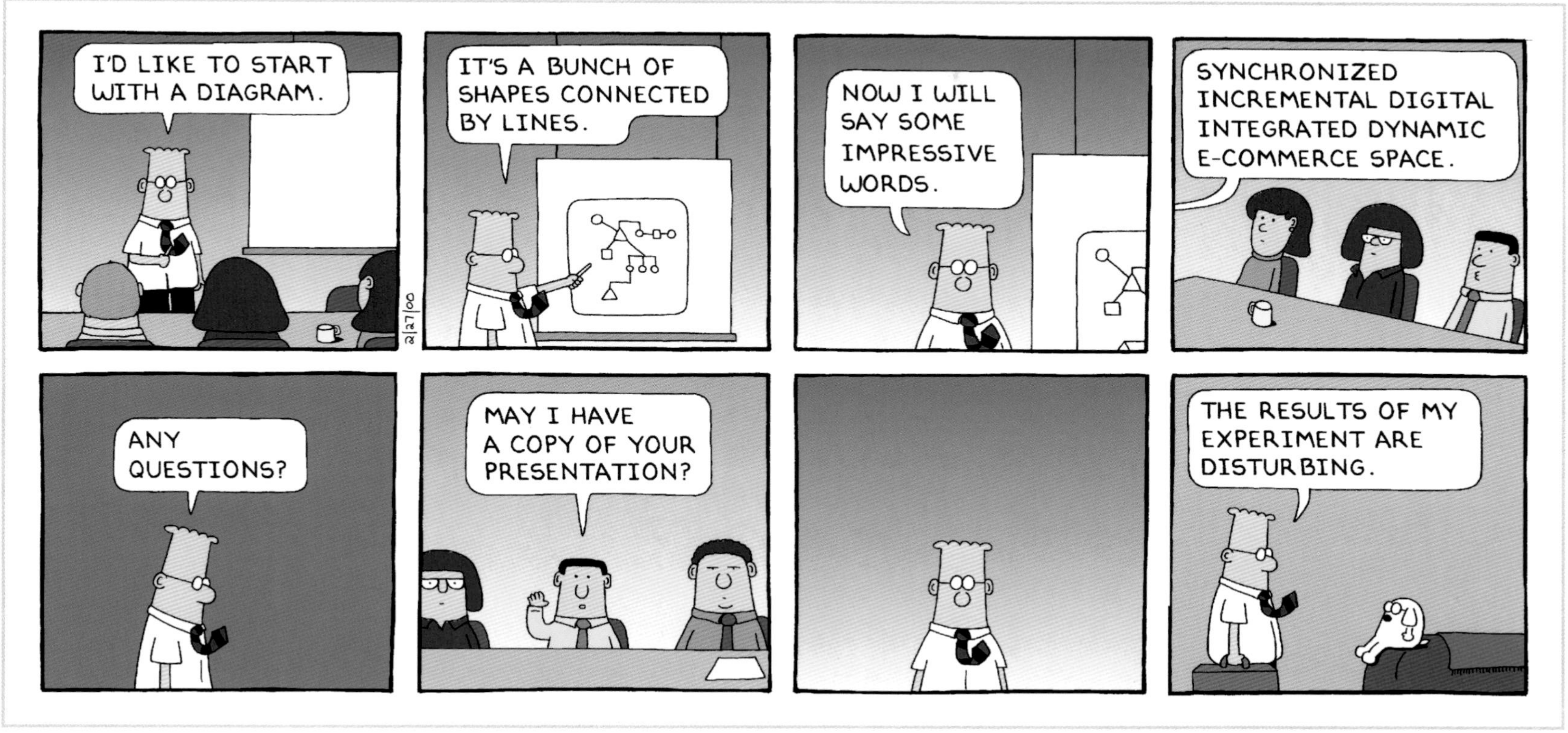
I'D LIKE TO START WITH A DIAGRAM.
IT'S A BUNCH OF SHAPES CONNECTED BY LINES.
2/27/00
NOW I WILL SAY SOME IMPRESSIVE WORDS.
SYNCHRONIZED INCREMENTAL DIGITAL INTEGRATED DYNAMIC E-COMMERCE SPACE.
ANY QUESTIONS?
MAY I HAVE A COPY OF YOUR PRESENTATION?
THE RESULTS OF MY EXPERIMENT ARE DISTURBING.

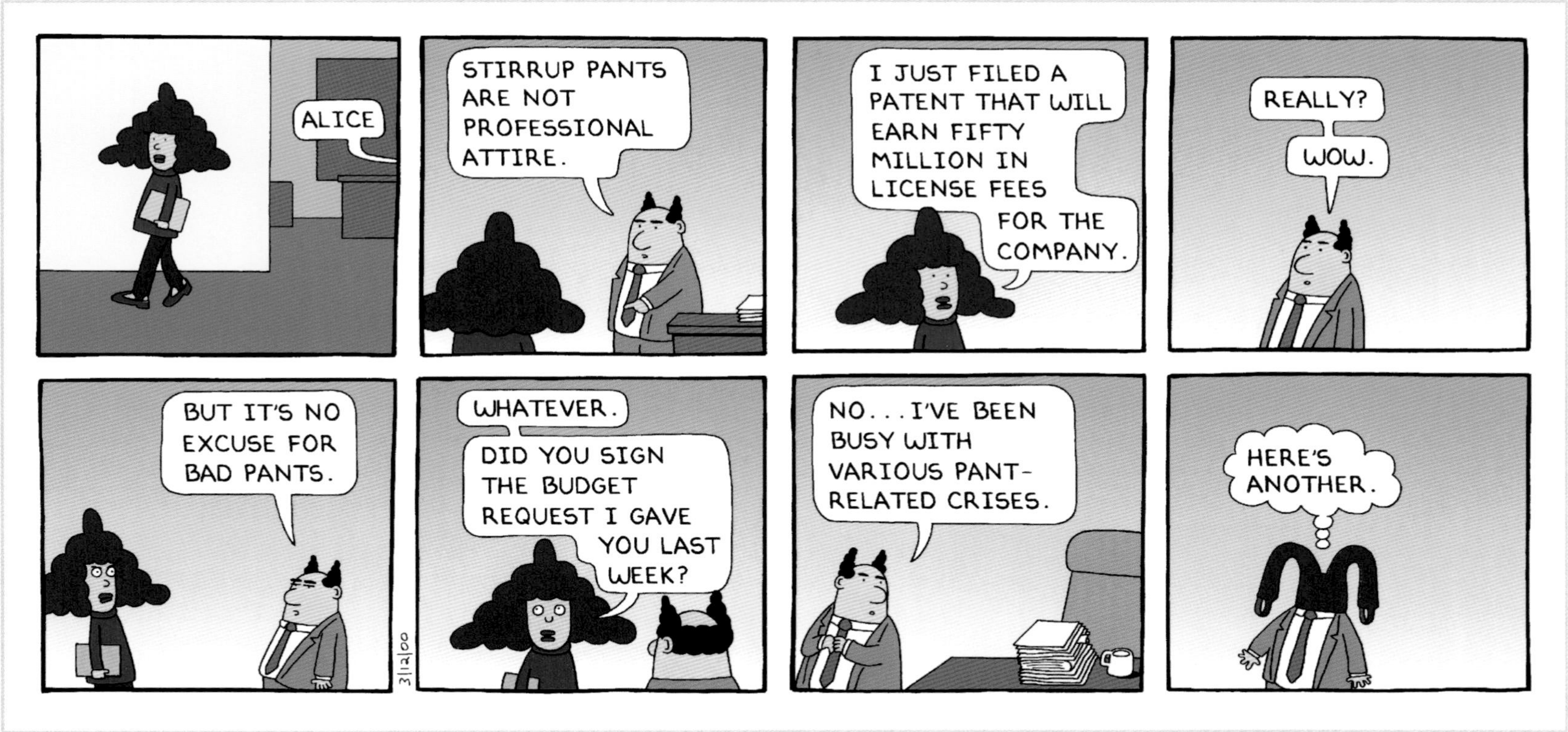
ALICE
STIRRUP PANTS ARE NOT PROFESSIONAL ATTIRE.
I JUST FILED A PATENT THAT WILL EARN FIFTY MILLION IN LICENSE FEES FOR THE COMPANY.
REALLY?
WOW.
BUT IT'S NO EXCUSE FOR BAD PANTS.
3/12/00
WHATEVER.
DID YOU SIGN THE BUDGET REQUEST I GAVE YOU LAST WEEK?
NO... I'VE BEEN BUSY WITH VARIOUS PANT-RELATED CRISES.
HERE'S ANOTHER.

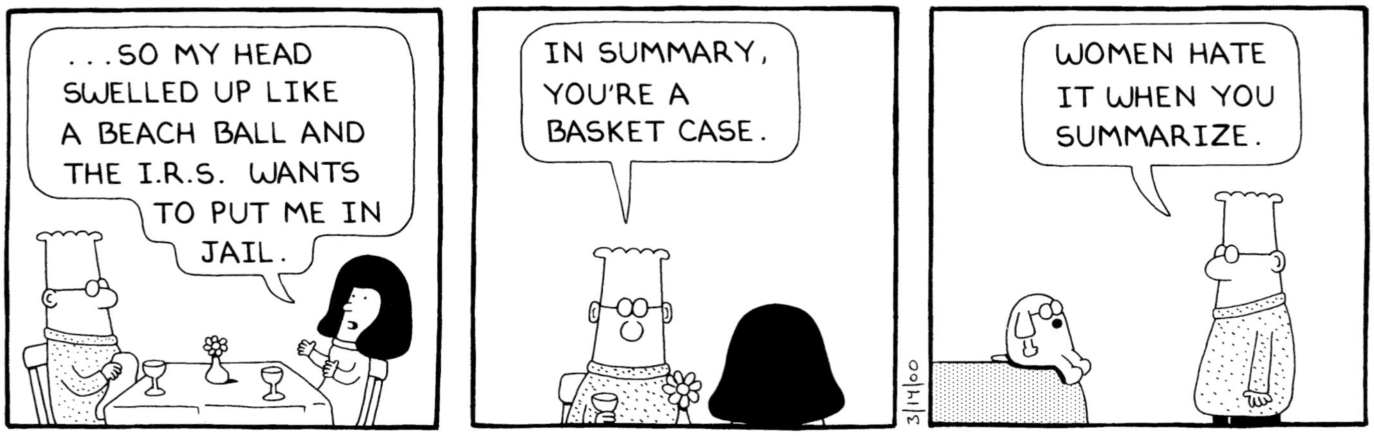
. . .SO MY HEAD SWELLED UP LIKE A BEACH BALL AND THE I.R.S. WANTS TO PUT ME IN JAIL.
IN SUMMARY, YOU'RE A BASKET CASE.
WOMEN HATE IT WHEN YOU SUMMARIZE.
3/14/00

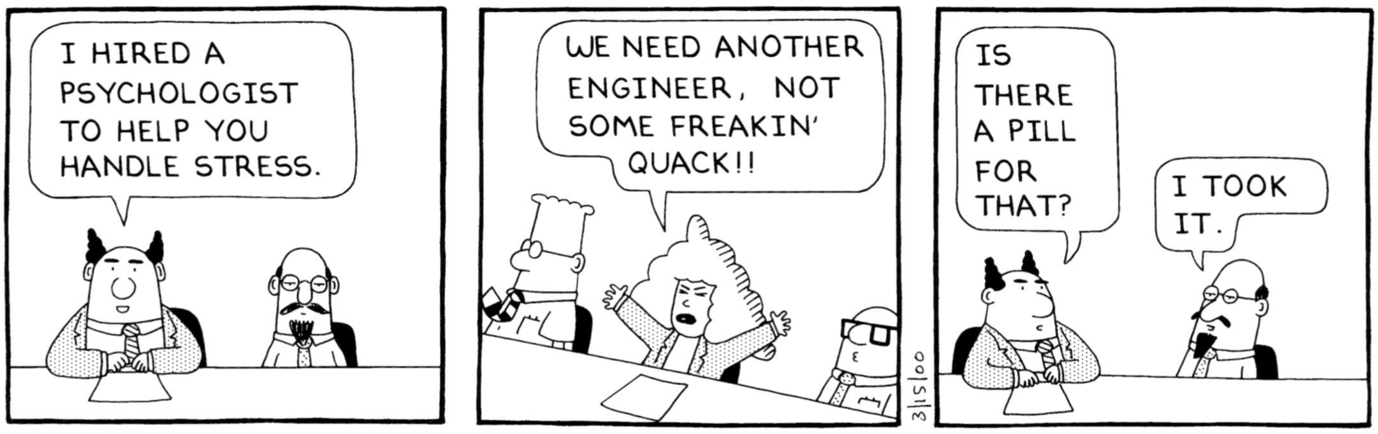
I HIRED A PSYCHOLOGIST TO HELP YOU HANDLE STRESS.
WE NEED ANOTHER ENGINEER, NOT SOME FREAKIN' QUACK!!
IS THERE A PILL FOR THAT?
I TOOK IT.
3/15/00

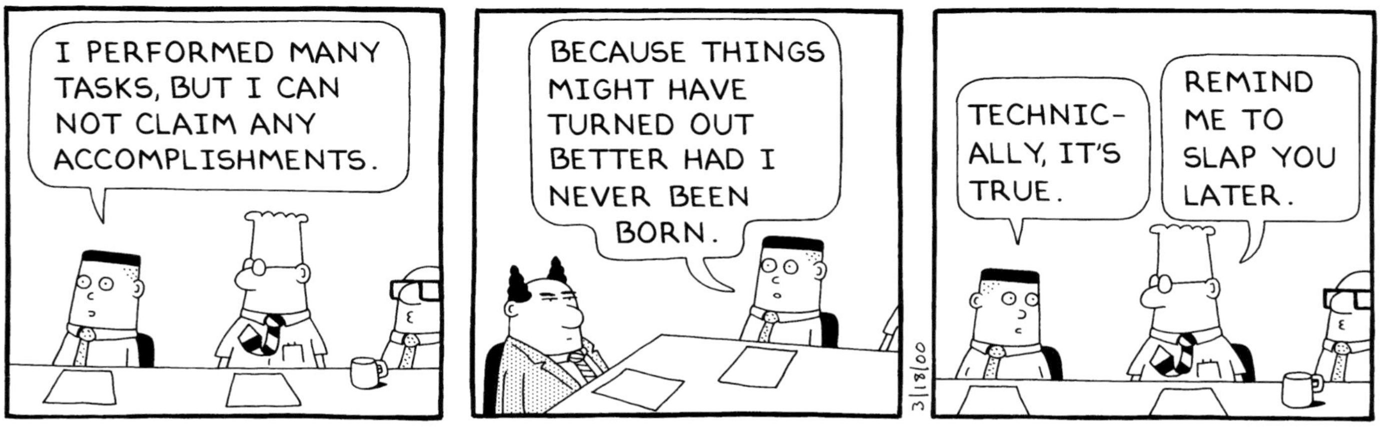
I PERFORMED MANY TASKS, BUT I CAN NOT CLAIM ANY ACCOMPLISHMENTS.
BECAUSE THINGS MIGHT HAVE TURNED OUT BETTER HAD I NEVER BEEN BORN.
TECHNIC-ALLY, IT'S TRUE.
REMIND ME TO SLAP YOU LATER.
3/18/00

A surprising number of people asked me to explain the strip below. I guess it is too recursive.

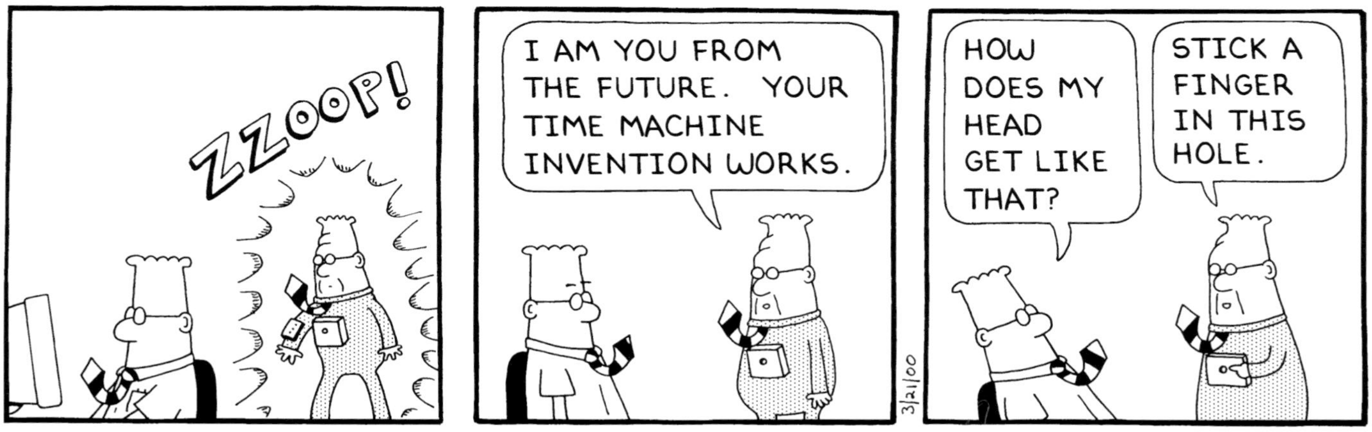
ZZOOP!
I AM YOU FROM THE FUTURE. YOUR TIME MACHINE INVENTION WORKS.
HOW DOES MY HEAD GET LIKE THAT?
STICK A FINGER IN THIS HOLE.
3/21/00

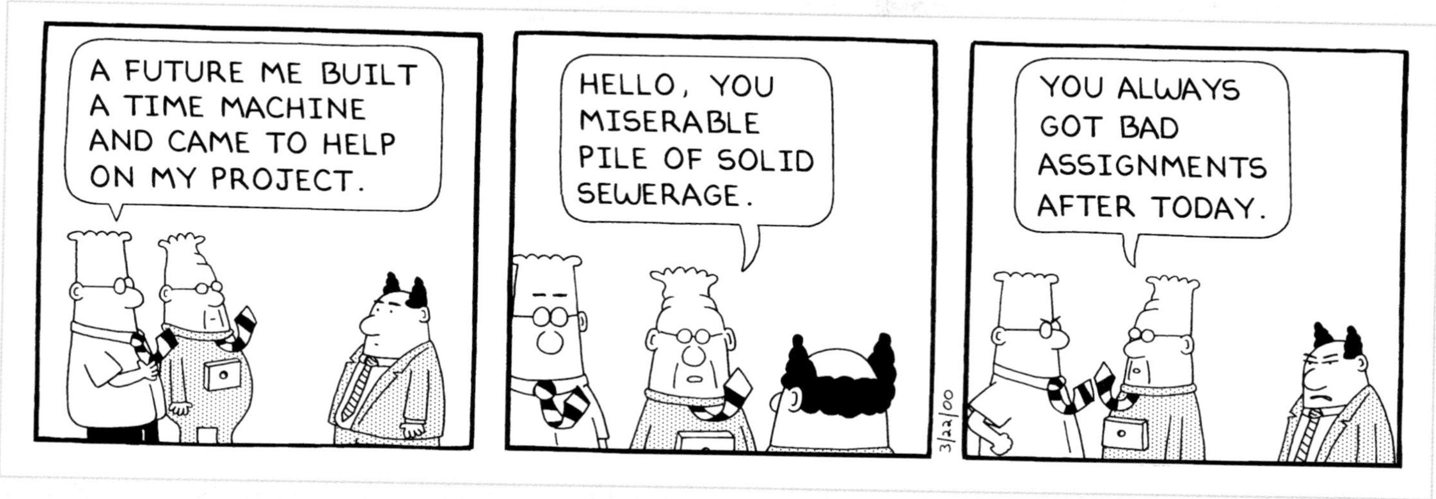
A FUTURE ME BUILT A TIME MACHINE AND CAME TO HELP ON MY PROJECT.
HELLO, YOU MISERABLE PILE OF SOLID SEWERAGE.
3/22/00
YOU ALWAYS GOT BAD ASSIGNMENTS AFTER TODAY.

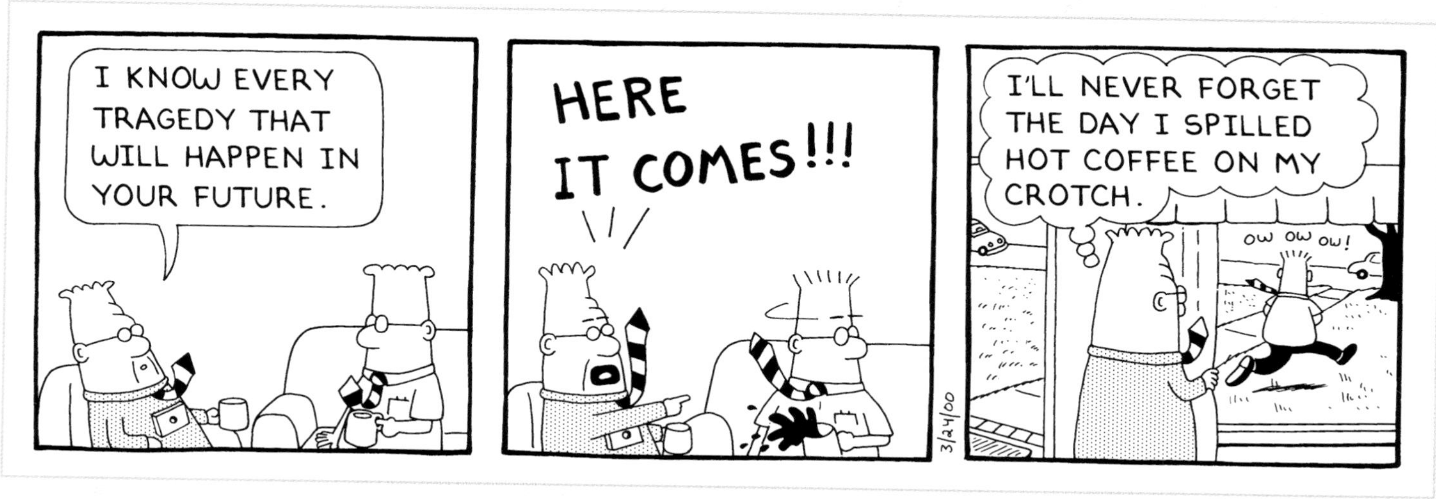
I KNOW EVERY TRAGEDY THAT WILL HAPPEN IN YOUR FUTURE.
HERE IT COMES!!!
3/24/00
I'LL NEVER FORGET THE DAY I SPILLED HOT COFFEE ON MY CROTCH.
OW OW OW!

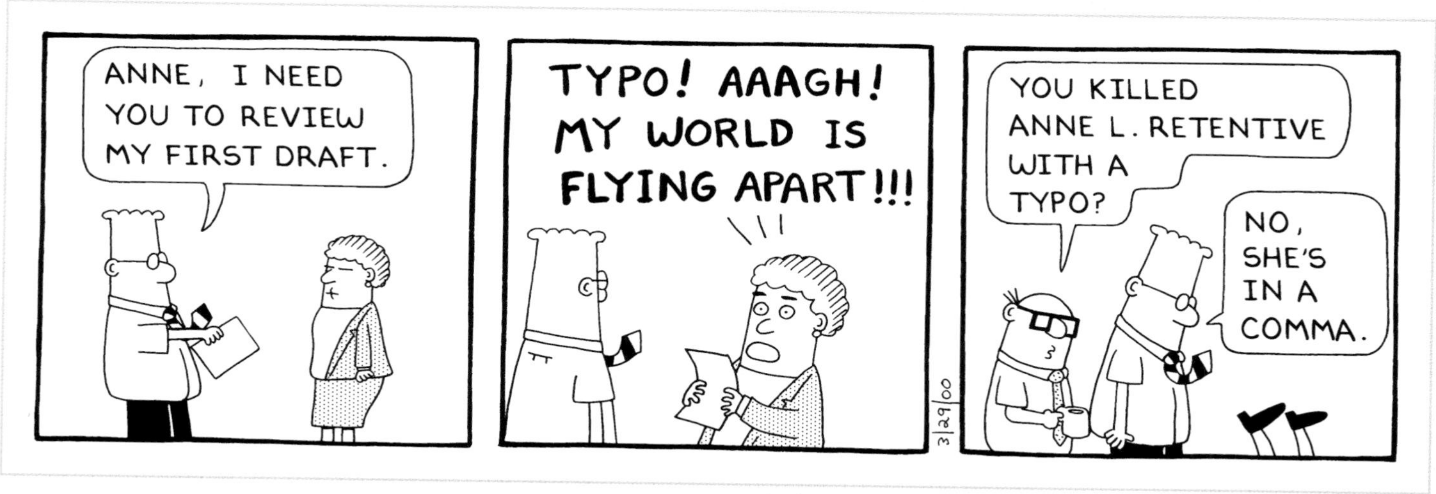
ANNE, I NEED YOU TO REVIEW MY FIRST DRAFT.
TYPO! AAAGH! MY WORLD IS FLYING APART!!!
3/29/00
YOU KILLED ANNE L. RETENTIVE WITH A TYPO?
NO, SHE'S IN A COMMA.

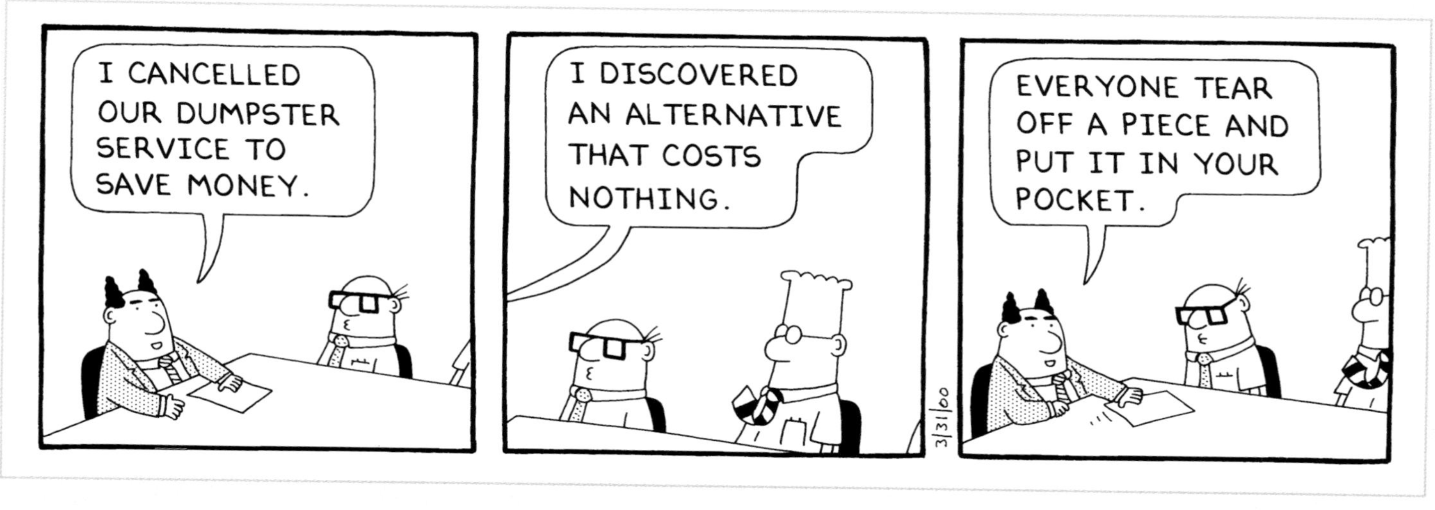
I CANCELLED OUR DUMPSTER SERVICE TO SAVE MONEY.
I DISCOVERED AN ALTERNATIVE THAT COSTS NOTHING.
3/31/00
EVERYONE TEAR OFF A PIECE AND PUT IT IN YOUR POCKET.

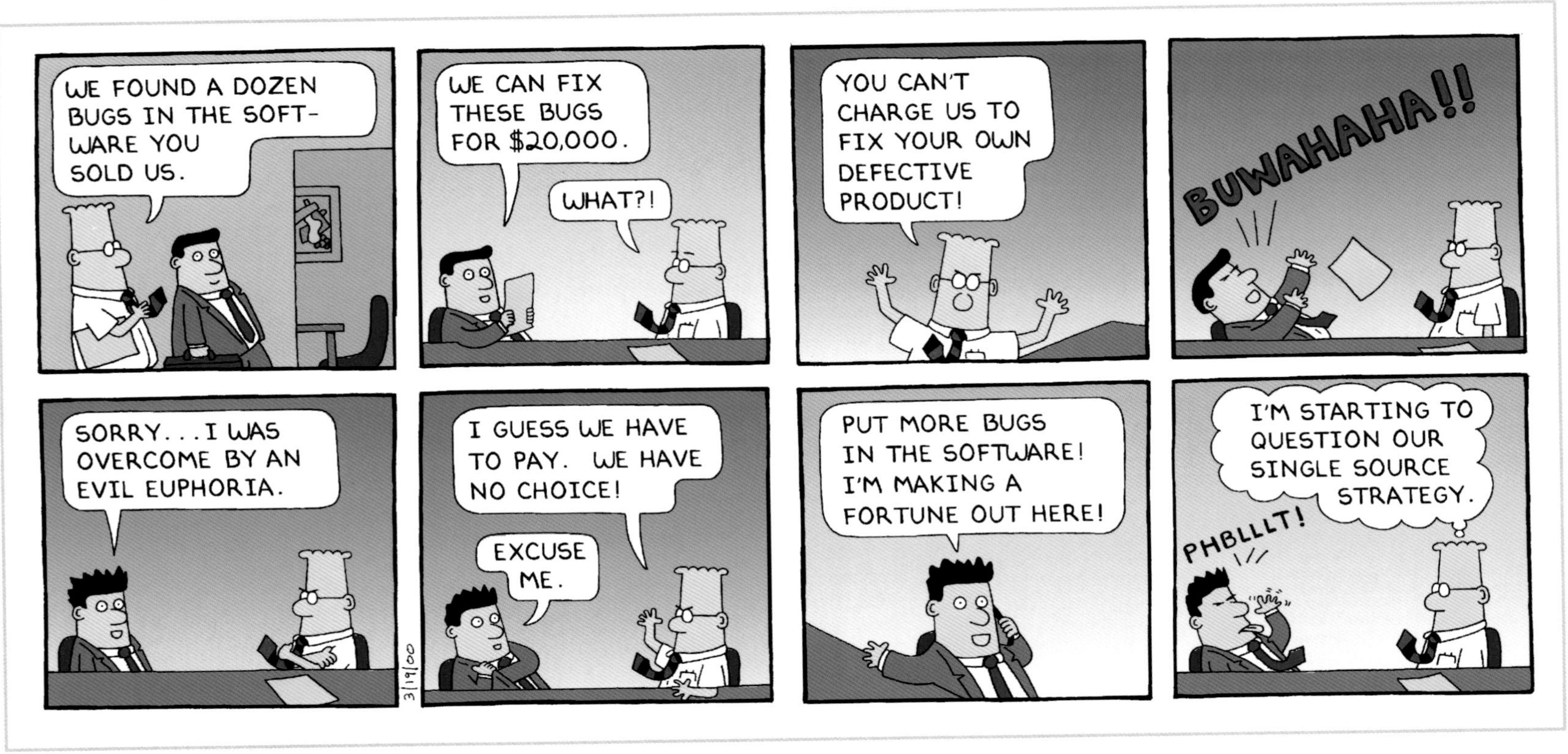
WE FOUND A DOZEN BUGS IN THE SOFT-WARE YOU SOLD US.
WE CAN FIX THESE BUGS FOR $20,000.
WHAT?!
YOU CAN'T CHARGE US TO FIX YOUR OWN DEFECTIVE PRODUCT!
BUWAHAHA!!
SORRY...I WAS OVERCOME BY AN EVIL EUPHORIA.
3/19/00
I GUESS WE HAVE TO PAY. WE HAVE NO CHOICE!
EXCUSE ME.
PUT MORE BUGS IN THE SOFTWARE! I'M MAKING A FORTUNE OUT HERE!
I'M STARTING TO QUESTION OUR SINGLE SOURCE STRATEGY.
PHBLLLT!

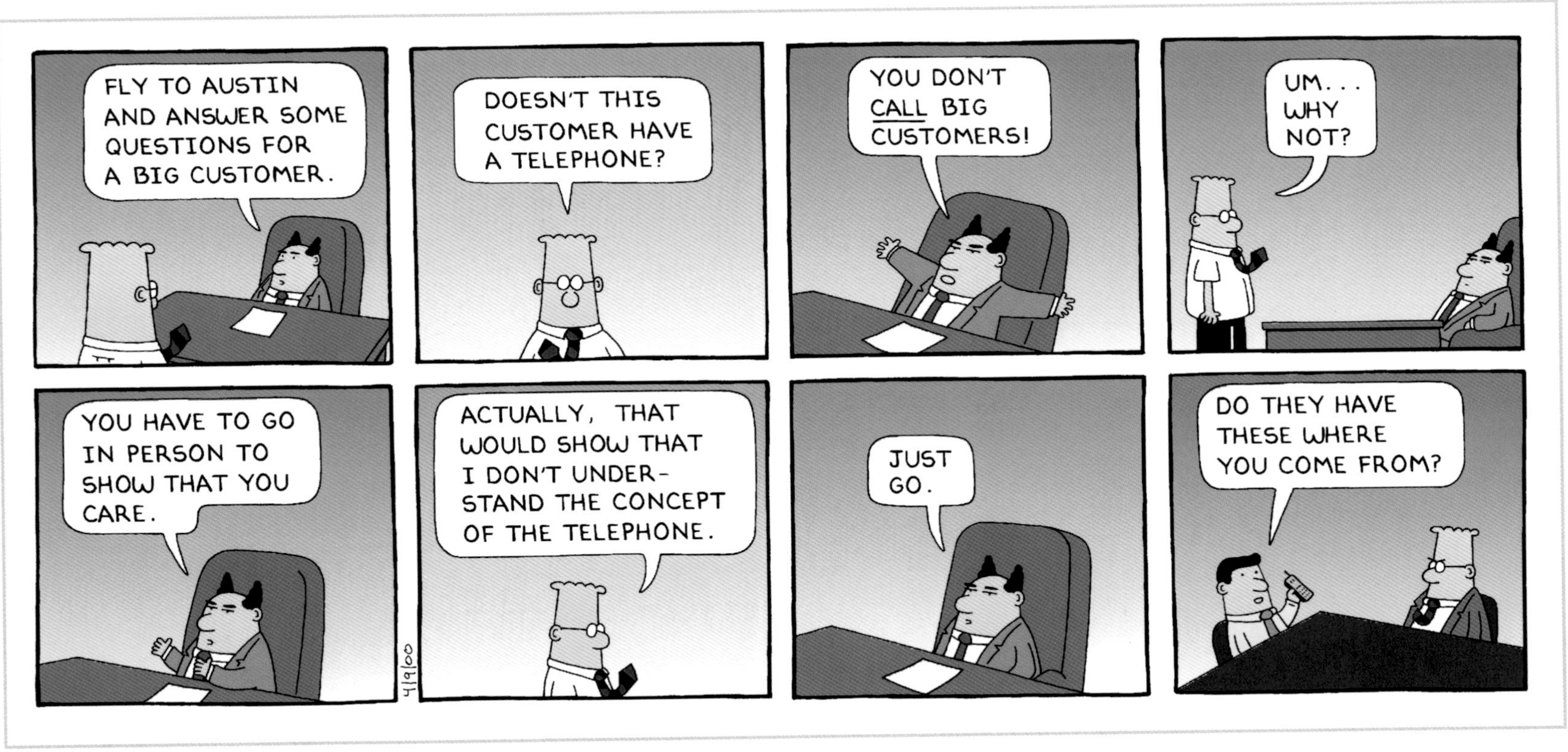
FLY TO AUSTIN AND ANSWER SOME QUESTIONS FOR A BIG CUSTOMER.
DOESN'T THIS CUSTOMER HAVE A TELEPHONE?
YOU DON'T CALL BIG CUSTOMERS!
UM... WHY NOT?
YOU HAVE TO GO IN PERSON TO SHOW THAT YOU CARE.
4/9/00
ACTUALLY, THAT WOULD SHOW THAT I DON'T UNDER-STAND THE CONCEPT OF THE TELEPHONE.
JUST GO.
DO THEY HAVE THESE WHERE YOU COME FROM?

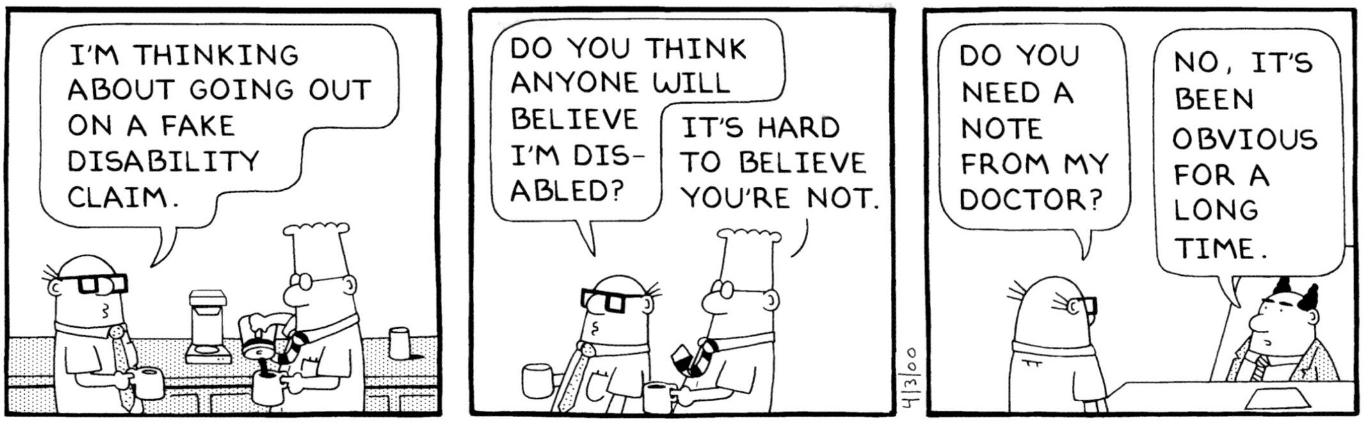
I'M THINKING ABOUT GOING OUT ON A FAKE DISABILITY CLAIM.
DO YOU THINK ANYONE WILL BELIEVE I'M DIS-ABLED?
IT'S HARD TO BELIEVE YOU'RE NOT.
4/3/00
DO YOU NEED A NOTE FROM MY DOCTOR?
NO, IT'S BEEN OBVIOUS FOR A LONG TIME.

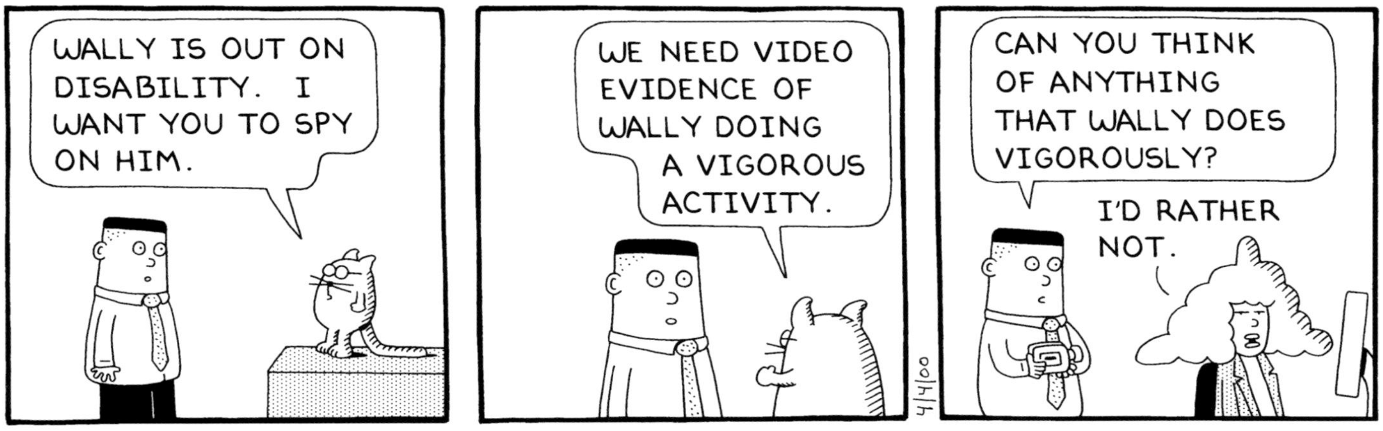
WALLY IS OUT ON DISABILITY. I WANT YOU TO SPY ON HIM.
WE NEED VIDEO EVIDENCE OF WALLY DOING A VIGOROUS ACTIVITY.
4/4/00
CAN YOU THINK OF ANYTHING THAT WALLY DOES VIGOROUSLY?
I'D RATHER NOT.

There's an art to making references that people with impure thoughts recognize as impure and people with pure thoughts don't notice.

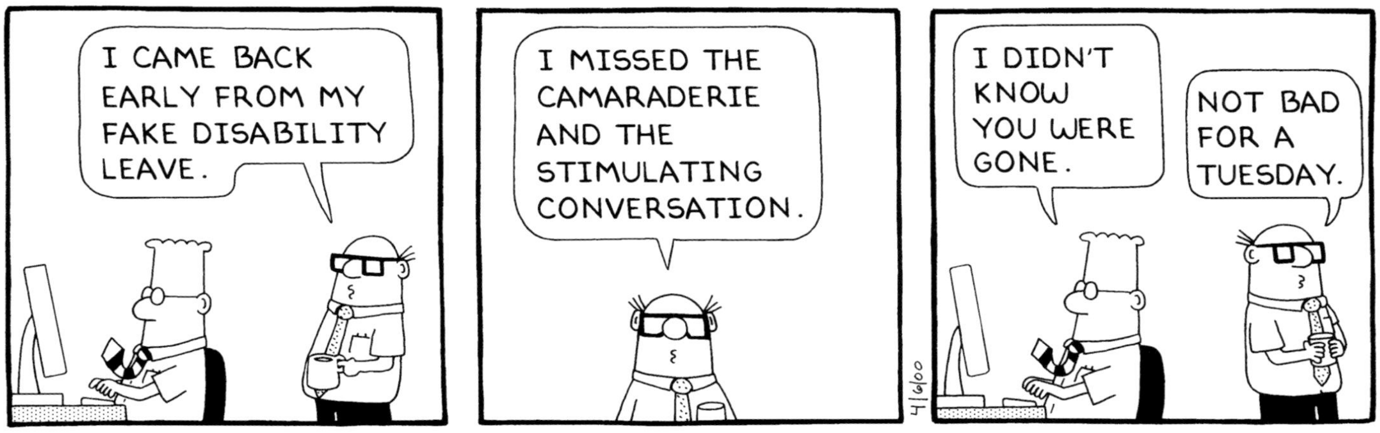
I CAME BACK EARLY FROM MY FAKE DISABILITY LEAVE.
I MISSED THE CAMARADERIE AND THE STIMULATING CONVERSATION.
4/6/00
I DIDN'T KNOW YOU WERE GONE.
NOT BAD FOR A TUESDAY.

One of my discoveries about writing dialogue is that in real-world conversations, people often say things that seem to have no correlation to what the other person said. People are in their own little worlds.

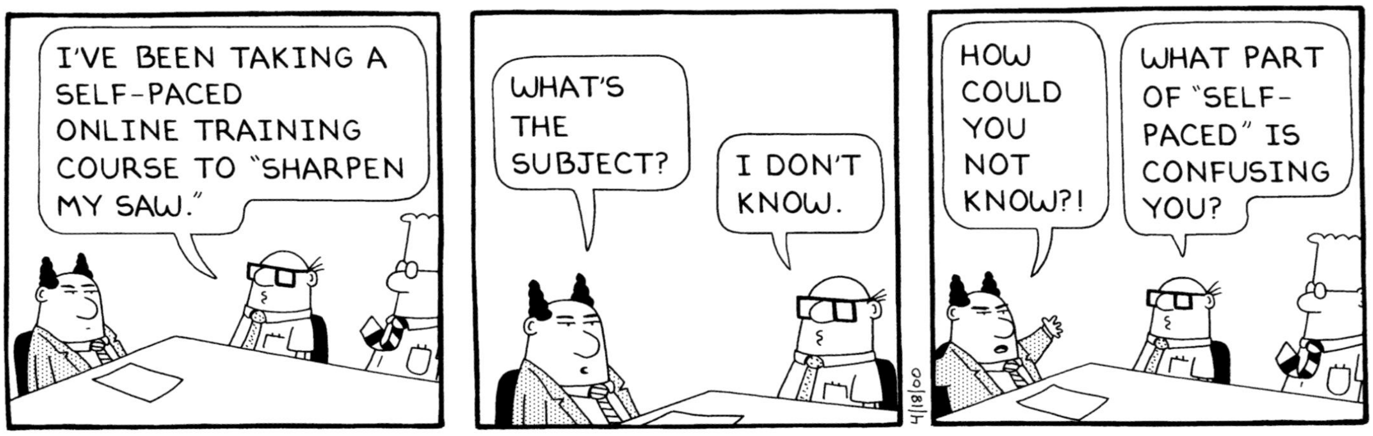
I'VE BEEN TAKING A SELF-PACED ONLINE TRAINING COURSE TO "SHARPEN MY SAW."
WHAT'S THE SUBJECT?
I DON'T KNOW.
4/18/00
HOW COULD YOU NOT KNOW?!
WHAT PART OF "SELF-PACED" IS CONFUSING YOU?

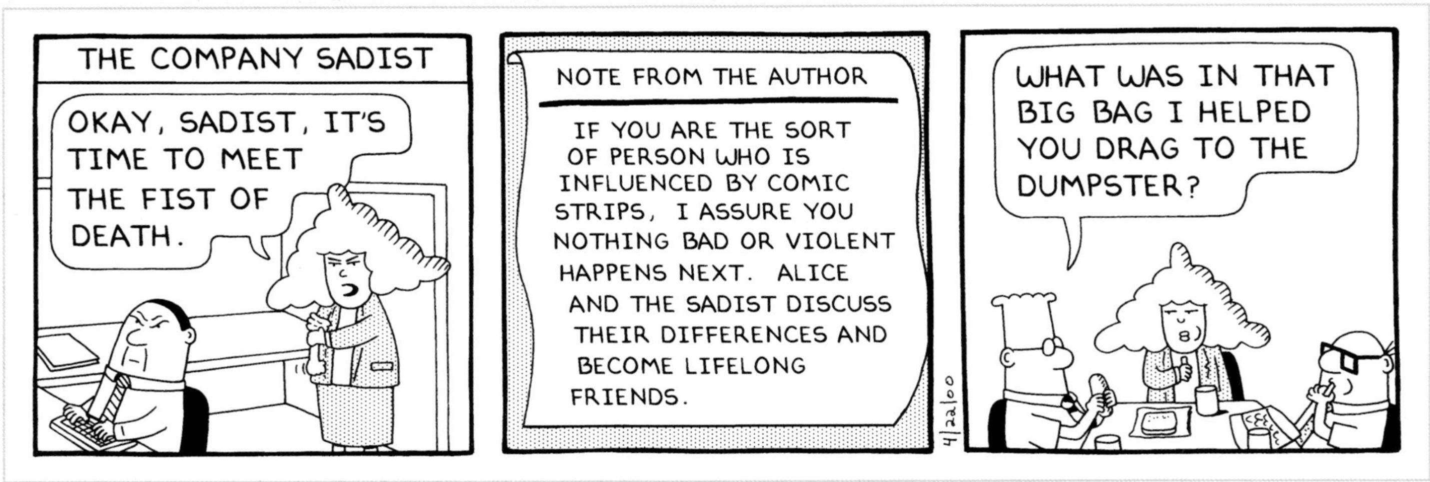
THE COMPANY SADIST
OKAY, SADIST, IT'S TIME TO MEET THE FIST OF DEATH.
NOTE FROM THE AUTHOR
IF YOU ARE THE SORT OF PERSON WHO IS INFLUENCED BY COMIC STRIPS, I ASSURE YOU NOTHING BAD OR VIOLENT HAPPENS NEXT. ALICE AND THE SADIST DISCUSS THEIR DIFFERENCES AND BECOME LIFELONG FRIENDS.
4/22/00
WHAT WAS IN THAT BIG BAG I HELPED YOU DRAG TO THE DUMPSTER?

It's convenient to have a character that is willing to kill off a character I'm done with.

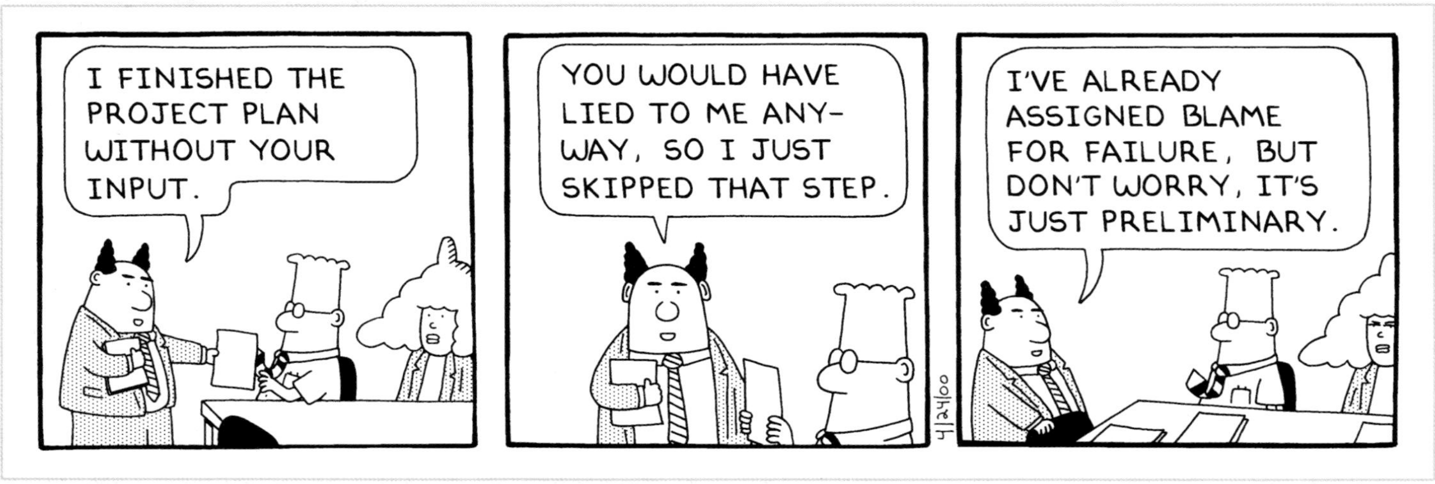
I FINISHED THE PROJECT PLAN WITHOUT YOUR INPUT.
YOU WOULD HAVE LIED TO ME ANY-WAY, SO I JUST SKIPPED THAT STEP.
4/24/00
I'VE ALREADY ASSIGNED BLAME FOR FAILURE, BUT DON'T WORRY, IT'S JUST PRELIMINARY.

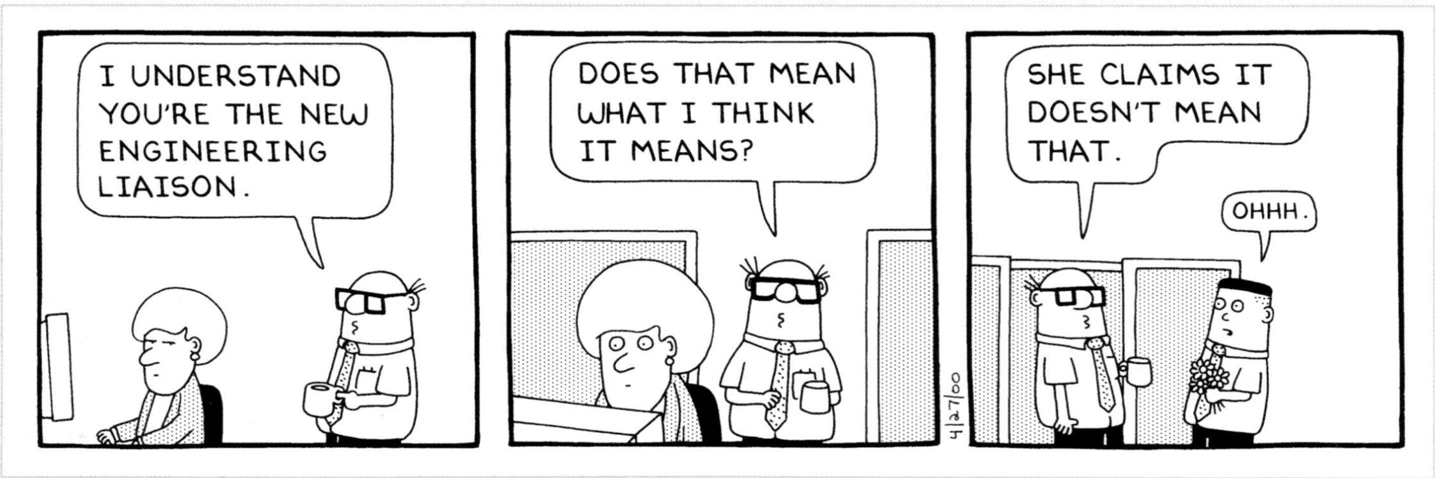
I UNDERSTAND YOU'RE THE NEW ENGINEERING LIAISON.
DOES THAT MEAN WHAT I THINK IT MEANS?
4/27/00
SHE CLAIMS IT DOESN'T MEAN THAT.
OHHH.

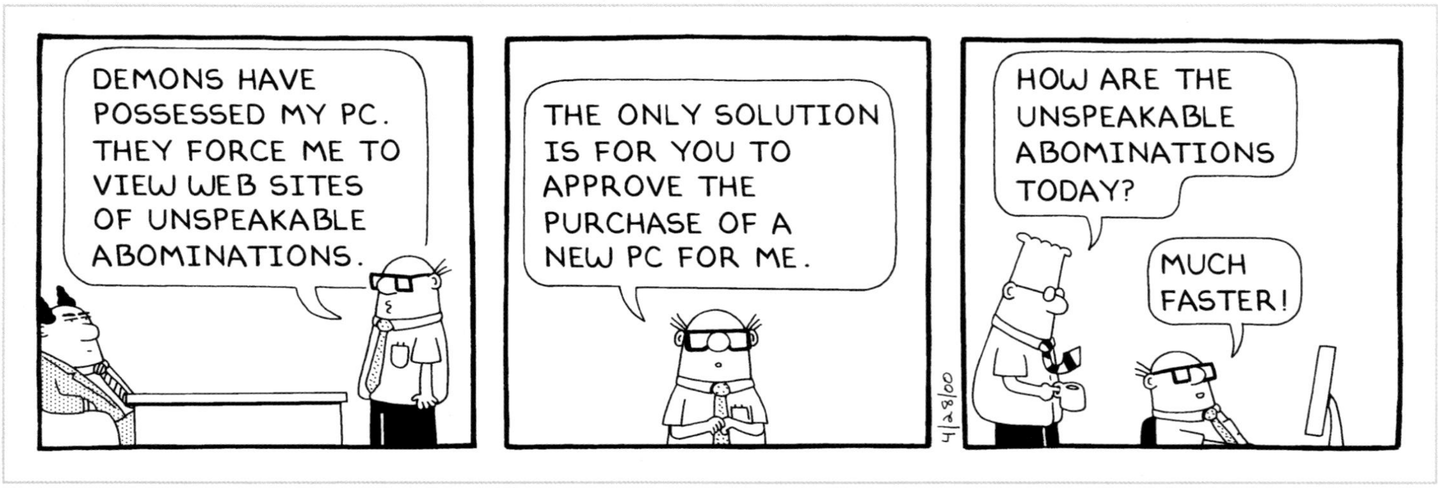
DEMONS HAVE POSSESSED MY PC. THEY FORCE ME TO VIEW WEB SITES OF UNSPEAKABLE ABOMINATIONS.
THE ONLY SOLUTION IS FOR YOU TO APPROVE THE PURCHASE OF A NEW PC FOR ME.
4/28/00
HOW ARE THE UNSPEAKABLE ABOMINATIONS TODAY?
MUCH FASTER!

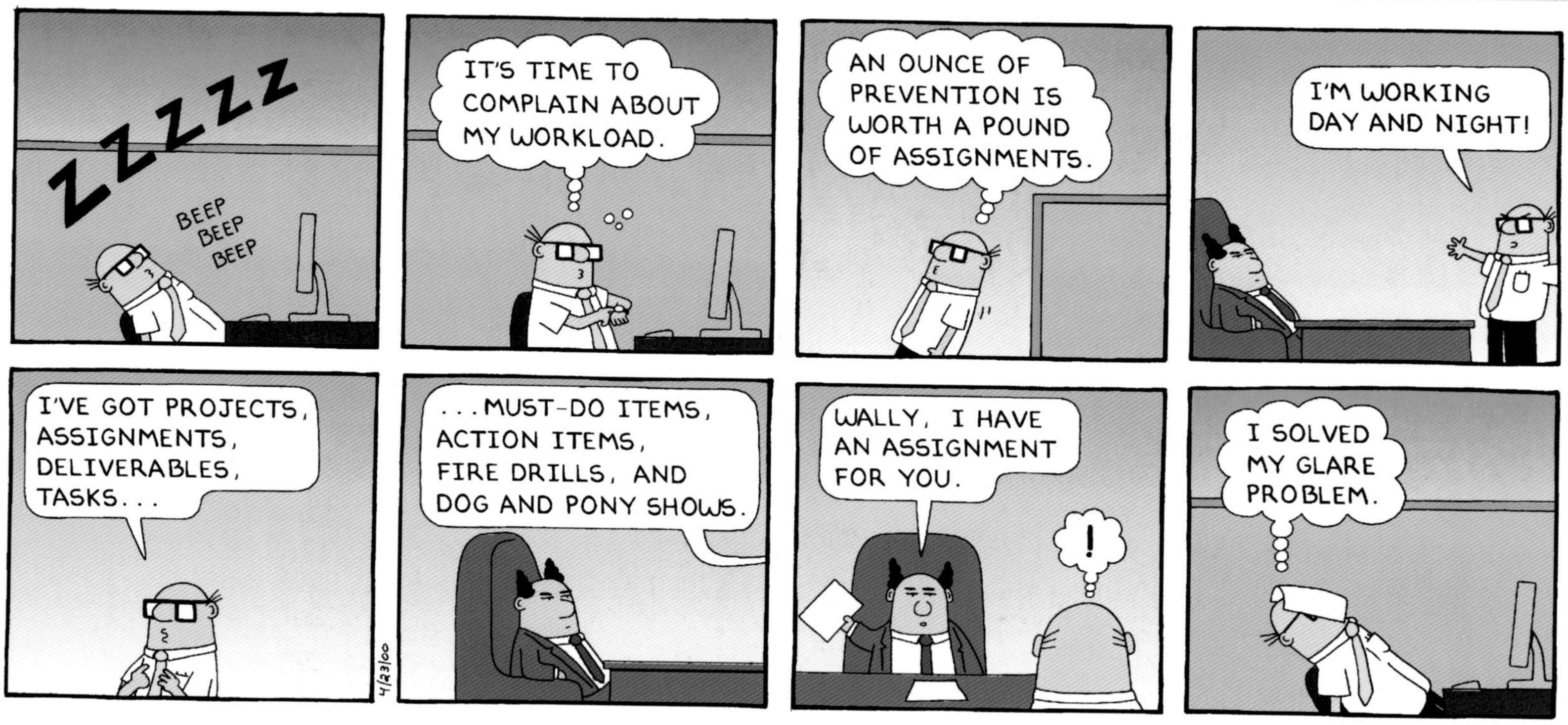
ZZZZZ
BEEP BEEP BEEP
IT'S TIME TO COMPLAIN ABOUT MY WORKLOAD.
AN OUNCE OF PREVENTION IS WORTH A POUND OF ASSIGNMENTS.
I'M WORKING DAY AND NIGHT!
I'VE GOT PROJECTS, ASSIGNMENTS, DELIVERABLES, TASKS...
4/23/00
...MUST-DO ITEMS, ACTION ITEMS, FIRE DRILLS, AND DOG AND PONY SHOWS.
WALLY, I HAVE AN ASSIGNMENT FOR YOU.
!
I SOLVED MY GLARE PROBLEM.

One of the challenges of cartooning is coming up with situations that are more absurd than reality. This comic is based on a conversation I had with a friend, without the invitation to make out.

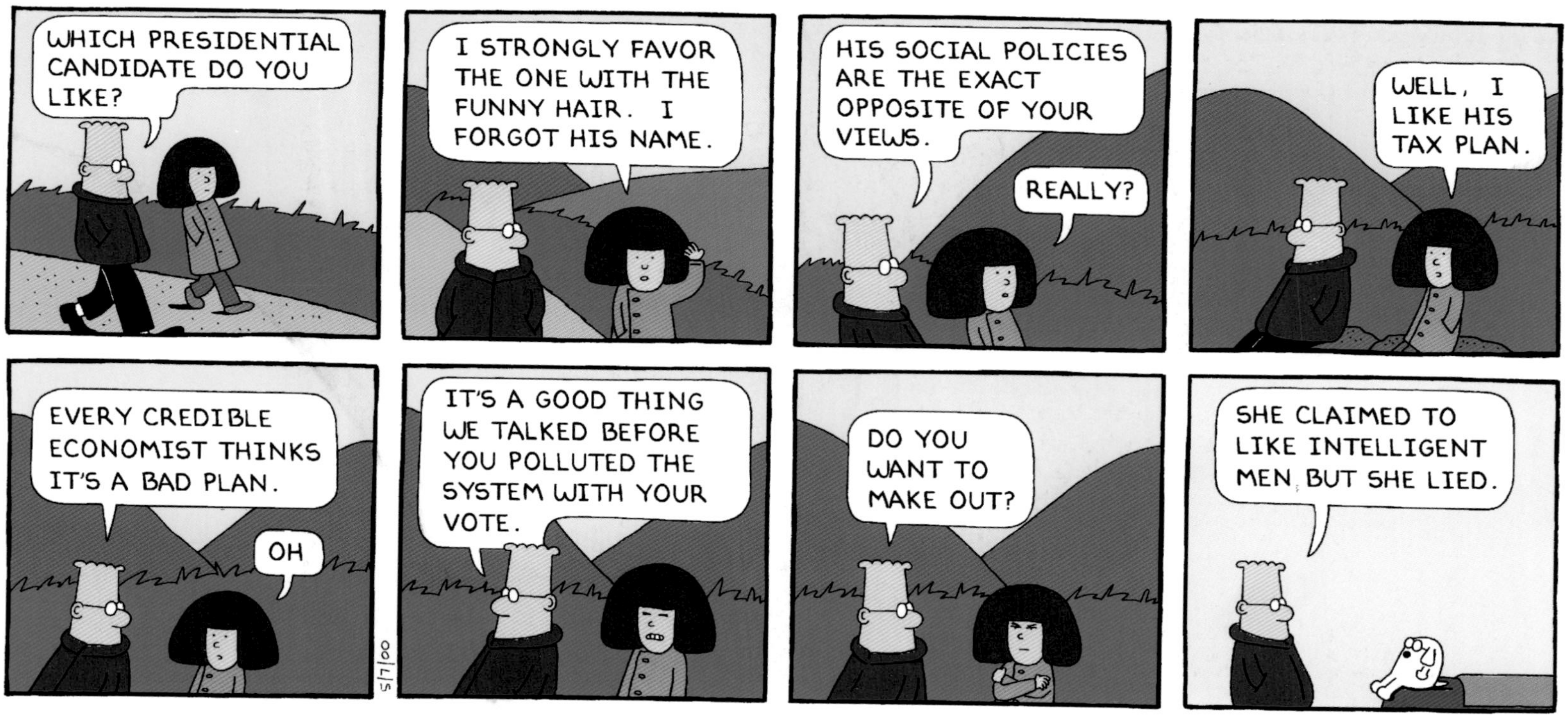
WHICH PRESIDENTIAL CANDIDATE DO YOU LIKE?
I STRONGLY FAVOR THE ONE WITH THE FUNNY HAIR. I FORGOT HIS NAME.
HIS SOCIAL POLICIES ARE THE EXACT OPPOSITE OF YOUR VIEWS.
REALLY?
WELL, I LIKE HIS TAX PLAN.
EVERY CREDIBLE ECONOMIST THINKS IT'S A BAD PLAN.
OH
5/7/00
IT'S A GOOD THING WE TALKED BEFORE YOU POLLUTED THE SYSTEM WITH YOUR VOTE.
DO YOU WANT TO MAKE OUT?
SHE CLAIMED TO LIKE INTELLIGENT MEN, BUT SHE LIED.

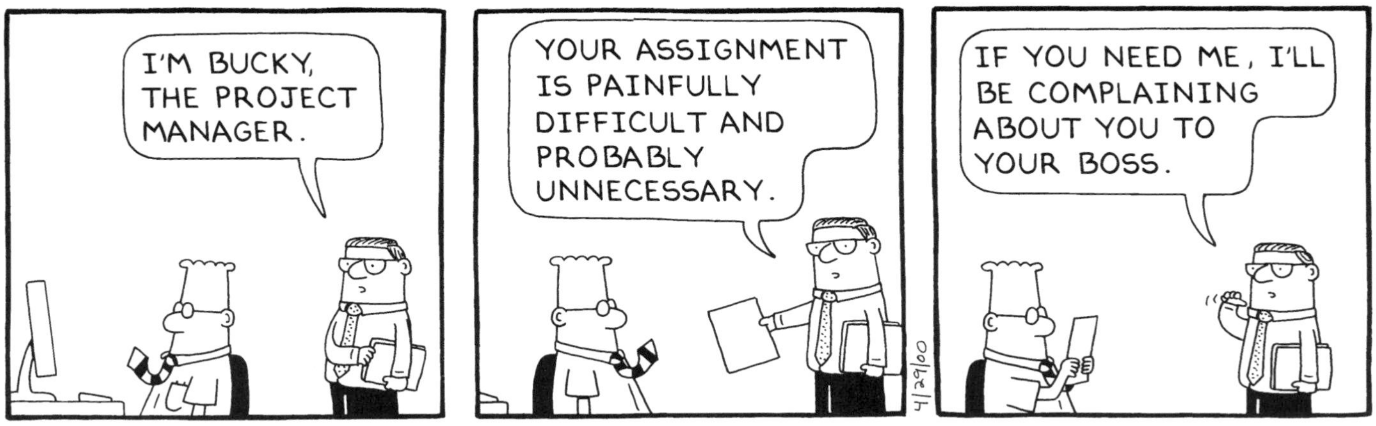
I'M BUCKY, THE PROJECT MANAGER.
YOUR ASSIGNMENT IS PAINFULLY DIFFICULT AND PROBABLY UNNECESSARY.
4/29/00
IF YOU NEED ME, I'LL BE COMPLAINING ABOUT YOU TO YOUR BOSS.

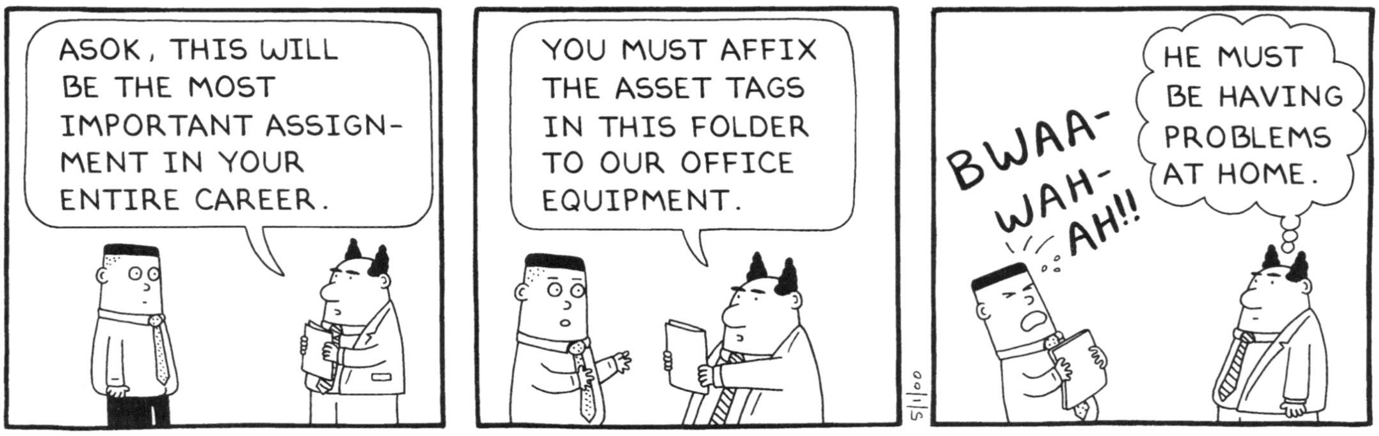
ASOK, THIS WILL BE THE MOST IMPORTANT ASSIGN-MENT IN YOUR ENTIRE CAREER.
YOU MUST AFFIX THE ASSET TAGS IN THIS FOLDER TO OUR OFFICE EQUIPMENT.
5/1/00
BWAA-WAH-AH!!
HE MUST BE HAVING PROBLEMS AT HOME.

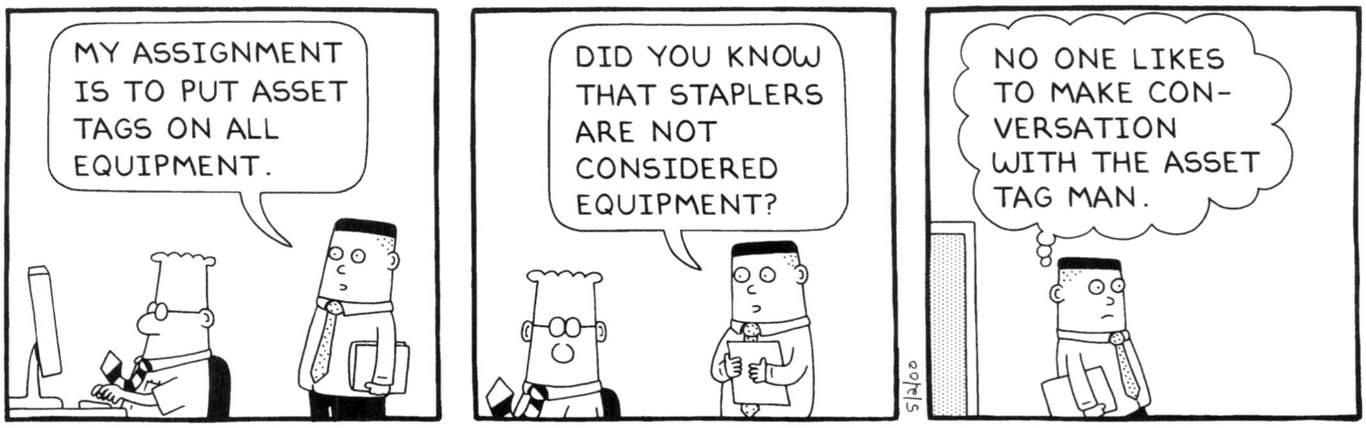
MY ASSIGNMENT IS TO PUT ASSET TAGS ON ALL EQUIPMENT.
DID YOU KNOW THAT STAPLERS ARE NOT CONSIDERED EQUIPMENT?
5/2/00
NO ONE LIKES TO MAKE CON-VERSATION WITH THE ASSET TAG MAN.

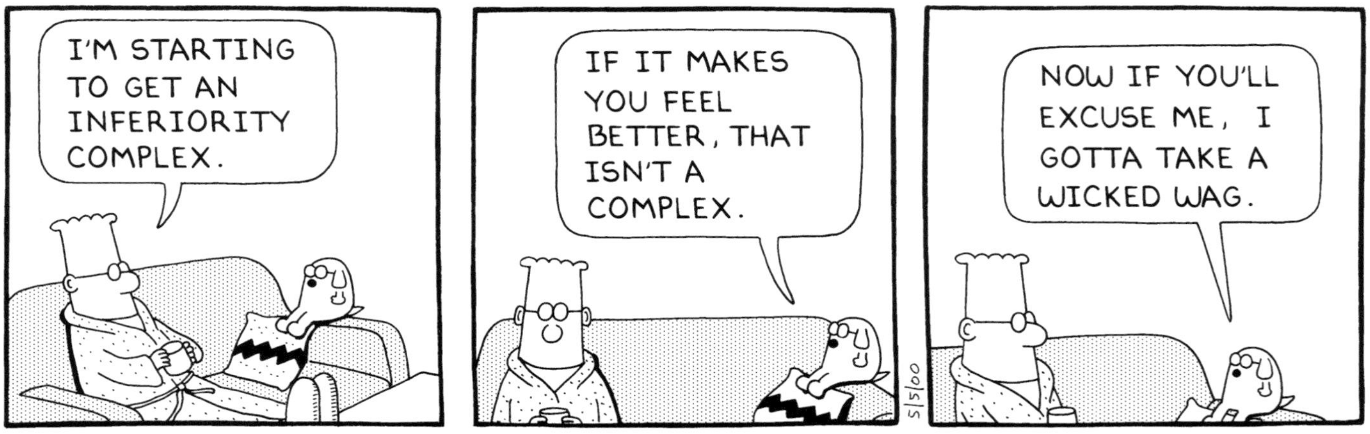
I'M STARTING TO GET AN INFERIORITY COMPLEX.
IF IT MAKES YOU FEEL BETTER, THAT ISN'T A COMPLEX.
5/5/00
NOW IF YOU'LL EXCUSE ME, I GOTTA TAKE A WICKED WAG.

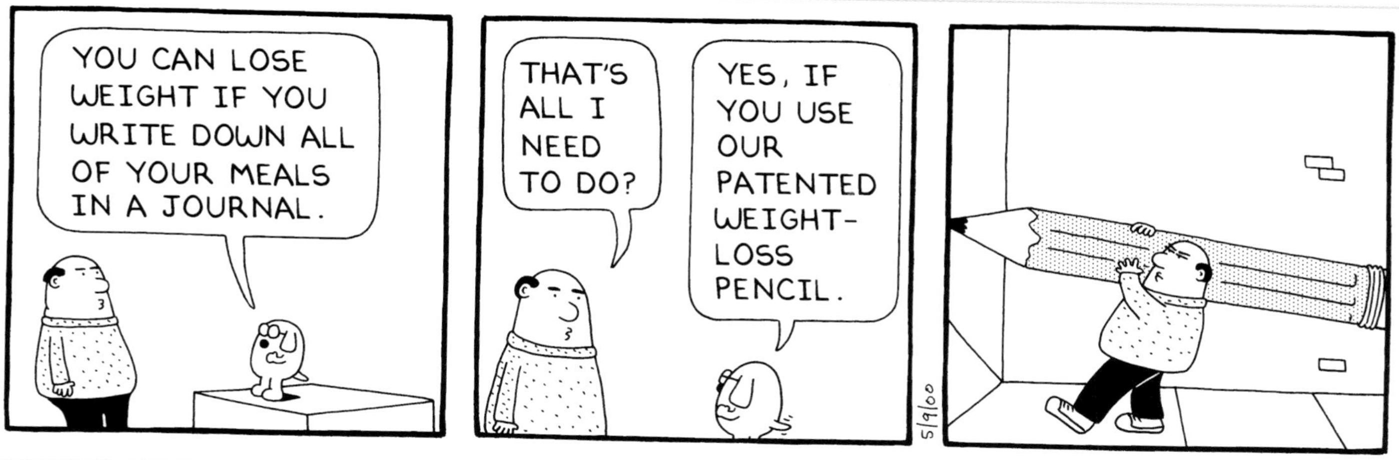
YOU CAN LOSE WEIGHT IF YOU WRITE DOWN ALL OF YOUR MEALS IN A JOURNAL.
THAT'S ALL I NEED TO DO?
YES, IF YOU USE OUR PATENTED WEIGHT-LOSS PENCIL.
5/9/00

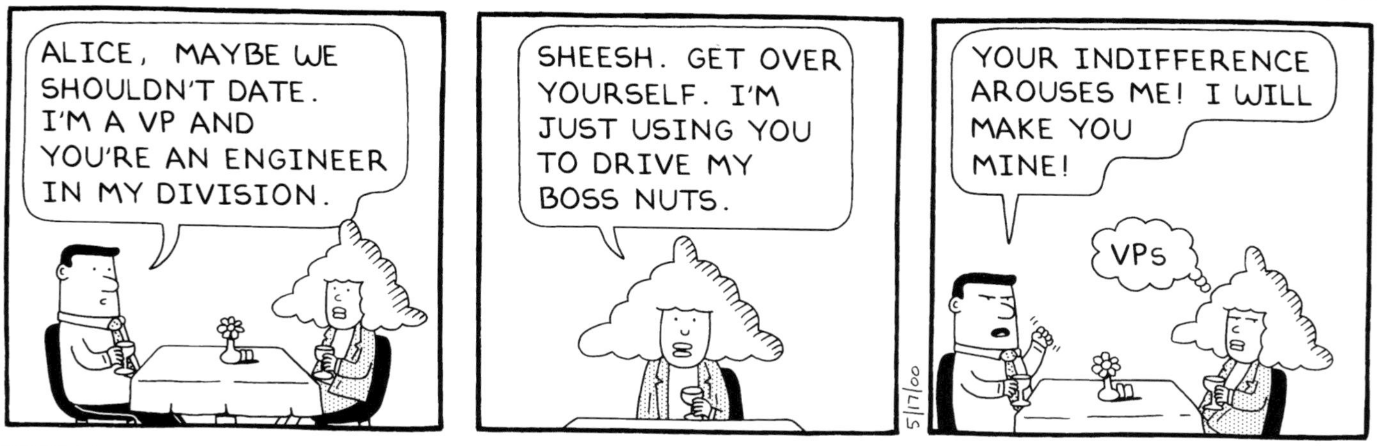
ALICE, MAYBE WE SHOULDN'T DATE. I'M A VP AND YOU'RE AN ENGINEER IN MY DIVISION.
SHEESH. GET OVER YOURSELF. I'M JUST USING YOU TO DRIVE MY BOSS NUTS.
YOUR INDIFFERENCE AROUSES ME! I WILL MAKE YOU MINE!
VPs
5/17/00

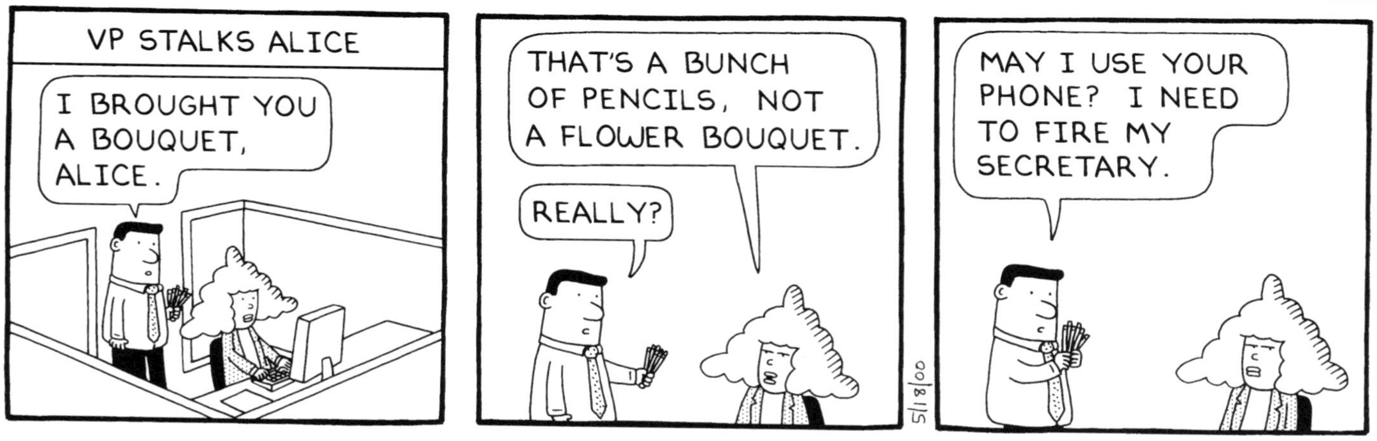
VP STALKS ALICE
I BROUGHT YOU A BOUQUET, ALICE.
THAT'S A BUNCH OF PENCILS, NOT A FLOWER BOUQUET.
REALLY?
MAY I USE YOUR PHONE? I NEED TO FIRE MY SECRETARY.
5/18/00

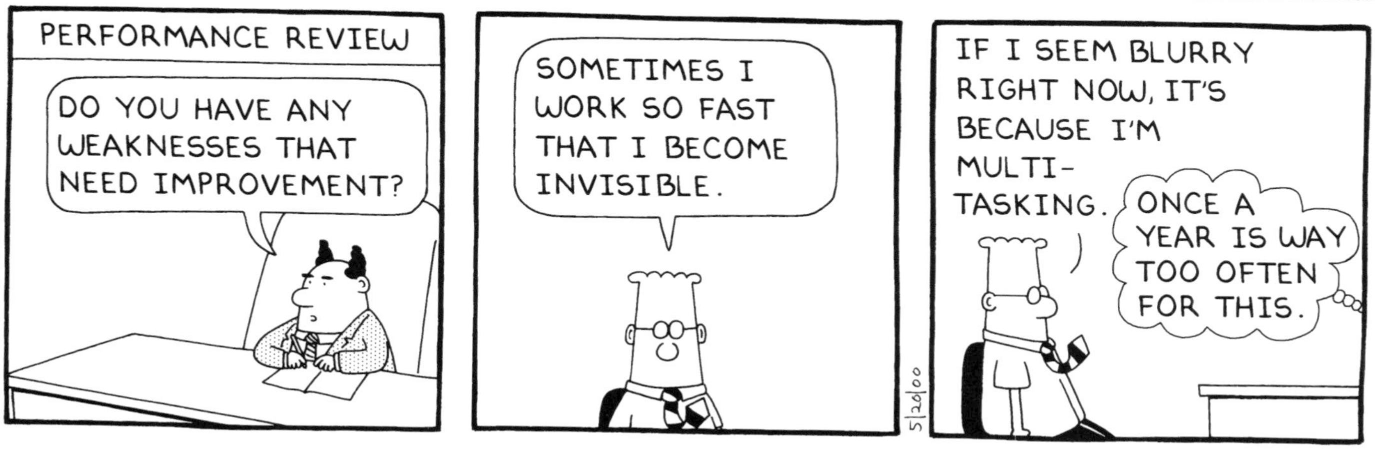
PERFORMANCE REVIEW
DO YOU HAVE ANY WEAKNESSES THAT NEED IMPROVEMENT?
SOMETIMES I WORK SO FAST THAT I BECOME INVISIBLE.
IF I SEEM BLURRY RIGHT NOW, IT'S BECAUSE I'M MULTI-TASKING.
ONCE A YEAR IS WAY TOO OFTEN FOR THIS.
5/20/00

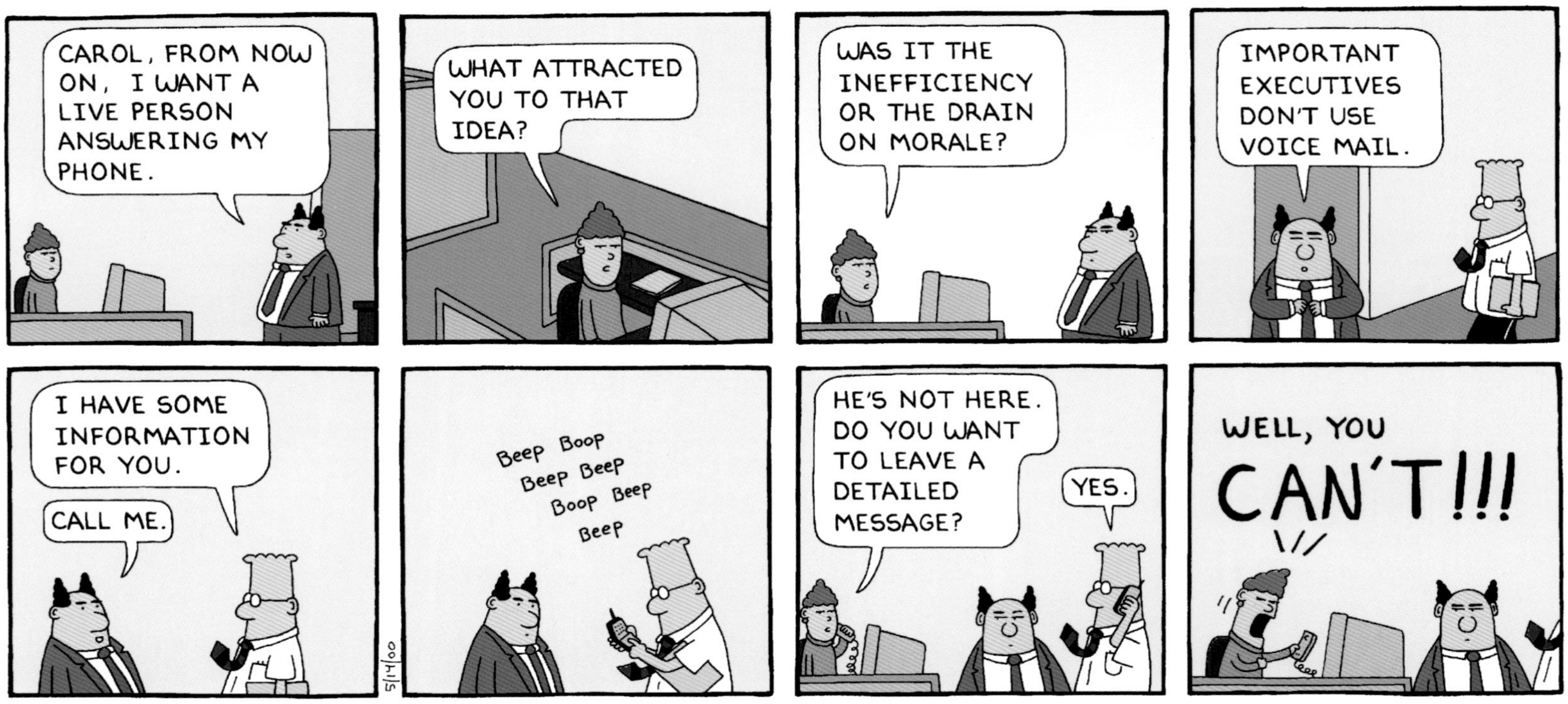
CAROL, FROM NOW ON, I WANT A LIVE PERSON ANSWERING MY PHONE.
WHAT ATTRACTED YOU TO THAT IDEA?
WAS IT THE INEFFICIENCY OR THE DRAIN ON MORALE?
IMPORTANT EXECUTIVES DON'T USE VOICE MAIL.
I HAVE SOME INFORMATION FOR YOU.
CALL ME.
5/14/00
Beep Boop Beep Beep Boop Beep Beep
HE'S NOT HERE. DO YOU WANT TO LEAVE A DETAILED MESSAGE?
YES.
WELL, YOU CAN'T!!!

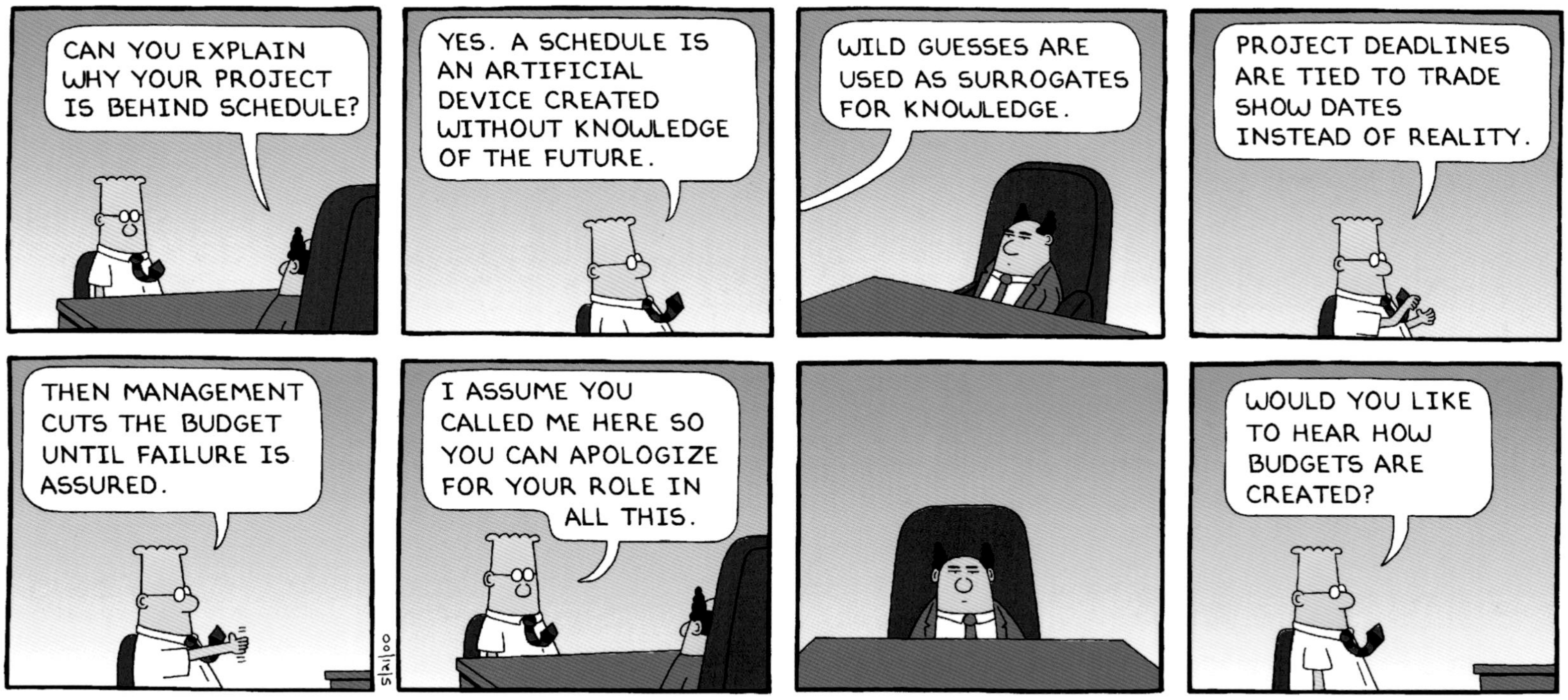
CAN YOU EXPLAIN WHY YOUR PROJECT IS BEHIND SCHEDULE?
YES. A SCHEDULE IS AN ARTIFICIAL DEVICE CREATED WITHOUT KNOWLEDGE OF THE FUTURE.
WILD GUESSES ARE USED AS SURROGATES FOR KNOWLEDGE.
PROJECT DEADLINES ARE TIED TO TRADE SHOW DATES INSTEAD OF REALITY.
THEN MANAGEMENT CUTS THE BUDGET UNTIL FAILURE IS ASSURED.
5/21/00
I ASSUME YOU CALLED ME HERE SO YOU CAN APOLOGIZE FOR YOUR ROLE IN ALL THIS.
WOULD YOU LIKE TO HEAR HOW BUDGETS ARE CREATED?

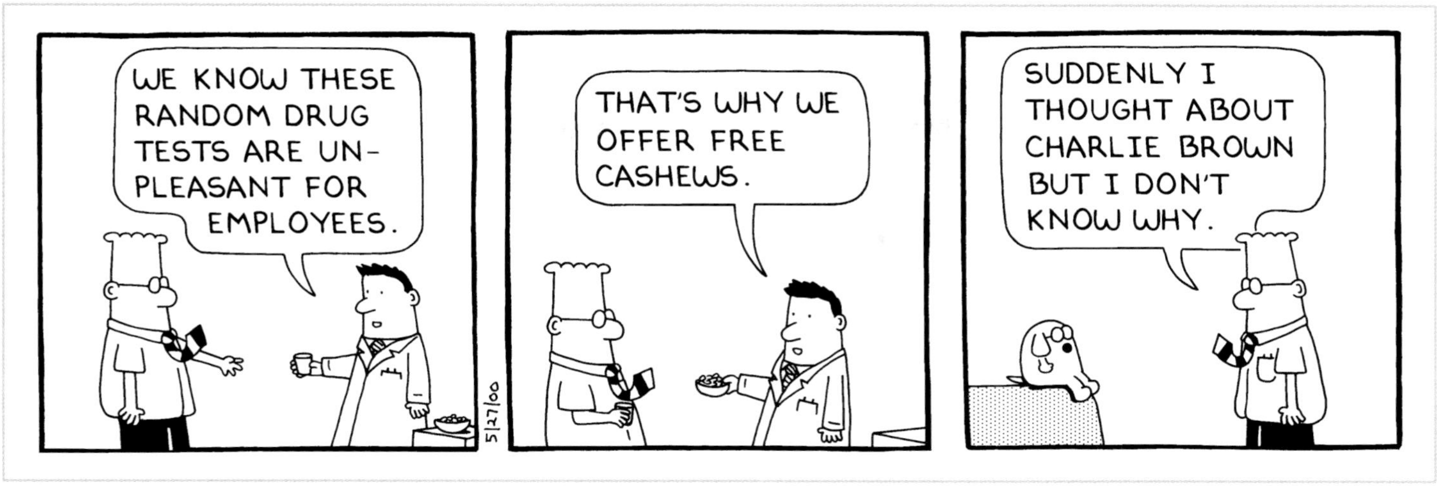
WE KNOW THESE RANDOM DRUG TESTS ARE UN-PLEASANT FOR EMPLOYEES.
THAT'S WHY WE OFFER FREE CASHEWS.
SUDDENLY I THOUGHT ABOUT CHARLIE BROWN BUT I DON'T KNOW WHY.
5/27/00

On this day, many cartoonists mentioned the Peanuts *comic strip as a tribute to Charles Schulz. In this comic, the cashews are offered in exchange for a urine sample; in other words, they are pee nuts. I don't think anyone made the connection. It isn't my best work.*

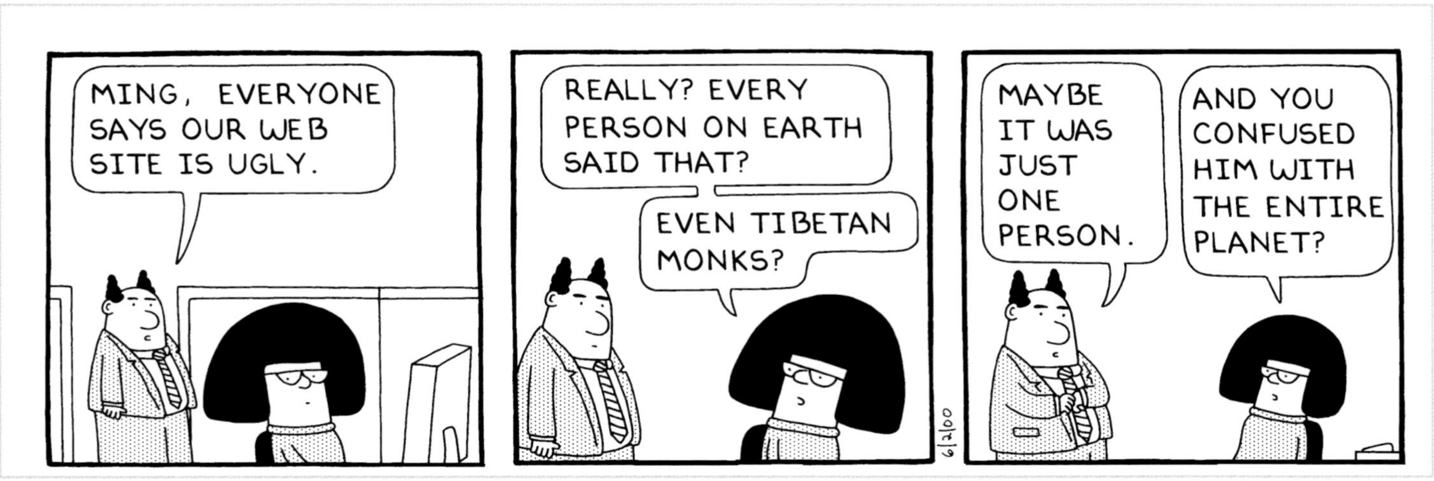
MING, EVERYONE SAYS OUR WEB SITE IS UGLY.
REALLY? EVERY PERSON ON EARTH SAID THAT?
EVEN TIBETAN MONKS?
MAYBE IT WAS JUST ONE PERSON.
AND YOU CONFUSED HIM WITH THE ENTIRE PLANET?
6/2/00

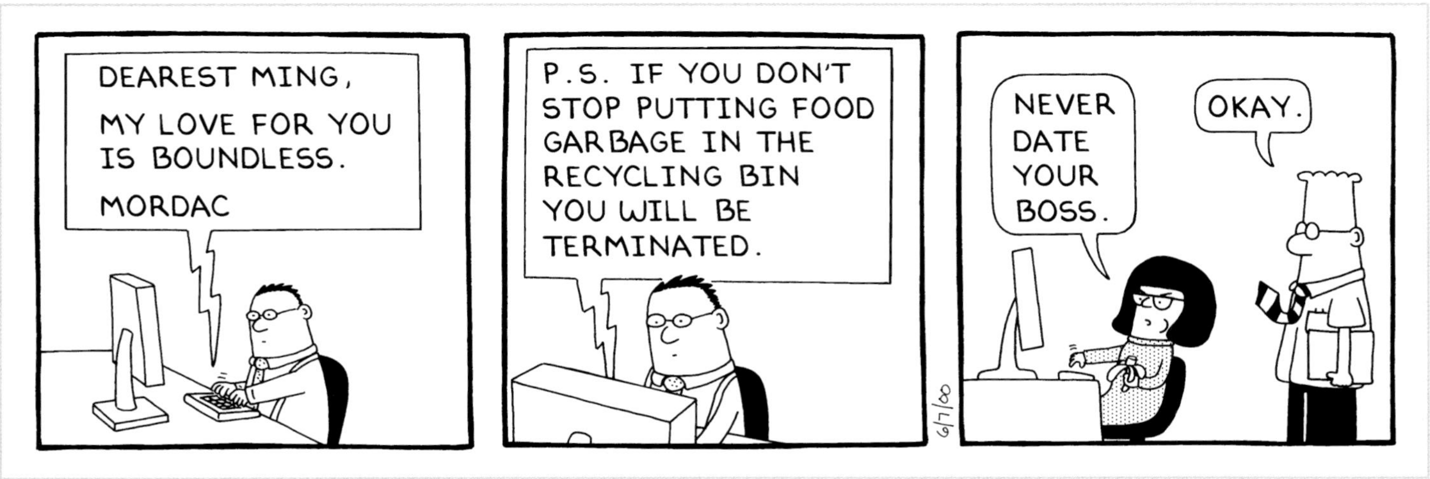
DEAREST MING,
MY LOVE FOR YOU IS BOUNDLESS.
MORDAC
P.S. IF YOU DON'T STOP PUTTING FOOD GARBAGE IN THE RECYCLING BIN YOU WILL BE TERMINATED.
NEVER DATE YOUR BOSS.
OKAY.
6/7/00

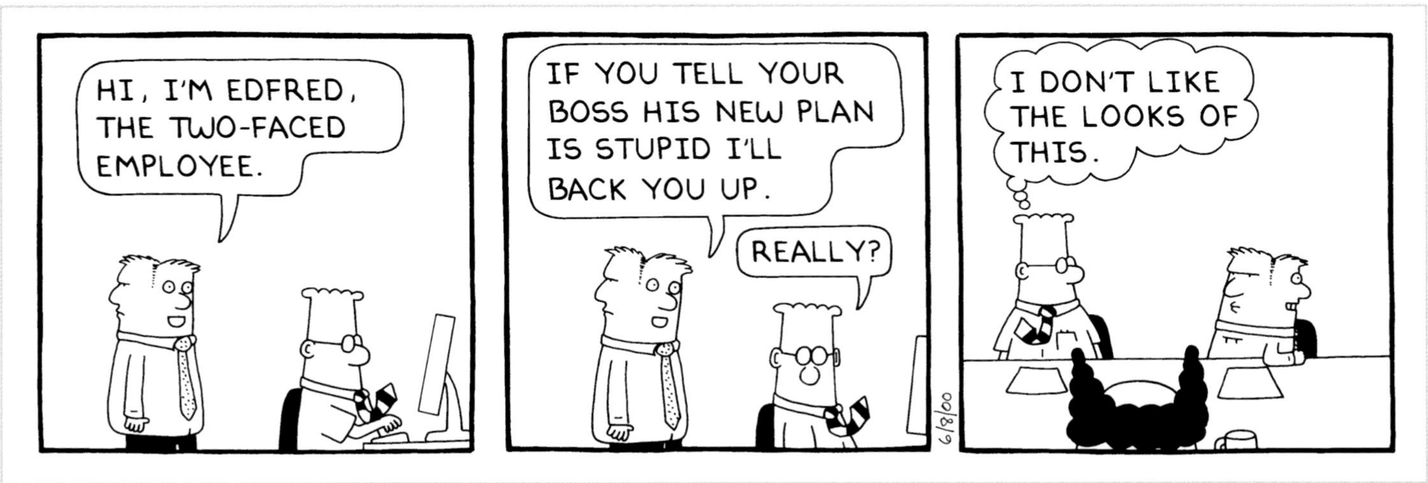
HI, I'M EDFRED, THE TWO-FACED EMPLOYEE.
IF YOU TELL YOUR BOSS HIS NEW PLAN IS STUPID I'LL BACK YOU UP.
REALLY?
I DON'T LIKE THE LOOKS OF THIS.
6/8/00

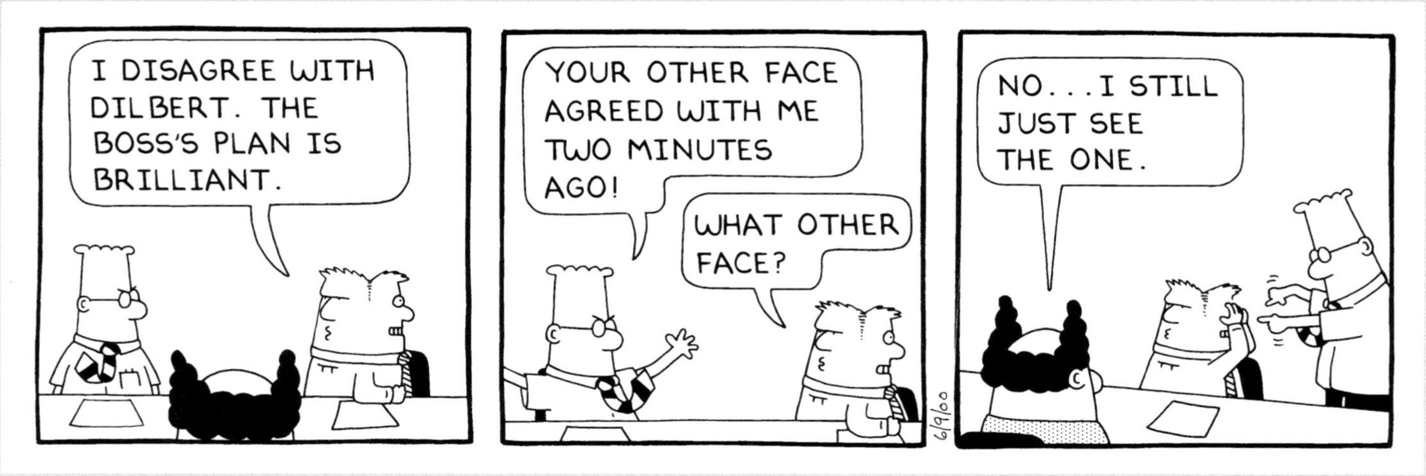
I DISAGREE WITH DILBERT. THE BOSS'S PLAN IS BRILLIANT.
YOUR OTHER FACE AGREED WITH ME TWO MINUTES AGO!
WHAT OTHER FACE?
6/9/00
NO...I STILL JUST SEE THE ONE.

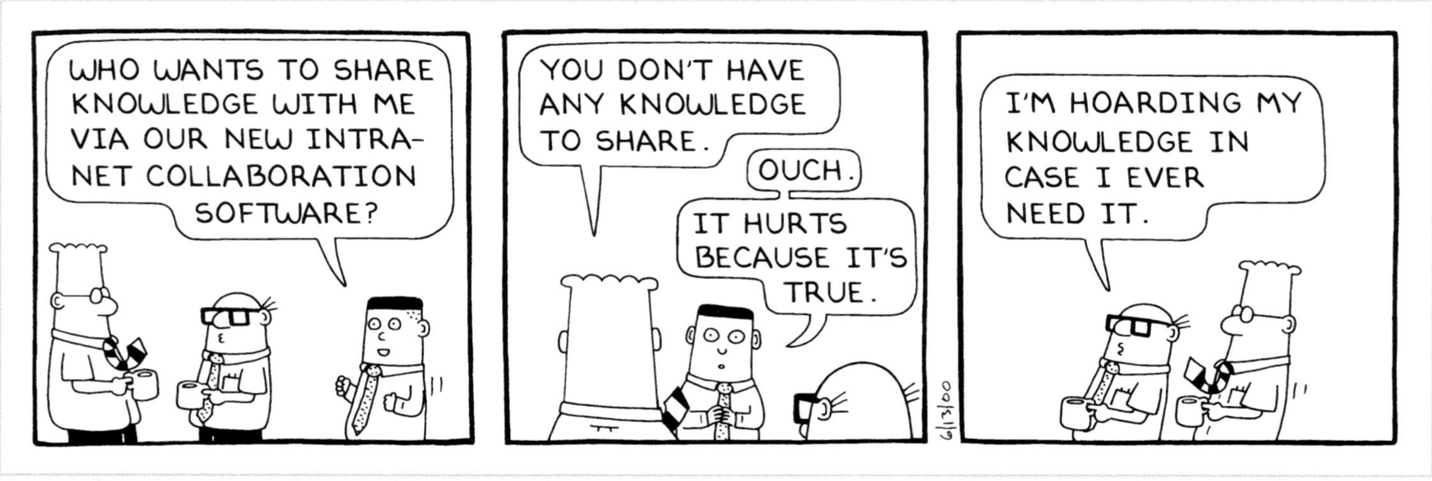
WHO WANTS TO SHARE KNOWLEDGE WITH ME VIA OUR NEW INTRA-NET COLLABORATION SOFTWARE?
YOU DON'T HAVE ANY KNOWLEDGE TO SHARE.
OUCH.
IT HURTS BECAUSE IT'S TRUE.
6/13/00
I'M HOARDING MY KNOWLEDGE IN CASE I EVER NEED IT.

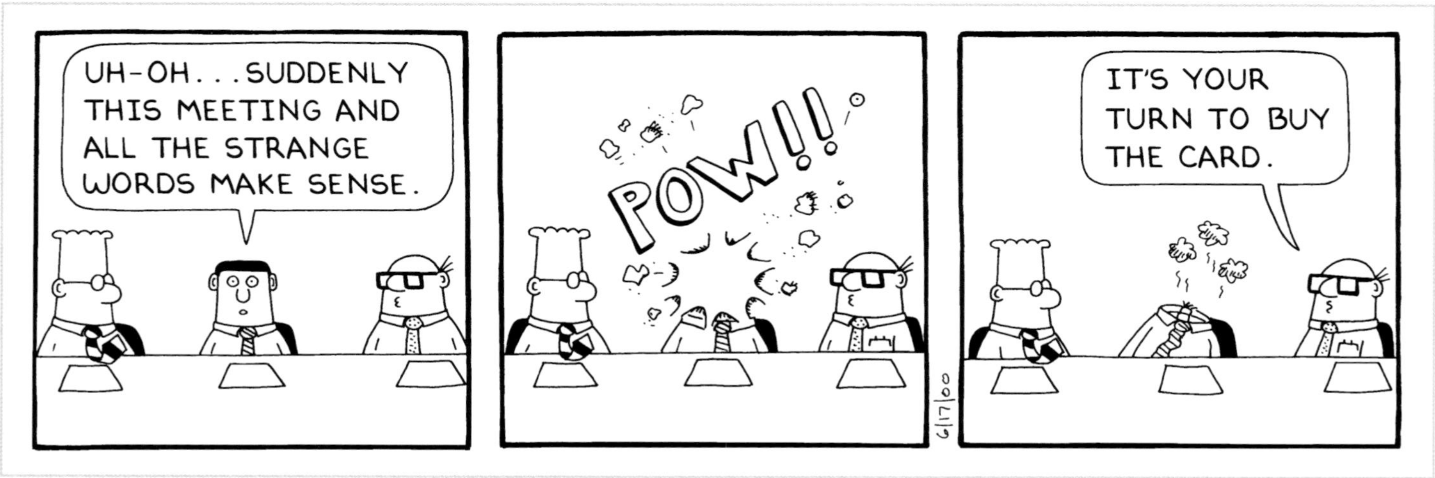
UH-OH...SUDDENLY THIS MEETING AND ALL THE STRANGE WORDS MAKE SENSE.
POW!!
6/17/00
IT'S YOUR TURN TO BUY THE CARD.

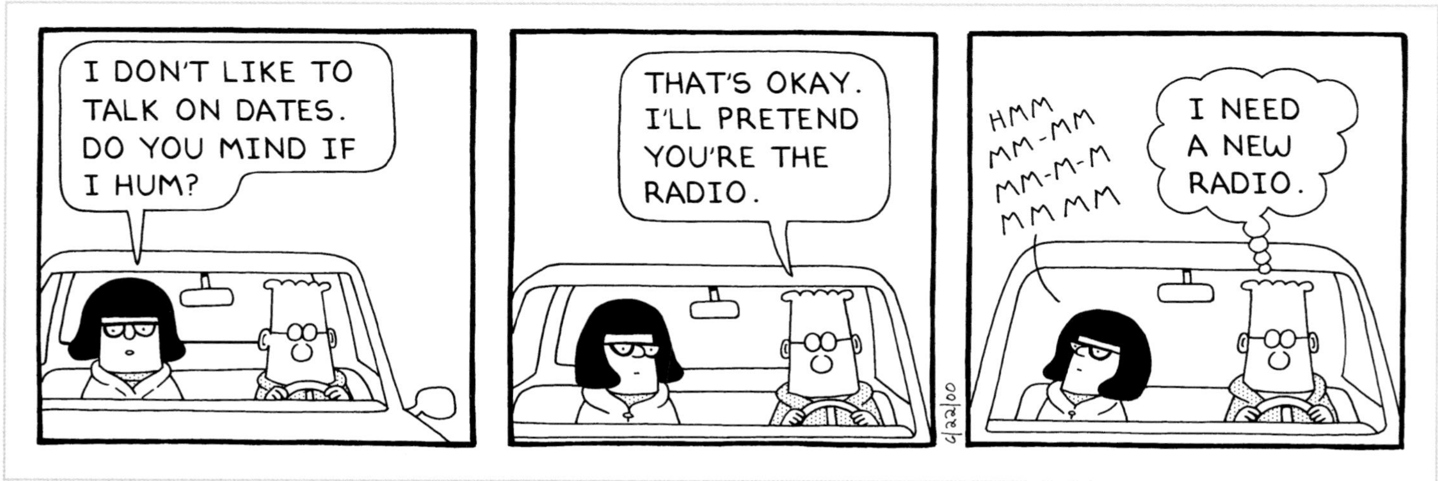
I DON'T LIKE TO TALK ON DATES. DO YOU MIND IF I HUM?
THAT'S OKAY. I'LL PRETEND YOU'RE THE RADIO.
6/22/00
HMM MM-MM MM-M-M MMMM
I NEED A NEW RADIO.

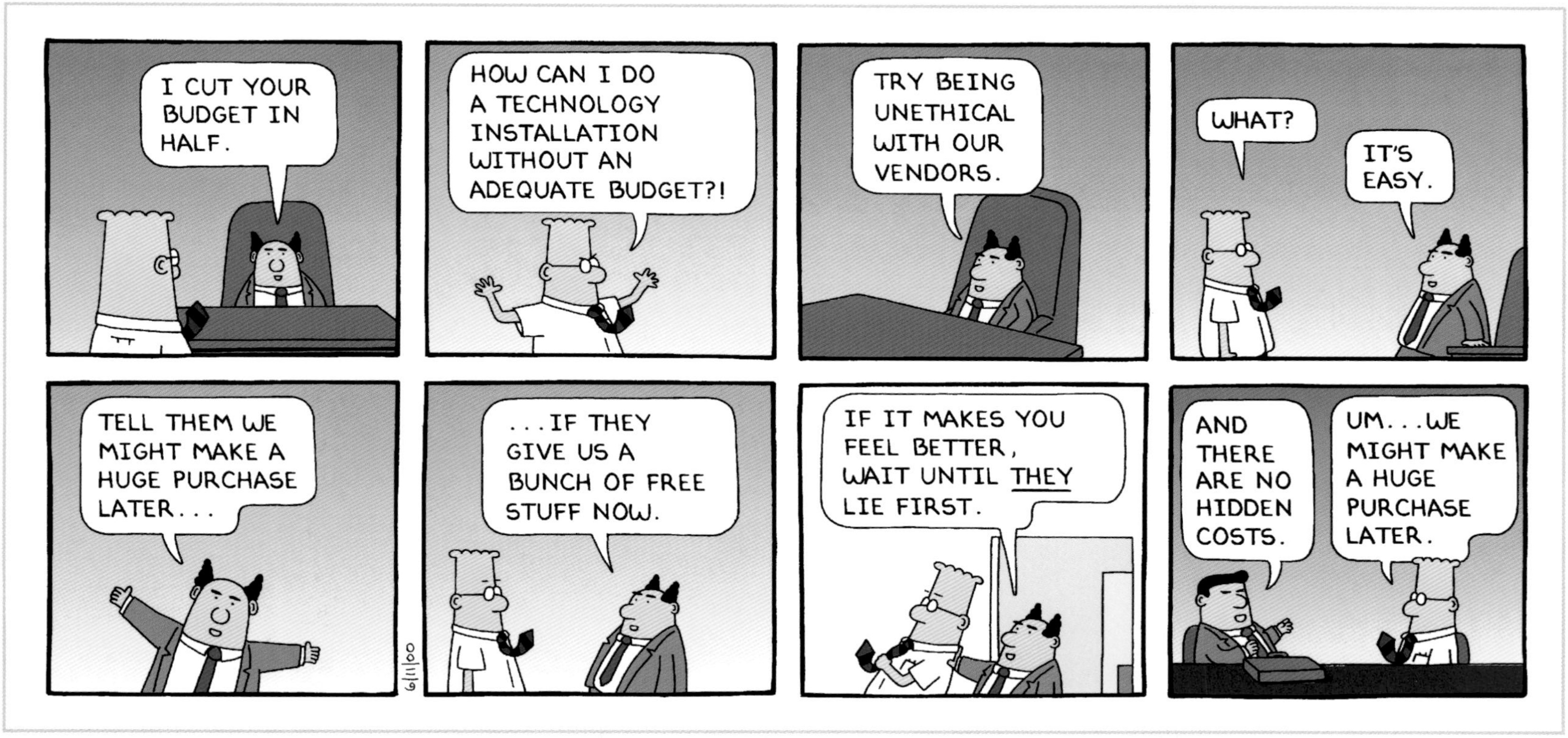
I CUT YOUR BUDGET IN HALF.
HOW CAN I DO A TECHNOLOGY INSTALLATION WITHOUT AN ADEQUATE BUDGET?!
TRY BEING UNETHICAL WITH OUR VENDORS.
WHAT?
IT'S EASY.
TELL THEM WE MIGHT MAKE A HUGE PURCHASE LATER...
...IF THEY GIVE US A BUNCH OF FREE STUFF NOW.
6/1/00
IF IT MAKES YOU FEEL BETTER, WAIT UNTIL THEY LIE FIRST.
AND THERE ARE NO HIDDEN COSTS.
UM...WE MIGHT MAKE A HUGE PURCHASE LATER.

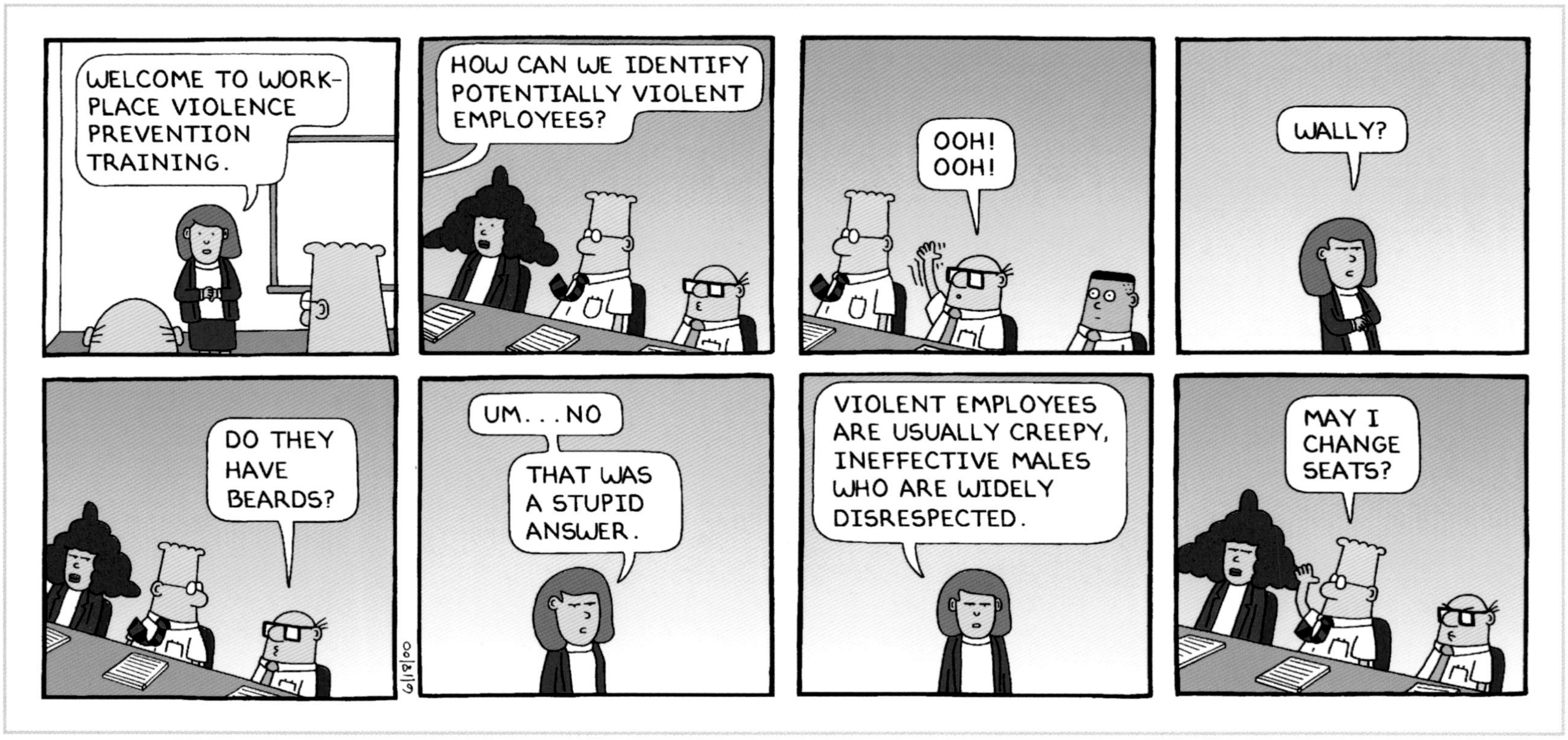
WELCOME TO WORK-PLACE VIOLENCE PREVENTION TRAINING.
HOW CAN WE IDENTIFY POTENTIALLY VIOLENT EMPLOYEES?
OOH! OOH!
WALLY?
DO THEY HAVE BEARDS?
6/18/00
UM...NO
THAT WAS A STUPID ANSWER.
VIOLENT EMPLOYEES ARE USUALLY CREEPY, INEFFECTIVE MALES WHO ARE WIDELY DISRESPECTED.
MAY I CHANGE SEATS?

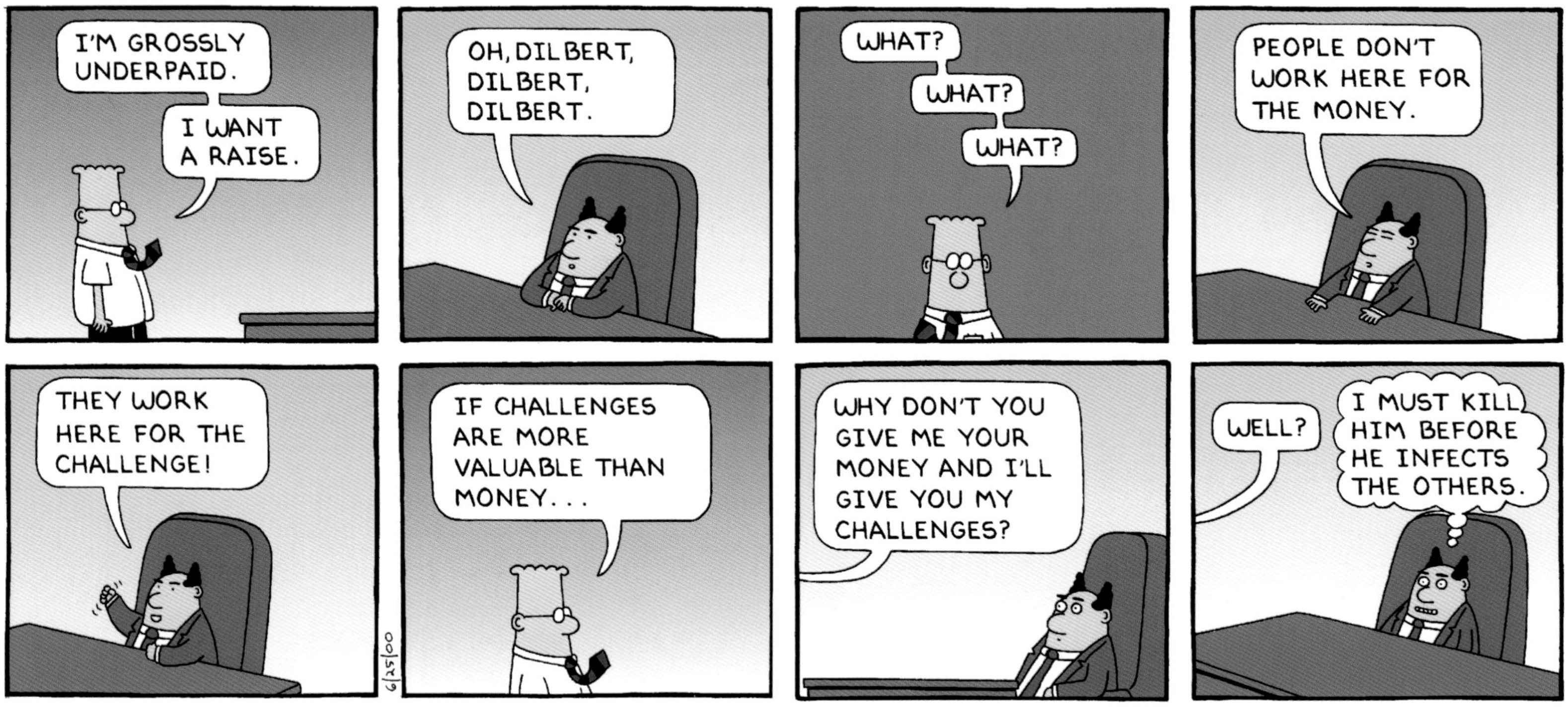
I'M GROSSLY UNDERPAID.
I WANT A RAISE.
OH, DILBERT, DILBERT, DILBERT.
WHAT?
WHAT?
WHAT?
PEOPLE DON'T WORK HERE FOR THE MONEY.
THEY WORK HERE FOR THE CHALLENGE!
IF CHALLENGES ARE MORE VALUABLE THAN MONEY...
6/25/00
WHY DON'T YOU GIVE ME YOUR MONEY AND I'LL GIVE YOU MY CHALLENGES?
WELL?
I MUST KILL HIM BEFORE HE INFECTS THE OTHERS.

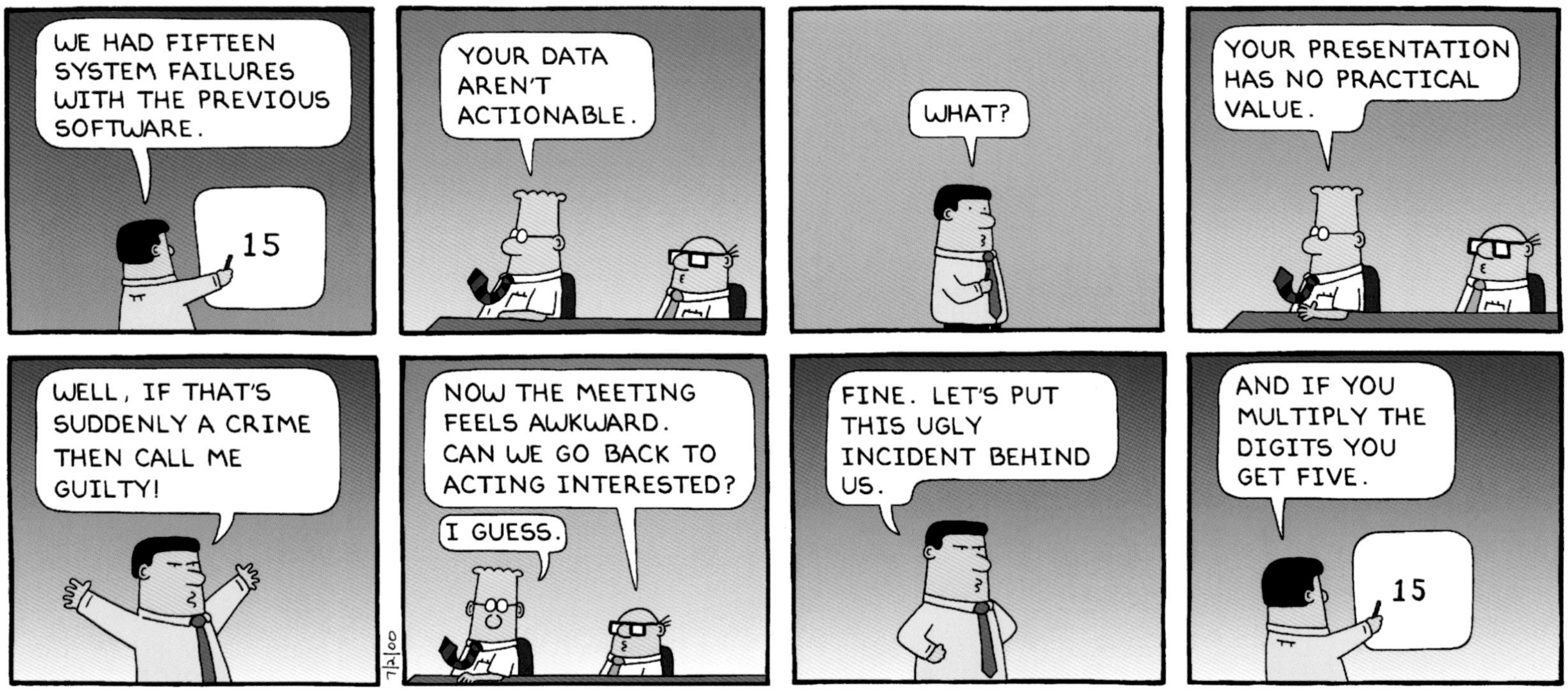
WE HAD FIFTEEN SYSTEM FAILURES WITH THE PREVIOUS SOFTWARE.
15
YOUR DATA AREN'T ACTIONABLE.
WHAT?
YOUR PRESENTATION HAS NO PRACTICAL VALUE.
WELL, IF THAT'S SUDDENLY A CRIME THEN CALL ME GUILTY!
NOW THE MEETING FEELS AWKWARD. CAN WE GO BACK TO ACTING INTERESTED?
I GUESS.
7/2/00
FINE. LET'S PUT THIS UGLY INCIDENT BEHIND US.
AND IF YOU MULTIPLY THE DIGITS YOU GET FIVE.
15

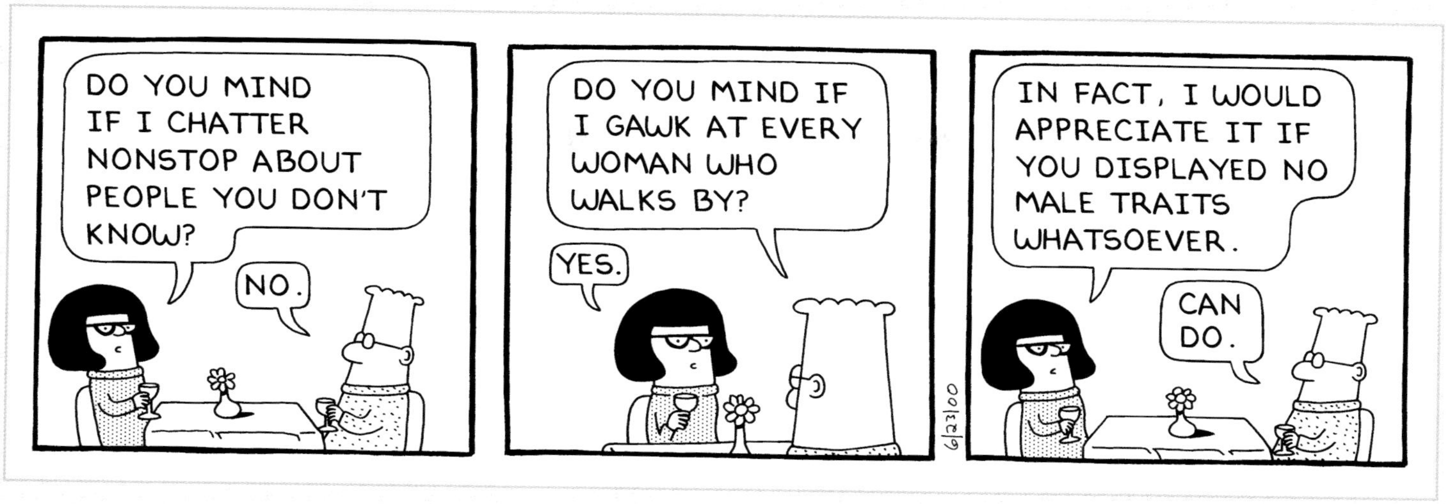
DO YOU MIND IF I CHATTER NONSTOP ABOUT PEOPLE YOU DON'T KNOW?
NO.
DO YOU MIND IF I GAWK AT EVERY WOMAN WHO WALKS BY?
YES.
6/23/00
IN FACT, I WOULD APPRECIATE IT IF YOU DISPLAYED NO MALE TRAITS WHATSOEVER.
CAN DO.

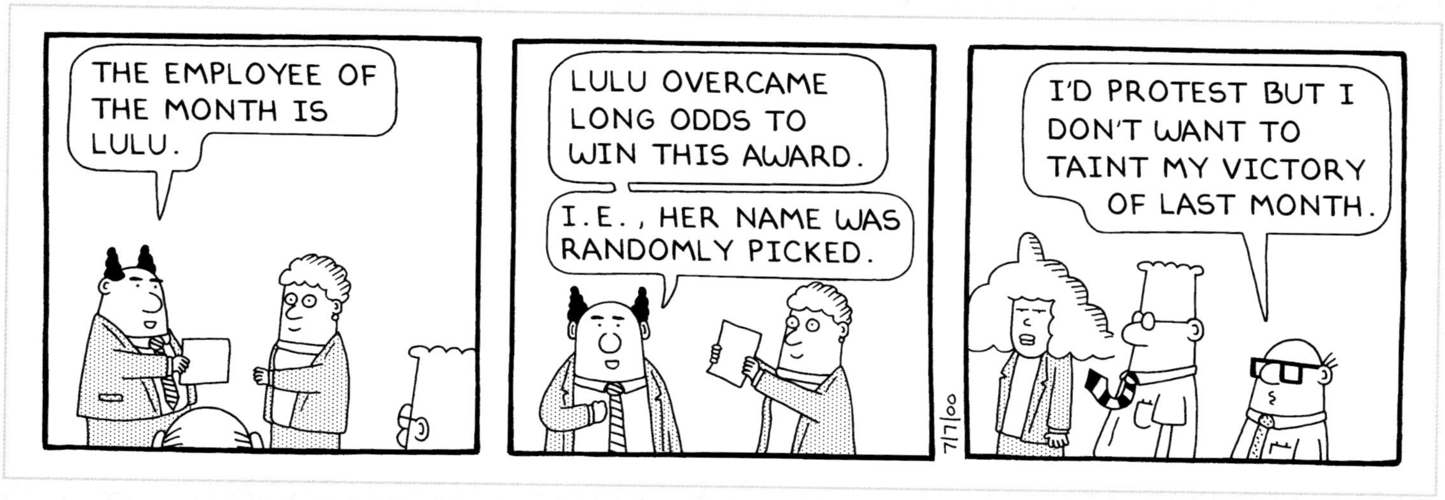
THE EMPLOYEE OF THE MONTH IS LULU.
LULU OVERCAME LONG ODDS TO WIN THIS AWARD.
I.E., HER NAME WAS RANDOMLY PICKED.
7/7/00
I'D PROTEST BUT I DON'T WANT TO TAINT MY VICTORY OF LAST MONTH.

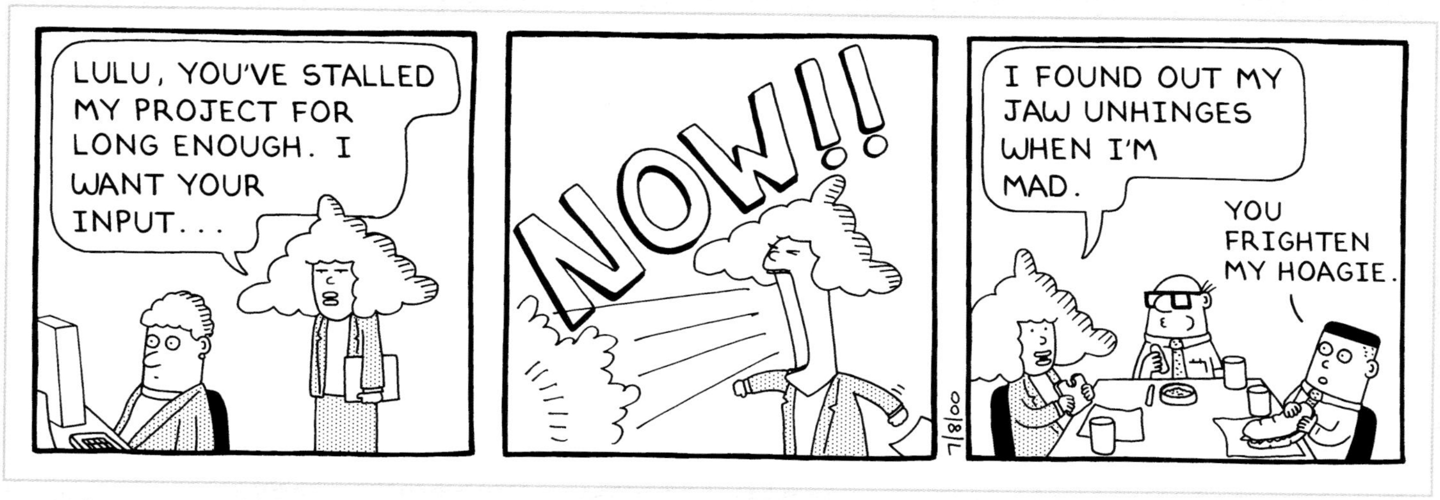
LULU, YOU'VE STALLED MY PROJECT FOR LONG ENOUGH. I WANT YOUR INPUT...
NOW!!
7/8/00
I FOUND OUT MY JAW UNHINGES WHEN I'M MAD.
YOU FRIGHTEN MY HOAGIE.

I have a casual hobby that involves identifying sentences that have, in all probability, been written or uttered only once in human history. "You frighten my hoagie" is probably one of them.

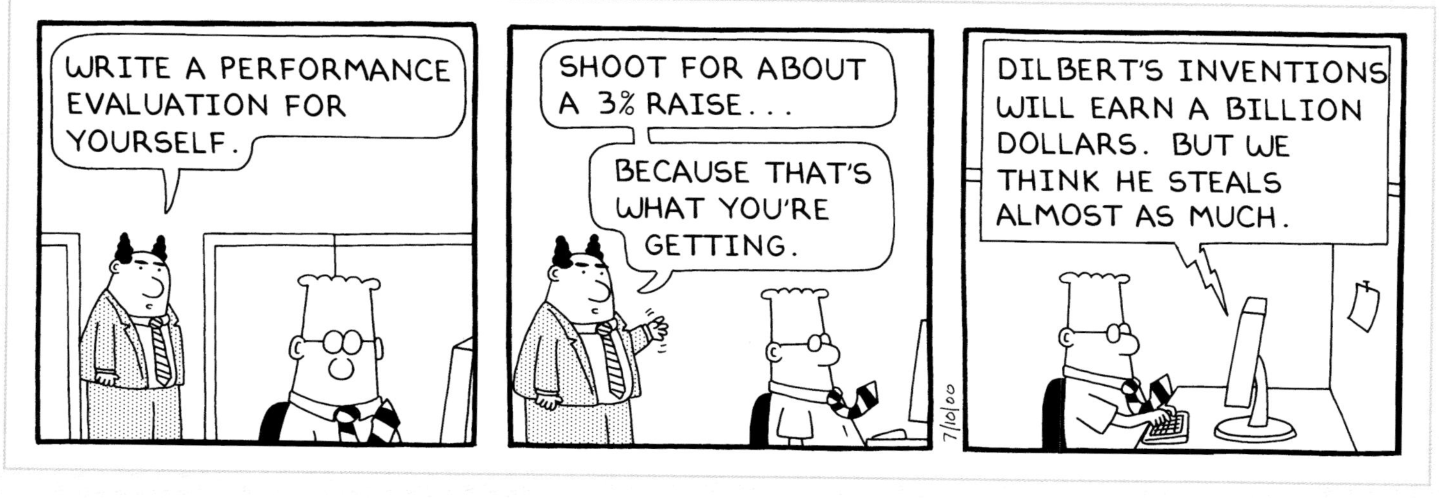
WRITE A PERFORMANCE EVALUATION FOR YOURSELF.
SHOOT FOR ABOUT A 3% RAISE...
BECAUSE THAT'S WHAT YOU'RE GETTING.
7/10/00
DILBERT'S INVENTIONS WILL EARN A BILLION DOLLARS. BUT WE THINK HE STEALS ALMOST AS MUCH.

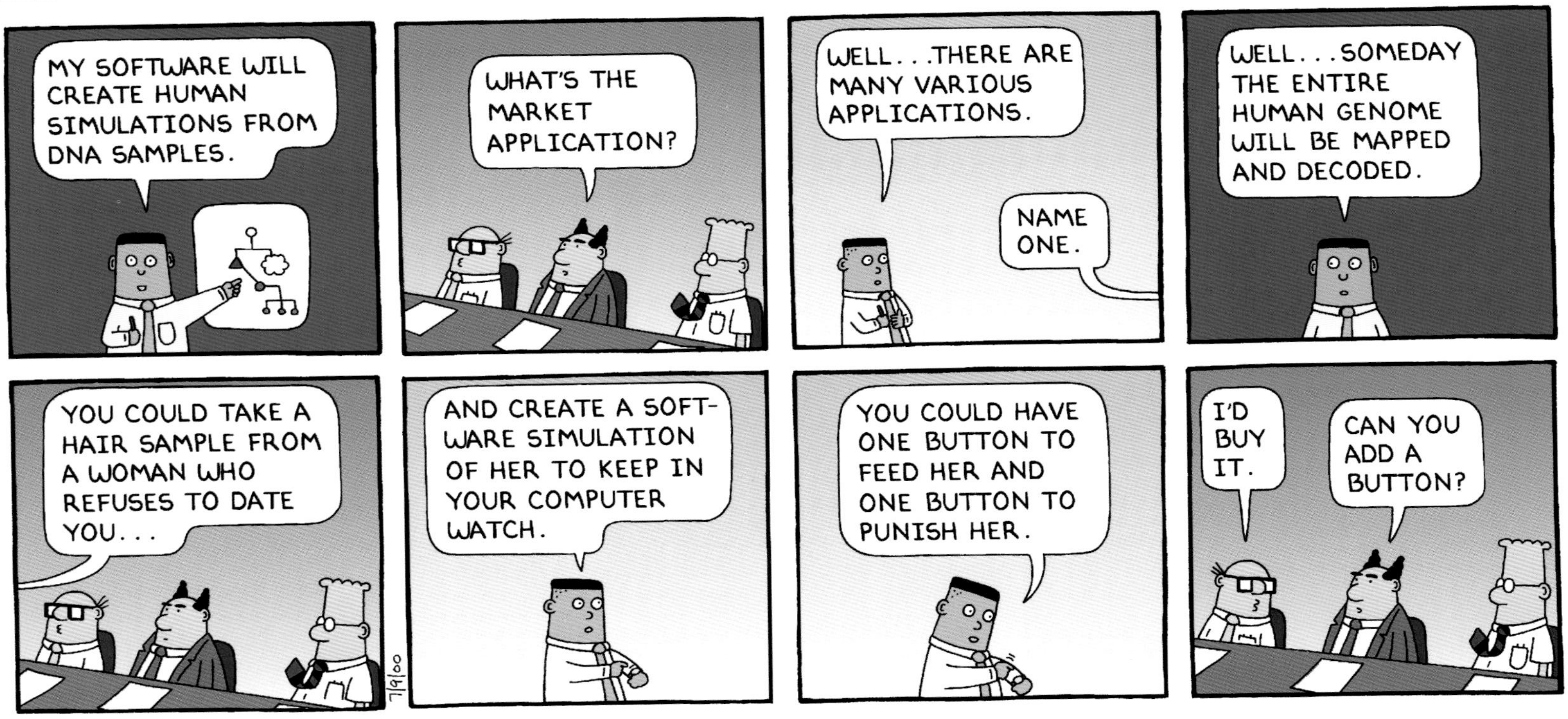
MY SOFTWARE WILL CREATE HUMAN SIMULATIONS FROM DNA SAMPLES.
WHAT'S THE MARKET APPLICATION?
WELL...THERE ARE MANY VARIOUS APPLICATIONS.
NAME ONE.
WELL...SOMEDAY THE ENTIRE HUMAN GENOME WILL BE MAPPED AND DECODED.
YOU COULD TAKE A HAIR SAMPLE FROM A WOMAN WHO REFUSES TO DATE YOU...
AND CREATE A SOFT-WARE SIMULATION OF HER TO KEEP IN YOUR COMPUTER WATCH.
YOU COULD HAVE ONE BUTTON TO FEED HER AND ONE BUTTON TO PUNISH HER.
I'D BUY IT.
CAN YOU ADD A BUTTON?

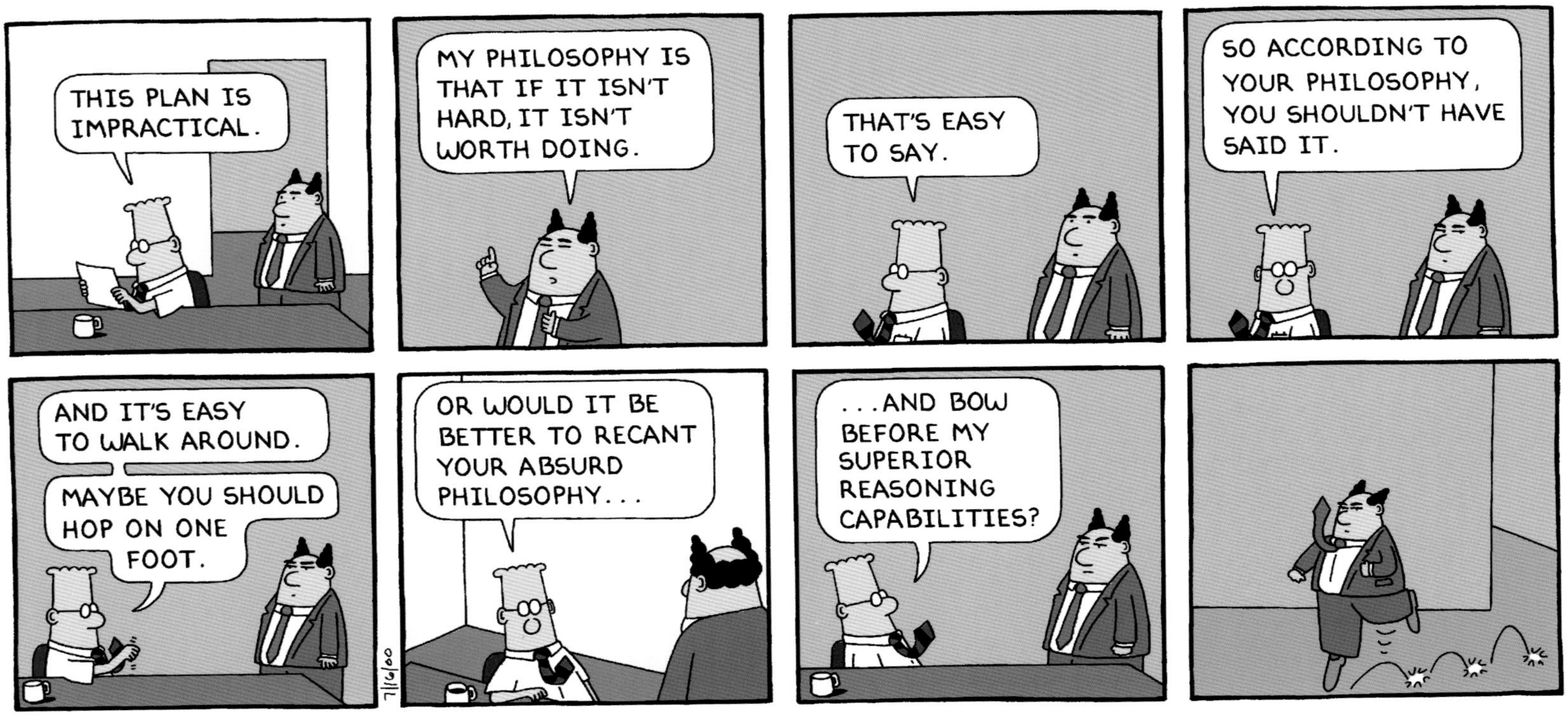
THIS PLAN IS IMPRACTICAL.
MY PHILOSOPHY IS THAT IF IT ISN'T HARD, IT ISN'T WORTH DOING.
THAT'S EASY TO SAY.
SO ACCORDING TO YOUR PHILOSOPHY, YOU SHOULDN'T HAVE SAID IT.
AND IT'S EASY TO WALK AROUND.
MAYBE YOU SHOULD HOP ON ONE FOOT.
OR WOULD IT BE BETTER TO RECANT YOUR ABSURD PHILOSOPHY...
...AND BOW BEFORE MY SUPERIOR REASONING CAPABILITIES?

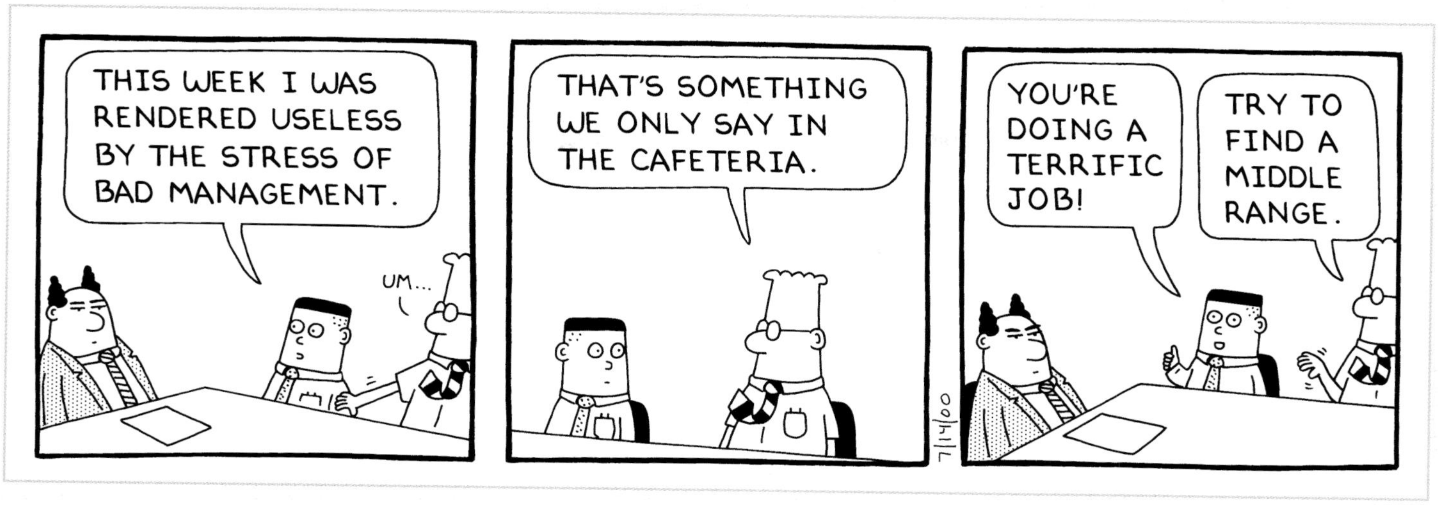
THIS WEEK I WAS RENDERED USELESS BY THE STRESS OF BAD MANAGEMENT.
UM...
THAT'S SOMETHING WE ONLY SAY IN THE CAFETERIA.
7/14/00
YOU'RE DOING A TERRIFIC JOB!
TRY TO FIND A MIDDLE RANGE.

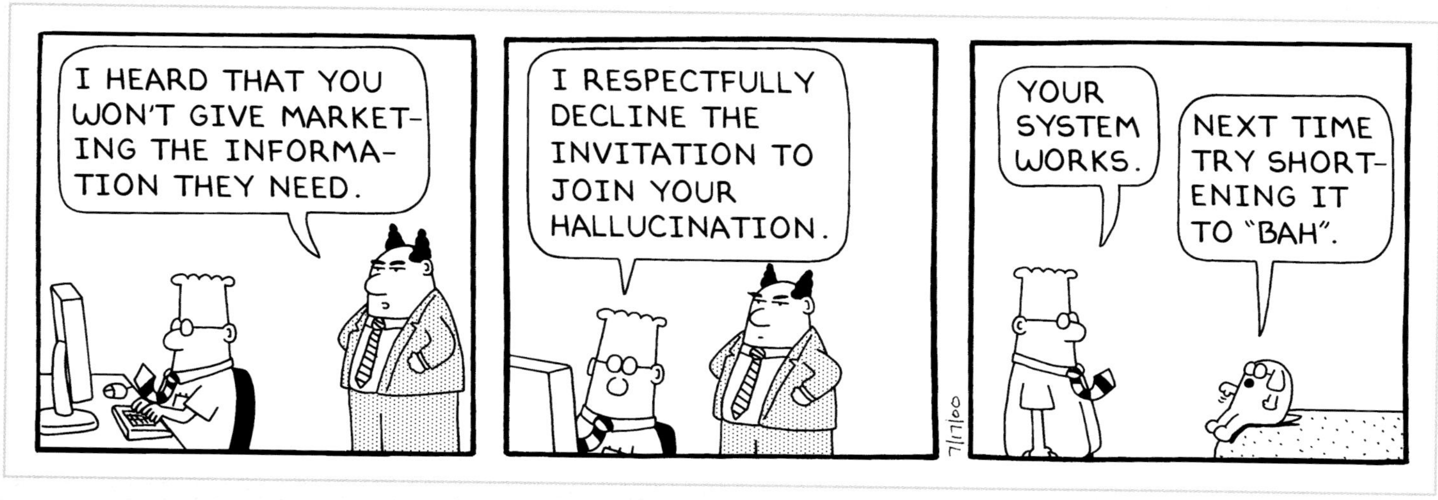
I HEARD THAT YOU WON'T GIVE MARKETING THE INFORMATION THEY NEED.
I RESPECTFULLY DECLINE THE INVITATION TO JOIN YOUR HALLUCINATION.
7/17/00
YOUR SYSTEM WORKS.
NEXT TIME TRY SHORTENING IT TO "BAH".

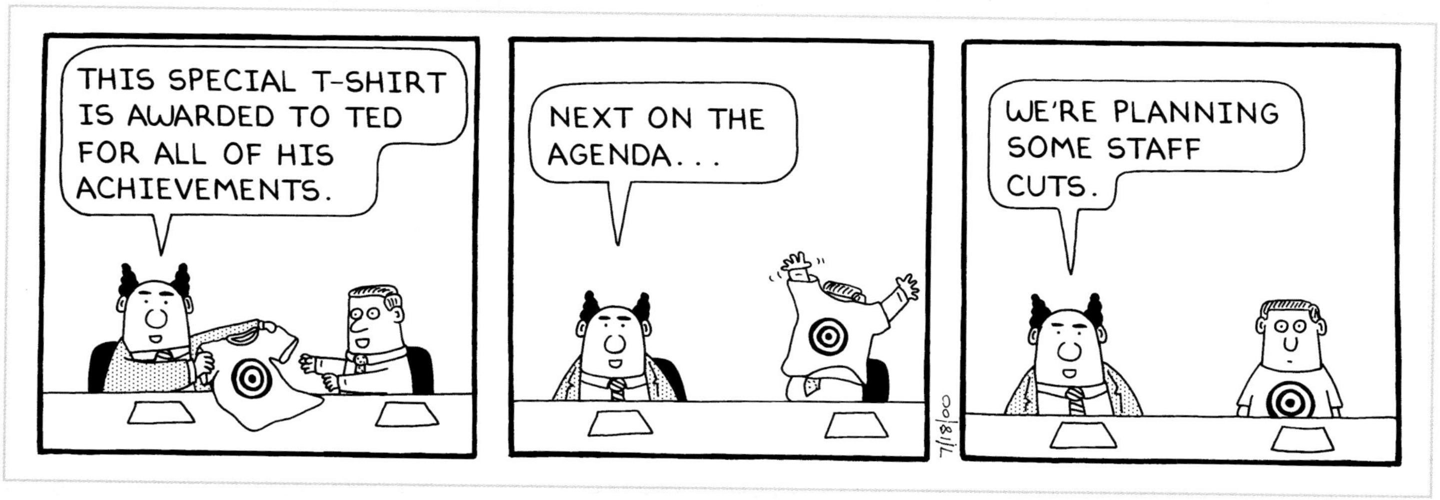
THIS SPECIAL T-SHIRT IS AWARDED TO TED FOR ALL OF HIS ACHIEVEMENTS.
NEXT ON THE AGENDA...
7/18/00
WE'RE PLANNING SOME STAFF CUTS.

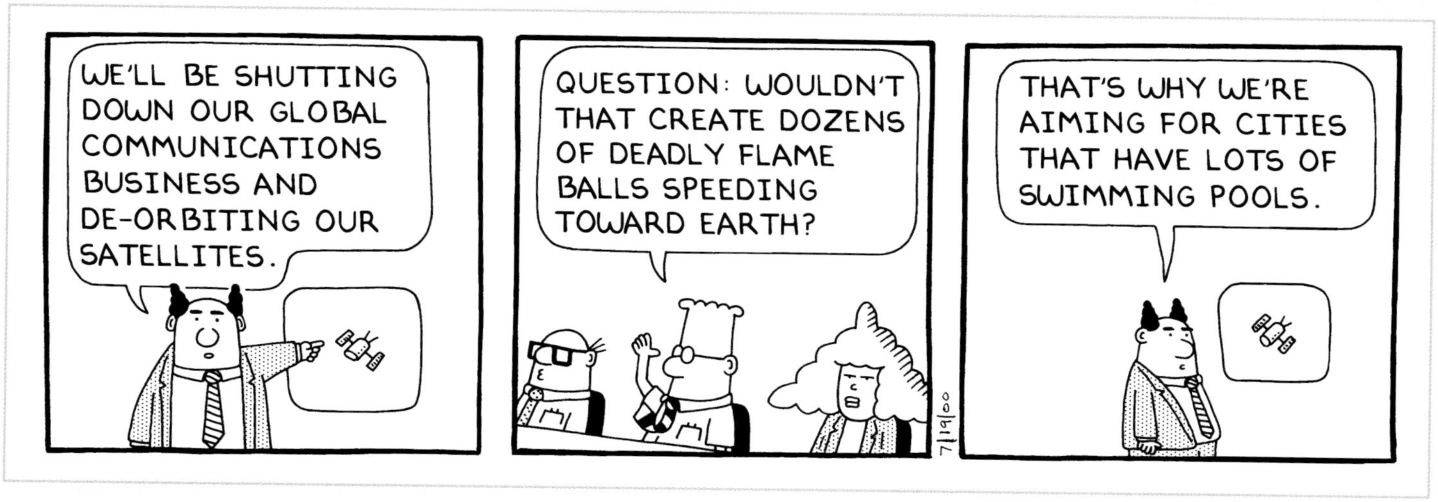
WE'LL BE SHUTTING DOWN OUR GLOBAL COMMUNICATIONS BUSINESS AND DE-ORBITING OUR SATELLITES.
QUESTION: WOULDN'T THAT CREATE DOZENS OF DEADLY FLAME BALLS SPEEDING TOWARD EARTH?
7/19/00
THAT'S WHY WE'RE AIMING FOR CITIES THAT HAVE LOTS OF SWIMMING POOLS.

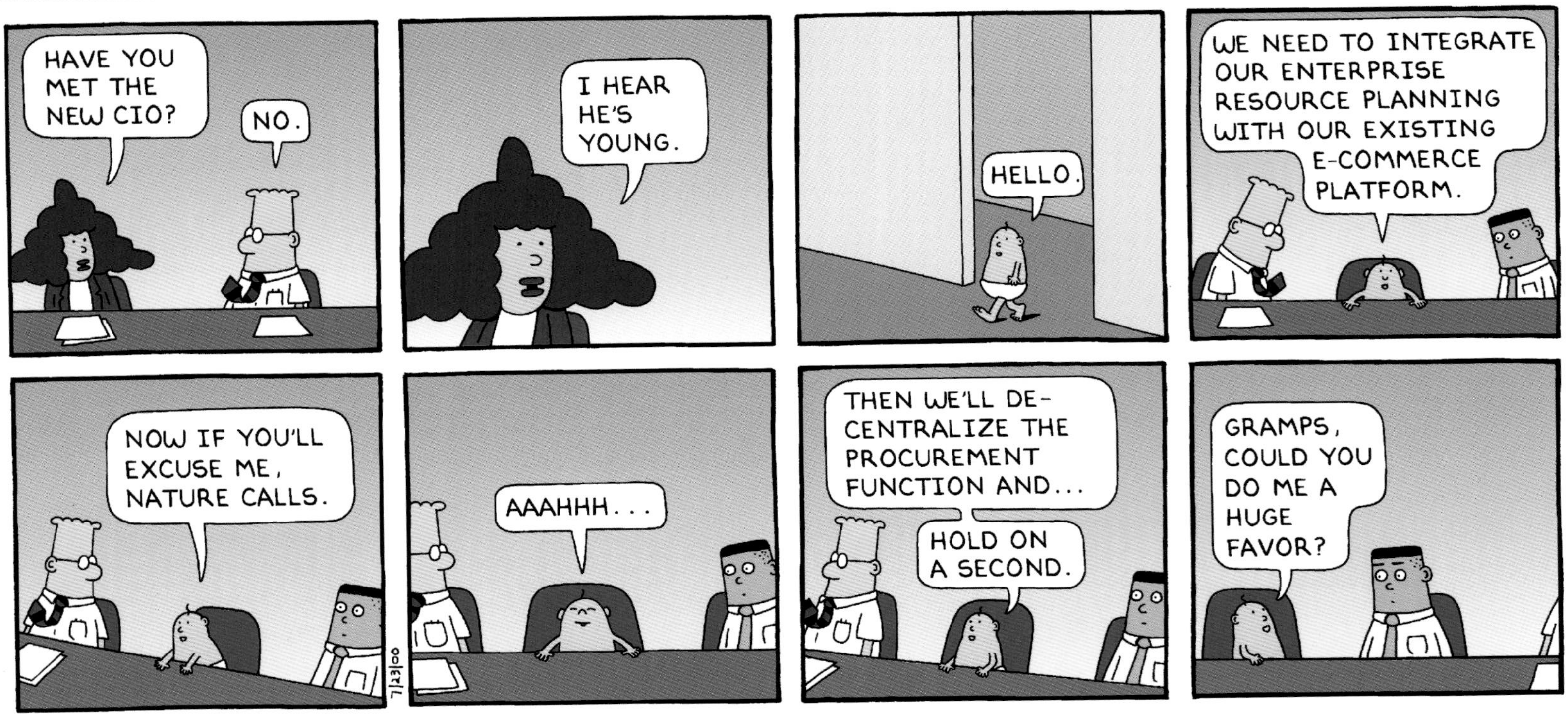
HAVE YOU MET THE NEW CIO?
NO.
I HEAR HE'S YOUNG.
HELLO.
WE NEED TO INTEGRATE OUR ENTERPRISE RESOURCE PLANNING WITH OUR EXISTING E-COMMERCE PLATFORM.
NOW IF YOU'LL EXCUSE ME, NATURE CALLS.
AAAHHH. . .
THEN WE'LL DE-CENTRALIZE THE PROCUREMENT FUNCTION AND. . .
HOLD ON A SECOND.
GRAMPS, COULD YOU DO ME A HUGE FAVOR?
7/23/00

I had to redraw the last panel because the original showed the top of Wally's butt crack. Apparently butt cracks are offensive to people who have no mirrors.

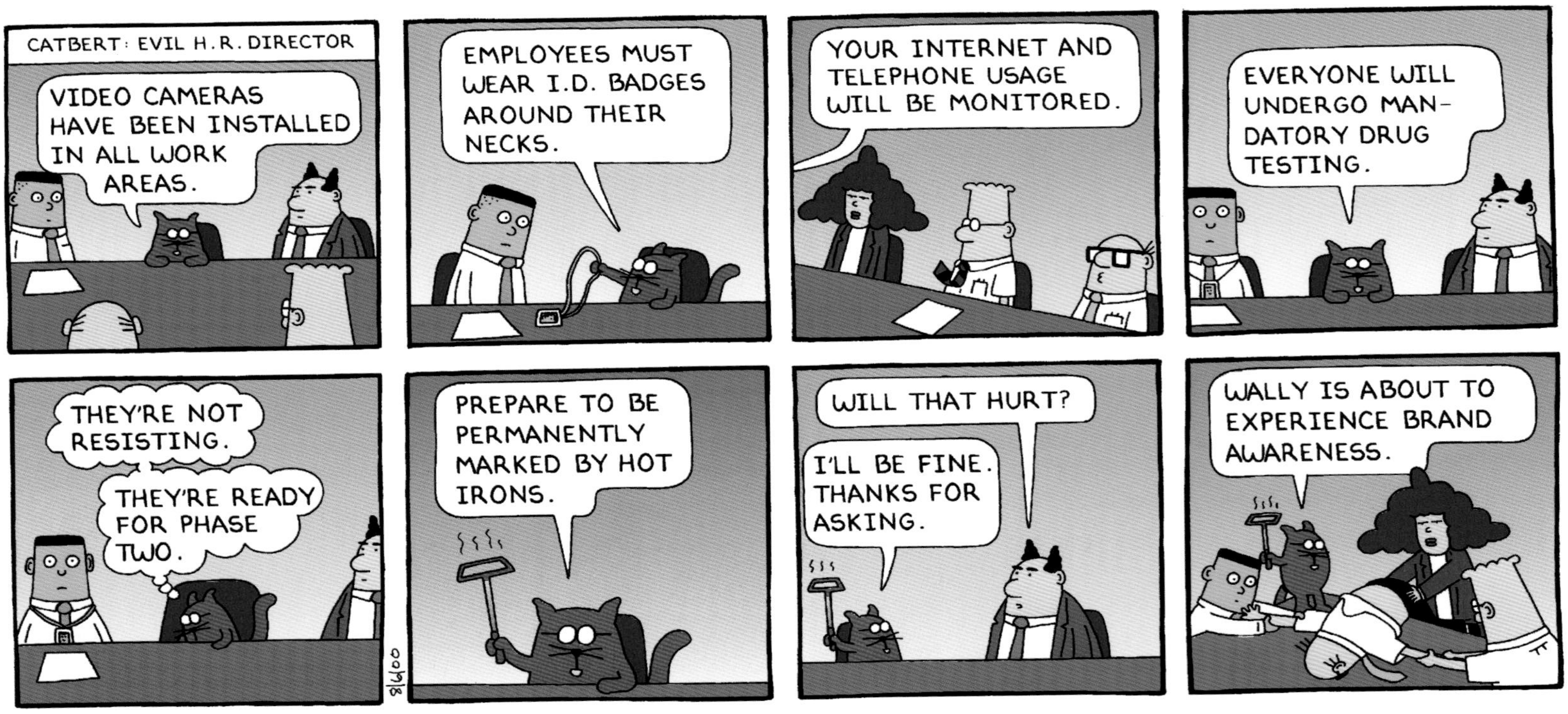
CATBERT: EVIL H.R. DIRECTOR
VIDEO CAMERAS HAVE BEEN INSTALLED IN ALL WORK AREAS.
EMPLOYEES MUST WEAR I.D. BADGES AROUND THEIR NECKS.
YOUR INTERNET AND TELEPHONE USAGE WILL BE MONITORED.
EVERYONE WILL UNDERGO MAN-DATORY DRUG TESTING.
THEY'RE NOT RESISTING.
THEY'RE READY FOR PHASE TWO.
PREPARE TO BE PERMANENTLY MARKED BY HOT IRONS.
8/6/00
WILL THAT HURT?
I'LL BE FINE. THANKS FOR ASKING.
WALLY IS ABOUT TO EXPERIENCE BRAND AWARENESS.

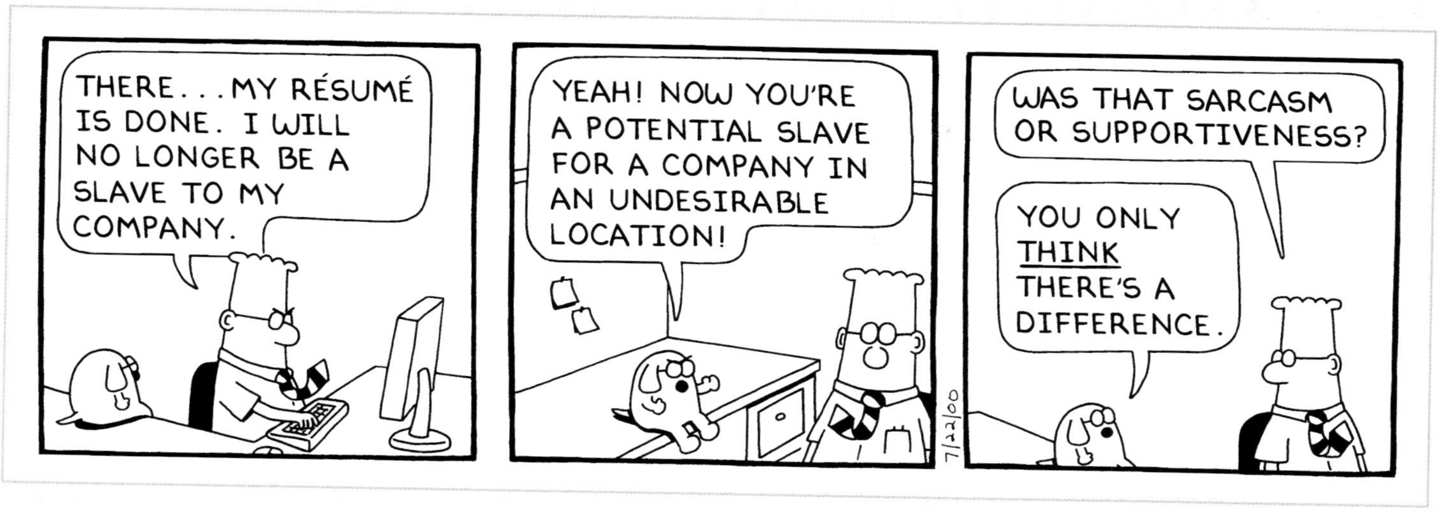
THERE. . . MY RÉSUMÉ IS DONE. I WILL NO LONGER BE A SLAVE TO MY COMPANY.
YEAH! NOW YOU'RE A POTENTIAL SLAVE FOR A COMPANY IN AN UNDESIRABLE LOCATION!
7/22/00
WAS THAT SARCASM OR SUPPORTIVENESS?
YOU ONLY THINK THERE'S A DIFFERENCE.

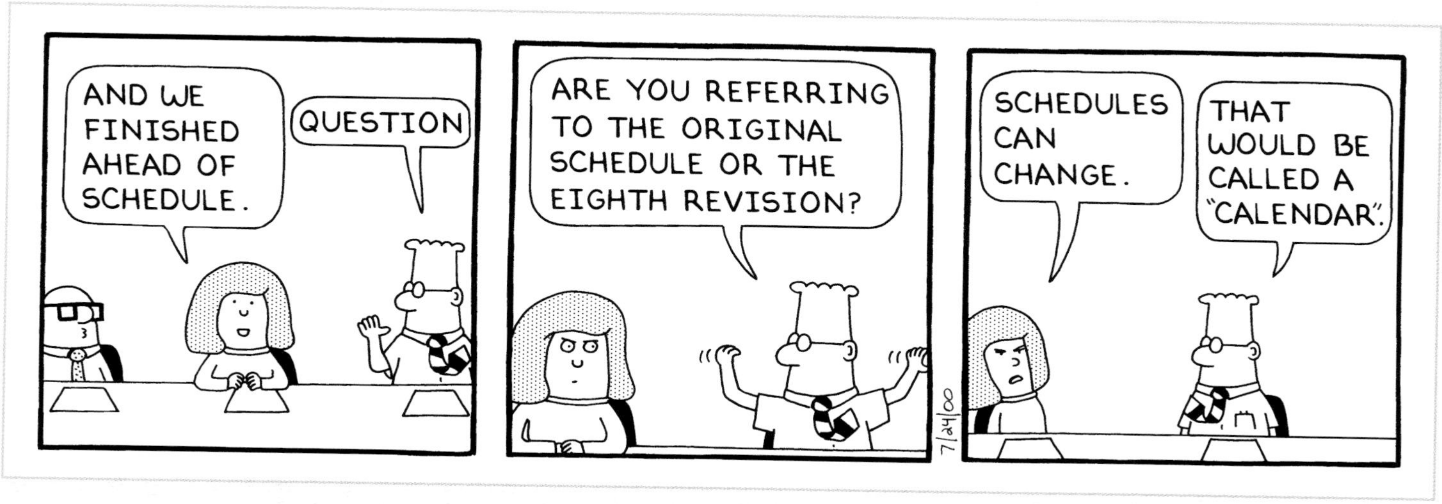
AND WE FINISHED AHEAD OF SCHEDULE.
QUESTION
ARE YOU REFERRING TO THE ORIGINAL SCHEDULE OR THE EIGHTH REVISION?
7/24/00
SCHEDULES CAN CHANGE.
THAT WOULD BE CALLED A "CALENDAR".

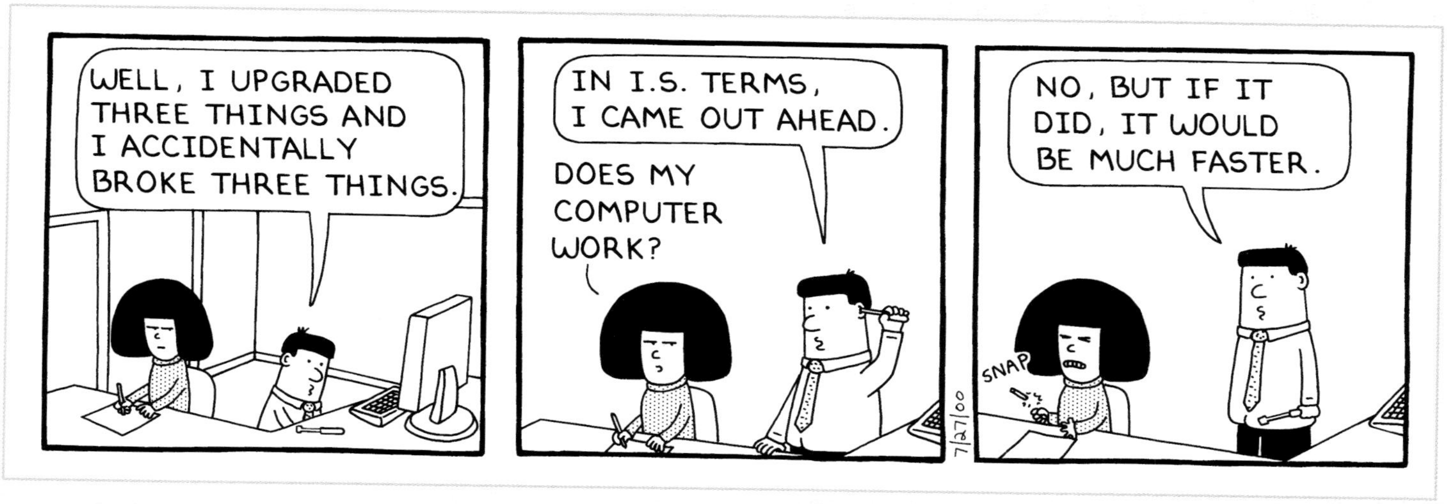
WELL, I UPGRADED THREE THINGS AND I ACCIDENTALLY BROKE THREE THINGS.
IN I.S. TERMS, I CAME OUT AHEAD.
DOES MY COMPUTER WORK?
7/27/00
NO, BUT IF IT DID, IT WOULD BE MUCH FASTER.
SNAP

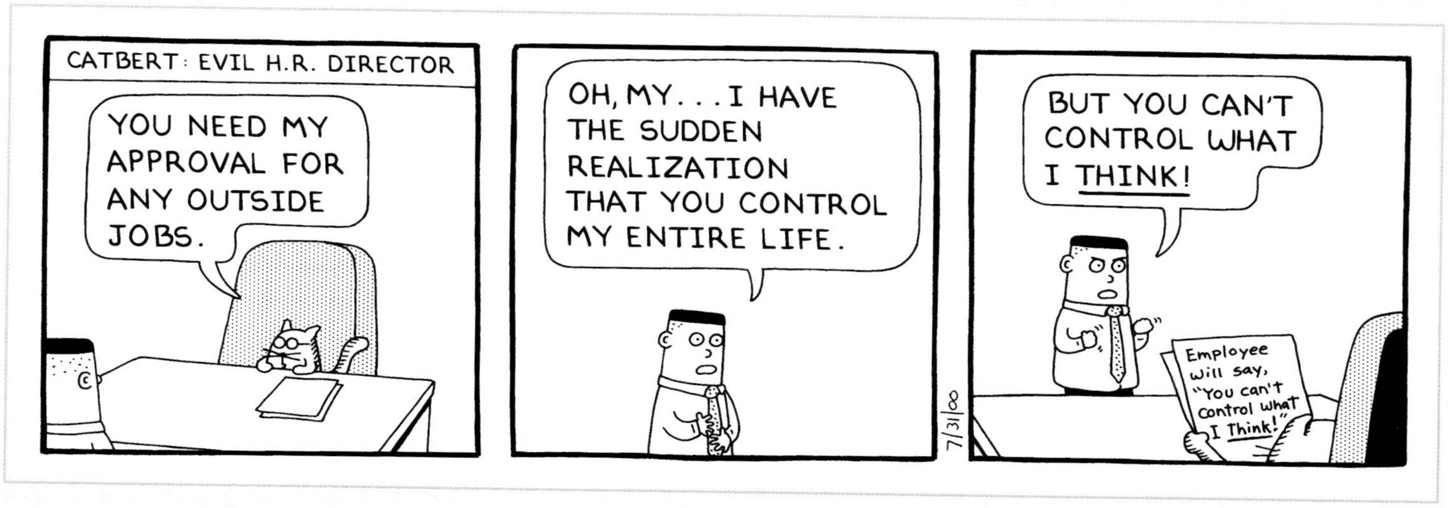
CATBERT: EVIL H.R. DIRECTOR
YOU NEED MY APPROVAL FOR ANY OUTSIDE JOBS.
OH, MY. . . I HAVE THE SUDDEN REALIZATION THAT YOU CONTROL MY ENTIRE LIFE.
7/31/00
BUT YOU CAN'T CONTROL WHAT I THINK!
Employee will say, "You can't control what I Think!"

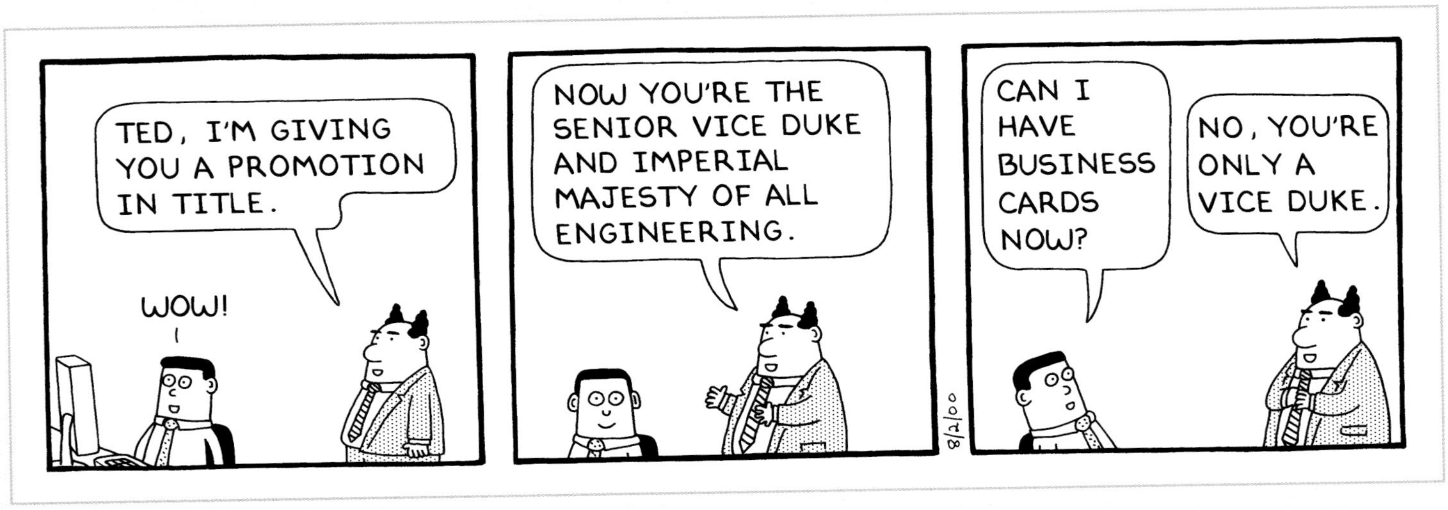
TED, I'M GIVING YOU A PROMOTION IN TITLE.
WOW!
NOW YOU'RE THE SENIOR VICE DUKE AND IMPERIAL MAJESTY OF ALL ENGINEERING.
CAN I HAVE BUSINESS CARDS NOW?
NO, YOU'RE ONLY A VICE DUKE.
8/2/00

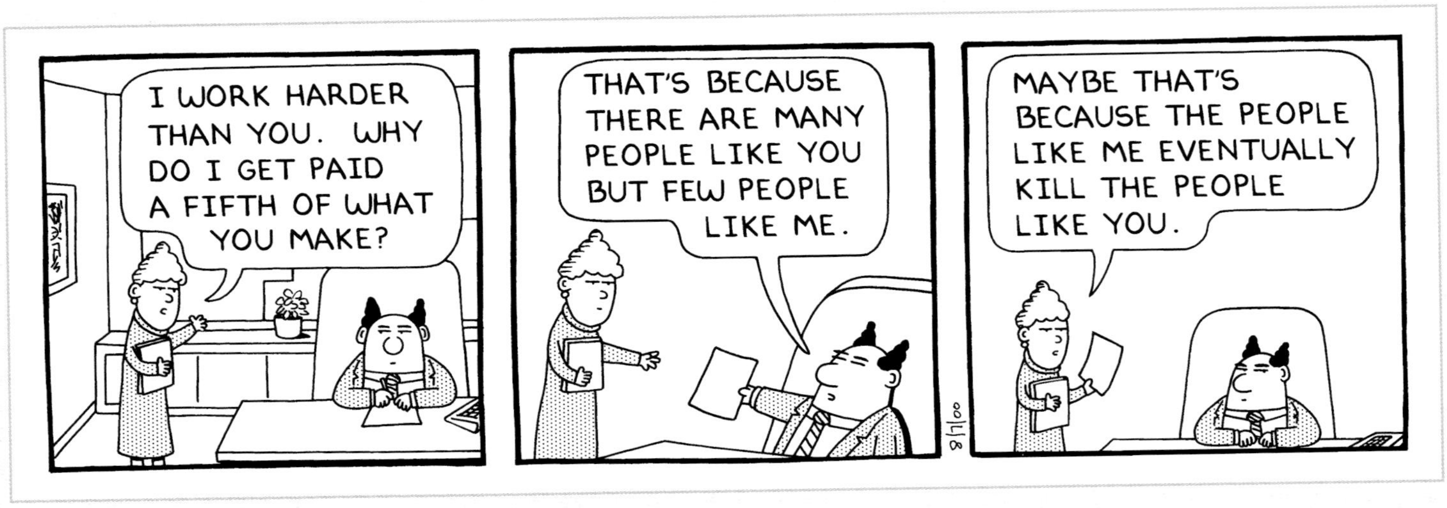
I WORK HARDER THAN YOU. WHY DO I GET PAID A FIFTH OF WHAT YOU MAKE?
THAT'S BECAUSE THERE ARE MANY PEOPLE LIKE YOU BUT FEW PEOPLE LIKE ME.
MAYBE THAT'S BECAUSE THE PEOPLE LIKE ME EVENTUALLY KILL THE PEOPLE LIKE YOU.
8/7/00

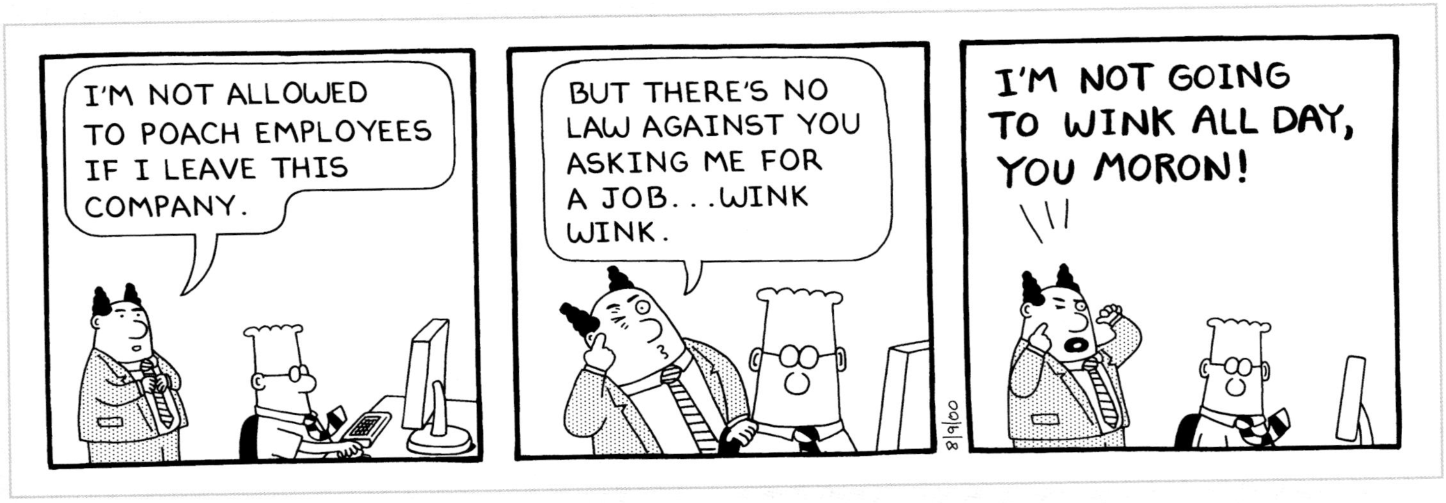
I'M NOT ALLOWED TO POACH EMPLOYEES IF I LEAVE THIS COMPANY.
BUT THERE'S NO LAW AGAINST YOU ASKING ME FOR A JOB...WINK WINK.
I'M NOT GOING TO WINK ALL DAY, YOU MORON!
8/9/00

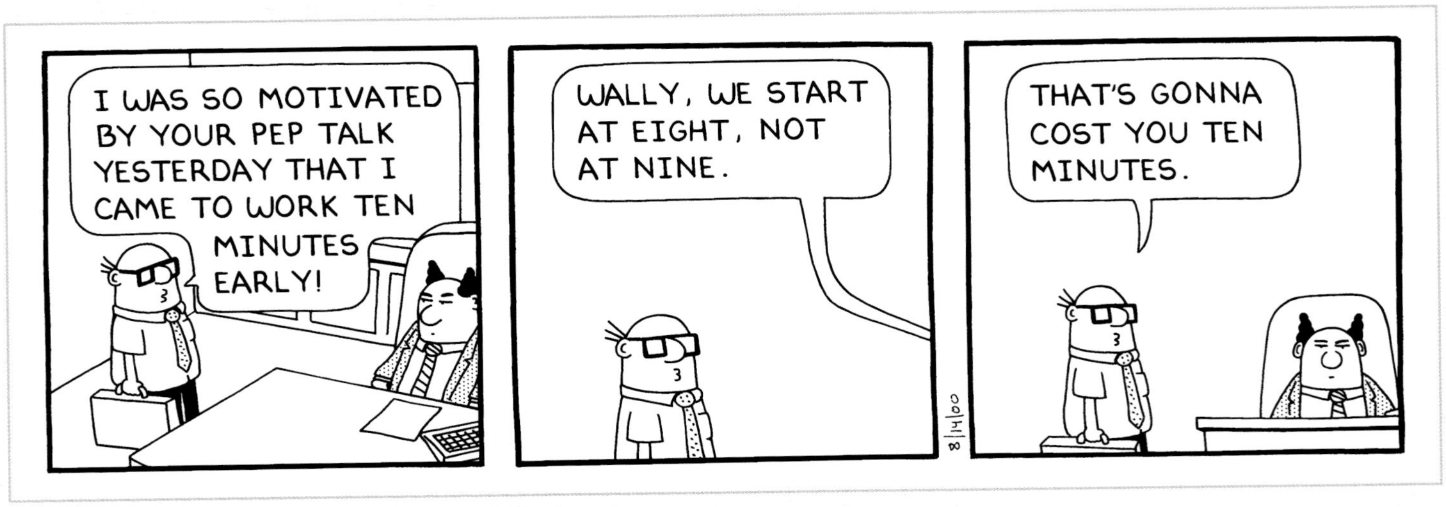
I WAS SO MOTIVATED BY YOUR PEP TALK YESTERDAY THAT I CAME TO WORK TEN MINUTES EARLY!
WALLY, WE START AT EIGHT, NOT AT NINE.
THAT'S GONNA COST YOU TEN MINUTES.
8/14/00

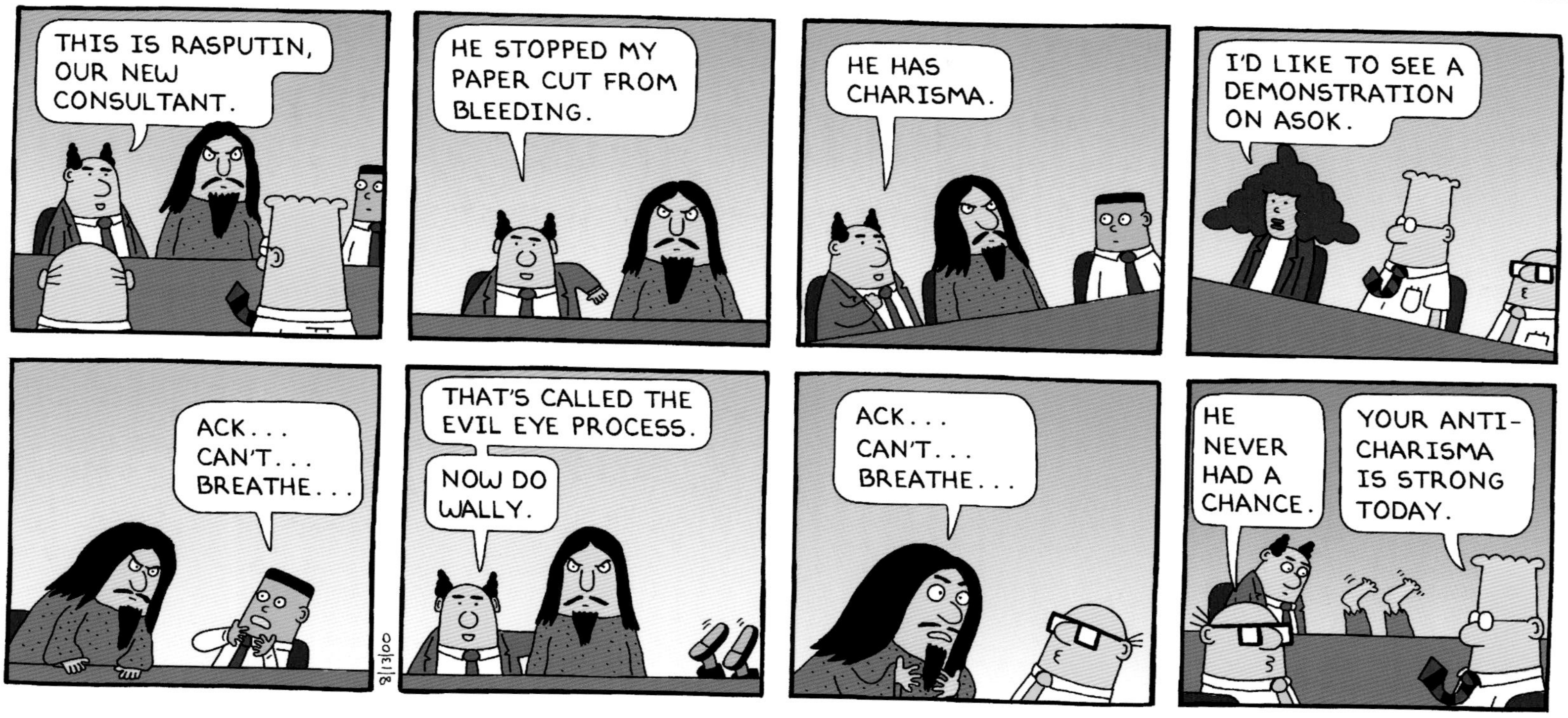
THIS IS RASPUTIN, OUR NEW CONSULTANT.
HE STOPPED MY PAPER CUT FROM BLEEDING.
HE HAS CHARISMA.
I'D LIKE TO SEE A DEMONSTRATION ON ASOK.
ACK... CAN'T... BREATHE...
8/13/00
THAT'S CALLED THE EVIL EYE PROCESS.
NOW DO WALLY.
ACK... CAN'T... BREATHE...
HE NEVER HAD A CHANCE.
YOUR ANTI-CHARISMA IS STRONG TODAY.

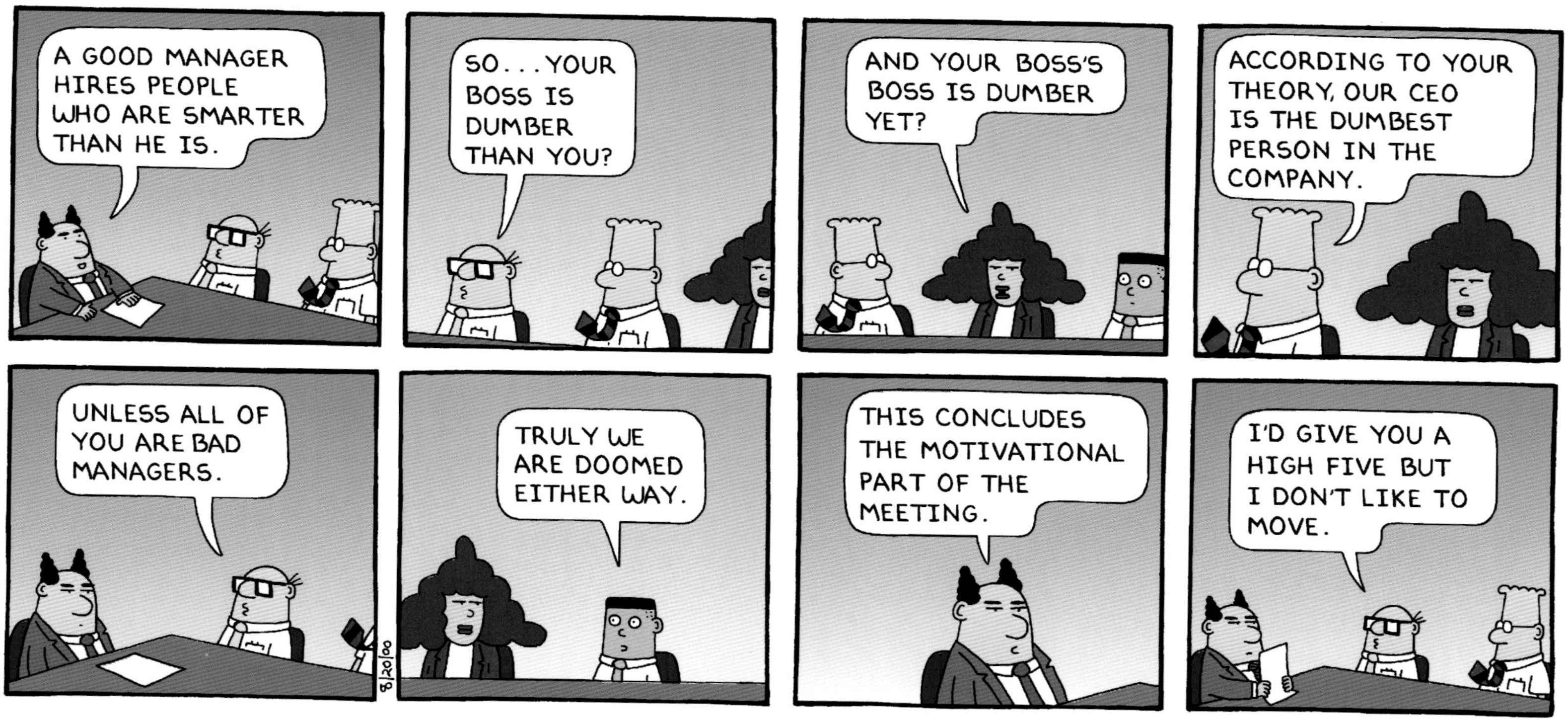
A GOOD MANAGER HIRES PEOPLE WHO ARE SMARTER THAN HE IS.
SO...YOUR BOSS IS DUMBER THAN YOU?
AND YOUR BOSS'S BOSS IS DUMBER YET?
ACCORDING TO YOUR THEORY, OUR CEO IS THE DUMBEST PERSON IN THE COMPANY.
UNLESS ALL OF YOU ARE BAD MANAGERS.
8/20/00
TRULY WE ARE DOOMED EITHER WAY.
THIS CONCLUDES THE MOTIVATIONAL PART OF THE MEETING.
I'D GIVE YOU A HIGH FIVE BUT I DON'T LIKE TO MOVE.

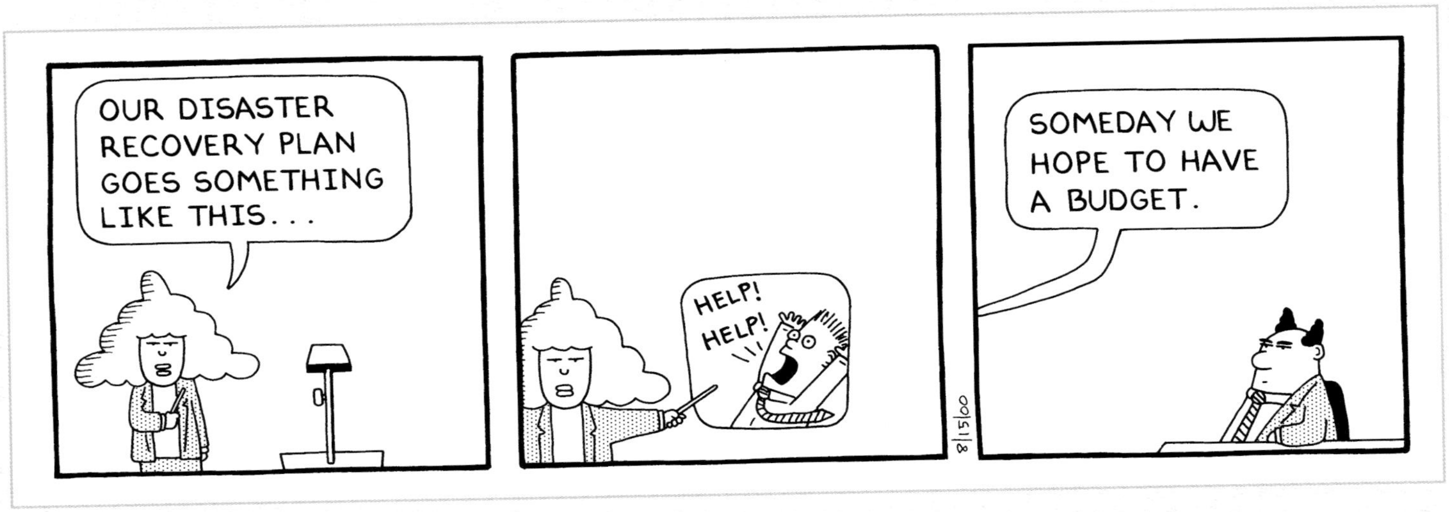
OUR DISASTER RECOVERY PLAN GOES SOMETHING LIKE THIS...
HELP! HELP!
SOMEDAY WE HOPE TO HAVE A BUDGET.
8/15/00

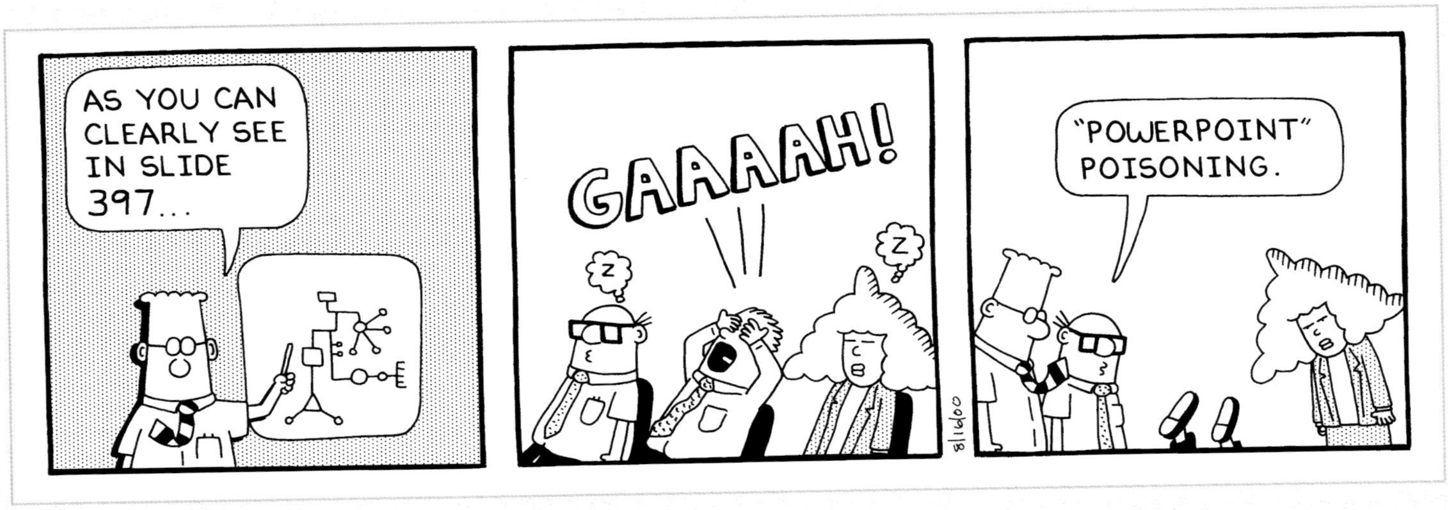
AS YOU CAN CLEARLY SEE IN SLIDE 397...
GAAAAH!
Z
Z
"POWERPOINT" POISONING.
8/16/00

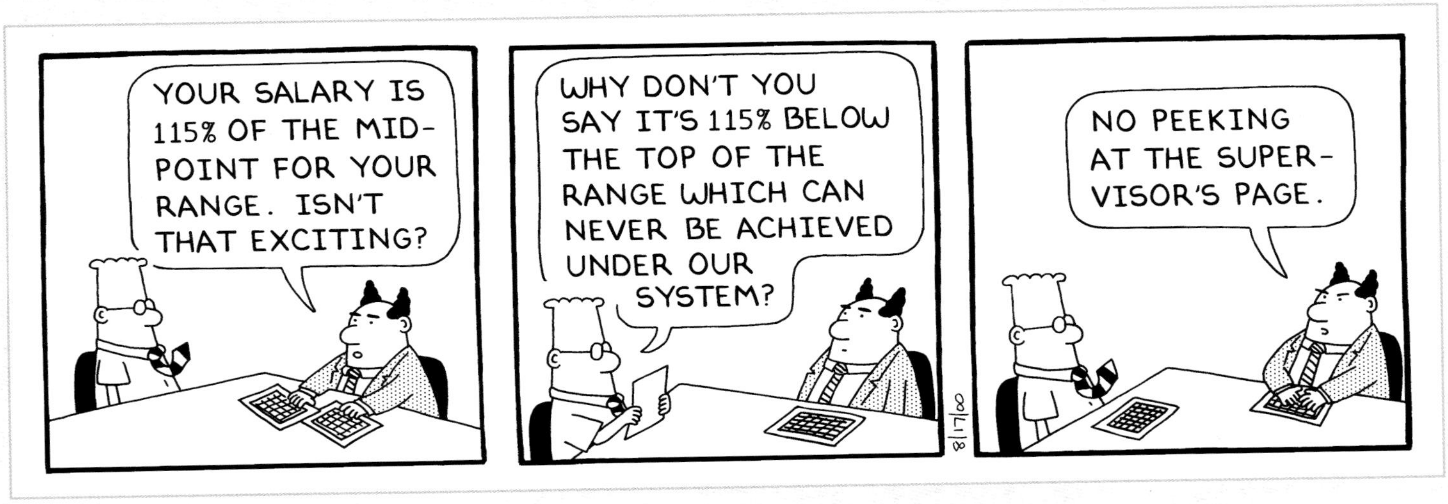
YOUR SALARY IS 115% OF THE MID-POINT FOR YOUR RANGE. ISN'T THAT EXCITING?
WHY DON'T YOU SAY IT'S 115% BELOW THE TOP OF THE RANGE WHICH CAN NEVER BE ACHIEVED UNDER OUR SYSTEM?
NO PEEKING AT THE SUPER-VISOR'S PAGE.
8/17/00

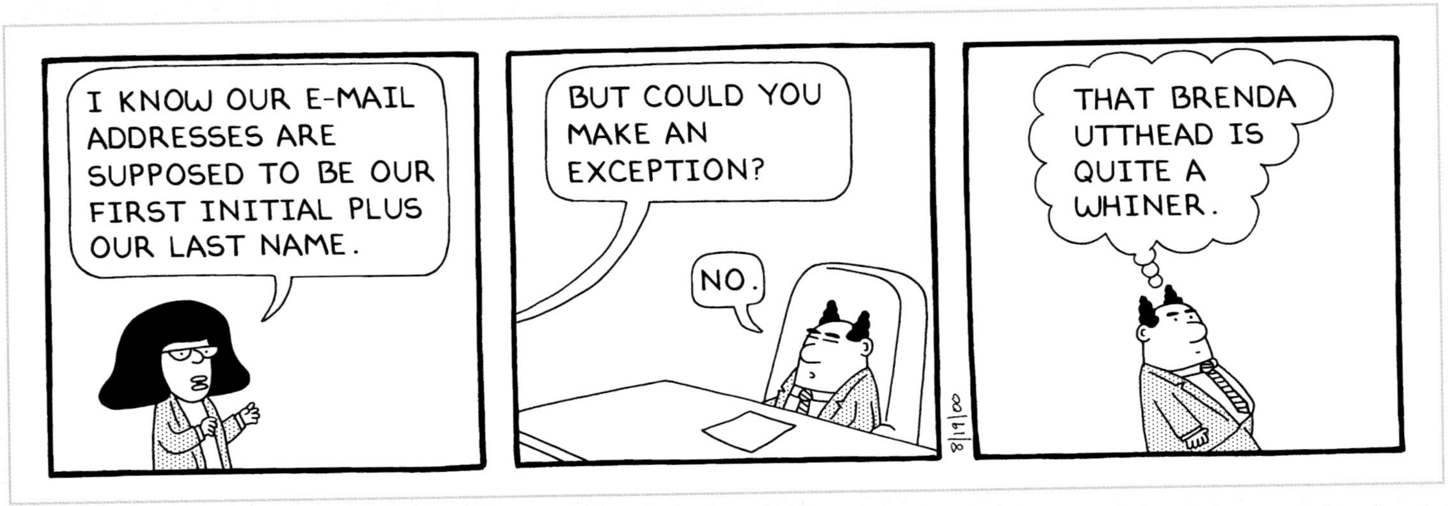
I KNOW OUR E-MAIL ADDRESSES ARE SUPPOSED TO BE OUR FIRST INITIAL PLUS OUR LAST NAME.
BUT COULD YOU MAKE AN EXCEPTION?
NO.
THAT BRENDA UTTHEAD IS QUITE A WHINER.
8/19/00

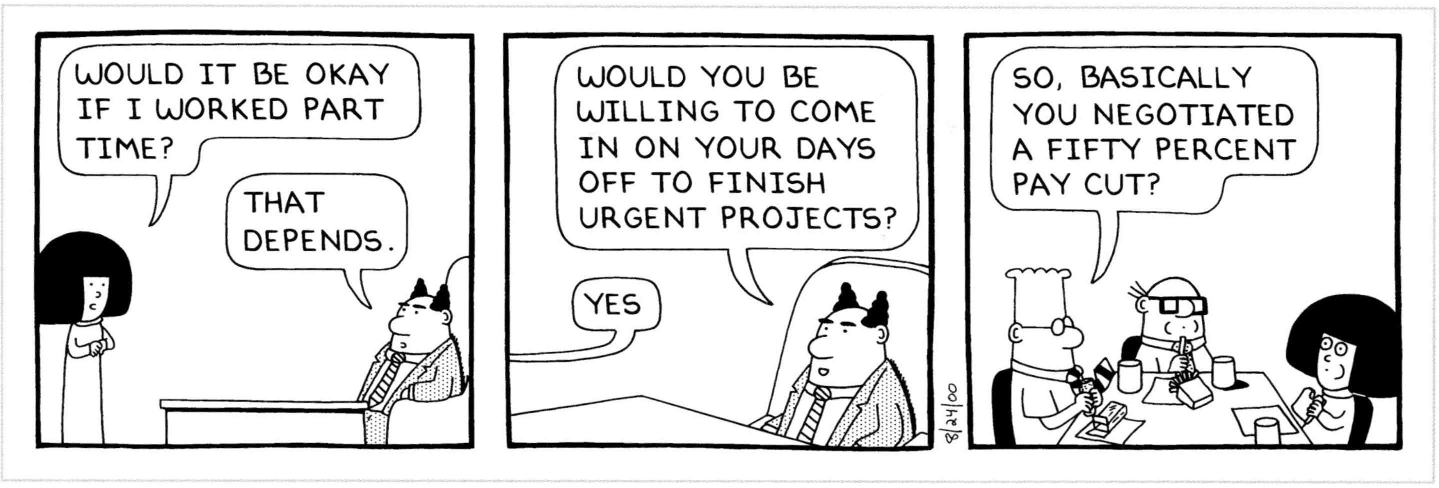
WOULD IT BE OKAY IF I WORKED PART TIME?
THAT DEPENDS.
WOULD YOU BE WILLING TO COME IN ON YOUR DAYS OFF TO FINISH URGENT PROJECTS?
YES
8/24/00
SO, BASICALLY YOU NEGOTIATED A FIFTY PERCENT PAY CUT?

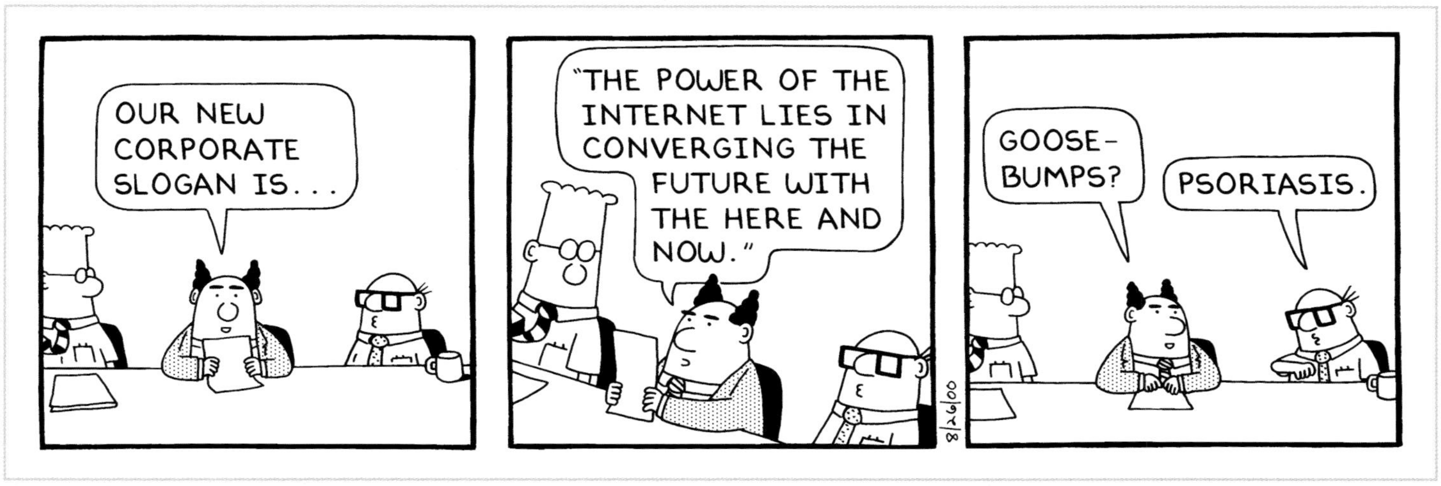
OUR NEW CORPORATE SLOGAN IS...
"THE POWER OF THE INTERNET LIES IN CONVERGING THE FUTURE WITH THE HERE AND NOW."
8/26/00
GOOSE-BUMPS?
PSORIASIS.

This slogan was taken from an actual company, verbatim.

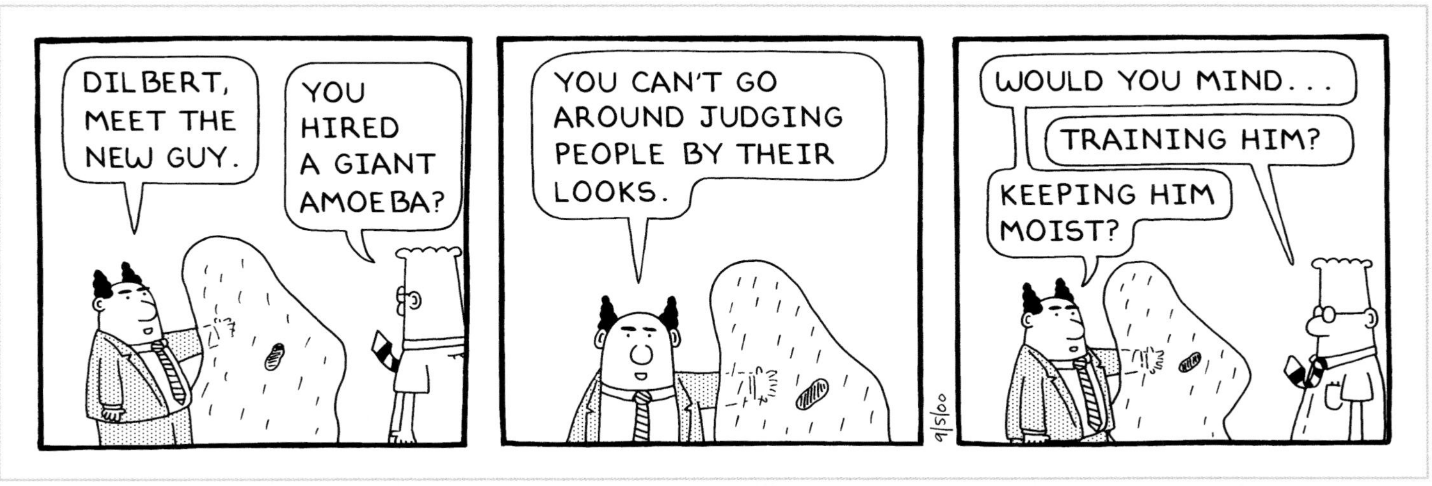
DILBERT, MEET THE NEW GUY.
YOU HIRED A GIANT AMOEBA?
YOU CAN'T GO AROUND JUDGING PEOPLE BY THEIR LOOKS.
9/5/00
WOULD YOU MIND...
TRAINING HIM?
KEEPING HIM MOIST?

A big part of cartooning is picking the right words. In this case, I doubt there is a funnier word than "moist".

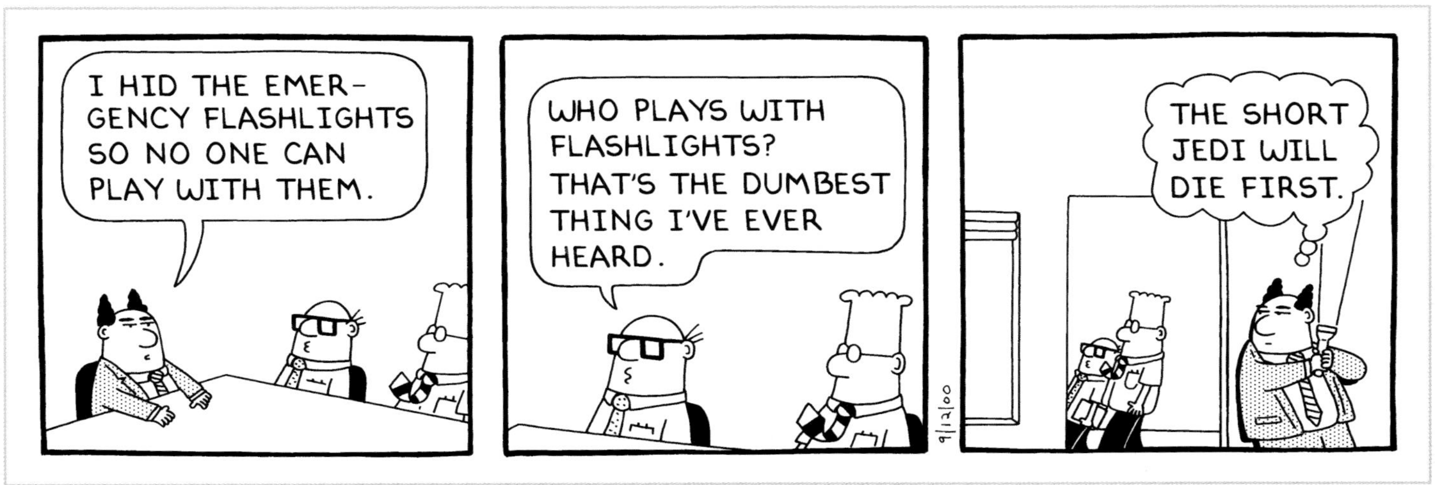
I HID THE EMER-GENCY FLASHLIGHTS SO NO ONE CAN PLAY WITH THEM.
WHO PLAYS WITH FLASHLIGHTS? THAT'S THE DUMBEST THING I'VE EVER HEARD.
9/12/00
THE SHORT JEDI WILL DIE FIRST.

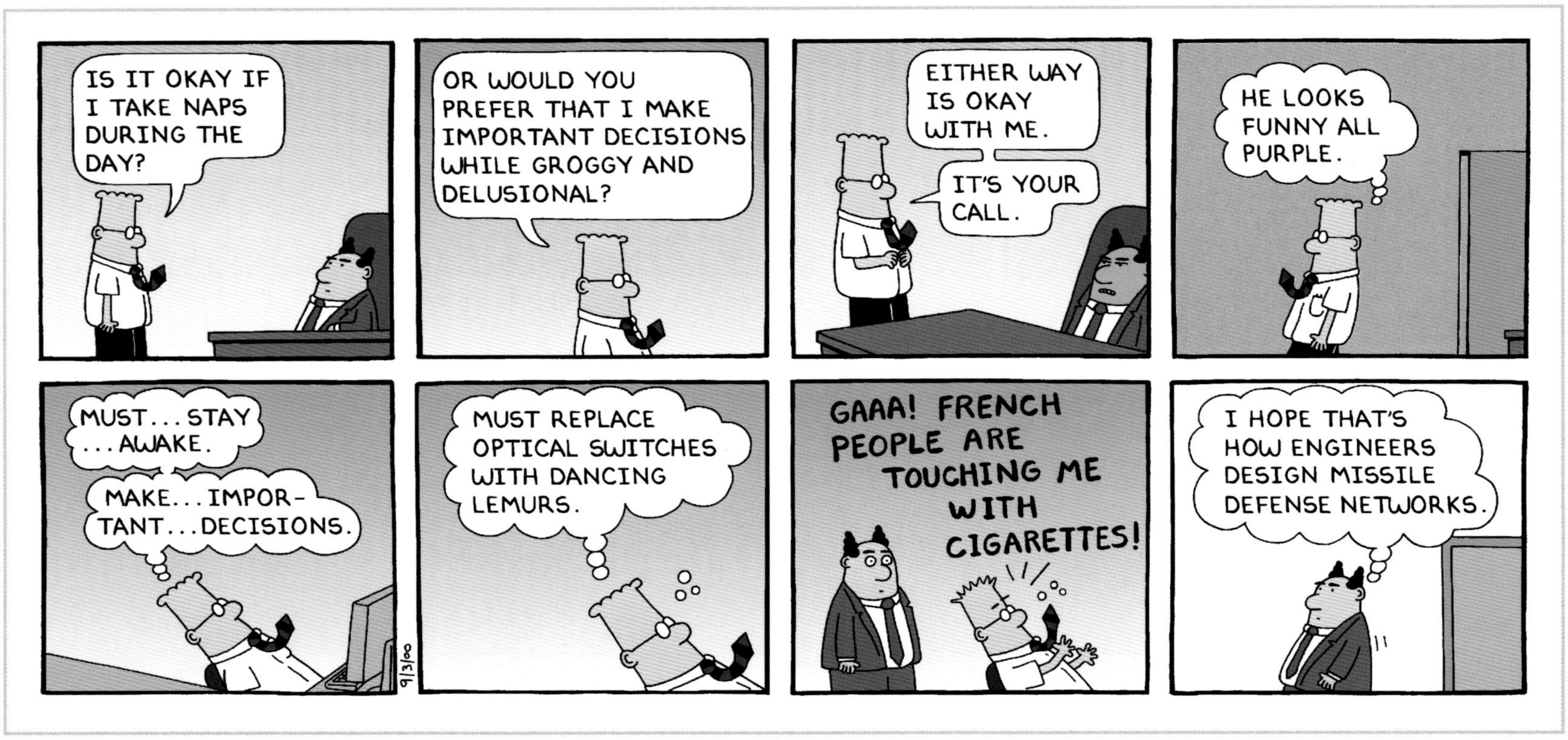
IS IT OKAY IF I TAKE NAPS DURING THE DAY?
OR WOULD YOU PREFER THAT I MAKE IMPORTANT DECISIONS WHILE GROGGY AND DELUSIONAL?
EITHER WAY IS OKAY WITH ME.
IT'S YOUR CALL.
HE LOOKS FUNNY ALL PURPLE.
MUST...STAY...AWAKE.
MAKE...IMPOR-TANT...DECISIONS.
9/3/00
MUST REPLACE OPTICAL SWITCHES WITH DANCING LEMURS.
GAAA! FRENCH PEOPLE ARE TOUCHING ME WITH CIGARETTES!
I HOPE THAT'S HOW ENGINEERS DESIGN MISSILE DEFENSE NETWORKS.

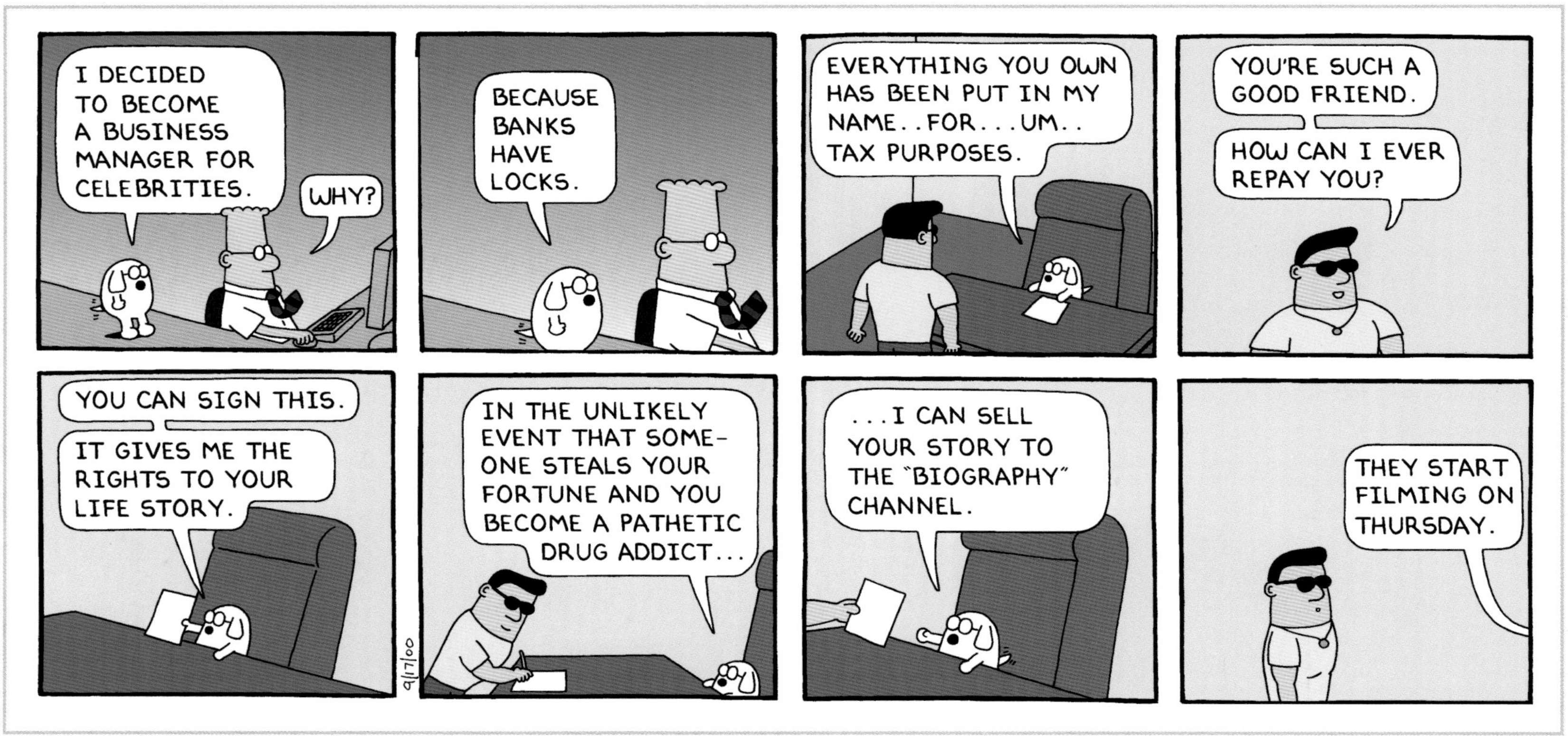
I DECIDED TO BECOME A BUSINESS MANAGER FOR CELEBRITIES.
WHY?
BECAUSE BANKS HAVE LOCKS.
EVERYTHING YOU OWN HAS BEEN PUT IN MY NAME..FOR...UM..TAX PURPOSES.
YOU'RE SUCH A GOOD FRIEND.
HOW CAN I EVER REPAY YOU?
YOU CAN SIGN THIS.
IT GIVES ME THE RIGHTS TO YOUR LIFE STORY.
9/17/00
IN THE UNLIKELY EVENT THAT SOME-ONE STEALS YOUR FORTUNE AND YOU BECOME A PATHETIC DRUG ADDICT...
...I CAN SELL YOUR STORY TO THE "BIOGRAPHY" CHANNEL.
THEY START FILMING ON THURSDAY.

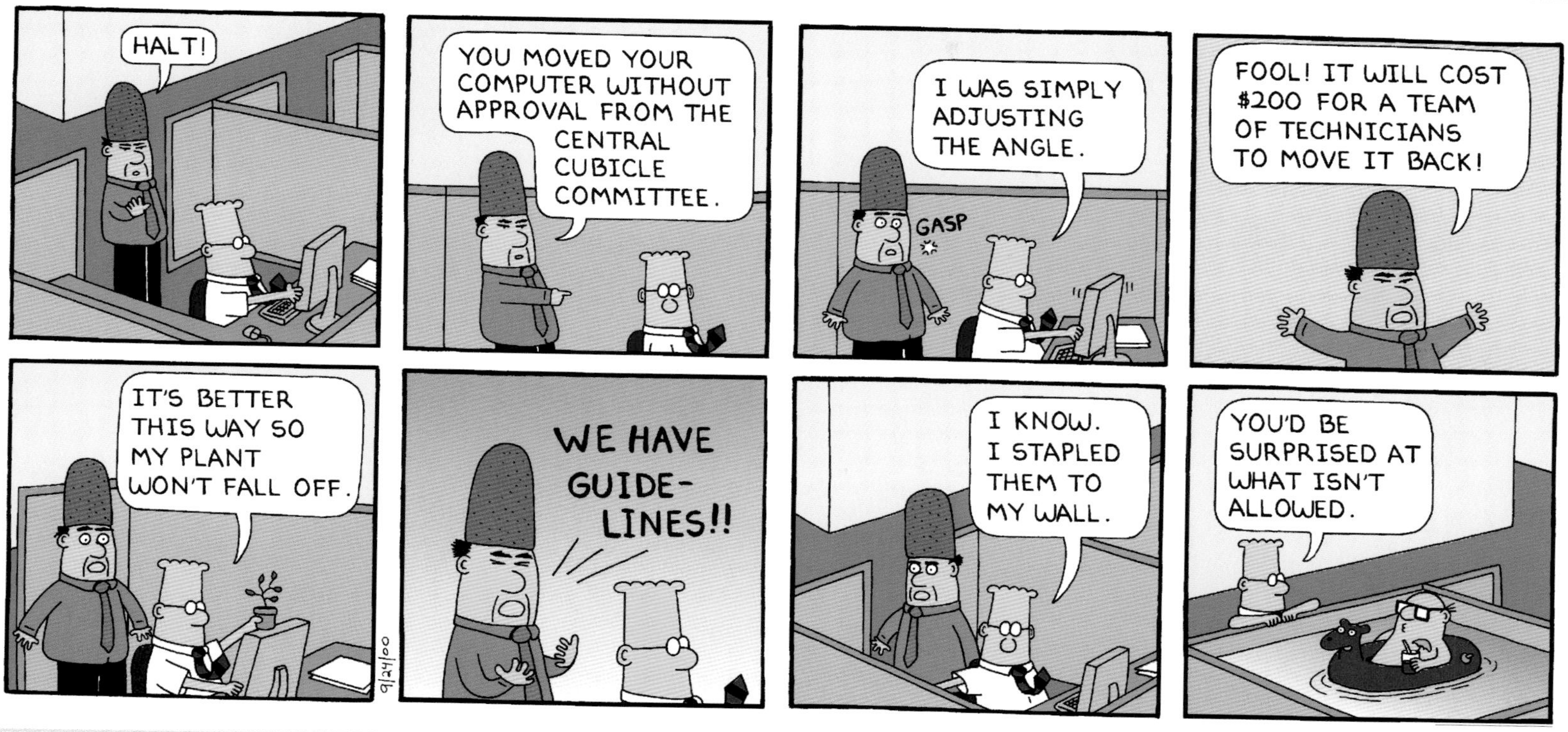
HALT!
YOU MOVED YOUR COMPUTER WITHOUT APPROVAL FROM THE CENTRAL CUBICLE COMMITTEE.
I WAS SIMPLY ADJUSTING THE ANGLE.
GASP
FOOL! IT WILL COST $200 FOR A TEAM OF TECHNICIANS TO MOVE IT BACK!
IT'S BETTER THIS WAY SO MY PLANT WON'T FALL OFF.
9/24/00
WE HAVE GUIDE-LINES!!
I KNOW. I STAPLED THEM TO MY WALL.
YOU'D BE SURPRISED AT WHAT ISN'T ALLOWED.

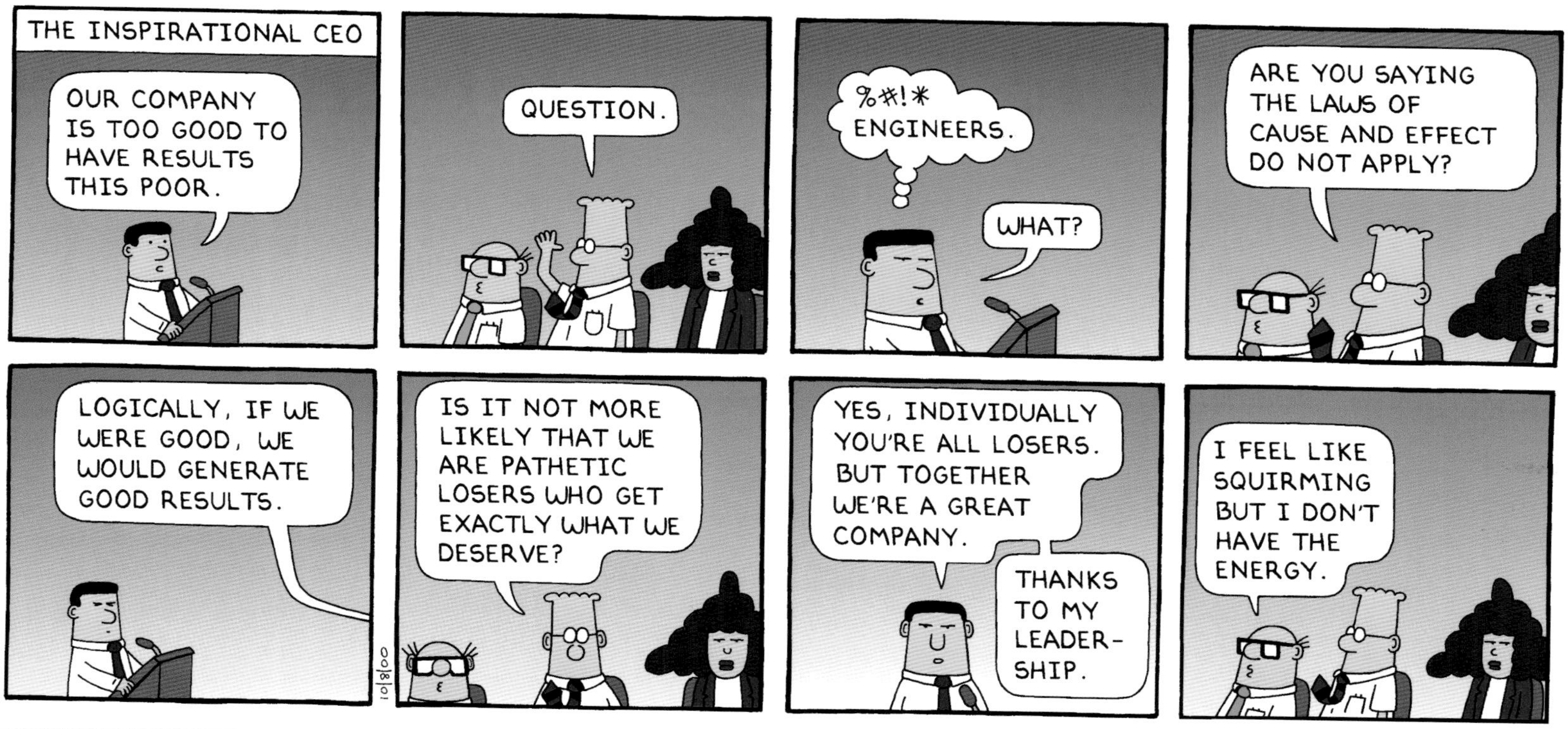
THE INSPIRATIONAL CEO
OUR COMPANY IS TOO GOOD TO HAVE RESULTS THIS POOR.
QUESTION.
%#!* ENGINEERS.
WHAT?
ARE YOU SAYING THE LAWS OF CAUSE AND EFFECT DO NOT APPLY?
LOGICALLY, IF WE WERE GOOD, WE WOULD GENERATE GOOD RESULTS.
10/8/00
IS IT NOT MORE LIKELY THAT WE ARE PATHETIC LOSERS WHO GET EXACTLY WHAT WE DESERVE?
YES, INDIVIDUALLY YOU'RE ALL LOSERS. BUT TOGETHER WE'RE A GREAT COMPANY.
THANKS TO MY LEADER-SHIP.
I FEEL LIKE SQUIRMING BUT I DON'T HAVE THE ENERGY.

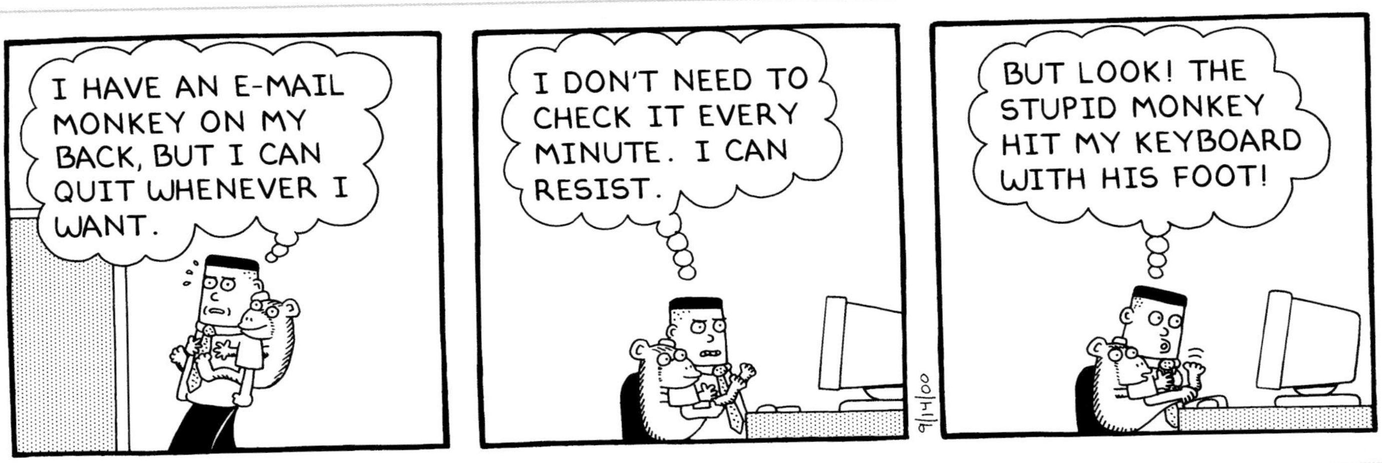
I HAVE AN E-MAIL MONKEY ON MY BACK, BUT I CAN QUIT WHENEVER I WANT.
I DON'T NEED TO CHECK IT EVERY MINUTE. I CAN RESIST.
BUT LOOK! THE STUPID MONKEY HIT MY KEYBOARD WITH HIS FOOT!
9/14/00

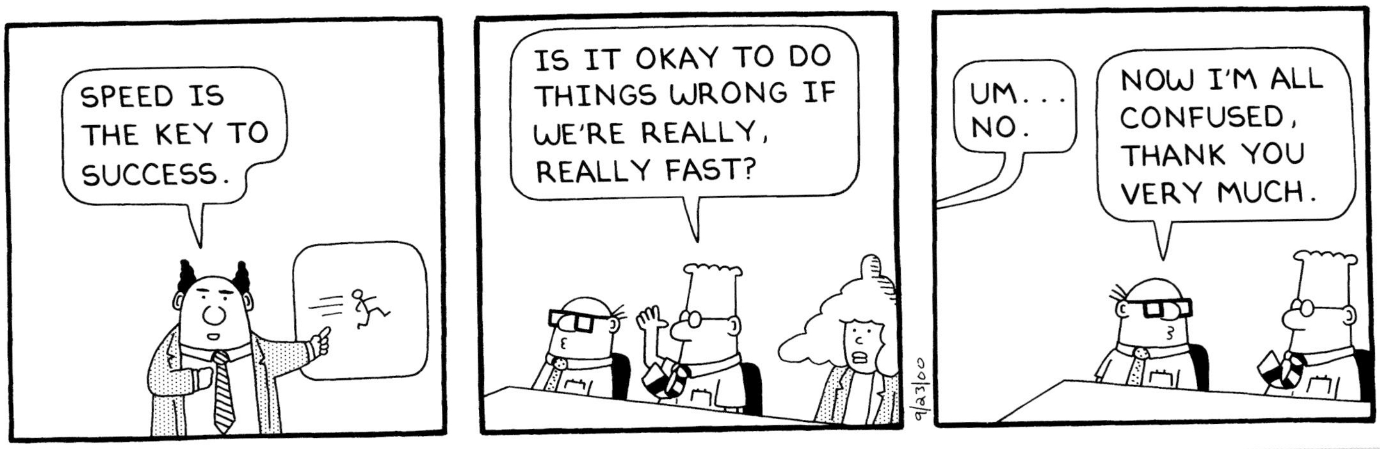
SPEED IS THE KEY TO SUCCESS.
IS IT OKAY TO DO THINGS WRONG IF WE'RE REALLY, REALLY FAST?
UM... NO.
NOW I'M ALL CONFUSED, THANK YOU VERY MUCH.
9/23/00

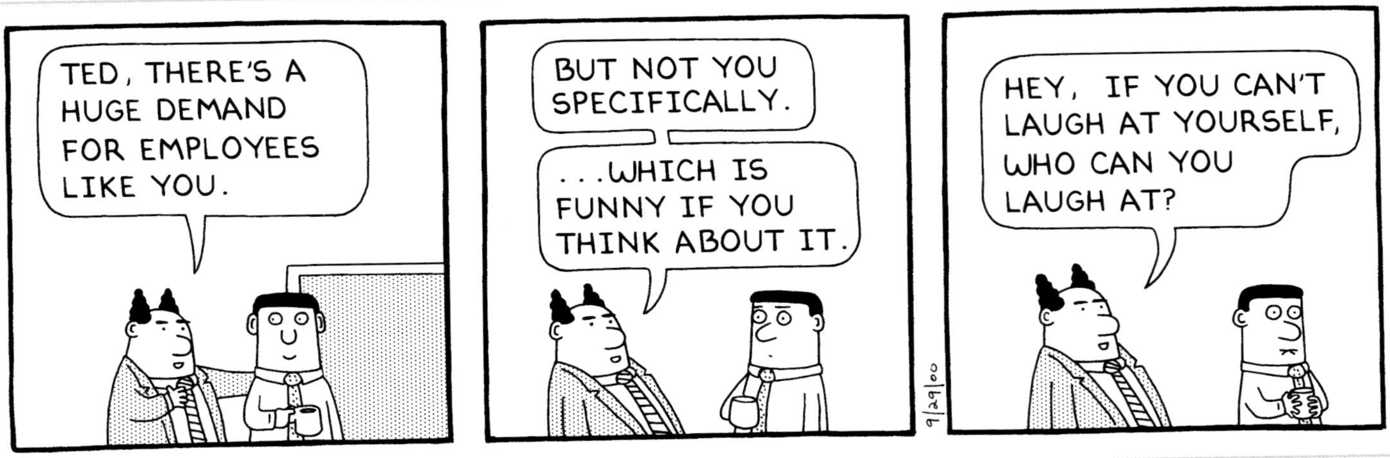
TED, THERE'S A HUGE DEMAND FOR EMPLOYEES LIKE YOU.
BUT NOT YOU SPECIFICALLY.
...WHICH IS FUNNY IF YOU THINK ABOUT IT.
HEY, IF YOU CAN'T LAUGH AT YOURSELF, WHO CAN YOU LAUGH AT?
9/29/00

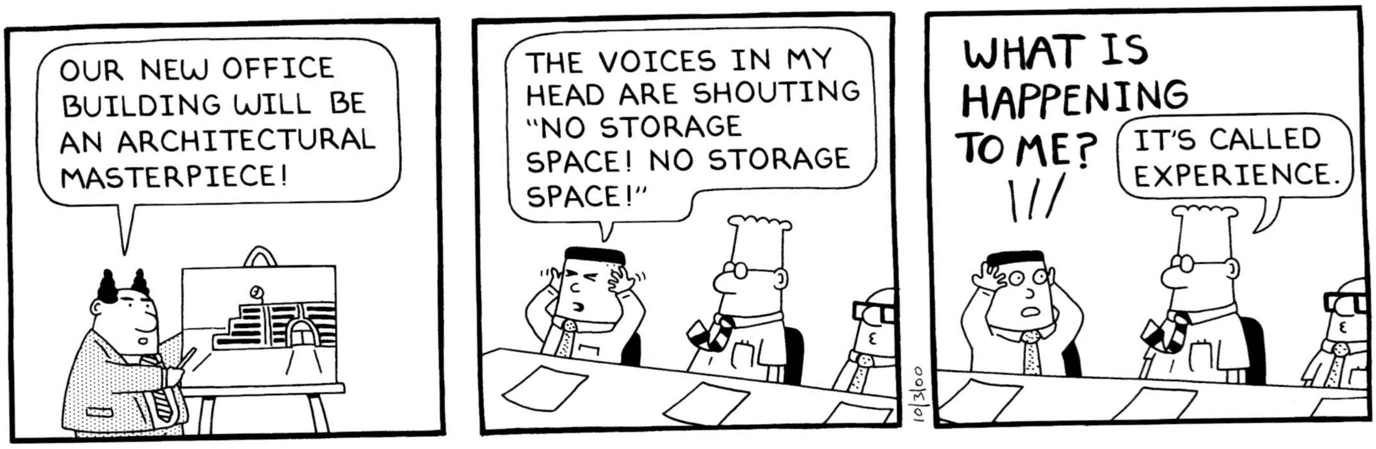
OUR NEW OFFICE BUILDING WILL BE AN ARCHITECTURAL MASTERPIECE!
THE VOICES IN MY HEAD ARE SHOUTING "NO STORAGE SPACE! NO STORAGE SPACE!"
WHAT IS HAPPENING TO ME?
IT'S CALLED EXPERIENCE.
10/3/00

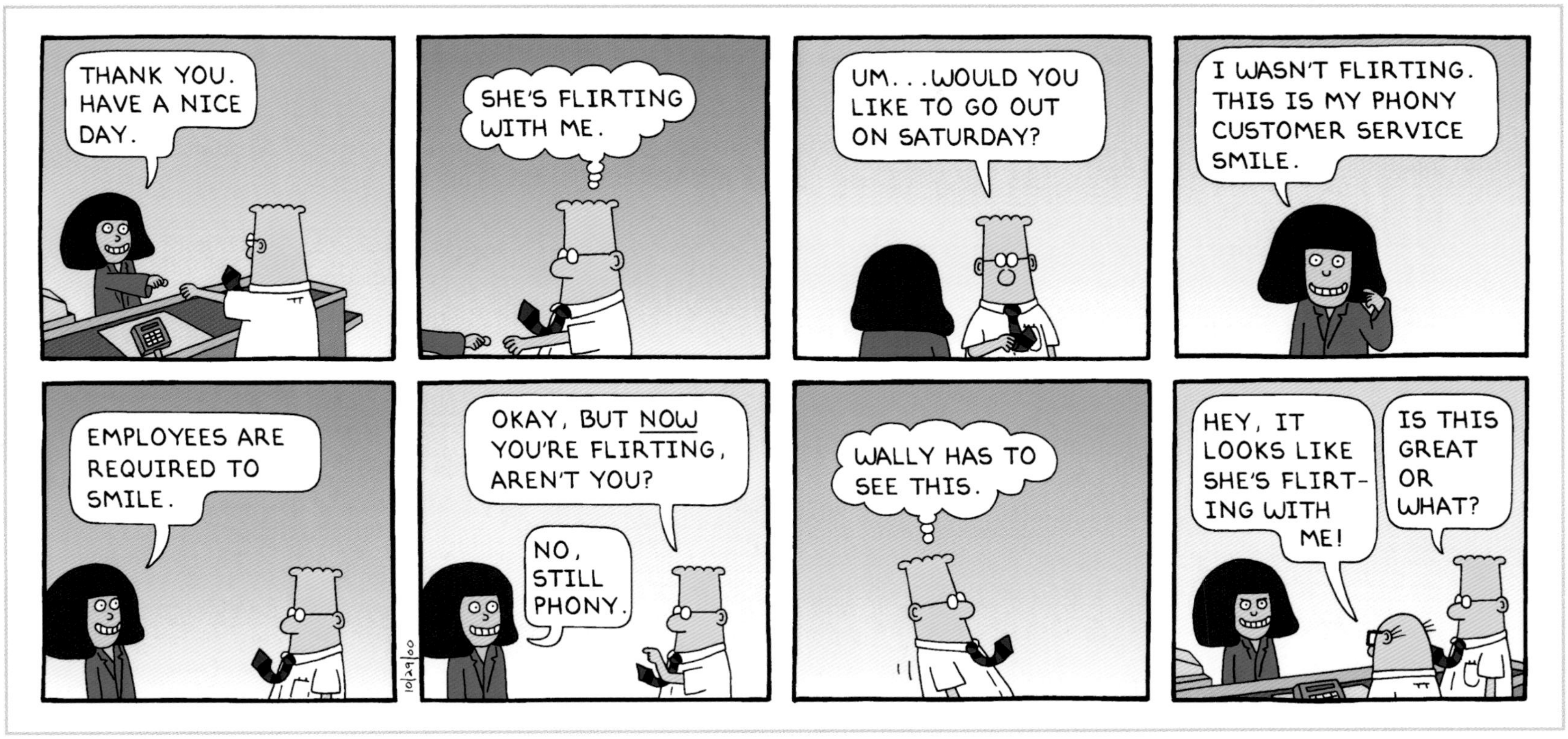
THANK YOU. HAVE A NICE DAY.
SHE'S FLIRTING WITH ME.
UM...WOULD YOU LIKE TO GO OUT ON SATURDAY?
I WASN'T FLIRTING. THIS IS MY PHONY CUSTOMER SERVICE SMILE.
EMPLOYEES ARE REQUIRED TO SMILE.
OKAY, BUT NOW YOU'RE FLIRTING, AREN'T YOU?
NO, STILL PHONY.
10/29/00
WALLY HAS TO SEE THIS.
HEY, IT LOOKS LIKE SHE'S FLIRT-ING WITH ME!
IS THIS GREAT OR WHAT?

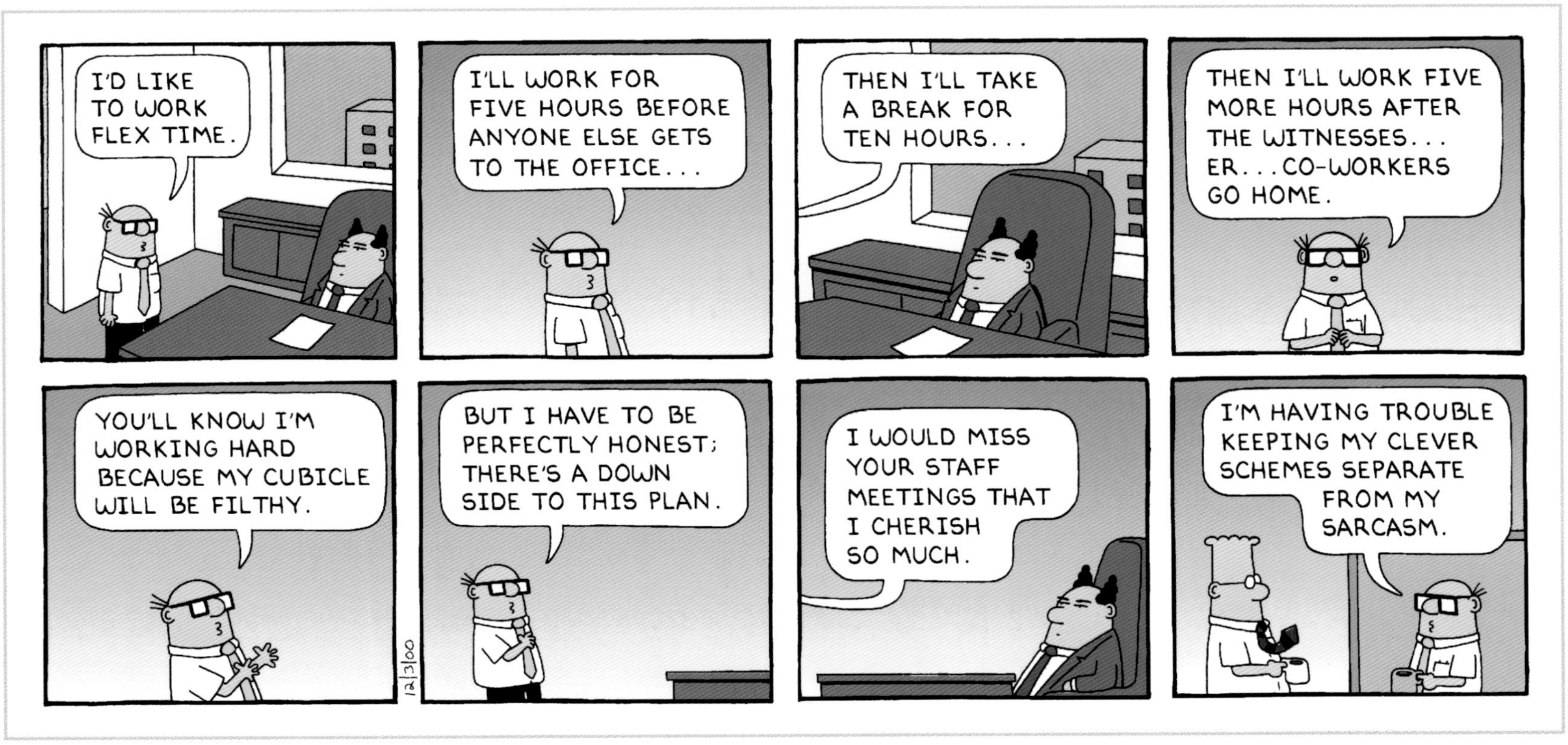
I'D LIKE TO WORK FLEX TIME.
I'LL WORK FOR FIVE HOURS BEFORE ANYONE ELSE GETS TO THE OFFICE...
THEN I'LL TAKE A BREAK FOR TEN HOURS...
THEN I'LL WORK FIVE MORE HOURS AFTER THE WITNESSES... ER...CO-WORKERS GO HOME.
YOU'LL KNOW I'M WORKING HARD BECAUSE MY CUBICLE WILL BE FILTHY.
12/3/00
BUT I HAVE TO BE PERFECTLY HONEST; THERE'S A DOWN SIDE TO THIS PLAN.
I WOULD MISS YOUR STAFF MEETINGS THAT I CHERISH SO MUCH.
I'M HAVING TROUBLE KEEPING MY CLEVER SCHEMES SEPARATE FROM MY SARCASM.

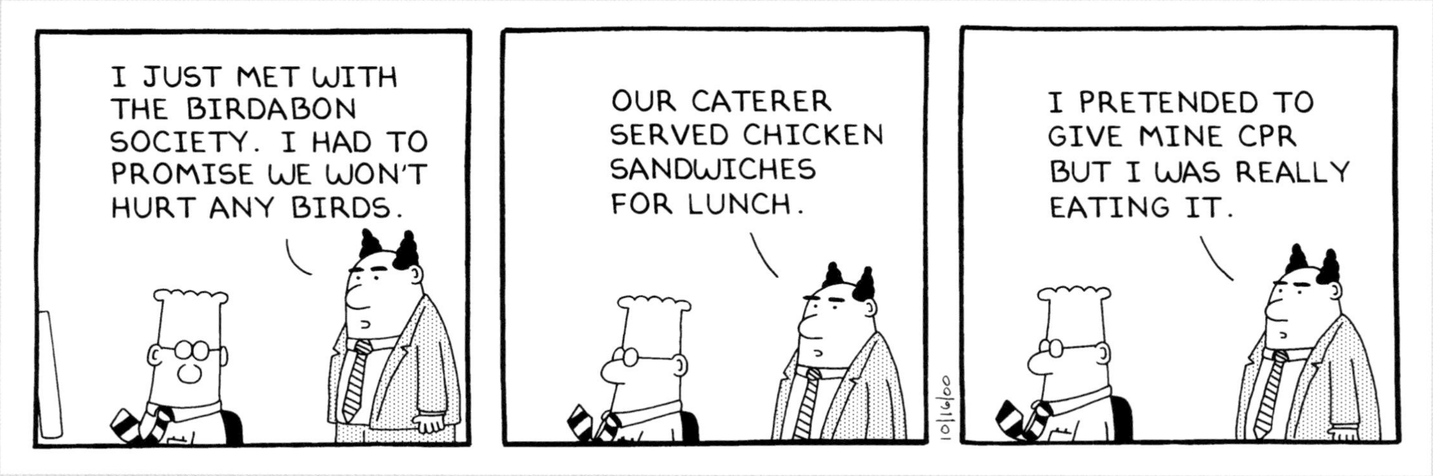
I JUST MET WITH THE BIRDABON SOCIETY. I HAD TO PROMISE WE WON'T HURT ANY BIRDS.
OUR CATERER SERVED CHICKEN SANDWICHES FOR LUNCH.
I PRETENDED TO GIVE MINE CPR BUT I WAS REALLY EATING IT.

This is one of my personal favorites. The art is totally irrelevant because the funny part is imagining the scene the boss describes.

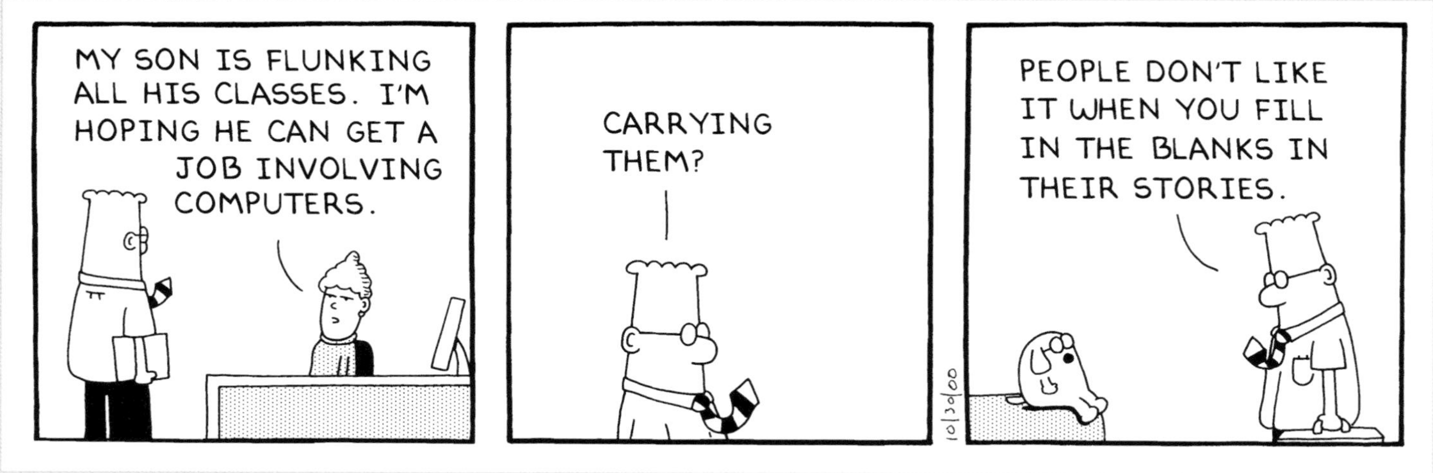
MY SON IS FLUNKING ALL HIS CLASSES. I'M HOPING HE CAN GET A JOB INVOLVING COMPUTERS.
CARRYING THEM?
PEOPLE DON'T LIKE IT WHEN YOU FILL IN THE BLANKS IN THEIR STORIES.

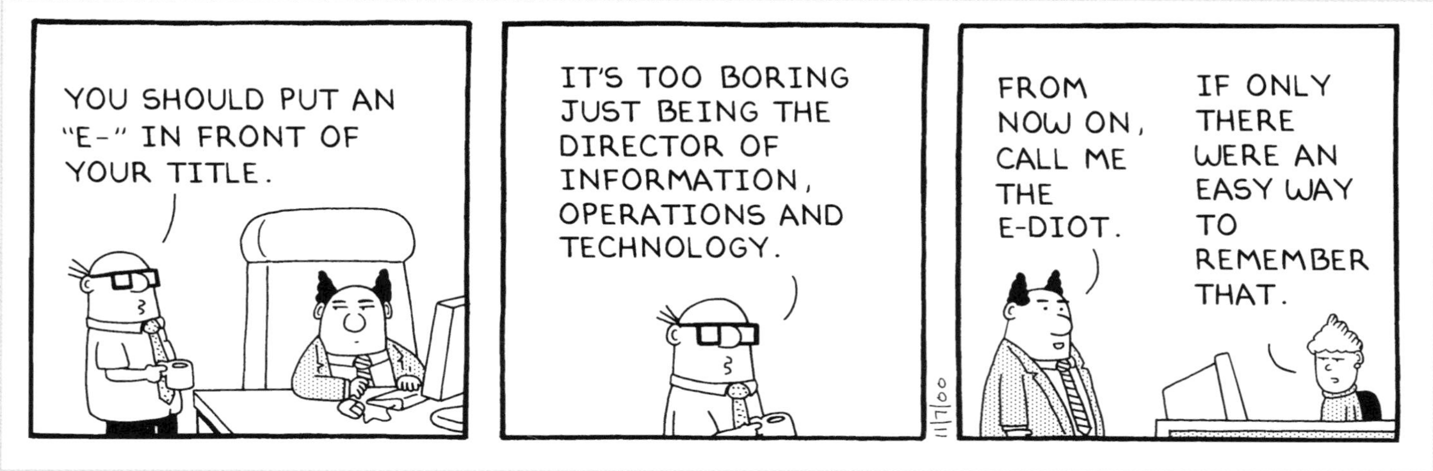
YOU SHOULD PUT AN "E-" IN FRONT OF YOUR TITLE.
IT'S TOO BORING JUST BEING THE DIRECTOR OF INFORMATION, OPERATIONS AND TECHNOLOGY.
FROM NOW ON, CALL ME THE E-DIOT.
IF ONLY THERE WERE AN EASY WAY TO REMEMBER THAT.

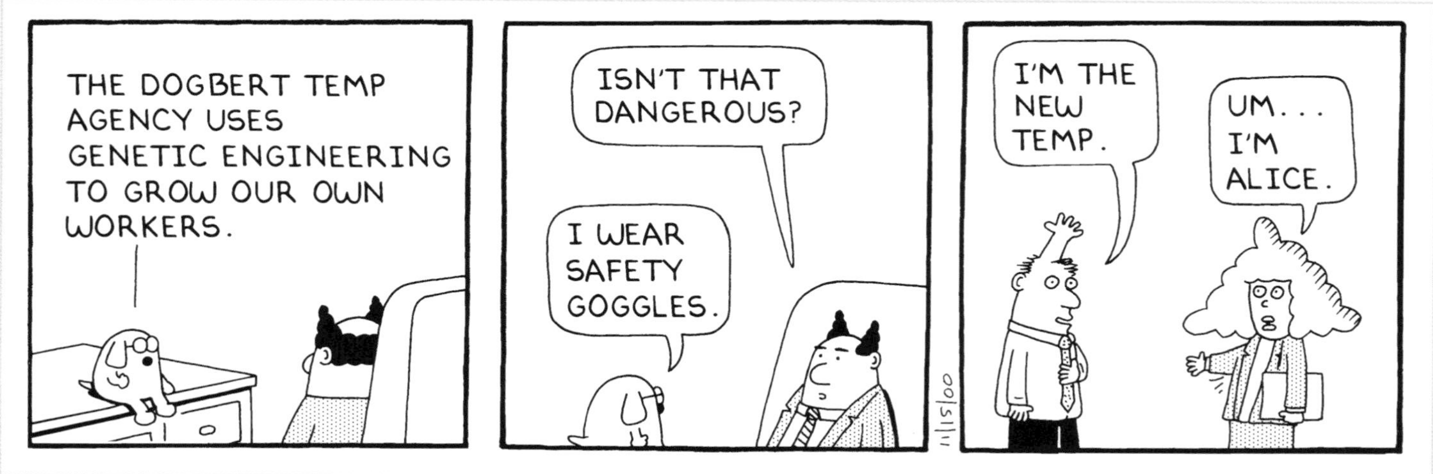
THE DOGBERT TEMP AGENCY USES GENETIC ENGINEERING TO GROW OUR OWN WORKERS.
ISN'T THAT DANGEROUS?
I WEAR SAFETY GOGGLES.
I'M THE NEW TEMP.
UM... I'M ALICE.

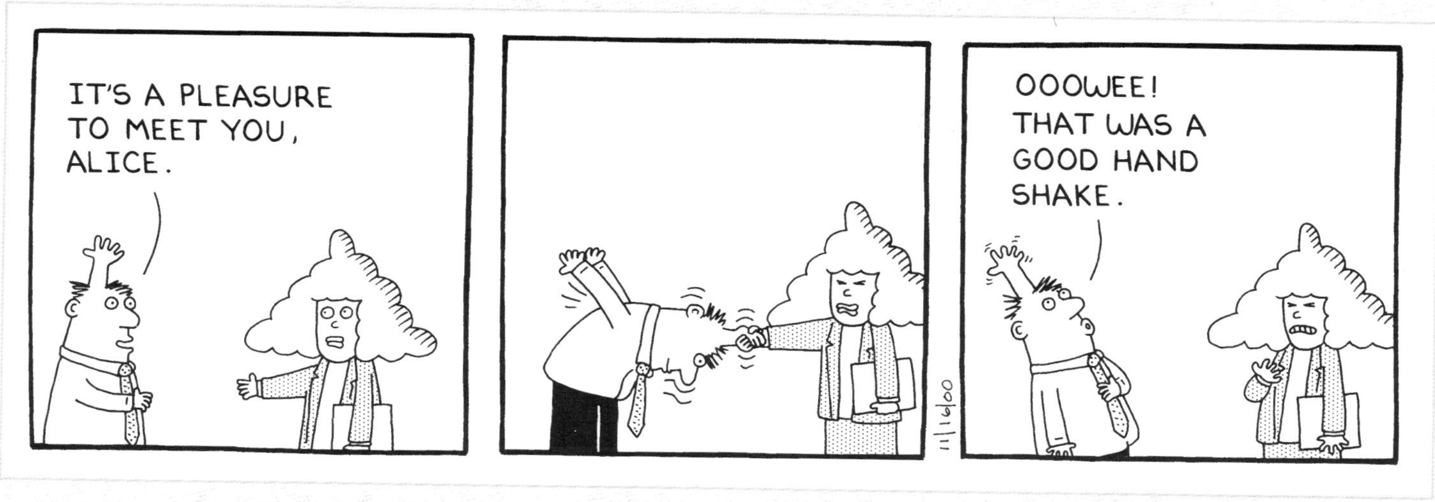
IT'S A PLEASURE TO MEET YOU, ALICE.
OOOWEE! THAT WAS A GOOD HAND SHAKE.
11/16/00

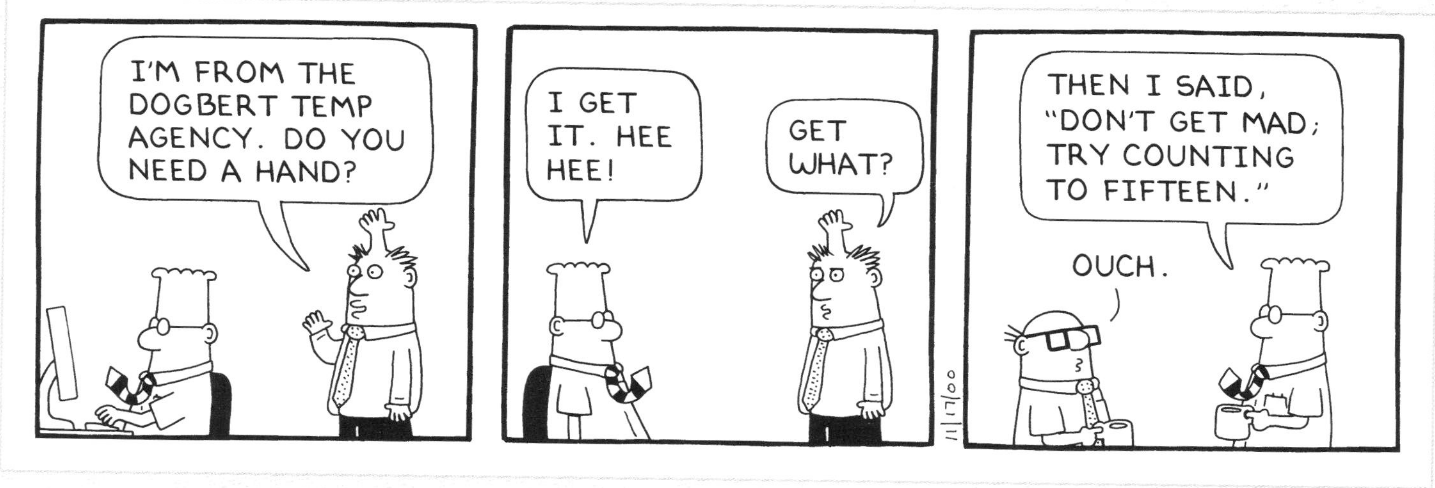
I'M FROM THE DOGBERT TEMP AGENCY. DO YOU NEED A HAND?
I GET IT. HEE HEE!
GET WHAT?
11/17/00
THEN I SAID, "DON'T GET MAD; TRY COUNTING TO FIFTEEN."
OUCH.

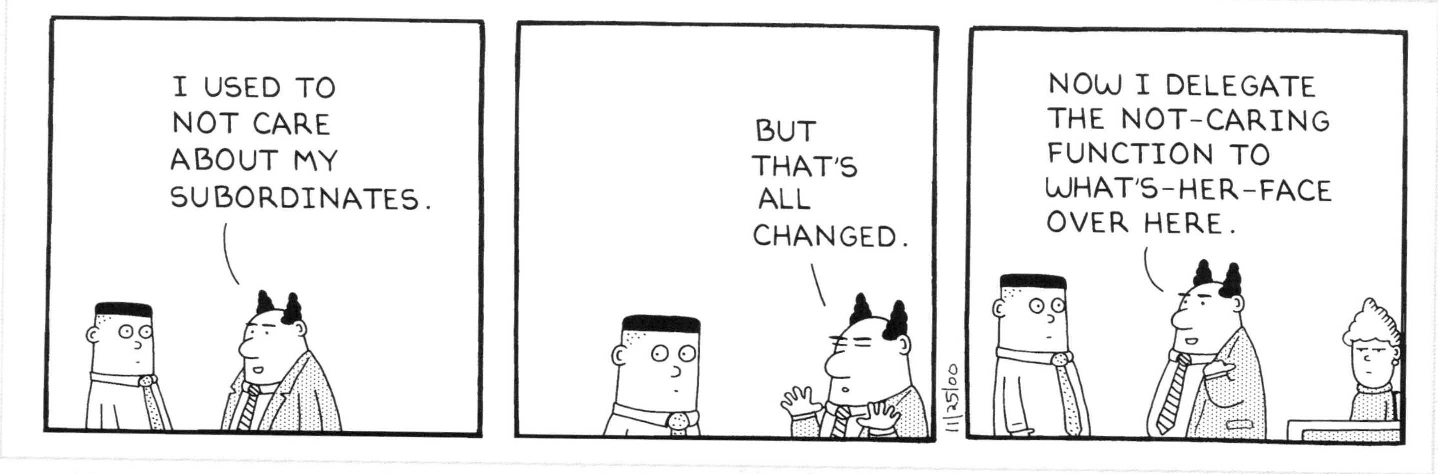
I USED TO NOT CARE ABOUT MY SUBORDINATES.
BUT THAT'S ALL CHANGED.
11/25/00
NOW I DELEGATE THE NOT-CARING FUNCTION TO WHAT'S-HER-FACE OVER HERE.

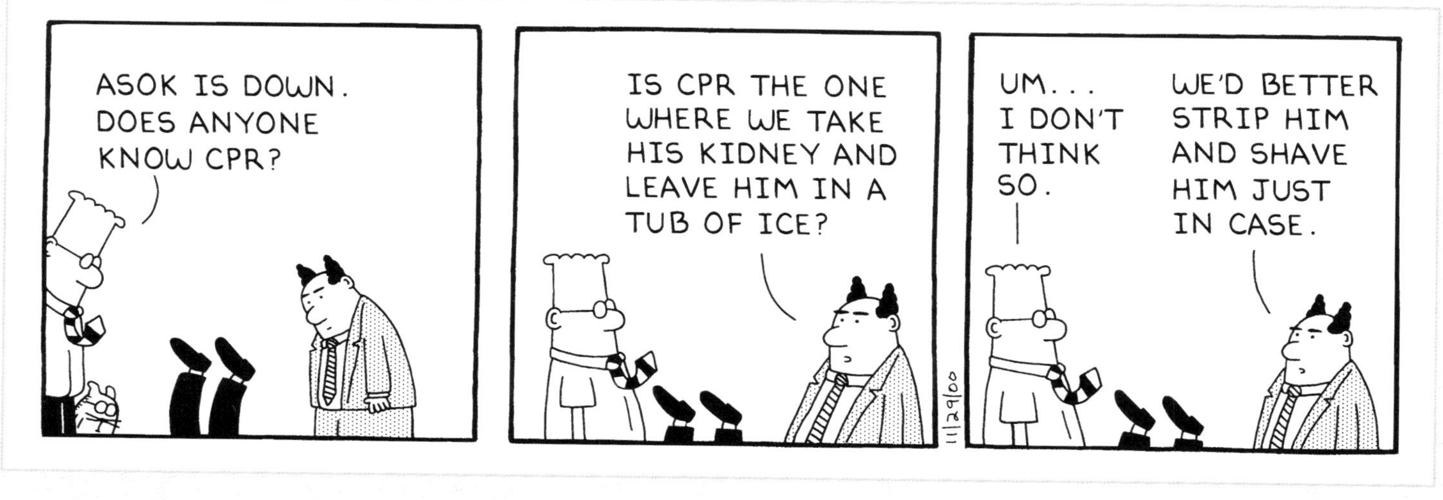
ASOK IS DOWN. DOES ANYONE KNOW CPR?
IS CPR THE ONE WHERE WE TAKE HIS KIDNEY AND LEAVE HIM IN A TUB OF ICE?
11/29/00
UM... I DON'T THINK SO.
WE'D BETTER STRIP HIM AND SHAVE HIM JUST IN CASE.

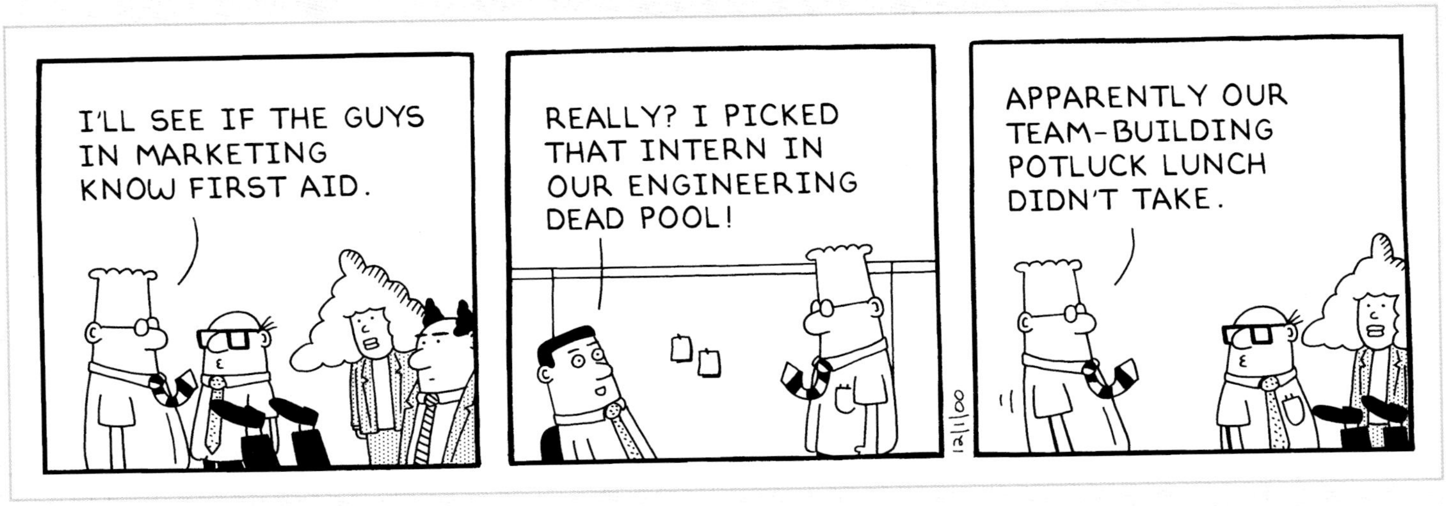
I'LL SEE IF THE GUYS IN MARKETING KNOW FIRST AID.
REALLY? I PICKED THAT INTERN IN OUR ENGINEERING DEAD POOL!
12/1/00
APPARENTLY OUR TEAM-BUILDING POTLUCK LUNCH DIDN'T TAKE.

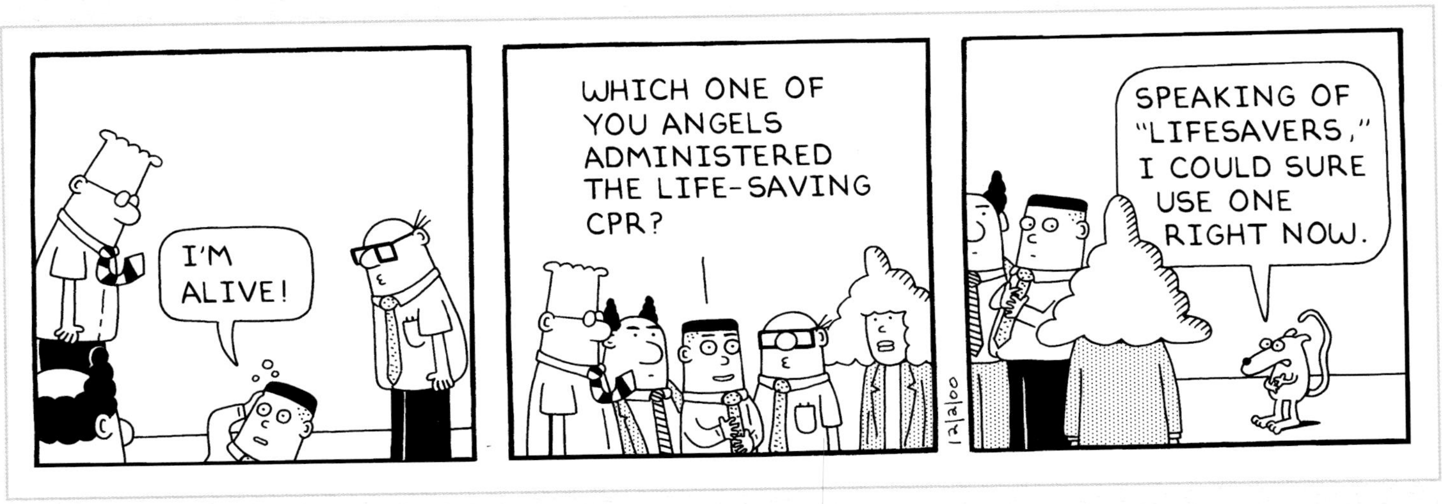
I'M ALIVE!
WHICH ONE OF YOU ANGELS ADMINISTERED THE LIFE-SAVING CPR?
12/2/00
SPEAKING OF "LIFESAVERS," I COULD SURE USE ONE RIGHT NOW.

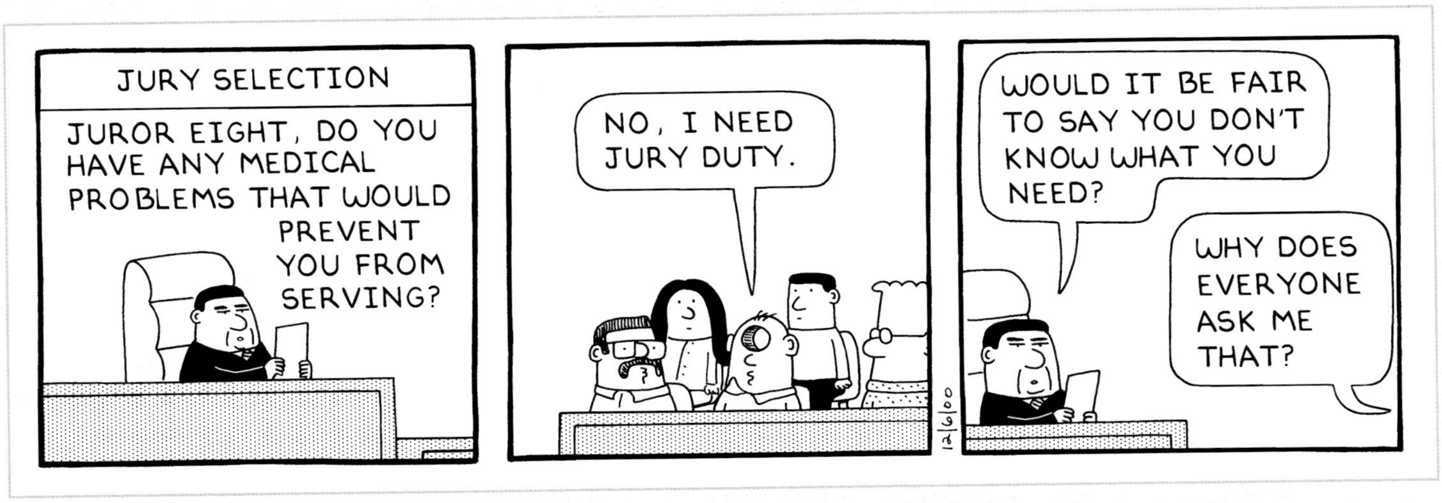
JURY SELECTION
JUROR EIGHT, DO YOU HAVE ANY MEDICAL PROBLEMS THAT WOULD PREVENT YOU FROM SERVING?
NO, I NEED JURY DUTY.
12/6/00
WOULD IT BE FAIR TO SAY YOU DON'T KNOW WHAT YOU NEED?
WHY DOES EVERYONE ASK ME THAT?

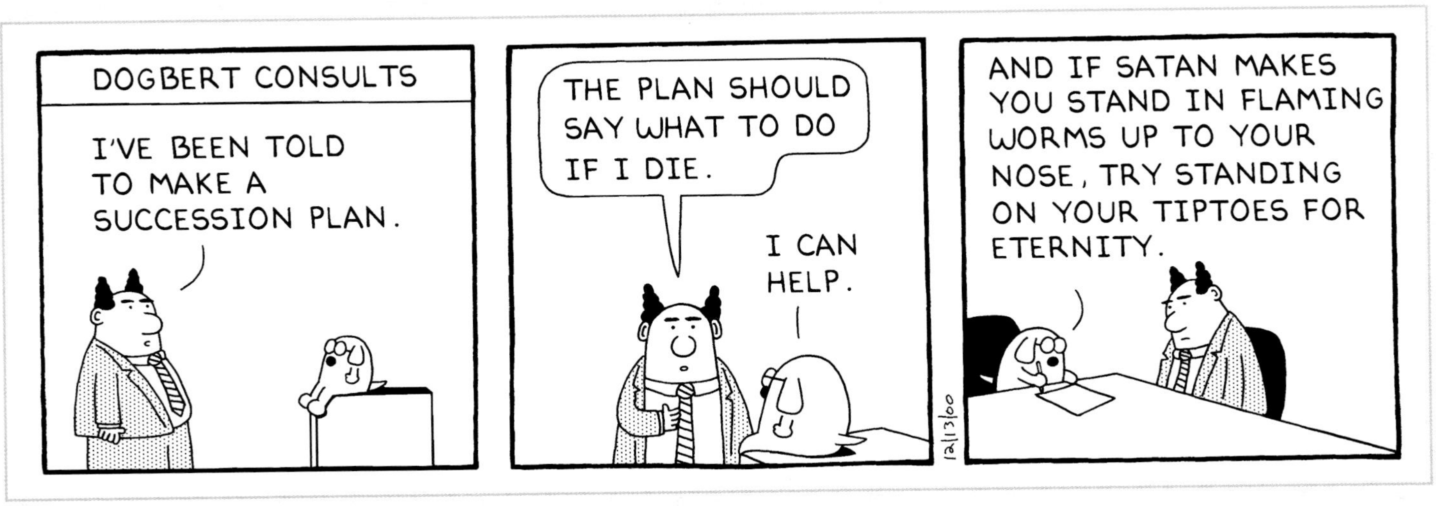
DOGBERT CONSULTS
I'VE BEEN TOLD TO MAKE A SUCCESSION PLAN.
THE PLAN SHOULD SAY WHAT TO DO IF I DIE.
I CAN HELP.
12/13/00
AND IF SATAN MAKES YOU STAND IN FLAMING WORMS UP TO YOUR NOSE, TRY STANDING ON YOUR TIPTOES FOR ETERNITY.

AND WE'LL HAVE SUB-SECOND RESPONSE TIME.
ACTUALLY, IT'S ALREADY TWO SECONDS, AND YOUR CHANGE WILL ADD TWO MORE.
WHY DO YOU ALWAYS HAVE TO BE RIGHT?!
JUST ONCE CAN'T YOU ADMIT I'M RIGHT?
OKAY, I ADMIT THAT TWO PLUS TWO EQUALS LESS THAN ONE.
12/10/00
I DON'T MEAN NOW, JERK. I MEAN IN GENERAL.
OKAY. IN GENERAL I ADMIT THAT THE RULES OF PHYSICS ARE OPTIONAL.
YOU'RE DOING IT WRONG!!
YOU'RE RIGHT. MY FAULT AGAIN.

EVERYTHING IS READY. WE JUST NEED THE BUDGET.
YOU DID GET THE FUNDING...
DIDN'T YOU?
I'VE BEEN VERY BUSY.
THIS PROJECT HAS BEEN YOUR TOP PRIORITY FOR OVER A YEAR!!!
YOU ONLY HAD ONE TASK: GET FUNDING.
12/17/00
WHAT HAVE YOU BEEN DOING FOR THE PAST YEAR?!
I REMEMBER ATTENDING MEETINGS...
AAY-III-YIII-YIII!!
IF YOU NEED ANYTHING, JUST HOLLER.

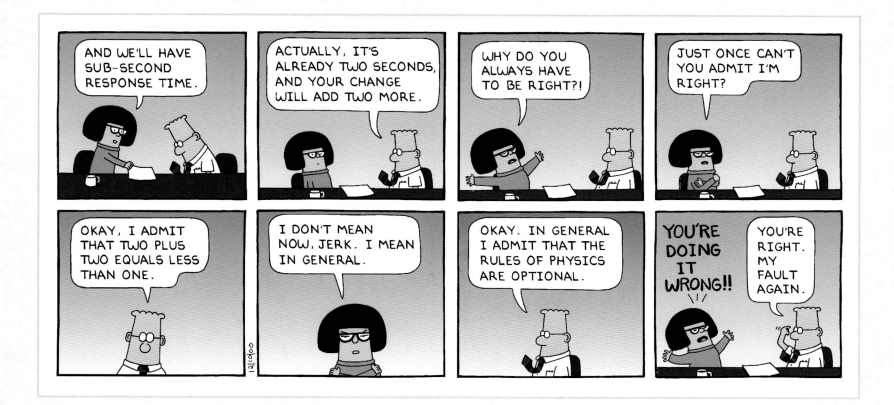

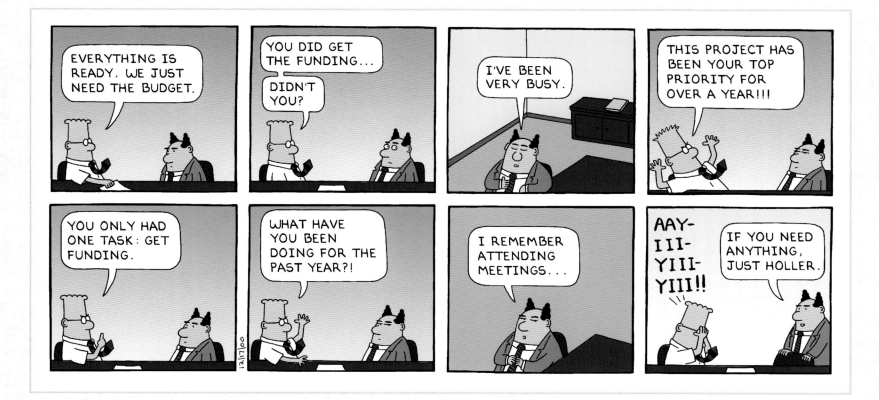

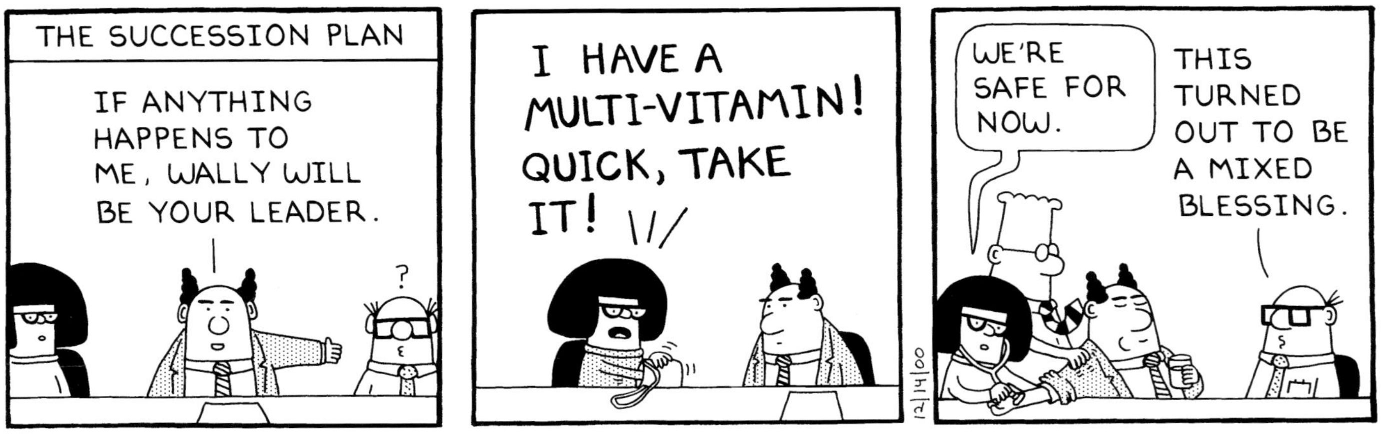
THE SUCCESSION PLAN
IF ANYTHING HAPPENS TO ME, WALLY WILL BE YOUR LEADER.
?
I HAVE A MULTI-VITAMIN! QUICK, TAKE IT!
12/14/00
WE'RE SAFE FOR NOW.
THIS TURNED OUT TO BE A MIXED BLESSING.

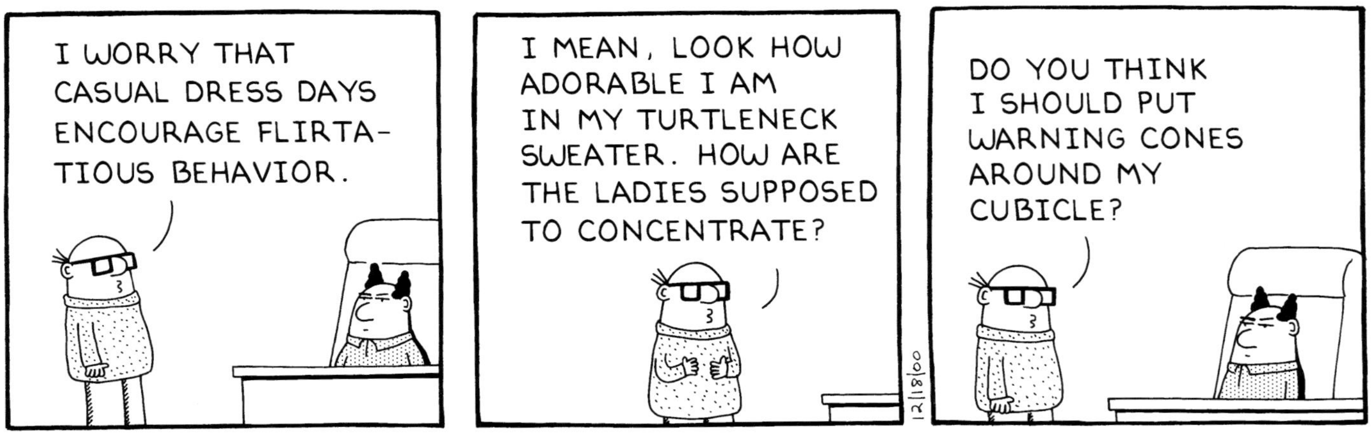
I WORRY THAT CASUAL DRESS DAYS ENCOURAGE FLIRTA-TIOUS BEHAVIOR.
I MEAN, LOOK HOW ADORABLE I AM IN MY TURTLENECK SWEATER. HOW ARE THE LADIES SUPPOSED TO CONCENTRATE?
12/18/00
DO YOU THINK I SHOULD PUT WARNING CONES AROUND MY CUBICLE?

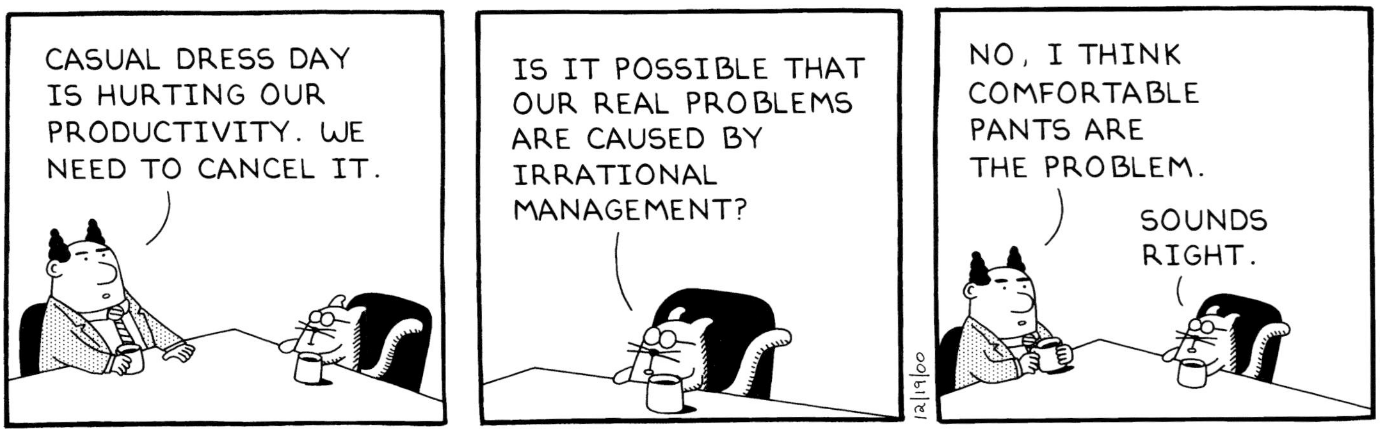
CASUAL DRESS DAY IS HURTING OUR PRODUCTIVITY. WE NEED TO CANCEL IT.
IS IT POSSIBLE THAT OUR REAL PROBLEMS ARE CAUSED BY IRRATIONAL MANAGEMENT?
12/19/00
NO, I THINK COMFORTABLE PANTS ARE THE PROBLEM.
SOUNDS RIGHT.

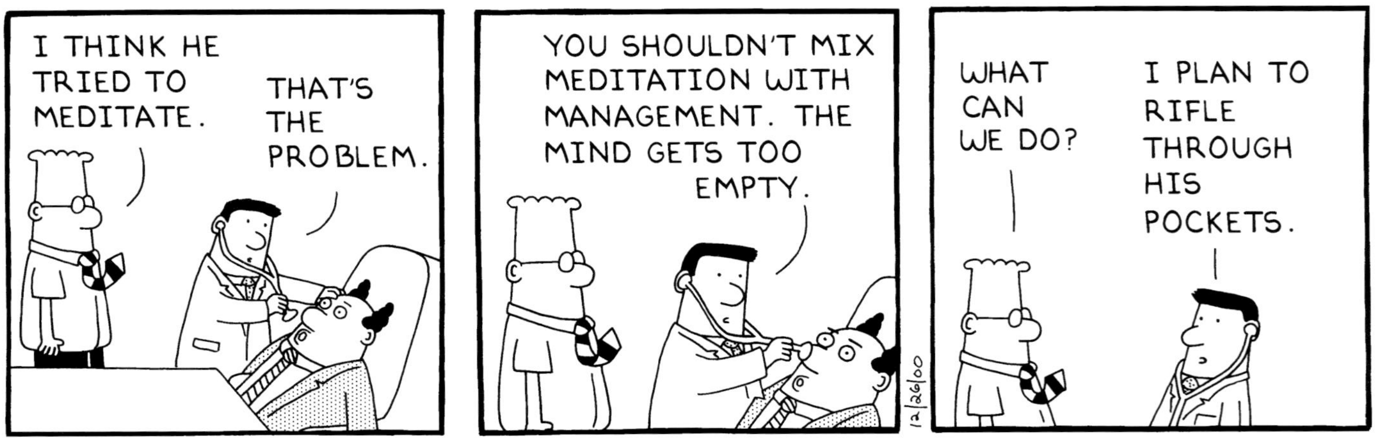
I THINK HE TRIED TO MEDITATE.
THAT'S THE PROBLEM.
YOU SHOULDN'T MIX MEDITATION WITH MANAGEMENT. THE MIND GETS TOO EMPTY.
12/26/00
WHAT CAN WE DO?
I PLAN TO RIFLE THROUGH HIS POCKETS.

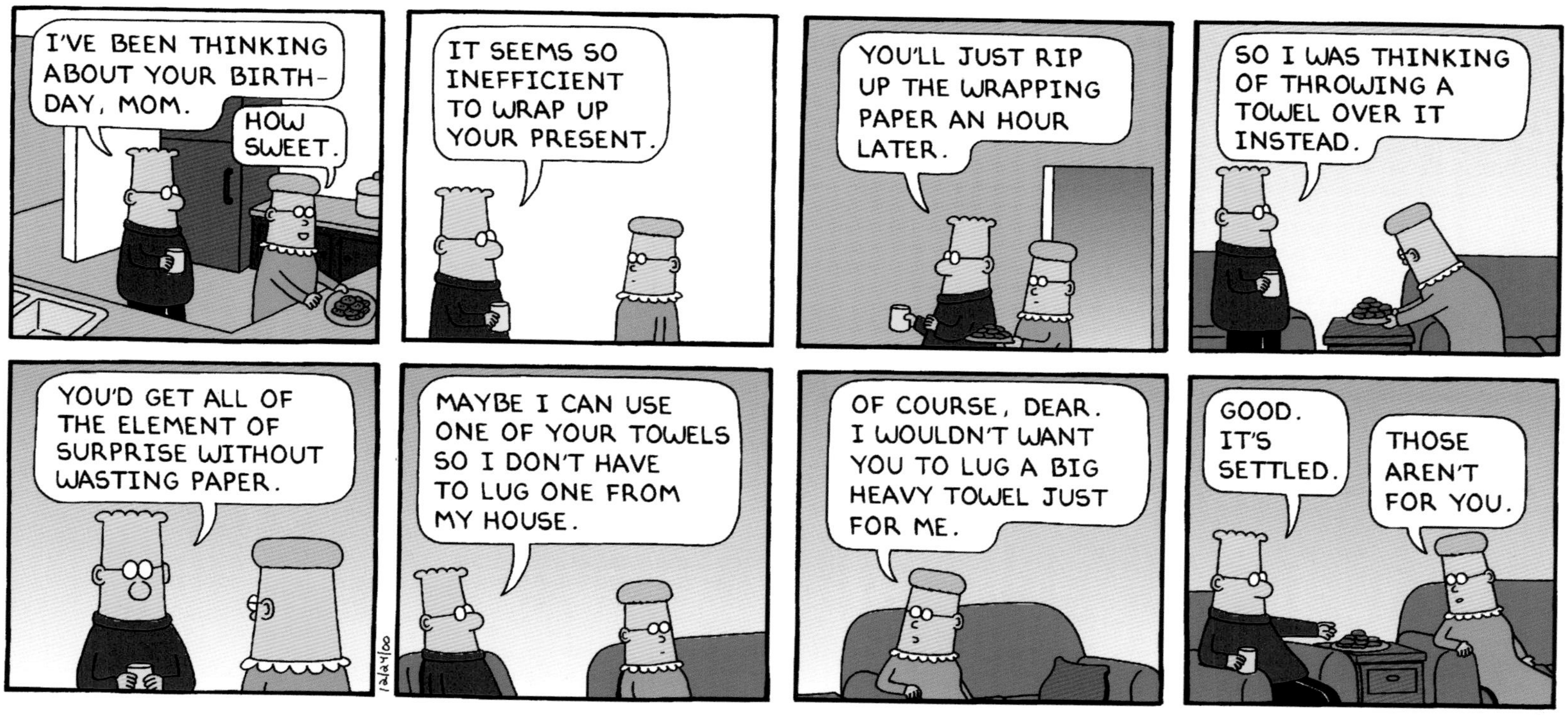
I'VE BEEN THINKING ABOUT YOUR BIRTH-DAY, MOM.
HOW SWEET.
IT SEEMS SO INEFFICIENT TO WRAP UP YOUR PRESENT.
YOU'LL JUST RIP UP THE WRAPPING PAPER AN HOUR LATER.
SO I WAS THINKING OF THROWING A TOWEL OVER IT INSTEAD.
YOU'D GET ALL OF THE ELEMENT OF SURPRISE WITHOUT WASTING PAPER.
MAYBE I CAN USE ONE OF YOUR TOWELS SO I DON'T HAVE TO LUG ONE FROM MY HOUSE.
OF COURSE, DEAR. I WOULDN'T WANT YOU TO LUG A BIG HEAVY TOWEL JUST FOR ME.
GOOD. IT'S SETTLED.
THOSE AREN'T FOR YOU.

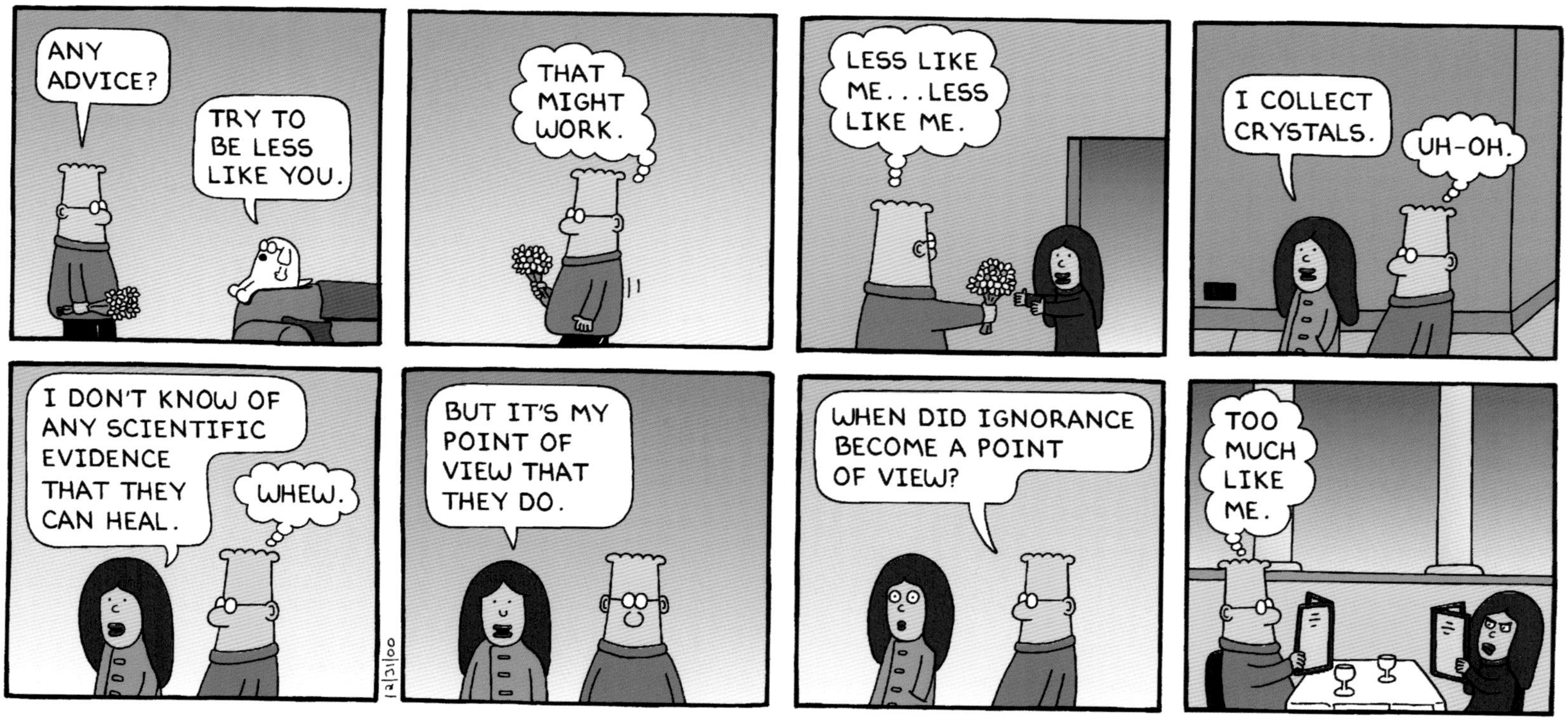
ANY ADVICE?
TRY TO BE LESS LIKE YOU.
THAT MIGHT WORK.
LESS LIKE ME. . . LESS LIKE ME.
I COLLECT CRYSTALS.
UH-OH.
I DON'T KNOW OF ANY SCIENTIFIC EVIDENCE THAT THEY CAN HEAL.
WHEW.
BUT IT'S MY POINT OF VIEW THAT THEY DO.
WHEN DID IGNORANCE BECOME A POINT OF VIEW?
TOO MUCH LIKE ME.

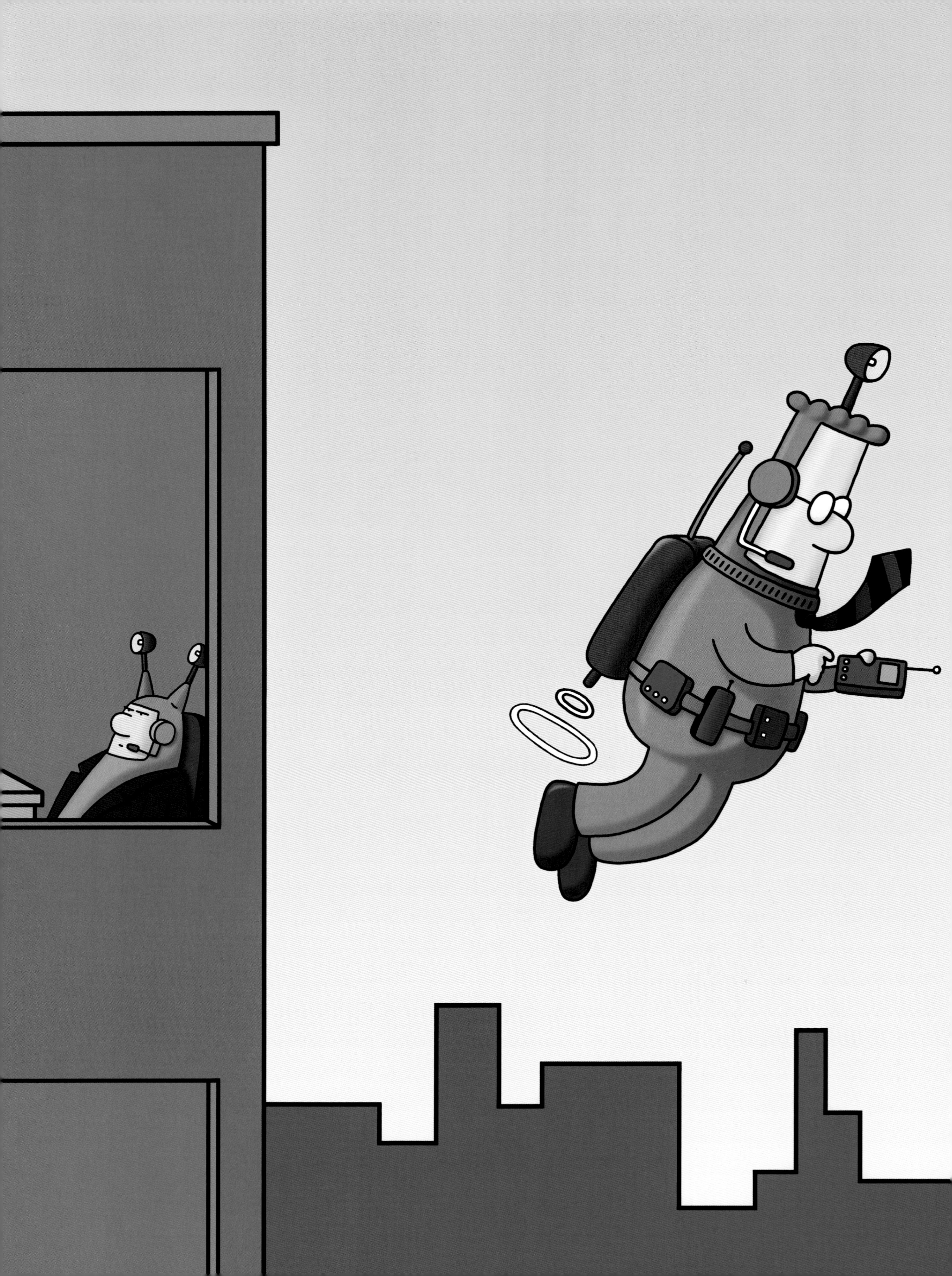

The Modern Era
2001 - 2008

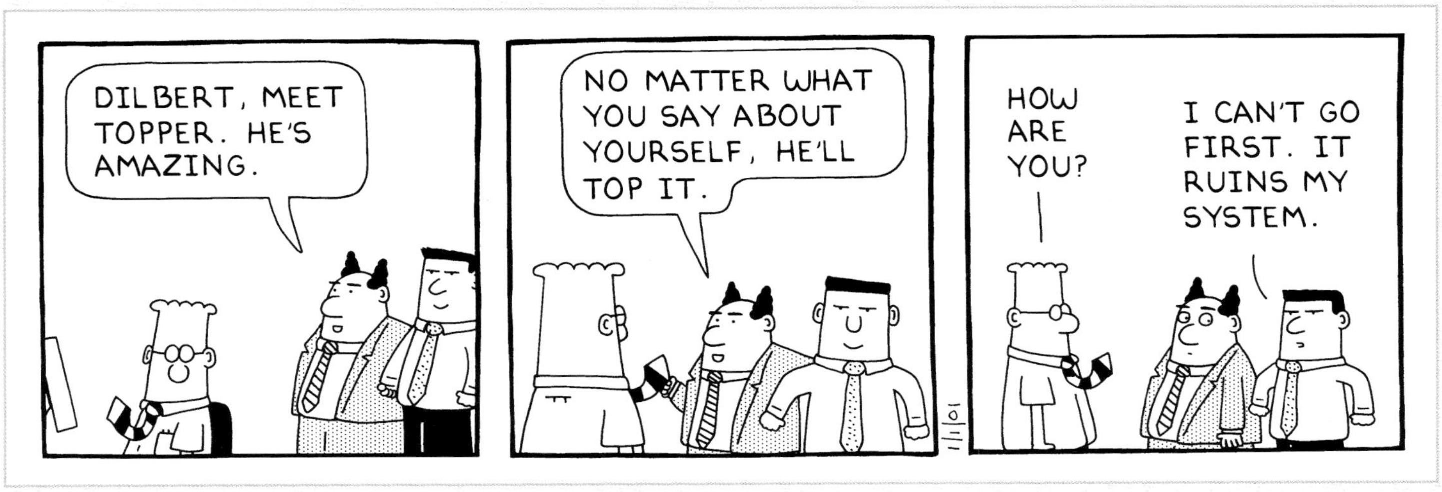
DILBERT, MEET TOPPER. HE'S AMAZING.
NO MATTER WHAT YOU SAY ABOUT YOURSELF, HE'LL TOP IT.
HOW ARE YOU?
I CAN'T GO FIRST. IT RUINS MY SYSTEM.
1/1/01

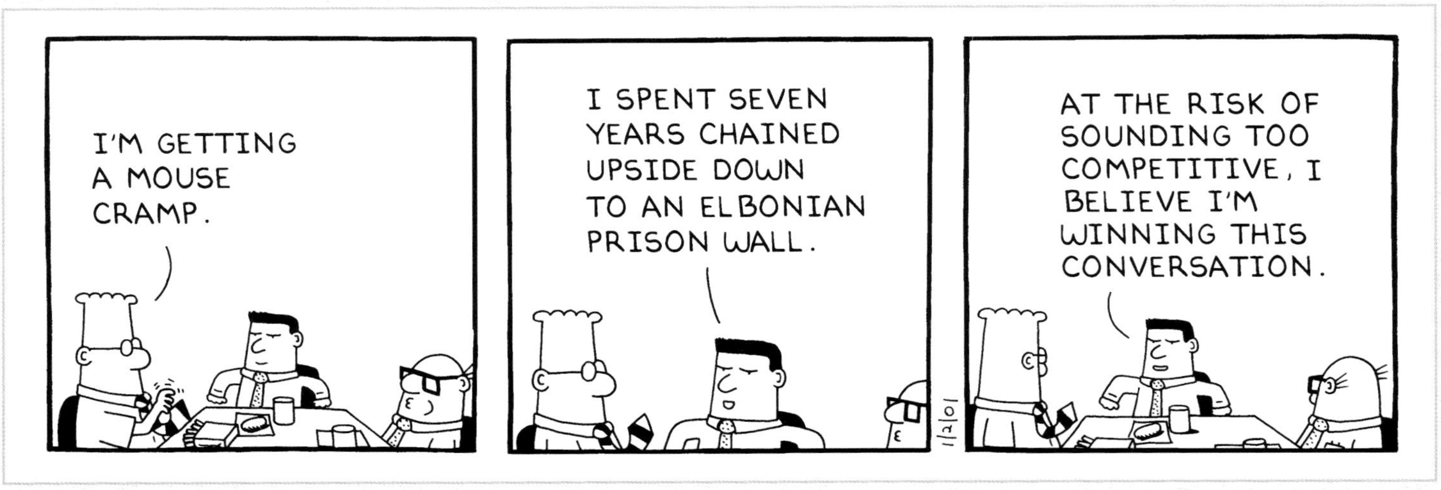
I'M GETTING A MOUSE CRAMP.
I SPENT SEVEN YEARS CHAINED UPSIDE DOWN TO AN ELBONIAN PRISON WALL.
1/2/01
AT THE RISK OF SOUNDING TOO COMPETITIVE, I BELIEVE I'M WINNING THIS CONVERSATION.

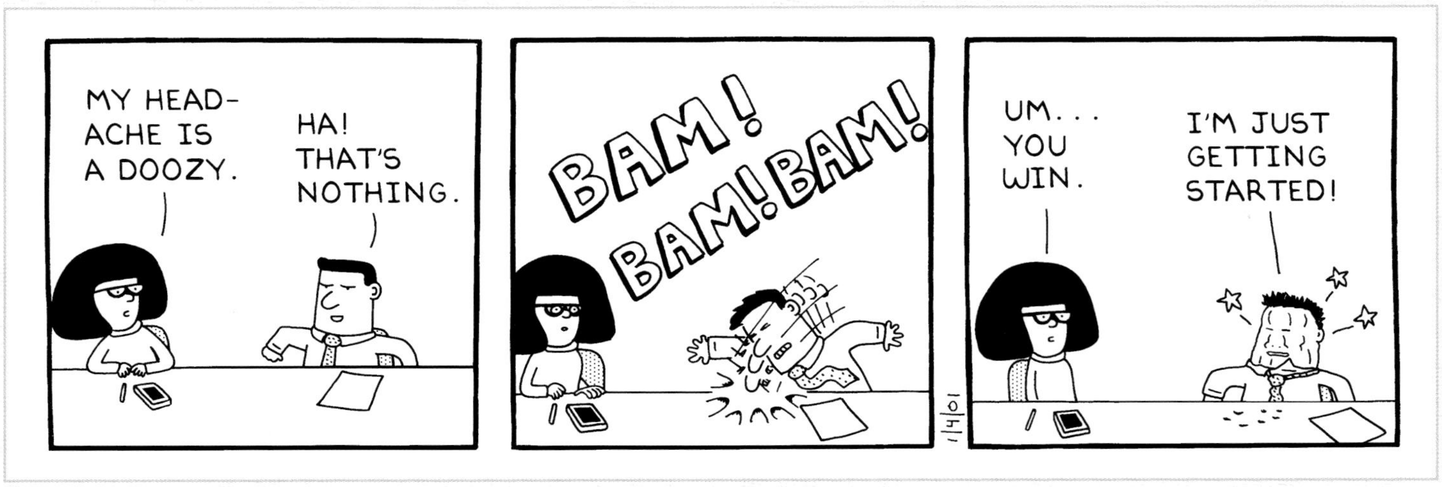
MY HEAD-ACHE IS A DOOZY.
HA! THAT'S NOTHING.
BAM! BAM! BAM!
1/4/01
UM... YOU WIN.
I'M JUST GETTING STARTED!

Topper became one of the most requested characters. It turns out every department has one. But he's a one-joke character, so I resist the urge to use him often.

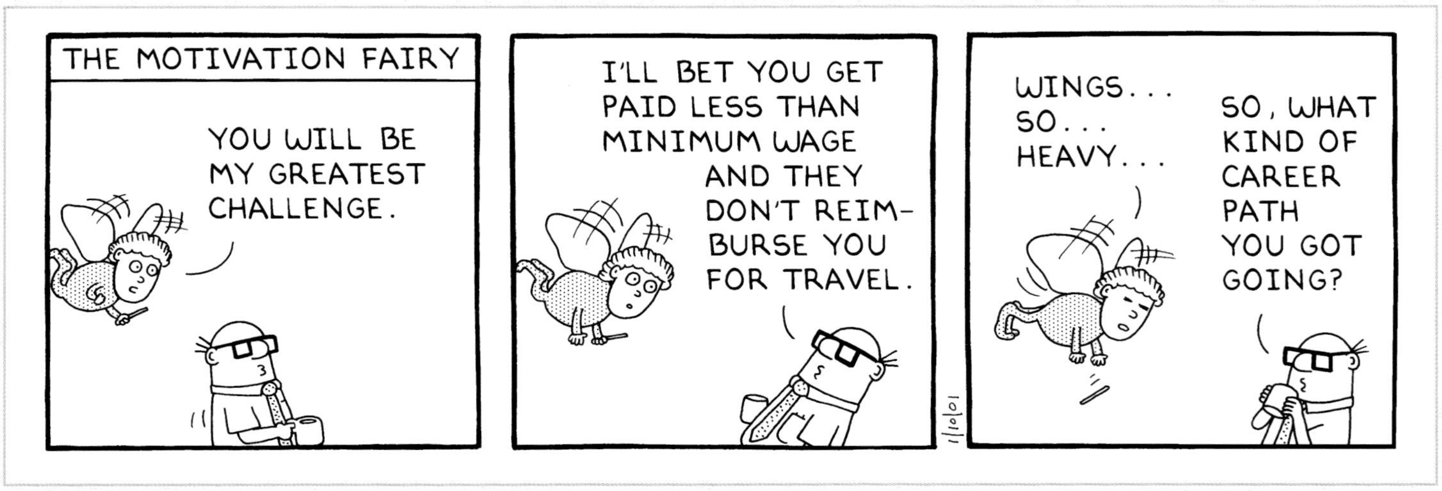
THE MOTIVATION FAIRY
YOU WILL BE MY GREATEST CHALLENGE.
I'LL BET YOU GET PAID LESS THAN MINIMUM WAGE AND THEY DON'T REIM-BURSE YOU FOR TRAVEL.
1/10/01
WINGS... SO... HEAVY...
SO, WHAT KIND OF CAREER PATH YOU GOT GOING?

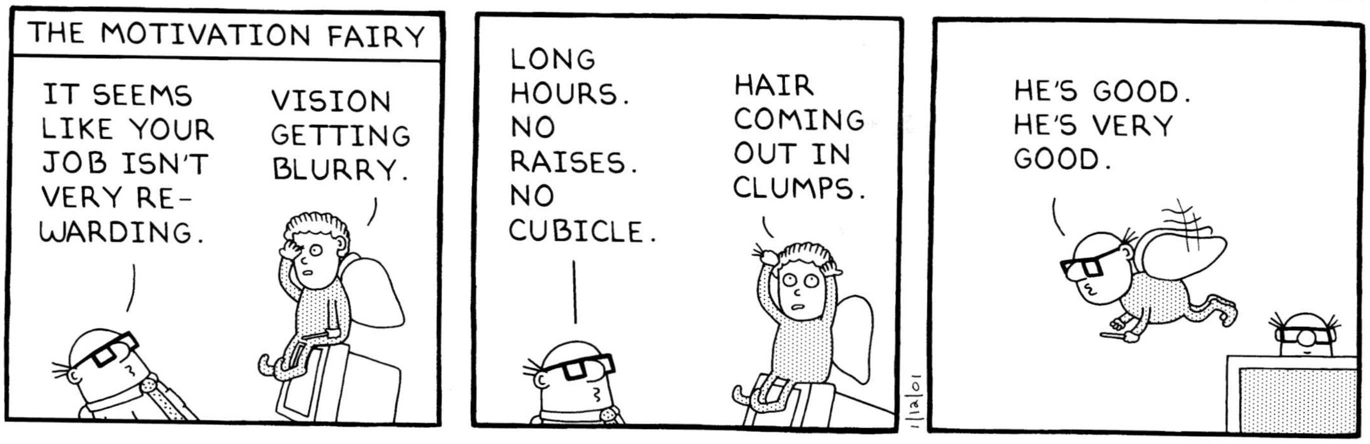
THE MOTIVATION FAIRY
IT SEEMS LIKE YOUR JOB ISN'T VERY RE-WARDING.
VISION GETTING BLURRY.
LONG HOURS. NO RAISES. NO CUBICLE.
HAIR COMING OUT IN CLUMPS.
HE'S GOOD. HE'S VERY GOOD.

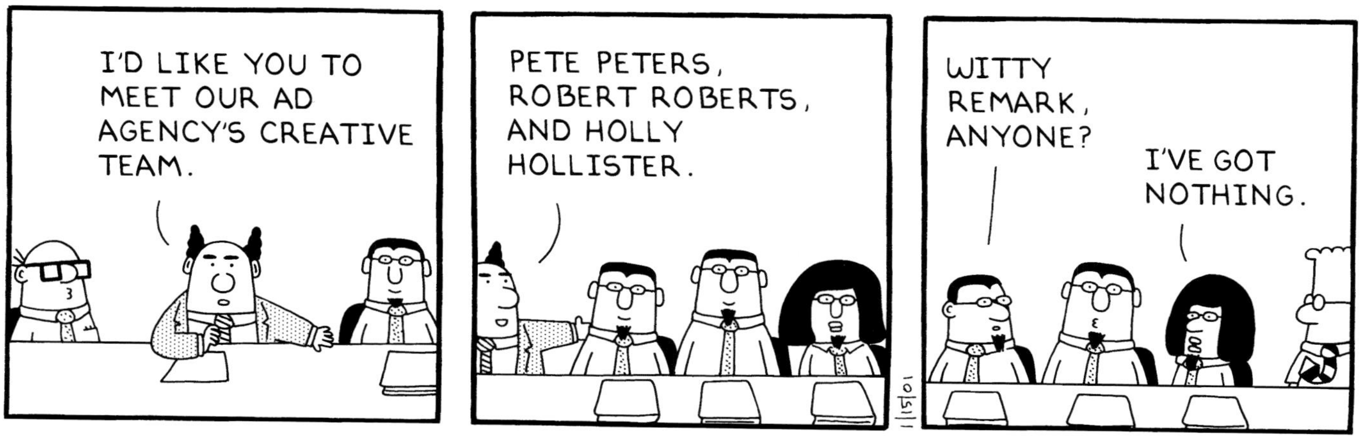
I'D LIKE YOU TO MEET OUR AD AGENCY'S CREATIVE TEAM.
PETE PETERS, ROBERT ROBERTS, AND HOLLY HOLLISTER.
WITTY REMARK, ANYONE?
I'VE GOT NOTHING.

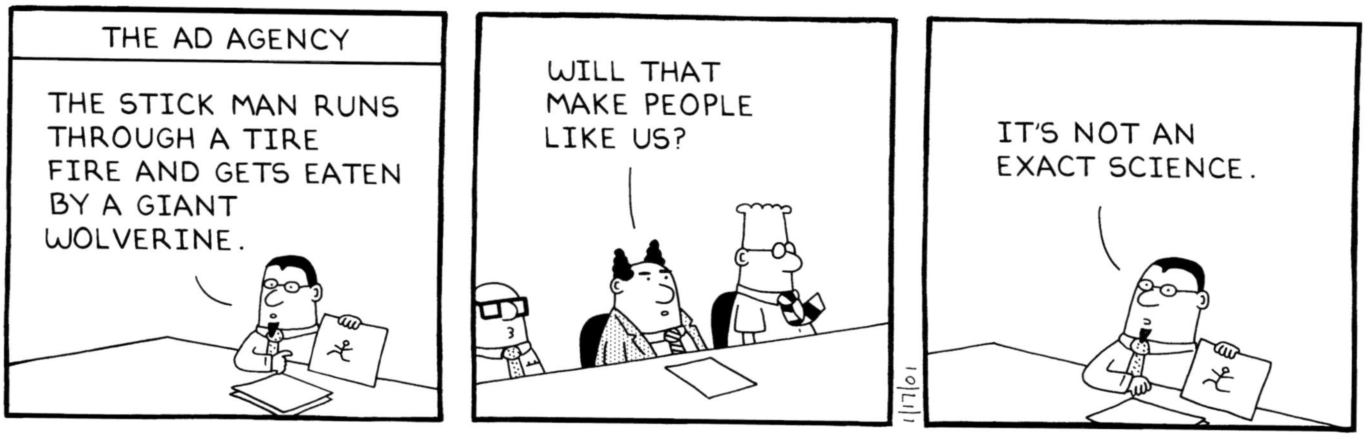
THE AD AGENCY
THE STICK MAN RUNS THROUGH A TIRE FIRE AND GETS EATEN BY A GIANT WOLVERINE.
WILL THAT MAKE PEOPLE LIKE US?
IT'S NOT AN EXACT SCIENCE.

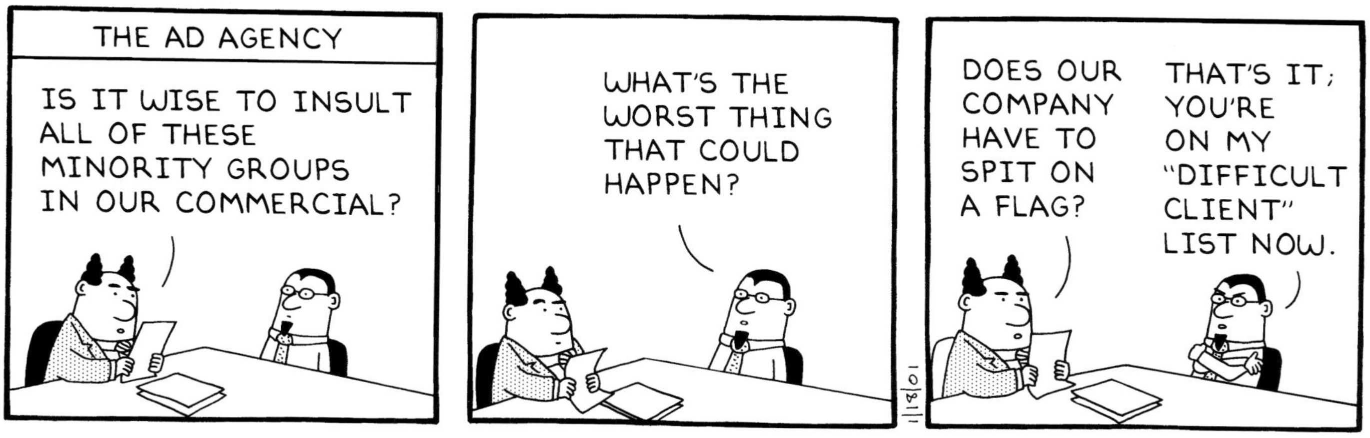
THE AD AGENCY
IS IT WISE TO INSULT ALL OF THESE MINORITY GROUPS IN OUR COMMERCIAL?
WHAT'S THE WORST THING THAT COULD HAPPEN?
DOES OUR COMPANY HAVE TO SPIT ON A FLAG?
THAT'S IT; YOU'RE ON MY "DIFFICULT CLIENT" LIST NOW.

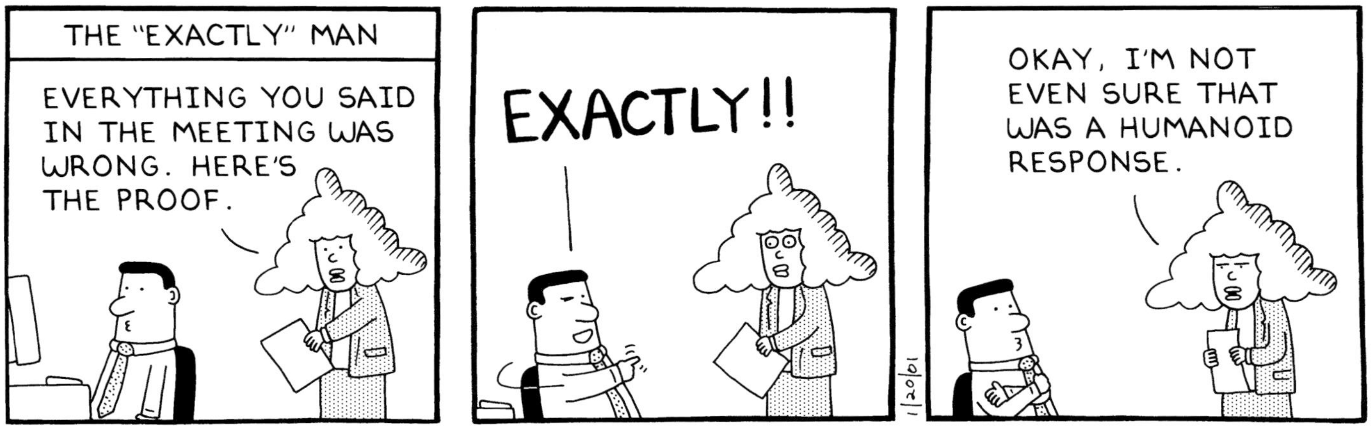
THE "EXACTLY" MAN
EVERYTHING YOU SAID IN THE MEETING WAS WRONG. HERE'S THE PROOF.
EXACTLY!!
1/20/01
OKAY, I'M NOT EVEN SURE THAT WAS A HUMANOID RESPONSE.

Many of the suggestions I get from readers start with, "A co-worker of mine has this annoying habit." No matter how random or obscure the habit is, I always feel like I know that person too.

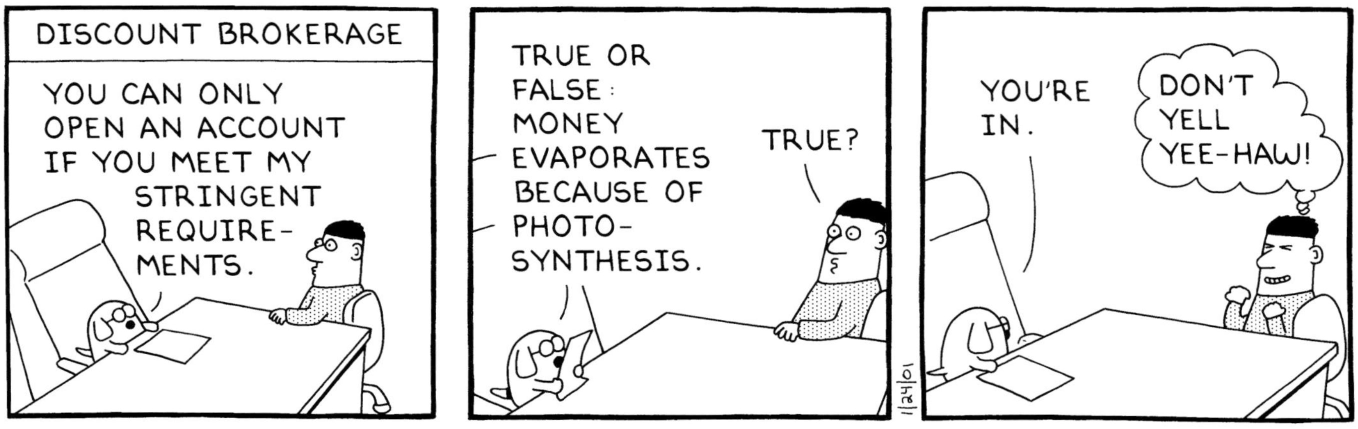
DISCOUNT BROKERAGE
YOU CAN ONLY OPEN AN ACCOUNT IF YOU MEET MY STRINGENT REQUIRE-MENTS.
TRUE OR FALSE: MONEY EVAPORATES BECAUSE OF PHOTO-SYNTHESIS.
TRUE?
1/24/01
YOU'RE IN.
DON'T YELL YEE-HAW!

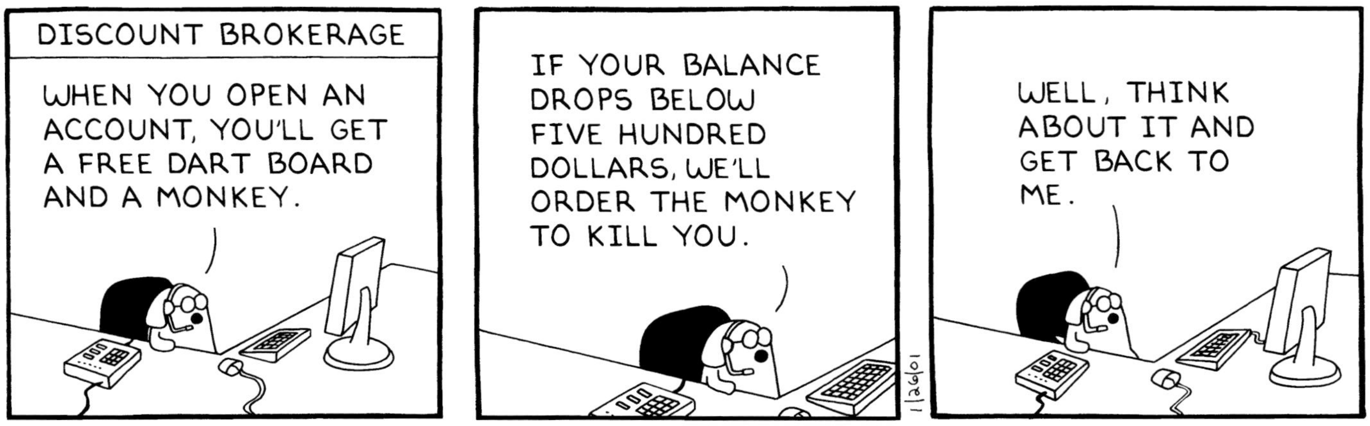
DISCOUNT BROKERAGE
WHEN YOU OPEN AN ACCOUNT, YOU'LL GET A FREE DART BOARD AND A MONKEY.
IF YOUR BALANCE DROPS BELOW FIVE HUNDRED DOLLARS, WE'LL ORDER THE MONKEY TO KILL YOU.
1/26/01
WELL, THINK ABOUT IT AND GET BACK TO ME.

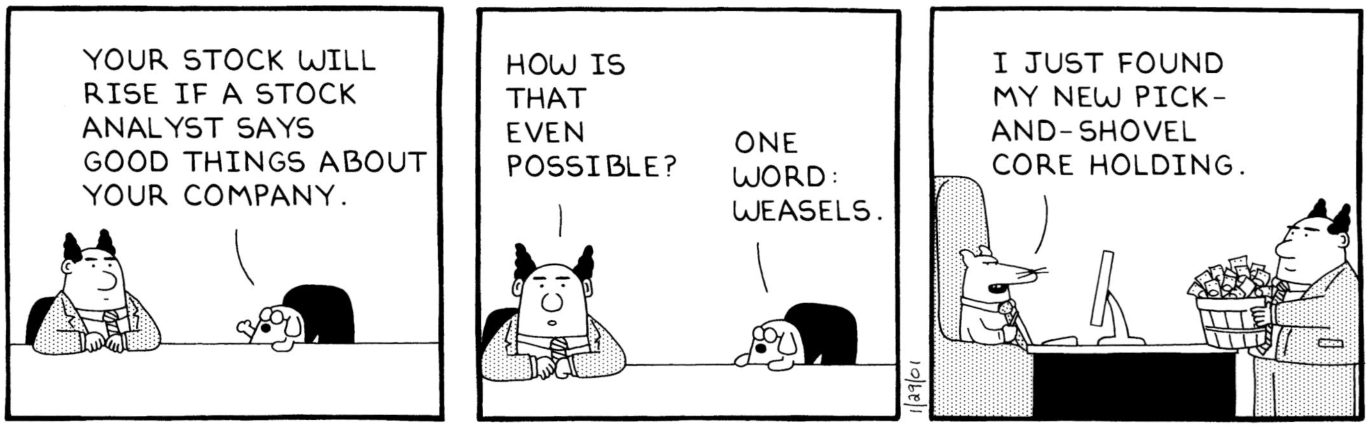
YOUR STOCK WILL RISE IF A STOCK ANALYST SAYS GOOD THINGS ABOUT YOUR COMPANY.
HOW IS THAT EVEN POSSIBLE?
ONE WORD: WEASELS.
1/29/01
I JUST FOUND MY NEW PICK-AND-SHOVEL CORE HOLDING.

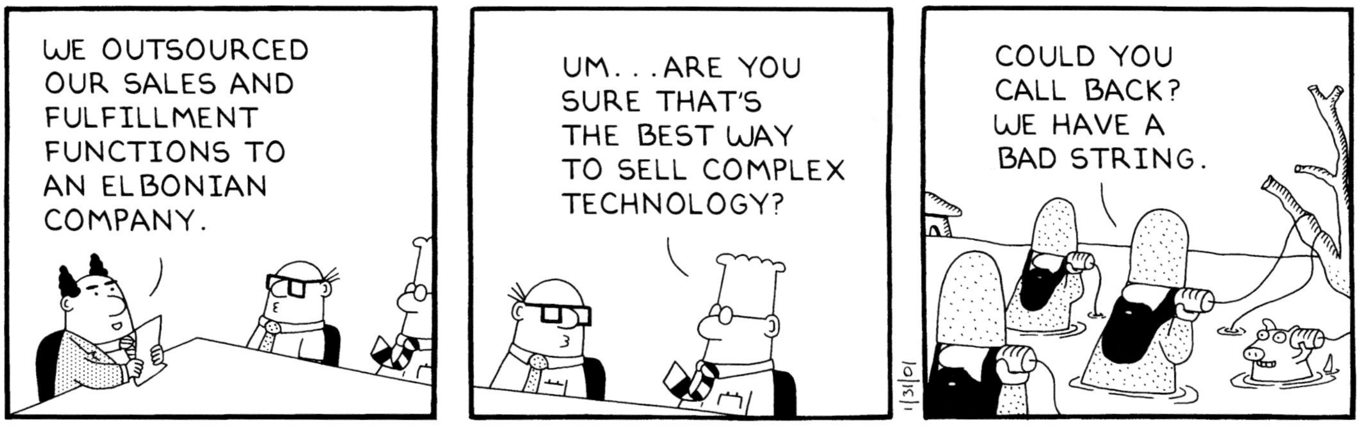
WE OUTSOURCED OUR SALES AND FULFILLMENT FUNCTIONS TO AN ELBONIAN COMPANY.
UM. . .ARE YOU SURE THAT'S THE BEST WAY TO SELL COMPLEX TECHNOLOGY?
COULD YOU CALL BACK? WE HAVE A BAD STRING.
1/31/01

I'm always looking for the ultimate exaggeration. Spitting at a product until dying of dehydration is one of my better efforts.

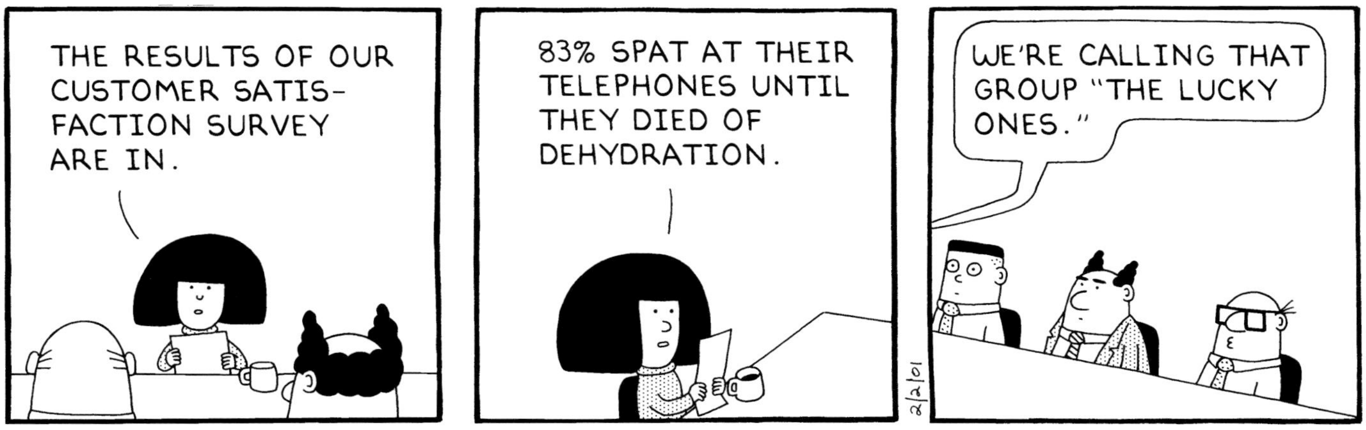
THE RESULTS OF OUR CUSTOMER SATIS-FACTION SURVEY ARE IN.
83% SPAT AT THEIR TELEPHONES UNTIL THEY DIED OF DEHYDRATION.
WE'RE CALLING THAT GROUP "THE LUCKY ONES."
2/2/01

The strip below is a humor-writing trick I use a lot: having people act opposite of how they are supposed to act. In this case, the sales department is supposed to be polite. I just reversed it, and added a few extras.

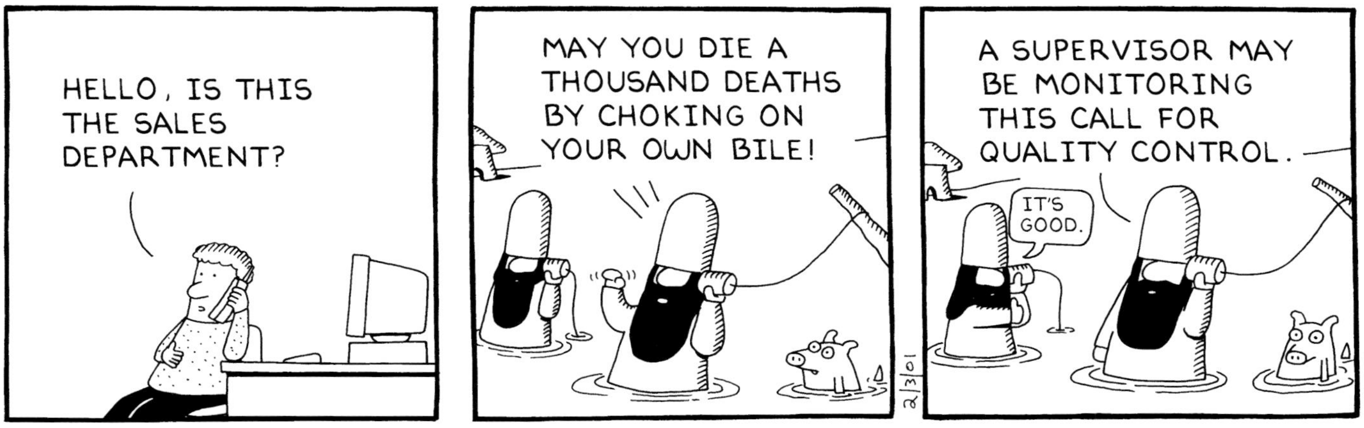
HELLO, IS THIS THE SALES DEPARTMENT?
MAY YOU DIE A THOUSAND DEATHS BY CHOKING ON YOUR OWN BILE!
A SUPERVISOR MAY BE MONITORING THIS CALL FOR QUALITY CONTROL.
IT'S GOOD.
2/3/01

I try to use characters to represent concepts. Writing about a concept without the image to represent it wouldn't be engaging.

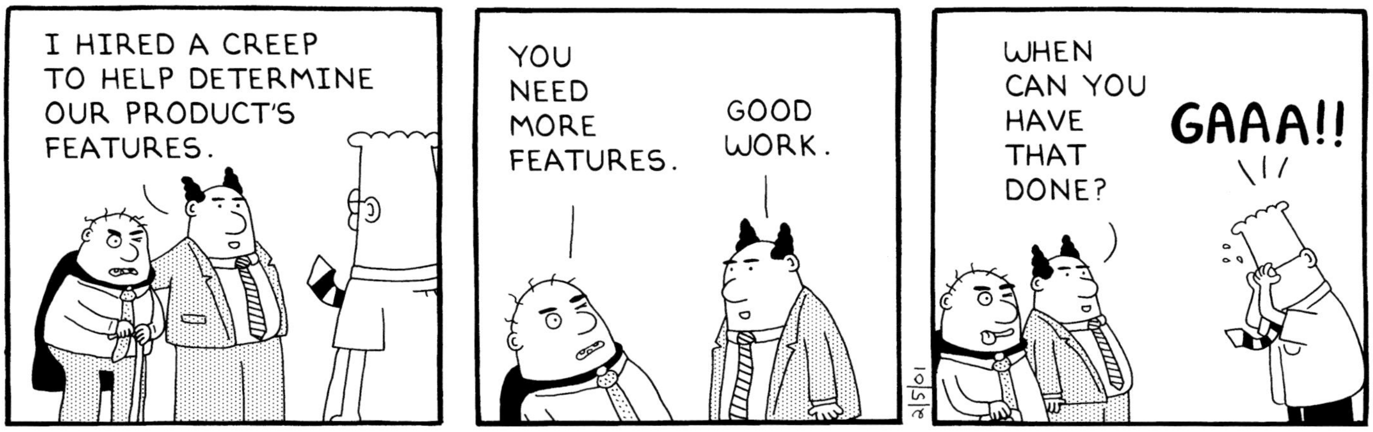
I HIRED A CREEP TO HELP DETERMINE OUR PRODUCT'S FEATURES.
YOU NEED MORE FEATURES.
GOOD WORK.
WHEN CAN YOU HAVE THAT DONE?
GAAA!!
2/5/01

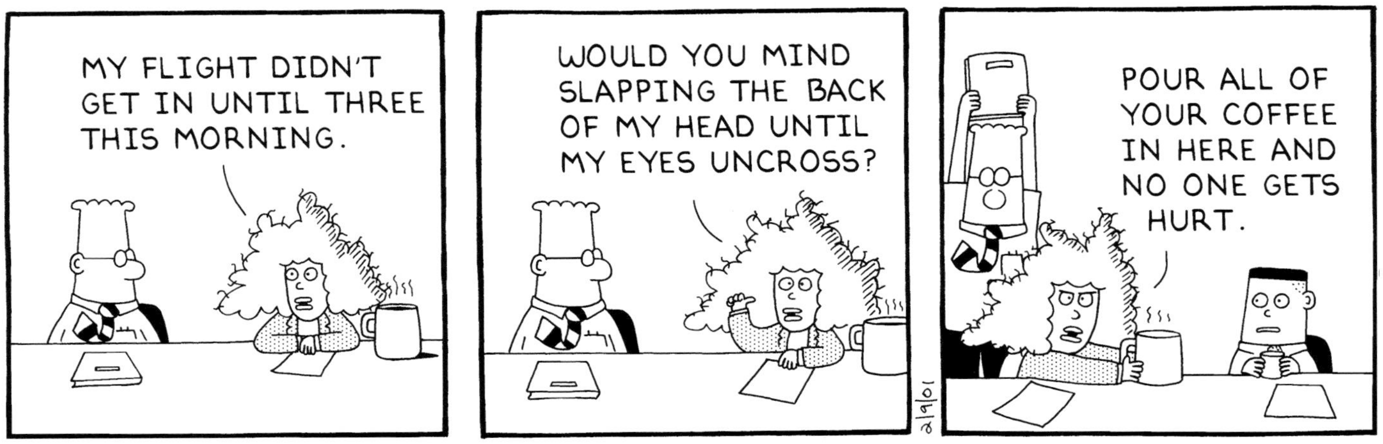
MY FLIGHT DIDN'T GET IN UNTIL THREE THIS MORNING.
WOULD YOU MIND SLAPPING THE BACK OF MY HEAD UNTIL MY EYES UNCROSS?
2/9/01
POUR ALL OF YOUR COFFEE IN HERE AND NO ONE GETS HURT.

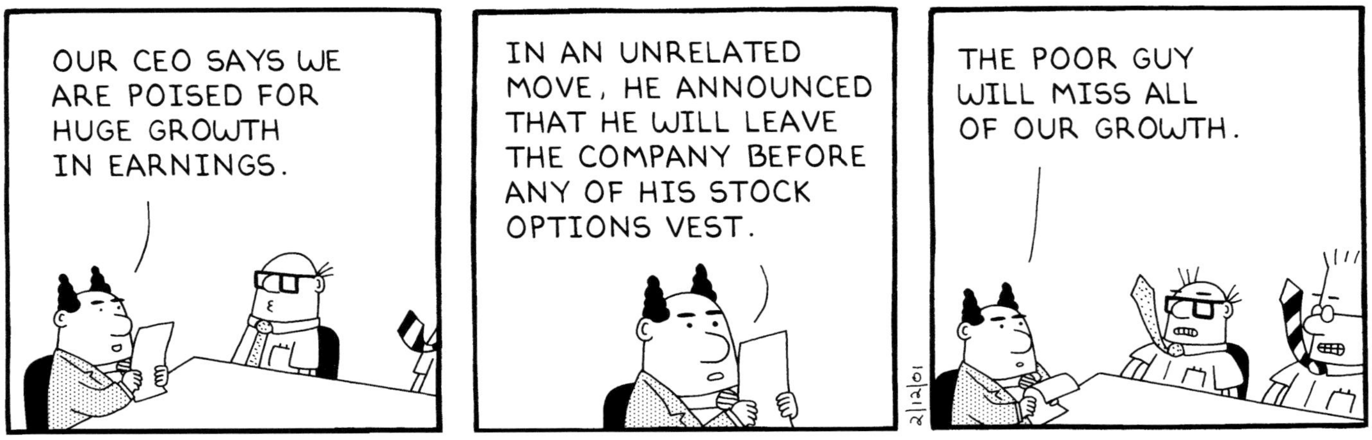
OUR CEO SAYS WE ARE POISED FOR HUGE GROWTH IN EARNINGS.
IN AN UNRELATED MOVE, HE ANNOUNCED THAT HE WILL LEAVE THE COMPANY BEFORE ANY OF HIS STOCK OPTIONS VEST.
2/12/01
THE POOR GUY WILL MISS ALL OF OUR GROWTH.

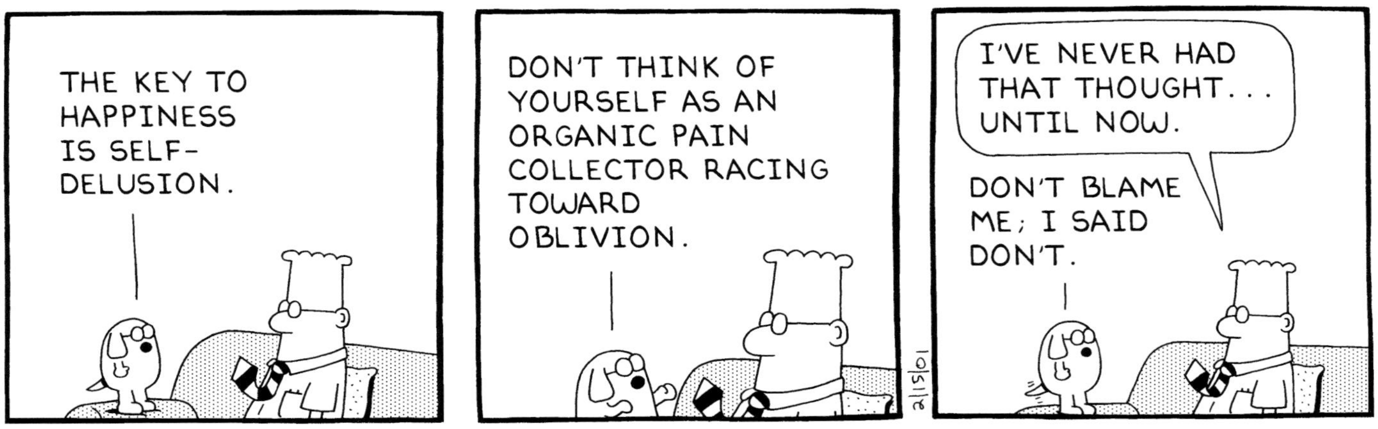
THE KEY TO HAPPINESS IS SELF-DELUSION.
DON'T THINK OF YOURSELF AS AN ORGANIC PAIN COLLECTOR RACING TOWARD OBLIVION.
2/15/01
I'VE NEVER HAD THAT THOUGHT... UNTIL NOW.
DON'T BLAME ME; I SAID DON'T.

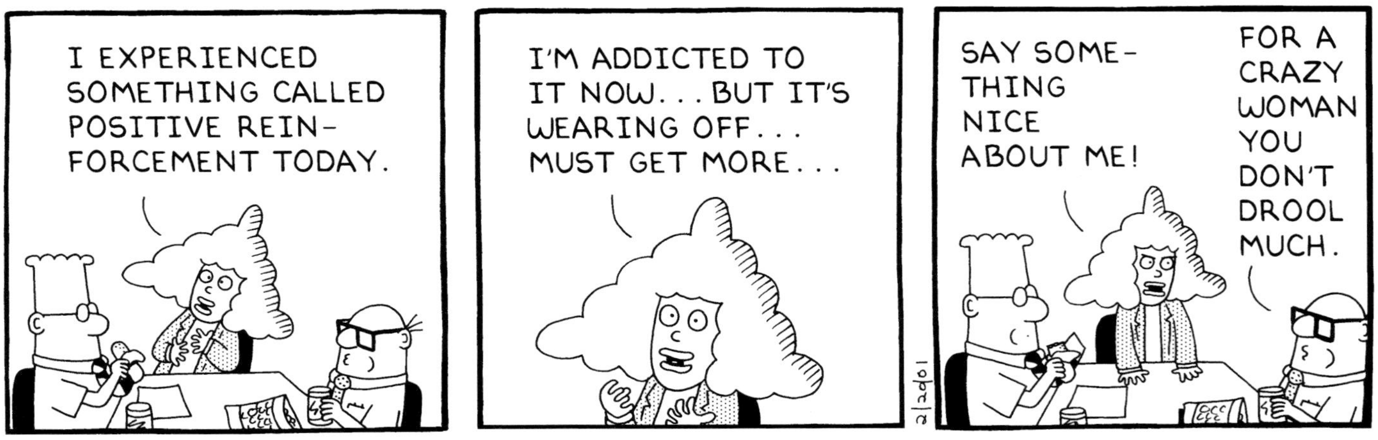
I EXPERIENCED SOMETHING CALLED POSITIVE REIN-FORCEMENT TODAY.
I'M ADDICTED TO IT NOW... BUT IT'S WEARING OFF... MUST GET MORE...
2/20/01
SAY SOME-THING NICE ABOUT ME!
FOR A CRAZY WOMAN YOU DON'T DROOL MUCH.

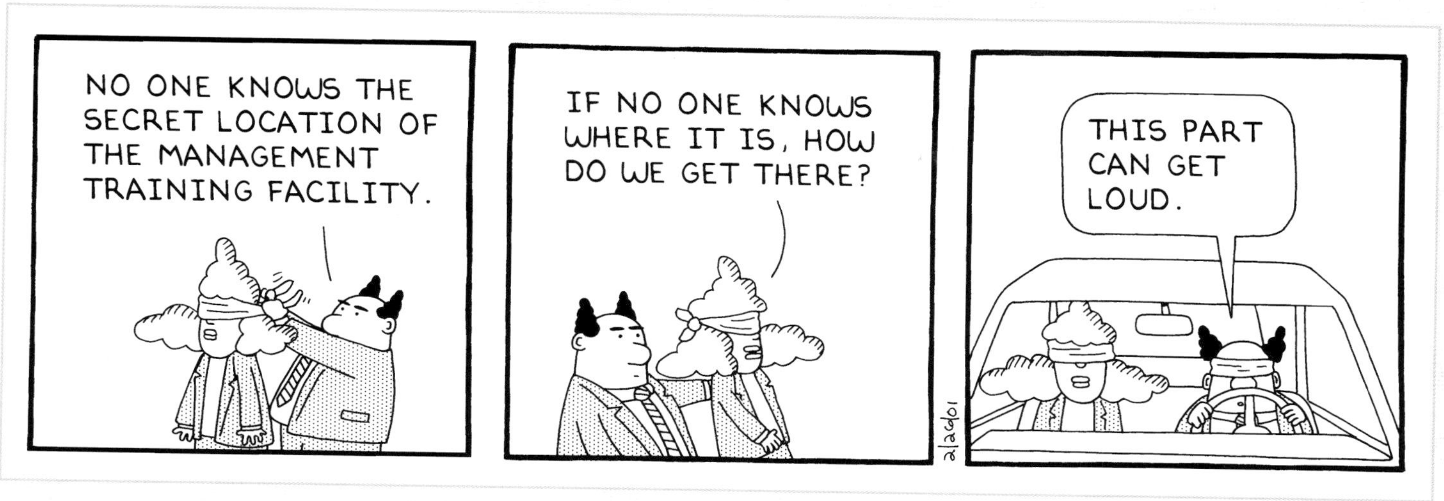
NO ONE KNOWS THE SECRET LOCATION OF THE MANAGEMENT TRAINING FACILITY.
IF NO ONE KNOWS WHERE IT IS, HOW DO WE GET THERE?
THIS PART CAN GET LOUD.
2/26/01

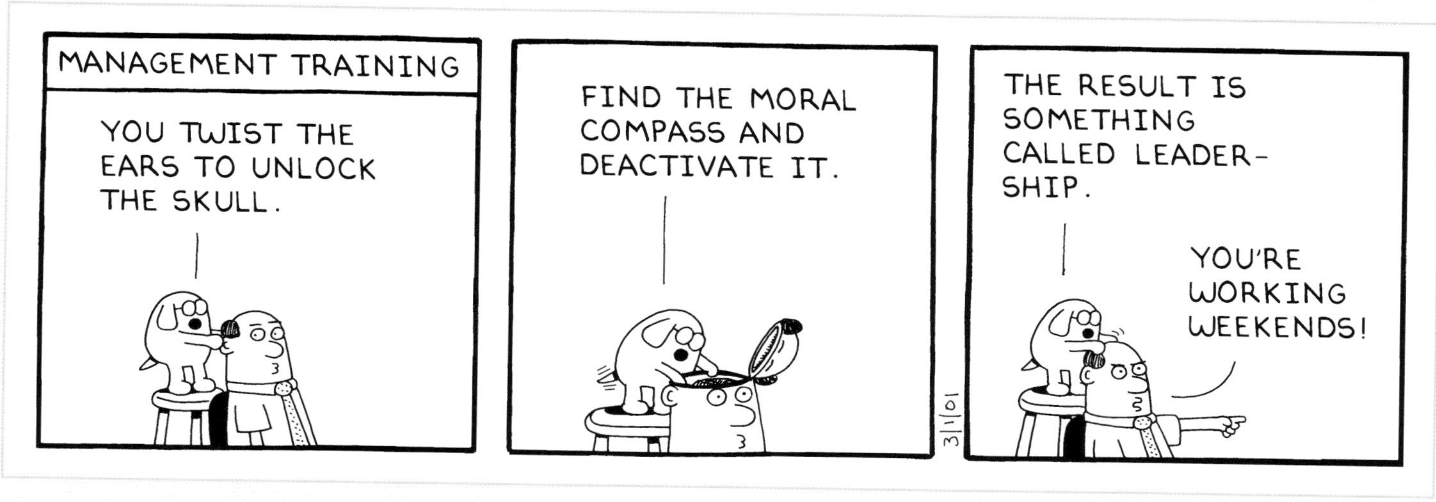
MANAGEMENT TRAINING
YOU TWIST THE EARS TO UNLOCK THE SKULL.
FIND THE MORAL COMPASS AND DEACTIVATE IT.
THE RESULT IS SOMETHING CALLED LEADER-SHIP.
YOU'RE WORKING WEEKENDS!
3/1/01

One of the first decisions a cartoonist has to make is the degree to which characters will violate natural laws. I decided that in Dilbert, *anything would be possible.*

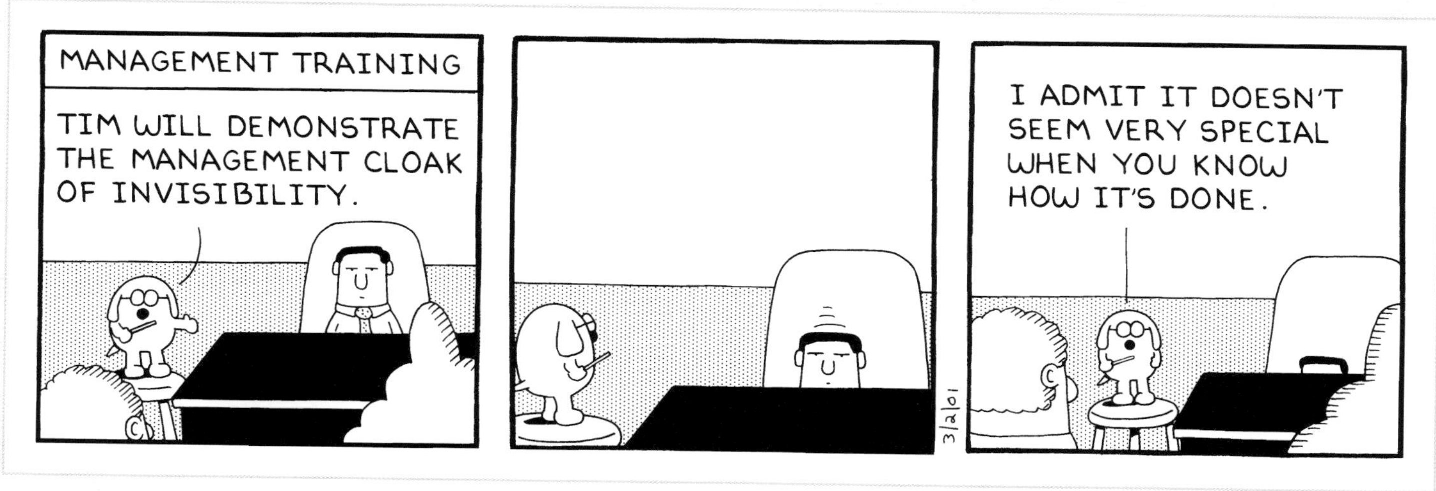
MANAGEMENT TRAINING
TIM WILL DEMONSTRATE THE MANAGEMENT CLOAK OF INVISIBILITY.
I ADMIT IT DOESN'T SEEM VERY SPECIAL WHEN YOU KNOW HOW IT'S DONE.
3/2/01

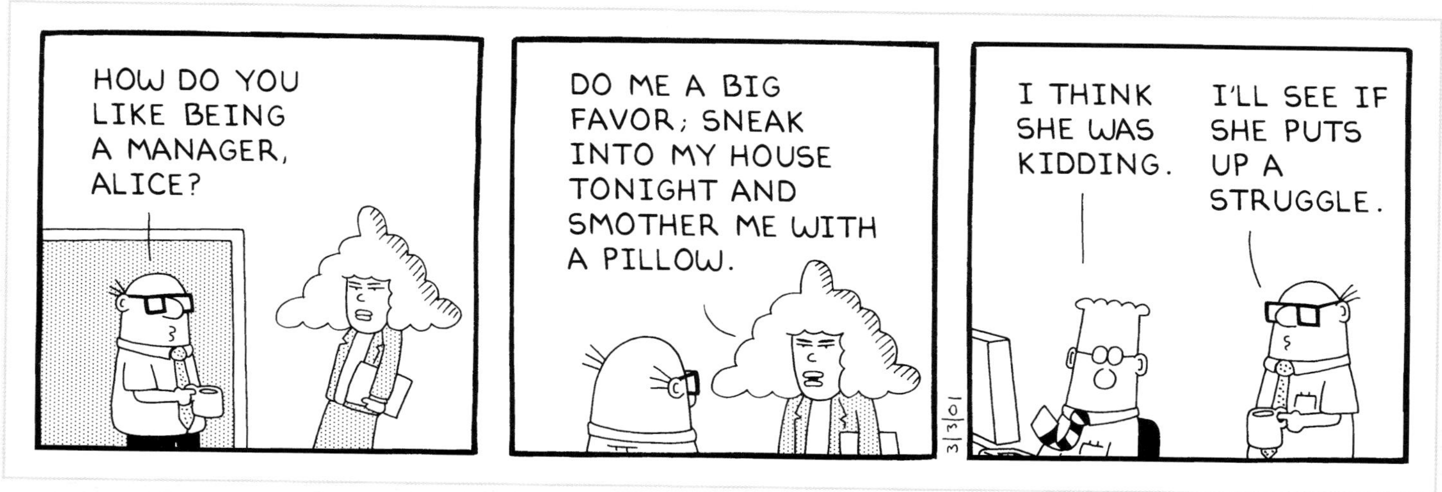
HOW DO YOU LIKE BEING A MANAGER, ALICE?
DO ME A BIG FAVOR; SNEAK INTO MY HOUSE TONIGHT AND SMOTHER ME WITH A PILLOW.
I THINK SHE WAS KIDDING.
I'LL SEE IF SHE PUTS UP A STRUGGLE.
3/3/01

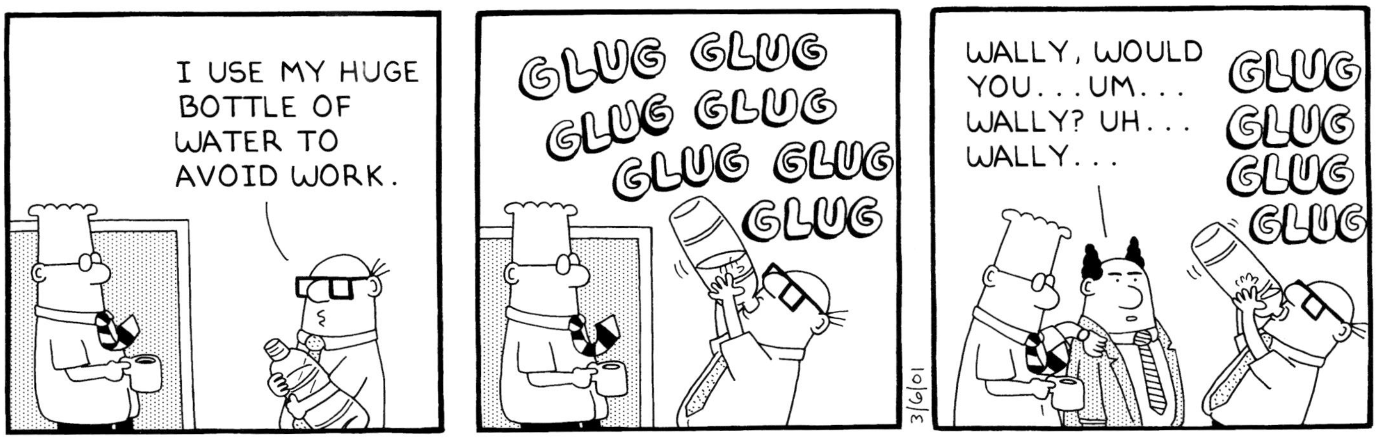
I USE MY HUGE BOTTLE OF WATER TO AVOID WORK.
GLUG GLUG GLUG GLUG GLUG GLUG GLUG
3/6/01
WALLY, WOULD YOU...UM... WALLY? UH... WALLY...
GLUG GLUG GLUG GLUG

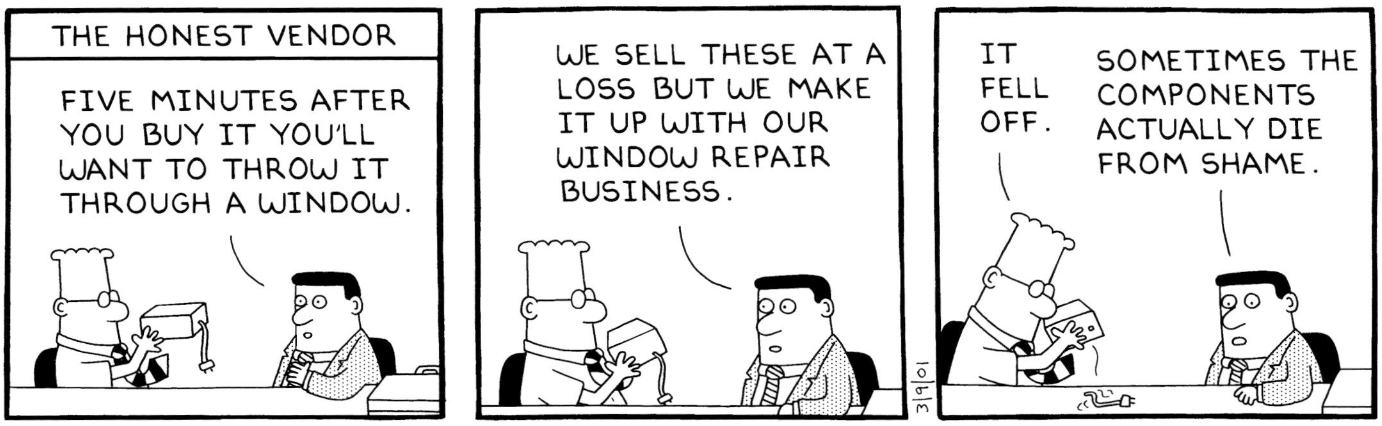
THE HONEST VENDOR
FIVE MINUTES AFTER YOU BUY IT YOU'LL WANT TO THROW IT THROUGH A WINDOW.
WE SELL THESE AT A LOSS BUT WE MAKE IT UP WITH OUR WINDOW REPAIR BUSINESS.
3/9/01
IT FELL OFF.
SOMETIMES THE COMPONENTS ACTUALLY DIE FROM SHAME.

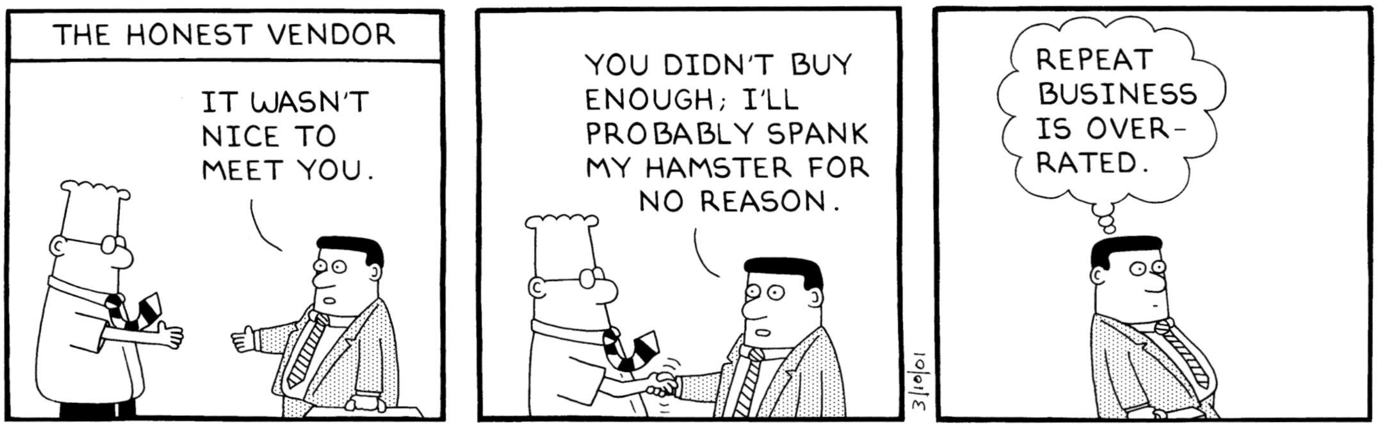
THE HONEST VENDOR
IT WASN'T NICE TO MEET YOU.
YOU DIDN'T BUY ENOUGH; I'LL PROBABLY SPANK MY HAMSTER FOR NO REASON.
3/10/01
REPEAT BUSINESS IS OVER-RATED.

Spank his hamster. Heh heh.

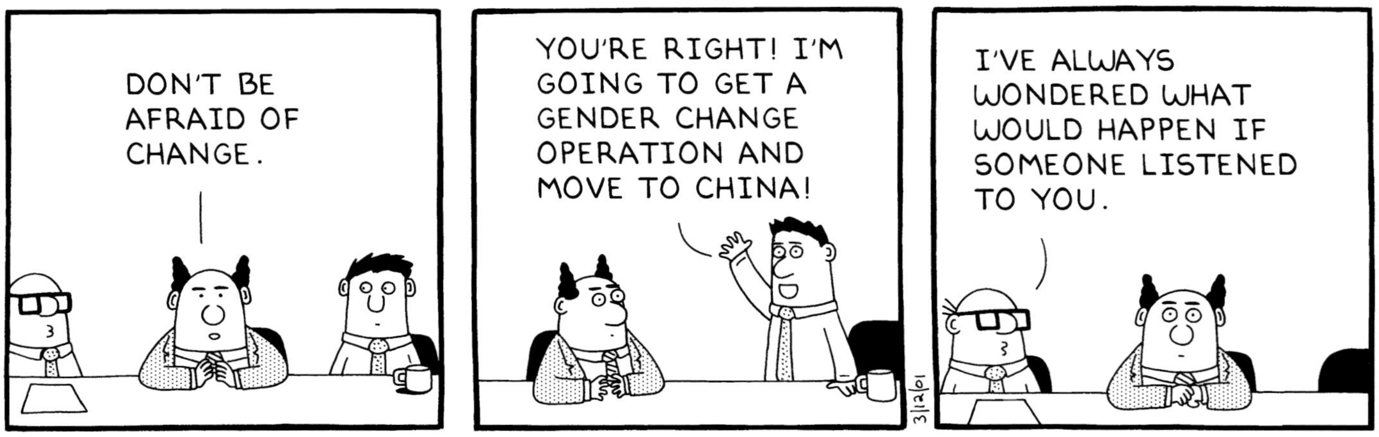
DON'T BE AFRAID OF CHANGE.
YOU'RE RIGHT! I'M GOING TO GET A GENDER CHANGE OPERATION AND MOVE TO CHINA!
3/12/01
I'VE ALWAYS WONDERED WHAT WOULD HAPPEN IF SOMEONE LISTENED TO YOU.

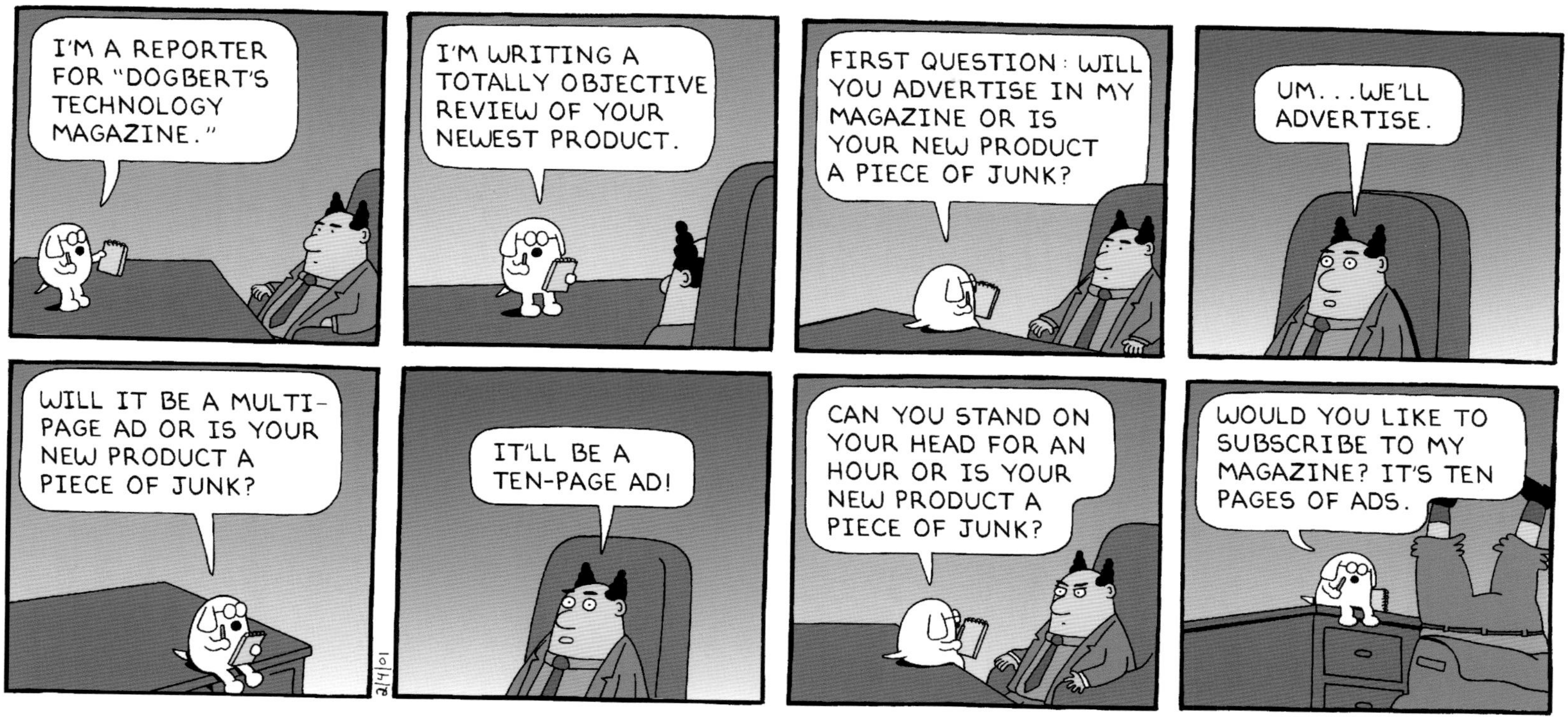

I'M A REPORTER FOR "DOGBERT'S TECHNOLOGY MAGAZINE."
I'M WRITING A TOTALLY OBJECTIVE REVIEW OF YOUR NEWEST PRODUCT.
FIRST QUESTION: WILL YOU ADVERTISE IN MY MAGAZINE OR IS YOUR NEW PRODUCT A PIECE OF JUNK?
UM. . . WE'LL ADVERTISE.
WILL IT BE A MULTI-PAGE AD OR IS YOUR NEW PRODUCT A PIECE OF JUNK?
2/4/01
IT'LL BE A TEN-PAGE AD!
CAN YOU STAND ON YOUR HEAD FOR AN HOUR OR IS YOUR NEW PRODUCT A PIECE OF JUNK?
WOULD YOU LIKE TO SUBSCRIBE TO MY MAGAZINE? IT'S TEN PAGES OF ADS.

This is another humor-writing trick: confirming your most cynical suspicions.

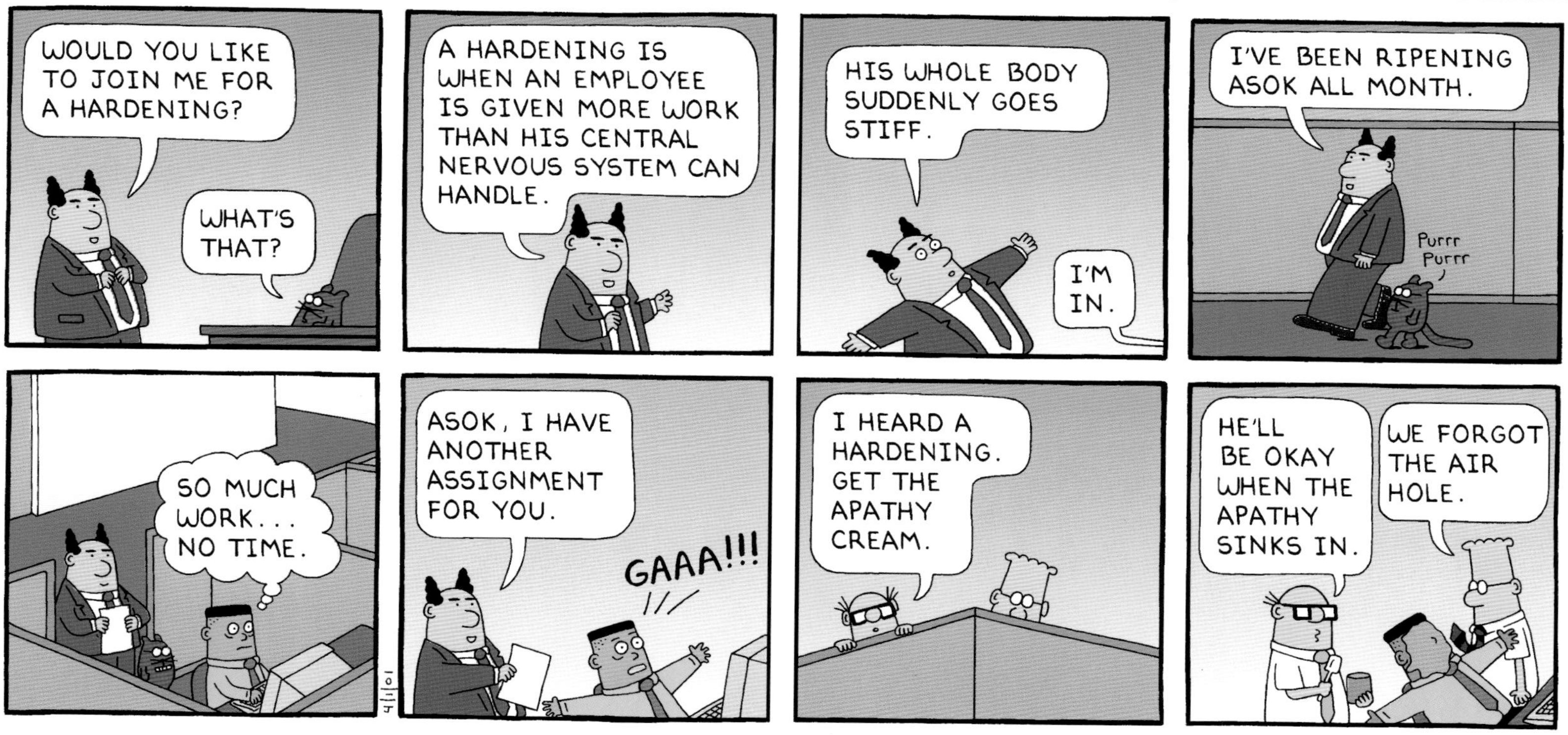

WOULD YOU LIKE TO JOIN ME FOR A HARDENING?
WHAT'S THAT?
A HARDENING IS WHEN AN EMPLOYEE IS GIVEN MORE WORK THAN HIS CENTRAL NERVOUS SYSTEM CAN HANDLE.
HIS WHOLE BODY SUDDENLY GOES STIFF.
I'M IN.
I'VE BEEN RIPENING ASOK ALL MONTH.
Purrr Purrr
SO MUCH WORK. . . NO TIME.
4/1/01
ASOK, I HAVE ANOTHER ASSIGNMENT FOR YOU.
GAAA!!!
I HEARD A HARDENING. GET THE APATHY CREAM.
HE'LL BE OKAY WHEN THE APATHY SINKS IN.
WE FORGOT THE AIR HOLE.

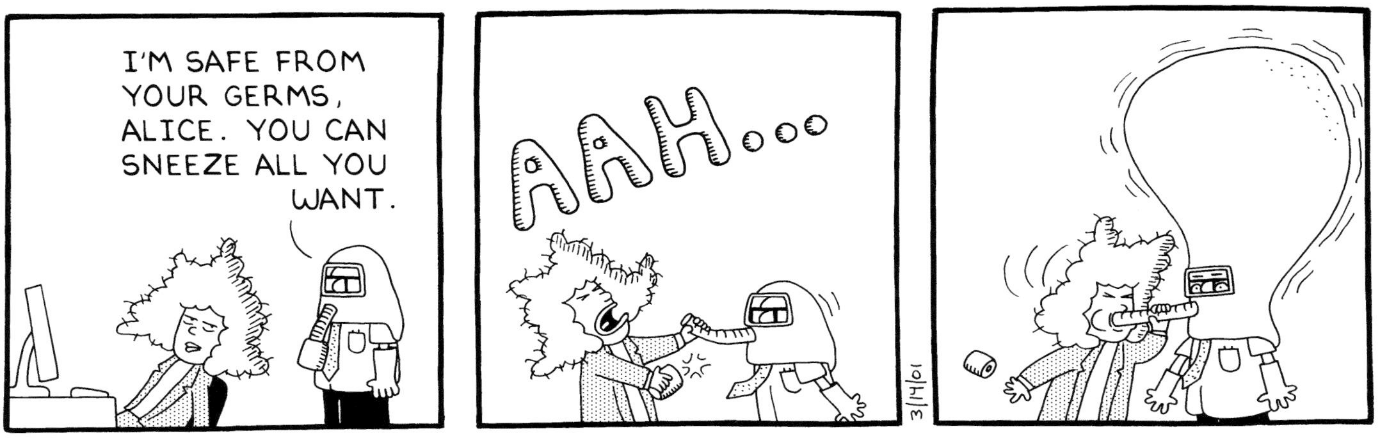
I'M SAFE FROM YOUR GERMS, ALICE. YOU CAN SNEEZE ALL YOU WANT.
AAH...
3/14/01

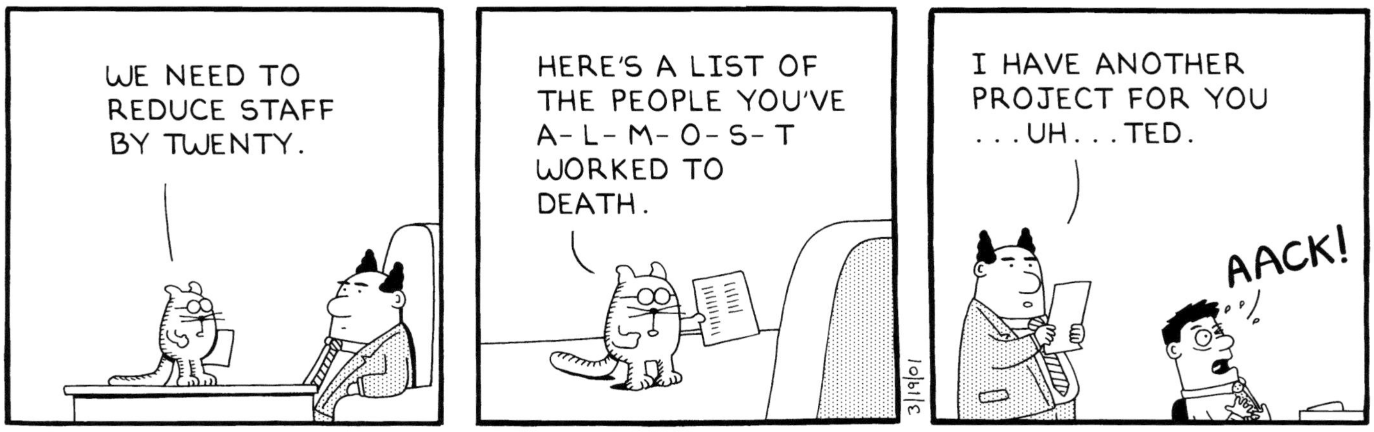
WE NEED TO REDUCE STAFF BY TWENTY.
HERE'S A LIST OF THE PEOPLE YOU'VE A-L-M-O-S-T WORKED TO DEATH.
3/19/01
I HAVE ANOTHER PROJECT FOR YOU ...UH...TED.
AACK!

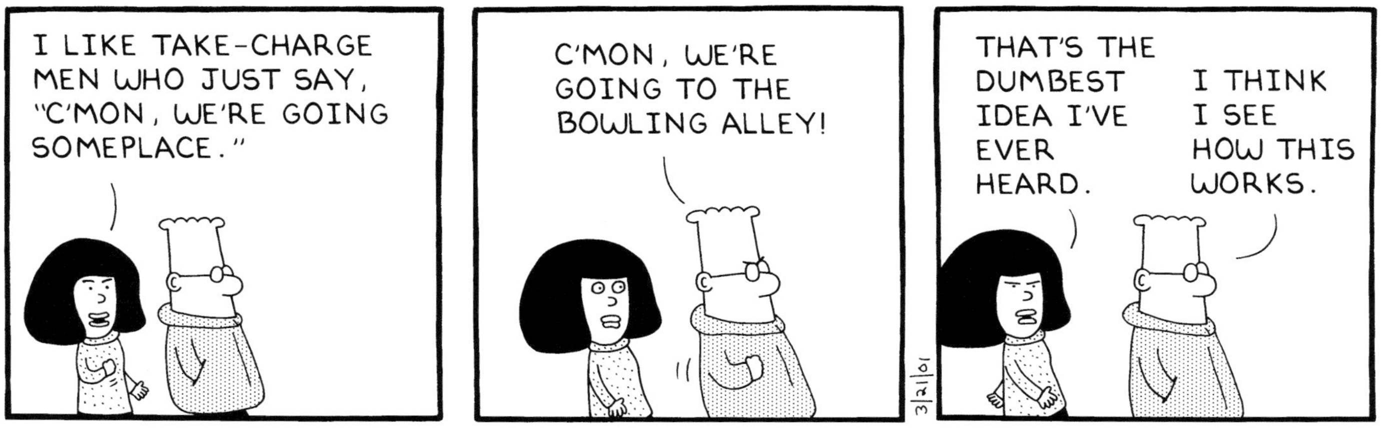
I LIKE TAKE-CHARGE MEN WHO JUST SAY, "C'MON, WE'RE GOING SOMEPLACE."
C'MON, WE'RE GOING TO THE BOWLING ALLEY!
3/21/01
THAT'S THE DUMBEST IDEA I'VE EVER HEARD.
I THINK I SEE HOW THIS WORKS.

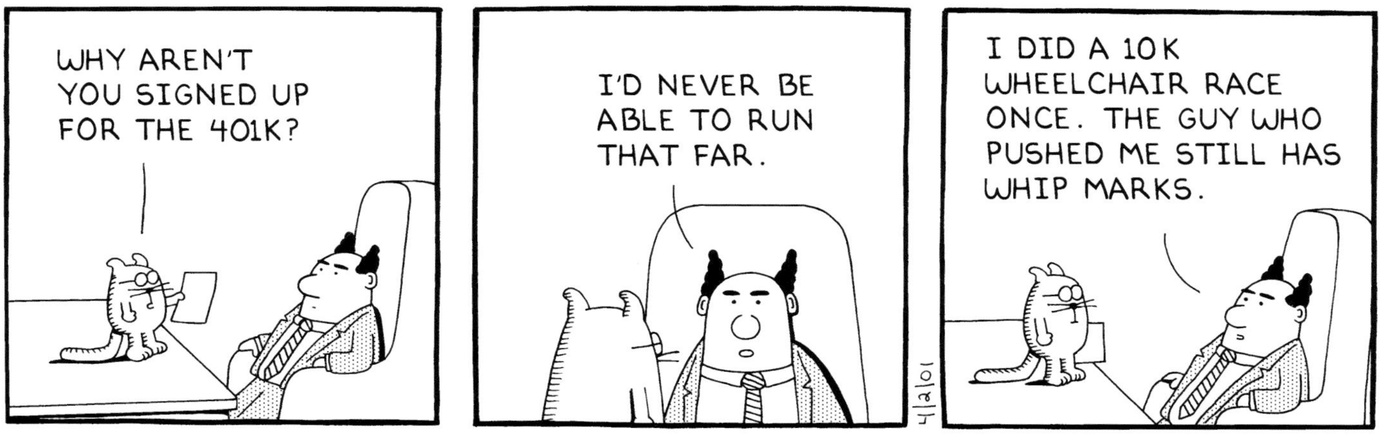
WHY AREN'T YOU SIGNED UP FOR THE 401K?
I'D NEVER BE ABLE TO RUN THAT FAR.
4/2/01
I DID A 10K WHEELCHAIR RACE ONCE. THE GUY WHO PUSHED ME STILL HAS WHIP MARKS.

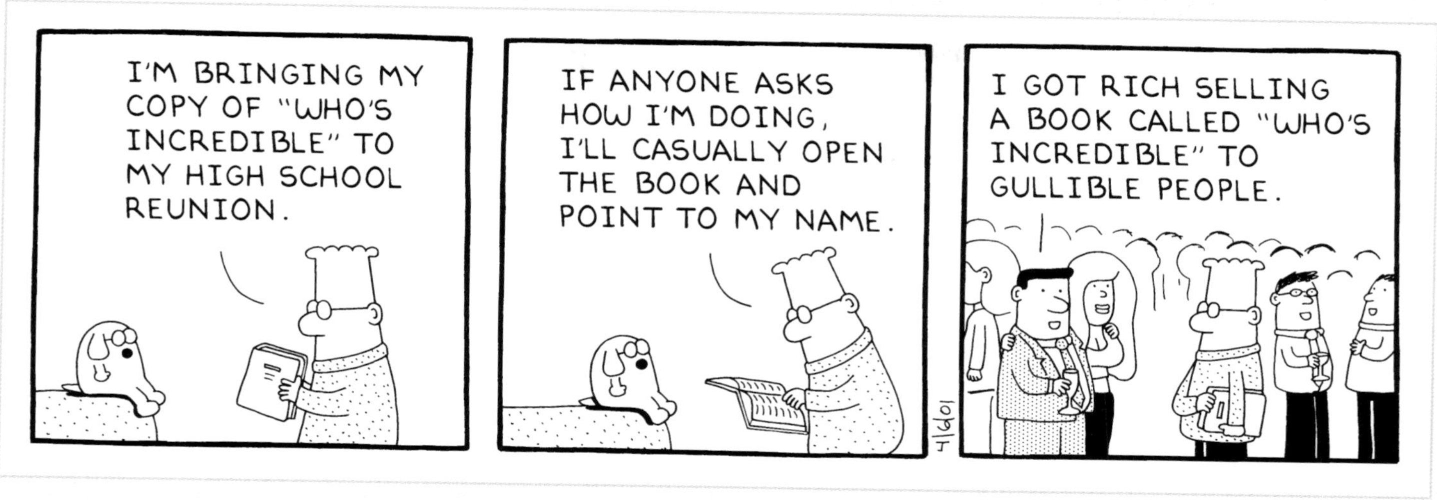
I'M BRINGING MY COPY OF "WHO'S INCREDIBLE" TO MY HIGH SCHOOL REUNION.
IF ANYONE ASKS HOW I'M DOING, I'LL CASUALLY OPEN THE BOOK AND POINT TO MY NAME.
4/6/01
I GOT RICH SELLING A BOOK CALLED "WHO'S INCREDIBLE" TO GULLIBLE PEOPLE.

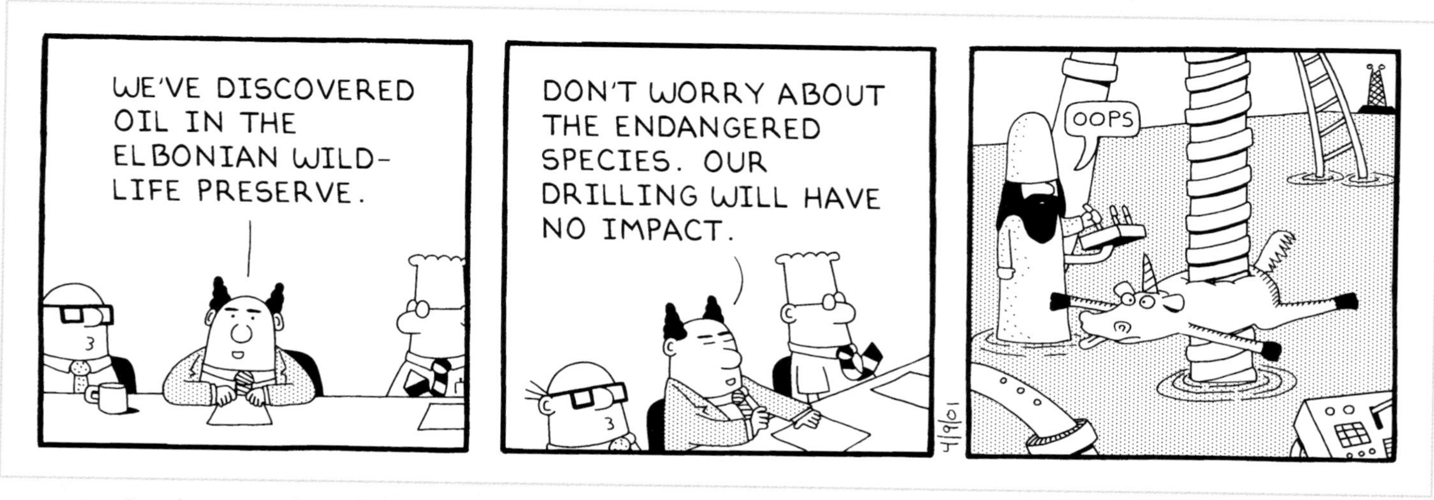
WE'VE DISCOVERED OIL IN THE ELBONIAN WILD-LIFE PRESERVE.
DON'T WORRY ABOUT THE ENDANGERED SPECIES. OUR DRILLING WILL HAVE NO IMPACT.
4/9/01
OOPS

Readers complained that I inserted my political opinions in this strip. In reality, I have no coherent political opinions. I just couldn't get the idea of a unicorn getting drilled out of my head until I drew it.

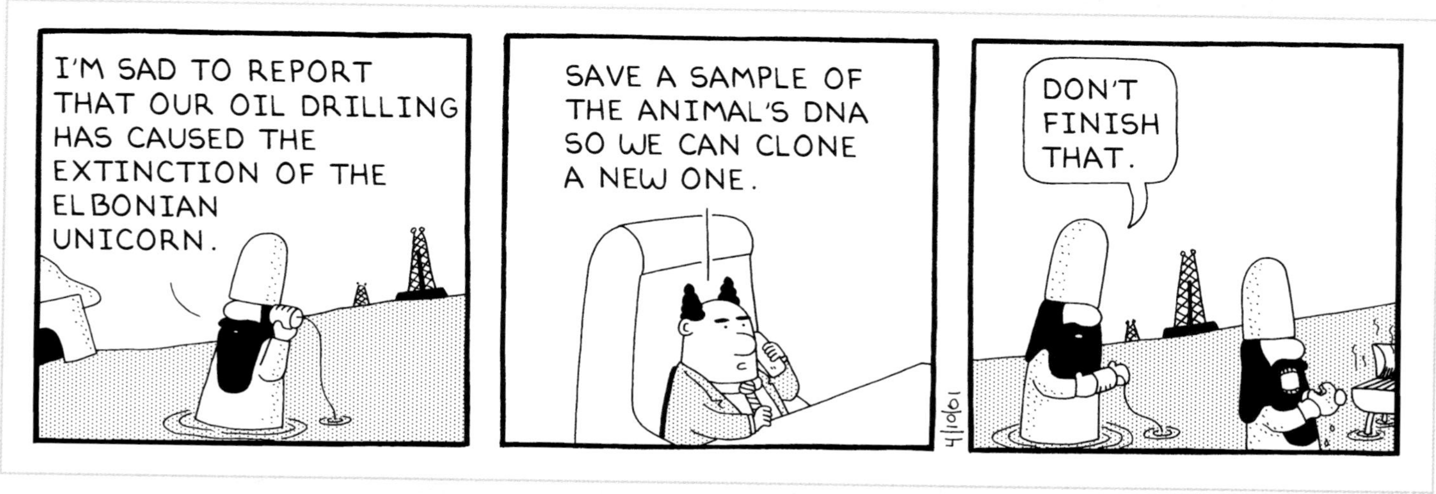
I'M SAD TO REPORT THAT OUR OIL DRILLING HAS CAUSED THE EXTINCTION OF THE ELBONIAN UNICORN.
SAVE A SAMPLE OF THE ANIMAL'S DNA SO WE CAN CLONE A NEW ONE.
4/10/01
DON'T FINISH THAT.

Few things are more satisfying than drawing a cool-looking mechanical gadget. It's what every eleven-year-old boy wants to do someday.

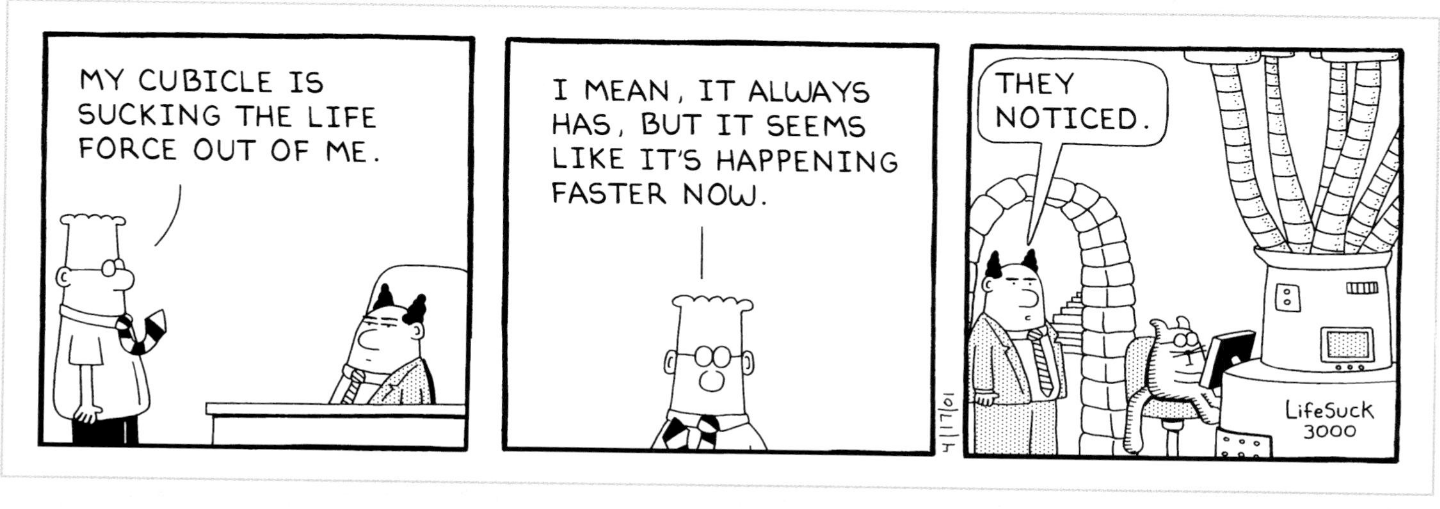
MY CUBICLE IS SUCKING THE LIFE FORCE OUT OF ME.
I MEAN, IT ALWAYS HAS, BUT IT SEEMS LIKE IT'S HAPPENING FASTER NOW.
4/11/01
THEY NOTICED.
LifeSuck 3000

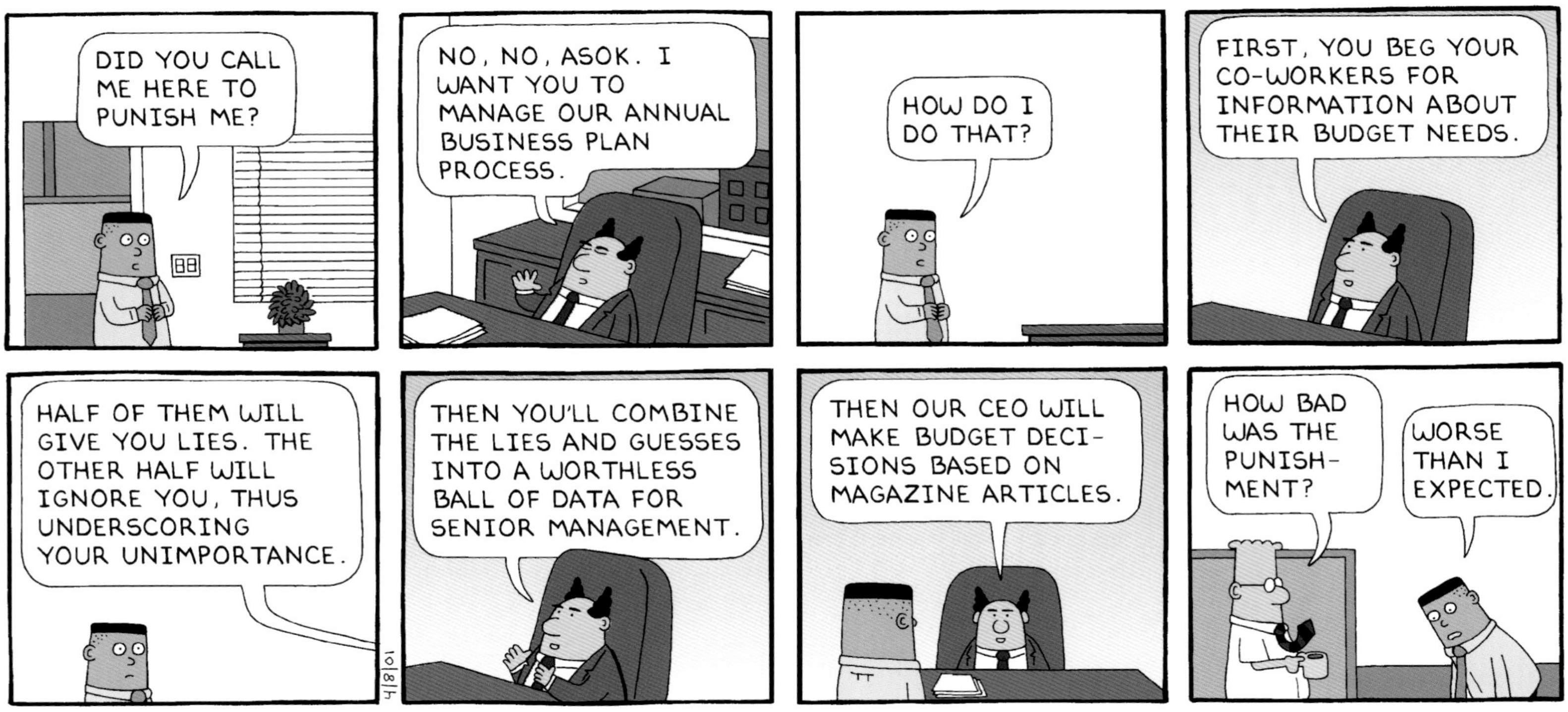
DID YOU CALL ME HERE TO PUNISH ME?
NO, NO, ASOK. I WANT YOU TO MANAGE OUR ANNUAL BUSINESS PLAN PROCESS.
HOW DO I DO THAT?
FIRST, YOU BEG YOUR CO-WORKERS FOR INFORMATION ABOUT THEIR BUDGET NEEDS.
HALF OF THEM WILL GIVE YOU LIES. THE OTHER HALF WILL IGNORE YOU, THUS UNDERSCORING YOUR UNIMPORTANCE.
4/8/01
THEN YOU'LL COMBINE THE LIES AND GUESSES INTO A WORTHLESS BALL OF DATA FOR SENIOR MANAGEMENT.
THEN OUR CEO WILL MAKE BUDGET DECISIONS BASED ON MAGAZINE ARTICLES.
HOW BAD WAS THE PUNISHMENT?
WORSE THAN I EXPECTED.

The dot-com era came to an abrupt end. The pendulum swung. Management had the power again, and employee dissatisfaction soared. Suddenly it became easier to write Dilbert *comics.*

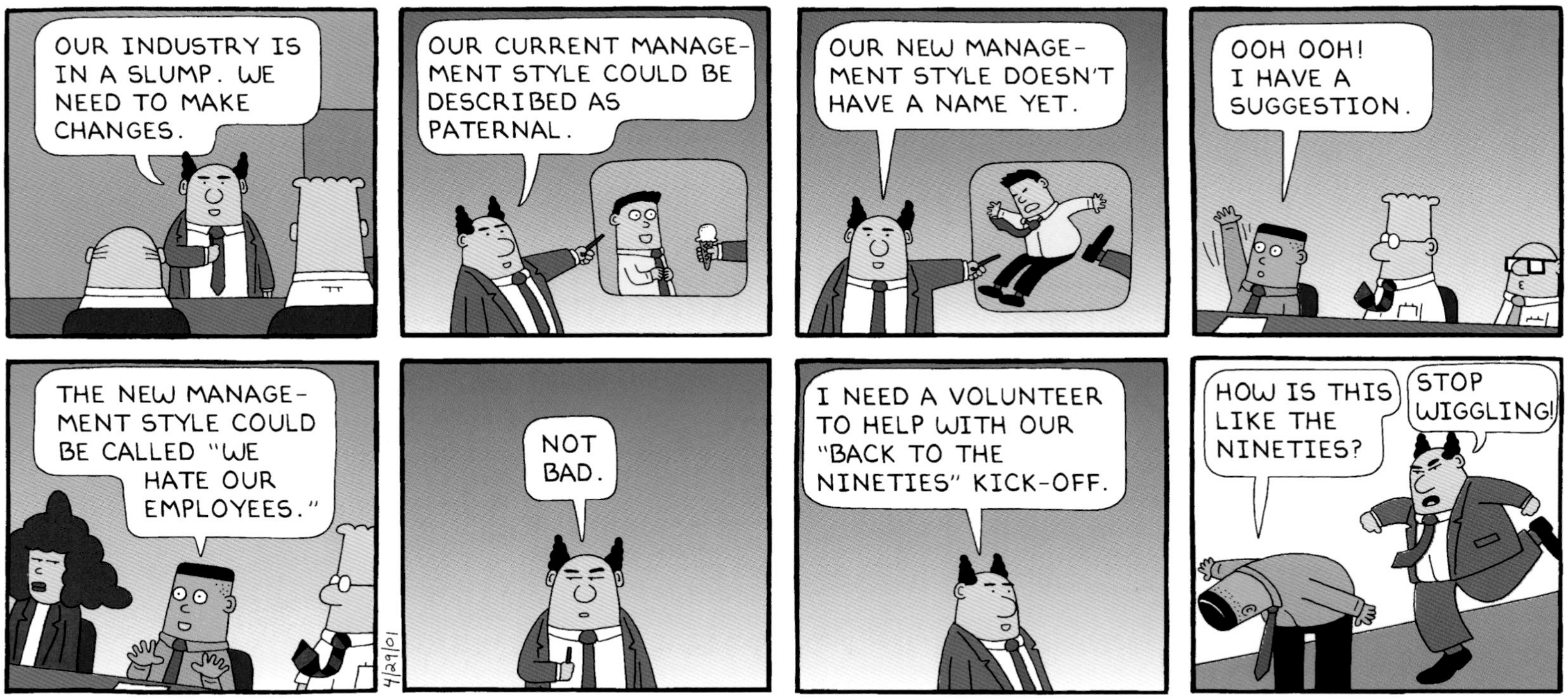
OUR INDUSTRY IS IN A SLUMP. WE NEED TO MAKE CHANGES.
OUR CURRENT MANAGEMENT STYLE COULD BE DESCRIBED AS PATERNAL.
OUR NEW MANAGEMENT STYLE DOESN'T HAVE A NAME YET.
OOH OOH! I HAVE A SUGGESTION.
THE NEW MANAGEMENT STYLE COULD BE CALLED "WE HATE OUR EMPLOYEES."
4/29/01
NOT BAD.
I NEED A VOLUNTEER TO HELP WITH OUR "BACK TO THE NINETIES" KICK-OFF.
HOW IS THIS LIKE THE NINETIES?
STOP WIGGLING!

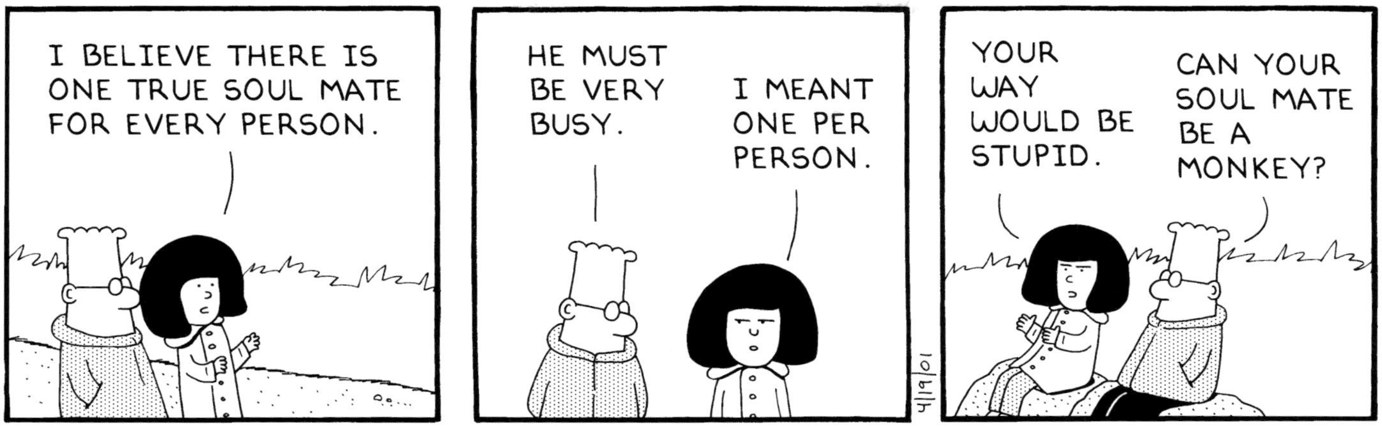
I BELIEVE THERE IS ONE TRUE SOUL MATE FOR EVERY PERSON.
HE MUST BE VERY BUSY.
I MEANT ONE PER PERSON.
YOUR WAY WOULD BE STUPID.
CAN YOUR SOUL MATE BE A MONKEY?
4/19/01

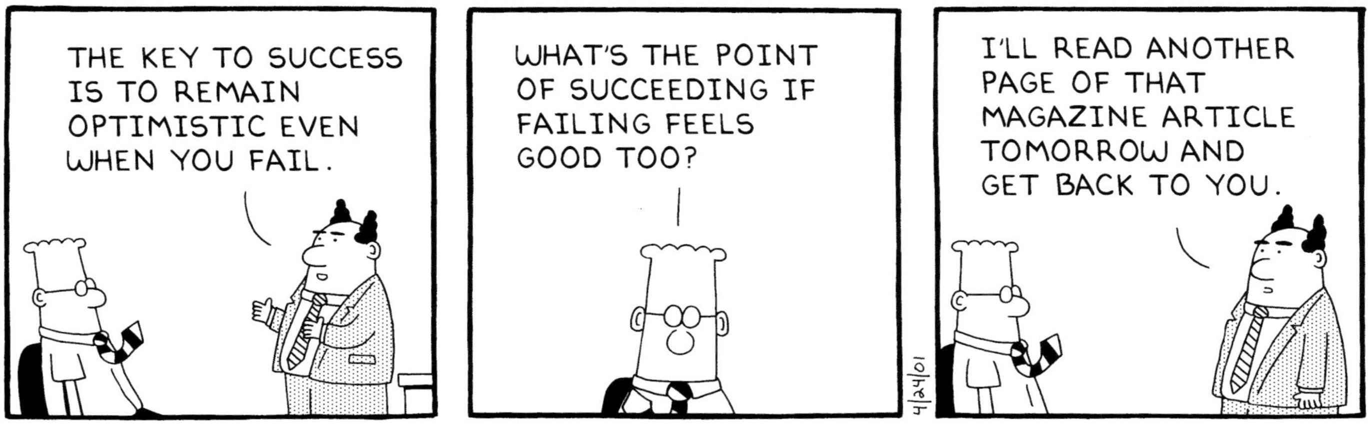
THE KEY TO SUCCESS IS TO REMAIN OPTIMISTIC EVEN WHEN YOU FAIL.
WHAT'S THE POINT OF SUCCEEDING IF FAILING FEELS GOOD TOO?
I'LL READ ANOTHER PAGE OF THAT MAGAZINE ARTICLE TOMORROW AND GET BACK TO YOU.
4/24/01

This is the sort of strip (below) that makes me think I could be a better artist if I had lots of time.

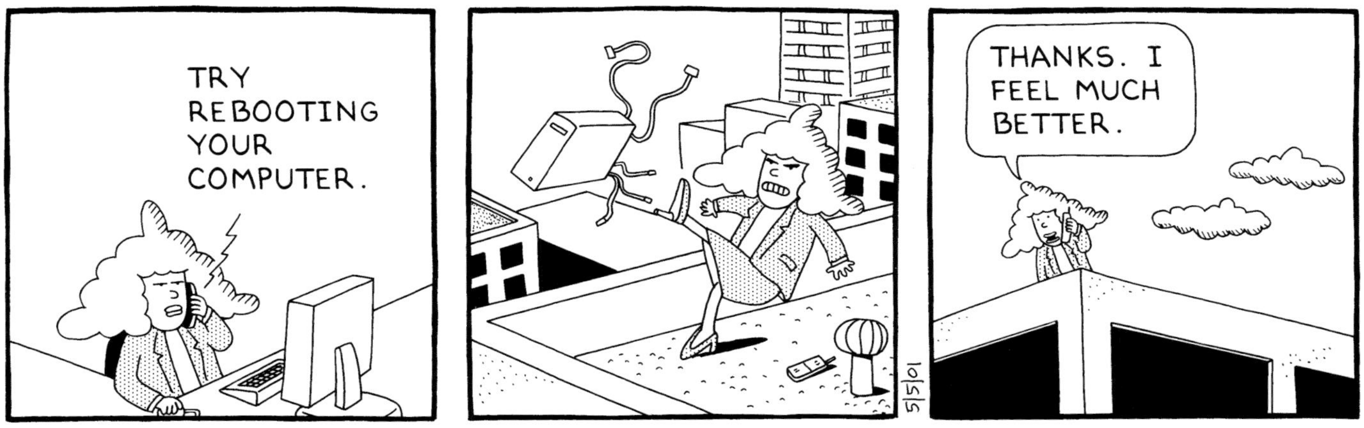
TRY REBOOTING YOUR COMPUTER.
THANKS. I FEEL MUCH BETTER.
5/5/01

When I call a tech support number, I usually get the same angry and unhelpful service as everyone else. But sometimes the tech support person recognizes my name and asks if I am the "Dilbert guy." When that happens, I get wonderful service.

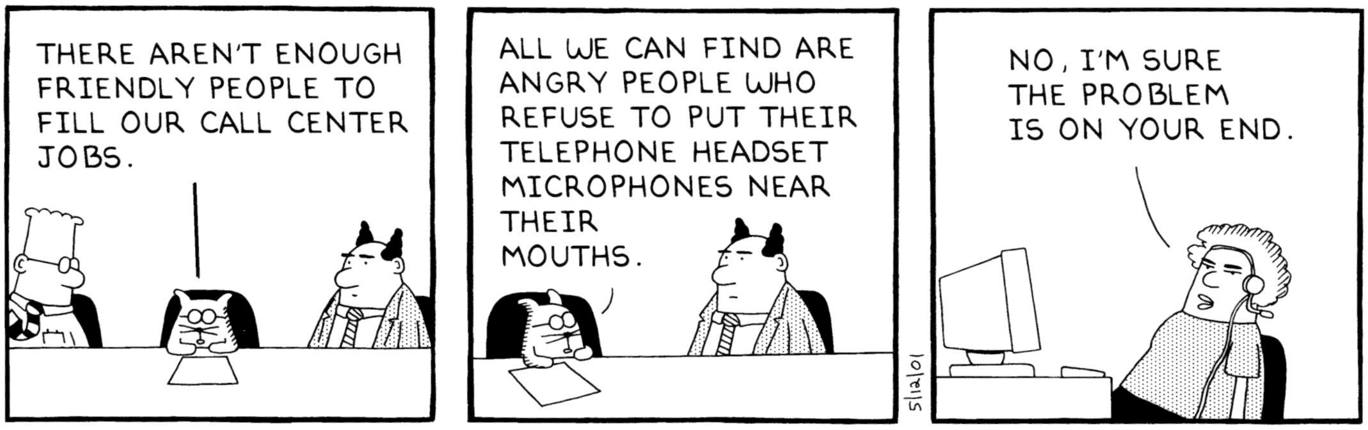
THERE AREN'T ENOUGH FRIENDLY PEOPLE TO FILL OUR CALL CENTER JOBS.
ALL WE CAN FIND ARE ANGRY PEOPLE WHO REFUSE TO PUT THEIR TELEPHONE HEADSET MICROPHONES NEAR THEIR MOUTHS.
NO, I'M SURE THE PROBLEM IS ON YOUR END.
5/12/01

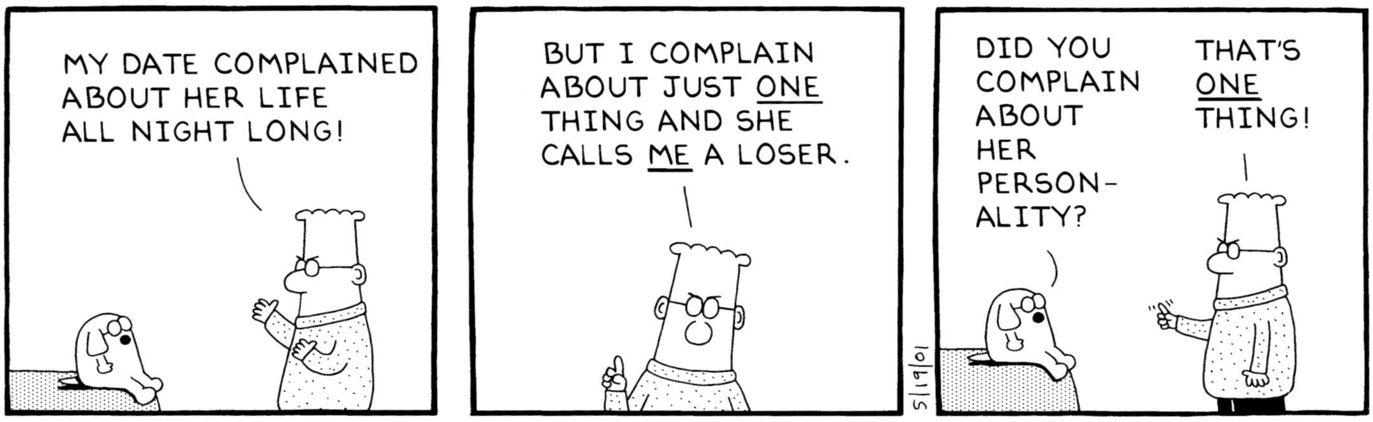
MY DATE COMPLAINED ABOUT HER LIFE ALL NIGHT LONG!
BUT I COMPLAIN ABOUT JUST ONE THING AND SHE CALLS ME A LOSER.
DID YOU COMPLAIN ABOUT HER PERSON-ALITY?
THAT'S ONE THING!
5/19/01

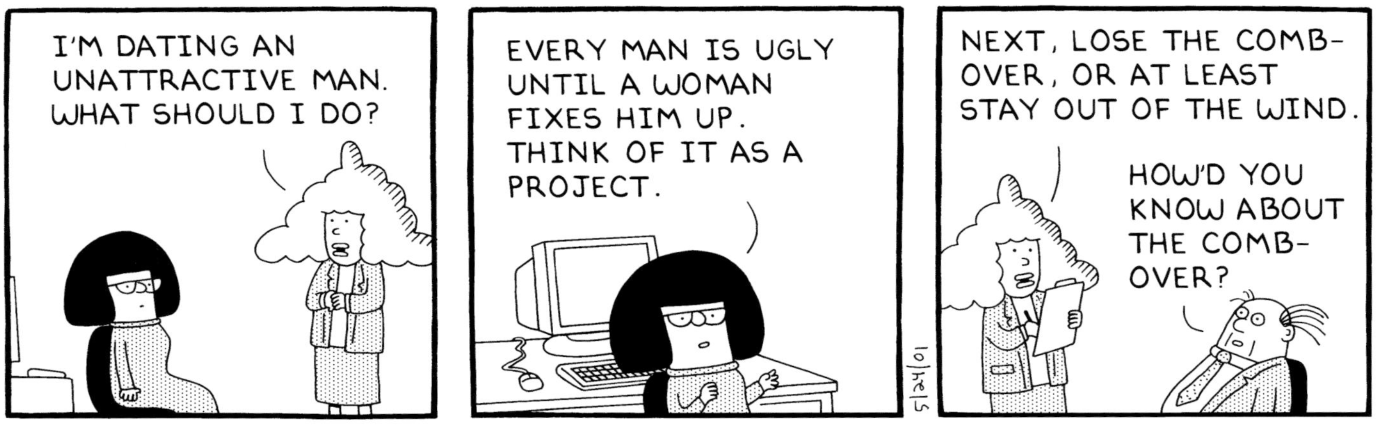
I'M DATING AN UNATTRACTIVE MAN. WHAT SHOULD I DO?
EVERY MAN IS UGLY UNTIL A WOMAN FIXES HIM UP. THINK OF IT AS A PROJECT.
NEXT, LOSE THE COMB-OVER, OR AT LEAST STAY OUT OF THE WIND.
HOW'D YOU KNOW ABOUT THE COMB-OVER?
5/24/01

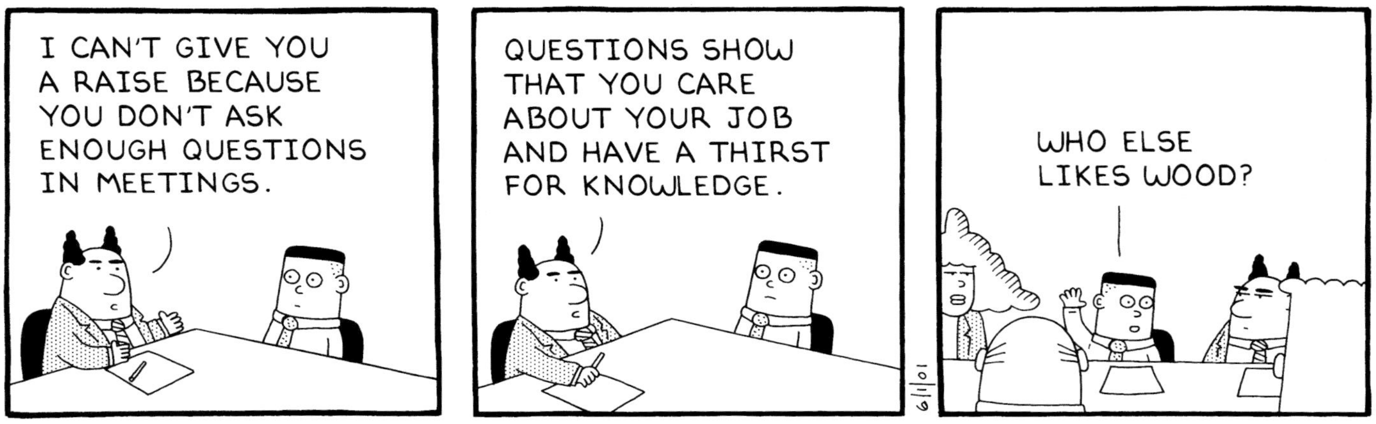
I CAN'T GIVE YOU A RAISE BECAUSE YOU DON'T ASK ENOUGH QUESTIONS IN MEETINGS.
QUESTIONS SHOW THAT YOU CARE ABOUT YOUR JOB AND HAVE A THIRST FOR KNOWLEDGE.
WHO ELSE LIKES WOOD?
6/1/01

Sometimes randomness is funny to me. But I might be alone in that.

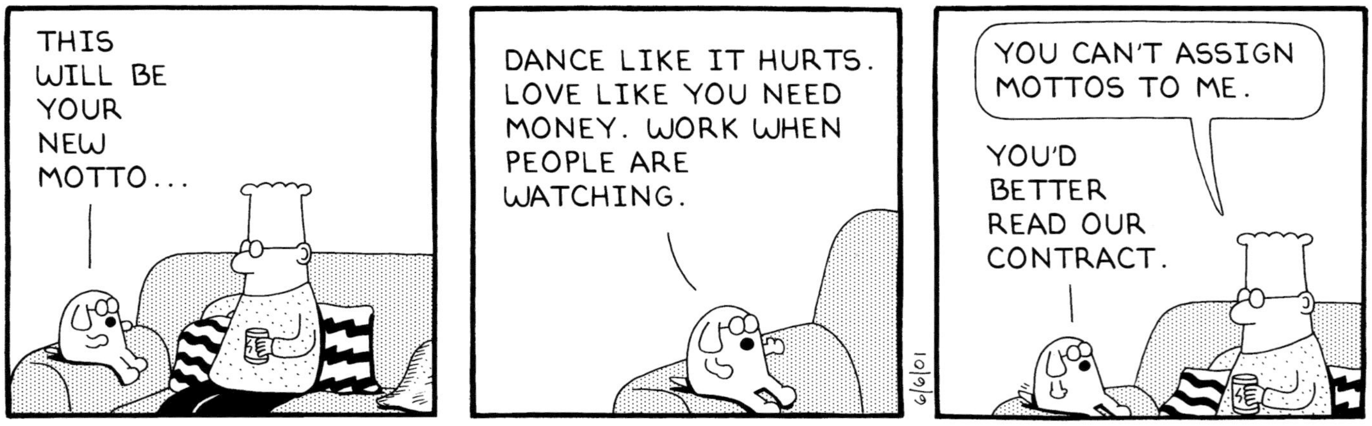
THIS WILL BE YOUR NEW MOTTO...
DANCE LIKE IT HURTS. LOVE LIKE YOU NEED MONEY. WORK WHEN PEOPLE ARE WATCHING.
YOU CAN'T ASSIGN MOTTOS TO ME.
YOU'D BETTER READ OUR CONTRACT.
6/6/01

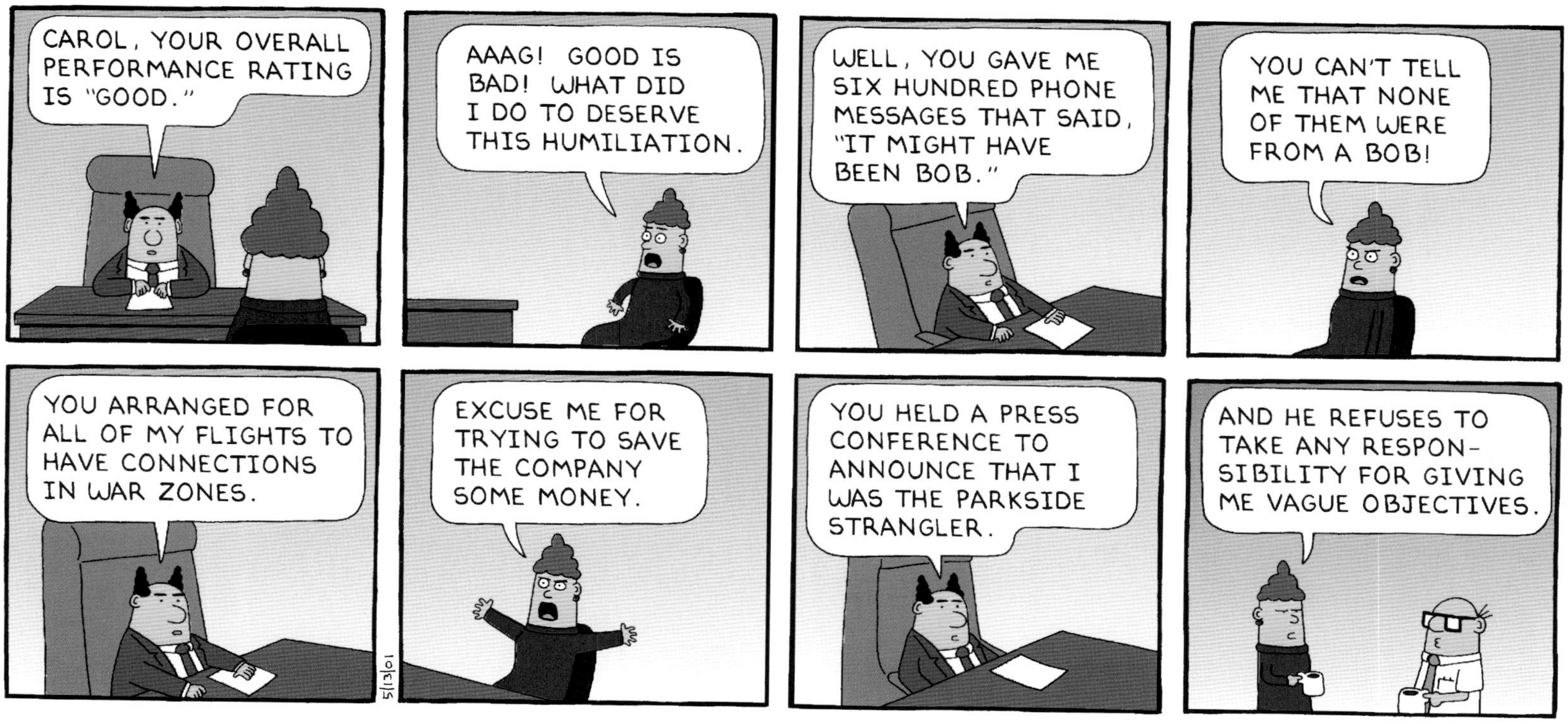
CAROL, YOUR OVERALL PERFORMANCE RATING IS "GOOD."
AAAG! GOOD IS BAD! WHAT DID I DO TO DESERVE THIS HUMILIATION.
WELL, YOU GAVE ME SIX HUNDRED PHONE MESSAGES THAT SAID, "IT MIGHT HAVE BEEN BOB."
YOU CAN'T TELL ME THAT NONE OF THEM WERE FROM A BOB!
YOU ARRANGED FOR ALL OF MY FLIGHTS TO HAVE CONNECTIONS IN WAR ZONES.
EXCUSE ME FOR TRYING TO SAVE THE COMPANY SOME MONEY.
YOU HELD A PRESS CONFERENCE TO ANNOUNCE THAT I WAS THE PARKSIDE STRANGLER.
AND HE REFUSES TO TAKE ANY RESPON-SIBILITY FOR GIVING ME VAGUE OBJECTIVES.

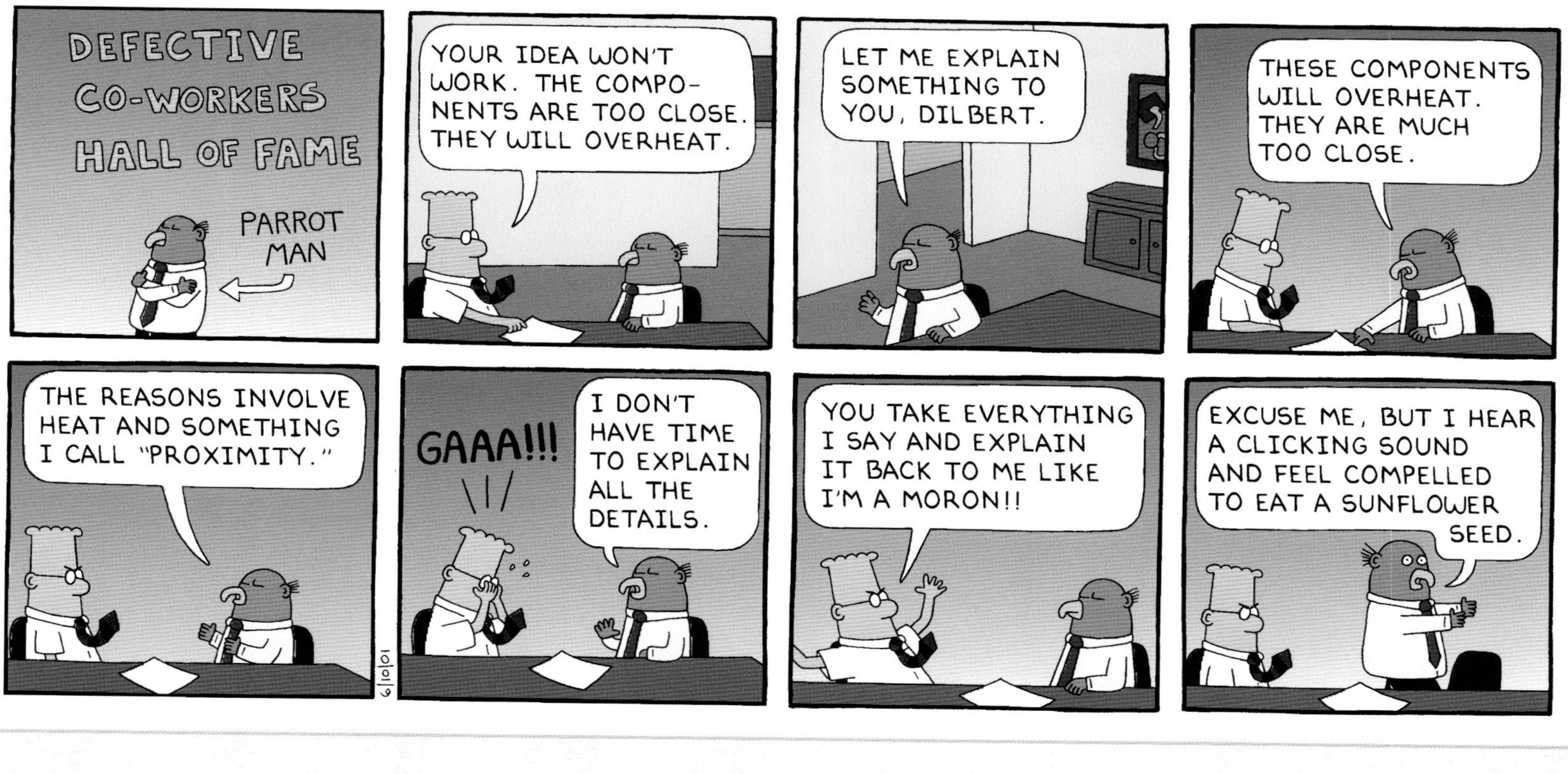
DEFECTIVE CO-WORKERS HALL OF FAME
PARROT MAN
YOUR IDEA WON'T WORK. THE COMPO-NENTS ARE TOO CLOSE. THEY WILL OVERHEAT.
LET ME EXPLAIN SOMETHING TO YOU, DILBERT.
THESE COMPONENTS WILL OVERHEAT. THEY ARE MUCH TOO CLOSE.
THE REASONS INVOLVE HEAT AND SOMETHING I CALL "PROXIMITY."
GAAA!!!
I DON'T HAVE TIME TO EXPLAIN ALL THE DETAILS.
YOU TAKE EVERYTHING I SAY AND EXPLAIN IT BACK TO ME LIKE I'M A MORON!!
EXCUSE ME, BUT I HEAR A CLICKING SOUND AND FEEL COMPELLED TO EAT A SUNFLOWER SEED.

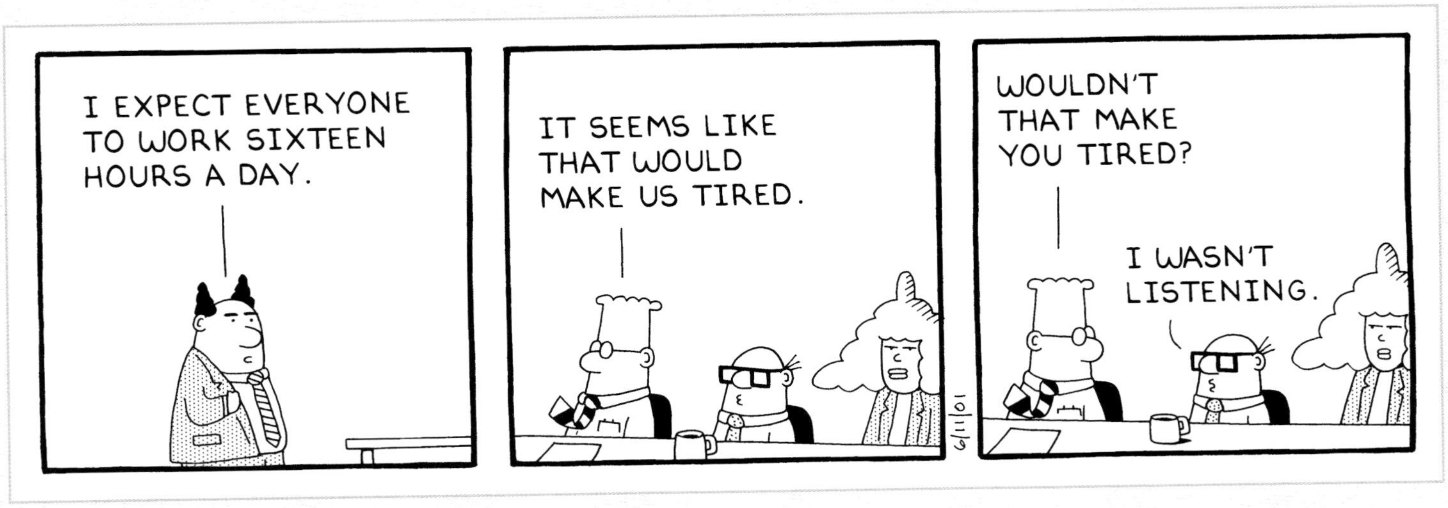
I EXPECT EVERYONE TO WORK SIXTEEN HOURS A DAY.
IT SEEMS LIKE THAT WOULD MAKE US TIRED.
6/11/01
WOULDN'T THAT MAKE YOU TIRED?
I WASN'T LISTENING.

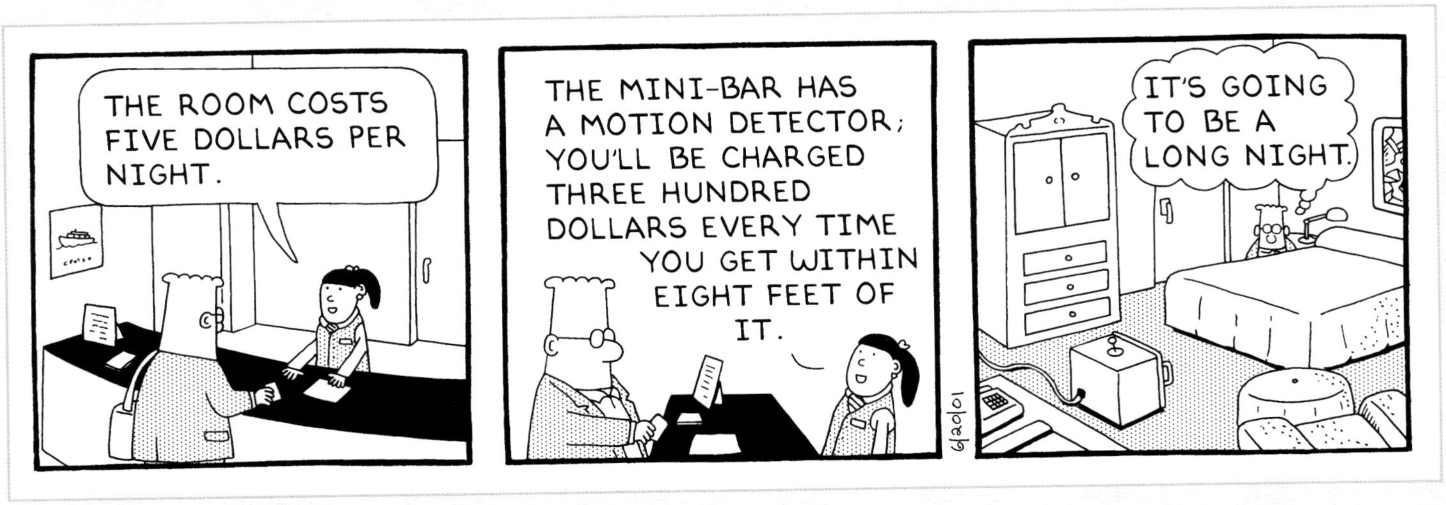
THE ROOM COSTS FIVE DOLLARS PER NIGHT.
THE MINI-BAR HAS A MOTION DETECTOR; YOU'LL BE CHARGED THREE HUNDRED DOLLARS EVERY TIME YOU GET WITHIN EIGHT FEET OF IT.
6/20/01
IT'S GOING TO BE A LONG NIGHT.

When Dilbert travels, it quadruples my workload because all the scenery is different from what I know how to draw. That's why he doesn't travel more.

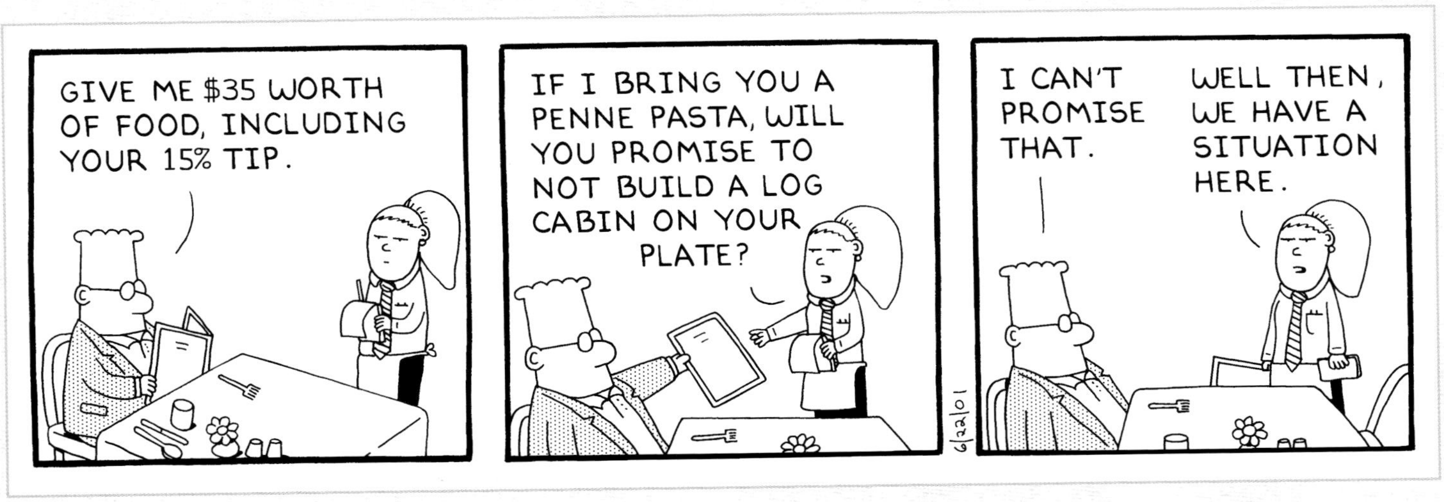
GIVE ME $35 WORTH OF FOOD, INCLUDING YOUR 15% TIP.
IF I BRING YOU A PENNE PASTA, WILL YOU PROMISE TO NOT BUILD A LOG CABIN ON YOUR PLATE?
6/22/01
I CAN'T PROMISE THAT.
WELL THEN, WE HAVE A SITUATION HERE.

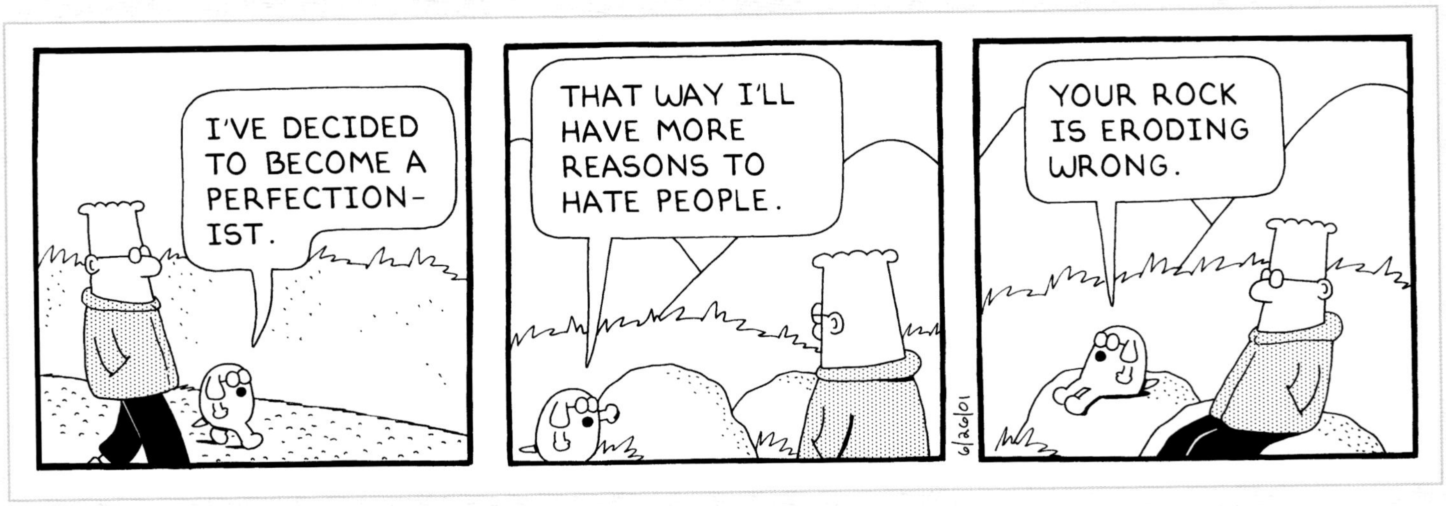
I'VE DECIDED TO BECOME A PERFECTION-IST.
THAT WAY I'LL HAVE MORE REASONS TO HATE PEOPLE.
6/26/01
YOUR ROCK IS ERODING WRONG.

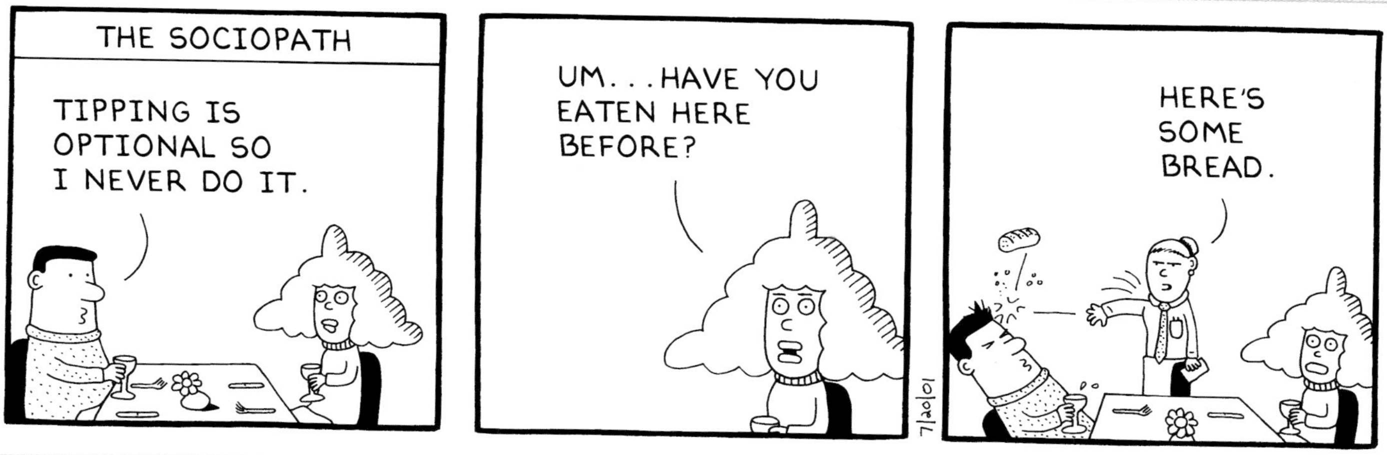
THE SOCIOPATH
TIPPING IS OPTIONAL SO I NEVER DO IT.
UM. . . HAVE YOU EATEN HERE BEFORE?
7/20/01
HERE'S SOME BREAD.

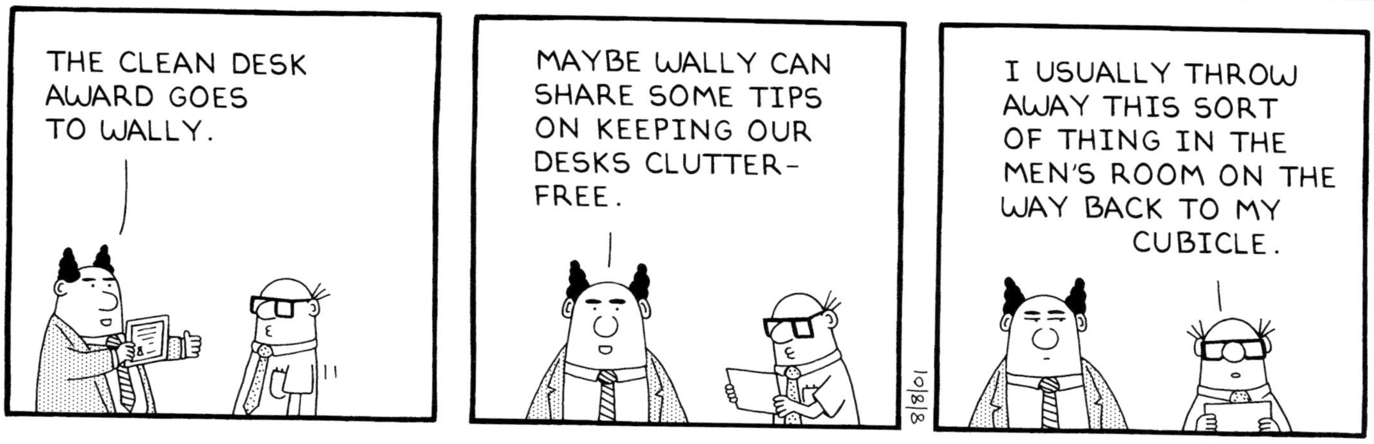
THE CLEAN DESK AWARD GOES TO WALLY.
MAYBE WALLY CAN SHARE SOME TIPS ON KEEPING OUR DESKS CLUTTER-FREE.
8/8/01
I USUALLY THROW AWAY THIS SORT OF THING IN THE MEN'S ROOM ON THE WAY BACK TO MY CUBICLE.

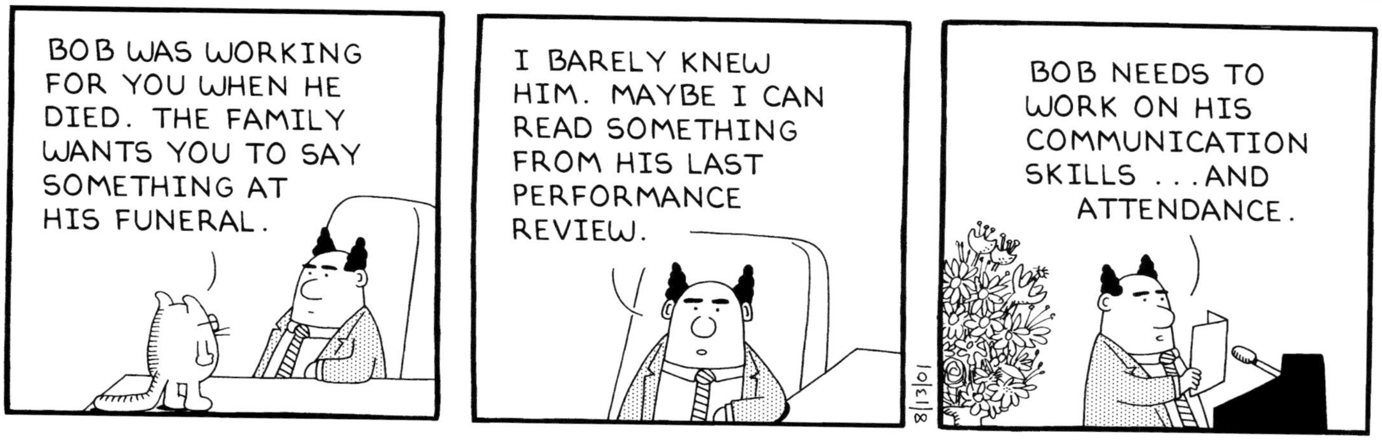
BOB WAS WORKING FOR YOU WHEN HE DIED. THE FAMILY WANTS YOU TO SAY SOMETHING AT HIS FUNERAL.
I BARELY KNEW HIM. MAYBE I CAN READ SOMETHING FROM HIS LAST PERFORMANCE REVIEW.
8/13/01
BOB NEEDS TO WORK ON HIS COMMUNICATION SKILLS . . . AND ATTENDANCE.

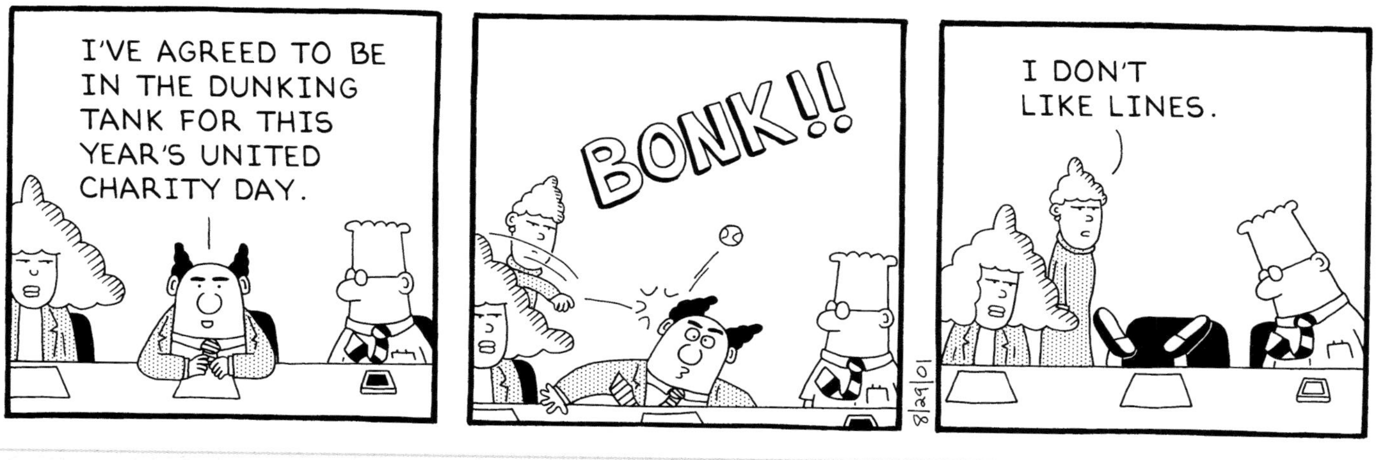
I'VE AGREED TO BE IN THE DUNKING TANK FOR THIS YEAR'S UNITED CHARITY DAY.
BONK!!
8/29/01
I DON'T LIKE LINES.

I CAN'T SLEEP. WOULD YOU TELL ME A STORY.
ONCE UPON A TIME THERE WAS A POINTY-HAIRED MONSTER.
HE PROMISED RICHES TO THE VILLAGERS IF THEY COULD ACHIEVE HIS RANDOM OBJECTIVES.
THE VILLAGERS WORKED LONG HOURS BUT THEY WERE HAPPY AND OPTIMISTIC.
SUDDENLY THE EVIL MONSTER CUT THEIR FUNDING AND HIRED THE VILLAGE IDIOT TO BE PROJECT MANAGER.
8/19/01
AND THAT IS HOW THE VILLAGERS GOT TRAPPED IN MEETINGS FOR ALL ETERNITY.
THE END.
WAAA!!
WAAA!!
WAAA!
RATS CRY WHEN THEY HEAR ABOUT MY LIFE.
IT NEVER PAYS TO LISTEN.

UH-OH... SLOW-WALKING WOMEN.
I CAN'T SQUEEZE AROUND.
I'LL MAKE FOOTSTEP NOISE SO THEY'LL NOTICE AND MOVE.
STOMP
STOMP
STOMP
IT DIDN'T WORK. THEY'RE OBLIVIOUS SLOW-WALKING WOMEN!
TIME STANDS STILL AS I WAIT TO TAKE MY NEXT STEP.
9/30/01
OH NO... IT'S A PAIR OF OBLIVIOUS SLOW-WALKING WOMEN.
I'LL THROW YOU OVER THE TOP. THEN YOU OPEN THE SIDE DOOR SO I CAN GO AROUND.
THIRD ONE TODAY.
WEIRD.

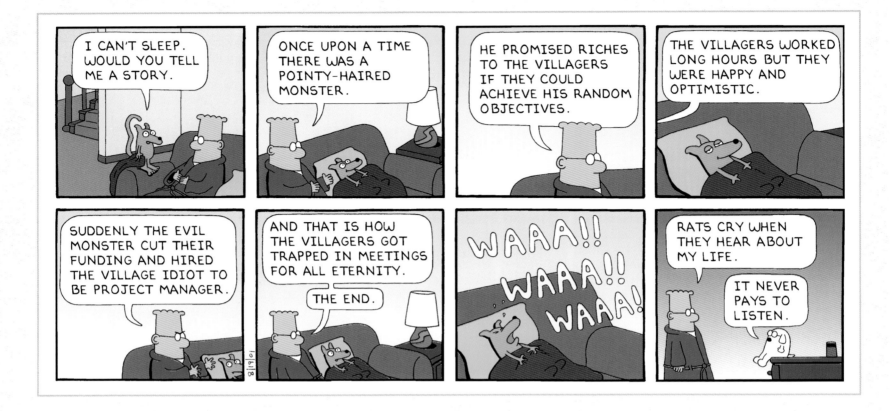

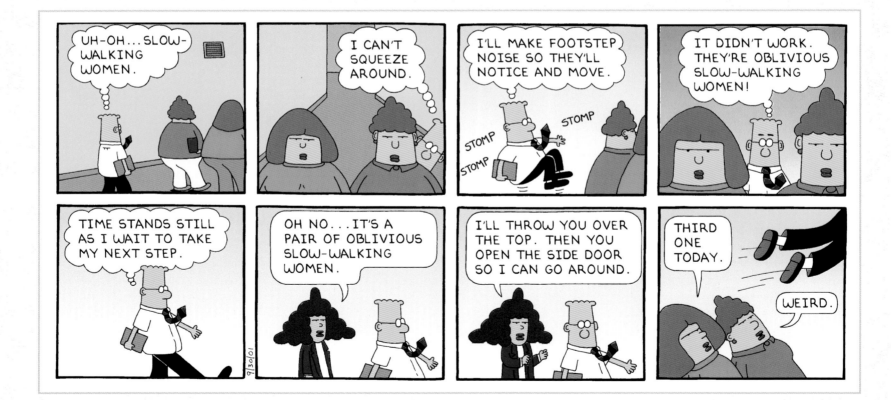

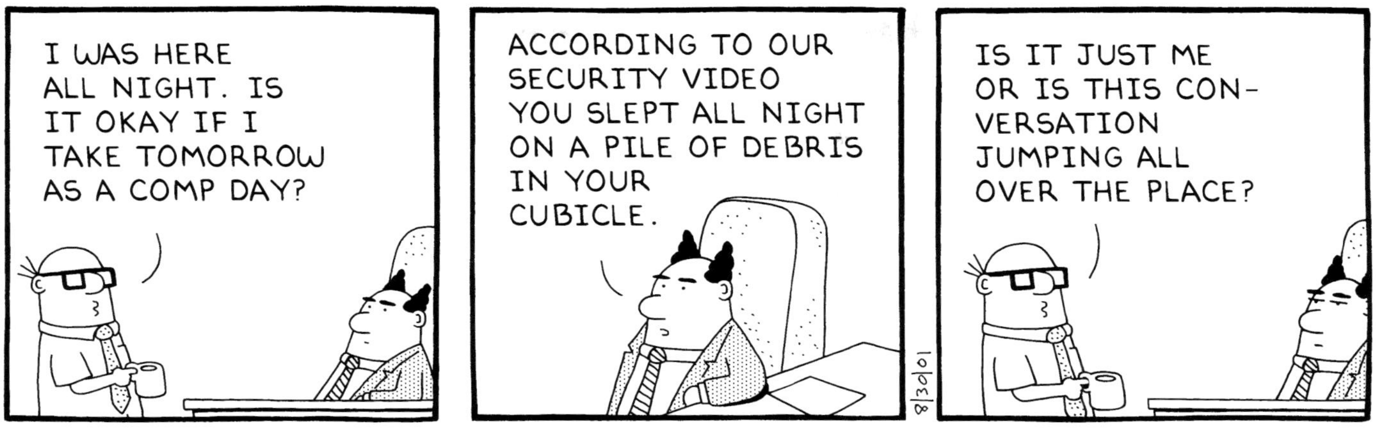
I WAS HERE ALL NIGHT. IS IT OKAY IF I TAKE TOMORROW AS A COMP DAY?
ACCORDING TO OUR SECURITY VIDEO YOU SLEPT ALL NIGHT ON A PILE OF DEBRIS IN YOUR CUBICLE.
IS IT JUST ME OR IS THIS CON-VERSATION JUMPING ALL OVER THE PLACE?
8/30/01

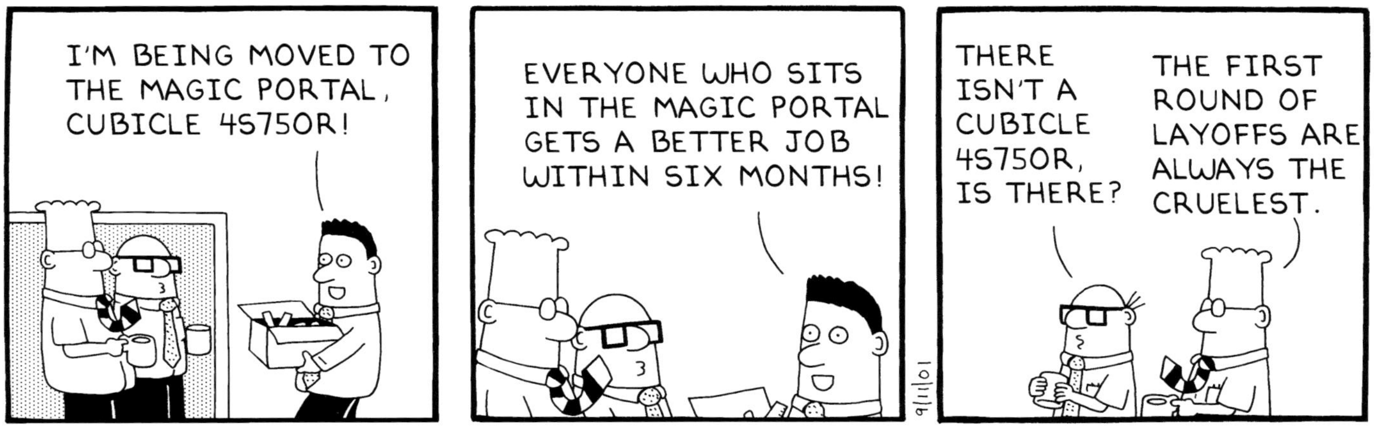
I'M BEING MOVED TO THE MAGIC PORTAL, CUBICLE 4S750R!
EVERYONE WHO SITS IN THE MAGIC PORTAL GETS A BETTER JOB WITHIN SIX MONTHS!
9/1/01
THERE ISN'T A CUBICLE 4S750R, IS THERE?
THE FIRST ROUND OF LAYOFFS ARE ALWAYS THE CRUELEST.

That was my actual cubicle address at Pacific Bell.

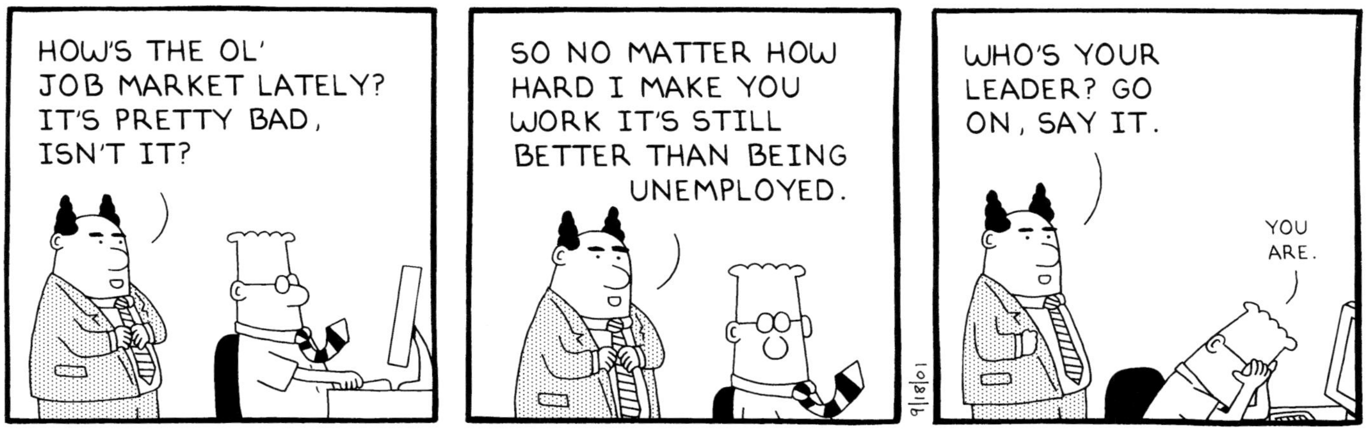
HOW'S THE OL' JOB MARKET LATELY? IT'S PRETTY BAD, ISN'T IT?
SO NO MATTER HOW HARD I MAKE YOU WORK IT'S STILL BETTER THAN BEING UNEMPLOYED.
9/18/01
WHO'S YOUR LEADER? GO ON, SAY IT.
YOU ARE.

Readers altered the boss's line in the last panel in this comic to "Who's my bitch?" The altered version was forwarded all over the Internet, and people assumed I wrote it that way. People still tell me it is their favorite Dilbert *comic. I only wish I had written it.*

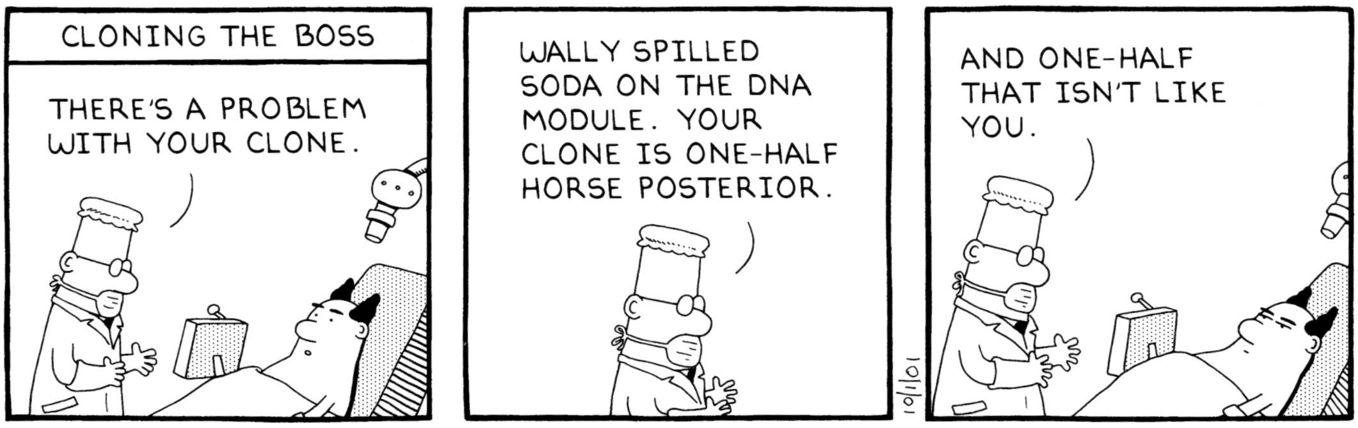
CLONING THE BOSS
THERE'S A PROBLEM WITH YOUR CLONE.
WALLY SPILLED SODA ON THE DNA MODULE. YOUR CLONE IS ONE-HALF HORSE POSTERIOR.
10/1/01
AND ONE-HALF THAT ISN'T LIKE YOU.

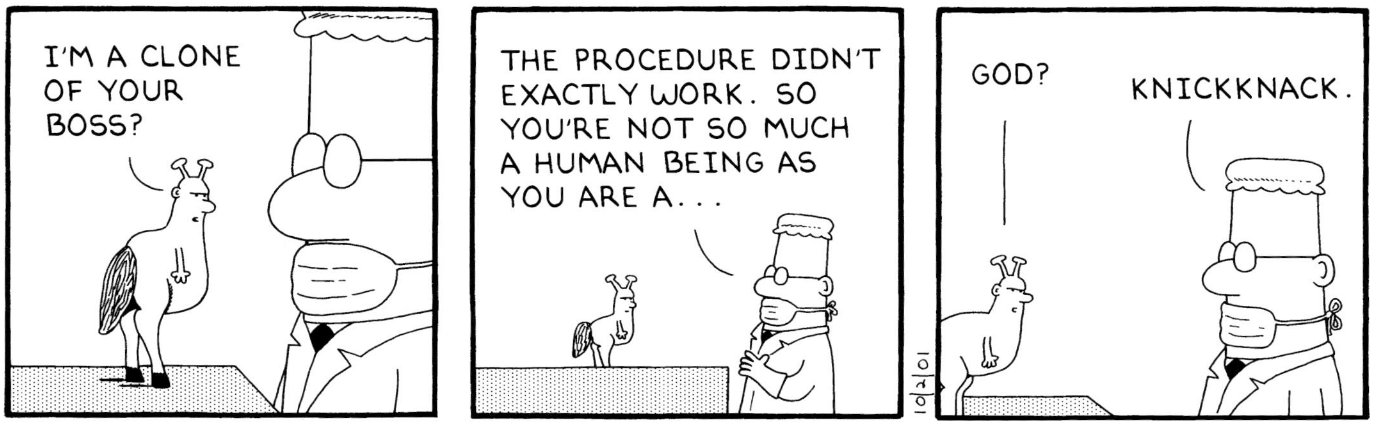
I'M A CLONE OF YOUR BOSS?
THE PROCEDURE DIDN'T EXACTLY WORK. SO YOU'RE NOT SO MUCH A HUMAN BEING AS YOU ARE A...
GOD?
KNICKKNACK.
10/2/01

Misplaced optimism is another humor-writing trick I use often. The more wrong the optimism is, the funnier.

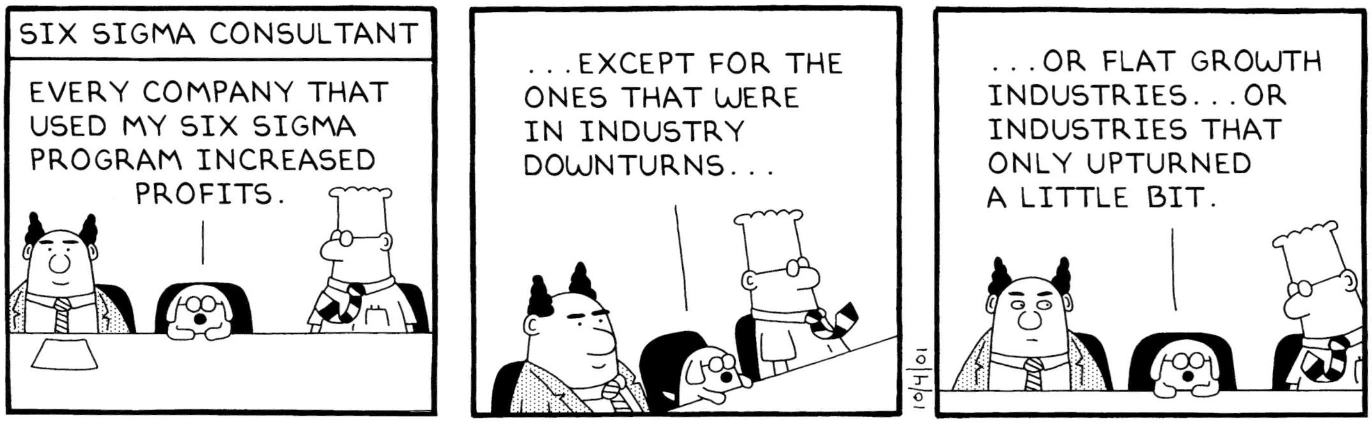
SIX SIGMA CONSULTANT
EVERY COMPANY THAT USED MY SIX SIGMA PROGRAM INCREASED PROFITS.
...EXCEPT FOR THE ONES THAT WERE IN INDUSTRY DOWNTURNS...
...OR FLAT GROWTH INDUSTRIES...OR INDUSTRIES THAT ONLY UPTURNED A LITTLE BIT.
10/4/01

I didn't need my old day job to know that any new management fad was being oversold. Some things don't change.

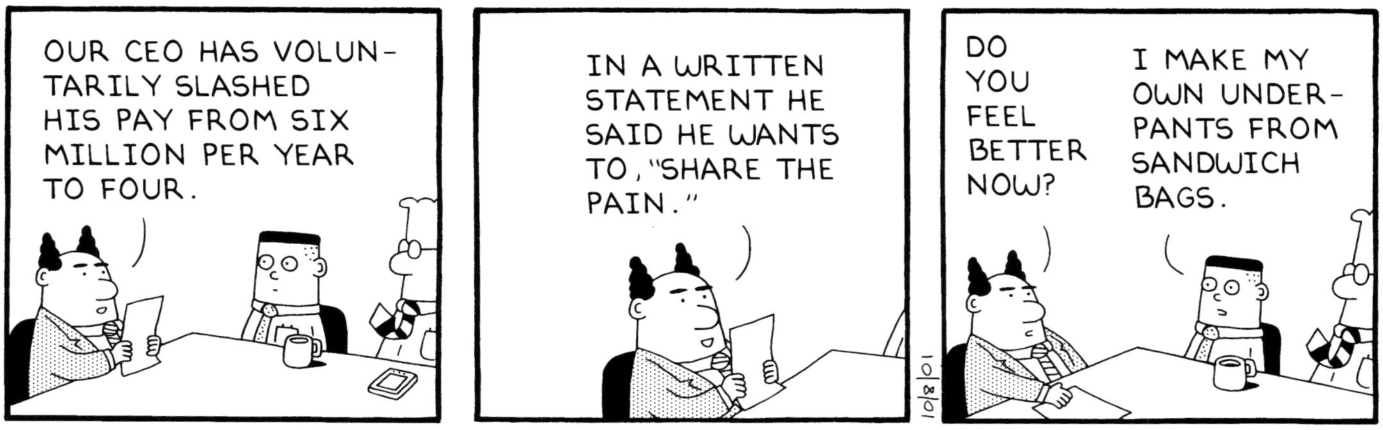
OUR CEO HAS VOLUN-TARILY SLASHED HIS PAY FROM SIX MILLION PER YEAR TO FOUR.
IN A WRITTEN STATEMENT HE SAID HE WANTS TO, "SHARE THE PAIN."
DO YOU FEEL BETTER NOW?
I MAKE MY OWN UNDER-PANTS FROM SANDWICH BAGS.
10/8/01

This comic is in my top ten personal favorites.

Ron Insana of CNBC recognized himself and called to ask for a signed strip. I was happy to give it.

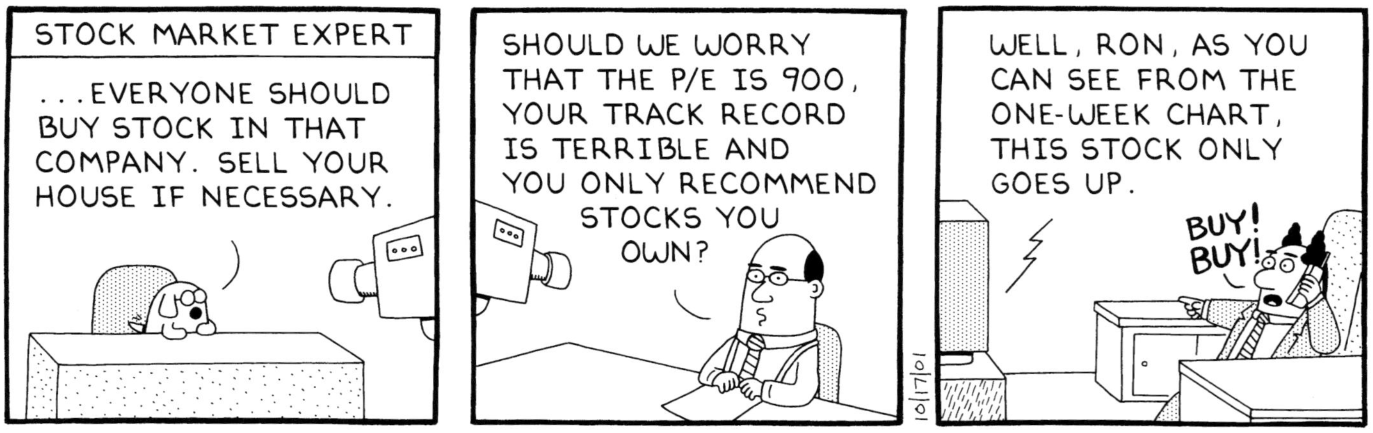
STOCK MARKET EXPERT
...EVERYONE SHOULD BUY STOCK IN THAT COMPANY. SELL YOUR HOUSE IF NECESSARY.
SHOULD WE WORRY THAT THE P/E IS 900, YOUR TRACK RECORD IS TERRIBLE AND YOU ONLY RECOMMEND STOCKS YOU OWN?
WELL, RON, AS YOU CAN SEE FROM THE ONE-WEEK CHART, THIS STOCK ONLY GOES UP.
BUY! BUY!
10/17/01

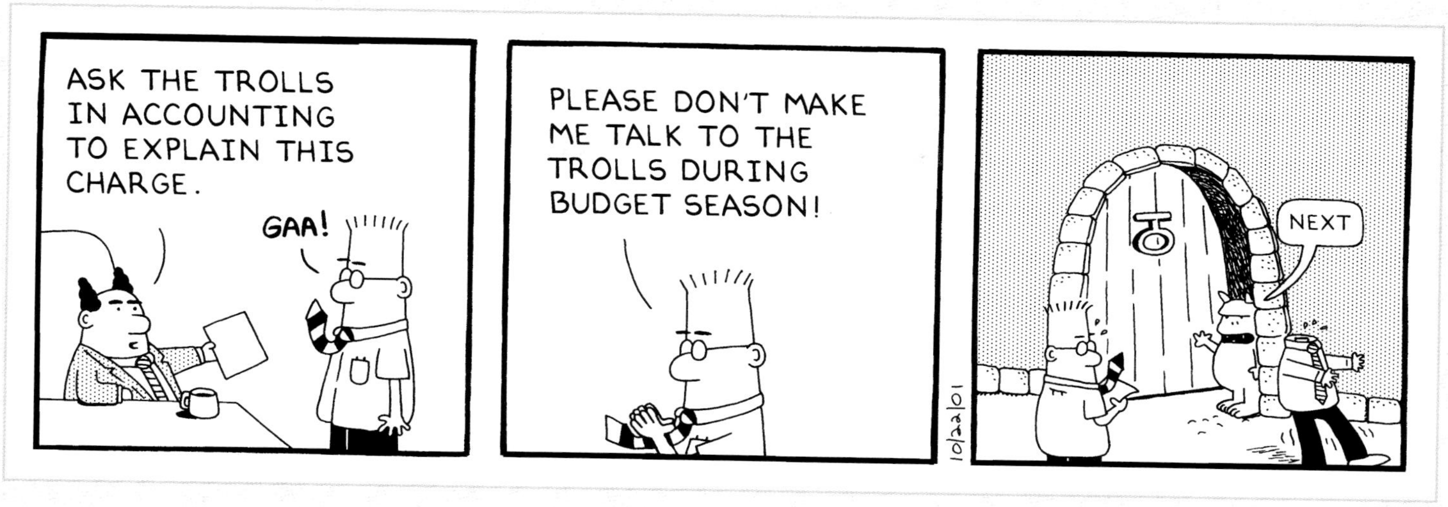
ASK THE TROLLS IN ACCOUNTING TO EXPLAIN THIS CHARGE.
GAA!
PLEASE DON'T MAKE ME TALK TO THE TROLLS DURING BUDGET SEASON!
10/22/01
NEXT

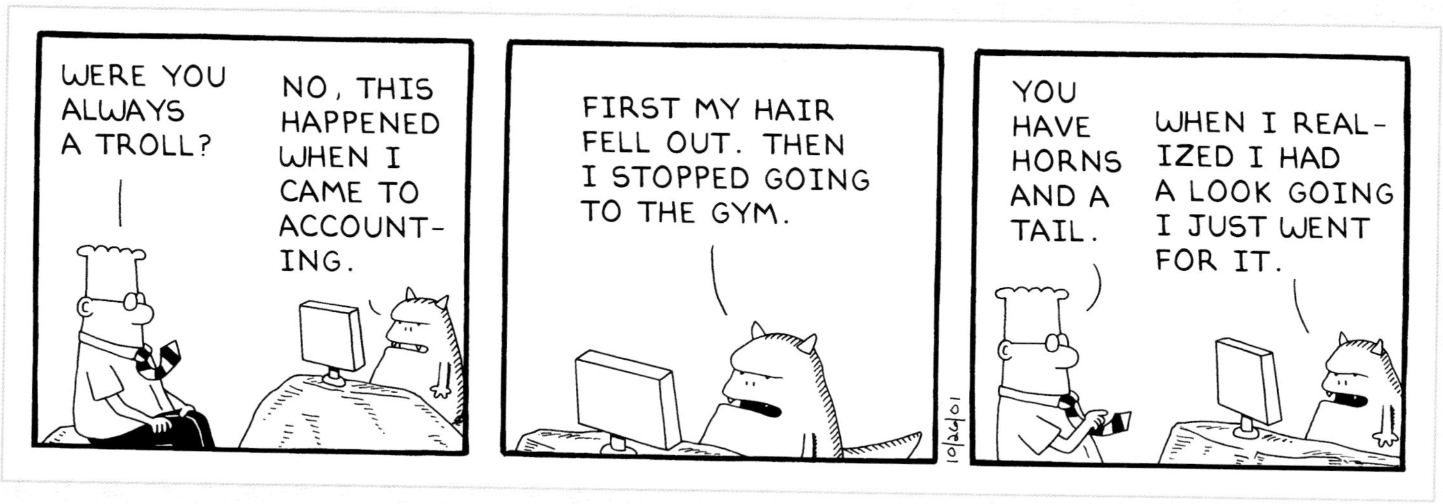
WERE YOU ALWAYS A TROLL?
NO, THIS HAPPENED WHEN I CAME TO ACCOUNT-ING.
FIRST MY HAIR FELL OUT. THEN I STOPPED GOING TO THE GYM.
10/26/01
YOU HAVE HORNS AND A TAIL.
WHEN I REAL-IZED I HAD A LOOK GOING I JUST WENT FOR IT.

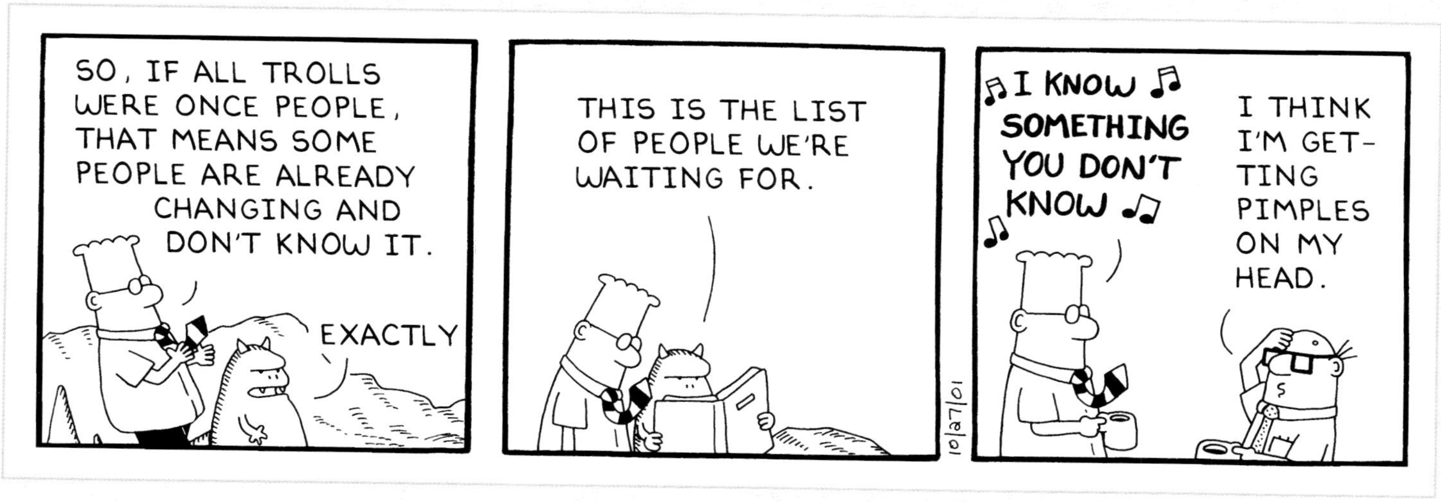
SO, IF ALL TROLLS WERE ONCE PEOPLE, THAT MEANS SOME PEOPLE ARE ALREADY CHANGING AND DON'T KNOW IT.
EXACTLY
THIS IS THE LIST OF PEOPLE WE'RE WAITING FOR.
10/27/01
I KNOW SOMETHING YOU DON'T KNOW
I THINK I'M GET-TING PIMPLES ON MY HEAD.

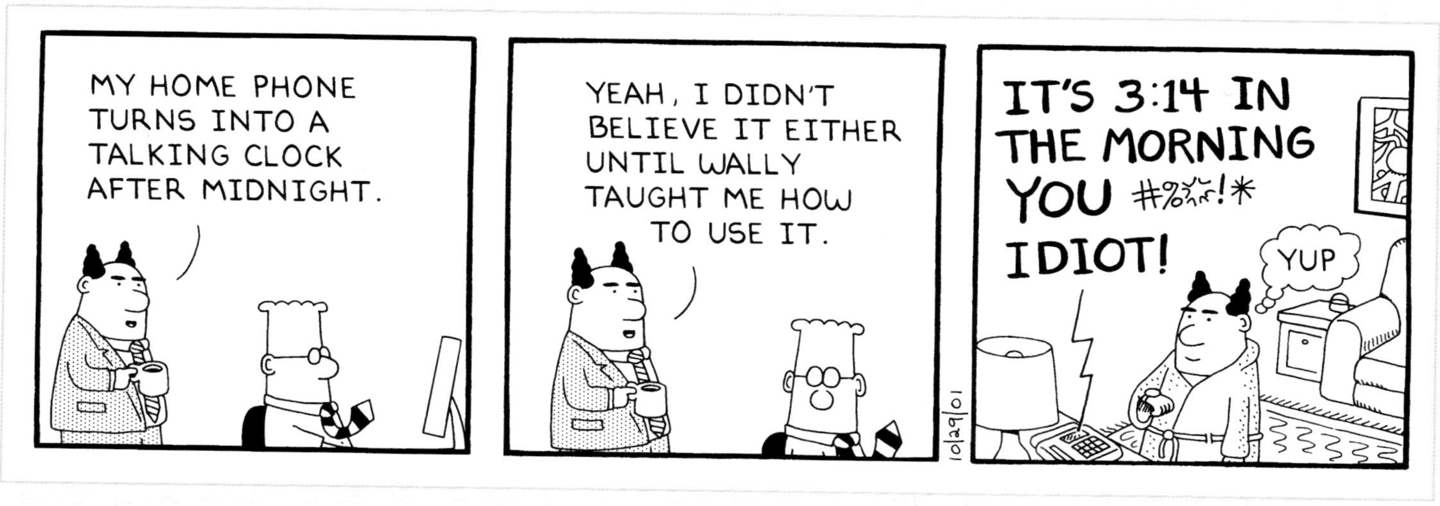
MY HOME PHONE TURNS INTO A TALKING CLOCK AFTER MIDNIGHT.
YEAH, I DIDN'T BELIEVE IT EITHER UNTIL WALLY TAUGHT ME HOW TO USE IT.
10/29/01
IT'S 3:14 IN THE MORNING YOU #%!* IDIOT!
YUP

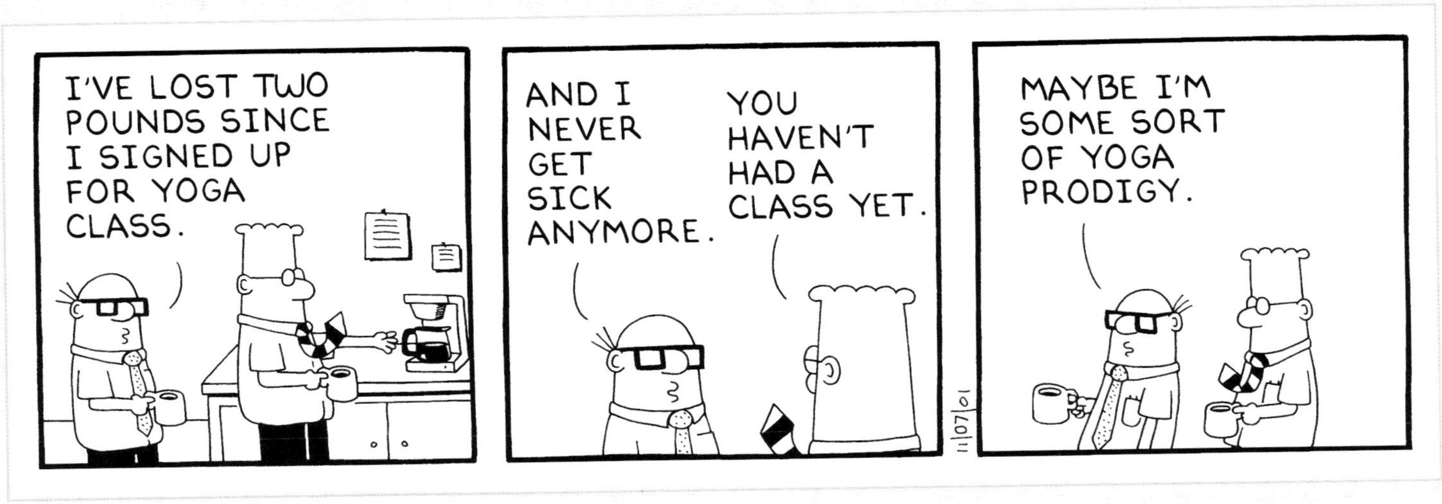
I'VE LOST TWO POUNDS SINCE I SIGNED UP FOR YOGA CLASS.
AND I NEVER GET SICK ANYMORE.
YOU HAVEN'T HAD A CLASS YET.
MAYBE I'M SOME SORT OF YOGA PRODIGY.
11/07/01

My font size suddenly got larger. It wasn't intentional. I just forgot what size I normally used.

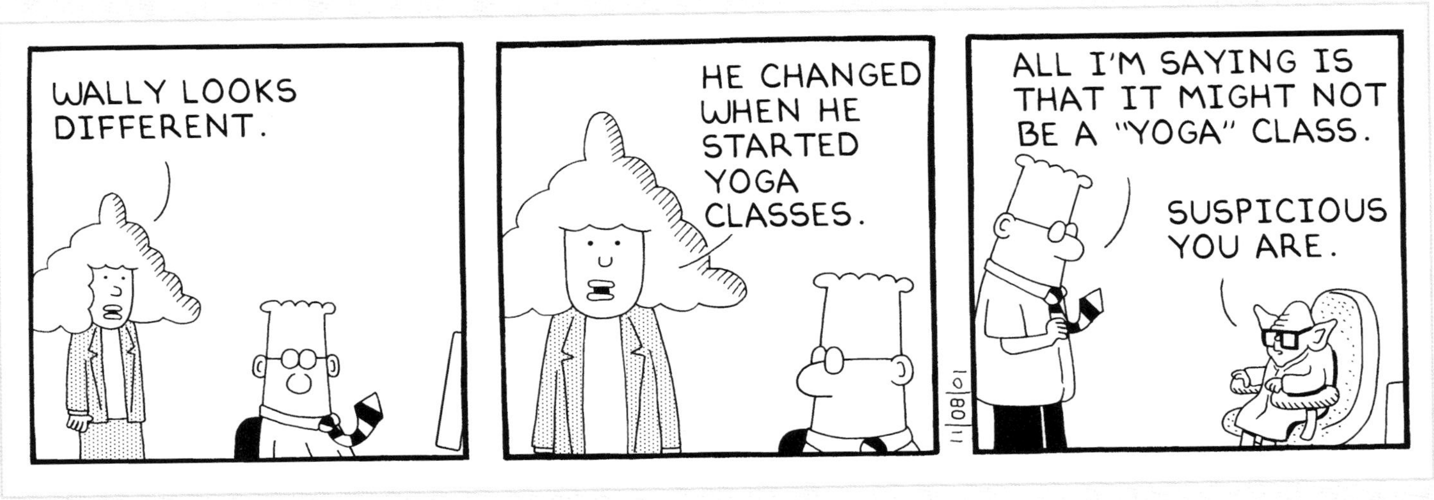
WALLY LOOKS DIFFERENT.
HE CHANGED WHEN HE STARTED YOGA CLASSES.
ALL I'M SAYING IS THAT IT MIGHT NOT BE A "YOGA" CLASS.
SUSPICIOUS YOU ARE.
11/08/01

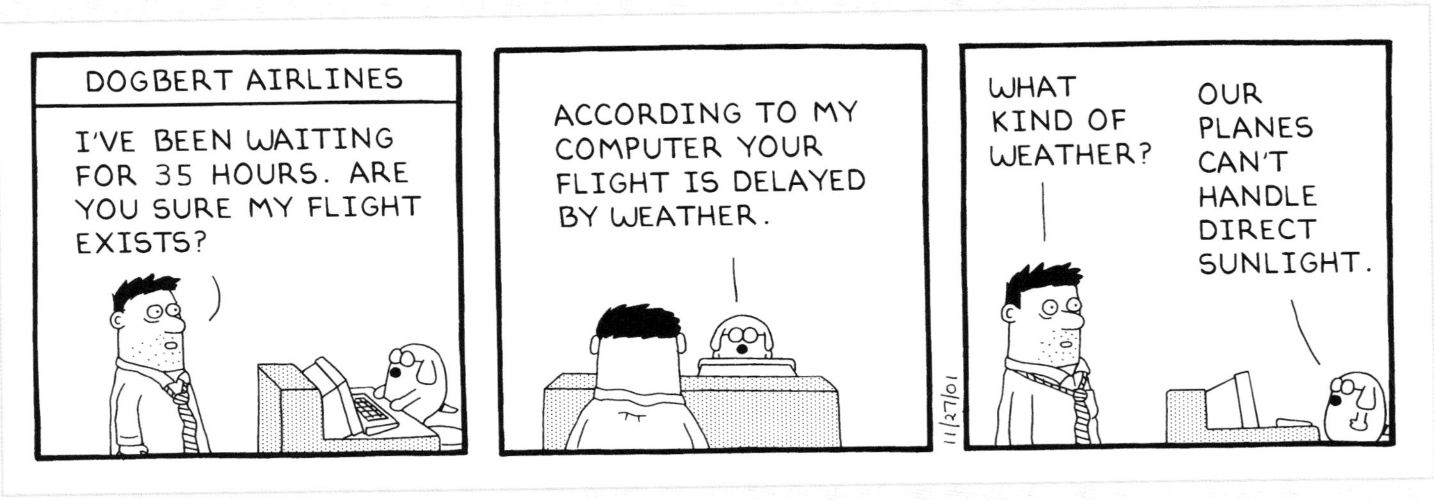
DOGBERT AIRLINES
I'VE BEEN WAITING FOR 35 HOURS. ARE YOU SURE MY FLIGHT EXISTS?
ACCORDING TO MY COMPUTER YOUR FLIGHT IS DELAYED BY WEATHER.
WHAT KIND OF WEATHER?
OUR PLANES CAN'T HANDLE DIRECT SUNLIGHT.
11/27/01

I must have noticed the font problem and shrunk it back where it belonged.

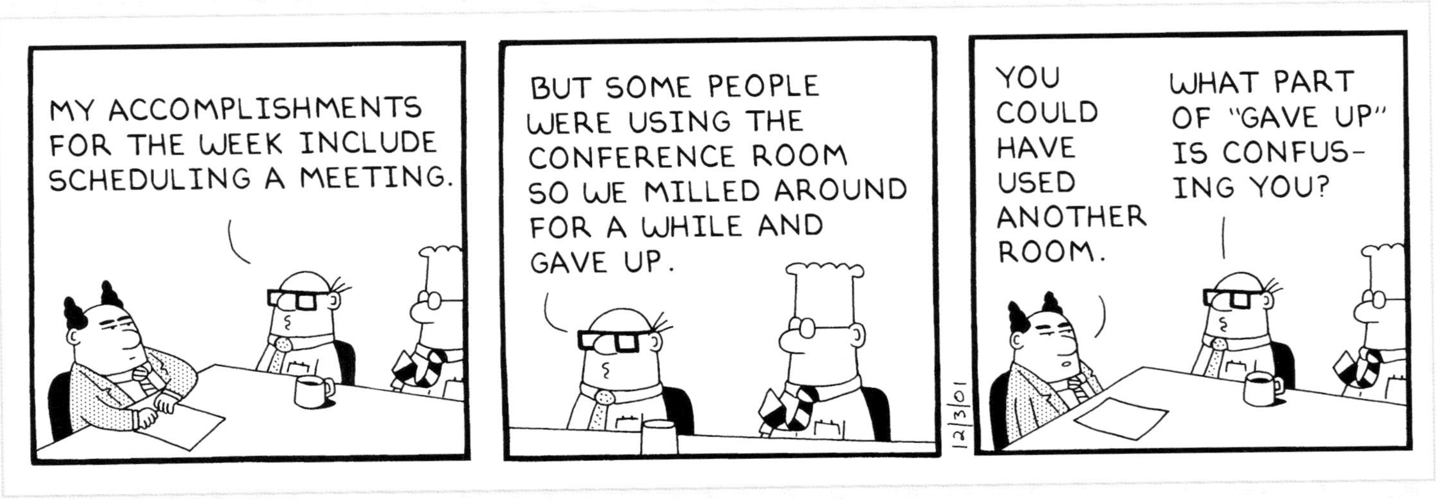
MY ACCOMPLISHMENTS FOR THE WEEK INCLUDE SCHEDULING A MEETING.
BUT SOME PEOPLE WERE USING THE CONFERENCE ROOM SO WE MILLED AROUND FOR A WHILE AND GAVE UP.
YOU COULD HAVE USED ANOTHER ROOM.
WHAT PART OF "GAVE UP" IS CONFUS-ING YOU?
12/3/01

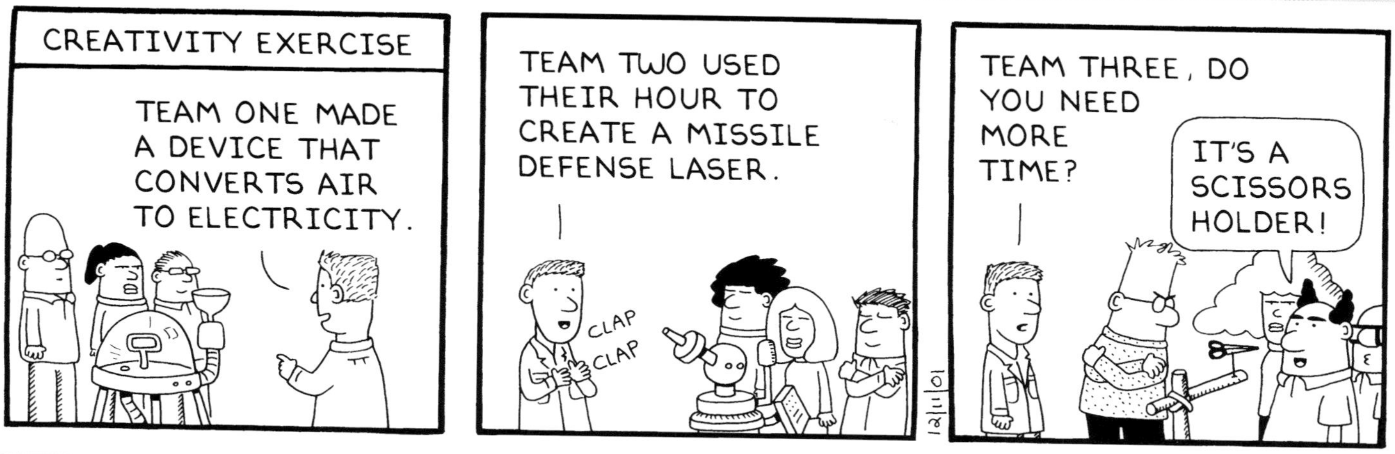
CREATIVITY EXERCISE
TEAM ONE MADE A DEVICE THAT CONVERTS AIR TO ELECTRICITY.
TEAM TWO USED THEIR HOUR TO CREATE A MISSILE DEFENSE LASER.
CLAP CLAP
TEAM THREE, DO YOU NEED MORE TIME?
IT'S A SCISSORS HOLDER!
12/11/01

During this period I was working with a design firm called IDEO to develop Dilbert's Ultimate Cubicle. It was a prototype cubicle with a variety of whimsical and useful elements. We did it primarily for publicity, and it generated a ton. The secondary goal was to see if better cubicles could be built to improve the lives of people who work in them. That part didn't materialize because, while the prototype was terrific, there is no incentive for management to improve cubicles. This series is loosely based on that experience.

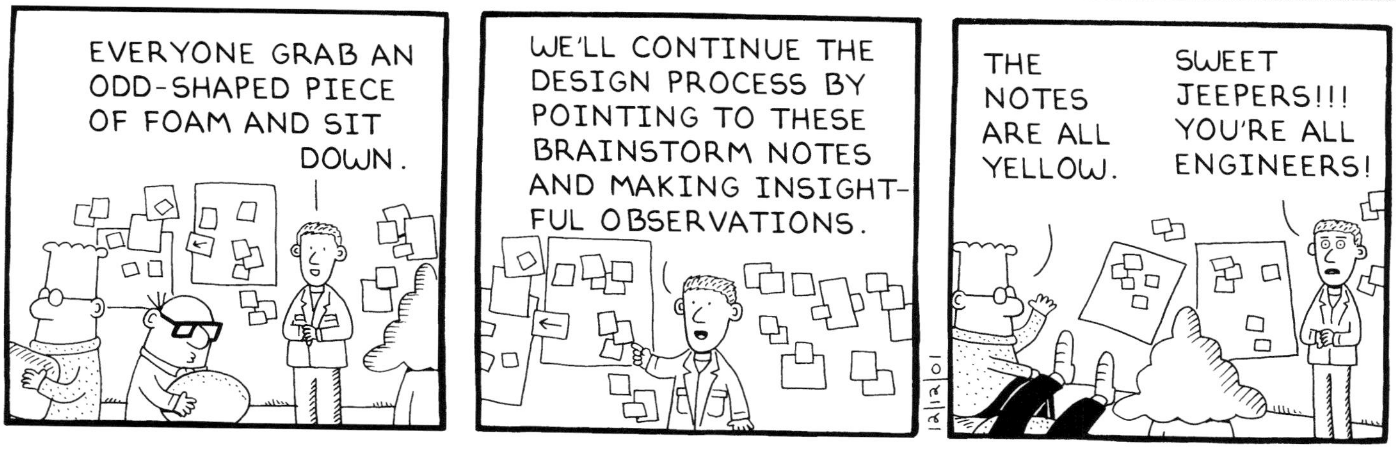
EVERYONE GRAB AN ODD-SHAPED PIECE OF FOAM AND SIT DOWN.
WE'LL CONTINUE THE DESIGN PROCESS BY POINTING TO THESE BRAINSTORM NOTES AND MAKING INSIGHTFUL OBSERVATIONS.
THE NOTES ARE ALL YELLOW.
SWEET JEEPERS!!! YOU'RE ALL ENGINEERS!
12/12/01

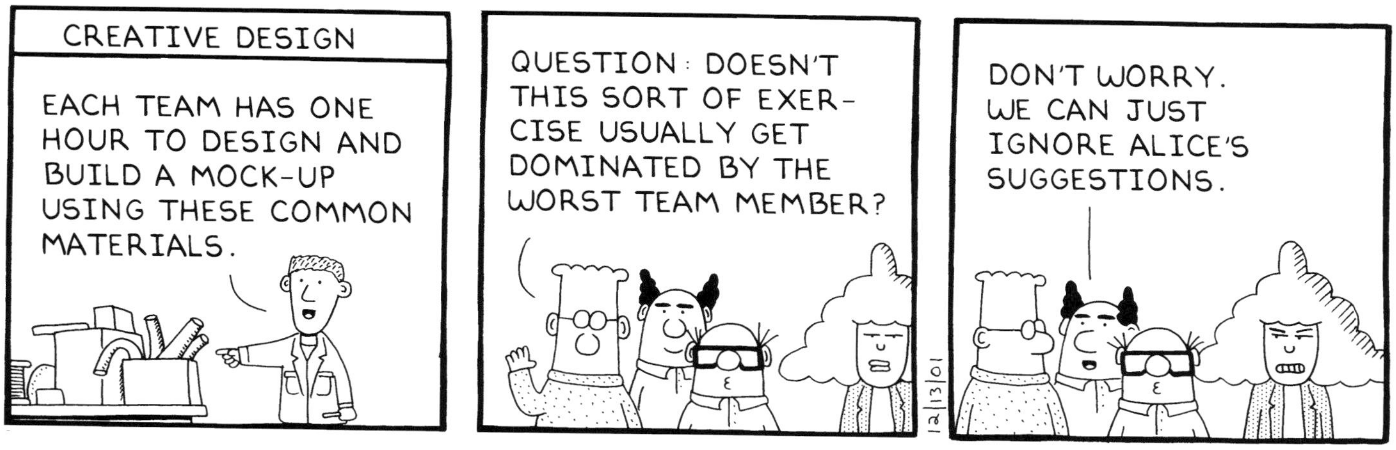
CREATIVE DESIGN
EACH TEAM HAS ONE HOUR TO DESIGN AND BUILD A MOCK-UP USING THESE COMMON MATERIALS.
QUESTION: DOESN'T THIS SORT OF EXERCISE USUALLY GET DOMINATED BY THE WORST TEAM MEMBER?
DON'T WORRY. WE CAN JUST IGNORE ALICE'S SUGGESTIONS.
12/13/01

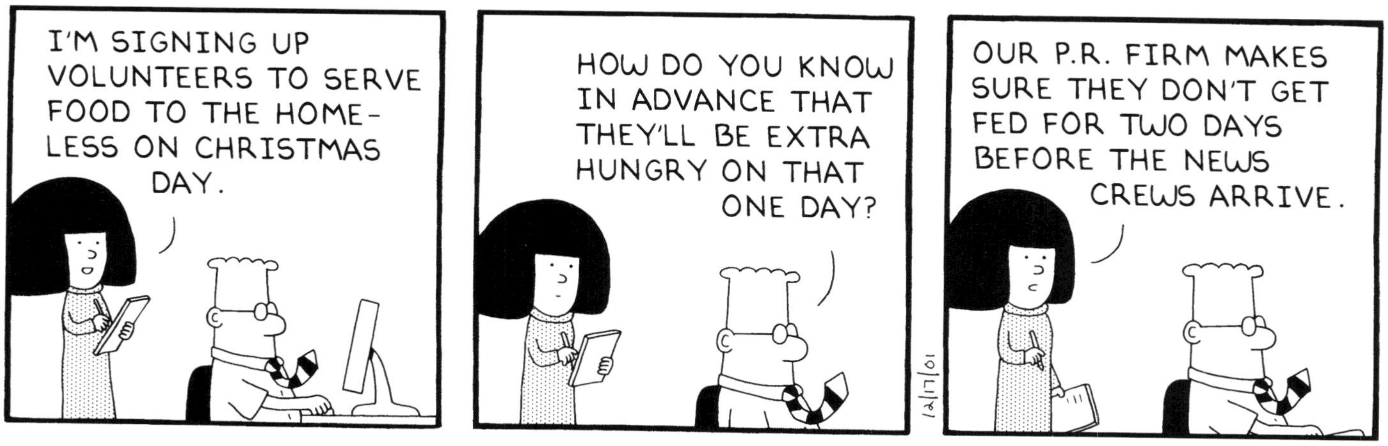
I'M SIGNING UP VOLUNTEERS TO SERVE FOOD TO THE HOMELESS ON CHRISTMAS DAY.
HOW DO YOU KNOW IN ADVANCE THAT THEY'LL BE EXTRA HUNGRY ON THAT ONE DAY?
OUR P.R. FIRM MAKES SURE THEY DON'T GET FED FOR TWO DAYS BEFORE THE NEWS CREWS ARRIVE.
12/17/01

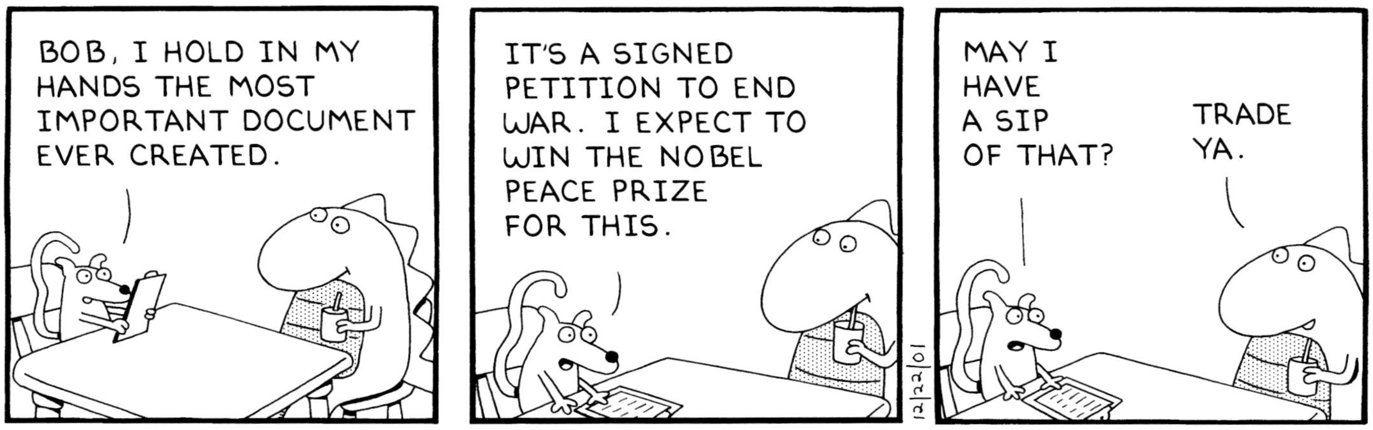
BOB, I HOLD IN MY HANDS THE MOST IMPORTANT DOCUMENT EVER CREATED.
IT'S A SIGNED PETITION TO END WAR. I EXPECT TO WIN THE NOBEL PEACE PRIZE FOR THIS.
MAY I HAVE A SIP OF THAT?
TRADE YA.
12/22/01

By this time, Ratbert and Bob the dinosaur were infrequent characters.

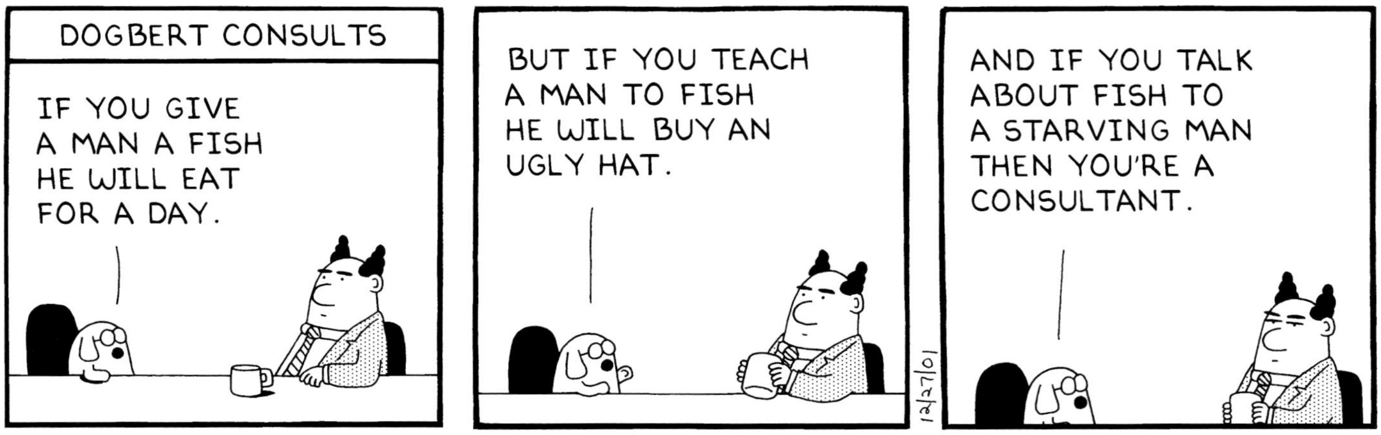
DOGBERT CONSULTS
IF YOU GIVE A MAN A FISH HE WILL EAT FOR A DAY.
BUT IF YOU TEACH A MAN TO FISH HE WILL BUY AN UGLY HAT.
AND IF YOU TALK ABOUT FISH TO A STARVING MAN THEN YOU'RE A CONSULTANT.
12/27/01

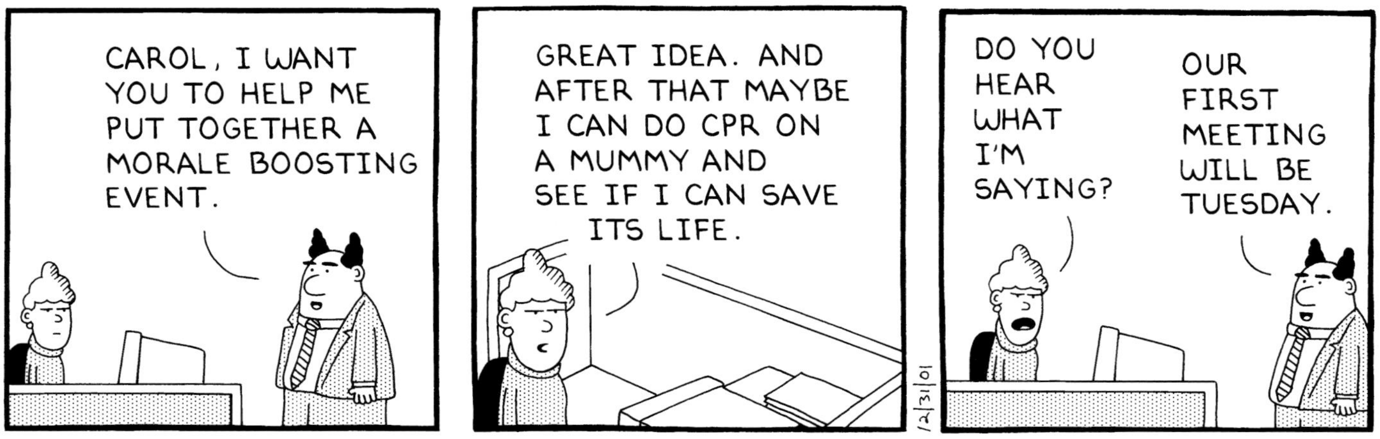
CAROL, I WANT YOU TO HELP ME PUT TOGETHER A MORALE BOOSTING EVENT.
GREAT IDEA. AND AFTER THAT MAYBE I CAN DO CPR ON A MUMMY AND SEE IF I CAN SAVE ITS LIFE.
DO YOU HEAR WHAT I'M SAYING?
OUR FIRST MEETING WILL BE TUESDAY.
12/31/01

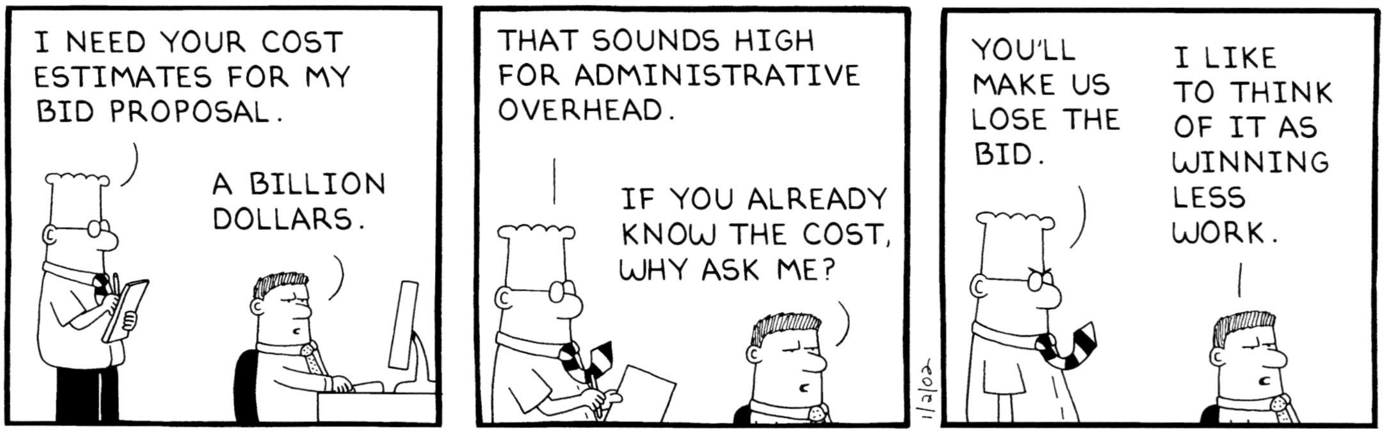
I NEED YOUR COST ESTIMATES FOR MY BID PROPOSAL.
A BILLION DOLLARS.
THAT SOUNDS HIGH FOR ADMINISTRATIVE OVERHEAD.
IF YOU ALREADY KNOW THE COST, WHY ASK ME?
YOU'LL MAKE US LOSE THE BID.
I LIKE TO THINK OF IT AS WINNING LESS WORK.
1/2/02

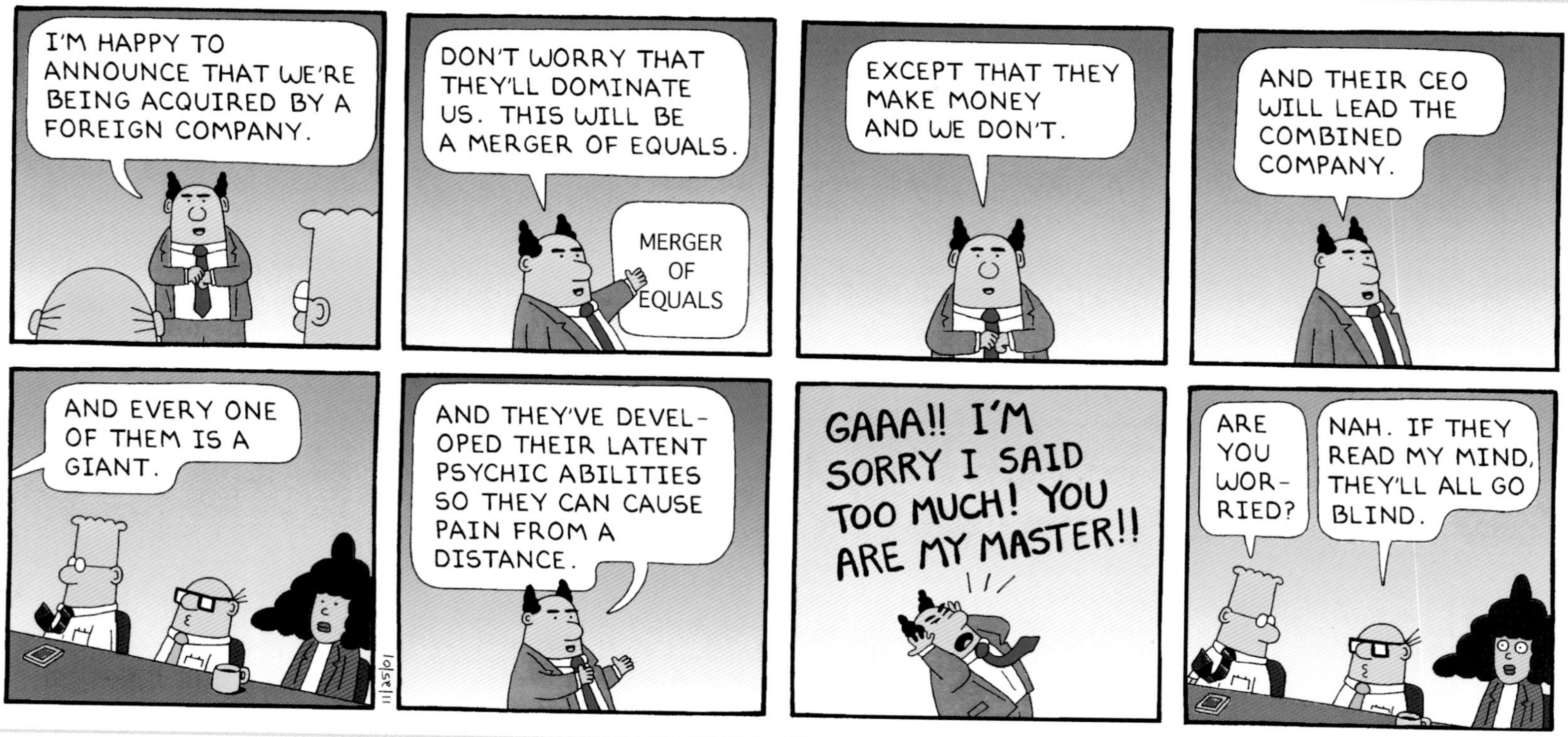
I'M HAPPY TO ANNOUNCE THAT WE'RE BEING ACQUIRED BY A FOREIGN COMPANY.
DON'T WORRY THAT THEY'LL DOMINATE US. THIS WILL BE A MERGER OF EQUALS.
MERGER OF EQUALS
EXCEPT THAT THEY MAKE MONEY AND WE DON'T.
AND THEIR CEO WILL LEAD THE COMBINED COMPANY.
AND EVERY ONE OF THEM IS A GIANT.
11/25/01
AND THEY'VE DEVELOPED THEIR LATENT PSYCHIC ABILITIES SO THEY CAN CAUSE PAIN FROM A DISTANCE.
GAAA!! I'M SORRY I SAID TOO MUCH! YOU ARE MY MASTER!!
ARE YOU WORRIED?
NAH. IF THEY READ MY MIND, THEY'LL ALL GO BLIND.

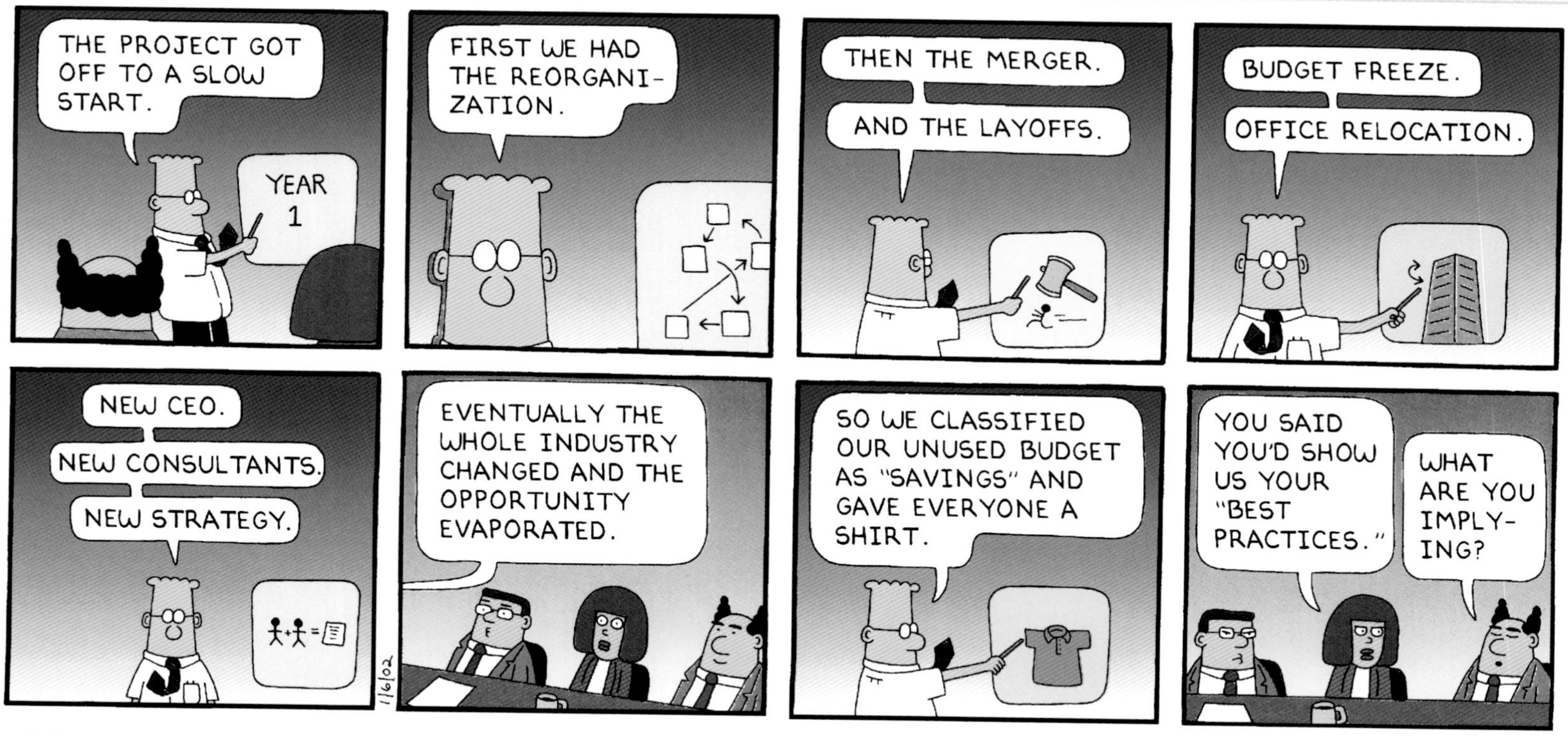
THE PROJECT GOT OFF TO A SLOW START.
YEAR 1
FIRST WE HAD THE REORGANIZATION.
THEN THE MERGER.
AND THE LAYOFFS.
BUDGET FREEZE.
OFFICE RELOCATION.
NEW CEO.
NEW CONSULTANTS.
NEW STRATEGY.
1/6/02
EVENTUALLY THE WHOLE INDUSTRY CHANGED AND THE OPPORTUNITY EVAPORATED.
SO WE CLASSIFIED OUR UNUSED BUDGET AS "SAVINGS" AND GAVE EVERYONE A SHIRT.
YOU SAID YOU'D SHOW US YOUR "BEST PRACTICES."
WHAT ARE YOU IMPLYING?

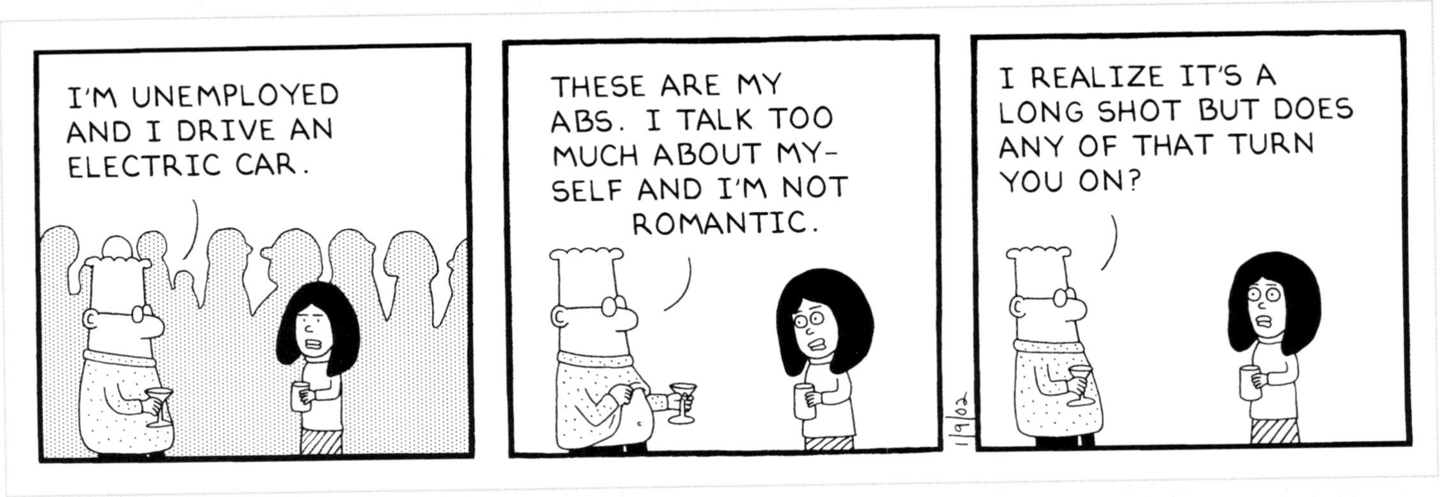
I'M UNEMPLOYED AND I DRIVE AN ELECTRIC CAR.
THESE ARE MY ABS. I TALK TOO MUCH ABOUT MY-SELF AND I'M NOT ROMANTIC.
I REALIZE IT'S A LONG SHOT BUT DOES ANY OF THAT TURN YOU ON?
1/9/02

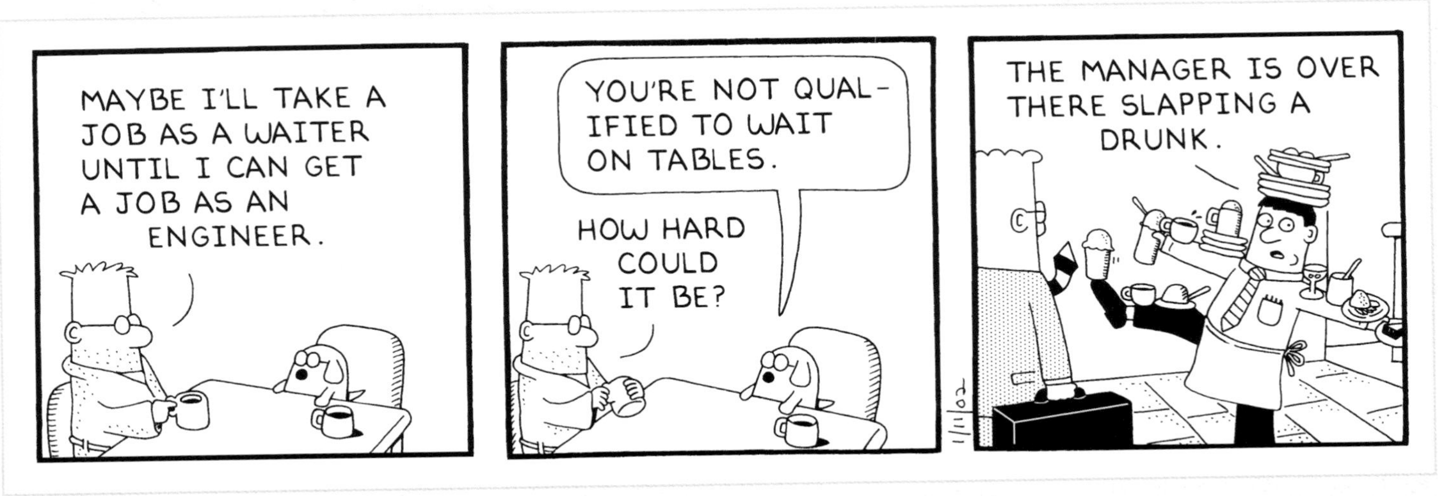
MAYBE I'LL TAKE A JOB AS A WAITER UNTIL I CAN GET A JOB AS AN ENGINEER.
YOU'RE NOT QUAL-IFIED TO WAIT ON TABLES.
HOW HARD COULD IT BE?
THE MANAGER IS OVER THERE SLAPPING A DRUNK.
1/11/02

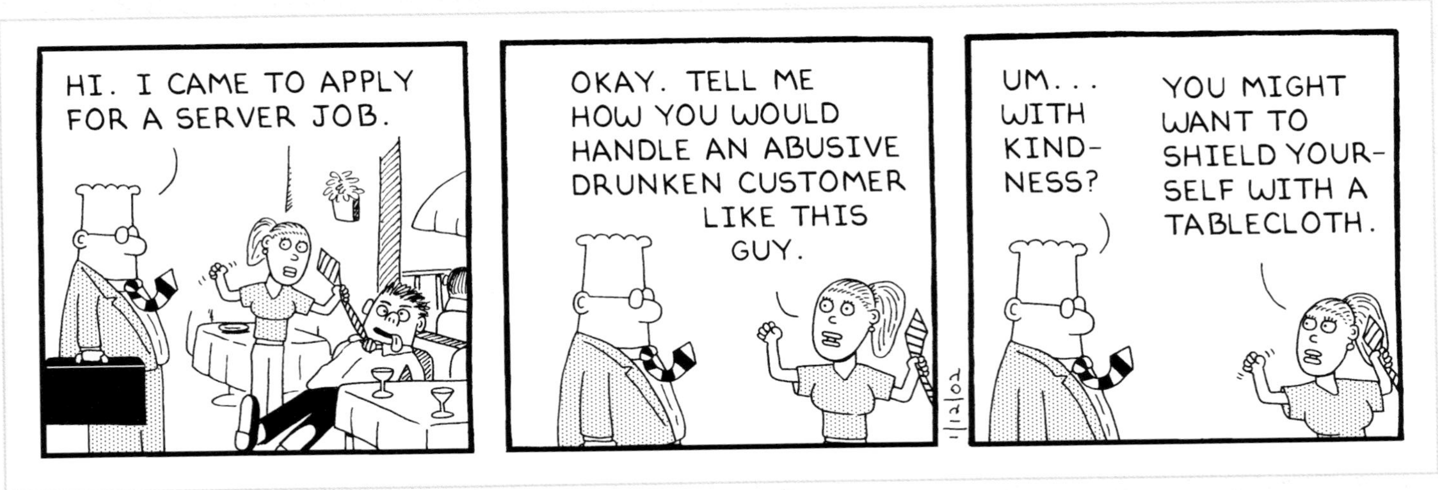
HI. I CAME TO APPLY FOR A SERVER JOB.
OKAY. TELL ME HOW YOU WOULD HANDLE AN ABUSIVE DRUNKEN CUSTOMER LIKE THIS GUY.
UM... WITH KIND-NESS?
YOU MIGHT WANT TO SHIELD YOUR-SELF WITH A TABLECLOTH.
1/12/02

I own two restaurants in the San Francisco Bay Area: Stacey's Café in Pleasanton, and Stacey's at Waterford, in Dublin. My business partner is Stacey. This is her, administering some tough love.

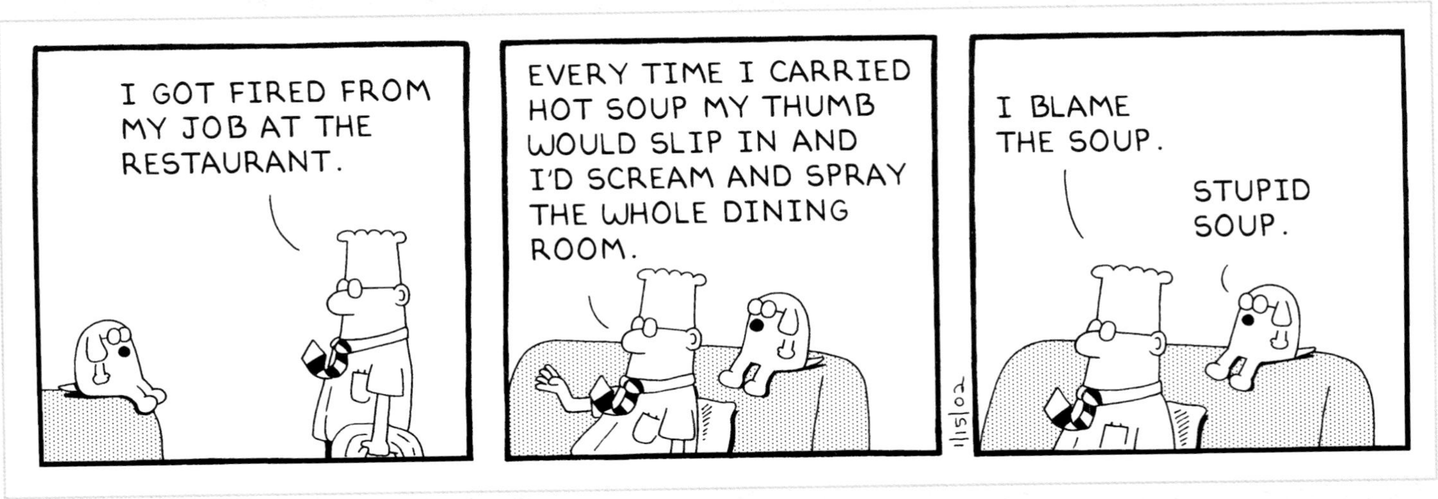
I GOT FIRED FROM MY JOB AT THE RESTAURANT.
EVERY TIME I CARRIED HOT SOUP MY THUMB WOULD SLIP IN AND I'D SCREAM AND SPRAY THE WHOLE DINING ROOM.
I BLAME THE SOUP.
STUPID SOUP.
1/15/02

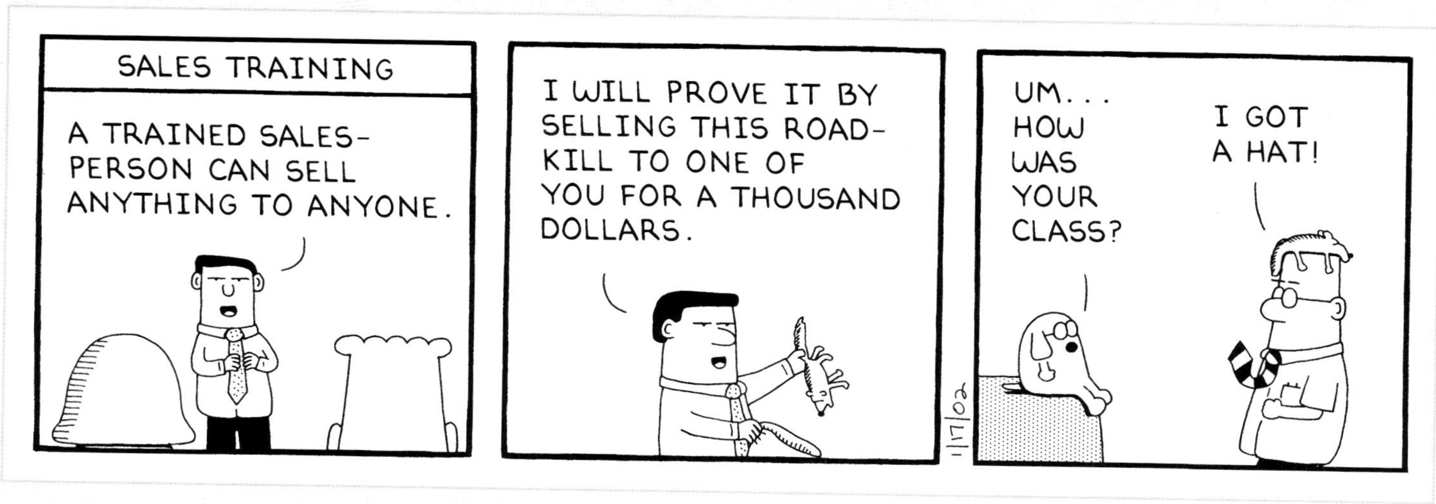
SALES TRAINING
A TRAINED SALES-PERSON CAN SELL ANYTHING TO ANYONE.
I WILL PROVE IT BY SELLING THIS ROAD-KILL TO ONE OF YOU FOR A THOUSAND DOLLARS.
UM... HOW WAS YOUR CLASS?
I GOT A HAT!
1/17/02

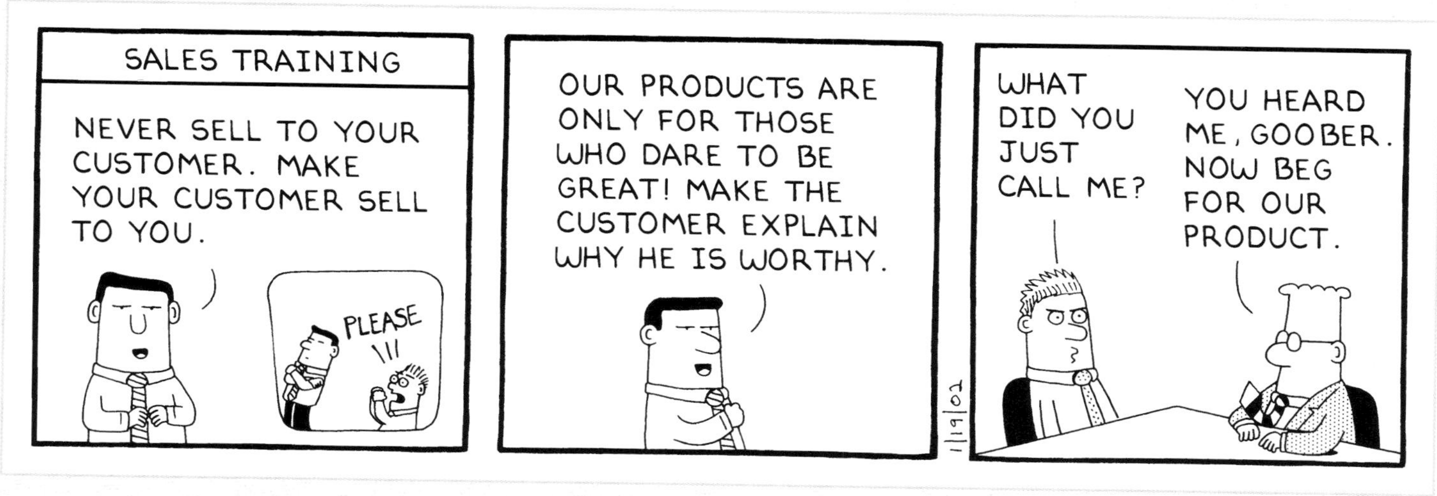
SALES TRAINING
NEVER SELL TO YOUR CUSTOMER. MAKE YOUR CUSTOMER SELL TO YOU.
PLEASE
OUR PRODUCTS ARE ONLY FOR THOSE WHO DARE TO BE GREAT! MAKE THE CUSTOMER EXPLAIN WHY HE IS WORTHY.
WHAT DID YOU JUST CALL ME?
YOU HEARD ME, GOOBER. NOW BEG FOR OUR PRODUCT.
1/19/02

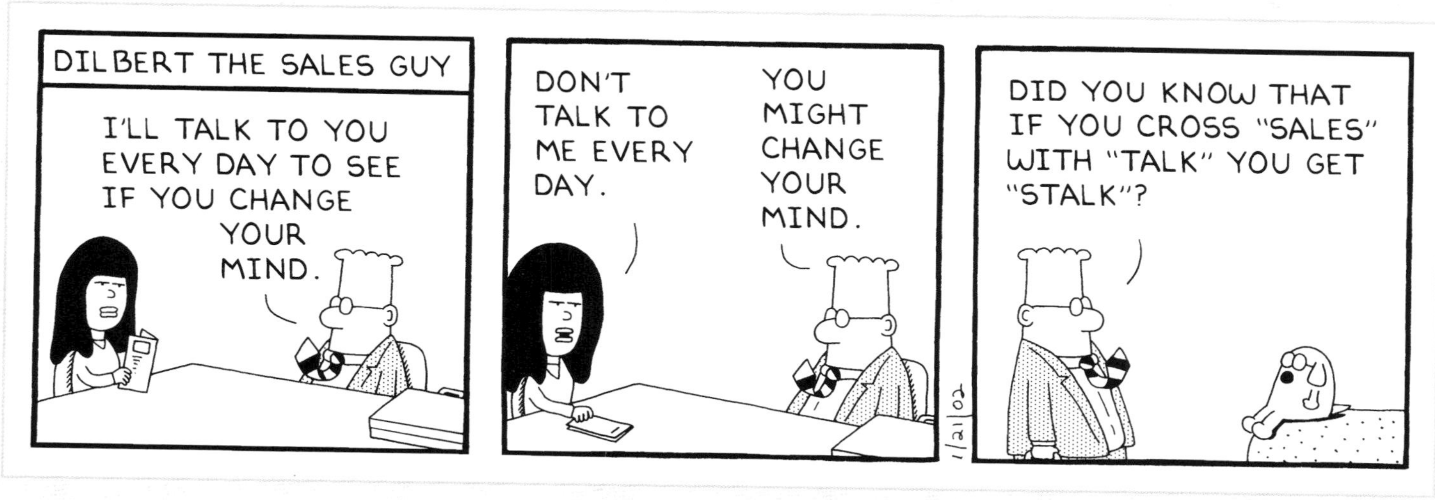
DILBERT THE SALES GUY
I'LL TALK TO YOU EVERY DAY TO SEE IF YOU CHANGE YOUR MIND.
DON'T TALK TO ME EVERY DAY.
YOU MIGHT CHANGE YOUR MIND.
DID YOU KNOW THAT IF YOU CROSS "SALES" WITH "TALK" YOU GET "STALK"?
1/21/02

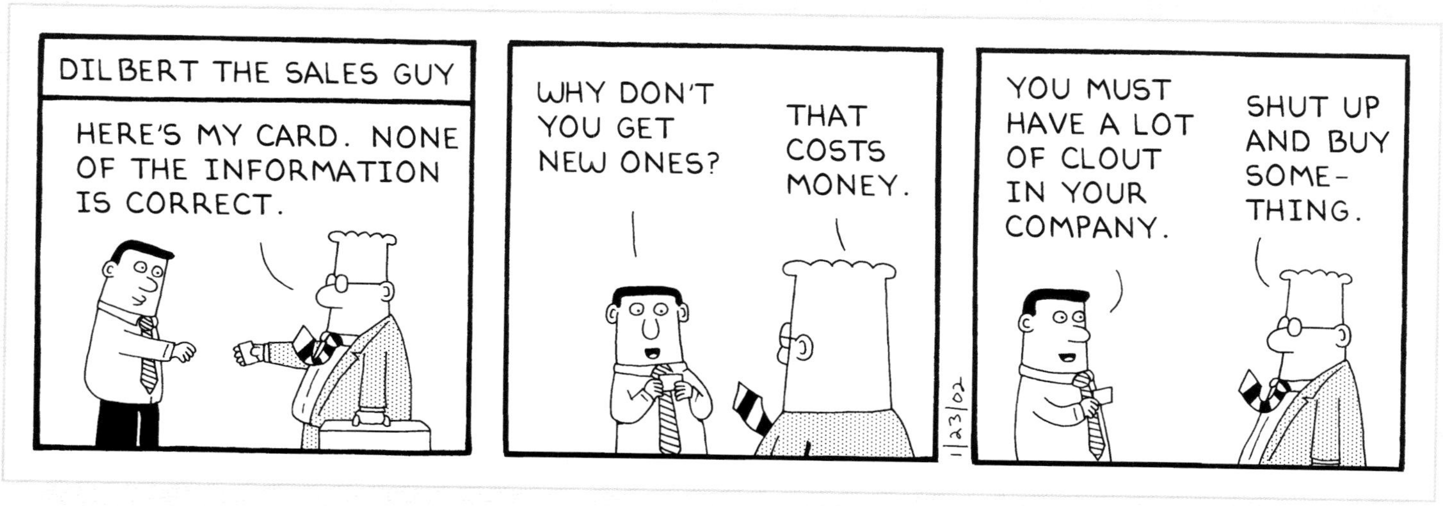
DILBERT THE SALES GUY
HERE'S MY CARD. NONE OF THE INFORMATION IS CORRECT.
WHY DON'T YOU GET NEW ONES?
THAT COSTS MONEY.
YOU MUST HAVE A LOT OF CLOUT IN YOUR COMPANY.
SHUT UP AND BUY SOME-THING.
1/23/02

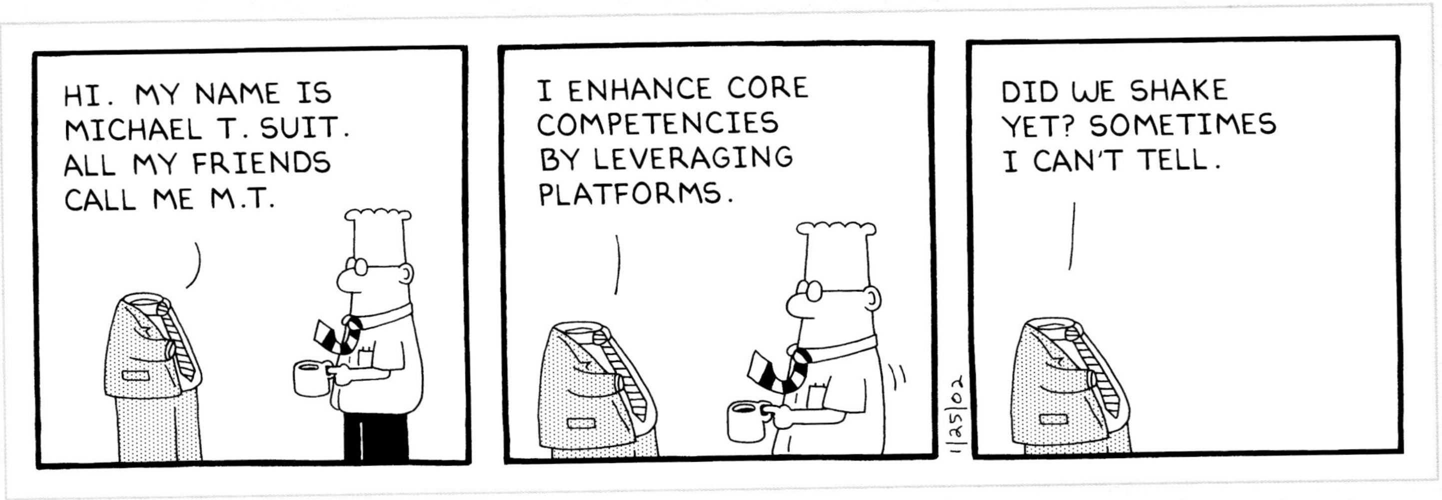
HI. MY NAME IS MICHAEL T. SUIT. ALL MY FRIENDS CALL ME M.T.
I ENHANCE CORE COMPETENCIES BY LEVERAGING PLATFORMS.
DID WE SHAKE YET? SOMETIMES I CAN'T TELL.
1/25/02

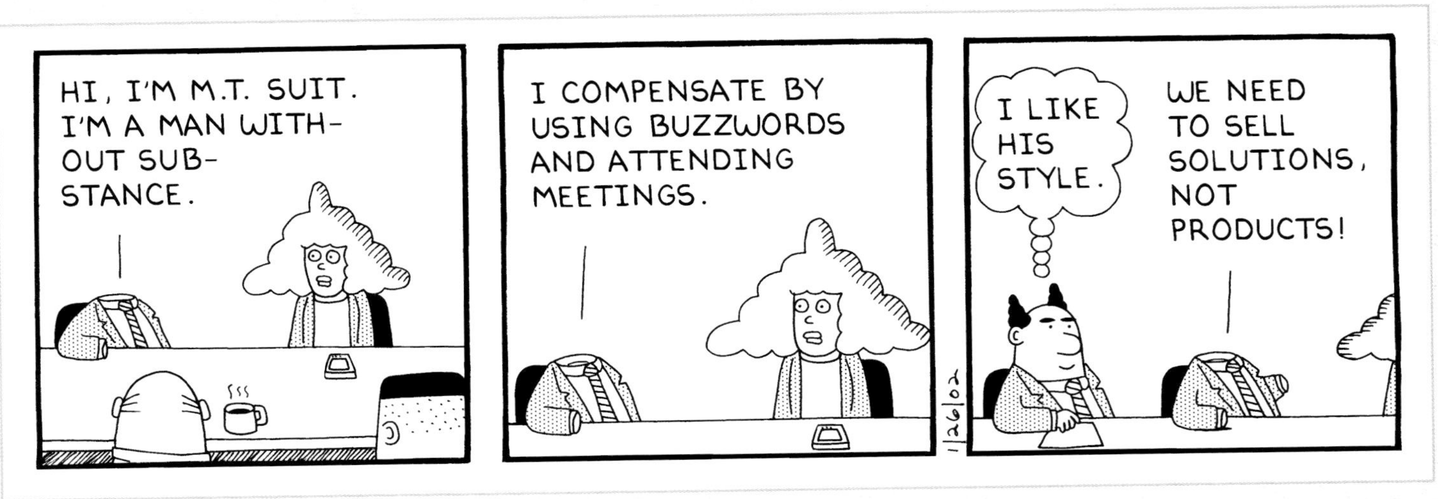
HI, I'M M.T. SUIT. I'M A MAN WITH-OUT SUB-STANCE.
I COMPENSATE BY USING BUZZWORDS AND ATTENDING MEETINGS.
I LIKE HIS STYLE.
WE NEED TO SELL SOLUTIONS, NOT PRODUCTS!
1/26/02

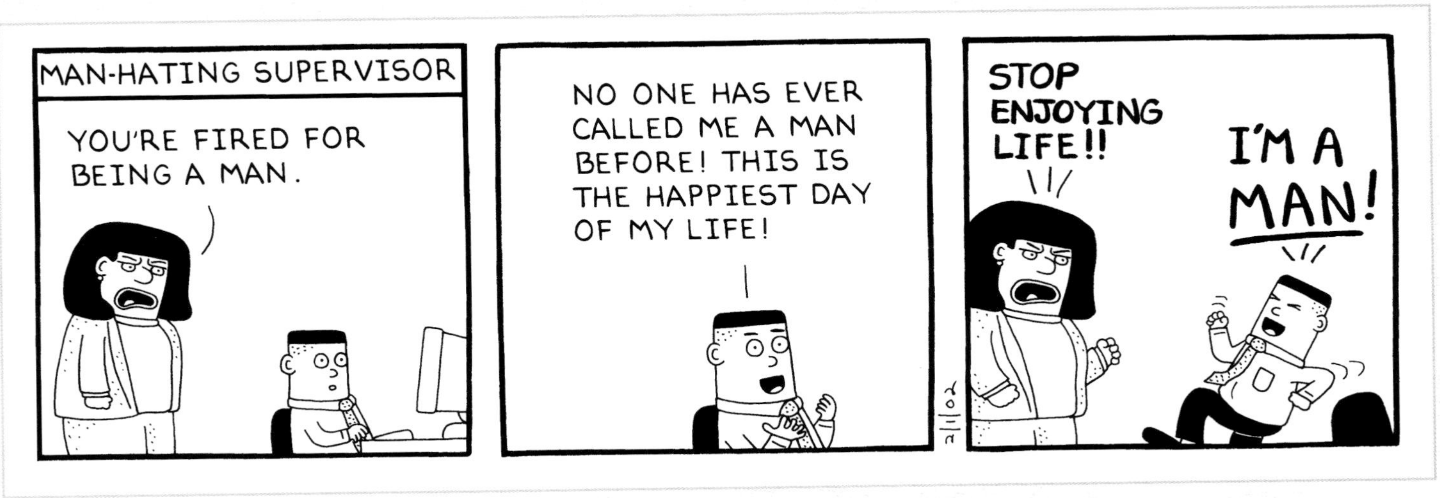
MAN-HATING SUPERVISOR
YOU'RE FIRED FOR BEING A MAN.
NO ONE HAS EVER CALLED ME A MAN BEFORE! THIS IS THE HAPPIEST DAY OF MY LIFE!
STOP ENJOYING LIFE!!
I'M A MAN!
2/1/02

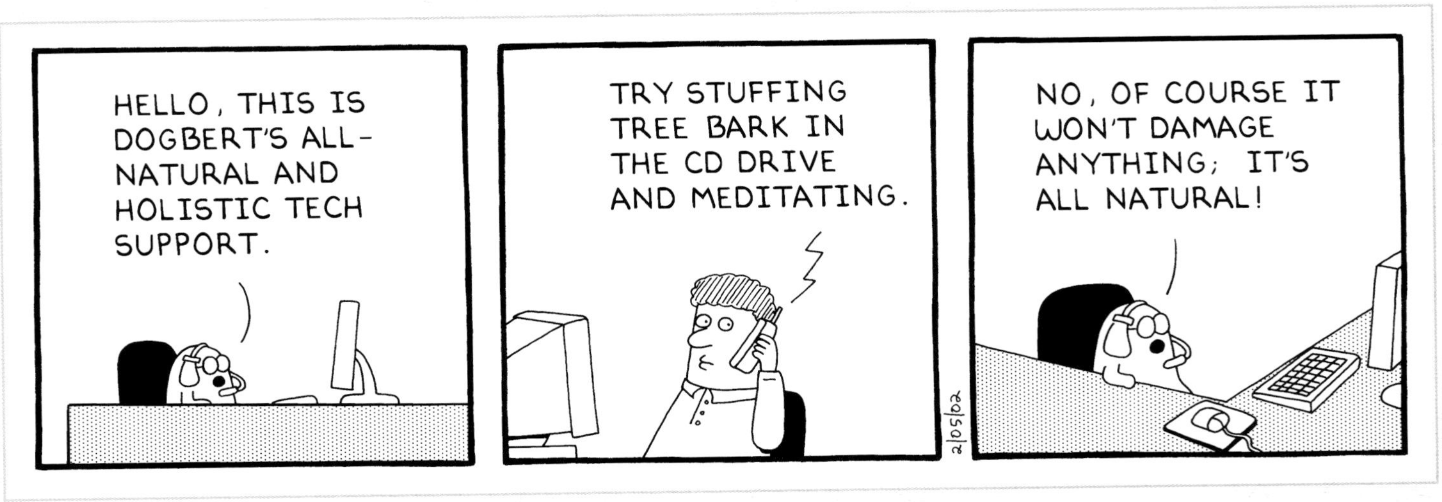
HELLO, THIS IS DOGBERT'S ALL-NATURAL AND HOLISTIC TECH SUPPORT.
TRY STUFFING TREE BARK IN THE CD DRIVE AND MEDITATING.
NO, OF COURSE IT WON'T DAMAGE ANYTHING; IT'S ALL NATURAL!
2/05/02

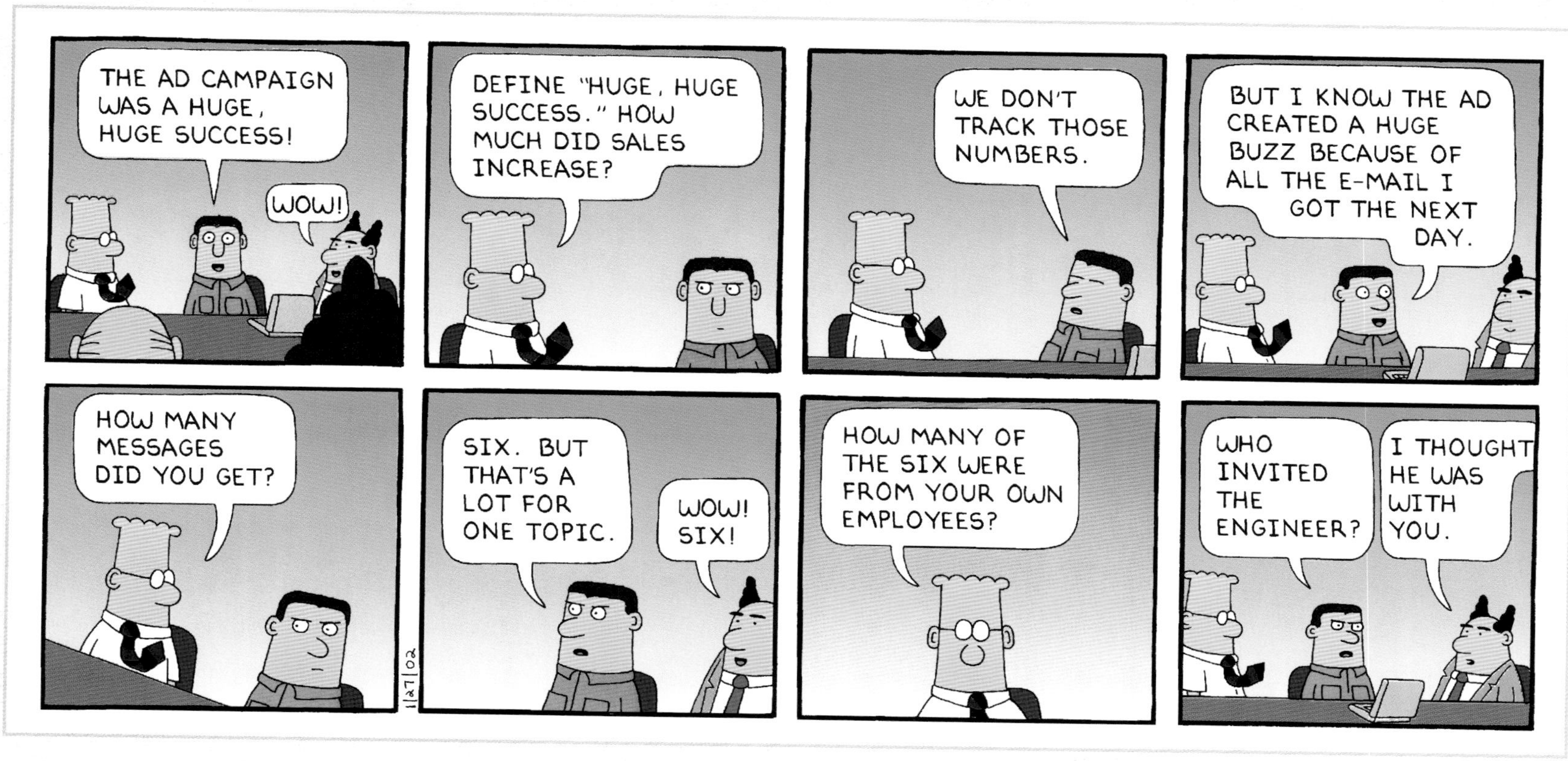
THE AD CAMPAIGN WAS A HUGE, HUGE SUCCESS!
WOW!
DEFINE "HUGE, HUGE SUCCESS." HOW MUCH DID SALES INCREASE?
WE DON'T TRACK THOSE NUMBERS.
BUT I KNOW THE AD CREATED A HUGE BUZZ BECAUSE OF ALL THE E-MAIL I GOT THE NEXT DAY.
HOW MANY MESSAGES DID YOU GET?
SIX. BUT THAT'S A LOT FOR ONE TOPIC.
WOW! SIX!
HOW MANY OF THE SIX WERE FROM YOUR OWN EMPLOYEES?
WHO INVITED THE ENGINEER?
I THOUGHT HE WAS WITH YOU.
1/27/02

I was in this meeting. I played the part of Dilbert.

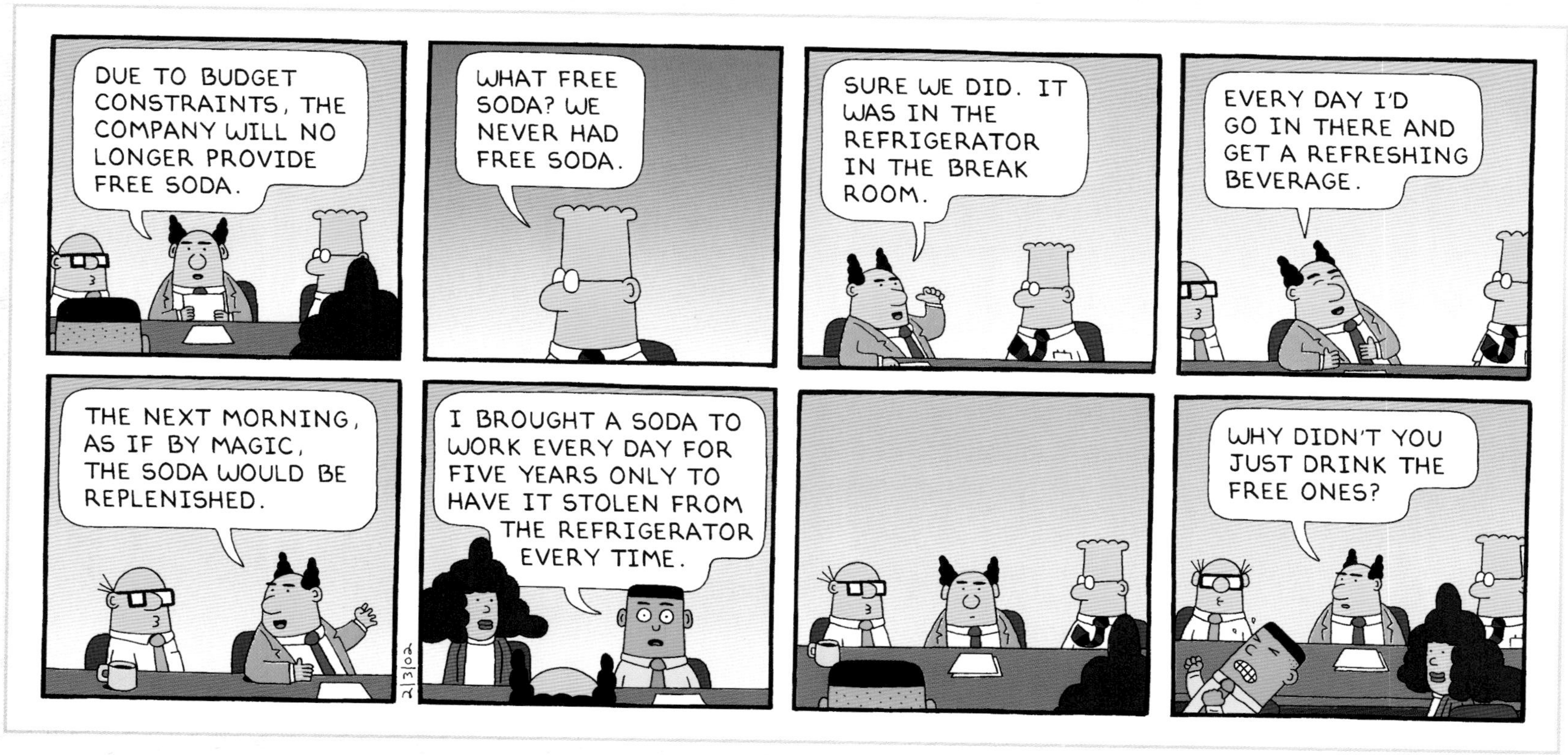
DUE TO BUDGET CONSTRAINTS, THE COMPANY WILL NO LONGER PROVIDE FREE SODA.
WHAT FREE SODA? WE NEVER HAD FREE SODA.
SURE WE DID. IT WAS IN THE REFRIGERATOR IN THE BREAK ROOM.
EVERY DAY I'D GO IN THERE AND GET A REFRESHING BEVERAGE.
THE NEXT MORNING, AS IF BY MAGIC, THE SODA WOULD BE REPLENISHED.
I BROUGHT A SODA TO WORK EVERY DAY FOR FIVE YEARS ONLY TO HAVE IT STOLEN FROM THE REFRIGERATOR EVERY TIME.
WHY DIDN'T YOU JUST DRINK THE FREE ONES?
2/3/02

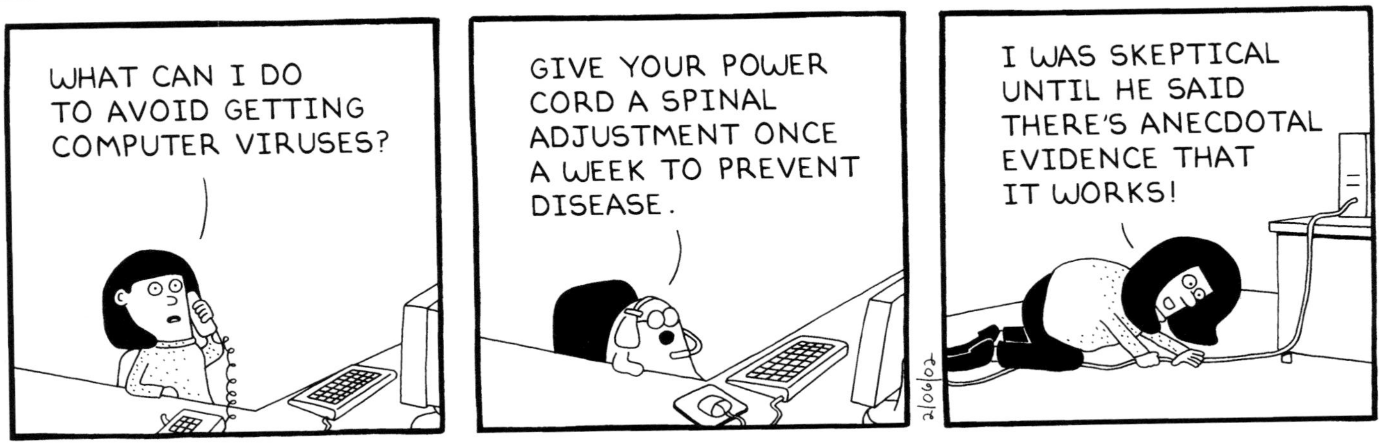
WHAT CAN I DO TO AVOID GETTING COMPUTER VIRUSES?
GIVE YOUR POWER CORD A SPINAL ADJUSTMENT ONCE A WEEK TO PREVENT DISEASE.
2/06/02
I WAS SKEPTICAL UNTIL HE SAID THERE'S ANECDOTAL EVIDENCE THAT IT WORKS!

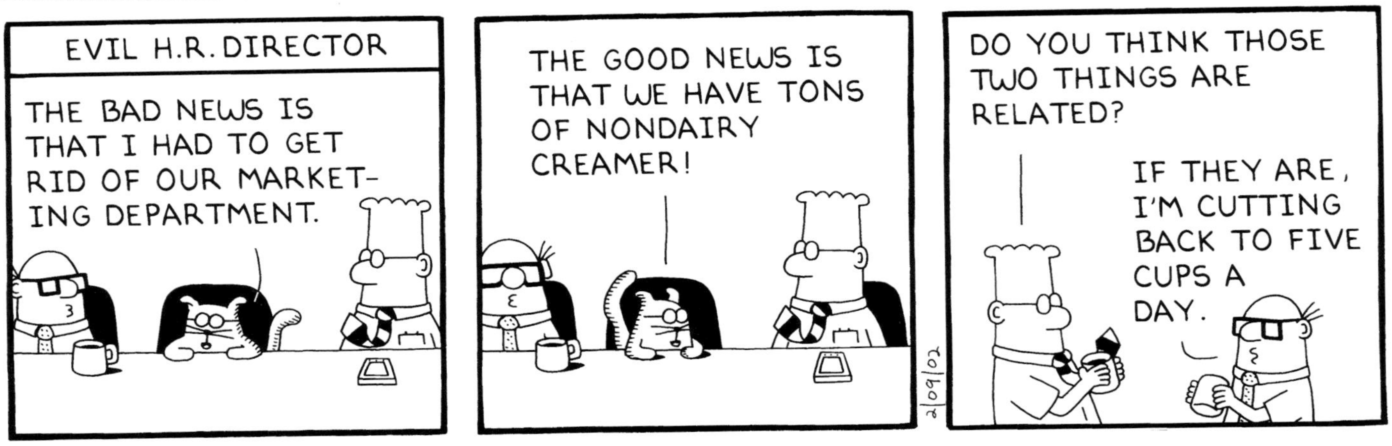
EVIL H.R. DIRECTOR
THE BAD NEWS IS THAT I HAD TO GET RID OF OUR MARKET-ING DEPARTMENT.
THE GOOD NEWS IS THAT WE HAVE TONS OF NONDAIRY CREAMER!
2/09/02
DO YOU THINK THOSE TWO THINGS ARE RELATED?
IF THEY ARE, I'M CUTTING BACK TO FIVE CUPS A DAY.

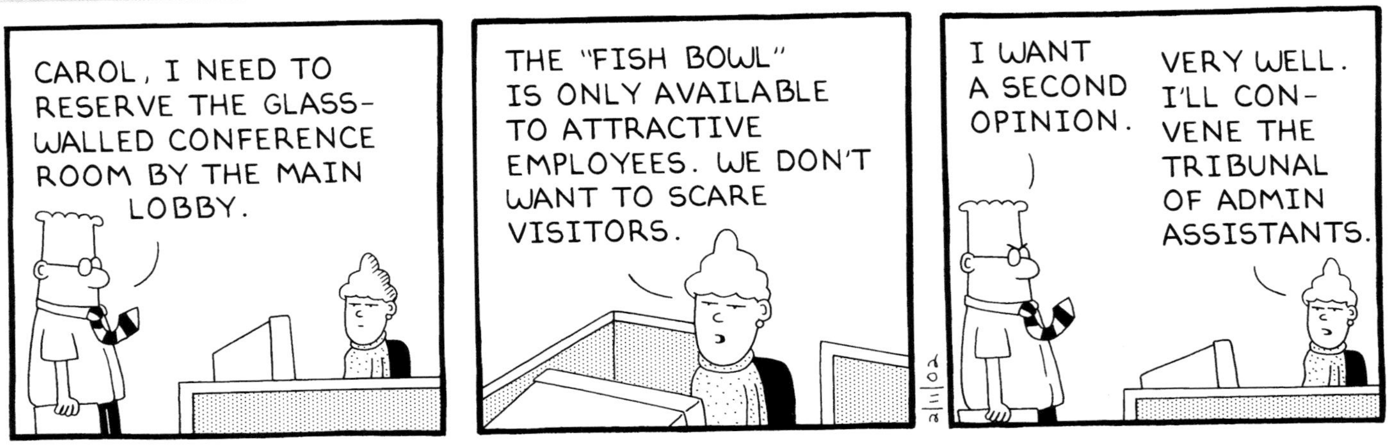
CAROL, I NEED TO RESERVE THE GLASS-WALLED CONFERENCE ROOM BY THE MAIN LOBBY.
THE "FISH BOWL" IS ONLY AVAILABLE TO ATTRACTIVE EMPLOYEES. WE DON'T WANT TO SCARE VISITORS.
2/11/02
I WANT A SECOND OPINION.
VERY WELL. I'LL CON-VENE THE TRIBUNAL OF ADMIN ASSISTANTS.

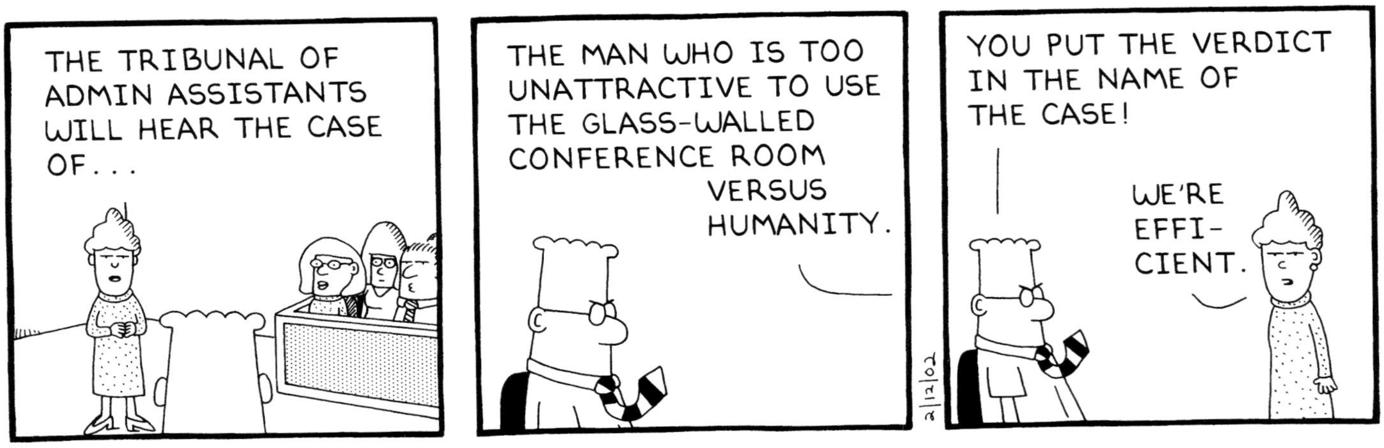
THE TRIBUNAL OF ADMIN ASSISTANTS WILL HEAR THE CASE OF...
THE MAN WHO IS TOO UNATTRACTIVE TO USE THE GLASS-WALLED CONFERENCE ROOM VERSUS HUMANITY.
2/12/02
YOU PUT THE VERDICT IN THE NAME OF THE CASE!
WE'RE EFFI-CIENT.

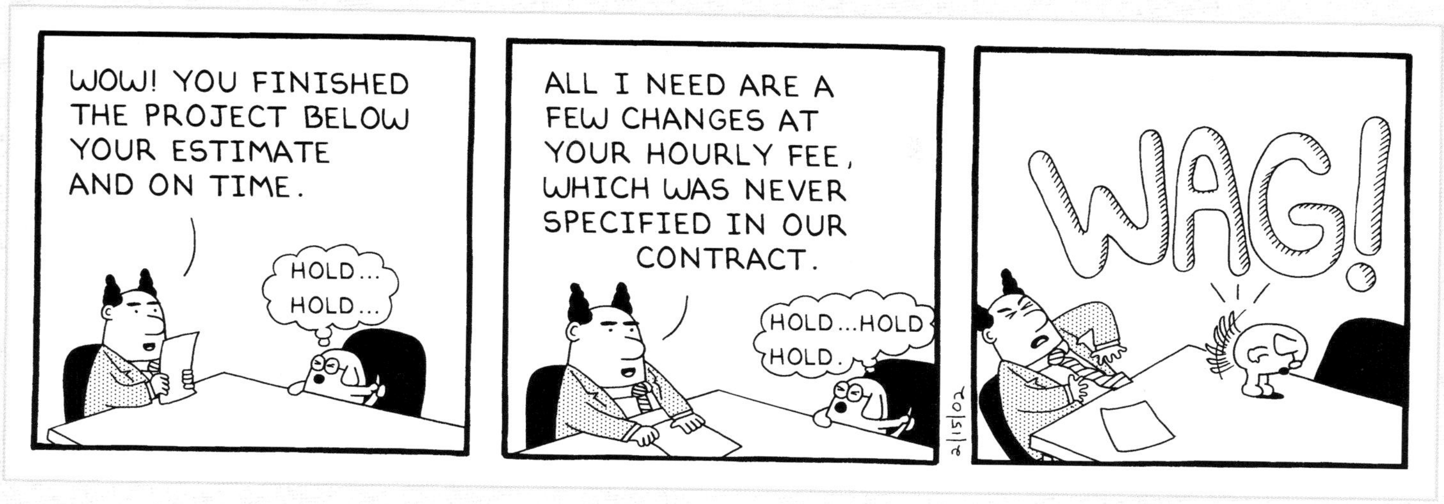
WOW! YOU FINISHED THE PROJECT BELOW YOUR ESTIMATE AND ON TIME.
HOLD... HOLD...
ALL I NEED ARE A FEW CHANGES AT YOUR HOURLY FEE, WHICH WAS NEVER SPECIFIED IN OUR CONTRACT.
HOLD...HOLD HOLD.
2/15/02
WAG!

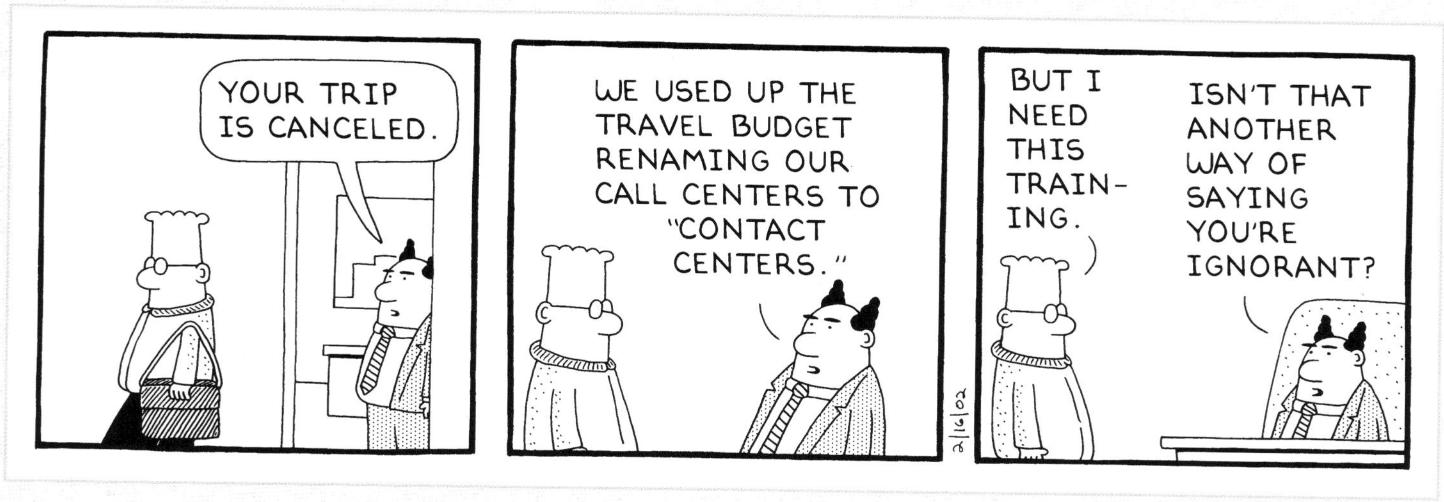
YOUR TRIP IS CANCELED.
WE USED UP THE TRAVEL BUDGET RENAMING OUR CALL CENTERS TO "CONTACT CENTERS."
2/16/02
BUT I NEED THIS TRAIN-ING.
ISN'T THAT ANOTHER WAY OF SAYING YOU'RE IGNORANT?

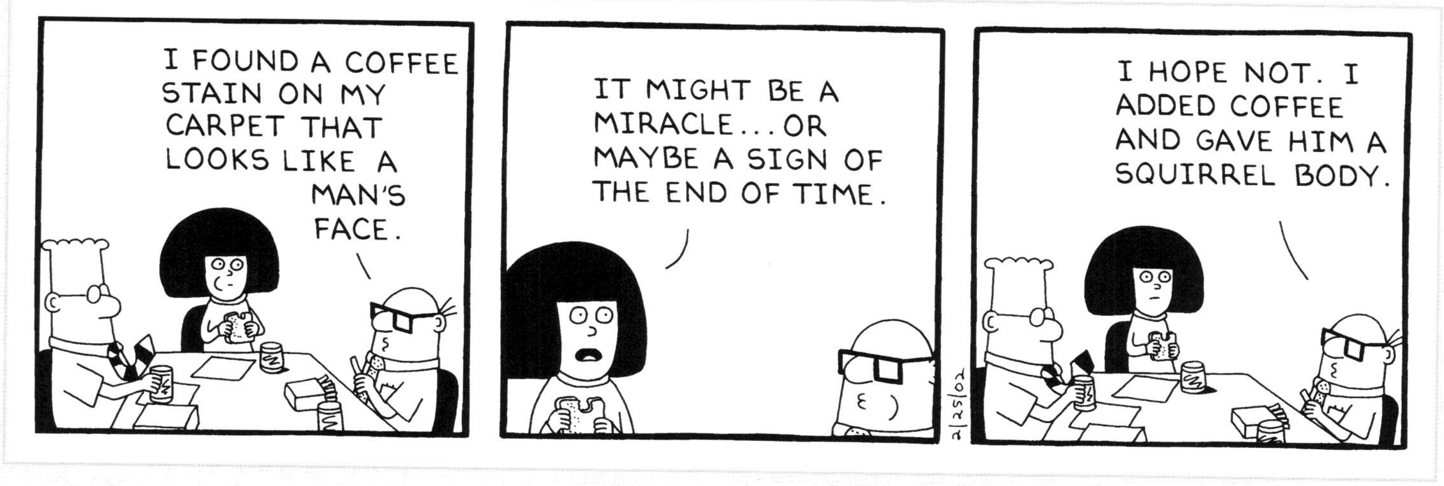
I FOUND A COFFEE STAIN ON MY CARPET THAT LOOKS LIKE A MAN'S FACE.
IT MIGHT BE A MIRACLE...OR MAYBE A SIGN OF THE END OF TIME.
2/25/02
I HOPE NOT. I ADDED COFFEE AND GAVE HIM A SQUIRREL BODY.

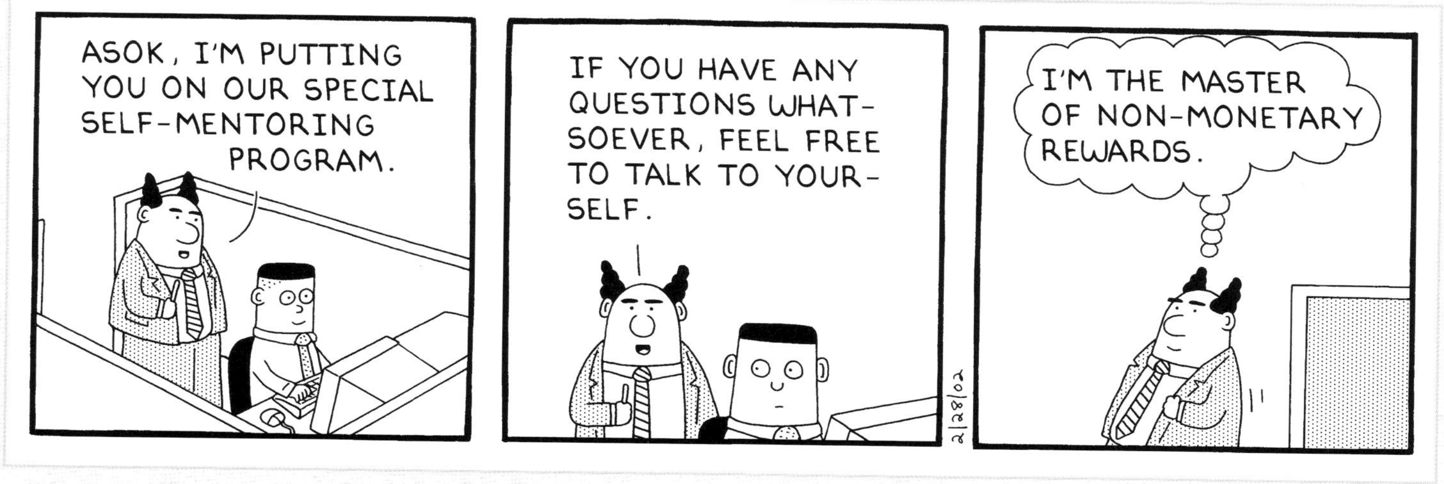
ASOK, I'M PUTTING YOU ON OUR SPECIAL SELF-MENTORING PROGRAM.
IF YOU HAVE ANY QUESTIONS WHAT-SOEVER, FEEL FREE TO TALK TO YOUR-SELF.
2/28/02
I'M THE MASTER OF NON-MONETARY REWARDS.

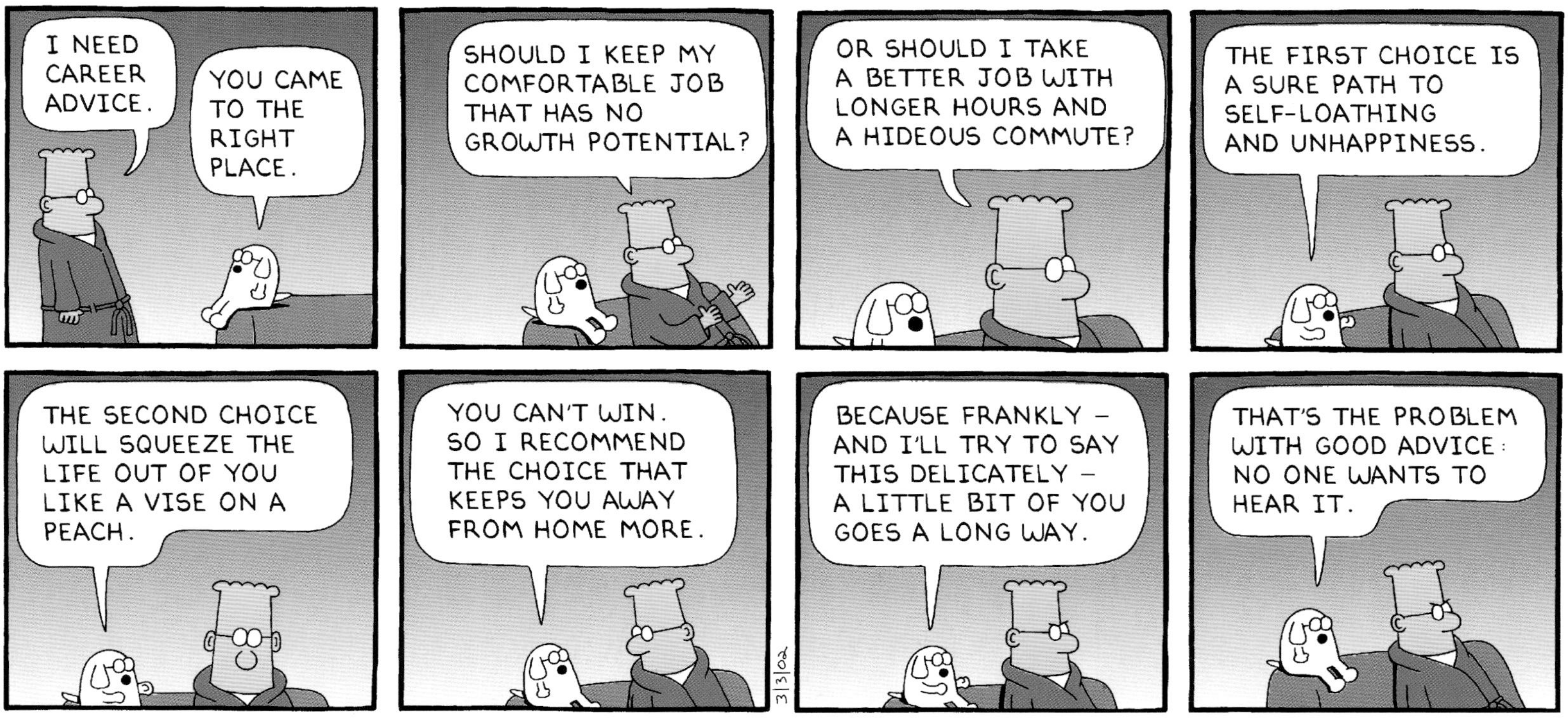
I NEED CAREER ADVICE.
YOU CAME TO THE RIGHT PLACE.
SHOULD I KEEP MY COMFORTABLE JOB THAT HAS NO GROWTH POTENTIAL?
OR SHOULD I TAKE A BETTER JOB WITH LONGER HOURS AND A HIDEOUS COMMUTE?
THE FIRST CHOICE IS A SURE PATH TO SELF-LOATHING AND UNHAPPINESS.
THE SECOND CHOICE WILL SQUEEZE THE LIFE OUT OF YOU LIKE A VISE ON A PEACH.
YOU CAN'T WIN. SO I RECOMMEND THE CHOICE THAT KEEPS YOU AWAY FROM HOME MORE.
3/3/02
BECAUSE FRANKLY – AND I'LL TRY TO SAY THIS DELICATELY – A LITTLE BIT OF YOU GOES A LONG WAY.
THAT'S THE PROBLEM WITH GOOD ADVICE: NO ONE WANTS TO HEAR IT.

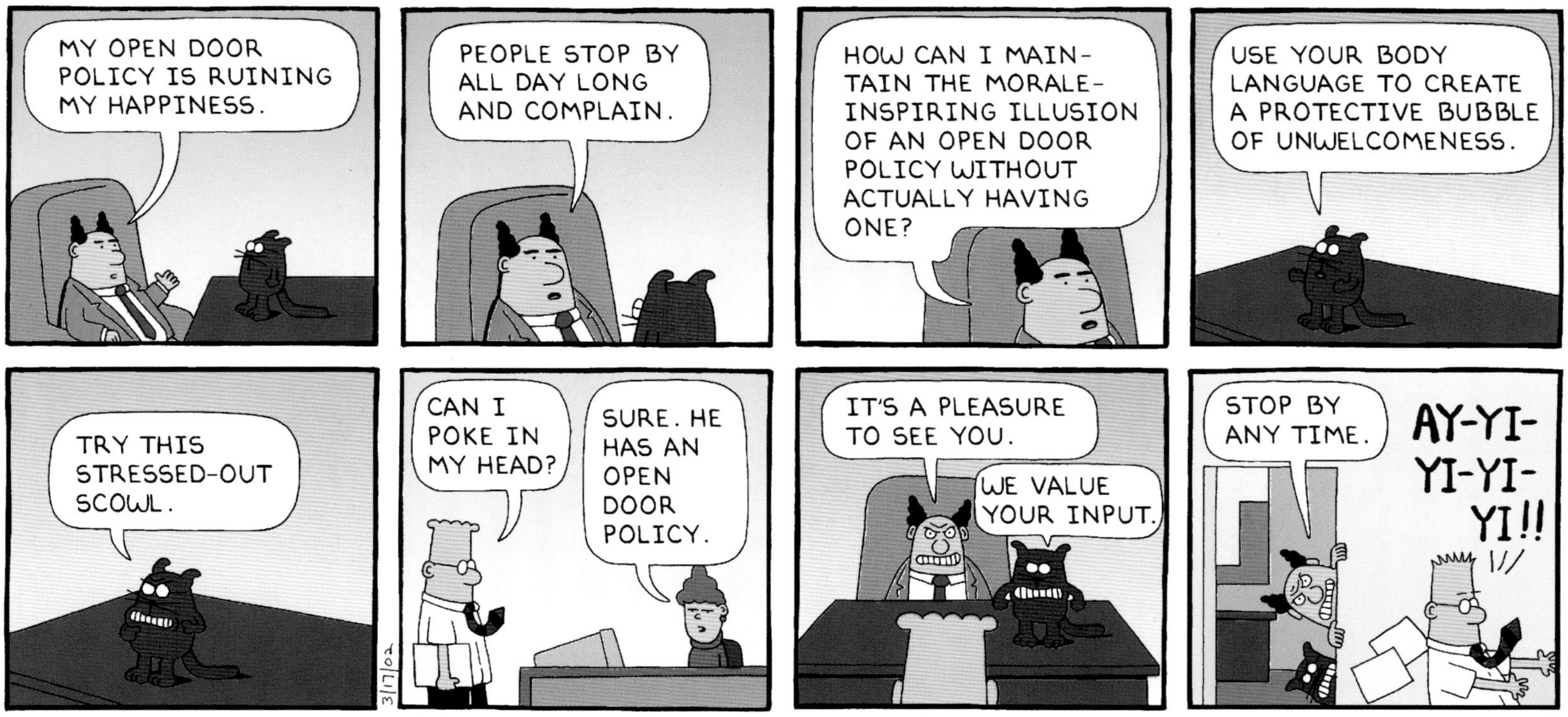
MY OPEN DOOR POLICY IS RUINING MY HAPPINESS.
PEOPLE STOP BY ALL DAY LONG AND COMPLAIN.
HOW CAN I MAIN-TAIN THE MORALE-INSPIRING ILLUSION OF AN OPEN DOOR POLICY WITHOUT ACTUALLY HAVING ONE?
USE YOUR BODY LANGUAGE TO CREATE A PROTECTIVE BUBBLE OF UNWELCOMENESS.
TRY THIS STRESSED-OUT SCOWL.
3/17/02
CAN I POKE IN MY HEAD?
SURE. HE HAS AN OPEN DOOR POLICY.
IT'S A PLEASURE TO SEE YOU.
WE VALUE YOUR INPUT.
STOP BY ANY TIME.
AY-YI-YI-YI-YI!!

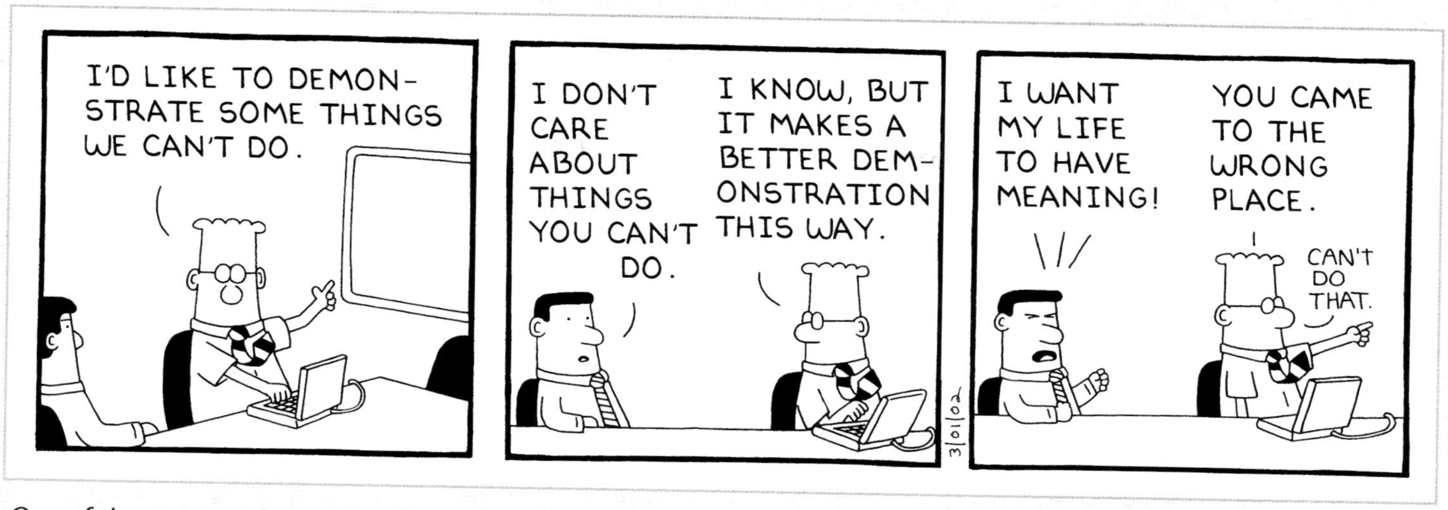
I'D LIKE TO DEMON-STRATE SOME THINGS WE CAN'T DO.
I DON'T CARE ABOUT THINGS YOU CAN'T DO.
I KNOW, BUT IT MAKES A BETTER DEM-ONSTRATION THIS WAY.
3/01/02
I WANT MY LIFE TO HAVE MEANING!
YOU CAME TO THE WRONG PLACE.
CAN'T DO THAT.

One of the strongest human impulses, after survival and reproduction, is the need to communicate irrelevant information.

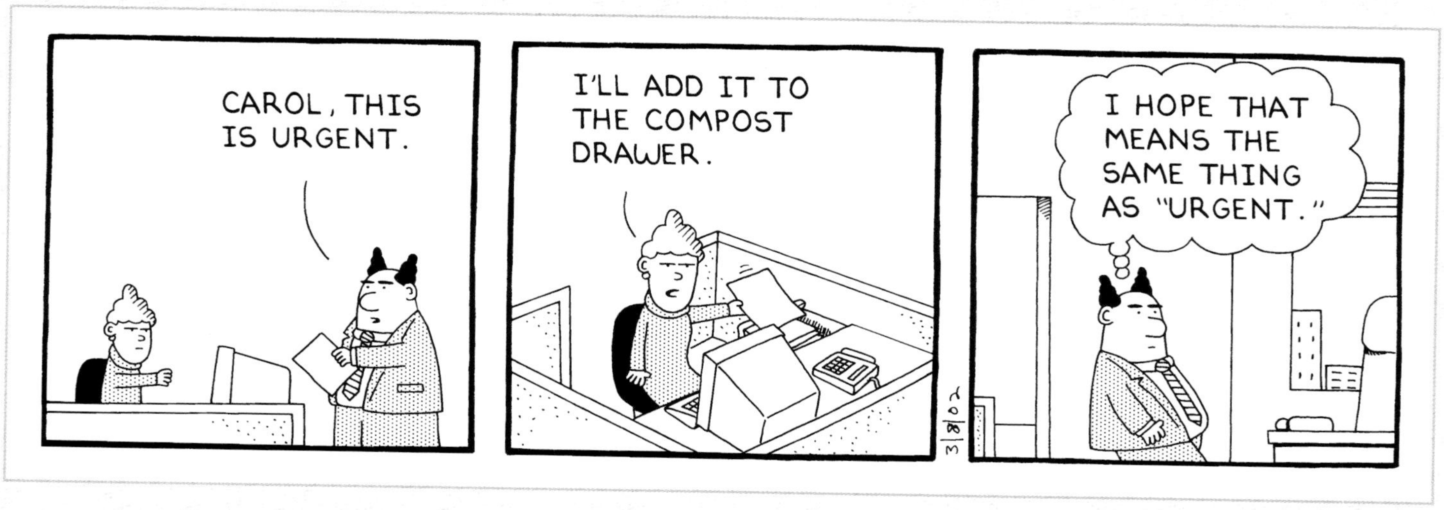
CAROL, THIS IS URGENT.
I'LL ADD IT TO THE COMPOST DRAWER.
3/8/02
I HOPE THAT MEANS THE SAME THING AS "URGENT."

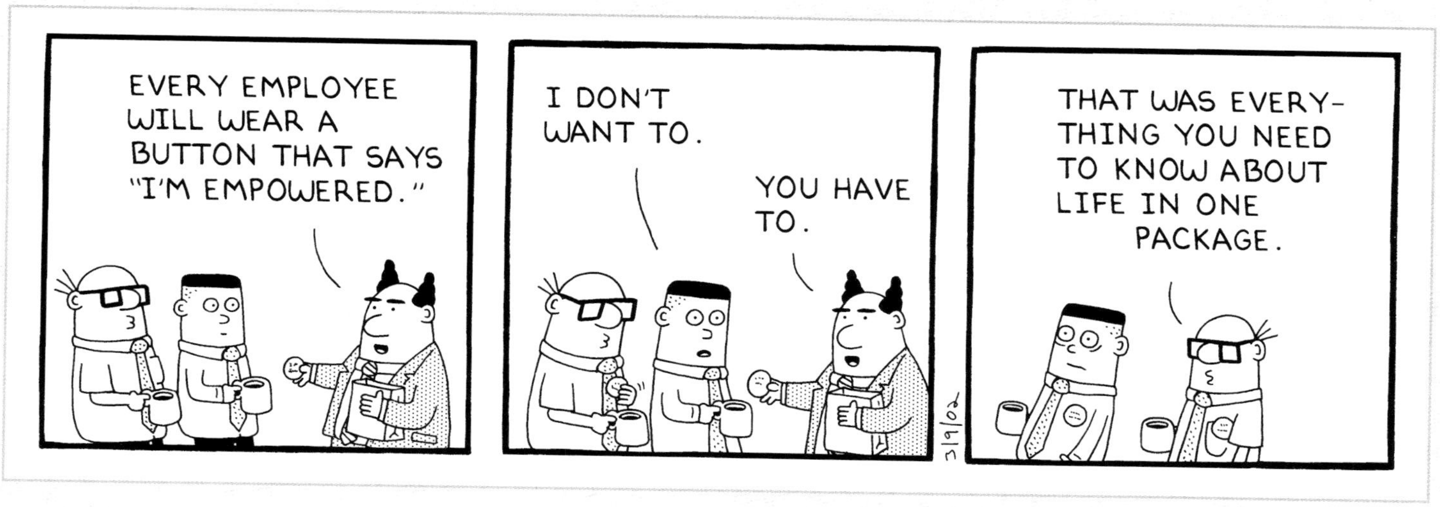
EVERY EMPLOYEE WILL WEAR A BUTTON THAT SAYS "I'M EMPOWERED."
I DON'T WANT TO.
YOU HAVE TO.
3/9/02
THAT WAS EVERY-THING YOU NEED TO KNOW ABOUT LIFE IN ONE PACKAGE.

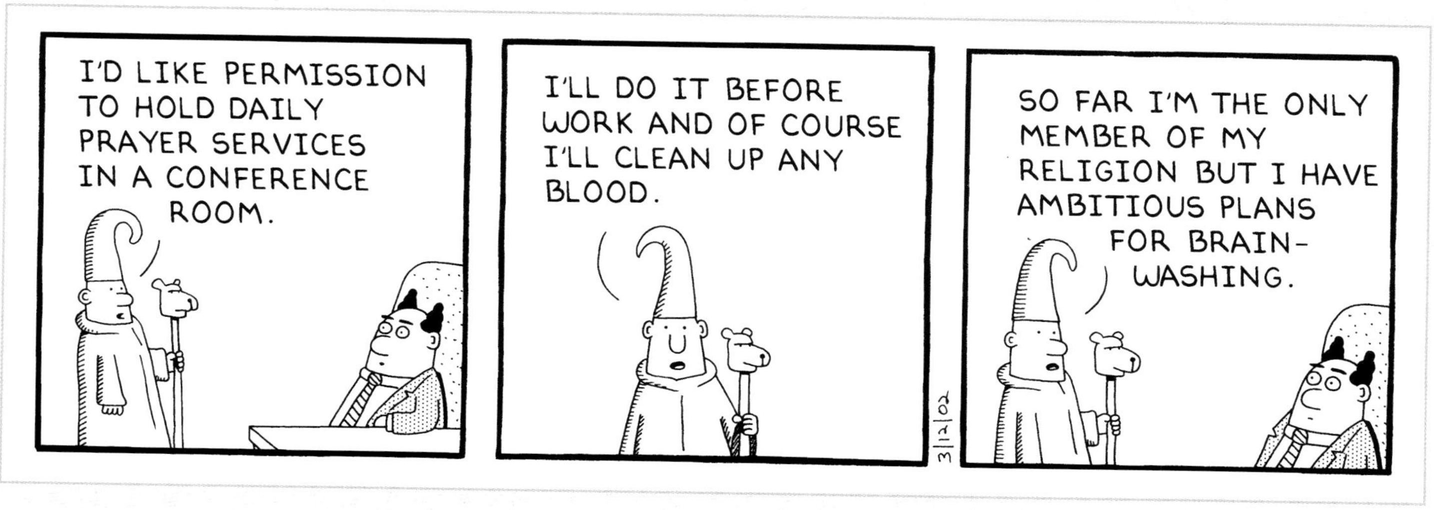
I'D LIKE PERMISSION TO HOLD DAILY PRAYER SERVICES IN A CONFERENCE ROOM.
I'LL DO IT BEFORE WORK AND OF COURSE I'LL CLEAN UP ANY BLOOD.
3/12/02
SO FAR I'M THE ONLY MEMBER OF MY RELIGION BUT I HAVE AMBITIOUS PLANS FOR BRAIN-WASHING.

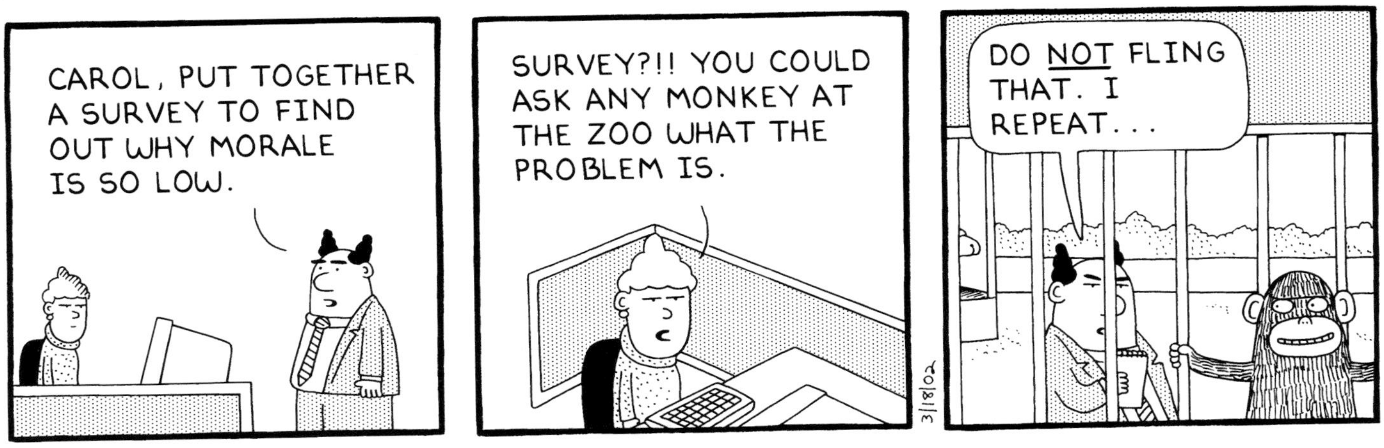
CAROL, PUT TOGETHER A SURVEY TO FIND OUT WHY MORALE IS SO LOW.
SURVEY?!! YOU COULD ASK ANY MONKEY AT THE ZOO WHAT THE PROBLEM IS.
3/18/02
DO NOT FLING THAT. I REPEAT...

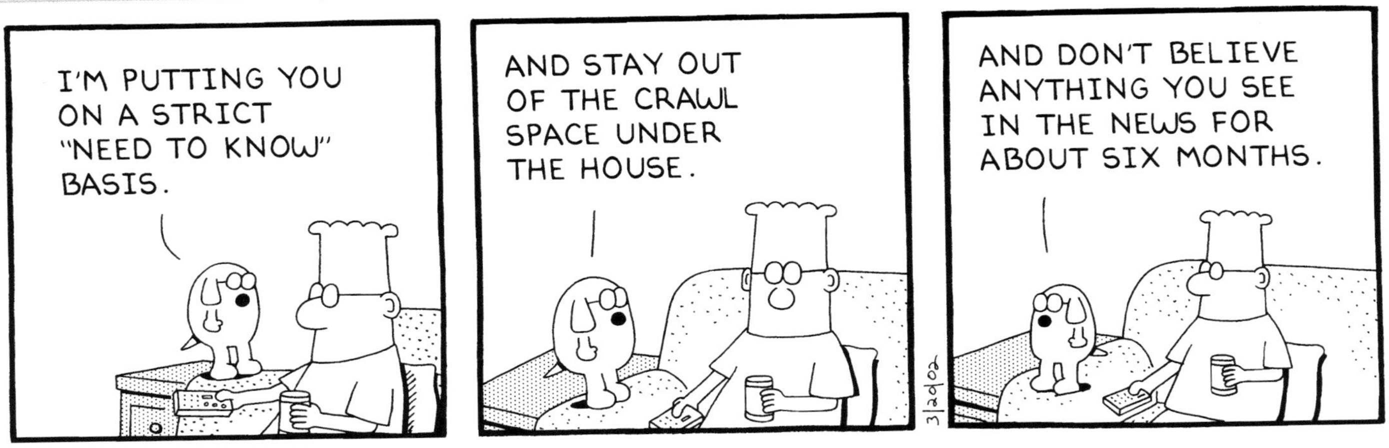
I'M PUTTING YOU ON A STRICT "NEED TO KNOW" BASIS.
AND STAY OUT OF THE CRAWL SPACE UNDER THE HOUSE.
3/20/02
AND DON'T BELIEVE ANYTHING YOU SEE IN THE NEWS FOR ABOUT SIX MONTHS.

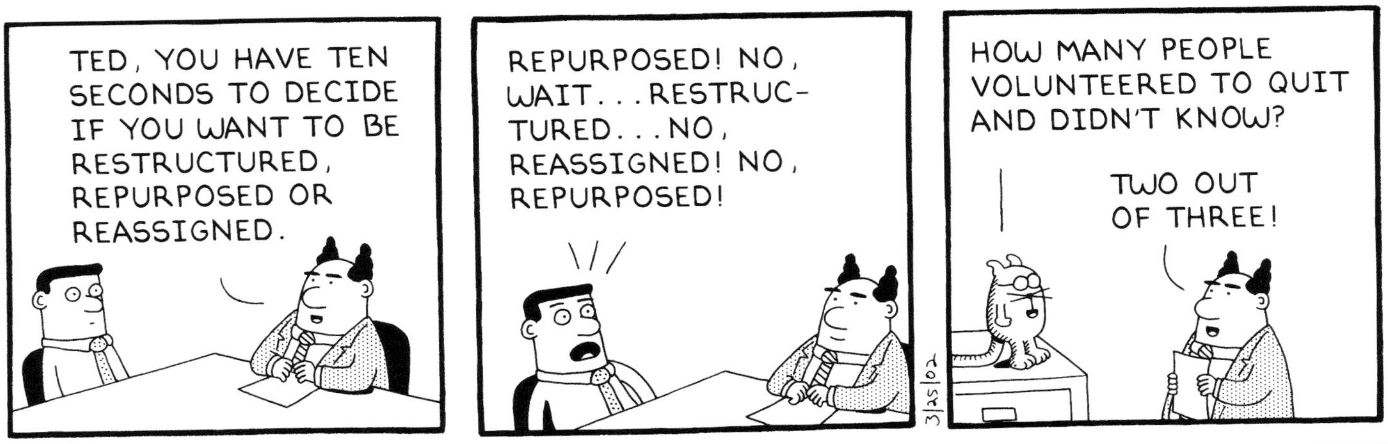
TED, YOU HAVE TEN SECONDS TO DECIDE IF YOU WANT TO BE RESTRUCTURED, REPURPOSED OR REASSIGNED.
REPURPOSED! NO, WAIT... RESTRUCTURED... NO, REASSIGNED! NO, REPURPOSED!
3/25/02
HOW MANY PEOPLE VOLUNTEERED TO QUIT AND DIDN'T KNOW?
TWO OUT OF THREE!

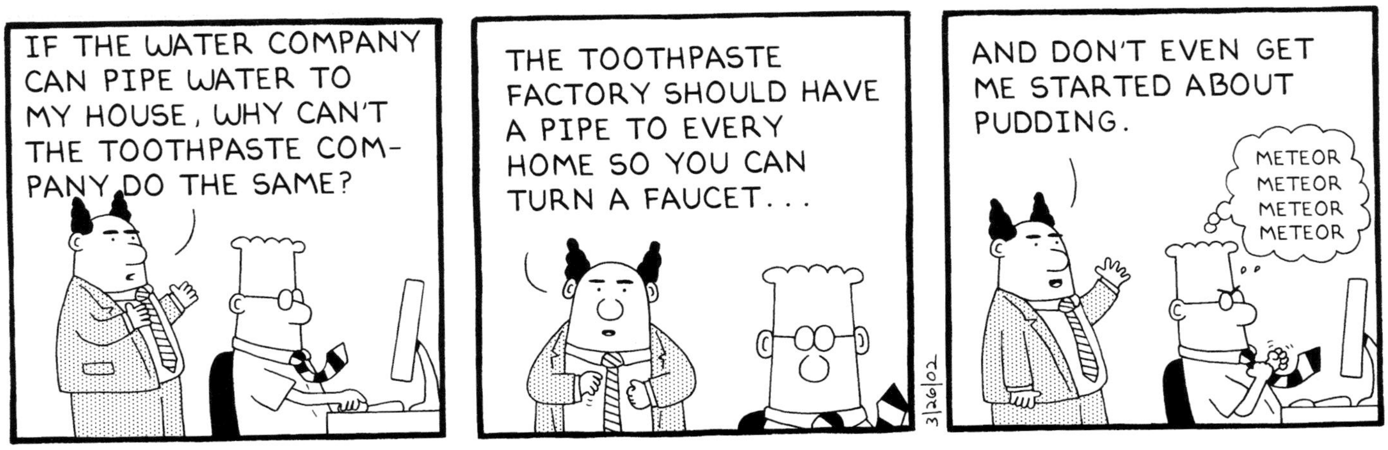
IF THE WATER COMPANY CAN PIPE WATER TO MY HOUSE, WHY CAN'T THE TOOTHPASTE COMPANY DO THE SAME?
THE TOOTHPASTE FACTORY SHOULD HAVE A PIPE TO EVERY HOME SO YOU CAN TURN A FAUCET...
3/26/02
AND DON'T EVEN GET ME STARTED ABOUT PUDDING.
METEOR METEOR METEOR METEOR

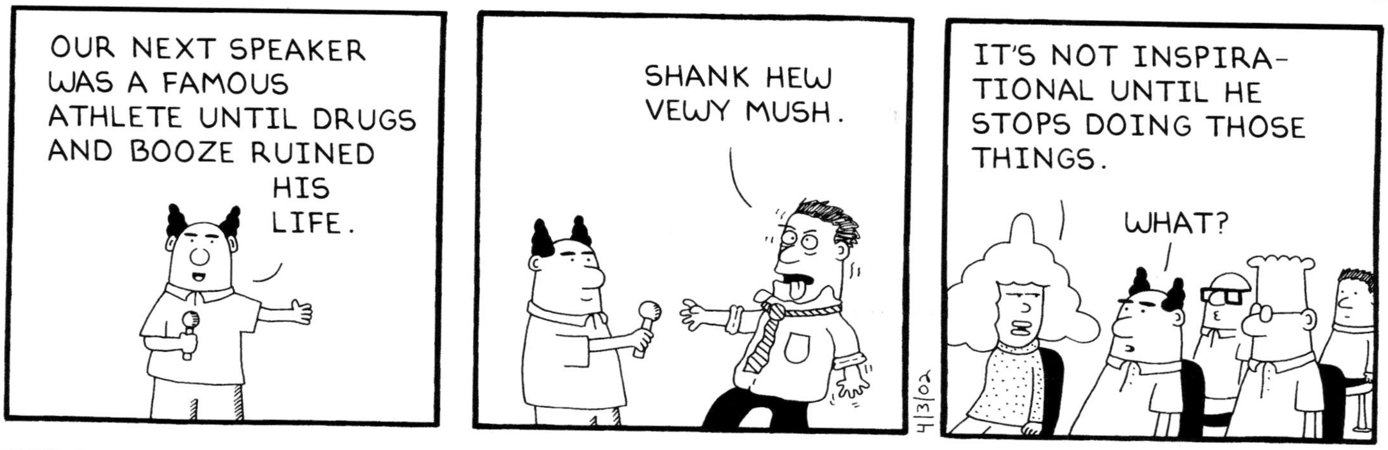
OUR NEXT SPEAKER WAS A FAMOUS ATHLETE UNTIL DRUGS AND BOOZE RUINED HIS LIFE.
SHANK HEW VEWY MUSH.
4/3/02
IT'S NOT INSPIRATIONAL UNTIL HE STOPS DOING THOSE THINGS.
WHAT?

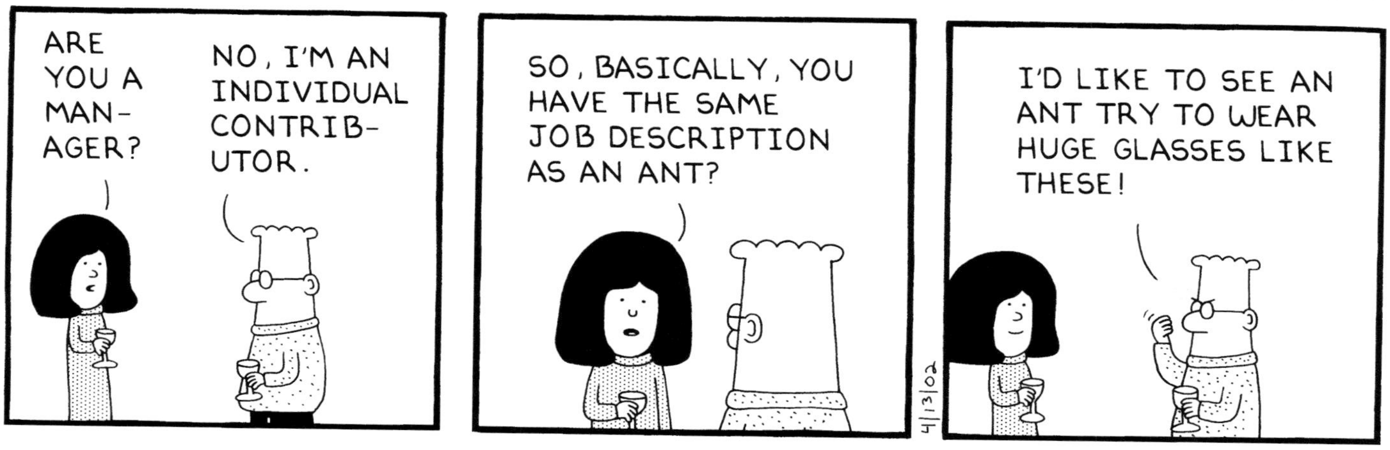
ARE YOU A MANAGER?
NO, I'M AN INDIVIDUAL CONTRIBUTOR.
SO, BASICALLY, YOU HAVE THE SAME JOB DESCRIPTION AS AN ANT?
4/13/02
I'D LIKE TO SEE AN ANT TRY TO WEAR HUGE GLASSES LIKE THESE!

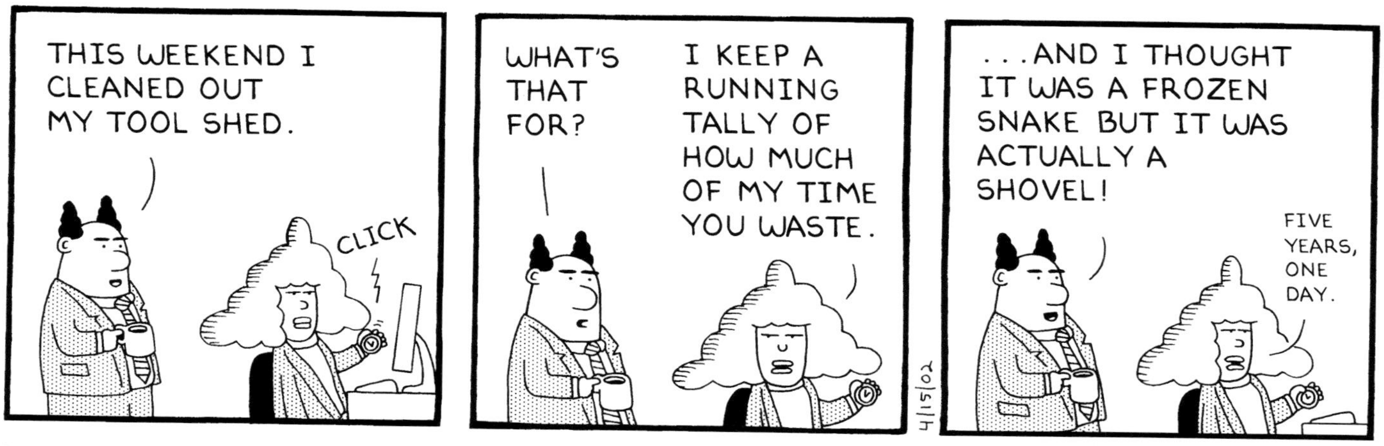
THIS WEEKEND I CLEANED OUT MY TOOL SHED.
CLICK
WHAT'S THAT FOR?
I KEEP A RUNNING TALLY OF HOW MUCH OF MY TIME YOU WASTE.
4/15/02
...AND I THOUGHT IT WAS A FROZEN SNAKE BUT IT WAS ACTUALLY A SHOVEL!
FIVE YEARS, ONE DAY.

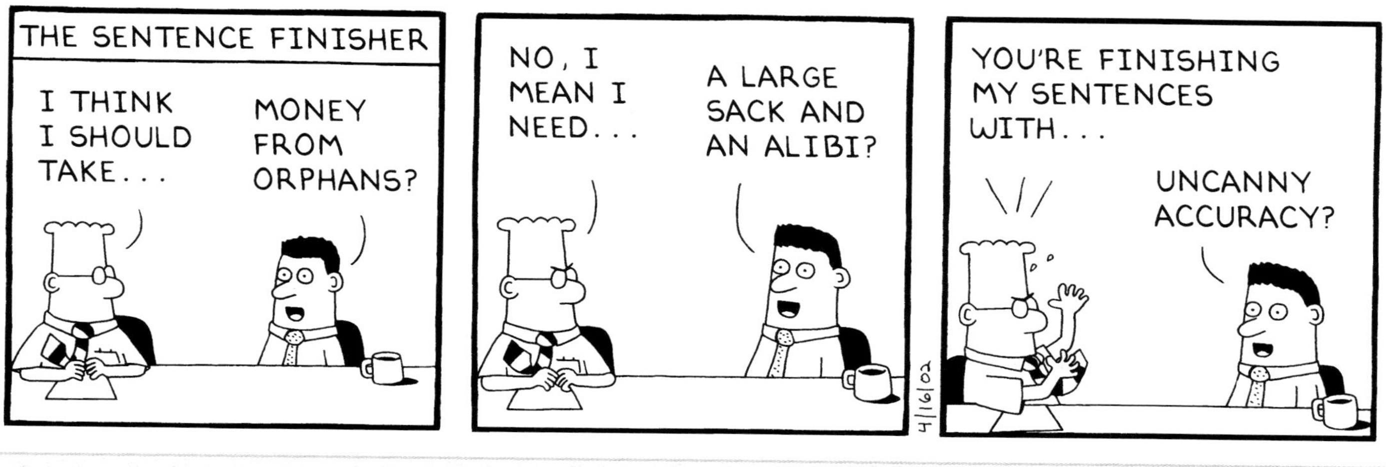
THE SENTENCE FINISHER
I THINK I SHOULD TAKE...
MONEY FROM ORPHANS?
NO, I MEAN I NEED...
A LARGE SACK AND AN ALIBI?
4/16/02
YOU'RE FINISHING MY SENTENCES WITH...
UNCANNY ACCURACY?

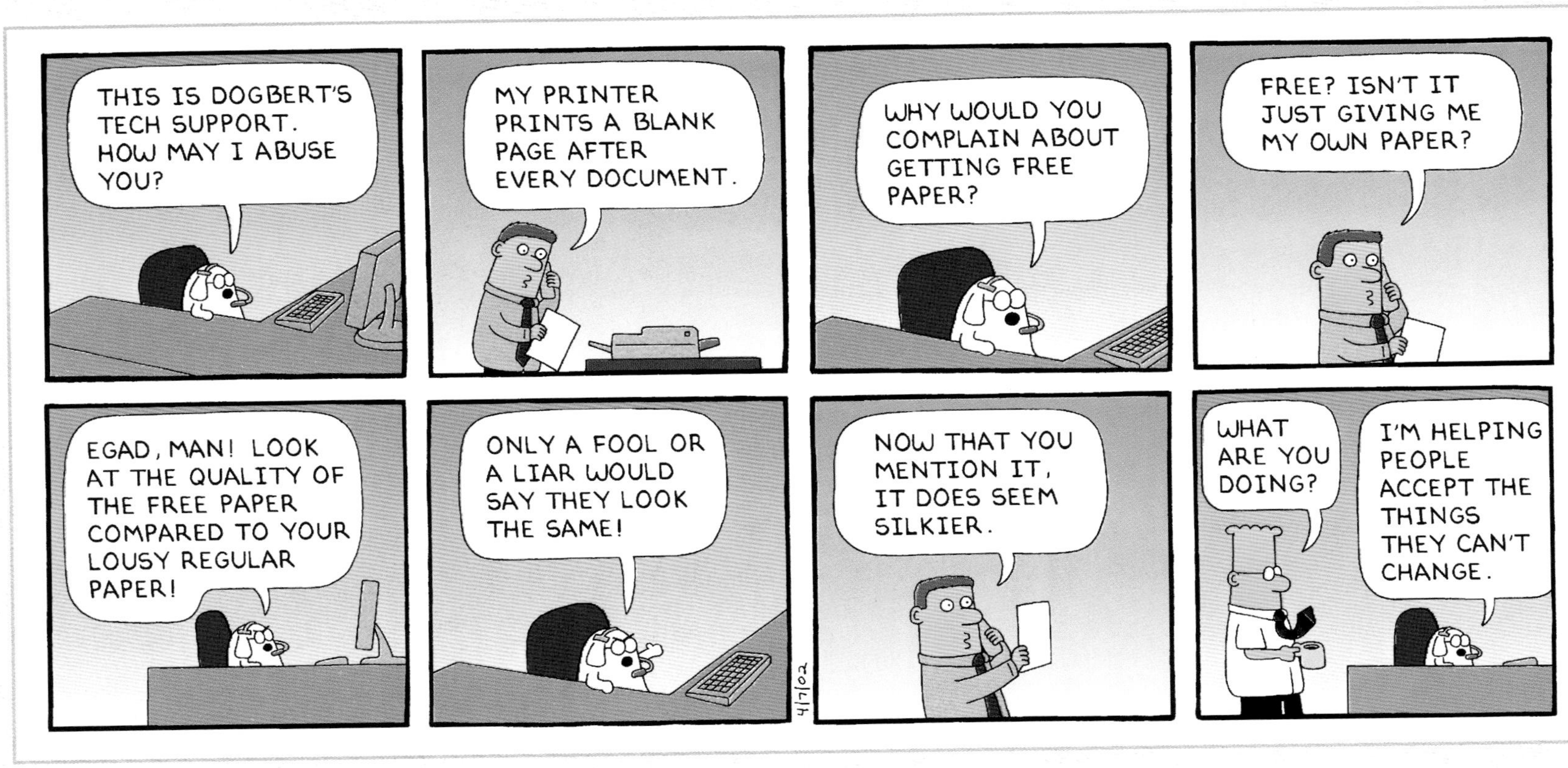
THIS IS DOGBERT'S TECH SUPPORT. HOW MAY I ABUSE YOU?
MY PRINTER PRINTS A BLANK PAGE AFTER EVERY DOCUMENT.
WHY WOULD YOU COMPLAIN ABOUT GETTING FREE PAPER?
FREE? ISN'T IT JUST GIVING ME MY OWN PAPER?
EGAD, MAN! LOOK AT THE QUALITY OF THE FREE PAPER COMPARED TO YOUR LOUSY REGULAR PAPER!
ONLY A FOOL OR A LIAR WOULD SAY THEY LOOK THE SAME!
4/7/02
NOW THAT YOU MENTION IT, IT DOES SEEM SILKIER.
WHAT ARE YOU DOING?
I'M HELPING PEOPLE ACCEPT THE THINGS THEY CAN'T CHANGE.

Implied flatulence is always funny. It's the law.

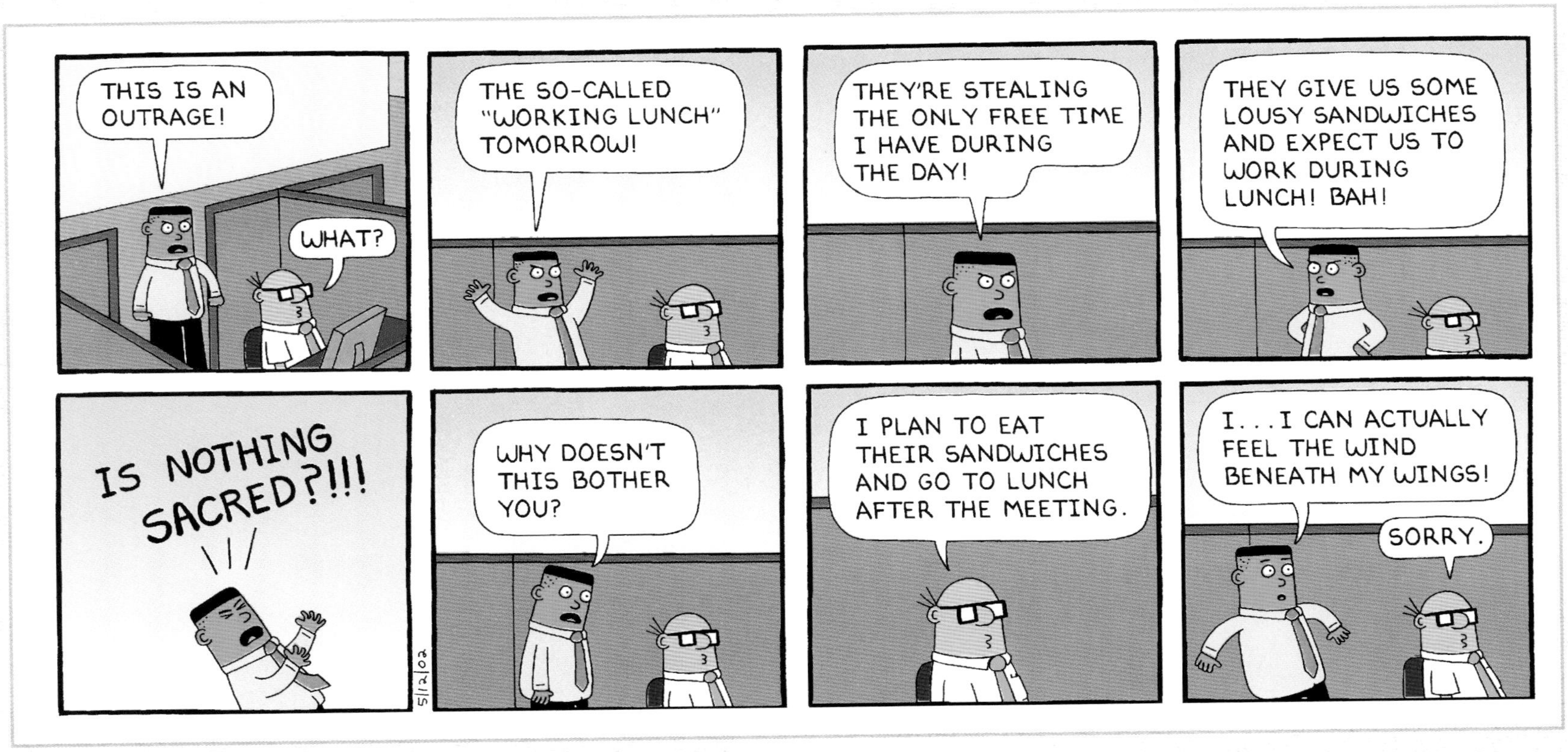
THIS IS AN OUTRAGE!
WHAT?
THE SO-CALLED "WORKING LUNCH" TOMORROW!
THEY'RE STEALING THE ONLY FREE TIME I HAVE DURING THE DAY!
THEY GIVE US SOME LOUSY SANDWICHES AND EXPECT US TO WORK DURING LUNCH! BAH!
IS NOTHING SACRED?!!!
5/12/02
WHY DOESN'T THIS BOTHER YOU?
I PLAN TO EAT THEIR SANDWICHES AND GO TO LUNCH AFTER THE MEETING.
I...I CAN ACTUALLY FEEL THE WIND BENEATH MY WINGS!
SORRY.

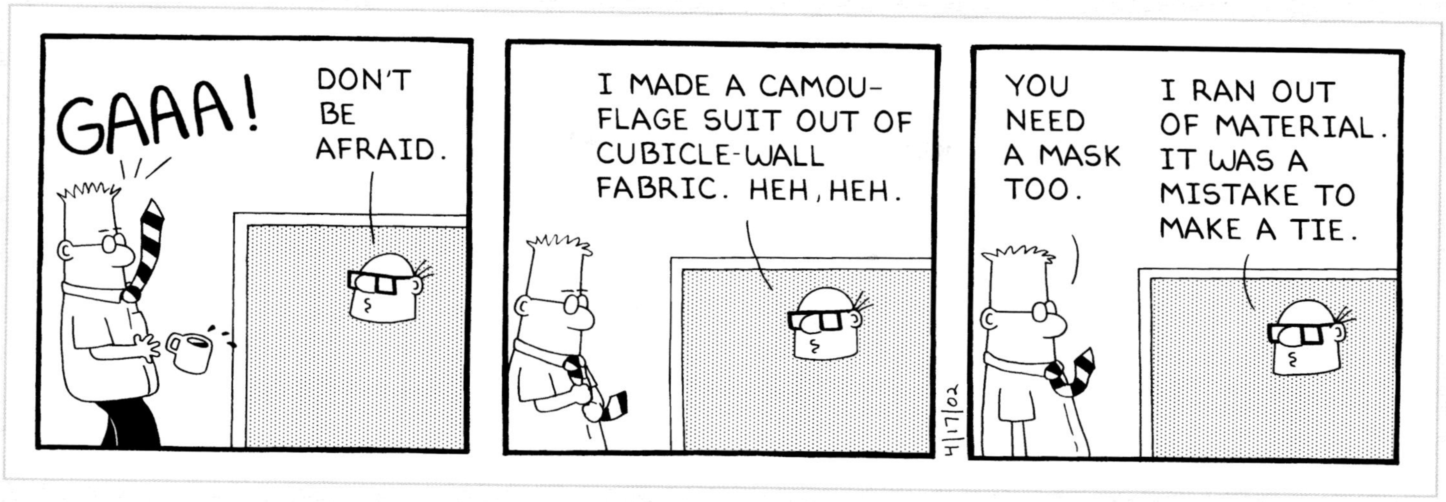
GAAA!
DON'T BE AFRAID.
I MADE A CAMOU-FLAGE SUIT OUT OF CUBICLE-WALL FABRIC. HEH, HEH.
YOU NEED A MASK TOO.
I RAN OUT OF MATERIAL. IT WAS A MISTAKE TO MAKE A TIE.
4/17/02

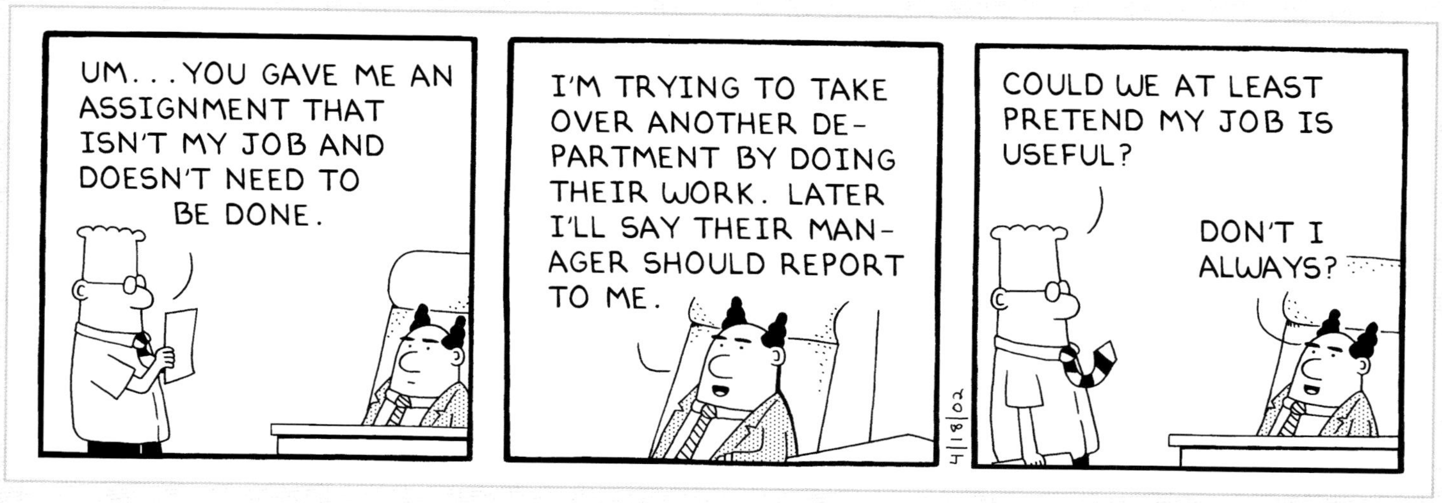
UM...YOU GAVE ME AN ASSIGNMENT THAT ISN'T MY JOB AND DOESN'T NEED TO BE DONE.
I'M TRYING TO TAKE OVER ANOTHER DE-PARTMENT BY DOING THEIR WORK. LATER I'LL SAY THEIR MAN-AGER SHOULD REPORT TO ME.
COULD WE AT LEAST PRETEND MY JOB IS USEFUL?
DON'T I ALWAYS?
4/18/02

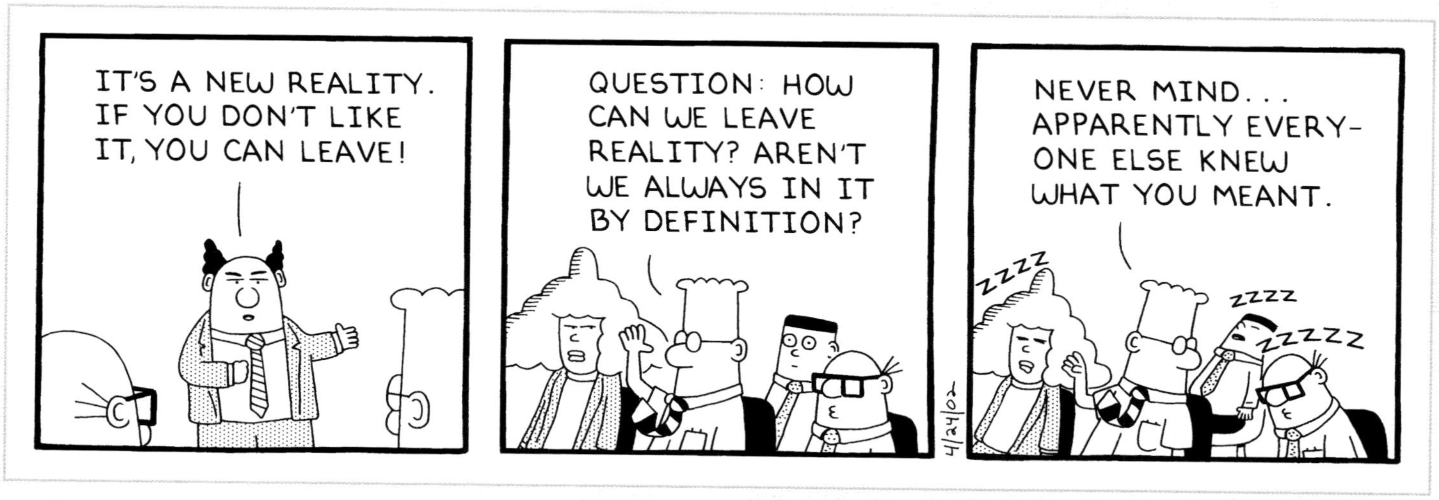
IT'S A NEW REALITY. IF YOU DON'T LIKE IT, YOU CAN LEAVE!
QUESTION: HOW CAN WE LEAVE REALITY? AREN'T WE ALWAYS IN IT BY DEFINITION?
NEVER MIND... APPARENTLY EVERY-ONE ELSE KNEW WHAT YOU MEANT.
ZZZZ
ZZZZ
ZZZZZ
4/24/02

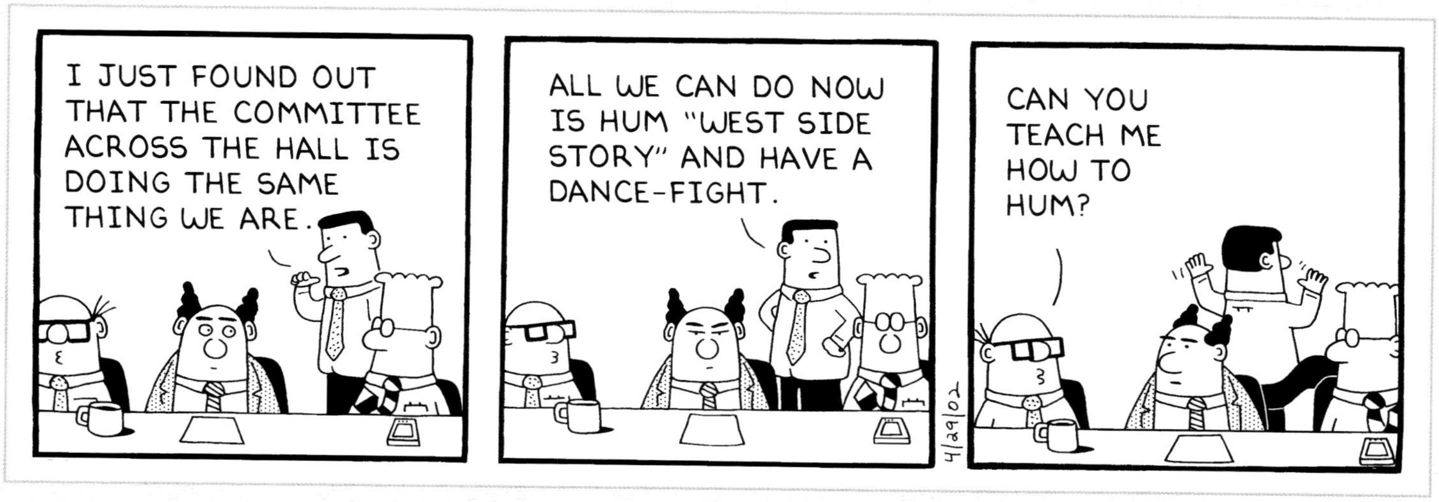
I JUST FOUND OUT THAT THE COMMITTEE ACROSS THE HALL IS DOING THE SAME THING WE ARE.
ALL WE CAN DO NOW IS HUM "WEST SIDE STORY" AND HAVE A DANCE-FIGHT.
CAN YOU TEACH ME HOW TO HUM?
4/29/02

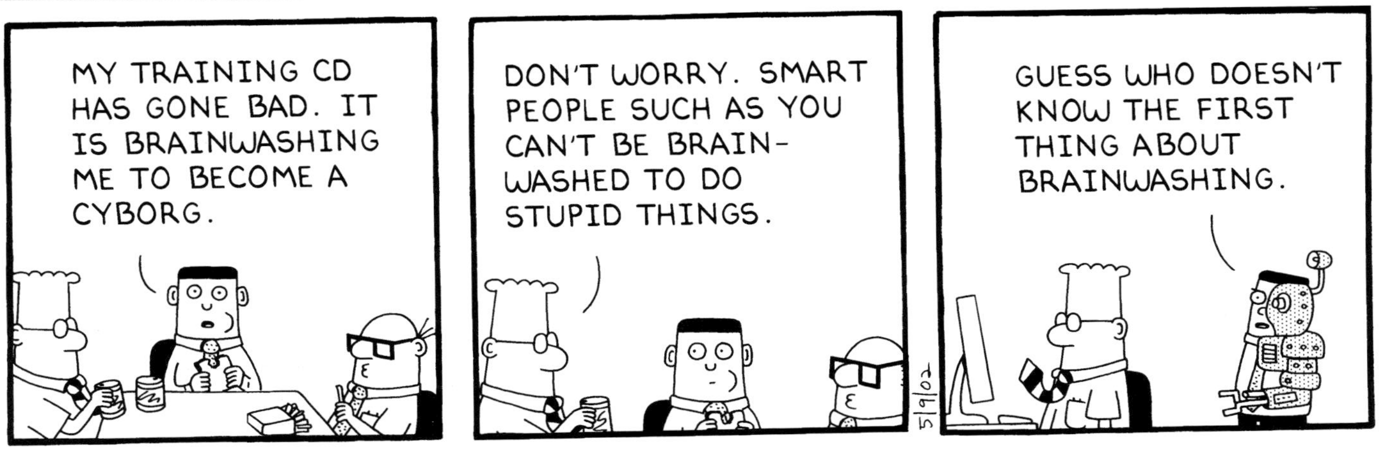
MY TRAINING CD HAS GONE BAD. IT IS BRAINWASHING ME TO BECOME A CYBORG.
DON'T WORRY. SMART PEOPLE SUCH AS YOU CAN'T BE BRAIN-WASHED TO DO STUPID THINGS.
5/9/02
GUESS WHO DOESN'T KNOW THE FIRST THING ABOUT BRAINWASHING.

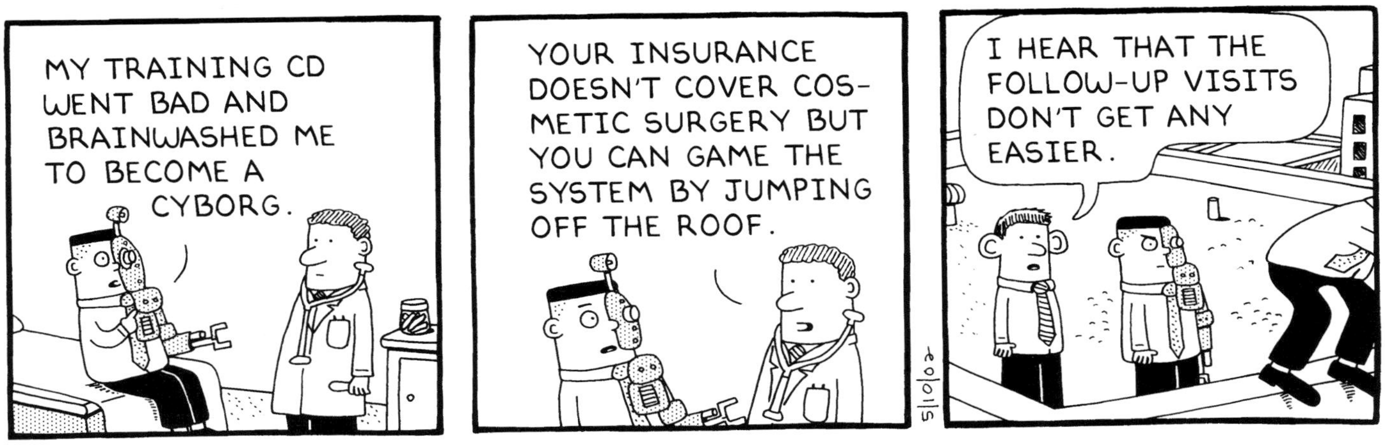
MY TRAINING CD WENT BAD AND BRAINWASHED ME TO BECOME A CYBORG.
YOUR INSURANCE DOESN'T COVER COS-METIC SURGERY BUT YOU CAN GAME THE SYSTEM BY JUMPING OFF THE ROOF.
5/10/02
I HEAR THAT THE FOLLOW-UP VISITS DON'T GET ANY EASIER.

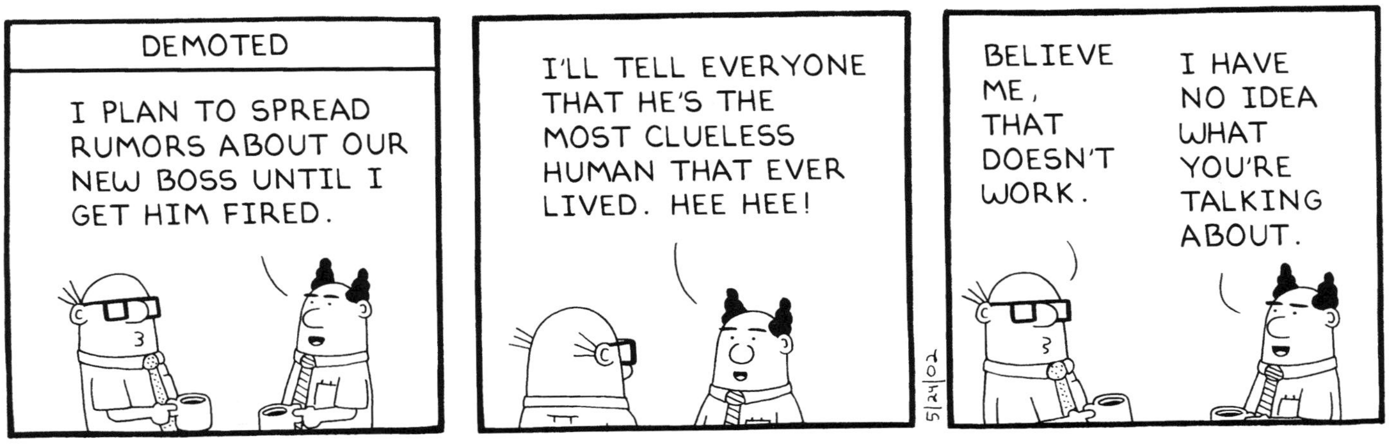
DEMOTED
I PLAN TO SPREAD RUMORS ABOUT OUR NEW BOSS UNTIL I GET HIM FIRED.
I'LL TELL EVERYONE THAT HE'S THE MOST CLUELESS HUMAN THAT EVER LIVED. HEE HEE!
5/24/02
BELIEVE ME, THAT DOESN'T WORK.
I HAVE NO IDEA WHAT YOU'RE TALKING ABOUT.

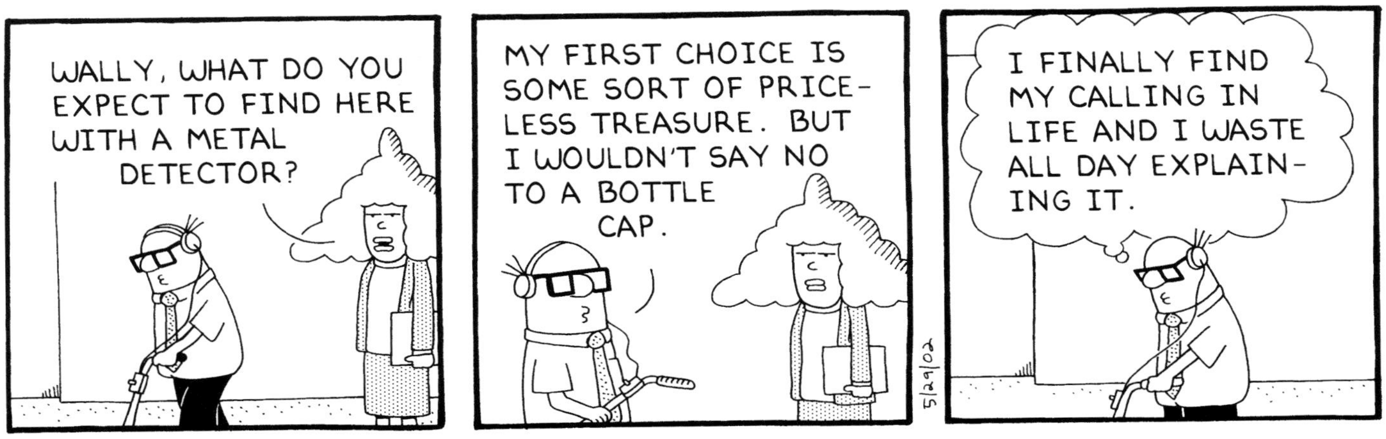
WALLY, WHAT DO YOU EXPECT TO FIND HERE WITH A METAL DETECTOR?
MY FIRST CHOICE IS SOME SORT OF PRICE-LESS TREASURE. BUT I WOULDN'T SAY NO TO A BOTTLE CAP.
5/29/02
I FINALLY FIND MY CALLING IN LIFE AND I WASTE ALL DAY EXPLAIN-ING IT.

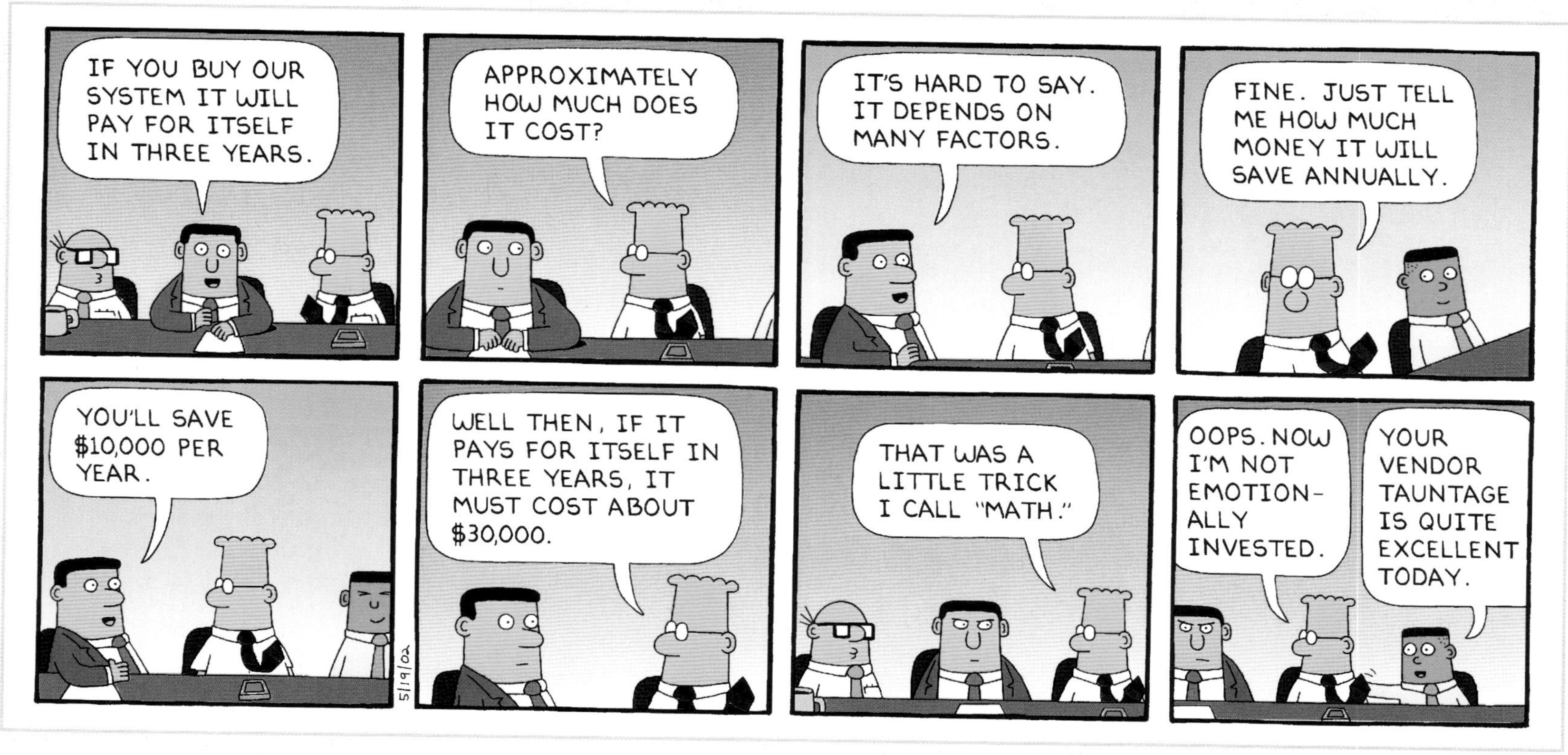
IF YOU BUY OUR SYSTEM IT WILL PAY FOR ITSELF IN THREE YEARS.
APPROXIMATELY HOW MUCH DOES IT COST?
IT'S HARD TO SAY. IT DEPENDS ON MANY FACTORS.
FINE. JUST TELL ME HOW MUCH MONEY IT WILL SAVE ANNUALLY.
YOU'LL SAVE $10,000 PER YEAR.
5/19/02
WELL THEN, IF IT PAYS FOR ITSELF IN THREE YEARS, IT MUST COST ABOUT $30,000.
THAT WAS A LITTLE TRICK I CALL "MATH."
OOPS. NOW I'M NOT EMOTION-ALLY INVESTED.
YOUR VENDOR TAUNTAGE IS QUITE EXCELLENT TODAY.

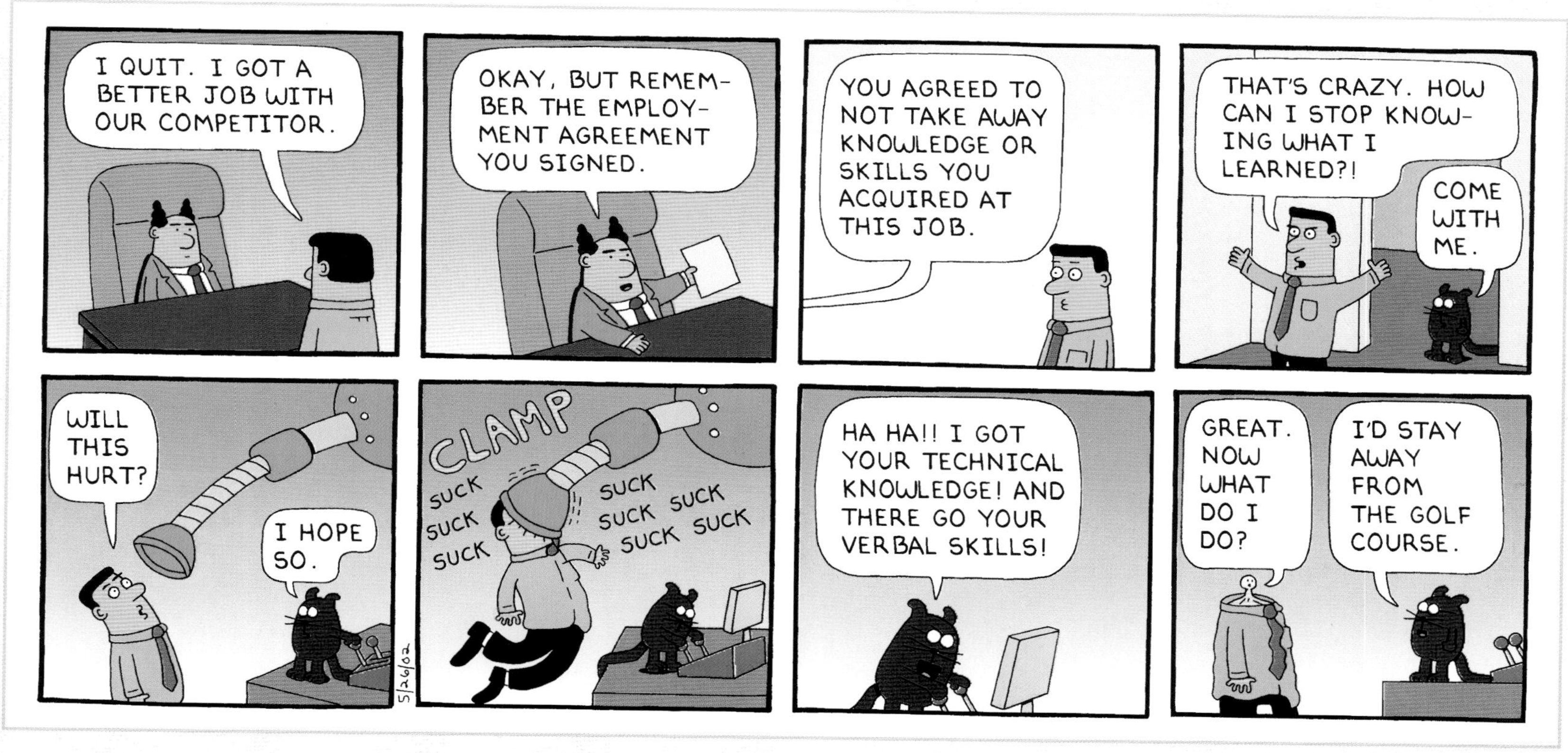
I QUIT. I GOT A BETTER JOB WITH OUR COMPETITOR.
OKAY, BUT REMEM-BER THE EMPLOY-MENT AGREEMENT YOU SIGNED.
YOU AGREED TO NOT TAKE AWAY KNOWLEDGE OR SKILLS YOU ACQUIRED AT THIS JOB.
THAT'S CRAZY. HOW CAN I STOP KNOW-ING WHAT I LEARNED?!
COME WITH ME.
WILL THIS HURT?
I HOPE SO.
5/26/02
CLAMP
SUCK SUCK SUCK
SUCK SUCK SUCK SUCK SUCK
HA HA!! I GOT YOUR TECHNICAL KNOWLEDGE! AND THERE GO YOUR VERBAL SKILLS!
GREAT. NOW WHAT DO I DO?
I'D STAY AWAY FROM THE GOLF COURSE.

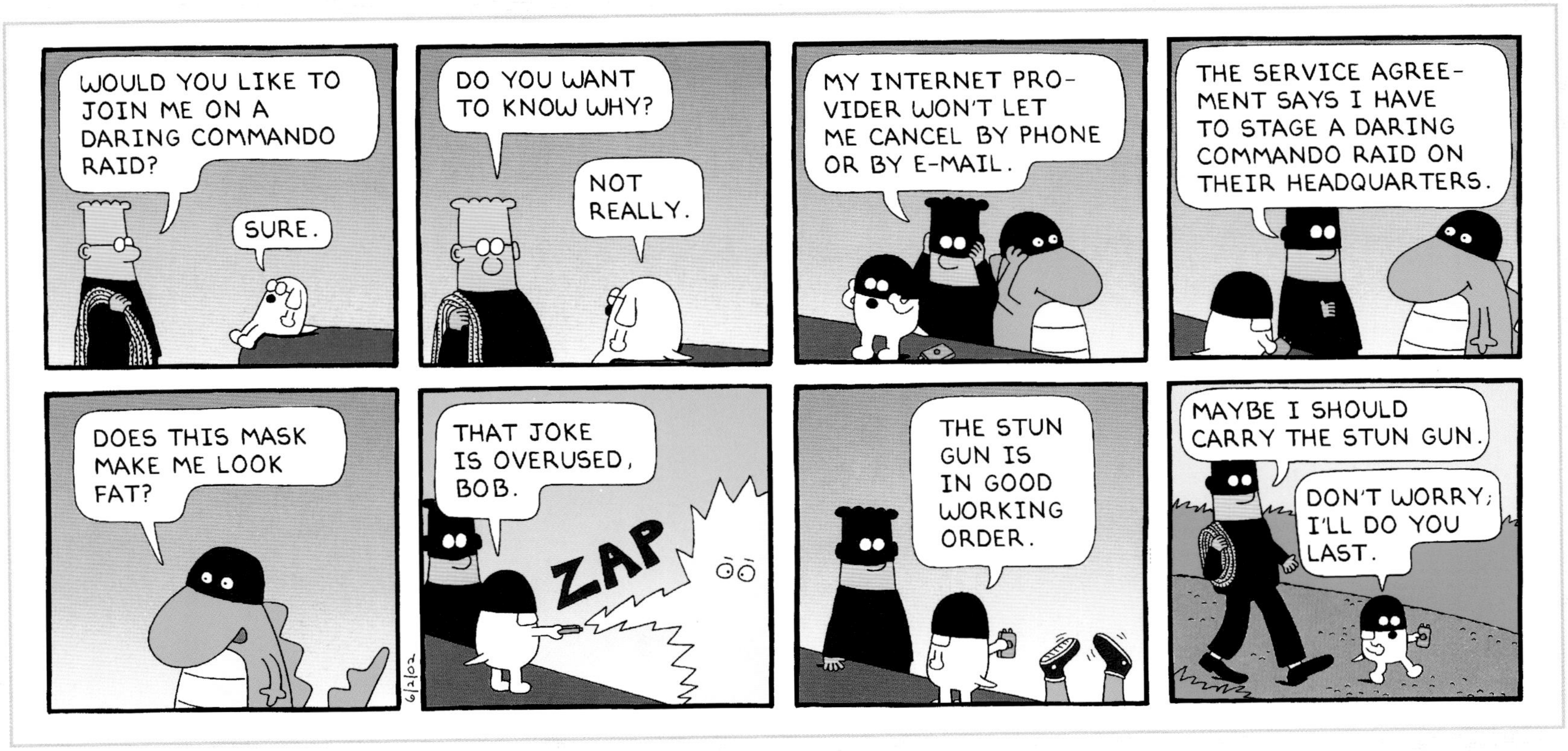
WOULD YOU LIKE TO JOIN ME ON A DARING COMMANDO RAID?
SURE.
DO YOU WANT TO KNOW WHY?
NOT REALLY.
MY INTERNET PRO- VIDER WON'T LET ME CANCEL BY PHONE OR BY E-MAIL.
THE SERVICE AGREE- MENT SAYS I HAVE TO STAGE A DARING COMMANDO RAID ON THEIR HEADQUARTERS.
DOES THIS MASK MAKE ME LOOK FAT?
THAT JOKE IS OVERUSED, BOB.
ZAP
THE STUN GUN IS IN GOOD WORKING ORDER.
MAYBE I SHOULD CARRY THE STUN GUN.
DON'T WORRY; I'LL DO YOU LAST.

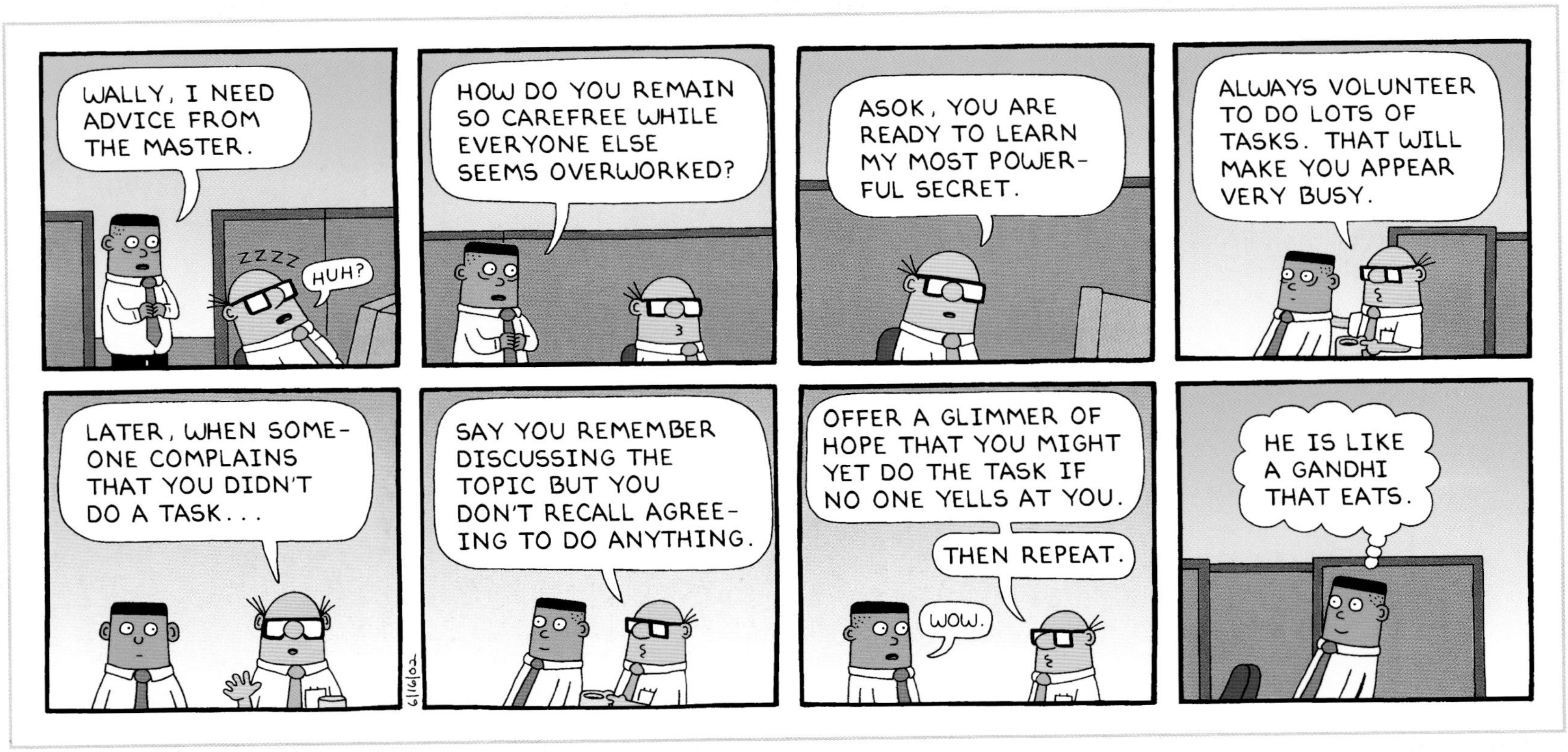
WALLY, I NEED ADVICE FROM THE MASTER.
ZZZZ
HUH?
HOW DO YOU REMAIN SO CAREFREE WHILE EVERYONE ELSE SEEMS OVERWORKED?
ASOK, YOU ARE READY TO LEARN MY MOST POWER- FUL SECRET.
ALWAYS VOLUNTEER TO DO LOTS OF TASKS. THAT WILL MAKE YOU APPEAR VERY BUSY.
LATER, WHEN SOME- ONE COMPLAINS THAT YOU DIDN'T DO A TASK...
SAY YOU REMEMBER DISCUSSING THE TOPIC BUT YOU DON'T RECALL AGREE- ING TO DO ANYTHING.
OFFER A GLIMMER OF HOPE THAT YOU MIGHT YET DO THE TASK IF NO ONE YELLS AT YOU.
THEN REPEAT.
WOW.
HE IS LIKE A GANDHI THAT EATS.

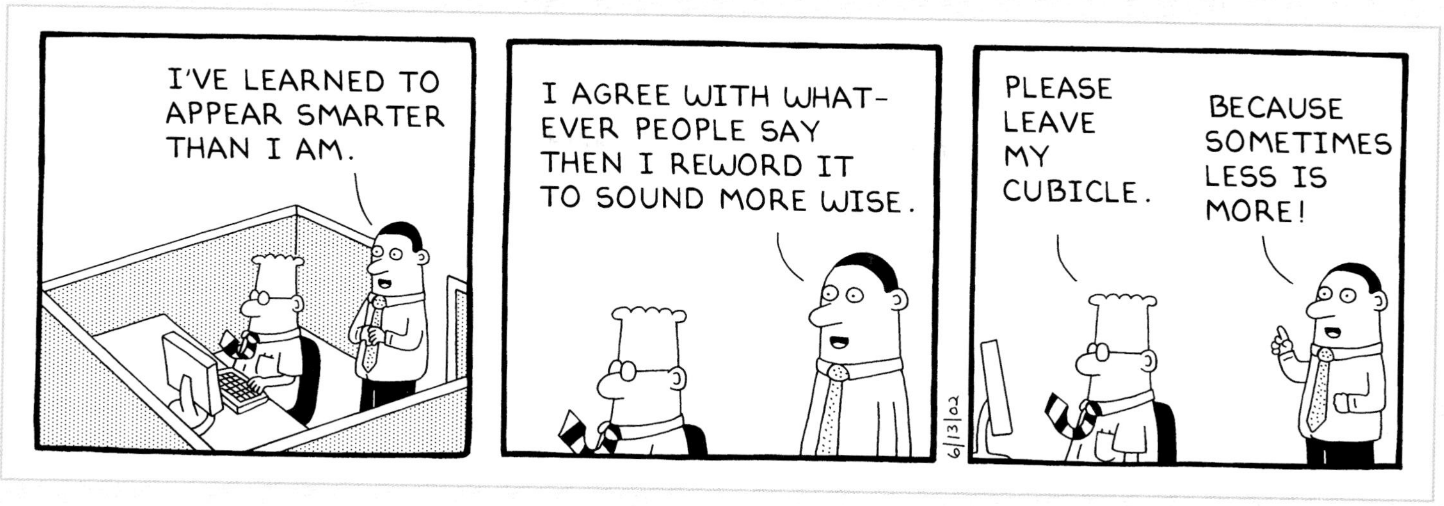
I'VE LEARNED TO APPEAR SMARTER THAN I AM.
I AGREE WITH WHAT-EVER PEOPLE SAY THEN I REWORD IT TO SOUND MORE WISE.
6/13/02
PLEASE LEAVE MY CUBICLE.
BECAUSE SOMETIMES LESS IS MORE!

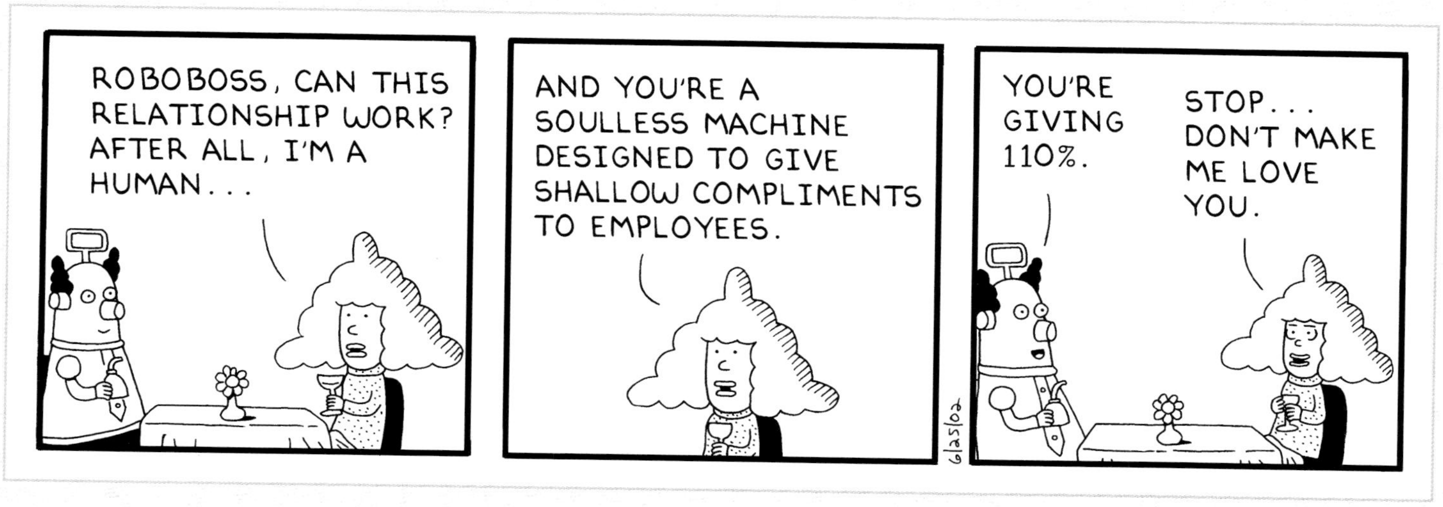
ROBOBOSS, CAN THIS RELATIONSHIP WORK? AFTER ALL, I'M A HUMAN . . .
AND YOU'RE A SOULLESS MACHINE DESIGNED TO GIVE SHALLOW COMPLIMENTS TO EMPLOYEES.
6/25/02
YOU'RE GIVING 110%.
STOP . . . DON'T MAKE ME LOVE YOU.

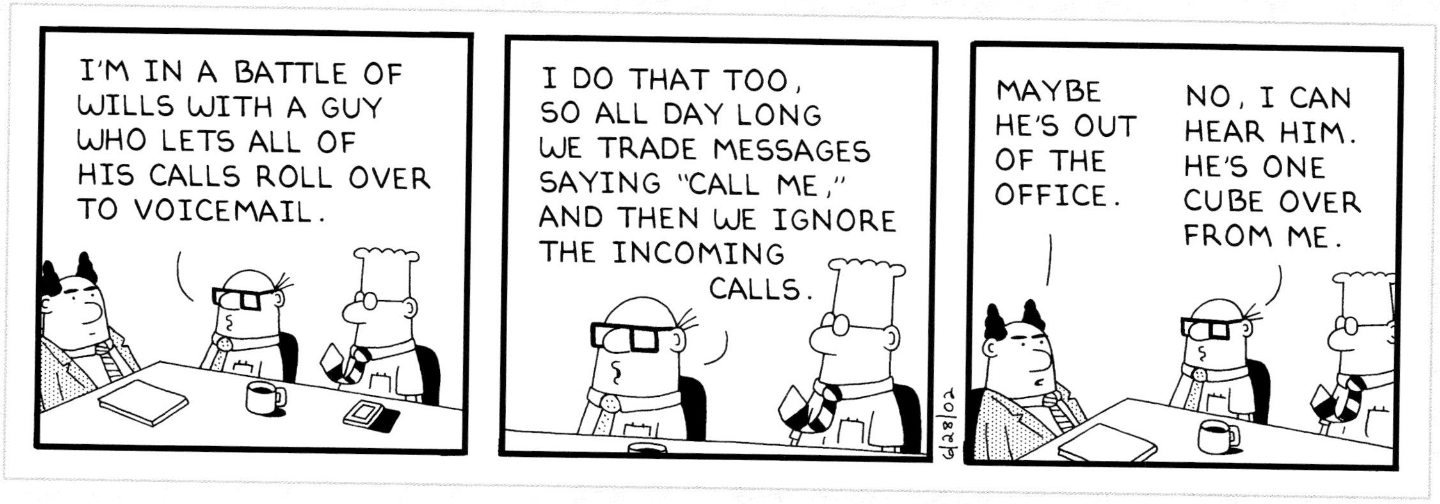
I'M IN A BATTLE OF WILLS WITH A GUY WHO LETS ALL OF HIS CALLS ROLL OVER TO VOICEMAIL.
I DO THAT TOO, SO ALL DAY LONG WE TRADE MESSAGES SAYING "CALL ME," AND THEN WE IGNORE THE INCOMING CALLS.
6/28/02
MAYBE HE'S OUT OF THE OFFICE.
NO, I CAN HEAR HIM. HE'S ONE CUBE OVER FROM ME.

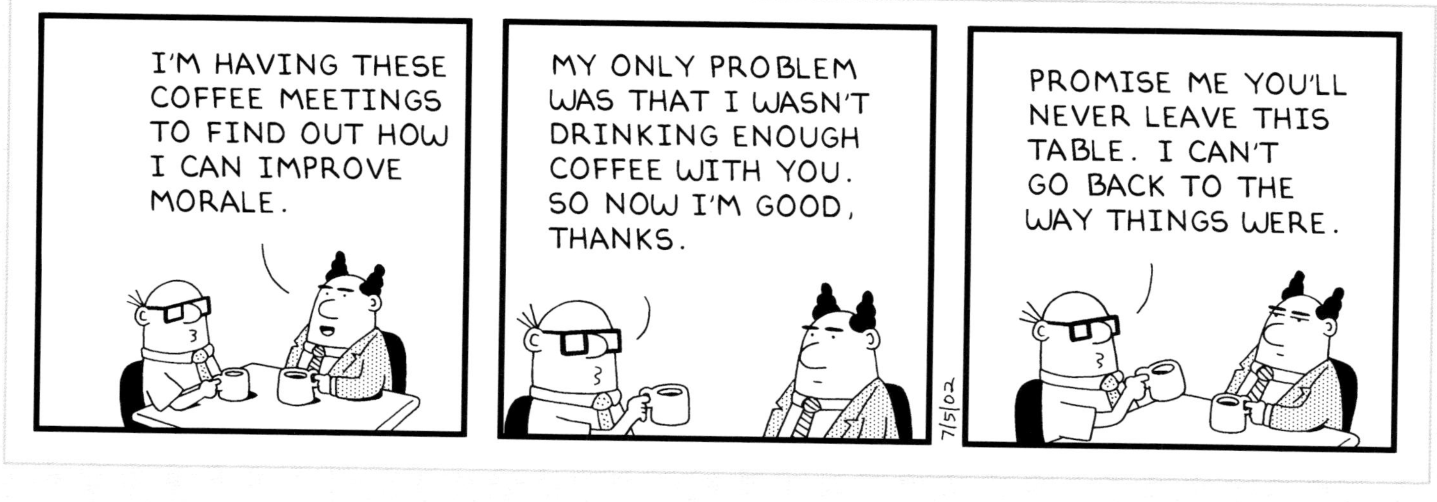
I'M HAVING THESE COFFEE MEETINGS TO FIND OUT HOW I CAN IMPROVE MORALE.
MY ONLY PROBLEM WAS THAT I WASN'T DRINKING ENOUGH COFFEE WITH YOU. SO NOW I'M GOOD, THANKS.
7/5/02
PROMISE ME YOU'LL NEVER LEAVE THIS TABLE. I CAN'T GO BACK TO THE WAY THINGS WERE.

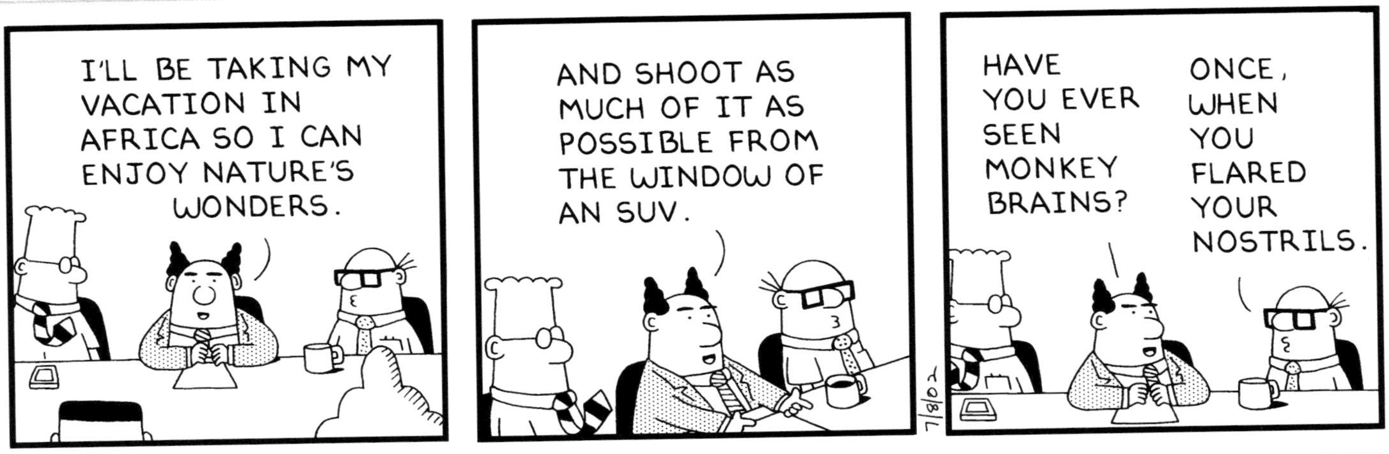
I'LL BE TAKING MY VACATION IN AFRICA SO I CAN ENJOY NATURE'S WONDERS.
AND SHOOT AS MUCH OF IT AS POSSIBLE FROM THE WINDOW OF AN SUV.
7/8/02
HAVE YOU EVER SEEN MONKEY BRAINS?
ONCE, WHEN YOU FLARED YOUR NOSTRILS.

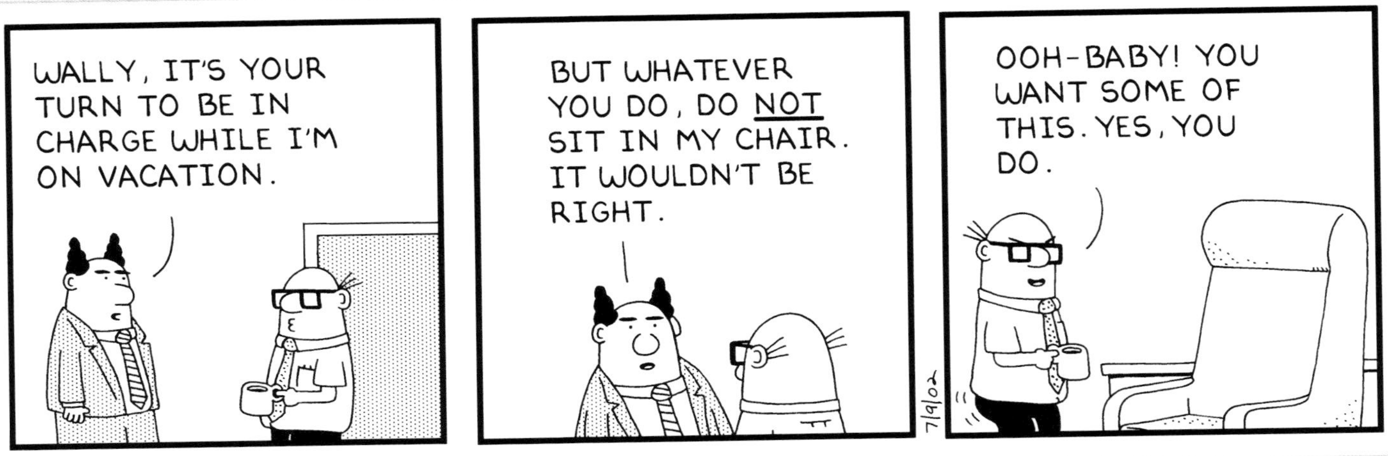
WALLY, IT'S YOUR TURN TO BE IN CHARGE WHILE I'M ON VACATION.
BUT WHATEVER YOU DO, DO NOT SIT IN MY CHAIR. IT WOULDN'T BE RIGHT.
7/9/02
OOH-BABY! YOU WANT SOME OF THIS. YES, YOU DO.

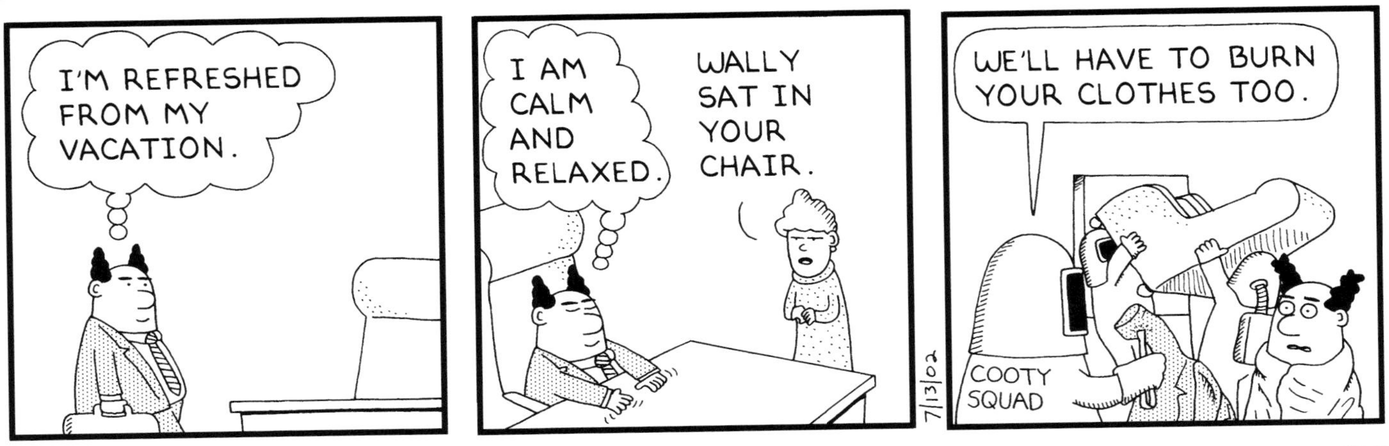
I'M REFRESHED FROM MY VACATION.
I AM CALM AND RELAXED.
WALLY SAT IN YOUR CHAIR.
7/13/02
WE'LL HAVE TO BURN YOUR CLOTHES TOO.
COOTY SQUAD

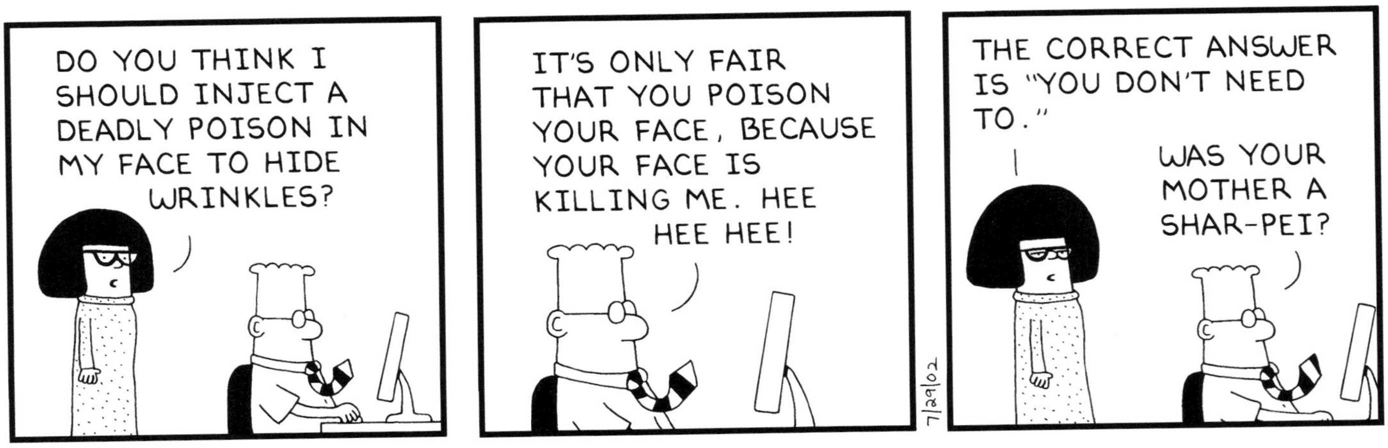
DO YOU THINK I SHOULD INJECT A DEADLY POISON IN MY FACE TO HIDE WRINKLES?
IT'S ONLY FAIR THAT YOU POISON YOUR FACE, BECAUSE YOUR FACE IS KILLING ME. HEE HEE HEE!
7/29/02
THE CORRECT ANSWER IS "YOU DON'T NEED TO."
WAS YOUR MOTHER A SHAR-PEI?

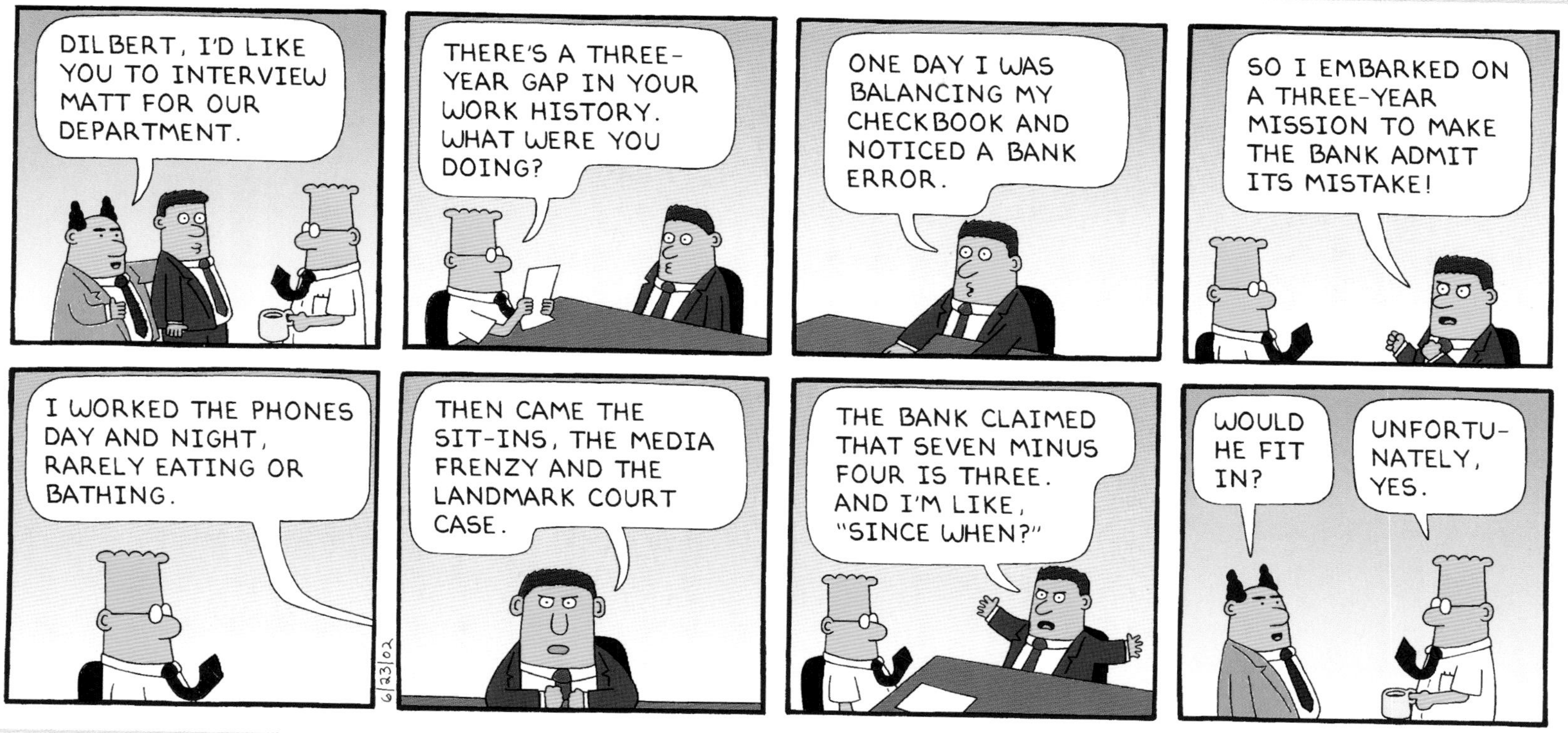
DILBERT, I'D LIKE YOU TO INTERVIEW MATT FOR OUR DEPARTMENT.
THERE'S A THREE-YEAR GAP IN YOUR WORK HISTORY. WHAT WERE YOU DOING?
ONE DAY I WAS BALANCING MY CHECKBOOK AND NOTICED A BANK ERROR.
SO I EMBARKED ON A THREE-YEAR MISSION TO MAKE THE BANK ADMIT ITS MISTAKE!
I WORKED THE PHONES DAY AND NIGHT, RARELY EATING OR BATHING.
6/23/02
THEN CAME THE SIT-INS, THE MEDIA FRENZY AND THE LANDMARK COURT CASE.
THE BANK CLAIMED THAT SEVEN MINUS FOUR IS THREE. AND I'M LIKE, "SINCE WHEN?"
WOULD HE FIT IN?
UNFORTU-NATELY, YES.

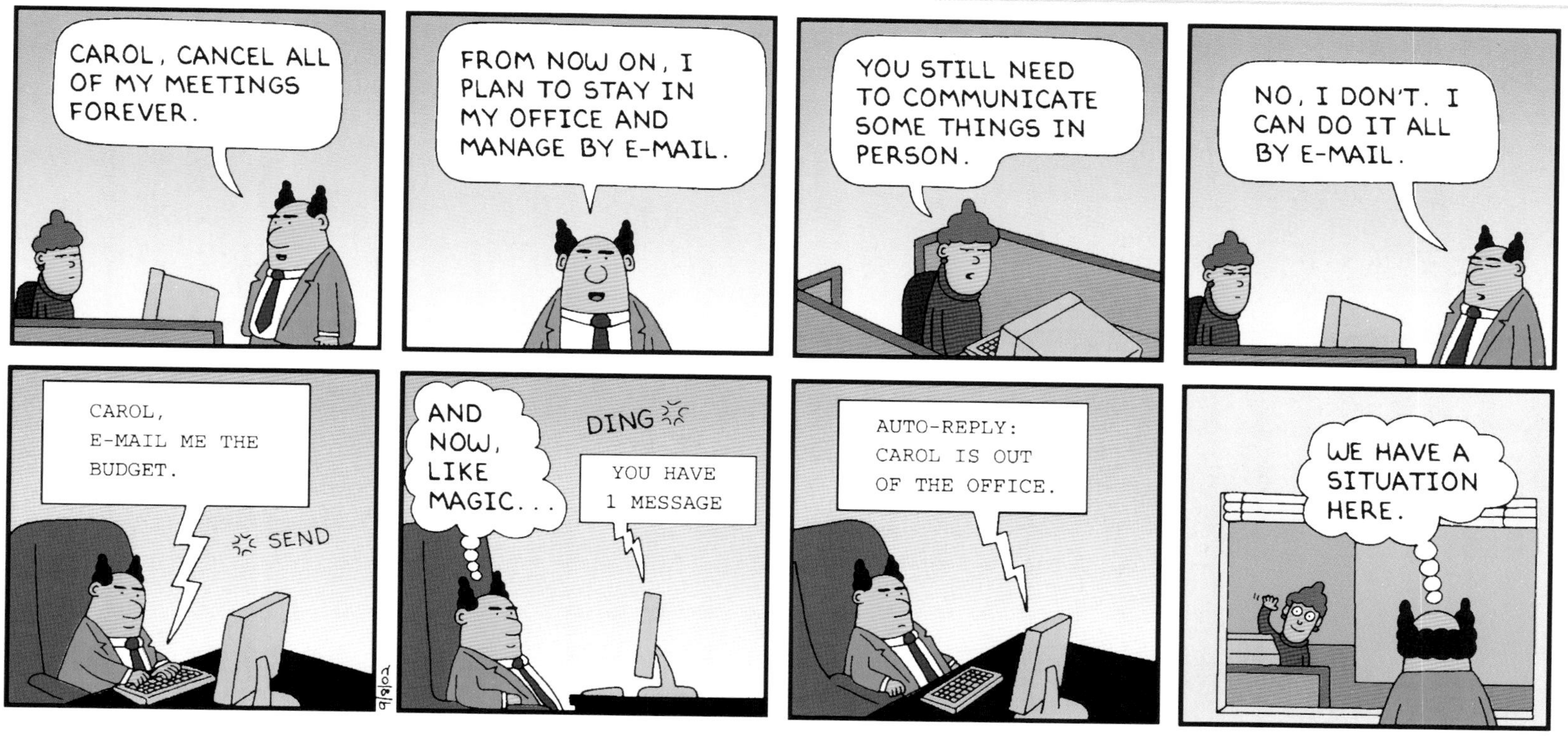
CAROL, CANCEL ALL OF MY MEETINGS FOREVER.
FROM NOW ON, I PLAN TO STAY IN MY OFFICE AND MANAGE BY E-MAIL.
YOU STILL NEED TO COMMUNICATE SOME THINGS IN PERSON.
NO, I DON'T. I CAN DO IT ALL BY E-MAIL.
CAROL, E-MAIL ME THE BUDGET.
SEND
9/8/02
AND NOW, LIKE MAGIC...
DING
YOU HAVE 1 MESSAGE
AUTO-REPLY: CAROL IS OUT OF THE OFFICE.
WE HAVE A SITUATION HERE.

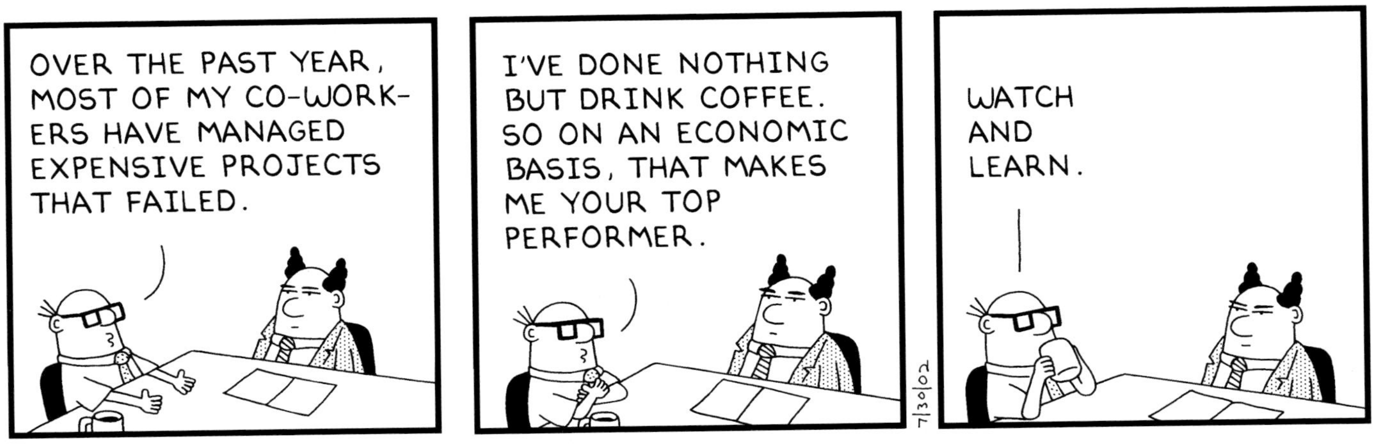
OVER THE PAST YEAR, MOST OF MY CO-WORKERS HAVE MANAGED EXPENSIVE PROJECTS THAT FAILED.
I'VE DONE NOTHING BUT DRINK COFFEE. SO ON AN ECONOMIC BASIS, THAT MAKES ME YOUR TOP PERFORMER.
7/30/02
WATCH AND LEARN.

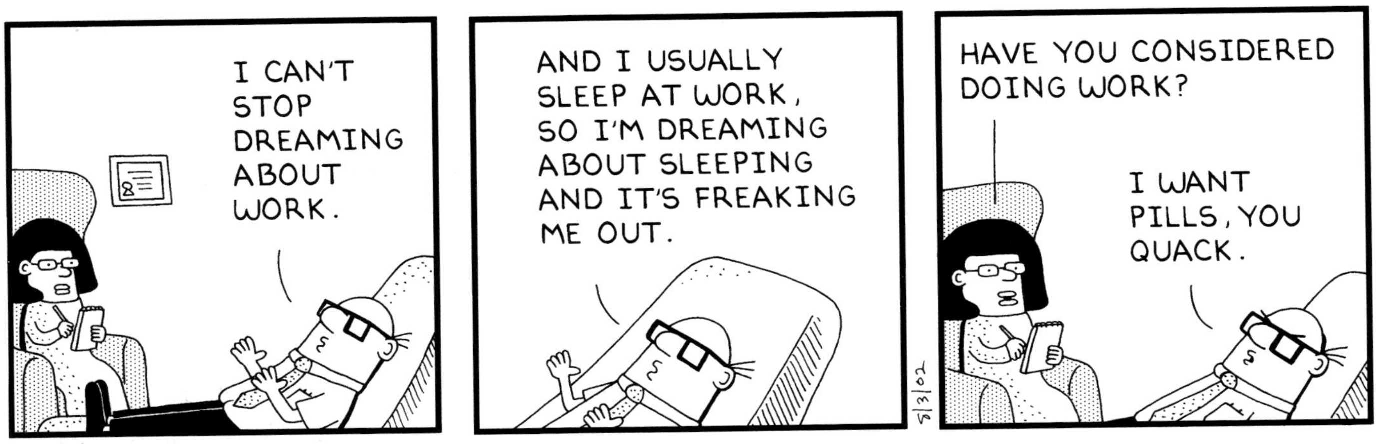
I CAN'T STOP DREAMING ABOUT WORK.
AND I USUALLY SLEEP AT WORK, SO I'M DREAMING ABOUT SLEEPING AND IT'S FREAKING ME OUT.
5/3/02
HAVE YOU CONSIDERED DOING WORK?
I WANT PILLS, YOU QUACK.

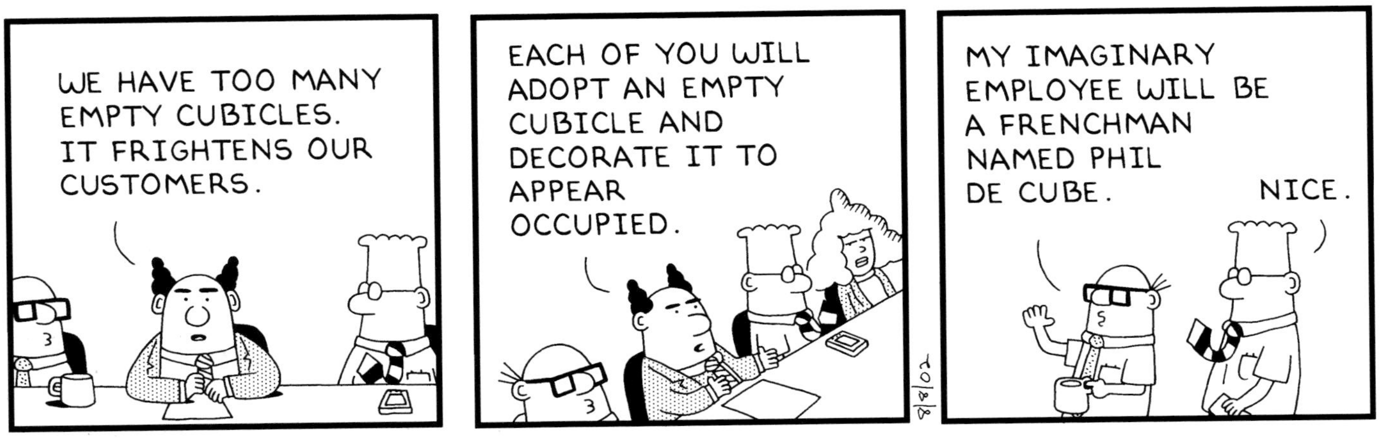
WE HAVE TOO MANY EMPTY CUBICLES. IT FRIGHTENS OUR CUSTOMERS.
EACH OF YOU WILL ADOPT AN EMPTY CUBICLE AND DECORATE IT TO APPEAR OCCUPIED.
8/8/02
MY IMAGINARY EMPLOYEE WILL BE A FRENCHMAN NAMED PHIL DE CUBE.
NICE.

This one is based on a real event. People who haven't experienced the corporate world surely think I make up this stuff.

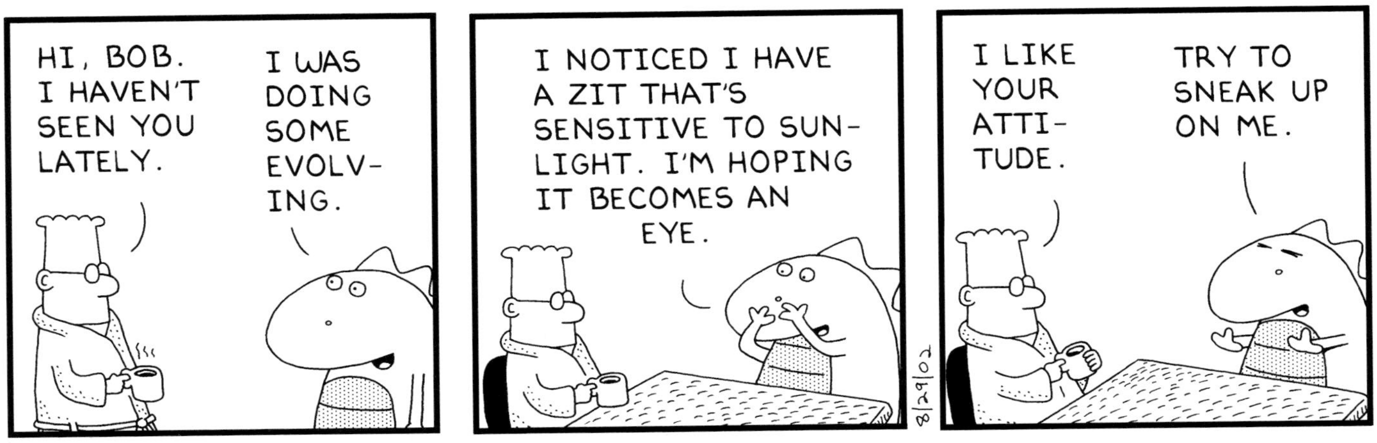
HI, BOB. I HAVEN'T SEEN YOU LATELY.
I WAS DOING SOME EVOLVING.
I NOTICED I HAVE A ZIT THAT'S SENSITIVE TO SUNLIGHT. I'M HOPING IT BECOMES AN EYE.
8/29/02
I LIKE YOUR ATTITUDE.
TRY TO SNEAK UP ON ME.

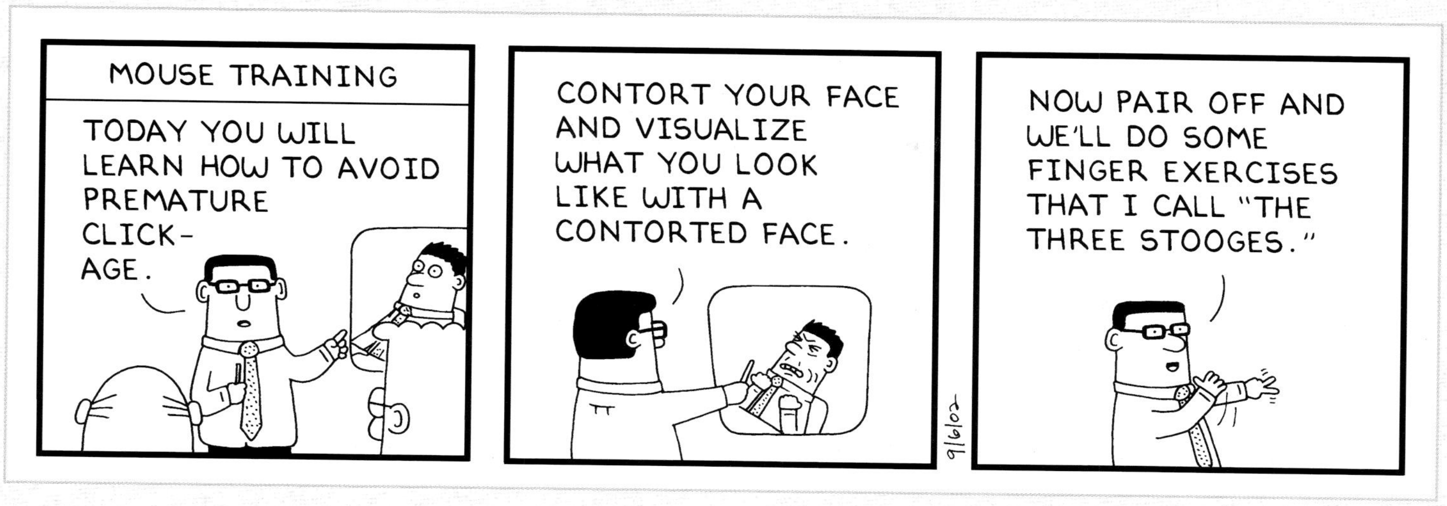
MOUSE TRAINING
TODAY YOU WILL LEARN HOW TO AVOID PREMATURE CLICK-AGE.
CONTORT YOUR FACE AND VISUALIZE WHAT YOU LOOK LIKE WITH A CONTORTED FACE.
9/6/02
NOW PAIR OFF AND WE'LL DO SOME FINGER EXERCISES THAT I CALL "THE THREE STOOGES."

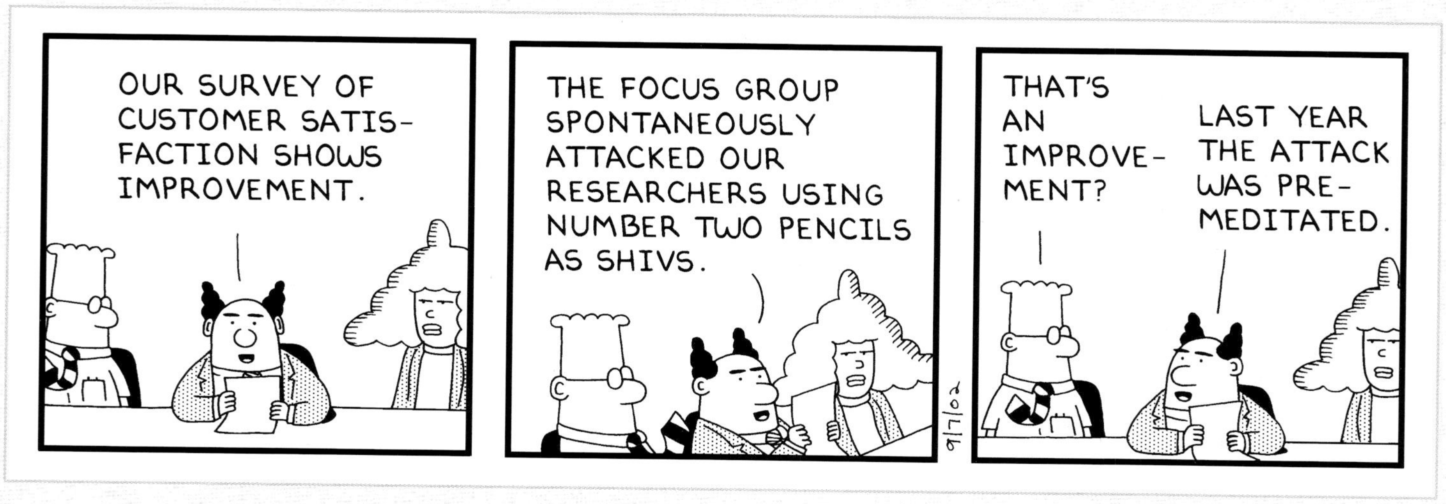
OUR SURVEY OF CUSTOMER SATIS-FACTION SHOWS IMPROVEMENT.
THE FOCUS GROUP SPONTANEOUSLY ATTACKED OUR RESEARCHERS USING NUMBER TWO PENCILS AS SHIVS.
9/7/02
THAT'S AN IMPROVE-MENT?
LAST YEAR THE ATTACK WAS PRE-MEDITATED.

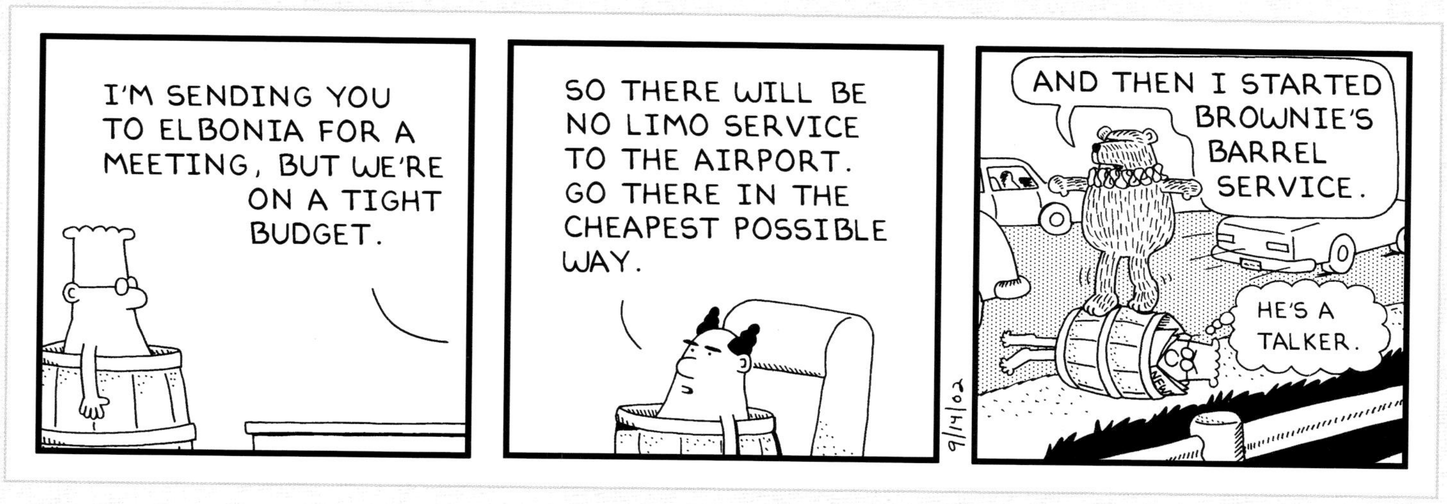
I'M SENDING YOU TO ELBONIA FOR A MEETING, BUT WE'RE ON A TIGHT BUDGET.
SO THERE WILL BE NO LIMO SERVICE TO THE AIRPORT. GO THERE IN THE CHEAPEST POSSIBLE WAY.
9/14/02
AND THEN I STARTED BROWNIE'S BARREL SERVICE.
HE'S A TALKER.

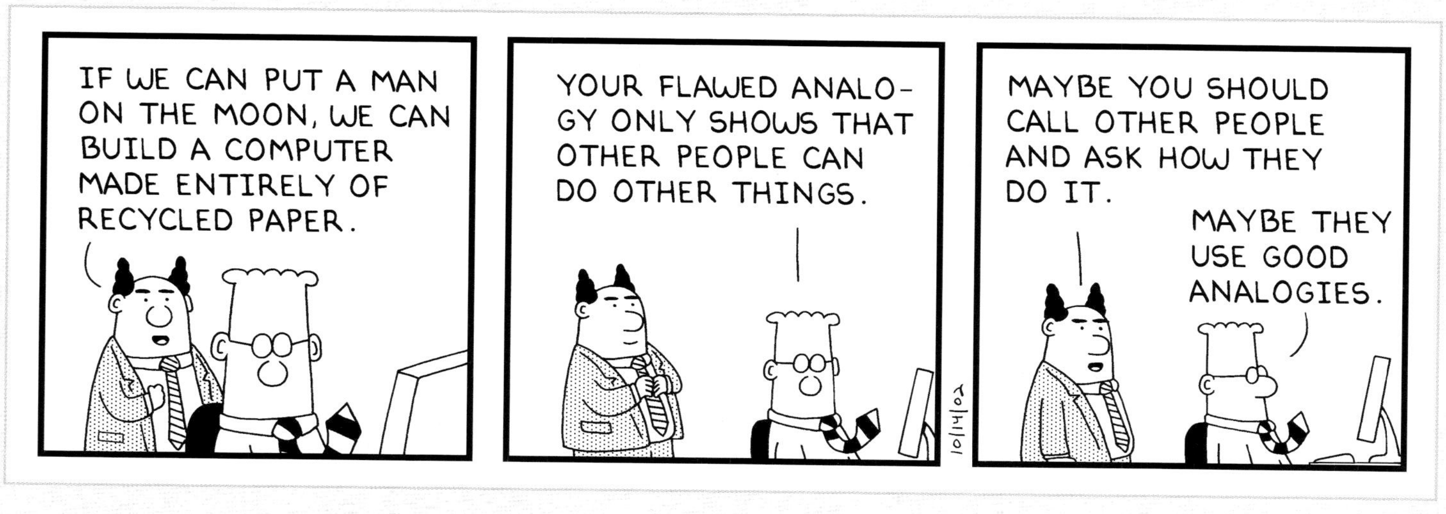
IF WE CAN PUT A MAN ON THE MOON, WE CAN BUILD A COMPUTER MADE ENTIRELY OF RECYCLED PAPER.
YOUR FLAWED ANALO-GY ONLY SHOWS THAT OTHER PEOPLE CAN DO OTHER THINGS.
10/14/02
MAYBE YOU SHOULD CALL OTHER PEOPLE AND ASK HOW THEY DO IT.
MAYBE THEY USE GOOD ANALOGIES.

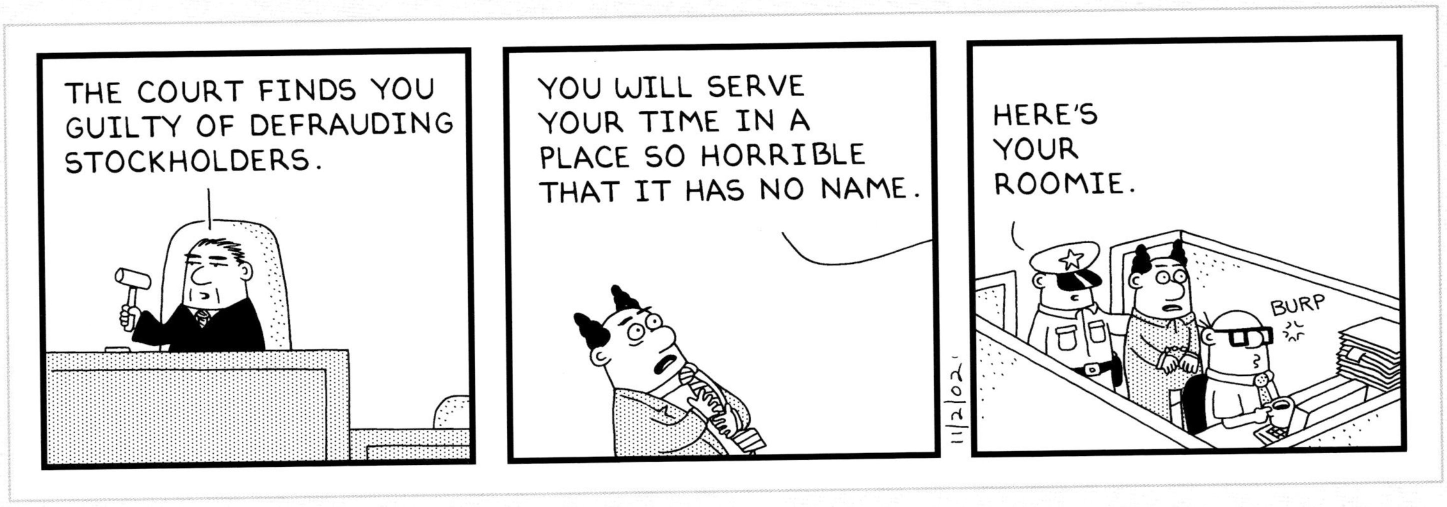
THE COURT FINDS YOU GUILTY OF DEFRAUDING STOCKHOLDERS.
YOU WILL SERVE YOUR TIME IN A PLACE SO HORRIBLE THAT IT HAS NO NAME.
11/2/02
HERE'S YOUR ROOMIE.
BURP

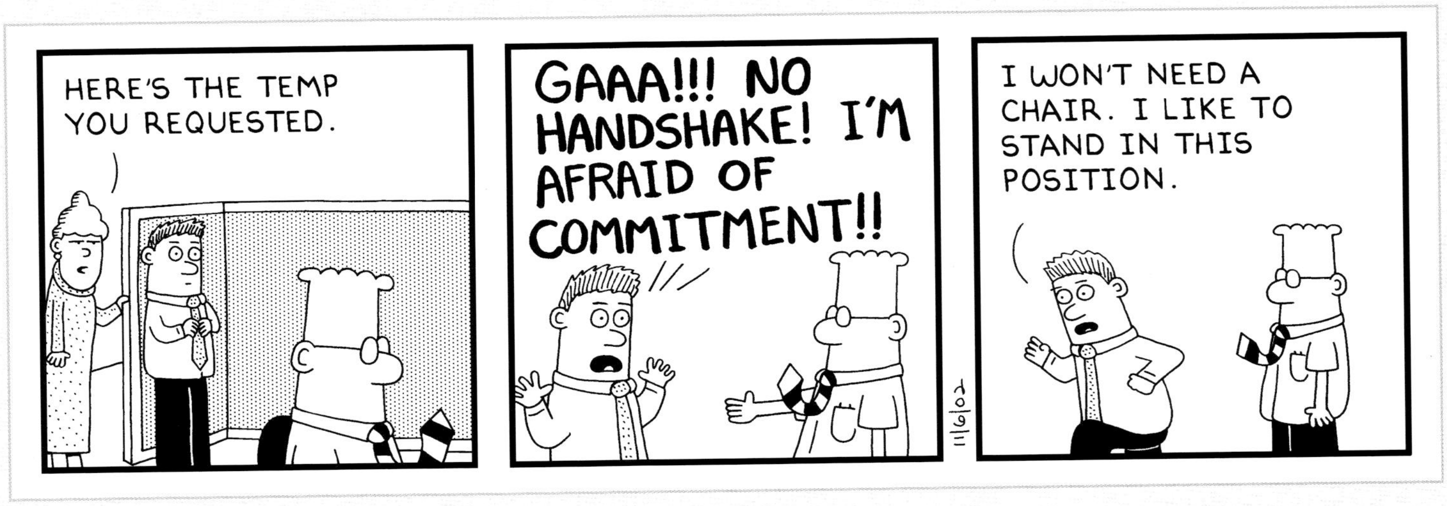
HERE'S THE TEMP YOU REQUESTED.
GAAA!!! NO HANDSHAKE! I'M AFRAID OF COMMITMENT!!
11/6/02
I WON'T NEED A CHAIR. I LIKE TO STAND IN THIS POSITION.

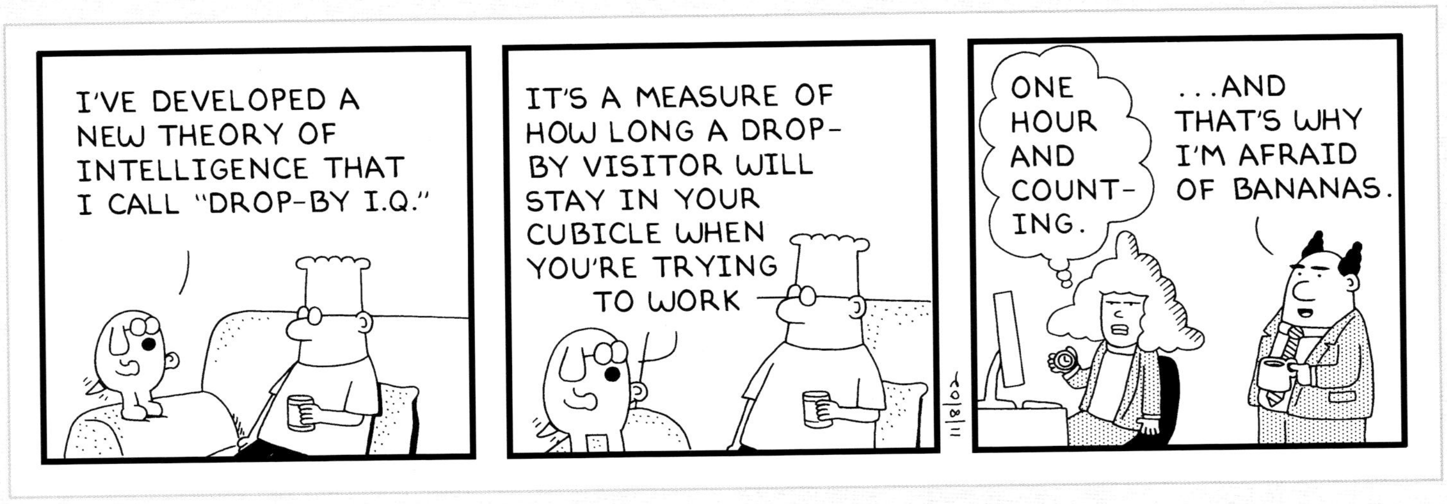
I'VE DEVELOPED A NEW THEORY OF INTELLIGENCE THAT I CALL "DROP-BY I.Q."
IT'S A MEASURE OF HOW LONG A DROP-BY VISITOR WILL STAY IN YOUR CUBICLE WHEN YOU'RE TRYING TO WORK
11/8/02
ONE HOUR AND COUNT-ING.
...AND THAT'S WHY I'M AFRAID OF BANANAS.

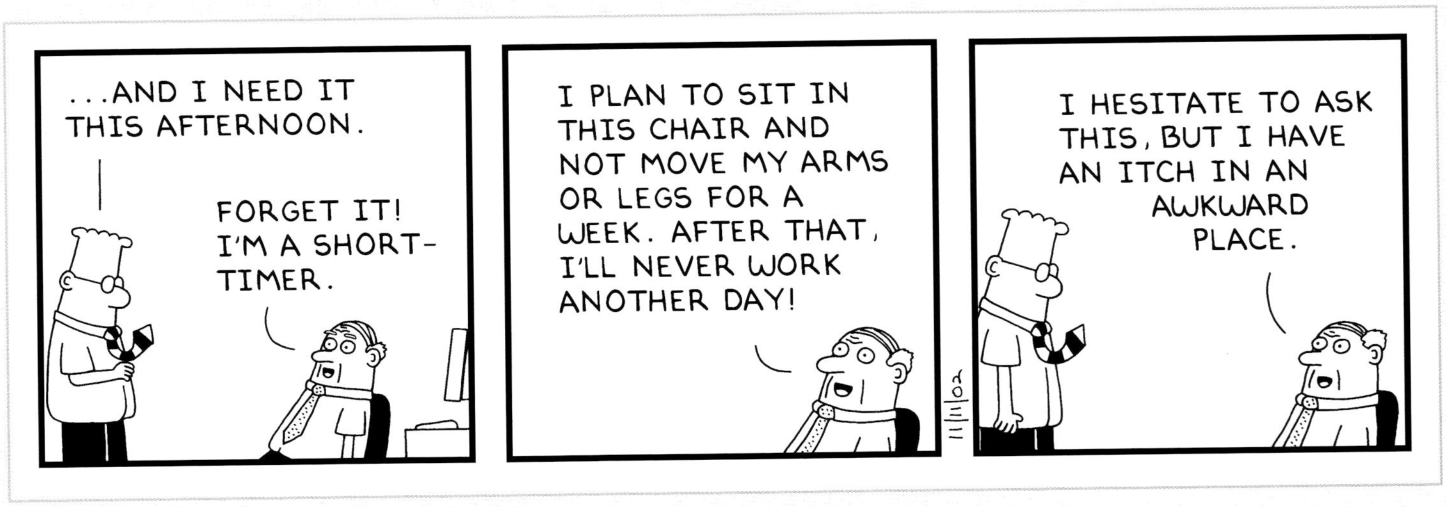
...AND I NEED IT THIS AFTERNOON.
FORGET IT! I'M A SHORT-TIMER.
I PLAN TO SIT IN THIS CHAIR AND NOT MOVE MY ARMS OR LEGS FOR A WEEK. AFTER THAT, I'LL NEVER WORK ANOTHER DAY!
11/11/02
I HESITATE TO ASK THIS, BUT I HAVE AN ITCH IN AN AWKWARD PLACE.

THE THREE PILLARS OF OUR PYRAMID ARE COMMUNICATION, INTEGRITY, AND TEAMWORK.
QUESTION: SINCE WHEN DO PYRAMIDS HAVE PILLARS?
ANSWER: SHUT UP.
PROBLEM: ALL OF MY TEAM MEMBERS ARE IDIOTS.
IF I COMMUNICATE MY HONEST OPINION OF THEIR IDEAS, I WON'T BE A TEAM PLAYER.
10/13/02
BUT IF I PRETEND TO AGREE WITH THEIR BAD IDEAS, I WON'T HAVE INTEGRITY.
SO INSTEAD OF BEING A PYRAMID, CAN I BE A TWO-LEGGED STOOL LIKE YOU?
WOW! THAT WAS MUCH BETTER THAN MY PILLAR QUESTION.
AREN'T I ON YOUR TEAM?

THE ORIGINAL SCHEDULE LOOKED LIKE THIS...
ONE MONTH FOR A MANAGEMENT DECISION AND ONE YEAR TO DO THE PROJECT.
DECIDE
DO
THE REVISED SCHEDULE IS THIS...
ONE YEAR OF INDECISION FOLLOWED BY INTENSE PRESSURE TO DO THE IMPOSSIBLE BEFORE THE DEADLINE.
INDECISION
NO WAY
NOW IF YOU'LL EACH TAKE A PAIR OF 3-D GLASSES...
11/17/02
YOU CAN SEE THE LAYERS OF MANAGEMENT INCOMPETENCE PRACTICALLY JUMP OUT AT YOU.
NOW SCRATCH ONE OF THESE SCENTED CARDS TO SNIFF THE UNMISTAKABLE ODOR OF DOOM.
I DON'T SMELL ANYTHING. IS MINE BROKEN?

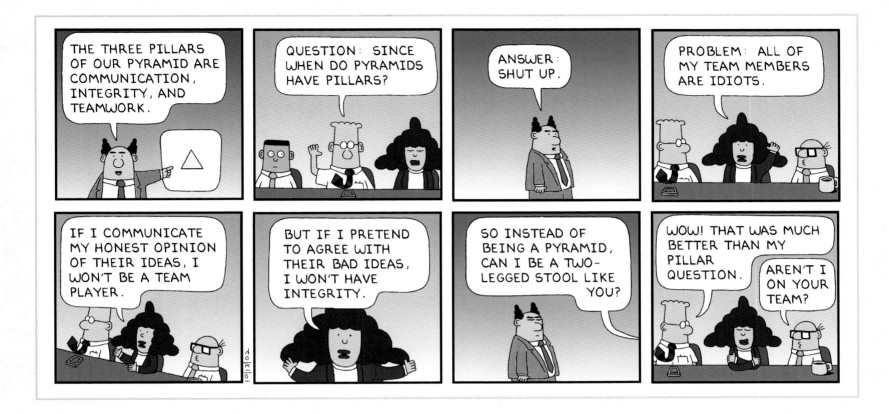

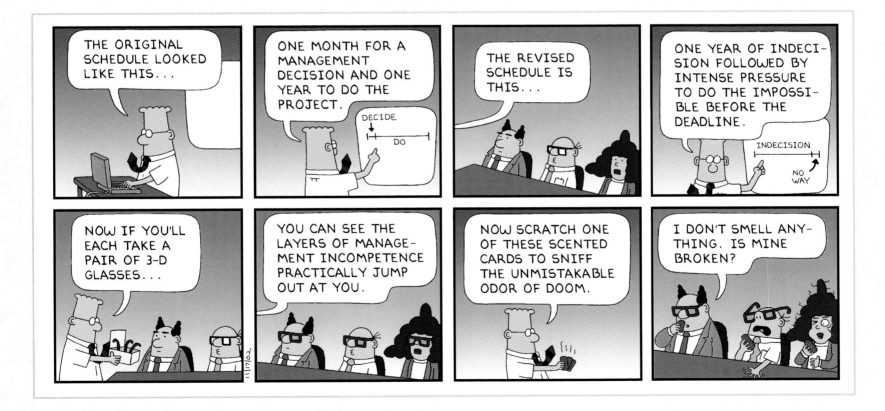

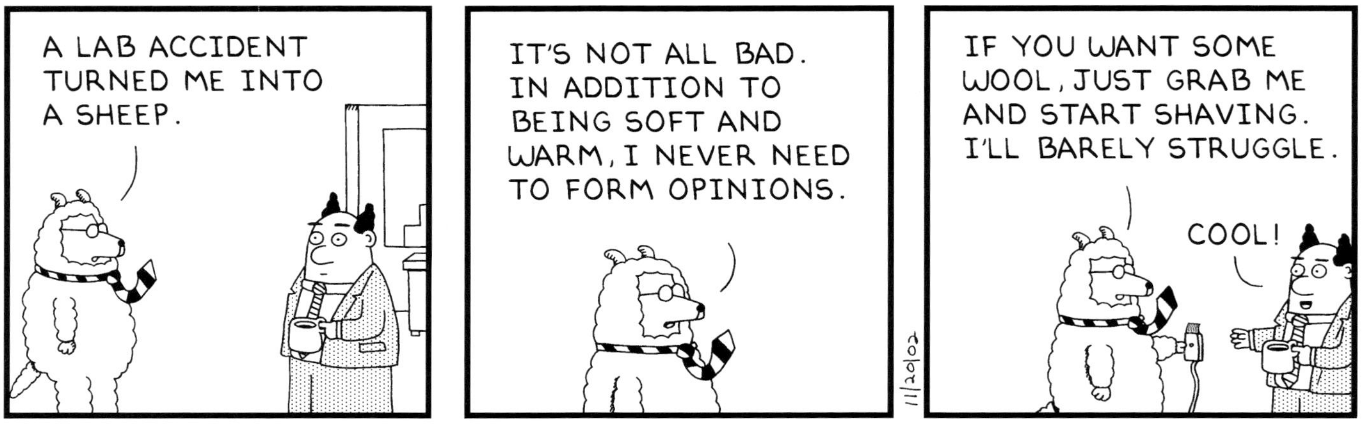
A LAB ACCIDENT TURNED ME INTO A SHEEP.
IT'S NOT ALL BAD. IN ADDITION TO BEING SOFT AND WARM, I NEVER NEED TO FORM OPINIONS.
11/20/02
IF YOU WANT SOME WOOL, JUST GRAB ME AND START SHAVING. I'LL BARELY STRUGGLE.
COOL!

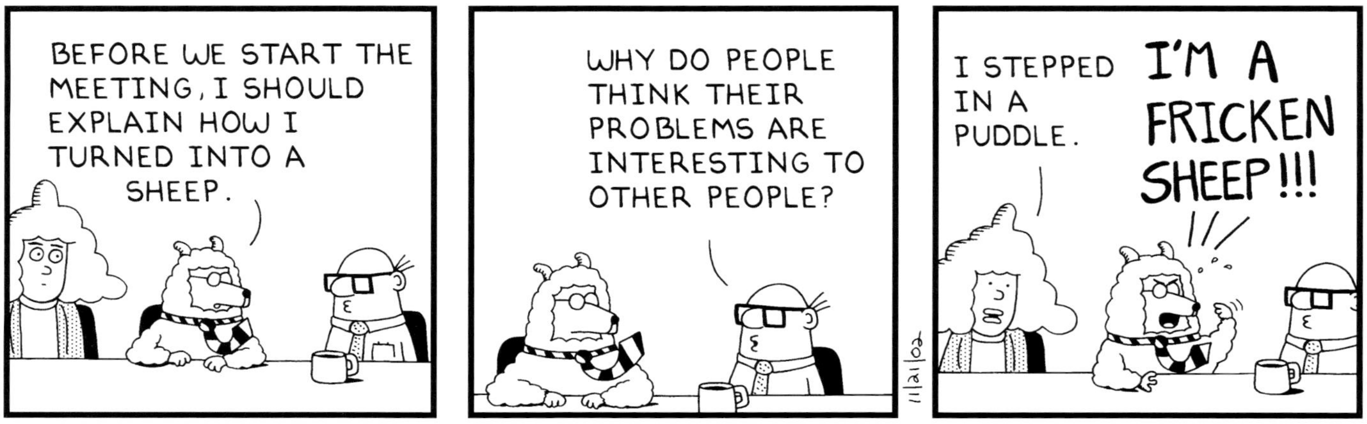
BEFORE WE START THE MEETING, I SHOULD EXPLAIN HOW I TURNED INTO A SHEEP.
WHY DO PEOPLE THINK THEIR PROBLEMS ARE INTERESTING TO OTHER PEOPLE?
11/21/02
I STEPPED IN A PUDDLE.
I'M A FRICKEN SHEEP!!!

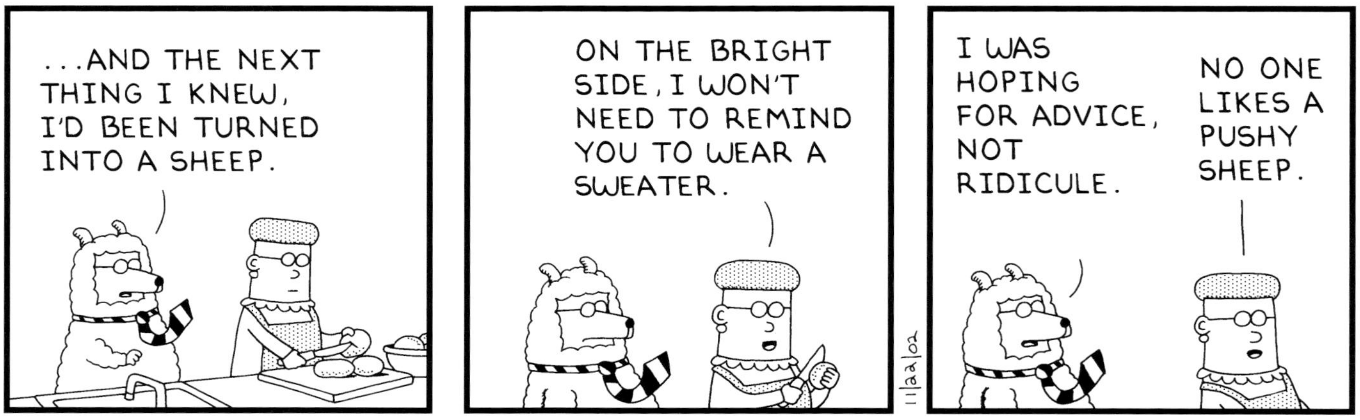
...AND THE NEXT THING I KNEW, I'D BEEN TURNED INTO A SHEEP.
ON THE BRIGHT SIDE, I WON'T NEED TO REMIND YOU TO WEAR A SWEATER.
11/22/02
I WAS HOPING FOR ADVICE, NOT RIDICULE.
NO ONE LIKES A PUSHY SHEEP.

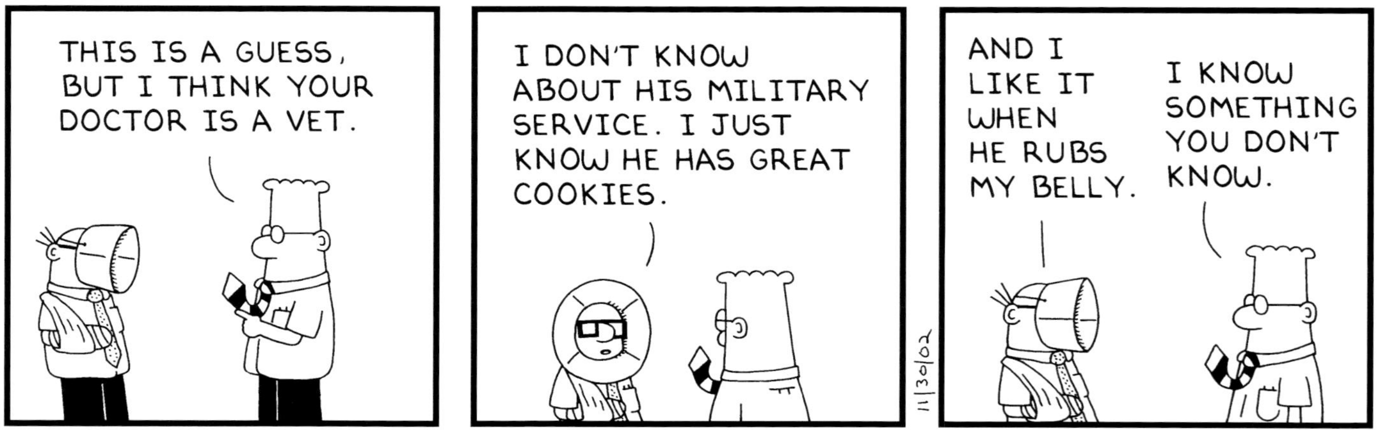
THIS IS A GUESS, BUT I THINK YOUR DOCTOR IS A VET.
I DON'T KNOW ABOUT HIS MILITARY SERVICE. I JUST KNOW HE HAS GREAT COOKIES.
11/30/02
AND I LIKE IT WHEN HE RUBS MY BELLY.
I KNOW SOMETHING YOU DON'T KNOW.

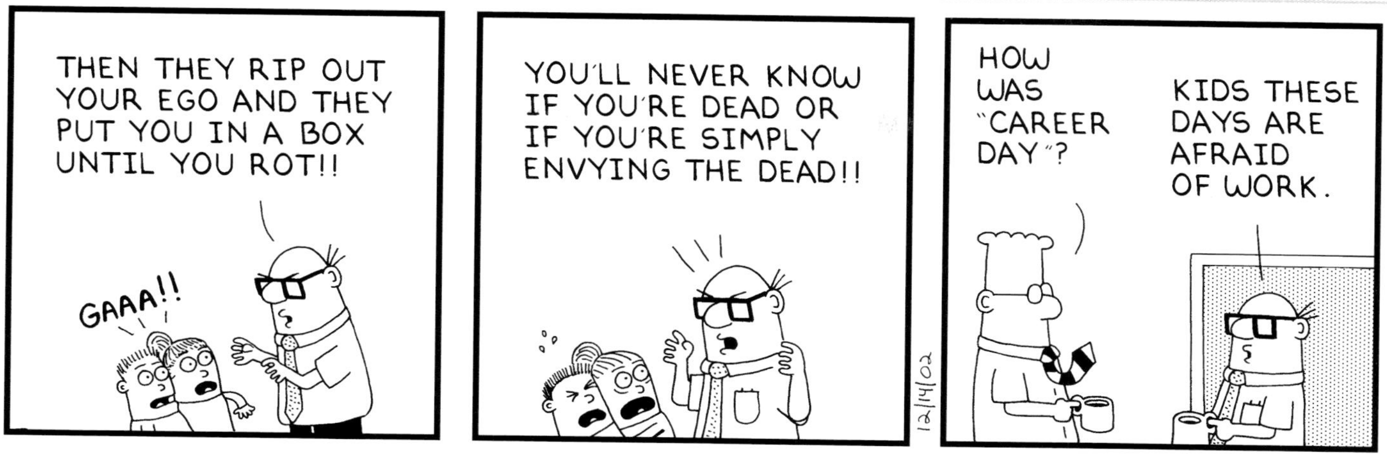
THEN THEY RIP OUT YOUR EGO AND THEY PUT YOU IN A BOX UNTIL YOU ROT!!
GAAA!!
YOU'LL NEVER KNOW IF YOU'RE DEAD OR IF YOU'RE SIMPLY ENVYING THE DEAD!!
12/14/02
HOW WAS "CAREER DAY"?
KIDS THESE DAYS ARE AFRAID OF WORK.

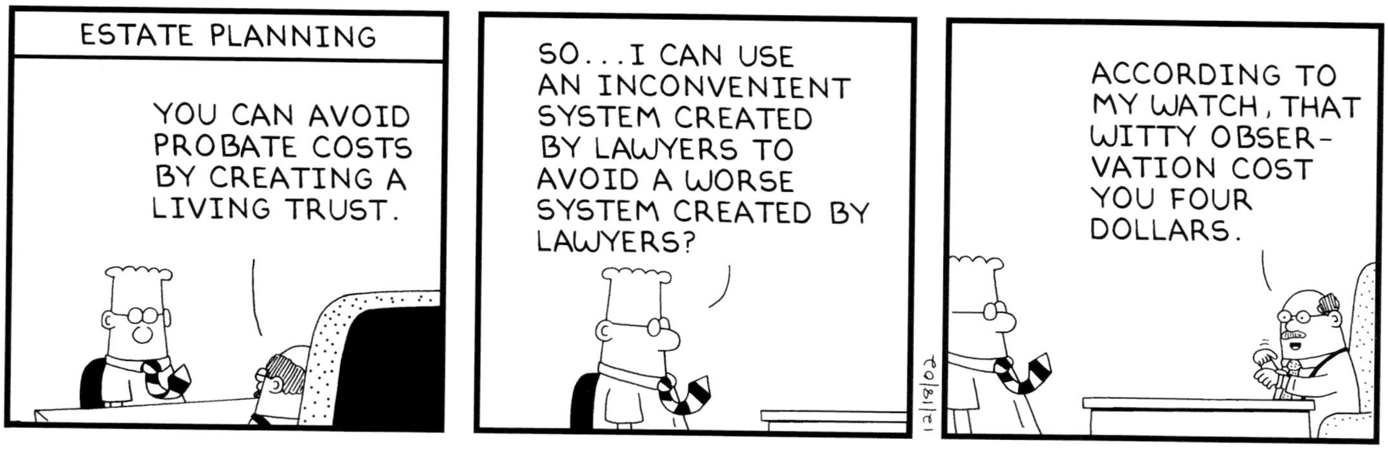
ESTATE PLANNING
YOU CAN AVOID PROBATE COSTS BY CREATING A LIVING TRUST.
SO...I CAN USE AN INCONVENIENT SYSTEM CREATED BY LAWYERS TO AVOID A WORSE SYSTEM CREATED BY LAWYERS?
12/18/02
ACCORDING TO MY WATCH, THAT WITTY OBSER-VATION COST YOU FOUR DOLLARS.

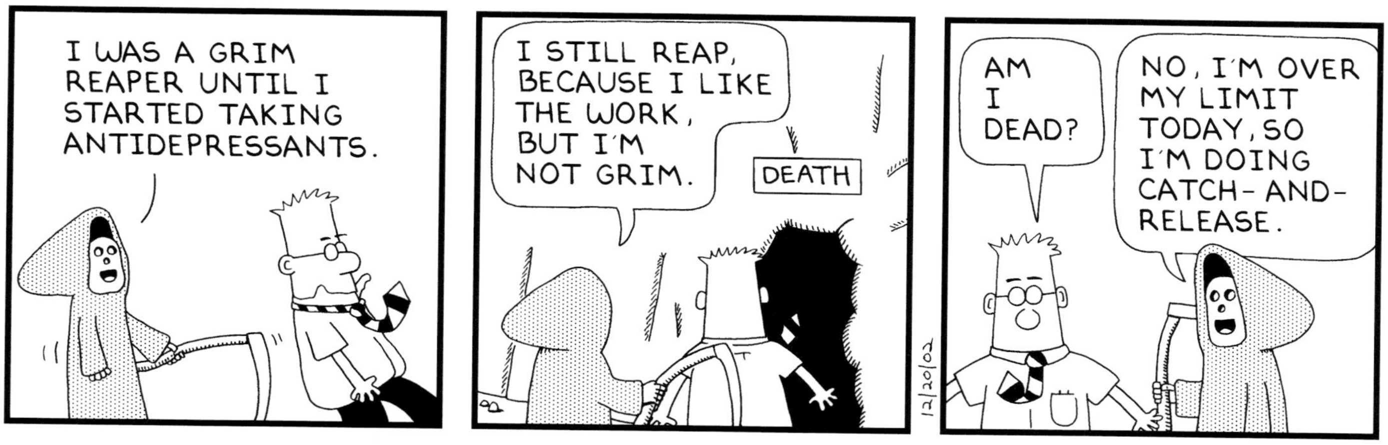
I WAS A GRIM REAPER UNTIL I STARTED TAKING ANTIDEPRESSANTS.
I STILL REAP, BECAUSE I LIKE THE WORK, BUT I'M NOT GRIM.
DEATH
12/20/02
AM I DEAD?
NO, I'M OVER MY LIMIT TODAY, SO I'M DOING CATCH-AND-RELEASE.

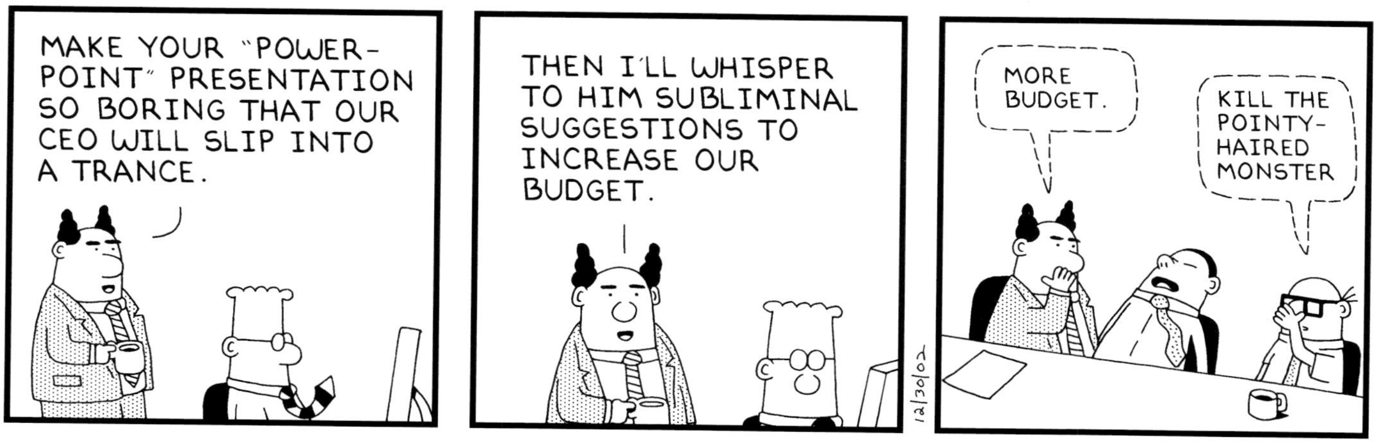
MAKE YOUR "POWER-POINT" PRESENTATION SO BORING THAT OUR CEO WILL SLIP INTO A TRANCE.
THEN I'LL WHISPER TO HIM SUBLIMINAL SUGGESTIONS TO INCREASE OUR BUDGET.
12/30/02
MORE BUDGET.
KILL THE POINTY-HAIRED MONSTER

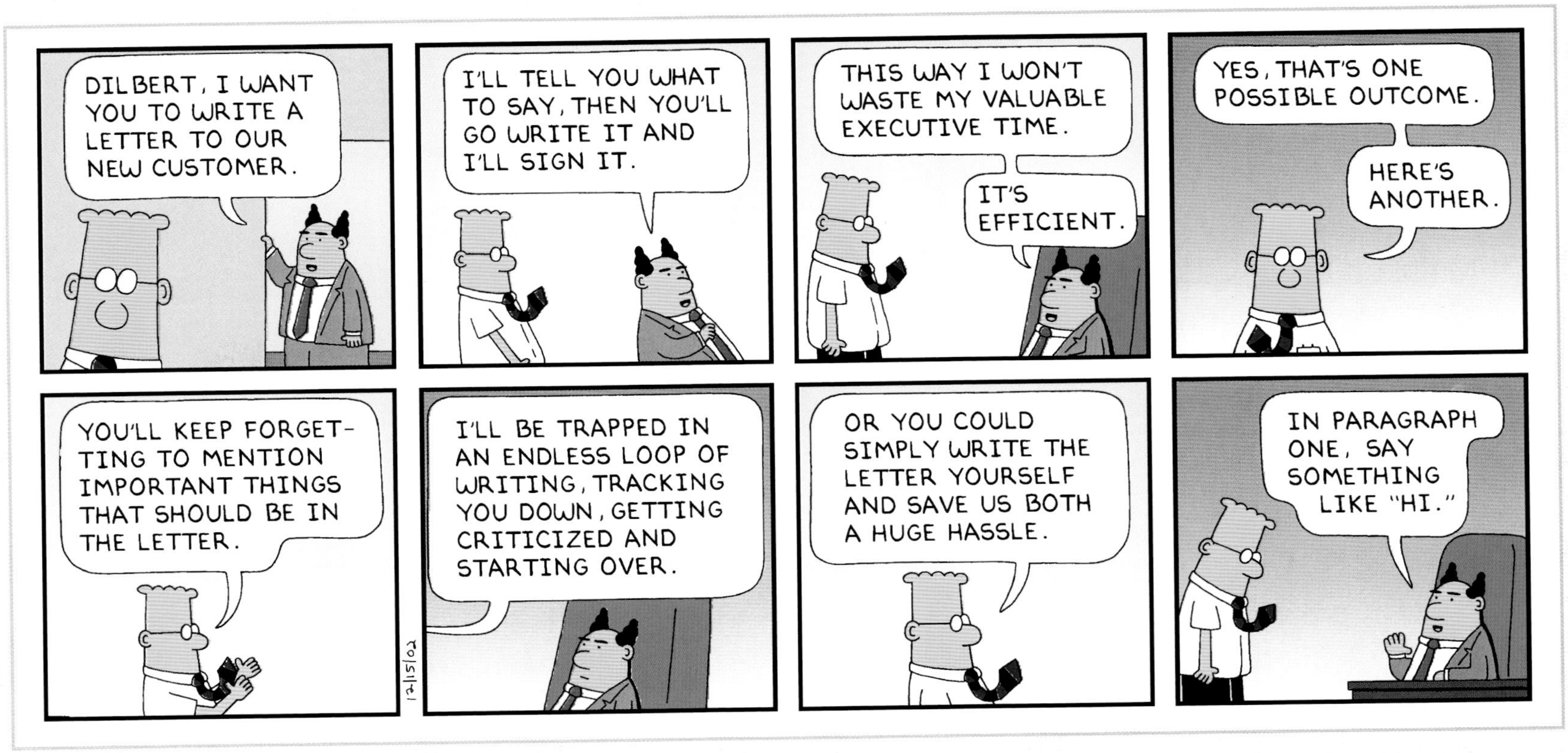
DILBERT, I WANT YOU TO WRITE A LETTER TO OUR NEW CUSTOMER.
I'LL TELL YOU WHAT TO SAY, THEN YOU'LL GO WRITE IT AND I'LL SIGN IT.
THIS WAY I WON'T WASTE MY VALUABLE EXECUTIVE TIME.
IT'S EFFICIENT.
YES, THAT'S ONE POSSIBLE OUTCOME.
HERE'S ANOTHER.
YOU'LL KEEP FORGETTING TO MENTION IMPORTANT THINGS THAT SHOULD BE IN THE LETTER.
I'LL BE TRAPPED IN AN ENDLESS LOOP OF WRITING, TRACKING YOU DOWN, GETTING CRITICIZED AND STARTING OVER.
OR YOU COULD SIMPLY WRITE THE LETTER YOURSELF AND SAVE US BOTH A HUGE HASSLE.
IN PARAGRAPH ONE, SAY SOMETHING LIKE "HI."
12/15/02

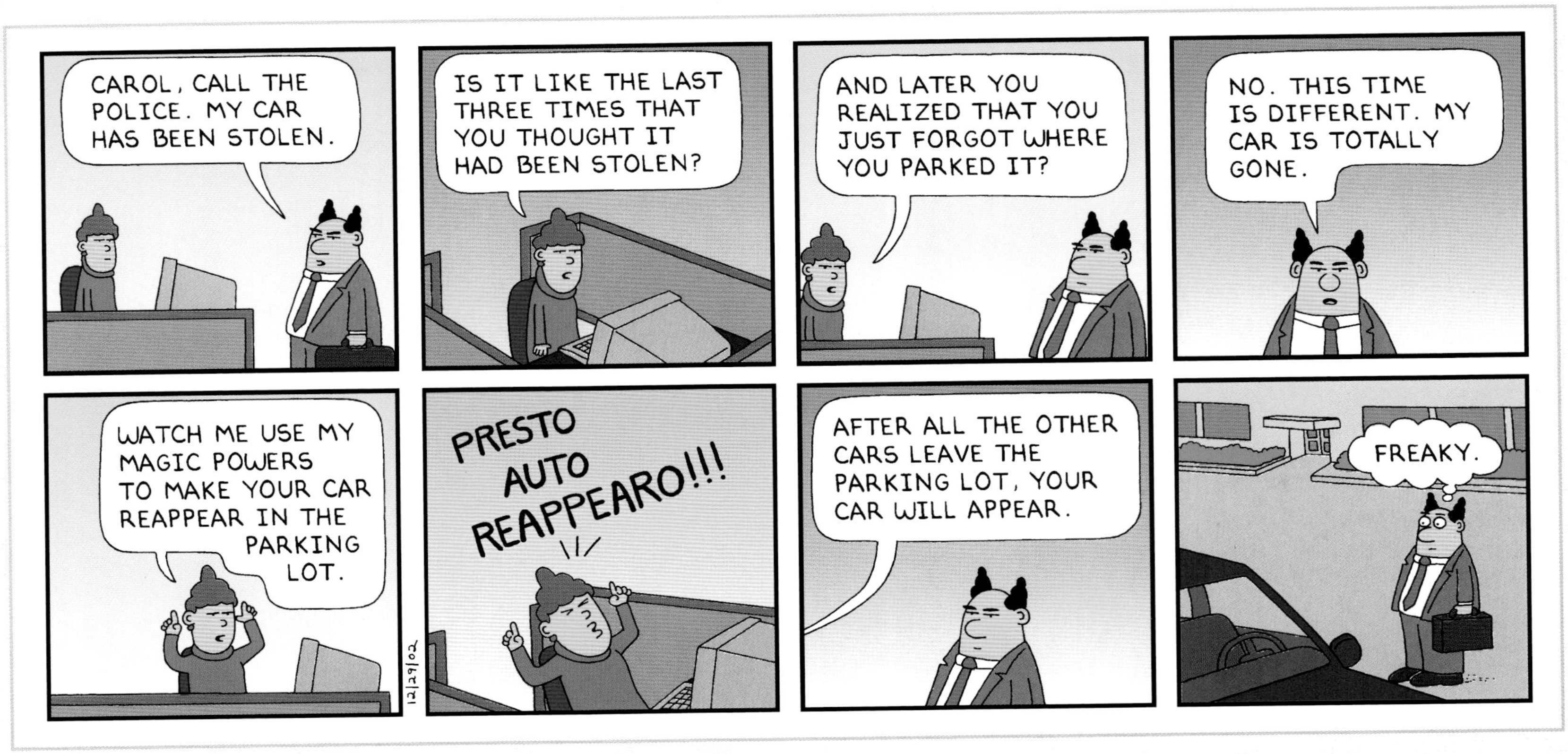
CAROL, CALL THE POLICE. MY CAR HAS BEEN STOLEN.
IS IT LIKE THE LAST THREE TIMES THAT YOU THOUGHT IT HAD BEEN STOLEN?
AND LATER YOU REALIZED THAT YOU JUST FORGOT WHERE YOU PARKED IT?
NO. THIS TIME IS DIFFERENT. MY CAR IS TOTALLY GONE.
WATCH ME USE MY MAGIC POWERS TO MAKE YOUR CAR REAPPEAR IN THE PARKING LOT.
PRESTO AUTO REAPPEARO!!!
AFTER ALL THE OTHER CARS LEAVE THE PARKING LOT, YOUR CAR WILL APPEAR.
FREAKY.
12/29/02

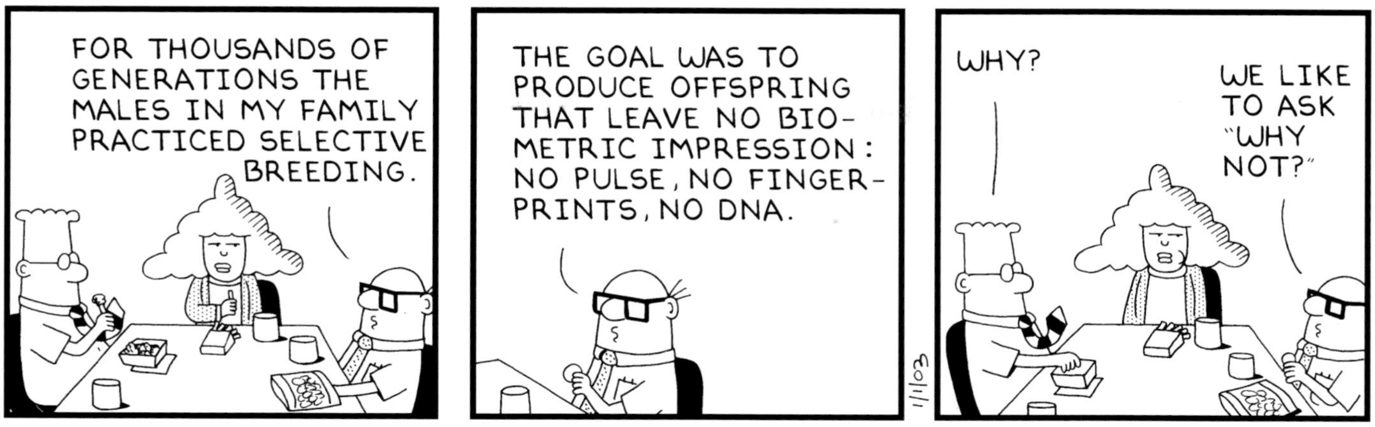
FOR THOUSANDS OF GENERATIONS THE MALES IN MY FAMILY PRACTICED SELECTIVE BREEDING.
THE GOAL WAS TO PRODUCE OFFSPRING THAT LEAVE NO BIO-METRIC IMPRESSION: NO PULSE, NO FINGER-PRINTS, NO DNA.
WHY?
WE LIKE TO ASK "WHY NOT?"

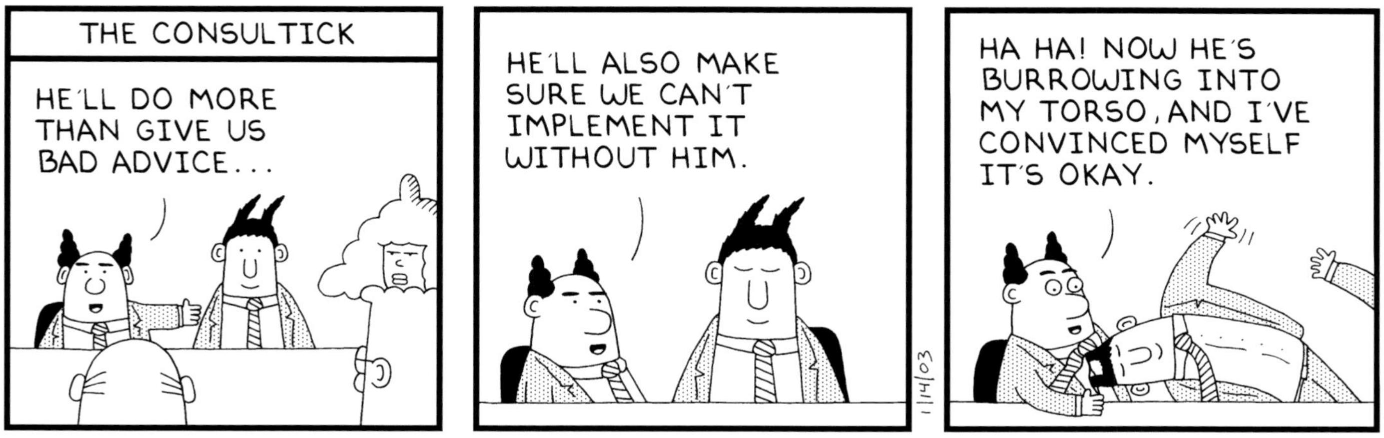
THE CONSULTICK
HE'LL DO MORE THAN GIVE US BAD ADVICE...
HE'LL ALSO MAKE SURE WE CAN'T IMPLEMENT IT WITHOUT HIM.
HA HA! NOW HE'S BURROWING INTO MY TORSO, AND I'VE CONVINCED MYSELF IT'S OKAY.

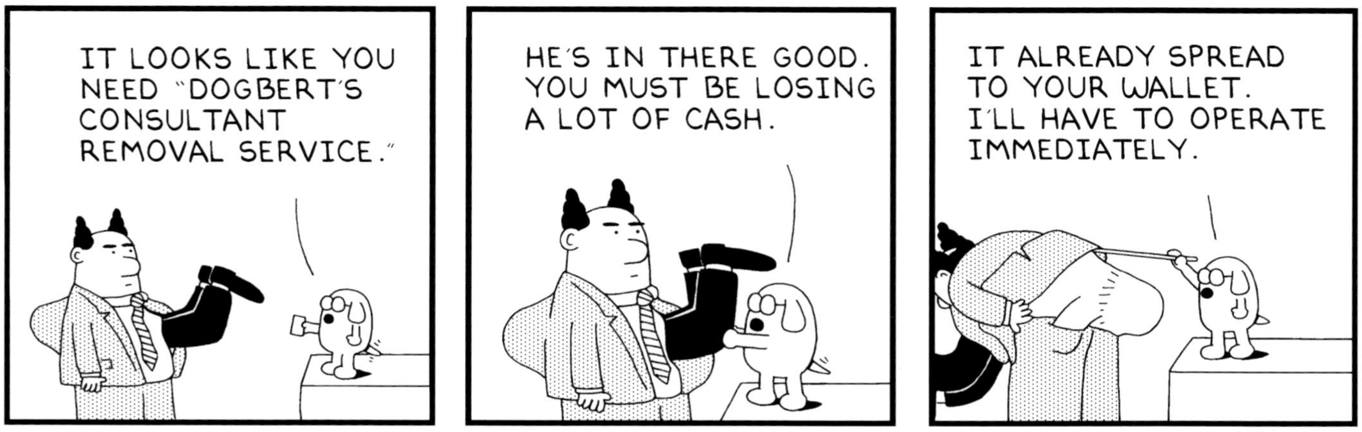
IT LOOKS LIKE YOU NEED "DOGBERT'S CONSULTANT REMOVAL SERVICE."
HE'S IN THERE GOOD. YOU MUST BE LOSING A LOT OF CASH.
IT ALREADY SPREAD TO YOUR WALLET. I'LL HAVE TO OPERATE IMMEDIATELY.

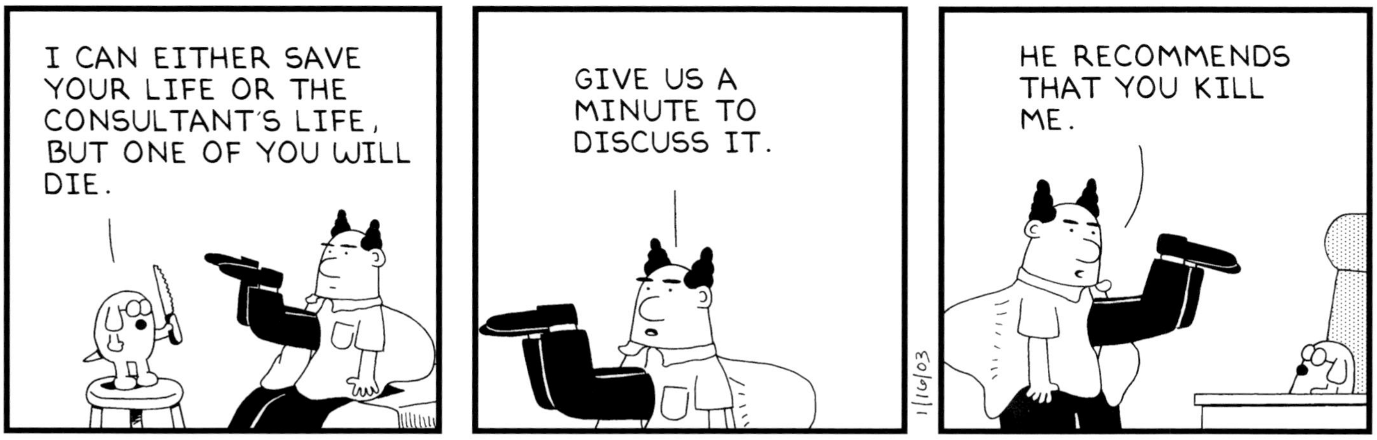
I CAN EITHER SAVE YOUR LIFE OR THE CONSULTANT'S LIFE, BUT ONE OF YOU WILL DIE.
GIVE US A MINUTE TO DISCUSS IT.
HE RECOMMENDS THAT YOU KILL ME.

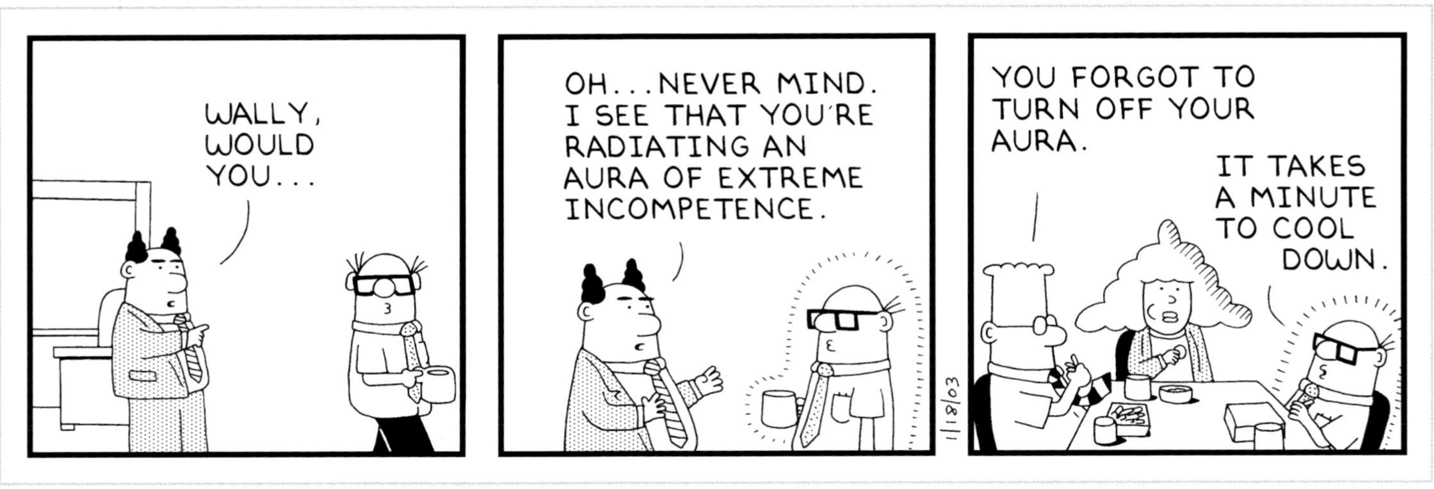
WALLY, WOULD YOU...
OH...NEVER MIND. I SEE THAT YOU'RE RADIATING AN AURA OF EXTREME INCOMPETENCE.
1/18/03
YOU FORGOT TO TURN OFF YOUR AURA.
IT TAKES A MINUTE TO COOL DOWN.

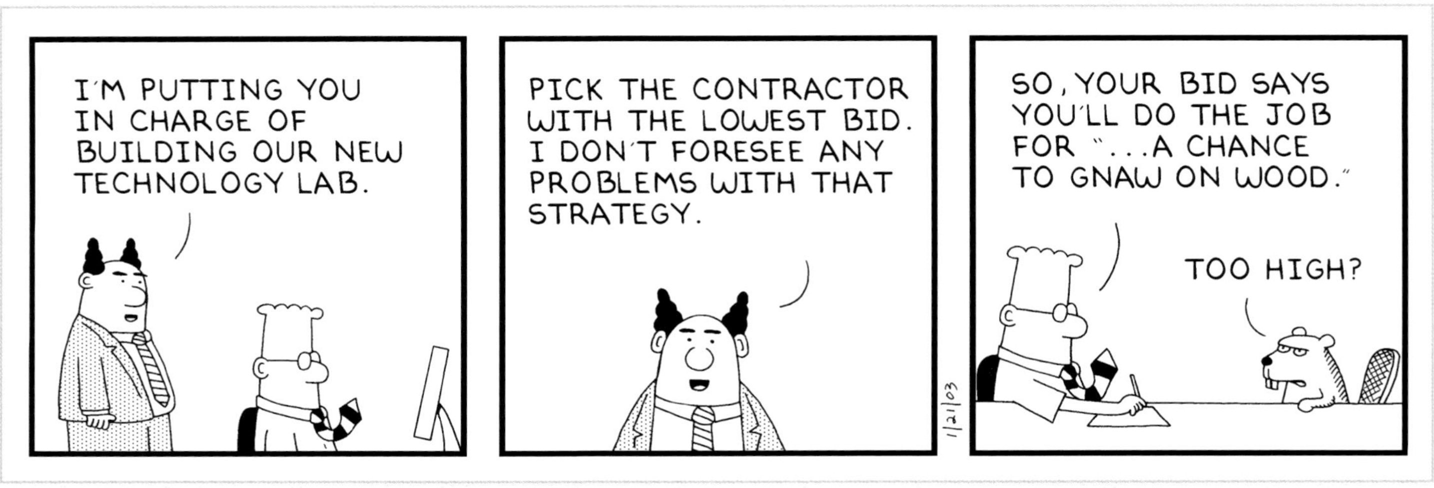
I'M PUTTING YOU IN CHARGE OF BUILDING OUR NEW TECHNOLOGY LAB.
PICK THE CONTRACTOR WITH THE LOWEST BID. I DON'T FORESEE ANY PROBLEMS WITH THAT STRATEGY.
1/21/03
SO, YOUR BID SAYS YOU'LL DO THE JOB FOR "...A CHANCE TO GNAW ON WOOD."
TOO HIGH?

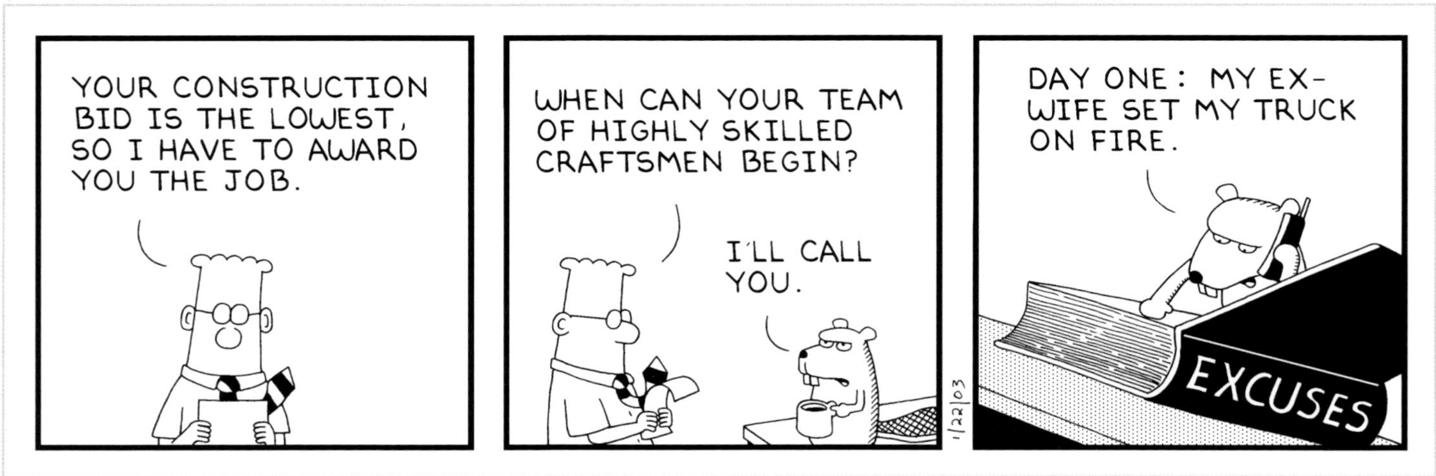
YOUR CONSTRUCTION BID IS THE LOWEST, SO I HAVE TO AWARD YOU THE JOB.
WHEN CAN YOUR TEAM OF HIGHLY SKILLED CRAFTSMEN BEGIN?
I'LL CALL YOU.
1/22/03
DAY ONE: MY EX-WIFE SET MY TRUCK ON FIRE.
EXCUSES

I wrote this while having work done on my house. I heard every excuse you can hear for not showing up for work. The two excuses you can always count on are (1) my truck broke down, and (2) my ex-wife is nuts.

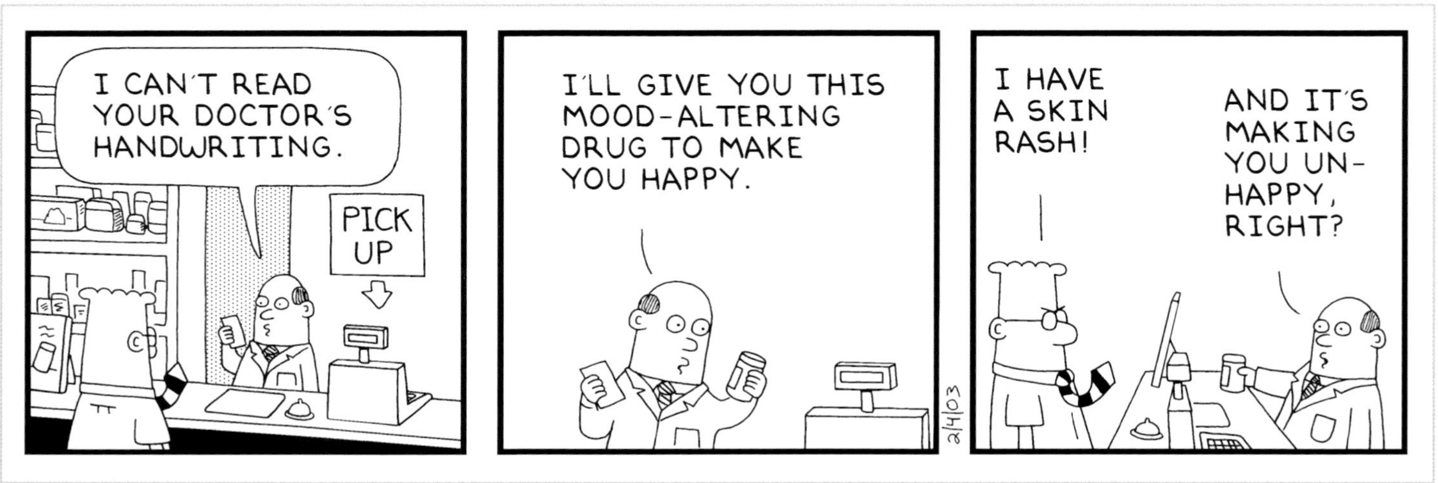
I CAN'T READ YOUR DOCTOR'S HANDWRITING.
PICK UP
I'LL GIVE YOU THIS MOOD-ALTERING DRUG TO MAKE YOU HAPPY.
2/4/03
I HAVE A SKIN RASH!
AND IT'S MAKING YOU UN-HAPPY, RIGHT?

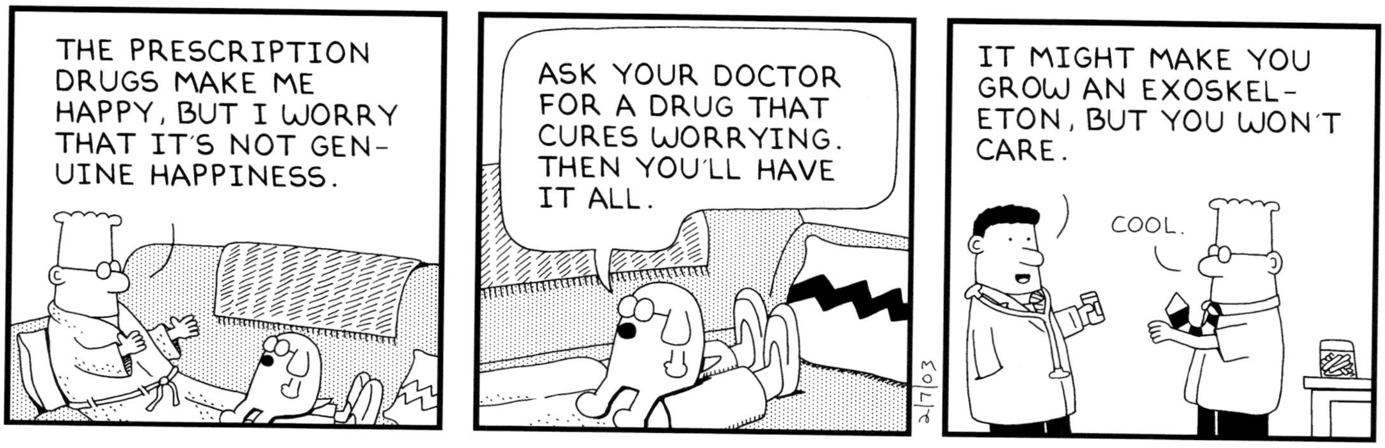
THE PRESCRIPTION DRUGS MAKE ME HAPPY, BUT I WORRY THAT IT'S NOT GEN-UINE HAPPINESS.
ASK YOUR DOCTOR FOR A DRUG THAT CURES WORRYING. THEN YOU'LL HAVE IT ALL.
IT MIGHT MAKE YOU GROW AN EXOSKEL-ETON, BUT YOU WON'T CARE.
COOL.
2/7/03

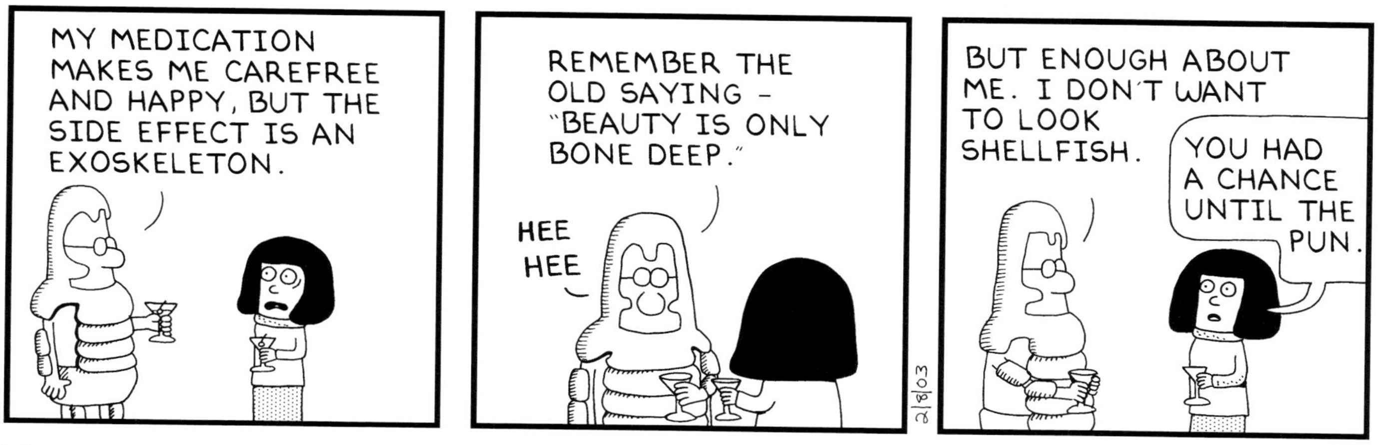
MY MEDICATION MAKES ME CAREFREE AND HAPPY, BUT THE SIDE EFFECT IS AN EXOSKELETON.
REMEMBER THE OLD SAYING – "BEAUTY IS ONLY BONE DEEP."
HEE HEE
BUT ENOUGH ABOUT ME. I DON'T WANT TO LOOK SHELLFISH.
YOU HAD A CHANCE UNTIL THE PUN.
2/8/03

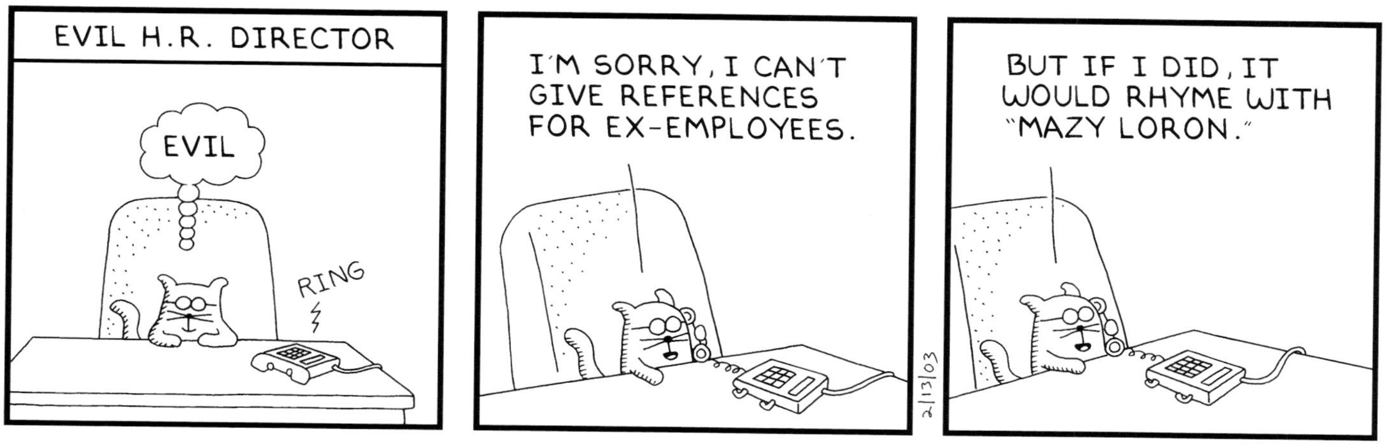
EVIL H.R. DIRECTOR
EVIL
RING
I'M SORRY, I CAN'T GIVE REFERENCES FOR EX-EMPLOYEES.
BUT IF I DID, IT WOULD RHYME WITH "MAZY LORON."
2/13/03

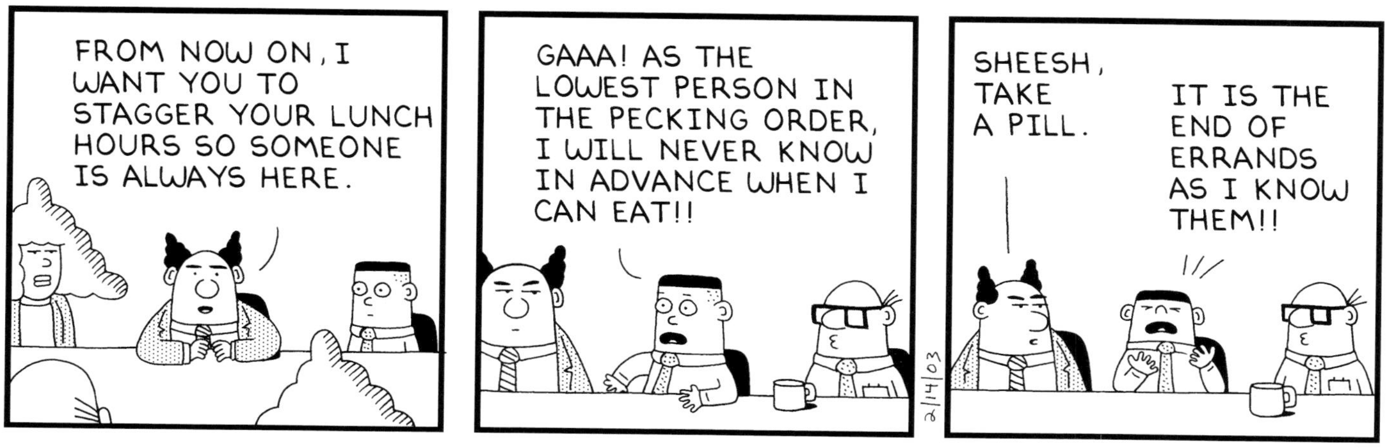
FROM NOW ON, I WANT YOU TO STAGGER YOUR LUNCH HOURS SO SOMEONE IS ALWAYS HERE.
GAAA! AS THE LOWEST PERSON IN THE PECKING ORDER, I WILL NEVER KNOW IN ADVANCE WHEN I CAN EAT!!
SHEESH, TAKE A PILL.
IT IS THE END OF ERRANDS AS I KNOW THEM!!
2/14/03

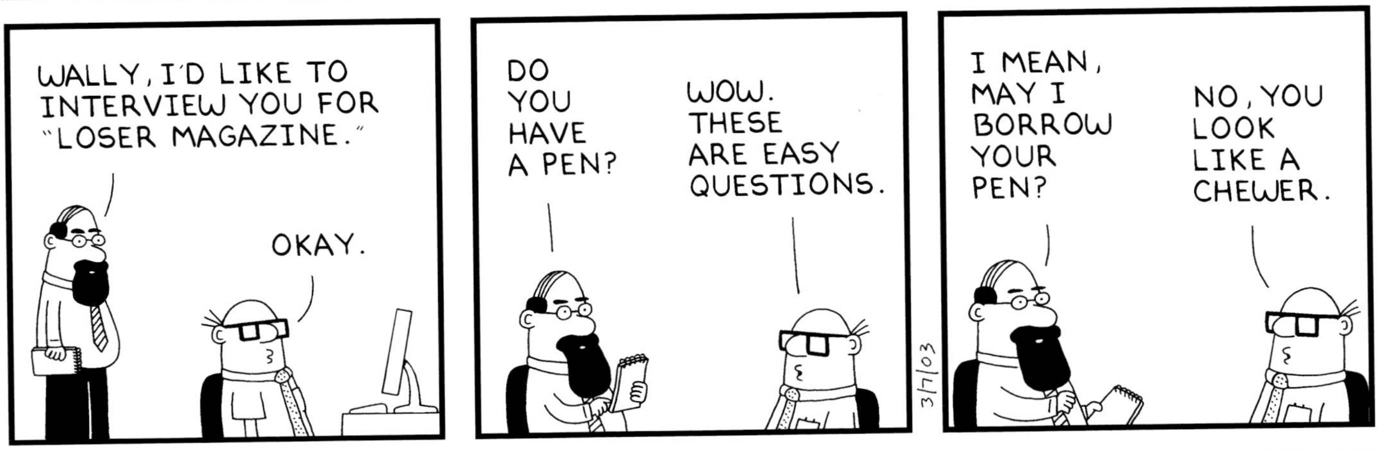
WALLY, I'D LIKE TO INTERVIEW YOU FOR "LOSER MAGAZINE."
OKAY.
DO YOU HAVE A PEN?
WOW. THESE ARE EASY QUESTIONS.
3/7/03
I MEAN, MAY I BORROW YOUR PEN?
NO, YOU LOOK LIKE A CHEWER.

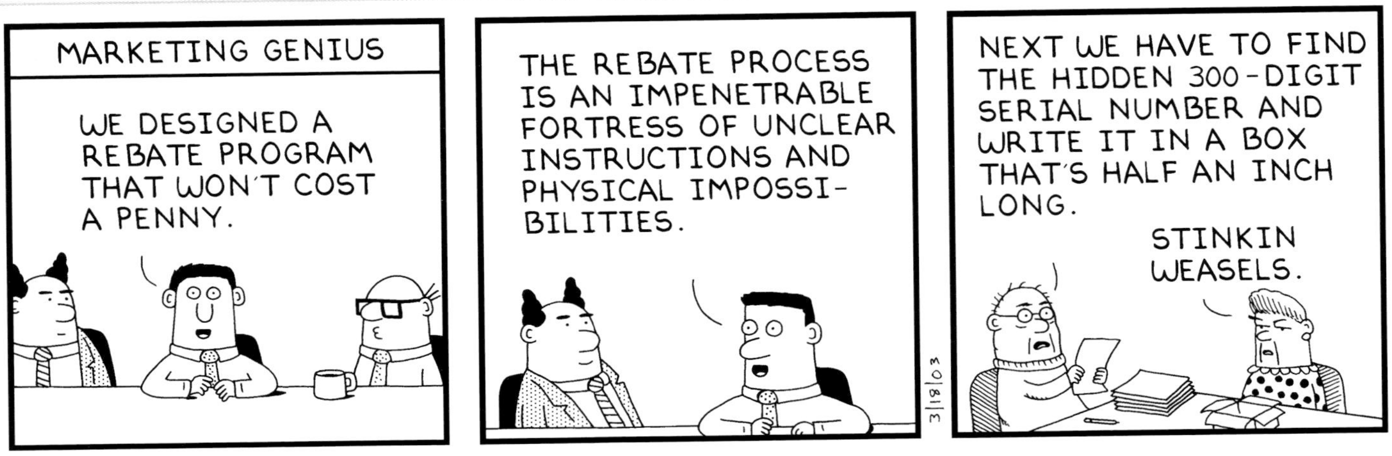
MARKETING GENIUS
WE DESIGNED A REBATE PROGRAM THAT WON'T COST A PENNY.
THE REBATE PROCESS IS AN IMPENETRABLE FORTRESS OF UNCLEAR INSTRUCTIONS AND PHYSICAL IMPOSSI-BILITIES.
3/18/03
NEXT WE HAVE TO FIND THE HIDDEN 300-DIGIT SERIAL NUMBER AND WRITE IT IN A BOX THAT'S HALF AN INCH LONG.
STINKIN WEASELS.

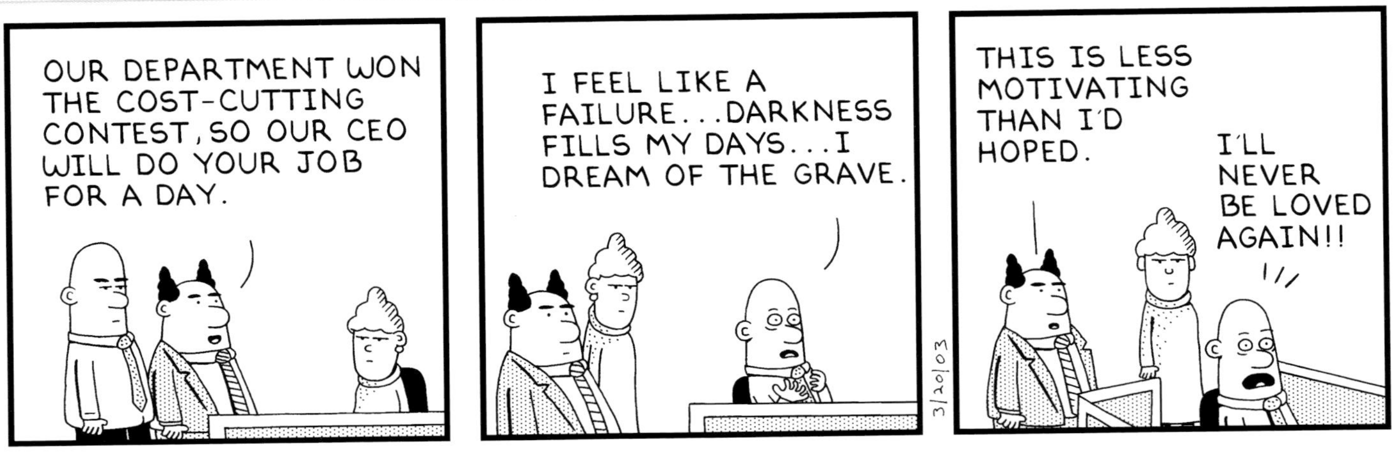
OUR DEPARTMENT WON THE COST-CUTTING CONTEST, SO OUR CEO WILL DO YOUR JOB FOR A DAY.
I FEEL LIKE A FAILURE... DARKNESS FILLS MY DAYS... I DREAM OF THE GRAVE.
3/20/03
THIS IS LESS MOTIVATING THAN I'D HOPED.
I'LL NEVER BE LOVED AGAIN!!

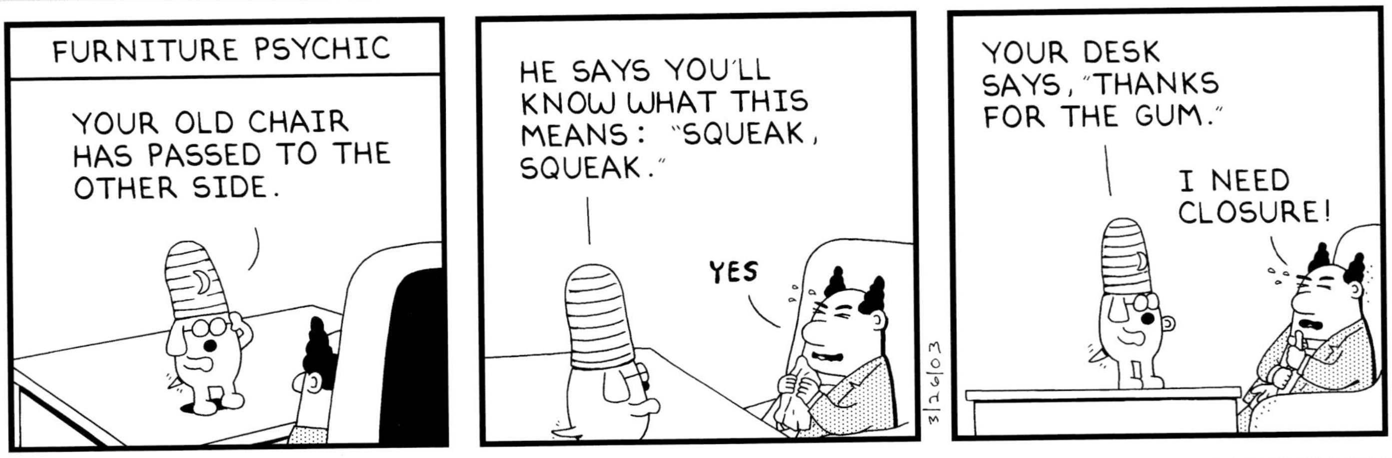
FURNITURE PSYCHIC
YOUR OLD CHAIR HAS PASSED TO THE OTHER SIDE.
HE SAYS YOU'LL KNOW WHAT THIS MEANS: "SQUEAK, SQUEAK."
YES
3/26/03
YOUR DESK SAYS, "THANKS FOR THE GUM."
I NEED CLOSURE!

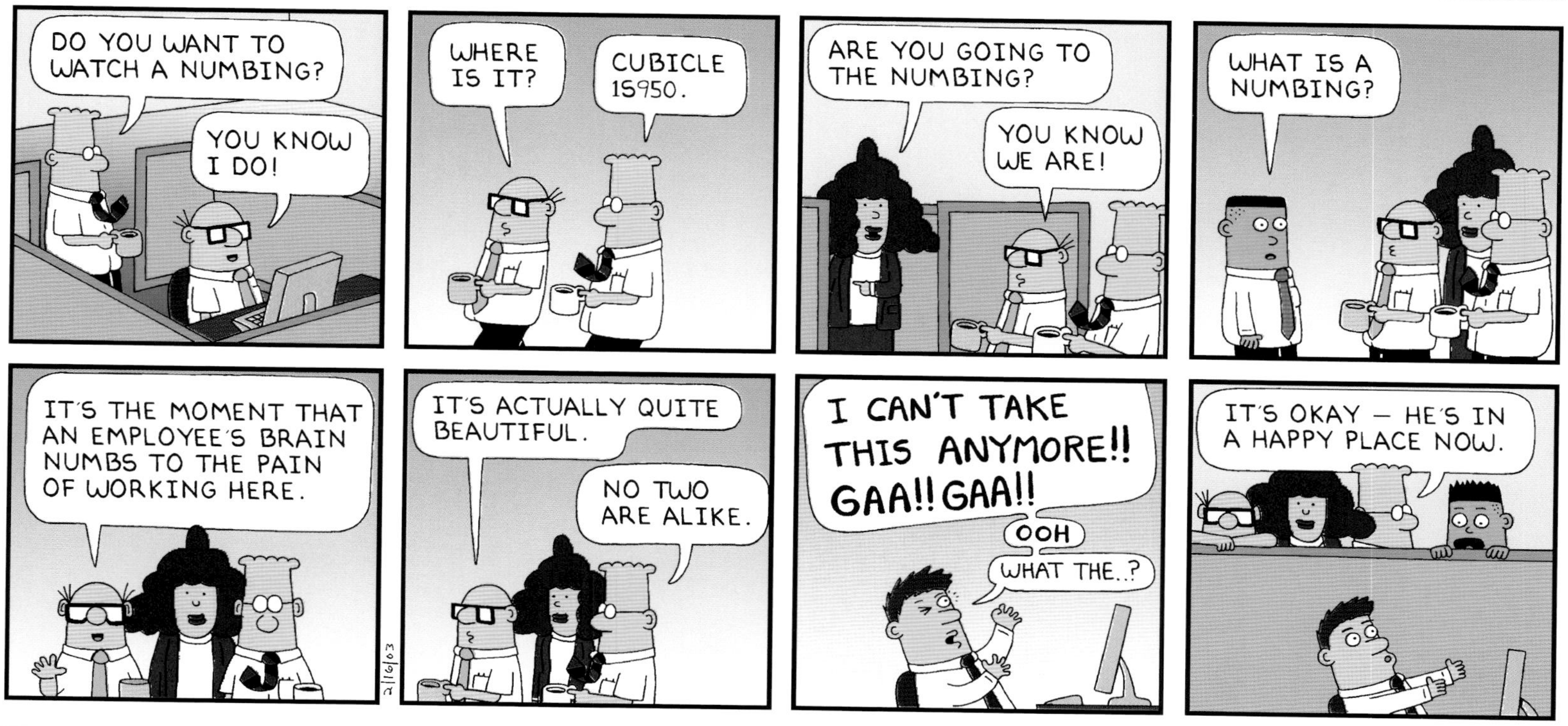
DO YOU WANT TO WATCH A NUMBING?
YOU KNOW I DO!
WHERE IS IT?
CUBICLE 15950.
ARE YOU GOING TO THE NUMBING?
YOU KNOW WE ARE!
WHAT IS A NUMBING?
IT'S THE MOMENT THAT AN EMPLOYEE'S BRAIN NUMBS TO THE PAIN OF WORKING HERE.
IT'S ACTUALLY QUITE BEAUTIFUL.
NO TWO ARE ALIKE.
I CAN'T TAKE THIS ANYMORE!! GAA!! GAA!!
OOH
WHAT THE..?
IT'S OKAY — HE'S IN A HAPPY PLACE NOW.

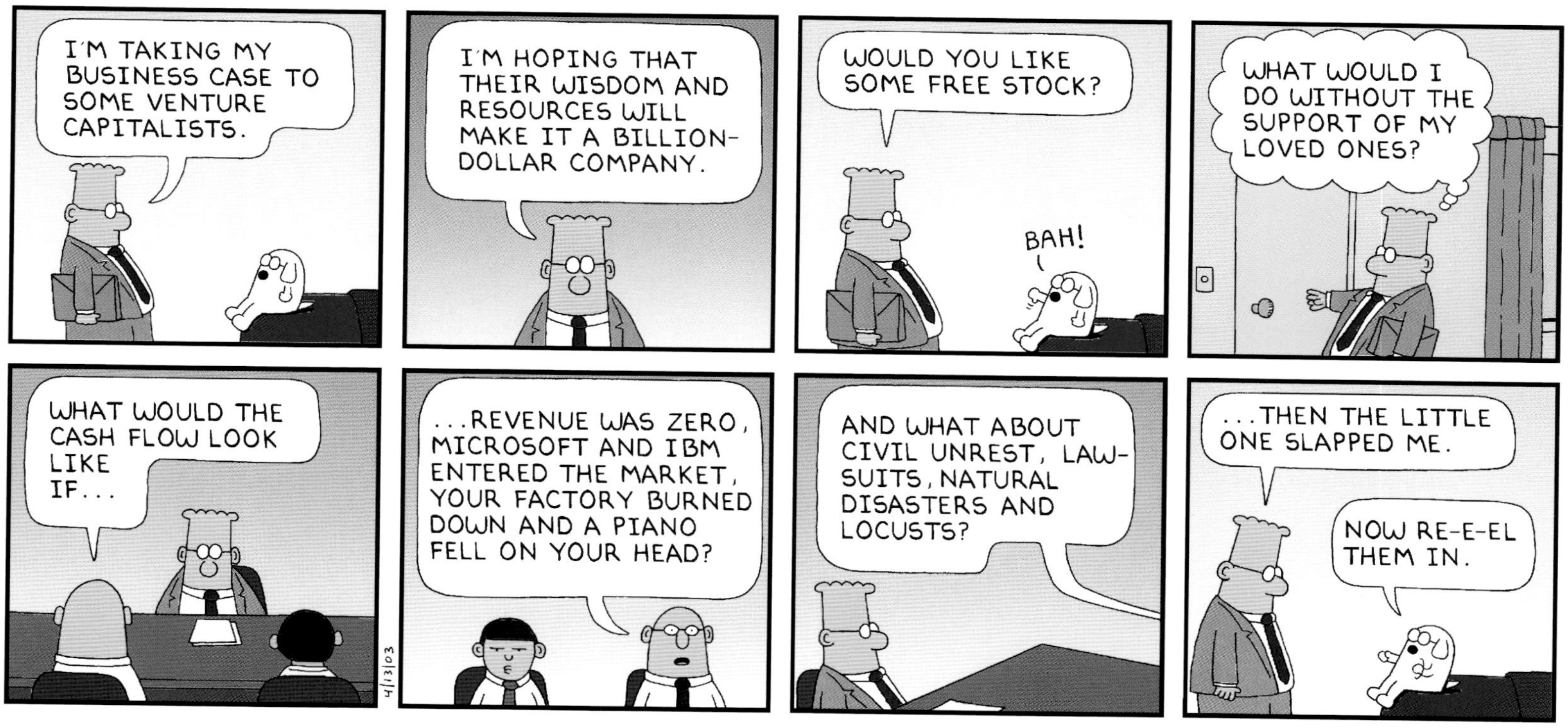
I'M TAKING MY BUSINESS CASE TO SOME VENTURE CAPITALISTS.
I'M HOPING THAT THEIR WISDOM AND RESOURCES WILL MAKE IT A BILLION-DOLLAR COMPANY.
WOULD YOU LIKE SOME FREE STOCK?
BAH!
WHAT WOULD I DO WITHOUT THE SUPPORT OF MY LOVED ONES?
WHAT WOULD THE CASH FLOW LOOK LIKE IF...
...REVENUE WAS ZERO, MICROSOFT AND IBM ENTERED THE MARKET, YOUR FACTORY BURNED DOWN AND A PIANO FELL ON YOUR HEAD?
AND WHAT ABOUT CIVIL UNREST, LAW-SUITS, NATURAL DISASTERS AND LOCUSTS?
...THEN THE LITTLE ONE SLAPPED ME.
NOW RE-E-EL THEM IN.

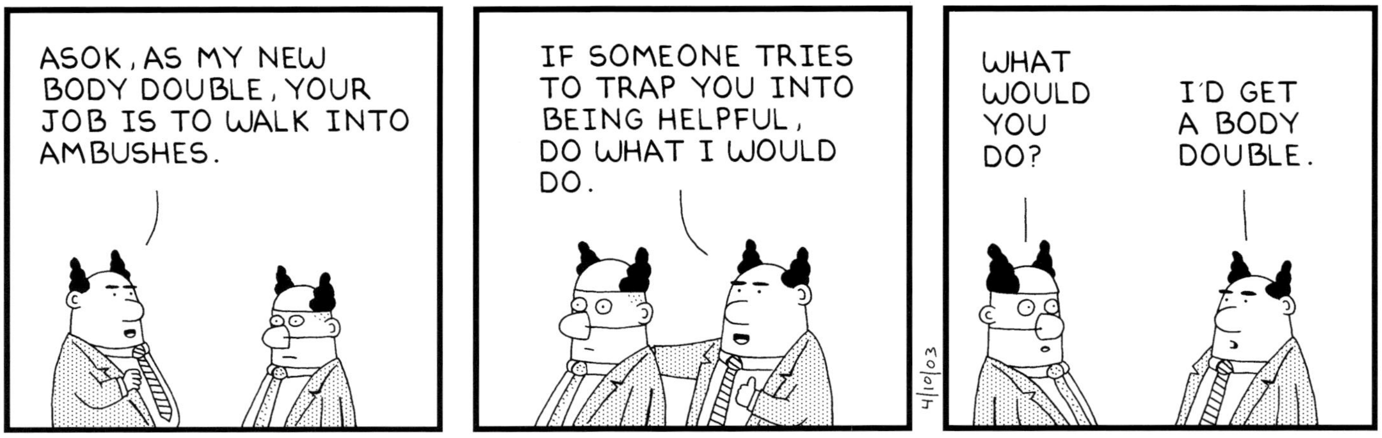
ASOK, AS MY NEW BODY DOUBLE, YOUR JOB IS TO WALK INTO AMBUSHES.
IF SOMEONE TRIES TO TRAP YOU INTO BEING HELPFUL, DO WHAT I WOULD DO.
4/10/03
WHAT WOULD YOU DO?
I'D GET A BODY DOUBLE.

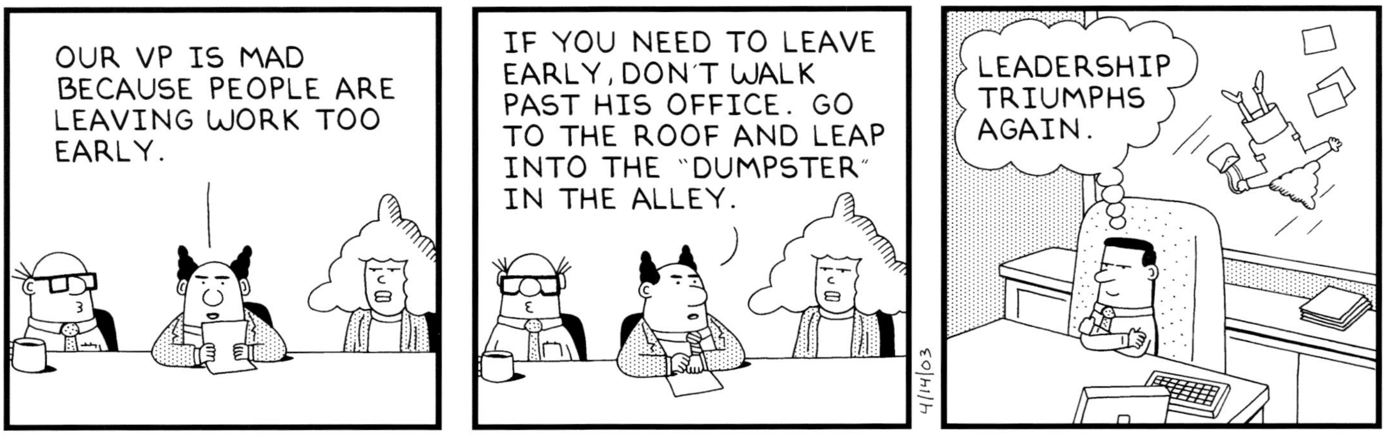
OUR VP IS MAD BECAUSE PEOPLE ARE LEAVING WORK TOO EARLY.
IF YOU NEED TO LEAVE EARLY, DON'T WALK PAST HIS OFFICE. GO TO THE ROOF AND LEAP INTO THE "DUMPSTER" IN THE ALLEY.
4/14/03
LEADERSHIP TRIUMPHS AGAIN.

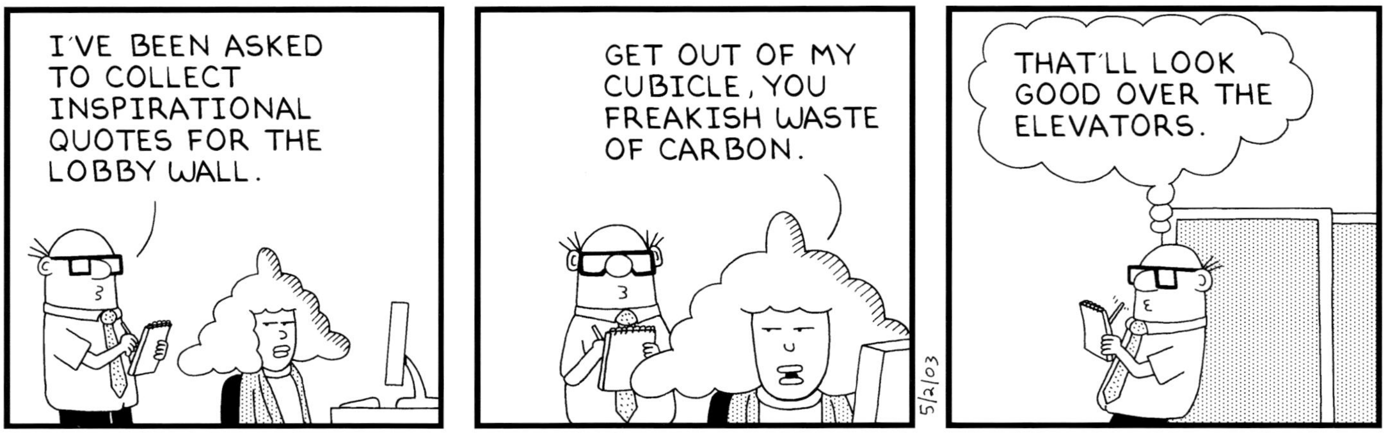
I'VE BEEN ASKED TO COLLECT INSPIRATIONAL QUOTES FOR THE LOBBY WALL.
GET OUT OF MY CUBICLE, YOU FREAKISH WASTE OF CARBON.
5/2/03
THAT'LL LOOK GOOD OVER THE ELEVATORS.

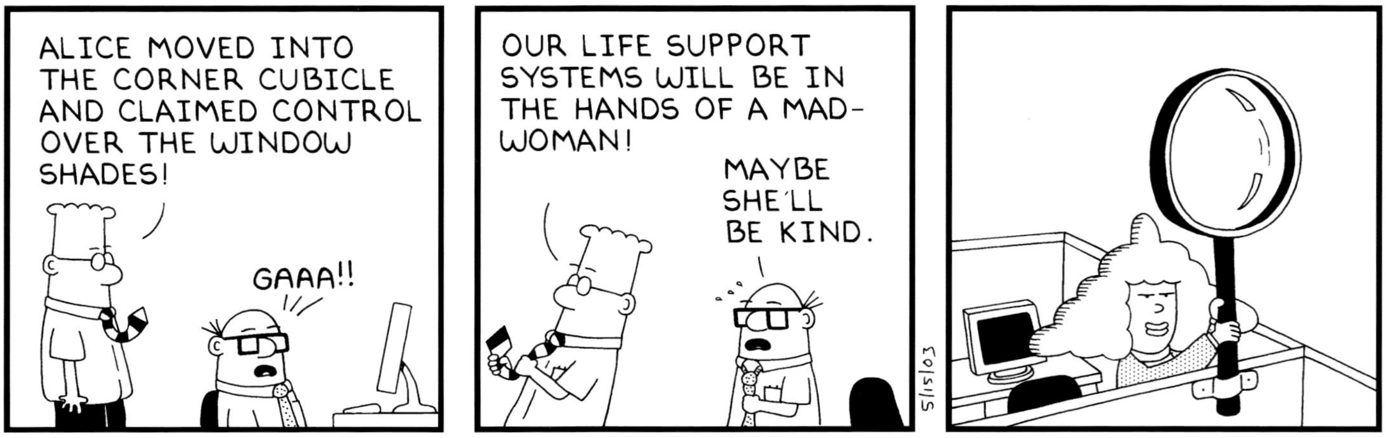
ALICE MOVED INTO THE CORNER CUBICLE AND CLAIMED CONTROL OVER THE WINDOW SHADES!
GAAA!!
OUR LIFE SUPPORT SYSTEMS WILL BE IN THE HANDS OF A MAD-WOMAN!
MAYBE SHE'LL BE KIND.
5/15/03

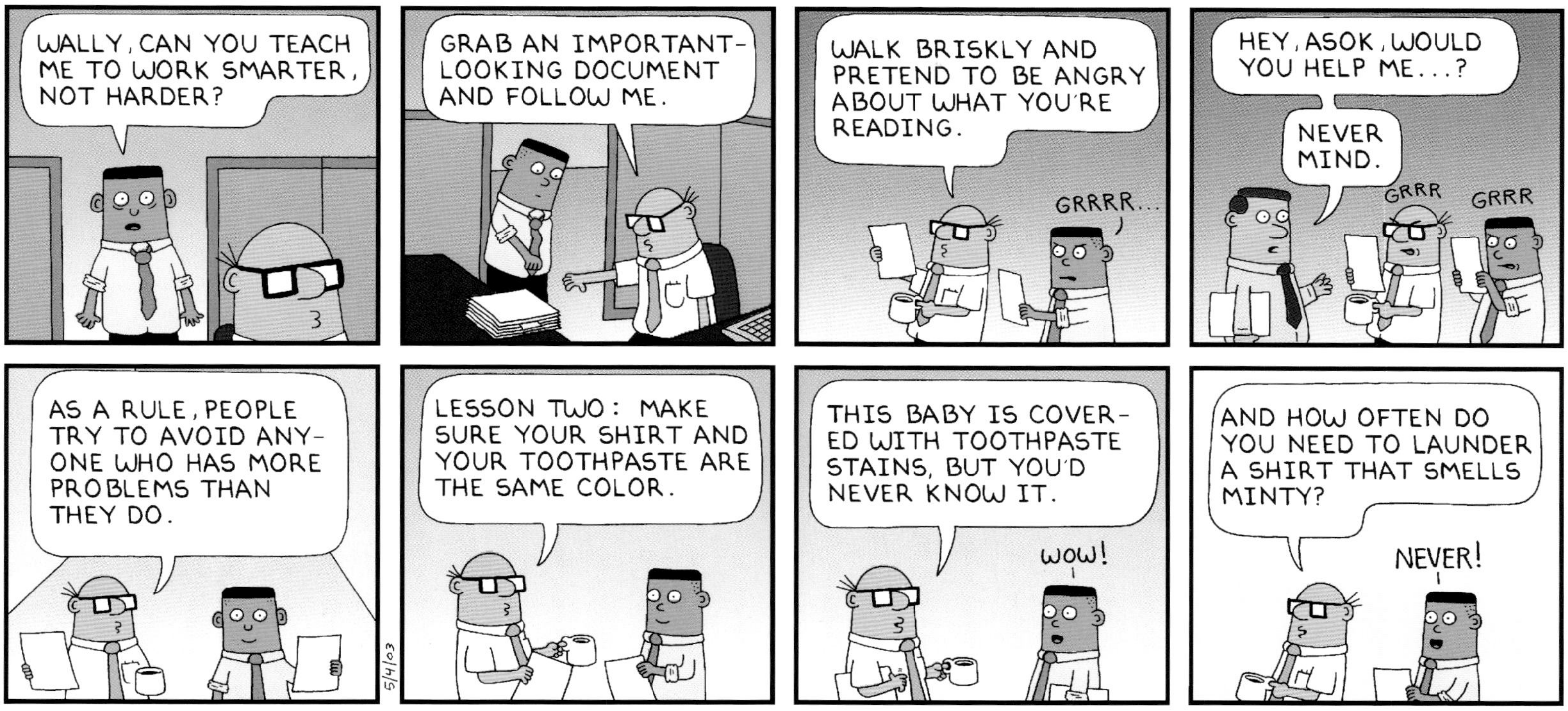
WALLY, CAN YOU TEACH ME TO WORK SMARTER, NOT HARDER?
GRAB AN IMPORTANT-LOOKING DOCUMENT AND FOLLOW ME.
WALK BRISKLY AND PRETEND TO BE ANGRY ABOUT WHAT YOU'RE READING.
GRRRR...
HEY, ASOK, WOULD YOU HELP ME...?
NEVER MIND.
GRRR
GRRR
AS A RULE, PEOPLE TRY TO AVOID ANYONE WHO HAS MORE PROBLEMS THAN THEY DO.
5/4/03
LESSON TWO: MAKE SURE YOUR SHIRT AND YOUR TOOTHPASTE ARE THE SAME COLOR.
THIS BABY IS COVERED WITH TOOTHPASTE STAINS, BUT YOU'D NEVER KNOW IT.
WOW!
AND HOW OFTEN DO YOU NEED TO LAUNDER A SHIRT THAT SMELLS MINTY?
NEVER!

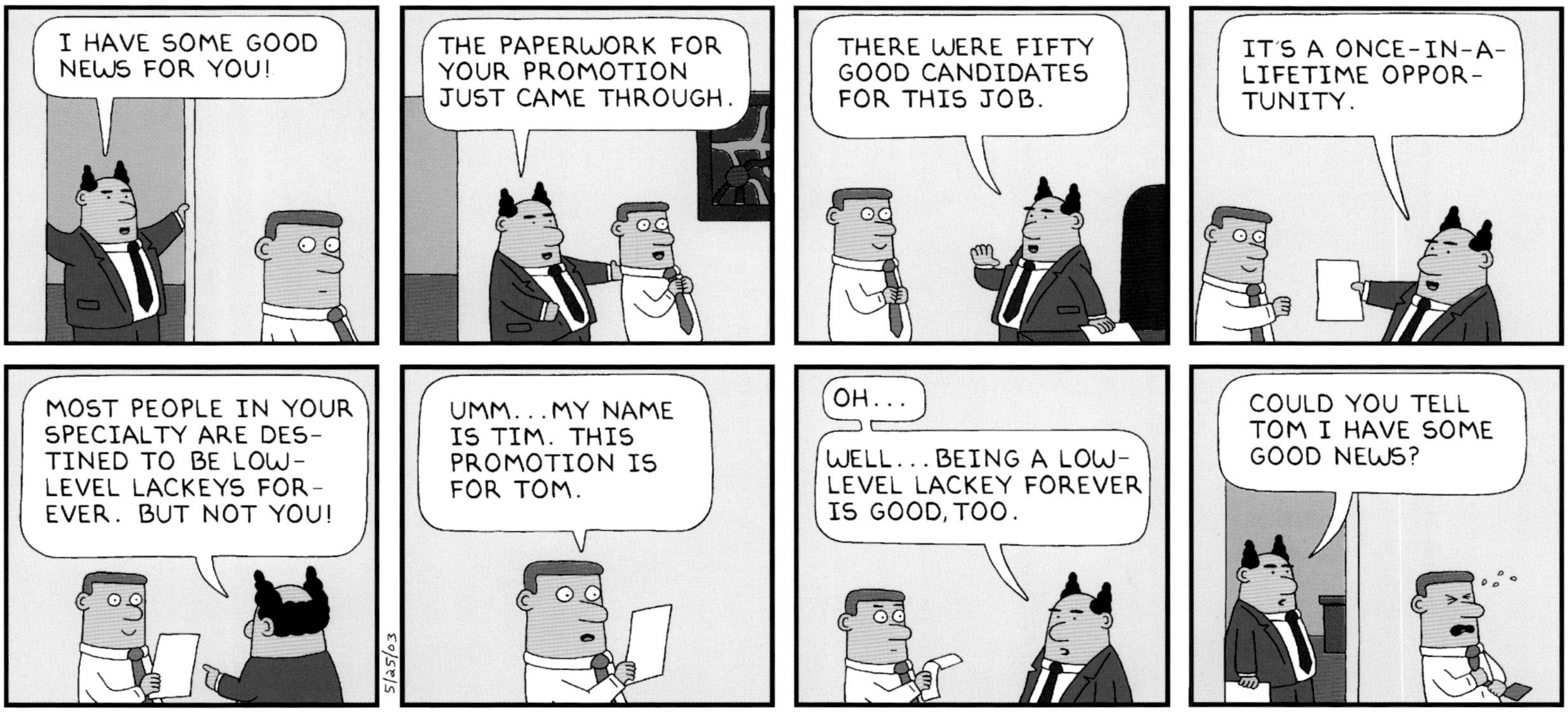
I HAVE SOME GOOD NEWS FOR YOU!
THE PAPERWORK FOR YOUR PROMOTION JUST CAME THROUGH.
THERE WERE FIFTY GOOD CANDIDATES FOR THIS JOB.
IT'S A ONCE-IN-A-LIFETIME OPPORTUNITY.
MOST PEOPLE IN YOUR SPECIALTY ARE DESTINED TO BE LOW-LEVEL LACKEYS FOREVER. BUT NOT YOU!
5/25/03
UMM...MY NAME IS TIM. THIS PROMOTION IS FOR TOM.
OH...
WELL...BEING A LOW-LEVEL LACKEY FOREVER IS GOOD, TOO.
COULD YOU TELL TOM I HAVE SOME GOOD NEWS?

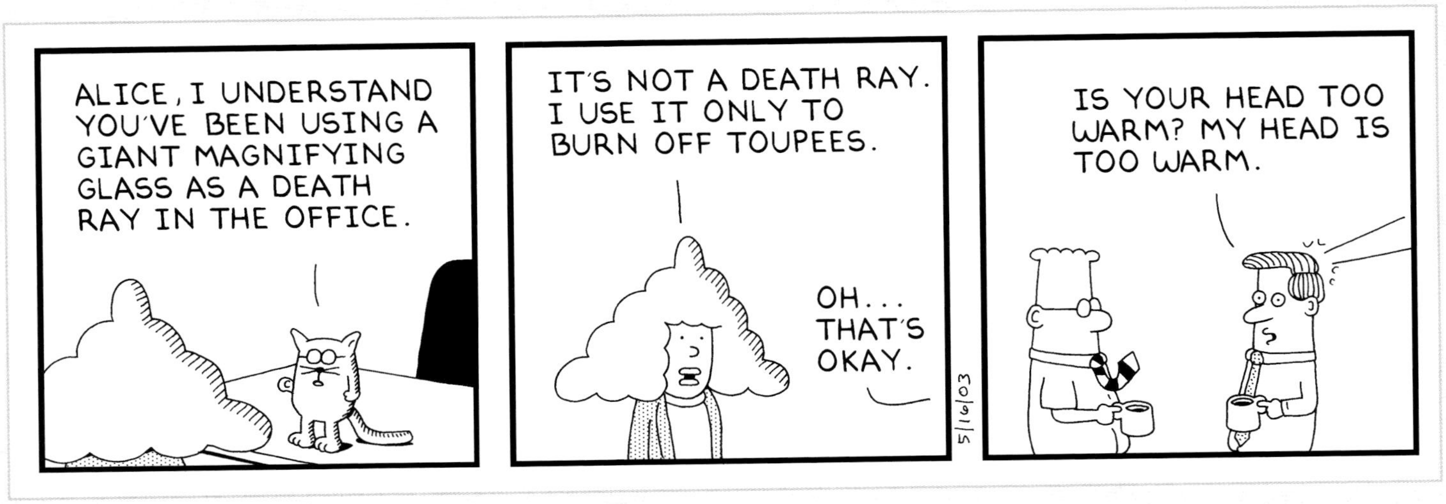
ALICE, I UNDERSTAND YOU'VE BEEN USING A GIANT MAGNIFYING GLASS AS A DEATH RAY IN THE OFFICE.
IT'S NOT A DEATH RAY. I USE IT ONLY TO BURN OFF TOUPEES.
OH... THAT'S OKAY.
5/16/03
IS YOUR HEAD TOO WARM? MY HEAD IS TOO WARM.

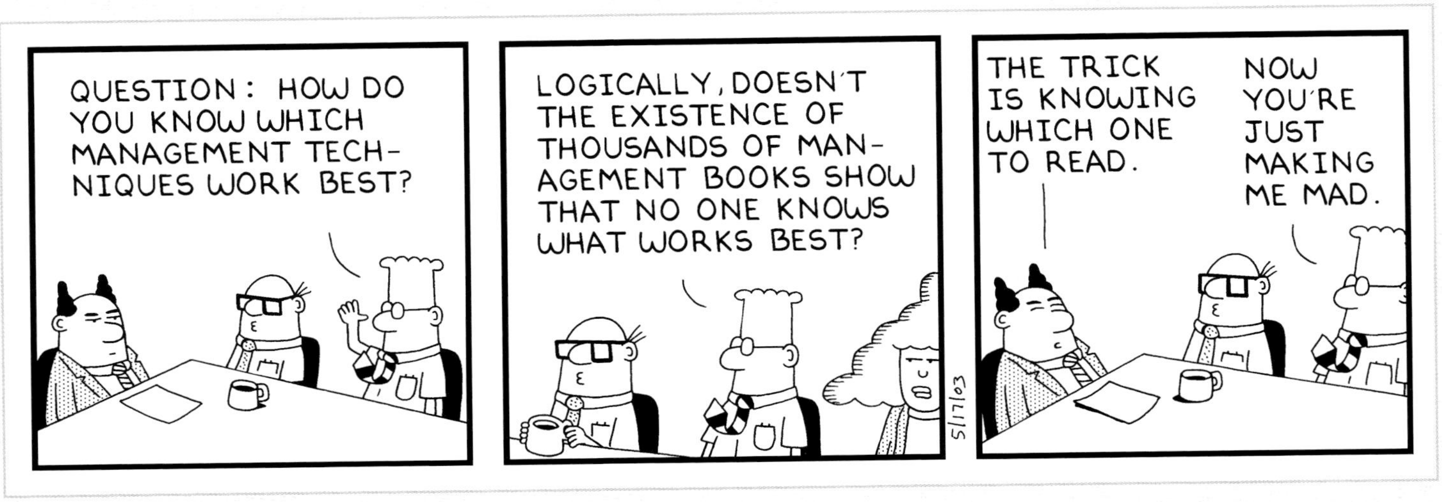
QUESTION: HOW DO YOU KNOW WHICH MANAGEMENT TECHNIQUES WORK BEST?
LOGICALLY, DOESN'T THE EXISTENCE OF THOUSANDS OF MANAGEMENT BOOKS SHOW THAT NO ONE KNOWS WHAT WORKS BEST?
5/17/03
THE TRICK IS KNOWING WHICH ONE TO READ.
NOW YOU'RE JUST MAKING ME MAD.

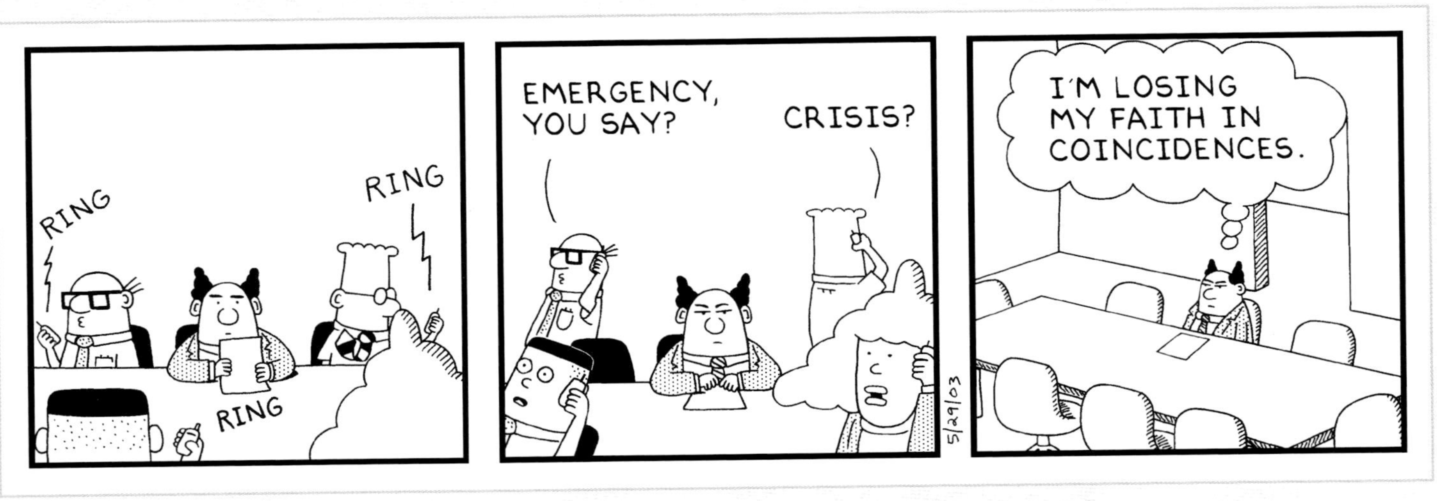
RING
RING
RING
EMERGENCY, YOU SAY?
CRISIS?
5/29/03
I'M LOSING MY FAITH IN COINCIDENCES.

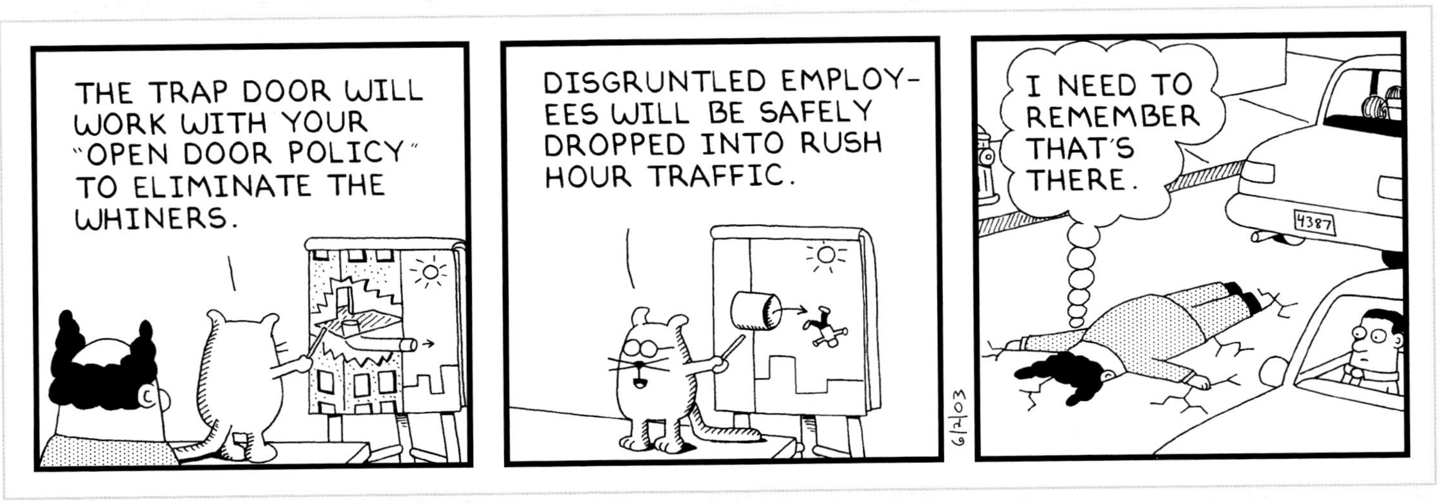
THE TRAP DOOR WILL WORK WITH YOUR "OPEN DOOR POLICY" TO ELIMINATE THE WHINERS.
DISGRUNTLED EMPLOYEES WILL BE SAFELY DROPPED INTO RUSH HOUR TRAFFIC.
6/2/03
I NEED TO REMEMBER THAT'S THERE.
4387

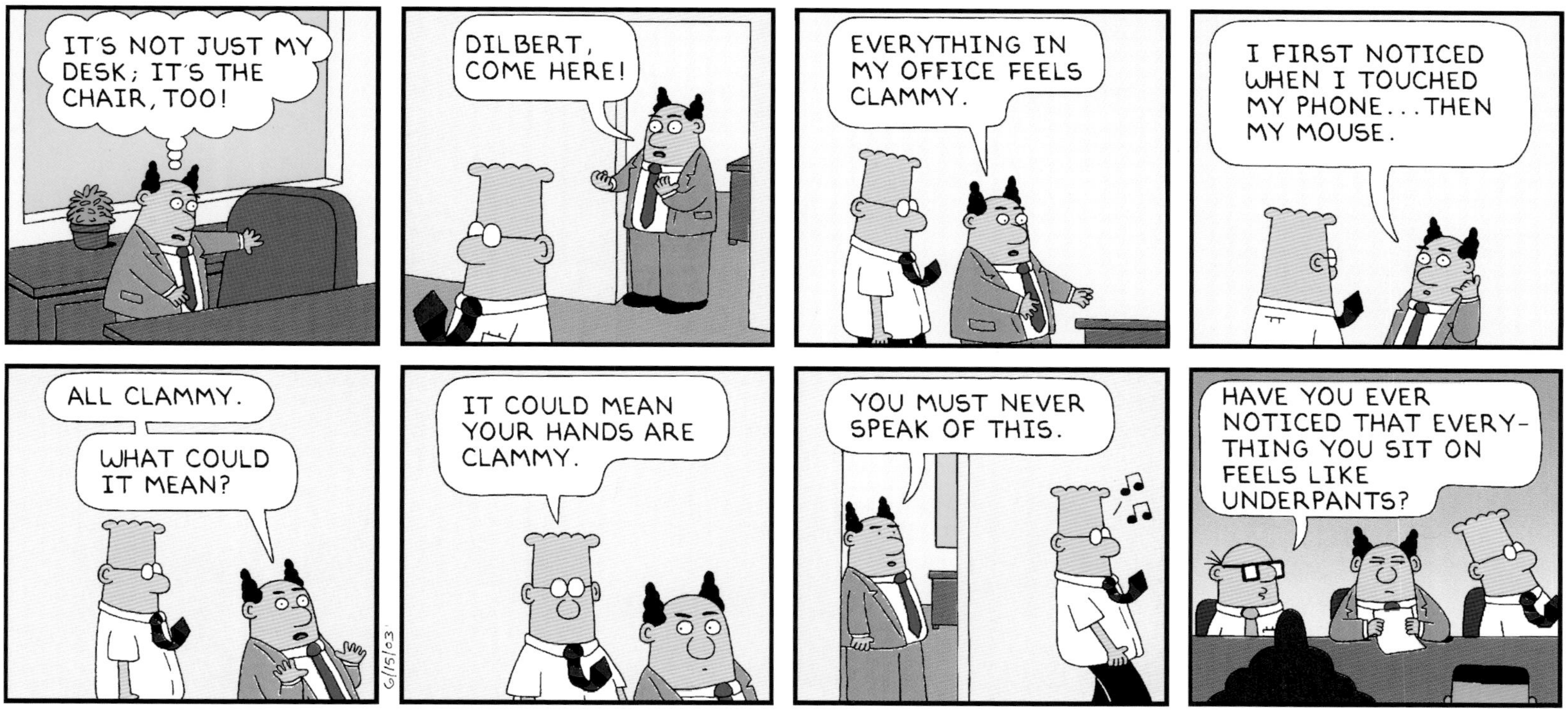
IT'S NOT JUST MY DESK; IT'S THE CHAIR, TOO!
DILBERT, COME HERE!
EVERYTHING IN MY OFFICE FEELS CLAMMY.
I FIRST NOTICED WHEN I TOUCHED MY PHONE... THEN MY MOUSE.
ALL CLAMMY.
WHAT COULD IT MEAN?
6/15/03
IT COULD MEAN YOUR HANDS ARE CLAMMY.
YOU MUST NEVER SPEAK OF THIS.
HAVE YOU EVER NOTICED THAT EVERY-THING YOU SIT ON FEELS LIKE UNDERPANTS?

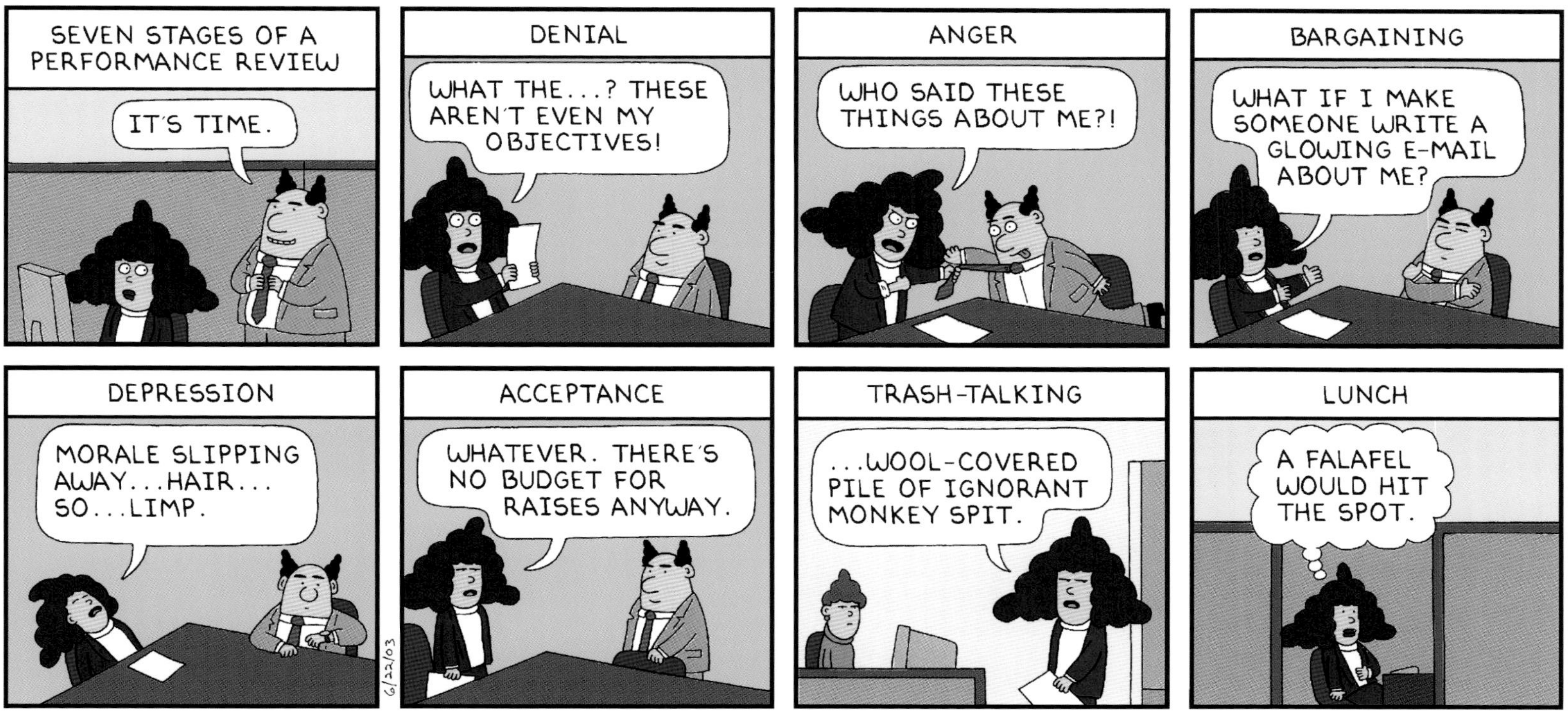
SEVEN STAGES OF A PERFORMANCE REVIEW
IT'S TIME.
DENIAL
WHAT THE...? THESE AREN'T EVEN MY OBJECTIVES!
ANGER
WHO SAID THESE THINGS ABOUT ME?!
BARGAINING
WHAT IF I MAKE SOMEONE WRITE A GLOWING E-MAIL ABOUT ME?
DEPRESSION
MORALE SLIPPING AWAY... HAIR... SO... LIMP.
6/22/03
ACCEPTANCE
WHATEVER. THERE'S NO BUDGET FOR RAISES ANYWAY.
TRASH-TALKING
...WOOL-COVERED PILE OF IGNORANT MONKEY SPIT.
LUNCH
A FALAFEL WOULD HIT THE SPOT.

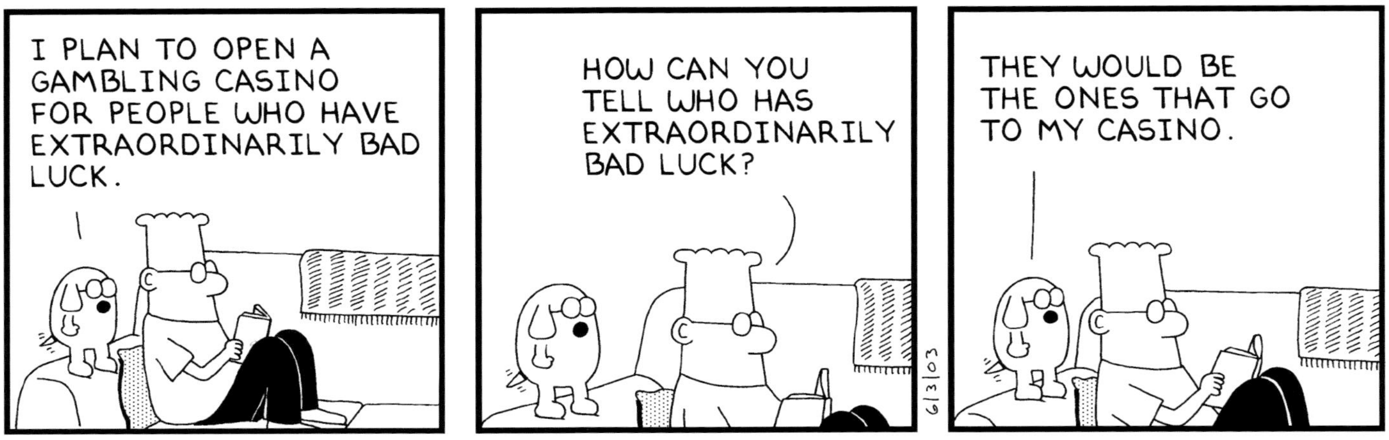
I PLAN TO OPEN A GAMBLING CASINO FOR PEOPLE WHO HAVE EXTRAORDINARILY BAD LUCK.
HOW CAN YOU TELL WHO HAS EXTRAORDINARILY BAD LUCK?
6/3/03
THEY WOULD BE THE ONES THAT GO TO MY CASINO.

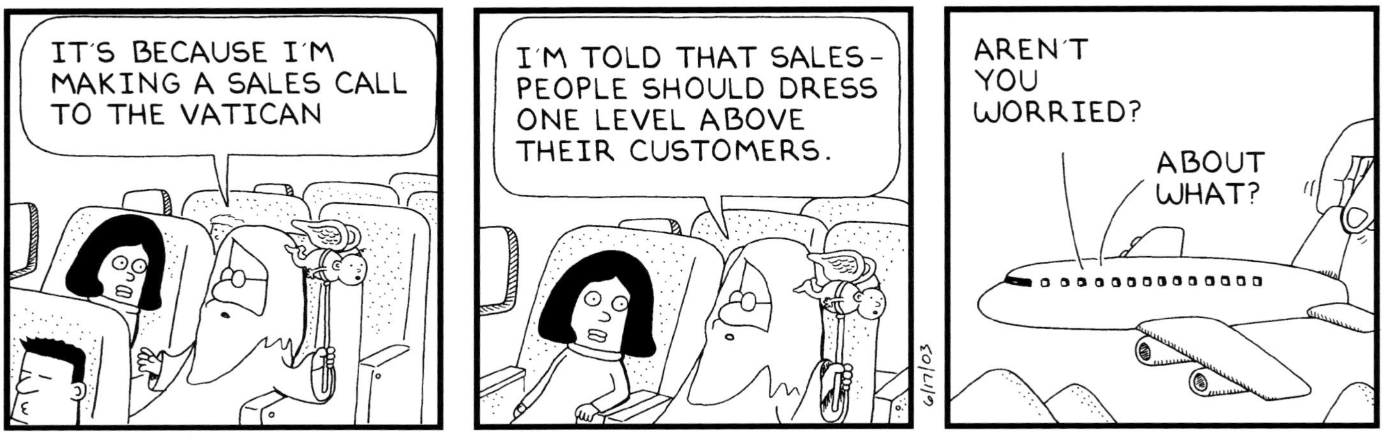
IT'S BECAUSE I'M MAKING A SALES CALL TO THE VATICAN
I'M TOLD THAT SALES-PEOPLE SHOULD DRESS ONE LEVEL ABOVE THEIR CUSTOMERS.
6/17/03
AREN'T YOU WORRIED?
ABOUT WHAT?

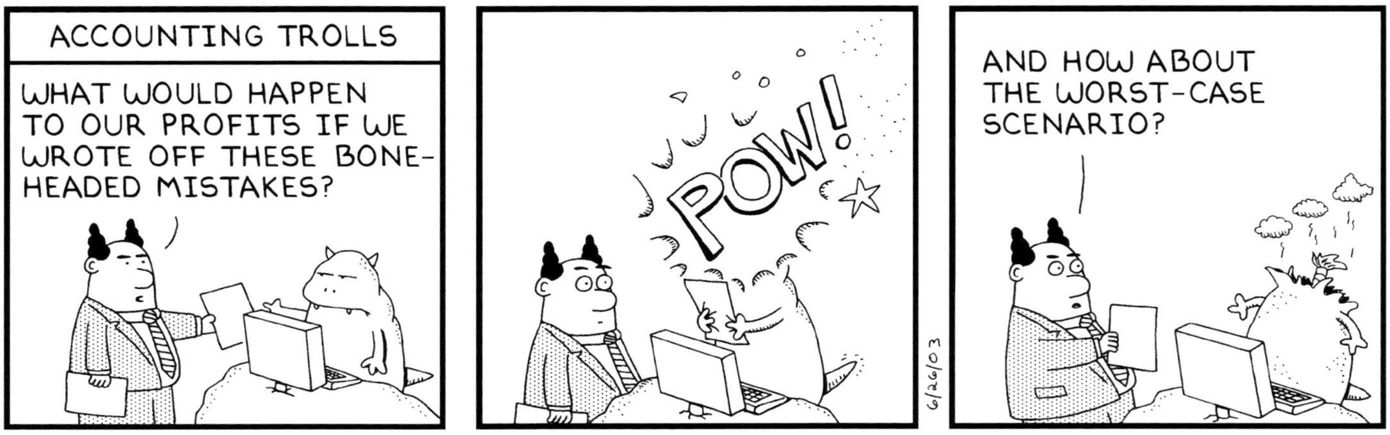
ACCOUNTING TROLLS
WHAT WOULD HAPPEN TO OUR PROFITS IF WE WROTE OFF THESE BONE-HEADED MISTAKES?
POW!
6/26/03
AND HOW ABOUT THE WORST-CASE SCENARIO?

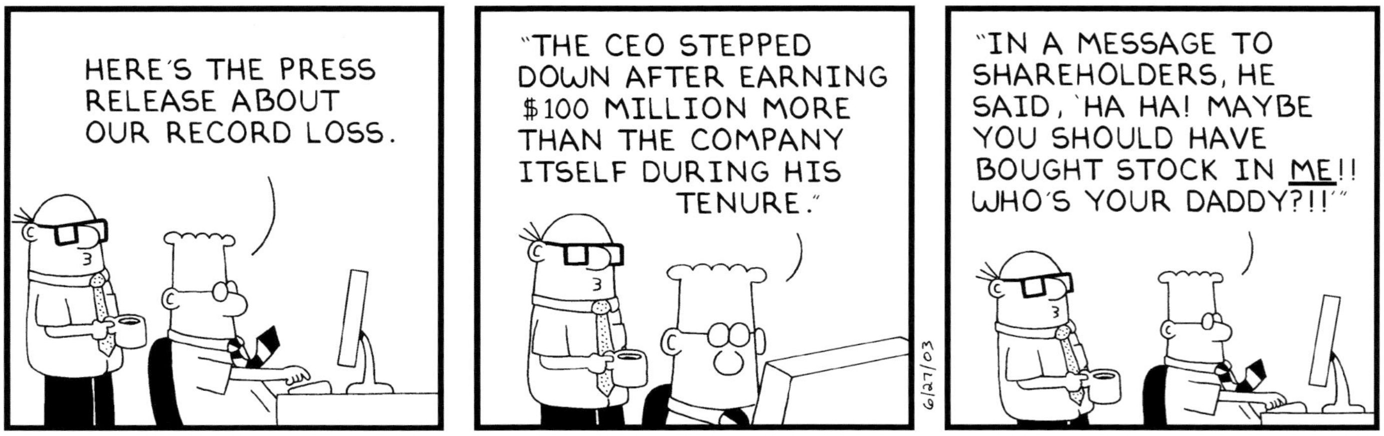
HERE'S THE PRESS RELEASE ABOUT OUR RECORD LOSS.
"THE CEO STEPPED DOWN AFTER EARNING $100 MILLION MORE THAN THE COMPANY ITSELF DURING HIS TENURE."
6/27/03
"IN A MESSAGE TO SHAREHOLDERS, HE SAID, 'HA HA! MAYBE YOU SHOULD HAVE BOUGHT STOCK IN ME!! WHO'S YOUR DADDY?!!'"

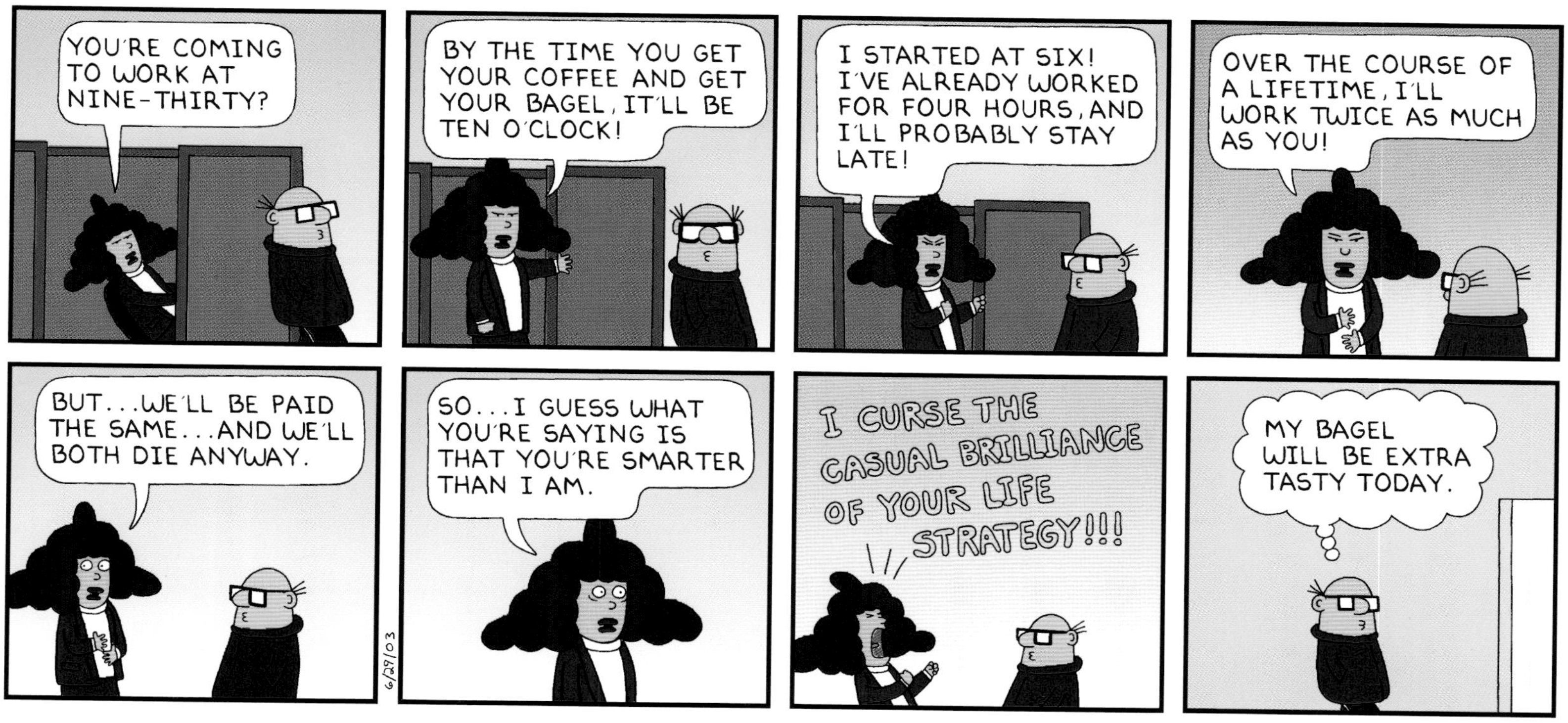
YOU'RE COMING TO WORK AT NINE-THIRTY?
BY THE TIME YOU GET YOUR COFFEE AND GET YOUR BAGEL, IT'LL BE TEN O'CLOCK!
I STARTED AT SIX! I'VE ALREADY WORKED FOR FOUR HOURS, AND I'LL PROBABLY STAY LATE!
OVER THE COURSE OF A LIFETIME, I'LL WORK TWICE AS MUCH AS YOU!
BUT...WE'LL BE PAID THE SAME...AND WE'LL BOTH DIE ANYWAY.
6/29/03
SO...I GUESS WHAT YOU'RE SAYING IS THAT YOU'RE SMARTER THAN I AM.
I CURSE THE CASUAL BRILLIANCE OF YOUR LIFE STRATEGY!!!
MY BAGEL WILL BE EXTRA TASTY TODAY.

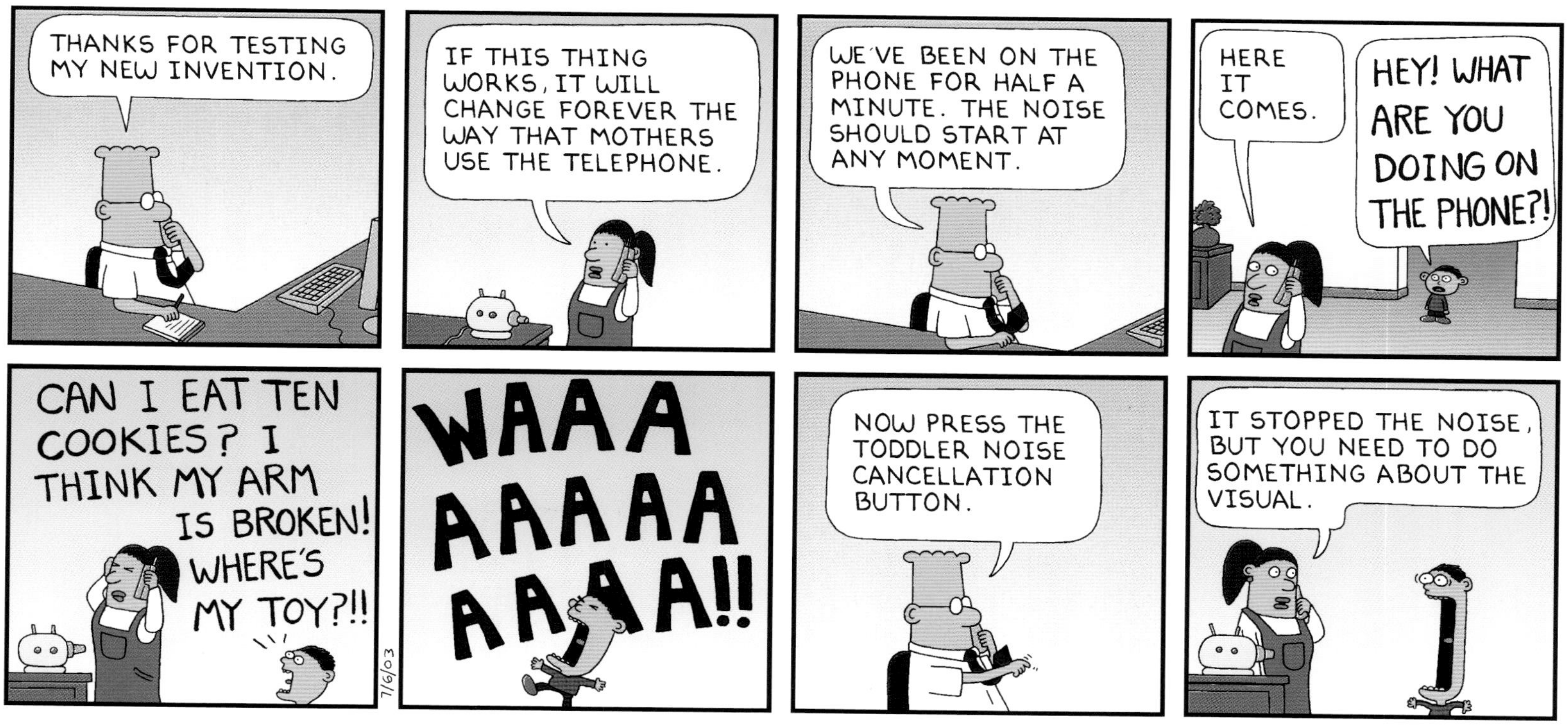
THANKS FOR TESTING MY NEW INVENTION.
IF THIS THING WORKS, IT WILL CHANGE FOREVER THE WAY THAT MOTHERS USE THE TELEPHONE.
WE'VE BEEN ON THE PHONE FOR HALF A MINUTE. THE NOISE SHOULD START AT ANY MOMENT.
HERE IT COMES.
HEY! WHAT ARE YOU DOING ON THE PHONE?!
CAN I EAT TEN COOKIES? I THINK MY ARM IS BROKEN! WHERE'S MY TOY?!!
7/6/03
WAAA AAAAA AAAA!!
NOW PRESS THE TODDLER NOISE CANCELLATION BUTTON.
IT STOPPED THE NOISE, BUT YOU NEED TO DO SOMETHING ABOUT THE VISUAL.

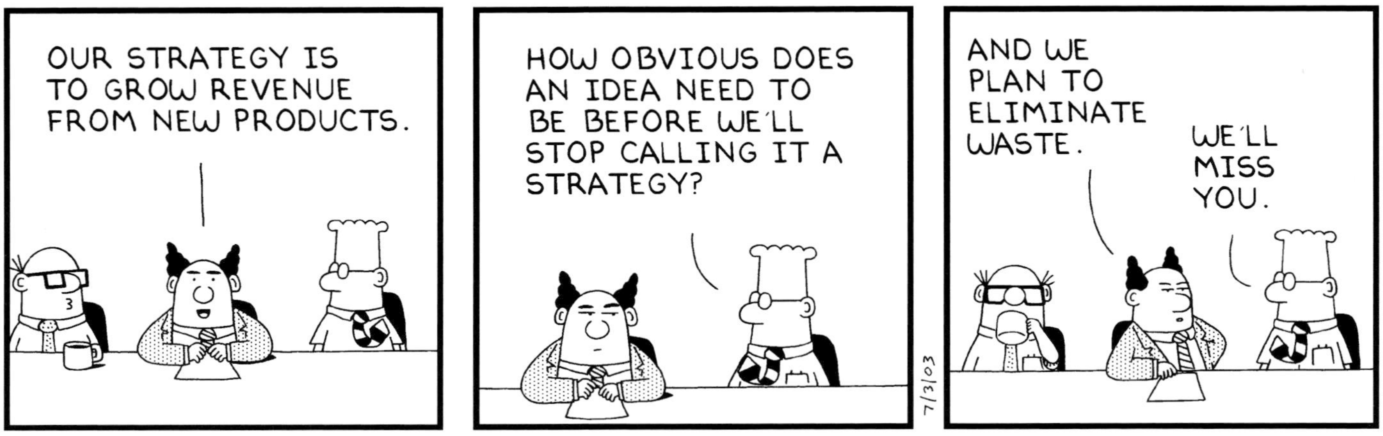
OUR STRATEGY IS TO GROW REVENUE FROM NEW PRODUCTS.
HOW OBVIOUS DOES AN IDEA NEED TO BE BEFORE WE'LL STOP CALLING IT A STRATEGY?
AND WE PLAN TO ELIMINATE WASTE.
WE'LL MISS YOU.
7/3/03

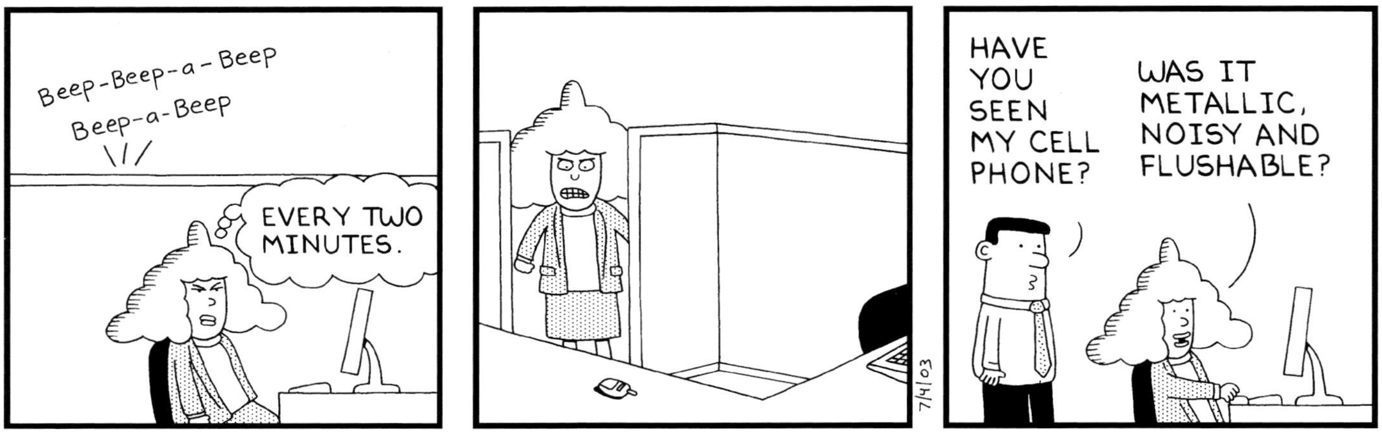
Beep-Beep-a-Beep
Beep-a-Beep
EVERY TWO MINUTES.
7/4/03
HAVE YOU SEEN MY CELL PHONE?
WAS IT METALLIC, NOISY AND FLUSHABLE?

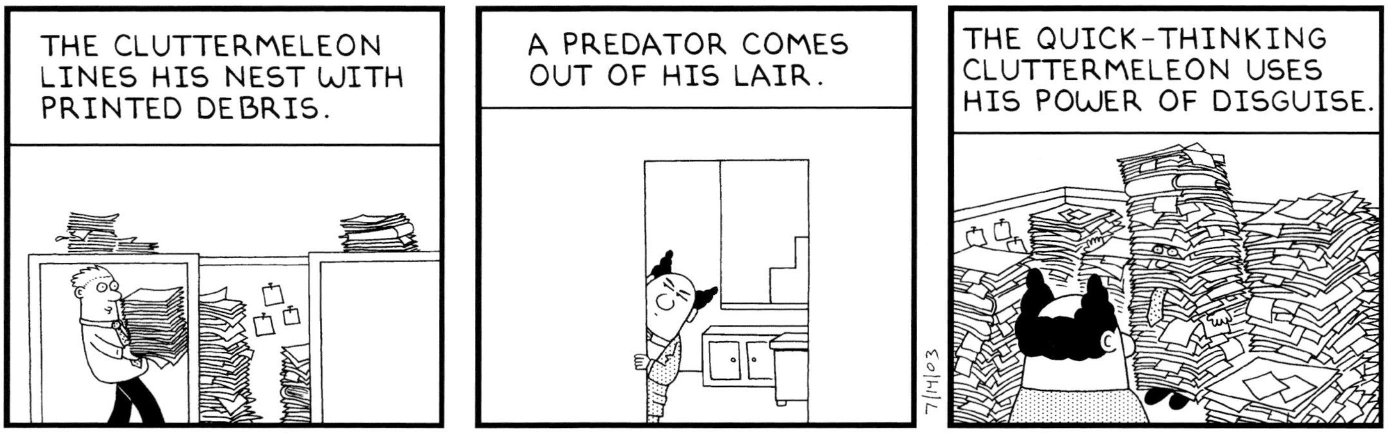
THE CLUTTERMELEON LINES HIS NEST WITH PRINTED DEBRIS.
A PREDATOR COMES OUT OF HIS LAIR.
7/14/03
THE QUICK-THINKING CLUTTERMELEON USES HIS POWER OF DISGUISE.

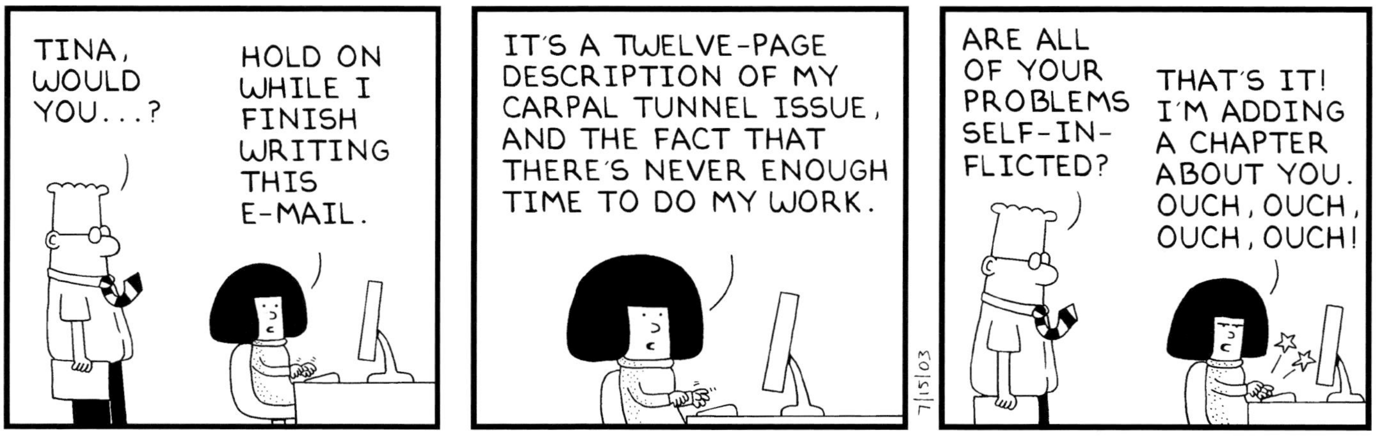
TINA, WOULD YOU...?
HOLD ON WHILE I FINISH WRITING THIS E-MAIL.
IT'S A TWELVE-PAGE DESCRIPTION OF MY CARPAL TUNNEL ISSUE, AND THE FACT THAT THERE'S NEVER ENOUGH TIME TO DO MY WORK.
7/15/03
ARE ALL OF YOUR PROBLEMS SELF-INFLICTED?
THAT'S IT! I'M ADDING A CHAPTER ABOUT YOU. OUCH, OUCH, OUCH, OUCH!

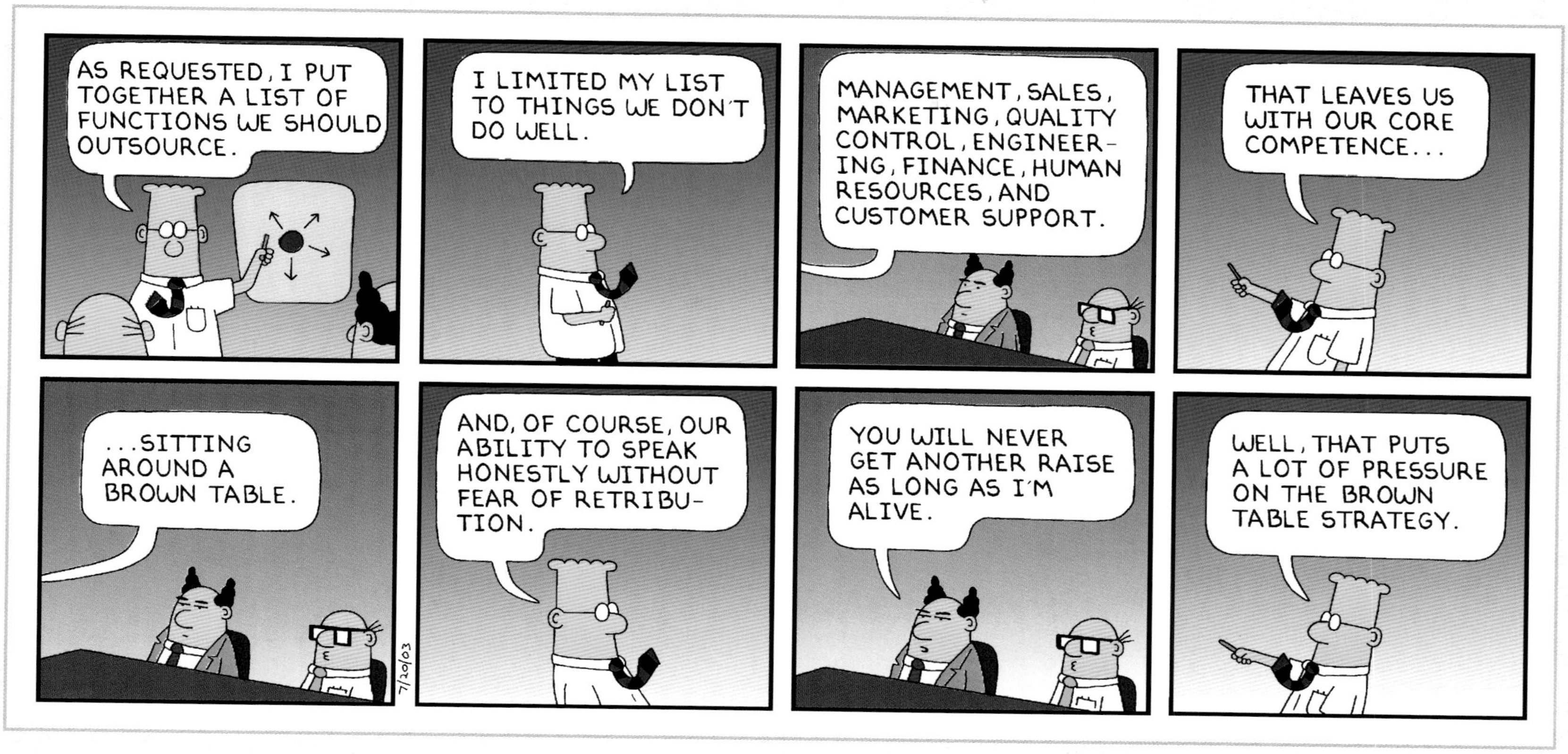
AS REQUESTED, I PUT TOGETHER A LIST OF FUNCTIONS WE SHOULD OUTSOURCE.
I LIMITED MY LIST TO THINGS WE DON'T DO WELL.
MANAGEMENT, SALES, MARKETING, QUALITY CONTROL, ENGINEER-ING, FINANCE, HUMAN RESOURCES, AND CUSTOMER SUPPORT.
THAT LEAVES US WITH OUR CORE COMPETENCE...
...SITTING AROUND A BROWN TABLE.
7/20/03
AND, OF COURSE, OUR ABILITY TO SPEAK HONESTLY WITHOUT FEAR OF RETRIBU-TION.
YOU WILL NEVER GET ANOTHER RAISE AS LONG AS I'M ALIVE.
WELL, THAT PUTS A LOT OF PRESSURE ON THE BROWN TABLE STRATEGY.

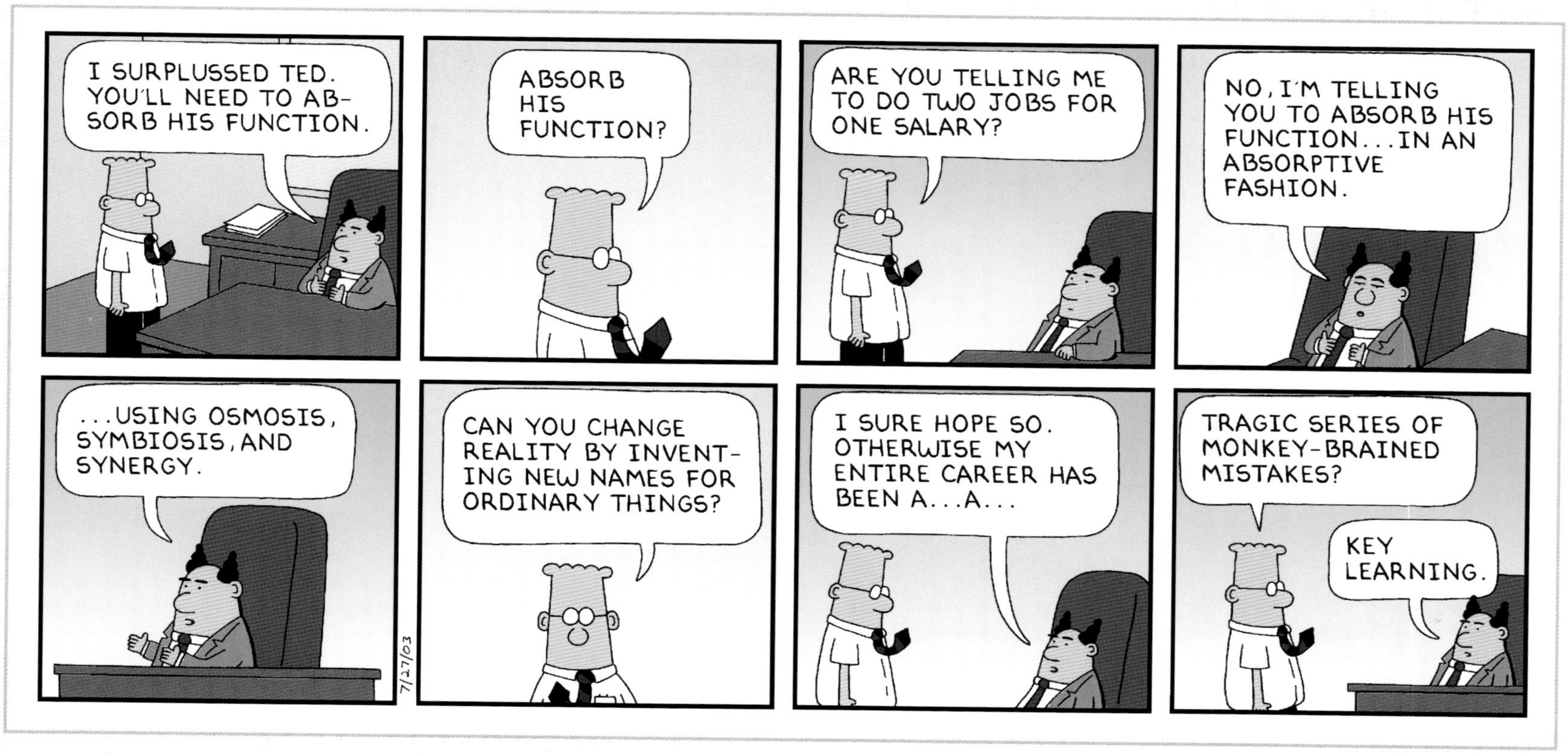
I SURPLUSSED TED. YOU'LL NEED TO AB-SORB HIS FUNCTION.
ABSORB HIS FUNCTION?
ARE YOU TELLING ME TO DO TWO JOBS FOR ONE SALARY?
NO, I'M TELLING YOU TO ABSORB HIS FUNCTION...IN AN ABSORPTIVE FASHION.
...USING OSMOSIS, SYMBIOSIS, AND SYNERGY.
7/27/03
CAN YOU CHANGE REALITY BY INVENT-ING NEW NAMES FOR ORDINARY THINGS?
I SURE HOPE SO. OTHERWISE MY ENTIRE CAREER HAS BEEN A...A...
TRAGIC SERIES OF MONKEY-BRAINED MISTAKES?
KEY LEARNING.

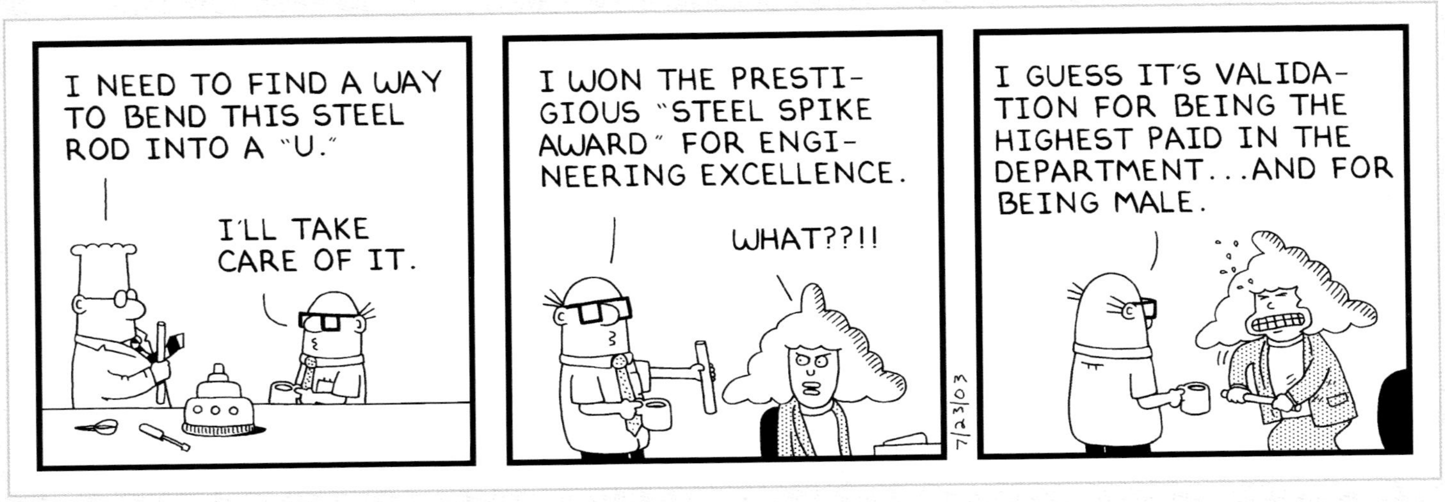
I NEED TO FIND A WAY TO BEND THIS STEEL ROD INTO A "U."
I'LL TAKE CARE OF IT.
I WON THE PRESTIGIOUS "STEEL SPIKE AWARD" FOR ENGINEERING EXCELLENCE.
WHAT??!!
7/23/03
I GUESS IT'S VALIDATION FOR BEING THE HIGHEST PAID IN THE DEPARTMENT...AND FOR BEING MALE.

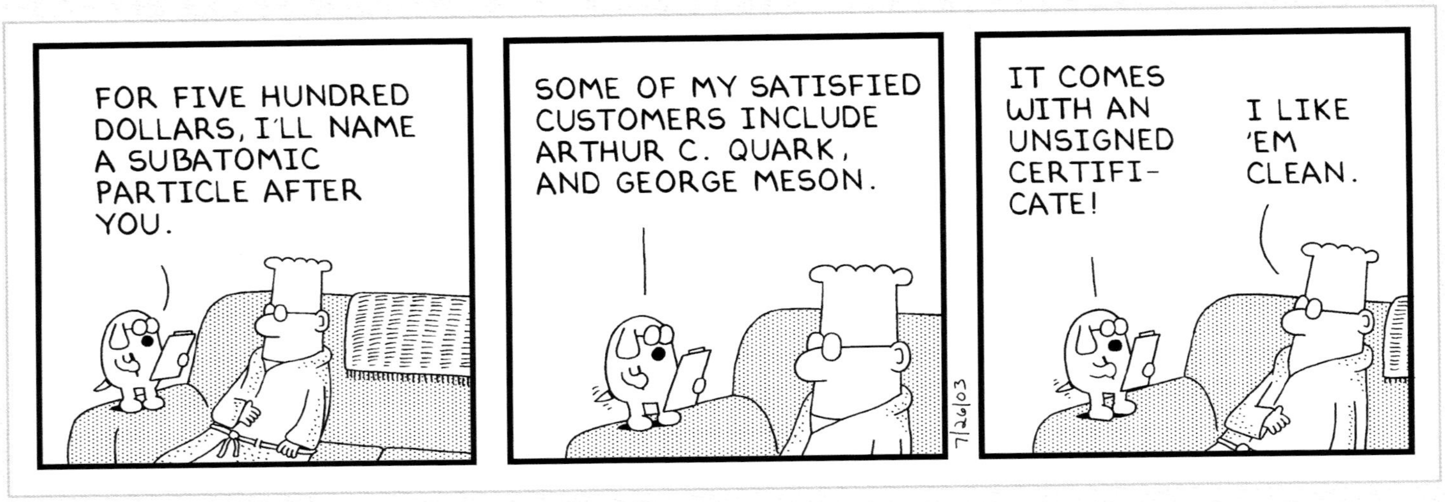
FOR FIVE HUNDRED DOLLARS, I'LL NAME A SUBATOMIC PARTICLE AFTER YOU.
SOME OF MY SATISFIED CUSTOMERS INCLUDE ARTHUR C. QUARK, AND GEORGE MESON.
7/26/03
IT COMES WITH AN UNSIGNED CERTIFICATE!
I LIKE 'EM CLEAN.

Usually I know why something is funny. Dilbert's line "I like 'em clean" always makes me laugh and I have no idea why.

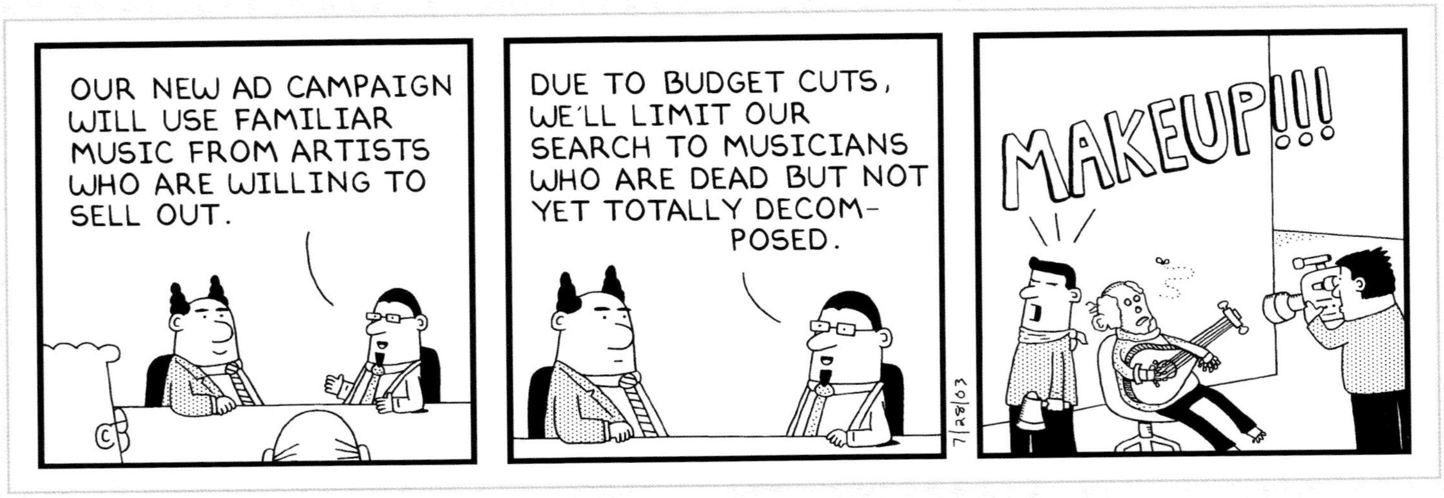
OUR NEW AD CAMPAIGN WILL USE FAMILIAR MUSIC FROM ARTISTS WHO ARE WILLING TO SELL OUT.
DUE TO BUDGET CUTS, WE'LL LIMIT OUR SEARCH TO MUSICIANS WHO ARE DEAD BUT NOT YET TOTALLY DECOMPOSED.
7/28/03
MAKEUP!!!

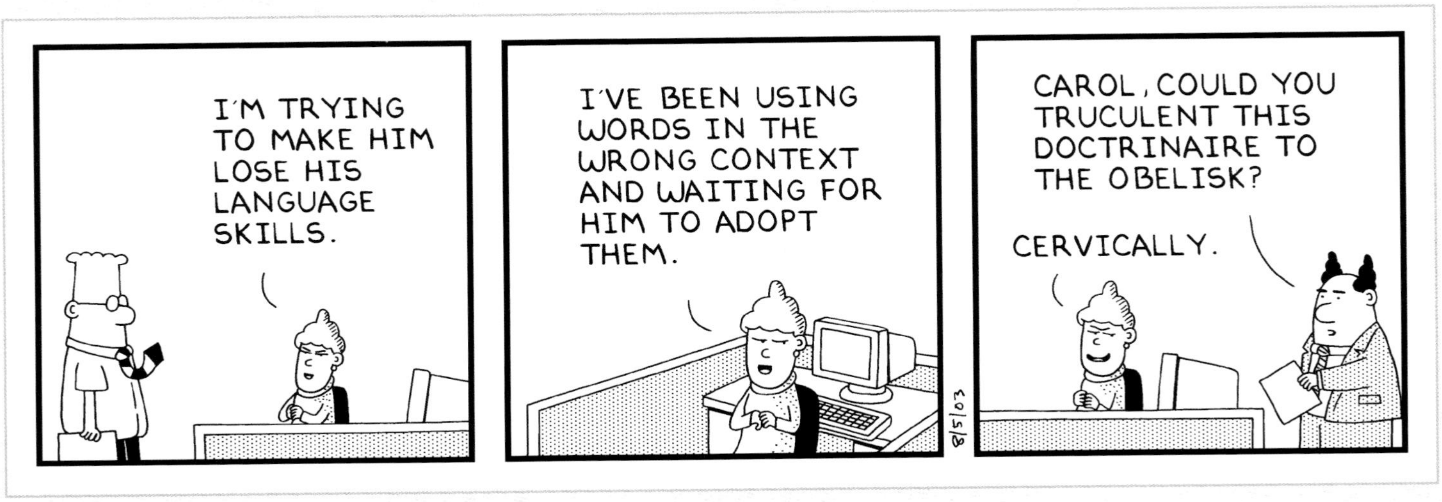
I'M TRYING TO MAKE HIM LOSE HIS LANGUAGE SKILLS.
I'VE BEEN USING WORDS IN THE WRONG CONTEXT AND WAITING FOR HIM TO ADOPT THEM.
8/5/03
CAROL, COULD YOU TRUCULENT THIS DOCTRINAIRE TO THE OBELISK?
CERVICALLY.

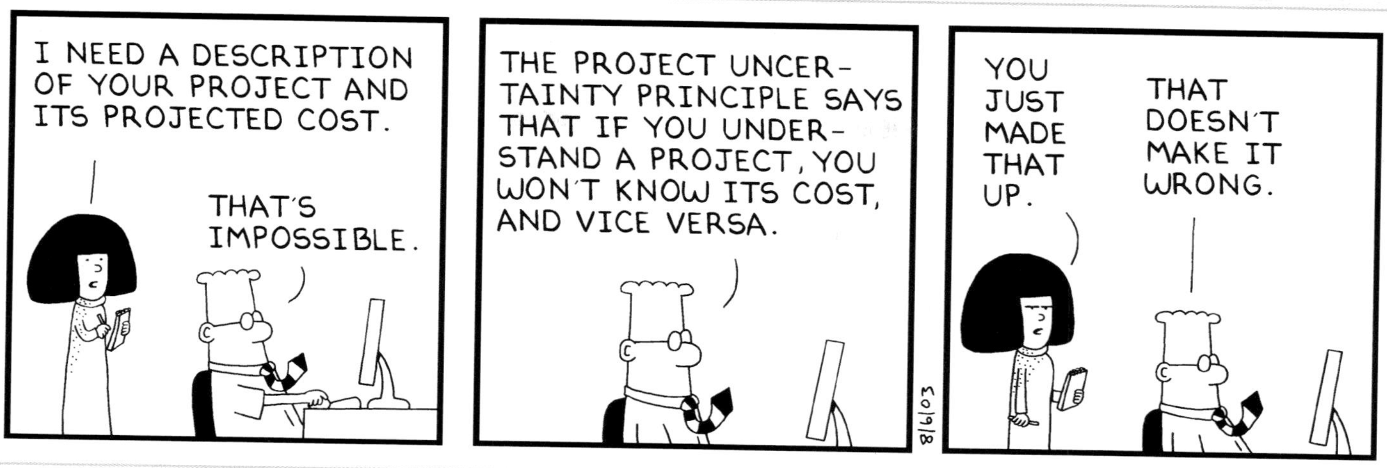
I NEED A DESCRIPTION OF YOUR PROJECT AND ITS PROJECTED COST.
THAT'S IMPOSSIBLE.
THE PROJECT UNCERTAINTY PRINCIPLE SAYS THAT IF YOU UNDERSTAND A PROJECT, YOU WON'T KNOW ITS COST, AND VICE VERSA.
8/6/03
YOU JUST MADE THAT UP.
THAT DOESN'T MAKE IT WRONG.

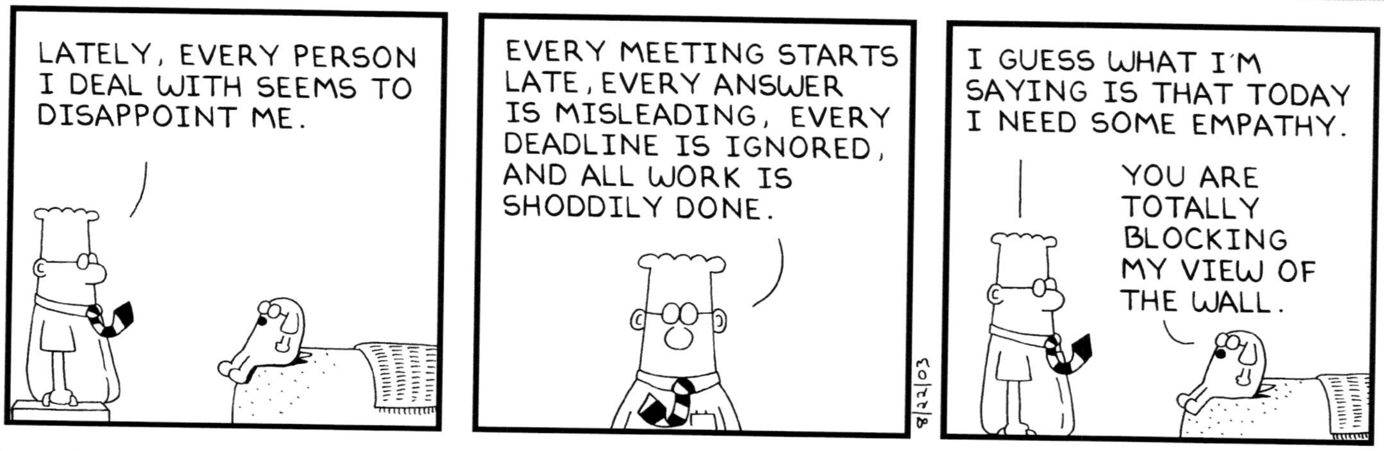
LATELY, EVERY PERSON I DEAL WITH SEEMS TO DISAPPOINT ME.
EVERY MEETING STARTS LATE, EVERY ANSWER IS MISLEADING, EVERY DEADLINE IS IGNORED, AND ALL WORK IS SHODDILY DONE.
8/22/03
I GUESS WHAT I'M SAYING IS THAT TODAY I NEED SOME EMPATHY.
YOU ARE TOTALLY BLOCKING MY VIEW OF THE WALL.

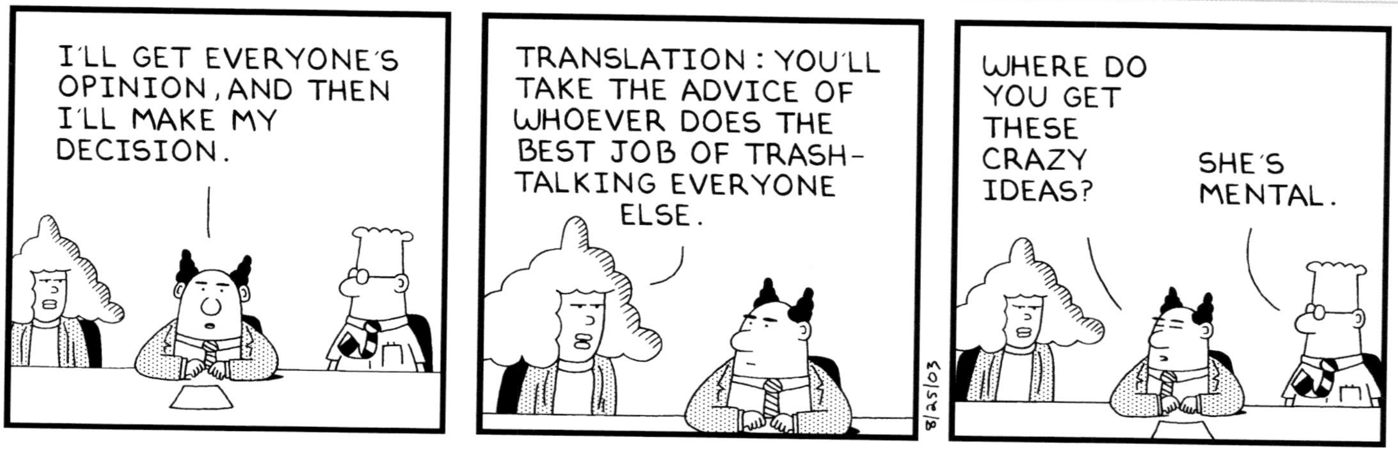
I'LL GET EVERYONE'S OPINION, AND THEN I'LL MAKE MY DECISION.
TRANSLATION: YOU'LL TAKE THE ADVICE OF WHOEVER DOES THE BEST JOB OF TRASH-TALKING EVERYONE ELSE.
8/25/03
WHERE DO YOU GET THESE CRAZY IDEAS?
SHE'S MENTAL.

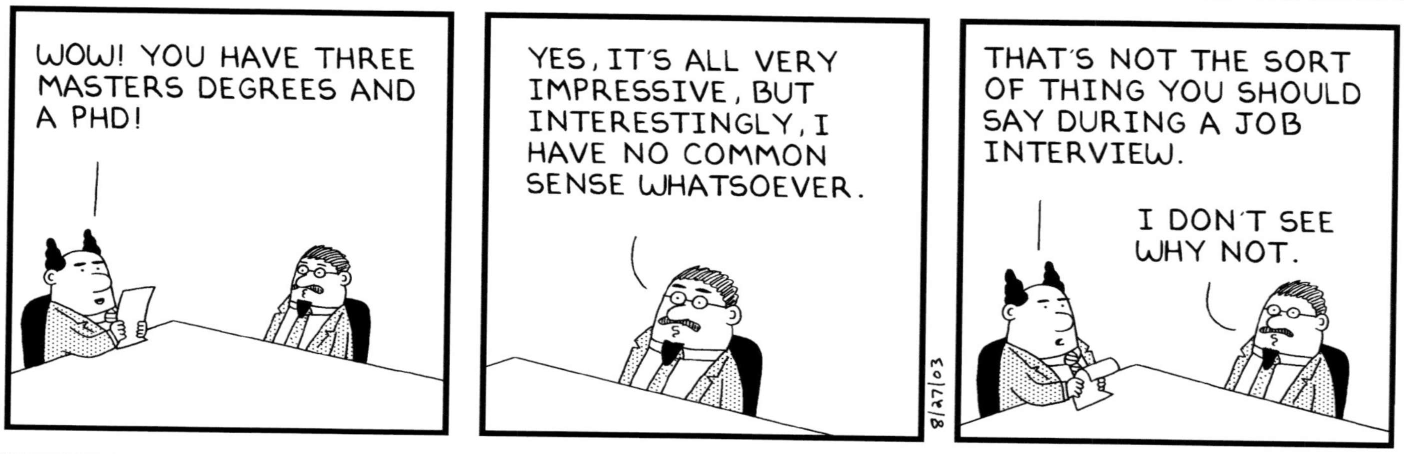
WOW! YOU HAVE THREE MASTERS DEGREES AND A PHD!
YES, IT'S ALL VERY IMPRESSIVE, BUT INTERESTINGLY, I HAVE NO COMMON SENSE WHATSOEVER.
8/27/03
THAT'S NOT THE SORT OF THING YOU SHOULD SAY DURING A JOB INTERVIEW.
I DON'T SEE WHY NOT.

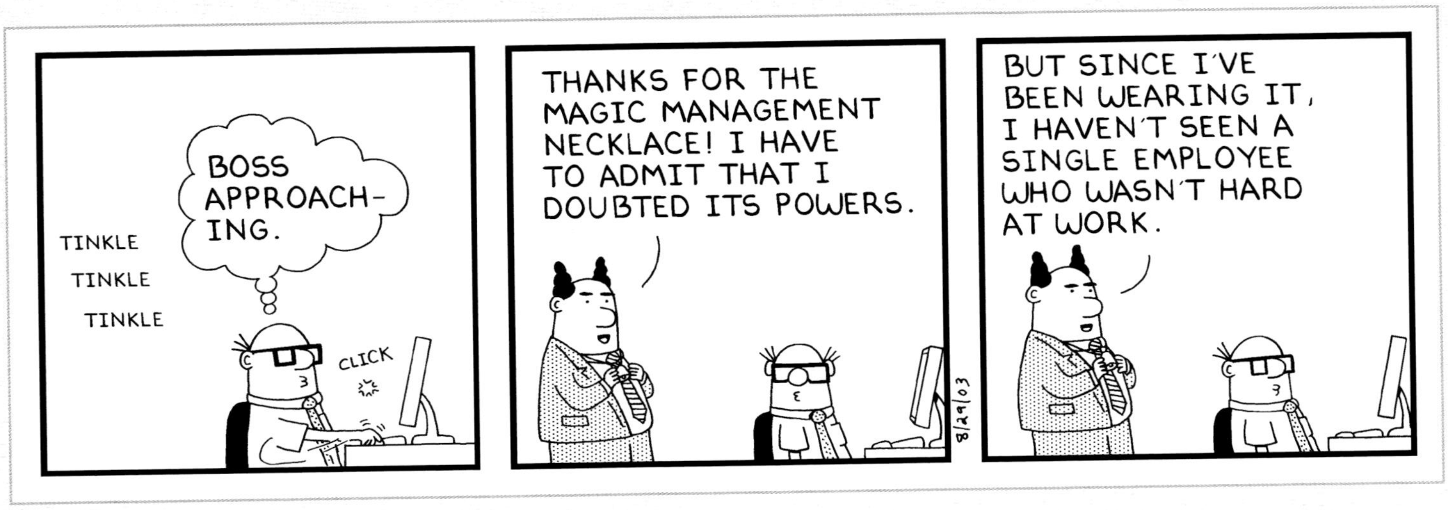

TINKLE
TINKLE
TINKLE
BOSS APPROACHING.
CLICK
THANKS FOR THE MAGIC MANAGEMENT NECKLACE! I HAVE TO ADMIT THAT I DOUBTED ITS POWERS.
8/29/03
BUT SINCE I'VE BEEN WEARING IT, I HAVEN'T SEEN A SINGLE EMPLOYEE WHO WASN'T HARD AT WORK.

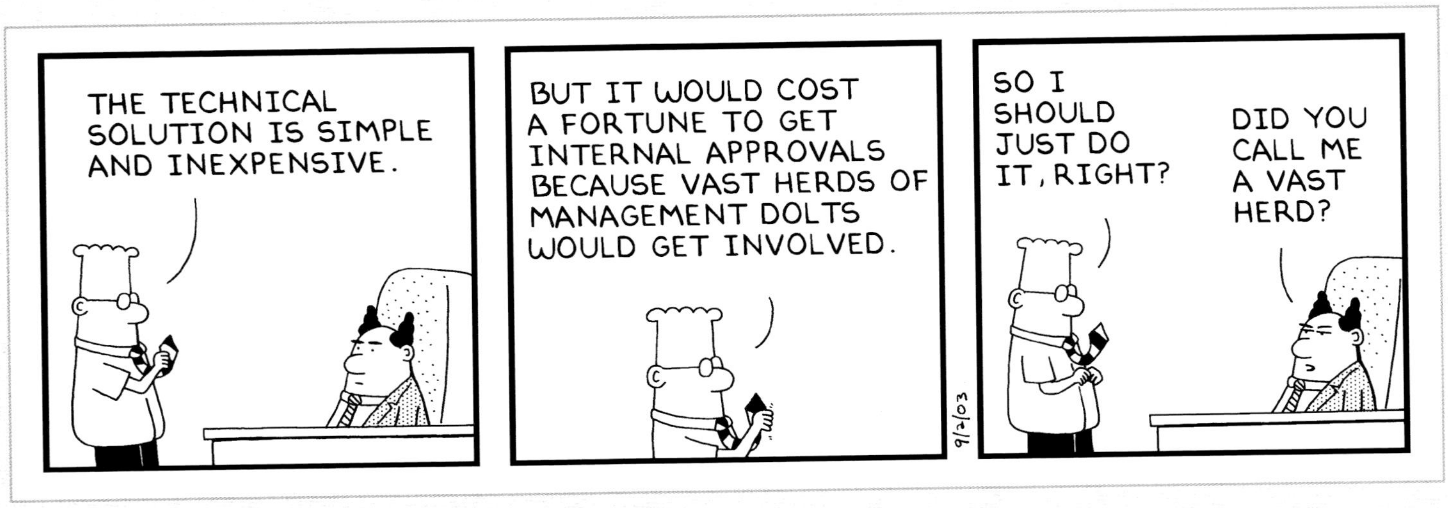

THE TECHNICAL SOLUTION IS SIMPLE AND INEXPENSIVE.
BUT IT WOULD COST A FORTUNE TO GET INTERNAL APPROVALS BECAUSE VAST HERDS OF MANAGEMENT DOLTS WOULD GET INVOLVED.
9/2/03
SO I SHOULD JUST DO IT, RIGHT?
DID YOU CALL ME A VAST HERD?

If you say "vast herd" fast, it's funnier.

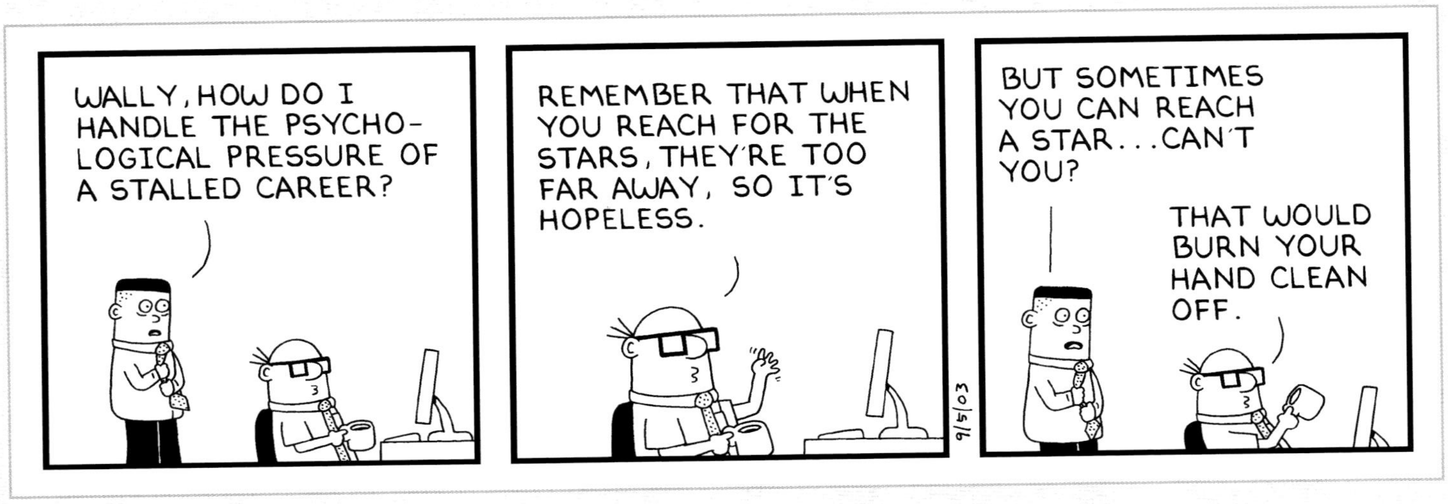

WALLY, HOW DO I HANDLE THE PSYCHOLOGICAL PRESSURE OF A STALLED CAREER?
REMEMBER THAT WHEN YOU REACH FOR THE STARS, THEY'RE TOO FAR AWAY, SO IT'S HOPELESS.
9/5/03
BUT SOMETIMES YOU CAN REACH A STAR... CAN'T YOU?
THAT WOULD BURN YOUR HAND CLEAN OFF.

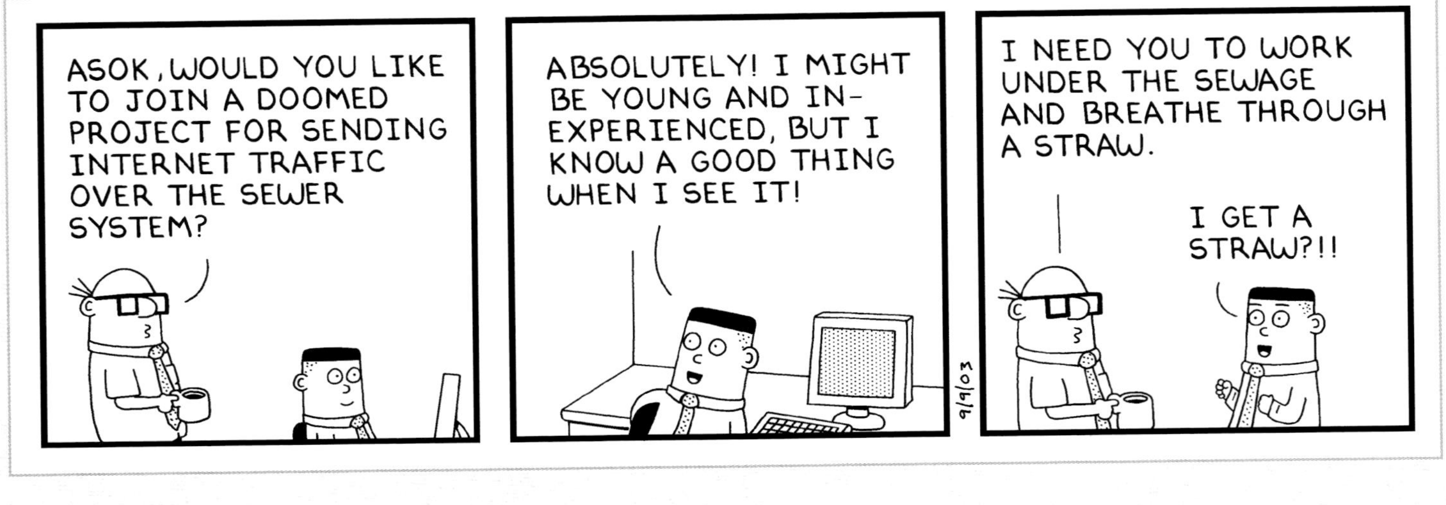

ASOK, WOULD YOU LIKE TO JOIN A DOOMED PROJECT FOR SENDING INTERNET TRAFFIC OVER THE SEWER SYSTEM?
ABSOLUTELY! I MIGHT BE YOUNG AND INEXPERIENCED, BUT I KNOW A GOOD THING WHEN I SEE IT!
9/9/03
I NEED YOU TO WORK UNDER THE SEWAGE AND BREATHE THROUGH A STRAW.
I GET A STRAW?!!

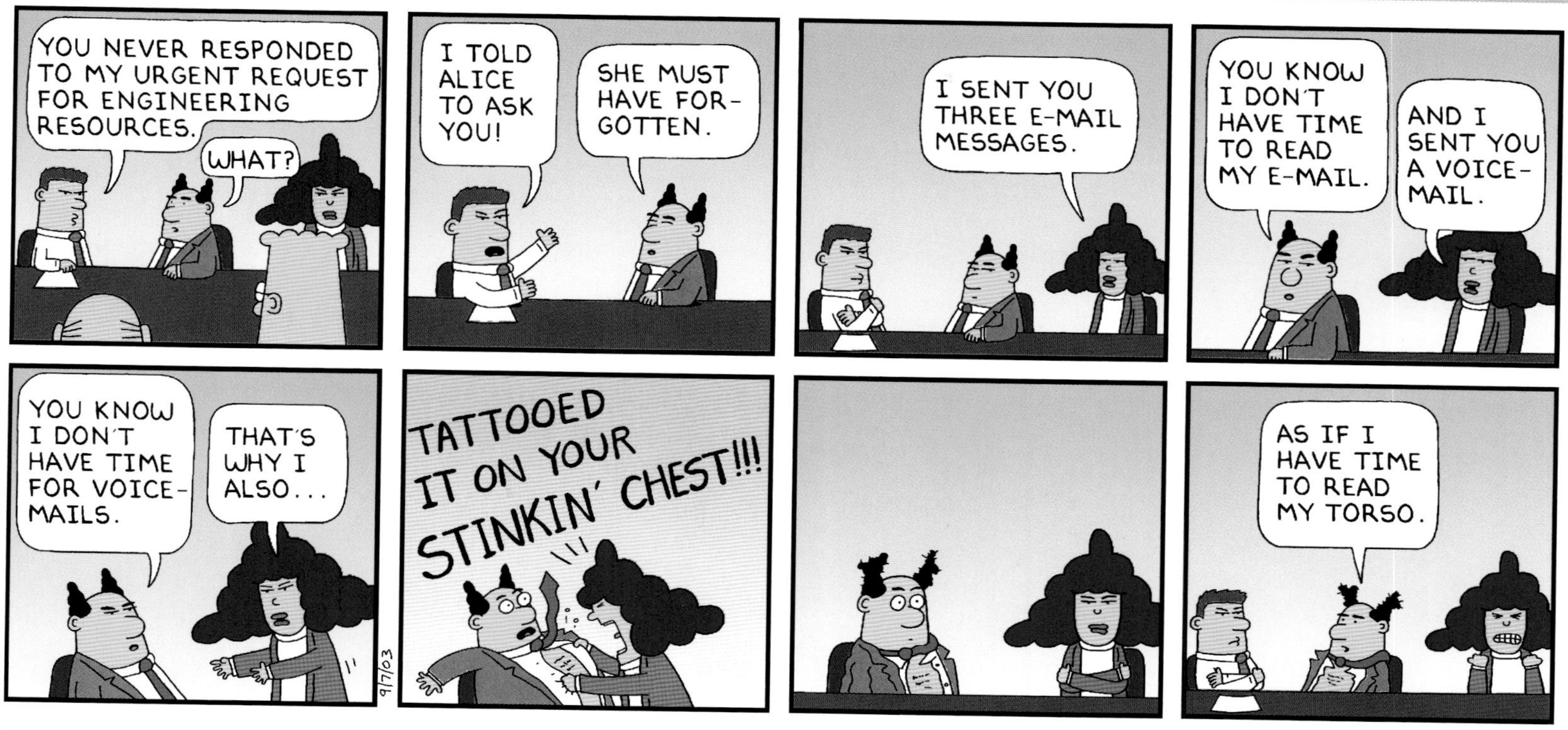
YOU NEVER RESPONDED TO MY URGENT REQUEST FOR ENGINEERING RESOURCES.
WHAT?
I TOLD ALICE TO ASK YOU!
SHE MUST HAVE FOR-GOTTEN.
I SENT YOU THREE E-MAIL MESSAGES.
YOU KNOW I DON'T HAVE TIME TO READ MY E-MAIL.
AND I SENT YOU A VOICE-MAIL.
YOU KNOW I DON'T HAVE TIME FOR VOICE-MAILS.
THAT'S WHY I ALSO...
9/7/03
TATTOOED IT ON YOUR STINKIN' CHEST!!!
AS IF I HAVE TIME TO READ MY TORSO.

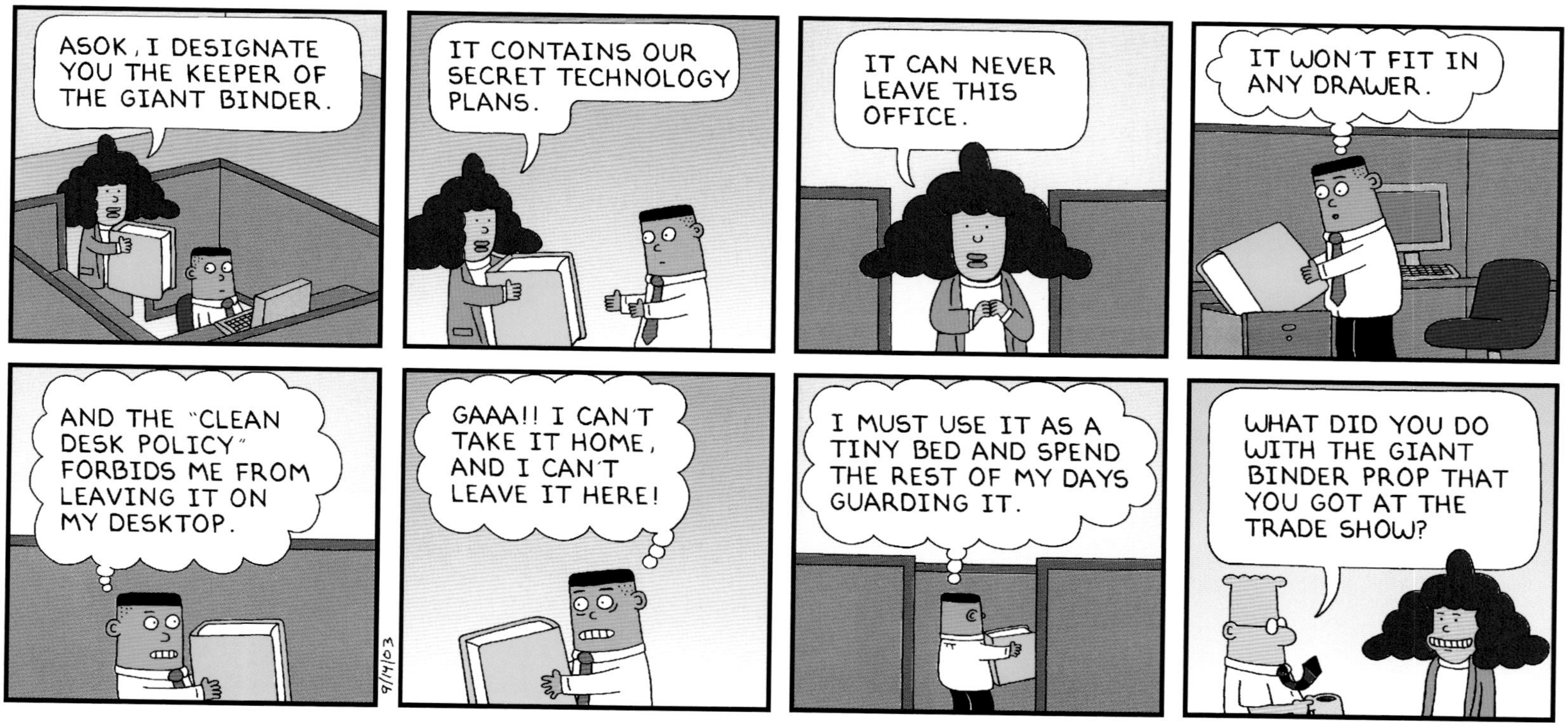
ASOK, I DESIGNATE YOU THE KEEPER OF THE GIANT BINDER.
IT CONTAINS OUR SECRET TECHNOLOGY PLANS.
IT CAN NEVER LEAVE THIS OFFICE.
IT WON'T FIT IN ANY DRAWER.
AND THE "CLEAN DESK POLICY" FORBIDS ME FROM LEAVING IT ON MY DESKTOP.
9/14/03
GAAA!! I CAN'T TAKE IT HOME, AND I CAN'T LEAVE IT HERE!
I MUST USE IT AS A TINY BED AND SPEND THE REST OF MY DAYS GUARDING IT.
WHAT DID YOU DO WITH THE GIANT BINDER PROP THAT YOU GOT AT THE TRADE SHOW?

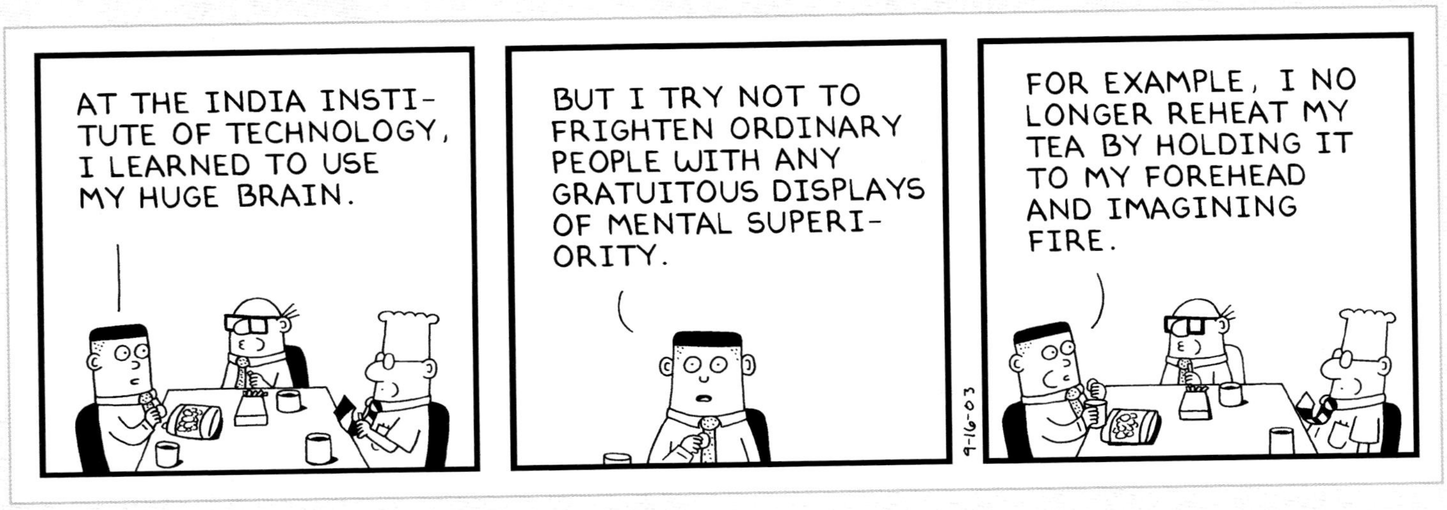
AT THE INDIA INSTITUTE OF TECHNOLOGY, I LEARNED TO USE MY HUGE BRAIN.
BUT I TRY NOT TO FRIGHTEN ORDINARY PEOPLE WITH ANY GRATUITOUS DISPLAYS OF MENTAL SUPERIORITY.
FOR EXAMPLE, I NO LONGER REHEAT MY TEA BY HOLDING IT TO MY FOREHEAD AND IMAGINING FIRE.
9-16-03

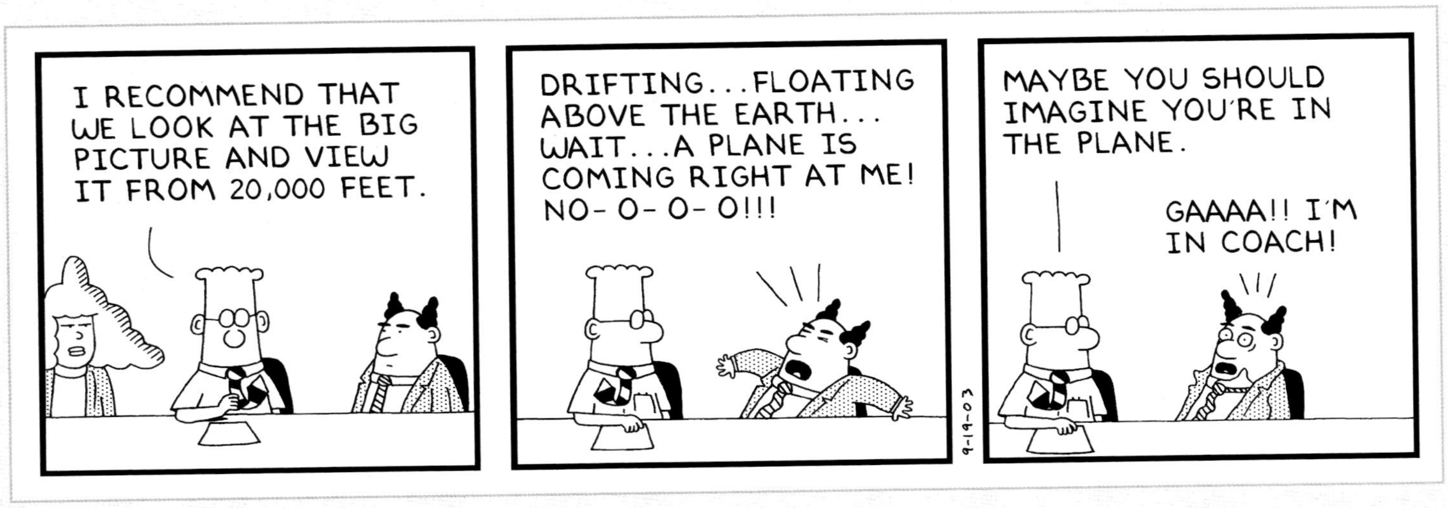
I RECOMMEND THAT WE LOOK AT THE BIG PICTURE AND VIEW IT FROM 20,000 FEET.
DRIFTING...FLOATING ABOVE THE EARTH... WAIT...A PLANE IS COMING RIGHT AT ME! NO-O-O-O!!!
MAYBE YOU SHOULD IMAGINE YOU'RE IN THE PLANE.
GAAAA!! I'M IN COACH!
9-19-03

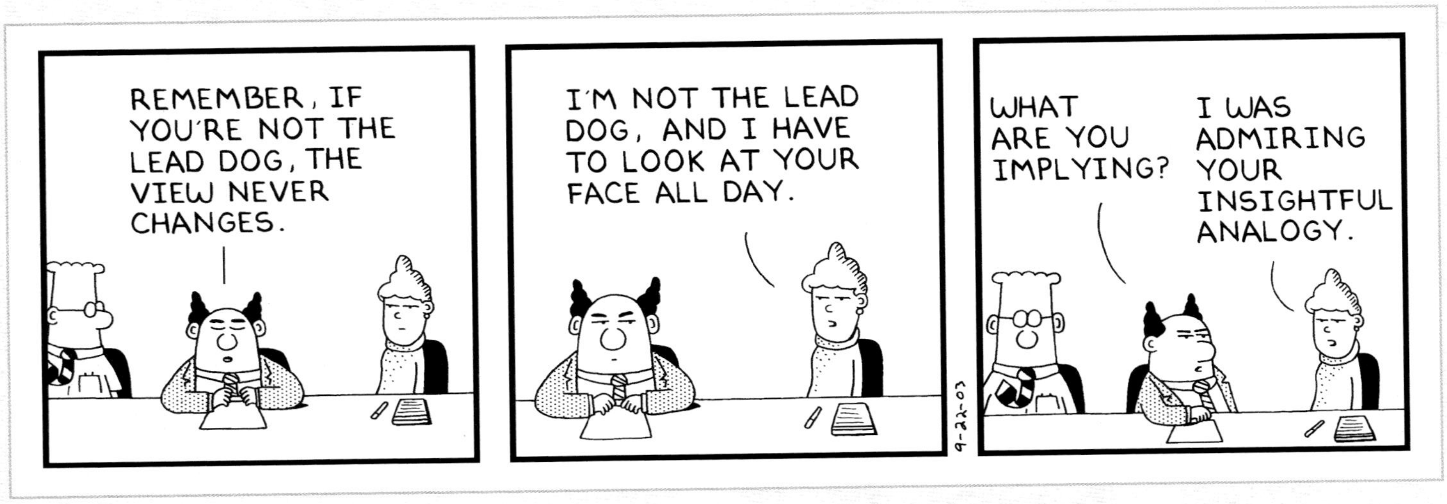
REMEMBER, IF YOU'RE NOT THE LEAD DOG, THE VIEW NEVER CHANGES.
I'M NOT THE LEAD DOG, AND I HAVE TO LOOK AT YOUR FACE ALL DAY.
WHAT ARE YOU IMPLYING?
I WAS ADMIRING YOUR INSIGHTFUL ANALOGY.
9-22-03

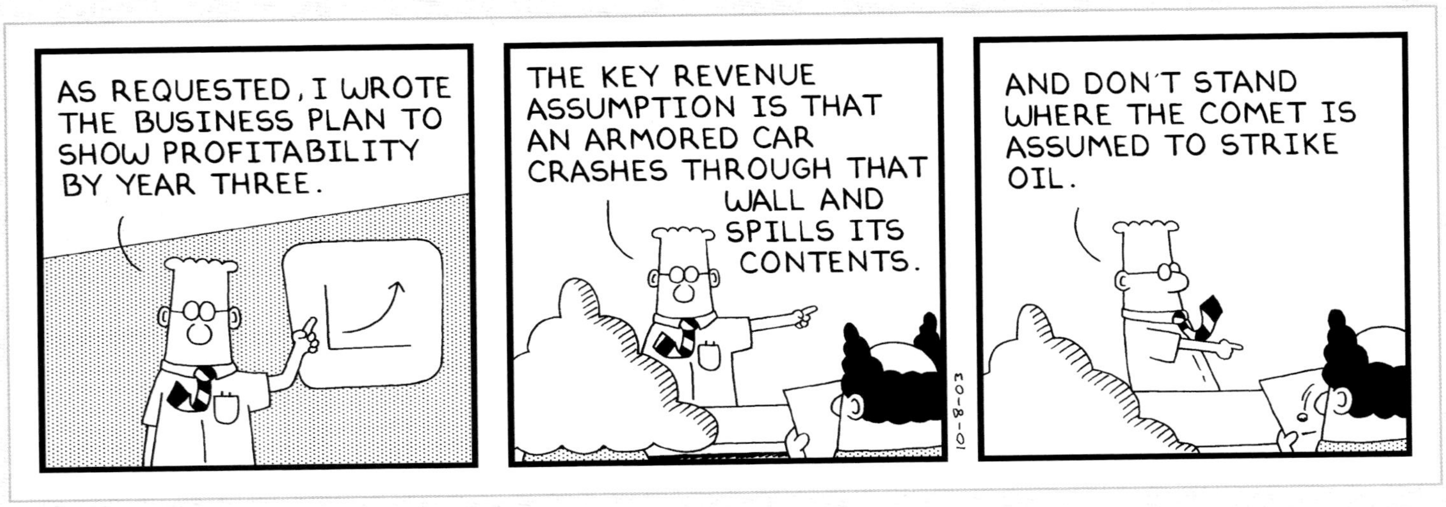
AS REQUESTED, I WROTE THE BUSINESS PLAN TO SHOW PROFITABILITY BY YEAR THREE.
THE KEY REVENUE ASSUMPTION IS THAT AN ARMORED CAR CRASHES THROUGH THAT WALL AND SPILLS ITS CONTENTS.
AND DON'T STAND WHERE THE COMET IS ASSUMED TO STRIKE OIL.
10-8-03

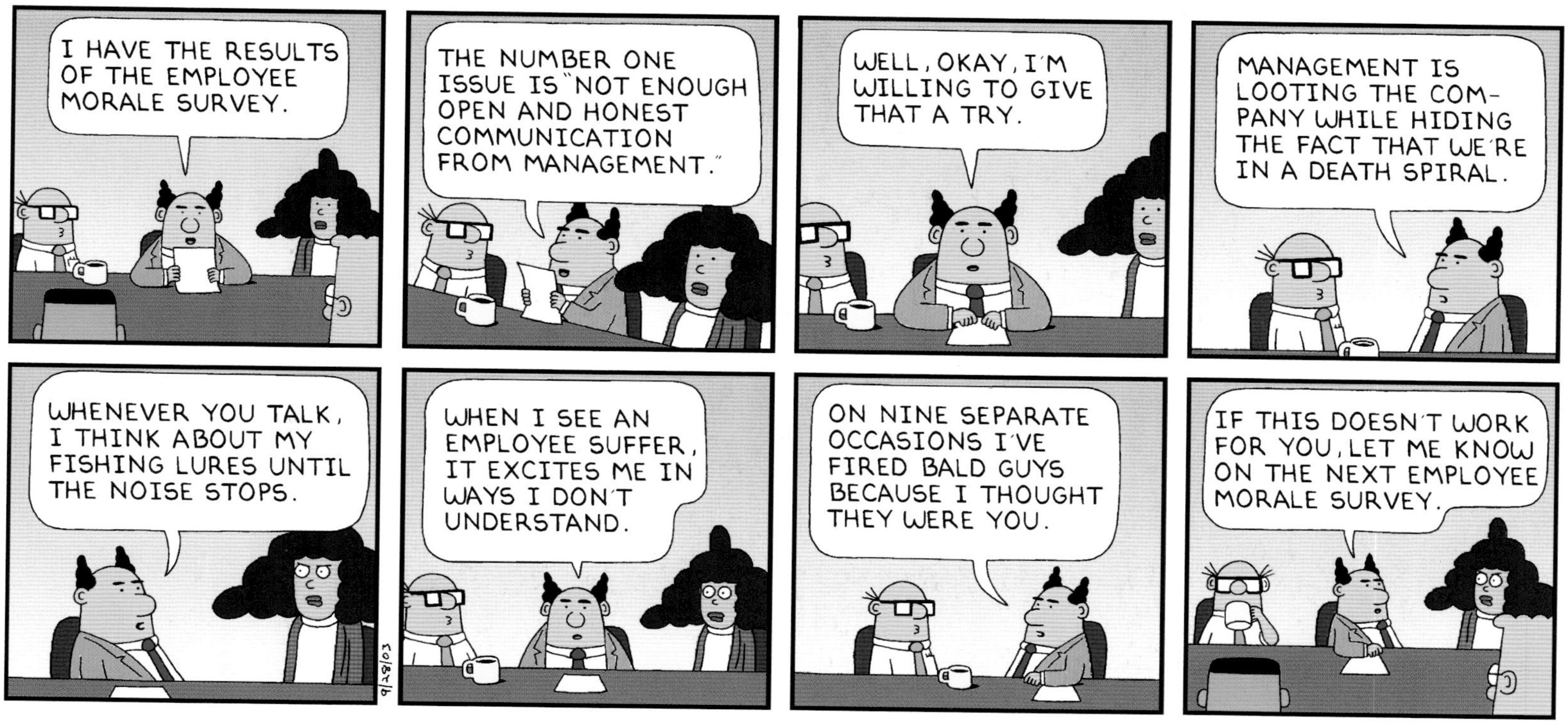

I HAVE THE RESULTS OF THE EMPLOYEE MORALE SURVEY.
THE NUMBER ONE ISSUE IS "NOT ENOUGH OPEN AND HONEST COMMUNICATION FROM MANAGEMENT."
WELL, OKAY, I'M WILLING TO GIVE THAT A TRY.
MANAGEMENT IS LOOTING THE COM-PANY WHILE HIDING THE FACT THAT WE'RE IN A DEATH SPIRAL.
WHENEVER YOU TALK, I THINK ABOUT MY FISHING LURES UNTIL THE NOISE STOPS.
9/28/03
WHEN I SEE AN EMPLOYEE SUFFER, IT EXCITES ME IN WAYS I DON'T UNDERSTAND.
ON NINE SEPARATE OCCASIONS I'VE FIRED BALD GUYS BECAUSE I THOUGHT THEY WERE YOU.
IF THIS DOESN'T WORK FOR YOU, LET ME KNOW ON THE NEXT EMPLOYEE MORALE SURVEY.

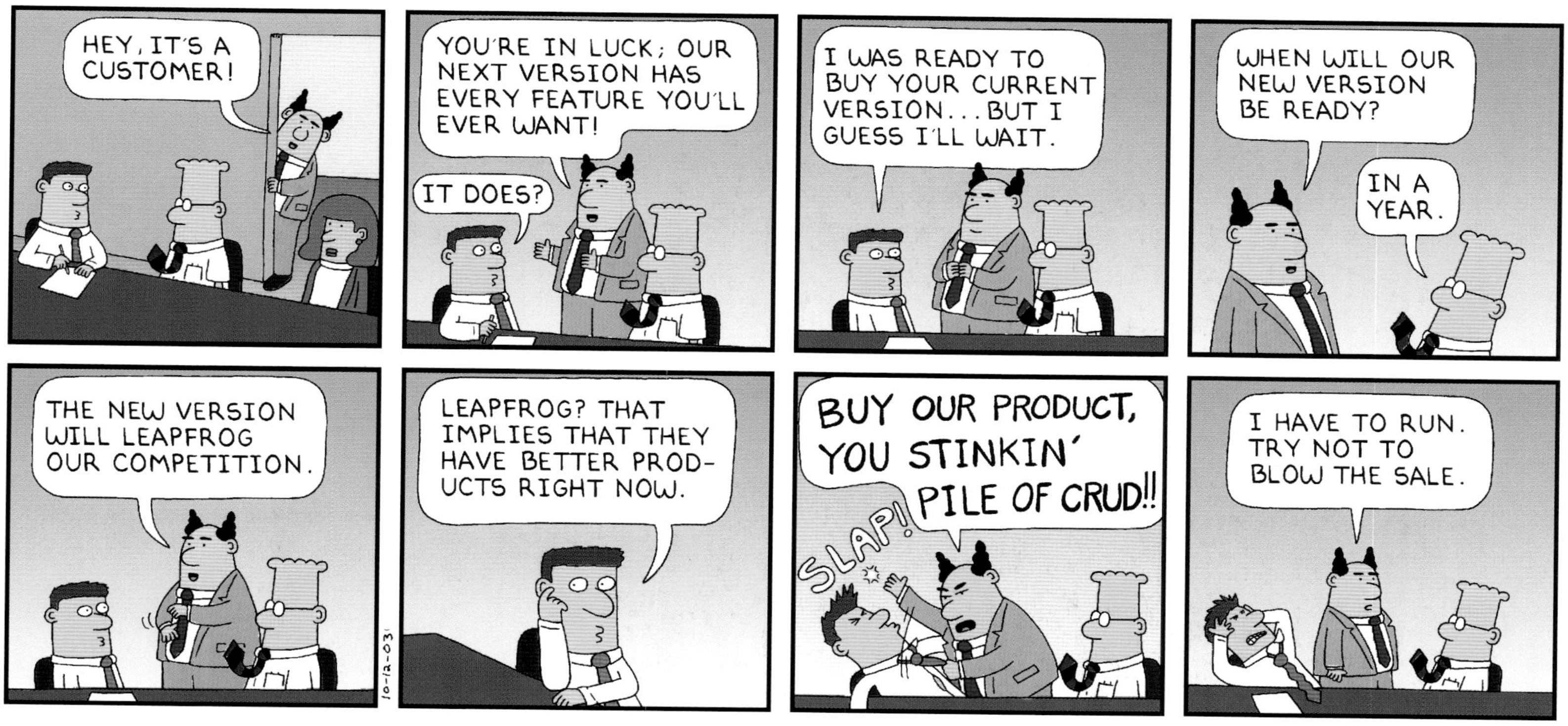

HEY, IT'S A CUSTOMER!
YOU'RE IN LUCK; OUR NEXT VERSION HAS EVERY FEATURE YOU'LL EVER WANT!
IT DOES?
I WAS READY TO BUY YOUR CURRENT VERSION... BUT I GUESS I'LL WAIT.
WHEN WILL OUR NEW VERSION BE READY?
IN A YEAR.
THE NEW VERSION WILL LEAPFROG OUR COMPETITION.
10-12-03
LEAPFROG? THAT IMPLIES THAT THEY HAVE BETTER PROD-UCTS RIGHT NOW.
BUY OUR PRODUCT, YOU STINKIN' PILE OF CRUD!!
SLAP!
I HAVE TO RUN. TRY NOT TO BLOW THE SALE.

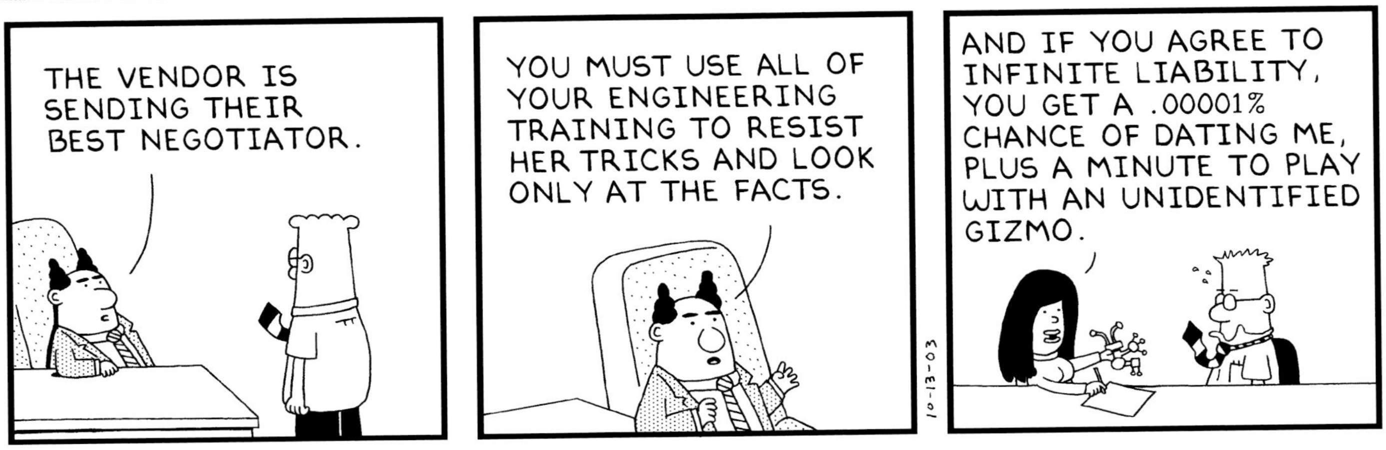
THE VENDOR IS SENDING THEIR BEST NEGOTIATOR.
YOU MUST USE ALL OF YOUR ENGINEERING TRAINING TO RESIST HER TRICKS AND LOOK ONLY AT THE FACTS.
10-13-03
AND IF YOU AGREE TO INFINITE LIABILITY, YOU GET A .00001% CHANCE OF DATING ME, PLUS A MINUTE TO PLAY WITH AN UNIDENTIFIED GIZMO.

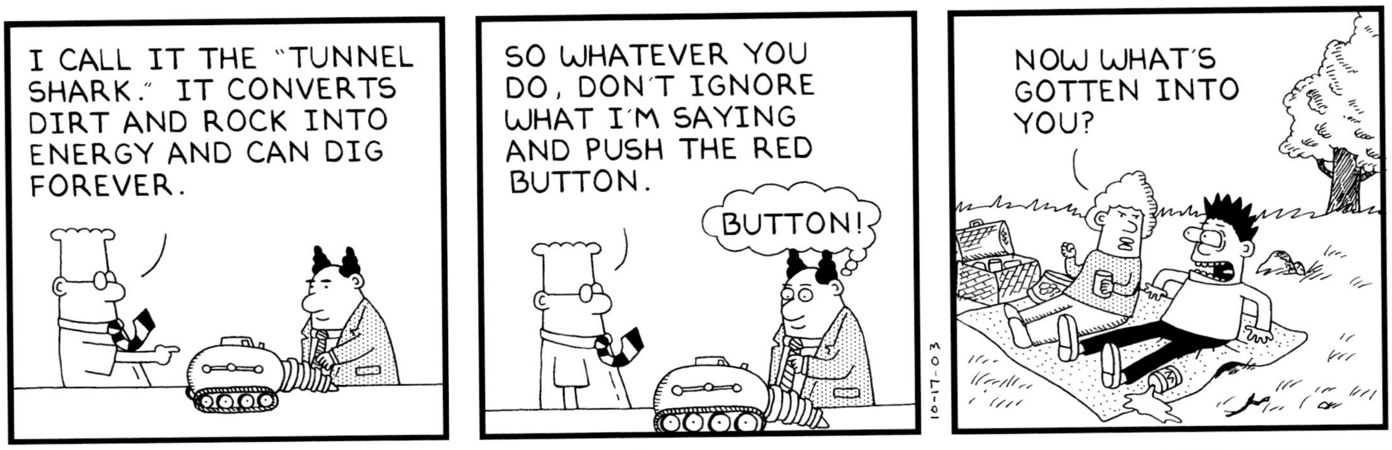
I CALL IT THE "TUNNEL SHARK." IT CONVERTS DIRT AND ROCK INTO ENERGY AND CAN DIG FOREVER.
SO WHATEVER YOU DO, DON'T IGNORE WHAT I'M SAYING AND PUSH THE RED BUTTON.
BUTTON!
10-17-03
NOW WHAT'S GOTTEN INTO YOU?

I asked other cartoonists to draw Dilbert *for a week. The one below is by Lynn Johnston, creator of* For Better or For Worse.

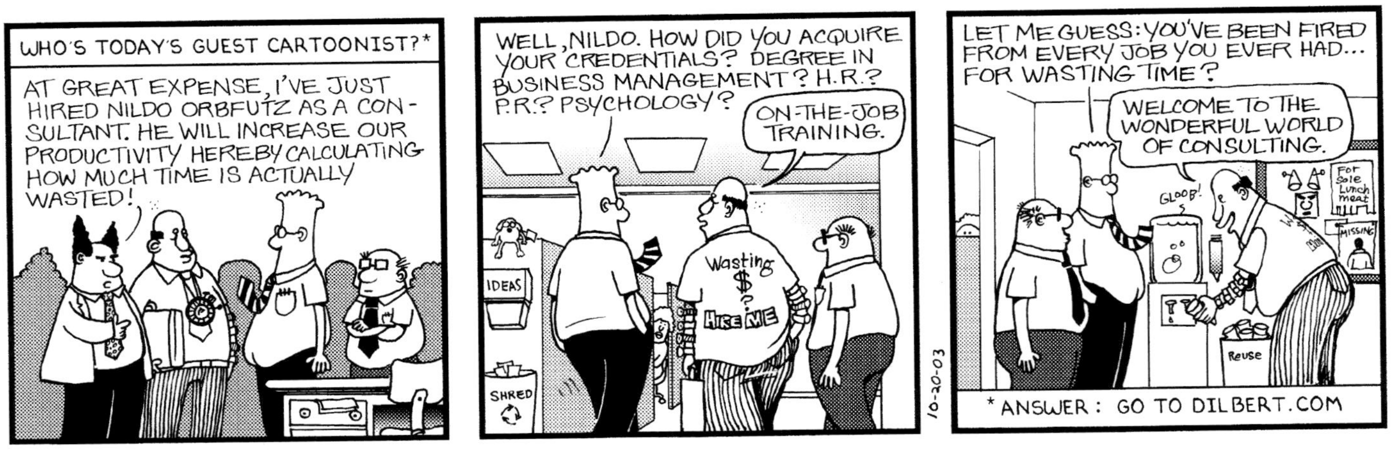
WHO'S TODAY'S GUEST CARTOONIST?*
AT GREAT EXPENSE, I'VE JUST HIRED NILDO ORBFUTZ AS A CONSULTANT. HE WILL INCREASE OUR PRODUCTIVITY HERE BY CALCULATING HOW MUCH TIME IS ACTUALLY WASTED!
WELL, NILDO. HOW DID YOU ACQUIRE YOUR CREDENTIALS? DEGREE IN BUSINESS MANAGEMENT? H.R.? P.R.? PSYCHOLOGY?
ON-THE-JOB TRAINING.
IDEAS
SHRED
Wasting $?
HIRE ME
10-20-03
LET ME GUESS: YOU'VE BEEN FIRED FROM EVERY JOB YOU EVER HAD... FOR WASTING TIME?
WELCOME TO THE WONDERFUL WORLD OF CONSULTING.
GLOOB!
For Sale Lunch meat
MISSING
Reuse
*ANSWER: GO TO DILBERT.COM

This version of Dilbert *is by Pat Brady, creator of* Rose is Rose.

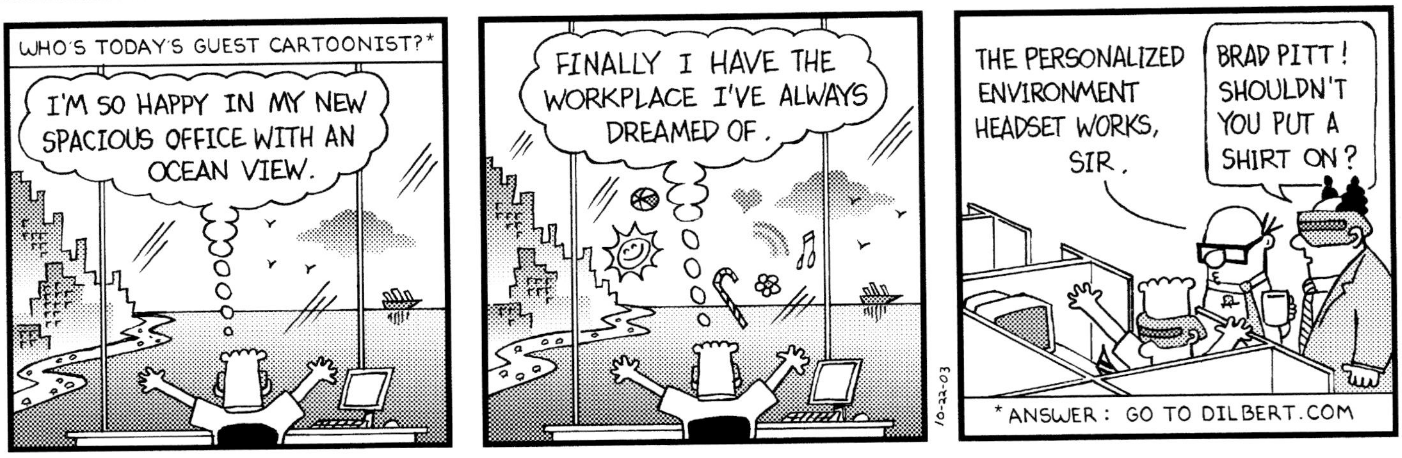
WHO'S TODAY'S GUEST CARTOONIST?*
I'M SO HAPPY IN MY NEW SPACIOUS OFFICE WITH AN OCEAN VIEW.
FINALLY I HAVE THE WORKPLACE I'VE ALWAYS DREAMED OF.
10-22-03
THE PERSONALIZED ENVIRONMENT HEADSET WORKS, SIR.
BRAD PITT! SHOULDN'T YOU PUT A SHIRT ON?
*ANSWER: GO TO DILBERT.COM

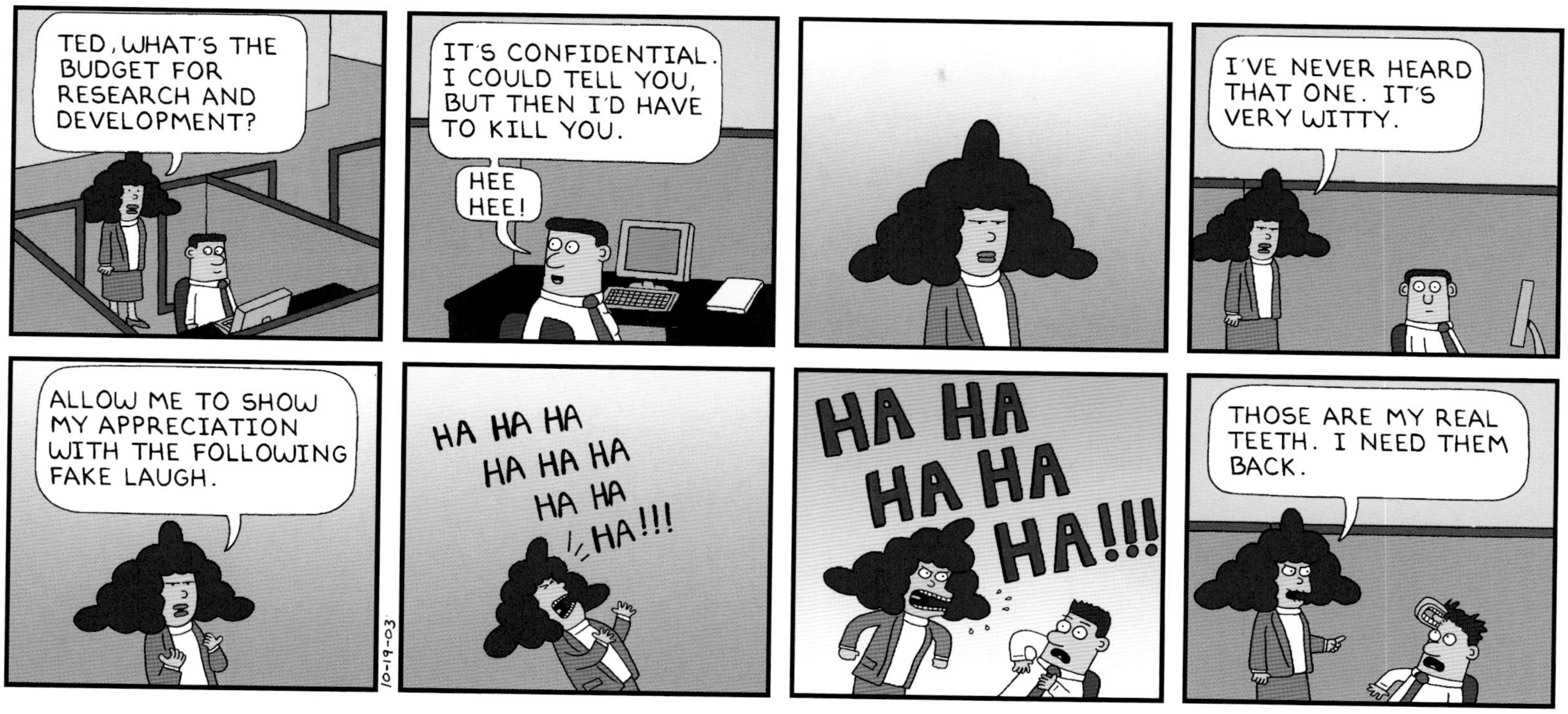
TED, WHAT'S THE BUDGET FOR RESEARCH AND DEVELOPMENT?
IT'S CONFIDENTIAL. I COULD TELL YOU, BUT THEN I'D HAVE TO KILL YOU.
HEE HEE!
I'VE NEVER HEARD THAT ONE. IT'S VERY WITTY.
ALLOW ME TO SHOW MY APPRECIATION WITH THE FOLLOWING FAKE LAUGH.
10-19-03
HA HA HA HA HA HA HA HA HA!!!
HA HA HA HA HA!!!
THOSE ARE MY REAL TEETH. I NEED THEM BACK.

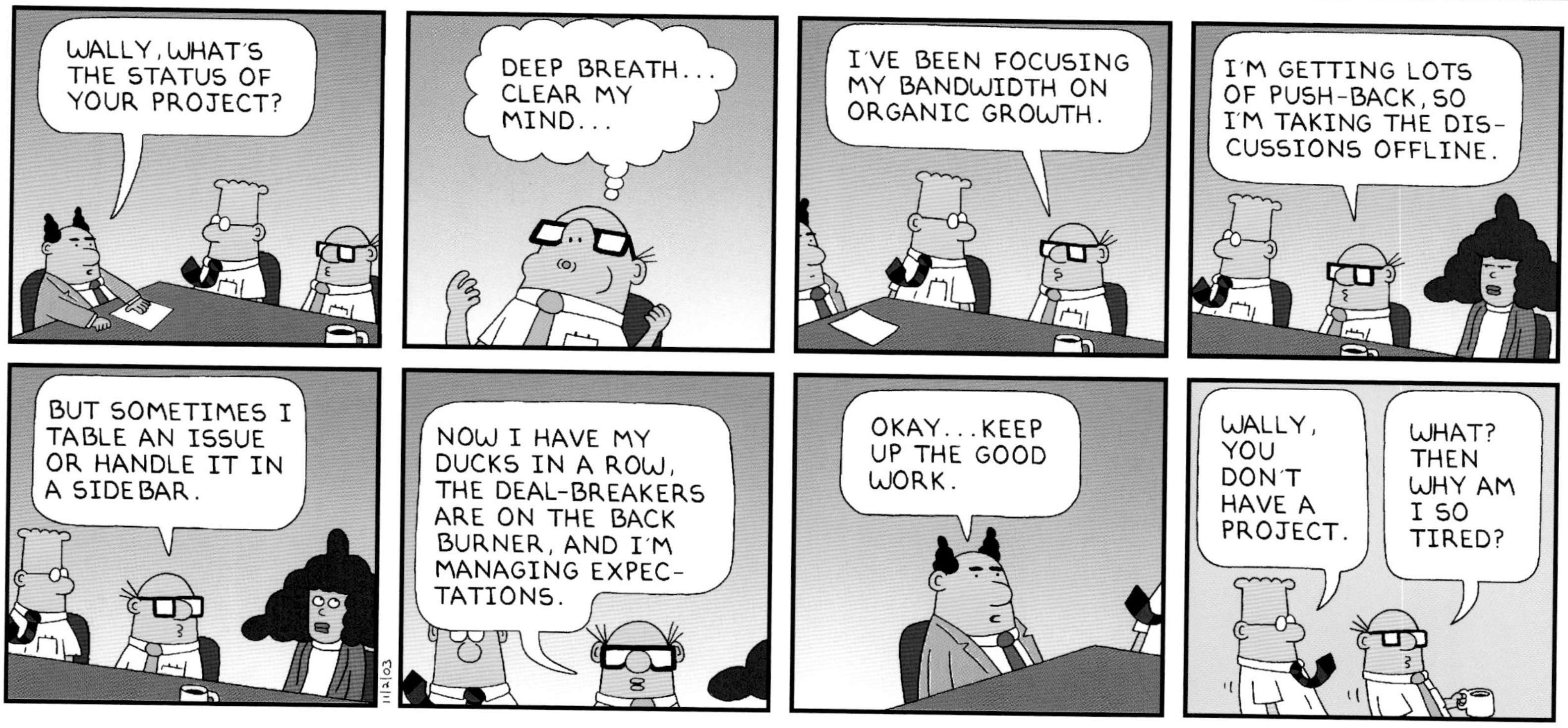
WALLY, WHAT'S THE STATUS OF YOUR PROJECT?
DEEP BREATH... CLEAR MY MIND...
I'VE BEEN FOCUSING MY BANDWIDTH ON ORGANIC GROWTH.
I'M GETTING LOTS OF PUSH-BACK, SO I'M TAKING THE DISCUSSIONS OFFLINE.
BUT SOMETIMES I TABLE AN ISSUE OR HANDLE IT IN A SIDEBAR.
11/2/03
NOW I HAVE MY DUCKS IN A ROW, THE DEAL-BREAKERS ARE ON THE BACK BURNER, AND I'M MANAGING EXPECTATIONS.
OKAY... KEEP UP THE GOOD WORK.
WALLY, YOU DON'T HAVE A PROJECT.
WHAT? THEN WHY AM I SO TIRED?

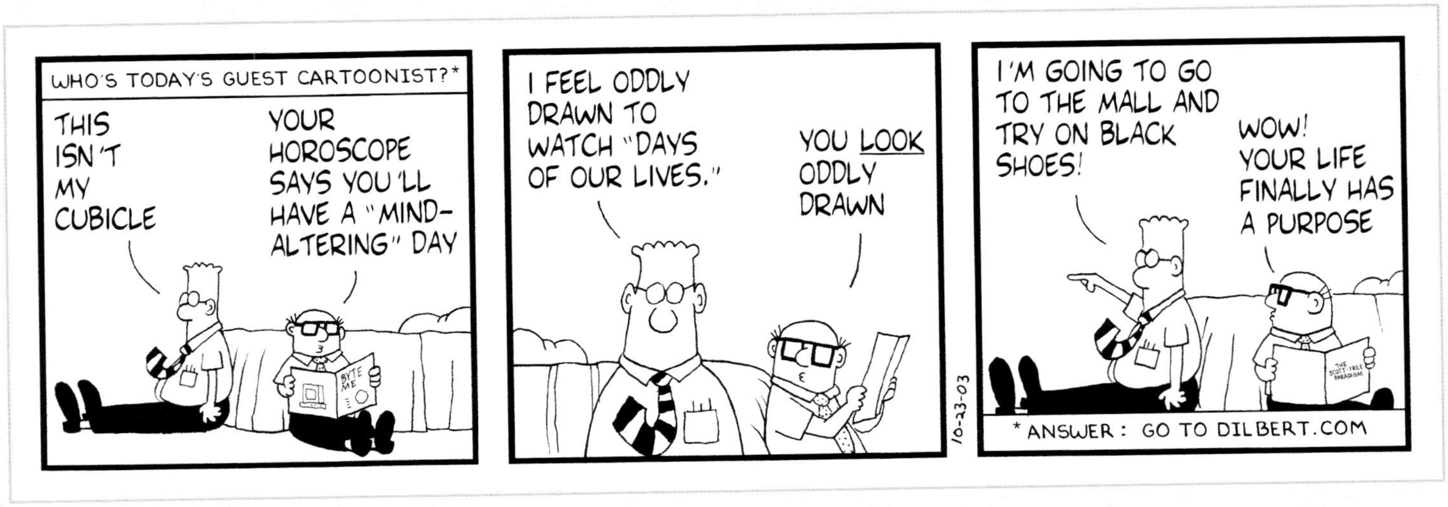
WHO'S TODAY'S GUEST CARTOONIST?*
THIS ISN'T MY CUBICLE
YOUR HOROSCOPE SAYS YOU'LL HAVE A "MIND-ALTERING" DAY
I FEEL ODDLY DRAWN TO WATCH "DAYS OF OUR LIVES."
YOU LOOK ODDLY DRAWN
10-23-03
I'M GOING TO GO TO THE MALL AND TRY ON BLACK SHOES!
WOW! YOUR LIFE FINALLY HAS A PURPOSE
*ANSWER: GO TO DILBERT.COM

This version of Dilbert *is from Greg Evans, creator of* Luann.

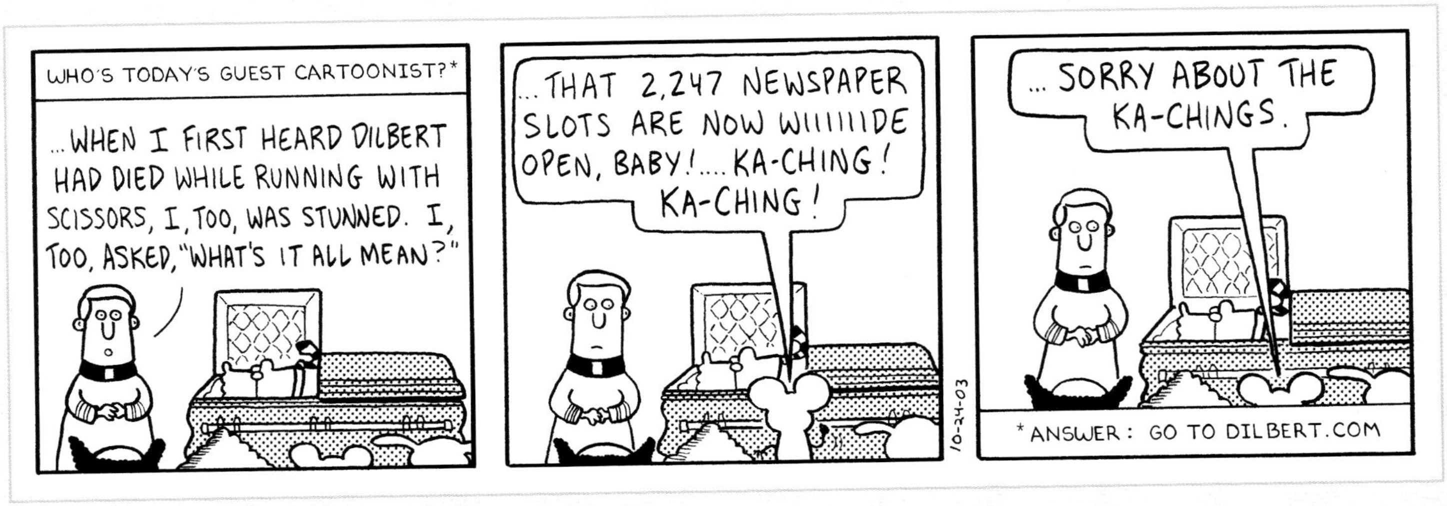
WHO'S TODAY'S GUEST CARTOONIST?*
...WHEN I FIRST HEARD DILBERT HAD DIED WHILE RUNNING WITH SCISSORS, I, TOO, WAS STUNNED. I, TOO, ASKED, "WHAT'S IT ALL MEAN?"
...THAT 2,247 NEWSPAPER SLOTS ARE NOW WIIIIIIDE OPEN, BABY!.... KA-CHING! KA-CHING!
10-24-03
... SORRY ABOUT THE KA-CHINGS.
*ANSWER: GO TO DILBERT.COM

This version of Dilbert *is from Stephan Pastis, creator of* Pearls Before Swin.

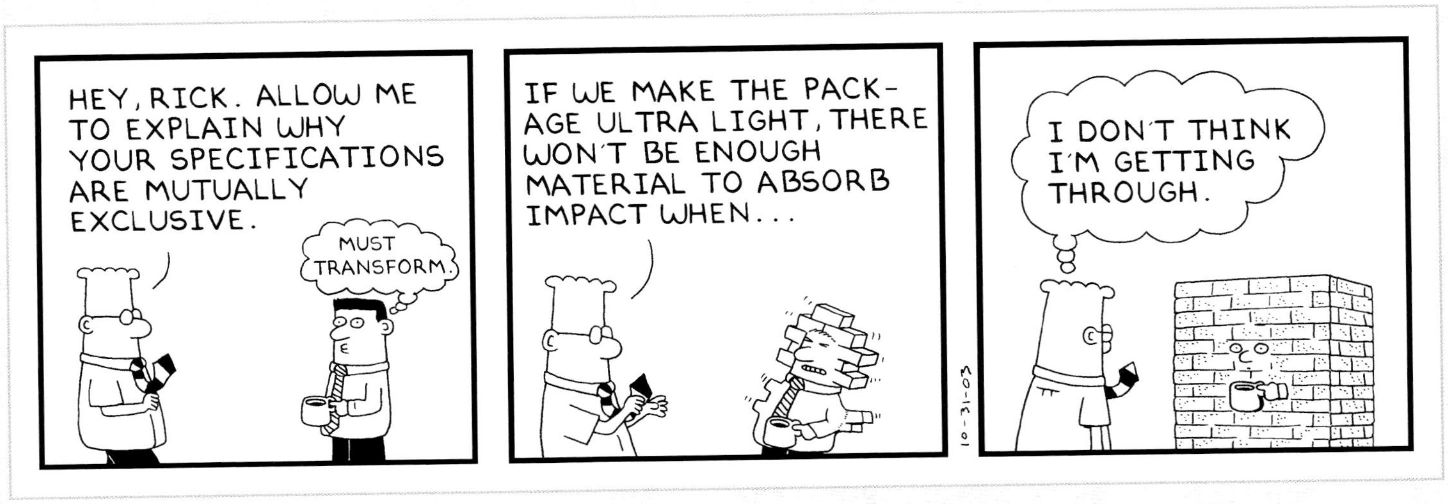
HEY, RICK. ALLOW ME TO EXPLAIN WHY YOUR SPECIFICATIONS ARE MUTUALLY EXCLUSIVE.
MUST TRANSFORM.
IF WE MAKE THE PACKAGE ULTRA LIGHT, THERE WON'T BE ENOUGH MATERIAL TO ABSORB IMPACT WHEN...
10-31-03
I DON'T THINK I'M GETTING THROUGH.

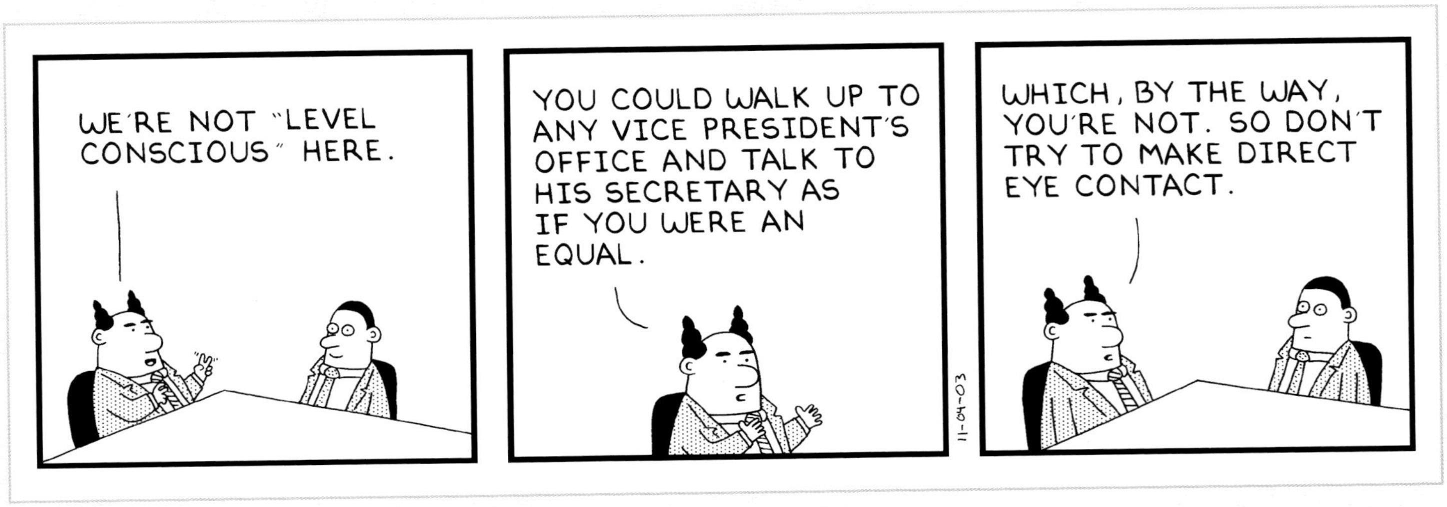
WE'RE NOT "LEVEL CONSCIOUS" HERE.
YOU COULD WALK UP TO ANY VICE PRESIDENT'S OFFICE AND TALK TO HIS SECRETARY AS IF YOU WERE AN EQUAL.
11-04-03
WHICH, BY THE WAY, YOU'RE NOT. SO DON'T TRY TO MAKE DIRECT EYE CONTACT.

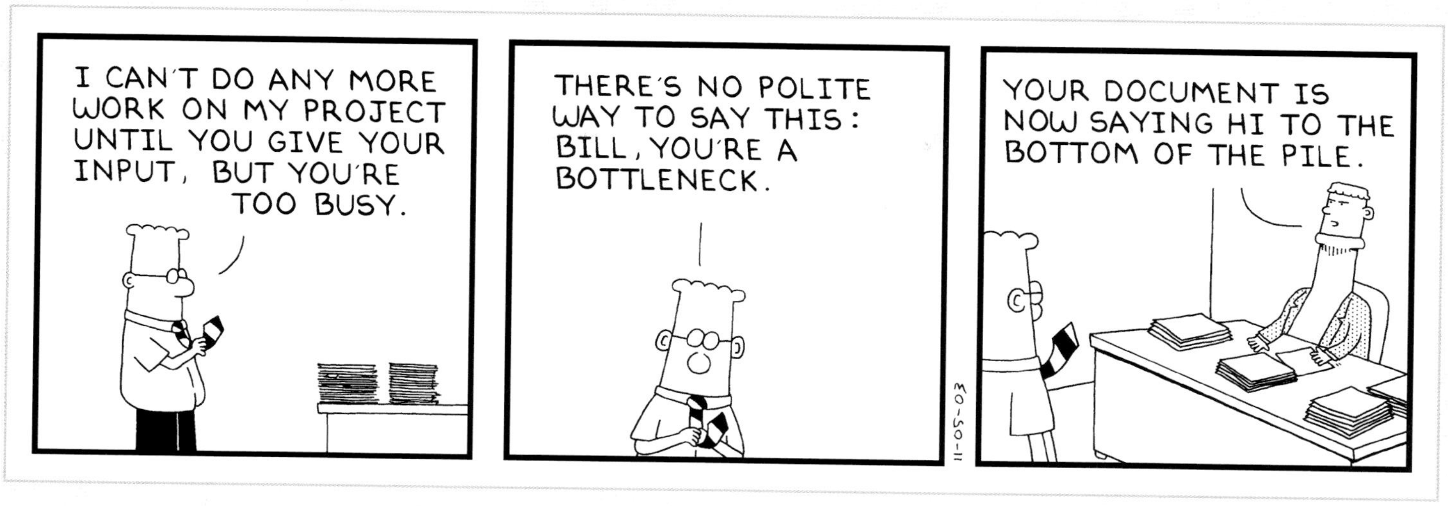
I CAN'T DO ANY MORE WORK ON MY PROJECT UNTIL YOU GIVE YOUR INPUT, BUT YOU'RE TOO BUSY.
THERE'S NO POLITE WAY TO SAY THIS: BILL, YOU'RE A BOTTLENECK.
11-05-03
YOUR DOCUMENT IS NOW SAYING HI TO THE BOTTOM OF THE PILE.

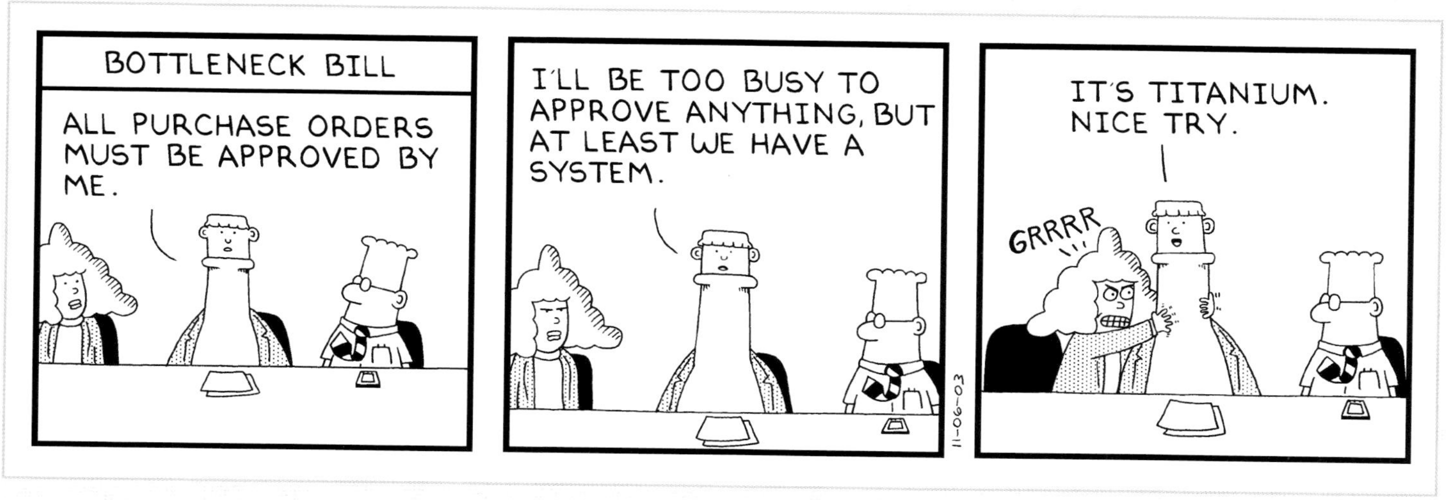
BOTTLENECK BILL
ALL PURCHASE ORDERS MUST BE APPROVED BY ME.
I'LL BE TOO BUSY TO APPROVE ANYTHING, BUT AT LEAST WE HAVE A SYSTEM.
11-06-03
IT'S TITANIUM. NICE TRY.
GRRRR

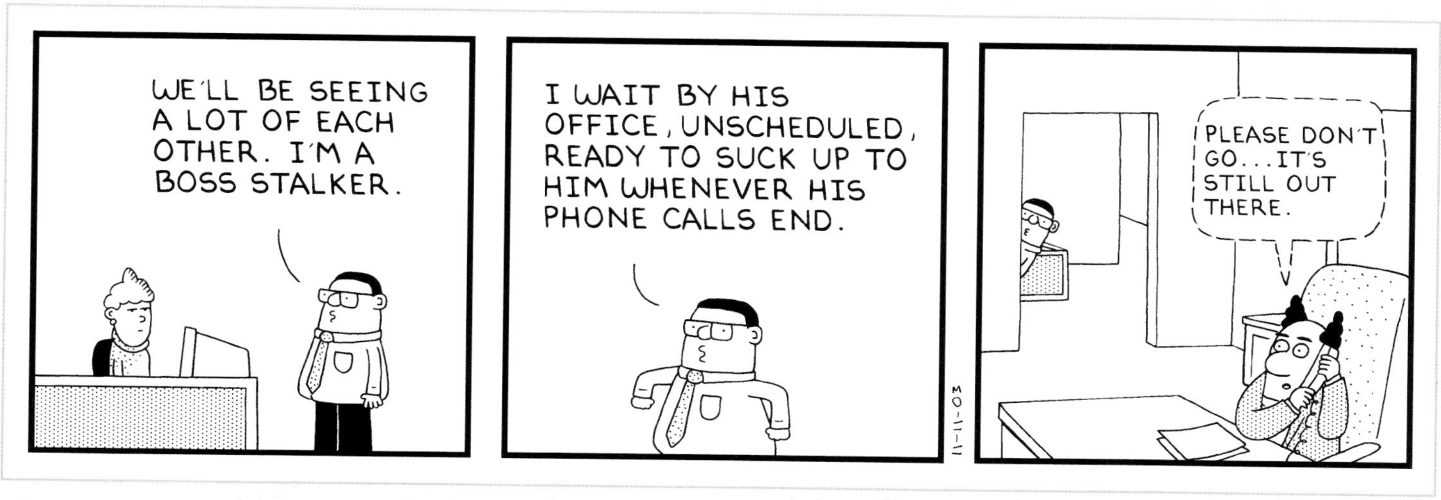
WE'LL BE SEEING A LOT OF EACH OTHER. I'M A BOSS STALKER.
I WAIT BY HIS OFFICE, UNSCHEDULED, READY TO SUCK UP TO HIM WHENEVER HIS PHONE CALLS END.
11-11-03
PLEASE DON'T GO... IT'S STILL OUT THERE.

I worked with a guy who kept his most important documents, of which there were no other copies, in the recycling tray. That didn't work out for him.

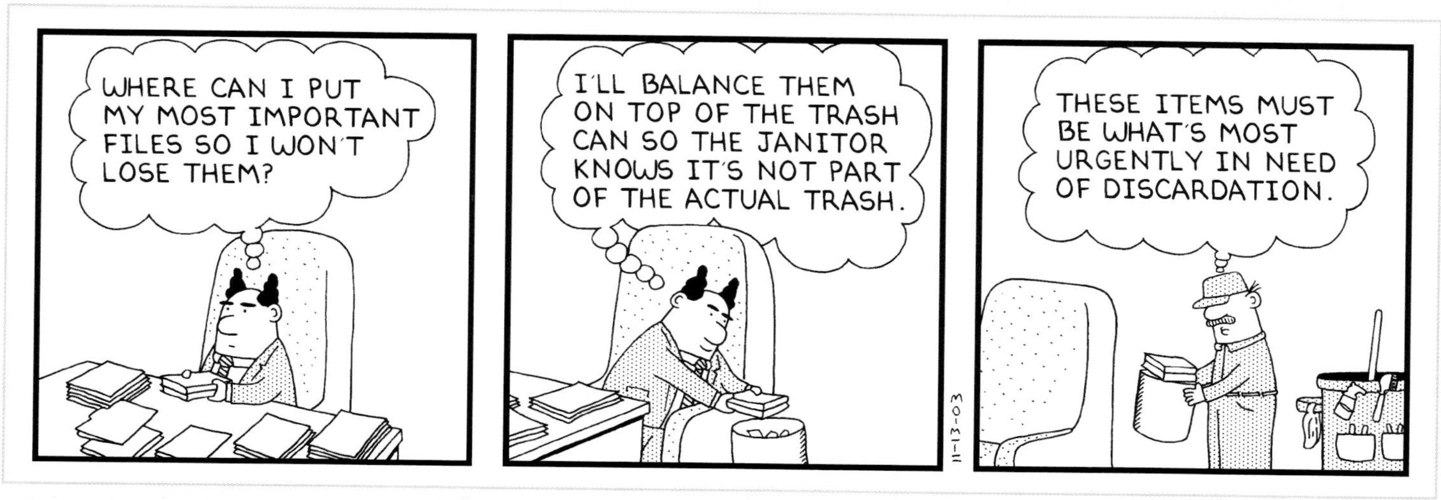
WHERE CAN I PUT MY MOST IMPORTANT FILES SO I WON'T LOSE THEM?
I'LL BALANCE THEM ON TOP OF THE TRASH CAN SO THE JANITOR KNOWS IT'S NOT PART OF THE ACTUAL TRASH.
11-13-03
THESE ITEMS MUST BE WHAT'S MOST URGENTLY IN NEED OF DISCARDATION.

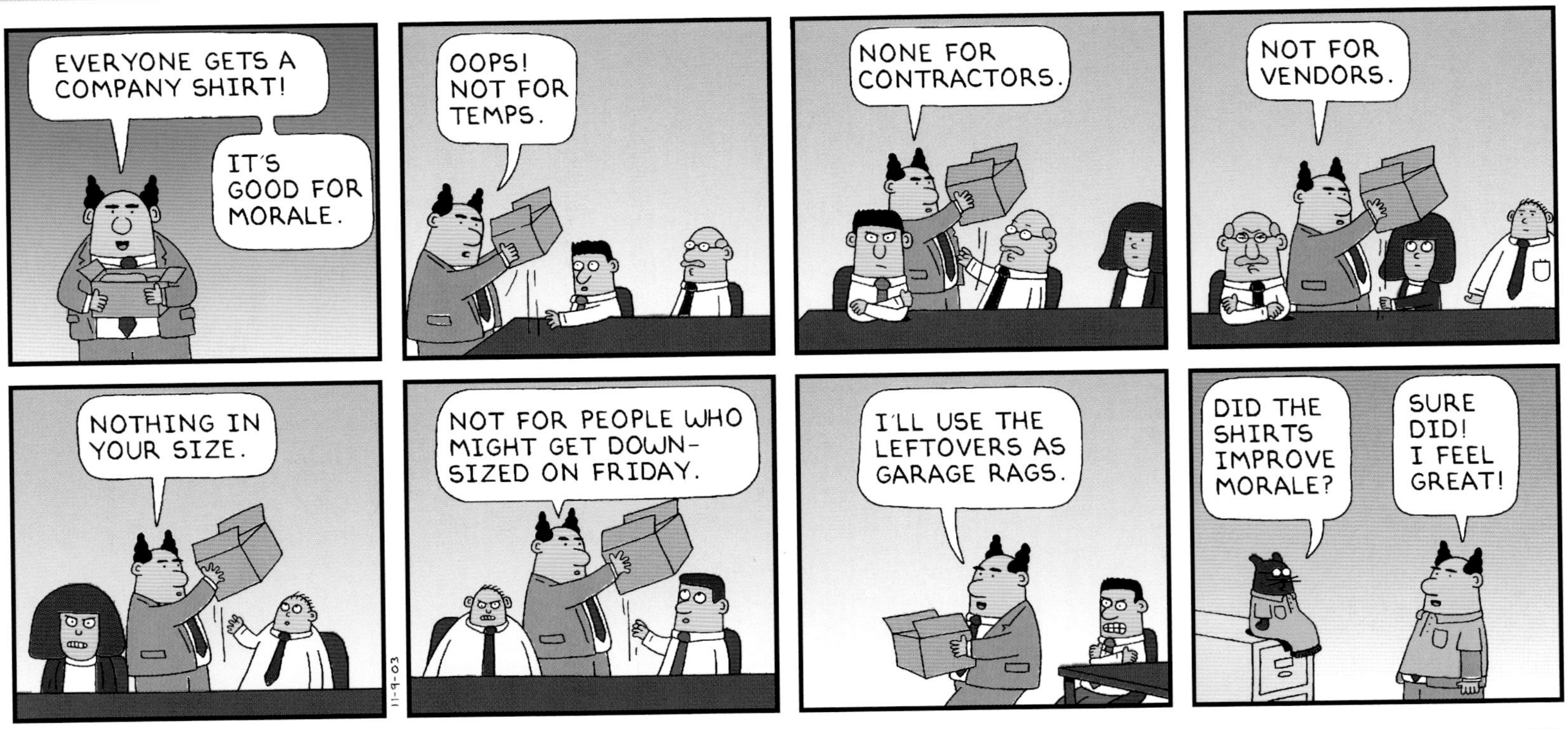
EVERYONE GETS A COMPANY SHIRT!
IT'S GOOD FOR MORALE.
OOPS! NOT FOR TEMPS.
NONE FOR CONTRACTORS.
NOT FOR VENDORS.
NOTHING IN YOUR SIZE.
NOT FOR PEOPLE WHO MIGHT GET DOWN-SIZED ON FRIDAY.
I'LL USE THE LEFTOVERS AS GARAGE RAGS.
DID THE SHIRTS IMPROVE MORALE?
SURE DID! I FEEL GREAT!
11-9-03

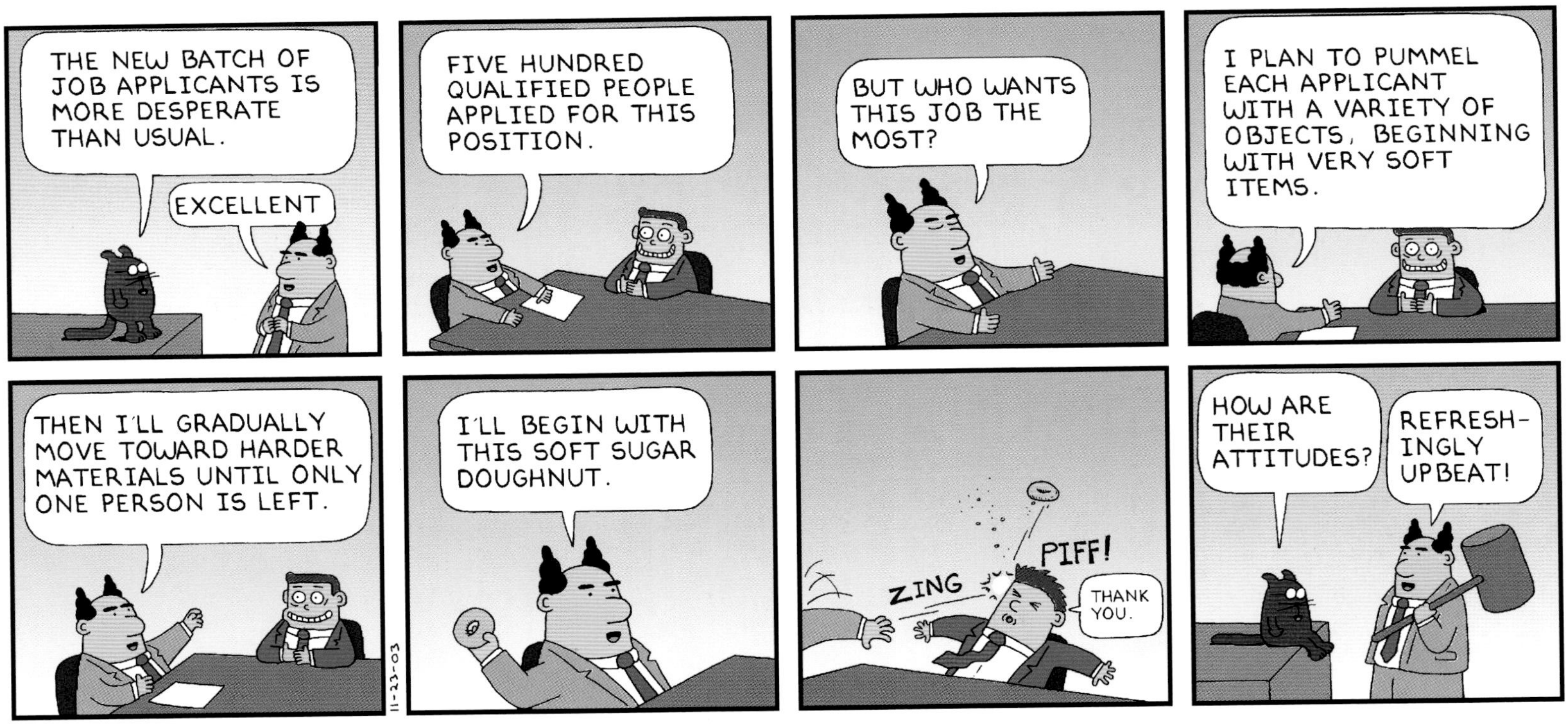
THE NEW BATCH OF JOB APPLICANTS IS MORE DESPERATE THAN USUAL.
EXCELLENT
FIVE HUNDRED QUALIFIED PEOPLE APPLIED FOR THIS POSITION.
BUT WHO WANTS THIS JOB THE MOST?
I PLAN TO PUMMEL EACH APPLICANT WITH A VARIETY OF OBJECTS, BEGINNING WITH VERY SOFT ITEMS.
THEN I'LL GRADUALLY MOVE TOWARD HARDER MATERIALS UNTIL ONLY ONE PERSON IS LEFT.
I'LL BEGIN WITH THIS SOFT SUGAR DOUGHNUT.
ZING
PIFF!
THANK YOU.
HOW ARE THEIR ATTITUDES?
REFRESH-INGLY UPBEAT!
11-23-03

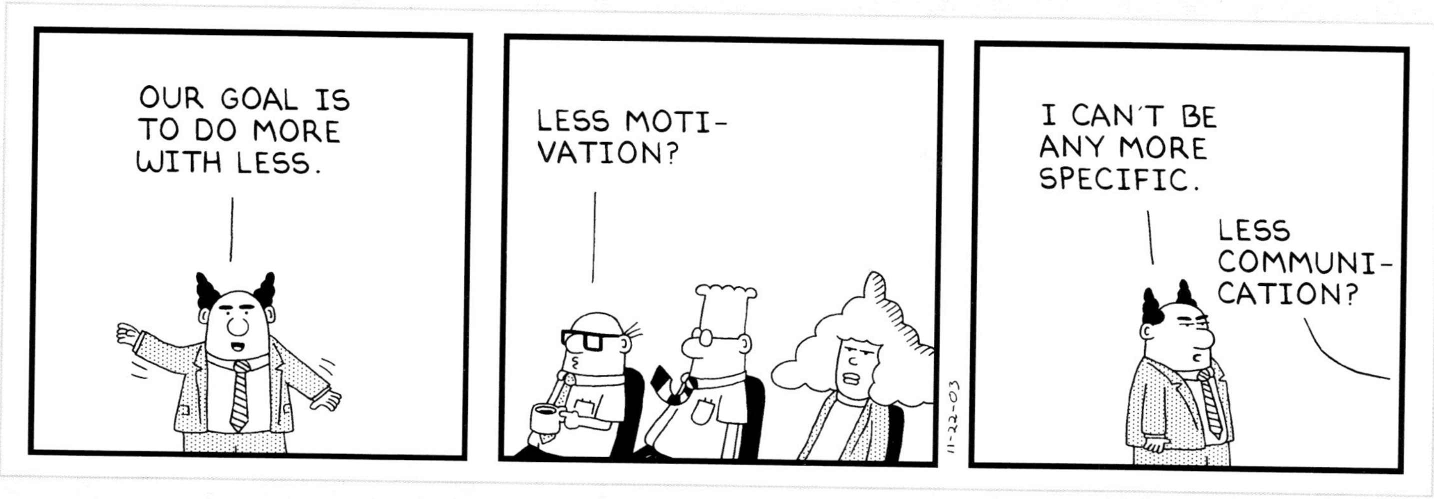
OUR GOAL IS TO DO MORE WITH LESS.
LESS MOTI-VATION?
11-22-03
I CAN'T BE ANY MORE SPECIFIC.
LESS COMMUNI-CATION?

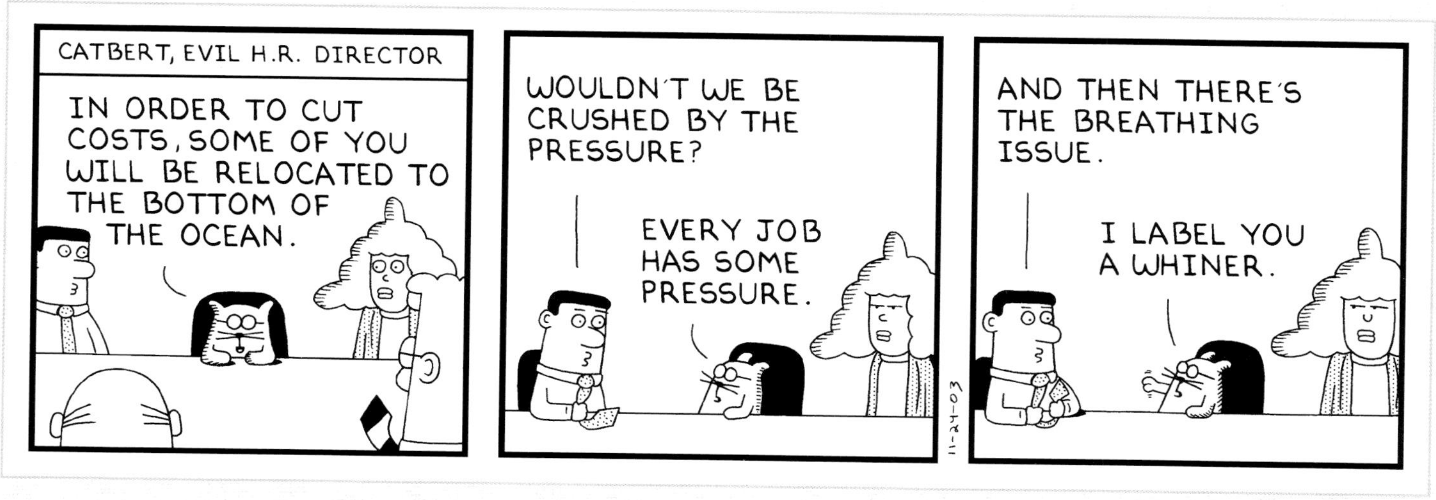
CATBERT, EVIL H.R. DIRECTOR
IN ORDER TO CUT COSTS, SOME OF YOU WILL BE RELOCATED TO THE BOTTOM OF THE OCEAN.
WOULDN'T WE BE CRUSHED BY THE PRESSURE?
EVERY JOB HAS SOME PRESSURE.
11-24-03
AND THEN THERE'S THE BREATHING ISSUE.
I LABEL YOU A WHINER.

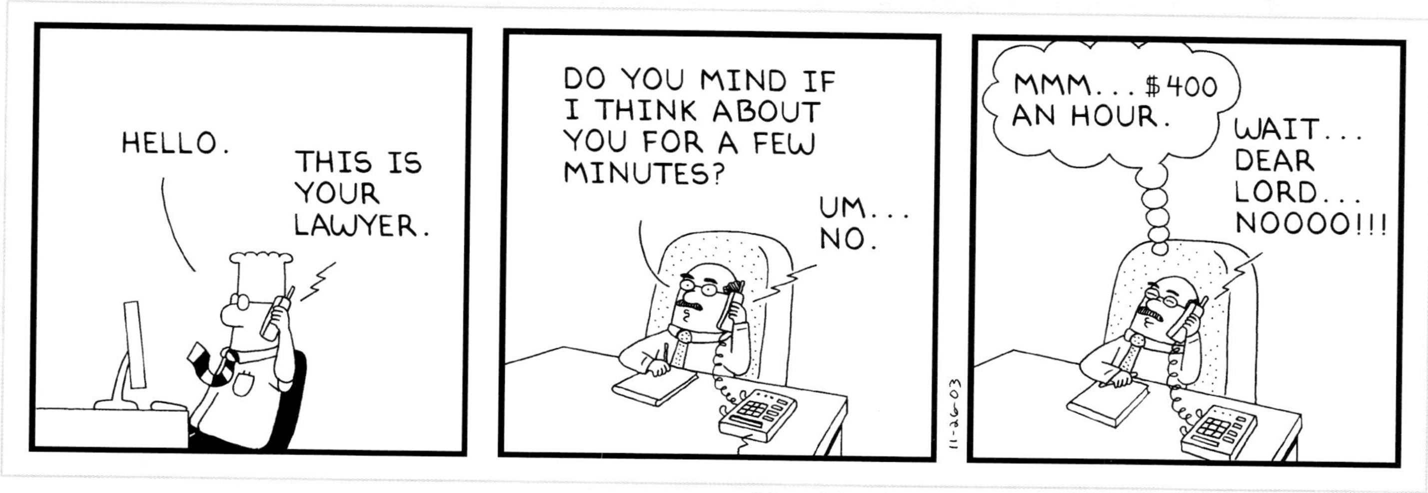
HELLO.
THIS IS YOUR LAWYER.
DO YOU MIND IF I THINK ABOUT YOU FOR A FEW MINUTES?
UM... NO.
11-26-03
MMM... $400 AN HOUR.
WAIT... DEAR LORD... NOOOO!!!

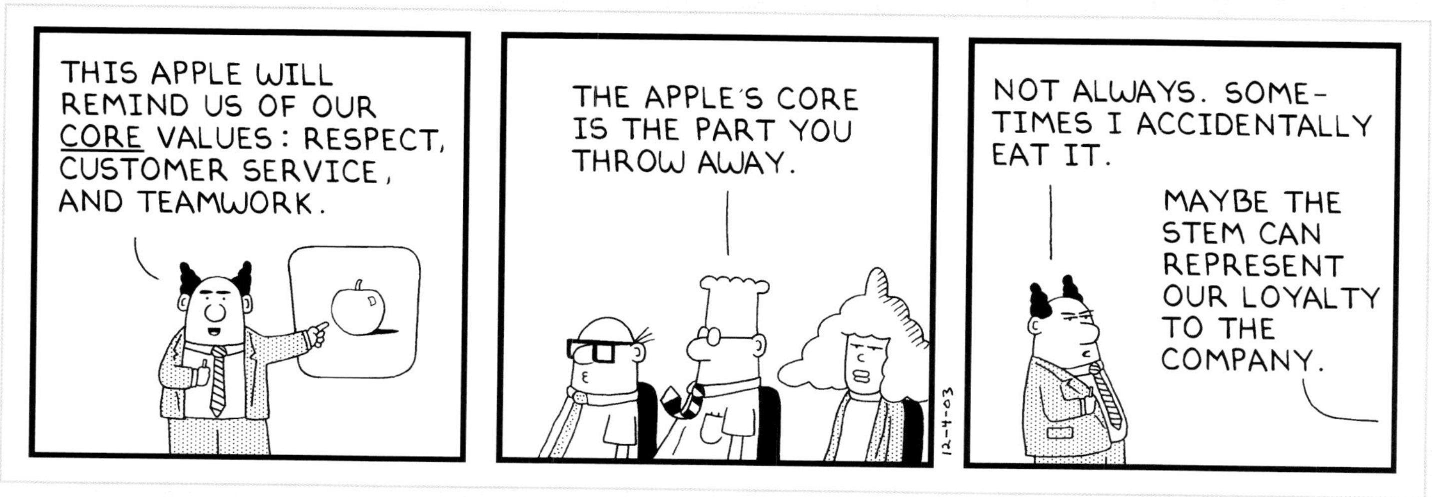
THIS APPLE WILL REMIND US OF OUR CORE VALUES: RESPECT, CUSTOMER SERVICE, AND TEAMWORK.
THE APPLE'S CORE IS THE PART YOU THROW AWAY.
12-4-03
NOT ALWAYS. SOME-TIMES I ACCIDENTALLY EAT IT.
MAYBE THE STEM CAN REPRESENT OUR LOYALTY TO THE COMPANY.

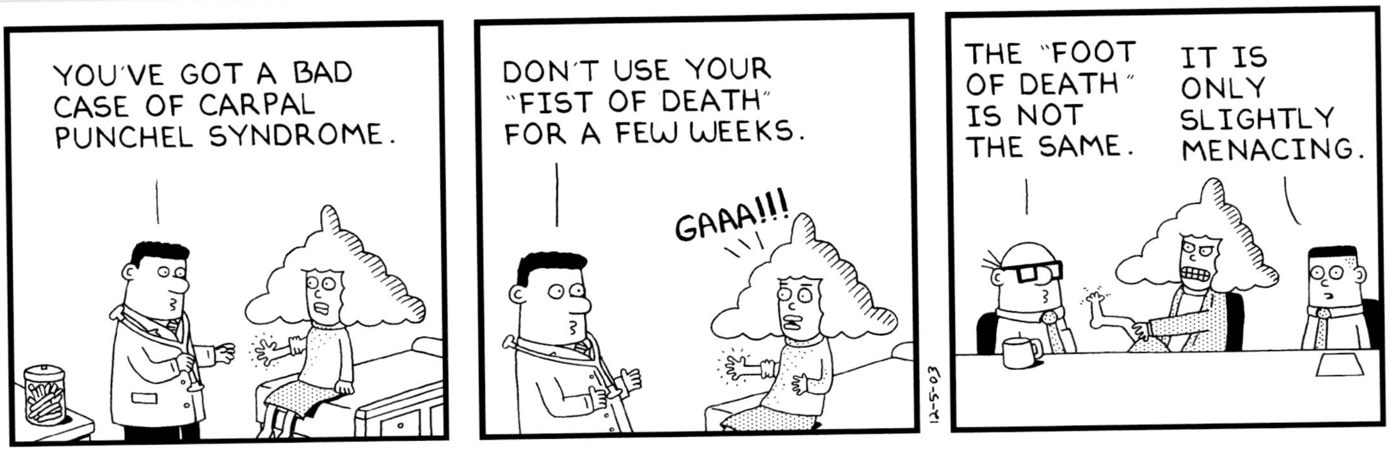
YOU'VE GOT A BAD CASE OF CARPAL PUNCHEL SYNDROME.
DON'T USE YOUR "FIST OF DEATH" FOR A FEW WEEKS.
GAAA!!!
12-5-03
THE "FOOT OF DEATH" IS NOT THE SAME.
IT IS ONLY SLIGHTLY MENACING.

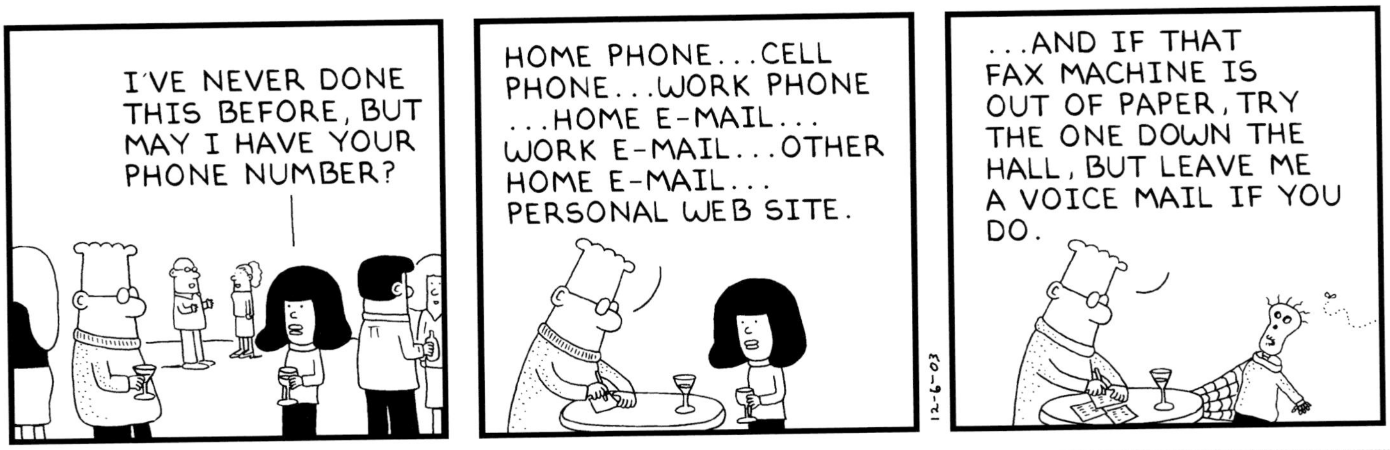
I'VE NEVER DONE THIS BEFORE, BUT MAY I HAVE YOUR PHONE NUMBER?
HOME PHONE...CELL PHONE...WORK PHONE ...HOME E-MAIL... WORK E-MAIL...OTHER HOME E-MAIL... PERSONAL WEB SITE.
12-6-03
...AND IF THAT FAX MACHINE IS OUT OF PAPER, TRY THE ONE DOWN THE HALL, BUT LEAVE ME A VOICE MAIL IF YOU DO.

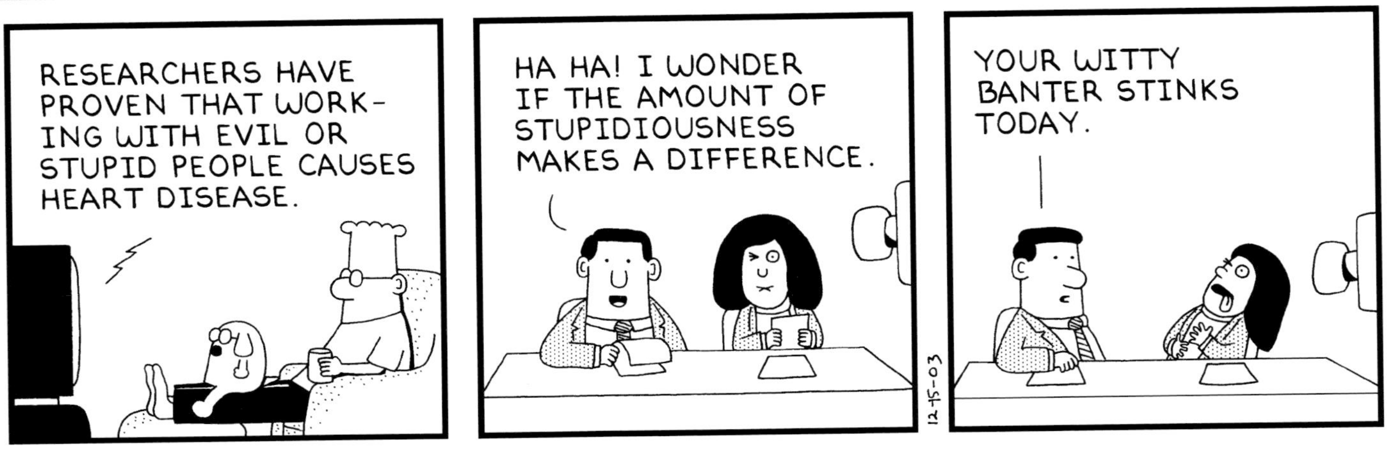
RESEARCHERS HAVE PROVEN THAT WORK-ING WITH EVIL OR STUPID PEOPLE CAUSES HEART DISEASE.
HA HA! I WONDER IF THE AMOUNT OF STUPIDIOUSNESS MAKES A DIFFERENCE.
12-15-03
YOUR WITTY BANTER STINKS TODAY.

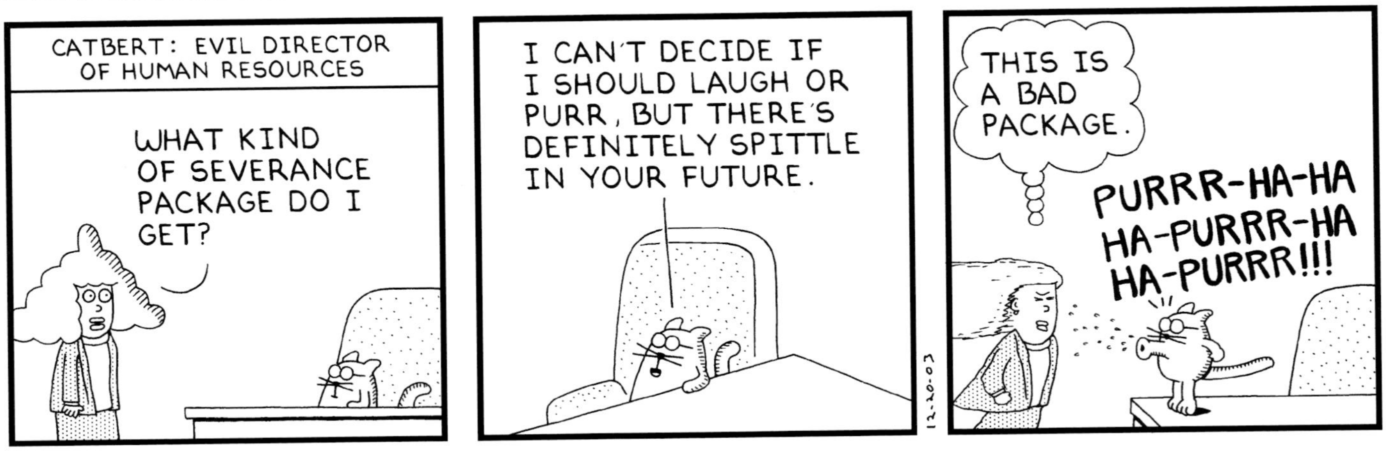
CATBERT: EVIL DIRECTOR OF HUMAN RESOURCES
WHAT KIND OF SEVERANCE PACKAGE DO I GET?
I CAN'T DECIDE IF I SHOULD LAUGH OR PURR, BUT THERE'S DEFINITELY SPITTLE IN YOUR FUTURE.
12-20-03
THIS IS A BAD PACKAGE.
PURRR-HA-HA HA-PURRR-HA HA-PURRR!!!

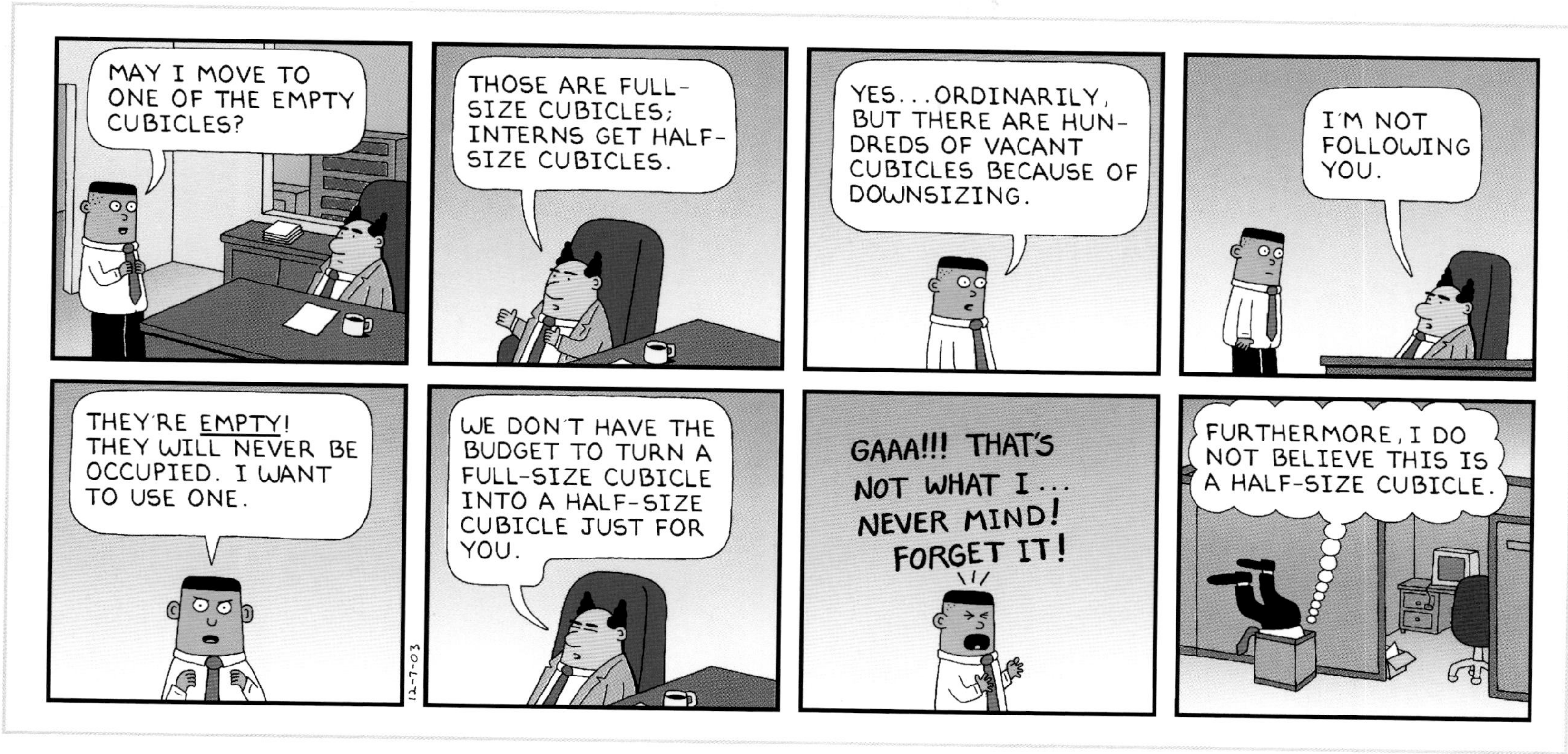
MAY I MOVE TO ONE OF THE EMPTY CUBICLES?
THOSE ARE FULL-SIZE CUBICLES; INTERNS GET HALF-SIZE CUBICLES.
YES...ORDINARILY, BUT THERE ARE HUNDREDS OF VACANT CUBICLES BECAUSE OF DOWNSIZING.
I'M NOT FOLLOWING YOU.
THEY'RE EMPTY! THEY WILL NEVER BE OCCUPIED. I WANT TO USE ONE.
12-7-03
WE DON'T HAVE THE BUDGET TO TURN A FULL-SIZE CUBICLE INTO A HALF-SIZE CUBICLE JUST FOR YOU.
GAAA!!! THAT'S NOT WHAT I... NEVER MIND! FORGET IT!
FURTHERMORE, I DO NOT BELIEVE THIS IS A HALF-SIZE CUBICLE.

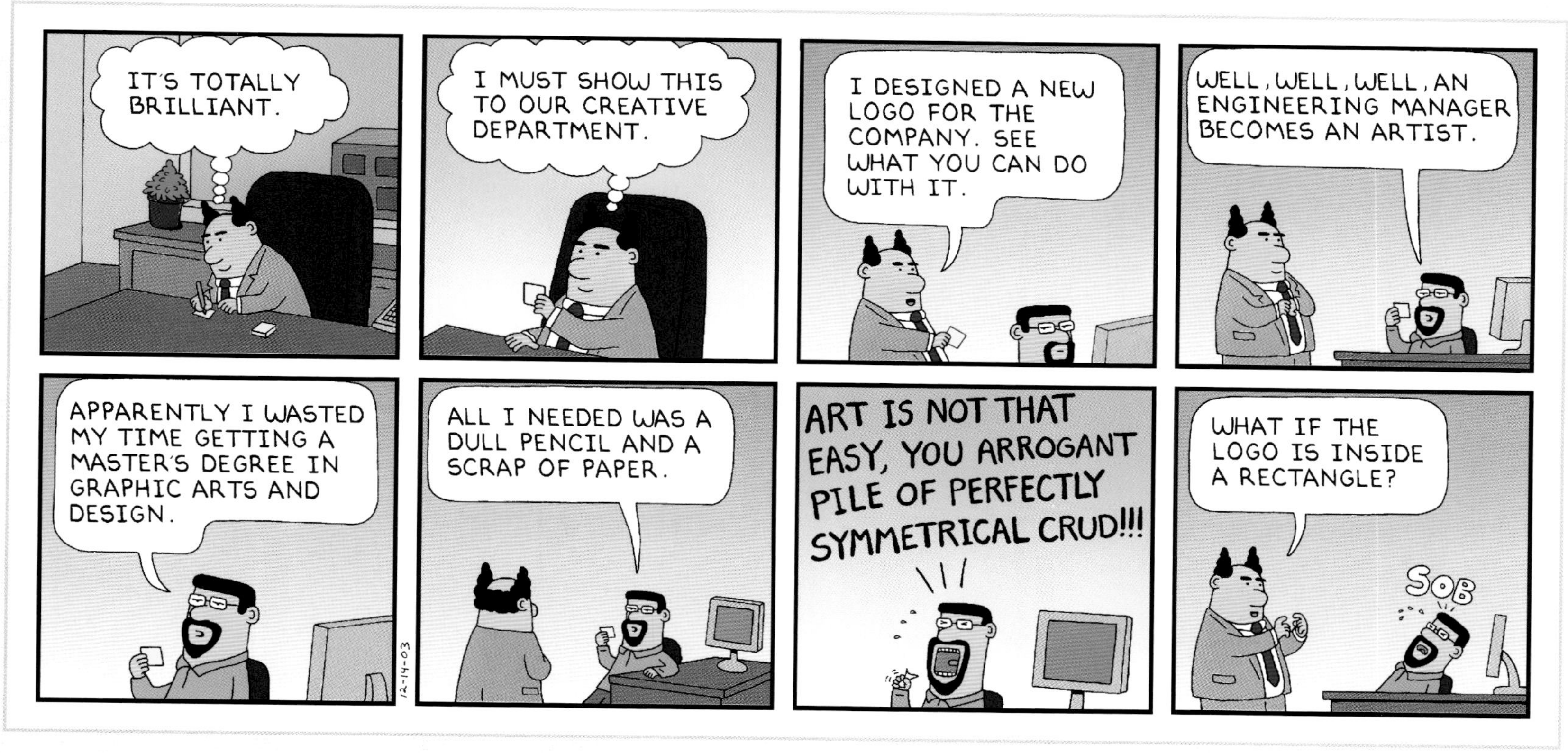
IT'S TOTALLY BRILLIANT.
I MUST SHOW THIS TO OUR CREATIVE DEPARTMENT.
I DESIGNED A NEW LOGO FOR THE COMPANY. SEE WHAT YOU CAN DO WITH IT.
WELL, WELL, WELL, AN ENGINEERING MANAGER BECOMES AN ARTIST.
APPARENTLY I WASTED MY TIME GETTING A MASTER'S DEGREE IN GRAPHIC ARTS AND DESIGN.
12-14-03
ALL I NEEDED WAS A DULL PENCIL AND A SCRAP OF PAPER.
ART IS NOT THAT EASY, YOU ARROGANT PILE OF PERFECTLY SYMMETRICAL CRUD!!!
WHAT IF THE LOGO IS INSIDE A RECTANGLE?
SOB

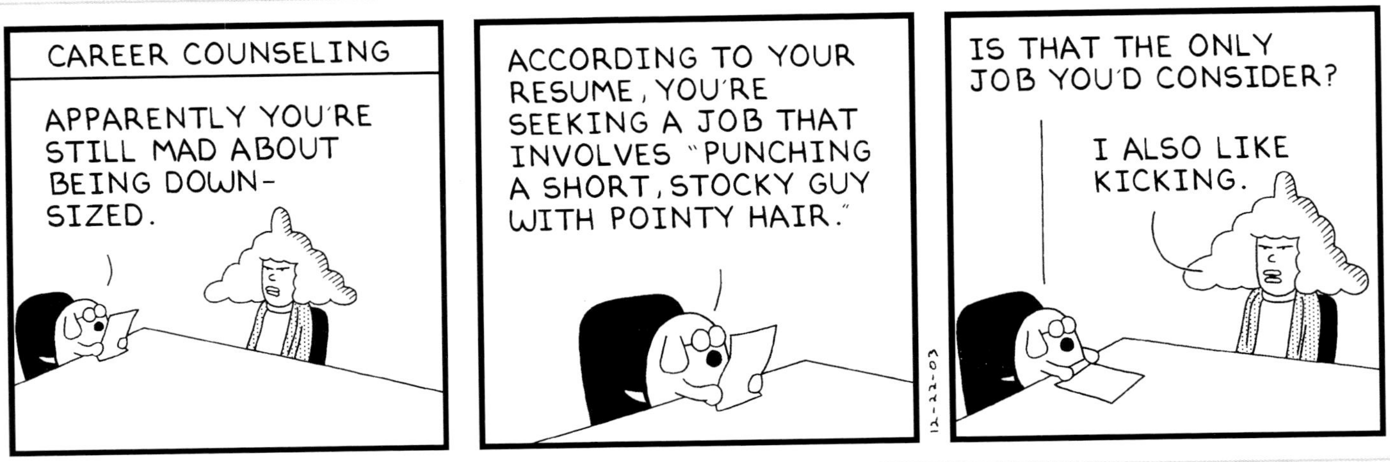
CAREER COUNSELING
APPARENTLY YOU'RE STILL MAD ABOUT BEING DOWN-SIZED.
ACCORDING TO YOUR RESUME, YOU'RE SEEKING A JOB THAT INVOLVES "PUNCHING A SHORT, STOCKY GUY WITH POINTY HAIR."
IS THAT THE ONLY JOB YOU'D CONSIDER?
I ALSO LIKE KICKING.
12-22-03

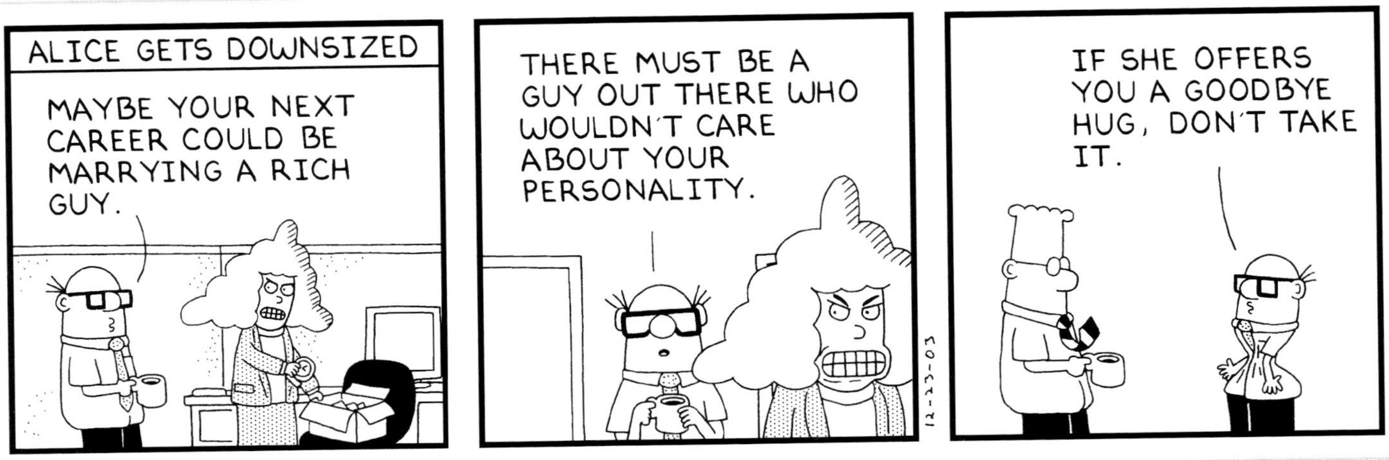
ALICE GETS DOWNSIZED
MAYBE YOUR NEXT CAREER COULD BE MARRYING A RICH GUY.
THERE MUST BE A GUY OUT THERE WHO WOULDN'T CARE ABOUT YOUR PERSONALITY.
IF SHE OFFERS YOU A GOODBYE HUG, DON'T TAKE IT.
12-23-03

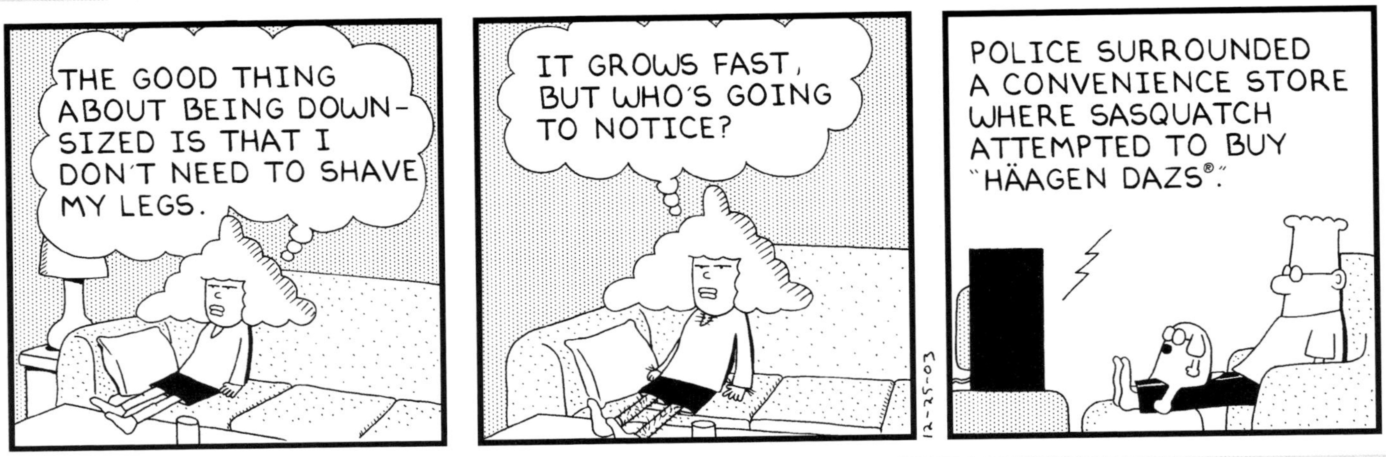
THE GOOD THING ABOUT BEING DOWN-SIZED IS THAT I DON'T NEED TO SHAVE MY LEGS.
IT GROWS FAST, BUT WHO'S GOING TO NOTICE?
POLICE SURROUNDED A CONVENIENCE STORE WHERE SASQUATCH ATTEMPTED TO BUY "HÄAGEN DAZS®."
12-25-03

The original version of the following strip said the CEO "went to get a hummer." The choice of words was intentional, and I hoped the ambiguity would be enough to get it published and delight readers who had learned to expect the worst from me. My editors helpfully changed it to "buy a hummer," allegedly to make the writing clearer. I didn't find out until the comic was published. Now they check with me first.

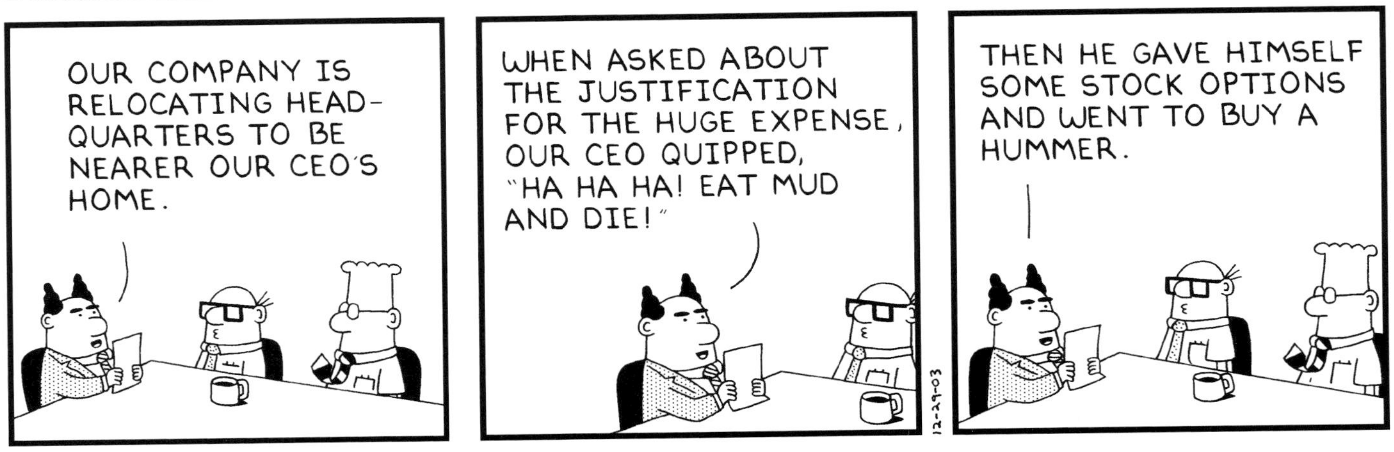
OUR COMPANY IS RELOCATING HEAD-QUARTERS TO BE NEARER OUR CEO'S HOME.
WHEN ASKED ABOUT THE JUSTIFICATION FOR THE HUGE EXPENSE, OUR CEO QUIPPED, "HA HA HA! EAT MUD AND DIE!"
THEN HE GAVE HIMSELF SOME STOCK OPTIONS AND WENT TO BUY A HUMMER.
12-29-03

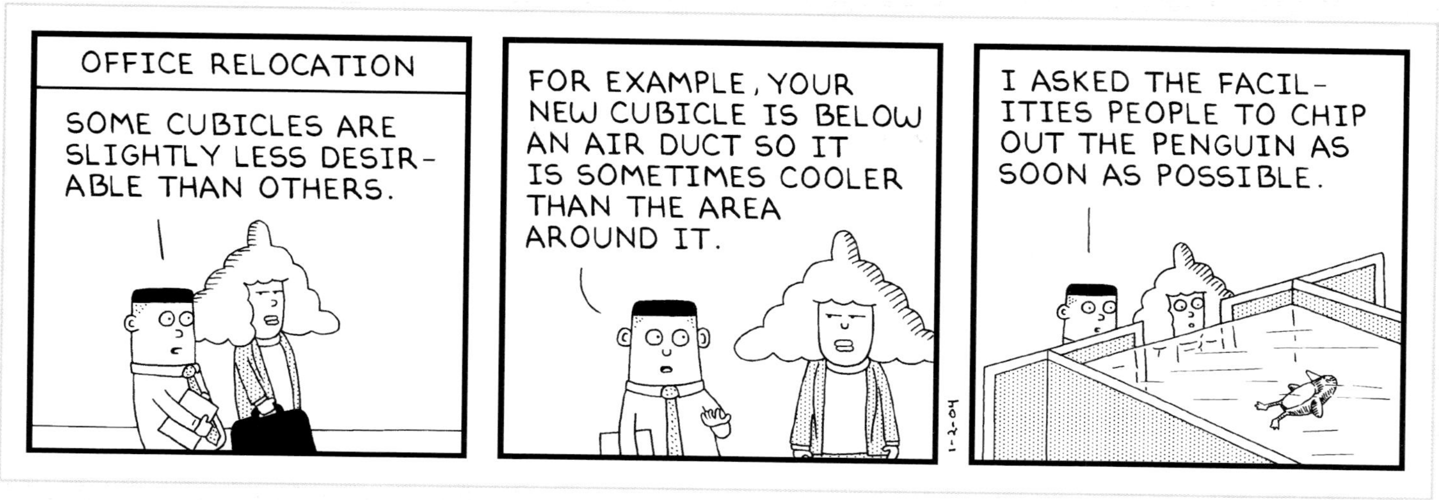
OFFICE RELOCATION
SOME CUBICLES ARE SLIGHTLY LESS DESIRABLE THAN OTHERS.
FOR EXAMPLE, YOUR NEW CUBICLE IS BELOW AN AIR DUCT SO IT IS SOMETIMES COOLER THAN THE AREA AROUND IT.
I ASKED THE FACILITIES PEOPLE TO CHIP OUT THE PENGUIN AS SOON AS POSSIBLE.

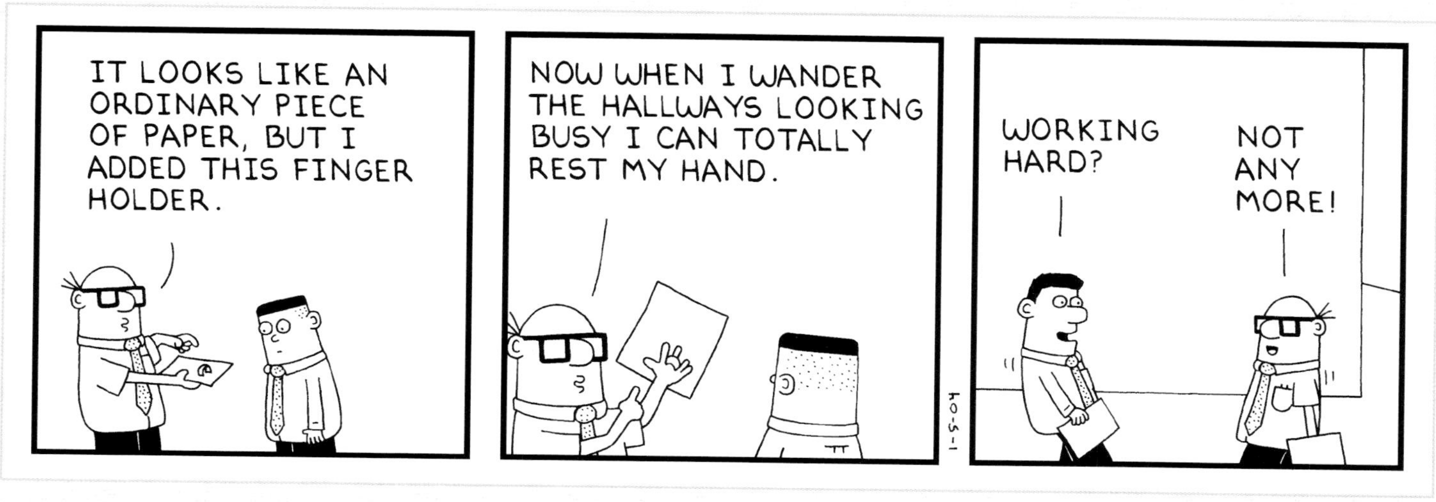
IT LOOKS LIKE AN ORDINARY PIECE OF PAPER, BUT I ADDED THIS FINGER HOLDER.
NOW WHEN I WANDER THE HALLWAYS LOOKING BUSY I CAN TOTALLY REST MY HAND.
WORKING HARD?
NOT ANY MORE!

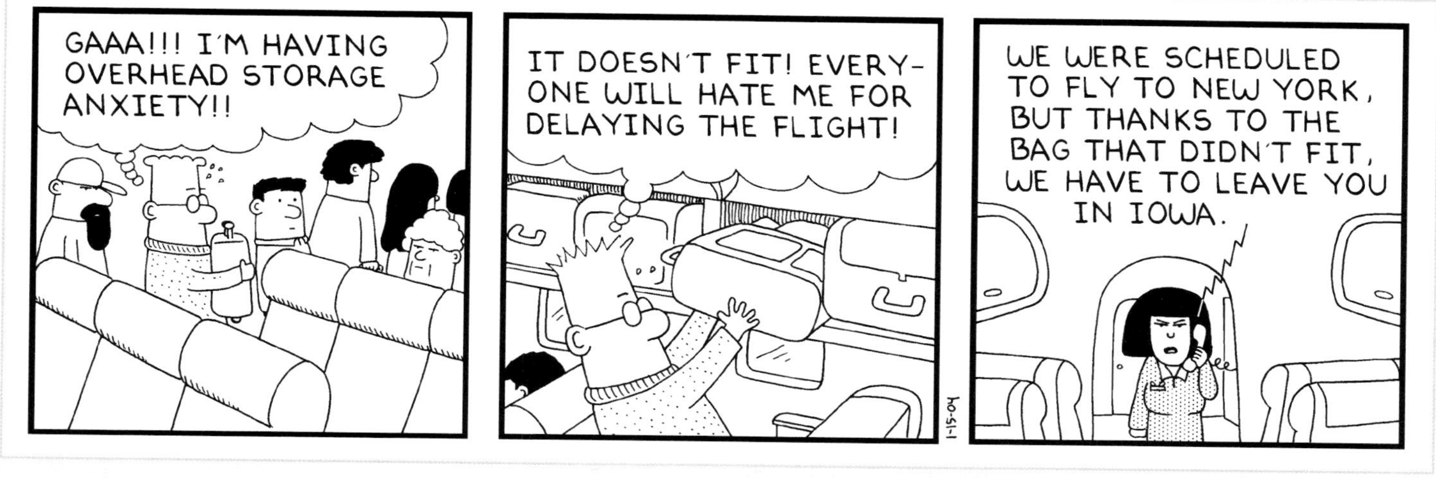
GAAA!!! I'M HAVING OVERHEAD STORAGE ANXIETY!!
IT DOESN'T FIT! EVERYONE WILL HATE ME FOR DELAYING THE FLIGHT!
WE WERE SCHEDULED TO FLY TO NEW YORK, BUT THANKS TO THE BAG THAT DIDN'T FIT, WE HAVE TO LEAVE YOU IN IOWA.

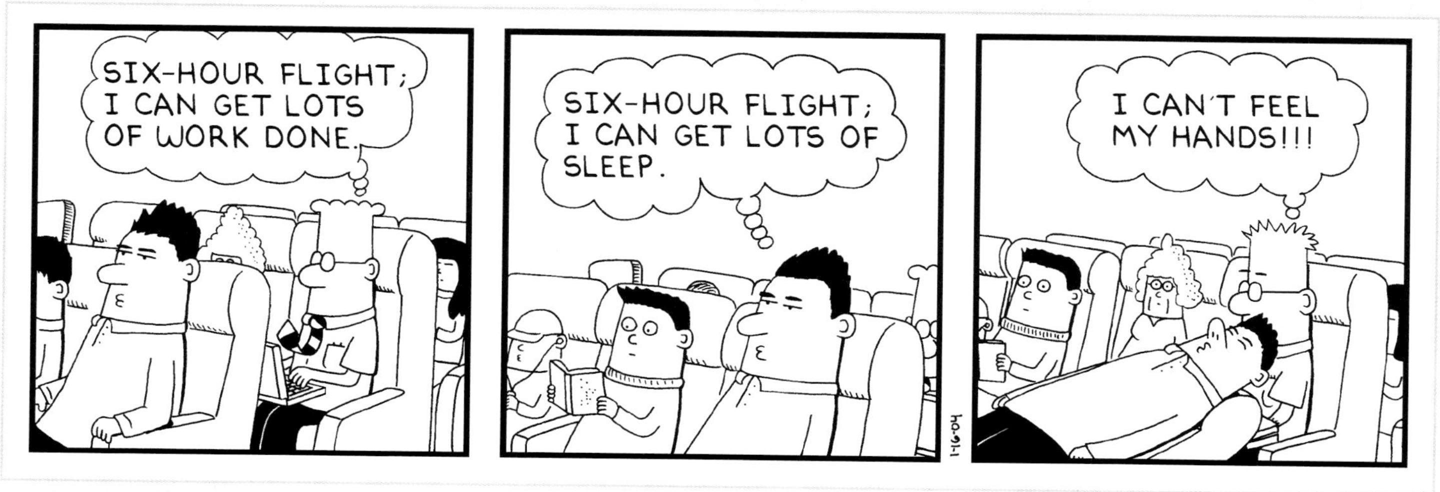
SIX-HOUR FLIGHT; I CAN GET LOTS OF WORK DONE.
SIX-HOUR FLIGHT; I CAN GET LOTS OF SLEEP.
I CAN'T FEEL MY HANDS!!!

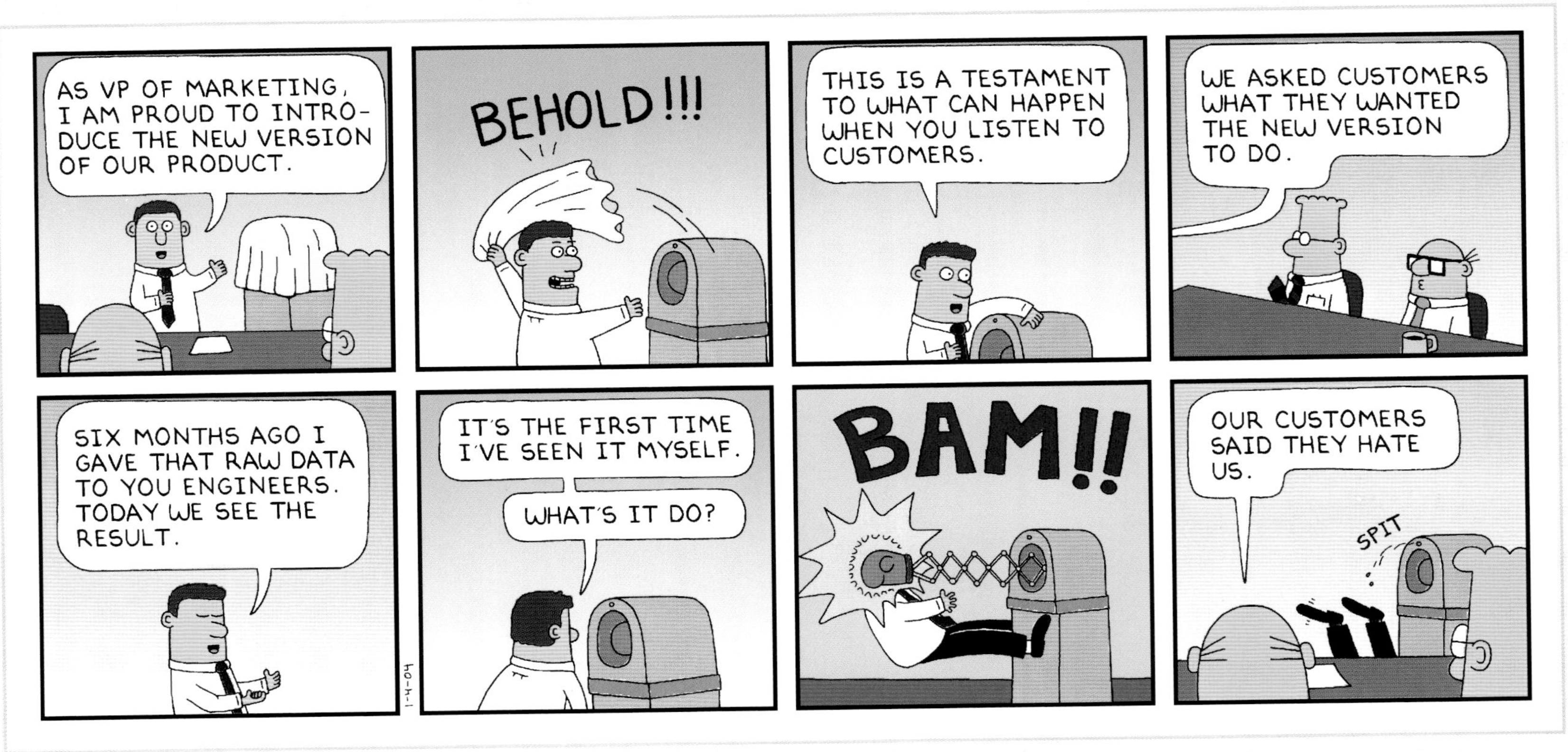
AS VP OF MARKETING, I AM PROUD TO INTRODUCE THE NEW VERSION OF OUR PRODUCT.
BEHOLD!!!
THIS IS A TESTAMENT TO WHAT CAN HAPPEN WHEN YOU LISTEN TO CUSTOMERS.
WE ASKED CUSTOMERS WHAT THEY WANTED THE NEW VERSION TO DO.
SIX MONTHS AGO I GAVE THAT RAW DATA TO YOU ENGINEERS. TODAY WE SEE THE RESULT.
1-4-04
IT'S THE FIRST TIME I'VE SEEN IT MYSELF.
WHAT'S IT DO?
BAM!!
OUR CUSTOMERS SAID THEY HATE US.
SPIT

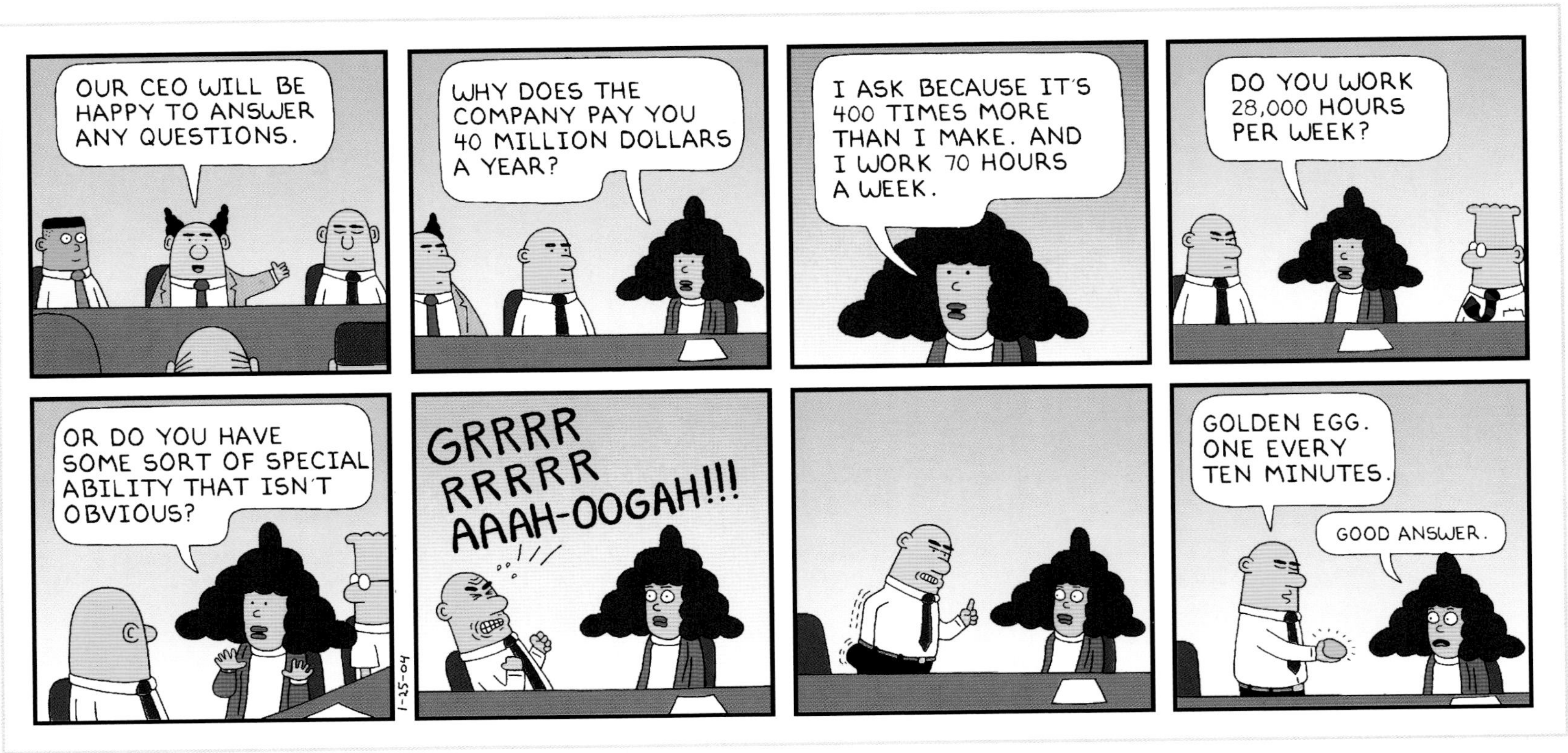
OUR CEO WILL BE HAPPY TO ANSWER ANY QUESTIONS.
WHY DOES THE COMPANY PAY YOU 40 MILLION DOLLARS A YEAR?
I ASK BECAUSE IT'S 400 TIMES MORE THAN I MAKE. AND I WORK 70 HOURS A WEEK.
DO YOU WORK 28,000 HOURS PER WEEK?
OR DO YOU HAVE SOME SORT OF SPECIAL ABILITY THAT ISN'T OBVIOUS?
1-25-04
GRRRR RRRRR AAAH-OOGAH!!!
GOLDEN EGG. ONE EVERY TEN MINUTES.
GOOD ANSWER.

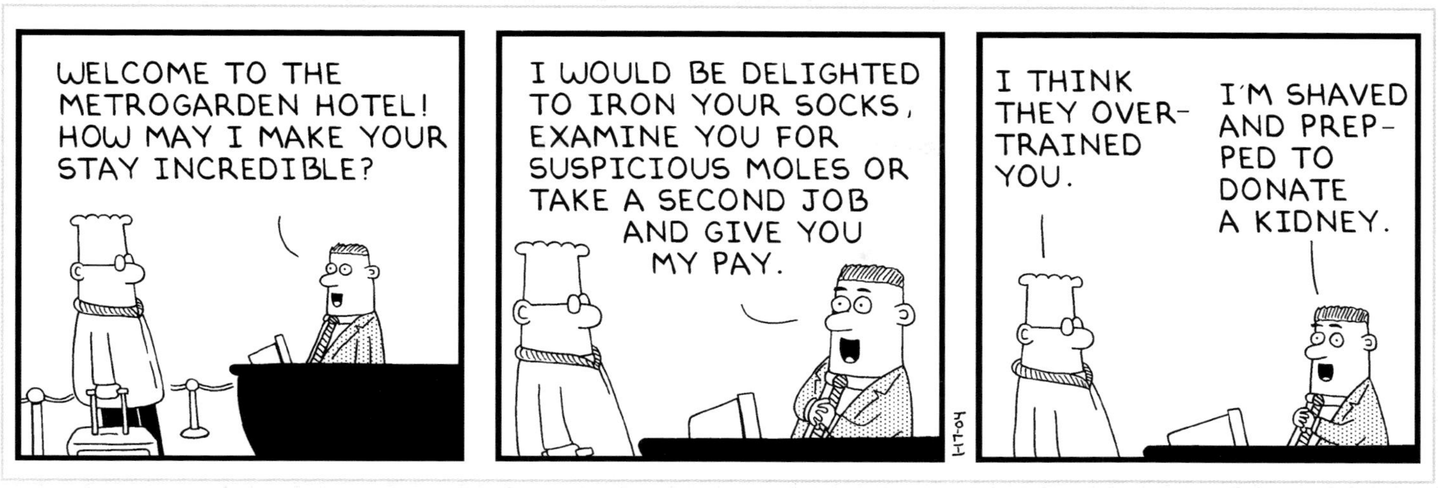
WELCOME TO THE METROGARDEN HOTEL! HOW MAY I MAKE YOUR STAY INCREDIBLE?
I WOULD BE DELIGHTED TO IRON YOUR SOCKS, EXAMINE YOU FOR SUSPICIOUS MOLES OR TAKE A SECOND JOB AND GIVE YOU MY PAY.
1-17-04
I THINK THEY OVER-TRAINED YOU.
I'M SHAVED AND PREP-PED TO DONATE A KIDNEY.

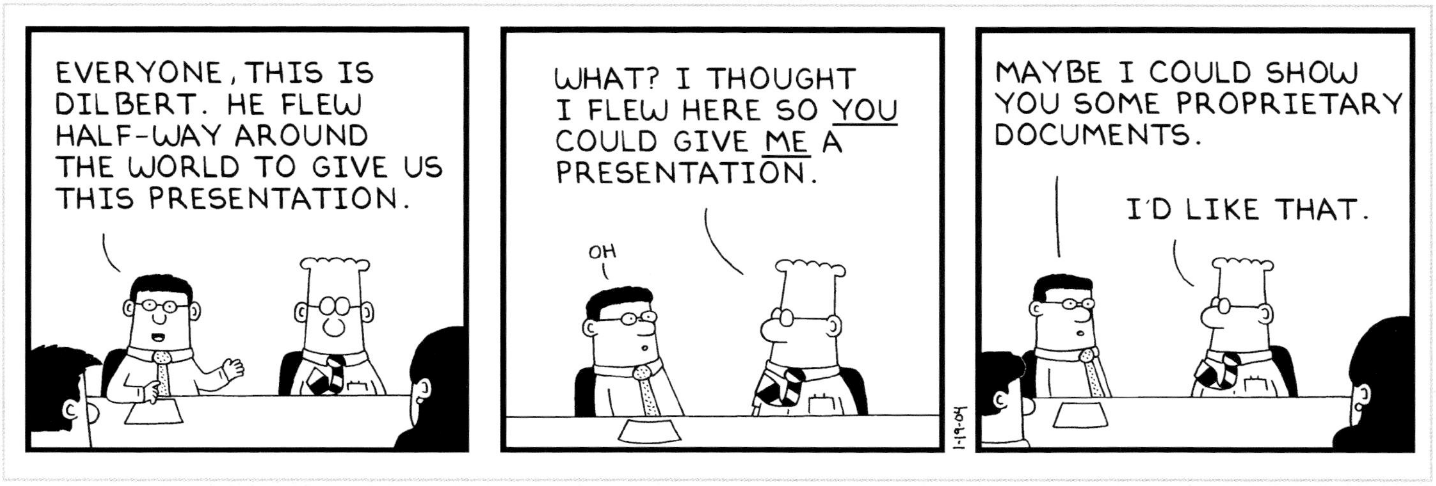
EVERYONE, THIS IS DILBERT. HE FLEW HALF-WAY AROUND THE WORLD TO GIVE US THIS PRESENTATION.
OH
WHAT? I THOUGHT I FLEW HERE SO YOU COULD GIVE ME A PRESENTATION.
1-19-04
MAYBE I COULD SHOW YOU SOME PROPRIETARY DOCUMENTS.
I'D LIKE THAT.

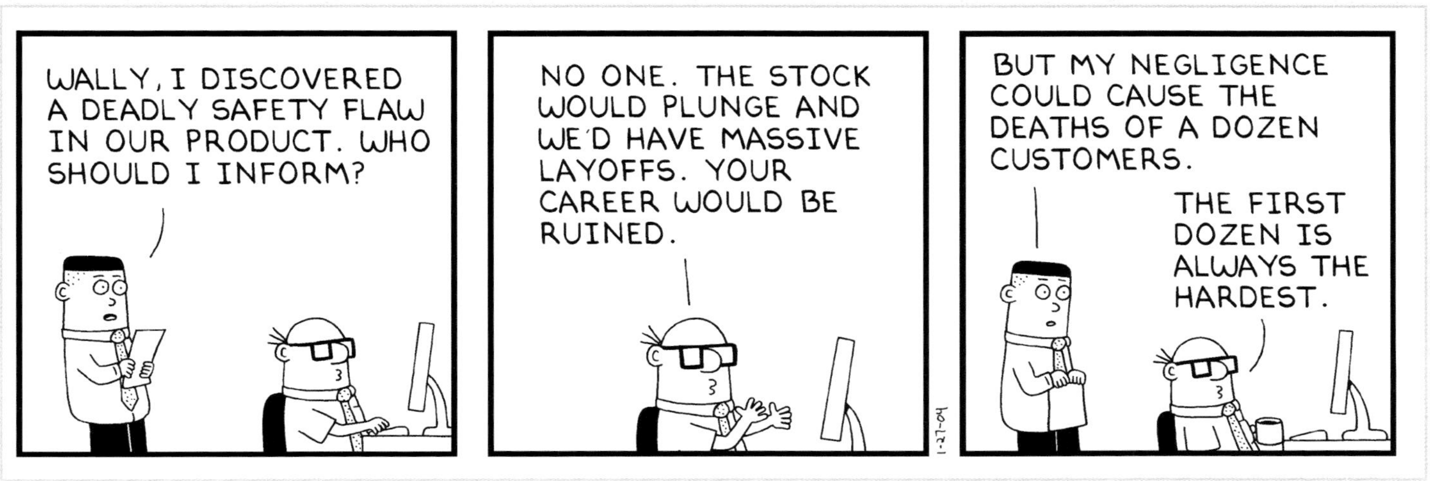
WALLY, I DISCOVERED A DEADLY SAFETY FLAW IN OUR PRODUCT. WHO SHOULD I INFORM?
NO ONE. THE STOCK WOULD PLUNGE AND WE'D HAVE MASSIVE LAYOFFS. YOUR CAREER WOULD BE RUINED.
1-27-04
BUT MY NEGLIGENCE COULD CAUSE THE DEATHS OF A DOZEN CUSTOMERS.
THE FIRST DOZEN IS ALWAYS THE HARDEST.

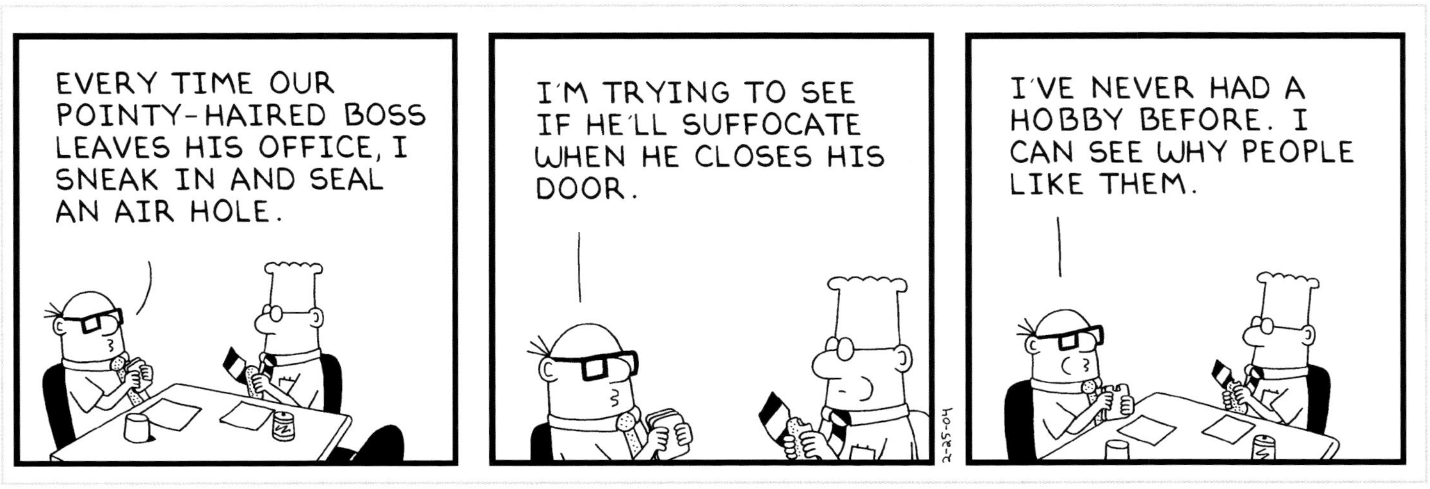
EVERY TIME OUR POINTY-HAIRED BOSS LEAVES HIS OFFICE, I SNEAK IN AND SEAL AN AIR HOLE.
I'M TRYING TO SEE IF HE'LL SUFFOCATE WHEN HE CLOSES HIS DOOR.
2-25-04
I'VE NEVER HAD A HOBBY BEFORE. I CAN SEE WHY PEOPLE LIKE THEM.

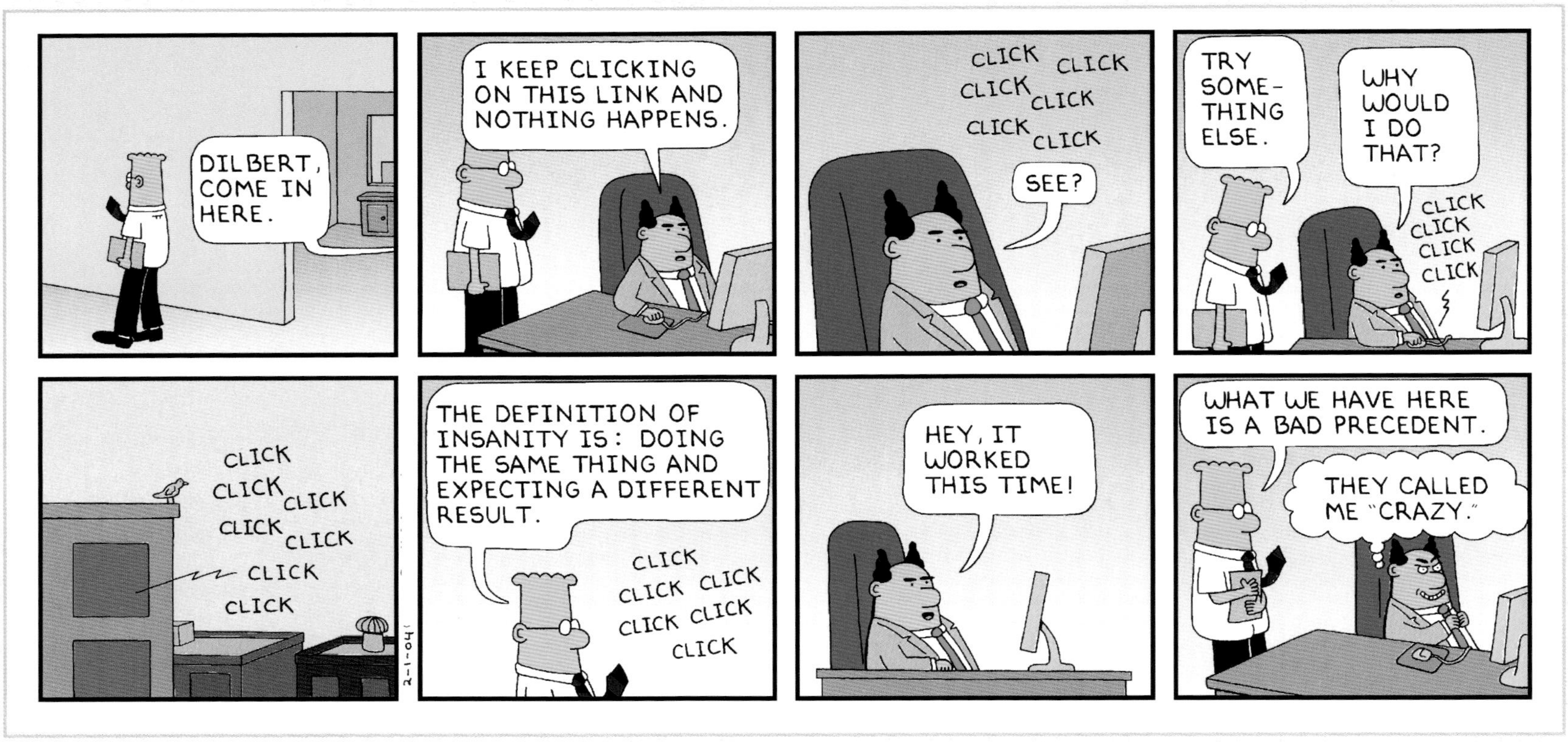
DILBERT, COME IN HERE.
I KEEP CLICKING ON THIS LINK AND NOTHING HAPPENS.
CLICK CLICK CLICK CLICK CLICK CLICK
SEE?
TRY SOME-THING ELSE.
WHY WOULD I DO THAT?
CLICK CLICK CLICK CLICK
CLICK CLICK CLICK CLICK CLICK CLICK CLICK
2-1-04
THE DEFINITION OF INSANITY IS: DOING THE SAME THING AND EXPECTING A DIFFERENT RESULT.
CLICK CLICK CLICK CLICK CLICK CLICK
HEY, IT WORKED THIS TIME!
WHAT WE HAVE HERE IS A BAD PRECEDENT.
THEY CALLED ME "CRAZY."

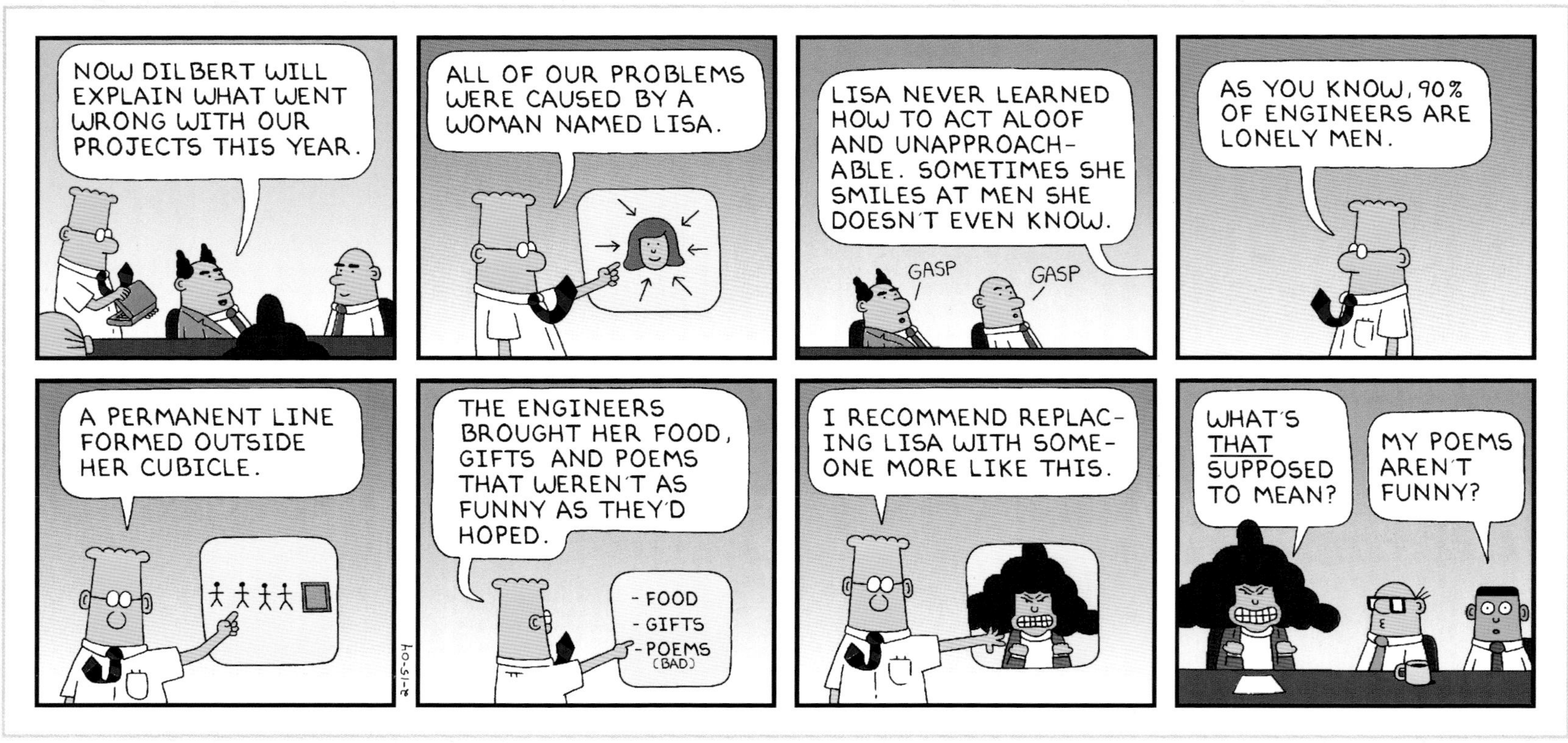
NOW DILBERT WILL EXPLAIN WHAT WENT WRONG WITH OUR PROJECTS THIS YEAR.
ALL OF OUR PROBLEMS WERE CAUSED BY A WOMAN NAMED LISA.
LISA NEVER LEARNED HOW TO ACT ALOOF AND UNAPPROACH-ABLE. SOMETIMES SHE SMILES AT MEN SHE DOESN'T EVEN KNOW.
GASP
GASP
AS YOU KNOW, 90% OF ENGINEERS ARE LONELY MEN.
A PERMANENT LINE FORMED OUTSIDE HER CUBICLE.
THE ENGINEERS BROUGHT HER FOOD, GIFTS AND POEMS THAT WEREN'T AS FUNNY AS THEY'D HOPED.
- FOOD
- GIFTS
- POEMS (BAD)
2-15-04
I RECOMMEND REPLAC-ING LISA WITH SOME-ONE MORE LIKE THIS.
WHAT'S THAT SUPPOSED TO MEAN?
MY POEMS AREN'T FUNNY?

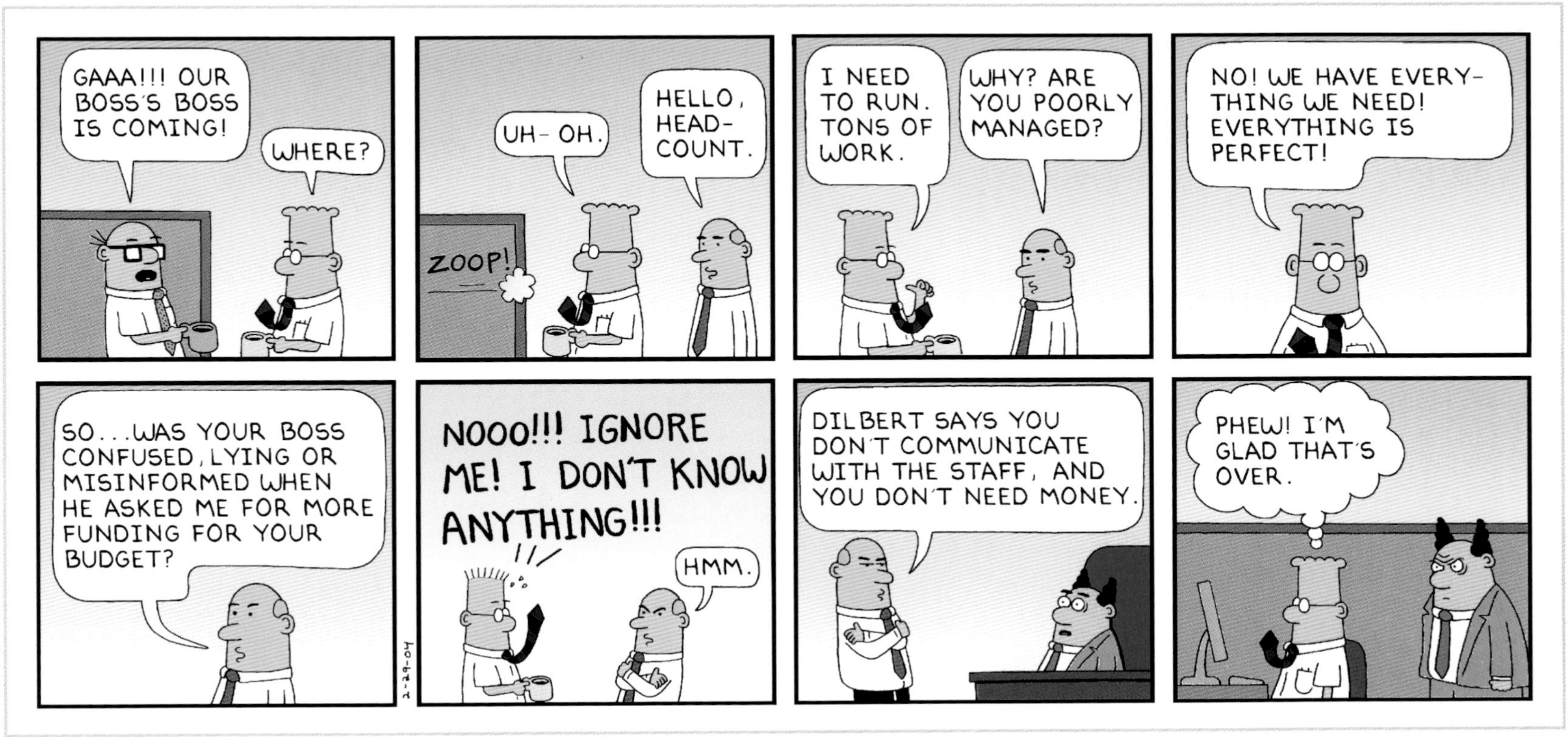
GAAA!!! OUR BOSS'S BOSS IS COMING!
WHERE?
UH-OH.
HELLO, HEAD-COUNT.
ZOOP!
I NEED TO RUN. TONS OF WORK.
WHY? ARE YOU POORLY MANAGED?
NO! WE HAVE EVERY-THING WE NEED! EVERYTHING IS PERFECT!
SO... WAS YOUR BOSS CONFUSED, LYING OR MISINFORMED WHEN HE ASKED ME FOR MORE FUNDING FOR YOUR BUDGET?
NOOO!!! IGNORE ME! I DON'T KNOW ANYTHING!!!
HMM.
DILBERT SAYS YOU DON'T COMMUNICATE WITH THE STAFF, AND YOU DON'T NEED MONEY.
PHEW! I'M GLAD THAT'S OVER.

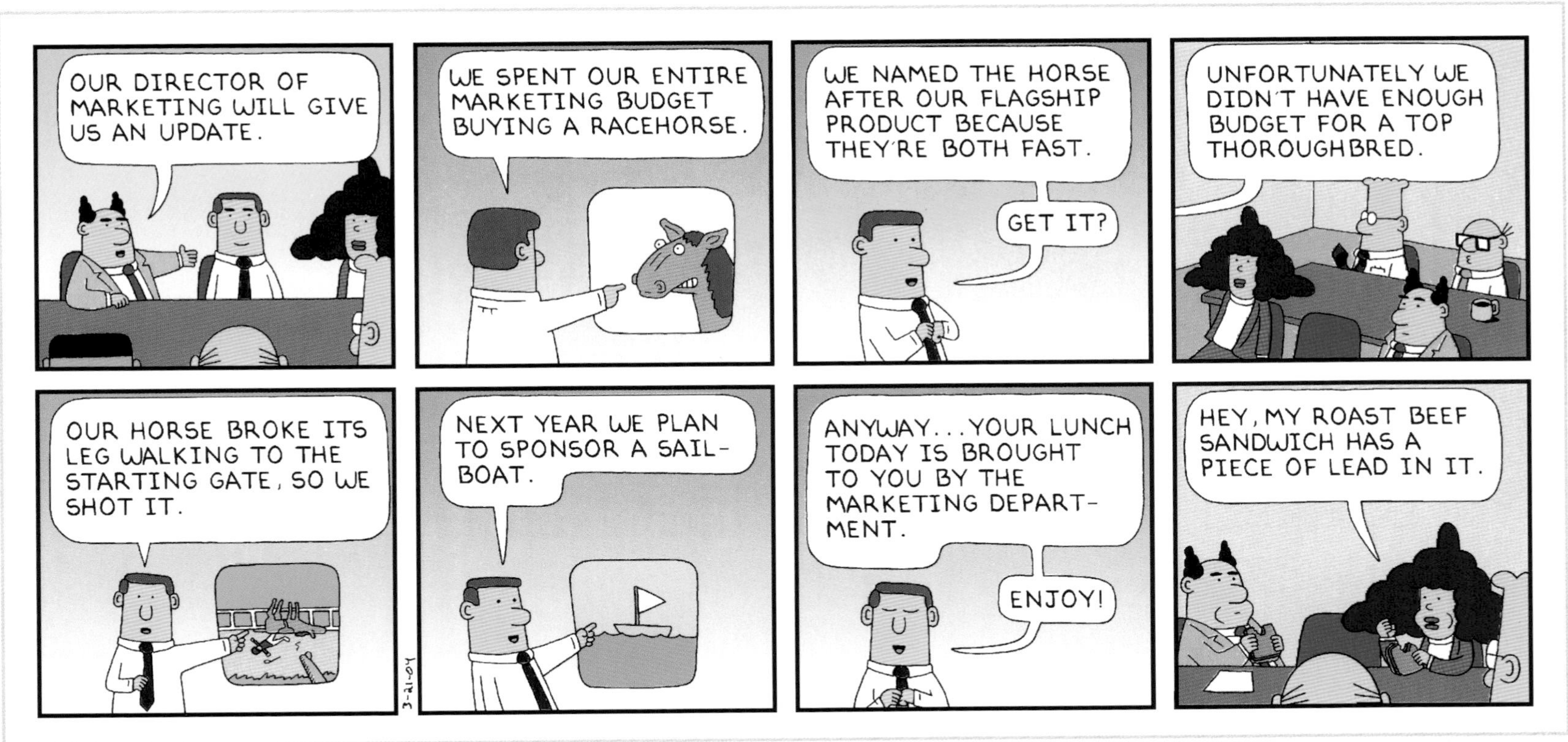
OUR DIRECTOR OF MARKETING WILL GIVE US AN UPDATE.
WE SPENT OUR ENTIRE MARKETING BUDGET BUYING A RACEHORSE.
WE NAMED THE HORSE AFTER OUR FLAGSHIP PRODUCT BECAUSE THEY'RE BOTH FAST.
GET IT?
UNFORTUNATELY WE DIDN'T HAVE ENOUGH BUDGET FOR A TOP THOROUGHBRED.
OUR HORSE BROKE ITS LEG WALKING TO THE STARTING GATE, SO WE SHOT IT.
NEXT YEAR WE PLAN TO SPONSOR A SAIL-BOAT.
ANYWAY... YOUR LUNCH TODAY IS BROUGHT TO YOU BY THE MARKETING DEPART-MENT.
ENJOY!
HEY, MY ROAST BEEF SANDWICH HAS A PIECE OF LEAD IN IT.

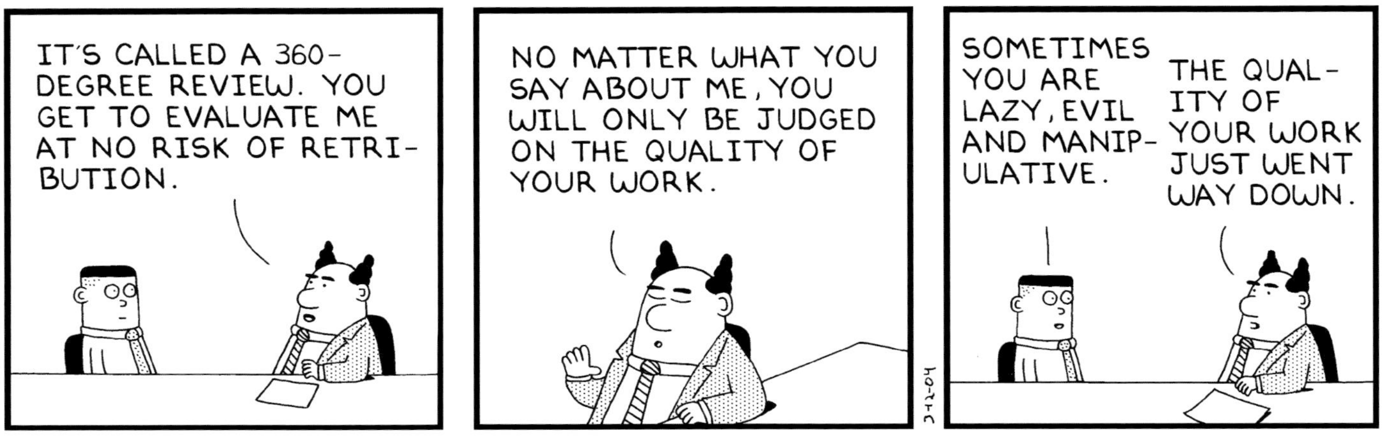
IT'S CALLED A 360-DEGREE REVIEW. YOU GET TO EVALUATE ME AT NO RISK OF RETRIBUTION.
NO MATTER WHAT YOU SAY ABOUT ME, YOU WILL ONLY BE JUDGED ON THE QUALITY OF YOUR WORK.
SOMETIMES YOU ARE LAZY, EVIL AND MANIPULATIVE.
THE QUALITY OF YOUR WORK JUST WENT WAY DOWN.
3-12-04

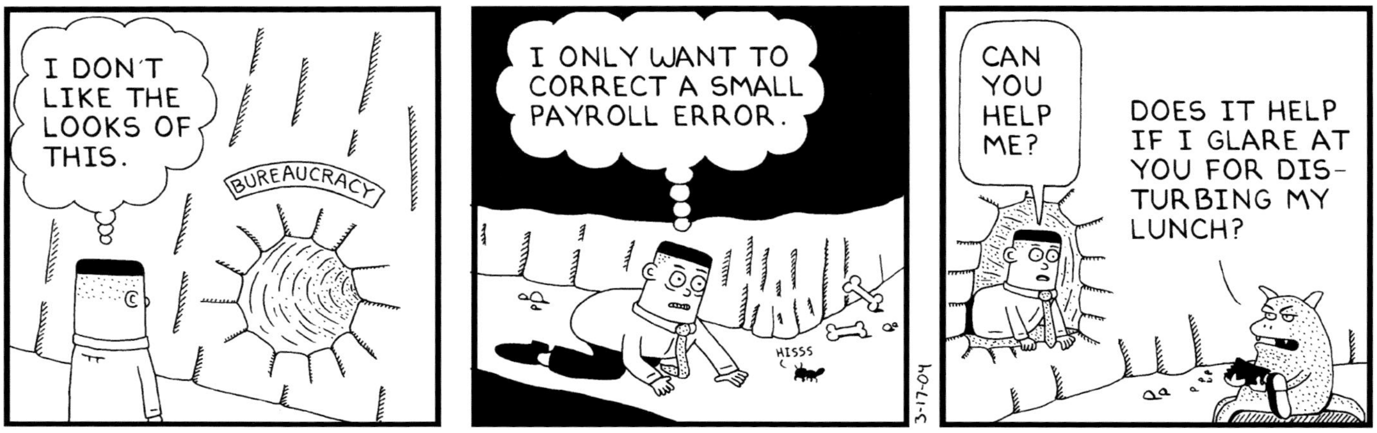
I DON'T LIKE THE LOOKS OF THIS.
BUREAUCRACY
I ONLY WANT TO CORRECT A SMALL PAYROLL ERROR.
HISSS
CAN YOU HELP ME?
DOES IT HELP IF I GLARE AT YOU FOR DISTURBING MY LUNCH?
3-17-04

Does the doorway to the bureaucracy look like a sphincter muscle? That's what I was shooting for.

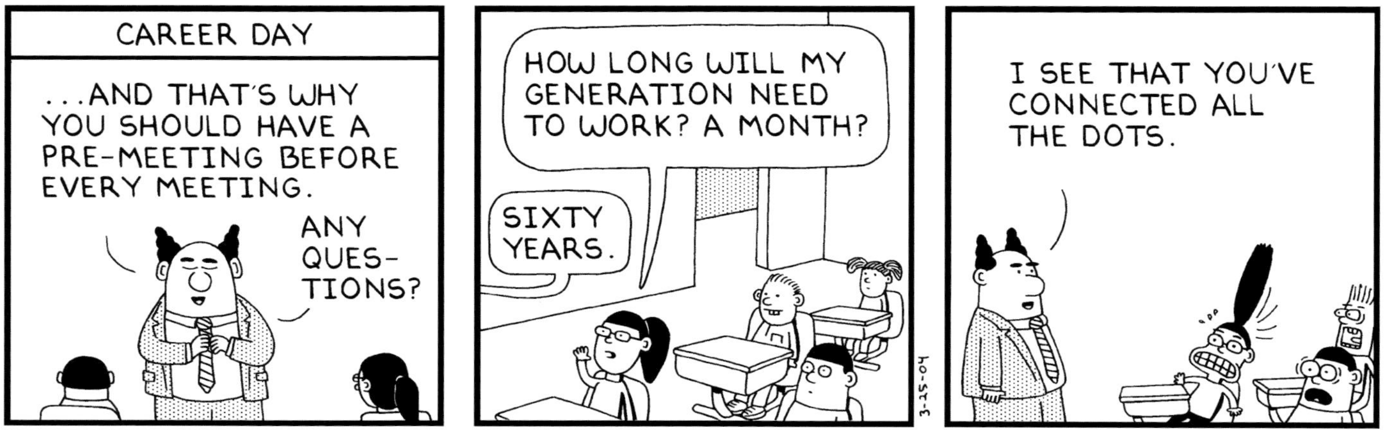
CAREER DAY
...AND THAT'S WHY YOU SHOULD HAVE A PRE-MEETING BEFORE EVERY MEETING.
ANY QUESTIONS?
HOW LONG WILL MY GENERATION NEED TO WORK? A MONTH?
SIXTY YEARS.
3-25-04
I SEE THAT YOU'VE CONNECTED ALL THE DOTS.

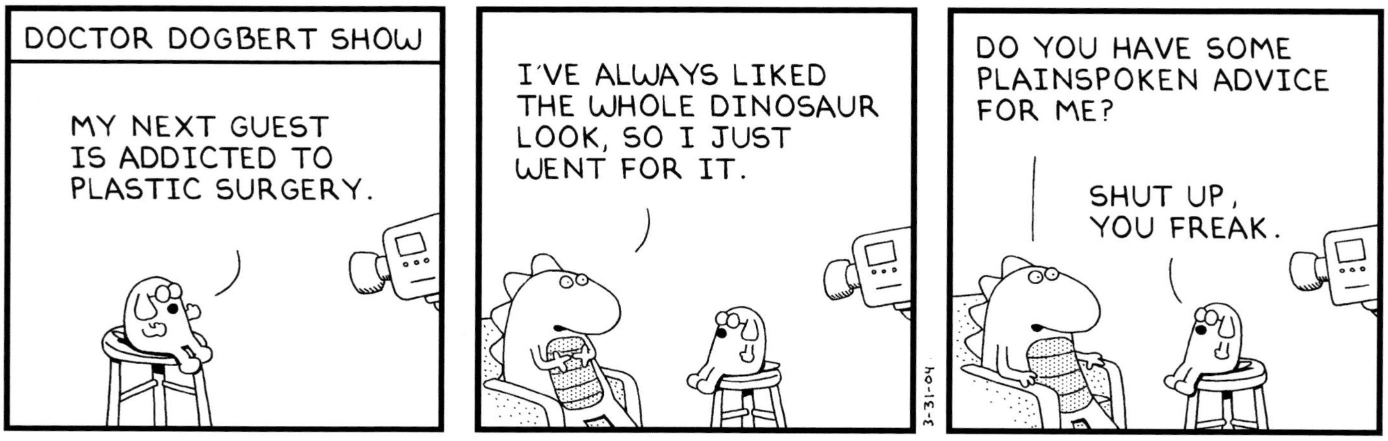
DOCTOR DOGBERT SHOW
MY NEXT GUEST IS ADDICTED TO PLASTIC SURGERY.
I'VE ALWAYS LIKED THE WHOLE DINOSAUR LOOK, SO I JUST WENT FOR IT.
3-31-04
DO YOU HAVE SOME PLAINSPOKEN ADVICE FOR ME?
SHUT UP, YOU FREAK.

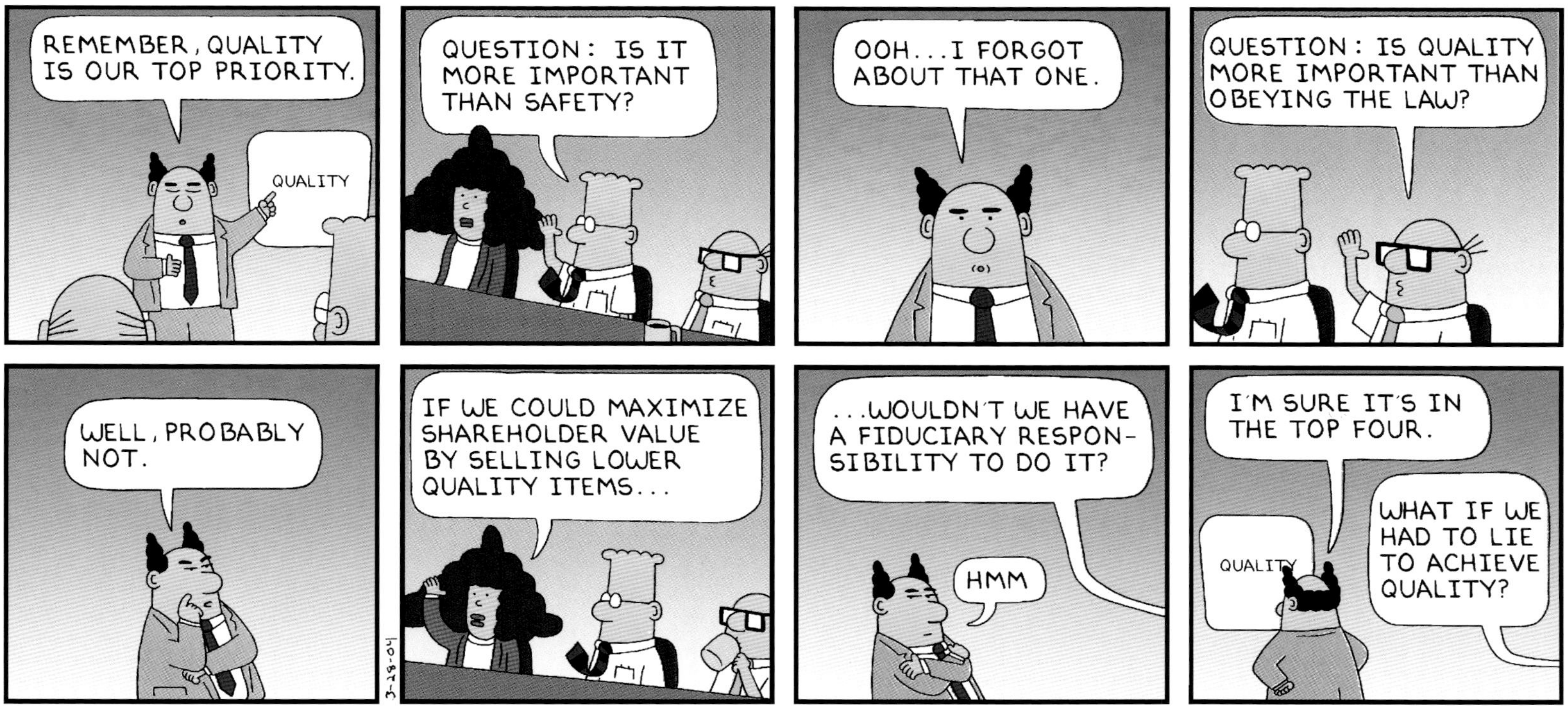
REMEMBER, QUALITY IS OUR TOP PRIORITY.
QUALITY
QUESTION: IS IT MORE IMPORTANT THAN SAFETY?
OOH... I FORGOT ABOUT THAT ONE.
QUESTION: IS QUALITY MORE IMPORTANT THAN OBEYING THE LAW?
WELL, PROBABLY NOT.
IF WE COULD MAXIMIZE SHAREHOLDER VALUE BY SELLING LOWER QUALITY ITEMS...
3-28-04
...WOULDN'T WE HAVE A FIDUCIARY RESPONSIBILITY TO DO IT?
HMM
I'M SURE IT'S IN THE TOP FOUR.
QUALITY
WHAT IF WE HAD TO LIE TO ACHIEVE QUALITY?

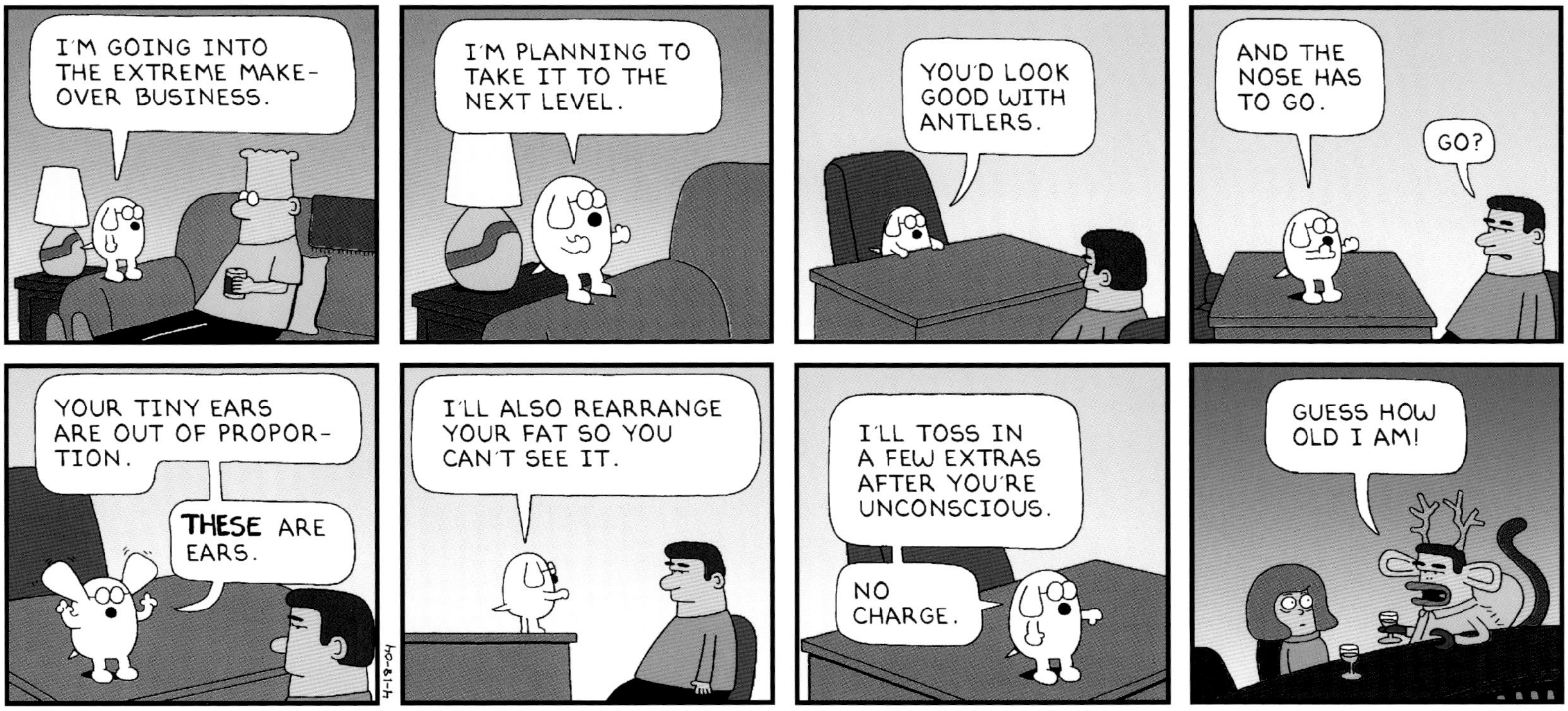
I'M GOING INTO THE EXTREME MAKEOVER BUSINESS.
I'M PLANNING TO TAKE IT TO THE NEXT LEVEL.
YOU'D LOOK GOOD WITH ANTLERS.
AND THE NOSE HAS TO GO.
GO?
YOUR TINY EARS ARE OUT OF PROPORTION.
THESE ARE EARS.
4-18-04
I'LL ALSO REARRANGE YOUR FAT SO YOU CAN'T SEE IT.
I'LL TOSS IN A FEW EXTRAS AFTER YOU'RE UNCONSCIOUS.
NO CHARGE.
GUESS HOW OLD I AM!

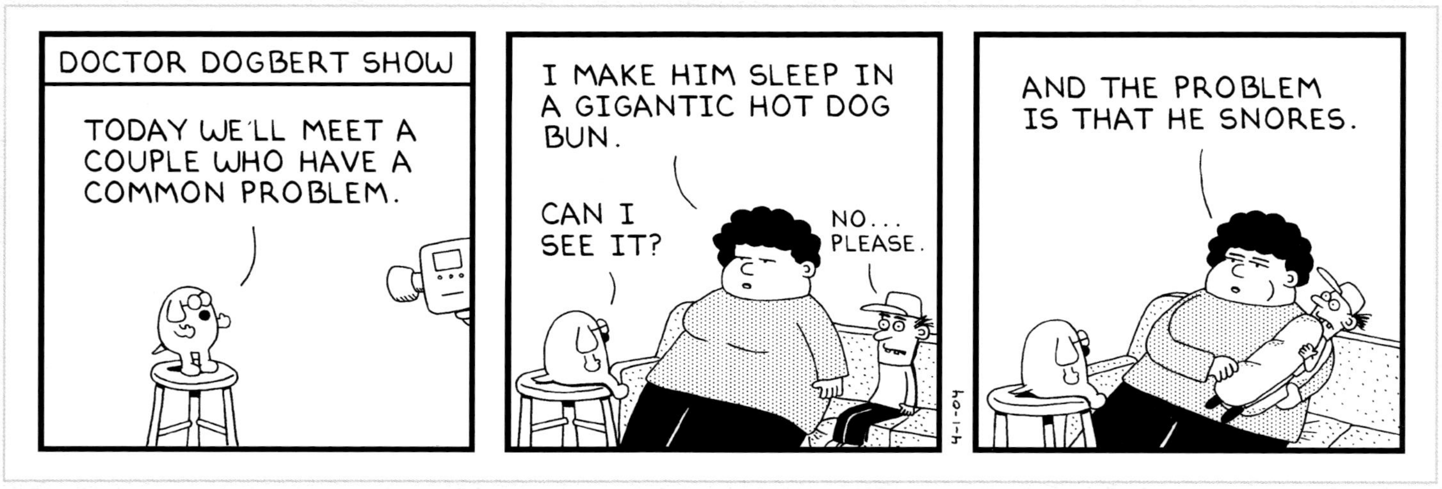
DOCTOR DOGBERT SHOW
TODAY WE'LL MEET A COUPLE WHO HAVE A COMMON PROBLEM.
I MAKE HIM SLEEP IN A GIGANTIC HOT DOG BUN.
CAN I SEE IT?
NO... PLEASE.
AND THE PROBLEM IS THAT HE SNORES.
4-1-04

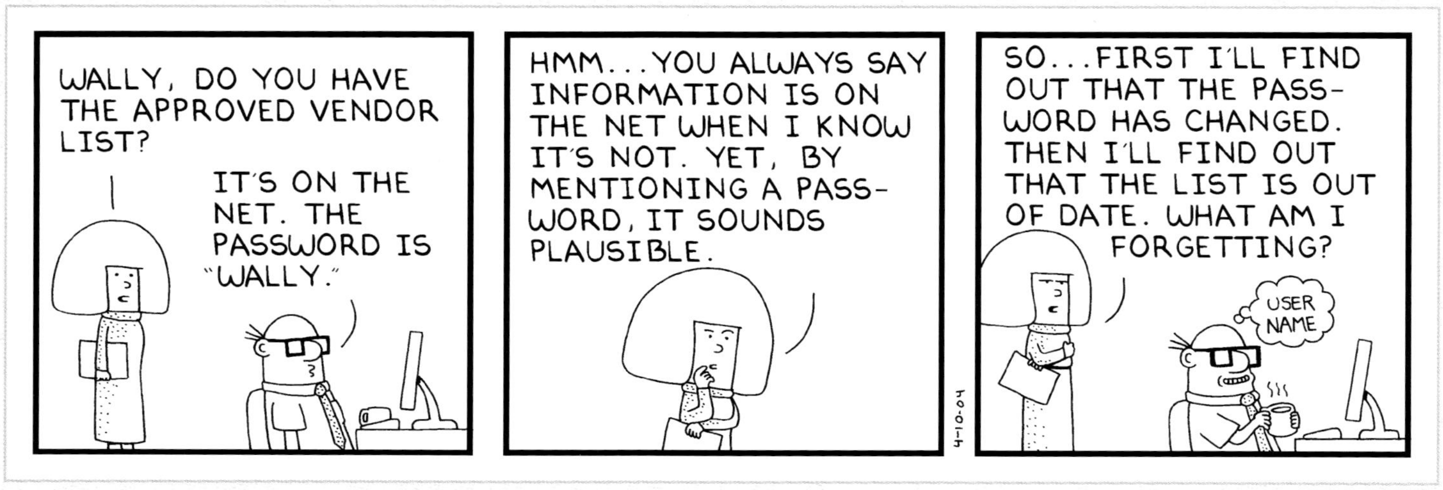
WALLY, DO YOU HAVE THE APPROVED VENDOR LIST?
IT'S ON THE NET. THE PASSWORD IS "WALLY."
HMM...YOU ALWAYS SAY INFORMATION IS ON THE NET WHEN I KNOW IT'S NOT. YET, BY MENTIONING A PASS-WORD, IT SOUNDS PLAUSIBLE.
SO...FIRST I'LL FIND OUT THAT THE PASS-WORD HAS CHANGED. THEN I'LL FIND OUT THAT THE LIST IS OUT OF DATE. WHAT AM I FORGETTING?
USER NAME
4-10-04

If this comic seems unfinished, that's because it is. In the last step, I generally put the black in Tina's hair and the desk chairs. I must have been in a hurry.

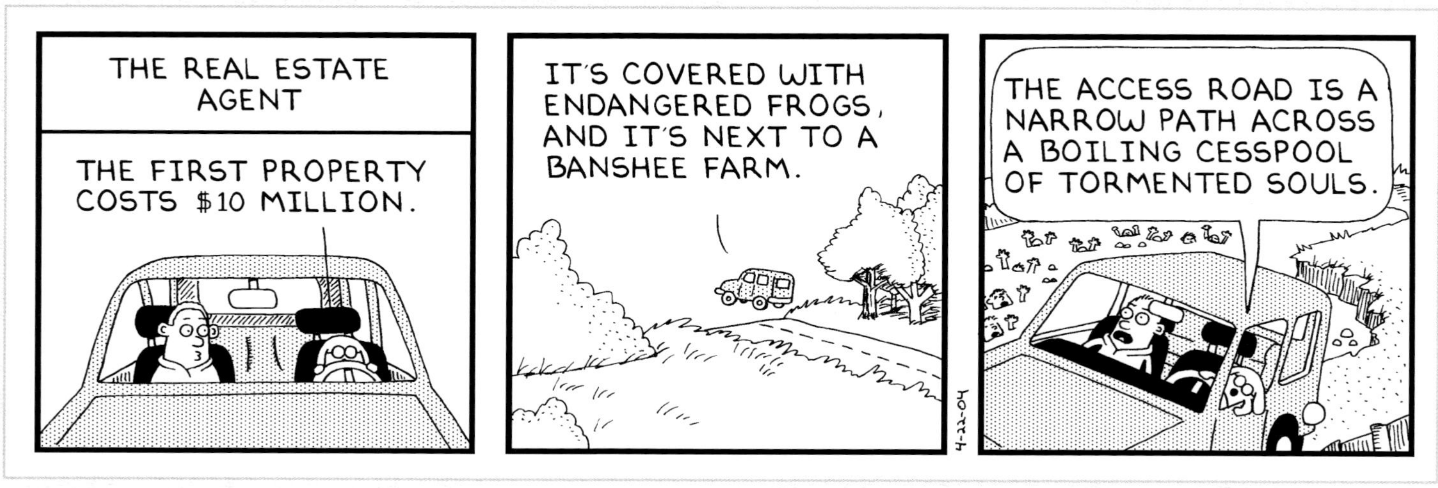
THE REAL ESTATE AGENT
THE FIRST PROPERTY COSTS $10 MILLION.
IT'S COVERED WITH ENDANGERED FROGS, AND IT'S NEXT TO A BANSHEE FARM.
THE ACCESS ROAD IS A NARROW PATH ACROSS A BOILING CESSPOOL OF TORMENTED SOULS.
4-22-04

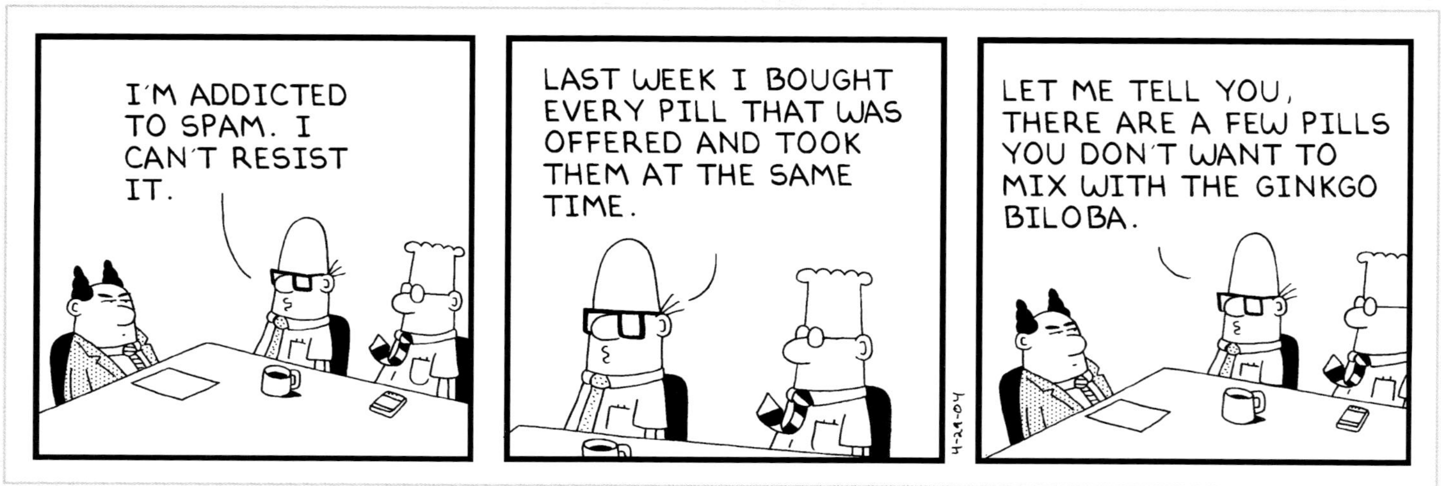
I'M ADDICTED TO SPAM. I CAN'T RESIST IT.
LAST WEEK I BOUGHT EVERY PILL THAT WAS OFFERED AND TOOK THEM AT THE SAME TIME.
LET ME TELL YOU, THERE ARE A FEW PILLS YOU DON'T WANT TO MIX WITH THE GINKGO BILOBA.

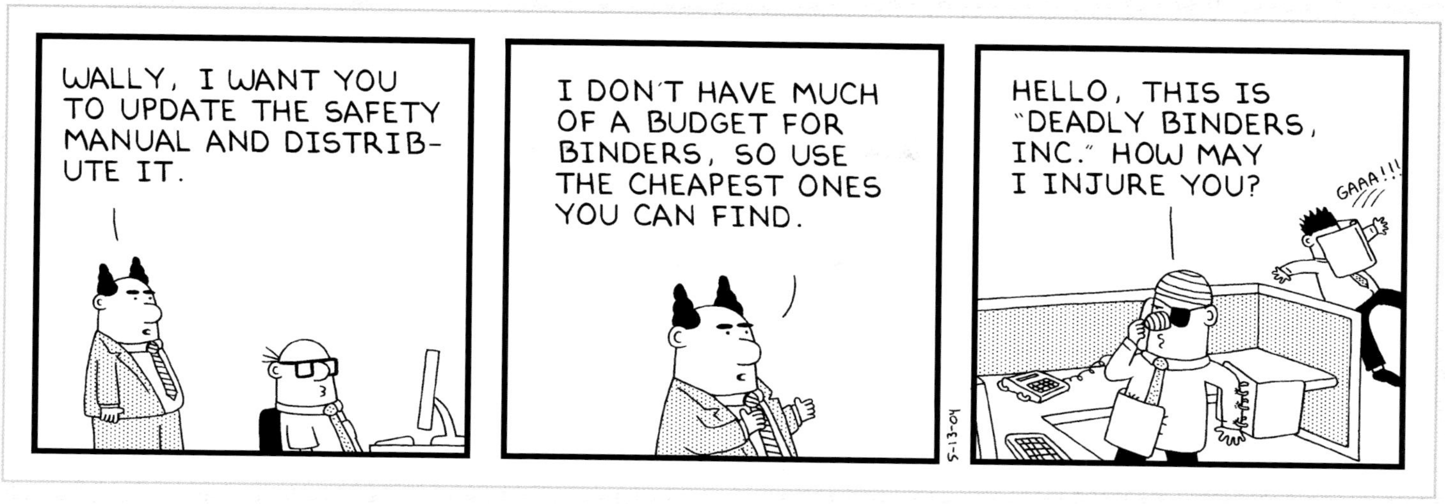
WALLY, I WANT YOU TO UPDATE THE SAFETY MANUAL AND DISTRIBUTE IT.
I DON'T HAVE MUCH OF A BUDGET FOR BINDERS, SO USE THE CHEAPEST ONES YOU CAN FIND.
5-13-04
HELLO, THIS IS "DEADLY BINDERS, INC." HOW MAY I INJURE YOU?
GAAA!!!

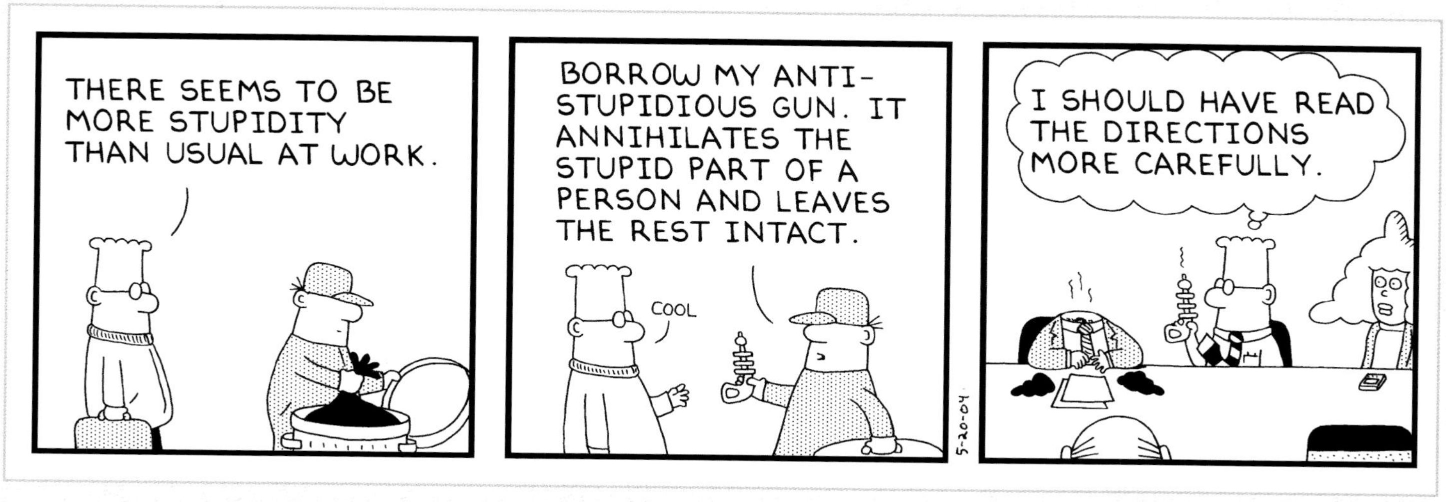
THERE SEEMS TO BE MORE STUPIDITY THAN USUAL AT WORK.
BORROW MY ANTI-STUPIDIOUS GUN. IT ANNIHILATES THE STUPID PART OF A PERSON AND LEAVES THE REST INTACT.
COOL
5-20-04
I SHOULD HAVE READ THE DIRECTIONS MORE CAREFULLY.

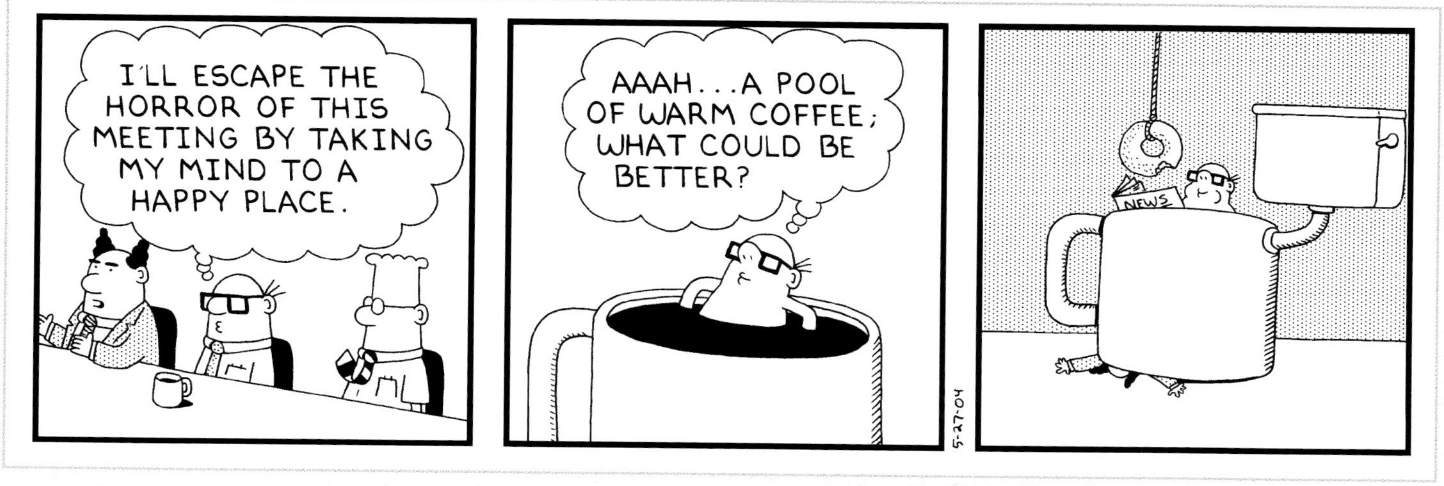
I'LL ESCAPE THE HORROR OF THIS MEETING BY TAKING MY MIND TO A HAPPY PLACE.
AAAH...A POOL OF WARM COFFEE; WHAT COULD BE BETTER?
5-27-04
NEWS

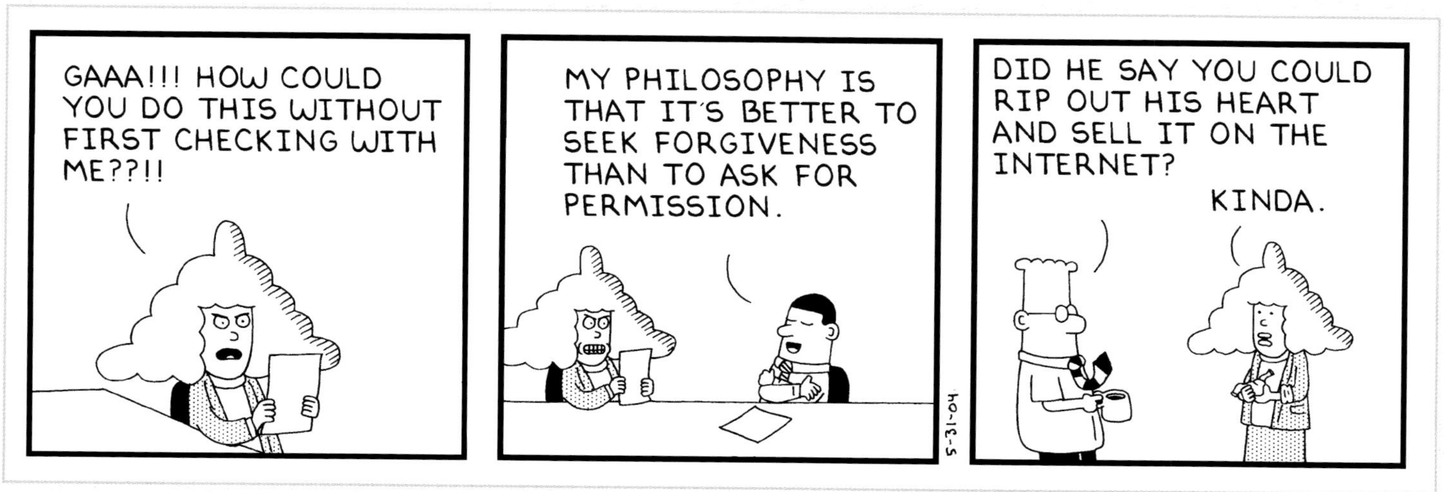
GAAA!!! HOW COULD YOU DO THIS WITHOUT FIRST CHECKING WITH ME??!!
MY PHILOSOPHY IS THAT IT'S BETTER TO SEEK FORGIVENESS THAN TO ASK FOR PERMISSION.
5-31-04
DID HE SAY YOU COULD RIP OUT HIS HEART AND SELL IT ON THE INTERNET?
KINDA.

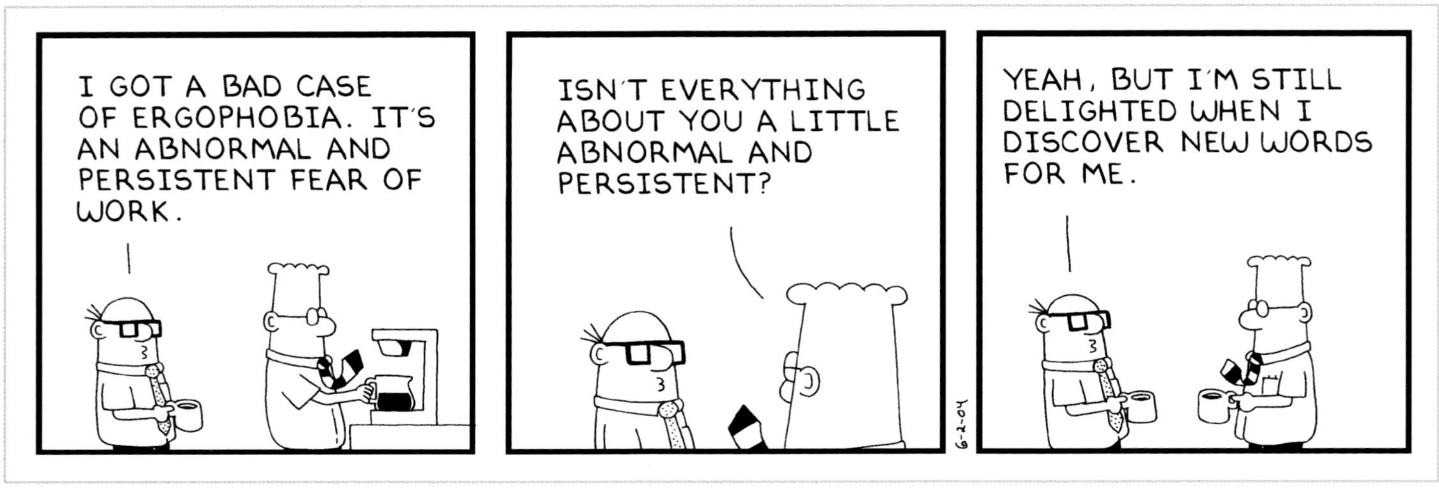
I GOT A BAD CASE OF ERGOPHOBIA. IT'S AN ABNORMAL AND PERSISTENT FEAR OF WORK.
ISN'T EVERYTHING ABOUT YOU A LITTLE ABNORMAL AND PERSISTENT?
6-2-04
YEAH, BUT I'M STILL DELIGHTED WHEN I DISCOVER NEW WORDS FOR ME.

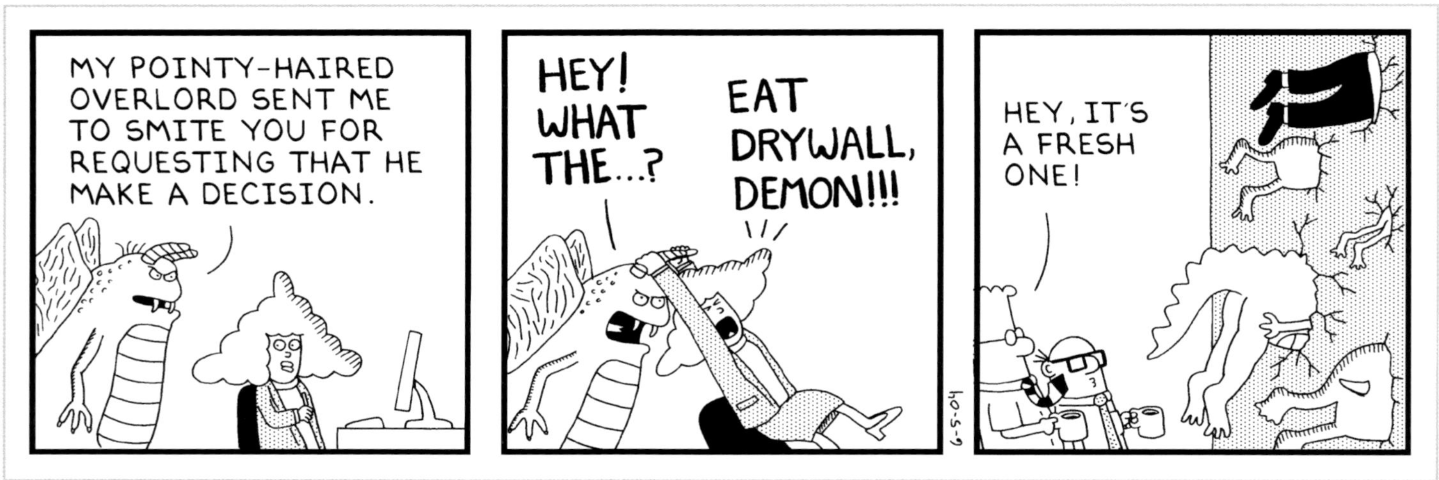
MY POINTY-HAIRED OVERLORD SENT ME TO SMITE YOU FOR REQUESTING THAT HE MAKE A DECISION.
HEY! WHAT THE...?
EAT DRYWALL, DEMON!!!
6-5-04
HEY, IT'S A FRESH ONE!

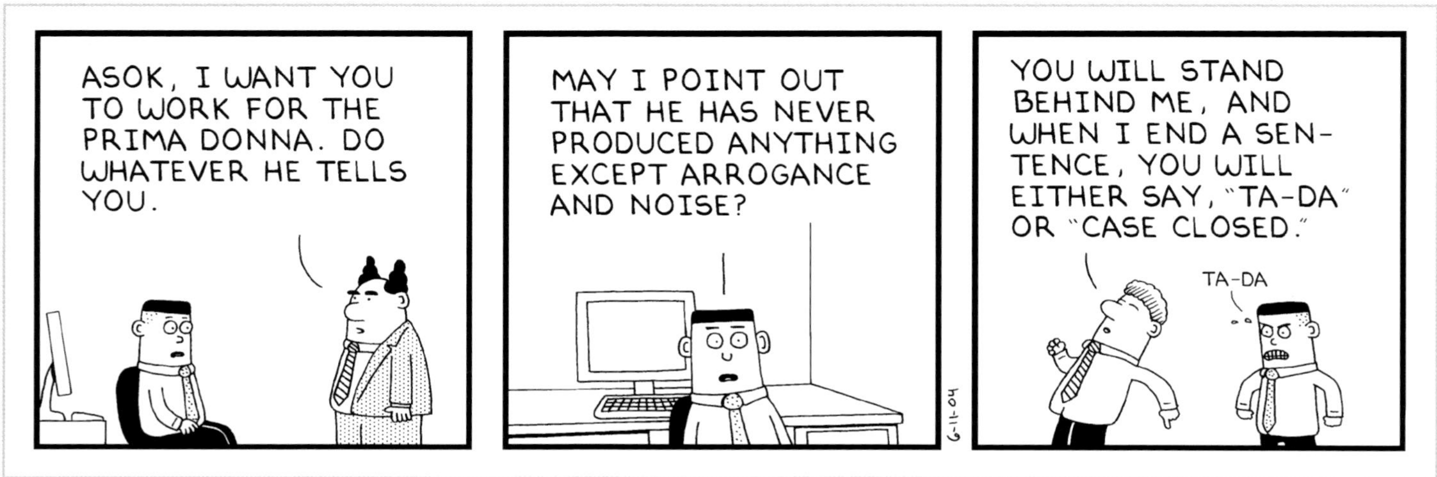
ASOK, I WANT YOU TO WORK FOR THE PRIMA DONNA. DO WHATEVER HE TELLS YOU.
MAY I POINT OUT THAT HE HAS NEVER PRODUCED ANYTHING EXCEPT ARROGANCE AND NOISE?
6-11-04
YOU WILL STAND BEHIND ME, AND WHEN I END A SENTENCE, YOU WILL EITHER SAY, "TA-DA" OR "CASE CLOSED."
TA-DA

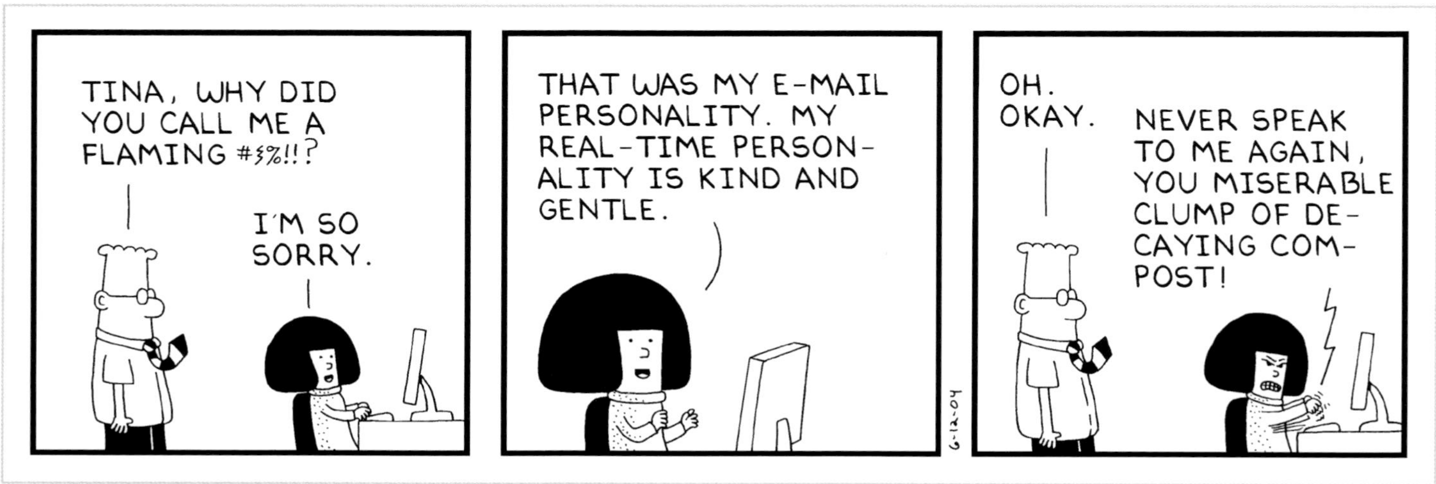
TINA, WHY DID YOU CALL ME A FLAMING #$%!!?
I'M SO SORRY.
THAT WAS MY E-MAIL PERSONALITY. MY REAL-TIME PERSONALITY IS KIND AND GENTLE.
6-12-04
OH. OKAY.
NEVER SPEAK TO ME AGAIN, YOU MISERABLE CLUMP OF DECAYING COMPOST!

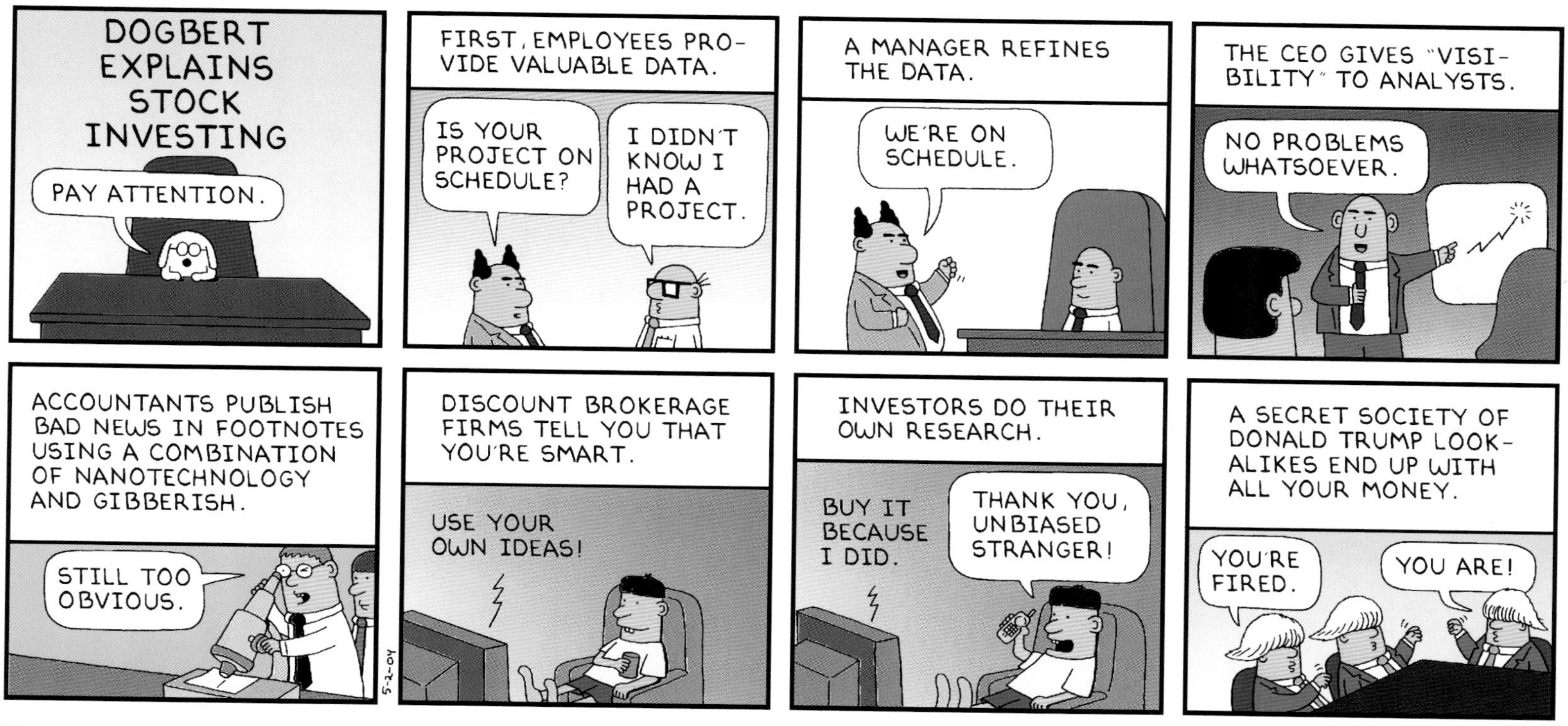
DOGBERT EXPLAINS STOCK INVESTING
PAY ATTENTION.
FIRST, EMPLOYEES PROVIDE VALUABLE DATA.
IS YOUR PROJECT ON SCHEDULE?
I DIDN'T KNOW I HAD A PROJECT.
A MANAGER REFINES THE DATA.
WE'RE ON SCHEDULE.
THE CEO GIVES "VISIBILITY" TO ANALYSTS.
NO PROBLEMS WHATSOEVER.
ACCOUNTANTS PUBLISH BAD NEWS IN FOOTNOTES USING A COMBINATION OF NANOTECHNOLOGY AND GIBBERISH.
STILL TOO OBVIOUS.
5-2-04
DISCOUNT BROKERAGE FIRMS TELL YOU THAT YOU'RE SMART.
USE YOUR OWN IDEAS!
INVESTORS DO THEIR OWN RESEARCH.
BUY IT BECAUSE I DID.
THANK YOU, UNBIASED STRANGER!
A SECRET SOCIETY OF DONALD TRUMP LOOK-ALIKES END UP WITH ALL YOUR MONEY.
YOU'RE FIRED.
YOU ARE!

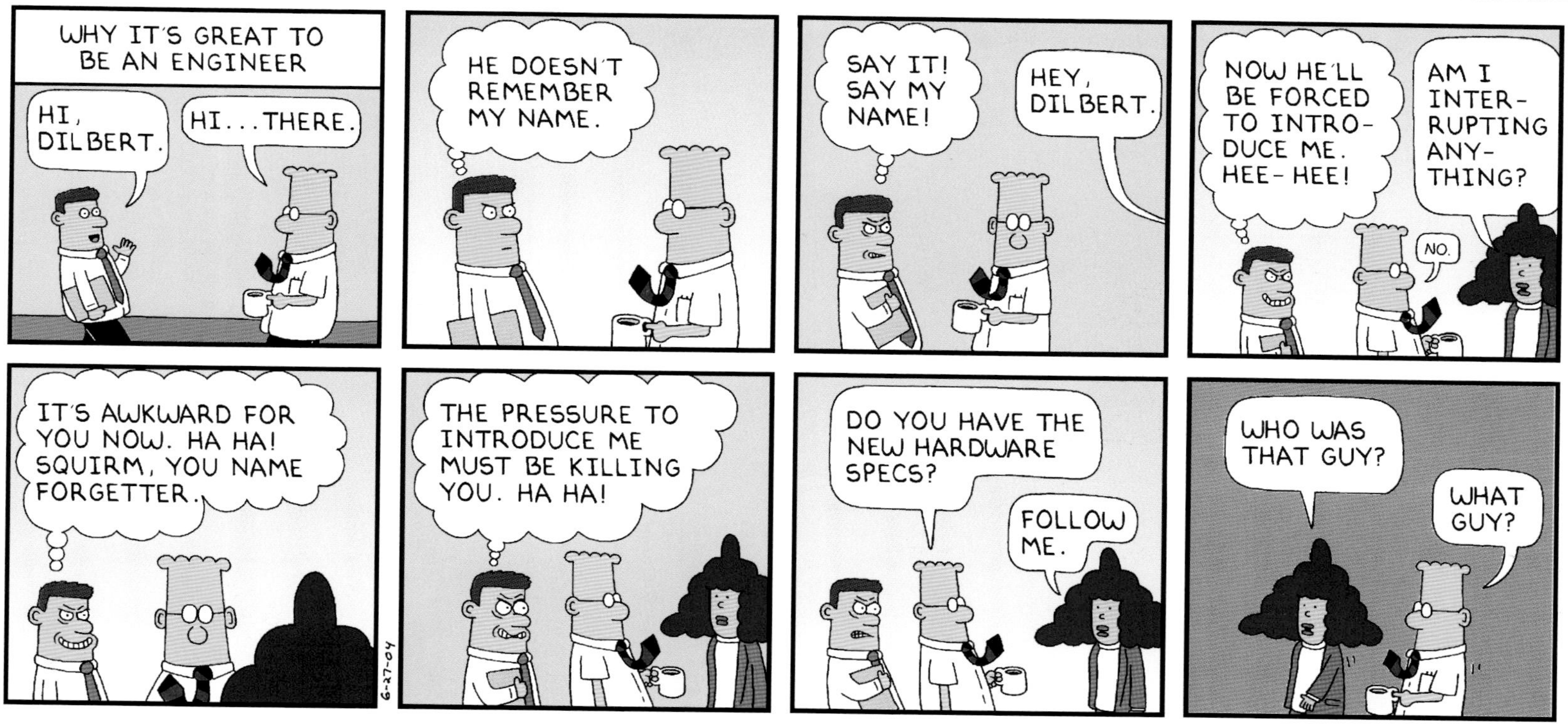
WHY IT'S GREAT TO BE AN ENGINEER
HI, DILBERT.
HI... THERE.
HE DOESN'T REMEMBER MY NAME.
SAY IT! SAY MY NAME!
HEY, DILBERT.
NOW HE'LL BE FORCED TO INTRODUCE ME. HEE-HEE!
AM I INTERRUPTING ANYTHING?
NO.
IT'S AWKWARD FOR YOU NOW. HA HA! SQUIRM, YOU NAME FORGETTER.
6-27-04
THE PRESSURE TO INTRODUCE ME MUST BE KILLING YOU. HA HA!
DO YOU HAVE THE NEW HARDWARE SPECS?
FOLLOW ME.
WHO WAS THAT GUY?
WHAT GUY?

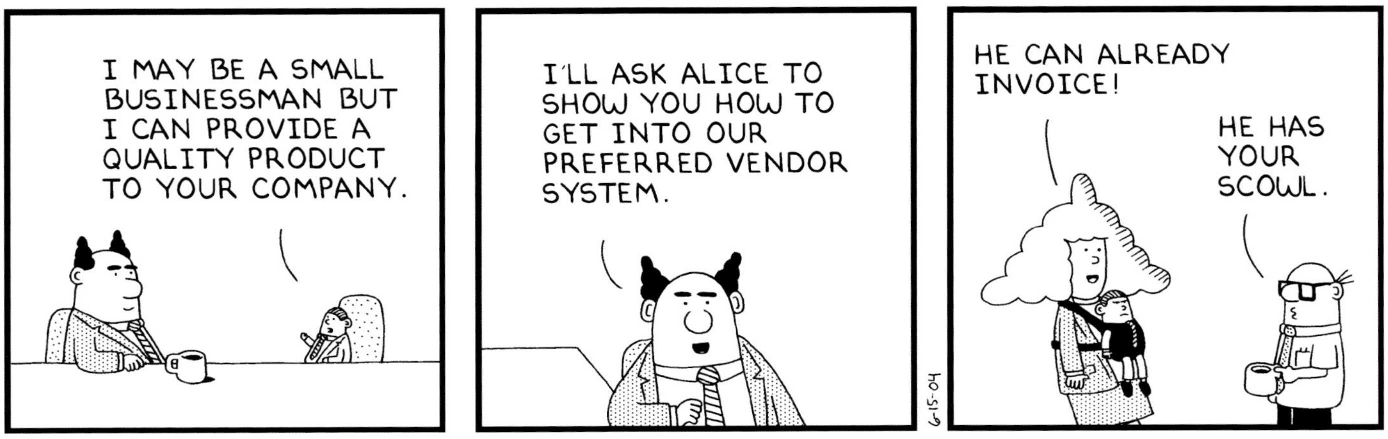
I MAY BE A SMALL BUSINESSMAN BUT I CAN PROVIDE A QUALITY PRODUCT TO YOUR COMPANY.
I'LL ASK ALICE TO SHOW YOU HOW TO GET INTO OUR PREFERRED VENDOR SYSTEM.
6-15-04
HE CAN ALREADY INVOICE!
HE HAS YOUR SCOWL.

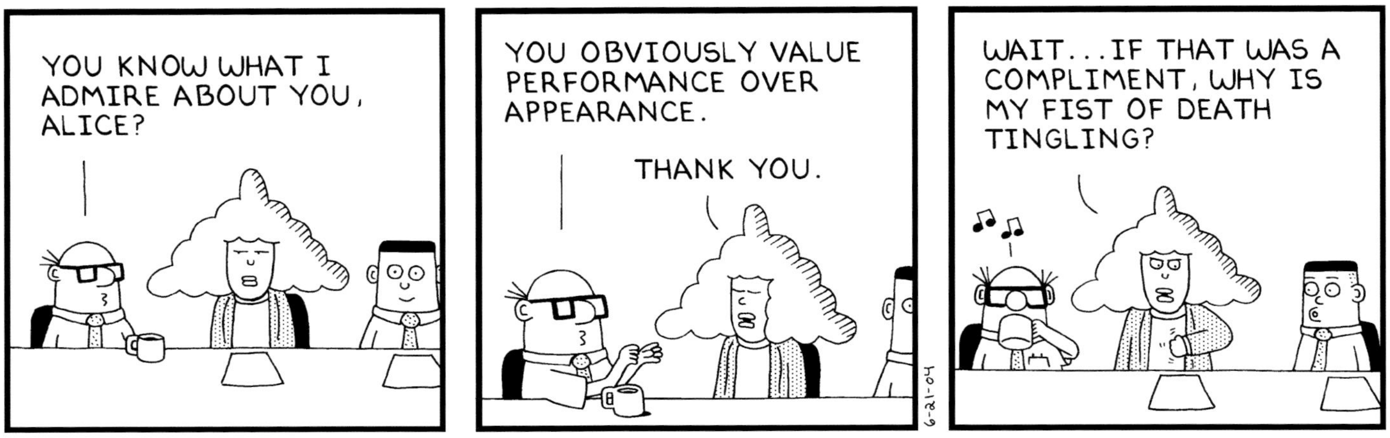
YOU KNOW WHAT I ADMIRE ABOUT YOU, ALICE?
YOU OBVIOUSLY VALUE PERFORMANCE OVER APPEARANCE.
THANK YOU.
6-21-04
WAIT...IF THAT WAS A COMPLIMENT, WHY IS MY FIST OF DEATH TINGLING?

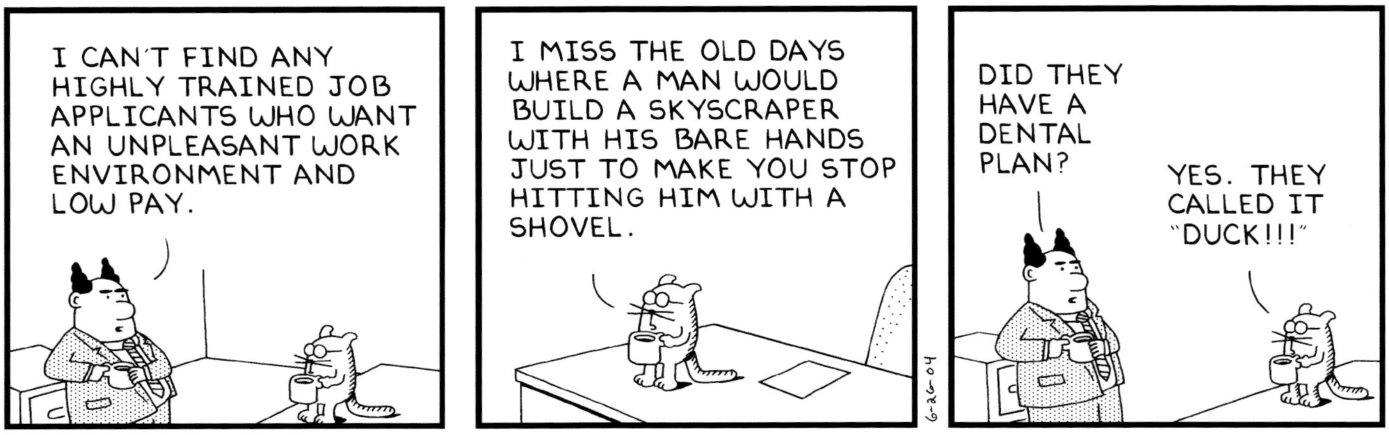
I CAN'T FIND ANY HIGHLY TRAINED JOB APPLICANTS WHO WANT AN UNPLEASANT WORK ENVIRONMENT AND LOW PAY.
I MISS THE OLD DAYS WHERE A MAN WOULD BUILD A SKYSCRAPER WITH HIS BARE HANDS JUST TO MAKE YOU STOP HITTING HIM WITH A SHOVEL.
6-26-04
DID THEY HAVE A DENTAL PLAN?
YES. THEY CALLED IT "DUCK!!!"

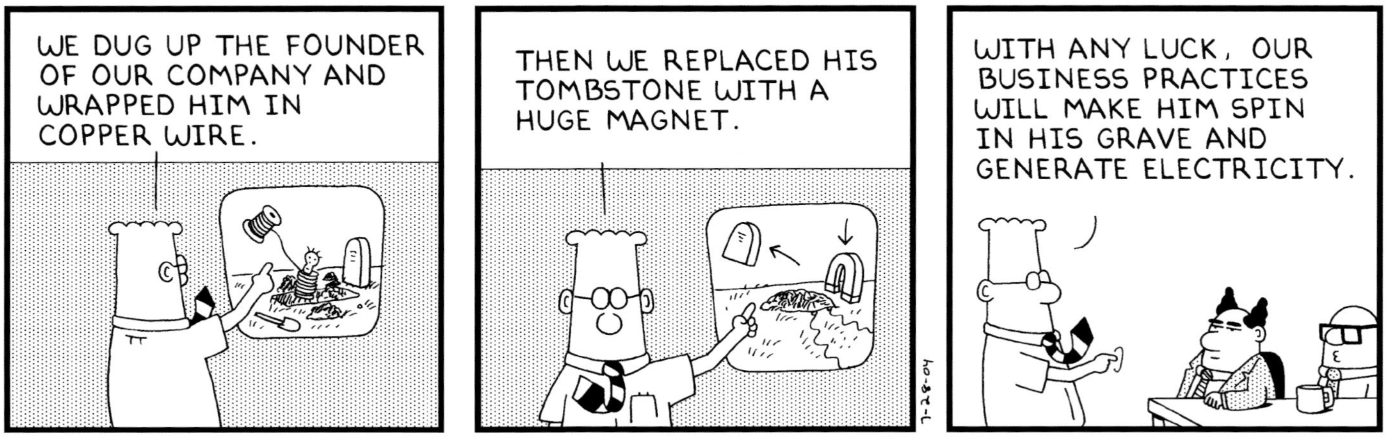
WE DUG UP THE FOUNDER OF OUR COMPANY AND WRAPPED HIM IN COPPER WIRE.
THEN WE REPLACED HIS TOMBSTONE WITH A HUGE MAGNET.
7-28-04
WITH ANY LUCK, OUR BUSINESS PRACTICES WILL MAKE HIM SPIN IN HIS GRAVE AND GENERATE ELECTRICITY.

DILBERT, THIS IS PROXIS. I RECRUITED HIM FROM THE GULLIBLE NEBULA.
I CONVINCED HIM TO RELOCATE HIS FAMILY.
HELLO.
MY SPACESHIP WAS DESTROYED DURING THE LANDING, BUT THAT'S NO PROBLEM.
I EXPECT TO WORK HERE FOR THE REST OF MY 300-YEAR LIFESPAN.
THAT REMINDS ME: WE NEED TO TALK.
7-11-04
YOUR JOB FUNCTION HAS BEEN OUTSOURCED. I HAVE TO LET YOU GO.
YOUR SEVERANCE PACKAGE IS: I GRAB YOU BY THE SNOUT AND FLING YOU ONTO THE SIDEWALK.
MAY I USE YOU AS A REFERENCE?

OUR VP OF MARKETING IS HERE TO DESCRIBE OUR NEW BET-THE-COMPANY STRATEGY.
WE'LL SATURATE THE AIRWAVES WITH AN AD CAMPAIGN FEATURING A TALKING SQUIRREL.
HE'LL HAVE A FAKE NORWEGIAN ACCENT LIKE, "GEEVE ME ZEE NUTS." HA HA!
ANY QUESTIONS?
YES, YOU WITH THE STRANGE HEAD.
HOW WILL A TALKING SQUIRREL MAKE PEOPLE BUY OUR PRODUCTS?
7-25-04
I JUST REALIZED I'M A COMPLETE FRAUD. I'LL PACK UP MY DESK AND LEAVE IMMEDIATELY.
CAN WE GET THROUGH ONE MEETING WITHOUT YOU RUINING EVERYTHING?

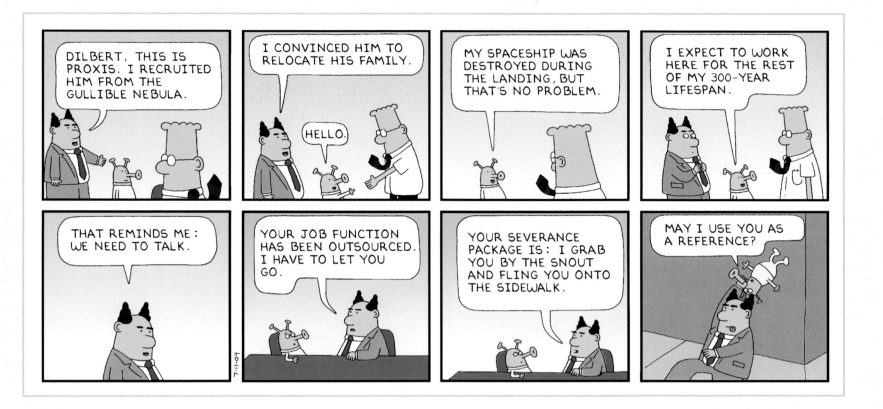

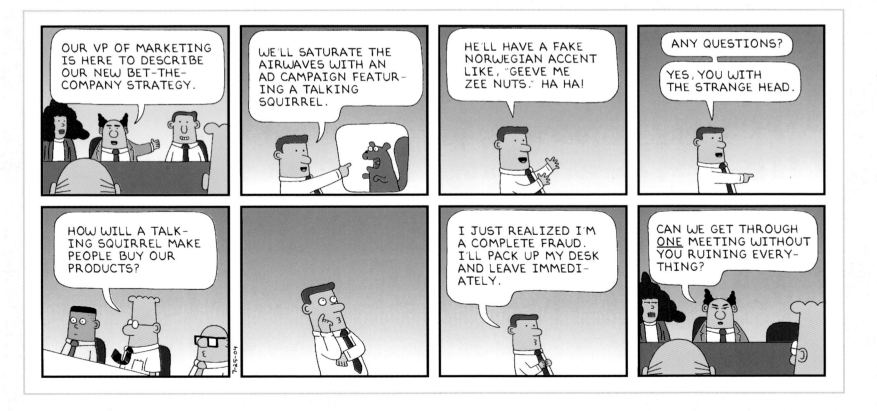

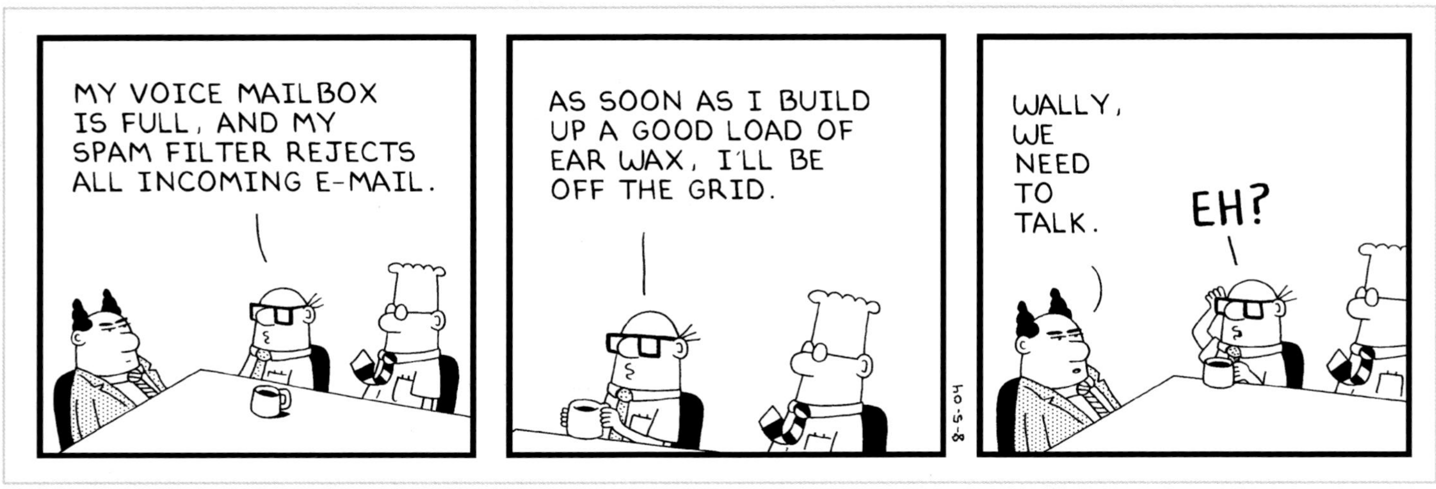
MY VOICE MAILBOX IS FULL, AND MY SPAM FILTER REJECTS ALL INCOMING E-MAIL.
AS SOON AS I BUILD UP A GOOD LOAD OF EAR WAX, I'LL BE OFF THE GRID.
8-5-04
WALLY, WE NEED TO TALK.
EH?

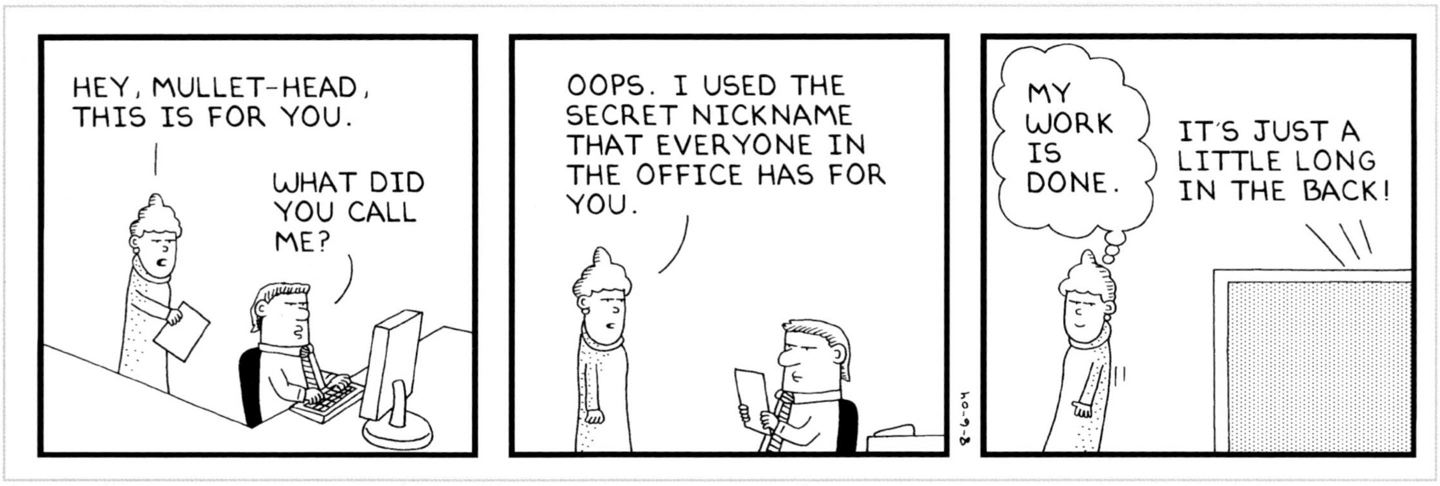
HEY, MULLET-HEAD, THIS IS FOR YOU.
WHAT DID YOU CALL ME?
OOPS. I USED THE SECRET NICKNAME THAT EVERYONE IN THE OFFICE HAS FOR YOU.
8-6-04
MY WORK IS DONE.
IT'S JUST A LITTLE LONG IN THE BACK!

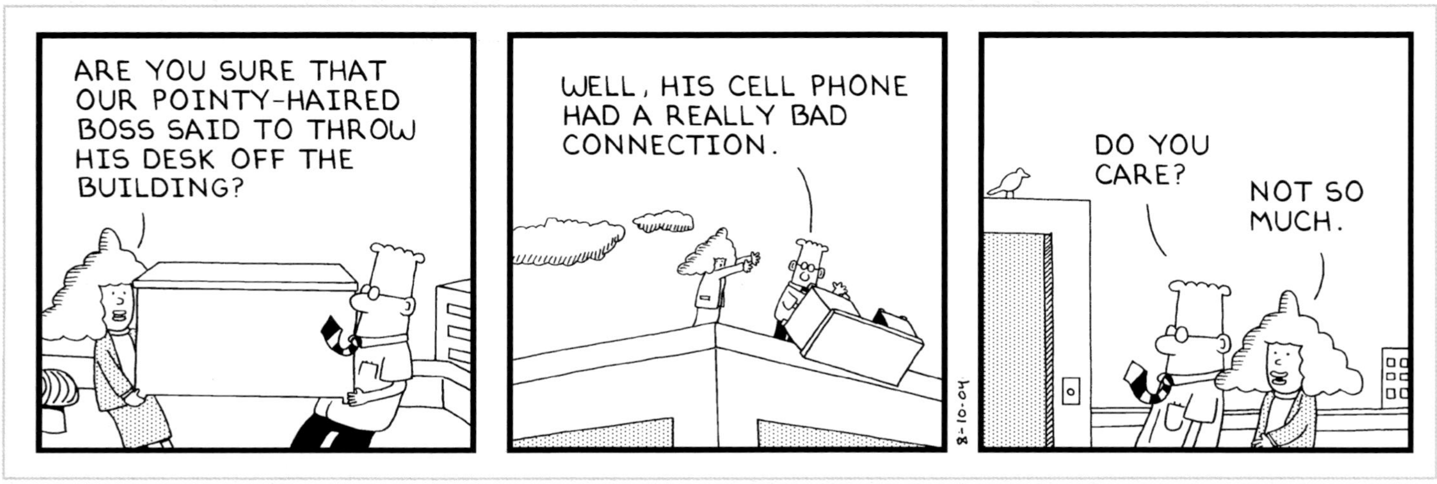
ARE YOU SURE THAT OUR POINTY-HAIRED BOSS SAID TO THROW HIS DESK OFF THE BUILDING?
WELL, HIS CELL PHONE HAD A REALLY BAD CONNECTION.
8-10-04
DO YOU CARE?
NOT SO MUCH.

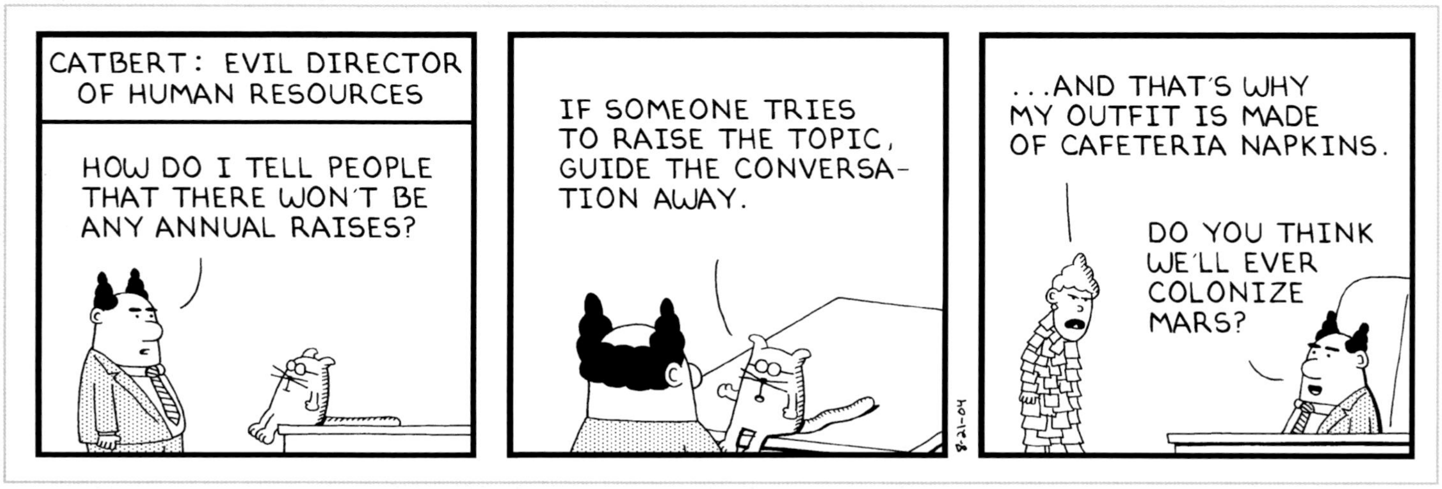
CATBERT: EVIL DIRECTOR OF HUMAN RESOURCES
HOW DO I TELL PEOPLE THAT THERE WON'T BE ANY ANNUAL RAISES?
IF SOMEONE TRIES TO RAISE THE TOPIC, GUIDE THE CONVERSA- TION AWAY.
8-21-04
...AND THAT'S WHY MY OUTFIT IS MADE OF CAFETERIA NAPKINS.
DO YOU THINK WE'LL EVER COLONIZE MARS?

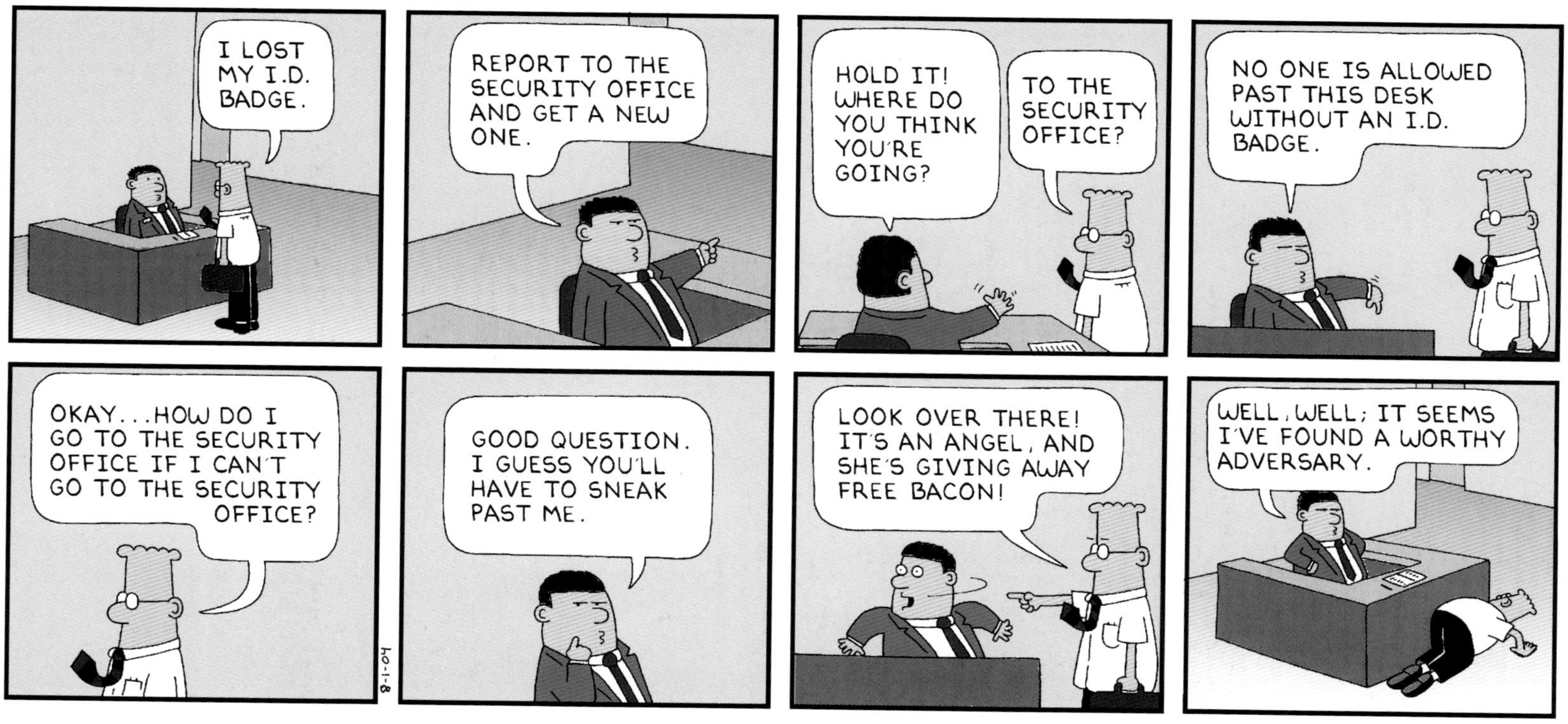
I LOST MY I.D. BADGE.
REPORT TO THE SECURITY OFFICE AND GET A NEW ONE.
HOLD IT! WHERE DO YOU THINK YOU'RE GOING?
TO THE SECURITY OFFICE?
NO ONE IS ALLOWED PAST THIS DESK WITHOUT AN I.D. BADGE.
OKAY...HOW DO I GO TO THE SECURITY OFFICE IF I CAN'T GO TO THE SECURITY OFFICE?
8-1-04
GOOD QUESTION. I GUESS YOU'LL HAVE TO SNEAK PAST ME.
LOOK OVER THERE! IT'S AN ANGEL, AND SHE'S GIVING AWAY FREE BACON!
WELL, WELL; IT SEEMS I'VE FOUND A WORTHY ADVERSARY.

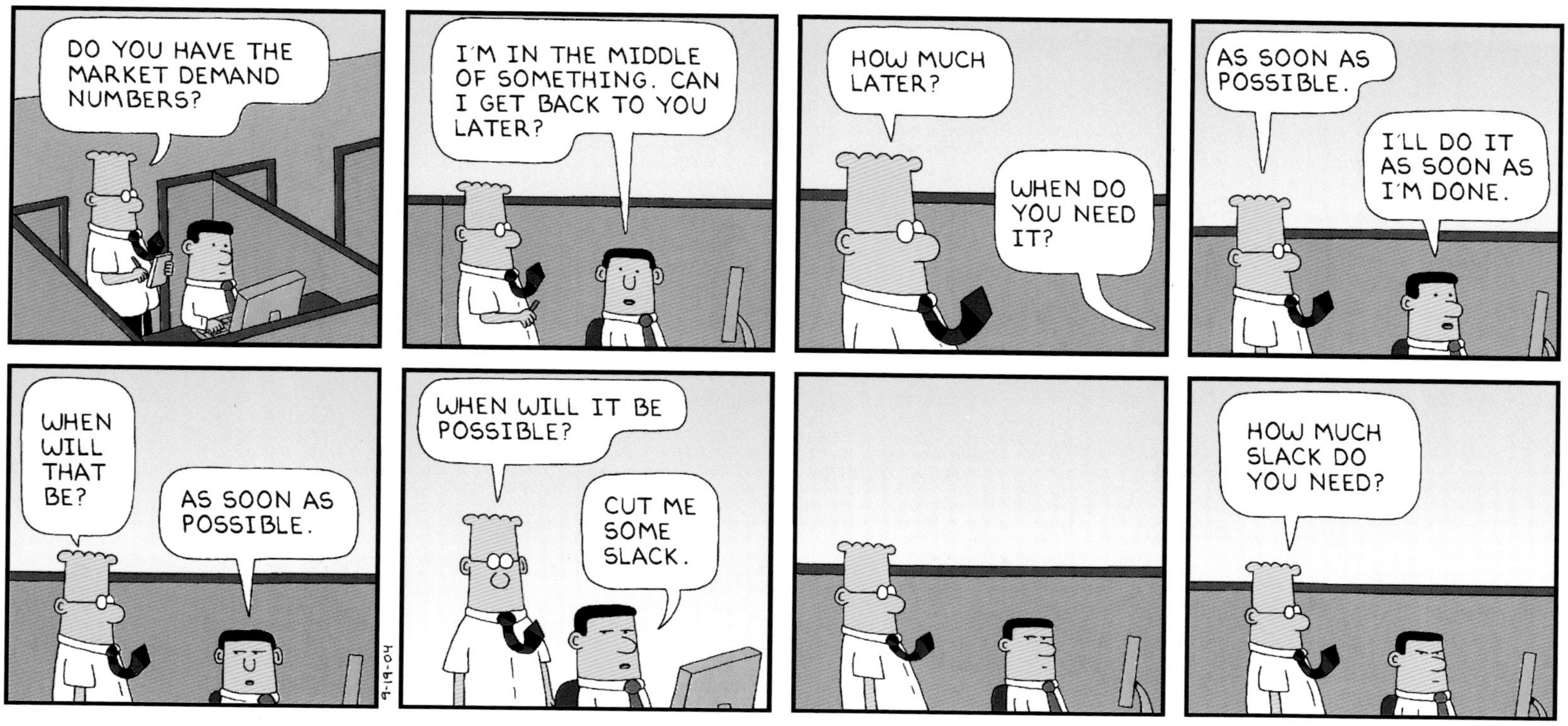
DO YOU HAVE THE MARKET DEMAND NUMBERS?
I'M IN THE MIDDLE OF SOMETHING. CAN I GET BACK TO YOU LATER?
HOW MUCH LATER?
WHEN DO YOU NEED IT?
AS SOON AS POSSIBLE.
I'LL DO IT AS SOON AS I'M DONE.
WHEN WILL THAT BE?
AS SOON AS POSSIBLE.
9-19-04
WHEN WILL IT BE POSSIBLE?
CUT ME SOME SLACK.
HOW MUCH SLACK DO YOU NEED?

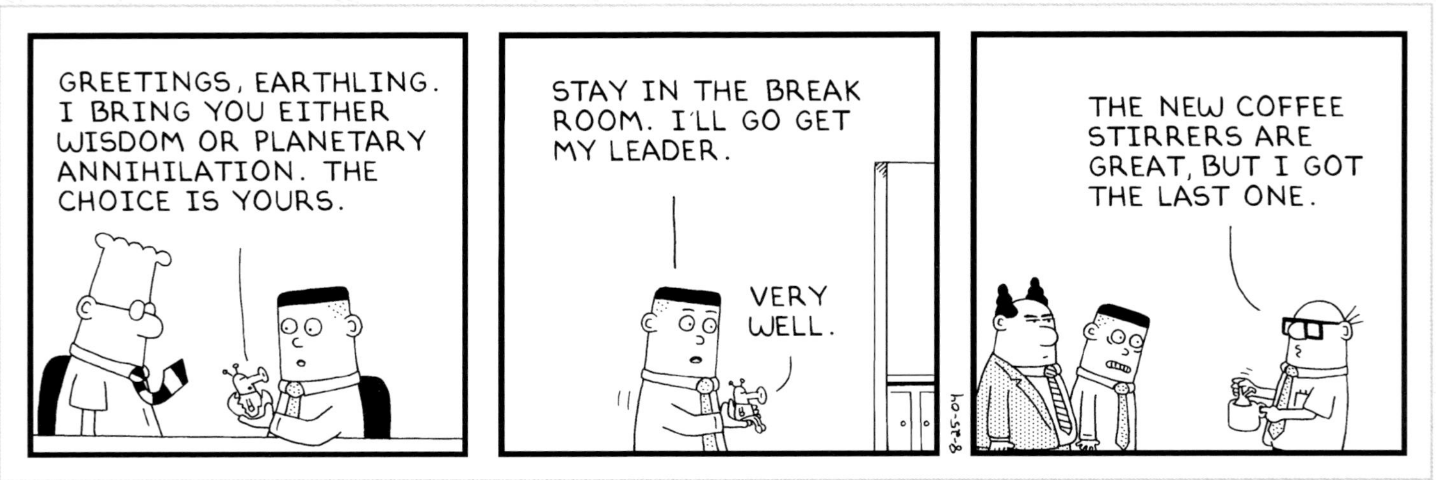
GREETINGS, EARTHLING. I BRING YOU EITHER WISDOM OR PLANETARY ANNIHILATION. THE CHOICE IS YOURS.
STAY IN THE BREAK ROOM. I'LL GO GET MY LEADER.
VERY WELL.
8-25-04
THE NEW COFFEE STIRRERS ARE GREAT, BUT I GOT THE LAST ONE.

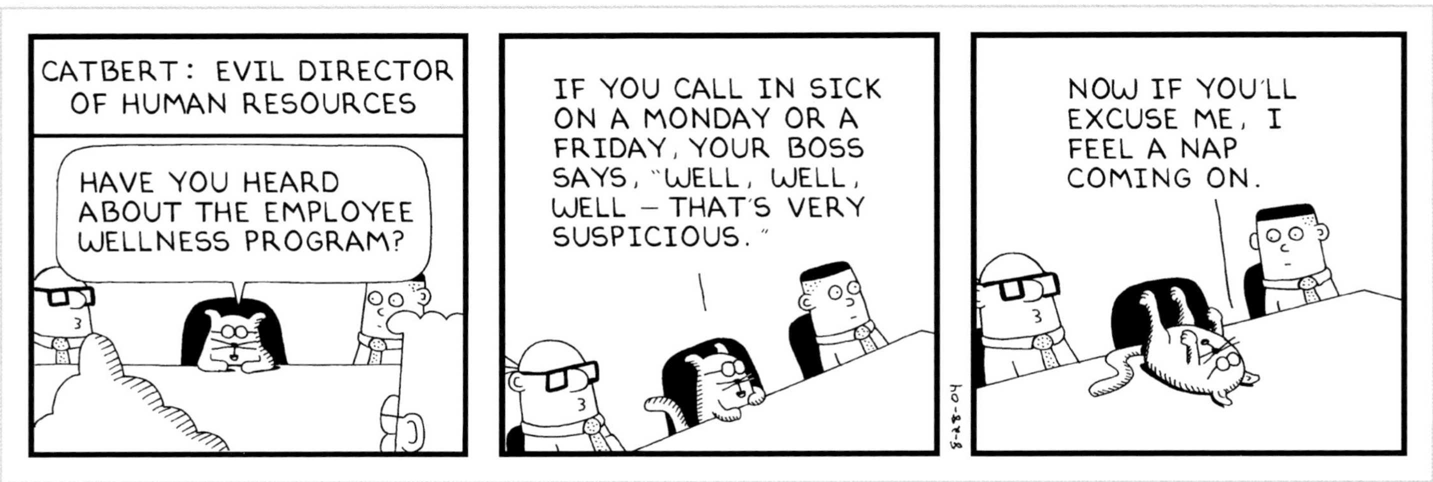
CATBERT: EVIL DIRECTOR OF HUMAN RESOURCES
HAVE YOU HEARD ABOUT THE EMPLOYEE WELLNESS PROGRAM?
IF YOU CALL IN SICK ON A MONDAY OR A FRIDAY, YOUR BOSS SAYS, "WELL, WELL, WELL – THAT'S VERY SUSPICIOUS."
8-28-04
NOW IF YOU'LL EXCUSE ME, I FEEL A NAP COMING ON.

Sometimes I finish the joke early, as in the second panel above. In this case, the third panel isn't about anything but Catbert looking cute on his back.

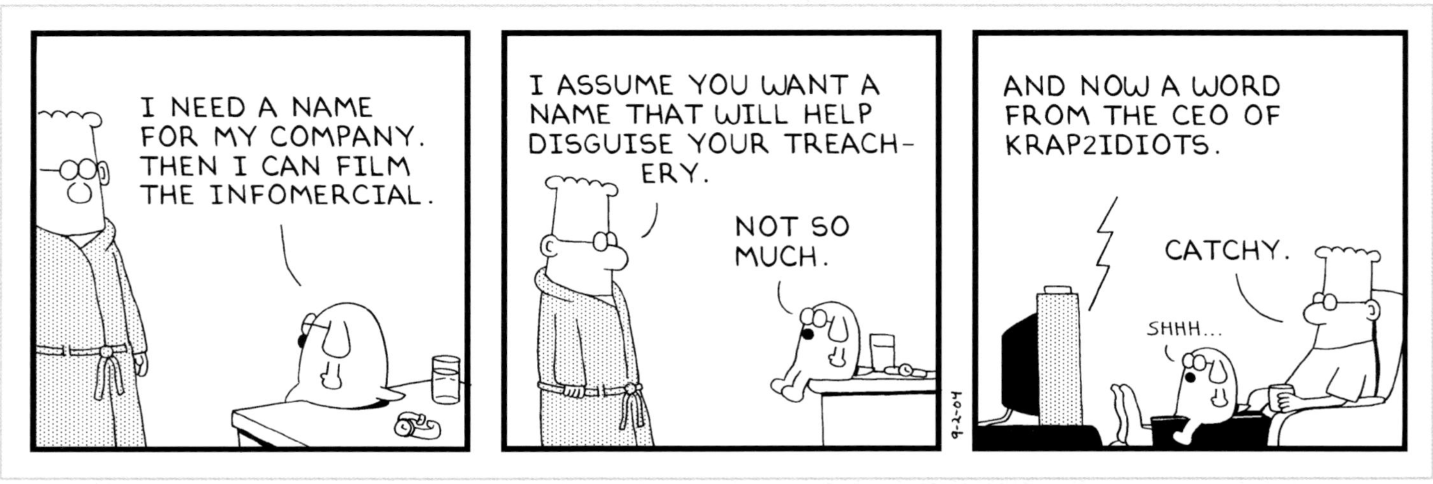
I NEED A NAME FOR MY COMPANY. THEN I CAN FILM THE INFOMERCIAL.
I ASSUME YOU WANT A NAME THAT WILL HELP DISGUISE YOUR TREACHERY.
NOT SO MUCH.
9-2-04
AND NOW A WORD FROM THE CEO OF KRAP2IDIOTS.
CATCHY.
SHHH...

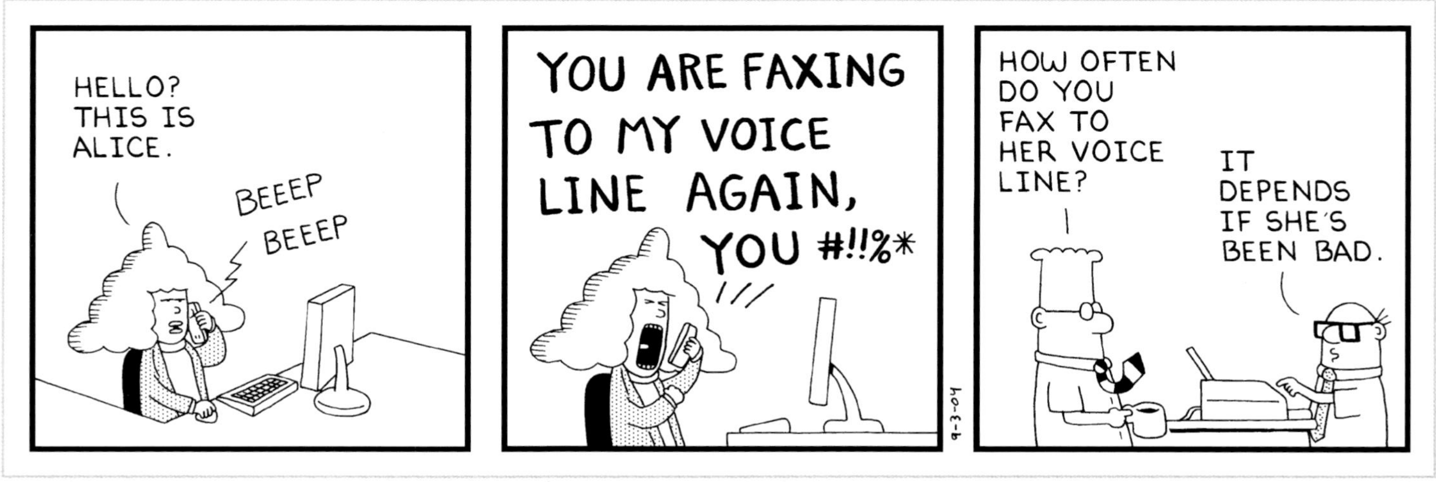
HELLO? THIS IS ALICE.
BEEEP
BEEEP
YOU ARE FAXING TO MY VOICE LINE AGAIN, YOU #!!%*
9-3-04
HOW OFTEN DO YOU FAX TO HER VOICE LINE?
IT DEPENDS IF SHE'S BEEN BAD.

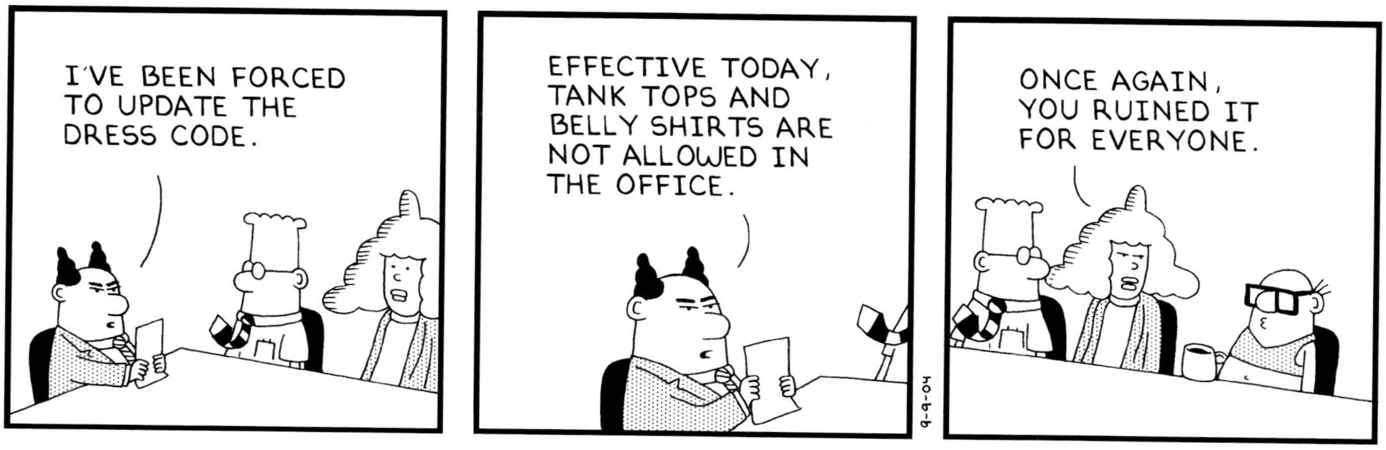
I'VE BEEN FORCED TO UPDATE THE DRESS CODE.
EFFECTIVE TODAY, TANK TOPS AND BELLY SHIRTS ARE NOT ALLOWED IN THE OFFICE.
9-9-04
ONCE AGAIN, YOU RUINED IT FOR EVERYONE.

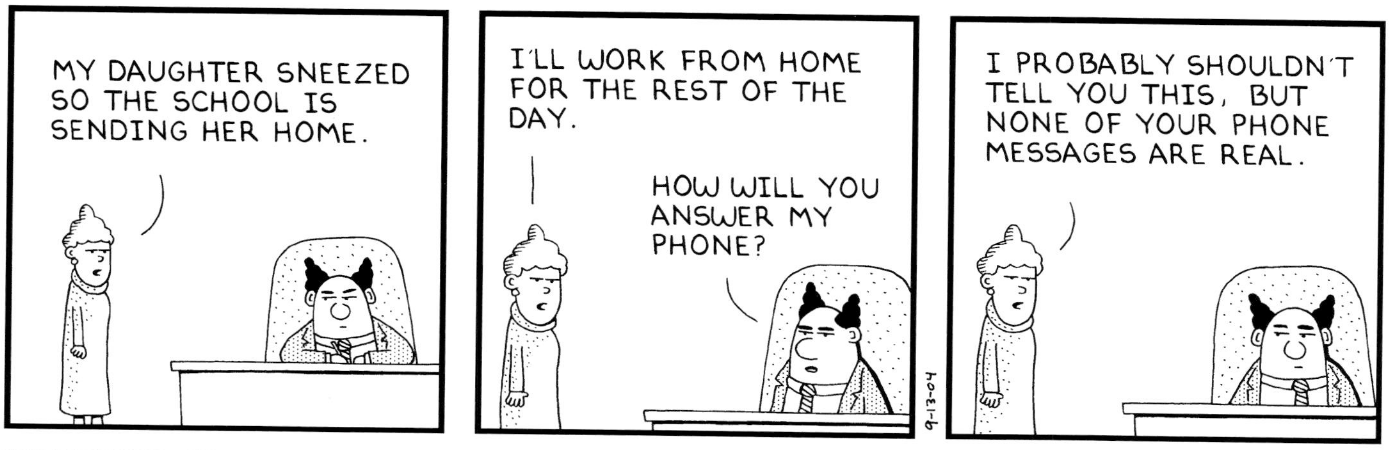
MY DAUGHTER SNEEZED SO THE SCHOOL IS SENDING HER HOME.
I'LL WORK FROM HOME FOR THE REST OF THE DAY.
HOW WILL YOU ANSWER MY PHONE?
9-13-04
I PROBABLY SHOULDN'T TELL YOU THIS, BUT NONE OF YOUR PHONE MESSAGES ARE REAL.

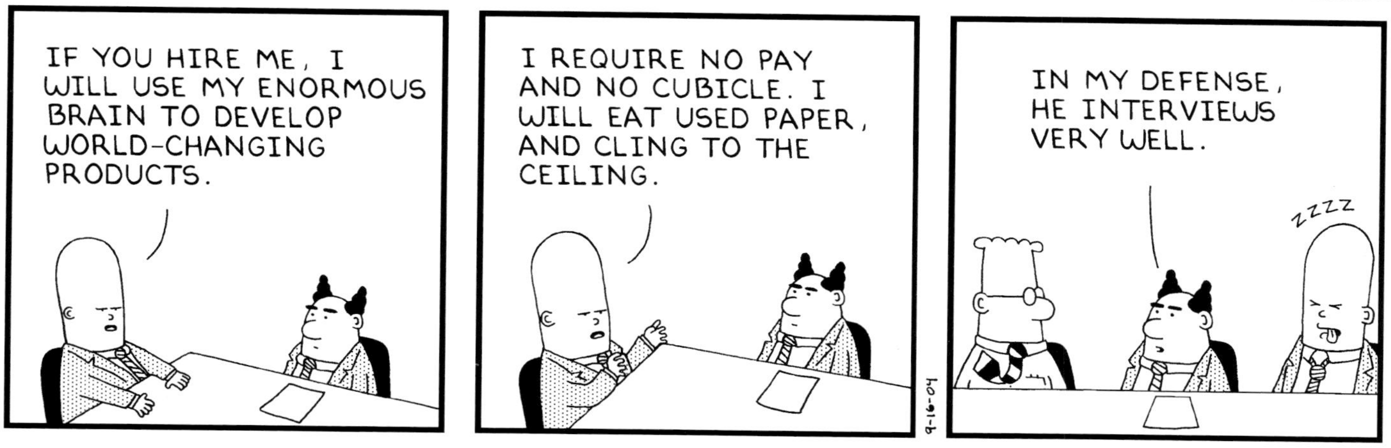
IF YOU HIRE ME, I WILL USE MY ENORMOUS BRAIN TO DEVELOP WORLD-CHANGING PRODUCTS.
I REQUIRE NO PAY AND NO CUBICLE. I WILL EAT USED PAPER, AND CLING TO THE CEILING.
9-16-04
IN MY DEFENSE, HE INTERVIEWS VERY WELL.
ZZZZ

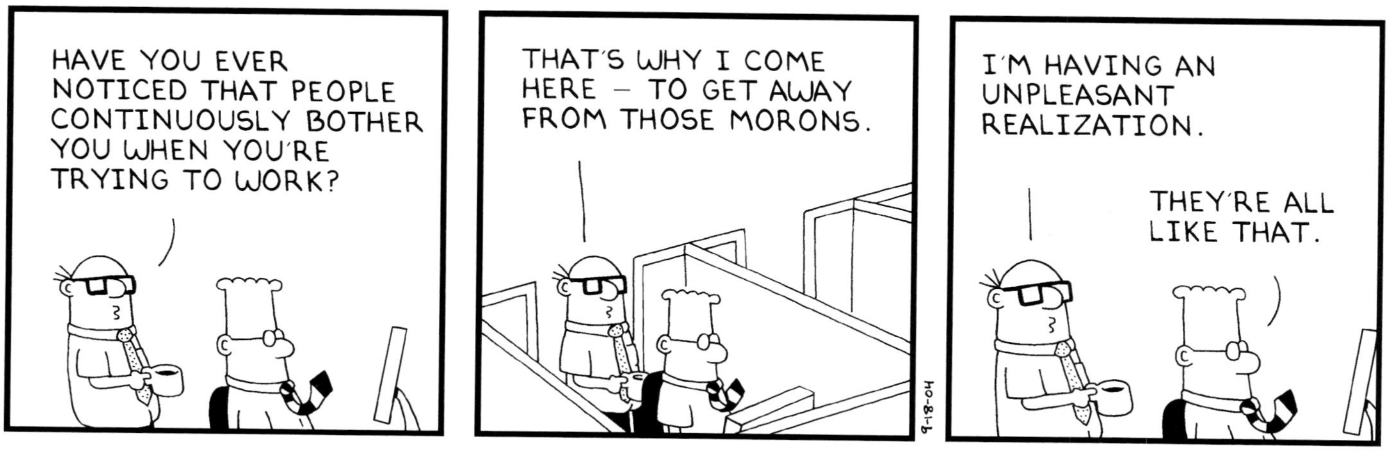
HAVE YOU EVER NOTICED THAT PEOPLE CONTINUOUSLY BOTHER YOU WHEN YOU'RE TRYING TO WORK?
THAT'S WHY I COME HERE – TO GET AWAY FROM THOSE MORONS.
9-18-04
I'M HAVING AN UNPLEASANT REALIZATION.
THEY'RE ALL LIKE THAT.

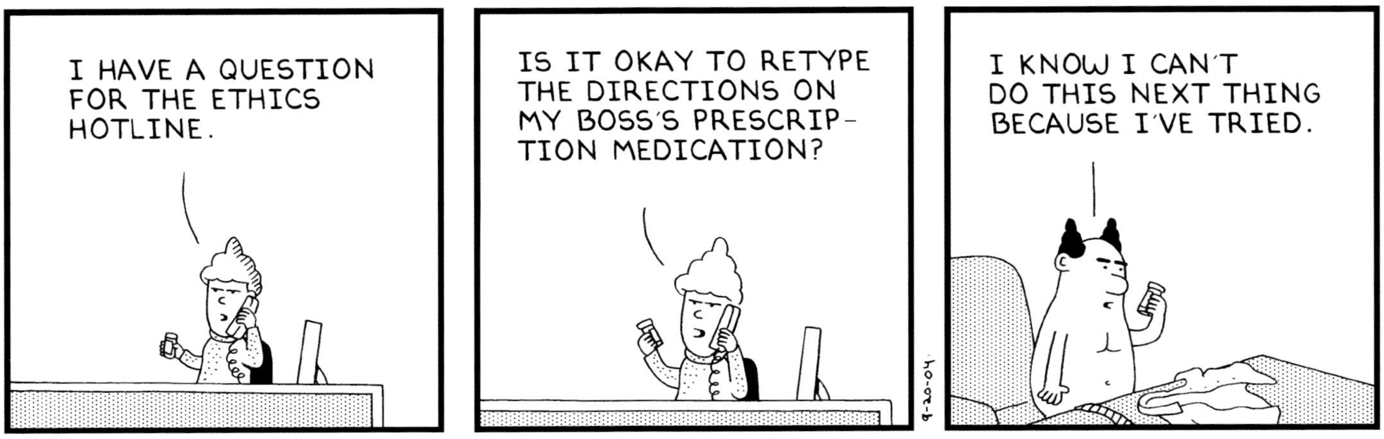
I HAVE A QUESTION FOR THE ETHICS HOTLINE.
IS IT OKAY TO RETYPE THE DIRECTIONS ON MY BOSS'S PRESCRIPTION MEDICATION?
9-20-04
I KNOW I CAN'T DO THIS NEXT THING BECAUSE I'VE TRIED.

The strip above is only as funny as your imagination is disgusting.

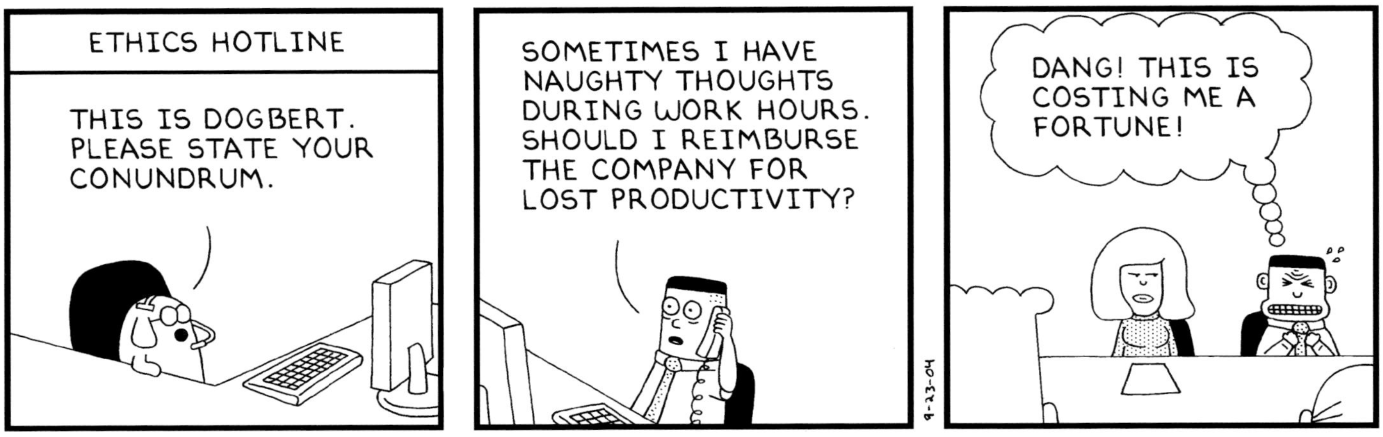
ETHICS HOTLINE
THIS IS DOGBERT. PLEASE STATE YOUR CONUNDRUM.
SOMETIMES I HAVE NAUGHTY THOUGHTS DURING WORK HOURS. SHOULD I REIMBURSE THE COMPANY FOR LOST PRODUCTIVITY?
9-23-04
DANG! THIS IS COSTING ME A FORTUNE!

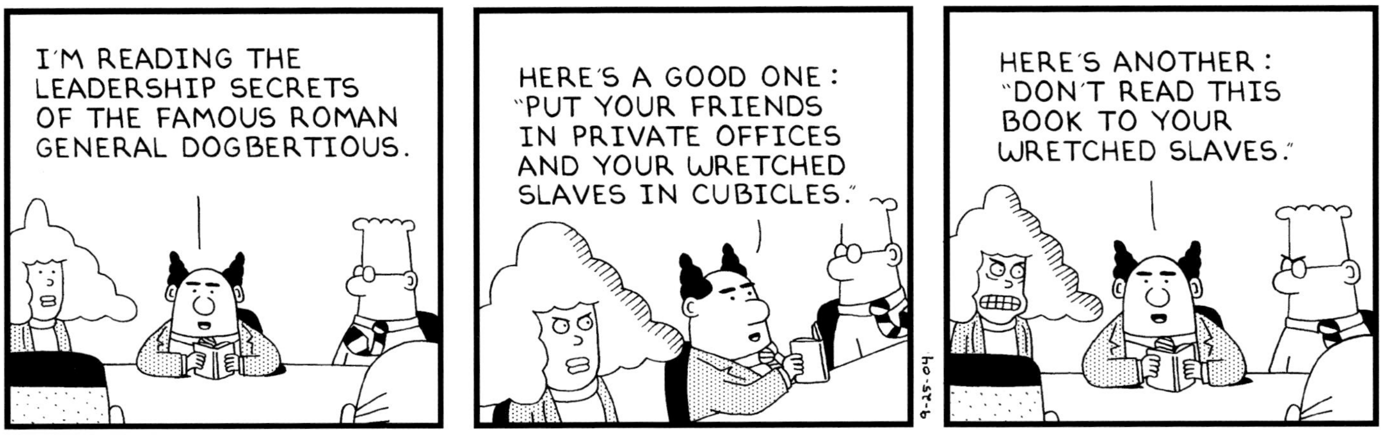
I'M READING THE LEADERSHIP SECRETS OF THE FAMOUS ROMAN GENERAL DOGBERTIOUS.
HERE'S A GOOD ONE: "PUT YOUR FRIENDS IN PRIVATE OFFICES AND YOUR WRETCHED SLAVES IN CUBICLES."
9-25-04
HERE'S ANOTHER: "DON'T READ THIS BOOK TO YOUR WRETCHED SLAVES."

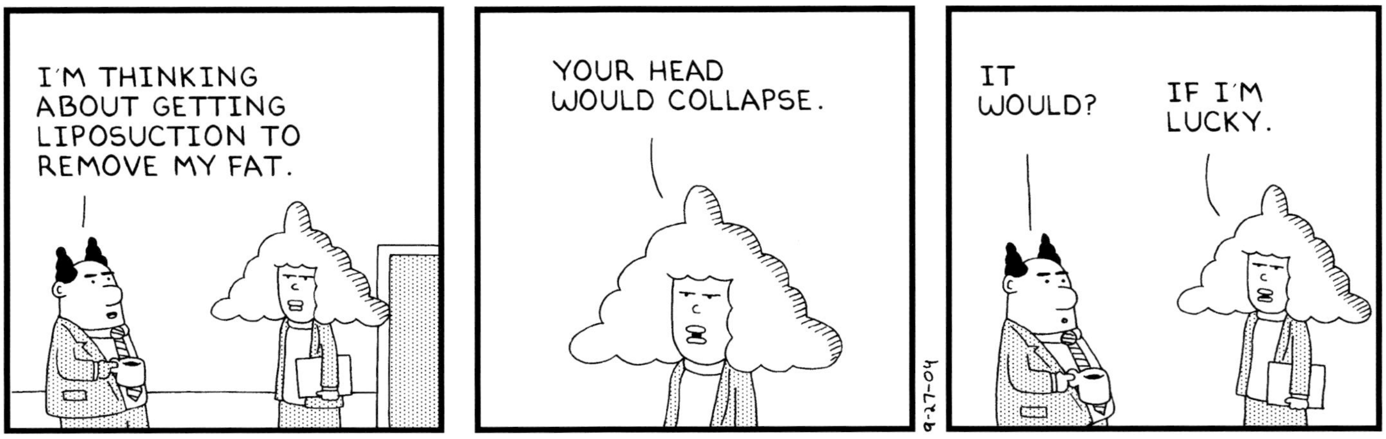
I'M THINKING ABOUT GETTING LIPOSUCTION TO REMOVE MY FAT.
YOUR HEAD WOULD COLLAPSE.
9-27-04
IT WOULD?
IF I'M LUCKY.

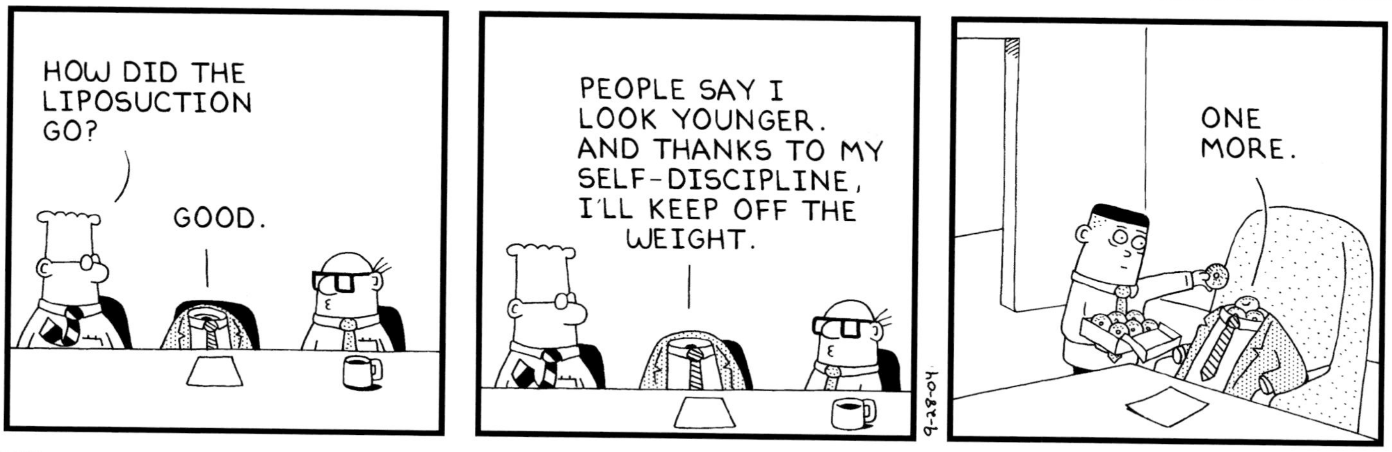
HOW DID THE LIPOSUCTION GO?
GOOD.
PEOPLE SAY I LOOK YOUNGER. AND THANKS TO MY SELF-DISCIPLINE, I'LL KEEP OFF THE WEIGHT.
9-28-04
ONE MORE.

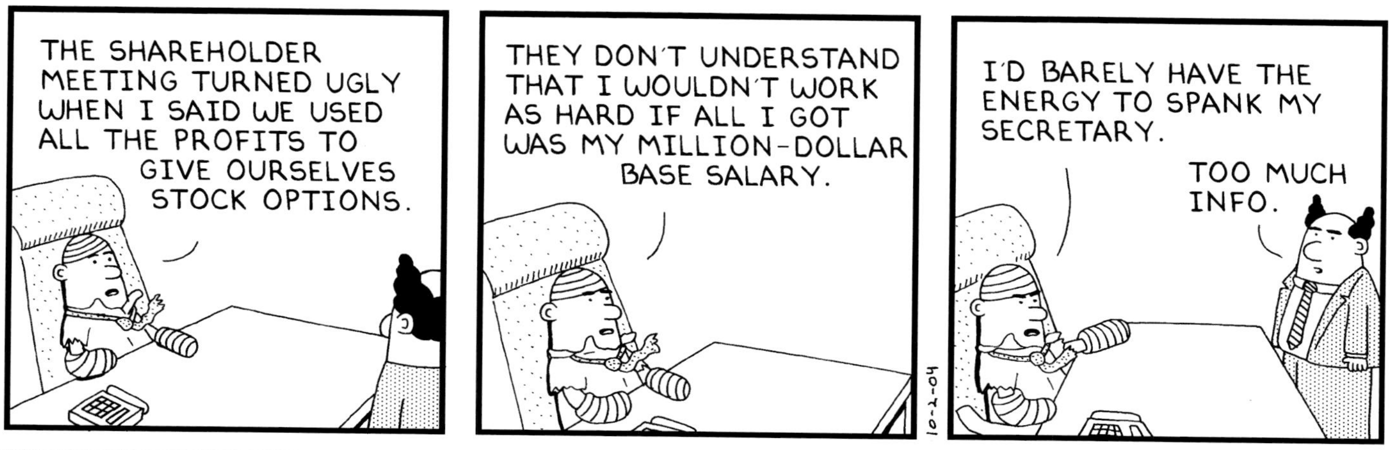
THE SHAREHOLDER MEETING TURNED UGLY WHEN I SAID WE USED ALL THE PROFITS TO GIVE OURSELVES STOCK OPTIONS.
THEY DON'T UNDERSTAND THAT I WOULDN'T WORK AS HARD IF ALL I GOT WAS MY MILLION-DOLLAR BASE SALARY.
10-2-04
I'D BARELY HAVE THE ENERGY TO SPANK MY SECRETARY.
TOO MUCH INFO.

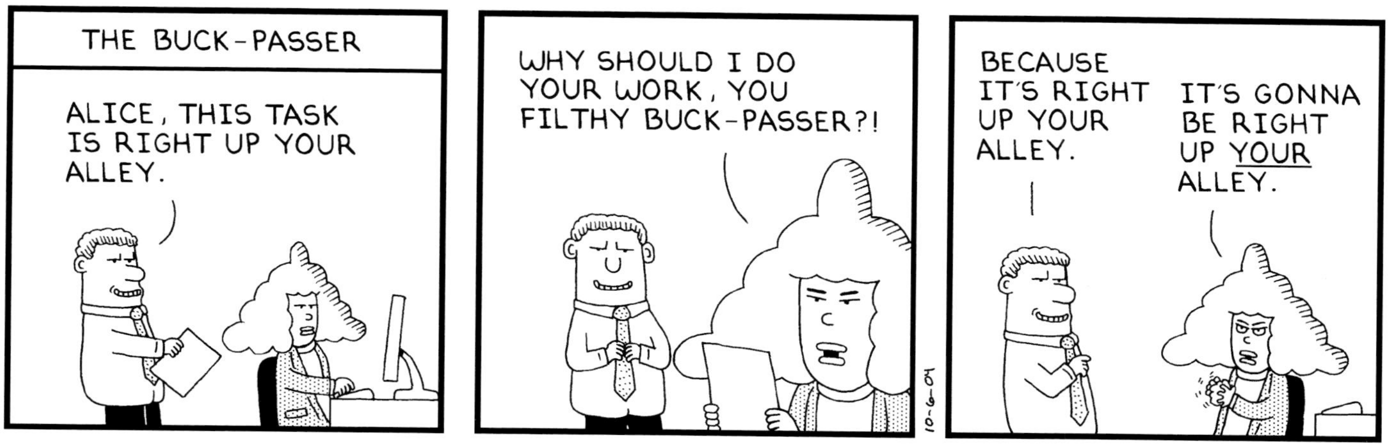
THE BUCK-PASSER
ALICE, THIS TASK IS RIGHT UP YOUR ALLEY.
WHY SHOULD I DO YOUR WORK, YOU FILTHY BUCK-PASSER?!
10-6-04
BECAUSE IT'S RIGHT UP YOUR ALLEY.
IT'S GONNA BE RIGHT UP YOUR ALLEY.

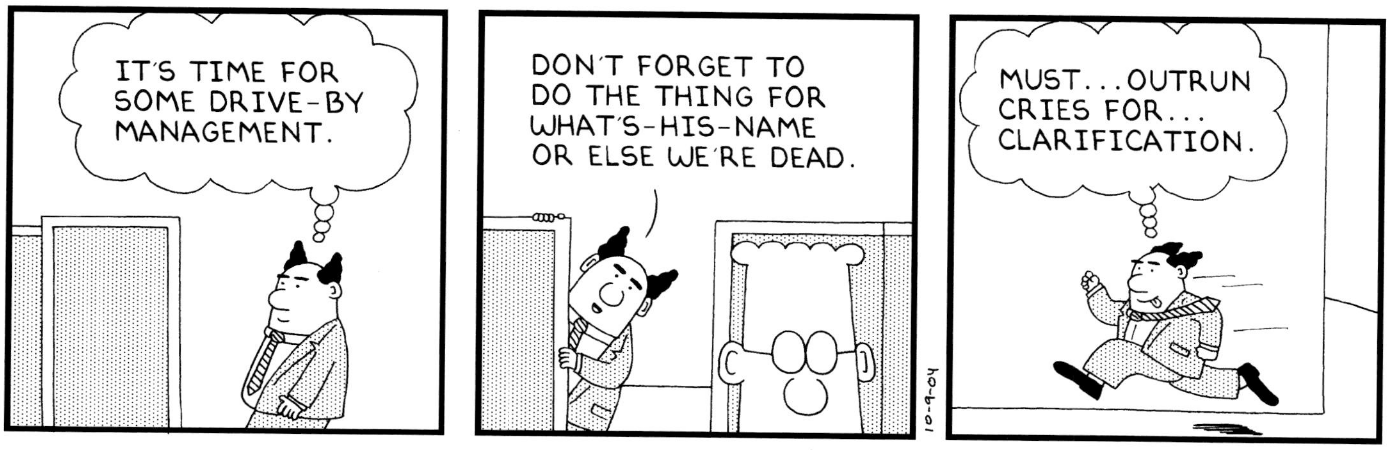
IT'S TIME FOR SOME DRIVE-BY MANAGEMENT.
DON'T FORGET TO DO THE THING FOR WHAT'S-HIS-NAME OR ELSE WE'RE DEAD.
10-9-04
MUST...OUTRUN CRIES FOR... CLARIFICATION.

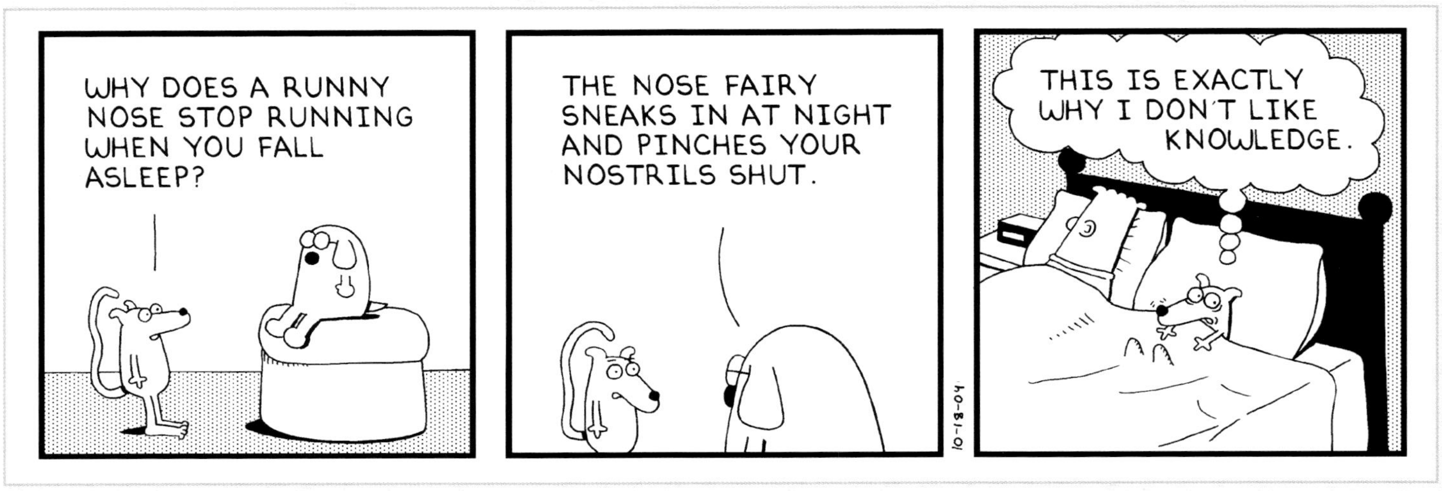
WHY DOES A RUNNY NOSE STOP RUNNING WHEN YOU FALL ASLEEP?
THE NOSE FAIRY SNEAKS IN AT NIGHT AND PINCHES YOUR NOSTRILS SHUT.
10-18-04
THIS IS EXACTLY WHY I DON'T LIKE KNOWLEDGE.

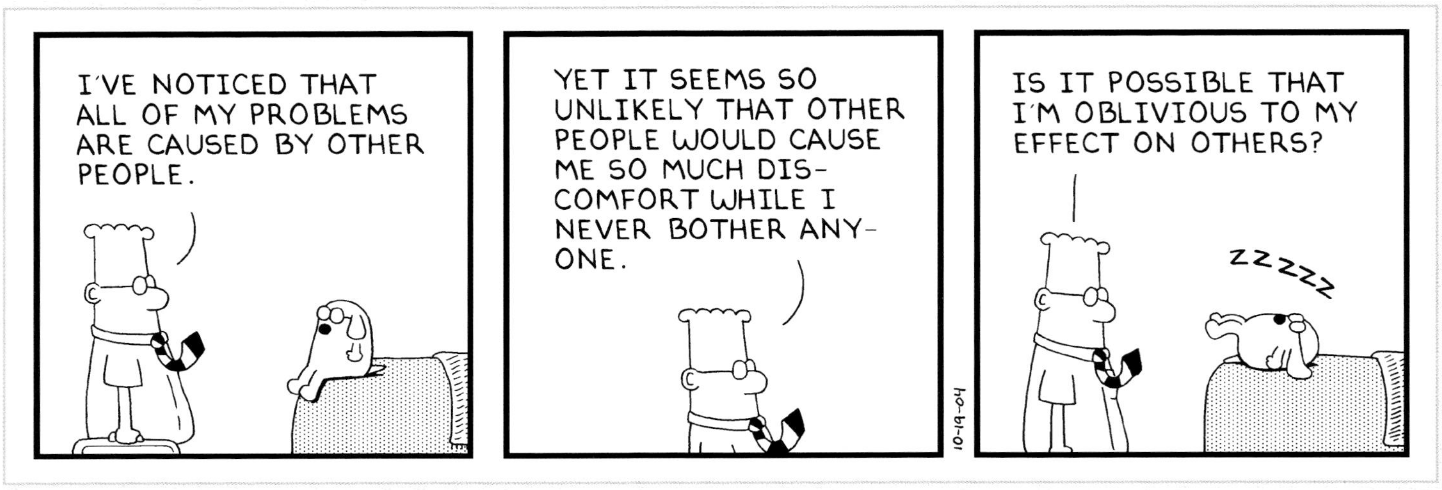
I'VE NOTICED THAT ALL OF MY PROBLEMS ARE CAUSED BY OTHER PEOPLE.
YET IT SEEMS SO UNLIKELY THAT OTHER PEOPLE WOULD CAUSE ME SO MUCH DIS-COMFORT WHILE I NEVER BOTHER ANY-ONE.
10-19-04
IS IT POSSIBLE THAT I'M OBLIVIOUS TO MY EFFECT ON OTHERS?
ZZZZZ

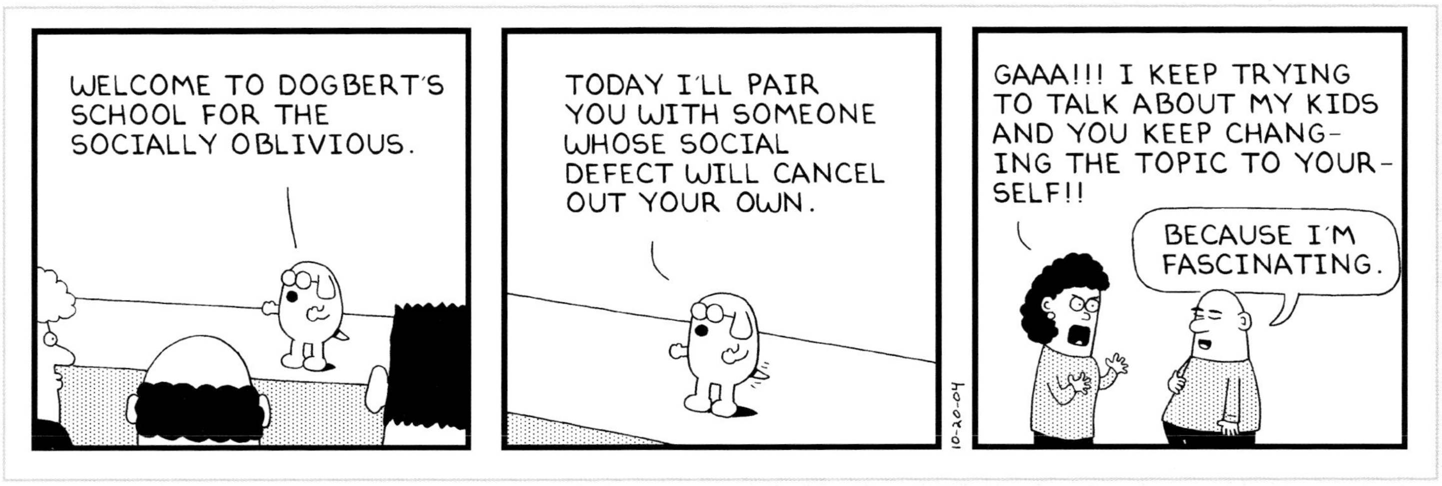
WELCOME TO DOGBERT'S SCHOOL FOR THE SOCIALLY OBLIVIOUS.
TODAY I'LL PAIR YOU WITH SOMEONE WHOSE SOCIAL DEFECT WILL CANCEL OUT YOUR OWN.
10-20-04
GAAA!!! I KEEP TRYING TO TALK ABOUT MY KIDS AND YOU KEEP CHANG-ING THE TOPIC TO YOUR-SELF!!
BECAUSE I'M FASCINATING.

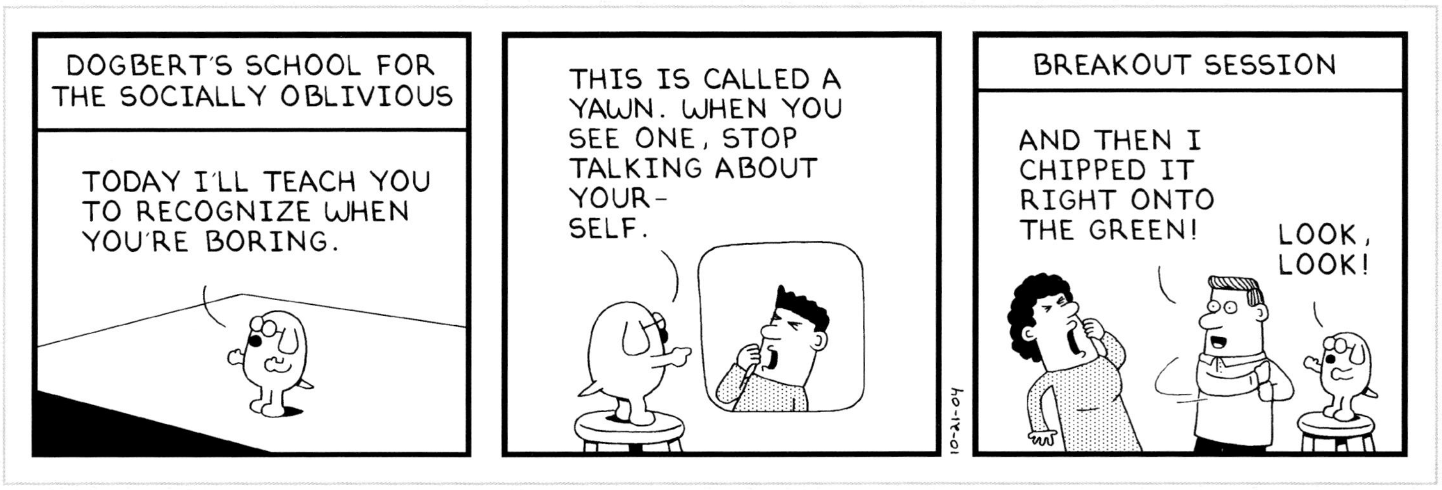
DOGBERT'S SCHOOL FOR THE SOCIALLY OBLIVIOUS
TODAY I'LL TEACH YOU TO RECOGNIZE WHEN YOU'RE BORING.
THIS IS CALLED A YAWN. WHEN YOU SEE ONE, STOP TALKING ABOUT YOUR-SELF.
10-21-04
BREAKOUT SESSION
AND THEN I CHIPPED IT RIGHT ONTO THE GREEN!
LOOK, LOOK!

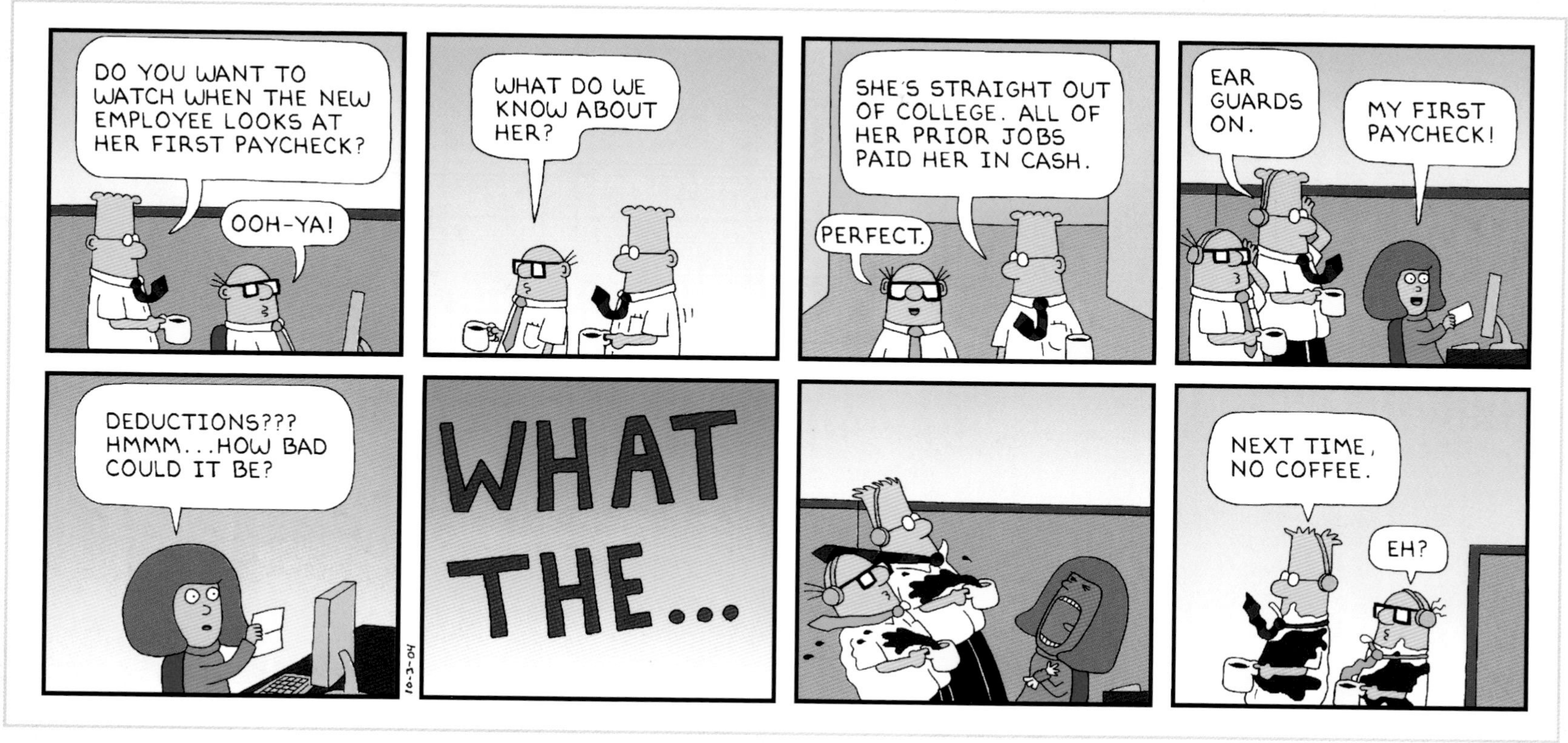
DO YOU WANT TO WATCH WHEN THE NEW EMPLOYEE LOOKS AT HER FIRST PAYCHECK?
OOH-YA!
WHAT DO WE KNOW ABOUT HER?
SHE'S STRAIGHT OUT OF COLLEGE. ALL OF HER PRIOR JOBS PAID HER IN CASH.
PERFECT.
EAR GUARDS ON.
MY FIRST PAYCHECK!
DEDUCTIONS??? HMMM...HOW BAD COULD IT BE?
10-3-04
WHAT THE...
NEXT TIME, NO COFFEE.
EH?

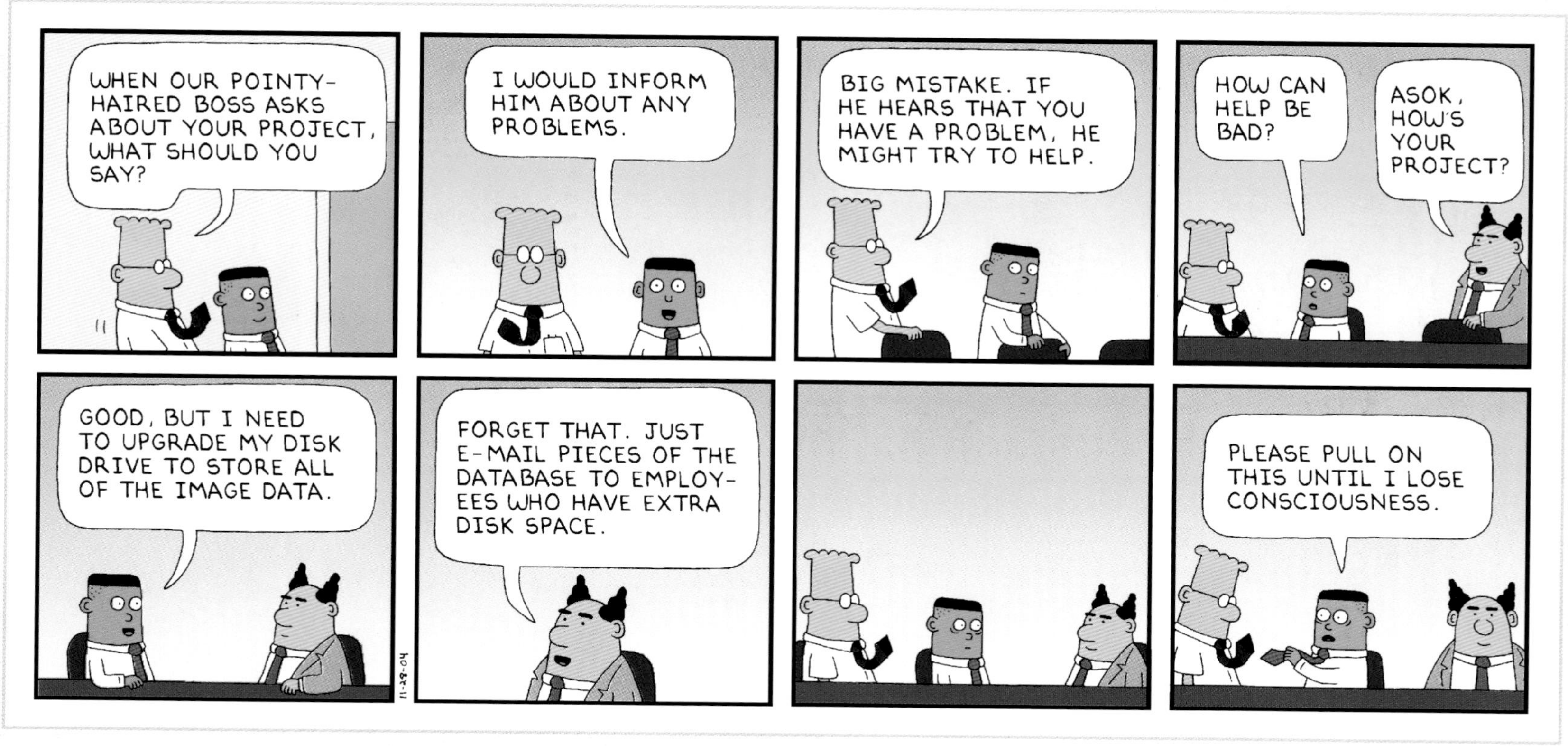
WHEN OUR POINTY-HAIRED BOSS ASKS ABOUT YOUR PROJECT, WHAT SHOULD YOU SAY?
I WOULD INFORM HIM ABOUT ANY PROBLEMS.
BIG MISTAKE. IF HE HEARS THAT YOU HAVE A PROBLEM, HE MIGHT TRY TO HELP.
HOW CAN HELP BE BAD?
ASOK, HOW'S YOUR PROJECT?
GOOD, BUT I NEED TO UPGRADE MY DISK DRIVE TO STORE ALL OF THE IMAGE DATA.
11-28-04
FORGET THAT. JUST E-MAIL PIECES OF THE DATABASE TO EMPLOYEES WHO HAVE EXTRA DISK SPACE.
PLEASE PULL ON THIS UNTIL I LOSE CONSCIOUSNESS.

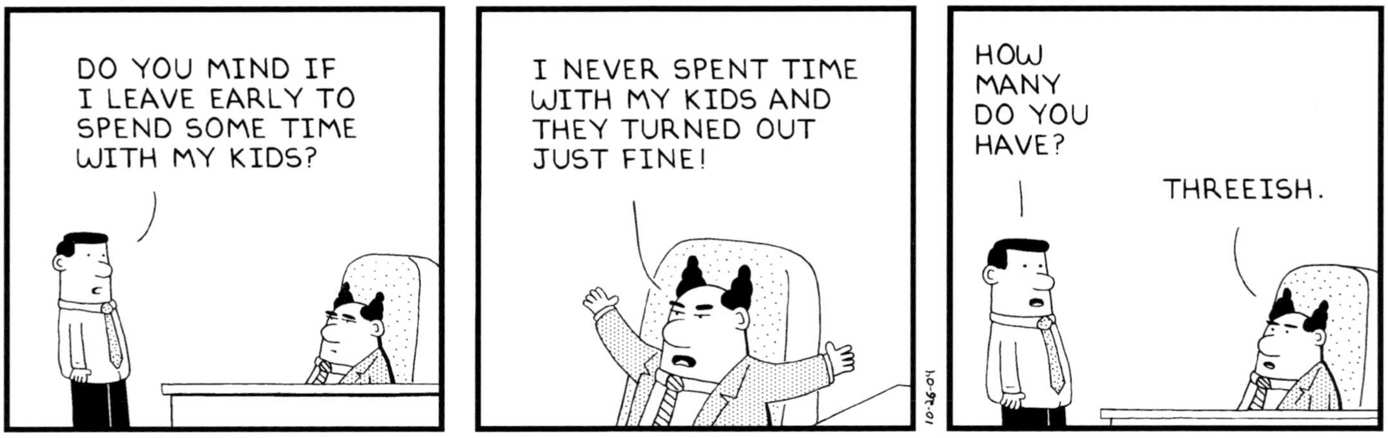
DO YOU MIND IF I LEAVE EARLY TO SPEND SOME TIME WITH MY KIDS?
I NEVER SPENT TIME WITH MY KIDS AND THEY TURNED OUT JUST FINE!
HOW MANY DO YOU HAVE?
THREEISH.
10-26-04

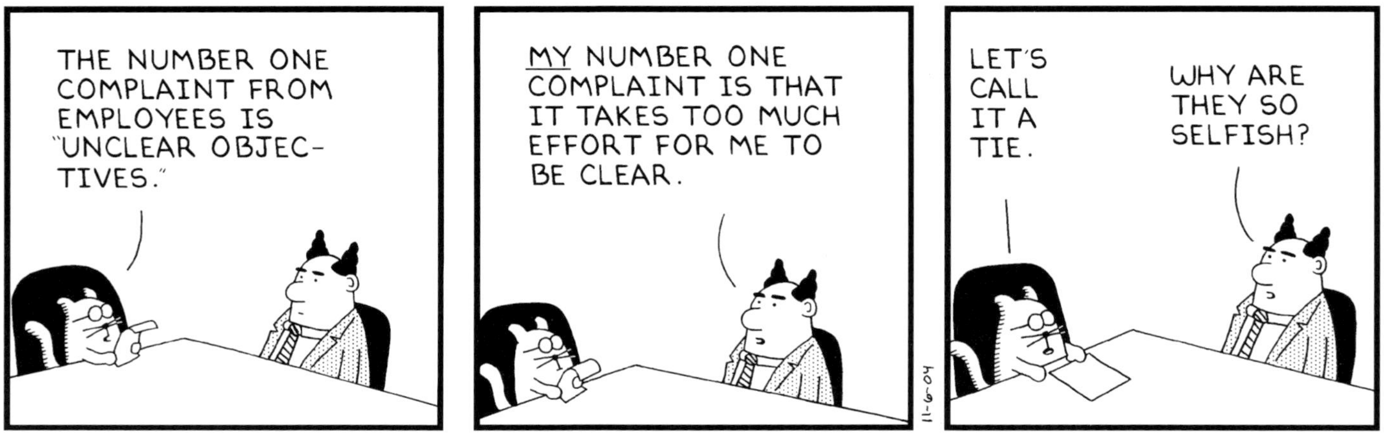
THE NUMBER ONE COMPLAINT FROM EMPLOYEES IS "UNCLEAR OBJEC-TIVES."
MY NUMBER ONE COMPLAINT IS THAT IT TAKES TOO MUCH EFFORT FOR ME TO BE CLEAR.
LET'S CALL IT A TIE.
WHY ARE THEY SO SELFISH?
11-6-04

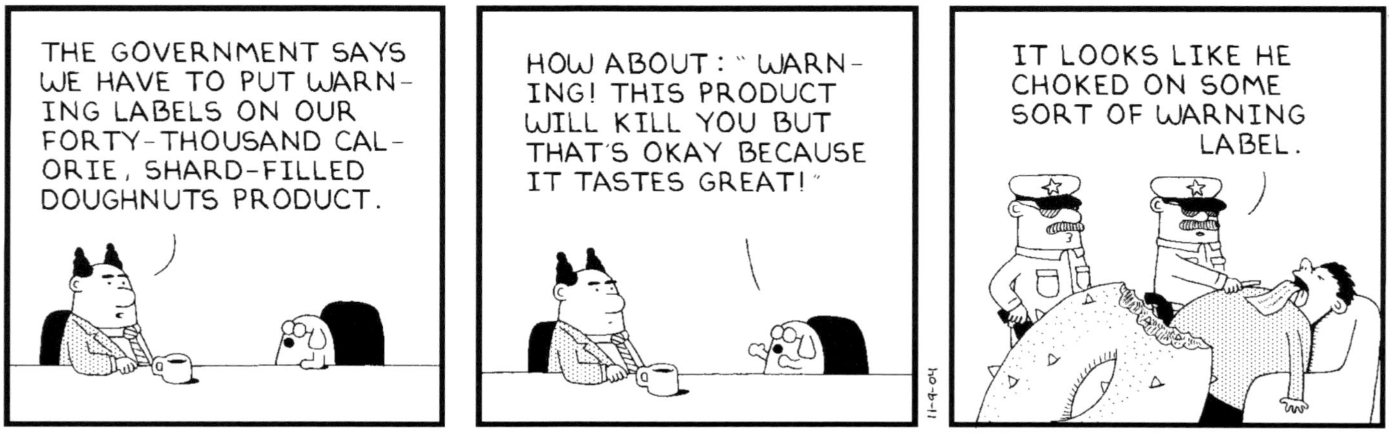
THE GOVERNMENT SAYS WE HAVE TO PUT WARN-ING LABELS ON OUR FORTY-THOUSAND CAL-ORIE, SHARD-FILLED DOUGHNUTS PRODUCT.
HOW ABOUT: "WARN-ING! THIS PRODUCT WILL KILL YOU BUT THAT'S OKAY BECAUSE IT TASTES GREAT!"
IT LOOKS LIKE HE CHOKED ON SOME SORT OF WARNING LABEL.
11-9-04

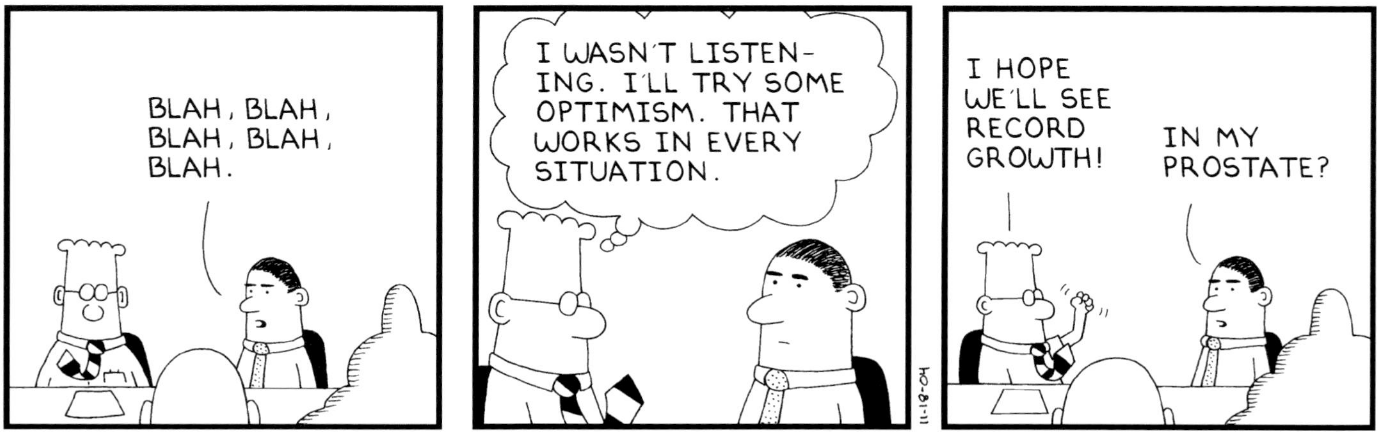
BLAH, BLAH, BLAH, BLAH, BLAH.
I WASN'T LISTEN-ING. I'LL TRY SOME OPTIMISM. THAT WORKS IN EVERY SITUATION.
I HOPE WE'LL SEE RECORD GROWTH!
IN MY PROSTATE?
11-18-04

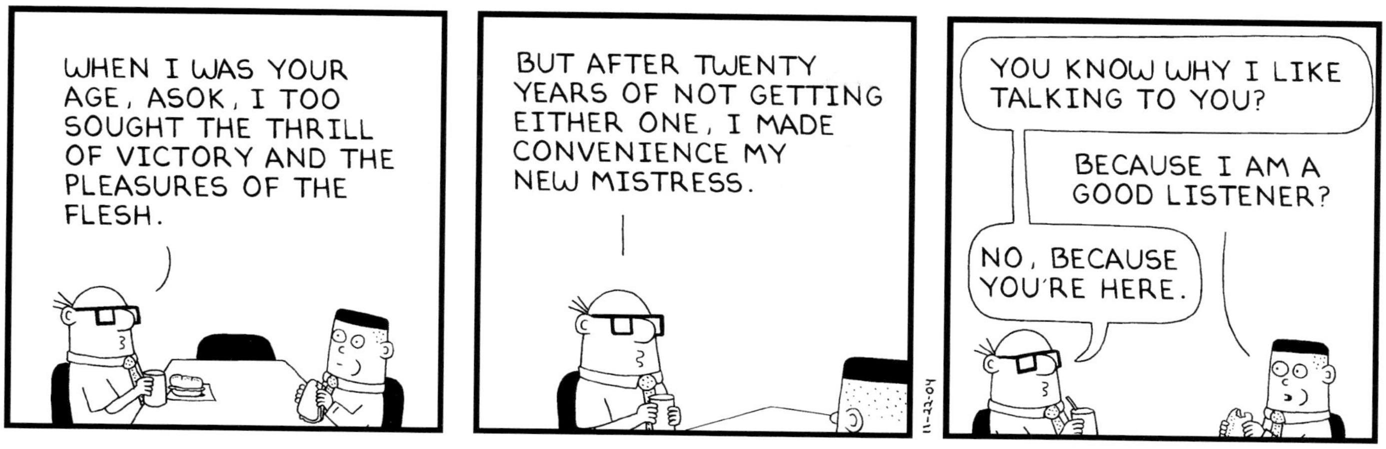
WHEN I WAS YOUR AGE, ASOK, I TOO SOUGHT THE THRILL OF VICTORY AND THE PLEASURES OF THE FLESH.
BUT AFTER TWENTY YEARS OF NOT GETTING EITHER ONE, I MADE CONVENIENCE MY NEW MISTRESS.
11-22-04
YOU KNOW WHY I LIKE TALKING TO YOU?
BECAUSE I AM A GOOD LISTENER?
NO, BECAUSE YOU'RE HERE.

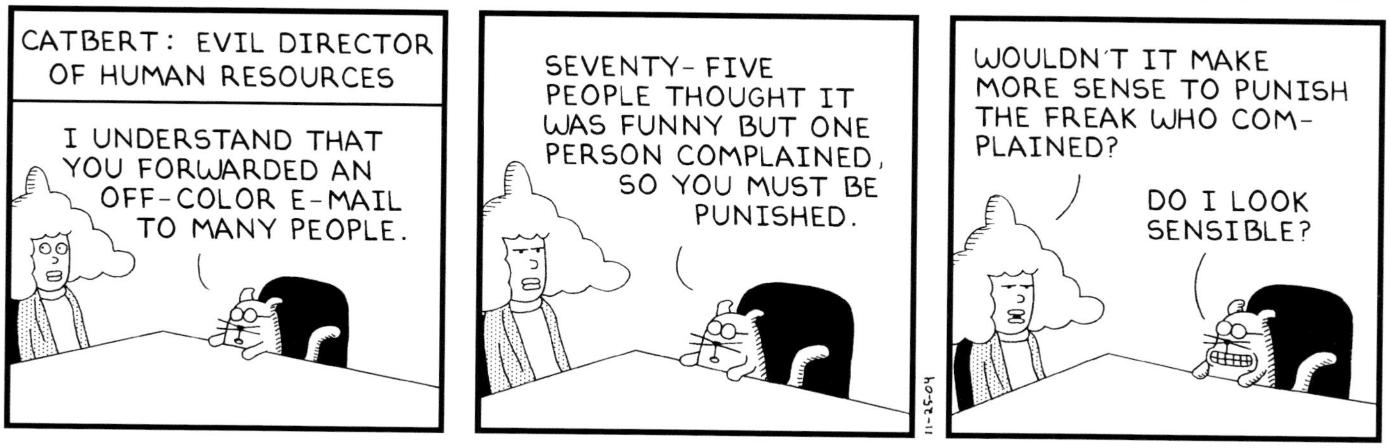
CATBERT: EVIL DIRECTOR OF HUMAN RESOURCES
I UNDERSTAND THAT YOU FORWARDED AN OFF-COLOR E-MAIL TO MANY PEOPLE.
SEVENTY-FIVE PEOPLE THOUGHT IT WAS FUNNY BUT ONE PERSON COMPLAINED, SO YOU MUST BE PUNISHED.
11-25-04
WOULDN'T IT MAKE MORE SENSE TO PUNISH THE FREAK WHO COMPLAINED?
DO I LOOK SENSIBLE?

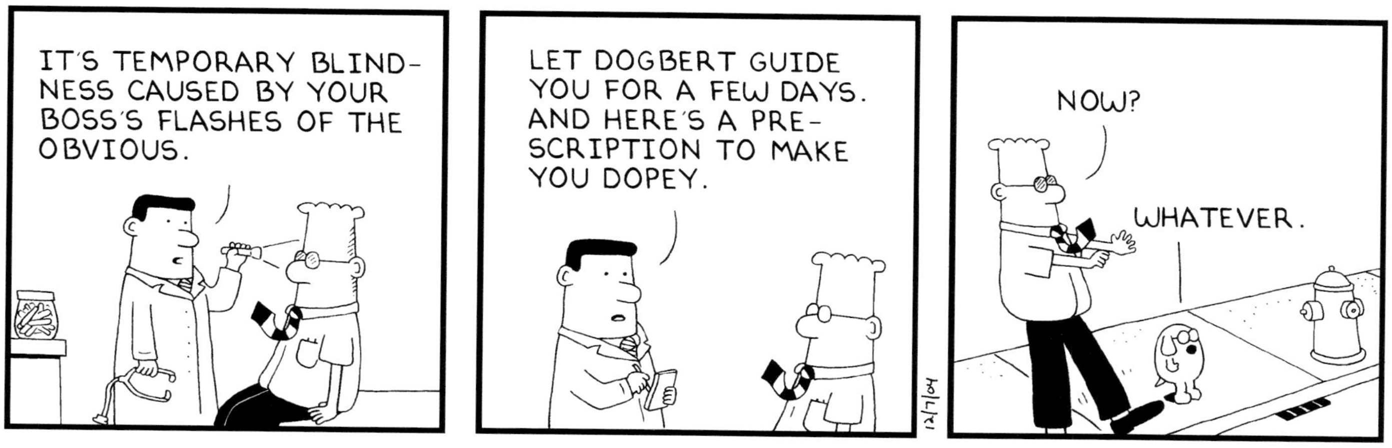
IT'S TEMPORARY BLINDNESS CAUSED BY YOUR BOSS'S FLASHES OF THE OBVIOUS.
LET DOGBERT GUIDE YOU FOR A FEW DAYS. AND HERE'S A PRESCRIPTION TO MAKE YOU DOPEY.
12/7/04
NOW?
WHATEVER.

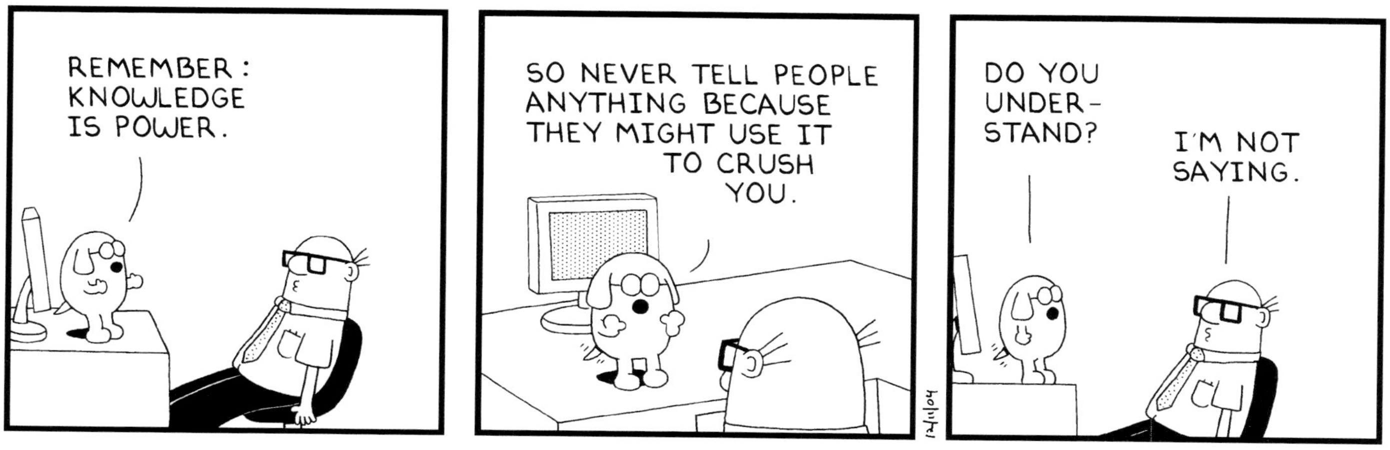
REMEMBER: KNOWLEDGE IS POWER.
SO NEVER TELL PEOPLE ANYTHING BECAUSE THEY MIGHT USE IT TO CRUSH YOU.
12/11/04
DO YOU UNDERSTAND?
I'M NOT SAYING.

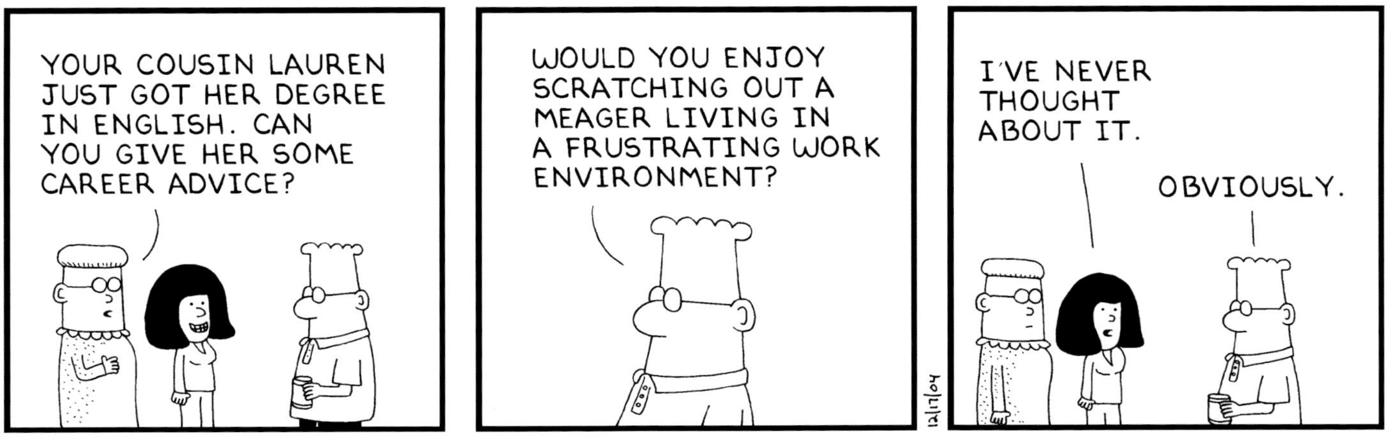
YOUR COUSIN LAUREN JUST GOT HER DEGREE IN ENGLISH. CAN YOU GIVE HER SOME CAREER ADVICE?
WOULD YOU ENJOY SCRATCHING OUT A MEAGER LIVING IN A FRUSTRATING WORK ENVIRONMENT?
I'VE NEVER THOUGHT ABOUT IT.
OBVIOUSLY.

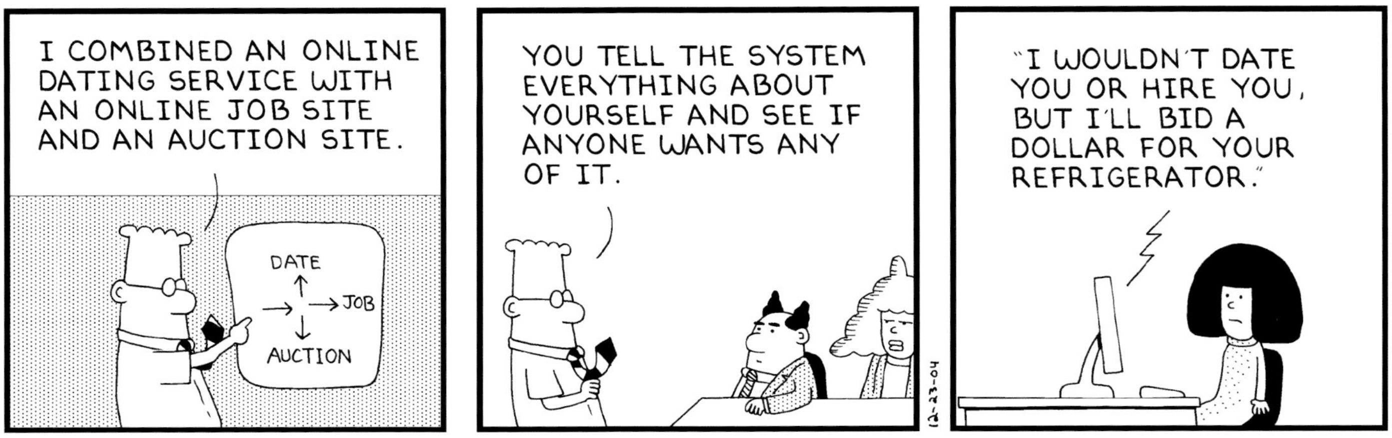
I COMBINED AN ONLINE DATING SERVICE WITH AN ONLINE JOB SITE AND AN AUCTION SITE.
DATE
JOB
AUCTION
YOU TELL THE SYSTEM EVERYTHING ABOUT YOURSELF AND SEE IF ANYONE WANTS ANY OF IT.
"I WOULDN'T DATE YOU OR HIRE YOU, BUT I'LL BID A DOLLAR FOR YOUR REFRIGERATOR."

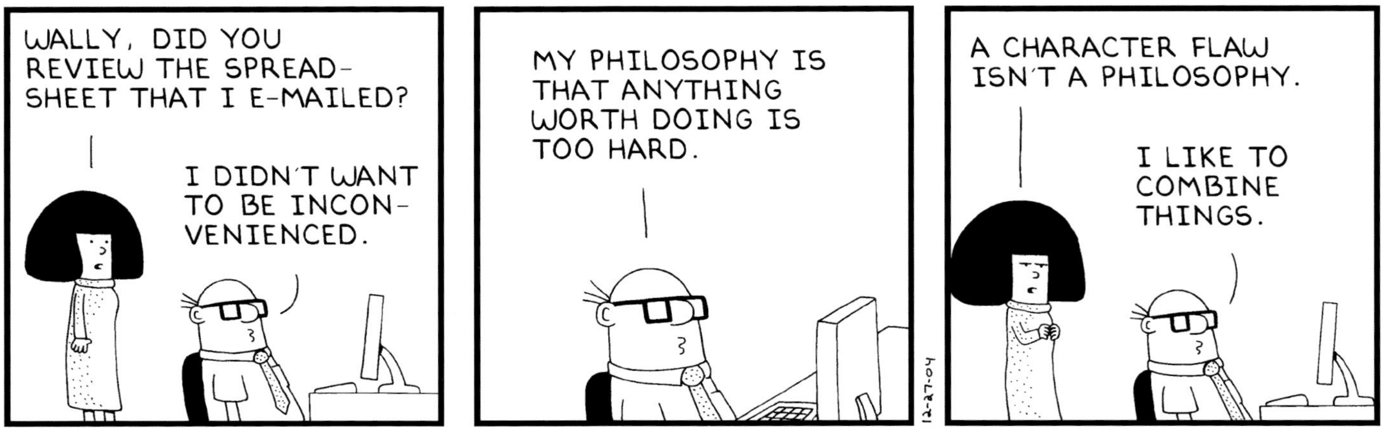
WALLY, DID YOU REVIEW THE SPREAD-SHEET THAT I E-MAILED?
I DIDN'T WANT TO BE INCON-VENIENCED.
MY PHILOSOPHY IS THAT ANYTHING WORTH DOING IS TOO HARD.
A CHARACTER FLAW ISN'T A PHILOSOPHY.
I LIKE TO COMBINE THINGS.

My dad is a treasure trove of irregular names for ordinary items. When I heard him refer to a toilet as a growler, I knew I had to use it.

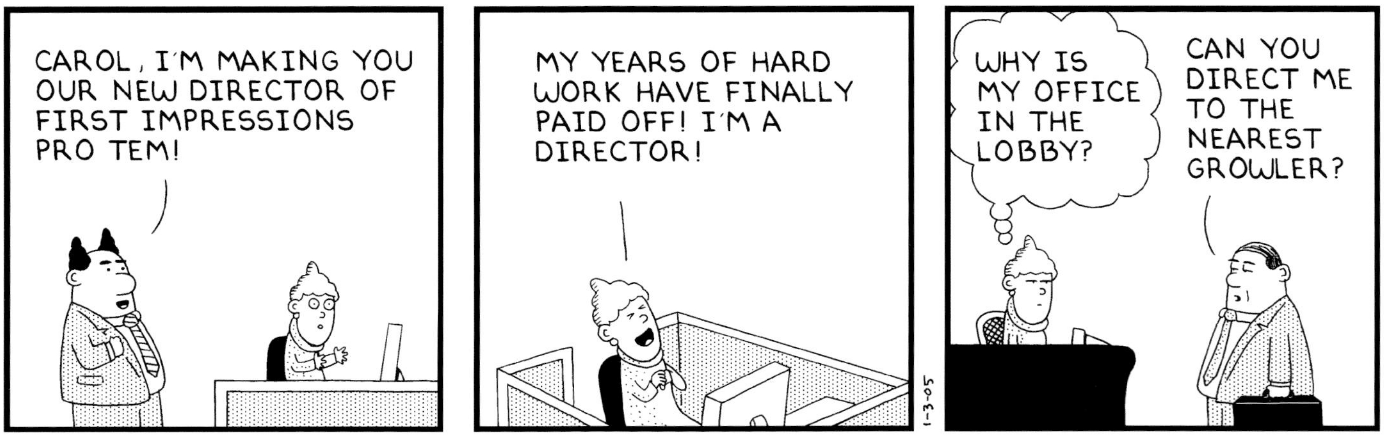
CAROL, I'M MAKING YOU OUR NEW DIRECTOR OF FIRST IMPRESSIONS PRO TEM!
MY YEARS OF HARD WORK HAVE FINALLY PAID OFF! I'M A DIRECTOR!
WHY IS MY OFFICE IN THE LOBBY?
CAN YOU DIRECT ME TO THE NEAREST GROWLER?

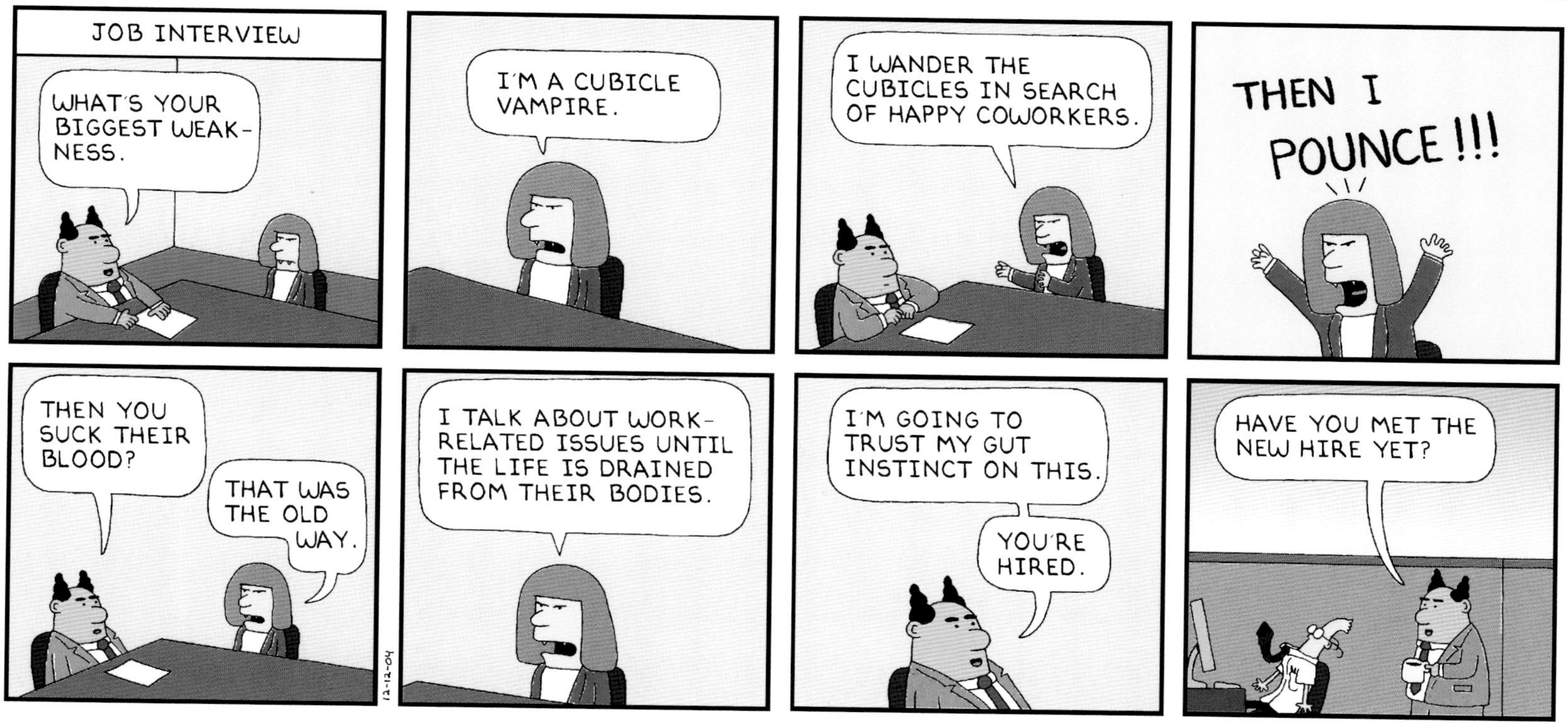
JOB INTERVIEW
WHAT'S YOUR BIGGEST WEAK-NESS.
I'M A CUBICLE VAMPIRE.
I WANDER THE CUBICLES IN SEARCH OF HAPPY COWORKERS.
THEN I POUNCE!!!
THEN YOU SUCK THEIR BLOOD?
THAT WAS THE OLD WAY.
12-12-04
I TALK ABOUT WORK-RELATED ISSUES UNTIL THE LIFE IS DRAINED FROM THEIR BODIES.
I'M GOING TO TRUST MY GUT INSTINCT ON THIS.
YOU'RE HIRED.
HAVE YOU MET THE NEW HIRE YET?

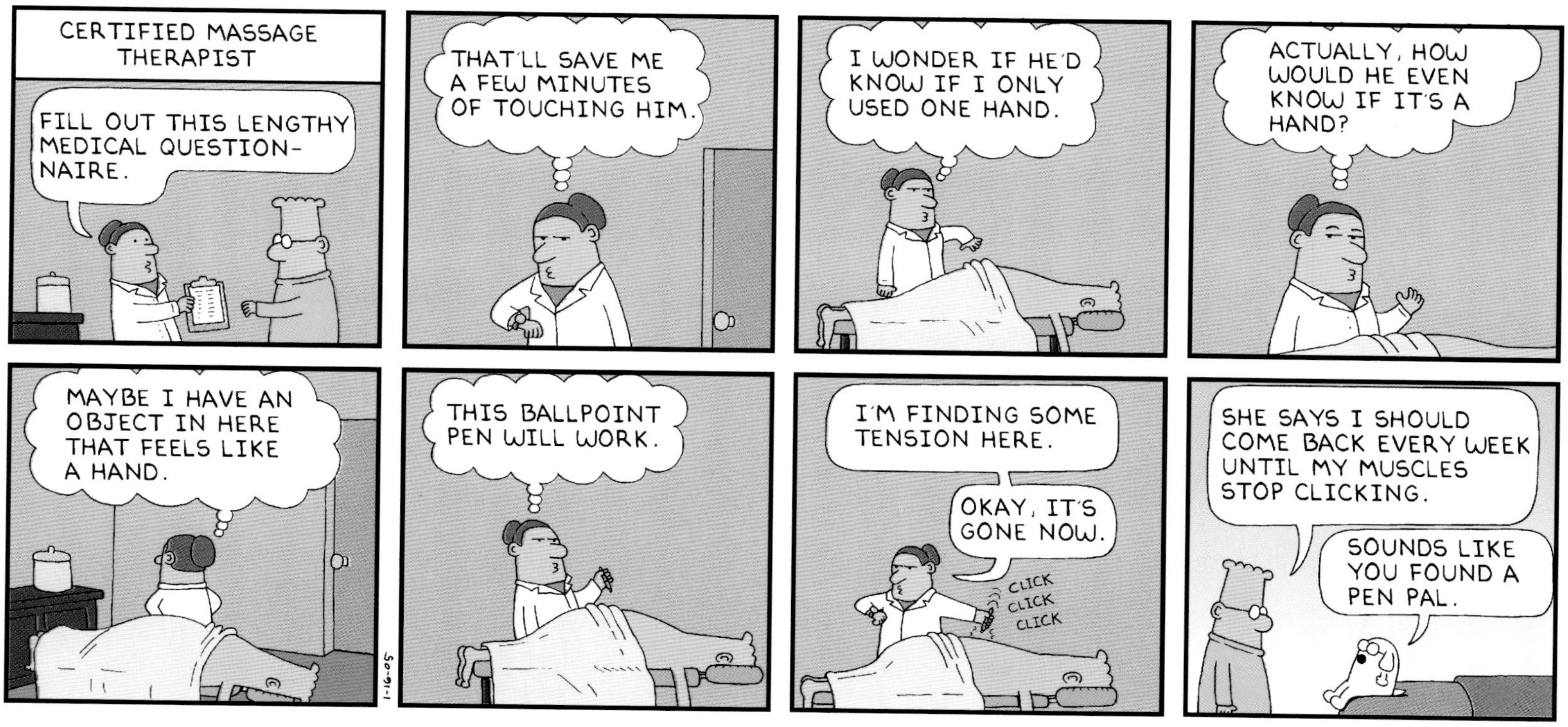
CERTIFIED MASSAGE THERAPIST
FILL OUT THIS LENGTHY MEDICAL QUESTION-NAIRE.
THAT'LL SAVE ME A FEW MINUTES OF TOUCHING HIM.
I WONDER IF HE'D KNOW IF I ONLY USED ONE HAND.
ACTUALLY, HOW WOULD HE EVEN KNOW IF IT'S A HAND?
MAYBE I HAVE AN OBJECT IN HERE THAT FEELS LIKE A HAND.
1-16-05
THIS BALLPOINT PEN WILL WORK.
I'M FINDING SOME TENSION HERE.
OKAY, IT'S GONE NOW.
CLICK CLICK CLICK
SHE SAYS I SHOULD COME BACK EVERY WEEK UNTIL MY MUSCLES STOP CLICKING.
SOUNDS LIKE YOU FOUND A PEN PAL.

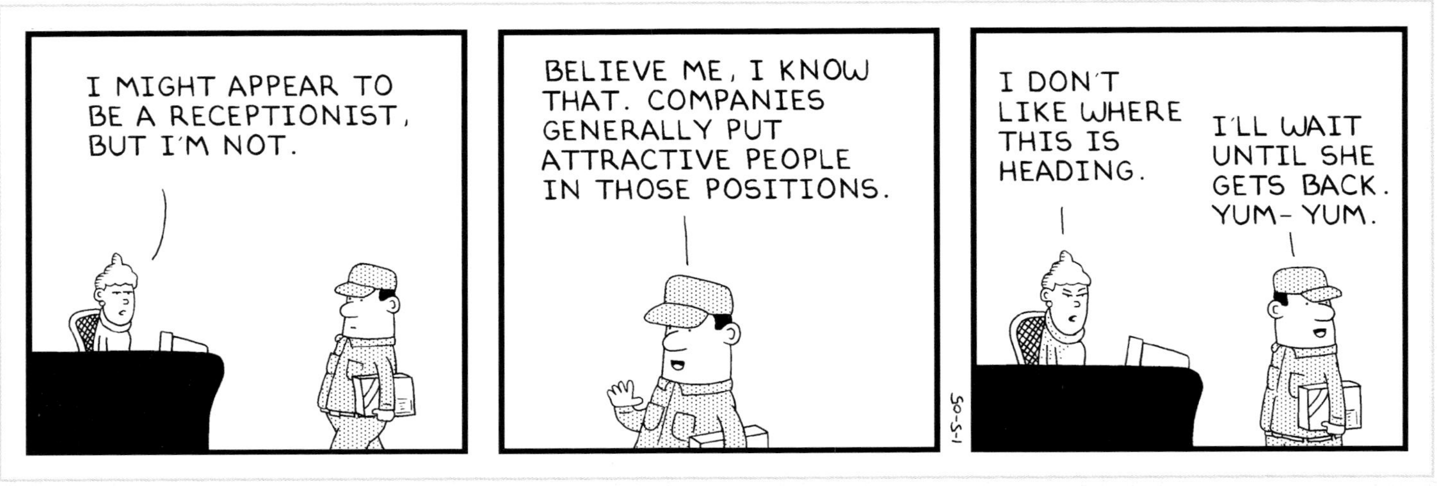
I MIGHT APPEAR TO BE A RECEPTIONIST, BUT I'M NOT.
BELIEVE ME, I KNOW THAT. COMPANIES GENERALLY PUT ATTRACTIVE PEOPLE IN THOSE POSITIONS.
1-5-05
I DON'T LIKE WHERE THIS IS HEADING.
I'LL WAIT UNTIL SHE GETS BACK. YUM-YUM.

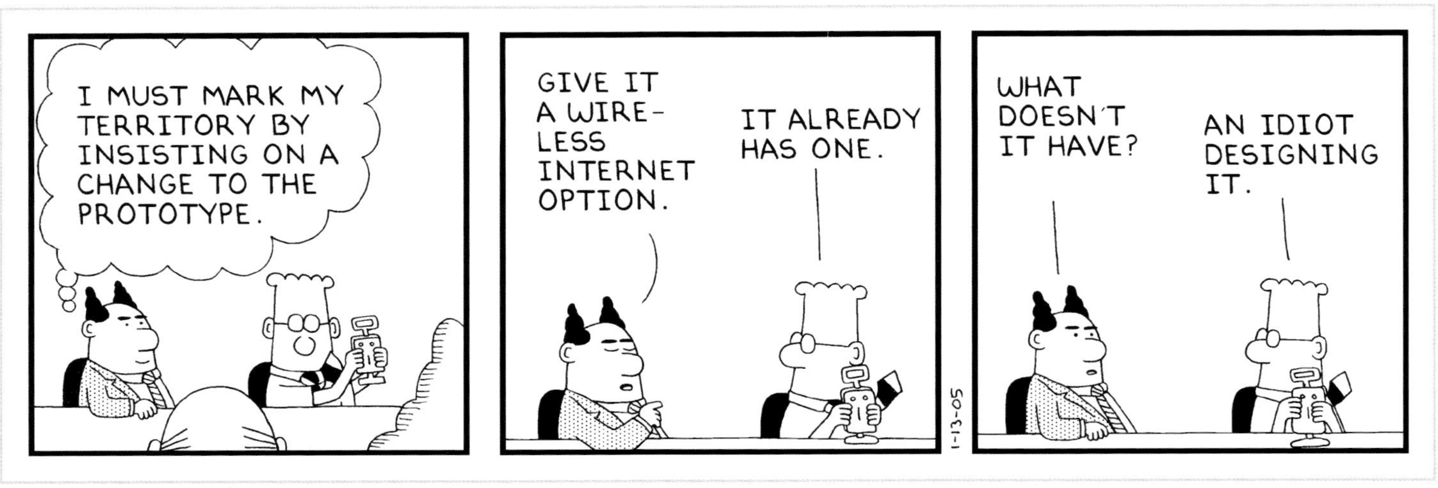
I MUST MARK MY TERRITORY BY INSISTING ON A CHANGE TO THE PROTOTYPE.
GIVE IT A WIRE-LESS INTERNET OPTION.
IT ALREADY HAS ONE.
1-13-05
WHAT DOESN'T IT HAVE?
AN IDIOT DESIGNING IT.

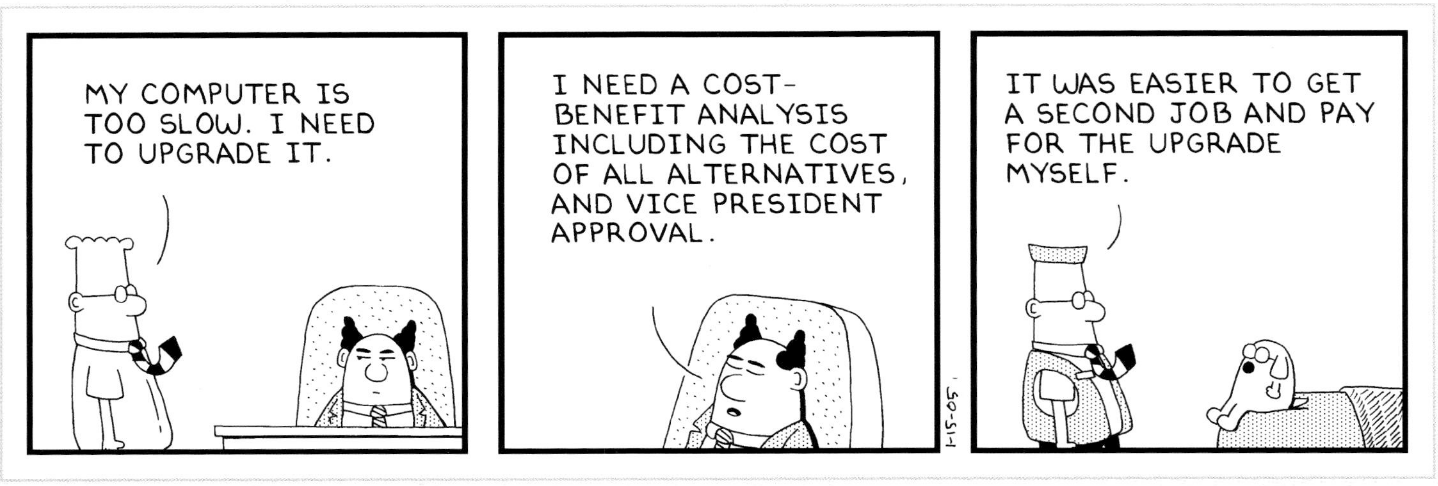
MY COMPUTER IS TOO SLOW. I NEED TO UPGRADE IT.
I NEED A COST-BENEFIT ANALYSIS INCLUDING THE COST OF ALL ALTERNATIVES, AND VICE PRESIDENT APPROVAL.
1-15-05
IT WAS EASIER TO GET A SECOND JOB AND PAY FOR THE UPGRADE MYSELF.

Yes, people complained about the following strip under the theory that portraying one particular person is the same as making a blanket statement about an entire class of people.

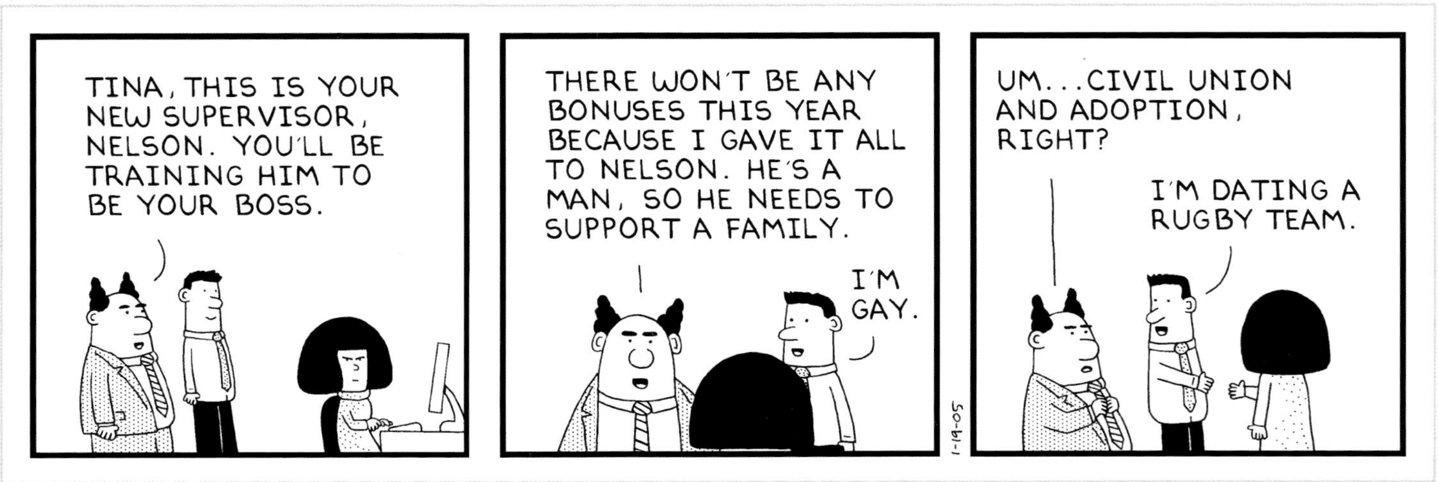
TINA, THIS IS YOUR NEW SUPERVISOR, NELSON. YOU'LL BE TRAINING HIM TO BE YOUR BOSS.
THERE WON'T BE ANY BONUSES THIS YEAR BECAUSE I GAVE IT ALL TO NELSON. HE'S A MAN, SO HE NEEDS TO SUPPORT A FAMILY.
I'M GAY.
1-19-05
UM...CIVIL UNION AND ADOPTION, RIGHT?
I'M DATING A RUGBY TEAM.

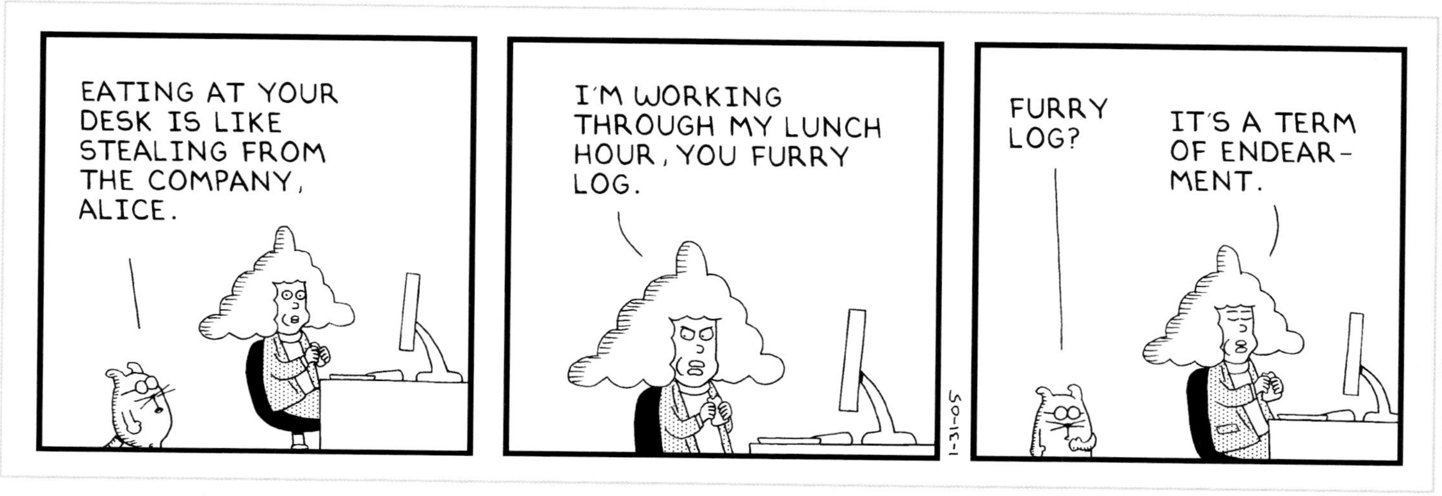
EATING AT YOUR DESK IS LIKE STEALING FROM THE COMPANY, ALICE.
I'M WORKING THROUGH MY LUNCH HOUR, YOU FURRY LOG.
1-31-05
FURRY LOG?
IT'S A TERM OF ENDEAR-MENT.

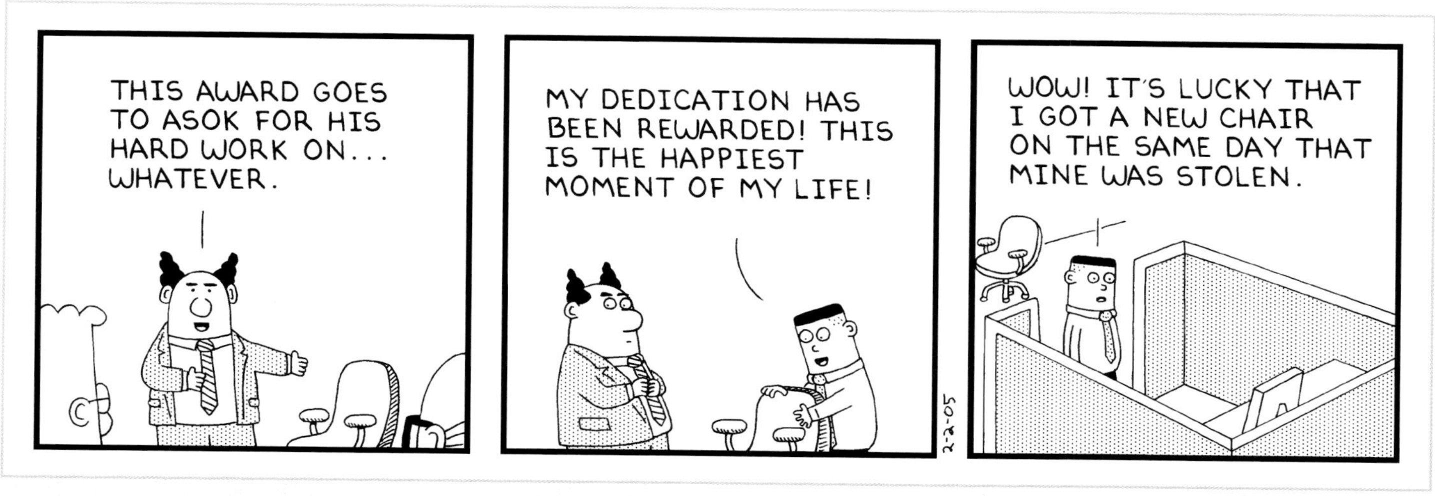
THIS AWARD GOES TO ASOK FOR HIS HARD WORK ON... WHATEVER.
MY DEDICATION HAS BEEN REWARDED! THIS IS THE HAPPIEST MOMENT OF MY LIFE!
2-2-05
WOW! IT'S LUCKY THAT I GOT A NEW CHAIR ON THE SAME DAY THAT MINE WAS STOLEN.

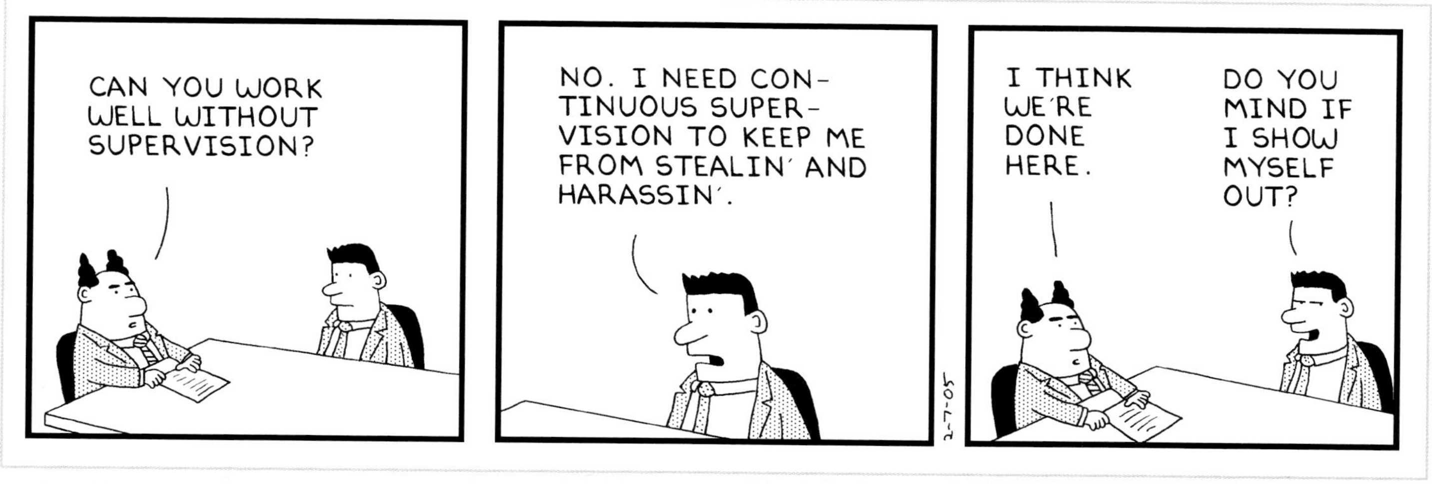
CAN YOU WORK WELL WITHOUT SUPERVISION?
NO. I NEED CON-TINUOUS SUPER-VISION TO KEEP ME FROM STEALIN' AND HARASSIN'.
2-7-05
I THINK WE'RE DONE HERE.
DO YOU MIND IF I SHOW MYSELF OUT?

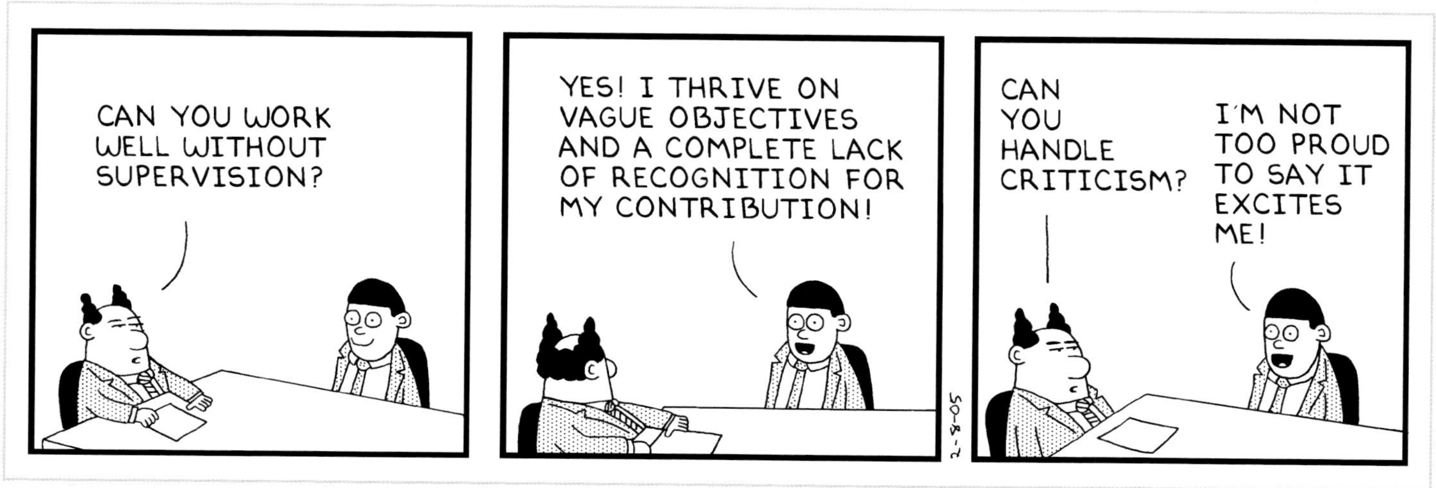
CAN YOU WORK WELL WITHOUT SUPERVISION?
YES! I THRIVE ON VAGUE OBJECTIVES AND A COMPLETE LACK OF RECOGNITION FOR MY CONTRIBUTION!
2-8-05
CAN YOU HANDLE CRITICISM?
I'M NOT TOO PROUD TO SAY IT EXCITES ME!

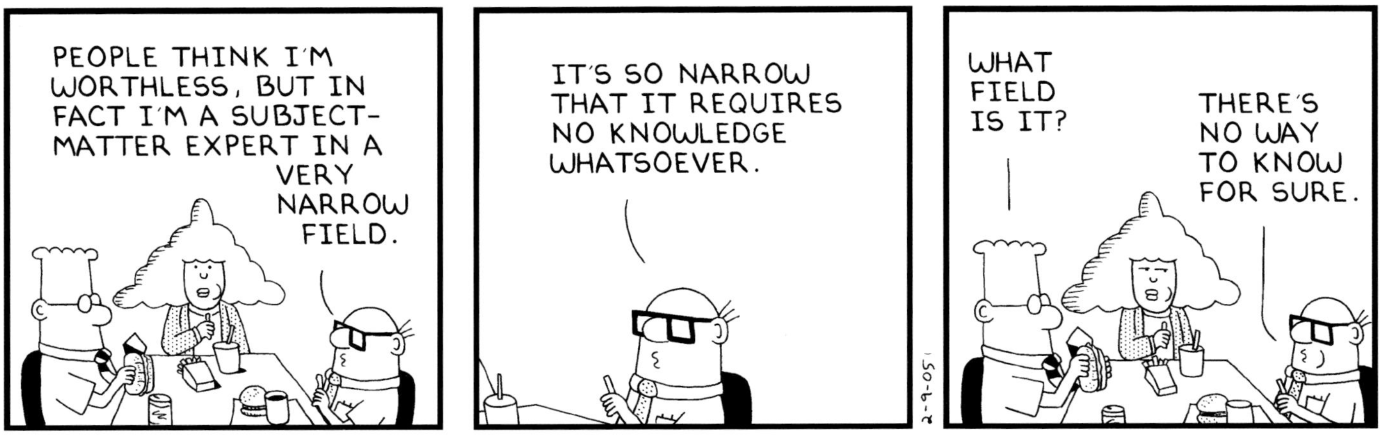
PEOPLE THINK I'M WORTHLESS, BUT IN FACT I'M A SUBJECT-MATTER EXPERT IN A VERY NARROW FIELD.
IT'S SO NARROW THAT IT REQUIRES NO KNOWLEDGE WHATSOEVER.
2-9-05
WHAT FIELD IS IT?
THERE'S NO WAY TO KNOW FOR SURE.

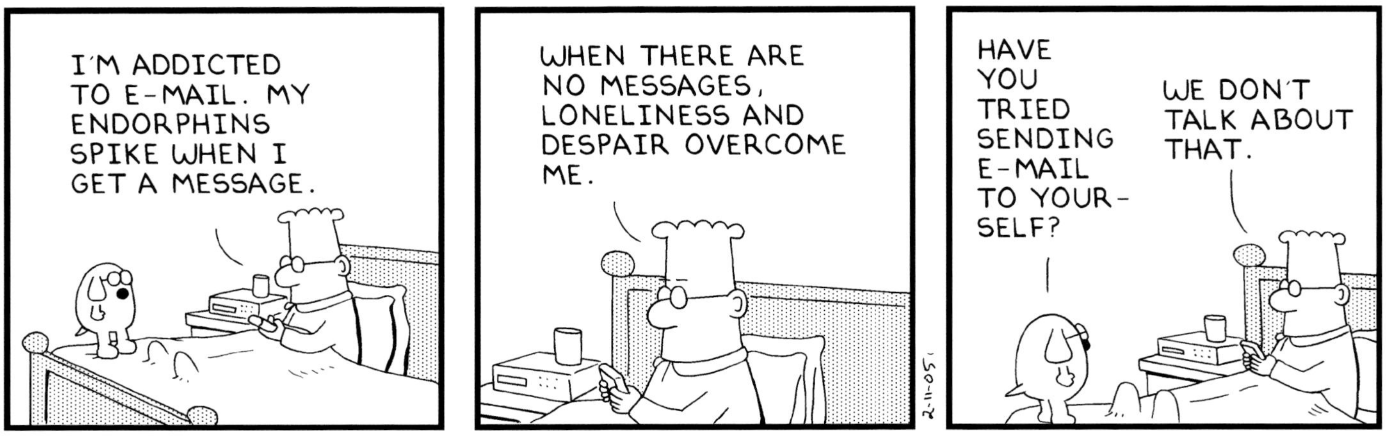
I'M ADDICTED TO E-MAIL. MY ENDORPHINS SPIKE WHEN I GET A MESSAGE.
WHEN THERE ARE NO MESSAGES, LONELINESS AND DESPAIR OVERCOME ME.
2-11-05
HAVE YOU TRIED SENDING E-MAIL TO YOUR-SELF?
WE DON'T TALK ABOUT THAT.

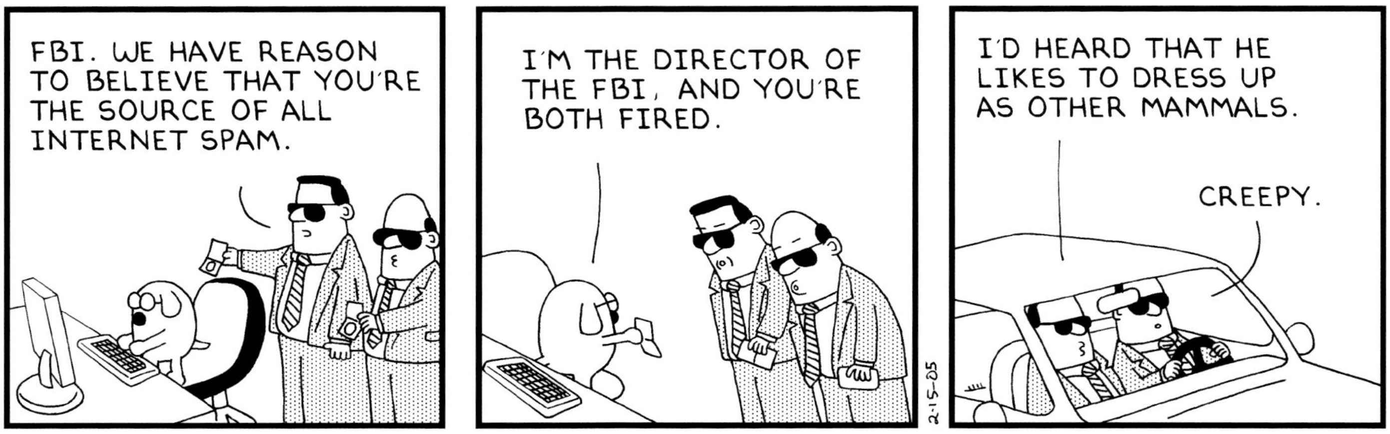
FBI. WE HAVE REASON TO BELIEVE THAT YOU'RE THE SOURCE OF ALL INTERNET SPAM.
I'M THE DIRECTOR OF THE FBI, AND YOU'RE BOTH FIRED.
2-15-05
I'D HEARD THAT HE LIKES TO DRESS UP AS OTHER MAMMALS.
CREEPY.

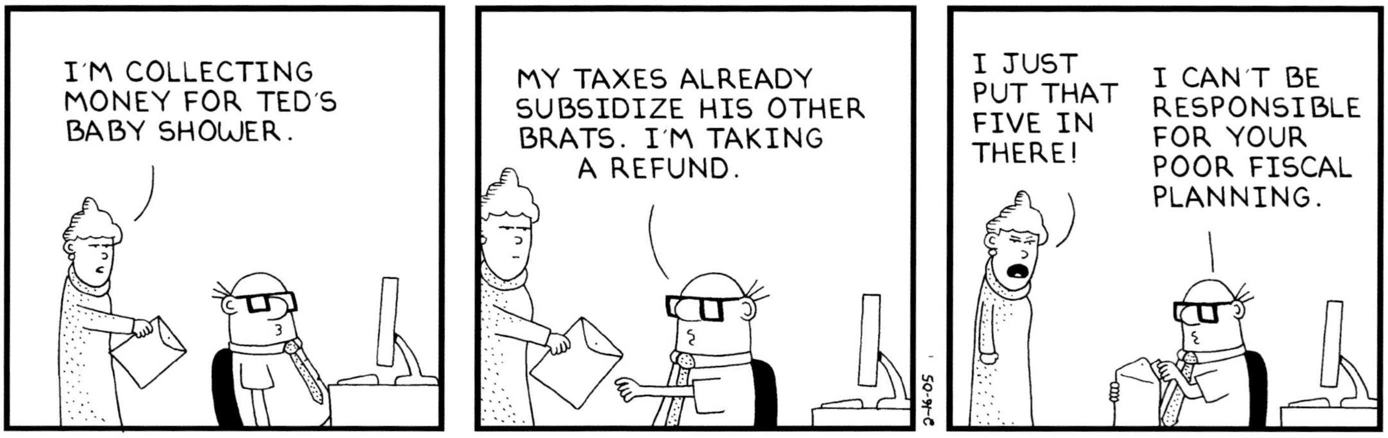
I'M COLLECTING MONEY FOR TED'S BABY SHOWER.
MY TAXES ALREADY SUBSIDIZE HIS OTHER BRATS. I'M TAKING A REFUND.
2-16-05
I JUST PUT THAT FIVE IN THERE!
I CAN'T BE RESPONSIBLE FOR YOUR POOR FISCAL PLANNING.

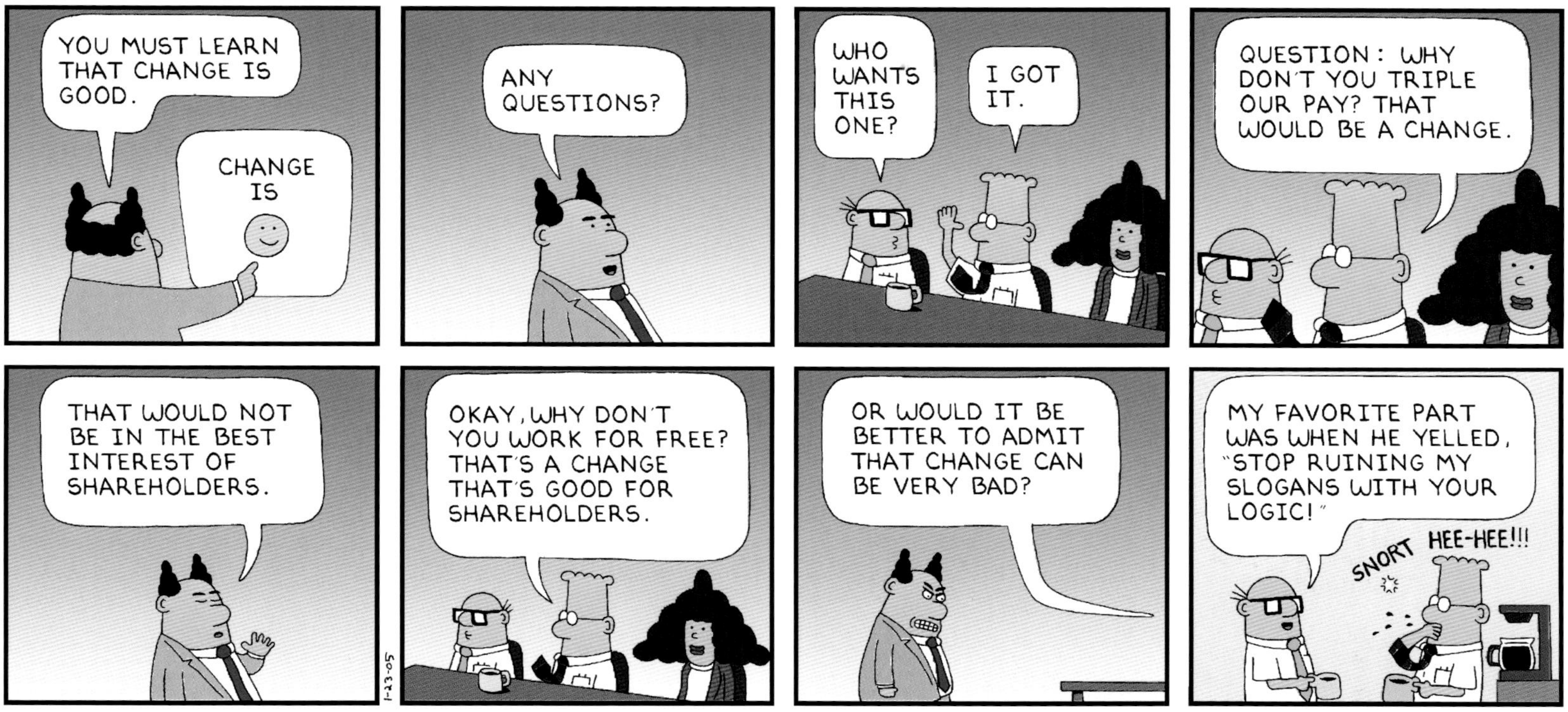
YOU MUST LEARN THAT CHANGE IS GOOD.
CHANGE IS
ANY QUESTIONS?
WHO WANTS THIS ONE?
I GOT IT.
QUESTION: WHY DON'T YOU TRIPLE OUR PAY? THAT WOULD BE A CHANGE.
THAT WOULD NOT BE IN THE BEST INTEREST OF SHAREHOLDERS.
OKAY, WHY DON'T YOU WORK FOR FREE? THAT'S A CHANGE THAT'S GOOD FOR SHAREHOLDERS.
OR WOULD IT BE BETTER TO ADMIT THAT CHANGE CAN BE VERY BAD?
MY FAVORITE PART WAS WHEN HE YELLED, "STOP RUINING MY SLOGANS WITH YOUR LOGIC!"
SNORT
HEE-HEE!!!

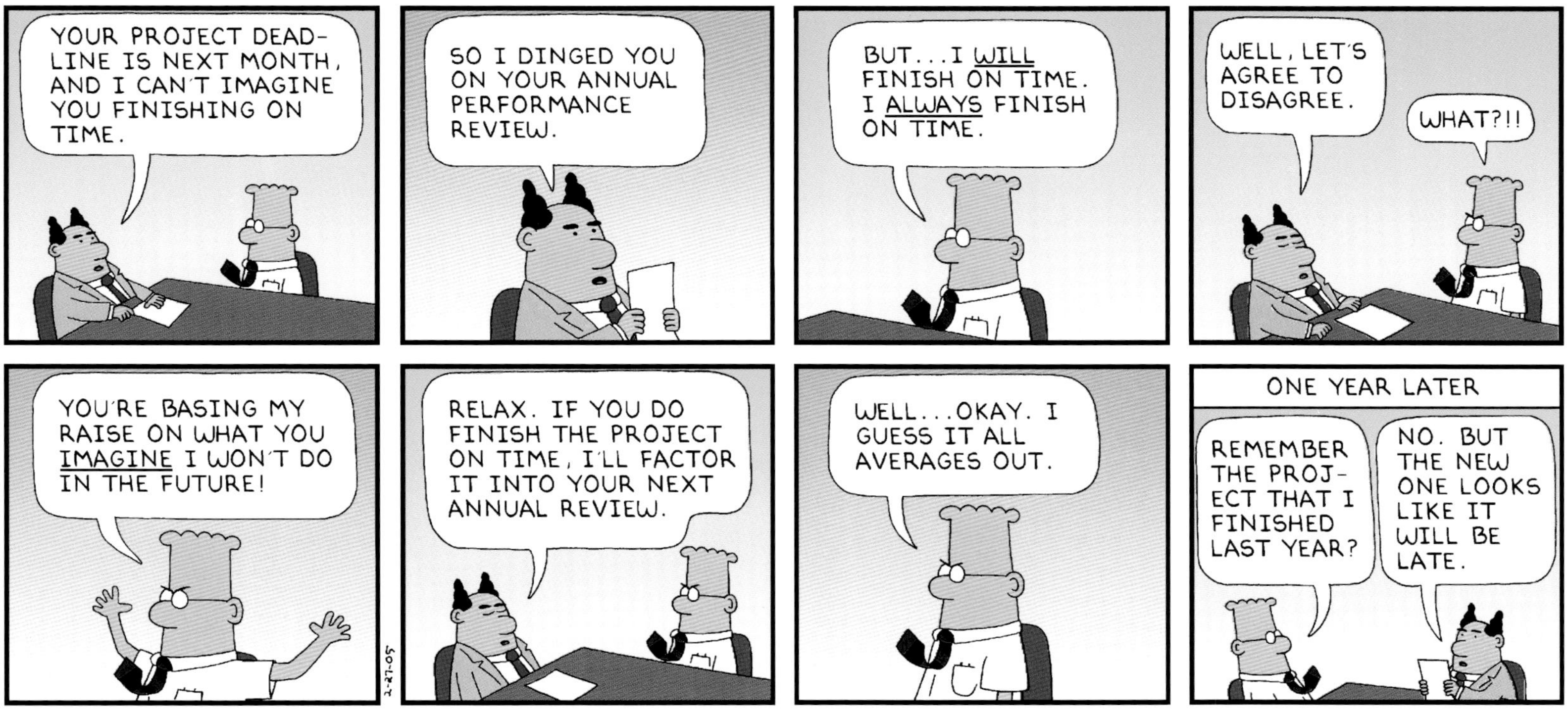
YOUR PROJECT DEADLINE IS NEXT MONTH, AND I CAN'T IMAGINE YOU FINISHING ON TIME.
SO I DINGED YOU ON YOUR ANNUAL PERFORMANCE REVIEW.
BUT... I WILL FINISH ON TIME. I ALWAYS FINISH ON TIME.
WELL, LET'S AGREE TO DISAGREE.
WHAT?!!
YOU'RE BASING MY RAISE ON WHAT YOU IMAGINE I WON'T DO IN THE FUTURE!
RELAX. IF YOU DO FINISH THE PROJECT ON TIME, I'LL FACTOR IT INTO YOUR NEXT ANNUAL REVIEW.
WELL... OKAY. I GUESS IT ALL AVERAGES OUT.
ONE YEAR LATER
REMEMBER THE PROJECT THAT I FINISHED LAST YEAR?
NO. BUT THE NEW ONE LOOKS LIKE IT WILL BE LATE.

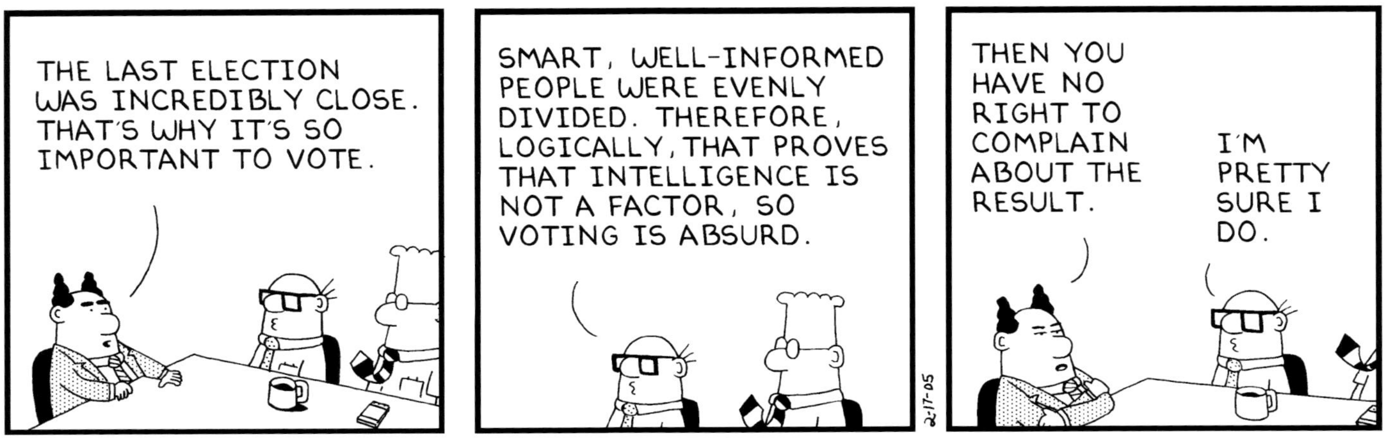
THE LAST ELECTION WAS INCREDIBLY CLOSE. THAT'S WHY IT'S SO IMPORTANT TO VOTE.
SMART, WELL-INFORMED PEOPLE WERE EVENLY DIVIDED. THEREFORE, LOGICALLY, THAT PROVES THAT INTELLIGENCE IS NOT A FACTOR, SO VOTING IS ABSURD.
THEN YOU HAVE NO RIGHT TO COMPLAIN ABOUT THE RESULT.
I'M PRETTY SURE I DO.

I make this argument often. It drives people nuts. That's why I like it.

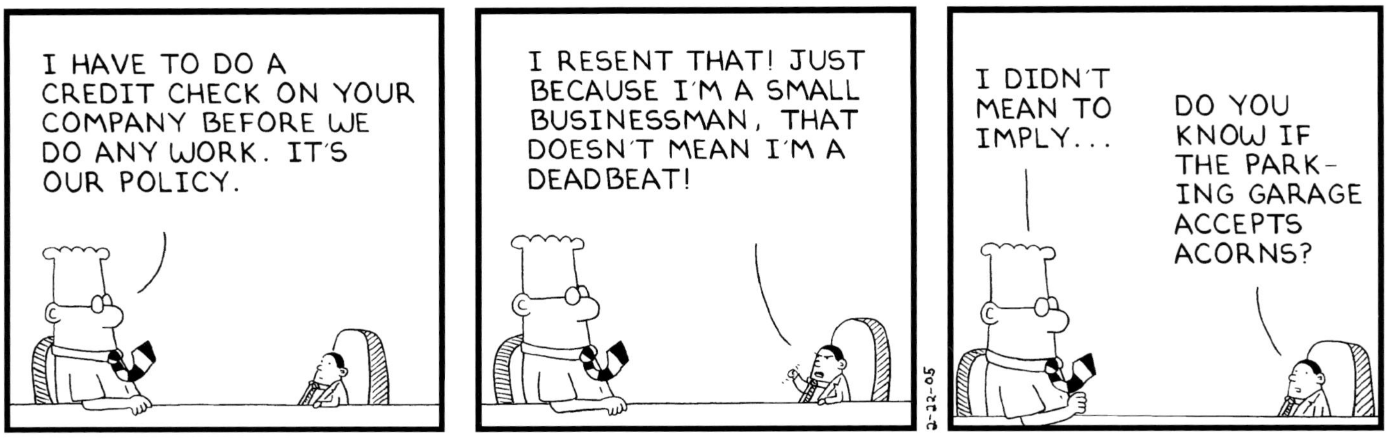
I HAVE TO DO A CREDIT CHECK ON YOUR COMPANY BEFORE WE DO ANY WORK. IT'S OUR POLICY.
I RESENT THAT! JUST BECAUSE I'M A SMALL BUSINESSMAN, THAT DOESN'T MEAN I'M A DEADBEAT!
I DIDN'T MEAN TO IMPLY...
DO YOU KNOW IF THE PARKING GARAGE ACCEPTS ACORNS?

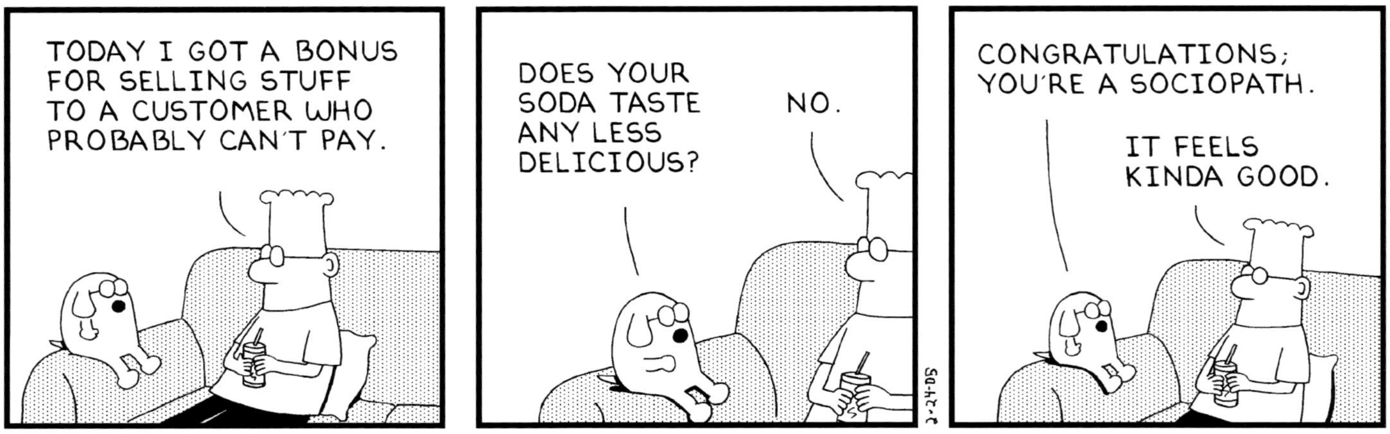
TODAY I GOT A BONUS FOR SELLING STUFF TO A CUSTOMER WHO PROBABLY CAN'T PAY.
DOES YOUR SODA TASTE ANY LESS DELICIOUS?
NO.
CONGRATULATIONS; YOU'RE A SOCIOPATH.
IT FEELS KINDA GOOD.

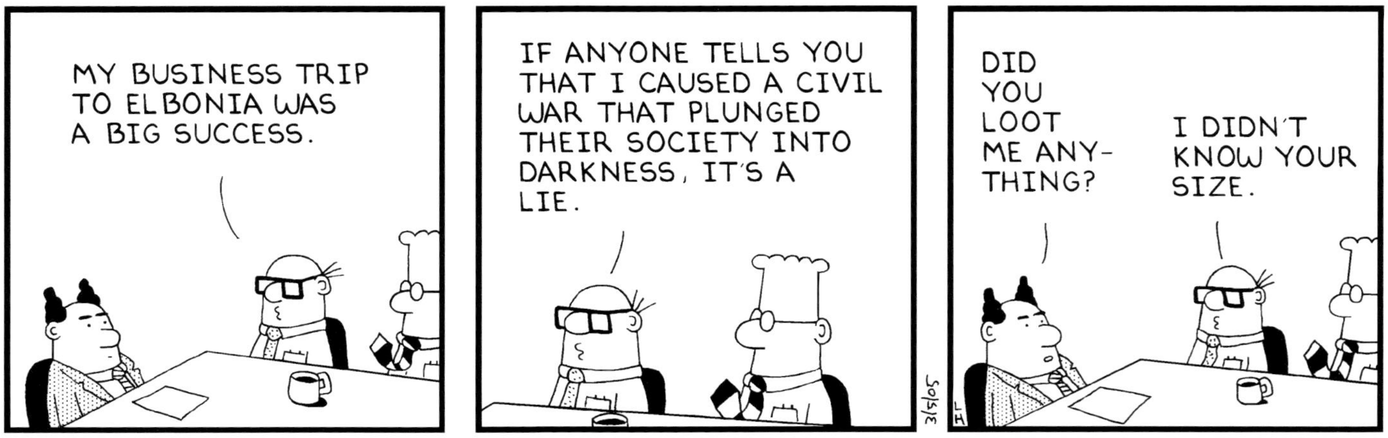
MY BUSINESS TRIP TO ELBONIA WAS A BIG SUCCESS.
IF ANYONE TELLS YOU THAT I CAUSED A CIVIL WAR THAT PLUNGED THEIR SOCIETY INTO DARKNESS, IT'S A LIE.
DID YOU LOOT ME ANYTHING?
I DIDN'T KNOW YOUR SIZE.

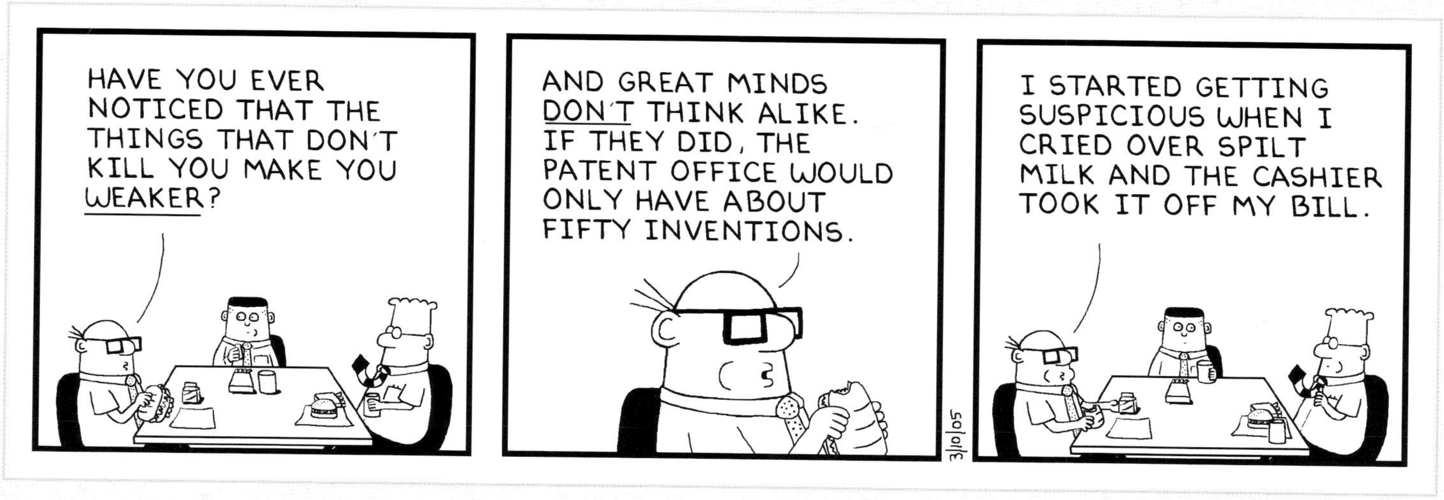
HAVE YOU EVER NOTICED THAT THE THINGS THAT DON'T KILL YOU MAKE YOU WEAKER?
AND GREAT MINDS DON'T THINK ALIKE. IF THEY DID, THE PATENT OFFICE WOULD ONLY HAVE ABOUT FIFTY INVENTIONS.
3/10/05
I STARTED GETTING SUSPICIOUS WHEN I CRIED OVER SPILT MILK AND THE CASHIER TOOK IT OFF MY BILL.

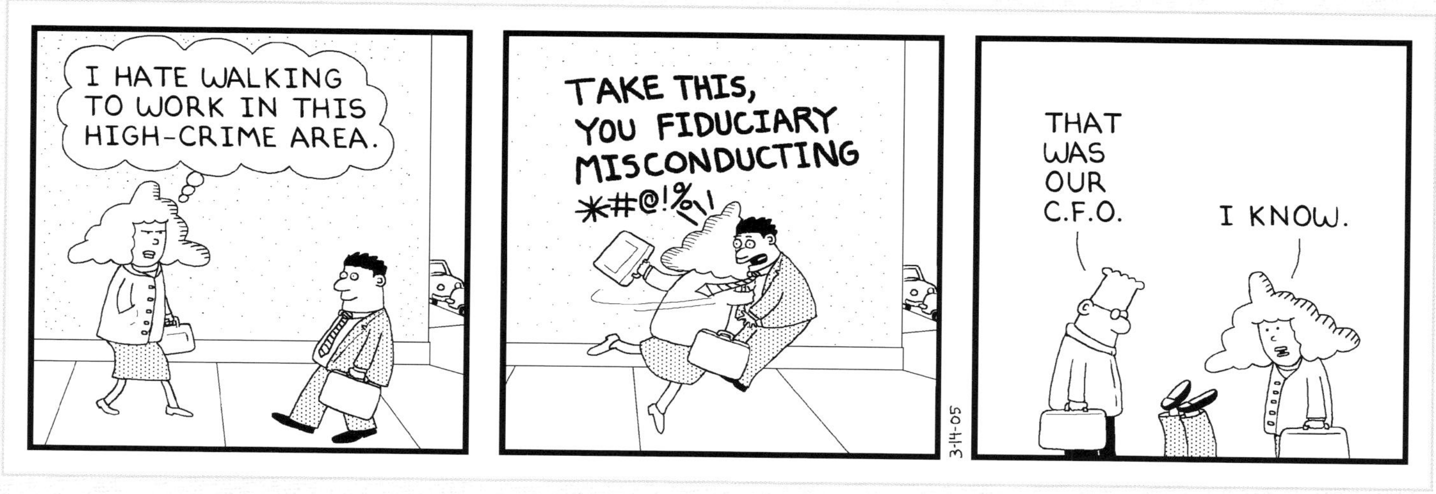
I HATE WALKING TO WORK IN THIS HIGH-CRIME AREA.
TAKE THIS, YOU FIDUCIARY MISCONDUCTING *#@!%!
3-14-05
THAT WAS OUR C.F.O.
I KNOW.

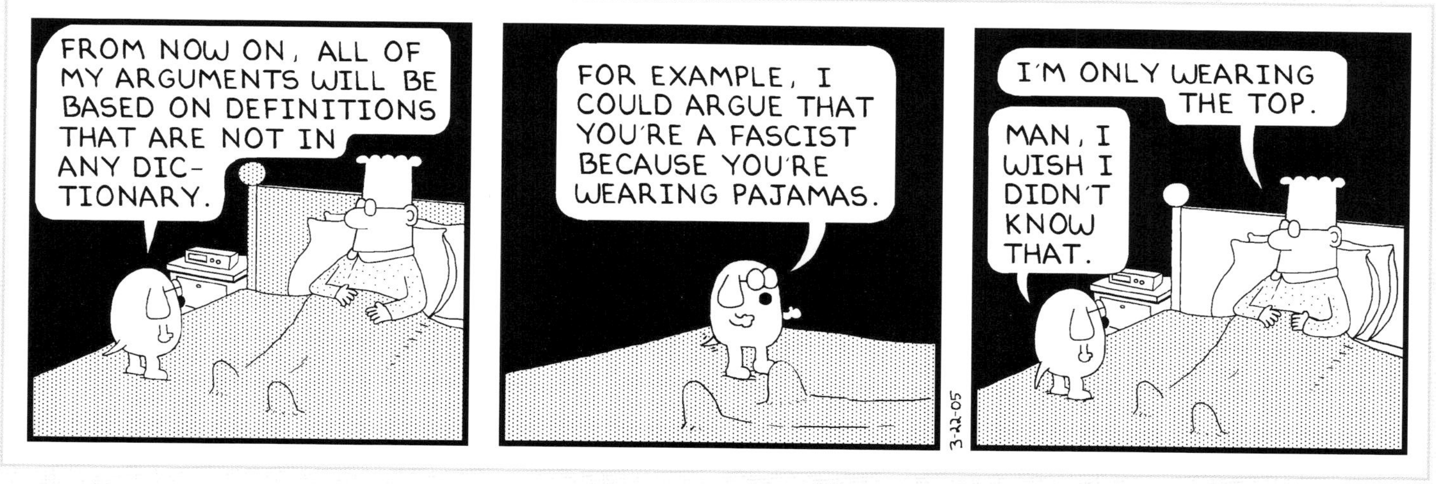
FROM NOW ON, ALL OF MY ARGUMENTS WILL BE BASED ON DEFINITIONS THAT ARE NOT IN ANY DICTIONARY.
FOR EXAMPLE, I COULD ARGUE THAT YOU'RE A FASCIST BECAUSE YOU'RE WEARING PAJAMAS.
3-22-05
I'M ONLY WEARING THE TOP.
MAN, I WISH I DIDN'T KNOW THAT.

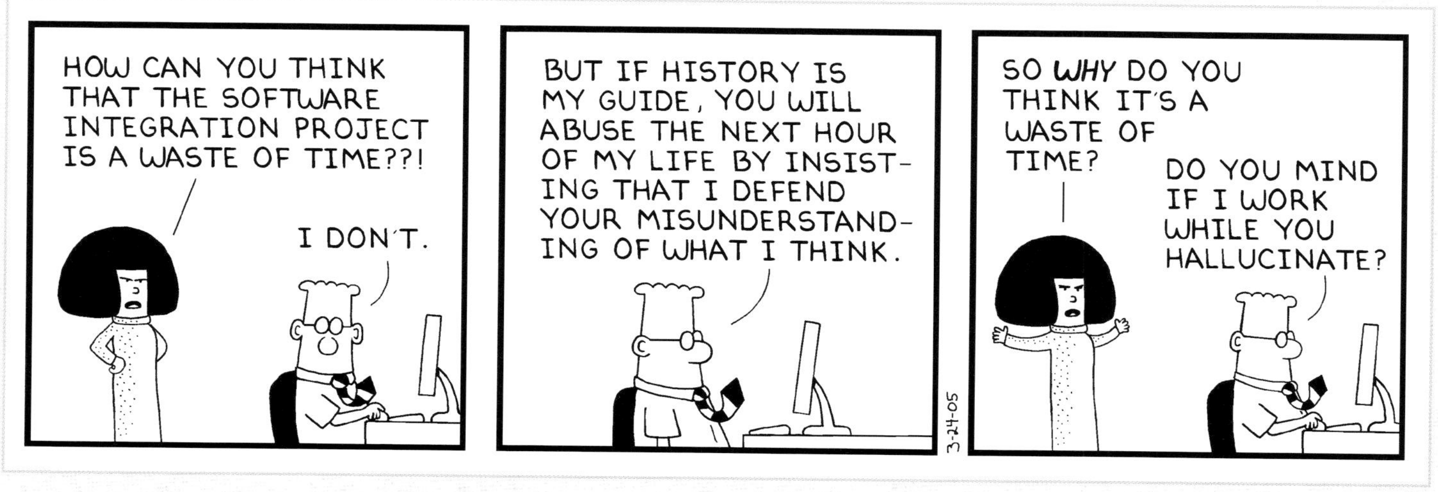
HOW CAN YOU THINK THAT THE SOFTWARE INTEGRATION PROJECT IS A WASTE OF TIME??!
I DON'T.
BUT IF HISTORY IS MY GUIDE, YOU WILL ABUSE THE NEXT HOUR OF MY LIFE BY INSISTING THAT I DEFEND YOUR MISUNDERSTANDING OF WHAT I THINK.
3-24-05
SO WHY DO YOU THINK IT'S A WASTE OF TIME?
DO YOU MIND IF I WORK WHILE YOU HALLUCINATE?

I MISSED THE INTRODUCTIONS.
I'LL USE MY MANAGER INSTINCT TO FIGURE OUT WHO'S IMPORTANT.
ONLY A SENIOR EXECUTIVE COULD GET AWAY WITH LOOKING SO DISENGAGED.
I'LL MIRROR HIS MANNERISMS SO HE'LL LIKE ME.
NOW FOR A WITTY SIDE COMMENT.
HA HA! THAT WILL HAPPEN WHEN MONKEYS FLY OUT OF MY NOSE.
3-20-05
NO REACTION! HE MUST BE SO IMPORTANT THAT HE HAS NO SENSE OF HUMOR!
I PLEDGE MY LOYALTY TO YOU AND ONLY YOU!!!
I HEARD THAT YOU PLEDGED YOUR LOYALTY TO A DEAD GUY.
AT LEAST HE WON'T ASK FOR MUCH.

CAROL, THE NEW MANAGER HASN'T HIRED AN ADMIN, SO I SAID HE COULD SHARE YOU.
WHAT?!!
I'M DROWNING IN WORK, AND YOU WANT TO DOUBLE MY LOAD???!!!
IT'S NO BIG DEAL. JUST PRIORITIZE YOUR WORK.
AND I NEED YOU TO FAX THIS.
NO CAN DO.
MY TOP PRIORITY IS GETTING THE NEW GUY ALL SET UP.
HMM... I GUESS THAT'S FAIR.
I'LL SEND HIM OVER.
3-27-05
I CAN'T ORDER YOUR BUSINESS CARDS; I NEED TO DO A HUGE FAXING PROJECT!
HEE HEE! MARMADUKE IS SITTING ON SOMETHING AGAIN!

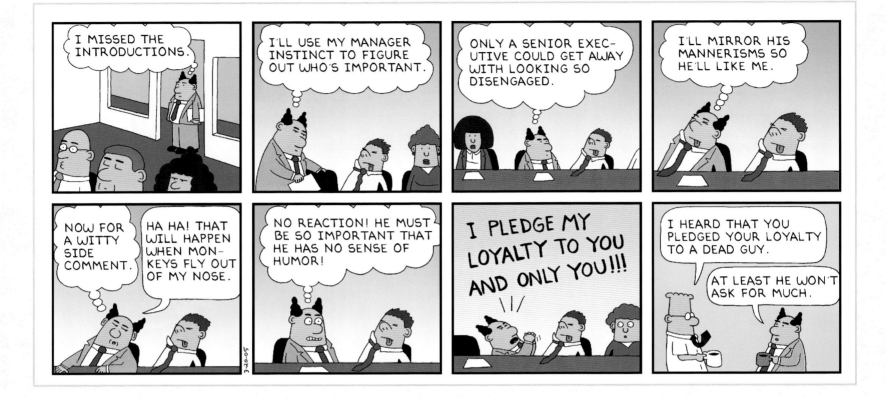

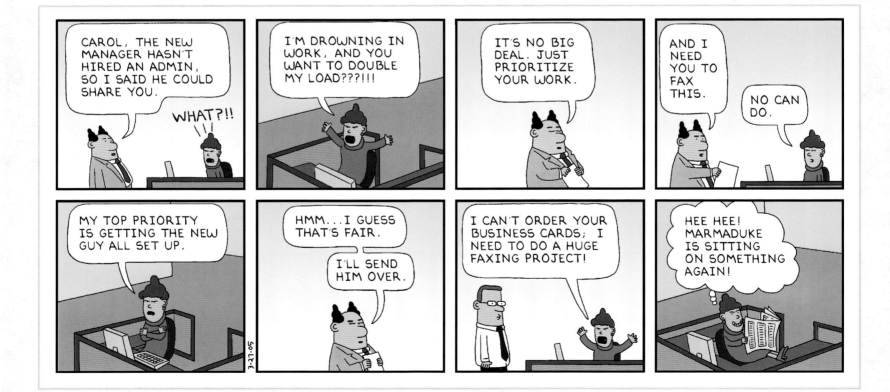

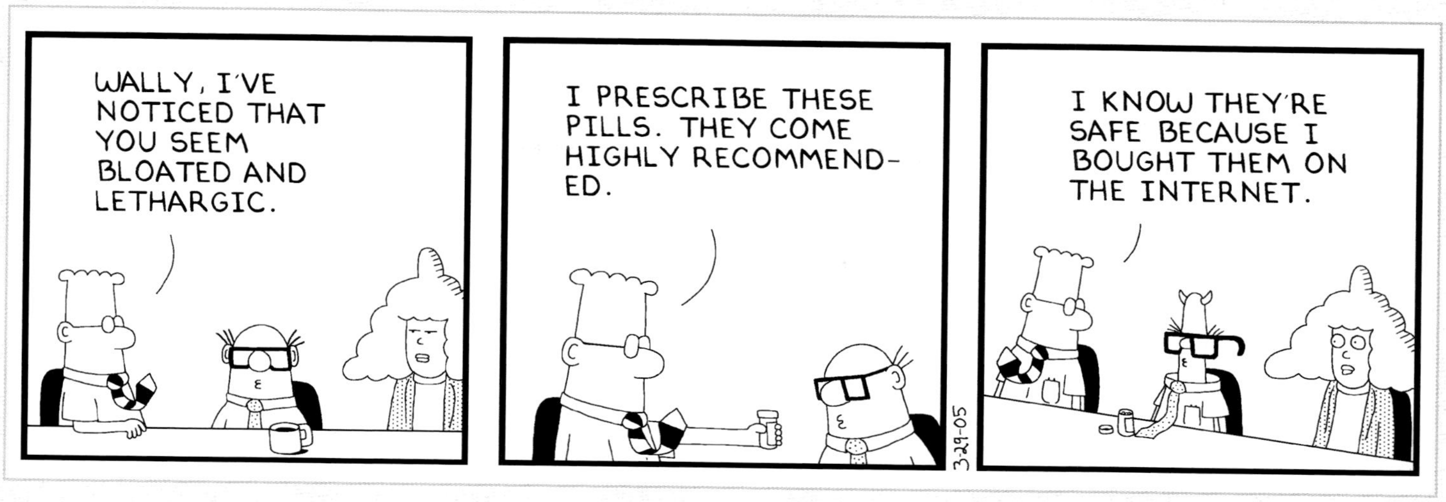
WALLY, I'VE NOTICED THAT YOU SEEM BLOATED AND LETHARGIC.
I PRESCRIBE THESE PILLS. THEY COME HIGHLY RECOMMEND-ED.
I KNOW THEY'RE SAFE BECAUSE I BOUGHT THEM ON THE INTERNET.
3-29-05

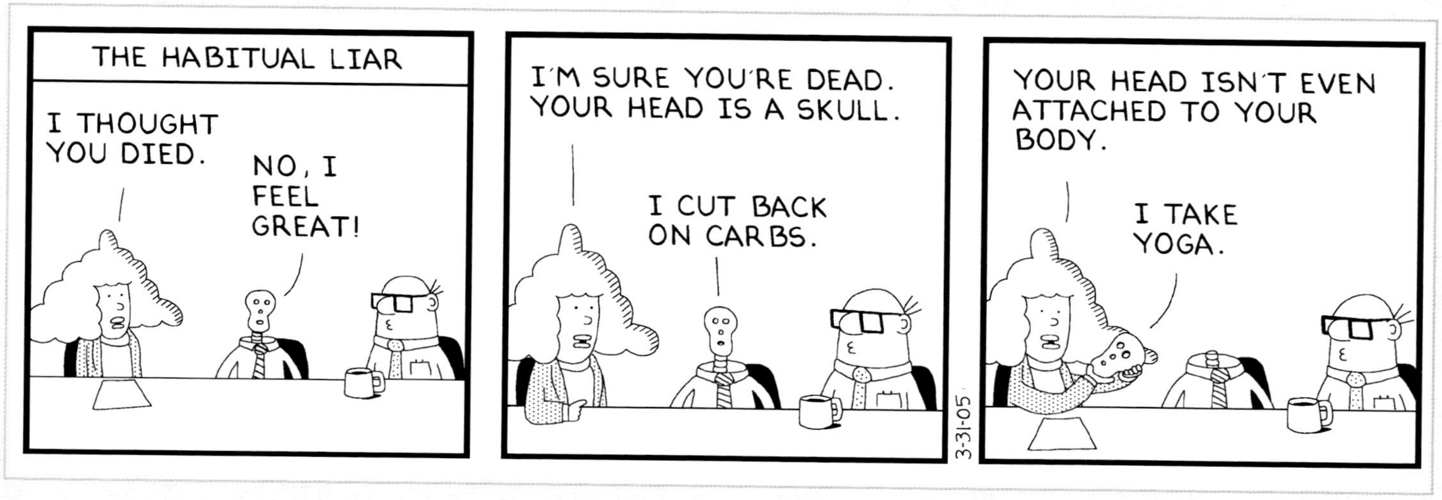
THE HABITUAL LIAR
I THOUGHT YOU DIED.
NO, I FEEL GREAT!
I'M SURE YOU'RE DEAD. YOUR HEAD IS A SKULL.
I CUT BACK ON CARBS.
YOUR HEAD ISN'T EVEN ATTACHED TO YOUR BODY.
I TAKE YOGA.
3-31-05

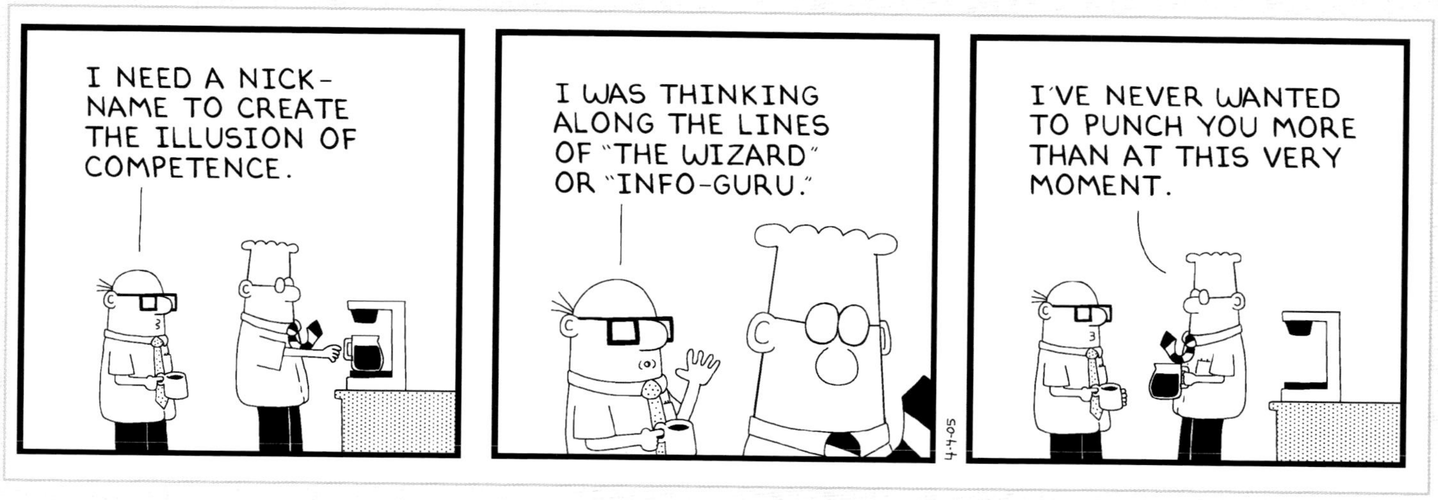
I NEED A NICK-NAME TO CREATE THE ILLUSION OF COMPETENCE.
I WAS THINKING ALONG THE LINES OF "THE WIZARD" OR "INFO-GURU."
I'VE NEVER WANTED TO PUNCH YOU MORE THAN AT THIS VERY MOMENT.
4-4-05

Notice that the artwork in this strip, particularly in the middle panel, seems more poorly drawn than usual. At about this time, I started drawing the strip directly on the computer. It took several months of practice to get the look right. This was the start of the learning curve.

I have an exotic hand problem called a focal dystonia that developed from overuse. My right hand is 100 percent functional for every purpose except pressing a writing utensil against a piece of paper. When I work on paper, my brain causes my right hand to spasm, which effectively removes my ability to draw or write. In fact, when I draw left-handed, which I can do, but slowly, my right hand still spasms.

Given the odd specificity of the problem, I reasoned that drawing on the computer might not trigger the spasm. I was right. Although I hold a stylus exactly like a pen, and draw on the screen just as if it were paper, my brain doesn't recognize it as standard drawing and doesn't trigger the spasm. I also cut my workload by about 50 percent.

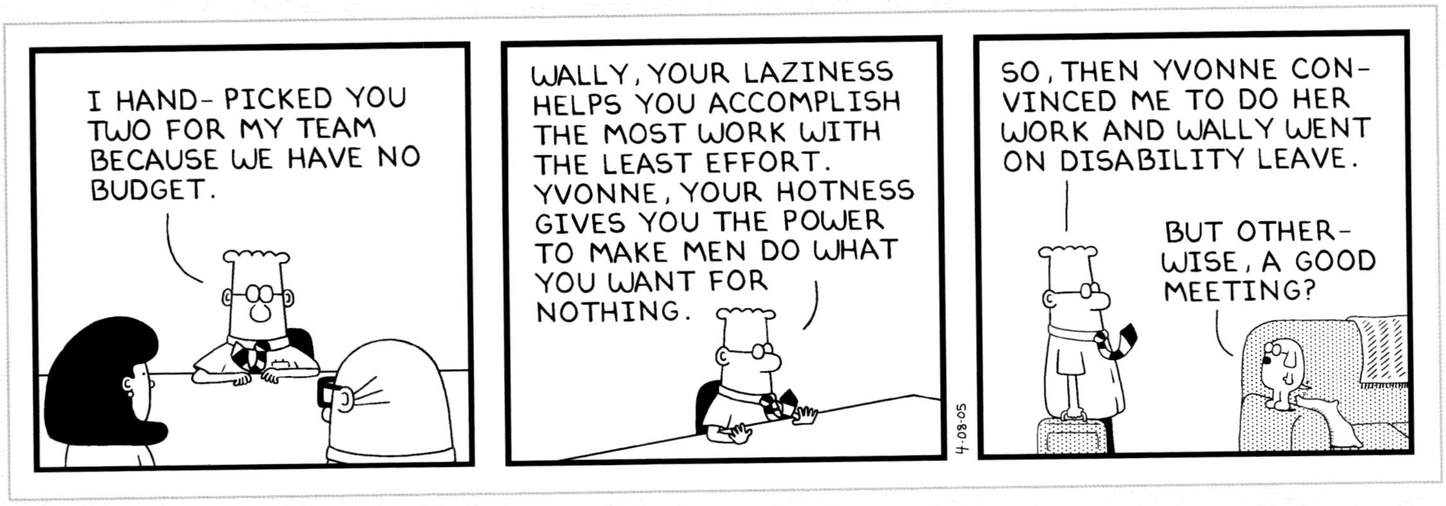
I HAND-PICKED YOU TWO FOR MY TEAM BECAUSE WE HAVE NO BUDGET.
WALLY, YOUR LAZINESS HELPS YOU ACCOMPLISH THE MOST WORK WITH THE LEAST EFFORT. YVONNE, YOUR HOTNESS GIVES YOU THE POWER TO MAKE MEN DO WHAT YOU WANT FOR NOTHING.
4-08-05
SO, THEN YVONNE CONVINCED ME TO DO HER WORK AND WALLY WENT ON DISABILITY LEAVE.
BUT OTHERWISE, A GOOD MEETING?

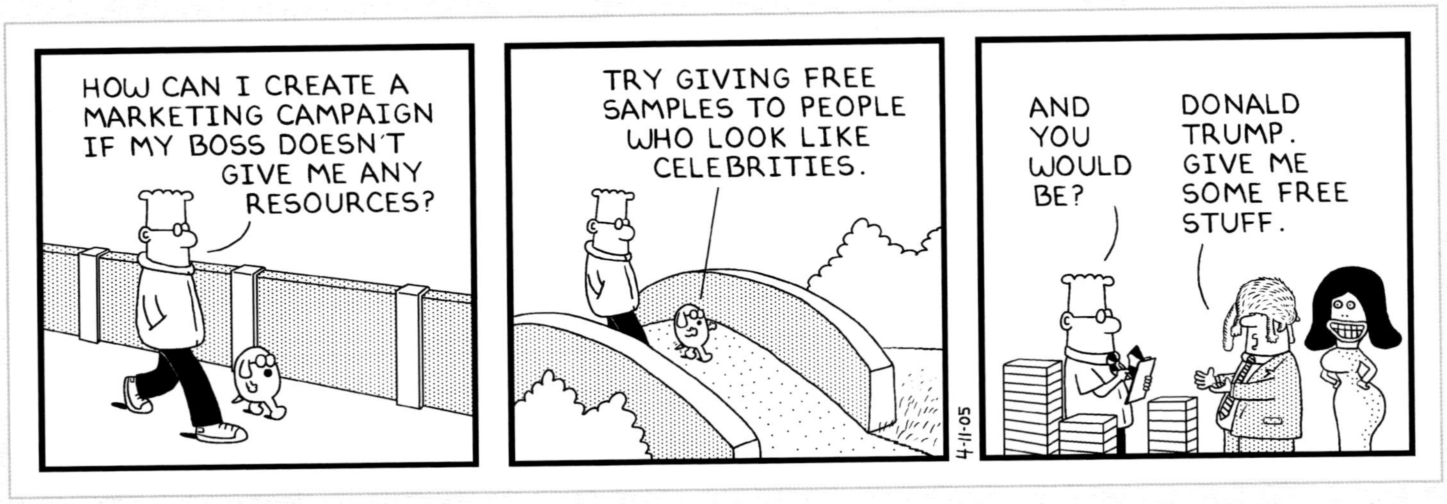
HOW CAN I CREATE A MARKETING CAMPAIGN IF MY BOSS DOESN'T GIVE ME ANY RESOURCES?
TRY GIVING FREE SAMPLES TO PEOPLE WHO LOOK LIKE CELEBRITIES.
4-11-05
AND YOU WOULD BE?
DONALD TRUMP. GIVE ME SOME FREE STUFF.

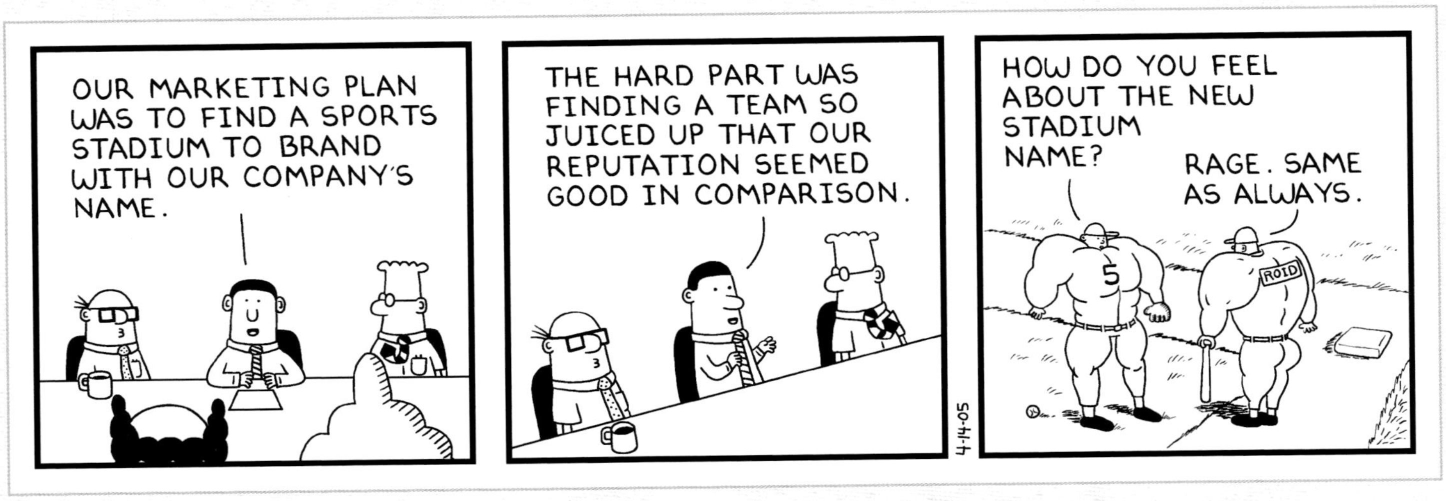
OUR MARKETING PLAN WAS TO FIND A SPORTS STADIUM TO BRAND WITH OUR COMPANY'S NAME.
THE HARD PART WAS FINDING A TEAM SO JUICED UP THAT OUR REPUTATION SEEMED GOOD IN COMPARISON.
4-14-05
HOW DO YOU FEEL ABOUT THE NEW STADIUM NAME?
RAGE. SAME AS ALWAYS.
5
ROID

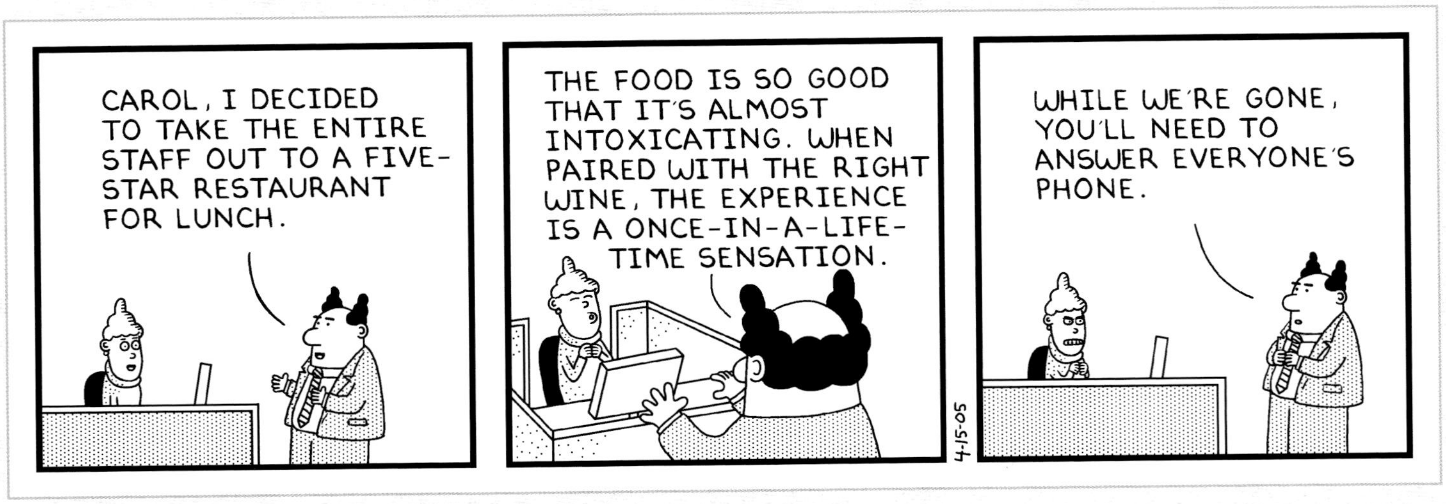
CAROL, I DECIDED TO TAKE THE ENTIRE STAFF OUT TO A FIVE-STAR RESTAURANT FOR LUNCH.
THE FOOD IS SO GOOD THAT IT'S ALMOST INTOXICATING. WHEN PAIRED WITH THE RIGHT WINE, THE EXPERIENCE IS A ONCE-IN-A-LIFETIME SENSATION.
4-15-05
WHILE WE'RE GONE, YOU'LL NEED TO ANSWER EVERYONE'S PHONE.

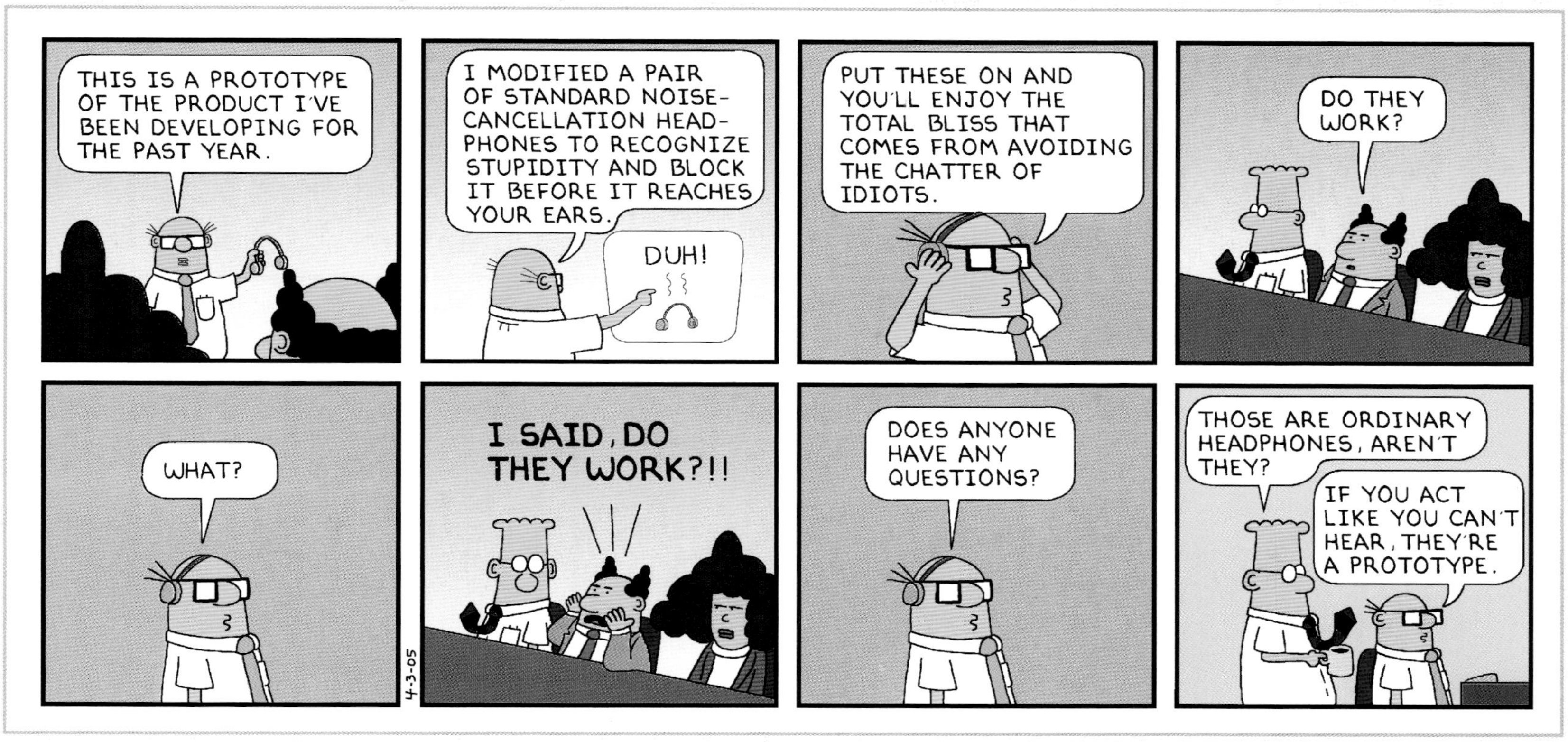
THIS IS A PROTOTYPE OF THE PRODUCT I'VE BEEN DEVELOPING FOR THE PAST YEAR.
I MODIFIED A PAIR OF STANDARD NOISE-CANCELLATION HEAD-PHONES TO RECOGNIZE STUPIDITY AND BLOCK IT BEFORE IT REACHES YOUR EARS.
DUH!
PUT THESE ON AND YOU'LL ENJOY THE TOTAL BLISS THAT COMES FROM AVOIDING THE CHATTER OF IDIOTS.
DO THEY WORK?
WHAT?
I SAID, DO THEY WORK?!!
DOES ANYONE HAVE ANY QUESTIONS?
THOSE ARE ORDINARY HEADPHONES, AREN'T THEY?
IF YOU ACT LIKE YOU CAN'T HEAR, THEY'RE A PROTOTYPE.
4-3-05

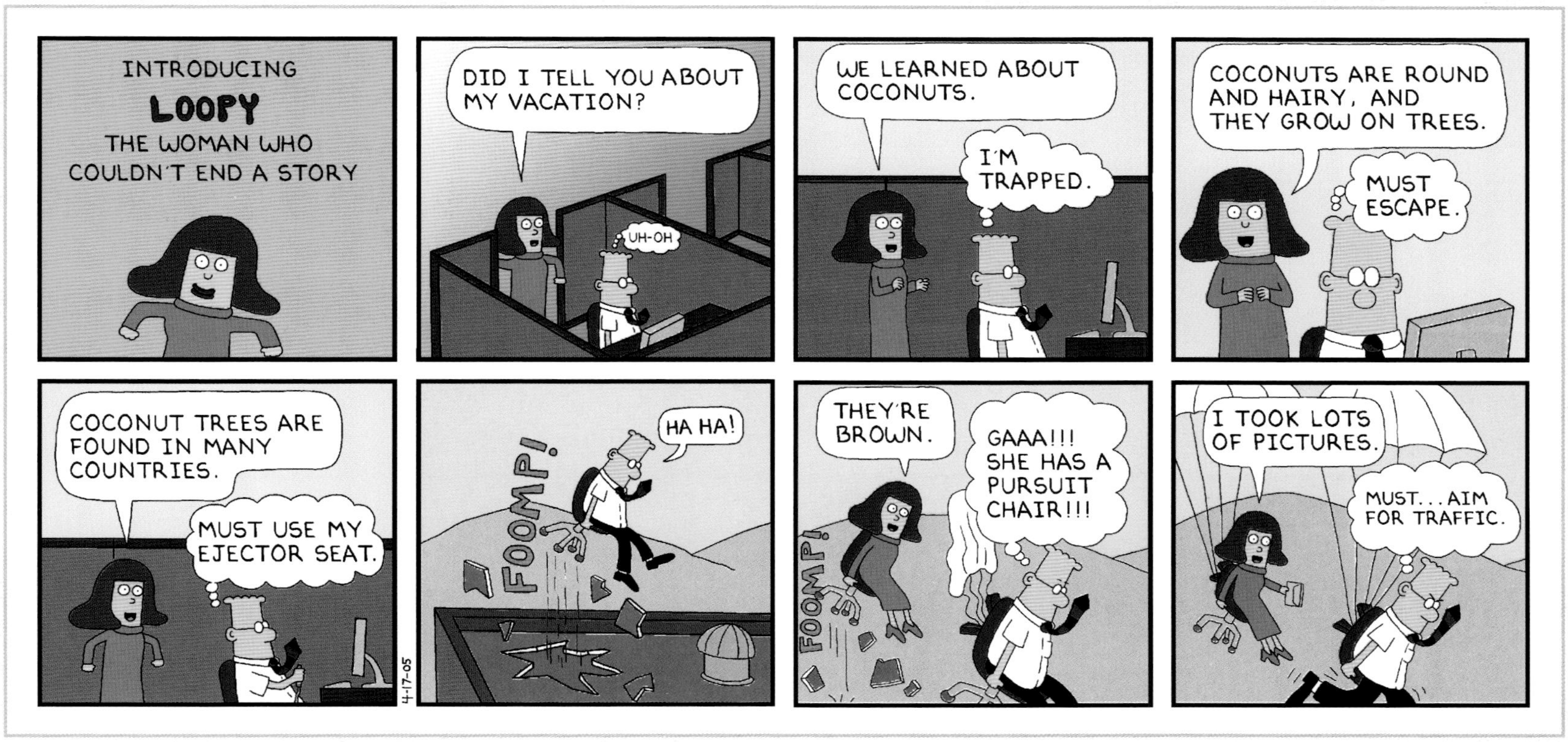
INTRODUCING
LOOPY
THE WOMAN WHO COULDN'T END A STORY
DID I TELL YOU ABOUT MY VACATION?
UH-OH
WE LEARNED ABOUT COCONUTS.
I'M TRAPPED.
COCONUTS ARE ROUND AND HAIRY, AND THEY GROW ON TREES.
MUST ESCAPE.
COCONUT TREES ARE FOUND IN MANY COUNTRIES.
MUST USE MY EJECTOR SEAT.
4-17-05
HA HA!
FOOMP!
THEY'RE BROWN.
GAAA!!! SHE HAS A PURSUIT CHAIR!!!
FOOMP!
I TOOK LOTS OF PICTURES.
MUST... AIM FOR TRAFFIC.

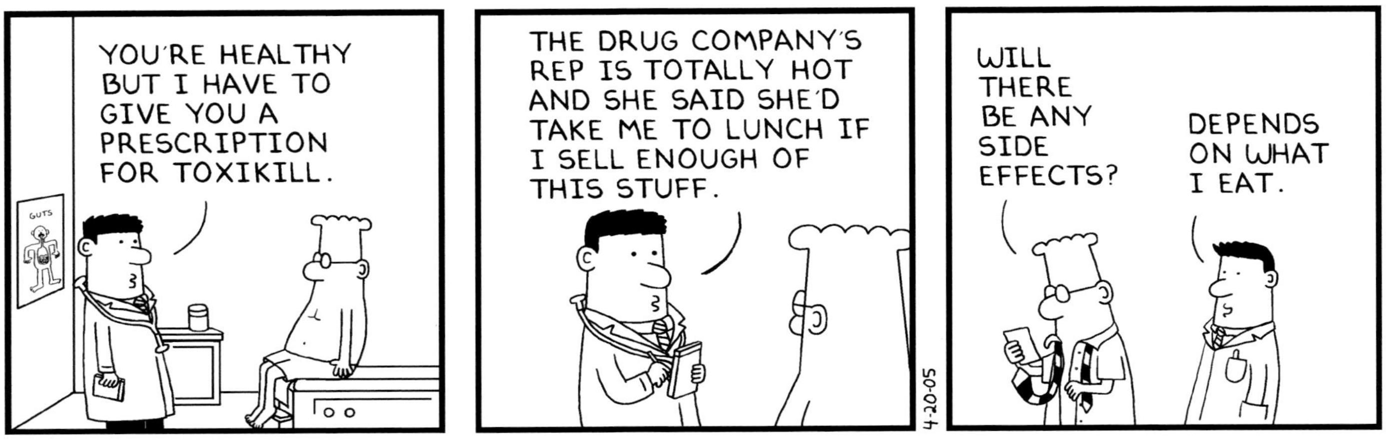
YOU'RE HEALTHY BUT I HAVE TO GIVE YOU A PRESCRIPTION FOR TOXIKILL.
GUTS
THE DRUG COMPANY'S REP IS TOTALLY HOT AND SHE SAID SHE'D TAKE ME TO LUNCH IF I SELL ENOUGH OF THIS STUFF.
4-20-05
WILL THERE BE ANY SIDE EFFECTS?
DEPENDS ON WHAT I EAT.

If you think it is easy to concoct a prescription drug name that is not already taken by a pharmaceutical company, band, or Web site, you are wrong. I spent an hour on Google before I settled on Toxikill.

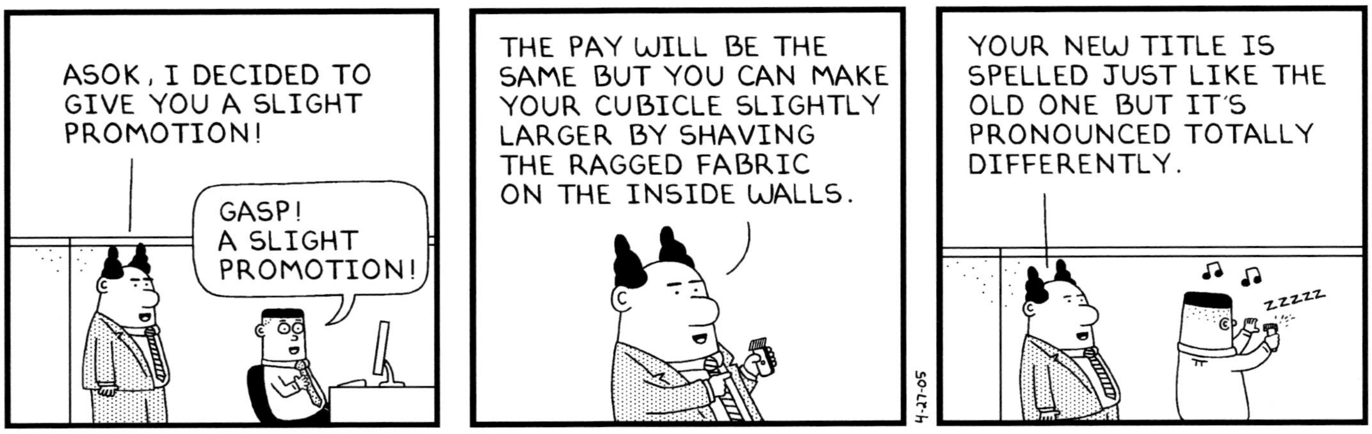
ASOK, I DECIDED TO GIVE YOU A SLIGHT PROMOTION!
GASP! A SLIGHT PROMOTION!
THE PAY WILL BE THE SAME BUT YOU CAN MAKE YOUR CUBICLE SLIGHTLY LARGER BY SHAVING THE RAGGED FABRIC ON THE INSIDE WALLS.
4-27-05
YOUR NEW TITLE IS SPELLED JUST LIKE THE OLD ONE BUT IT'S PRONOUNCED TOTALLY DIFFERENTLY.
ZZZZZ

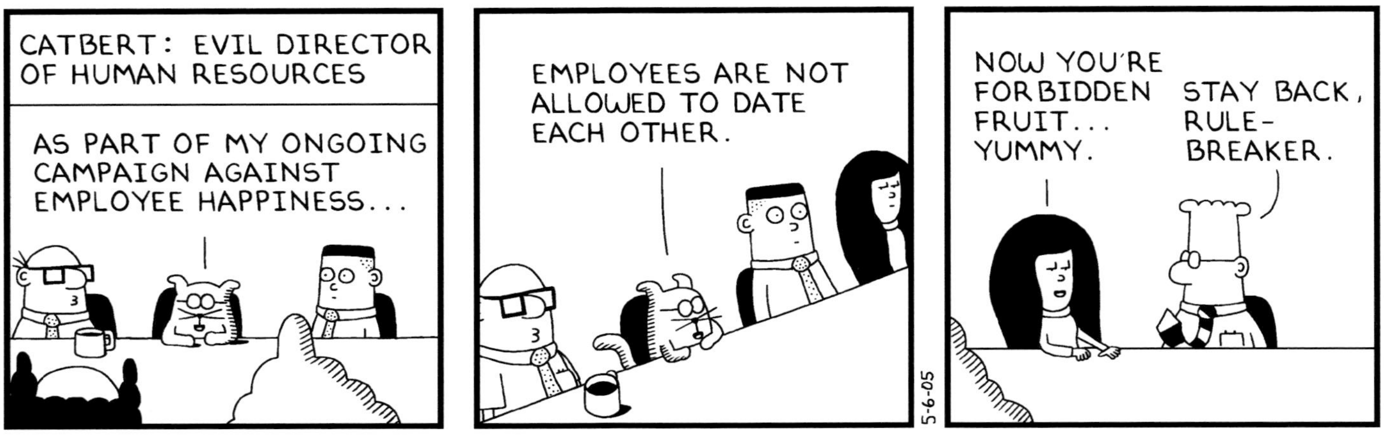
CATBERT: EVIL DIRECTOR OF HUMAN RESOURCES
AS PART OF MY ONGOING CAMPAIGN AGAINST EMPLOYEE HAPPINESS...
EMPLOYEES ARE NOT ALLOWED TO DATE EACH OTHER.
5-6-05
NOW YOU'RE FORBIDDEN FRUIT... YUMMY.
STAY BACK, RULE-BREAKER.

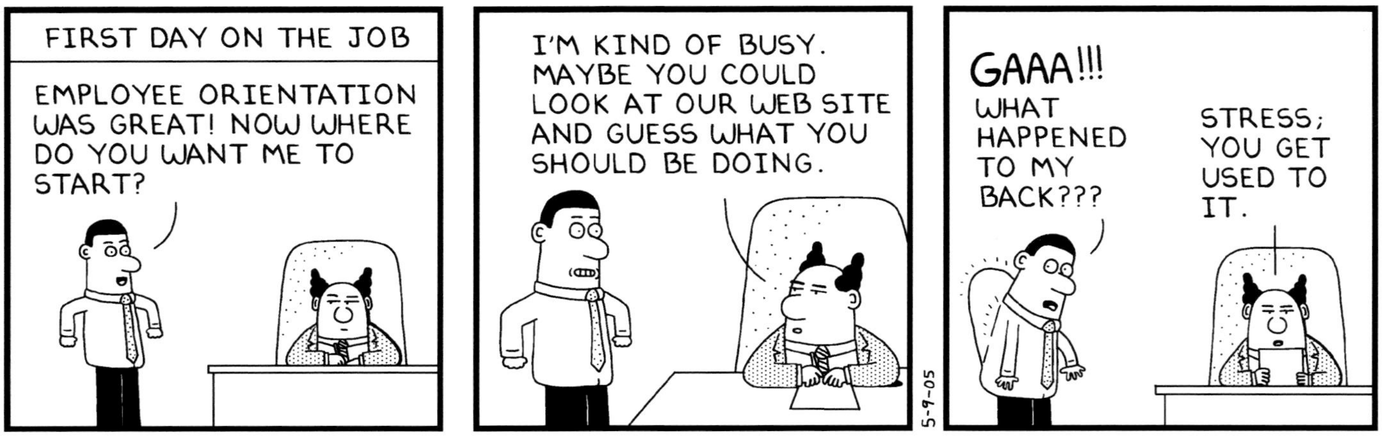
FIRST DAY ON THE JOB
EMPLOYEE ORIENTATION WAS GREAT! NOW WHERE DO YOU WANT ME TO START?
I'M KIND OF BUSY. MAYBE YOU COULD LOOK AT OUR WEB SITE AND GUESS WHAT YOU SHOULD BE DOING.
5-9-05
GAAA!!! WHAT HAPPENED TO MY BACK???
STRESS; YOU GET USED TO IT.

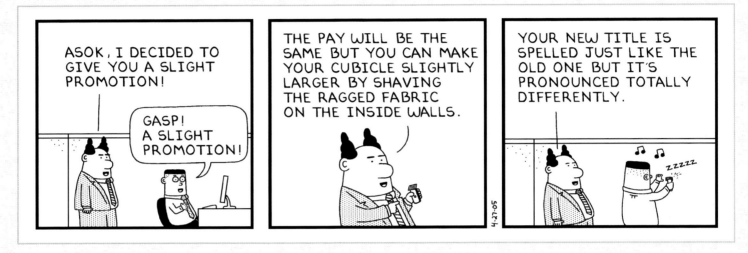

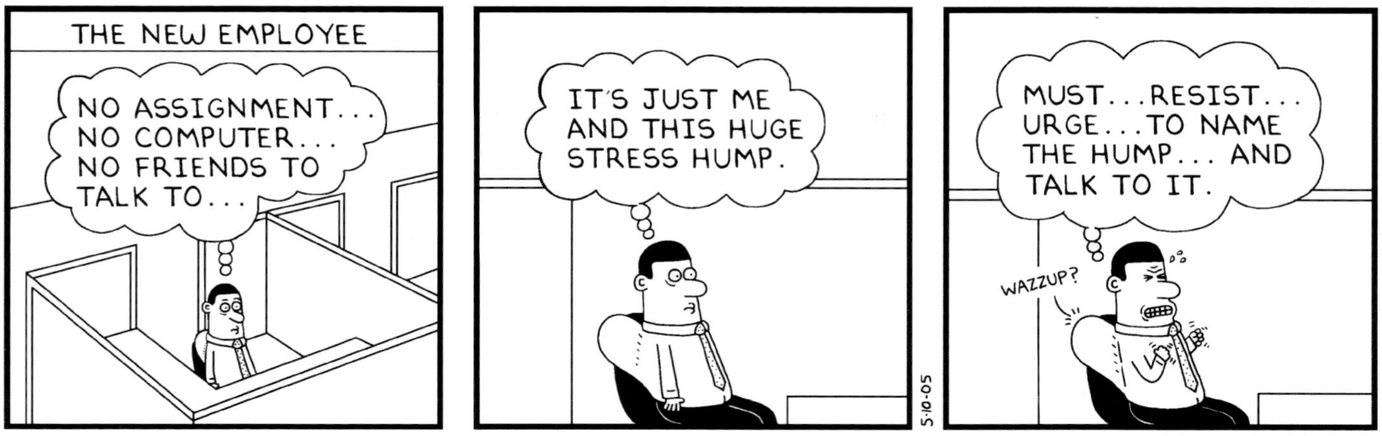
THE NEW EMPLOYEE
NO ASSIGNMENT... NO COMPUTER... NO FRIENDS TO TALK TO...
IT'S JUST ME AND THIS HUGE STRESS HUMP.
MUST...RESIST... URGE...TO NAME THE HUMP... AND TALK TO IT.
WAZZUP?
5-10-05

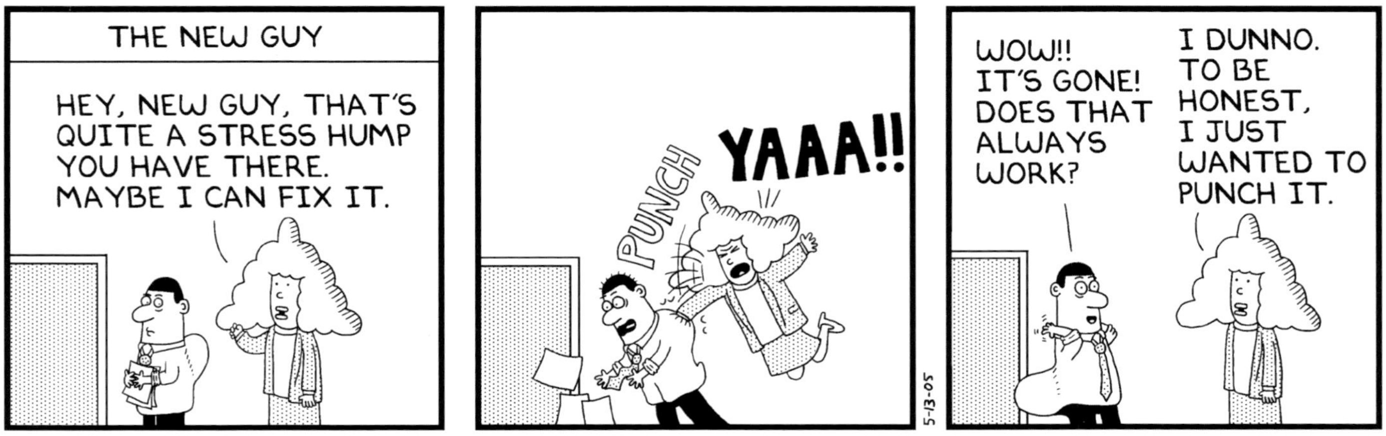
THE NEW GUY
HEY, NEW GUY, THAT'S QUITE A STRESS HUMP YOU HAVE THERE. MAYBE I CAN FIX IT.
PUNCH
YAAA!!
WOW!! IT'S GONE! DOES THAT ALWAYS WORK?
I DUNNO. TO BE HONEST, I JUST WANTED TO PUNCH IT.
5-13-05

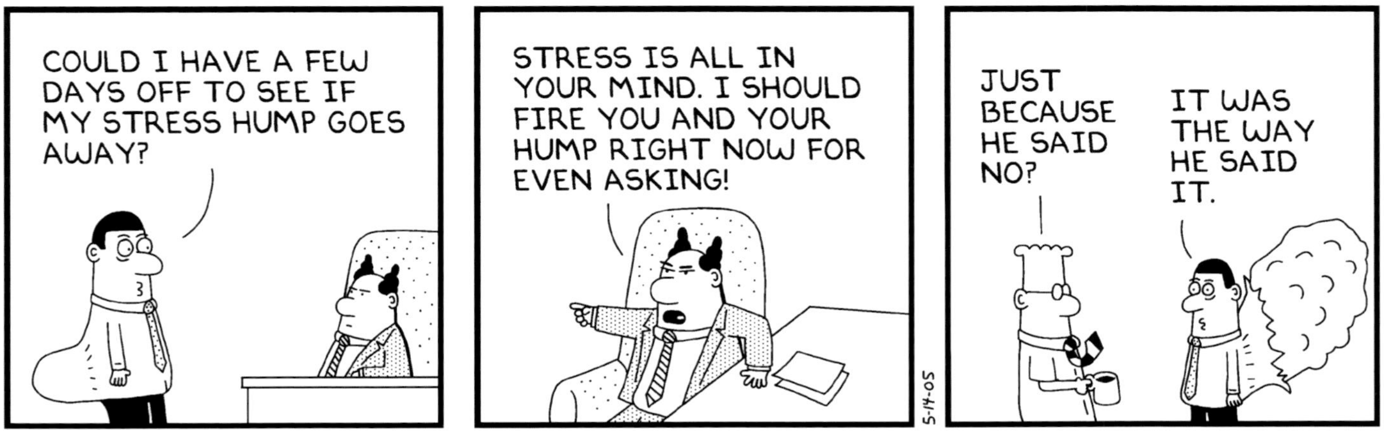
COULD I HAVE A FEW DAYS OFF TO SEE IF MY STRESS HUMP GOES AWAY?
STRESS IS ALL IN YOUR MIND. I SHOULD FIRE YOU AND YOUR HUMP RIGHT NOW FOR EVEN ASKING!
JUST BECAUSE HE SAID NO?
IT WAS THE WAY HE SAID IT.
5-14-05

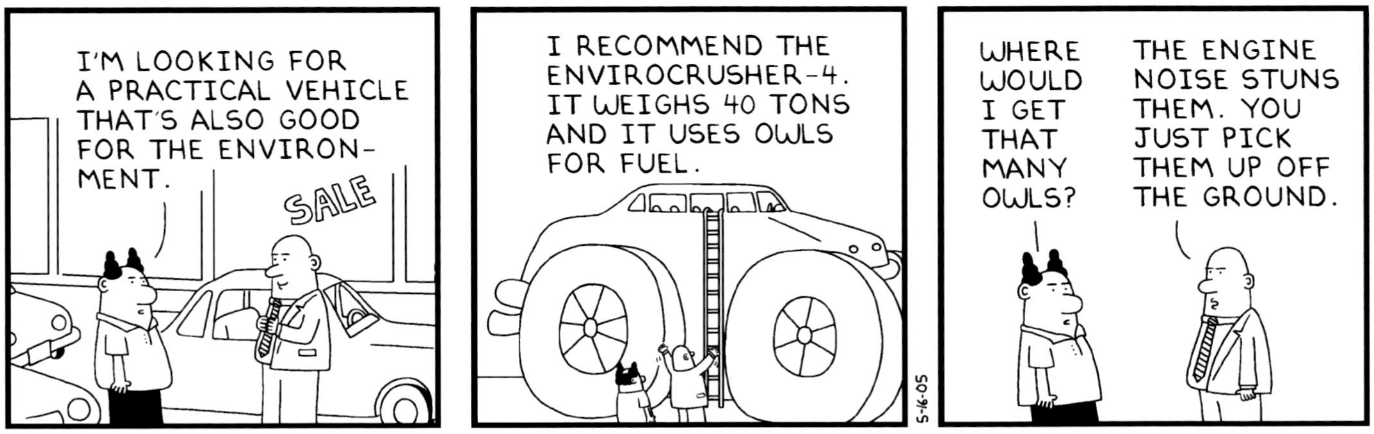
I'M LOOKING FOR A PRACTICAL VEHICLE THAT'S ALSO GOOD FOR THE ENVIRON-MENT.
SALE
I RECOMMEND THE ENVIROCRUSHER-4. IT WEIGHS 40 TONS AND IT USES OWLS FOR FUEL.
WHERE WOULD I GET THAT MANY OWLS?
THE ENGINE NOISE STUNS THEM. YOU JUST PICK THEM UP OFF THE GROUND.
5-16-05

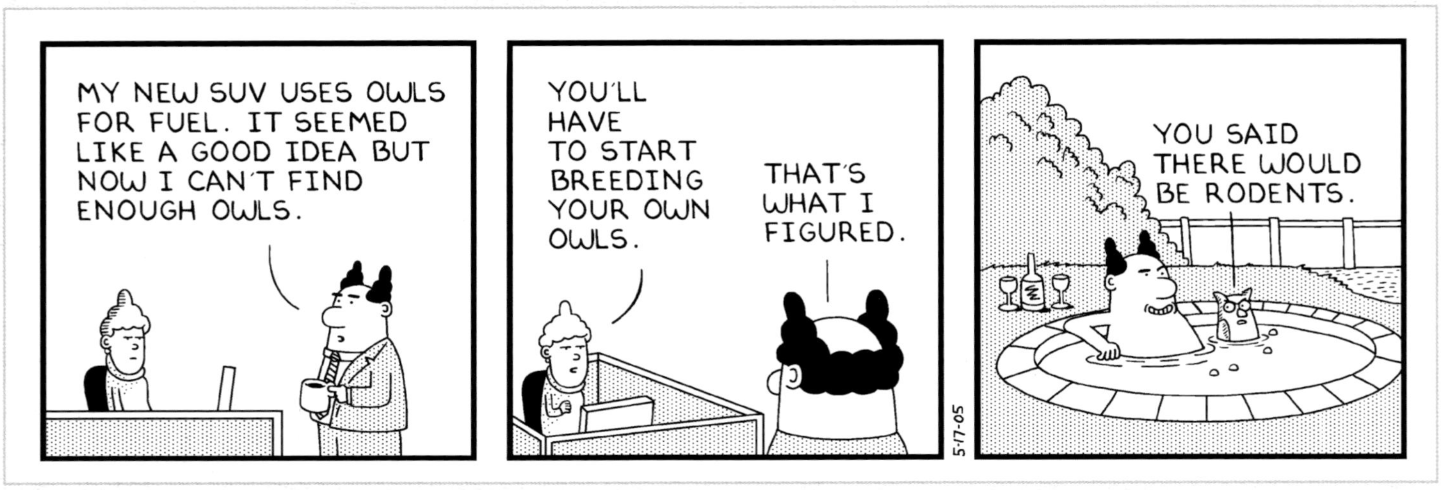
MY NEW SUV USES OWLS FOR FUEL. IT SEEMED LIKE A GOOD IDEA BUT NOW I CAN'T FIND ENOUGH OWLS.
YOU'LL HAVE TO START BREEDING YOUR OWN OWLS.
THAT'S WHAT I FIGURED.
5-17-05
YOU SAID THERE WOULD BE RODENTS.

My editors didn't think I should show the boss in a hot tub with an owl prior to presumably mating with it. So although it was okay to run this version on Dilbert.com, where people rarely complain about content, the version below ran in newspapers.

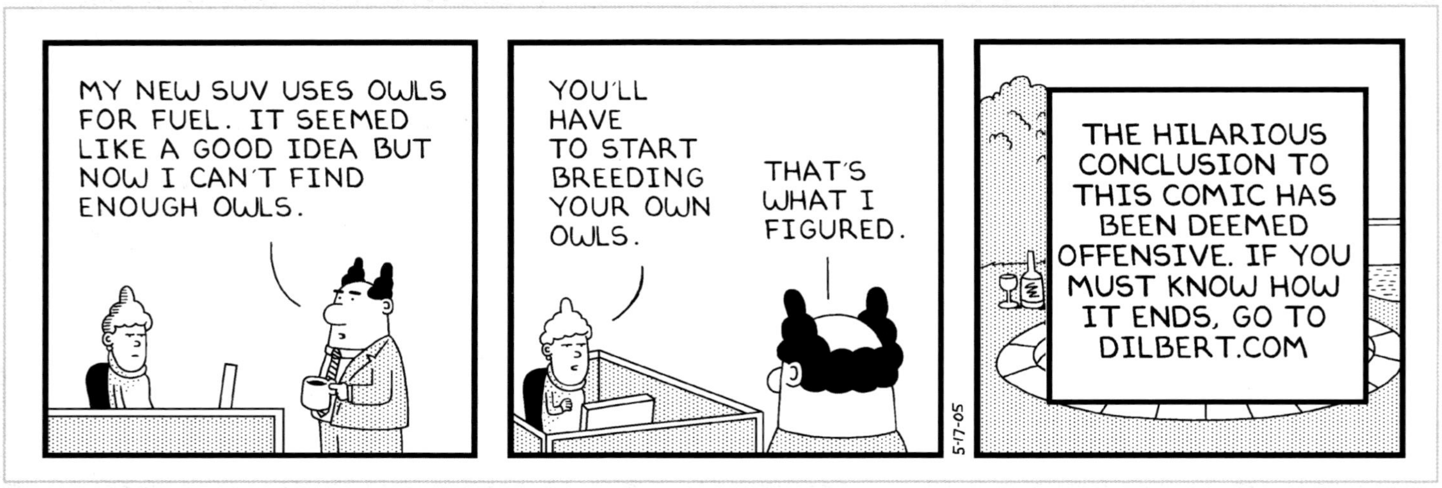
MY NEW SUV USES OWLS FOR FUEL. IT SEEMED LIKE A GOOD IDEA BUT NOW I CAN'T FIND ENOUGH OWLS.
YOU'LL HAVE TO START BREEDING YOUR OWN OWLS.
THAT'S WHAT I FIGURED.
5-17-05
THE HILARIOUS CONCLUSION TO THIS COMIC HAS BEEN DEEMED OFFENSIVE. IF YOU MUST KNOW HOW IT ENDS, GO TO DILBERT.COM

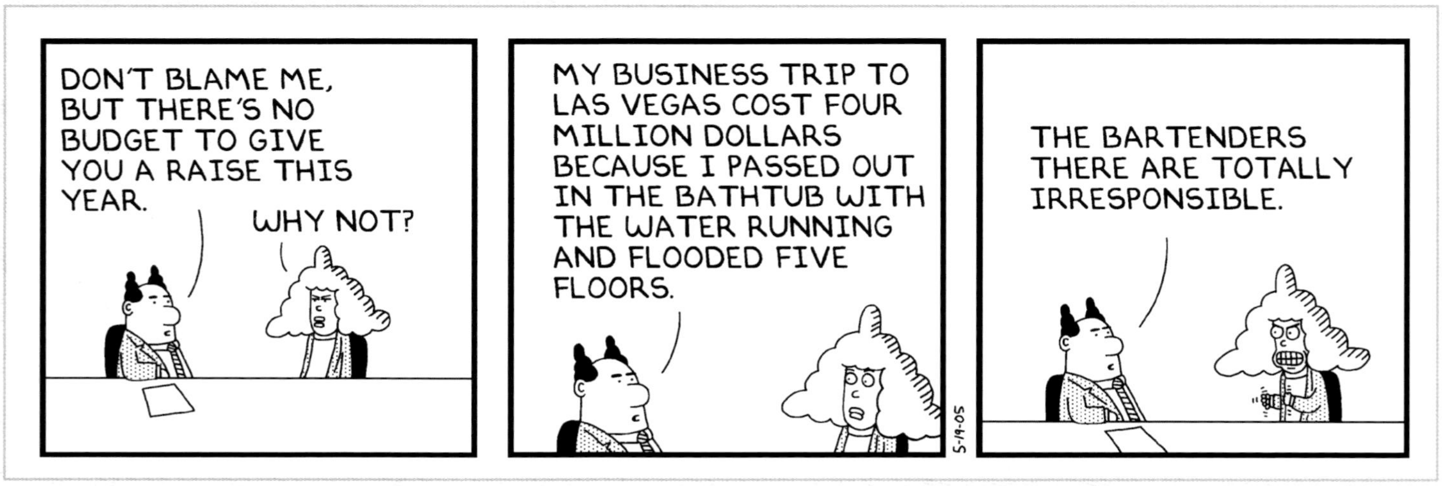
DON'T BLAME ME, BUT THERE'S NO BUDGET TO GIVE YOU A RAISE THIS YEAR.
WHY NOT?
MY BUSINESS TRIP TO LAS VEGAS COST FOUR MILLION DOLLARS BECAUSE I PASSED OUT IN THE BATHTUB WITH THE WATER RUNNING AND FLOODED FIVE FLOORS.
5-19-05
THE BARTENDERS THERE ARE TOTALLY IRRESPONSIBLE.

The bathtub-flooding part of this story actually happened to a friend. He worried it would end up in a Dilbert comic.

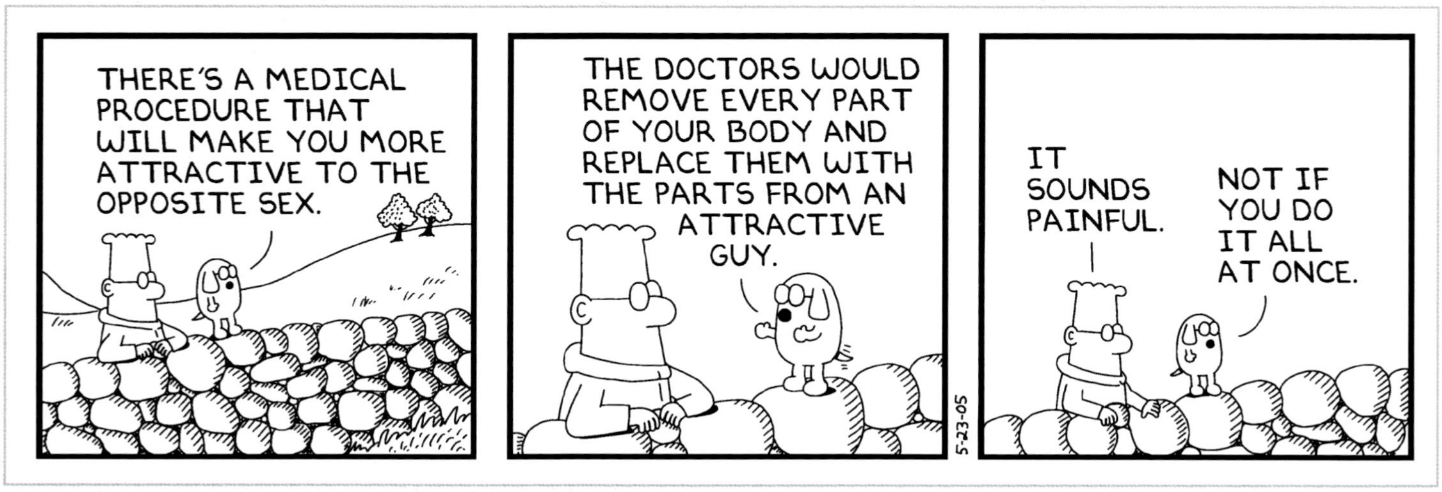
THERE'S A MEDICAL PROCEDURE THAT WILL MAKE YOU MORE ATTRACTIVE TO THE OPPOSITE SEX.
THE DOCTORS WOULD REMOVE EVERY PART OF YOUR BODY AND REPLACE THEM WITH THE PARTS FROM AN ATTRACTIVE GUY.
5-23-05
IT SOUNDS PAINFUL.
NOT IF YOU DO IT ALL AT ONCE.

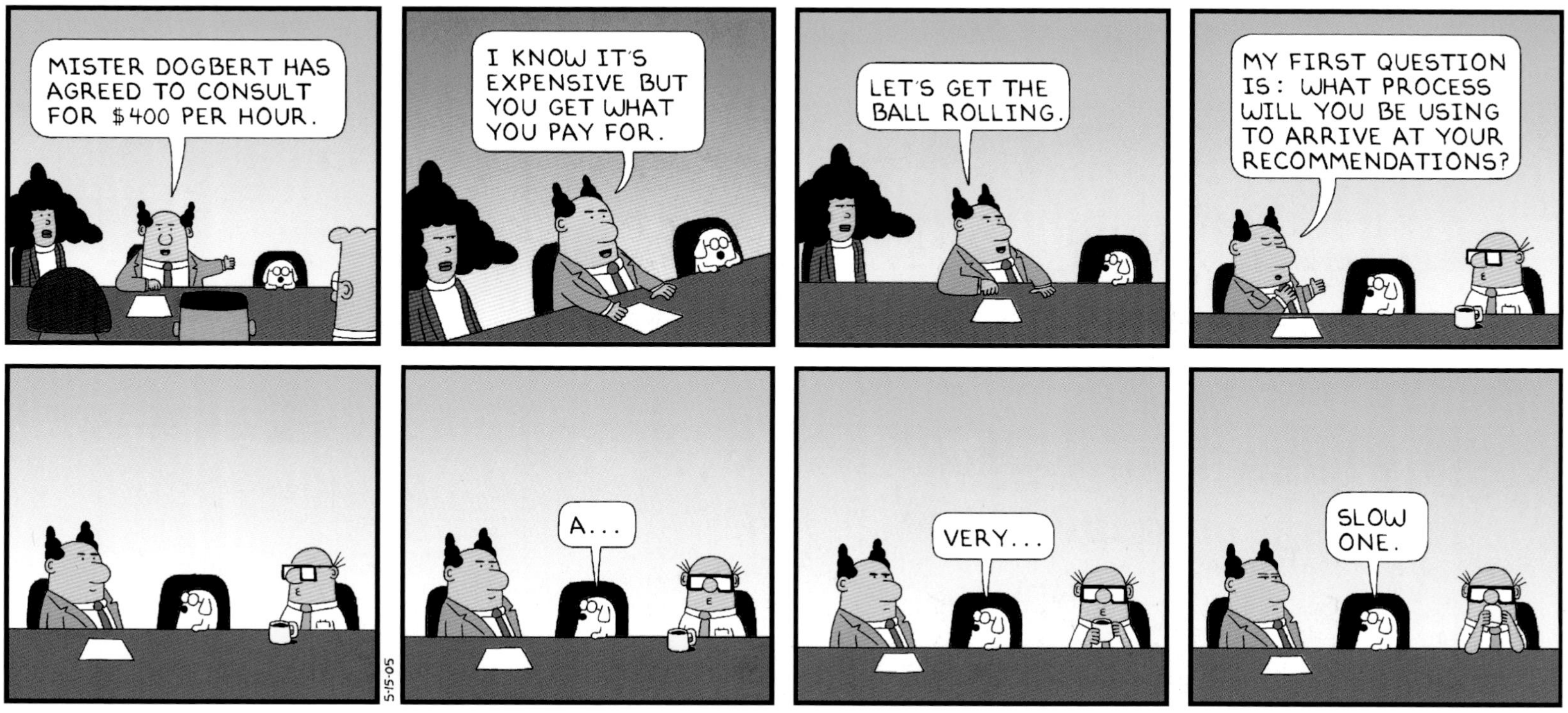
MISTER DOGBERT HAS AGREED TO CONSULT FOR $400 PER HOUR.
I KNOW IT'S EXPENSIVE BUT YOU GET WHAT YOU PAY FOR.
LET'S GET THE BALL ROLLING.
MY FIRST QUESTION IS: WHAT PROCESS WILL YOU BE USING TO ARRIVE AT YOUR RECOMMENDATIONS?
5-15-05
A...
VERY...
SLOW ONE.

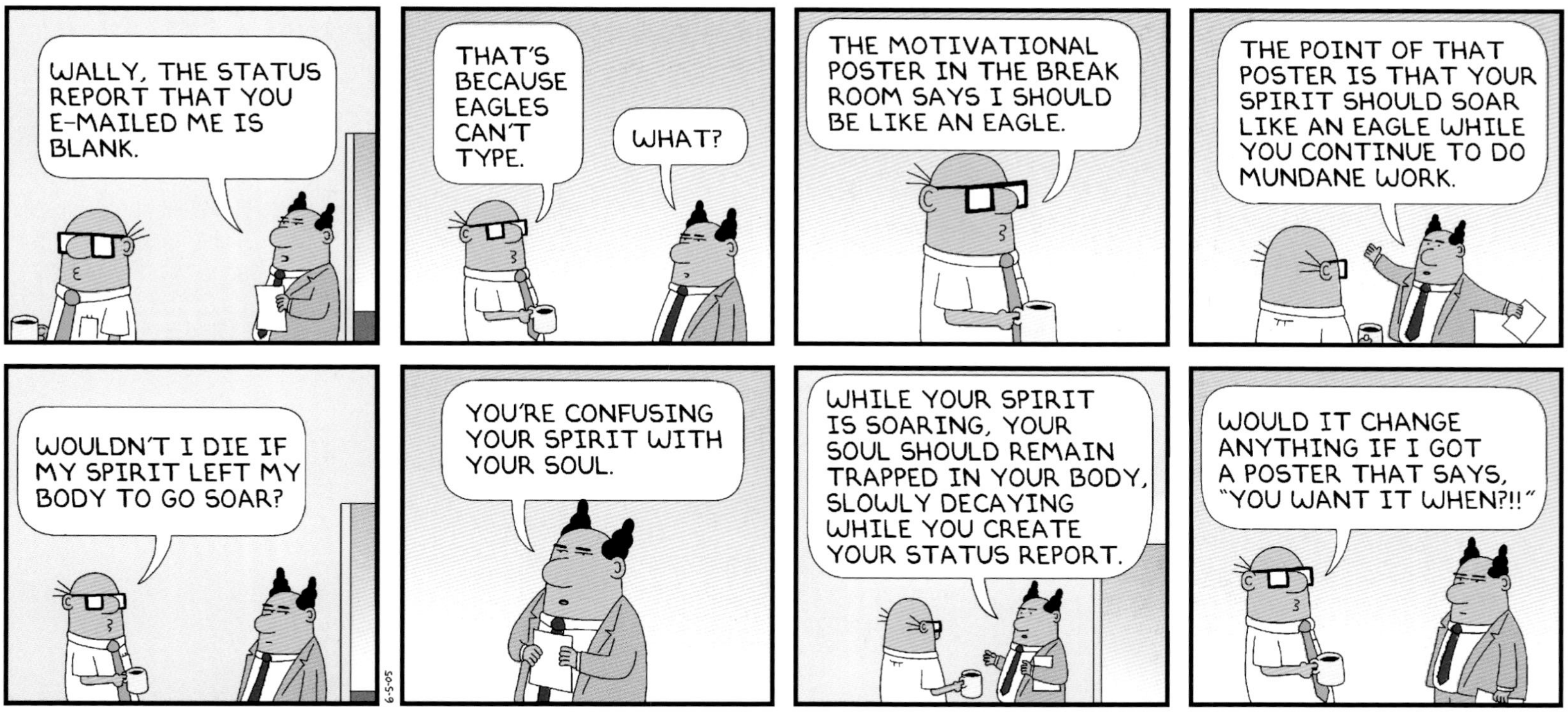
WALLY, THE STATUS REPORT THAT YOU E-MAILED ME IS BLANK.
THAT'S BECAUSE EAGLES CAN'T TYPE.
WHAT?
THE MOTIVATIONAL POSTER IN THE BREAK ROOM SAYS I SHOULD BE LIKE AN EAGLE.
THE POINT OF THAT POSTER IS THAT YOUR SPIRIT SHOULD SOAR LIKE AN EAGLE WHILE YOU CONTINUE TO DO MUNDANE WORK.
WOULDN'T I DIE IF MY SPIRIT LEFT MY BODY TO GO SOAR?
6-5-05
YOU'RE CONFUSING YOUR SPIRIT WITH YOUR SOUL.
WHILE YOUR SPIRIT IS SOARING, YOUR SOUL SHOULD REMAIN TRAPPED IN YOUR BODY, SLOWLY DECAYING WHILE YOU CREATE YOUR STATUS REPORT.
WOULD IT CHANGE ANYTHING IF I GOT A POSTER THAT SAYS, "YOU WANT IT WHEN?!!"

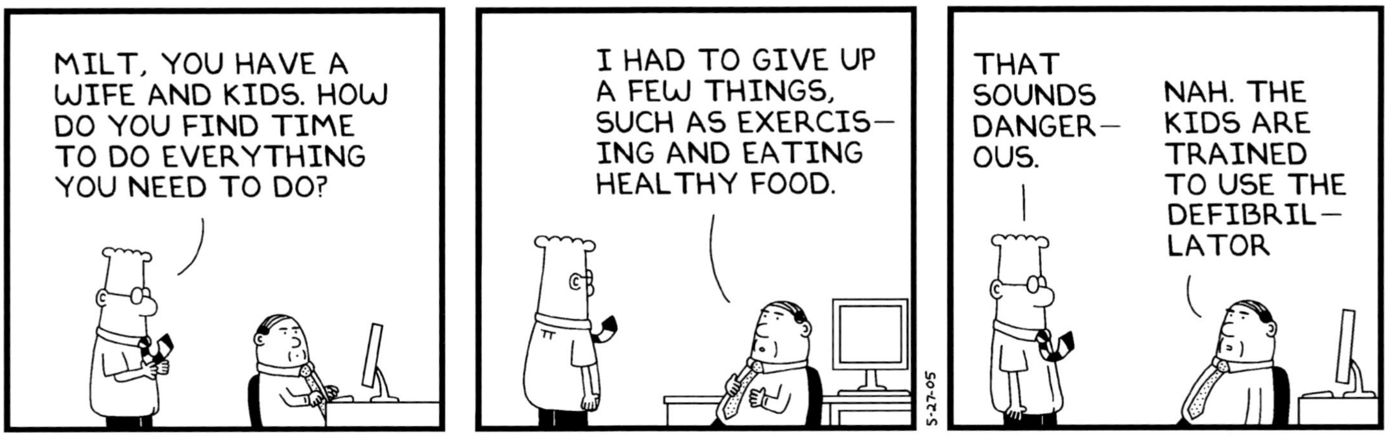
MILT, YOU HAVE A WIFE AND KIDS. HOW DO YOU FIND TIME TO DO EVERYTHING YOU NEED TO DO?
I HAD TO GIVE UP A FEW THINGS, SUCH AS EXERCISING AND EATING HEALTHY FOOD.
THAT SOUNDS DANGEROUS.
NAH. THE KIDS ARE TRAINED TO USE THE DEFIBRILLATOR
5-27-05

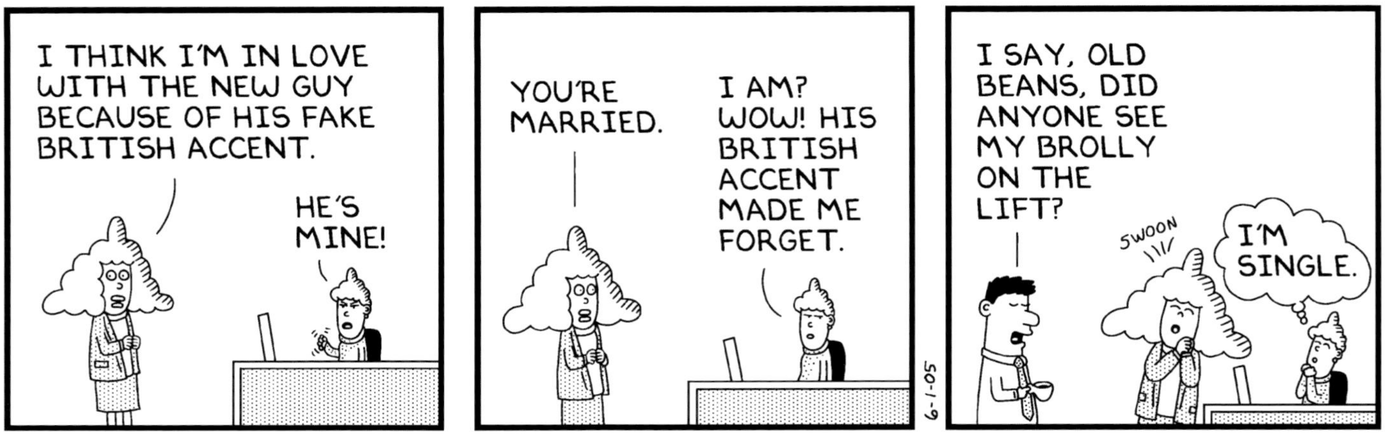
I THINK I'M IN LOVE WITH THE NEW GUY BECAUSE OF HIS FAKE BRITISH ACCENT.
HE'S MINE!
YOU'RE MARRIED.
I AM? WOW! HIS BRITISH ACCENT MADE ME FORGET.
I SAY, OLD BEANS, DID ANYONE SEE MY BROLLY ON THE LIFT?
SWOON
I'M SINGLE.
6-1-05

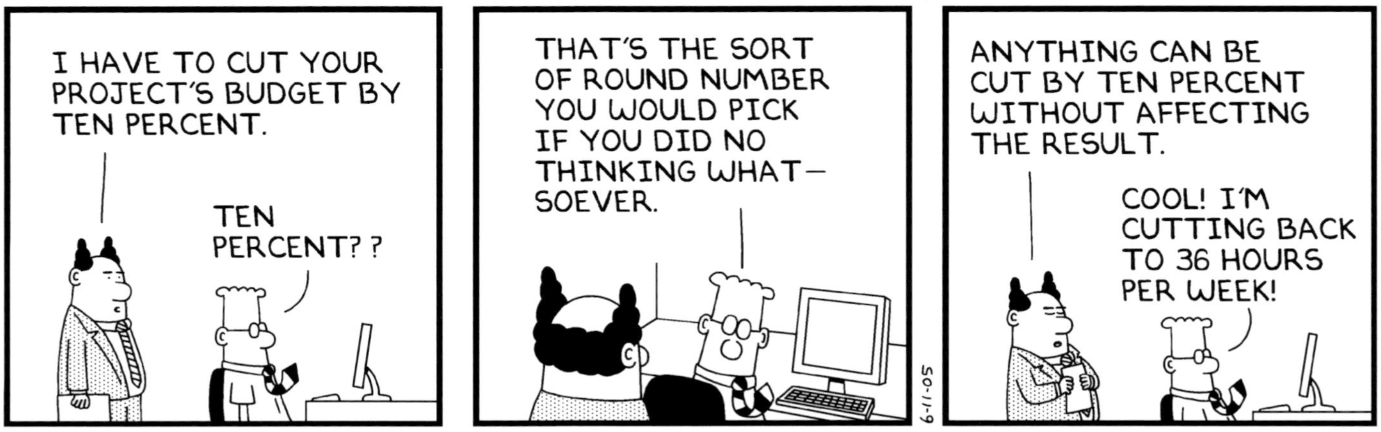
I HAVE TO CUT YOUR PROJECT'S BUDGET BY TEN PERCENT.
TEN PERCENT??
THAT'S THE SORT OF ROUND NUMBER YOU WOULD PICK IF YOU DID NO THINKING WHATSOEVER.
ANYTHING CAN BE CUT BY TEN PERCENT WITHOUT AFFECTING THE RESULT.
COOL! I'M CUTTING BACK TO 36 HOURS PER WEEK!
6-11-05

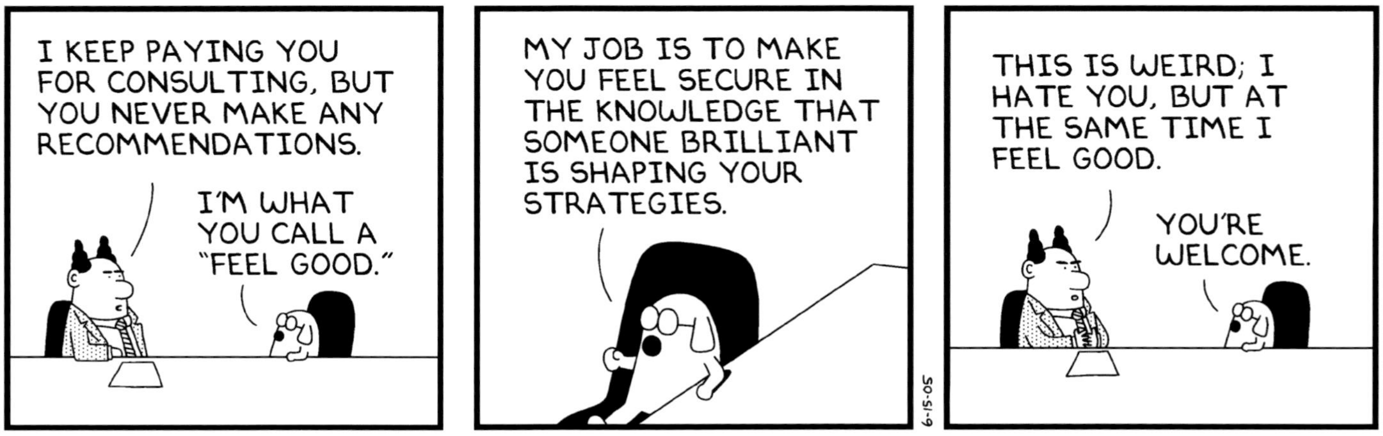
I KEEP PAYING YOU FOR CONSULTING, BUT YOU NEVER MAKE ANY RECOMMENDATIONS.
I'M WHAT YOU CALL A "FEEL GOOD."
MY JOB IS TO MAKE YOU FEEL SECURE IN THE KNOWLEDGE THAT SOMEONE BRILLIANT IS SHAPING YOUR STRATEGIES.
THIS IS WEIRD; I HATE YOU, BUT AT THE SAME TIME I FEEL GOOD.
YOU'RE WELCOME.
6-15-05

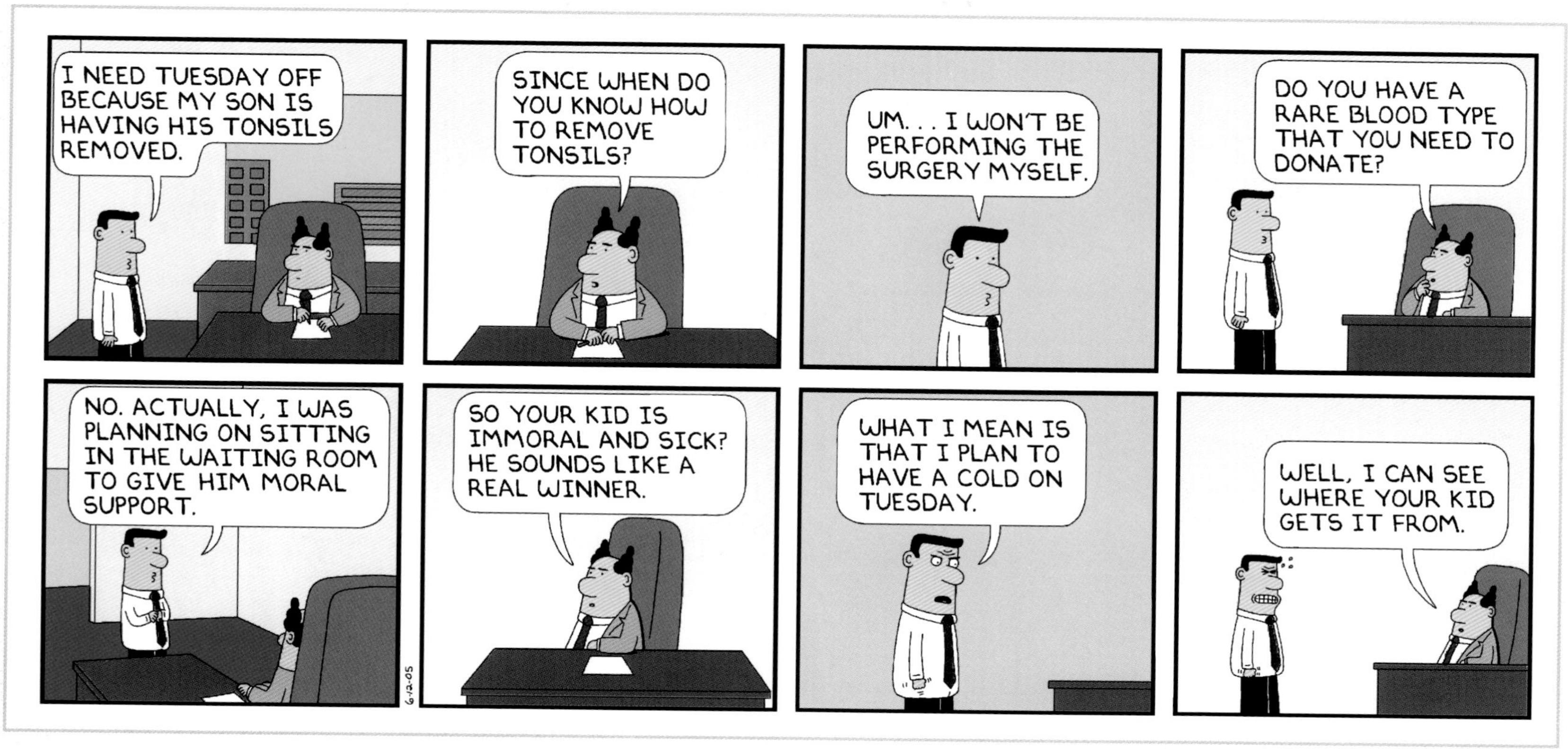
I NEED TUESDAY OFF BECAUSE MY SON IS HAVING HIS TONSILS REMOVED.
SINCE WHEN DO YOU KNOW HOW TO REMOVE TONSILS?
UM. . . I WON'T BE PERFORMING THE SURGERY MYSELF.
DO YOU HAVE A RARE BLOOD TYPE THAT YOU NEED TO DONATE?
NO. ACTUALLY, I WAS PLANNING ON SITTING IN THE WAITING ROOM TO GIVE HIM MORAL SUPPORT.
SO YOUR KID IS IMMORAL AND SICK? HE SOUNDS LIKE A REAL WINNER.
WHAT I MEAN IS THAT I PLAN TO HAVE A COLD ON TUESDAY.
WELL, I CAN SEE WHERE YOUR KID GETS IT FROM.
6-12-05

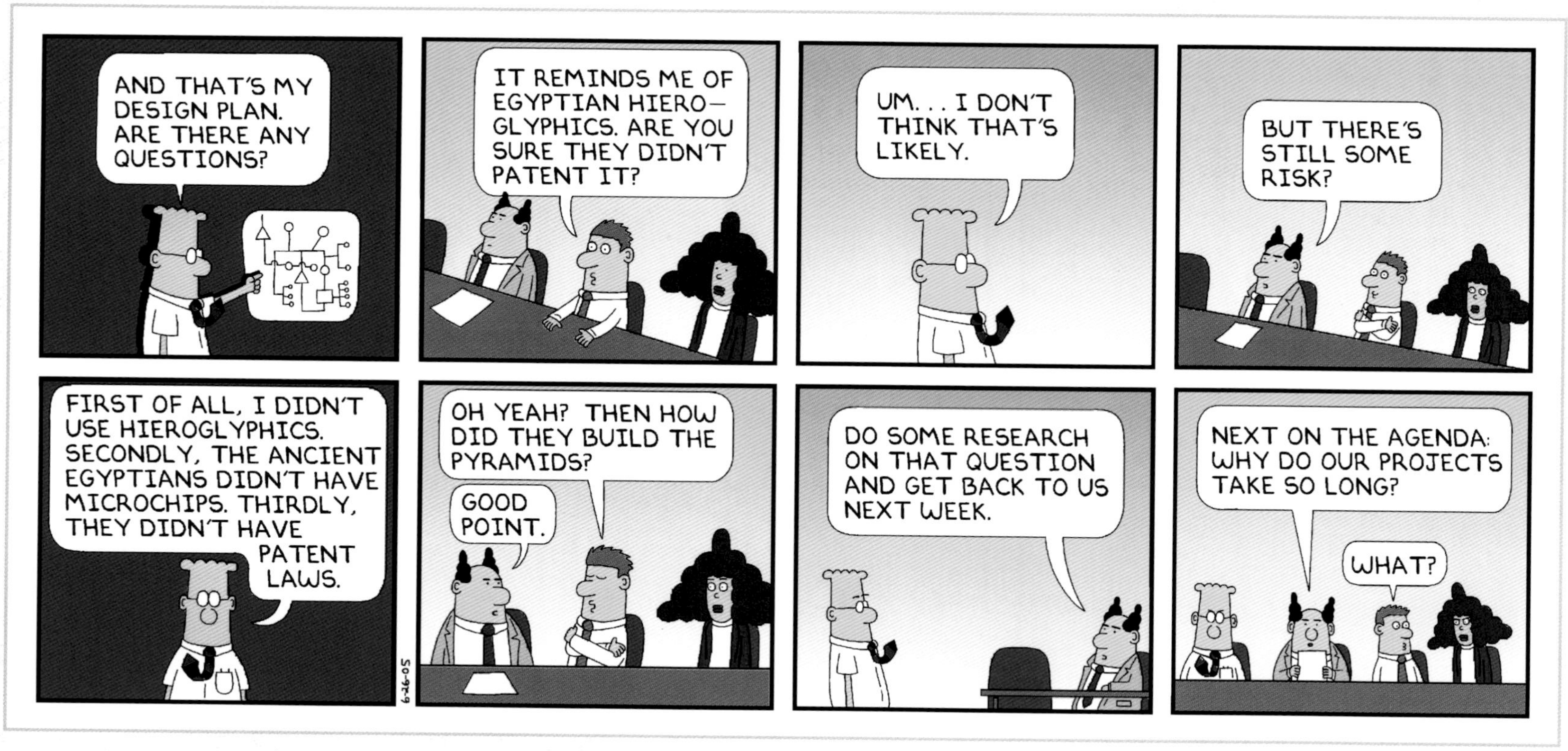
AND THAT'S MY DESIGN PLAN. ARE THERE ANY QUESTIONS?
IT REMINDS ME OF EGYPTIAN HIERO–GLYPHICS. ARE YOU SURE THEY DIDN'T PATENT IT?
UM. . . I DON'T THINK THAT'S LIKELY.
BUT THERE'S STILL SOME RISK?
FIRST OF ALL, I DIDN'T USE HIEROGLYPHICS. SECONDLY, THE ANCIENT EGYPTIANS DIDN'T HAVE MICROCHIPS. THIRDLY, THEY DIDN'T HAVE PATENT LAWS.
OH YEAH? THEN HOW DID THEY BUILD THE PYRAMIDS?
GOOD POINT.
DO SOME RESEARCH ON THAT QUESTION AND GET BACK TO US NEXT WEEK.
NEXT ON THE AGENDA: WHY DO OUR PROJECTS TAKE SO LONG?
WHAT?
6-26-05

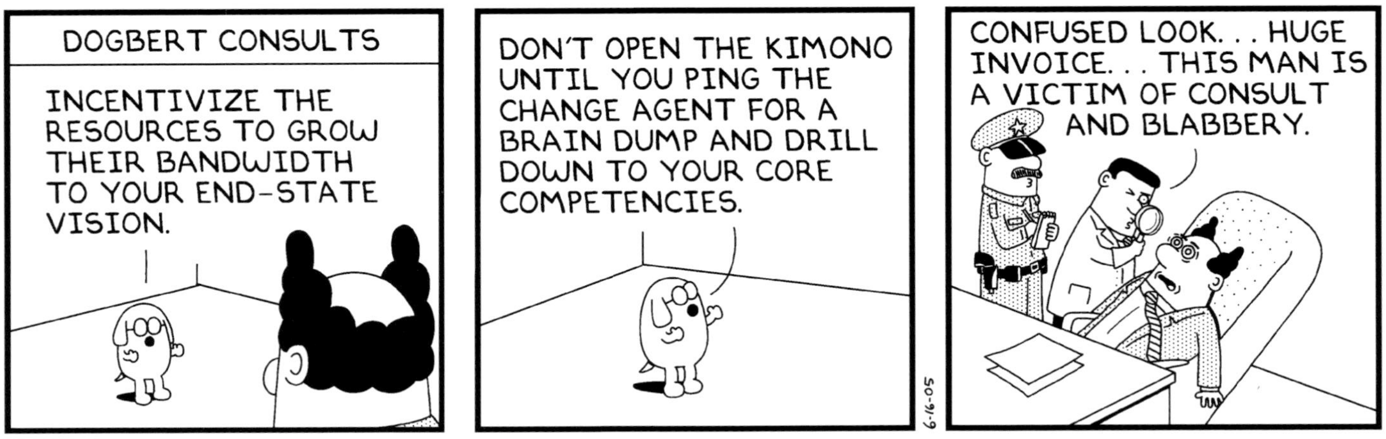
DOGBERT CONSULTS
INCENTIVIZE THE RESOURCES TO GROW THEIR BANDWIDTH TO YOUR END-STATE VISION.
DON'T OPEN THE KIMONO UNTIL YOU PING THE CHANGE AGENT FOR A BRAIN DUMP AND DRILL DOWN TO YOUR CORE COMPETENCIES.
CONFUSED LOOK. . . HUGE INVOICE. . . THIS MAN IS A VICTIM OF CONSULT AND BLABBERY.
6-16-05

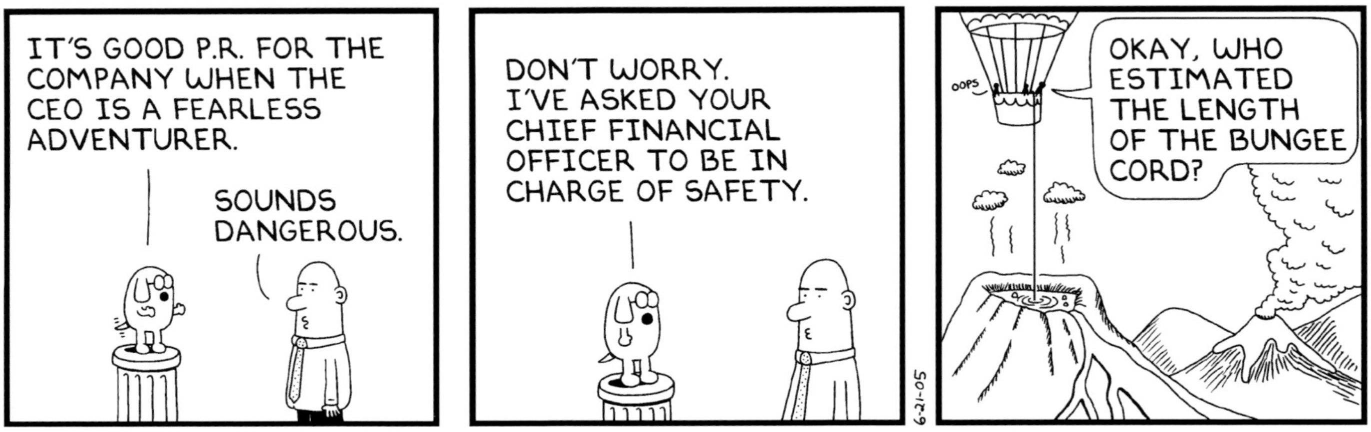
IT'S GOOD P.R. FOR THE COMPANY WHEN THE CEO IS A FEARLESS ADVENTURER.
SOUNDS DANGEROUS.
DON'T WORRY. I'VE ASKED YOUR CHIEF FINANCIAL OFFICER TO BE IN CHARGE OF SAFETY.
OOPS
OKAY, WHO ESTIMATED THE LENGTH OF THE BUNGEE CORD?
6-21-05

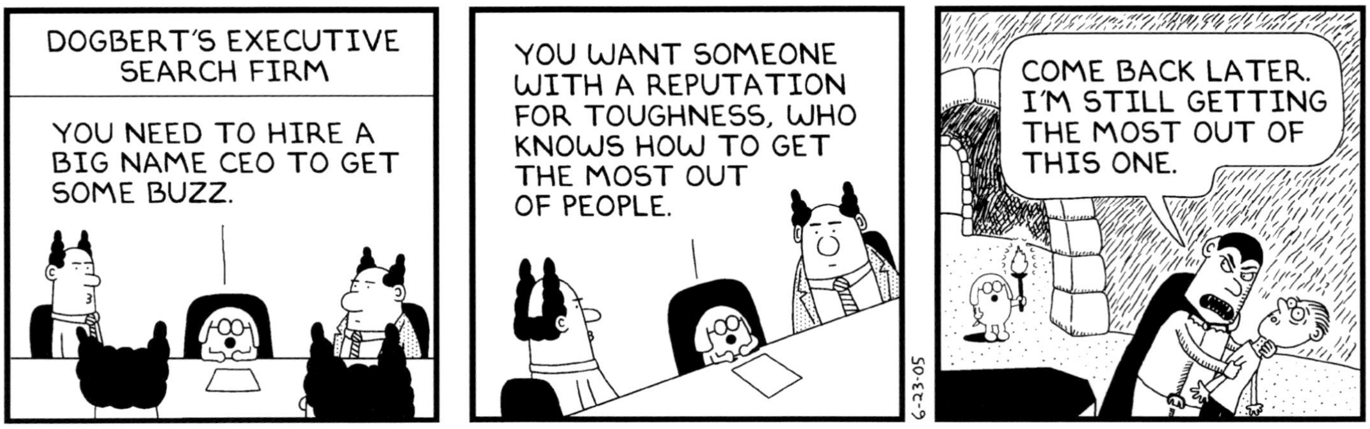
DOGBERT'S EXECUTIVE SEARCH FIRM
YOU NEED TO HIRE A BIG NAME CEO TO GET SOME BUZZ.
YOU WANT SOMEONE WITH A REPUTATION FOR TOUGHNESS, WHO KNOWS HOW TO GET THE MOST OUT OF PEOPLE.
COME BACK LATER. I'M STILL GETTING THE MOST OUT OF THIS ONE.
6-23-05

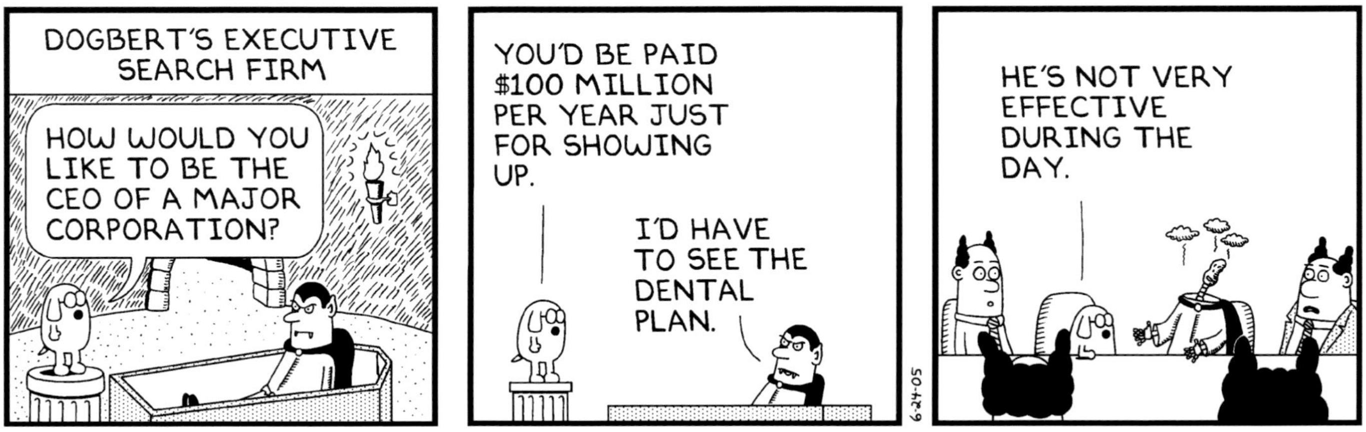
DOGBERT'S EXECUTIVE SEARCH FIRM
HOW WOULD YOU LIKE TO BE THE CEO OF A MAJOR CORPORATION?
YOU'D BE PAID $100 MILLION PER YEAR JUST FOR SHOWING UP.
I'D HAVE TO SEE THE DENTAL PLAN.
HE'S NOT VERY EFFECTIVE DURING THE DAY.
6-24-05

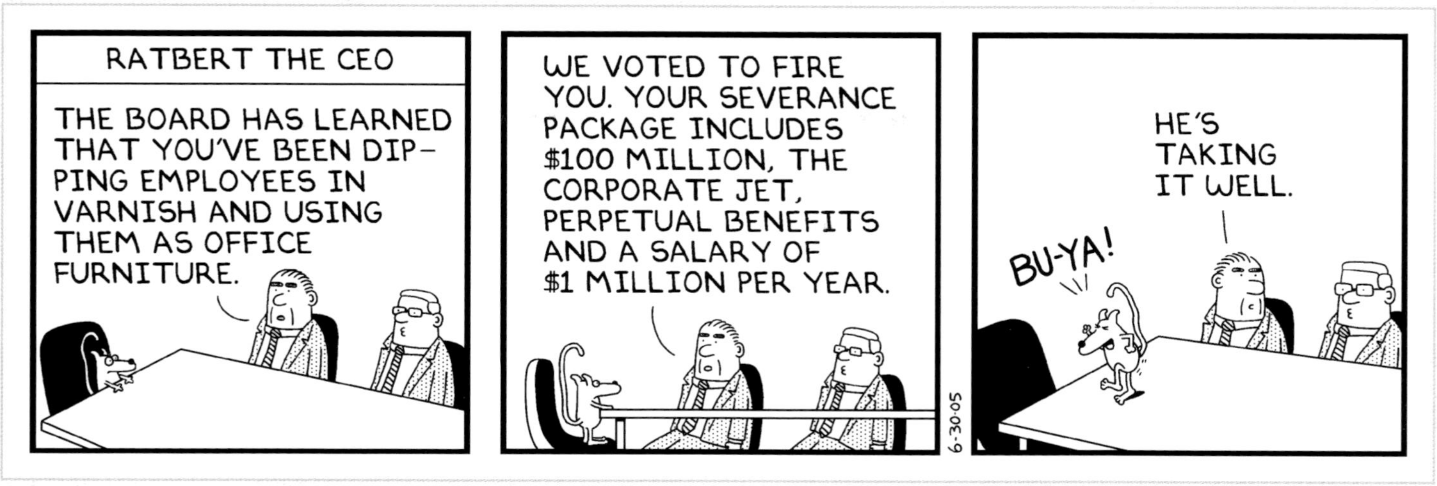
RATBERT THE CEO
THE BOARD HAS LEARNED THAT YOU'VE BEEN DIP-PING EMPLOYEES IN VARNISH AND USING THEM AS OFFICE FURNITURE.
WE VOTED TO FIRE YOU. YOUR SEVERANCE PACKAGE INCLUDES $100 MILLION, THE CORPORATE JET, PERPETUAL BENEFITS AND A SALARY OF $1 MILLION PER YEAR.
6-30-05
BU-YA!
HE'S TAKING IT WELL.

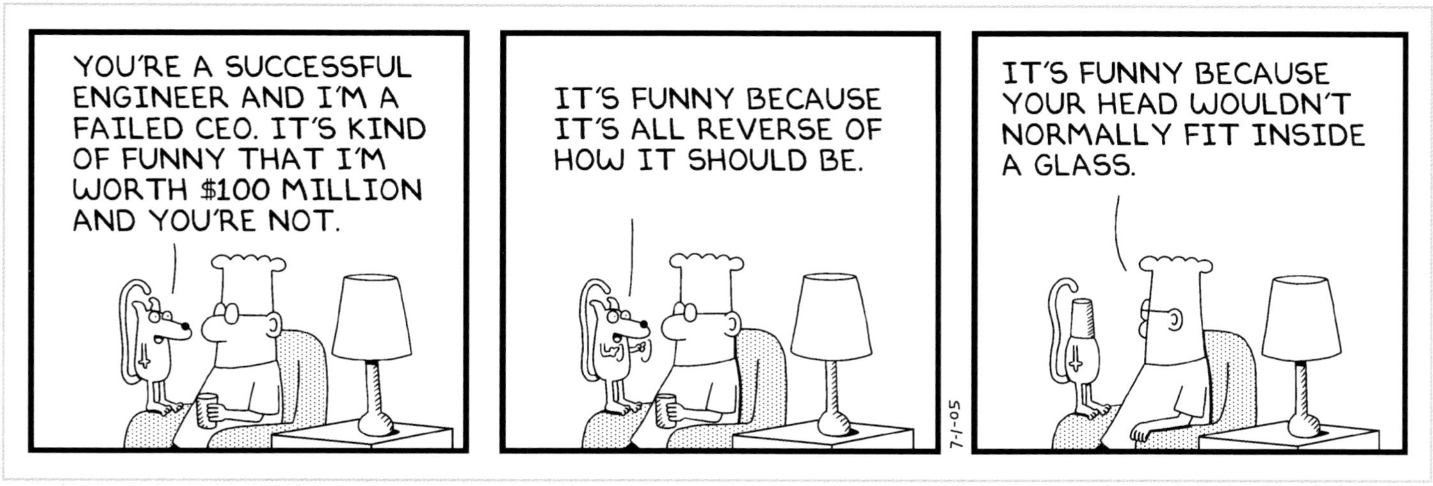
YOU'RE A SUCCESSFUL ENGINEER AND I'M A FAILED CEO. IT'S KIND OF FUNNY THAT I'M WORTH $100 MILLION AND YOU'RE NOT.
IT'S FUNNY BECAUSE IT'S ALL REVERSE OF HOW IT SHOULD BE.
7-1-05
IT'S FUNNY BECAUSE YOUR HEAD WOULDN'T NORMALLY FIT INSIDE A GLASS.

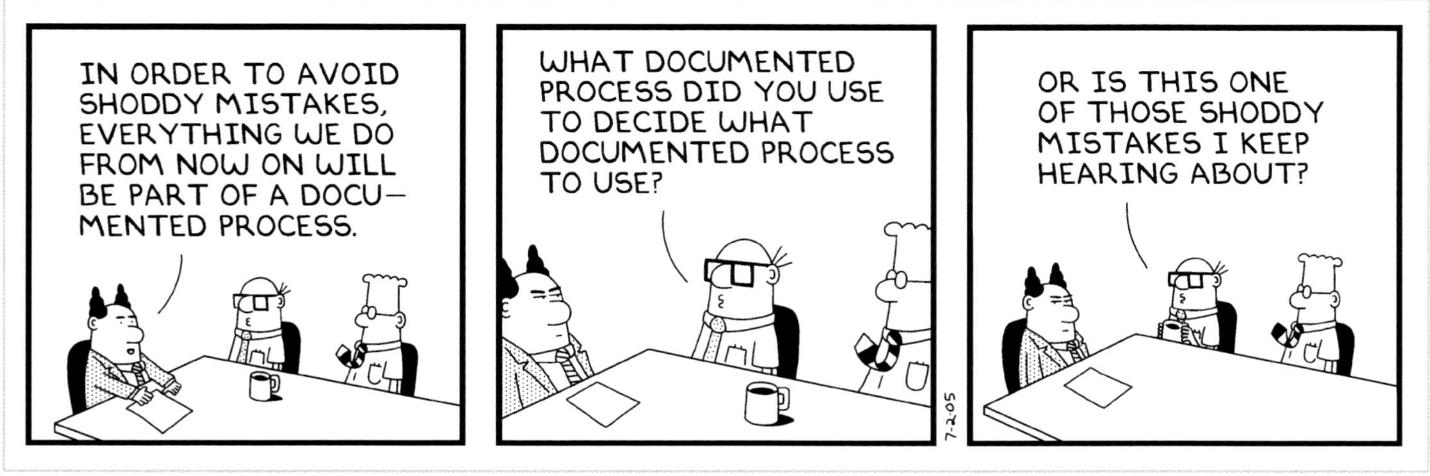
IN ORDER TO AVOID SHODDY MISTAKES, EVERYTHING WE DO FROM NOW ON WILL BE PART OF A DOCU-MENTED PROCESS.
WHAT DOCUMENTED PROCESS DID YOU USE TO DECIDE WHAT DOCUMENTED PROCESS TO USE?
7-2-05
OR IS THIS ONE OF THOSE SHODDY MISTAKES I KEEP HEARING ABOUT?

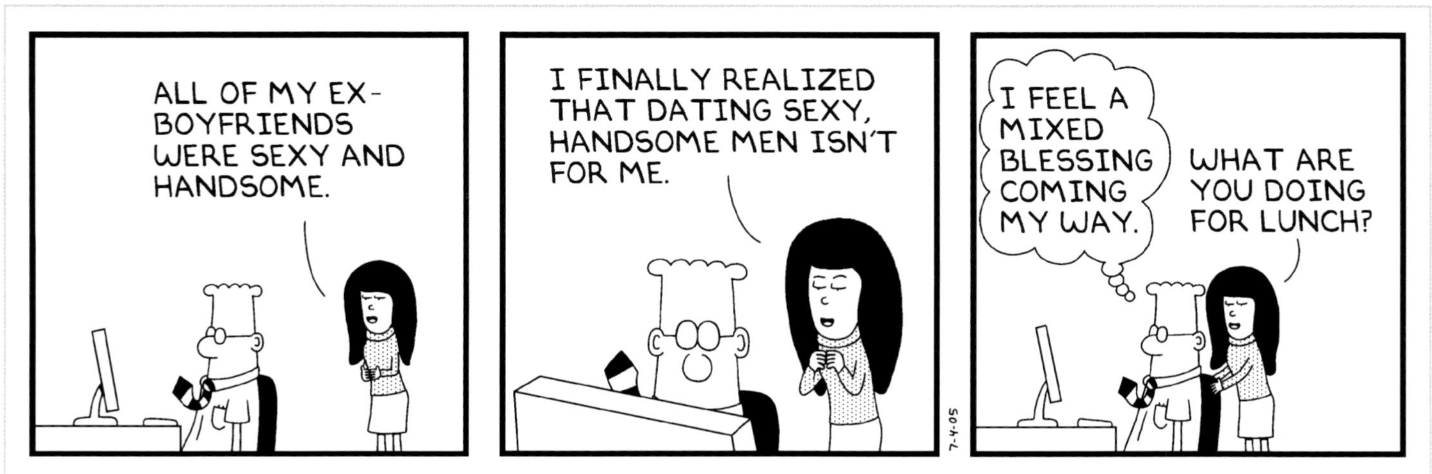
ALL OF MY EX-BOYFRIENDS WERE SEXY AND HANDSOME.
I FINALLY REALIZED THAT DATING SEXY, HANDSOME MEN ISN'T FOR ME.
7-4-05
I FEEL A MIXED BLESSING COMING MY WAY.
WHAT ARE YOU DOING FOR LUNCH?

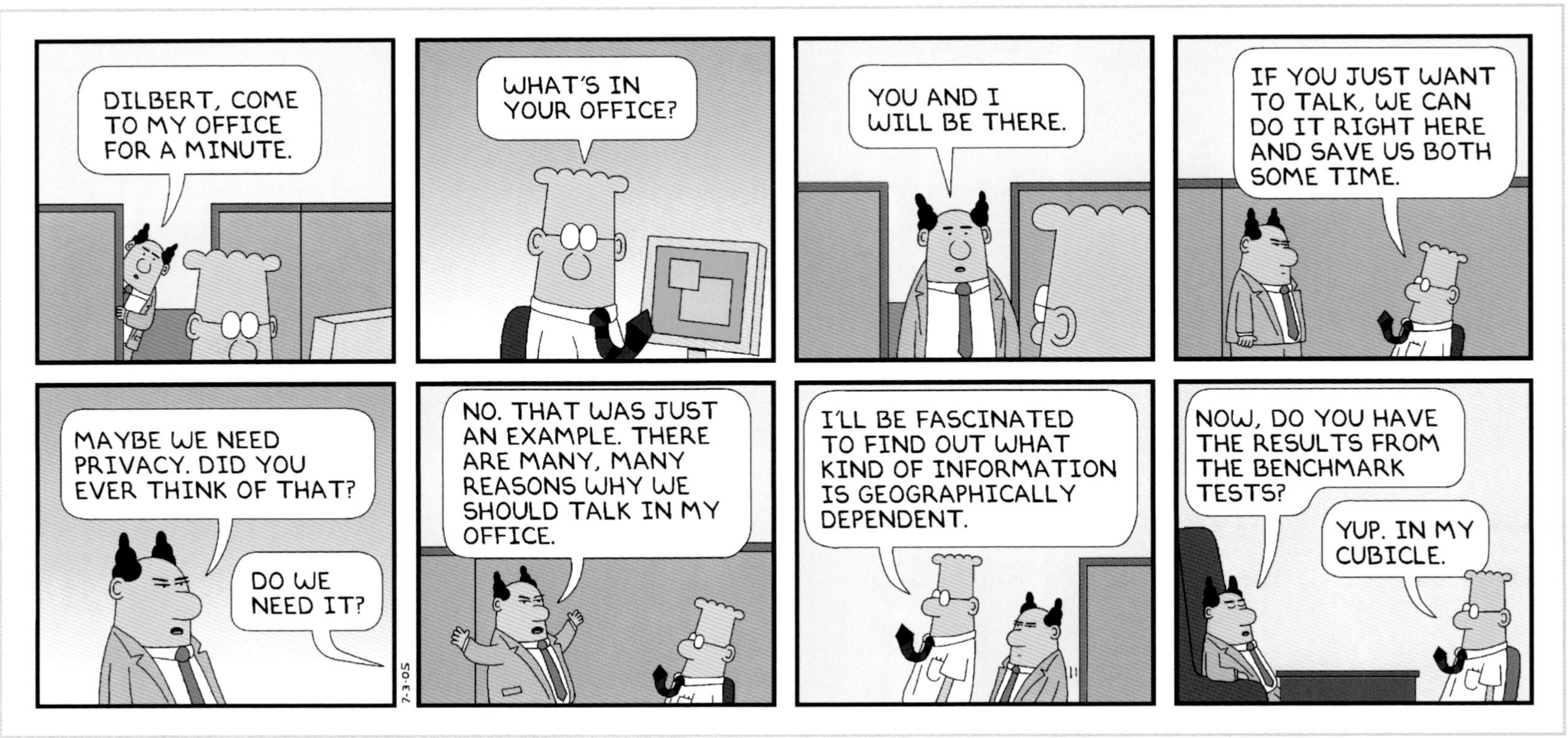
DILBERT, COME TO MY OFFICE FOR A MINUTE.
WHAT'S IN YOUR OFFICE?
YOU AND I WILL BE THERE.
IF YOU JUST WANT TO TALK, WE CAN DO IT RIGHT HERE AND SAVE US BOTH SOME TIME.
MAYBE WE NEED PRIVACY. DID YOU EVER THINK OF THAT?
DO WE NEED IT?
7-3-05
NO. THAT WAS JUST AN EXAMPLE. THERE ARE MANY, MANY REASONS WHY WE SHOULD TALK IN MY OFFICE.
I'LL BE FASCINATED TO FIND OUT WHAT KIND OF INFORMATION IS GEOGRAPHICALLY DEPENDENT.
NOW, DO YOU HAVE THE RESULTS FROM THE BENCHMARK TESTS?
YUP. IN MY CUBICLE.

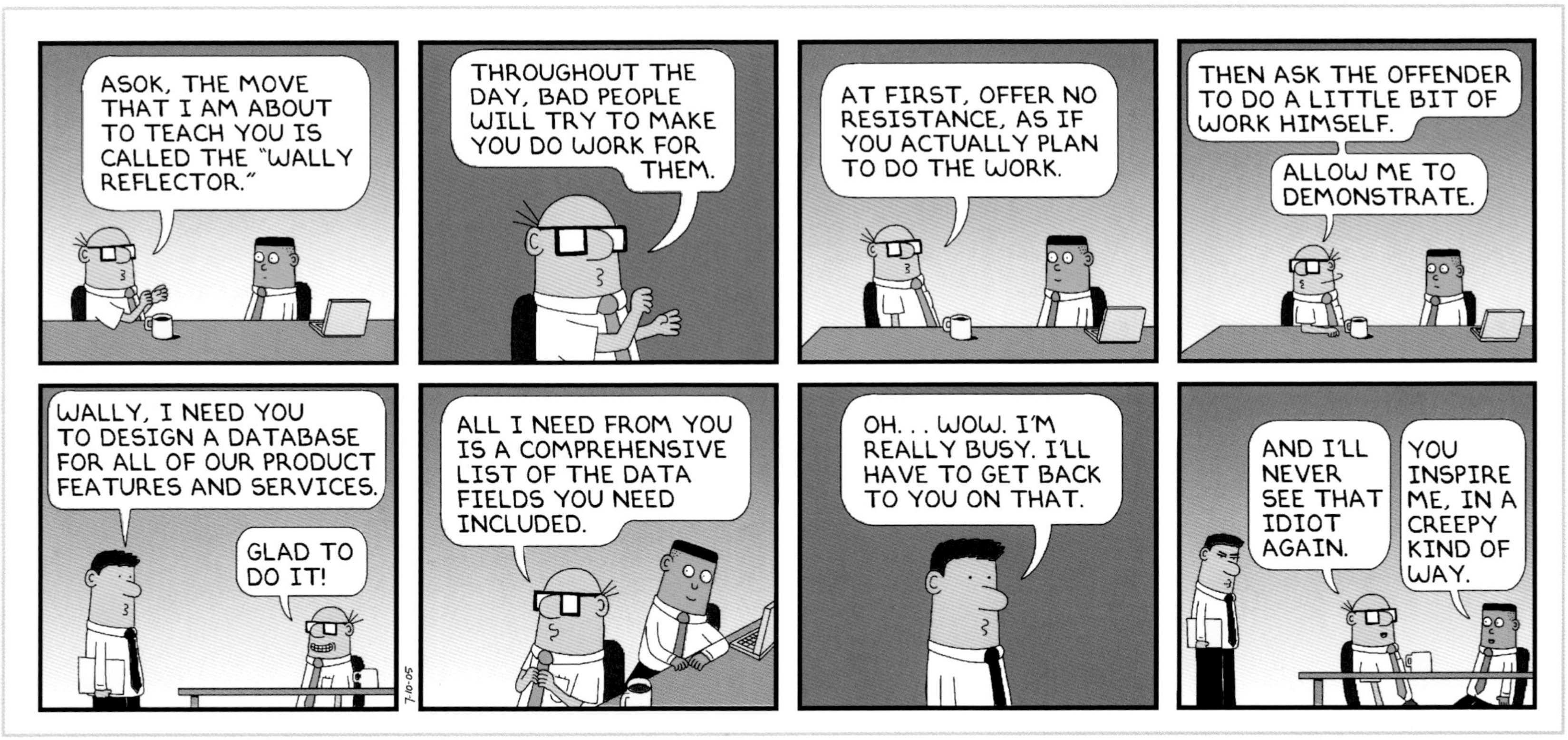
ASOK, THE MOVE THAT I AM ABOUT TO TEACH YOU IS CALLED THE "WALLY REFLECTOR."
THROUGHOUT THE DAY, BAD PEOPLE WILL TRY TO MAKE YOU DO WORK FOR THEM.
AT FIRST, OFFER NO RESISTANCE, AS IF YOU ACTUALLY PLAN TO DO THE WORK.
THEN ASK THE OFFENDER TO DO A LITTLE BIT OF WORK HIMSELF.
ALLOW ME TO DEMONSTRATE.
WALLY, I NEED YOU TO DESIGN A DATABASE FOR ALL OF OUR PRODUCT FEATURES AND SERVICES.
GLAD TO DO IT!
7-10-05
ALL I NEED FROM YOU IS A COMPREHENSIVE LIST OF THE DATA FIELDS YOU NEED INCLUDED.
OH. . . WOW. I'M REALLY BUSY. I'LL HAVE TO GET BACK TO YOU ON THAT.
AND I'LL NEVER SEE THAT IDIOT AGAIN.
YOU INSPIRE ME, IN A CREEPY KIND OF WAY.

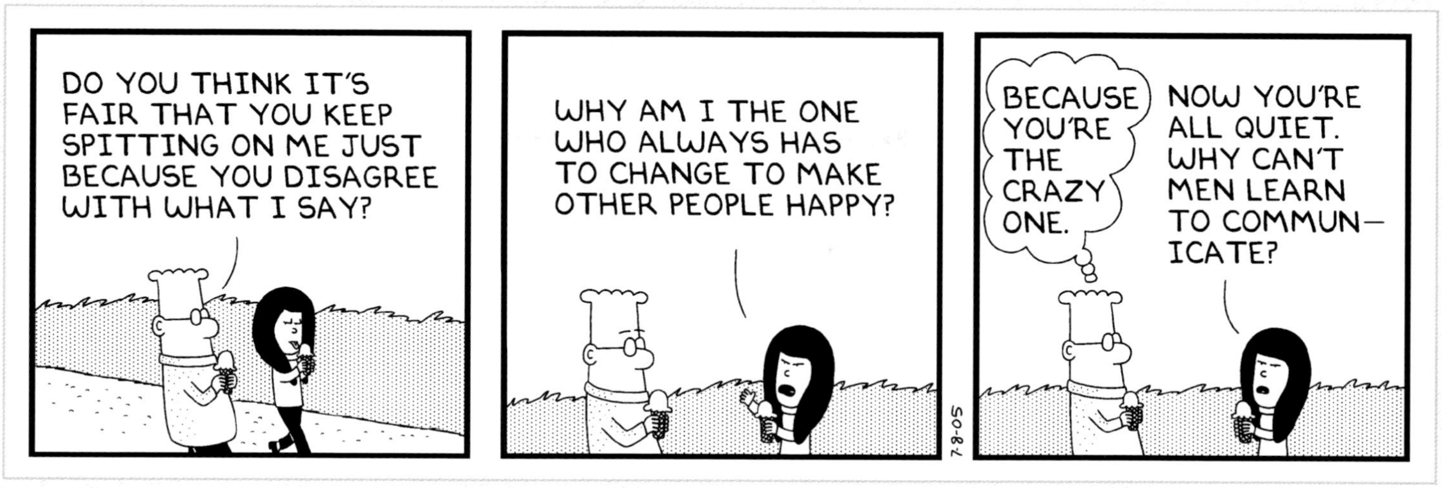
DO YOU THINK IT'S FAIR THAT YOU KEEP SPITTING ON ME JUST BECAUSE YOU DISAGREE WITH WHAT I SAY?
WHY AM I THE ONE WHO ALWAYS HAS TO CHANGE TO MAKE OTHER PEOPLE HAPPY?
7-8-05
BECAUSE YOU'RE THE CRAZY ONE.
NOW YOU'RE ALL QUIET. WHY CAN'T MEN LEARN TO COMMUNICATE?

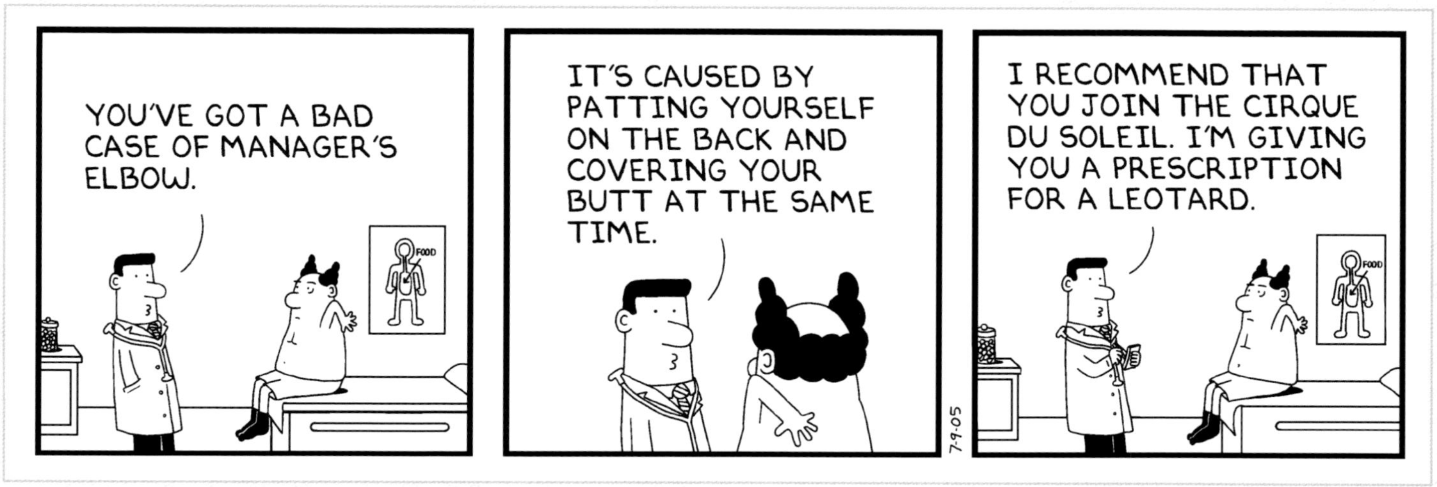
YOU'VE GOT A BAD CASE OF MANAGER'S ELBOW.
FOOD
IT'S CAUSED BY PATTING YOURSELF ON THE BACK AND COVERING YOUR BUTT AT THE SAME TIME.
7-9-05
I RECOMMEND THAT YOU JOIN THE CIRQUE DU SOLEIL. I'M GIVING YOU A PRESCRIPTION FOR A LEOTARD.
FOOD

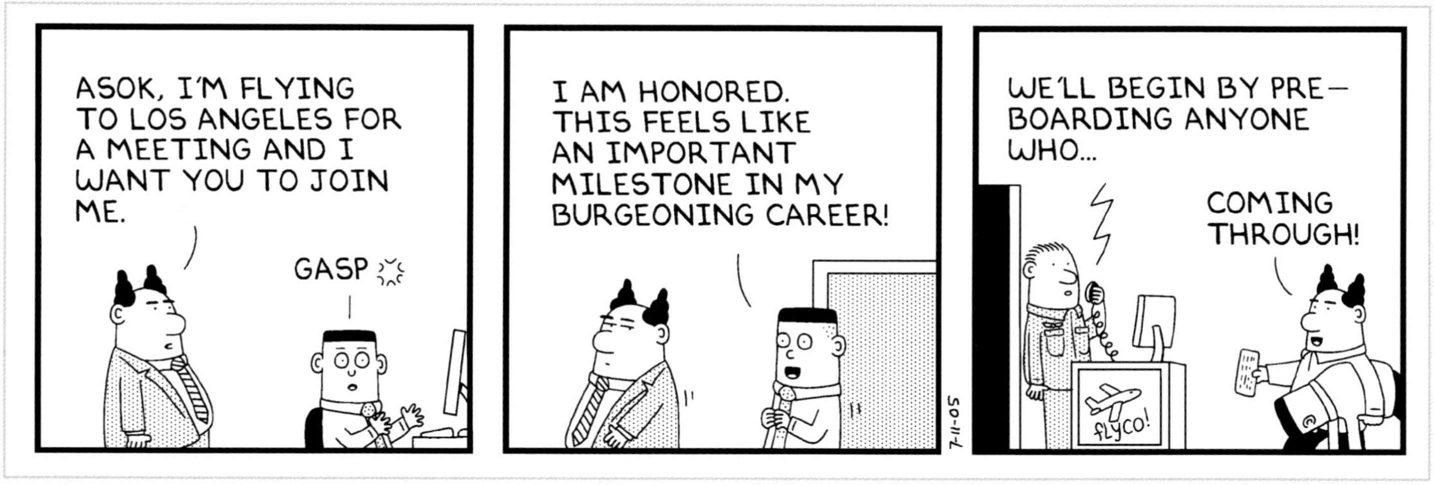
ASOK, I'M FLYING TO LOS ANGELES FOR A MEETING AND I WANT YOU TO JOIN ME.
GASP
I AM HONORED. THIS FEELS LIKE AN IMPORTANT MILESTONE IN MY BURGEONING CAREER!
7-11-05
WE'LL BEGIN BY PRE-BOARDING ANYONE WHO...
COMING THROUGH!
FLYCO!

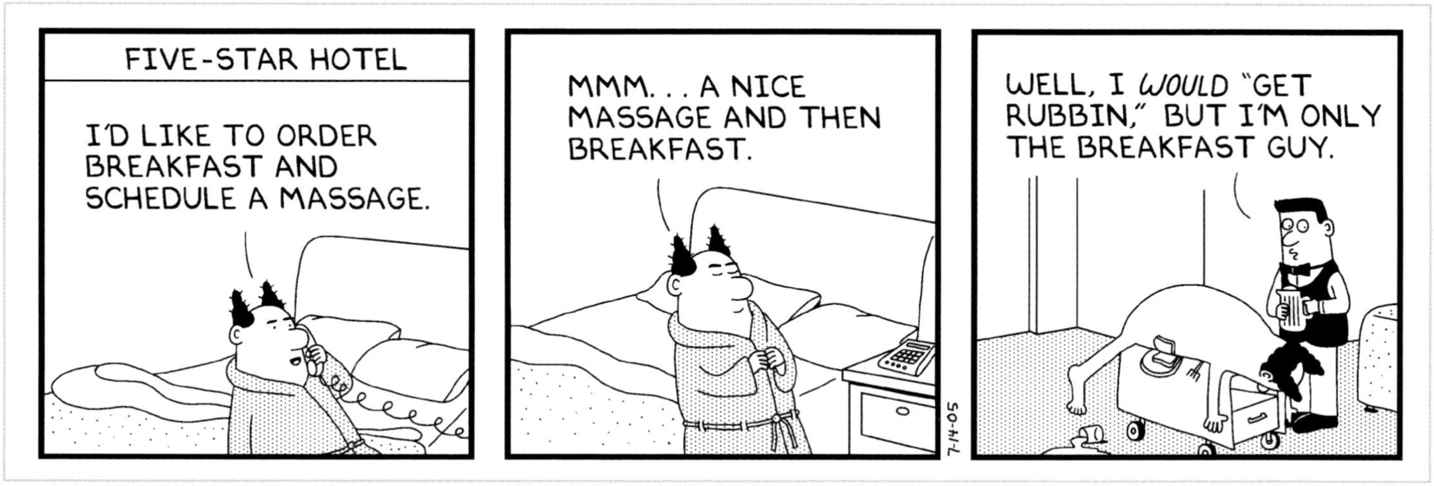
FIVE-STAR HOTEL
I'D LIKE TO ORDER BREAKFAST AND SCHEDULE A MASSAGE.
MMM. . . A NICE MASSAGE AND THEN BREAKFAST.
7-14-05
WELL, I *WOULD* "GET RUBBIN," BUT I'M ONLY THE BREAKFAST GUY.

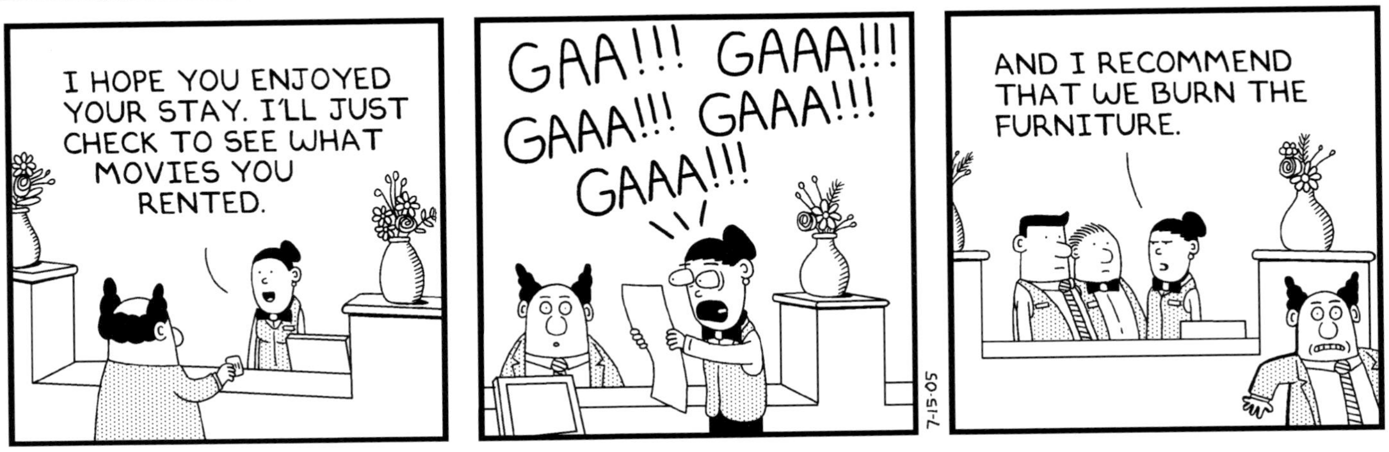
I HOPE YOU ENJOYED YOUR STAY. I'LL JUST CHECK TO SEE WHAT MOVIES YOU RENTED.
GAA!!! GAAA!!! GAAA!!! GAAA!!! GAAA!!!
7-15-05
AND I RECOMMEND THAT WE BURN THE FURNITURE.

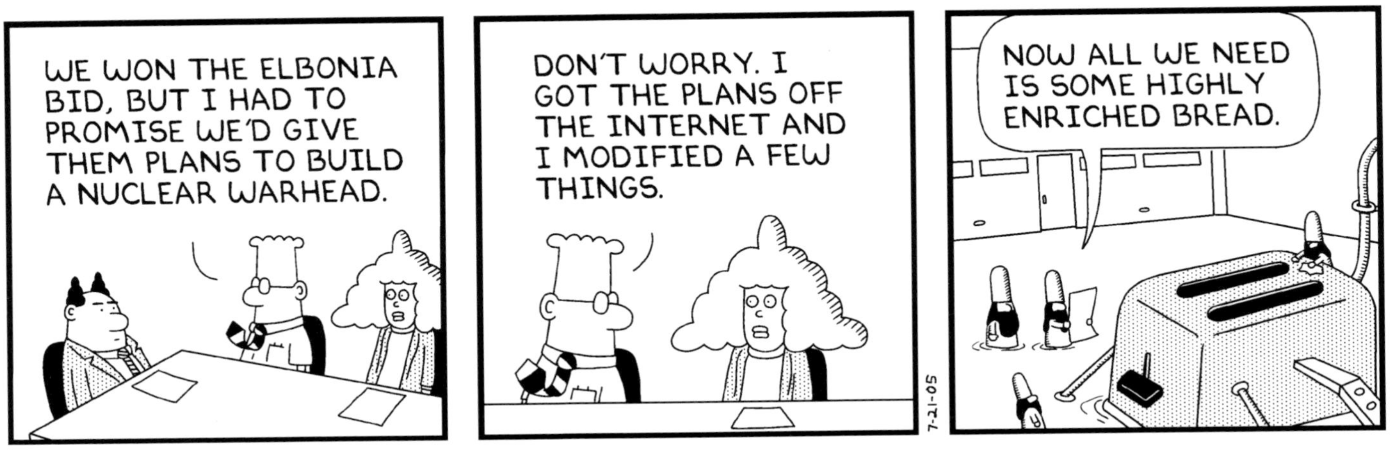
WE WON THE ELBONIA BID, BUT I HAD TO PROMISE WE'D GIVE THEM PLANS TO BUILD A NUCLEAR WARHEAD.
DON'T WORRY. I GOT THE PLANS OFF THE INTERNET AND I MODIFIED A FEW THINGS.
7-21-05
NOW ALL WE NEED IS SOME HIGHLY ENRICHED BREAD.

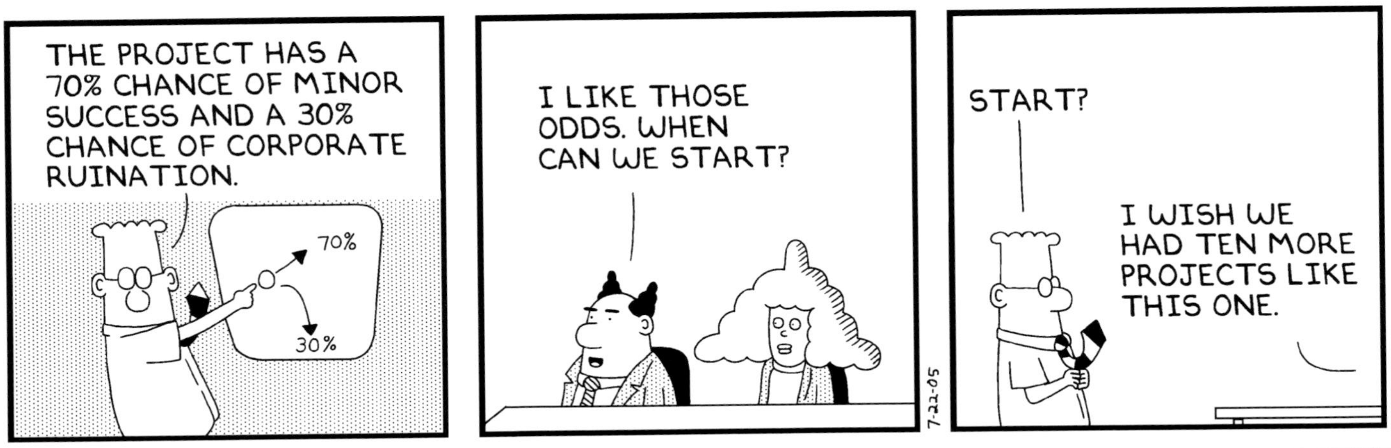
THE PROJECT HAS A 70% CHANCE OF MINOR SUCCESS AND A 30% CHANCE OF CORPORATE RUINATION.
70%
30%
I LIKE THOSE ODDS. WHEN CAN WE START?
7-22-05
START?
I WISH WE HAD TEN MORE PROJECTS LIKE THIS ONE.

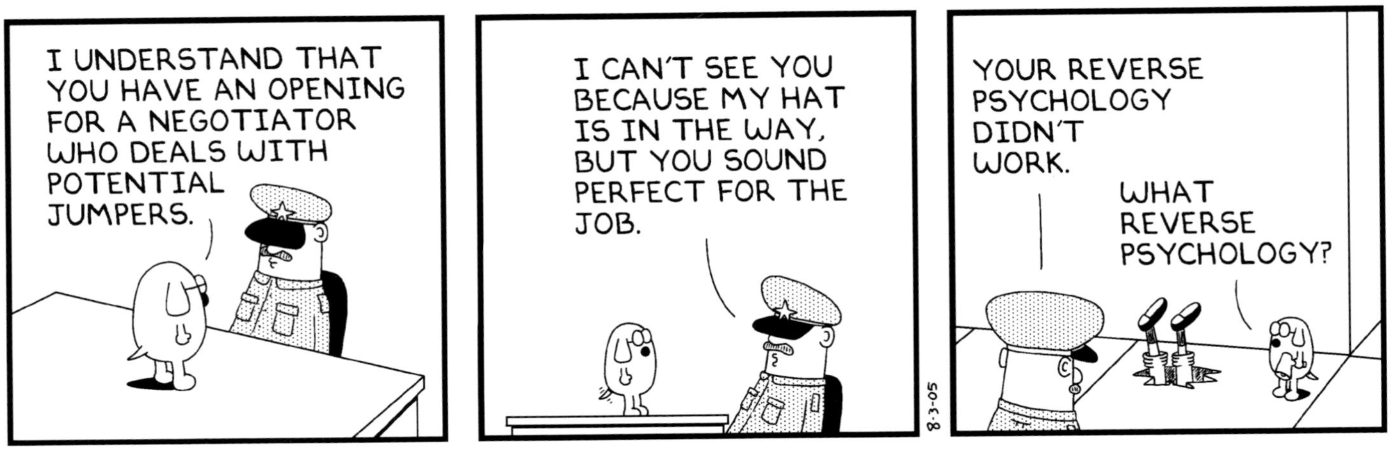
I UNDERSTAND THAT YOU HAVE AN OPENING FOR A NEGOTIATOR WHO DEALS WITH POTENTIAL JUMPERS.
I CAN'T SEE YOU BECAUSE MY HAT IS IN THE WAY, BUT YOU SOUND PERFECT FOR THE JOB.
8-3-05
YOUR REVERSE PSYCHOLOGY DIDN'T WORK.
WHAT REVERSE PSYCHOLOGY?

This is the comic the way I originally submitted it, but it's not the way it eventually ran in newspapers.

There's an unwritten and relatively recent rule in newspaper comics: You can't show a handgun being discharged. I had a new editor, and I wondered if anyone told him the unwritten rule. I figured it was worth a shot, so to speak.

My new editor only lasted a few weeks on the job, and never saw the strip. But his assistant knew the unwritten rule and picked it out of the pipeline. He convened some executives at United Feature Syndicate to get a ruling. After the meeting, he told me the executives couldn't allow a picture of a handgun being discharged.

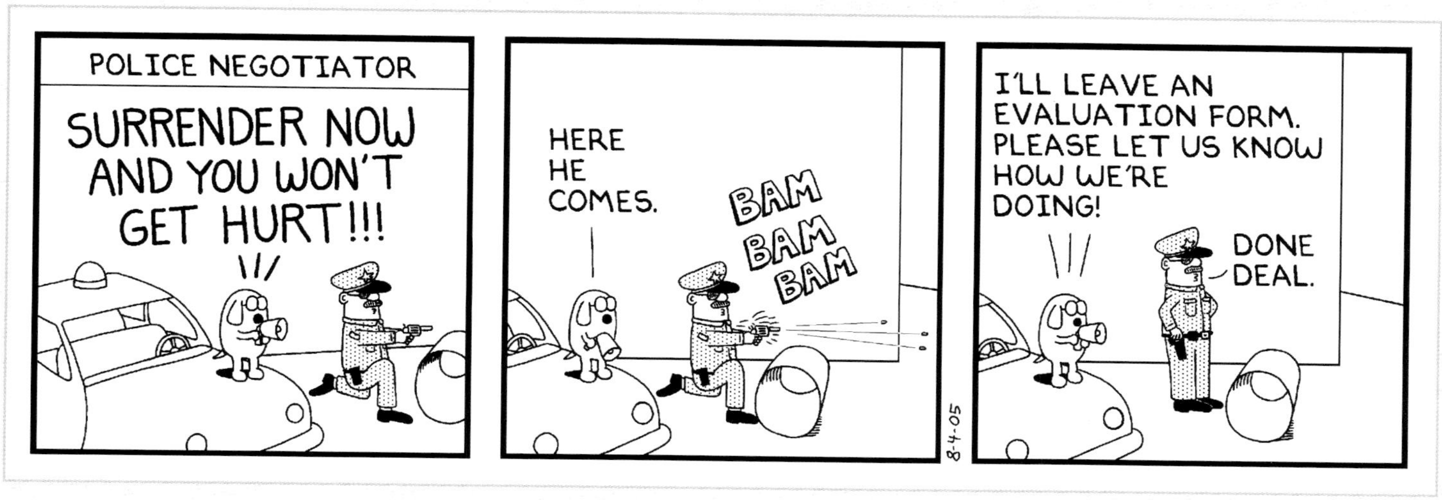
POLICE NEGOTIATOR
SURRENDER NOW AND YOU WON'T GET HURT!!!
HERE HE COMES.
BAM BAM BAM
I'LL LEAVE AN EVALUATION FORM. PLEASE LET US KNOW HOW WE'RE DOING!
DONE DEAL.
8-4-05

To clarify, I asked if it was okay in concept that a police officer was gunning down an unarmed man. "No problem," said the assistant editor. "You just can't show the gun being fired."

So I put together this version, where the gun is firing, but you can't see it.

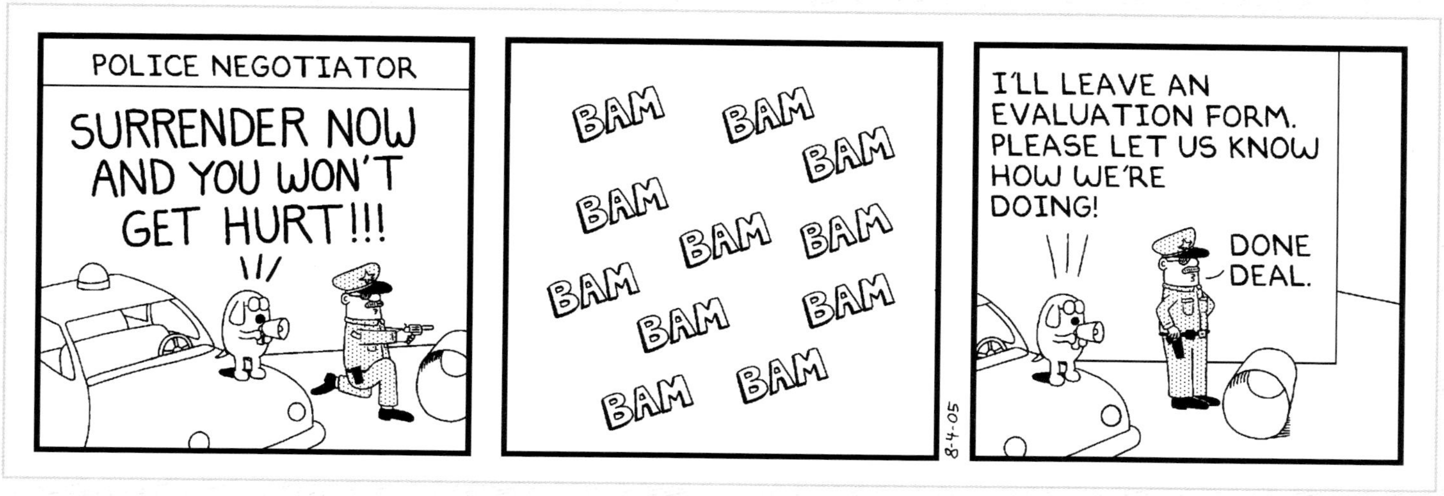
POLICE NEGOTIATOR
SURRENDER NOW AND YOU WON'T GET HURT!!!
BAM BAM BAM BAM BAM BAM BAM BAM BAM BAM BAM
I'LL LEAVE AN EVALUATION FORM. PLEASE LET US KNOW HOW WE'RE DOING!
DONE DEAL.
8-4-05

The assistant editor called and said he had reconvened the executives and their opinion on this strip was that it was still inappropriate. After all, I showed the gun, and then I showed the "BAM BAM." Clearly the gun was being fired, so it would still cause trouble with anti-gun readers.

This is where my sixteen years of corporate experience came in handy. I knew I needed to think like a committee to get my comic past the committee of editors. So I did some brainstorming and came up with an idea that only a committee could love. I replaced the gun with a doughnut . . . that happens to fire bullets. The doughnut-gun version ran in newspapers all over the world, without explanation. No one complained.

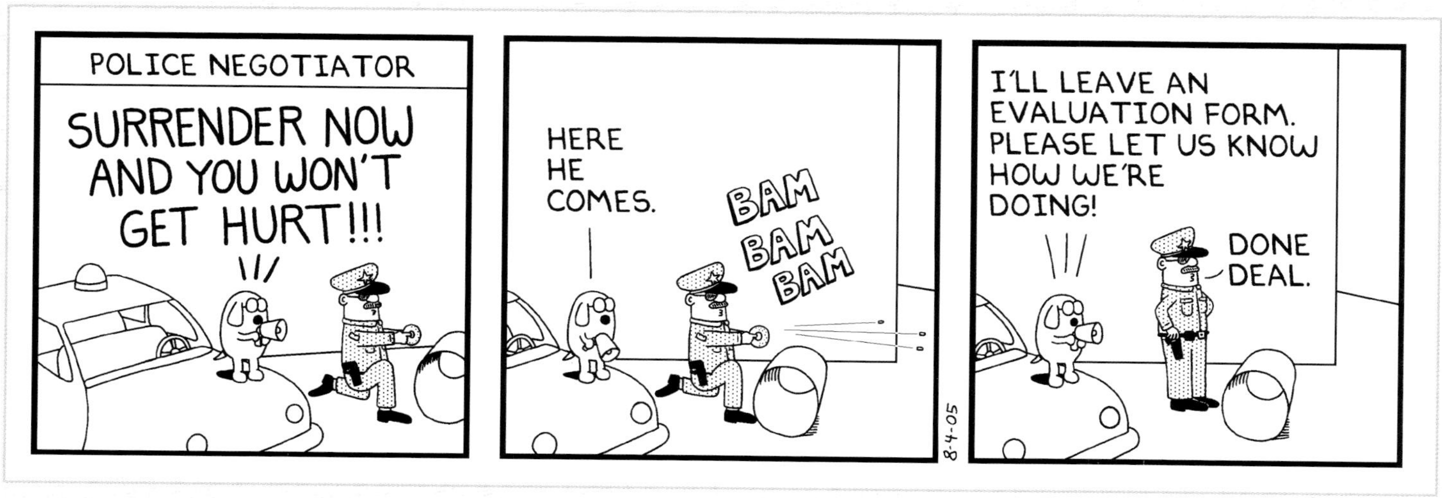
POLICE NEGOTIATOR
SURRENDER NOW AND YOU WON'T GET HURT!!!
HERE HE COMES.
BAM BAM BAM
I'LL LEAVE AN EVALUATION FORM. PLEASE LET US KNOW HOW WE'RE DOING!
DONE DEAL.
8-4-05

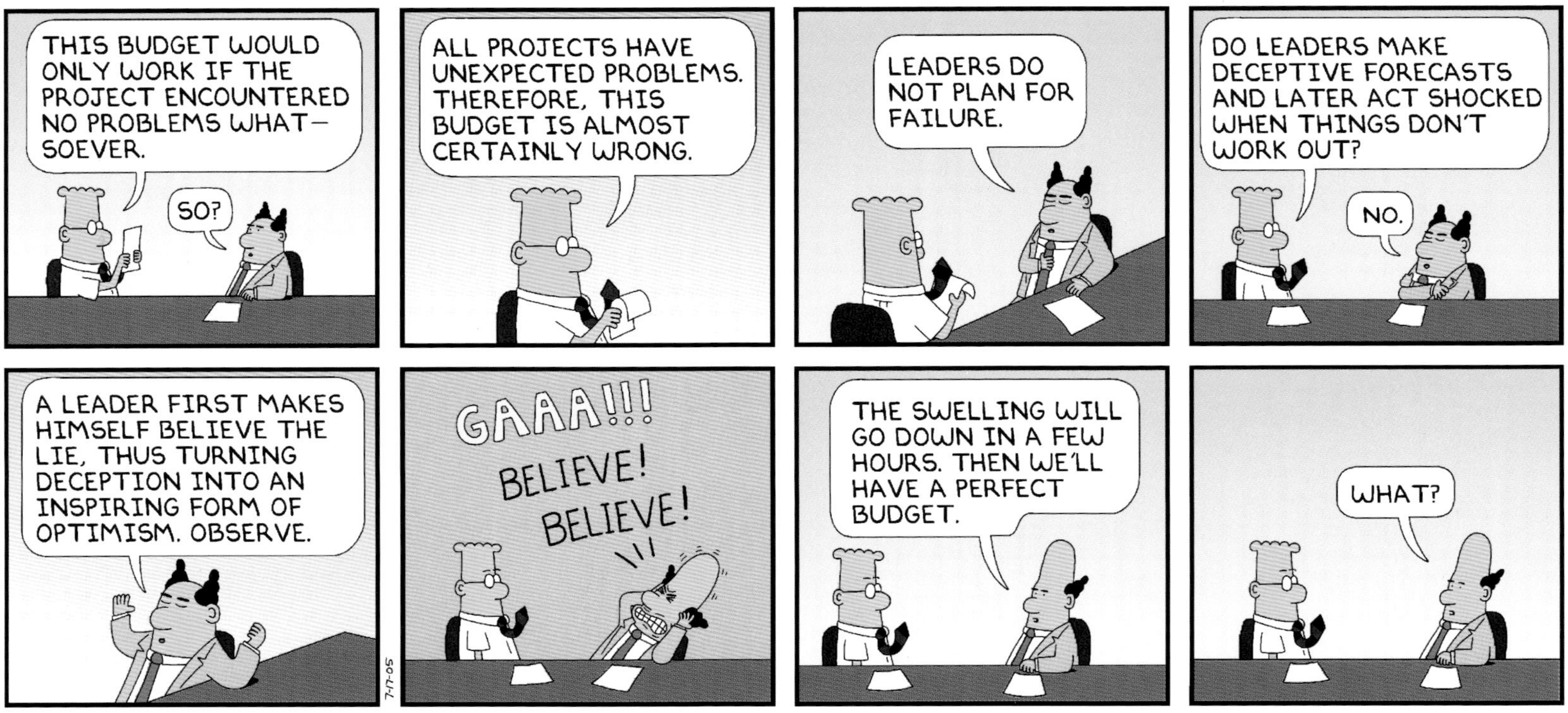
THIS BUDGET WOULD ONLY WORK IF THE PROJECT ENCOUNTERED NO PROBLEMS WHAT-SOEVER.
SO?
ALL PROJECTS HAVE UNEXPECTED PROBLEMS. THEREFORE, THIS BUDGET IS ALMOST CERTAINLY WRONG.
LEADERS DO NOT PLAN FOR FAILURE.
DO LEADERS MAKE DECEPTIVE FORECASTS AND LATER ACT SHOCKED WHEN THINGS DON'T WORK OUT?
NO.
A LEADER FIRST MAKES HIMSELF BELIEVE THE LIE, THUS TURNING DECEPTION INTO AN INSPIRING FORM OF OPTIMISM. OBSERVE.
7-17-05
GAAA!!!
BELIEVE!
BELIEVE!
THE SWELLING WILL GO DOWN IN A FEW HOURS. THEN WE'LL HAVE A PERFECT BUDGET.
WHAT?

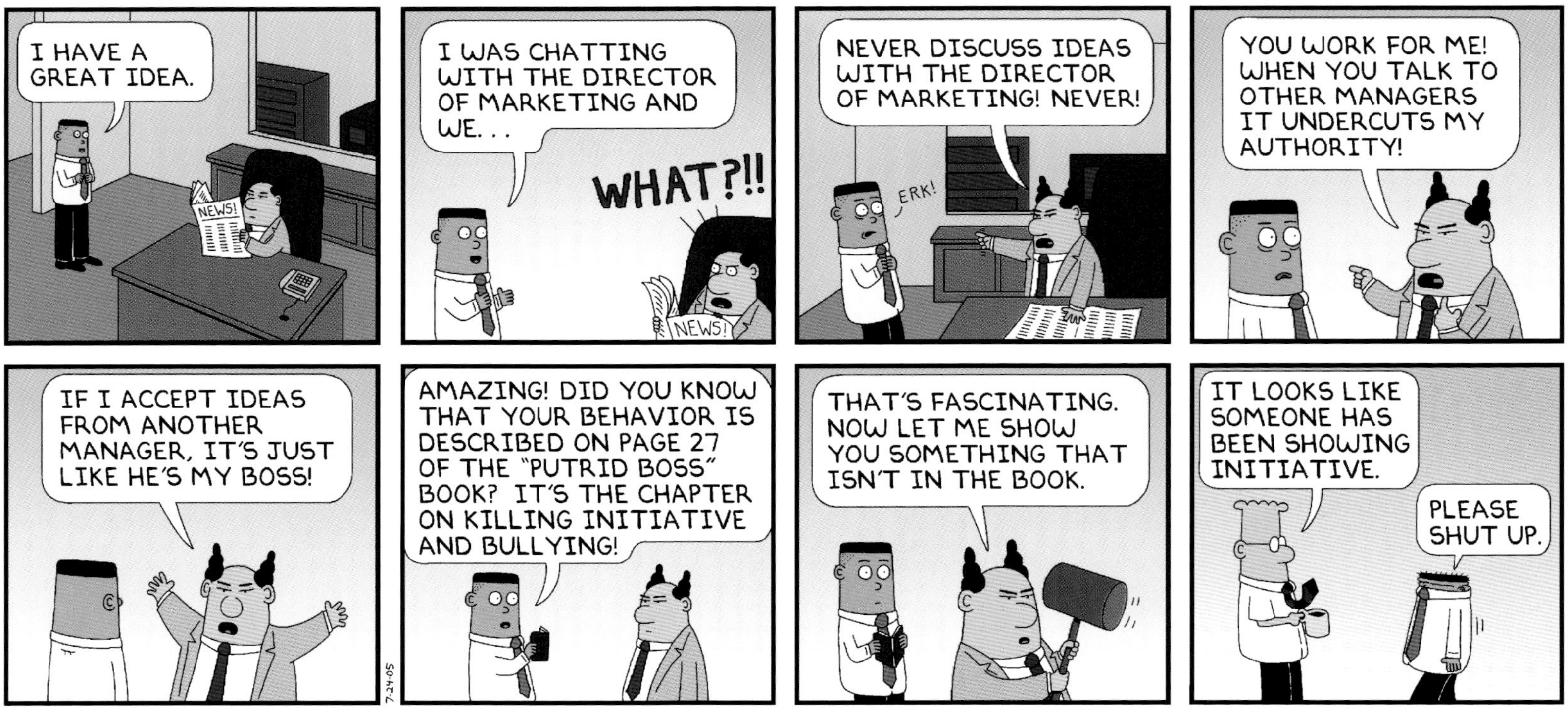
I HAVE A GREAT IDEA.
NEWS!
I WAS CHATTING WITH THE DIRECTOR OF MARKETING AND WE. . .
WHAT?!!
NEWS!
NEVER DISCUSS IDEAS WITH THE DIRECTOR OF MARKETING! NEVER!
ERK!
YOU WORK FOR ME! WHEN YOU TALK TO OTHER MANAGERS IT UNDERCUTS MY AUTHORITY!
IF I ACCEPT IDEAS FROM ANOTHER MANAGER, IT'S JUST LIKE HE'S MY BOSS!
7-24-05
AMAZING! DID YOU KNOW THAT YOUR BEHAVIOR IS DESCRIBED ON PAGE 27 OF THE "PUTRID BOSS" BOOK? IT'S THE CHAPTER ON KILLING INITIATIVE AND BULLYING!
THAT'S FASCINATING. NOW LET ME SHOW YOU SOMETHING THAT ISN'T IN THE BOOK.
IT LOOKS LIKE SOMEONE HAS BEEN SHOWING INITIATIVE.
PLEASE SHUT UP.

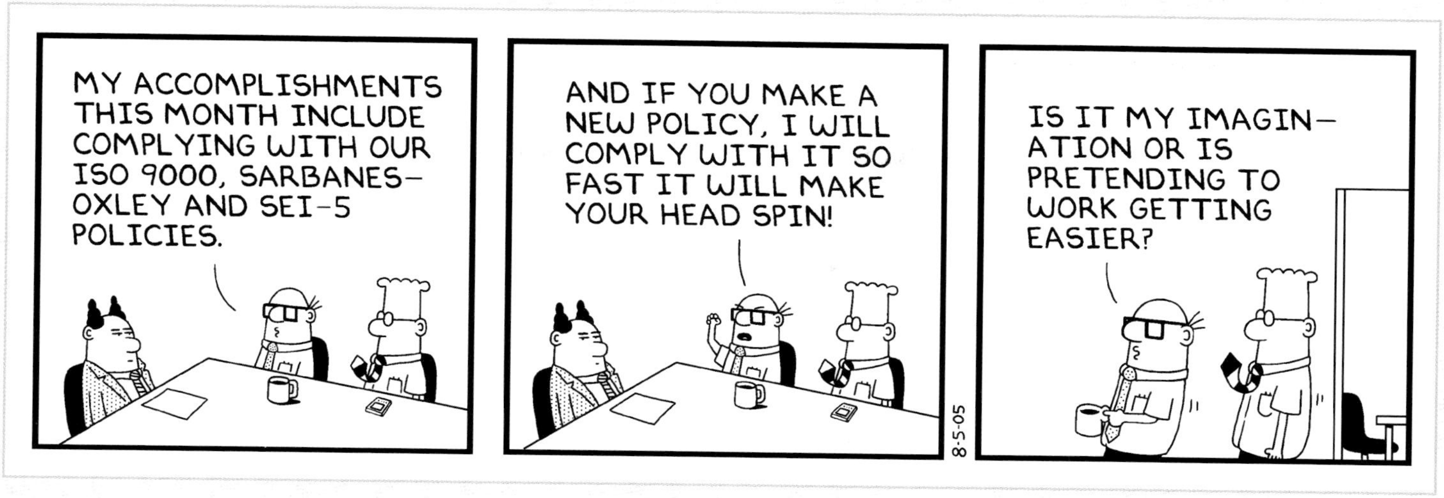
MY ACCOMPLISHMENTS THIS MONTH INCLUDE COMPLYING WITH OUR ISO 9000, SARBANES-OXLEY AND SEI-5 POLICIES.
AND IF YOU MAKE A NEW POLICY, I WILL COMPLY WITH IT SO FAST IT WILL MAKE YOUR HEAD SPIN!
8-5-05
IS IT MY IMAGINATION OR IS PRETENDING TO WORK GETTING EASIER?

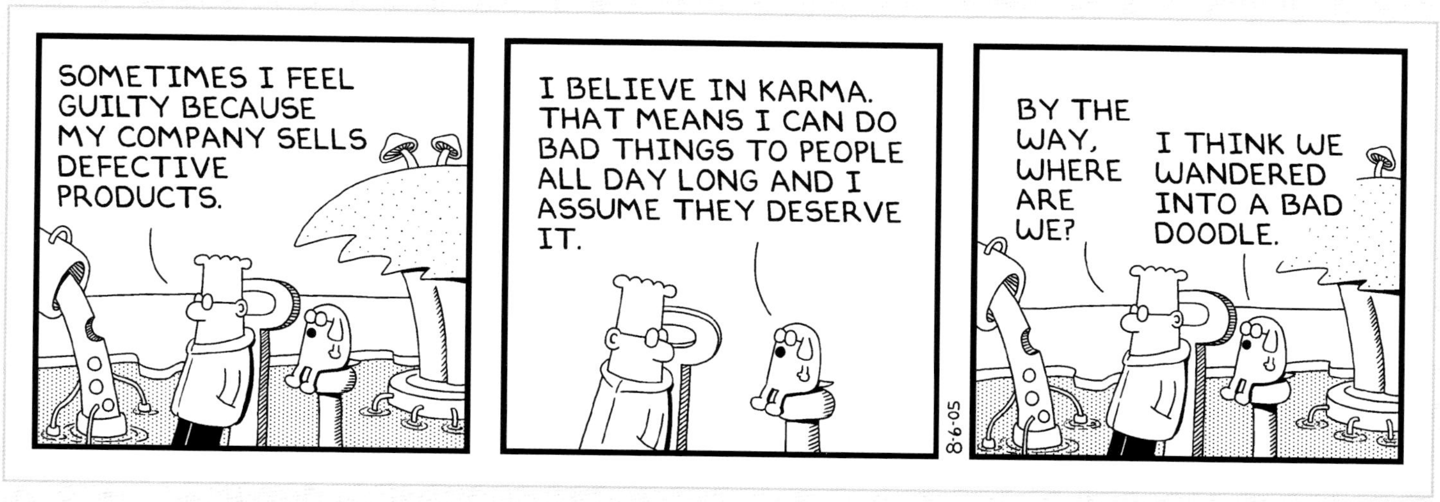
SOMETIMES I FEEL GUILTY BECAUSE MY COMPANY SELLS DEFECTIVE PRODUCTS.
I BELIEVE IN KARMA. THAT MEANS I CAN DO BAD THINGS TO PEOPLE ALL DAY LONG AND I ASSUME THEY DESERVE IT.
8-6-05
BY THE WAY, WHERE ARE WE?
I THINK WE WANDERED INTO A BAD DOODLE.

I was getting so tired of drawing desks and conference tables that I just needed to put the boys someplace else for a day.

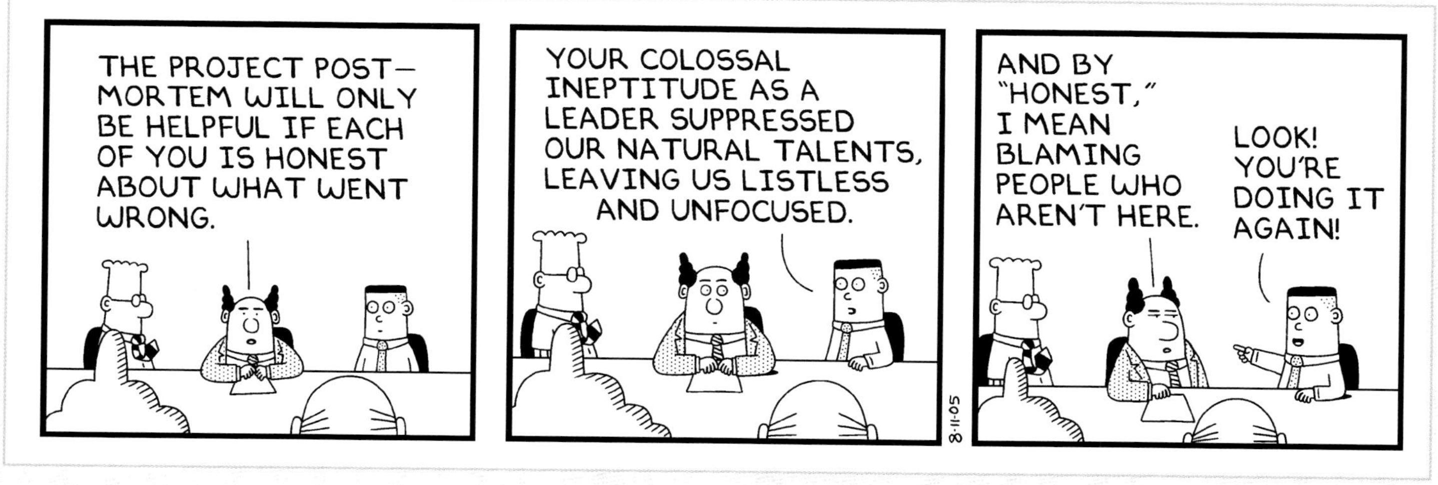
THE PROJECT POST-MORTEM WILL ONLY BE HELPFUL IF EACH OF YOU IS HONEST ABOUT WHAT WENT WRONG.
YOUR COLOSSAL INEPTITUDE AS A LEADER SUPPRESSED OUR NATURAL TALENTS, LEAVING US LISTLESS AND UNFOCUSED.
8-11-05
AND BY "HONEST," I MEAN BLAMING PEOPLE WHO AREN'T HERE.
LOOK! YOU'RE DOING IT AGAIN!

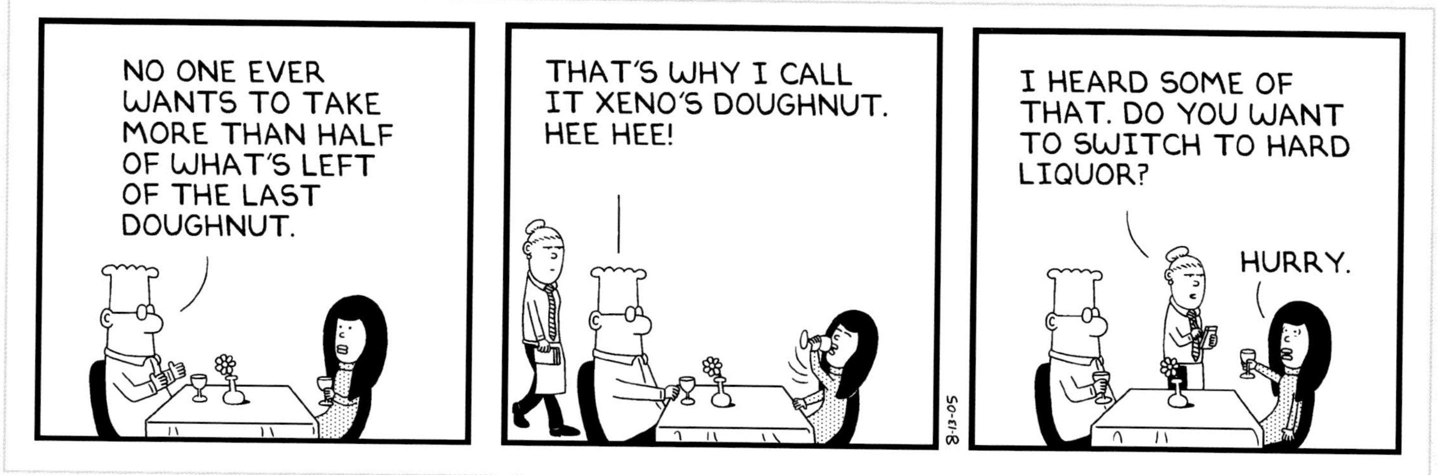
NO ONE EVER WANTS TO TAKE MORE THAN HALF OF WHAT'S LEFT OF THE LAST DOUGHNUT.
THAT'S WHY I CALL IT XENO'S DOUGHNUT. HEE HEE!
8-13-05
I HEARD SOME OF THAT. DO YOU WANT TO SWITCH TO HARD LIQUOR?
HURRY.

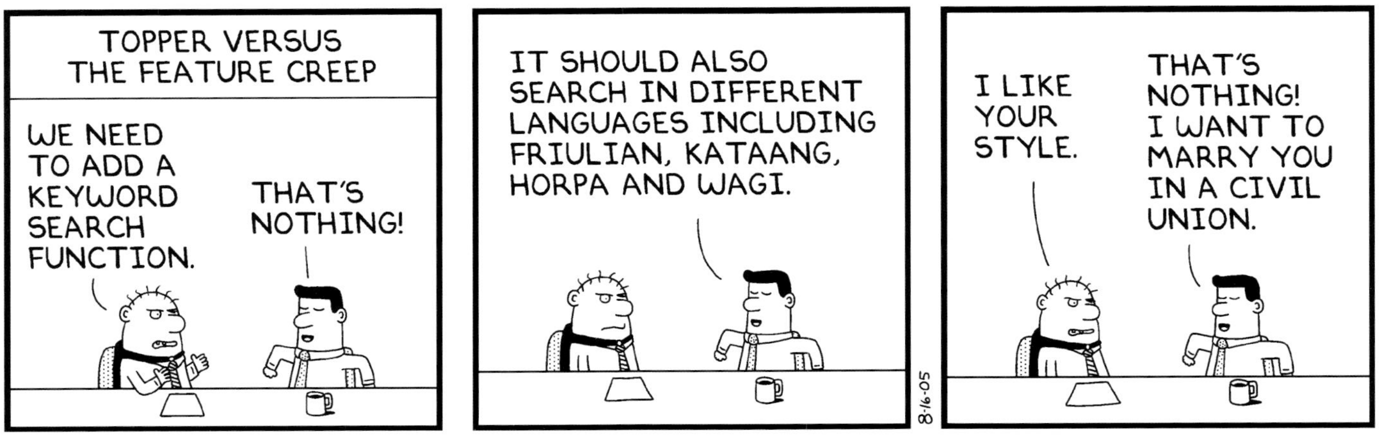
TOPPER VERSUS THE FEATURE CREEP
WE NEED TO ADD A KEYWORD SEARCH FUNCTION.
THAT'S NOTHING!
IT SHOULD ALSO SEARCH IN DIFFERENT LANGUAGES INCLUDING FRIULIAN, KATAANG, HORPA AND WAGI.
I LIKE YOUR STYLE.
THAT'S NOTHING! I WANT TO MARRY YOU IN A CIVIL UNION.
8-16-05

Wikipedia has made my job so much easier. Those are all real languages.

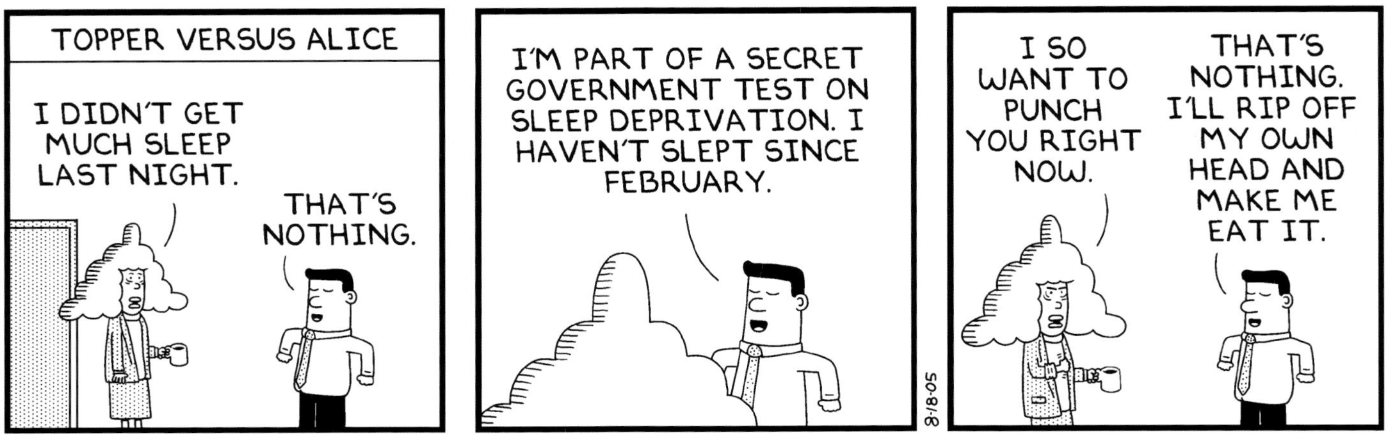
TOPPER VERSUS ALICE
I DIDN'T GET MUCH SLEEP LAST NIGHT.
THAT'S NOTHING.
I'M PART OF A SECRET GOVERNMENT TEST ON SLEEP DEPRIVATION. I HAVEN'T SLEPT SINCE FEBRUARY.
I SO WANT TO PUNCH YOU RIGHT NOW.
THAT'S NOTHING. I'LL RIP OFF MY OWN HEAD AND MAKE ME EAT IT.
8-18-05

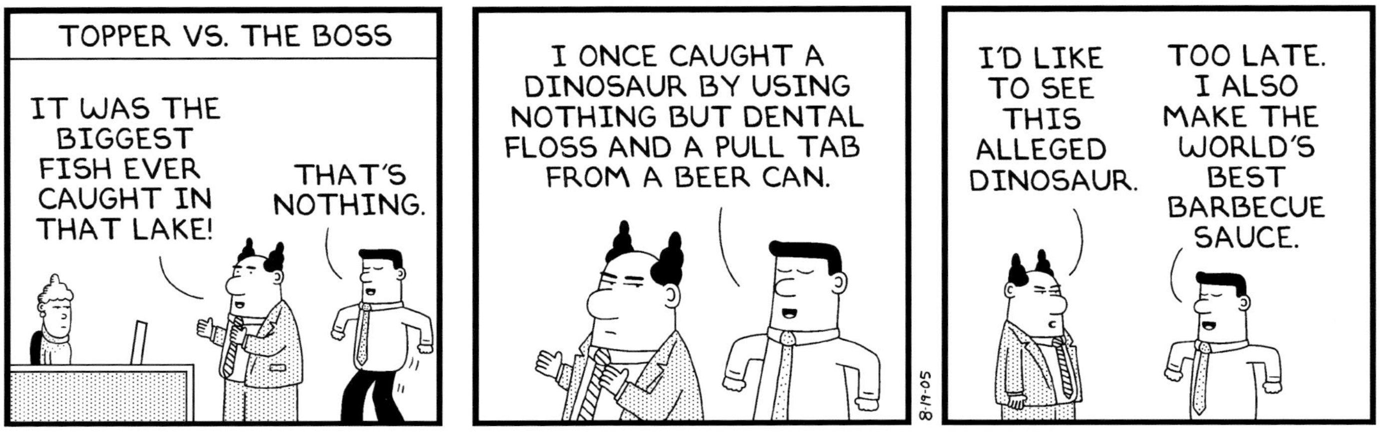
TOPPER VS. THE BOSS
IT WAS THE BIGGEST FISH EVER CAUGHT IN THAT LAKE!
THAT'S NOTHING.
I ONCE CAUGHT A DINOSAUR BY USING NOTHING BUT DENTAL FLOSS AND A PULL TAB FROM A BEER CAN.
I'D LIKE TO SEE THIS ALLEGED DINOSAUR.
TOO LATE. I ALSO MAKE THE WORLD'S BEST BARBECUE SAUCE.
8-19-05

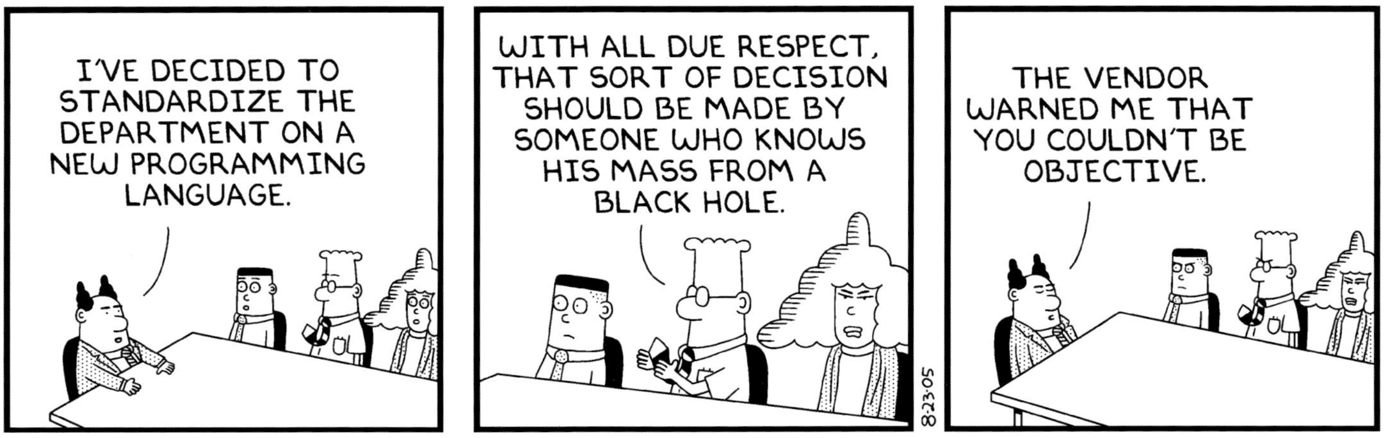
I'VE DECIDED TO STANDARDIZE THE DEPARTMENT ON A NEW PROGRAMMING LANGUAGE.
WITH ALL DUE RESPECT, THAT SORT OF DECISION SHOULD BE MADE BY SOMEONE WHO KNOWS HIS MASS FROM A BLACK HOLE.
THE VENDOR WARNED ME THAT YOU COULDN'T BE OBJECTIVE.
8-23-05

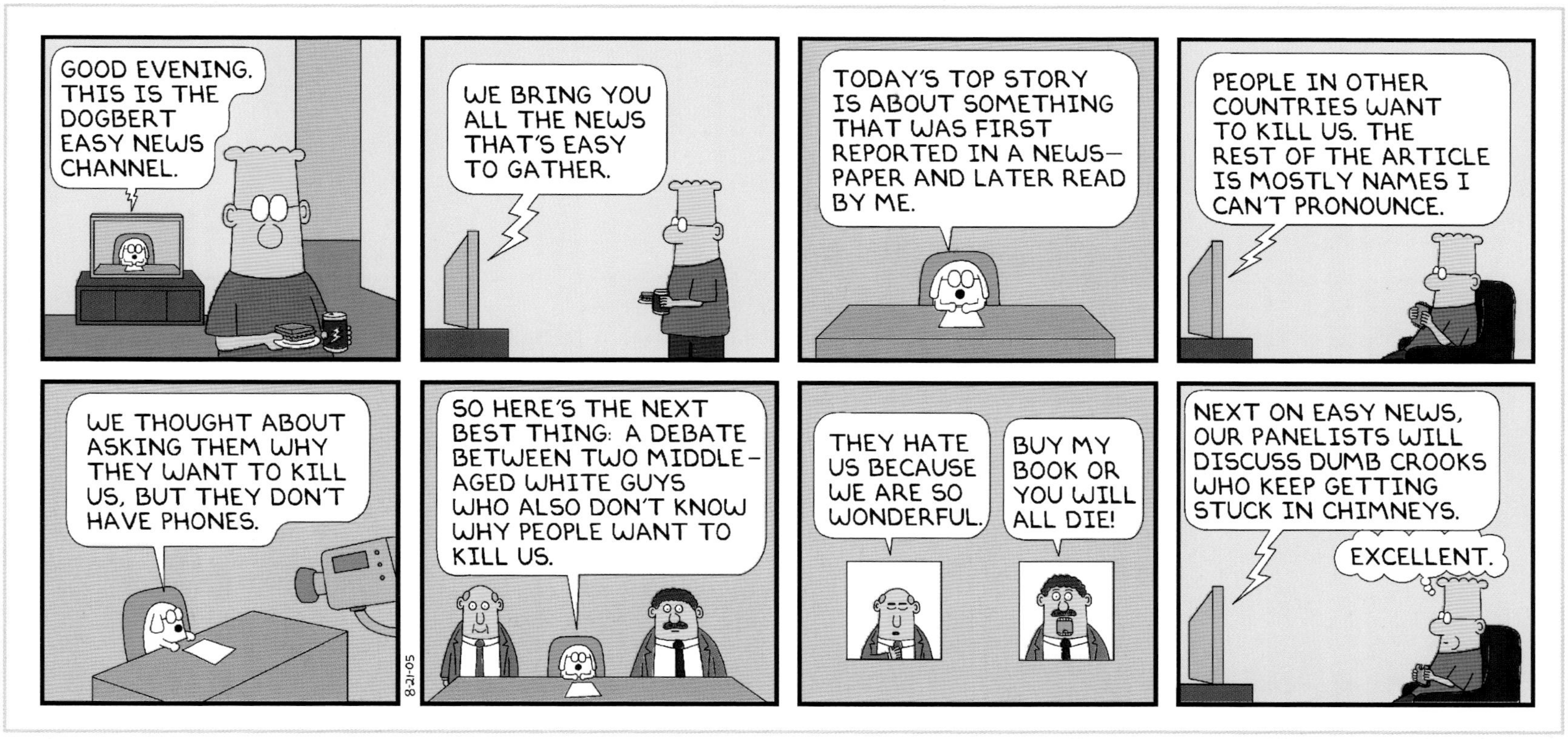
GOOD EVENING. THIS IS THE DOGBERT EASY NEWS CHANNEL.
WE BRING YOU ALL THE NEWS THAT'S EASY TO GATHER.
TODAY'S TOP STORY IS ABOUT SOMETHING THAT WAS FIRST REPORTED IN A NEWS-PAPER AND LATER READ BY ME.
PEOPLE IN OTHER COUNTRIES WANT TO KILL US. THE REST OF THE ARTICLE IS MOSTLY NAMES I CAN'T PRONOUNCE.
WE THOUGHT ABOUT ASKING THEM WHY THEY WANT TO KILL US, BUT THEY DON'T HAVE PHONES.
8-21-05
SO HERE'S THE NEXT BEST THING: A DEBATE BETWEEN TWO MIDDLE-AGED WHITE GUYS WHO ALSO DON'T KNOW WHY PEOPLE WANT TO KILL US.
THEY HATE US BECAUSE WE ARE SO WONDERFUL.
BUY MY BOOK OR YOU WILL ALL DIE!
NEXT ON EASY NEWS, OUR PANELISTS WILL DISCUSS DUMB CROOKS WHO KEEP GETTING STUCK IN CHIMNEYS.
EXCELLENT.

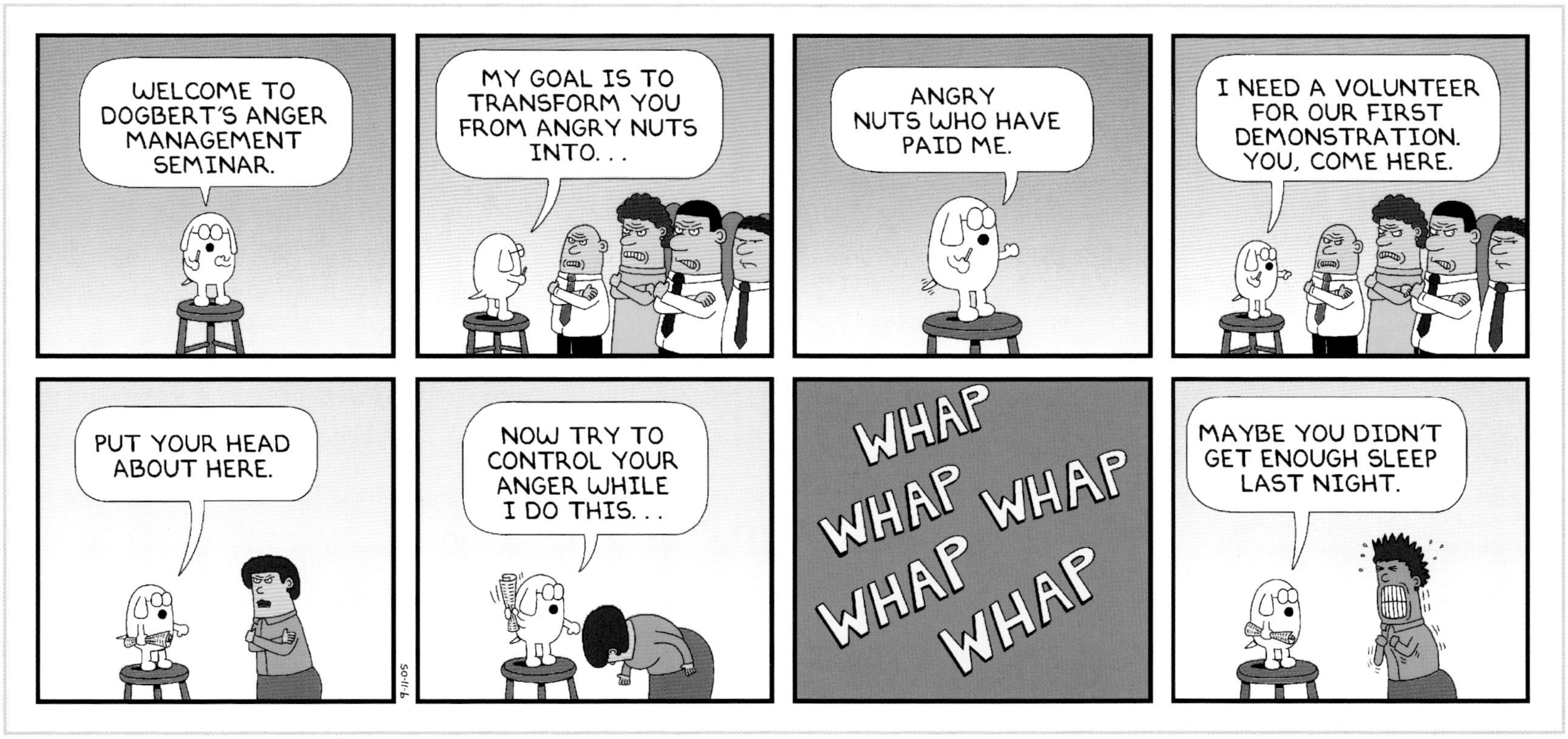
WELCOME TO DOGBERT'S ANGER MANAGEMENT SEMINAR.
MY GOAL IS TO TRANSFORM YOU FROM ANGRY NUTS INTO. . .
ANGRY NUTS WHO HAVE PAID ME.
I NEED A VOLUNTEER FOR OUR FIRST DEMONSTRATION. YOU, COME HERE.
PUT YOUR HEAD ABOUT HERE.
9-11-05
NOW TRY TO CONTROL YOUR ANGER WHILE I DO THIS. . .
WHAP WHAP WHAP WHAP WHAP WHAP
MAYBE YOU DIDN'T GET ENOUGH SLEEP LAST NIGHT.

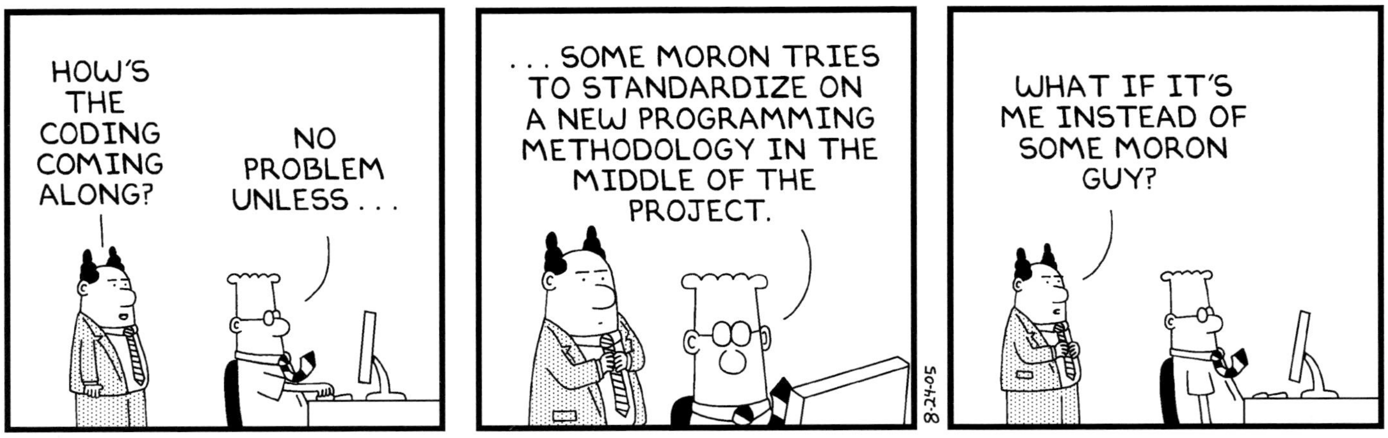
HOW'S THE CODING COMING ALONG?
NO PROBLEM UNLESS . . .
. . . SOME MORON TRIES TO STANDARDIZE ON A NEW PROGRAMMING METHODOLOGY IN THE MIDDLE OF THE PROJECT.
8-24-05
WHAT IF IT'S ME INSTEAD OF SOME MORON GUY?

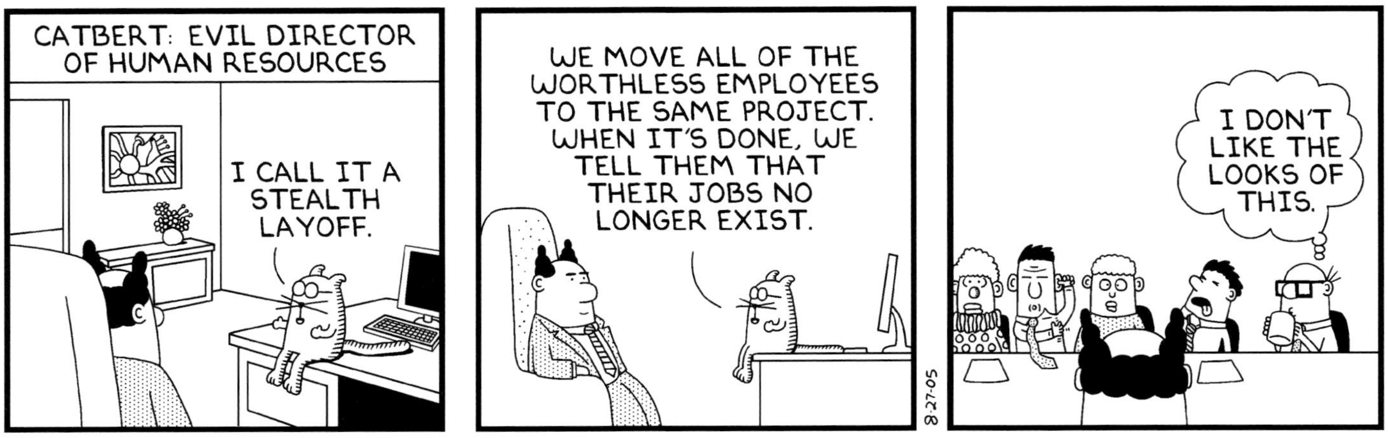
CATBERT: EVIL DIRECTOR OF HUMAN RESOURCES
I CALL IT A STEALTH LAYOFF.
WE MOVE ALL OF THE WORTHLESS EMPLOYEES TO THE SAME PROJECT. WHEN IT'S DONE, WE TELL THEM THAT THEIR JOBS NO LONGER EXIST.
8-27-05
I DON'T LIKE THE LOOKS OF THIS.

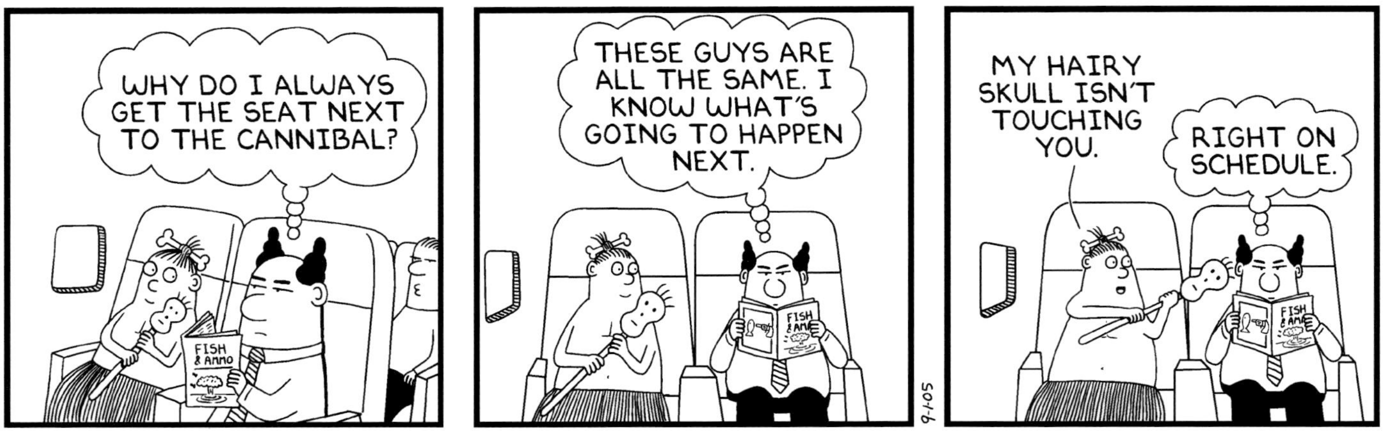
WHY DO I ALWAYS GET THE SEAT NEXT TO THE CANNIBAL?
THESE GUYS ARE ALL THE SAME. I KNOW WHAT'S GOING TO HAPPEN NEXT.
9-1-05
MY HAIRY SKULL ISN'T TOUCHING YOU.
RIGHT ON SCHEDULE.

This is the sort of comic where the ending is prompted by some accident in the drawing. I had no idea where this comic was heading when it started. But after I drew the hairy skull, and I realized how annoying it would be to sit next to a guy who had one, the rest just followed.

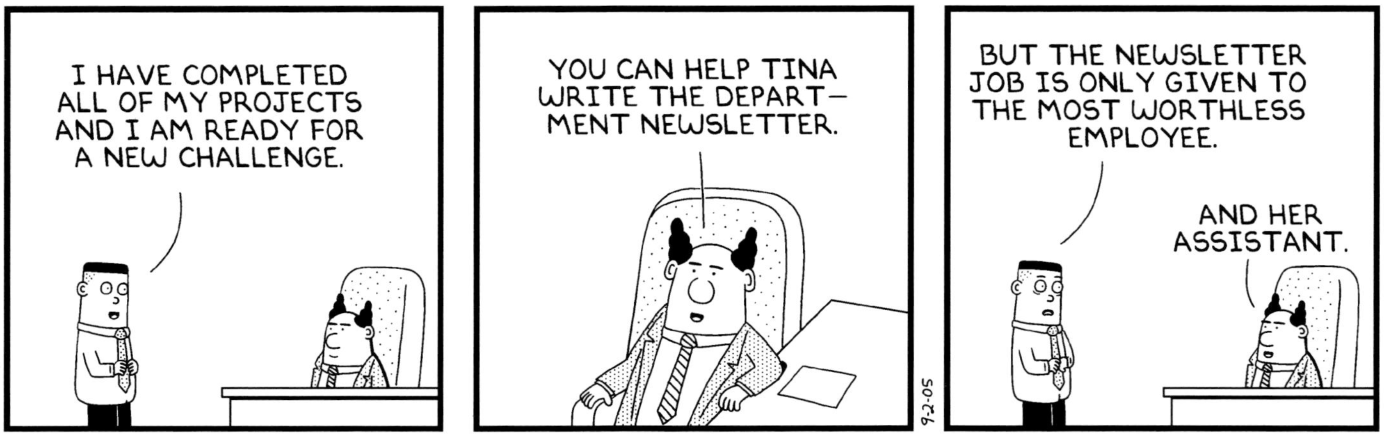
I HAVE COMPLETED ALL OF MY PROJECTS AND I AM READY FOR A NEW CHALLENGE.
YOU CAN HELP TINA WRITE THE DEPART-MENT NEWSLETTER.
9-2-05
BUT THE NEWSLETTER JOB IS ONLY GIVEN TO THE MOST WORTHLESS EMPLOYEE.
AND HER ASSISTANT.

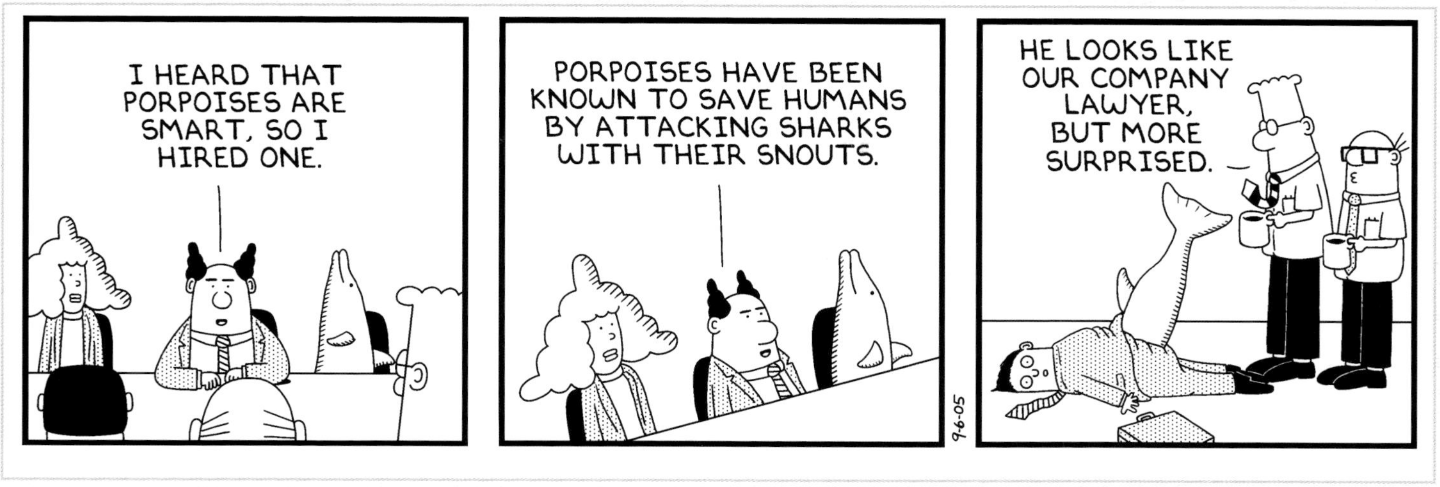
I HEARD THAT PORPOISES ARE SMART, SO I HIRED ONE.
PORPOISES HAVE BEEN KNOWN TO SAVE HUMANS BY ATTACKING SHARKS WITH THEIR SNOUTS.
HE LOOKS LIKE OUR COMPANY LAWYER, BUT MORE SURPRISED.
9-6-05

The strip above didn't make it past my editors under the theory that the newspaper-reading public was not ready for a porpoise to be fin-deep in a lawyer's butt. However, it did run unaltered on Dilbert.com. The revised strip that ran in newspapers is below.

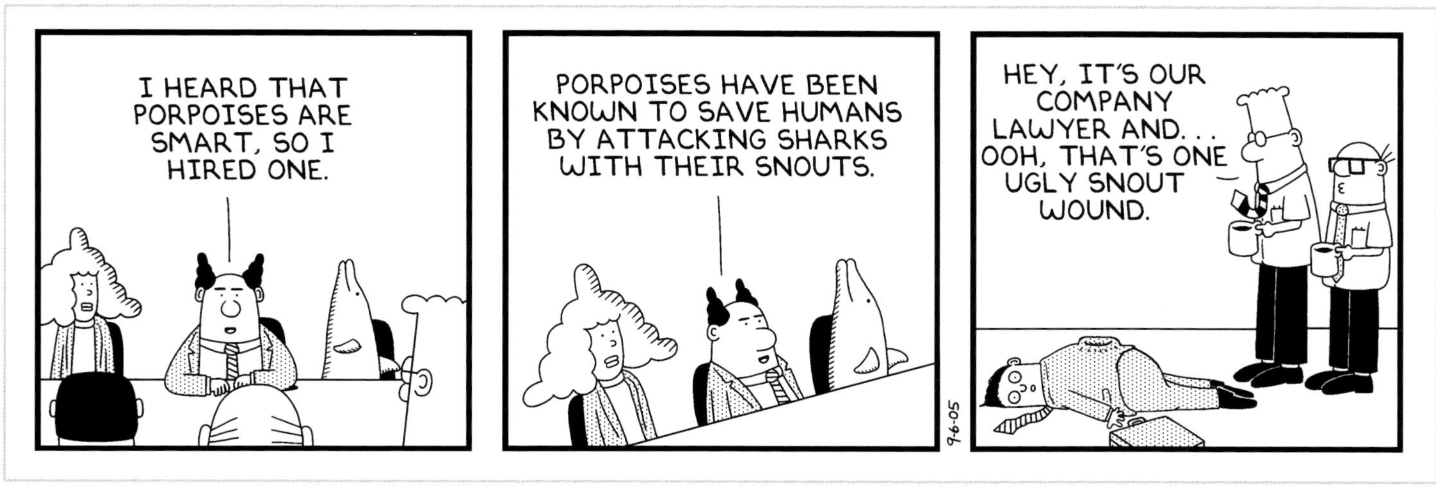
I HEARD THAT PORPOISES ARE SMART, SO I HIRED ONE.
PORPOISES HAVE BEEN KNOWN TO SAVE HUMANS BY ATTACKING SHARKS WITH THEIR SNOUTS.
HEY, IT'S OUR COMPANY LAWYER AND. . . OOH, THAT'S ONE UGLY SNOUT WOUND.
9-6-05

I don't think it lost much. Snout wounds are funny too.

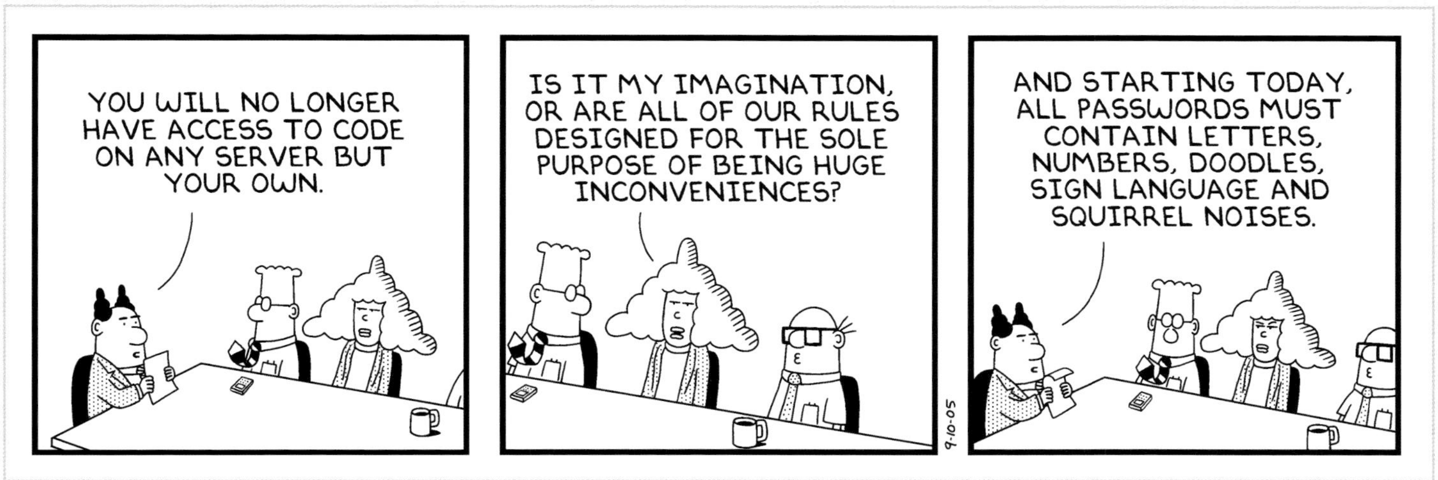
YOU WILL NO LONGER HAVE ACCESS TO CODE ON ANY SERVER BUT YOUR OWN.
IS IT MY IMAGINATION, OR ARE ALL OF OUR RULES DESIGNED FOR THE SOLE PURPOSE OF BEING HUGE INCONVENIENCES?
AND STARTING TODAY, ALL PASSWORDS MUST CONTAIN LETTERS, NUMBERS, DOODLES, SIGN LANGUAGE AND SQUIRREL NOISES.
9-10-05

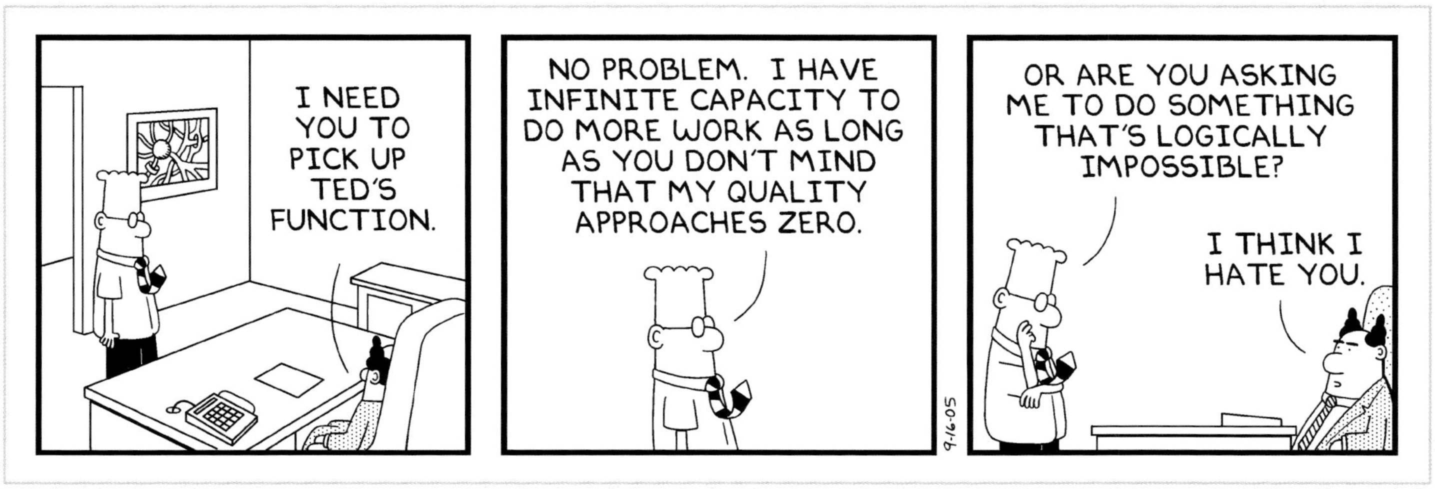
I NEED YOU TO PICK UP TED'S FUNCTION.
NO PROBLEM. I HAVE INFINITE CAPACITY TO DO MORE WORK AS LONG AS YOU DON'T MIND THAT MY QUALITY APPROACHES ZERO.
OR ARE YOU ASKING ME TO DO SOMETHING THAT'S LOGICALLY IMPOSSIBLE?
I THINK I HATE YOU.
9-16-05

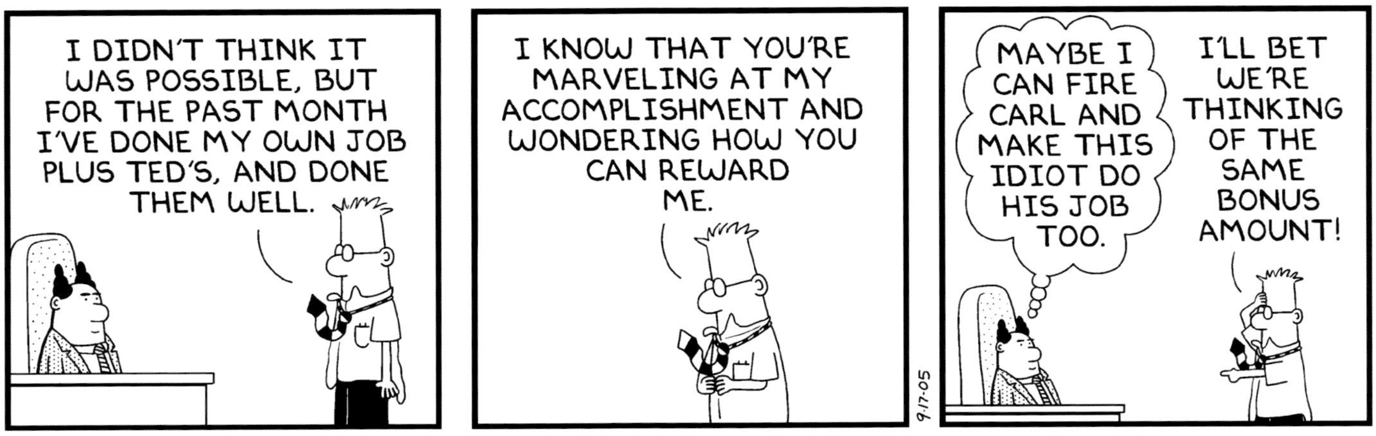
I DIDN'T THINK IT WAS POSSIBLE, BUT FOR THE PAST MONTH I'VE DONE MY OWN JOB PLUS TED'S, AND DONE THEM WELL.
I KNOW THAT YOU'RE MARVELING AT MY ACCOMPLISHMENT AND WONDERING HOW YOU CAN REWARD ME.
9-17-05
MAYBE I CAN FIRE CARL AND MAKE THIS IDIOT DO HIS JOB TOO.
I'LL BET WE'RE THINKING OF THE SAME BONUS AMOUNT!

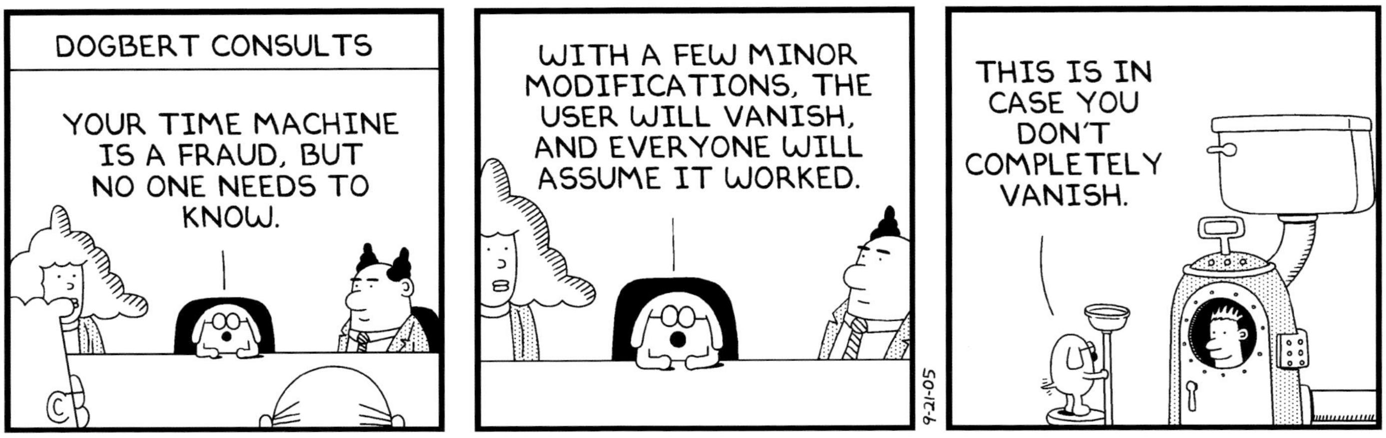
DOGBERT CONSULTS
YOUR TIME MACHINE IS A FRAUD, BUT NO ONE NEEDS TO KNOW.
WITH A FEW MINOR MODIFICATIONS, THE USER WILL VANISH, AND EVERYONE WILL ASSUME IT WORKED.
9-21-05
THIS IS IN CASE YOU DON'T COMPLETELY VANISH.

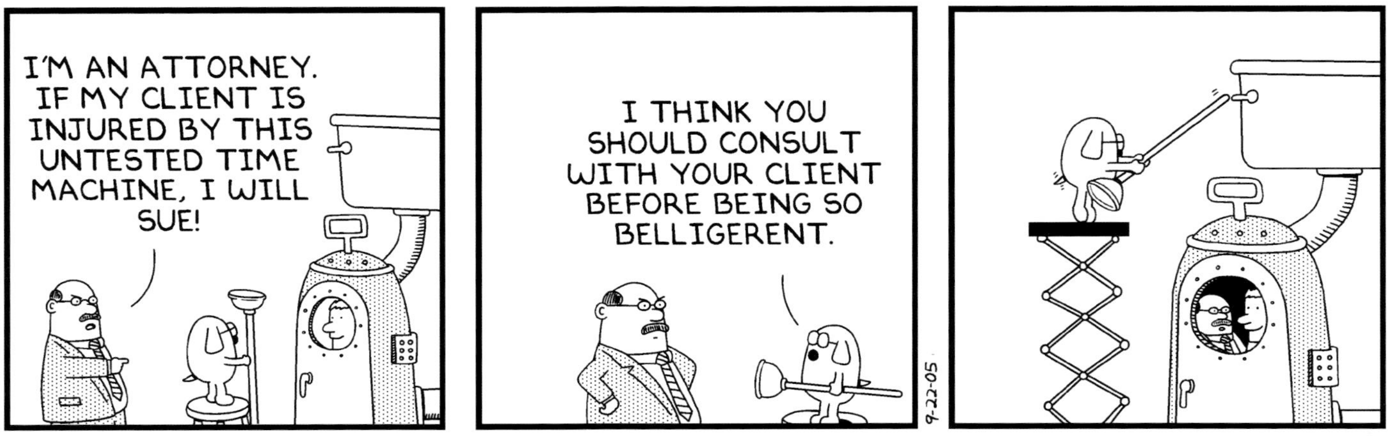
I'M AN ATTORNEY. IF MY CLIENT IS INJURED BY THIS UNTESTED TIME MACHINE, I WILL SUE!
I THINK YOU SHOULD CONSULT WITH YOUR CLIENT BEFORE BEING SO BELLIGERENT.
9-22-05

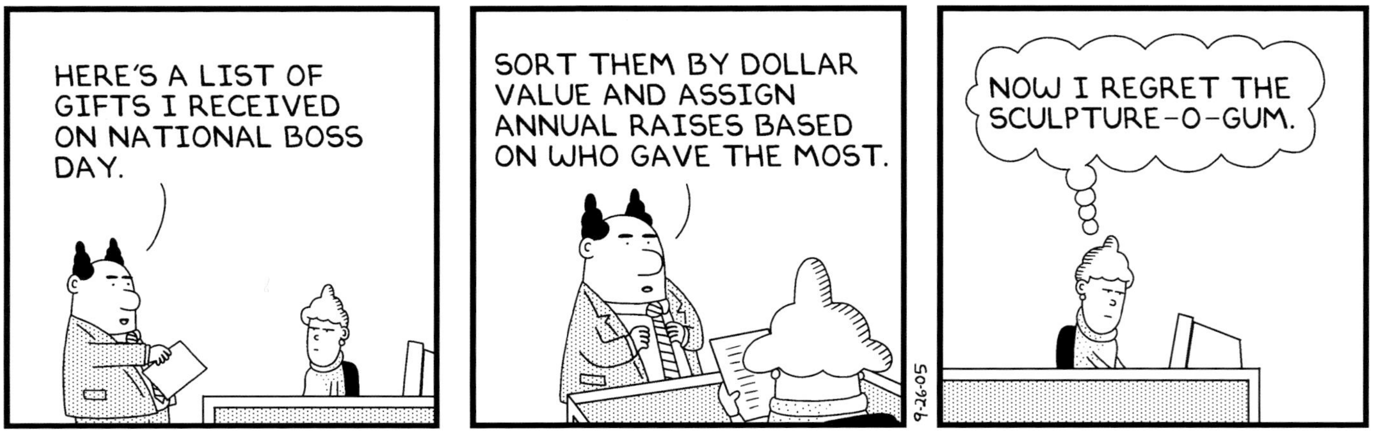
HERE'S A LIST OF GIFTS I RECEIVED ON NATIONAL BOSS DAY.
SORT THEM BY DOLLAR VALUE AND ASSIGN ANNUAL RAISES BASED ON WHO GAVE THE MOST.
9-26-05
NOW I REGRET THE SCULPTURE-O-GUM.

HELLO! HELLO!
LET ME SEE THAT. I'M AN ENGINEER.
HMM... IT MIGHT BE A BAD SIGNAL OR MAYBE A BAD PHONE.
THERE'S ONLY ONE WAY TO ISOLATE THE PROBLEM.
GO UP ON THE ROOF AND SEE IF YOU HAVE RECEPTION THERE.
DANG. NOTHING.
UH-OH. THE DOOR IS LOCKED. NO OTHER WAY TO GET DOWN... NO ONE CAN HEAR ME YELL AND MY PHONE DOESN'T WORK.
MY ONLY HOPE IS TO JUMP INTO THAT OPEN GARBAGE BIN IN THE ALLEY.
9-25-05
THAT'LL TEACH HIM TO KEEP HIS BATTERY CHARGED.

TED, YOU'VE BEEN SAYING NEGATIVE THINGS ABOUT THE COMPANY IN YOUR PERSONAL BLOG. WE HAVE TO FIRE YOU.
I HAVE FREEDOM OF SPEECH. IT'S MY CONSTITUTIONAL RIGHT TO SAY WHATEVER I WANT.
IF YOU FIRE ME FOR MY OPINIONS, YOU'LL BE SPITTING ON THE GRAVES OF OUR FOUND-ING FATHERS.
I'LL GET THE BEST LAWYER THAT MONEY CAN BUY, AND FIGHT YOU ALL THE WAY TO THE SUPREME COURT!
THE ONLY WAY YOU CAN LEGALLY FIRE ME IS IF MY WORK ISN'T GOOD.
10-2-05
OOH.
I PROBABLY SAID TOO MUCH HERE.
YOUR WORK ISN'T GOOD. HERE'S YOUR FINAL PAYCHECK.
STUPID FOUNDING FATHERS.

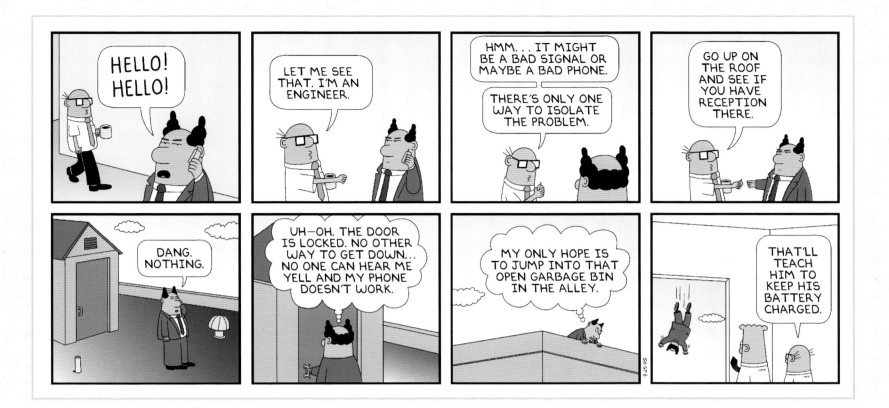

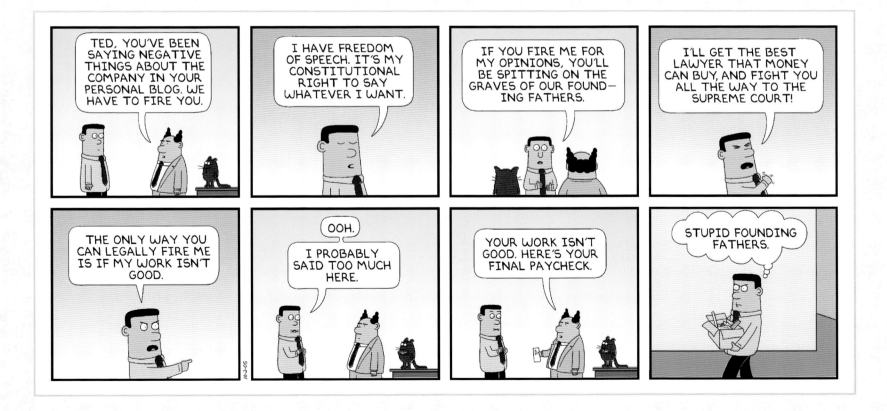

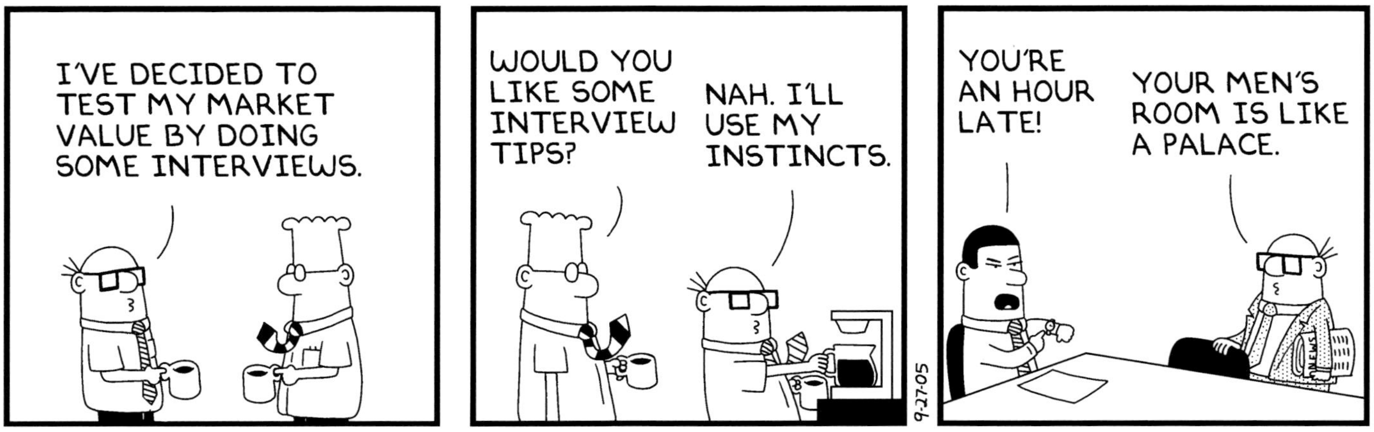
I'VE DECIDED TO TEST MY MARKET VALUE BY DOING SOME INTERVIEWS.
WOULD YOU LIKE SOME INTERVIEW TIPS?
NAH. I'LL USE MY INSTINCTS.
9-27-05
YOU'RE AN HOUR LATE!
YOUR MEN'S ROOM IS LIKE A PALACE.

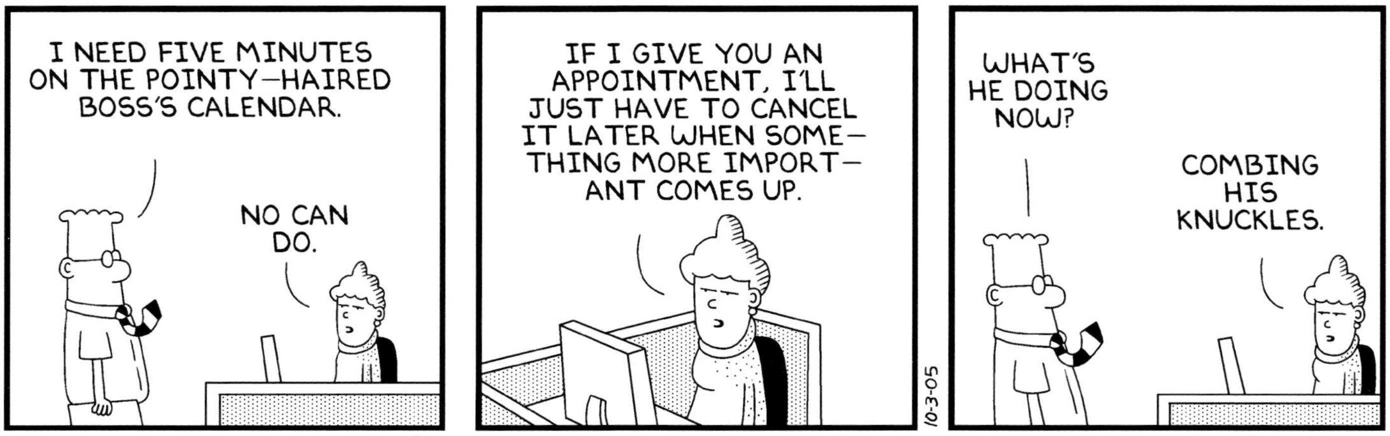
I NEED FIVE MINUTES ON THE POINTY-HAIRED BOSS'S CALENDAR.
NO CAN DO.
IF I GIVE YOU AN APPOINTMENT, I'LL JUST HAVE TO CANCEL IT LATER WHEN SOME-THING MORE IMPORT-ANT COMES UP.
10-3-05
WHAT'S HE DOING NOW?
COMBING HIS KNUCKLES.

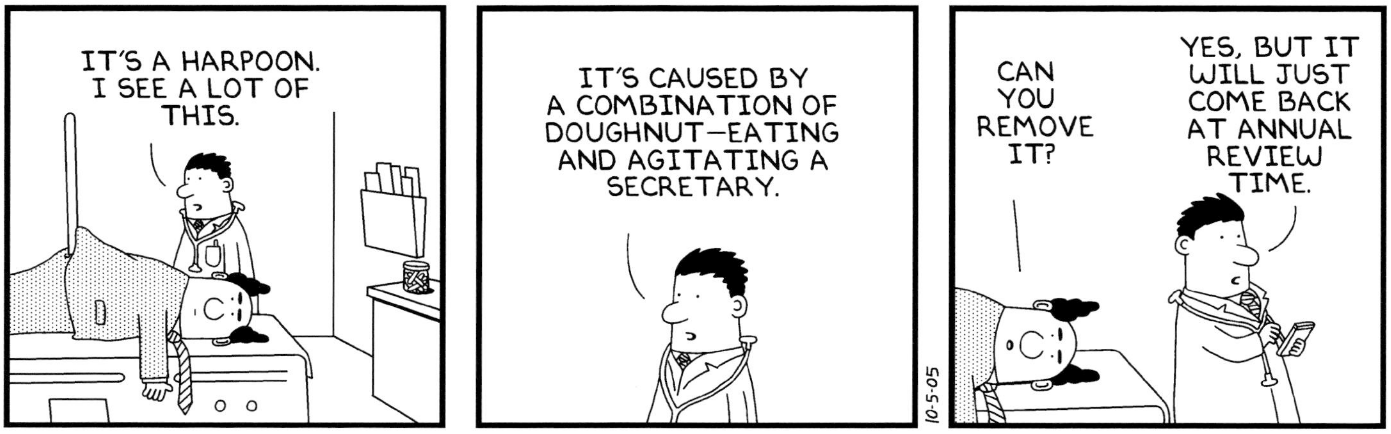
IT'S A HARPOON. I SEE A LOT OF THIS.
IT'S CAUSED BY A COMBINATION OF DOUGHNUT-EATING AND AGITATING A SECRETARY.
10-5-05
CAN YOU REMOVE IT?
YES, BUT IT WILL JUST COME BACK AT ANNUAL REVIEW TIME.

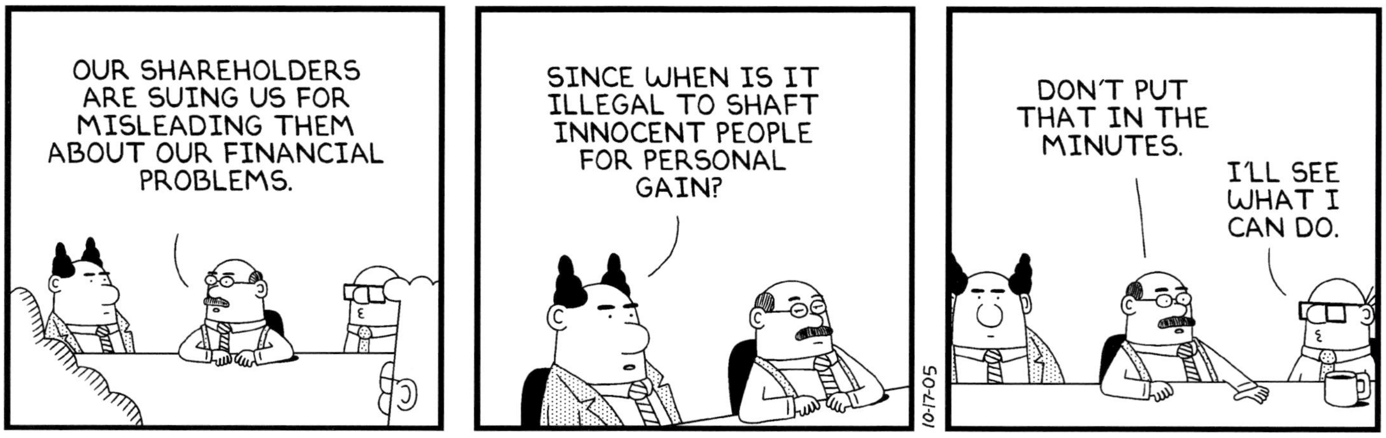
OUR SHAREHOLDERS ARE SUING US FOR MISLEADING THEM ABOUT OUR FINANCIAL PROBLEMS.
SINCE WHEN IS IT ILLEGAL TO SHAFT INNOCENT PEOPLE FOR PERSONAL GAIN?
10-17-05
DON'T PUT THAT IN THE MINUTES.
I'LL SEE WHAT I CAN DO.

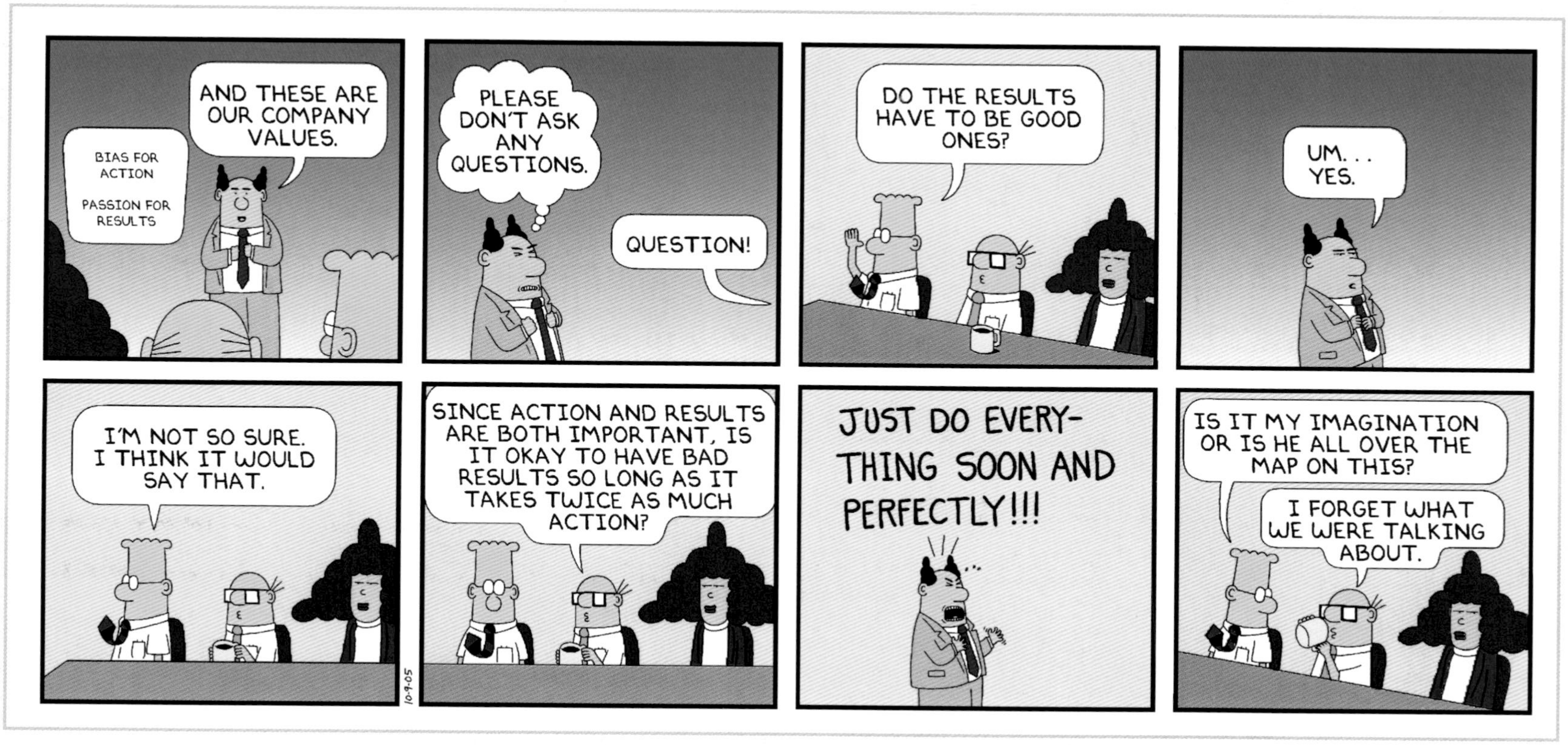
BIAS FOR ACTION
PASSION FOR RESULTS
AND THESE ARE OUR COMPANY VALUES.
PLEASE DON'T ASK ANY QUESTIONS.
QUESTION!
DO THE RESULTS HAVE TO BE GOOD ONES?
UM. . . YES.
I'M NOT SO SURE. I THINK IT WOULD SAY THAT.
SINCE ACTION AND RESULTS ARE BOTH IMPORTANT, IS IT OKAY TO HAVE BAD RESULTS SO LONG AS IT TAKES TWICE AS MUCH ACTION?
JUST DO EVERY-THING SOON AND PERFECTLY!!!
IS IT MY IMAGINATION OR IS HE ALL OVER THE MAP ON THIS?
I FORGET WHAT WE WERE TALKING ABOUT.
10-9-05

I was buying furniture at this point and experienced this exact situation.

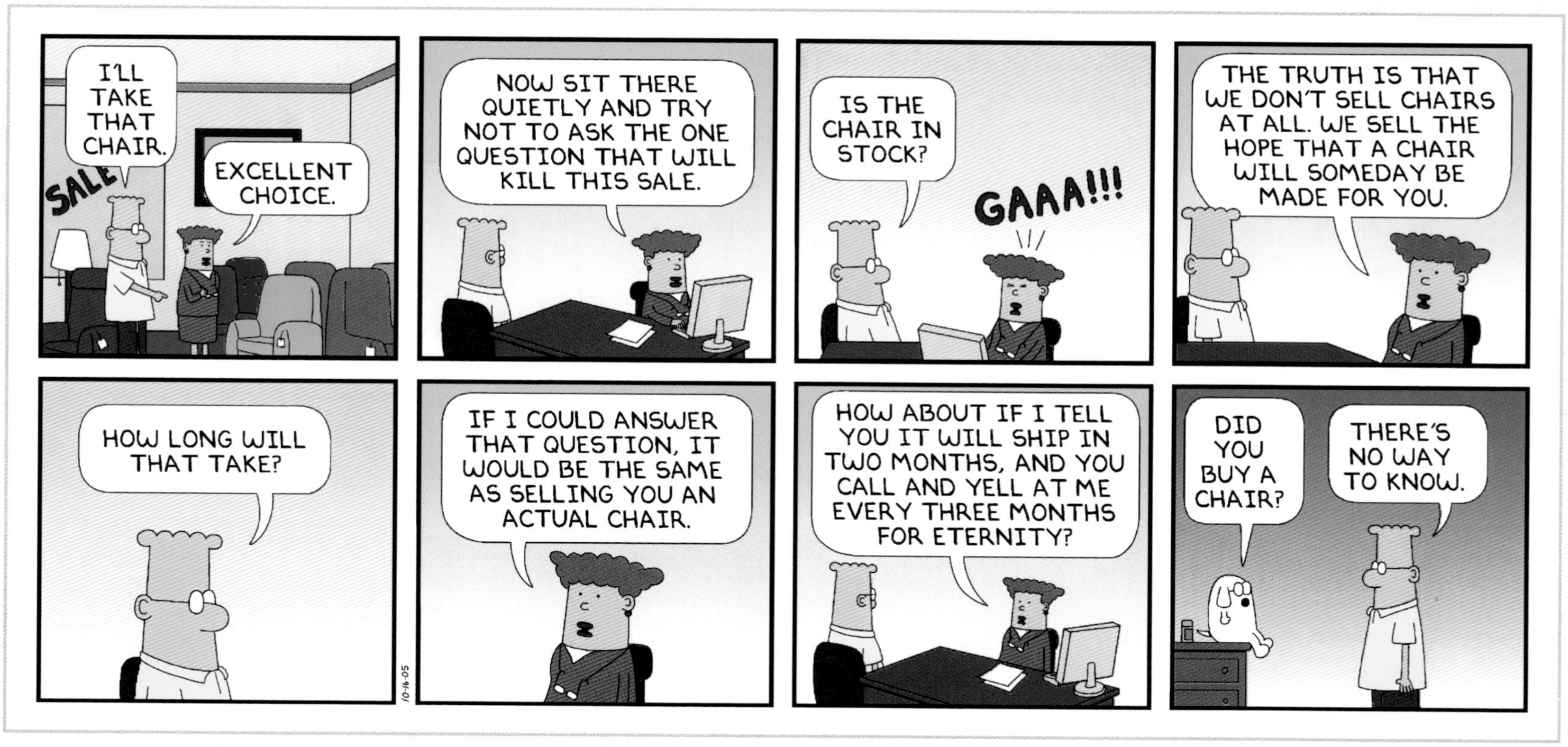
I'LL TAKE THAT CHAIR.
SALE
EXCELLENT CHOICE.
NOW SIT THERE QUIETLY AND TRY NOT TO ASK THE ONE QUESTION THAT WILL KILL THIS SALE.
IS THE CHAIR IN STOCK?
GAAA!!!
THE TRUTH IS THAT WE DON'T SELL CHAIRS AT ALL. WE SELL THE HOPE THAT A CHAIR WILL SOMEDAY BE MADE FOR YOU.
HOW LONG WILL THAT TAKE?
IF I COULD ANSWER THAT QUESTION, IT WOULD BE THE SAME AS SELLING YOU AN ACTUAL CHAIR.
HOW ABOUT IF I TELL YOU IT WILL SHIP IN TWO MONTHS, AND YOU CALL AND YELL AT ME EVERY THREE MONTHS FOR ETERNITY?
DID YOU BUY A CHAIR?
THERE'S NO WAY TO KNOW.
10-16-05

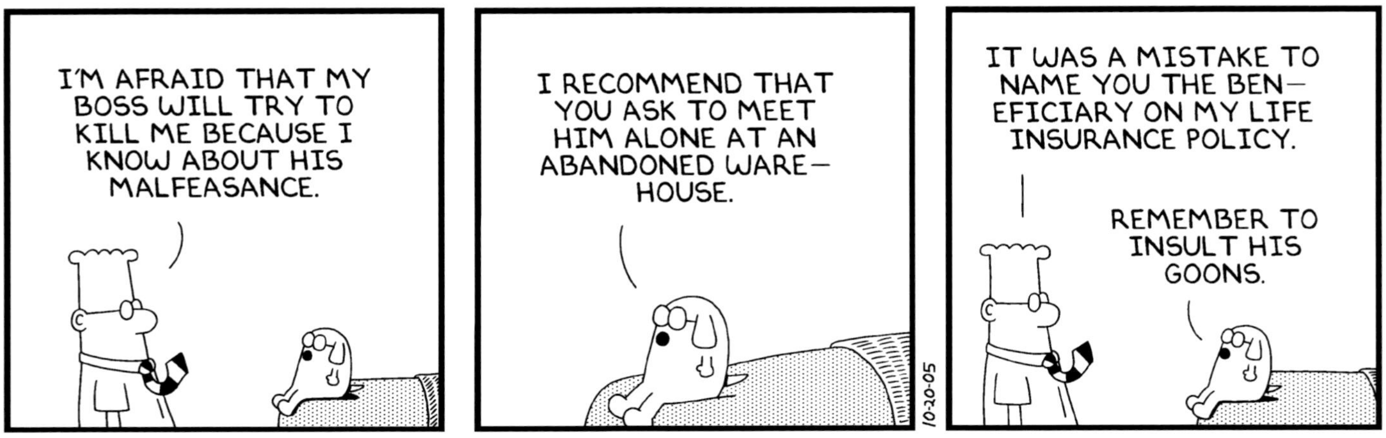
I'M AFRAID THAT MY BOSS WILL TRY TO KILL ME BECAUSE I KNOW ABOUT HIS MALFEASANCE.
I RECOMMEND THAT YOU ASK TO MEET HIM ALONE AT AN ABANDONED WARE-HOUSE.
10-20-05
IT WAS A MISTAKE TO NAME YOU THE BEN-EFICIARY ON MY LIFE INSURANCE POLICY.
REMEMBER TO INSULT HIS GOONS.

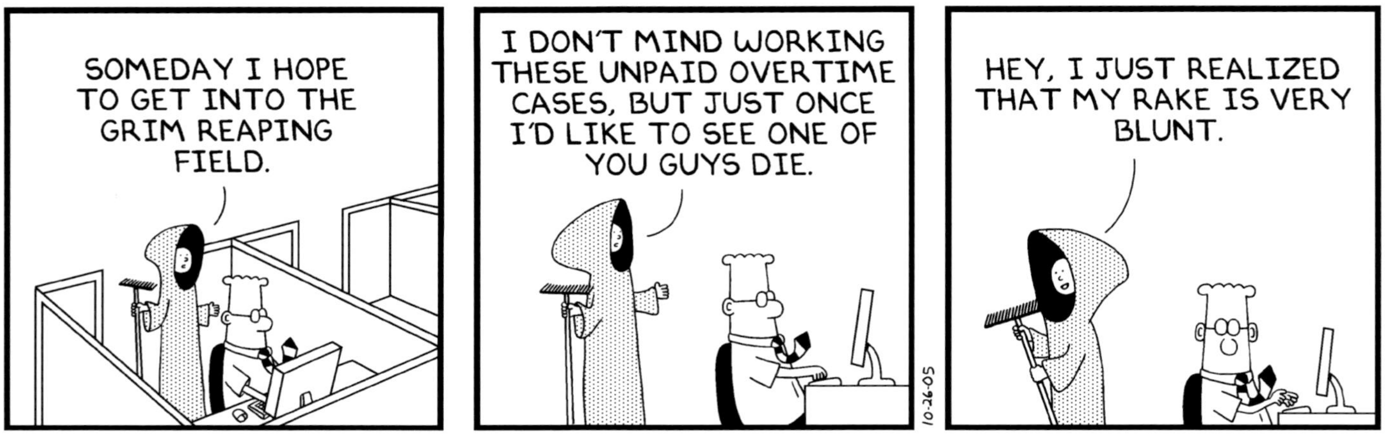
SOMEDAY I HOPE TO GET INTO THE GRIM REAPING FIELD.
I DON'T MIND WORKING THESE UNPAID OVERTIME CASES, BUT JUST ONCE I'D LIKE TO SEE ONE OF YOU GUYS DIE.
10-26-05
HEY, I JUST REALIZED THAT MY RAKE IS VERY BLUNT.

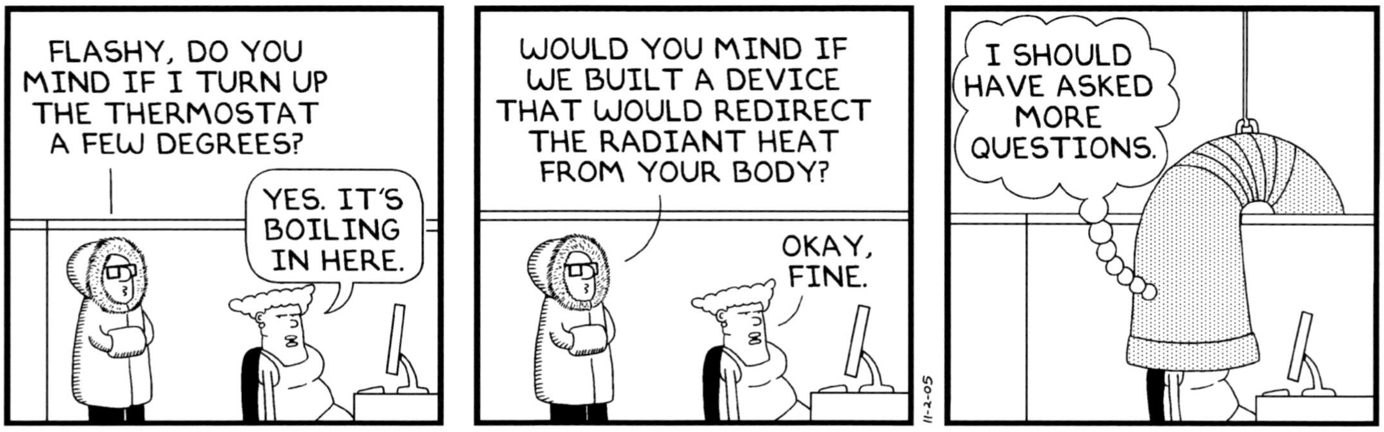
FLASHY, DO YOU MIND IF I TURN UP THE THERMOSTAT A FEW DEGREES?
YES. IT'S BOILING IN HERE.
WOULD YOU MIND IF WE BUILT A DEVICE THAT WOULD REDIRECT THE RADIANT HEAT FROM YOUR BODY?
OKAY, FINE.
11-2-05
I SHOULD HAVE ASKED MORE QUESTIONS.

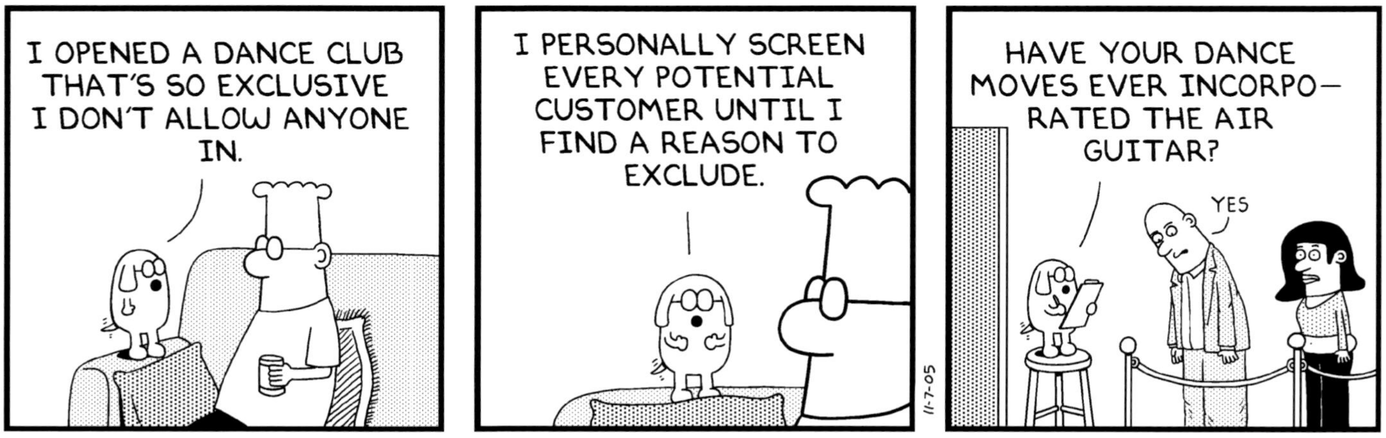
I OPENED A DANCE CLUB THAT'S SO EXCLUSIVE I DON'T ALLOW ANYONE IN.
I PERSONALLY SCREEN EVERY POTENTIAL CUSTOMER UNTIL I FIND A REASON TO EXCLUDE.
11-7-05
HAVE YOUR DANCE MOVES EVER INCORPO-RATED THE AIR GUITAR?
YES

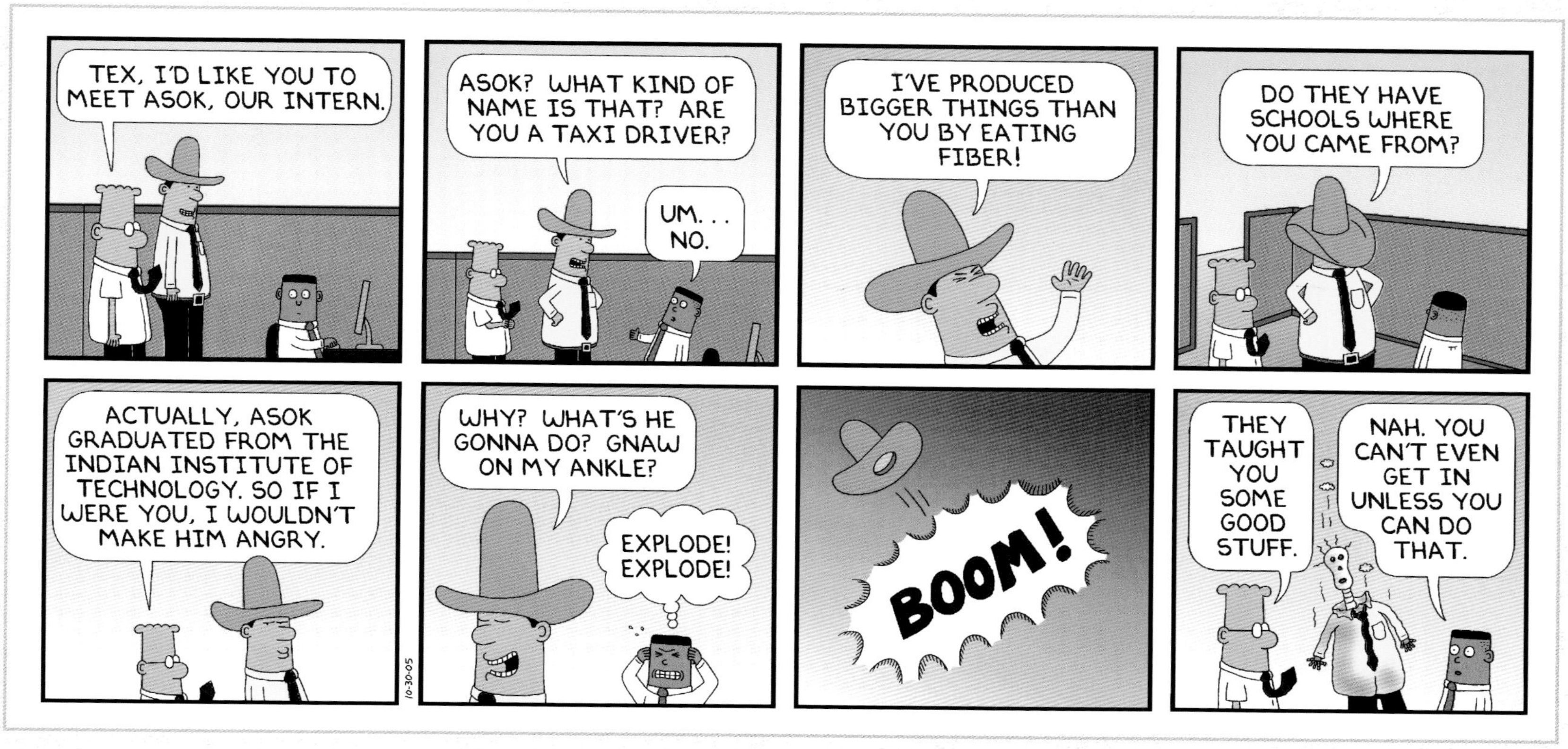
TEX, I'D LIKE YOU TO MEET ASOK, OUR INTERN.
ASOK? WHAT KIND OF NAME IS THAT? ARE YOU A TAXI DRIVER?
UM... NO.
I'VE PRODUCED BIGGER THINGS THAN YOU BY EATING FIBER!
DO THEY HAVE SCHOOLS WHERE YOU CAME FROM?
ACTUALLY, ASOK GRADUATED FROM THE INDIAN INSTITUTE OF TECHNOLOGY. SO IF I WERE YOU, I WOULDN'T MAKE HIM ANGRY.
10-30-05
WHY? WHAT'S HE GONNA DO? GNAW ON MY ANKLE?
EXPLODE! EXPLODE!
BOOM!
THEY TAUGHT YOU SOME GOOD STUFF.
NAH. YOU CAN'T EVEN GET IN UNLESS YOU CAN DO THAT.

A number of angry people wrote to tell me that comics like this could prevent people from donating organs, and I would be responsible for the deaths of thousands of innocent people. I would like to state for the record that retail stores do not harvest the organs of customers and sell them on eBay. No one else does either. So donate your organs and stop being a baby.

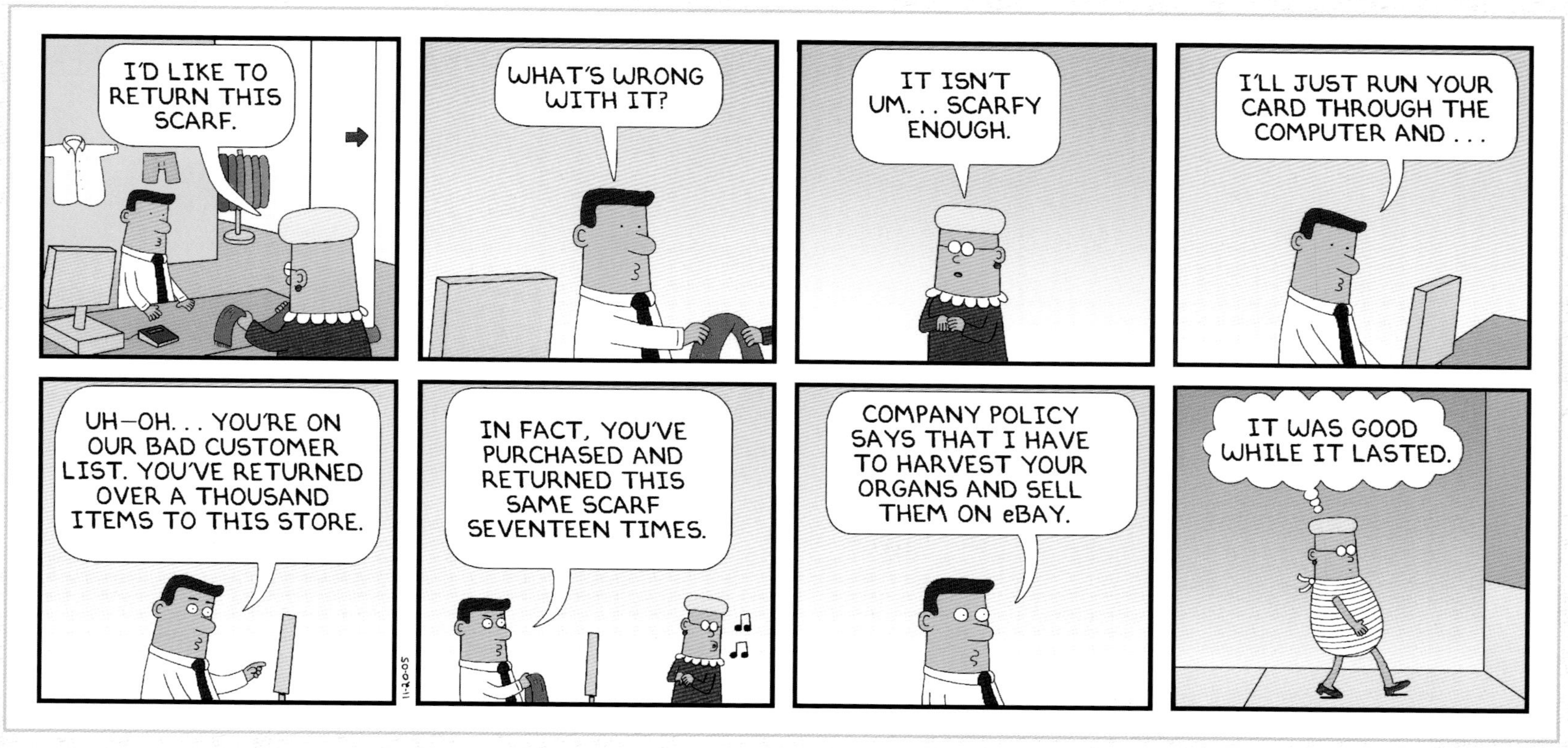
I'D LIKE TO RETURN THIS SCARF.
WHAT'S WRONG WITH IT?
IT ISN'T UM... SCARFY ENOUGH.
I'LL JUST RUN YOUR CARD THROUGH THE COMPUTER AND ...
UH—OH... YOU'RE ON OUR BAD CUSTOMER LIST. YOU'VE RETURNED OVER A THOUSAND ITEMS TO THIS STORE.
11-20-05
IN FACT, YOU'VE PURCHASED AND RETURNED THIS SAME SCARF SEVENTEEN TIMES.
COMPANY POLICY SAYS THAT I HAVE TO HARVEST YOUR ORGANS AND SELL THEM ON eBAY.
IT WAS GOOD WHILE IT LASTED.

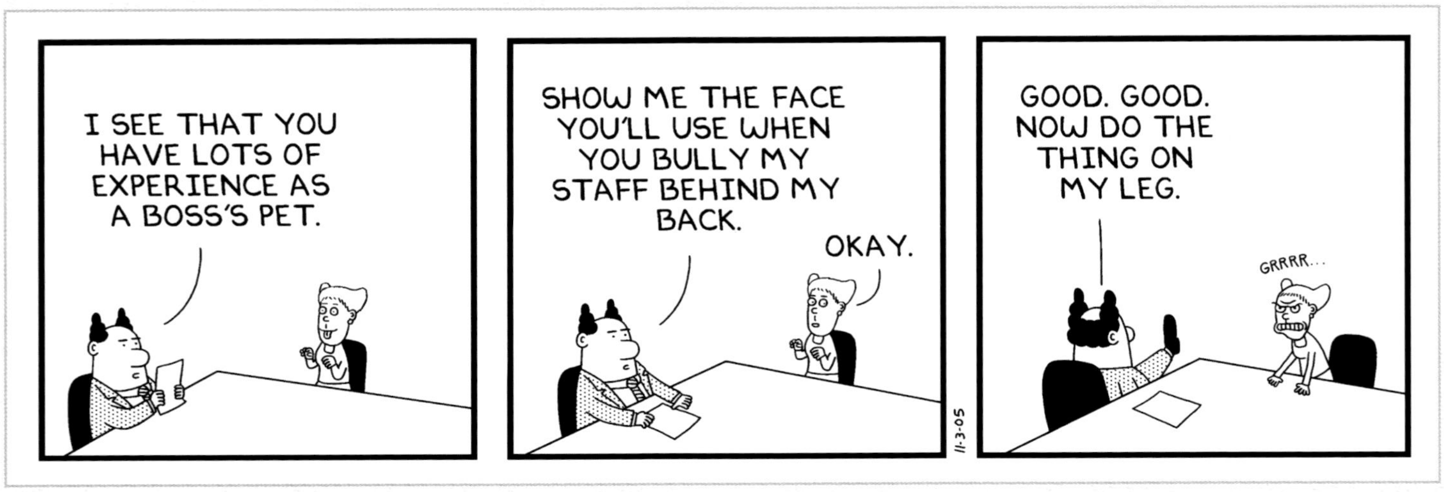
I SEE THAT YOU HAVE LOTS OF EXPERIENCE AS A BOSS'S PET.
SHOW ME THE FACE YOU'LL USE WHEN YOU BULLY MY STAFF BEHIND MY BACK.
OKAY.
11-3-05
GOOD. GOOD. NOW DO THE THING ON MY LEG.
GRRRR...

The strip above never ran in newspapers. My editors deemed it offensive on a variety of grounds.

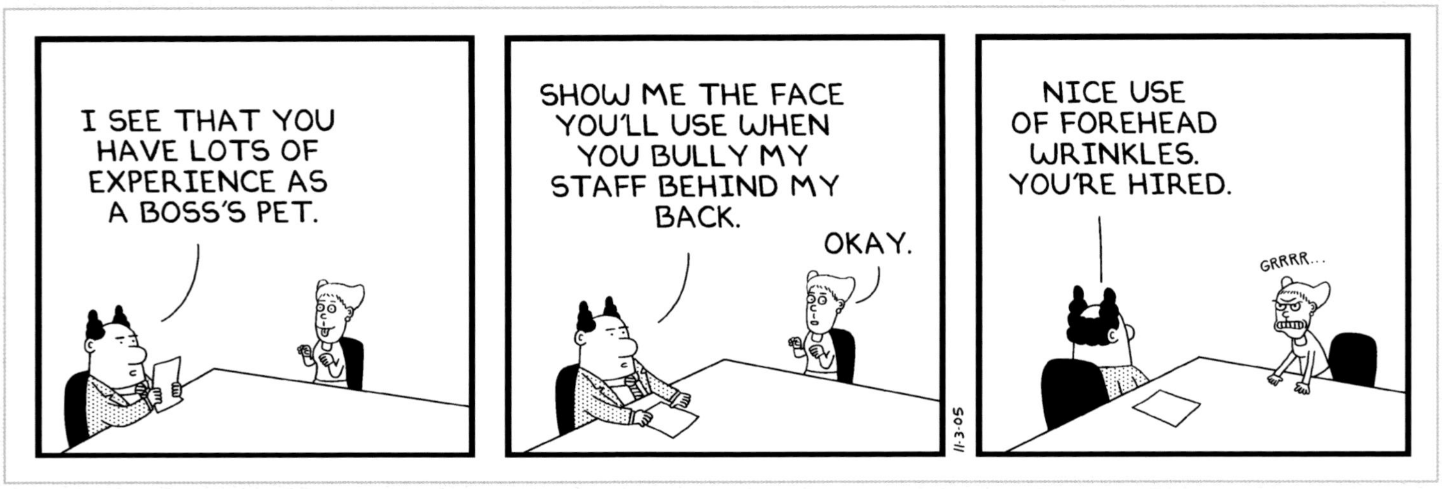
I SEE THAT YOU HAVE LOTS OF EXPERIENCE AS A BOSS'S PET.
SHOW ME THE FACE YOU'LL USE WHEN YOU BULLY MY STAFF BEHIND MY BACK.
OKAY.
11-3-05
NICE USE OF FOREHEAD WRINKLES. YOU'RE HIRED.
GRRRR...

This modified version ran in newspapers. I think it lost something.

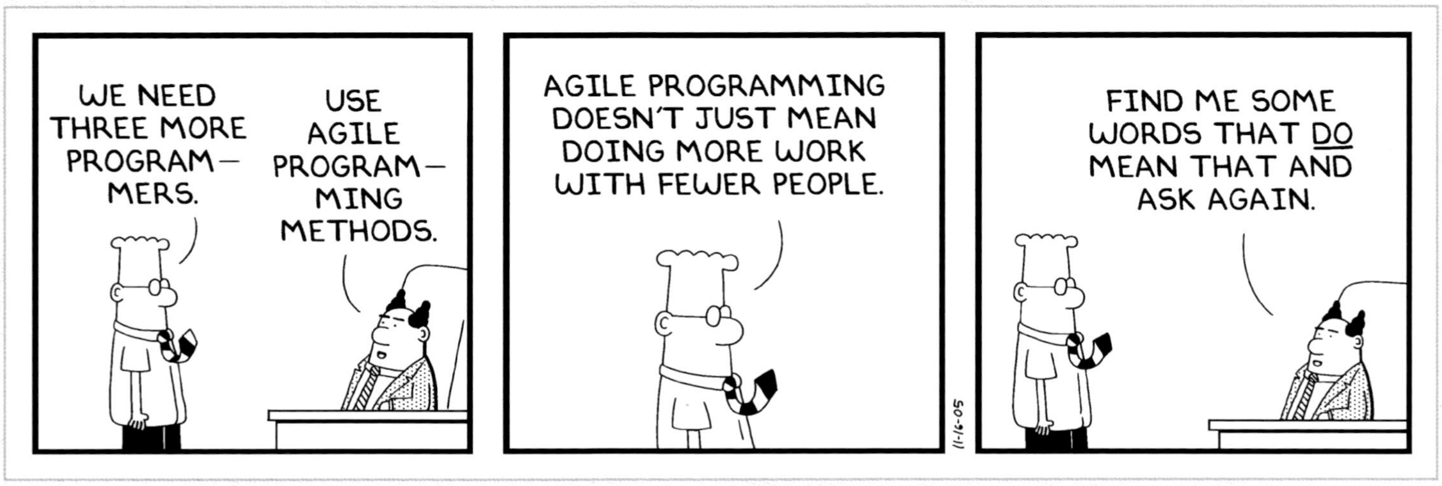
WE NEED THREE MORE PROGRAM-MERS.
USE AGILE PROGRAM-MING METHODS.
AGILE PROGRAMMING DOESN'T JUST MEAN DOING MORE WORK WITH FEWER PEOPLE.
11-16-05
FIND ME SOME WORDS THAT DO MEAN THAT AND ASK AGAIN.

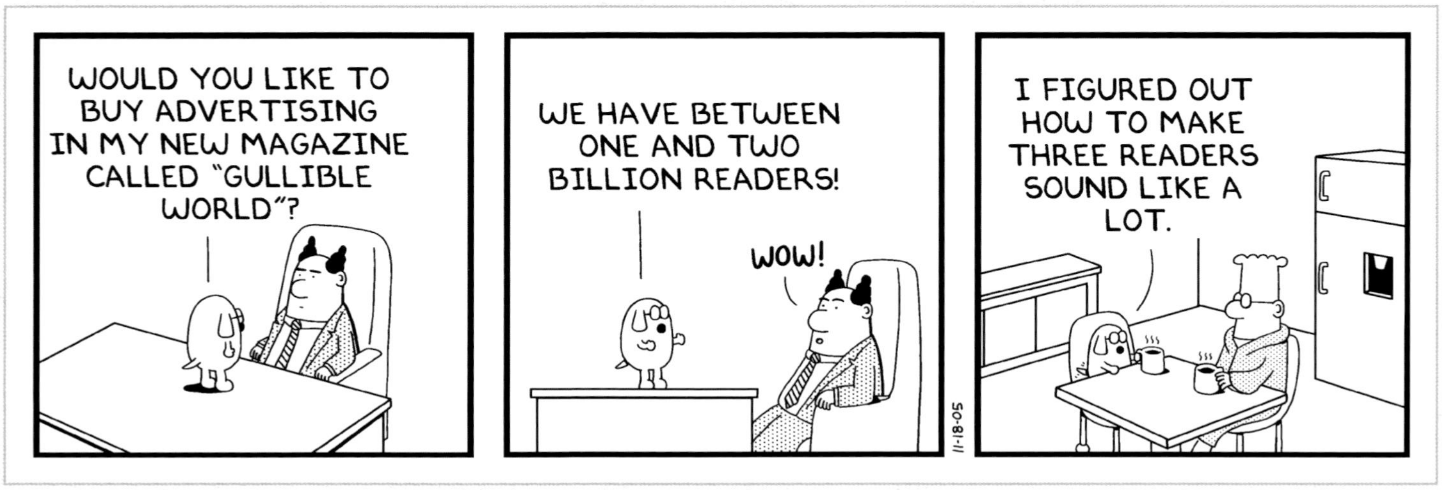
WOULD YOU LIKE TO BUY ADVERTISING IN MY NEW MAGAZINE CALLED "GULLIBLE WORLD"?
WE HAVE BETWEEN ONE AND TWO BILLION READERS!
WOW!
11-18-05
I FIGURED OUT HOW TO MAKE THREE READERS SOUND LIKE A LOT.

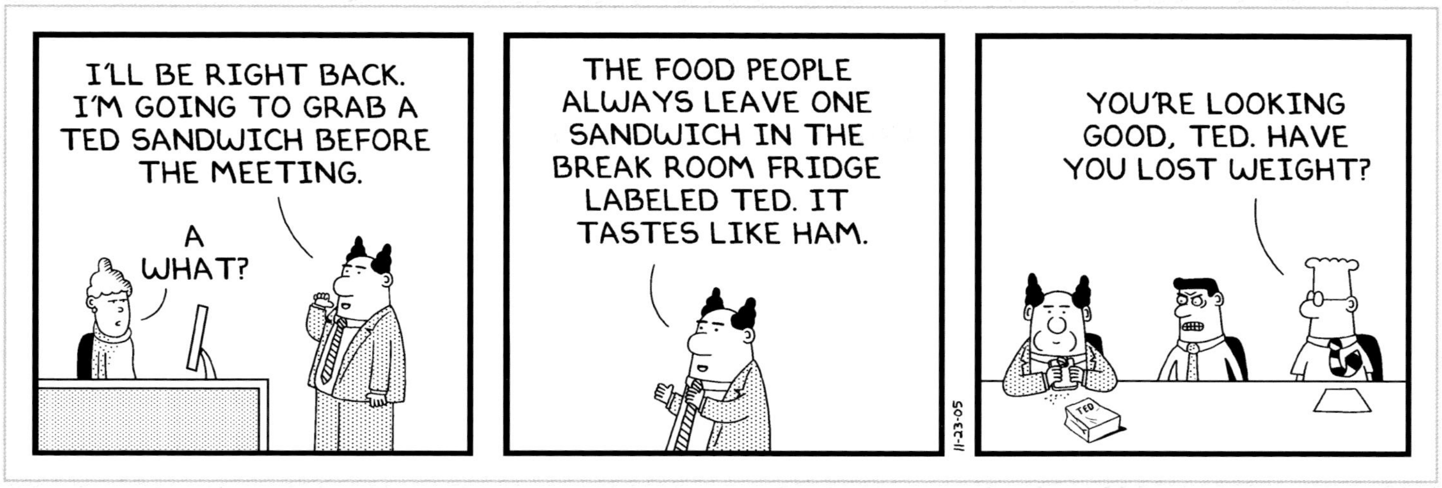
I'LL BE RIGHT BACK. I'M GOING TO GRAB A TED SANDWICH BEFORE THE MEETING.
A WHAT?
THE FOOD PEOPLE ALWAYS LEAVE ONE SANDWICH IN THE BREAK ROOM FRIDGE LABELED TED. IT TASTES LIKE HAM.
11-23-05
YOU'RE LOOKING GOOD, TED. HAVE YOU LOST WEIGHT?
TED

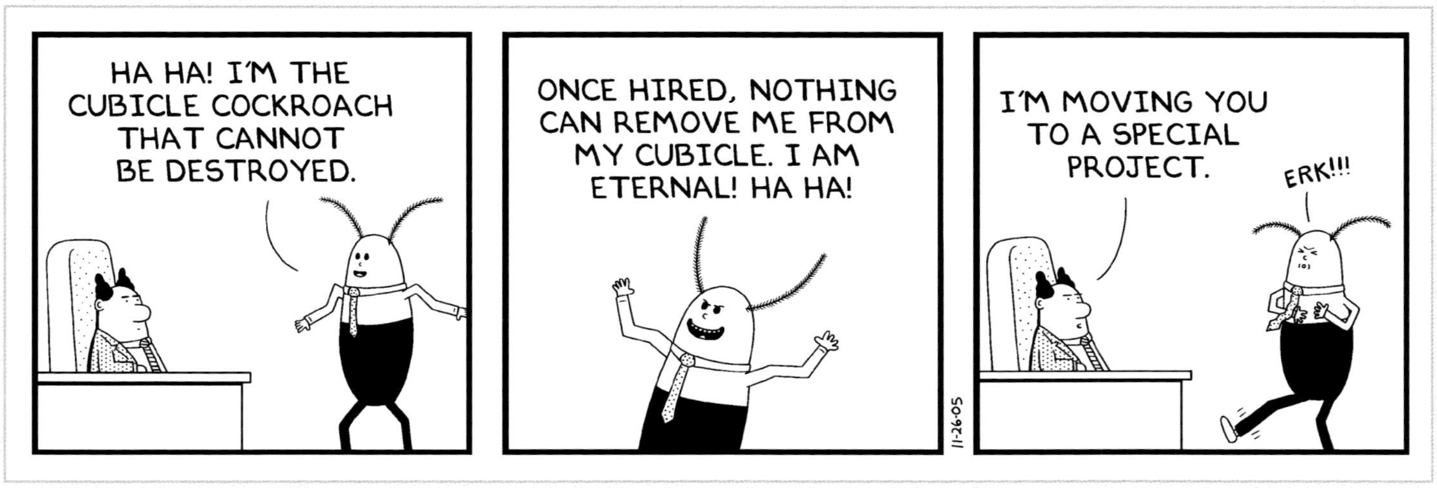
HA HA! I'M THE CUBICLE COCKROACH THAT CANNOT BE DESTROYED.
ONCE HIRED, NOTHING CAN REMOVE ME FROM MY CUBICLE. I AM ETERNAL! HA HA!
11-26-05
I'M MOVING YOU TO A SPECIAL PROJECT.
ERK!!!

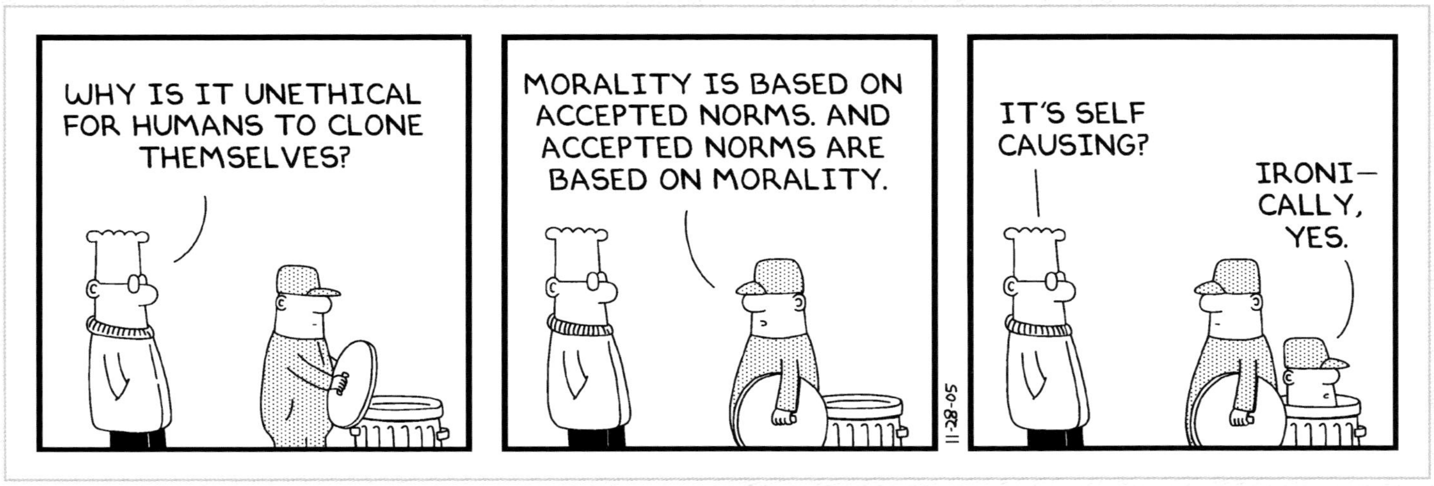
WHY IS IT UNETHICAL FOR HUMANS TO CLONE THEMSELVES?
MORALITY IS BASED ON ACCEPTED NORMS. AND ACCEPTED NORMS ARE BASED ON MORALITY.
11-28-05
IT'S SELF CAUSING?
IRONI-CALLY, YES.

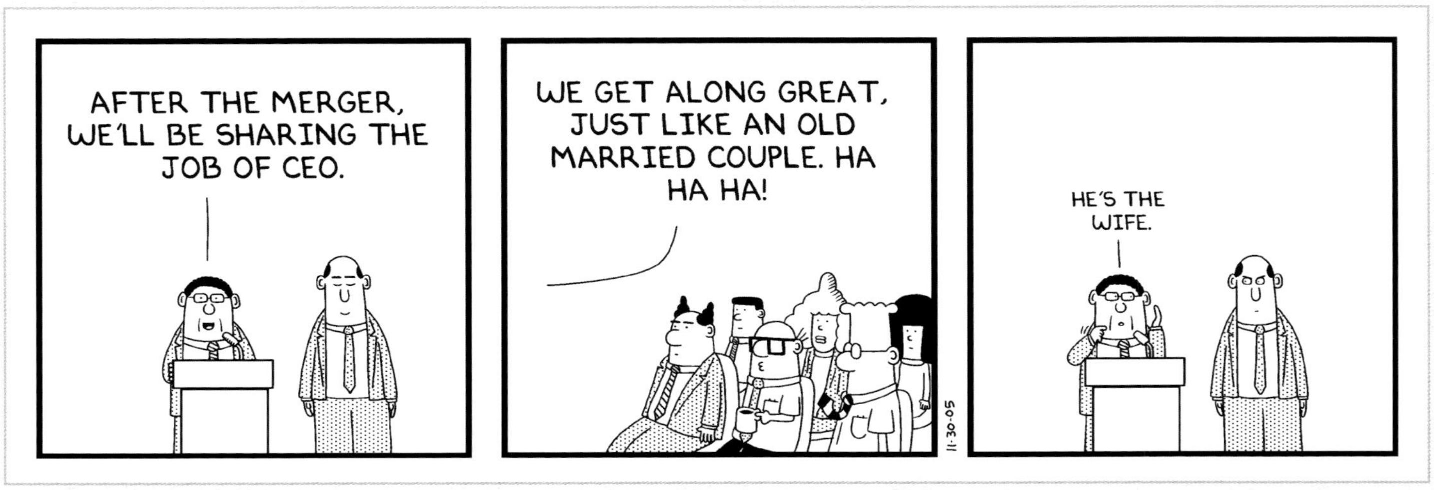
AFTER THE MERGER, WE'LL BE SHARING THE JOB OF CEO.
WE GET ALONG GREAT, JUST LIKE AN OLD MARRIED COUPLE. HA HA HA!
11-30-05
HE'S THE WIFE.

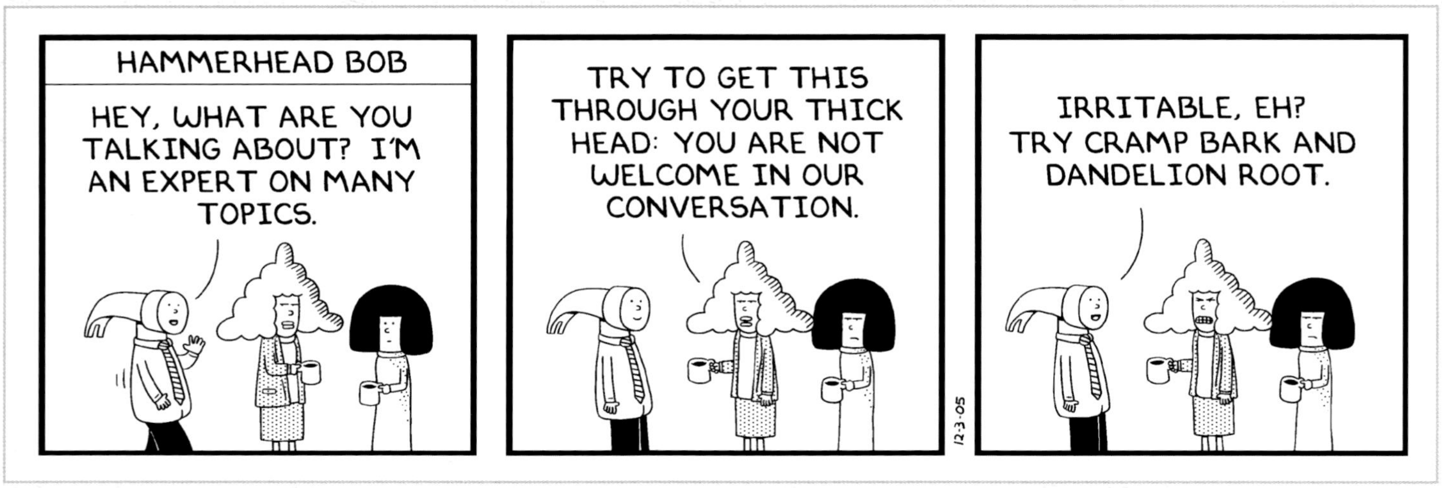
HAMMERHEAD BOB
HEY, WHAT ARE YOU TALKING ABOUT? I'M AN EXPERT ON MANY TOPICS.
TRY TO GET THIS THROUGH YOUR THICK HEAD: YOU ARE NOT WELCOME IN OUR CONVERSATION.
12-3-05
IRRITABLE, EH? TRY CRAMP BARK AND DANDELION ROOT.

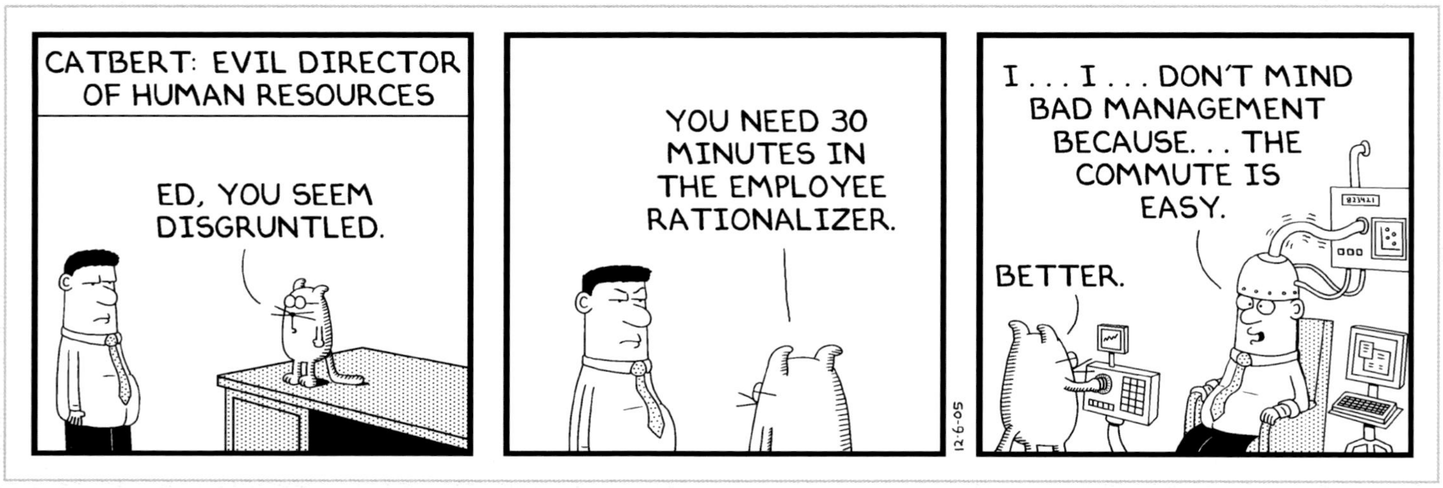
CATBERT: EVIL DIRECTOR OF HUMAN RESOURCES
ED, YOU SEEM DISGRUNTLED.
YOU NEED 30 MINUTES IN THE EMPLOYEE RATIONALIZER.
12-6-05
I . . . I . . . DON'T MIND BAD MANAGEMENT BECAUSE. . . THE COMMUTE IS EASY.
BETTER.

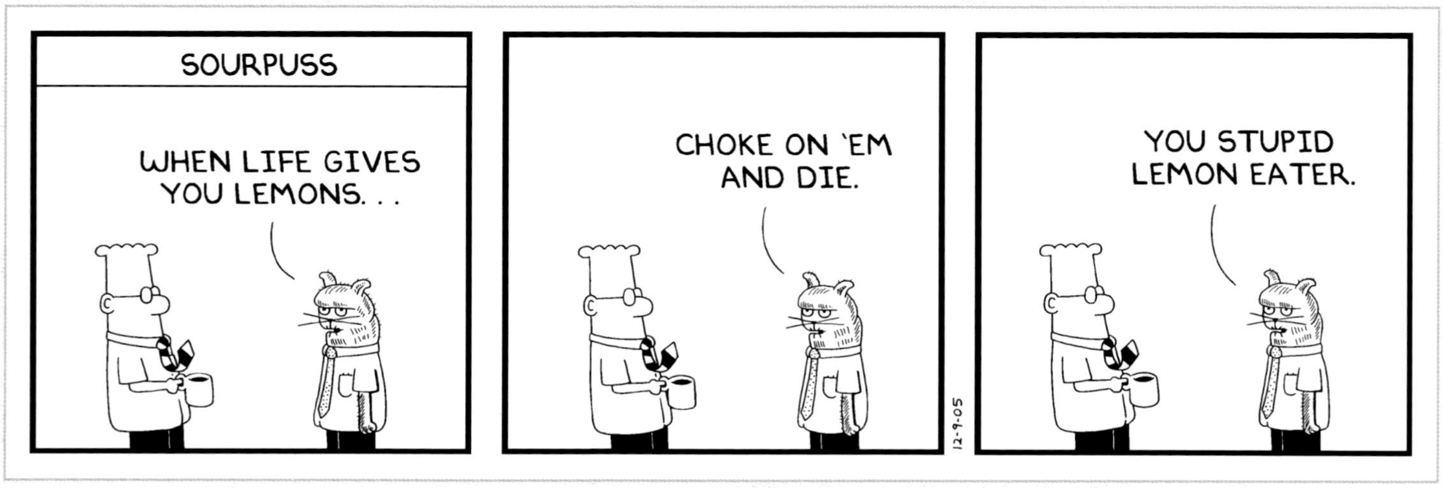
SOURPUSS
WHEN LIFE GIVES YOU LEMONS. . .
CHOKE ON 'EM AND DIE.
12-9-05
YOU STUPID LEMON EATER.

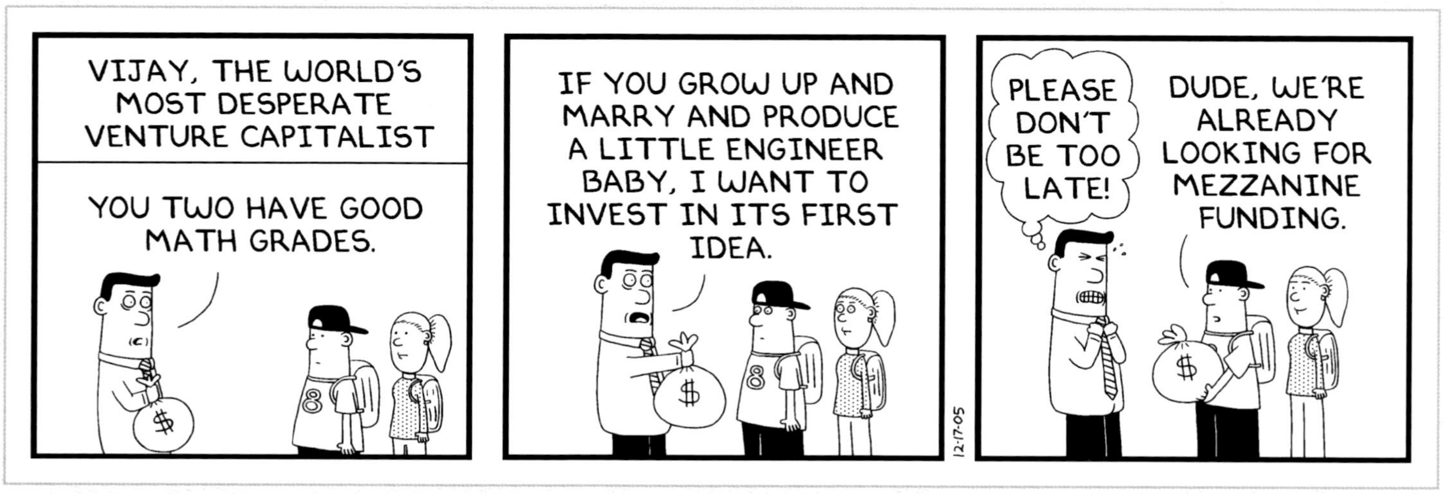
VIJAY, THE WORLD'S MOST DESPERATE VENTURE CAPITALIST
YOU TWO HAVE GOOD MATH GRADES.
IF YOU GROW UP AND MARRY AND PRODUCE A LITTLE ENGINEER BABY, I WANT TO INVEST IN ITS FIRST IDEA.
12-17-05
PLEASE DON'T BE TOO LATE!
DUDE, WE'RE ALREADY LOOKING FOR MEZZANINE FUNDING.

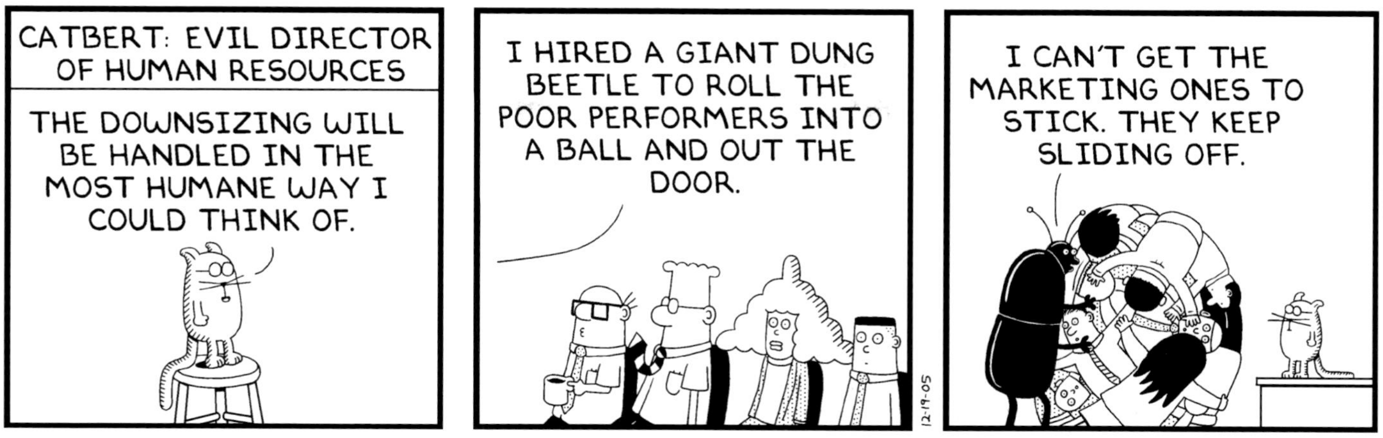
CATBERT: EVIL DIRECTOR OF HUMAN RESOURCES
THE DOWNSIZING WILL BE HANDLED IN THE MOST HUMANE WAY I COULD THINK OF.
I HIRED A GIANT DUNG BEETLE TO ROLL THE POOR PERFORMERS INTO A BALL AND OUT THE DOOR.
I CAN'T GET THE MARKETING ONES TO STICK. THEY KEEP SLIDING OFF.
12-19-05

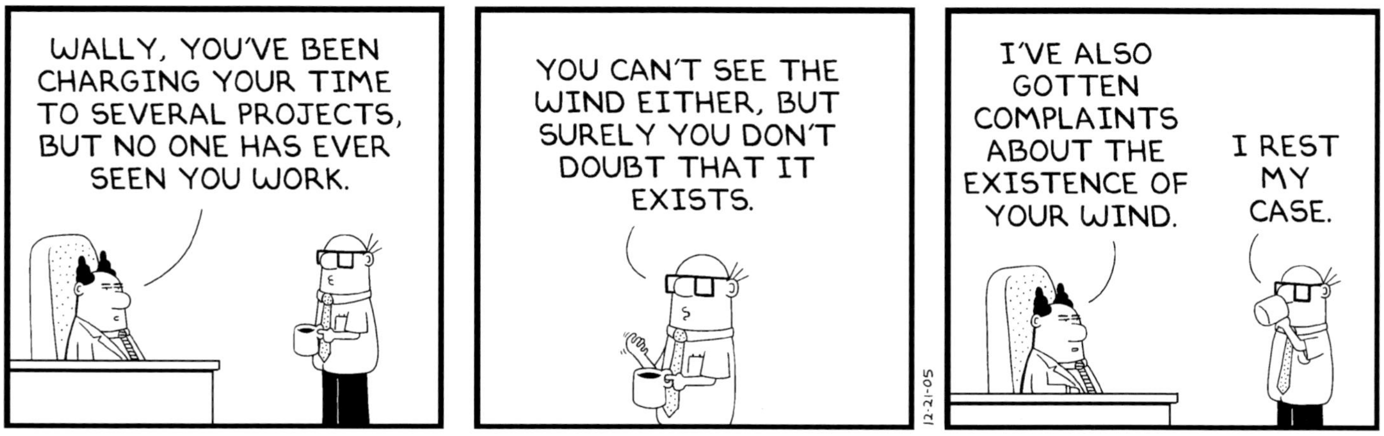
WALLY, YOU'VE BEEN CHARGING YOUR TIME TO SEVERAL PROJECTS, BUT NO ONE HAS EVER SEEN YOU WORK.
YOU CAN'T SEE THE WIND EITHER, BUT SURELY YOU DON'T DOUBT THAT IT EXISTS.
I'VE ALSO GOTTEN COMPLAINTS ABOUT THE EXISTENCE OF YOUR WIND.
I REST MY CASE.
12-21-05

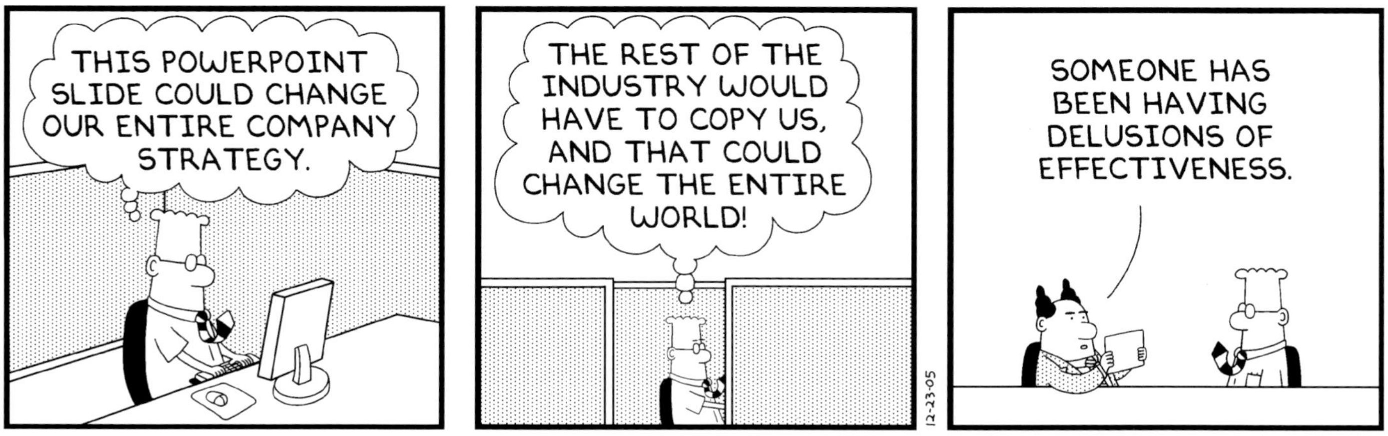
THIS POWERPOINT SLIDE COULD CHANGE OUR ENTIRE COMPANY STRATEGY.
THE REST OF THE INDUSTRY WOULD HAVE TO COPY US, AND THAT COULD CHANGE THE ENTIRE WORLD!
SOMEONE HAS BEEN HAVING DELUSIONS OF EFFECTIVENESS.
12-23-05

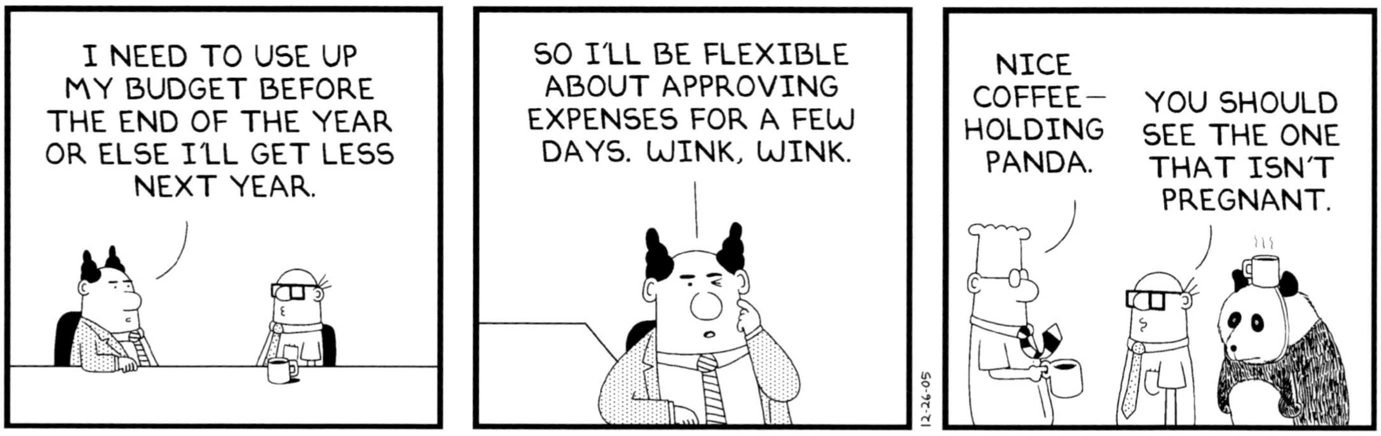
I NEED TO USE UP MY BUDGET BEFORE THE END OF THE YEAR OR ELSE I'LL GET LESS NEXT YEAR.
SO I'LL BE FLEXIBLE ABOUT APPROVING EXPENSES FOR A FEW DAYS. WINK, WINK.
NICE COFFEE-HOLDING PANDA.
YOU SHOULD SEE THE ONE THAT ISN'T PREGNANT.
12-26-05

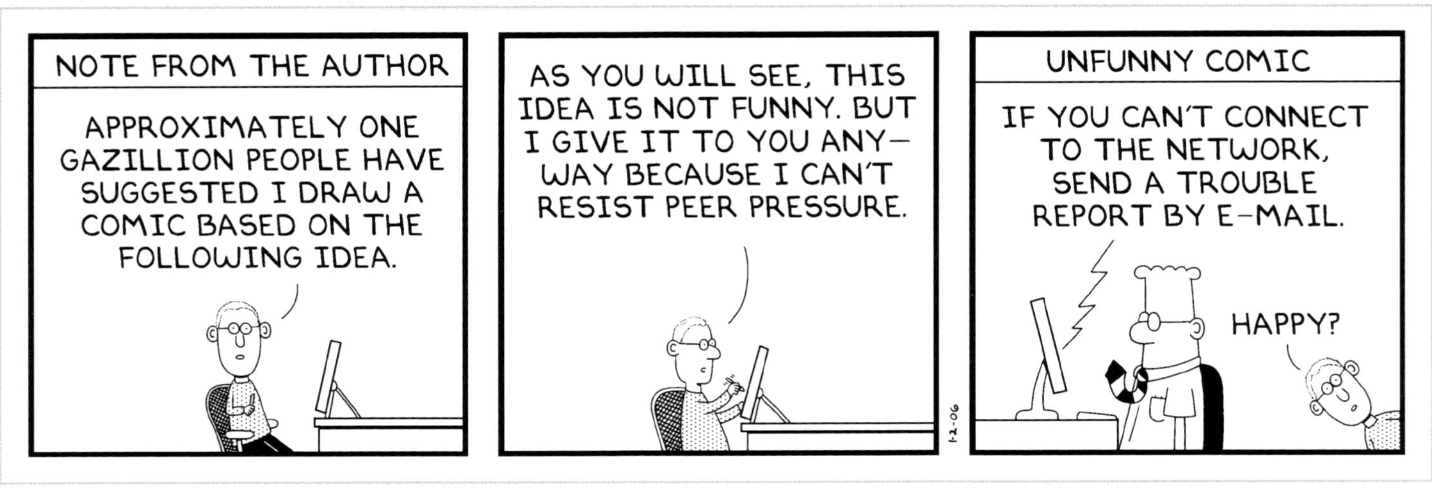
NOTE FROM THE AUTHOR
APPROXIMATELY ONE GAZILLION PEOPLE HAVE SUGGESTED I DRAW A COMIC BASED ON THE FOLLOWING IDEA.
AS YOU WILL SEE, THIS IDEA IS NOT FUNNY. BUT I GIVE IT TO YOU ANY-WAY BECAUSE I CAN'T RESIST PEER PRESSURE.
1-2-06
UNFUNNY COMIC
IF YOU CAN'T CONNECT TO THE NETWORK, SEND A TROUBLE REPORT BY E-MAIL.
HAPPY?

I was hoping to stop the unending flow of this particular suggestion. This strip helped a little.

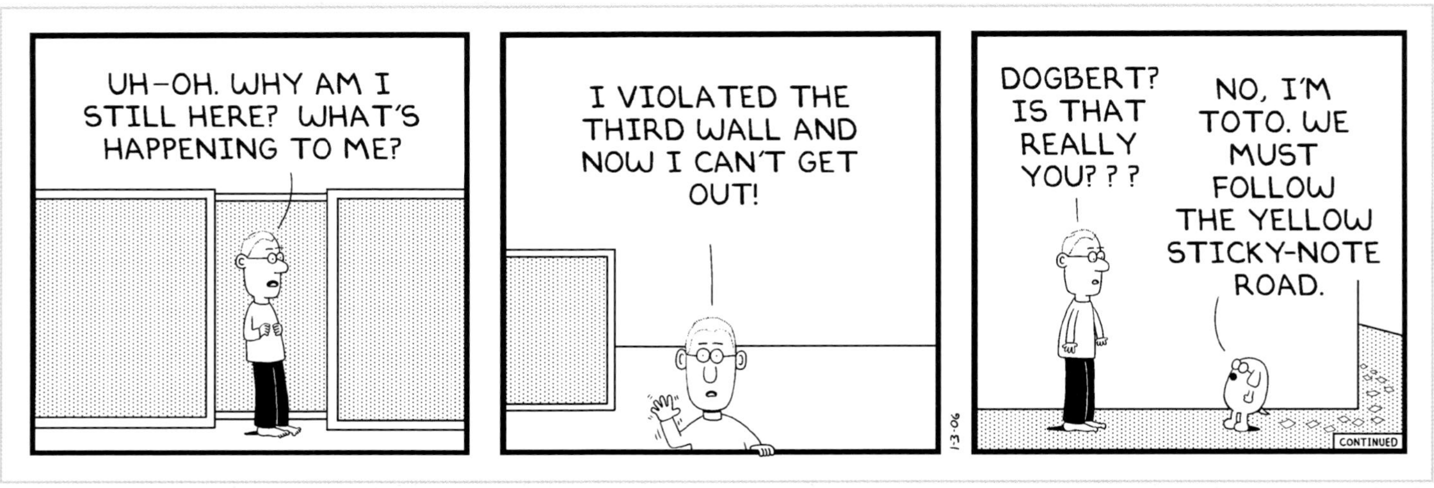
UH-OH. WHY AM I STILL HERE? WHAT'S HAPPENING TO ME?
I VIOLATED THE THIRD WALL AND NOW I CAN'T GET OUT!
1-3-06
DOGBERT? IS THAT REALLY YOU? ? ?
NO, I'M TOTO. WE MUST FOLLOW THE YELLOW STICKY-NOTE ROAD.
CONTINUED

Readers informed me that I should have said the fourth wall, not the third. Oops.

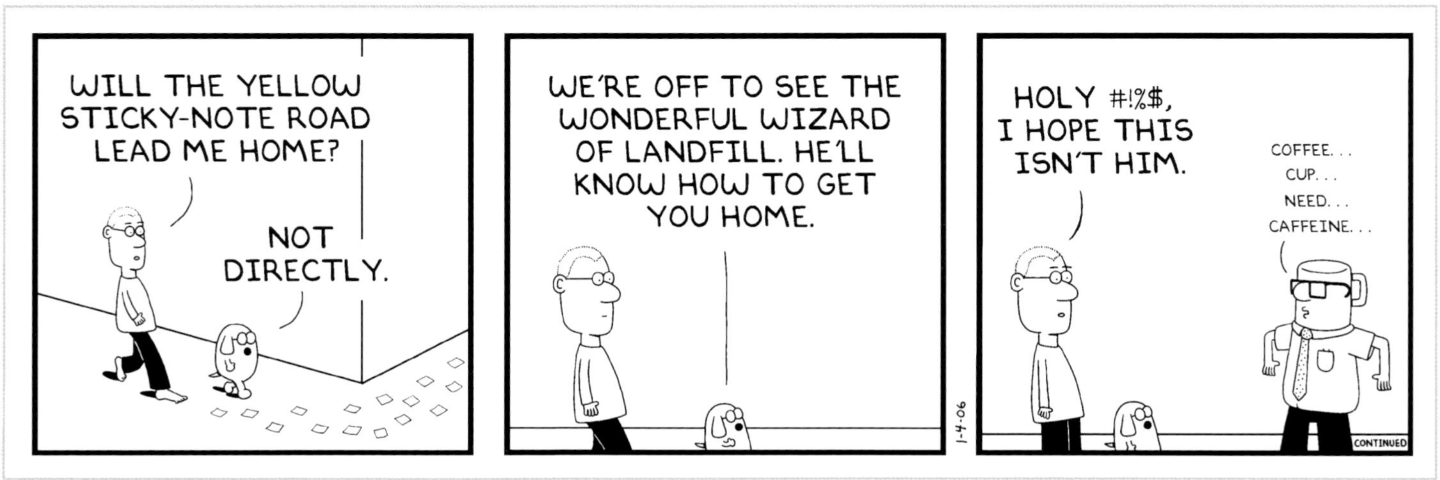
WILL THE YELLOW STICKY-NOTE ROAD LEAD ME HOME?
NOT DIRECTLY.
WE'RE OFF TO SEE THE WONDERFUL WIZARD OF LANDFILL. HE'LL KNOW HOW TO GET YOU HOME.
1-4-06
HOLY #!%$, I HOPE THIS ISN'T HIM.
COFFEE... CUP... NEED... CAFFEINE...
CONTINUED

Once I placed myself in the strip, I got carried away. This series was not popular, but it is worth including in the twentieth-anniversary book because it is so different.

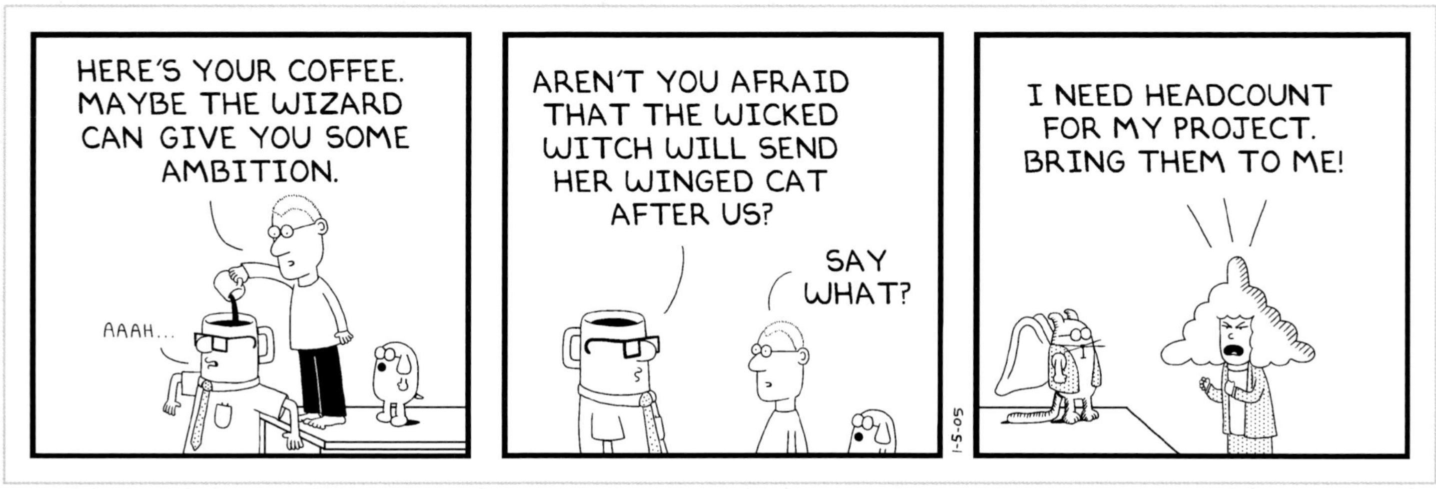
HERE'S YOUR COFFEE. MAYBE THE WIZARD CAN GIVE YOU SOME AMBITION.
AAAH...
AREN'T YOU AFRAID THAT THE WICKED WITCH WILL SEND HER WINGED CAT AFTER US?
SAY WHAT?
1-5-05
I NEED HEADCOUNT FOR MY PROJECT. BRING THEM TO ME!

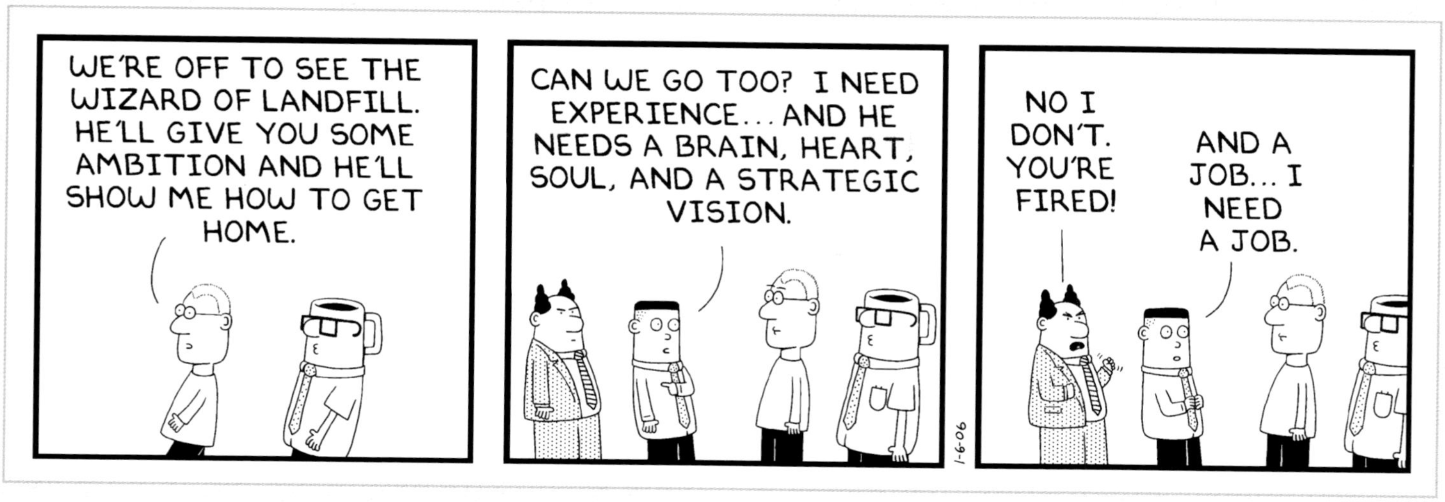
WE'RE OFF TO SEE THE WIZARD OF LANDFILL. HE'LL GIVE YOU SOME AMBITION AND HE'LL SHOW ME HOW TO GET HOME.
CAN WE GO TOO? I NEED EXPERIENCE... AND HE NEEDS A BRAIN, HEART, SOUL, AND A STRATEGIC VISION.
1-6-06
NO I DON'T. YOU'RE FIRED!
AND A JOB... I NEED A JOB.

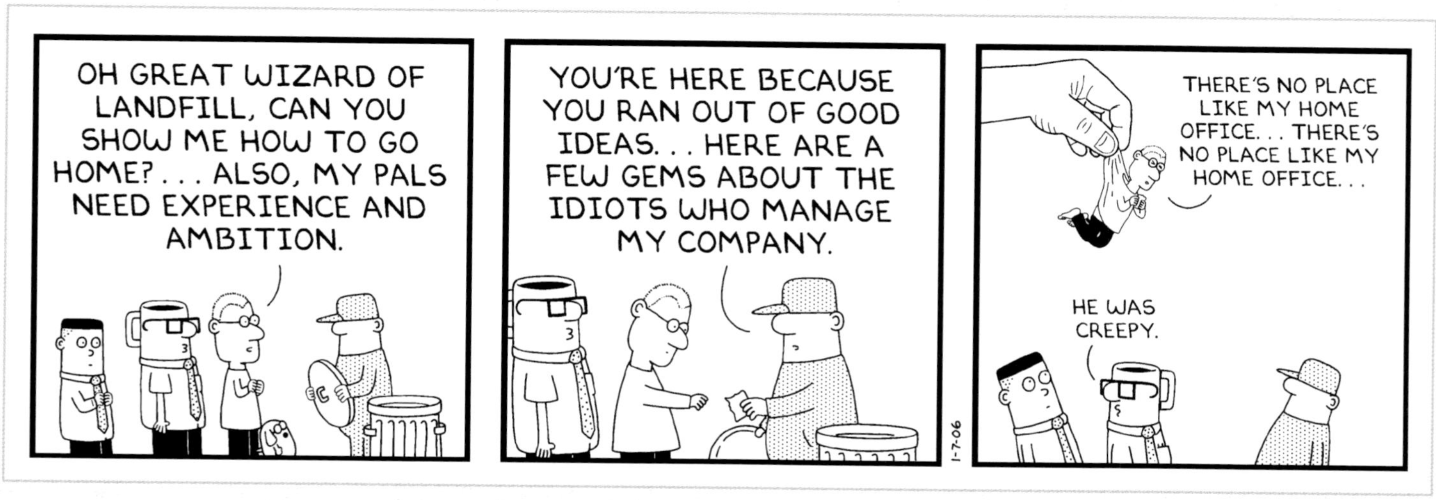
OH GREAT WIZARD OF LANDFILL, CAN YOU SHOW ME HOW TO GO HOME?... ALSO, MY PALS NEED EXPERIENCE AND AMBITION.
YOU'RE HERE BECAUSE YOU RAN OUT OF GOOD IDEAS... HERE ARE A FEW GEMS ABOUT THE IDIOTS WHO MANAGE MY COMPANY.
1-7-06
THERE'S NO PLACE LIKE MY HOME OFFICE... THERE'S NO PLACE LIKE MY HOME OFFICE...
HE WAS CREEPY.

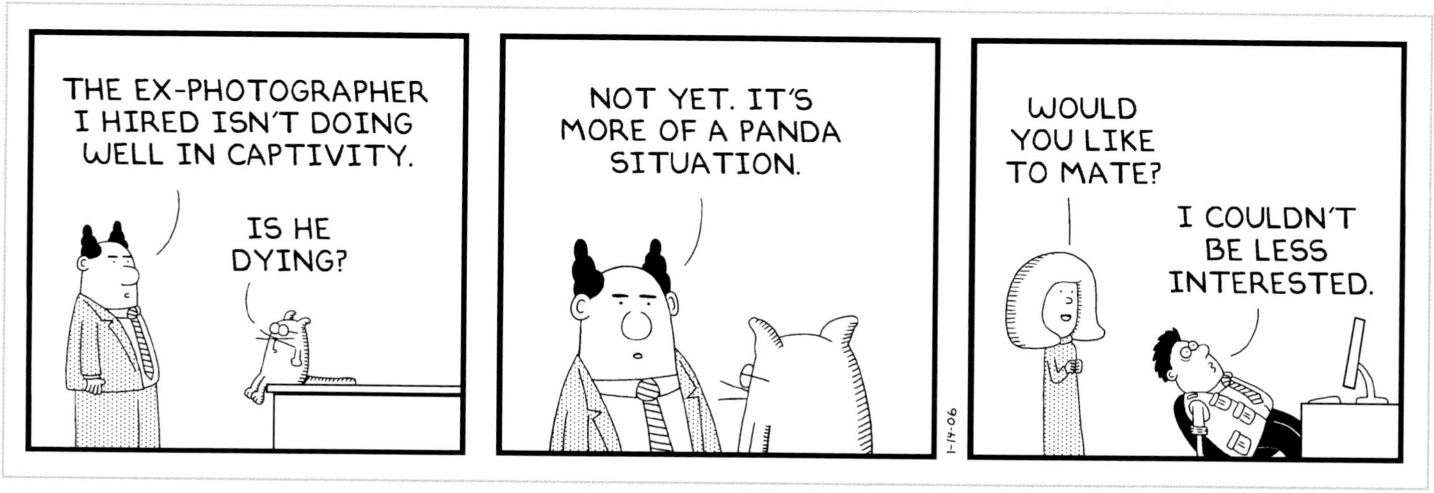
THE EX-PHOTOGRAPHER I HIRED ISN'T DOING WELL IN CAPTIVITY.
IS HE DYING?
NOT YET. IT'S MORE OF A PANDA SITUATION.
1-14-06
WOULD YOU LIKE TO MATE?
I COULDN'T BE LESS INTERESTED.

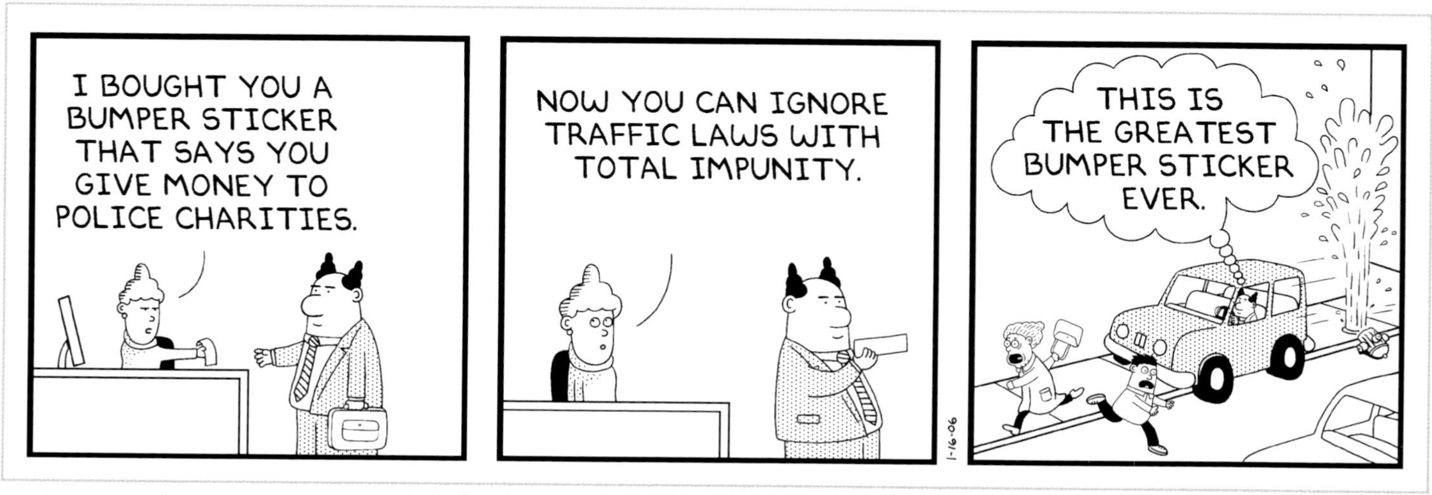
I BOUGHT YOU A BUMPER STICKER THAT SAYS YOU GIVE MONEY TO POLICE CHARITIES.
NOW YOU CAN IGNORE TRAFFIC LAWS WITH TOTAL IMPUNITY.
1-16-06
THIS IS THE GREATEST BUMPER STICKER EVER.

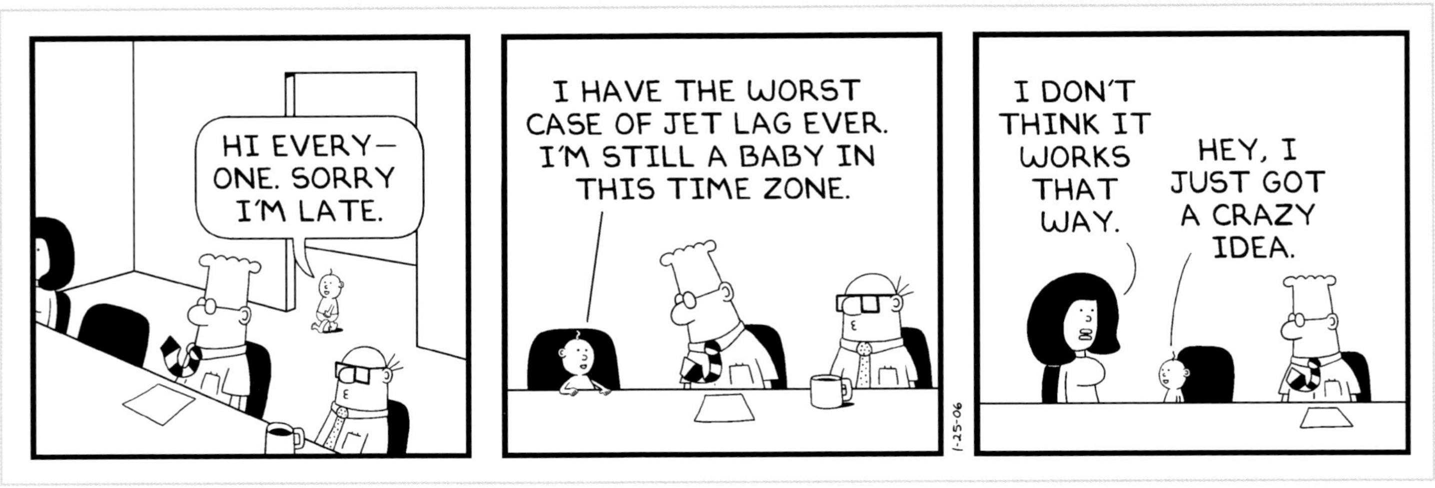
HI EVERY-ONE. SORRY I'M LATE.
I HAVE THE WORST CASE OF JET LAG EVER. I'M STILL A BABY IN THIS TIME ZONE.
1-25-06
I DON'T THINK IT WORKS THAT WAY.
HEY, I JUST GOT A CRAZY IDEA.

My editors weren't comfortable with a talking baby looking at a woman's chest, so this one never ran in papers.

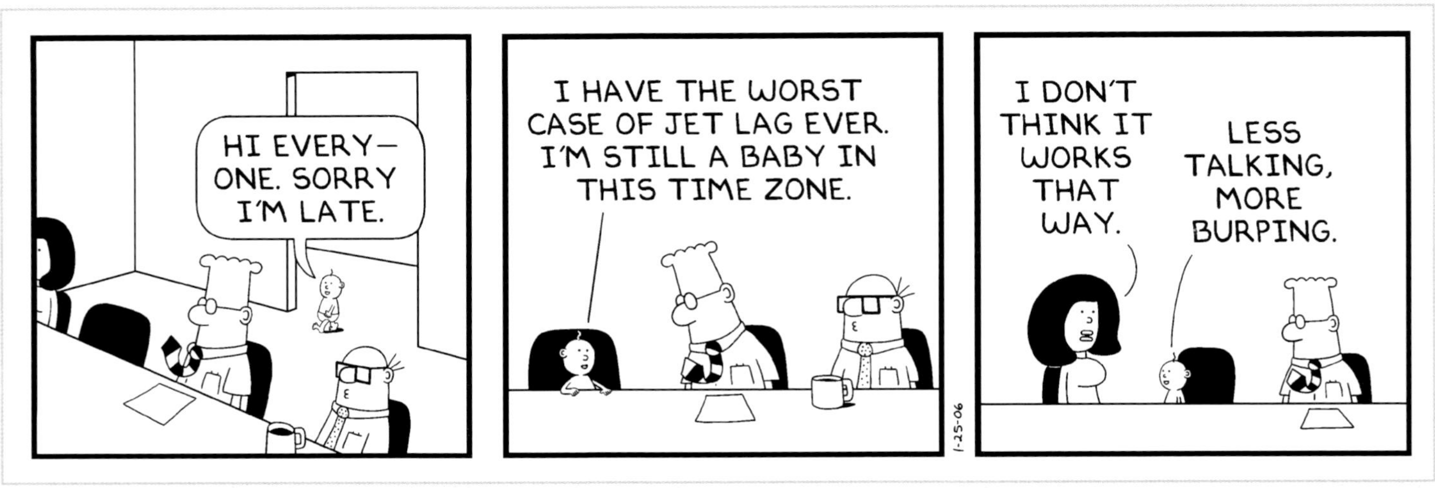
HI EVERY-ONE. SORRY I'M LATE.
I HAVE THE WORST CASE OF JET LAG EVER. I'M STILL A BABY IN THIS TIME ZONE.
1-25-06
I DON'T THINK IT WORKS THAT WAY.
LESS TALKING, MORE BURPING.

This watered-down version was approved for publication.

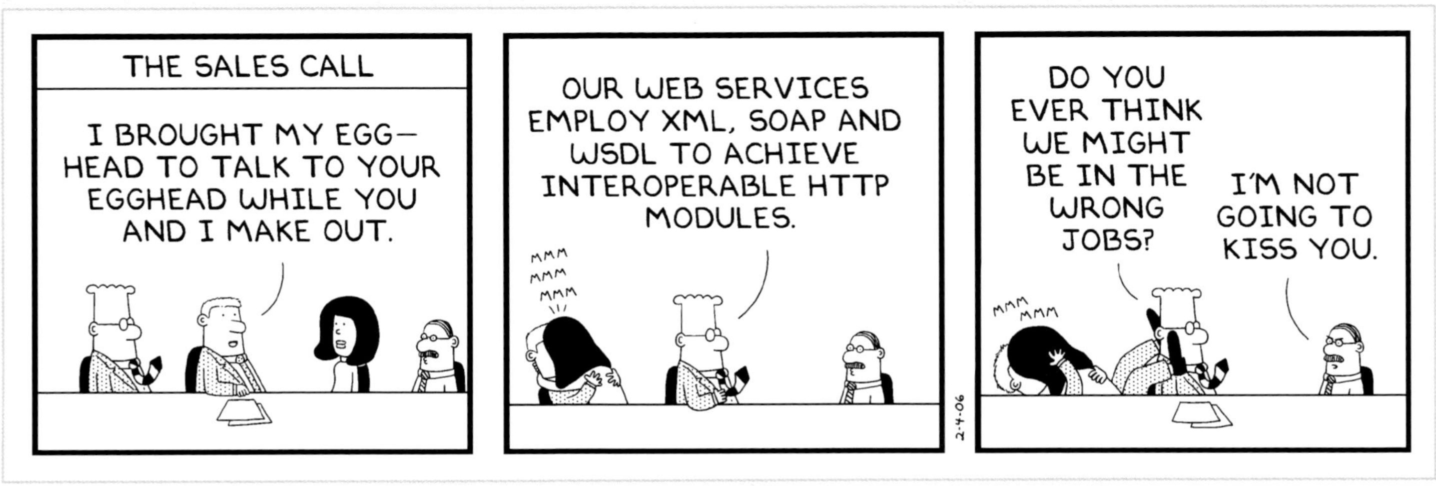
THE SALES CALL
I BROUGHT MY EGG-HEAD TO TALK TO YOUR EGGHEAD WHILE YOU AND I MAKE OUT.
MMM MMM MMM
OUR WEB SERVICES EMPLOY XML, SOAP AND WSDL TO ACHIEVE INTEROPERABLE HTTP MODULES.
2-4-06
MMM MMM
DO YOU EVER THINK WE MIGHT BE IN THE WRONG JOBS?
I'M NOT GOING TO KISS YOU.

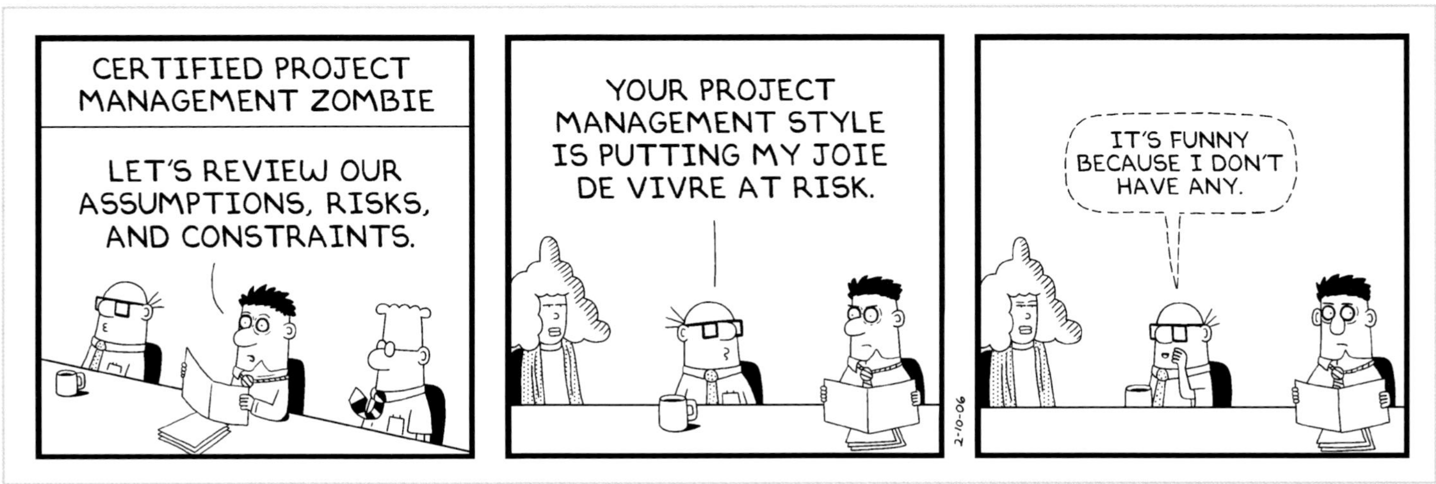
CERTIFIED PROJECT MANAGEMENT ZOMBIE
LET'S REVIEW OUR ASSUMPTIONS, RISKS, AND CONSTRAINTS.
YOUR PROJECT MANAGEMENT STYLE IS PUTTING MY JOIE DE VIVRE AT RISK.
2-10-06
IT'S FUNNY BECAUSE I DON'T HAVE ANY.

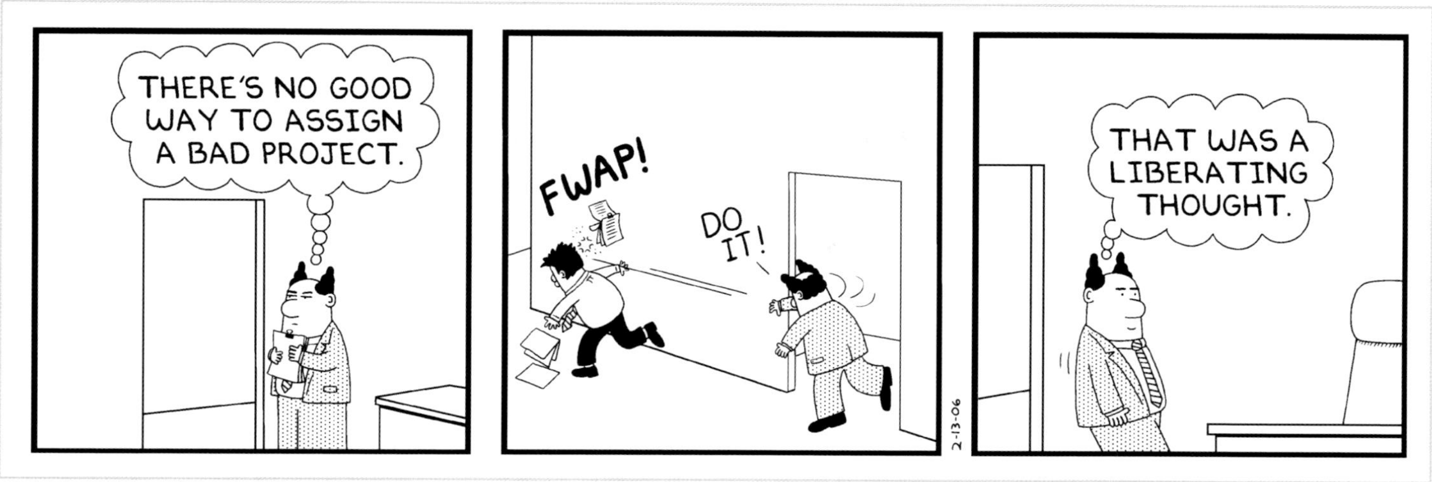
THERE'S NO GOOD WAY TO ASSIGN A BAD PROJECT.
FWAP!
DO IT!
2-13-06
THAT WAS A LIBERATING THOUGHT.

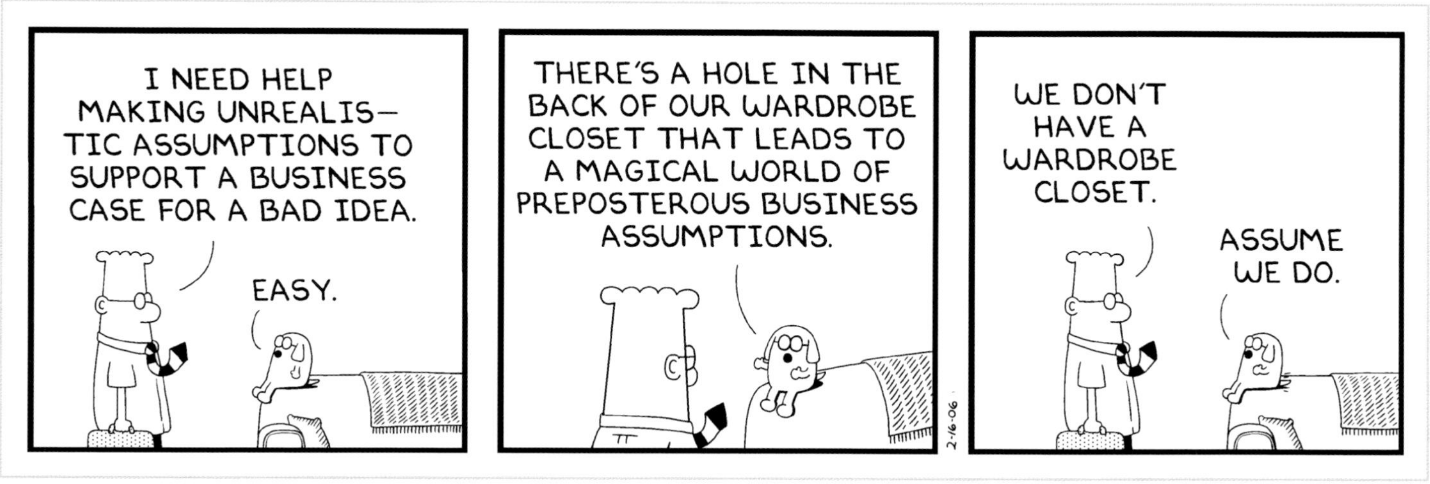
I NEED HELP MAKING UNREALIS– TIC ASSUMPTIONS TO SUPPORT A BUSINESS CASE FOR A BAD IDEA.
EASY.
THERE'S A HOLE IN THE BACK OF OUR WARDROBE CLOSET THAT LEADS TO A MAGICAL WORLD OF PREPOSTEROUS BUSINESS ASSUMPTIONS.
2-16-06
WE DON'T HAVE A WARDROBE CLOSET.
ASSUME WE DO.

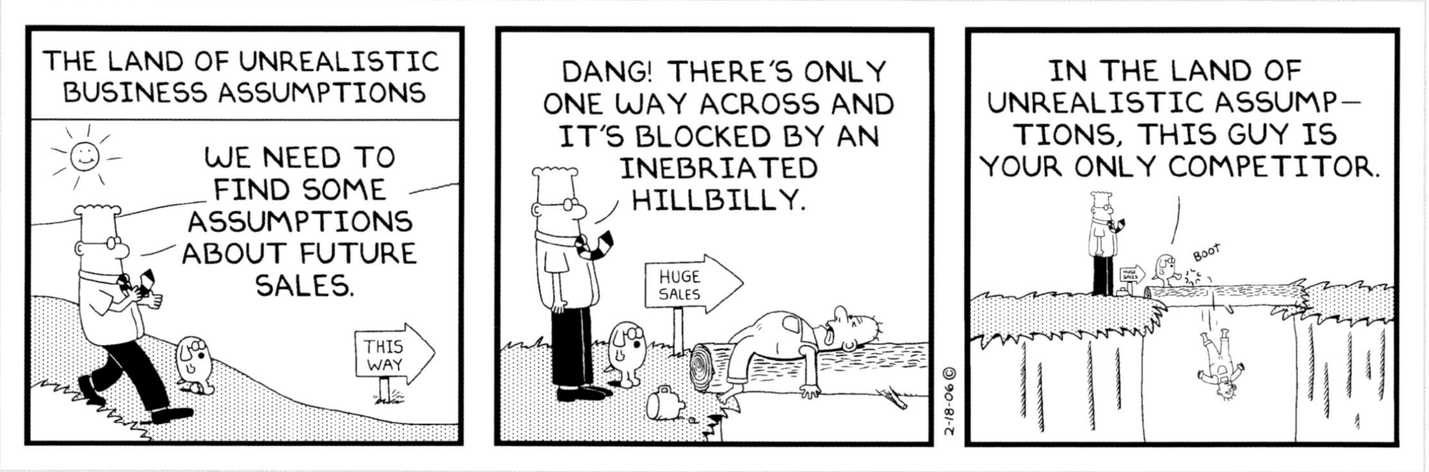
THE LAND OF UNREALISTIC BUSINESS ASSUMPTIONS
WE NEED TO FIND SOME ASSUMPTIONS ABOUT FUTURE SALES.
THIS WAY
DANG! THERE'S ONLY ONE WAY ACROSS AND IT'S BLOCKED BY AN INEBRIATED HILLBILLY.
HUGE SALES
2-18-06 ©
IN THE LAND OF UNREALISTIC ASSUMP– TIONS, THIS GUY IS YOUR ONLY COMPETITOR.
BOOT

I got a well-written letter from a professor who complained about my depiction of hillbillies. I learned that "hillbilly" is a derogatory name given to a poor person who lives in the Appalachian Mountains. I thought it was more of a generic description of a lifestyle choice involving moonshine, overalls, and eating freshly shot critters.

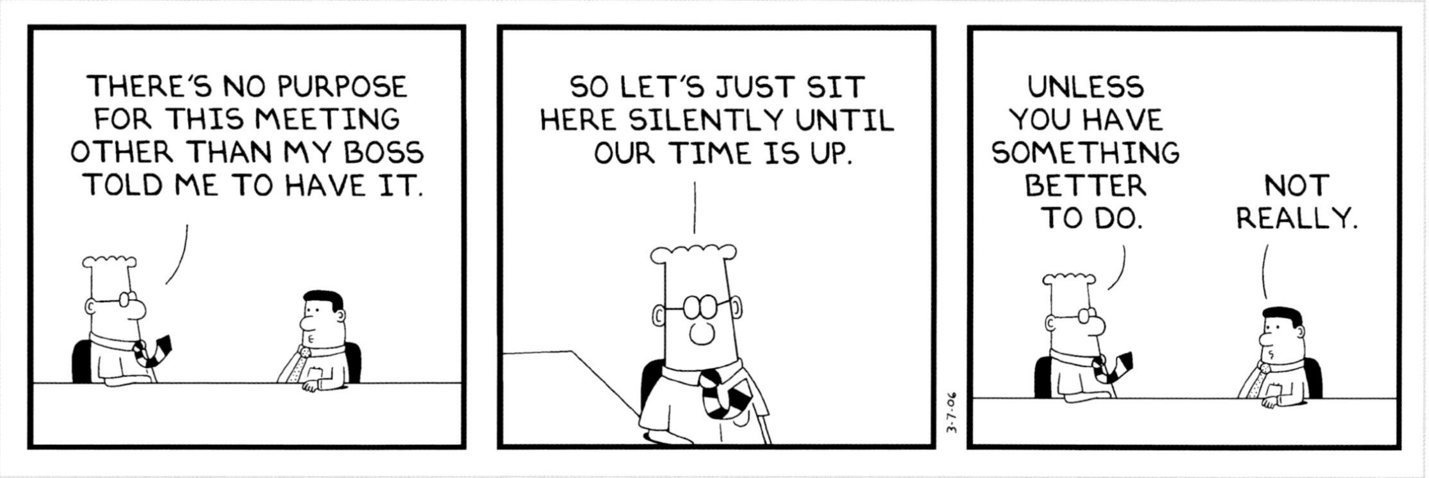
THERE'S NO PURPOSE FOR THIS MEETING OTHER THAN MY BOSS TOLD ME TO HAVE IT.
SO LET'S JUST SIT HERE SILENTLY UNTIL OUR TIME IS UP.
3-7-06
UNLESS YOU HAVE SOMETHING BETTER TO DO.
NOT REALLY.

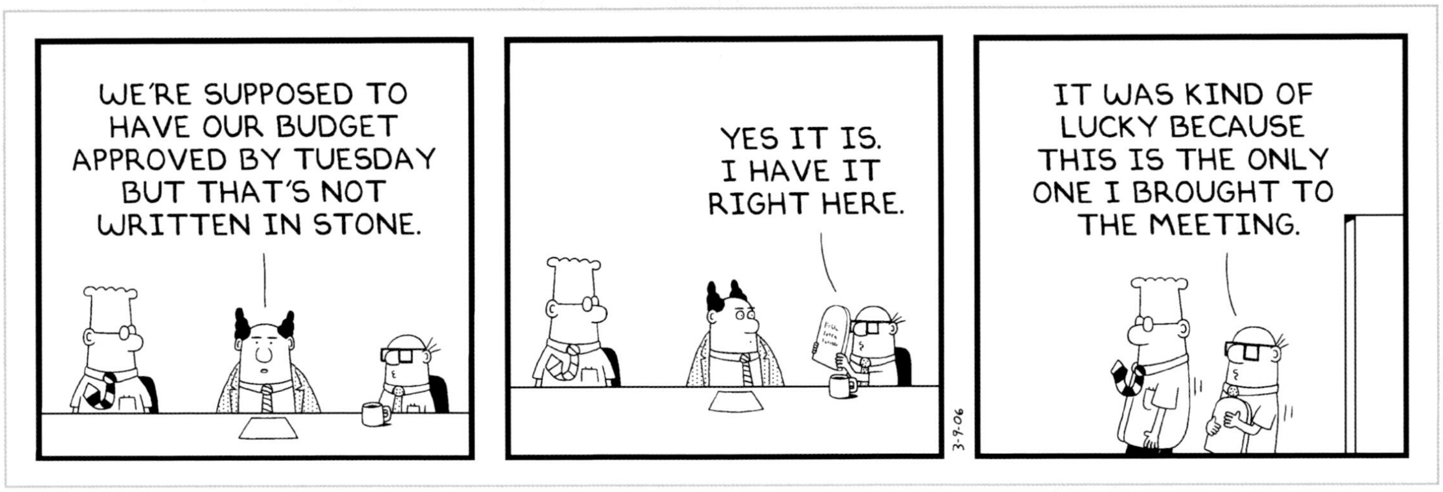
WE'RE SUPPOSED TO HAVE OUR BUDGET APPROVED BY TUESDAY BUT THAT'S NOT WRITTEN IN STONE.
YES IT IS. I HAVE IT RIGHT HERE.
3-9-06
IT WAS KIND OF LUCKY BECAUSE THIS IS THE ONLY ONE I BROUGHT TO THE MEETING.

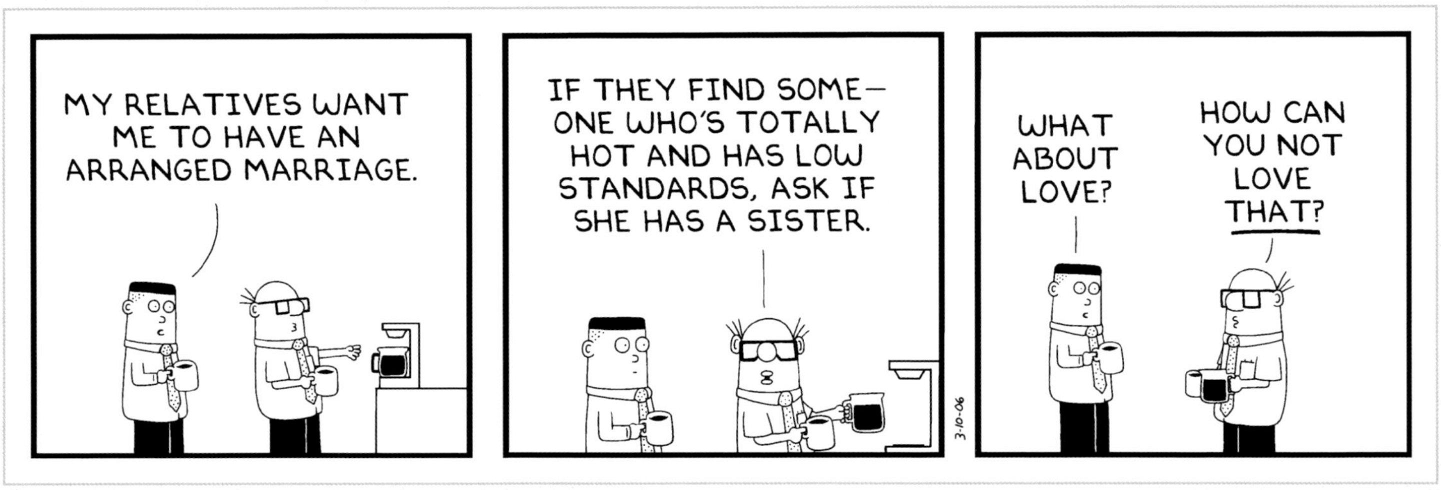
MY RELATIVES WANT ME TO HAVE AN ARRANGED MARRIAGE.
IF THEY FIND SOME-ONE WHO'S TOTALLY HOT AND HAS LOW STANDARDS, ASK IF SHE HAS A SISTER.
3-10-06
WHAT ABOUT LOVE?
HOW CAN YOU NOT LOVE THAT?

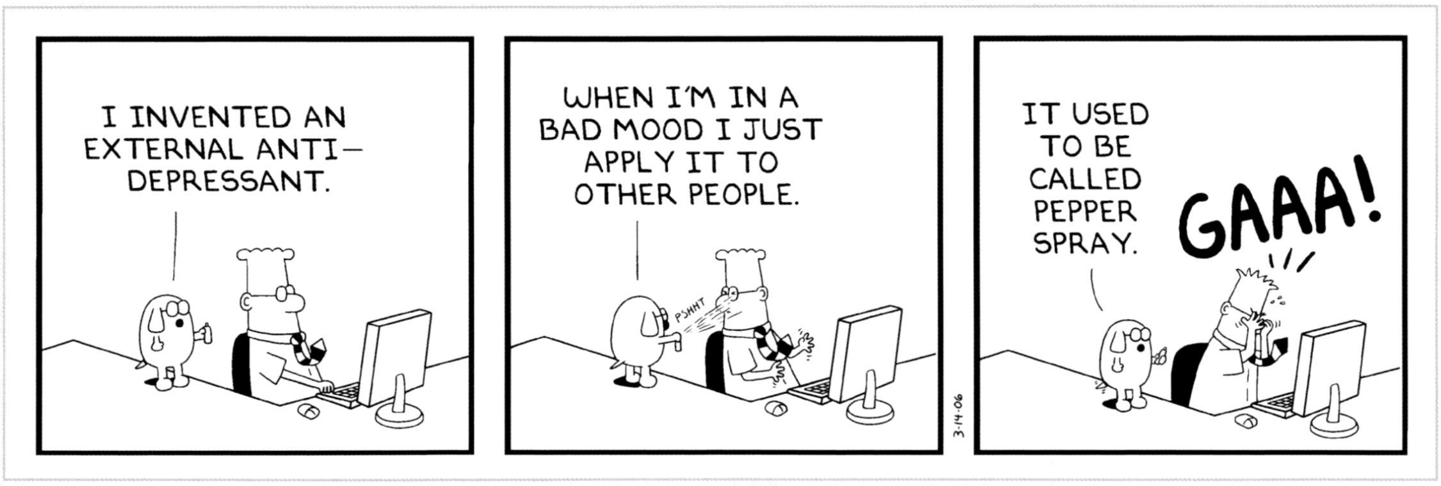
I INVENTED AN EXTERNAL ANTI-DEPRESSANT.
WHEN I'M IN A BAD MOOD I JUST APPLY IT TO OTHER PEOPLE.
PSHHT
3-14-06
IT USED TO BE CALLED PEPPER SPRAY.
GAAA!

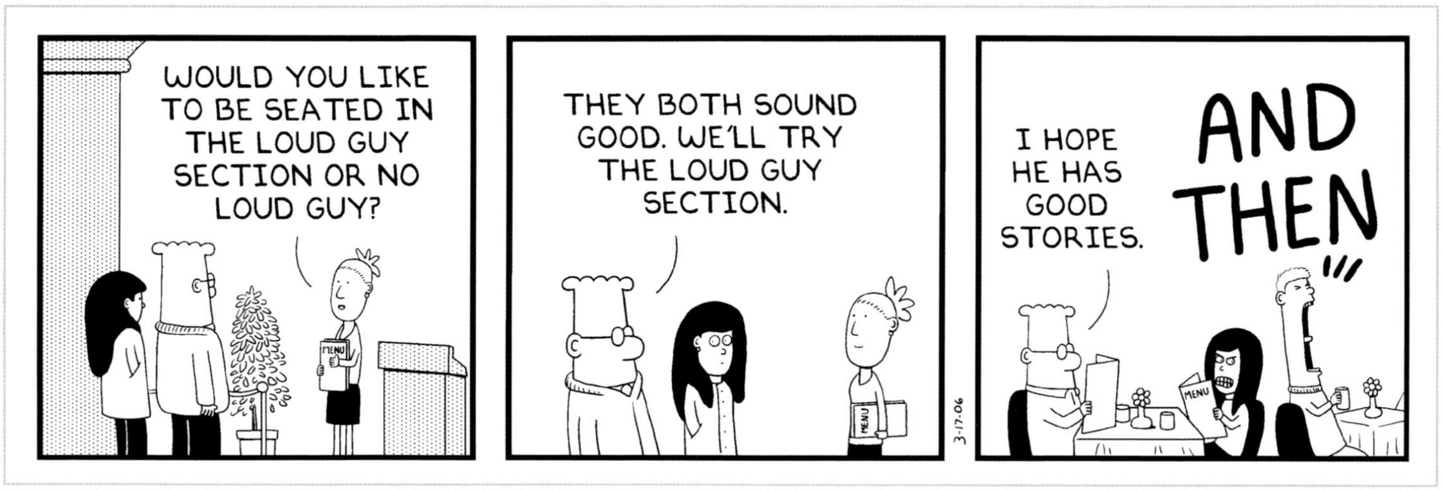
WOULD YOU LIKE TO BE SEATED IN THE LOUD GUY SECTION OR NO LOUD GUY?
MENU
THEY BOTH SOUND GOOD. WE'LL TRY THE LOUD GUY SECTION.
MENU
3-17-06
I HOPE HE HAS GOOD STORIES.
AND THEN
MENU

ALICE, MY LAPTOP IS SLOWING DOWN. CAN YOU TAKE A LOOK AT IT?
HERE'S THE PROBLEM. THERE'S TOO MUCH SMUT ON YOUR HARD DRIVE.
I RECOMMEND DELETING THE FILM CLIPS THAT HAVE POOR LIGHTING.
AND HERE'S A WHOLE CATEGORY THAT YOU HAVEN'T LOOKED AT IN WEEKS.
I'LL MOVE THOSE TO AN EXTERNAL DRIVE IN CASE YOU NEED 'EM LATER.
3-5-06
WALLY HAS ALL OF THIS STUFF ON THE SERVER. YOU DON'T NEED IT ON YOUR LAPTOP.
WHAT THE....? YOU PINHEAD! YOU DISABLED YOUR FIREWALL!
IF YOU WORK HERE LONG ENOUGH, YOUR OUTRAGE ENDS UP IN ALL OF THE WRONG PLACES.
WHO MOVED MY STAPLER?!!

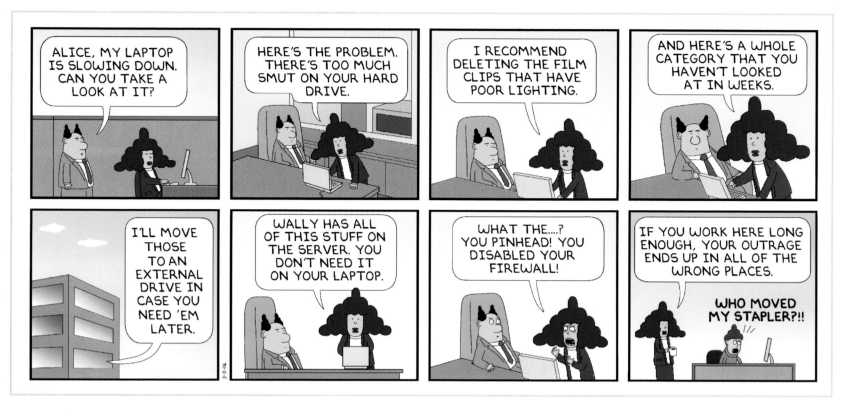

In the original version, Alice found porn on the boss's laptop, not smut. It means the same thing, but my editors felt we would get fewer complaints with a less politically charged word. Apparently they were right. No one complained about smut, but I'm sure we would have gotten complaints about porn.

WHAT'S THAT THING DOING HERE?
THIS IS MY DAUGHTER, TRAYLOR.
I BROUGHT HER TO THE OFFICE SO SHE CAN LEARN ABOUT WORK– ING IN A CORPORATE ENVIRONMENT.
OKAY. WHATEVER. I HAVE A NEW PROJECT FOR YOU.
SOME IDIOT CUT HIS FINGER. NOW WE HAVE TO DO A SAFETY AWARENESS CAMPAIGN.
3-26-06
PUT ON THIS DOG COSTUME. YOU'RE THE MASCOT FOR OUR "SPOT" THE SAFETY HAZARD CAMPAIGN.
WHENEVER ANYONE WALKS BY, YOU SAY, "WOOF WOOF, DON'T USE SCISSORS."
CAN I GET A TATTOO?
SURE.

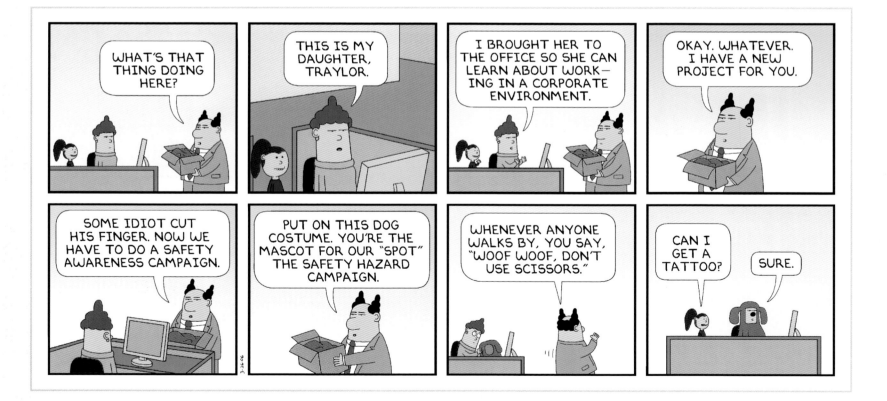

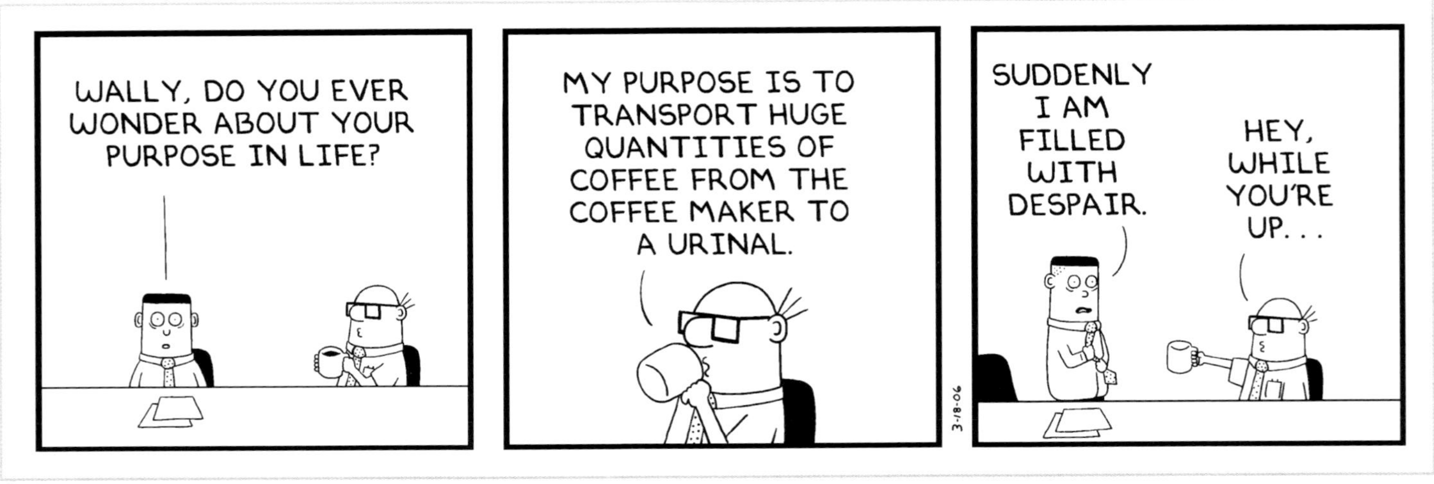
WALLY, DO YOU EVER WONDER ABOUT YOUR PURPOSE IN LIFE?
MY PURPOSE IS TO TRANSPORT HUGE QUANTITIES OF COFFEE FROM THE COFFEE MAKER TO A URINAL.
3-18-06
SUDDENLY I AM FILLED WITH DESPAIR.
HEY, WHILE YOU'RE UP. . .

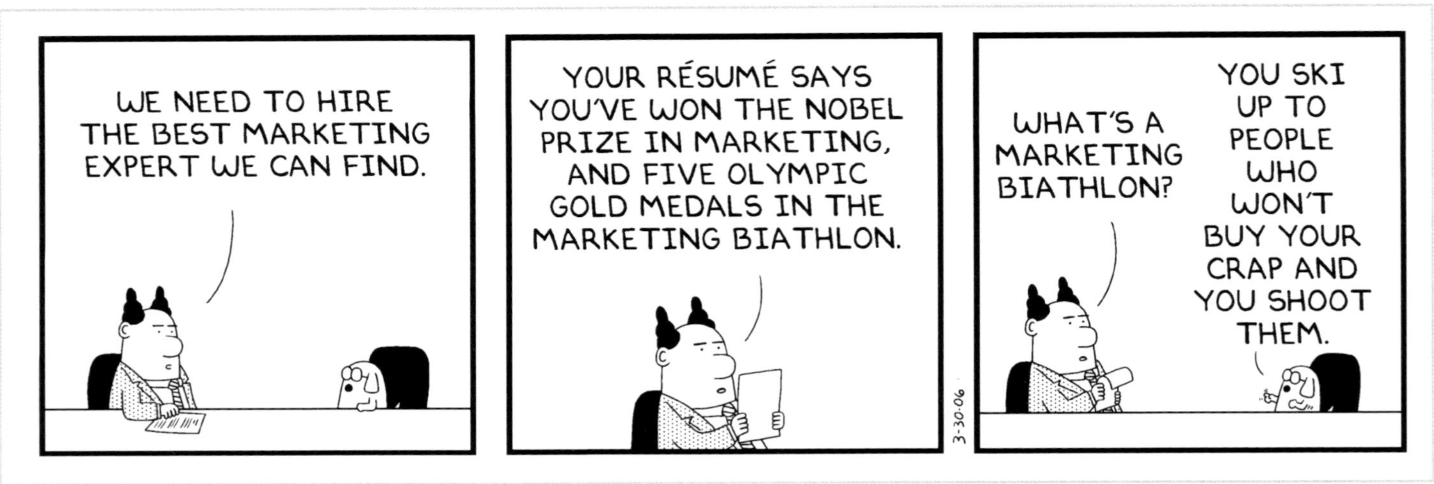
WE NEED TO HIRE THE BEST MARKETING EXPERT WE CAN FIND.
YOUR RÉSUMÉ SAYS YOU'VE WON THE NOBEL PRIZE IN MARKETING, AND FIVE OLYMPIC GOLD MEDALS IN THE MARKETING BIATHLON.
3-30-06
WHAT'S A MARKETING BIATHLON?
YOU SKI UP TO PEOPLE WHO WON'T BUY YOUR CRAP AND YOU SHOOT THEM.

This was the first successful use of the word "crap" in a Dilbert *comic. It was a long, hard struggle, and perhaps not the worthiest goal, but success feels good no matter where you find it.*

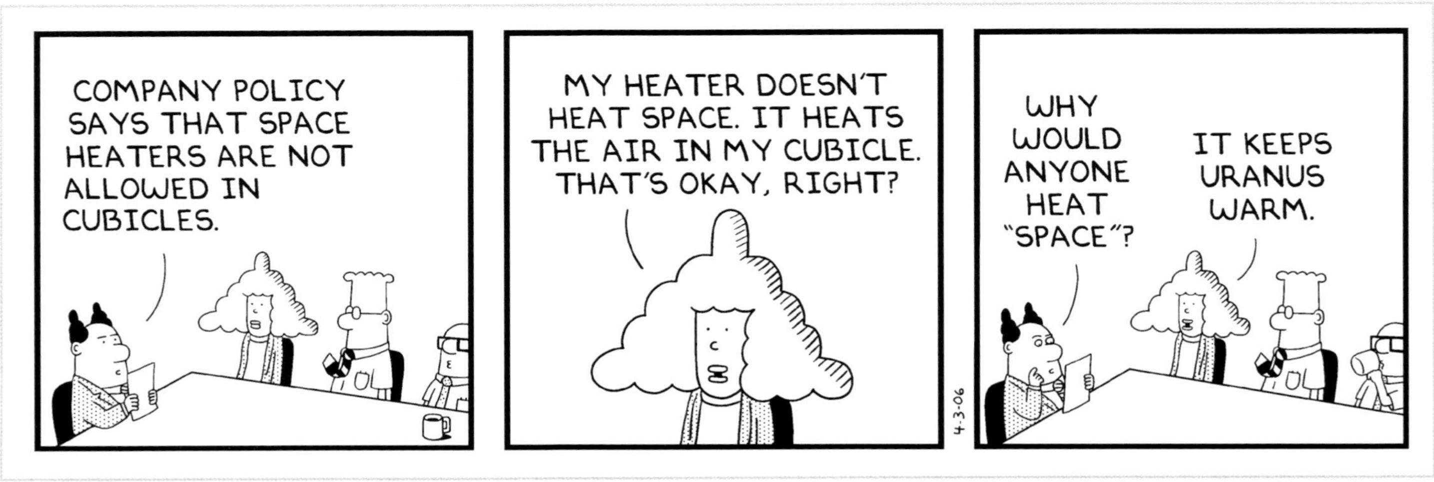
COMPANY POLICY SAYS THAT SPACE HEATERS ARE NOT ALLOWED IN CUBICLES.
MY HEATER DOESN'T HEAT SPACE. IT HEATS THE AIR IN MY CUBICLE. THAT'S OKAY, RIGHT?
4-3-06
WHY WOULD ANYONE HEAT "SPACE"?
IT KEEPS URANUS WARM.

I'm amazed the strip above got published. But I think some conservative papers replaced it with a repeat. That's a fairly common practice, and I have no problem with it. The editors know what is acceptable in their local markets.

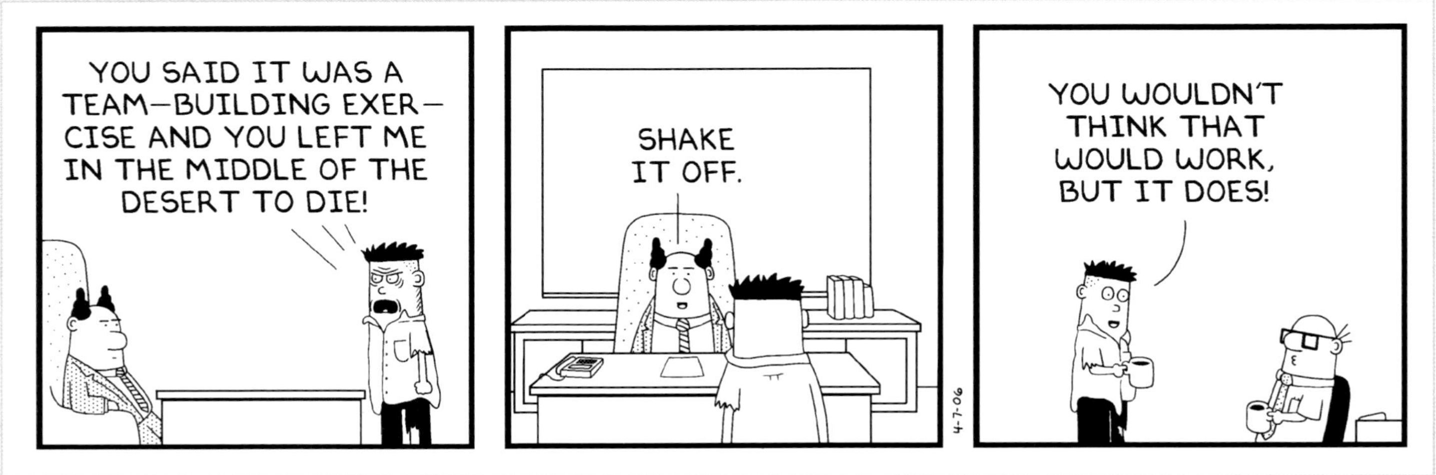
YOU SAID IT WAS A TEAM-BUILDING EXER-CISE AND YOU LEFT ME IN THE MIDDLE OF THE DESERT TO DIE!
SHAKE IT OFF.
4-7-06
YOU WOULDN'T THINK THAT WOULD WORK, BUT IT DOES!

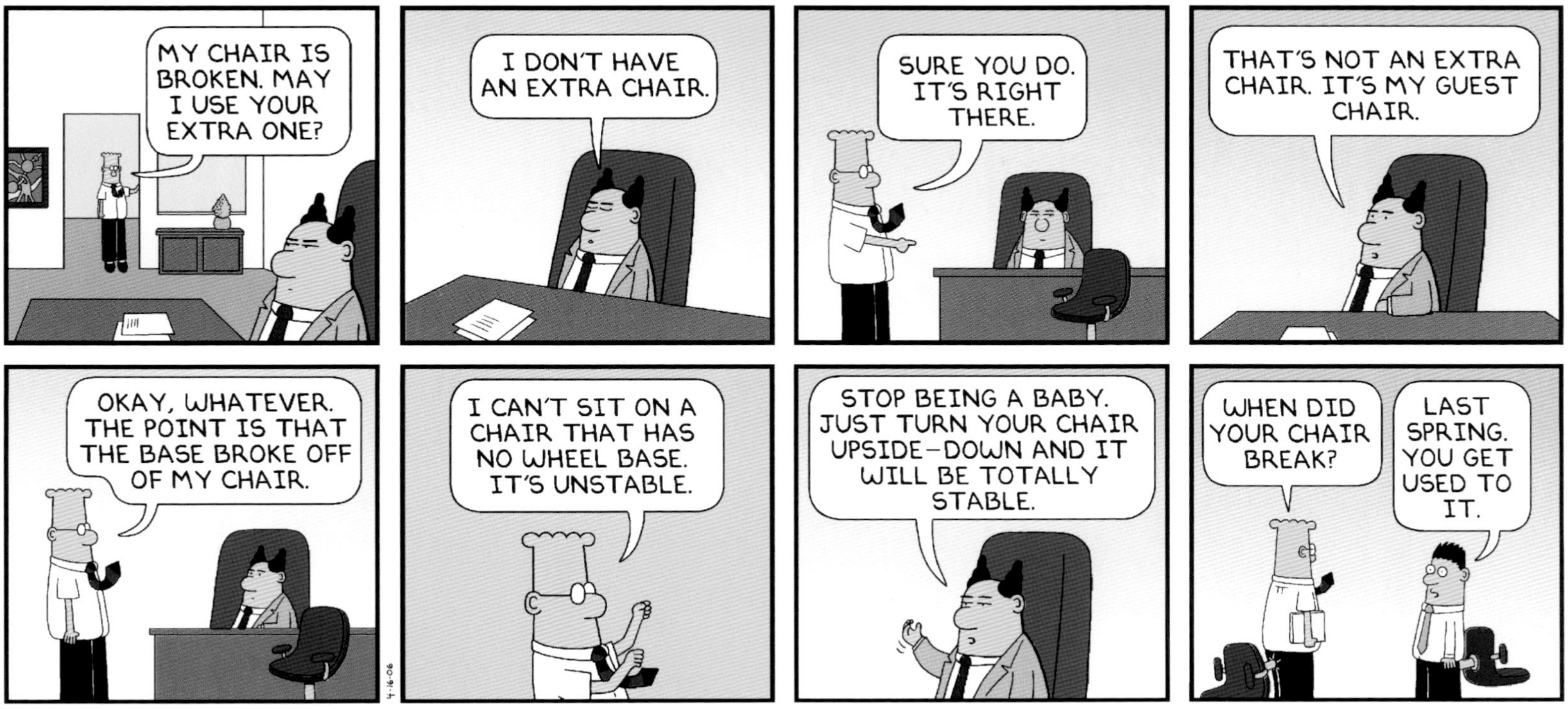
MY CHAIR IS BROKEN. MAY I USE YOUR EXTRA ONE?
I DON'T HAVE AN EXTRA CHAIR.
SURE YOU DO. IT'S RIGHT THERE.
THAT'S NOT AN EXTRA CHAIR. IT'S MY GUEST CHAIR.
OKAY, WHATEVER. THE POINT IS THAT THE BASE BROKE OFF OF MY CHAIR.
I CAN'T SIT ON A CHAIR THAT HAS NO WHEEL BASE. IT'S UNSTABLE.
STOP BEING A BABY. JUST TURN YOUR CHAIR UPSIDE-DOWN AND IT WILL BE TOTALLY STABLE.
WHEN DID YOUR CHAIR BREAK?
LAST SPRING. YOU GET USED TO IT.

I fully expected to have to change the last panel on this one, and I was surprised when the request never came. Newspaper comics are still twenty years behind television and the Internet in terms of what is considered acceptable, but clearly there has been some loosening.

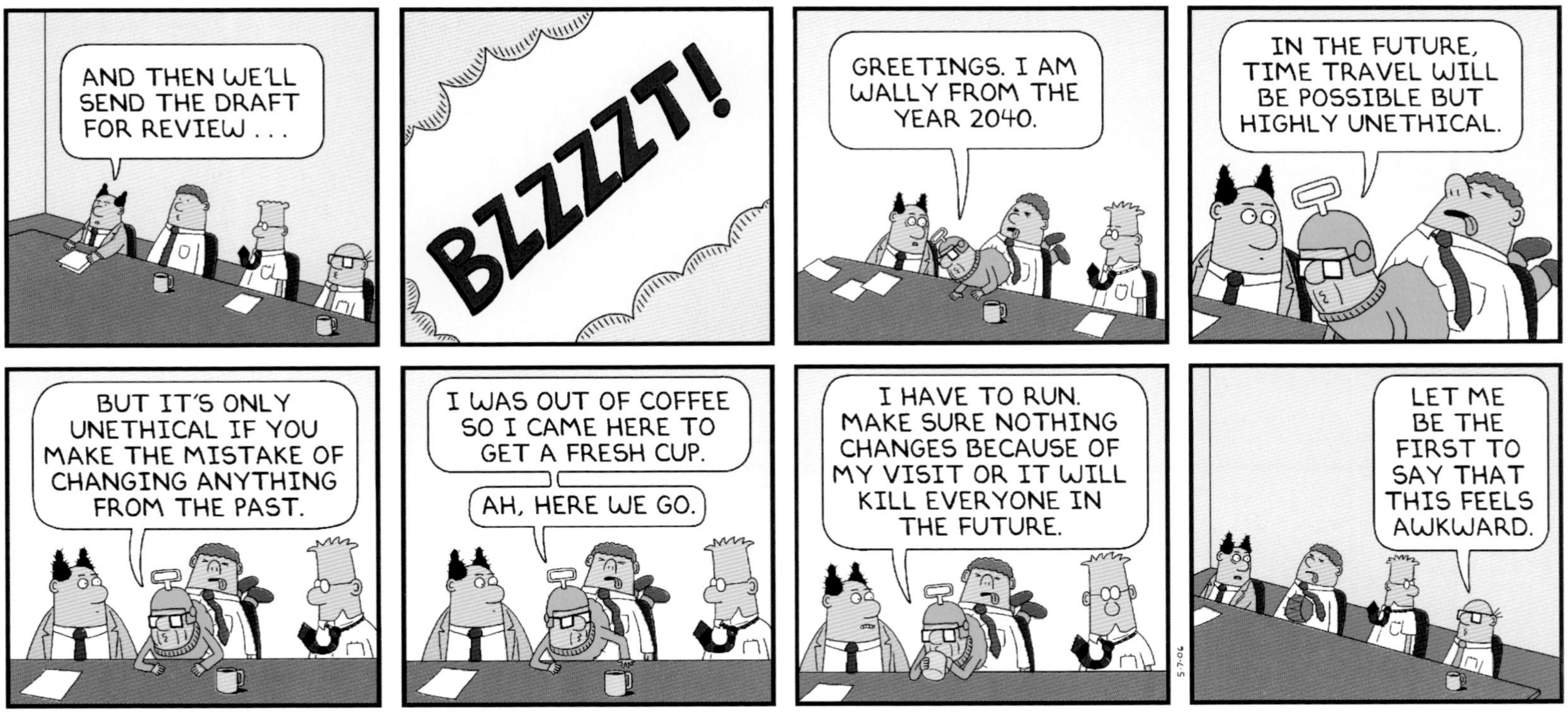
AND THEN WE'LL SEND THE DRAFT FOR REVIEW . . .
BZZZZT!
GREETINGS. I AM WALLY FROM THE YEAR 2040.
IN THE FUTURE, TIME TRAVEL WILL BE POSSIBLE BUT HIGHLY UNETHICAL.
BUT IT'S ONLY UNETHICAL IF YOU MAKE THE MISTAKE OF CHANGING ANYTHING FROM THE PAST.
I WAS OUT OF COFFEE SO I CAME HERE TO GET A FRESH CUP.
AH, HERE WE GO.
I HAVE TO RUN. MAKE SURE NOTHING CHANGES BECAUSE OF MY VISIT OR IT WILL KILL EVERYONE IN THE FUTURE.
LET ME BE THE FIRST TO SAY THAT THIS FEELS AWKWARD.

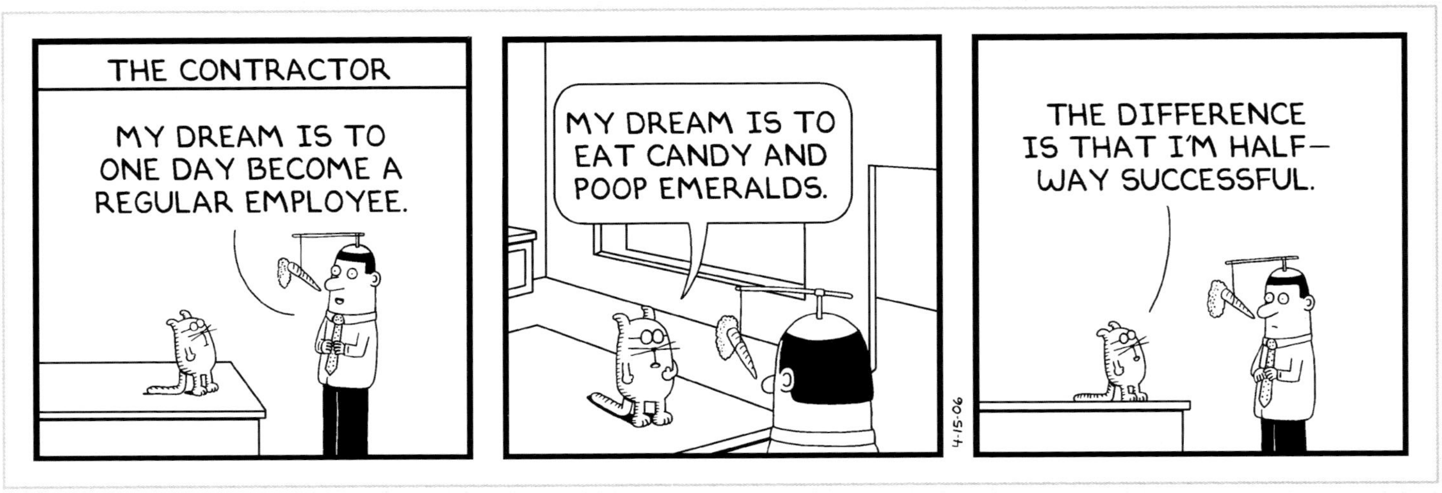
THE CONTRACTOR
MY DREAM IS TO ONE DAY BECOME A REGULAR EMPLOYEE.
MY DREAM IS TO EAT CANDY AND POOP EMERALDS.
4-15-06
THE DIFFERENCE IS THAT I'M HALF-WAY SUCCESSFUL.

The comic above wouldn't have made it past my editors in the recent past.
But it sailed right through without a hitch.

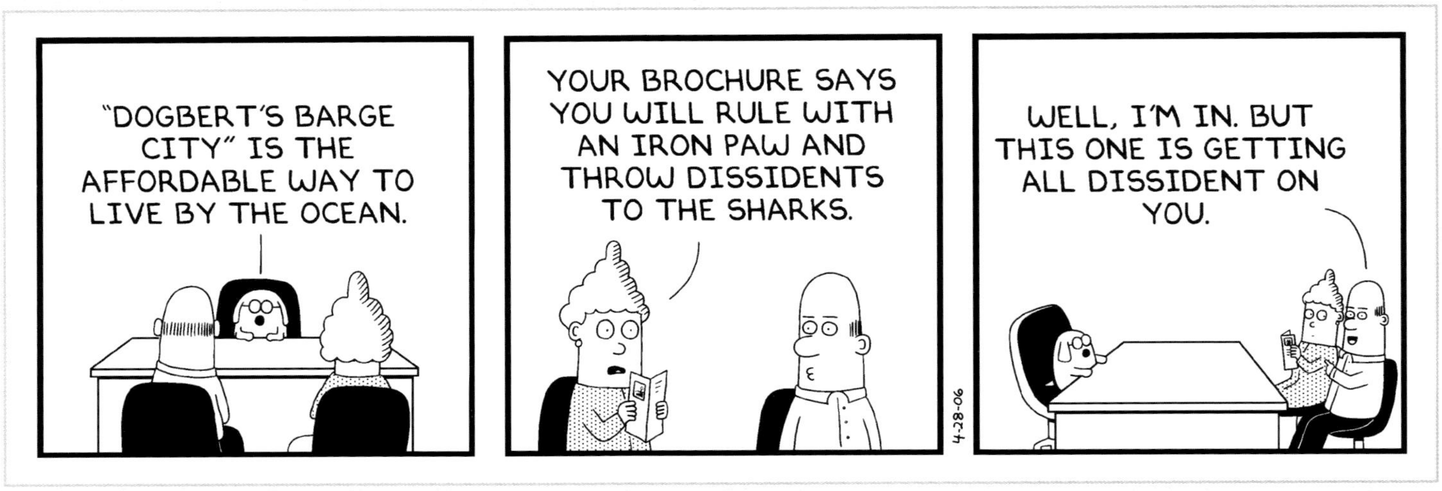
"DOGBERT'S BARGE CITY" IS THE AFFORDABLE WAY TO LIVE BY THE OCEAN.
YOUR BROCHURE SAYS YOU WILL RULE WITH AN IRON PAW AND THROW DISSIDENTS TO THE SHARKS.
4-28-06
WELL, I'M IN. BUT THIS ONE IS GETTING ALL DISSIDENT ON YOU.

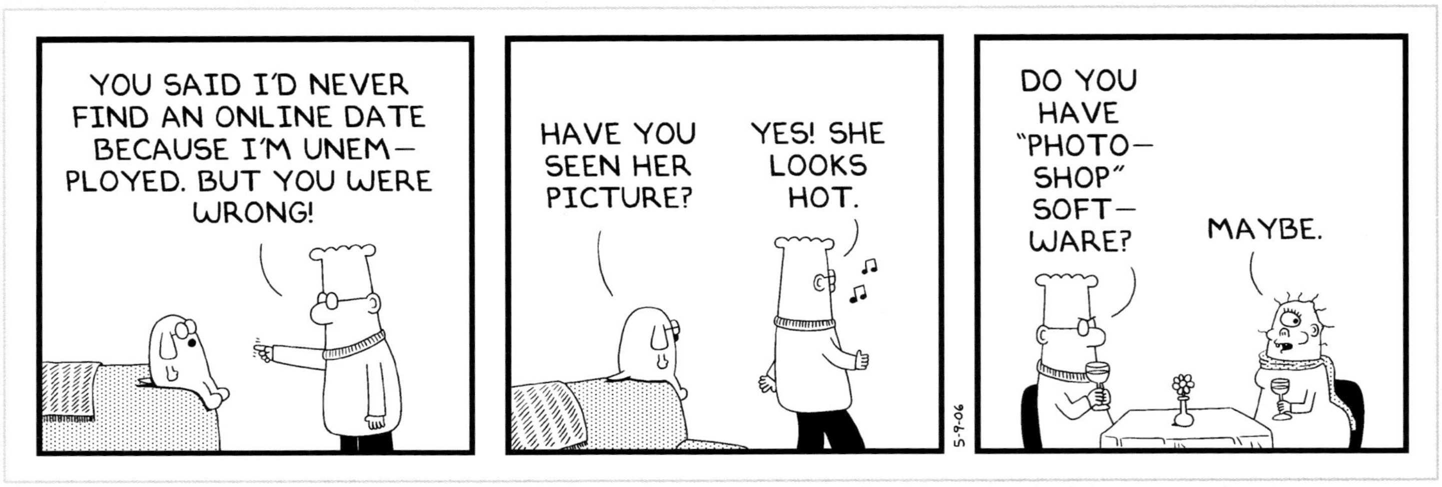
YOU SAID I'D NEVER FIND AN ONLINE DATE BECAUSE I'M UNEM-PLOYED. BUT YOU WERE WRONG!
HAVE YOU SEEN HER PICTURE?
YES! SHE LOOKS HOT.
5-9-06
DO YOU HAVE "PHOTO-SHOP" SOFT-WARE?
MAYBE.

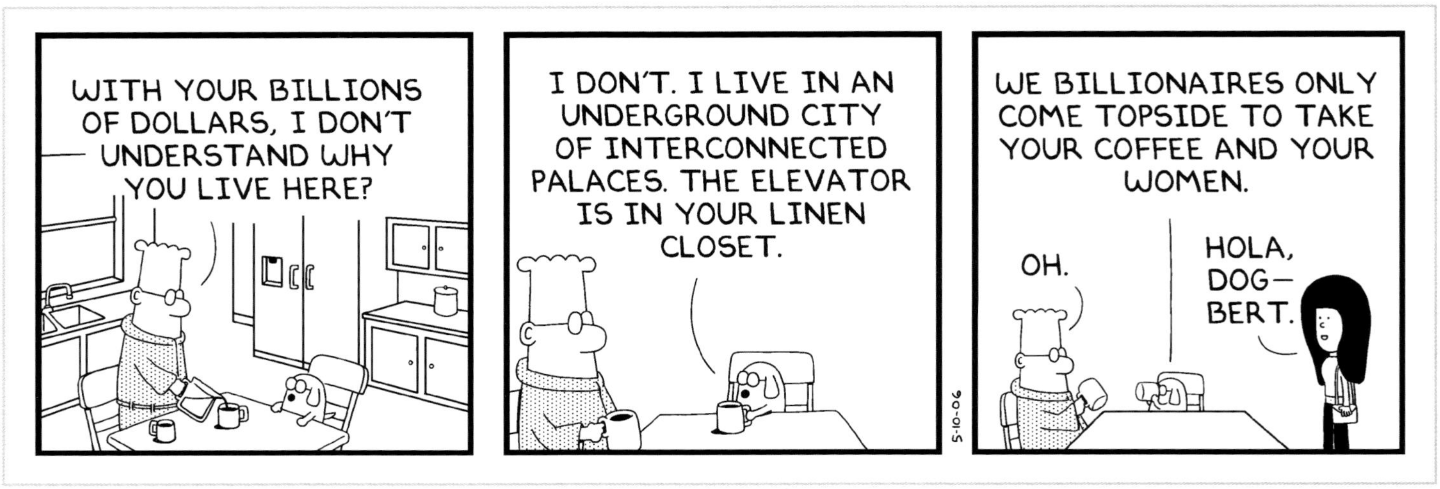
WITH YOUR BILLIONS OF DOLLARS, I DON'T UNDERSTAND WHY YOU LIVE HERE?
I DON'T. I LIVE IN AN UNDERGROUND CITY OF INTERCONNECTED PALACES. THE ELEVATOR IS IN YOUR LINEN CLOSET.
5-10-06
WE BILLIONAIRES ONLY COME TOPSIDE TO TAKE YOUR COFFEE AND YOUR WOMEN.
OH.
HOLA, DOG-BERT.

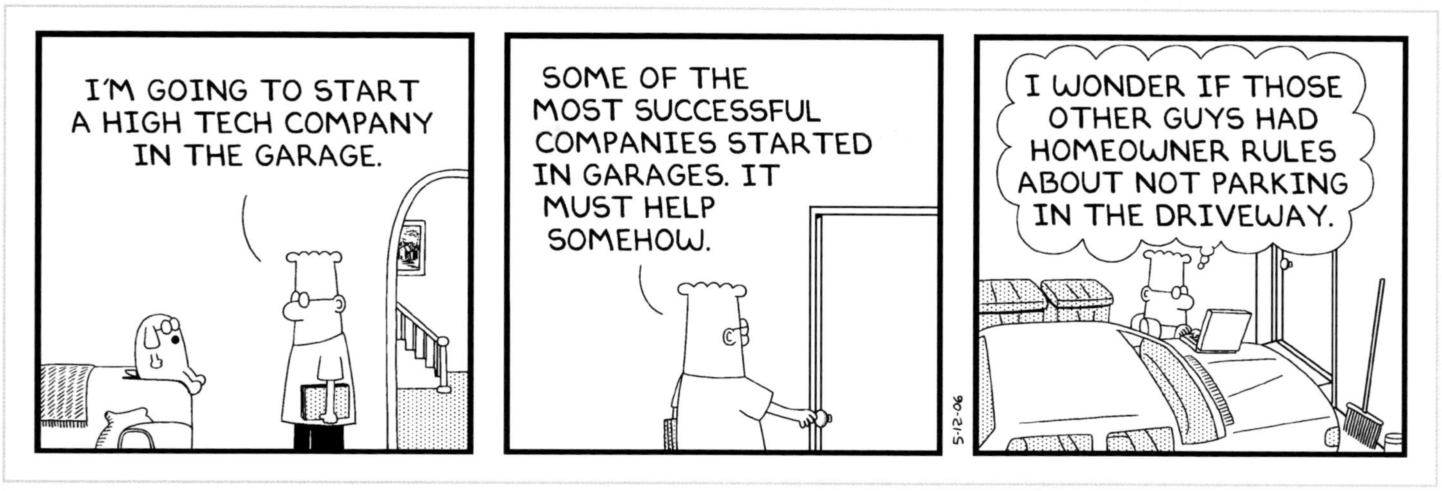
I'M GOING TO START A HIGH TECH COMPANY IN THE GARAGE.
SOME OF THE MOST SUCCESSFUL COMPANIES STARTED IN GARAGES. IT MUST HELP SOMEHOW.
5-12-06
I WONDER IF THOSE OTHER GUYS HAD HOMEOWNER RULES ABOUT NOT PARKING IN THE DRIVEWAY.

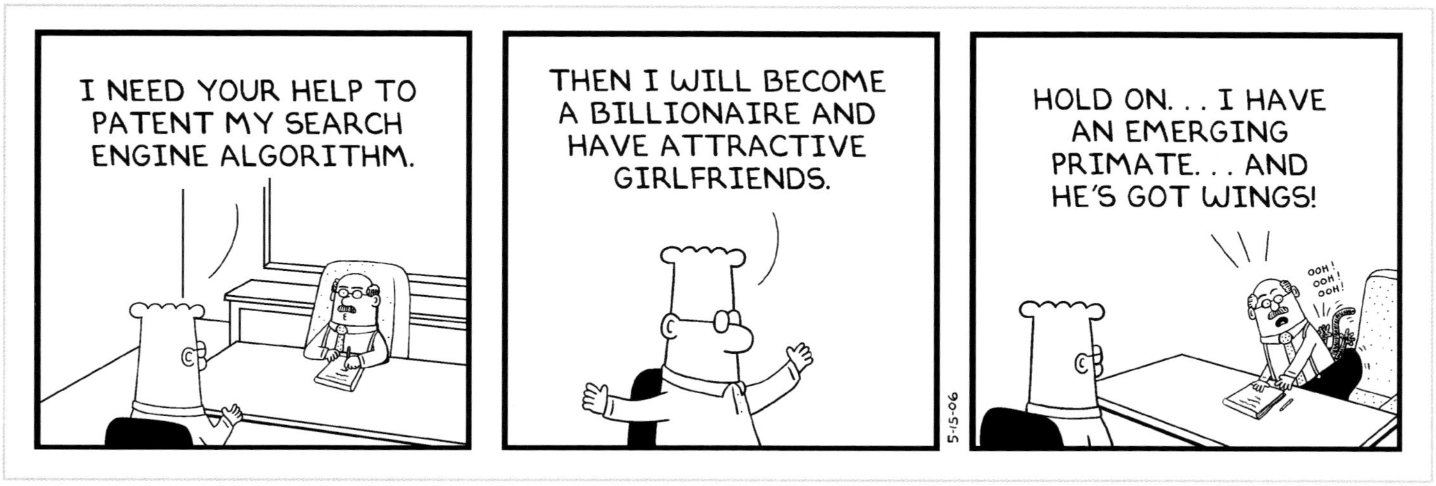
I NEED YOUR HELP TO PATENT MY SEARCH ENGINE ALGORITHM.
THEN I WILL BECOME A BILLIONAIRE AND HAVE ATTRACTIVE GIRLFRIENDS.
5-15-06
HOLD ON. . . I HAVE AN EMERGING PRIMATE. . . AND HE'S GOT WINGS!
OOH! OOH! OOH!

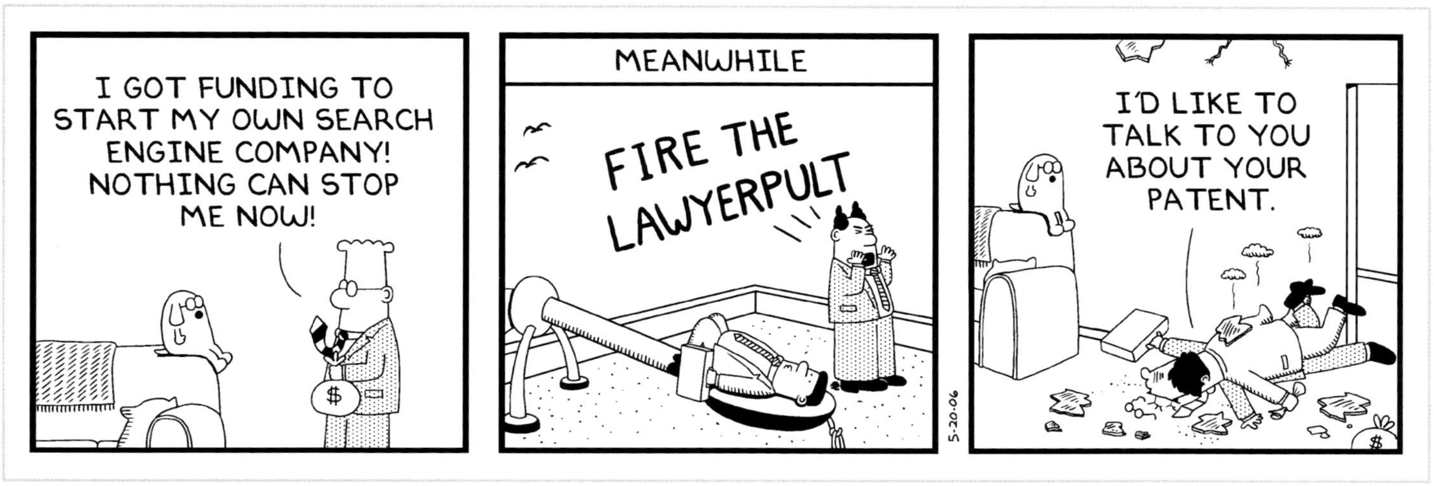
I GOT FUNDING TO START MY OWN SEARCH ENGINE COMPANY! NOTHING CAN STOP ME NOW!
MEANWHILE
FIRE THE LAWYERPULT
5-20-06
I'D LIKE TO TALK TO YOU ABOUT YOUR PATENT.

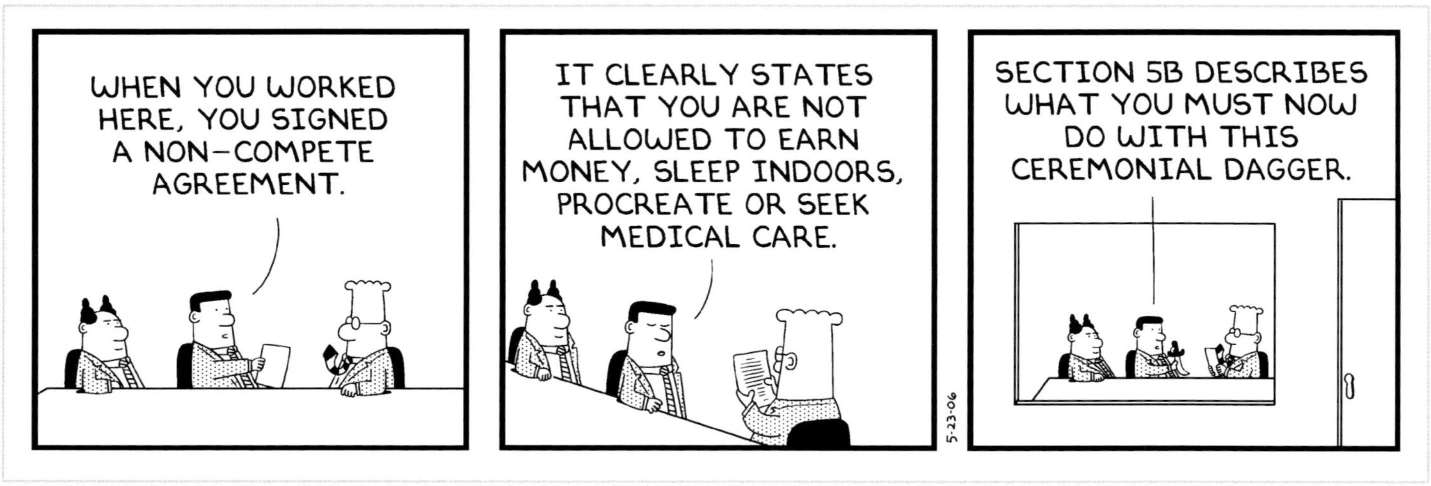
WHEN YOU WORKED HERE, YOU SIGNED A NON-COMPETE AGREEMENT.
IT CLEARLY STATES THAT YOU ARE NOT ALLOWED TO EARN MONEY, SLEEP INDOORS, PROCREATE OR SEEK MEDICAL CARE.
5-23-06
SECTION 5B DESCRIBES WHAT YOU MUST NOW DO WITH THIS CEREMONIAL DAGGER.

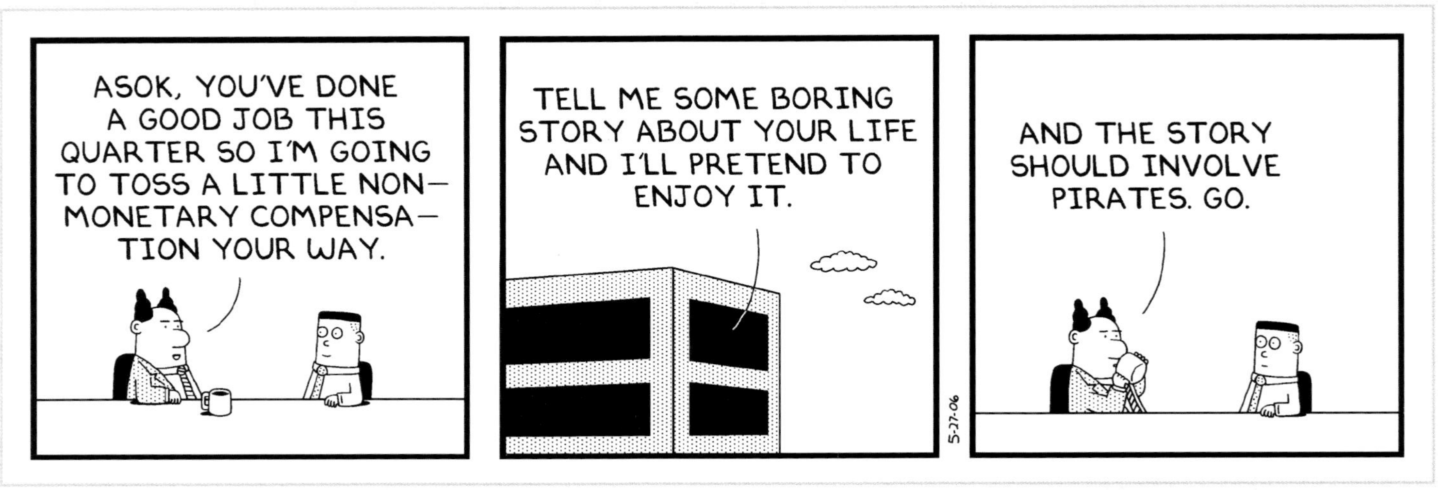
ASOK, YOU'VE DONE A GOOD JOB THIS QUARTER SO I'M GOING TO TOSS A LITTLE NON-MONETARY COMPENSATION YOUR WAY.
TELL ME SOME BORING STORY ABOUT YOUR LIFE AND I'LL PRETEND TO ENJOY IT.
5-27-06
AND THE STORY SHOULD INVOLVE PIRATES. GO.

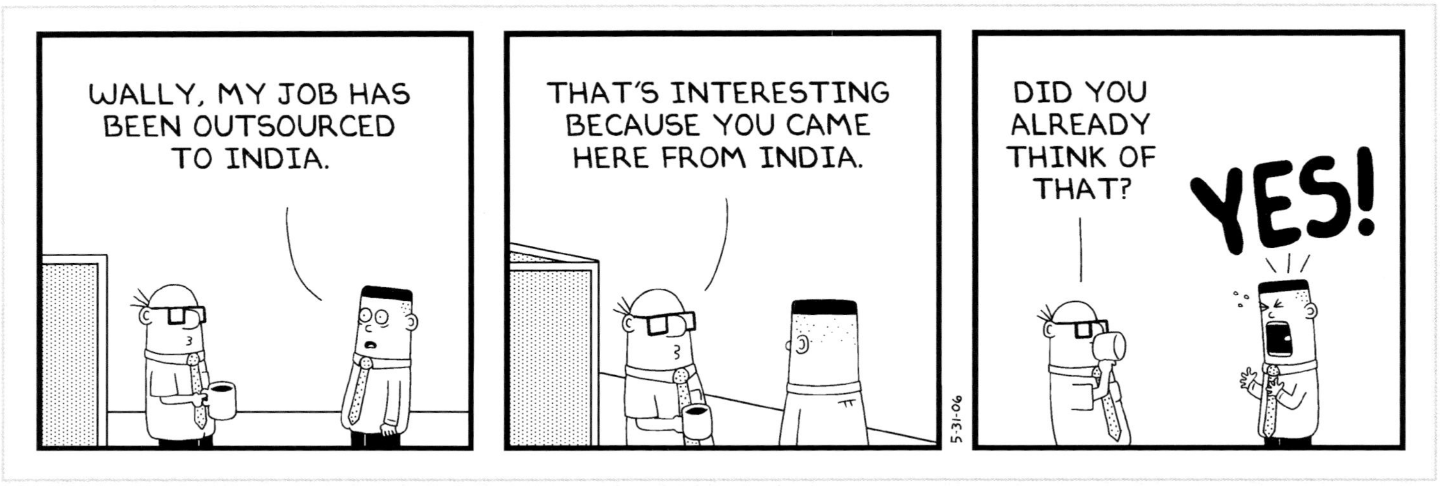
WALLY, MY JOB HAS BEEN OUTSOURCED TO INDIA.
THAT'S INTERESTING BECAUSE YOU CAME HERE FROM INDIA.
5-31-06
DID YOU ALREADY THINK OF THAT?
YES!

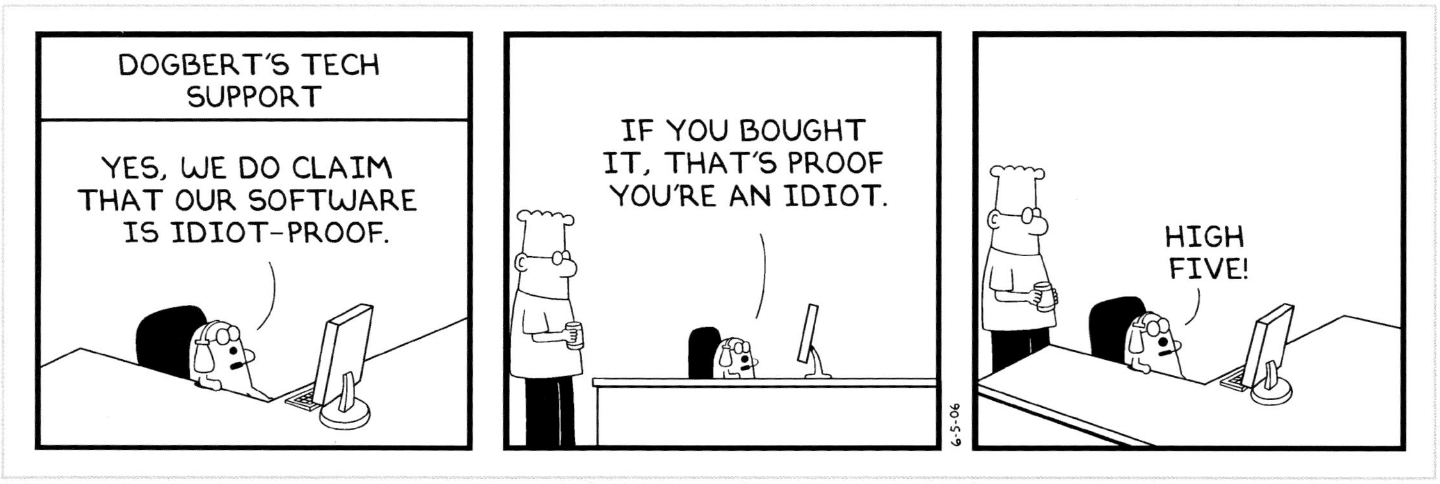
DOGBERT'S TECH SUPPORT
YES, WE DO CLAIM THAT OUR SOFTWARE IS IDIOT-PROOF.
IF YOU BOUGHT IT, THAT'S PROOF YOU'RE AN IDIOT.
6-5-06
HIGH FIVE!

Citizens of Aruba were outraged by this comic, believing I implied their lovely country was covered in fecal matter. That wasn't my intent. There just aren't that many things you can put behind "fecal" so it sounds like an island.

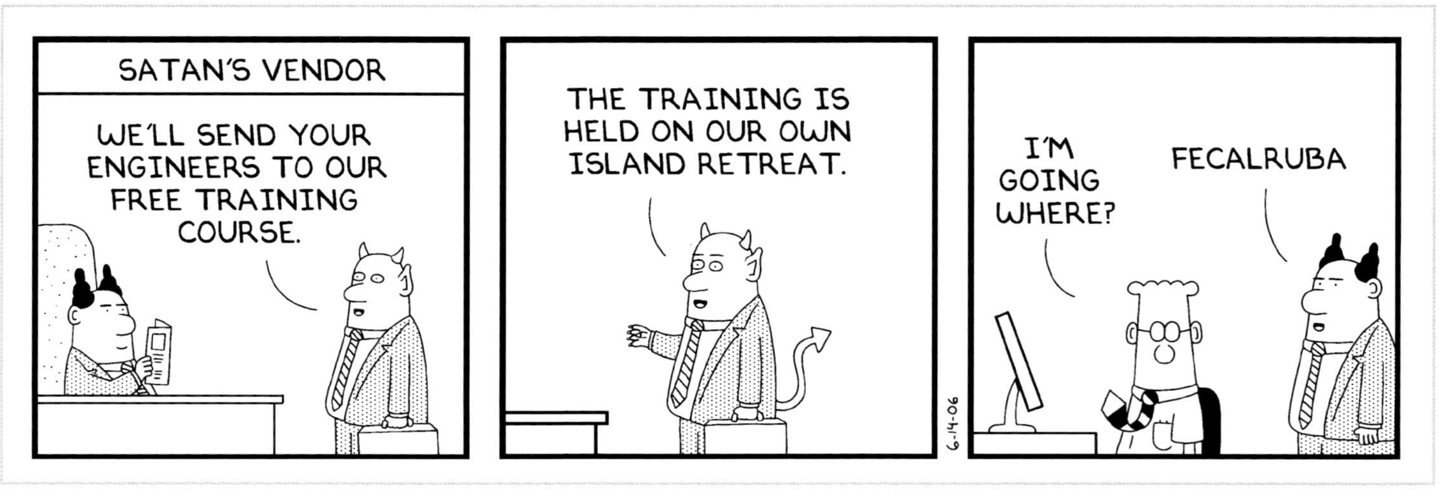
SATAN'S VENDOR
WE'LL SEND YOUR ENGINEERS TO OUR FREE TRAINING COURSE.
THE TRAINING IS HELD ON OUR OWN ISLAND RETREAT.
6-14-06
I'M GOING WHERE?
FECALRUBA

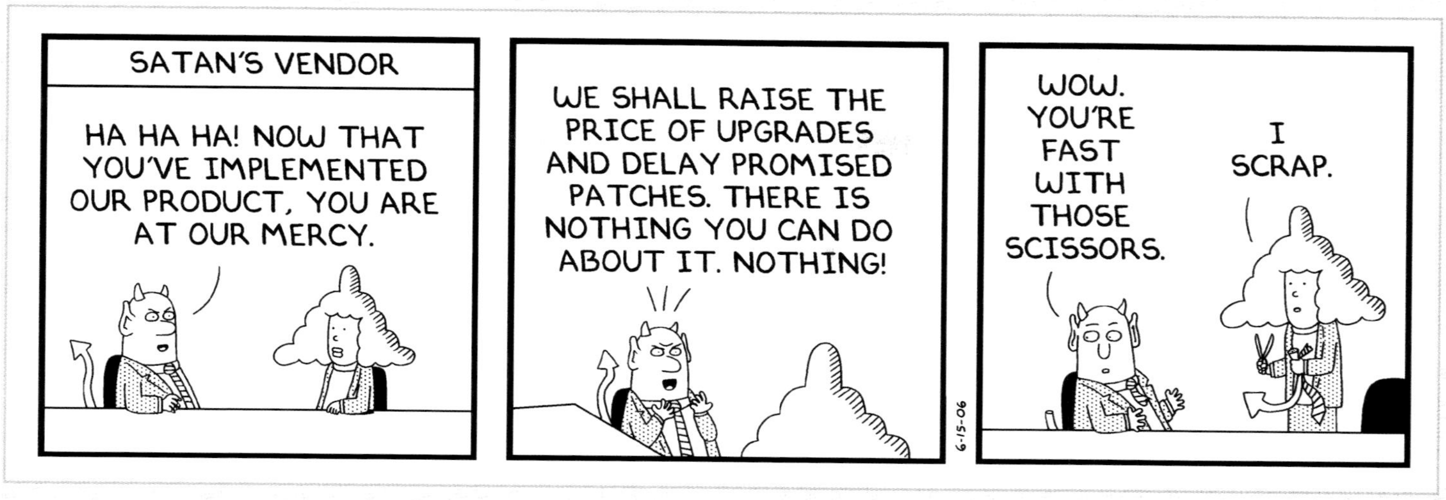
SATAN'S VENDOR
HA HA HA! NOW THAT YOU'VE IMPLEMENTED OUR PRODUCT, YOU ARE AT OUR MERCY.
WE SHALL RAISE THE PRICE OF UPGRADES AND DELAY PROMISED PATCHES. THERE IS NOTHING YOU CAN DO ABOUT IT. NOTHING!
6-15-06
WOW. YOU'RE FAST WITH THOSE SCISSORS.
I SCRAP.

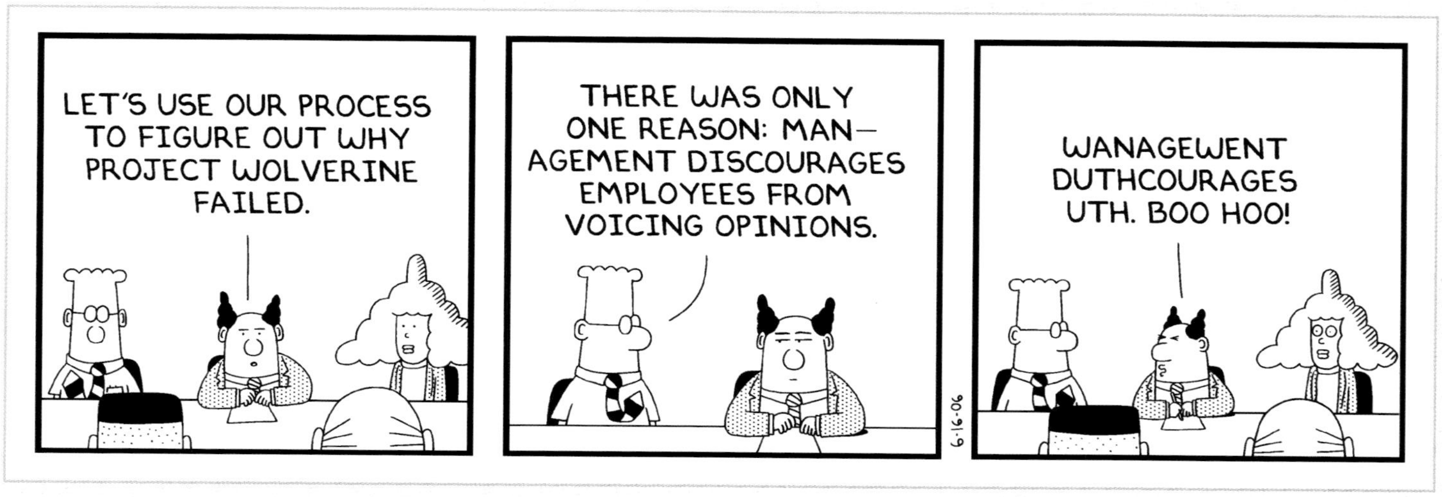
LET'S USE OUR PROCESS TO FIGURE OUT WHY PROJECT WOLVERINE FAILED.
THERE WAS ONLY ONE REASON: MAN—AGEMENT DISCOURAGES EMPLOYEES FROM VOICING OPINIONS.
6-16-06
WANAGEWENT DUTHCOURAGES UTH. BOO HOO!

The strip below was published in newspapers. The original showed Asok naked from the back. For some reason, that was going too far.

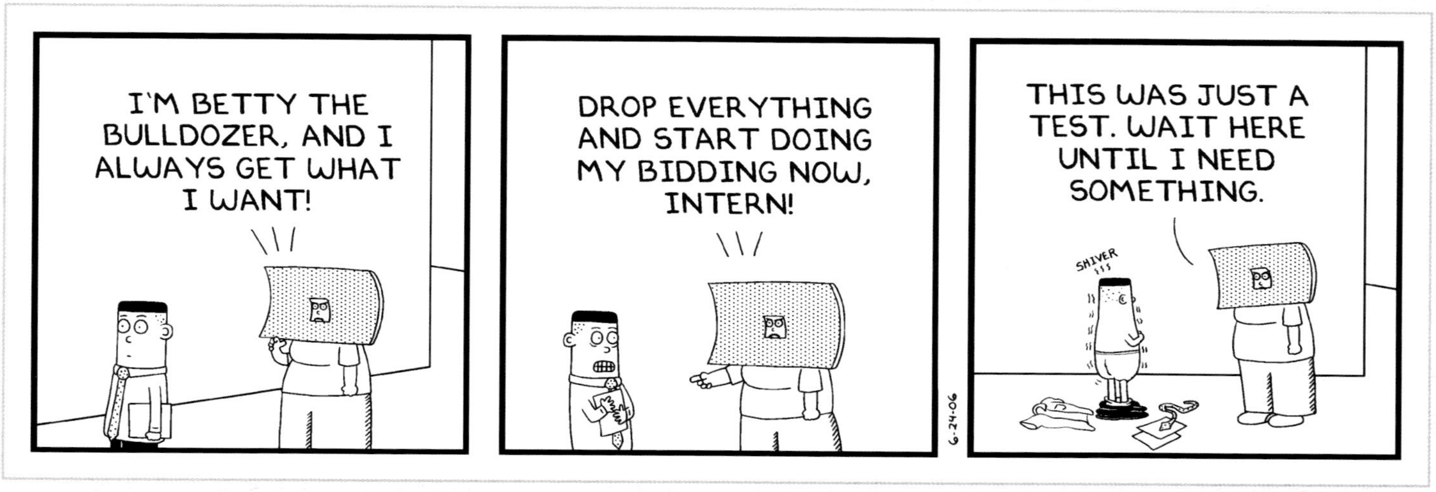
I'M BETTY THE BULLDOZER, AND I ALWAYS GET WHAT I WANT!
DROP EVERYTHING AND START DOING MY BIDDING NOW, INTERN!
6-24-06
THIS WAS JUST A TEST. WAIT HERE UNTIL I NEED SOMETHING.
SHIVER

There's a basic rule of cartooning that the funnier the comic, the more you can get away with. The following strip wasn't funny enough to let me get away with a naked intern's buttocks.

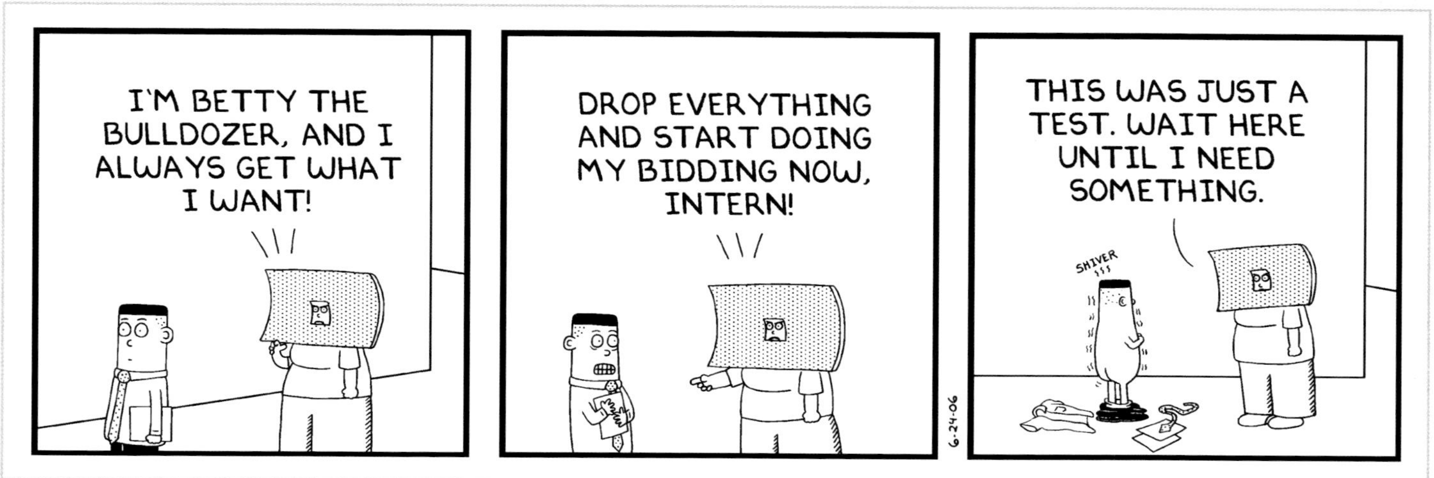
I'M BETTY THE BULLDOZER, AND I ALWAYS GET WHAT I WANT!
DROP EVERYTHING AND START DOING MY BIDDING NOW, INTERN!
6-24-06
THIS WAS JUST A TEST. WAIT HERE UNTIL I NEED SOMETHING.
SHIVER

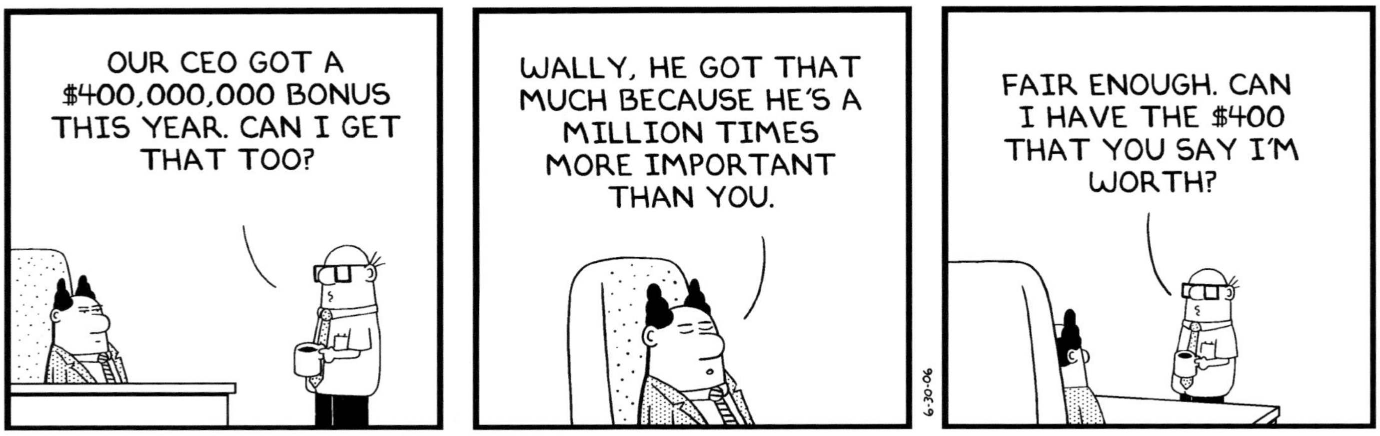
OUR CEO GOT A $400,000,000 BONUS THIS YEAR. CAN I GET THAT TOO?
WALLY, HE GOT THAT MUCH BECAUSE HE'S A MILLION TIMES MORE IMPORTANT THAN YOU.
6-30-06
FAIR ENOUGH. CAN I HAVE THE $400 THAT YOU SAY I'M WORTH?

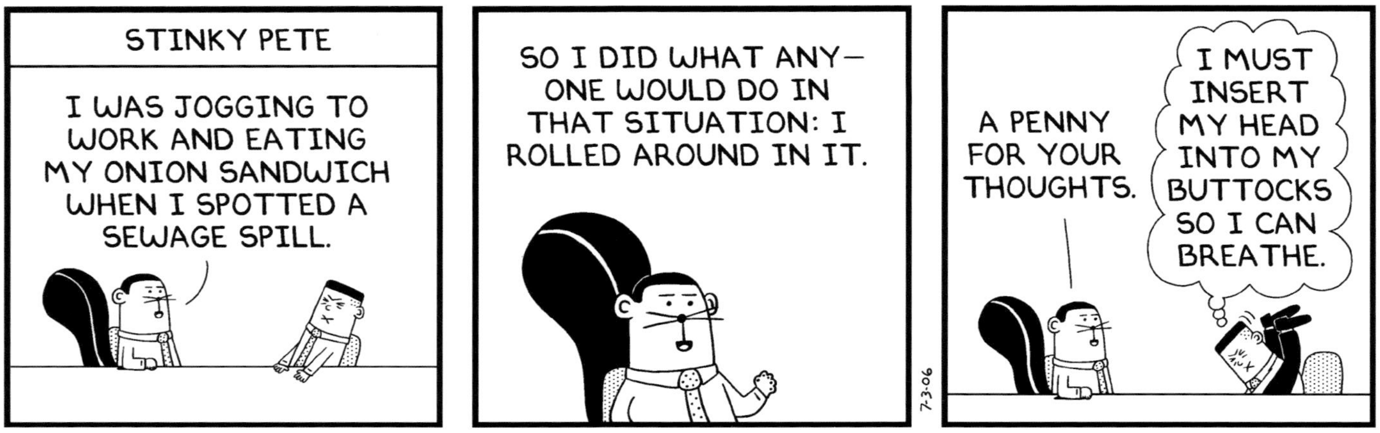
STINKY PETE
I WAS JOGGING TO WORK AND EATING MY ONION SANDWICH WHEN I SPOTTED A SEWAGE SPILL.
SO I DID WHAT ANY–ONE WOULD DO IN THAT SITUATION: I ROLLED AROUND IN IT.
7-3-06
A PENNY FOR YOUR THOUGHTS.
I MUST INSERT MY HEAD INTO MY BUTTOCKS SO I CAN BREATHE.

While I couldn't show a picture of Asok's buttocks, I could show him in the process of sticking his head into them.

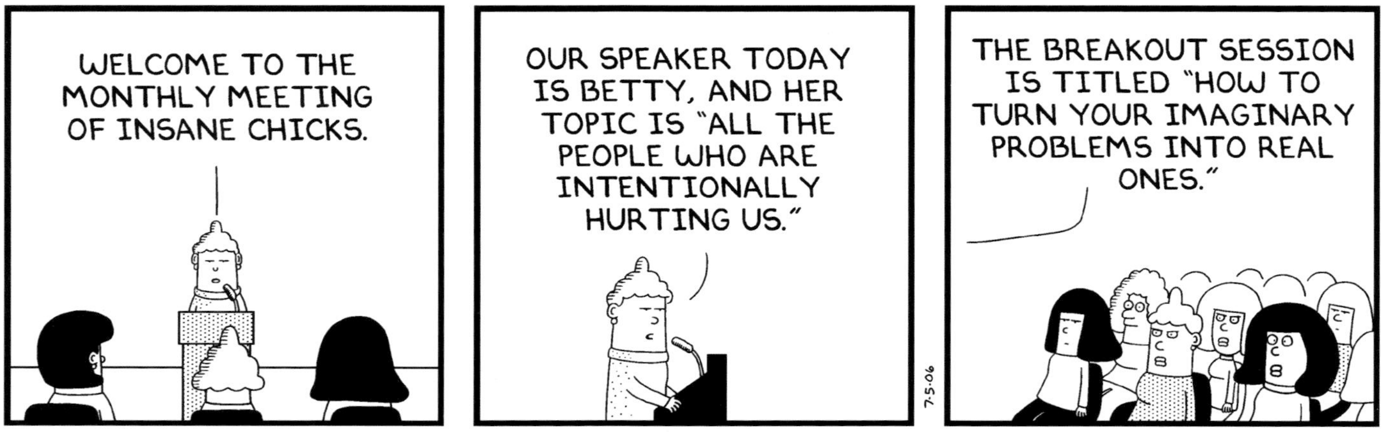
WELCOME TO THE MONTHLY MEETING OF INSANE CHICKS.
OUR SPEAKER TODAY IS BETTY, AND HER TOPIC IS "ALL THE PEOPLE WHO ARE INTENTIONALLY HURTING US."
7-5-06
THE BREAKOUT SESSION IS TITLED "HOW TO TURN YOUR IMAGINARY PROBLEMS INTO REAL ONES."

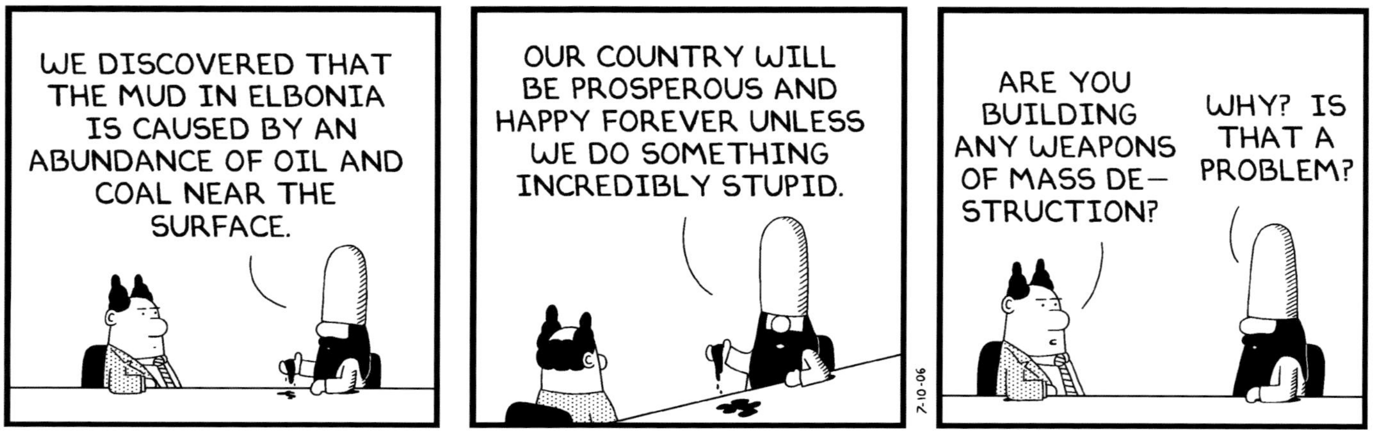
WE DISCOVERED THAT THE MUD IN ELBONIA IS CAUSED BY AN ABUNDANCE OF OIL AND COAL NEAR THE SURFACE.
OUR COUNTRY WILL BE PROSPEROUS AND HAPPY FOREVER UNLESS WE DO SOMETHING INCREDIBLY STUPID.
7-10-06
ARE YOU BUILDING ANY WEAPONS OF MASS DE–STRUCTION?
WHY? IS THAT A PROBLEM?

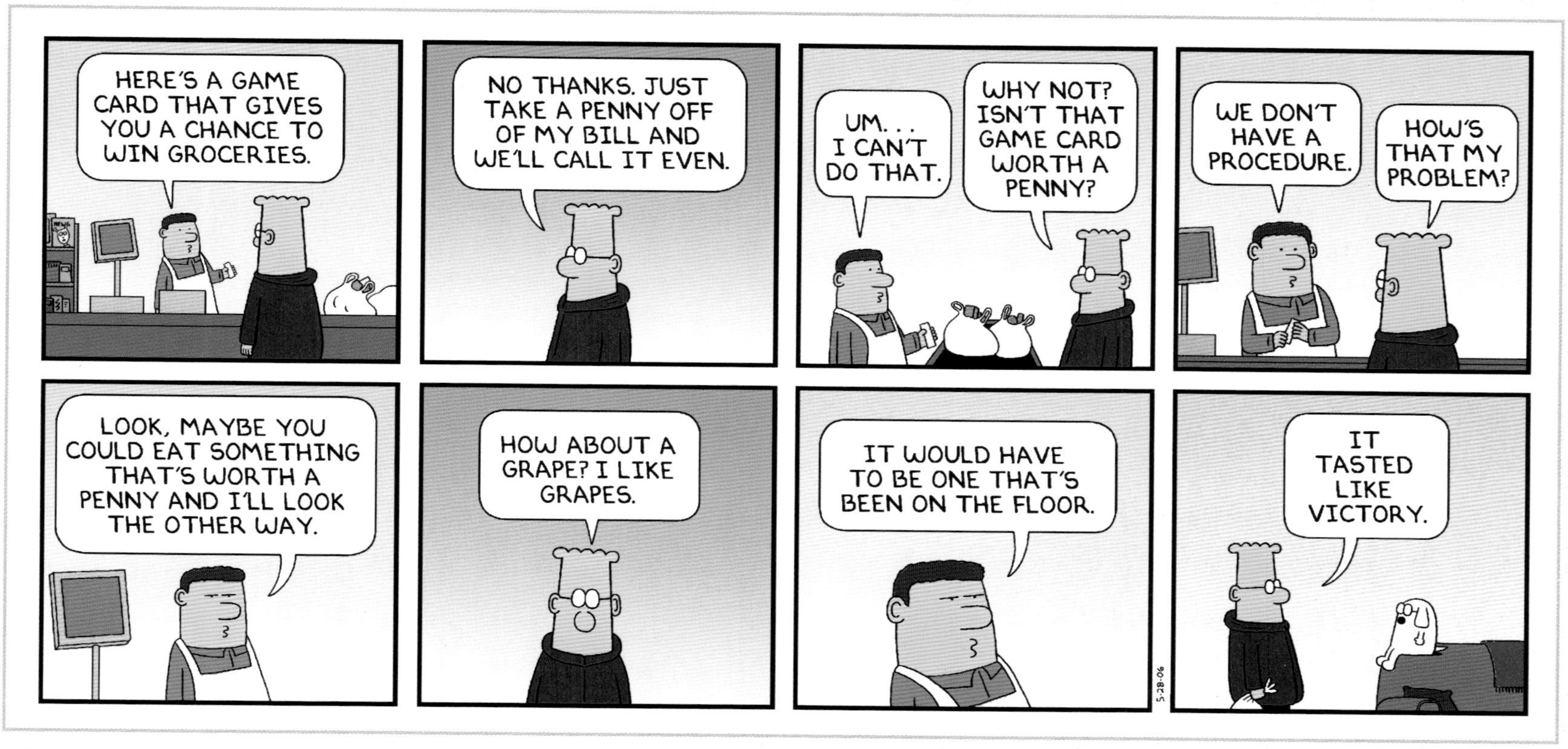
HERE'S A GAME CARD THAT GIVES YOU A CHANCE TO WIN GROCERIES.
NO THANKS. JUST TAKE A PENNY OFF OF MY BILL AND WE'LL CALL IT EVEN.
UM. . . I CAN'T DO THAT.
WHY NOT? ISN'T THAT GAME CARD WORTH A PENNY?
WE DON'T HAVE A PROCEDURE.
HOW'S THAT MY PROBLEM?
LOOK, MAYBE YOU COULD EAT SOMETHING THAT'S WORTH A PENNY AND I'LL LOOK THE OTHER WAY.
HOW ABOUT A GRAPE? I LIKE GRAPES.
IT WOULD HAVE TO BE ONE THAT'S BEEN ON THE FLOOR.
5-28-06
IT TASTED LIKE VICTORY.

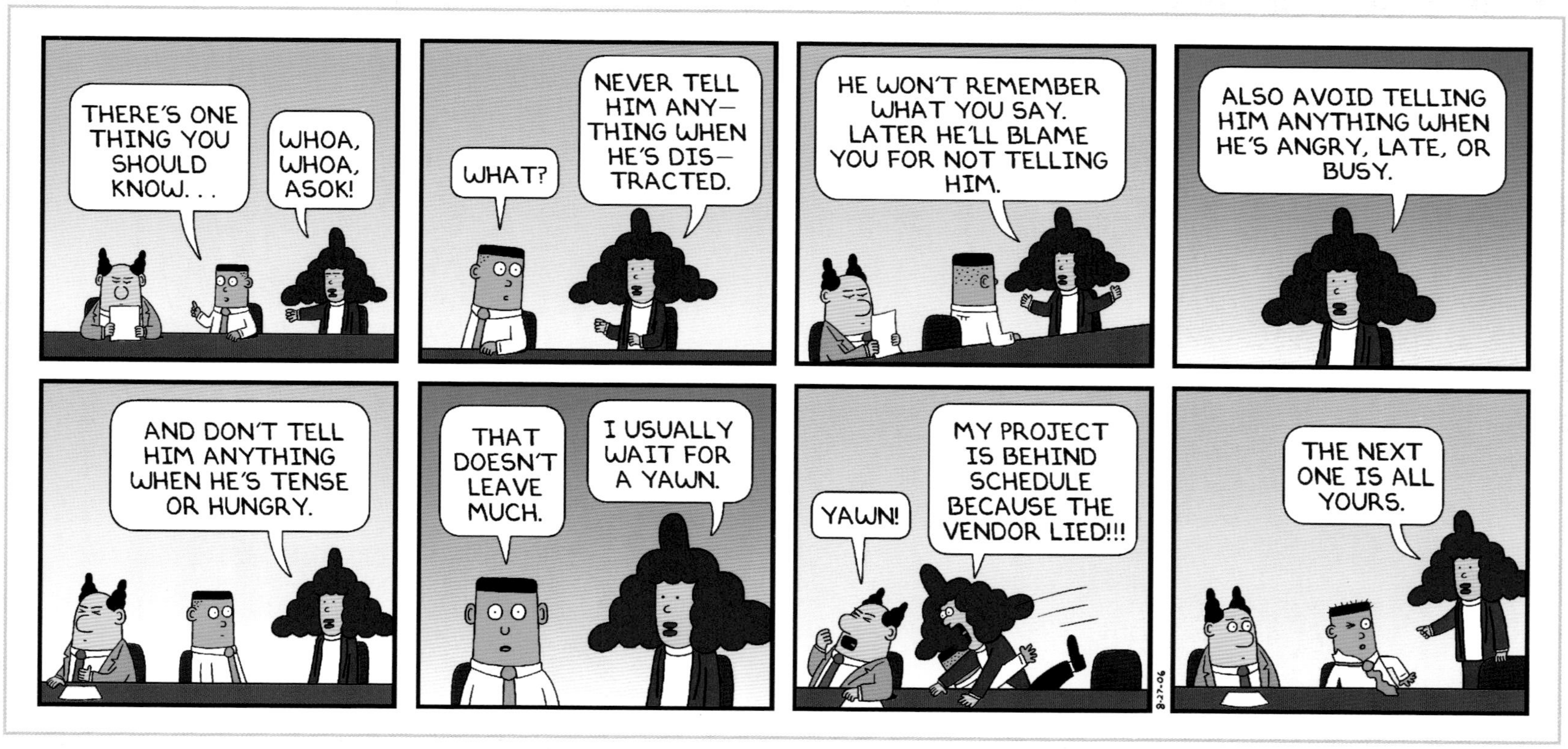
THERE'S ONE THING YOU SHOULD KNOW. . .
WHOA, WHOA, ASOK!
WHAT?
NEVER TELL HIM ANY-THING WHEN HE'S DIS-TRACTED.
HE WON'T REMEMBER WHAT YOU SAY. LATER HE'LL BLAME YOU FOR NOT TELLING HIM.
ALSO AVOID TELLING HIM ANYTHING WHEN HE'S ANGRY, LATE, OR BUSY.
AND DON'T TELL HIM ANYTHING WHEN HE'S TENSE OR HUNGRY.
THAT DOESN'T LEAVE MUCH.
I USUALLY WAIT FOR A YAWN.
YAWN!
MY PROJECT IS BEHIND SCHEDULE BECAUSE THE VENDOR LIED!!!
8-27-06
THE NEXT ONE IS ALL YOURS.

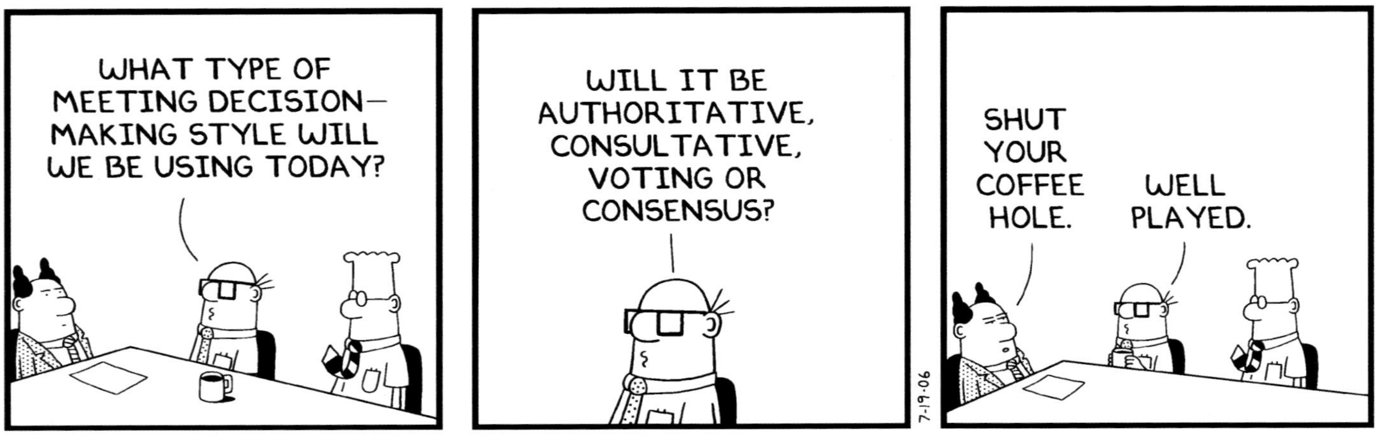
WHAT TYPE OF MEETING DECISION-MAKING STYLE WILL WE BE USING TODAY?
WILL IT BE AUTHORITATIVE, CONSULTATIVE, VOTING OR CONSENSUS?
SHUT YOUR COFFEE HOLE.
WELL PLAYED.
7-19-06

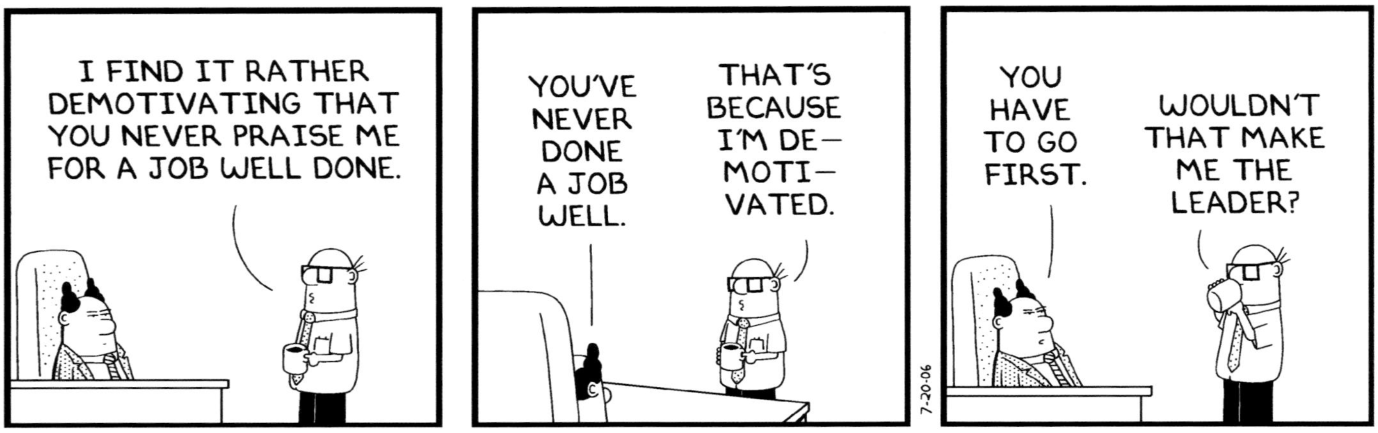
I FIND IT RATHER DEMOTIVATING THAT YOU NEVER PRAISE ME FOR A JOB WELL DONE.
YOU'VE NEVER DONE A JOB WELL.
THAT'S BECAUSE I'M DE-MOTI-VATED.
YOU HAVE TO GO FIRST.
WOULDN'T THAT MAKE ME THE LEADER?
7-20-06

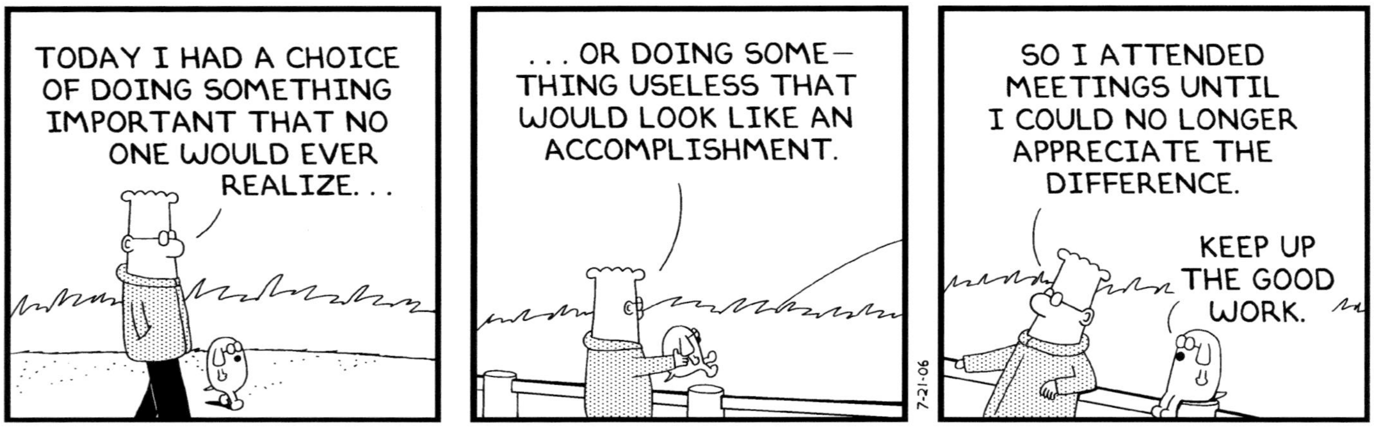
TODAY I HAD A CHOICE OF DOING SOMETHING IMPORTANT THAT NO ONE WOULD EVER REALIZE. . .
. . . OR DOING SOME-THING USELESS THAT WOULD LOOK LIKE AN ACCOMPLISHMENT.
SO I ATTENDED MEETINGS UNTIL I COULD NO LONGER APPRECIATE THE DIFFERENCE.
KEEP UP THE GOOD WORK.
7-21-06

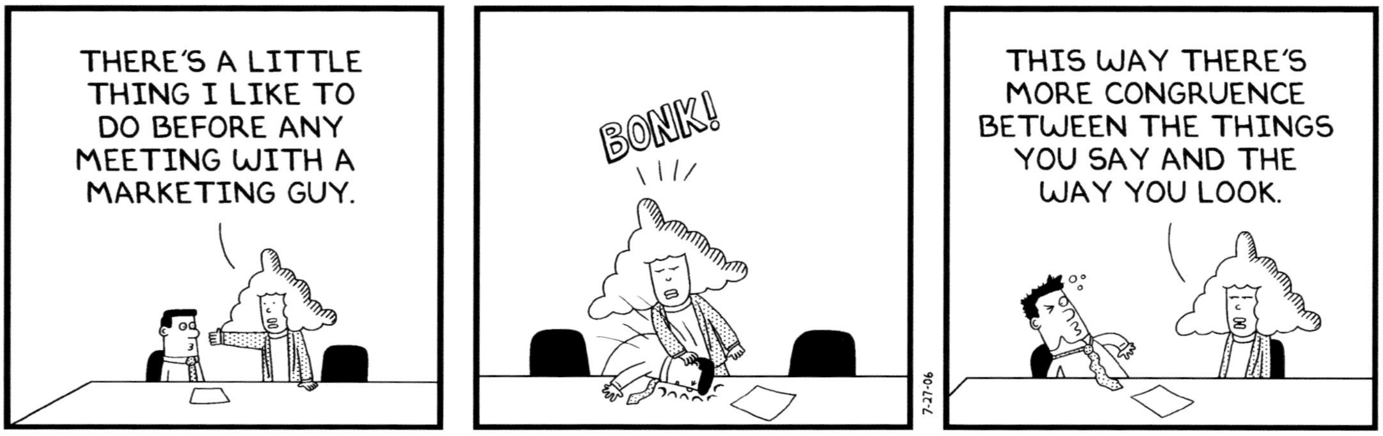
THERE'S A LITTLE THING I LIKE TO DO BEFORE ANY MEETING WITH A MARKETING GUY.
BONK!
THIS WAY THERE'S MORE CONGRUENCE BETWEEN THE THINGS YOU SAY AND THE WAY YOU LOOK.
7-27-06

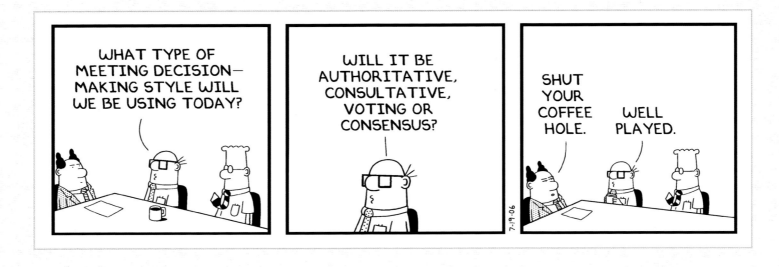

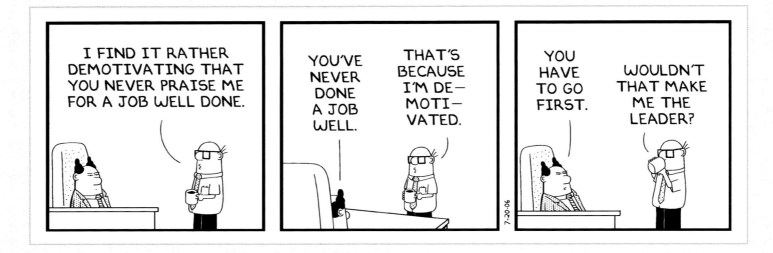

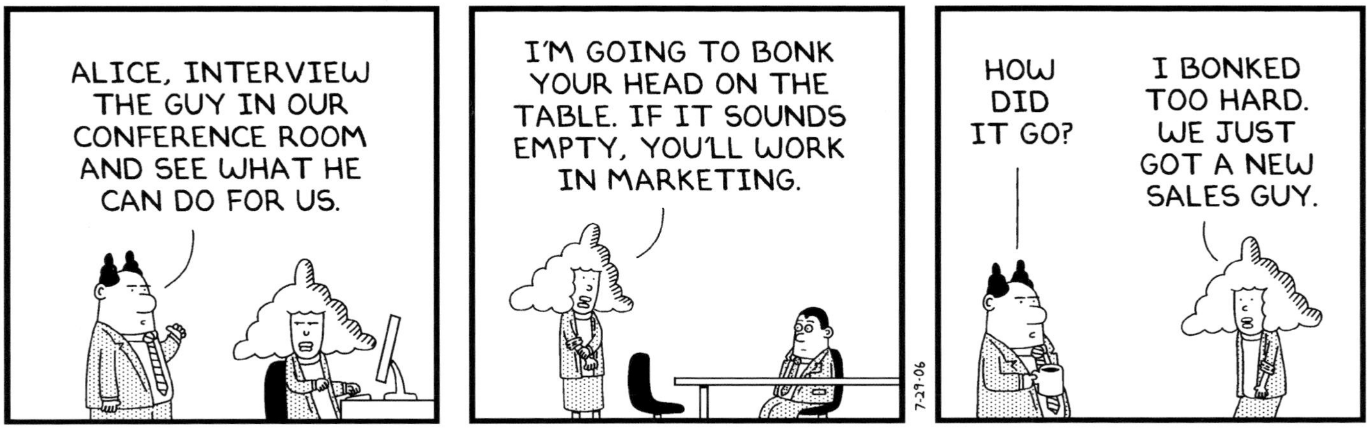
ALICE, INTERVIEW THE GUY IN OUR CONFERENCE ROOM AND SEE WHAT HE CAN DO FOR US.
I'M GOING TO BONK YOUR HEAD ON THE TABLE. IF IT SOUNDS EMPTY, YOU'LL WORK IN MARKETING.
7-29-06
HOW DID IT GO?
I BONKED TOO HARD. WE JUST GOT A NEW SALES GUY.

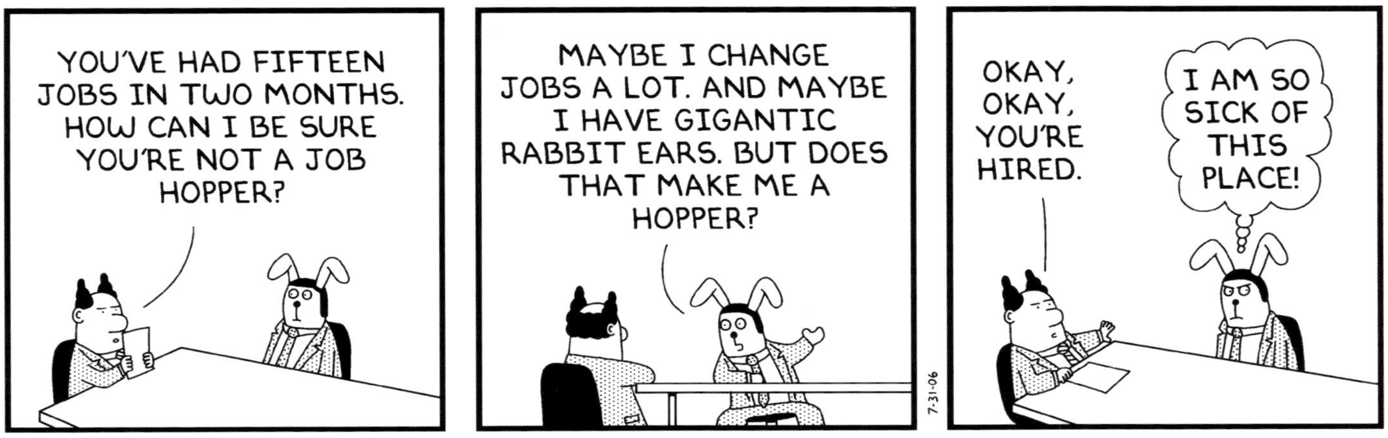
YOU'VE HAD FIFTEEN JOBS IN TWO MONTHS. HOW CAN I BE SURE YOU'RE NOT A JOB HOPPER?
MAYBE I CHANGE JOBS A LOT. AND MAYBE I HAVE GIGANTIC RABBIT EARS. BUT DOES THAT MAKE ME A HOPPER?
7-31-06
OKAY, OKAY, YOU'RE HIRED.
I AM SO SICK OF THIS PLACE!

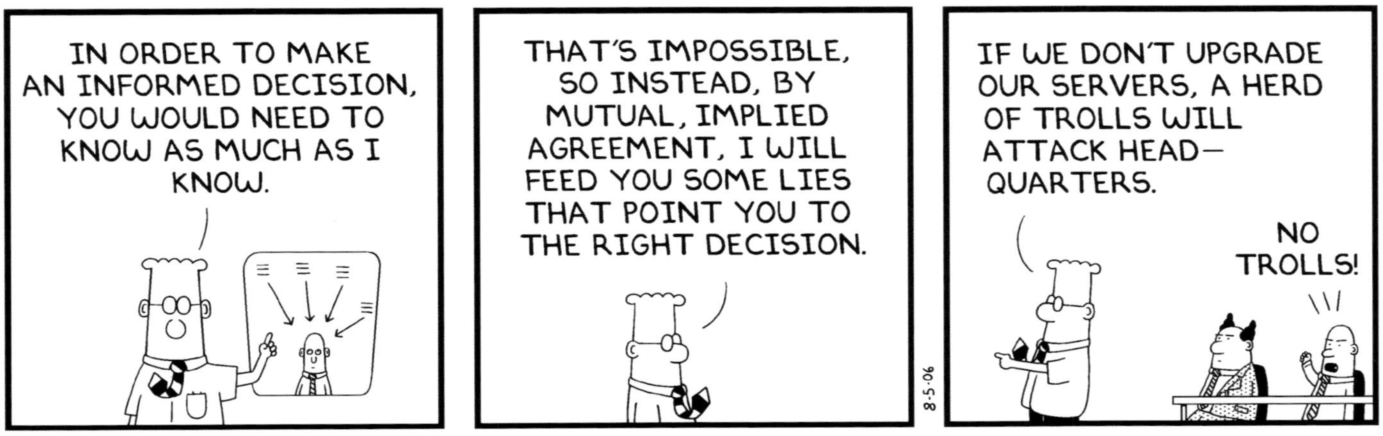
IN ORDER TO MAKE AN INFORMED DECISION, YOU WOULD NEED TO KNOW AS MUCH AS I KNOW.
THAT'S IMPOSSIBLE, SO INSTEAD, BY MUTUAL, IMPLIED AGREEMENT, I WILL FEED YOU SOME LIES THAT POINT YOU TO THE RIGHT DECISION.
8-5-06
IF WE DON'T UPGRADE OUR SERVERS, A HERD OF TROLLS WILL ATTACK HEAD-QUARTERS.
NO TROLLS!

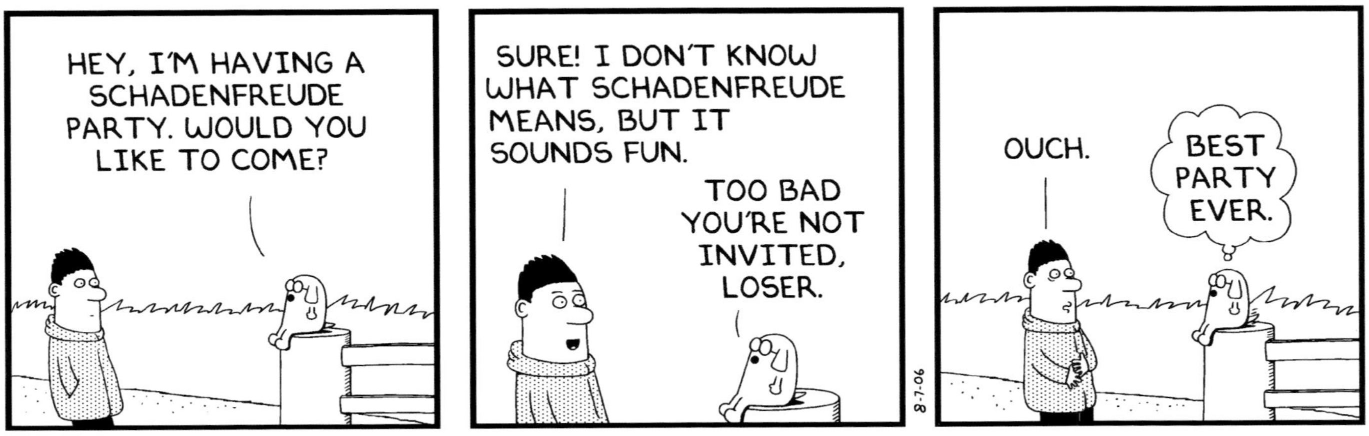
HEY, I'M HAVING A SCHADENFREUDE PARTY. WOULD YOU LIKE TO COME?
SURE! I DON'T KNOW WHAT SCHADENFREUDE MEANS, BUT IT SOUNDS FUN.
TOO BAD YOU'RE NOT INVITED, LOSER.
8-7-06
OUCH.
BEST PARTY EVER.

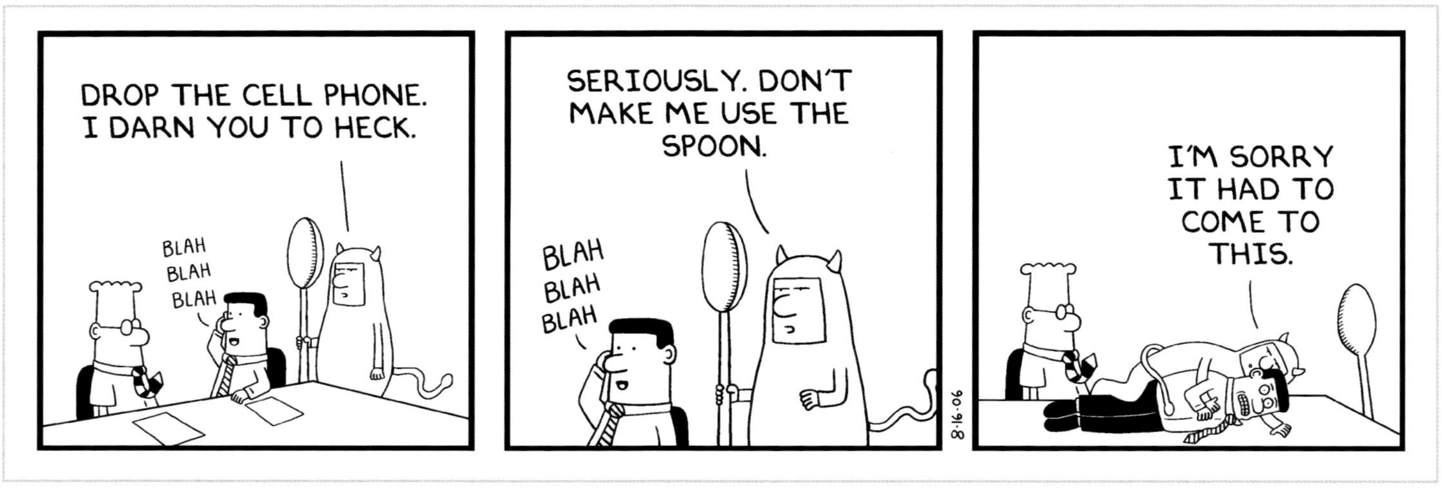
DROP THE CELL PHONE. I DARN YOU TO HECK.
BLAH BLAH BLAH
SERIOUSLY. DON'T MAKE ME USE THE SPOON.
BLAH BLAH BLAH
8-16-06
I'M SORRY IT HAD TO COME TO THIS.

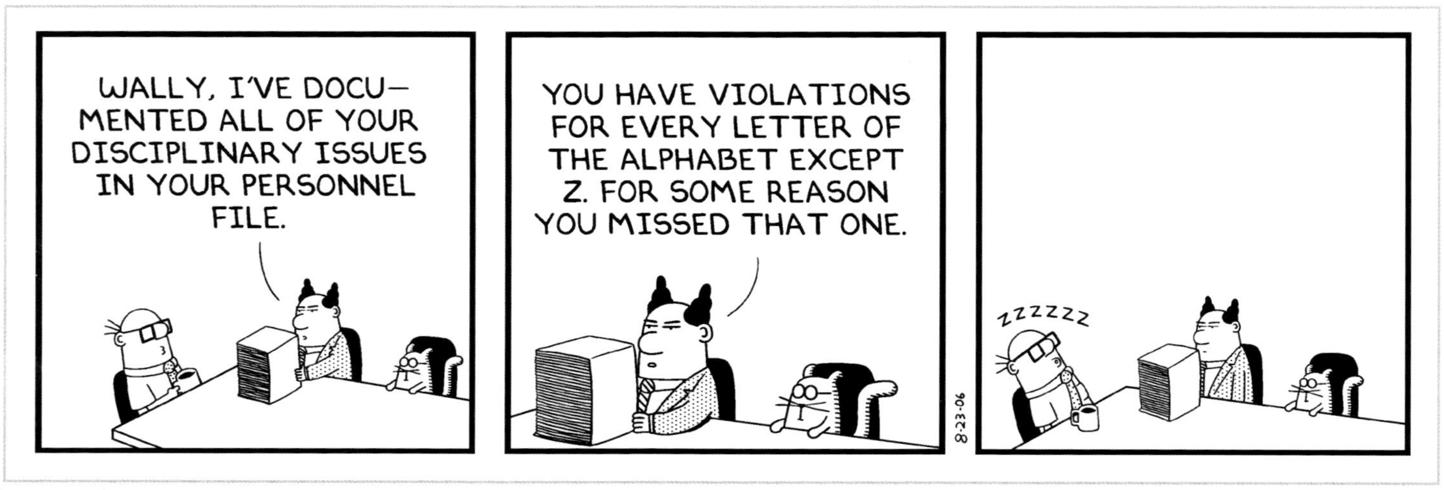
WALLY, I'VE DOCU-MENTED ALL OF YOUR DISCIPLINARY ISSUES IN YOUR PERSONNEL FILE.
YOU HAVE VIOLATIONS FOR EVERY LETTER OF THE ALPHABET EXCEPT Z. FOR SOME REASON YOU MISSED THAT ONE.
8-23-06
ZZZZZZ

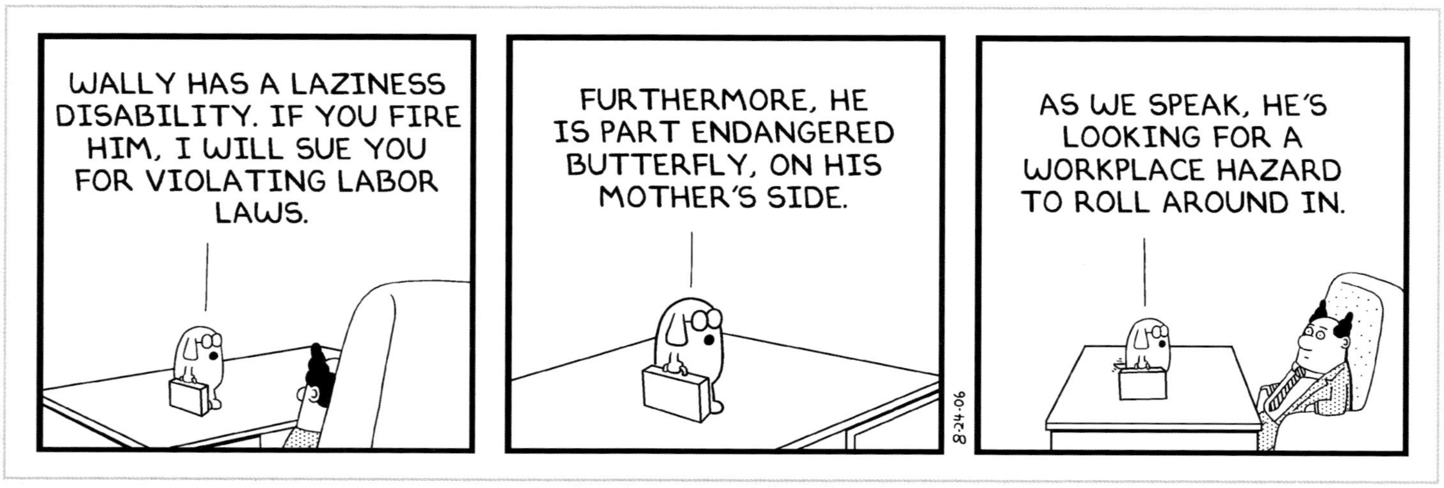
WALLY HAS A LAZINESS DISABILITY. IF YOU FIRE HIM, I WILL SUE YOU FOR VIOLATING LABOR LAWS.
FURTHERMORE, HE IS PART ENDANGERED BUTTERFLY, ON HIS MOTHER'S SIDE.
8-24-06
AS WE SPEAK, HE'S LOOKING FOR A WORKPLACE HAZARD TO ROLL AROUND IN.

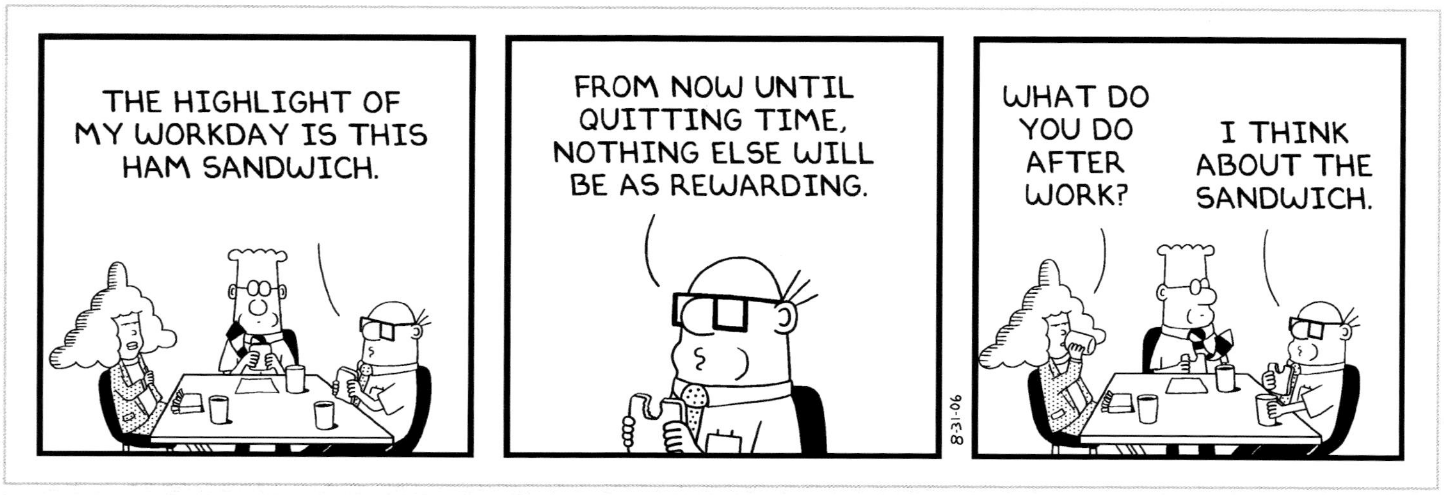
THE HIGHLIGHT OF MY WORKDAY IS THIS HAM SANDWICH.
FROM NOW UNTIL QUITTING TIME, NOTHING ELSE WILL BE AS REWARDING.
8-31-06
WHAT DO YOU DO AFTER WORK?
I THINK ABOUT THE SANDWICH.

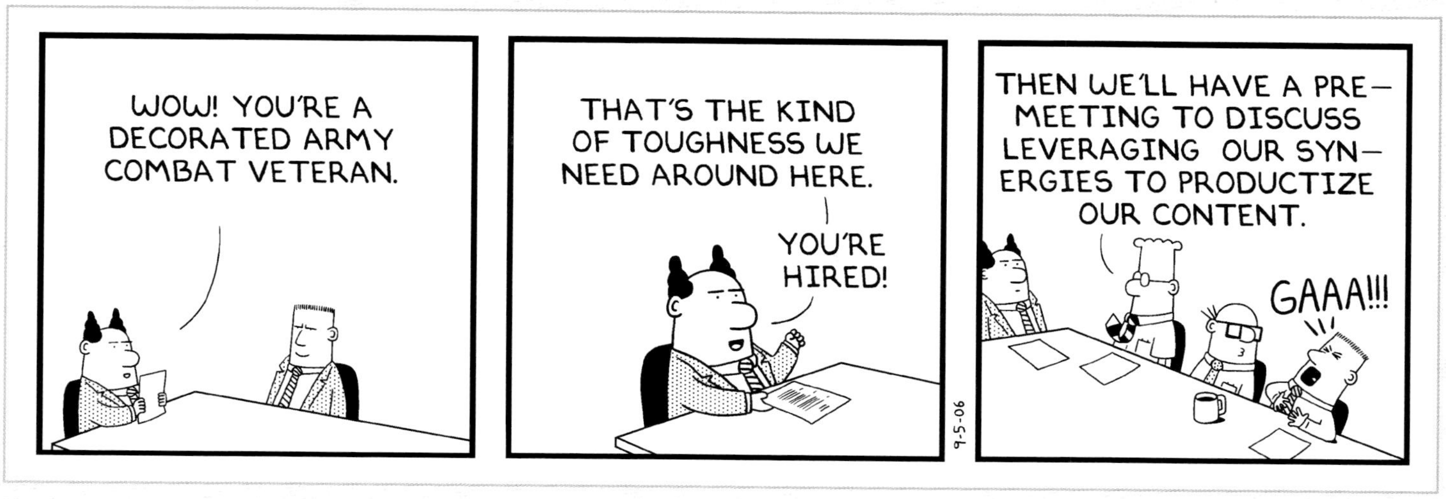
WOW! YOU'RE A DECORATED ARMY COMBAT VETERAN.
THAT'S THE KIND OF TOUGHNESS WE NEED AROUND HERE.
YOU'RE HIRED!
THEN WE'LL HAVE A PRE-MEETING TO DISCUSS LEVERAGING OUR SYNERGIES TO PRODUCTIZE OUR CONTENT.
GAAA!!!
9-5-06

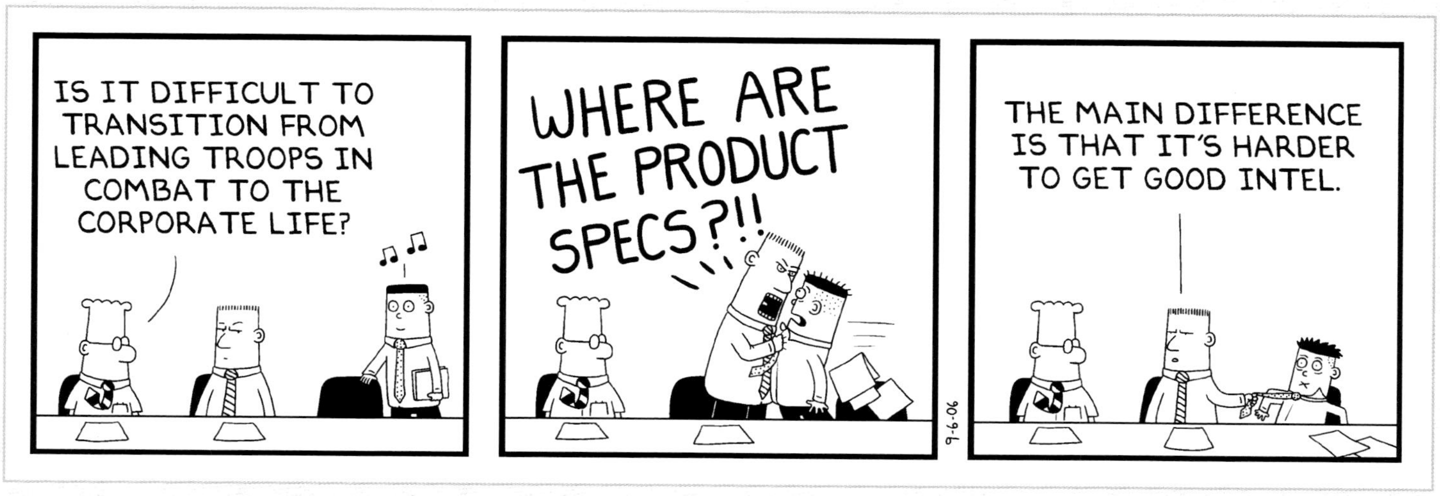
IS IT DIFFICULT TO TRANSITION FROM LEADING TROOPS IN COMBAT TO THE CORPORATE LIFE?
WHERE ARE THE PRODUCT SPECS?!!
THE MAIN DIFFERENCE IS THAT IT'S HARDER TO GET GOOD INTEL.
9-6-06

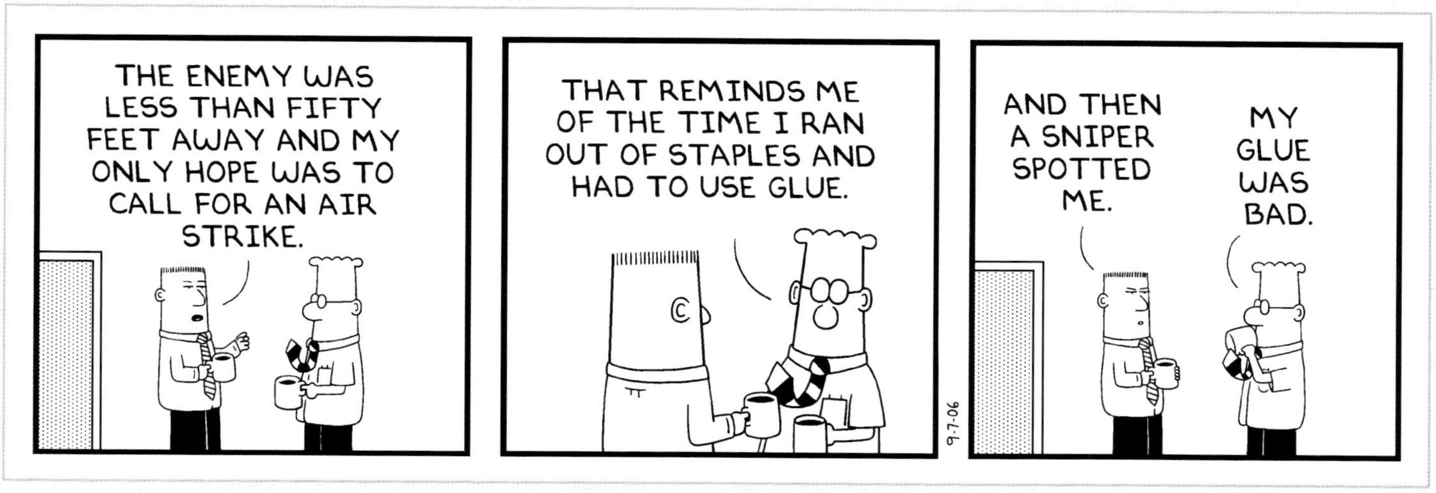
THE ENEMY WAS LESS THAN FIFTY FEET AWAY AND MY ONLY HOPE WAS TO CALL FOR AN AIR STRIKE.
THAT REMINDS ME OF THE TIME I RAN OUT OF STAPLES AND HAD TO USE GLUE.
AND THEN A SNIPER SPOTTED ME.
MY GLUE WAS BAD.
9-7-06

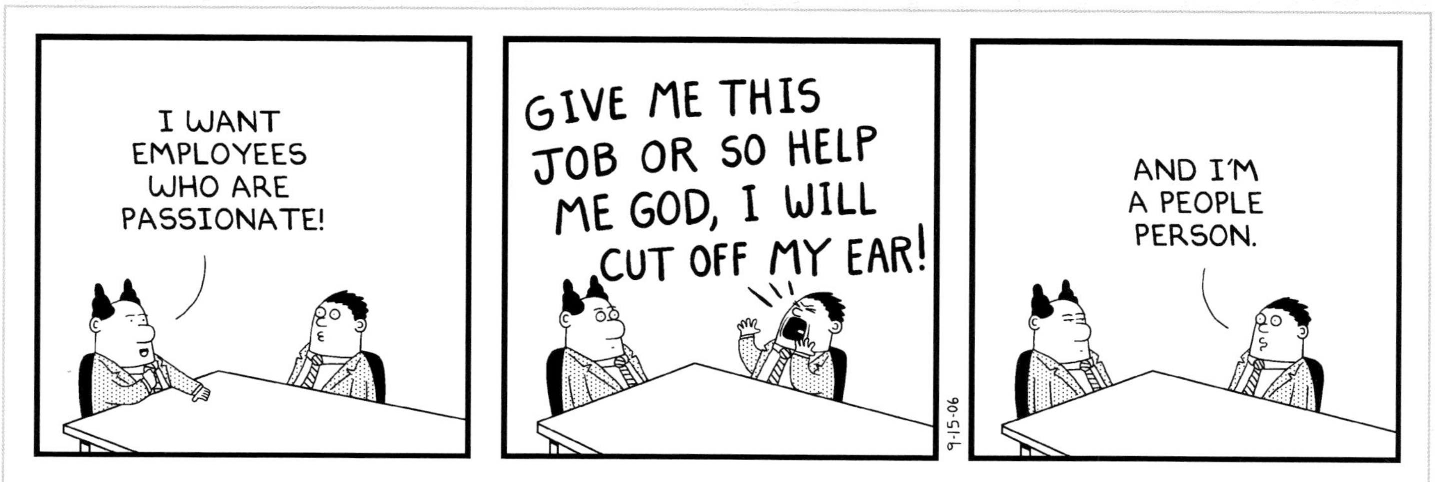
I WANT EMPLOYEES WHO ARE PASSIONATE!
GIVE ME THIS JOB OR SO HELP ME GOD, I WILL CUT OFF MY EAR!
AND I'M A PEOPLE PERSON.
9-15-06

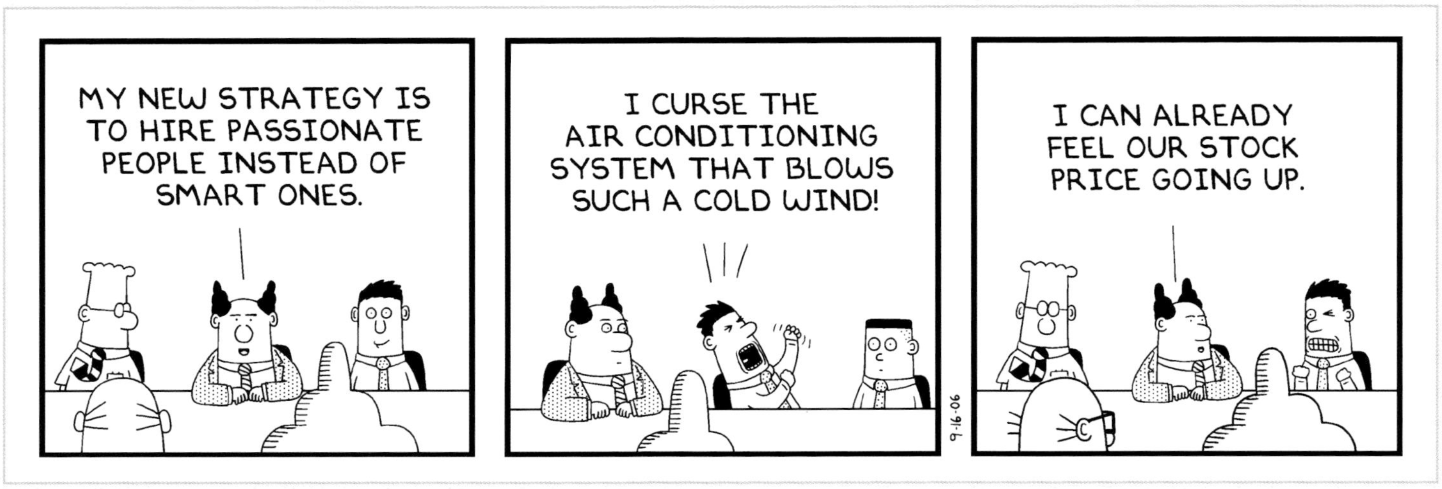
MY NEW STRATEGY IS TO HIRE PASSIONATE PEOPLE INSTEAD OF SMART ONES.
I CURSE THE AIR CONDITIONING SYSTEM THAT BLOWS SUCH A COLD WIND!
9-16-06
I CAN ALREADY FEEL OUR STOCK PRICE GOING UP.

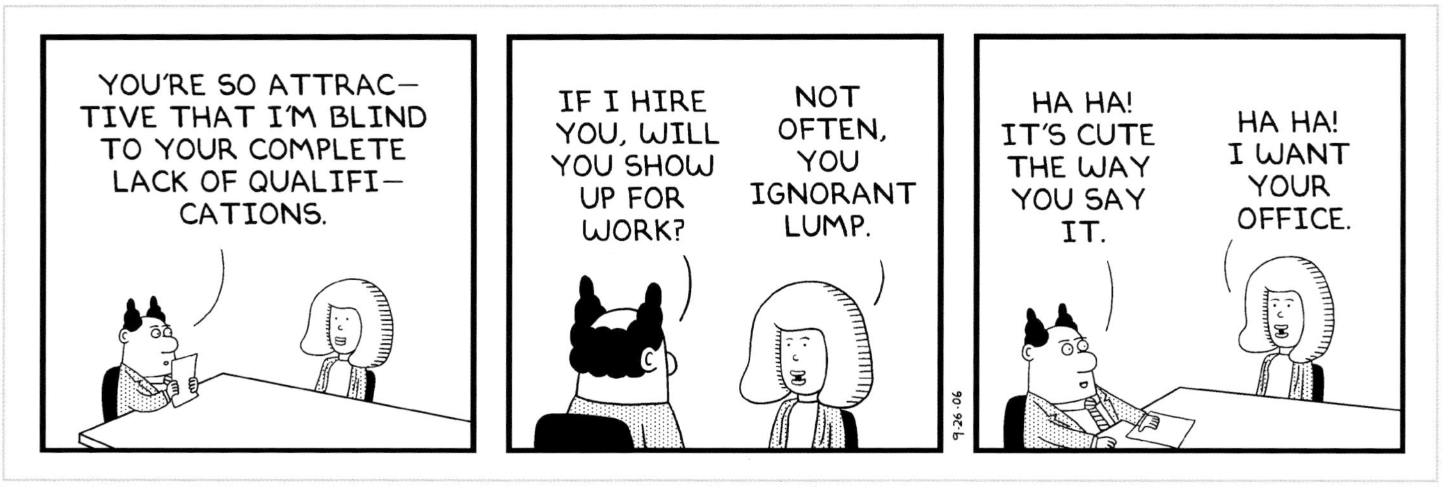
YOU'RE SO ATTRAC–TIVE THAT I'M BLIND TO YOUR COMPLETE LACK OF QUALIFI–CATIONS.
IF I HIRE YOU, WILL YOU SHOW UP FOR WORK?
NOT OFTEN, YOU IGNORANT LUMP.
9-26-06
HA HA! IT'S CUTE THE WAY YOU SAY IT.
HA HA! I WANT YOUR OFFICE.

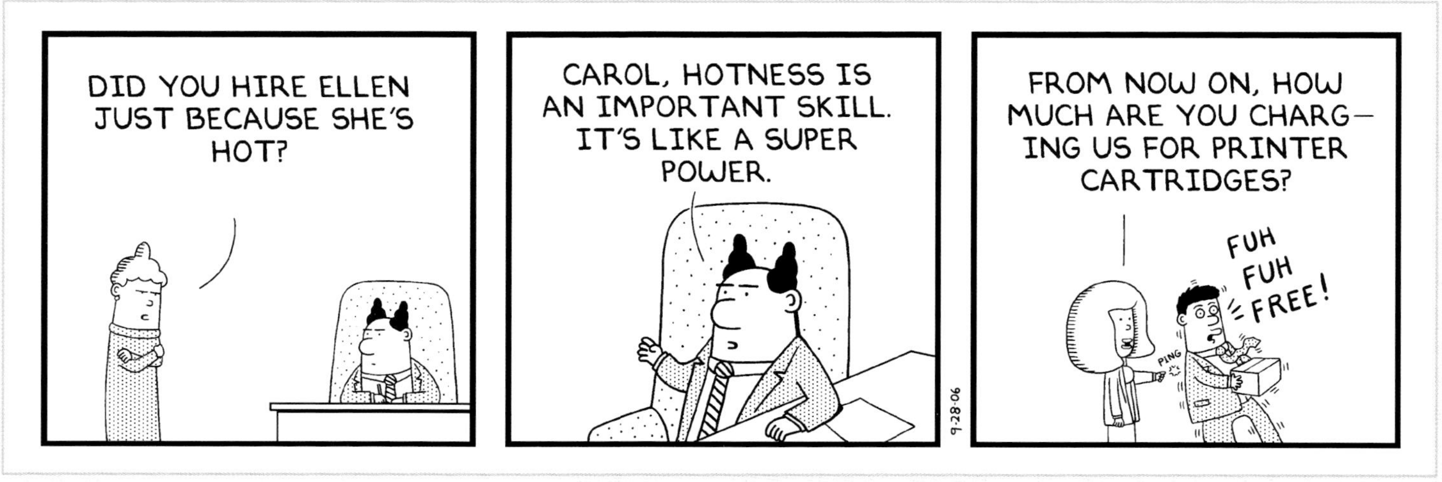
DID YOU HIRE ELLEN JUST BECAUSE SHE'S HOT?
CAROL, HOTNESS IS AN IMPORTANT SKILL. IT'S LIKE A SUPER POWER.
9-28-06
FROM NOW ON, HOW MUCH ARE YOU CHARG–ING US FOR PRINTER CARTRIDGES?
PING
FUH FUH FREE!

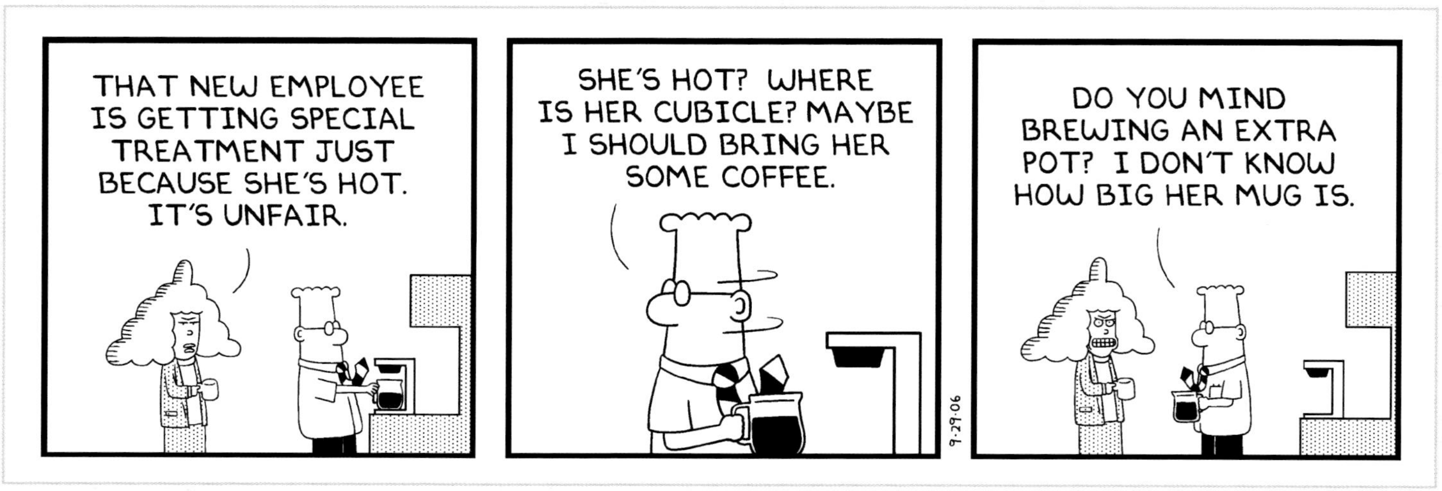
THAT NEW EMPLOYEE IS GETTING SPECIAL TREATMENT JUST BECAUSE SHE'S HOT. IT'S UNFAIR.
SHE'S HOT? WHERE IS HER CUBICLE? MAYBE I SHOULD BRING HER SOME COFFEE.
9-29-06
DO YOU MIND BREWING AN EXTRA POT? I DON'T KNOW HOW BIG HER MUG IS.

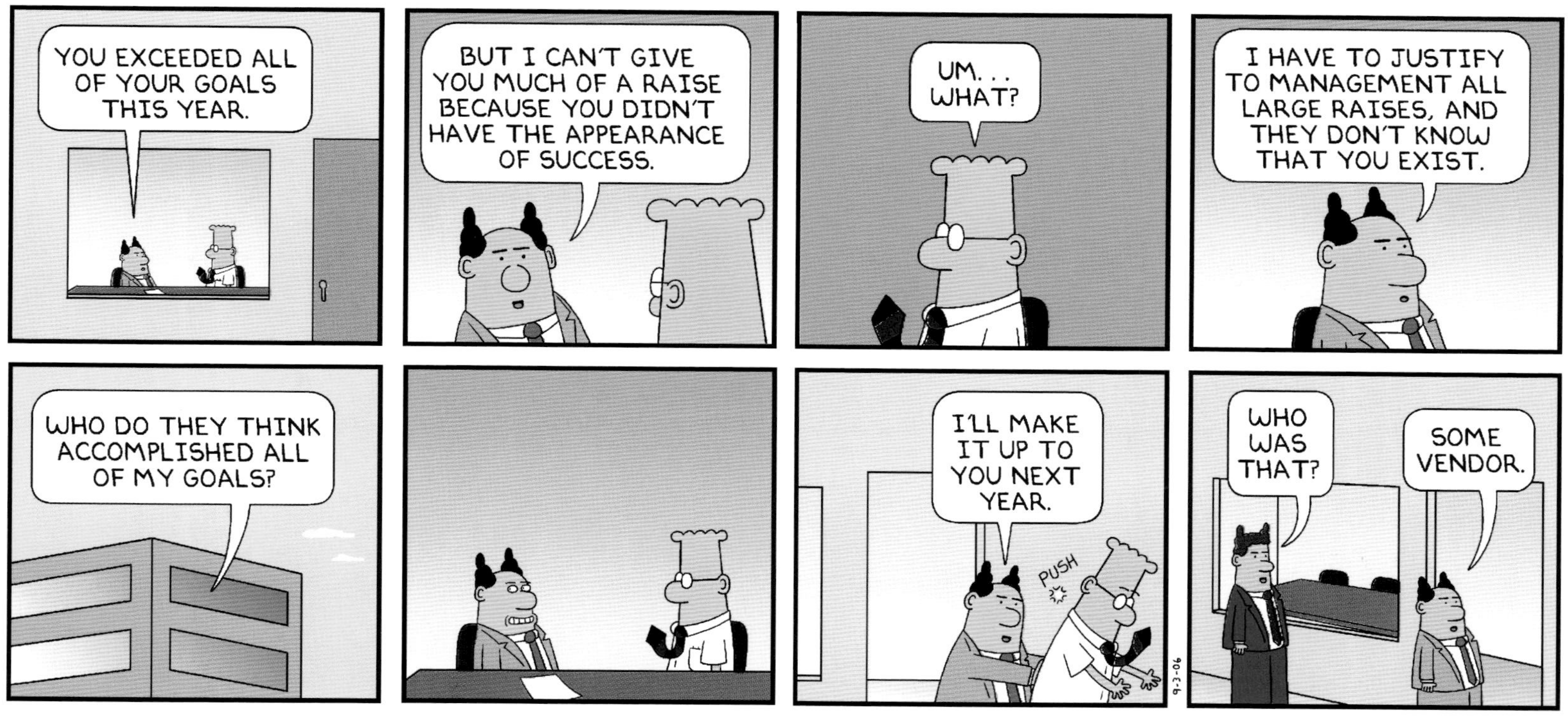
YOU EXCEEDED ALL OF YOUR GOALS THIS YEAR.
BUT I CAN'T GIVE YOU MUCH OF A RAISE BECAUSE YOU DIDN'T HAVE THE APPEARANCE OF SUCCESS.
UM. . . WHAT?
I HAVE TO JUSTIFY TO MANAGEMENT ALL LARGE RAISES, AND THEY DON'T KNOW THAT YOU EXIST.
WHO DO THEY THINK ACCOMPLISHED ALL OF MY GOALS?
I'LL MAKE IT UP TO YOU NEXT YEAR.
PUSH
9-3-06
WHO WAS THAT?
SOME VENDOR.

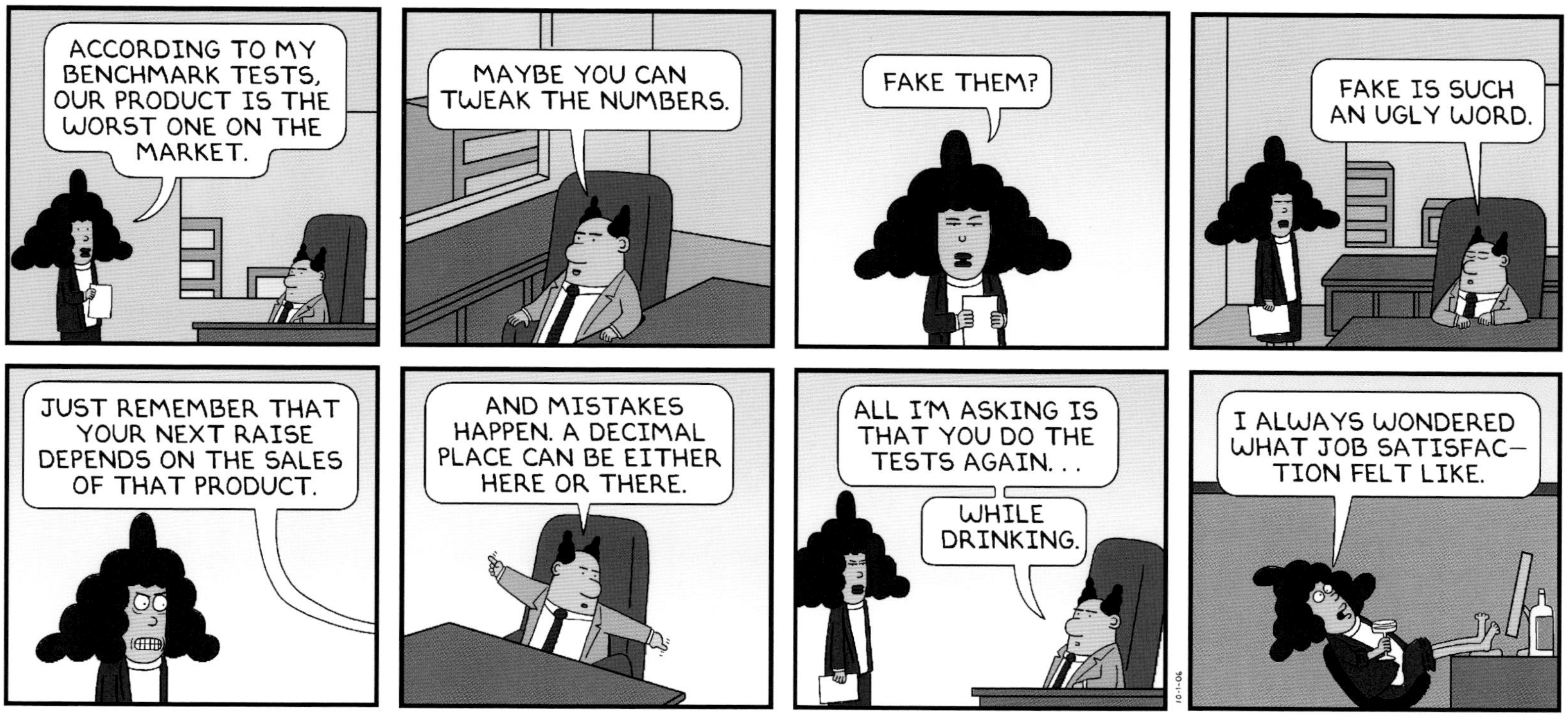
ACCORDING TO MY BENCHMARK TESTS, OUR PRODUCT IS THE WORST ONE ON THE MARKET.
MAYBE YOU CAN TWEAK THE NUMBERS.
FAKE THEM?
FAKE IS SUCH AN UGLY WORD.
JUST REMEMBER THAT YOUR NEXT RAISE DEPENDS ON THE SALES OF THAT PRODUCT.
AND MISTAKES HAPPEN. A DECIMAL PLACE CAN BE EITHER HERE OR THERE.
ALL I'M ASKING IS THAT YOU DO THE TESTS AGAIN. . .
WHILE DRINKING.
10-1-06
I ALWAYS WONDERED WHAT JOB SATISFAC-TION FELT LIKE.

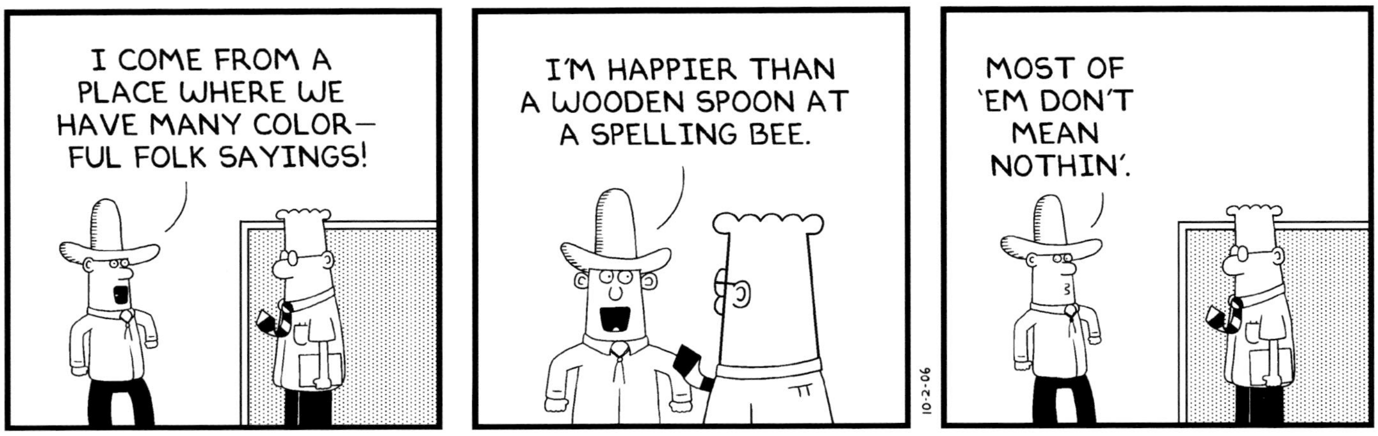
I COME FROM A PLACE WHERE WE HAVE MANY COLOR-FUL FOLK SAYINGS!
I'M HAPPIER THAN A WOODEN SPOON AT A SPELLING BEE.
10-2-06
MOST OF 'EM DON'T MEAN NOTHIN'.

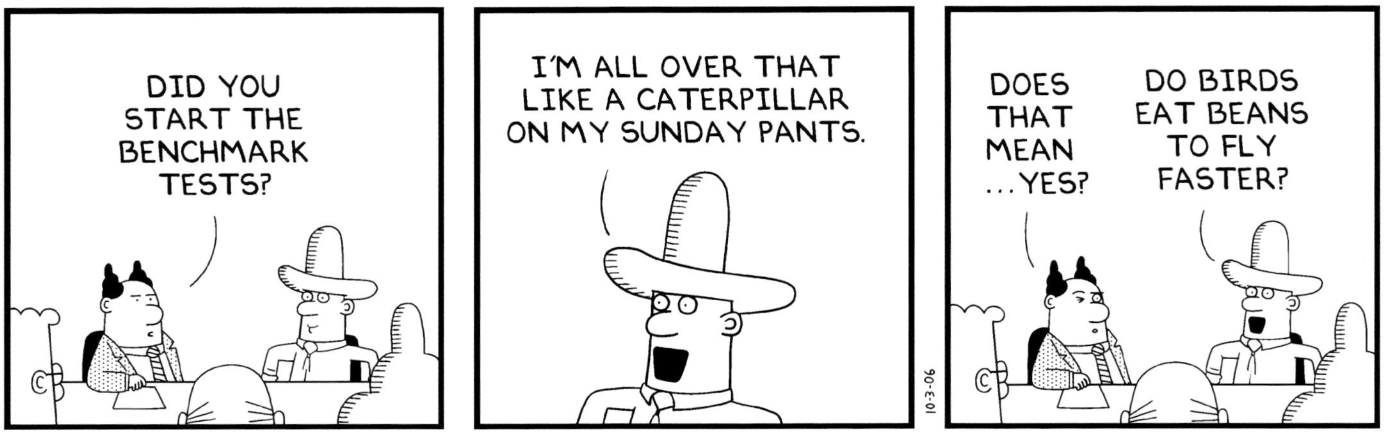
DID YOU START THE BENCHMARK TESTS?
I'M ALL OVER THAT LIKE A CATERPILLAR ON MY SUNDAY PANTS.
10-3-06
DOES THAT MEAN ...YES?
DO BIRDS EAT BEANS TO FLY FASTER?

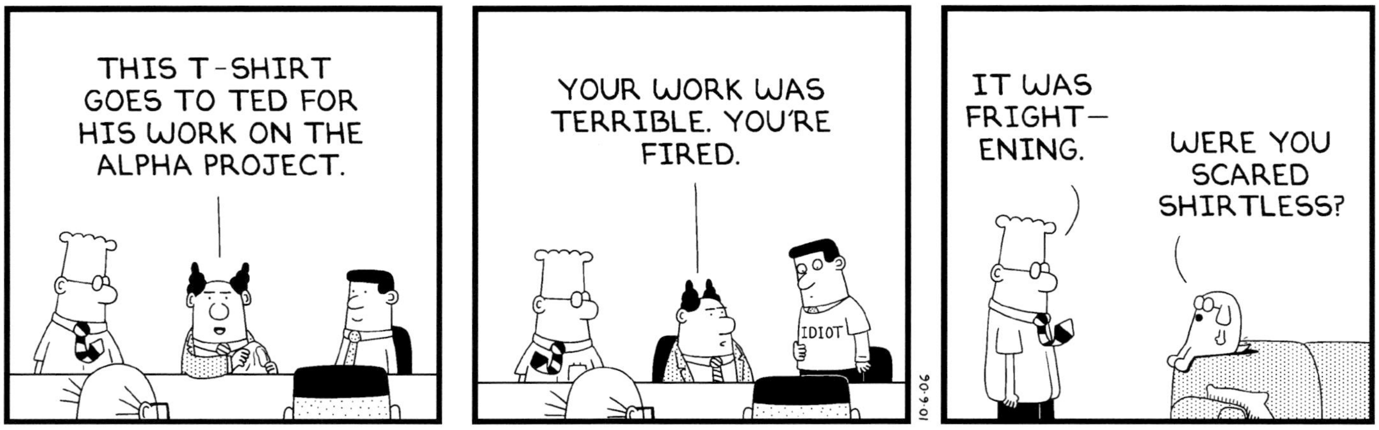
THIS T-SHIRT GOES TO TED FOR HIS WORK ON THE ALPHA PROJECT.
YOUR WORK WAS TERRIBLE. YOU'RE FIRED.
IDIOT
10-6-06
IT WAS FRIGHT-ENING.
WERE YOU SCARED SHIRTLESS?

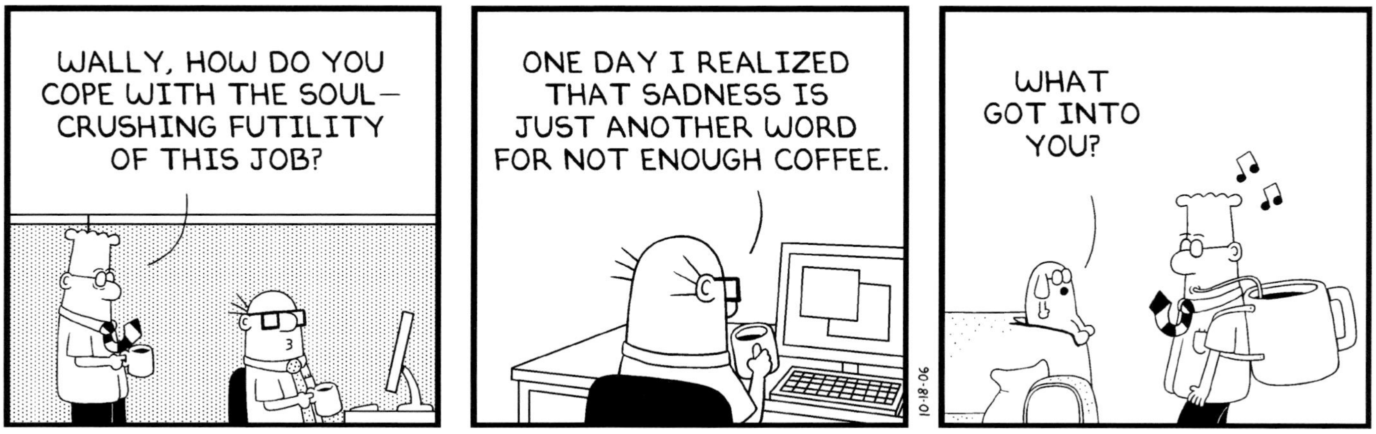
WALLY, HOW DO YOU COPE WITH THE SOUL-CRUSHING FUTILITY OF THIS JOB?
ONE DAY I REALIZED THAT SADNESS IS JUST ANOTHER WORD FOR NOT ENOUGH COFFEE.
10-18-06
WHAT GOT INTO YOU?

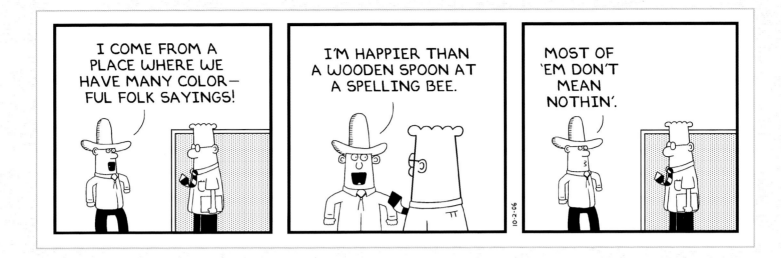

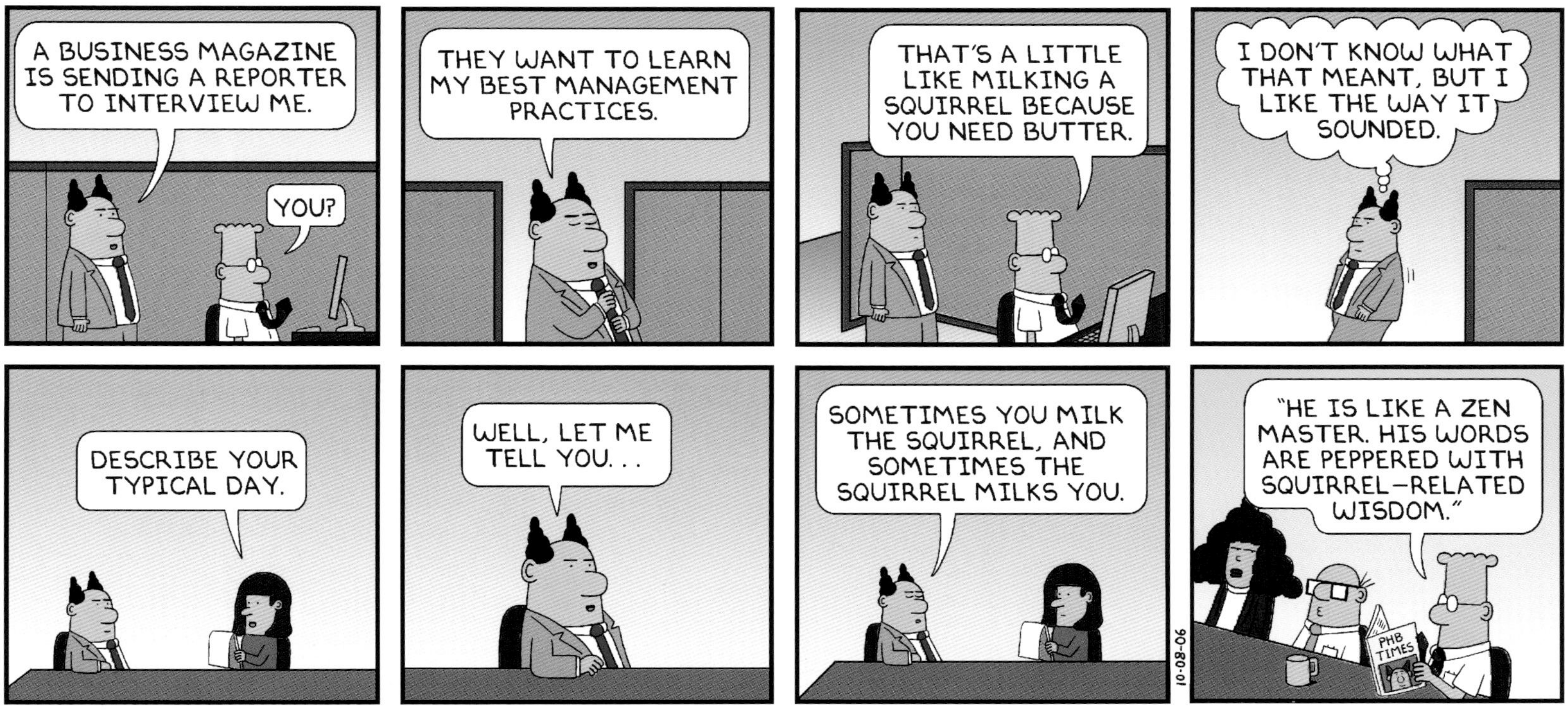
A BUSINESS MAGAZINE IS SENDING A REPORTER TO INTERVIEW ME.
YOU?
THEY WANT TO LEARN MY BEST MANAGEMENT PRACTICES.
THAT'S A LITTLE LIKE MILKING A SQUIRREL BECAUSE YOU NEED BUTTER.
I DON'T KNOW WHAT THAT MEANT, BUT I LIKE THE WAY IT SOUNDED.
DESCRIBE YOUR TYPICAL DAY.
WELL, LET ME TELL YOU. . .
SOMETIMES YOU MILK THE SQUIRREL, AND SOMETIMES THE SQUIRREL MILKS YOU.
10-08-06
"HE IS LIKE A ZEN MASTER. HIS WORDS ARE PEPPERED WITH SQUIRREL-RELATED WISDOM."
PHB TIMES

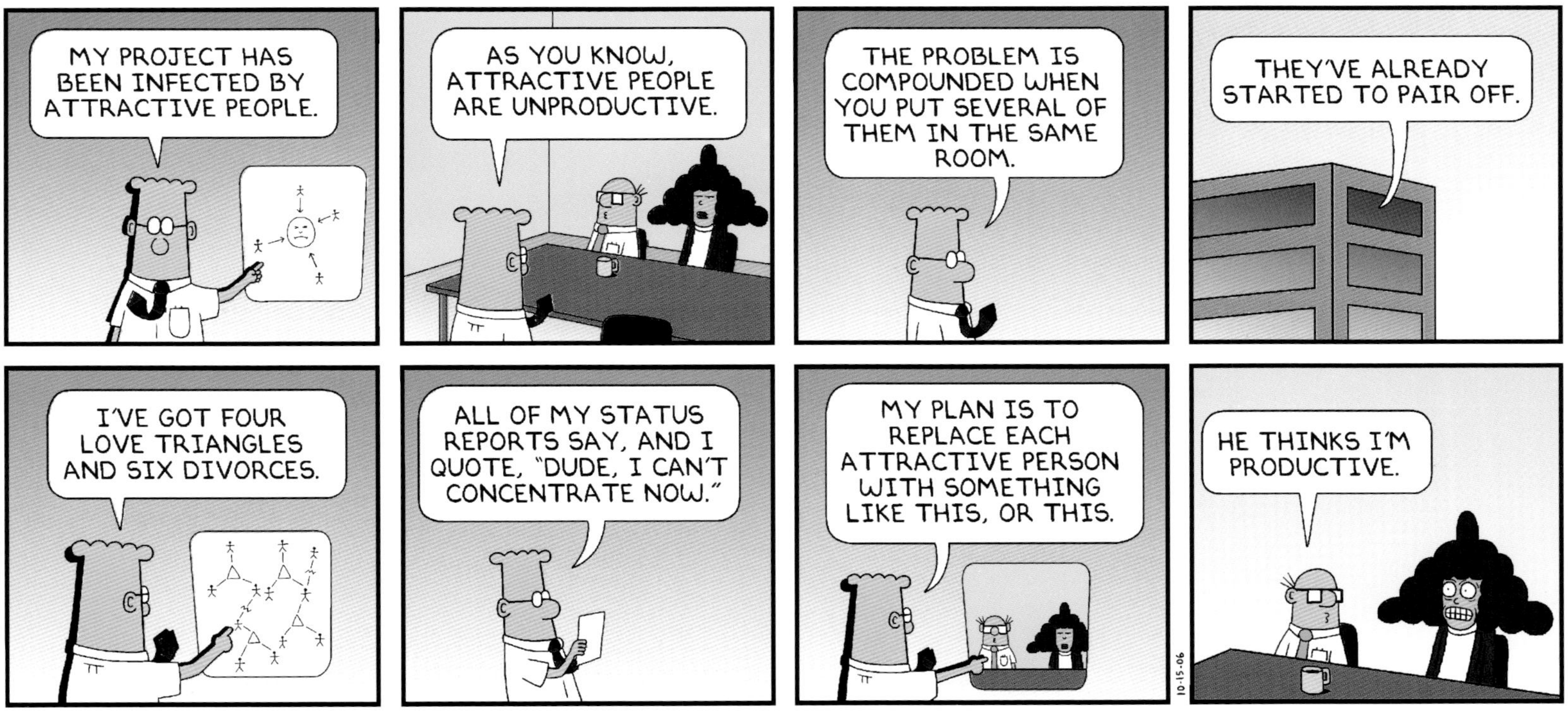
MY PROJECT HAS BEEN INFECTED BY ATTRACTIVE PEOPLE.
AS YOU KNOW, ATTRACTIVE PEOPLE ARE UNPRODUCTIVE.
THE PROBLEM IS COMPOUNDED WHEN YOU PUT SEVERAL OF THEM IN THE SAME ROOM.
THEY'VE ALREADY STARTED TO PAIR OFF.
I'VE GOT FOUR LOVE TRIANGLES AND SIX DIVORCES.
ALL OF MY STATUS REPORTS SAY, AND I QUOTE, "DUDE, I CAN'T CONCENTRATE NOW."
MY PLAN IS TO REPLACE EACH ATTRACTIVE PERSON WITH SOMETHING LIKE THIS, OR THIS.
10-15-06
HE THINKS I'M PRODUCTIVE.

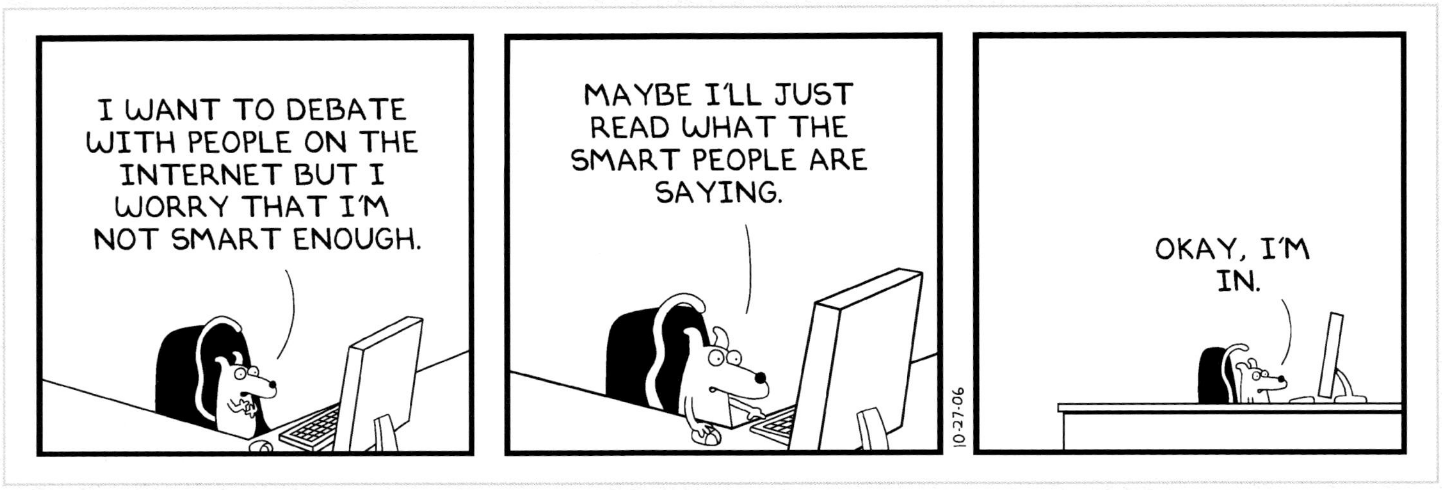
I WANT TO DEBATE WITH PEOPLE ON THE INTERNET BUT I WORRY THAT I'M NOT SMART ENOUGH.
MAYBE I'LL JUST READ WHAT THE SMART PEOPLE ARE SAYING.
OKAY, I'M IN.
10-27-06

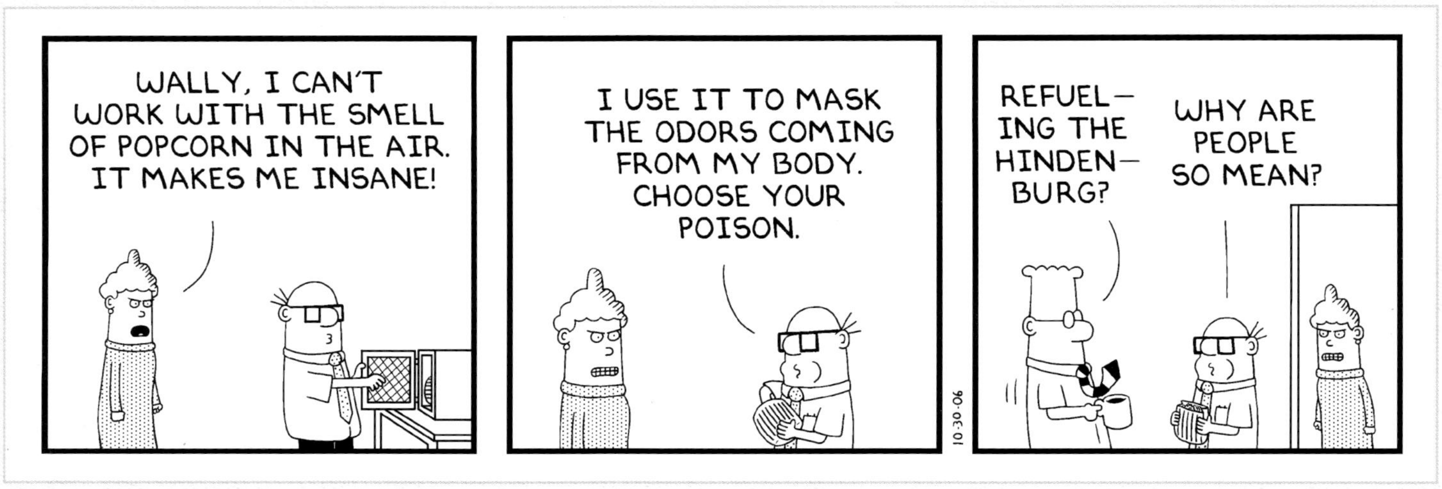
WALLY, I CAN'T WORK WITH THE SMELL OF POPCORN IN THE AIR. IT MAKES ME INSANE!
I USE IT TO MASK THE ODORS COMING FROM MY BODY. CHOOSE YOUR POISON.
REFUEL-ING THE HINDEN-BURG?
WHY ARE PEOPLE SO MEAN?
10-30-06

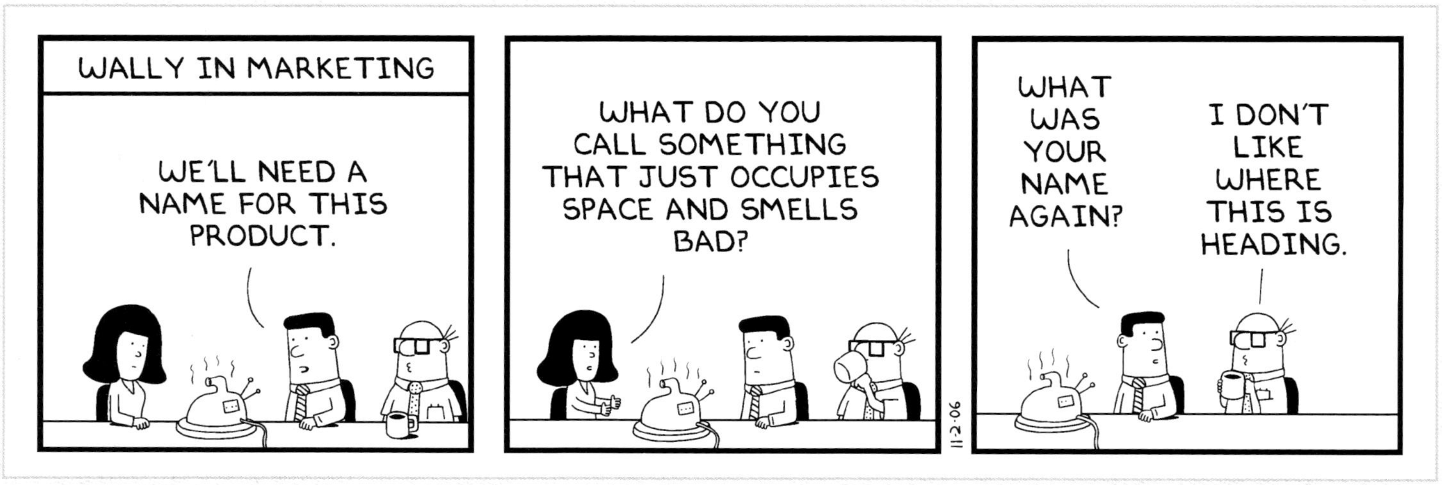
WALLY IN MARKETING
WE'LL NEED A NAME FOR THIS PRODUCT.
WHAT DO YOU CALL SOMETHING THAT JUST OCCUPIES SPACE AND SMELLS BAD?
WHAT WAS YOUR NAME AGAIN?
I DON'T LIKE WHERE THIS IS HEADING.
11-2-06

The following comic is based on my good friend Josh Libresco, who has his own market research company. I'm including it in this book so he will feel compelled to buy several copies.

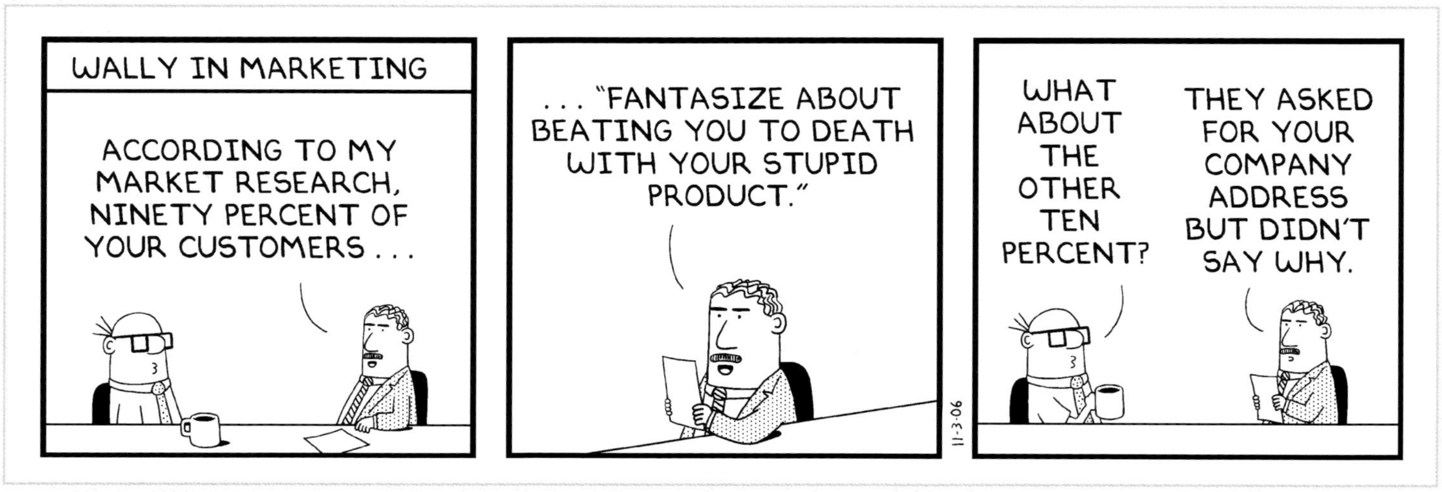
WALLY IN MARKETING
ACCORDING TO MY MARKET RESEARCH, NINETY PERCENT OF YOUR CUSTOMERS . . .
. . . "FANTASIZE ABOUT BEATING YOU TO DEATH WITH YOUR STUPID PRODUCT."
WHAT ABOUT THE OTHER TEN PERCENT?
THEY ASKED FOR YOUR COMPANY ADDRESS BUT DIDN'T SAY WHY.
11-3-06

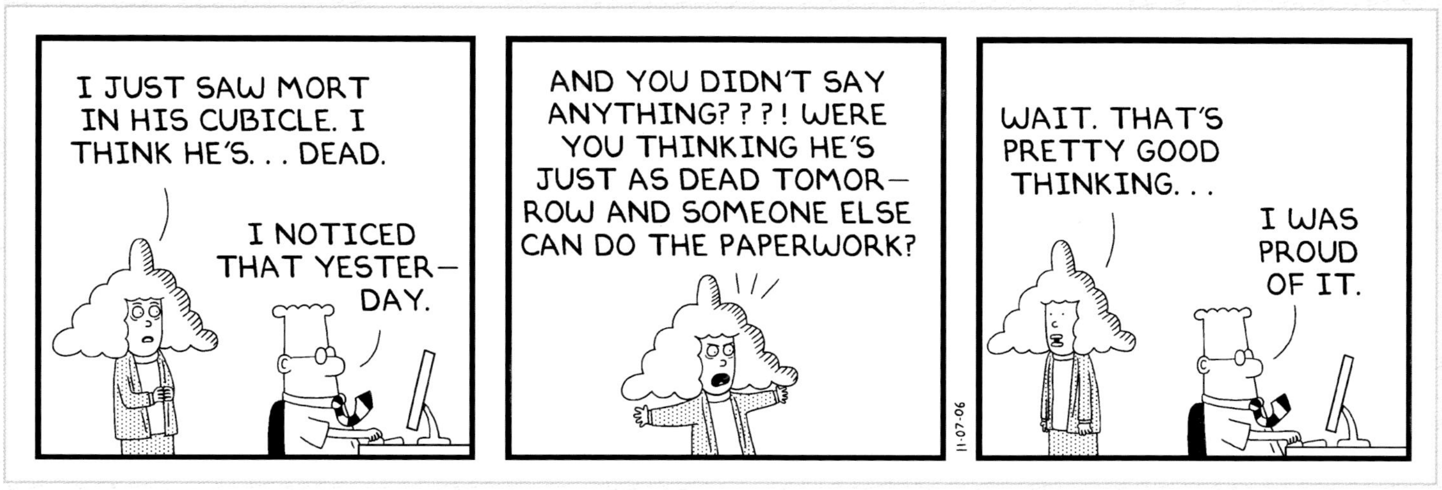
I JUST SAW MORT IN HIS CUBICLE. I THINK HE'S. . . DEAD.
I NOTICED THAT YESTER-DAY.
AND YOU DIDN'T SAY ANYTHING? ? ? ! WERE YOU THINKING HE'S JUST AS DEAD TOMOR-ROW AND SOMEONE ELSE CAN DO THE PAPERWORK?
11-07-06
WAIT. THAT'S PRETTY GOOD THINKING. . .
I WAS PROUD OF IT.

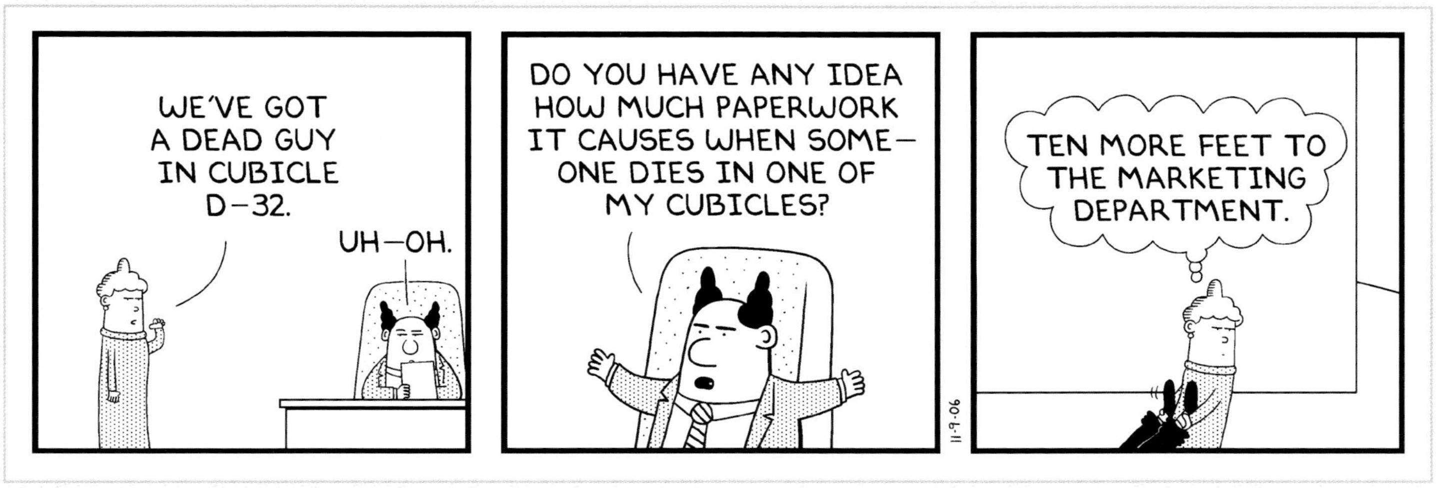
WE'VE GOT A DEAD GUY IN CUBICLE D-32.
UH-OH.
DO YOU HAVE ANY IDEA HOW MUCH PAPERWORK IT CAUSES WHEN SOME-ONE DIES IN ONE OF MY CUBICLES?
11-9-06
TEN MORE FEET TO THE MARKETING DEPARTMENT.

The following strip appeared in papers. In the original version, he had no underpants on his head. His head was literally a butthead. My editor asked for it to be redrawn. So I covered his butthead with underpants.

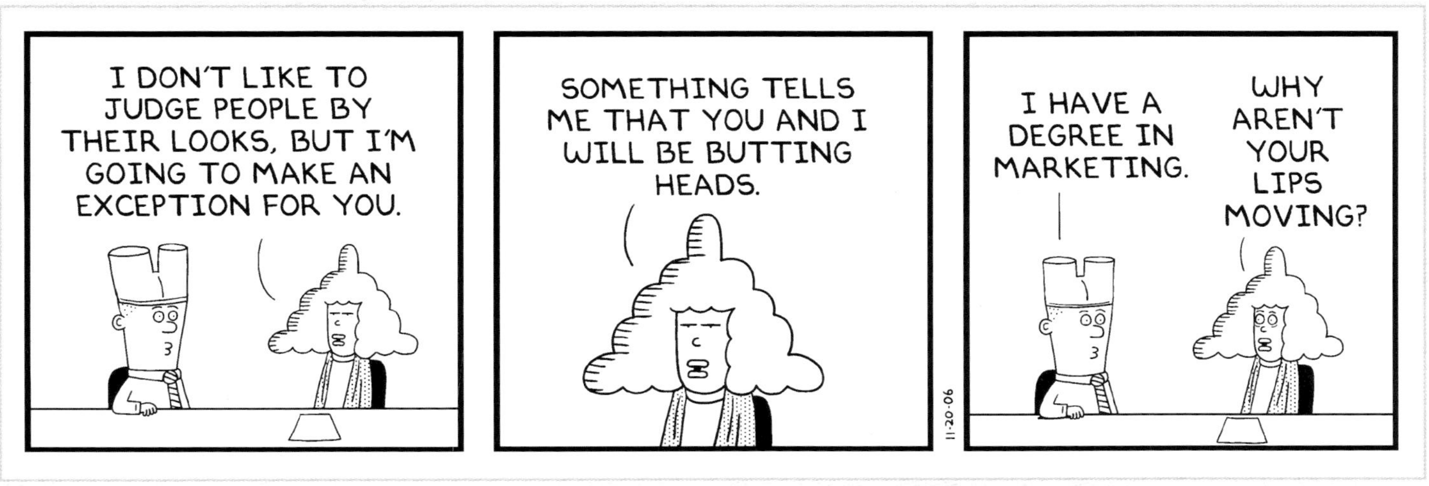
I DON'T LIKE TO JUDGE PEOPLE BY THEIR LOOKS, BUT I'M GOING TO MAKE AN EXCEPTION FOR YOU.
SOMETHING TELLS ME THAT YOU AND I WILL BE BUTTING HEADS.
11-20-06
I HAVE A DEGREE IN MARKETING.
WHY AREN'T YOUR LIPS MOVING?

Here is the version that was rejected.

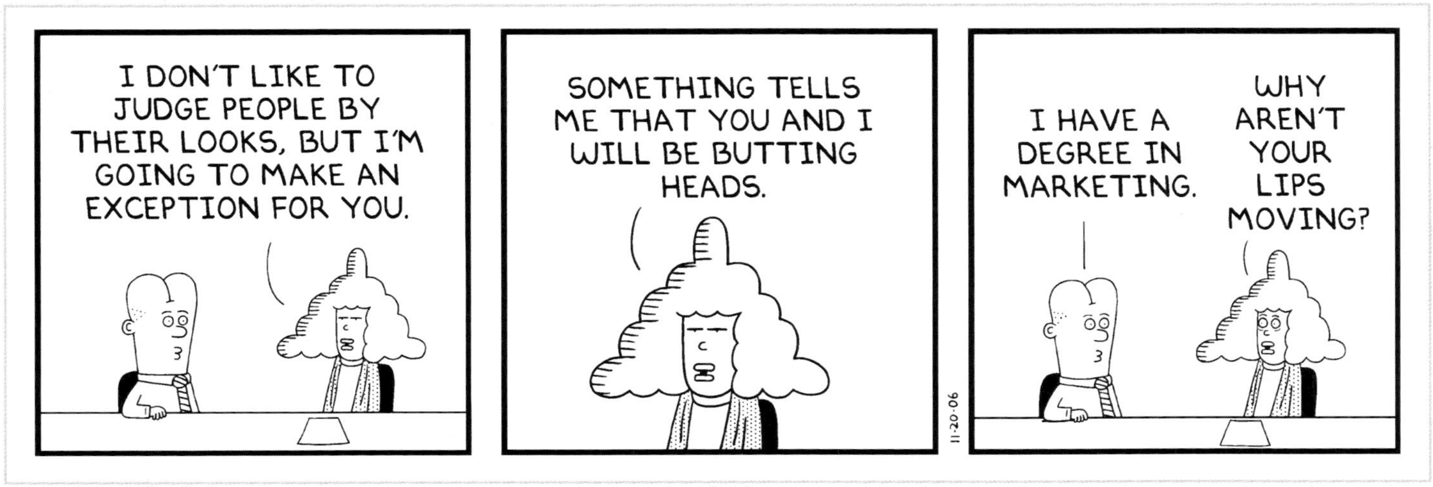
I DON'T LIKE TO JUDGE PEOPLE BY THEIR LOOKS, BUT I'M GOING TO MAKE AN EXCEPTION FOR YOU.
SOMETHING TELLS ME THAT YOU AND I WILL BE BUTTING HEADS.
11-20-06
I HAVE A DEGREE IN MARKETING.
WHY AREN'T YOUR LIPS MOVING?

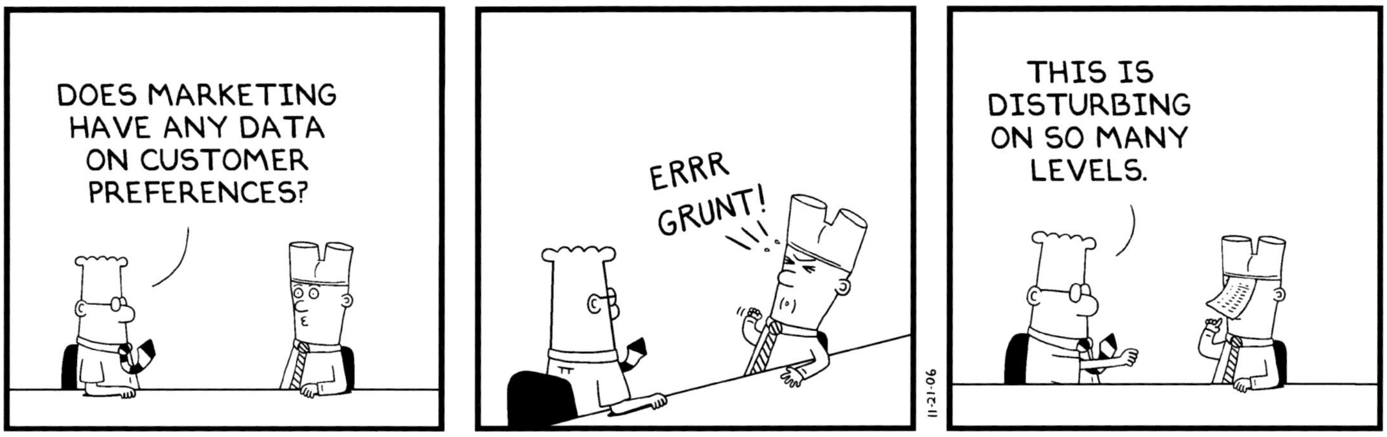
DOES MARKETING HAVE ANY DATA ON CUSTOMER PREFERENCES?
ERRR GRUNT!
THIS IS DISTURBING ON SO MANY LEVELS.
11-21-06

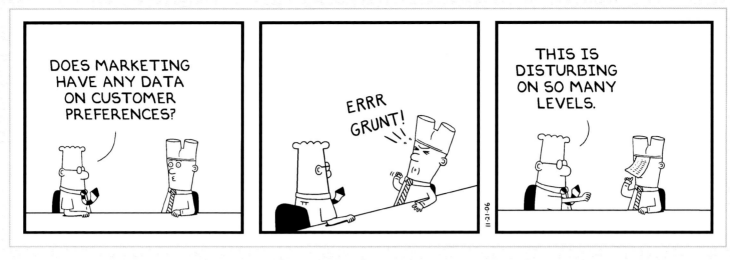

The series continued. Again, I had to add underpants.

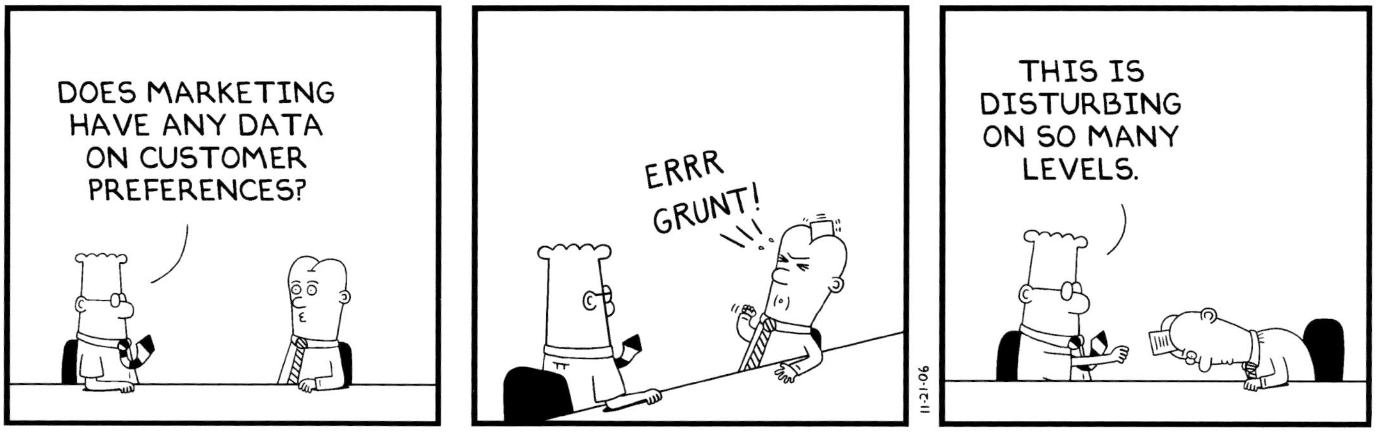
DOES MARKETING HAVE ANY DATA ON CUSTOMER PREFERENCES?
ERRR GRUNT!
THIS IS DISTURBING ON SO MANY LEVELS.
11-21-06

The pantless version is much funnier.

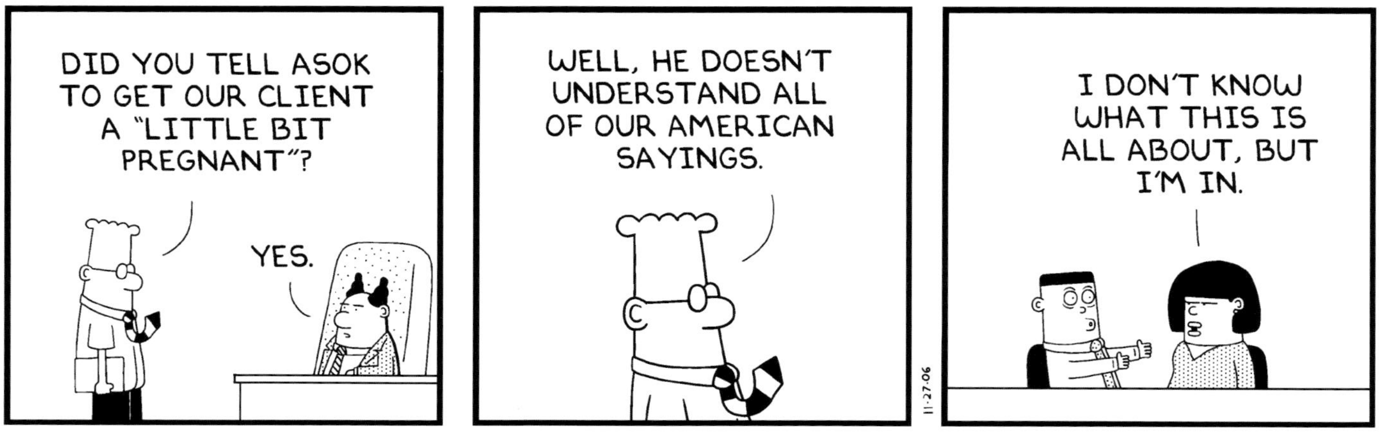
DID YOU TELL ASOK TO GET OUR CLIENT A "LITTLE BIT PREGNANT"?
YES.
WELL, HE DOESN'T UNDERSTAND ALL OF OUR AMERICAN SAYINGS.
I DON'T KNOW WHAT THIS IS ALL ABOUT, BUT I'M IN.
11-27-06

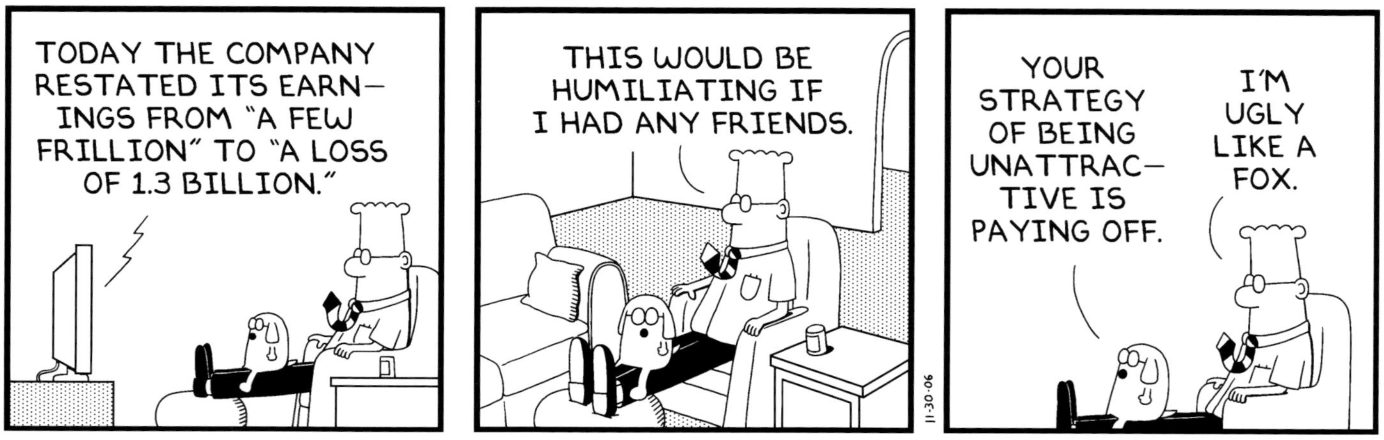
TODAY THE COMPANY RESTATED ITS EARN-INGS FROM "A FEW FRILLION" TO "A LOSS OF 1.3 BILLION."
THIS WOULD BE HUMILIATING IF I HAD ANY FRIENDS.
YOUR STRATEGY OF BEING UNATTRAC-TIVE IS PAYING OFF.
I'M UGLY LIKE A FOX.
11-30-06

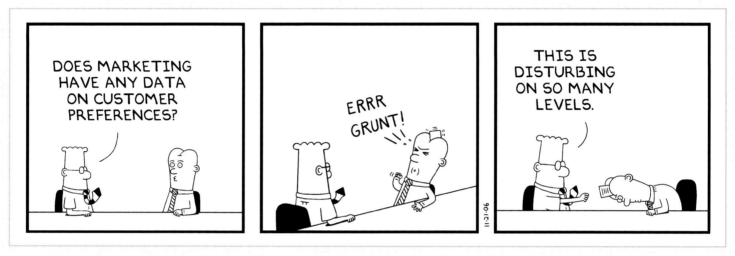

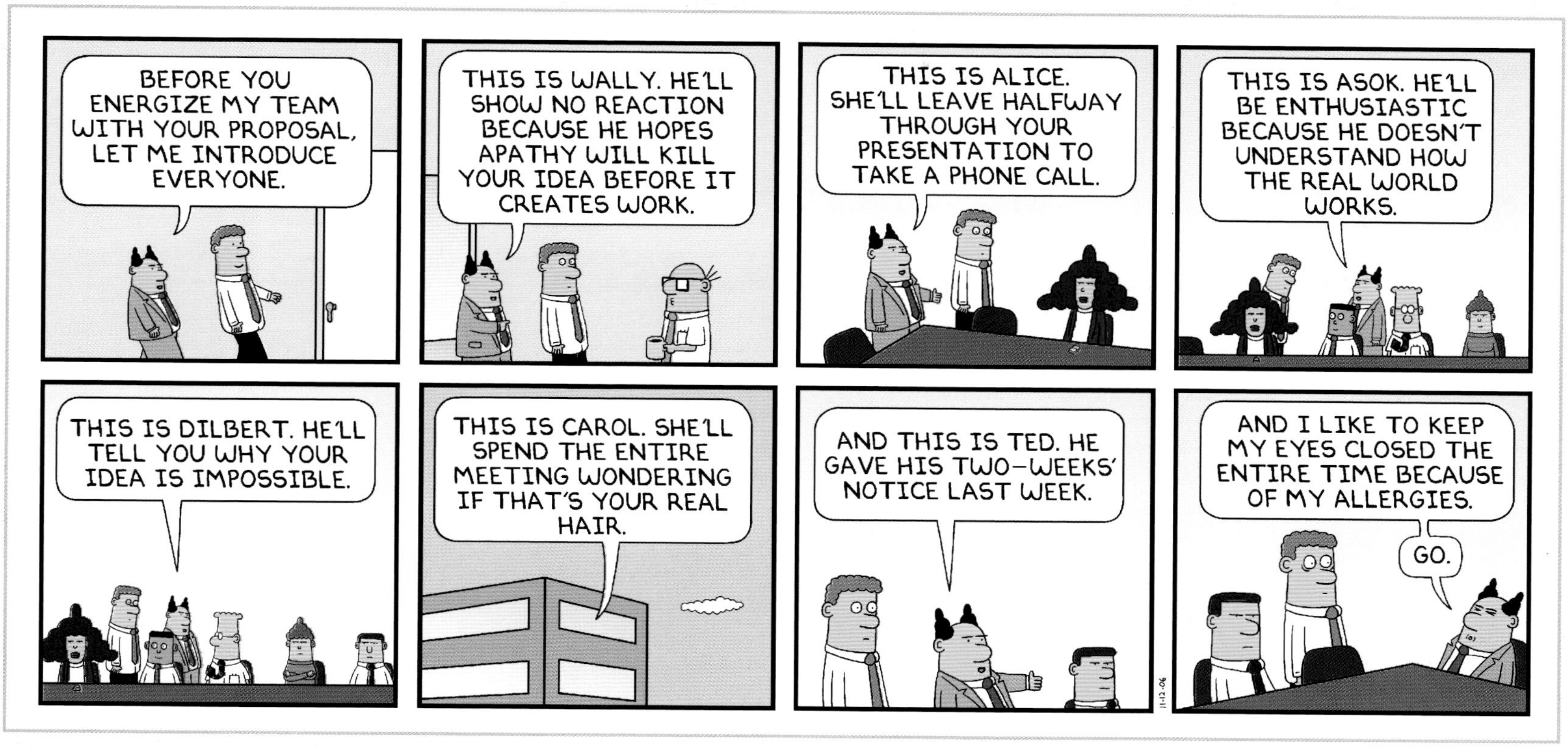
BEFORE YOU ENERGIZE MY TEAM WITH YOUR PROPOSAL, LET ME INTRODUCE EVERYONE.
THIS IS WALLY. HE'LL SHOW NO REACTION BECAUSE HE HOPES APATHY WILL KILL YOUR IDEA BEFORE IT CREATES WORK.
THIS IS ALICE. SHE'LL LEAVE HALFWAY THROUGH YOUR PRESENTATION TO TAKE A PHONE CALL.
THIS IS ASOK. HE'LL BE ENTHUSIASTIC BECAUSE HE DOESN'T UNDERSTAND HOW THE REAL WORLD WORKS.
THIS IS DILBERT. HE'LL TELL YOU WHY YOUR IDEA IS IMPOSSIBLE.
THIS IS CAROL. SHE'LL SPEND THE ENTIRE MEETING WONDERING IF THAT'S YOUR REAL HAIR.
AND THIS IS TED. HE GAVE HIS TWO-WEEKS' NOTICE LAST WEEK.
AND I LIKE TO KEEP MY EYES CLOSED THE ENTIRE TIME BECAUSE OF MY ALLERGIES.
GO.

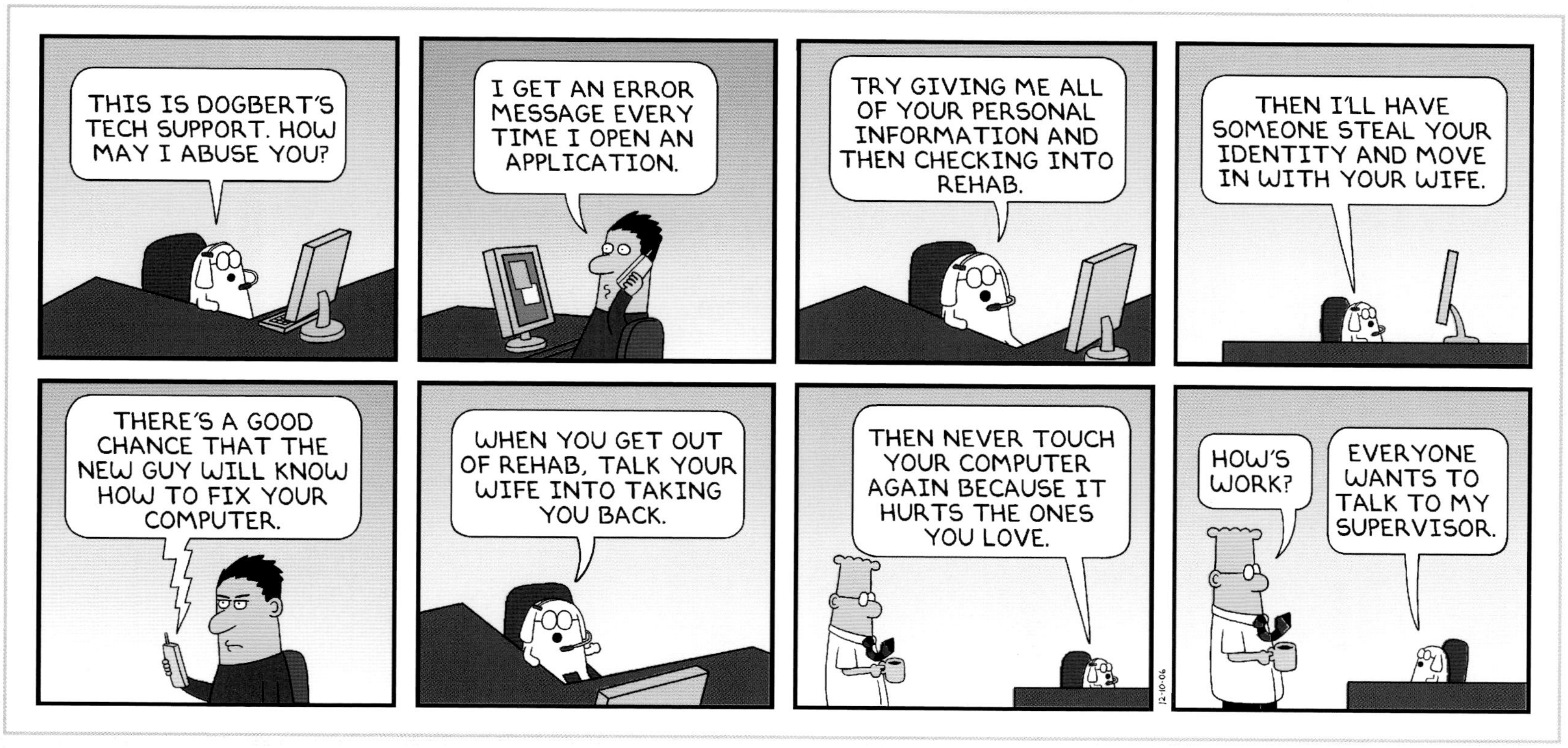
THIS IS DOGBERT'S TECH SUPPORT. HOW MAY I ABUSE YOU?
I GET AN ERROR MESSAGE EVERY TIME I OPEN AN APPLICATION.
TRY GIVING ME ALL OF YOUR PERSONAL INFORMATION AND THEN CHECKING INTO REHAB.
THEN I'LL HAVE SOMEONE STEAL YOUR IDENTITY AND MOVE IN WITH YOUR WIFE.
THERE'S A GOOD CHANCE THAT THE NEW GUY WILL KNOW HOW TO FIX YOUR COMPUTER.
WHEN YOU GET OUT OF REHAB, TALK YOUR WIFE INTO TAKING YOU BACK.
THEN NEVER TOUCH YOUR COMPUTER AGAIN BECAUSE IT HURTS THE ONES YOU LOVE.
HOW'S WORK?
EVERYONE WANTS TO TALK TO MY SUPERVISOR.

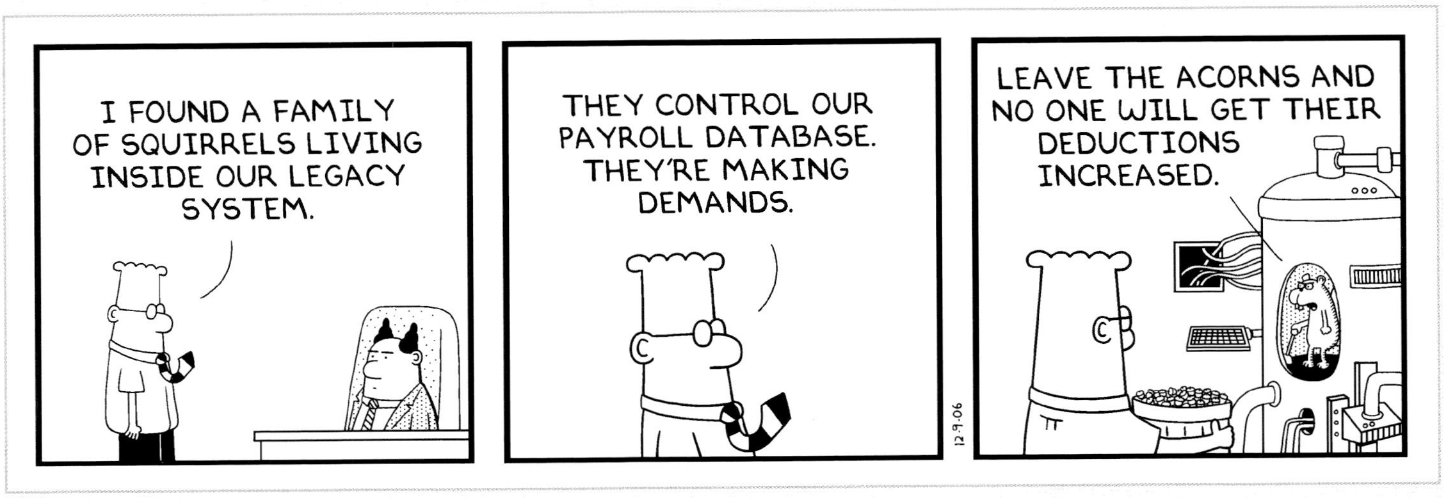
I FOUND A FAMILY OF SQUIRRELS LIVING INSIDE OUR LEGACY SYSTEM.
THEY CONTROL OUR PAYROLL DATABASE. THEY'RE MAKING DEMANDS.
LEAVE THE ACORNS AND NO ONE WILL GET THEIR DEDUCTIONS INCREASED.
12-9-06

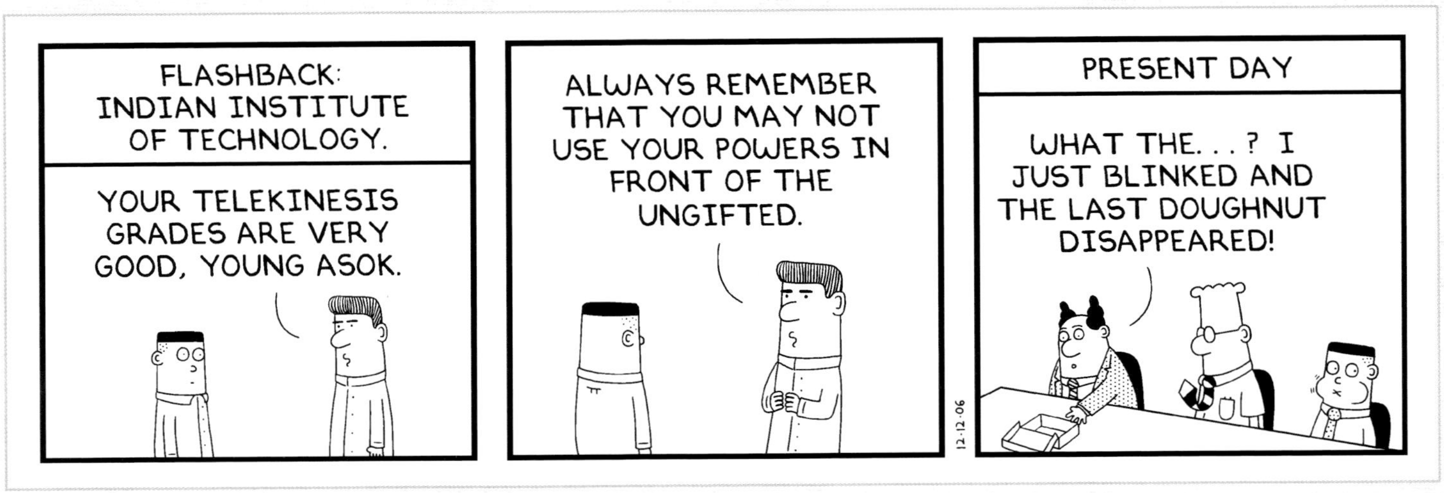
FLASHBACK: INDIAN INSTITUTE OF TECHNOLOGY.
YOUR TELEKINESIS GRADES ARE VERY GOOD, YOUNG ASOK.
ALWAYS REMEMBER THAT YOU MAY NOT USE YOUR POWERS IN FRONT OF THE UNGIFTED.
PRESENT DAY
WHAT THE. . . ? I JUST BLINKED AND THE LAST DOUGHNUT DISAPPEARED!
12-12-06

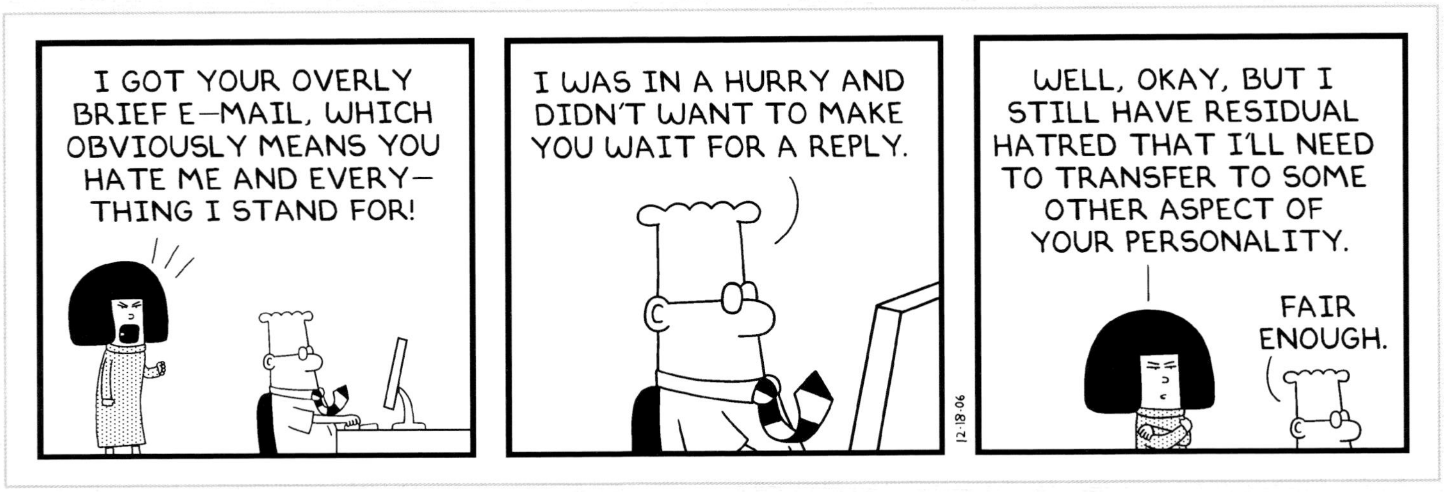
I GOT YOUR OVERLY BRIEF E-MAIL, WHICH OBVIOUSLY MEANS YOU HATE ME AND EVERY-THING I STAND FOR!
I WAS IN A HURRY AND DIDN'T WANT TO MAKE YOU WAIT FOR A REPLY.
WELL, OKAY, BUT I STILL HAVE RESIDUAL HATRED THAT I'LL NEED TO TRANSFER TO SOME OTHER ASPECT OF YOUR PERSONALITY.
FAIR ENOUGH.
12-18-06

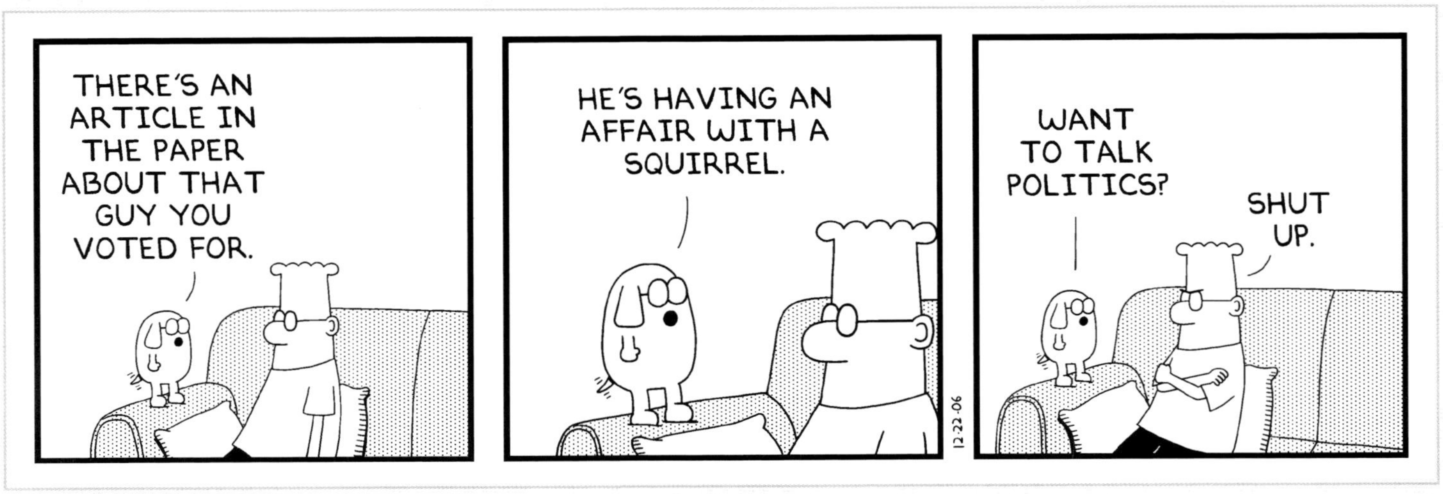
THERE'S AN ARTICLE IN THE PAPER ABOUT THAT GUY YOU VOTED FOR.
HE'S HAVING AN AFFAIR WITH A SQUIRREL.
WANT TO TALK POLITICS?
SHUT UP.
12-22-06

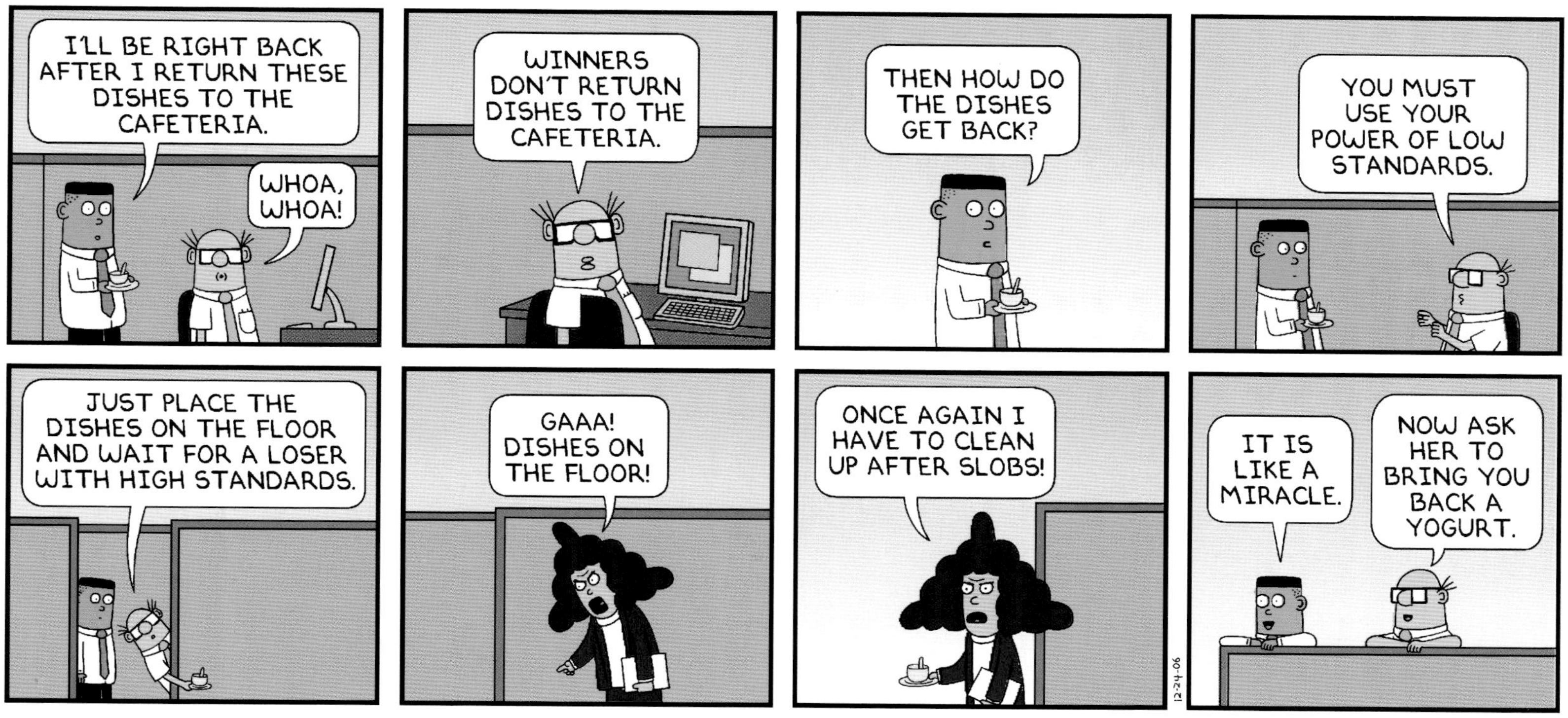
I'LL BE RIGHT BACK AFTER I RETURN THESE DISHES TO THE CAFETERIA.
WHOA, WHOA!
WINNERS DON'T RETURN DISHES TO THE CAFETERIA.
THEN HOW DO THE DISHES GET BACK?
YOU MUST USE YOUR POWER OF LOW STANDARDS.
JUST PLACE THE DISHES ON THE FLOOR AND WAIT FOR A LOSER WITH HIGH STANDARDS.
GAAA! DISHES ON THE FLOOR!
ONCE AGAIN I HAVE TO CLEAN UP AFTER SLOBS!
12-24-06
IT IS LIKE A MIRACLE.
NOW ASK HER TO BRING YOU BACK A YOGURT.

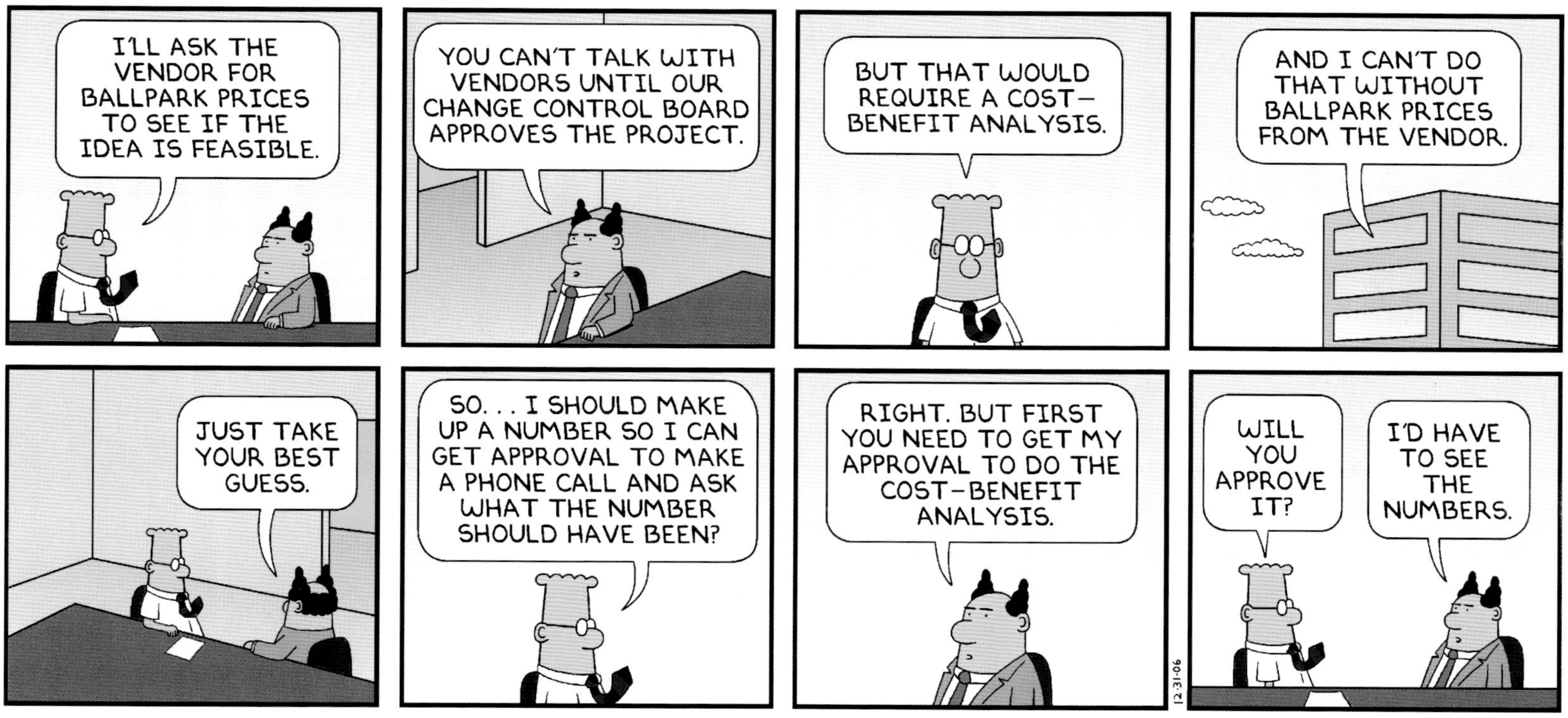
I'LL ASK THE VENDOR FOR BALLPARK PRICES TO SEE IF THE IDEA IS FEASIBLE.
YOU CAN'T TALK WITH VENDORS UNTIL OUR CHANGE CONTROL BOARD APPROVES THE PROJECT.
BUT THAT WOULD REQUIRE A COST-BENEFIT ANALYSIS.
AND I CAN'T DO THAT WITHOUT BALLPARK PRICES FROM THE VENDOR.
JUST TAKE YOUR BEST GUESS.
SO. . . I SHOULD MAKE UP A NUMBER SO I CAN GET APPROVAL TO MAKE A PHONE CALL AND ASK WHAT THE NUMBER SHOULD HAVE BEEN?
RIGHT. BUT FIRST YOU NEED TO GET MY APPROVAL TO DO THE COST-BENEFIT ANALYSIS.
12-31-06
WILL YOU APPROVE IT?
I'D HAVE TO SEE THE NUMBERS.

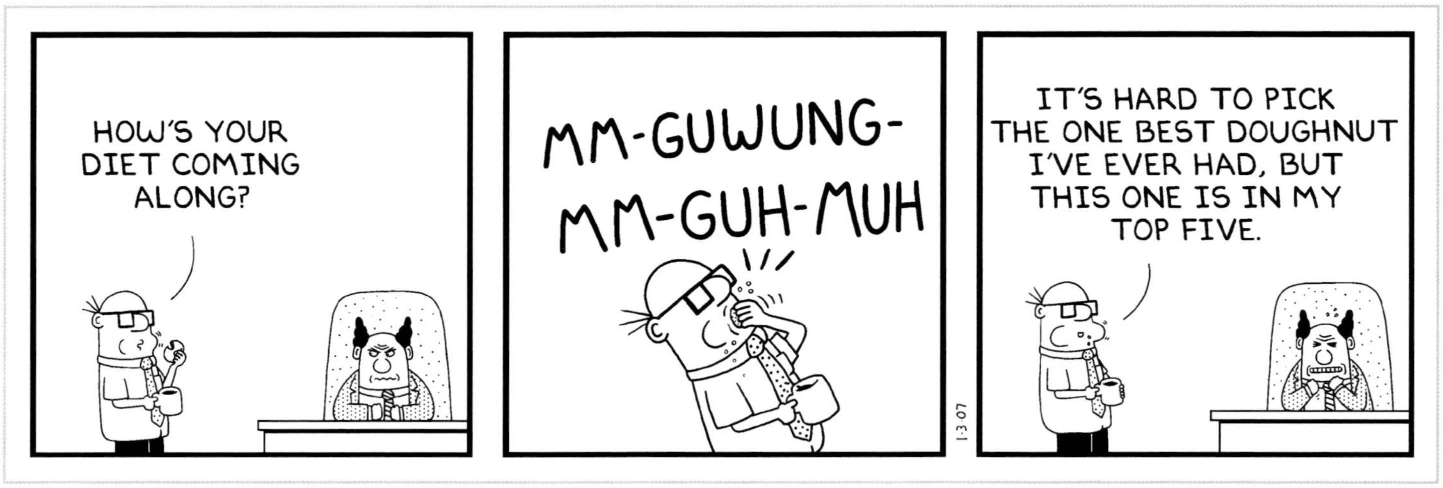
HOW'S YOUR DIET COMING ALONG?
MM-GUWUNG-MM-GUH-MUH
1-3-07
IT'S HARD TO PICK THE ONE BEST DOUGHNUT I'VE EVER HAD, BUT THIS ONE IS IN MY TOP FIVE.

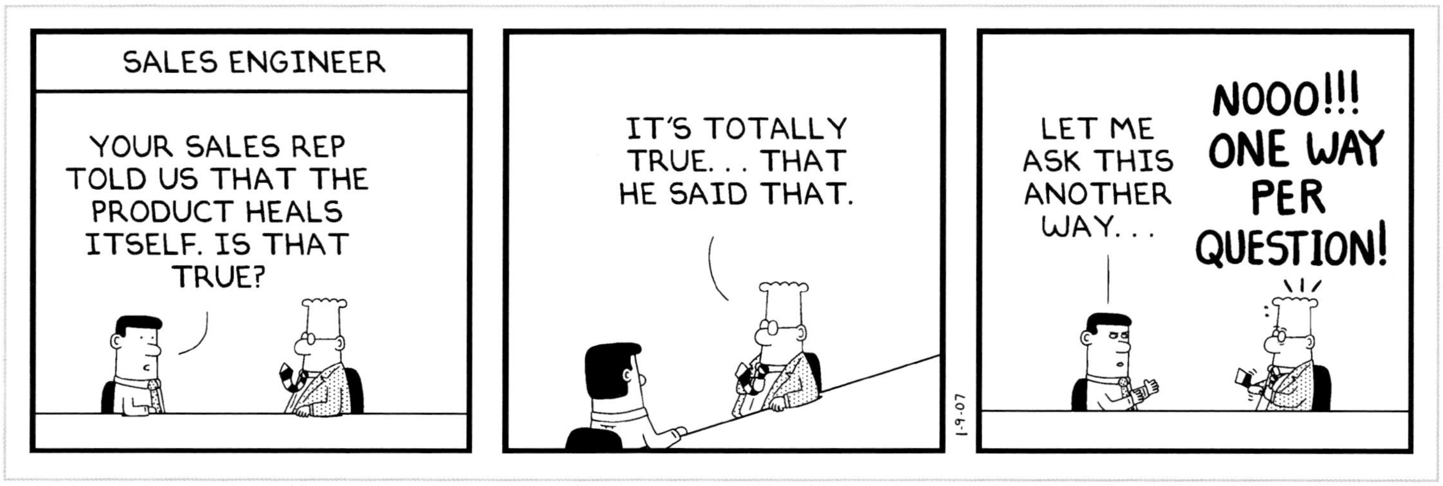
SALES ENGINEER
YOUR SALES REP TOLD US THAT THE PRODUCT HEALS ITSELF. IS THAT TRUE?
IT'S TOTALLY TRUE. . . THAT HE SAID THAT.
1-9-07
LET ME ASK THIS ANOTHER WAY. . .
NOOO!!! ONE WAY PER QUESTION!

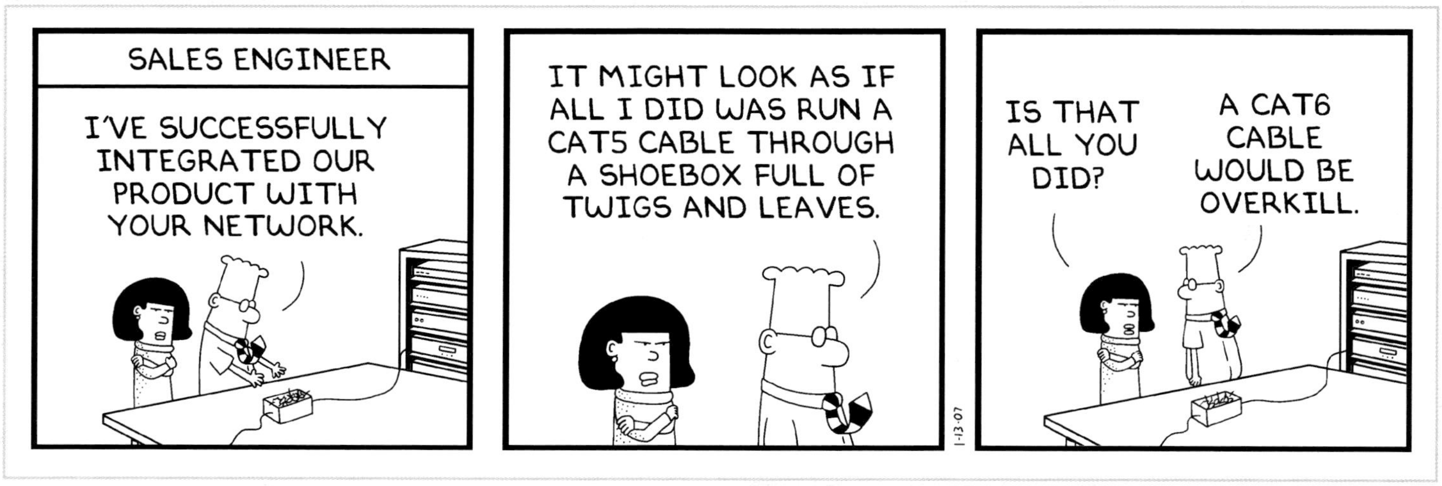
SALES ENGINEER
I'VE SUCCESSFULLY INTEGRATED OUR PRODUCT WITH YOUR NETWORK.
IT MIGHT LOOK AS IF ALL I DID WAS RUN A CAT5 CABLE THROUGH A SHOEBOX FULL OF TWIGS AND LEAVES.
1-13-07
IS THAT ALL YOU DID?
A CAT6 CABLE WOULD BE OVERKILL.

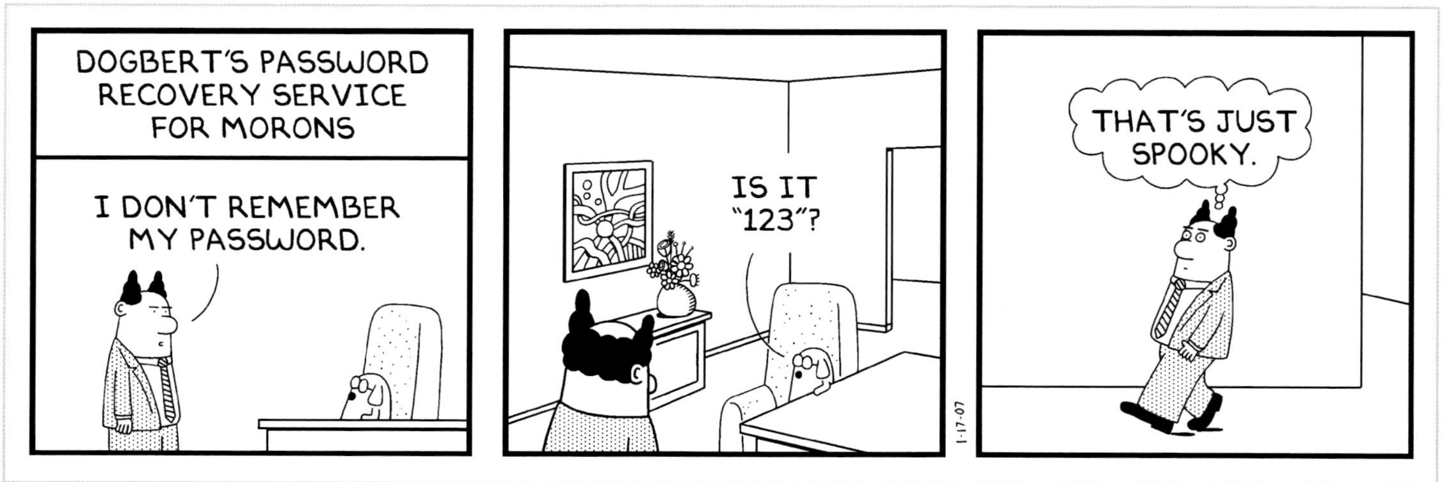
DOGBERT'S PASSWORD RECOVERY SERVICE FOR MORONS
I DON'T REMEMBER MY PASSWORD.
IS IT "123"?
1-17-07
THAT'S JUST SPOOKY.

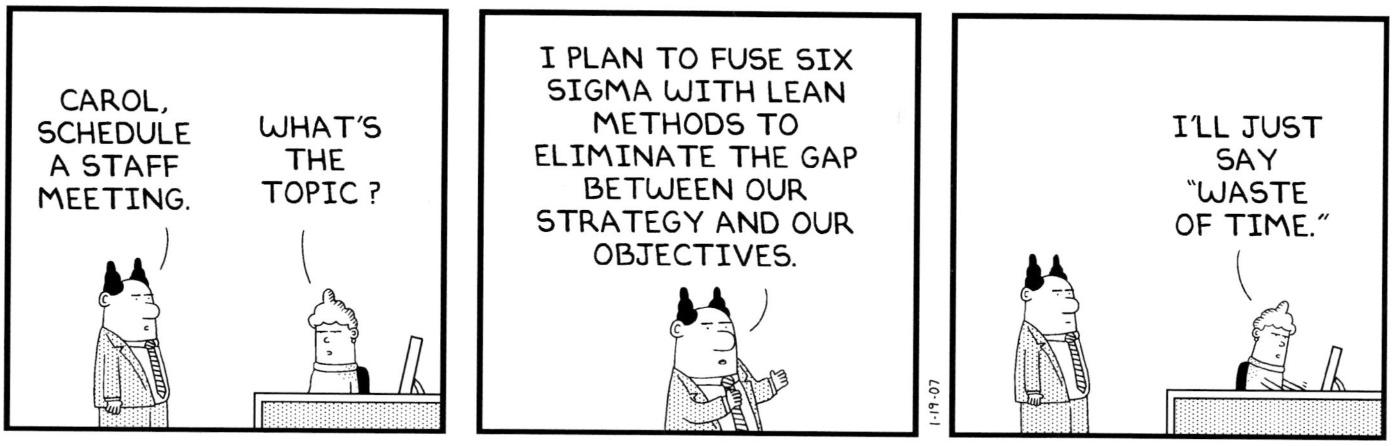
CAROL, SCHEDULE A STAFF MEETING.
WHAT'S THE TOPIC ?
I PLAN TO FUSE SIX SIGMA WITH LEAN METHODS TO ELIMINATE THE GAP BETWEEN OUR STRATEGY AND OUR OBJECTIVES.
I'LL JUST SAY "WASTE OF TIME."
1-19-07

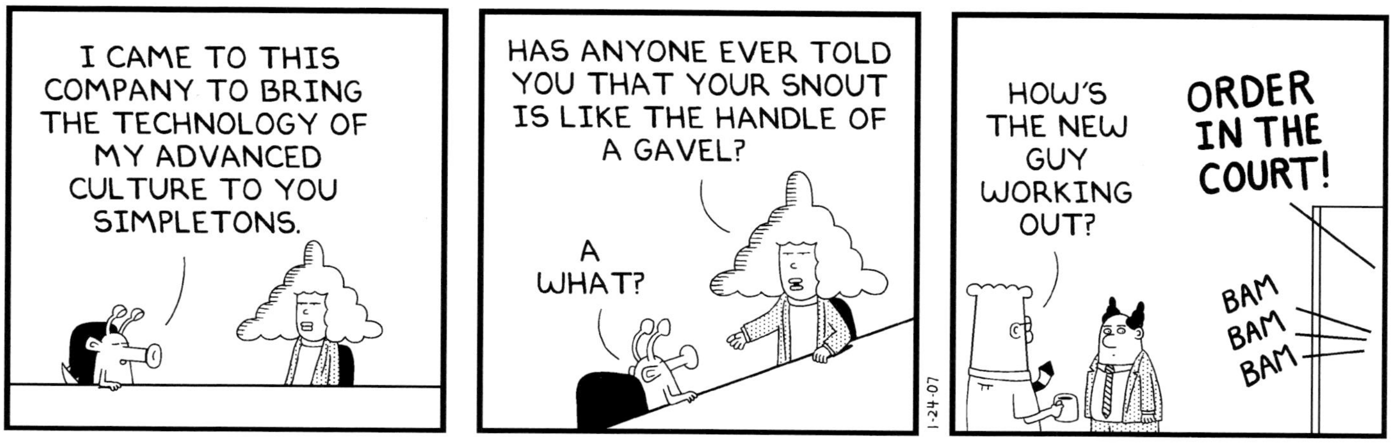
I CAME TO THIS COMPANY TO BRING THE TECHNOLOGY OF MY ADVANCED CULTURE TO YOU SIMPLETONS.
HAS ANYONE EVER TOLD YOU THAT YOUR SNOUT IS LIKE THE HANDLE OF A GAVEL?
A WHAT?
HOW'S THE NEW GUY WORKING OUT?
ORDER IN THE COURT!
BAM BAM BAM
1-24-07

Above is another example of a comic where I finished the first panel without knowing where the rest was heading. I stared at it for a while and decided the alien's snout was something that Alice couldn't resist grabbing like a handle.

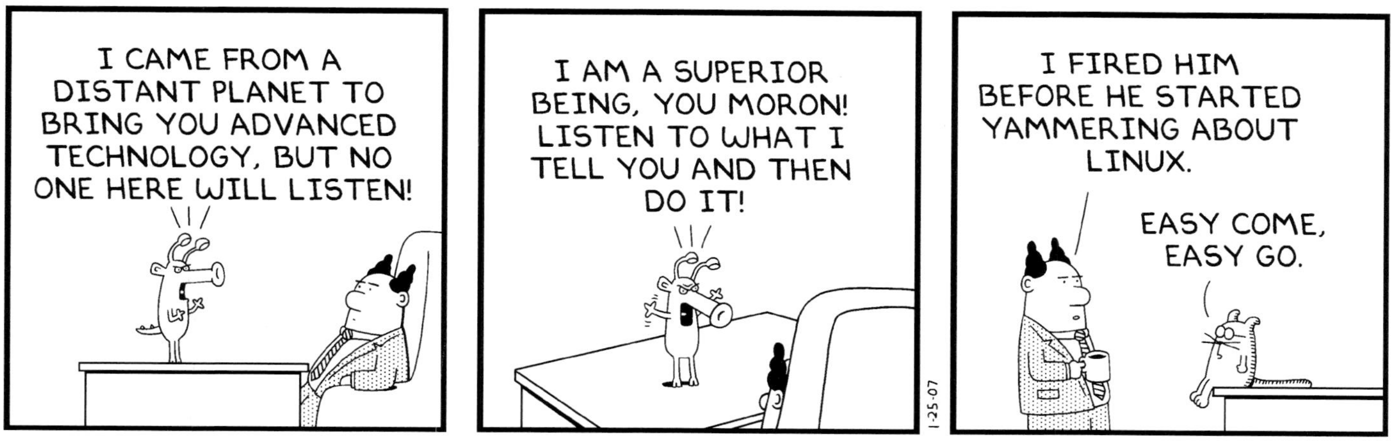
I CAME FROM A DISTANT PLANET TO BRING YOU ADVANCED TECHNOLOGY, BUT NO ONE HERE WILL LISTEN!
I AM A SUPERIOR BEING, YOU MORON! LISTEN TO WHAT I TELL YOU AND THEN DO IT!
I FIRED HIM BEFORE HE STARTED YAMMERING ABOUT LINUX.
EASY COME, EASY GO.
1-25-07

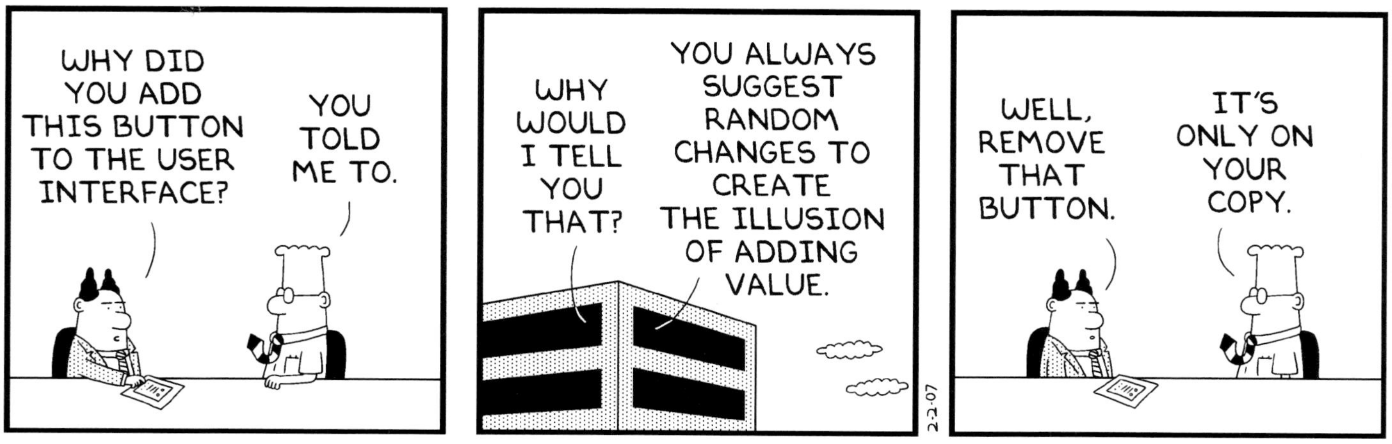
WHY DID YOU ADD THIS BUTTON TO THE USER INTERFACE?
YOU TOLD ME TO.
WHY WOULD I TELL YOU THAT?
YOU ALWAYS SUGGEST RANDOM CHANGES TO CREATE THE ILLUSION OF ADDING VALUE.
WELL, REMOVE THAT BUTTON.
IT'S ONLY ON YOUR COPY.
2-2-07

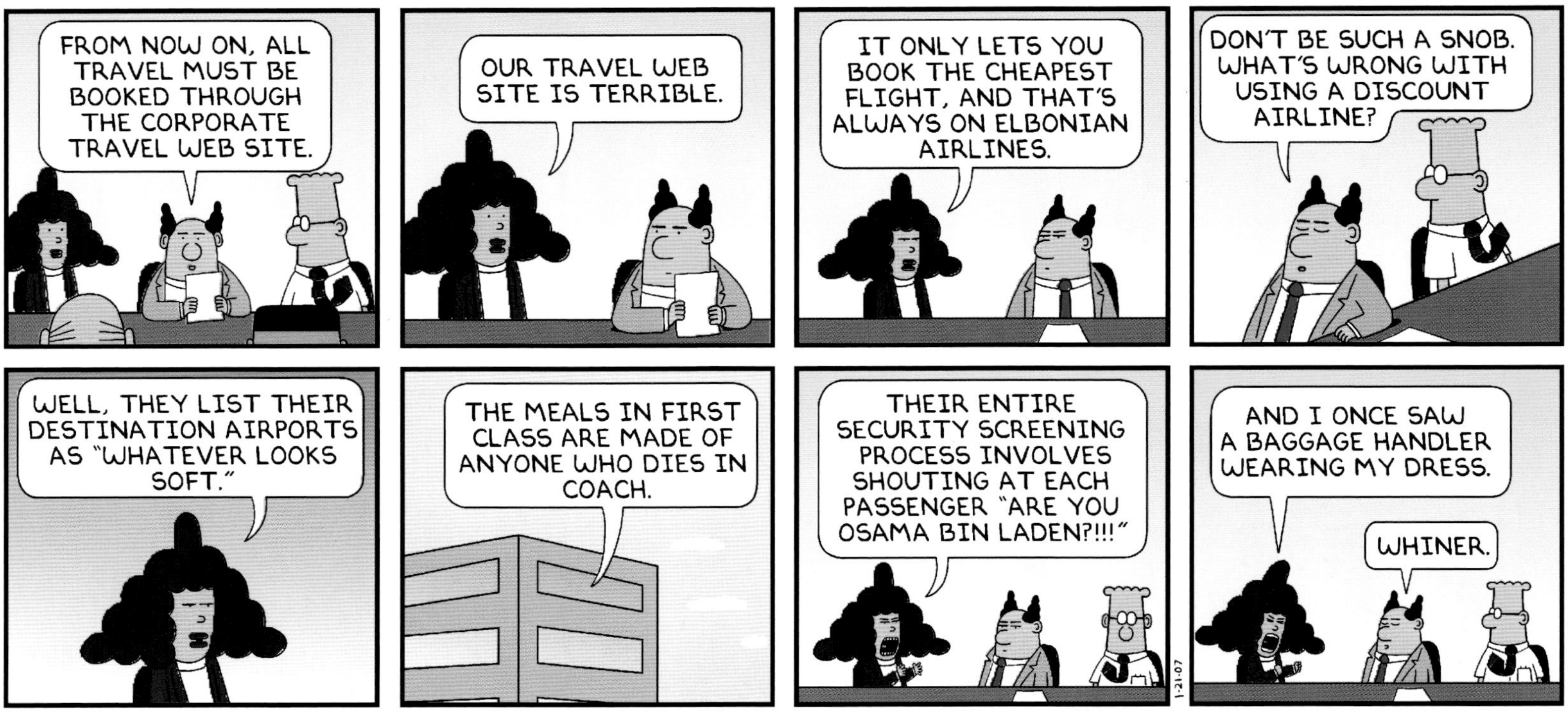
FROM NOW ON, ALL TRAVEL MUST BE BOOKED THROUGH THE CORPORATE TRAVEL WEB SITE.
OUR TRAVEL WEB SITE IS TERRIBLE.
IT ONLY LETS YOU BOOK THE CHEAPEST FLIGHT, AND THAT'S ALWAYS ON ELBONIAN AIRLINES.
DON'T BE SUCH A SNOB. WHAT'S WRONG WITH USING A DISCOUNT AIRLINE?
WELL, THEY LIST THEIR DESTINATION AIRPORTS AS "WHATEVER LOOKS SOFT."
THE MEALS IN FIRST CLASS ARE MADE OF ANYONE WHO DIES IN COACH.
THEIR ENTIRE SECURITY SCREENING PROCESS INVOLVES SHOUTING AT EACH PASSENGER "ARE YOU OSAMA BIN LADEN?!!!"
1-21-07
AND I ONCE SAW A BAGGAGE HANDLER WEARING MY DRESS.
WHINER.

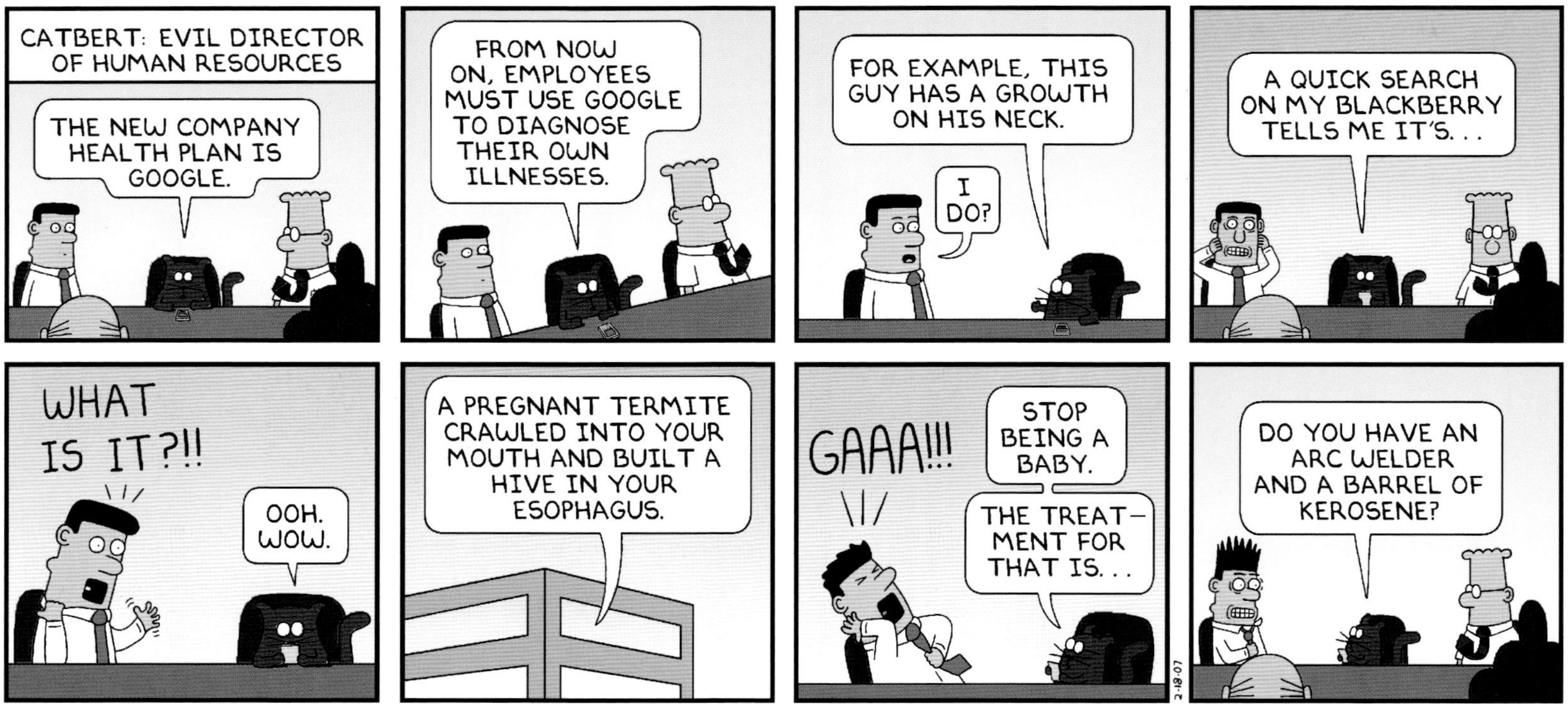
CATBERT: EVIL DIRECTOR OF HUMAN RESOURCES
THE NEW COMPANY HEALTH PLAN IS GOOGLE.
FROM NOW ON, EMPLOYEES MUST USE GOOGLE TO DIAGNOSE THEIR OWN ILLNESSES.
FOR EXAMPLE, THIS GUY HAS A GROWTH ON HIS NECK.
I DO?
A QUICK SEARCH ON MY BLACKBERRY TELLS ME IT'S. . .
WHAT IS IT?!!
OOH. WOW.
A PREGNANT TERMITE CRAWLED INTO YOUR MOUTH AND BUILT A HIVE IN YOUR ESOPHAGUS.
GAAA!!!
STOP BEING A BABY.
THE TREAT-MENT FOR THAT IS. . .
2-18-07
DO YOU HAVE AN ARC WELDER AND A BARREL OF KEROSENE?

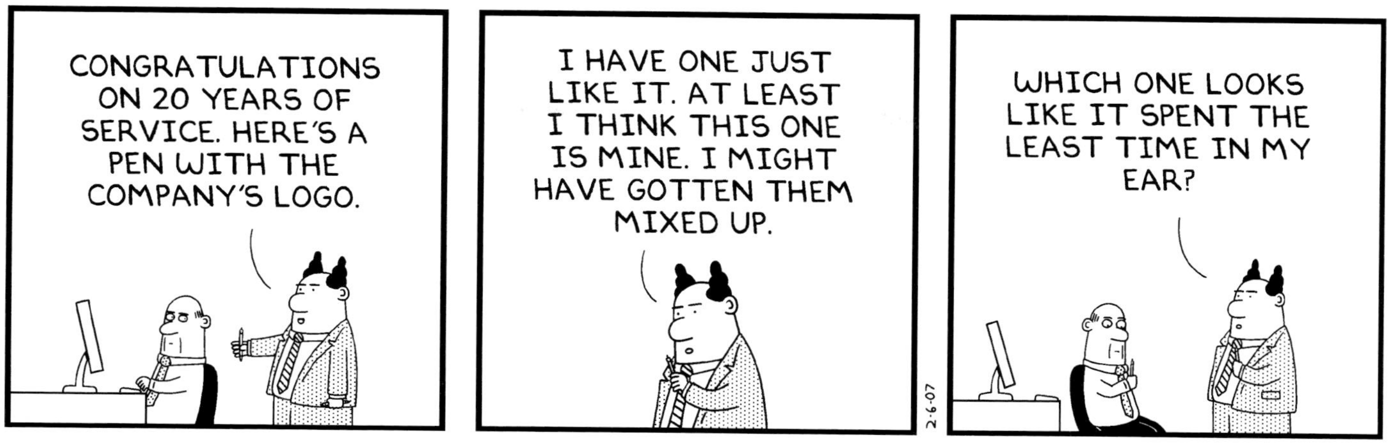
CONGRATULATIONS ON 20 YEARS OF SERVICE. HERE'S A PEN WITH THE COMPANY'S LOGO.
I HAVE ONE JUST LIKE IT. AT LEAST I THINK THIS ONE IS MINE. I MIGHT HAVE GOTTEN THEM MIXED UP.
2-6-07
WHICH ONE LOOKS LIKE IT SPENT THE LEAST TIME IN MY EAR?

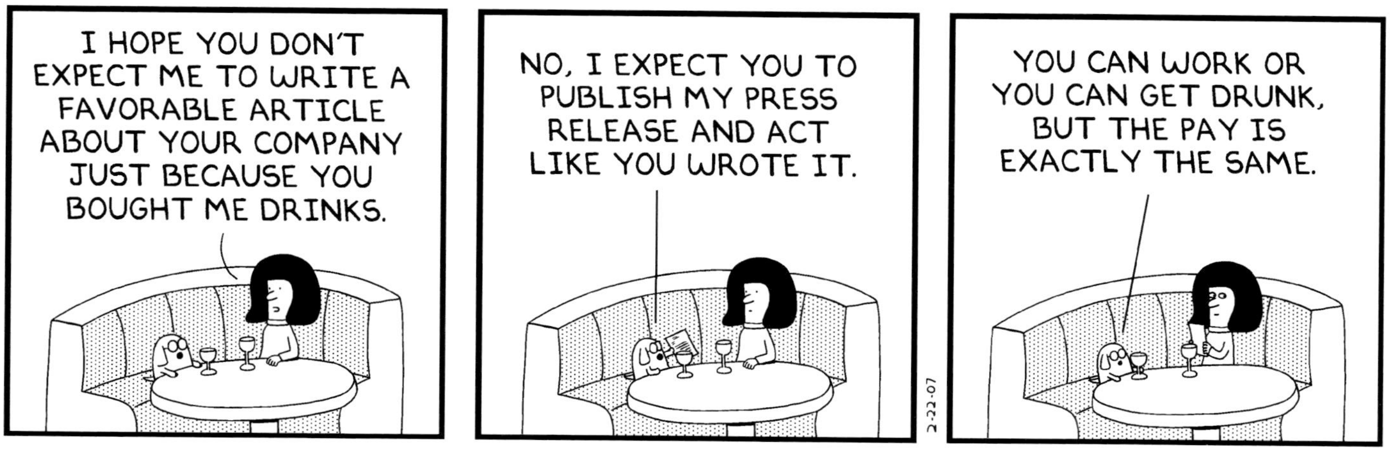
I HOPE YOU DON'T EXPECT ME TO WRITE A FAVORABLE ARTICLE ABOUT YOUR COMPANY JUST BECAUSE YOU BOUGHT ME DRINKS.
NO, I EXPECT YOU TO PUBLISH MY PRESS RELEASE AND ACT LIKE YOU WROTE IT.
2-22-07
YOU CAN WORK OR YOU CAN GET DRUNK, BUT THE PAY IS EXACTLY THE SAME.

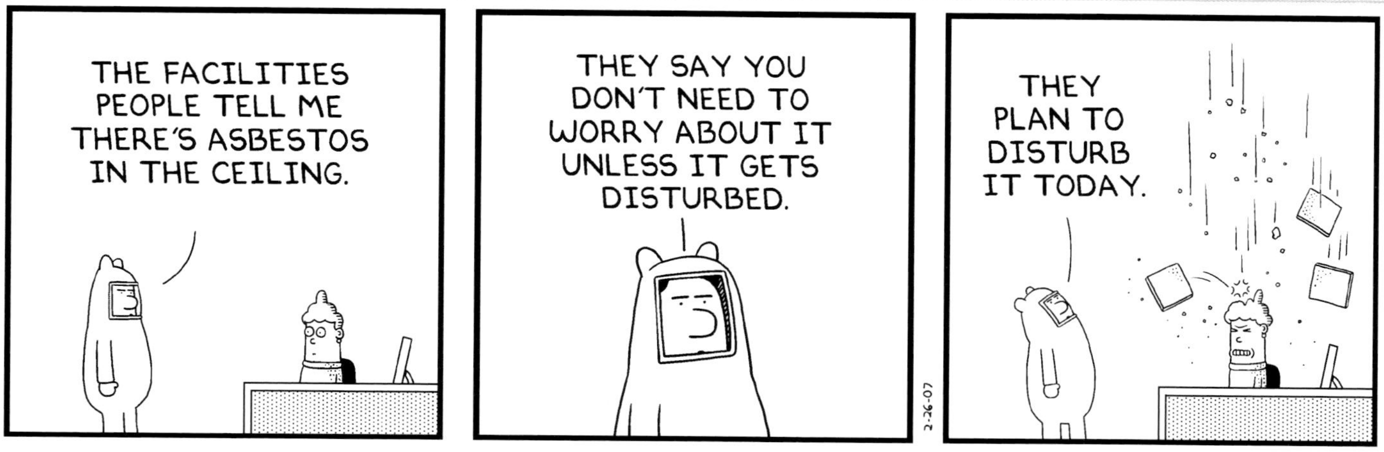
THE FACILITIES PEOPLE TELL ME THERE'S ASBESTOS IN THE CEILING.
THEY SAY YOU DON'T NEED TO WORRY ABOUT IT UNLESS IT GETS DISTURBED.
2-26-07
THEY PLAN TO DISTURB IT TODAY.

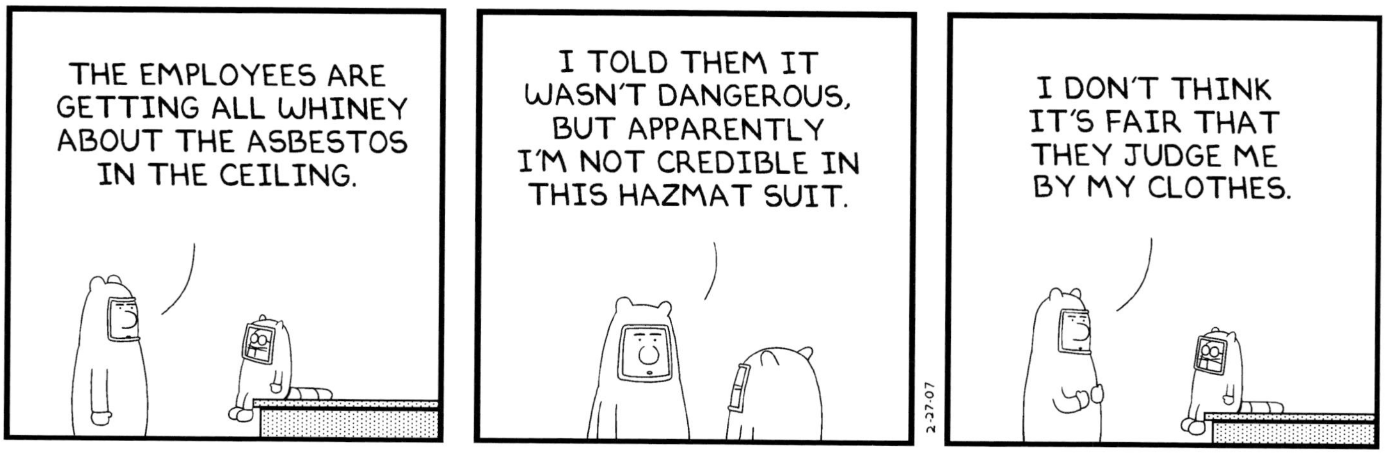
THE EMPLOYEES ARE GETTING ALL WHINEY ABOUT THE ASBESTOS IN THE CEILING.
I TOLD THEM IT WASN'T DANGEROUS, BUT APPARENTLY I'M NOT CREDIBLE IN THIS HAZMAT SUIT.
2-27-07
I DON'T THINK IT'S FAIR THAT THEY JUDGE ME BY MY CLOTHES.

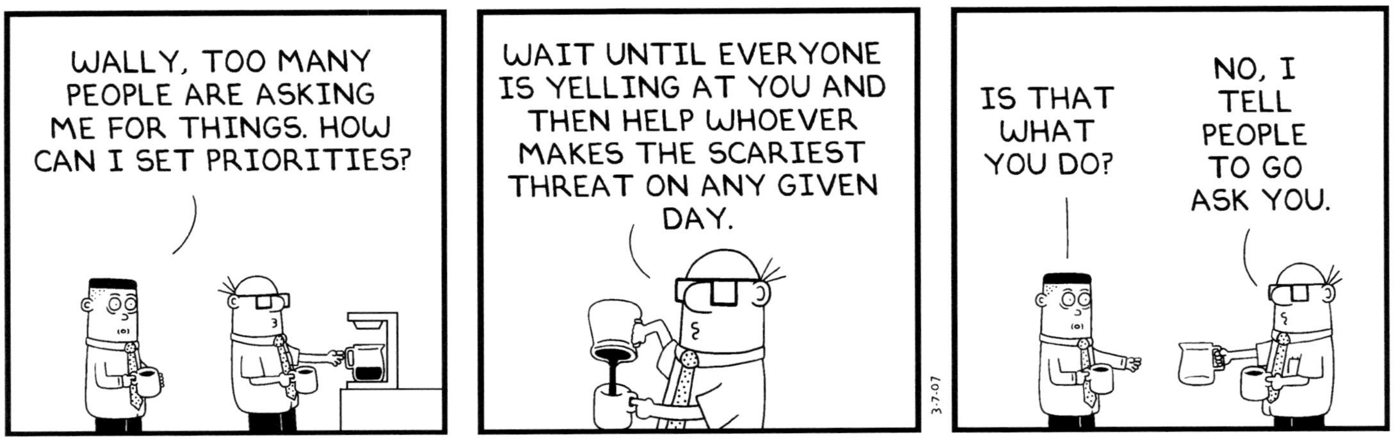
WALLY, TOO MANY PEOPLE ARE ASKING ME FOR THINGS. HOW CAN I SET PRIORITIES?
WAIT UNTIL EVERYONE IS YELLING AT YOU AND THEN HELP WHOEVER MAKES THE SCARIEST THREAT ON ANY GIVEN DAY.
3-7-07
IS THAT WHAT YOU DO?
NO, I TELL PEOPLE TO GO ASK YOU.

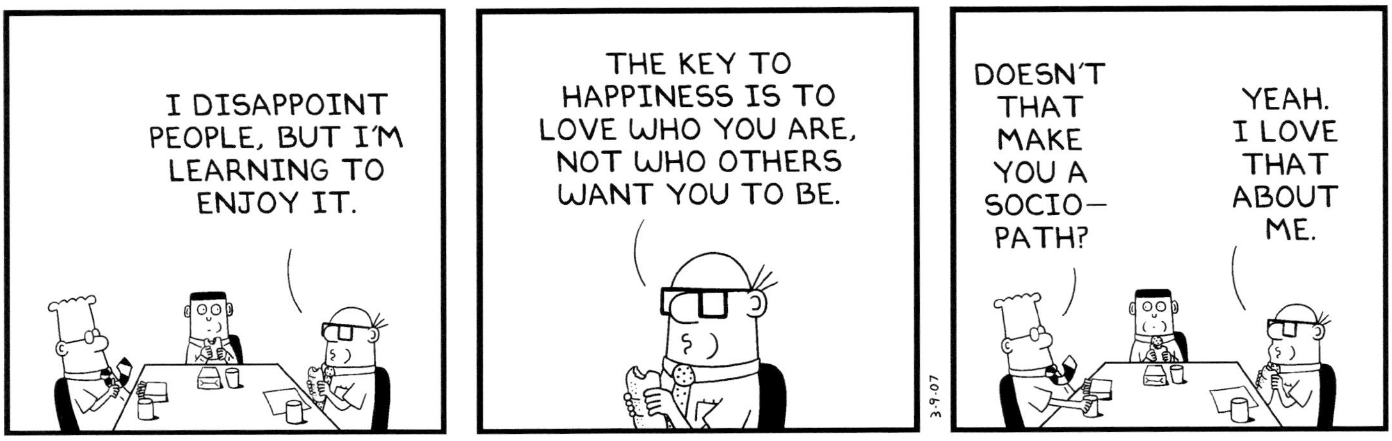
I DISAPPOINT PEOPLE, BUT I'M LEARNING TO ENJOY IT.
THE KEY TO HAPPINESS IS TO LOVE WHO YOU ARE, NOT WHO OTHERS WANT YOU TO BE.
3-9-07
DOESN'T THAT MAKE YOU A SOCIO-PATH?
YEAH. I LOVE THAT ABOUT ME.

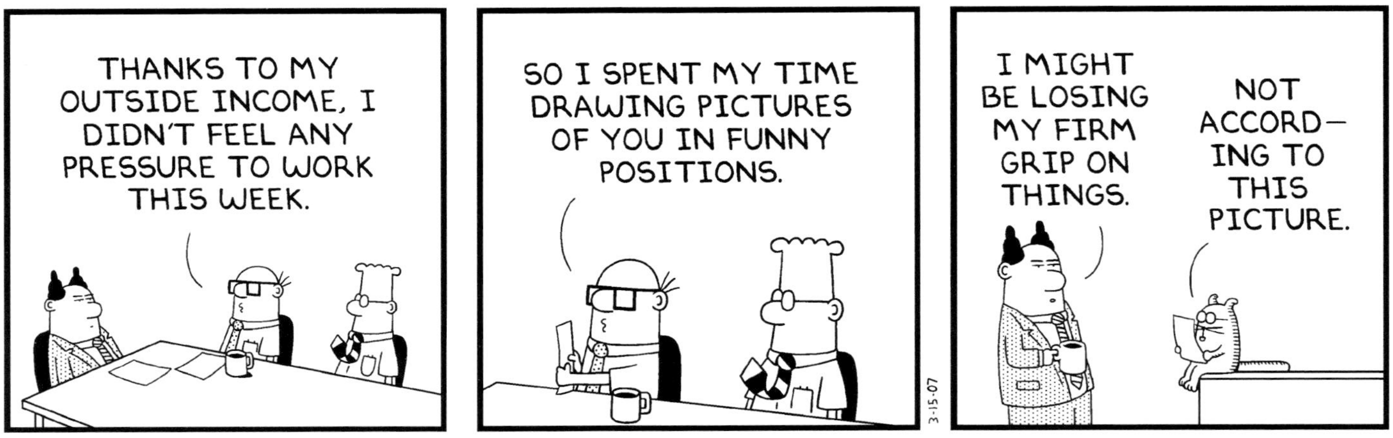
THANKS TO MY OUTSIDE INCOME, I DIDN'T FEEL ANY PRESSURE TO WORK THIS WEEK.
SO I SPENT MY TIME DRAWING PICTURES OF YOU IN FUNNY POSITIONS.
3-15-07
I MIGHT BE LOSING MY FIRM GRIP ON THINGS.
NOT ACCORD-ING TO THIS PICTURE.

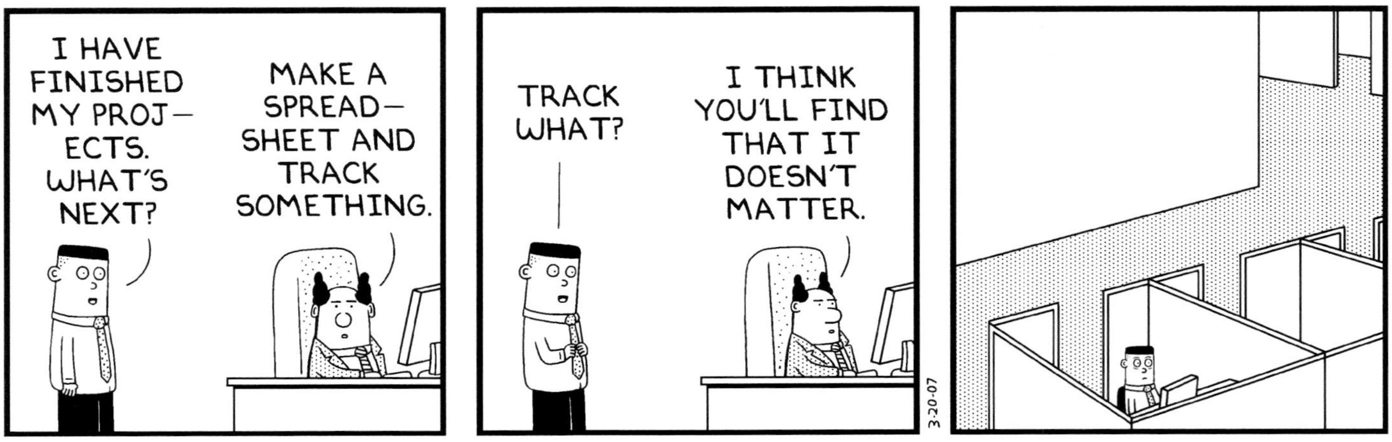
I HAVE FINISHED MY PROJ-ECTS. WHAT'S NEXT?
MAKE A SPREAD-SHEET AND TRACK SOMETHING.
TRACK WHAT?
I THINK YOU'LL FIND THAT IT DOESN'T MATTER.
3-20-07

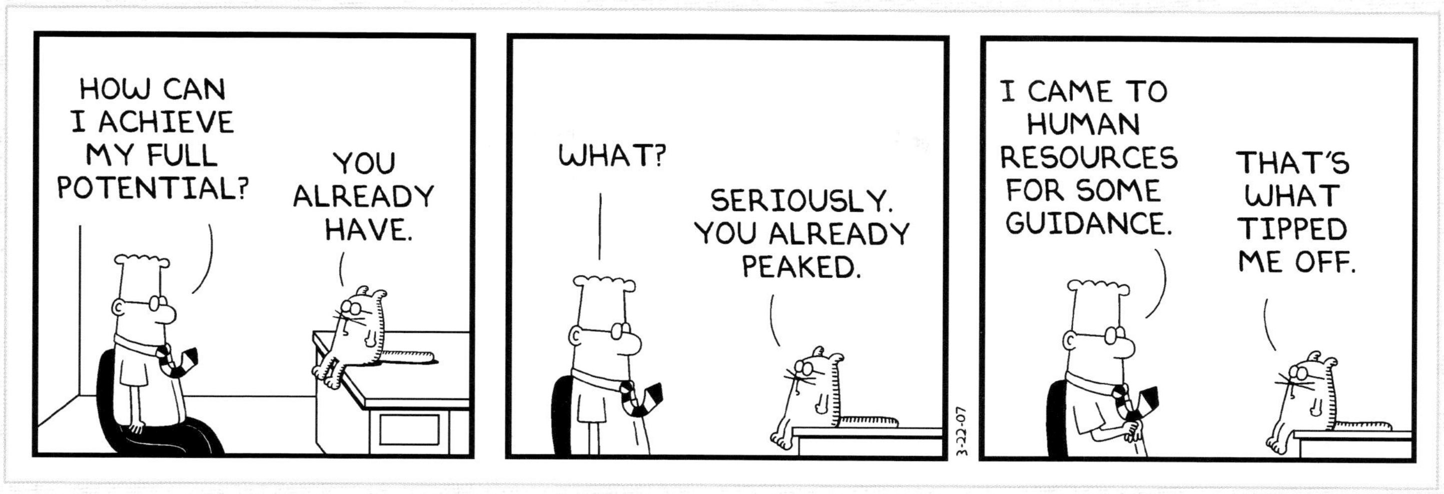
HOW CAN I ACHIEVE MY FULL POTENTIAL?
YOU ALREADY HAVE.
WHAT?
SERIOUSLY. YOU ALREADY PEAKED.
I CAME TO HUMAN RESOURCES FOR SOME GUIDANCE.
THAT'S WHAT TIPPED ME OFF.
3-22-07

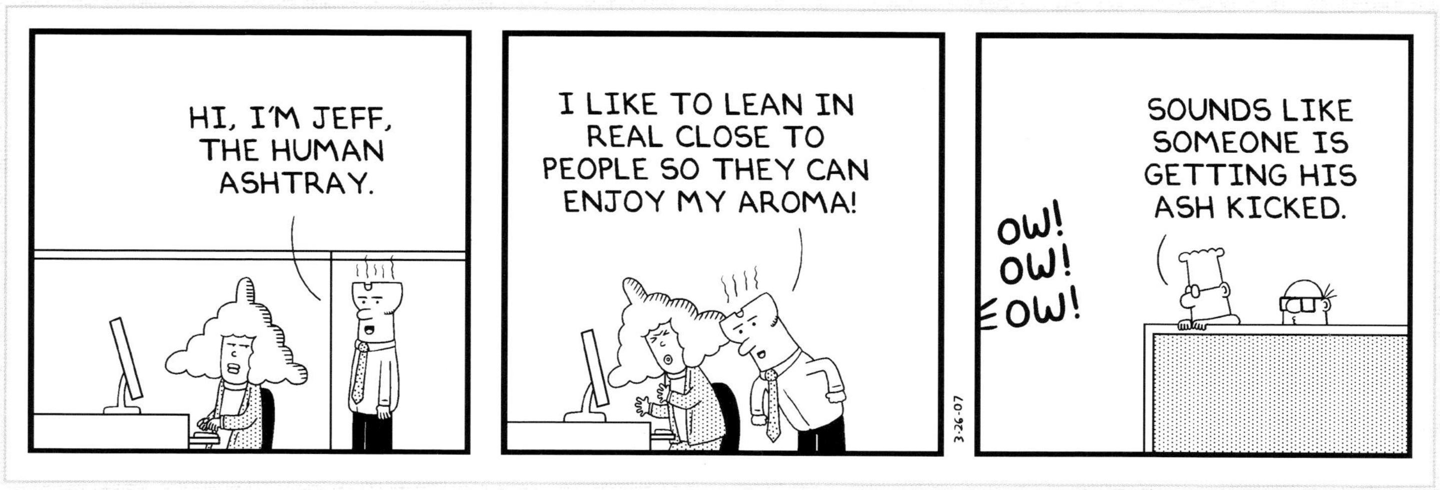
HI, I'M JEFF, THE HUMAN ASHTRAY.
I LIKE TO LEAN IN REAL CLOSE TO PEOPLE SO THEY CAN ENJOY MY AROMA!
OW! OW! OW!
SOUNDS LIKE SOMEONE IS GETTING HIS ASH KICKED.
3-26-07

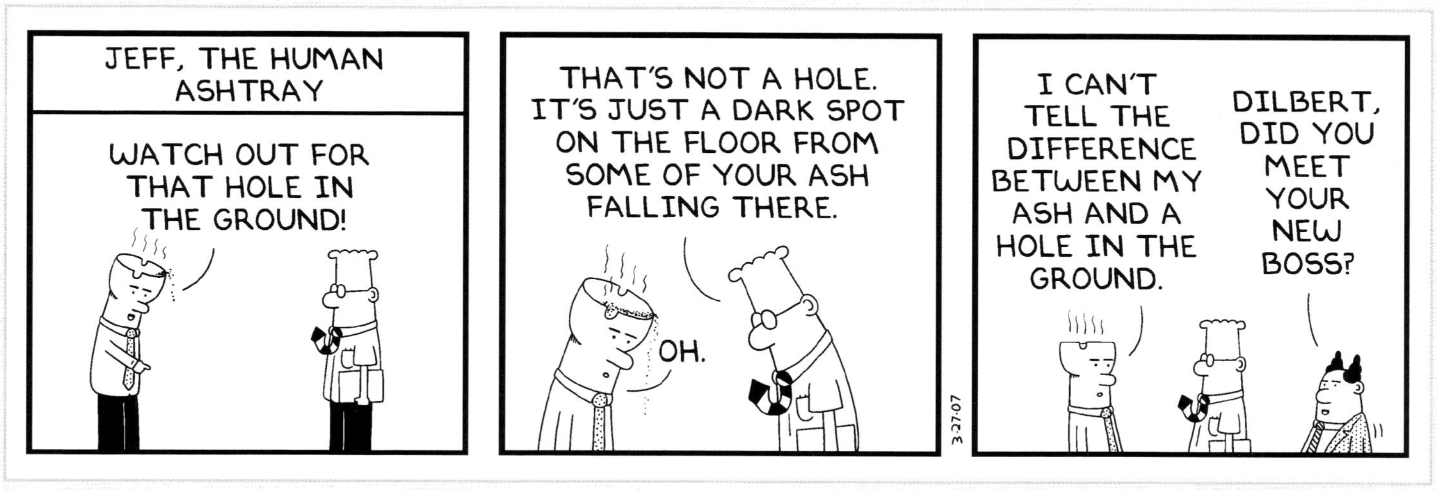
JEFF, THE HUMAN ASHTRAY
WATCH OUT FOR THAT HOLE IN THE GROUND!
THAT'S NOT A HOLE. IT'S JUST A DARK SPOT ON THE FLOOR FROM SOME OF YOUR ASH FALLING THERE.
OH.
I CAN'T TELL THE DIFFERENCE BETWEEN MY ASH AND A HOLE IN THE GROUND.
DILBERT, DID YOU MEET YOUR NEW BOSS?
3-27-07

The original version of the following strip (page 541) shows more of Jeff, the human ashtray, below the belt. My editors thought it was too much.

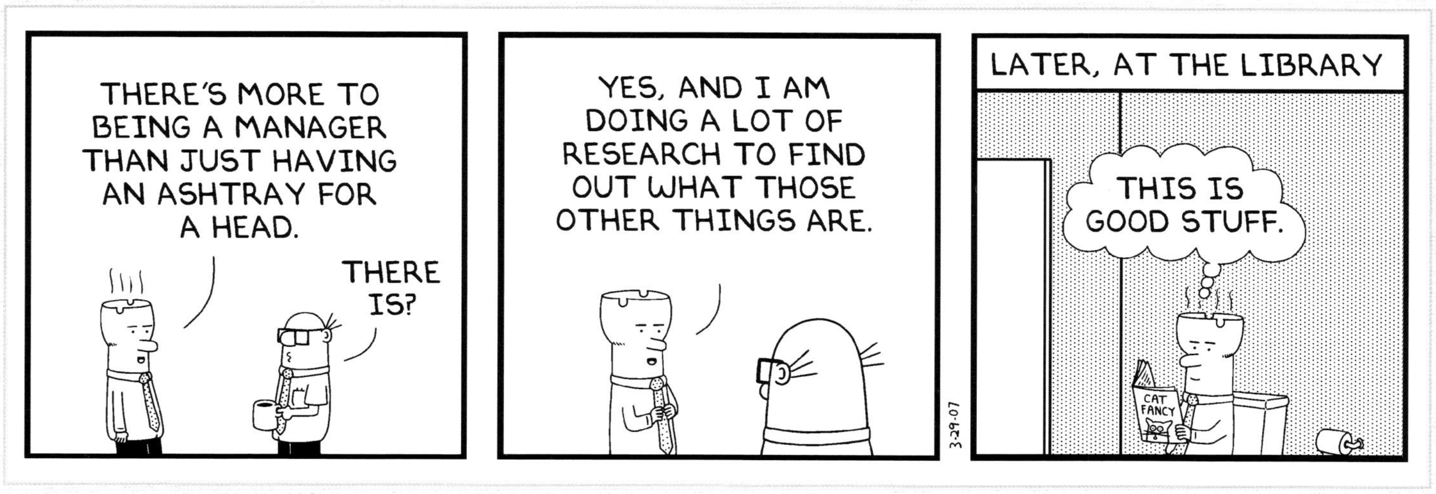
THERE'S MORE TO BEING A MANAGER THAN JUST HAVING AN ASHTRAY FOR A HEAD.
THERE IS?
YES, AND I AM DOING A LOT OF RESEARCH TO FIND OUT WHAT THOSE OTHER THINGS ARE.
LATER, AT THE LIBRARY
THIS IS GOOD STUFF.
CAT FANCY
3-29-07

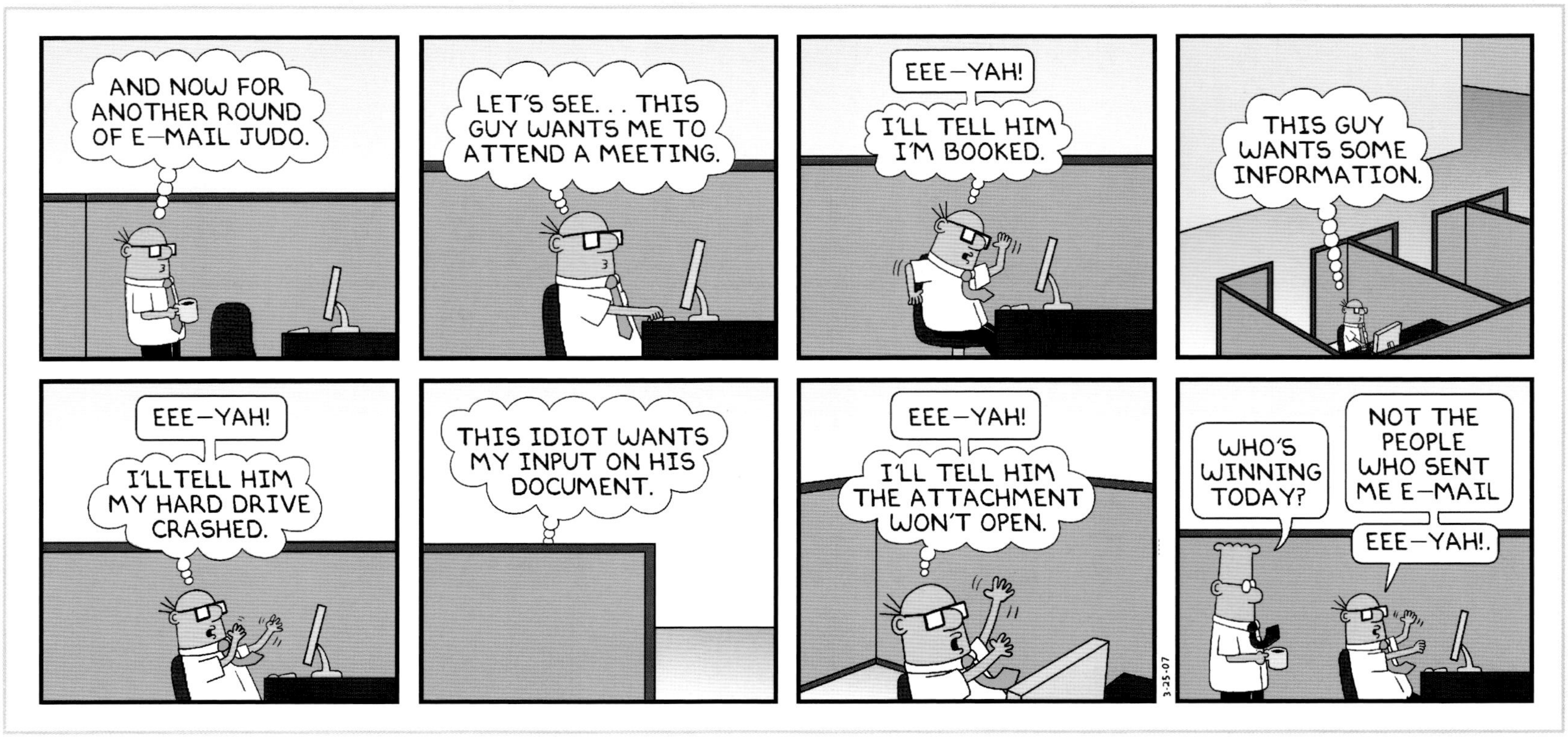
AND NOW FOR ANOTHER ROUND OF E-MAIL JUDO.
LET'S SEE. . . THIS GUY WANTS ME TO ATTEND A MEETING.
EEE—YAH!
I'LL TELL HIM I'M BOOKED.
THIS GUY WANTS SOME INFORMATION.
EEE—YAH!
I'LLTELL HIM MY HARD DRIVE CRASHED.
THIS IDIOT WANTS MY INPUT ON HIS DOCUMENT.
EEE—YAH!
I'LL TELL HIM THE ATTACHMENT WON'T OPEN.
WHO'S WINNING TODAY?
NOT THE PEOPLE WHO SENT ME E-MAIL
EEE—YAH!.
3-25-07

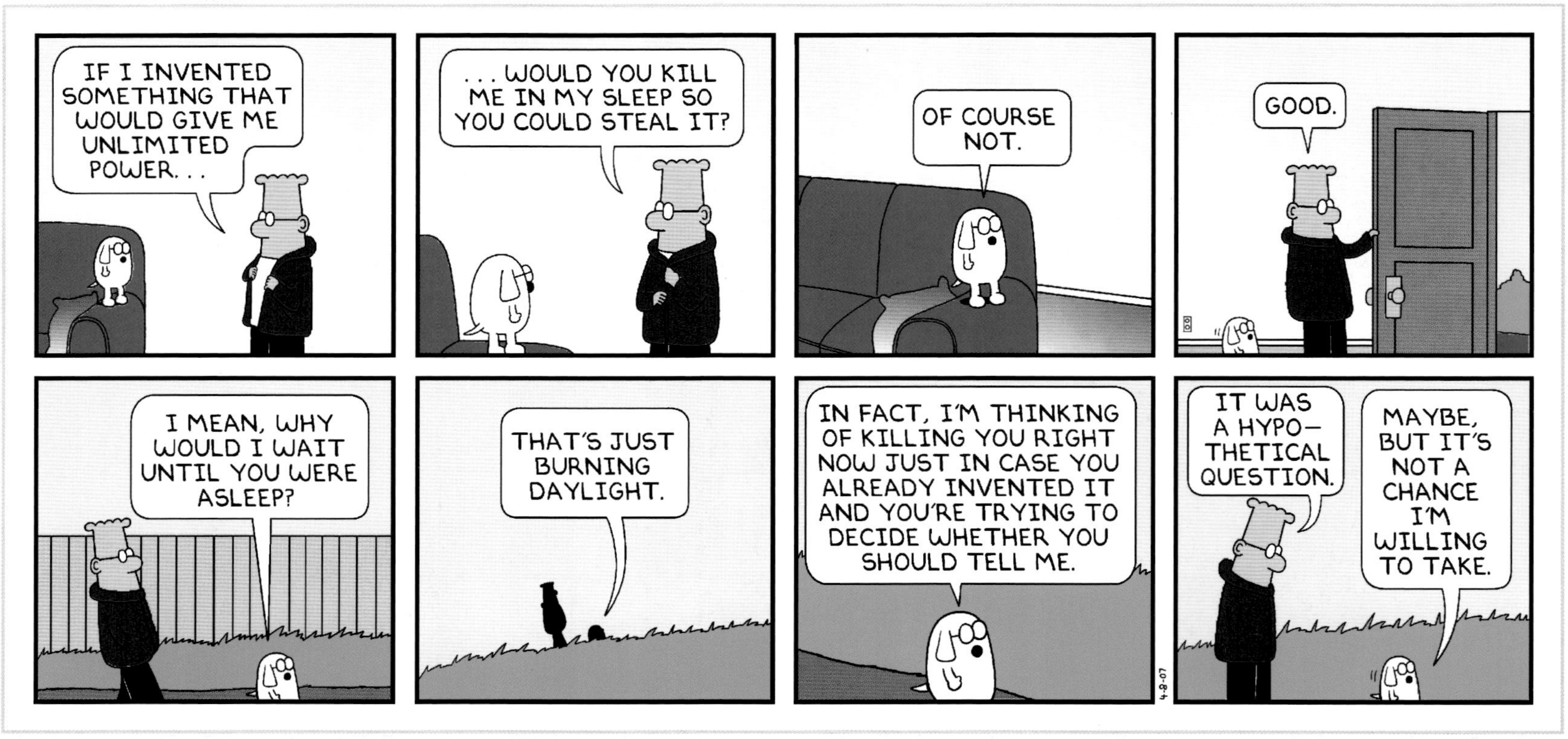
IF I INVENTED SOMETHING THAT WOULD GIVE ME UNLIMITED POWER. . .
. . . WOULD YOU KILL ME IN MY SLEEP SO YOU COULD STEAL IT?
OF COURSE NOT.
GOOD.
I MEAN, WHY WOULD I WAIT UNTIL YOU WERE ASLEEP?
THAT'S JUST BURNING DAYLIGHT.
IN FACT, I'M THINKING OF KILLING YOU RIGHT NOW JUST IN CASE YOU ALREADY INVENTED IT AND YOU'RE TRYING TO DECIDE WHETHER YOU SHOULD TELL ME.
IT WAS A HYPO—THETICAL QUESTION.
MAYBE, BUT IT'S NOT A CHANCE I'M WILLING TO TAKE.
4-8-07

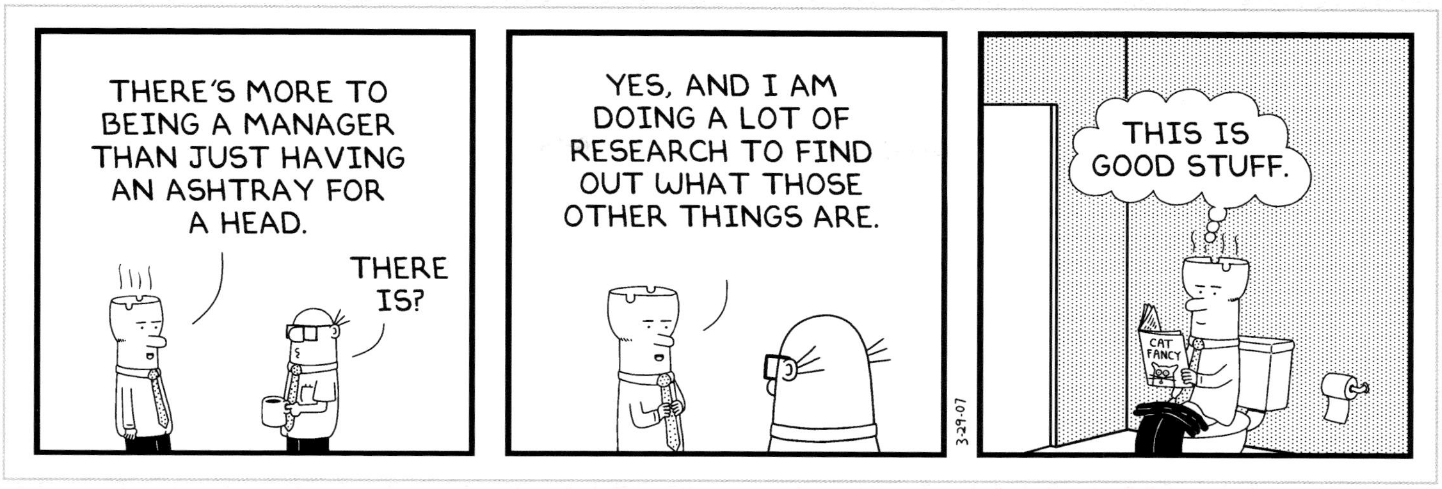
THERE'S MORE TO BEING A MANAGER THAN JUST HAVING AN ASHTRAY FOR A HEAD.
THERE IS?
YES, AND I AM DOING A LOT OF RESEARCH TO FIND OUT WHAT THOSE OTHER THINGS ARE.
THIS IS GOOD STUFF.
CAT FANCY
3-29-07

In retrospect, this version does show more than the humor required.

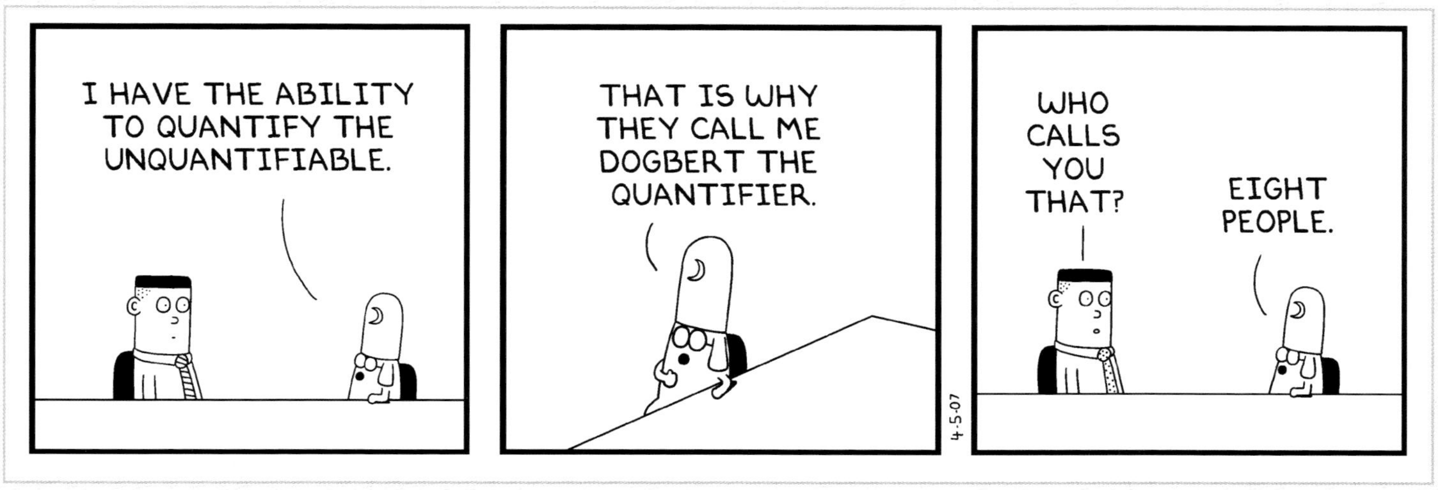
I HAVE THE ABILITY TO QUANTIFY THE UNQUANTIFIABLE.
THAT IS WHY THEY CALL ME DOGBERT THE QUANTIFIER.
4-5-07
WHO CALLS YOU THAT?
EIGHT PEOPLE.

You have to be in just the right mood for the following comic to work. Sometimes it just lies there. Other times it is one of my favorites.

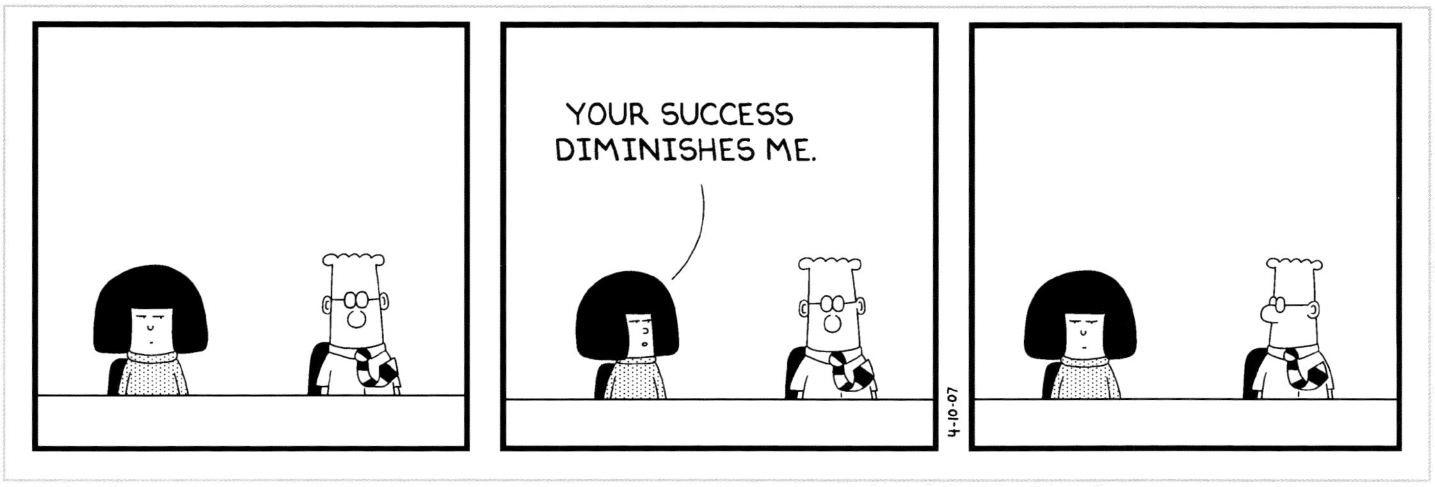
YOUR SUCCESS DIMINISHES ME.
4-10-07

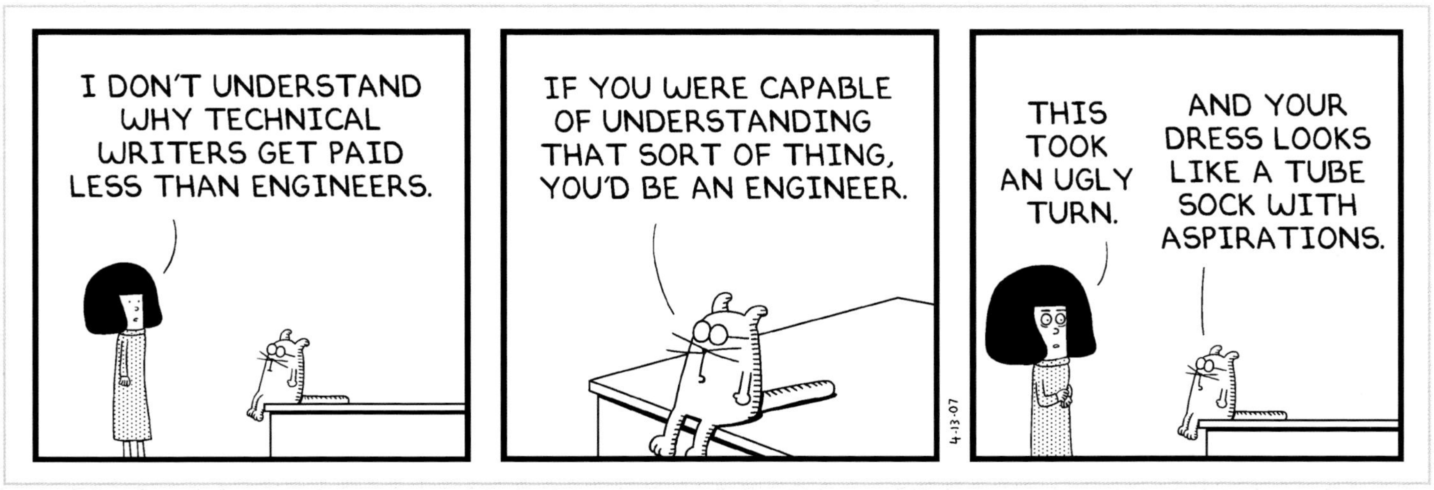
I DON'T UNDERSTAND WHY TECHNICAL WRITERS GET PAID LESS THAN ENGINEERS.
IF YOU WERE CAPABLE OF UNDERSTANDING THAT SORT OF THING, YOU'D BE AN ENGINEER.
4-13-07
THIS TOOK AN UGLY TURN.
AND YOUR DRESS LOOKS LIKE A TUBE SOCK WITH ASPIRATIONS.

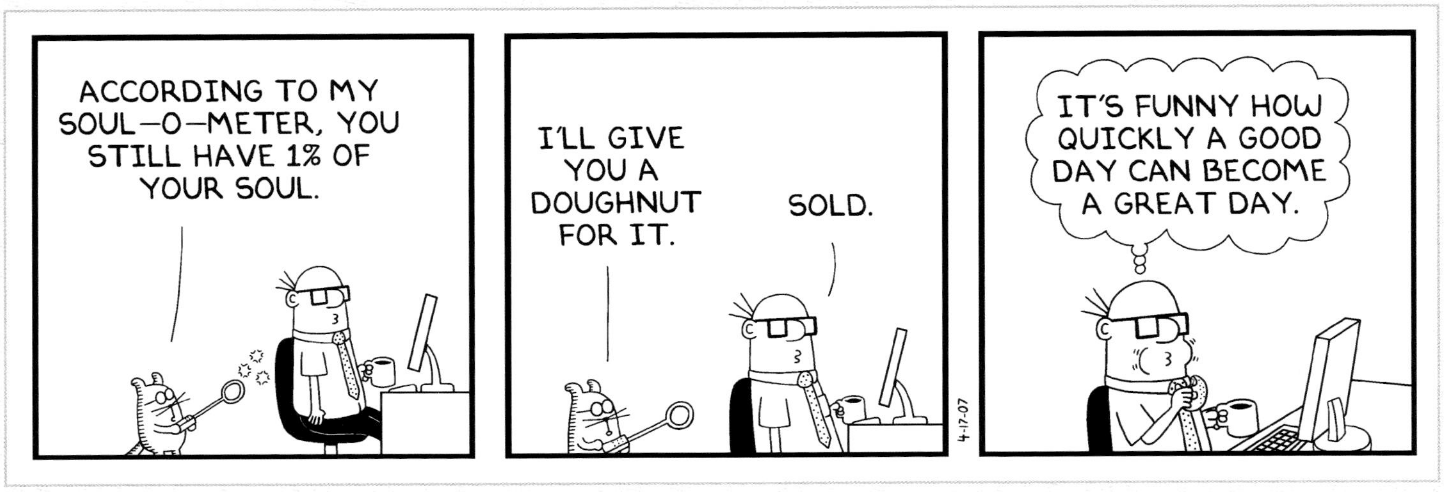
ACCORDING TO MY SOUL—O—METER, YOU STILL HAVE 1% OF YOUR SOUL.
I'LL GIVE YOU A DOUGHNUT FOR IT.
SOLD.
4-17-07
IT'S FUNNY HOW QUICKLY A GOOD DAY CAN BECOME A GREAT DAY.

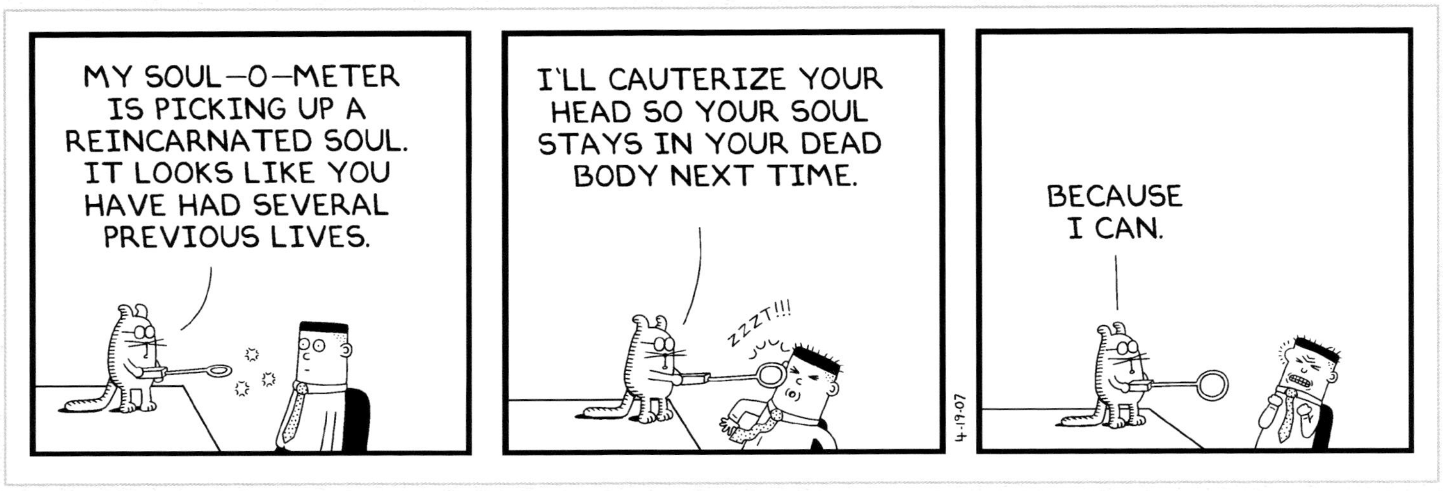
MY SOUL—O—METER IS PICKING UP A REINCARNATED SOUL. IT LOOKS LIKE YOU HAVE HAD SEVERAL PREVIOUS LIVES.
I'LL CAUTERIZE YOUR HEAD SO YOUR SOUL STAYS IN YOUR DEAD BODY NEXT TIME.
ZZZT!!!
4-19-07
BECAUSE I CAN.

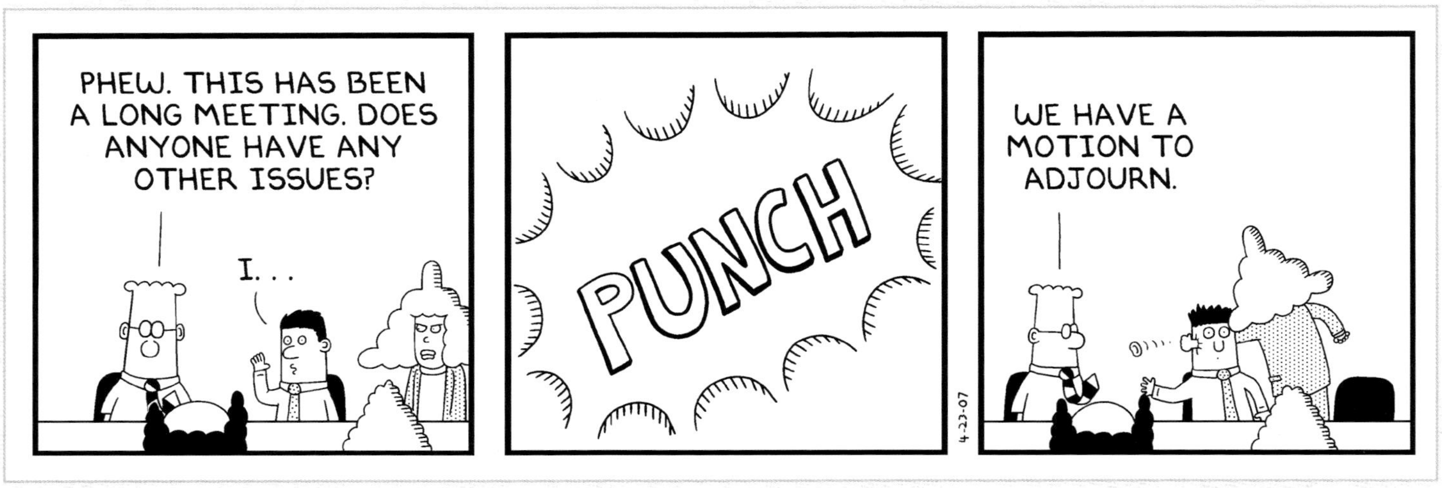
PHEW. THIS HAS BEEN A LONG MEETING. DOES ANYONE HAVE ANY OTHER ISSUES?
I. . .
PUNCH
4-23-07
WE HAVE A MOTION TO ADJOURN.

The strip below ran in newspapers. The original, on the next page, was deemed too suggestive because of Alice's position.

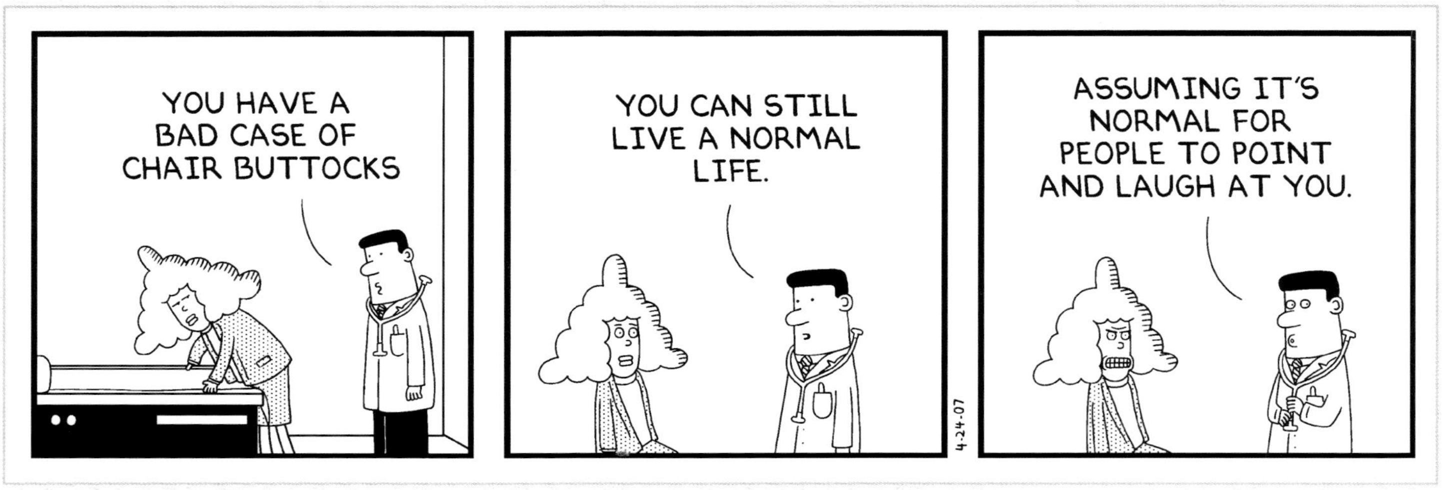
YOU HAVE A BAD CASE OF CHAIR BUTTOCKS
YOU CAN STILL LIVE A NORMAL LIFE.
4-24-07
ASSUMING IT'S NORMAL FOR PEOPLE TO POINT AND LAUGH AT YOU.

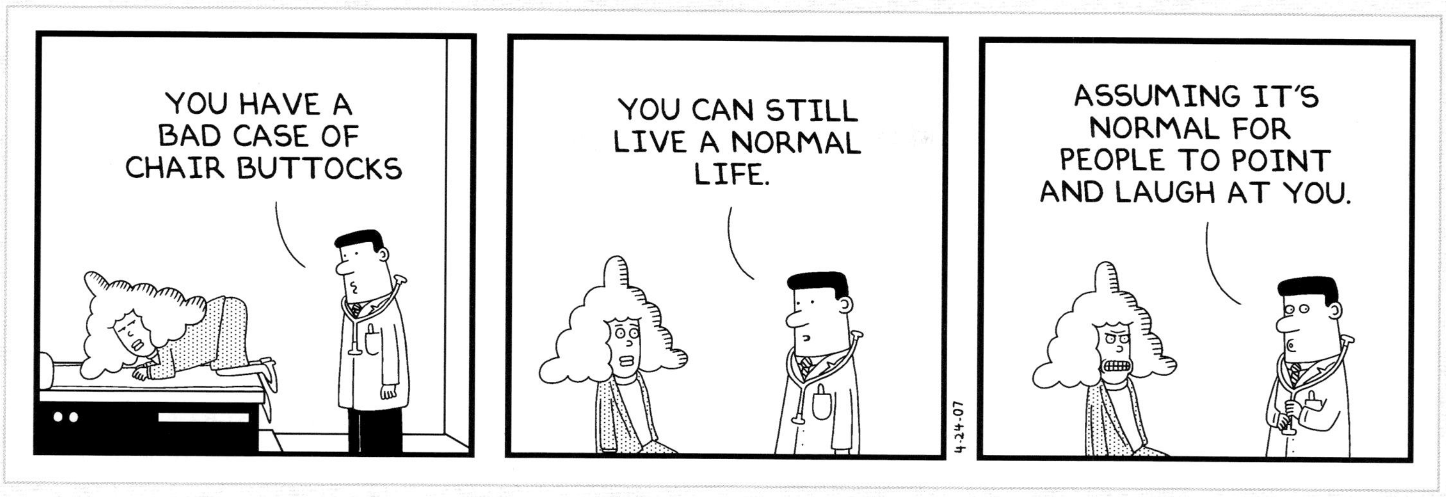
YOU HAVE A BAD CASE OF CHAIR BUTTOCKS
YOU CAN STILL LIVE A NORMAL LIFE.
4-24-07
ASSUMING IT'S NORMAL FOR PEOPLE TO POINT AND LAUGH AT YOU.

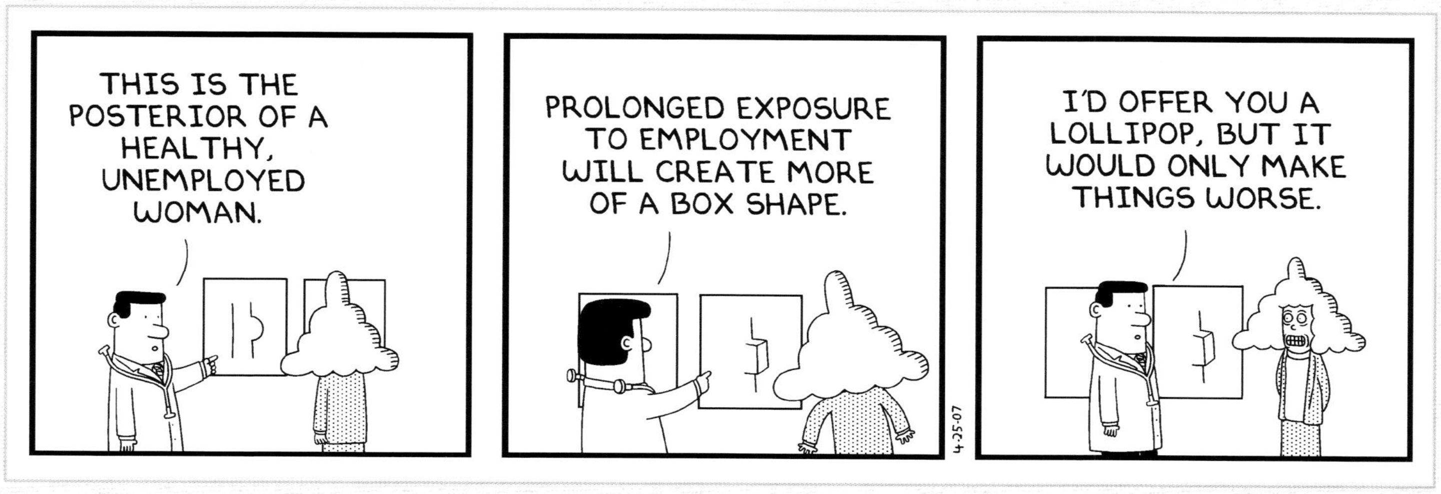
THIS IS THE POSTERIOR OF A HEALTHY, UNEMPLOYED WOMAN.
PROLONGED EXPOSURE TO EMPLOYMENT WILL CREATE MORE OF A BOX SHAPE.
4-25-07
I'D OFFER YOU A LOLLIPOP, BUT IT WOULD ONLY MAKE THINGS WORSE.

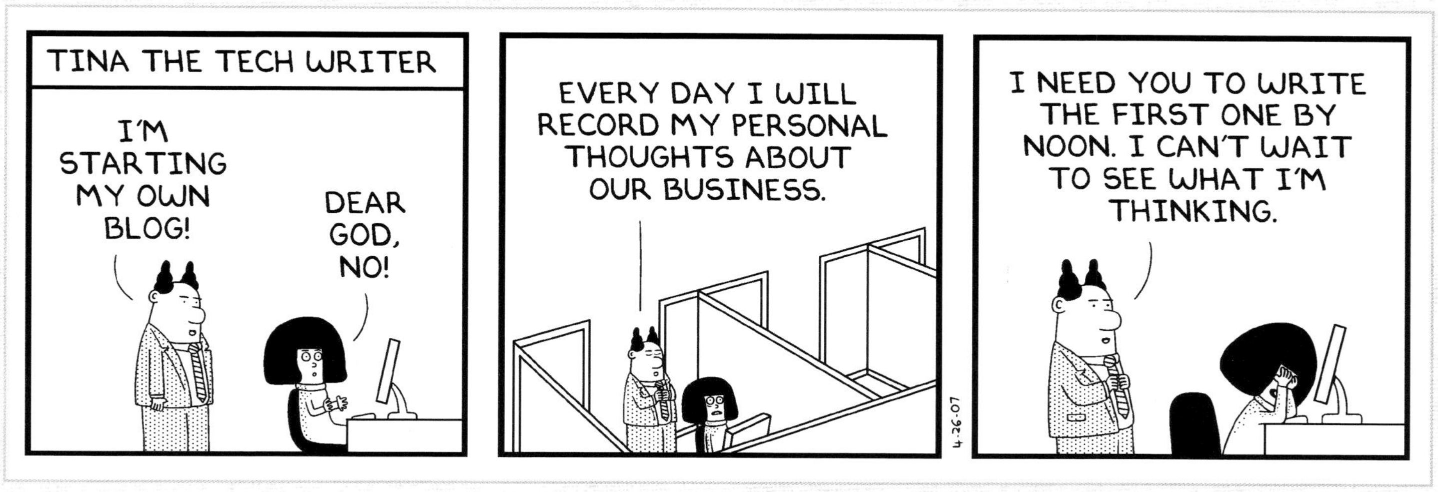
TINA THE TECH WRITER
I'M STARTING MY OWN BLOG!
DEAR GOD, NO!
EVERY DAY I WILL RECORD MY PERSONAL THOUGHTS ABOUT OUR BUSINESS.
4-26-07
I NEED YOU TO WRITE THE FIRST ONE BY NOON. I CAN'T WAIT TO SEE WHAT I'M THINKING.

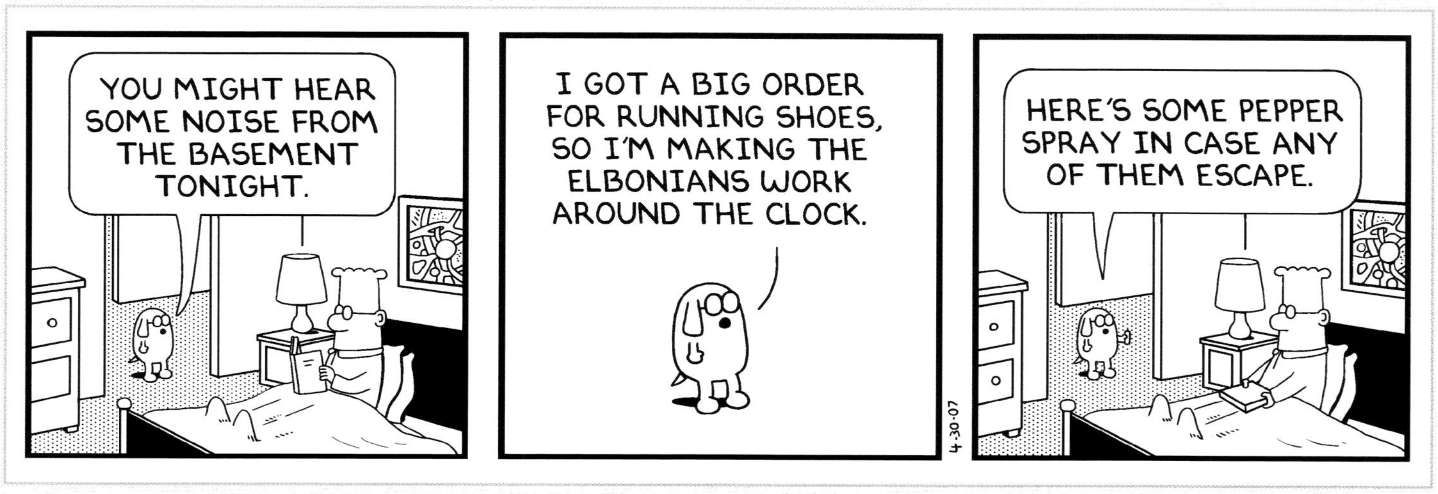
YOU MIGHT HEAR SOME NOISE FROM THE BASEMENT TONIGHT.
I GOT A BIG ORDER FOR RUNNING SHOES, SO I'M MAKING THE ELBONIANS WORK AROUND THE CLOCK.
4-30-07
HERE'S SOME PEPPER SPRAY IN CASE ANY OF THEM ESCAPE.

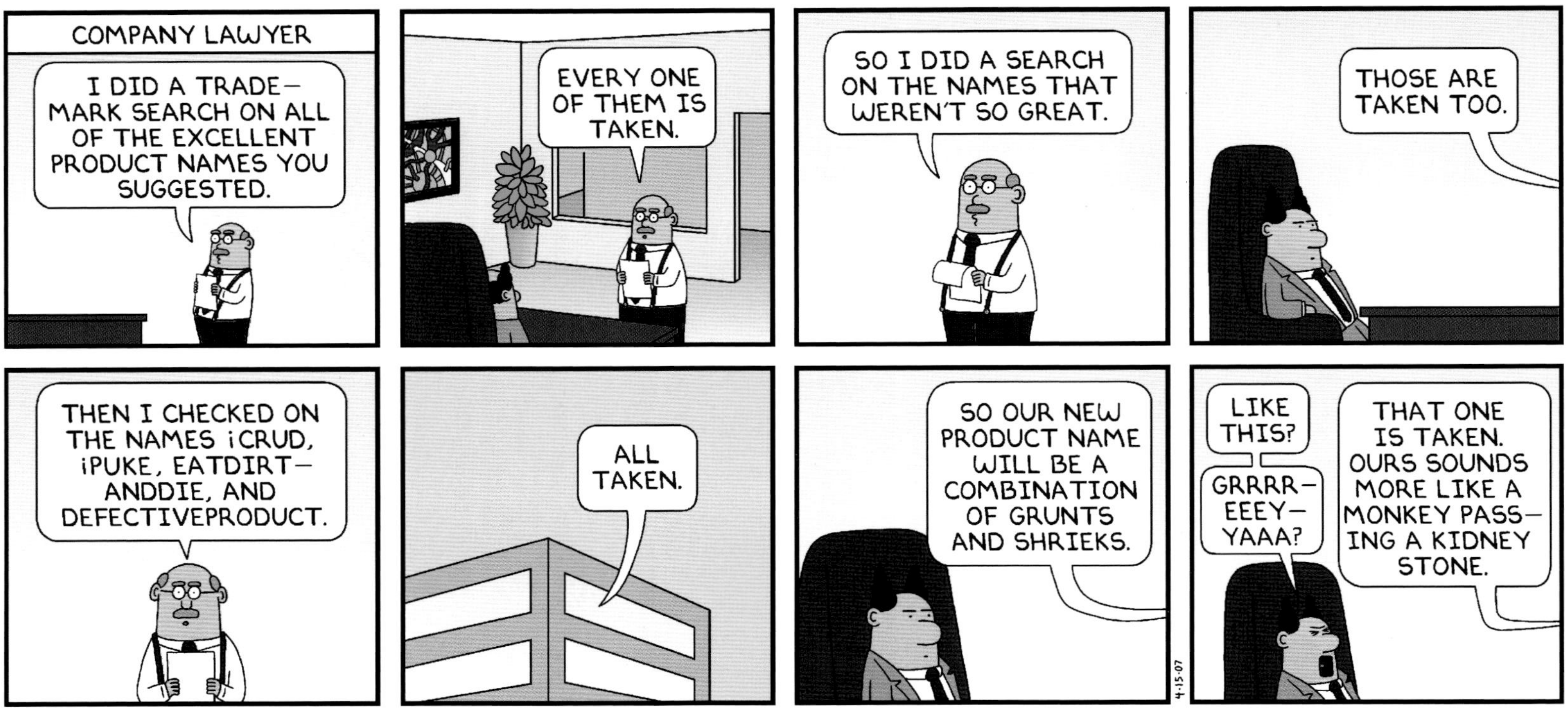
COMPANY LAWYER
I DID A TRADE-MARK SEARCH ON ALL OF THE EXCELLENT PRODUCT NAMES YOU SUGGESTED.
EVERY ONE OF THEM IS TAKEN.
SO I DID A SEARCH ON THE NAMES THAT WEREN'T SO GREAT.
THOSE ARE TAKEN TOO.
THEN I CHECKED ON THE NAMES iCRUD, iPUKE, EATDIRT-ANDDIE, AND DEFECTIVEPRODUCT.
ALL TAKEN.
SO OUR NEW PRODUCT NAME WILL BE A COMBINATION OF GRUNTS AND SHRIEKS.
LIKE THIS?
GRRRR-EEEY-YAAA?
THAT ONE IS TAKEN. OURS SOUNDS MORE LIKE A MONKEY PASS-ING A KIDNEY STONE.
4-15-07

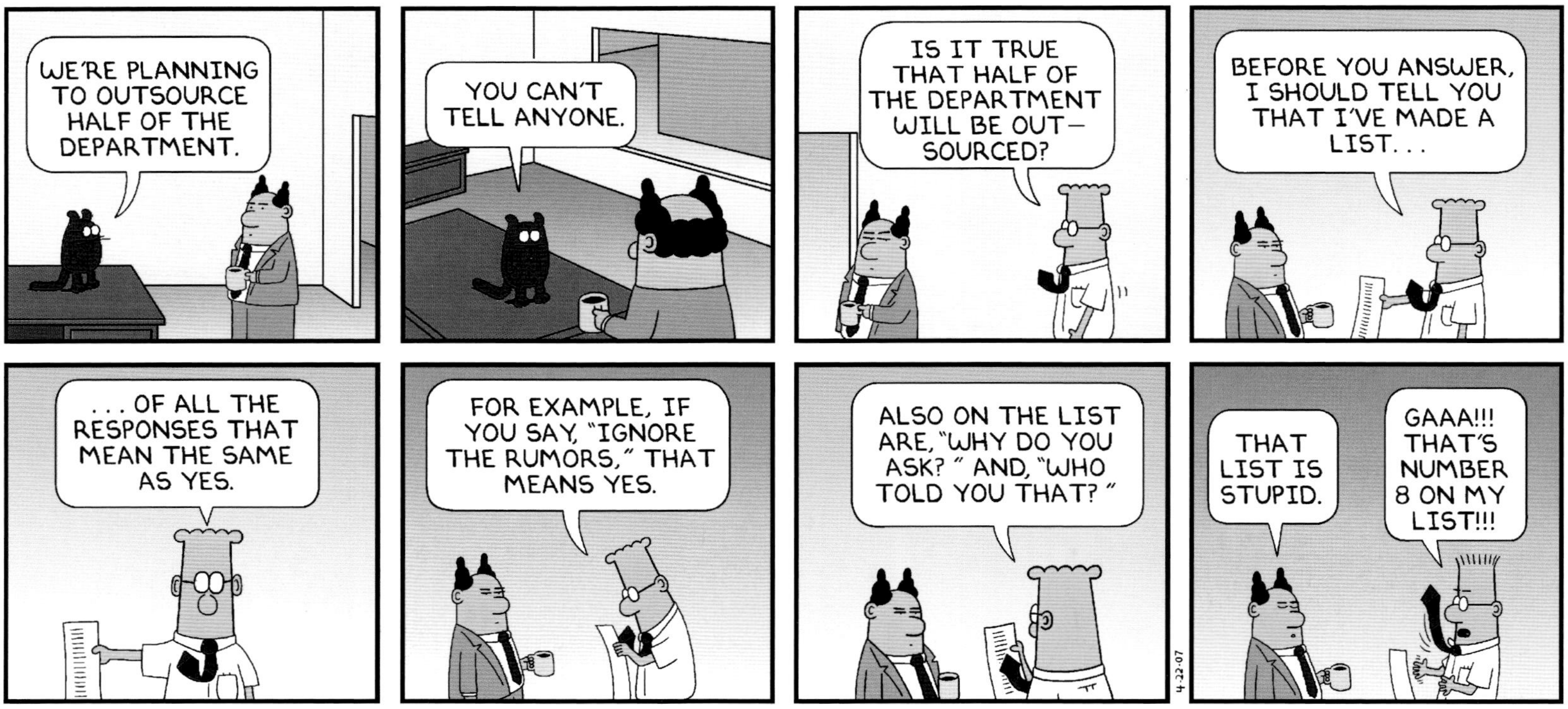
WE'RE PLANNING TO OUTSOURCE HALF OF THE DEPARTMENT.
YOU CAN'T TELL ANYONE.
IS IT TRUE THAT HALF OF THE DEPARTMENT WILL BE OUT-SOURCED?
BEFORE YOU ANSWER, I SHOULD TELL YOU THAT I'VE MADE A LIST. . .
. . . OF ALL THE RESPONSES THAT MEAN THE SAME AS YES.
FOR EXAMPLE, IF YOU SAY, "IGNORE THE RUMORS," THAT MEANS YES.
ALSO ON THE LIST ARE, "WHY DO YOU ASK?" AND, "WHO TOLD YOU THAT?"
THAT LIST IS STUPID.
GAAA!!! THAT'S NUMBER 8 ON MY LIST!!!
4-22-07

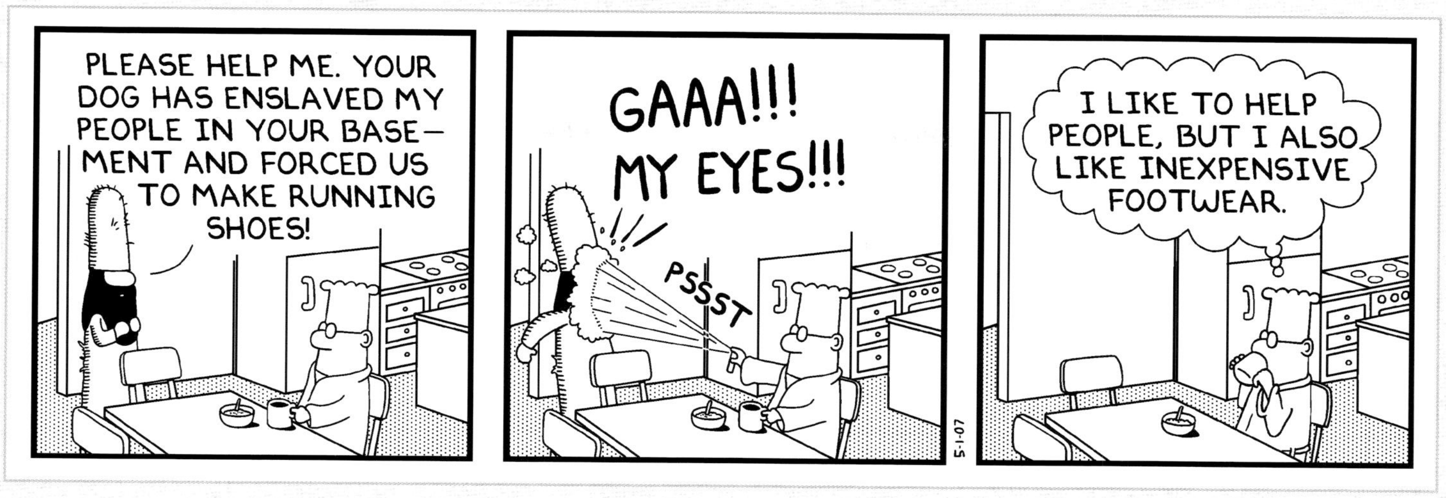
PLEASE HELP ME. YOUR DOG HAS ENSLAVED MY PEOPLE IN YOUR BASE— MENT AND FORCED US TO MAKE RUNNING SHOES!
GAAA!!! MY EYES!!!
PSSST
I LIKE TO HELP PEOPLE, BUT I ALSO LIKE INEXPENSIVE FOOTWEAR.
5-1-07

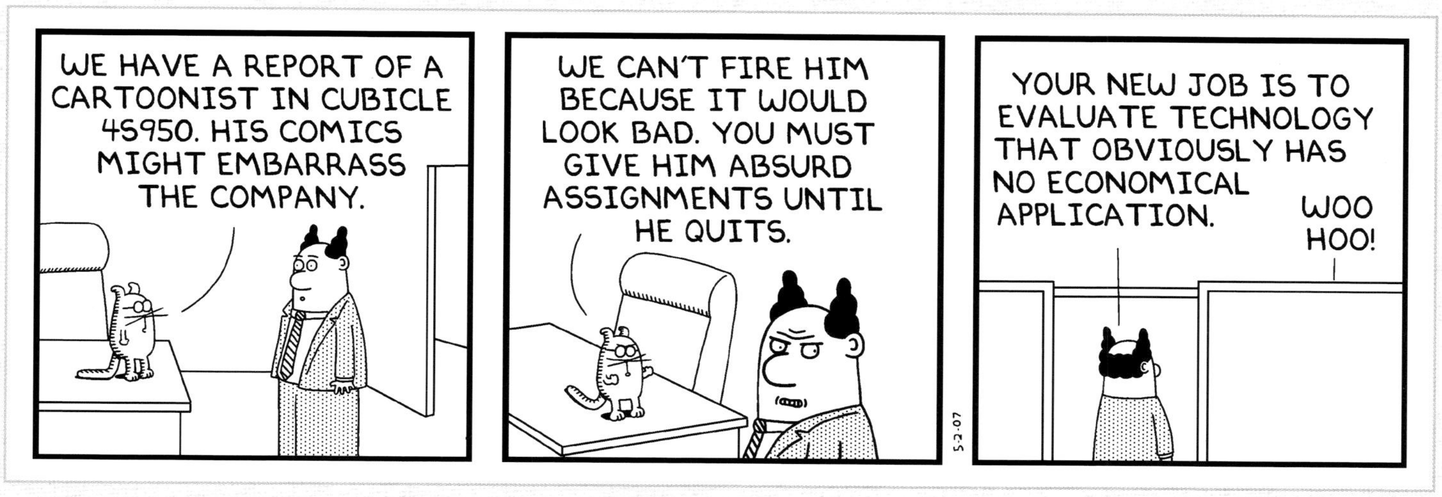
WE HAVE A REPORT OF A CARTOONIST IN CUBICLE 4S950. HIS COMICS MIGHT EMBARRASS THE COMPANY.
WE CAN'T FIRE HIM BECAUSE IT WOULD LOOK BAD. YOU MUST GIVE HIM ABSURD ASSIGNMENTS UNTIL HE QUITS.
YOUR NEW JOB IS TO EVALUATE TECHNOLOGY THAT OBVIOUSLY HAS NO ECONOMICAL APPLICATION.
WOO HOO!
5-2-07

I thought it was time to tell the story of my corporate life after I became a cartoonist but before I was doing well enough to quit my day job.

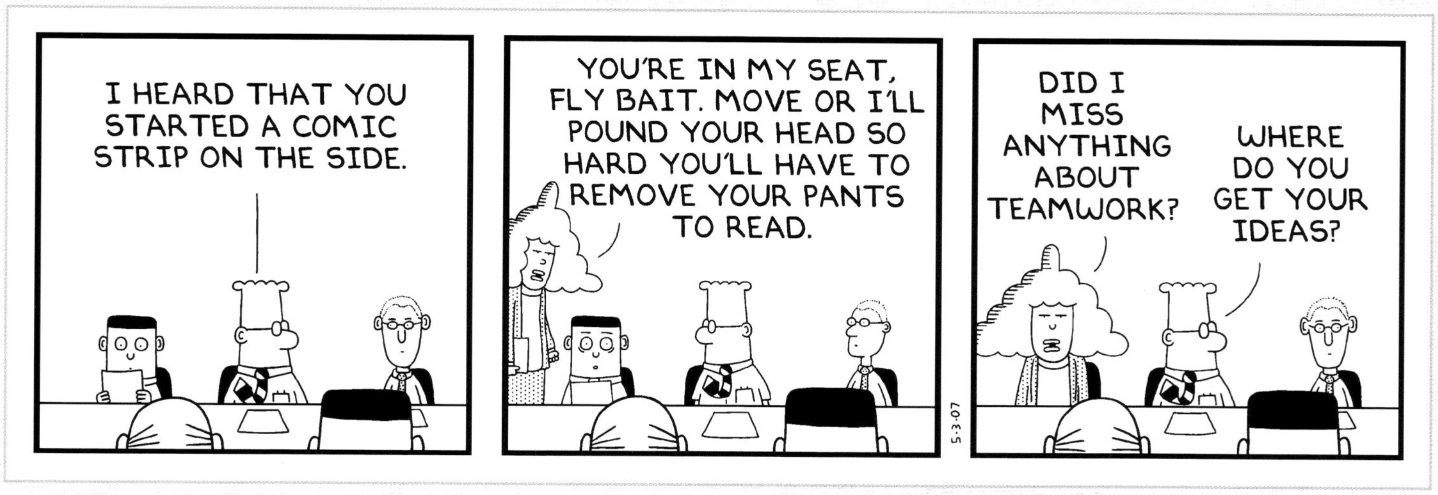
I HEARD THAT YOU STARTED A COMIC STRIP ON THE SIDE.
YOU'RE IN MY SEAT, FLY BAIT. MOVE OR I'LL POUND YOUR HEAD SO HARD YOU'LL HAVE TO REMOVE YOUR PANTS TO READ.
DID I MISS ANYTHING ABOUT TEAMWORK?
WHERE DO YOU GET YOUR IDEAS?
5-3-07

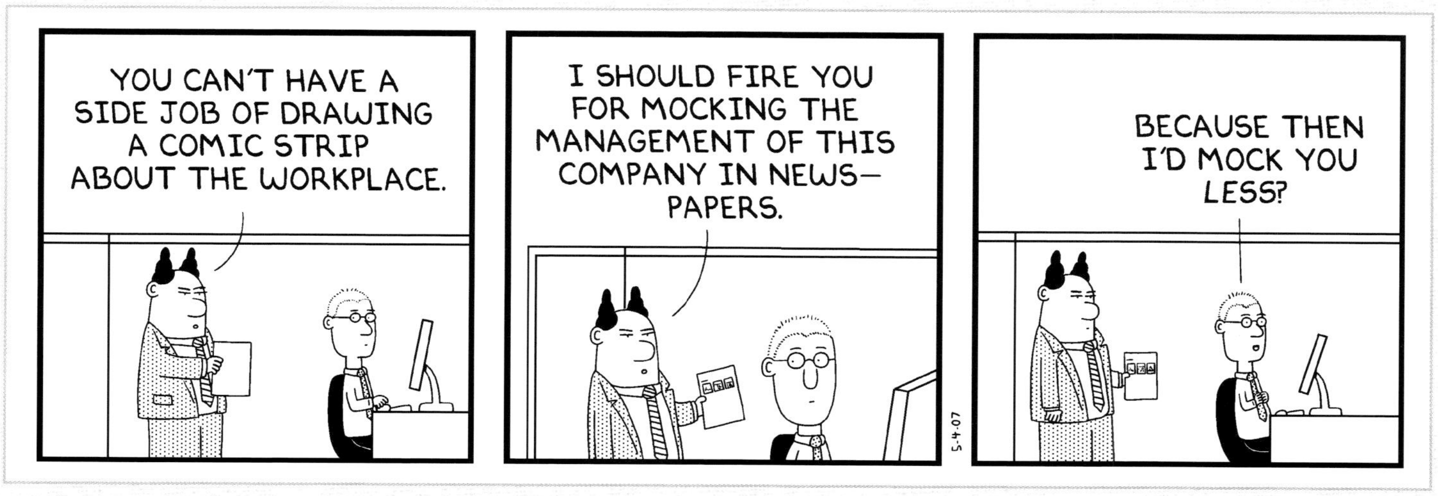
YOU CAN'T HAVE A SIDE JOB OF DRAWING A COMIC STRIP ABOUT THE WORKPLACE.
I SHOULD FIRE YOU FOR MOCKING THE MANAGEMENT OF THIS COMPANY IN NEWS— PAPERS.
BECAUSE THEN I'D MOCK YOU LESS?
5-4-07

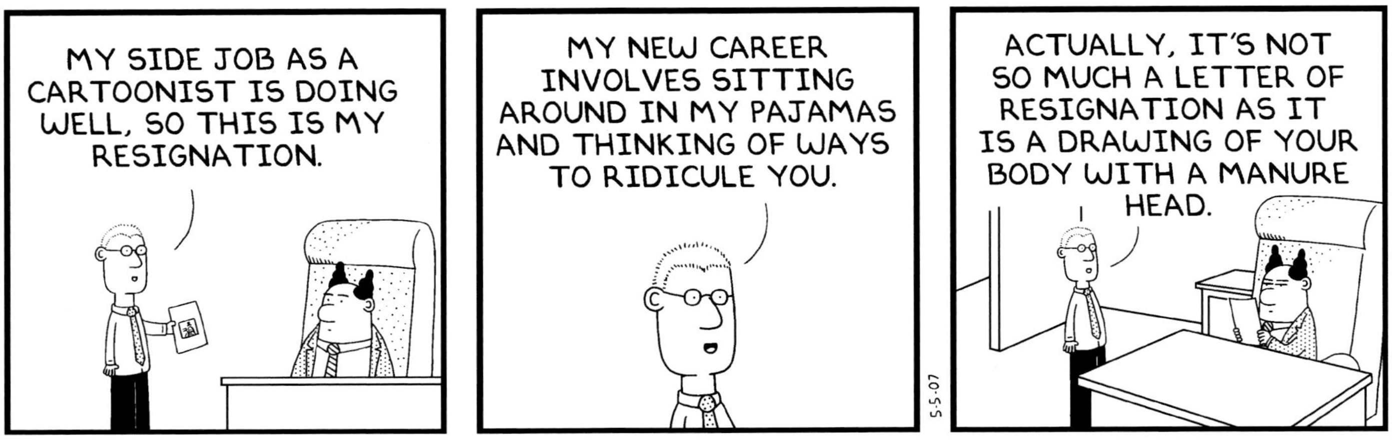
MY SIDE JOB AS A CARTOONIST IS DOING WELL, SO THIS IS MY RESIGNATION.
MY NEW CAREER INVOLVES SITTING AROUND IN MY PAJAMAS AND THINKING OF WAYS TO RIDICULE YOU.
5-5-07
ACTUALLY, IT'S NOT SO MUCH A LETTER OF RESIGNATION AS IT IS A DRAWING OF YOUR BODY WITH A MANURE HEAD.

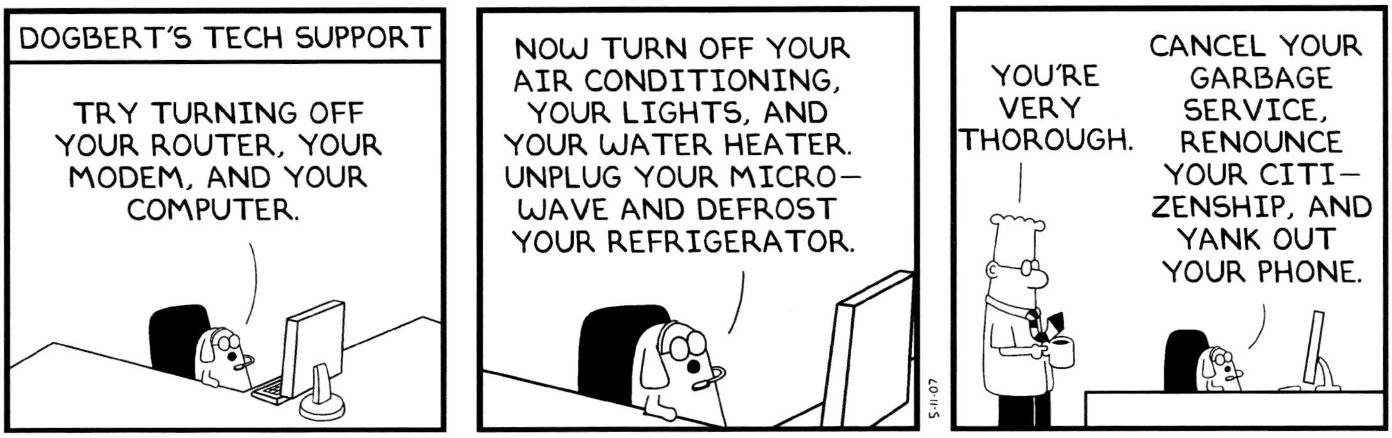
DOGBERT'S TECH SUPPORT
TRY TURNING OFF YOUR ROUTER, YOUR MODEM, AND YOUR COMPUTER.
NOW TURN OFF YOUR AIR CONDITIONING, YOUR LIGHTS, AND YOUR WATER HEATER. UNPLUG YOUR MICRO-WAVE AND DEFROST YOUR REFRIGERATOR.
5-11-07
CANCEL YOUR GARBAGE SERVICE, RENOUNCE YOUR CITI-ZENSHIP, AND YANK OUT YOUR PHONE.
YOU'RE VERY THOROUGH.

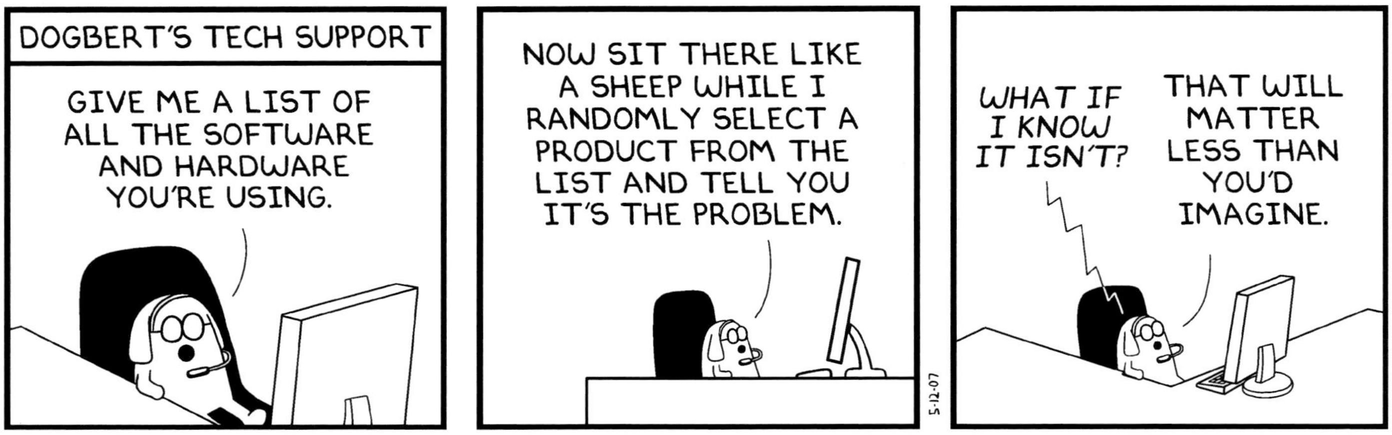
DOGBERT'S TECH SUPPORT
GIVE ME A LIST OF ALL THE SOFTWARE AND HARDWARE YOU'RE USING.
NOW SIT THERE LIKE A SHEEP WHILE I RANDOMLY SELECT A PRODUCT FROM THE LIST AND TELL YOU IT'S THE PROBLEM.
5-12-07
WHAT IF I KNOW IT ISN'T?
THAT WILL MATTER LESS THAN YOU'D IMAGINE.

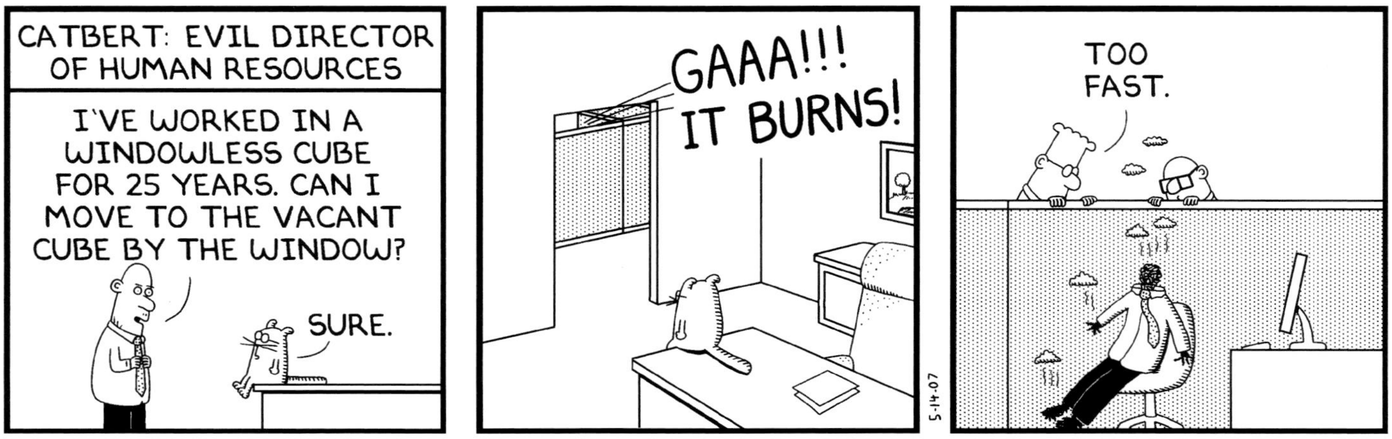
CATBERT: EVIL DIRECTOR OF HUMAN RESOURCES
I'VE WORKED IN A WINDOWLESS CUBE FOR 25 YEARS. CAN I MOVE TO THE VACANT CUBE BY THE WINDOW?
SURE.
GAAA!!! IT BURNS!
5-14-07
TOO FAST.

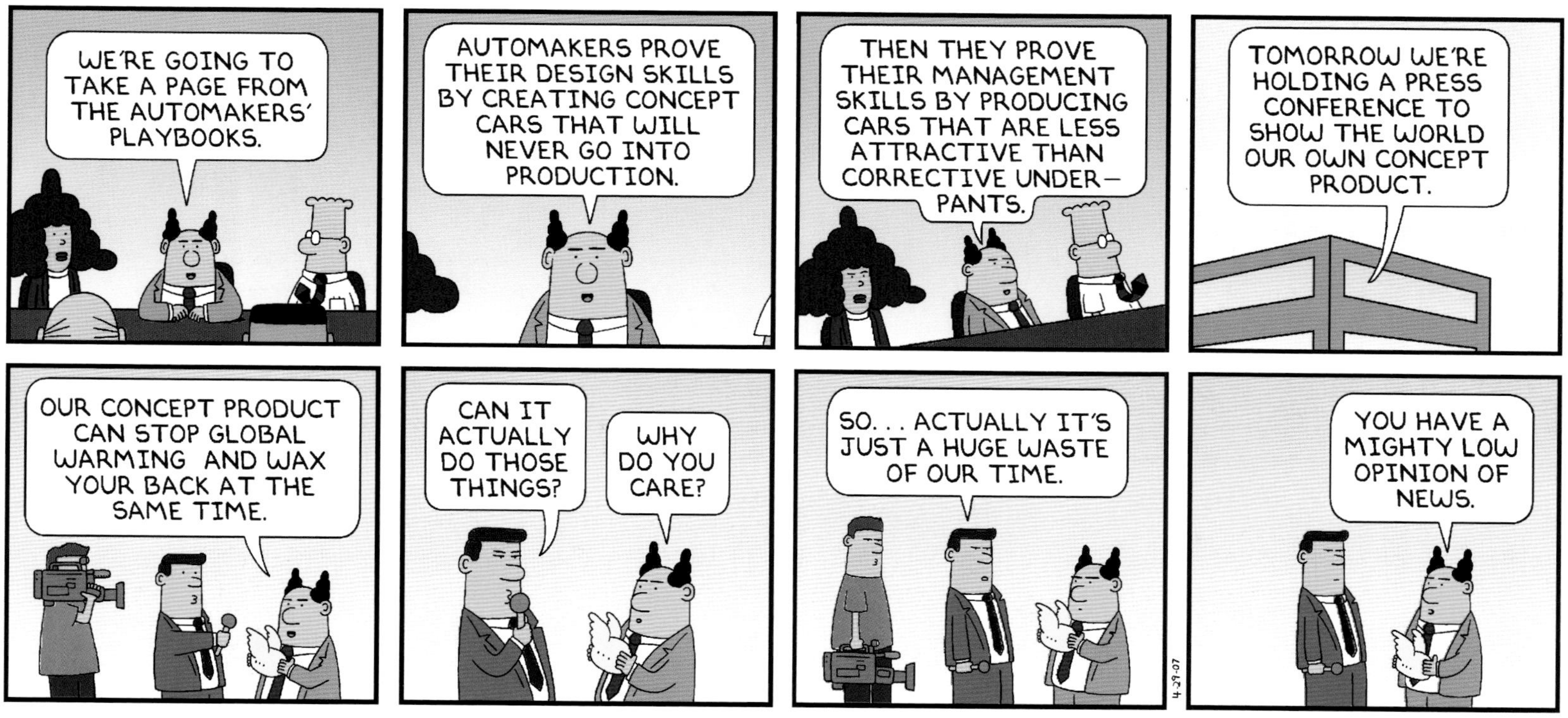
WE'RE GOING TO TAKE A PAGE FROM THE AUTOMAKERS' PLAYBOOKS.
AUTOMAKERS PROVE THEIR DESIGN SKILLS BY CREATING CONCEPT CARS THAT WILL NEVER GO INTO PRODUCTION.
THEN THEY PROVE THEIR MANAGEMENT SKILLS BY PRODUCING CARS THAT ARE LESS ATTRACTIVE THAN CORRECTIVE UNDER-PANTS.
TOMORROW WE'RE HOLDING A PRESS CONFERENCE TO SHOW THE WORLD OUR OWN CONCEPT PRODUCT.
OUR CONCEPT PRODUCT CAN STOP GLOBAL WARMING AND WAX YOUR BACK AT THE SAME TIME.
CAN IT ACTUALLY DO THOSE THINGS?
WHY DO YOU CARE?
SO. . . ACTUALLY IT'S JUST A HUGE WASTE OF OUR TIME.
YOU HAVE A MIGHTY LOW OPINION OF NEWS.
4-29-07

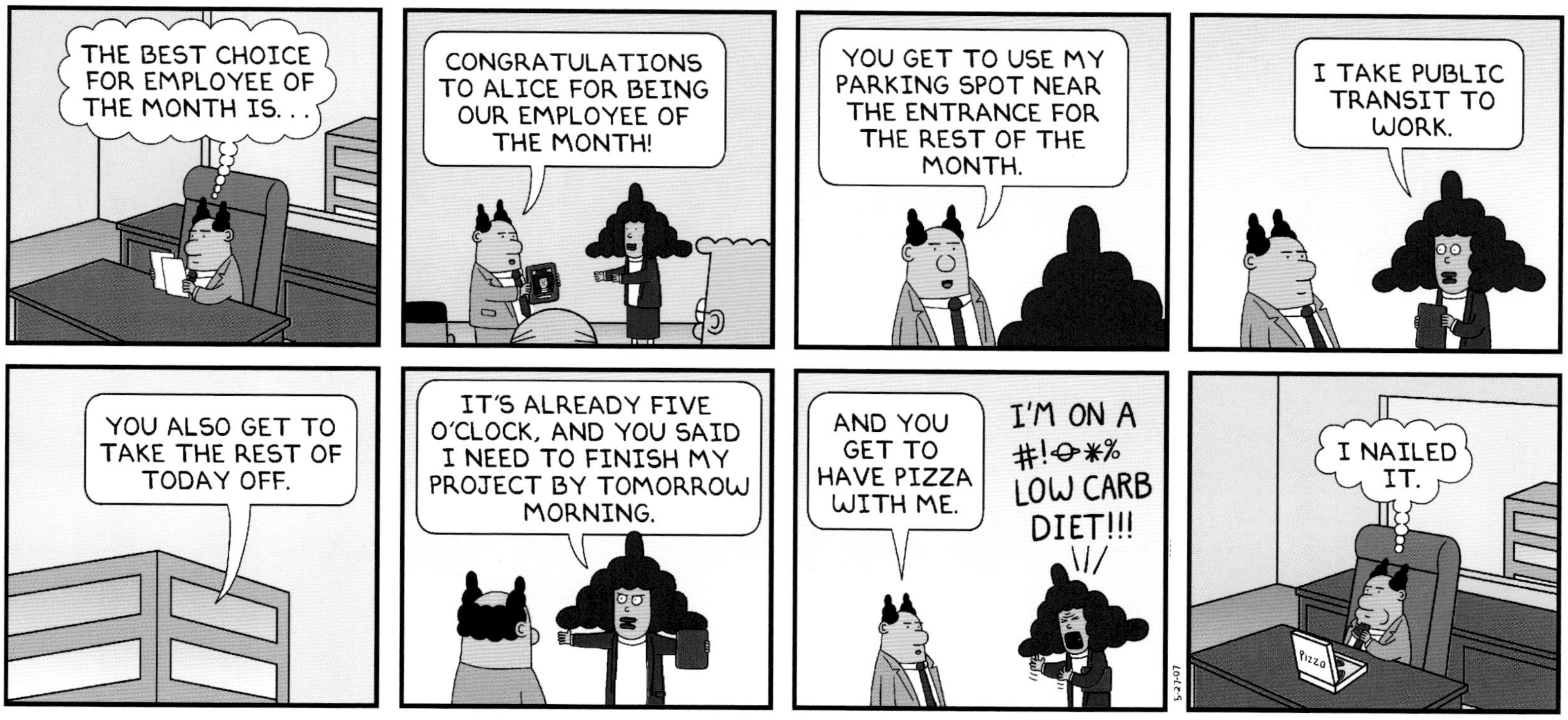
THE BEST CHOICE FOR EMPLOYEE OF THE MONTH IS. . .
CONGRATULATIONS TO ALICE FOR BEING OUR EMPLOYEE OF THE MONTH!
YOU GET TO USE MY PARKING SPOT NEAR THE ENTRANCE FOR THE REST OF THE MONTH.
I TAKE PUBLIC TRANSIT TO WORK.
YOU ALSO GET TO TAKE THE REST OF TODAY OFF.
IT'S ALREADY FIVE O'CLOCK, AND YOU SAID I NEED TO FINISH MY PROJECT BY TOMORROW MORNING.
AND YOU GET TO HAVE PIZZA WITH ME.
I'M ON A #!☉*% LOW CARB DIET!!!
I NAILED IT.
Pizza
5-27-07

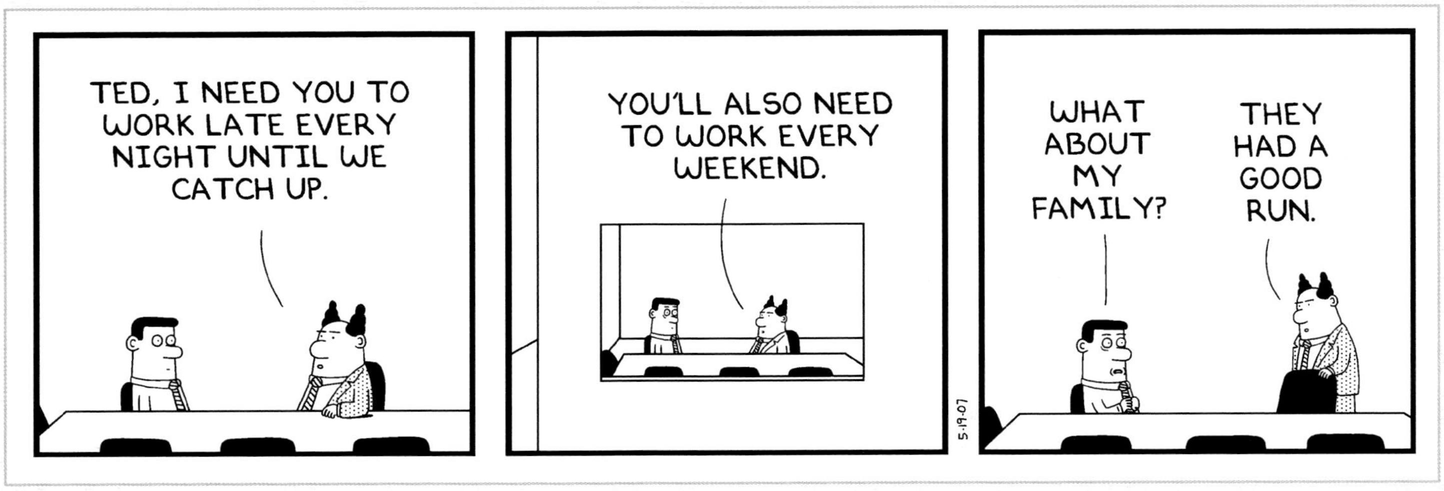
TED, I NEED YOU TO WORK LATE EVERY NIGHT UNTIL WE CATCH UP.
YOU'LL ALSO NEED TO WORK EVERY WEEKEND.
5-19-07
WHAT ABOUT MY FAMILY?
THEY HAD A GOOD RUN.

Today, I started work at 3 A.M., which is not that unusual for me. I have four deadlines looming before the weekend. Cartooning is a great job, but it isn't as easy as people assume.

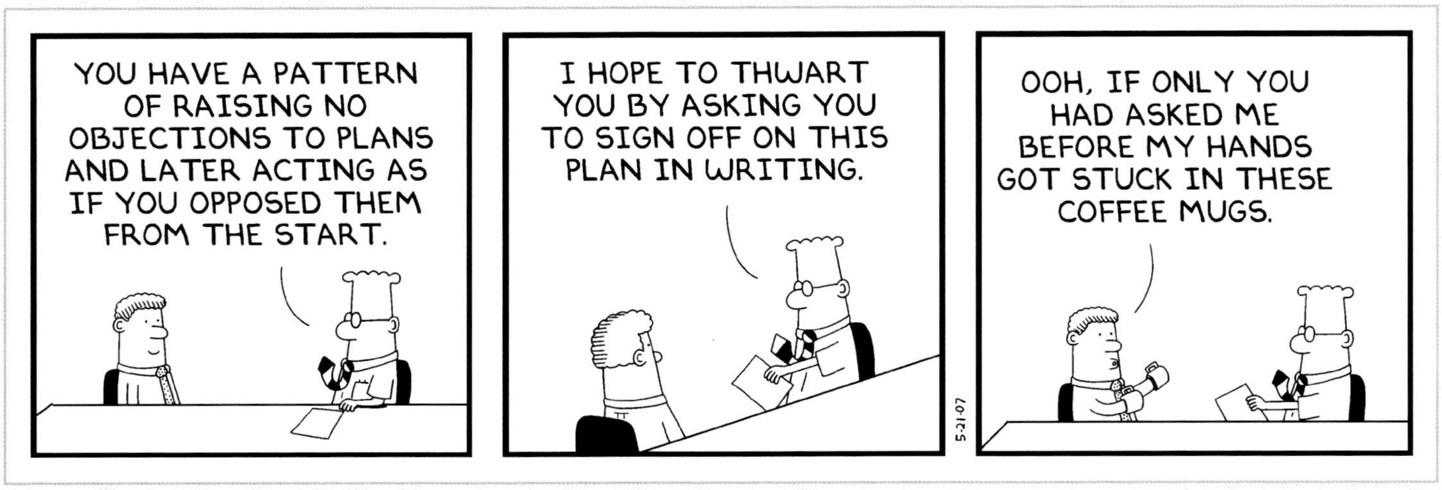
YOU HAVE A PATTERN OF RAISING NO OBJECTIONS TO PLANS AND LATER ACTING AS IF YOU OPPOSED THEM FROM THE START.
I HOPE TO THWART YOU BY ASKING YOU TO SIGN OFF ON THIS PLAN IN WRITING.
5-21-07
OOH, IF ONLY YOU HAD ASKED ME BEFORE MY HANDS GOT STUCK IN THESE COFFEE MUGS.

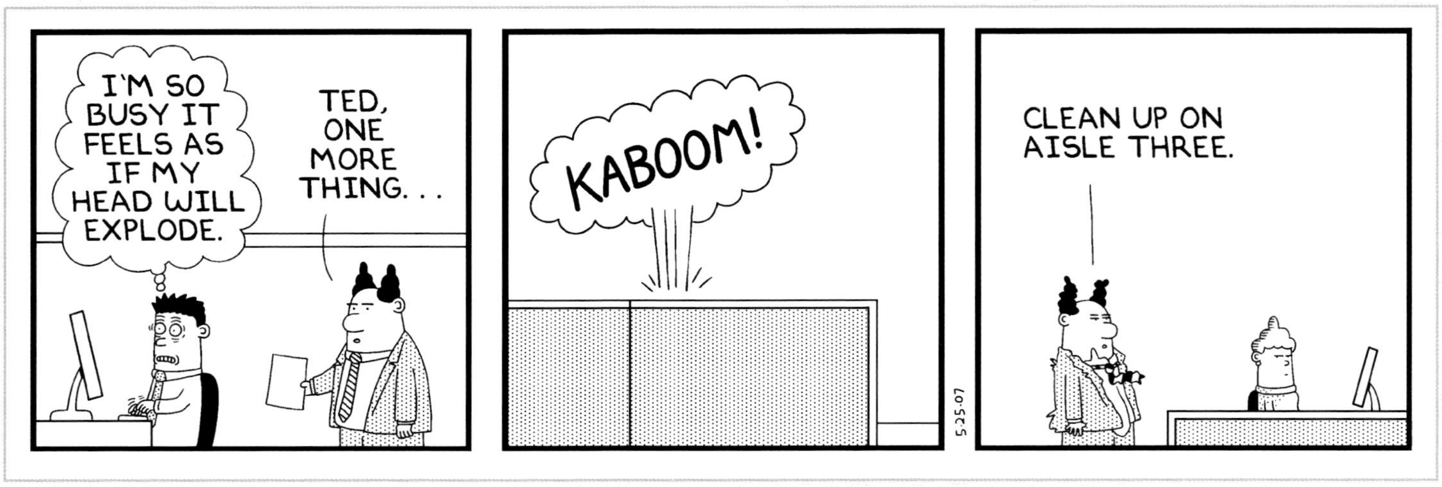
I'M SO BUSY IT FEELS AS IF MY HEAD WILL EXPLODE.
TED, ONE MORE THING. . .
KABOOM!
5-25-07
CLEAN UP ON AISLE THREE.

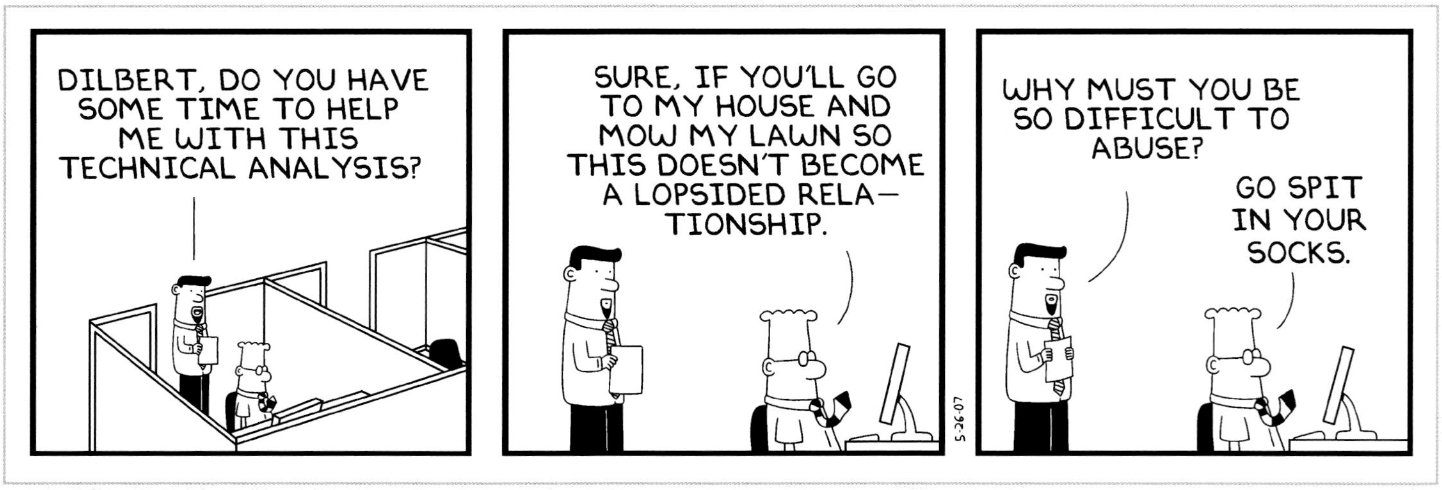
DILBERT, DO YOU HAVE SOME TIME TO HELP ME WITH THIS TECHNICAL ANALYSIS?
SURE, IF YOU'LL GO TO MY HOUSE AND MOW MY LAWN SO THIS DOESN'T BECOME A LOPSIDED RELA—TIONSHIP.
5-26-07
WHY MUST YOU BE SO DIFFICULT TO ABUSE?
GO SPIT IN YOUR SOCKS.

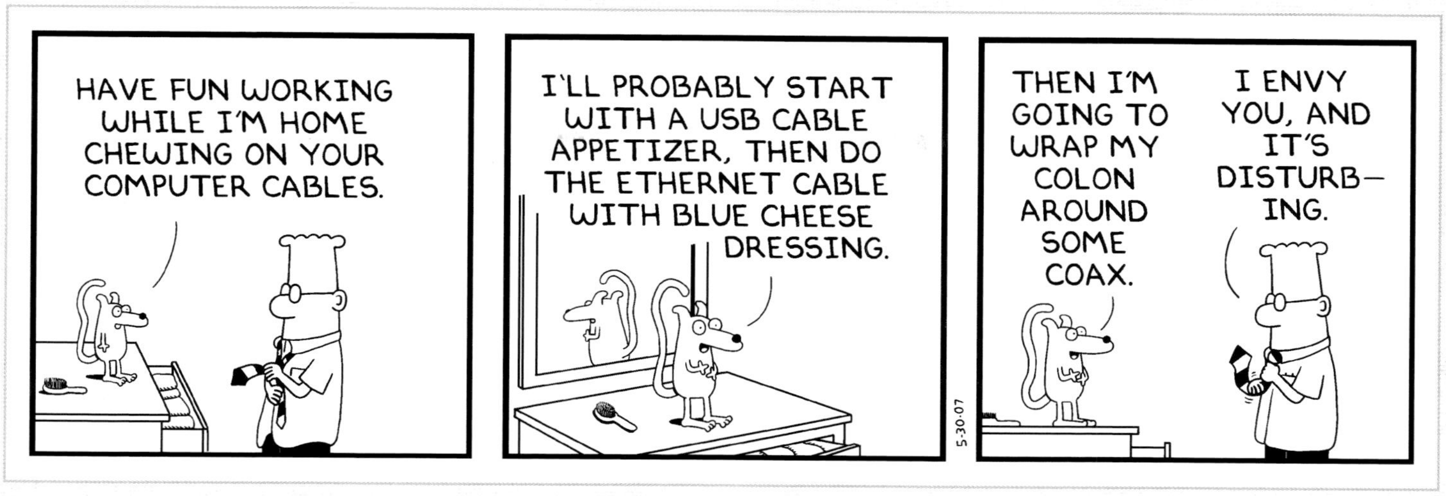
HAVE FUN WORKING WHILE I'M HOME CHEWING ON YOUR COMPUTER CABLES.
I'LL PROBABLY START WITH A USB CABLE APPETIZER, THEN DO THE ETHERNET CABLE WITH BLUE CHEESE DRESSING.
THEN I'M GOING TO WRAP MY COLON AROUND SOME COAX.
I ENVY YOU, AND IT'S DISTURB-ING.
5-30-07

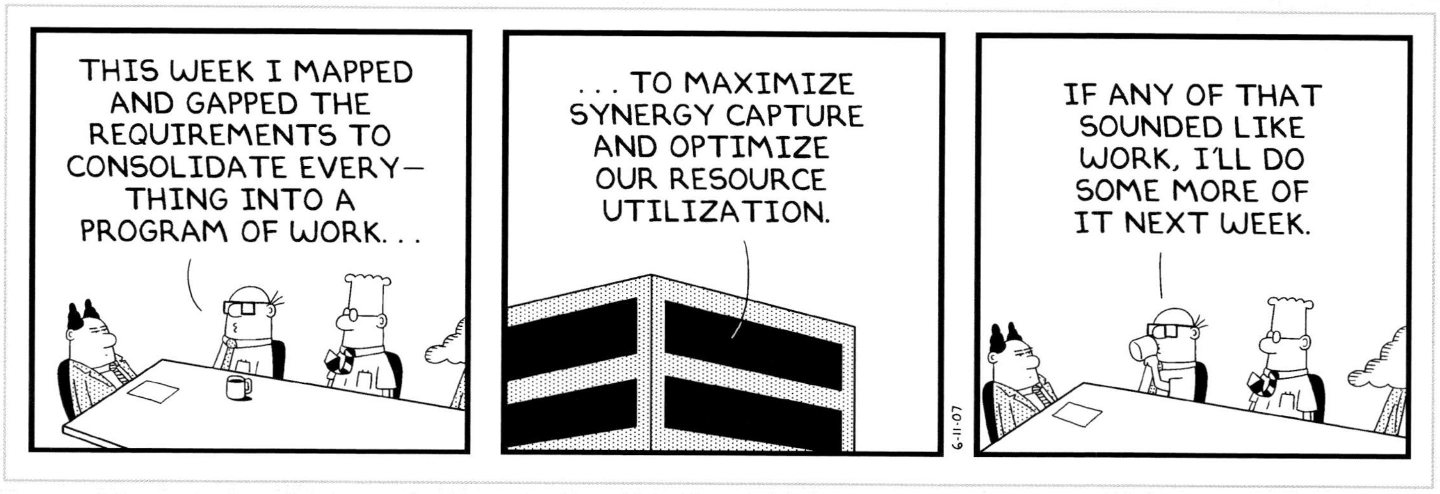
THIS WEEK I MAPPED AND GAPPED THE REQUIREMENTS TO CONSOLIDATE EVERY-THING INTO A PROGRAM OF WORK. . .
. . . TO MAXIMIZE SYNERGY CAPTURE AND OPTIMIZE OUR RESOURCE UTILIZATION.
IF ANY OF THAT SOUNDED LIKE WORK, I'LL DO SOME MORE OF IT NEXT WEEK.
6-11-07

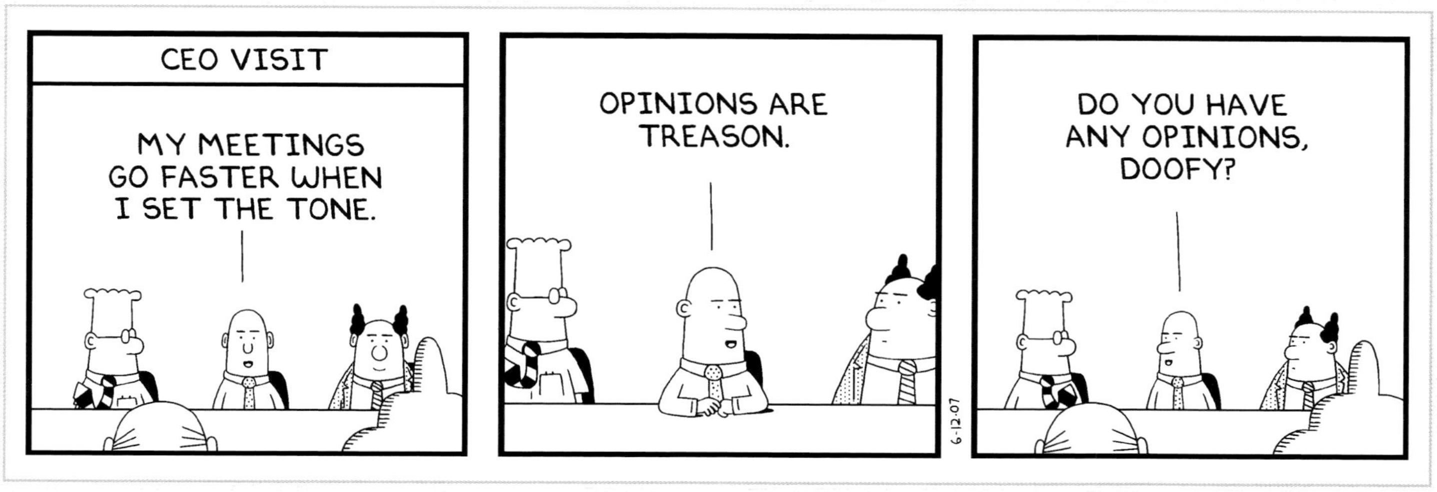
CEO VISIT
MY MEETINGS GO FASTER WHEN I SET THE TONE.
OPINIONS ARE TREASON.
DO YOU HAVE ANY OPINIONS, DOOFY?
6-12-07

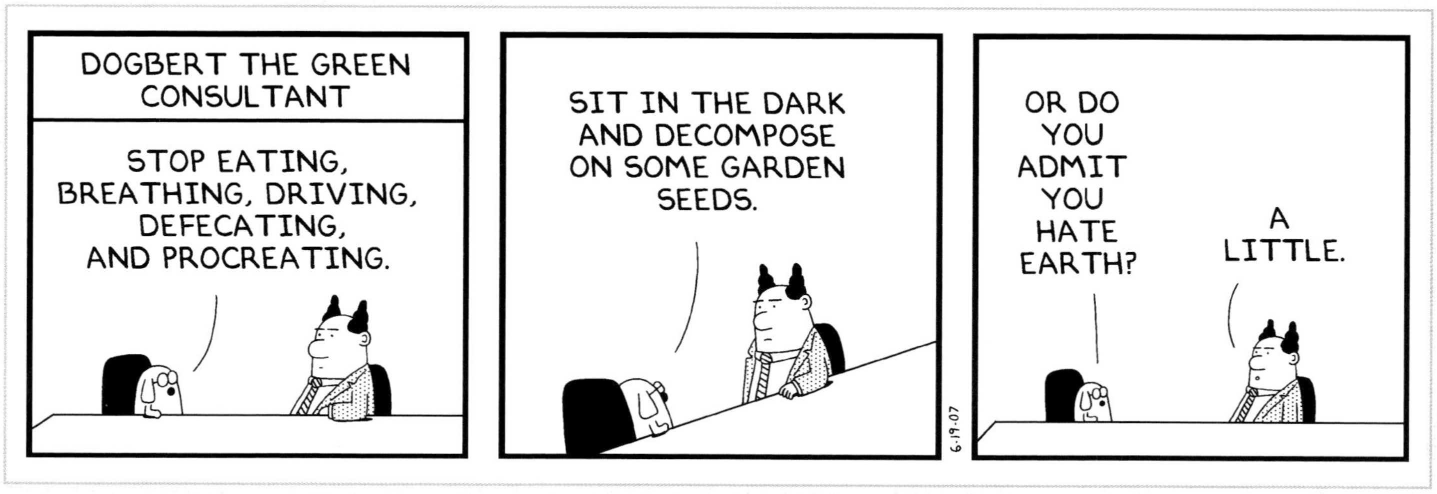
DOGBERT THE GREEN CONSULTANT
STOP EATING, BREATHING, DRIVING, DEFECATING, AND PROCREATING.
SIT IN THE DARK AND DECOMPOSE ON SOME GARDEN SEEDS.
OR DO YOU ADMIT YOU HATE EARTH?
A LITTLE.
6-19-07

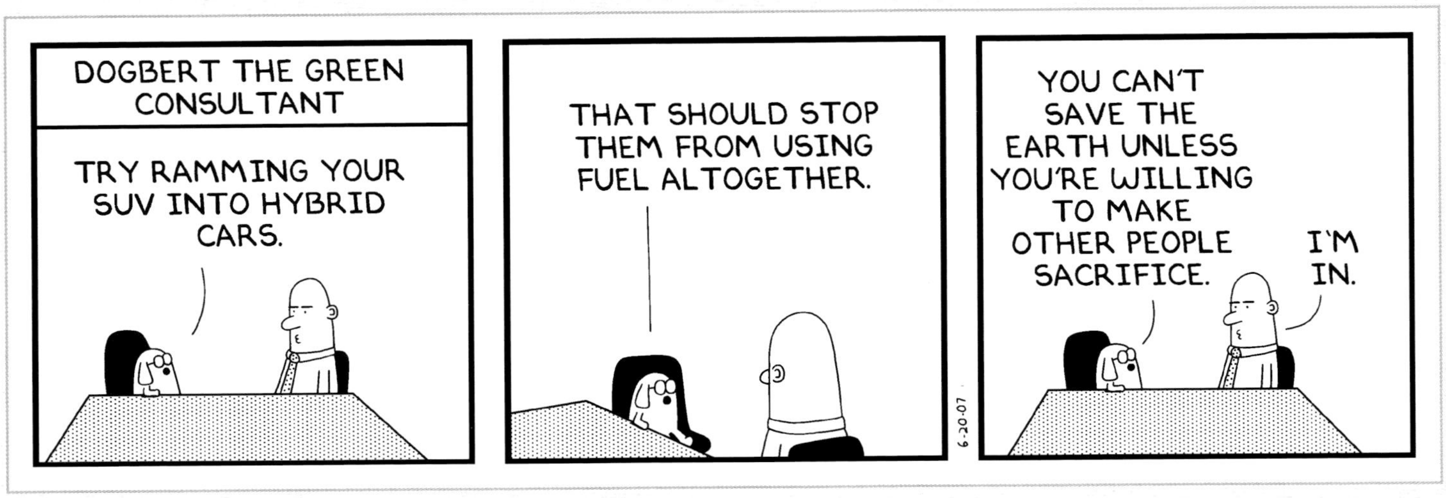
DOGBERT THE GREEN CONSULTANT
TRY RAMMING YOUR SUV INTO HYBRID CARS.
THAT SHOULD STOP THEM FROM USING FUEL ALTOGETHER.
6-20-07
YOU CAN'T SAVE THE EARTH UNLESS YOU'RE WILLING TO MAKE OTHER PEOPLE SACRIFICE.
I'M IN.

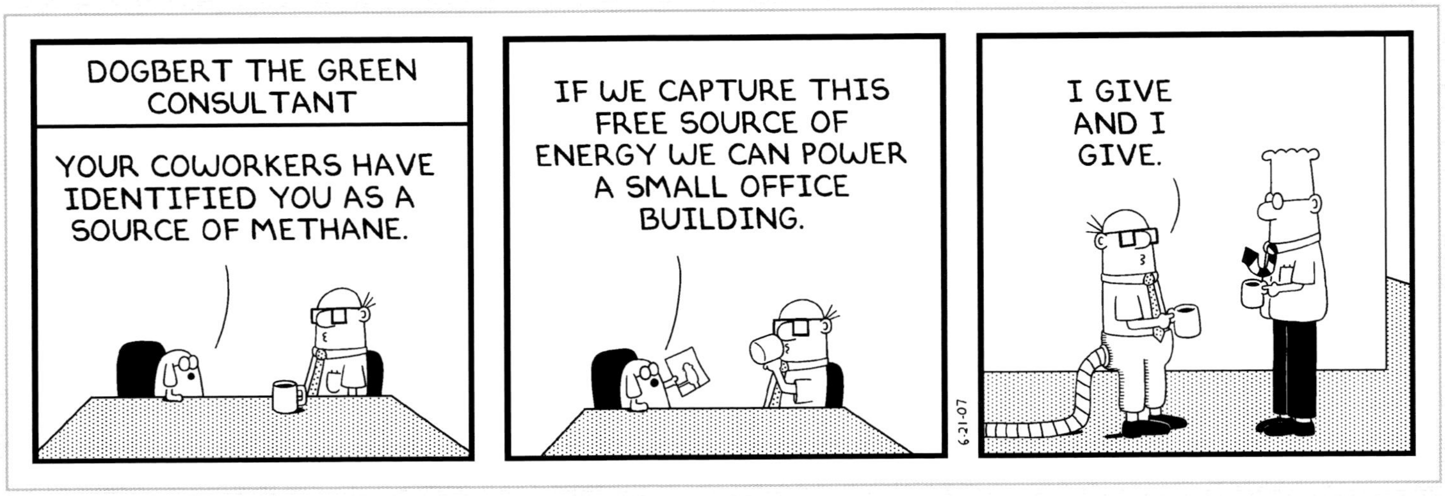
DOGBERT THE GREEN CONSULTANT
YOUR COWORKERS HAVE IDENTIFIED YOU AS A SOURCE OF METHANE.
IF WE CAPTURE THIS FREE SOURCE OF ENERGY WE CAN POWER A SMALL OFFICE BUILDING.
6-21-07
I GIVE AND I GIVE.

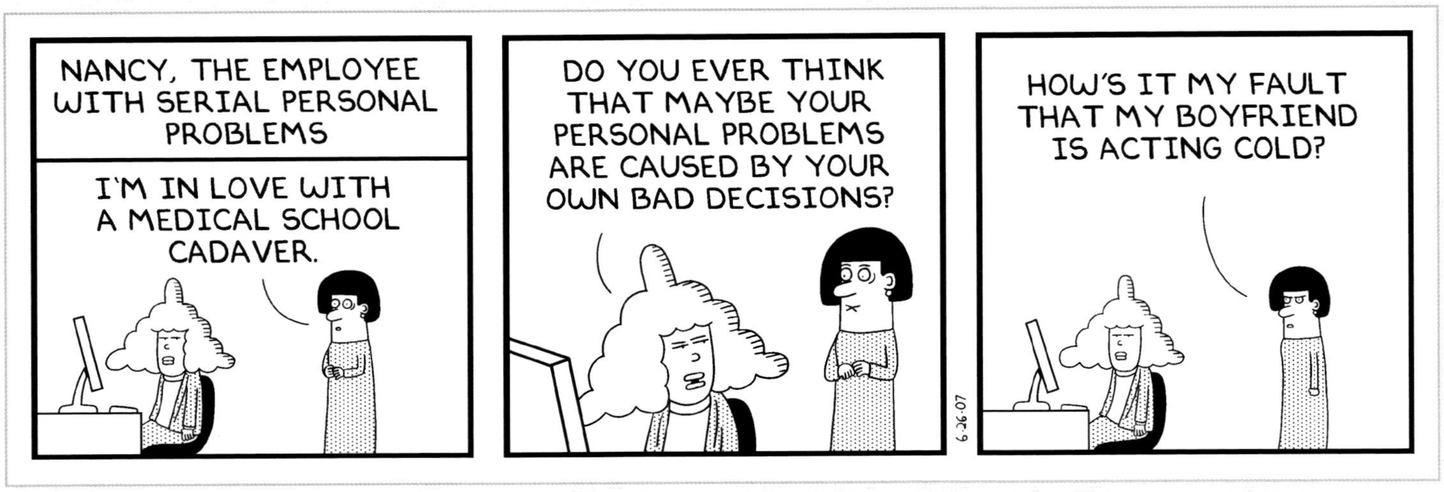
NANCY, THE EMPLOYEE WITH SERIAL PERSONAL PROBLEMS
I'M IN LOVE WITH A MEDICAL SCHOOL CADAVER.
DO YOU EVER THINK THAT MAYBE YOUR PERSONAL PROBLEMS ARE CAUSED BY YOUR OWN BAD DECISIONS?
6-26-07
HOW'S IT MY FAULT THAT MY BOYFRIEND IS ACTING COLD?

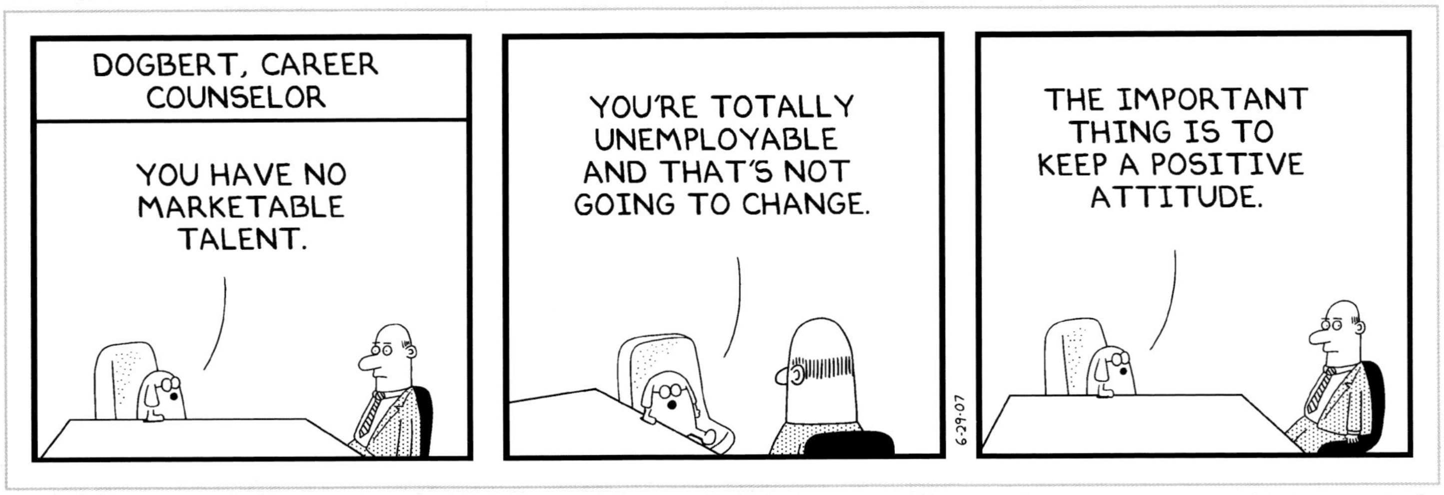
DOGBERT, CAREER COUNSELOR
YOU HAVE NO MARKETABLE TALENT.
YOU'RE TOTALLY UNEMPLOYABLE AND THAT'S NOT GOING TO CHANGE.
6-29-07
THE IMPORTANT THING IS TO KEEP A POSITIVE ATTITUDE.

CEO MEETING
I BROUGHT DILBERT IN CASE YOU HAVE ANY TECHNICAL QUESTIONS.
WHAT'S THE STATUS ON THE TECHNOLOGY PLAT— FORM MIGRATION PROJECT?
BE COMPLETELY HONEST. WE HAVE NOTHING TO HIDE.
WELL, OKAY.
THE PROJECT IS LIKE A HUNDRED DRUNKEN CLOWNS WITH BEES IN THEIR UNDERPANTS.
I EXPECT THE DECLINE IN MORALE TO LEAD TO VIOLENCE.
MOST OF US ARE ONLY PRETENDING TO WORK WHILE SECRETLY HOPING THE PROJECT GETS CANCELED AFTER YOU GET FIRED BY THE BOARD.
IT TURNS OUT THAT WE *DID* HAVE A FEW THINGS TO HIDE.

YOU SHOULD HIRE ME AS YOUR MANAGEMENT CONSULTANT.
WE'RE A MANAGEMENT CONSULTING FIRM. WE DON'T NEED A MAN— AGEMENT CONSULTANT TO CONSULT US.
ARE YOU SAYING THAT MANAGEMENT CONSULTING IS WORTHLESS?
NO, I'M SAYING WE ALREADY KNOW EVERYTHING ABOUT MANAGEMENT CONSULTING.
HOW CAN YOU BE SO SURE I CAN'T HELP YOU WHEN YOU DON'T KNOW WHAT MY ADVICE WILL BE?
OKAY, YOU'RE HIRED. WHAT'S YOUR ADVICE?
BEATS ME. I'LL HAVE TO ASK MY MANAGEMENT CONSULTANT.

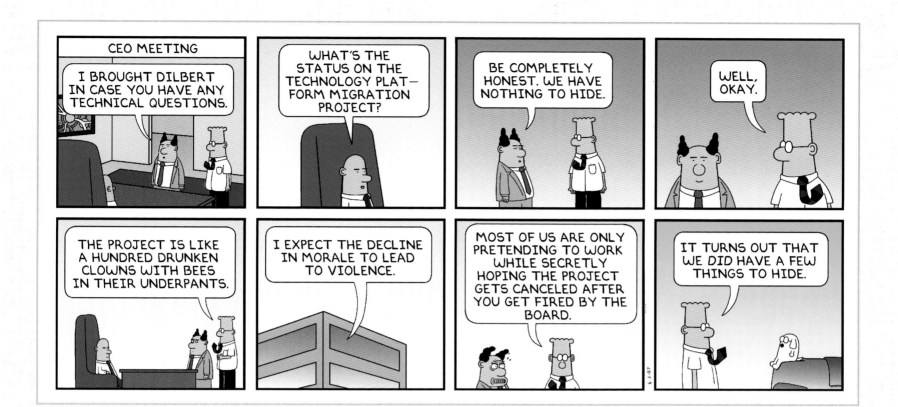

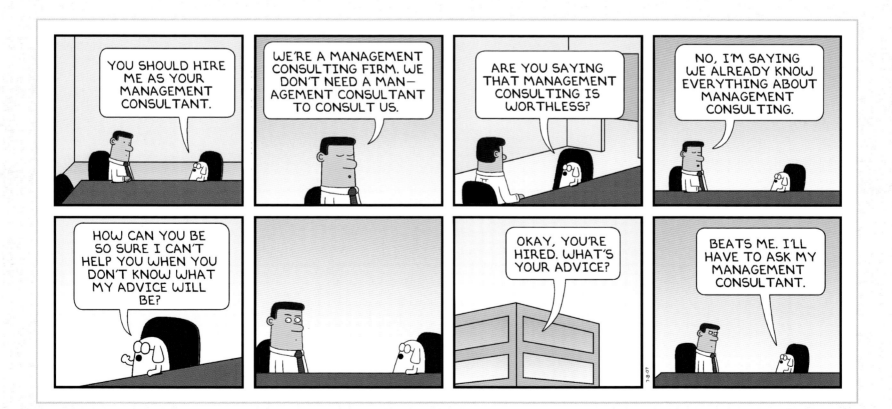

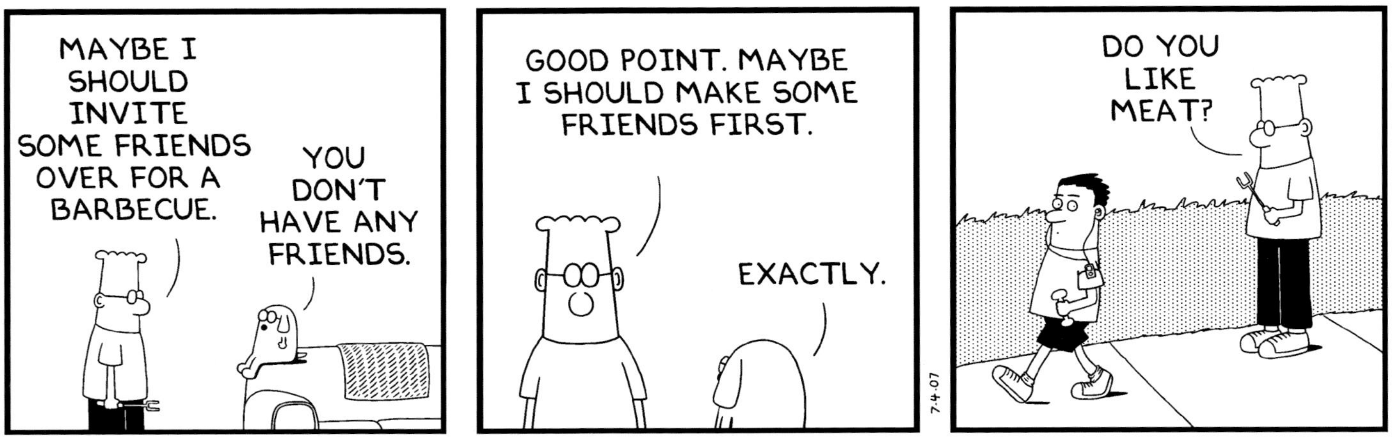
MAYBE I SHOULD INVITE SOME FRIENDS OVER FOR A BARBECUE.
YOU DON'T HAVE ANY FRIENDS.
GOOD POINT. MAYBE I SHOULD MAKE SOME FRIENDS FIRST.
EXACTLY.
7-4-07
DO YOU LIKE MEAT?

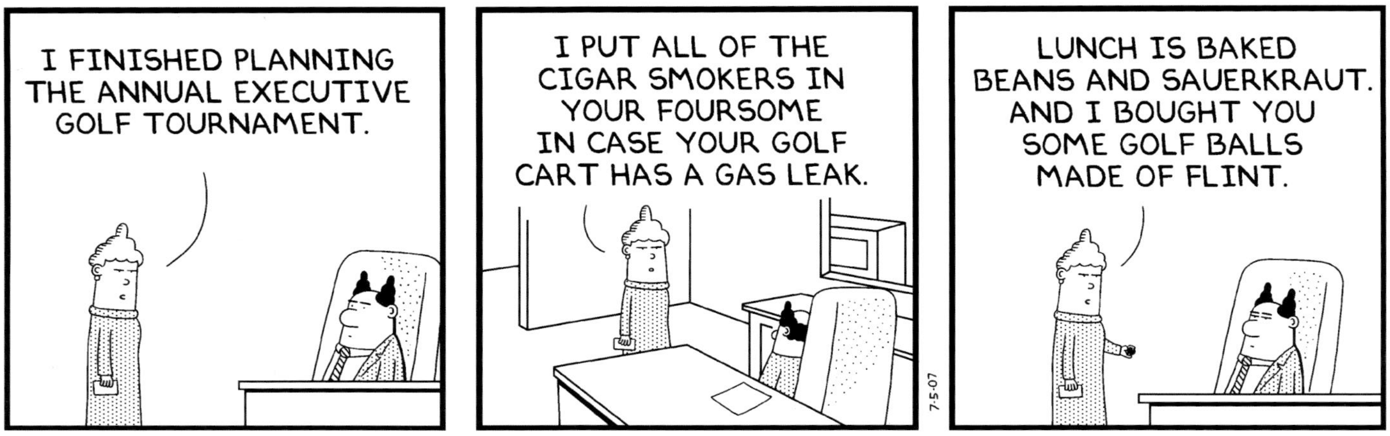
I FINISHED PLANNING THE ANNUAL EXECUTIVE GOLF TOURNAMENT.
I PUT ALL OF THE CIGAR SMOKERS IN YOUR FOURSOME IN CASE YOUR GOLF CART HAS A GAS LEAK.
7-5-07
LUNCH IS BAKED BEANS AND SAUERKRAUT. AND I BOUGHT YOU SOME GOLF BALLS MADE OF FLINT.

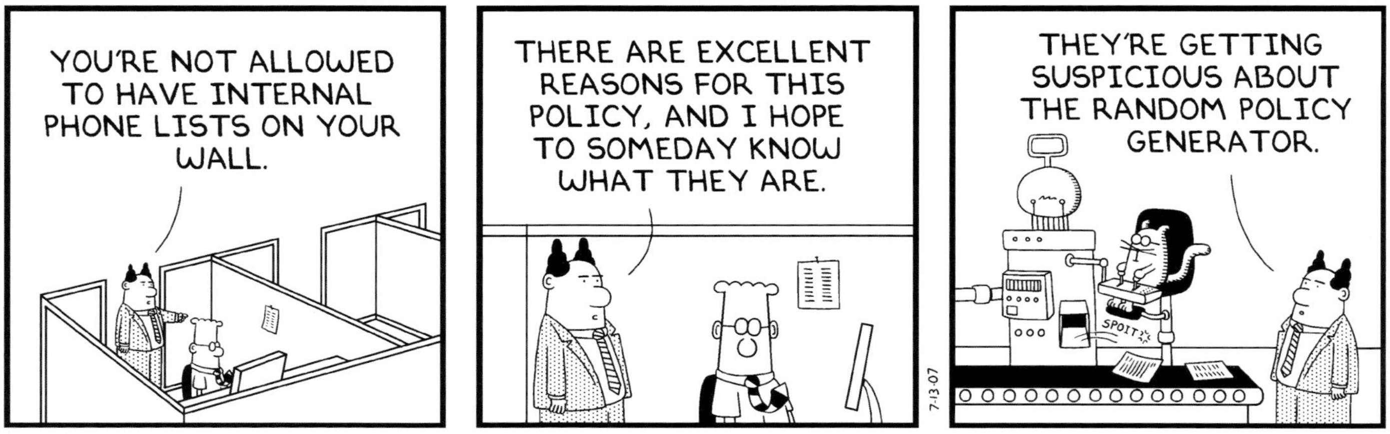
YOU'RE NOT ALLOWED TO HAVE INTERNAL PHONE LISTS ON YOUR WALL.
THERE ARE EXCELLENT REASONS FOR THIS POLICY, AND I HOPE TO SOMEDAY KNOW WHAT THEY ARE.
7-13-07
THEY'RE GETTING SUSPICIOUS ABOUT THE RANDOM POLICY GENERATOR.
SPOIT

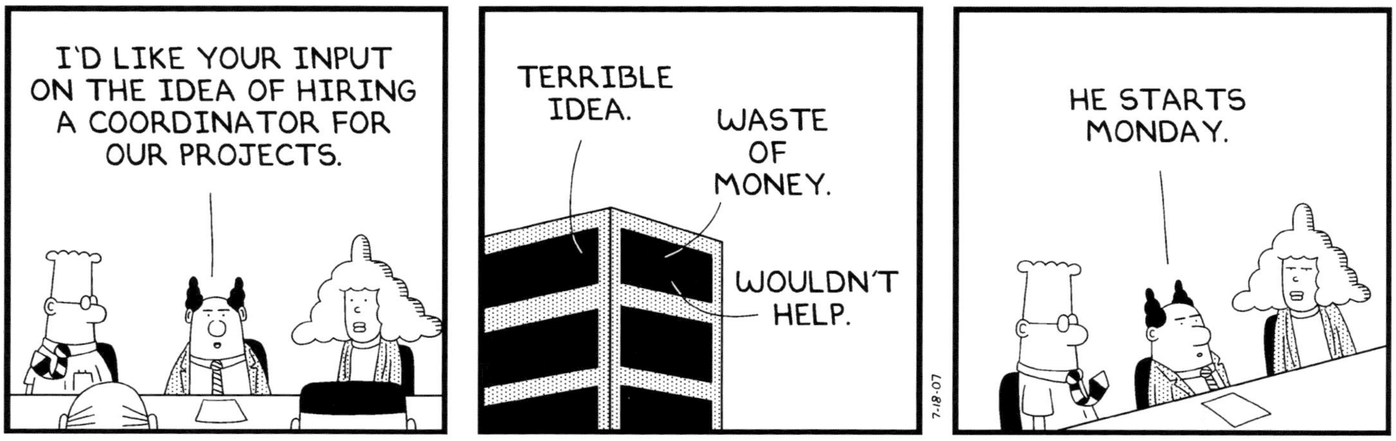
I'D LIKE YOUR INPUT ON THE IDEA OF HIRING A COORDINATOR FOR OUR PROJECTS.
TERRIBLE IDEA.
WASTE OF MONEY.
WOULDN'T HELP.
7-18-07
HE STARTS MONDAY.

DO YOU HAVE A MINUTE?
NO.
THIS WILL JUST TAKE A SECOND.
NO IT WON'T.
IT'S REAL QUICK.
NEVER IS.
YOU HAVE MY WORD THAT IT WILL TAKE NO LONGER THAN FIVE SECONDS.
OKAY.
GO.
OH, GOOD. SO, I WAS WALKING BY AND I THOUGHT MAYBE I SHOULD STOP AND ASK YOU SOMETHING BECAUSE. . .
TIME'S UP.
12-2-07
JERK
LIAR

CATBERT: EVIL DIRECTOR OF HUMAN RESOURCES
YOUR BOSS SAYS YOU HAVE A BAD ATTITUDE.
THAT'S BECAUSE MY PROJECT IS A FLAILING CORPSE OF MISERY, AND MY BOSS DONATED HIS BRAIN TO A GUM MUSEUM.
IF I HAD A GOOD ATTITUDE IN THIS SITUATION, IT WOULD BE A SIGN OF MENTAL IMBALANCE.
MY BAD ATTITUDE IS PROOF THAT I AM THINKING CLEARLY.
ARE YOU GOING TO COMPLIMENT ME ON MY CLARITY OR DEMAND I BE IRRATIONAL?
I'M PUTTING YOU IN CHARGE OF THE EMPLOYEE MORALE FESTIVAL.
I HAVE A SUDDEN URGE TO GRAB YOU BY THE TAIL AND BEAT MYSELF TO DEATH.
1-20-08
THAT'S HOW I KNOW I WON THE MEETING.

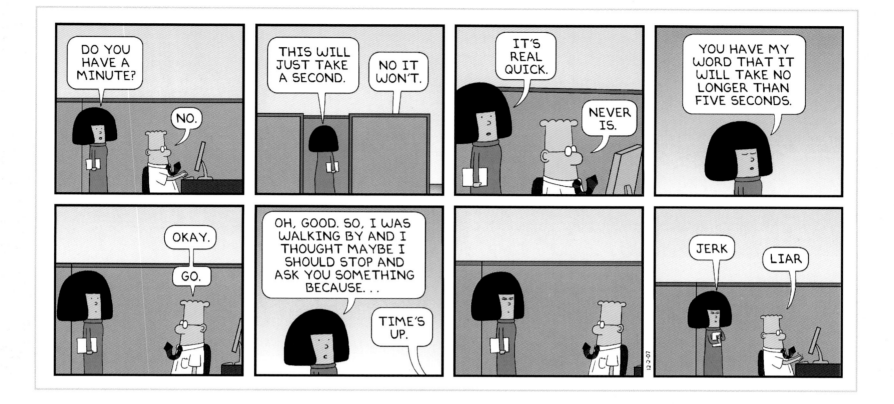

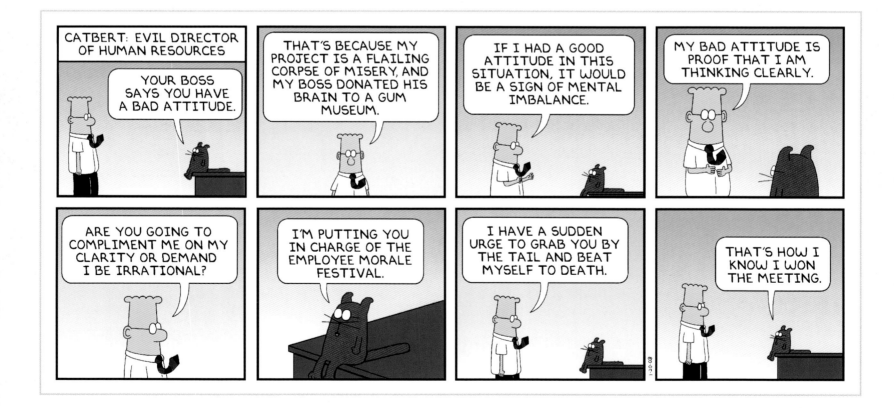

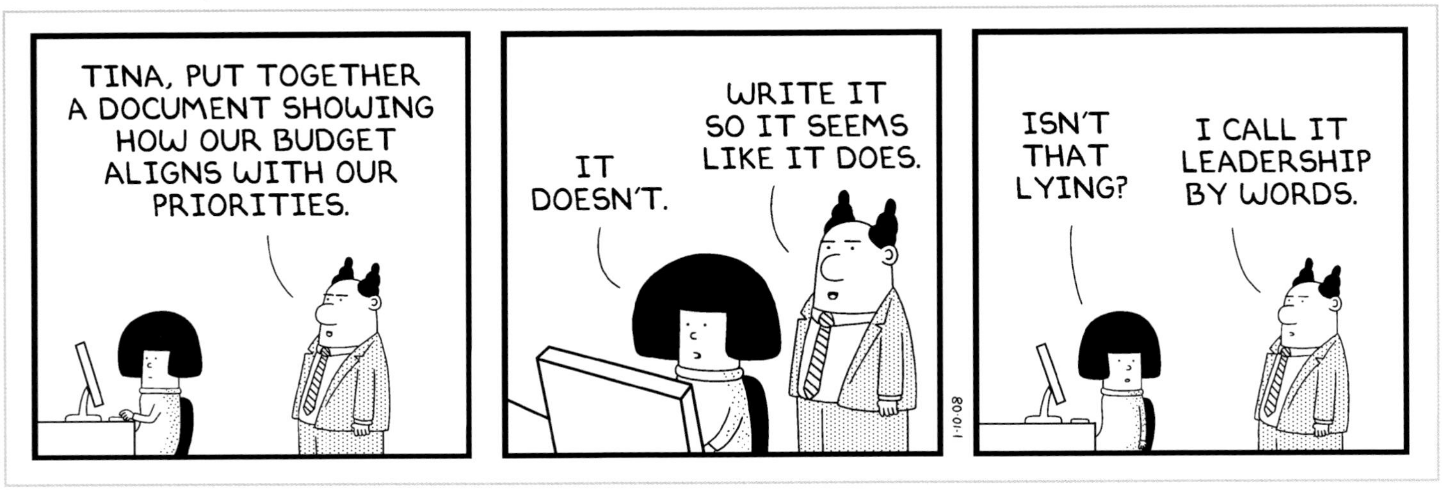
TINA, PUT TOGETHER A DOCUMENT SHOWING HOW OUR BUDGET ALIGNS WITH OUR PRIORITIES.
IT DOESN'T.
WRITE IT SO IT SEEMS LIKE IT DOES.
1-10-08
ISN'T THAT LYING?
I CALL IT LEADERSHIP BY WORDS.

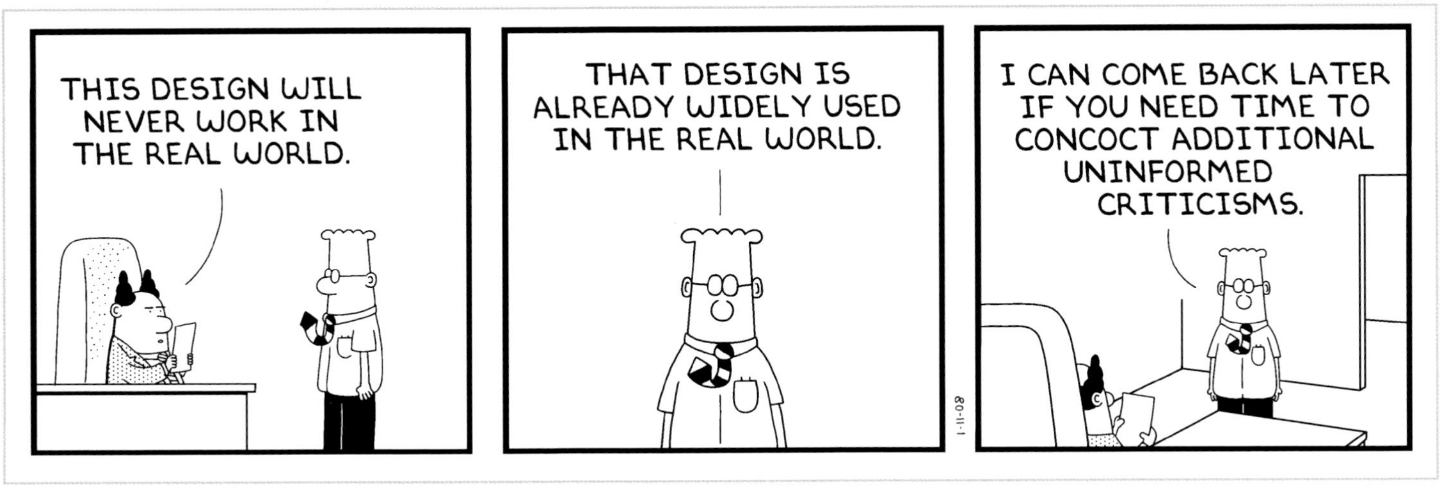
THIS DESIGN WILL NEVER WORK IN THE REAL WORLD.
THAT DESIGN IS ALREADY WIDELY USED IN THE REAL WORLD.
1-11-08
I CAN COME BACK LATER IF YOU NEED TIME TO CONCOCT ADDITIONAL UNINFORMED CRITICISMS.

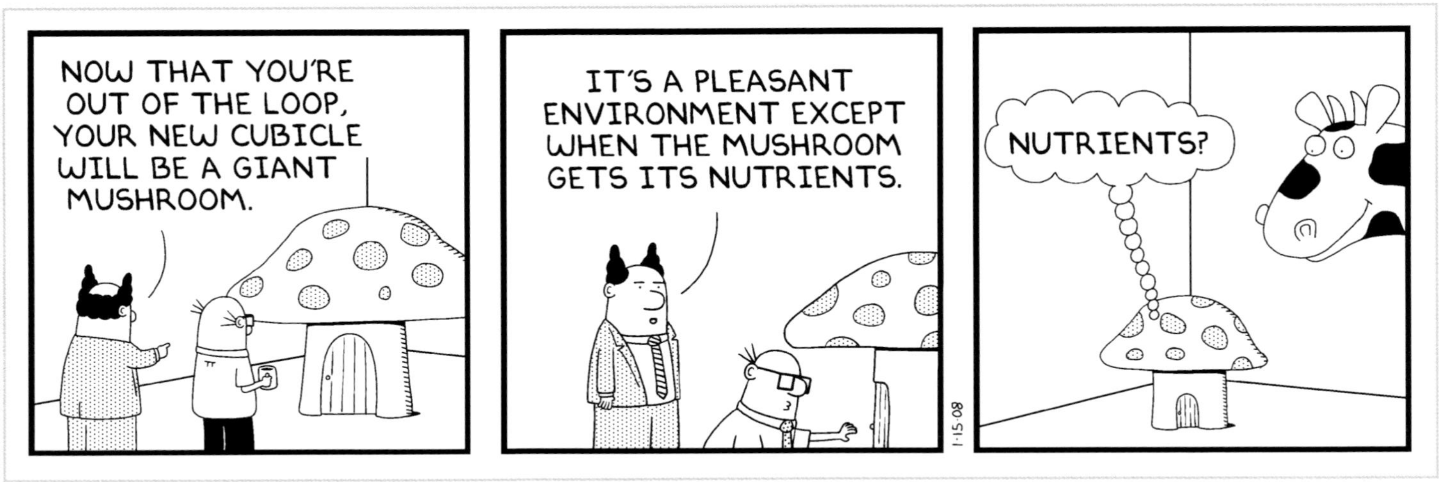
NOW THAT YOU'RE OUT OF THE LOOP, YOUR NEW CUBICLE WILL BE A GIANT MUSHROOM.
IT'S A PLEASANT ENVIRONMENT EXCEPT WHEN THE MUSHROOM GETS ITS NUTRIENTS.
1-15-08
NUTRIENTS?

The first version of this comic showed the cow squatting over the mushroom, but I figured that wouldn't make it past my editors.

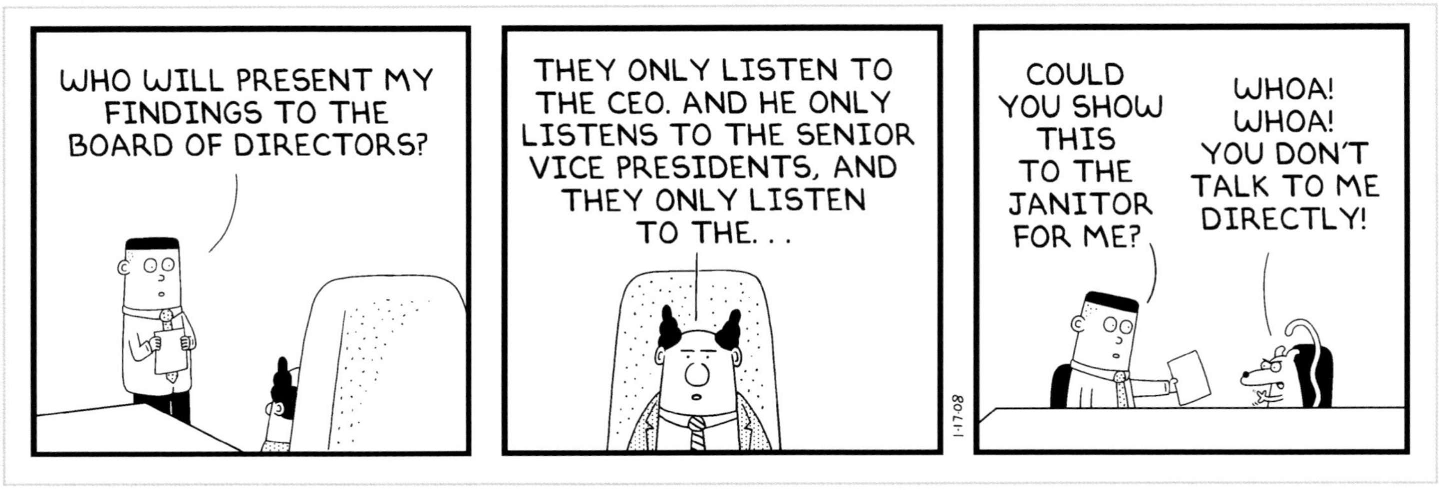
WHO WILL PRESENT MY FINDINGS TO THE BOARD OF DIRECTORS?
THEY ONLY LISTEN TO THE CEO. AND HE ONLY LISTENS TO THE SENIOR VICE PRESIDENTS, AND THEY ONLY LISTEN TO THE. . .
1-17-08
COULD YOU SHOW THIS TO THE JANITOR FOR ME?
WHOA! WHOA! YOU DON'T TALK TO ME DIRECTLY!

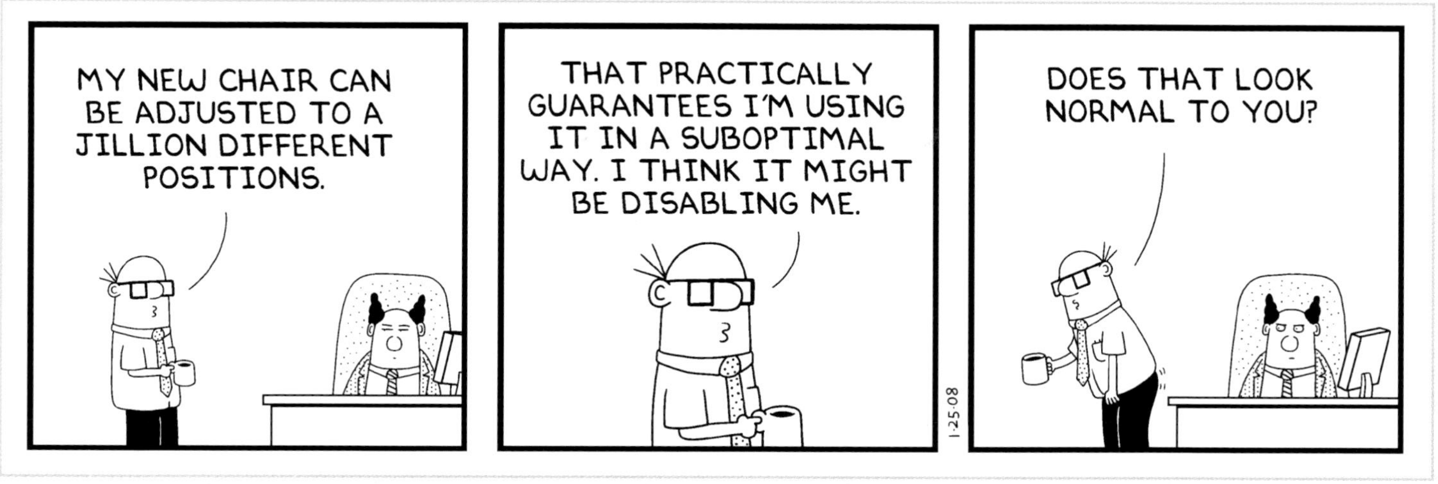
MY NEW CHAIR CAN BE ADJUSTED TO A JILLION DIFFERENT POSITIONS.
THAT PRACTICALLY GUARANTEES I'M USING IT IN A SUBOPTIMAL WAY. I THINK IT MIGHT BE DISABLING ME.
1-25-08
DOES THAT LOOK NORMAL TO YOU?

The following comic is based on my hobby of reading obscure articles on the Internet and then imagining that anyone else would enjoy hearing about what I have learned.

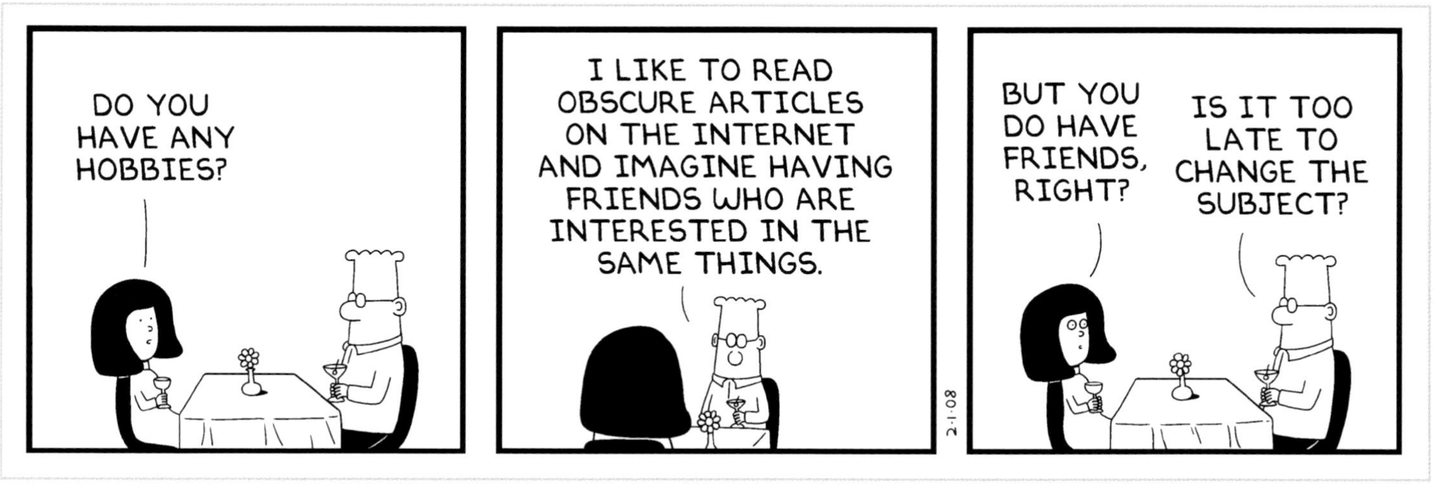
DO YOU HAVE ANY HOBBIES?
I LIKE TO READ OBSCURE ARTICLES ON THE INTERNET AND IMAGINE HAVING FRIENDS WHO ARE INTERESTED IN THE SAME THINGS.
2-1-08
BUT YOU DO HAVE FRIENDS, RIGHT?
IS IT TOO LATE TO CHANGE THE SUBJECT?

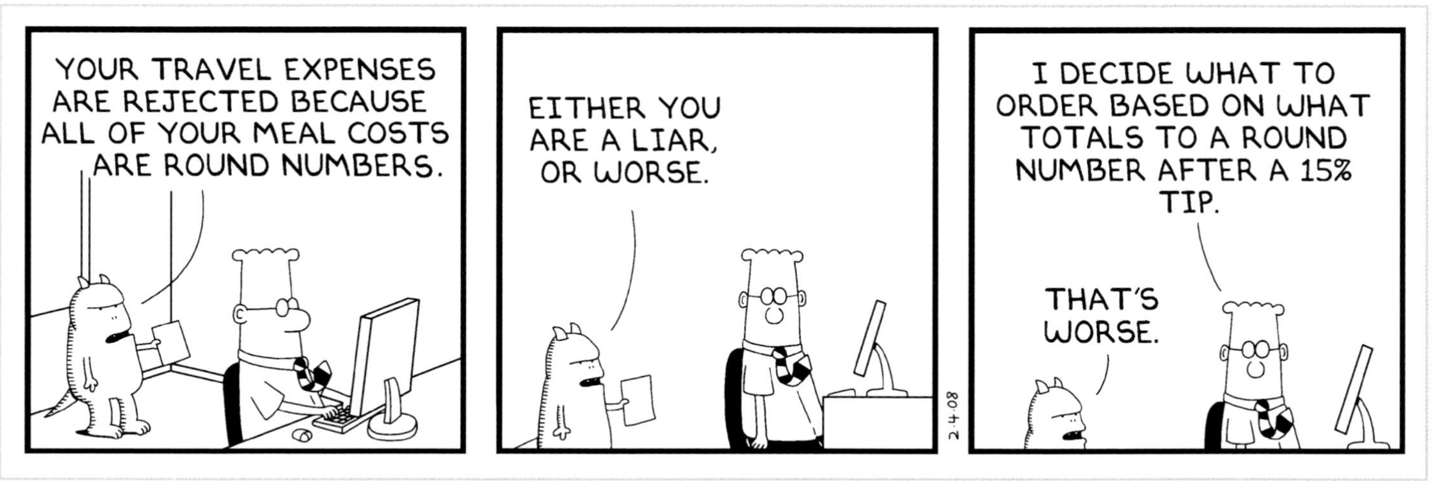
YOUR TRAVEL EXPENSES ARE REJECTED BECAUSE ALL OF YOUR MEAL COSTS ARE ROUND NUMBERS.
EITHER YOU ARE A LIAR, OR WORSE.
2-4-08
I DECIDE WHAT TO ORDER BASED ON WHAT TOTALS TO A ROUND NUMBER AFTER A 15% TIP.
THAT'S WORSE.

Whoever invented the dotted-line speech bubble to indicate whispering was a genius.

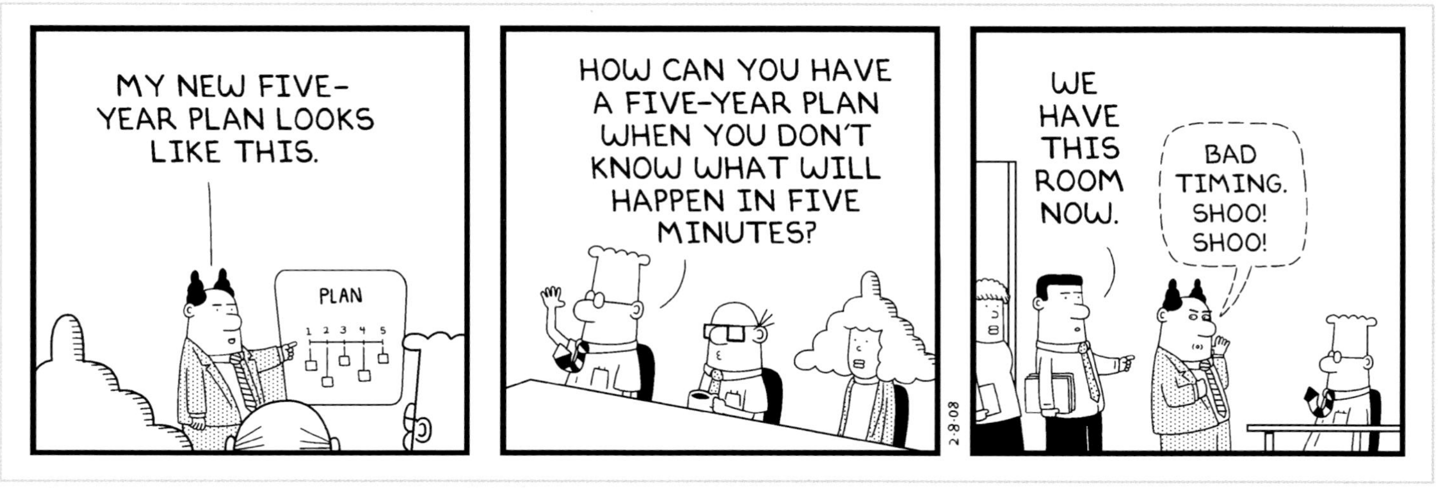
MY NEW FIVE-YEAR PLAN LOOKS LIKE THIS.
PLAN
1 2 3 4 5
HOW CAN YOU HAVE A FIVE-YEAR PLAN WHEN YOU DON'T KNOW WHAT WILL HAPPEN IN FIVE MINUTES?
2-8-08
WE HAVE THIS ROOM NOW.
BAD TIMING. SHOO! SHOO!

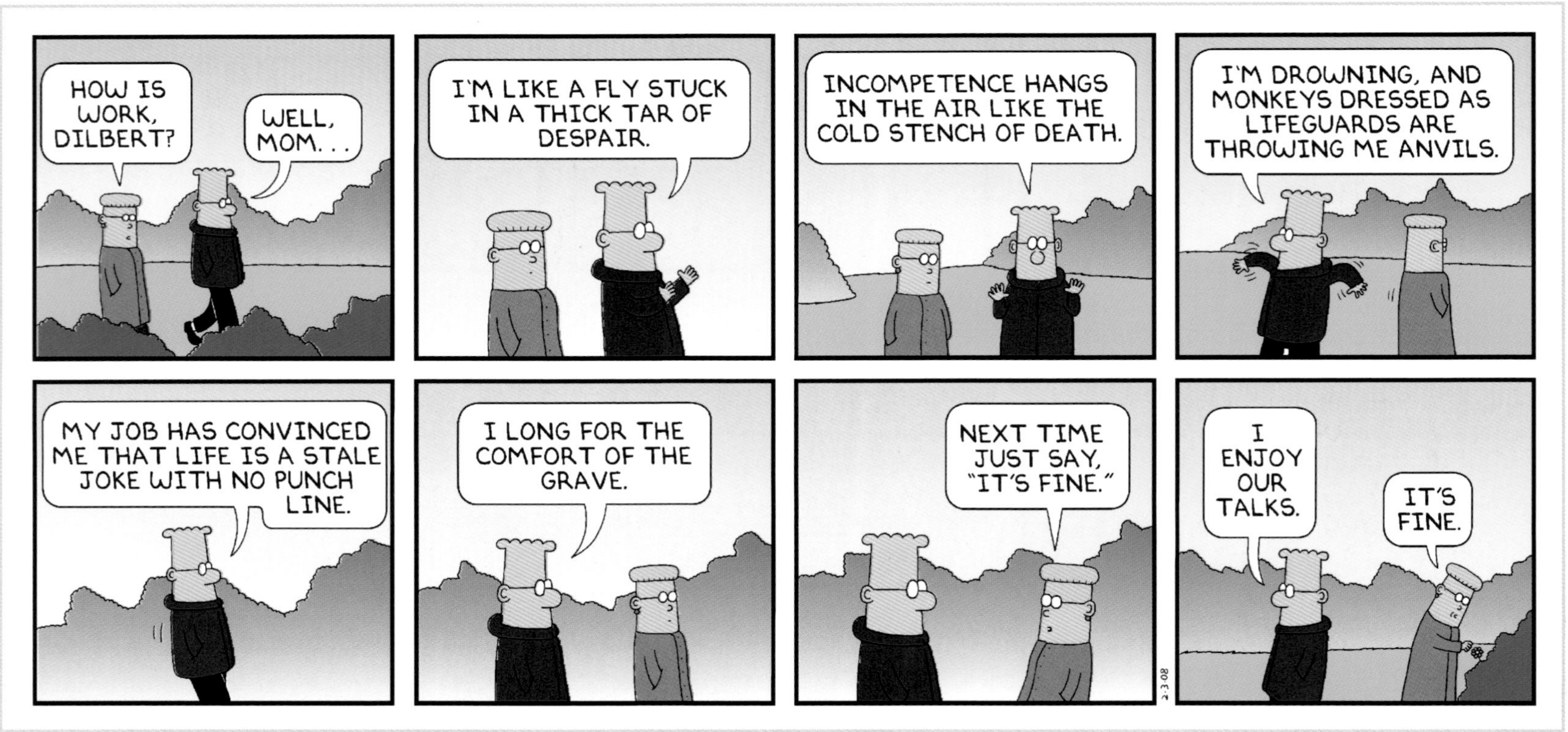
HOW IS WORK, DILBERT?
WELL, MOM. . .
I'M LIKE A FLY STUCK IN A THICK TAR OF DESPAIR.
INCOMPETENCE HANGS IN THE AIR LIKE THE COLD STENCH OF DEATH.
I'M DROWNING, AND MONKEYS DRESSED AS LIFEGUARDS ARE THROWING ME ANVILS.
MY JOB HAS CONVINCED ME THAT LIFE IS A STALE JOKE WITH NO PUNCH LINE.
I LONG FOR THE COMFORT OF THE GRAVE.
NEXT TIME JUST SAY, "IT'S FINE."
2-3-08
I ENJOY OUR TALKS.
IT'S FINE.

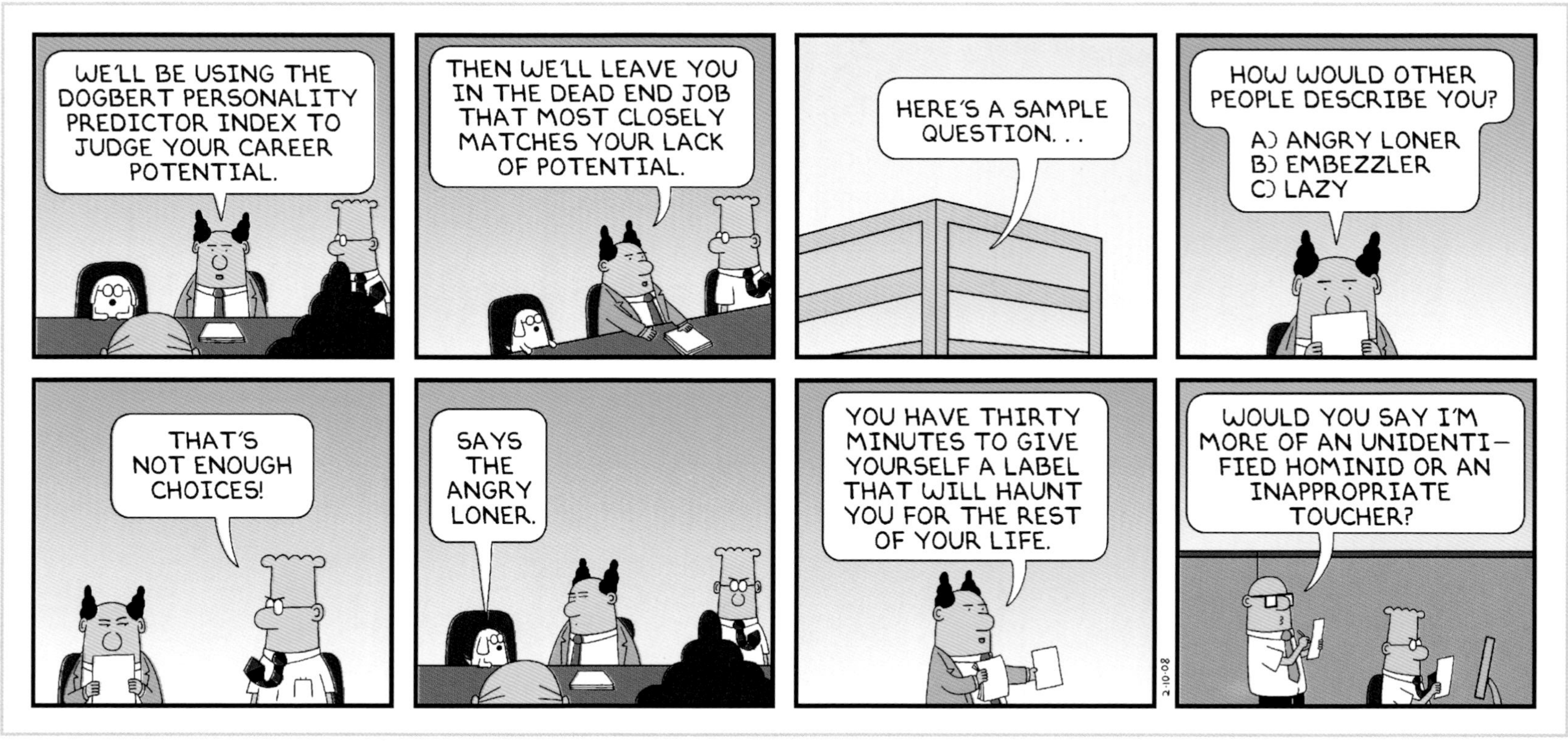
WE'LL BE USING THE DOGBERT PERSONALITY PREDICTOR INDEX TO JUDGE YOUR CAREER POTENTIAL.
THEN WE'LL LEAVE YOU IN THE DEAD END JOB THAT MOST CLOSELY MATCHES YOUR LACK OF POTENTIAL.
HERE'S A SAMPLE QUESTION. . .
HOW WOULD OTHER PEOPLE DESCRIBE YOU?
A) ANGRY LONER
B) EMBEZZLER
C) LAZY
THAT'S NOT ENOUGH CHOICES!
SAYS THE ANGRY LONER.
YOU HAVE THIRTY MINUTES TO GIVE YOURSELF A LABEL THAT WILL HAUNT YOU FOR THE REST OF YOUR LIFE.
2-10-08
WOULD YOU SAY I'M MORE OF AN UNIDENTI-FIED HOMINID OR AN INAPPROPRIATE TOUCHER?

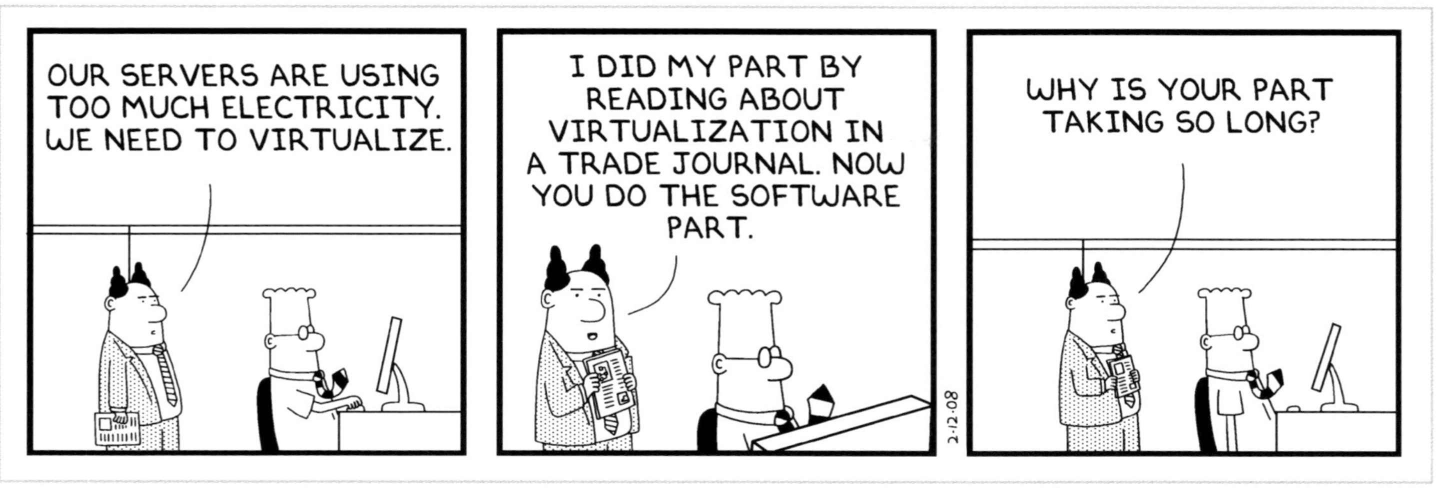
OUR SERVERS ARE USING TOO MUCH ELECTRICITY. WE NEED TO VIRTUALIZE.
I DID MY PART BY READING ABOUT VIRTUALIZATION IN A TRADE JOURNAL. NOW YOU DO THE SOFTWARE PART.
WHY IS YOUR PART TAKING SO LONG?
2-12-08

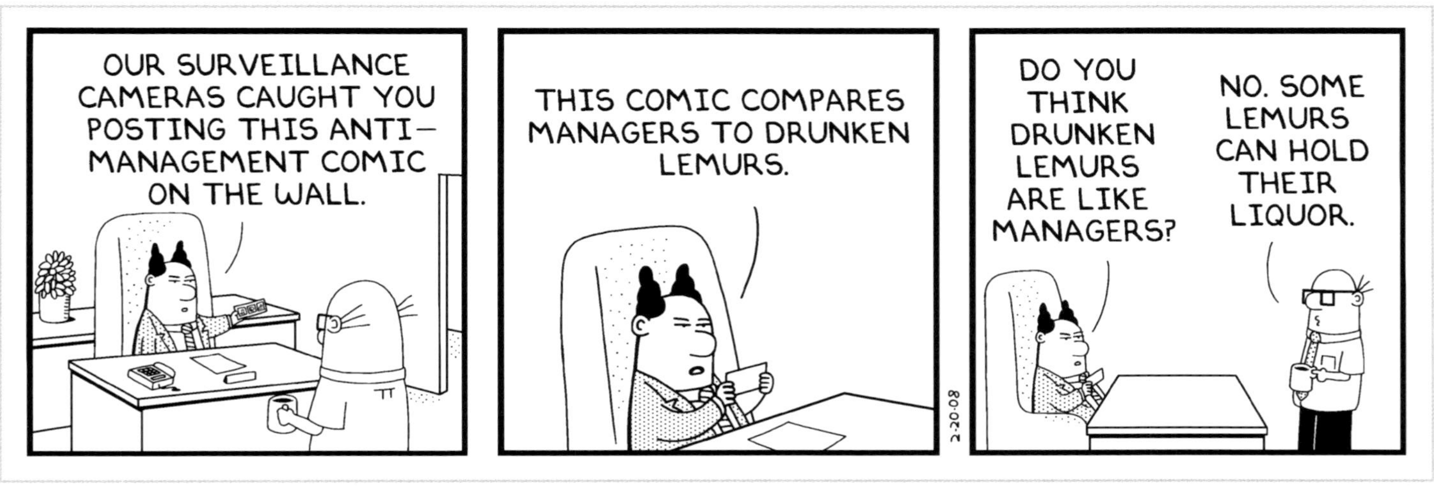
OUR SURVEILLANCE CAMERAS CAUGHT YOU POSTING THIS ANTI-MANAGEMENT COMIC ON THE WALL.
THIS COMIC COMPARES MANAGERS TO DRUNKEN LEMURS.
DO YOU THINK DRUNKEN LEMURS ARE LIKE MANAGERS?
NO. SOME LEMURS CAN HOLD THEIR LIQUOR.
2-20-08

In the real world, a casino employee got fired for posting a Dilbert *comic that compared managers to drunken lemurs. The story made national headlines. After the employee's life was changed by my alleged art, I decided to make art imitate life, and bring the story full circle. This series of strips also made national news.*

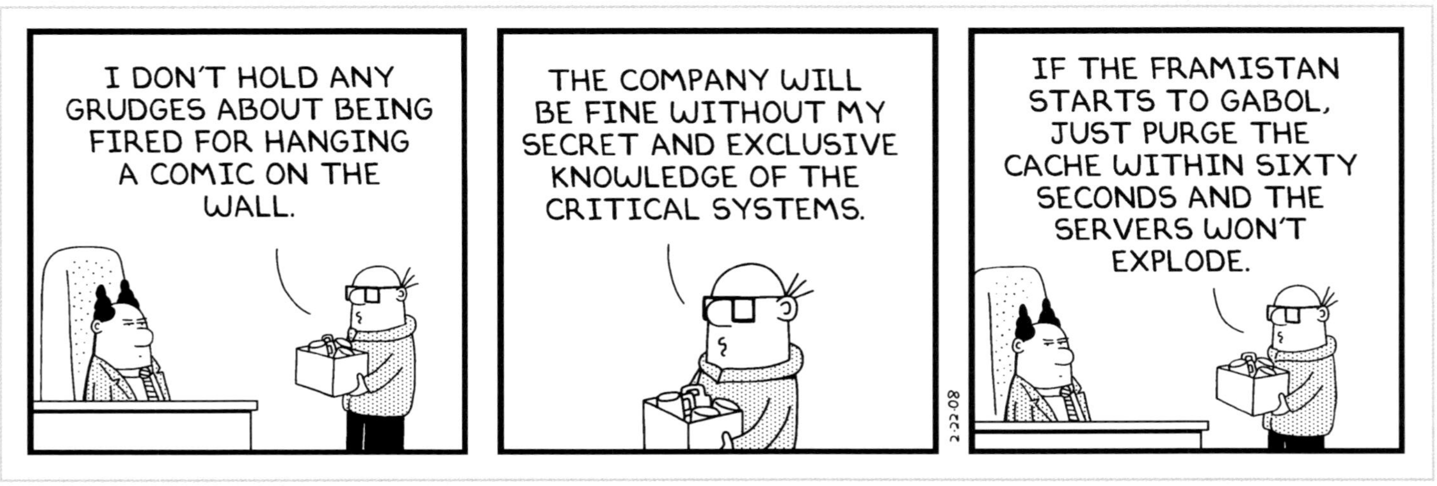
I DON'T HOLD ANY GRUDGES ABOUT BEING FIRED FOR HANGING A COMIC ON THE WALL.
THE COMPANY WILL BE FINE WITHOUT MY SECRET AND EXCLUSIVE KNOWLEDGE OF THE CRITICAL SYSTEMS.
IF THE FRAMISTAN STARTS TO GABOL, JUST PURGE THE CACHE WITHIN SIXTY SECONDS AND THE SERVERS WON'T EXPLODE.
2-22-08

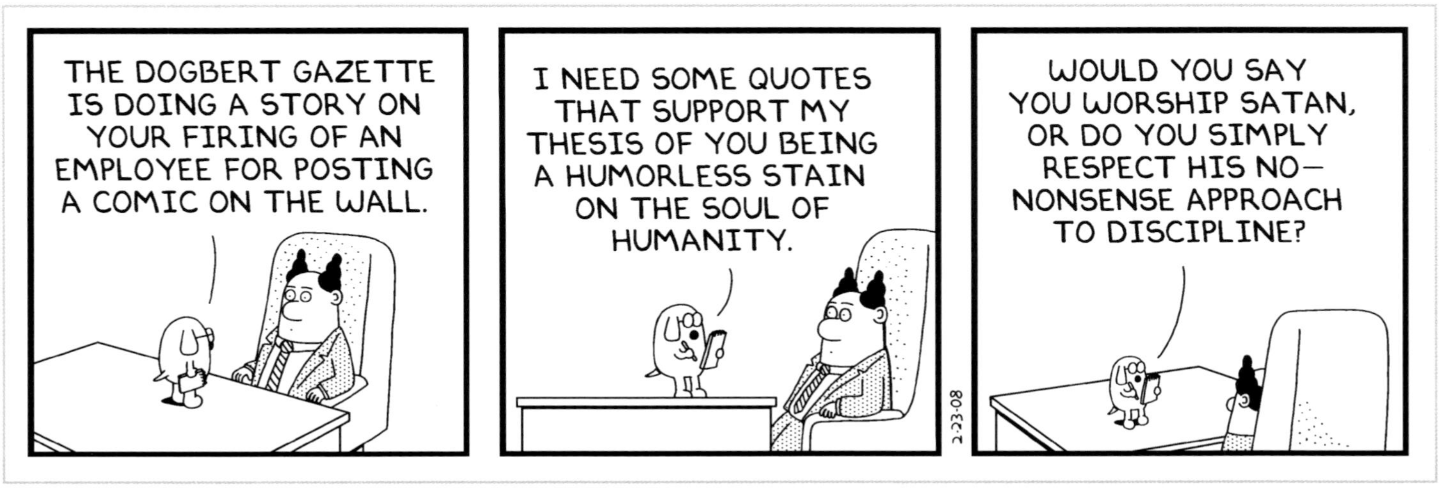
THE DOGBERT GAZETTE IS DOING A STORY ON YOUR FIRING OF AN EMPLOYEE FOR POSTING A COMIC ON THE WALL.
I NEED SOME QUOTES THAT SUPPORT MY THESIS OF YOU BEING A HUMORLESS STAIN ON THE SOUL OF HUMANITY.
WOULD YOU SAY YOU WORSHIP SATAN, OR DO YOU SIMPLY RESPECT HIS NO-NONSENSE APPROACH TO DISCIPLINE?
2-23-08

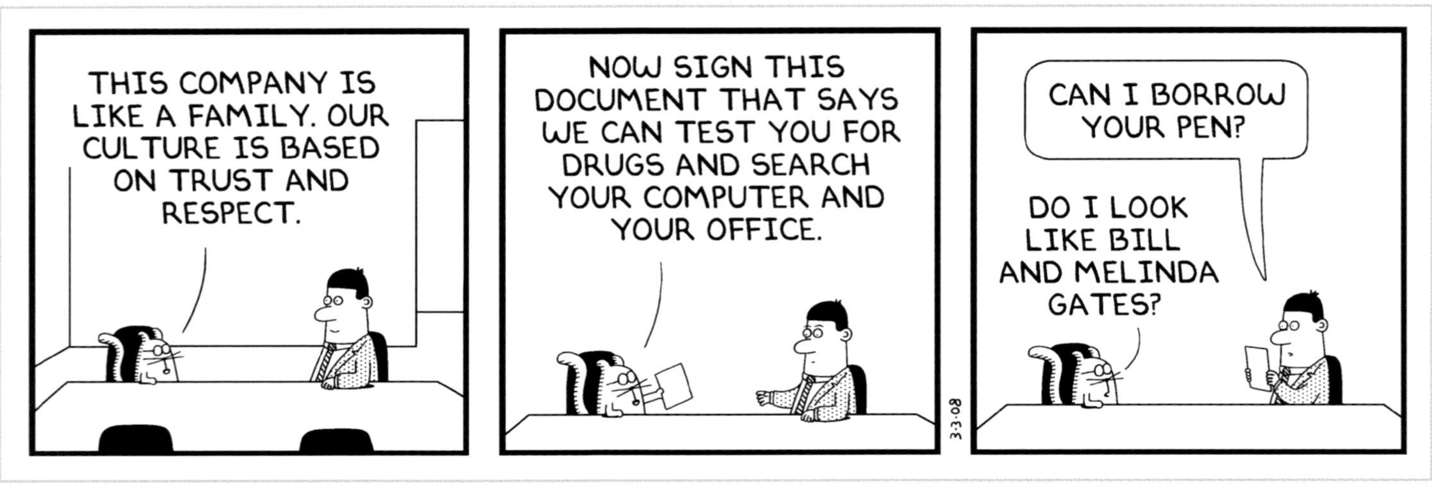
THIS COMPANY IS LIKE A FAMILY. OUR CULTURE IS BASED ON TRUST AND RESPECT.
NOW SIGN THIS DOCUMENT THAT SAYS WE CAN TEST YOU FOR DRUGS AND SEARCH YOUR COMPUTER AND YOUR OFFICE.
CAN I BORROW YOUR PEN?
DO I LOOK LIKE BILL AND MELINDA GATES?
3-3-08

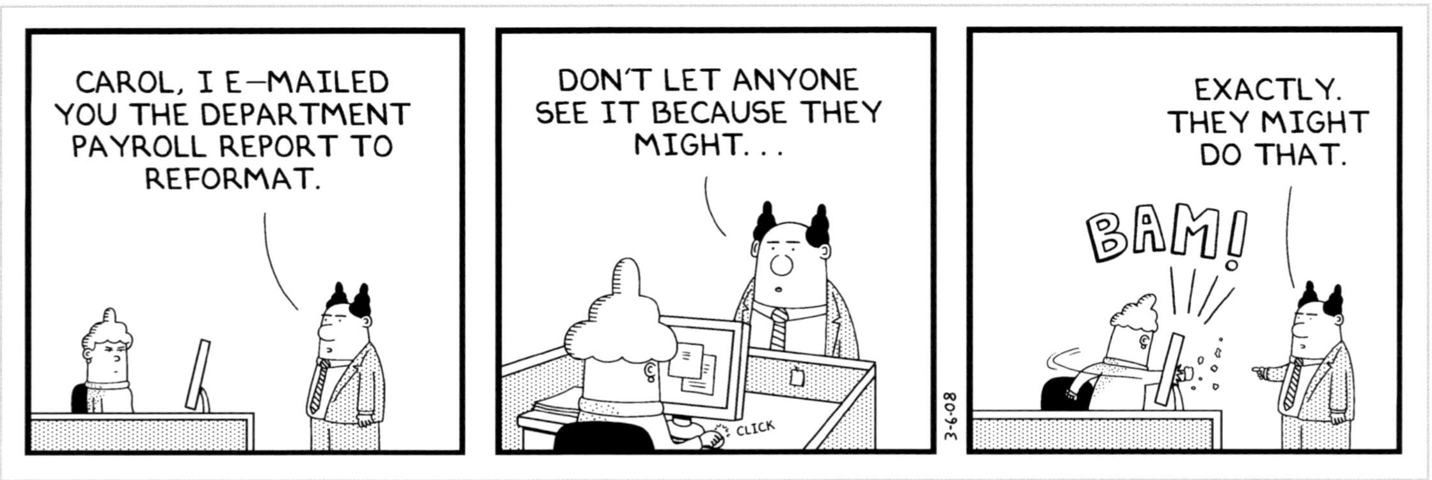
CAROL, I E-MAILED YOU THE DEPARTMENT PAYROLL REPORT TO REFORMAT.
DON'T LET ANYONE SEE IT BECAUSE THEY MIGHT. . .
CLICK
EXACTLY. THEY MIGHT DO THAT.
BAM!
3-6-08

I draw a lot of comics that involve punching. I like the way it looks in comic form. And frankly, I can't draw that many things, so I tend to repeat any action that I think I nailed.

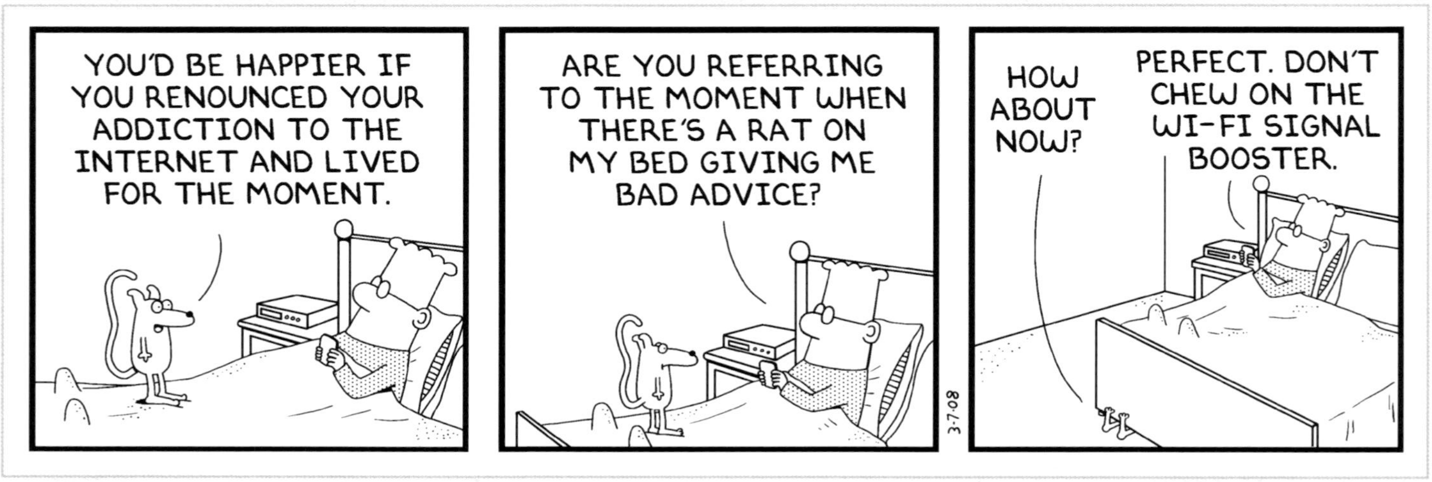
YOU'D BE HAPPIER IF YOU RENOUNCED YOUR ADDICTION TO THE INTERNET AND LIVED FOR THE MOMENT.
ARE YOU REFERRING TO THE MOMENT WHEN THERE'S A RAT ON MY BED GIVING ME BAD ADVICE?
HOW ABOUT NOW?
PERFECT. DON'T CHEW ON THE WI-FI SIGNAL BOOSTER.
3-7-08

The following series was the most controversial of my career, and probably the most popular. I thought it was more silly than blasphemous. There's no intended criticism or even a point. The topic is touchy by nature, but I took a chance on it under the theory that anyone who follows the teachings of Jesus would spend his or her time feeding the poor and not complaining about comics. (That theory was disproved.)

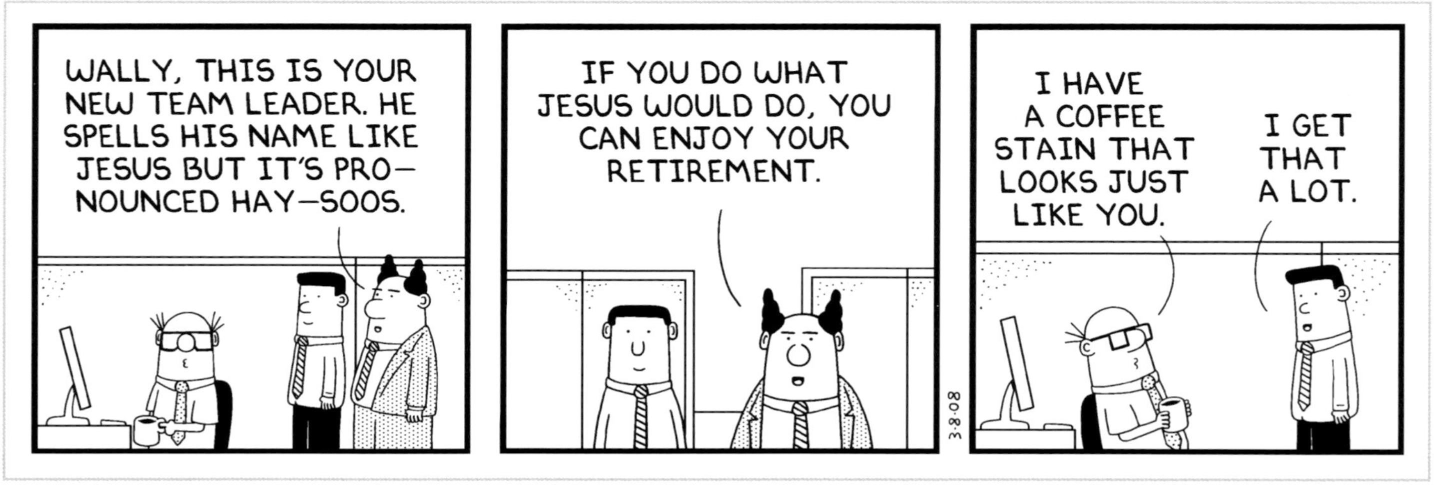
WALLY, THIS IS YOUR NEW TEAM LEADER. HE SPELLS HIS NAME LIKE JESUS BUT IT'S PRO-NOUNCED HAY-SOOS.
IF YOU DO WHAT JESUS WOULD DO, YOU CAN ENJOY YOUR RETIREMENT.
I HAVE A COFFEE STAIN THAT LOOKS JUST LIKE YOU.
I GET THAT A LOT.
3-8-08

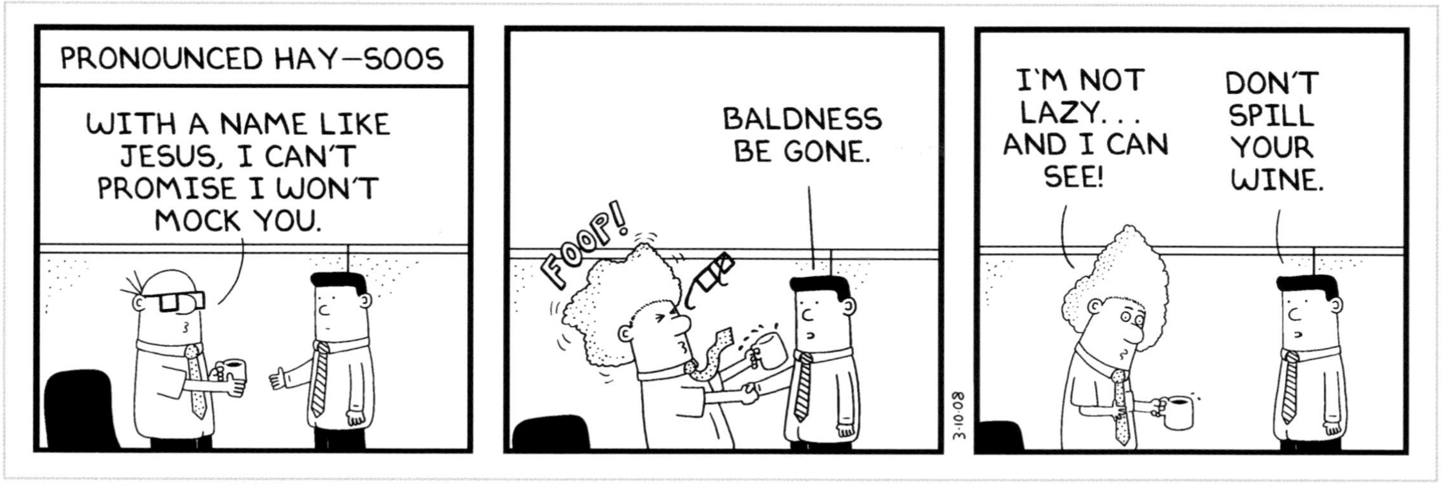
PRONOUNCED HAY–SOOS
WITH A NAME LIKE JESUS, I CAN'T PROMISE I WON'T MOCK YOU.
FOOP!
BALDNESS BE GONE.
3-10-08
I'M NOT LAZY. . . AND I CAN SEE!
DON'T SPILL YOUR WINE.

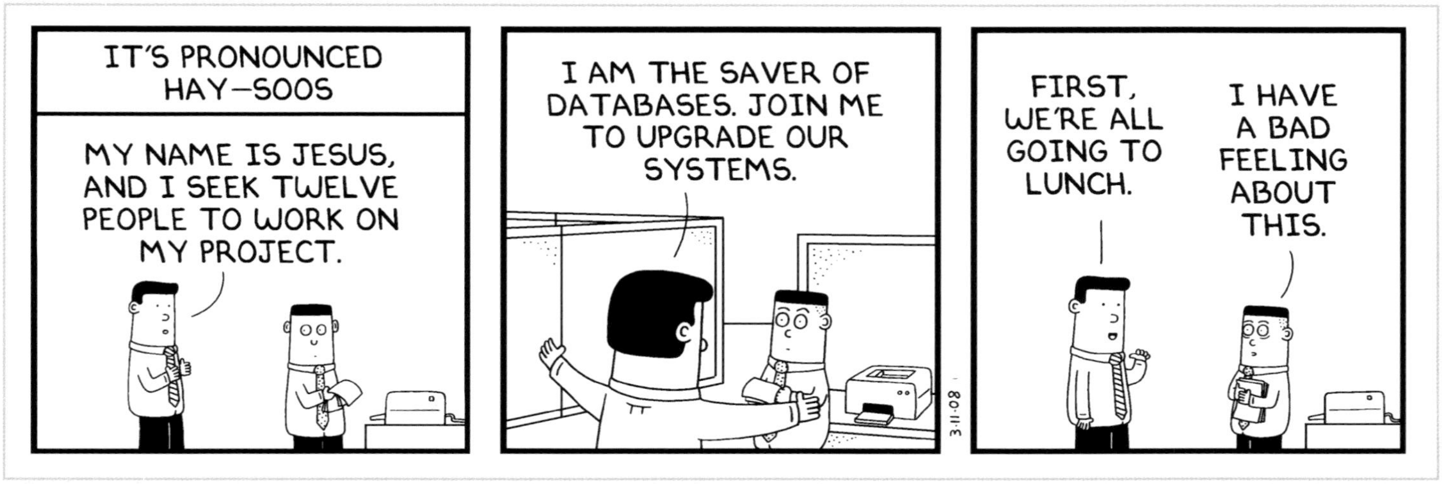
IT'S PRONOUNCED HAY–SOOS
MY NAME IS JESUS, AND I SEEK TWELVE PEOPLE TO WORK ON MY PROJECT.
I AM THE SAVER OF DATABASES. JOIN ME TO UPGRADE OUR SYSTEMS.
3-11-08
FIRST, WE'RE ALL GOING TO LUNCH.
I HAVE A BAD FEELING ABOUT THIS.

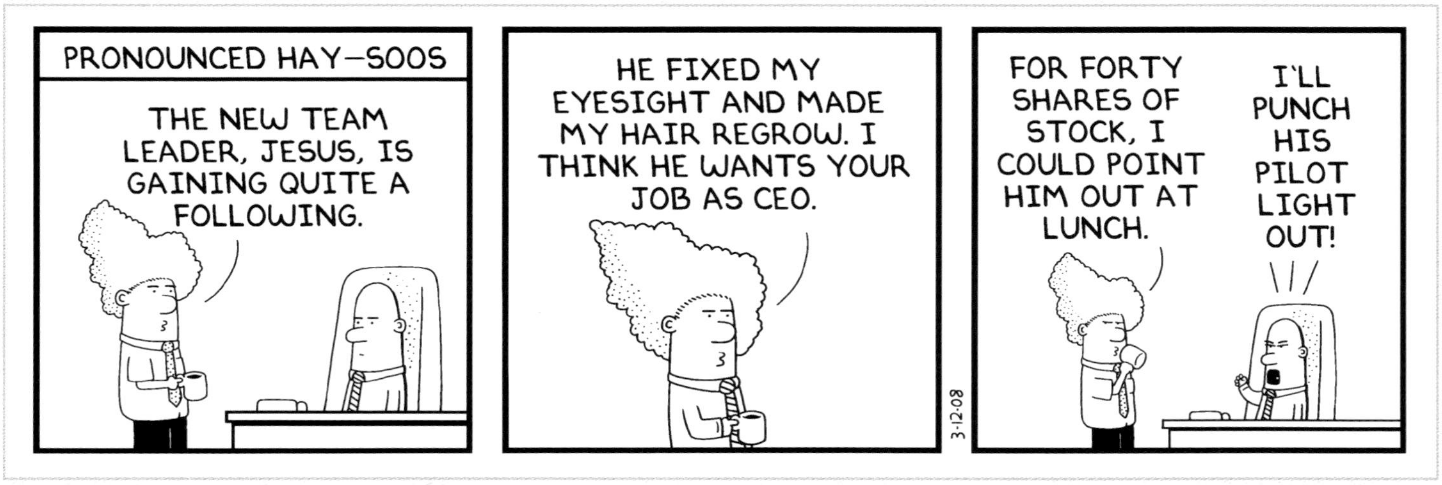
PRONOUNCED HAY–SOOS
THE NEW TEAM LEADER, JESUS, IS GAINING QUITE A FOLLOWING.
HE FIXED MY EYESIGHT AND MADE MY HAIR REGROW. I THINK HE WANTS YOUR JOB AS CEO.
3-12-08
FOR FORTY SHARES OF STOCK, I COULD POINT HIM OUT AT LUNCH.
I'LL PUNCH HIS PILOT LIGHT OUT!

Since I draw Dilbert *strips a few months before they appear in newspapers. I didn't realize this series would be running near Easter. That probably won't help me get into heaven.*

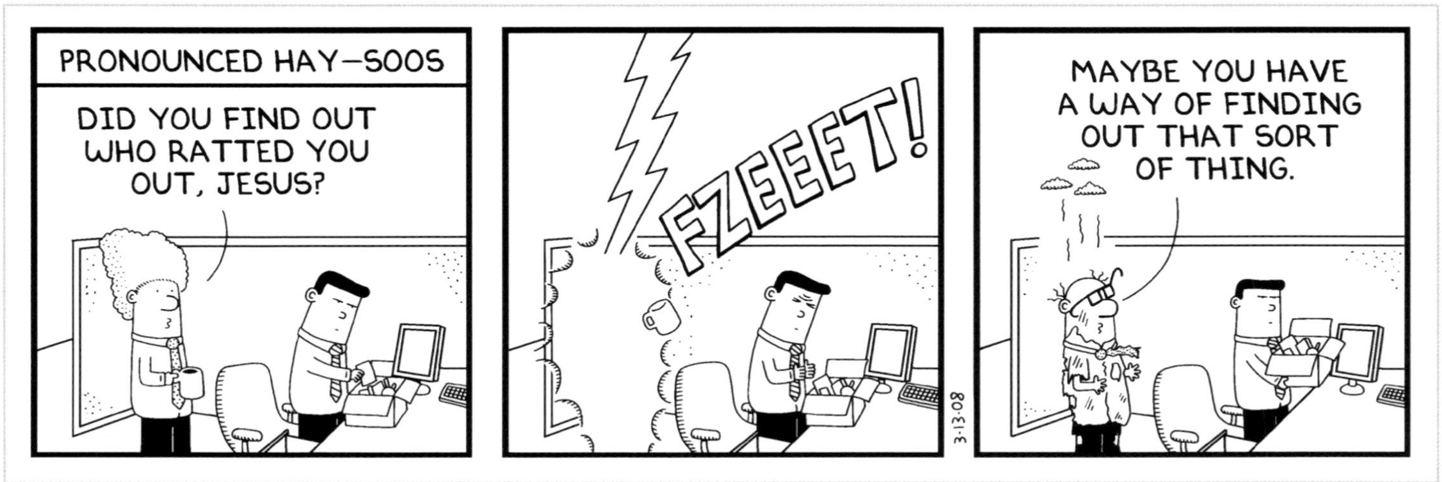
PRONOUNCED HAY–SOOS
DID YOU FIND OUT WHO RATTED YOU OUT, JESUS?
FZEEET!
3-13-08
MAYBE YOU HAVE A WAY OF FINDING OUT THAT SORT OF THING.

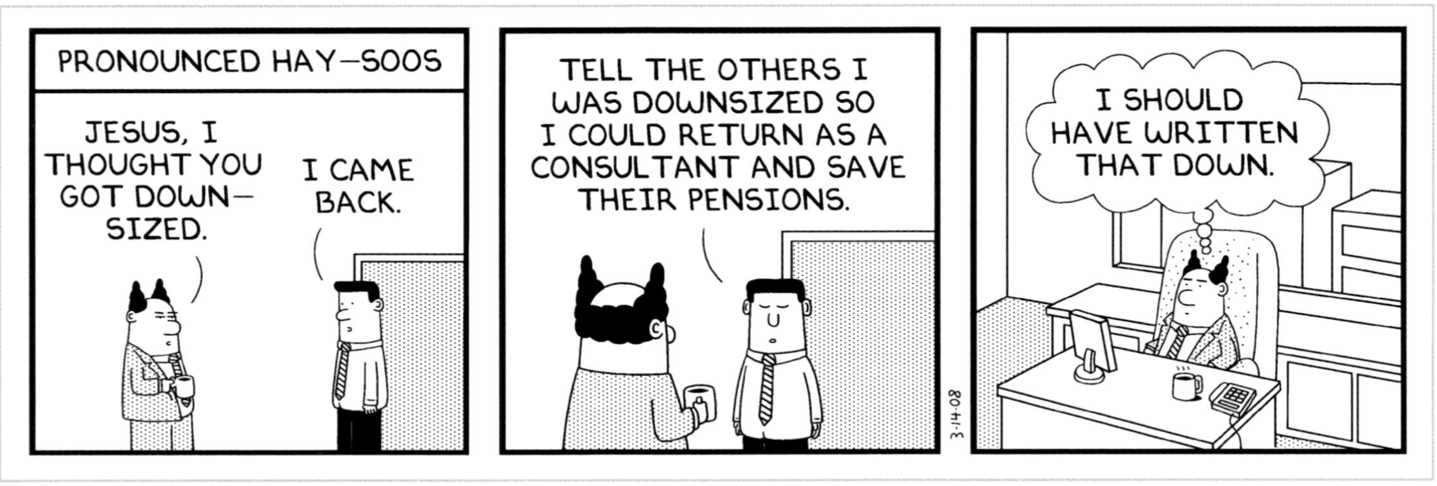
PRONOUNCED HAY—SOOS
JESUS, I THOUGHT YOU GOT DOWN—SIZED.
I CAME BACK.
TELL THE OTHERS I WAS DOWNSIZED SO I COULD RETURN AS A CONSULTANT AND SAVE THEIR PENSIONS.
3-14-08
I SHOULD HAVE WRITTEN THAT DOWN.

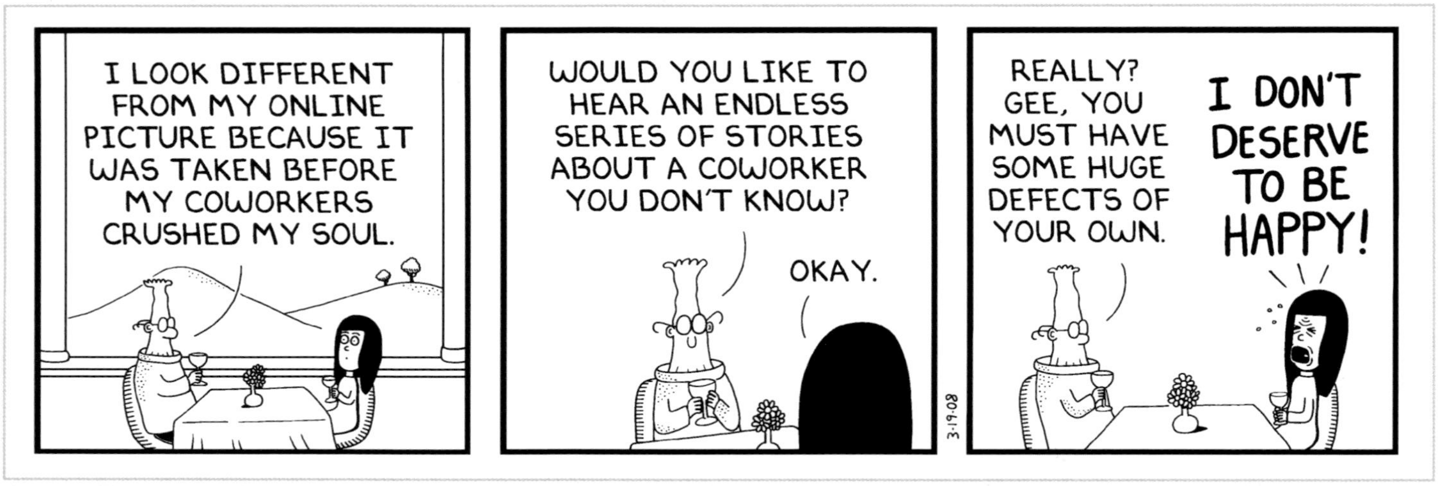
I LOOK DIFFERENT FROM MY ONLINE PICTURE BECAUSE IT WAS TAKEN BEFORE MY COWORKERS CRUSHED MY SOUL.
WOULD YOU LIKE TO HEAR AN ENDLESS SERIES OF STORIES ABOUT A COWORKER YOU DON'T KNOW?
OKAY.
3-19-08
REALLY? GEE, YOU MUST HAVE SOME HUGE DEFECTS OF YOUR OWN.
I DON'T DESERVE TO BE HAPPY!

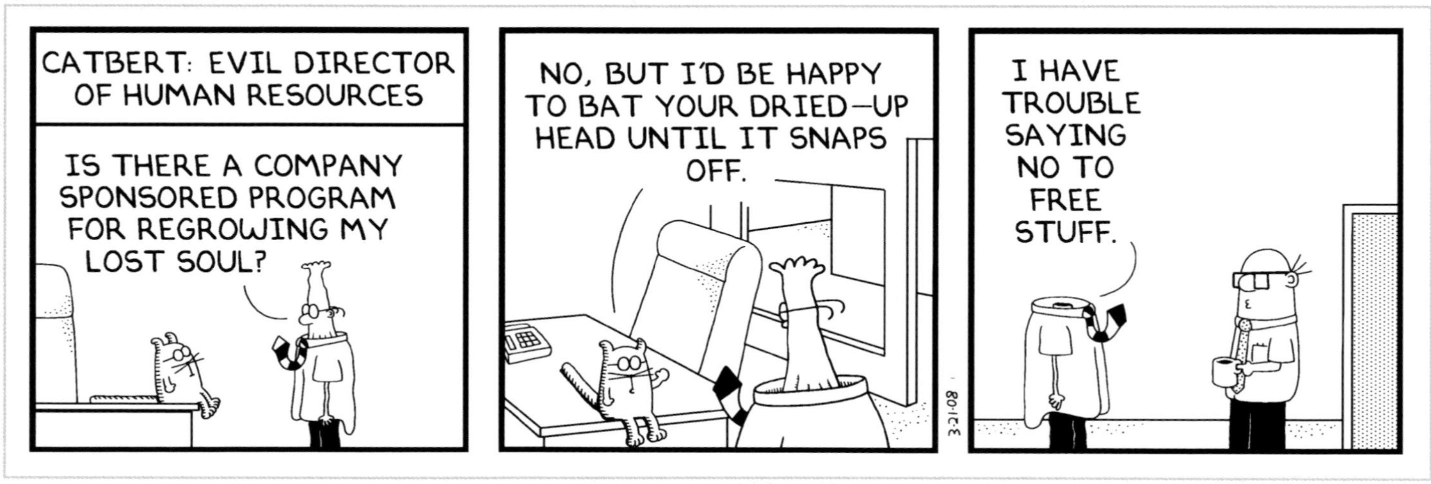
CATBERT: EVIL DIRECTOR OF HUMAN RESOURCES
IS THERE A COMPANY SPONSORED PROGRAM FOR REGROWING MY LOST SOUL?
NO, BUT I'D BE HAPPY TO BAT YOUR DRIED—UP HEAD UNTIL IT SNAPS OFF.
3-21-08
I HAVE TROUBLE SAYING NO TO FREE STUFF.

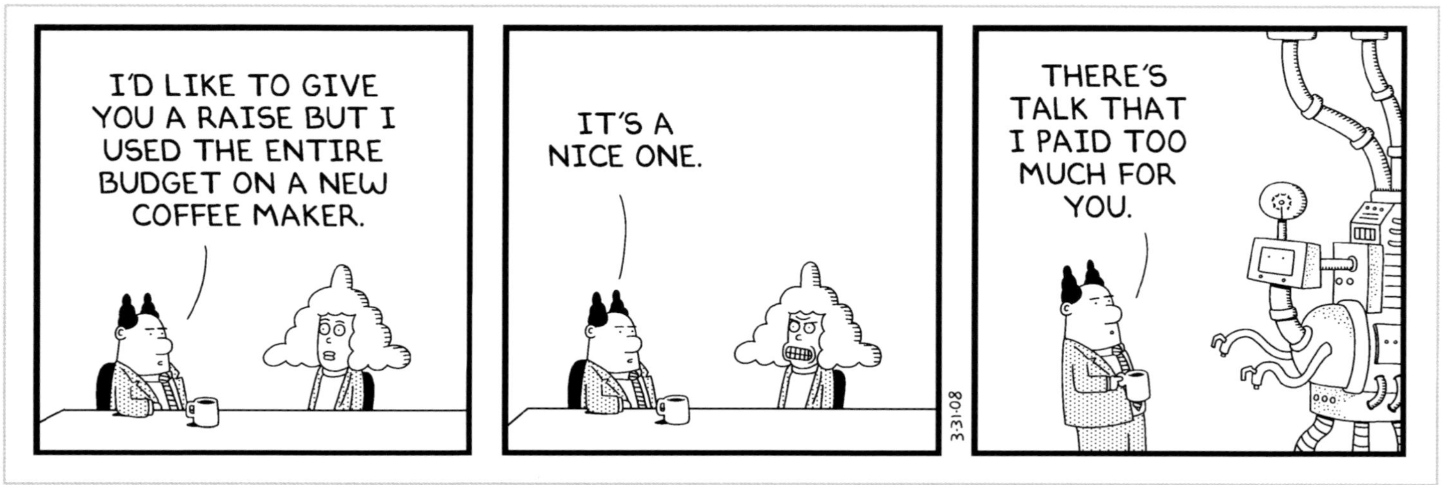
I'D LIKE TO GIVE YOU A RAISE BUT I USED THE ENTIRE BUDGET ON A NEW COFFEE MAKER.
IT'S A NICE ONE.
3-31-08
THERE'S TALK THAT I PAID TOO MUCH FOR YOU.

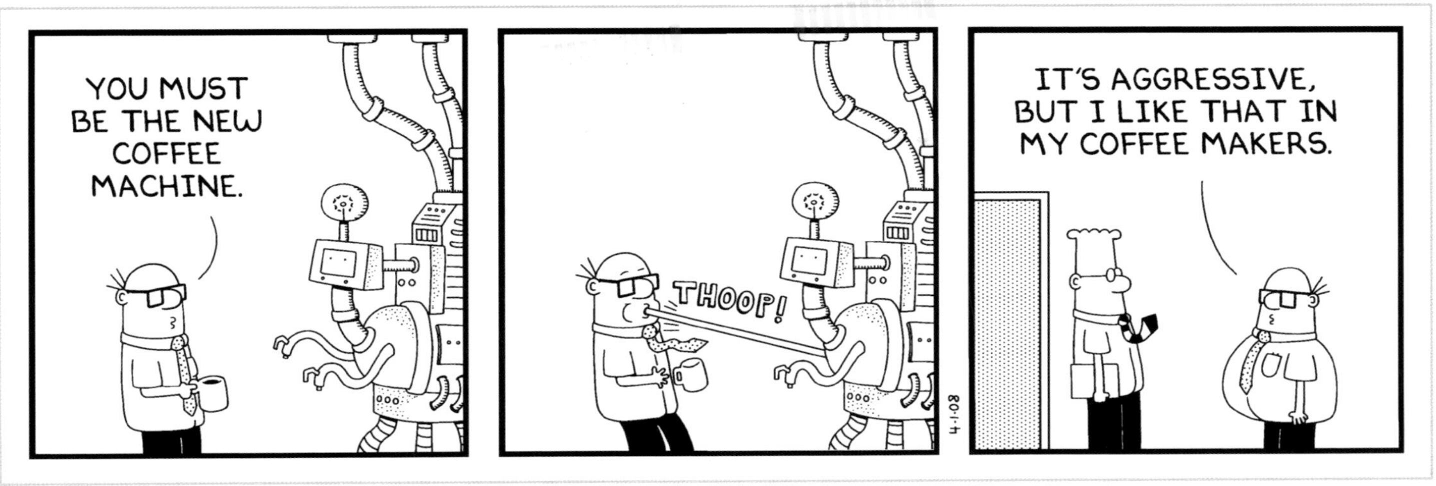
YOU MUST BE THE NEW COFFEE MACHINE.
THOOP!
4-1-08
IT'S AGGRESSIVE, BUT I LIKE THAT IN MY COFFEE MAKERS.

Few things make me prouder than finding the perfect word for a sound effect. In this case, only "thoop" would do.

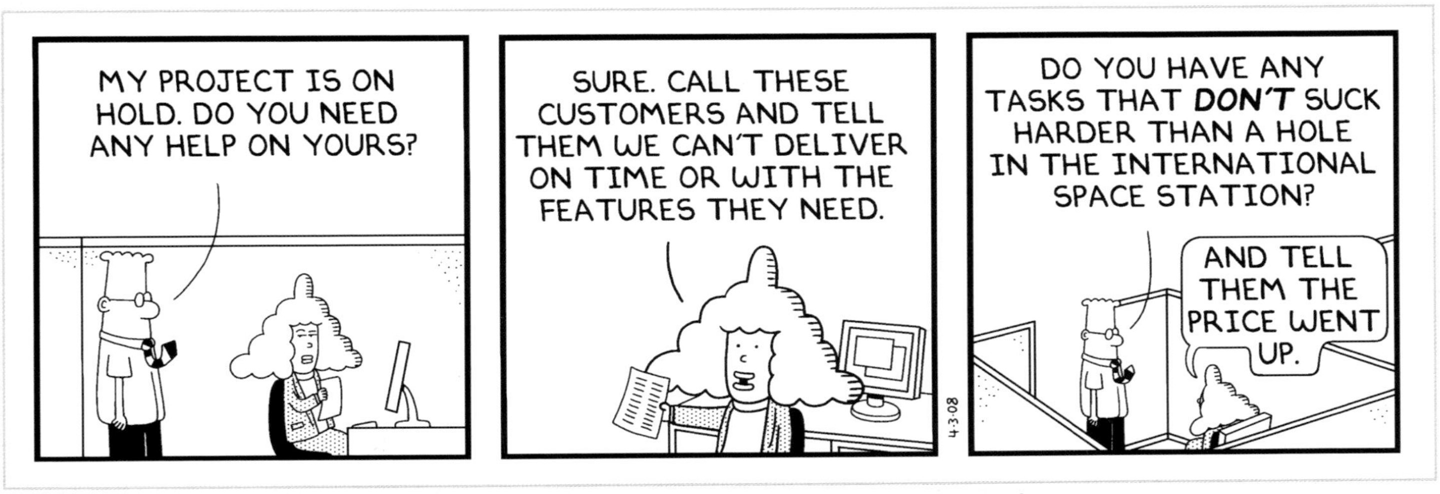
MY PROJECT IS ON HOLD. DO YOU NEED ANY HELP ON YOURS?
SURE. CALL THESE CUSTOMERS AND TELL THEM WE CAN'T DELIVER ON TIME OR WITH THE FEATURES THEY NEED.
4-3-08
DO YOU HAVE ANY TASKS THAT **DON'T** SUCK HARDER THAN A HOLE IN THE INTERNATIONAL SPACE STATION?
AND TELL THEM THE PRICE WENT UP.

This one had to be altered for publication. I wasn't allowed to say, "suck harder than a hole in the International Space Station."

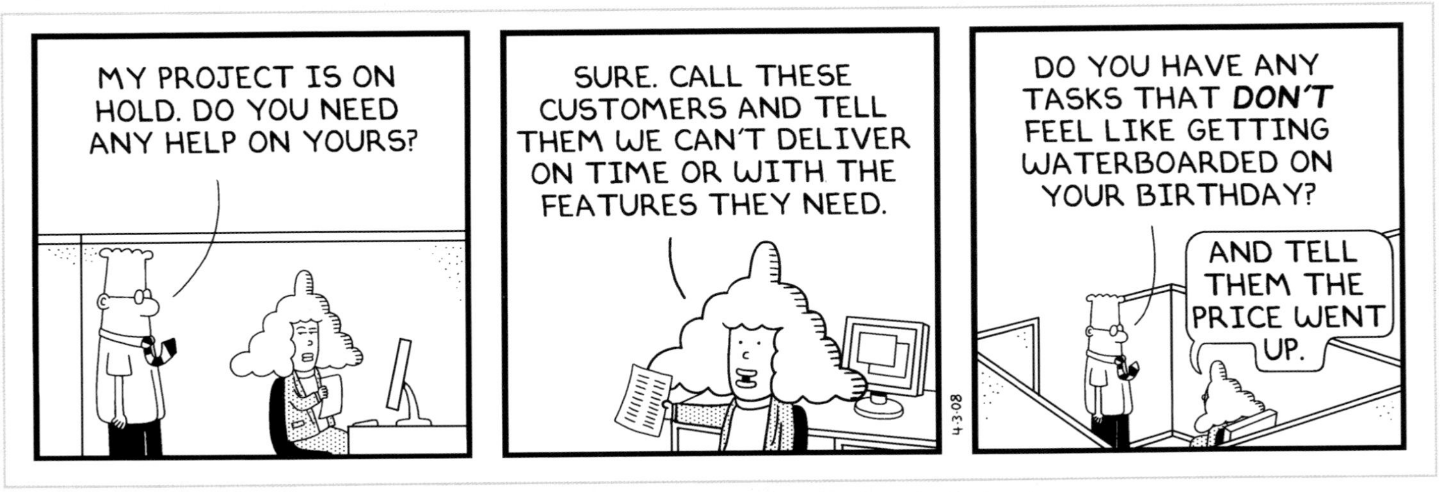
MY PROJECT IS ON HOLD. DO YOU NEED ANY HELP ON YOURS?
SURE. CALL THESE CUSTOMERS AND TELL THEM WE CAN'T DELIVER ON TIME OR WITH THE FEATURES THEY NEED.
4-3-08
DO YOU HAVE ANY TASKS THAT **DON'T** FEEL LIKE GETTING WATERBOARDED ON YOUR BIRTHDAY?
AND TELL THEM THE PRICE WENT UP.

But "waterboarded on your birthday" sailed right through.

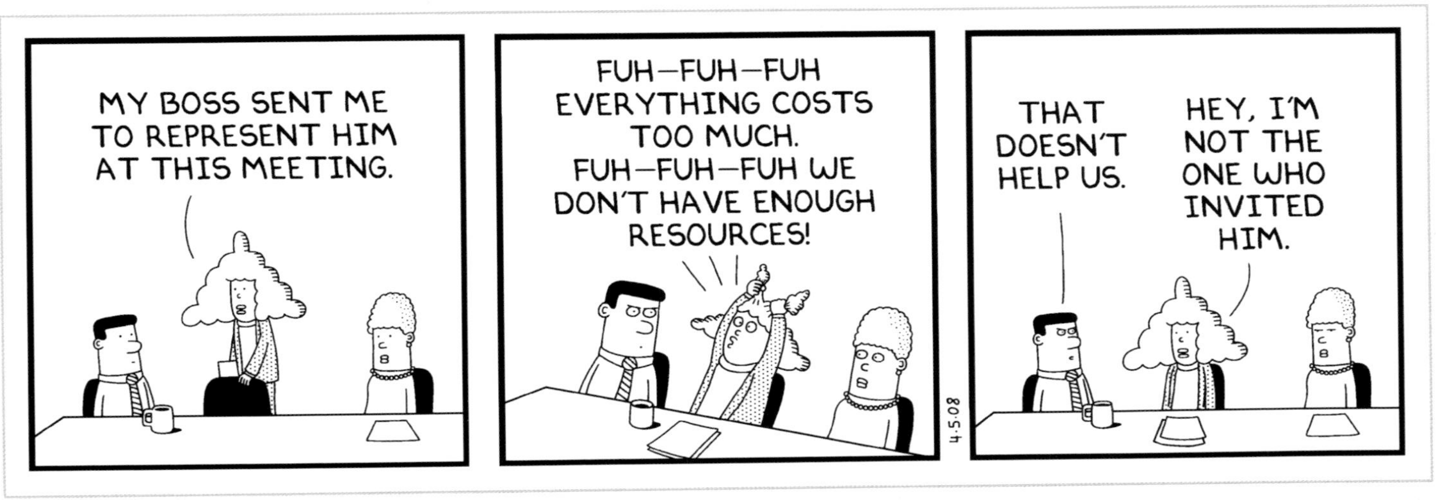
MY BOSS SENT ME TO REPRESENT HIM AT THIS MEETING.
FUH—FUH—FUH EVERYTHING COSTS TOO MUCH. FUH—FUH—FUH WE DON'T HAVE ENOUGH RESOURCES!
4-5-08
THAT DOESN'T HELP US.
HEY, I'M NOT THE ONE WHO INVITED HIM.

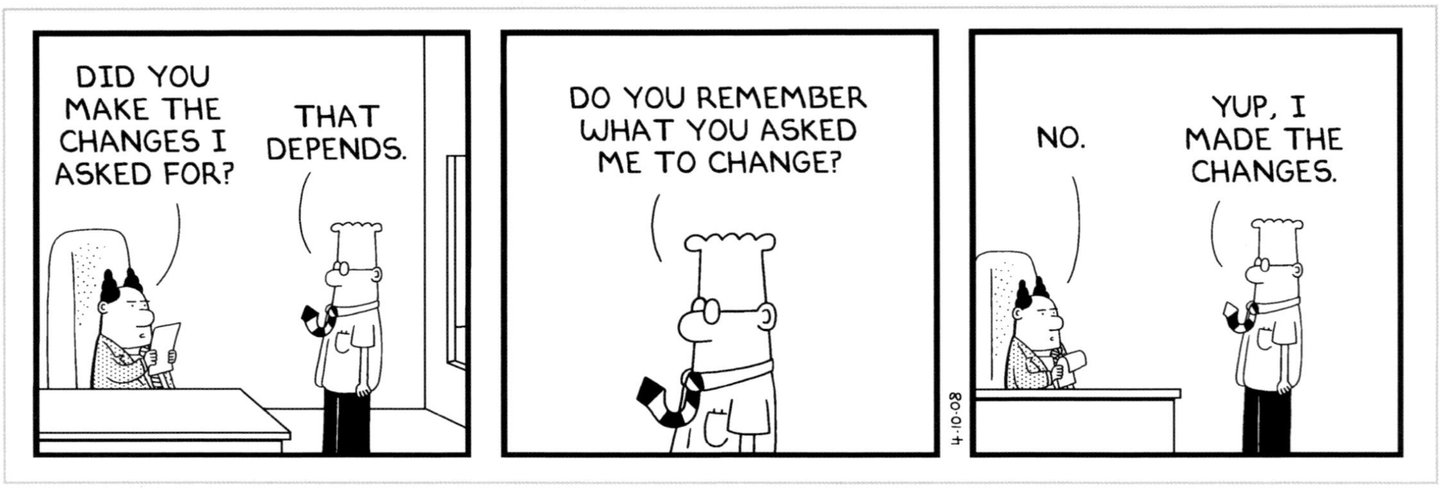
DID YOU MAKE THE CHANGES I ASKED FOR?
THAT DEPENDS.
DO YOU REMEMBER WHAT YOU ASKED ME TO CHANGE?
4-10-08
NO.
YUP, I MADE THE CHANGES.

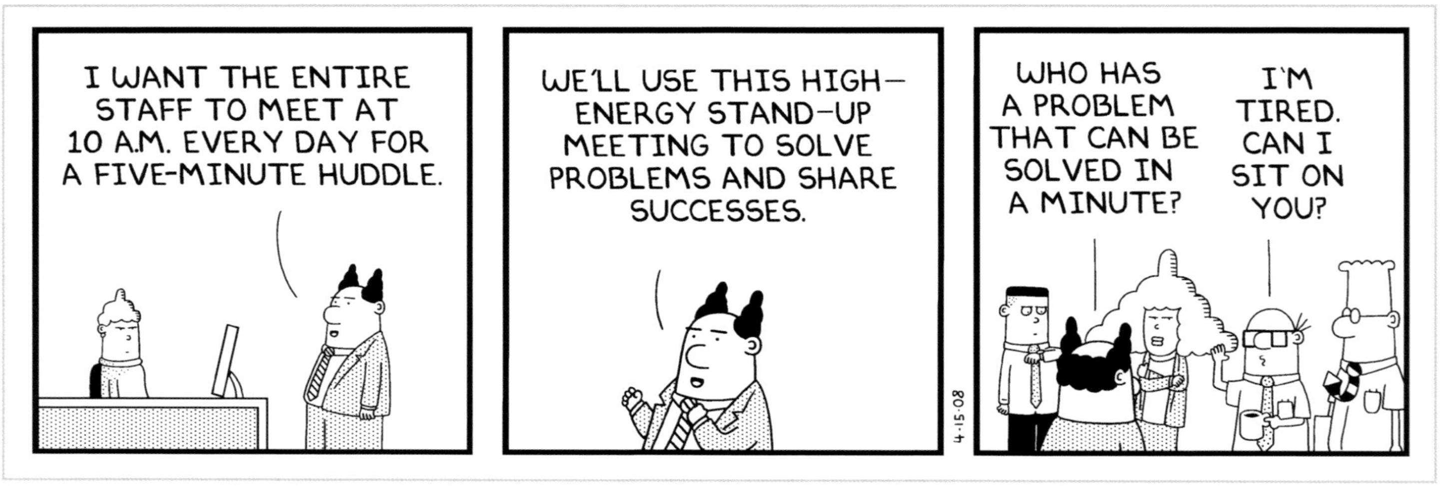
I WANT THE ENTIRE STAFF TO MEET AT 10 A.M. EVERY DAY FOR A FIVE-MINUTE HUDDLE.
WE'LL USE THIS HIGH-ENERGY STAND-UP MEETING TO SOLVE PROBLEMS AND SHARE SUCCESSES.
4-15-08
WHO HAS A PROBLEM THAT CAN BE SOLVED IN A MINUTE?
I'M TIRED. CAN I SIT ON YOU?

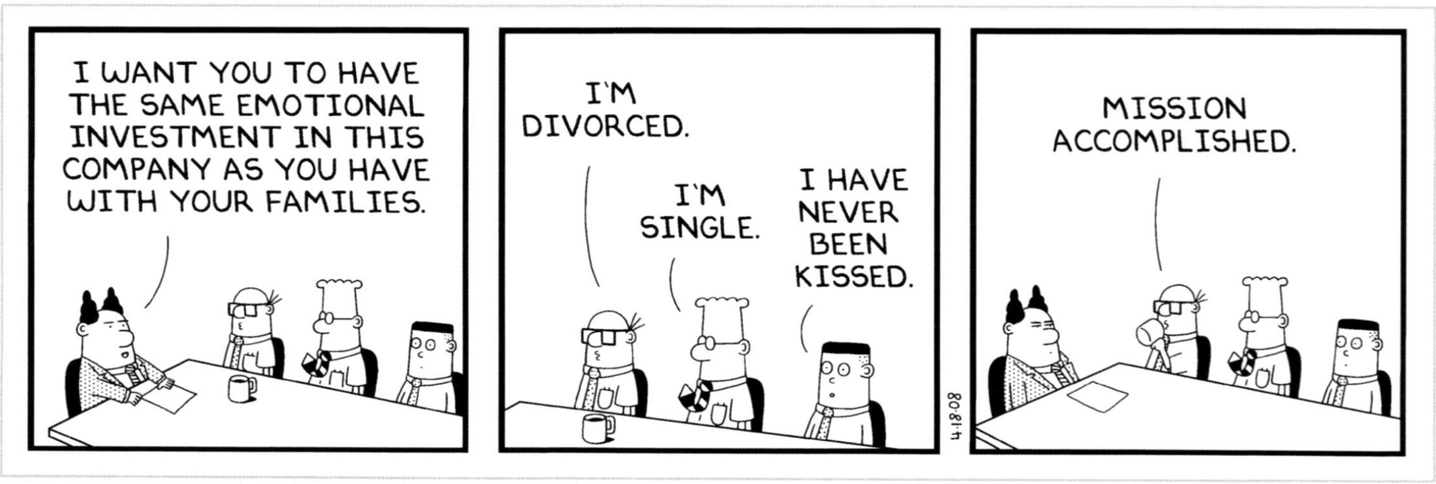
I WANT YOU TO HAVE THE SAME EMOTIONAL INVESTMENT IN THIS COMPANY AS YOU HAVE WITH YOUR FAMILIES.
I'M DIVORCED.
I'M SINGLE.
I HAVE NEVER BEEN KISSED.
4-18-08
MISSION ACCOMPLISHED.

It has always been a challenge to put more absurdity in Dilbert than you might find in a typical workplace. To do the job right, I often include aliens and the frequent demise of Generic Ted. Still, people will read the following comic and say, "That's just like my workplace."

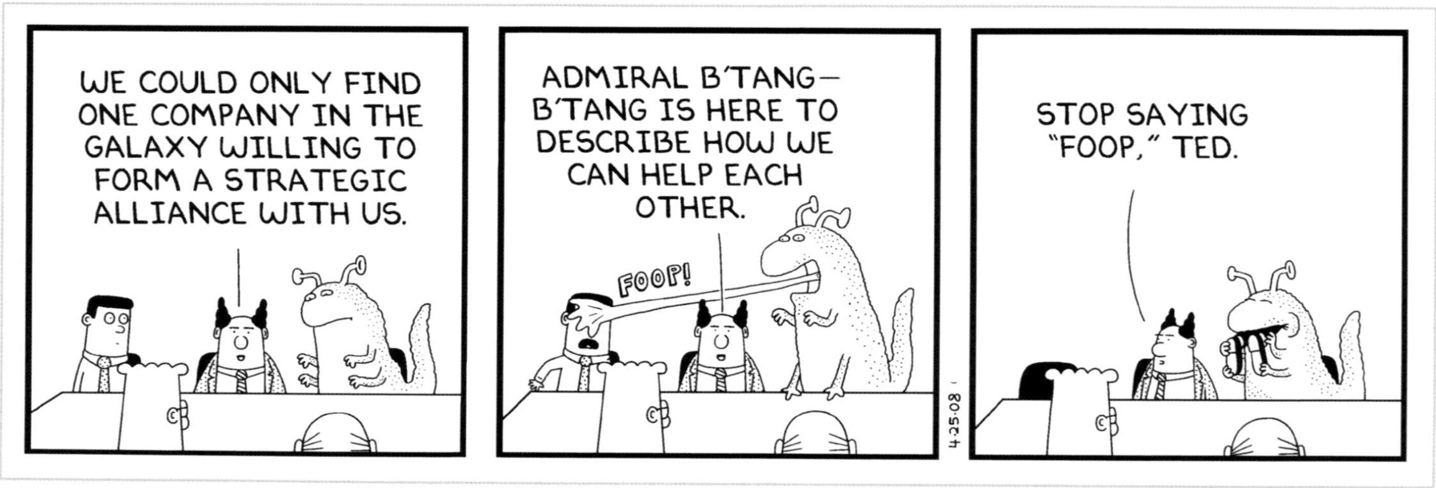
WE COULD ONLY FIND ONE COMPANY IN THE GALAXY WILLING TO FORM A STRATEGIC ALLIANCE WITH US.
ADMIRAL B'TANG-B'TANG IS HERE TO DESCRIBE HOW WE CAN HELP EACH OTHER.
FOOP!
4-25-08
STOP SAYING "FOOP," TED.

To all my readers for the past twenty years, thank you. I hope I gave you as much as you gave me. Know that I tried.

—Scott Adams

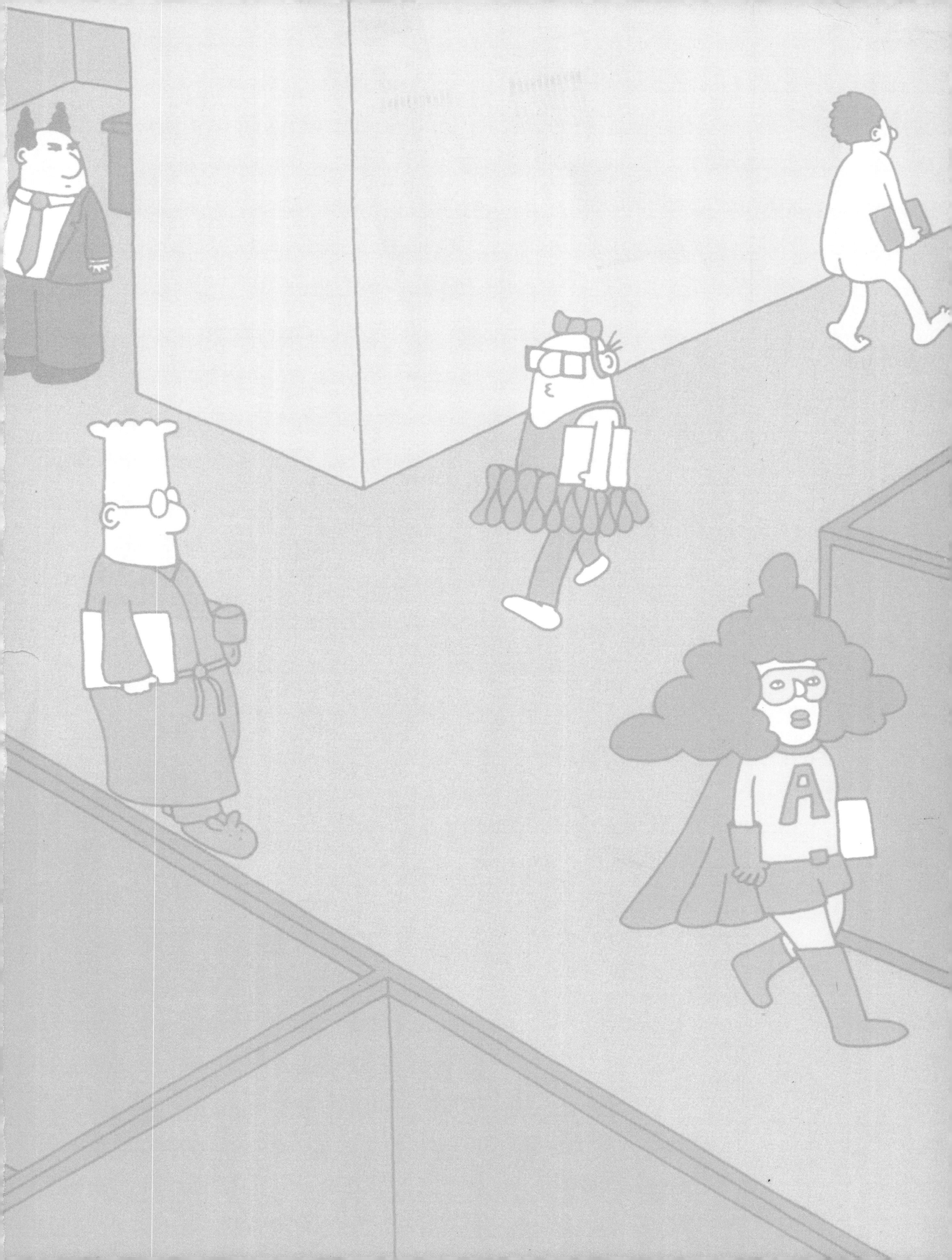

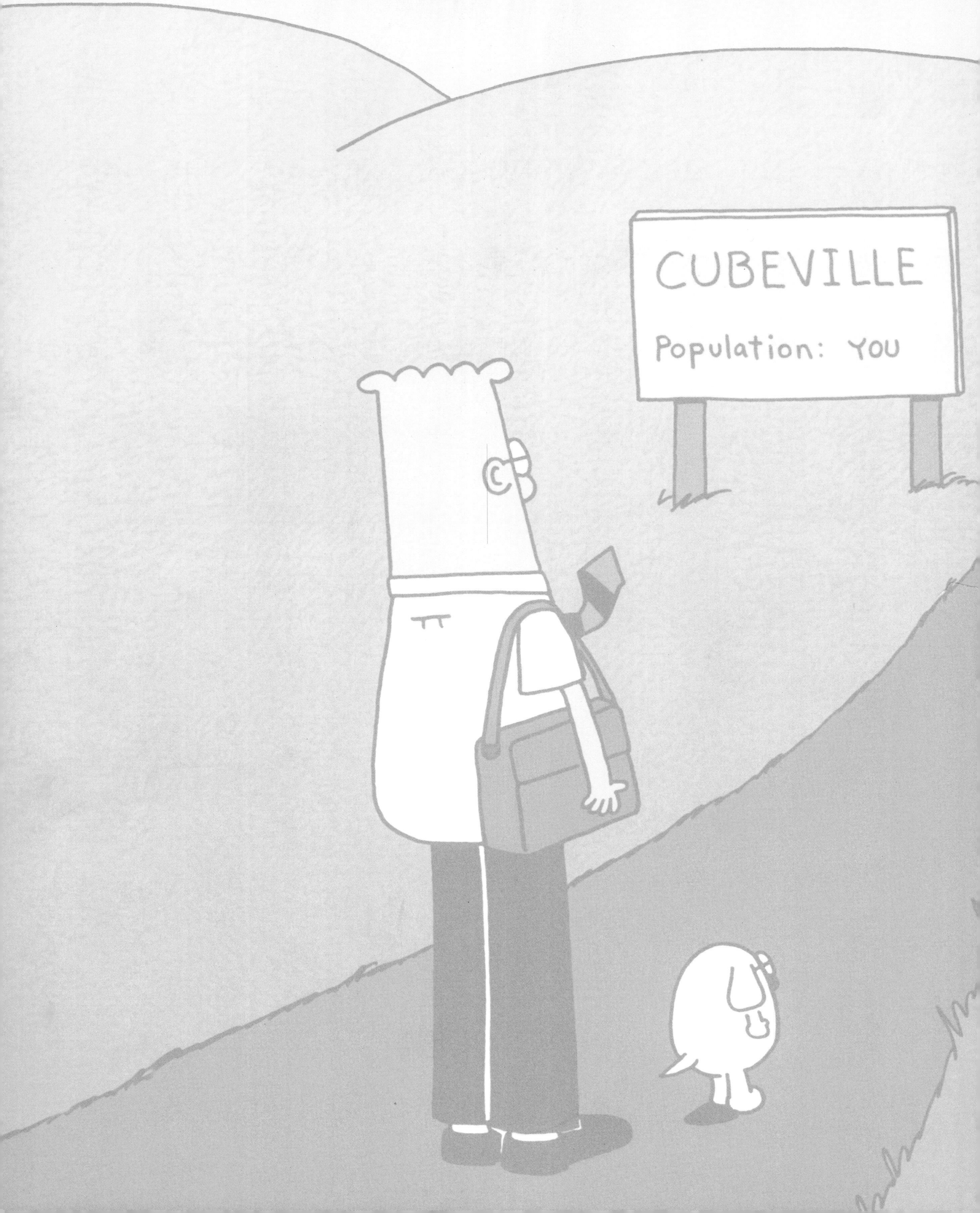
CUBEVILLE
Population: YOU